WITHDRAWN

Older Americans Information Directory

2008

Seventh Edition

Older Americans Information Directory

Associations & Organizations • Continuing Education
Government Programs • Health Resources
Assisted Living Facilities • Independent Living Centers
Legal Aid Resources • Travel & Recreation

A SEDGWICK PRESS Book

Grey House Publishing

PUBLISHER:	Leslie Mackenzie
EDITORIAL DIRECTOR:	Laura Mars-Proietti
PRODUCTION MANAGER:	Karen Stevens
PRODUCTION ASSISTANTS:	Anthony Del Vecchio, Karynn Kettinq, Alicia Miles, Sarah Miles
MARKETING DIRECTOR:	Jessica Moody

A Sedgwick Press Book
Grey House Publishing, Inc.
185 Millerton Road
Millerton, NY 12546
518.789.8700
FAX 518.789.0545
www.greyhouse.com
e-mail: books @greyhouse.com

While every effort has been made to ensure the reliability of the information presented in this publication, Grey House Publishing neither guarantees the accuracy of the data contained herein nor assumes any responsibility for errors, omissions or discrepancies. Grey House accepts no payment for listing; inclusion in the publication of any organization, agency, institution, publication, service or individual does not imply endorsement of the editors or publisher.

Errors brought to the attention of the publisher and verified to the satisfaction of the publisher will be corrected in future editions.

Except by express prior written permission of the Copyright Proprietor no part of this work may be copied by any means of publication or communication now known or developed hereafter including, but not limited to, use in any directory or compilation or other print publication, in any information storage and retrieval system, in any other electronic device, or in any visual or audio-visual device or product.

This publication is an original and creative work, copyrighted by Grey House Publishing, Inc. and is fully protected by all applicable copyright laws, as well as by laws covering misappropriation, trade secrets and unfair competition.

Grey House has added value to the underlying factual material through one or more of the following efforts: unique and original selection; expression; arrangement; coordination; and classification.

Grey House Publishing, Inc. will defend its rights in this publication.

Copyright © 2008 Grey House Publishing, Inc.
All rights reserved
First edition published 1994
Seventh edition published 2008

Printed in the USA
Older Americans information directory. – 1st ed. (1994)-

   v. ; 27.5 cm.
   Biennial
   Includes index.
   ISSN: 1072-477X

1. Aged—Services for—United States—Directories. 2. Aged—United States—Information services—Directories. I. Gale Research Inc. II. Grey House Publishing, Inc.

HV1457.O42
362.6/025/73   94660686
ISBN 13: 978-1-59237-357-4

Table of Contents

Introduction

Articles
Aging and Your Eyes ix
Alcohol Use and Abuse xii
Arthritis Advice xiv
Cancer Facts for People Over 50 xviii
Depression: Don't Let the Blues Hang Around xxi
Diabetes in Older People – A Disease You Can Manage xxv
Forgetfulnes: It's Not Always What You Think xxviii
Hearing Loss xxxi
High Blood Pressure xxxiv
HIV, AIDS, and Older People xxxvii
Mourning the Death of a Spouse xli
Hiring a Home Care Provider xliv
10 Factors to Consider When Choosing a Medicare Health Plan xlv

National Organizations & Federal Agencies 1

State Organizations & Government Agencies 37

Awards, Honors & Prizes 231

Continuing Education 239

Disability Aids & Assistive Devices
    Automobile 266
    Bath 270
    Bed 273
    Chairs 273
    Communication 274
    Cushions & Wedges 287
    Dressing Aids 290
    Health Aids 291
    Hearing Aids 294
    Hobbies & Sports 295
    Home Aids 295
    Kitchen & Eating Aids 297
    Lifts, Ramps & Elevators 301
    Scooters 306
    Stationery 309
    Walking Aids 311
    Wheelchairs 313
    Wheelchair Accessories 317

Health Conditions: Associations, Publications, Research Centers, Web Sites
    Aging 320

AIDS	393
Allergies	408
Alzheimer's Disease	413
Arthritis	443
Cancer	457
Death & Bereavement	518
Depression & Mental Health	521
Diabetes	527
Hearing Impaired	541
Heart Disease	584
Hypertension	589
Impotence	591
Incontinence	592
Parkinson's Disease	594
Stroke	601
Substance Abuse	607
Visually Impaired	635

Assisted Living Facilities
State Listings 681

Independent Living Centers
State Listings 813

Legal Aid Resources
State Listings 863

Libraries & Information Centers
State Listings 904

Print Resources for Older Americans
Publishers 947

Travel
Transportation 951
State Programs 954
Tours & Services 957

Appendix 1
Glossary of Health & Medical Terms 963
Appendix 2
Glossary of Legal Terms 969

Entry Name Index 979
Geographic Index 1067
Subject Index 1121

Introduction

This seventh edition of *Older Americans Information Directory* could not be more timely. Questions that are currently on the minds of all Americans – especially those pertaining to the economy and health care, are on the minds of older Americans with a concern that intensifies each day, as more and more "baby boomers" reach retirement. How to find and pay for needed support services? How to deal with health issues? How to be effective self-advocates? How to understand changing legal situations? How to manage financial issues? How to find ways to keep your mind and body active and involved?

This comprehensive reference work answers these questions and more for the 37.3 million older Americans that the U.S. Census recorded in 2006. It will continue to provide answers for the 40 million seniors projected in 2010 (15% increase) and the 55 million seniors projected in 2020 (36% increase). This generation of older Americans is living longer, staying healthier, and getting smarter, than their counterparts of just 20 years ago. *Older Americans Information Directory* is designed to help this growing population find the resources they need to continue leading long, happy, healthy and productive lives.

CONTENT

Listings: *Older Americans Information Directory* includes 12,060 listings, 11,051 fax numbers, 4,868 emails and 6,638 web sites. The listings are thoughtfully organized into 12 major chapters, including *Organizations, Agencies, Awards, Continuing Education, Disability Aids, Health Conditions, Living Facilities, Legal Resources, Libraries* and *Print Resources*. Each listing includes current contact information, key personnel, and helpful descriptions.

Articles: Following this Introduction are 11 valuable articles, reprinted from the National Institute on Aging. They are written in easy to understand language, on topics relevant to a majority of aging Americans, from *Aging and Your Eyes* to *Mourning the Death of a Spouse*. In addition, you'll find two articles from ElderLaw on *Medicare* and *Home Health Care*. See the Table of Contents for the complete list.

Appendices: This edition includes two helpful appendices. The first is a *Glossary of Health & Medical Terms,* with 65 terms that define language found throughout this and other publications, as well as terms used by professionals in the field. The second is a *Glossary of Legal Terms,* that includes 22 in-depth definitions designed to demystify terms used by lawyers and others regarding legal situations that many older Americans are likely to find themselves in.

Indexes: Three indexes offer additional ways to access this Directory's content. The *Entry Index* is an alphabetical list of all 12,060 entries herein. The *Geographic Index* lists all Agencies, Associations, Facilities, and Organizations by state. The *Subject Index* organizes appropriate listings by more than 100 categories, from Elder Abuse to Wills.

WINNER OF TWO AWARDS
We are pleased to announce that *Older Americans Information Directory* won the **2007 National Mature Media Award**, presented by the Mature Market Resource Center. This

is the third consecutive edition of the Directory that has been recognized for "the best in advertising, marketing and educational materials for older adults."

Older American Information Directory has also been awarded the **2007 National Health Information Award**, presented by the Health Information Resource Center, "Honoring the Nation's Best Consumer Health Information Programs and Materials," presented in the class of: Health Promotion/Disease and Injury Prevention Information.

This data is also available as **Older Americans Information Directory – Online Database**. Using powerful search and retrieval software, this interactive Online Database quickly accesses the information in the print version, searchable by dozens of criteria. Visit www.greyhouse.com for a free search and more infomation.

As always, we welcome your comments and suggestions for the next edition.

Aging and Your Eyes

Are you holding the newspaper farther away from your eyes than you used to? Join the crowd — age can bring changes that affect your eyesight. Some changes are more serious than others, but no matter what the problem, there are things you can do to protect your vision. The key is to have regular eye exams so you can find problems early.

Five Steps to Protect Your Eyesight

- Have your eyes checked every 1 or 2 years by an eye care professional. This can be an ophthalmologist or optometrist. He or she should put drops in your eyes to enlarge (dilate) your pupils. This is the only way to find some eye diseases, such as diabetic retinopathy, that have no early signs or symptoms. If you wear glasses, they should be checked too.

- Find out if you are at high risk for eye disease. Are you over age 65? Are you African-American and over age 40? Do you or people in your family have diabetes or eye disease? If so, you need to have a dilated eye exam.

- Have regular physical exams to check for diseases like diabetes and high blood pressure. These diseases can cause eye problems if not treated.

- See an eye care professional right away if you suddenly cannot see or everything looks dim or if you see flashes of light. Also see an eye care professional if you have eye pain, fluid coming from the eye, double vision, redness, or swelling of your eye or eyelid.

- Wear sunglasses that block ultraviolet (UV) radiation and a hat with a wide brim when outside. This will protect your eyes from too much sunlight, which can raise your risk of getting cataracts.

Eye Problems

Some eye problems do not threaten your eyesight. Others are more serious diseases and can lead to blindness.

Common Eye Problems

The following common eye complaints can be treated easily. Sometimes they can be signs of more serious problems.

- **Presbyopia** (prez-bee-OH-pee-uh) is a slow loss of ability to see close objects or small print. It is a normal process that happens as you get older. Holding the newspaper at arm's length is a sign of presbyopia. You might also get headaches or tired eyes when you read or do other close work. Reading glasses usually fix the problem.

- **Floaters** are tiny specks or "cobwebs" that seem to float across your eyes. You might notice them in well-lit rooms or outdoors on a bright day. Floaters can be a normal part of aging. Sometimes they are a sign of a more serious eye problem such as retinal detachment. If you see many new floaters and/or flashes of light *see your eye care professional right away*. This is considered a medical emergency.

- **Tearing** (or having too many tears) can come from being sensitive to light, wind, or temperature changes. Protecting your eyes, by wearing sunglasses for example, may solve the problem. Sometimes, tearing may mean a more serious eye problem, such as an infection or a blocked tear duct. Your eye care professional can treat both of these conditions.

- **Eyelid problems** can come from different diseases or conditions. Common eyelid problems include red and swollen eyelids, itching, tearing, being sensitive to light, and crusting of eyelashes during sleep. This condition is called blepharitis (ble-fa-RI-tis) and may be treated with warm compresses. Other less common eyelid problems, such as swelling or growths, can be treated with medicine or surgery.

Eye Diseases and Disorders

The following eye problems can lead to vision loss and blindness. Often they have few or no symptoms. Having regular eye exams is the best way to protect yourself. If your eye care professional finds a problem early there are things you can do to keep your eyesight.

- **Cataracts** are cloudy areas in the eye's lens causing loss of eyesight. Cataracts often form slowly without any symptoms. Some stay small and don't change eyesight very much. Others may become large or dense and harm vision. Cataract surgery can help. Your eye care professional can watch for changes in your cataract over time to see if you need surgery. Cataract surgery is very safe. It is one of the most common surgeries done in the United States.

- **Corneal diseases and conditions** can cause redness, watery eyes, pain, lower vision, or a halo effect. The cornea is the clear, dome-shaped "window" at the front of the eye. Disease, infection, injury, and other things can hurt the cornea. Some corneal conditions are more common in older people. Treatments for corneal problems can be simple. You may just need to change your eyeglass prescription and use eye drops. In severe cases, corneal transplantation is the treatment. It generally works well and is safe.

- **Dry eye** happens when tear glands don't work well. You may feel itching, burning, or have some vision loss. Dry eye is more common as people get older, especially among women. Your eye care professional may tell you to use a home humidifier, or special eye drops (artificial tears), or ointments to treat dry eye. In serious cases special contact lenses or surgery may help.

- **Glaucoma** comes from too much fluid pressure inside the eye. Over time, the pressure can hurt the optic nerve. This leads to vision loss and blindness. Most people with glaucoma have no early symptoms or pain from the extra pressure. You can protect yourself by having regular eye exams through dilated pupils. Treatment may be prescription eye drops, medicines that you take by mouth, laser treatment, or surgery.

- **Retinal disorders** are a leading cause of blindness in the United States. The retina is a thin tissue that lines the back of the eye and sends light signals to the brain. Retinal disorders that affect aging eyes include:

    - *Age-related macular degeneration (AMD).* AMD affects the part of the retina (the macula) that gives you sharp central vision. Over time, AMD can ruin the sharp vision needed to see objects clearly and to do common tasks like driving and reading. In some cases, AMD can be treated with lasers. Photodynamic therapy uses a drug and strong light to slow the progress of AMD. Another treatment uses injections. Ask your eye care professional if you have signs of AMD. Also ask if you should be taking special dietary supplements that may lower your chances of its getting worse.

    - *Diabetic retinopathy.* This is a problem that may appear if you have diabetes. It happens when small blood vessels stop feeding the retina as they should. It develops slowly and there are no early warning signs. Laser surgery and a treatment called vitrectomy can help. Studies show that keeping blood sugar under control can prevent diabetic retinopathy or slow its progress. If you have diabetes be sure to have an eye exam through dilated pupils at least once a year.

    - *Retinal detachment.* This is when the retina separates from the back of the eye. When this happens, you may see more floaters or light flashes in your eye, either all at once or over time. Or it may seem as though there is a curtain in front of your eyes. If you have any of these symptoms, see your eye care professional at once. ***This is a medical emergency.*** With surgery or laser treatment, doctors often can bring back all or part of your eyesight.

Low Vision

Low vision affects some people as they age. Low vision means you cannot fix your eyesight with glasses, contact lenses, medicine, or surgery. It can get in the way of your normal daily routine. You may have low vision if you:

- have trouble seeing well enough to do everyday tasks like reading, cooking, or sewing;

- can't recognize the faces of friends or family;

- have trouble reading street signs; or

- find that lights don't seem as bright as usual.

If you have any of these problems, ask your eye care professional to test you for low vision. There are special tools and aids to help people with low vision read, write, and manage daily living tasks. Lighting can be changed to suit your needs. You also can try large-print reading materials, magnifying aids, closed-circuit televisions, audio tapes, electronic reading machines, and computers that use large print and speech.

Other simple changes also may help:

- Write with bold, black felt-tip markers.
- Use paper with bold lines to help you write in a straight line.
- Put colored tape on the edge of your steps to help you keep from falling.
- Install dark-colored light switches and electrical outlets that you can see easily against light-colored walls.
- Use motion lights that turn on by themselves when you enter a room. These may help you avoid accidents caused by poor lighting.
- Use telephones, clocks, and watches with large numbers; put large-print labels on the microwave and stove.

For More Information

National Eye Institute (NEI)
National Institutes of Health
2020 Vision Place
Bethesda, MD 20892-3655
301-496-5248
www.nei.nih.gov

For more information about health and aging, contact:

National Institute on Aging Information Center
P.O. Box 8057
Gaithersburg, MD 20898-8057
800-222-2225 (toll-free)
800-222-4225 (TTY/toll-free)
www.nia.nih.gov

To order publications (in English or Spanish) or sign up for regular email alerts, visit www.nia.nih.gov/HealthInformation.

Visit NIHSeniorHealth.gov (www.nihseniorhealth.gov), a senior-friendly website from the National Institute on Aging and the National Library of Medicine. This website has health information for older adults. There are also special features that make it simple to use. For example, you can click on a button to have the text read out loud or to make the type larger.

National Institute on Aging
U. S. Department of Health and Human Services
National Institutes of Health
October 2005 (Reprinted March 2007)

Reprinted from NIA-National Institute on Aging
www.nia.nih.gov

Alcohol Use and Abuse

Anyone at any age can have a drinking problem. Great Uncle George may have always liked his liquor, so his family may not see that his drinking behavior is getting worse as he gets older. Grandma Betty was a teetotaler all her life-she started having a drink each night to help her get to sleep after her husband died. Now no one realizes that she needs a couple of drinks to get through each day.

These are common stories. The fact is that families, friends, and health care professionals often overlook their concerns about older people's drinking. Sometimes trouble with alcohol in older people is mistaken for other conditions that happen with age. But alcohol use deserves special attention. Because the aging process affects how the body handles alcohol, the same amount of alcohol can have a greater effect as a person grows older. Over time, someone whose drinking habits haven't changed may find she or he has a problem.

Facts About Alcohol and Aging

- Some research has shown that as people age they become more sensitive to alcohol's effects. In other words, the same amount of alcohol can have a greater effect on an older person than on someone who is younger.

- Some medical conditions, such as high blood pressure, ulcers, and diabetes, can worsen with alcohol use.

- Many medicines-prescription, over-the-counter, or herbal remedies-can be dangerous or even deadly when mixed with alcohol. This is a special worry for older people because the average person over age 65 takes at least two medicines a day. If you take any medicines, ask your doctor or pharmacist if you can safely drink alcohol. Here are some examples:

- Aspirin can cause bleeding in the stomach and intestines; the risk of bleeding is higher if you takeaspirin while drinking alcohol.

- Cold and allergy medicines (antihistamines) often make people sleepy; when combined with alcohol this drowsiness can be worse.

- Alcohol used with large doses of the pain killer acetaminophen can raise the risk of liver damage.

- Some medicine, such as cough syrups and laxatives, have a high alcohol content.

Effects of Alcohol

Even drinking a small amount of alcohol can impair judgment, coordination, and reaction time. It can increase the risk of work and household accidents, including falls and hip fractures. It also adds to the risk of car crashes.

Heavy drinking over time also can cause certain cancers, liver cirrhosis, immune system disorders, and brain damage. Alcohol can make some medical concerns hard for doctors to find and treat. For example, alcohol causes changes in the heart and blood vessels. These changes can dull pain that might be a warning sign of a heart attack. Drinking also can make older people forgetful and confused. These symptoms could be mistaken for signs of Alzheimer's disease. For people with diabetes, drinking affects blood sugar levels.

People who abuse alcohol also may be putting themselves at risk for serious conflicts with family, friends, and coworkers. The more heavily they drink, the greater the chance for trouble at home, at work, with friends, and even with strangers.

How to Know if Someone Has a Drinking Problem

There are two patterns of drinking: early and late onset. Some people have been heavy drinkers for many years. But, as with great Uncle George, over time the same amount of liquor packs a more powerful punch. Other people, like Grandma Betty, develop a drinking problem later in life. Sometimes this is due to major life changes like shifts in employment, failing health, or the death of friends or loved ones. Often these life changes can bring loneliness, boredom, anxiety, and depression. In fact, depression in older adults often goes along with alcohol misuse. At first, a drink seems to bring relief from stressful situations. Later on, drinking can start to cause trouble.

Not everyone who drinks regularly has a drinking problem, and not all problem drinkers drink every day. You might want to get help if you or a loved one:

- Drink to calm your nerves, forget your worries, or reduce depression.
- Gulp down drinks.
- Frequently have more than one drink a day. (A standard drink is one 12-ounce bottle or can of beer or a wine cooler, one 5-ounce glass of wine, or 1.5 ounces of 80-proof distilled spirits.)
- Lie about or try to hide drinking habits.
- Hurt yourself, or someone else, while drinking.
- Need more alcohol to get high.
- Feel irritable, resentful, or unreasonable when not drinking.
- Have medical, social, or financial worries caused by drinking.

Getting Help

Studies show that older problem drinkers are as able to benefit from treatment as are younger alcohol abusers. To get help, talk to your doctor. He or she can give you advice about your health, drinking, and treatment options. Your local health department or social services agencies can also help.

There are many types of treatments available. Some, such as 12-step help programs, have been around a long time. Others include getting alcohol out of the body (detoxification); taking prescription medicines to help prevent a return to drinking once you have stopped; and individual and/or group counseling. Newer programs teach people with drinking problems to learn which situations or feelings trigger the urge to drink as well as ways to cope without alcohol. Because the support of family members is important, many programs also counsel married couples and family members as part of the treatment process. Programs may also link individuals with important community resources.

Scientists continue to study alcohol's effects on people and to look for new ways to treat alcoholism. This research will increase the chance for recovery and improve the lives of problem drinkers.

The National Institute on Alcohol Abuse and Alcoholism, part of the National Institutes of Health, recommends that people over age 65 who choose to drink have no more than one drink a day. Drinking at this level usually is not associated with health risks.

For More Information

National Institute on Alcohol Abuse and Alcoholism (NIAAA)
5635 Fishers Lane MSC 9304
Bethesda, MD 20892-9304
301-443-3860
www.niaaa.nih.gov

For more information on health and aging, contact:

National Institute on Aging Information Center
P.O. Box 8057
Gaithersburg, MD 20898-8057
800-222-2225 (toll-free)
800-222-4225 (TTY toll-free)

To order publications (in English or Spanish) or sign up for regular email alerts, visit: www.nia.nih.gov/HealthInformation/Publications.

The National Institute on Aging website is www.nia.nih.gov.

Visit NIHSeniorHealth.gov (www.nihseniorhealth.gov), a senior-friendly website from the National Institute on Aging and the National Library of Medicine. This simple-to-use website features popular health topics for older adults. It has large type and a 'talking' function that reads the text out loud.

National Institute on Aging
U. S. Department of Health and Human Services
National Institutes of Health
September 2002 (Reprinted September 2005)

Reprinted from NIA-National Institute on Aging
www.nia.nih.gov

Arthritis Advice

Arthritis is not just a word doctors use when they talk about painful, stiff joints. In fact, there are many kinds of arthritis, each with different symptoms and treatments. Most types of arthritis are chronic. That means they can go on for a long period of time.

Arthritis can attack joints in almost any part of the body. Some forms of arthritis cause changes you can see and feel—swelling, warmth, and redness in your joints. In some the pain and swelling last only a short time, but are very bad. Other types cause less troublesome symptoms, but still slowly damage your joints.

Common Kinds of Arthritis

Arthritis is one of the most common diseases in this country. Millions of adults and half of all people age 65 and older are troubled by this disease. Older people most often have osteoarthritis, rheumatoid arthritis, or gout.

Osteoarthritis (OA) is the most common type of arthritis in older people. OA starts when cartilage begins to become ragged and wears away. Cartilage is the tissue that pads bones in a joint. At OA's worst, all of the cartilage in a joint wears away, leaving bones that rub against each other. You are most likely to have OA in your hands, neck, lower back, or the large weight-bearing joints of your body, such as knees and hips.

OA symptoms can range from stiffness and mild pain that comes and goes with activities like walking, bending, or stooping to severe joint pain that keeps on even when you rest or try to sleep. Sometimes OA causes your joints to feel stiff when you haven't moved them in a while, like after riding in the car. But the stiffness goes away when you move the joint. In time OA can also cause problems moving joints and sometimes disability if your back, knees, or hips are affected.

What causes OA? Growing older is what most often puts you at risk for OA. Other than that, scientists think the cause depends on which part of the body is involved. For example, OA in the hands or hips may run in families. OA in the knees can be linked with being overweight. Injuries or overuse may cause OA in joints such as knees, hips, or hands.

Rheumatoid Arthritis (RA) is an *autoimmune* disease. In RA, that means your body attacks the lining of a joint just as it would if it were trying to protect you from injury or disease. For example, if you had a splinter in your finger, the finger would become *inflamed*—painful, red, and swollen. RA leads to *inflammation* in your joints. This inflammation causes pain, swelling, and stiffness that lasts for hours. This can often happen in many different joints at the same time. You might not even be able to move the joint. People with RA often don't feel well. They may be tired or run a fever. People of any age can develop RA, and it is more common in women.

RA can attack almost any joint in the body, including the joints in the fingers, wrists, shoulders, elbows, hips, knees, ankles, feet, and neck. If you have RA in a joint on one side of the body, the same joint on the other side of your body will probably have RA also. RA not only destroys joints. It can also attack organs such as the heart, muscles, blood vessels, nervous system, and eyes.

Gout is one of the most painful forms of arthritis. An attack can begin when crystals of uric acid form in the connective tissue and/or joint spaces. These deposits lead to swelling, redness, heat, pain, and stiffness in the joint. Gout attacks often follow eating foods like shellfish, liver, dried beans, peas, anchovies, or gravy. Using alcohol, being overweight, and certain medications may also make gout worse. In older people, some blood pressure medicines can also increase your chance of a gout attack.

Gout is most often a problem in the big toe, but it can affect other joints, including your ankle, elbow, knee, wrist, hand, or other toes. Swelling may cause the skin to pull tightly around the joint and make the area red or purple and very tender. Your doctor might suggest blood tests and x-rays. He or she might also take a sample of fluid from your joint while you are having an attack.

Other forms of arthritis include psoriatic arthritis (in people with the skin condition psoriasis), ankylosing spondylitis (which mostly affects the spine), reactive arthritis (arthritis that occurs as a reaction to another illness in the body), and arthritis in the temporomandibular joint (where the jaw joins the skull).

Warning Signs

You might have some form of arthritis if you have:

- Lasting joint pain,
- Joint swelling,
- Joint stiffness,
- Tenderness or pain when touching a joint,
- Problems using or moving a joint normally, or
- Warmth and redness in a joint.

If any one of these symptoms lasts longer than 2 weeks, see your regular doctor or a rheumatologist. If you have a fever, feel physically ill, suddenly have a swollen joint, or have problems using your joint, see your doctor sooner. Your health care provider will ask questions about your symptoms and do a physical exam. He or she may take x rays or do lab tests before suggesting a treatment plan.

Treating Arthritis

Each kind of arthritis is handled a little differently, but there are some common treatment choices. Rest, exercise, eating a healthy, well-balanced diet, and learning the right way to use and protect your joints are key to living with any kind of arthritis. The right shoes and a cane can help with pain in the feet, knees, and hips when walking. You can also find gadgets to help you open jars and bottles or to turn the door knobs in your house more easily.

In addition, there are also medicines that can help with the pain and swelling. Acetaminophen can safely ease arthritis pain. Some NSAIDs (**n**onsteroidal **a**nti-**i**nflammatory **d**rugs), like ibuprofen and naproxen, are sold without a prescription. Other NSAIDs must be prescribed by a doctor. But in 2005, the U.S. Food and Drug Administration (FDA) warned people about the possible side effects of some NSAIDs, both those sold with or without a prescription. You should read the warnings on the package or insert that comes with the drug. Talk to your doctor about if and how you should use acetaminophen or NSAIDs for your arthritis pain. You can also check with the FDA for more information about these drugs.

Some treatments are special for each common type of arthritis.

Osteoarthritis. Medicines can help you control OA pain. Rest and exercise will make it easier for you to move your joints. Keeping your weight down is a good idea. If pain from OA in your knee is very bad, your doctor might give you shots in the joint. This can help you to move your knee and get about without pain. Some people have surgery to repair or replace damaged joints.

Rheumatoid Arthritis. With treatment, the pain and swelling from RA will get better, and joint damage might slow down or stop. You may find it easier to move around, and you will just feel better. In addition to pain and anti-inflammatory medicines, your doctor might suggest anti-rheumatic drugs, called DMARDs (**d**isease-**m**odifying **a**ntirheumatic **d**rugs). These can slow damage from the disease. Medicines like prednisone, known as corticosteroids, can ease swelling while you wait for DMARDs to take effect. Another type of drug, biologic response modifiers, blocks the damage done by the immune system. They sometimes help people with mild-to-moderate RA when other treatments have not worked.

Gout. If you have had an attack of gout, talk to your doctor to learn why you had the attack and how to prevent future attacks. The most common treatment for an acute attack of gout uses NSAIDs or corticosteroids like prednisone. This reduces swelling, so you may start to feel better within a few hours after treatment. The attack usually goes away fully within a few days. If you have had several attacks, your doctor can prescribe medicines to prevent future ones.

Exercise Can Help

Along with taking the right medicine and properly resting your joints, exercise is a good way to stay fit, keep muscles strong, and control arthritis symptoms. Daily exercise, such as walking or swimming, helps keep joints moving, lessens pain, and makes muscles around the joints stronger.

Three types of exercise are best if you have arthritis:

- *Range-of-motion exercises,* like dancing, relieve stiffness, keep you flexible, and help you keep moving your joints.
- *Strengthening exercises,* such as weight training, will keep or add to muscle strength. Strong muscles support and protect your joints.

- *Aerobic or endurance exercises,* like bicycle riding, make your heart and arteries healthier, help prevent weight gain, and improve the overall working of your body. Aerobic exercise also may lessen swelling in some joints.

The National Institute on Aging (NIA) has a free 80-page booklet on how to start and stick with a safe exercise program. The Institute also has a 48-minute companion video. See the last panel of this Age Page for more information. Before beginning any exercise program, talk with your doctor or health care worker.

Other Things to Do

Along with exercise and weight control, there are other ways to ease the pain around joints. You might find comfort by applying heat or cold, soaking in a warm bath, or swimming in a heated pool.

Your doctor may suggest surgery when damage to your joints becomes disabling or when other treatments do not help with pain. Surgeons can repair or replace these joints with artificial (man-made) ones. In the most common operations, doctors replace hips and knees.

Unproven Remedies

Many people with arthritis try remedies that have not been tested or proven helpful. Some of these, such as snake venom, are harmful. Others, such as copper bracelets, are harmless, but also unproven.

How can you tell that a remedy may be unproven?

- The remedy claims that a treatment, like a lotion or cream, works for all types of arthritis and other diseases,
- Scientific support comes from only one research study, or
- The label has no directions for use or warning about side effects.

Areas for Further Research

Recent studies suggest that Chinese acupuncture may ease OA pain for some people. Others try dietary supplements, such as glucosamine and chondroitin. Research now shows that these two dietary supplements may help lessen your OA pain. Scientists are studying alternative treatments, such as these two supplements, to find out how they work and if they keep the joint changes caused by arthritis from getting worse. More information is needed before anyone can be sure.

Talk to Your Doctor

Most importantly, do not take for granted that your pain and arthritis are just part of growing older normally. You and your doctor can work together to safely lessen the pain and stiffness that might be troubling you and to prevent more serious damage to your joints.

For More Information

Here are some helpful Federal and non-Federal resources.

NationalCenter for Complementary and Alternative Medicine
NCCAM Clearinghouse
P.O. Box 7923
Gaithersburg, MD 20898
888-644-6226 (toll-free)
866-464-3615 (TTY/toll-free)
www.nccam.nih.gov

National Institute of Arthritis and Musculoskeletal and Skin Diseases
NIAMS Information Clearinghouse
1 AMS Circle
Bethesda, MD 20892-3675
877-22-NIAMS (877-226-4267, toll-free)
301-565-2966 (TTY)
www.niams.nih.gov

American College of Rheumatology/Association of Rheumatology Health Professionals
1800 Century Place
Suite 250
Atlanta, GA 30345-4300
404-633-3777
www.rheumatology.org

Arthritis Foundation
P.O. Box 7669
Atlanta, GA 30357-0669
800-568-4045 (toll-free)
or check the telephone directory for your local chapter
www.arthritis.org

To get the NIA's exercise book or video or for more information on health and aging, contact:

National Institute on Aging Information Center
P.O. Box 8057

Gaithersburg, MD 20898-8057
800-222-2225 (toll-free)
800-222-4225 (TTY/toll-free)
www.nia.nih.gov

To order publications (in English or Spanish) or sign up for regular email alerts, visit www.nia.nih.gov/HealthInformation.

Visit NIHSeniorHealth.gov (www.nihseniorhealth.gov), a senior-friendly website from the National Institute on Aging and the National Library of Medicine. This website has health information for older adults. There are also special features that make it simple to use. For example, you can click on a button to have the text read out loud or to make the type larger.

National Institute on Aging
U. S. Department of Health and Human Services
Public Health Service
National Institutes of Health
May 2005 (Reprinted April 2007)

Reprinted from NIA-National Institute on Aging
www.nia.nih.gov

Cancer Facts for People Over 50

Cancer strikes people of all ages, but you are more likely to get cancer as you get older, even if no one in your family has had it. The good news is that cancer death rates are going down. No matter what your age, the chances of surviving cancer are better today than ever before.

What Is Cancer?

There are many kinds of cancer but they all begin when cells in a part of the body become abnormal and start making more cells. These extra cells form a mass of tissue called a growth or tumor. If the tumor gets bigger, it can hurt nearby tissues and organs. Cancer cells also can break away and spread to other parts of the body.

When cancer is found early, treatment is more likely to work. Early treatment often can shrink or destroy the tumor and stop it from growing and spreading. It may help to get regular checkups and to know the symptoms of cancer.

What Symptoms Should I Watch For?

Cancer can cause many different symptoms. Here are some things to watch for:

- A thickening or lump in the breast or any other part of the body
- A new mole or a change in an existing mole
- A sore that does not heal
- Hoarseness or a cough that does not go away
- Changes in bowel or bladder habits
- Discomfort after eating
- A hard time swallowing
- Weight gain or loss with no known reason
- Unusual bleeding or discharge
- Feeling weak or very tired

Most often, these symptoms are not due to cancer. They may be caused by non-cancerous (benign) tumors or other problems. If you are having any of these symptoms or other changes in your health, you should see a doctor as soon as possible.

Don't wait to feel pain. In its early stages, cancer usually doesn't cause pain.

What Regular Tests Should I Have?

It is important to have regular tests to check for cancer long before you might notice anything wrong. Checking for cancer when you don't have symptoms is called screening. Screening may involve a physical exam, lab tests, or tests to look at internal organs.

Medicare now covers a number of screening tests for cancer. For more information, call the Medicare toll-free help line at 800-633-4227.

Before recommending a screening test, your doctor will ask about your age, past medical problems, family medical problems, general health, and lifestyle. You may want to talk about your concerns or questions with your doctor so that together you can weigh the pros and cons of screening tests.

If you are 50 or older, the following is a list of some screening tests that check for some specific cancers:

Breast Cancer: *Clinical Breast Exam* — during a clinical breast exam, a doctor or other health care professional checks the breasts and underarms for lumps or other changes that could be a sign of breast cancer. Although primarily diagnosed in women, breast cancer can happen to men as well.

Breast Cancer: *Mammogram* — a special x-ray of the breast that often can find cancers too small for a woman or her doctor to feel. A woman's risk of breast cancer goes up as she gets older. The National Cancer Institute (NCI) says that women in their 40s or older should have a screening mammogram every 1 to 2 years.

Cervical Cancer: *Pap Test* — the doctor gently scrapes cells from the cervix (the lower part of the uterus or womb) and vagina. The cells are sent to a lab to see if they are abnormal. The NCI recommends that all women have a Pap test at least once every 3 years. However, if you are age 65 or older, talk with your doctor about whether you still need to get Pap tests.

Cervical cancer is caused by a virus, called the human papilloma virus (HPV), which can stay in the body for many years.

Cervical and Other Cancers: *Pelvic Exam* — the doctor checks the uterus, vagina, ovaries, and rectum for any changes in shape or size. During a pelvic exam, an instrument called a speculum is used to widen the vagina so that the upper part of the vagina and the cervix can be seen.

Colorectal Cancer: *Fecal Occult Blood Test* — stool samples are put on special cards and sent to a lab. In the lab, they are looked at under a microscope to see if there is occult (hidden) blood, which can be a sign of cancer. Studies show that if you have a fecal occult blood test every 1 or 2 years between the ages of 50 and 80, you can lower your chance of dying from colorectal cancer. Most cases of colorectal cancer are diagnosed in people over age 50.

Colorectal Cancer: *Sigmoidoscopy* — the doctor uses a thin, flexible tube with a light to look inside the lower part of the colon and rectum for growths or abnormal areas. Studies show that sigmoidoscopy, done once every 5 years, can save lives.

Colorectal Cancer: *Colonoscopy* — although like a sigmoidoscopy, this test looks at the whole colon. Some doctors recommend a colonoscopy every 10 years.

Mouth and Throat Cancers: *Oral Exams* — are used by doctors and dentists to detect cancer early by looking at the lips, tongue, mouth, and throat to see if there are any abnormal changes.

Prostate Cancer: *Digital Rectal Exam* — the doctor puts a gloved finger into the rectum and feels the prostate through the wall of the rectum. If the doctor feels hard or lumpy areas, they may be a sign of cancer. Prostate cancer is the most common cancer in American men — especially men over age 65. Researchers are working to find the best screening test for prostate cancer.

Prostate Cancer: *Prostate Specific Antigen (PSA) Test* — measures the amount of PSA in the blood. If the PSA level is higher than average, it may mean that prostate cancer cells are present. PSA levels also may be high in men who have other prostate problems. Researchers are studying ways to make the PSA test more accurate.

Skin Cancer: *Skin Exams* — are routine exams of the skin that can help find skin cancer early. Skin cancer is the most common form of cancer in the United States.

If a screening test does show a growth or abnormal change, it doesn't always mean that you have cancer. You may need more tests. A biopsy is the only sure way to know whether the problem is cancer. In a biopsy, a small piece of tissue is taken from the abnormal area and looked at under a microscope to check for cancer cells. If tests show you have cancer, you should talk with your doctor and decide how to treat it as soon as possible.

How Is Cancer Treated?

There are a number of cancer treatments. These include surgery, radiation therapy, and chemotherapy (anticancer drugs). Recently, doctors have also been using biological therapy for some cancers. Some biological therapies help the body's own defenses kill cancer cells. Other biological therapies block the chain of events in and around cancer cells so that they die or stop growing.

People with cancer often see different specialists. These may include a medical oncologist (specialist in cancer treatment), a surgeon, a radiation oncologist (specialist in radiation therapy), and others. The doctor may talk with you about using one type of treatment alone or two or more treatments together. Your choice of treatment depends on the type of cancer you have, where it is in the body, and the stage it is at. You and your doctor will also take into account your overall health and any specific health problems you may have.

You may have heard that older people cannot have the same treatments as younger people with cancer. But studies show that treatments used in younger adults are often safe and work just as well in older adults.

Before starting treatment, you may want another doctor to go over the diagnosis and treatment plan. This is called getting a second opinion. Some insurance companies require a second opinion; others may pay for a second opinion if you ask for one.

Some cancer patients take part in studies of new treatments. These studies — called clinical trials — are meant to find out whether new treatments are safe and whether they work or work better than other treatments. If you are a cancer patient and are interested in taking part in a clinical trial, talk with your doctor. You can find out about current clinical trials for cancer from the NCI's Cancer Information Service, see the 'For More Information' section.

Cancer Facts for People Over 50

Can Cancer Be Prevented?

Although your chances of getting cancer go up as you get older, there are things that you can do to prevent it. Experts think that about two-thirds of all cancers may be linked to things we can control, especially use of tobacco and what we eat and drink. Having a lot of contact with some chemicals, metals, or pesticides (weed killers and insect killers) can also make your risk of cancer higher. You can lower your risk of cancer in several ways:

- *Do not use tobacco products.* Tobacco causes cancer. In fact, smoking tobacco, using smokeless tobacco, and passive smoking (often breathing other people's tobacco smoke) cause a third of all cancer deaths in the United States each year.

- *Avoid sunburns.* Too much ultraviolet radiation from the sun and from other sources — such as sunlamps and tanning booths — damages your skin and can cause skin cancer.

- *Eat right.* Have at least five servings of fruits and vegetables each day. Also cut down on fatty foods and eat plenty of fiber.

- *Keep your weight down.* People who are very overweight are more likely to get cancers of the prostate, pancreas, uterus, colon, and ovary. Older women who are overweight are more likely to develop breast cancer.

- *Stay active.* Studies show that exercise can help lower your chance of getting breast and colon cancer and perhaps other cancers too. The National Institute on Aging has more information on exercise for people age 50 and older, see the "For More Information" section.

- *If you drink alcohol, don't have more than one or two drinks a day.* Drinking large amounts of alcohol raises the risk of cancers of the mouth, throat, esophagus, and larynx. People who smoke cigarettes and drink alcohol have an especially high risk of getting these cancers.

- *Follow work and safety rules to avoid dangerous contact with materials that cause cancer.*

For More Information

The Cancer Information Service (CIS), a program of the National Cancer Institute, can provide accurate, up-to-date information about cancer. Information specialists can answer your questions in English, Spanish, and on TTY equipment. The number is easy to remember: 800-4-CANCER (800-422-6237, toll-free) or 800-332-8615 (TTY/toll-free). You can get answers to your questions online through the CIS instant messaging service on NCI's website at www.cancer.gov. Click on "LiveHelp online chat".

For more information about health and aging, contact:

National Institute on Aging Information Center
P.O. Box 8057
Gaithersburg, MD 20898-8057
800-222-2225 (toll-free)
800-222-4225 (TTY/toll-free)
www.nia.nih.gov

To order publications (in English or Spanish) or sign up for regular email alerts, visit www.nia.nih.gov/HealthInformation.

Visit NIHSeniorHealth.gov (www.nihseniorhealth.gov), a senior-friendly website from the National Institute on Aging and the National Library of Medicine. This website has health information for older adults. There are also special features that make it simple to use. For example, you can click on a button to have the text read out loud or to make the type larger.

National Institute on Aging
U. S. Department of Health and Human Services
National Institutes of Health
October 2005 (Reprinted April 2007)

Reprinted from NIA-National Institute on Aging
www.nia.nih.gov

Depression: Don't Let the Blues Hang Around

Everyone feels blue now and then. It's part of life. But if you no longer enjoy activities that you usually like, you may have a more serious problem. Being depressed, without letup, can change the way you think and feel. Doctors call this "clinical depression."

Being "down in the dumps" over a period of time is not a normal part of getting older. But it is a common problem, and medical help may be needed. For most people, depression will get better with treatment. "Talk" therapy, medicine, or other treatment methods can ease the pain of depression. You do not need to suffer.

There are many reasons why depression in older people is often missed or untreated. As a person ages, the signs of depression are much more varied than at younger ages. It can appear as increased tiredness, or it can be seen as grumpiness or irritability. Depression can be tricky to recognize in older adults. Confusion or attention problems caused by depression can sometimes look like Alzheimer's disease or other brain disorders.

Mood changes and signs of depression can be caused by medicines older people may take for arthritis, high blood pressure, or heart disease. It can be hard for a doctor to detect depression. The good news is that people who are depressed usually feel better with the right treatment.

What Causes Depression?

There is no one cause of depression. For some people, a single event can bring on the illness. Depression often strikes people who felt fine but who suddenly find they are dealing with a death in the family or a serious illness. For some people, changes in brain chemistry can affect mood and cause depression. Sometimes those under a lot of stress, like caregivers, can feel depressed. Others become depressed for no clear reason.

People with serious illnesses, such as cancer, diabetes, heart disease, stroke, or Parkinson's disease, sometimes become depressed. They worry about how their illness will change their lives. They might be tired and not able to deal with something that makes them sad. Treatment for depression helps them manage their depressive symptoms and improves their quality of life.

Genetics, too, can play a role. Studies show that depression may run in families. Children of depressed parents may be at a higher risk for depression. And, depression tends to be a disorder that occurs more than once. Many older people who have been depressed in the past will be at an increased risk.

What to Look For

How do you know when you need help? After all, as you age, you may have to face problems that could cause anyone to feel "depressed." Perhaps you are dealing with the death of a loved one or friend. Maybe you are having a tough time getting used to retirement and you feel lonely. Possibly you have a chronic illness. Or, you might feel like you have lost control over your life.

After a period of feeling sad, older people usually adjust and regain their emotional balance. But, if you are suffering from clinical depression and don't get help, your depression might last for weeks, months, or even years. Here is a list of the most common signs of depression. If you have several of these, and they last for more than 2 weeks, see a doctor.

- An "empty" feeling, ongoing sadness, and anxiety
- Tiredness, lack of energy
- Loss of interest or pleasure in everyday activities, including sex
- Sleep problems, including trouble getting to sleep, very early morning waking, and sleeping too much
- Eating more or less than usual
- Crying too often or too much
- Aches and pains that don't go away when treated
- A hard time focusing, remembering, or making decisions
- Feeling guilty, helpless, worthless, or hopeless
- Being irritable
- Thoughts of death or suicide; a suicide attempt

If you are a family member, friend, or health care provider of an older person, watch for clues. Sometimes depression can hide behind a smiling face. A depressed person who lives alone may appear to feel better when someone stops by to say hello. The symptoms may seem to go away. But, when someone is very depressed, the symptoms usually come back.

Don't ignore the warning signs. If left untreated, serious depression can lead to suicide. Listen carefully if someone of any age complains about being depressed or says people don't care. That person may really be asking for help.

Getting Help

The first step is to accept that you or your family member needs help. You may not be comfortable with the subject of mental illness. Or, you might feel that asking for help is a sign of weakness. You might be like many older people, their relatives, or friends, who believe that a depressed person can quickly "snap out of it" or that some people are too old to be helped. They are wrong.

A health care provider can help you. Once you decide to get medical advice, start with your family doctor. The doctor should check to see if your depression could be caused by a health problem (such as hypothyroidism or vitamin B12 deficiency) or a medicine you are taking. After a complete exam, your doctor may suggest you talk to a mental health worker, such as a social worker, mental health counselor, psychologist, or psychiatrist. Doctors specially trained to treat depression in older people are called geriatric psychiatrists.

Don't avoid getting help because you may be afraid of how much treatment might cost. Often, only short-term psychotherapy (talk therapy) is needed. It is usually covered by insurance. Also, some community mental health centers may offer treatment based on a person's ability to pay.

Be aware that some family doctors may not understand about aging and depression. If your doctor is unable or unwilling to help, you may want to talk to another health care provider.

Are you the relative or friend of a depressed older person who won't go to a doctor for treatment? Try explaining how treatment may help the person feel better. In some cases, when a depressed person can't or won't go to the doctor's office, the doctor or mental health specialist can start by making a phone call. A telephone call can't take the place of the personal contact needed for a complete medical checkup, but it might inspire the person to go for treatment.

Treating Depression

Your doctor or mental health expert can often treat your depression successfully. Different therapies seem to work for different people. For instance, support groups can provide new coping skills or social support if you are dealing with a major life change. A doctor might suggest that you go to a local senior center, volunteer service, or nutrition program.

Several kinds of talk therapies are useful as well. One method might help give you a more positive outlook on life. Always thinking about the sad things in your life or what you have lost might have led to your depression. Another method works to improve your relations with others to give you more hope about your future.

Getting better takes time, but with support from others and treatment you will get a little better each day.

Antidepressant drugs (medicine to treat depression) can also help. These medications can improve your mood, sleep, appetite, and concentration. There are several types of antidepressants available. Some of these medicines can take up to 12 weeks before you feel like they are working. Your doctor may want you to continue medications for 6 months or more after your symptoms disappear.

Some antidepressants can cause unwanted side effects, although newer medicines have fewer side effects. Any antidepressant should be used with great care to avoid this problem. Remember:

- The doctor needs to know about all prescribed and over-the-counter medications, vitamins, or herbal supplements you are taking.

- The doctor should also be aware of any other physical problems you have.

- Be sure to take antidepressants in the proper dose and on the right schedule.

Electroconvulsive therapy (ECT) can also help. Don't be misled by the way some movies and books have portrayed ECT (also called electroshock therapy). They do not give a true picture. ECT may be recommended when medicines can't be tolerated or when a quick response is needed. ECT is given as a series of treatments over a few weeks. Like other antidepressant therapies, follow-up treatment is often needed to help prevent a return of depression.

Help from Family and Friends

Family and friends can play an important role in treatment. You can help your relative or friend stay with the treatment plan. If needed, make appointments for the person or go along to the doctor, mental health expert, or support group.

Be patient and understanding. Get your relative or friend to go on outings with you or to go back to an activity that he or she once enjoyed. Encourage the person to be active and busy, but not to take on too much at one time.

Preventing Depression

What can be done to lower the risk of depression? How can people cope? There are a few steps you can take. Try to prepare for major changes in life, such as retirement or moving from your home of many years. One way to do this is to try and keep friendships over the years. Friends can help ease loneliness if you lose a spouse. You can also develop a hobby. Hobbies may help keep your mind and body active. Stay in touch with family. Let them help you when you feel very sad. If you are faced with a lot to do, try to break it up into smaller jobs that are easy to finish.

Exercise can also help prevent depression or lift your mood if you are already depressed. Older people who are depressed can gain mental as well as physical benefits from mild forms of exercise like walking outdoors or in shopping malls. Gardening, dancing, and swimming are other good forms of exercise. Pick something you like to do. Begin with 10-15 minutes a day, and increase the time as you are able. Being physically fit and eating a balanced diet may help avoid illnesses that can bring on disability or depression.

Remember, with treatment, most people will find that positive thoughts will gradually replace the negative thoughts that resulted from depression. Expect your mood to improve slowly. Feeling better takes time. But it can happen.

For More Information

American Association for Geriatric Psychiatry
7910 Woodmont Avenue, Suite 1050
Bethesda, MD 20814-3004
301-654-7850
www.aagpgpa.org

American Psychological Association
750 First Street, NE
Washington, DC 20002-4242
800-374-2721 (toll-free)
www.apa.org

Depression and Bipolar Support Alliance
730 N. Franklin St., Suite 501
Chicago, IL 60610-7224
800-826-3632 (toll-free)
www.dbsalliance.org

National Alliance for the Mentally Ill
Colonial Place Three
2107 Wilson Boulevard, Suite 300
Arlington, VA 22201-3042
800-950-6264 (toll-free)
www.nami.org

National Institute of Mental Health
6001 Executive Blvd., Room 8184, MSC 9663
Bethesda, MD 20892-9663
866-615-6464 (for publications/toll-free)
301-443-4513
866-415-8051 (TTY, toll-free)
www.nimh.nih.gov

National Mental Health Association
2000 N. Beauregard St.
6th Floor
Alexandria, VA 22311
800-969-6642 (toll-free)
800-433-5959 (TTY/toll-free)
www.nmha.org

For information about depression and Alzheimer's patients and caregivers, contact:

Alzheimer's Disease Education and Referral (ADEAR) Center
P.O. Box 8250
Silver Spring, MD 20907-8250
800-438-4380 (toll-free)
www.alzheimers.nia.nih.gov

For more information on health and aging contact:

National Institute on Aging Information Center
P.O. Box 8057
Gaithersburg, MD 20898-8057
800-222-2225 (toll-free)
800-222-4225 (TTY/toll-free)
www.nia.nih.gov

To order publications in (English or Spanish) or sign up for regular email alerts, go to www.nia.nih.gov/HealthInformation.

Visit NIHSeniorHealth.gov (www.nihseniorhealth.gov), a senior-friendly website from the National Institute on Aging and the National Library of Medicine. This simple-to-use website has health information for older adults. It has large type and a talking function that "reads" the text out loud.

National Institute on Aging
U. S. Department of Health and Human Services
Public Health Service
National Institutes of Health
Reprinted 2006

Reprinted from NIA-National Institute on Aging
www.nia.nih.gov

Diabetes in Older People - A Disease You Can Manage

Diabetes is a serious disease. People get diabetes when their blood glucose level, sometimes called blood sugar, is too high. Diabetes can lead to dangerous health problems, such as having a heart attack or a stroke. The good news is that there are things you can do to take control of diabetes and prevent its problems. And, if you are worried about getting diabetes, there are things you can do to lower your risk.

What is Diabetes?

Our bodies change the food we eat into glucose. Insulin helps turn glucose into energy that "fuels" our cells. If you have diabetes, your body does not make insulin, does not use insulin the right way, or both. That means there is too much glucose in the blood. Doctors who specialize in taking care of people with diabetes are called endocrinologists.

Types of Diabetes

There are two kinds of diabetes. In type 1 diabetes, the body does not make insulin. It develops most often in children and young adults but can happen at any age.

Type 2 diabetes is the most common kind. You may have heard it called adult-onset diabetes. In type 2 diabetes, the body makes insulin but doesn't use it the right way. Your chance of getting type 2 diabetes is higher if you are overweight, inactive, and/or have a family history of diabetes.

Symptoms

Sometimes people with type 2 diabetes don't even know they have it. People with untreated diabetes often feel tired, hungry, or thirsty. They may lose weight, urinate often, or have trouble with their eyes, such as blurred vision. They may also get skin infections or heal slowly from cuts and bruises. See your doctor right away if you have one or more of these symptoms.

Diabetes can cause problems with your heart, blood vessels, eyes, kidneys, nerves, teeth, and gums. People with type 2 diabetes also may be more at risk for Alzheimer's disease. Researchers are studying this connection now.

There is a lot we don't know about diabetes and how best to manage it. But there is a lot we do know. For example, we know that careful control of your weight, glucose, blood pressure, and cholesterol can help prevent or delay diabetes and problems caused by it. Exercise can also help.

Pre-diabetes

Many people have "pre-diabetes." This means their glucose levels are higher than normal but not high enough to be called diabetes. People with pre-diabetes are at high risk for developing type 2 diabetes, heart disease, and stroke.

Pre-diabetes is a serious problem, but there are things you can do. For example, losing weight by exercising and eating healthy foods can work to prevent or delay diabetes in older adults.

Tests for Diabetes

If you have symptoms of diabetes, your doctor will check your blood glucose levels. The most common test for diabetes is called the fasting glucose test. This blood test measures your glucose after you have nothing to eat or drink (that's called fasting) for at least 8 hours, usually overnight. Another blood test, called the oral glucose tolerance test, checks your glucose after fasting overnight and then again 2 hours after you have a sugary drink. Your doctor may want you to have the test for diabetes twice to make sure of the results.

Managing Diabetes

When you have diabetes, your body does not use or make insulin properly. Your doctor may prescribe pills, insulin, other injectable medicines, or a combination of these to help control your blood glucose levels. Insulin can be taken by shots/injections, with an insulin pump, or even inhaled.

In addition, you can keep control of your diabetes by:

- **Tracking your glucose levels.** Very high glucose levels or very low glucose levels (called hypoglycemia) are dangerous health emergencies.

Talk to your doctor about how you can check your glucose levels at home.

- **Making healthy food choices.** Learn how different foods affect your glucose levels. Think about foods you like that will also help you lose weight. Let your doctor know if you want help with meal planning.
- **Getting exercise.** Daily exercise can help improve glucose levels in older people with diabetes. Ask your doctor to help you plan an exercise program.
- **Keeping track of how you are doing.** Talk to your doctor about how well your diabetes care plan is working. Make sure you know how often you need to check your glucose levels.

Your doctor may want you to see other health care providers who can help you manage some of the extra problems caused by diabetes. He or she can also give you a schedule for tests you may need. Talk to your doctor about what you can do to stay healthy. Here are some things to keep in mind:

- **Have yearly eye exams.** Finding and treating eye problems early may keep your eyes healthy.
- **Check your kidneys yearly.** Diabetes can be hard on your kidneys. A urine and blood test will show if your kidneys are okay.
- **Get flu shots and a pneumonia vaccine.** A yearly flu shot will help keep you healthy. If you're over 65, make sure you have had a pneumonia shot. Talk with your doctor to see if you should get another one.
- **Check your cholesterol.** At least once a year, get a blood test to check your cholesterol as well as your triglyceride levels. High levels may increase your risk for heart problems.
- **Care for your teeth and gums.** Your teeth and gums need to be checked by a dentist to avoid serious problems twice a year.
- **Find out your average blood glucose level.** At least twice a year, get a blood test called the A1C test. The result will tell you your average glucose level for the past 2 to 3 months.
- **Protect your skin.** Keep your skin clean and use skin softeners for dryness. Take care of minor cuts and bruises to prevent infections.
- **Look at your feet.** Take time to look at your feet every day for any red patches. If you have sores, blisters, breaks in the skin, infections, or build-up of calluses see your doctor. Your doctor may also tell you to see a foot doctor called a podiatrist.
- **Watch your blood pressure.** Get your blood pressure checked regularly.

Medicare Can Help

Medicare will pay to help you learn how to care for your diabetes. It will also pay for some diabetes tests, supplies, special shoes, foot exams, eye tests, and help with meal planning.

For more information about what Medicare covers, call 1-800-MEDICARE (1-800-633-4227) or visit their website, www.medicare.gov/Health/Diabetes.asp.

For More Information:

Here are some helpful Federal and non Federal resources:

American Diabetes Association
1701 North Beauregard Street
Alexandria, VA 22311
1-800-DIABETES (1-800-342-2383)
www.diabetes.org

National Diabetes Education Program
One Diabetes Way
Bethesda, MD 20892-3560
1-800-438-5383
www.ndep.nih.gov

National Diabetes Information Clearinghouse (NDIC)
National Institute of Diabetes and Digestive and Kidney Diseases
One Information Way
Bethesda, MD 20892-3560
1-800-860-8747
www.diabetes.niddk.nih.gov

For more information on health and aging, contact:

National Institute on Aging Information Center
P.O. Box 8057
Gaithersburg, MD 20898-8057
1-800-222-2225
1-800-222-4225 (TTY)

Visit www.nia.nih.gov/HealthInformation to order publications (in English or Spanish) or sign up for regular email alerts.

Visit NIHSeniorHealth.gov (www.nihseniorhealth.gov), a senior-friendly website from the National Institute on Aging and the National Library of Medicine. This website has health information for older adults. There are also special features that make it simple to use. For example, you can click on a button to have the text read out loud or to make the type larger.

National Institute on Aging
U. S. Department of Health and Human Services
Public Health Service
National Institutes of Health
August 2007

Reprinted from NIA-National Institute on Aging
www.nia.nih.gov

Forgetfulness: It's Not Always What You Think

Many older people worry about becoming more forgetful. They think forgetfulness is the first sign of Alzheimer's disease (AD). In the past, memory loss and confusion were considered a normal part of aging. However, scientists now know that most people remain both alert and able as they age, although it may take them longer to remember things.

A lot of people experience memory lapses. Some memory problems are serious, and others are not. People who have serious changes in their memory, personality, and behavior may suffer from a form of brain disease called dementia. Dementia seriously affects a person's ability to carry out daily activities. AD is one of many types of dementia.

The term dementia describes a group of symptoms that are caused by changes in brain function. Dementia symptoms may include:

- asking the same questions repeatedly,
- becoming lost in familiar places,
- being unable to follow directions,
- getting disoriented about time, people, and places, and
- neglecting personal safety, hygiene, and nutrition.

People with dementia lose their abilities at different rates. Dementia is caused by many conditions. Some conditions that cause dementia can be reversed, and others cannot. Further, many different medical conditions may cause symptoms that seem like AD, but are not. Some of these medical conditions may be treatable. Reversible conditions can be caused by a high fever, dehydration, vitamin deficiency and poor nutrition, bad reactions to medicines, problems with the thyroid gland, or a minor head injury. Medical conditions like these can be serious and should be treated by a doctor as soon as possible.

Sometimes older people have emotional problems that can be mistaken for dementia. Feeling sad, lonely, worried, or bored may be more common for older people facing retirement or coping with the death of a spouse, relative, or friend. Adapting to these changes leaves some people feeling confused or forgetful. Emotional problems can be eased by supportive friends and family, or by professional help from a doctor or counselor.

The two most common forms of dementia in older people are AD and multi infarct dementia (sometimes called vascular dementia). These types of dementia are irreversible, which means they cannot be cured. In AD, nerve cell changes in certain parts of the brain result in the death of a large number of cells. Symptoms of AD begin slowly and become steadily worse. As the disease progresses, symptoms range from mild forgetfulness to serious impairments in thinking, judgment, and the ability to perform daily activities. Eventually, patients may need total care.

In multi infarct dementia, a series of strokes or changes in the brain's blood supply may result in the death of brain tissue. The location in the brain where the strokes occur and the severity of the strokes determine the seriousness of the problem and the symptoms that arise. Symptoms usually begin abruptly and progress in a step-wise fashion with repeated strokes. At this time, there is no way to reverse damage that has already been caused by a stroke. However, treatment to prevent further strokes is very important.

Diagnosis

People who are worried about memory problems should see their doctor. If the doctor believes that the problem is serious, then a thorough physical, neurological, and psychiatric evaluation may be recommended. A complete medical examination for memory loss may include gathering information about the person's medical history, including use of prescription and over the counter medicines, diet, past medical problems, and general health. Because a correct diagnosis depends on recalling these details accurately, the doctor also may ask a family member for information about the person.

Tests of blood and urine may be done to help the doctor find any problems. There are also tests of mental abilities (tests of memory, problem solving, counting, and language). A brain CT scan may assist the doctor in ruling out a curable disorder. A scan also may show signs of normal age related changes in the brain. It may be necessary to have another scan at a later date to see if there have been further changes in the brain.

Multi infarct dementia and AD can exist together, making it hard for the doctor to diagnose either one specifically. Scientists once thought that multi infarct dementia and other types of vascular dementia caused most cases of irreversible mental impairment. They now believe that most older people with irreversible dementia have Alzheimer's disease.

Treatment

Even if the doctor diagnoses an irreversible form of dementia, much still can be done to treat the patient and help the family cope. A person with dementia should be under a doctor's care, and may see a neurologist, psychiatrist, family doctor, internist, or geriatrician. The doctor can treat the patient's physical and behavioral problems and answer the many questions that the person or family may have.

For some people in the early and middle stages of AD, the drugs tacrine (Cognex, which is still available but no longer actively marketed by the manufacturer), donepezil (Aricept), rivastigmine (Exelon), and galantamine (Razadyne, formerly known as Reminyl) are prescribed to possibly delay the worsening of some of the disease's symptoms. Another drug, memantine (Namenda), has been approved for treatment of moderate to severe AD. Doctors believe it is very important for people with multi infarct dementia to try to prevent further strokes by controlling high blood pressure, monitoring and treating high blood cholesterol and diabetes, and not smoking.

Many people with dementia need no medication for behavioral problems. But for some people, doctors may prescribe medications to reduce agitation, anxiety, depression, or sleeping problems. These troublesome behaviors are common in people with dementia. Careful use of doctor prescribed drugs may make some people with dementia more comfortable and make caring for them easier.

A healthy diet is important. Although no special diets or nutritional supplements have been found to prevent or reverse AD or multi infarct dementia, a balanced diet helps maintain overall good health. In cases of multi infarct dementia, improving the diet may play a role in preventing more strokes.

Family members and friends can assist people with dementia in continuing their daily routines, physical activities, and social contacts. People with dementia should be kept up-to-date about the details of their lives, such as the time of day, where they live, and what is happening at home or in the world. Memory aids may help in the day to day living of patients in the earlier stages of dementia. Some families find that a big calendar, a list of daily plans, notes about simple safety measures, and written directions describing how to use common household items are useful aids.

Advice for Today

Scientists are working to develop new drugs that someday may slow, reverse, or prevent the damage caused by AD and multi infarct dementia. In the meantime, people who have no dementia symptoms can try to keep their memory sharp.

Some suggestions include developing interests or hobbies and staying involved in activities that stimulate both the mind and body. Giving careful attention to physical fitness and exercise also may go a long way toward keeping a healthy state of mind. Limiting the use of alcoholic beverages is important, because heavy drinking over time can cause permanent brain damage.

Many people find it useful to plan tasks; make "things to do" lists; and use notes, calendars, and other memory aids. They also may remember things better by mentally connecting them to other meaningful things, such as a familiar name, song, or lines from a poem.

Stress, anxiety, or depression can make a person more forgetful. Forgetfulness caused by these emotions usually is temporary and goes away when the feelings fade. However, if these feelings last for a long period of time, getting help from a professional is important. Treatment may include counseling or medication, or a combination of both.

Some physical and mental changes occur with age in healthy people. However, much pain and suffering can be avoided if older people, their families, and their doctors recognize dementia as a disease, not part of normal aging.

For More Information

The Alzheimer's Disease Education and Referral (ADEAR) Center is a service of the National Institute on Aging, part of the Federal Government's National Institutes of Health. The Center provides information to health professionals, patients and their families, and the public:

ADEAR Center
P.O. Box 8250
Silver Spring, MD 20907-8250
800-438-4380

e-mail: adear@nia.nih.gov
www.alzheimers.nia.nih.gov

The Alzheimer's Association is a nonprofit organization supporting AD research and offering information and support services to people with AD and their families.

Alzheimer's Association
225 North Michigan Avenue
Suite 1700
Chicago, IL 60601-7633
800-272-3900 (toll-free)
www.alz.org

Information about community resources is available from State and Area Agencies on Aging:

Eldercare Locator
800-677-1116 (toll-free)
www.eldercare.gov

For more information on health and aging, contact:

National Institute on Aging Information Center
P.O. Box 8057
Gaithersburg, MD 20898-8057
1-800-222-2225 (toll-free)
1-800-222-4225 (TTY toll-free)
www.nia.nih.gov

To order publications (in English or Spanish) or sign up for regular e-mail alerts, go to www.nia.nih.gov/HealthInformation.

Visit NIHSeniorHealth.gov, a senior-friendly website from the National Institute on Aging and the National Library of Medicine. This simple-to-use website features popular health topics for older adults. It has large type and a talking function that "reads" the text out loud.

National Institute on Aging
U.S. Department of Health and Human Services
Public Health Service
National Institutes of Health
August 2006

Hearing Loss

About one-third of Americans between the ages of 65 and 74 have hearing problems. About half the people who are 85 and older have hearing loss. Whether a hearing loss is small (missing certain sounds) or large (being profoundly deaf), it is a serious concern. If left untreated, problems can get worse.

Hearing loss can affect your life in many ways. You may miss out on talks with friends and family. On the telephone, you may find it hard to hear what the caller is saying. At the doctor's office, you may not catch the doctor's words.

Sometimes hearing problems can make you feel embarrassed, upset, and lonely. It's easy to withdraw when you can't follow a conversation at the dinner table or in a restaurant. It's also easy for friends and family to think you are confused, uncaring, or difficult, when the problem may be that you just can't hear well.

If you have trouble hearing, there is help. Start by seeing your doctor. Depending on the type and extent of your hearing loss, there are many treatment choices that may help. Hearing loss does not have to get in the way of your ability to enjoy life.

How Do I Know if I Have a Hearing Loss?

See your doctor if you:

- Have trouble hearing over the telephone,
- Find it hard to follow conversations when two or more people are talking,
- Need to turn up the TV volume so loud that others complain,
- Have a problem hearing because of background noise,
- Sense that others seem to mumble, or
- Can't understand when women and children speak to you.

What Should I Do?

If you have trouble hearing, see your doctor. Sometimes the diagnosis and treatment can take place in the doctor's office. Or your doctor may refer you to an **otolaryngologist** (oh-toh-layr-ehn-GOL-luh-jist), a doctor who specializes in the ear, nose, and throat. The otolaryngologist will take a medical history, ask if other family members have hearing problems, do a thorough exam, and suggest any needed tests. You may be referred to an **audiologist** (aw-dee-AH-luh-jist). Audiologists are health care professionals trained to measure hearing. The audiologist will use an audiometer to test your ability to hear sounds of different pitch and loudness. These tests are painless. Audiologists can help if you need a hearing aid. They can help select the best hearing aid for you and help you learn to get the most from it.

What Causes Hearing Loss?

Hearing loss can have many different causes, including the aging process, ear wax buildup, exposure to very loud noises over a long period of time, viral or bacterial infections, heart conditions or stroke, head injuries, tumors, certain medicines, and heredity.

What Different Types of Hearing Loss Are There?

Presbycusis (prez-bee-KYOO-sis) is age-related hearing loss. It becomes more common in people as they get older. People with this kind of hearing loss may have a hard time hearing what others are saying or may be unable to stand loud sounds. The decline is slow. Just as hair turns gray at different rates, presbycusis can develop at different rates. It can be caused by **sensorineural** (sen-soh-ree-NOO-ruhl) hearing loss. This type of hearing loss results from damage to parts of the inner ear, the auditory nerve, or hearing pathways in the brain. Presbycusis may be caused by aging, loud noise, heredity, head injury, infection, illness, certain prescription drugs, and circulation problems such as high blood pressure. The degree of hearing loss varies from person to person. Also, a person can have a different amount of hearing loss in each ear.

Tinnitus (tih-NIE-tuhs) accompanies many forms of hearing loss, including those that sometimes come with aging. People with tinnitus may hear a ringing, roaring, or some other noise inside their ears. Tinnitus may be caused by loud noise, hearing loss, certain medicines, and other health problems, such as allergies and problems in the heart and blood vessels. Often it is unclear why the ringing happens. Tinnitus can come and go, it can stop completely, or it can stay. Some medicines may help ease the problem. Wearing a hearing aid makes it easier for some people to hear the sounds they need to hear by making them louder. Maskers, small devices that use sound to make tinnitus less noticeable, help other people. Music also can be soothing and can sometimes mask the sounds caused by the condition. It also helps to avoid things that might make tinnitus worse, like smoking, alcohol, and loud noises.

Conductive hearing loss happens when something blocks the sounds that are carried from the eardrum (tympanic membrane) to the inner ear. Ear wax buildup, fluid in the middle ear, abnormal bone growth, a punctured eardrum, or a middle ear infection can cause this type of hearing loss. If ear wax blockage is a problem for you, the American Academy of Otolaryngology-Head and Neck Surgery suggests using mild treatments, such as mineral oil, baby oil, glycerin, or commercial ear drops to soften ear wax. If you think you may have a hole in your eardrum, however, you should see your doctor.

How Can I Help a Person with Hearing Loss?

Here are some tips you can use when talking with someone who has a hearing problem:

- Face the person and talk clearly.
- Speak at a reasonable speed; do not hide your mouth, eat, or chew gum.
- Stand in good lighting and reduce background noises.
- Use facial expressions or gestures to give useful clues.
- Repeat yourself if necessary, using different words.
- Include the hearing-impaired person when talking. Talk with the person, not about the person, when you are with others. This helps keep the hearing-impaired person from feeling alone and excluded.
- Be patient; stay positive and relaxed.
- Ask how you can help.

What Can I Do if I Have Trouble Hearing?

- Let people know that you have trouble hearing.
- Ask people to face you, and to speak more slowly and clearly; also ask them to speak without shouting.
- Pay attention to what is being said and to facial expressions or gestures.
- Let the person talking know if you do not understand.
- Ask people to reword a sentence and try again.

What Devices or Treatments Can Help?

What will help you depends on your hearing problem. Some common solutions include:

- **Hearing aids.** These are small devices you wear in or behind your ear. Hearing aids can help some kinds of hearing loss by making sounds louder. However, they sometimes pick up background noises - for example, traffic noise in the street or people talking at other tables in a crowded restaurant. This can affect how well you hear in certain situations. Before buying a hearing aid, check to find out if your insurance will cover the cost.

  There are many kinds of hearing aids. An audiologist can help fit you with the hearing aid that will work best for you. You can ask the audiologist about having a trial period to try out a few different aids.

  Remember, when you buy a hearing aid, you are buying a product and a service. Find a hearing aid dealer (called a dispenser) who has the patience and skill to help you during the month or so it takes to get used to the new hearing aid.

  You may need to have several fittings of your hearing aid, and you will need to get directions on how to use it. Hearing aids use batteries, which you will need to change on a regular basis. They also may need repairs from time to time. Buy a hearing aid that has only the features you need.

- **Assistive/Adaptive Devices.** There are many products that can help you live well with less-than-perfect hearing. The list below includes some examples of the many choices:

- **Telephone amplifying devices** range from a special type of telephone receiver that makes sounds louder to special phones that work with hearing aids.
- **TV and radio listening systems** can be used with or without hearing aids. You do not have to turn the volume up high.
- **Assistive listening devices** are available in some public places such as auditoriums, movie theaters, churches, synagogues, and meeting places.
- **Alerts** such as doorbells, smoke detectors, and alarm clocks can give you a signal that you can see or a vibration that you can feel. For example, a flashing light could let you know someone is at the door or that the phone is ringing.

- **Cochlear implants.** If your deafness is severe, a doctor may suggest cochlear implants. In this surgery, the doctor puts a small electronic device under the skin behind the ear. The device sends the message past the non-working part of the inner ear and on to the brain. This process helps some people hear. These implants are not helpful for all types of deafness or hearing loss.

For More Information

There are many things you can do about hearing loss. The first step is to check with your doctor. You also can get more information from the following groups:

National Institute on Deafness and Other Communication Disorders (NIDCD)
NIDCD Information Clearinghouse
National Institutes of Health
31 Center Drive, MSC 2320
Bethesda, MD 20892-2320
Phone: 1-800-241-1044 (toll-free)
TTY: 1-800-241-1055
www.nidcd.nih.gov

American Academy of Otolaryngology-Head and Neck Surgery, Inc. (AAO-HNS)
1 Prince Street
Alexandria, VA 22314-3357
Phone: 703-836-4444
TTY: 703-519-1585
www.entnet.org

American Speech-Language-Hearing Association (ASHA)
10801 Rockville Pike
Rockville, MD 20852
Phone: 1-800-638-8255 (toll-free/voice/TTY)
www.asha.org

American Tinnitus Association (ATA)
P.O. Box 5
Portland, OR 97207-0005
Phone: 1-800-634-8978 (toll-free)
www.ata.org

Self Help for Hard of Hearing People, Inc. (SHHH)
7910 Woodmont Avenue
Suite 1200
Bethesda, MD 20814
Phone: 301-657-2248
TTY: 301-657-2249
www.shhh.org

Laurent Clerc National Deaf Education Center
Gallaudet University
800 Florida Avenue, NE
Washington, DC 20002-3695
Phone: 202-651-5000 (voice and TTY)

For more information on health and aging, contact:

National Institute on Aging Information Center
P.O. Box 8057
Gaithersburg, MD 20898-8057
1-800-222-2225
1-800-222-4225 (TTY)

To order publications (in English or Spanish) or sign up for e-mail alerts, visit www.niapublications.org.

The National Institute on Aging website is www.nia.nih.gov.

Visit NIHSeniorHealth.gov (www.nihseniorhealth.gov), a senior-friendly website from the National Institute on Aging and the National Library of Medicine. The simple-to-use website features popular health topics for older adults. It has large type and a "talking" function that reads the text out loud.

National Institute on Aging
U. S. Department of Health and Human Services
National Institutes of Health
September 2002 (Reprinted August 2005)

Reprinted from NIA-National Institute on Aging
www.nia.nih.gov

High Blood Pressure

You can have high blood pressure, or *hypertension,* and still feel just fine. That's because high blood pressure does not cause signs of illness that you can see or feel. But, high blood pressure, sometimes called "the silent killer," is a major health problem. If high blood pressure isn't controlled with lifestyle changes and medicine, it can lead to stroke, heart disease, eye problems, or kidney failure.

What Is Blood Pressure?

Blood pressure is the force of blood pushing against the walls of arteries. When the doctor measures your blood pressure the results are given in two numbers. The first number, called *systolic pressure,* measures the pressure when your heart beats. The second number, called *diastolic pressure,* measures the pressure while your heart relaxes between beats. Normal blood pressure is a systolic pressure of less than 120 and a diastolic pressure of less than 80.

Do You Have High Blood Pressure?

One reason to have regular visits to the doctor is to have your blood pressure checked. The doctor will say your blood pressure is high when it measures 140/90 or higher at two or more checkups. He or she may ask you to check your blood pressure at home at different times of the day. If the pressure stays high, the doctor may suggest medicine, changes in your diet, and exercise.

What Do The Numbers Mean?		
	Systolic	**Diastolic**
Normal Blood Pressure	Less than 120	Less than 80
High Blood Pressure	140 or more	90 or more
Prehypertension	Between 120-139	Between 80-89
Isolated Systolic Hypertension	140 or more	Less than 90

You could have *prehypertension* if your blood pressure is only slightly higher than normal - for example, the first number (systolic) is between 120 and 139 or the second number (diastolic) is between 80 and 89. Prehypertension can put you at risk for developing high blood pressure. Your doctor will probably want you to make changes in your day-to-day habits to try and lower your blood pressure.

What If Just the First Number Is High?

For older people, the first number (systolic) often is 140 or greater, but the second number (diastolic) is less than 90. This problem is called isolated systolic hypertension. Isolated systolic hypertension is the most common form of high blood pressure in older people, and it can lead to serious health problems. It is treated in the same way as regular high blood pressure. If your systolic pressure is 140 or higher, ask your doctor how you can lower it.

Some Risks You Can't Change

Anyone can get high blood pressure. But some people have a greater chance of having it because of things they can't change. These are:

- **Age.** The chance of having high blood pressure increases as you get older.
- **Gender.** Before age 55, men have a greater chance of having high blood pressure. Women are more likely to have high blood pressure after menopause.
- **Family history.** High blood pressure tends to run in some families.
- **Race.** African-Americans are at increased risk for high blood pressure.

How Can I Control My Blood Pressure?

More than half of Americans over age 60 and about three-fourths of those 70 years of age and older have high blood pressure. The good news is blood pressure can be controlled in most people. To start, there are many lifestyle changes you can make to lower your risk of high blood pressure, including:

- **Keep a healthy weight.** Being overweight adds to your risk of high blood pressure. Ask your doctor if you need to lose weight.

- **Exercise every day.** Moderate exercise can lower your risk of high blood pressure. Try to exercise at least 30 minutes a day most days of the week. Check with your doctor before starting an exercise plan if you have a long-term health problem or are over 50 and have been inactive.
- **Eat a healthy diet.** A diet rich in fruits, vegetables, whole grains, and low-fat dairy products may help to lower blood pressure. Ask your doctor about following a healthy diet.
- **Cut down on salt.** Many Americans eat more salt (sodium) than they need. Most of the salt comes from processed food (for example, soup and baked goods). A low-salt diet might help lower your blood pressure. Talk with your doctor about eating less salt.
- **Drink less alcohol.** Drinking alcohol can affect your blood pressure. Most men shouldn't have more than two drinks a day; most women should not drink more than one drink a day.
- **Don't smoke.** Smoking increases your risk for high blood pressure and heart disease. If you smoke, quit.
- **Manage stress.** People react to stress in different ways. For some, stress can cause their blood pressure to go up. Talk to your doctor about how you can lower stress. Exercise and getting a good night's sleep can help.

If these lifestyle changes don't control your high blood pressure, your doctor will prescribe medicine. You may try several kinds before finding the one that works best for you. Medicine can control your blood pressure, but it can't cure it. You may need to take medicine for the rest of your life. You and your doctor can plan together how to manage your blood pressure.

High Blood Pressure Facts

High blood pressure is serious because it can lead to major health problems. If you have high blood pressure, remember:

- High blood pressure may not make you feel sick, but it is serious. See a doctor to treat it.
- You can lower your blood pressure by changing your day-to-day habits and by taking medicine, if needed.
- If you take high blood pressure medicine, making some lifestyle changes may help lower the dose you need.
- If you are already taking blood pressure medicine and your blood pressure is less than 120/80, that's good. It means medicine and lifestyles changes are working. If another doctor asks if you have high blood pressure, the answer is, "Yes, but it is being treated."
- Tell your doctor about all the drugs you take. Don't forget to mention over-the-counter drugs, vitamins, and dietary supplements. They may affect your blood pressure. They also can change how well your blood pressure medicine works.
- Blood pressure pills should be taken at the same time each day. For example, take your medicine in the morning with breakfast or in the evening after brushing your teeth. If you miss a dose, do not double the dose the next day.
- Know what your blood pressure should be. Don't take more of your blood pressure medicine than your doctor prescribes. Very low blood pressure is not good, either.
- Do not stop taking your high blood pressure medicine unless your doctor tells you to stop. Do not skip a day or take half a pill. Remember to refill your medicine before you run out of pills.
- Taking your blood pressure at home:
  - There are many blood pressure home monitors for sale. Ask your doctor, nurse, or pharmacist to see what monitor you need and show you how to use it
  - Avoid smoking, exercise, and caffeine 30 minutes before taking your blood pressure.
  - Make sure you are sitting with your feet on the floor and your back is against something.
  - Relax quietly for 5 minutes before checking your blood pressure.
  - Keep a list of your blood pressure numbers to share with your doctor, physician's assistant, or nurse. Take your home monitor to the doctor's office to make sure your monitor is working right.

For More Information

Here are some helpful Federal and non-Federal resources.

National Heart, Lung, and Blood Institute
Health Information Center
P.O. Box 30105
Bethesda, MD 20824-0105
301-592-8573
240-629-3255 (TTY)
www.nhlbi.nih.gov

National Library of Medicine
MedlinePlus
Search for: "High Blood Pressure"
www.medlineplus.gov

American Heart Association
7272 Greenville Avenue
Dallas, TX 75231
800-242-8721 (toll-free)
www.americanheart.org

For more information on health and aging, contact:

National Institute on Aging Information Center
P.O. Box 8057
Gaithersburg, MD 20898-8057
800-222-2225 (toll-free)
800-222-4225 (TTY/toll-free)
www.nia.nih.gov
www.nia.nih.gov/Espanol

To sign up for regular email alerts about new publications and other information from the NIA, go to www.nia.nih.gov/HealthInformation.

Visit NIHSeniorHealth (www.nihseniorhealth.gov), a senior-friendly website from the National Institute on Aging and the National Library of Medicine. This website has health information for older adults. Special features make it simple to use. For example, you can click on a button to have the text read out loud or to make the type larger.

National Institute on Aging
U.S. Department of Health and Human Services
Public Health Service
National Institutes of Health
September 2007

Reprinted from NIA-National Institute on Aging
www.nia.nih.gov

HIV, AIDS, and Older People

Grace was dating again. George, a close family friend she had known for a long time, was starting to stay overnight more and more often. Because she was past childbearing age, Grace didn't think about using condoms. And because she had known George for so long, she didn't think to ask him about his sexual history. So, Grace was shocked when she tested positive for HIV.

What Is HIV? What Is AIDS?

Like most people, you probably have heard a lot about HIV and AIDS. You may have thought that these diseases weren't your problem and that only younger people have to worry about them. But anyone at any age can get HIV/AIDS.

HIV (short for human immunodeficiency virus) is a virus that damages the immune system-the system your body uses to fight off diseases. HIV infection leads to a much more serious disease called AIDS (acquired immunodeficiency syndrome). When the HIV infection gets in your body, your immune system can weaken. This puts you in danger of getting other life-threatening diseases, infections, and cancers. When that happens, you have AIDS. AIDS is the last stage of HIV infection. If you think you may have HIV, it is very important to get tested. Today there are drugs that can help your body keep the HIV in check and fight against AIDS.

What Are the Symptoms of HIV/AIDS?

Many people have no symptoms when they first become infected with HIV. It can take as little as a few weeks for minor, flu-like symptoms to show up, or more than 10 years for more serious symptoms to appear. Signs of HIV include headache, cough, diarrhea, swollen glands, lack of energy, loss of appetite and weight loss, fevers and sweats, repeated yeast infections, skin rashes, pelvic and abdominal cramps, sores in the mouth or on certain parts of the body, or short-term memory loss.

Getting Tested for HIV/AIDS

- It can take as long as 3 to 6 months after the infection for the virus to show up in your blood.
- Your health care provider can test your blood for HIV/AIDS. If you don't have a health care provider, check your local phone book for the phone number of a hospital or health center where you can get a list of test sites.
- Many health care providers who test for HIV also can provide counseling.
- In most states the tests are private, and you can choose to take the test without giving your name.

You can now also test your blood at home. The "Home Access Express HIV-1 Test System" is made by the Home Access Health Corporation. You can buy it at the drug store. It is the only HIV home test system approved by the Food and Drug Administration (FDA) and legally sold in the United States. Other HIV home test systems and kits you might see on the Internet or in magazines or newspapers have not been approved by FDA and may not always give correct results.

How Do People Get HIV and AIDS?

Anyone, at any age, can get HIV and AIDS. HIV usually comes from having unprotected sex or sharing needles with an infected person, or through contact with HIV-infected blood. No matter your age, you may be at risk if:

- *You are sexually active and do not use a latex or polyurethane condom.* You can get HIV/AIDS from having sex with someone who has HIV. The virus passes from the infected person to his or her partner in blood, semen, and vaginal fluid. During sex, HIV can get into your body through any opening, such as a tear or cut in the lining of the vagina, vulva, penis, rectum, or mouth. Latex condoms can help prevent an infected person from transferring the HIV virus to you. (Natural condoms do not protect against HIV/AIDS as well as the latex and polyurethane types.)

- *You do not know your partner's drug and sexual history.* What you don't know can hurt you. Even though it may be hard to do, it's very important to ask your partner about his or her sexual history and drug use. Here are some questions to ask: Has your partner been tested for HIV/AIDS? Has he or she had a number of different sex partners? Has your partner ever had unprotected sex with someone who has shared needles? Has he or she injected drugs or shared needles with someone else? Drug users are not the only people who might share needles. For example, people with diabetes who inject insulin or draw blood to test glucose levels might share needles.

- *You have had a blood transfusion or operation in a developing country at any time.*
- *You had a blood transfusion in the United States between 1978 and 1985.*

Is HIV/AIDS Different in Older People?

A growing number of older people now have HIV/AIDS. About 19 percent of all people with HIV/AIDS in this country are age 50 and older. This is because doctors are finding HIV more often than ever before in older people, and because improved treatments are helping people with the disease live longer.

But there may even be many more cases than we know about. Why? One reason may be that doctors do not always test older people for HIV/AIDS and so may miss some cases during routine check-ups. Another may be that older people often mistake signs of HIV/AIDS for the aches and pains of normal aging, so they are less likely than younger people to get tested for the disease. Also, they may be ashamed or afraid of being tested. People age 50 and older may have the virus for years before being tested. By the time they are diagnosed with HIV/AIDS, the virus may be in the late stages.

The number of HIV/AIDS cases among older people is growing every year because:

- Older Americans know less about HIV/AIDS than younger people. They do not always know how it spreads or the importance of using condoms, not sharing needles, getting tested for HIV, and talking about it with their doctor.
- Health care workers and educators often do not talk with middle-age and older people about HIV/AIDS prevention.
- Older people are less likely than younger people to talk about their sex lives or drug use with their doctors.
- Doctors may not ask older patients about their sex lives or drug use, or talk to them about risky behaviors.

Facts About HIV/AIDS

You may have read or heard things that are not true about how you get HIV/AIDS. Here are the FACTS:

- You cannot get HIV through casual contact such as shaking hands or hugging a person with HIV/AIDS.
- You cannot get HIV from using a public telephone, drinking fountain, restroom, swimming pool, Jacuzzi, or hot tub.
- You cannot get HIV from sharing a drink.
- You cannot get HIV from being coughed or sneezed on by a person with HIV/AIDS.
- You cannot get HIV from giving blood.
- You cannot get HIV from a mosquito bite.

Anyone facing a serious disease like HIV/AIDS may become very depressed. This is a special problem for older people, who may have no strong network of friends or family who can help. At the same time, they also may be coping with other diseases common to aging such as high blood pressure, diabetes, or heart problems. As the HIV/AIDS gets worse, many will need help getting around and caring for themselves. Older people with HIV/AIDS need support and understanding from their doctors, family, and friends.

HIV/AIDS can affect older people in yet another way. Many younger people who are infected turn to their parents and grandparents for financial support and nursing care. Older people who are not themselves infected by the virus may find they have to care for their own children with HIV/AIDS and then sometimes for their orphaned or HIV-infected grandchildren. Taking care of others can be mentally, physically, and financially draining. This is especially true for older caregivers. The problem becomes even worse when older caregivers have AIDS or other serious health problems. Remember, it is important to get tested for HIV/AIDS early. Early treatment increases the chances of living longer.

HIV/AIDS in People of Color and Women

The number of HIV/AIDS cases is rising in people of color across the country. About half of all people with HIV/AIDS are African American or Hispanic.

The number of cases of HIV/AIDS for women has also been growing over the past few years. The rise in the number of cases in women of color age 50 and older has been especially steep. Most got the virus from sex with infected partners. Many others got HIV through shared needles. Because women may live longer than men, and because of the rising divorce rate, many widowed, divorced, and separated women are dating these days. Like older men, many older women may be at risk because they do not know how HIV/AIDS is spread. Women who no longer worry about getting pregnant may be less likely to use a condom and to practice safe sex. Also, vaginal dryness and thinning often occurs as women age; when that happens, sexual activity can lead to small cuts and tears that raise the risk for HIV/AIDS.

Treatment and Prevention

There is no cure for HIV/AIDS. But if you become infected, there are drugs that help keep the HIV virus in check and slow the spread of HIV in the body. Doctors are now using a combination of drugs called HAART *(highly active antiretroviral therapy)* to treat HIV/AIDS. Although it is not a cure, HAART is greatly reducing the number of deaths from AIDS in this country.

Prevention. Remember, there are things you can do to keep from getting HIV/AIDS. Practice the steps below to lower your risk:

- If you are having sex, make sure your partner has been tested and is free of HIV. Use male or female condoms (latex or polyurethane) during sexual intercourse.
- Do not share needles or any other equipment used to inject drugs.
- Get tested if you or your partner had a blood transfusion between 1978 and 1985.
- Get tested if you or your partner has had an operation or blood transfusion in a developing country at any time.

Resources

Health agencies in most cities offer HIV testing. The following national organizations have information about HIV/AIDS.

Centers for Disease Control and Prevention (CDC)
National AIDS Hotline
1-800-342-AIDS
(operates 24 hours a day, 7 days a week)
1-800-344-7432 for Spanish
1-800-243-7889 (TTY)
www.cdc.gov

CDC National Prevention Information Network
P. O. Box 6003
Rockville, Maryland 20849-6003
1-800-458-5231
1-800-243-7012 (TTY)
www.cdcnpin.org/scripts/index.asp

National Institute of Allergy and Infectious Diseases (NIAID)
Office of Communications and Public Liaison
6610 Rockledge Drive, MSC 6612
Bethesda, MD 20892-6612
301-496-5717
www.niaid.nih.gov

AIDSinfo
P.O. Box 6303
Rockville, MD 20849-6303
1-800-HIV-0440 (1-800-448-0440)
Monday to Friday, 12:00 p.m. to 5:00 p.m. Eastern Time
1-888-480-3739 (TTY/TDD)
www.aidsinfo.nih.gov

National Association on HIV Over Fifty
23 Miner Street
Boston, MA 02215-3318
www.hivoverfifty.org

Senior Action in a Gay Environment (SAGE)
305 7th Avenue
16th Floor
New York, NY 10001
212-741-2247
www.sageusa.org

For more information on health and aging, contact:

National Institute on Aging Information Center
P.O. Box 8057
Gaithersburg, MD 20898-8057
1-800-222-2225
1-800-222-4225 (TTY)

To order publications (in English or Spanish) online, visit www.nia.nih.gov/HealthInformation/Publications

Visit NIHSeniorHealth.gov (www.nihseniorhealth.gov), a senior-friendly website from the National Institute on Aging and the National Library of Medicine. This website features popular health topics for older adults. It is simple to use, has large type, and a 'talking' function that reads text aloud.

National Institute on Aging
U. S. Department of Health and Human Services
Public Health Service
National Institutes of Health
June 2004

Reprinted from NIA-National Institute on Aging
www.nia.nih.gov

Mourning the Death of a Spouse

When your spouse dies, your world changes. You are in mourning-feeling grief and sorrow at the loss. You may feel numb, shocked, and fearful. You may feel guilty for being the one who is still alive. If your spouse died in a nursing home, you may wish that you had been able to care for him or her at home. At some point, you may even feel angry at your spouse for leaving you. All these feelings are normal. There are no rules about how you should feel. There is no right or wrong way to mourn.

When you grieve, you can feel both physical and emotional pain. People who are grieving often cry easily and can have:

- trouble sleeping
- little interest in food
- problems with concentration
- a hard time making decisions

If you are grieving, in addition to dealing with feelings of loss, you may also need to put your own life back together. This can be hard work. During this time, you may be surprised by some of your feelings, but they are a part of mourning. Some people may feel better sooner than they expect. Others may take longer. As time passes, you may still miss your spouse, but for most people the intense pain will lessen. There will be good and bad days. You will know that you are feeling better when the good days begin to outnumber the bad.

For some people, mourning can go on so long that it becomes unhealthy. This can be a sign of serious depression and anxiety. If your sadness stays with you and keeps you from carrying on with your day-to-day life, talk to your doctor.

What Can You Do?

At the start of your grieving, you may find that taking care of details and keeping busy helps. For a while, family and friends may be around. But there comes a time when you will have to face your new life alone.

Here are some ideas to keep in mind:

- *Take care of yourself.* Grief can be hard on your health. Try to eat right, exercise, and get enough sleep. Avoid bad habits such as drinking too much alcohol or smoking that can put your health at risk. Be sure to take your medicines as your doctor ordered. Remember to see the doctor for your usual visits.

- *Talk to caring friends.* Let your family and friends know when you want to talk about your husband or wife. It may help to be with people who let you say what you're feeling.

- *Join a grief support group.* Sometimes it helps to talk to people who are also grieving. Check with hospitals, religious groups, and local government agencies to find out about support groups.

- *Try not to make any major changes right away.* It's a good idea to wait for a while before making big decisions like moving or changing jobs.

- *See your doctor.* If you're having trouble taking care of your everyday activities, like getting dressed or fixing meals, talk to your doctor.

- *Don't think you have to handle your grief alone.* Sometimes short-term talk therapy with a counselor can help.

- *Remember your children are grieving, too.* You may find that your relationship with your children has changed. It will take time for the whole family to adjust to life without your spouse.

- *Remember-mourning takes time.* It's common to have rollercoaster emotions for a while.

Do Men and Women Feel the Same Way?

Andrew, age 73, felt like the wind had been knocked out of him when his wife died. He began sleeping all day and staying up at night watching TV. Meals were mostly snacks like cookies and chips. He knew it wasn't healthy, but he didn't know what to do. Across town, Alice woke up in a panic. It had been 5 weeks since Jeff, her husband of 41 years, died. She cared for him during his long illness. How was she going to cope with the loneliness?

Men and women share many of the same feelings when their spouse dies. Both may deal with the pain of loss and both may worry about the future. But because many couples divide their household chores, there can also be differences. For example, one person may pay bills, clean house, and handle car repairs. The other person may cook meals, file income taxes, and mow the lawn. This splitting up of jobs works well until there is one person who has to do it all.

Some men are at a loss when it comes to doing household chores. But these jobs can be learned over time. Men are sometimes surprised when they're widowed. For those men who are both widowed and retired, grief may cause depression. If you or any family member is having this problem, see your doctor. Treatment can help.

Facing the future without a husband can be scary for some women. Many have never lived alone. Some women will worry about money. Women who have never paid bills or balanced a checkbook will need to learn about managing money.

Women may also worryabout feeling safe. It's a good idea to make sure there are working locks on the doors and windows. If you need help, ask your family or friends. You'll need to get in the habit of taking care of your house and car. It takes time, but it can be done.

Taking Charge of Your Life

After years of being part of a couple, it can be upsetting to be alone. Many people find it helps to have things to do every day. Write down your weekly plans. You might:

- Take a walk with a friend.
- Go to the library to check out books.
- Volunteer at a local school as a tutor or playground aide.
- Join a community exercise class or a senior swim group.
- Be part of a chorus.
- Meet with old friends.
- Sign up for bingo or bridge at a nearby recreation center.
- Think about a part-time job.
- Join a bowling league or a sewing group.
- Offer to watch your grandchildren or a neighbor's child.
- Consider adopting a pet.

Some widowed people lose interest in cooking and eating. It may help to have a noon meal at a senior center, cafeteria, or with friends. When home, some people find that turning on a radio or TV during meals helps with loneliness. For information on nutrition and cooking for one, see the *General Nutrition Resource List for Seniors* at www.nal.usda.gov/fnic/pubs/olderadults.htm or look for helpful books at your local library or bookstore.

Is There More To Do?

When you feel stronger, you may need to think about:

- Writing a new will.
- Looking into a durable power of attorney for legal matters and a power of attorney for health care in case you are unable to make your own medical decisions.
- Putting any joint assets (such as a house or car) in your name.
- Checking on your health insurance as well as your current life, car, and homeowner's insurance.
- Signing up for Medicare by your 65th birthday.
- Paying state and federal taxes.

When you are ready, go through your husband's or wife's clothes and other personal items. It may be hard to give away these belongings. Instead of parting with everything at once, you might make three piles: one to keep, one to give away, and one "not sure." Ask your children to help. Think about setting aside items like clothing, a watch, favorite book, or picture to give to your children or grandchildren as personal reminders of your spouse.

What About Going Out?

Lillian felt lost. Widowed at age 71, she kept seeing the same couples that she and her husband, Ray, had always liked. But without Ray she felt out of place. How could she enjoy going out when she felt like a "fifth-wheel"?

Having a social life can be hard. It may be scary to think about going to parties alone. It can be hard to think about coming home alone. It may be even harder to think about dating. Some people miss the feeling of closeness and affection that marriage brings.

Here are some things to remember:

- Go slowly. There's no rush.
- It's okay to make the first move when it comes to planning things to do.
- Try group activities. Invite friends for a pot luck dinner or go to a senior center.
- With married friends, think about informal outings like walks or movies rather then "couples" events that remind you of the past.
- Find an activity you like. You may have fun and meet people who like to do the same thing.
- Remember that friendship can come in many forms.

Don't Forget

Take care of yourself. Get help from your family or professionals if you need it. Be open to new experiences. Don't feel guilty if you laugh at a joke or enjoy a visit with a friend. You are adjusting to life without your spouse.

For More Information

Centers for Medicare & Medicaid Services
7500 Security Boulevard
Baltimore, MD 21244
800-633-4227 (toll-free)
877-486-2048 (TTY/toll-free)
www.medicare.gov

Eldercare Locator
800-677-1116 (toll-free)
www.eldercare.gov

USA.gov
www.usa.gov/Topics/Seniors.shtml

Social Security Administration
6401 Security Boulevard
Baltimore, MD 21235
800-772-1213 (toll-free)
800-325-0778 (TTY/toll-free)
www.socialsecurity.gov

US Department of Agriculture
Food and Nutrition Information Center
10301 Baltimore Avenue, Room 105
301-504-5719
301-504-6856 (TTY)
www.nal.usda.gov

For more information on health and aging, including nutrition, exercise, and sleep, contact:

National Institute on Aging
Information Center
P.O. Box 8057
Gaithersburg, MD 20898-8057
800-222-2225 (toll-free)
800-222-4225 (TTY/toll-free)
www.nia.nih.gov

Visit www.nia.nih.gov/HealthInformation to order publications (in English or Spanish) or sign up for regular email alerts.

Visit NIHSeniorHealth.gov (www.nihseniorhealth.gov), a senior-friendly website from the National Institute on Aging and the National Library of Medicine. This website has health information for older adults. There are also special features that make it simple to use. For example, you can click on a button to have the text read out loud or to make the type larger.

National Institute on Aging
U.S. Department of Health and Human Services
Public Health Service
National Institutes of Health
January 2007

Reprinted from NIA-National Institute on Aging
www.nia.nih.gov

Hiring a Home Care Provider

Most people prefer to be cared for in their home rather than a nursing home, but finding a home care provider for you or a loved one can be daunting. The following are some things to keep in mind when looking for a caregiver.

Level of care. The first thing to consider is what level of care is needed. This will determine what type of caregiver to hire and how much the caregiver will cost. Home care providers can range from someone who offers companionship to someone who provides medical services. You can also hire a geriatric care manager to evaluate your or your loved one's needs and review the available options. To find a geriatric care manager in your area, visit the Web site of the National Association of Professional Geriatric Care Managers at http://www.findacaremanager.org.

Write a job description. Once you have established what type of caregiver you need, you can write a job description. The description should list all the services you need a caregiver to provide, such as bathing, dressing, eating, bill paying, transportation, household chores, or physical therapy.

Decide whether to use an agency or hire independently. There are several advantages to using an agency to find a caregiver. An agency screens caregivers for you, takes care of paperwork, and provides backup workers and insurance, among other things. The disadvantages are that you may not get to choose your caregiver or have the same caregiver every day. In addition, the agency may limit what the caregiver can do for you. If you decide not to go through an agency, you will need to carefully screen caregivers. You will also need to make sure you pay employment taxes and unemployment insurance.

Locate a caregiver. Contact your local agency on aging to find information on home health care agencies in your area. You can call the Eldercare Locator toll-free at 1-800-677-1116 or go to http://www.eldercare.gov to find the area agency on aging near you. There are thousands of private home care agencies around the nation. If you are hiring a caregiver on your own, other resources for finding help include getting a referral from a friend, looking in the Yellow Pages, or advertising for help at a senior center or in the newspaper.

Consider adult day care. Adult day care facilities provide care and companionship outside of the home and give seniors the chance to interact with peers. Facilities can provide social or therapeutic activities. You can pair adult day care with a home caregiver to allow you or your loved one a few hours outside the house.

Get financial help. The cost of home health care will vary depending on the type of help that is needed - the more skilled the help, the more expensive the cost. Personal-care assistants may earn between $7.50 and $15 an hour while more skilled aides may make $16 to $25 an hour or more. Medicare and Medicaid may provide some coverage of the medical portion of home health care. To find out more about what Medicare pays for, elder abuse hotline if you suspect abuse.

For more information about finding a home care provider, visit the National Association for Home Care & Hospice (NAHC).

© 2007 ElderLawNet, Inc., www.elderlawanswers.com. Reprinted with permission.

10 Factors to Consider When Choosing a Medicare Drug Plan

Choosing a Medicare drug plan (Medicare Part D) requires evaluating more factors than just the cost of the monthly premium. In fact, a beneficiary may conclude that the plan with the cheapest monthly premium may not be the best value. Moreover, the experience with Medicare Advantage (private Medicare managed care plans) suggests that premiums will change in future years as plan sponsors abandon their least profitable plans.

The following checklist of factors to consider is based on a similar checklist developed by the Center for Medicare Advocacy.

1. Formulary: The "formulary" is the roster of drugs the plan covers and will pay for. Does the plan include the particular prescription drugs that the beneficiary needs - or anticipates needing - and how much will they cost? Of course, a beneficiary cannot predict drug needs for unanticipated medical conditions. Although drug plans may discontinue coverage or increase the cost of any particular drug, they must continue to cover participants currently taking a discontinued drug until the end of the year.

2. Exceptions process: A plan may grant an "exception" to its formulary if a beneficiary is using or is prescribed a medically necessary drug that is not on the plan's formulary. What is the plan's process for granting these exceptions?

3. Transition process: What are the plan's rules for temporarily providing drugs that are not covered by the plan during a "transition" period? How long is this period?

4. Utilization management tools: To what extent does the plan attempt to steer beneficiaries to lower-cost drugs? For example, does the plan require that a beneficiary try certain medications before covering a costlier drug prescribed by the beneficiary's doctor? Does the plan charge different co-payment amounts for generic and brand-name drugs or for different drugs? What are the cost-sharing requirements for the beneficiary's current drugs?

5. Quantity limitations: Is there a limit on the number of prescriptions a beneficiary may receive in a month? Are there limits on the number of pills or other dosages available in a single prescription?

6. Deductible: Will the annual deductible be the standard $250 or lower? Does the total cost of the drugs that the beneficiary currently takes at least meet the deductible plus a year's worth of premium payments? (AARP has created a calculator for beneficiaries to determine potential savings under the drug benefit.)

7. Pharmacy: Will the beneficiary be able to buy drugs covered under the plan at his or her customary pharmacy? If the beneficiary is in a long-term care facility, is the facility's pharmacy included in the plan's network? Does the plan have preferred and non-preferred pharmacies within its network and does it require beneficiaries to pay more for using a non-preferred pharmacy?

8. Mail order option: Are beneficiaries allowed or required to use mail-order? Is there a price difference for mail-order purchases?

9. Plan sponsor: Is the plan sponsor a known, reliable entity?

10. Coordination with state program: How do the plan's benefits coordinate with any State Pharmaceutical Assistance Program?

© 2007 ElderLawNet, Inc., www.elderlawanswers.com. Reprinted with permission.

National Organizations & Federal Agencies/General

This chapter includes main offices of national organizations and Federal agencies that provide general information useful for all older Americans. These listings cover such issues as retirement, housing, health insurance, finances, daycare, transportation and advocacy. This chapter also includes listings for associations of various health professionals that older Americans depend on. A number of Canadian associations appear at the end of the section.

General

1 Administration on Aging (AoA)
US Department of Health & Human Services
One Massachusetts Ave
Suites 4100 + 5100
Washington, DC 20201
202-619-0724
800-677-1116
Fax: 202-357-3555
e-mail: aoainfo@aoa.hhs.gov
http://www.aoa.gov

Josefina G Carbonell, Assistant Secretary for Aging

The AoA is the Federal agency dedicated to policy development, planning and the delivery of supportive home and community-based services to older persons and their caregivers.

2 Administration on Aging: Office of Field Operations
One Massachusetts Ave
Suite 4100 + 5100
Washington, DC 20201
202-401-4634
http://SC
TDD 022-520-08

Josefina G Carbonell, Assistant Secretary for Aging

Supervises the regional offices of the Administration on Aging. Assures that the Older American Act requirements are carried out.

3 Administration on Aging: Office of Program Development
One Massachusetts Ave
Suite 4100 + 5100
Washington, DC 20201
202-401-4634
800-677-1116
Fax: 202-690-7203
http://www.aoa.gov

Josefina G Carbonell, Assistant Secretary for Aging

4 Administration on Aging: Office of State and Community Programs
One Massachusetts Ave
Suite 4100 + 5100
Washington, DC 20201
202-401-4634
800-677-1116
Fax: 202-690-7203
http://www.aoa.gov

Josefina G Carbonell, Assistant Secretary for Aging

Provides program reporting and analysis.

5 Administration on Developmental Disabilities
US Department of Health & Human Services
200 Independence Avenue SW
Washington, DC 20201
202-619-0257
877-696-6775
Fax: 202-690-7203
http://www.dhhs.gov

Deborah McFadden, Commissioner
Will Wolstein, Deputy Commissioner
Michael O Leavitt, CEO

Works with state governments, local communities and the private sector to promote self sufficiency and protect the rights of individuals with developmental disabilities.

6 Air Force Aid Society
241 18th Street S
Suite 202
Arlington, VA 22202-3409
703-607-3134
800-769-8951
Fax: 703-607-3022
e-mail: dvosburg@afas.org
http://www.afas.org

Lt Gen John Hopper Jr, CEO
John R Buehler, President

Collects and holds funds to relieve the distress of active, retired and selected Reserve Air Force personnel and their dependents, including those of deceased personnel. Operates through local units on all major US Air Force installations worldwide. Education Loan programs are offered to members, to assist in financing postsecondary education; education grants are also offered to dependent children of active duty, retired and deceased Air Force members.

7 America's Health Insurance Plans
601 Pennsylvania Avenue NW
South Building, Suite 500
Washington, DC 20004
202-778-3200
Fax: 202-331-7487
e-mail: ahip@ahip.org
http://www.hiaa.org

Karen Ignagni, President/CEO

HIAA is a trade association representing the interests of the privately-insured health care system. HIAA also provides information and publications on health care issues, including continuation of group health benefits, major medical, and Medicare supplements.

8 American Academy of Ambulatory Care Nursing
East Holy Avenue
PO Box 56
Pitman, NJ 08071
609-256-2350
800-262-6877
Fax: 856-589-7463
e-mail: aaacn@ajj.com
http://www.aaacn.org

Kitty Shulman, MSN, RNC, Director/Treasurer
Charlene Williams MBA, President
Cynthia R Nowicki Hnatiuk EdD, Executive Director

Nurses with administrative/management responsibilities in ambulatory care. To improve the quality and efficiency of ambulatory care through continuing education programs. Program goals are to enhance the leadership and supervisory skills of nurse administrators, and improve members' abilities to influence organizational decisions. Conducts skill building workshops; provides educators to members' groups for in-service educational programs.

9 American Academy of Nurse Practitioners
PO Box 12846
Austin, TX 78711-2846
512-442-4262
Fax: 512-442-6469
e-mail: admin@aanp.org
http://www.aanp.org

Judith Dempster-Gonzalez, Executive Director

Groups (2000) and individuals (1600) promoting high standards of health care delivered by nurse practitioners. Acts as a forum to enhance the identity and continuity of nurse practitioners. Addresses national and state legislative issues that affect members; acts as a resource center on legislative activity. Supports continuing education programs. Encourages research in the field. Compiles statistics.

National Organizations & Federal Agencies/General

10   **American Academy of Nursing**
888 17th St, NW
Suite 800
Washington, DC 20006   202-777-1170
Fax: 202-777-0107
e-mail: info@aannet.org
http://www.aannet.org

Pamela Mitchell PhD, President
Catherine Gilliss, DNSC/RN/FAAC, President-Elect
Diana J Mason, PhD/RN/FAAN, Secretary

Purposes are to: advance new concepts in nursing and health care; identify and explore issues in health, the professions and society that concern nursing; examine interrelationships among the segments within nursing and the interaction among nurses as these affect the development of the nursing profession; identify and propose resolutions to issues and problems confronting nursing and health, including alternative plans for implementation. Sponsors symposia.

1973

11   **American Academy of Oral and Maxillofacial Radiology**
PO Box 1010
Evans, GA 0809-1010   706-721-2607
Fax: 706-721-6276
e-mail: mshrout@mail.mcg.edu
http://www.aaomr.org

Laurie C Carter, DDS/PhD, President
Michael K Shrout DMD, Executive Director

Dentists and other professionals who specialize in oral and maxillofacial radiology in clinical practice, teaching or research. Serves as authoritative body on radiation hygiene and hazards for the American Dental Association.

12   **American Academy of Otolaryngology: Head and Neck Surgery**
1 Prince Street
Alexandria, VA 22314-3357   703-836-4444
Fax: 703-683-5100
e-mail: info@entnet.org
http://www.entnet.org

Jerome C Goldstein, Executive VP
Tom Harlow, Finance Executive

Professional society of medical doctors specializing in otolaryngology (diseases of the ear, nose and throat) and head and neck surgery. Represents otolaryngology in governmental and socio-economic areas and provides high-quality medical education for otolaryngologists. Coordinates Combined Otolaryngological Spring Meetings for ten national otolaryngological societies. Operates job information exchange service and museum.

13   **American Alliance for Health: Physical Education, Recreation and Dance**
1900 Association Drive
Reston, VA 20191-1502   703-476-3400
800-213-7193
Fax: 703-476-9527
e-mail: evp@aahperd.org
http://www.aahperd.org

Michael Davis, CEO

Students and educators in physical education, dance, health, athletics, safety education, recreation and outdoor education. Purpose is to improve its fields of education at all levels through such services as consultation, periodicals and special publications, leadership development, determination of standards and research. Sponsors placement service.

14   **American Assembly for Men in Nursing**
11 Cornell Road
Latham, NY 12110-1402   518-782-9400
800-724-6976
Fax: 518-782-9530
e-mail: aamn@aamn.org
http://www.nysna.org

Linda O'Brien, Presidnet
Karen A Ballard, President-Elect
Lorna Stewart, VP

Registered nurses. Works to: help eliminate prejudice in nursing; interest men in the nursing profession; provide opportunities for the discussion of common problems; encourage education and promote further professional growth; advise and assist in areas of professional inequity; help develop sensitivities to various social needs; promote the principles and practices of positive health care. Acts as a clearinghouse for information on men in nursing. Conducts educational programs.

15   **American Association for Adult and Continuing Education**
10111 Martin Luther King Jr Highway
Suite 200C
Bowie, MD 20720   301-459-6261
Fax: 301-459-6241
e-mail: aaace10@aol.com
http://www.aaace.org

Cle Anderson, Association Manager
Amy Rose, EdD, President
Douglas Smith, EdD, President-Elect

To honor the learner who serves as an exemplar for adult education students throughout the nation. See Continuing Education chapter for specific opportunities by state.

16   **American Association for Respiratory Care**
9425 N Macarthur Boulevard
Suite 100
Irving, TX 75063-4799   972-243-2272
Fax: 972-484-2720
e-mail: info@aarc.org
http://www.aarc.org

Kathy Blackmon, Programs Coordinator
Sam Giordano, Executive Director

Allied health society of respiratory care technicians and therapists employed by hospitals, skilled nursing facilities, home care companies, group practices, educational institutions, and municipal organizations. To encourage, develop, and provide educational programs for persons interested in the profession of respiratory care; and to advance the science of respiratory care.

17   **American Association of Colleges of Nursing**
1 Dupont Circle NW
Suite 530
Washington, DC 20036-1135   202-463-6930
Fax: 202-785-8320
http://www.aacn.nche.edu

Jennifer Ahern, Deputy Executive Director
Geraldine Bednash, Executive Director
Stephen C Shannon, President/CEO

Institutions offering baccalaureate and/or graduate degrees in nursing. Seeks to advance the practice of professional nursing by improving the quality of baccalaureate and graduate programs, promoting research, and developing academic leaders. Works with other professional nursing organizations and organizations in other health professions to evaluate and improve health care. Conducts educational programs on masters and doctoral nursing education and faculty practice; sponsors executive development series for new and aspiring deans of nursing.

18   **American Association of Colleges of Osteopathic Medicine**
5550 Friendship Boulevard
Suite 310
Chevy Chase, MD 20815-7231   301-968-4100
Fax: 301-968-4101
http://www.aacom.org

Stephen C Shannon DO MPH, President/CEO
Anna M Naranjo MA, Executive Assistant
Douglas Wood, Administrator

Osteopathic medical colleges. Operates centralized application service; monitors and works with Congress and other government agencies in the planning of health care programs. Gathers statistics on osteopathic medical students, faculty, and diplomates.

National Organizations & Federal Agencies/General

19 **American Association of Critical Care Nurses**
101 Columbia
Aliso Viejo, CA 92656-4109
949-362-2000
800-899-2226
Fax: 949-362-2020
e-mail: info@aacn.org
http://www.aacn.org
Dorrie Fontaine RN DNSc FAAN, President
Wanda L Johanson RN MN, CEO

Professional critical care nurses. Established to provide continuing education programs for nurses specializing in critical care and to develop standards of nursing care of critically ill patients. Conducts educational programs. Offers certification program for critical care nurses.

20 **American Association of Managed Care Nurses**
4435 Waterfront Drive
Suite 101
Glen Allen, VA 23060-3393
804-747-9698
Fax: 804-747-5316
e-mail: sreed@aamcn.org
http://www.aamcn.org
Michelle Martin, Secretary
LaNita Knocke, RN/BS/CMCN, President-Elect
Sheryl A Riley, RN/OCN/CMCN, President

Managed health care professionals, including registered nurses, licensed practical nurses, and nurse practitioners. Seeks to enhance the abilities of members to meet the future needs of the managed health care profession through education. Provides courses towards certification in managed care nursing.

21 **American Association of Nurse Anesthetists**
222 South Prospect Ave
Park Ridge, IL 60068-4037
847-692-7050
Fax: 847-692-6968
e-mail: info@aana.com
http://www.aana.com
Jeffrey M Beutler CRNA MS, Executive Director
Wanda O Wilson, CRNA/PhD, President
Jackie S Rowles, President-Elect

Certified Registered Nurse Anesthetists (CRNAs) are anesthesia specialists who administer 65% of the 26 million anesthetics given to patients each year in the United States. CRNAs are also the sole anesthesia providers in 65% of rural hospitals in which many of them would have to close their doors without CRNAs anesthesia services. CRNAs have been providing anesthesia care for over 100 years.

22 **American Association of Occupational Health Nurses**
2920 Brandywine Road
Suite 100
Atlanta, GA 30341-5539
770-455-7757
Fax: 770-455-7271
e-mail: ann@aaohn.org
http://www.aaohn.org
Richard Kowalski, President
Kay N Campbell, President-Elect
Ann Cox, Executive Director

Registered professional nurses employed by business and industrial firms; nurse educators, nurse editors, nurse writers, and others interested in occupational health nursing. Promotes and sets standards for the profession. Provides and approves continuing education; maintains governmental affairs program; offers placement service.

23 **American Association of Office Nurses**
109 N Kinderkamack Road
Montvale, NJ 07645-1312
201-391-2600
800-457-7504
Fax: 201-573-8543
e-mail: aaonmail@aaon.org
http://www.aaon.org
Debra L Wagener RN, President

Nurses working primarily in physicians' offices. Promotes improvement of the image of the office nurse. Encourages professional growth and development; facilitates exchange of information among members. Provides continuing education opportunities. Issues publications.

24 **American Association of Physician Specialists**
5550 West Executive Drive
Suite 400
Tampa, FL 33609
813-433-2277
Fax: 813-830-6599
e-mail: ncooper@aapsga.org
http://www.aapsga.org
William J Carbone, CEO
Nadine Simone, Executive Assistant

For osteopathic and allopathic physicians. Provides a clinically recognized mechanism for speciality certification of physicians with advance training.

25 **American Association of Retired Veterinarians**
PO Box 4826
Ithaca, NY 14852-4826
607-533-4114
Walter Martin MD, Contact

Individuals with a degree in veterinary medicine who are retired or considering retiring, and their spouses. Seeks to advance the science and art of veterinary medicine. Encourages friendship among those in the profession. Promotes social and professional lives of retired veterinarians. Attempts to assist future retirees in achievement of their goals in retirement life. Organizes group trips and cruises.
1986

26 **American Association of Retirement Communities**
c/o Center for Economic Development
700 Pelham Road N
Jacksonville, AL 36265-1602
256-782-5700
800-517-3847
Fax: 334-242-4203
e-mail: aarc@.jsu.edu
http://www.the-aarc.org
Chris Elliott, Executive Director
Beth Alexander, President/CEO

Works to promote retirement as an industry. Assists local officials in developing strategies to attract retirees to communities. Provides information about the retirement market and educates local officials on the economic benefits of retirees to a community. Facilitates planning for growth and the increased demand for services which accompany increased retiree population.

27 **American Baptist Homes and Hospitals Association**
PO Box 851
Valley Forge, PA 19482
610-768-2411
800-222-3872
Fax: 610-768-2470
http://www.nationalministries.org
Aundreia Alexander, Director

Retirement facilities (80), nursing homes and hospitals (31), and children's homes and special services (23). Provides special programs and educational events for member institutions. Offers consulting network program for member facilities. Compiles statistics.

28 **American Bar Association**
750 N Lake Shore Drive
Chicago, IL 60611-3152
312-988-5000
800-285-2221
Fax: 312-988-6219
e-mail: info@abanet.org
http://www.abanet.org
Dr Wright Riggins, Executive Director

Attorneys in good standing of the bar of any state. Conducts research and educational projects and activities to: encourage professional improvement; provide public services; improve the administration of civil and criminal justice; increase the availability of legal services to the public. Sponsors Law Day USA. Administers many standing and special committees. See Legal Resources chapter for specific state resources.

National Organizations & Federal Agencies/General

29 **American Benefits Council**
1212 New York Avenue NW
Suite 1250
Washington, DC 20005-3987
202-289-6700
Fax: 202-289-4582
e-mail: info@abcstaff.org
http://www.americanbenefitscouncil.org

James A Kline, President
Lynn D Dudley, VP/Senior Counsel

Represents Fortune 500 companies on federal employee benefits policy issues.
1967

30 **American Board of Internal Medicine**
510 Walnut Street
Suite 1700
Philadelphia, PA 19106-3699
215-446-3500
800-441-2246
Fax: 215-446-3590
e-mail: request@abim.org
http://www.abim.org

Christine K Cassel, MD, President
Kenneth Polonsky, MD, Secretary/Treasurer

Certification board established to determine the qualifications of, administer examinations to, and certify as specialists in internal medicine those doctors meeting its standards of clinical competence. Board members are elected from certified leaders in internal medicine. The board has certified approximately 121,000 internists and 54,000 subspecialist diplomates and issued 10,000 recertification certificates.
1936

31 **American Board of Perianesthesia Nursing Certification**
475 Riverside Drive
6th Fl
New York, NY 10115
800-622-7262
Fax: 212-367-4256
e-mail: abpanc@proexam.org
http://www.cpancapa.org

Ann Beldia Smith, MSN/RN/CAPA, President
Phoebe Conklin, BS/RN/CPAN, President-Elect
Maria Anderson, BSN/RN/CPAN, Secretary/Treasurer

Administers examination to individuals wishing to attain post-anesthesia nursing certification.

32 **American College Health Association**
PO Box 28937
Baltimore, MD 21240-8937
410-859-1500
Fax: 410-859-1510
e-mail: acha@access.digex.net
http://www.acha.org

Doyle E Randol, Executive Director
Lesley Sacher, President

Institutions (930) and individuals (2500). Provides an organization in which institutions of higher education and interested individuals may work together to promote health in its broadest aspects for students and all other members of the college community. Offers continuing education programs for health professionals. Maintains placement listings for physicians and other personnel seeking positions in college health. Compiles statistics. Conducts seminars and training programs. See Continuing Education chapter for specific educational opportunities.

33 **American College of Clinical Pharmacology**
3 Ellinwood Court
New Hartford, NY 13413-1101
315-768-6117
Fax: 315-768-6119
e-mail: accp1ssu@aol.com
http://www.accp1.org

Gilbert J Buckart, President
Susan Ulrich RpH, Executive Director

Strives to be the premier professional society with the size, influence, and diversity of membership consistent with the breadth of the discipline of clinical pharmacology. Provides educational programs and forum for membership, health professionals, students, and the public. Assists in the development and dissemination of basic and clinical knowledge to improve rational drug use and patient outcomes. Serves as a forum for active public debate to influence scientific, regulatory, and public health policy issues. Provides opportunities to influence future directions of the College. Supports and encourages the discovery and development efforts designed to provide improved therapeutic modalities.

34 **American College of Legal Medicine**
1100 E Woodfield Road
Suite 550
Schaumburg, IL 60173-4946
847-969-0283
800-433-9137
Fax: 847-517-7229
e-mail: info@adm.org
http://www.aclm.org

Bruce H Siedberg, President
Wendy J Weiser, Executive Director
Bradley Mettson, Manager

For persons interested in degrees in medicine, dentistry, and law. Promotes and advances the field of legal medicine or medical jurisprudence; arranges for meetings with medical, legal, and professional groups and legislative, judicial, and enforcement bodies interested in any province where law and medicine are contiguous; fosters and encourages centers for study and research in the field of legal medicine and publishes materials pertaining to legal medicine.

35 **American College of Trust and Estate Counsel**
3415 S Sepulveda Boulevard
Suite 330
Los Angeles, CA 90034-6032
310-398-1888
Fax: 310-572-7280
http://www.actec.org

Gerry Vogt, Executive Director

Attorneys specializing in probate law. Sends delegates to American Bar Association's Real Property, Probate, and Trust Law Section; maintains liaison with other organizations involved in probate law. See Legal Resources chapter for specific legal resources by state.

36 **American Correctional Health Services Association**
250 Gatsby Place
Alpharetta, GA 30022
937-586-3708
877-918-1842
Fax: 770-650-5789
e-mail: admin@achsa.org
http://www.corrections.com/achsa

Royanne Schissel RN, President
Clyde E Maxwell Jr, President-Elect
Mary Raines, Secretary

Health care providers, individuals, or organizations interested in improving the quality of correctional health services. Aims are: to promote the provision of health services to incarcerated persons consistent in quality and quantity with acceptable health care practices; to promote and encourage continuing education and provide technical and professional guidance for correctional health care personnel; to establish a forum for the sharing and discussion of correctional health care issues. Conducts conferences on correctional health care management, nursing, mental health, juvenile corrections, dentistry, and related subjects. Maintains placement service.

37 **American Council of Life Insurers**
101 Constitution Ave, NW
Suite 700
Washington, DC 20001
202-624-2000
877-674-4659
http://www.acli.com

Frank Keating, President/CEO

National Organizations & Federal Agencies/General

National trade association that represents the interests of legal reserve life insurance companies in legislative, regulatory and judicial matters at the federal, state and municipal levels of government and at the NAIC. Its member companies hold more than 90 percent of the life insurance force in the United States.

38 **American Counseling Association**
5999 Stevenson Avenue
Alexandria, VA 22304-3304
703-823-9800
800-347-6647
Fax: 800-473-2329
http://www.counseling.org
TDD 703-823-6862

Brian Canfield, President
Richard Yep, Executive Director

Counseling professionals in elementary and secondary schools, higher education, community agencies and organizations, rehabilitation programs, government, industry, business, private practice, career counseling, and mental health counseling. Conducts professional development institutes and provides liability insurance.
1952

39 **American Dental Society of Anesthesiology**
211 E Chicago Avenue
Suite 780
Chicago, IL 60611-6983
312-664-8270
877-255-3742
Fax: 312-642-9713
e-mail: adsahome@mac.com
http://www.adsahome.org

Joseph E Carlisle DMD, President
Karen E Crowley MS/DDS, President-Elect
R Knight Charlton, Executive Director

Members are dentists and physicians interested in the study and advancement of dental anesthesiology.

40 **American Federation of School Administrators**
1101 17th Street NW
Suite 408
Washington, DC 20036-4720
202-986-4209
Fax: 202-986-4211
e-mail: afsa@admin.org
http://www.admin.org

Jill Levy, National President
Diann Woodard, Executive VP
Roch Girard, Secretary

Principals, vice-principals, directors, supervisors, and administrators involved in pedagogical education. Purposes are to: achieve the highest goals in education; maintain and improve standards, benefits, and conditions for personnel without regard to color, race, sex, background, or national origin; obtain job security; protect seniority and merit; cooperate with all responsible organizations in education; promote understanding, participation, and support of the public, communities, and agencies; be alert to resist attacks and campaigns that would create or entrench a spoils system; promote democratic society by supporting full educational opportunities for every child and student in the nation.
1971

41 **American Health Care Association**
1201 L Street NW
Washington, DC 20005-4046
202-842-4444
Fax: 202-842-3860
http://www.ahca.org

Paul R Willging, Executive VP
Dave Kyllo, VP

Federation of state associations of long-term health care facilities. Promotes standards for professionals in long-term health care delivery and quality care for patients and residents in a safe environment. Focuses on issues of availability, quality, affordability, and fair payment. Operates as liaison with governmental agencies, Congress, and professional associations. Compiles statistics.

42 **American Holistic Nurses Association**
323 N San Francisco St
Suite 201
Flagstaff, AZ 86001
928-526-2196
800-278-2462
Fax: 928-526-2752
e-mail: info@ahna.org
http://www.ahna.org

Jeanne Crawford, Executive Director
Carla Mariano, President
Luia M Thornton, President-Elect

Members of the AHNA embrace holistic nursing as a lifestyle and as a profession. Realizing that true healing comes from within, holistic nurses must first heal themselves before they can facilitate the healing of others. Members work in all arenas of nursing to facilitate the integration of holistic nursing principles into nursing education, clinical practice and nursing research.
1981

43 **American Kinesiotherapy Association**
118 College Drive #5142
Hattiesburg, MS 39406
800-296-2582
Fax: 216-615-3355
e-mail: ccbkt@akta.org
http://www.akta.org

Jon Vonderhaar, President

Professional society of kinesiotherapists, and associate and student members with interest in physical and mental rehabilitation and adapted physical education. Kinesiotherapists use kinesiology (the study of human movement) to design and implement therapeutic exercise to meet the rehabilitative needs of persons with disease, injury, and/or physical disorders.) Goal is to promote the profession of kinseotheraphy by working toward public recognition of kinesiotherapy and to pursue and support legislative concerns of the profession. Works to maintain and advance the standard of care through educational opportunities.g
1946

44 **American Licensed Practical Nurses Association**
1090 Vermont Avenue NW
Suite 1200
Washington, DC 20005-4954
202-289-6790
Fax: 202-682-0168

Paul M Tendler, Contact
Felecia Jones, Executive VP

Licensed practical nurses. Promotes the practical nursing profession; lobbies and maintains relations with the government on issues and legislation that may have an impact on LPNs. Conducts continuing education classes. Facilitates discussion of issues affecting the nursing and health professions.

45 **American Medical Association**
515 N State Street
Chicago, IL 60610-4320
312-464-5000
800-621-8335
Fax: 312-464-4184
http://www.ama-assn.org

E Ratcliffe Anderson Jr MD, Executive VP
Michael D Maves, CEO

County medical societies and physicians. Disseminates scientific information to members and the public. Informs members on significant medical and health legislation on state and national levels and represents the profession before Congress and governmental agencies. Cooperates in setting standards for medical schools, hospitals, residency programs, and continuing medical education courses. Offers physician placement service and counseling on practice management problems. Operates library which lends material and provides specific medical information to physicians. Ad-hoc committees are formed for such topics as health care planning and principles of medical ethics.

National Organizations & Federal Agencies/General

46 **American Medical Association Alliance**
515 N State Street
Floor 9
Chicago, IL 60610-4325
312-464-4470
Fax: 312-464-5020
e-mail: amaa@ama-assn.org
http://http://www.amaalliance.org

Jo Posselt, Executive Director
Ben Mindell, Manager

Members are spouses of physicians. Serves as the volunteer arm of the American Medical Association. Promotes the goals of the medical profession and works to meet public health needs. Raises more than $2 million annually for the American Medical Association Education and Research Foundation, which provides assistance to medical schools and students.

47 **American Medical Informatics Association**
4915 Street Elmo Avenue
Suite 401
Bethesda, MD 20814
301-657-1291
Fax: 301-657-1296
e-mail: mail@amia.org
http://www.amia.org

Daniel R Masys, MD, President
Joyce A Mitchell PhD, President-Elect
Blackford Middleton, Treasurer

Medical personnel, physicians, physical scientists, engineers, data processors, researchers, educators, hospital administrators, nurses, medical record administrators, and computer professionals. Objectives are: to apply advanced systems and information technologies to scientific, literary, and educational activities; to promote excellence in health care; to promote patient care, teaching, research, and health administration.
1990

48 **American Medical Rehabilitation Providers Association (AMRPA)**
1710 N Street NW
Washington, DC 20036-2907
202-223-1920
888-346-4624
Fax: 202-223-1925
e-mail: czollar@13x.com
http://www.amrpa.org

Kathleen Yosko, President/CEO
Carolyn Zollar, VP

AMRPA has emerged from the traditions of medical rehabilitation and stands poised to renew the power of collective advocacy.

49 **American Mental Health Counselors Association**
801 N Fairfax Street
Suite 304
Alexandria, VA 22314-1775
703-548-6002
800-326-2642
Fax: 703-548-4775
e-mail: amhca@prodigy.net
http://www.AMHCA.org

Carol Staben-Burroughs, President
Gail Mears, President-Elect
W Mark Hamilton MD, Executive Director/CEO

Professional counselors employed in mental health services; students. Aims to: deliver quality mental health services to children, youth, adults, families, and organizations; improve the availability and quality of counseling services through licensure and certification, training standards, and consumer advocacy. Supports specialty and special interest networks. Fosters communication among members. A division of the American Counseling Association.

50 **American Nephrology Nurses' Association**
PO Box 56
Pitman, NJ 08071
856-256-2320
Fax: 609-589-7463
e-mail: anna@mail.ajj.com
http://www.inurse.com/~ANNA

Lesley C Dinwiddie MSN RN, President
Mike Cunningham, Executive Director

Registered nurses, physicians, dietitians, social workers, and technicians. Promotes continuing education of members at national, regional, and local levels.

51 **American Nurses Association**
8515 Georgia Ave
Suite 400
Silver Springs, MD 20910
202-651-7000
800-274-4262
Fax: 202-651-7001
http://www.nursingworld.org

Barbara A Blakeney, President

Member associations representing registered nurses. Sponsors American Nurses Foundation (for research), American Academy of Nursing.

52 **American Occupational Therapy Association**
4720 Montgomery Lane
Bethesda, MD 20824-1220
301-652-2682
Fax: 301-652-7711
e-mail: praota@aota.org
http://www.aota.org
TDD 800-377-8555

Penelope A Moyers, President
Florence Clark, VP
Sheri Montgomery, Secretary

Registered occupational therapists and certified occupational therapy assistants who provide services to people whose lives have been disrupted by physical injury or illness, developmental problems, the aging process, or social or psychological difficulties. Occupational therapy focuses on the active involvement of the patient in specially designed therapeutic tasks and activities to improve function, performance capacity, and the ability to cope with demands of daily living. Conducts research and educational programs and compiles statistics.

53 **American Physiological Society**
US Department of Health & Human Services
9650 Rockville Pike
Bethesda, MD 20814-3991
301-634-7164
Fax: 301-634-7241
http://www.the-aps.org

Hannah V Carey, President

Professional society of physiologists.

54 **American Psychiatric Nurses Association**
1555 Wilson Boulevard
Suite 602
Arlington, VA 22209-2429
703-243-2443
866-243-2443
Fax: 703-243-3390
e-mail: info@apna.org
http://www.apna.org

Nicholas Croce, Jr MS, Executive Director

Provides leadership to advance psychiatric mental health nursing practice, improve mental health care for families, individuals, groups and communities, and shape health policy for the delivery of mental health services.

55 **American Psychoanalytic Association**
309 E 49th Street
New York, NY 10017-1601
212-752-0450
Fax: 212-593-0571
e-mail: centraloffice@apsa.org
http://www.apsa.org

K Lynne Moritz MD, President
Prudence Gourguechon MD, President-Elect

Psychoanalysts who have graduated from or are currently attending an accredited institute. Seeks to establish and maintain standards for the training of psychoanalysts and for the practice of psychoanalysis; fosters the integration of psychoanalysis with other branches of medicine; encourages research. Conducts twice yearly national meetings.
1911

National Organizations & Federal Agencies/General

56 **American Psychological Society**
1010 Vermont Avenue NW
Suite 1100
Washington, DC 20005-4907   202-783-2077
Fax: 202-783-2083
e-mail: aps@aps.washington.dc.us
http://www.psychologicalscience.org
Alan G Kraut, Executive Director

Scientists and academics. Works for the advancement of the discipline of psychology and the promotion of human welfare through research and application. Conducts research programs; educates policy makers on the role human behavior plays in societal problems; offers liability insurance plans.
1988

57 **American Radiological Nurses Association**
7794 Grow Drive
Pensacola, FL 32514   850-474-7292
Fax: 850-484-8762
e-mail: arna@rsna.org
http://www.arna.net
Betty Rohr, Executive Secretary

Radiological nurses. Seeks to provide, promote, and maintain continuity of quality patient care through education, standards of care, professional growth, and collaboration with other health care providers.

58 **American Registry of Pathology**
14th Street & Alaska Avenue N
Washington, DC 20306   202-782-2143
Fax: 202-782-4567
http://www.afip.org
Donald West King, Executive Director
William Gardners, CEO

Engages in cooperative enterprises in medical research and education with the Armed Forces Institute of Pathology. Functions as a fiscal agent in the management of research grants and monies derived from tuition fees publications and contributions. Serves as a link between, and encourages cooperation among, the military and civilian medical, dental, and veterinary communities for the mutual benefit of military and civilian medicine. Provides personnel and other services. Offers 38 continuing medical education courses annually. Bestows annual John Hill Brinton Award in recognition of outstanding young researcher, John Shaw Billings Lifetime Achievement Award to senior AFIP staff member, Callender-Binford fellowships.
1921

59 **American Society for Geriatric Dentistry**
211 E Chicago Avenue
Floor 5
Chicago, IL 60611-2668   312-440-2660
Fax: 312-440-2824
Janet A Yellowitz DMD, President

Devoted to the maintenance and improvement of the oral health of the elderly. Promotes the continuing education of the practitioner of geriatric dentistry; auxiliary and nursing home administrators and personnel; hygienists, nurses, and students. Maintains speakers' bureau.

60 **American Society for Laser Medicine and Surgery**
2100 Stewart Avenue
Suite 240
Wausau, WI 54401-1709   715-845-9283
Fax: 715-848-2493
e-mail: information@aslms.org
http://www.aslms.org
Roy G Geronemus, President
Richard O Gregory MD, Secretary
Dianne Dalsky, Executive Director

Physicians, physicists, and other scientists; nurses, dentists, podiatrists, veterinarians, and other paramedical personnel; technicians and commercial representatives concerned with the medical applications of lasers. Facilitates exchange of information concerning lasers.

61 **American Society for Parenteral and Enteral Nutrition**
8630 Fenton Street
Suite 412
Silver Spring, MD 20910-3828   301-587-6315
800-727-4567
Fax: 301-587-2365
e-mail: aspen@access.digex.net
http://www.nutritioncare.org
Vincent W Vanek, President
Robin Kriegel CAE, Executive Director
Stephen A Mcclave MD, VP

Physicians, dietitians, nurses, pharmacists, and members of the industry. Works to promote quality patient care, education, and research in the field of nutrition and metabolic support in all health care settings. Educates health care professionals. Conducts postgraduate courses and research programs; compiles statistics.
1983

62 **American Society of Colon and Rectal Surgeons**
85 W Algonquin Road
Suite 550
Arlington Heights, IL 60005-4460   847-290-9184
Fax: 847-290-9203
e-mail: ascrs@execadmin.com
http://www.fascrs.org
W Douglas Wong MD, President
Anthony Senegore MD, President-Elect
Paula Sue Bekwith MD, VP

Represents more than 1000 board certified colon and rectal surgeons and other surgeons dedicated to advancing and promoting the science and practice of the treatment of patients with diseases and disorders affecting the colon, rectum and anus.

63 **American Society of General Surgeons**
PO Box 4834
Englewood, CO 80155   303-771-5948
800-998-8322
Fax: 303-771-2550
e-mail: asgs-info@theasgs.org
http://www.theasgs.org
J Barry McKernan, MD, FACS, President
Robert W Sewell, MD, FACS, President-Elect
Guy R Nicastri, MD, FACS, Treasurer/Secretary

The ASGS represents the socioeconomic, political, scientific, and professional interests of General Surgeon specialists.

64 **American Society of Internal Medicine**
1011 Pennsylvania Avenue NW
Suite 800
Washington, DC 20006-1813   202-835-2746
Fax: 202-835-0443
Alan R Nelson, Executive VP

Professional society of physicians specializing in internal medicine. Is concerned with the social, economic, and political factors affecting the delivery of high quality care. Focuses on the delivery and financing of medical care in areas including access to care, appropriate reform of American health care system, medical and public education, issues affecting the elderly, private and public sector, health insurance and reimbursement, managed care, documentation of physician performance, and medical technology and computerization aimed at maintaining and promoting high quality medical care at a reasonable cost.

65 **American Society of Maxillofacial Surgeons**
444 E Algonquin Road
Arlington Heights, IL 60005-4654   847-228-3338
Fax: 847-228-6509
e-mail: admin@maxface.org
http://www.maxface.org
Catherine A Hay, Executive Director

Professional society of doctors of medicine and doctors of dental surgery who have at least five years of recognized graduate training and experience in maxillofacial surgery. Seeks to stimulate and advance knowledge of the science and art of maxillofacial surgery and improve and elevate the standard of practice.

National Organizations & Federal Agencies/General

66 **American Society of Neuroradiology**
2210 Midwest Road
Suite 207
Oak Brook, IL 60523-8205
630-574-0220
Fax: 630-574-0661
e-mail: asnrgant@interaccess.com
http://www.asnr.org

Charles M Strother MD, President
Patricia A Huggins MD, VP
James B Gantenberg, FACHE, Executive/CEO

Neuroradiologists who spend at least half of their time practicing neuroradiology. Fosters education, basic science research, and communication in neuroradiology.
1962

67 **American Society of Peri-Anesthesia Nurses**
10 Melrose Avenue
Suite 110
Cherry Hill, NJ 08003-3696
856-616-9600
877-737-9696
Fax: 856-616-9601
e-mail: aspan@aspan.org
http://www.aspan.org

Susan Fossum, BSN,RN,CPAN, President
Lois Schick, VP/President-Elect
Gene Near,BSN,RN,CPAN, Secretary

Nurses practicing in all phases of ambulatory surgery, preanesthesia and post anesthesia care. Promotes quality and cost effective care for patients, their families, and the community through public and professional education, research and standards of practice. Offers continuing education programs.
1980

68 **American Society of Plastic Surgeons**
444 E Algonquin Road
Arlington Heights, IL 60005-4664
847-228-9900
Fax: 847-228-7485
http://www.plasticsurgery.org

Richard A D'Amio, MD, President
John W Canady, MP, President-Elect
Philip C Haeck, MD, Treasurer

Professional society of plastic surgeons. Works in cooperation with the Plastic Surgery Educational Foundation to promote optimal care for plastic surgery patients through research, service, and education activities. Sponsors public/patient education program, clinical symposia, and professional development workshops. Acts as a liaison between members, government and medical organizations. Conducts charitable activities.intains speakers' bureau; compiles statistics.
1931

69 **American Society of Post-Anesthesia Nurses**
10 Melrose Ave
Suite 110
Cherry Hill, NJ 08003
856-616-9600
877-737-9696
Fax: 856-616-9601
e-mail: aspan@aspan.org
http://www.aspan.org

Susan Fossum, President
Lois Schick, VP/President-Elect
Gene Near, Secretary

Post-anesthesia nurses. Promotes upgrading of standards of postanesthesia patient care and the professional growth of licensed nurses involved in the care of patients in the immediate postanesthesia period. Provides forum for exchange of knowledge and ideas on patient care; facilitates cooperation among postanesthesia nurses and physicians and other medical personnel; encourages specialization and research in the field. Promotes public awarenessnd understanding of the care of postanesthesia patients. Conducts courses.

70 **American Society of Retired Dentists**
20283 State Road 7
Suite 300
Boca Raton, FL 33498-6903
561-395-2773

71 **American Society of Tropical Medicine and Hygiene**
60 Revere Drive
Suite 500
Northbrook, IL 60062-1591
847-480-9592
Fax: 847-480-9282
e-mail: astmh@astmh.org
http://www.astmh.org

Claire Panosian, MD/DTM+H, President
Thomas E Wellems, MD/PhD, President-Elect
George V Hillyer, Secretary/Treasurer

Professional society of physicians and scientists interested in tropical medicine and hygiene, including the areas of arbovirology, entomology, medicine, nursing, parasitology, immunology, infectious disease and travelers' health.
1903

72 **American Thoracic Society**
61 Broadway
Floor 4
New York, NY 10006-2704
212-315-6441
Fax: 212-315-6498
http://www.thoracic.org

David H Ingbar MD, President
Jo Rae Wright PhD, President-Elect
J Randall Curtis, VP

International Professional and scientific Society for respiratory and critical care medicine. Seeks to prevent and fight respiratory diseases through research, education and advocacy. Also serves as the medical section of the American Lung Association.
1905

73 **American Yoga Association**
PO Box 19986
Sarasota, FL 34276-2986
941-927-4977
Fax: 941-921-9844
e-mail: info@americanyogaassociation.org
http://www.americanyogaassociation.org

Alice Christensen, Founder/Executive Director
Patricia Rockwood, Publications Director

Promotes the practice of yoga as a practical and effective tool for physical, mental, and emotional health and well-being. Teaches all facets of classical yoga with emphasis on breathing, exercise, and relaxation/meditation. Has specially designed programs for the elderly Easy Does It Fitness, which includes workshops for health professionals and other fitness trainers throughout the country. Also offers a Stress Management Program to businesses.ses and organizations throughout the country. Conducts classes, seminars, lectures, workshops. Offers free introductory classes to interested groups. Distributes instructional materials on teaching safe beginner yoga practices and practical nutrition and the benefits of yoga in treating common health problems. Has engaged in local, state, and federally funded research to evaluate the effects of classical yoga practice.

74 **Armed Forces Benefit Association**
909 N Washington Street
Alexandria, VA 22314-1556
703-549-4455
800-776-2322
Fax: 703-706-5961
e-mail: info@afba.com

Ed Eberhart, President

Active and retired military personnel. Informs members of current legislation and benefits for military staff. Sponsors group insurance, discounts on merchandise, and group medical and dental care. Bestows honorary memberships.

75 **Army Distaff Foundation**
1200 Oregon Avenue NW
Washington, DC 20015-1543
202-541-0105
800-541-HALL
Fax: 202-364-2856

Calvert Benedict, Executive Director

Provides retirement housing and health care services to active and retired military officers, and their relatives. Operates Knollwood, a military retirement community with independent apartment, as well as assisted living and nursing care.

National Organizations & Federal Agencies/General

76 **Army Emergency Relief**
200 Stovall Street
Alexandria, VA 22332
703-428-0000
866-878-6378
Fax: 703-325-7183
http://www.aerhq.org

E C Meyer General, President
Robert Foley, Executive Director

A private organization whose primary purpose is to relieve distress of members of the Army (active and retired) and their dependents, and to provide assistance to needy spouses and orphans of deceased Army members; a secondary purpose is to make available educational assistance (scholarships) unmarried dependent children of soldiers (active, retired, or deceased) who need such assistance to pursue undergraduate studies.

1942

77 **Asian American Center for Justice**
American Citizens for Justice
1140 Connecticut Ave NW
Suite 1200
Washington, DC 20036
202-296-2300
Fax: 202-296-2318
e-mail: acjoffice@aol.com

Asian Pacific Americans and other individuals concerned with discrimination against ethnic groups. Works to combat and prevent racial intolerance. Operates the Asian American Center for Justice. Monitors legislation and law enforcement. Community education of Asian Pacific American history and culture. See Legal Resources chapters for specific state resources.

78 **Assisted Living Federation of America**
1650 King Street
Suite 602
Alexandria, VA 22314
703-894-1805
Fax: 703-894-1831
e-mail: info@alfa.org
http://www.alfa.org

Richard Grimes, MED, CAE, President/CEO
Evrett Benton, Chair

79 **Association for Assessment in Counseling**
5999 Stevenson Avenue
Alexandria, VA 22304-3304
703-823-9800
800-347-6647
Fax: 703-823-0252

Mark Pope MD, President
John L Jaco, Executive Director
Richard Yep, Executive Director

A division of the American Counseling Association. School and college counselors, career counselors, rehabilitation counselors, private practice counselors and counselor educators. Supports counselors with information and advice that will help them use assessments appropriately. Provides: information on trends, issues, and advances in assessment; reviews and evaluations of new or revised tests; guidelines and position papers on topics such as responsible test use, application of minimum competency tests, and performance assessments.

80 **Association for Gerontology in Higher Education**
1220 L St. NW
Suite 901
Washington, DC 20005-1527
202-289-9806
Fax: 202-289-9824
http://www.aghe.org

Marie Bernard, President
Marilyn Gugliucci, President-Elect
Margaret Perkinson, Treasurer

Higher education institutions which offer, on a national level, gerontological education and research programs. Promotes and encourages education and training of persons preparing for research or careers in gerontology, and works to increase public awareness of the needs of such training. Provides base for continuing cooperation with public officials, voluntary organizations, national associations, and others interested in aging and education. See Continuing Education chapters for specific state opportunities.

1974

81 **Association for Professionals in Infection Control and Epidemiology**
1275 K Street NW
Suite 1000
Washington, DC 20005-4021
202-789-1890
Fax: 202-789-1899
e-mail: apicinfo@apic.org
http://www.apic.org

Denise Murphey, President
Janet Frain, President-Elect
James Marx, Treasurer

Physicians, microbiologists, nurses, epidemiologists, medical technicians, sanitarians, and pharmacists. Purpose is to improve patient care by improving the profession of infection control through the development of educational programs and standards. Promotes quality research and standardization of practices and procedures. Develops communications among members, and assesses and influences legislation related to the field. Conducts seminars at local level.

1972

82 **Association for Spiritual, Ethical and Religious Values in Counseling**
5999 Stevenson Avenue
Alexandria, VA 22304-3304
703-823-9800
800-347-6647
Fax: 703-823-0252
http://www.aservic.org

Michael Briggs, President
Mike Robinson, President-Elect
Grant Hayes, Treasurer

A division of American Counseling Association. Counselors and other human development professionals who are convinced that religious, spiritual and other human values are essential to the full development of the person and to the discipline of counseling. Strives to understand and find ways to integrate religious, spiritual and other values in counseling and other developmental processes.

83 **Association of Black Nursing Faculty**
5823 Queens Cove
Lisle, IL 60532-3164
630-969-3809
Fax: 630-969-3895
e-mail: sallen@tuckerpub.com
http://www.abnnc.org

Bess Stewart MD, President
Sallie Tucker-Allen, Executive Director

Black nursing faculty teaching in nursing programs accredited by the National League for Nursing. Works to promote health-related issues and educational concerns of interest to the black community and ABNF. Serves as a forum for communication and the exchange of information among members; develops strategies for expressing concerns to other individuals, institutions, and communities. Assists members in professional development; develops and sponsors continuing education activities; fosters networking and guidance in employment and recruitment activities. Promotes health-related issues of legislation, government programs, and community activities. Supports black consumer advocacy issues. Encourages research. Maintains speakers' bureau and hall of fame. Offers charitable program and placement services. Compiles statistics, offers a computer-assisted job bank and research group information.

84 **Association of Brethren Caregivers**
1451 Dundee Avenue
Elgin, IL 60120-1674
847-742-5100
800-323-8039
Fax: 847-742-6103
e-mail: abc@brethren.org
http://www.brethren.org/abc

Kathy Reid, Executive Director
Stan Noffsinger, Religious Leader

The Association of Brethren Caregivers fosters the ministry of giving and receiving care through the development of resources, programs, events and leadership that connect persons and communities in their lifelong journeys toward wholeness.

National Organizations & Federal Agencies/General

85 **Association of Former Intelligence Officers**
6723 Whittier Avenue
Suite 303a
Mc Lean, VA 22101-4522
703-790-0320
800-234-6717
Fax: 703-790-0264
e-mail: afio@afio.com
http://www.afio.com

S Eugene Poteat, President
Elizabeth Van Croft, Executive Director

US citizens who have served in any agency or department involved in US intelligence; individuals of good character who support the position that the US needs an adequate intelligence capability. Promotes public understanding and support of a strong and responsible national intelligence establishment. Believes reliable intelligence is essential to the cause of peace and national security. Provides research assistance to writers and scholars in the field; provides speakers for schools and professional and civic groups. Encourages the teaching of intelligence at high schools, universities, and colleges. Offers interviews on intelligence and intelligence-related issues. Maintains placement service and speakers' bureau.
1975

86 **Association of Personal Historians**
146 W 57th Street
Suite 45D
New York, NY 10019-3301
212-586-1533
e-mail: letticestuart@verizon.net
http://www.personalhistorians.org

Paula Stahel, President
Pat McNees, Vice President
Adrienne Johns, Treasurer

The Association of Personal Historians is an organization whose members are dedicated to helping others preserve their personal histories and life stories. The purpose of the Association is to advance the profession of assisting individuals, organizations and communities to preserve their histories, life stories and memories.

87 **Association of Retired Americans**
6505 E 82nd Street
Suite 130
Indianapolis, IN 46250-5507
317-915-2500
800-806-6160
Fax: 317-915-2510
http://www.ara-usa.org

Richard Dellinger, Chairman/CEO

Senior Americans, age 45 or more interested in enhancing their lives through group benefits. Purpose is to offer a program of high quality, low-cost benefits and services to members. Services available through ARA are: discounts on prescriptions, eyeglasses, and hearing aids; low interest credit cards; discounts on lodging, car rental, tours, cruises, and airfare; insurance benefits.
1972

88 **Association of the United States Army**
2425 Wilson Boulevard
Arlington, VA 22201-3326
703-841-4300
800-336-4570
Fax: 703-525-9039
e-mail: ausainfo@ausa.org
http://www.ausa.org

Gordon R Sullivan, President/CEO

Professional society of: active, retired, and reserve military personnel; West Point and Army ROTC cadets; civilians interested in national defense. Seeks to advance the security of the United States and consolidate the efforts of all who support the United States Army as an indispensable instrument of national security. Conducts industrial symposia for manufacturers of Army weapons and equipment, and those in the Department of the Army who plan, develop, test, and use weapons and equipment. Symposia subjects have included guided missiles, army aviation, electronics and communication, telemedicine, vehicles, and armor. Sponsors monthly PBS TV series America's Army.
1950

89 **B'nai B'rith Senior Citizens Housing Committe (BBSCHC)**
2020 K Street NW
7th Floor
Washington, DC 20006-1828
202-857-6600
Fax: 202-857-1099
e-mail: seniors@bnaibrith.org
http://www.bnaibrith.org

Mark D Olshan, Director
Eugene Fogel, Associate Director

This national center for Housing and Services sponsors housing and travel for senior citizens.

90 **Baromedical Nurses Association**
PO Box 531190
San Diego, CA 92153
303-918-9686
Fax: 619-651-7543
http://www.hyperbaricnurses.org

Justin Everts, President
Kathy Furnas, VP
Robin Ortega, Secretary

Registered nurses practicing baromedicine (hyperbaric medicine), involved in research related to baromedical nursing, completing basic orientation in baromedicine, or contributing to literature on baromedicine or baromedical nursing. Defines, develops, and promotes the status and standards of baromedical nursing and maintains speakers' bureau.

91 **Beverly Foundation**
566 El Dorado Street
Suite 100
Pasadena, CA 91101
626-792-2292
Fax: 626-792-6117
e-mail: info@beverlyfoundation.org
http://www.beverlyfoundation.org

Develops education and research programs and policy studies to facilitate long-term health care and supportive services and life quality of people with chronic-care needs, particularly older adults, their families, and caregivers. The focus is on optimal functional independence and an informed public. Unrestricted income is derived from product sales, interest, dividends, donations, and grants. Restricted funds are sought to support new program developments which focus on improving service systems and methods of long-term care. Sells educational materials to health care industry. Maintains library.

92 **Bureau of Naval Personnel**
Retired Activities Branch
5720 Integrity Drive
Millington, TN 38055-0000
901-874-5195
866-827-5672
Fax: 901-874-5556
e-mail: Mill_RetiredActivities@navy.mil
http://http://www.npc.navy.mil/channels

The mission of Retired Activities Branch at Navy Personnel Command (NPC) is to keep the retired community apprised of their benefits and provide customer services to our retirees and their families.

93 **Capital Assistance Program for Elderly and Persons with Disabilities**
Federal Transit Administration
400 7th Street SW
Washington, DC 20590
202-366-4043
Fax: 202-366-3472
http://www.fta.dot.gov
TTY 800-877-8339

James S Simpson, Administrator
Sandy Bushue, Deputy Administrator
Susan E Schruth, Assoc Admin Program Management

To provide financial assistance in meeting the transportation needs of elderly persons and persons with disabilities where public transportation services are unavailable, insufficient, or inappropriate.

National Organizations & Federal Agencies/General

94　Caregiver Alliance
180 Montgomery Street
Suite 1100
San Francisco, CA 94108
415-434-3388
800-445-8106
Fax: 414-434-3508
e-mail: info@caregiver.org
http://www.caregiver.org

Kathy Murphy, President
Kathryn Lee, Vice President
Kathleen Kelly, MPA, Executive Director

Good information with resources and hotline numbers. Family Caregivers Alliance suports and assists caregivers of brain-impaired adults through education services, research and advocacy.
　　　　1977

95　Caring Connections
1700 Diagonal Road
Suite 625
Alexandria, VA 22314
703-647-6685
800-658-8898
Fax: 703-837-1233
e-mail: consumers@nhpco.org
http://www.caringinf.org

Merikokeb Wondafrash, Program Assist Consumer Programs

Caring Connections, a program of the National Hospice and Palliative Care Organization (NHPCO), is a national consumer engagement initiative to improve care at the end of life, supported by a grant from The Robert Wood Johnson Foundation. Caring Connections provides free brochures on a wide range of end-of-life topics including advance care planning, caregiving, hospice and palliative care, grief and loss, and pain. State-specific advance directives for all 50 states and the District of Columbia are also available. Consumers can access the free brochures and state-specific advance directives by calling our Helpline or by visiting our website.

96　Catholic Charities USA (CCUSA)
66 Canal Center Plaza
Suite 600
Alexandria, VA 22314
703-549-1390
Fax: 703-549-1656
http://www.catholiccharitiesusa.org

Rev Larry Snyder, President
John Keightley, Executive VP
Jean Beil, Senior VP

CCUSA is a network of organizations offering nationwide services to older people, including counseling, homemaker and caregiver services, emergency assistance, group homes, and institutional care.

97　Catholic Golden Age (CGA)
National Headquarters
Olyphant, PA 18447
800-836-5699
Fax: 570-586-7721
e-mail: cgaemail@aol.com
http://www.catholicgoldenage.org

CGA sponsors charitable work and helps older people meet their social, physical, economic, intellectual and spiritual needs.

98　Center for Adult Learning and Educational Credentials
1 Dupont Circle NW
Suite 250
Washington, DC 20036-1141
202-939-9300
Fax: 202-775-8578
http://www.acenet.edu

David Ward, President

Professional educators providing support and guidance in the development of policies, procedures and evaluation for post secondary educational institutions. See Coninuing Education chapter for specific opportunities by state.
　　　　1918

99　Center for Medical Ethics and Mediation
PO Box 8110
San Diego, CA 92138-6110
619-296-7268
Fax: 619-296-7268
e-mail: cmem@flash.net
http://www.cmem.org

Robert J Wagener, President
Joe Ventura CPA, Partner

Provides training, education, and consultation services to health and legal professionals, health care consumers, and the general public in matters related to health, health care, law, alternative dispute resolution, and ethics. Trains institutional ethics committees to employ alternative forms of dispute resolution in ethics consultations, including mediation and other collaborative facilitation models. Conducts research and educational programs.

100　Center for the Advancement of State Community Services Programs (CASCSP)
National Association of State Units on Aging (NAUSA)
1201 15th St, NW Suite 350
Washington, DC 20005
202-898-2578
Fax: 202-898-2583
e-mail: info@nasua.org
http://www.nasua.org

Patricia Polansky, President
Irene Collins, First VP
Deborah Armstrong, Seretary

The Center provides information and support for community-based care for older people.

101　Center for the Rights of the Terminally Ill
PO Box 54246
Hurst, TX 76054-4246
817-656-5143
e-mail: crti@eaze.net

Opposition to euthanasia and infanticide, and the study of Right to Die court cases, patients' rights, suicide, death and dying, death education, care of the elderly, and protection of vulnerable patients.

102　Centers for Medicare and Medicaid Services (CMS)
7500 Security Boulevard
Baltimore, MD 21244-1850
410-786-3000
877-267-2323
Fax: 202-690-7675
http://www.cms.hhs.gov

Mark B McClellan, MD, PhD, Administrator
Leslie V Norfolk, Esq, Deputy Administrator

CMS, part of the Federal Government, administers health insurance through Medicare and Medicaid. CMS regulates hospitals, nursing homes, and home health agencies.

103　Centro Gerontologico Latino
75 Maiden Lane
Suite 208
New York, NY 10038-4810
212-402-5474
Fax: 212-402-5473
e-mail: info@gerolatino.org
http://www.gerolatino.org

Mario E Tapia, President/CEO

Works to improve the quality of life of Hispanic seniors. Provides Thanksgiving meals to needy families; operates cable television show in Manhattan, NY. Writes question and answer column in New York paper El Diario to provide information to Hispanic seniors.
　　　　1991

104　Children of Aging Parents
PO Box 167
Richboro, PA 18954
800-227-7294
http://www.caps4caregivers.org

Brian M Duke MHA, President

Provides information and emotional support to caregivers of older people. Serves as a national clearinghouse for information on resources and issues dealing with older people.

11

National Organizations & Federal Agencies/General

1977

105 Christian Association of PrimeTimers
PO Box 777
St Charles, IL 60174
800-443-0227
Fax: 630-443-0087
http://www.christianprimetimers.org
Roland S Johnson, President
Marc Whitmore, Chief Executive Officer

The purpose of this ministry is to provide money-saving values for its members while promoting traditional values in our society, including superior products and services. It encourages prime-timers (seniors) to use their talents and acquired wisdom for the benefit of their community. The Christian Association of PrimeTimers has been referred to as the Christian alternative to the American Association of Retired Persons.

1994

106 City of Hope
1500 Duarte Road
Duarte, CA 91010-3012
626-256-4673
800-423-7119
Fax: 626-301-8115
http://www.cityofhope.org
Michael A Friedman, President/CEO
Theodore G Krontinis MD, Executive VP
Anna B Pawlowska MD

Supports the National Pilot Medical Center and the Beckman Research Institute, which are engaged in treatment, research, and medical education in catastrophic diseases including cancer; leukemia; blood, heart and lung diseases; certain hereditary maladies; and metabolic disorders, such as diabetes. Patient care is available on a national and nonsectarian basis. Provides physician referrals. Offers free consulting service to doctors and hospitals. Seeks to influence medicine and science through 80 pilot research programs. From its staff and 200 laboratories, during the past decade over 3000 original findings have emerged in diseases treated as well as studies in diabetes, Alzheimer's disease, AIDS, Huntington's disease, genetics, and brain and nerve function. Receives nationwide support from nearly 500 chartered auxiliaries in over 230 cities, 32 states and Washington, DC, and from management, labor, fraternal and benevolent organizations, individuals, and special campaigns.

1913

107 Civil Rights Compliance Activities
US Department Office of Civil Rights
Hubert H Humphrey Building
200 Independence Ave SW, Room 506-F
Washington, DC 20201
202-619-0403
800-368-1019
Fax: 202-619-3818
http://www.hhs.gov/ocr
TDD 800-537-7697
Winston Wilkinson, Director

To eliminate unlawful discrimination and ensure equal opportunities for beneficiaries and potential beneficiaries of Federal financial assistance provided by the Department of Health and Human Services (HHS), as well as eliminate unlawful discrimination against those involved in programs and activities conducted by HHS on the basis of any individual's disabilities. The Office for Civil Rights (OCR) enforces various civil rights laws and regulations.

108 Civil Rights of Institutionalized Persons Division
US Department of Justice
Special Litigation Section
950 Pennsylvania Avenue NW
Washington, DC 20530
202-514-6255
877-218-5228
Fax: 202-514-0212
e-mail: askdoj@usdoj.gov
http://www.usdoj.gov
Michael B Mukasey, Attorney General

To initiate actions for redress in cases involving deprivations of rights of institutionalized persons secured and protected by the Constitution or laws of the United States. To provide equal utilization of any public facility owned or operated by any State or subdivision thereof, without regard to race, religion, or national origin.

109 Clearinghouse on Abuse and Neglect of the Elderly (CANE)
University of Delaware
297 Graham Hall
Newark, DE 19716
302-831-3525
e-mail: CANE-UD@udel.edu
http://www.elderabusecenter.org

CANE, funded by the Administration on Aging, is a database of elder abuse materials and resources operated by the University of Delaware's National Center on Elder Abuse.

110 Clearinghouse on Disability Information (CDI)
Office for Special Education & Rehab Service
400 Maryland Avenue SW
Washington, DC 20202-7100
202-245-7468
Fax: 202-245-7638
e-mail: john.hager@ed.gov
http://www.ed.gov
Hudson La Force III, COO
Margaret Spellings, U.S Secretary Of Education
David Dunn, Chief Of Staff

Provide information and data regarding the location, provision, and availability of services and programs for persons with disabilities. Staff is trained to serve as experts in referring requests to other sources of disability-related information, if necessary.

111 Client Assistance Program: Office of Program Operations
220 I Street NE
Suite 130
Washington, DC 20002
202-547-0198
800-638-0243
Fax: 202-547-2083
e-mail: jcooney@uls-dc.com
http://www.uls-dc.com/cap
Joseph Cooney, Contact

Programs in each state provide information and assistance to individuals seeking or receiving services under the Rehabilitation Act of 1973.

112 Coalition for Economic Survival (CES)
514 Shatto Place
Suite 270
Los Angeles, CA 90020-1784
323-656-4410
Fax: 213-252-4422
e-mail: contactces@earthlink.net
http://www.cesinaction.org
Larry Gross, Executive Director
Alison Dickson, Deputy Director
Jessica Gudiel, Tenant Organizer

Supports senior citizens in economic concerns such as affordable housing, rent control, repairs and tenants rights.

1973

113 Commission on Law and Aging
American Bar Association
740 15th Street NW
Washington, DC 20005-1022
202-662-1000
Fax: 202-662-1032
e-mail: abaaging@abanet.org
http://www.abanet.org/aging
Charles P Sabatino, Executive Director
Erica F Wood, Assistant Director
Holly Robinson, Associate Director

The Commission examines and responds to law-related needs of older people. It makes referrals and maintains a listing of legal aid offices where older people can get free or low-cost legal assistance. See Legal Resources chapter for specific state resources.

National Organizations & Federal Agencies/General

114 **Continuing Care Accreditation Commission**
1730 Rhode Island Avenue NW
Suite 209
Washington, DC 20036-3120
202-587-5001
866-888-1122
Fax: 202-587-5009
http://www.carf.org
Christine McDonell, Acting Managing Director
Amanda Birch, Manager
Brian J Boon PhD, President

Offers lists of continuing care facilities across the country, grouped by region to the public; resources and publications also available pertaining to the elderly and treatment facilities.
1985

115 **Council for Health & Human Services Ministries**
United Church of Christ
700 Prospect Avenue E
Cleveland, OH 44115-1131
216-861-5000
Fax: 216-736-2251
e-mail: chhsm@ucc.org
http://WWW.chhsm.org
Bryan W Sickbert, President/CEO
Darrell Boyd, Associate Director
La Verne Council

Health and human service institutions related to the United Church of Christ. Seeks to study, plan, and implement a program in health and human services; assist members in developing and providing quality services and in financing institutional and noninstitutional health and human service ministries; stimulate awareness of and support for these programs; inform the UCC of policies that affect the needs, problems, and conditions of patients; cooperate with interdenominational agencies and others in the field. Maintains placement service and hall of fame. Compiles statistics; provides specialized education programs.

116 **Council of Better Business Bureau**
BBBOnLine
4200 Wilson Boulevard
8th Floor
Arlington, VA 22203
703-276-0100
Fax: 703-525-8277
http://www.bbbonline.org
Steven J Cole, President/CEO
Charlie Underhill, Executive Vice President
Steven A Salter, VP BBBOnLine

BBBOnLine's mission is to promote trust and confidence on the Internet through the BBBOnLine Reliability and Privacy Seal Programs. BBBOnLine's web site seal programs allows companies with web sites to display the seals once they have been evaluated and confirmed to meet the program requirements.

117 **Deafness and Communicative Disorders**
Rehabilitation Services Administration-DVDB
US Department of Education
330 C Street SW, MES Bldg #3228
Washington, DC 20202
202-205-9152
Fax: 202-205-9340
e-mail: annette.reichman@ed.gov
http://www.ed.gov/about/offices
Annette Reichman, Chief

Promotes improved and expanded rehabilitation services for deaf and hard of hearing people, individuals with speech or language impairments, and individuals who are deaf-blind.

118 **Demonstration Grants to States with Respect to Alzheimer's Disease, Health Resources & Services**
US Department of Health & Human Services
200 Independence Avenue SW
Washington, DC 20201
202-619-0257
877-696-6775
Fax: 301-594-2511
http://www.dhhs.gov
Lori Stalbaum, Program Officer

To assist states in carrying out demonstration projects for planning, establishing, and operating programs for: Program Development-Coordinate with public and private organizations the development and operations of diagnosis, treatment, care management, respite care, legal counseling, and education services provided within the state to individuals with Alzheimer's disease and related disorders, families of those individuals, and care giving provi.

119 **Department of Veterans Affairs**
Office of Public Affairs
Washington, DC 20420
800-827-1000
http://www.va.gov
James B Peake, Secretary Of Veterans Affairs
Thomas G Bowman, Chief Of Staff

The VA, part of the Federal Government, provides benefits for eligible veterans and their families in outpatient clinics, medical centers, and nursing homes across the US.

120 **Dermatology Nurses' Association**
PO Box 56
Pitman, NJ 08071
856-256-2330
800-454-4362
Fax: 856-589-7463
e-mail: dndo@ajj.com
http://dna.inurse.com
Robin Weber, President
Joan L Johnson, Director

Established to develop and foster the highest standards of dermatologic nursing care, enhance professional growth through education and research, facilitate communication among members, and promote interdisciplinary collaboration.
1981

121 **Devonshire Acres**
1330 North Sidney Avenue
Drawer 392
Sterling, CO 80751
http://www.chancellorhealthcare.com

122 **Diplomatic and Consular Officers, Retired**
1801 F Street NW
Washington, DC 20006-4406
202-682-0500
800-344-9127
Fax: 202-842-3295
e-mail: dacor@ix.netcom.com
http://www.dacorbacon.org
Richard McKee, Executive Director

Active and retired Foreign Service members who have served in officer positions.
1950

123 **Eldercare Initiative in Consumer Law (EICL)**
National Consumer Law Center
77 Summer Street, 10th Floor
Boston, MA 02110
617-542-8010
Fax: 617-542-8028
e-mail: ncic@consumerlaw.org
http://www.consumerlaw.org

The Initiative provides assistance on legal issues of older people. See Legal Resources for specific resources by state.

124 **Eldercare Locator**
National Association of Area Agencies on Aging
1112 16th Street NW
Suite 100
Washington, DC 20036-4827
202-872-0057
800-677-1116
http://www.eldercare.gov
Helen Eltzeroth, Manager

Eldercare Locator links those who need assistance with state and local area agencies on aging and community-based organizations that serve older adults and their caregivers.

National Organizations & Federal Agencies/General

125 **Elderly People or Persons with Disabilities Housing**
National Law Housing Project
614 Grand Ave. Ste 320
Oakland, CA 94610
510-251-9400
Fax: 510-451-2300
e-mail: nhlp@nhlp.org
http://www.nhlp.org

Gideon Anders, Executive Director
Susan Stern, Development Director

HUD originally made direct loans and subsequently made capital grants to nonprofit sponsors for the construction or substantial rehabilitation of rental housing for elderly people or persons with disabilities. In 1990, this program was revised into the supportive housing for elderly people and for persons with disabilities programs. Financial assistance is now in the form of a capital advance for 40 years that is non-repayable and interest-free so long as the project is available for low-income elderly persons and rental assistance is provided through a 20-year renewable contract to subsidize shortfalls in project income from dwelling unit rents.

126 **Emergency Nurses Association**
915 Lee Street
Des Plaines, IL 60016-6513
847-460-4100
800-900-9659
Fax: 847-460-4001
e-mail: enainfo@ena.org
http://www.ena.org

Denise King, RN MSN CEN, President
David Westman, Executive Director
Bill Briggs, President-Elect

Registered nurses, licensed practical nurses, and licensed vocational nurses; emergency medical technicians or nurses and members of allied health fields engaged or interested in emergency patient care. Objectives are: to promote emergency nursing and to establish standards in the field; to work with other health-related organizations toward the improvement of emergency care; to serve as a resource for emergency nursing education and research. Seeks to identify and address emergency nursing issues. Disseminates educational and research information in the field. Sponsors: Emergency Nursing Core Curriculum; Standards of Emergency Nursing Practice; Emergency Nursing Pediatric Course; Trauma Nursing Core Course.

127 **Employee Benefits Security Administration**
US Department of Labor
Frances Perkins Building
200 Constitution Avenue NW
Washington, DC 20210
202-254-7013
866-487-2365
http://www.dol.gov/ebsa
TTY 877-889-5627

Ann L Combs, Assistant Secretary
Alan D Lebowitz, Dpty Asst Secretary Program Ops
Bradford P Campbell, Deputy Asst Secretary Policy

EBSA protects the integrity of pensions, health plans, and other employee benefits for more than 150 million people.

128 **Employment Discrimination: Age**
Equal Employment Opportunity Commission
1801 L Street NW
Washington, DC 20507
202-663-4900
800-669-4000
Fax: 202-663-4912
e-mail: info@ask.eeoc.gov
http://www.eeoc.gov
TTY 800-669-6820

Leslie E Silverman, Commissioner
Stuart J Ishimaru, Commissioner
Christine M Griffin, Commissioner

To prohibit arbitrary age discrimination of people over the age of 40, in hiring and other employment practices, promote the employment of older workers based on ability rather than age, and help employers and employees find ways to meet problems arising from the impact of age on employment.

129 **Employment Discrimination: Disabled**
Equal Employment Opportunity Commission
1801 L Street NW
Washington, DC 20507
202-663-4900
800-669-4000
Fax: 202-663-4912
e-mail: info@ask.eeoc.gov
http://www.eeoc.gov
TTY 202-663-4494

Leslie E Silverman, Commissioner
Stuart J Ishimaru, Commissioner
Christine M Griffin, Commissioner

To provide for enforcement of the Federal prohibition against employment discrimination by private employers and state and local governments against qualified individuals with disabilities.

130 **Equal Employment Opportunity Commission**
1801 L Street NW
Washington, DC 20507
202-663-4264
800-872-3362
Fax: 202-663-4912

Leslie E Silverman, Commissioner
Stuart J Ishimaru, Commissioner
Christine M Griffin, Commissioner

Provides information on and accepts and investigates charges of discrimination based on age, sex, race, color, etc. Spanish-speaking operator available.

131 **Equal Employment Opportunity: Civil Rights Division**
US Department of Justice
950 Pennsylvania Avenue NW
Washington, DC 20530
202-514-4713
Fax: 202-514-1116
http://www.usdoj.gov

Wan J Kim, Assistant Attorney General

To enforce federal laws providing equal employment opportunities for all without regard to race, religion, national origin, sex, and disability.

132 **Experience Works**
2200 Clarenon Boulevard
Suite 1000
Arlington, VA 22201-2540
703-522-7272
866-397-9757
Fax: 703-522-0141
http://www.experienceworks.org

133 **Families USA Foundation**
1201 New York Ave, NW
Suite 1100
Washington, DC 20005-3117
202-628-3030
Fax: 202-347-2417
e-mail: info@familiesusa.org
http://www.familiesusa.org

Ronald F Pollack, Executive Director
Philippe Villers, President

Works with those involved in health care and long-term care reform through reports and other materials.

134 **Federal Council on the Aging: Office of the Secretary**
US Department of Health & Human Services
200 Independence Avenue SW
Washington, DC 20201
202-619-0257
877-696-6775
Fax: 202-690-7203

Michael O Leavitt, CEO

Council was created to advise the President, Secretary of Health and Human Services, Commissioner on Aging, and Congress on matters relating to the special needs of older Americans. It is composed of 15 members appointed by the President, with the approval of the Senate. Members are representatives of older Americans, national organizations with an interest in aging, business, labor, and the general public.

National Organizations & Federal Agencies/General

135 Federal Trade Commission
600 Pennsylvania Avenue NW
Washington, DC 20580
202-326-2222
877-382-4387
http://www.ftc.gov

Pamela Jones Harbour, Commissioner
Jon Liebowitz, Commissioner
William E Kovacic, Commissioner

The FTC site includes news and alerts, consumer protection and anti-trust information, including how these issues apply to older Americans.

136 Fifty-Plus Lifelong Fitness
Lifelong Fitness Alliance
658 Bair Island Rd Suite 200
Redwood City, CA 94063
650-361-8282
Fax: 650-361-8885
e-mail: info@lifelongfitnessalliane.org
http://www.50plus.org

Anne W Cribbs, Managng Director
Jim Warren, President
Tony Abbis, VP

Fifty Plus is a nonprofit organization whose mission is to promote an active lifestyle for older people. The organization started at Stanford University as an outgrowth of some medical research on the value of exercise for older persons. It currently has approximately 2,000 members across the US. Fifty Plus sponsors fitness activities such as walks, runs and hikes for seniors. It organized runs, walks and get togethers in various regions.
1979

137 Food Donation Program: Food Distribution Center
USDA Food and Nutrition Service
3101 Park Center Drive
Alexandria, VA 22302
703-305-2062
Fax: 703-305-2908
http://www.fns.usda.gov

Roberto Salazar, Administrator
George A Braley, Associate Administrator

To improve the diets of school and preschool children, the elderly, needy persons in charitable institutions, and other individuals in need of food assistance, and to increase the market for domestically produced foods acquired under surplus removal or price support operations.

138 Food and Drug Administration
5600 Fishers Lane
Rockville, MD 20857
888-463-6332
http://www.fda.gov

Andrew C von Eschenbach, MD, Acting Commissioner

The FDA is responsible for protecting the public health by assuring the safety, efficacy, and security of human and veterinary drugs, biological products, medical devices, our nation's food supply, cosmetics, and products that emit radiation.

139 Foster Grandparent Program
Senior Corps
1201 New York Avenue NW
Washington, DC 20525
202-606-5000
Fax: 202-606-3472
e-mail: info@cns.gov
http://www.cns.gov

Tess Scannell, Director

The Foster Grandparent Program connects volunteers age 60 and over with children and young people with exceptional needs. Volunteers mentor, support and help some of the most vulnerable children in the United States.

140 Foundation Aiding the Elderly (FATE)
PO Box 254849
Sacramento, CA 95865-4849
916-481-8558
877-481-8558
Fax: 916-481-8329
e-mail: caroleh@4fate.org
http://www.4fate.org

Carole Herman, Founder/President

Assists the public with relatives and friends in long-term care nursing homes. Provides awareness of the existence of, and potential for abuse, neglect, and lack of dignity of the elderly in nursing homes. Initiates action to make improvements. Raises funds for the grassroots efforts to end nursing home abuse.
1980

141 Fund for Assuring an Independent Retirement
100 Indiana Avenue NW
Suite 813
Washington, DC 20001-2144
202-393-4695
Fax: 202-737-1540
http://www.nalc.org

Fredric V Rolando, Executive VP
William H Young, President
Gary H Mullins, VP

Coalition of 22 organizations whose 7 million members are employed by or retired from the federal government. Seeks to protect the wages and benefits of such members. Conducts research and political education programs and analyzes legislative proposals for the benefit of member organizations and Congress.

142 Genesis Institute
10220 N Nevada Street
Suite 280
Spokane, WA 99218-3117
509-467-7913
Fax: 509-467-0344
e-mail: hutchinsd@aol.com
http://www.genesisinstitute.org

Dave Hutchins, Co-Founder/Executive Director
Ray Hopkins, Co-Founder/Associate Director
Cathy Hutchins, Manager

Exists to care for human souls, guided by the fixed point of biblical revelation. All Genesis training ministries seek to enable and encourage the Christian Community to this end. Offers a variety of courses designed for Christian leaders and layworkers, including the elderly population.

143 Grandparents Rights Organization
100 W Long Lake Road
Suite 250
Bloomfield Hills, MI 48304-2721
248-646-7191
Fax: 248-646-9722
e-mail: rsvlaw@aol.com
http://www.grandparentsrights.org

Richard S Victor, Founder/Executive Director

Conducts educational and advocacy activities aimed at preserving and fostering the child-grandparent relationship in cases where grandparents have been denied the right to visit their grandchildren. Conducts research programs; compiles statistics.
1984

144 Gray Panthers
1612 K St, NW
Suite 300
Washington, DC 20006
202-737-6637
800-280-5362
Fax: 202-737-1160
e-mail: info@graypanthers.org
http://www.graypanthers.org

Maggie Kuhn, Founder

Consciousness-raising activist group of older adults and young people. Aims to combat ageism - the discrimination against persons on the basis of chronological age. Believes that both the old and the young have much to contribute to make our society more just and humane. Advises, acts as catalyst for, and organizes local groups of young, middle-aged, and older persons to work on issues of their choosing.: national health care, affordable housing, environmental preservation, peace, ending discrimination, education, economic and tax justice and social justice.
1970

National Organizations & Federal Agencies/General

145 **H2U: Health, Happiness, You**
One Park Plaza
Building 1-4E
Nashville, TN 37203
800-771-0428
Fax: 615-344-5757
e-mail: h2u@hcahealthcare.com
http://www.h2u.com

Mary Ann Hodge, Executive Director

Healthcare organization dedicated to empowering adults to live healthier, more fulfilling lives. Members receive many national and local benefits, including a quarterly color magazine filled with tips on leading a healthy life, a monthly newsletter and on-line access to the H2U Health Risk Assessment. Dues are $15.00 per year. H2U also produces an employee-based health program that promotes wellness and safety in the workplace.

146 **HEATH Resource Center**
2134 G St, NW
Washington, DC 20052-0019
202-973-0904
800-544-3284
Fax: 202-994-3365
e-mail: askheath@gwu.edu
http://www.heath.gwu.edu

Dr Lynda West, Principal Investigator
Dr Joel Gomez, Co-Principal Investigator
Donna Martinez, Director

Sponsored by the President's Committee on Employment of People with Disabilities. Provides information on education and accommodations for the disabled in work settings. Also offers referral to local sources. Newsletter and resource papers available.

147 **Health Promotion Institute**
National Council on the Aging
1901 L St, NW
4th Floor
Washington, DC 20036
202-479-1200
800-373-4906
Fax: 202-479-0735
e-mail: questions@noca.org
http://www.ncoa.org

James Firman, President/CEO

Promotes physical, mental and emotional health, as well as social and spiritual well-being.
1950

148 **Hemlock Society USA**
PO Box 101810
Denver, CO 80250-1810
303-639-1202
800-247-7421
Fax: 303-639-1224
e-mail: hemlock@hemlock.org
http://www.hemlock.org

Arthur Metcalfe, Chairman
Paul Spiers PhD, President
Marsha Temple, CEO

Hemlock has grown into a significant pressure group for physician-assisted dying in America. Hemlock has two objectives: to change the law to permit physician aid in dying and to help people plan for a peaceful death. Education and community service is done by the Hemlock Foundation, a 501(c)(3) organization.
1980

149 **Home Equity Conversion Mortgages: Office of Insured Single Family Housing**
US Department of Housing and Urban Development
451 7th Street SW
Washington, DC 20410
202-708-1112
Fax: 202-708-3537
http://www.hud.gov/offices
TTY 202-708-1455

Alphonso Jackson, Secretary
John W Cox, CFO

To enable elderly home-owners, 62 years or older, to convert equity in their homes to monthly streams of income or lines of credit.

150 **Home Healthcare Nurses Association (HHNA)**
7794 Grow Drive
Pensacola, FL 32514-7072
202-547-3540
800-558-4462
Fax: 850-484-8762
e-mail: hhna_info@nhac.org
http://www.hhna.org

Belinda E Puetz, Administrator

Works to develop and promote the specialty of home healthcare nursing. Provides a forum for members to exchange information; influences public policy affecting the practice; fosters excellence in practice.
1993

151 **Hospice Association of America**
228 7th Street SE
Washington, DC 20003-4306
202-547-7424
Fax: 202-547-3540
e-mail: djh@nahc.org
http://www.nahc.org

Val J Halamandaris, President
Elaine D Stephens, Chair
Michele A Quirolo, Vice Chair

Hospices, home health agencies, community cancer centers, and interested health care professionals. Promotes concept of hospice, a philosophy of health care which is expressed through the provision of a variety of medical and nonmedical services to terminally ill patients and their families. Technical assistance, educational programs, publications, and representation of industry issues to state and federal governments. Maintains speakers' bureau. Compiles statistics.
1982

152 **Hospice Foundation of America (HFA)**
1621 Connecticut Ave, NW
Suite 300
Washington, DC 20009-1164
202-638-5419
800-854-3402
Fax: 202-638-5312
e-mail: david@hospicefoundation.org
http://www.hospicefoundation.org

Jack D Gordon, Chairman/CEO
David Abrams, President

Works to promote the philosophy and application of hospice care for terminally ill people and improve the American health system. Advocates the hospice concept of care; offers professional development and educational programs; sponsors research on ethical issues; participates in public policy initiatives; provides technical assistance to hospices.

153 **Hospital Audiences**
548 Broadway
Floor 3
New York, NY 10012-3950
212-575-7676
Fax: 212-575-7669
e-mail: hai@aol.com
http://www.hospitalaudiences.org

Michael Jon Spencer, Founder/Executive Director
Max Daniels, Manager

Service recipients include people with mental and physical disabilities, the frail elderly, youth at risk of HIV and violence or in detention, mentally retarded/developmentally disabled persons, homeless single adults and families, and persons with HIV/AIDS. Promotes the cultural enrichment of these individuals by arranging access to cultural experiences, and by presenting music, dance, and theater events for people from health/human service facilities. Develops daily living skills through hands-on participation in the arts. Provides prevention education/skill building to persons at high risk regarding critical public health issues, such as HIV/AIDS and youth violence.
1969

National Organizations & Federal Agencies/General

154 **Housing for the Elderly or Disabled**
Office of Elderly and Assisted Housing
451 7th Street SW
Washington, DC 20410 202-708-1112
Fax: 202-708-2583
http://www.hud.gov
TTY 202-708-1455
Alphonso Jackson, Secretary
Roy A Bernardi, Deputy Secretary
Marcella E Belt, Chief Executive Officer

To provide for rental or cooperative housing and related facilities (such as central dining) for the elderly (62 years or older) or disabled and supportive housing for the elderly.

155 **International Association for the Study of Pain**
IASP Secretariat
111 Queen Anne Ave North
Suite 501
Seattle, WA 98109-4955 206-283-0311
Fax: 206-283-9403
e-mail: iaspdesk@juno.com
http://www.iasp-pain.org
Gerald F Gebhart, President-Elect
Troels S Jensen MD PhD, President
Herald Breivik MD DMSc, Secretary

Scientists, physicians, and other health professionals interested in pain research and therapy. Encourages research on pain mechanisms and syndromes; seeks to improve management of patients with acute and chronic pain. Promotes education and training in the field of pain; informs the public of results of current research. Fosters development of an international data bank, adoption of a uniform classification and definition regarding pain and pain syndromes, and creation of a uniform records system on information relating to pain mechanisms, syndromes, and management. Promotes the formation of national associations for the study and treatment of pain.
Number of Members: 6,500

156 **International Association of Biomedical Gerontology**
University of NE Medical Center
984635 Nebraska Medical Center
Omaha, NE 68198-4635 402-559-4416
Fax: 402-559-7330
Denham Harman MD, President

157 **International Psychogeriatric Association**
550 Frontage Road
Suite 3759
Northfield, IL 60093 847-501-3310
Fax: 847-501-3317
e-mail: membership@ipa-online.org
http://www.ipa-online.org
Joel Sadavoy, President
Helen Fung-kum Chiu, President-Elect
Susan M Oster, Executive Director

Health care professionals and scientists with an interest in the behavioral and biological aspects of mental health in the elderly. Works to keep members abreast of developments in research and clinical practice in the field of geriatric mental health. Conducts research programs.

158 **International Rehabilitation Medicine Association**
133 Moursund Avenue
Room A-221
Houston, TX 77030 713-799-5086
Fax: 713-799-5058
Donna Jones, Executive Director

Medical professionals interested in the use of rehabilitation medicine.
1968

159 **International Society for Quality of Life Studies**
Pamplin College of Business
1800 Kraft Drive
Suite 111
Blacksburg, VA 24060-6370 540-231-5110
Fax: 540-961-4162
e-mail: ISQOLS@vt.edu
http://www.isqols.org
M Joseph Sirgy, Executive Director
Valerie Moller, President
Robert Cummins, President-Elect

Seeks to stimulate research in quality of life studies. Conductional resarch and educational programs.

160 **International Society for Traumatic Stress Studies**
60 Revere Drive
Suite 500
Northbrook, IL 60062-1591 847-480-9028
Fax: 847-480-9282
e-mail: istss@istss.org
http://www.istss.org
Stuart Turner, President
Ulrich Schnyder PhD, VP

Professionals who treat individuals suffering from traumatic stress. (Traumatic stress is a medical term applied to persons who experience severe mental or emotional reactions to extraordinary stressful situations such as war, crime, natural disasters, and high-stress occupations.) Conducts research in the treatment of these cases; disseminates information. Holds seminars. Bestows awards.

161 **International Society of Psychiatric Consultation Liaison Nurses**
2810 Crossroads Drive
Suite 3800
Madison, WI 53718 608-443-2463
866-330-7227
Fax: 608-443-2474
http://www.ispn-psych.org/html/ispcln.html
Geraldine S Pearson, President
Mary Jo Regan-Kubinski, President
Peggy Dulaney, Secretary

Nurses engaged in the practice of, or with an interest in, psychiatric consultation liaison nursing. Promotes development of psychiatric consultation nursing as a subspecialty of psychiatric and mental health nursing. Seeks to advance understanding of mind-body interaction in healing and wellness. Facilitates communication among members and serves as a clearinghouse on psychiatric consultation liaison nursing. Makes available networking opportunities and professional conference discounts to members.
1963

162 **Judge Advocates Association**
8109 Overlake Court
Fairfax Stanton, VA 22039 703-474-7691
e-mail: jaa@jaa.org
http://www.jaa.org
CDR Jeffrey C Good, President
Col Timothy J Ott, VP
MG John Altenburg, President-Elect

Active, reserve, retired and former Judge Advocates of the Army, Navy, Air Force, Marine Corps, and Coast Guard. Assists in developing of military law and an efficient military legal and judicial system.
1943

163 **Mature Market Resource Center**
1850 W Winchester Road
Suite 213
Libertyville, IL 60048-5355 847-816-8660
800-828-8225
Fax: 847-816-8662
e-mail: maturemkt@aol.com
Maria Tuthill, Associate Director

National Organizations & Federal Agencies/General

Acts as a clearinghouse of resources for the mature market. Provides research and information on new trends and discoveries in senior health and fitness. Produces resource books. National Senior Health and Fitness Day and various Mature Fitness Awards USA.

164 **Meals on Wheels Association of America**
203 S Union Street
Alexandria, VA 22314-3355
703-548-5558
Fax: 703-548-8024
http://www.mowaa.org

Enid A Borden, CEO/President

Provides home delivery of meals, improving the quality of life for low-income, elderly, homebound and disabled.
1973

165 **Medic Alert Foundation International**
1323 Colorado Avenue
Turlock, CA 95382-2018
209-668-3333
800-432-5378
Fax: 209-669-2489

Paul Kortschak, CEO

Provides information on registering with Medic Alert (personal medical emergency services) and ordering alert emblem (bracelet). Free registration form and catalog are available. Hours: 24 hours per day/seven days per week.
1956

166 **Medical Library Association**
65 E Wacker Place
Suite 1900
Chicago, IL 60601-7246
312-419-9094
Fax: 312-419-8950
e-mail: info@mlahq.org
http://www.mlanet.org

Mark E Funk, President
Mary L Ryan, President-Elect
Carla J Funk, Executive Director

A nonprofit, educational organization of more than 1,100 institutions and 3,600 individual members in the health sciences information field, committed to educating health information professionals, supporting health information research, promoting access to the world's health sciences information, and working to ensure that the best health information is available to all. See Libraries chapter for state listings.

167 **Medicare Hospital Insurance**
Health Care Financing Administration
200 Independence Avenue SW
Washington, DC 20201
202-690-6726
877-696-6775
Fax: 202-690-7203

Thomas A Scully, President

To provide hospital insurance protection for covered services to any person 65 or above, to certain disabled persons, and to individuals with chronic renal disease.

168 **Medicare Rights Center**
1460 Broadway
17th Floor
New York, NY 10036-7306
212-869-3850
Fax: 212-869-3532
http://www.medicarerights.org

Diane Archer, Executive Director
Robert M Hayes, President

Seeks to ensure the rights of senior citizens and people with disabilities to quality, affordable health care. Provides counseling services to Medicare beneficiaries with health insurance problems and questions; compiles information on inquiries to detect issues and systemic problems in Medicare claims administration. Educates beneficiaries, advocates, providers, and social workers about developments in Medicare law and how to handle problems. Monitors trends and changes in Medicare laws, regulations, and guidelines.

169 **Military Benefit Association**
14605 Avion Parkway
PO Box 221110
Chantilly, VA 20151-1104
703-968-6200
800-336-0100
Fax: 703-968-6423
e-mail: mbabarnum@aol.com
http://www.militarybenefit.org

Roy L Gibson, President
Annette Lape, Manager

The objects and purposes of this Association shall be the promotion of the welfare of its members; the advancement and safeguarding of their economic interets; and generally to encourage and promote better financial conditions for its members through cooperative enterprises.
1956

170 **Military Officers Association of America (MOAA)**
201 N Washington Street
Alexandria, VA 22314-2539
703-549-2311
800-234-6622
Fax: 703-838-8173
e-mail: msc@moaa.org
http://www.moaa.org

Norbert R Ryan Jr, President/CEO
Marv Harris, Public Relations Director
Col Glenn Zauber, CFO

Men and women who are or have been commissioned or warrant officers in any component of the Army, Navy, Air Force, Marine Corps, Coast Guard, National Oceanic and Atmospheric Administration, and Public Health Service. Supports strong national defense and represents and assists members and their dependents and survivors with retirement issues and benefits. Sponsors educational assistance program, survivor assistance, travel, and insurance.iree employment services.
1929

171 **Military Order of the World Wars**
435 N Lee Street
Alexandria, VA 22314-2348
703-683-4911
877-320-3774
Fax: 703-683-4501
e-mail: mowwhq@aol.com
http://www.militaryorder.net

Brion V Chabot, Preciding Officer
Roger C Bultman, Cheif Staff

Commissioned officers and warrant officers who served in the active or reserve components of any of the uniformed services. Promotes patriotic education in schools. Supports Junior and Senior ROTC programs and Boy Scouts and Girl Scouts of America.

172 **Mortgage Insurance and Rental Housing foe Elderly**
Office of Multifamily Development
Department of Housing and Urban Development
451 7th Street SW
Washington, DC 20410
202-708-1142
Fax: 202-708-2583
http://www.hud.gov

Alphonso Jackson, Secretary
Roy A Bernardi, Deputy Secretary
Marcella E Belt, Chief Executive Officer

To provide good quality rental housing for the elderly.

173 **NIH: Environmental Health Sciences**
US Department of Health & Human Services
111 TW Alexander Drive
Research Triangle Park
Triangle Park, NC 27709
919-541-0049
http://www.niehs.nih.gov.home.htm

Conducts and supports research on potential environmental contributors to human illnesses and dysfunction, including asthma, alzheimer's, bronchitis, cancer, lead poisoning.

National Organizations & Federal Agencies/General

174 **NIH: Heart, Lung & Blood Institute**
US Department of Health & Human Services
PO Box 30105
Bethesda, MD 20824-0105
301-592-8573
Fax: 240-629-3246
e-mail: nhlbinfo@nhlbi.nih.gov
http://www.nhlbi.nih.gov
TTY 240-629-3246
Elizabeth G Nabel, MD, Director

The mission is to improve meaning of one American people by supporting and understanding research to prevent, detect, diagnose and treat diseases of heart, lungs, blood vessels, and sleep disorders.

175 **NIH: National Eye Institute**
2020 Vision Place
Bethesda, MD 20892
301-496-5248
Fax: 301-402-1065
http://www.nei.nih.gov
Paul A Sieving, Director

The NEI attempts to discover safe and effective methods to prevent, diagnose, and treat diseases and disorders of the visual system. In this way the Institute helps to prevent, reduce, and possibly even eleiminate blindness and visual impairment.

176 **NIH: National Institute of Dental and Cracial Research**
US Department of Health & Human Services
31 Center Drive
MSC 2290
Bethesda, MD 20892-2190
301-496-4261
Fax: 301-480-4098
e-mail: nidcrinfo@mail.gov
http://www.nidcr.nih.gov
Lawrence A Tabak, DDS, PhD, Director
Dushanka V Kleinman, DDS, MScD, Deputy Director
Thomas G Murphy, Acting Executive Officer

Our mission is to improve oral, dental and craniofacial health through research, research training, and the dissemination of health information.

177 **NIH: National Institute of Osteoporosis and Related Bone Diseases**
US Department of Health & Human Services
1 AMS Circle
Bethesda, MD 20892
301-495-4484
877-226-4267
Fax: 301-718-6366
e-mail: niamsbonceinfo@mail.nih.gov
http://www.osteo.org
Susan Whittier, Project Director
Doris Myklebust, Secretary/Treasurer

The NIH/Osteoporosis and Related Bone Diseases National Resource Center provides patients, health professionals, and the public with an important link to resources and information on metabolic bone diseases such as osteoporosis. Paget's disease of bone, osteogenesis imperfecta, and primary hyperarathyroidism. Specific populations include the elderly, men, women, adolescents, and minorities. The Resource Center offers materials in English, Spanish, Chinese, Korean, Lao, Cambodian and Vietnamese. The center offers links to selected resources, information packet publications, electronic newsletters and support groups.

178 **NIH: National Institute on Aging**
US Department of Health & Human Services
31 Center Drive, MSC 2292
Building 31, Room 5C27
Bethesda, MD 20892
301-496-1752
800-222-2225
Fax: 301-496-1072
e-mail: nidcdinfo@nidcd.nih.gov
http://www.nia.nih.gov
TTY 800-222-4225
Richard J Hodes, MD, Director

Concerned with the health problems of older Americans. The Center offers free printed materials, including fact sheets about going to the hospital and about prostate problems.

179 **NIH: National Institute on Deafness and Communication Disorders**
US Department of Health & Human Services
31 Center Drive
MSC 2320
Bethesda, MD 20892-2320
301-496-7243
800-241-1044
Fax: 301-907-8830
e-mail: nidcdinfo@nidcd.nih.gov
http://www.nidcd.nih.gov
TDD 800-241-1055
TTY 301-402-0252
James F Battey, Jr., MD, PhD, Director

Our mission is to uncover new knowledge that will lead to better health for everyone.

180 **National AFL-CIO Cope Retiree Program**
815 16th Street NW
3rd Floor
Washington, DC 20006-4101
202-637-5294
Fax: 202-637-5107
John Sweeney, President

Retirees promoting organized labor unions
1970

181 **National Academy for Teaching and Learning About Aging**
University of North Texas
PO Box 310919
Denton, TX 76203
940-565-3450
Fax: 940-565-3141
http://www.unt.edu/natla
Don Louis PhD, Interim Director

Professionals interested in aging education. Promotes communication among generations.
1983

182 **National Academy of Elder Law Attorneys**
1604 N Country Club Road
Tucson, AZ 85716-3119
520-881-4005
Fax: 520-325-7925
e-mail: info@naela.com
http://www.naela.org
Laury L Adsit, Director
Stuart Zimring, President
Susan McMahon, Exeucutive Director

Practicing attorneys, law professors, and others interested in the provision of legal services to the elderly. Promotes technical expertise and education for legal services addressing the needs of the elderly and their families.
1987

183 **National Adult Day Services Association**
2519 Connecticut Avenue NW
Washington, DC 20008
800-558-5301
Fax: 202-783-2255
e-mail: info@nadsa.org
http://www.nadsa.org
Beth Meyer-Arnold, Chair
Roberta Merkle, Chair-Elect
Christine Powers, Secretary

Adult daycare practitioners; health and social service planners; individuals involved in planning and providing services for older persons. Promotes and enhances adult daycare programs; provides services and activities for disabled older persons on a long-term basis; provides training and technical assistance and consultation services for daycare personnel; organizes funding; develops statndards and guidelines for adult daycare programs; encourages adult daycare centers to participate in local area health planning activities to heighten the effectiveness of adult daycare. Plans and conducts training events for annual meeting and related conferences; maintains annotated bibliography; lobbies for approved public policy positions; surveys state adult daycare regulations and legislation.

National Organizations & Federal Agencies/General

184 **National Association for Hispanic Elderly**
243 E Colorado Boulevard
Suite 300
Pasadena, CA 91101
626-564-1988
Fax: 626-564-2659
http://www.anppm.org

Dr Carmela G Lacayo, President/CEO

185 **National Association for Home Care and Hospice (NAHC)**
228 Seventh Street SE
Washington, DC 20003-4306
202-547-7424
Fax: 202-547-3540
e-mail: exec@nahc.org
http://www.nahc.org

Elaine D Stephens, Chair
Michele A Quirolo, Vice Chair
Denise Palsgaard, Secretary

Providers of home health care, hospice, and homemaker-home health aide services; interested individuals and organizations. Develops and promotes high standards of patient care in home care services. Seeks to affect legislative and regulatory processes concerning home care services; gathers and disseminates home care industry data; develops public relations strategies; works to increase political visibility of home care services. Interprets home care services to governmental and private sector bodies affecting the delivery and financing of such services. Provides legal and accounting consulting services; conducts market research and compiles statistics. Offers members insurance discounts. Sponsors educational programs for organizations and individuals concerned with home care services.

186 **National Association for Senior Living Industries**
4340 E West Highway
Suite 401
Bethesda, MD 20814-4471
301-657-0270
Fax: 301-656-0989
e-mail: nasli@paimgmt.com

Ann Loew, Association Director
Susan Gorin, Executive Director

Businesses, associations, governmental agencies, and interested professionals. Seeks to improve the quality of life for senior citizens through educational and developmental programs. Offers networking for those who provide products and services to senior adults.
1985

187 **National Association of Activity Professionals**
PO Box 5530
Sevierville, TN 37864-5530
865-429-0717
Fax: 865-453-9914
e-mail: info@thenaap.com
http://www.thenaap.com

Charles T Taylor, Executive Director
Diane Mockbee, President
Brenda Scott, VP

An organization of individuals who provide activity programming for the residents of long-term care facilitites, retirement living communities, adult day care centers, and other primarily geriatric setting. Members provide individualized therapeutic and restorative activities. NAAP provides excellence in support services to activity professionals through education, advocacy, technical assistance, promotion of standards, fostering of research, and peer and industry relations. NAAP represents the interests of activity directors, assistants, educators, and consultants certified for practice by a variety of certification bodies.

188 **National Association of Area Agencies on Aging**
1730 Rhode Island Avenue NW
Washington, DC 20036
202-872-0888
Fax: 202-872-0057
http://www.n4a.org

Charles Sisson, President
Lynn Kellogg, First Vice President
John Wanat, Second Vice President

NoA is the umbrella organization for the AoA-funded Area Agencies on Aging. The association administers the AoA sponsored Eldercare Locator. See State chapter for state agencies.

189 **National Association of Counselors**
303 W Cypress Street
San Antonio, TX 78212-5512
210-271-0781
800-486-3676
Fax: 210-225-8450

Marvin T Deane, CEO
Del Martinez, Manager

Real estate counselors. Promotes the advancement of real estate counseling. Monitors legislation in the field; develops new counseling forms; conducts educational programs.

190 **National Association of County Aging Programs**
25 Massachusetts Ave, NW
Washington, DC 20001-2028
202-393-6226
Fax: 202-737-0480
e-mail: smarkwoo@naco.org
http://www.naco.org

Eric Coleman, President
Valerie Brown, 1st VP
Teresa Altemus, 2nd VP

Affiliated with the National Association of Counties. Assists counties in their plans for providing services to the aging of the community. See State chapter for county and state programs.
1935

191 **National Association of Directors of Nursing Administration in Long Term Care**
Reed Hartman Tower
11353 Reed Hartman Hwy Suite 210
Cincinnati, OH 45241
513-791-3679
800-222-0539
Fax: 513-791-3699
e-mail: info@nadona.org
http://www.nadona.org

Sherrie Dornberger, President
Robin Storey, VP

Directors, assistant directors, and former directors of nursing in long term care. Goals are: to create and establish an acceptable ethical standard for practices in long term care nursing administration; to promote and encourage research in the profession; to develop and provide a consistent program of education and certification for the positions of director, associate director, and assistant director; to promote a positive image of the long term health care industry. Encourages members to share concerns and experiences; sponsors research programs. Advocates legislation pertaining to the practice of professional nursing. Maintains speakers' bureau.
1986

192 **National Association of Government Communicators (NAGC)**
201 Park Washington Court
Falls Church, VA 22046
703-538-1787
Fax: 703-241-5603
e-mail: info@nagc.com
http://www.nagc.com

Gene Rose, President
George Selby, President-Elect
John S Verrico, Director Communications

Promotes communication between national, state and local government in conjunction with a greater public awareness
1976

193 **National Association of Military Widows**
4023 25th Road N
Arlington, VA 22207-3903
703-527-4565
800-842-3451
Fax: 703-354-4380
http://www.militarywidows.org

Patricia D Shecter, President
Marilyn Savage, President-Elect
Etta Brown, Secretary

National Organizations & Federal Agencies/General

Formed to serve the interests of women whose husbands died while on active duty, of a service connected illness, during disability, or regular retirement from the armed forces.

194 **National Association of Nutrition and Aging Services Programs (NANASP)**
1612 K Street NW
Suite 400
Washington, DC 20006
202-682-6899
Fax: 202-223-2099
e-mail: cross@matzblancato.com
http://www.nanasp.org

Sharon TerHaar, President
Timothy Hockett, First VP
Keith Schildt PhD, 2nd VP

NANASP, a membership organization, supports a broad range of nutrition and related services for community-dwelling older people by training nutrition providers and advocating for older people.

195 **National Association of Older Worker Employment**
National Council on the Aging
1901 L St, NW
4th Floor
Washington, DC 20036
202-479-1200
800-867-2755
Fax: 202-479-0735
http://www.ncoa.org

James Firman, President/CEO

Works toward the goal that all individuals, regardless of age, be allowed to utilize their skills and talents as productive and contributing members of the work force.

196 **National Association of Partners in Education**
4040 Fairfax Parkway
Alexandria, VA 22312-1164
703-696-4412
Fax: 703-588-3702
e-mail: napehq@napehq.org
http://www.napehq.org

Daniel W Merenda, President/CEO

To provide leadership in the formation and growth of effective partnerships that ensure success for all students., leading texts in the field of partnerships, and national survey and research projects. Membership includes 2.6 million volunteers involved in 200,000 partnerships nationwide.
1988

197 **National Association of Physician Nurses**
900 S Washington Street
Suite G13
Falls Church, VA 22046-4009
703-237-8616
Fax: 703-533-1153

Ruth Ludeman, Executive Director

Professional organizations for nurses who work in private practice.

198 **National Association of Professional Geriatric Care Managers (PGCM)**
1604 N Country Club Road
Tucson, AZ 85716-3119
520-881-8008
Fax: 520-325-7925
http://www.caremanager.org

Monika White, President
Linda Fodrini-Johnson, President-Elect
Kaaren Boothroyd, Executive Director

Information resource for those interested in the field of geriatriccare while supporting quality care and services for the elderly.
1985

199 **National Association of Retired Federal Employees**
606 N Washington Street
Alexandria, VA 22314-1914
703-838-7760
800-627-3394
Fax: 703-838-7785
e-mail: natlhq@narfe.org
http://www.narfe.org

Charles L Fallis, President

Retired US Government civilian and District of Columbia employees, their spouses, persons drawing annuities as survivors of retired US government employees, present employees eligible for optional retirement, and federal employees. Seeks to: serve annuitants and potential annuitants and their survivors under the retirement laws; sponsor and support beneficial legislation; promote the general welfare of civil service annuitants and their families. Association is also interested in preretirement programs, especially in federal and district government agencies, and in broad field of problems of the aged and aging.
1921

200 **National Association of Senior Companion Project Directors**
2001 S State Street
51500
Salt Lake City, UT 84190-2300
801-468-2775
Fax: 801-468-2852
e-mail: info@nascpd.org
http://www.nascpd.org

Lynne Browne-Zounces, President

Works to address the needs of SCP project directors. Fosters communication between project directors, organizations, and agencies serving the SCP and the Corporation for National Service offices. Encourages the support and exchange of services among programs benefiting the aging. Seeks to prevent duplication and maximize the quality and level of services. Expands and promotes opportunities for senior companions worldwide. Assists is preserving government funding for SCP projects; works for increased stipends for volunteers. Works with Washington representatives on behalf of legislative changes, offers professional training and development, conducts surveys, operates speakers' bureau and compiles statistics.

201 **National Association of State Retirement Administrators**
693 W Nye Lane
Carson City, NV 89703-1527
775-687-4200
866-473-7768
Fax: 775-687-5131
e-mail: dbilyeu@nvpers.org
http://www.nvpers.org

Dana K Bilyeu, Executive Director

Administrators of statewide public employee retirement systems. Encourages nationwide review of pension and retirement programs; sponsors conferences; provides technical and information services.
1947

202 **National Association of State Units on Aging**
1201 15th Street NW
Washington, DC 20005-2842
202-898-2578
Fax: 202-898-2583
e-mail: staff@nasua.org
http://www.nasua.org

Irene Collins, First VP
James Toews, Second VP
Deborah Armstrong, Secretary

Offers support, information and technical assistance to state units on aging.
1990

203 **National Association of State Veterans Homes**
5211 Auth Road
Suitland, MD 20746
301-899-7908
Fax: 301-899-8186
e-mail: info@hasvh.org
http://www.hasvh.org

Gary Robertson, President

National Organizations & Federal Agencies/General

State supported veterans homes. Seeks to: maintain high standards of domiciliary, nursing home, and hospital care for veterans and eligible family members; provide a clearinghouse for techniques and expertise in veteran care and in the management of these institutions; represent the veterans' needs before Congress and the Veterans Administration. Encourages continued federal financial support for building state facilities and for providing care for veterans currently living in state homes. Works to sustain current veterans' benefits. Assists other states in establishing homes. Compiles statistics.
1952

204 **National Association of Veterans Program Administrators**
600 S Clyde Morris Boulevard
Daytona Beach, FL 32114-3966
386-226-6350
Fax: 386-226-6951
e-mail: sshorr@mail.ccf.edu
http://www.navpa.org

Faith DesLauriers, President
Les Bakke, VP

Devoted to promoting professional competency and efficiency through an association of members and others associated with and involved in Veterans Education Assistance Programs. Offers membership to those directly employed in veterns affairs or those genuinely interested in and supportive of the goals of the Association.
1975

205 **National Board for Certified Counselors**
3 Terrace Way
Suite D
Greensboro, NC 27403-3660
336-547-0607
800-398-5389
Fax: 336-547-0017
e-mail: nbcc@nbcc.org
http://www.nbcc.org

Thomas Clawson, Executive Director
Susan Eubanks, Associate Executive Director

Sets professional counselor credentialing standards.
1982

206 **National Caucus and Center on Black Aged**
1220 L Street NW
Suite 800
Washington, DC 20005-2410
202-637-8400
Fax: 202-347-0895
e-mail: info@ncba-aged.org
http://www.ncba-aged.org

Karyne Jones-Conley, President/CEO
Elias Hussein, Executive VP

Seeks to improve living conditions for low-income elderly Americans, particularly blacks. Advocates changes in federal and state laws in improving the economic, health, and social status of low-income senior citizens. Promotes community awareness of problems and issues effecting low-income aging population. Operates an employment program involving 2000 older persons in 14 states. Sponsors, owns, and manages rental housing for the elderly. Conducts training and intern programs in nursing home administration, long-term care, housing management, and commercial property maintenance.
1970

207 **National Center for Voluntary Leadership in Aging**
National Council on the Aging
1901 L St, NW 4th Floor
Washington, DC 20036
202-479-1200
800-867-2755
Fax: 202-479-0735
http://http://www.ncoa.org

James Firman, President/CEO

Links and assists volunteers serving on boards, commissions and committees of organizations seeking to meet the needs of older adults and their families.

208 **National Center on Arts and the Aging**
1901 L St, NW 4th Floor
Washington, DC 20036
202-479-1200
Fax: 202-479-0735
http://www.ncoa.org

James Firman, President
Sylvia Rigss Liroff, Coordinator

A program of the National Council on the Aging. Seeks to stimulate a national awareness of the importance of the arts as part of the programs available to older adults and to ensure older adults equal access to the arts and art education. Acts as a national clearinghouse for program and funding resources; collects, organizes, and disseminates information and develops materials in response to requests from the field; cooperates with public and private institutions and agencies to assure older persons maximum access to and participation in the arts; acts as arts and aging consultant.

209 **National Center on Elder Abuse**
C/O Center For Community Research And Services
University Of Delaware
297 Graham Hall
Newark, DE 19716
302-831-3525
Fax: 302-831-4225
e-mail: NCEA@nasua.org
http://www.elderabusecenter.org

Sara Aravanis, Director

A national resource for elder rights, law enforcement and legal professionals, public policy leaders, researchers, and the public. The Center's mission is to promote understanding, knowledge sharing, and action on elder abuse, neglect, and exploitation.

210 **National Citizens Coalition for Nursing Home Reform**
1828 L Street NW
Suite 801
Washington, DC 20036-5104
202-332-2276
Fax: 202-332-2949
e-mail: nccnhr@nccnhr.org
http://www.nursinghomeaction.org

Alice H Hedt, Executive Director
Alison Hirschel, President
Sherry Huff Culp, VP

National, state and local consumer/citizen groups and individuals seeking nursing home and board and care reform. Seeks to provide a consumer voice at the national, state, and local levels in the development and implementation of the long-term care system. Publishes monthly newsletter and consumer books and materials.u consisting of advocates from around the country. Serves as a clearinghouse for information on nursing home and board care issues, and publishes consumer books and pamphlets. Maintains speakers' bureau; conducts research and advocacy programs.

211 **National Coalition on Rural Aging**
409 3rd Street SW
Suite 200
Washington, DC 20024-3212
202-479-1200
Fax: 202-479-0735

Kristin Duke, Director
James P Firman, CEO

Works toward improving and increasing services to the elderly living in rural areas.
1978

212 **National Committee for Quality Healthcare**
601 13th Street NW
Suite 500 North
Washington, DC 20005
202-783-1300
Fax: 202-783-3434
e-mail: ncqhc@crols.com
http://www.ncqhc.org

Catherine E McDermott, President/CEO

National Organizations & Federal Agencies/General

Coalition of health care professionals and organizations principally involved in the health care industry; includes hospitals, physicians, health maintenance organizations, nursing homes, manufacturers of health care equipment, investment bankers, architects, contractors, and accountants. Works to maintain and strengthen quality health care in the US.

213 **National Committee for Responsive Philanthropy**
2001 S Street NW
Suite 620
Washington, DC 20009-1165
202-387-9177
Fax: 202-332-5084
e-mail: ncrp@aol.com
http://www.ncrp.org

Aaron Dorfman, Executive Director

Organization representing low income, minorities, women, consumers, environmentalists, older Americans, youth, and others working for social change and the public interest who are concerned about the lack of philanthropic giving to organizations working for social change or progressive issues. Works with leaders in the philanthropic community and the recipients of philanthropic giving to increase public accountability by philanthropies. Also works to increase access to philanthropy's monies for those groups representing critical public needs. Initiates efforts to facilitate access to charity drives in the workplace. Is concerned with the giving patterns of private foundations, United Way, and corporations with philanthropic programs. Conducts research; compiles statistics; publicizes reports; organizes local alternatives to United Way.

1976

214 **National Committee for the Prevention of Elder Abuse**
1612 K Street NW
Washington, DC 20006-2802
202-682-4140
Fax: 202-223-2099
e-mail: ncpea@verizon.net
http://www.preventelderabuse.org

Randolph W Thompson, President
Georgia Anetzberger, VP
Chayo Reyes, Treasurer

An association of researchers, practitioners, educators, and advocates dedicated to protecting the safety, security, and dignity of Americas' most vulnerable citizens. Established to achieve a clearer understanding of abuse and provide direction and leadership to prevent it.

1988

215 **National Committee to Preserve Social Security and Medicare (NCPSSM)**
10 G Street NE
Suite 600
Washington, DC 20004
202-216-0420
800-966-1935
Fax: 202-216-0451
e-mail: general@ncpssm.org
http://www.ncpssm.org

Barbara Kennelly, President

An advocacy and education membership organization, works to protect and enhance Federal programs vital to seniors' health and economic well-being.

216 **National Conference on Public Employee Retirement Systems**
444 N Capitol Street NW
Suite 221
Washington, DC 20001-1512
202-624-1456
877-202-5706
Fax: 202-624-1439
e-mail: info@ncpers.org
http://www.ncpers.org

Robert Podgorny, President
Pat McElligott, VP

Dedicated to the protection and preservation of retirement benefits for all public sector employees and retirees. Founded to protect public employees against an action by the federal government that would have wiped out public pension systems, namely, mandatory Social Security coverage of non-covered state and local government employees.

1941

217 **National Council of Social Security Management Associations**
418 C St, NE
Washington, DC 20002
202-547-8530
Fax: 202-547-8532
e-mail: president@ncssma.org
http://www.ncssma.org

Greg Heineman, President
Bethany Paradis, Vice President
Ron Mitchell, Executive Officer

Managers and supervisors of the 1350 Social Security field offices and teleservice centers in the US and Puerto Rico. Purposes are to represent the interests of members before Congress, the media, and agency heads and to improve the image and professionalism of federal employees. Has conducted research on federal employee pay and retirement benefits. Maintains speakers' bureau.

Number of Members: 3,200

218 **National Council on Child Abuse (NCCAFV)**
1025 Connecticut Avenue NW
Suite 1000
Washington, DC 20036-5417
202-429-6695
Fax: 831-655-3930
e-mail: info@nccafv.org
http://www.nccafv.org

Alan Davis, President/Secretary
Mary Ellen Rood MS, Executive VP

Works to prevent elder abuse and all forms of family violence including child abuse and spouse/partner abuse. NCCAFI provides information through its website and referrals for services upon request.

1984

219 **National Council on Disability**
1331 F Street NW
Suite 1050
Washington, DC 20004-1162
202-272-2004
Fax: 202-272-2022
http://www.ncd.gov

Mike Collins, Executive Director

Federal agency led by 15 members appointed by the President of the United States and confirmed by the United States Senate. The overall purpose of the National Council is to promote policies, programs, practices and procedures that guarantee equal opportunity for all people with disabilities, regardless of the nature of severity of the disability; and to empower people with disabilities to achieve economic self-sufficiency, independent living andd integration into all aspects of society.

220 **National Council on the Aging**
1901 L St, NW
4th Floor
Washington, DC 20036
202-479-1200
800-424-9046
Fax: 202-479-0735
e-mail: info@ncoa.org
http://www.ncoa.org
TDD 202-479-6674

James Firman, President

A comprehensive aging network membership association for professionals and volunteers who provide services to older persons and their families. For more than 40 years, NCOA has been at the forefront of advocacy, policy, education and model program development on issues affecting the quality of life for older Americans.

221 **National Emergency Medicine Association**
306 W Joppa Road
Baltimore, MD 21204-4048
410-494-0300
800-332-6362
Fax: 410-494-0725
http://www.nemahealth.org

Thomas Blair, Chair
Patricia Brookhart, Treasurer
Suzanne Levin, Secretary

National Organizations & Federal Agencies/General

Provides information and referral for emergency medical services. Free information packet and transcripts of the Heart of the Matter radio program are available.

222 National Endowment for the Arts: Office for Special Constituencies
1100 Pennsylvania Avenue NW
Suite 605
Washington, DC 20004-2501
202-682-5400
Fax: 202-682-5651

Paula Terry, Coordinator
Dana Gioia, CEO

Offer cultural organizations information on how to make programs accessible to older adults and individuals with various disabilities.

223 National Family Caregivers Association (NFCA)
10400 Connecticut Avenue
Suite 500
Kensington, MD 20895-3944
301-942-6430
800-896-3650
Fax: 301-942-2302
e-mail: info@nfcacares
http://www.nfcacares.org

Suzanne Geffen Mintz, Co-Founder/President

Supports family caregivers, providing assistance and information, free membership for family caregivers.

224 National Federation for Specialty Nursing Organizations
PO Box 56
Pitman, NJ 08071
856-256-2333
Fax: 609-589-7463
e-mail: nfsno@mail.ajj.com

Cynthia Nowicki, Executive Director
Anthony Jannetti, Manager

Nursing specialty organizations representing approximately 400,000 individuals. Provides a forum for the discussion of issues of mutual concern to members; attempts to gain more input in the establishment of nursing standards. Sponsors Nurse in Washington Internship.

225 National Federation of Licensed Practical Nurses
605 Poole Drive
Garner, NC 27529-5203
919-779-0046
Fax: 919-779-5642
e-mail: jbeal@mgmt4u.com
http://www.nflpn.org

Irene Bruns, LPN, President
Charlene Barbour, Executive Director

Federation of state associations of licensed practical and vocational nurses. Aims to: preserve and foster the ideal of comprehensive nursing care for the ill and aged; improve standards of practice; secure recognition and effective utilization of LPNs; further continued improvement in the education of LPNs. Acts as clearinghouse for information on practical nursing and cooperates with other groups concerned with better patient care.an program.
1949

226 National Gerontological Nursing Association
7794 Growing Drive
Pensacola, FL 32514
850-473-1174
800-723-0560
Fax: 850-484-8762
e-mail: ngna@puetzamc.org
http://www.ngna.org

Belinda Puetz, Executive Director
Deborah Blanchard, Chapter Services
Judith Hertz, PhD RN, President

An organization of nurses specializing in care of older adults, informs the public on health issues affecting older people, supports education for nurses and other health care practitioners, and provides a forum to discuss topics such as nutrition in long-term care facilities and elder law for nurses.

227 National Health Information Center
Office of Disease Prevention and Health Promotion
PO Box 1133
Washington, DC 20013-1133
301-565-4167
800-336-4797
Fax: 301-984-4256
http://www.health.gov/nhic/

Rachel Langston, Manager

Aids consumers and health professionals in locating health information; provides referrals to national organizations. Free literature is available; some publications for sale. Hours: 9:00 a.m. to 5:30 p.m. Monday-Friday.

228 National Hispanic Council on Aging
734 15th St, NW
Suite 1050
Washington, DC 20036-1854
202-347-9733
Fax: 202-347-9735
e-mail: nhcoa@nhcoa.org
http://www.nhcoa.org

Yanira Cruz MPH, President/CEO

A national organization providing advocacy, education, and information for older Hispanic people.

229 National Indian Council on Aging
10501 Montgomery Boulevard NE
Suite 210
Albuquerque, NM 87111-3846
505-292-2001
Fax: 505-292-1922
e-mail: dave@nicoa.org
http://www.nicoa.org

Clifford Doxtator, Chairman
James DeLaCruz, Vice Chair
Harriet Rhoades, Secretary

Native Americans. Seeks to bring about improved, comprehensive services to the Indian and Alaska native elderly. Objectives are to act as a focal point for the articulation of the needs of the Indian elderly; to disseminate information on Indian aging programs; to provide technical assistance and training opportunities to tribal organizations in the development of their programs. Conducts research on the needs of Indian elderly.
1976

230 National Information and Referral Support Center (NIRSC)
1225 I Street NW
Suite 725
Washington, DC 20005-3914
202-898-2578
Fax: 202-898-2583
http://www.nasua.org

Provides technical assistance, consultation, and training to State and Area Agencies on Aging and to local information and referral providers funded under the Older Americans Act.

231 National Institute of Senior Housing
National Council on the Aging
1901 L St, NW
4th Floor
Washington, DC 20036
202-479-1200
Fax: 202-479-0735
e-mail: info@ncoa.org
http://www.ncoa.org
TDD 202-479-6674

James P Firman, EdD, President/CEO
Ronald W Schoeffler, EdD, Executive Director
Richard Burman, Chief Operating Officer

The National Council on Aging (NCOA) is dedicated to improving the health and independence of older persons and increasing their continuing contributions to communities, society, and future generations. NCOA is a 501(c)3 organization.
Number of Members: 3,800

National Organizations & Federal Agencies/General

232 **National Institute on Adult Daycare**
National Council on the Aging
409 3rd Street SW
Suite 200
Washington, DC 20024-3212
202-479-1200
800-867-2755
Fax: 202-479-0735
James Firman, President/CEO

The only national organization providing a focal point for adult daycare at the national level.

233 **National Institute on Age, Work and Retirement**
National Council on the Aging
1901 L St, NW
4th Floor
Washington, DC 20036
202-479-1200
Fax: 202-479-0735
e-mail: info@ncoa.org
http://www.ncoa.org
James P Firman, President/CEO

Promotes opportunities for middle-aged and older workers. Provides information on organizations serving older workers and technical assistance to older worker program directors. Conducts research on work/retirement behavior and attitudes. Advises corporations on employment practices and retirement planning programs.

234 **National Institute on Community-Based Long-Term Care**
National Council on the Aging
1901 L St, NW
4th Floor
Washington, DC 20036
202-479-1200
800-867-2755
Fax: 202-479-0735
James Firman, President/CEO

A unit of the National Council on the Aging. Seeks to promote a comprehensive long-term care system that will integrate home-and community-based services, enabling older adults to live in their own homes as long as it is medically, socially, and economically feasible. Serves as information clearinghouse for long-term care professionals. Advocates public policies that support home and community-based services. Maintains speake.rs' bureau; offers educational sessions; compiles statistics.

235 **National Institute on Financial Issues and Services for Elders**
National Council on the Aging
1901 L St, NW
4th Floor
Washington, DC 20036
202-479-1200
800-867-2755
Fax: 202-479-0735
James Firman, President/CEO

Assists professionals who provide financial assistance to older persons.

236 **National Institutes of Health**
US Department of Health & Human Services
9000 Rockville Pike
Bethesda, MD 20892
301-496-4000
e-mail: NIHinfo@od.nih.gov
http://www.nih.gov
TTY 301-402-9612
Elias A Zerhouni, MD, Director

NIH is the steward of medical and behavioral research for the Nation. Its mission is science in pursuit of fundamental knowledge about the nature and behavior of living systems and the application of that knowledge to extend healthy life and reduce the burdens of illness and disability. There are various divisions of the NIH that deal with specific health issues; see separate NIH listings.

237 **National Interfaith Coalition on Aging**
National Council on the Aging
409 3rd Street SW
Suite 200
Washington, DC 20024-3212
202-479-1200
800-867-2755
Fax: 202-479-0735
James Firman, President/CEO

Promotes dialogue and cooperative effort among organizations and individuals about the spiritual concerns and well-being of older Americans.

238 **National Jewish Medical and ResearchCenter**
1400 Jackson Street
Denver, CO 80206-2762
303-388-4461
800-222-LUNG
Fax: 303-270-2165
e-mail: lungline@njc.org
http://www.nationaljewish.org
Michael Salem, President/CEO
Ron Berge, Executive VP/COO

A recorded message prompts caller according to specific needs. A registered nurse is available to provide information on respiratory diseases and offers tips on how to cope with them. Offers referrals to doctors in the caller's area. Free literature is available. Hours: 8:00 a.m. to 5:00 p.m. Monday-Friday.
1978

239 **National Legal Support for Elderly People with Mental Disabilities Project**
1101 15th Street NW
Suite 1212
Washington, DC 20005
202-457-5730
Fax: 202-223-0409
e-mail: info@bazelon.org
http://www.bazelon.org
TDD 202-467-4232
Robert Bernstein, Executive Director

Project focuses on legal issues of older people, training legal aid lawyers, organizing workshops, and providing information on legal issues facing older people with mental disabilities.

240 **National Long-Term Care Ombudsman Resource Center (NLTCORC)**
ORC Office
1828 L Street NW, Suite 801
Washington, DC 20036
202-332-2275
Fax: 202-332-2949
e-mail: ombudcenter@ncnhr.org
http://www.ltcombudsman.org
Alice H Hedt, NCCNHR, Executive Director
Lori Smetanka, Director

Operated by the NCCNHR in collaboration with the National Association of State Units on Aging. The Center support groups under Federal mandate to identify and resolve residents' problems at long-term care facilities.

241 **National Long-Term Care Resource Center**
420 Delaware St, SE
MMC 729
Minneapolis, MN 55455
612-624-6151
Fax: 612-624-2196
http://www.hsr.umn.edu

Assists State and Area Agencies on Aging and other community-based service agencies to monitor, develop, and refine community long-term care systems through legal reform.

242 **National Mental Health Association**
2000 N Beauregard Street
6th Floor
Alexandria, VA 22311-1739
703-684-7722
800-969-6642
Fax: 703-684-5968
e-mail: intoctr@nmha.org
http://www.nmha.org
David L Shern, President/CEO
Kate Gaston, VP
1909

National Organizations & Federal Agencies/General

243 **National Network for the Disabled**
PO Box 3574
Gardena, CA 90247-7274
310-638-5717
Fax: 310-638-5986

Linda Walls, Founder/President

Offers networking, companionship, and supoprt for the elderly and parents of disabled children.

244 **National Old Timers Auto Racing Club**
4 Rita Drive
Bethel, CT 06801-3025
203-791-8536

Pete Poodiack, Executive Director

Sanctions 25+ year old open wheel, stock car and modified exhibitions and memorabilia. Museum at Flemington Fairgrounds.

245 **National Old-Time Fiddlers' Association**
115 W Idaho Street
Weiser, ID 83672-1945
208-414-0255
800-437-1280
Fax: 208-414-0256
e-mail: notfc@ruralnetwork.net
http://fiddlecontest.com

Layna Hafer, Manager

Dedicated to the coordination of the states in the revival and preservation of old time fiddle music.
1953 Number of Members: 600

246 **National Organization for Albinism and Hypopigmentation**
PO Box 959
East Hampstead, NH 03826
603-887-2310
800-473-2310
Fax: 603-887-6049
e-mail: info@albinism.org
http://www.albinism.org

Michael McGowan, President

NOAH provides information and support regarding albinism and related conditions, promotes public and professional education about these conditions, and encourages research and funding that will lead to improved diagnosis and management of albinism. NOAH provides networking for those with special interests related to albinism, such as minority groups and Hermansky-Pudlak syndrome.
1982

247 **National Organization for Victim Assistance**
510 King Street
Suite 424
Alexandria, VA 22314
703-535-6682
800-879-6682
Fax: 703-535-5500
http://www.trynova.org

Carol Lavery, President
Jeannette M Adkins, MEd, Executive Director

NOVA's mission is to promote rights and services for victims of crime and crisis everywhere.

248 **National Organization of HIV over Fifty**
SW Boulevard Family Health Care Services
340 Southwest Boulevard
Kansas City, KS 66103-2150
816-421-5263
Fax: 913-722-2542
e-mail: janepfosler@mindspring.com
http://www.HIVoverfifty.org

Jim Campbell, President
Paul Quin, VP

The mission of this organization is to promote the availability of a full range of educational, prevention, service, and health care programs for persons over age 50 years affected by HIV.

249 **National Organization on Disability (NOD)**
910 16th Street NW
Suite 600
Washington, DC 20006-2916
202-293-5960
800-248-ABLE
Fax: 202-293-7999
http://www.nod.org
TDD 202-293-5968

Michael Deland, President
Charles Dey, VP/Director

Recorded message requests name, address, and type of information desired. Provides information on NOD programs and offers referrals to organizations and agencies concerned with specific disabilities. Free information packet and fact sheets are available. Hours: 24 hours per day/ seven days per week.

250 **National Osteoporosis Foundation**
1232 22nd Street NW
Washington, DC 20037-1216
202-223-2226
800-231-4222
Fax: 202-223-2237
e-mail: nofmail@nof.org
http://www.nof.org

Judith Cranford, Executive Director
Alice Page, Manager

A national voluntary health organization dedicated to reducing the widespread prevalence of osteoporosis. (Osteoporosis is an excessive loss of bone tissue which often results in fractures of the hip, spine, and wrist.) Seeks to: increase public awareness and knowledge about osteoporosis; provide information about osteoporosis to sufferers and their families; educate physicians and allied health professionals; advocate for increased governmental. support for research on osteoporosis; and support basic biomedical, epidemiological, clinical, behavioral, and social research and research training. Sponsors Research Grant Award program; conducts public and professional education programs.

251 **National People's Action**
110 N Milwaukee Avenue
Chicago, IL 60622-4103
312-243-3038
Fax: 312-243-7044
e-mail: hn1742@connectinc.com
http://www.npa-us.org

Emira Palacios, Co-Chairperson
Alicia Mendoza, Manager

Coalition of neighborhood organizations, unions, senior citizens' groups, and churches concerned with investment in and revitalization of individual neighborhoods. Lobbies for increased involvement on issues concerning: housing; credit and lending policies; community development funds; drugs; utility rates; health care costs. Organizes low- and moderate-income people and was instrumental in passage of legislation.sure Act and the Community Reinvestment Act.

252 **National Prison Hospice Association**
PO Box 4623
Boulder, CO 80306-4623
303-448-8051
Fax: 303-544-9875
e-mail: npha@npha.org
http://www.npha.org

Fleet Maull, President
Phyllis Taylor, VP
Felice Owens, Treasurer

Promotes hospice care for terminally ill inmates and those facing the prospect of dying in prison. Hospice is a comfort-oriented care that allows seriously ill and dying patients to die with dignity and humanity with as little pain as possible.
1991

253 **National Program on Women and Aging**
Brandeis University
The Heller School for Social Policy and Management
Institute on Assetts and Social Policy, MS 035
Waltham, MA 02454-9110
781-736-3826
800-929-1995
http://www.brandeis.edu/heller/national

National Organizations & Federal Agencies/General

Focuses on older women's issues and provides policy analysis, research, and assistance to the network of Administration and Aging-funded State and Area Agencies on Aging. The Center provides information and publications on women's health, caregiving, income security, and housing as well as prevention of crime and violence toward older women.

254 **National Rehabilitation Information Center (NARIC)**
8201 Corporate Drive
Suite 600
Landover, MD 20785
301-459-5900
800-346-2742
Fax: 301-459-4263
e-mail: naricinfo@heitechservices.com
http://www.naric.com

Mark Odum, Director

Provides information on disabilities, rehabilitation, and related issues. Performs database searches for a small fee. Free information packet is available; publication for sale. Hours: 8:00 a.m. to 5:00 p.m. Monday-Friday.

255 **National Resource Center on Native American Aging (NRCNAA)**
PO Box 9037
Grand Forks, ND 58202-9037
701-777-3848
Fax: 701-777-6779
http://www.med.und.nodak.edu/depts/rural/nrcnaa

The Resource Center, funded by the Administration on Aging, provides support, advocacy, and information for older Native Americans, including American Indians, Alaska Natives, and Native Hawaiians.

256 **National Resource Center on Supportive Housing & Home Modifications**
USC Andrus Gerontology Center
3715 McClintock Avenue
Los Angeles, CA 90089-0191
213-740-1364
Fax: 213-740-7069
e-mail: homemods@usc.edu
http://www.homemods.org

Jon Pynoos PhD, Director

Contact the center for information on government-assisted housing, assisted living policies, home modifications for older people, training and education courses, and technical assistance.

257 **National Retired Teachers Association**
A Division of AARP (NRTA)
601 E Street NW
Washington, DC 20049
202-434-2277
Fax: 202-434-2320
http://www.aarp.org

Horace B Deets, Executive Director
William D Novelli, CEO

Retired or current teachers who are 50 years of age or older
1947

258 **National Rural Health Association**
521 E 63rd Street
Kansas City, MO 64111
816-756-3140
Fax: 816-756-3144
http://www.nrharural.org

Alan Morgan, CEO
Rob McVay, Director Of Operations/CFO

Non-profit, professional organization targeting health care problems unique to rural areas and serving as a liaison between rural health care providers and older people.

259 **National Senior Citizens Law Center**
3435 Wilshire Boulevard
Suite 2860
Los Angeles, CA 90010-2029
213-639-0930
Fax: 213-639-0934
http://www.nsclc.org

Paul Nathanson, Executive Director
Edward Spurgeon, President
Michael Kelly, VP

Legal services support center specializing in the legal problems of the elderly poor. Acts as advocate on behalf of elderly, poor clients in litigation and administrative affairs. Sponsors conferences and workshops on areas of the law affecting the elderly. See Legal Resources chapter for specific state resorces.

260 **National Senior Games Association**
PO Box 82059
Baton Rouge, LA 70884-2059
225-766-6800
Fax: 225-766-9115
http://www.nationalseniorgames.org

Phil Godfrey, President/CEO

Non-profit organization promoting healthy lifestyles for older people through education, fitness, and sports.

261 **National Senior Service Corps**
1201 New York Avenue NW
Washington, DC 20525
202-606-5000
Fax: 202-606-3472
http://www.cns.gov

Volunteers from all different backgrounds of at least 55 years of age, involved in community needs. Local projects are organized and include healthcare, schools, courts and day dare.

262 **National Senior Service Corps Directors Associations**
4958 Butterworth Place NW
Washington, DC 20016-4354
202-244-2244
Fax: 202-244-2322

Alan G Lopatin, President

Directors of voluntary programs involving senior citizens, including foster grandparent, senior companion, and community service initiatives. Promotes involvement of senior citizens in community life. Coordinates members' activities and facilitates communication and cooperation among members; conducts research and educational programs; makes available children's services; compiles statistics.

263 **National Senior Women's Tennis Association**
171 Jennings Road
Cold Spring Harbor, NY 11724-1008
516-367-3746
e-mail: carolyn@carolynnichols.com
http://www.nswta.com

Carolyn Nichols, President
Pat Greer, Secretary/Executive Assistant
Ann Nunziata, Treasurer

Our mission is to increase awareness and participation in Senior Women's Tennis through augmenting current programs and creating and implementing new, innovative programs.

Number of Members: 1,200

264 **National Tax Association**
725 15th Street NW
Suite 600
Washington, DC 20005-2139
202-737-3325
Fax: 202-737-7308
e-mail: natltax@aol.com
http://www.ntanet.org

Ranjana Madhusudtian, President
James Poterba, First VP
Charmaine J Wright, Secretary

Government and corporate tax officials, accountants, consultants, economists, attorneys, teachers, and others interested in the field of taxation. Promotes scientific, nonpolitical study of taxation; encourages better understanding of the common interests of national, state, and local governments in matters of taxation and public finance. Membership benefits: National Tax Journal, Annual Conference on Taxation, Spring Symposium, NTA Forum and Special Conferences and Symposiums.

National Organizations & Federal Agencies/General

265 **National Urban League**
120 Wall Street
8th Floor
New York, NY 10005
212-558-5300
Fax: 212-344-5332
e-mail: info@nul.org
http://www.nul.org

Marc H Morial, President/CEO
Chandra Y Anderson, Senior VP Of Development
Paul Wycisk, Senior VP/CFO

Non-profit, community service organization helping older African Americans through advocacy and service programs which include health awareness, nutrition, housing, and intergenerational activities.

266 **National Women's Health Network**
514 10th Street NW
Suite 400
Washington, DC 20004-1410
202-347-1140
Fax: 202-347-1168
http://www.nwhn.org

Cynthia Pearson, Executive Director

An advocacy organization giving women a greater voice in the health care system in the United States. It is the only such membership organization and has a 20-year history of accomplishments on behalf of all women. Its clearinghouse of women's health information helps women make well-informed decisions. Also monitors federal legislation to ensure that women's needs are not overlooked.

267 **Naval Submarine League**
PO Box 1146
Annandale, VA 22003-9146
703-256-0891
877-280-7827
Fax: 703-642-5815
e-mail: nslops@starpower.net
http://www.navalsubleague.com

J Guy Reynolds, President
Bruce B Engelhardt, USN, VP
C Michael Garverick, Executive Director

Active and retired submariners, submarine industry employees, and other individuals interested in promoting a strong submarine force. Provides service and support to the active duty submarine force personnel. Seeks to educate the public on the need for a strong submarine force. Provides speakers, films, and slides to civic groups. Conducts annual closed sessions for members. Sponsors writing competitions and special awards.
1982

268 **Navy Mutual Aid Association**
29 Carpenter Road
Arlington, VA 22212
866-428-3191
Fax: 703-945-1441

Philip J Coady, President

Quasi-official mutual insurance organization for active and retired Navy, Marine Corps, Coast Guard, National Oceanic and Atmospheric Administration, and Public Health Service personnel.

269 **Navy Retired Activities Branch**
5720 Integrity Drive
Millington, TN 38055-6220
901-874-4307
800-255-8950
Fax: 901-874-2611
e-mail: p625@persnet.navy.mil
http://www.npc.navy.mil/commandsupport/

John W Townes III, Deputy Chief

A program of the US Department of the Navy. Manages the Survivor Benefit Plan, Secretary of the Navy Retiree Council, Retired Activities Offices, REtiree Casualty Assistance, Armed Forces Retirement Home. Aids retirees and survivors with problems regarding benefits and entitlements.
1978

270 **Navy Seabee Veterans of America**
555 Fairview Street
Creve Coeur, IL 61610-3237
309-699-7344
800-732-2335
Fax: 309-699-1201
e-mail: jimw133@aol.com
http://www.nsva.org

David J Buchanan, Commander
W.R. "Bear Holland", Vice Commander at Large

Veterans of the Naval Construction Forces and the Navy Civil Engineer Corps.

271 **Non-Discrimination in Federally Assisted Programs**
Office of Fair Housing and Equal Opportunity
451 7th Street SW
Room 5214
Washington, DC 20410
202-708-1112
Fax: 202-708-1251
e-mail: turner_x_.russell@hud.gov
http://www.hud.gov

Turner Russell, Contact
Marcella Belt, CEO

The Age Discrimination Act of 1975, as amended, is designed to prohibit discrimination on the basis of age in programs or activities receiving Federal financial assistance. The Act, however, permits federally assisted programs and activities and recipients of Federal funds to continue to use certain age distinctions and factors other than age that meet requirements of the Act and the regulation.

272 **Non-Discrimination in the Community Development Block Grant Program**
Asst Secretary for Fair Housing Equal Opportunity
451 7th Street SW
Room 5214
Washington, DC 20410
202-619-1112
Fax: 202-708-1425
e-mail: turner_x_.russell@hud.gov
http://www.hud.gov

Turner Russell, Contact
Marella Belt, CEO

Any individual feeling aggrieved because of an alleged discriminatory action in a Title I program on the basis of race, color, national origin, handicap, or age may file a complaint with the Department of Housing and Urban Development.

273 **Nurse Healers-Professional Associates International**
Box 419
Craryville, NJ 12521
518-325-1185
877-32N-HPAI
Fax: 509-693-3537
e-mail: nh-pai@therapeutic-touch.org
http://www.therapeutic-touch.org

Official organization of Therapeutic Touch, sets the standards for the practice and teaching of Therapeutic Touch. An international network of members interested in healing. It facilitates the exchange of research findings, teaching strategies, and new developments in this area. The human being is viewed as a complex, dynamic whole, and healing is seen as the means of restoring the integrity of the mind, body and spirit.
1977

274 **Nurses Christian Fellowship**
PO Box 7895
6400 Schroeder Road
Madison, WI 53707-7895
608-274-9001
Fax: 608-274-7882
e-mail: information@ivcf.org
http://www.ivcf.org

Mary Thompson, Director
Alec Hill, President

National Organizations & Federal Agencies/General

Professional organization and ministry of and for nurses and nursing students. Concerned for the nurse 'as a whole person,' and advocates quality care. Seeks to 'bring the good news of Jesus Christ to nursing education and practice.' Christian faith and contemporary nursing issues. Local activities include Bible studies, fellowship groups, conferences, prayer groups, and person-to-person training for student leaders, advisers, and volunteer staff.

1952

275 Office of Disability: Social Security Administration
Social Security Administration
Windsor Park Building
6401 Security Boulevard
Baltimore, MD 21235
410-965-3424
800-772-1213
Fax: 410-965-6503
http://www.ssa.gov
TTY 800-325-0778

Jo Anne B Barnhart, Commissioner
Nancy A McCullough, Senior Executive Officer
Veronica B Henderson, Executive Secretary

The Office of Disability pays disability under two programs: the Social Security Disability Insurance Program and the Supplemental Security Income (SSI) program. The office aids in application, decides disability and then determines benefits.

276 Office of Supplemental Security Income
US Department of Health & Human Services
Windsor Park Building
6401 Security Boulevard
Baltimore, MD 21235
410-965-4512
Fax: 410-965-9063
http://www.ssa.gov

Jo Anne B Barnhart, Commissioner

Supplemental Security Income (SSI) is run by Social Security but financed by the general revenue funds of the US Treasury. Any US citizen who is blind, disabled, or 65 or older is eligible.

277 Old Lesbians Organizing for Change
PO Box 5853
Athens, OH 45701
713-869-1482
Fax: 713-802-2989
e-mail: info@oloc.org
http://www.oloc.org

Arden Eversmeyer, Founder/President

Lesbians 60 years or older. Serves as a network to reduce ageism. Exchanges information on diversity of races, ethnicities, class backgrounds, and histories of members. Develops and disseminates educational materials on ageism and how to combat discrimination.

278 Older Women's League
3300 N Fairfax Drive
Suite 218
Arlington, VA 22201
703-812-7990
800-825-3695
Fax: 703-812-0687
e-mail: owlinfo@owl-national.org
http://www.owl-national.org

Ellen Bruce, President
Donna Wagner, Vice President

As the only national grassroots membership organization to focus solely on issues unique to women as they age, OWL strives to improve the status and quality of life for midlife and older women. OWL is a nonprofit, nonpartisan organization that accomplishes its work through research, education, and advocacy activities conducted through a chapter network. Now in its 23rd year, OWL provides a strong and effective voice for midlife and older women.

1980

279 Oley Foundation for Home Parenteral and Enteral Nutrition
214 Hun Memorial A-28
Albany, NY 12208
518-262-5079
800-776-OLEY
Fax: 518-262-5528
e-mail: bishopj@mail.amc.edu
http://www.oley.org

Rick Davis, President
Laura Ellis, VP
Michael Medwar, Secretary

Supports care of those who require tube or IV feedings at home.

1983

280 Over the Hill Gang International
1515 North Tejon St
Colorado Springs, CO 80907
719-389-0022
Fax: 719-389-0024
e-mail: info@othgi.com
http://www.othgi.com

Arthur P Foley, Director
Denise B Foley, Manager

Individuals 50 years of age and older who enjoy the camaraderie of skiing and other recreational activities with friends and share a spirit of adventure. Goal is to promote active sports, fitness, and the fellowship of individuals 50 years and older. Primarily a ski organization, but has expanded to include other sports such as biking, hiking, and golf. Sponsors adventure tours throughout the US, Europe, and the southern hemisphere. sponsored fund-raising projects to support the Colorado Ski Museum.

1977

281 PRIDE Foundation
Promote Real Independence for the Disabled/Elderly
391 Long Hill Road
Box 1293
Groton, CT 06340-1293
860-445-7320
800-332-9122
Fax: 860-445-1448
e-mail: sewtique@aol.com
http://www.sewtiqueonline.com

Evelyn S Kennedy, President/Proprietor

Is a nonprofit organization whose primary objective is to provide assistance for disabled and elderly persons. The purpose is to suggest solutions in the areas of homemaking, independence in dressing, personal grooming, and fashionable apparel. Consulting services are provided to families, agencies, and health organizations dealing with special needs of special persons.

282 Part A Title III: Ombudsman Services for Older Individuals
US Department of Health & Human Services
330 Independence Avenue SW
Washington, DC 20201
202-401-4634
Fax: 202-619-3757

Josefina G Carbonell, CEO

To assist State Agencies on Aging and Area Agencies on Aging to carry out programs for the provision of long-term care ombudsman services for older individuals.

283 Part A Title VI: Grants to Indian Tribes and Part B Title VI: Grants to Native Hawaiians
US Department of Health & Human Services
330 Independence Avenue SW
Washington, DC 20201
202-619-2957
Fax: 202-619-3759
http://www.acf.hss.gov

Quanah Crossland Stamps, Commissioner
Josefina G Carbonell ASA, Assistant Secretary
Edwin Walker PDASA, Deputy Assistant Secretary

To promote the delivery of supportive services, including nutrition services, to Native Americans, Alaskan Natives, and Native Hawaiians, 60 years and older. Services are comparable to services provided under title III of the Older Americans Act of 1965, as amended. Tribes also have the authority to define Indians under 60 years of age as 'older Indian' for eligibility purposes.

National Organizations & Federal Agencies/General

284 **Part B Title III: Grants for Supportive Services and Senior Centers**
US Department of Health & Human Services
330 Independence Avenue SW
Washington, DC 20201
202-401-4634
Fax: 202-619-3759

Josefina G Carbonell, CEO

To assist State Agencies on Aging and Area Agencies on Aging to foster the development of community-based systems of services for persons 60 and over via statewide planning, area planning, and provision of supportive services, including multi-purpose senior centers.

285 **Part C Title III: Nutrition Services**
US Department of Health & Human Services
330 Independence Avenue SW
Washington, DC 20201
202-401-4634
Fax: 202-619-3759

Josefina G Carbonell, CEO

To provide grants to states to support nutritious meals, nutrition education, and other appropriate nnutrition services for individuals 60 and over and their spouses, especially those older individuals with the greatest social need or those with the greatest economic need; and in certain cases under age 60, if the individual is disabled and resides with and accompanies an older individual. Meals may be served in a congregate setting or delivered.

286 **Part F Title 111: Preventive Health Services Special Programs for the Aging**
US Department of Health & Human Services
200 Independence Avenue SW
Washington, DC 20201
202-619-0257
877-696-6775
e-mail: secretary@hhs.gov
http://www.hhs.gov

Mike Leavitt, Secretary
Alex Michael Azar II, Deputy Secretary
Rich McKeown, Chief of Staff

To assist State Agencies on Aging and Area Agencies on Aging to carry out programs with repect to preventive health services and health promotion for older individuals, especially those living in areas of States that are medically underserved and in which there are a large number of older individuals who have the greatest economic need for the services.

287 **Part G Title 111: Prevention of Abuse, Neglect and Exploitation of Older Individuals**
US Department of Health & Human Services
200 Independence Avenue SW
Washington, DC 20201
202-619-0257
877-696-6775
e-mail: secretary@hhs.gov
http://www.hhs.gov

Mike Leavitt, Secretary
Alex Michael Azar II, Deputy Secretary
Rich McKeown, Chief of Staff

To assist State Agencies on Aging and Area Agencies on Aging to carry out programs with repect to the prevention of abuse, neglect, and exploitation of older individuals.

288 **Pension Research Council (PRC)**
Wharton School, University of Pennsylvania
3620 Locust Walk, 3000 SH-DH
Philadelphia, PA 19104
215-898-7620
Fax: 215-573-3418
e-mail: prc@wharton.upenn.edu
http://www.pensionresearchcouncil.org

Olivia S Mitchell, Executive Director
Michael O Pansini, Owner

Sponsors nonpartisan, interdisciplinary research on the entire range of private and social retirement security and related benefit plans in the United States and around the world. Affiliated with the Wharton School of the University of Pennsylvania, and is supported by contributions from industry, insurance companies, banks, and pension consultants. Conducts interpretive studies of broad scope.
1952

289 **Pension Rights Center**
1350 Connecticut Avenue NW
Suite 206
Washington, DC 20036-1739
202-296-3776
Fax: 202-833-2472
e-mail: pnsnrights@aol.com
http://www.pensionrights.org

Karen W Ferguson, Director

Public interest group whose purpose is to protect and promote the pension rights of workers, retirees, and their families and to develop solutions to the nation's retirement income problems. Represents workers and retirees' interests before government agencies and Congress.

290 **Pension to Veterans, Surviving Spouses, and Children**
US Department of Veterans Affairs
810 Vermont Avenue NW
Washington, DC 20420
202-273-7210
Fax: 202-233-2807
http://www.va.gov

Honorable James B Peake, Secretary Veterans Affairs
Thomas G Bowman, Chief of Staff
Honorable Gordan H Mansfield, Deputy Secretary

To assist needy surviving spouses and children of deceased war-time veterans whose deaths were not due to service.

291 **People Animals Love**
4900 Massachusetts Avenue NW
Suite 330
Washington, DC 20016
202-966-2171
Fax: 202-966-2172
e-mail: palinfo@peopleanimalslove.com
http://www.peopleanimalslove.com

Earl O Strimple DVM, Founder/Chairman
Louann Mackowiak, President
Joseph S Cavarretta CAE, Executive Director

PAL is a nonprofit organization that brings people and animals together, brightening the lives of the lonely, easing the pain of the sick, and enriching the world of at-risk children.

292 **People's Medical Society**
PO Box 868
Allentown, PA 18105
610-770-1670
e-mail: cbi@peoplesmed.org
http://www.peoplesmed.org

Charles B Inlander, President

The People's Medical Society has been an important advisor to the Health Care Financing Administration on Medicare issues and an important health resource for many major news organizations.
1983

293 **Personal Census Search: Data User Services Division**
US Department of Commerce, Bureau of the Census
4700 Silver Hill Road Washington Place
Suitland, MD 20746
301-763-0287

Pamela Hout, CEO

To provide a source of data for proof of age or relationship for individuals in need of such information based on census records. These records may be the only recourse if the birth was not registered and if generally acceptable proofs, such as affidavits from the doctor or midwife who attended the birth, family Bible records, or baptismal certification are not available. Personal information from census records of 1920 and later is confidential.

294 **President's Committee for People with Intellectual Disabilities (PCPID)**
Administration for Children and Families
Aerospace Center, Suite 701
370 L'Enfant Promenade SW
Washington, DC 20447
202-619-0634
Fax: 202-205-9519
e-mail: satwater@acf.hhs.gov
http://www.acf.hhs.gov

Sally Atwater, Executive Director

National Organizations & Federal Agencies/General

Advises and assists the President and the Secretary of Health and Human Services on issues related to mental retardation. Evaluates national, state and local programs for individuals who are mentally retarded.

295 Pro Literacy Worldwide
1320 Jamesville Avenue
Syracuse, NY 13210-4241
315-422-9121
888-528-2224
Fax: 315-422-6369
e-mail: info@proliteracy.org
http://www.proliteracy.org
David C Harvey, President/CEO

Supports worldwide adult literacy. Programs include speaking, reading, writing and computational skills. Provides reading materials and resources for those with limited reading abilities.

296 Profit Sharing/401(k) Council of America
20 N Wacker Drive
Suite 3700
Chicago, IL 60606-3103
312-419-1863
Fax: 312-419-1864
e-mail: psca@psca.org
http://www.psca.org
David L Wray, President

Sponsors sharing information and working together to preserve a favorable regulatory environment for profit sharing and 401(K) plans. Collects best practices information and shares it with members through faxes, publications, conferences and a technical assistance hotline. Also, supports plan sponsors and participants in Washington through Congressional lobbying.

297 Protecting Adult Welfare (PAW)
17400 Marilla St.
Northridge, CA 91325
818-998-5400
800-506-4999
Fax: 775-871-6544
http://www.pawfoundation.org
Phillip Berman PhD, Chairman
William Margold, President

Encourages awareness and the protection of adult welfare through telephone help lines, peer counseling and enlightenment seminars.
1995

298 Railroad Retirement Board (RRB)
844 N Rush Street
Chicago, IL 60611-1275
312-787-3923
800-772-4258
Fax: 312-751-4923
http://www.rrb.gov
TDD 312-751-4701
Kenneth P Boehne, CFO

Administers comprehensive retirement-survivor and unemployment-sickness benefit programs for the Nation's railroad workers and their families. Participates in the administration of the Social Security Act and the Health Insurance for the Aged Act insofar as they affect railroad retirement beneficiaries. Note: Any local chapter can be reached by calling the 800# above.

299 Rascal Insurance Services
Electric Mobility Corporation
World Headquarters
591 Mantua Blvd
Sewell, NJ 08080
877-282-1447
e-mail: emcinsurance@electricmobility.com
http://www.rascalinsurance.com
Michael Johns, Director

Rascal Insurance Services is one of the nation's leading providers of power mobility equipment and distributor of the Rascal powerchair and scooter. Call for further information.

300 Rebuilding Together with Christmas in April
1536 16th Street NW
Washington, DC 20036-1402
202-483-9083
800-473-4229
Fax: 202-483-9081
e-mail: general_mail@christmasinapril.com
http://www.christmasinapril.org
Patty Riley Johnson, President/CEO

Sponsors research and educational programs concerning the elderly. Offers housing rehabilitation for low-income, elderly, and handicapped people.
1988

301 Respiratory Nursing Society
708 Gladstone CR
Maryville, TN 37804
850-474-8869
888-330-4767
Fax: 850-484-8762
e-mail: msat@aol.com
Casey Norris BSN MSN, President
Mary Findeisen PhD RN RRT, President-Elect

Nurses who care for clients with pulmonary dysfunction, and who are interested in the promotion of pulmonary health. Fosters the personal and professional development of respiratory nurses, and quality care of their clients. Provides educational opportunities and promotes research in the field.

302 Retired Enlisted Association (TREA)
1111 S Abilene Court
Aurora, CO 80012-4950
303-752-0660
800-338-9337
Fax: 303-752-0835
e-mail: editor@trea.org
http://www.TREA.org
David Washington, National President
Sharon Rhatican, Executive Director

Provides services to any enlisted person, retired from an active or reserve component of the Armed Forces, either for length of service or permanent medical disability. Active Duty, Reserve and National Guard enlisted personnel with 10 or more years retirement creditable service are also eligible for membership. compensation, Veterans Administration disability compensation, and cost-of-living allowances; encouraging the addition of national cemeteries; keeping medical facilities open. Sponsors cultural and social activities for members through local chapters. Conducts seminars and sponsors travel and insurance programs.
1963

303 Retired Military Police Association
PO Box 25343
Fayetteville, NC 28314-5005
910-867-4292
e-mail: rmpamack@aol.com
Mack H Mullins, Executive Director

Retired military police personnel. Works with active duty military police and civilian police during catastrophes. Conducts reunions and special events. Performs volunteer work and charitable services.

304 Retired and Senior Volunteer Program
1201 New York Avenue NW
Washington, DC 20525
202-606-5000
Fax: 202-565-2789
e-mail: info@cns.gov
http://www.cns.gov
TTY 202-606-3472
Rosetta Freeman-Busby, State Director

Provides part-time, uncompensated service opportunities for persons age 55 or older. Participants serve a wide range of national and community needs, working with persons of all ages in community-based projects across America.

National Organizations & Federal Agencies/General

305 Retirement Industry Trust Association
4424 Montgomery Avenue
Suite 102
Bethesda, MD 20814-4435
301-652-5066
Fax: 301-913-9146
http://www.r-i-t-a.org

Paul Maxwell, President
David S O'Bryon, Executive Director
Scott McCartan, Treasurer

The goals of RITA are: to promote throguh legislative and regulatory lobbying activities, the interest of trustees, custodians, and administrators of self-directed retirement plans; to encourage the development and use of uniform procedures in the administration of self-directed retirement plans; to provide a forum for the exchange of general information about the efficient administration of self-directed retirement plans; to improve business conditions in the industry devoted to marketing self-directed retirement plans; to stimulate personal and professional development and education among RITA members and associates.

306 SPRY Foundation
3916 Rosemary Street
Chevy Chase, MD 20815
301-656-3405
Fax: 301-656-6221
e-mail: morganr@spry.org
http://www.spry.org

Sandy Markwood, Vice Chair; Secretary/Treasurer

Non-profit foundation that develops research and education programs to help older adults plan for a healthy and financially secure future.

307 Sears Mature Outlook
PO Box 9390
Des Moines, IA 50306
800-336-6330
Fax: 515-334-9247

Alison Poklop, Marketing Manager

Organization for individuals over 50 years of age, that offers store discounts, a magazine and newsletter of general interest articles.

308 Senate Special Committee on Aging
US Senate Special Committee on Aging
G-31 Dirksen Senate Office Building
Washington, DC 20510
202-224-5364
Fax: 202-224-8660
e-mail: mailbox@aging.senate.gov
http://www.aging.senate.gov

Sen Gordon Smith, Chairman

Covers nonlegislative health and aging issues in the Senate.

309 Senior Companion Program
Greater Washington Urban League
Executive Office
2901 14th Street NW
Washington, DC 20009
202-265-8200
Fax: 202-265-6122
e-mail: LUWGDBS@aol.com
http://www.gwul.org/deptgwul

Maudine R Cooper, President/CEO
Jerry A Moore III, Chair
Sharon E Smallwood-Gund, Secretary

Offers companionship and volunteer opportunities for those 60 years of age or older. Provides services to low-income elderly through mental healthcare of the terminally ill and acute care.
1938

310 Senior Job Bank
PO Box 30064
Savannah, GA 31410
888-501-0804
e-mail: founder@seniorjobbank.org
http://www.seniorjobbank.org

Eric Summers, Founder

Online resource that provides free job information and resource for members.

311 Senior Service America (SSA)
8403 Colesville Road
Suite 1200
Silver Spring, MD 20910
301-578-8900
Fax: 301-478-8859
e-mail: contact@ssa-i.org
http://www.seniorserviceamerica.org

Non-profit organization providing employment opportunities, conducting research programs and workshops, and publishing its research findings.

312 Small Business Administration (SBA)
Service Corps of Retired Executive Association
1110 Vermont Avenue NW
Washington, DC 20005-3544
202-606-4000
http://www.jba.gov

To utilize the management experience of retired and active business executives to counsel and train potential and existing small businesses. The business must be independently owned and operated, not dominant in its field, and conform to SBA size standards.

313 Social Security Administration
US Department of Health & Human Services
6401 Security Boulevard
Baltimore, MD 21235-6401
410-965-6114
800-772-1213
http://www.ssa.gov

Bill Vitek, Manager

The Social Security Administration administers a national program of contributory social insurance whereby employees, employers, and the self-employed pay contributions which are pooled in special trust funds. When earnings stop or are reduced because the worker retires, dies, or becomes disabled, monthly cash benefits are paid to partially replace the earnings the family has lost.

314 Social Security: Retirement Insurance
US Department of Health & Human Services
Office of Public Inquiries, Room 4100
Annex
Baltimore, MD 21235
410-965-2736
800-772-1213
Fax: 410-966-6166
http://www.hhs.gov

Mike Leavitt, Secretary
Alex Michael Azar II, Deputy Secretary
Rich McKeown, Chief of Staff

To replace part of the earnings lost due to retirement. Also, certain family members can receive benefits including: a wife or husband age 62 or over; a spouse at any age, if a child who is under age 16 or is disabled is in his or her care and is entitled to benefits based on the worker's record; unmarried children under age 18; unmarried adult offspring at any age if disabled before age 22; and divorced wives or husbands age 62 or over.

315 Social Security: Special Benefits for Persons Aged 72 & Older
US Department of Health & Human Services
Office of Public Inquiries, Room 4100
Annex
Baltimore, MD 21235
410-965-2736
800-772-1213
Fax: 410-966-6166
http://www.hhs.gov

Wade F Horn PhD, Assistant Secretary

To assure some regular income to certain persons age 72 and over who had little or no opportunity to earn Social Security protection during their working years. Individuals who reached age 72 before 1968 need no work credits under Social Security to be eligible for special payments. Those who reached age 72 in 1968 or later need some work credits to be eligible. The amount of work credit needed increases gradually each year.

316 Society for Advancement in Nursing
PO Box 307
New York, NY 10003
212-998-5335

Erline P McGriff, President

National Organizations & Federal Agencies/General

Nurses having earned a minimum of a baccalaureate degree in nursing. Seeks to make a distinction between educational preparation and practice toward professional and technical careers in nursing. Promotes establishment of new licensure procedures for professional practice that differ from current registered nurse licensure. Strives to serve as a unified voice promoting relevant issues in nursing and health. Maintains speakers' bureau. Presently inactive.

317 Society for Ambulatory Care Professionals
American Hospital Association
1 N Franklin Street
Chicago, IL 60606-4425
312-422-3000
Fax: 312-422-4577
http://www.sacp-net.org

Dick Davidson, President

Promotes and works towards the advancement of ambulatory and home health care
1986

318 Special Care Dentistry
401 N Michigan Avenue
Suite 2200
Chicago, IL 60611
312-527-6764
Fax: 312-673-6663
e-mail: scd@scdonline.org
http://www.scdonline.org

Burt Nussbaum, President
Ford Grant, Vice President
Janet Yellowitz, Secretary

SCD's mission is to promote the oral health of special needs patients. SCD is currently comprised of dental health professionals who are part of the component organizations: American Association of Hospital Dentists (AAHD) - Hospital based dental professionals, American Society for Geriatric Dentistry (ASGD) - Dental professionals who treat geriatric, homebound and cognitively impaired adults, and the Academy of Dentistry for Persons with Disabilities (ADPD) - Dental professionals who treat physically challenged individuals.

319 State Guard Association of the United States
PO Box 1416
Fayetteville, GA 30214-6416
770-460-1215
Fax: 770-460-1215
e-mail: director@sgaus.org
http://www.sgaus.org

Byers W Coleman, Executive Director

The mission is to foster and support the militia concept in the Constitution of the United States of America and to provide assistance and support to the duly authorized militia of the various states and territories.on on the history and mission of the militia and to advocate a viable state militia system.

320 Supportive Older Women's Network
2805 N 47th Street
Philadelphia, PA 19131-1540
215-477-6000
Fax: 215-477-6555
e-mail: info@sown.org
http://www.sown.org

Merle Drake MSS, Executive Director
Nancy Morrow MSW, Development Director
Leena Ritchie, Treasurer

Helps women (60+) to cope with aging issues through support groups, leadership training, consultation and newsletters. Telephone support groups for homebound women are also provided.

321 TIAA-CREF
730 3rd Avenue
New York, NY 10017-3207
212-490-9000
800-842-7782
Fax: 212-916-4840
http://www.tiaa-cref.org

Herbert M Allison, Jr, Chairman/President/CEO
Stephanie Cohen Glass, Dir Corporate Media Relations
Susan S Kozik, EVP Chief Technology Officer

Provides a nationwide portable pension system for over 2 million employees of some 8,000 colleges, universities, independent schools, and related nonprofit educational and research institutions.

322 Tax Counseling for the Elderly: Taxpayers Services
Internal Revenue Service, US Dept of the Treasury
500 N Capitol Street
Washington, DC 20221
202-874-6748
http://www.irs.gov

Mark W Everson, Commissioner

To authorize the Internal Revenue Service to enter into agreements with private or public nonprofit agencies or organizations; to establish a network of trained volunteers to provide free income tax information and return preparation assistance to elderly taxpayers, 60 years or older.

323 Thyroid Foundation of America
One Longfellow Place
Suite 1518
Boston, MA 02114
617-534-1500
800-832-8321
Fax: 617-534-1515
e-mail: info@allthyroid.org
http://www.allthyroid.org

Judy Pate, Administrative Director
Lawrence C Wood, President

The Thyroid Foundation of America provides education and support to thyroid patients and works to increase public awareness of thyroid disease.

324 US Commission on Civil Rights: Civil Rights Discrimination Complaints
624 9th Street NW
Washington, DC 20425
202-376-8513
800-552-6843
http://www.uscer.gov

Kenneth L Marcus, Staff Director

To serve as a national clearinghouse for information to the public in respect to discrimination or denials of equal protection because of race, color, religion, sex, age, handicap, or national origin; to hold public hearings and collect and study information on discrimination or denials of equal protection. To receive and refer complaints alleging denial of civil rights because of the aforementioned factors.

325 US Department of Education: Office of Civil Rights
400 Maryland Avenue SW
Washington, DC 20202
202-401-2000
800-421-3481
Fax: 202-205-9862
http://www.ed.gov

Margaret Spellings, CEO

Prohibits discrimination on the basis of disability in programs and activities funded by the Department of Education. Investigates complaints and provides technical assistance to individuals and entities with rights and responsibilities under Section 504.

326 US Department of Health & Human Services
200 Independence Avenue SW
Room 615F
Washington, DC 20201
202-690-7650
Fax: 202-690-7098
http://www.dhhs.gov

The Secretary advises the President on health, welfare, and income security plans, policies, and programs of the Federal Government. The Secretary directs Department staff in carrying out the approved programs and activities of the Department and promotes general public understanding of the Department's goals, programs, and objectives. The Secretary administers these functions through the Office of the Secretary and the 4 Operating Divisions.

National Organizations & Federal Agencies/General

327 **US Department of Housing & Urban Development: Fair Housing and Equal Opportunity Hotline**
451 7th Street SW
Washington, DC 20410
202-708-1112
800-669-9777
Fax: 202-708-3106
http://www.hud.gov
TDD 202-708-1455
TTY 202-708-1455

Alphonso Jackson, Secretary
Roy A Bernardi, Deputy Secretary

Receives calls from victims of housing discrimination related to race, age, gender, disability, ethnicity, or national origin.

328 **US Department of Justice**
Civil Rights Division
950 Pennsylvania Ave, NW
Washington, DC 20530-0001
202-514-2000
800-514-0301
Fax: 202-307-0595
http://www.usdoj.gov

William Reynolds, Assistant Attorney General
Merrialy Friedlander, Director

Coordinates the implementation by federal agencies of section 504 of the Rehabilitation Act of 1973, as amended, which prohibits discrimination on the basis of handicap in federally assisted programs and in programs and activities conducted by federal executive agencies.

329 **US Department of Labor: Office of Federal Contract Compliance Programs**
200 Constitution Avenue NW
Washington, DC 20210
202-693-5000
866-4US-ADOL
Fax: 202-693-1453
http://www.dol.gov/esa

Elaine L Chao, CEO

Prohibits discrimination on the basis of disability and requires federal contractors and sub-contractors with contracts of $2,500 or more to take affirmative action to employ and advance individuals with disabilities.

330 **US Department of Transportation**
400 7th Street SW
Washington, DC 20590
202-366-4000
Fax: 202-755-7687
http://www.dot.gov

Rodney Slater, Director
Norman Y Mineta, CEO

Enforces ADA provisions that require nondiscrimination in public and private mass transportation systems and services.

331 **US Department of Veterans Affairs**
810 Vermont Avenue NW
Washington, DC 20420
800-488-8244
http://www.va.gov

Honorable R James Nicholson, Secretary Veterans Affairs
Thomas G Bowman, Chief of Staff
Honorable Gordon H Mansfield, Deputy Secretary

The US Department of Veterans Affairs provides patient care and federal benefits to veterans and their dependents.

332 **US Library of Congress Handicapped Hotline**
1291 Taylor Street NW
Washington, DC 20542
202-707-5100
800-424-9100
Fax: 207-707-0712

Frank Cylke, Executive Director

Administers a national library service that provides braille and audio-recorded books and magazines on free loan to anyone who cannot read standard print because of visual or physical disabilities. Provides referrals to state and local libraries. Hours: 8:00 a.m. to 4:30 p.m. Monday-Friday.

333 **US Office of Personnel Management**
1900 E Street NW
Washington, DC 20415
202-606-1800
888-767-6738
http://www.opm.gov

Constance Horner, Director
Claudio Benedi, Manager

Establishes policies for employment of the handicapped within the federal service. Administers a merit system for the federal employment that includes recruiting, examining, training, and promoting people on the basis of knowledge and skills, regardless of sex, race, religion or other factors.

334 **USA Next United Seniors Association**
PO Box 2038
Purcellville, VA 20132
703-359-6500
800-887-2872
Fax: 703-359-6510
e-mail: info@usanext.org
http://www.usanext.org

Charles W Jarvis, Chairman/Cheif Executive

Seeks to educate senior citizens about Social Secutiry, Medicare and other related issues.

335 **United Methodist Association of Health and Welfare Ministries (UMA)**
407B Corporate Center Drive
Vandalia, OH 45377-1165
937-415-3624
800-411-9901
Fax: 937-222-7364
e-mail: uma@umassociaton.org
http://www.umassociation.org

Merle L Griffith MD, President/CEO

Promotes communication between Methodist hospitals, ministries, retirement homes and family and youth associations

1940

336 **Vestibular Disorders Association**
PO Box 13305
Portland, OR 97213-0305
800-837-8428
Fax: 503-229-8064
e-mail: veda@vestibular.org
http://www.vestibular.org

Claire E Haddad, President
John A Niemitz, VP
Lisa Haven, Executive Director

This Association is a non profit organization that provides information to people with vestibular disorders, such as Labyrinthitis, BPPV, Meniere's Disease, and Perilymph Fistula.

1983

337 **Veterans Information and Assistance**
US Department of Veterans Affairs
810 Vermont Avenue NW
Washington, DC 20420
800-488-8244
http://www.va.gov

Honorable James Peake, Secretary Veterans Affairs
Thomas G Bowman, Chief of Staff
Honorable Gordon H Mansfield, Deputy Secretary

To provide all necessary information and assistance to potential claimants and other interested parties concerning veterans benefits and to provide a single point where this assistance can be obtained.

338 **Veterans Prosthetic Appliance, Rehabilitation and Prosthetics**
US Department of Veterans Affairs
810 Vermont Avenue NW
Room 542
Washington, DC 20420
202-273-5400

R James Nicholson, CEO

National Organizations & Federal Agencies/Canada

To provide, through purchase and/or fabrication, prosthetic and related appliances, equipment, and services to disabled veterans so that they may live and work as productive citizens.

339 Vietnamese Senior Citizens Association
6131 Willston Drive
Falls Church, VA 22044-3002 703-532-0267
Linh Quang Vien, President

Vietnamese individuals 50 years of age and older. Offers social and cultural assistance and fellowship to members. Seeks to preserve and develop Vietnamese culture, traditions, and customs. Sponsors community events including the Tet festival (a celebration of the Vietnamese New Year) and ceremonies commemorating Vietnamese national heroes and deceased relatives of members. Holds annual Christmas party. Maintains cemetery for members. Sponsors speakers and organizes trips.

340 Visiting Nurse Association of America
900 19th Street NW
Suite 200
Washington, DC 20006 202-384-1420
Fax: 202-384-1444
e-mail: vnaa@vnaa.org
http://www.vnaa.org

Voluntary, nonprofit home health care agencies. Develops competitive strength among community-based nonprofit visiting nurse organizations; works to strengthen business resources and economic programs through contracting, marketing, governmental affairs and publications.

341 Volunteers for Abused/Neglected Children
1705 DeSales St NW #300
Washington, DC 20036 202-328-2191
Fax: 202-265-6682
e-mail: nahdcasa@worldnet.att.net
http://www.voladv.org
Anne Radd, Director

Recruit, train, assign and manage volunteers to speak up for abused and neglected children who are in the court system.

342 Weatherization Assistance for Low-Income Persons: Conservation and Renewable Energy
US Dept of Energy, Weatherization Assist Program
2000 14th Street NW
Suite 300 East
Washington, DC 20009 202-673-6700
877-337-3463
Fax: 202-673-6725
http://www.eere.energy.gov
Charles J Clinton, Director
Carl E Williams, Weatherization Program Manager

To insulate the dwellings of low-income persons, particularly the elderly and disabled, in order to conserve needed energy and aid those persons least able to afford highter utility costs.

343 Windward Foundation
55 Windward Lane
Klickitat, WA 98670-9710 509-369-2000
800-369-4646
Fax: 509-369-2004
e-mail: windward@gorge.net
http://www.windward.org
Walter Patrick, Executive Director

Promotes self-reliance among homeless persons, single parents, and senior citizens through remedial work and hands-on programs. Focus includes: food, communication, and personal growth. Maintains library of books, periodicals, and archival materials on self-reliance skills and crafts. Bestows scholarships; conducts research.
1998

344 Workmen's Benefit Fund of the USA
399 Conklin St
Suite 310
Farmingdale, NY 11735-2614 516-938-6060
Fax: 516-706-9020
e-mail: info@wbfusa.com
http://www.wbfusa.com

Fraternal benefit life insurance society.
1984

345 World Institute on Disability
510 16th Street
Suite 100
Oakland, CA 94612-1520 510-763-4100
Fax: 510-763-4109
e-mail: wid@wid.org
http://www.wid.org
Deborah Kaplan, Executive Director
Kathy Martinez, Deputy Director

Policy issues affecting the disabled community, including personal assistance services, AIDS and disability, telecommunications, general disability policy, independent living, studies of attendant services, attitudes toward people with disabilities, leadership development, independent living program effectiveness, health insurance needs, and quality of life issues.
1983

Canada

346 Abbotsford Seniors' Association
33889 Essendene Avenue
Abbotsford BC, ZZ V2S 2H6 604-853-4014
Fax: 604-853-4031
e-mail: janner47@yahoo.com
http://www.abbotsfordseniorsassoc.com
John Larcheder, President
Patricia Edwards, Secretary

Provides recreational facilities for the seniors in the area.

347 Advocacy Centre for the Elderly
701, 2 Carlton Street
Toronto ON, ZZ M5B 1J3 416-598-2656
Fax: 416-598-7924
http://www.advocacycentreelderly.org

Provides legal services to low income seniors in the Greater Metropolitan Toronto Area. Also provides public legal education & law reform services provincially.

348 Age & Opportunity Inc.
200, 280 Smith Street
Winnipeg MS, ZZ R3C 1K2 204-956-6440
Fax: 204-946-5667
e-mail: info@ageopportunity.mb.ca
http://www.ageopportunity.mb.ca
Michelle Ranville, CEO
Nico Velthuys, Business Manager
Stacy Miller, Manager Community Services

Age & Opportunity is a social service agency that offers life-enhancing programs and services to older adults.

349 Association of Mature Canadians
366 Bay Street
7th Floor
Toronto ON, ZZ M5H 4B2 416-601-0429
Fax: 416-601-0308
e-mail: service@maturecanadians.ca
http://www.maturecanadians.ca
Robert Bruce, Executive Director

Supports members, through education and communication, by addressing changing lifestyle and health care needs in a socially and financially responsible way.

National Organizations & Federal Agencies/Canada

350 **CARP Canada's Association for the Fifty-Plus**
1304 27 Queen Street E
Toronto ON, ZZ M5C 2M6
416-363-8478
Fax: 416-363-8747
e-mail: advocacy@50plus.com
http://www.carp.ca

Lillian Morgenthau, President/Co-Founder
Murray Morgenthau, Executive Director/Co-Founder

Promotes the rights & quality of life of older Canadians through advocacy, education, information & CARP recommended services.

351 **Carefirst Seniors & Community Services Association**
501 3601 Victoria Park Avenue
Toronto ON, ZZ M1W 3Y3
416-502-2323
Fax: 416-502-2382
e-mail: info@carefirstseniors.com
http://www.carefirstseniors.com

Helen Leung, Executive Director

Small local charitable organization.

352 **Help the Aged**
205 1300 Carling Avenue
Ottawa ON, ZZ K1Z 7L2
613-232-0727
Fax: 613-232-7625
e-mail: info@helptheaged.ca
http://www.helptheaged.ca

To improve the quality of life of the elderly poor, support their independence and inclusion, and provide services and programs to relieve distress, poverty and sickness.

353 **Institute for Life Course and Aging**
University of Toronto
222 College Street
Suite 106
Toronto ON, ZZ M5T 3J1
416-978-0377
Fax: 416-978-4771
http://www.aging.utoronto.ca

Prof Lynn McDonald, Director
Susan Murphy, Administration

To conduct interdisciplinary research on the biological, psychological and social dimensions of the life course and aging; to provide graduate and post-graduate education on the life course and aging.

354 **NWT Seniors' Society**
103 4916-46th Avenue
Yellowknife NT, ZZ X1A 1L2
867-920-7444
Fax: 867-920-7601
e-mail: seniors@tamarack.nt.ca
http://www.nwtseniorssociety.ca

Barbara Hood, Executive Director
Beatrice Campbell, President

Promotes the independence and well-being of older citizens through the provision of programs and services in partnership with responsible government and other organizations.

355 **National Institute for the Care of the Elderly**
222 College Street
Suite 106
Toronto ON, ZZ M5T 3J1
416-978-0545
Fax: 416-978-4771
e-mail: info@nicenet.ca
http://www.nicenet.ca

Lynn McDonald PhD, Scientific Director
Anthony P Lombardo MA PhD, Network Manager

NICE is an international network of researchers, practitioners, students and seniors dedicated to improving the care of older adults, both in Canada and abroad.

356 **National Pensioners & Senior Citizens Federation**
44-2nd Avenue
Trenton ON, ZZ K8V 5M6
613-394-0739
e-mail: mitchell2@sympatico.ca
http://www.npscf.org

Art Field, President
Joyce Mitchell, Secretary

The National Pensioners and Senior Citizens Federation is an organization devoted entirely to the welfare and best interests of Canada's elderly.

357 **Older Women's Network**
80 Lothian Avenue
Etobicoke ON, ZZ M8Z 4K5
416-239-7252

Provides growth experience for older adults in group setting.

State Organizations & Government Agencies/Alabama

This chapter is arranged by state, and includes both private and governmental agencies. Within each state section, there are general resources on state, county and, often, city levels. These resources cover general issues, such as retirement, housing, health insurance, finances, daycare, transportation and advocacy. Resources for specific issues are included in other chapters, although some overlap does occur: Continuing Education; Assisted Living; Independent Living; Legal Aid; Libraries; and Health Conditions.

Alabama

358 Alabama Client Assistance Program
2129 East South Boulevard
Montgomery, AL 36116-2455
334-281-8780
800-441-7607
Fax: 334-281-1973
http://www.rehab.state.al.us
Lamona Lucas, Director
Steve Shivers, President

Mission is to enable Alabama's disabled population to achieve their maximum potential.

359 Alabama Department of Education: Disability Determination Service
PO Box 830300
Birmingham, AL 35283
205-989-2100
Fax: 205-989-2296
Linda T Bell, Medical Relations Officer
Olivia Fralish, Medical Relations Officer

360 Alabama Department of Public Health
201 Monroe Street
PO Box 303017
Montgomery, AL 36104
334-206-5300
866-264-4073
http://www.adph.org
Claude Fox, State Health Officer
Donald Williamson, Manager

The purpose of the Alabama Department of Public Health is to provide caring, high quality and professional services for the improvement and protection of the public's health through disease prevention and the assurance of public health services to resident and transient populations of the state regardless of social circumstances or the ability to pay.

361 Alabama Department of Rehabilitation Services
2129 SE Boulevard
Montgomery, AL 36116
334-281-8780
800-441-7607
Fax: 334-281-1973
http://www.rehab.state.al.us
Steve Shives, Commissioner
Jim Harris III, Assistant Commissioner

Mission is to enable Alabama's disabled population to achieve their maximum potential.

362 Alabama Department of Retirement Systems
135 South Union Street
PO Box 302150
Montgomery, AL 36104
334-832-4140
800-214-2158
Fax: 334-240-3032
http://www.rsa.state.al.us
David G Bronner, CEO

Safekeepers of the pensions for thousands of Alabamians. It is our constant goal to seek and secure the best investments and services for our membership.

363 Alabama Department of Revenue
50 N Ripley Street
Montgomery, AL 36132
334-242-1170
800-353-2540
http://www.ador.state.al.us
Cynthia Underwood, Acting Commissioner
Lewis A Easterly, Department Secretary

Mission is to efficiently and effectively administer the revenue laws in an equitable, courteous and professional manner to fund the governmental services for the citizens of Alabama.

364 Alabama Department of Senior Services
770 Washington Avenue
RSA Plaza Suite 470
Montgomery, AL 36130
334-242-5743
877-425-2243
Fax: 334-242-5594
e-mail: ageline@adss.alabama.gov
http://www.adss.state.al.us/
Irene B Collins, Executive Director

A cabinet level state agency that administers programs for senior citizens and people with disabilities. The department was originally establised by the Alabama Legislature in 1957 as the Alabama Commission on Aging.

365 Alabama Department of Veteran Affairs
770 Washington Avenue
RSA Plaza, Suite 530
Montgomery, AL 36130
334-242-5077
Fax: 334-242-5102
http://www.va.state.al.us
Frank Wilkes, Manager

Mission is to promote awareness, assist eligible veterans, their families, and survivors to receive from the US Federal and State Governments and and all benefits to which they may be entitled under existing or future laws to be enacted.

366 Alabama Developmental Disability Council
RSA Union Building
100 N Union Street
PO Box 301410
Montgomery, AL 36130-1410
334-242-3973
800-232-2158
Fax: 334-242-0797
e-mail: addpc@mh.state.al.us
http://www.acdd.org
Elmyra Jones, Executive Director
Cheryl Bartlett PhD, Planning/QA Specialist
Shunqulla Moore, Office Manager

Serves Alabama's disabled population and representatives of all service provider agencies that serve people with disabilities. The Council generates a state plan and identifies priority areas for service planning.
Number of Members: 36

367 Alabama Disabilities Advocacy Program
PO Box 870395
Tuscaloosa, AL 35487-0395
205-348-4928
800-826-1675
Fax: 205-348-3909
e-mail: adap@adap.ua.edu
http://www.adap.net
TDD 205-348-4928
Ellen Gillespie, Director
James Tucker, Associate Director
Angie Allen, Case Advocate

The Alabama Disabilities Advocacy Program (ADAP) is the federally mandated, statewide, 'Protection, and Advocacy' system serving eligible individuals with disabilities in Alabama. ADAP has four program components: protection and advocacy for persons with developmental disabilities (PADD), protection and advocacy for individuals with mental illness (PAIMT), protection and advocacy of individual rights (PAIR), and protection and advocacy for assistive technology (PAAT).

State Organizations & Government Agencies/Alabama

368 **Alabama Protection & Advocacy for Persons with Mental Illness**
PO Box 870395
Tuscaloosa, AL 35487-0395
205-348-4928
800-826-1675
Fax: 205-348-3909
e-mail: adap@adap.ua.edu
http://www.adap.net
TDD 205-348-4928
TTY 800-826-1675

Ellen Gillespie, Director
James Tucker, Associate Director
Angie Allen, Case Advocate

Mission is to provide quality, legally based advocacy services to Alabamians with disabilities in order to protect, promote and expand their rights.

369 **Alabama Radio Reading Service Network**
650 11th Street S
Birmingham, AL 35294
205-934-6576
Fax: 205-934-5075
http://www.wbhm.org/ARRS

Philip Habeeb, Executive Director

The objectives and activities of the Service is to bring printed matter to all in the state of Alabama that are physically handicapped or physically impaired.

370 **Alabama State Department of Human Resources**
50 North Ripley Street
Montgomery, AL 36130
334-242-1310
Fax: 334-353-1115
e-mail: ogapi@dhr.alabama.gov
http://www.dhr.state.al.us

Dr. Page Walley, Commissioner

The mission of the Alabama Department of Human Resources is to partner with communities to promote family stability and provide for the safety and self sufficency Alabamians.

371 **Alabama Tombigbee Regional Commission**
107 Broad Street
Camden, AL 36726-2122
334-682-4234
800-762-6329
Fax: 334-682-4205
http://www.alarc.org/atrc

John Clyde Riggs, Executive Director
Evelyn Morton, Administrative Assistant

Founded in 1970, it was created because local government leaders from ten counties in Southwest Alabama believe that the physical, economic and social well-being of the entire region and its individual communities depends on continuing area-wide cooperation and the sharing of many policies, plans and services.

372 **Alabama Workers Compensation Division**
Department of Industrial Relations
649 Monroe Street
Montgomery, AL 36131
334-242-2868
800-528-5166
Fax: 334-361-3143
e-mail: don.fisher@dir.alabama.gov
http://www.dir.alabama.gov

Phyllis Kennedy, Director
Donald K Fisher, Assistant Director

This division humanizes the Alabama workplace through its protective effort for employees and employers. It administers the Alabama Workers' Compensation (WC) law providing compensation for job related injuries and occupational diseases. In doing so, safety in the workplace is encouraged and expanded for all workers.

373 **East Alabama Commission: Agency on Aging**
PO Box 2186
Anniston, AL 36202-2186
256-237-6741
800-239-6741
Fax: 256-237-6763
http://www.carpdc.org

Randy Frost, Director Senior Services
Bill Curtis, Executive Director

Serves Tallapoosa County, Calhoun County, Etowah County, Cleburne County, Randolph County, Talladega County, Clay County, Coosa County, Chambers County, and Cherokee County.

374 **Governor's Committee on Employment of Persons with Disabilities**
Division of Rehabilitation Service
PO Box 11586
Montgomery, AL 36111
334-281-8780
Fax: 334-613-3893
http://www.rehab.state.al.us

Lamona Lucas, Director
Steve Shivers, President

375 **Home Care Association of Alabama**
PO Box 3238
Montgomery, AL 36109
334-395-9949
877-395-9949
Fax: 334-395-9959
e-mail: executivedirector@homecarealabama.org
http://www.homecarealabama.org

Melanie Golson, Executive Director

The Home Care Association of Alabama was formed to provide a unified voice for home care providers, supporting the concept that the home environment plays a significant role in promoting well being and facilitating the healing process.

376 **Jefferson County Office of Senior Citizens**
2601 Highland Avenue South
Birmingham, AL 35205-1707
205-325-1416
Fax: 205-325-1429
http://www.jeffco.jccal.org

Bettye Fine Collins, Commissioner
William M Voigt, Executive Director

Serves as a portal to care, accessing multiple services needs, determining eligibility, and purchasing services through conracts.

377 **Lee Russell Council of Governments: Area Agency on Aging**
2207 Gateway Drive
Opelika, AL 36801-6834
334-749-5264
800-243-5463
Fax: 334-749-6582
e-mail: sburnett@coa.state.al.us
http://www.lrcog.com

Suzanne Burnette, Executive Director
Jackie Pinkard, Aging Director

Area Agency on Aging. Medicaid Waiver Program. Title V.

378 **Montgomery Area Council on Aging**
115 E Jefferson Street
Montgomery, AL 36104-3654
334-263-0532
Fax: 334-240-6769
http://www.macoa.org

Richard R Heinzman, Executive Director
Mary Hughes, Development Director

MACOA promotes independent, dignified, and meaningful living for senior citizens through a variety of programs that offer hope, care, sustenance, and opportunity to more than 2,500 seniors each month. MACOA's activities provide the warmth of family and home along with hope, motivation, enjoyment, and means to live independently.

379 **North Central Alabama Regional Council of Governments: Area Agency on Aging**
PO Box C
216 Jackson Street SE
Decatur, AL 35601
256-355-4515
Fax: 256-351-1380
http://www.narcog.org

C. Ronald Matthews, Executive Director
Ben Armstrong, GIS Planner
Ann Bell, Nutrition Aid/Secretarial Aid

NARCOG is the North-central Regional Council of Governments. NARCOG's Board of Directors consists of representatives from 7 participating member governments.

State Organizations & Government Agencies/Alabama

380 Northwest Alabama Council of Governments: Area Agency on Aging
PO Box 2603
103 Student Drive
Muscle Shoals, AL 35661
256-389-0500
Fax: 256-389-0599
e-mail: kjones@nwscc.cc.al.us
http://www.nacolg.com
Keith Jones, Executive Director
Mayor Ed Crouch, Chairman Of The Board

The Northwest Alabama Council of Local Governments is not a municipal government, county government, a part of the federal government or a regulator agency. NACOLG is a regional council of governments established to deal with problems that cross the city lines, country lines or the whole region such as transportation, aging services, community/economic development and planning. Our membership is comprised of five county governments of Colbert, Lauderdale, Franklin, Marion and Winston and the thirty-three (33) municipal governments within these counties.

381 Protection & Advocacy for Persons with Developmental Disabilities
University of Alabama
PO Box 870395
Tuscaloosa, AL 35487-0395
205-348-4928
800-826-1675
Fax: 205-348-3909
e-mail: adap@adap.ua.edu
http://www.adap.net
TDD 205-348-4928
Ruben Cook, Director
Ellen Gillespie, Executive Director

Mission is to provide quality, legally-based advocacy services to Alabamians with disabilities in order to protect, promote and expand their rights.

382 RSVP Athens Limestone County
409 West Washington Street
PO Box 852
Athens, AL 35612
256-232-7207
Fax: 256-232-8842
e-mail: bruth@al-rsvp.com
http://www.al-rsvp.com
Betty M Ruth, Executive Director
Barbara G McMeans, Reading Coordinator
Bobbie Brooks, Volunteer Coordinator

RSVP offers men and women exciting opportunities for personal development and satisfaction by providing volunteer programs that offer outlets for their energy and creativity while serving in their community.

383 RSVP Baldwin County
Kiwanis Club of Bay Minette
300 N Hoyle Avenue
PO Box 0607
Bay Minette, AL 36507-4501
334-937-6764
334-937-6764
Fax: 334-937-6765
TDD 334-937-6765
Faye Robinson, Director

We have 8-10 senior volunteers helping with beach clean up yearly at Gulf Shores. This benefits not only the residents but visitors also. Our senior volunteers also plant and maintain gardens and trees, and are involved in recycling, environmental education, local museums, and working with the handicapped.

384 RSVP Birmingham Area
3600 8th Avenue S
Suite 200
Birmingham, AL 35222-3279
205-251-0296
Fax: 205-251-0298
e-mail: pmsbs@bellsouth.net
Cheryl Rainey, Director

The Retired and Senior Volunteer Program (RSVP) provides opportunities for people 55 and over to make a difference in their community through volunteer service. RSVP volunteers contribute aywhere from a few to over forty hours a week, serving through schools, day care centers, police departments, hospitals and other nonprofit and public organizations to help meet critical community needs. RSVP offers maximum flexibility and choice to its volunteers. RSVP matches the personal interests and skills of older Americans with opportunities to help solve community problems and offers supplemental insurance while on duty, and on-the-job training from the agency or organization where volunteers are placed.

385 RSVP Calhoun County
16 Public Square W
Suite 6
Jacksonville, AL 36265
256-435-5091
Fax: 256-435-5410
e-mail: calhounrsvp@cableone.net
http://www.seniorservice.org/calhoun_rsvp
Denise Rucker, Acting Director

The Retired and Senior Volunteer Program (RSVP) provides opportunities for people 55 and over to make a difference in their community through volunteer service. RSVP volunteers contribute anywhere from a few to over forty hours a week, serving through schools, day care centers, police departments, hospitals and other nonprofit and public organizations to help meet critical community needs. RSVP offers a maximum flexibility and choice to its volunteers. RSVP matches the personal interests and skills of older Americans with opportunities to help solve community problems and offers suplemental insurance while on duty, and on-the-job training from the agency or organization where volunteers are placed.

386 RSVP Dallas County
PO Box 987
Selma, AL 36702-0987
334-874-2514
Fax: 334-874-2564
e-mail: valperry@zebra.net
http://www.joinseniorservice.org
John Davis, Contact

Provides opportunities for people 55 and over to make a difference in their community through volunteer service. RSVP volunteers contribute anywhere from a few to over forty hours a week, serving through schools, day care centers, police departments, hospitals and other nonprofit and public organizations to help meet critcal community needs. RSVP matches the personal interests and skills of older Americans with opportunities to help solve community problems and offers supplemental insurance while on duty, and on-the-job training from the agency or organization where volunteers are placed.

387 RSVP Escambia County
Courthouse Annex, Room 405
100 Henderson Street
Brewton, AL 36441
251-867-0255
Fax: 251-867-1982
Amy Cooley, Director

The Retired and Senior Volunteer Program (RSVP) provides opportunities for people 55 and over to make a difference in their community through volunteer service. RSVP volunteers contribute anywhere from a few to over forty hours a week, serving through schools, day care centers, police departments, hospitals and other nonprofit and public organizations to help meet critical community needs. RSVP offers a maximum flexibility and choice to its volunteers. RSVP matches the personal interests and skills of older Americans with opportunities to help solve community problems and offers supplemental insurance while on duty, and on-the-job-training from the agency or organization where volunteers are placed.

State Organizations & Government Agencies/Alabama

388   RSVP Etowah County
800 Forrest Avenue
Room 219
Gadsden, AL 35901-3672   256-549-8147
                                  Fax: 256-549-5351
                              e-mail: rsvpian@aol.com
                              http://www.etowahcounty.org
Traci Pondick, Director

The Retired and Senior Volunteer Program (RSVP) provides opportunities for people 55 and over to make a difference in their community through volunteer service. RSVP volunteers contribute anywhere from a few to over forty hours a week, serving through schools, day care centers, police departments, hospitals and other nonprofit and public organizations to help meet critical community needs. RSVP offers maximum flexibility and choice to its volunteers. RSVP matches the personal interests and skills of older Americans with opportunities to help solve community problems and offers supplemental insurance while on duty, and on-the-job training from the agency or organization where volunteers are placed.

389   RSVP Greene County
PO Box 656
Eutaw, AL 35462   205-372-1501
                                  Fax: 205-372-0499
                          e-mail: greenecco@mindspring.com
                          http://www.joinseniorservice.org
Susie Morrow, Contact

Provides opportunities for 55 people and over to make a difference in their community through volunteer service. RSVP volunteers contribute anywhere from a few to over forty hours a week, serving through schools, day care centers, police departments, hospitals and other nonprofit and public organizations to help meet critical community needs. RSVP matches the personal interests and skills of older Americans with opportunities to help solve community problems and offers supplemental insurance while on duty, and on-the-job training from the agency or organization where volunteers are placed.

390   RSVP Houston Henry Geneva Counties
501 N Foster Street
Dothan, AL 36303-4546   334-836-1300
                                  Fax: 334-836-1301
                              e-mail: diannesvp1@aol.com
                          http://www.joinseniorservice.org
Dianne Marshburn, Contact

Provides opportunities for people 55 and over to make a difference in their community through volunteer service. RSVP volunteers contribute anywhere from a few to over forty hours a week, serving through schools, day care centers, police departments, hospitals and other nonprofit and public organizations to help meet critical community needs. RSVP matches the personal interests and skills of older American with opportunities to help solve community problems and offers supplemental insurance while on duty, pre-service orientation, and on-the-job training from the agency or organization where volunteers are placed.

391   RSVP Lee & Russell Counties
211 Samford Avenue
Opelika, AL 36801   334-749-0226
                                  Fax: 334-749-9195
                      e-mail: easersvpdirector@mindspring.com
                              http://www.seniorcorps.gov
Bridget Woodyard, Director

The Retired and Senior Volunteer Program (RSVP) provides opportunities for people 55 and over to make a difference in their community through volunteer service. RSVP volunteers contribute anywhere from a few to over forty hours a week, serving through schools, day care centers, police departments, hospitals and other nonprofit and public organizations to help meet critical community needs. RSVP offers maximum flexibility and choice to its volunteers. RSVP matches the personal interests and skills of older Americans with opportunities to help solve community problems and offers supplemental insurance while on duty, and on-the-job training from the agency or organization where volunteers are placed.

392   RSVP Marshall County
1805 Gunter Avenue
Suite A-1
Guntersville, AL 35976-2150   256-571-7734
                                  Fax: 256-571-7775
                              e-mail: jeanann@mcrsvp.org
                              http://www.seniorcorps.gov
Jean-Ann Moon, Director

The Retired and Senior Volunteer Program (RSVP) provides opportunities for people 55 and over to make a difference in their community through volunteer service. RSVP volunteers contribute anywhere from a few to over forty hours a week, serving through schools, day care centers, police departments, hospitals and other nonprofit and public organizations to help meet critical community needs. RSVP offers maximum flexibility and choice to its volunteers. RSVP matches the personal interests and skills of older Americans with opportunities to help solve community problems and offers supplemental insurance while on duty, and on-the-job training from the agency or organizations where volunteers are placed.

393   RSVP Mobile
304 Bay Shore Avenue
Mobile, AL 36607-2058   251-574-7787
                                  Fax: 251-574-7789
                              e-mail: rsvpmobile@zebra.net
                              http://www.seniorcorps.gov
Terri Grodsky, Director

The Retired and Senior Volunteer Program (RSVP) provides opportunities for people 55 and over to make a difference in their community through volunteer service. RSVP volunteers contribute anywhere from a few to over forty hours a week, serving through schools, day care centers, police departments, hospitals and other nonprofit and public organizations to help meet critical community needs. RSVP offers maximum flexibility and choice to its volunteers. RSVP matches the personal interests and skills of older Americans with opportunities to help solve community problems and offers supplemental insurance while on duty, and on-the-job training from the agency or organization where volunteers are placed.

394   RSVP Monroe/Cone-Cuh County
PO Box 688
Monroeville, AL 36461   251-575-3159
                                  Fax: 251-575-9381
                          e-mail: slbradley40@hotmail.com
                          http://www.joinseniorservice.org
Sarah Bradley, Contact

Provides opportunities for people 55 and over to make a difference in their community through volunteer service. RSVP volunteers contribute anywhere from a few to over forty hours a week, serving through schools, day care centers, police departments, hospitals and other nonprofit and public organizations to help meet critical community needs. RSVP matches the personal interests and skills of older Americans with opportunities to help solve community problems and offers supplemental insurance while on duty, and on-the-job training from the agency or organization where volunteers are placed.

395   RSVP Pike County
217 Pierson Street
Troy, AL 36081-2125   334-566-6158
                                  Fax: 334-670-3914
                              e-mail: pikersvp@troycable.net
                              http://www.seniorcorps.gov
Tammy S Lockley, Contact

Provides opportunities for people 55 and over to make a difference in their community through volunteer service. RSVP volunteers contribute anywhere from a few to over forty hours a week, serving through schools, day care centers, police departments, hospitals and other nonprofit and public organizations to help meet critical community needs. RSVP matches the personal interests and skills of older Americans with opportunities to help solve community problems and offers supplemental insurance while on duty, and on-the-job training from the agency or organization where volunteers are placed.

State Organizations & Government Agencies/Alaska

396 RSVP Southwest Alabama
137 Adams Avenue
PO Box 127
Thomasville, AL 36784
334-636-5827
Fax: 334-636-5893
e-mail: sasrsvp@pinebelt.net
http://www.joinseniorservice.org

Donna Phillips, Director

Provides volunteer opportunities for Clark County senior citizens and volunteer service for the community.

397 RSVP Tallapossa & Coosa Counties
1675 Cherokee Road
PO Box 699
Alexander City, AL 35011
256-215-4351
Fax: 256-234-0384
e-mail: Ccummins@cacc.cc.al.us
http://www.seniorcorps.gov

Carley Cummins, Director

The Retired and Senior Volunteer Program (RSVP) provides opportunities for people 55 and over to make a difference in their community through volunteer service. RSVP volunteers contribute anywhere from a few to over forty hours a week, serving through schools, day care centers, police departments, hospitals and other nonprofit and public organizations to help meet critical community needs. RSVP offers maximum flexibility and choice to its volunteers. RSVP matches the personal interests and skills of older Americans with opportunities to help solve community problems and offers supplemental insurance while on duty, on-the-job training from the agency or organization where volunteers are placed.

398 Railroad Retirement Board: Alabama District Office
950 22nd Street N
Birmingham, AL 35203-1134
205-731-0019
Fax: 205-731-0026
e-mail: birmingham@rrb.gov
http://www.rrb.gov/pdf/field/birmingham.pdf

Catherine A Leyser, Customer Service Comments

The Railroad Board is an independent agency in the executive branch of the Federal Government. The primary function is to administer comprehensive retirement-survivor and unemployment sickness benefit programs for the nation's railroad workers and their families.

399 South Central Alabama Development Commission: Area Agency on Aging
5900 Carmichael Place
Montgomery, AL 36117-2345
334-244-6903
800-762-6329
Fax: 334-270-0038
e-mail: sylvia.bowers@adss.alabama.gov
http://www.scadc.state.al.us

Sylvia Bowers, Director
Ladine Collins, Finance Director

A public quasi-governmental agency that provides aging, planning and GIS, economic and community development services to its member governments.

400 TARCOG: Area Agency on Aging
5075 Research Drive NW
Huntsville, AL 35805-5912
256-830-0818
Fax: 256-830-0843
e-mail: tarcog@adss.state.al.us
http://www.alarc.org/tarcog

Bob Culver, Executive Director
Nancy Hollingsworth, Administrative Secretary
Nancy Robertson, Director, Aging Programs

TARCOG provides many services to the region's elderly population. The AAA plans and manages a system of in-home and community services to help seniors maintain their independence and dignity, and it administers federal, state, local and private funds to support those services.

401 Volunteer Center of Morgan County
708 6th Avenue SE
Decatur, AL 35601
256-355-8628
Fax: 256-355-8726
e-mail: mkbraddock@vcomc.org
http://www.vcomc.org

Mary K Braddock, Executive Director
Jessica Nelson, Special Events Coordinator
Yolanda Dunbar, Programs Coordinator

Recruits, trains, and interviews volunteers and refers them to qualified community agencies requesting such services. Holds 2-3 training sessions per year. Sponsors Taste of Valley festival.

402 Volunteers of America Southeast
600 Azalea Road
Mobile, AL 36609-1590
251-666-4431
800-859-4431
Fax: 251-666-2836
http://www.voasoutheast.org

Wallace T Davis, PhD, President/CEO
Porter Sue Simpson, Director Of Affiliates

Volunteers of America Southeast makes every effort to create a community of care that enables individuals to live as independently as possible for as long as possible. We provide for individuals who are 62 years of age and older with a low income an opportunity to live in a safe, comfortable, and affordable setting.

403 West Alabama Planning and Development Council: Area Agency on Aging
4200 Highway 69 North Suite 1
PO Box 509
North Port, AL 35476
205-333-2990
800-239-4049
Fax: 205-333-2713
e-mail: warc@adss.alabama.gov
http://www.warc.info/areadevelop

Robert B Lake, Executive Director

One of the primary functions of the WARC is to assist the region's counties and municipalities with obtaining funds for projects that stimulate economic development in the region and improve the area's quality of life. The majority of these activities are coordinated with the Alabama Department of Economic and Community Affairs.

Alaska

404 Alaska Client Assistance Program (CAP)
2900 Boniface Parkway
Suite 100
Anchorage, AK 99504-3132
907-333-2211
Fax: 907-333-1186
e-mail: akcap@alaska.com
http://http://home.gci.net~alaskacap
TDD 800-004-7TTY

Pam Stratton, Executive Director

CAP is Alaska's Client Assist Program. We are an ombudsman/advocacy service which provides information, help and individualized advocacy.

405 Alaska Commission on Aging
PO Box 110693
150 Third Street 103
Juneau, AK 99811-0693
907-465-4879
Fax: 907-465-1398
e-mail: denise.daniello@alaska.gov
http://www.alaskaaging.org

Denise Daniello, Executive Director
Frank B Appel, Chairman
MaryAnn VandeCastle, H&Ss Planner II

The mission of the Alaska Commission on Aging is to promote the dignity and independence of senior Alaskans, and to assist them in leading useful and meaningful lives.

State Organizations & Government Agencies/Alaska

406 Alaska Department of Military and Veterans Affairs
PO Box 5800 Camp Denali Camp Denali
Fort Richardson, AK 99505-5800   907-428-6003
Fax: 907-428-6019
e-mail: fmvawebmaster@ak-prepared.com
http://www.ak.prepared.com/dmva
Major Craig Campbell, Commissioner
Mr. John Cramer, Acting Deputy Commissioner
BG Thomas H Katkus, Assistant Adjutant General

407 Alaska Department of Revenue
PO Box 110400
333 W Willoughby 11th Floor SOB
Juneau, AK 99811-0400   907-465-2300
Fax: 907-465-2389
http://www.revenue.state.ak.us
Jerry Burnett, Director
Carol Gamez, Administrative Manager
Dorie Choquette, Procurement Officer

The mission of the Department of Revenue is to collect and invest funds for public purposes. The mission of the Office of the Commissioner is to provide support and policy direction to the divisions in the department.

408 Alaska Disability Law Center
3330 Arctic Boulevard
Suite 103
Anchorage, AK 99503   907-344-1002
800-478-1234
Fax: 907-349-1002
e-mail: akpa@dlcak.org
http://www.dlcak.org
TTY 907-565-1002
David C Fleurant, Executive Director

An independent non-profit organization that provides legal advocacy services for people with disabilities anywhere in Alaska. DLC is designated under federal law as the Sate of Alaska's "Protection and Advocacy" (P&A) agency.

409 Alaska Division of Mental Health and Developmental Disabilities
350 Main Street Room 404
PO Box 110601
Juneau, AK 99811-0601   907-465-3030
Fax: 907-465-3068
http://www.state.ak.us
Karleen K Jackson, Commissioner
Bill Hogan, Deputy Commissioner
Bill Streur, Deputy Commissioner

The Division plans for and provides appropriate prevention, treatment and support for families impacted by mental disorders or developmental disabilities while maximizing self-determination. Community based services are provided by grantees. Inpatient services are provided in two facilities.

410 Alaska Division of Retirement & Benefits
PO Box 110203
Juneau, AK 99811   907-465-4460
800-821-2251
Fax: 907-465-3086
http://www.state.ak.us/drb
Pat Shier, Director

Mission is to deliver benefits to members in accordance with legal requirements.

411 Alaska Division of Vocational Rehabilitation
801 W 10th Street
Suite A
Juneau, AK 99801-1894   907-465-2814
800-478-2815
Fax: 907-465-2856
e-mail: dawn.hamilton@alaska.gov
http://http://labor.state.ak.us/dvr/home.htm
Cheryl Walsh, Director

Our mission is to assist individuals with disabilities to obtain and maintain employment.

412 Alaska Governor's Committee on Employment and Rehabilitation of People with Disabilities
801 West 10th Street
Suite A
Juneau, AK 99801-1894   907-465-2814
800-478-2815
Fax: 907-465-2856
http://www.labor.state.ak.us/govscomm
Becky Simpson, Chairperson

The primary purpose of the Governor's Committee is to carry on a continuing program to promote the employment and rehabilitation of citizens of the State of Alaska who have disabilities. The Committee creates statewide interest in the rehabilitation and employment of people with disabilities by advocating for a comprehensive statewide system for access to assistive technology and by obtaining and maintaining cooperation with public and private groups and individuals in this field.

413 Alaska Statewide Independent Living Council
1057 West Fireweed Lane
Suite 206
Anchorage, AK 99503   907-263-2011
888-294-7452
Fax: 907-263-2012
e-mail: preinhart.silc@aci.net
http://www.alaskasilc.org
TDD 907-263-2011
Patrick Reinhart, Executive Director
Yronelly Sanchez, Project Coordinator

The Alaska Statewide Independent Living is committed to promoting a philosophy of consumer control, peer support, self help, self determination, equal access, and individual and systems advocacy, in order to maximize leadership, empowerment, independence, productivity, and to support full inclusion and integration of individuals with disabilities into the mainstream of American society.

414 Alaska Welcomes You
7321 Branche Drive
Anchorage, AK 99518-2573   907-349-6301
Fax: 907-563-5946

Corporation that researches and inspects accommodations, restaurants, parks, fishing activities, flight seeing activities, cruises and other Alaskan activities for guests who are mobility impaired.

415 Alaska Workers Compensation Board
Department of Labor
PO Box 25512
Juneau, AK 99811   907-465-2790
Fax: 907-465-2797
Paul Lisankie, Director

The Workers Compensation Division is the administrative arm of the Workers' Compensation Board. Its basic purpose is to ensure that Alaska workers who suffer injury or disease from their employment receive medical care and cash wage benefits during disablement through their employers or their employers' insurance companies. The board schedules cases for hearing and issue orders, including formal board sessions.

416 Alaskans Commission on Aging
PO Box 110693
150 Third Street #103
Juneau, AK 99811-0693   907-465-3250
Fax: 907-465-1398
e-mail: maryann.vandecastle@alaska.gov
http://www.alasaaging.org
Denise Daniello, Executive Director
Maryann CandeCastle, H&SS Planner II
Leslie Bullock, H&SS Planner I

Statewide services.

State Organizations & Government Agencies/Arizona

417 **Assistive Technology of Alaska**
2217 E Tudor Road
Suite 4
Anchorage, AK 99507-1068
907-563-2599
800-723-2852
Fax: 907-563-0699
http://www.atla.biz
TTY 907-561-2592

Kathy Privratsky, Executive Director
Richard Sanders, Program Manager
Mystie Rail, Marketing & Media Specialist

Statewide program to promote assistive technology devices and sources for persons of all ages with all disabilities. Referral and informational services offered about devices, where to obtain them and their cost.

418 **Disability Determination Services**
619 E Ship Creek Avenue
Suite 305
Anchorage, AK 99501
907-562-0460
800-577-3334
Fax: 907-777-8181

Sandra Kelley, Chief

Our mission is to make disability determinations for people with severe disabilities who apply for Social Security Disability Insurance and/or Supplemental Security Income.

419 **Fairbanks Senior Center**
1424 Moore Street
Fairbanks, AK 99701
907-452-6417
Fax: 907-452-6423

Barbara Stevens, Executive Director

Provides community service opportunities for persons age 55 and older. Provide community service opportunities for seniors to work with children one on one.

420 **Farthest North Club of the Deaf**
Deaf Community Services (DCS)
475 Hall Street
Fairbanks, AK 99701-4969
907-456-5913
800-847-0939
Fax: 907-456-2604
e-mail: dcs@polarnet.com
http://www.ptialaska..net/~padcs

Doug Cluff, DCS Director

Supports the rights of the deaf. Promotes deaf social activities.

421 **Kenai Senior Connection**
361 Senior Court
Kenai, AK 99611-6861
907-283-4156
Fax: 907-283-3200
e-mail: rcraig@ci.kenai.ak.us
http://www.ci.kenai.ak.us/seniorcenter

Rachel Craig, Senior Services Director

We strive to serve as a community focal point for senior services where adults 60+ come together for fellowship and program participation, to engage in opportunities for dignity and personal growth, to improve and enrich their quality of life, to support the needs of older individuals, to enhance their independence and to broaden their involvement within the community.

422 **Social Security: Juneau Disability Determination Services**
801 W 10th Street
Suite 200
Juneau, AK 99801-1878
907-465-2814

Gale Finnott, Executive Director

423 **State of Alaska, Department of Health &Social Services**
Division of Senior & Disabilities Services
240 Main Street
Suite 601
Juneau, AK 99811-0680
907-465-3372
866-465-3165
Fax: 907-465-1170
e-mail: shanna_reimer@health.state.ak.us
http://www.hss.state.ak.us/dsds
TTY 907-465-5430

Rod Moline PhD, Director
Shanna Reimer, Administrative Assistant

The mission of the Division Of Senior and Disabilities Services is to promote independence of Alaska seniors and people with physical and developmental disabilites.

Arizona

424 **Arizona Aging and Adult Administration**
1789 W Jefferson Street
Code 950A
Phoenix, AZ 85007-3202
602-542-4446
800-432-4040
Fax: 602-542-6575
e-mail: contactdaas@azdes.gov
http://www.azdes.gov/aaa

Rex Critchfield, Manager

Arizona's designated State Unit on Aging. The Older Americans Act provides the Aging and Adult Administration with its authority. Works to advocacte for and on behalf of at-risk and older persons. Also develops and impliments a comprehensive service delivery system that most accurately reflects the needs of their local communities.

425 **Arizona Area Agency on Aging: Region One**
1366 E Thomas Road
Suite 108
Phoenix, AZ 85014-5739
602-264-2255
888-783-7500
Fax: 602-230-9132
e-mail: kasunic@aaaphx.org
http://www.aaaphx.org

Mary Lynn Kasunic, President

The Area Agency on Aging serves senior citizens and adults 18 to 59 with disabilities through a variety of home and community based programs including home delivered meals, adult day health care, home care, trasportation and legal assistance.

426 **Arizona Department of Aging**
1400 W Washington Street
Suite 950A
Phoenix, AZ 85007-2900
602-542-4446
800-482-8049
Fax: 602-542-6575

Richard Littler, Director

427 **Arizona Department of Economic Security**
1717 W Jefferson Street
Room 119
Phoenix, AZ 85007-3295
602-542-5678
Fax: 602-542-5339
http://www.azdes.gov

Liz Baker, Communications Director
Fernando Vender, Chief Public Information Officer
Kevan Kaighn, Public Information Officer

The Department of Economic Security is a human service agency providing services in six areas: Aging and Community Services, Benefits and Medical Eligibility, Child Support Enforcement, Children and Family Services, Developmental Disabilities and Employment and Rehabilitation Services.

State Organizations & Government Agencies/Arizona

428 **Arizona Department of Family Health Services**
150 North 18th Avenue
Phoenix, AZ 85007-2670
602-542-1000
Fax: 602-542-0883

Susan Gerard, Director

429 **Arizona Department of Revenue**
PO Box 52138
Phoenix, AZ 85072-2138
602-255-3381
800-352-4090
Fax: 602-542-3756
http://www.revenue.state.az.us

Gale Garriott, Director

430 **Arizona Department of Veterans Services**
3333 N Central Avenue
Suite 1048
Phoenix, AZ 85012-2457
602-627-3281
Fax: 602-627-3285
http://www.azdvs.gov

Richard Gregg Maxon, Director
Mike Klier, Deputy Director

431 **Arizona Disability Determination Services**
3310 N 19th Avenue
Phoenix, AZ 85015-5760
602-264-2644
800-352-0409
Fax: 602-274-2908

The DARS Division for Disability Determination Services (DDS), funded entirely through the Social Security Administration (SSA), makes disability determinations for persons with severe disabilities who apply for Social Security Disability and/or Supplemental Security Income.

432 **Arizona Inter Tribal Council**
2214 North Central Avenue
Suite 100
Phoenix, AZ 85004
602-258-4822
Fax: 602-258-4825
http://www.itcaonline.com

John R Lewis, Executive Director
Alberta C Tippeconnic, Assistant Director
Alice Morgan, Finance Officer

The pupose of the ITCA is to provide the member tribes with the means for action on matters that affect them collectively and individually, to promote tribal sovereignty and to strengthen tribal governments.

433 **Arizona Public Safety Personnel Retirement System**
3010 E Camelback Road
Suite 200
Phoenix, AZ 85016-4416
602-255-5575
Fax: 602-255-5572
e-mail: jhacking@psprs.com
http://www.psprs.com

Tracey Peterson CPA, CFE, Chief Operating Officer
Rob Brown PhD, CFA, Chief Investment Officer

434 **Arizona Railroad Retirement Board**
1201 S Alma School Road
Mesa, AZ 85210-2097
480-610-5590
Fax: 480-610-5988
http://www.rrb.gov

Gale Bowman, Representative

An independent agency in the executive branch of the Federal Government. The RRB's primary function is to administer comprehensive retirement-survivor and unemployment sickness benefit programs to the nation's railroad workers and their families.

435 **Arizona Retirement System**
3300 North Central Avenue
Phoenix, AZ 85012-0250
602-240-2000
Fax: 602-240-2090
http://www.azasrs.gov

Paul Matson, Director
Anthony Guarino, Deputy Director/COO
Gary R Dokes, Chief Investment Officer

A leading state benefit plan administrator in the areas of core member service funded status, investment performance, and operational effectiveness.

436 **Arizona Workers Compensation Board**
Industrial Commission
800 West Washington Street
Phoenix, AZ 85007-2934
602-542-4653
800-544-6488
Fax: 602-542-3070
e-mail: webmaster@ica.state.az.us
http://www.ica.state.az.us

Larry Etchechury, Director
Teresa Hilton, Commission Secretary

The mission statement of the Industrial Commission is to efficiently administer and effectively enforce all applicable laws and regulations not specifically delegated to others, relative to the protection of life, health, safety, and welfare of employees within the State.

437 **Governor's Council on Developmental Disabilities**
3839 N Third Street
Suite 306 (SCO74Z)
Phoenix, AZ 85012
602-277-4986
Fax: 602-277-4454
e-mail: fkahn@azdes.gov
http://www.azgcdd.org
TTY 602-277-4949

Frank Kahn, Executive Director
Cynthia Gafford, Executive Assistant/Contracts Mg
Laura Wilson, Planner III

The purpose of the Council is to advocate for and assure that individuals with developmental disabilities and their families participate in the design of and have access to culturally competent services, supports and provides opportunities to become integrated and included in the community.

438 **Navajo Area Agency on Aging: Division of Health**
PO Box 1390
Window Rock, AZ 86515-1390
928-871-6868
Fax: 928-871-6793
e-mail: contactdaas@azdes.gov
http://www.azdes.gov/aaa/regions

The mission of the NAAA is to provide aging related services in the areas of the greatest need and to the greatest number of Navajo elders, without jeopardizing quality of services.

439 **Northern Arizona Council of Governments Area Agency on Aging**
119 E Aspen Avenue
Flagstaff, AZ 86001-5222
928-774-1895
877-521-3500
Fax: 928-774-1895
e-mail: aaadir@nacod.org
http://www.nacog.org

Kenneth Sweet, Executive Director

The NACOG Area Agency on Aging, Region III, serves clients in the four Northern Counties of Arizona, excluding the reservations. We are part of a national network of organizations, established under the Older Americans Act of 1965 to respond to the needs of Older Adults. There are more then 650 Area Agencies on Aging throughout the United States.

440 **Pima Council on Aging**
8467 E Broadway
Tucson, AZ 85710
520-790-7262
Fax: 520-790-7577
e-mail: help@pcoa.org
http://www.pcoa.org

Jim Murphy, Executive Director

State Organizations & Government Agencies/Arizona

Mission is to promote dignity and respect for aging, and to advocate for independence in the lives of Pima County's older adults and their families, now and for generations to come.

441 Pinal/Gila Council for Senior Citizens
8969 W. McCartney Rd.
Casa Grande, AZ 85222
520-836-2758
800-293-9393
Fax: 520-421-2033
Olivia Guerrero, Executive Director

442 RSVP East Valley Retired & Senior Volunteer Program
247 N MacDonald
Mesa, AZ 85201
480-775-1466
Fax: 480-833-6282
e-mail: eastvalleyrsvp@mindspring.com
Fran White, Volunteer Services Director

RSVP links the skills and talents of persons 55 and over with needs in the East Valley communities of Chandler, Gilbert, Guadalupe, Mesa and Tempe. Volunteers serve hospitals, schools, food banks, museums, literacy programs, police and fire departments, libraries, etc. Volunteers who register with RSVP receive supplemental accident/liability insurance while traveling to volunteer assignments and mileage and meal reimbursement. The program is Free.

443 RSVP Gila Pinal
C/O CAAG Historic Belmont
271 Main Street
Superior, AZ 85273
520-689-5004
Fax: 520-689-5020
e-mail: CAAG@Goodnet.com
Joan Phillips, Director

The Retired and Senior Volunteer Program (RSVP) provides opportunities for people 55 and over to make a difference in their community through volunteer service. RSVP volunteers contribute anywhere from a few to over forty hours a week, serving through schools, day care centers, police departments, hospitals and other nonprofit and public organizations to help meet critical community needs. RSVP offers maximum flexibility and choice to its volunteers. RSVP matches the personal interests and skills of older Americans with opportunities to help solve community problems and offers supplemental insurance while on duty, on-the-job training from the agency or organization where volunteers are placed. The following Counties are served: Gila, Pinal.

444 RSVP Maricopa County
1366 E Thomas Road
Suite 108
Phoenix, AZ 85014-5739
602-264-7787
Fax: 602-230-9132
e-mail: rsvp1@aaaphx.org
Lesle Garner, Director

The Retired and Senior Volunteer Program (RSVP) provides opportunities for people 55 and over to make a difference in their community through volunteer service. RSVP volunteers contribute anywhere from a few to over forty hours a week, serving through schools, day care centers, police departments, hospitals and other nonprofit and public organizations to help meet critical community needs. RSVP offers maximum flexibility and choice to its volunteers. RSVP matches the personal interests and skills of older Americans with opportunities to help solve community problems and offers supplemental insurance while on duty, on-the-job training from the agency or organization where volunteers are placed.

445 RSVP Northern Arizona
PO Box 5063
Flagstaff, AZ 86011
928-523-6584
Fax: 520-523-9189
e-mail: liane.sims@nau.edu
Liane Sims, Project Director

The Retired and Senior Volunteer Program (RSVP) provides opportunities for people 55 and over to make a difference in their community through volunteer service. RSVP volunteers contribute anywhere from a few to over forty hours a week, serving through schools, day care centers, police departments, hospitals and other nonprofit and public organizations to help meet critical community needs. RSVP offers maximum flexibility and choice to its volunteers. RSVP matches the personal interests and skills of older Americans with opportunities to help solve community problems and offers supplemental insurance while on duty, and on-the-job training from the agency or organization where volunteers are placed.

446 RSVP Southeastern Arizona
300 W Stewart Street
PO Box 399
Willcox, AZ 85643
520-384-0665
Fax: 520-384-0038
e-mail: wilcap@ctc.net
Nancy Clark, Director

The Retired and Senior Volunteer Program (RSVP) provides opportunities for people 55 and over to make a difference in their community through volunteer service. RSVP volunteers contribute anywhere from a few to over forty hours a week, serving through schools, day care centers, police departments, hospitals and other nonprofit and public organizations to help meet critical community needs. RSVP offers maximum flexibility and choice to its volunteers. RSVP matches the personal interests and skills of older Americans with opportunities to help solve community problems and offers supplemental insurance while one duty, and on-the-job training from the agency or organization where volunteers are placed. The following Counties are served: Cochise, Graham, Greenlee, and Santa Cruz.

447 RSVP Tucson
8467 E Broadway Boulevard
Tucson, AZ 85710
520-790-7262
Fax: 520-790-7577
Cecilia Salaz, Director

The Retired and Senior Volunteer Program (RSVP) provides opportunities for people 55 and over to make a difference in their community through volunteer service. RSVP volunteers contribute anywhere from a few to over forty hours a week, serving through schools, day care centers, police departments, hospitals and other nonprofit and public organizations to help meet critical community needs. RSVP offers maximum flexibility and choice to its volunteers. RSVP matches the personal interests and skills of older Americans with opportunities to help solve community problems and offers supplemental insurance while on duty, on-the-job training from the agency or organization where volunteers are placed. The following County is served: Pima.

448 RSVP Western Arizona
224 South Third Avenue
Yuma, AZ 85364
928-782-1886
Fax: 928-329-4248
Judy Tripp, Director

The Retired and Senior Volunteer Program (RSVP) provides opportunities for people 55 and over to make a difference in their community through volunteer service. RSVP volunteers contribute anywhere from a few to over forty hours a week, serving through schools, day care centers, police departments, hospitals and other nonprofit and public organizations to help meet critical community needs. RSVP offers maximum flexibility and choice to its volunteers. RSVP matches the personal interests and skills of older Americans with opportunities to help solve community problems and offers supplemental insurance while on duty, on-the-job training from the agency or organization where volunteers are placed. The following Counties are served: La Paz, Mohave, Yuma.

449 Retired Activities Office: Phoenix Affairs Office
Navy & Marine Corps, Reserve Readiness Center
1201 N 35th Avenue
Phoenix, AZ 85009-3398
602-353-3033
Fax: 602-278-4993
e-mail: nmcrephx@cnrf.navy.mil

State Organizations & Government Agencies/Arkansas

The RAO serves as a link between local retired military and the active-duty community which provides assistance to retired military. It provides installation commanders with a means of providing more effective services and improving communication for the local retired community. The RAO is staffed and operated by volunteer retired military who assist other retired members, their families and survivors to receive entitled services and benefits. Through newsletters, seminars and appreciation days, the RAO supports quality of life issues throughout the retirement years to their fellow service members.

450 SEAGO Area: Agency on Aging
118 Arizona Street
Bisbee, AZ 85603-1800
520-432-6012
800-686-1431
Fax: 520-432-6069
e-mail: info@seago.org
http://www.seago.org
Rich Gaar, Executive Director

Operates home and community based services through contract providers. Assist individuals seeking information about services for disabled and elders. Assist with Medicare and other benefit programs.

451 Senior Citizens of Patagonia
100 Quiroga Street
PO Box 1121
Patagonia, AZ 85624
520-394-2494

The mission of the Senior Citizens of Patagonia is to provide transportation, social, educational and nutritional support for the senior citizens of the Patagonia/Sonoita area.

452 Verde Valley Senior Citizens Association
500 East Cherry Street
Cottonwood, AZ 86326
928-634-5450
e-mail: info@vvseniors.org
http://www.verdevalleyseniorcenter.com
Elaine Bremmer, Executive Director
Michelle Stone, Assistant To The Director

The Verde Valley Senior Center's primary objective is to enrich the lives of senior citizens and Verde Valley communities by providing wholesome meals, safe, convenient transportation and promoting a variety of social and recreational activities for all to enjoy.

453 Western Arizona Council of Governments: Area Agency on Aging
224 S 3rd Avenue
Yuma, AZ 85364-2224
928-782-1886
800-782-188
Fax: 928-329-4248
e-mail: aaa@wacog.com
http://www.wacog.com
Jill Harrison, Aging Director

Arkansas

454 Arkansas Advocates for Nursing Home Residents
PO Box 22421
Little Rock, AR 72221-2421
501-450-9619
Fax: 501-371-9681
http://www.aanhr.org
Nancy Allison, President
Rich Huddleston, Executive Director

AANHR is a nonprofit organization dedicated to protecting and improving the quality of care and life for Arkansas residents in long term care facilities.

455 Arkansas Aging Foundation
706 S Pulaski Street
Little Rock, AR 72201-3927
501-376-6083
Fax: 501-376-6084

Works to maintain the independence of older people. Provides health promotion and disease prevention information.

456 Arkansas Assistive Technology Projects
Increasing Capabilities Access Network
26 Corporate Hill Dr
Little Rock, AR 72205
501-666-8868
800-828-2799
Fax: 501-666-5319
http://www.arkansas-ican.org
Barbara Gullet, Executive Director

A consumer responsive statewide program promoting assistive technology devices and sources for persons of all ages with all disabilities. Referral and information services provide information about devices, where to obtain them and their cost.

457 Arkansas Department of Aging
PO Box 1437
Slot S-530
Little Rock, AR 72203
501-682-2441
Fax: 870-683-8155
e-mail: tatus@arkansas.gov
http://www.arkansas.gov/dhs/aging
Herb Sanderson, Director

458 Arkansas Department of Finance and Administration
1515 W 7th Street
Suite 600
Little Rock, AR 72201-3940
501-686-9745
Fax: 501-324-9070
http://www.state.ar.us/dfa
Janet Grard, Network General Manager

459 Arkansas Department of Human Services: Division of Aging and Adult Services
PO Box 1437
Slot S-530
Little Rock, AR 72203-1437
501-682-2441
Fax: 501-682-8155
e-mail: herb.sanderson@arkansas.gov
http://www.arkansas.gov/shs/aging
Herb Sanderson, Director

460 Arkansas Department of Public Employees Retired Systems
2301 S University Avenue
Little Rock, AR 72204
501-671-2000
800-682-7377
http://www.uaex.edu/indus/state.office
Ivory W Lyles, Associate Vice President

461 Arkansas Department of Veterans Affairs
2200 Fort Roots Drive
Bldg 65 Room 119
North Little Rock, AR 72114
501-370-3820
Fax: 501-370-3829
e-mail: adva@arkansas.gov
http://www.veterans.arkansas.gov
David Fletcher, Director
Doyle Batey, Deputy Director

The mission of the Arkansas Department of Veterans Affairs is to provide assistance to veterans and their dependents in acquiring state and federal benefits to which they are entitled to by virtue of ther service to this country. We maintain a claims and appeals section in the VA Regional Office and operate two veterans' homes and one veterans' cemetary. We also provide support and training to the seventy-five (75) county veterans' service officers.

462 Arkansas Developmental Disability Council
5800 West 10th Street
Suite 805
Little Rock, AR 72204
501-661-2589
800-462-0599
Fax: 501-661-2399
e-mail: mary.edwards@arkansas.gov
http://www.ddcouncil.org
Mary L Edwards, Council Coordinator
Lee C Russell, Information Officer

State Organizations & Government Agencies/Arkansas

The Arkansas Governor's Developmental Disabilities Council supports people with developmental disabilities in the achievement of independence, productivity, integration, and inclusion in the community.

463 Arkansas Disability Determinations for SSA
701 S Pulaski Street
Little Rock, AR 72201-3926
501-682-3030
800-482-9950
Fax: 501-682-7553
http://www.arkansas.gov/ddssa
Arthur Boutiette, Executive Director

464 Arkansas Division of Aging & Adult Services
PO Box 1437
Little Rock, AR 72203-1437
501-682-2441
Fax: 501-682-8155
Herb Sanderson, Manager

465 Arkansas Division of Developmental Disabilities Services
PO Box 1437 Slot N501
Donaghey Plaza North
Little Rock, AR 72203-1437
501-682-8678
Fax: 501-682-8380
http://www.arkansas.gov/dhs/ddds
Traci Harris, Program Administrator

State agency to assist persons with developmental disabilities and their family in obtaining appropriate assistance and services.

466 Arkansas Division of Services for the Blind
700 Main Street
PO Box 3237
Little Rock, AR 72203-3237
501-682-5463
800-960-9270
Fax: 501-682-0366
http://www.arkansas.gov.dhs/dsb/newdsb
TDD 501-682-0093
Mrs. Sharon Berry, Vice-Chairman

Dedicated to the independence of Arkansans who are blind or visually impaired and is committed to the principal that these individuals have the right to make informed choices regarding where they live, where they work, how they participate in the community, and how they interact with others.

467 Arkansas Rehabilitation Services
1616 Brookwood Drive
Little Rock, AR 72202
501-296-1600
800-330-0632
Fax: 501-686-2830
http://www.arsinfo.org
Mike Beebe, Governor
William L Walker Jr., Director
Robert Trevino, Commissioner

Offers total rehabilitative care making the patient understand the problems to which they will need to adjust, what abilities they have and what types of assistance or equipment they will need, and what resources in the community can help with their return to independent living. The staff is dedicated to providing the kind of specialized treatment necessary for those constantly changing needs.

468 Arkansas Teacher Retirement System
1400 West Third Street
Little Rock, AR 72201-1833
501-682-1517
800-666-2877
Fax: 501-682-1944
e-mail: info@artrs.gov
http://www.atrs.state.ar.us
Paul Doane, Cheif Executive Officer
Gail Bolden, Chief Operating Officer
Suzanne Davenport, Chief Financial Officer

The Arkansas Teacher Retirement System was established by Act 266 of 1937 to provide retirement benefits to the employees of the state's education community. Operation of the system began on July 1, 1937 as a reserve system, whereby a financial base derived from employer and employee contributions, and income from investments, pay future benefits.

469 Central Arkansas Area: Agency on Aging
320 Trailwood Drive
Po Box 831
Heber Springs, AR 72543
501-362-2413
800-482-6359
Fax: 501-362-8571
e-mail: info@care-link.org
http://www.care-link.org
Elaine Eubank, President/CEO
Beth Landon, VP Community Services

Services include home care, hospice, information and assistance, case management, home-delivered meals, senior centers, transportation, employment, and adult day care.

470 Cleburne County Aging Program
320 Trailwood Drive
PO Box 831
Heber Springs, AR 72543
501-362-2413
Fax: 501-362-8571
e-mail: ccap1@cox-internet.com
http://www.cox-internet.com/seniorcenter
Ed Hass, Executive Director
Ron Cantrell, Assistant Director/Finance Dir.

The Senior Center serves as a resource for senior adults to find services in the community to meet their needs. Meals are provided to the homebound senior adults who are unable to obtain or prepare meals due to disability or age; mid-day meals are planned by a registered dietitian to meet one-third of the recommended daily allowance for senior adults; activities are planned to provide education and recreational opportunities for senior adults at the center; transportation services are designed to provide access for senior adults to doctors, drug stores grocery shopping, nursing homes, utility companies, local government offices and other appointments as well as the senior center.

471 East Arkansas Area: Agency on Aging
2005 E Highland Drive
Jonesboro, AR 72403-5035
870-930-2239
800-467-3278
Fax: 870-930-2255
e-mail: dmonehan@eaaaa.org
http://www.e4aonline.com
Ed Doman, Director
James Doman, Executive Director

The mission of the East Arkansas Area Agency on Aging is to provide leadership relative to aging issues on behalf of older persons in East Arkansas, and to carry out a wide range of functions in planning, coordination, and service delivery such as that the older persons are assisted in leading independent, meaningful, and dignified lives in their own homes and communities as long as possible.

472 Northwest Arkansas Area: Agency on Aging
1510 Rock Springs Road
PO Box 1795
Harrison, AR 72602-1795
870-741-1144
800-432-9721
Fax: 870-741-6214
e-mail: dplumlee@aaanwar.org
http://www.aaanwar.org
Jerry Mitchell, Executive Director
Mary Patrick, Deputy Director

A private, nonprofit organization dedicated to enhancing the lives of senior citizens and helping them to continue living at home as long as possible. The agency offers a wide array of home and community based services with a mix of federal and state funding, private contributions and private pay.

State Organizations & Government Agencies/Arkansas

473 **RSVP East Arkansas**
PO Box 5035
Jonesboro, AR 72403-5035
870-930-2229
800-205-6787
Fax: 870-930-2234
http://www.seniorservices.org/ear_rsvp
Nian Peeler, Director

The Retired and Senior Volunteer Program (RSVP) provides opportunities for people 55 and over to make a difference in their community through volunteer service. RSVP volunteers contribute anywhere from a few to over forty hours a week, serving through schools, day care centers, police departments, hospitals and other nonprofit and public organizations to help meet critical community needs. RSVP offers maximum flexibility and choice to its volunteers. RSVP matches the personal interests and skills of older Americans with opportunities to help solve community problems and offers supplemental insurance while on duty, on-the-job training from the agency or organizaton where volunteers are placed. The following Counties are served: Clay, Crittenden, Cross, Lawrence, Lee, Randolph, St. Francis.

474 **RSVP Garland County**
126 Oriole Street
Hot Springs, AR 71901-3047
501-623-6830
Fax: 501-623-2750
Norma McLain, Director

RSVP enriches life for persons 55 years of age and over through volunteer service. The program provides a way for them to stay involved in their community by sharing their knowledge and addressing community needs.

475 **RSVP Greater Texarkana Arkansas**
E 3rd & Walnut Street
PO Box 2711
Texarkana, AR 75504
870-779-4983
Fax: 870-774-3170
Ermer J Pondexter, Director

The Retired and Senior Volunteer Program (RSVP) provides opportunities for people 55 and over to make a difference in their community through volunteer service. RSVP volunteers contribute anywhere from a few to over forty hours a week, serving through schools, day care centers, police departments, hospitals and other nonprofit and public organizations to help meet critical community needs. RSVP offers maximum flexibility and choice to its volunteers. RSVP matches the personal interests and skills of older Americans with opportunities to help solve community problems and offers supplemental insurance while on duty, on-the-job training from the agency or organization where volunteers are placed. The following Counties are served: Hempstead, Howard, Little River, Lafayette, Miller, Nevada, Sevier.

476 **RSVP Jefferson County**
211 West 3rd Avenue
Suite 125
Pine Bluff, AR 71601
870-534-2156
Fax: 870-534-8005
Denise Grace, Director

The Retired and Senior Volunteer Program (RSVP) provides opportunities for people 55 and over to make a difference in their community through volunteer service. RSVP volunteers contribute anywhere from a few to over forty hours a week, serving through schools, day care centers, police departments, hospitals and other nonprofit and public organizations to help meet critical community needs. RSVP offers maximum flexibility and choice to its volunteers. RSVP matches the personal interests and skills of older Americans with opportunities to help solve community problems and offers supplemental insurance while on duty, on-the-job training from the agency or organization where volunteers are placed. The following County is served: Jefferson.

477 **RSVP North Central Arkansas**
PO Box 2578
Batesville, AR 72503-2578
501-793-8900
Fax: 501-793-4258
e-mail: slamons@cei.net
Sue Lamons

The Retired and Senior Volunteer Program (RSVP) provides opportunities for people 55 and over to make a difference in their community through volunteer service. RSVP volunteers contribute anywhere from a few to over forty hours a week, serving through schools, day care centers, police departments, hospitals and other nonprofit and public organizations to help meet critical community needs. RSVP offers maximum flexibility and choice to its volunteers. RSVP matches the personal interests and skills to older Americans with opportunities to help solve community problems and offers supplemental insurance while on duty, on-the-job training from the agency or organization where volunteers are placed. The following Counties are served: Cleburne, Independence, Izard, Jackson, Sharp, Stone, White, Woodruff.

478 **RSVP Northwest Arkansas**
506 East Spruce
PO Box 778
Rogers, AR 72757
501-636-7301
Fax: 479-636-7312
Deborah Courtney, Director

The Retired and Senior Volunteer Program (RSVP) provides opportunities for people 55 and over to make a difference in their community through volunteer service. RSVP volunteers contribute anywhere from a few to over forty hours a week, serving through schools, day care centers, police departments, hospitals and other nonprofit and public organizations to help meet critical community needs. RSVP offers maximum flexibility and choice to its volunteers. RSVP matches the personal interests and skills of older Americans with opportunities to help solve community problems and offers supplemental insurance while on duty, on-the-job training from the agency or organization where volunteers are placed. The following County is served: Washington.

479 **RSVP Stutgart North Arkansas**
425 S Main Street
Stuttgart, AR 72160
870-673-8584
Fax: 870-673-8585
e-mail: RSVP@futura.net
Jo Rowe, Project Director

We live in a small, rural town and our approximatly 200 wonderful retired and senior volunteers are involved in many varied activities including gardening, education, tree-planting, beautification, pollution control and prevention, recycling, and working with parks and museums.

480 **RSVP Tri-County**
824 Camp Street
El Dorado, AR 71730-4316
870-864-7083
Fax: 870-864-7085
Linda Fitts, Director

The Retired and Senior Volunteer Program (RSVP) provides opportunities for people 55 and over to make a difference in their community through volunteer service. RSVP volunteers contribute anywhere from a few to over forty hours a week, serving thourgh schools, day care centers, police departments, hospitals and other nonprofit and public organizations to help meet critical community needs. RSVP offers maximum flexibility and choice to its volunteers. RSVP matches the personal interests and skills to older Americans with opportunities to help solve community problems and offer supplemental insurance while on duty, on-the-job training from the agency or organization where volunteers are placed.

481 **RSVP West Arkansas**
401 N 13th Street
Fort Smith, AR 72903
479-783-4155
Fax: 479-782-2269
e-mail: westark_rsvp@juno.com
Susie Reehl, Director

State Organizations & Government Agencies/California

The Retired and Senior Volunteer Program (RSVP) provides opportunities for people 55 and over to make a difference in their community through volunteer service. RSVP volunteers contribute anywhere from a few to over forty hours a week, serving through schools, day care centers, police departments, hospitals and other nonprofit and public organizations to help meet critical community needs. RSVP offers maximum flexibility and choice to its volunteers. RSVP matches the personal interests and skills of older Americans with opportunities to help solve problems and offers supplemental insurance while on duty, on-the-job training from the agency or organization where volunteers are placed. The following Counties are served: Crawford, Sebastian, Adair Oklahoma.

482 RSVP of Central Arkansas
PO Box 5936
North Little Rock, AR 72119-5936
501-604-4527
Fax: 501-604-4528
e-mail: staff@rsvpccnark.org
http://www.rsvpccnark.org

Jacqulyn G Hale, Executive Director

The Retired and Senior Volunteer Program (RSVP) provides opportunities for people 55 and over to make a difference in their community through volunteer service. RSVP volunteers contribute anywhere from a few to over forty hours a week, serving though schools, day care centers, police departments, hospitals and other nonprofit and public organizations to help meet critical community needs. RSVP offers maximum flexibility and choice to its volunteers. RSVP matches the personal interests and skills to older Americans with opportunities to help solve community problems and offer supplemental insurance while on duty, on-the-job training from the agency or organization where volunteers are placed.

483 Railroad Retirement Board: Arkansas District Office
1200 Cherry Brook Drive
Suite 500
Little Rock, AR 72211-4122
501-324-5241
Fax: 501-324-7159
e-mail: littlerock@rrb.gov
http://www.rrb.gov

Terri S. Morgan, Chief Information Officer

484 Senior Specialists Agency on Aging
905 W Grand Avenue
Hot Springs, AR 71913-3438
501-321-2811
800-467-2170
Fax: 501-321-2650
e-mail: info@seniorspecialists.org
http://www.seniorspecialists.org

Timothy Herr, Director
Bette Fancher, Director Community Relations
Glenda Chumn, Director Health Services

Serves seniors in the counties of Clark, Conway, Garland, Hot Spring, Johnson, Montgomery, Perry Pike, and Yell in West Central Arkansas. They provide information and assistance, in home personal care, hospice care, a Senior Companion Volunteer Program, and are the primary funding source for 15 senior adult centers. Their goal is to assist seniors to lead independent, meaningful and dignified lives.

485 Southeast Arkansas Area: Agency on Aging
709 East Eighth Avenue
PO Box 8569
Pine Bluff, AR 71611-8569
870-543-6300
800-264-3260
Fax: 870-534-2152
http://www.aaasca.org
TDD 870-534-3268

Betty M Bradshaw, President/CEO

Quality home and community services throughout Southeast Arkansas. Services include skilled and personal home care, transportation, senior center services, home delivered meals, case management and housing.

486 Southwest Arkansas Area: Agency on Aging
600 Columbia 11 East
Magnolia, AR 71753
870-234-7410
800-272-2127
Fax: 870-234-6804
e-mail: dkendrick@aaaswa.net
http://www.agewithdignity.com
TDD 800-336-5575

David Sneed, Executive Director

A nonprofit organization serving adults age 60 or older, family caregivers, agencies and organizations working with seniors. It is part of a national netowrk of more then 650 area agencies on aging throughout the United States.

487 Western Arkansas Area: Agency on Aging
524 Garrison Avenue
PO Box 1724
Fort Smith, AR 72902-1724
479-783-5550
800-737-1827
Fax: 501-783-0029
e-mail: areaagency@agingwest.org
http://www.agingwest.org

Jim Medley MSW, Executive Director

488 White River Area: Agency on Aging
3998 Harrison Street
Po Box 2637
Batesville, AR 72501
870-612-3000
800-382-3205
Fax: 870-793-3971
http://www.wraaa.com
TDD 800-382-3205

Ed Haas, Executive Director

A non-profit organization that provides services to older persons to help them remain independent and in their own homes.

California

489 Alameda County Area: Agency on Aging
Department of Adult and Aging Services
6955 Foothill Boulevard, Suite 300
Oakland, CA 94605
510-577-1900
Fax: 510-577-1965
http://www.alamedasocialservices.org

Linda Kretz, Director

The Alameda County Social Services Department of Adult and Aging Servicese strives to be consumer focused and accessible to the community. The Department offers a coordinated service delivery system that protects, supports, and advocates for an aging population, particularly those with disabilities.

490 American Federation of the Blind: San Francisco Chapter
44 Montgomery Street
Suite 1305
San Francisco, CA 94104
415-392-4845
Fax: 415-392-0383
e-mail: sanfran@afb.net
http://www.afb.org

Gil Johnson, Executive Director

The American Federation for the Blind (AFB) is a national nonprofit that expands possibilities for people with vision loss.

491 Area 1 Agency on Aging
3300 Glenwood Street
Eureka, CA 95501
707-442-3763
Fax: 707-442-3714
http://www.a1aa.org

Nancy Gregory, President
Tom Rowe, Vice President
Donna Chambers, Executive Director

State Organizations & Government Agencies/California

Area 1 Agency on Aging (A1AA) advocates, plans, coordinates, develops, and delivers a range of senior, information, volunteer and caregiver services in Humboldt and Del Norte Counties. Our mission is to provide leadership and guidance in supporting an older person's ability to lead a dignified, safe, healthy and independent life and to provide leadership and resources that support volunteers as they make positive changes in our community.

492   Area 12 Agency on Aging
13975 Mono Way
Suite E
Sonora, CA 95370-4709
209-532-6272
800-510-2020
Fax: 209-532-6501
e-mail: info@area12.org
http://www.area12.org

Linda Zach, Executive Director
Pauline White, Assistant Director

Mission is to provide leadership on issues whiach affect the quality of life for older persons and to pormote citizenship involvement in planning and delivering programs and services necessary to ensure maximum independence and dignity for older individuals and functionally impaired adults.

493   Area 4 Agency on Aging
2260 Park Towne Circle
Suite 100
Sacramento, CA 95825
916-486-1876
Fax: 916-486-9454
e-mail: mail@a4aa.com
http://www.a4aa.com

Deanna Lea, Executive Director
Pat McVicar, Assistant Director
David Soto, Senior Program Manager

Our mission is to provide leadership on issues which affect the quality of life for older persons and to promote citizenship involvement in planning and delivering programs and services necessary to ensure maximum independence and dignity for older individuals and functionally impaired adults.

494   Arthritis Foundation: Northeastern California Chapter
3040 Explorer Drive
Suite 1
Sacramento, CA 95827-2729
916-368-5599
800-571-3456
Fax: 916-368-5596
e-mail: info.necca@arthritis.org
http://www.arthritis.org

Mark Warren, Chapter President

Provides a wide range of services to persons with arthritis and their families. Offers physician referral and assistance in locating medical aids and self-help devices for arthritis. Classes by Arthritis Foundation certified instructors in self-help, exercise and aquatics.

495   Bureau of Naval Personnel: California Retired Affairs Office
Naval Air Weapons Station
Code 75H000D, 1 Administration Circle
China Lake, CA 93555-6001
760-939-0978
Fax: 760-939-3227

Capt. Mark G Storch, Commander

The RAO serves as a link between local retired military and the active-duty community which provides assistance to retired military. It provides installation commanders with a means of providing more effective services and improving communication for the local retired community. The RAO is staffed and operated by volunteer retired military who assist other retired members, their families and survivors to receive entitled services and benefits. Through newsletters, seminars and appreciation days, the RAO supports quality of life issues throughout the retirement years to their fellow service members.

496   Bureau of Naval Personnel: Fleet and Family Support Center
Building 259, Code N93R23
3005 Corbina Alley, Suite 1
San Diego, CA 92136-5190
619-556-7404
Fax: 619-556-7435

Carl E Weiscopf, Director

Fleet and Family Support Center serves active duty, reserved and retired Department of Defense service and family members that are currently residing or expect to reside in the greater San Diego area.

497   Bureau of Naval Personnel: San Diego Retired Activities Office
Naval Amphibious Base Coronado
Code 00C
Coronado San Diego, CA 92155-5000
619-437-2780
Fax: 619-437-2107

The RAO serves as a link between local retired military and the active-duty community which provides assistance to retired military. It provides installation commanders with a means of providing more effective services and improving communication for the local retired community. The RAO is staffed and operated by volunteer retired military who assist other retired members, their families and survivors to receive entitled services and benefits. Through newsletters, seminars and appreciation days, the RAO supports quality of life issues throughout the retirement years to their fellow service members.

498   California Agency of Health & Welfare: Department of Rehabilitation
PO Box 944222
Sacramento, CA 94244-2220
916-324-1313
Fax: 916-263-7474
e-mail: publicaffairs@dor.ca.gov
http://www.rehab.cahwnet.gov

Candace Gilmore, CFO

The California Department of Rehabilitation works in partnership with consumers and other stakeholders to provide services and advocacy resulting in employment, independent living and equality for individuals with disabilities.

499   California Agency of Health and Welfare: Department of Aging
1300 National Drive
Suite 200
Sacramento, CA 95834-1992
916-419-7500
Fax: 916-298-2268
e-mail: webmaster@aging.ca.gov
http://www.aging.ca.gov

John Carr, Office External Affairs
Lora Connolly, Manager

The California Department of Aging (CDA) administers programs that serve older adults, adults with disabilities, family caregivers, and residents in long-term care facilities throughout the state.

500   California Aging Services
1315 I Street
Suite 100
Sacramento, CA 95814-2912
916-392-5111
Fax: 916-428-4250
http://www.aging.org

Anne Burns Johnson, President/CEO
Linda Mcguire, Assistant to President
Jack Chrsity, Director Public Policy

The leading advocate and resource for the state's 400 nonprofit providers of quality senior living and care.

501   California American/Asian Elderly Society
138 Waverly Place
San Francisco, CA 94108
415-397-8322
Fax: 415-397-8322

Hy Man Phong, President

State Organizations & Government Agencies/California

502 California Association for Older Americans
325 Clementina Street
San Francisco, CA 94103-3009
415-541-9629
Fax: 415-896-0358
Shirley Bierly, Director

Organization offers educational lectures on senior issues, has information and referral service, networks with a multitude of organizations in California, primarily San Francisco and Bay area. Publishes 'Senior Power', a quarterly newsletter distributed nationwide.

503 California Association of Area Agencies on Aging
Ventura County Area Agency on Aging
980 North Street
Suite 2200
Sacramento, CA 95814
916-446-2800
Fax: 916-534-9111
http://www.c4a.info
Clay Kempf, President
Barbara Swanson, Vice President
Wendy Moore, Secretary

Lead in developing a statewide, comprehensive, and integrated home and community-based service system that supports dignity, diversity, and choice for older persons and persons with disabilities, their caregivers, and families.

504 California Association of Homes andServices for the Aging
1315 I Street
Suite 100
Sacramento, CA 95814-2912
916-392-5111
Fax: 916-428-4250
http://www.aging.org
David B Ferguson, Board Chair
Gregory Bearce, Vice Chair
Winthrop Marshall, Secretary

It is the mission of the Aging Services of California, formerly the California Association of Homes and Services for the Aging, to advance housing and services for older adults and to support and inspire its members through advocacy, education, research and services enabling them to meet changing needs of their clients and communities.

505 California Client Assistance Program
830 K Street Mall
Second Floor, Room 220
Sacramento, CA 95814
916-322-5066
800-952-5544
Fax: 916-323-0385
e-mail: smentkowski@rehab.cawnet.gov
TTY 800-598-3273
Sheila Conlon Mentkowski, Chief

The Client Assistance Program is an advocacy program for present, past, or prospective clients of the California Department of Rehabilitation, and other agencies which receive funding under the auspices of the Federal Rehabilitation Act.

506 California Commission on Aging
1300 National Drive
Suite 173
Sacramento, CA 95834
916-419-7591
Fax: 916-419-7596
e-mail: ccoa@ccoa.ca.gov
http://www.CalAging.org
Sandra Fitzpatrick, Executive Director

Principal Advocacy Organization for California seniors and advisor to the governor, state legislature and state departments on senior issues.

507 California Department of Aging
1300 National Drive
Suite 200
Sacramento, CA 95834-1992
916-419-7500
800-735-2929
Fax: 916-928-2268
e-mail: webmaster@aging.ca.gov
http://www.aging.ca.gov
Chris Arnold, Director
Lora Connolly, Manager

The California Department of Aging (CDA) administers programs that serve older adults, adults with disabilities, family caregivers, and residents in long-term care facilities throughout the State. The Department administers funds allocated under the federal Older Americans Act, the Older, Californians Act, and throughout the Medi-Cal program.

508 California Department of Aging and Adult Services
686 E Mill Street
San Bernardino, CA 92415-0640
909-891-3900
Fax: 909-891-3919
http://http://hss.co.san-bernadino.ca.us/daas
TDD 949-387-2423
Mary Sawicki, Director

The Department of Aging and Adult Services offer a wide variety of programs designed to help the senior, disabled, and at-risk adults in our county.

509 California Department of Aging: Children and Community Services
PO Box 201056
Stockton, CA 95201-3006
209-468-2202
Fax: 209-468-2207
Dave Erb, Executive Director

510 California Department of Alcohol and Drug Programs: Resource Center
1700 K Street
Sacramento, CA 95811
916-327-3728
800-879-2772
Fax: 916-323-1270
e-mail: resourcecenter@adp.ca.gov
http://www.adp.ca.gov
Renee Zito, Director

To lead efforts to reduce alcoholism, drug addition and problem gambling in California by developing, administering and supporting prevention, treatment and recovery programs. Distributes free information and publications about alcohol and other drugs. Requests for treatment are referred to county alcohol and drug programs.

511 California Department of Rehabilitation
830 K Street
Sacramento, CA 95814-3510
916-263-7365
e-mail: publicaffairs@dor.ca.gov
http://www.dor.ca.gov/public
Tony Sauer, Director

Assists people with disabilities, particularly those with severe disabilities, in obtaining and retaining meaningful employment and living independently in their communities. The Department develops, purchases, provides and advocates for programs and services in vocational rehabilitation, habilitation and independent living with a priority on serving persons with all disabilities, especially those with the most severe disabilities.

512 California Department of Veterans Affairs
1227 O Street
Sacramento, CA 95814
916-653-2158
800-952-5626
Fax: 916-653-2456
e-mail: cadva@ns.net
http://www.cdva.ca.gov
Thomas Johnson, Secretary
Roger Brautigan, Undersecretary
Jack Kirwan, Manager

State Organizations & Government Agencies/California

The mission of the California Department of Veterans Affairs is to promote and administer the benefits, programs, and services provided by the grateful state of California to its deserving veterans, their dependents and survivors.

513 California Developmental Disability Council
1507 21st Street
Suite 210
Sacramento, CA 95811   916-322-8481
866-802-0514
Fax: 916-443-4957
e-mail: council@scdd.ca.gov
http://www.scdd.ca.gov
Alan Kerzin, Executive Director

The State Council on Developmental Disabilities (SCDD) is established by state and federal law as an independent state agency to ensure that people with developmental disabilities and their families receive the services and support they need.

514 California Franchise Tax Board
3321 Power Inn Road
Sacramento, CA 95826-3893   916-845-6500
800-852-5711
http://www.ftb.ca.gov
John Chiang, State Controller And Chair
Dr. Judy Chu, Vice Chair
Michael C Genest, Director Of Finance

The purpose of the Franchise Tax Board is to collect the proper amount of tax revenue, and operate other programs entrusted to us, at the least cost; serve the public by continually improving the quality of our products and services; and perform in a manner warranting the highest degree of public confidence in our integrity, efficiency and fairness.

515 California Governor's Committee on Employment of People with Disabilities
800 Capitol Mall
MIC 41
Sacramento, CA 95814   916-654-8055
800-695-0350
Fax: 916-654-9821
http://www.disabilityemployment.org
TTY 916-654-9820
Catherine K Baird, Executive Director
Charlie Kaplan, Associate Director
Kim Carey, Special Assist to Executive Dir

The Governor's Committee is responsible for providing leadership to increase the numbers of people with disabilities in the California worksforce.

516 California Latino Council of the Deaf and Hard of Hearing
PO Box 65591
Los Angeles, CA 90065   562-634-4112
Fax: 562-630-5391
e-mail: CLCDHH@aol.com
http://www.deafvision.net/clc/
TTY 562-634-4112
Mark D Apodaca, President

CLCDHH's mission is to promote leadership, advocacy, education, and to address the needs of the Deaf and Hard of Hearing Latino Community.

517 California Protection & Advocacy for Persons With Disabilities
100 Howe Avenue
Suite 185N
Sacramento, CA 95825-8219   916-488-9950
800-776-5746
Catherine Blakemore, Executive Director

518 California Public Employees' Retirement System
Lincoln Plaza Complex
400 Q Street
Sacramento, CA 95811   916-326-3829
888-225-7377
Fax: 916-326-3410
http://www.calpers.ca.gov
TTY 916-795-3240
Rob Feckner, President
Robert F Carlson, Vice President
Fred Buenrostro, Chief Executive Officer

Provides retirement and health benefits programs and services, and administers other programs dedicated to protecting the financial security of our members.

519 California Seniors Council
234 Santa Cruz Avenue
Aptos, CA 95003-4438   831-688-0400
Fax: 831-688-1225
e-mail: clayk@seniorscouncil.org
http://www.seniorscouncil.org
Clay Kempf, Executive Director
Patty Talbott, Associate Director
Jan Shirchild, Program Coordinator

It is the mission of the Seniors Council to enable older persons to function with independence and dignity in their homes and in the community to their fullest capacity.

520 California State Board of Equalization
3221 Power Inn Road
Suite 210
Sacramento, CA 95826-3889   916-227-6600
800-400-7115
Fax: 916-227-6641
http://www.boe.ca.gov
TDD 800-735-2929
Ramon J Hirsig, Executive Director

The mission of the State Board of Equalization is to serve the public through fair, effective, and efficient tax administration.

521 California State Teachers Retirement System
PO Box 15275
Sacramento, CA 95851   916-229-3870
800-228-5453
Fax: 916-229-3879
http://www.calstrs.com
TTY 916-229-3541
Jack Ehnes, Chief Executive Officer
Peggy Plett, Deputy CEO/Benefits & Services
Christine Ford, Chief Financial Officer

522 California Workers Compensation Board
455 Golden Gate Avenue, 2nd Floor
PO Box 429003
San Francisco, CA 94102   415-703-5011
800-736-7401
Fax: 415-703-5027
http://www.dir.ca.gov/dwc
Carrie Nevans, Administrative Director
Susan Hamilton, Presiding Judge

Division of Workers' Compensation mission is to minimize the adverse impact of work related injuries on California employees and employers.

523 Central Coast Commission for Senior Citizens
528 S Broadway
Santa Maria, CA 93454-5109   805-925-9554
800-510-2020
Fax: 805-925-9555
e-mail: seniors@slonet.org
http://www.centralcoastseniors.org
Joyce Lippman, Director

State Organizations & Government Agencies/California

The Central Coast Commission for Senior Citizens-Area Agency on Aging (AAA) is a non-profit organization responsible for allocating federal and state dollars to local agencies to insure their supportive, nutrition and health promotion services to older adults in San Luis Obispo and Santa Barbara Counties are availiable.

524　City of Los Angeles Department of Aging
600 S Spring Street
Suite 900
Los Angeles, CA 90014-1955　　　323-357-0311
　　　　　　　　　　　　　　　800-634-6516
　　　　　　　　　　　　　Fax: 213-485-8225
　　　　　　　　　e-mail: age.webinfo@lacity.org
　　　　　　　　　　http://www.lacity.org/doa
Faye Washington, Director

Mission is to improve the quality of life, independence, health and dignity of the City's older population by managing community based senior programs that are comprehensive, coordinated and accessible, and to advocacte for the needs of older citizens.

525　Contra Costa County Office on Aging
2530 Arnold Drive
Suite 300
Martinez, CA 94553-4068　　　　925-335-8720
　　　　　　　　　　　　　　Fax: 925-335-8717
　　　　　　　　　　　　　　TDD 925-313-1730
Lennis Lyon, Program Manager

526　Costa Mesa Senior Center
695 West 19th Street
Costa Mesa, CA 92627　　　　　949-645-2356
　　　　　　　　　　　　　Fax: 949-645-4804
　　　　　e-mail: CostaMesaSeniorCenter@yahoo.com
　　　　　　　　　http://www.cmseniorcenter.org
Aviva Goelman, Executive Director
Darryl Kim, Program Director
Cecilia Zhang, Fiscal Officer

The multipurpose Center is governed by the independent nonprofit Costa Mesa Senior Corporation. The mission of the Corporation and the Center is to maximize the quality of life among the older adult population of Costa Mesa and surrounding communities through provision of programs that will: promote dignity and self-esteem; foster independence and self-determination; facilitate social interaction and involvement in community life; and dispel stereotypical and negative myths about aging.

527　Council on Aging of Silicon Valley
2115 the Alameda
San Jose, CA 95126-1141　　　　408-296-8290
　　　　　　　　　　　　　　　800-510-2020
　　　　　　　　　　　　　Fax: 408-249-8918
　　　　　　　　　　　e-mail: info@sccoa.org
　　　　　　　　　　　http://www.careaccess.org
Stephen Schmoll, Executive Director

Senior services and referral in Silicon Valley California.

528　Diablo Valley Foundation for the Aging
Rossmoor Shopping Plaza
1936 Tice Valley Boulevard
Walnut Creek, CA 94595-2203　　925-945-8040
　　　　　　　　　　　　　Fax: 925-458-8025
　　　　　　　　　　e-mail: contactus@dv-fa.org
　　　　　　　　　http://www.foundationforaging.org
Judith Hartman, Chairperson
Mario Beria, Vice Chairperson
Laverne Gordon, Secretary

Our mission is to provide that support as your professional relative, enabling you to live with optimal independence and freedom. Whatever they might be, DVFA has the solutions to keep you or the one you love living in comfort.

529　Disability Determination Services: LosAngeles West Branch
PO Box 60999
Los Angeles, CA 90060-0999　　　213-736-7500
　　　　　　　　　　　　http://www.ssa.gov/disability
Ken A Rasmussen, Professional Relations

Our purpose is to give individual attention to each individual claim in the highest professional manner and to achieve this purpose, an adjunctive team obtains and evaluates current, precise medical and other information in a timely, unbiased and thorough manner.

530　Disability Determination Services: Central Support Services Branch
1000 G Street
Suite 500
Sacramento, CA 95814-0892　　　916-322-3532
　　　　　　　　　　　　　http://www.ssa.gov

Our purpose is to give individual attention to each individual claim in the highest professional manner and to achieve this purpose, an adjunctive team obtains and evaluates current, precise medical and other information in a timely, unbiased and thorough manner.

531　Disability Determination Services: La Jolla Branch
PO Box 85501
San Diego, CA 92186-5501　　　619-278-4550
　　　　　　　　　　　　http://www.ssa.gov/disability

Our purpose is to give individual attention to each individual claim in the highest professional manner and to achieve this purpose, an adjunctive team obtains and evaluates current, precise medical and other information in a timely, unbiased and thorough manner.

532　Disability Determination Services: Los Angeles South Branch
PO Box 60396
Los Angeles, CA 90060-0396　　　213-736-4086
　　　　　　　　　　　　http://www.ssa.gov/disability
Lisa Jeffers, Professional Relations

Our purpose is to give individual attention to each individual claim in the highest professional manner and to achieve this purpose, an adjunctive team obtains and evaluates current, precise medical and other information in a timely, unbiased and thorough manner.

533　Disability Determination Services: Oakland Branch
PO Box 24225
Oakland, CA 94623-1225　　　　510-622-3506
　　　　　　　　　　　　http://www.ssa.gov/disability

Our purpose is to give individual attention to each individual claim in the highest professional manner and to achieve this purpose, an adjunctive team obtains and evaluates current, precise medical and other information in a timely, unbiased and thorough manner.

534　Disability Determination Services: Roseville Branch
PO Box 619020
Roseville, CA 95678-9861　　　916-774-4100
　　　　　　　　　　　　Fax: 916-774-4162
　　　　　　　　　　http://www.ssa.gov/disability
Gina N Garcia, Profeesional Relations

Our purpose is to give individual attention to each individual claim in the highest professional manner and to achieve this pupose, an adjunctive team obtains and evaluates current, precise medical and other information in a timely, unbiased and thorough manner.

535　Disability Determination Services: Sacramento Branch
PO Box 997120
Sacramento, CA 95899-7120　　　916-263-5000
　　　　　　　　　　　　Fax: 916-263-5310
　　　　　　　　　　http://www.ssa.gov/disability

State Organizations & Government Agencies/California

Our purpose is to give individual attention to each individual claim in the highest professional manner and, to achieve this purpose, an adjunctive team obtains and evaluates current, precise medical and other information in a timely, unbiased and thorough manner

536 Disability Determination Services: San Diego Branch
PO Box 85326
San Diego, CA 92186-5326   619-278-4300
http://www.ssa.gov/disability
Our purpose is to give individual attention to each individual claim in the highest professional manner and to achieve this purpose, an adjunctive team obtains and evaluates current, precise medical and other information in a timely, unbiased and thorough manner.

537 Disability Evaluations Division: SierraBranch
PO Box 1072
Fresno, CA 93714-1072   559-440-5377
Fax: 800-869-0195
Celeste Fox, Professional Relations

538 East Los Angeles Service Center
133 North Sunol Drive
Los Angeles, CA 90063   323-260-2806
Fax: 323-266-6457
http://www.ladcss.org/srvc
Catherine Garcia, Director

It is the mission of Community and Senior Services to provide comprehensive human services to residents of Los Angeles County in partnership with communities, businesses and public and private agencies.

539 El Dorado County Area: Agency on Aging
937 Spring Street
Placerville, CA 95667-4543   530-621-6150
800-510-2020
Fax: 530-642-9233
http://www.co.el-dorado.ca.us
Doug Nowka, Director

The Area Agency on Aging is responsible for the administration of senior programs for El Dorado County residents 60 years of age and older. The Area Agency on Aging develops and impliments the Area Plan for Senior Services in El Dorado County.

540 Elder Care Alliance
2361 E 29th Street
Oakland, CA 94606-3511   510-434-2800
Fax: 510-434-2806
e-mail: info@eldercarealliance.org
http://www.eldercarealliance.org
Susan Edwards, VP Of Operations & Marketing
Pat Copass, Director Of Marketing
Ted Goad, VP Human Resources

Is a nonprofit, faith-centered organization dedicated to providing care services to meet the needs of older adults. We are committed to serving and enriching the physical, emotional, and spiritual well-being of older adults through a network of professional, faith-centered care communities and services.

541 Fresno Madera Area: Agency on Aging
3845 North Clark Street
Suite 103
Fresno, CA 93726-4812   559-453-6494
800-510-2020
Fax: 559-453-4779
e-mail: admin@fmaaa.org
http://www.fmaaa.org
Jo Johnson, Exective Director
Madera County, Fresno County, Fresno.

542 Gray Panthers of Central Contra Costa
Po Box 5722
Concord, CA 04524   925-254-4165
e-mail: donscopp@earthlink.net
http://www.gpcal.org
Ralph Copperman, Convenor
Joan Weber, Co-Convenor

Contra Costa chapter of a national orgazation of intergenerational activists dedicated to social change. Takes on societal issues such as peace, healthcare, jobs and housing, fighting to change laws and attitudes for social justice.

543 Gray Panthers of East Bay/Berkeley
1403 Addison Street
Berkeley, CA 94702-1902   510-548-9696
Fax: 510-548-9697
e-mail: graypanthersberk@aol.com
http://www.gpcal.org
Margot Smith, Director

The first 'Network' of friends gathered to look at the common problems faced by retirees - loss of income, loss of contact with associates and loss of one of our society's most distinguishing social roles, one's job. They also discovered a new kind of freedom in their retirement - the freedom to speak personally and passionately about what they believed in.

544 Gray Panthers of Long Beach
C/O Long Beach Senior Center
1150 East 4th Street
Long Beach, CA 90802   562-570-3500
Fax: 202-737-1160
e-mail: jfscoville@yahoo.com
http://www.gpcal.org
Teresa Munoz, Chairperson
Julia Scoville, Director

Long Beach chapter of a national organization of intergenerational activists dedicated to social change. Takes on societal issues such as peace, healthcare, jobs, and housing from an intergenerational perspective, and fights to change laws and attitudes toward social justice.

545 Gray Panthers of Marin County
PO Box 583
Fairfax, CA 94930   415-453-1550
Fax: 415-332-5929
e-mail: yvettewakefield@yahoo.com
http://http://graypanthers.org
Yvette Wakefield, Convenor

Marin county chapter of a national organization of intergenerational activists dedicated to social change. Takes on societal problems such as peace, healthcare, jobs, and housing, and fights to change laws and attitudes for social justice.

546 Gray Panthers of Orange County
331 N Olive Street
Orange, CA 92866-1039   717-542-8662
Fax: 202-737-1160
e-mail: info@graypanthers.org
http://www.graypanthers.org
Maxine Quirk, Director

Orange County Chapter of a national organization of intergenerational activists dedicated to social change. Takes on society's toughest problems such as peace, healthcare, jobs, and housing, and fights to change laws and attitudes towards social justice.

547 Gray Panthers of Sacramento
PO Box 19438
Sacramento, CA 95819   916-344-4772
Fax: 916-332-5980
e-mail: joanblee@sbcglobal.net
http://www.gpcal.org
Joan B Lee, Chairperson

Sacramento chapter of a national organization of intergeneraltional activists didicated to social change. Takes on societal problems such as peace, healthcare, jobs, and housing, and fights to change laws and attitudes toward social justice.

State Organizations & Government Agencies/California

548 Gray Panthers of San Fernando Valley
10825 Woodward Avenue
Sunland, CA 91040-2535
818-353-1162
Fax: 202-737-1160
e-mail: shawkes@turn.org
http://www.graypanthers.org
Sigrid Hawkes, Director

San Fernando Valley chapter of a national organization of intergenerational activists dedicated to social change. Takes on societal issues such as peace, healthcare, jobs, and housing, and fights to change laws and attitudes for social justice.

549 Gray Panthers of San Francisco
1182 Market Street
Room 203
San Francisco, CA 94102-4916
415-552-8800
Fax: 415-552-8801
e-mail: graypanther-sf@sbcglobal.net
http://www.graypantherssf.igc.org
Sonia Segal, Convenor

Multigenerational activist group who support peace, health care, social security, nutrition, housing, and local issues that impact all citizens.

550 Gray Panthers of Santa Barbara
5110A Cathedral Oaks Road
Santa Barbara, CA 93111
805-967-7171
Fax: 805-967-3771
e-mail: jasinskicj@aol.com
http://www.graypanthers.com
Chen Jasinski, Convenors

Santa Barbara chapter of a national organizatio of intergenerational activists dedicated to social change. Takes on societal issues such as peace, healthcare, jobs, and housing, and fights to change laws and attitudes toward social justice.

551 Gray Panthers of South Bay
PO Box 7138
Torrance, CA 90504-8538
310-217-9202
Fax: 310-329-1455
e-mail: graypanthers.southbay@earthlink.net
http://www.graypanthers.org
Jim Dawson, Convenor

South Bay chapter of a national organization of intergeneraltional activists dedicated to social change. Takes on societal issues such as peace, healthcare, jobs, and housing, and fights to change laws and attitudes toward social justice.

552 Gray Panthers of Southern Alameda County
1328 Via El Monte
San Lorenzo, CA 94580-2224
510-278-2094
Fax: 202-737-1160
e-mail: james.fortsyth@sbc.global.net
http://www.graypanthers.org
Betty L Moose, Director

Southern Alameda County chapter of a national organization of intergenerational activists dedicated to social change. Takes on societal issues such as peace, healthcare, jobs, and housing, and fights to change laws and attitudes toward social justice.

553 Greater Valley Physicians Medical Group
2219 S Hacienda Boulevard
Suite 101
Hacienda Heights, CA 91745
626-961-2461
Fax: 626-330-5392
http://www.drkaran.yourmd.com
Pankaj K Karan MD, Contact

554 HomeAid Orange County
17744 Sky Park Circle
Suite 170
Irvine, CA 92614
949-553-9510
Fax: 949-224-1855
e-mail: info@homeaidoc.org
http://www.homeaidoc.org
Richard Hunsaker, President
Scott Larson, Executive Director
Gina Cunningham, Director Development

555 Imperial County Area Agency on Aging
1331 S Clark Rd.
Bld 11
El Centro, CA 92243
760-339-6450
800-510-2020
e-mail: aaa24director@imperialcounty.net
http://www.co.imperial.ca.us
Norma Saikhon, Public Administrator
Rebecca Sanchez, Manager/Director

Our mission is to provide leadership at the local level in developing systems of home and community based services that maintain 'least restrictive' home like environments. In particular, emphasis shall be placed on coordinating with local systems to enable individuals to live with maximum independence and dignity in their homes and communities through the development of comprehensive and coordinated systems of home and community care.

556 Jewish Communal Retirees Association of Los Angeles
13834 Califa Street
Van Nuys, CA 91401-4306
818-786-3687
Charles Mesnick, President

Voluntary association of retired Jewish communal professionals. Sponsors community projects such as the publication of a comprehensive listing of agencies and organizations which provide services for seniors in the fields of housing, medical, recreation, legal, and citizenship.

557 Kern County Aging And Adult Services
5357 Truxtun Avenue
Bakersfield, CA 93309
661-868-1000
800-510-2020
Fax: 661-868-1001
e-mail: aginginfo@co.kern.ca.us
http://www.co.kern.ca.us/aas
Eddy Laine, Director
Kathy Lemon, Manager

Committed to providing community-based services to ensure seniors and disabled adults remain safely in their homes. We strive to preserve the dignity of older adults and persons with disabilities.

558 Kings Tulare Area: Agency on Aging
1920 W Princeton Avenue
Suite A
Visalia, CA 93277-4400
559-730-2553
800-321-2462
Fax: 209-730-4220
http://www.ktaaa.org
TDD 209-730-2557
John Davis, Director

The Area Agency on Aging coordinates senior programs for Kinds and Tulare County residents 60 years of age and older.

559 La Palma Recreation & Community Services
7821 Walker Street
La Palma, CA 90623-1720
714-690-3350
Fax: 714-522-2967
Jan Hobson, Executive Director

Offers adults fifty years and older the opportunity to meet new friends, learn new things, and have fun. Features games, bingo, cards, fundraising activities, guest speakers, potluck luncheons, and community services.

State Organizations & Government Agencies/California

560 **La Quinta Senior Center**
City of La Quinta
PO Box 1504
La Quinta, CA 92247-1504 760-564-0096
Fax: 760-564-5004
http://www.la-quinta.org
Caroline Doran, Manager
Christina Calderon, Coordinator

The La Quinta Senior Center is a community focal point offering a wide range of services to adults 55 years of age or older. The Center offers a variety of classes, seminars, special events and weekly programs.

561 **Los Angeles County Area Agency on Aging**
3333 Wilshire Boulevard
Suite 400
Los Angeles, CA 90010 213-738-4004
Cynthia Banks, Director

The Area Agency on Aging plans, develops and delivers services for seniors (60 years and older) and for adults (18-59 years) with disabilities and long-term care needs.

562 **Los Angeles Disability Determination Services**
PO Box 60396
Los Angeles, CA 90060-0396 213-736-4086

Our purpose is to give individual attention to each individual claim in the highest professional manner and to achieve this purpose, an adjunctive team obtains and evaluates current, precise medical and other information in a timely, unbiased and thorough manner.

563 **Marin County: Area Agency on Aging**
Division of Aging
10 N San Pedro Road
Suite 1012
San Rafael, CA 94903-4155 415-499-7396
800-834-4777
e-mail: angeinfo@mailbox.lacity.org
Ellen Caulfield, Director
Nick Trunzo, Executive Director

564 **Marin Senior Coordinating Council(Whistlestop)**
930 Tamalpais Avenue
San Rafael, CA 94901-3325 415-454-1551
Fax: 415-456-1581
e-mail: info@thewhistlestop.org
http://www.thewhistlestop.org
Don Morgan, Executive Director
Rebecca Lack, Executive Assistant
Betty Dietz, Programs & Resource Coordinator

For senior citizens in Marin County, CA. Works to improve the quality of life for senior citizens through nutritional, transportation, educational, recreational, information and referral services.

565 **Meals on Wheels of Culver Palms**
4153 Overland Avenue
Culver City, CA 90230-4118 310-253-6700
http://www.mealcall.org/meals-on-wheels/ca
Frances M Stronks, Executive Director

To deliver high quality, nutritious meals to the homes of persons in the Culver City/Palms/Marina Del Rey area who are incapacitated due to age, convalescence or disability.

566 **Merced County Area Agency for Aging**
851 W 23rd Street
Merced, CA 95340-3611 209-385-7550
800-834-1122
Fax: 209-384-8102
http://www.co.merced.ca.us/aaa
Ana Pagan, Director
Rick Bungcayao, Manager

Mission is to work in partnership with the community to provide for the protection, care and support of families and individuals, and to promote personal responsibility and self-sufficiency.

567 **Merced Senior Community Center**
755 West 15th Street
Merced, CA 95340 209-385-8803

568 **North Coast Opportunities: Area Agency on Aging**
413a N State Street
Ukiah, CA 95482-4421 707-462-1954
800-606-5550
Fax: 707-462-0191
e-mail: info@ncoinc.org
http://www.ncoinc.org
Roberta Green, Director
Nancy Powers-Stone, Executive Director

North Coast Opportunities (NCO) pledges to be a leader in developing and providing human services that strengthen our community.

569 **Office for Aging and Community Services: Monterey County Department of Social Services**
713 La Guardia Street
Suite A
Salinas, CA 93905 831-755-3403
Fax: 831-783-7021
e-mail: remarkmr@co.moonterey.ca.us
http://www.co.monterey.ca.us/dss/aaa
TDD 408-755-8490
Marie Glavin, Director

570 **Office of Public Affairs, Social Security Administration**
San Francisco Regional Public Affairs Office
PO Box 4201
Richmond, CA 94804 510-970-8430
800-772-1213
Fax: 510-970-8218
e-mail: sf.rpa@ssa.gov
http://www.socialsecurity.gov
Leslie S Walker, Regional Communications Director
Lowell Kepke, Deputy Director
Kathleen Wiegand, Senior Public Affairs Specialist

The San Francisco Regional Public Affairs Office responds to regional media inquiries relating to the Social Security and Supplemental Security Income programs.

571 **Older Women's League of Ohlone**
346 Hanover Avenue
401
Oakland, CA 94606 207-581-2385
e-mail: cberk@ix.netcom.com
http://www.owl.national.org
Cleo Berkum, Executive Director

The Older Women's League of California is co-creator with Congress of California Seniors of this Women's Issues Section. This organization advocates for mid-life and older women. A community-based, private, nonprofit organization, OWL accomplishes its work through research, education and advocacy activities conducted by a chapter network across the county.

572 **Orange County Area: Agency on Aging**
1300 S Grand Avenue
Building B
Santa Ana, CA 92705-4434 714-567-7500
800-510-2020
Fax: 714-567-5021
e-mail: officeonaging@ocgov.com
http://www.officeonaging.ocgov.com
TDD 714-567-7500
Karen Roper, Executive Director

Orange Countie's Office on Aging serves as the lead advocate for 400,000 older adults residing in the county, with a specific focus on low-income ethnic minorities. As an advocate, the Office on Aging is responsible for understanding the needs of Orange County's older adults and utilizing the federal funding and programs availiable to meet those requirements. In addition, the office on Aging is charged with directing or participating in coalitions to drive new ideas, services, and legislation in support of Older Adults.

State Organizations & Government Agencies/California

573 Orange County Korean Community Service Center
9884 Garden Grove Boulevard
Garden Grove, CA 92644   714-636-7400
                             Fax: 714-636-7990
e-mail: ockoreancenters@aol.com

This community center assists newly arriving Korean immigrants, with an emphasis on seniors, by helping with everyday problems such as translating mail and other paper work. The Center also helps needy families with its Healthy Family Program and Medi-Cal. The disabled and seniors can also get help in applying for SSA, SSI, MSI, Medicare, CAPI and Renter's Assistance.

574 PSA 2 Area Agency On Aging
PO Box 1400
Yreka, CA 96097-1400   530-842-1687
                             Fax: 530-842-4804
Dennis Dudley, Director
Barbara Swanson, Executive Director

575 Passages Adult Resource Center-Area Agency on Aging
California State University
2491 Carmichael Drive
Suite 400
Chico, CA 95928   530-898-5923
                            800-822-0109
                            Fax: 530-898-4870
e-mail: passages@csuchico.edu
http://www.passagescenter.org
Joe Cobery, Director

The AAA is responsible for planning and administering services for seniors (60+) in the five counties of Butte, Colusa, Glenn, Plumas and Tehama. Some services, such as the Information and Assistance and the Long Term Care Ombudsman Program, are provided directly by the staff at PASSAGES Adult Resouce Center, other services, including congregate meals, home-delivered meals, transportation, legal assistance and in-home services, are provided through contracts with community agencies.

576 RSVP All Peoples Christian Center
822 E 20th Street
Los Angeles, CA 90011-1104 213-747-6357
                             Fax: 213-747-0541
e-mail: tmoran@allpeoplescc.org
http://www.allpeoplescc.org
Sandra Bryant, Executive Director
Sheryl Johnson, Executive Assistant

The Retired and Senior Volunteer Program (RSVP) provides opportunities for people 55 and over to make a difference in their community through volunteer service. RSVP volunteers contribute anywhere from a few to over forty hours a week, serving through schools, day care centers, police departments, hospitals and other nonprofit and public organizations to help meet critical community needs. RSVP offers maximum flexibility and choice to its volunteers. RSVP matches the personal interests and skills of older Americans with opportunities to help solve community problems and offers supplemental insurance while on duty, and on-the-job training from the agency or organization where volunteers are placed. The following County is served: Los Angeles.

577 RSVP Central Coast
660 Pismo Street
San Luis Obispo, CA 93401-3945 805-544-8740
                                 Fax: 805-544-9146
e-mail: slorsvp@slonet.org
http://www.seniorservice.org/slo_rsvp
Richard Gruner, Executive Director

RSVP helps people 55 years and over find service opportunities in their home communities. RSVP participants serve from a few to over forty hours a week in organizations that range from hospitals and youth recreation centers to local police stations and education facilities. RSVP involves seniors in service that matches their personal interests and makes use of their skills and lifelong experiences.

578 RSVP City of Burbank
1301 W Olive Avenue
PO Box 6459
Burbank, CA 91506-2217   818-238-5370
                             Fax: 818-238-5388
e-mail: dcall@ci.burbank.ca.us
http://www.seniorservice.org/burbank_rsvp
Dee Call, Director

The Retired and Senior Volunteer Program (RSVP) provides opportunities for people 55 and over to make a difference in their community through volunteer service. RSVP volunteers contribute anywhere from a few to over forty hours a week, serving through schools, day care centers, police departments, hospitals and other nonprofit and public organizations to help meet critical community needs. RSVP offers maximum flexibility and choice to its volunteers. RSVP matches the personal interests and skills of older Americans with opportunities to help solve community problems and offers supplemental insurance while on duty, on-the-job training from the agency or organization where volunteers are placed. The following County is served: Los Angeles.

579 RSVP Coachella Valley
73750 Catalina Way
Palm Desert, CA 92260-2906 760-340-4312
                             Fax: 760-340-9585
e-mail: rcooa.aging.fferguso@co.riverside.ca.us
Fran Ferguson, Executive Director

The Retired and Senior Volunteer Program (RSVP) provides opportunities for people 55 and over to make a difference in their community through volunteer service. RSVP volunteers contribute anywhere from a few to over forty hours a week, serving through schools, day care centers, police departments, hospitals and other nonprofit and public organizations to help meet critical community needs. RSVP offers maximum flexibility and choice to its volunteers. RSVP matches the personal interests and skills of older Americans with opportunities to help solve community problems and offer supplemental insurance while on duty, on-the-job training from the agency or organization where volunteers are placed. The following County is served: Riverside.

580 RSVP Culver City
4095 Overland Avenue
Culver City, CA 90230   310-253-6704
                             Fax: 310-253-6711
e-mail: Vholtdoby@aol.com
http://www.culvercity.org/senior/rsvp.asp
Bobbie Lanham, Director

The Retired and Senior Volunteer Program (RSVP) provides opportunities for people 55 and over to make a difference in their community through volunteer service. RSVP volunteers contribute anywhere from a few to over forty hours a week, serving through schools, day care centers, police departments, hospitals and other nonprofit and public organizations to help meet critical community needs. RSVP offers maximum flexibility and choice to its volunteers. RSVP matches the personal interests and skills of older Americans with opportunities to help solve community problems and offers supplemental insurance while on duty, on-the-job training from the agency or organization where volunteers are placed. The following County is served: Los Angeles.

581 RSVP Fresno
1900 Mariposa Mall
Suite 114
Fresno, CA 93721-2525   559-237-3101
                            866-476-7787
                            Fax: 559-237-6860
e-mail: ccaples@vcfresno.org
http://www.volunteercenteroffresno.org
Cathy Caples, Executive Director
Dennis Daggett, Accountant
Nicole Tucker, Bookkeeper

State Organizations & Government Agencies/California

The mission of the Volunteer Center of Fresno County is to serve as the leader for the community by matching volunteer resources with volunteer opportunities. By assuming a leadership role in this effort, the Volunteer Center facilitates, coordinates, and evaluates the process to successfully recruit and retain potential volunteers while in addition to administering internal core programs. The Center supports community-based agencies during the planning and implementation of volunteer projects. The heart of the Volunteer Center's mission is to cultivate a community conscience that promotes the spirit, the value and the dignity of volunteerism. The following Counties are served: Fresno, Madera, Merced.

582 RSVP Greater East Los Angeles
4848 E Colonia De Las Rosas
Los Angeles, CA 90022-1313
323-265-9592
Fax: 323-263-9856
e-mail: casarsvo@netzero.net

Elia Serrano, Director

The Retired and Senior Volunteer Program (RSVP) provides opportunities for people 55 and over to make a difference in their community through volunteer service. RSVP volunteers contribute anywhere from a few to over forty hours a week, serving through schools, day care centers, police departments, hospitals and other nonprofit and public organizations to help meet critical community needs. RSVP offers maximum flexibility and choice to its volunteers. RSVP matches the personal interests and skills of older Americans with opportunities to help solve community problems and offers supplemental insurance while on duty, on-the-job training from the agency or organization where volunteers are placed. The following County is served: Los Angeles.

583 RSVP Humboldt/Del Norte Counties
3300 Glenwood Street
Eureka, CA 95501-3463
707-442-3711
Fax: 707-442-3714
e-mail: vcor@wcinet.net
http://www.a1aa.org/vcor

Pam Zeutenhorst, Director

The Retired and Senior Volunteer Program (RSVP) provides opportunities for people 55 and over to make a difference in their community through volunteer service. RSVP volunteers contribute anywhere from a few to over forty hours a week, serving through schools, day care centers, police departments, hospitals and other nonprofit and public organizations to help meet critical community needs. RSVP offers maximum flexibility and choice to its volunteers. RSVP matches the personal interests and skills of older Americans with opportunities to help solve community problems and offers supplemental insurance while on duty, on-the-job training from the agency or organization where volunteers are placed. The following Counties are served: Del Norte, Humboldt.

584 RSVP Kings/Tulare Counties
3500 W Mineral King Avenue
Suite C
Visalia, CA 93291
559-730-2551
Fax: 559-730-2575

Linda Herrera, Director

The Retired and Senior Volunteer Program (RSVP) provides opportunities for people 55 and over to make a difference in their community through volunteer service. RSVP volunteers contribute anywhere from a few to over forty hours a week, serving through schools, day care centers, police departments, hospitals and other nonprofit and public organizations to help meet critical community needs. RSVP offers maximum flexibility and choice to its volunteers. RSVP matches the personal interests and skills of older Americans with opportunities to help solve community problems and offers supplemental insurance while on duty, on-the-job training from the agency or organization where volunteers are placed. The following Counties are served: Kings, Tulare.

585 RSVP Lake/Mendocino Counties
413 N State Street
Ukiah, CA 95482-4421
707-462-2596
800-606-5550
Fax: 707-462-0191
e-mail: tbartolomei@ncoinc.org
http://www.mendovolunteers.com

Tami Bartolomei, Director

Provides help to their communities by feeding the hungry without compensation. There are no education, experience or income requirements for participation. Benefits include free supplemental insurance. Serves Lake and Mendocino counties.

586 RSVP Long Beach
3801 E Willow Street
Long Beach, CA 90815-1734
562-506-2801
Fax: 562-424-3915
e-mail: djrsvplb@hotmail.com
http://www.seniorservice.org/longbeach_rsvp

Diane L Johnson, Director

The Retired and Senior Volunteer Program (RSVP) provides opportunities for people 55 and over to make a difference in their community through volunteer service. RSVP volunteers contribute anywhere from a few to over forty hours a week, serving through schools, day care centers, police departments, hospitals and other nonprofit and public organizations to help meet critical community needs. RSVP offers maximum flexibility and choice to its volunteers. RSVP matches the personal interests and skills of older Americans with opportunities to help solve community problems and offers supplemental insurance while on duty, on-the-job training from the agency or organization where volunteers are placed. The following County served is Los Angeles.

587 RSVP Los Angeles Parks
6671 Yucca Street
Los Angeles, CA 90028-4756
323-461-4363
Fax: 323-913-4701

Jacqueline Raycraft, Director

The Retired and Senior Volunteer Program (RSVP) provides opportunities for people 55 and over to make a difference in their community through volunteer service. RSVP volunteers contribute anywhere from a few to over forty hours a week, serving through schools, day care centers, police departments, hospitals and other nonprofit and public organizations to help meet critical community needs. RSVP offers maximum flexibility and choice to its volunteers. RSVP matches the personal interests and skills with older Americans with opportunities to help solve community problems and offers supplemental insurance while on duty, on-the-job training from the agency or organization where volunteers are placed. The following County is served: Los Angeles.

588 RSVP Nevada County
471 Sutton Way
Suite 202
Grass Valley, CA 95945-4106
530-271-0255
Fax: 530-271-0849
http://http://a4aa.com/html/rsvp.html

Sara Morrison, Director

Recruits and places senior volunteers in meaningful volunteer assigments in community and non profit agencies. The following County is served: Nevada.

589 RSVP Northern Santa Clara County
450 Bryant Street
Palo Alto, CA 94301-1701
650-326-5362
Fax: 650-326-3048
e-mail: rsvp@avenidas.org

David Whitman, Director

State Organizations & Government Agencies/California

The Retired and Senior Volunteer Program (RSVP) provides opportunities for people 55 and over to make a difference in their community through volunteer service. RSVP volunteers contribute anywhere from a few to over forty hours a week, serving through schools, day care centers, police departments, hospitals and other nonprofit and public organizations to help meet critical community needs. RSVP offers maximum flexibility and choice to its volunteers. RSVP matches the personal interests and skills of older Americans with opportunities to help solve community problems and offers supplemental insurance while on duty, on-the-job training from the agency or organization where volunteers are placed. The following County is served: Santa Clara.

590 RSVP Oakland
900 Fallon Street
Room 514
Oakland, CA 94607-4808   510-464-3176
                            Fax: 510-464-3177
Josephine Lopez, Director

The Retired and Senior Volunteer Program (RSVP) provides opportunities for people 55 and over to make a difference in their community through volunteer service. RSVP volunteers contribute anywhere from a few to over forty hours a week, serving through schools, day care centers, police departments, hospitals and other nonprofit and public organizations to help meet critical community needs. RSVP offers maximum flexibility and choice to its volunteers. RSVP matches the personal interests and skills of older Americans with opportunities to help solve community problems and offers supplemental insurance while on duty, on-the-job training from the agency or organization where volunteers are placed. The following County is served: Alameda.

591 RSVP Ojai County
111 W Santa Ana Street
PO Box 621
Ojai, CA 93023   805-646-7787
                            Fax: 805-646-1748
         e-mail: rsvpojai@helpofojai.org
         http://www.seniorservices.org/ojai_rsvp
Kathleen M Tarrats, Director

The Retired and Senior Volunteer Program (RSVP) provides opportunities for people 55 and over to make a difference in their community through volunteer service. RSVP volunteers contribute anywhere from a few to over forty hours a week, serving through schools, day care centers, police departments, hospitals and other nonprofit and public organizations to help meet critical community needs. RSVP offers maximum flexibility and choice to its volunteers. RSVP matches the personal interests and skills of older Americans with opportunities to help solve community problems and offers supplemental insurance while on duty, on-the-job training from the agency or organization where volunteers are placed. The following County is served: Ventura.

592 RSVP Oxnard County
Wilson Senior Center
350 North C Street
Oxnard, CA 93030-4646   805-385-8023
                            Fax: 805-385-7494
         e-mail: rsvp@ci.oxnard.ca.us
         http://www.ci.oxnard.ca.us
Marysue Eastlake, Director

The City of Oxnard Senior Services sponsors the Oxnard Retired and Senior Volunteer Program (RSVP). Through RSVP, men and women 55 and older are putting their life experience to work for their communities.

593 RSVP Pomona Valley
2120 Foothill Boulevard
Suite 115
La Verne, CA 91750-2949   909-593-7511
                            Fax: 909-596-8445
         e-mail: rsvp@linkling.com
         http://www.rsvphelps.org
Bobbie Hill, President
Eileen Brown, RSVP Director

RSVP provides guidance to volunteer service opportunities for adults over the age of 55 who would like to use their interests and skills to meet critical community needs while enriching their own lives with a high quality volunteer experience.

594 RSVP Sacramento County
3727 Marconi Avenue
Sacramento, CA 95821   916-875-3631
                            Fax: 916-875-3799
         e-mail: anders1@co.sacramento.ca.us
         http://www.rsvpsacramento.org
Laureen Anderson, Director

Volunteer assignments for persons 55 years of age and older with nonprofit and public agencies within the community. Staff assists volunteers in finding an assignment consistent with their interests and skills. RSVP volunteers are covered (during volunteer activities) under a supplemental accident and liability insurance. They may also receive limited mileage reimbursement if needed. Any public agency or private nonprofit organization may request volunteers through RSVP. The following Counties are served: Placer, Sacramento, Yolo.

595 RSVP San Bernardino County
150 W. 1st Street
175
Claremont, CA 91711   909-482-0355
                            Fax: 909-624-1294
Patricia Henry, Director

The Retired and Senior Volunteer Program (RSVP) helps individuals age 55 and older put their skills and life experience to work for their communities. RSVP volunteers serve from a few hours to forty hours a week. They do just about everything - from tutoring children and building homes for low-income families, to teaching computer skills and testing for water safety. However they choose to serve, RSVP volunteers meet critical community needs. The following County is served: San Bernardino.

596 RSVP San Fernando/Santa Clarita Valleys
8134 Van Nuys Boulevard
Suite 200
Panorama, CA 91402   818-908-5070
                            Fax: 818-908-5147
Caren C Lea, Director

Our small but active corps of senior volunteers provide environmental education to our surrounding community by serving as docent tour leaders at the L.A. Zoo, Tillman Japanese Garden, Autry Western Heritage Museum, Pacific Asia Museum, Geltz Center, and others. They also serve as office volunteers, coordinating the work at Habitat for Humanity.

597 RSVP Santa Barbara
35 West Victoria Street
Santa Barbara, CA 93101-3127   805-963-0474
                               Fax: 805-963-0475
         e-mail: RogerHand@webtv.net
Roger Hand, Director

The Retired and Senior Volunteer Program (RSVP) provides opportunities for people 55 and over to make a difference in their community through volunteer service. RSVP volunteers contribute anywhere from a few to over forty hours a week, serving through schools, day care centers, police departments, hospitals and other nonprofit and public organizations to help meet critical community needs. RSVP offers maximum flexibility and choice to its volunteers. RSVP matches the personal interests and skills of older Americans with opportunities to help solve community problems and offers supplemental insurance while on duty, on-the-job training from the agency or organization where volunteers are placed. The following County is served: Santa Barbara.

598 RSVP Shast and Tehama Counties
200 Mercury Oaks Drive
Redding, CA 96003   530-226-3033
                            Fax: 530-225-5178
         e-mail: jessica.cunningham@chw.edu
         http://www.shastarsvp.org
Jessica Cunningham, Director

State Organizations & Government Agencies/California

The Retired and Senior Volunteer Program (RSVP) provides opportunities for people 55 and over to make a difference in their community through volunteer service. RSVP volunteers contribute anywhere from a few to over forty hours a week, serving though schools, day care centers, police departments, hospitals and other nonprofit and public organizations to help meet critical community needs. RSVP offers maximum flexibility and choice to its volunteers. RSVP matches the personal interests and skills to older Americans with opportunities to help solve community problems and offer supplemental insurance while on duty, on-the-job training from the agency or organization where volunteers are placed.

599 RSVP Sonoma County
153 Stony Circle
Suite 100
Santa Rosa, CA 95401-9516
707-573-3399
Fax: 707-573-3380

Laurie Parrish, Director

The Retired and Senior Volunteer Program (RSVP) provides opportunities for people 55 and over to make a difference in their community through volunteer service. RSVP volunteers contribute anywhere from a few to over forty hours a week, serving through schools, day care centers, police departments, hospitals and other nonprofit and public organizations to help meet critical community needs. RSVP offers maximum flexibility and choice to its volunteers. RSVP matches the personal interests and skills of older Americans with opportunities to help solve community problems and offers supplemental insurance while on duty, and on-the-job training from the agency or organization where volunteers are placed. The following County is served: Sonoma.

600 RSVP South Bay County
1339 Post Avenue
Torrance, CA 90802
310-320-3322
Fax: 310-320-3949
e-mail: rsvpsouthbay@sbcglobal.net
http://http://rsvpsv.org

Thomas White, Executive Director

RSVP of South Bay is a nonprofit agency that is funded in part by the Corporation for National Service and matched in dollars by corporations, foundations, clubs and individuals donors in the community. The mission of RSVP of South Bay is to utilize the skills of senior volunteers in meeting the educational, environmental, health, public safety and other identified needs of the South Bay community.

601 RSVP Thousand Oaks/Conejo Valley
1385 E Janss Road
Thousand Oaks, CA 91362
805-381-2742
Fax: 805-495-5430
e-mail: rsvp@crpd.org

Cindy Powers, Director

The Retired and Senior Volunteer Program (RSVP) provides opportunities for people 55 and over to make a difference in their community through volunteer service. RSVP volunteers contribute anywhere from a few to over forty hours a week, serving through schools, day care centers, police departments, hospitals and other nonprofit and public organizations to help meet critical community needs. RSVP offers maximum flexibility and choice to its volunteers. RSVP matches the personal interests and skills of older Americans with opportunities to help solve community problems and offers supplemental insurance while on duty, on-the-job training from the agency or organization where volunteers are placed. The following County is served: Ventura.

602 RSVP Visalia Volunteer
310 N Locust Street
Visalia, CA 93291-4944
559-713-4481
Fax: 559-713-4831

Richard De Ocio, Director

The Retired and Senior Volunteer Program (RSVP) provides opportunities for people 55 and over to make a difference in their community through volunteer service. RSVP volunteers contribute anywhere from a few to over forty hours a week, serving through schools, day care centers, police departments, hospitals and other nonprofit and public organizations to help meet critical community needs. RSVP offers maximum flexibility and choice to its volunteers. RSVP matches the personal interests and skills of older Americans with opportunities to help solve community problems and offers supplemental insurance while on duty, and on-the-job training from the agency or organization where volunteers are placed. The following County served is: Tulare.

603 RSVP West Valley of San Bernardino County
150 West 1st Street
175
Claremont, CA 91711-0908
909-482-0355
Fax: 909-624-1294

Patricia Henny, Director

Providing a wide range of interesting volunteer opportunities for seniors aged 55 years of age and older in the cities of: Bloomington, Chino, Chino Hills, Colton, Fontana, Grand Terrace, Montclair, Mt Baldy Village, Ontario, Rancho Cucamonga, Rialto, Upland.

604 RSVP Western Riverside County
418 E Florida Avenue
Hemet, CA 92543
951-929-0423
Fax: 951-652-0064
e-mail: rsvp@ccuw.org
http://www.ccuw.org

Kristie McCormack, Director

RSVP, a part of Senior Corps, offers meaningful volunteer opportunities for the active senior 55 and better. There are many volunteer opportunities to serve your interest right in the community in which you live.

605 Railroad Retirement Board-California District Office
801 I Street
Room 205
Sacramento, CA 95814-2559
916-498-6654
Fax: 916-498-6659
e-mail: sacramento@rrb.gov
http://www.rrb.gov/field/do/sacr.asp

Daniel L Williams, Representative
Shelly Rouillard, Executive Director

606 Rancho Bernardo Joslyn Senior Center
18402 W Bernardo Drive
San Diego, CA 92127-3018
858-487-9324
Fax: 858-487-9235
http://www.rbernardo.com/seniors/joslyn

Betsy Macomber, President
Arlene Cawthorne, Vice President
Sandie Dewane, Executive Director

A member-supported, non-profit organization dedicated to enhancing the well-being and quality of life of men and women 50 years of age and older. It has been serving the RB area for 12 years. The Center offers a wide range of activities and services.

607 Region 9: Administration on Aging (AoA)
US Department of Health & Human Services
50 United Nations Plaza
Room 455
San Francisco, CA 94102
415-437-8780
800-422-6237
Fax: 415-437-8782
http://www.aoa.gov

David Ishida, Regional Administrator
Josefina G Carbonell ASA, Assistant Secretary
Edwin Walker PDASA, Deputy Assistant Secretary

Region includes American Samoa, Arizona, California, CNMI, Guam, Hawaii, and Nevada. Through this network, older persons in each community have access to supportive and nutrition services. Persons age 60 and over may participate, and priority is given to the elderly with greatest economic or social needs.

State Organizations & Government Agencies/California

608 Retired Activities Office
Naval Base San Diego
306 Corbina Alley, Suite 1
San Diego, CA 92136-5190
619-556-7359
Fax: 619-556-7435
e-mail: nrswrao@navy.mil
http://www.cnrsw.navy.mil/internal/rao
Rene Trevino, RA, AIA, Executive Director

The Retired Activities Office (RAO) was established under the Department of Navy Retired Activities Program mandated by the Secretary of the Navy as well as the Chief of Naval Operations Directives. The services provided by RAO are varied and important to the retired community. All retirees and their families are encouraged to use these services to save time and money as well. We provide peace of mind.

609 San Diego County Area: Agency on Aging
9089 Clairemont Mesa Boulevard
Suite 104
San Diego, CA 92123-1225
858-492-1090
800-422-8885
Fax: 858-492-9284
Daniel Laver, Director
Veronica Braun, President

610 San Diego Hebrew Homes
211 Saxony Road
Encinitas, CA 92024-2791
760-632-0081
Fax: 760-942-0894
e-mail: pferris@seacrestvillage.org
http://ww.seacrestvillage.com
Pam Ferris, President/CEO
Robin Israel, VP Fund Development
Carolyn Brooking, Corporate Director Marketing

Offers services and support that reflect sincere dedication to seniors.

611 San Francisco Commission on the Aging
875 Stevenson Street
Floor 3
San Francisco, CA 94103
415-355-3555
Fax: 415-355-6785
http://www.sfgov.org/daas
Darrick Lam, Executive Director
Shireen McSpudden, Deputy Director of Programs

The Department of Aging and Adult Services (DAAS) is the Area Agency on Aging for the City and County of San Francisco. In this capacity, DAAS is specifically charged with planning, coordinating, providing and advocactingfor community-based services for older adults and adults with disabilities.

612 Santa Cruz Volunteer Center
1010 Emeline Avenue
Building C
Santa Cruz, CA 95060
831-427-5070
Fax: 831-423-6267
e-mail: scruz@scvolunteercenter.org
http://www.scvolunteercenter.com
Karen Delaney, Executive Director

The mission is accomplished by operating two types of programs: those designed to recruit and orient volunteers for placement in other nonprofit agencies; and those providing direct services to address specific needs by the Board, using volunteer services.

613 Senior Citizens of Shasta County
2290 Benton Drive
Redding, CA 96003-2152
530-241-9759
Robert Haase, President

For persons age 50 and older. Promotes social interaction among members. Sponsors card games, craft activities, dances, library, and exercise classes. Conducts charitable activities.

614 Senior Gleaners
1951 Bell Avenue
Sacramento, CA 95838-3039
916-925-3240
800-585-1530
Fax: 916-568-1528
e-mail: sgi@seniorgleaners.org
http://www.seniorgleaners.org
Edie Harmon, President
Felix Barrera, 1st Vice President

Our mission is to alleviate hunger among the poor and elderly and to glean surplus foods, at low or no cost, from every available source, for distribution among the needy members and other charitable organizations in a fair and equitable manner.

615 Solano Napa: Agency on Aging
400 Contra Costa St.
Vallejo, CA 94590-5721
707-644-6612
800-510-2020
Fax: 707-644-7905
http://www.aaans.org
Leanne Martinsen, Executive Director
Doug Hansen, Fiscal Director

Our Area Agency on Aging (AAA) serves Napa and Solano counties. It is one of 33 similar programs in California. Our role is to plan, coordinate and advocate for the development of local programs to meet the needs of older persons.

616 Sonoma County Task Force for the Homeless
3315 Airway Drive
Santa Rosa, CA 95403
707-575-4484
Fax: 707-575-4494
e-mail: sctfhmls#pacbell.net
http://www.sonomacountyhomeless.org
Nick Stewart, Chair
Gail Brownell, Vice-Chair
Dannielle Danforth, Treasurer

The Sonoma County Task Force for the Homeless is a catalyst and leadership resource bringing the community together to: promote affordable housing; prevent homelessness; assist people who are homeless.

617 Spiritual Fitness Division (CREDO Southwest)
3670 Surface Navy Blvd
Building 330
San Diego, CA 92136
619-556-2826
Fax: 619-532-1441
e-mail: spiritualfitnesscenter@navy.mil
http://www.cnrsw.navy.mil

Clients are active or retired personnel of the Sea Services (USN, USMC, USCG) and their family members. Provides workshops and retreats that address a variety of problems, including personal conflicts, substance abuse, and parenting difficulties. Seeks to create an atmosphere where maximum personal and spiritual growth can occur in a short time. Promotes continued growth in interpersonal skills. Conducts retreat programs and discussion groups.

618 Stanislaus County Department of Aging and Veteran Services
121 Downey Avenue
Suite 102
Modesto, CA 95354
209-558-7380
Fax: 209-558-8648
http://www.c4a.info
Carolyn Hebenstreich, Manager

Our mission is to lead in developing a statewide, comprehensive, and integrated home and community-based service system that supports dignity, diversity, and choice for older persons with disabilities, their caregivers, and families.

619 Sunset Hall Program at Bethany Towers
1745 N Gramercy Place
Los Angeles, CA 90028
323-962-5277
Fax: 323-962-5208
e-mail: sunsethall@sunsethall.org
http://www.sunsethall.org
Wendy Caputo, Executive Director

State Organizations & Government Agencies/Colorado

A non-profit program for free thinking elders who continue to share independence fo spirit and involvement in the world. Our mission is to create a sense of community and a caring supportive environment.

620 Ventura County Area Agency on Aging
646 County Square Drive
Suite 100
Ventura, CA 93003
805-477-7300
800-510-2020
Fax: 805-477-7312
http://http://aaa.countyofventura.org
Victoria Jump, Executive Director

The responsibility of the Ventura County Area Agency on Aging is to Ventura County's sixty-plus population including those with different social and cultural needs; to foster and support self-determination and independence among the older population; and to provide leadership in the development of community-based system of care. The mission is accomplished through a network of education, advocacy, problem solving, program planning, and funding.

621 Volunteer Center
2401 Shadelands Drive
Suite 112
Walnut Creek, CA 94598
925-472-5760
Fax: 925-472-5780
e-mail: info@helpnow.org
http://www.helpnow.org
Lorraine Meuleners, Executive Director

The mission of the Volunteer Center is to harness the power of volunteerism in Contra Costa and Alameda Counties and assist volunteers in building a lifelong commitment to community service.

622 Volunteer Center Orange County
1901 E 4th Street
Suite 100
Santa Ana, CA 92705-3918
714-953-5757
Fax: 714-834-0585
e-mail: info@volunteercenter.org
http://www.volunteercenter.org
Daniel McQuaid, President/CEO
Stephanie McCormick, Chief Operating Officer

The Volunteer Centers of California and its network of Volunteer Centers participate in Citizens Corps and Homeland Security in collaboration with emergency first responders and statewide disaster organizations. Volunteer Centers specialize in practicing spontaneous volunteers in recovery and clean-up volunteer positions during a disaster.

623 Volunteer Center of Kern County
1400 Chester Avenue
Suite J
Bakersfield, CA 93301
661-397-9787
Fax: 661-397-9780
e-mail: bratliffvc@yahoo.com
http://www.volunteercenter.info
Sarah Webb, President
Sherry Bullock, Vice President
Brenda Ratliff, Executive Director

To promote volunteerism as a means of fostering increased citizen involvement in the community and enabling public and private nonprofit agencies to enhance or maintain needed human services.

624 Volunteer Exchange
14120 Beach Boulevard
Suite 210
Westminster, CA 92683-4454
714-899-6845
Fax: 714-899-6851
e-mail: volntrex@aol.com
http://www.ocvolunteerexchange.com
Mary Yorba, Executive Director

Volunteer recruitment and referral organization for Orange County, CA. Misty's closet assists low income women re-entering the job market.

625 Volunteers of America Bay Area
1601 Harbor Bay Parkway
Suite 150
Alameda, CA 94502-3014
510-473-0500
Fax: 510-473-9225
http://www.voaba.org
John R Bailey, President/CEO
Kerry Beuthin, Director Developement
Jacqueline Kidd, Director Of Human Resources

Volunteers of America Bay Area is a diverse, creative ministry of service founded on spiritual values with unique programs designed to assist, treat and help empower people to transform the quality of their lives and expand their opportunities.

626 West Hollywood Senior Center: Jewish Family Service
7377 Santa Monica Boulevard
Room B
West Hollywood, CA 90046-6620
323-851-8202
Fax: 323-876-6140
http://www.la4senors.com/west_hollywood
Susan Alexman, LCSW, Director

For seniors over the age of 55. Provides multi-service programs, counseling, case management, and recreational activities.

Colorado

627 Alpine Area Agency on Aging
NW Colorado Council of Governments
249 Warren Avenue Po Box 2308
Silverthorne, CO 80498-2308
970-468-0295
Fax: 970-468-1208
e-mail: gjs@nwc.cog.co.us
http://www.nwc.cog.co.us
Jean Hammes, Program Director
Steve Getz, Director, Energy Mgmt. Program
Gary Severson, Executive Director

NWCCOG's Alpine Area Agency on Aging (AAAA) is the designated regional planning and service agency for services to seniors in Region XII. Federal Older Americans Act funds are used in conjunction with state, county, and local funds to develop and implement a comprehensive and coordinated system of service to the elderly in the region.

628 Boulder County Aging Services Division
3482 N Broadway
Po Box 471
Boulder, CO 80306
303-441-3570
Fax: 303-441-4550
e-mail: bcaa@co.boulder.co.us
http://www.co.boulder.co.us/cs.ag/
Rosemary Williams MSW, Manager

Advocates for, plans, coordinates and funds services for older adults and their families by administering the Area Agency on Aging, contracting and providing services in the areas of nutrition, transportation, legal services, information and referral, health promotion, elder abuse prevention, and home health care.

629 Colorado Aging and Adult Services
1575 Sherman Street
Denver, CO 80203
303-866-2800
303-866-3851
Fax: 303-866-2696
http://www.cdhs.state.co.us/aas
TTY 303-866-2850

The Division of Aging and Adult Services (AAS) will efficiently and effectively provide human services in support of independent living, self sufficiency, safety and dignity goals. These goals are on behalf of adults age 18 and over who have disabilities or functional impairments or are otherwise at risk. As a Division, we act upon Colorado Department of Human Service's vision to be the nation's leader in helping individuals, families and communities to be safe and independent.

State Organizations & Government Agencies/Colorado

630 **Colorado Association of Homes & Services for the Aging**
1888 Sherman Street
Suite 610
Denver, CO 80203
303-837-8834
Fax: 303-837-8836
e-mail: Karen@CAHSA.org
http://www.cahsa.org

Laura Landwirth, Executive Director
Karen Simmering, Director Of Operations
Carole Hull, Assisted Living Consultant

The Colorado Association of Homes and Services for the Aging (CAHSA) is the state's largest and oldest nonprofit organization representing providers of housing and health-related service options to Colorado's elderly. CAHSA advocates public policy initiatives that support individual rights, quality care, equitable access and reimbursement for seniors. CAHSA is the state affiliate for two national organizations, the Assisted Living Federation of America (ALFA) and the American Association of Homes and Services for the Aging (AAHSA).

Number of Members: 250

631 **Colorado Client Assistance Program**
The Legal Center for People with Disabilities
455 Sherman Street
Suite 130
Denver, CO 80203-4403
303-722-0300
800-288-1376
Fax: 303-722-0720

Geoff Peterson, Coordinator
David L Gies, Executive Director

Assists people with disabilities who are seeking or receiving services from the Colorado Division of Vocational Rehabilitation.

632 **Colorado Department of Aging**
1575 Sherman Street
10th Floor
Denver, CO 80203-1702
303-866-2800
888-866-4243
Fax: 303-866-2696
http://www.cdhs.state.co.us/aas

Rita Barreras, Manager
Joan Pinamont, Manager

The Division of Aging and Adult Services (AAS) will efficiently and effectively provide human services in support of independent living, self-sufficiency, safety, and dignity goals.

633 **Colorado Department of Revenue**
1375 Sherman Street
Denver, CO 80261
303-757-9972
303-866-3091
http://www.revenue.state.co.us

Joan Oma, Pmt, Manager

634 **Colorado Department of Social Services: Division of Vocational Rehabilitation**
1575 Sherman Street
4th Floor
Denver, CO 80203
303-866-4150
866-870-4595
Fax: 303-866-4905
e-mail: voc.rehab@state.co.us
http://www.cdhs.state.co.us/dvr/hm

635 **Colorado Department of Social Services: Division of Older American Programs**
110 16th Street
Suite 200
Denver, CO 80202-5204
303-894-2882
Fax: 303-620-4191

636 **Colorado Developmental Disability Council**
3401 Quebec Street
Suite 6009
Denver, CO 80207
720-941-0176
Fax: 720-941-2880
e-mail: coppc@ol.com
http://www.coddc.org

Donald St. Louise, Director

The mission of the CDDC is to advocate in collaboration with and on behalf of peple with developmental disabilities for the establishment and implimentation of public policy which will further their independence, productivity and integration.

637 **Colorado Disability Determination Services**
2530 South Parker Road
Suite 500
Aurora, CO 80014-1641
303-368-4100
Fax: 303-752-5692
http://www.cdhs.state.co.us

Vicki L Johnson, Director

Disability Determination Services (DSS) is the State Agency that makes the disability decisions for Social Security.

638 **Colorado Division of Mental Health**
3824 W Princeton Cir.
Denver, CO 80236-3197
303-866-7466
Fax: 303-866-7428
http://www.cdhs.state.co.us/dmh/

George Kawamura, Director
Keith Lagrenade, CEO

Mission is to ensure culturally competent, comprehensive care that promotes individual, family, and community resiliency and recovery. This is accomplished through providing to the public mental health system expertise in policy, program development, evaluation, quality improvement, training, consultation and resource acquistion.

639 **Colorado Mountain College Senior Nutrition Program**
831 Grand Avenue
Glenwood Springs, CO 81601-3961
970-945-2446
800-621-8559
Fax: 970-947-8488
e-mail: gstephenson@coloradomtn.edu
http://www.coloradomtn.edu

Gwen Stephenson, Director

Rural nutrition program for the elderly focusing around eight Congregate Meal sites within Garfield county. Our goal is to provide nutritious meals for the seniors of Garfield coutny, especially those who are rural, low income, frial and disabled.

640 **Colorado Protection & Advocacy for Persons with Disabilities**
Legal Center for People with Disabilities
455 Sherman Street
Suite 130
Denver, CO 80203-4403
303-722-0300
800-288-1376
Fax: 303-722-0720

Mary Ann Harvey, Director
Carol Coover-Clark, Owner

The Legal Center is an independent public interest non-profit specializing in civil rights and discrimination issues. We protect the human, civil, and legal rights of people with mental and physical disabilities, people with HIV, and older people throughout Colorado.

641 **Colorado Public Employees Retirement Association**
1300 Logan Street
Po Box 5800
Denver, CO 80203-2309
303-832-9550
800-759-7372
Fax: 303-863-3819
http://www.copera.org/pera

Meredith Williams, Manager

Mission is to promote long-term financial security for our members while maintaining the stability of the fund.

State Organizations & Government Agencies/Colorado

642 Colorado Workers Compensation Board
633 17th Street
Suite 400
Denver, CO 80202-3660
303-318-8700
888-390-7936
Fax: 303-318-8710
e-mail: workers.comp@state.co.us
http://www.coworkforce.com

Bob Summers, Director

The Colorado Division of Worker's Compensation is the state office responsible for administering and enforcing the worker's compensation law in this state. In doing so, it recognizes the intent of the Colorado General Assembly to ensure the quick and efficient delivery of disability and medical benefits to injured workers, at a reasonable cost to employers.

643 Denver Regional Council of Governments Area Agency on Aging
1290 Broadway
Suite 700
Denver, CO 80203
303-455-1000
Fax: 303-480-6790
e-mail: drcog@drcog.org
http://www.drcog.org

Jennifer Schaufele, Executive Director
Jayla Sanchez-Warren, Director
Roxie Ronsen, Administrative Officer

The Denver Regional Council of Governments (DRCOG) is proud of its focus on quality-of-life issues. These include mobility, service to older adults, environmental concerns, planning for the future, public safety, and the provision of information for sound decision-making.

644 East Central Colorado: Area Agency on Aging
128 Colorado Avenue
Po Box 28
Stratton, CO 80836-1152
719-348-5562
800-825-0208
Fax: 719-348-5887
e-mail: aging@prairiedevelopment.com
http://http://ecaaa.tripod.com

Terry Baylie, Director
Maryjo Downey, Executive Director

The East Central Area on Aging, is among 16 designated Area Agencies on Aging within the state of Colorado. Through federal Older Americans Act grant funds, allocated to the Region via the East Central Council of Local Governments (ECCOG) the area agencies utilizes these funds in conjunction with state, county, and local funds to plan for, monitor and fund an array of home and community based services and programs

645 Eastern Colorado Services for the Disabled
Po Box 1682
617 South 10th Street
Sterling, CO 80751-3168
970-522-7121
Fax: 970-522-1173
e-mail: ramona@escdd.org
http://www.easterncoloradoservices.org

Ramona Proctor, Executive Director
Traci Schrade, Finance Director

Eastern Colorado Services for the Developmentally Disabled Inc. is a community centered board serving developmentally disabled persons in 10 rural counties, covering 17,514 square miles. Programs include infant/toddler services, adult community integrated employment, community participation vocational training, sheltered employment, personal and social skills training, residential services supporting life services, and family resource services

646 Elderhaus
Adult Day Programs
605 South Shields Street
Fort Collins, CO 80521-3539
970-221-0406
Fax: 970-221-9965
e-mail: elderhas@frii.com
http://http://elderhaus.org/family.php

Joanne Johnsen, Executive Director
Rose Luna, Assistant Director

Providing quality affordable day programs and services to adults with special needs in a safe, pleasant environment through qualified staff and to provide relief and support to caregivers.

647 Huerfano Las Animas: Area Agency on Aging
200 East First Street
Trinidad, CO 81082-3003
719-846-4401
Fax: 719-846-4402

Walter DeGurse, Director
Robert Valdez, Manager

648 Iron Workers Local 24 Retirees Club International Association of Ironworkers
501 West 4th Avenue
Denver, CO 80223
303-623-5386
Fax: 303-825-0645
e-mail: dueslocal24@worldnet.att.net
http://www.ironworkers.org

Joseph Trujillo, President

Ironworkers are the people who make the shell of large office and government buildings
Number of Members: 140,000

649 Kit Carson And Lincoln Counties RSVP
317 Maint Street
Po Box 233
Flagler, CO 80815
719-765-4671
Fax: 719-765-4079
e-mail: rsvp@esrta.com
http://www.kitcarsoncounty.org/kcc_files/rsvp

Melody Maskus, Director

Our senior volunteers are very proud of their participation in the preservation and renovation of Flagler Hospital, now used as a community library and town of Flagler offices as well as a small museum. This has benefitted the entire community. They are also involved in recycling and park improvements.

650 Longmont Meals on Wheels
910 Longs Peak Avenue
Longmont, CO 80501
303-772-0540
Fax: 303-651-8413
e-mail: longmontmeals@yahoo.com
http://www.longmontmeals.org

Gary Grizzard, President

While providing hot, nutritious meals for seniors and for individuals unable to prepare their own meals, it is the mission of Longmont Meals on Wheels to serve our community by seeking to: promote client health through good nutrition and social interaction; facilitate independence; expand the reach of our program through responsible stewardship and effective communication; foster a sense of community with our clients, volunteers and neighbors.

651 Lyons Golden Gang
335 Railroad Ave. #B
Po Box 1091
Lyons, CO 80540-1091
303-823-6771
http://www.lyons-colorado.com

Diane H Briggle, Administrator
Neice Pralguske, Contact

Lyons Golden Gang provides nutritious meals on Tuesday, Wednesday and Friday at the Walt Self Senior Housing main building on 335 Railroad Avenue. Meals are also provided to the homes of those who are ill, disabled or elderly on Tuesday through Friday. A donation of $2.25 is asked from everyone, but the fee can be adjusted. For further information and to make reservations, call Niece Pralguske at 303-823-6125.

652 Pikes Peak Area: Agency on Aging
15 S 7th Street
Colorado Springs, CO 80905-1501
719-471-7080
Fax: 719-471-1226
http://www.ppacg.org/cms/index.php

Robert MacDonald, Executive Director
Barb Louricas, Office Manager

State Organizations & Government Agencies/Colorado

The Pikes Peak Area Council of Governments (PPACG) is a voluntary organization of municipal and county governments serving a regional community.

653 RSVP Adams-Arapahoe
2360 West 90th Avenue
Federal Heights, CO 80260-6700
303-426-4408
Fax: 303-426-0014
e-mail: info@seniorhub.org
http://www.seniorhub.org

Tom Rapp, Director
Linda Lassley, Volunteer Coordinator

A non-profit resource center for seniors. Our mission is to advance the quality of life for older adults through advocacy, community partnerships, and a variety of direct services planned to sustain their independence.

654 RSVP Boulder County
951 Arapahoe Avenue
Suite 10
Boulder, CO 80302
303-443-1933
Fax: 303-443-1899
e-mail: rsvp@rsvpboulder.com
http://www.rsvpboulder.org

Maureen Ewing, Executive Director

To provide seniors in Boulder County the opportunity to contribute to their communities in meaningful ways through volunteerism and to promote independence and comfort of seniors and adults with disabilities.

655 RSVP Colorado West
300 N Cascade
Suite 4
Montrose, CO 81402-3502
970-249-9639
Fax: 970-249-3574
e-mail: rsvpcw@qwest.net
http://http://conseniorcorps.org/rsvp/colorado

Neil Pratt, Executive Director

To enlist the time, talent and lifetime experience of persons age 55+ in the meaningful volunteer service that enhances both community and volunteer lives in Delta, Montrose, Gunnison and San Miguel Counties.

656 RSVP High County
1402 Blake Avenue
Glenwood Springs, CO 81601
970-945-7486
Fax: 970-945-6240
e-mail: stewart@coloradomtn.edu
http://www.coloradomtn.edu

Colorado Mountain College senior programs provide a variety of services to older citizens in Garfield County

657 RSVP Jefferson County Seniors Resource Center
3227 Chase Street
Denver, CO 80212-7033
303-238-8151
Fax: 303-238-8497
e-mail: rwingate@scraging.org
http://www.srcaging.org

John Zabwa, President/CEO
Kathleen Stapleton, Board Chairman

The Retired and Senior Volunteer Program (RSVP) helps people age 55 and older put their skills and life experiences to work in their communities. RSVP is a network of nonprofit agencies in Jefferson County that helps older adults find opportunities to address community needs through volunteer service.

658 RSVP Otero Bent-Crowley Counties
13 W 3rd Street, Room 110
PO Box 494
La Junta, CO 81050-0494
719-383-3164
Fax: 719-383-4607
e-mail: rsvplj@ria.net

John Boerger, Director

Our senior volunteers plant and maintain vegetable and flower gardens and work with the Forest Service to identify plants along trails and keep the trails clean.

659 RSVP Pueblo
230 N Union Avenue
Pueblo, CO 81003-4207
719-545-8900
Fax: 719-544-7831

Gloria Valdez, Director

The Retired and Senior Volunteer Program (RSVP) provides opportunities for people 55 and over to make a difference in their community through volunteer service. RSVP volunteers contribute anywhere from a few to over forty hours a week, serving through schools, day care centers, police departments, hospitals and other nonprofit and public organizations to help meet critical community needs. RSVP offers maximum flexibility and choice to its volunteers. RSVP matches the personal interests and skills of older Americans with opportunities to help solve community problems and offers supplemental insurance while on duty, on-the-job training from the agency or organization where volunteers are placed. The following County is served: Pueblo.

660 RSVP Rural Resort Region
551 Broadway
PO Box 660
Eagle, CO 81631
970-328-8818
Fax: 970-328-8829
e-mail: volntrec@eagle-county.com
http://www.easi.org

Jackie Allen-Benson, Director

The Retired and Senior Volunteer Program (RSVP) provides opportunities for people 55 and over to make a difference in their community through volunteer service. RSVP volunteers contribute anywhere from a few to over forty hours a week, serving through schools, day care centers, police departments, hospitals and other nonprofit and public organizations to help meet critical community needs. RSVP offers maximum flexibility and choice to its volunteers. RSVP matches the personal interests and skills of older Americans with opportunities to help solve community problems and offers supplemental insurance while on duty, and on-the-job training from the agency or organization where volunteers are placed. The following Counties are served: Eagle and Summitt.

661 RSVP San Luis Valley
409 Trinchera
San Luis, CO 81144-1120
719-672-0331
Fax: 719-672-3043
e-mail: patt@slvmhc.org
http://www.slvmhc.org

Fernando A Martinez, Executive Director
Mary E Trujillo, Assistant Executive Director

The Retired and Senior Volunteer Program (RSVP) provides opportunities for people 55 and over to make a difference in their community through volunteer service. RSVP volunteers contribute anywhere from a few to over forty hours a week, serving through schools, day care centers, police departments, hospitals and other nonprofit and public organizations to help meet critical community needs. RSVP offers maximum flexibility and choice to its volunteers. RSVP matches the personal interests and skills of older Americans with opportunities to help solve community problems and offers supplemental insurance while on duty, on-the-job training from the agency or organization where volunteers are placed. The following Counties are served: Alamosa, Conejos, Costilla, Mineral, Rio Grande, Saguache.

662 RSVP VOA Colorado Branch
905 North College Avenue
Fort Collins, CO 80524
970-472-9630
Fax: 970-472-8393
e-mail: larimervoa@frii.com
http://www.voacolorado.org

Diane Stobnicke, Manager

State Organizations & Government Agencies/Connecticut

The Retired and Senior Volunteer Program (RSVP) provides opportunities for people 55 and over to make a difference in their community through volunteer service. RSVP volunteers contribute anywhere from a few to over forty hours a week, serving though schools, day care centers, police departments, hospitals and other nonprofit and public organizations to help meet critical community needs. RSVP offers maximum flexibility and choice to its volunteers. RSVP matches the personal interests and skills to older Americans with opportunities to help solve community problems and offer supplemental insurance while on duty, on-the-job training from the agency or organization where volunteers are placed.

663 **RSVP VOA Denver**
2525 16th Street
Suite 1110
Denver, CO 80211
303-477-2340
Fax: 303-964-9603
e-mail: voadenrsvp@aol.com
http://www.voacolorado.org

Erin Kruse, Project Manager

RSVP is designed to create a positive and meaningful experience for individuals like you. We are an association of volunteers 55 and better who individually and collectively make a significant, positive impact on our community. Whether you are delivering a hot meal to a homebound senior, reading to an elementary-school child, planting trees in a wildlife preserve or fulfilling one of hundreds of other volunteer opportunities you make a difference!

664 **RSVP Weld County**
UNC Central Campus
Campus Box 67
Greeley, CO 80639
970-351-2588
Fax: 970-351-2581
e-mail: linda.akers@unco.edu
http://www.unco.edu/nhs/rsvp

Linda Akers MSW, Director
Terrie McKellar, Volunteer Coordinator
Debbie Sherin, Administrative Aid

Provides opportunities for persons over 55 to become involved in significant and worthwhile volunteer service to their communities and administers serveral community service programs.

665 **Railroad Retirement Board: Colorado District Office**
721 19th Street Room 177
Po Box 8869
Denver, CO 80201-8869
303-844-4311
Fax: 303-844-2609
http://www.rrb.gov/field/do_denv.asp

Joseph Gray, Manager

The Railroad Retirement Board (RRB) is an independent agency in the executive branch of the Federal Government. The RRB's primary function is to administer comprehensive retirement-survivor and unemployment-sickness benefit programs for the nation's railroad workers and their families, under the Railroad Retirement and Railroad Unemployment Insurance Acts.

666 **Region 8: Administration on Aging (AoA)**
US Department of Health & Human Services
1961 Stout Street
Room 353
Denver, CO 80294
303-844-2951
Fax: 303-844-2943
http://www.aoa.gov

Percy Devine, Regional Administrator
Josefina G Carbonell ASA, Assistant Secretary
Edwin Walker PDASA, Deputy Assistant Secretary

Region includes Colorado, Montana, North Dakota, South Dakota, Utah, and Wyoming.

667 **Region Ten Area: Agency on Aging**
300 N Cascade Avenue
Montrose, CO 81402
970-249-2436
Fax: 970-249-2488
e-mail: lee@region10.net
http://www.region10.net

Paul Gray, Executive Director
Lee Bartlett, Program Director

A non profit alliance of government and business that has become the regional source center for businesses and residents.

668 **San Juan Basin Area: Agency on Aging**
281 Sawyer Drive
Durango, CO 81301
970-259-1967
Fax: 970-382-8925

Heather Kostelnik, ASU Contact
Jim Snyder, Field Contact

The Area Agency on Aging develops and delivers services for seniors (60 years and older) and for adults (18-59 years) with disabilities and long-term care needs.

669 **South Central Colorado Seniors**
1116 3rd Street
Alamosa, CO 81101
719-589-4511
Fax: 719-589-2343
e-mail: SLVSCCS@amigo.net

Dan Gutierrez, Director

South Central Colorado Seniors sponsors the San Luis Valley Nutrition Program.

670 **Teller Senior Coalition**
PO Box 6956
Woodland Park, CO 80866-6956
719-687-3330
Fax: 719-687-6155
e-mail: info@tellerseniorcoalition.org
http://www.tellerseniorcoalition.org

Phyllis Sisolak, Executive Director
Carolynne Forster, Managing Director

The Teller Senior Coalition (TSC) was organized when the Teller County Commissioners decided that senior services be privatized. TSC was organized by interested seniors and community leaders to continue vital programs: daily hot meals, transportation, education, information and handy man services. TSC is currently the only organization in Teller County to offer all of these important services. We have received the IRS designation of 501(c)(3) non-profit organization. Our misison is to assist Teller County senior citizens in living a full and active life with dignity and independence.

671 **Upper Arkansas Area: Agency on Aging**
139 E 3rd Street
Salida, CO 81201-2612
719-539-3341
Fax: 719-539-7431
e-mail: aaareg13@amigo.net
http://www.vaacog.com

Stephen Holland, Director

The Upper Arkansas Area Agency on Aging will assist seniors (60+) through the region in maintaining health, dignity, independence, and quality of life through education, advocacy, coordination and delivery of services and programs.

Connecticut

672 **Bureau of Naval Personnel: Connecticut Retired Activities Office**
Naval Sub Base, New London
Building 83, PO Box 93
Groton, CT 06349-5000
860-694-3284
Fax: 860-694-4695

Capt Mark S Ginda, Commanding Officer
CDR Philip McKenna, Jr, Executive Officer

State Organizations & Government Agencies/Connecticut

The RAO serves as a link between local retired military and the active-duty community which provides assistance to retired military. It provides installation commanders with a means of providing more effective services and improving communication for the local retired community. The RAO is staffed and operated by volunteer retired military who assist other retired members, their families and survivors to receive entitled services and benefits. Through newsletters, seminars and appreciation days, the RAO supports quality of life issues throughout the retirement years to their fellow service members.

673 Bureau of Rehabilitation Services: Disability Determination Services
25 Sigourney Street
11-Th Floor
Hartford, CT 06106
860-424-4844
800-537-2549
Fax: 860-424-4850
e-mail: amy.porter@po.state.ct.us
http://ww.brs.state.ct.us

Amy Porter, Project Director

Provides vocational rehabilitation, independent living and social security disability determination services to persons with disabilities.

674 Connecticut Association of Not-for-Profit Providers for the Aging
1340 Worthington Ridge
Berlin, CT 06450-7137
860-828-2903
Fax: 860-828-8694
e-mail: canpfa@canpfa.org
http://www.canpfa.org

Mag Morelli, President

CANPFA promotes a vision of the world in which every community offers an integrated and coordinated continuum of high quality, affordable health care, housing and community based services.

675 Connecticut Board of Education and Services for the Blind
184 Windsor Avenue
Windsor, CT 06095-4536
860-602-4000
Fax: 860-602-4020
http://www.ct.gov/besb/site

Keith Maynard, Plant Manager

676 Connecticut Client Assistance Program
60B Weston Street
Hartford, CT 06120-1551
860-297-4300
800-842-7303
Fax: 860-566-8714
http://www.ct.gov/opapd/cwp

James McGaughey, Executive Director

The Mission of the Office of Protection and Advocacy for Persons with Disabilities is to advance the cause of equal rights for persons with disabilities and their families

677 Connecticut Commisson on Aging
210 Capitol Avenue
509
Hartford, CT 06106-5041
860-240-5200
860-240-5204
Fax: 860-240-5204
e-mail: commission.aging@po.state.ct.us
http://www.cga.ct.gov/coa
TDD 860-566-7772

Julie Evans Starr, Executive Director

The mission is to advocate on behalf of elderly persons in Connecticut by regularly monitoring their status, assessing the impact of current and proposed initiatives, and conducting activities which promote the interest of these individuals and to report to the Govenor and the Legislature.

678 Connecticut Council On DevelopmentalDisabilities
460 Capitol Avenue
Hartford, CT 06106-1308
860-418-6160
860-653-1134
Fax: 800-418-6003
http://www.ct.gov/ctcdd/cwp

Edward T Preneta, Director

679 Connecticut Department of Aging
175 Main Street
Hartford, CT 06106-1861
860-247-2732

Mary Ellen Klinick, Commissioner
Bruce Douglas, Executive Director

680 Connecticut Department of Revenue
25 Sigourney Street
Hartford, CT 06106-5032
860-297-5962
http://www.state.ct.us/drs/cwp

Gene Gavin, Manager

The mission of the Connecticut Department of Revenue Services (DRS) is to administer the tax laws of the State of Connecticut and collect the tax revenues in the most cost effective manner.

681 Connecticut Disability Determination Serices
25 Sigourney Street
11th Floor
Hartford, CT 06106
860-424-4844
800-537-2549
Fax: 860-566-1795
e-mail: evelyn.knight@po.state.ct.us
http://www.brs.state.ct.us/contactus.htm

Jan S Gilbert, Professional Relations

682 Connecticut Protection & Advocacy for Persons with Disabilities
60B Weston Street
Hartford, CT 06120-1551
860-297-4300
800-842-7303
Fax: 860-566-8714
http://www.ct.gov/opapd/site

James McGaughey, Executive Director

Consumer information for persons with disabilities.

683 Connecticut State of Veterans Affairs Department of Rocky Hill: Hospital Services Program
287 West Street
Rocky Hill, CT 06067-3501
860-721-5818
800-550-0000
Fax: 860-721-5919
e-mail: linda.schwartz@po.state.ct.us
http://www.state.ct.us/ctva

Dr Linda Spooner Schwartz RN, Commissioner
Charlie Williams, Chief Of Staff

Rocky Hill provides quality long-term care services for our veterans.

684 Connecticut Teachers Retirement Board
21 Grand Street
Hartford, CT 06106-1500
860-241-8400
800-504-1102
Fax: 860-525-6018
e-mail: trb.webmaster@po.state.ct.us
http://www.ct.gov/trb

Clare H Barnett, Chairperson
Darlene Perez, Administrator

Mission is to adequate funding to pay all benefits, to effectively administer the Retirement System; to protect and administer the statutory rights and benefits of members of the State Teacher's Retirement System; and to provide pre/post retirement services.

State Organizations & Government Agencies/Connecticut

685 **East Coast Assistance Dogs**
PO Box 831
Torrington, CT 06790
860-489-6550
Fax: 860-489-3791
e-mail: ecad1@aol.com
http://www.ecad1.org
Lucille A Picard, Founder/Administrator/Instructor
Dale Picard, Founder/Instructor

Our mission is to enable people with disabilities to gain greater independence and mobility through the use of specially trained dogs.

686 **Eastern Connecticut Area: Agency on Aging**
4 Broadway
3rd Floor
Norwich, CT 06360-2315
860-887-3561
800-690-6998
Fax: 860-886-4736
http://www.seniorresourcesec.org
Joan Wessell, Executive Director
Nancy Krodel, Assistant Director

Mission is to provide information and services to the aging population, their families and care providers.

687 **Hartford Area Social Security Office**
20 Church Street
Floor One
Hartford, CT 06103-3290
860-493-1857
800-772-1213
TDD 860-525-4697

688 **North Central Area Agency on Aging**
2 Hartford Square West
Suite 101
Hartford, CT 06106-5129
860-724-6443
800-994-9422
Fax: 860-251-6107
e-mail: carmen.reyes@ncaaact.org
http://www.geocities.com/ncaaaus
Carmen Y Reyes, Executive Director

Goal is to provide good quality of life for seniors by ensuring that the have access to quality and cost effective services.

689 **RSVP Central Connecticut**
147 W Main Street
PO Box 578
New Britain, CT 06050
860-224-7117
Fax: 860-224-8365
e-mail: rsvpnb@juno.com
Diane Briggs, Director
Marjorie Spinney, Coordinator
Arnold Schwartz, Chariman, Board Of Directors

The Retired and Senior Volunteer Program (RSVP) provides opportunities to persons 55 years of age and older to participate in their communities by sharing their knowledge and skills through meaningful volunteer experiences. Connecticut has twelve RSVP programs that connect 55+ seniors with community organizations that need their assistance. Volunteers provide valuable services in day care centers, nursing homes, hospice programs, hospitals home health agencies and schools with mentoring and tutoring programs, and as community organizers for special projects. The following Counties are served: Hartford, New Haven.

690 **RSVP Central Naugatuck Valley**
232 N Elm Street
Waterbury, CT 06702
203-575-4220
Fax: 203-575-4318
http://www.newopportunitiesinc.org/elderly
Melissa L Zwang, Director

The Retired and Senior Volunteer Program (RSVP) provides opportunities for people 55 and over to make a difference in their community through volunteer service. RSVP volunteers contribute anywhere from a few to over forty hours a week, serving through schools, day care centers, police departments, hospitals and other nonprofit and public organizations to help meet critical community needs. RSVP offers maximum flexibility and choice to its volunteers. RSVP matches the personal interests and skills of older Americans with opportunities to help solve community problems and offers supplemental insurance while on duty, on-the-job training from the agency or organization where volunteers are placed. The following Counties are served: New Haven, Litchfield.

691 **RSVP Eastern Fairfield County**
263 Golden Hill Street
Bridgeport, CT 06604-4112
203-576-8048
Fax: 203-576-8330
e-mail: rsvphqsw@juno.com
Michael Bower, Contact

The Retired and Senior Volunteer Program (RSVP) provides opportunities to persons 55 years of age and older to participate in their communities by sharing their knowledge and skills through meaningful volunteer experiences. Connecticut has twelve RSVP programs that connect 55+ seniors with community organizations that need their assistance. Volunteers provide valuable services in day care centers, nursing homes, hospice programs, hospitals, homehealth agencies and schools with mentoring and tutoring programs, and as community organizers for special projects. The following County is served: Fairfield.

692 **RSVP Greater Bristol**
98 Summer Street
Bristol, CT 06010
860-584-9533
Fax: 860-582-5224
e-mail: rsvp.bristol.ct@snet.net
Patricia Malone, Director

The Retired and Senior Volunteer Program (RSVP) provides opportunities to persons 55 years of age and older to participate in their communities by sharing their knowledge and skills through meaningful volunteer experiences. Connecticut has twelve RSVP programs that connect 55+ seniors with community organizations that need their assistance. Volunteers provide valuable services in day care centers, nursing homes, hospice programs, hospitals, home health agencies and schools with mentoring and tutoring programs, and as community organizers for special projects. The following Counties are served: Hartford, Litchfield.

693 **RSVP Greater Hartford**
555 Windsor Street
Hartford, CT 06120-2418
860-560-5760
Fax: 860-560-5508
e-mail: marywi@crtet.org
http://www.seniorservice.org/greater_hartford
Mary Wilcox, Director

The Greater Hartford Retired and Senior Volunteer Program (RSVP) offers unique opportunities for people, aged 55 and older to offer their talents, knowledge and life experiences to their communities, while enjoying self-fulfillment and interaction with other volunteers who have similar interests. The following Counties are served Hartford, Tolland.

694 **RSVP Mid State**
381 Main Street
PO Box 187
Middletown, CT 06457
860-347-0236
Fax: 860-346-9187
e-mail: midstatersvp@stlukeshome.org
Tara L Gill, Director

The Retired and Senior Volunteer Program (RSVP) provides opportunities for people 55 and over to make a difference in their community through volunteer service. RSVP volunteers contribute anywhere from a few to over forty hours a week, serving through schools, day care centers, police departments, hospitals and other nonprofit and public organizations to help meet critical community needs. RSVP offers maximum flexibility and choice to its volunteers. RSVP matches the personal interests and skills of older Americans with opportunities to help solve community problems and offers supplemental insurance while on duty, and on-the-job training from the agency or organization where volunteers are placed. The folliwng County is served: Middlesex.

695 RSVP Northern Fairfield County
2 Terrace Place
Danbury, CT 06810-6631
203-792-8200
Fax: 203-748-2563

Ellen Melville, Director

RSVP of Northern Fairfield County matches the skills and talents of adults age 55 and over with a wide variety of volunteer opportunities in our community. RSVP volunteers use their life experiences and skills to answer the call of their neighbors in need through enhancing and supporting services provided by area agencies and nonprofit organizations. The following County is served: Fairfield.

696 RSVP Southern New London
83 Huntington Street
New London, CT 06320
860-444-0006
Fax: 860-444-0059
e-mail: cvisco@tvcca.org
http://www.tvcca.org/services

Deborah Monahan, Executive Director
Kathleen McCarty, Board Chairperson

RSVP provides a variety of volunteer opportunities for retired and senior persons of any income level, age 55 and older. RSVP volunteers provide vital services to their communities utilizing their skills and life long experience. Volunteer benefits include secondary accident and liability insurance and, where possible, transportation reimbursement, as available to and from volunteer assignment stations.

697 RSVP Southwestern Connecticut
98 S Main Street
Norwalk, CT 06854-3126
203-899-2442
Fax: 203-899-2430
e-mail: tklein@neon-norwalk.org
http://www.rsvpswct.org

Teri Klein, Project Director
Annie Dubosse, Outreach Coordinator
Madeline Bollmann, Administrative Assistant

Recruits and places volunteers age 55 and over in programs that benefit the community and themselves. Matches individual interests, skills and life experience with productive volunteer positions.

698 RSVP Windham-Tolland Counties
C/O Killingly Community Center
185 Broad Street
Room 215
Danielson, CT 06239
860-444-0006
Fax: 860-444-0059
e-mail: cvisco@tvcca.org

Cathy Visco, Director

Provides volunteer opportunities to individuals 55 years of age and older. Volunteers provide services that help to meet the needs of their communtiy. The following Counties are served: Tolland, Windham.

699 South Central Connecticut Agency on Aging
One Long Wharf Drive
New Haven, CT 06511
203-785-8533
800-994-9422
Fax: 203-933-7078
http://www.agencyounginc.scc.org

Neysa Stallmann Guerino, Executive Director
Truth South, Owner

Care management, volunteer opportunities, CHOICES, funding, planning and advocacy on behalf of older americans in New Haven-Fairfield County.

700 Volunteer Center of United Way for Capital Area
30 Laurel Street
Hartford, CT 06106-1341
860-493-1100
Fax: 860-493-1199
http://www.uwcact.org

Susan B Dunnn, President/CEO

Referral service for potential volunteers. Works to train volunteer managers, develop volunteer programs for the corporate community, and broker noncash resources of for-profit organizations to nonprofit agencies.

701 Western Connecticut Area: Agency on Aging
84 Progress Lane
Waterbury, CT 06705-3859
203-757-5449
800-994-9422
Fax: 203-757-4081
e-mail: westernctaca@sbcglobal.net
http://www.wcaaa.org

Bermer Ridenhour, Vice President
Dolores Winans, Secretary
Kay V Bergin, Treasurer

The Western CT Area Agency on Aging develops, manages and provides comprehensive services for seniors, caregivers and individuals with disabilities in order to maintain their independence and quality of life.

Delaware

702 Delaware Assistive Technology Initiative
University of Delaware
DuPont Hospital for Children
PO Box 269
Wilmington, DE 19899-0269
302-651-6790
800-870-3284
Fax: 302-651-6793
e-mail: dati@asel.udel.edu
http://www.dati.org
TDD 302-651-6794

Beth Mineo Mollica PhD, Director
Kia Bergman, Information/Outreach Coordinator
Linda Kelly, Staff Assistant

Funded by the US Department of Education, National Institute on Disability and Rehabilitation Research as one of the Tech Act projects, the DATI focuses on improving public awareness, public access to information, funding for assistive technology devices and services, training and technical assistance, and coordination of statewide activities. The project has established Assistive Technology Resource Centers in each of Delaware's three countiesand is open to the public.

703 Delaware Association of Nonprofit Homes for the Aging
1175 McKee Road
Dover, DE 19901
302-674-8030
Fax: 302-674-8650

Represents not-for-profit nursing homes, continuing care retirement communities, assisted living and senior housing facilities, and community service organizations operating in Delaware.

State Organizations & Government Agencies/Delaware

704   Delaware Client Assistance Program
United Cerebral Palsy
245 E Camden-Wyoming Avenue
Camden, DE 19934   302-698-9336
                        800-640-9336
                        Fax: 302-698-9338
                        e-mail: capucp@magpage.com
Melissa Shahan, Director

Provides advocacy services for persons involved with programs covered under the Rehabilitation Act of 1973 as amended, information and referrals on Ad A, Title I.

705   Delaware Commission of Veterans Affairs
802 Silver Lake Boulevard
Suite 100
Dover, DE 19904-2488   302-739-2792
                        800-344-9900
                        Fax: 302-739-2794
                        e-mail: adavila@state.de.us
                        http://www.veteransaffairs.delaware.gov
Antonio Davila, Executive Director

The Delaware Commission of Veterans Affairs (DCVA) was established in 1987 to provide assistance to Delaware's veterans, their spouses and dependent children.

706   Delaware Council for Persons with Disabiities
410 Federal Street
Suite 1
Dover, DE 19901-3640   302-739-3613
                        Fax: 302-739-6704
                        http://http://scpd.delaware.gov
Kyle Hodges, Manager

The mission of the State Counicl for Persons with Disabilities is to unite, in one Council, disability advocates and State agency policy makers to ensure that individuals with disabilities are empowered to become fully integrated within the community.

707   Delaware Department of Education
401 Federal Street
Suite #2
Dover, DE 19901-3639   302-735-4000
                        Fax: 302-739-4654
                        e-mail: dedoc@doe.k12.de.us
                        http://www.doe.state.de.us
Dr. Pascal D Forgione Jr, Superintendent
Harriet N Smith-Windsor, Executive Director

A publicly funded state agency that gives information about local facilities and administers supplemental funds for visually handicapped students in local schools. It also maintains special teachers of sight conservation and braille programs for both children and adults.

708   Delaware Department of Health and Social Services: Division for the Visually Impaired
300 Cornell Drive
Suites 3A And A4
Wilmington, DE 19801   302-577-2083
                        Fax: 302-577-2081
                        http://www.dhss.delaware.gov/dhss/dvi
Cynthia B Lovell, Director

The Division for the Visually Impaired is the State's oldest agency dating from 1909. Mission is to improve the quality of life for Delaware's citizens by promoting health and well being, fostering self-sufficiency, and protecting vulnerable populations.

709   Delaware Developmental Disability Council
410 Federal Street
Dover, DE 19901   302-739-3333
                        Fax: 302-739-2015
                        e-mail: pat.maichel@state.de.us
                        http://http://ddc.delaware.gov
Patricia Maichle, Executive Director

The mission of the Delaware Developmental Disabilities Council is to promote and embrace inclusion, equality and empowerment.

710   Delaware Disability Determination Services
Po Box 15711
Wilmington, DE 19885-5711   302-324-7600
                            Fax: 866-373-8089
                        http://www.delawareworks.com/dvr/services/dds
Marc Young, Deputy Director

The Disability Determination Services Unit of DVR is a state administered federal program that serves Delawareans who are unable to work because of a disability. The DDS develops, adjudicates, and processes disability claims of residents for Social Security disability benefits.

711   Delaware Division of Revenue
820 N French Street
Wilmington, DE 19801-3530   302-577-8686
                            800-292-7826
                            Fax: 302-577-8202
                        http://http://revenue.delaware.gov
Patrick T. Carter, Director

As the primary revenue collector for the State, the mission of the Division of Revenue is to collect 100% of the taxes and other revenues required by law, no more and no less, and to do so in a manner that creates the highest possible level of satisfaction on the part of the public with the competence, courtesy, effectiveness, and efficiency of the Division.

712   Delaware Division of Services for Aging Adults with Physical Disabilities
1901 N Dupont Highway
New Castle, DE 19720-1160   302-577-4791
                            800-223-9074
                            Fax: 302-255-4445
                            e-mail: dsaapdinfo@state.de.us
                        http://www.dhss.delaware.gov/dhss/dsaapd
Eleanor Cain, Director
Allan Zaback, Manager

Carries out a broad range of activities on behalf of older persons and adults with physical disabilities in Delaware.

713   Delaware Protection & Advocacy for Persons with Disabilities
100 W 10th Street
Wilmington, DE 19801   302-575-0660
                        Fax: 302-575-0840
                        http://www.declasi.org
Christopher White, Executive Director

A private, non-profit law firm dedicated to the equal justice for all. We provide civil legal services to assist clients in becoming self sufficient and meeting basic needs with dignity. Our clients include members of our community who have low incomes, who have disabilities, or who are age 60 and over.

714   Delaware Workers Compensation Board
4425 N Market Street
Wilmington, DE 19802-1307   302-761-8085
                        http://www.delawareworks.com
Harold E Stafford, Manager

The Office of Worker's Compensation administers and enforces state laws, rules and regulations regarding industrial accidents and illnesses.

715   Modern Maturity Center
1121 Forrest Avenue
Dover, DE 19904-3308   302-734-1200
                        Fax: 302-674-1265
                        http://www.modern-maturity.org
Ed McNamara, President
Elizabeth Carlson, First Vice President
Carolyn Fredericks, Chief Executive Officer

The mission of the Modern Maturity Center is to provide programs and services that will enhance the quality of life, with dignity and respect, for older adults.

State Organizations & Government Agencies/District of Columbia

716 **RSVP New Castle County**
1901 North DuPont Highway
Chas Debnam Building
New Castle, DE 19720
302-255-9675
Fax: 302-255-4465
http://www.dhss.delaware.gov/dhss
Vincent P Meconi, Secretary
Karryl H McManus, Deputy Secretary

To improve the quality of life for Delaware's citizens by promoting health and well being, foster self-sufficiency, and protection vulnerable populations.

717 **RSVP Sussex County**
546 S Bedford Street
Georgetown, DE 19947-1852
302-856-5815
Fax: 302-856-5255
http://www.dhss.delaware.gov/dhss/sov/rsvpsusse
Maryann Hook, Director

The Retired and Senior Volunteer Program (RSVP) provides opportunities for people 55 and over to make a difference in their community through volunteer service. RSVP volunteers contribute anywhere from a few to over forty hours a week, serving through schools, day care centers, police departments, hospitals and other nonprofit and public organizations to help meet critical community needs. RSVP offers maximum flexibility and choice to its volunteers. RSVP matches the personal interests and skills of older Americans with opportunities to help solve community problems and offers supplemental insurance while on duty, on-the-job training from the agency or organization where volunteers are placed. The following County is served: Sussex.

District of Columbia

718 **American Association of Homes & Services for the Aging**
2519 Connecticut Avenue NW
Washington, DC 20008-1520
202-783-2242
Fax: 202-783-2255
e-mail: info@aahsa.org
http://www.aahsa.org
William L Minnix Jr DMin, President/CEO
Daniel Smith, VP

Serve two million people every day through mission-driven, not-for-profit organizations dedicated to provide continuum of aging services: adult day services, home health, community services, senior housing, assisted living residences, continuing care retirement communities, and nursing homes.

719 **Bureau of Naval Personnel: District of Columbia Retired Affairs Office**
Navy Family Service Center
Naval Station Anacostia, Building 150
2791 Brookley Avenue SW
Washington, DC 20373
202-433-6150
Fax: 202-433-6138
e-mail: david.rowe@navy.mil

The RAO serves as a link between local retired military and the active-duty community which provides assistance to retired military. It provides installation commanders with a means of providing more effective services and improving communication for the local retired community. The RAO is staffed and operated by volunteer retired military who assist other retired members, their families and survivors to receive entitled services and benefits. Through newsletters, seminars and appreciation days, the RAO supports quality of life issues throughout the retirement years to their fellow service members.

720 **Disability Determination Division**
810 1st Street NE
Room 8019
Washington, DC 20002-4227
202-442-8516
Fax: 202-442-8501
Sandra K Brown, Acting Medical Relations Officer

721 **District of Columbia Association of Nonprofit Services for the Aging**
c/o Baptist Senior Adult Ministries
1330 Massachusetts Avenue NW
Washington, DC 20005-4155
202-504-3400
Fax: 202-638-0649
Francis S Smith, Executive Director

722 **District of Columbia Office on Aging**
441 4th Street NW
Suite 900S
Washington, DC 20001-2714
202-724-5622
Fax: 202-724-4979
http://http://dcoa.dc.gov/dcoa
Francis S Smith, Executive Director

Serves the District of Columbia residents 60 years of age and older. Contact the Information and Assistance Unit for more information about innovative programs and services offered by the Office.

723 **District of Columbia Rehabilitation Services**
810 First Street NE
Washington, DC 20001-3706
202-442-8400
http://www.rsa.dhs.dc.gov/rsa
James Clark, Supervisor

A private, nonprofit organization that offers contracts for health services, social evaluation, individual counseling, referral to community services, college programs and more for the visually impaired. The staff includes nine full-time employees.

724 **District of Columbia Retirement Board**
900 7th Street NW
Second Floor
Washington, DC 20001
202-343-3200
Fax: 202-535-1414
http://www.dcrb.dc.gov/dcrb
Eric Stanchfield, Executive Director
Sheila Morgan-Johnson, Chief Investment Officer

The mission of the DC Retirement Board is to invest, control and manage the assets of the Teachers' Retirement Fund and the Police Officers' and Firefighters' Retirement Fund.

725 **District of Columbia Worker Compensation Board**
64 New York Avenue NE
2nd Floor
Washington, DC 20002
202-671-1394
http://www.does.dc.gov
Francis Smith, Executive Director

The Compensation Review Board (CRB) in accordance with Administrative Police Issuance, replaces the Office of the Director in providing administrative appellate review and dispostion of workers' and disability compensation claims arising under the DC Workers' Compensation Act.

726 **Generations United**
1331 H Street NW
Suite 900
Washington, DC 20005-4752
202-289-3979
Fax: 202-289-3952
e-mail: gu@gu.org
http://www.gu.org
Donna M Butts, Executive Director

Generations United (GU) is the national membership organization focused solely on improving the lives of children, youth, and older people through intergenerational strategies, programs, and public policies. Our mission is to improve the lives of children, youth, and older people through intergenerational collaboration, public polices, and programs for the enduring benefit of all.

727 **Gray Panthers Metropolitan**
1424 9th Street NW
Washington, DC 20001-3344
202-347-9541
Fax: 202-347-9541
e-mail: gpanther@capaccess.org
http://www.angelfire.com/pe/dcgreypanthers

State Organizations & Government Agencies/Florida

Advocates for adequate standard of living for the elderly and youth. Addresses health care reform issues. Seeks sufficient retirement income and security for all. Supports peace and justice issues which include jobs and antinuclear actions.

728 **Information, Protection & Advocacy for Persons with Disabilities**
220 I Street NE
Suite 130
Washington, DC 20002
202-547-0198
Fax: 202-547-2083
e-mail: jbrown@uls-dc.org
http://www.uls.dc.org

Jane Brown Esq, Executive Director

Offers services and support for persons with disabilities in the Washington, DC area.

400 pages

729 **Mayor's Committee on Persons with Disabilities**
810 First Street NE
Room 10015
Washington, DC 20002
202-442-8673
Fax: 202-442-8742

Rhonda Stewart, Contact

The Committee acts in an advisory capacity to the Mayor on programs, services, facilities and activities which impact on citizens with disabilities in the District of Columbia. The Committee concerns itself with advocacy issues related to an inclusive delivery system for services to persons with disabilities.

730 **National Citizen's Coalition for Nursing Home Reform (NCCNHR)**
1828 L Street NW
Suite 801
Washington, DC 20036
202-332-2276
Fax: 202-332-2949
http://www.nccnhr.org

Alice H Hedt, Executive Director
William F Benson, President

NCCNHR provides information on nursing home reform, promotes quality standards, and works to empower residents.

Florida

731 **ARC Gateway**
3932 North 10th Avenue
Pensacola, FL 32503-2806
850-434-2638
Fax: 850-438-2180
e-mail: info@arc-gateway.org
http://www.arc-gateway.org

Monroe Watley, President
Linda Bloom, Vice-President
Kathy Anthony, Treasurer

To increase the opportunities for all persons with, or at risk of, development disabilities, to choose where, how and with whom, they live, learn, work and play.

732 **Alliance for Aging**
9500 S Dadeland Boulevard
Suite 400
Miami, FL 33156-2867
305-670-6500
Fax: 305-670-6516
http://www.allianceforaging.org

Max B Rothman, President/CEO
Rhina Jaar, Executive Assistant
Jessica Perez, Receptionist

The Alliance for Aging is a private not-for-profit, agency part of a nationwide network of more then 650 Area Agencies on Aging. A volunteer Board of Directors governs the Alliance. Operating funds are received through federal, state and local grants, as well as private donations from individuals, corporations and special initiatives.

733 **Assistive Technology Educational Network of Florida**
1207 Mellonville Avenue
Sanford, FL 32771
407-688-2201
800-558-6580
Fax: 407-320-2379
e-mail: diane_penn@scps.k12.fl.us
http://www.aten.scps.k12.fl.us

Mark Cerasale, Administrator
Diane Penn MA, Technology Specialist
Dee Enright, Executive Secretary

Provides state-wide information, awareness, and training for students, family members, teachers and other professionals; a quarterly newsletter and a network of specialists (Local Assistive Technology Specialists) trained by ATEN to provide support at the district level.

734 **Brevard County Community Services Council**
3600 W King Street
Cocoa, FL 32926-4150
321-639-8770
Fax: 321-636-8446
e-mail: info@communityservicescouncil.org
http://www.communityservicescouncil.org

Cindy Flackmeier, President/CEO
Janice Wiese, Program Director
Mickey Belson, Program Director

Community Services Council of Brevard is a private not for profit organization dedicated to helping seniors enjoy happy, healthy, and secure lives. The mission of Community Services Council is to develop solutions to community problems and to promote and maintain independence and maximize the quality of life for the citizens of Brevard County, particularly the elderly and disabled adults.

735 **Broward County Area: Agency on Aging**
5345 NW 35th Avenue
Fort Lauderdale, FL 33309-7012
954-714-3456
Fax: 305-497-1586

Edith Lederberg, Director

736 **Broward Meals on Wheels**
3810 Inverray Blvd.
Suite 305
Lauderhill, FL 33319
954-731-8770
Fax: 954-731-7131
e-mail: bmow@bmow.com
http://www.bmow.com

Peggy Miller, Executive Director
Ann Chickowsky, Nutrition Care Manager
Ken Beers, Operations Manager

Mission is to provide essential services that improve health, reduce isolation and promote independent living for seniors.

737 **Bureau of Naval Personnel: Florida Retired Affairs Office-Jacksonville**
Family Service Center
Naval Air Station
Box 2
Jacksonville, FL 32212-5000
904-542-2345
http://www.nasjax.navy.mil

Capt Chip Dobson, Commanding Officer
Capt Chuck Tamblyn, Executive Officer

The RAO serves as a link between local retired military and the active-duty community which provides assistance to retired military. It provides installation commanders with a means of providing more effective services and improving communication for the local retired community. The RAO is staffed and operated by volunteer retired military who assist other retired members, their families and survivors to receive entitled services and benefits. Through newsletters, seminars and appreciation days, the RAO supports quality of life issues throughout the retirement years to their fellow service members.

State Organizations & Government Agencies/Florida

738 Bureau of Naval Personnel: Milton Retired Activities Office
Fleet and Family Support Center
Naval Air Station Whiting Field
7511 USS Enterprise Street
Milton, FL 32570
850-623-7177
Fax: 850-623-7735
Eugene Jackson, Contact

The RAO serves as a link between local retired military and the active-duty community which provides assistance to retired military. It provides installation commanders with a means of providing more effective services and improving communication for the local retired community. The RAO is staffed and operated by volunteer retired military who assist other retired members, their families and survivors to receive entitled services and benefits. Through newsletters and seminars and appreciation days, the RAO supports quality of life issues throughout the retirement years to their fellow service members.

739 Bureau of Naval Personnel: Orlando Retired Activities Office
Naval Traing Center
Building 2024, Box 931660
2500 Leahy Avenue
Orlando, FL 32893-1600
407-646-4204
800-225-8950
Fax: 407-646-4213
e-mail: rao8@juno.com

The RAO serves as a link between local retired military and the active-duty community which provides assistance to retired military. It provides installation commanders with a means of providing more effective services and improving communication for the local retired community. The RAO is staffed and operated by volunteer retired military who assist other retired members, their families and survivors to receive entitled services and benefits. Through newsletters and seminars and appreciation days, the RAO supports quality of life issues throughout the retirement years to their fellow service members.

740 Bureau of Naval Personnel: Pensacola Retired Activities Office
Naval Air Station
Building 625
Pensacola, FL 32508
850-452-5990
Fax: 850-452-5118
Diana Hooker, Executive Director

The RAO serves as a link between local retired military and the active-duty community which provides assistance to retired military. It provides installation commanders with a means of providing more effective services and improving communication for the local retired community. The RAO is staffed and operated by volunteer retired military personnel who assist other retired members, their families and survivors to receive entitled services andbenefits. Through newsletters and seminars and appreciation days, the RAO supports quality of life issues throughout the retirement years to their fellow service members.

741 Coalition for Independent Living Options
6800 Forest Hill Boulevard
West Palm Beach, FL 33413
561-966-4288
800-683-7337
Fax: 561-641-6619
http://www.cilo.org
TTY 561-641-6538
Shelley Gottsagen, Executive Director

The purpose is to have an advocacy organization for children and adults with disabilities.

742 Department of Health & Rehabilitative Services
4042 Bald Cypress Way
Tallahassee, FL 32399-6570
850-245-4250
Fax: 850-922-6969
http://www.doh.state.fl.us/environment

Offers counseling and referrals on rehabilitation facilities.

743 East Central Florida Area: Agency on Aging
1011 N Wymore Road
Suite 105
Winter Park, FL 32789-1737
407-623-1075
800-262-2243
Fax: 407-623-1084
Judith G Thames, Director
Jeffrey Jones, Manager

744 Fifty Five Years & Up
701 SW 27th Avenue
Suite 1203
Miami, FL 33135
305-642-5520
Fax: 305-642-5549
e-mail: 55yearsandup@msn.com
http://www.55yearsandup.com
Jose Marmol, Vice President

745 Florida Association of Homes for the Aging
1812 Riggins Road
Tallahassee, FL 32308
904-671-3700
Fax: 904-671-3790
e-mail: info@faha.org
http://www.faha.org
Janegayle Boyd, President/CEO

The mission of the Florida Association of Homes for the Aging is to represent and promote the common interests of continuing care retirement communities, assisted living facilities, nursing homes, and affordable supportive housing members through advocacy, education, leadership development and shared services to enhance their ability to serve older or disabled adults.

Number of Members: 500

746 Florida Client Assistance Program
2728 Centerview Drive
Suite 102
Tallahassee, FL 32301-5092
850-488-9071
800-342-0823
Fax: 850-488-8640
http://www.advocacycenter.org
Gary Weston, Executive Director

The Advocacy Center for Persons with Disabilities, Inc., is a non-profit organization providing Protection and Advocacy services in the state of Florida. Our mission is to advance the quality of life, dignity, equality, self-determination, and freedom of choice of persons with disabilities through collaboration, education, advocacy , as well as legal and legislative strategies.

747 Florida Council on Aging
1018 Thomasville Road
Suite 110
Tallahassee, FL 32303-8701
850-222-8877
Fax: 850-222-2575
e-mail: mlduggar@aol.com
http://www.fcoa.org
Dave Lynn, President

The Florida Council on Aging is committed to serving Florida's diverse aging interests through education, information-sharing and advocacy.x

748 Florida Department of Administration: State Retirement Commission
2737 Centerview Drive
Suite 10
Tallahassee, FL 32399
850-414-4615
Fax: 850-488-5290
Sandra Bell, Manager

749 Florida Department of Aging
1317 Winewood Boulevard
Suite 2
Tallahassee, FL 32399-6570
850-488-8922
Fax: 850-922-4193
Larry Polivka, Assistant Secretary
Chris Shoemaker, Executive Director

State Organizations & Government Agencies/Florida

750 **Florida Department of Children, Families and Elderly Services**
1317 Winewood Boulevard
Tallahassee, FL 32399-6570
850-487-1111
Fax: 850-922-2993
http://www.myflorida.com/cf_web
Paul Keith, President

The Florida Department of Children and Families' mission is to protect vulnerable children and adults, to promote strong, economically self-sufficient families, and to advance personal and family recovery and resiliency from mental illness and substance addiction. Our Adult Services Program provides services for frail, elderly and disabled adults who are at risk or are victims of abuse, neglect, or exploitation and disabled adults who need assistance to remain in their own homes in the community.

751 **Florida Department of Elder Affairs Program of Aging and Adult Services**
4040 Esplanade Way
Tallahassee, FL 32399-7000
850-414-2000
Fax: 850-414-2004
http://http://elderaffairs.state.fl.us
Carole Green, Manager
Susan Tucker, Deputy Secretary
Joan L Spainhower, Communications Director

An agency designated by Flordia voters to be in charge of issues concerning older Flordians. Its purpose is to serve elders in every aspect possible to help them keep their self-sufficiency and self determination. The Department implements a variety of innovative programs for long term care. Recognizing that the majority of Flordia's elders are active and independent and want to remain that way aslong as possible.

752 **Florida Department of Mental Health and Rehabilitative Services**
1317 Winewood Boulevard
Tallahassee, FL 32399-6570
850-414-4615
Fax: 850-487-2239
Dr. Ira Rose, Director
Sandra Bell, Manager

753 **Florida Department of Revenue**
5050 West Tennessee Street
Tallahassee, FL 32399
850-414-4615
http://sun6.dms.state.fl.us/dor
Lisa Echeverri, Executive Director

Mission of the Florida Department of Revenue is to serve citizens with respect, concern, and professionalism. To make complying with tax and child support laws easy and understandable. To administer the laws fairly and consistently and to provide excellent service efficiently and at the lowest possible cost.

754 **Florida Department of Veterans Affairs**
4040 Esplanade Way
Suite 152
Tallahassee, FL 32399-0950
850-487-1533
Fax: 850-488-4001
http://www.floridavets.org
LeRoy Collins Jr, Executive Director
Earl Daniell, Chief of Staff
Courtney Heidelberg, Public Relations Manager

Our mission is to help Florida veterans, their families and survivors to improve their health and economic well-being through quality benefits information, advocacy, education and long term health services.

755 **Florida Developmental Disabilities Council**
124 Marriott Drive
Suite 230
Tallahassee, FL 32301-2981
850-488-4180
800-580-7801
Fax: 850-922-6702
e-mail: fddc@fddc.org
http://www.fddc.org
K Joseph Krieger, Director
Debra Dowds, Executive Director

Promotes innovative programs and practices that prevent disabilities and improve the quality of life for people with disabilities and thier families. Participates in statewide and nationwide advocacy.

756 **Florida Division of Vocational Rehabilitation**
2002 Old Saint Augustine Road
Building A
Tallahassee, FL 32301-4862
850-245-3399
800-451-4327
Fax: 850-921-7215
http://www.rehabworks.org
Bill Palmer, Director

State agency serving individuals with physical or mental disabilities that interfere with them keeping or maintaining employment.

757 **Florida Dog Guides F.T.D.**
PO Box 20662
2016 27th Street East
Bradenton, FL 32408
941-748-8245
800-520-4589
Fax: 941-747-0969
e-mail: adogs@floridadogguidesftd.org
http://www.floridadogguidesftd.org
TDD 941-748-8245

Deaf and hard of hearing individuals interested in working with and providing trained certified hearing dogs for the deaf. Sponsors state-wide dog shows and canine good citizen testing. Provides deaf awareness and advocacy.

758 **Florida Protection & Advocacy for Persons with Disabilities**
2728 Centerview Drive
Suite 102
Tallahassee, FL 32301-5069
850-488-9071
800-342-0823
Fax: 850-488-8640
http://www.advocacycenter.org
Gary Weston, Executive Director

The Advocacy Center for Persons with Disabilities is a non-profit organization providing Protection and Advocacy services in the State of Florida.

759 **Florida Retirement Division**
PO Box 9000
Tallahassee, FL 32315-9000
805-488-5540
866-738-2366
Fax: 850-921-0371
http://www.myflorida.com/retirement
Sarabeth Snuggs, Division Director

The Florida Retirement System enables our citizens to meet their financial needs and enjoy their retirement. The quality of life of our citizens should not be hindered after they reach retirement, but should empower them to spend or save their earnings, as they deem appropriate. The strong financial health of the FRS pension plan ensures the integrity of our state's pension now and in the future.

Number of Members: 600,000

760 **Gray Panthers of North Dade**
861 N Venetian Drive
Miami, FL 33139-1012
305-374-8240
e-mail: info@graypanthers.org
http://www.graypanthers.org
Dorothy Fleisher, Director

A national organization of intergenerational activists dedicated to social change.

761 **Gray Panthers of South Dade**
10725 SW 82nd Avenue
Miami, FL 33256
305-595-0594
Fax: 305-273-9664
e-mail: saxe@bellsouth.net
http://www.graypanthers.org
Norman Saxe, Convener

State Organizations & Government Agencies/Florida

A network of independent activisits bound together by our passion for social justice. We are a loosely coordinated set of networks bound only by our passionate comnmitment to speak truth to power.

762 Heart of Florida United Way Volunteer Center
Dr. Nelson Ying Center
1940 Traylor Boulevard
Orlando, FL 32804-4714
407-835-0900
Fax: 407-835-1959
http://www.hfuw.org
Robert H Brown, President/CEO
Troy Robinson, VP Resource

Affects community-wide change by linking leaders of businesses and nonprofit organization together. Programs include Volunteer Management Training, volunteer recruitment, corporate volunteerism, community involvement projects, volunteer recognition, and educational resources.

763 Meals on Wheels
2801 S Financial Court
Suite 1001
Sanford, FL 32773-6418
407-333-8877
Fax: 407-829-2468
http://www.mealsetc.org
David R Billsborough, President

The mission of Meals on Wheels is to enhance the quality of life for elder Seminole County residents by providing appetizing, nutritious meals, and support services which permit seniors to maintain independence and dignity.

764 Miami Dade County Retired and Senior Volunteer Program
4500 NW Biscayne Blvd.
Suite 320
Miami, FL 33137
305-576-2511
Fax: 305-375-4501
e-mail: Bsosa@miamidade.gov
http://www.miamidade.gov/dhs
Beba Sosa, President
Alexander Penelas, CEO

Miami Dade County's Department of Human Services (DHS) provides volunteer service opportunities in their home communities. This program is available to people 55 years and older. Participants serve up to forty hours a week in organizations that range from hospitals and youth recreation centers to local police stations and education facilities. Seniors are matched by their personal interests, skills, and lifelong experiences.

765 North Florida Area: Agency on Aging
2414 Mahan Drive
Tallahassee, FL 32308-5302
850-488-0055
866-467-4624
Fax: 850-922-2420
e-mail: aaanf@elderaffairs.org
http://www.aaanf.org
Janice D Wise, Executive Director
Norma Adams, Fiscal Administrator
Linda Burns, Office Manager

The mission of the Area Agency on Aging for North Florida is to plan, coordinate and advocate for programs and services which promote the independence, dignity, health and well being of seniors and caregivers.

766 Northeast Florida Area: Agency on Aging
4401 Wisconnett Blvd
2nd Floor
Jacksonville, FL 32210
904-777-2106
Fax: 352-388-6400
Elizabeth Lee, Director
Linda Levin, Manager

767 Osceola County Council on Aging
1099 Shady Lane
Kissimmee, FL 34744-6107
407-846-8532
Fax: 407-846-8550
http://www,occoa.org
Beverly Hoagland, Executive Director

The Osceols County Council on Aging is a private, non-profit agency dedicated to providing services and housing to promote the physical, mental and social well-being of seniors, at risk youth, adults with disabilities and their care givers in our community. Our goals are to help frail citizens maintain their independence and dignity in an effort to avoid being institutionalized and to provide active seniors with volunteer, recreational and socialactivities to keep them involved and fulfilled.

768 Palm Beach Treasure Coast Area: Agency on Aging
1764 N Congress Avenue
Suite 201
West Palm Beach, FL 33409-5189
561-697-7250
Fax: 561-697-7250
Vivian Pfau, Office Of The CEO

Administers public funds, private grants, and donations for senior services. Promotes independence, dignity, health and wellbeing of older people. Advocates, plans and coordinates programs benefitting senior citizens.

769 RSVP Alachua County
218 SE 24th St
Bldg B
Gainesville, FL 32641
352-264-6735
Fax: 352-264-6703
Ann Snavely, Director

Mission is to offer citizens 55 years of age and greater, challenging and rewarding volunteer opportunities in order to significantly and positively impact our communities.

770 RSVP Big Bend
2518 W Tennessee Street
Tallahassee, FL 32304
850-921-5554
Fax: 850-921-0082
http://www.ecsbigbend.org
Elma Haley, Executive Director

The Retired and Senior Volunteer Program (RSVP) provides opportunities for people 55 and over to make a difference in their community through volunteer service. RSVP volunteers contribute anywhere from a few to over forty hours a week, serving through schools, day care centers, police departments, hospitals and other nonprofit and public organizations to help meet critical community needs. RSVP offers maximum flexibility and choice to its volunteers. RSVP matches the personal interests and skills of older Americans with opportunities to help solve community problems and offers supplemental insurance while on duty, and on-the-job training from the agency or organization where volunteers are placed. The following Counties are served: Franklin, Gadsden, Jefferson, Leon, Liberty, Madison, Suwannee, Taylor, Wakulla.

771 RSVP Broward County
4701 NW 33rd Avenue
Ft Lauderdale, FL 33309-6807
954-484-7117
Fax: 954-484-8292
e-mail: administration@seniorvolunteerservices.org
http://www.seniorvolunteerservices.org
Edward Gray, Program Director

The Retired and Senior Volunteer Program (RSVP) provides opportunities for people 55 and over to make a difference in their community through volunteer service. RSVP volunteers contribute anywhere from a few to over forty hours a week, serving though schools, day care centers, police departments, hospitals and other nonprofit and public organizations to help meet critical community needs. RSVP offers maximum flexibility and choice to its volunteers. RSVP matches the personal interests and skills to older Americans with opportunities to help solve community problems and offer supplemental insurance while on duty, on-the-job training from the agency or organization where volunteers are placed.

State Organizations & Government Agencies/Florida

772 **RSVP Central Panhandle**
103 W Nebraska St
Bonifay, FL 32425-2132   850-547-2511
                Fax: 850-547-2511
e-mail: juliebielinski@hotmail.com
http://www.newlifestyles.com/facility
Julie Prevatt Bielinski, Director

The Retired and Senior Volunteer Program (RSVP) provides opportunities for people 55 and over to make a difference in their community through volunteer service. RSVP volunteers contribute anywhere from a few to over forty hours a week, serving through schools, day care centers, police departments, hospitals and other nonprofit and public organizations to help meet critical community needs. RSVP offers maximum flexibility and choice to its volunteers. RSVP matches the personal interests and skills of older Americans with opportunities to help solve community problems and offers supplemental insurance while on duty, on-the-job training from the agency or organization where volunteers are placed. The following Counties are served: Calhoun, Holmes, Jackson, Walton, Washington.

773 **RSVP Citrus County**
2804 W Marc Knighton Court
Lecanto, FL 34461-7718   352-527-5900
                Fax: 352-527-5908
e-mail: catherine.pearson@bocc.citrus.fl.us
http://www.citruscountyfl.org
Catherine Pearson, Director

The RSVP mission is to provide meaningful volunteer opportunities for people 55 and over who bring vast experience, skills, and interests from diverse economic, educational and social backgrounds to serve on a regular basis at sites throughout Citrus County.

774 **RSVP Collier County**
801 8th Avenue South
Naples, FL 34102   239-774-8833
                Fax: 239-732-2604
e-mail: rsvp@colliergov.net
http://www.aps.naples.net
Sharon Downey, Project Director

Provides an opportunity for seniors and retirees aged 55 years and older to make a difference in their community. Your individual interests, skills & knowledge are matched to a volunteer effort that is most suitable for you. RSVP represents over a hundred different non-profit agencies, schools and county government. You can be placed in a meaningful and satisfying position with one of the agencies that needs your help, the expertise & experience

775 **RSVP Duval County**
150 E 1st Street
Jacksonville, FL 32206-5002   904-630-0998
                Fax: 904-630-0511
Sally S Robson, Director

We have 35 senior volunteers involved in bulk mailings for education, solicitations, beautification of their apartment buildings, grounds and senior centers and helping Habitat-For-Humanity building homes, family selection and committee. They also serve as docents at the local museums and zoo. The following County served is: Duval.

776 **RSVP Flagler County**
4750 E Moody Blvd.
Suite 233
Bunnell, FL 32136   386-437-7449
                Fax: 386-437-9997
e-mail: flaglerrsvp@yahoo.com
http://www.flaglervolunteer.org
Suzy Rutherford, Volunteer Coordinator

The Retired and Senior Volunteer Program (RSVP) provides opportunities for people 55 and over to make a difference in their community through volunteer service. RSVP volunteers contribute anywhere from a few to over forty hours a week, serving through schools, day care centers, police departments, hospitals and other nonprofit and public organizations to help meet critical community needs. RSVP offers maximum flexibility and choice to its volunteers. RSVP matches the personal interests and skills of older Americans with the opportunities to help solve community problems and offers supplemental insurance while on duty, on-the-job training from the agency or organization where volunteers are placed. The following County is served: Flagler.

777 **RSVP Hernando County**
801 N Broad Street
Brooksville, FL 34601-2203   352-796-1425
                Fax: 352-797-9952
Darlene Wilson, Director

The Retired and Senior Volunteer Program (RSVP) provides opportunities for people 55 and over to make a difference in their community through volunteer service. RSVP volunteers contribute anywhere from a few to over forty hours a week, serving through schools, day care centers, police departments, hospitals and other nonprofit and public organizations to help meet critical community needs. RSVP offers maximum flexibility and choice to its volunteers. RSVP matches the personal interests and skills of older Americans with opportunities to help solve community problems and offers supplemental insurance while on duty, on-the-job training from the agency or organization where volunteers are placed. The following County is served: Hernando.

778 **RSVP Hillsborough County**
601 E Kennedy Boulevard
25th Floor
Tampa, FL 33602-4156   813-272-5031
                Fax: 813-272-7145
Freddie Hudson, Director

Provides services to seniors including insurance, travel and meal allowances.

779 **RSVP Indian River County**
694 14th Street
Vero Beach, FL 32960   561-569-0760
                Fax: 561-778-7272
Nancy Anderson, Director

Provides opportunities for people 55 and over to make a difference in their community through volunteer service. RSVP volunteers contribute anywhere from a few to over forty hours a week, serving through schools, day care centers, police departments, hospitals and other nonprofit and public organizations to help meet critical community needs. RSVP matches the personal interests and skills of older Americans with opportunities to help solve community problems and offers supplemental insurance while on duty, and on-the-job training from the agency or organization where volunteers are placed.

780 **RSVP Lake County Senior Citizens Mid Florida Community Services**
1211 Penn Street
Leesburg, FL 34748   352-365-1995
                Fax: 352-326-2164
Otis Maxson, Executive Director

The Retired and Senior Volunteer Program (RSVP) provides opportunities for people 55 and over to make a difference in their community through volunteer service. RSVP volunteers contribute anywhere from a few to over forty hours a week, serving through schools, day care centers, police departments, hospitals and other nonprofit and public organizations to help meet critical community needs. RSVP offers maximum flexibility and choice to its volunteers. RSVP matches the personal interests and skills of older Americans with opportunities to help solve community problems and offers supplemental insurance while on duty, on-the-job training from the agency or organization where volunteers are placed.

State Organizations & Government Agencies/Florida

781 RSVP Lee County
3600 Evans Avenue
Fort Myers, FL 33901
941-275-1881
Fax: 941-275-1077
e-mail: friend@peganet.com

Tricia Molzow, Director

For two years, over 200 of our volunteers have worked at planting trees and creating butterfly gardens in our community. Recently some of them, in cooperation with Lee Memorial Hospital, are creating Horticulture Therapy Gardens. Others work at nature centers and historical/preservation societies. The following County is served: Lee.

782 RSVP Manatee North Sarasota Counties
4140 20th Street West
Bradenton, FL 34205
941-749-3001
Fax: 941-748-8957

Natalie Schiff, Director

The Retired and Senior Volunteer Program (RSVP) provides opportunities for people 55 and over to make a difference in their community through volunteer service. RSVP volunteers contribute anywhere from a few to over forty hours a week, serving through schools, day care centers, police departments, hospitals and other nonprofit and public organizations to help meet critical community needs. RSVP offers maximum flexibility and choice to its volunteers. RSVP matches the personal interests and skills of older Americans with opportunities to help solve community problems and offers supplemental insurance while on duty, on-the-job training from the agency or organization where volunteers are placed. The following Counties are served: Manatee, Sarasota.

783 RSVP Marion County
3001 SW College Rd
Ocala, FL 34474
352-654-5444
Fax: 352-371-1547
e-mail: boothd@cf.edu

Dian Booth, Contact

The Retired and Senior Volunteer Program (RSVP) provides opportunities for people 55 and over to make a difference in their community through volunteer service. RSVP volunteers contribute anywhere from a few to over forty hours a week, serving through schools, day care centers, police departments, hospitals and other nonprofit and public organizations to help meet critical community needs. RSVP offers maximum flexibility and choice to its volunteers. RSVP matches the personal interests and skills to older Americans with opportunities to help solve community problems and offers supplemental insurance while on duty, on-the-job training from the agency or organization where volunteers are placed. The following County is served: Marion.

784 RSVP Martin County
PO Box 362
50 Kindred Street Suite 207
Stuart, FL 34994-3033
772-220-4472
Fax: 772-220-7771
e-mail: chodnett@martinvolunteers.org
http://www.martinvolunteers.org/rsvp

Carol L Hodnett, Director
Anne Lalley, Project Coordinator

The Retired and Senior Volunteer Program (RSVP) provides opportunities for people 55 and over to make a difference in their community through volunteer service. RSVP volunteers contribute anywhere from a few to over forty hours a week, serving through schools, day care centers, police departments, hospitals and other nonprofit and public organizations to help meet critical community needs. RSVP offers maximum flexibility and choice to its volunteers. RSVP matches the personal interests and skills of older Americans with opportunities to help solve community problems and offers supplemental insurance while on duty, on-the-job training from the agency or organization where volunteers are placed. The following County is served: Martin.

785 RSVP Okaloosa County
207 Hospital Drive NE
Fort Walton Beach, FL 32548-5066
850-833-9165
Fax: 850-833-9174

Vicki Baldwin, Director

Recruits volunteers 60 and older to donate time and effort to worthy causes. Volunteer opportunities are available in schools, convalescent homes, libraries, Council on Aging, American Red Cross, American Cancer Society, and many more. The following County is served: Okaloosa.

786 RSVP Palm Beach County
1764 N Congress Avenue
Suite 201
West Palm Beach, FL 33409-5189
561-684-5885
Fax: 561-697-7250
e-mail: burbank@elderaffairs.org
http://www.joinseniorservice.org

Joyce Edison, Volunteer Specialist

The Retired and Senior Volunteer Program (RSVP) is an active group of volunteers 55 years of age or older putting their experience, skills, talents, and wisdom towards finding solutions to our community's concerns.

787 RSVP Pasco County
7227 Land O' Lakes Boulevard
Land O' Lakes, FL 34638
813-794-2207
Fax: 813-794-2794

Holly Rockhill, Director

The Retired and Senior Volunteer Program (RSVP) provides opportunities for people 55 and over to make a difference in their community through volunteer service. RSVP volunteers contribute anywhere from a few to over forty hours a week, serving through schools, day care centers, police departments, hospitals and other nonprofit and public organizations to help meet critical community needs. RSVP offers maximum flexibility and choice to its volunteers. RSVP matches the personal interests and skills of older Americans with opportunities to help solve community problems and offers supplemental insurance while on duty, on-the-job training from the agency or organization where volunteers are placed. The following County is served: Pasco.

788 RSVP Pinellas County
3443 1st Avenue N
St Petersburg, FL 33713-8516
727-327-8690
Fax: 727-321-9612
e-mail: grose@poc-inc.org
http://www.poc-inc.org

Gregg E Rose, RSVP Program Director

The Retired and Senior Volunteer Program of Pinellas County, Florida, provides meaningful and satisfying volunteer opportunities for individuals 55 years of age and older by matching their skills, experience, and knowledge with the addressing of unmet needs and critical issues within the community. Volunteers are currently placed in 130 not-for-profit agencies, hospitals, schools, nursing care facilities, and governmental programs throughoutPinellas County.

789 RSVP Santa Rosa
6294 Buckskin Drive
Milton, FL 32570
850-983-5220
Fax: 850-983-5225
e-mail: murielrsvpsrc@mchsi.com
http://www.rsvpsantarosa.org

Col. Jerry Goebel, President
Juther Meredith, Vice President
Rob Baker, Treasurer

State Organizations & Government Agencies/Florida

The Retired and Senior Volunteer Program (RSVP) provides opportunities for people 55 and over to make a difference in their community through volunteer service. RSVP volunteers contribute anywhere from a few to over forty hours a week, serving though schools, day care centers, police departments, hospitals and other nonprofit and public organizations to help meet critical community needs. RSVP offers maximum flexibility and choice to its volunteers. RSVP matches the personal interests and skills to older Americans with opportunities to help solve community problems and offer supplemental insurance while on duty, on-the-job training from the agency or organization where volunteers are placed.

790 RSVP Sarasota/Charlotte Counties
3600 Evens Avenue
Fort Myers, FL 33901
239-275-4427
Fax: 239-275-8344

Marge Slepica, Directro

The Retired and Senior Volunteer Program (RSVP) matches local problems with people age 55 and older who are willing to help. RSVP volunteers choose how and when they want to serve. Volunteers do whatever their skills and interests lead them to do. The program provides the senior volunteers with accident, liability and excess auto insurance. The coverage is in effect from the time the volunteer leaves home to go to the volunteer site until the volunteer returns home. The following Counties are served: Charlotte, Sarasota.

791 RSVP St John's County
40 Orange Street
St Augustine, FL 32084-3693
904-826-2181
Fax: 904-826-4903

Cheryl Freeman, Director

Committed to supplying volunteers who are experienced in life and business with satisfying opportunities to meet critical community needs. Over 500 volunteers 55 years and older serve in more than 60 locations in St Johns county, Florida.

792 RSVP St Lucie County
1909 Delaware Avenue
Ft Pierce, FL 34947
561-468-5824
Fax: 561-468-5220

Provides opportunities for people 55 and over to make a difference in their community through volunteer service. RSVP volunteers contribute anywhere from a few to over forty hours a week, serving through schools, day care centers, police departments, hospitals and other nonprofit and public organizations to help meet critical community needs. RSVP matches the personal interests and skills of older Americans with opportunities to help solve community problems and offers supplemental insurance while on duty, and on-the-job training from the agency or organization where volunteers placed.

793 RSVP Volunteer Services of United Way Palm Beach County
2600 Quantum Boulevard
Boynton Beach, FL 33426-8627
561-375-6680
Fax: 561-375-6666
e-mail: vwaypbc@gate.net
http://www.unitedwaypbc.org

Robert Palinn, Program Director

Designed to engage persons 55 and older iun volunteer service to meet critical community needs and to provide a high quality experience that will enrich the lives of volunteers. There is no minimum of time required for volunteering.

794 RSVP Volusia County
160 N Beach Street
PO Box 671
Daytona Beach, FL 32115
386-253-4700
888-252-6110
Fax: 386-253-6300
http://www.coaiaa.org

Gail Camputaro, Executive Director

The Retired and Senior Volunteer Program (RSVP) provides opportunities for people 55 and over to make a difference in their community through volunteer service. RSVP volunteers contribute anywhere from a few to over forty hours a week, serving through schools, day care centers, police departments, hospitals and other nonprofit and public organizations to help meet critical community needs. RSVP offers maximum flexibility and choice to its volunteers. RSVP matches the personal interests and skills of older Americans with opportunities to help solve community problems and offers supplemental insurance while on duty, on-the-job training from the agency or organization where volunteers are placed. The following County is served: Volusia.

795 Railroad Retirement Board: JacksonvilleDistrict Office
550 Water Street
Suite 330
Jacksonville, FL 32202-5122
904-232-2546
800-808-0772
Fax: 904-232-2874
http://www.rrb.gov

Henry G Crowe, Representative

The Railroad Retirement Board is an independent agency in the executive branch of the Federal Government. The RRB's primary function is to administer comprehensive retirement-survivor and unemployment-sickness benefit programs for the nation's railroad workers and their families, under the Railroad Retirement and Railroad Unemployment Insurance Acts.

796 Sanford Senior Center
401 E Seminole Boulevard
Sanford, FL 32771
407-302-1010
Fax: 407-302-1090
e-mail: eltonhek@ci.sanford.fl.us
http://www.ci.sanford.fl.us

Kim Eltonhead, Manager

Meeting the needs of senior citizens.

797 Seminole County Volunteer Program
Seminole Community College
100 Weldon Boulevard
PO Box 951636
Lake Mary, FL 32795-1636
407-323-4440
800-424-8867
Fax: 407-323-8001
e-mail: rsvpsem@aol.com
http://www.scvp.org

Patricia Shields, Director

Seminole County Volunteer Program is dedicated to improving the quality of life in Seminole County, Florida. Through innovative partnerships and collaborations, we provide skilled volunteers who positively impact: education, environment public safety, health and human needs.

798 Senior Solutions of Southwest Florida
2285 1st Street
Fort Myers, FL 33901-2959
239-332-4233
Fax: 239-332-3596
http://www.seniorsolutions.org

Leigh Wade, Director

799 Seniors First
5395 L B McLeod Road
Orlando, FL 32811-2952
407-292-0177
Fax: 407-292-2773
e-mail: info@seniorsfirstinc.com
http://www.seniorsfirstinc.com

Jon Dunwell, Chairman
George Royal, 1st Vice Chair
Melvin Pittman, 2nd Vice Chair

Senior First enhances the quality of life for Orange County senior citizens by maintaining their independence and dignity through nutrition, home improvement, and support services which assist seniors in need.

State Organizations & Government Agencies/Florida

800 Social Security: Miami Disability Determination
Division Of Disability Determinations
Po Box 839001
Miami, FL 33283
305-596-3020
800-223-6820
Fax: 856-534-4018

V Kincaid, Manager

The Division of Disability Determinations (DDD) is responsible for making decisions regarding the medical eligibility of Florida citizens applying for disability benefits under the federal Social Security and Supplemental Security Income programs, and the state Medically Needy program.

801 Social Security: Orlando Disability Determination
PO Box 144040
Orlando, FL 32814
407-897-2970
800-342-2065
Fax: 407-897-6497

Jim May, Manager

The Division of Disability Determination (DDD) is responsible for making decisions regarding the medical eligibility of Florida citizens applying for disability benefits under the federal Social Security and Supplemental Security Income programs, and the state Medically Needy program.

802 Social Security: Tallahassee Disability Determination
227 N Bronough Street
Suite 2070
Tallahassee, FL 32301-1380
850-942-8978
800-772-1213
Fax: 850-942-8980
http://www.ssa.gov

Rosie M Steele, District Manager

Administers the Title II and Title XVII disability programs. To be insured for Title II benefits, applicants must have worked in covered employment for at least five of the last ten years prior to becoming disabled. To be eligible for Title XVII disability benefits, applicants must meet an income and resource test. For retirement Title II beneficiaries must be 65 or 62 for early retirement. Title XVI recipients must be 65.

803 Social Security: Tampa Disability Determination
PO Box 155503
Tampa, FL 33684
813-983-3000
800-223-1172
Fax: 813-983-3030

Alan Shaffren, Program Administrator

The Division of Disability Determinations (DDD) is responsible for making decisions regarding the medical eligibility of Florida citizens applying for disability benefits under the federal Social Security and Supplemental Security Income programs, and the state Medically Needy program.

804 Tampa Bay Regional Planning Council-Area Agency on Aging
9455 Koger Boulevard N
St Petersburg, FL 33702-2480
727-521-5151
Fax: 727-570-5118

Sally D Gronda, Director

805 US Railroad Retirement Board: Tampa District Office
Timberlake Federal Building
500 E Zack Street Suite 300
Tampa, FL 33602
813-228-2695
Fax: 813-228-2939
e-mail: tampa@rrb.gov
http://www.rrb.gov

Virginia W Earl, District Manager

This office handles general inquiries from beneficiaries receiving Railroad Retirement benefits. The office takes applications from eligible employees, their spouses, their survivers for retirement and survivor benefits.

806 United Way of Central Florida
5605 US Highway 98 S
PO Box 1357
Highland City, FL 33846
863-648-1500
Fax: 863-648-1535
e-mail: info@uwcf.org
http://www.uwcf.org

Terry Worthington, President
Sandi Honeycutt, Executive Assistant
Susan Clayton Black, Director Communications/Mktg

United Way of Central Florida is focused on kids, families and wellness. We deal with social issues collectively, leveraging investments to create solutions that bring results for our community.

807 Volunteer Jacksonville
6817 Southpoint Parkway
Suite 1902
Jacksonville, FL 32216-6299
904-332-6767
Fax: 904-332-6722
e-mail: vj@volunteerjacksonville.org
http://www.volunteerjacksonville.org

Judy Smith, President/CEO
Krista Winfield-Estes, Vice President/COO

We inspire, connect, engage, and support volunteers who make a difference in our community.

808 West Central Florida Area: Agency on Aging
5905 Breckenridge Parkway
Suite F
Tampa, FL 33610-4239
813-225-1300
800-963-5337
Fax: 813-623-1342

Maureen Kelly, President/CEO
Gloria D Schuyler, COO

The West Central Florida Area Agency on Aging is a private, non-profit ccorporation which adminsters public funds, private grants and donations for senior services in Hillsborough, Polk, Manatee, Highlands and Hardee Counties.

809 William Beardall Senior Center
800 S Delaney Avenue
Orlando, FL 32801-3897
407-246-2637
Fax: 407-246-4114
e-mail: kiersten.freeman@cityoforlando.net
http://www.cityoforlando.net

Kiersten Freeman, Manager

City recreation center for seniors.

810 Winter Springs Senior Center
400 N Edgemon Avenue
Winter Springs, FL 32708-2539
407-327-6697

Susie Coffman, Executive Director

To provide those services that enhance and enrich the quality of life of its citizens. To ensure the most effective, economic and innovative approach to this end, we shall maintain the highest standard of integrity, ethics and professionalism both personally and publicly.

811 Workers Compensation Board Florida
200 East Gainses Street
Tallahassee, FL 32399-0300
850-413-3100
Fax: 850-487-3232
http://www.fldfs.com

Tanner Holloman, Manager

State Organizations & Government Agencies/Georgia

Georgia

812 AARP Southeast Regional Office
AARP
999 Peachtree Street
Suite 1650
Atlanta, GA 30309-4421
404-888-0077
Fax: 404-888-0902
e-mail: kmitchell@aarp.org
http://www.aarp.org
TTY 916-446-2680

Ken Mitchells, Director

A resource for AARP members in the states of Alabama, Florida, Georgia, Kentucky, Maryland, Mississippi, North Carolina, South Carolina, Tennessee, Virginia, and West Virginia, as well as the District of Columbia, Puerto Rico and the Virgin Islands. Hours are 9-5 Monday through Friday.

813 ADA Technical Assistance Program
1419 Mayson Street
Atlanta, GA 30324
404-541-9001
800-949-4232
Fax: 404-541-9002
http://www.sedbtac.org

Amy Oliveras, Administrative Assistant
Joseph Addo, Owner

One of ten regional centers funded by NIDRR, to provide information and technical assistance to assist in voluntary compliance with the Americans with Disabilities Act.

814 Atlanta Regional Commission: Aging Services Division
3715 Northside Parkway NW
Atlanta, GA 30327-2806
404-463-3100
Fax: 404-364-9380

Shelley Caplan, Project Director

815 Bureau of Naval Personnel: Retired Activities Office
Fleet and Family Support Center
1000 Halsey Avenue Code 016/ Bldg 80
Marietta, GA 30060-5099
678-655-6060
Fax: 678-925-6060

Janine Bemis, Site Manager

The RAO serves as a link between local retired military and the active-duty community which provides assistance to retired military. It provides installation commanders with a means of providing more effective services and improving communication for the local retired community. The RAO is staffed and operated by volunteer retired military who assist other retired members, their families and survivors to receive entitled services and benefits. Through newsletters and seminars and appreciation days, the RAO supports quality of life issues throughout the retirement years to their fellow service members.

816 Central Savannah River Regional Area:Agency on Aging
3023 Riverwatch Parkway
Suite A
Augusta, GA 30907-2016
706-210-2000
Fax: 706-210-2006
http://www.csrardc.org/csra

Jeannette G Cummings, Director
Andy Crosson, Manager

The CSRA RDC is a public-sector, non-profit planning and development agency that serves a 13 county and 41 city region in the eastern portion of central Georgia.

817 Chattahoochee Flint Area: Agency on Aging
PO Box 110
Franklin, GA 30217
706-675-6721

Robert C Buchanan, Director
Henry Booker, Manager

818 Coastal Georgia Regional Development Center Area: Agency on Aging
127 f Street
Po Box 1917
Brunswick, GA 31521-1917
912-264-7363
Fax: 912-262-2313
e-mail: info@coastalgeorgiardc.org
http://www.coastalgeorgiardc.org

Dan Coty, Chairman

819 DHR Division of Aging Services
2 Peachtree Street NW
9th Floor
Atlanta, GA 30303-3181
404-657-5258
Fax: 404-657-5285

Maria Greene, Director

820 Georgia Advocacy Office
150 E Ponce De Leon Avenue
Suite 430
Decatur, GA 30030
404-885-1234
800-537-2329
Fax: 404-378-0031
e-mail: info@thegao.org
http://www.thegao.org

Ruby Moore, Executive Director

Protection and advocacy services for Georgians with developmental disabilities.

821 Georgia Association of Homes and Services for the Aging
607 Peachtree Street NE
Atlanta, GA 30308-2226
404-872-9191
Fax: 404-872-1737
e-mail: gahsa@gahsa.org
http://www.gahsa.org

Walter Coffey, President/CEO
Jacque Thornton, Senior Vice President
Barry Lastinger, Events Coordinator

Provides services to seniors, including affordable and ethical long-termcare for older Georgians.

Number of Members: 100

822 Georgia Client Assistance Program
Division of Rehabilitation Services
755 Commerce Drive
Decatur, GA 30030
404-638-5200
800-822-9727
Fax: 404-638-5201
http://www.vocrehabga.org

Helps eligible persons with complaints, appeals and understanding available benefits under the 1992 Rehabilitation Act Amendments and Title I of the Americans with Disabilities Act. CAP investigates complaints, mediates conflict, represents complainants in appeals, provides legal services if warranted, advocates for due process, identifies and recommends solutions to system problems, & advises of benefits available under the 1992 Rehab Act Amendments and Americans with Disabilities Act.

823 Georgia Department of Aging
878 Peachtree Street NE
Apt 318
Atlanta, GA 30309-3933
404-206-6000
Fax: 404-730-7950

Fred McGinnis, Director
Wanda Rucker, Manager

824 Georgia Department of Labor: Disability Adjudication Section
PO Box 57
Stone Mountain, GA 30086
678-476-7000
Fax: 678-476-7377
e-mail: Bruce.Johnston@ssa.gov
http://www.vocrehabga.org

Bruce Johnston, Manager Professional Relations

State Organizations & Government Agencies/Georgia

825 Georgia Department of Revenue
491 Laney-Walker Blvd.
Augusta, GA 30901
706-821-2476
Fax: 706-731-7956
http://www.dor.ga.gov

Scott Stephens, Manager

826 Georgia Department of Veterans Service
Floyd Memorial Building
Suite E-367
Atlanta, GA 30334
404-656-5940
Fax: 404-657-1288
e-mail: rroby@vs.state.ga.us

Rick Roby, Senior Veterans Claim Councelor

Mission of the Department of Veterans Service is to serve the some 700,000 plus-veterans residing in Georgia, their dependents and survivors in all matters pertaining to veterans benefits.

827 Georgia Division of Mental Health: Developmental Disabilities & Addictive Diseases
2 Peachtree Street NW
22nd Floor
Atlanta, GA 30303
404-657-2252
Fax: 404-657-1137
http://www.dhr.state.ga.us

Karl H Schwarzkopf PhD, Director

The Division of MHDDAD serves people of all ages, and those with the most severe problems. The MHDDAD regional offices are the contact points for people needing treatment for mental illness or substance abuse problems, support services for people with mental retardation, or substance abuse prevention services.

828 Georgia Employees' Retirement System
2 Northside 75
Suite 300
Atlanta, GA 30318-7778
404-350-6300
800-805-4609
Fax: 404-350-6310
http://www.ersga.org

Michael J Nehf, Executive Director
Ray Higgins, Chief Operating Officer
Sheila Jenkins, Sr Director Benefits/Legislation

The mission of ERS is to be the guardian of the retirement systems it administers for the ultimate benefit of the members, retirees, beneficiaries of those systems. This mission is accomplished through ERS' core responsibilities which include pension administration; the collection, reconciliation and disbursement of contributions for the welfare of the members, retirees and beneficiaries of the plans; and the sound and secure investment of the retirement funds.

829 Georgia Office of Aging
Two Peachtree Street NW
Suite 9385
Atlanta, GA 30303-3142
404-657-5258
866-552-4464
Fax: 404-657-5285
http://www.aging.dhr.georgia.gov

Maria Greene, Executive Director

The Division of Aging Services (DAS) continuously seeks to improve the effectiveness and efficiency of services. We fully comply with the requirements of the Older Americans Act to ensure that services are properly and effectively adminstered to meet the needs of elderly Georgians.

830 Georgia State Board of Workers' Compansation
1 CNN Center NW
Suite 1000
Atlanta, GA 30303-2762
404-656-3875
800-533-0682
Fax: 404-651-9467

Stan Carter, Executive Director
Thomas M Risko, Chief Financial Officer

The State Board of Workers Compensation serves over a quarter of a million employers in Georgia and over 3,8 million workers. The State Board is funded by assessments from insurance companies and self-insured employers. An employee that is injured on the job and is covered by the law may be eligible for replacement of a portion of lost wages, medical payments, vocational rehabilitation services and other benefits.

831 Georgia Teachers Retirement System
2 Northside 75 NW
Suite 100
Atlanta, GA 30318-7778
404-352-6500
800-352-0650
Fax: 404-352-4885
http://www.trsga.com

Jeffrey L Ezell, Executive Director
Stephen J Boyers, Chief Financial Officer
R David McCleskey, Chief Operating Officer

TRS administers the fund from which teachers in the state's public schools, many employees of the University System of Georgia, and certain others designated employees in educational-related work environments receive retirement benefits.

832 Govenor's Council on Developmental Disabilities
2 Peachtree Street
Suite 26-240
Atlanta, GA 30303-3181
404-657-2126
888-275-4233
Fax: 404-657-2123
e-mail: info@gcdd.org
http://www.gcdd.org

Eric Jacobson, Executive Director

The mission of the Govenor's Council on Developmental Disabilities is to collaborate with Georgia citizens, public and private advocacy organizations, and policy makers to positively influence public policies that enhance the quality of life for people with developmental disabilities and their families. The Council provides collaboration through information and advocacy activities, program implementaion and funding, and public policy analysis.

833 Gwinnett Council for Seniors
186 E Pike St
Po Box 933
Lawrenceville, GA 30045
770-822-5147
Fax: 770-979-9370

Marie Goff, Manager

Seniors dedicated to helping other seniors in ways vital to seniors' benefit and welfare.

834 Heart of Georgia Altamaha AAA
331 W Parker Street
Baxley, GA 31513
912-367-3648
Fax: 912-367-3640
e-mail: heartoga@bellsouth.net
http://www.hogardc.com

Gail H Thompson, Director

The basic mission of the RDC is to provide professional advice and assistance to its member governments in the areas of comprehensive planning, community and economic development, historic preservation, local government and administration, and management, aging, and workforce investment

835 Heart of Georgia Area: Agency on Aging
PO Box 663
605 Daughtry Avenue
Mc Rae, GA 31055
229-868-5938
Fax: 229-868-6220

Robert F Williams, Director
Susan Yawn, Manager

Basic mission is to provide professional advice and assistance to its member governments in the areas of comprehensive planning, community and economic development, historic preservation, local government administration, and management, aging services, and workforce investment.

State Organizations & Government Agencies/Georgia

836 Helen Keller National Center for Deaf & Blind Southeast Regional Office
1003 Virginia Avenue
Suite 104
Atlanta, GA 30354-1366
404-766-9625
Fax: 404-766-3447
e-mail: MW4HKNC@aol.com
http://www.hknc.org

Joseph McNulty, Executive Director
Susan Lascek, Supervisor Regional Reps

HKNC regional reps provide consultation and technical assistance to people with deaf-blindness and their families, and to public and private education and adult service agencies in their region. They locate, assist, and refer individuals to the most appropriate programs for services, if needed.

837 Henry County Council on Aging
140 Henry Parkway
McDonough, GA 30253
770-288-6000
Fax: 770-954-2164
http://www.co.henry.ga.us

Jason Harper, Chairman
Warren Holder, District 1 Commissioner
Elizabeth Mathis, District 2 Commissioner

Provides services to seniors.

838 Legacy Link
PO Box 2534
Gainesville, GA 30503-2534
770-538-2650
800-845-5465
Fax: 770-538-2660
e-mail: pvfreeman@dhr.state.ga.us
http://www.legacylink.org

Pat Viles Freeman, Executive Director

Wide variety of services for seniors and persons with disabilities in 13-county region. Volunteer opportunities and employment training services available for 55 years and older. The information source for seniors, their families and others who care. Legacy Link is an Area Agency on Aging.

839 Middle Flint Regional Development Center Area: Agency on Aging
220 West Lamar Street
Americus, GA 31709
229-931-2909
Fax: 229-931-2745
e-mail: swalls@middleflintrdc.org
http://www.middleflintrdc.org

Don ten Bensel, Executive Director
Sarah Walls, Assistant Executive Director
Grace Howell, Executive Secretary

Regional Development Centers are multi-county planning and development agencies serving municipal and county governments in different areas of a state.

840 Middle Georgia Regional Development Center Area: Agency on Aging
175 Emery Highway
Suite C
Macon, GA 31217-3679
478-751-6160
Fax: 478-751-6517
e-mail: info@mgrdc.org
http://www.mgrdc.org

Ralph Nix, Executive Director
Sandi Glore, Office Manager

Regional Development Centers are multi-county planning and development agencies serving municipal and county governments in different areas of a state.

841 Northeast Georgia Area: Agency on Aging
305 Research Drive
Athens, GA 30605-2725
706-369-5650
Fax: 706-369-5792
e-mail: negrdc@negrdc.org
http://www.negrdc.org

Jim Dove, Executive Director
Carol Cofer, WIA Director

The Area Agency on Aging (AAA) contracts with counties, private organizations, senior centers, attorneys at law, and non-profit organizations to provide services to the elderly.

842 RSVP Albany County
309 Pine Avenue
Albany, GA 31701-2532
229-432-1131
800-282-6612
Fax: 229-438-0408
http://www.sowegacoa.org

Tina Strassenberg, Director

The Retired and Senior Volunteer Program (RSVP) provides opportunities for people 55 and over to make a difference in their community through volunteer service. RSVP volunteers contribute anywhere from a few to over forty hours a week, serving though schools, day care centers, police departments, hospitals and other nonprofit and public organizations to help meet critical community needs. RSVP offers maximum flexibility and choice to its volunteers. RSVP matches the personal interests and skills to older Americans with opportunities to help solve community problems and offer supplemental insurance while on duty, on-the-job training from the agency or organization where volunteers are placed.

843 RSVP Coosa Valley
3 Riverside Parkway
PO Box 5263
Rome, GA 30161-3042
706-291-6648
Fax: 706-235-2842
e-mail: debbiem@roman.net

Debbie Martin, Director

The Retired and Senior Volunteer Program (RSVP) provides opportunities for people 55 and over to make a difference in their community through volunteer service. RSVP volunteers contribute anywhere from a few to over forty hours a week, serving through schools, day care centers, police departments, hospitals and other nonprofit and public organizations to help meet critical community needs. RSVP offers maximum flexibility and choice to its volunteers. RSVP matches the personal interests and skills of older Americans with opportunities to help solve community problems and offers supplemental insurance while on duty, on-the-job training from the agency or organization where volunteers are placed. The following Counties are served: Bartow, Catoosa, Chattoga, Dade, Floyd, Gordon, Haralson, Paulding, Polk, Walker.

844 RSVP Northeast Georgia
135 Hoyt Street
Athens, GA 30601
706-549-4850
Fax: 706-549-7786
http://www.athenscommunitycouncilonaging.org

Kathryn Fowler, Executive Director

The Retired Senior Volunteer Program (RSVP) is part of Senior Corps, a network of national service programs that provides older Americans the opportunity to apply to their life experience to meeting community needs. RSVP volunteers serve in a diverse range of nonprofit organizations, public agencies, and faith-based groups. Among other activities, they mentor children, volunteer in hospitals, deliver meals to homebound elderly persons, assist atthe State Botanical Gardens, and lend their business skills to community groups that provide critical social services. The following Counties are served: Barrow, Clarke, Elbert, Greene, Jackson, Madison, Morgan, Oconee, Oglethorpe, Walton.

845 RSVP Savannah
618 W Anderson Street
PO Box 1353
Savannah, GA 31415-5420
912-234-7842
Fax: 912-238-2977
e-mail: rsvpfgp@earthlink.net

Debbie W Walker, Director

The Retired and Senior Volunteer Program (RSVP) helps seniors age 55 years and older put their skills and life experience to work for their communities. RSVP volunteers serve from a few hours to forty hours a week. RSVP volunteers meet critical community needs. The following Counties are served: Bacon, Bryan, Camden, Chatham, Effingham, Glynn, Liberty, Long, McIntosh, Pierce, Wayne.

846 Railroad Retirement Board: Georgia District Office
401 W Peachtree Street
Atlanta, GA 30308-3519
404-331-2841
Fax: 404-331-1629
e-mail: atlanta@rrb.gov
http://www.rrb.gov/field/do_atla.asp
Lyndon J Lang, Representative

847 Region 4: Administration on Aging (AoA)
US Department of Health & Human Services
Atlanta Federal Center
61 Forsyth Street SW, Suite 5M69
Atlanta, GA 30303-8909
404-562-7600
Fax: 404-562-7598
http://www.aoa.gov
Terry Powell, Administrative Officer

Region includes Alabama, Florida, Georgia, Kentucky, Mississippi, North Carolina, South Carolina, and Tennessee. Through this network, older persons in each community have access to supportive and nutrition services. Persons age 60 and over may participate, and priority is given to the elderly with greatest economic or social needs.

848 ResCare Home Care
3020 N Patterson Street
Valdosta, GA 31602-2797
229-244-8854
800-894-3715
Fax: 229-244-0979
http://www.rescarehomecare.com
Ellen Goldberg, Regional Director

Southern Home Care Services has provided professional nursing, personal care homemaking and respite services in the home, the hospitals, and long term care facilities. We are committed to providing the quality and attention that our clients deserve. Delivering service with compassion and respect is our goal.

849 Retired Affairs Office: Kings Bay Office
Fleet and Family Support Center
Naval Submarine Base (QL11)
1063 USS Tennessee Avenue
Kings Bay, GA 31547-2606
912-573-4718
Fax: 912-573-2042
http://www.subasekb.navy.mil/retiree.htm
Capt Michael McKinnon, Commanding Officer

The Kings Bay Retired Affairs Office is a central point for all military retirees to get information on issues that affect them. The RAO is designed to reseach questions, give reliable answers and refer personnel to appropriate service providers. It serves as a valuable link to help retirees and their family members obtain the rights, benefits, and privileges they are entitled to.

850 Social Security: Atlanta Disability Determination
2630 Martin Luther King Jr Drive SW
Suite A
Atlanta, GA 30311-1605
404-691-7460
http://www.ssa.gov/atlanta/southeast
Evan Lucas, Manager

851 Southeast Georgia Regional Development Center Area: Agency on Aging (SEGA)
1725 S Georgia Parkway E
Waycross, GA 31501
912-285-6097
Fax: 912-285-6126
http://www.segardc.org
Lace Futch, Executive Director
Lisa Cribb, Deputy Executive Director

Mission is to develop a comprehensive, coordinated system of services to promote the independence and continued well being of older residents.

852 Sowega Council on Aging: Georgia Division of Aging Services
1105 Palmyra Road
Albany, GA 31701-1933
229-432-1124
Fax: 229-483-0995
e-mail: info@sowegacoa.org
http://www.sowegacoa.org
Kay H Hind, Director

Plans, develops, and implements programs and activities that relate to or impact those people sixty years of age or older in southwest Georgia.

853 Walton County Senior Citizens Council
PO Box 764
Roswell, GA 30077
770-267-6589
Fax: 770-267-6540
Margie S Searcy, Executive Director

For individuals aged 60 and over. Provides services to the elderly so that they may live an independent life. Services include congregate meals, home delivered meals, transportation, continuing education, information and referral, recreation, and screening.

Hawaii

854 Assistive Technology Resource Centers of Hawaii
414 Kuwili Street
Suite 104
Honolulu, HI 96817
808-532-7110
800-645-3007
Fax: 808-532-7120
e-mail: atrc-info@atrc.org
http://www.atrc.org
Barbara Fischlowitz-Leong, Project Director

Provides information and referral to anyone interested in assistive technology devices and services. Operates eight equipment loan banks. Provides training to consumer and professional groups including self-advocacy skills for consumers and family members. Works to ensure that schools, vocational rehabilitation agencies and health insurers provide assessments, funding and training in the use of assistive technology devices and services for their clients. Low-interest loan programs available.

855 Bureau of Naval Personnel: Hawaii Retired Activities Office
Fleet and Family Support Center
850 Ticonderoga Street
Suite 300
Pearl Harbor, HI 96860-5100
808-473-4222
Fax: 808-471-4755
http://www.greatlifehawaii.com

Assistance is provided to retirees, their survivors and family members in obtaining their rights and benefits. The office also holds an Annual Retired Activities Seminar; and publishes a Retired Activities Biannual Newsletter.

856 Communications & Disabilities Action Board
919 Ala Moana Boulevard
Room 101
Honolulu, HI 96814-4920
808-586-8121
Fax: 808-586-8219
e-mail: dcab@doh.hawaii.gov
http://http://hawaii.gov/health/dcab
Francine Wai, Executive Director

857 Disability Determination Branch
PO Box 2458
Honolulu, HI 96804-2458
808-973-2244
Fax: 888-337-3910
e-mail: ann.look@ssa.gov
http://www.ssa.gov
Ann A Look, Professional Relations

State Organizations & Government Agencies/Hawaii

858 Hawaii County Office of Aging
101 Aupuni Street
Suite 342
Hilo, HI 96720-4262
808-961-8600
Fax: 808-961-8603
e-mail: hcoa@hcoahawaii.org
http://www.hawaii-country.com

Alan Parker, Director

Serves to represent the County of Hawaii in the planning, coordination, advocacy, and administration of programs for older persons in the county.

859 Hawaii Department of Adult Mental Health
1250 Punchbowl Street
Room 256
Honolulu, HI 96813
808-536-4686
Fax: 805-586-4745
http://www.hawaii.gov/health/mental-health

Dr. Nalene Andratti, Director
John Woods, Manager

Seeks to improve the mental health of Hawaii's people by reducing the prevalance of emotional disorders, and mental illness. Services include mental health education, treatment and rehabilitation through community-based mental health centers, and an in-patient state hospital facility for the mentally-ill, including those referred through courts and the criminal justice system.

860 Hawaii Department of Defense: Office of Veterans Services
459 Patterson Road
E-Wing Room 1-A103
Honolulu, HI 96819
808-433-0420
Fax: 808-433-0385
e-mail: ovs@ovs.hawaii.gov
http://www.dod.state.hi.us/ovs

Edward R Cruickshank, Director

Objectives are to assist veterans in obtaining State and federal entitlements, to supply the latest information on veterans' issues and to provide advice and support to veterans making the transition back into civilian life.

861 Hawaii Department of Health: Commission on Persons with Disabilities
919 Ala Moana Boulevard
Suite 101
Honolulu, HI 96814-4920
808-586-8121
Fax: 808-586-8129

Francine Wai, Executive Director

862 Hawaii Department of Health: Disability and Communication Access Board
919 Ala Moana Boulevard
Room 101
Honolulu, HI 96814-4920
808-586-8121
Fax: 808-586-8129
e-mail: dcab@doh.hawaii.gov
http://www.hawaii.gov/health/dcab
TDD 808-586-8130

Francine Wai, Executive Director

Provides information and referral on services for people with disabilities.

863 Hawaii Disability Compensation Division: Department of Labor and Indian Relations
830 Punchbowl Street
Room 211
Honolulu, HI 96813-5095
808-586-9174
Fax: 808-586-9219

Gary Hamada, Administrator

Administers Hawaii Workers Compensation and Temporary disability information programs prepaid health care.

864 Hawaii Disability Rights Center
900 Fort Street Mall
Suite 1040
Honolulu, HI 96813
808-949-2922
800-882-1057
Fax: 808-949-2928
e-mail: info@hawaiidisability.org
http://www.hawaiidisabilityrights.org

Harry Smith, President

HDRC is the designated Client Assist Program (CAP) and Protection and Advocacy (P&A) system for Hawaii's estimated 180,000 residents with disabilities. We strive to serve as many individuals with disabilities with as many different legal rights issues as our resources will allow.

865 Hawaii Executive Office on Aging
250 South Hotel Street
Suite 109
Honolulu, HI 96813-2831
808-586-0100
800-468-4644
Fax: 808-586-0185
e-mail: eoa@doh.hawaii.gov
http://www4.hawaii.gov/eoa

Marilyn R Seely, Director
Pat Sasaki, Manager

Mission of the Executive office on Aging (EOA) is to assure the well-being of the states 230,000 adults, age 60 and older.

866 Hawaii Planning Council on Developmental Disabilities
919 Ala Moana Boulevard
Room 101
Honolulu, HI 96814-4920
808-586-8121
Fax: 808-586-8129
e-mail: dcab@doh.hawaii.gov
http://www.hawaii.gov/health/dcab

Francine Wai, Executive Director

Consists of 25 Hawaii residents appointed by the Governor. The council addresses the needs of the people with developmental disabilities: specifically, develops a state plan that sets the priorities for persons with developmental disabilities.

867 Hawaii State Council on Developmental Disabilities
919 Ala Moana Boulevard
Suite 113
Honolulu, HI 96814
808-586-8100
Fax: 808-586-7543
e-mail: council@hiddc.org
http://www.hiddc.org

Waynette Cabral, Executive Administrator
Debbie Miyasaka-Gushiken, Community/Legislative Liason

The mission of the Council is to support with developmental disabilities to control their own destiny and determine the quality of life they desire.

868 Hawaii State Employees' Retirement System
201 Merchant Street
Suite 1400
Honolulu, HI 96813
808-586-1735
Fax: 808-587-5766
http://www4.hawaii.gov

David Shimabukuro, Administrator
Wesley Machida, Assistant Administrator

Public employees pension fund.

869 Honolulu County Elderly Affairs Division
Standard Finance Building
715 South King Street
Suite 200
Honolulu, HI 96813-3021
808-768-7705
Fax: 808-527-6895
e-mail: information@elderlyaffairs.com
http://www.elderlyaffairs.com
TDD 808-527-6300

Karen Miyake, County Executive

State Organizations & Government Agencies/Idaho

The Elderly Affairs Division (EAD) is an area agency on aging established by the Older Americans Act 1965. Serving Oahu, its mission is to develop systems of home and community-based services that assist older persons in leading independent, meaningful, and dignified lives.

870 Kauai County Office of Elderly Affairs
4444 Rice Street
Suite 330
Lihue, HI 96766-1386   808-281-4470
                          Fax: 808-241-5113
                   e-mail: coksvp@aloha.net
                      http://www.kauai.gov

Eleanor J Lloyd, Director

Purpose is to plan, support, and advocate for programs to promote the well-being of Kauai's older adults and to address and respond to the priority needs of all seniors.

871 Maui County Office on Aging: Department of Housing and Human Concerns
200 South High Street
9th Floor
Wailuku, HI 96793-2155   808-270-7755
                          Fax: 808-270-7870
          e-mail: mayors.office@mauicounty.gov
                    http://www.co.maui.hi.us

Charmaine M Tavaras, Director

An Area Agency on Aging under the madates of the Older Americans Act reauthorized in 2000.

872 RSVP Hawaii County
865 Piilani Street
Suite 101
Hilo, HI 96720   808-961-8730
                          Fax: 808-961-8709
                e-mail: rsvp@co.hawaii.hi.us
                http://www.hawaii-county.com

Patricia Engelhard, Director
Pamela Mizuno, Deputy Director

The Retired and Senior Volunteer Program (RSVP) provides opportunities for people 55 and over to make a difference in their community through volunteer service. RSVP volunteers contribute anywhere from a few to over forty hours a week, serving thourgh schools, day care centers, police departments, hospitals and other nonprofit and public organizations to help meet critical community needs. RSVP offers maximum flexibility and choice to its volunteers. RSVP matches the personal interests and skills to older Americans with opportunities to help solve community problems and offer supplemental insurance while on duty, on-the-job training from the agency or organization where volunteers are placed.

873 RSVP Kauai
4444 Rice Street
Suite 105
Lihue, HI 96766-1340   808-241-6412
                          Fax: 808-241-6409

RSVP provides volunteer opportunities for persons 55+ and older to remain as active, contributing members of the community through volunteer involvement.

874 RSVP Maui County
Kaunoa Senior Center
401 Alakapa Place
Paia, HI 96779-9736   808-270-7308
                          Fax: 808-270-8037
              e-mail: dana.acosta@co.maui.hi.is

Dana Acosta, Director

For the senior who is still too young to retire, RSVP allows the community to continue benefitting from the retired senior volunteer's expertise and services while providing opportunities for the senior volunteer to remain active in community life. Senior volunteers are matched with qualified agencies according to their interests or areas of expertise. The following Counties are served: Lanai, Maui, Molokai, Kalawao.

875 RSVP Oahu
600 Kapiolani Blvd.
Suite 305
Honolulu, HI 96819-2218   808-586-5191
                          Fax: 808-536-7237
                  e-mail: oahursvp@pixi.com

Marc Delorme, Director

The Retired and Senior Volunteer Program (RSVP) provides opportunities for people 55 and over to make a difference in their community through volunteer service. RSVP volunteers contribute anywhere from a few to over forty hours a week, serving through schools, day care centers, police departments, hospitals and other nonprofit and public organizations to help meet critical community needs. RSVP offers maximum flexibility and choice to its volunteers. RSVP matches the personal interests and skills of older Americans with opportunities to help solve community problems and offers supplemental insurance while on duty, on-the-job training from the agency or organization where volunteers are placed.

Idaho

876 Area Two: Agency on Aging
124 New 6th Street
Lewiston, ID 83501-2133   208-743-5580
                             800-877-3206
                          Fax: 208-746-5456
           e-mail: s.shrepshire@acommunityaction
                      http://www.caanid.org

Jenny Zorens, Director
Sabrina Shrapshire, Community Services Supervisor

Non Profit Social Service Agency

877 Caribou County Senior Citizens Center
60 S Main Street
Soda Springs, ID 83276-1426   208-547-3007

Ronda South, Executive Director

878 Disability Determination Services
1505 McKinney Street
Po Box 21
Boise, ID 83704-8533   208-327-7333
                             800-626-2681
                          Fax: 208-327-7331
              e-mail: rmadsen@labor.idaho.gov
                http://http://labor.idaho/gov

Roger Madsen, Director

879 Eastern Idaho Special Services Agency Area: Agency on Aging
357 Constitution Way
Idaho Falls, ID 83402   208-522-5391
                             800-632-4813
                          Fax: 208-522-5453
                    e-mail: choyt@eicap.org
                       http://www.eicao.org

Russell Spain, Director
James L Hall, Executive Director

An agency helping to empower all people in all communities to achieve maximum self-sufficiency and independence.

880 Homedale Senior Center
224 West Idaho
PO Box 848
Homedale, ID 83628   208-337-3020
                          Fax: 208-337-5065

Shirley McAbee, Director

Offers senior programs.

State Organizations & Government Agencies/Idaho

881 Idaho Commission On Aging
3380 Americana Terrace
Suite 120
Boise, ID 83706
208-334-3833
877-471-2777
Fax: 208-334-3033
e-mail: ktoryanski@aging.idaho.gov
http://www.idahoaging.com
Kim Wherry Toryanski, Adminstrator

882 Idaho Commission on Aging
3380 Americana Terrace
Suite 120
Boise, ID 83706-2500
208-334-3833
877-471-2777
Fax: 208-334-3033
e-mail: ktoryansi@aging.idaho.gov
http://www.idahoaging.com
Kim Wherry Toryanski, Administrator
Sarah Scott, Manager

The Idaho Commission on Aging (ICOA) is the sole state agency designated under the Older Americans Act to administer programs and services for Idahoans 60 years of age and older.

883 Idaho Council on Developmental Disabilities
802 W Bannock Street
Suite 308
Boise, ID 83702-5840
208-334-2178
800-544-2433
Fax: 208-334-3417
e-mail: info@icdd.idaho.gov
http://www.state.id.us/icdd
TDD 208-334-2179
Marilyn B Sword, Executive Director

The Council provides public education and awareness about developmental disabilities, promotes quality in-service supports for people with disabilities and their families; monitors and evaluates policies, plans and services provided by public agencies; encourages citizen participation in policymaking; and promotes innovative programs and projects through grants.

884 Idaho Developmental Disability Council
450 West State Street
9th Floor
Boise, ID 83720
208-334-0618
Fax: 208-334-3417
http://www.healthandwelfare.idaho.gov
Dick Schultz, Deputy Director

Mission is to protect and promote the health, welfare and safety of Idahoans.

885 Idaho Division Of Veterans Services
320 Collins Road
Boise, ID 83702
208-334-3513
Fax: 208-334-2627
http://www.veterans.idaho.gov
Dave Brasuell, Administrator

886 Idaho Industrial Commission
317 Main Street
Boise, ID 83702-7274
208-334-6000
Fax: 208-334-2321
e-mail: mgale@iic.idaho.gov
http://www.iic.idaho.gov
Regulates Idsho workers compensation. Offers rehabilitation to workers injured in idaho.

887 Idaho Mental Health Center
1720 Westgate Drive
Boise, ID 83704-7164
208-334-0800
800-600-6474
Fax: 208-334-0828
http://www.healthandwelfare.idaho.gov
Dr. Gary Payne, Director

888 Idaho Office on Aging
PO Box 1238
Twin Falls, ID 83303-1238
208-732-6221
800-680-0274
Fax: 208-736-2126
e-mail: info@csi.edu
http://www.csi.edu
Richard F Boyd, Director
Jim Fields, Executive Director

889 Idaho State Tax Commission
800 Park Boulevard Plaza
Boise, ID 83722
208-334-7660
800-972-7660
http://http://tax.idaho.gov
Mission is to provide courteous, quality services and to administer the state's tax laws in a fair, timely, and cost effective manner to benefit Idaho and its citizens.

890 North Idaho College Area: Agency on Aging
1221 Ironwood Drive
Suite 102
Coeur d'Alene, ID 83814
208-667-3179
800-786-5536
Fax: 208-667-5938
e-mail: infoassist@agingadultsvcs.org
http://www.aaani.org
Pearl Bouchard, AAS Director
Bobbie Sailor, Assistant Director

Dedicated to protection, independence and dignity of individuals through advocacy and service.

891 RSVP Lewiston
1424 Main Street
PO Box 1585
Lewiston, ID 83501-1907
208-746-7787
Fax: 208-743-9573
e-mail: rsvp@lewiston.com
Eva Mathewson, Director
Barbara Bush, Executive Director

Most of our senior volunteers are involved with recycling, including four who haul recycle materials to drop points. We have several who beautify and educate as Master Gardeners and others who work to keep the public flower beds maintained in a small town. We have volunteers involved and educating at local museums, our county extension agency, and working for Habitat for Humanity. The following Counties are served: Clearwater, Idaho, Latah, Lewis, Nez Perce.

892 RSVP Magic Valley
315 Falls Avenue
PO Box 1238
Twin Falls, ID 83303
208-736-2122
Fax: 208-736-2126
e-mail: ooarsvp@micron.net
http://http://officeonaging.csi.edu/rsvp
Jim Fields, Director

The Retired adn Senior Volunteer Program (RSVP) invites adults age 55 and over to use their life experience and job-related skills to answer the call of their neighbors in need. Giving anywhere from a few to over forty hours per week, RSVP volunteers help solve serious problems in their communities.

893 RSVP North Idaho
1221 Ironwood Drive
Suite 102
Coeur d'Alene, ID 83814-1402
208-667-3179
800-786-5536
Fax: 208-667-5938
e-mail: rsvp@agingadultsvcs.org

The Retired and Senior Volunteer Program (RSVP) provides opportunities for people 55 and over to make a difference in their community through volunteer service. RSVP volunteers contribute anywhere from a few to over forty hours a week, serving through schools, day care centers, police departments, hospitals and other nonprofit and public organizations to help meet critical community needs. RSVP offers maximum flexibility and choice to its volunteers. RSVP matches the personal interests and skills of older Americans with opportunities to help solve community problems and offers supplemental insurance while on duty, on-the-job training from the agency or organization where volunteers are placed. The following Counties are being served: Benewah, Bonner, Boundary, Kootenai, Shoshone.

894 **RSVP Treasure Valley**
1607 W Jefferson Street
Boise, ID 83702-5111
208-345-4357
Fax: 208-336-0880
Sharlene Brown, Project Director

Retired and Senior Volunteer Program invites adults age 55 and over to use their life experience and skills to answer the call of their neighbors in need.

895 **Rimrock Senior Center**
525 Main Street
PO Box 453
Grand View, ID 83624
208-834-2808
Fax: 208-834-2808
e-mail: kemond@sageidaho.com
Carolyn Larson, Coordinator

Supports and promotes the interests of local senior citizens.

896 **Sage Community Resources**
125 E 50th St
Garden City, ID 83714
208-322-7033
800-859-0324
Fax: 208-322-3569
http://www.sageidaho.com
Kathy Simko, President
Wendy Alloway, Executive Assistant

897 **Southeast Idaho Council of Governments: Area Agency on Aging**
214 E Center
Po Box 6079
Pocatello, ID 83205
208-233-4032
800-526-8129
Fax: 208-233-4841
Robert Perky, Executive Director

Illinois

898 **Adams County RSVP**
1301 South 48th Street
Quincy, IL 62305
217-641-4961
Fax: 217-641-4900
e-mail: gosney@jwcc.edu
Sarah Bonness, Director

The purpose of Retired and Senior Volunteer Program (RSVP) is to provide a variety of opportunities for retired persons age 55 or older to participate more fully in the life of their community through significant volunteer service.

899 **American Association of Retired Persons: Midwest Region Office**
1750 W Bryn Mawr Avenue
Suite 600
Chicago, IL 60631-3548
773-714-9800
Fax: 773-714-9927
http://www.aarp.org
TTY 916-446-2680
Judy Comstock, Director

A resource for AARP members in the states of Illinois, Indiana, Iowa, Michigan, Minnesota, Nebraska, North Dakota, Ohio, South Dakota, and Wisconsin. Hours 9-5, Monday through Friday.

900 **Area Agency on Aging for Lincolnland**
3100 Montvale Drive
Suite C
Springfield, IL 62704
217-787-9234
800-252-2918
Fax: 217-787-6290
e-mail: info@aginglinc.org
http://www.aginglinc.org
Julie Hubbard, Executive Director

The Area Agency on Aging for Lincolnland is dedicated to helping older adults maintain dignity, health, and independence. Many services and programs are offered to support older adults and family caregivers in a twelve county area.

901 **Attorney General's Office: Disability Rights Bureau**
100 W Randolph Street
Chicago, IL 60601-3218
312-814-3000
800-964-3013
Fax: 312-814-1656
http://www.ag.state.il.us
Lisa Madigan, Attorney General

Information on Illinois' Comprehensive Health Insurance Plan and architectural accessibility. Enforcement of Illinois' access law and standards. Information on initiatives such as: 'Opening the Courthouse Doors to People with Disabilities;' accessing effective communication in a medical setting and addressing the abuse, neglect or financial exploitation of people with disabilities. Other information and referrals.

902 **Bureau of Naval Personnel: Illinois Retired Activities Office**
Fleet and Family Support Center
Naval Training Center, Building 42, Room 118
2601A Paul Jones Street
Great Lakes, IL 60088-5125
847-688-3603
888-231-0714
Fax: 847-688-2827

The RAO serves as a link between local retired military and the active-duty community which provides assistance to retired military. It provides installation commanders with a means of providing more effective services and improving communication for the local retired community. The RAO is staffed and operated by volunteer retired military who assist other retired members, their families and survivors to receive entitled services and benefits. Through newsletters and seminars and appreciation days, the RAO supports quality of life issues throughout the retirement years to their fellow service members.

903 **Central Illinois Agency on Aging (CIAA)**
700 Hamilton Boulevard
Peoria, IL 61603-3617
309-674-2071
Fax: 309-674-3639
e-mail: anita@ciaoa.com
http://www.ciaoa.com
TDD 309-674-1831
Joanne Thomas, Director

CIAA is a private not-for-profit agency that focuses its services on adults age 60 or older who live in Fulton, Marshall, Peoria, Stark, Tazewell and Woodford Counties. CIAA assists older adults by: Advocating on their behalf; Coordinating services to make them easy to find and use; Developing programs to serve the older population; Funding other local agencies to provide for important needs.

904 **Charleston Area Senior Center**
720 6th Street
Charleston, IL 61920-2147
217-348-8410
Fax: 217-345-1194
Marilyn Strangeman, Manager

Recruits persons age 55 and over to volunteer within non profit agencies and organizations within Coles County IL.

State Organizations & Government Agencies/Illinois

905 **Chicago Department of Senior Services**
30 N Lasalle
Suite 2320
Chicago, IL 60602 312-744-5770
Fax: 312-744-6777
e-mail: seniorservices@cityofchicago.org
TDD 312-744-6777
Joyce Gallagher, Commissioner

906 **Coles County Council on Aging**
204 S 21st Street
Mattoon, IL 61938-3897 217-234-3311
Fax: 217-234-3410
e-mail: lifespancenter@yahoo.com
http://www.colescouncilonaging.org
Dee Braden, Executive Director
Marylin Strangeman, Administrative Assistant

The mission of the Coles County Council on Aging is to enhance quality of life by promoting independence, dignity, self-fulfillment and health for older adults in Coles County through advocacy, education and provision of appropriate community-based services.

907 **Coles County Telecare**
Coles County Council on Aging
204 S 21st Street
Mattoon, IL 61938-3869 217-234-3311
Fax: 217-234-3410
e-mail: lifespancenter@yahoo.com
http://www.colescouncilonaging.org
Dee Braden, Executive Director
Marilyn Strangeman, Administrative Assistant

Senior infromation and assistance Assist with filling out forms, giving information and reffering to other agencies.

908 **Community Health Charities of Illinois**
307 North Michigan Avenue
Suite 800
Chicago, IL 60601 312-360-0382
800-299-6842
Fax: 312-360-0388
e-mail: info@healthcharities.org
http://www.healthcharitiesillinois.org
Barbara Boden, President/CEO
Laurence Kaufman, VP Institutional Development

The mission of Community Health Charities is to provide every employee the opportunity to support medical research, health education and patient services through charitable giving in the workplace. Our goal is to advise employers and individuals the convenience of 'one-stop' health support, but with the ability to direct donations to the specific member health charities that you want to support. Contributions are used for research, patient services, and education.

909 **Dial-A-Ride Rural Public Transportation**
204 S 21st Street
Mattoon, IL 61938-3869 217-234-3311
800-500-5505
Fax: 217-234-3410
e-mail: lifespancenter@yahoo.com
http://www.colescouncilonaging.org
Dee Braden, Executive Director
Marilyn Strangeman, Administrative Assistant

Provides transportation not only to older adults, but also to persons with disabilities and all age groups of the general public. The program, which currently owns eleven wheelchair accessible buses, offers Coles County residents access to community resources while promoting independence and mobility.

910 **East Central Illinois Area: Agency on Aging**
1003 Maple Hill Road
Bloomington, IL 61704-9327 309-829-2065
800-888-4456
Fax: 309-829-2065
e-mail: aginginfo@eciaaa.org
http://www.eciaaa.org
Mike O'Donnell, Executive Director
Susan H Redman, Deputy Director

A non-profit organization authorized to plan and administer services to enable older adults to live in their homes with dignity and safety as long as possible with appropriate supportive services, prevent unnecessary institutionalization and uphold their rights.

911 **Egyptian Area: Agency on Aging**
200 E Plaza Drive
Carterville, IL 62918-1982 618-985-8311
888-895-3306
Fax: 618-985-8315
e-mail: egyptianaaa@midamer.net
http://www.egyptianaaa.org
John M Smith, Executive Director

As Area Agencies in Illiois it is our mission to promote the well-being of senior adults and assisting them in maintaining their independence in the community.

912 **Equip for Equality Central/Southern Illinois**
235 South Fifth Street
PO Box 276
Springfield, IL 62705 217-544-0464
800-758-0464
Fax: 217-523-0720
e-mail: contactus@equipforequality.org
http://www.equipforequality.org
TTY 800-610-2779
Zena Naiditch, President/CEO
Marsha D Koelliker, Director Public Policy

The mission of Equip for Equality is to advance the human and civil rights of children and adults with physical and mental disabilities in Illinois. It is the only statewide, cross-disability, comprehensive advocacy organization providing self-advocacy assistance, legal services, and disability rights education while also engaging in public policy and legislative advocacy and conducting abuse investigations and other oversight activities.

913 **Equip for Equality Northeastern Region**
20 North Michigan Avenue
Suite 300
Chicago, IL 60602 312-341-0022
800-537-2632
Fax: 312-341-0295
e-mail: contactus@equipforequality.org
http://www.equipforequality.org
TTY 800-610-2779
Zena Naiditch, President/CEO
Marsha D Koelliker, Director Public Policy

The mission of Equip for Equality is to advance the human and civil rights of children and adults with physical and mental disabilities in Illinois. It is the only statewide, cross-disability, comprehensive advocacy organization providing self-advocacy assistance, legal services, and disability rights education while also engaging in public policy and legislative advocacy and conducting abuse investigations and other oversight activities.

914 **Equip for Equality Northwestern Region**
1617 Second Avenue
Suite 210
Rock Island, IL 61204 309-786-6868
800-758-6869
Fax: 309-786-2393
e-mail: contactus@equipforequality.org
http://www.equipforequality.org
TTY 800-610-2779
Zena Naiditch, President/CEO
Marsha D Koelliker, Director Public Policy

The mission of Equip for Equality is to advance the human and civil rights of children and adults with physical and mental disabilities in Illinois. It is the only statewide, cross-disability, comprehensive advocacy organization providing self-advocacy assistance, legal services, and disability rights education while also engaging in public policy and legislative advocacy and conducting abuse investigations and other oversight activities.

State Organizations & Government Agencies/Illinois

915 Family Caregiver Resource Center
Coles County Council on Aging
204 S 21st Street
Mattoon, IL 61938-3869
217-234-3311
Fax: 217-234-3410
e-mail: lifespancenter@yahoo.com
http://www.colescouncilonaging.org
Dee Braden, Executive Director
Marilyn Strangeman, Administrative Assistant

Provides information and support to persons caring for individuals over sixty years of age, and grandparents raising grandchildren, through counseling services, support groups, training workshops, literature and other resources.

916 Homemaker Program
Coles County Council on Aging
204 S 21st Street
Mattoon, IL 61938-3869
217-234-3311
Fax: 217-234-3410
e-mail: lifespancenter@yahool.com
http://www.colescouncilonaging.org
Dee Braden, Executive Director
Marilyn Strangeman, Administrative Assistant

Provides a variety of personal assistance services to eligible individuals. These services include housekeeping, errands, respite, laundry, meal preparation, personal care tasks, and home budgeting and money management. Through the provision of these services older adults are enabled to remain in their homes safely, and prevent or postpone unnecessary or premature institutionalization.

917 Illinios Department of Revenue
101 W Jefferson Street
Springfield, IL 62702-5145
217-782-3128
http://www.revenue.state.il.us
Geraldine Conrad, Manager

918 Illinois Assistive Technology Project
1 West Old State Capitol Plaza
Suite 100
Springfield, IL 62701-1224
217-522-7985
800-852-5110
Fax: 217-522-8067
e-mail: wgunther@iltech.org
http://www.iltech.org
TTY 217-522-9966
Wilhelmina Gunther, Executive Director
Sue Castles, Loan Program Coordinator

Directed by and for people with disabilities and their family members. As a federally mandated program, IATP strives to break down barriers and change policies that make getting and using technology difficult. IATP offers solutions to help people find what is available in products and services that will best meet their needs, where to find it, and how to get it.

919 Illinois Client Assistance Program (CAP)
100 N First Street
1st Floor West
Springfield, IL 62702
217-782-5374
800-641-3929
e-mail: dhscap@dhs.state.il.us
http://www.dhs.state.il.us/ors/cap
Cynthia Grothaus, Manager

Client Assist Programs (CAPs) provide information and assistance to individuals seeking or receiving vocational rehabilitation services under the Rehabilitation Act, including assistance in pursuing administrative, legal, and other appropriate remedies.

920 Illinois Council on Developmental Disability
100 W Randolph Street
Suite 10-600
Chicago, IL 60601
312-814-2080
Fax: 312-814-7441
e-mail: sromano@mail.state.il.us
http://www.state.il.us/agency/icdd
TTY 888-261-2717
Sheila T Romano EdD, Executive Director
Sandy Thurston Ryan, Director Program/Planning

ICDD is responsible for investing in new programs to improve the delivery of services and supports to individuals with developmental disabilities and their families in Illinois. The Council focuses on education, employment, transportation, community living, health care and other areas so that people with developmental disabilities can enjoy their lives to the fullest extent possible. Just as importantly, ICDD works to build the capabilities of individuals, families and communities, enabling each to become more self-sufficient through the Developmental Disabilities Assistance and Bill of Rights Act (DD Act).

921 Illinois Department of Human Services: Office of Rehabilitation Services
PO Box 19429
Springfield, IL 62794-9429
217-782-2000
800-843-6154
Fax: 217-785-5753
e-mail: dhs.ors@illinois.gov
http://www.dhs.state.il.us

Mission is to assist our customers to achieve maximum self-sufficiency, independence and health through the provision of seamless, integrated services for individuals, families and communities.

922 Illinois Department of Mental Health and Developmental Disabilities
401 Stratton Office
Springfield, IL 62765
217-782-2000
Fax: 217-524-0835
http://www.dhs.state.il.us
Jess McDonald, Director

923 Illinois Department of Rehabilitation Services
PO Box 19250
Springfield, IL 62794-9250
217-782-2000
800-843-6154
Fax: 217-785-1574
http://www.dhs.state.il.us
Dorothy Homeier, Chief Program Services

The state's lead agency serving individuals with disabilities. DRS works in partnership with people with disabilities and their families to assist them in making informed choices to achieve full community participation through employment, education, and independent living opportunities.

924 Illinois Department of Veterans Affairs
833 South Spring Street
Po Box 19432
Springfield, IL 62794-9432
217-782-6641
800-437-9824
Fax: 217-524-0344
http://www.state.il.us/agency/dva
Tammy Duckworth, Director
Sergio Estrada Jr, Assistant Director

Mission is to assist veterans and their dependents and survivors in obtaining the benefits they are entitled to under the laws of the United States, and the State of Illinois, or any other governmental agency

State Organizations & Government Agencies/Illinois

925 Illinois Department on Aging
421 East Capitol Avenue
Suite 100
Springfield, IL 62701-1789
217-785-3356
Fax: 217-785-4477
e-mail: ilsenior@aging.state.il.us
http://www.state.il.us/aging
TDD 800-252-8966

Charles D Johnson, Director
Michael Gelder, Deputy Director
Nikki Smith PhD, Director Communications/Outreach

Serves and advocates for older Illinoisans and their caregivers by administering programs and promoting partnerships that encourage independence, dignity and quality of life.

926 Illinois Workers Compensation Board
100 W Randolph Street
Suite 8-200
Chicago, IL 60601-3227
312-814-6500
Fax: 312-814-6523
http://www.iwcc.il.gov/boards

John Hallock Jr, Director

Board assists the IWCC in formulating policies, setting priorities, and developing administrative goals.

927 Life Services Network of Illinois: Springfield
2 Lawrence Square
Springfield, IL 62704-2581
217-789-1677
Fax: 217-789-1778
e-mail: info@lsni.org
http://www.lsni.org

Dennis R Bozzi, President
Tess Kwiatkowski, Executive Vice President
Kirk Riva, VP Public Policy

Life Services Network of Illinois (LSN), a statewide trade association, has represented providers of the complete continuum of services for older adults, including nursing facilities, assisted living, senior housing and home and community based services. Our success as an association is founded in our commitment to helping our members overcome obstacles while identifying future opportunities for their success. This philosophy is what makes LSN and our members unique and successful.

928 Lifescape Community Services
705 Kilburn Avenue
Rockford, IL 61101-6537
815-963-1609
800-779-1189
Fax: 815-963-1627
e-mail: marketing@lifescapeservices.com
http://www.lifescapeservices.com

Carol Green, Executive Director

To promote independent living and enhance the quality of life for individuals by providing affordable nutrition and other services, with an emphasis on the aging population.

929 Little Brothers: Friends of the Elderly
28 E Jackson Blvd
Suite 405
Chicago, IL 60604
312-786-1032
Fax: 312-786-1067
e-mail: mcolleran.net@littlebrothers.org
http://www.littlebrothers.org

Mary Colleran, Development Director
Liz Drew, National Executive Director

Provides companionship and special assistance to low-income individuals over 70 years of age.

930 Mattoon Area Senior Center: Coles Council on Aging
204 S 21st Street
Mattoon, IL 61938-3869
217-234-3311
Fax: 217-234-3410
e-mail: lifespancenter@yahoo.com
http://www.colescouncilonaging.org

Dee Braden, Executive Director

The senior centers provide area older adults not only a place to meet, share and learn from others, but also opportunities to grow, develop and achieve. The centers also are a source for information. A wide variety of recreational and educational programs are routinely offered at the two senior centers. Both centers also serve as congregate meal sites for EIU's Peace Meal program.

931 Midland Area: Agency on Aging
PO Box 1420
434 S. Poplar St
Centralia, IL 62801-9121
618-532-1853
Fax: 618-532-5259
http://www.midlandaaa.org

Deborah Kuiken, Executive Director

932 Northeastern Illinois Area: Agency on Aging
PO Box 809
Kankakee, IL 60901
815-939-0727
800-528-2000
Fax: 815-939-0022
e-mail: info@ageguide.org
http://http://ageguide.org

Charles Johnson, Director
Lucia West Jones, Executive Director

A not-for-profit agency that plans and coordinates a comprehensive network of services for persons 60+ in the fastest growing areas in the State.

933 Northwestern Illinois Area: Agency on Aging
2576 Charles Street
Rockford, IL 61108-1652
815-226-4901
800-542-8402
Fax: 815-226-8984
e-mail: niaaa@nwilaaa.org
http://www.nwilaaa.org

Janet Ellis, Director

Area agency on aging serving nine counties of northwestern Illinois.

934 Oasis Logan County Senior Center
501 Pulaski Street
Lincoln, IL 62656-2705
217-732-6132
Fax: 217-732-5844

Dominic Dalapaos, Director

Individuals of age 55 and over in Logan County, IL. Provides socialization, education, and health services for senior citizens.

935 RSVP Champaign
Stevick Senior Center
48 E Main Street
Champaign, IL 61820-3630
217-359-6500
Fax: 217-359-6550

John Hosteny, Director

Anyone age 55 or over can choose from over 180 Retired Senior Volunteer Program stations to contribute his/her time, skills or professional services to the community. For those who volunteer, RSVP offers mileage and meal reimbursement if needed, insurance, placement assistance and well-deserved recognition.

936 RSVP Decatur
788 E Clay Street
Decatur, IL 62521-2613
217-428-6616
Fax: 217-428-7256
e-mail: lbaker@doveinc.org

Lore Baker, Director

State Organizations & Government Agencies/Illinois

The Retired and Senior Volunteer Program (RSVP) provides opportunities for people 55 and over to make a difference in their community through volunteer service. RSVP volunteers contribute anywhere from a few to over forty hours a week, serving through schools, day care centers, police departments, hospitals and other nonprofit and public organizations to help meet critical community needs. RSVP offers maximum flexibility and choice to its volunteers. RSVP matches the personal interests and skills of older Americans with opportunities to help solve community problems and offers supplemental insurance while on duty, on-the-job training from the agency or organization where volunteers are placed. The following County is served: Macon.

937 RSVP Joliet
203 N Ottawa Street
Joliet, IL 60432-4006
815-723-3405
Fax: 815-723-3452
e-mail: stthomas@cidov.org
http://www.cc-doj.org

Sr Ellen Thomas, Director
Kathy McGowan, Executive Director

Helping people age 55 and older find volunteer opportunities in their home and communities by matching their personal interests and experience with the needs of an organization. The following Counties are served: Cook, Dupage, Ford, Grundy, Kendall, Kankakee, Iroquois, Will.

938 RSVP Kane McHenry Counties
3519N Richmond Road
Johnsburg, IL 60051
815-344-3555
Fax: 815-344-3593
e-mail: ddanitz@seniorservicesassoc.org

Deborah Danitz, RSVP Director
Rita Bouldin, Manager

RSVP engages people age 55 and older in a diverse range of volunteer activities including food pantries, transporting homebound seniors, and delivering meals.

939 RSVP Lake County
106 S Sheridan Road
Waukegan, IL 60085-5610
847-249-4330
Fax: 847-249-4393

Janet Crane, Director

The Retired and Senior Volunteer Program (RSVP) provides opportunities for people 55 and over to make a difference in their community through volunteer service. RSVP volunteers contribute anywhere from a few to over forty hours a week, serving through schools, day care centers, police departments, hospitals and other nonprofit and public organizations to help meet critical community needs. RSVP offers maximum flexibility and choice to its volunteers. RSVP matches the personal interests and skills of older Americans with opportunities to help solve community problems and offers supplemental insurance while on duty, on-the-job training from the agency or organization where volunteers are placed. The following County is served: Lake.

940 RSVP Maple Lawn
700 N Main Street
Eureka, IL 61530-1085
309-467-2337
Fax: 309-467-9097
e-mail: beth@maple_lawn.com
http://www.maple-lawn.com

Marj Bachman, Mission Outreach Director

The program is relatively new. Currently, our volunteers are working on doing repairs and weatherizing the homes of elderly and disabled people in our community. The following Counties are served: Livingston, Marshall, Woodford.

941 RSVP Peoria/Tazewell Counties
3100 N Knoxville Avenue
Suite 15
Peoria, IL 61603-1038
309-682-8521
Fax: 309-682-8524
e-mail: rsvp@rsvpvolunteers.org
http://www.rsvpvolunteers.org

Jan Sweikert, Director

The Retired and Senior Volunteer Program (RSVP) provides opportunities for people 55 and over to make a difference in their community through volunteer service. RSVP volunteers contribute anywhere from a few to over forty hours a week, serving though schools, day care centers, police departments, hospitals and other nonprofit and public organizations to help meet critical community needs. RSVP offers maximum flexibility and choice to its volunteers. RSVP matches the personal interests and skills to older Americans with opportunities to help solve community problems and offer supplemental insurance while on duty, on-the-job training from the agency or organization where volunteers are placed.

942 RSVP Program CEFA Economic Opportunity Corporation
1805 S Banker Street
PO Box 928
Effingham, IL 62401-0928
217-342-2193
Fax: 217-342-4701
e-mail: rschneiderjon@effingham.net
http://www.cefseoc.org/rsvp

Paul White, Chief Executive Officer

Offers persons of retirement age the opportunities to participate more fully in their communities through many forms of volunteer services and productive work.

943 RSVP Rock Island
729 34th Avenue
Rock Island, IL 61201-5950
309-793-4425
Fax: 309-793-6807
e-mail: shartung@wiaaa.org
http://www.wiaaa.org/rsvp

Suzanne Hartung, Director

RSVP recruits, orients and places senior volunteers (age 55 and older) in public and not-for-profit programs and agencies. RSVP staff has an established record of matching the needs of nonprofit organizations with volunteers who can help. Over 109 not-for-profit community organizations and governmental entities submit job descriptions to RSVP staff, who then recruit, interview and match volunteers to the specific job requests. The following Counties are served: Bureau, Henderson, Henry, Know, LaSalle, McDonough, Mercer, Putnam, Rock Island, Warren.

944 RSVP Triton College Volunteer Program
2000 Fifth Avenue
River Grove, IL 60171-1907
708-456-0300
Fax: 708-583-3778
e-mail: kderesinn@triton.cc.il.us
http://www.triton.cc.il.us

Patricia Granados, EdD, President
Katherine Deresinski, Program Director

RSVP (Triton College Volunteer Program) is a unique nationwide volunteer program sponsored locally by Triton College. It offers active adults the opportunity to use their talents and experience in service to the community. Public and nonprofit organizations urgently need people who are willing to share their interests and skills with others. RSVP members are able to serve on a monthly or weekly basis. You may be able to serve in one or more ongoing efforts. The number of hours you serve is flexible (the average is one to four hours a week). These hours make a big difference to those you help.

State Organizations & Government Agencies/Illinois

945 RSVP YWCA Senior Services
905 N Main Street
Normal, IL 61761-1590
309-454-1451
Fax: 309-454-1454
http://www.ywca.org

Tarry Plattner, Director
Sandy Holcomb, Assistant Director

YWCA-RSVP helps individuals age 55 and older put their skills and life experiences to work for their community. RSVP facilitates senior volunteerism through carefully matched placement and follow-up support.

946 Rachel's Place Adult Day Care
309 West Park
Aurora, IL 60506
630-896-9022

Adult day service provides a protective and stimulating environment for older adults who are in need of daytime supervision. The elderly profit from the array of services offered, while their caregivers receive respite from the pressures and demands of caring for an elderly relative or friend. Participants benefit from a structured environment, companionship, nutritious meals and a variety of activities under the supervision of professional staff.

947 Railroad Retirement Board: Chicago District Office
844 N Rush Street
9th Floor
Chicago, IL 60611-2092
312-751-4500
Fax: 312-751-7136
e-mail: chicago@rrb.gov
http://www.rrb.gov

Robert J Eggart, Representative

An independent agency in the executive branch of the Federal Government. The primary function is to administer comprehensive retirement-survivor and unemployment sickness benefit programs for the nation's railroad workers and their families

948 Railroad Retirement Board: Decatur District Office
132 S Water Street
Suite 517
Decatur, IL 62523-1397
217-423-9747
Fax: 217-423-7872
e-mail: decatur@rrb.gov
http://www.rrb.gov

James L McFadden, Representative

An independent agency in the executive branch of the Federal Government. Its primary function is to administer comprehensive retirement-survivor and unemployment sickness benefit programs for the nation's railroad workers and their families.

949 Railroad Retirement Board: Joliet District Office
PO Box 457
63 West Jefferson Street
Joliet, IL 60434
815-740-2101
Fax: 815-740-2139
e-mail: joliet@rrb.gov
http://www.rrb.gov

Rachel Veerman, Contact Representative
Rosemary K Cupples, Contact Representative

Federal agency administering the RR Retirement Act N,E, ILL suburbs.

950 Railroad Retirement Board: Survivor Division
Bureau of Survivor Benefits
844 N Rush Street
Room 1100
Chicago, IL 60611-1275
312-787-3923
http://www.rrb.gov

Provides assistance to widows of railroad workers.

951 Region 5: Administration on Aging (AoA)
US Department of Health & Human Services
233 N Michigan Avenue
Room 790
Chicago, IL 60601-5519
312-353-3141
Fax: 312-886-8533
http://www.aoa.gov

Larry Brewster, Regional Administrator
Fran Wersells, Aging Program Specialist
Robert Demsch, Program Assistant

Region includes Illinois, Indiana, Michigan, Minnesota, Ohio, and Wisconsin.

952 Retired & Senior Volunteer Program of Hull House Chicago
1030 W Van Buren
Chicago, IL 60607
312-906-8600
800-448-0083
Fax: 312-235-5287
e-mail: bbarr@hullhouse.org
http://www.hullhouse.org

Clarence N Wood, President/CEO
Mischelle Causey-Drake, Chief Operations Officer
Andrew Abrahms, Chief Development Officer

Volunteers serve as tutors and mentors, friendly visitors, clerical assistants, receptionists, nutrition aides, patient care workers, volunteer pharmacist, museum guides, and telephone operators.

953 Retired & Senior Volunteer Program of Northern DuPage Counties
2121 S Goebbert Road
Arlington Hights, IL 60005-1814
847-228-1320
Fax: 847-228-1327
e-mail: rsvp@volunteerinfo.net
http://www.volunteerinfo.net

Mary Fitzgibbons, Executive Director

Help people age 55 and over find volunteer opportunities in their community. We match skills and interests for meaningful assignments.

954 Senior Community Service Employment Program (Title V)
PO Box 298
Karnak, IL 62956-0298
618-634-2201
Fax: 618-634-9551

Cheryl Vanderford, Executive Director

955 Senior Services of Central Illinois
701 W Mason Street
Springfield, IL 62702-2498
217-528-4035
Fax: 217-528-9322
e-mail: kschainker@ssoci.org
http://www.ssoci.org

Karen Schainker, Executive Director
Angela M Oliver, Development Director

Specializes in non-medical services to individuals age 60+ nutrition, transportation, counseling, information, elder abuse/crime support, volunteer opportunities, and programs/activities, which prevent premature institutionalization. The following Counties are served: Logan, Mason, Menard, Sangamon.

956 Seniors Action Service Caring Home Aid Program
1114 Church Street
Evanston, IL 60201
847-864-7274
Fax: 847-864-7295
http://www.seniorsactionservice.org

Nancy L Anderson, Executive Director

Places companions and homemakers in homes of elderly and infirm people. Also offers training for caregivers through the Senior Care Careers program.

State Organizations & Government Agencies/Indiana

957 **Shawnee Development Council**
530 West Washington Street
PO Box 298
Karnak, IL 62956-0298
618-634-2201
800-526-0844
Fax: 618-634-9551
e-mail: sdcinc@shawneedevelopment.org
Cheryl Vanderford, Executive Director

Provides a variety of volunteer opportunities for retired persons aged 55 and older to participate more fully in the life of their community through significant volunteer service. The program encourages older adults to remain active by utilizing their skills, experience and talents to the benefit of others.

958 **Social Security Springfield Disability Determination**
PO Box 19250
Springfield, IL 62794-9429
217-785-0218
800-225-3607
http://www.ssa.gov/chicago/dds.htm
TTY 217-782-5734
Ann P Robert, Deputy Director

The Social Security Disability program provides benefits to persons with severe disabilities whose impairments prevent them form performing gainful work.

959 **Southeastern Illinois Area Agency on Aging**
516 Market Street
Mount Carmel, IL 52863-1558
612-262-2306
800-635-8544
Fax: 618-262-4967
e-mail: sciaoa@verizon.net
http://www.state.il.us/aging
Yvonne Hutchings, Executive Director

Our mission is to serve and advocate for older Illinoisans and their caregivers by administering programs and promoting partnerships that encourage independence, dignity, and quality of life. Counties served: Crawford, Edwards, Hamilton, Jasper, Lawrence, Richland, Wabash, Wayne, and White.

960 **Southwestern Illinois Area Agency on Aging**
2365 Country Road
Belleville, IL 62221-2571
618-222-2561
800-326-3221
Fax: 618-222-2567
e-mail: ask@answersonaging.com
http://www.answersonaging.com
Joy Paeth, Chief Executive Officer

Our mission is to serve and advocate for older Illinoisans and their caregivers by administering programs and promoting partnerships that encourage independence, dignity, and quality of life. Counties served: Bond, Clinton, Madison, Monroe, Randolph, St. Clair, and Washington.

961 **West Central Illinois Area: Agency on Aging**
1125 Hampshire Street
Quincy, IL 62301-3026
217-223-7094
800-252-9027
Fax: 217-222-1220
e-mail: info@wciagingnetwork.org
http://www.wciagingnetwork.org
Lynn Niewohner, Director

Our mission is to serve and advocate for older Illinoisans and their caregivers by administering programs and promoting partnerships that encourage independence, dignity, and quality of life.

962 **Western Illinois Area: Agency on Aging**
729 34th Avenue
Rock Island, IL 61201-5911
309-793-6800
800-322-1051
Fax: 309-793-6807
TDD 309-793-6800
Greta Brooks, Director

Our mission is to server and advocate for older Illinoisans and their caregivers by administering programs and promoting partnerships that encourage independence, dignity, and quality of life.

Indiana

963 **Adams County Council on Aging**
313 W Jefferson Street
Room 120
Decatur, IN 46733-1656
260-724-5316
e-mail: accoa@onlyinternet.net
http://www.co.adams.in.us
Sharon Tester, Director

Provides information and referral, transportation assistance, outreach, and advocacy to individuals over 60 years of age.

964 **Aging And Community Service Of South CenTral Indiana**
1531 13th Street
Suite G900
Columbus, IN 47201-1302
812-372-6918
866-644-6407
Fax: 812-372-7846
http://www.agingandcommunityservices.org
Diane Cantrell, Director

Plan, develop and coordinate a comprehensive system of services for the elderly and disabled persons at risk of institutionalization.

965 **Aging and In-Home Services**
2927 Lake Avenue
Fort Wayne, IN 46805-5414
260-745-1200
800-552-3662
Fax: 260-456-1066
e-mail: dmccormick@agingihs.org
http://www.agingihs.org
Diann McCormick, President

The mission of Aging and In-Home Services of Northeast Indiana is to promote independence, dignity, and advocacy for all older adults and persons with disabilities. Counties served: Adams, Allen, DeKalb, Huntington, LaGrange, Noble, Steuben, Wells and Whitley.

966 **Area 1 Northwest Indiana Community ActioN Corp.**
5518 Calumet Avenue
Hammond, IN 46320-2017
219-937-3500
800-826-7871
Fax: 219-931-5501
http://www.agingihs.org/areaagencies.htm
Gary Olund, CEO

967 **Area 10 Agency on Aging**
7500 W Reeves Road
Bloomington, IN 47404-9688
812-876-3383
800-844-1010
Fax: 812-876-9922
e-mail: area10@area10.bloomington.in.us
http://www.bloomington.in.us
Jewel Echelbarger, Executive Director

Multi service agency for Older Americans in Monroe and Owen Counties. Information and Assistance, Home and Community Based Services, Caregiver Support, Transportation, plus Health and Nutrition, Fitness and Housing. Respecting the dignity and independence of each individual.

968 **Area 12 Council on Aging**
13091 Benedict Drive
Dillsboro, IN 47018
812-432-5200
800-742-5001
Fax: 812-432-3822
http://www.lifetime-resources.org
Sally Beckley, Director

Programs are designed to meet the growing needs of people in the communities we serve. Senior citizens, individuals with disabilities, caregivers, concerned neighbors, and the community at large will find services, resources or referrals to meet their needs.

State Organizations & Government Agencies/Indiana

969 Area 13 Agency on Aging: Older Hoosier Programs
1019 N 4th Street
Po Box 314
Vincennes, IN 47591-2355
812-888-4292
800-742-9002
Fax: 812-888-4566

Anne Jacoby, Director

970 Area 15 Hoosier Uplands Agency on Aging
521 W Main Street
Mitchell, IN 47446-1410
812-849-4457
800-333-2451
Fax: 812-849-4467
e-mail: bktarr@hoosieruplands.org
http://www.hoosieruplands.org

John Fultz, Chairman
Martha Fields, Vice-Chairperson

A local non-profit agency based in southern Indiana that serves as an Area Agency on Aging, Community Action Agency, licensed Home Health Care and Hospital Care and Hospice agency, and Community Housing Development Organization.

971 Area 2 Agency on Aging: Real Services
PO Box 1835
1151 S Michigan Street
South Bend, IN 46601
574-233-8205
800-552-7928
Fax: 219-284-2691
http://www.realservicesinc.com

Rebecca Zaseck, Director

Provides in-home and community services to the elderly, disabled and low-income.

972 Area 4 Agency on Aging and Community Services
PO Box 4727
660 North 36th Street
Lafayette, IN 47903-4727
765-447-7683
800-382-7556
Fax: 765-447-6862

Fay Ebrite, Director
Ken Green, President

A not-for-profit organization committed to providing a better quality of life for elderly, disabled and disadvantaged citizens of all ages.

973 Area 5 Agency on Aging and Community Services
1801 Smith St.
Suite 300
Logansport, IN 46947-2152
574-722-4451
800-654-9421
Fax: 219-722-3447
http://www.areafive.com

Michael Meagher, Director

An independent not-for-profit organization, governed by a volunteer board of directors, dedicated to meeting the needs of the elderly, disabled, and disadvantaged members of the communities we serve.

974 Area 9 Agency on Aging
520 S 9th St
Suite 100
Richmond, IN 47374-4227
765-966-1795
800-458-9345
Fax: 765-962-1190
http://www.iue.edu/administration/area9

Tony Shepherd, Executive Director
Kathy Bridgford, Director Of Administration

To assist older persons and disablied individuals of all ages in leading independent, meaningful and dignified lives in their own homes and communities for as long as possible.

975 Boone County Senior Services Foundation
515 Crown Pointe Dr.
Lebanon, IN 46052-2116
765-482-5220
Fax: 765-482-5239
e-mail: bcssi@booneseninor.org

Susan T Ritz, Executive Director
Sonya Shoup, Director Of Operations

Social service agency whose mission is to make it possible for the elderly of Boone county, Indiana, to live out their lives with accomplishment and dignity within the enviroment of their own choice. This is accomplished through a variety of services.

976 Central Indiana Council on Aging
4755 Kingsway Drive
Suite 200
Indianapolis, IN 46205-1560
317-254-5465
800-489-9550
Fax: 317-254-5494
e-mail: contact@cicoa.org
http://www.cicoa.org

John D Kinman, Senior Vice President
Ellen White Quigley, Deputy Mayor Community Affairs

Helps build communities that enable older persons and those of any age with a disability to live with the greatest possible independence, dignity and quality of life.

977 Fort Wayne EASI
3024 Fairfield Avenue
Suite 110
Ft Wayne, IN 46807-1697
260-458-2005
Fax: 260-458-2549
e-mail: captainj@aol.com
http://http://easi.org

Jean Joley, Contact

This program, made possible by the Corporation for National and Community Service, provides funding and support for selected older Americans to serve as technical and administrative consultants to organizations around the United States in establishing self sufficient Senior Environment Corps.

978 Indiana Aging Division
PO Box 7083
Indianapolis, IN 46207-7083
317-233-4454
Fax: 317-233-4693
e-mail: wpoindexter@fssa.state.in.us
http://www.in.gov/fssa

Anne Murphy, Chief Of Staff

The Indiana Division of Aging (IDA) provides a broad range of in-home and community based services to older adults and persons of all ages with disabilities. Services provided focus on prevention, early intervention, protection and advocacy. The Division collaborates with communities, local organizations, and other units of government to provide services to individuals and their families.

979 Indiana Association of Area Agencies on Aging
Aging and Community Services
1531 13th Street, Suite G900
Columbus, IN 47201-1302
812-372-6918
866-644-6407
Fax: 812-372-7846
e-mail: dcantrell@areaxi.org
http://www.agingandcommunityservices.org

Diane Cantrell, Executive Director

The Indiana Association of Area Agency on Aging (IAAAA) advocates for quality programs and services for older adults and persons with disabilities.

980 Indiana Department of Aging and Community Services
251 N Illinois Street
Indianapolis, IN 46204-1927
317-232-7800
800-545-7764
Fax: 615-453-0861

Cathy Boggs, Executive Director

Offers information on state-wide programs for the elderly.

State Organizations & Government Agencies/Indiana

981 Indiana Department of Health Veteran's Home
3851 N River Road
West Lafayette, IN 47906-3762
765-463-1502
Fax: 765-497-8004
http://www.in.gov/isdh

Judy Hahn, Executive Director

Supports Indiana's economic prosperity and quality of life by promoting, protecting and providing for the health of Hoosiers in their communities.

982 Indiana Department of Revenue
100 N Senate Avenue
Indianapolis, IN 46204-2253
317-233-4018
Fax: 317-233-2329
http://www.in.gov/dor
TDD 317-232-4952

983 Indiana Department of Veterans Affairs
302 W Washington Street
Room E120
Indianapolis, IN 46204-2761
317-232-3910
800-400-4520
Fax: 317-232-7721
http://www.in.gov/dva

Charles T Applegate, Executive Director

Remains focused on aiding and assisting "Hoosier" veterans and qualified family members or survivors, who are eligible for benefits or advantages provided by Indiana and the US government.

984 Indiana Developmental Disability Council
143 W Market Street
Suite 404
Indianapolis, IN 46204-2801
317-232-7770
Fax: 317-233-3712
e-mail: gpcpd@gpcpd.org
http://www.in.gov/gpcpd
TDD 317-232-7771

Suellen Jackson-Boner, Manager

Promotes public policy which leads to the independence, productivity, and inclusion of people with disabilities.

985 Indiana Disability Determination Bureau
PO Box 7069
Indianapolis, IN 46207-7069
317-396-2000
800-622-4968
http://www.in.gov
TDD 800-252-0573

Peter Bisbecos, Director
Dave Gootee, Deputy Director

The Division of Disability and Rehabilitative Services (DDRS) exists to inform, protect and serve individuals with disabilities and their families in need of human services, resources, or support to attain employment and self-sufficiency or to maintain independence.

986 Indiana Governor's Planning Council for People with Disabilities
150 West Market Street
Suite 628
Indianapolis, IN 46204
317-232-7770
Fax: 317-233-3712
e-mail: gpcpd@gpcpd.org
http://www.in.gov/gpcpd

Suellen Jackson-Boner, Manager

Mission is to promote public policy which leads to the independence, productivity and inclusion of people with disabilities in all aspects of society.

987 Indiana Protection & Advocacy Services
4701 North Keystone Avenue
Suite 222
Indianapolis, IN 46205
317-722-5555
800-622-4845
Fax: 317-722-5564
e-mail: dward@ipas.in.gov
http://www.in-gov.ipas

Karen Pedevilla, Education & Training Director

To see that the human, legal and civil rights of people with disabilities are affirmed. Congress established protection and advocacy (P&A) systems in each state. Indiana Protection & Advocacy Services provides advocacy for Indiana citizens. IPAS proudly serves people with disabilities, helping them exercise their rights, as well as providing training and resources to ensure their inclusion in the life of our communities.

988 Indiana Public Employee's Retirement Fund
143 W Market Street
Suite 602
Indianapolis, IN 46204-2801
317-822-0033
888-526-1687

E Victor Indiano, Partner

989 Indiana Teachers Retirement Fund
150 W Market Street
Suite 300
Indianapolis, IN 46204-2885
317-232-3860
888-286-3544
Fax: 317-233-0914
http://www.in.gov/trf
TDD 317-233-3306

E Victor Indiano, Partner

Mission is to prudently manage the Fund in accordance with fiduciary standards, provide quality benefits, and deliver a high level of service to our members, while demonstrating responsibility to the citizens of the state.

990 Life Stream Services
1701 Pilgrim Boulevard
Po Box 308
Yorktown, IN 47396
765-759-1121
800-589-1121
Fax: 765-759-0060
e-mail: mail@lifestreaminc.org
http://www.lifestreaminc.org

Kenneth Adkins, President/CEO
Jim Allbaugh, VP Of Operations

Working together to improve and extend the quality of life for persons at risk of losing their independence. Services offered include home delivered meals, transportation, care management, homemaker, home health aide, senior cafes, information and assistance.

991 Madison County RSVP
125 E 13th Street
Anderson, IN 46016-1700
765-641-2470
Fax: 765-641-2194
e-mail: rsvp@and.lib.in.us
http://www.and.lib.in.us

Judy Kratzner, Director RSVP

The Retired and Senior Volunteer Program (RSVP) provides opportunities for people 55 and over to make a difference in their community through volunteer service. RSVP volunteers contribute anywhere from a few to over forty hours a week, serving thourgh schools, day care centers, police departments, hospitals and other nonprofit and public organizations to help meet critical community needs. RSVP offers maximum flexibility and choice to its volunteers. RSVP matches the personal interests and skills to older Americans with opportunities to help solve community problems and offer supplemental insurance while on duty, on-the-job training from the agency or organization where volunteers are placed.

992 RSVP Crawford-Perry-Spencer
302 Main Street
PO Box 336
Tell City, IN 47586-0336
812-547-3435
Fax: 812-547-3466
e-mail: rsvp@lhdc.dubois.net

Sharon Jean Schulte, Director

State Organizations & Government Agencies/Indiana

The Retired and Senior Volunteer Program (RSVP) provides opportunities for people 55 and over to make a difference in their community through volunteer service. RSVP volunteers contribute anywhere from a few to over forty hours a week, serving through schools, day care centers, police departments, hospitals and other nonprofit and public organizations to help meet critical community needs. RSVP offers maximum flexibility and choice to its volunteers. RSVP matches the personal interests and skills of older Americans with opportunities to help solve community problems and offers supplemental insurance while on duty, on-the-job training from the agency or organization where volunteers are placed. The following Counties are served: Crawford, Perry, Spencer.

993 RSVP Daviess County Indiana
501 Burkhart Drive
PO Box 648
Washington, IN 47501
812-254-1996
Fax: 812-254-1996
e-mail: rsvp1@rtccom.net
http://www.seniorcorps.gov

Susan Ballengee, Executive Director

The Retired and Senior Volunteer Program (RSVP) provides opportunities for people 55 and over to make a difference in their community through volunteer service. RSVP volunteers contribute anywhere from a few to over forty hours a week, serving thourgh schools, day care centers, police departments, hospitals and other nonprofit and public organizations to help meet critical community needs. RSVP offers maximum flexibility and choice to its volunteers. RSVP matches the personal interests and skills to older Americans with opportunities to help solve community problems and offer supplemental insurance while on duty, on-the-job training from the agency or organization where volunteers are placed.

994 RSVP Dearborn County
PO Box 4194
Lawrenceburg, IN 47025-4194
812-539-4005
Fax: 812-539-2362
e-mail: info@myrsvp.org
http://www.myrsvp.org

Mary Lewis, Executive Director

The Retired and Senior Volunteer Program (RSVP) provides opportunities for people 55 and over to make a difference in their community through volunteer service. RSVP volunteers contribute anywhere from a few to over forty hours a week, serving through schools, day care centers, police departments, hospitals and other nonprofit and public organizations to help meet critical community needs. RSVP offers maximum flexibility and choice to its volunteers. RSVP matches the personal interests and skills of older Americans with opportunities to help solve community problems and offers supplemental insurance while on duty, on-the-job training from the agency or organization where volunteers are placed. The following Counties are served: Dearborn, Ohio, Ripley, Switzerland.

995 RSVP Dekalb-Noble-Steuben Counties
107 West 5th Street
Auburn, IN 46706
260-925-0917
Fax: 260-925-1732
e-mail: rsvp@locl.net

Patti J Sheppard, Director

The Retired and Senior Volunteer Program (RSVP) provides opportunities for people 55 and over to make a difference in their community through volunteer service. RSVP volunteers contribute anywhere from a few to over forty hours a week, serving through schools, day care centers, police departments, hospitals and other nonprofit and public organizations to help meet critical community needs. RSVP offers maximum flexibility and choice to its volunteers. RSVP matches the personal interests and skills of older Americans with opportunities to help solve community problems and offers supplemental insurance while on duty, on-the-job training from the agency or organization where volunteers are placed The following Counties are served DeKalb, Noble, Steuben.

996 RSVP Dubois-Pike-Warrick Counties
607 3rd Avenue
PO Box 279
Jasper, IN 47547-0729
812-482-2233
Fax: 812-482-1071
e-mail: rsvptricap@psci.net

Mary E Beckman, Director

The Retired and Senior Volunteer Program (RSVP) provides opportunities for people 55 and over to make a difference in their community through volunteer service. RSVP volunteers contribute anywhere from a few to over forty hours a week, serving through schools, day care centers, police departments, hospitals and other nonprofit and public organizations to help meet critical community needs. RSVP offers maximum flexibility and choice to its volunteers. RSVP matches the personal interests and skills of older Americans with opportunities to help solve community problems and offers supplemental insurance while on duty, on-the-job training from the agency or organization where volunteers are placed. The following Counties are Dubois, Gibson, Pike, Warrick.

997 RSVP Elkhart County
201 South Second
Elkhart, IN 46516
260-925-0917
Fax: 260-925-1732
e-mail: rsvp@loci.net

Karen Kandlstorfer, Contact

Provides opportunities for people 55 and over to make a difference in their community through volunteer service. RSVP volunteers contribute anywhere from a few to over forty hours a week, serving through schools, day care centers, police departments, hospitals and other nonprofit and public organizations to help meet critical community needs. RSVP matches the personal interests and skills of older Americans with opportunities to help solve community problems and offers supplemental insurance while on duty, on-the-job training from the agency or organization where volunteers are placed.

998 RSVP Fulton
625 Pontiac Street
Rochester, IN 46975-1340
574-223-3716
Fax: 574-223-4962
e-mail: rsvpmona@yahoo.com

Mona Elsea, Director

The Retired and Senior Volunteer Program (RSVP) provides opportunities for people 55 and over to make a difference in their community through volunteer service. RSVP volunteers contribute anywhere from a few to over forty hours a week, serving through schools, day care centers, police departments, hospitals and other nonprofit and public organizations to help meet critical community needs. RSVP offers maximum flexibility and choice to its volunteers. RSVP matches the personal interests and skills of older Americans with opportunities to help solve community problems and offers supplemental insurance while on duty, on-the-job training from the agency or organization where volunteers are placed. The following County served: Fulton.

999 RSVP Hancock-Henry-Rush
615 West SR 38
PO Box 449
New Castle, IN 47362-0449
765-521-7414
Fax: 765-521-7415
e-mail: smcamis@icapcaa.org

Susan McAmis, Director

State Organizations & Government Agencies/Indiana

The Retired and Senior Volunteer Program (RSVP) provides opportunities for people 55 and over to make a difference in their community through volunteer service. RSVP volunteers contribute anywhere from a few to over forty hours a week, serving through schools, day care centers, police departments, hospitals and other nonprofit and public organizations to help meet critical community needs. RSVP offers maximum flexibility and choice to its volunteers. RSVP matches the personal interests and skills to older Americans with opportunities to help solve community problems and offers supplemental insurance while on duty, on-the-job training from the agency or organization where volunteers are placed. The following Counties are served: Hancock, Henry, Rush.

1000 **RSVP Indianapolis**
901 S Shelby Street
Room 324
Indianapolis, IN 46203-1151
317-791-5941
Fax: 317-791-5945
e-mail: cac-rsvp@uindy.edu

Kyle Ciresi, Director

The Retired and Senior Volunteer Program (RSVP) provides opportunities for people 55 and over to make a difference in their community through volunteer service. RSVP volunteers contribute anywhere from a few to over forty hours a week, serving through schools, day care centers, police departments, hospitals and other nonprofit and public organizations to help meet critical community needs. RSVP offers maximum flexibility and choice to its volunteers. RSVP matches the personal interests and skills of older Americans wit opportunities to help solve community problems and offers supplemental insurance while on duty, on-the-job training from the agency or organization where volunteers are placed. The following Counties are served: Marion, Johnson.

1001 **RSVP Jefferson County**
512 West Main Street
Madison, IN 47250-3718
812-265-3950
Fax: 812-273-6676
e-mail: vcopelan@tls.net

Vickie Copeland, Director

RSVP volunteers serve in organizations that range from hospitals and youth recreational centers to local police stations and education facilities. In all, RSVP helps seniors find volunteer positions with more than 75 organizations.

1002 **RSVP Knox County**
1019 N Fourth Street Room 305
Po Box 314
Vincennes, IN 47591
812-888-5879
Fax: 812-888-4566
e-mail: pdreiman@vinu.edu

Patty Dreiman, Director

RSVP volunteers provide a wide range of important community services in areas such as homeland security, public safety, health, education, the environment and elder care. They may tutor children in reading and math, respond to natural disasters, help to build houses, model parenting skills to teen parents, participate in neighborhood watch programs, plant community gardens, deliver meals, or help community organizations operate more efficiently.hatever your interests and background, there is certainly an RSVP opportunity to match!

1003 **RSVP LaPorte County**
6919 Indianapolis Blvd.
Hammond, IN 46324
219-844-5174
Fax: 219-844-4885

Thomas Szawara, Director

The Retired and Senior Volunteer Program (RSVP) provides opportunities for people 55 and over to make a difference in their community through volunteer service. RSVP volunteers contribute anywhere from a few to over forty hours a week, serving through schools, day care centers, police departments, hospitals and other nonprofit and public organizations to help meet critical community needs. RSVP offers maximum flexibility and choice to its volunteers. RSVP matches the personal interests and skills of older Americans with opportunities to help solve community problems and offers supplemental insurance while on duty, on-the-job training from the agency or organization where volunteers are placed. The following Counties are served: LaPorte, Starke.

1004 **RSVP Lake County**
6919 Indianapolis Blvd
Hammond, IN 46324-2205
219-844-5174
Fax: 219-844-4885
e-mail: byurko@catholic-charities.org

Betty A Yurko, Contact

Provides opportunities for people 55 and over to make a difference in their community through volunteer service. RSVP volunteers contribute anywhere from a few to over forty hours a week, serving through schools, day care centers, police departments, hospitals and other nonprofit and public organizations to help meet critical community needs. RSVP matches the personal interests and skills of older Americans with opportunities to help solve community problems and offers supplemental insurance while on duty, on-the-job training from the agency or organization where volunteers are placed.

1005 **RSVP Madison County**
125 E 13th Street
Anderson, IN 46016-1700
765-641-2470
Fax: 765-641-2194
e-mail: rsvp@and.lib.in.us
http://www.and.lib.in.us

Judy Kratzner, Manager

Our mission is to utilize the skills, knowledge, and services of older adults through promotion of volunteerism in agencies that strive to improve the health, safety, education, and quality of life of all generations, present, and future, in Madison County, Indiana.

1006 **RSVP Monroe Owen Counties**
7500 W Reeves Road
Bloomington, IN 47404-9688
812-876-3383
Fax: 812-876-9922
e-mail: ssarin-rsvp@area10-bloomington.in.us
http://www.area10.bloomington.in.us

Shalini Sarin, Executive Director

The Retired and Senior Volunteer Program (RSVP) provides opportunities for people 55 and over to make a difference in their community through volunteer service. RSVP volunteers contribute anywhere from a few to over forty hours a week, serving through schools, day care centers, police departments, hospitals and other nonprofit and public organizations to help meet critical community needs. RSVP offers maximum flexibility and choice to its volunteers. RSVP matches the personal interests and skills of older Americans with opportunities to help solve community problems and offers supplemental insurance while on duty, on-the-job training from the agency or organization where volunteers are placed.

1007 **RSVP Putnam County**
Po Box 1018
30 No 7th Street Suite 105
Terre Haute, IN 47808
812-232-1264
Fax: 812-232-9634
e-mail: rsvp@ccrtc.com

Monica Van Hook, Director

State Organizations & Government Agencies/Indiana

Provides opportunities for people 55 and over to make a difference in their community through volunteer service. RSVP volunteers contribute anywhere from a few to over forty hours a week, serving through schools, day care centers, police departments, hospitals and other nonprofit and public organizations to help meet critical community needs. RSVP matches the personal interests and skills of older Americans with opportunities to help solve community problems and offers supplemental insurance while on duty, on-the-job training from the agency or organization where volunteers are placed.

1008 RSVP South Central Indiana RSVP
702 E Market Street
New Albany, IN 47150-2916
812-948-1815
Fax: 812-948-9249
e-mail: rsvp@interfaithinc.org
Ceil Sperzel, Program Director

Recruits retirees to volunteer in all helping agencies, using the skills and availability of our seniors to help address community needs.

1009 RSVP St. Joseph County
1817 Miami Street
South Bend, IN 46613
574-234-3111
Fax: 574-289-1034
e-mail: pclaeys@ccfwsb.org
http://www.diocesefwsb.org/charity
Pam Claeys, Director

The Retired and Senior Volunteer Program (RSVP) provides opportunities for people 55 and over to make a difference in their community through volunteer service. RSVP volunteers contribute anywhere from a few to over forty hours a week, serving through schools, day care centers, police departments, hospitals and other nonprofit and public organizations to help meet critical community needs. RSVP offers maximum flexibility and choice to its volunteers. RSVP matches the personal interests and skills of older Americans with opportunities to help solve community problems and offers supplemental insurance while on duty, on-the-job training from the agency or organization where volunteers are placed.

1010 RSVP Valparaiso
1005 Campbell Street
PO Box 246
Valparaiso, IN 46385-4262
219-464-1028
Fax: 219-464-0012
e-mail: Jbolin@niia.net
Joyce Bollin, Director

The Retired and Senior Volunteer Program (RSVP) provides opportunities for people 55 and over to make a difference in their community through volunteer service. RSVP volunteers contribute anywhere from a few to over forty hours a week, serving through schools, day care centers, police departments, hospitals and other nonprofit and public organizations to help meet critical community needs. RSVP offers maximum flexibility and choice to its volunteers. RSVP matches the personal interests and skills of older Americans with opportunities to help solve community problems and offers supplemental insurance while on duty, on-the-job training from the agency or organization where volunteers are placed.

1011 RSVP Wayne County
City of Richmond, Park Department
1600 S 2nd Street
Richmond, IN 47374-6882
765-983-7309
Fax: 765-983-7386
e-mail: myoung@ci.richmond.in.us
http://www.ci.richmond.in.us
Martha Young, Director

The Retired and Senior Volunteer Program (RSVP) provides opportunities for people 55 and over to make a difference in their community through volunteer service. RSVP volunteers contribute anywhere from a few to over forty hours a week, serving through schools, day care centers, police departments, hospitals and other nonprofit and public organizations to help meet critical community needs. RSVP offers maximum flexibility and choice to its volunteers. RSVP matches the personal interests and skills of older Americans with opportunities to help solve community problems and offers supplemental insurance while on duty, and on-the-job training from the agency or organization where volunteers are placed. The following County is served: Wayne.

1012 Railroad Retirement Board District Office
50 S Meridian Street
Suite 303
Indianapolis, IN 46204-3538
317-226-6111
Fax: 317-226-5374
http://www.rrb.gov/field/do_indi.asp
Robert Braitman, Manager

An independent agency in the executive branch of the Federal Government. The primary function is to administer comprehensive retirement-survivor and unemployment-sickness benefit programs for the nation's railroad workers and their families.

1013 South Central Indiana Council for Aging and Aged
Po Box 995
426 Bank Street Suite 100
New Albany, IN 47151-0995
812-948-8330
888-948-8330
Fax: 812-948-9701
e-mail: information@lsr14.org
http://www.lifespanresources.org
Keith E Stormes, Executive Director
Earlene Bennett, Executive Assistant

Provides assistance with case management, information and referral to various services for persons who are aging or developmentally disabled. Provides assistance with home health care, personal assistance, home-delivered and congregate meals, adult day care, respite care for families, and prescriptions. Counties served: Clark, Floyd, Harrison, Scott.

1014 Southwestern Indiana Regional Council on Aging
16 West Virginia Street
PO Box 3938
Evansville, IN 47737-3938
812-464-7800
800-253-2188
Fax: 812-464-7811
e-mail: swirca@swirca.org
http://www.swirca.org
Robert J Patrow, Executive Director

Volunteers aged 60 years or older in Evansville, IN. Provides a variety of opportunities for persons 60 years or older to participate more fully in the life of their community through significant volunteer service. Distributes teddy bears to abused, neglected, disabled, and underprivileged children. The following Counties are served: Gibson, Perry, Posey, Vanderburgh and Warrick.

1015 West Central Indiana Economic Development District Area Agency On Aging And Disabled
PO Box 359
Terre Haute, IN 47808
812-238-1561
800-489-1561
Fax: 812-238-1564
http://www.westcentralin.com
Merve Nolot, Executive Director
Gloria Wetnigit, Quality Assurance Coordinator

we serve a 6-county area with only one major metro area; five counties are 80% or more rural. We serve the 60+ population and birth to death disabled providing home and community based services.

State Organizations & Government Agencies/Iowa

Iowa

1016 Area 14 Agency on Aging
210 Russell Street
Creston, IA 50801-2412
641-782-4040
800-262-0378
Fax: 641-782-4519
e-mail: areaxiv@mddc.com
http://www.areaxivaaa.org
Steve Bolie, Executive Director

Mission is to lead, advocacte, and serve as well as plan and coordinate resources in the provision of services to older persons in central Iowa, their families, caregivers, or representatives enabling elders to lead independent, meaningful and dignified lives in the least restrictive environment.

1017 Elderbridge Agency on Aging
22 N Georgia Avenue
Suite 216
Mason City, IA 50401-3435
641-424-0678
800-243-0678
Fax: 641-424-2927
e-mail: elderbridge@elderbridge.org
http://www.elderbridge.org
Lahoma Counts, Executive Director

Elderbridge is a non-profit organization funded through federal Older Americans Act and State of Iowa General Revenue funds, and contributions.

1018 Hawkeye Valley Area: Agency on Aging
2101 Kimball Ave.
Suite 320
Waterloo, IA 50702
319-272-2244
800-779-8707
Fax: 319-272-2455
http://www.hvaaa.org

Agency provides planning, advocacy, funding for senior programs and services. Funded services include: Meals on Wheels, Senior Dining, Adult Day Care, Case Management and Transportation.

1019 Heritage Area: Agency on Aging
6301 Kirkwood Boulevard SW
Po Box 2068
Cedar Rapids, IA 52406
319-398-5559
800-332-5394
Fax: 319-398-5533
e-mail: heritage@kirkwood.cc.ia.us
http://www.kirkwood.edu
Elizabeth Selk, Director
Tarin Allen, Case Manager

Agency provides planning, advocacy, funding for senior programs and services in a seven county area. Funded services include: Meals on Wheels, Senior Dining, Adult Day Care, Case Management and Transportation.

1020 Iowa Client Assistance Program
Locust Street Office
Des Moines, IA 50309
515-281-3957
Fax: 515-242-6119
http://www.iowa.gov/dhr/pd/client_assis_program
Harietta Helland, Disability Consultant

Information and referral on disability issues.

1021 Iowa Commission of Veterans Affairs
7105 NW 70th Avenue
Johnston, IA 50131-1824
515-242-5331
Fax: 515-242-5659
e-mail: info@idva.state.ia.us
http://www.iowava.org
Patrick Palmersheim, CEO

1022 Iowa Commission on Persons with Disabilities
Lucas State Office Building
Second Floor
Des Moines, IA 50319
515-242-6172
888-219-0471
Fax: 515-242-6119
e-mail: dhr.disabilities@iowa.gov
http://www.state.ia.us/dhr
TTY 888-219-0471
Jill Fulitano-Avery, Administrator

The Division of Persons with Disabilities exists to promote the employment of Iowans with disabilities and reduce barriers to employment by providing information, referral, assessment and guidance, training, and negotiation services to employers and citizens with disabilities.

1023 Iowa Department of Elder Affairs
510 E 12th Street
Suite 2
Des Moines, IA 50319-9025
515-725-3333
800-532-3213
Fax: 515-242-3300
http://www.iowa.gov/elderaffairs
Mark A Haverland, Executive Director

1024 Iowa Department of Human Rights: Deaf Services Commissions
Department Of Human Rights, 2nd Floor
Lucas State Office Building
Des Moines, IA 50319
515-281-3164
888-221-3724
Fax: 515-242-6119
http://www.iowa.gov/dhr/ds
Kathryn Baumann-Reese, Administrator

1025 Iowa Department of Revenue & Finance
Hoover Building
1305 E Walnut
Des Moines, IA 50319
515-281-3114
800-367-3388
Fax: 800-572-3943
e-mail: idr@iowa.gov
http://www.iowa.gov/tax
Mark R Schuling, Director

1026 Iowa Developmental Disability Council
617 E Second Street
Des Moines, IA 50309
515-281-9082
800-452-1936
Fax: 515-281-9087
http://www.state.ia.us/ddcouncil
Becky Maddy Harker, Executive Director

The Council identifies, develops and promotes public policy and support practices through capacity building, advocacy, and systems change activities. The purpose is to ensure that people with developmental disabilities and their families are included in planning, decision making, and development of policy related to services and supports that affect their quality of life and full participation in communities of their choice.

1027 Iowa Division of MHMRDD: Office of Human Services
Hoover
Des Moines, IA 50319
515-281-5874
Fax: 515-281-4597
http://www.dhs.state.ia.us
Kevin W Concannon, Director

1028 Iowa Program for Assistive Technology
Center for Disabilities and Development
100 Hawkins Drive, Room S295
Iowa City, IA 52242-1011
319-356-0550
800-331-3027
Fax: 319-384-5139
http://www.iowaat.orginfotech
TTY 877-686-0032
Jane Gay, Director

State Organizations & Government Agencies/Iowa

The Iowa Program for Assistive Technology (IPAT) is Iowa's grant project under the Assistive Technology Act (ATA) of 1998. IPAT's goals are to promote and create systems change in the state with regards to assistive technology (AT) and it's use. IPAT works with consumers and family members, service providers, and state and local agencies/organizations to promote assistive technology through awareness, training, and policy work. IPAT accomplishes this through five specific goal areas: education, employment, health, community living and recreation, telecommunication and information and technology.

1029 Iowa Protection & Advocacy for the Disabled
950 Office Park Road
Suite 221
West Des Moines, IA 50265-2548
515-278-2502
800-779-2502
Fax: 515-278-0539
e-mail: info@ipna.org
http://www.ipna.org

Sylvia Piper, Executive Director
Karen M Wilson, President

A federally funded program that will protect and advocate for the human and legal rights that ensure individuals with disabilities and/or mental illness a free, appropriate public education, employment opportunities and residence or treatment in the least restrictive environment or method and for freedom from stigma.

1030 Iowa Workers Compensation
1000 E Grand Avenue
Des Moines, IA 50319-1020
515-281-5387
800-562-4692
Fax: 515-281-6501
e-mail: iwd.dwc@iwd.iowa.gov
http://www.iowaworkforce.org/wc

Christopher Godfrey, Commissioner

1031 Lucas County Health Center
1200 N 7th Street
Chariton, IA 50049-1210
641-774-3000
800-404-3111
Fax: 641-774-3233
http://www.lchcia.com

Linda Neer, Director

Lucas County Health Center Volunteer Services plays an important role in the local community. Volunteer Services has four areas of focus: volunteer placement, a personal emergency response program, insurance education, and low-cost food distribution. LCHC Volunteer Services is designed to match volunteers with opportunities for the mutual benefit of all involved.

1032 RSVP Black Hawk
2101 Kimball Avenue
Suite 121
Waterloo, IA 50702-5057
319-272-2250
Fax: 319-272-1958
e-mail: station1@sbtek.net
http://www.rsvpserves.com

Sheila Bohr, Director

The Retired and Senior Volunteer Program (RSVP) provides opportunities for people 55 and over to make a difference in their community through volunteer service. RSVP volunteers contribute anywhere from a few to over forty hours a week, serving through schools, day care centers, police departments, hospitals and other nonprofit and public organizations to help meet critical community needs. RSVP offers maximum flexibility and choice to its volunteers. RSVP matches the personal interests and skills of older Americans with opportunities to help solve community problems and offers supplemental insurance while on duty, on-the-job training from the agency or organization where volunteers are placed. The following County is served: Black Hawk.

1033 RSVP Carroll County
514 North Court Street
Carroll, IA 51401-2752
712-792-4212
Fax: 712-792-1957
e-mail: crsvp@hotmail.com

Debra S Fahn, Director

The Retired and Senior Volunteer Program (RSVP) provides opportunities for people 55 and over to make a difference in their community through volunteer service. RSVP volunteers contribute anywhere from a few to over forty hours a week, serving through schools, day care centers, police departments, hospitals and other nonprofit and public organizations to help meet critical community needs. RSVP offers maximum flexibility and choice to its volunteers. RSVP matches the personal interests and skills of older Americans with opportunities to help solve community problems and offers supplemental insurance while on duty, on-the-job training from the agency or organization where volunteers are placed. The following County is served: Carroll.

1034 RSVP Clarinda
CTC Campus
PO Box 338
Clarinda, IA 51632
712-542-2161
Fax: 712-542-2012
e-mail: rsvp01@heartland.net

Lucille Lawrence, Director

The Retired and Senior Volunteer Program (RSVP) provides opportunities for people 55 and over to make a difference in their community through volunteer service. RSVP volunteers contribute anywhere from a few to over forty hours a week, serving through schools, day care centers, police departments, hospitals and other nonprofit and public organizations to help meet critical community needs. RSVP offers maximum flexibility and choice to its volunteers. RSVP matches the personal interests and skills of older Americans with opportunities to help solve community problems and offers supplemental insurance while on duty, on-the-job training from the agency or organization where volunteers are placed. The following Counties are served: Montgomery, Page, Taylor.

1035 RSVP Clinton County
315 South 2nd Street
Clinton, IA 52732-4214
563-243-7787
Fax: 563-244-4757
e-mail: tlmrsvp@hotmail.com

Tamara Meyer, Director

The Retired and Senior Volunteer Program (RSVP) provides opportunities for people 55 and over to make a difference in their community through volunteer service. RSVP volunteers contribute anywhere from a few to over forty hours a week, serving through schools, day care centers, police departments, hospitals and other nonprofit and public organizations to help meet critical community needs. RSVP offers maximum flexibility and choice to its volunteers. RSVP matches the personal interests and skills of older Americans with opportunities to help solve community problems and offers supplemental insurance while on duty, on-the-job training from the agency or organization where volunteers are placed. The following County is served: Clinton.

1036 RSVP Dubuque County
350 N Grandview Avenue
Dubuque, IA 52001-6388
563-589-2622
Fax: 563-557-2813
http://www.newlifestyles.com/facility

Deb Bell, Director

RSVP of Dubuque County provides persons age 55 and older opportunities to enhance their lives and their community through volunteer service.

State Organizations & Government Agencies/Iowa

1037 RSVP Fort Dodge
617 Central Avenue
Fort Dodge, IA 50501-3811   515-573-3477
Fax: 515-576-4766
e-mail: jnemitz@fortdodgeiowa.org
http://www.fortdodgeiowa.org
Jeanine Nemitz, Executive Director

The Retired and Senior Volunteer Program (RSVP) provides opportunities for people 55 and over to make a difference in their community through volunteer service. RSVP volunteers contribute anywhere from a few to over forty hours a week, serving through schools, day care centers, police departments, hospitals and other nonprofit and public organizations to help meet critical community needs. RSVP offers maximum flexibility and choice to its volunteers. RSVP matches the personal interests and skills to older Americans with opportunities to help solve community problems and offers supplemental insurance while on duty, on-the-job training from the agency or organization where volunteers are placed. The following County is served: Webster.

1038 RSVP Hamilton Wright Counties
749 2nd Street
Webster City, IA 50595-1426   515-832-2525
Fax: 515-832-9640
e-mail: wcrsvp@hotmail.com
Joan Van Deer, Executive Director

The Retired and Senior Volunteer Program (RSVP) provides opportunities for people 55 and over to make a difference in their community through volunteer service. RSVP volunteers contribute anywhere from a few to over forty hours a week, serving through schools, day care centers, police departments, hospitals and other nonprofit and public organizations to help meet critical community needs. RSVP offers maximum flexibility and choice to its volunteers. RSVP matches the personal interests and skills of older Americans with opportunities to help solve community problems and offers supplemental insurance while on duty, on-the-job training from the agency or organization where volunteers are placed. The following Counties are served: Hamilton, Wright.

1039 RSVP Henry County
407 S White Street
Mt Pleasant, IA 52641-2262   319-385-6523
Fax: 319-385-6731
e-mail: bateschbalk@hchc.org
http://www.healthyhenrycounty.org
Karen Bates Chabal, Director
Nancy Hahn, Coordinator

The Retired and Senior Volunteer Program (RSVP) provides opportunities for people 55 and over to make a difference in their community through volunteer service. RSVP volunteers contribute anywhere from a few to over forty hours a week, serving through schools, day care centers, police departments, hospitals and other nonprofit and public organizations to help meet critical community needs. RSVP offers maximum flexibility and choice to its volunteers. RSVP matches the personal interests and skills of older Americans with opportunities to help solve community problems and offers supplemental insurance while on duty, on-the-job training from the agency or organization where volunteer is placed. The following County is served: Henry.

1040 RSVP Johnson County
28 S Linn Street
Iowa City, IA 52240-3920   319-356-5218
Fax: 319-356-5417
e-mail: jcook@elderservicesiowa.com
Joan Cook, Director

This program recruits and links persons 55 and older with volunteer opportunities that meet critical community needs while providing a high quality experience that enriches the lives of both volunteers and those they serve. The following Counties are served: Des Moines, Iowa, Johnson, Muscatine.

1041 RSVP Linn County
1026 A Avenue NE
PO Box 3026
Cedar Rapids, IA 52406-3026   319-369-8774
Fax: 319-369-7965
e-mail: rsvp@crstlukes.com
Sarah S Case, Director

The Retired and Senior Volunteer Program (RSVP) provides opportunities for people 55 and over to make a difference in their community through volunteer service. RSVP volunteers contribute anywhere from a few to over forty hours a week, serving through schools, day care centers, police departments, hospitals and other nonprofit and public organizations to help meet critical community needs. RSVP offers maximum flexibility and choice to its volunteers. RSVP matches the personal interests and skills of older Americans with opportunities to help solve community problems and offers supplemental insurance while on duty, on-the-job training from the agency or organization where volunteers are placed. The following County is served: Linn.

1042 RSVP North Central Iowa
C/O Waldorf College
106 South Sixth Street
Forest City, IA 50436   641-585-2450
800-292-1903
Fax: 641-585-8194
e-mail: hanson@waldorf.edu
http://www.waldorf.edu/services
Elaine Hanson, Director

The Retired and Senior Volunteer Program (RSVP) provides opportunities for people 55 and over to make a difference in their community through volunteer service. RSVP volunteers contribute anywhere from a few to over forty hours a week, serving through schools, day care centers, police departments, hospitals and other nonprofit and public organizations to help meet critical community needs. RSVP offers maximum flexibility and choice to its volunteers. RSVP matches the personal interests and skills of older Americans with opportunities to help solve community problems and offers supplemental insurance while on duty, on-the-job training from the agency or organization where volunteers are placed. The following Counties are served: Poweshiek, Tama.

1043 RSVP North Lee County
811 Avenue E
PO Box 386
Fort Madison, IA 52627-0386   319-372-7700
Fax: 319-372-8661
e-mail: jbergman@fortmadison-ia.com
http://www.newlifestyles.com
Jean Bergman, Director

The Retired and Senior Volunteer Program (RSVP) provides opportunities for people 55 and over to make a difference in their community through volunteer service. RSVP volunteers contribute anywhere from a few to over forty hours a week, serving through schools, day care centers, police departments, hospitals and other nonprofit and public organizations to help meet critical community needs. RSVP offers maximum flexibility and choice to its volunteers. RSVP matches the personal interests and skills of older Americans with opportunities to help solve community problems and offers supplemental insurance while on duty, on-the-job training from the agency or organization where volunteers are placed.

1044 RSVP Northeast Iowa
202 Winnebago Street
Decorah, IA 52101-1812   563-382-3717
Fax: 563-382-4524
e-mail: rsvp@decorah.lib.ia.us
http://www2.decorah.lib.ia.us/RSVP/index.htm
Kathy Barloon, Director

State Organizations & Government Agencies/Iowa

The Retired and Senior Volunteer Program (RSVP) provides opportunities for people 55 and over to make a difference in their community through volunteer service. RSVP volunteers contribute anywhere from a few to over forty hours a week, serving through schools, day care centers, police departments, hospitals and other nonprofit and public organizations to help meet critical community needs. RSVP offers maximum flexibility and choice to its volunteers. RSVP matches the personal interests and skills of older Americans with opportunities to help solve community problems and offers supplemental insurance while on duty, on-the-job training from the agency or organization where volunteers are placed. The following Counties are served: Allamakee, Bremer, Chickasaw, Clayton, Fayette, Howard, Winneshiek.

1045 RSVP Ottumwa
217 E Main Street
PO Box 308
Ottumwa, IA 52501-0308
641-683-1161
Fax: 641-682-3466
e-mail: pseals@ottumwaiowa.com

Patsy Seals, Director

The Retired and Senior Volunteer Program (RSVP) provides opportunities for people 55 and over to make a difference in their community through volunteer service. RSVP volunteers contribute anywhere from a few to over forty hours a week, serving through schools, day care centers, police departments, hospitals and other nonprofit and public organizations to help meet critical community needs. RSVP offers maximum flexibility and choice to its volunteers. RSVP matches the personal interests and skills of older Americans with opportunities to help solve community problems and offers supplemental insurance while on duty, on-the-job training from the agency or organization where volunteers are placed.

1046 RSVP Pottawattamie Mills Counties
915 North 16th Street
Council Bluffs, IA 51501
712-322-4017
Fax: 712-322-8572
e-mail: rsvp@loesshills.redcross.org
http://www.loesshills.redcross.org

Chris Reed, Director

Retired and Senior Volunteer Program of Pottawattamie and Mills Counties will engage persons 55 and older in volunteer service to meet critical community needs and to provide a high quality experience that will enrich the lives of volunteers.

1047 RSVP Story Marshall Counties
617 Pennsylvania Avenue
Story City, IA 50248-1241
515-733-4917
Fax: 515-733-4448
e-mail: rsvp@isunet.net

Kalen Petersen, Director

The Retired and Senior Volunteer Program (RSVP) provides opportunities for people 55 and over to make a difference in their community through volunteer service. RSVP volunteers contribute anywhere from a few to over forty hours a week, serving through schools, day care centers, police departments, hospitals and other nonprofit and public organizations to help meet critical community needs. RSVP offers maximum flexibility and choice to its volunteers. RSVP matches the personal interests and skills of older Americans with opportunities to help solve community problems and offers supplemental insurance while on duty, on-the-job training from the agency or organization where volunteers are placed.

1048 RSVP United Way of Central Iowa
1111 Ninth Street
Suite 100
Des Moines, IA 50314-2527
515-246-6500
Fax: 515-246-6522
e-mail: contactus@unitedwaydm.org
http://www.unitedwaydm.org

Shannon Cofield, President
Kirk Irwin, Chief Operating Officer
Shirley Burgess, Volunteer Engagement Director

United Way of Central Iowa will be the leader and catalyst for community change in the business of caring.

1049 RSVP Woodbury County
715 Douglas Street
Sioux City, IA 51101-1021
712-252-1861
Fax: 712-255-1352

Johnalyn Platt, Director
Janice Klimiades, Chief Executive Officer

The Retired and Senior Volunteer Program (RSVP) provides opportunities for people 55 and over to make a difference in their community through volunteer service. RSVP volunteers contribute anywhere from a few to over forty hours a week, serving through schools, day care centers, police departments, hospitals and other nonprofit and public organizations to help meet critical community needs. RSVP offers maximum flexibility and choice to its volunteers. RSVP matches the personal interests and skills of older Americans with the opportunities to help solve community problems and offers supplemental insurance while on duty, on-the-job training from the agency or organization where volunteers are placed.

1050 Railroad Retirement Board: Iowa District Office
210 Walnut Street
Deferal Building Room 921
Des Moines, IA 50309-2136
515-284-4344
Fax: 515-284-4616
e-mail: desmonies@rrb.gov
http://www.rrb.gov

Carol Laird, Manager

An independent agency in the executive branch of the Federal Government. Primary function is to administer comprehensive retirement-survivor and unemployment-sickness benefit programs for the nations railroad workers and their families.

1051 SCORE of Tulsa
Council Bluffs Chaimber Of Commerce
Po Box 1565
Council Bluffs, IA 51502-1565
712-325-1000
Fax: 712-322-5698

Jim Killerlam, Chairperson

Retired businesspeople in southwestern Iowa. Provides consulting services to individuals wishing to start a new business or who have problems with established businesses. Conducts business education seminars.
Number of Members: 11,500

1052 Scenic Valley Area: Agency on Aging
3505 Stoneman Road
Dubuque, IA 52002-5305
563-588-3970
Fax: 563-588-1952
http://www.scenicvalley.org

Linda McDonald, Manager

Provides information and assistance and to arrange services for seniors age 60 and older.

1053 Seneca Area Agency on Aging
117 N Cooper Street
Suite 2
Ottumwa, IA 52501
641-682-2270
800-642-6522
Fax: 641-682-2445
e-mail: seneca@seneca-aaa.org
http://www.seneca-aaa.org

Connie Holland, Director

Our mission is to advocate for and provide assistance to older persons in a non-discriminatory manner, working toward fostering and maintaining independence while preserving the dignity of each individual and focusing on their quality of life.

State Organizations & Government Agencies/Kansas

1054 Siouxland Aging Services
2301 Pierce Street
Sioux City, IA 51104-3850
712-279-6900
800-798-6916
Fax: 712-233-3415
e-mail: siouxlandaging@siouxlandaging.org
http://www.siouxlandaging.org
Rhonda Sims, Office Manager/Information
Pat Rasco, Case Management
Ann De Boom, Manager

Area IV Agency on Aging.

1055 Southeast Iowa Area: Agency on Aging
509 Jefferson Street
Burlington, IA 52601-5427
319-752-5433
800-292-1268
Fax: 319-754-7030
http://www.southeastiowaagingservices.com
Dennis Zegarax, Executive Director

A planning and funding agency whose purpose is to fund services which enable older persons to remain as independent as possible in the least restrictive environment.

1056 Southwest 8 Senior Services
300 West Broadway
Suite 240
Council Bluffs, IA 51503
712-328-2540
800-432-9209
Fax: 712-328-6899
http://www.southwest8.org
Barbara Morrison, Executive Director
Judy Roane, Fiscal Director
Kelly Butts, Director Development

We provide a broad range of programs that support seniors, caregivers and their families in the eight counties of Iowa: Cass, Fremont, Harrison, Mills, Montgomery, Page, Pottawattamie, and Shelby. From in-home services like home-delivered meals and housecleaning to information about Medicare and drug cards to family caregiver support for seniors and their loved ones, we can help. The nation-wide network is there to work with seniors and their families in finding services that will allow them to remain independent and in their own homes for as long as possible.

Kansas

1057 Beach Center on Families and Disability
University of Kansas
3111 Haworth Hall
Lawrence, KS 66044
785-864-7600
Fax: 785-864-7605
e-mail: beach@dole.lsi.ukans.edu
http://www.beachcenter.org
TTY 785-864-3434
Susan Bashinski, Assistant Research Professor

A federally funded center that conducts research and training in the factors that contribute to the successful functioning of families with members who have disabilities.

1058 Butler County Department on Aging
110 E Augusta Avenue
Augusta, KS 67019
316-775-0500
800-279-3655
Fax: 316-775-0555
http://www.bucoks.com/depts/aging
Connie Rausch, Director
Brenda Louthan, Assistant Director/Program Mgr

The Department on Aging serves nearly 10,000 Butler County citizens, age 60 and older. We are committed to helping the frail and elderly who choose to remain at home, by providing a link to in-home services. Our goal is to promote independence, health, self-care, and self-value for the elders who reside in Butler County.

1059 Central Plains Area: Agency on Aging
510 N Main Street
Suite 502
Wichita, KS 67203-3725
316-660-7298
Fax: 316-383-7757
http://www.cpaaa.org
Annette Graham, Executive Director
Davalyne Osbourn, Infomation Specialists
Teresa Hatfield, Information Specialists

Central Plains Area Agency on Aging is one of eleven Area Agencies on Aging (AAA's) in Kansas. Its service area is Harvey, Sedgwick, and Butler Counties and it has the highest number of older people of any AAA in the state; approximately 84,737 people aged 60 and over. Services provided include case management, in-home and community services, information, assistance and volunteer services.

1060 Disability Rights Center Of Kansas
635 S.W. Harrison Street
Suite 100
Topeka, KS 66603-3726
785-273-9661
877-776-1541
Fax: 785-273-9414
e-mail: info@ksadv.org
http://http://drckansas.org
Tim Voth, Intake Coordinator
Rocky Nichols, Executive Director

Legal, administrative and other advocacy to protect the rights of persons with disabilities.

1061 East Central Kansas Area: Agency on Aging
132 S Main Street
Ottawa, KS 66067-2327
785-242-7200
800-633-5621
Fax: 785-242-7202
e-mail: eckaaa@eckaaa.state.ks.us
http://www.agingkansas.org/aaa/psa7.htm
Elizabeth Maxwell, Executive Director

A non-profit corporation which receives funds from the federal, state and local governments, client fees, and private resources. It was founded in 1973 and has a successful history of meeting the needs of the rural elderly. The Area Agency is responsible for providing and coordinating services for persons age sixty and over.

1062 Harvey County Department on Aging
800 N Main Street
Po Box 687
Newton, KS 67114-1807
316-284-6880
Fax: 316-284-6856
e-mail: khannemann@harveycounty.com
http://www.harveycounty.com
Kathryn Hannemann, Director

Provides services to Harvey County's seniors aged 60 and older. Commited to helping the frail and elderly who choose to remain at home by providing home and community based services, their goal is to promote level of choice, independence and self-care.

1063 Kansas Association of Area Agencies on Aging
Johnson County Area Agency on Aging
11811 S Sunset Drive
Suite 300
Olathe, KS 66061-7056
913-715-8861
888-214-4404
Fax: 913-715-8825
http://www.agingkansas.org
TTY 913-894-8822
Linda White, Director

The Johnson County Area Agency on Aging is part of Johnson County Human Services and Aging and is responsible for planning and implementing services for persons 60 years of age and older in Johnson County, Kansas. The goal of the Johnson County Area Agency on Aging is to provide a wide range of services that help older adults maintain independence and dignity in their own homes and in the community.

State Organizations & Government Agencies/Kansas

1064 Kansas Client Assistance Program
Disability Rights Center of Kansas
635 SW Harrison, Suite 100
Topeka, KS 66603
785-273-9661
877-776-1541
e-mail: info@drckansas.org
http://www.drckansas.org

Rocky Nichols, Executive Director

CAP assists anyone with a disability that is interested in applying for and receiving services from rehabilitation programs, projects or facilities funded under the Rehabilitation Act.

1065 Kansas Commission on Disability Concerns
1000 Sw Jackson St.
Suite 100
Topeka, KS 66612-1877
785-296-1722
800-295-5232
Fax: 785-296-6809
http://www.kcdinfo.com
TDD 800-295-5232

Martha Gabehart, Executive Director
Pat Eakes, Legislative Liaison

KCDC believes that all people with disabilities are entitled to be equal partners in Kansas society. The purpose is to involve all sentiments of the Kansas Community through legislative advocacy, education and resource networking to ensure full and equal citizenship for all Kansas with disabilities.

1066 Kansas Commission on Veterans Affairs
Jayhawk Tower 700 SW Jackson
Room 701
Topeka, KS 66603-3743
785-296-3976
Fax: 785-296-1462
e-mail: kcva002@ink.org
http://www.kcva.org

Eugene Wages, Director
George Webb, Executive Director

1067 Kansas Department of Human Resources: Commission on Disabilities Concern
1000 SW Jackson Street Suite 100
Topeka, KS 66612-1354
785-296-1772
800-295-5232
Fax: 785-296-3490
e-mail: mgaehart@kansascommerce.com
http://http://kdoch.state.ks.us

Martha K Gabehart, Executive Director

For years the Kansas Commission on Disability Concerns (KCDC) has focused on enhancing employment opportunities for people with disabilities. Though we have expanded over the years to include activities that deal with education, housing, transportation and personal care assistance, employment remains a continuous part of our activities.

1068 Kansas Department of Revenue
915 SW Harrison Street
Topeka, KS 66625
785-296-3959
877-526-7738
Fax: 785-291-3614
http://www.ksrevenue.org
TDD 785-296-6461

Gary J Daniels, CEO

1069 Kansas Department of Social and Rehabilitation Services
915 SW Harrison Street
Topeka, KS 66612
785-296-3959
Fax: 785-296-2173
http://www.srskansas.org

Laura Howard, Deputy Secretary

Mission is to protect children and promote adult self-sufficiency

1070 Kansas Department on Aging
503 S Kansas Avenue
Topeka, KS 66603-9800
785-296-4986
800-432-3535
Fax: 785-296-0256
http://www.k4s.org/kdoa/default.htm

Wilda Davidson, Customer Relations Director

Provides information on services available to seniors within Kansas.

1071 Kansas Developmental Disability Council
Docking State Office
Building 141
Topeka, KS 66612-1570
785-296-2608
Fax: 785-296-2861
http://www.kcdd.org

Jane Rhys, Executive Director
Donna Beauchamp, Council Chair

Mission is to ensure the opportunity to make choices regarding participation in society and quality of life for individuals with developmental disabilities.

1072 Kansas Employment Services and Job Training Program Liaison
Kansas Department of Human Resources
401 SW Topeka Boulevard
Topeka, KS 66603-3151
785-296-7874
Fax: 785-293-5112

Steve Kelly, Manager

1073 Kansas Mental Health & Retardation Service
Docking State Office Building
915 SW Harrison, 10th Floor East
Topeka, KS 66612-1570
785-296-7272
Fax: 785-296-6142
e-mail: sxxe@srskansas.org
http://www.srskansas.org

Steven Erikson, Director

Agencies are mandated to protect and advocate for the rights of people with mental illnesses and to investigate reports of abuse and neglect in facilities that care for or treat individuals with mental illness.

1074 Kansas Public Employees Retirement System
611 S Kansas Avenue
Topeka, KS 66603-3803
785-296-6166
888-275-5737
Fax: 785-296-6638
e-mail: kpers@kpers.org
http://www.kpers.org

Glenn Deck, President

1075 Kansas Specialty Dog Service
124 W 7th Street
216
Washington, KS 66968-2222
785-325-2258
Fax: 785-325-2258
e-mail: ksds@washingtonks.net
http://www.gdui.org/ksds

Karen Price, Chief Executive Officer
Lori Haber, Development Coordinator
Michelle Woerner, Training Department Coordinator

1076 National Federation of the Blind of Kansas
11905 Mohawk Lane
Shawnee Mission, KS 66209-1038
913-339-9341
Fax: 913-339-6031
e-mail: susan.stanzel@kc.rr.com
http://www.nfbks.org

Donna J Wood, President
Susan L Stanzel, First Vice President
Tom Page, Second Vice President

Works for complete equality and integration of the blind in society. Provides support and information services.

State Organizations & Government Agencies/Kansas

1077 **National Silver-Haired Congress: Kansas Department on Aging**
503 S Kansas Avenue
Topeka, KS 66603-3404
785-296-4986
800-432-3535
Fax: 785-296-0256
e-mail: wwwmail@aging.state.ks.us
http://www.agingkansas.org

A grassroots initiative that promotes support of issues involving older adults and intergenerational concerns. It is not a lobbying effort, and policy is not created by a board in a top down manner. It has been designed as an educational effort administered by and for older adults. To serve, you must be at least 60 years old at the time of filing as a candidate for election.

1997

1078 **North Central Flint Hills Area: Agency on Aging**
401 Houston Street
Manhattan, KS 66502-6135
785-776-9294
800-432-2703
Fax: 785-776-9479
e-mail: ncfhaaa@ncfhaaa.com
http://www.agingkansas.org/aaa

Julie Govert Walter, Executive Director

Works in partnership with local senior citizens, county aging organizations and state and federal agencies to plan, coordinate and sponsor a wide variety of programs and services to keep older Kansas active, healthy and independent.

1079 **Northeast Kansas Area: Agency on Aging**
526 Oregon Street
Hiawatha, KS 66434-2222
785-742-7152
800-883-2549
Fax: 785-742-7154
e-mail: nekaaa@hotmail.com
http://www.k4s.org

Jim Beckwith, Executive Director

Northeast Kansas Area Agency on Aging is a single point of entry for senior citizens in a 7 county area. Services range from in-home help, insurance counseling, information to educational programs. We serve senior citizens 60 and over. Some in-home services cost a minimal amount while others are no cost.

1080 **Northwest Kansas Area: Agency on Aging**
1300 North 78th Street
Suite 100
Kansas City, KS 66112-1540
913-573-8532
888-661-1444
Fax: 913-573-8577
e-mail: janwilliams@wycokck.org
http://www.agingkansas.org/aaa/psa1.htm

Jan Williams, Director

Provides needs and services to Senior Adults. Acts as an advocacte for their interests, and to provide a means for Senior Adults to gain and maintain direct input into decision-making processes.

1081 **RSVP Barton County**
1125 Williams
Great Bend, KS 67530
620-792-1614
Fax: 620-792-3305
e-mail: warrenma@bartonccc.edu
http://www.seniorservice.org

Mary Lou Warren, Director

Barton RSVP can help you find a volunteer opportunity that will use your talents, skills and experiences in many areas, including literacy, in-home assistance, natural emergencies and more.

1082 **RSVP Butler County**
510 E Augusta Avenue
Augusta, KS 67010-2100
316-775-0500
Fax: 316-775-0555
http://www.bucoks.com

Melody Gault, RSVP Project Director

The Retired and Senior Volunteer Program (RSVP) provides opportunities for people 55 and over to make a difference in their community through volunteer service. RSVP volunteers contribute anywhere from a few to over forty hours a week, serving though schools, day care centers, police departments, hospitals and other nonprofit and public organizations to help meet critical community needs. RSVP offers maximum flexibility and choice to its volunteers. RSVP matches the personal interests and skills to older Americans with opportunities to help solve community problems and offer supplemental insurance while on duty, on-the-job training from the agency or organization where volunteers are placed.

1083 **RSVP Finney County**
907 N Tenth Street
Garden City, KS 67846-5209
620-275-5566
Fax: 620-275-2285
e-mail: finneycountyrsvp@sbcglobal.net
http://www.seniorcenterfc.com/RSVP.html

Marty Dinkel, Director

The Retired and Senior Volunteer Program (RSVP) provides opportunities for people 55 and over to make a difference in their community through volunteer service. RSVP volunteers contribute anywhere from a few to over forty hours a week, serving through schools, day care centers, police departments, hospitals and other nonprofit and public organizations to help meet critical community needs. RSVP offers maximum flexibility and choice to its volunteers. RSVP matches the personal interests and skills of older Americans with opportunities to help solve community problems and offers supplemental insurance while on duty, on-the-job training from the agency or organization where volunteers are placed. The following County served is: Finney.

1084 **RSVP Ford County**
Dodge City Community College
2501 N 14 Street
Dodge City, KS 67801-2733
620-227-7077
Fax: 620-227-5117
e-mail: dallen@dc3.edu
http://www.seniorservice.org/dodge_city_rsvp

Debbie Allen, Director

Places persons age 55 and older in volunteer roles that match their skills and personal interests. Our volunteers serve at over 80 work stations. The following Counties are served: Clark, Edwards, Ford, Gray, Hodgeman, Meade.

1085 **RSVP Harvey County**
Harvey County Courthouse
800 North Main Street
Newton, KS 67114-1807
316-284-6881
Fax: 316-284-6856
e-mail: rbarrera@harveycounty.com
http://www.seniorcorps.org

Rosa Barrera, Director

The Retired and Senior Volunteer Program (RSVP) provides opportunities for people 55 and over to make a difference in their community through volunteer service. RSVP volunteers contribute anywhere from a few to over forty hours a week, serving through schools, day care centers, police departments, hospitals and other nonprofit and public organizations to help meet critical community needs. RSVP offers maximum flexibility and choice to its volunteers. RSVP matches the personal interests and skills of older Americans with opportunities to help solve community problems and offers supplemental insurance while on duty, on-the-job training from the agency or organization where volunteers are placed.

1086 **RSVP Johnson County**
9707 Metcalf Avenue
3rd Floor
Overland Park, KS 66212-2219
913-341-1792
Fax: 913-341-0275
e-mail: info@vcjc.org
http://www.vcjc.org

Elaine Perrilla, Executive Director
Cara Dickerson, RSVP Director

State Organizations & Government Agencies/Kansas

RSVP of Johnson County partners with approximately 150 agencies across the metro area. Volunteers are giving their time and expertise by delivering meals to homebound individuals, assisting teachers, making quilts for children in hospitals, cashiering at hospital gift shops, tutoring students, and much more. The following Counties are served: Johnson.

1087 RSVP Northwest Kansas
Colby Community College
165 Fike Park
PO Box 803
Colby, KS 67701-2447
785-462-6744
Fax: 785-462-6283
e-mail: rsvp@colby.cc.ks.us
http://www.newlifestyles.com

Laura Withington, Director

The Retired and Senior Volunteer Program (RSVP) provides opportunities for people 55 and over to make a difference in their community through volunteer service. RSVP volunteers contribute anywhere from a few to over forty hours a week, serving through schools, day care centers, police departments, hospitals and other nonprofit and public organizations to help meet critical community needs. RSVP offers maximum flexibility and choice to its volunteers. RSVP matches the personal interests and skills of older Americans with opportunities to help solve community problems and offers supplemental insurance while on duty, on-the-job training from the agency or organization where volunteers are placed. The following Counties are served: Logan, Phillips, Sheridan, Thomas.

1088 RSVP Pratt County
619 N Main Street
Pratt, KS 67124-1661
620-672-7811
Fax: 620-672-9323
e-mail: prattrsvp@sbcglobal.net

Nancy Badders, Director

The Retired and Senior Volunteer Program (RSVP) provides opportunities for people 55 and over to make a difference in their community through volunteer service. RSVP volunteers contribute anywhere from a few to over forty hours a week, serving through schools, day care centers, police departments, hospitals and other nonprofit and public organizations to help meet critical community needs. RSVP offers maximum flexibility and choice to its volunteers. RSVP matches the personal interests and skills of older Americans with opportunities to help solve community problems and offers supplemental insurance while on duty, on-the-job training from the agency or organization where volunteers are placed. The following Counties are served: Barber, Kiowa, Pratt.

1089 RSVP Reno County
815 N Walnut
Hutchinson, KS 67501-5831
620-665-4960
Fax: 620-665-4965
e-mail: volunteercenter@hutchcc.edu
http://www.hutch.edu/rsvp

Debbie Berndsen, Director
Leah Winkel, Assistant Director
Cyndi Fredericks, Recruitment Coordinator

The Retired and Senior Volunteer Program (RSVP) provides opportunities for people 55 and over to make a difference in their community through volunteer service. RSVP volunteers contribute anywhere from a few to over forty hours a week, serving thourgh schools, day care centers, police departments, hospitals and other nonprofit and public organizations to help meet critical community needs. RSVP offers maximum flexibility and choice to its volunteers. RSVP matches the personal interests and skills to older Americans with opportunities to help solve community problems and offer supplemental insurance while on duty, on-the-job training from the agency or organization where volunteers are placed.

1090 RSVP Riley County
205 South 4th Street
Suite 1K
Manhattan, KS 66502-5923
785-776-7787
Fax: 785-776-0704

Lori Bishop, Executive Director

The Retired and Senior Volunteer Program (RSVP) provides opportunities for people 55 and over to make a difference in their community through volunteer service. RSVP volunteers contribute anywhere from a few to over forty hours a week, serving through schools, day care centers, police departments, hospitals and other nonprofit and public organizations to help meet critical community needs. RSVP offers maximum flexibility and choice to its volunteers. RSVP matches the personal interests and skills of older Americans with opportunities to help solve community problems and offers supplemental insurance while on duty, on-the-job training from the agency or organization where volunteers are placed. The following Counties are served: Clay, Marshall, Pottawatomie, Riley, Washington.

1091 RSVP Saline County
239 N Santa Fe Avenue
Salina, KS 67401-2317
785-823-3128
Fax: 785-823-3819
e-mail: rsvp@salhelp.org
http://www.salhelp.org/volunteerconnection

Nancy Klostermeyer, Director

The Retired and Senior Volunteer Program (RSVP) provides opportunities for people 55 and over to make a difference in their community through volunteer service. RSVP volunteers contribute anywhere from a few to over forty hours a week, serving through schools, day care centers, police departments, hospitals and other nonprofit and public organizations to help meet critical community needs. RSVP offers maximum flexibility and choice to its volunteers. RSVP matches the personal interest and skills of older Americans with opportunities to help solve community problems and offers supplemental insurance while on duty, on-the-job training from the agency or organization where volunteers are placed. The following County is served: Saline.

1092 RSVP Southeast Kansas
3740 S Santa Fe
Chanute, KS 66720
620-431-3902
Fax: 620-431-1409
e-mail: pallen@tvds.org

Patty Allen, RSVP Director

Volunteer Program for those 55 years of age or older. Seventy volunteer stations are available where volunteers can serve to make a positive impact in their community.

1093 RSVP Wyandotte County
434 Minnesota Avenue
PO Box 17-1042
Kansas City, KS 66117
913-371-3674
Fax: 913-371-2718
e-mail: cedwards@unitedway-wyco.org
http://www.unitedway-wyco.org

Chandra Edwards, Director

The Retired and Senior Volunteer Program (RSVP) provides opportunities for people 55 and over to make a difference in their community through volunteer service. RSVP volunteers contribute anywhere from a few to over forty hours a week, serving through schools, day care centers, police departments, hospitals and other nonprofit and public organizations to help meet critical community needs. RSVP offers maximum flexibility and choice to its volunteers. RSVP matches the personal interests and skills of older Americans with opportunities to help solve community problems and offers supplemental insurance while on duty, on-the-job training from the agency or organization where volunteers are placed. The following County is served: Wyandotte.

1094 Railroad Retirement Board: Kansas
271 West 3rd Street N
Suite 4010
Wichita, KS 67202-1294
620-287-5973
800-808-0772
Fax: 316-687-3572
e-mail: wichita@rrb.gov
http://www.rrb.gov

Mark Thomson, Representative

State Organizations & Government Agencies/Kentucky

The Railroad Retirement Board (RRB) is an independent agency in the executive branch of the Federal Government. The RRB's primary function is to administer comprehensive retirement-survivor and unemployment-sickness benefit programs for the nation's railroad workers and their families, under the Railroad Retirement and Railroad Umemployment Insurance Acts. In connection with the retirement program, the RRB has administrative responsibilities under the Social Security Act for certain benefit payments and railroad workers' Medicare coverage.

1095 South Central Kansas Area Agency on Aging
304 S Summit
Po Box 1122
Arkansas City, KS 67005-1122
620-442-0268
800-362-0264
Fax: 620-442-0296
e-mail: info@skcaaa.org
http://www.sckaaa.org

Betty Londeen, Executive Director

The role of the agency is to plan, coordinate and to adovocate for the development of comprehensive service delivery system to meet the needs of older persons living in Planning and Service area no 10, Chautauqua, Cowley, Elk, Greenwood, Harper, Kingman, McPherson, Reno, Rice and Summer counties.

1096 Southeast Kansas Area: Agency on Aging
1 W Ash
Chanute, KS 66720-1010
620-431-2980
800-794-2440
Fax: 620-431-2988
e-mail: sekaaa@hotmail.com
http://www.agingkansas.org/aaa

John Green, Administrator

The general purpose of the Southeast Kansas Area Agency on Aging is to assess the needs of persons 60 years of age or older and plan the delivery of priority service programs.

Kentucky

1097 Barren River Area Development District
177 Graham Av
Bowling Green, KY 42101
270-781-2381
800-598-2381
Fax: 270-842-0768
http://www.bradd.org

Debbie McCartey, Executive Director

1098 Big Sandy Area Development District
110 Resource Court
Prestonsburg, KY 41653
606-886-2374
800-737-2723
Fax: 606-886-3382
e-mail: sandy.runyon@bigsandy.org
http://www.bigsandy.org

Sandy Runyon, Executive Director

AÆmulti-county organization charged with planning, promoting, and coordinating programs for regional economic and social development.

1099 Bluegrass Area Agency on Aging
699 Perimeter Drive
Lexington, KY 40517
859-269-8021
866-229-0018
Fax: 859-269-7917
e-mail: aging@bglife.com
http://www.newlifestyles.com

Lenny Stoltz, II, Executive Director

As a part of a national network, our role is to develop and coordinate a comprehensive service delivery system to meet the needs of seniors in Central Kentucky. Counties served: Anderson, Bourbon, Boyle, Clark, Estill, Fayette, Franklin, Garrard, Harrison, Jessamine, Lincoln, Madison, Mercer, Nicholas, Powell, Scott and Woodford.

1100 Buffalo Trace Area Agency on Aging
201 Government Street, Suite 300
PO Box 460
Maysville, KY 41056
606-564-6894
800-998-4347
Fax: 606-564-0955
http://www.btadd.com

Caroline Ullery, Aging Planner

Buffalo Trace Area Development District is a state designated Area Agency on Aging and part of a National Network on Aging under the direction of the US Administration on Aging and under the supervision of the Kentucky Office of Aging Services. An Area Agency on Aging holds the responsibility of implementing the Older Americans Act of 1965, as amended, and charged with the responsibility of identifying the needs of the elderly, addressing those needs as well as serving as an advocate on behalf of all Older Americans at the local level. Counties served: Bracken, Fleming, Lewis, Mason, and Robertson.

1101 Community Action Council: Lexington Fayette Jessamine Counties
710 West High Street
PO Box 11610
Lexington, KY 40576
859-223-4600
Fax: 859-244-2219
e-mail: bgeran@commaction.org

Jack E Burch, Executive Director

The Retired and Senior Volunteer Program serves community organizations, historic sites, health care facilities, and more by placing volunteers at locations throughout Fayette and Jessamine counties. The volunteers serve as mentors, tutors and caregivers for at-risk children and youth or fill the needs of nonprofits by providing a helping hand.

1102 Cumberland Valley Area: Agency on Aging
342 Old Whitley Road
Po Box 1740
London, KY 40743-1740
606-864-7391
Fax: 606-878-7361
http://http://chfs.ky.gov/agencies/os

Andrew Meadors, Executive Director

Home to most of the states human services and health care programs.

1103 Department for Disability Determination Services
PO Box 1000
Frankfort, KY 40602-1000
800-928-8050
e-mail: margaret.trinkle@ssa.gov
http://www.ssa.gov/disability

Margaret Trinkle, Manager

The Kentucky Disability Determination Services (DDS) is a division of the the Department of Labor and Workforce Development fully funded by the Federal Government, and is responsible for developing medical evidence and making the determination on whether residents of Kentucky are or are not disabled under Social Security disability law.

1104 Disabled American Veterans
3725 Alexandria Pike
Cold Spring, KY 41076-1799
859-441-7300
877-426-2838
Fax: 859-441-1416
http://www.dav.org

Bradley S Barton, Chairman
Raymond E Dempsey, Vice-Chairman
Arthur H Wilson, Secretary

An organization of disabled veterans who are focused on building better lives for disabled veterans and their families.

1105 FIVCO Area: Agency on Aging
3000 Louisa St
Catlettsburg, KY 41129
606-929-1366
Fax: 606-327-0023
http://www.fivco.org

Sherry McDavid, Executive Director
Tom Saylor, Associate Director

State Organizations & Government Agencies/Kentucky

1106 Gateway Area Development District
110 Lake Park Drive
Morehead, KY 40351
606-780-0090
Fax: 606-780-0111
http://www.gwadd.org

Gail K Wright, Executive Director
Regina Back, Aging Director

1107 Green River Area: Agency on Aging
3860 Highway 60 West
Owensboro, KY 42301
270-926-4433
Fax: 270-684-0714
e-mail: jitenshah@at.gradd.com
http://www.gradd.com

Jiten Shah, Executive Director

The mission of the Green River Area Development District (GRADD) is to afford local governments and citizens a regional forum to identify issues and opportunities, and to provide leadership in planning and implementing programs to improve the quality of life in our district.

1108 Kentucky Cabinet for Education, Arts and The Humanities: Commission for the Deaf and Hearing Impaired
632 Versailles Road
Frankfort, KY 40601-3858
502-573-2604
800-372-2907
Fax: 502-573-3594

Bobbie Beth Scoggine, Executive Director

1109 Kentucky Cabinet for Workforce Development: Department for the Blind
209 St. Claire Street
PO Box 757
Frankfort, KY 40602-0757
502-564-4754
800-321-6668
Fax: 502-564-2951
e-mail: blind@ky.gov
http://www.blind.ky.gov
TDD 502-564-2929

Stephen Johnson, Executive Director

Our mission is to provide opportunities for employment and independence to individuals with visual disabilities. We offer services to assist their effort to become more independent and productive in the workplace, community, school, and home.

1110 Kentucky Client Assistance Program
209 St. Claire Street
5th Floor
Frankfort, KY 40601
502-564-8035
800-633-6283
Fax: 502-564-1566
e-mail: vickil.staggs@mail.state.ky.us
http://http://kycap.ky.gov

Gerry Gordon-Brown, CAP Director

Provides information, advice and advocacy on benefits available from rehabilitation programs to individuals with disabilities.

1111 Kentucky Council on Developmental Disabilities
100 Fair Oaks Lane
4E-F
Frankfort, KY 40621
502-564-7841
877-367-5332
Fax: 502-564-9826
e-mail: shelley.runkle@ky.gov
http://www.chfs.ky.gov/kcdd

Pat Sybold, Executive Director
Leslie Mason, Program Administrator
Vicki Goins, Internal Policy Analyst

The Kentucky Council on Developmental Disabilities is to create change through visonary leadership and advocacy so that people have choices and control over their own lives.

1112 Kentucky Department of Veterans Affairs
1111 Louisville Road (NGAKY Bldg.)
Frankfort, KY 40601
502-564-9203
Fax: 502-564-9240
http://www1.va.gov/vso

Pamela Luce, Manager

Goal is to provide excellence in patient care, veteran's benefits and customer satisfaction. We have reformed our department internally and are striving for high quality, prompt and seamless service to veterans. Our department's employees continue to offer their dedication and commitment to help veterans gtet the service they have earned. Our nations veterans deserve NO less.

1113 Kentucky Department of Workers Claims
657 Chamberlain Avenue
Frankfort, KY 40601-6117
502-564-5550
Fax: 502-564-5732
e-mail: debora.wingate.ky.gov
http://www.labor.ky.gov/workersclaims

Dwight T Lovan, Executive Director

1114 Kentucky Division of Mental Health
Cabinet for Human Resources
100 Fair Oaks Lane
4E-D
Frankfort, KY 40621-0001
502-564-5777
Fax: 502-564-9010
e-mail: mapennington@mail.state.ky.us
http://http://mhmr.ky.gov/mhsas/default.asp

Donna Hillman, Director
Lisa Rice, Assistant Director

The Department of Mental Health and Mental Retardation Services contracts with fourteen regional community mental health and mental retardation boards to provide an array of community based mental health services, operates four psychiatric hospitals and contracts with a fifth hospital for 100 adult beds.

1115 Kentucky Office of Aging Services
Cabinet for Families and Children
275 E Main Street
5W-A
Frankfort, KY 40621
502-564-6930
Fax: 502-564-4595
http://www.chfs.ky.gov

Jerry Whitley, Director

Home to most of the state's human services and health care programs.

1116 Kentucky Protection & Advocacy Division
100 Fair Oaks Lane
Third Floor
Frankfort, KY 40601
502-564-2967
800-372-2988
Fax: 502-564-0848
http://www.kypa.net/drupal

Maureen Fitzgerald, Executive Director

Protecting the rights of persons with disabilities in Kentucky providing information and referral, training, and technical assistance.

1117 Kentucky Retirement Systems
Perimeter Park West
1260 Louisville Road
Frankfort, KY 40601-6124
502-696-8800
800-928-4646
Fax: 502-696-8822
e-mail: krs.mail@kyret.com
http://www.kyret.com

Robert M Burnside, Executive Director
Gerri D Miller, Chief Benefits Officer
William Thielen, Chief Operations Officer

Kentucky Retirement Systems is responsible for the investment of funds and administration of benefits for over 267,000 state and local governement employees in the Commonwealth of Kentucky. These employees include state employees, state police officers, city and county employees, as well as nonteaching staff of local school boards and regional universities.

State Organizations & Government Agencies/Kentucky

1118 Kentucky Revenue Cabinet
501 High Street
Frankfort, KY 40620
502-564-4581
Fax: 502-564-3685
http://www.state.ky.us/agencies/revenue
Bonnie Lee, Executive Director

1119 Kentucky River Area: Agency on Aging
917 Perry Park Road
Hazard, KY 41701
606-436-3158
Fax: 606-436-2144
e-mail: peggy@kradd.org
http://www.kradd.org/aging
Peggy Koll, Human Services Director

Serves Lee, Breathett, Ousley, Wolfe, Leidue, Perry, Knott, Letcher counties elderly populations.

1120 Kentucky Teachers Retirement System
479 Versailles Road
Frankfort, KY 40601-3800
502-848-8500
800-618-1687
Fax: 502-573-0199
e-mail: ktrs.info@ky.gov
http://www.ktrs.ky.gov
Gary Harbin, President

1121 Kentuckyiana Regional Planning &Development Agency (KIPDA)
11520 Commonwealth Drive
Louisville, KY 40299-2340
502-266-6084
Fax: 502-266-5047
e-mail: kipda.trans@ky.gov
http://www.kipda.org
TDD 800-648-6056
Jack Scriber, Executive Director
Tom Pope, Director Finance

KIPDA provides regional planning, review and technical services in the areas of public administration, social services and transportation as well as community ridesharing programs. KIPDA also coordinates services for persons 60 years of age and over. KIPDA is designated by the Kentucky State Clearinghouse as the regional review agency for virtually all applications for federal and/or state funds made by organizations or governments within the state of Kentucky.

1122 Lake Cumberland Area Development District Area: Agency on Aging
PO Box 1570
Russell Springs, KY 42642-1570
270-866-4200
Fax: 270-866-2044
e-mail: cindy.branscum@mail.state.ky.us
http://http://lcadd.org
Cindy Branseum, Elderly Services Diretor
Joyce Flowers, Homecare Coordinator
Donna Diaz, Executive Director

Helps frail and elderly remain at home provding in home and community based services.

1123 Lincoln Trail Area: Agency on Aging
613 College Street Road
PO Box 604
Elizabethtown, KY 42702-0604
270-769-2393
800-264-0393
Fax: 270-769-2993
e-mail: nancy@ltadd.org
http://www.ltadd.org
Nancy Addington, Director

Our mission is to build the capacity of its members to help older persons and persons with disabilities live with dignity and choices in their homes and communities for as long as possible. The following Counties are served: Breckinridge, Grayson, Hardin, Larue, Marion, Nelson, Washington.

1124 Metro United Way
334 E Broadway
PO Box 4488
Louisville, KY 40204-0488
502-583-2821
877-566-2821
Fax: 502-583-0330
e-mail: info@metrounitedway.org
http://www.metrounitedway.org
TDD 502-589-4259
Joseph P Tolan, President

1125 North Kentucky Area Development District
22 Spiral Drive
Florence, KY 41042-1300
859-283-1885
Fax: 859-283-8178
e-mail: nkadd@nkadd.org
http://www.nakadd.org
John Mays, Manager
Area Agency on Aging

1126 Purchase Area Development District
PO Box 588
Mayfield, KY 42066
270-247-7171
Fax: 270-251-6110

1127 RSVP Audubon Area
1650 W 2nd Street
Drawer 107
Owensboro, KY 42301
270-683-1589
Fax: 270-683-1580
e-mail: cferrell@audubon-area.com
http://www.audubon-area.com
Cindy Ferrell, Director

The Retired and Senior Volunteer Program (RSVP) provides opportunities for people 55 and over to make a difference in their community through volunteer service. RSVP volunteers contribute anywhere from a few to over forty hours a week, serving through schools, day care centers, police departments, hospitals and other nonprofit and public organizations to help meet critical community needs. RSVP offers maximum flexibility and choice to its volunteers. RSVP matches the personal interests and skills of older Americans with opportunities to help solve community problems and offers supplemental insurance while on duty, on-the-job training from the agency or organization where volunteers are placed. The following Counties are served: Daviess, Hancock, Henderson, McLean, Ohio, Union, Webster.

1128 RSVP Brighton Center
799 Ann Street
PO Box 325
Newport, KY 41072
859-491-8303
Fax: 859-491-8702
e-mail: dmilavec@brightoncenter.com
http://www.brightoncenter.com
Deborah Rose-Milavec, Director

To create opportunities for individuals and families to reach self-sufficiency through family support services, education and leadership throughout the communities of Northern Kentucky. We will achieve this mission by creating an environment which rewards excellence and innovation, encourages mutual respect and maximizes resources.

1129 RSVP Central Kentucky
617 N Mulberry Street
Suite 4
Elizabethtown, KY 42701-1940
270-737-0669
Fax: 270-234-8764
e-mail: ckrsvp@aol.com
Judy Cedarholm, Director

State Organizations & Government Agencies/Louisiana

The Retired and Senior Volunteer Program (RSVP) provides opportunities for people 55 and over to make a difference in their community through volunteer service. RSVP volunteers contribute anywhere from a few to over forty hours a week, serving through schools, day care centers, police departments, hospitals and other nonprofit and public organizations to help meet critical community needs. RSVP offers maximum flexibility and choice to its volunteers. RSVP matches the personal interests and skills of older Americans with opportunities to help solve community problems and offers supplemental insurance while on duty, on-the-job training from the agency or organization where volunteers are placed. The following Counties are served: Breckinridge, Grayson, Hardin, Larue, Nelson.

1130 RSVP Hickman-McCracken Counties
1400 H C Mathis Drive
Paducah, KY 42001   270-442-8993
                       Fax: 270-443-8609
e-mail: seniorcenter@ci.paducah.ky.us
Ann Ponder Simpson, Director

Our mission is to provide an affordable and positive comprehensive system of recreation programs designed to enhance the quality of life for the residents of the City of Paducah as well as surrounding communities. We will strive to organize and implement leisure pursuits that promote the mental, social, and physical well being of all actively or passively participating citizens regardless of socioeconomic background, race, creed or religion.

1131 RSVP Louisville Metro Community Action Partnership
1200 S 3rd Street
Louisville, KY 40203-2906   502-574-1157
                             Fax: 502-637-6814
e-mail: sarah.richie@loukymetro.org
http://www.louisvilleky.gov
Kimberly Bunton, Interim Executive Director
Sarah Richie, Social Svc Program Supervisor

Provides opportunities for persons 55 and over to have a continuing positive impact on their community through meaningful volunteer projects.

1132 RSVP Mason County
115 1/2 E Third Street
Maysville, KY 41056   606-564-5511
                         Fax: 606-564-5512
e-mail: rsvp@magy-UKY.campuswix.net
Pat Stephenson, Director

RSVP helps people age 55 and older find volunteer service opportunities in their communities. RSVP particiapants serve from a few to over forty hours a week in organizations that range from hospital and youth centers to local service agencies and education facilities. RSVP involves seniors in service that matches their personal interests and makes use of their skills and lifelong experiences.

1133 Railroad Retirement Board: Kentucky District Office
PO Box 3705
Louisville, KY 40201-3705   502-582-5208
                             Fax: 502-582-5518
e-mail: luisville@rrb.gov
Gene Guyhan, Manager

1134 Senior Citizens of Whitley County
107 S 4th Street
Williamsburg, KY 40769-1221   606-549-5600
Virginia Hayes, Director

Provides information and referral service, meals, transportation, escorts, and domestic services for people over the age of 60.

1135 Senior Services of Northern Kentucky
1032 Madison Avenue
Covington, KY 41011-3172   859-491-0522
                            Fax: 859-491-4590
e-mail: bdouglas@seniorservices.nky.org
http://www.seniorservicesnky.org
Barbara Gunn, President/CEO
Lonnie E Fields, VP Finance/Administration
Marianne Burke, VP Client Services

Senior Services of Northern Kentucky provides a vital role in keeping older adults healthy, by providing healthy nutrition (Meals on Wheels), education programs on health and wellness, transportation for medical appointments and a wide array of social services. By keeping the elderly healthy they can remain a vital part of their community and can continue to live in their own home.

1136 Social Security: Louisville Disability Determination
PO Box 1061
Louisville, KY 40201-1061   502-582-6690

Louisiana

1137 Beauregard Council on Aging
PO Box 534
Deridder, LA 70634   337-463-6578
                        Fax: 337-463-7431
e-mail: CLGBCOA@aol.com
http://www.beau.org
Connie Granger, Executive Director

The Beauregard Council on Aging is a multipurpose center whose total program is to provide development and delivery of services for persons sixty years of age and over and/or their spouse. The center also serves as a community resource for information, referral and training in the field of aging. We operate under the Governor's Office of Elderly Affairs. The program is funded by both federal and state funds. The BCOA is a non-discriminating agency that encourages participation of low-income, minority, socially needy, and the handicapped. However, anyone sixty years of age or older is eligible for our services.

1138 Bienville Area: Agency on Aging
112 Courthouse Drive
Arcadia, LA 71001-3617   318-263-8936
                           Fax: 318-263-9774
Gertie Baker, Manager

1139 Bossier Council on Aging Area: Agency on Aging
706 Bearkat Drive
Bossier City, LA 71111-4566   318-741-8303
                              800-256-8993
                         Fax: 318-741-7490
Mary Ann Rankin, Executive Director

1140 Bureau of Naval Personnel: Louisiana Retired Activities Office
Fleet and Family Support Center
2300 General Meyer Avenue
Code N 83
New Orleans, LA 70142-5007   504-678-2134
                            Fax: 504-678-9024

The RAO serves as a link between local retired military and the active-duty community which provides assistance to retired military. It provides installation commanders with a means of providing more effective services and improving communication for the local retired community. The RAO is staffed and operated by volunteer retired military who assist other retired members, their families and survivors to receive entitled services and benefits. Through newsletters, seminars and appreciation days, the RAO supports quality of life issues throughout the retirement years to their fellow service members.

State Organizations & Government Agencies/Louisiana

1141 Caddo Council on Aging
4015 Greenwood Road
Shreveport, LA 71109-6422
318-632-2090
800-256-3003
Fax: 318-632-2095

Maryalice Rountree, Executive Director

1142 Cajun Area: Agency on Aging
1304 Bertrand Drive
Suite F6
Lafayette, LA 70506-9106
337-572-8940
800-738-2256
Fax: 337-237-7756

Shannon Broussard, Manager

1143 Calcasieu Council of Aging
3950 Highway 14
Lake Charles, LA 70607
337-474-2583
800-223-5872
Fax: 337-474-6563
http://www.calcoa.org

Sonya Caraway, Director

It is the sole purpose of the Calcasieu Council of Aging to assist older adults in order to remain independent in their own homes.

1144 Caldewell Parish Council on Aging
PO Box 1498
Columbia, LA 71418-1498
318-649-0107
Fax: 318-649-7600
e-mail: dottie@caldwellcoa.org
http://www.caldwellcoa.org

Dottie Etheridge, Executive Director
Monica Pauley, Assistant Director

Congregate Meals, Home Delivered Meals, Recreation, Information and Assistance, Homemaker Services, Transportation, Medication Mangement, Nutrition Counseling, Nutrition Education, Legal Assistance are some of the services offered.

1145 Cameron Council on Aging
PO Box 8801
Lake Charles, LA 70606-8801
337-775-5668
e-mail: dinahtoby@aol.com

Dinah Landry, Executive Director

Cameron Council on Aging program helps older people to remain health, find jobs, discover new ways to continue contributing to society after retirement, and take advantage of government and private benefits programs that can improve the quality of their lives.

1146 Capital Area: Agency on Aging
PO Box 86430
Baton Rouge, LA 70879-6430
225-923-8000
Fax: 225-923-8030

1147 Claiborne Voluntary Council on Aging
608 E 4th Street
PO Box 480
Homer, LA 71040-3530
318-927-6922
Fax: 318-927-1070
e-mail: clab@bayou.com

Josephine Miller, Executive Director

Services are for persons over 60 years of age.

1148 De Soto Council on Aging Area: Agency on Aging
1004 Polk Street
Mansfield, LA 71052-2523
318-872-2691
Fax: 318-872-9473

Sharron Procell, Executive Director

1149 Disability Determination Services
5905 Florida Boulevard
Suite 3
Baton Rouge, LA 70806-4335
225-925-4613
Fax: 225-925-1831

Lonnie Beverly, Manager

1150 Disability Determination Services: Shreveport Branch
2920 Knight Street
Shreveport, LA 71105-2483
318-869-6400
Fax: 318-869-6406
e-mail: Robbie.Day@ssa.gov

Robbie Day, Professional Relations
Wayne Parker, Administrator

1151 East Baton Rouge Council on Aging
5790 Florida Boulevard
Baton Rouge, LA 70806-4244
225-923-8000
Fax: 985-923-8030

Johnny Dykes, Executive Director

1152 Franklin Parish Council on the Aging
714 Adams Street
Winnsboro, LA 71295-3318
318-435-7579
800-613-4710
Fax: 318-435-3518
e-mail: fpcoa@3G.quik.com

Barbara Copes, Director

Dedicated to improving the health and independence of older persons and increasing their continuing contributions to communities, society, and future generations.

1153 Jefferson Council on Aging
6640 Riverside Drive
Suite 140
Metairie, LA 70003-7110
504-888-5880
Fax: 504-888-5887
e-mail: medwards@jcoa.net
http://www.jcoa.net

Michael Edwards, Administrative Director
Thomas Laughlin, CEO

Area Agency on Aging.

1154 Lafourche Council on Aging
1612 Highway 182
PO Box 500
Raceland, LA 70394
985-537-3446
Fax: 985-537-6995
e-mail: laf.coadirector@mobiletel.com

Charlene Rodriguez, Director

Service organization for senior citizens in Lafourche Parish, LA. Conducts charitable activities.

1155 Lincoln Council on Aging
109 S Sparta Street
Ruston, LA 71270-4528
318-255-5070
Fax: 318-255-5076

Michelle Wright, Executive Director

1156 Louisiana Assistive Technology Access Network
3042 Old Forge Drive
Baton Rouge, LA 70808
225-925-9500
800-270-6185
Fax: 225-925-9560
http://www.latan.org

Julie Nesbit, President/CEO
Clara Pourciau, Assistant Director
Cyndi Mabry, Public Information Officer

LATAN assists individuals with disabilities to achieve a higher quality of life and greater independence through increased access to assistive technology as part of their daily lives.

1157 Louisiana Client Assistance Program
210 Okeefe Avenue
Suite 700
New Orleans, LA 70112-1806
504-522-2337
800-960-7705
Fax: 504-522-5507
e-mail: adcc@advocacyla.org

Susan Howard, Director

State Organizations & Government Agencies/Louisiana

Programs in each state provide information and assistance to individuals seeking or receiving service under the Rehabilitation Act of 1973.

1158 Louisiana Department of Aging
Office of Elderly Affairs
4550 North Boulevard
2nd Floor
Baton Rouge, LA 70806-4013
225-383-4761
Fax: 504-342-7100

Richard Collins, Director
George Nelson Jr, President

1159 Louisiana Department of Revenue
8490 Picardy Avenue
Baton Rouge, LA 70809-3731
225-383-4761
http://www.rev.state.la.us

George Nelson Jr, President

1160 Louisiana Department of Veterans Affairs
PO Box 94095
Baton Rouge, LA 70804-9095
225-383-4761
Fax: 225-922-0511

George Nelson Jr, President

1161 Louisiana Developmental Disability Council
647 Main Street
PO Box 3455
Baton Rouge, LA 70821-3455
225-342-6804
800-450-8108
Fax: 225-342-1970
e-mail: swinchel@dhh.la.gov
http://www.laddc.org

Sandee Winchell, Executive Director

The mission of the Council is to assure that all persons with developmental disabilities receive the best services, the most appropriate assistance, and the opportunities necessary to enable them to achieve their maximum potential through increased self determination, independence, producitivity, integration, and inclusion.

1162 Louisiana Employee's Retirement Department
PO Box 44213
Baton Rouge, LA 70804-4213
225-922-0600
800-256-3000
Fax: 225-922-0595

Bob Borden, Executive Director

1163 Louisiana Protection & Advocacy for Persons with Disabilities
210 Okeefe Avenue
Suite 700
New Orleans, LA 70112-1806
504-525-4361
Fax: 504-522-5507

Ronald Wilson

1164 Louisiana Teachers Retirement System
PO Box 94123
Baton Rouge, LA 70804-9123
225-925-6446
Fax: 225-925-3944

Maureen Westgard, Manager

1165 Louisiana Workers Compensation Board
1001 North 23rd Street
PO Box 94040
Baton Rouge, LA 70802-9040
225-342-7555
800-756-7123
Fax: 225-342-5665
e-mail: owca@ldol.state.la.us
http://www.ldol.state.la.us

From workplace safety consultation to medical examinations OWCA is working to keep Louisiana businesses safe.

1166 Madison Council on Aging
PO Box 1229
Tallulah, LA 71284-1229
318-574-4101
Fax: 318-574-4118

Sandra Thompson, Executive Director

1167 Morehouse Council on Aging
PO Box 1471
Bastrop, LA 71221-1471
318-283-0845
Fax: 318-283-0833

Reggie DeFreese, Executive Director

1168 Natchitoches Parish Council on Aging
220 E 5th Street
Natchitoches, LA 71457-5817
318-357-3250
Fax: 318-357-2424

Norma Metoyer, Manager

1169 New Orleans Council on Aging
PO Box 19067
New Orleans, LA 70179
504-821-4121
Fax: 504-821-1222

Howard Rodgers, Executive Director

1170 North Delta-Area Agency on Aging
2115 Justice Street
Monroe, LA 71201-3617
318-387-2572
Fax: 318-387-9054

David Creed, Manager

1171 Ouachita Council on Aging
PO Box 7418
Monroe, LA 71211
318-387-0535
Fax: 318-322-0545
e-mail: aging@centurytel.net
TDD 318-324-0607

Lynda McGehee, Executive Director
Shirley Cagle, Assistant Director

Responsible for carrying out a wide range of functions relative to advocacy, planning, coordination, inter-agency linkage, information sharing, brokering, monitoring, and evaluation designed to lead to the development or enhancement of comprehensive and coordinated community based system to serve all areas in Ouachita Parish.

1172 Plaquemines Council on Aging
27419 Highway 29
PO Box 189
Port Sulphur, LA 70083-0189
985-564-3220
Fax: 985-564-3338
e-mail: plaqcoal@bellsouth.net
http://plaqueminesparish.com

Yvette Glass, Director

Plaquemines Council on Aging was established to provide a variety of services to persons 60 years of age or older residing in Plaquemines Parish.

1173 Protection & Advocacy of Individual Rights
Advocacy Center for the Elderly and Disabled
1010 Common Street
Suite 2600
New Orleans, LA 70112
504-522-2337
800-960-7705
Fax: 504-522-7705
e-mail: advocacycenter@advocacyla.org
http://www.advocacyla.org

Lois Simpson, Executive Director
Elizabeth Smith, Controller

The Advocacy Center believes in the dignity of every life, and in the freedom of all people to experience the highest degree of self-determination. Embracing this philosophy, the Advocacy Center protects and advocates for the human and legal rights of persons living in Louisiana who are elderly or disabled.

State Organizations & Government Agencies/Louisiana

1174 RSVP Baton Rouge
5790 Florida Boulevard
Baton Rouge, LA 70806-4244
225-923-8000
Fax: 225-923-8030

Johnny Dykes, Executive Director

The Retired and Senior Volunteer Program (RSVP) provides opportunities for people 55 and over to make a difference in their community through volunteer service. RSVP volunteers contribute anywhere from a few to over forty hours a week, serving thourgh schools, day care centers, police departments, hospitals and other nonprofit and public organizations to help meet critical community needs. RSVP offers maximum flexibility and choice to its volunteers. RSVP matches the personal interests and skills to older Americans with opportunities to help solve community problems and offer supplemental insurance while on duty, on-the-job training from the agency or organization where volunteers are placed.

1175 RSVP Caddo-Bossier Counties
4017 Greenwood Road
Shreveport, LA 71109-6422
318-632-2112
Fax: 318-632-2134
e-mail: tmicheelsccoa@sport.rr.com

Teresa Micheels, Director

The Retired and Senior Volunteer Program (RSVP) provides opportunities for people 55 and over to make a difference in their community through volunteer service. RSVP volunteers contribute anywhere from a few to over forty hours a week, serving through schools, day care centers, police departments, hopsitals and other nonprofit and public organizations to help meet critical community needs. RSVP offers maximum flexibility and choice to its volunteers. RSVP matches the personal interests and skills of older Americans with opportunities to help solve community problems and offers supplemental insurance while on duty, on-the-job training from the agency or organization where volunteers are placed. The following Counties are served: Bossier, Caddo, De Soto.

1176 RSVP Calcasieu Parish
2017 Oak Park Boulevard
Lake Charles, LA 70601-4810
337-721-4020
Fax: 337-437-3397
http://www.cppj.net

Adele Mart, Director

The mission of this program is to create and maintain senior citizen volunteer service opportunities within the Parish for active and healthy seniors residing in Parish.

1177 RSVP Jefferson Parish
1221 Elmwood Park Boulevard
Suite 402
Harahan, LA 70123-2337
504-736-6164
Fax: 225-667-3046
e-mail: creine@jeffparish.net

Chriszelda Reine, Director

RSVP provides a variety of opportunities for retired individuals and seniors to help their community and benefit from performing useful services. Volunteers work in hospitals, offices, nursing homes, day care centers, schools. They also receive limited insurance and expense reimbursement.

1178 RSVP Lafayette
501 Saint John Street
Lafayette, LA 70501-5709
337-234-9936
Fax: 337-234-9932
e-mail: rsvp_laf@bellsouth.net
http://www.seniorservice.org

Rose Ann Meynard, Director

The Retired and Senior Volunteer Program (RSVP) provides opportunities for people 55 and over to make a difference in their community through volunteer service. RSVP volunteers contribute anywhere from a few to over forty hours a week, serving through schools, day care centers, police departments, hospitals and other nonprofit and public organizations to help meet critical community needs. RSVP offers maximum flexibility and choice to its volunteers. RSVP matches the personal interests and skills of older Americans with opportunities to help solve community problems and offers supplemental insurance while on duty, on-the-job training from the agency or organization where volunteers are placed. The following County is served: Lafayette.

1179 RSVP Lincoln Parish
1400 Oakdale Street
Ruston, LA 71270-6342
318-255-2215
Fax: 318-255-2170
e-mail: lincolnrsvp@usa.com

Chyree A Dean, Director

The Retired and Senior Volunteer Program (RSVP) provides opportunities for people 55 and over to make a difference in their community through volunteer service. RSVP volunteers contribute anywhere from a few to over forty hours a week, serving through schools, day care centers, police departments, hospitals and other nonprofit and public organizations to help meet critical community needs. RSVP offers maximum flexibility and choice to its volunteers. RSVP matches the personal interests and skills of older Americans with opportunities to help solve community problems and offers supplemental insurance while on duty, on-the-job training from the agency or organization where volunteers are placed. The following Counties are served: Bienville, Lincoln.

1180 RSVP Natchitoches Parish
415 Trudeau Street
Natchitoches, LA 71457-4444
318-357-2203
Fax: 318-352-0629
e-mail: nppjocs@cox-internet.com

Laura Lewis, Director

The Retired and Senior Volunteer Program (RSVP) provides opportunities for people 55 and over to make a difference in their community through volunteer service. RSVP volunteers contribute anywhere from a few to over forty hours a week, serving through schools, day care centers, police departments, hospitals and other nonprofit and public organizations to help meet critical community needs. RSVP offers maximum flexibility and choice to its volunteers. RSVP matchese the personal interests and skills of older Americans with opportunities to help solve community problems and offers supplemental insurance while on duty, on-the-job training from the agency or organization where volunteers are placed. The following County is served: Natchitoches.

1181 RSVP New Orleans
2475 Canal Street
Suite 400
New Orleans, LA 70119-6543
504-821-4121
Fax: 504-821-1222
e-mail: rsvp@nocoa.org
http://www.nocoa.org

Tamika L Warmington, Director

RSVP provides a link between those 55 years and older who wish to volunteer in the community and agencies that need the wisdom and talents of these volunteers with benefits such as insurance and recognition events.

1182 RSVP Ouachita Parish
4502 Bon Aire Drive
Monroe, LA 71203-3113
318-345-3716
Fax: 318-345-1992
e-mail: massey@ulm.edu

Rita Massey, Director

State Organizations & Government Agencies/Louisiana

The Retired and Senior Volunteer Program (RSVP) provides opportunities for people 55 and over to make a difference in their community through volunteer service. RSVP volunteers contribute anywhere from a few to over forty hours a week, serving through schools, day care centers, police departments, hospitals and other nonprofit and public organizations to help meet critical community needs. RSVP offers maximum flexibility and choice to its volunteers. RSVP matches the personal interests and skills of older Americans with opportunities to help solve community problems and offers supplemental insurance while on duty, on-the-job training from the agency or organization where volunteers are placed. The following County is served: Ouachita.

1183 RSVP Rapides Parish
204 Chester Street
Alexandria, LA 71301-6511
318-442-2405
Fax: 318-448-0824
e-mail: rrsvp@aol.com

Pat Hebert, Executive Director

The Retired and Senior Volunteer Program (RSVP) provides opportunities for people 55 and over to make a difference in their community through volunteer service. RSVP volunteers contribute anywhere from a few to over forty hours a week, serving through schools, day care centers, police departments, hospitals and other nonprofit and public organizations to help meet critical community needs. RSVP offers maximum flexibility and choice to its volunteers. RSVP matches the personal interests and skills of older Americans with opportunities to help solve community problems and offers supplemental insurance while on duty, on-the-job training from the agency or organization where volunteers are placed. The following County is served: Rapides.

1184 RSVP River Parishes
107 Maryland Drive
Suite B
Luling, LA 70070-2163
985-785-1037
Fax: 985-785-1950
e-mail: fcairersvp@stcharlesgov.net
http://www.stcharlesgov.net

Fay L Caire, Director

The purpose of RSVP is to enable older Americans aged 55 and over to contribute to their communities through volunteer service, to enhance the lives of the volunteers and those whom they serve, and to provide communities valuable services. RSVP utilizes the vast talents of older volunteers willing to share their experiences, abilities, and skills in responding to a wide variety of community needs. The following Counties are served: St. Charles, St. James, St. John the Baptist.

1185 Railroad Retirement Board: District Office
501 Magazine Street
Suite 1045
New Orleans, LA 70130-3399
504-589-2597
Fax: 504-589-4899

Paul Sosricki, Representative

1186 Red River Council on Aging
PO Box 688
Coushatta, LA 71019
318-932-5721
Fax: 318-932-9572

Mary Wailes, Executive Director

1187 St Charles Council on Aging
626 Pine Street
Suite A
Hahnville, LA 70057-2358
985-783-3008
Fax: 985-783-1996
e-mail: information@stcharlescoa.com
http://www.stcharlesgov.net

Margaret Powe, Executive Director
Elizabeth Thomas, Administrative Manager Finance
April Keller, Administrative Assistant

Serve senior citizens sixty and older in St Charles Parish.

1188 St John Area: Agency on Aging
PO Box 512
Reserve, LA 70084
985-652-3660
Fax: 985-651-4933

Barbara Gralapp, Executive Director

1189 St John Parish Council on Aging
1801 West Airline Highway
La Place, LA 70068
985-652-9569
866-437-5262
Fax: 985-651-4933
e-mail: info@stjohnla.us

Nickie Monica, Parish President
Stacey Cador, Director Human Resources

Dedicated to improving the health and independence of older persons and increasing their continuing contributions to communities, society, and future generations.

1190 St. Bernard Council on Aging
8201a W Judge Perez Drive
Chalmette, LA 70043-1611
504-278-7335
Fax: 504-278-6522
e-mail: stbernardcoa@yahoo.com

Susan McNeal, Director

Dedicated to improving the health and independence of older persons and increasing their continuing contributions to communities, society, and future generations.

1191 St. James Parish Department of Human Resources
PO Box 87
Convent, LA 70723
225-562-2307
Fax: 504-562-2425

Dianne Braithwaite, Manager

1192 St. Tammany Council on Aging
PO Box 171
Covington, LA 70434
985-892-0377
800-256-2823
Fax: 985-892-2014
e-mail: coast@coastseniors.org
http://www.coastseniors.org

Mary Toti, Executive Director
Len Beech, Senior Services Operations Mgr
Crystal Richard, Programs Manager

Coasts helps seniors stay healthy with nutrition services; stay active with wellness and recreation activities; stay alive with medical alert program; and stay informed with classes and presentations.

1193 Tensas Council on Aging
PO Box 726
Saint Joseph, LA 71366
318-766-3770
Fax: 318-766-3774
e-mail: tenscoa@yahoo.com

Clarissa C Newman, Executive Director

1194 Terrebonne Council on Aging
995 W Tunnel Boulevard
Houma, LA 70360-5557
985-868-7701
Fax: 985-868-7806
e-mail: tcoainfo@tcoa-la.org

Diana N Edmonson, Executive Director

1195 Volunteers Of AmericaGreater New Orleans Retired Seniors Volunteer Program
Volunteers of American GNO - North Shore Office
823 Carroll Street
Suite B
Mandeville, LA 70448
985-674-0488
Fax: 985-674-0336
e-mail: ezornman@voagno.org

Elizabeth Zornman, RSVP Director

State Organizations & Government Agencies/Maine

RSVP offers volunteers 55 and older a variety of volunteer opportunities addressing critical needs here in St. Tammany Parish. We are dedicated to helping seniors remain active and involved by providing a high quality volunteer experience. Volunteer assignments offer variety, flexibility, and the opportunity to make a difference right here in your own community.

1196 Webster Area: Agency on Aging
PO Box 913
Minden, LA 71058
318-371-3056
800-256-2853
Fax: 318-424-4748

Dathene Brown, Manager

1197 West Carroll Council on Aging
PO Box 1058
Oak Grove, LA 71263-1058
318-428-4217
Fax: 318-428-2097

Brenda Hagan, Executive Director

1198 Winn Council on Aging
211 E Main Street
Winnfield, LA 71483
318-628-2186
Fax: 318-628-2111
e-mail: winncoa@kricket.net

Joyce McElroy, Director

To serve senior citizens over age 60 and help them stay in their own homes.

Maine

1199 Aroostook Area: Agency on Aging
PO Box 1288
Presque Isle, ME 04769-1288
207-764-3396
800-539-1786
Fax: 207-764-6182

Stephen Farnham, Executive Director

1200 Bureau of Naval Personnel: Retired Activities Office
400 Foxtrot Avenue
Naval Air Station, Box 26
Brunswick, ME 04011-5004
207-921-2609
Fax: 207-921-2617
e-mail: FSC-RAO@nasb.navy.mil

Mary Hipkins, Relocation Counselor

The RAO serves as a link between local retired military and the active duty community which provides assistance to retired military. It provides installation commanders with a means of providing more effective services and improving communication for the local retired community. The RAO is staffed and operated by volunteer retired military who assist other retired members, their families and survivors to receive entitled services and benefits. Through newsletters, seminars and appreciation days the RAO supports quality of life issues throughout the retirement years to their fellow service members.

1201 Central Maine Area: Agency on Aging
PO Box 248
Gardiner, ME 04345
207-622-9212
800-639-1553
Fax: 207-622-7857

Muriel Scott, Executive Director

1202 Disability Determination Services
Arsenal Street Extension
Augusta, ME 04330
207-287-7900
Fax: 207-287-7964

Robin Upton-Sukeforth, Professional Relations

1203 Eastern Area Agency on Aging
450 Essex Street
Bangor, ME 04401
800-432-7812
Fax: 207-941-2869
e-mail: info@caaa.org
http://www.EAAA.org
TTY 207-992-0150

Noelle Merrill, Executive Director

It is the mission of Eastern Agency on Aging to be the best source of information, options, and services for people as they grow older. To listen carefully, respect individual choice, and value independence. To be responsive to the changing needs of older people, families, and their communities.

1204 Freeport Elders Association
49 Park Street
Freeport, ME 04032-1319
207-865-6462

Patricia Guild, President

Senior citizens information and services.

1205 Maine Assistive Technology Projects
University of Maine at Augusta
University Heights
Augusta, ME 04330
207-622-3000
Fax: 207-772-1302

Kathleen Powers, Project Director

A statewide program promoting assistive technology devices and services for persons of all ages with all disabilities.

1206 Maine Association of Retirees (MAR)
180 Maine Avenue
Farmingdale, ME 04344
207-582-1960
800-535-6555
Fax: 207-582-4764
e-mail: mgarten@adelphia.net
http://www.maineretirees.org

Florence Hoover, Executive Director

Nonprofit organization exists solely to work to protect and/or expand the rights and benefits of Maine's retirees.

1207 Maine Bureau of Elder and Adult Services
11 State House Station
Augusta, ME 04333
207-287-9200
Fax: 207-624-5361

Christine Gianopoulos, Director

1208 Maine Department of Defense, Veterans and Emergency Management
Camp Keyes
Augusta, ME 04333
207-626-4271
Fax: 207-626-4509
http://www.state.me.us/va/defense

Frank Soares, Director

The Department of Defense, Veterans and Emergency Management coordinates and administers the discharge of Maine State Government's responsibility relating to military, veterans and civil emergency preparedness through the authorization, planning, provision of resources, administration, operation and audit of activities in these areas.

1209 Maine Department of Human Services: Bureau of Elder and Adult Services
35 Anthony Avenue
11 State House Station
Augusta, ME 04333-0011
207-624-5335
800-262-2232
Fax: 207-624-5361
http://www.maine.gov/dhhs/beas
TTY 888-720-1925

Diana Scully, Director
Elizabeth Gattine, Legal Services Consultant
Mary Walsh, Manager Community Programs

We promote programs and services for older adults, their families and for the people with disabilities.

State Organizations & Government Agencies/Maine

1210 Maine Department of Labor: Bureau of Employment Security
Veterans' Employment Service
20 Union Street
Augusta, ME 04333
207-287-3788
Fax: 207-624-6499

Valerie Landry, Manager

1211 Maine Department of Labor: Bureau of Rehabilitation Services
150 State House Station
Augusta, ME 04333-0150
207-624-5950
800-698-4440
Fax: 207-624-5980
e-mail: jill.c.duson@maine.gov
http://www.maine.gov/rehab
TTY 888-755-0023

Jill C Duson, Executive Director

BRS works to bring about full access to employment, independence and community integration for people with disabilities.

1212 Maine Developmental Disability Council
Building 205 Room 313
Augusta, ME 04330
207-287-4213
Fax: 207-287-8001
e-mail: rebecca.weinstein@state.me.us

Julia Bell, Executive Director

1213 Maine Revenue Services
24 State House Station
Augusta, ME 04333
207-287-2076
Fax: 207-624-9694
e-mail: webmaster_tax@state.me.us
http://www.state.me.us/revenue

Anthony J Neves, Executive Director

1214 Maine State Retirement System
State House Station 46
Augusta, ME 04333
207-287-3461
Fax: 207-287-1032

Kay Evans, Manager

1215 Maine Worker's Compensation Board
27 State House Station
Augusta, ME 04333
207-287-3751
Fax: 207-287-7198

Paul R Dionne, Executive Director

1216 RSVP Aroostook
33 Davis Street
PO Box 1288
Presque Isle, ME 04769-2218
207-764-6184
800-439-1789
Fax: 207-764-6182
e-mail: eleanorreese@aroostookaging.org
http://www.aroostookaging.org

Eleanor Reese, Director

The mission of the Aroostook Agency on Aging is improving the quality of life and promoting the well-being of older people in our communities.

1217 RSVP Penquis Coastal
170 Pleasant Street
Suite A
Rockland, ME 04841
207-596-0361
800-585-1605
Fax: 207-594-2695
http://www.penquiscap.org

Jennifer Hill, Director
Ann Smarella, Membership Director
Patricia Ott, Division Manager RSVP

The Retired and Senior Volunteer Program (RSVP) provides opportunities for people 55 and over to make a difference in their community through volunteer service. RSVP volunteers contribute anywhere from a few to over forty hours a week, serving through schools, day care centers, police departments, hospitals and other nonprofit and public organizations to help meet critical community needs. RSVP offers maximum flexibility and choice to its volunteers. RSVP matches the personal interests and skills of older Americans with opportunities to help solve community problems and offers supplemental insurance while on duty, on-the-job training from the agency or organization where volunteers are placed. The following Counties are served: Knox, Lincoln, Waldo.

1218 RSVP Southern Maine
136 US Route 1
Scarborough, ME 04074-9055
207-396-6500
800-427-7411
Fax: 207-883-8249
e-mail: kmurray@smaaa.org
http://www.smaaa.org
TDD 207-883-0532

Ken Murray, Director

The Retired and Senior Volunteer Program (RSVP) provides opportunities for people 55 and over to make a difference in their community through volunteer service. RSVP volunteers contribute anywhere from a few to over forty hours a week, serving through schools, day care centers, police departments, hospitals and other nonprofit and public organizations to help meet critical community needs. RSVP offers maximum flexibility and choice to its volunteers. RSVP matches the personal interests and skills of older Americans with opportunities to help solve community problems and offers supplemental insurance while on duty, on-the-job training from the agency or organization where volunteers are placed. The following Counties are served: Cumberland, York.

1219 Senior Spectrum
One Weston Court
Suite 203
Augusta, ME 04330-4644
207-622-9212
800-639-1553
Fax: 207-622-7857
e-mail: feedback@seniorspectrum.com

Muriel Scott, President/CEO

Provides information and assistance, respite care, adult day programs, Meals on Wheels, benefits counseling, home care services, and social activities for seniors.

1220 Seniors Plus
8 Falcon Road
PO Box 659
Lewiston, ME 04243-0659
207-795-4010
800-427-1241
Fax: 207-795-4009
http://www.seniorsplus.org
TTY 207-795-7232

Pam Allen, Executive Director
Robert Chick, Treasurer

Seniors Plus believes in maintaining the independence, dignity and quality of life of older adults. Seniors Plus will work consistently to remove barriers and strive to provide services in a reliable and coordinated manner.

1221 Southern Maine Area Agency on Aging
136 Route US One
Scarborough, ME 04074
207-396-6500
800-427-7411
Fax: 207-883-8249
e-mail: smaaa@smaaa.org
http://www.smaaa.org
TTY 207-883-0532

Larry Gross, Executive Director
Debbie DiDominicus, Deputy Director
Margaret Brown, Development Director

State Organizations & Government Agencies/Maryland

Mission of Southern Maine Agency on Aging is to assure that older people living in Southern Maine, especially those who are frail, living alone, or have low incomes, receive the support necessary to maintain their independence in the community.

1222 United Way of Eastern Maine
24 Springer Drive
Bangor, ME 04401-3655
207-941-2800
Fax: 207-941-2805
e-mail: janeto@unitedwayem.org
http://www.unitdwayem.org

Eric Buch, President
Carol Colson, VP Resource Development
Laura Mitchell, Director Communications

Our mission is to improve the lives of people in Eastern Maine by mobilizing the caring power of people and communities. We bring together human, financial and strategic resources to strengthen children and families, support seniors, meet people's basic needs, and promote self-sufficiency for all people.

1223 Western-Area Agency on Aging
PO Box 659
Lewiston, ME 04243
207-795-4010
800-427-1241
Fax: 207-795-4009

Pam Allen, Executive Vice President

Maryland

1224 Allegany County Area: Agency on Aging
19 Frederick Street
Cumberland, MD 21502-2309
301-777-5970
Fax: 301-722-0937
e-mail: HRDC@allaonet.org
TDD 800-735-2258

Dan Lewallen, Director
Leslie Colbrese, Manager

Cumberland, Allegany County.

1225 Anne Arundel County Area: Agency on Aging
101 Crain Highway NW
Glen Burnie, MD 21061-3014
410-222-6711
800-492-2499
Fax: 410-222-6817
TDD 410-222-6825

Carol R Baker PhD, Director

Anne Arundel County, Glen Burnie.

1226 Anne Arundel County Department of Aging and Disabilities
Heritage Complex
2666 Riva Road
Annapolis, MD 21401-7345
410-222-4464
800-492-2499
Fax: 410-222-4360
e-mail: info_and_assistance@aacounty.org
http://www.aacounty.org/aging
TDD 410-222-4355
TTY 410-222-4355

Virginia A Thomas, CFA, Director
Sandra Berkeley, Director I & A Program

The Department of Aging provides a number of programs for both older persons and persons with disabilities.

1227 Baltimore City Commission on Aging, Retirement Education: CARE
118 N Howard Street
7th Floor
Baltimore, MD 21201-3424
410-396-4932
Fax: 410-385-0381

Neetu Dhawn-Gray, Director
John P Stewart, Executive Director

1228 Baltimore County Department of Aging
611 Central Avenue
Towson, MD 21204-4299
410-887-3094
Fax: 410-887-2159
e-mail: aginginfo@co.ba.md.us
http://www.baltimorecountyonline.info
TDD 410-887-3787

Betty Evans, Manager/Information/Assistant
Sue Green, Special Project Manager
Arnold Eppel, Manager

Provides a wide arraay of services to older seniors: nationally accredited senior centers, information and assistance, outreach, employment, housing, caregiver support, transportation, nutrition sites, and educational and informational booklets.

1229 Bureau of Health Professions, Health Resources and Services Administration
5600 Fishers Lane
Room 8-05
Rockville, MD 20857
301-443-5794
Fax: 301-443-2111
http://www.bhpr.hrsa.gov

Michelle Snyder, Associate Administrator

The Bureau of Health Professions (BHPr), Health Resources and Services Administration, improves the health status of the population by providing national leadership in the development, distribution and retention of a diverse, culturally competent health workforce that provides the highest quality care of all. Makes Grants to health professions training programs and supports scholarships, educational loans and loan repayment programs for certain health professionals.

1230 Bureau of Naval Personnel: Maryland Retired Activities Office
Fleet and Family Support Center
United States Naval Academy
Annapolis, MD 21402-5073
410-293-2641
Fax: 410-293-5380
http://www.usna.edu/familyservices

The RAO serves as a link between local retired military and the active-duty community which provides assistance to retired military. It provides installation commanders with a means of providing more effective services and improving communication for the local retired community. The RAO is staffed and operated by volunteer retired military who assist other retired members, their families and survivors to receive entitled services and benefits. Through newsletters, seminars and appreciation days, the RAO supports quality of life issues throughout the retirement years to their fellow service members.

1231 Bureau of Naval Personnel: Patuxent Retired Activities Office
Fleet and Family Support Center
Naval Air Station
Building 2090
Patuxent River, MD 20670-2090
301-757-1885
Fax: 301-342-4802

The RAO serves as a link between local retired military and the active-duty community which provides assistance to retired military. It provides installation commanders with a means of providing more effective services and improving communication for the local retired community. The RAO is staffed and operated by volunteer retired military who assist other retired members, their families and survivors to receive entitled services and benefits. Through newsletters, seminars and appreciation days, the RAO supports quality of life issues throughout the retirement years to their fellow service members.

1232 Carroll County Bureau of Aging
7 School House Avenue
Westminster, MD 21157-4566
410-876-3363
Fax: 301-848-4848
TDD 410-848-5355

Janet B Flora, Director

Westminster, Carroll County.

State Organizations & Government Agencies/Maryland

1233 Cecil County Department of Aging
214 North Street
Elkton, MD 21921-5513
410-996-5295
Fax: 410-620-9483
e-mail: stwigg@ccgov.org
http://www.ccgov.org

Susan Twigg, Director
Mary Kahoe, Sr Information Assistance

Serves Cecil county residents sixty years and older

1234 Charles County Department of Community Service Aging Division
Hc 1
Box 1144
Port Tobacco, MD 20677-9801
301-934-9305
Fax: 301-934-0126
http://www.charlescounty.org

Karen L Lehman Cieplak, Division Chief
Margaret Cheseldine, Director

Charles County, Port Tobacco.

1235 Department of Disabilities and Special Needs
217 E Redwood Street
Baltimore, MD 21202
410-767-3660
800-637-4113
http://www.mdod.maryland.gov
TTY 410-767-3660

Kristen Cox, Secretary
Diane McComb, Deputy Secretary
John Brennan, Chief of Staff

The mission of the Department of Disabilities is to empower individuals with disabilities to achieve their personal and professional goals in the communities where they live.

1236 Frederick County Commission on Aging
520 N Market Street
Frederick, MD 21701-5243
301-694-1061
Fax: 301-631-3554
e-mail: deptofaging@fredco-md.net
http://www.co.frederick.md.us
TDD 301-694-1672

Jennifer Short, Manager

Local Area Agency on Aging.

1237 Harford County Office on Aging
145 N Hickory Avenue
Bel Air, MD 21014-3239
410-638-3025
Fax: 410-638-3069

James Macgill, Director
Carol Lienhart, Executive Director

Harford County, Bel Air.

1238 Health & Housing Association Mid-Atlantic Nonprofit
10280 Old Columbia Road
Suite 220
Columbia, MD 21046
410-381-1176
Fax: 410-381-0240
e-mail: info@malifespan.org
http://www.manpha.org

Isabella Firth, President
Danna Kauffman, VP Government Relations
Heather Udell, Corporate Director Marketing

1239 MAC Area: Agency on Aging
1504 Riverside Drive
Salisbury, MD 21801-6740
410-742-0505
Fax: 410-742-0525

Margaret Bradford, Executive Director

Worcester County, Soverset County, Wicomico County, Dorchester County, Salisbury.

1240 Maryland Association of Area Agencies on Aging
Baltimore City Commission on Aging
10 N Calvert Street
Suite 300
Baltimore, MD 21202-1868
410-396-2273
Fax: 410-545-1539
e-mail: john.stewart@baltimorecity.gov
http://www.mdcounties.org

John P Stewart, Executive Director

A nonprofit organization representing 19 Area Agencies and all jurisdictions, serves as a visible and effective advocate for older adults within the substate jurisdictions of Maryland, educating about aging issues in order to obtain an adequate and appropriate system of services in Maryland.

1241 Maryland Client Assistance Program
2301 Argonne Drive
Baltimore, MD 21218-1628
410-554-9361
800-638-6243
Fax: 410-554-9362

Beth Lash, Manager

Helps individuals with disabilities understand the rehabilitation process and receives appropriate and quality services from the Division of Rehabilitation Services and other programs and facilities providing services under the Rehabilitation Act of 1973.

1242 Maryland Department of Aging
301 W Preston Street
Suite 1007
Baltimore, MD 21201-2393
410-767-1100
Fax: 410-333-7943

Rosalie Abrams, Director
Jean Roesser, Manager

1243 Maryland Developmental Disability Council
217 E Redwood Street
Suite 1300
Baltimore, MD 21202
410-767-3670
800-305-6441
Fax: 410-333-3686
http://www.md-council.org

Brian Cox, Executive Director
Catherine Lyle, Deputy Director
Angela Castillo-Epps, Director Comunications/Policy

The Maryland Developmental Disabilities Council is a public policy organization comprised of people with disabilities and family members who are joined by state officials, service providers and other designated partners. The Council is an independent, self-governing organization that represents the interests of people with developmental disabilities and their families.

1244 Maryland Disability Determination Services
Division of Rehabilitation Services
PO Box 6338
Timonium, MD 21094-6338
410-308-4360
800-492-4283
Fax: 410-308-4550
e-mail: md.dd.timonium.dds@ssa.gov
http://www.dors.state.md.us

Kathi Thompson, Director

The Maryland Disability Determination Services (DDS) claims examiners, staff physicians and psychologists determine the eligibility of Maryland applicants for Social Security Administration's (SSA) two disability programs.

1245 Maryland Protection & Advocacy Agency
Maryland Disability Law Center
Walbert Building, Suite 400
1800 North Charles Street
Baltimore, MD 21201
410-727-6352
800-233-7201
Fax: 410-727-6389
e-mail: virginiak@mdlcbalto.org
http://www.mdlcbalto.org
TDD 410-727-6387

Virginia Knowlton, Executive Director

State Organizations & Government Agencies/Maryland

MDLC is the Protection and Advocacy organization for Maryland. MDLC mission is to ensure that people with disabilities are accorded the full rights and entitlements afforded to them by state and federal law.

1246 Maryland State Retirement and Pension System
120 E Baltimore Street
Baltimore, MD 21202
410-625-5555
800-492-5909
Fax: 410-333-7550
e-mail: sra@sra.state.md.us
http://www.sra.state.md.us
TDD 410-625-5535
TTY 410-625-5535

R Dean Kenderdine, Interim Executive Director
Anne M Burdowski, Director Communications/Policy
Dale E Markel, Chief Information Officer

Our mission is to administer the survivor, disability, and retirement benefits of the System's participants, and to ensure that sufficient assets are available to fund the benefits when due.

1247 Maryland Veterans Commission
31 Hopkins Plaza
Suite 110
Baltimore, MD 21201-2826
410-333-4428
Fax: 410-333-1071

1248 Maryland Workers Compensation Board
10 E Baltimore Street
Baltimore, MD 21202-1630
410-864-5100
Fax: 410-864-5101

1249 Montgomery County Government: Division of Elder Affairs
101 Monroe Street
Rockville, MD 20850-2580
301-217-2240
Fax: 301-217-1495
TDD 301-217-1246

Elizabeth Boehner, Director

Montgomery County, Rockville.

1250 Office of Retirement and Survivors
US Department of Health & Human Services
Windsor Park Building
6401 Security Boulevard
Baltimore, MD 21235
800-772-1213
Fax: 410-965-8582
http://www.ssa.gov
TTY 800-325-0778

Jo Anne B Barnhart, Commissioner

The Office of Retirement and Survivors Insurance determines benefits to those ages 62 and older and to members of families where the primary income person is deceased.

1251 Office of Supplemental Security Income: Social Security Administration
US Department of Health and Human Services
Windsor Park Building
6401 Security Boulevard
Baltimore, MD 21235
410-965-2736
800-772-1213
Fax: 410-965-9063
http://www.ssa.gov
TTY 800-325-0778

Jo Anne B Barnhart, Commissioner

To insure a minimum level of income to persons who have attained age 65 or are blind or disabled, whose income and resources are below specified levels.

1252 Prince George's County Bureau of Aging
5012 Rhode Island Avenue
Hyattsville, MD 20781-2037
301-699-2800
Fax: 301-699-2857
TDD 301-277-0076

Sue Ward, Director
Nancie Park, Manager

Hyattsville, Prince Georges County.

1253 Queen Anne's County Department of Aging
104 Powell Street
Centreville, MD 21617-1027
410-758-3900
Fax: 410-758-4489

Sue Leager, Director
Dave Williams, Administrator

Queen Anne's County, Grasonville, Crumpton, Centreville, Stevensville.

1254 RSVP Allegany County
71 Baltimore Street, 3rd Floor
PO Box 1308
Cumberland, MD 21501-1308
301-724-7116
Fax: 301-724-1044
e-mail: volunteercenter@allconet.org

Deborah K Miller, Director

The Retired and Senior Volunteer Program (RSVP) provides opportunities for people 55 and over to make a difference in their community through volunteer service. RSVP volunteers contribute anywhere from a few to over forty hours a week, serving through schools, day care centers, police departments, hospitals and other nonprofit and public organizations to help meet critical community needs. RSVP offers maximum flexibility and choice to its volunteers. RSVP matches the personal interests and skills of older Americans with opportunities to help solve community problems and offers supplemental insurance while on duty, on-the-job training from the agency or organization where volunteers are placed. The following Counties are served: Allegany, Garrett of Maryland, Mineral of West Virginia.

1255 RSVP Baltimore City
5610 Harford Road
Baltimore, MD 21214
410-361-9401
Fax: 410-254-8421

Daphne Hicks, Director

The Retired and Senior Volunteer Program (RSVP) provides opportunities for people 55 and over to make a difference in their community through volunteer service. RSVP volunteers contribute anywhere from a few to over forty hours a week, serving thourgh schools, day care centers, police departments, hospitals and other nonprofit and public organizations to help meet critical community needs. RSVP offers maximum flexibility and choice to its volunteers. RSVP matches the personal interests and skills to older Americans with opportunities to help solve community problems and offer supplemental insurance while on duty, on-the-job training from the agency or organization where volunteers are placed.

1256 RSVP Hagerstown
140 West Franklin Street
Fourth Floor
Hagerstown, MD 21740
301-790-0275
Fax: 301-739-4957
http://www.wccoaging.org

Hannah S Cramer, RSVP Director

The Retired and Senior Volunteer Program (RSVP) provides opportunities for people 55 and over to make a difference in their community through volunteer service. RSVP volunteers contribute anywhere from a few to over forty hours a week, serving thourgh schools, day care centers, police departments, hospitals and other nonprofit and public organizations to help meet critical community needs. RSVP offers maximum flexibility and choice to its volunteers. RSVP matches the personal interests and skills to older Americans with opportunities to help solve community problems and offer supplemental insurance while on duty, on-the-job training from the agency or organization where volunteers are placed.

1257 RSVP Lower Eastern Shore
1504 Riverside Drive
Salisbury, MD 21801-6740
410-742-0505
Fax: 410-742-0525
e-mail: hlrrsvp@intercom.net

Hazel L Ricker, Director

State Organizations & Government Agencies/Massachusetts

To offer individuals age 55 and older meaningful volunteer service opportunities that strengthens the well being of both the volunteer and the community. The following Counties are served: Dorchester, Somerset, Wicomico, Worcester.

1258 RSVP Montgomery County
401 Hungerford Drive
1st Floor
Rockville, MD 20850-4154
240-777-2610
Fax: 240-777-2601
http://www.montgomerycountymd.gov/volunteer
Ann Evans, RSVP Project Director

The Retired and Senior Volunteer Program (RSVP) provides opportunities for people 55 and over to make a difference in their community through volunteer service. RSVP volunteers contribute anywhere from a few to over forty hours a week, serving though schools, day care centers, police departments, hospitals and other nonprofit and public organizations to help meet critical community needs. RSVP offers maximum flexibility and choice to its volunteers. RSVP matches the personal interests and skills to older Americans with opportunities to help solve community problems and offer supplemental insurance while on duty, on-the-job training from the agency or organization where volunteers are placed.

1259 RSVP Prince George's County
Department of Family Services
5012 Rhode Island Avenue
Hyattsville, MD 20781-2037
301-699-2797
Fax: 301-699-2857
e-mail: imyles@co.pg.md.us
Ivin D Myles, Contact

RSVP helps people aged 55 years and older put their skills and life experiences to work in their communities. Volunteers serve from just a few hours to up to 20 hours each week in a variety of roles which include: mentoring students in schools, supporting and providing services to community and government agencies, leading exercises and assisting with food preparation in Senior Centers, visitng home bound elderly persons, assisting seniors with health insurance problems and acting as tax counselors.

1260 RSVP St. Mary's County
Office on Aging
41780 Baldridge Street
PO Box 653
Leonardtown, MD 20650-0653
301-475-4507
Fax: 301-475-4503
e-mail: Jayne.Hunsinger@co.saint-marys.md.us
http://www.saint-marys.md.us
Jayne Hunsinger, Director

The Retired and Senior Volunteer Program (RSVP) provides opportunities for people 55 and over to make a difference in their community through volunteer service. RSVP volunteers contribute anywhere from a few to over forty hours a week, serving through schools, day care centers, police departments, hospitals and other nonprofit and public organizations to help meet critical community needs. RSVP offers maximum flexibility and choice to its volunteers. RSVP matches the personal interests and skills of older Americans with opportunities to help solve community problems and offers supplemental insurance while on duty, on-the-job training from the agency or organization where volunteers are placed. The following County is served: Saint Mary's.

1261 Railroad Retirement Board: Maryland District Office
George H Falkin
Building 31
Baltimore, MD 21201
410-962-2550
Fax: 410-962-9835
Casey N Gresey, Representative

1262 Social Security: Baltimore Disability Determination
2301 Argonne Drive
Baltimore, MD 21218-1628
410-965-8882
David Fouts MD

1263 St. Mary's County Office on Aging
PO Box 653
Leonardtown, MD 20650
301-475-4200
Fax: 301-475-4503
e-mail: jennie.page@co.saint-marys.md.us
http://www.co.saint-marys.md.us
Lori Jennings-Harris, Director
Jennie Page, Deputy Director

The St. Mary's County Department of Aging provides a wide variety of programs and services to the county's senior residents. Activities range from social and recreational programs to the direct support of essential services, such as nutrition, health, and in-home services.

1264 Washington County Commission on Aging
9 Public Square
Hagerstown, MD 21740-5510
301-790-0275
Fax: 301-739-4957
Fredrick Otto, Director
Susan MacDonald, Executive Director

Massachusetts

1265 Adams Council on Aging
Adams Community Center
20 E Street
Adams, MA 01220-2300
413-743-8333
Fax: 413-743-8334
http://www.adamsma.virtualtownhall.net
Barbara St. Pierre, Director

The Adams Council on Aging (CoA) is a town department. It was organized to develop a comprehensive network of in-home and community-based services and supportive programs for people sixty years of age and over in the Town of Adams.

1266 Baypath Senior Citizens Services
PO Box 2625
Framingham, MA 01703-2625
508-620-0840
800-287-7284
Fax: 508-872-6449
Jeanne McCann, Director

Framingham, Dover, Hudson, Ashland, Marlborough, Wayland, Sherborn, Northborough, Hopkinton, Southboro, Holliston, Natick, Sudbury, Westborough.

1267 Bernardston Council on Aging
38 Church Street
PO Box 504
Bernardston, MA 01337-0504
413-648-9616
Fax: 413-648-9318
e-mail: bernpi@crocker.com
Dianne Salls, CoA Director
Martha Jane Shaw, Senior Center Director

Serves senior citizens in Bernardston, Northfield, and Leyden, MA. Provides hot meals, social programs, and information regarding health and legislative issues affecting senior citizens. Sponsors counseling program for personal and family problems. Open-Northfield- Monday-Tuesday, Thursday: 8am through 1pm Bernardston- Wednesday and Friday: 8am through 1pm.

1268 Beverly Council on Aging
Senior Community Center
90 Colon Street
Beverly, MA 01915-3604
978-921-6017
Fax: 978-927-8397
http://www.bevelyma.gov
Mary Ann Holak, Director

State Organizations & Government Agencies/Massachusetts

A municipal agency concerned with planning, coordinating, and funding community services at the Center, as well as advocating for elders. The Beverly Council on Aging (BCOA) is a federally mandated program to promote a healthier and happier lifestyle for seniors. Services/Activities: Monthly Newsletter, Health Clinics, Transportation, Meals, Adaptive Equipment Exchange, Outreach, Meals on Wheels, Home Visits, Tax Assistance, Birthday Celebrations, Notary Public, Holiday/Theme Parties, Volunteer Awards Event, Annual Dinners, Senior of the Year Award, Cultural Events, Computer Instruction/Internet Access, Trips, Shows, Library, Game Room, Line and Ballroom Dancing, Luncheons, Arts & Crafts, Card Games, Live Bands, BINGO.

1269 Boston Commission on Affairs of the Elderly
1 City Hall Plaza
Room 271
Boston, MA 02201
617-635-4366
Fax: 617-635-3213
e-mail: elderly@cityofboston.gov
http://www.cityofboston.gov/elderly
TDD 617-635-4599
TTY 617-635-4599

Eliza Greenberg, Commissioner

The mission of the Commission on Affairs of the Elderly is to enhance the quality of life for Boston's senior citizens through planning, coordinating, and monitoring the delivery of services to the elderly in an efficient and effective manner.

1270 Bristol Elder Services
182 North Main Street
Fall River, MA 02720
508-675-2101
Fax: 508-679-0320
e-mail: info@bristolelder.org
http://www.bristolelder.org
TTY 508-646-9704

Margaret Pilkington, Ombudsman Program Director
Nancy Viverios, Nutrition Program Assist Dir

1271 Cape & Islands Senior Corps
68 Route 134
South Dennis, MA 02660-3710
508-394-4630
Fax: 508-394-3712
e-mail: Mary.Carchrie@escci.org
http://www.escci.org

Mary D Carchrie, Director

Dedicated to promoting the welfare and enhancing the quality of life of elders, as well as helping them to maintain maximum independence and dignity. Our organization works with the community to identify and respond to the needs, problems, and concerns of elders and their families.

1272 Central Massachusetts Agency on Aging
360 W Boylston Street
West Boylston, MA 01583-2365
508-852-5539
Fax: 508-852-5425
e-mail: cmaaging@seniorconnection.org
http://www.seniorconnection.org
TDD 508-852-5539

Robert P Dwyer PhD, Executive Director

Boylston, Worcester County, Middlesex County.

1273 Chelsea-Revere-Winthrop Elder Services Area: Agency on Aging
PO Box 189
Revere, MA 02151
781-286-0550
Fax: 781-286-8831

James Cunningham Jr, Director

Revere, Chelsea, Winthrop.

1274 Coastline Elderly Services
1646 Purchase Street
New Bedford, MA 02740-6819
508-999-6400
800-243-4636
Fax: 508-993-6510
TDD 508-993-6400

Charles Sisson, Director

Fairhaven.

1275 Community Action Commission of Cape Cod & Islands
115 Enterprise Road
Hyannis, MA 02601-2212
508-771-1727
800-845-1999
Fax: 508-775-7488

Cheryl Bartlett, Executive Director

Senior citizens in the Cape Cod, MA area. Evaluates the quality of senior citizens' lives and advocates their rights regarding transportation, housing, nutrition, entitlements, and nursing home care. Offers public education programs on human service issues. Works to further favorable legislation at the state level, especially concerning health care issues.

1276 Dalton Council on Aging
Dalton Community Center
400 Main Street
Dalton, MA 01226-1605
413-684-2000
Fax: 413-684-6107
e-mail: dcoa@bcn.net

Susan Jacobs, Director

Appointed board of 11 citizens responsible for providing information to and referral for Dalton, MA residents 60 years of age and older and their families.

1277 Elder Service Plan of the North Shore
62 Market Street
Lynn, MA 01901
781-595-4717
Fax: 781-595-5479

Carol Suleski, Executive Director

Elder Service Plans are part of PACE (Programs of All-inclusive Care for the Elderly). These plans provide comprehensive medical and social services to frail elders so that they can live in their communities instead of in nursing homes.

1278 Elder Services of Berkshire County
66 Wendell Avenue
Pittsfield, MA 01201-6306
413-499-9346
800-544-5242
Fax: 413-442-6443
e-mail: esbc@esbci.org
http://www.esbci.org
TDD 413-499-0524

Robert P Dean, Executive Director
Louisa Weeden, Executive Secretary
Catherin R May, Manager

Offers in home and community services to provide Berkshire elders the opportunity to live with dignity, independence and self determination, and to achieve the highest possible quality of life.

1279 Elder Services of Cape Cod and the Islands
68 Route 134
South Dennis, MA 02660-3710
508-394-4630
800-244-4630
Fax: 508-394-3712

Leslie E Scheer, Director

South Dennis, Barnstable County, Dukes County, Nantucket County.

1280 Franklin County Home Care Corporation
330 Montague City Road
Suite 1
Turners Falls, MA 01376-2529
413-773-5555
800-732-4636
Fax: 413-772-1084
e-mail: info@fchcc.org
http://www.fchcc.org

Roseann Martoccia, Director
Bette Jenks, Information/Referral

Area Agency on Aging and Aging Services Access Point serving the Franklin County and Worth Quabbin region of Massachesetts.

State Organizations & Government Agencies/Massachusetts

1281 Friends of the Pepperell Seniors
18 River Road
PO Box 1555
Pepperell, MA 01463-3555
978-433-0326
Fax: 978-433-0347
Sharon Mercurio, Director

To better the lives of the senior citizens of Pepperell by raising funds that sponsor and support activities that contribute to their health and well-being and to essential items for the Pepperell Senior Center through the Pepperell Council on Aging.

1282 Greater Lynn Senior Services (GLSS)
8 Silsbee Street
Lynn, MA 01901-1485
781-596-8222
Fax: 781-599-8033
TDD 617-592-7370
Vince Lique, Director

1283 Greater Springfield Senior Services
66 Industry Avenue
Springfield, MA 01104-3362
413-781-8800
800-649-3641
Fax: 413-781-0632
TDD 413-781-8800
Patricia Clark, Director
Elaine Massery, Executive Director

1284 HESSCO Elder Services
One Merchant Street
Sharon, MA 02067-1662
781-784-4944
800-243-4636
Fax: 781-784-4922
e-mail: info@hessco.org
http://www.hessco.org
TDD 508-543-2611
TTY 781-784-4944
Mary Jean McDermott, Executive Director

At HESSCO Elder Services we've dedicated ourselves to finding solutions to help those over sixty take full advantage of their later years. Our goal is to make it easier for older individuals and their families to access a comprehensive system of health and supportive services.

1285 Hampshire Community Action Commission
557 E Hampton Road
Northampton, MA 01060
413-582-4245
Fax: 413-582-4202
e-mail: ldesmond@hcac.org
Linda Desmond, Director

The Retired and Senior Volunteer Program of Hampshire and Franklin County invite people over 55 years of age to share their skills of a lifetime with their community in very needed programs throughout the two-county area.

1286 Hearing Rehabilitation Foundation
35 Medford Street
Somerville, MA 02143-4242
617-628-4537
e-mail: hearf@aol.com
http://www.hearf.org
Geoff Plant, PhD, President

1287 Highland Valley Elder Services
320 Riverside Drive
Florence, MA 01062-2700
413-586-2000
800-322-0551
Fax: 413-584-7076
e-mail: qll@highlandvalley.org
Robert Gallant, Director

Northampton, Hampshire County, Hampden County.

1288 Jewish Community Relations Council of Greater Boston
126 High Street
Boston, MA 02110-2700
617-457-8600
Fax: 617-988-6255
e-mail: info@jcrcboston.org
http://www.jcrcboston.org
Alan Ronkin, Deputy Director

Human rights organization working on behalf of Jews and political prisoners in the former Soviet Union. Membership is concentrated in New England and upper New York state area, but group operates on a national level. Primary purpose is to work toward the emigration of Jews from the former USSR, and provide Jews remaining in the former Soviet Union with religious, cultural, moral and financial support.

1289 MAB Community Services
200 Ivy Street
Brookline, MA 02446-3907
617-738-5110
800-682-9200
Fax: 617-738-1247
http://www.mabcommunity.org
Barbara Salisbury, Chief Executive Officer
Brenda English, Chief Operations Officer
Cynthia Canham, Director Development

MAB Community Services is dedicated to working with individuals with disabilities to eliminate barriers and create opportunities.

1290 Massachusetts Assistive Technology Partnership
MATP Center
1295 Boylston Street
Suite 310
Boston, MA 02215-3407
617-355-7820
800-848-8867
Fax: 617-345-6345
Judy Brewer, Project Director

A statewide program promoting assistive technology devices and services for persons with all disabilities.

1291 Massachusetts Client Assistance Program
1 Ashburton Place
Room 1305
Boston, MA 02108-1518
617-727-9640
Fax: 671-727-0965
e-mail: blygargar@web.state.ma.us

1292 Massachusetts Department of Elder Affairs
1 Ashburton Place
Room 517
Boston, MA 02108-1518
617-727-7750
800-882-2003
Fax: 617-727-9368

1293 Massachusetts Department of Revenue
PO Box 7010
Boston, MA 02204
617-887-6367
800-392-6089
http://www.dor.state.ma.us
Alan LeBovidge, Commissioner
Sheila Le Blanc, Senior Deputy Commissioner

The mission of the Massachusetts Department of Revenue is to achieve maximum compliance with the tax, child support and municipal finance laws of the Commonwealth. In meeting its mission, the Department is dedicated to enforcing these laws in a fair, impartial and consistent manner by providing professional and courteous service to all its customers.

1294 Massachusetts Developmental Disabilities Council
600 Washington Street
Room 670
Boston, MA 02111-1704
617-727-6374
Fax: 617-727-1179

Group of citizens which analyzes needs of people with severe, lifelong disabilities and works to improve public policy. MDDC produces several publications and has committees and a grants program to study and advocate for changes in the service system.

State Organizations & Government Agencies/Massachusetts

1295 Massachusetts Disability Determination Services
110 Chauncy Street
Boston, MA 02111-1794
617-727-1600
Fax: 617-654-7575

1296 Massachusetts Executive Office of Health and Human Services
Commission for the Deaf and Hard of Hearing
210 South Street
5th Floor
Boston, MA 02111-2725
617-695-7500
800-882-1155
Fax: 617-695-7599

1297 Massachusetts Executive Office for Administration and Finance
Teacher's Retirement Board
69 Canal Street
Suite 3
Boston, MA 02114-2006
617-727-3661
Fax: 617-727-9797

Joan Schloss, CEO

1298 Massachusetts Executive Office of Health and Human Services
Department of Veteran Services
100 Cambridge Street
Suite 1002
Boston, MA 02114-2533
617-727-3570
Fax: 617-727-5903

1299 Massachusetts Executive Office of Health and Human Services
Commission for the Blind
88 Kingston Street
Boston, MA 02111-2228
617-727-5550
800-392-6450
Fax: 617-727-5960

1300 Massachusetts Protection & Advocacy Organization
Disability Law Center
11 Beacon Street, Suite 925
Boston, MA 02108
617-723-8455
800-872-9992
Fax: 617-723-9125
e-mail: mail@dlc-ma.og
http://www.dlc-ma.org
TTY 800-381-0577

Christine Griffen, Executive Director

To provide legal advocacy on disability issues that promote the fundamental rights of all people with disabilities to participate fully and equally in the social and economic life of Massachusetts.

1301 Massachusetts Social Security Region 1 Administration
10 Causeway Street
1st Floor, Room 148
Boston, MA 02222
800-772-1213
Fax: 410-965-6503
http://www.ssa.gov/boston
TTY 800-325-0778

Manuel J Vaz, Regional Commissioner

To advance the economic security of the nation's people through compassionate and vigilant leadership in shaping and managing America's Social Security programs.

1302 Mystic Valley Elder Services
300 Commercial Street
Malden, MA 02148-7312
781-324-7705
Fax: 781-324-1369

Marsha Webster, Director
Daniel O Leary, Manager

Everett, Malden, Medford, Melrose, North Reading, Reading, Stoneham, Wakefield.

1303 New Bedford Council on Aging
572 Pleasant Street
PO Box 7658
New Bedford, MA 02742-7658
508-991-6250
Fax: 508-979-1797
TDD 508-979-1796

Dorothy J Koczera, Executive Director
Felicitia Monteiro, Coordinator

Agency serves area senior citizens through health education and recreation programs. Operates 2 senior centers. Outreach Benefits Counselor does home visits to shut-ins to assist with health benefits.

1304 North Shore Elder Services
152 Sylvan Street
Danvers, MA 01923-3568
978-750-4540
Fax: 978-750-8053
TDD 758-750-4540

Janet McAveeney, Director
Paul Lanzikos, Executive Director

The North Shore is a rental retirement community offering a senior living experience for value-conscious seniors that is truly outstanding. There is no endowment, no long-term commitment, no paying for assistance services which may not be necessary. Assisted living services are available through Regency At Home Care Services, Ltd. as an option, if needed.

1305 Northfield Senior Center
Town Hall
69 Main Street
Northfield, MA 01360
413-498-2186
Fax: 413-498-5115

Joanne Balzarini, Director

Individuals in Franklin County, MA serving senior citizens.

1306 Old Colony Planning Council Area: Agency on Aging
70 School Street
Brockton, MA 02301-4097
508-583-1833
Fax: 508-559-8768

Patricia Goggin, Director
Pasquale Ciaramella, Manager

1307 Operation ABLE of Greater Boston
131 Tremont Street
Suite 301
Boston, MA 02111-1336
617-542-4180
Fax: 617-542-4187
e-mail: ABLE@operationable.net
http://www.operationable.net

Joan Cirillo, Executive Director

Promotes employment and training opportunities for men and women 45 years of age and older. Services include job referral and placement, PC training, partnerships with the business community, and advocacy aimed at quality job opportunities for midlife to older job seekers.

1308 PXE International
4301 Connecticut Avenue NW
Suite 404
Washington, DC 20008-2369
202-362-9599
Fax: 202-966-8553
e-mail: info@pxe.org
http://www.pxe.org

Patrick F Terry, President
Lionel G Bercovitch, MD, Scientific/Medical Chair

Offers vital services to those with pseudoxanthoma elasticum, a connective tissue disorder causing calcification of connective tissue in various places throughout the body, often affecting the membrane behind the eye.

State Organizations & Government Agencies/Massachusetts

1309 **Quincy Retirement Board**
1250 Hancock Street
Suite 506S
Quincy, MA 02169
617-376-1075
Fax: 617-376-1149
e-mail: emasterson@ci.quincy.ma.us
http://www.ci.quincy.ma.us

Edward J Masterson, Executive Director
Marguerite Lightbourne, Deputy Director

Our mission is to enhance the services we provide to our members.

1310 **RSVP Berkshire**
330 North Avenue
Pittsfield, MA 01201-6302
413-499-9345
Fax: 413-442-0422
e-mail: rsvp@berkshire.net

Normalyn Powers, Director

The Retired and Senior Volunteer Program (RSVP) provides opportunities for people 55 and over to make a difference in their community through volunteer service. RSVP volunteers contribute anywhere from a few to over forty hours a week, serving through schools, day care centers, police departments, hospitals and other nonprofit and public organizations to help meet critical community needs. RSVP offers maximum flexibility and choice to its volunteers. RSVP matches the personal interests and skills of older Americans with opportunities to help solve community problems and offers supplemental insurance while on duty, on-the-job training from the agency or organization where volunteers are placed. The following County is served: Berkshire.

1311 **RSVP Boston**
One City Hall Plaza
Room 271
Boston, MA 02201-1020
617-635-4366
Fax: 617-635-3213

Francesca Johnnene, Director

The Retired and Senior Volunteer Program (RSVP) provides opportunities for people 55 and over to make a difference in their community through volunteer service. RSVP volunteers contribute anywhere from a few to over forty hours a week, serving through schools, day care centers, police departments, hospitals and other nonprofit and public organizations to help meet critical community needs. RSVP offers maximum flexibility and choice to its volunteers. RSVP matches the personal interests and skills of older Americans with opportunities to help solve community problems and offers supplemental insurance while on duty, on-the-job training from the agency or organization where volunteers are placed. The following County is served: Suffolk.

1312 **RSVP Chicopee-Holyoke-Ludlow**
152 Center Street
Chicopee, MA 01013-1611
413-612-0219
Fax: 413-612-0220
e-mail: lornorton@valleyopp.com

Lorraine Norton, Director

Our volunteers are people who don't want to sit around being bored and growing old. Our paid staff of three, recruit people fifty-five and over to volunteer their time and share their talents in human service programs within their own communities.

1313 **RSVP Fall River-Taunton**
264 Griffin Street
Fall River, MA 02724-2702
508-679-0041
Fax: 508-324-7503
e-mail: Bleary@cfcinc.org
http://www.CFCINC.org

William Leary, Director

The Retired and Senior Volunteer Program (RSVP) provides opportunities for people 55 and over to make a difference in their community through volunteer service. RSVP volunteers contribute anywhere from a few to over forty hours a week, serving through schools, day care centers, police departments, hospitals and other nonprofit and public organizations to help meet critical community needs. RSVP offers maximum flexibility and choice to its volunteers. RSVP matches the personal interests and skills of older Americans with opportunities to help solve community problems and offers supplemental insurance while on duty, on-the-job training from the agency or organization where volunteers are placed. The following County is served: Bristol.

1314 **RSVP Greater Lawrence-Haverhill**
264 Essex Street
Lawrence, MA 01840-1516
978-686-9407
Fax: 978-794-9953
e-mail: rsvp@merrimackvalleychamber.com

Guy Kelley, Jr, Director

The Retired and Senior Volunteer Program (RSVP) provides opportunities for people 55 and over to make a difference in their community through volunteer service. RSVP volunteers contribute anywhere from a few to over forty hours a week, serving through schools, day care centers, police departments, hospitals and other nonprofit and public organizations to help meet critical community needs. RSVP offers maximum flexibility and choice to its volunteers. RSVP matches the personal interests and skills of older Americans with opportunities to help solve community problems and offers supplemental insurance while on duty, on-the-job training from the agency or organization where volunteers are placed. The following County is served: Essex.

1315 **RSVP Lowell**
Community Teamwork
167 Dutton Street
Lowell, MA 01852-1803
978-459-0551
Fax: 978-970-1483
e-mail: lbrown@cometeam.org

Karen Frederick, Executive Director
Rob Buckel, Director Volunteers

Retired and Senior Volunteers use their skills and lifetime experiences to address community problems. They may tutor young people in need of a little extra help with their school work. The RSVP Volunteers may deliver meals on wheels, or visit elderly patients who are hospitalized or in nursing homes. RSVP volunteers are 55 years of age or older with no income limits.

1316 **RSVP Mayflower of Plymouth County**
34 Main Street Extension
3rd Floor
Plymouth, MA 02360-3329
508-746-7787
Fax: 508-746-7795
e-mail: MayflowerRSVP@verizon.net

Joan E Thompson, Director

The Retired and Senior Volunteer Program (RSVP) provides opportunities for people 55 and over to make a difference in their community through volunteer service. RSVP volunteers contribute anywhere from a few to over forty hours a week, serving through schools, day care centers, police departments, hospitals and other nonprofit and public organizations to help meet critical community needs. RSVP offers maximum flexibility and choice to its volunteers. RSVP matches the personal interests and skills of older Americans with opportunites to help solve community problems and offers supplemental insurance while on duty, on-the-job training from the agency or organization where volunteers are placed. The following County is served: Plymouth.

1317 **RSVP Norfolk County**
614 High Street
PO Box 310
Dedham, MA 02026-1897
781-329-5728
Fax: 781-326-6480
e-mail: rsvp@norfolkcounty.org
http://www.norfolkcounty.org

Tammy E Colbert, Director

State Organizations & Government Agencies/Massachusetts

The Norfolk County Retired and Senior Volunteer Program (RSVP) invites adults age 55 and over to use their life experience and skills to answer the call of their neighbors in need.

1318 RSVP Senior Care North Shore
5 Blackburn Center
Gloucester, MA 01930-2259   978-281-1750
Fax: 978-281-1753
http://www.seniorcareinc.org
Kay Bierwiler, Executive Director

Our mission is to provide and coordinate services to elders, enabling them to live independently at home and remain part of their community.

1319 RSVP Springfield
Urban League of Springfield
756 State Street
Springfield, MA 01109-4112   413-739-7211
Fax: 413-732-9364
e-mail: andrew6503@aol.com
Beverlye Blanchard Zebrowski, Director

The Retired and Senior Volunteer Program (RSVP) provides opportunities for people 55 and over to make a difference in their community through volunteer service. RSVP volunteers contribute anywhere from a few to over forty hours a week, serving through schools, day care centers, police departments, hospitals and other nonprofit and public organizations to help meet critical community needs. RSVP offers maximum flexibility and choice to its volunteers. RSVP matches the personal interests and skills of older Americans with opportunities to help solve community problems and offers supplemental insurance while on duty, on-the-job training from the agency or organization where volunteers are placed. The following County is served: Hampden.

1320 RSVP Worcester Area
128 Providence Street
Suite 208
Worcester, MA 01604-5433   508-799-1884
Fax: 508-799-8073
e-mail: rsvp@ci.worcester.ma.us
http://www.ci.worcester.ma.us
Denise L Herror, Director

RSVP connects people age 55 and over with opportunities that address compelling community needs.

1321 Railroad Retirement Board Dsitrict Office
PO Box 2448
Boston, MA 02130   617-223-8550
Fax: 617-223-8551
e-mail: boston@rrb.gov
Raymond P Fecteau, Manager

1322 Region 1: Administration on Aging (AoA)
US Department of Health & Human Services
John F Kennedy Building
Room 2075
Boston, MA 02203   212-565-1158
Fax: 617-565-4511
http://www.aoa.gov
Dan Quirk, Regional Administrator
Josefina G Carbonell ASA, Assistant Secretary
Edwin Walker PDASA, Deputy Assistant Secretary

Region includes Connecticut, Maine, Massachusetts, New Hampshire, Rhode Island, and Vermont. Through this network, older persons in each community have access to supportive and nutrition services. Persons age 60 and over may participate, and priority is given to the elderly with greatest economic or social needs.

1323 Scituate Council on Aging
Catherine McGowan Senior Center
27 Brook Street
Scituate, MA 02066-1309   781-545-8722
Fax: 781-545-2806
http://www.scituatecaregiver.org
Joan Wright, Director
Mary Dean, Program Coordinator

Promotes and provides social services and activities for senior citizens in Scituate, MA.

1324 Senior Home Care Services
5 Blackburn Center
Gloucester, MA 01930   978-281-1750
Fax: 978-281-1753
e-mail: srcare@seniorcareinc.org
http://www.seniorcareinc.org
TDD 978-468-1193
TTY 978-282-1836
Johnstone D Trott, President
George Nickless, Vice President
Kay Bierwiler, Interim Executive Director

SeniorCare offers short and long-term services that make it easier for elders to remain in the comfort of their own homes. Services may include: homemaking, shopping, personal care, meal preparation, laundry, caregiver, respite and personal emergency response systems. We also offer several enhanced programs for frail elders who might otherwise be facing long-term institutional placement.

1325 Service Opportunities After Retirement (SOAR)
492 Waltham Street
West Newton, MA 02465-1920   617-969-5906
Fax: 617-964-3975
e-mail: jlatorre-stiller@ncscweb.org
http://www.soar-ma.org
Janice Latorre-Stilelr, Director

SOAR's mission is to help meet community needs in Ashland, Framingham, Natick, Newton, Wayland, Wellesley and Weston, through unpaid volunteerism, by recruiting, training, supporting, rewarding and retaining people over age 55 who share their skills, experience and expertise in such a way that both the community and the individuals are enriched.

1326 Shrewsbury Senior Center
98 Maple Avenue
Shrewsbury, MA 01545-5349   508-841-8640
Fax: 508-841-8641
http://www.shrewsbury-ma.gov/councilaging
Sharon M Yager, Director
Vicky Pelligrino, Assistant Director

The Shrewsbury Senior Center is under the auspices of the Shrewsbury Council on Aging (SCOA), a human service department of the town, which serves the needs and issues of Shrewsbury's seniors, age 60 and over, or families with senior issues.

1327 Somerville Cambridge Elder Services
61 Medford Street
Somerville, MA 02143-3429   617-628-2601
Fax: 617-628-1085
e-mail: sces@eldercare.org
http://www.eldercare.org
TDD 617-628-1705
John O'Neill, Director

Elderly home care agency.

1328 South Shore Elder Services
159 Bay State Drive
Braintree, MA 02184-5203   781-848-3910
Fax: 781-843-8279
e-mail: eflynn@sselder.org
http://www.sselder.org
Edward J Flynn Jr, Director

1329 Urban Medical Group
545A Centre Street
Jamaica Plain, MA 02130-2075   617-522-5464
Fax: 617-524-2966
http://www.urbanmedicalgroup.org
Susan L Kaufman, Executive Director
Emily Brower, Administrative Director

Our mission is to provide a lifetime of compassionate, continuous, high-quality primary care to adults. We strive to ensure every patient's dignity and independence.

State Organizations & Government Agencies/Michigan

1330 Wellfleet Council on Aging
715 Old Kings Highway
Wellfleet, MA 02667-8013
508-349-0313
Fax: 508-349-0319
http://www.wellfleetma.org

Suzanne Grout Thomas, Director
Linda Balch, Outreach Director

Dedicated to improving the health and independence of older persons and increasing their continuing contributions to communities, societies, and future generations.

1331 West Suburban Elder Services
125 Walnut Street
Watertown, MA 02472-4052
617-926-4100
800-243-4636
Fax: 781-926-9897
TDD 617-926-5717

Carol Oram, Director
Susan E Temper, Executive Director

Watertown, Belmont, Brookline, Needham, Newton, Waltham, Wellesley, Weston.

1332 WestMass Elder Care
4 Valley Mill Road
Holyoke, MA 01040-5887
413-538-9020
800-462-2301
Fax: 413-538-6258

Priscilla Chalmers, Director

Holyoke, Chicopee.

1333 Workers Compensation Board Massachusetts
600 Washington Street
Floor 7
Boston, MA 02111-1704
617-261-0035
Fax: 617-727-6477
http://www.state.ma.us/dia

James J Campbell, Director

1334 Yarmouth Council on Aging
528 Forest Road
South Yarmouth, MA 02673-2842
508-394-7606
Fax: 508-398-4810
http://www.yarmouth.ma.us/council

Karen Marciante, Director

The Council on Aging is in charge of assessing the needs of the elderly, offering programs to seniors, and servicing the Town's aging population.

Michigan

1335 1B Area: Agency on Aging
29100 Northwestern Highway
Southfield, MI 48034-1046
248-213-6704
800-852-7795
Fax: 248-948-9691
http://www.aaa1b.org

Jenny Jarvis, Director Communications
Sandra Reminga, Executive Director

A nonprofit organization serving the needs of older adults, persons with disabilities and family caregivers residing in the counties of Livingston, Macomb, Monroe, Oakland, St Clair, Washtenaw. Committed to helping individuals remain living in their own home or residence of choice by providing access to home care services.

1336 A Friend's House Adult Day Services
15945 Canal
PO Box 380290
Clinton Township, MI 48038
586-412-8494
Fax: 586-412-8084
e-mail: csmseniors@csmacomb.org
http://www.csmacomb.org

Joyce McCracken LPN, Program Coordinator

Supervised, daytime care and activities for physically and/or memory-impaired adults; respite, monthly support group, counseling and care consultation for caregiving families.

1337 A Friend's House Adult Day Services: Romeo
Agape Center
347 South Main
Clinton Township, MI 48038
586-336-6839
Fax: 586-336-6843
e-mail: csmseniors@csmacomb.org
http://www.csmacomb.org

Lisa Gornowicz, Activities Coordinator
Suzanne Szczepanski-White, Director Senior Services

Supervised, daytime care and activities for memory-impaired adults; respite, counseling and care consultation for caregiving families.

1338 A Friend's House Adult Day Services: Warren
14200 Eleven Mile
Warren, MI 48089
586-777-8700
Fax: 586-777-8740
e-mail: csmseniors@csmacomb.org
http://www.csmacomb.org

Adrianna Scobie, Site Coordinator
Suzanne Szczaoabsju-White, Director Senior Services

Supervised, daytime care and activities for physically and/or memory-impaired adults; respite, monthly support groups, counseling and care consultation for caregiving families.

1339 Alpena Regional Medical Center Auxiliary
1501 W Chisholm Street
Alpena, MI 49707-1498
989-356-7390
800-556-8842
Fax: 989-356-7305

John McVeety, Administrator

Volunteers in northeastern Michigan who assist local hospital with community health programs. Conducts fundraising activities.

1340 Alzheimer's Association: South Central Michigan Chapter
107 Aprill Drive
Suite 1
Ann Arbor, MI 48103-1956
734-677-3081
800-337-3827
Fax: 734-677-3091
http://www.alzmigreatlakes.org

Elizabeth Longley, President/CEO
Kim DeHart Walsh, Program Director
Al Esper, Development Officer

Families and friends of Alzheimer's Disease patients, interested others. Provides advocacy, education, and support services. Supports research efforts. Offers support group programs, educational workshops, and video rental. Maintains speakers' bureau and lending library.

1341 Area Agency on Aging of Western Michigan, (AAAWM)
1279 Cedar Street NE
Grand Rapids, MI 49503-1378
616-456-5664
Fax: 616-456-5692
http://www.oaawm.org

Thomas Czerwinski, Director
Jackie O'Connor, Assistant Director

Grand Rapids, Allegan County, Ionia County, Kent County, Lake County, Mason County, Montcalm County, Newaygo County, Osceola County, Mecosta County.

1342 Bay County Council on Aging
1116 Frankford Avenue
Panama City, FL 32401-1861
850-769-3468
Fax: 850-872-2151
e-mail: baycouncil@bellsouth.net
http://www.baycouncilonaging.org

Elizabeth N Coulliette, Executive Director
Karen Coffman, Assistant Director

State Organizations & Government Agencies/Michigan

The organization provides services to the elderly of Bay County enabling senior adults to be healthy, active and independent in the lifestyles they choose. Bay County Council on Aging offers numerous programs which assist older persons in need.

1343 Blueprint for Aging
5361 Mcauley Drive
PO Box 995
Ann Arbor, MI 48106
734-712-3625
Fax: 734-712-7765
e-mail: jkind@csswashtenaw.org

Jill L Kind, Contact

The Blueprint for Aging is a diverse coalition of community members and representatives from over 40 public and nonprofit organizations who have actively worked for over five years to assist Washentaw County in becoming more responsive to its older residents.

1344 Bureau of Naval Personnel: Michigan Retired Activities Office
Marine Reserve Center
7600 East Jefferson Avenue
Detroit, MI 48214
313-824-1650
Fax: 313-824-2770

The RAO serves as a link between local retired military and the active-duty community which provides assistance to retired military. It provides installation commanders with a means of providing more effective services and improving communication for the local retired community. The RAO is staffed and operated by volunteer retired military who assist other retired members, their families and survivors to receive entitled services and benefits. Through newsletters and seminars and appreciation days, the RAO supports quality of life issues throughout the retirement years to their fellow service members.

1345 Charlevoix County Commission on Aging
110 E Main Street
East Jordan, MI 49727
231-536-5300
Fax: 231-237-0105
http://www.charlevoixcounty.org

Susan Bergmann, RN, BSN, Director
Barbara Shools, RN, Program Coordinator

Adult day services, activities, music and exercise, BINGO, games, outings, socialization, healthy snacks, personal care, nail and hair care, foot care.

1346 Chicago Social Security Management Association
44400 Van Dyke Avenue
Sterling Heights, MI 48314
586-997-0740
Fax: 586-997-3961
e-mail: Kenneth.Tash@ssa.gov
http://www.ncssma.org

Ken Tash, Area 3 Representative

CSSMA is a professional organization of Chicago Region field management staff dedicated to the enhancement and improvement of the overall operation of the programs administered by SSA and to futhering the best interests and general welfare of all field personnel.

1347 Detroit Area: Agency on Aging
220 Bagley Street
Detroit, MI 48226-1400
313-446-4444
Fax: 313-222-5308

Paul Bridgewater, Director

Detroit, Wayne County, Harper Woods, Highland Park, Grosse Pointe Park, Grosse Pointe, Grosse Pointe Woods, Grosse Pointe Farms, Grosse Pointe Shores, Hamtramck.

1348 Gray Panthers Metro Detroit
PO Box 37033
Oak Park, MI 48237
248-669-6343
Fax: 202-737-1160
e-mail: beelock47@comcast.net
http://www.graypanthersmetrodetroit.org

Randy Block, Co-Director
Ethel Schwartz, Co-Director

Intergenerational social justice group which invites activists of all ages to work together to: challenge descrimination based on race, sex or age; to work for social and economic justice, universal health care and peace.

1349 Gray Panthers of Huron Valley
1803 Cayuga Place
Ann Arbor, MI 48104-4720
734-663-6248
e-mail: juncar5575@sbcglobal.com
http://www.graypanthers.org

June Rusten, Director

Intergenerational social justice group which invites activists of all ages to work together to challenge descrimination based on race, sex or age; to work for social and economic justice, universal health care and peace.

1350 Iron Workers Local 25 Retirees Club of the International Association
25150 Trans X Drive
PO Box 965
Novi, MI 48376
248-344-9494
Fax: 248-344-4851

Jim Hamric, Manager

Represents members' interests; conducts lobbying activities. Provides assistance programs for retirees.

1351 Mature Minglers Senior Center: Senior Adult Services and Programs
7273 Wing Lake Road
Bloomfield Hills, MI 48301-3772
810-932-6235
Fax: 248-932-6243

Christine Tvaroha, Supervisor

Community service organization for seniors in Bloomfield Hills, Bloomfield Township, Orchard Lake, and West Bloomfield, MI.

1352 Michigan Association of Area Agencies on Aging
115 W Allegan Street
Suite 610
Lansing, MI 48933-1783
517-482-2871
Fax: 517-886-1305

Mary Ablan, Director

Provide supportive services that enable older adults to live with independence and dignity in a setting of their choice.

1353 Michigan Association of Homes and Services for the Aging
6512 Centurion Drive
Suite 380
Lansing, MI 48917-8248
517-323-3687
Fax: 517-323-4569
http://www.mahsahome.org

David Herbel, President/CEO
Karlene Ketola, MSA, VP Member Services

We create the future of aging services, advocate for service excellence, deliver member value, promote a continuum of service.

1354 Michigan Association of Retired School Personnel
PO Box 23214
Lansing, MI 48909-3214
517-337-1757
Fax: 517-337-8560
e-mail: staff-marsp@marsp.org
http://www.marsp.org

Bonnie J Carpenter, Executive Director

Represents and promotes the interests of retired school personnel.

1355 Michigan Bureau of Workers' Disability Compensation
PO Box 30016
Lansing, MI 48909
517-322-1296
Fax: 517-322-1808
e-mail: jack.wheatley@cis.state.mi.us
http://www.cis.state.mi.us/wkrcomp

Jack Wheatley, Director

State Organizations & Government Agencies/Michigan

The Bureau of Workers' Disability Compensation's mission is to administer the Act in order to facilitate timely benefit payments to injured employees at a reasonable cost to employers.

1356 Michigan Client Assistance Program
Michigan Protection and Advocacy Service
4095 Legacy Pkwy Suite 500
Lansing, MI 48933-1700
517-487-1755
800-292-5896
Fax: 517-487-0827
e-mail: jbrown@mpas.org
http://www.mpas.org

Jeanette Brown, Employment Advocacy Director
Elmer L Cerano, Executive Director

1357 Michigan Department of Community Health
HIV/AIDS Prevention & Intervention Section
3423 N Logan Martin Luther King Jr Boulevard
Lansing, MI 48901
517-373-3654
Fax: 517-335-8395

Loretta Davis-Satterla, Director Division HI
Bobbie Butler, Manager

Gives general public and high-risk education grants supporting educational materials, programs and a hotline.

1358 Michigan Department of Human Services
PO Box 30037
Lansing, MI 48909
517-373-2035
Fax: 517-335-6101
e-mail: dhsweb@michigan.gov
http://www.michigan.gov/dhs
TDD 517-373-8071

Marianne Udow, Director
Laura Champagne, Chief Deputy Director Operations

The Department of Human Services (DHS) is Michigan's public assistance, child and family welfare agency. DHS directs the operations of public assistance and service programs through a network of 100 county Department of Human Service offices around the state.

1359 Michigan Department of Management and Budget: Bureau of Retirement Systems
PO Box 30171
Lansing, MI 48909-7671
517-373-3654
800-381-5111
Fax: 517-322-6988

Bobbie Butler, Manager

1360 Michigan Department of Military Affairs Bureau of State Operations and Veterans' Affairs
2500 S Washington Avenue
Lansing, MI 48913
517-483-5500
Fax: 517-483-5822

Gordon Stump, Manager

1361 Michigan Department of Treasury
430 W Allegan Street
Lansing, MI 48922
517-373-3200
800-487-7000
e-mail: treasIndTax@michigan.gov
http://www.treas.state.mi.us

Jay Rising, CEO

1362 Michigan Developmental Disability Council
1033 South Washington Avenue
Lansing, MI 48910
517-334-6123
Fax: 517-334-7353
e-mail: vanhornr@michigan.gov
http://www.michigan.gov
TDD 517-334-7354

Vendella Collins, Executive Director

Our mission is to support people with developmental disabilities to achieve life dreams.

1363 Michigan Office of Services to the Aging
7109 W Saginaw Highway
1st Floor
Lansing, MI 48917-1120
517-373-8230
Fax: 989-343-4092
e-mail: OSADirector@michigan.gov
http://www.miseniors.net

Sharon L Gire, Director
Carol Dye, Administrative Assistant
Peggy Brey, Deputy Director

Provides services and advocacy to the aging in Michigan.

1364 Michigan Office on Aging
611 W Ottawa Street
3rd Floor
Lansing, MI 48933-1070
517-373-8230
Fax: 517-373-4092

Sharon L Gire, Executive Director

1365 Michigan Rehabilitation Services
PO Box 30010
Lansing, MI 48909-7510
517-887-9370
800-292-5896
Fax: 517-373-0565

Peter P Griswold, State Director
Marlene Malloy, Executive Director

A state and federally funded program that helps persons with disabilities prepare for and find a job that matches their interests and abilities. Assistance is also available to workers with disabilities who are having difficulty keeping a job. A person is eligible for MRS services if he or she has a disability, is unemployed and needs vocational rehabilitation services to prepare for and find a job.

1366 Michigan Society of Gerontology
PO Box 4055
East Lansing, MI 48826-4055
616-887-2920
Fax: 616-887-8586
e-mail: info@msginfor.org
http://www.msginfo.org

Bob Schlueter, President
Jeff Dwyer, Vice President

A voluntary organization made up of Michigan citizens who are concerned with education, research, action and service on behalf of older people in Michigan. MSG provides a multi-disciplinary forum for the exchange of ideas among diverse groups of professionals and students.

1367 Michigan Workers Compensation Board
201 N Washington Square
Lansing, MI 48933-1321
517-322-1296
Fax: 517-322-1808

1368 Northeast Michigan Community Services Region 9 Area: Agency on Aging
2375 Gordon Road
Alpena, MI 49707-4627
989-356-3474
Fax: 989-358-6604
http://www.nemcsa.org

Laurie Sauer, Director
John Swise, CEO

Services provided to Alcona, Alpena, Arenac, Cheboygan, Crawford, Iasco, Montmorency, Ogernaw, Oscoda, Otsego, Presque Isle and Roscommon Counties.

1369 RSVP Genesee-Shiawassee Counties
2421 Corunna Road
Room 118
Flint, MI 48503-3358
810-760-1092
Fax: 810-760-5388
e-mail: rsvpfnt@aol.com

Karen Reid Zimmermann, Director

State Organizations & Government Agencies/Michigan

The Retired and Senior Volunteer Program (RSVP) provides opportunities for people 55 and over to make a difference in their community through volunteer service. RSVP volunteers contribute anywhere from a few to over forty hours a week, serving through schools, day care centers, police departments, hospitals and other nonprofit and public organizations to help meet critical community needs. RSVP offers maximum flexibility and choice to its volunteers. RSVP matches the personal interests and skills of older Americans with opportunities to help solve community problems and offers supplemental insurance while on duty, on-the-job training from the agency or organization where volunteers are placed. The following Counties are served: Genesee, Shiawassee.

1370 RSVP Ingham
6545 Mercantile Way
Lansing, MI 48911-5990
517-887-6116
Fax: 517-887-7313
e-mail: rsvp@rsvptansing.com
http://www.volunteerwisdom.com
Janet Clark, Executive Director

The Retired and Senior Volunteer Program (RSVP) provides opportunities for people 55 and over to make a difference in their community through volunteer service. RSVP volunteers contribute anywhere from a few to over forty hours a week, serving thorough schools, day care centers, police departments, hospitals and other nonprofit and public organizations to help meet critical community needs. RSVP offers maximum flexibility and choice to its volunteers. RSVP matches the personal interests and skills to older Americans with opportunities to help solve community problems and offer supplemental insurance while on duty, on-the-job training from the agency or organization where volunteers are placed.

1371 RSVP Jackson County
407 S Mechanic Street
Jackson, MI 49201-2331
517-782-4616
Fax: 517-782-2693
e-mail: rsvpcss@dmci.net
Pamela McCrum, Director

The Retired and Senior Volunteer Program (RSVP) provides opportunities for people 55 and over to make a difference in their community through volunteer service. RSVP volunteers contribute anywhere from a few to over forty hours a week, serving through schools, day care centers, police departments, hospitals and other nonprofit and public organizations to help meet critical community needs. RSVP offers maximum flexibility and choice to its volunteers. RSVP matches the personal interests and skills of older Americans with opportunities to help solve community problems and offers supplemental insurance while on duty, on-the-job training from the agency or organization where volunteers are placed. The following County is served: Jackson.

1372 RSVP Kent County
14 Ionia SW
Suite One
Grand Rapids, MI 49503-4150
616-459-9509
Fax: 616-459-9906
e-mail: ginniblanchard@sbcglobal.net
Ginni Blanchard, Director
Eliza Bivins, Program Coordinator
Kathy Smith, Program Assistant

The Retired and Senior Volunteer Program (RSVP) provides opportunities for people 55 and over to make a difference in their community through volunteer service. RSVP volunteers contribute anywhere from a few to over forty hours a week, serving through schools, day care centers, police departments, hospitals and other nonprofit and public organizations to help meet critical community needs. RSVP offers maximum flexibility and choice to its volunteers. RSVP matches the personal interests and skills of older Americans with opportunities to help solve community problems and offers supplemental insurance while on duty, on-the-job training from the agency or organization where volunteers are placed. The following County is served: Kent.

Number of Members: 1,100

1373 RSVP Macomb
PO Box 380290
Clinton Township, MI 48038
586-412-8054
Fax: 586-412-8084
e-mail: csmseniors@csmacomb.org
http://www.csmacomb.org
Susan Szczepanski-White, Director Senior Services
Sue Kearney, Volunteer Coordiantor

The Retired and Senior Volunteer Program (RSVP) provides opportunities for people 55 and over to make a difference in their community through volunteer service. RSVP volunteers contribute anywhere from a few to over forty hours a week, serving though schools, day care centers, police departments, hospitals and other nonprofit and public organizations to help meet critical community needs. RSVP offers maximum flexibility and choice to its volunteers. RSVP matches the personal interests and skills to older Americans with opportunities to help solve community problems and offer supplemental insurance while on duty, on-the-job training from the agency or organization where volunteers are placed.

1374 RSVP Marquette County
200 W Spring Street
Marquette, MI 49855-4630
906-226-4180
Fax: 906-226-4188
e-mail: kherrala@mqtcty.org
http://www.co.marquette.ci.mi
Kathy Herrala, Director

The Retired and Senior Volunteer Program (RSVP) provides opportunities for people 55 and over to make a difference in their community through volunteer service. RSVP volunteers contribute anywhere from a few to over forty hours a week, serving though schools, day care centers, police departments, hospitals and other nonprofit and public organizations to help meet critical community needs. RSVP offers maximum flexibility and choice to its volunteers. RSVP matches the personal interests and skills to older Americans with opportunities to help solve community problems and offer supplemental insurance while on duty, on-the-job training from the agency or organization where volunteers are placed.

1375 RSVP Mecosta/Lake/Osceola
14485 Northland Drive
Big Rapids, MI 49307-2368
231-796-4848
Fax: 231-796-7864
e-mail: rsvp@tucker-usa.com
Sandra Dalrymple, Director

Provides opportunities for people 55 and over to make a difference in their community through volunteer service. RSVP volunteers contribute anywhere from a few to over forty hours a week, serving through schools, day care centers, police departments, hospitals and other nonprofit and public organizations to help meet critical community needs. RSVP matches the personal interests and skills of older Americans with opportunities to help solve community problems and offers supplemental insurance while on duty, on-the-job training from the agency or organization where volunteers are placed.

1376 RSVP Oakland County
18310 W 12 Mile Road
Southfield, MI 48076-2670
248-559-1147
Fax: 248-559-2309
e-mail: mastenh@cssoc.org
Herschell T Masten, Director

The Retired and Senior Volunteer Program (RSVP) provides opportunities for people 55 and over to make a difference in their community through volunteer service. RSVP volunteers contribute anywhere from a few to over forty hours a week, serving through schools, day care centers, police departments, hospitals and other nonprofit and public organizations to help meet critical community needs. RSVP offers maximum flexibility and choice to its volunteers. RSVP matches the personal interests and skills of older Americans with opportunities to help solve community problems and offers supplemental insurance while on duty, on-the-job training from the agency or organization where volunteers are placed. The following County is served: Oakland.

State Organizations & Government Agencies/Michigan

1377 RSVP Ostego County
590 E Fifth
PO Box 1025
Gaylord, MI 49735
989-732-6232
Fax: 989-732-8080
e-mail: rsvp@freeway.net

Tami Phillipps, Director

The Retired and Senior Volunteer Program (RSVP) provides opportunities for people 55 and over to make a difference in their community through volunteer service. RSVP volunteers contribute anywhere from a few to over forty hours a week, serving through schools, day care centers, police departments, hospitals and other nonprofit and public organizations to help meet critical community needs. RSVP offers maximum flexibility and choice to its volunteers. RSVP matches the personal interests and skills of older Americans with opportunities to help solve community problems and offers supplemental insurance while on duty, on-the-job training from the agency or organization where volunteers are placed. The following County is served: Ostego.

1378 RSVP Wayne County
9851 Hamilton Avenue
Detroit, MI 48202-1424
313-883-7764
Fax: 313-883-0601
e-mail: emahaffy@csswayne.org

Essie Mahaffy, Director

The Retired and Senior Volunteer Program (RSVP) provides opportunities for people 55 and over to make a difference in their community through volunteer service. RSVP volunteers contribute anywhere from a few to over forty hours a week, serving through schools, day care centers, police departments, hospitals and other nonprofit and public organizations to help meet critical community needs. RSVP offers maximum flexibility and choice to its volunteers. RSVP matches the personal interests and skills of older Americans with opportunities to help solve community problems and offers supplemental insurance while on duty, on-the-job training from the agency or organization where volunteers are placed. The following County is served: Wayne.

1379 Railroad Retirement Board: Michigan District Office
McNaunara Federal
Building 447w
Detroit, MI 48226
313-226-6221
Fax: 313-226-4233

Michael A Jansen, Representative

1380 Region 14 Council on Aging
255 W Sherman Boulevard
Muskegon Heights, MI 49444-1450
231-739-5858
800-442-0054
Fax: 616-739-4452

Dee Scott, Executive Director

Muskegon, Muskegon County, Oceana County, Ottawa County, Muskegon Heights.

1381 Region Four Area: Agency on Aging
2919 Division Street
Saint Joseph, MI 49085-2436
269-983-0177
800-442-2803
Fax: 616-983-5218

Robert Dolsen, Director
Lynn Kellogg, CEO

St. Joseph, Van Buren County, Berrien County, Cass County.

1382 Region Seven Area: Agency on Aging
1615 S Euclid Avenue
Bay City, MI 48706-3319
989-893-4506
800-858-1637
Fax: 989-893-2651
e-mail: region_7@michigan.gov
http://www.region7aaa.org

Drew Orvash, Assistant Director
Bruce King, Executive Director

Bay County, Gladwin County, Clare County, Gratiot County, Huron County, Isabella County, Midland County, Saginaw County, Sanilac County, Tuscola County.

1383 Region Two Area: Agency on Aging
102 North Main Street
PO Box 189
Brooklyn, MI 49230
517-467-2204
800-335-7881
Fax: 517-467-9113
http://www.r2aaa.org

Lisa Tinsley, Executive Director

The Region 2 Area Agency on Aging office administers programs that help the elderly maintain their health and independence in their homes and communities. Counties served: Jackson, Hillsdale, Lenawee.

1384 Right to Life of Michigan
2340 Porter Street SW
Grand Rapids, MI 49519-2261
616-532-2300
Fax: 616-532-3461
e-mail: info@rtl.org
http://www.rtl.org

Barb Listing, President

Right to Life of Michigan is a nonpartisan, nonsectarian, nonprofit organization of diverse and caring people united to protect the precious gift of human life from fertilization to natural death.

1385 Senior Alliance Area Agency on Aging
3850 2nd Street
Suite 201
Wayne, MI 48184-1755
734-722-2830
Fax: 734-722-2836
e-mail: info@tsalink.org
http://www.thesenioralliance.org

Bob Brown, Executive Director
Lori Vail, Program Manager

To coordinate a comprehensive network of services in Western and Southern Wayne County to enable older persons to function as independently as possible in the community environment which best suits their needs. To provide the advocacy, programming, planning, contracting, funding, and personnel necessary to accomplish the foregoing purpose.

1386 Senior Companion Program of Macomb
PO Box 380290
Clinton Township, MI 48038
586-412-8286
Fax: 586-412-8084
e-mail: csmseniors@csmacomb.org
http://www.csmacomb.org

Mary Ann Spisak, Volunteer Coordinator

Volunteer service opportunities with hourly stipend for income-eligible adults age 60 or older; non-medical support for homebound adults.

1387 Senior Services
Joseph J Dunnigan Parkway
918 Jasper Street
Kalamazoo, MI 49001
269-382-0515
Fax: 269-382-3189
http://www.seniorservices1.org

Robert W Littke PhD, President/CEO
Donald M Ryan FCBA, CFRM, Director Fund Development
John Grilo, Director Clinical Programs

A 501(c)(3) Agency to provide over 21 services assisting the elderly to remain living at home, safely, independently and with dignity.

1388 Tri-County Office on Aging
5303 S Cedar Street
Lansing, MI 48911-3800
517-887-1440
800-405-9141
Fax: 517-887-8071
e-mail: info@tcoa.org
http://www.tcoa.org

Marion Owen, Executive Director

State Organizations & Government Agencies/Minnesota

Our mission is to promote and preserve the independence and dignity of the aging population.

1389 Valley Area: Agency on Aging
711 N Saginaw Street
Room 325
Flint, MI 48503-1758
810-239-7671
Fax: 313-239-8869

Valaria Conerly, Director

Flint, Shiawassee County, Genesee County, Lapeer County.

1390 Waterford Senior Center
3621 Pontiac Lake Road
Waterford, MI 48328
248-682-9450
Fax: 248-738-4710

Lannette Amon, Executive Director

Multi purpose senior center offering programs and services to those 55 years and older. Goal is to assist them to maintain independence and enhance their quality of life.

Minnesota

1391 Arrowhead Area: Agency on Aging
330 Canal Park Drive
Duluth, MN 55802-2316
218-722-5545
800-232-0707
Fax: 218-529-7592

Anne Tellett, Director
John Chell, Executive VP

Duluth, Cook County, Lake County, St. Louis County, Carlton County, Aitkin County, Itasca County, Koochiching County.

1392 Bureau of Naval Personnel: Minnesota Retired Activities Office
Naval Reserve Readiness Command Region Sixteen
715 Apollo Avenue
Minneapolis, MN 55450-2113
612-713-1578
http://www.navyreserve.navy.mil

Capt Victor Yanega, III, Commanding Officer
CDR David H Ryan, Executive Officer

The RAO serves as a link between local retired military and the active-duty community which provides assistance to retired military. It provides installation commanders with a means of providing more effective services and improving communication for the local retired community. The RAO is staffed and operated by volunteer retired military who assist other retired members, their families and survivors to receive entitled services and benefits. Through newsletters, seminars and appreciation days, the RAO supports quality of life issues throughout the retirement years to their fellow service members.

1393 Cass County Council on Aging
4100 8th Street SW
Backus, MN 56435
218-947-3702
Fax: 218-547-2440
http://www.co.cass.mn.us

Pat Lahti, Director

The Council on Aging provides information and referral services with senior services and agencies. The Council deals with issues of concern with seniors and with senior clubs in the area. The Council coordinates transportation services for those 60 years and over who sign up through the Council office and demonstrate need.

1394 Central Minnesota Council on Aging
2700 1st Street North
Suite 307
St. Cloud, MN 56303
320-253-9349
800-333-2433
Fax: 320-253-9576
e-mail: gail@cmcoa.org
http://www.cmcoa.org

Ann Dorsey, Contact
Peggy Reiland, Contact

The Central Minnesota Council on Aging is a non-profit organization and designated by the Minnesota Board on Aging as the Area Agency on Aging, to serve the counties of Benton, Cass, Chisago, Crow Wing, Isanti, Kanabec, Mille Lacs, Morrison, Pine Sherburne, Stearns, Todd, Wadena, and Wright. The Central Minnesota Council on Aging is committed to maintaining the highest level of independence with older people by developing and coordinating community care, reducing isolation and improving access to services.

1395 Communicating for Seniors
PO Box 677
Fergus Falls, MN 56538
218-739-3241
800-432-3276
Fax: 218-739-3832
http://www.selfemploymentcountry.org

Provides general information on health-related matters for the elderly, particularly in the area of insurance. Offers group Medicare supplement to members. Offers free brochure and other materials for sale. Hours: 8:00 a.m. to 4:30 p.m. Monday-Friday.

1396 Department of Employment and Economic Development
MN Workforce Center
320 W 2nd Street
Suite 205
Duluth, MN 55802-1409
218-723-4698
800-657-3947
Fax: 218-723-4721
e-mail: Ken.Norstrud@state.mn.us
TTY 218-723-4725

Ken Norstrud, Rehabilitation Area Manager

Our mission is to support the economic success of individual's, businesses, and communities by improving opportunities for growth.

1397 Disability Determination Services
Minnesota Dept of Employment and Economic Dvlpment
121 E Seventh Place
Suite 300
Saint Paul, MN 55101
651-296-5179
800-657-3858
Fax: 651-297-1650
e-mail: Cory.Kissell@state.mn.us
http://www.deed.state.mn/dds
TDD 651-297-4045
TTY 651-297-4045

Cory Kissell, Public Relations Officer

The Disability Determination Services Office assists the federal Social Security Administration (SSA) in determining if Minnesota applicants meet federal criteria for disability cash benefits under the SSA's Social Security Disability Insurance (SSDI) or Supplemental Security Income (SSI) programs.

1398 East Central Regional Development Commission Area on Aging
PO Box 147
Mora, MN 55051
320-679-4065
Fax: 320-679-4120

Herman Bakker, Director
Robert Voss, Owner

Mora, Mille Lacs County, Kanabec County, Isanti County, Pine County, Chisago County, Isle Onamia.

1399 Gray Panthers of Twin Cities
3249 Hennepin Avenue S
Suite 220
Minneapolis, MN 55408-3493
612-822-1011
e-mail: info@graypantherstwincities.org
http://www.graypantherstwincities.org

Sally Brown, Co-Director
Jane Hanger-Seeley, Co-Director

Our mission is work for social and economic justice and peace for all people.

State Organizations & Government Agencies/Minnesota

1400 **Happy Old Timers Senior Center**
405 6th Street
Hawley, MN 56549-4601   218-483-4681
Laurence Legler, President

Promotes and provides social services for senior citizens in Hawley, MN.

1401 **Headwaters Area: Agency on Aging**
PO Box 906
Bemidji, MN 56619   218-751-3108
       Fax: 218-751-3695
Alan Goldberg, Director

Bemidji, Lake of the Woods County, Clearwater County, Hubbard County, Beltrami County.

1402 **Metropolitan Area Agency on Aging**
2365 N McKnight Road
North St. Paul, MN 55109   651-641-8612
       Fax: 651-641-8618
       http://www.tcaging.org
Dawn Simonson, Executive Director

1403 **Mid-Minnesota Area: Agency on Aging**
333 W 6th Street
Willmar, MN 56201   320-235-8504
       800-450-8608
       Fax: 612-235-4329
Lorraine Patton, Director

Willmar, Kandiyohi County, Meeker County, McLeod County, Renville County.

1404 **Minnesota Board on Aging**
444 Lafayette Road N
Saint Paul, MN 55155-3843   651-296-2770
       800-882-6262
       Fax: 651-297-7855
Jim Varpness, Executive Director

A state unit on aging for the state of Minnesota. Funds 14 area agencies on aging throughout the state that provide services at the local level. The mission is to keep older people in their homes or places of residence for as long as possible.

1405 **Minnesota Council on Disability**
121 E 7th Lace
Suite 107
Saint Paul, MN 55101   651-296-6785
       800-945-8913
       Fax: 651-296-5935
Joan Willshire, Executive Director

1406 **Minnesota Department of Labor & Industry Workers Compensation Division**
443 Lafayette Road North
Saint Paul, MN 55155-4307   651-284-5005
       800-342-5354
       Fax: 651-284-5720
       e-mail: dli.workcomp@state.mn.us
       http://www.doli.state.mn.us
       TTY 651-297-4198
Scott Brener, Commissioner

To reduce the impact of work related injuries for employees and employers. Advice is given and questions answered on the toll-free number.

1407 **Minnesota Department of Revenue**
Mail Station 5510
Saint Paul, MN 55146   651-296-3781
       http://www.taxes.state.mn.us

1408 **Minnesota Department of Veterans Affairs**
20 12th Street W
Saint Paul, MN 55155-2006   651-296-2562
       Fax: 651-296-3954
Bernie Melter, CEO

1409 **Minnesota Governor's Council on Developmental Disabilities**
370 Centennial Office Building
658 Cedar Street
Saint Paul, MN 55155   651-296-4018
       877-348-0505
       Fax: 651-297-7200
       e-mail: admin.dd@state.mn.us
       http://www.mnddc.org
Colleen Wieck PhD, Executive Director

The mission of the Minnesota Governor's Council on Developmental Disabilities is to provide information, education, and training to build knowledge, develop skills, and change attitudes that will lead to increased independence, productivity, self determination, integration and inclusion (IPSII) for people with developmental disabilities and their families.

1410 **Minnesota Health & Housing Alliance**
2550 University Avenue W
Suite 350S
Saint Paul, MN 55114-1900   651-645-4545
       800-462-5368
       Fax: 651-645-0002
       e-mail: gkvenvold@mhha.com
       http://www.mhha.com
Gayle M Kvenvold, President/CEO
Barbara Averill, Director Communications/PR

MHHA promotes excellence and innovation in older adult services. We serve our members through advocacy, public information, education, products and services related to the aging services field and networking opportunities.

1411 **Minnesota Indian Area: Agency on Aging**
PO Box 217
Cass Lake, MN 56633   218-335-8585
       Fax: 218-335-6562
Luella Seelye, Director
Ardith Morrow, Manager

1412 **Minnesota Mental Health Division**
Human Services Building
444 Lafayette Road N
Saint Paul, MN 55155-3802   651-296-3848
Edwin Swenson, Director
Roberta Opheim, Manager

Oversees the provision of services to people with mental illness in the state of Minnesota. Services are provided on the local level through a network of 87 county social service departments.

1413 **Minnesota Public Employees Retirement Association**
514 St Peter Street
Room 200
Saint Paul, MN 55155   651-296-7460
       Fax: 651-297-2547
Mary Vanek, Manager

1414 **Minnesota STAR Program**
50 Sherburne Avenue
Room 309
Saint Paul, MN 55155   651-201-2640
       800-652-3529
       Fax: 651-282-6671
       e-mail: star.program@state.mn.us
       http://www.admin.state.mn.us
       TDD 651-296-9478
Chuck Rassbach, Executive Director

The STAR Program was established as Minnesota's Tech Act Project to plan and coordinate assistive technology (AT) information and services for the citizens of Minnesota with disabilities. The STAR Program serves as an advocate for federal and state assistive technology policy and legislation, builds assistive technology capacity in state government and helps assure statewide assistive technology services.

State Organizations & Government Agencies/Minnesota

1415 Minnesota State Council on Disability
121 7th Place E
Suite 145
Saint Paul, MN 55101-2188
651-296-6785
Fax: 651-296-5935
http://www.disability.state.mn.us
Joan Willshire, Executive Director

1416 Minnesota Teachers Retirement Association
60 Empire Drive
Suite 400
Saint Paul, MN 55103
651-296-2409
800-657-3669
Fax: 651-297-5999
e-mail: laurie.hacking@state.mn.us
http://www.tra.state.mn.us
TTY 800-627-3529
Laurie Fiori Hacking, Executive Director
Luther Thompson PhD, JD, Assistant Executive Director
John Wicklund, Assistant Executive Director

The mission of the Teachers Retirement Association is to enhance the quality of life for Minnesota teachers and their beneficiaries and to assist them in planning for an independent and financially secure retirement. To this end we are committed to the improvement of our customer services. Among the services provided to our customers are counseling members on retirement issues, maintaining member data, administering funds, communicating accurate information and delivering benefits.

1417 Minnestoa Retirement System
175 W Lafayette Frontage Road
Saint Paul, MN 55107-1488
651-296-2761
800-657-5757
Fax: 651-297-5238
David Bergstrom, Executive Director

1418 Paynesville Area Senior Center
1105 W Main Street
Paynesville, MN 56362-1000
320-243-4799
Fax: 320-243-5146
e-mail: pareactr@lakedale.link.net
Inez Jones, Director

Provides services and recreational activities for seniors.

1419 RSVP Aiken-Carlton Counties
1003 Cloquet Avenue
Suite 102
Cloquet, MN 55720-1694
218-879-9238
Fax: 218-879-1196
e-mail: jhatfield@monetbroadband.net
Jill Hatfield, Director

The Retired and Senior Volunteer Program (RSVP) provides opportunities for people 55 and over to make a difference in their community through volunteer service. RSVP volunteers contribute anywhere from a few to over forty hours a week, serving through schools, day care centers, police departments, hospitals and other nonprofit and public organizations to help meet critical community needs. RSVP offers maximum flexibility and choice to its volunteers. RSVP matches the personal interests and skills of older Americans with opportunities to help solve community problems and offers supplemental insurance while on duty, on-the-job training from the agency or organization where volunteers are placed. The following Counties are served: Aiken, Carlton.

1420 RSVP Anoka County
Government Center
2100 Third Avenue
Anoka, MN 55303-5049
763-422-7090
e-mail: diane.pokorney@co.anoka.mn.us
http://www.co.anoka.mn.us
Diane Pokorney, Coordinator

The Retired and Senior Volunteer Program (RSVP) provides opportunities for people 55 and over to make a difference in their community through volunteer service.

1421 RSVP Arrowhead County
702 Third Avenue South
Virginia, MN 55792-2775
218-748-7328
800-662-5711
Fax: 218-749-2944
e-mail: bebnet@acoa.org
Bonnie Ebnet, Director

RSVP engages older individuals in volunteer service to meet critical community needs and to provide a high quality experience to enrich the lives of volunteers. The following Counties are served: Cook, Lake, St. Louis.

1422 RSVP Eldercircle
10 NW 5th Street
Grand Rapids, MN 55744-2660
218-326-3175
Fax: 218-326-7965
e-mail: valerie@eldercircle.org
Valerie Jensen, Director

The Retired and Senior Volunteer Program (RSVP) provides opportunities for people 55 and over to make a difference in their community through volunteer service. RSVP volunteers contribute anywhere from a few to over forty hours a week, serving through schools, day care centers, police departments, hospitals and other nonprofit and public organizations to help meet critical community needs. RSVP offers maximum flexibility and choice to its volunteers. RSVP matches the personal interests and skills of older Americans with opportunities to help solve community problems and offers supplemental insurance while on duty, on-the-job training from the agency or organization where volunteers are placed.

1423 RSVP Greater Twin Cities
2021 E Hennepin Avenue
Suite 200
Minneapolis, MN 55413-2188
612-617-7833
Fax: 612-331-6772
e-mail: kobrien@voamn.org
Kelly O'Brien, Director

The Retired and Senior Volunteer Program (RSVP) provides opportunities for people 55 and over to make a difference in their community through volunteer service. RSVP volunteers contribute anywhere from a few to over forty hours a week, serving through schools, day care centers, police departments, hospitals and other nonprofit and public organizations to help meet critical community needs. RSVP offers maximum flexibility and choice to its volunteers. RSVP matches the personal interests and skills of older Americans with opportunities to help solve community problems and offers supplemental insurance while on duty, on-the-job training from the agency or organization where volunteers are placed.

1424 RSVP Heartland
PO Box 36
Cosmos, MN 56228
320-877-7244
Fax: 320-877-7483
e-mail: suep@heartlnadcaa.org
Sue Peterson, Director

Invites adults age 55 and over to use their life experiences and skills to answer the call of their neighbors in need. Giving anywhere from 4 to 40 hours per week helps solve serious problems in their communities.

1425 RSVP Mahube Community Council
PO Box 747
Detroit Lakes, MN 56502-0747
218-847-1385
Fax: 218-847-1388
e-mail: jhaack@mahube.org
http://www.mahube.org
John Haack, Director
Leah Pigatti, Executive Director

The Retired and Senior Volunteer Program (RSVP) helps individuals 55 and older put their skills and life experiences to work for their communities. The following Counties are served: Becker, Clearwater, Hubbard, Mahnomen.

State Organizations & Government Agencies/Minnesota

1426 **RSVP Red River Valley**
University of Minnesota
2900 University Avenue
Crookston, MN 56716-5000
218-281-8288
800-232-6466
Fax: 218-281-8250
e-mail: dpatenau@umn.edu
http://www.umcrookston.edu

Deanna Patenaude, Director

The Retired and Senior Volunteer Program (RSVP) provides opportunities for people 55 and over to make a difference in their community through volunteer service. RSVP volunteers contribute anywhere from a few to over forty hours a week, serving though schools, day care centers, police departments, hospitals and other nonprofit and public organizations to help meet critical community needs. RSVP offers maximum flexibility and choice to its volunteers. RSVP matches the personal interests and skills to older Americans with opportunities to help solve community problems and offer supplemental insurance while on duty, on-the-job training from the agency or organization where volunteers are placed.

1427 **RSVP Semcac**
PO Box 549
Rushford, MN 55971-9123
507-864-7741
Fax: 507-864-2440
e-mail: sharon.rustad@semcac.org

Sharon Rustad, Director

The Retired and Senior Volunteer Program (RSVP) provides opportunities for people 55 and over to make a difference in their community through volunteer service. RSVP volunteers contribute anywhere from a few to over forty hours a week, serving through schools, day care centers, police departments, hospitals and other nonprofit and public organizations to help meet critical community needs. RSVP offers maximum flexibility and choice to its volunteers. RSVP matches the personal interests and skills of older Americans with opportunities to help solve community problems and offers supplemental insurance while on duty, on-the-job training from the agency or organization where volunteers are placed. The following Counties are served: Dodge, Fillmore, Houston, Mower, Stelle.

1428 **RSVP Southern Tri-County**
1659 1/2 Main Street
Albert Lea, MN 56007-1868
507-377-7433
Fax: 507-377-2879
e-mail: bspande.volunteer@charterinternet.net

Beth Spande, Director

The Retired and Senior Volunteer Program (RSVP) provides opportunities for people 55 and over to make a difference in their community through volunteer service. RSVP volunteers contribute anywhere from a few to over forty hours a week, serving through schools, day care centers, police departments, hospitals and other nonprofit and public organizations to help meet critical community needs. RSVP offers maximum flexibility and choice to its volunteers. RSVP matches the personal interests and skills of older Americans with opportunities to help solve community problems and offers supplemental insurance while on duty, on-the-job training from the agency or organization where volunteers are placed. The following Counties are served: Faribault, Freeborn, Martin.

1429 **RSVP Todd-Wadena-Otter Tail-Wilkin**
109 South Walker Avenue
PO Box L
New York Mills, MN 56567-4104
218-385-2900
Fax: 218-385-4544
e-mail: katieq@otwcac.org

Kathryn Quittschreiber, Director

The Retired and Senior Volunteer Program (RSVP) provides opportunities for people 55 and over to make a difference in their community through volunteer service. RSVP volunteers contribute anywhere from a few to over forty hours a week, serving through schools, day care centers, police departments, hospitals and other nonprofit and public organizations to help meet critical community needs. RSVP offers maximum flexibility and choice to its volunteers. RSVP matches the personal interests and skills of older Americans with opportunities to help solve community problems and offers supplemental insurance while on duty, on-the-job training from the agency or organization where volunteers are placed. The following Counties are served: Otter Tail, Todd, Wadena, Wilkin.

1430 **RSVP Volunteer Services**
Crow Wing Social Services
204 Laurel Street
Suite 11
Brainerd, MN 56401-3545
218-824-1345
Fax: 218-824-1346
e-mail: RSVP@co.crow-wing.mn.us
http://www.co.crow-wing.mn.us

Mike Koecheler, Executive Director
Mari Jo Renstrom, Program Assistant

Our mission is connecting those in need with those able to help through volunteer service. Enhance the lives of the volunteers and those whom they serve. Provide communities with valuable services.

1431 **RSVP West Central Minnesota**
411 Industrial Park Boulevard
Elbow Lake, MN 56531
218-685-4486
Fax: 218-685-6741
e-mail: rsvp@co.grant.mn.us
http://www.wcmca.org

Karen Alvstand, Director
Steve Nagle, Executive Director

The Retired and Senior Volunteer Program (RSVP) provides opportunities for people 55 and over to make a difference in their community through volunteer service. RSVP volunteers contribute anywhere from a few to over forty hours a week, serving thourgh schools, day care centers, police departments, hospitals and other nonprofit and public organizations to help meet critical community needs. RSVP offers maximum flexibility and choice to its volunteers. RSVP matches the personal interests and skills to older Americans with opportunities to help solve community problems and offer supplemental insurance while on duty, on-the-job training from the agency or organization where volunteers are placed.

1432 **Railroad Retirement Board: Duluth Minnesota District Office**
515 W 1st Street
Duluth, MN 55802-1392
218-720-5301
Fax: 218-720-5315
e-mail: duluth@rrb.gov

Ron Ellefson, Representative

1433 **Railroad Retirement Board: St. Paul Minnesota District Office**
180 5th Street E
Suite 195
Saint Paul, MN 55101-1640
651-290-3491
Fax: 651-290-3076
e-mail: stpaul@rrb.gov

Brian P Running, Representative

1434 **Region Nine Area: Agency on Aging**
PO Box 3367
Mankato, MN 56002-3367
507-387-5643
800-450-5643
Fax: 507-387-7105
e-mail: lindag@rndc.mankato.mn.us
http://www.rndc.org

Linda Giersdorf, Director
Reggie Edwards, Executive Director

Provides area-wide advocacy and leadership regarding aging on behalf of older persons. Provides information, assistance and referral on services for older adults and their families. Serves the following counties: Sibley County, Le Sueur County, Waseca County, Faribault County, Martin County, Watonwan County, Brown County, Nicollet County, Blue Earth County.

1435 **Southeast Minnesota Area: Agency on Aging**
421 SW Avenue
201
Rochester, MN 55902
507-288-6944
800-333-2433
Fax: 507-288-4823
e-mail: semaaa@semaaarochestermn.org
TDD 800-657-3529

Connie Bagley, Director

Rochester, Rice County, Steele County, Freeborn County, Goodhue County, Dodge County, Mower County, Wabasha County, Olmsted County, Fillmore County, Winona County, Houston County. Community based services for the frail senior citizen. Meals on wheels, chore, advocates education, information and assistance, health insurance counseling, transportation.

1436 **Southeast Regional Service Center for Hearing Impaired People**
Olmstead County Human Services Building
2116 Campus Drive SE
Suite 32
Rochester, MN 55904-4713
507-285-7295
Fax: 507-280-5531
TTY 507-285-7172

Jeff Erickson, Executive Officer

Sponsors services to the deaf and hard of hearing. Provides interpreter referral, message relay, vocational rehabilitation, assistance in dealing with agencies, and loans of materials.

1437 **Southeast Senior Federation**
PO Box 376
West Concord, MN 55985
507-527-2799
866-851-7755
Fax: 507-527-2799
e-mail: semnsf@lakes.com
http://www.southeastseniors.org

Helen Aase, President

Strives to find solutions to problems confronting elderly persons.

1438 **Southeastern Minnesota Area: Agency on Aging**
421 SW First Avenue
Room 201
Rochester, MN 55902
507-288-6944
800-333-2433
Fax: 507-288-4823
e-mail: connie@semaaarochestermn.org

Connie J Bagley, Director

Information and personal assistance. Plans programs for senior citizens in 11 county area. Coordinates federal and state grant funding. Medicare and Insurance assistance.

1439 **Southwest Area: Agency on Aging**
2401 Broadway Avenue
Suite 2
Slayton, MN 56172-1167
507-836-8547
800-333-2433
Fax: 507-836-8866

Maddy Forsgberg, Director

Slayton, Lincoln County, Lyon County, Murray County, Redwood County, Pipestone County, Cottonwood County, Jackson County, Nobles County, Rock County.

1440 **United Way 211**
424 W Superior Street
Suite 402
Duluth, MN 55802-1590
218-726-4770
800-543-7709
Fax: 218-726-4778
e-mail: info@unitedwayduluth.org
http://www.unitedwayduluth.org

Paula Reed, President
Anita Gille, Director Events/Marketing

Our mission is to lead a united effort to strengthen our community by mobilizing resources to improve people's lives.

1441 **Upper Minnesota Valley Area Agency on Aging**
323 W Schlieman Avenue
Appleton, MN 56208-1229
320-289-1981
800-752-1983
Fax: 320-289-1983
e-mail: regbwaaa@umvrdc.org
http://www.umvrdc.org

Connie Nygard, Director
Paul Michaelson, Executive Director

Appleton, Big Stone County, Lac qui Parle County, Yellow Medicine County, Swift County, Chippewa County.

1442 **West Central Area: Agency on Aging**
PO Box 726
Fergus Falls, MN 56538
218-739-4617
800-333-2433
Fax: 218-739-4618
e-mail: reg4aaa@prtel.com

Margaret Babcock, Director
Mark Tysver, Manager

Becker County, Clay County, Douglas County, Grant County, Otter Tail County, Pope County, Stevens County, Traverse County, Wilkin County.

Mississippi

1443 **Area Agency on Aging of Southern Mississippi**
1020 32nd Avenue
Gulfport, MS 39501
228-868-2326
800-444-8014
Fax: 228-868-2311

Jane Kennedy, Director
Leslie Newcomb, Executive Director

1444 **Central Mississippi Area: Agency on Aging**
1170 Lakeland Drive
Jackson, MS 39216-4701
601-981-1516
Fax: 601-981-1515

Bettye Burgess, Director

1445 **East Central Area: Agency on Aging**
PO Box 499
Newton, MS 39345
601-683-2007
800-264-2007
Fax: 601-683-7873

Myrtle Burton, Director
Bill Richardson, Executive Director

Area agency on Aging for Clarke, Lasper, Kemper, Lauderdale, Leake, Neshoba, Newton, Scott, and Smith Counties in East Central Mississippi. Provides a comprehensive system of home- and community-based services and elder rights protection at the local level. Services include, but not limited to, congregate and home delivered meals; transportation; homemaker services; information, referral, and outreach; insurance counseling, ombudsman services (long-term care facilities); legal assistance; case managment; emergency response; and Title V employment (55+). Services and programs are designed to meet the needs of priority target groups, including those persons aged 60+; low income 60+; rural 60+; minority 60+; and low-income minority 60+.

State Organizations & Government Agencies/Mississippi

1446 Mississippi Association of Area Agencies on Aging
110 S Wall Street
Natchez, MS 39120-3477
601-446-6044
Fax: 601-446-6071
http://www.smpdd.com

Barry Dixon, Director

The Area Agency on Aging serves as the public advocate for the development and implementation of comprehensive and coordinated home and community based care systems responsive to the current needs and future growth of the aging population.

1447 Mississippi Client Assistance Program: Easter Seals Society
3226 N State Street
Jackson, MS 39216-4005
601-362-2585

Presley Posey, Executive Director

1448 Mississippi Commission for Veterans Affairs
4607 Lindbergh Drive
Jackson, MS 39209-3855
601-354-7205
Fax: 601-354-6060

Adrian Grice, Manager

1449 Mississippi Department of Mental Health
239 N Lamar Street
Jackson, MS 39201-1328
601-359-1288
Fax: 601-359-6295
TDD 601-359-6230

Albert Hendricks PhD, Director
Herb Loving, Executive Director

1450 Mississippi Department of Rehabilition Services for the Blind
PO Box 5314
Jackson, MS 39296-5314
601-364-2700
Fax: 601-364-2677

1451 Mississippi Developmental Disability Council
1001 Robert E Lee Building
239 North Lamar Street
Jackson, MS 39201
601-359-1270
Fax: 601-359-5330
e-mail: info@cdd.ms.gov
http://www.cdd.ms.gov
TDD 601-359-6230

Edwin Butler, Executive Director
Grenaye Sullivan, Administrative Assistant

The Mississippi Council on Developmental Disabilities is a body of advocates, appointed by the Governor, who promote quality of life for people with developmental disabilities, their families, and the community at large. Improvement in quality of life is provided through initiatives that have potential for replication, thus creating systemic change.

1452 Mississippi Division of Aging and Adult Services
Mississippi Department of Human Services
750 N State Street
Jackson, MS 39202
601-359-4929
800-948-3090
http://www.mdhs.state.ms.us

Marion Dunn-Tutor, PhD, Director

The mission of the Division of Aging and Adult Services is to protect the right of older citizens while expanding their opportunities and access to quality services. Our vision is for each older citizen to live the best life possible. The Division of Aging and Adult Services plans, coordinates and advocates for, and ensures the provision of services to all older Mississippians.

1453 Mississippi Office of Disability & Determination Services
Mississippi Department of Rehabilitation Services
PO Box 1698
Jackson, MS 39215-1698
601-853-5100
800-443-1000
Fax: 601-853-5451
http://www.mdrs.state.ms.us
TTY 601-853-5100

H S McMillan, Executive Director
Sheila Browning, Deputy Director
Jo Ann Summers, Interim Deputy Director

The Office of Disability Determination Services (ODDS), funded entirely through the Social Security Administration, establishes eligibility of Mississippians with severe disabilities that apply for Social Security Disability Insurance and/or Supplemental Security Income.

1454 Mississippi Public Employees Retirement Systems
429 Mississippi Street
Jackson, MS 39201-1005
601-359-3589
800-444-7377
Fax: 601-359-2285

Denise Mounger, Executive Director

1455 Mississippi State Tax Commission
1577 Springridge Road
PO Box 1033
Jackson, MS 39215-1033
601-923-7000
Fax: 601-923-7318
http://www.mstc.state.ms.us

Keith Hicks, Manager

Provides state income and business tax forms and information.

1456 Natchez-Adams Council on Aging
800 Washington Street
Natchez, MS 39120-3566
601-442-5082
Fax: 601-445-6650

Sabrena Bartley, Executive Director

Plans and renders services to aging citizens in Natchez and Adams Counties.

1457 North Central Area: Agency on Aging
711 B South Applegate
Winona, MS 38967
662-283-2675
888-427-0714
Fax: 662-283-5875
http://www.mdhs.state.ms.us/aas_agcy

Darlena Allen, Director

Our mission is to enhance the quality of life for older adults in the following counties: Attala, Carroll, Grenada, Holmes, Leflore, Montgomery, Yalobusha by ensuring that they have access to quality and cost effective services.

1458 North Delta Planning and Development District Area Agency on Aging
PO Box 1244
Clarksdale, MS 38614-1244
662-627-3401
800-523-6683
Fax: 662-627-6753

Marikay Wilson, Director
Glen Brown, Executive Director

1459 Northeast Mississippi Area: Agency on Aging
PO Box 600
Booneville, MS 38829
662-728-7038
800-745-6961
Fax: 662-728-7240
http://www.mdhs.state.ms.us/aas_agcy

Linda Presley, Director

Our mission is to make it easier for older persons to live independently in the comfort of their own surroundings - is not only cost effective, it is the preferred choice for millions of older adults nationwide. Counties served: Alcorn, Benton, Marshall, Prentiss, Tippah, and Tishomingo.

State Organizations & Government Agencies/Mississippi

1460 Preserve Sight Mississippi
5455 Executive Place
Jackson, MS 39206
601-362-6985
http://www.msblind.org
Lori Russell, Executive Director
To preserve sight and blindness.

1461 RSVP Adams County
800 Washington Street
Natchez, MS 39120-3566
601-442-5082
Fax: 601-445-6650
e-mail: janet@bkbank.com
Janet McNeely, Director
The Retired and Senior Volunteer Program (RSVP) provides opportunities for people 55 and over to make a difference in their community through volunteer service. RSVP volunteers contribute anywhere from a few to over forty hours a week, serving through schools, day care centers, police departments, hospitals and other nonprofit and public organizations to help meet critical community needs. RSVP offers maximum flexibility and choice to its volunteers. RSVP matches the personal interests and skills of older Americans with opportunities to help solve community problems and offers supplemental insurance while on duty, on-the-job training from the agency or organization where volunteers are placed. The following Counties are served: Adams, Washington.

1462 RSVP Attala County
PO Box 381
Kosciusko, MS 39090-0381
662-289-6964
Fax: 662-289-6964
e-mail: atcorsvp@bellsouth.net
Pam Comfort, Director
The Retired and Senior Volunteer Program (RSVP) provides opportunities for people 55 and over to make a difference in their community through volunteer service. RSVP volunteers contribute anywhere from a few to over forty hours a week, serving through schools, day care centers, police departments, hospitals and other nonprofit and public organizations to help meet critical community needs. RSVP offers maximum flexibility and choice to its volunteers. RSVP matches the personal interests and skills of older Americans with opportunities to help solve community problems and offers supplemental insurance while on duty, on-the-job training from the agency or organization where volunteers are placed. The following County is served: Attala.

1463 RSVP Clarksdale
c/o Coahoma
115 Desoto Avenue
PO Drawer 1445
Clarksdale, MS 38614-4385
601-627-7838
Fax: 662-624-4915
e-mail: mooregale61@yahoo.com
Bennie Bumper, Contact
We have about 33 senior volunteers who regularly recycle cans & newspapers, and plant and maintain gardens for product and beautification of the local community.

1464 RSVP Hancock County
1928 Depot Way
PO Box 248
Bay St Louis, MS 39520-4326
228-467-9204
Fax: 228-466-0300
e-mail: rsvphancock@mail.com
Jo Ann Lagasse, Director
Provides opportunities for people 55 and over to make a difference in their community through volunteer service. RSVP volunteers contribute anywhere from a few to over forty hours a week, serving through schools, day care centers, police departments, hospitals and other nonprofit and public organizations to help meet critical community needs. RSVP matches the personal interests and skills of older Americans with opportunities to help solve community problems and offers supplemental insurance while on duty, on-the-job training from the agency or organization where volunteers are placed.

1465 RSVP Harrison County
842 Commerce Street
Gulfport, MS 39507-3321
228-896-0412
Fax: 228-896-0414
e-mail: skordek@co.harrison.ms.us
Mary Cavanaugh, Director
The Retired and Senior Volunteer Program (RSVP) provides opportunities for people 55 and over to make a difference in their community through volunteer service. RSVP volunteers contribute anywhere from a few to over forty hours a week, serving through schools, day care centers, police departments, hospitals and other nonprofit and public organizations to help meet critical community needs. RSVP offers maximum flexibility and choice to its volunteers. RSVP matches the personal interests and skills of older Americans with opportunities to help solve community problems and offers supplemental insurance while on duty, on-the-job training from the agency or organization where volunteers are placed. The following County is served: Harrison.

1466 RSVP Lafayette County
107 Courthouse Square
Oxford, MS 38655
662-232-2377
Fax: 662-232-2377
e-mail: rsvp@dixie-net.com
Jeff Dalton, Director
Rosemary Austin, Secretary
RSVP helps people ages 55 and older find service opportunities in their home communities. RSVP participants serve from a few to over forty hours a week in private nonprofit organizations. RSVP involves seniors in services that match their personal interests and make use of their skills and lifelong experiences.

1467 RSVP Laurel-Jones County
433 Arco Lane
Laurel, MS 39440
601-425-5100
Fax: 601-425-9830
e-mail: rsvpmerlin.ebicom.net
Elma Portero, Project Director
RSVP volunteers choose how and where they want to serve. Many continue to do the type of work they have enjoyed earlier in life, while others try something completely different. As a RSVP volunteer, you might mentor at-risk youth, make hospital visits, check blood pressure, clean grounds, or help people recover from natural disasters.

1468 RSVP Lee County
PO Box 28
Tupelo, MS 38802-0028
601-842-9511
Fax: 601-842-5575
e-mail: lift@tsixroads.com
Mary Marion, Contact
Provides opportunities for people 55 and over to make a difference in their community through volunteer service. RSVP volunteers contribute anywhere from a few to over forty hours a week, serving through schools, day care centers, police departments, hospitals and other nonprofit and public organizations to help meet critical community needs. RSVP matches the personal interests and skills of older Americans with opportunities to help solve community problems and offers supplemental insurance while on duty, on-the-job training from the agency or organization where volunteers are placed.

1469 RSVP Lowndes County
161 Maple Street
PO Box 5015
Columbus, MS 39704
662-328-2174
Fax: 662-328-7264
e-mail: rsvpcms@cableone.net
Rosemarie Hughes, Director

State Organizations & Government Agencies/Missouri

The Retired and Senior Volunteer Program (RSVP) provides opportunities for people 55 and over to make a difference in their community through volunteer service. RSVP volunteers contribute anywhere from a few to over forty hours a week, serving through schools, day care centers, police departments, hospitals and other nonprofit and public organizations to help meet critical community needs. RSVP offers maximum flexibility and choice to its volunteers. RSVP matches the personal interests and skills of older Americans with opportunities to help solve community problems and offers supplemental insurance while on duty, on-the-job training from the agency or organization where volunteers are placed. The following County is served: Lowndes.

1470 RSVP Meridian-Lauderdale Counties
1528 12th Avenue
PO Box 5204
Meridian, MS 39301-4353
601-483-4607
Fax: 601-483-7011
e-mail: msharpe357@aol.com

Mary L Sharpe, Director

The Retired and Senior Volunteer Program (RSVP) provides opportunities for people 55 and over to make a difference in their community through volunteer service. RSVP volunteers contribute anywhere from a few to over forty hours a week, serving through schools, day care centers, police departments, hospitals and other nonprofit and public organizations to help meet critical community needs. RSVP offers maximum flexibility and choice to its volunteers. RSVP matches the personal interests and skills of older Americans with opportunities to help solve community problems and offers supplemental insurance while on duty, on-the-job training from the agency or organization where volunteers are placed. The following County is served: Lauderdale.

1471 RSVP Simpson County
406 Main Street
Mendenhall, MS 39114-3358
601-847-4612
Fax: 601-847-1192
e-mail: shrrsvp@bellsouth.net

Billie J Brown, Director

The Retired and Senior Volunteer Program (RSVP) provides opportunities for people 55 and over to make a difference in their community through volunteer service. RSVP volunteers contribute anywhere from a few to over forty hours a week, serving through schools, day care centers, police departments, hospitals and other nonprofit and public organizations to help meet critical community needs. RSVP offers maximum flexibility and choice to its volunteers. RSVP matches the personal interests and skills of older Americans with opportunities to help solve community problems and offers supplemental insurance while on duty, on-the-job training from the agency or organization where volunteers are placed. The following County is served: Simpson.

1472 South Delta Planning and Development District
PO Box 1776
Greenville, MS 38702-1776
662-378-3831
Fax: 601-378-3834

Sylvia Jackson, Director
W O Williford, President

1473 Southern Mississippi Area Agency on Aging
2015a 15th Street
Gulfport, MS 39501-2022
228-868-2311
800-444-8014
Fax: 228-868-2550
http://www.smpdd.com

Barry Dixon, Director
Les Newcome, Executive Director

The Area Agency on Aging serves as the public advocate for the development and implementation of comprehensive and coordinated home and community based care systems responsive to the current needs and future growth of the aging population.

1474 Southwest Mississippi Area Agency on Aging
110 S Wall Street
Natchez, MS 39120-3477
601-446-6044
800-338-2049
Fax: 601-446-6071

Robert Maddox, Director
Wirt Peterson, Executive Director

1475 Three Rivers Area: Agency on Aging
PO Box B
Pontotoc, MS 38863
662-489-2415
Fax: 662-489-6815

Jane Mapp, Director
Randy Kelly, Executive Director

Missouri

1476 Able Commission
1008 Holloway Street
Rolla, MO 65401-2734
573-364-4357
Fax: 573-364-0223

Lynne Brennan-Howk, Administrator

Activities for citizens over 55 in multi-purpose senior center; arts and crafts; telephone reassurance programs for older and handicapped people living alone.

1477 Columbia Area Senior Center
Senior Services of Boone County
1121 Business Loop 70 E
Columbia, MO 65201
573-874-2050
Fax: 573-875-8864

Ferd Lightner, President

Senior citizens in the Columbia, MO area. Represents members' interests; conducts lobbying activities. Provides assistance programs for retirees.

1478 Disability Determination Services
1500 Southridge Drive
Suite B
Jefferson City, MO 65109-5674
573-751-2929
Fax: 573-526-3788

Dr. Don Gann, Director
Myra Rackers, Manager

1479 Disability Determination Services: Cape Girardeau
3014 Blattner Drive
Cape Girardeau, MO 63703-6363
573-290-5710
Fax: 573-290-5709

Michelle Scherer, Manager

1480 Disability Determination Services: Kansas City
8500 E Bannister Road
Kansas City, MO 64134-1841
816-325-1200
Fax: 816-325-1287

Pinkney Newell, Manager

1481 Disability Determination Services: Saint Louis
7545 S Lindbergh Boulevard
Suite 220
Saint Louis, MO 63125-4843
314-340-3718
Fax: 314-340-4615

1482 Disability Determination Services: Springfield
2530i S Campbell Avenue
Springfield, MO 65807-3598
417-888-4070
Fax: 417-888-4069

State Organizations & Government Agencies/Missouri

1483 Greater St. Louis Association of the Deaf
8816 Manchester Road
134
Saint Louis, MO 63144-2602
Fax: 314-664-8959
e-mail: info@gsland.org
http://www.gslad.org
TTY 314-298-2458
Jeff Prail, President
Greg Petersen, Vice President
Jason Roberts, Public Relations

GSLAD's mission is to provide social, charitable, athletic and educational opportunities for members of GSLAD and friends of the Deaf in the Metropolitan St. Louis area.

1484 Long Term Care Ombudsman Program
PO Box 3947
Springfield, MO 65808-3947
417-886-7878
Fax: 417-862-2129
e-mail: ccozarks@dialus.com
Connie Payne, Director
Todd Long, Manager

1485 Mid-America Regional Council of Aging Services
600 Broadway
Kansas City, MO 64105-1536
816-474-4240
Fax: 816-421-7758
Jacquelyn Moore, Director
David A Warm, Plant Manager

1486 Mid-East Area: Agency on Aging
2510 S Brentwood Boulevard
Saint Louis, MO 63144-2328
314-962-7999
800-243-6060
William Keel, Director

1487 Missouri Assisted Living Association
428 E Capitol Avenue
Suite 206
Jefferson City, MO 65101
573-635-8750
Fax: 573-634-7344
e-mail: info@malarcf.org
http://www.malarcf.org
Kevin Edmonds, President
Drew Stubblefield, Vice President
Kerri Hock, Executive Director

MALA provides comprehensive legislative and regulatory representation before the Missouri Legislature and the state agencies that regulate assisted living.

1488 Missouri Council of the Blind
5453 Chippewa Street
Saint Louis, MO 63109-1635
314-832-7172
800-342-5632
Fax: 314-832-7796
e-mail: moblind@mindspring.com
http://www.missouricounciloftheblind.org
Beverly Armstrong, Executive Director
Sandi Mackley, Administrative Assistant

Blind and visually impaired individuals united to improve conditions for the blind in the areas of employment, cultural opportunities, companionship, financial assistance, rehabilitation, and housing. Conducts legislative advocacy.

1489 Missouri Department of Mental Health
1706 E Elm Street
Jefferson City, MO 65101-4130
573-634-5165
http://www.modmh.state.mo.us
Keith Schafer, Director
Josh Campbell, Manager

1490 Missouri Department of Revenue
301 W High Street
Jefferson City, MO 65105
573-751-7191
http://www.dor.state.mo.us
Debbie Niederhelm, Manager

1491 Missouri Developmental Disability Council
Department of Mental Health
PO Box 687
Jefferson City, MO 65102
573-751-4054
John Solomon, Division Director
Kent Stalder, Manager

1492 Missouri Division on Aging
PO Box 570
Jefferson City, MO 65102
573-751-3082
Richard C Dunn, Manager

1493 Missouri Employees Retirement System
PO Box 268
Jefferson City, MO 65102
573-634-5290
800-392-6848
Fax: 573-634-7934
Steve Yoakum, Manager

1494 Missouri Protection & Advocacy Services
925 S Country Club Drive
Jefferson City, MO 65109-4510
573-893-3333
800-392-8667
Fax: 573-893-4231
e-mail: mopasjc@socket.net
http://www.members.socket.net/nmopasjc/MOP&A.ht
Shawn De Loyola, Executive Director

Advocacy services for persons with disabilities who meet eligibility criteria for any of five programs: Protection & Advocacy for Individuals with Mental Illness (PAIMI); Protection and Advocacy for individuals with Developmental Disabilities (PADD); Client Assistance Program (CAP) for persons encountering problems with rehab act agencies; Protection and Advocacy for Individual Rights (PAIR); and Protection and Advocacy for Assistive Technologyy (PAAT).

1495 RSVP Heartland
PO Box 116
Kirksville, MO 63501
660-665-8314
Fax: 660-665-8315
e-mail: sasirsvp@kvmo.net
Pat Selby, Director

Persons 55 years of age and older. Provides opportunities for volunteer service and community involvement; holds annual volunteer recognition banquet.

1496 RSVP Andrew County
101 South 4th Street
PO Box 7
Savannah, MO 64485
816-324-5634
Fax: 816-324-5634
e-mail: rsvp@ccp.com
Hope L Shipps, Contact

Provides opportunities for people 55 and over to make a difference in their community through volunteer service. RSVP volunteers contribute anywhere from a few to over forty hours a week, serving through schools, day care centers, police departments, hospitals and other nonprofit and public organizations to help meet critical community needs. RSVP matches the personal interests and skills of older Americans with opportunities to help solve community problems and offers supplemental insurance while on duty, on-the-job training from the agency or organization where volunteers are placed.

State Organizations & Government Agencies/Missouri

1497 RSVP Boone County
800 N Providence Road
Suite 105
Columbia, MO 65203-4300
573-442-7238
Fax: 573-874-1821
e-mail: bcca06@centurytel.net
http://www.bcca.missouri.org
Cynthia Jobe, Project Director
Virginia Nettleton, Project Assistant
Lori Shelton, Executive Director

The Retired and Senior Volunteer Program (RSVP) provides opportunities for people 55 and over to make a difference in their community through volunteer service. RSVP volunteers contribute anywhere from a few to over forty hours a week, serving though schools, day care centers, police departments, hospitals and other nonprofit and public organizations to help meet critical community needs. RSVP offers maximum flexibility and choice to its volunteers. RSVP matches the personal interests and skills to older Americans with opportunities to help solve community problems and offer supplemental insurance while on duty, on-the-job training from the agency or organization where volunteers are placed.

1498 RSVP Douglass Community Services
1100 Broadway
Hannibal, MO 63401-4225
573-221-3892
Fax: 573-221-6944
e-mail: sherryp@douglassonline.org
Sherry Perkins, Contact
Dave Dexheimer, Manager

Provides opportunities for people 55 and over to make a difference in their community through volunteer service. RSVP volunteers contribute anywhere from a few to over forty hours a week, serving through schools, day care centers, police departments, hospitals and other nonprofit and public organizations to help meet critical community needs. RSVP matches the personal interests and skills of older Americans with opportunities to help solve community problems and offers supplemental insurance while on duty, on-the-job training from the agency or organization where volunteers are placed.

1499 RSVP Dunklin County
313 West Main
Malden, MO 63863-1508
573-276-3716
Fax: 573-276-2512
e-mail: dunersvp@shelton.bbs.com
Frances Hughes, Contact
Christa Edmonds, Secretary

RSVP volunteers choose how and where they want to serve. Today more than 450,000 seniors participate in RSVP, making it one of the largest volunteer efforts in the nation. RSVP, is a cost effective way to solve critical problems in education, public safety, human needs and the environment.

1500 RSVP Grundy/Sullivan Counties
2901 Hoover Drive
PO Box 173
Trenton, MO 64683-0173
660-359-3836
Fax: 660-359-3058
e-mail: rsvp@lyn.net
Edna Foster, Director

RSVP provides volunteer opportunities for persons 55 and older. The purpose of RSVP is to enrich the lives of older adults through significant community service work. RSVP encourages seniors to bring a lifetime of talent, experiences, skills and hobbies to community projects and organizations needing volunteer talent.

1501 RSVP Harrison-Daviess Counties
1402 West Main
Bethany, MO 64424
660-425-7555
Fax: 660-425-6953
e-mail: hcrsvp@grm.net
Louise Akins, Director

Volunteers plant and maintain flowers for handicapped and elderly and at locations in the city of Bethany. They also work with youth, teaching them about gardening, beautification, and flower arranging.

1502 RSVP Heartland
201 N Elson Street, Suite 205
PO Box 116
Kirksville, MO 63501-2855
660-665-8314
Fax: 660-665-8315
e-mail: sasirsvp@kvmo.net
http://www.seniorservice.org/heartland
Pat Selby, Director

The Retired and Senior Volunteer Program (RSVP) provides volunteer opportunities for persons age 55 and older. The purpose of RSVP is to enrich the lives of older adults through significant community service. RSVP encourages seniors to bring a lifetime of talent, experiences, skills and hobbies to community projects and organizations needing volunteer talent.

1503 RSVP Jackson-Platte Counties
1021 Pennsylvania Avenue
Kansas City, MO 64105-1334
816-474-5111
Fax: 816-842-1007
e-mail: betsyphillips@hauw.org
Betsy Phillips, Director

The Retired and Senior Volunteer Program (RSVP) provides opportunities for people 55 and over to make a difference in their community through volunteer service. RSVP volunteers contribute anywhere from a few to over forty hours a week, serving through schools, day care centers, police departments, hospitals and other nonprofit and public organizations to help meet critical community needs. RSVP offers maximum flexibility and choice to its volunteers. RSVP matches the personal interests and skills of older Americans with opportunities to help solve community problems and offers supplemental insurance while on duty, on-the-job training from the agency or organization where volunteers are placed. The following Counties are served: Clay, Jackson, Platte.

1504 RSVP Jasper County
101 N Rangeline Road
Suite 2
Joplin, MO 64801-4132
417-627-0600
Fax: 417-627-9710
e-mail: rsvp_joplin@hotmail.com
http://www.thevantagepoint.org
Tina Jones, Director

The Retired and Senior Volunteer Program (RSVP) provides opportunities for people 55 and over to make a difference in their community through volunteer service. RSVP volunteers contribute anywhere from a few to over forty hours a week, serving though schools, day care centers, police departments, hospitals and other nonprofit and public organizations to help meet critical community needs. RSVP offers maximum flexibility and choice to its volunteers. RSVP matches the personal interests and skills to older Americans with opportunities to help solve community problems and offer supplemental insurance while on duty, on-the-job training from the agency or organization where volunteers are placed.

1505 RSVP Livingston County
1117 Washington
PO Box 445
Chillicothe, MO 64601
660-646-0010
Fax: 660-707-0708
e-mail: chillirsvp@sbcglobal.net
Patty Mefford, Director

Provides volunteer opportunities for persons age 55 and older. Our purpose is to enrich the lives of older adults through significant community sevice. More than 500 volunteers contribute nearly 100,000 hours of their time to meet community needs each year. The places they work and the jobs they do are as varied as the volunteers themselves.

State Organizations & Government Agencies/Missouri

1506 RSVP Mississippi County
106 S Washington Street
East Prairie, MO 63845-1526
573-649-5243
Fax: 573-649-2024
e-mail: mcrsvpsusan@bootheel.net
Susan Cartwright, Director

The Retired and Senior Volunteer Program (RSVP) provides opportunities for people 55 and over to make a difference in their community through volunteer service. RSVP volunteers contribute anywhere from a few to over forty hours a week, serving through schools, day care centers, police departments, hospitals and other nonprofit and public organizations to help meet critical community needs. RSVP offers maximum flexibility and choice to its volunteers. RSVP matches the personal interests and skills of older Americans with opportunities to help solve community problems and offers supplemental insurance while on duty, on-the-job training from the agency or organization where volunteers are placed. The following County is served: Mississippi.

1507 RSVP Northwest Missouri/Northeast Kansas
1412 N 3rd Street
PO Box 5094
Saint Joseph, MO 64505-2527
816-232-7779
Fax: 816-232-7029
e-mail: rsvp@inter-serv.org
http://www.inter-serv.org
Jerry Schwichtenberg, Director

Allows persons 55 years of age and over to remain an active important part of their community by placing the individual or group in meaningful volunteer positions through out Buchman, Clinton, Dekalb and Holt counties inMissouri and Doniphan County.

1508 RSVP Pemiscot County
1105 Carleton Avenue
Caruthersville, MO 63830
573-333-1380
Fax: 573-333-2382
Pat Thrasher, Contact

Provides opportunities for people 55 and over to make a difference in their community through volunteer service. RSVP volunteers contribute anywhere from a few to over forty hours a week, serving through schools, day care centers, police departments, hospitals and other nonprofit and public organizations to help meet critical community needs. RSVP matches the personal interests and skills of older Americans with opportunities to help solve community problems and offers supplemental insurance while on duty, on-the-job training from the agency or organization where volunteers are placed.

1509 RSVP Pettis-Saline Counties
515 S Kentucky Avenue
Sedalia, MO 65301-4263
660-826-4212
Fax: 660-827-0633
e-mail: rsvp@iland.net
Bob Milnor, Director

The Retired and Senior Volunteer Program (RSVP) provides opportunities for people 55 and over to make a difference in their community through volunteer service. RSVP volunteers contribute anywhere from a few to over forty hours a week, serving through schools, day care centers, police departments, hospitals and other nonprofit and public organizations to help meet critical community needs. RSVP offers maximum flexibility and choice to its volunteers. RSVP matches the personal interests and skills of older Americans with opportunities to help solve community problems and offers supplemental insurance while one duty, on-the-job training from the agency or organization where volunteers are placed. The following County is served: Pettis.

1510 RSVP Poplar Bluff-Altrusa Club
101 Oak Street
PO Box 666
Poplar Bluff, MO 63902
573-686-8624
Fax: 573-686-8605
e-mail: rsvp@tcmax.net
Marty Warner, Director

The Retired and Senior Volunteer Program (RSVP) provides opportunities for people 55 and over to make a difference in their community through volunteer service. RSVP volunteers contribute anywhere from a few to over forty hours a week, serving through schools, day care centers, police departments, hospitals and other nonprofit and public organizations to help meet critical community needs. RSVP offers maximum flexibility and choice to its volunteers. RSVP matches the personal interests and skills of older Americans with opportunities to help solve community problems and offers supplemental insurance while on duty, on-the-job training from the agency or organization where volunteers are placed. The following County is served: Butler.

1511 RSVP Quad Lakes Area of Missouri
206 S Baird Street
Clinton, MO 64735-2418
660-885-6512
Fax: 660-885-6522
e-mail: rsvp2day@iland.net
Carole Sue Hoefer, Contact

The Retired and Senior Volunteer Program (RSVP) provides opportunities for people 55 and over to make a difference in their community through volunteer service. RSVP volunteers contribute anywhere from a few to over forty hours a week, serving through schools, day care centers, police departments, hospitals and other nonprofit and public organizations to help meet critical community needs. RSVP offers maximum flexibility and choice to its volunteers. RSVP matches the personal interests and skills of older Americans with opportunities to help solve community problems and offers supplemental insurance while on duty, on-the-job training from the agency or organization where volunteers are placed.

1512 RSVP Scott-Cape Counties
105 N Main Street
Chaffee, MO 63740-1116
573-887-3664
Fax: 573-887-3664
e-mail: cscrsvp@showme.net
http://www.seniorcorps.com
Tina M McDowell, Director

Recruits volunteer aged 55 or older to help expand services in not-for-profit agencies who are stuggling with today's social issues. This agency connects them with volunteers and resources so that they may work as effectively and efficiently as possible to create positive change for our communities. Volunteers have an opportunity to continue to contribute their talents and skills to benefit other, thus, enhancing the quality of life for all.

1513 RSVP Springfield
627 North Glenstone
PO Box 3947
Springfield, MO 65808-3947
417-862-3595
Fax: 417-862-2129
e-mail: mgeiger@ccozarks.org
http://www.rsvp-springfield.net
Margaret Geiger, Director

The Retired and Senior Volunteer Program (RSVP) has a dual purpose of engaging persons 55 and older in volunteer service to meet critical community needs and to provide a high quality experience that will enrich the lives of the volunteer.

1514 RSVP St. Charles-Lincoln-Warren Counties
2724 Droste Road
St Charles, MO 63301-1504
636-724-7787
800-748-7865
Fax: 636-925-3810
Steve Lewis, Contact

Volunteers serve in a diverse range of nonprofit organizations, including schools, hospitals, food parties, homeless and abuse shelters, local governments, libraries, courts, law enforcement agencies, senior centers, pet adoption agencies, thrift stores and much more.

State Organizations & Government Agencies/Montana

1515 RSVP St. Louis
7601 Watson Road
Saint Louis, MO 63119-5001
314-918-2294
Fax: 314-962-4159
e-mail: aklostermann@ccstl.org
Amy Klostermann, Director

The Retired and Senior Volunteer Program (RSVP) provides opportunities for people 55 and over to make a difference in their community through volunteer service. RSVP volunteers contribute anywhere from a few to over forty hours a week, serving through schools, day care centers, police departments, hospitals and other nonprofit and public organizations to help meet critical community needs. RSVP offers maximum flexibility and choice to its volunteers. RSVP matches the personal interests and skills of older Americans with opportunities to help solve community problems and offers supplemental insurance while on duty, on-the-job training from the agency or organization where volunteers are placed. The following Counties are served: Saint Louis, Saint Louis City.

1516 Railroad Retirement Board: Kansas City Missouri District Office
601 E 12th Street
Kansas City, MO 64106-2818
816-426-5884
800-808-0772
Fax: 816-426-5334
e-mail: kansascity@rrb.gov
L Lang, Manager

1517 Railroad Retirement Board: St. Louis
1222 Spruce Street
Saint Louis, MO 63103-2818
314-539-6220
800-808-0772
Fax: 314-539-6229
e-mail: stlouis@rrb.gov
Michael Petry, Representative

1518 Region 7: Administration on Aging (AoA)
US Department of Health & Human Services
601 E 12th Street
Room 1731
Kansas City, MO 64106
816-426-3511
Fax: 816-426-3516
http://www.aoa.gov
Larry Brewster, Regional Administrator
Josefina G Carbonell ASA, Assistant Secretary
Edwin Walker PDASA, Deputy Assistant Secretary

Region includes Iowa, Kansas, Missouri, and Nebraska.

1519 Region Ten Area: Agency on Aging
PO Box 3990
Joplin, MO 64803-3990
417-781-7562
Fax: 417-781-1609
Linda Carlson, Director
Richard Russell, Manager

1520 Southwest Missouri Office on Aging (SWMOA)
1735 S Fort Avenue
Springfield, MO 65807-1204
417-862-0762
800-497-0822
Fax: 417-865-2683
e-mail: swmoa@swmoa.com
http://www.swmoa.com
Dorothy K Knowles, Executive Director

1521 St. Louis Area: Agency on Aging
634 N Grand Boulevard
Suite 721
Saint Louis, MO 63103-1002
314-612-5918
Fax: 314-552-2307
Barbara Selders, Director
David Sykora, Manager

1522 St. Louis Society for the Blind and Visually Impaired
8770 Manchester Road
Saint Louis, MO 63144-2724
314-968-9000
Fax: 314-968-9003
e-mail: info@slsbvi.org
http://www.slsbvi.org
David Ekin, Executive Director

Offers rehabilitation services for blind and visually impaired adults in St. Louis area. Contracts with local schools for services to school age students.

1523 UMKC Institute for Human Development
Health Sciences Building, 3rd Floor
2220 Holmes
Kansas City, MO 64108
816-235-1770
800-444-0821
Fax: 816-235-1762
e-mail: calkinsc@umkc.edu
http://www.ihd.umkc.edu
TTY 800-452-1185
Carl F Calkins PhD, Director

A statewide program promoting assistive technology devices and services for persons of all ages with all disabilities.

1524 VantAge Point Area: Agency on Aging-Region Ten
2701 South Bird Street
PO Box 3990
Joplin, MO 64803-3990
417-627-0600
Fax: 417-627-9710
e-mail: bev@thevantagepoint.org
http://www.thevantagepoint.org
Richard Russell, Executive Director

The VantAge Point is the information and resource center of the Area Agency on Aging, Region Ten. The VantAge Point/Area Agency provides a wide variety of services to seniors and their families.

1525 Workers Compensation Board Missouri
PO Box 58
Jefferson City, MO 65102
573-751-4231
Patricia Secrest, Manager

Montana

1526 Action for Eastern Montana
2030 North Merrill
PO Box 1309
Glendive, MT 59330-1309
406-377-3564
Fax: 406-377-3570
Penny Stras, Executive Director

Community action agency with a variety of assistance programs to low-income families and individuals; Head Start, family planning, employment training, housing, family counseling, crisis intervention, child care referral and training, domestic abuse services and shelter. We are more directly involved in the production of affordable housing. Counties covered: Carter, Custer, Daniels, Dawson, Fallon, Geld, McCone, Phillips, Powder River, Prairie, Richland, Roosevelt, Rosebud, Sheridan, Treasure, Valley and Wilbaux.

1527 Area Eight Agency on Aging
501 Bay Drive
Great Falls, MT 59404-3208
406-454-6990
Fax: 406-454-6991
Randy Barrett, Director

Aging Services provides services to Cascade County residents 60 and over, such as transportation, home attendants, Senior Companions, Medicaid waivers, Meals on Wheels, Ombudsman, Retired and Senior Volunteer Program, Foster Grandparent Program, insurance counseling, caregiver support, Reverse Annuities and Senior Centers, improving the quality of life in later years.

State Organizations & Government Agencies/Montana

1528 **Area Five Agency on Aging**
305 W Mercury Street
307
Butte, MT 59701-1659
406-782-5555
Fax: 406-563-3524

Joe Gilboy, Director

1529 **Area Four Agency on Aging**
PO Box 1717
Helena, MT 59624-1717
406-442-1552
800-356-6544
Fax: 406-449-6011

Charles W Briggs, Director

1530 **Area Nine Agency on Aging**
160 Kelly Road #A
Kalispell, MT 59901
406-758-5730
Fax: 406-758-5732

Jim Atkinson, Executive Director

1531 **Area One Agency on Aging**
111 W Bell Street
Glendive, MT 59330-1614
406-365-3364
TDD 406-365-3367

Lori Brengle, Director

1532 **Area Seven Agency on Aging**
PO Box 21838
Billings, MT 59104-1838
406-252-4812
800-758-4812
Fax: 406-252-4812

Darrell La Mere, Director

1533 **Area Two Agency on Aging**
1502 4th Street W
Roundup, MT 59072
406-323-1320
Fax: 406-323-3859
e-mail: areatwo@midrivers.com

Karen Erdie, Director

1534 **Disability Determination Services**
PO Box 4189
Helena, MT 59604-4189
406-444-3054
800-545-3054
Fax: 800-356-4410

Michelle Thibodeau, Manager

1535 **Flathead County Area Nine Agency on Aging**
2 2nd Street W
Havre, MT 59501-3434
406-265-5464
Fax: 406-265-5487

Jim Atkinson, Director
Evelyn Havskjold, Manager

1536 **Highwood Senior Citizens**
RR 1
Box 70
Highwood, MT 59450-9801
406-733-5141

Emma Otto, Manager

Promotes and provides social services for senior citizens in Highwood, MT.

1537 **Missoula Aging Services**
227 W Front Street
Missoula, MT 59802-4301
406-728-7682
Fax: 406-728-7687

Susan Kohler-Hurd, Director
Colleen Baldwin, Manager

1538 **Montana Advocacy Program**
PO Box 1681
Helena, MT 59624-1681
406-449-2344
800-245-4743
Fax: 406-449-2418
e-mail: advocate@mt.net
http://www.mt.ne./~advocate
TDD 800-245-4743

Bernadette Franks-Ongoy, Executive Director

Protects and advocates the human and legal rights of Montanans with mental and physical disabilities while advancing dignity, equality, and self-determination. Designated federal P&A, with AT, CAP, PADD, PAIMI and PAIR programs. Advocacy and legal services for abuse, neglect, rights violations, access, discrimination in employment, accommodations and housing, and assistance with vocational rehabilitation/visual services.

1539 **Montana Department of Administration: Teacher's Retirement Division**
1500 E 6th Avenue
Helena, MT 59601-4541
406-444-3134
Fax: 406-444-2641

David Senn, Manager

1540 **Montana Department of Aging**
Capitol Station
Room 219
Helena, MT 59620
406-444-3111
Fax: 406-444-5900

Hank Hudson, Aging Coordinator
Chuck Butler, Manager

1541 **Montana Department of Military Affairs: Division of Veteran's Affairs**
100 N Last Chance Gulch
Helena, MT 59620
406-841-3740
Fax: 406-841-3145

Joseph Foster, Manager

1542 **Montana Department of Retirement Administration**
PO Box 100131
Helena, MT 59620
406-444-3154
800-444-5428
Fax: 406-444-5428
e-mail: mpera@state.mt.us
http://www.discoveringmontana.com

Michael O'Connor, Manager

1543 **Montana Department of Revenue**
PO Box 5805
Helena, MT 59604-5805
406-444-6900
Fax: 406-444-3696
http://www.mt.gov/revenue
TDD 406-444-2830

Dan Vucks, Manager

1544 **Montana Department of Social and Rahabilitation Services**
PO Box 4210
Helena, MT 59604-4210
406-444-2590
877-296-1197
Fax: 406-444-3632

James Good, President
Joe Matthews, Manager

Offers services for the disabled.

1545 **Montana Developmental Disability Council**
PO Box 526
Helena, MT 59624
406-443-4332
866-443-4332
Fax: 406-443-4192
http://www.mctdd.org

Deborah Swingley, Executive Director
Dee Burrell, Grant/Contract Manager

State Organizations & Government Agencies/Montana

The goal of the Council is to increase the independence, productivity, inclusion and integration into the community of people with developmental disabilities through systemic change, capacity building and advocacy activities. The Council has attempted to meet this goal through a two-prong advocacy approach, our State Plan and our Grant Program.

1546 Montana Governor's Office on Aging
Capitol Station
Helena, MT 59620
406-444-3111
800-332-2272
Fax: 406-444-5529
TDD 406-444-1250

Hank Hudson, Director
Chuck Butler, Manager

1547 Montana Office on Aging
PO Box 4210
Helena, MT 59604-4210
406-444-4077
Fax: 406-444-7743
http://www.dphhs.state.mt.us/sltc

Charles Rehbein, Bureau Chief
Kelly Williams, Administrator

The Office of Aging provides information, assistance and education on many sujects; senior center and other community supports, home delivered and congregate meals, affordable legal resources for elderly citizens, health insurance counseling, pension and pre-retirement education, veterans benefit information and more.

1548 Montana Protection & Advocacy Agency
Montana Advocacy Program
400 North Park, 2nd Floor
PO Box 1681
Helena, MT 59624
406-449-2344
800-245-4743
Fax: 406-449-2418
e-mail: bernie@mtadv.org
http://www.mtadv.org
TDD 406-449-2344

Bernadette Franks-Ongoy, Executive Director
Liesl Beck, Advocacy Specialist

1549 North Central-Area Agency on Aging
323 S Main Street
Conrad, MT 59425-2335
406-271-7553
800-332-2272
Fax: 406-278-5262

Rhonda Wisner, Director
Deb Pate, Executive Director

1550 Northern Rocky Mountain Retiree Association
1637 Red Crow Road
Victor, MT 59875
406-961-3959
e-mail: jfreeman@bitterroot.net

James H Freeman, President

1551 RSVP Butte School District No 1
111 N Montana Street
Butte, MT 59701-9295
406-533-2508
Fax: 406-533-2520
e-mail: brennickml@butte.k12.mt.us
http://www.butte.k12.mt.us

Michele L Brennick, Director

Butte School District #1 RSVP offers opportunities for individuals 55 and better to make their communities safer, healthier, and stronger through service. The variety of opportunities for community service allows individuals to share their experiences, abilities and skills for the betterment of their community and themselves.

1552 RSVP Cascade County
PO Box 2486
Great Falls, MT 59403
406-454-6990
Fax: 406-454-6991
e-mail: volunteerpower@yahoo.com
http://www.co.cascade.mt.us

Audrey Finlayson, Director

AKA Cascade County Aging Services serves residents of Cascade Coundty in areas such as Information Assistance and Referral, State Health Insurance Program, Senior Companion, Foster Grandparents, Commodity Foods (part of the Retired and Senior Volunteer Program), Meals on Wheels, Reverse Annuity Mortgage, Home Attendant, Respite Care, Ombudsman, Senior Centers, Medicaid Waiver and Transportation.

1553 RSVP Dawson-Wibaux
323 E Barry Street
PO Box 1324
Glendive, MT 59330-2305
406-377-4716
Fax: 406-377-2022
e-mail: rsvp@midrivers.com
http://www.joinservice.org

Patricia Atwell, Director

The Retired and Senior Volunteer Program (RSVP) provides opportunities for people 55 and over to make a difference in their community through volunteer service. RSVP volunteers contribute anywhere from a few to over forty hours a week, serving through schools, day care centers, police departments, hospitals and other nonprofit and public organizations to help meet critical community needs. RSVP offers maximum flexibility and choice to its volunteers. RSVP matches the personal interests and skills of older Americans with opportunities to help solve community problems and offers supplemental insurance while on duty, on-the-job training from the agency or organization where volunteers are placed. The following Counties are served: Dawson, Wibaux.

1554 RSVP Fallon County
420 W Montana Avenue
PO Box 1025
Baker, MT 59313
406-778-2358
Fax: 406-778-2600
e-mail: bakrsvp@midrivers.com

Patricia Madler, Director

The Retired and Senior Volunteer Program (RSVP) provides opportunities for people 55 and over to make a difference in their community through volunteer service. RSVP volunteers contribute anywhere from a few to over forty hours a week, serving through schools, day care centers, police departments, hospitals and other nonprofit and public organizations to help meet critical community needs. RSVP offers maximum flexibility and choice to its volunteers. RSVP matches the personal interests and skills of older Americans with opportunities to help solve community problems and offers supplemental insurance while on duty, on-the-job training from the agency or organization where volunteers are placed. The following Counties are served: Carter, Fallon.

1555 RSVP Helena
Rocky Mountain Development Council
200 South Cruse Avenue
PO Box 1717
Helena, MT 59624
406-447-1680
Fax: 406-447-1629
e-mail: bthowell@rmdc.net
http://www.rmdc.net

Bonnie Howell, Director

The Retired and Senior Volunteer Program provides a variety of volunteer opportunities for people 55 or better so they can remain active and involved in their communities. Volunteers serve from a few hours per week doing such things as clerical work, tutoring, preparing bulk mailings and sewing quilts. Volunteers also assist at schools, libraries, hospitals, nursing homes and other nonprofit agencies where help is needed.

State Organizations & Government Agencies/Nebraska

1556 **RSVP Hill County**
Hill County Area Ten Agency on Aging
2 West Second Street
Havre, MT 59501-3434 406-265-5464
Fax: 406-265-3611
e-mail: rsvp@havremt.net
Alison Hecker, Director

The Retired and Senior Volunteer Program (RSVP) provides opportunities for people 55 and over to make a difference in their community through volunteer service. RSVP volunteers contribute anywhere from a few to over forty hours a week, serving through schools, day care centers, police departments, hospitals and other nonprofit and public organizations to help meet critical community needs. RSVP offers maximum flexibility and choice to its volunteers. RSVP matches the personal interests and skills of older Americans with opportunities to help solve community problems and offers supplemental insurance while on duty, on-the-job training from the agency or organization where volunteers are placed.

1557 **RSVP Miles City**
Miles Community College
374 I-90 Business Loop
PO Box 86
Miles City, MT 59301 406-234-0505
800-431-3975
Fax: 406-234-0554
e-mail: rsvp05@midrivers.com
Della Howell, Director

The Retired and Senior Volunteer Program (RSVP) provides opportunities for people 55 and over to make a difference in their community through volunteer service. RSVP volunteers contribute anywhere from a few to over forty hours a week, serving through schools, day care centers, police departments, hospitals and other nonprofit and public organizations to help meet critical community needs. RSVP offers maximum flexibility and choice to its volunteers. RSVP matches the personal interests and skills of older Americans with opportunities to help solve community problems and offers supplemental insurance while on duty, on-the-job training from the agency or organization where volunteers are placed.

1558 **RSVP Roosevelt County**
124 Custer
Wolf Point, MT 59201-1603 406-653-6282
Fax: 406-653-6206
e-mail: rsvp@rooseveltcounty.org
Doris Puchase, Director

The Retired and Senior Volunteer Program (RSVP) provides opportunities for people 55 and over to make a difference in their community through volunteer service. RSVP volunteers contribute anywhere from a few to over forty hours a week, serving through schools, day care centers, police departments, hospitals and other nonprofit and public organizations to help meet critical community needs. RSVP offers maximum flexibility and choice to its volunteers. RSVP matches the personal interests and skills of older Americans with opportunities to help solve community problems and offers supplemental insurance while on duty, on-the-job training from the agency or organization where volunteers are placed.

1559 **RSVP South Central Montana**
315 1/2 Main Street
Suite 1
Roundup, MT 59072 406-323-1403
Fax: 406-323-4403
e-mail: rdprsvp@midrivers.com
Shirlee Brillhart, Director

Placing individuals 55 of age and older in meaningful job opportunities in the community to do volunteer work.

1560 **RSVP Southwest Montana**
32 South Tracy Avenue
Bozeman, MT 59715-2813 406-587-5444
Fax: 406-582-8499
e-mail: kwelker@rsvpmt.org
http://www.rsvpmt.org
Kelly Welker, Director

The Retired and Senior Volunteer Program (RSVP) provides opportunities for people 55 and over to make a difference in their community through volunteer service. RSVP volunteers contribute anywhere from a few to over forty hours a week, serving through schools, day care centers, police departments, hospitals and other nonprofit and public organizations to help meet critical community needs. RSVP offers maximum flexibility and choice to its volunteers. RSVP matches the personal interests and skills of older Americans with opportunities to help solve community problems and offers supplemental insurance while on duty, on-the-job training from the agency or organization where volunteers are placed. The following Counties are served: Gallatin, Park.

1561 **RSVP Yellowstone County**
1309 16th Street West
Billings, MT 59102-3151 406-245-6177
Fax: 406-259-2849
e-mail: yccoarb@imt.net
http://www.yccoa.org
Ramona L Bruckner, Director
Margaret Schmittou, Volunteer Coordinator
Jayne Crocker, Volunteer Coordinator

The Yellowstone County Retired and Senior Volunteer Program connects adults, 55+, to critical identified community needs. Through volunteering, these seniors enjoy social interaction while continuing to use their wisdom, experience and skills to impact their communities.

1562 **Railroad Retirement Board: Montana District Office**
2900 4th Avenue N
Billings, MT 59101-1266 406-247-7375
Fax: 406-247-7379
e-mail: billings@rrb.gov
Ron Kaminski, District Manager
Judith Bell, Manager
Becky Jo Harris, Contact Representative

1563 **Ravalli County Council on Aging**
802 West Main Street
Hamilton, MT 59840-2853 406-363-5690
Fax: 406-363-0401
Amy Busch, Director

Individuals over 60 years of age. Promotes the well-being of senior citizens through nutrition programs, in-home and transportation services, legal advice, and friendship. Provides information and referral services. Offers blood pressure checks and hearing checks.

1564 **Workers Compensation Board Montana**
5 S Last Chance Gulch Street
Helena, MT 59601-4178 406-444-6534
Fax: 406-444-5963
Dr. Carl Swanson, Director

Nebraska

1565 **Aging Office of Western Nebraska**
1517 Broadway
Suite 122
Scottsbluff, NE 69361-3184 308-635-0851
800-682-5140
Fax: 308-635-2321
Victor Walker, Executive Director

1566 **Blue Rivers Area: Agency on Aging (BRAAAA)**
412 Grant Street
Beatrice, NE 68310-2922 402-223-1352
Fax: 402-228-3546
Larry Ossowski, Director

State Organizations & Government Agencies/Nebraska

1567 Community Action Partnership of Mid-Nebraska Volunteer Services
16 West 11th Street
PO Box 2288
Kearney, NE 68847
308-865-5365
Fax: 308-865-5681
e-mail: rsvp@mnca.net
http://www.mnca.net

Rose King, Director Volunteer Services

Consists of: Retired and Senior Volunteer, Senior Companion Volunteer Program and Kearney Area Interfaith Caregivers.

1568 Corrigan Senior Center
3819 X Street
Omaha, NE 68107-3177
402-731-7210

Betty Winscot, Manager

Provides activities for seniors.

1569 Decatur Senior Center
9th & Broadway Street
PO Box 43
Decatur, NE 68020
402-349-5525

Phyllis Smith, Manager

Provides activities for senior citizens.

1570 Disability Determinations
PO Box 82530
Lincoln, NE 68501-2530
402-471-2961
Fax: 402-471-3626

Douglas Willman, Administrator

1571 Division of Aging & Disability Services
Nebraska Health & Human Services System
PO Box 95044
Lincoln, NE 68509-5044
402-471-4623
800-942-7830
Fax: 402-471-4619
http://www.aasa.dshs.org

Joann Weis, Director

Our mission is we help people live better lives through effective health and human services.

1572 Eastern Nebraska Office on Aging
885 S 72nd Street
Omaha, NE 68114-4631
402-444-6554
Fax: 402-444-6504

Beverly Griffith, Director
Bob Brinker, Executive Director

1573 Lincoln Area: Agency on Aging (LAAA)
1001 O Street
Suite 101
Lincoln, NE 68508-3655
402-441-7022
Fax: 402-441-6524

June Pederson, Director
Deborah Batten, Public Information Officer

1574 Midland Area: Agency on Aging
PO Box 905
Hastings, NE 68902
402-463-4565
Fax: 402-463-1069
e-mail: maaa@alltel.net

Dick Bauer, Executive Director

1575 Midwest Geriatrics
7915 N 30th Street
Omaha, NE 68112-2418
402-827-6015
Fax: 402-827-6005
e-mail: cwyatt@shf.org
http://www.mgi-seniors.org

Steve Hess, President/CEO
Cathy A Wyatt, Director Public Relations

Our mission is to provide vision, strategic planning, leadership, and management services for its affiliates and other organizations to ensure the accomplishment of their respective missions.

1576 Nebraska Advocacy Services
134 S 13th Street
6th Floor
Lincoln, NE 68508-1903
402-474-3183
Fax: 402-474-3274
e-mail: nas@nas-pa.org
http://www.nebraskaadvocacyservices.com
TDD 402-474-3183

Timothy Shaw, Executive Director

The designated protection and Advocacy agency for the state of Nebraska for people with mental and physical disabilities. Direct assistance provided if issue is within broad case priorities. Sliding scale fee. Information and referral at no cost.

1577 Nebraska Assistive Technology Partnership
5143 South 48th Street
Suite C
Lincoln, NE 68516
402-471-0734
888-806-6287
Fax: 402-471-6052
e-mail: attp@nde.state.ne.us
http://www.nde.state.ne.us/ATP

Mark Schultz, Director
Lilly Blase, Program Coordinator
Nancy Noha, Information Specialist

The Assistive Technology Partnership (ATP) is dedicated to helping Nebraskan's with disabilities, their families and professionals obtain assistive technology devices and services.

1578 Nebraska Association of Area Agencies on Aging
South Central Nebraska Area Agency on Aging
Suttle Plaza
4623 2nd Avenue, Suite 4
Kearney, NE 68847-8348
308-234-1851
800-658-4320
Fax: 308-234-1853
e-mail: rod.horsley@hhss.state.ne.us
http://www.hhss.state.ne.us

Rod Horsley, Director

To advocate and provide supportive services and programs to the elderly, which will allow them to live as independently, and in their own homes, as long as possible.

1579 Nebraska Client Assistance Program
301 Centennial Mall S
Lincoln, NE 68508-2529
402-471-3656
800-742-7594
Fax: 402-471-0017

Victoria Rasmussen, Director

1580 Nebraska Commission For The Blind And Visually Impaired (NCBVI)
4600 Valley Road
Suite 100
Lincoln, NE 68510-4844
402-471-2891
Fax: 402-471-3009

Dr. Pearl Van Zandt, Director

Offers services for the totally blind, legally blind, visually impaired, mentally retarded blind and more with health, counseling, educational, recreational, rehabilitation, computer training and professional training services.

1581 Nebraska Department of Aging
PO Box 95044
Lincoln, NE 68509-5044
402-471-5185
Fax: 402-471-4619

Jacklyn Smith, Director
Arti Cover, Manager

State Organizations & Government Agencies/Nebraska

1582 Nebraska Department of Revenue
301 Centennial Mall S
Lincoln, NE 68508-2529
402-471-5729
http://www.nol.org/home/NDR

Tom Norris, Manager

1583 Nebraska Department of Veterans Affairs
PO Box 95083
Lincoln, NE 68509-5083
402-471-2458
Fax: 402-471-2491

1584 Northeast Nebraska Area: Agency on Aging
PO Box 1447
Norfolk, NE 68702-1447
402-370-3454
800-572-8368
Fax: 402-370-3279

Joann Forster, Director
Connie Cooper, Executive Director

1585 Papillion Senior Citizen Center
1001 Limerick Road
Papillion, NE 68046-3023
402-597-2059
e-mail: laura@sc.omhcoxmail.com

Laura Jean O'Connor, Executive Director

Papillion Senior Center serves healthy portions of food, friendship and fun to people age 60 and older and their guests.

1586 RSVP Adams-Webster Counties
815 West 3rd St
Hastings, NE 68901-5221
402-463-1454
Fax: 402-463-2911
e-mail: julie@hastingsrsvp.org

Julie Nash, Director

The Retired and Senior Volunteer Program (RSVP) provides opportunities for people 55 and over to make a difference in their community through volunteer service. RSVP volunteers contribute anywhere from a few to over forty hours a week, serving through schools, day care centers, police departments, hospitals and other nonprofit and public organizations to help meet critical community needs. RSVP offers maximum flexibility and choice to its volunteers. RSVP matches the personal interests and skills of older Americans with opportunities to help solve community problems and offers supplemental insurance while on duty, on-the-job training from the agency or organization where volunteers are placed.

1587 RSVP Chadron
270 Pine Street
PO Box 587
Chadron, NE 69337-2296
308-432-4200
Fax: 308-432-5799
e-mail: chad_rsvpfgp@yahoo.com

Ron Wineteer, Director

The Retired and Senior Volunteer Program (RSVP) provides opportunities for people 55 and over to make a difference in their community through volunteer service. RSVP volunteers contribute anywhere from a few to over forty hours a week, serving through schools, day care centers, police departments, hospitals and other nonprofit and public organizations to help meet critical community needs. RSVP offers maximum flexibility and choice to its volunteers. RSVP matches the personal interests and skills of older Americans with opportunities to help solve community problems and offers supplemental insurance while on duty, on-the-job training from the agency or organization where volunteers are placed.

1588 RSVP Crawford
337 2nd Street
Box 521
Crawford, NE 69339-1051
308-665-2350
Fax: 308-665-2350
e-mail: crawrsvp@bbc.net

Donna Brown, Director

The Retired and Senior Volunteer Program (RSVP) provides opportunities for people 55 and over to make a difference in their community through volunteer service. RSVP volunteers contribute anywhere from a few to over forty hours a week, serving through schools, day care centers, police departments, hospitals and other nonprofit and public organizations to help meet critical community needs. RSVP offers maximum flexibility and choice to its volunteers. RSVP matches the personal interests and skills of older Americans with opportunities to help solve community problems and offers supplemental insurance while on duty, on-the-job training from the agency or organization where volunteers are place.

1589 RSVP Lincoln Area
1001 O Street
Suite 101
Lincoln, NE 68508-2321
402-441-7026
Fax: 402-441-6104
e-mail: lhans@ci.lincoln.ne.us
http://www.ci.lincoln.ne.us

Lily Hans, Director

The Retired and Senior Volunteer Program (RSVP) provides opportunities for people 55 and over to make a difference in their community through volunteer service. RSVP volunteers contribute anywhere from a few to over forty hours a week, serving through schools, day care centers, police departments, hospitals and other nonprofit and public organizations to help meet critical community needs. RSVP offers maximum flexibility and choice to its volunteers. RSVP matches the personal interests and skills of older Americans with opportunities to help solve community problems and offers supplemental insurance while on duty, on-the-job training from the agency or organization where volunteers are placed.

1590 RSVP Ogallala City-Keith Counties
411 E 2nd Street
Ogallala, NE 69153-2631
308-284-6464
Fax: 308-284-6565
e-mail: ogarsvp@megavision.com
http://www.ogallala-ne.gov

Virginia L Steinke, Director

The Retired and Senior Volunteer Program (RSVP) provides opportunities for people 55 and over to make a difference in their community through volunteer service. RSVP volunteers contribute anywhere from a few to over forty hours a week, serving though schools, day care centers, police departments, hospitals and other nonprofit and public organizations to help meet critical community needs. RSVP offers maximum flexibility and choice to its volunteers. RSVP matches the personal interests and skills to older Americans with opportunities to help solve community problems and offer supplemental insurance while on duty, on-the-job training from the agency or organization where volunteers are placed.

1591 RSVP Richardson County
PO Box 35
Falls City, NE 68355
402-245-3778
Fax: 402-245-2210
e-mail: rsvp@centco.net

Carol Gentry, Director

The Retired and Senior Volunteer Program (RSVP) provides opportunities for people 55 and over to make a difference in their community through volunteer service. RSVP volunteers contribute anywhere from a few to over forty hours a week, serving through schools, day care centers, police departments, hospitals and other nonprofit and public organizations to help meet critical community needs. RSVP offers maximum flexibility and choice to its volunteers. RSVP matches the personal interests and skills of older Americans with opportunities to help solve community problems and offers supplemental insurance while on duty, on-the-job training from the agency or organization where volunteers are placed.

State Organizations & Government Agencies/Nevada

1592 **RSVP Sheriden County**
111 North Main Street
Box 454
Rushville, NE 69360-0454
308-327-2959
Fax: 308-327-2959
e-mail: scrsvpbv@gpcom.net
Barbara Van Kerrebrook, Director

We have a senior volunteer who addresses county schools and writes articles for public awareness on recycling. Others work on gardening and beautification, and educate in our local museums.

1593 **Railroad Retirement Board: Nebraska District Office**
PO Box 1415
Omaha, NE 68101
402-221-4641
Fax: 402-211-4669
L J Zward, Manager

1594 **Seward Aging Services**
105 B Street
PO Box 513
Milford, NE 68405
402-761-3593
http://www.connect.seward.org
Kathy Ruzicka, Director

To provide and develop activities and services which promote independent living among the older citizens of the county and aid families in finding ways to support the needs of the elderly by working with other service provides in the area.

1595 **South Central Nebraska Area Agency on Aging**
124 W 46th Street
Kearney, NE 68847-8348
308-234-1851
Fax: 308-234-1853
Donna Mayo, Director
Rod Horsley, Executive Director

1596 **West Central Nebraska Area: Agency on Aging**
115 N Vine Street
North Platte, NE 69101-5305
308-535-8195
Fax: 308-535-8190
Sandy Miller, Choices Program Supervisor
Linda Foreman, Manager

1597 **Workers Compensation Board Nebraska**
PO Box 98908
Lincoln, NE 68509-8908
402-471-6468
Fax: 402-471-1823
Dr. Carl Thompson, Director
Glenn Morton, Manager

Nevada

1598 **Bureau of Disability Adjudication**
Dept of Employment, Training and Rehabilitation
1050 E William Street
Suite 300
Carson City, NV 89701
775-687-4430
800-882-4430
Fax: 775-886-0119
http://www.detr.state.nv.us
Kraig Schutte, Manager

The Bureau of Disability Adjudication evaluates applications from individuals with permanent disabilities to determine if they are eligible for federal Supplemental Security Income (SSI) or Social Security Disability Insurance (SSDI).

1599 **Bureau of Naval Personnel: Nevada Retired Affairs Activities Office**
Family Service Center
Fallon Naval Air, NV 89496-5000
775-426-3333
Fax: 775-426-3340

1600 **Division for Aging Services**
3416 Goni Road
Suite 132
Carson City, NV 89706-7968
775-687-4210
Fax: 775-687-4264
http://www.nvaging.net
Gil Johnston, Unit Manager Elder Rights
Carol Fala, Administrator
Marcia Cuccaro, Unit Manager Resource

Develop, coordinate and deliver a comprehensive support service in order for seniors to lead independent, meaningful and dignified lives.

1601 **Division of Mental Health & Developmental Services**
505 E King Street
Suite 602
Carson City, NV 89701-3790
775-684-5943
Fax: 775-684-5966
Pat Hardy, Director
Carlos Brandenberg, Administrator

1602 **Nevada Assistive Technology Projects**
3656 Research Way
Suite 32
Carson City, NV 89706-7932
775-687-4452
Fax: 775-687-3292
e-mail: kpreston@dhr.state.nv.us
Kelly Preston, Contact
Todd Butterworth, Manager

1603 **Nevada Department of Business & Industry: Governor's Committee on Employment of People with Disabilities**
4600 Kietzke Lane
Suite A108
Reno, NV 89502
775-688-1111
Fax: 775-688-1113
http://www.state.nv.us/b&i/gb
Sydney H Wickliffe, CPA, Director

The Governor's Committee promotes employment of people with disabilities by enhancing resources available to business and industry to encourage new employment opportunities for disabled persons. This is encouraged by increasing public understanding of the value and productivity that disabled persons can bring to the workplace, and by providing training and assistance to both the disabled population and employers in accommodating the special needs of people with disabilities.

1604 **Nevada Department of Human Resources Rehabilitation Division: Bureau of Services to the Blind**
505 E King Street
Carson City, NV 89701-4761
775-884-6125
Fax: 775-687-5980

1605 **Nevada Department of Taxation**
1550 College Parkway
Suite 115
Carson City, NV 89706-7939
775-684-2030
Fax: 775-687-5981
http://www.state.nv.us/taxation
Paul Ferrin, Manager

1606 **Nevada Developmental Disability Council**
505 E King Street
Suite 502
Carson City, NV 89701-3705
775-687-4452
Fax: 445-687-3292
Todd Butterworth, Manager

State Organizations & Government Agencies/New Hampshire

1607 **Nevada Division for Aging Services**
3100 W Sahara Avenue
Suite 103
Las Vegas, NV 89102-6001
702-486-3545
Fax: 702-486-3572
e-mail: dasvegas@aging.nv.gov
http://www.nvaging.net

Carol Sala, Administrator
Bruce McAnnany, Manager

Services for seniors: In-Home Care, Homemaker, Group Home Care, Case Manager, Elder Abuse Investigations, Subsidized Taxi Cab Fare, Medicare Counseling, Information and Referral.

1608 **Nevada Protection & Advocacy Agency**
Nevada Disability Advocacy and Law Center
6039 Eldora Avenue
Suite C, Box 3
Las Vegas, NV 89146
702-257-8150
888-349-3843
Fax: 702-257-8170
e-mail: ndalc@ndalclv.org
http://www.ndalc.org
TDD 702-257-8160

Jack Mayes, Executive Director

The Nevada Disability Advocacy & Law Center (NDALC) is a private, nonprofit organization and serves as Nevada's federally-mandated protection and advocacy system for the human, legal, and service rights of individuals with disabilities.

1609 **Nevada Public Employees' Retirement System**
693 W Nye Lane
Carson City, NV 89703-1527
775-687-4200
Fax: 775-687-5131

Dana Bilyeu, Manager

1610 **Nevada Workers Compensation Board**
400 West King Street
Suite 400
Carson City, NV 89703
775-684-7270
Fax: 775-687-6305
http://www.doi.state.nv.us

Charles J Verre, Chief Administrative Officer

Providing workers compensation information, news, facts, and contact information for employees, employers, insurers, and medical providers. Find rules, statutes, forms and professional help relating to workplace injuries and disabilities in the state of Nevada.

1611 **RSVP Clark County**
531 N 30th Street
Las Vegas, NV 89101-3650
702-382-0721
Fax: 702-385-3206
e-mail: edermer@catholiccharities.com

Erica Dermer, Director

The Retired and Senior Volunteer Program (RSVP) provides opportunities for people 55 and over to make a difference in their community through volunteer service. RSVP volunteers contribute anywhere from a few to over forty hours a week, serving through schools, day care centers, police departments, hospitals and other nonprofit and public organizations to help meet critical community needs. RSVP offers maximum flexibility and choice to its volunteers. RSVP matches the personal interests and skills of older Americans with opportunities to help solve community problems and offers supplemental insurance while on duty, on-the-job training from the agency or organization where volunteers are placed.

1612 **RSVP NV Rural Counties**
444 E William Street
Suite 1
Carson City, NV 89701-4054
775-687-4680
Fax: 775-687-4494
e-mail: branded@rsvp.carson.city.nv.us
http://www.nevadaruralrsvp.org

Janice Ayers, Director

Serves age 50 and older. Commited to helping the frail and elderly who choose to remain at home by providing home and community based services, their goal is to promote level of choice, independence and self care.

1613 **RSVP Washoe County**
401 West Second Street
Suite 101
Reno, NV 89503
775-784-1807
Fax: 775-327-5015
e-mail: mary@unr.edu

Mary Brock, Executive Director

The Retired and Senior Volunteer Program (RSVP) of Washoe County is committed to volunteerism. It actively recruits and encourages people 55 years and older to volunteer and places them in local nonprofit or public agencies of their choice.

1614 **State of Nevada Client Assistance Program**
1755 E Plumb Lane
Suite 128
Reno, NV 89502-3689
702-786-6688
800-633-9879
Fax: 775-688-1627
e-mail: detrocap@nvdetz.org
http://http://detr.state.nv/rehab/reh_

William E Bauer PhD, Director

Provides information about all services under all Rehabilitation Acts and about all benefits under Title I of the Americans with Disabilities Act. Provides mediation, advocacy or representation regarding services made by agencies which provide services under the Rehabilitation Act. Services to the Blind and Visually Impaired, Vocational Rehabilitation, Centers for Independent Living.

New Hampshire

1615 **Disability Determination Unit**
PO Box 452
Concord, NH 03302-0452
603-271-3341
Fax: 603-271-1114
http://www.ed.state.nh.us

Peggy Vieira, Contact

Disability Determination Unit (DDU) determines whether or not an applicant is eligible for Medicaid benefits. Persons who are disabled or alleged disabled are eligible for DDU determination.

1616 **New England Gerontological Association**
1 Cutts Road
Durham, NH 03824-3102
603-772-2244
e-mail: etillock@aol.com
http://www.negaonline.org

Eugene E Tillock, EdD, Executive Director

Offers a broad range of service to individuals and providers of aging services in the New England Region.

1617 **New Hampshire Client Assistance Program**
Governor's Commission on Disability
57 Regional Drive
Concord, NH 03301-8518
603-271-4175
800-852-3405
e-mail: bill.hagy@nh.gov
http://www.state.nh.us/disability
TTY 603-271-2774

Bill Hagy, Director

CAP assists anyone with a disability that is interested in applying for and receiving services from rehabilitation programs, projects or facilities funded under the Rehabilitation Act.

State Organizations & Government Agencies/New Hampshire

1618 **New Hampshire Department of Mental Health**
State Office Park S
Concord, NH 03301
603-271-5000
Fax: 603-271-5058

Donald Shumway, Director
Paul Garmon, Contact

1619 **New Hampshire Department of Revenue**
PO Box 457
Concord, NH 03302
603-271-2191
800-735-2964
Fax: 603-271-6121
http://www.state.nh.us/revenue

G Phillip Blastos, Manager

1620 **New Hampshire Developmental Disabilities Council**
10 Ferry Street
Concord, NH 03301-5022
603-228-4100
Fax: 603-271-1156
e-mail: nhddcncl@aol.com
http://www.NHDDC.com

Clyde Terry, Executive Director
Michael Walden, Manager

Offers information, referral and support services to disabled persons.

1621 **New Hampshire Division of Developmental Services**
NH DHHS Division of Community Based Care Services
105 Pleasant Street
Concord, NH 03301-3857
603-271-5034
800-852-3345
Fax: 603-271-5166
e-mail: mcartas@dhhs.state.nh.us
http://www.dhhs.state.nh.us
TDD 800-735-2964

Paul Gorman, EdD, Director
Susan Fox, Director

The developmental services system will join with local communities to support individuals of all ages with developmental disabilities or acquired brain disorders and their families to experience as much freedom, choice, control and responsibility over the services and supports they receive as desired.

1622 **New Hampshire Division of Elderly and Adult Services**
DEAS Office Park South
129 Pleasant Street
Building 1
Concord, NH 03301-3852
603-271-4680
800-351-1888
Fax: 603-271-4643
e-mail: ckeane@dhhs.state.nh.us
http://www.dhhs.state.nh.us

Catherine Keane, Director
Mary Maggioncaida, Manager of Program Development
Susan Lombard, Director Operations

State agency on aging services; limited services to incapacitated adults, age 18 and older.

1623 **New Hampshire Governor's Commission on Disability**
57 Regional Drive
Concord, NH 03301-8518
603-271-2773
Fax: 603-271-2837

Micher Jenkins, Contact
Carol Nadeau, Executive Director

1624 **New Hampshire Health and Human Services: Elderly and Adult Services**
6 Hazen Drive
Concord, NH 03301-6510
603-271-4680
800-351-1888
Fax: 603-271-4643

1625 **New Hampshire Protection & Advocacy for Persons with Disabilities**
PO Box 19
Concord, NH 03302
603-228-0432
Fax: 603-225-2077

Donna Woodfin, Contact
Richard Cohen, Executive Director

1626 **New Hampshire Retirement System**
54 Regional Drive
Concord, NH 03301
603-410-3500
877-600-0158
Fax: 603-410-3501
e-mail: info@nhrs.org
http://www.nh.gov/retirement
TDD 800-735-2964

Charlton MacVeagh, Chairman
Robert Leggett, Executive Director

The New Hampshire Retirement System is a public employee pension plan. It is a defined benefit plan, which offers eligible retirees a secure lifetime pension. This website has general information about NHRS and describes the eligibility requirements for each of the benefits. Publishes a Retirement Connection newsletter.

Number of Members: 51,000

1627 **New Hampshire Veterans Council**
359 Lincoln Street
Manchester, NH 03103-4901
603-624-9230
800-622-9230
Fax: 603-624-9236

Dennis J Viola, Manager

1628 **New Hampshire for Human Rights**
163 Loudon Road
Concord, NH 03301-6053
603-271-2767
Fax: 271-633-

Ramond Sperry Jr, Contact
Katharine A Daly, Manager

Offers legal help and information for disabled persons who are discriminated against in the housing industry.

1629 **Northern New England Association of Homes and Services for the Aging**
345 Edward J Roy Drive
Suite 201
Manchester, NH 03104
603-626-3479
Fax: 603-626-3763
http://www.nneahsa.com

Laurence Knowles, President
Meg Miller LNHA, Executive Director

The mission of NNEAHSA is to promote the interests of its not-for-profit members in Maine, New Hampshire, and Vermont which provide healthy, affordable and ethical long term care to our older citizens through education, advocacy, representation and collaboration.

1630 **RSVP Carroll County**
Main Street
PO Box 1182
North Conway, NH 03860-1182
603-856-9331
Fax: 603-356-0100
e-mail: ccrsvp@fagnetworks.net

Bennie Jesseman, Director

The Retired and Senior Volunteer Program (RSVP) provides opportunities for people 55 and over to make a difference in their community through volunteer service. RSVP volunteers contribute anywhere from a few to over forty hours a week, serving through schools, day care centers, police departments, hospitals and other nonprofit and public organizations to help meet critical community needs. RSVP offers maximum flexibility and choice to its volunteers. RSVP matches the personal interests and skills of older Americans with opportunities to help solve community problems and offers supplemental insurance while on duty, on-the-job training from the agency or organization where volunteers are placed.

State Organizations & Government Agencies/New Jersey

1631 **RSVP Coos County**
30 Exchange Street
Berlin, NH 03570-1911
603-752-4103
Fax: 603-752-7607
e-mail: kmckenna@tccap.org

Kathryn McKenna, Project Director

The Retired and Senior Volunteer Program (RSVP) provides opportunities for people 55 and over to make a difference in their community through volunteer service. RSVP volunteers contribute anywhere from a few to over forty hours a week, serving through schools, day care centers, police departments, hospitals and other nonprofit and public organizations to help meet critical community needs. RSVP offers maximum flexibility and choice to its volunteers. RSVP matches the personal interests and skills of older Americans with opportunities to help solve community problems and offers supplemental insurance while on duty, on-the-job training from the agency or organization where volunteers are placed.

1632 **RSVP Merrimack County**
97 Pleasant Street
Concord, NH 03301-3852
603-224-3452
Fax: 603-224-0157

Nancy Spater, Executive Director

The Retired and Senior Volunteer Program (RSVP) provides opportunities for people 55 and over to make a difference in their community through volunteer service. RSVP volunteers contribute anywhere from a few to over forty hours a week, serving through schools, day care centers, police departments, hospitals and other nonprofit and public organizations to help meet critical community needs. RSVP offers maximum flexibility and choice to its volunteers. RSVP matches the personal interests and skills to older Americans with opportunities to help solve community problems and offer supplemental insurance while on duty, on-the-job training from the agency or organization where volunteers are placed.

1633 **RSVP Monadnock**
64 Main Street
Suite 301
Keene, NH 03431-3701
603-352-2088
Fax: 603-357-6896

Geraldine Liebert, Executive Director

The Retired and Senior Volunteer Program (RSVP) provides opportunities for people 55 and over to make a difference in their community through volunteer service. RSVP volunteers contribute anywhere from a few to over forty hours a week, serving through schools, day care centers, police departments, hospitals and other nonprofit and public organizations to help meet critical community needs. RSVP offers maximum flexibility and choice to its volunteers. RSVP matches the personal interests and skills to older Americans with opportunities to help solve community problems and offer supplemental insurance while on duty, on-the-job training from the agency or organization where volunteers are placed.

1634 **RSVP Portsmouth**
245 Middle Street
Portsmouth, NH 03801-5128
603-436-4310
Fax: 603-436-4937

The Retired and Senior Volunteer Program (RSVP) provides opportunities for people 55 and over to make a difference in their community through volunteer service. RSVP volunteers contribute anywhere from a few to over forty hours a week, serving through schools, day care centers, police departments, hospitals and other nonprofit and public organizations to help meet critical community needs. RSVP offers maximum flexibility and choice to its volunteers. RSVP matches the personal interests and skills to older Americans with opportunities to help solve community problems and offer supplemental insurance while on duty, on-the-job training from the agency or organization where volunteers are placed.

1635 **RSVP Southern New Hampshire**
PO Box 5040
Manchester, NH 03108-5040
603-668-8010
Fax: 603-645-6734

Gale Hennessy, Executive Director

The Retired and Senior Volunteer Program (RSVP) provides opportunities for people 55 and over to make a difference in their community through volunteer service. RSVP volunteers contribute anywhere from a few to over forty hours a week, serving though schools, day care centers, police departments, hospitals and other nonprofit and public organizations to help meet critical community needs. RSVP offers maximum flexibility and choice to its volunteers. RSVP matches the personal interests and skills to older Americans with opportunities to help solve community problems and offer supplemental insurance while on duty, on-the-job training from the agency or organization where volunteers are placed.

1636 **RSVP and the Volunteer Center**
10 Campbell Street
Lebanon, NH 03766-1341
603-448-1825
877-711-7787
Fax: 603-448-3906
e-mail: BRose-rsvp@gcscc.org
http://www.rsvptoday.org

Teresa M Volta, Director
Doreen Bowlin, Assistant Program Director

RSVP and the Volunteer Center build on the values of the past, to address the needs of the present, and strengthen our communities for the future, through volunteer service. Working with local nonprofits, we recruit, place, and support volunteers of all ages throughout northern Windsor County, VT, and Sullivan/Grafton Counties in NH. Our signature programs include: Good Morning! telephone reassurance, Bone Builders low impact lifting for elders.

1637 **Service Corp of Retired Executives: Portsmouth Chapter No. 185**
195 Commerce Way
Unit A
Portsmouth, NH 03801-3251
603-352-0320

RL Devoucoux, Chairperson

Retired business professionals. Provides free business counseling.

New Jersey

1638 **Atlantic County Division of Intergenerational Services, Office of Aging**
Department of Health and Human Services
Shoreview Building, Office 218
101 South Shore Road
Northfield, NJ 08225
609-645-5843
Fax: 609-645-5907
http://www.aclink.org/intergenerational

Marilu Gagnon, Director

The Division of Intergenerational Services addresses the needs of youth, families, disabled and senior citizens. Trained staff are available to provide such services as information and referral, outreach, case management and juvenile/family crisis intervention to eligible individuals.

1639 **Bergen County Division of Senior Services**
One Bergen Plaza
2nd Floor
Hackensack, NJ 07601
201-336-7400
Fax: 201-336-7424
e-mail: seniors@co.bergen.nj.us
http://www.co.bergen.nj.us

Anne Ciavaglia, Director

The Bergen County Division of Senior Services was established with a mission to serve as an advocate for older adults. It is a planning, coordinating and funding agency for senior programs and services.

State Organizations & Government Agencies/New Jersey

1640 Burlington County Office on Aging
County Office Building
Mount Holly, NJ 08060
609-265-5069
800-792-8890
Fax: 609-265-3725

Cecile Neidich, Acting Director
Jeanne Borkowski, Manager

1641 Burlington County Retired and Senior Volunteer Program
RR 530
Pemberton, NJ 08068
609-894-9311
Fax: 609-894-0587
e-mail: lbennett@bcc.edu

Linda Bennett, Director
Robert Massina, President

1642 Cape May County Department of Aging
3509 Route 9 S
Rio Grande, NJ 08242-1637
609-889-2722
Fax: 609-889-0344

Margaret Spencer, Director

1643 Commissioner Of Labor And WorkforceDeveloper
New Jersey Department of Labor And Workforce Development
Trenton, NJ 08625
609-292-2323
Fax: 609-633-9271
e-mail: cmycoff@dol.state.nj.us
http://www.state.nj.us/labor

David J Soolow, Commisioner
Michelle Richardson, Assistant Commissioner

1644 Cumberland County Office on Aging &Disabled
790 E Commerce Street
Bridgeton, NJ 08302-2269
856-453-2220
Fax: 856-453-8419

Misono Miller, Executive Director

1645 Division of Disability Determination Services
Point Plaza W, Bldg 2
6737 Capitol Boulevard S
PO Box 9303 MS 45550
Tumwater, WA 98501
360-664-7362
800-562-6074
Fax: 360-586-0851
TDD 888-583-6941

Martin A Jones MD, Director
Jim Yerxa, Assistant Director
Mary Gabriel, Regional Manager

To serve our customers by providing accurate and timely disability decisions through efficient use of public resources in accordance with Social Security Administration Regulations.

1646 Division of Disability Determinations New Brunswick
506 Jersey Avenue
PO Box 2671
New Brunswick, NJ 08901
732-246-5866
Fax: 732-246-5865
http://www.state.nj.us/labor

Barbara Trella, Professional Relations Officer

The Division of Disability Determinations (DDD) is responsible for making decisions regarding the medical eligibility of New Jersey citizens applying for disability benefits under the federal Social Security and Supplemental Security Income programs, and the state Medically Needed program. It is also responsible for conducting reviews of existing beneficiaries under the federal programs and determining continuing eligibility.

1647 Division of Disability Determinations: Newark
PO Box 649
Newark, NJ 07101
973-648-4062
Fax: 973-648-2128
http://www.state.nj.us/labor

Jean Connolly, Professional Relations Officer

The Division of Disability Determinations (DDD) is responsible for making decisions regarding the medical eligibility of New Jersey citizens applying for disability benefits under the federal Social Security and Supplemental Security Income programs, and the state Medically Needed program. It is also responsible for conducting reviews of existing beneficiaries under the federal programs and determining continuing eligibility.

1648 Gloucester County Department on Aging
PO Box 337
Woodbury, NJ 08096
856-232-4646
Fax: 856-232-6709
e-mail: cmorris@co.gloucester.nj.us
http://www.co.gloucester.nj.us

Anna Docimo, Executive Director

The Gloucester County Division of Senior Services is an active participant in the New Jersey EASE program, administering a broad range of home and community based services that focus on the needs of senior citizens throughout the County. The Division of Senior Services provides information and assistance to aid residents of Gloucester County 60 years of age or older and their families. Our mission is to promote accessible and high-quality health and senior services to help all seniors in Gloucester County attain optimal health and independence. We promote, support and protect-well being. We encourage informed choices that enhance quality of life for seniors.

1649 Gray Panthers of Northern New Jersey
2 Winthrop Place
Leonia, NJ 07605-1226
201-944-0676
Fax: 202-737-1160
e-mail: info@graypanthers.org
http://www.graypanthers.org

May Hollinshead, Executive Director
Ed Purtill, Vice Director

National organization of intergenerational activists dedicated to social change. Takes on societal issues such as peace, healthcare, jobs and housing from an intergenerational perspective and fights to change laws and attitudes toward social justice.

1650 Gray Panthers of Southern New Jersey
110 W Crystal Lake Avenue
Apt 119d
Haddonfield, NJ 08033-3111
856-858-6535
Fax: 202-737-1160
e-mail: quotaman7@aol.com
http://www.graypanthers.org

Irene DiRenza, Co-Director
Lew Wilkinson, Co-Director

National organization of intergenerational activists dedicated to social change. Takes on societal issues such as peace, healthcare, jobs and housing from an intergenerational perspective, and fights to change laws and attitudes toward social justice.

1651 Guardian Eldercare
161 Main Street
Suite 3
Hackensack, NJ 07601-7114
201-368-9680
Fax: 201-342-2373

Robert Ericksen MD, Contact
Richard Samuels, President

Guardian Eldercare endeavors to provide excellence in health care services while recognizing the dignity of each individual.

1652 Hammonton Senior Citizens Club
PO Box 1228
Hammonton, NJ 08037-5228
609-567-3200
e-mail: jcalder@mail.hammontongazette.com

Linda Sciullo, Manager

Promotes and provides Social Services for senior citizens in Hammonton, NJ.

State Organizations & Government Agencies/New Jersey

1653 **Holland Township Community Seniors**
80 County Road 627
Phillipsburg, NJ 08865-7622

Promotes and provides Social Services for senior citizens in Phillipsburg, NJ.

1654 **Hudson County Office on Aging**
595 County Avenue
Bldg 2
Secaucus, NJ 07094-2605
201-271-4322
877-222-3737
Fax: 201-271-4366
e-mail: jconnors@oel.state.nj.us

Carol Ann Wilson, Director
Edward Benoit, Manager

Jersey City, Hudson County.

1655 **Hunterdon County Division of Senior Services**
PO Box 2900
Flemington, NJ 08822-2900
908-788-1361
Fax: 908-806-4537
e-mail: aging@co.hunterdon.nj.us
http://www.co.hunterdon.nj.us

Mary Ann Rosenberger, Director
Richard Chrysalis, Spvsr Senior Citizens Activities

This office is the focal point for compiling and distributing information pertinent to the county's elderly population, its needs, and services implemented to meet those needs. The Division of Senior Services administers several programs including the State Health Program (SHIP), Care/Case Management, Mr. Fixit Program, Senior Health Services and Prevention Health Services. The Division contracts for the provision of a multitude of additional serices with qualified provider agencies, and diligently monitors the performance of these service providers to insure quality and ease of access by the seniors for these services.

1656 **Indo-American Connection**
51 Reading Road
Edison, NJ 08817-6637
732-906-0406

Purushottam Karra, Contact
Ramanlal V Shah, Contact
Uday Varma, Owner

1657 **Mine Hill Senior Citizens Good Years Club**
Baker Street
Mine Hill, NJ 07803
973-366-9031

Muriel Zimmerman, Contact
Barry Lewis Jr, Administrator

Senior citizens united for recreational opportunities.

1658 **Monmouth County Office on Aging**
21 Main & E Center
Freehold, NJ 07728
732-431-7450
Fax: 732-303-7649

John A Wanat, Executive Director

Senior citizens. Serves as an advocate for elderly citizens. Provides information and referral services.

1659 **Morris County Office on Aging**
PO Box 900
Morristown, NJ 07963
973-539-0377
877-222-3737
Fax: 973-285-6883
e-mail: divaging@oel.com
TDD 201-285-6855

Bonnie Kelly, Director
Walter Morris, Owner

Morris County, Morristown.

1660 **New Jersey Association of Non-Profit Homes for the Aging**
760 Alexander Road
Cn-1
Princeton, NJ 08540-6305
609-452-1161
Fax: 609-452-2907

June Duggan, President

1661 **New Jersey Client Assistance Program**
210 S Broad Street
3rd Floor
Trenton, NJ 08608-2404
609-292-9742
800-922-7233
Fax: 609-777-0187
http://www.njpanda.org

Sarah Mitchell, Director
Maritza Williams, Intake Coordinator

The Client Assistance Program (CAP) assists persons with disabilities who are seeking or receiving services from federally funded rehabilitation programs. CAP provides legal and nonlegal individuals and systems advocacy.

1662 **New Jersey Department of Aging**
S Broad and Front Streets
Trenton, NJ 08625
609-292-4833
Fax: 609-633-6609

Ruth Leader, Director

1663 **New Jersey Department of Community Affairs: Commission on Recreation for the Handicapped**
101 South Broad Street
PO Box 811
Trenton, NJ 08625-0811
609-984-6654
http://www.state.nj.us/dca/rec
TDD 609-278-0175

Susan Bass Levin, Commissioner

The Commission functions to promote and assist in the development and implementation of recreation and leisure services for individuals with disabilities in the communities of New Jersey.

1664 **New Jersey Department of Human Services: Commission for the Blind**
153 Halsey Street
Newark, NJ 07102-2807
973-648-4691
Fax: 973-648-7874

Margo Montague, Manager

1665 **New Jersey Department of Human Services: Deaf and Heard of Hearing Division**
PO Box 74
Trenton, NJ 08625
609-984-7281
Fax: 609-984-0390

Brian Shomo, Manager

1666 **New Jersey Department of Mental Health**
Labor Building
Trenton, NJ 08625
609-777-0700
Fax: 777-083-

Allen Kaufman, Director
Kevin Martone, Administrator

1667 **New Jersey Developmental Disability Council**
20 West State Street
Trenton, NJ 08625-0700
609-292-3745
Fax: 609-292-7114
http://www.njcdd.org

Dr. Alison Lozano, PhD, Director

State Organizations & Government Agencies/New Jersey

1668 New Jersey Division of Taxation
PO Box 281
Trenton, NJ 08695
609-292-6400
800-286-6613
Fax: 609-826-4500
http://www.state.nj.us/treasury/taxation
Robert K Thompson, Executive Director

1669 New Jersey Intergenerational Network
13 Roszel Road
Suite A104
Princeton, NJ 08540-6211
609-951-8600
Fax: 609-452-2907
Claire McNew, Owner

1670 New Jersey Protection & Advocacy for Persons with Disabilities
Trenton, NJ 08625
609-292-7260
Fax: 609-292-6610
Robert Nickolas, Director

1671 North Hanover Senior Citizen Club
41 Schoolhouse Road
Wrightstown, NJ 08562-2106
609-758-2617
Fax: 609-758-3016
William F King, President

Retired people. Promotes good fellowship among members; supports local charities; conducts social activities.

1672 Ocean County Office on Aging
3 Mott Place
Cn2191
Toms River, NJ 08753-7560
732-929-2091
Fax: 908-506-5019
Philip Rubenstein, Executive Director
Jane Maloney, Executive Director

Ocean County, Toms River.

1673 Passaic County Office on Aging
209 Totowa Road
Wayne, NJ 07470-3116
973-881-4950
877-222-3737
Fax: 973-686-7770
e-mail: maryk@passaiccopuntynj.org
John A Stuart CPP, Director
Mary Kuzinski, Executive Director

Hawthorne, Passaic County.

1674 Prevent Blindness New Jersey
984 Southford Road
Suite 4
Middlebury, CT 06762-3234
203-598-0529
800-850-2020
Fax: 203-598-0584
e-mail: pblindness@aol.com
http://www.preventblindness.org/NJ/
Individuals interested in preventing blindness and preserving sight through research and education programs.

1675 RSVP Atlantic City Chapter
123 Madison Avenue
Atlantic City, NJ 08401-5417
609-348-3060
Elinor Goldman, Director
Widellia Hernandez-Colon, Executive Director

The Retired and Senior Volunteer Program (RSVP) provides opportunities for people 55 and over to make a difference in their community through volunteer service. RSVP volunteers contribute anywhere from a few to over forty hours a week, serving though schools, day care centers, police departments, hospitals and other nonprofit and public organizations to help meet critical community needs. RSVP offers maximum flexibility and choice to its volunteers. RSVP matches the personal interests and skills to older Americans with opportunities to help solve community problems and offer supplemental insurance while on duty, on-the-job training from the agency or organization where volunteers are placed.

1676 RSVP Bergen County
10 Banta Place
Hackensack, NJ 07601-5612
201-487-0555
Fax: 201-487-1279
Leo Grigolia

The Retired and Senior Volunteer Program (RSVP) provides opportunities for people 55 and over to make a difference in their community through volunteer service. RSVP volunteers contribute anywhere from a few to over forty hours a week, serving though schools, day care centers, police departments, hospitals and other nonprofit and public organizations to help meet critical community needs. RSVP offers maximum flexibility and choice to its volunteers. RSVP matches the personal interests and skills to older Americans with opportunities to help solve community problems and offer supplemental insurance while on duty, on-the-job training from the agency or organization where volunteers are placed.

1677 RSVP Bergen County New Jersey
10 Banta Place
Hackensack, NJ 07601-5612
201-487-0555
Fax: 201-487-1279
e-mail: rsvpbc@idt.net
Mary Gildea, Director
Leo Grigolia

The Retired and Senior Volunteer Program (RSVP) provides opportunities for people 55 and over to make a difference in their community through volunteer service. RSVP volunteers contribute anywhere from a few to over forty hours a week, serving though schools, day care centers, police departments, hospitals and other nonprofit and public organizations to help meet critical community needs. RSVP offers maximum flexibility and choice to its volunteers. RSVP matches the personal interests and skills to older Americans with opportunities to help solve community problems and offer supplemental insurance while on duty, on-the-job training from the agency or organization where volunteers are placed.

1678 RSVP Burlington County
RR 530
Pemberton, NJ 08068
609-894-9311
Fax: 609-894-0587
Robert Massina, President

The Retired and Senior Volunteer Program (RSVP) provides opportunities for people 55 and over to make a difference in their community through volunteer service. RSVP volunteers contribute anywhere from a few to over forty hours a week, serving though schools, day care centers, police departments, hospitals and other nonprofit and public organizations to help meet critical community needs. RSVP offers maximum flexibility and choice to its volunteers. RSVP matches the personal interests and skills to older Americans with opportunities to help solve community problems and offer supplemental insurance while on duty, on-the-job training from the agency or organization where volunteers are placed.

1679 RSVP Camden County
6981 N Park Drive
Pennsauken, NJ 08109-4205
856-663-4773
Fax: 856-663-7182
e-mail: camdencountyrsvp@yahoo.com
Juanita Fuller, Director

State Organizations & Government Agencies/New Jersey

The Retired and Senior Volunteer Program (RSVP) provides opportunities for people 55 and over to make a difference in their community through volunteer service. RSVP volunteers contribute anywhere from a few to over forty hours a week, serving though schools, day care centers, police departments, hospitals and other nonprofit and public organizations to help meet critical community needs. RSVP offers maximum flexibility and choice to its volunteers. RSVP matches the personal interests and skills to older Americans with opportunities to help solve community problems and offer supplemental insurance while on duty, on-the-job training from the agency or organization where volunteers are placed.

1680 RSVP Cape May Chapter
4 Moore Road
Cape May Court House, NJ 08210-1654
609-886-3400
Fax: 609-889-0344
e-mail: ltaylorday@co.cape-may.nj.us
Linda Taylor-Day, Director

The Retired and Senior Volunteer Program (RSVP) provides opportunities for people 55 and over to make a difference in their community through volunteer service. RSVP volunteers contribute anywhere from a few to over forty hours a week, serving though schools, day care centers, police departments, hospitals and other nonprofit and public organizations to help meet critical community needs. RSVP offers maximum flexibility and choice to its volunteers. RSVP matches the personal interests and skills to older Americans with opportunities to help solve community problems and offer supplemental insurance while on duty, on-the-job training from the agency or organization where volunteers are placed.

1681 RSVP Cape May County
4 Moore Road
Cape May C H, NJ 08210-1654
609-886-3400
Fax: 609-889-0344
Linda Taylor-Day, Manager

The Retired and Senior Volunteer Program (RSVP) provides opportunities for people 55 and over to make a difference in their community through volunteer service. RSVP volunteers contribute anywhere from a few to over forty hours a week, serving though schools, day care centers, police departments, hospitals and other nonprofit and public organizations to help meet critical community needs. RSVP offers maximum flexibility and choice to its volunteers. RSVP matches the personal interests and skills to older Americans with opportunities to help solve community problems and offer supplemental insurance while on duty, on-the-job training from the agency or organization where volunteers are placed.

1682 RSVP Cumberland
790 E Commerce Street
Bridgeton, NJ 08302-2269
856-453-8066
Fax: 856-453-8419
Judy Truman, Project Director
Mary Barber, Secretary
Dianne Terry, Manager

The Retired and Senior Volunteer Program (RSVP) provides opportunities for people 55 and over to make a difference in their community through volunteer service. RSVP volunteers contribute anywhere from a few to over forty hours a week, serving though schools, day care centers, police departments, hospitals and other nonprofit and public organizations to help meet critical community needs. RSVP offers maximum flexibility and choice to its volunteers. RSVP matches the personal interests and skills to older Americans with opportunities to help solve community problems and offer supplemental insurance while on duty, on-the-job training from the agency or organization where volunteers are placed.

1683 RSVP Cumberland County Chapter
790 E Commerce Street
Bridgeton, NJ 08302-2269
856-453-8066
Fax: 856-453-8419
Judy Truman, Director
Dianne Terry, Manager

The Retired and Senior Volunteer Program (RSVP) provides opportunities for people 55 and over to make a difference in their community through volunteer service. RSVP volunteers contribute anywhere from a few to over forty hours a week, serving though schools, day care centers, police departments, hospitals and other nonprofit and public organizations to help meet critical community needs. RSVP offers maximum flexibility and choice to its volunteers. RSVP matches the personal interests and skills to older Americans with opportunities to help solve community problems and offer supplemental insurance while on duty, on-the-job training from the agency or organization where volunteers are placed.

1684 RSVP Essex Hudson Chapter
2 Gardner Road and Route 46 W
Fairfield, NJ 07004
973-575-0880
Fax: 973-575-8462
e-mail: rdonald@rcmetronj.org
Rita Donald, Director
Nancy Asaro, CEO

The Retired and Senior Volunteer Program (RSVP) provides opportunities for people 55 and over to make a difference in their community through volunteer service. RSVP volunteers contribute anywhere from a few to over forty hours a week, serving though schools, day care centers, police departments, hospitals and other nonprofit and public organizations to help meet critical community needs. RSVP offers maximum flexibility and choice to its volunteers. RSVP matches the personal interests and skills to older Americans with opportunities to help solve community problems and offer supplemental insurance while on duty, on-the-job training from the agency or organization where volunteers are placed.

1685 RSVP Goucester County
1400 Tanyard Road
Sewell, NJ 08080-4222
856-468-1742
Fax: 856-458-9462
e-mail: hantonucci@gccnj.edu
http://www.gloucestercountyvolunteers.org/rsvp
Helen Antonucci, Director

RSVP has enabled Americans 55 years and older to continue making significant contributions to their community. Our program links the talents and skills of retired persons with over 121 nonprofit organizations that serve all ages. The volunteer chooses the organization and capacity in which they will volunteer. Hours are arranged according to the individual's schedule and there are even limited opportunities to serve without leaving your home.

1686 RSVP Mercer County
1985 Pennington Road
Ewing, NJ 08618-1106
609-883-2880
Fax: 609-883-2024
e-mail: rsvpmc@yahoo.com
Marjory Bernhard, Director
Elanor Letcher, Executive Director

The Retired and Senior Volunteer Program (RSVP) provides opportunities for people 55 and over to make a difference in their community through volunteer service. RSVP volunteers contribute anywhere from a few to over forty hours a week, serving though schools, day care centers, police departments, hospitals and other nonprofit and public organizations to help meet critical community needs. RSVP offers maximum flexibility and choice to its volunteers. RSVP matches the personal interests and skills to older Americans with opportunities to help solve community problems and offer supplemental insurance while on duty, on-the-job training from the agency or organization where volunteers are placed.

1687 RSVP Middlesex County
PO Box 69
New Brunswick, NJ 08903
732-249-6330
Fax: 732-545-3606
Jocelyn Bobin, Director
Barry Smith, Executive Director

State Organizations & Government Agencies/New Jersey

The Retired and Senior Volunteer Program (RSVP) provides opportunities for people 55 and over to make a difference in their community through volunteer service. RSVP volunteers contribute anywhere from a few to over forty hours a week, serving though schools, day care centers, police departments, hospitals and other nonprofit and public organizations to help meet critical community needs. RSVP offers maximum flexibility and choice to its volunteers. RSVP matches the personal interests and skills to older Americans with opportunities to help solve community problems and offer supplemental insurance while on duty, on-the-job training from the agency or organization where volunteers are placed.

1688 RSVP Morris County
180 W Hanover Avenue
Morristown, NJ 07960-2620
973-538-7947
Fax: 973-984-7658

The Retired and Senior Volunteer Program (RSVP) provides opportunities for people 55 and over to make a difference in their community through volunteer service. RSVP volunteers contribute anywhere from a few to over forty hours a week, serving though schools, day care centers, police departments, hospitals and other nonprofit and public organizations to help meet critical community needs. RSVP offers maximum flexibility and choice to its volunteers. RSVP matches the personal interests and skills to older Americans with opportunities to help solve community problems and offer supplemental insurance while on duty, on-the-job training from the agency or organization where volunteers are placed.

1689 RSVP Morris County Chapter
180 W Hanover Avenue
Morristown, NJ 07960-2620
973-538-7947
Fax: 973-984-7658
e-mail: rsvpmorris@juno.com

Mary Fassnacht, Director

The Retired and Senior Volunteer Program (RSVP) provides opportunities for people 55 and over to make a difference in their community through volunteer service. RSVP volunteers contribute anywhere from a few to over forty hours a week, serving though schools, day care centers, police departments, hospitals and other nonprofit and public organizations to help meet critical community needs. RSVP offers maximum flexibility and choice to its volunteers. RSVP matches the personal interests and skills to older Americans with opportunities to help solve community problems and offer supplemental insurance while on duty, on-the-job training from the agency or organization where volunteers are placed.

1690 RSVP Ocean County
1027 Hooper Avenue
Toms River, NJ 08753-8363
732-286-5888
Fax: 732-914-2064

Renee Morris, Executive Director

The Retired and Senior Volunteer Program (RSVP) provides opportunities for people 55 and over to make a difference in their community through volunteer service. RSVP volunteers contribute anywhere from a few to over forty hours a week, serving though schools, day care centers, police departments, hospitals and other nonprofit and public organizations to help meet critical community needs. RSVP offers maximum flexibility and choice to its volunteers. RSVP matches the personal interests and skills to older Americans with opportunities to help solve community problems and offer supplemental insurance while on duty, on-the-job training from the agency or organization where volunteers are placed.

1691 RSVP Ocean County Chapter
PO Box 547
Toms River, NJ 08754
732-286-5888
Fax: 732-914-2064
e-mail: rsvp@superlink.net

Renee Morris, Director

The Retired and Senior Volunteer Program (RSVP) provides opportunities for people 55 and over to make a difference in their community through volunteer service. RSVP volunteers contribute anywhere from a few to over forty hours a week, serving though schools, day care centers, police departments, hospitals and other nonprofit and public organizations to help meet critical community needs. RSVP offers maximum flexibility and choice to its volunteers. RSVP matches the personal interests and skills to older Americans with opportunities to help solve community problems and offer supplemental insurance while on duty, on-the-job training from the agency or organization where volunteers are placed.

1692 RSVP Passaic County
209 Fairfield Road
Fairfield, NJ 07004-2420
973-575-0880
Fax: 973-575-8462

Nancy Asaro, Chief Executive Officer

The Retired and Senior Volunteer Program (RSVP) provides opportunities for people 55 and over to make a difference in their community through volunteer service. RSVP volunteers contribute anywhere from a few to over forty hours a week, serving though schools, day care centers, police departments, hospitals and other nonprofit and public organizations to help meet critical community needs. RSVP offers maximum flexibility and choice to its volunteers. RSVP matches the personal interests and skills to older Americans with opportunities to help solve community problems and offer supplemental insurance while on duty, on-the-job training from the agency or organization where volunteers are placed.

1693 RSVP Somerset County
PO Box 3000
Somerville, NJ 08876-1262
918-704-6338
Fax: 908-231-1813

The Retired and Senior Volunteer Program (RSVP) provides opportunities for people 55 and over to make a difference in their community through volunteer service. RSVP volunteers contribute anywhere from a few to over forty hours a week, serving though schools, day care centers, police departments, hospitals and other nonprofit and public organizations to help meet critical community needs. RSVP offers maximum flexibility and choice to its volunteers. RSVP matches the personal interests and skills to older Americans with opportunities to help solve community problems and offer supplemental insurance while on duty, on-the-job training from the agency or organization where volunteers are placed.

1694 RSVP Somerset County Chapter
N Bridge and High Street
Somerville, NJ 08876
908-704-6338
Fax: 908-231-1813
e-mail: fattal@co.somerset.nj.us

Carla Fattal, Director

The Retired and Senior Volunteer Program (RSVP) provides opportunities for people 55 and over to make a difference in their community through volunteer service. RSVP volunteers contribute anywhere from a few to over forty hours a week, serving though schools, day care centers, police departments, hospitals and other nonprofit and public organizations to help meet critical community needs. RSVP offers maximum flexibility and choice to its volunteers. RSVP matches the personal interests and skills to older Americans with opportunities to help solve community problems and offer supplemental insurance while on duty, on-the-job training from the agency or organization where volunteers are placed.

1695 RSVP Sussex-Warren
350 Marshall Street
Phillipsburg, NJ 08865-3273
908-454-7000
Fax: 908-859-0729
e-mail: ouellettec@norwescap.org

Carol R Ouellette, Contact
Laurie Cahill, Manager

State Organizations & Government Agencies/New Jersey

The Retired and Senior Volunteer Program (RSVP) provides opportunities for people 55 and over to make a difference in their community through volunteer service. RSVP volunteers contribute anywhere from a few to over forty hours a week, serving though schools, day care centers, police departments, hospitals and other nonprofit and public organizations to help meet critical community needs. RSVP offers maximum flexibility and choice to its volunteers. RSVP matches the personal interests and skills to older Americans with opportunities to help solve community problems and offer supplemental insurance while on duty, on-the-job training from the agency or organization where volunteers are placed.

1696 RSVP Sussex-Warren Chapter
350 Marshall Street
Phillipsburg, NJ 08865-3273   908-454-7000
                              Fax: 908-859-0729
                e-mail: ouellettec@norwescap.org
Carol Ouellette, Director
Laurie Cahill, Manager

The Retired and Senior Volunteer Program (RSVP) provides opportunities for people 55 and over to make a difference in their community through volunteer service. RSVP volunteers contribute anywhere from a few to over forty hours a week, serving though schools, day care centers, police departments, hospitals and other nonprofit and public organizations to help meet critical community needs. RSVP offers maximum flexibility and choice to its volunteers. RSVP matches the personal interests and skills to older Americans with opportunities to help solve community problems and offer supplemental insurance while on duty, on-the-job training from the agency or organization where volunteers are placed.

1697 RSVP Union County
80 W Grand Street
Elizabeth, NJ 07202-1447   908-354-3040
                              Fax: 908-354-2665
Karen M Ensle, President

The Retired and Senior Volunteer Program (RSVP) provides opportunities for people 55 and over to make a difference in their community through volunteer service. RSVP volunteers contribute anywhere from a few to over forty hours a week, serving though schools, day care centers, police departments, hospitals and other nonprofit and public organizations to help meet critical community needs. RSVP offers maximum flexibility and choice to its volunteers. RSVP matches the personal interests and skills to older Americans with opportunities to help solve community problems and offer supplemental insurance while on duty, on-the-job training from the agency or organization where volunteers are placed.

1698 RSVP Union County Chapter
80 W Grand Street
Elizabeth, NJ 07202-1447   908-354-6040
                              Fax: 908-354-2665
                   e-mail: lludmer@caunj.org
Laurie Ludmer, Director

The Retired and Senior Volunteer Program (RSVP) provides opportunities for people 55 and over to make a difference in their community through volunteer service. RSVP volunteers contribute anywhere from a few to over forty hours a week, serving though schools, day care centers, police departments, hospitals and other nonprofit and public organizations to help meet critical community needs. RSVP offers maximum flexibility and choice to its volunteers. RSVP matches the personal interests and skills to older Americans with opportunities to help solve community problems and offer supplemental insurance while on duty, on-the-job training from the agency or organization where volunteers are placed.

1699 Railroad Retirement Board: New Jersey District Office
20 Washington Plaza
Newark, NJ 07102-3127   973-645-3990
                              Fax: 973-645-3373
Merideth L Rogers, Representative

1700 Salem County Office on Aging
98 Market Street
Salem, NJ 08079   856-339-8622
                              Fax: 856-339-9268
                           http://www.salemco.org
Blanch Hogate, Director Health/Senior Services
Pamela S Pedrick, Executive Director
Sheri Hinchman, Assistant Executive Director

The Salem County Office on Aging provides Adult Protective Services to people age 60 and older or those disabled 18 and over.

1701 Senior Citizens Council of Union County
1187 Morris Avenue
Union, NJ 07083-5908   908-964-7555
                              Fax: 908-964-7607
Richard Stone, Executive Director

Senior citizens. Advocates for seniors. Provides information and referral services. Conducts 6 seminars per year; sponsors trips.

1702 Social Service Association
6 Station Plaza
Ridgewood, NJ 07450-3125   201-444-2980
                              Fax: 201-444-4987
Linda Gilman, Executive Director
Denise Vollkommer, Manager

Volunteers. Provides case management and financial assistance to help make families and individuals independent.

1703 Somerset County Office on Aging
614 1st Avenue
Raritan, NJ 08869-1308   908-704-6331
                              Fax: 908-253-0180
                              TDD 908-231-7168
Ruth M Reader, Executive Director
Perry Tchorni, Executive Director

Somerset County, Somerville.

1704 Sussex County Office on Aging
PO Box 709
Newton, NJ 07860   973-579-0555
                              Fax: 201-383-1124
Rosemarie C Agostini, Director
Mary Lou McCutcheon, Executive Director

Summit County, Newton.

1705 Union County Division on Aging
County Administration Building
4th Floor
Elizabeth, NJ 07207   908-527-4870
                                       800-792-8820
                              Fax: 908-527-4885
Philip H Pearlman, Director
Fran Benson, Executive Director

Elizabeth, Union County.

1706 Volunteer Center of Camden County
1212 Beacon Avenue
Pennsauken, NJ 08109   856-663-9356
                              Fax: 856-663-4879
Laurelle Cummings, Director

Offers information about a variety of volunteer opportunities in Camden County, including serving meals to the homebound, mentoring a child, gardening, clerical work and more.

1707 Volunteer Center of Monmouth County
191 Bath Avenue
Long Branch, NJ   732-728-1927
                              Fax: 732-728-9386
             e-mail: volunteercenter@fcsmonmouth.org
                          http://www.volunterme.org
Jane Frotten, Director

State Organizations & Government Agencies/New Mexico

The Volunteer Center promotes and recognizes volunteerism in Monmouth County by ensuring that interested people are aware of the variety of volunteer opportunities available.

1708 Warren County Division Of Senior ServiceS
165 County Rte 519 South
Belvidere, NJ 07823
908-475-6591
877-222-3737
Fax: 908-475-6588
TDD 908-689-6900
Susan Lennon, Executive Director
Warren County, Belvidere.

New Mexico

1709 City of Albuquerque-Bernalillo County:Department of Senior Affairs
714 7th Street SW
Albuquerque, NM 87102-3814
505-764-6400
Fax: 505-764-6465
http://www.cabq.gov/seniors
Mr Kim Perdue, Director
Jean Spalt, Senior Information Supervisor
Blanca Hise, Executive Director

A wide array of services and opportunities to enhance Bernalillo County seniors' quality of life. Providing services for active, healthy seniors and for frail, homebound elderly, the goal is to provide a continuum of care to keep seniors mentally and physically active and in their homes for as long as safely possible. Depending on the particular program, the minimum age varies from ages 50-60 years. Contributions requested for some services.

1710 Disability Determination Services
PO Box 4588
Albuquerque, NM 87196-4588
505-841-5600
Fax: 505-841-5724
Daniel Roper, Manager

1711 Eastern New Mexico Area: Agency on Aging
901 W 13th Street
Clovis, NM 88101-5552
505-769-1613
Fax: 505-769-3530
Frank White, Director
Nancy Arias, Executive Director

1712 Guadalupe County Nutrition
Hc 69
Box 550
Santa Rosa, NM 88435-9503
505-472-5377
Fax: 505-472-5377
Sylvia Maestas, Executive Director

1713 NCNMEDD-Area Agency on Aging
PO Box 5115
Santa Fe, NM 87502-5115
505-827-7313
Fax: 505-827-7414
http://www.m,localgov.net/northcentral/aging
Jenny Martinez, Director

1714 New Mexico Client Assistance Program
1720 Louisiana Boulevard NE
Suite 204
Albuquerque, NM 87110-7070
505-256-3100
800-432-4682
Fax: 505-256-3184
James Jackson, Executive Director

1715 New Mexico Committee on Concerns of the Handicapped
419 Old Santa Fe Trail
Santa Fe, NM 87503
505-986-4575
Fax: 505-827-6328
Dewight Capshaw, Manager

1716 New Mexico Department of Aging
224 E Palace Avenue
4th Floor
Santa Fe, NM 87501-2013
505-827-4012
Fax: 505-827-7649
Michelle Grishan, Director

1717 New Mexico Department of Taxation and Revenue
1100 S Saint Francis Drive
Santa Fe, NM 87505-4147
505-827-0700
Fax: 505-841-6326
http://www.state.nm.us/tax
John Chavez, Manager

1718 New Mexico Educational Retirement Board
PO Box 26129
Santa Fe, NM 87502
505-827-8030
Fax: 505-827-1855
Danny J Lyle, CEO

1719 New Mexico Governor's Committee on Concern of the Handicapped
491 Old Santa Fe Trail
Santa Fe, NM 87501-2753
505-986-4589
Fax: 505-827-6465
Paula Tackett, Executive Director

1720 New Mexico Protection & Advocacy for Persons with Disabilities
1720 Louisiana Boulevard NE
Albuquerque, NM 87110-7022
505-256-3100
800-432-4687
Fax: 505-256-3184
James Jackson, Director

1721 New Mexico Public Employees Retirement Board
PO Box 2123
Santa Fe, NM 87504-2123
505-827-4700
Fax: 505-827-4670

1722 New Mexico State Agency on Aging
224 E Palace Avenue
Santa Fe, NM 87501-2013
505-827-7640
Fax: 505-827-7649
Michelle Lujan Grishan, Director
Debbie Armstrong, Executive Director

1723 New Mexico Technology
435 Saint Michaels Drive
Building D
Santa Fe, NM 87505
505-954-8533
800-866-2253
Fax: 505-954-8608
e-mail: AWinnegar@state.nm.us
http://www.nmtap.com
Andrew Winnegar, Director Program

The New Mexico Technology Assistance Program (NMTAP) offers free services to New Mexicans with disabilities to help them get the assistive technology (AT) services they need.

1724 New Mexico Veterans Service Commission
PO Box 2324
Santa Fe, NM 87503
505-827-6300
Fax: 505-827-6372
John M Garcia, Manager

1725 New Mexico Workers Compensation Board
PO Box 27198
Albuquerque, NM 87125-7198
505-841-6000
Fax: 505-841-6060
Steven Kennedy, Director
Alan Varela, Manager

State Organizations & Government Agencies/New Mexico

1726 Office of Indian Affairs: Indian Area Agency on Aging
228 E Palace Avenue
Santa Fe, NM 87501-2000   505-827-6440
                             Fax: 505-827-6435
Gloria Martinez, Director
Brian Lee, Executive Director

1727 Quality Senior Services
PO Box 969
Mesilla, NM 88046   505-523-1782
                             Fax: 505-526-7723
Steve Duran, Executive Director

1728 RSVP Alamogordo City
1201 Puerto Rico Avenue
Alamogordo, NM 88310-5529   505-437-8703
                             Fax: 505-439-4160
              e-mail: jquintana@ci.alamogorda.nm.us
Joe Quintana, RSVP Director
G L Wiley, Owner
Suzanne Montegomery, SCP Coodinator

The Retired and Senior Volunteer Program (RSVP) provides opportunities for people 55 and over to make a difference in their community through volunteer service. RSVP volunteers contribute anywhere from a few to over forty hours a week, serving though schools, day care centers, police departments, hospitals and other nonprofit and public organizations to help meet critical community needs. RSVP offers maximum flexibility and choice to its volunteers. RSVP matches the personal interests and skills to older Americans with opportunities to help solve community problems and offer supplemental insurance while on duty, on-the-job training from the agency or organization where volunteers are placed.

1729 RSVP Artesia
PO Box 1310
Artesia, NM 88211-1310   505-746-3655
                             Fax: 505-746-3886
                 e-mail: acqretired@qwest.net
Louise Stuart, Contact

The Retired and Senior Volunteer Program (RSVP) provides opportunities for people 55 and over to make a difference in their community through volunteer service. RSVP volunteers contribute anywhere from a few to over forty hours a week, serving though schools, day care centers, police departments, hospitals and other nonprofit and public organizations to help meet critical community needs. RSVP offers maximum flexibility and choice to its volunteers. RSVP matches the personal interests and skills to older Americans with opportunities to help solve community problems and offer supplemental insurance while on duty, on-the-job training from the agency or organization where volunteers are placed.

1730 RSVP Carlsbad City
2814 San Jose Boulevard
PO Box 716
Carlsbad, NM 88220   505-887-0871
                             Fax: 505-885-1101
              e-mail: jmethola@carlsbadnm.com
Josie Methola, Director

Provides opportunities for people 55 and over to make a difference in their community through volunteer service. RSVP volunteers contribute anywhere from a few to over forty hours a week, serving through schools, day care centers, police departments, hospitals and other nonprofit and public organizations to help meet critical community needs. RSVP matches the personal interests and skills of older Americans with opportunities to help solve commmunity problems and offers supplemental insurance while on duty, on-the-job training from the agency or organization where volunteers are placed.

1731 RSVP Chaves County
131 W 2nd Street
Roswell, NM 88201-4703   505-623-3960
                             Fax: 505-624-6870
Ida Montoya, Executive Director

The Retired and Senior Volunteer Program (RSVP) provides opportunities for people 55 and over to make a difference in their community through volunteer service. RSVP volunteers contribute anywhere from a few to over forty hours a week, serving though schools, day care centers, police departments, hospitals and other nonprofit and public organizations to help meet critical community needs. RSVP offers maximum flexibility and choice to its volunteers. RSVP matches the personal interests and skills to older Americans with opportunities to help solve community problems and offer supplemental insurance while on duty, on-the-job training from the agency or organization where volunteers are placed.

1732 RSVP Curry County
816 N Main Street
Clovis, NM 88101-6661   505-763-6009
                             Fax: 505-763-3656
Lucinda Bonney, Executive Director

The Retired and Senior Volunteer Program (RSVP) provides opportunities for people 55 and over to make a difference in their community through volunteer service. RSVP volunteers contribute anywhere from a few to over forty hours a week, serving though schools, day care centers, police departments, hospitals and other nonprofit and public organizations to help meet critical community needs. RSVP offers maximum flexibility and choice to its volunteers. RSVP matches the personal interests and skills to older Americans with opportunities to help solve community problems and offer supplemental insurance while on duty, on-the-job training from the agency or organization where volunteers are placed.

1733 RSVP Grant County
PO Box 2990
Silver City, NM 88062-2990   505-388-2523
                             Fax: 505-388-5118
                  e-mail: grantrsvp@zianet.com
Kathy Gallardo, Contact

The Retired and Senior Volunteer Program (RSVP) provides opportunities for people 55 and over to make a difference in their community through volunteer service. RSVP volunteers contribute anywhere from a few to over forty hours a week, serving though schools, day care centers, police departments, hospitals and other nonprofit and public organizations to help meet critical community needs. RSVP offers maximum flexibility and choice to its volunteers. RSVP matches the personal interests and skills to older Americans with opportunities to help solve community problems and offer supplemental insurance while on duty, on-the-job training from the agency or organization where volunteers are placed.

1734 RSVP Los Alamos
1000 Oppenheimer Drive
Los Alamos, NM 87544-2386   505-662-8920
                             Fax: 505-661-7677
                 http://www.losalamos.com/lasc
Pauline Schneider, Executive Director

The Retired and Senior Volunteer Program (RSVP) provides opportunities for people 55 and over to make a difference in their community through volunteer service. RSVP volunteers contribute anywhere from a few to over forty hours a week, serving though schools, day care centers, police departments, hospitals and other nonprofit and public organizations to help meet critical community needs. RSVP offers maximum flexibility and choice to its volunteers. RSVP matches the personal interests and skills to older Americans with opportunities to help solve community problems and offer supplemental insurance while on duty, on-the-job training from the agency or organization where volunteers are placed.

1735 RSVP Luna County
800 S Granite Street
Deming, NM 88030-4566   505-546-8823
                             Fax: 505-546-4076

State Organizations & Government Agencies/New Mexico

The Retired and Senior Volunteer Program (RSVP) provides opportunities for people 55 and over to make a difference in their community through volunteer service. RSVP volunteers contribute anywhere from a few to over forty hours a week, serving though schools, day care centers, police departments, hospitals and other nonprofit and public organizations to help meet critical community needs. RSVP offers maximum flexibility and choice to its volunteers. RSVP matches the personal interests and skills to older Americans with opportunities to help solve community problems and offer supplemental insurance while on duty, on-the-job training from the agency or organization where volunteers are placed.

1736 RSVP McKinley County Francis Adult Care Services
2407 Boyd
Suite 11
Gallup, NM 87301   505-722-3565
                                           Fax: 505-863-7987
e-mail: francesadultcare@cnetco.com
Rachel A Sanchez, Director

We have about 50 volunteers working environmentally. There are many beautification projects underway, one of which has our seniors beautifying a section of land (each year) at UNM Gallup Branch College by planting trees, shrubs, flowers, etc. Others recycle and educate at museums.

1737 RSVP Metropolitan
714 7th Street SW
Albuquerque, NM 87102-3814   505-764-1612
                                           Fax: 505-764-1620
Barbara Baca, Manager

The Retired and Senior Volunteer Program (RSVP) provides opportunities for people 55 and over to make a difference in their community through volunteer service. RSVP volunteers contribute anywhere from a few to over forty hours a week, serving though schools, day care centers, police departments, hospitals and other nonprofit and public organizations to help meet critical community needs. RSVP offers maximum flexibility and choice to its volunteers. RSVP matches the personal interests and skills to older Americans with opportunities to help solve community problems and offer supplemental insurance while on duty, on-the-job training from the agency or organization where volunteers are placed.

1738 RSVP Mid Rio Grand
100 S Main Street
Artesia, NM 88211   505-746-3655
                                           Fax: 505-746-3886

The Retired and Senior Volunteer Program (RSVP) provides opportunities for people 55 and over to make a difference in their community through volunteer service. RSVP volunteers contribute anywhere from a few to over forty hours a week, serving though schools, day care centers, police departments, hospitals and other nonprofit and public organizations to help meet critical community needs. RSVP offers maximum flexibility and choice to its volunteers. RSVP matches the personal interests and skills to older Americans with opportunities to help solve community problems and offer supplemental insurance while on duty, on-the-job training from the agency or organization where volunteers are placed.

1739 RSVP San Juan County
4601 College Boulevard
Farmington, NM 87402-4609   505-566-3782
                                           Fax: 505-566-3122

The Retired and Senior Volunteer Program (RSVP) provides opportunities for people 55 and over to make a difference in their community through volunteer service. RSVP volunteers contribute anywhere from a few to over forty hours a week, serving though schools, day care centers, police departments, hospitals and other nonprofit and public organizations to help meet critical community needs. RSVP offers maximum flexibility and choice to its volunteers. RSVP matches the personal interests and skills to older Americans with opportunities to help solve community problems and offer supplemental insurance while on duty, on-the-job training from the agency or organization where volunteers are placed.

1740 RSVP Sandoval
PO Box 40
Bernalillo, NM 87004   505-771-7188
                                           Fax: 505-867-7259

The Retired and Senior Volunteer Program (RSVP) provides opportunities for people 55 and over to make a difference in their community through volunteer service. RSVP volunteers contribute anywhere from a few to over forty hours a week, serving though schools, day care centers, police departments, hospitals and other nonprofit and public organizations to help meet critical community needs. RSVP offers maximum flexibility and choice to its volunteers. RSVP matches the personal interests and skills to older Americans with opportunities to help solve community problems and offer supplemental insurance while on duty, on-the-job training from the agency or organization where volunteers are placed.

1741 RSVP Santa Fe City
PO Box 909, Senior Services
Santa Fe, NM 87504-0909   505-955-4760
                                           Fax: 505-955-4765
e-mail: kwslater-huff@santafenm.gov
http://www.santafenm.gov
Kristen Slater-Huff, RSVP Director
Cristy Montoya, Program Secretary

The Retired Senior Volunteer Program (RSVP) provides opportunities for people 55 and over to make a difference in their community through volunteer service. RSVP volunteers contribute anywhere from a few to over forty hours a week, serving thourgh schools, hospitals and other organizations to help meet critical community needs. RSVP offers maximum flexibility and choice to its volunteers. RSVP matches the personal interests and skills to older Americans with opportunities to help solve community problems and offer supplemental insurance while on duty, on-the-job training from the agency or organization where volunteers are placed.

1742 RSVP Sierra County
360 W 4th Avenue
Room 119
Truth or Consequences, NM 87901-2355   505-894-3045
                                           Fax: 505-894-3065
e-mail: jennieb@riolink.com
Jennie Bustamante, Project Director

The Retired and Senior Volunteer Program (RSVP) provides opportunities for people 55 and over to make a difference in their community through volunteer service. RSVP volunteers contribute anywhere from a few to over forty hours a week, serving though schools, day care centers, police departments, hospitals and other nonprofit and public organizations to help meet critical community needs. RSVP offers maximum flexibility and choice to its volunteers. RSVP matches the personal interests and skills to older Americans with opportunities to help solve community problems and offer supplemental insurance while on duty, on-the-job training from the agency or organization where volunteers are placed.

1743 RSVP Village of Ruidoso
501 Sudderth Drive
Ruidoso, NM 88345-6013   505-257-4565
                                           Fax: 505-630-9805
e-mail: vorscenter@zianet.com
Sandee K Jourden, Director

The Retired and Senior Volunteer Program (RSVP) provides opportunities for people 55 and over to make a difference in their community through volunteer service. RSVP volunteers contribute anywhere from a few to over forty hours a week, serving though schools, day care centers, police departments, hospitals and other nonprofit and public organizations to help meet critical community needs. RSVP offers maximum flexibility and choice to its volunteers. RSVP matches the personal interests and skills to older Americans with opportunities to help solve community problems and offer supplemental insurance while on duty, on-the-job training from the agency or organization where volunteers are placed.

State Organizations & Government Agencies/New York

1744 Railroad Retirement Board: New Mexico
300 San Mateo Boulevard NE
Suite 401
Albuquerque, NM 87108-1503
505-346-6405
Fax: 505-346-6407
e-mail: albuquerque@rrb.gov
Barbara E Aylaian, Representative

1745 Retired Senior Volunteer Program of Rio Grande
975 S Mesquite Street
Las Cruces, NM 88001-3670
505-528-3035
Fax: 505-528-3351

1746 Social Security: Santa Fe Disability Determination
604 W San Mateo Road
Santa Fe, NM 87505-4143
505-827-3500
Fax: 505-827-3746
e-mail: terryb@oscar.state.nm.us
Terry Brigance, Director
Domingo P Martinez, Manager

1747 Southwestern New Mexico Area: Agency on Aging
1151 Heather Street
Las Cruces, NM 88005
505-541-4200
800-497-3646
Fax: 505-541-4234
http://www.zianet.com/snmaa
Art Bardwell, Director

New York

1748 Albany County Department for Aging and the Handicapped
162 Washington Avenue
Albany, NY 12210-2304
518-447-7198
518-447-7177
Fax: 518-472-6923
Richard D Healy, Director
Vincent W Colonno, Manager

1749 Allegany County Office for the Aging
17 Court Street
Belmont, NY 14813-1001
585-268-9390
Fax: 585-268-9657
Kimberly Toot, Director

1750 Association of Belltel Retirees
PO Box 33
Cold Spring Harbor, NY 11724
800-261-9222
e-mail: association@belltelretirees.org
CW Jones, Contact

1751 Birchwood Volunteers In Partnership
4800 Bear Road
Liverpool, NY 13088-4604
315-457-9946
Fax: 315-457-8290
http://www.elderwood.com
Sharon Snyder, Director Volunteer Services
Kristin Russell, Administrator

1752 Broome County Office for Aging
PO Box 1766
Binghamton, NY 13902-1766
607-778-2411
Fax: 607-778-2316
e-mail: ofa@co.broome.ny.us
http://www.gcbroomecounty.com
Kathleen Bunnell, Director

1753 Buffalo Senior Center
PO Box 941
Buffalo, NY 82834
307-684-9551
Fax: 307-684-5585
e-mail: mwilde@wyoming.com
Bobbie Walseth, Executive Director

Community service organization providing congregate and home delivered meals, transportation, social activity coordination, adult day care and home care, nursing, and aging resource center.

1754 Care Givers of the Elderly Support Group
139 E Avenue
Suite 201
Rochester, NY 14604-2615
585-325-3145
Patricia Woods, Executive Director

1755 Cattaraugus County Department of Aging
1701 Lincoln Avenue
Suite 7610
Olean, NY 14760-1121
716-373-8032
800-462-2901
Fax: 585-372-4734
TDD 716-373-8032
John Searles, Director
Cherianne Wold, Manager

1756 Cayuga County Office of the Aging
160 Genesee Street
Auburn, NY 13021-3483
315-253-1226
Fax: 315-253-1151
Joan Gallo, Director
Nelsa Selover, Executive Director

1757 Center for the Study of Aging of Albany
106 Madison Avenue
Albany, NY 12208-3695
518-465-6927
Fax: 518-462-1339
e-mail: iapaas@aol.com
http://www.members.aol.com/iapaas
Sara Harris, Executive Director

Participants include behavioral scientists, educators, gerontologists, physicians, and other health professionals. Promotes education, research, and training; provides leadership in the field of health and fitness for older people. Includes: programs for volunteers and professionals in aging, gerontology, geriatrics, wellness, physical fitness, and mental health; consultant services include adult day care, nutrition, physical and mental fitness, nursing home, housing, and retirement; speakers' bureau. Develops national and international conferences on health, fitness, and prevention. Provides expert assistance in research, institutional and community program development, planning, and organization; offers consultation addressing the development of library resource centers and collections of books on aging. Conducts seminars and offers information and referral services.

1758 Chautauqua County Office for the Aging
7 N Erie Street
Mayville, NY 14757-1027
716-753-4471
Fax: 716-753-4477
Katie Smith, Director

1759 Chemung County Office for the Aging
425 Pennsylvania Avenue
Elmira, NY 14904-1762
607-737-5520
Fax: 607-737-5521
TDD 607-737-5347
Samuel David, Director

1760 Chenango County Area: Agency on Aging
5 Court Street
Norwich, NY 13815-1695
607-337-1414
Fax: 607-336-6551
Denise Newvine, Director
William E Evans, Manager

State Organizations & Government Agencies/New York

1761 Clinton County Office for the Aging
135 Margaret Street
Suite 105
Plattsburgh, NY 12901-2994
518-565-4620
Fax: 518-565-4812
http://www.clintoncountygov.com
Crystal L Carter, Director

1762 Columbia County Office for the Aging
325 Columbia Street
Hudson, NY 12534-1905
518-828-4258
Fax: 518-822-0010
e-mail: kal@govt.co.columbia.ny.us
Kit Ali, Director
Kathy Revene, Administrator

1763 Corporate Volunteers of New York
61 Chambers Street
New York, NY 10007-1208
212-332-4075
Peggy Crisalli, President
Corporate volunteers.

1764 Cortland County Area: Agency on Aging
60 Central Avenue
Cortland, NY 13045-2795
607-753-5060
Fax: 607-758-5528
e-mail: cdeloff@cortland-co.org
http://www.cortland-co.org
Carol DeLoff, Director
Services include: informative assistance, advocacy, legal services, senior centers, meals on wheels, benefits counseling, health insurance assistance, in-home services, volunteer services, home repairs, recreation, energy programs, consumer information.

1765 Delaware County Office for the Aging
6 Court Street
Delhi, NY 13753-1002
607-746-6333
Fax: 607-746-6227
Tom Briggs, Director

1766 Department of Aging & Youth
1519 Nye Road
Suite 3000
Lyons, NY 14489-9133
315-946-5624
Fax: 315-946-5649
e-mail: aging@co.wayne.ny.us
http://www.co.wayne.ny.us
Penny Shockley, Director
Martin Williams, Deputy Director
Kathy McGonigal, Executive Director

1767 Disability Determination Services
PO Box 165
Albany, NY 12201
518-473-9320
800-223-0032
Fax: 518-473-9286
James Caseo, Director

1768 Division of Disability Determinations
300 Cadman Plaza W
13th Floor
Brooklyn, NY 11201-2701
718-522-8015
Fax: 718-522-8272
Sandra Wapner, Manager

1769 Division of Disability Determinations-Endicott
PO Box 9009
Endicott, NY 13761-9009
607-785-9398
Fax: 716-741-4017
Wayne Davison, Owner

1770 Erie County Department of Senior Services
95 Franklin Street
Buffalo, NY 14202-3968
716-858-8526
Fax: 716-858-7259
TDD 800-622-1220
Pamela Krawezyk, Commissioner
Patricia Watson, Director Information/Referral

1771 Essex County Office for the Aging
100 Court Street
PO Box 217
Elizabethtown, NY 12932-3695
518-873-3695
800-562-3660
Fax: 518-873-3784
http://www.co.essex.ny.us
Patricia Bashaw, Director
The Essex County Office for the Aging develops and carries out a comprehensive and coordinated system of health, education, employment, and social services for the District's elderly population, who are 60 years of age and older.

1772 Fort Plain Senior Center
204 Canal Street
Fort Plain, NY 13339-1119
518-993-3432

1773 Franklin County Office for the Aging
125 Catherine Street
Malone, NY 12953-1826
518-481-1526
800-397-8686
Fax: 518-481-1635
Joel T Saumier, Director
The purpose of the Office on Aging is to provide centralized access to diverse programs and individualized services for older adults and their families so they can preserve their independence and quality of life.

1774 Friends and Relatives of Institutionalized Aged
18 John Street
Suite 905
New York, NY 10038-5118
212-732-4455
Fax: 212-732-6945
e-mail: fria@fria.org
http://www.fria.org
Amy Paul, Executive Director
To assist relatives and friends in finding long-term care facilities for older persons and obtaining good care for them in nursing homes.

1775 Fulton County Office for the Aging
19 N William Street
Johnstown, NY 12095-2115
518-736-5650
Fax: 518-762-0698
e-mail: asinglepl@telnet.net
http://www.fcofa.org
Kathryn Leitch, Director
Programs and services for older adults and their families. Meals, transportation, home care, case management, long-term care, employment, housing, information, and caregivers services.

1776 Genesee County Office for the Aging
2 Bank Street
Batavia, NY 14020-2202
585-343-1611
Fax: 585-344-8559
Connie Boyd, Director
Pamela Whitmore, Manager

1777 Gray Panthers of New York
165 W 86th Street
New York, NY 10024-3412
212-799-7572
Fax: 202-737-1160
e-mail: dbrown30@nyc.rr.com
http://www.graypanthers.org
Edna Greg, Director

State Organizations & Government Agencies/New York

Quality of life issues: Universal health care, secure and comfortable housing, employment and educational opportunities for all.

1778 Gray Panthers of Suffolk County
PO Box 1395
Ronkonkoma, NY 11779
631-471-6614
Fax: 202-737-1160
e-mail: info@graypanthers.org
http://www.graypanthers.org
Blanche Mulholland, Co-Director
George Reilly, Co-Director

1779 Greater Rochester Area Partnership for the Elderly
1530 E Avenue
Rochester, NY 14610-1670
585-256-4351
Fax: 585-256-4352
e-mail: info@grapelder.org
http://www.grapelder.org
Beverly McChesney, Manager

Professionals and interested persons who aspire to improve the quality of services for older people. Our three main objectives are professional development, networking, public and social policy advocacy.

1780 Greene County Aging Services
159 Jefferson Heights
Suite B1
Catskill, NY 12414-1237
518-943-5332
Fax: 518-943-0841

1781 Greene County Department for Aging
19 S Jefferson Avenue
Apt A
Catskill, NY 12414-2128
518-943-4250
Fax: 518-843-0841
Thomas Yandeau, Director
Michele Guerin, Manager

1782 Herkimer County Office for the Aging
109 Mary Street
Suite 1101
Herkimer, NY 13350-2924
315-867-1195
Fax: 315-867-1109
e-mail: ncofa@herkimercounty.org
http://www.herkimercounty.org
Mary Scanlon, Director

1783 Jefferson County Office for Aging
250 Arsenal Street
Watertown, NY 13601-2546
315-785-3191
Fax: 315-785-5095
Anthony Bova, Director
Steven Binion, Executive Director

1784 Jewish Association for Services for the Aged Manhattan District Service
132 W 31st Street
Floor 15
New York, NY 10001-3406
212-273-5200
Fax: 212-695-4206
http://www.jasa.org
David Warren, President
Aileen Gitelson, Chief Executive Officer

JASA's mission is to sustain and enrich the lives of the aging in New York metropolitan area so that they can remain in the community with dignity and autonomy.

1785 Lewis County Office for the Aging
PO Box 408
Lowville, NY 13367
315-376-5313
Fax: 315-376-5105
Thomas F Kington, Director
Michael Gunn, Executive Director

1786 Lighthouse International Ruth M. Shellens Library
111 E 59th Street
New York, NY 10022-1264
212-821-9682
Fax: 212-821-9687
e-mail: gaks@lighthouse.org
http://www.lighthouse.org
Gloria Aks, Director Information Resources

Research and education related rehabilitation services, orientation and mobility. Independent living services.

1787 Livingston County Office for Aging
8 Livingston County Campus
Mount Morris, NY 14510-1197
585-243-7520
Fax: 585-658-2962
Kaaren Smith, Director

1788 Madison County Office for the Aging
138 Dominic Bruno Boulevard
Canastota, NY 13032-3528
315-684-9424
Fax: 315-684-9597
Anthony Joseph, Director

1789 Meals on Wheels of Buffalo and Erie County Foundation
100 E Cascey Drive
Buffalo, NY 14206
716-822-2002
Thomas A Kurtz, Contact
Richard J Gehring, President

1790 Metropolitan Commission on Aging
421 Montgomery Street
13th Floor
Syracuse, NY 13202-2923
315-435-2362
Fax: 315-435-3129
Dale Parsons, Director
Marilyn L Pinsky, Manager

1791 Monroe County Office for the Aging and Adult Services
111 Westfall Road
Room 652
Rochester, NY 14620-4603
585-753-6280
Fax: 585-753-6281
http://www.monroecounty.gov
Corinda Crossdale, Director

The goal for the Office of the Aging and Adult Services is to promote a safe and independent lifestyle through timely and responsive systems of protective services, long-term care, quality nutrition and supportive in-home services through a consumer-focused and coordinated service delivery system that protects, supports, and advocates for older residents of Monroe County.

1792 Montgomery County Office for the Aging
380 Guy Park Avenue
Amsterdam, NY 12010-1055
518-843-2300
Fax: 518-843-7478
Lorraine Suliveres, Director
Eileen Broyles, Executive Director

1793 Nassau County Department of Senior Citizen Affairs
60 Charles Lindbergh Boulevard
Suite 260
Uniondale, NY 11553-3691
516-227-8987
Fax: 516-571-5978
e-mail: seniors@nassaucountyny.gov
http://http://co.nassau.ny.us/srcit/index.htm
Sharon Mullon, Commissioner

As the Area Agency on Aging for Nassau County, the Department provides more than 90 programs and services for the County's 257,000 senior citizens and their caregivers. These programs are designed to maintain seniors' safety in their homes and communities for as long as possible.

State Organizations & Government Agencies/New York

1794 New York City Department for the Aging
2 Lafayette Street
New York, NY 10007-1307
212-442-1322
Fax: 212-442-1095

Herbert W Stupp, Manager

1795 New York Client Assistance Program
99 Washington Avenue
Suite 1002
Albany, NY 12210-2810
518-473-7378
Fax: 518-474-2652
http://www.cac.state.ny.us

1796 New York Commission on Quality of Care and Advocacy for Persons with Disabilities
401 State Street
Schenectady, NY 12305-2397
518-381-7102
800-624-4143
Fax: 518-388-2860
http://www.cqcapd.state.ny.us
TDD 800-624-4143

Gary O'Brien, Chair

The New York State Commission on Quality of Care for the Mentally Disabled (CQC) and the New York State Office of Advocate for Persons with Disabilities (OAP wD) have been merged to form a new agency, the New York State Commission on Quality of Care and Advocacy for Persons with Disabilities (CQCAPD). CQCAPD serves people with mental disabilities and their families by providing independent oversight of the quality and cost-effectiveness of services provided by all mental hygiene programs in New York State.

1797 New York Department of Aging
112 State Street
Room 710
Albany, NY 12207-2018
518-447-7177
Fax: 518-447-7188
e-mail: vcolonno@albanycounty.com

Jane Gould, Director
Vincent Colonno, Manager

The mission of the New York State Office for the Aging is to help older New Yorkers to be as independent as possible for as long as possible through advocacy, development and delivery of cost effective policies, programs and services which support and empower the elderly and thier families, in partnership with the network of public and private organizations which serve them.

1798 New York Department of Taxation & Finance
WA Harriman Campus
Albany, NY 12227
518-457-3512
Fax: 518-457-2486
http://www.tax.state.ny.us

Linda Di Bernardo, Manager

1799 New York Developmental Disability Planning Council
155 Washington Avenue
Second Floor
Albany, NY 12210
518-486-7505
800-395-3372
Fax: 518-402-3505
e-mail: ddpc@ddpc.state.ny.us
http://www.ddpc.state.ny.us

Sheila M Carey, Executive Director
Anna Lobosco, Deputy Executive Director
Thomas Lee, Public Information Officer

The New York State Developmental Disabilities Planning Council (DDPC), in partnership with individuals with developmental disabilities, their families and communities, provides leadership by promoting policies, plans, and practices that: affirm dignity, value and worth; support full participation in society; uphold equality and self-determination; and promote access to research and information needed for informed-decision-making for all individuals with developmental disabilities and their families.

1800 New York Division of Veterans Affairs
Empire State Plaza
Albany, NY 12223
518-474-6784
800-635-6534
Fax: 518-473-0379

George Basher, Executive Director

1801 New York Office on Aging
2 Empire State Plaza
Albany, NY 12223-1251
518-474-5731
800-342-9871
Fax: 518-474-0608

Neal F Lane, Executive Directors

1802 New York State Association of Area Agencies on Aging
272 Broadway
Albany, NY 12204-2737
518-449-7080
Fax: 518-449-7055
e-mail: office@nysaaaa.org
http://www.nysaaaa.org

1803 New York State Coalition for the Aging
144 Hudson Avenue
Albany, NY 12210-1802
518-465-0641
Fax: 518-465-0405

Kathryn H Stoddard, Executive Director

Training, technical assistance, advocacy for senior services in NYS.

1804 New York State Commission for the Blind
40 N Pearl Street
Albany, NY 12207-2729
518-434-5973
Fax: 518-474-5819

Jack Ryan, Director
Thomas Roberts, Contact
Margaret Malicki, Manager

Offers services for the totally blind, legally blind, visually impaired, mentally retarded blind and more with health, counseling, educational, recreational, rehabilitation, computer training and professional training services.

1805 New York State Division of Disability Determinations
PO Box 5030
Buffalo, NY 14205-5030
716-847-5007
800-726-1353
http://www.otda.state.ny.us

Mario Musso, Director

The New York State Division of Disability Determinations adjudicates the claims of persons filing for disability benefits with the Social Security Administration.

1806 New York State Intergenerational Network
Generations Child and Adult Day Care
230 Coldwater Road
Rochester, NY 14624-2444
585-272-2100
Fax: 585-429-2100

Eve Moses, Executive Officer

1807 New York State Office for the Aging: Senior Citizens Hotline
Agency
Building 2
Albany, NY 12223
518-434-5973
800-342-9871
Fax: 518-474-1398

Margaret Malicki, Manager

Provides information on statewide services for the elderly.

State Organizations & Government Agencies/New York

1808 New York State Office of Advocate for Persons with Disabilities
1 Empire State Plaza
Suite 1001
Albany, NY 12223-1100
518-474-5567
800-943-2323
Fax: 518-473-6005
e-mail: disability information@oapwd.state.ny.us
http://www.state.ny.us.disabledadvocate
Gary O'Brien, Manager
Cathy Gonzalez, Information/Referral
Richard Warner, Contact

New York regional technical assistance provider.

1809 New York State Office of Mental Health
44 Holland Avenue
Albany, NY 12229
518-474-2568
800-597-8481
Fax: 518-474-2149
http://www.omh.state.ny.us
Sharon Carpinello, RN, PhD, Commissioner

Promoting the mental health of all New Yorkers with a particular focus on providing hope and recovery for adults with serious mental illness and children with serious emotional disturbances.

1810 New York Teachers Retirement System
10 Corporate Woods Drive
Albany, NY 12211-2395
518-465-4400
800-782-0289
Bill Phillips, Administrator

1811 Niagara County Office for the Aging
100 Davison Road
Lockport, NY 14094-3319
716-439-7600
Fax: 716-439-7661
Shirley Wayda, Director
Anthony Restaino, Manager

1812 Oneida County Office for the Aging
235 Elizabeth Street
Utica, NY 13501-2211
315-798-5456
Fax: 315-798-6444
Kenneth Abramczyk, Director
Michael Romano, Executive Director

1813 Ontario County Office for the Aging
3010 County Complex Drive
Canandaigua, NY 14424-9502
585-396-4040
Fax: 585-396-7490
e-mail: onofa@co.ontario.ny.us
http://www.co.ontario.ny.us/aging
Helen Sherman, Director

1814 Orange County Office for Aging
30 Matthews Street
Suite 201
Goshen, NY 10924-1985
845-291-2150
Fax: 845-291-2182
Nick Gerten, Director

1815 Orleans County Office for the Aging
14016 Route 31
Albion, NY 14411-9382
585-589-7000
Fax: 585-589-3193
e-mail: aging@orleansny.com
http://www.orleansny.com
Pamela S Canham, Assistant Director

Services to the elderly and their caregivers.

1816 Oswego County Office for the Aging
70 Bunner Street
Oswego, NY 13126-3357
315-349-3484
Fax: 315-349-3231
Mary Robbins, Director
Lawrence Schmidt, Manager

1817 Otsego County Office for the Aging
197 Main Street
Cooperstown, NY 13326-1128
607-547-4208
Fax: 607-547-6492
James Konstanty, Manager

1818 Perinton Retired Men's Club
1350 Turk Hill Road
Fairport, NY 14450-8795
585-223-5050
Fax: 585-223-4045
Bonnie Nohe, Assistant Senior Supervisor
James Donahue, Manager

1819 Prevent Blindness America New York City Division
149 Madison Avenue
Room 805
New York, NY 10016-6713
212-980-2020
Fax: 203-598-0584

Individuals interested in preventing blindness and preserving sight through research and education programs.

1820 Putnam County Office for Aging
110 Old Route 6
Building A
Carmel, NY 10512-2119
845-225-1034
Fax: 845-225-1915
William Huestis, Director

1821 RIDE Retired Individuals Driving Elderly
721 Columbia Street
Hudson, NY 12534-2509
518-822-8222
Fax: 518-828-0251
e-mail: jsvid@columbiaopportunitie.org
http://mbeigel@columbiaopportunities.org
Marcella Beigel, Director
Zoe Sena, Program Specialist/"R.I.D.E"

Volunteer transportation service for seniors only to health related destinations and appointments. Our website is www.rsvpcolumbiaopportunities.org

1822 RSVP Auburn
PO Box 5
Auburn, NY 13021
315-255-1733
Fax: 315-252-3669
Catherine M Catto, Executive Director

The Retired and Senior Volunteer Program (RSVP) provides opportunities for people 55 and over to make a difference in their community through volunteer service. RSVP volunteers contribute anywhere from a few to over forty hours a week, serving though schools, day care centers, police departments, hospitals and other nonprofit and public organizations to help meet critical community needs. RSVP offers maximum flexibility and choice to its volunteers. RSVP matches the personal interests and skills to older Americans with opportunities to help solve community problems and offer supplemental insurance while on duty, on-the-job training from the agency or organization where volunteers are placed.

1823 RSVP Broome
230 Main Street
Binghamton, NY 13905-2610
607-231-0726
Fax: 607-797-6188
Tammy Hodges, Executive Director

State Organizations & Government Agencies/New York

The Retired and Senior Volunteer Program (RSVP) provides opportunities for people 55 and over to make a difference in their community through volunteer service. RSVP volunteers contribute anywhere from a few to over forty hours a week, serving though schools, day care centers, police departments, hospitals and other nonprofit and public organizations to help meet critical community needs. RSVP offers maximum flexibility and choice to its volunteers. RSVP matches the personal interests and skills to older Americans with opportunities to help solve community problems and offer supplemental insurance while on duty, on-the-job training from the agency or organization where volunteers are placed.

1824 RSVP Capitol Region
135 Western Avenue
Albany, NY 12222
518-442-5585
Fax: 518-442-5326
Deborah Doolittle, Executive Director

The Retired and Senior Volunteer Program (RSVP) provides opportunities for people 55 and over to make a difference in their community through volunteer service. RSVP volunteers contribute anywhere from a few to over forty hours a week, serving though schools, day care centers, police departments, hospitals and other nonprofit and public organizations to help meet critical community needs. RSVP offers maximum flexibility and choice to its volunteers. RSVP matches the personal interests and skills to older Americans with opportunities to help solve community problems and offer supplemental insurance while on duty, on-the-job training from the agency or organization where volunteers are placed.

1825 RSVP Cattaraugus County
1701 Lincoln Avenue
Suite 7610
Olean, NY 14760-1121
716-373-8032
Fax: 716-372-4734
Cherianne Wold, Manager

The Retired and Senior Volunteer Program (RSVP) provides opportunities for people 55 and over to make a difference in their community through volunteer service. RSVP volunteers contribute anywhere from a few to over forty hours a week, serving though schools, day care centers, police departments, hospitals and other nonprofit and public organizations to help meet critical community needs. RSVP offers maximum flexibility and choice to its volunteers. RSVP matches the personal interests and skills to older Americans with opportunities to help solve community problems and offer supplemental insurance while on duty, on-the-job training from the agency or organization where volunteers are placed.

1826 RSVP Chautaqua
715 Falconer Street
Jamestown, NY 14701-1935
716-665-3038
Fax: 716-665-8073
Debra Basile, Executive Director

The Retired and Senior Volunteer Program (RSVP) provides opportunities for people 55 and over to make a difference in their community through volunteer service. RSVP volunteers contribute anywhere from a few to over forty hours a week, serving though schools, day care centers, police departments, hospitals and other nonprofit and public organizations to help meet critical community needs. RSVP offers maximum flexibility and choice to its volunteers. RSVP matches the personal interests and skills to older Americans with opportunities to help solve community problems and offer supplemental insurance while on duty, on-the-job training from the agency or organization where volunteers are placed.

1827 RSVP Chemung County
104 W 2nd Street
Elmira, NY 14901-2730
607-734-4161
Fax: 607-734-4166
Carol Lincoln, Manager

The Retired and Senior Volunteer Program (RSVP) provides opportunities for people 55 and over to make a difference in their community through volunteer service. RSVP volunteers contribute anywhere from a few to over forty hours a week, serving though schools, day care centers, police departments, hospitals and other nonprofit and public organizations to help meet critical community needs. RSVP offers maximum flexibility and choice to its volunteers. RSVP matches the personal interests and skills to older Americans with opportunities to help solve community problems and offer supplemental insurance while on duty, on-the-job training from the agency or organization where volunteers are placed.

1828 RSVP Chenago County
44 W Main Street
Norwich, NY 13815
607-336-6414
Fax: 607-336-6415
e-mail: rsvp@ofcinc.org
http://www.ofcinc.org
Linda Campbell, Program Director

the retired and senior volunteer program (rsvp) provides opportunities for peopel 55 and over to make a difference in thier community through volunteers service in non-profit agencies & organizations. RSVP volunteers decide how muh they want to serve. Some volunteer service opportunities are: food pantries and soup kitchens, thrift stores, animal shelter, museums, libraries, nursing homes and hospitals, senior meal delivery, Habitat for Humanity.

1829 RSVP Clinton County
16 Flynn Avenue
Plattsburgh, NY 12901-3742
518-566-0944
Fax: 518-566-0945
Sandy Sexton, Manager

The Retired and Senior Volunteer Program (RSVP) provides opportunities for people 55 and over to make a difference in their community through volunteer service. RSVP volunteers contribute anywhere from a few to over forty hours a week, serving though schools, day care centers, police departments, hospitals and other nonprofit and public organizations to help meet critical community needs. RSVP offers maximum flexibility and choice to its volunteers. RSVP matches the personal interests and skills to older Americans with opportunities to help solve community problems and offer supplemental insurance while on duty, on-the-job training from the agency or organization where volunteers are placed.

1830 RSVP Columbia County
721 Columbia Street
Hudson, NY 12534-2509
518-828-0251
Fax: 518-828-4614
e-mail: coirsvp@mronline.net
Marcella Beigel, Director

The Retired and Senior Volunteer Program (RSVP) provides opportunities for people 55 and over to make a difference in their community through volunteer service. RSVP volunteers contribute anywhere from a few to over forty hours a week, serving though schools, day care centers, police departments, hospitals and other nonprofit and public organizations to help meet critical community needs. RSVP offers maximum flexibility and choice to its volunteers. RSVP matches the personal interests and skills to older Americans with opportunities to help solve community problems and offer supplemental insurance while on duty, on-the-job training from the agency or organization where volunteers are placed.

1831 RSVP Cortland
10 Central Avenue
Cortland, NY 13045-2795
607-753-5057
Fax: 607-756-3478
e-mail: ccolasurdo@cortland-co.org
Cindy Colasurdo, Contact

State Organizations & Government Agencies/New York

The Retired and Senior Volunteer Program (RSVP) provides opportunities for people 55 and over to make a difference in their community through volunteer service. RSVP volunteers contribute anywhere from a few to over forty hours a week, serving though schools, day care centers, police departments, hospitals and other nonprofit and public organizations to help meet critical community needs. RSVP offers maximum flexibility and choice to its volunteers. RSVP matches the personal interests and skills to older Americans with opportunities to help solve community problems and offer supplemental insurance while on duty, on-the-job training from the agency or organization where volunteers are placed.

1832 RSVP Dutchess County
9 Vassar Street
Poughkeepsie, NY 12601-3022
845-485-8170
Fax: 845-473-1674
e-mail: rsvprog@aol.com

Mary Scala, Director

Recruits people 55 years of age and older to do volunteer work for nonprofit agencies.

1833 RSVP Erie County
95 Franklin Street
Buffalo, NY 14202-3925
716-858-7548
Fax: 716-858-7259

Patricia Dowling, Executive Director

The Retired and Senior Volunteer Program (RSVP) provides opportunities for people 55 and over to make a difference in their community through volunteer service. RSVP volunteers contribute anywhere from a few to over forty hours a week, serving though schools, day care centers, police departments, hospitals and other nonprofit and public organizations to help meet critical community needs. RSVP offers maximum flexibility and choice to its volunteers. RSVP matches the personal interests and skills to older Americans with opportunities to help solve community problems and offer supplemental insurance while on duty, on-the-job training from the agency or organization where volunteers are placed.

1834 RSVP Essex County
38 Park Place
Suite 3
Port Henry, NY 12974-1344
518-546-3565
Fax: 518-546-3079
e-mail: rsvp@bluemoo.net

Patsy McCaughin, Director
Dusti Pratt, Program Assistant
Annabelle Waite, Office Aide

The Retired and Senior Volunteer Program (RSVP) provides opportunities for people 55 and over to make a difference in their community through volunteer service. RSVP volunteers contribute anywhere from a few to over forty hours a week, serving though schools, day care centers, police departments, hospitals and other nonprofit and public organizations to help meet critical community needs. RSVP offers maximum flexibility and choice to its volunteers. RSVP matches the personal interests and skills to older Americans with opportunities to help solve community problems and offer supplemental insurance while on duty, on-the-job training from the agency or organization where volunteers are placed.

1835 RSVP Franklin County
355 West Main Street
Malone, NY 12953-1817
518-481-1528
Fax: 518-481-1878
e-mail: afleury@co.franklin.ny.us

Annette Fleury, Contact

Provides opportunities for people 55 and over to make a difference in their community through volunteer service. RSVP volunteers contribute anywhere from a few to over forty hours a week, serving through schools, day care centers, police departments, hospitals and other nonprofit and public organizations to help meet critical community needs. RSVP matches the personal interests and skills of older Americans with opportunities to help solve community problems and offers supplemental insurance while on duty, on-the-job training from the agency or organization where the volunteers are placed.

1836 RSVP Genesee County
2 Bank Street
Batavia, NY 14020-2202
585-343-1611
Fax: 585-344-8559

Pamela Whitmore, Manager

The Retired and Senior Volunteer Program (RSVP) provides opportunities for people 55 and over to make a difference in their community through volunteer service. RSVP volunteers contribute anywhere from a few to over forty hours a week, serving though schools, day care centers, police departments, hospitals and other nonprofit and public organizations to help meet critical community needs. RSVP offers maximum flexibility and choice to its volunteers. RSVP matches the personal interests and skills to older Americans with opportunities to help solve community problems and offer supplemental insurance while on duty, on-the-job training from the agency or organization where volunteers are placed.

1837 RSVP Greene County
159 Jefferson Heights
Catskill, NY 12414-1237
518-943-5332
Fax: 518-943-0841

The Retired and Senior Volunteer Program (RSVP) provides opportunities for people 55 and over to make a difference in their community through volunteer service. RSVP volunteers contribute anywhere from a few to over forty hours a week, serving though schools, day care centers, police departments, hospitals and other nonprofit and public organizations to help meet critical community needs. RSVP offers maximum flexibility and choice to its volunteers. RSVP matches the personal interests and skills to older Americans with opportunities to help solve community problems and offer supplemental insurance while on duty, on-the-job training from the agency or organization where volunteers are placed.

1838 RSVP Herkimer County
61 West Street
Ilion, NY 13357-1723
315-894-9917
Fax: 315-894-6313

David Bruce, Executive Director

The Retired and Senior Volunteer Program (RSVP) provides opportunities for people 55 and over to make a difference in their community through volunteer service. RSVP volunteers contribute anywhere from a few to over forty hours a week, serving though schools, day care centers, police departments, hospitals and other nonprofit and public organizations to help meet critical community needs. RSVP offers maximum flexibility and choice to its volunteers. RSVP matches the personal interests and skills to older Americans with opportunities to help solve community problems and offer supplemental insurance while on duty, on-the-job training from the agency or organization where volunteers are placed.

1839 RSVP Madison County
PO Box 1209
Morrisville, NY 13408-1209
315-655-2075
Fax: 315-684-9290

Liz Crofut, Manager

State Organizations & Government Agencies/New York

The Retired and Senior Volunteer Program (RSVP) provides opportunities for people 55 and over to make a difference in their community through volunteer service. RSVP volunteers contribute anywhere from a few to over forty hours a week, serving though schools, day care centers, police departments, hospitals and other nonprofit and public organizations to help meet critical community needs. RSVP offers maximum flexibility and choice to its volunteers. RSVP matches the personal interests and skills to older Americans with opportunities to help solve community problems and offer supplemental insurance while on duty, on-the-job training from the agency or organization where volunteers are placed.

1840 RSVP Monroe County
1900 S Clinton Avenue
Rochester, NY 14618-5621
585-244-8400
Fax: 585-244-9114
e-mail: bkosoff@lifespan-roch.org
Beth Kosoff, Contact
Ann Marie Cook, President

The Retired and Senior Volunteer Program (RSVP) provides opportunities for people 55 and over to make a difference in their community through volunteer service. RSVP volunteers contribute anywhere from a few to over forty hours a week, serving though schools, day care centers, police departments, hospitals and other nonprofit and public organizations to help meet critical community needs. RSVP offers maximum flexibility and choice to its volunteers. RSVP matches the personal interests and skills to older Americans with opportunities to help solve community problems and offer supplemental insurance while on duty, on-the-job training from the agency or organization where volunteers are placed.

1841 RSVP Nassau County
1550 Fulton Avenue
Mineola, NY 11501
516-571-3920
Fax: 516-571-4080
e-mail: lois.mcgloin@mail.co.nassau.ny.us
Lois McGloin, Contact
Kempton Hicks, Manager

The Retired and Senior Volunteer Program (RSVP) provides opportunities for people 55 and over to make a difference in their community through volunteer service. RSVP volunteers contribute anywhere from a few to over forty hours a week, serving though schools, day care centers, police departments, hospitals and other nonprofit and public organizations to help meet critical community needs. RSVP offers maximum flexibility and choice to its volunteers. RSVP matches the personal interests and skills to older Americans with opportunities to help solve community problems and offer supplemental insurance while on duty, on-the-job training from the agency or organization where volunteers are placed.

1842 RSVP New York City
105 E 22nd Street
New York, NY 10010-5495
212-674-7787
Fax: 212-598-4782
Chenita Dix, Executive Director

The Retired and Senior Volunteer Program (RSVP) provides opportunities for people 55 and over to make a difference in their community through volunteer service. RSVP volunteers contribute anywhere from a few to over forty hours a week, serving though schools, day care centers, police departments, hospitals and other nonprofit and public organizations to help meet critical community needs. RSVP offers maximum flexibility and choice to its volunteers. RSVP matches the personal interests and skills to older Americans with opportunities to help solve community problems and offer supplemental insurance while on duty, on-the-job training from the agency or organization where volunteers are placed.

1843 RSVP Niagara County
1302 Main Street
Niagara Falls, NY 14301-1118
716-285-8224
Fax: 716-285-8232
e-mail: rsvp@hanci.com
http://www.hanci.com
Prisiclla Dolling, Director
Dot Swift, Coordinator

The Retired and Senior Volunteer Program (RSVP) provides opportunities for people 55 and over to make a difference in their community through volunteer service. RSVP volunteers contribute anywhere from a few to over forty hours a week, serving though schools, day care centers, police departments, hospitals and other nonprofit and public organizations to help meet critical community needs. RSVP offers maximum flexibility and choice to its volunteers. RSVP matches the personal interests and skills to older Americans with opportunities to help solve community problems and offer supplemental insurance while on duty, on-the-job training from the agency or organization where volunteers are placed.

1844 RSVP Oneida County
220 Memorial Parkway
Utica, NY 13501
315-223-3973
Fax: 315-223-3975
e-mail: kjohnson@oneidacountyrsvp.org
http://www.oneida.countyrsvp.org
Kari Johnson, Director

Provides opportunities for people 55 and over to make a difference in their community through volunteer service. RSVP volunteers contribute anywhere form a few to over forty hours a week, serving through schools, day care centers, police departments, hospitals and other nonprofit and public organizations to help meet critical community needs. RSVP matches the personal interests and skills of older Americans with opportunities to help solve community problems and offers supplemental insurance while on duty, on-the-job training from the agency or organization where volunteers are placed.

1845 RSVP Orange County
30 Matthews Street
Goshen, NY 10924-1963
845-291-2100
Fax: 845-291-2182
e-mail: ofa@co.orange.ny.us
http://www.co.orange.ny.us
Mary Stuart, Coordinator
Richard E Rutteri, Manager

The Retired and Senior Volunteer Program (RSVP) provides opportunities for people 55 and over to make a difference in their community through volunteer service. RSVP volunteers contribute anywhere from a few to over forty hours a week, serving though schools, day care centers, police departments, hospitals and other nonprofit and public organizations to help meet critical community needs. RSVP offers maximum flexibility and choice to its volunteers. RSVP matches the personal interests and skills to older Americans with opportunities to help solve community problems and offer supplemental insurance while on duty, on-the-job training from the agency or organization where volunteers are placed.

1846 RSVP Putnam County
110 Old Route 6
Carmel, NY 10512-2119
845-621-0600
Fax: 845-621-0800

The Retired and Senior Volunteer Program (RSVP) provides opportunities for people 55 and over to make a difference in their community through volunteer service. RSVP volunteers contribute anywhere from a few to over forty hours a week, serving though schools, day care centers, police departments, hospitals and other nonprofit and public organizations to help meet critical community needs. RSVP offers maximum flexibility and choice to its volunteers. RSVP matches the personal interests and skills to older Americans with opportunities to help solve community problems and offer supplemental insurance while on duty, on-the-job training from the agency or organization where volunteers are placed.

State Organizations & Government Agencies/New York

1847 RSVP Rockland
185 North Main Street
Spring Valley, NY 10977   845-356-6818
Fax: 845-574-4498
e-mail: gzabusky@sunyrockland.edu
http://www.sunyrockland.edu/rsvp
Gerri Zabusky LMSW ACSW, Director
Susan Ball, Program Assistant

RSVP of Rockland County's mission is to match senior volunteers' skills with the needs of local nonprofit agencies.

1848 RSVP Saratoga County
152 W High Street
Ballston Spa, NY 12020-3528   518-884-4110
Fax: 518-884-4104

The Retired and Senior Volunteer Program (RSVP) provides opportunities for people 55 and over to make a difference in their community through volunteer service. RSVP volunteers contribute anywhere from a few to over forty hours a week, serving though schools, day care centers, police departments, hospitals and other nonprofit and public organizations to help meet critical community needs. RSVP offers maximum flexibility and choice to its volunteers. RSVP matches the personal interests and skills to older Americans with opportunities to help solve community problems and offer supplemental insurance while on duty, on-the-job training from the agency or organization where volunteers are placed.

1849 RSVP Schuyler County
208 W Broadway Street
Montour Falls, NY 14865-9602   607-535-7105
Fax: 607-535-6270
Beth Lask, Manager

The Retired and Senior Volunteer Program (RSVP) provides opportunities for people 55 and over to make a difference in their community through volunteer service. RSVP volunteers contribute anywhere from a few to over forty hours a week, serving though schools, day care centers, police departments, hospitals and other nonprofit and public organizations to help meet critical community needs. RSVP offers maximum flexibility and choice to its volunteers. RSVP matches the personal interests and skills to older Americans with opportunities to help solve community problems and offer supplemental insurance while on duty, on-the-job training from the agency or organization where volunteers are placed.

1850 RSVP Suffolk County
1 W Main Street
Smithtown, NY 11787-2629   631-979-9490
Fax: 631-979-9320
e-mail: porsino@optionline.net
http://www.rsvpsuffolk.org
Debra Weiner, Executive Director

The Retired and Senior Volunteer Program (RSVP) provides opportunities for people 55 and over to make a difference in their community through volunteer service. RSVP volunteers contribute anywhere from a few to over forty hours a week, serving though schools, day care centers, police departments, hospitals and other nonprofit and public organizations to help meet critical community needs. RSVP offers maximum flexibility and choice to its volunteers. RSVP matches the personal interests and skills to older Americans with opportunities to help solve community problems and offer supplemental insurance while on duty, on-the-job training from the agency or organization where volunteers are placed.

1851 RSVP Sullivan County
100 North Street
Monticello, NY 12701-1163   845-794-3000
Fax: 845-794-7409
e-mail: MaryJ.Inghrim@co.sullivan.ny.us
MaryJ Inghrim, RSVP Project Director
Elaine Finkle, RSVP Assistant

The Retired and Senior Volunteer Program (RSVP) provides opportunities for people 55 and over to make a difference in their community through volunteer service. RSVP volunteers contribute anywhere from a few to over forty hours a week, serving though schools, day care centers, police departments, hospitals and other nonprofit and public organizations to help meet critical community needs. RSVP offers maximum flexibility and choice to its volunteers. RSVP matches the personal interests and skills to older Americans with opportunities to help solve community problems and offer supplemental insurance while on duty, on-the-job training from the agency or organization where volunteers are placed.

1852 RSVP Tompkins County
121 W Court Street
Ithaca, NY 14850-4105   607-277-4545
Fax: 607-272-8060
Danielle Conte, Executive Director

The Retired and Senior Volunteer Program (RSVP) provides opportunities for people 55 and over to make a difference in their community through volunteer service. RSVP volunteers contribute anywhere from a few to over forty hours a week, serving though schools, day care centers, police departments, hospitals and other nonprofit and public organizations to help meet critical community needs. RSVP offers maximum flexibility and choice to its volunteers. RSVP matches the personal interests and skills to older Americans with opportunities to help solve community problems and offer supplemental insurance while on duty, on-the-job training from the agency or organization where volunteers are placed.

1853 RSVP Ulster County
PO Box 557
Stone Ridge, NY 12484   845-687-5274
Fax: 845-687-5273
e-mail: canzianc@sunyulster.edu
Catherine Canzian, Director

Mission is to engage men and women age 55 and better in meaningful volunteer service that strengthens the well being of both self and community.

1854 RSVP Wayne-Seneca-Ontario
159 Montezuma Street
Lyons, NY 14489-1228   315-946-7530
Fax: 315-946-7430
e-mail: annette@waynecap.org
Annette S Hawver, Contact
Janelle Cooper, Chief Executive Officer

The Retired and Senior Volunteer Program (RSVP) provides opportunities for people 55 and over to make a difference in their community through volunteer service. RSVP volunteers contribute anywhere from a few to over forty hours a week, serving though schools, day care centers, police departments, hospitals and other nonprofit and public organizations to help meet critical community needs. RSVP offers maximum flexibility and choice to its volunteers. RSVP matches the personal interests and skills to older Americans with opportunities to help solve community problems and offer supplemental insurance while on duty, on-the-job training from the agency or organization where volunteers are placed.

1855 RSVP of Warren and Washington Counties
696 Upper Glen Street
Queensbury, NY 12804   518-743-9158
Fax: 518-793-5784
e-mail: rsvp@tcuwny.org
http://www.tcuwny.org/rsvp.html
Nancy Talarski, Project Director

RSVP, the Retired and Senior Volunteer Program, serves as a clearinghouse for volunteers 55 and over who reside in Warren and Washington Counties. Currently we have 300 volunteers working in 70 different agencies in our service area. In addition, we have our own programs including Osteobusters, an exercise and education program, and a Medical Transport program that arranges rides for homebound people who need to get to physician appointments.

State Organizations & Government Agencies/New York

1856 Railroad Retirement Board-New York City
26 Federal Plaza
New York, NY 10278
212-264-9820
Fax: 212-742-7802
e-mail: newyork@rrb.gov

Rose I Jonas, Representative
Casey Gresey, Manager

1857 Railroad Retirement Board: Albany District Office
PO Box 529
Albany, NY 12201
518-431-4004
Fax: 518-431-4000
e-mail: albany@rrb.gov

Daniel Layton, Representative

1858 Railroad Retirement Board: Buffalo New York District Office
111 W Huron Street
Buffalo, NY 14202-2303
716-551-4141
Fax: 716-551-3802
e-mail: buffalo@rrb.gov

Philip C Dissek, Representative

1859 Railroad Retirement Board: Syracuse NewYork District Office
1400 Old Country Road
Suite 204
Westbury, NY 11590-5156
516-334-5940
Fax: 516-334-4763
e-mail: westbruy@rrb.gov

Marie Baran, Representative

1860 Ready Willing & Able
232 E 84th Street
New York, NY 10028-2902
212-628-5207
Fax: 212-249-5589
http://www.doe.org

George McDonald, President

1861 Ready Willing & Able: Gates
120 Gates Avenue
Brooklyn, NY 11216-1506
718-622-0634
Fax: 718-622-0877

1862 Region 2 and 3: Administration on Aging(AoA)
US Department of Health & Human Services
26 Federal Plaza
Room 38-102
New York, NY 10278
212-264-2976
Fax: 215-264-0114
http://www.aoa.gov

Dan Quirk, Regional Administrator
Josefina G Carbonell ASA, Assistant Secretary
Edwin Walker PDASA, Deputy Assistant Secretary

Regions include Delaware, District of Columbia, Maryland, New Jersey, New York, Pennsylvania, Puerto Rico, Virginia, Virgin Islands and West Virginia. Through this network, older persons in each community have access to supportive and nutrition services. Persons age 60 and over may participate, priority is given to the elderly with greatest economic or social needs.

1863 Region 2: Administration on Aging (AoA)
US Department of Health & Human Services
26 Federal Plaza
Room 38-102
New York, NY 10278
212-264-2976
Fax: 212-264-2162
http://www.aoa.gov

Region includes New Jersey, New York, Puerto Rico, and the Virgin Islands.

1864 Rensselaer County Department for the Aging
Ned Pattison Rensselaer County
1600 7th Avenue
Troy, NY 12180-3410
518-270-2730
Fax: 518-270-2736

Paul Tazbir, Director
Joseph Cybulski, Manager

1865 Retired Senior Volunteer Program of Steuben County
3 Pulteney Square E
Bath, NY 14810-1510
607-776-7813
Fax: 607-776-7813

Nan Hammas, Executive Director

1866 Rockland County Center for the Physically Handicapped
Jawonio Vocational Center
260 S Little Tor Road
New City, NY 10956-1616
845-634-4648
Fax: 845-634-7731
e-mail: jawonio@jawonio.org
http://www.jawonio.org
TDD 845-634-4672

Esther White, Contact
Paul Tendler, Administrator

Offers vocational evaluation, training, counseling and job placement services.

1867 Rockland County Office for Aging
Dr Robert Yeager Health Center
Building B
Pomona, NY 10970
845-364-2110
Fax: 845-364-2348

June Molof, Director
Marilyn Wekar, Senior Help Line

1868 Saratoga County Office for the Aging
40 South Street
Ballston Spa, NY 12020-1029
518-884-4742
Fax: 518-884-4104

Franklin C DeMarinis, Director
David Wickerham, Administrator

1869 Schenectady County Office for the Aging
117 Nott Terminal
Schenectady, NY 12307
518-382-8481
Fax: 518-382-8644

Nancy M DeLissio, Executive Director
Vickye Eckert, Executive Director

1870 Schoharie County Office for the Aging
113 Park Place
Suite 3
Schoharie, NY 12157
518-295-2001
Fax: 518-295-2015
e-mail: ofa@schohaire.ny.us
http://www.schohairecounty-ny.us

R Carol Coltrain, Director
Theresa Munford, Aging Services Supervisor
Rose Hook, Aging Services Supervisor

The Schoharie County Office for the Aging is committed to meeting the special needs of Schoharie County's senior population and friends who care for them. Schoharie County Office for the Aging offers service directly or through sub contracts, designed to maintain the quality of life to those age 60 and over.

1871 Schuyler County Office for the Aging
PO Box J
Montour Falls, NY 14865
607-535-7108
Fax: 607-535-2030

Richard Cole, Director
Robert Dunthy, Executive Director

State Organizations & Government Agencies/North Carolina

1872 **Seneca County Office for the Aging**
1 Dipronio Drive
Waterloo, NY 13165-1680
315-539-1765
Fax: 315-539-9479
e-mail: areardon@senecacounty.org
Angela M Reardon, Director

1873 **Seneca Nation of Indians Office for Aging**
1500 Route 438
Irving, NY 14081-9505
716-532-3341
Fax: 716-532-5077
Susan Pierce, Director

1874 **Senior Action in a Gay Environment**
105 7th Avenue
16th Floor
New York, NY 10001-6008
212-741-2247
Fax: 212-366-1947
e-mail: sageusa@aol.com
Terry Kaelber, Executive Director

The nation's largest and oldest social service and advocacy organization dedicated to LGBT seniors. SAGE serves New York City's senior LGBT population with social services, recreational programs, and community organizing, and provides advocacy and education about LGBT aging issues nationwide.

1875 **St. Lawrence County Office for Aging**
Sears Building
Canton, NY 13617
315-386-4730
Fax: 315-379-2300
John A Karlberg, Director
Barbara McBurnie, Manager

1876 **St. Regis Mohawk Office for the Aging**
St Regis Mohawk Indian Reservation
Hogansburg, NY 13655
518-358-2272
Fax: 518-358-3203
Darlene Sunday, Director
L David Jacobs, Manager

1877 **Steuben County Office for the Aging**
117 E Steuben Street
Bath, NY 14810-1636
607-776-1151
Fax: 607-776-7813
Linda Tetor, Director
Lisa Cogswell, Manager

1878 **Suffolk County Office for the Aging**
100 Veterans Memorial Highway
Hauppauge, NY 11788-5402
631-853-8200
Fax: 631-853-8225
Holly Rhodes-Teague, Director

1879 **Sullivan County Office for the Aging**
PO Box 5012
Monticello, NY 12701-5192
845-794-3872
Fax: 845-794-7409
e-mail: james.lyttle@co.sullivan.ny.us
James A Lyttle, Director

1880 **Tioga Opportunities Department on Aging**
231 Main Street
Owego, NY 13827-1628
607-687-4120
Fax: 607-687-4147
e-mail: aging@tiogaopp.org
http://www.tiogaopp.org
Martha Brennan, Director
Linda Dawson, Aging Services Coordinator
Carol Houssock, Manager

1881 **Warren Hamilton Counties Office for the Aging**
333 Glen Street
Glens Falls, NY 12801-3548
518-761-6347
Fax: 518-761-6353
e-mail: kellyc@co.warren.ny.us
http://www.co.warren.ny.us
TDD 518-662-1220
Candace Kelly, Director

The Warren-Hamilton Counties Office for the Aging is a bi-county governmental agency dedicated to maintaining seniors' independence and dignity. The OFA advocates for seniors and their families, providing support services, education and assistance in accessing available services.

1882 **Washington County Office for the Aging**
411 Lower Main Street
Hudson Falls, NY 12839-2661
518-746-2420
800-848-3303
Fax: 518-746-2418
Claire Murphy, Director

1883 **Wyoming County Office for the Aging**
76 N Main Street
Warsaw, NY 14569-1329
585-786-8833
800-836-0067
Fax: 585-786-8832
e-mail: officeaging@wyomingco.net
http://www.wyomingco.net
Sabrina Pribek, Director
Ang Proper, Executive Director

Serve residents of Wyoming County aged 60 and older by helping the frail and elderly who choose to remain at home by providing home and community based services.

1884 **Yates County Office for the Aging**
417 Liberty Street
Penn Yan, NY 14527-1100
315-536-5515
Fax: 315-536-8987
Julia K Teahan, Director

North Carolina

1885 **Albemarle Commission**
PO Box 646
Hertford, NC 27944
252-426-5753
Fax: 252-426-8482
e-mail: acaaap@simflex.com
Lynne Raisor, Director
Kay Rose, Manager

Funds aging services in Camden, Chowan, Gates, Byde, Pasquotank, Perquimans and Washington counties.

1886 **Camden County Senior Center**
117 North Highway 343
POB 190
Camden, NC 27921
252-338-1919
Fax: 252-331-5621
e-mail: msawyer@camdencountync.gov
http://www.camdencountync.gov
Michaelene P Sawyer, Director/Nutrition Site Manager

Sponsors congregate lunches and home delivered lunches five days a week for seniors 60+. Offers a complete exercise room for 50+ along with other activities such as table games, Senior Games, and crafts classes. Information and referral is available for legal aid services, Medicaid and Medicare along with Medicare PDP and health insurance, tax assistance. Telephone reassurance program for Camden County. Offers day trips to local areas of interest and weekend trips.

State Organizations & Government Agencies/North Carolina

1887 Centralina Area: Agency on Aging
PO Box 35008
Charlotte, NC 28235-5008
704-372-2416
Fax: 704-347-4710
e-mail: gwoody@centralina.;org
http://www.centralina.org
TDD 704-372-2416

Gayla S Woody, Administrator

Serves North Carolinians 60+ and older in Anson, Cabarrus, Goston, Irechell, Lincoln, Meddenburg, Rowan, Stanley and Union counties. Our goal is to provide assistance for older adults to stay independent as long as possible and identify needed resources to maintain quality of life.

1888 Disability Determination Services
PO Box 243
Raleigh, NC 27602
800-443-9360
Fax: 800-804-5509

1889 Eastern Carolina Council Area Agency onAging
PO Box 1717
New Bern, NC 28563-1717
252-638-3185
Fax: 252-638-3187
e-mail: tcedars@eccog.org
http://www.eccog.org

Tonya Cedars, Director
Joe McKinney, Executive Director

1890 Friends of the Senior Center
283 N 3rd Street
Albemarle, NC 28001-4011
704-986-3769
Fax: 704-986-3776
e-mail: bweemhoff@co.stanly.nc.us

Rebecca G Weemhoff, Contact

1891 Granville County Senior Center
PO Box 551
Oxford, NC 27565
919-693-1930
Fax: 919-693-5358

Kathy May, Executive Director

1892 High Country Region D Area: Agency on Aging
719A Greenway Road
PO Box 1820
Boone, NC 28607-1820
828-265-5434
Fax: 828-265-5439
e-mail: rherndon@regiond.org
http://www.regiond.org

Anita Davie, Director
Rick Herndon, Executive Director
Tonia Cook, AAA Program Assistant

The Area Agency on Aging plans, administers and advocates for the development of a comprehensive service delivery system to meet short and long-term needs of the elderly in this region. The following Counties are served: Alleghany, Ashe, Avery, Mitchell, Watauga, Wilkes, and Yancey.

1893 Isothermal Planning & Development Commission
PO Box 841
Rutherfordton, NC 28139
828-287-2281
Fax: 828-287-2735

Sybil Walker, Director

1894 Jackson County Department on Aging
59 Central Street
Sylva, NC 28779-5411
828-586-8562
Fax: 828-586-1120
e-mail: aging4@mchsi.com

Helen Bryson, Director

Provides services and assistance to the elderly.

1895 KerrTar Regional Council of Governments Area: Agency on Aging
PO Box 709
Henderson, NC 27536
252-492-8561
Fax: 252-492-9110

Stephen Norwood, Director

1896 McDowell Council on Aging
PO Box 1162
Marion, NC 28752-1162
828-652-4240

Dorothy Baldwin, Chairperson
Rod Birdsong, Executive Director

Promotes understanding of the special needs of older persons. Provides advocacy, information and referral, and other services.

1897 Meals on Wheels of Haywood County
486 E Marshall Street
Waynesville, NC 28786-3328
828-452-6620
Fax: 828-452-6686
e-mail: tbeaman@dsshaywood.org

Tony Beaman, CSWM, Director

Volunteers working to provide a nutritious meal five days a week to elderly or handicapped persons to prevent malnutrition or placement in a care facility.

1898 Meals on Wheels of Rowan
PO Box 1914
Salisbury, NC 28145-1914
704-633-1081

Kathy Rummage, Executive Administrator
Wayne Mullis, Owner

Volunteers working to serve a hot noonday meal to the homebound and elderly.

1899 Mid-Carolina Area: Agency on Aging
PO Box 1510
Fayetteville, NC 28302-1510
910-323-4191
800-662-7030
Fax: 252-323-9330

Margaret Hardee, Administrator
James Caldwell, Executive Director

1900 Mid-East Commission Area: Agency on Aging
PO Box 1787
Washington, NC 27889-1787
252-946-8043
Fax: 252-946-5489

Louisa Cox, Director
Tim Ware, President

1901 North Carolina Area: Agency on Aging
2101 Mail Service Center
Raleigh, NC 27699-2101
919-733-3983
Fax: 919-733-0443

Karen Gottivi, Manager

1902 North Carolina Assistive Technology Projects
1110 Navaho Drive
Suite 101
Raleigh, NC 27609-7322
919-872-2298
Fax: 919-850-2792
e-mail: capt@minespring.com/tilda ncapt
http://www.minesprig.com/tilda.nactp

Ricki Cook, Project Director
Toni Hiatt, Executive Director

A federally funded grant whose mission is to improve and expand access to assistive technology for North Carolinians of all ages and disability types. The project works in the areas of training, education, device try out, technical assistance, peer support and access to information. The project works to change systems which impede access to technology for people with disabilities. The project hosts an annual statewide expo featuring vendor exhibits and training workshops.

State Organizations & Government Agencies/North Carolina

1903 **North Carolina Association of Long Term Care Facilities**
4010 Barrett Drive
Suite 102
Raleigh, NC 27609-6622
919-787-3560
Fax: 919-783-5415

Lou Wilson, Executive Director

Rest home operators and employees, social workers, and other interested persons. Works to improve the care and service given by homes for the aged and family care homes.

1904 **North Carolina Association of Nonprofit Homes for the Aging**
3301 Womans Club Drive
Suite 145
Raleigh, NC 27612-4810
919-571-8333
Fax: 919-571-1297

Susan Williamson, Executive Director

1905 **North Carolina Client Assistance Program**
Division of Rehabilitation Services
2806 Mail Service Center
Raleigh, NC 27699-2806
919-855-3600
800-215-7227
Fax: 919-715-2456
e-mail: nccap@ncmail.net
http://www.cap.state.nc.us
TTY 919-855-3600

Kathy Brack, Director
Frank Ashfield, Client Advocate
Kathy Crow, Client Advocate

The North Carolina Client Assistance Program (CAP) is a federally funded program designed to assist individuals with disabilities in understanding and using rehabilitation services.

1906 **North Carolina Council on Developmental Disabilities**
3801 Lake Boone Trail
Suite 250
Raleigh, NC 27607-2969
919-510-0500
Fax: 919-420-7917
http://www.nc-ddc.org

Ken Long, Owner

1907 **North Carolina Department of Administration: Advocacy Council for Persons with Disabilities**
1318 Dale Street
Suite 100
Raleigh, NC 27605-1275
919-733-9250
Fax: 919-733-9173

Allison Bowen, Executive Director

1908 **North Carolina Department of Aging**
2101 MSC Taylor Hall 693 Palmer Drive
Raleigh, NC 27699-2101
919-733-3983
Fax: 919-733-0443

Karen Gottivi, Manager

1909 **North Carolina Department of Human Resources: Services for the Blind**
309 Ashe Avenue
Raleigh, NC 27606-2102
919-733-9822
Fax: 919-733-9769

Debbie Jackson, Executive Director

1910 **North Carolina Department of Revenue**
PO Box 25000
Raleigh, NC 27640-0640
919-733-3991
Fax: 919-733-5750
http://www.dor.state.nc.us

E Norris Tolson, Secretary

To administer the tax laws and collect the taxes due the state in an impartial, uniform, and efficient manner.

1911 **North Carolina Department of the State: Treasurer Division of Retirement Systems**
325 N Salisbury Street
1st Floor
Raleigh, NC 27603-1388
919-733-4191
Fax: 919-508-5350

Jack Pruitt, Executive Director

1912 **North Carolina Industrial Commission**
430 N Salisbury Street
Raleigh, NC 27603-5926
919-854-1322
Fax: 919-715-0282
http://www.comp.state.ny.us

J Howard Bunn Jr, Chairperson

1913 **North Carolina Retired Government Employees Association**
PO Box 10561
Raleigh, NC 27605
919-834-4652
800-356-1190
Fax: 919-834-4622

Ed Regan, Executive Director

Protects the general welfare of its members. Conducts lobbying.

1914 **North Carolina Senior Citizens Association**
PO Box 34
Fayetteville, NC 28302
910-323-3641
800-323-6525
Fax: 910-323-4343

Ben C Sutton, Executive VP

Represents the interests of senior citizens.

1915 **North Carolina Workers Compensation Board**
430 N Salisbury Street
Raleigh, NC 27603-5926
919-733-4820
Fax: 919-715-0282
http://www.comp.state.ny.us/

J Howard Bunn Jr, Director

1916 **Piedmont Triad Council of Governments Area: Agency on Aging**
2216 W Meadowview Road
Suite 201
Greensboro, NC 27407-3480
336-294-4950
Fax: 336-632-0457
e-mail: info@ptcog.org
http://www.ptcog.org

Randall Billings, Executive Director

1917 **Railroad Retirement Board: North Carolina District Office**
7508 E Independence Boulevard
Suite 120
Charlotte, NC 28227-9409
704-344-6118
Fax: 704-344-6429
e-mail: charlotte@rrb.gov

Shelia P Gary, Representative

1918 **Retired Military Police Association**
PO Box 25343
Fayetteville, NC 28314-5005
910-867-4292

1919 **Richmond County Council on the Aging**
225 S Lawrence Street
Rockingham, NC 28379-3633
910-997-4491

Ernest Watts, Executive Director

Provides services to county residents aged 60 years and older.

1920 **Senior Advisory Association of North Carolina**
PO Box 30037
Winston Salem, NC 27130
336-760-2348

Promotes and provides social services for senior citizens in Winston-Salem, NC.

State Organizations & Government Agencies/North Dakota

1921 **Upper Coastal Plain Area Agency on Aging**
1309 S Wesleyan Boulevard
PO Box 2748
Rocky Mount, NC 27802
252-446-0411
Fax: 252-446-5651
e-mail: hproctor@ucpcog.org
http://ww.ucpcog.org

Heather Proctor, Director
Selena Beaman, Aging Program Specialist

The AAA serves a five-county region; Edgecombe, Halifax, Nash, Northampton and Wilson Counties. Our agency coordinates services that help serve adults that remain in their homes-if that is their preference.

1922 **VOCAL-New Hanover County**
1906 Jumpin Run
Wilmington, NC 28403-5335
919-251-1203

Elbert Kring, Executive Officer

Conducts charitable activities.

1923 **Volunteer Center of Greater Durham**
136 E Chapel Hill Street
Durham, NC 27701-3202
919-688-8977
Fax: 919-682-0444

Amber Raggie, Executive Director

1924 **Western Piedmont Council of Governments**
Area Agency on Aging
736 4th Street SW
Hickory, NC 28602-3401
828-322-9191
Fax: 828-322-5991
e-mail: director@wpcog.org
http://www.wpcogaaa.org

R Douglas Taylor, Director
Sheila Weeks, Aging Director

The Western Piedmont Area Agency on Aging (AAA) is an organization working on behalf of older adults and their families in Alexander, Burke, Caldwell, and Catawba Counties, North Carolina.

North Dakota

1925 **Disability Determination Services**
600 S 2nd Street
Bismarck, ND 58504-5729
701-328-8700
Fax: 701-328-8709

Sue Bickel, Administrator

1926 **North Dakota Aging Services**
600 E Boulevard Avenue
Dept 325
Bismarck, ND 58505
701-328-4601
Fax: 701-328-4061
e-mail: dhsaging@state.nd.us
TDD 701-328-8968

Linda Wright, Executive Director

Provides programs and services to support older adults and persons with physical disabilities in their effort to live safely and productively in the least restrictive appropriate setting.

1927 **North Dakota Client Assistance Program**
600 S 2nd Street
Suite A1b
Bismarck, ND 58504-5729
701-328-8947
Fax: 701-328-8969
TDD 701-328-8968

1928 **North Dakota Department of Aging**
600 E Boulevard Avenue
Dept 325
Bismarck, ND 58505
701-328-2455
Fax: 701-328-4061
e-mail: dhsaging@state.nd.us

Bryan Klipfel, Manager

1929 **North Dakota Department of Veterans Affairs**
PO Box 9003
Fargo, ND 58106-9003
701-239-7165
Fax: 701-239-7166

Kathy Halgunseth, Manager

1930 **North Dakota Protection & Advocacy**
400 E Broadway Avenue
Suite 409
Bismarck, ND 58501-4071
701-328-2950
800-472-2670
Fax: 701-328-3934
e-mail: panda@atate.nd.us
http://www.ndpanda.org
TDD 800-366-6888

Teresa Larsen, Executive Director

The Protection and Advocacy Project (P&A) is a state agency whose purpose is to advocate for, and protect the legal rights of, people with disabilities.

1931 **North Dakota Public Employees Retirement System**
400 E Broadway Avenue
Bismarck, ND 58501-4038
701-852-2320
Fax: 701-328-3920

Gisele Thorson, Manager

1932 **North Dakota State Council on Developmental Disabilities**
600 E Boulevard Avenue
Bismarck, ND 58505
701-328-2455
Fax: 701-328-8969
e-mail: sowalt@state.nd.us

Bryan Klipfel, Manager

1933 **North Dakota State Tax Department**
600 E Boulevard Avenue
Bismarck, ND 58505
701-328-2455
Fax: 701-328-3700
http://www.state.nd.us/taxdpt
TDD 800-366-6888

Bryan Klipfel, Manager

1934 **North Dakota Teachers Retirement Fund**
PO Box 7100
Bismarck, ND 58507-7100
701-328-9885
Fax: 701-328-9897

Steve Chochrane, Executive Director

1935 **North Dakota Workers Compensation**
500 E Front Avenue
Bismarck, ND 58504-5689
701-328-3800
800-777-5033
Fax: 701-328-3820
e-mail: ndworkerscomp@web.state.nd.us
http://www.ndworkercomp@web.state.nd.us
TDD 701-328-3786

Sandy Blunt, CEO

1936 **RSVP Devils Lake Area**
128 4th Avenue NE
15
Devils Lake, ND 58301-2420
701-662-6767
Fax: 701-662-6779
e-mail: rsvp@stellarnet.com

Trudy Ertmann, Project Director

Provides opportunities for people 55 and over to make a difference in their community through volunteer service. RSVP volunteers contribute anywhere from a few to over forty hours a week, serving through schools, day care centers, police departments, hospitals and other nonprofit and public organizations to help meet critical community needs. RSVP matches the personal interests and skills of older Americans with opportunities to help solve community problems and offers supplemental insurance while on duty, on-the-job training from the agency or organization where volunteers are placed.

1937 RSVP North Central North Dakota
400 22nd Avenue NW
Minot, ND 58703-1031
701-852-3799
Fax: 701-857-8555

Miriam Smette, Executive Director

The Retired and Senior Volunteer Program (RSVP) provides opportunities for people 55 and over to make a difference in their community through volunteer service. RSVP volunteers contribute anywhere from a few to over forty hours a week, serving though schools, day care centers, police departments, hospitals and other nonprofit and public organizations to help meet critical community needs. RSVP offers maximum flexibility and choice to its volunteers. RSVP matches the personal interests and skills to older Americans with opportunities to help solve community problems and offer supplemental insurance while on duty, on-the-job training from the agency or organization where volunteers are placed.

1938 RSVP of Central North Dakota
1223 S 12th Street
Suite 4
Bismarck, ND 58504-6626
701-258-5436
Fax: 701-258-6771
e-mail: julie.eikamp@ndsu.edu
http://www.rsvp.ndsu.nodak.edu

Julie Eikamp, Project Director
Mary Siverson, Project Coordinator

The Retired and Senior Volunteer Program (RSVP) provides opportunities for people 55 and over to make a difference in their community through volunteer service. RSVP volunteers contribute anywhere from a few to over forty hours a week, serving though schools, day care centers, police departments, hospitals and other nonprofit and public organizations to help meet critical community needs. RSVP offers maximum flexibility and choice to its volunteers. RSVP matches the personal interests and skills to older Americans with opportunities to help solve community problems and offer supplemental insurance while on duty, on-the-job training from the agency or organization where volunteers are placed.

1939 Railroad Retirement Board: North Dakota District Office
PO Box 383
Fargo, ND 58107
701-239-5117
Fax: 701-239-5261
e-mail: fargo@rrb.gov

Debbie M Heibling, Representative

Ohio

1940 AARP Ohio Office
17 S High Street
Suite 800
Columbus, OH 43215-3467
614-224-9800
Fax: 614-224-9801
http://www.AARP.org/OH
TTY 614-224-9802

1941 Alzheimer's Association: Greater Cincinnati
644 Linn Street
Suite 1026
Cincinnati, OH 45203-1742
513-721-4284
Fax: 513-345-8446
http://www.alz.org/grtrcinc

Sue Wilke, Executive Director

1942 Area Two Area: Agency on Aging
6 S Patterson Boulevard
Dayton, OH 45402-2111
937-341-3000
800-258-7277
Fax: 937-341-3005
e-mail: AAA@info4seniors.org
http://www.info4seniors.org

Douglas McGarry, Director

Provides information and services to older persons and their caregivers in a nine county area in West Central Ohio.

1943 Association of Ohio Philanthropic Homes for the Aging
855 S Wall Street
Columbus, OH 43206-1921
614-444-2882
Fax: 614-444-2974
e-mail: info@aopha.org
http://www.aopha.org

John Alfano, President

1944 Avon Maximum Independent Living
11607 Euclid Avenue
Cleveland, OH 44106-4394
216-231-7221
Fax: 440-842-7890

Stephen Hansler, Contact

1945 Buckeye Hills-Hocking Valley Regional Development District
RR 1
Box 20
Marietta, OH 45750-9712
740-374-9436
800-331-2644
Fax: 740-374-8038

Cindy Farson, Director
Boyer Simcox, Executive Director

Marietta, Perry County, Hocking County, Morgan County, Athens County, Meigs County, Noble County, Washington County, Monroe County.

1946 Bureau of Disability Determination
Ohio Rehabilitation Services Commission
PO Box 359001
Columbus, OH 43235-9001
614-438-1502
800-282-4536
Fax: 614-438-1504
http://www.rsc.ohio.gov
TTY 800-282-4536

Kathleen M Johnson, Director

The Bureau of Disability Determination, in agreement with the Social Security Administration, is responsible for determining medical eligibility for Ohioans, Social Security Disability Insurance (SSDI) and Supplemental Security Income (SSI) claims. Although BDD is part of the Ohio Rehabilitation Services Commission, it's federally regulated and receives 100 percent of its funding from the Social Security Administration.

1947 CAP Darke County
1469 Sweitzer Street
Greenville, OH 45331
937-548-8143
Fax: 937-890-7629

Janey Christman, Director

Represents member's interests; conducts lobbying activities; sponsors social functions.

1948 Canton Negro Oldtimers
1844 Ira Turpin Way NE
Canton, OH 44705-1416
330-580-9098

State Organizations & Government Agencies/Ohio

1949 Carroll County Council on Aging
PO Box 14
Carrollton, OH 44615
330-627-7017
Fax: 330-627-7936

Susan Henderson, Director

Multi-purpose senior citizen center. Serving the Carrollton, Ohio area.

1950 Cedarville Senior Citizens
48 N Main Street
Cedarville, OH 45314-8557
937-766-5744

Jane Mills, President

1951 Central Ohio Area: Agency on Aging
272 S Gift Street
Columbus, OH 43215-4479
614-645-7250
Fax: 614-645-3884

Larke Recchie, Director
Cindy Farson, Executive Director

Delaware County, Fairfield County, Fayette County, Franklin County, Licking county, Madison County, Pickaway County, Union County, Columbus.

1952 Cincinnati Area: Council on Aging
644 Linn Street
Suite 110
Cincinnati, OH 45203-1720
513-721-7670
Fax: 513-721-0090
TDD 513-721-8379

Robert Logan, Director
Suzanne Burke, CEO

Cincinnati, Butler County, Hamilton County, Warren County, Clermont County, Clinton County.

1953 Columbus Volunteer Corps
City Hall W Broad Street
Room 12190
Columbus, OH 43215
614-645-6404
Fax: 614-645-5940

Pamela Farber, Administrator

Volunteers working for the city of Columbus, OH.

1954 Council for Older Adults
818 Bowtown Road
Delaware, OH 43015-9661
740-363-6677
Fax: 740-363-7588
http://www.growingolder.org

Robert Horrocks, Executive Director
Donna Meyer, Outreach Coordinator

Plans, coordinates, and funds services and events for seniors in Delaware County, OH.

1955 District Five Area: Agency on Aging
PO Box 1978
Mansfield, OH 44901-1978
419-524-4144
Fax: 419-522-9482

Patricia Brammer, Director
Judi Sauers, Executive Director

Mansfield, Seneca County, Wyandot County, Marion County, Huron County, Crawford County, Morrow County, Ashland County, Richland County, Knox County.

1956 District Seven Area: Agency on Aging
160 Dorsey Drive
Rio Grande, OH 45674-0500
740-245-5306
800-852-7277
Fax: 740-245-5979
http://www.aaa7.org
TTY 888-270-1550

Pamela Matura, Director

The Area Agency on Aging District 7 (AAA7) administers programs for the elderly funded by the state and federal governments. Our mission is to identify the needs of Southern Ohioans age 60 and over. The following ten counties are included in our District 7: Adams, Brown, Gallia, Highland, Jackson, Lawrence, Pike, Ross, Scioto, and Vinton.

1957 Highland County Senior Citizens
185 Muntz Street
Hillsboro, OH 45133-1421
937-393-4745
888-350-6551
Fax: 937-393-8797
e-mail: hcitizens@cinci.rr.com

Suzanne Hopkins, Executive Director

Persons over age 55. Sponsors services and activities for elderly people.

1958 Massillon Senior Citizens' Center
39 Lincoln Way W
Massillon, OH 44647-6581
330-837-2784
Fax: 330-832-9648

Nancy A Johnson, Director

Provides essential leisure services for the older adult citizens of Massillon and the surrounding area. Leisure Services of this division will be planned, coordinated and promoted to meet the current and future needs and desires of (primarily) older adults and (secondarily) the community at large. Programs will be provided in the most cost effective manner possible.

1959 Midway Community and Senior Citizens
37358 State Route 800
Sardis, OH 43946-9715
740-934-9751

Ruth Ann Ridgeway, Contact
Crystal Buegel, Principal

1960 Muskingum County Senior Services
1118 W Main Street
Zanesville, OH 43701-3148
740-452-0984
Fax: 740-452-0984

Margaret A Sowers, Executive Director
James Shiplett, President

Offers services to the senior citizens of Muskingum County, OH. Seeks to alleviate institutionalization.

1961 Northwestern Ohio Area: Agency on Aging
2155 Arlington Avenue
Toledo, OH 43609-1903
419-382-0624
Fax: 419-382-4560

Billie Johnson, Director

1962 Ohio Association of Area Agencies onAging
1335 Dublin Road
Suite 200a
Columbus, OH 43215-1066
614-481-3511
Fax: 614-481-3566
e-mail: oaaaa@ohioaging.org
http://www.ohioaging.org

Jane Taylor, Executive Director
Penny Lovett, Director of Education
Subha Lembach, Policy and Advocacy Coordinator

1963 Ohio Client Assistance Program
30 E Broad Street
Room 120
Columbus, OH 43215-3414
614-466-9956
Fax: 614-752-4197

Carolyn Knight, Administrator

State Organizations & Government Agencies/Ohio

1964 Ohio Department of Aging
50 W Broad Street
Floor 9
Columbus, OH 43215-3363
614-728-0253
Fax: 614-466-5741
e-mail: odamail@age.state.oh.us
http://www.goldenbuckeye.com
Traci Beil-Thomas, Deputy Director Communications

The department serves and represents about 2 million Ohioans age 60 and older. They advocate for the needs of all older citizens with emphasis on improving the quality of life, helping senior citizens live active, healthy, and independent lives, and promoting positive attitudes toward aging and older people. Committed to helping the frail elderly who choose to remain at home by providing home and community based services, the level of choice, inddependence and self-care.

1965 Ohio Department of Taxation
Estate Tax Division
1880 E Dublin Granville Road
Suite 200
Columbus, OH 43229-3523
614-895-6250
Fax: 614-895-6655
http://www.state.oh.us/tax
Gary Goodmanson, Contact

Administers Ohio's tax laws as efficiently as possible. Provides state income and business tax forms and information.

1966 Ohio Developmental Disability Council
8 E Long Street
12th Floor
Columbus, OH 43215-2914
614-466-5205
800-766-7426
Fax: 614-466-0298
e-mail: david.zwyer@dmr.state.oh.us
http://www.ddc.ohio.gov
TDD 614-644-5530
David Zwyer, Director

The Ohio DD Council is a planning and advocacy agency that strives to improve services for people with developmental disabilities and to include them more fully in their communities. Council uses grants to model changes in services, and pursues changes on the public policy level.

1967 Ohio Disabled American Veterans
65 S Front Street
Room 708
Columbus, OH 43215-4131
614-221-3582
Fax: 614-221-4822
Frank Williams, Manager

1968 Ohio Governor's Council on People with Disabilities
400 E Campus View Boulevard
Columbus, OH 43235-4604
614-438-1391
800-282-4536
Fax: 614-438-1274
e-mail: Lucille.Walls@rst.state.oh.us
http://www.gcpd.ohio.gov
TDD 800-282-4536
Lucille Walls, Executive Director

Advisory body to the governor and the legislature on issues that concern Ohioans with disabilities. State liaison to President's Committee on Employment of People with Disabilities and National Organization on Disability.

1969 Ohio Protection & Advocacy for Persons With Disabilities
8 E Long Street
5th Floor
Columbus, OH 43215-2914
614-466-7264
Fax: 614-644-1888
Carolyn S Knight, Executive Director

1970 Ohio Public Employees Retirement System
277 E Town Street
Columbus, OH 43215-4642
614-222-5684
Fax: 614-466-5837
Laurie Fiori Hacking, CEO

1971 Ohio School Employees Retirement System
45 N 4th Street
Columbus, OH 43215-3602
614-221-5853
Fax: 614-222-5808

1972 Oregon Senior Citizens' Center
5760 Bayshore Road
Oregon, OH 43618-1014
419-698-7078
Billie Derivan, Executive Director

1973 RSVP Akron
415 S Portage Path
Akron, OH 44320-2327
330-762-8645
Fax: 330-762-5571

The Retired and Senior Volunteer Program (RSVP) provides opportunities for people 55 and over to make a difference in their community through volunteer service. RSVP volunteers contribute anywhere from a few to over forty hours a week, serving though schools, day care centers, police departments, hospitals and other nonprofit and public organizations to help meet critical community needs. RSVP offers maximum flexibility and choice to its volunteers. RSVP matches the personal interests and skills to older Americans with opportunities to help solve community problems and offer supplemental insurance while on duty, on-the-job training from the agency or organization where volunteers are placed.

1974 RSVP Athensns
20 Kern Street
Athens, OH 45701-2698
740-593-7382
Fax: 740-593-8006
Alice Curtis, Executive Director

The Retired and Senior Volunteer Program (RSVP) provides opportunities for people 55 and over to make a difference in their community through volunteer service. RSVP volunteers contribute anywhere from a few to over forty hours a week, serving though schools, day care centers, police departments, hospitals and other nonprofit and public organizations to help meet critical community needs. RSVP offers maximum flexibility and choice to its volunteers. RSVP matches the personal interests and skills to older Americans with opportunities to help solve community problems and offer supplemental insurance while on duty, on-the-job training from the agency or organization where volunteers are placed.

1975 RSVP Belmont County
410 Fox Shannon Place
St Clairsville, OH 43950
740-695-0293
Fax: 740-695-9255
e-mail: jhartman@cacbelmont.org
http://www.cacbelmont.org
Judith Hartman, RSVP Coordinator

The Retired and Senior Volunteer Program (RSVP) provides opportunities for people 55 and over to make a difference in their community through volunteer service. RSVP volunteers contribute anywhere from a few to over forty hours a week, serving though schools, day care centers, police departments, hospitals and other nonprofit and public organizations to help meet critical community needs. RSVP offers maximum flexibility and choice to its volunteers. RSVP matches the personal interests and skills to older Americans with opportunities to help solve community problems and offer supplemental insurance while on duty, on-the-job training from the agency or organization where volunteers are placed.

State Organizations & Government Agencies/Ohio

1976 **RSVP Cincinnati Area**
1740 Glenway Avenue
Cincinnati, OH 45205-1354   513-354-5704
                                 Fax: 513-921-8222
                        e-mail: rsvp@fsmail.org
                        http://www.servingfamilies.org
Michael Dutle, RSVP Director

RSVP links the skills and experiences of mature human resources with community service organization needs. We partner with mature individuals and community service organizations whose priorities include making a significant and positive difference in our community. We provide opportunities for high quality experiences that enrich the lives of volunteers.

1977 **RSVP Clark County**
101 S Fountain Avenue
Springfield, OH 45502-1207   937-324-5705
                                 Fax: 937-324-9005

The Retired and Senior Volunteer Program (RSVP) provides opportunities for people 55 and over to make a difference in their community through volunteer service. RSVP volunteers contribute anywhere from a few to over forty hours a week, serving though schools, day care centers, police departments, hospitals and other nonprofit and public organizations to help meet critical community needs. RSVP offers maximum flexibility and choice to its volunteers. RSVP matches the personal interests and skills to older Americans with opportunities to help solve community problems and offer supplemental insurance while on duty, on-the-job training from the agency or organization where volunteers are placed.

1978 **RSVP Franklin County**
370 S 5th Street
Columbus, OH 43215-5408   614-221-6766
                                 Fax: 614-224-6866
Mari Lee Zuercher, President

The Retired and Senior Volunteer Program (RSVP) provides opportunities for people 55 and over to make a difference in their community through volunteer service. RSVP volunteers contribute anywhere from a few to over forty hours a week, serving though schools, day care centers, police departments, hospitals and other nonprofit and public organizations to help meet critical community needs. RSVP offers maximum flexibility and choice to its volunteers. RSVP matches the personal interests and skills to older Americans with opportunities to help solve community problems and offer supplemental insurance while on duty, on-the-job training from the agency or organization where volunteers are placed.

1979 **RSVP Gallia County**
235 Broadway Street
Jackson, OH 45640-1701   740-286-4918
Susan Rogers, Executive Director

The Retired and Senior Volunteer Program (RSVP) provides opportunities for people 55 and over to make a difference in their community through volunteer service. RSVP volunteers contribute anywhere from a few to over forty hours a week, serving though schools, day care centers, police departments, hospitals and other nonprofit and public organizations to help meet critical community needs. RSVP offers maximum flexibility and choice to its volunteers. RSVP matches the personal interests and skills to older Americans with opportunities to help solve community problems and offer supplemental insurance while on duty, on-the-job training from the agency or organization where volunteers are placed.

1980 **RSVP Harcatus**
1324 3rd Street NW
New Philadelphia, OH 44663-1306 330-364-9251
                                 Fax: 330-343-6526
Gail Baldwin, Executive Director

The Retired and Senior Volunteer Program (RSVP) provides opportunities for people 55 and over to make a difference in their community through volunteer service. RSVP volunteers contribute anywhere from a few to over forty hours a week, serving though schools, day care centers, police departments, hospitals and other nonprofit and public organizations to help meet critical community needs. RSVP offers maximum flexibility and choice to its volunteers. RSVP matches the personal interests and skills to older Americans with opportunities to help solve community problems and offer supplemental insurance while on duty, on-the-job training from the agency or organization where volunteers are placed.

1981 **RSVP Jefferson**
180 N 4th Street
Steubenville, OH 43952-4416   740-282-1661
                                 Fax: 740-282-1526

The Retired and Senior Volunteer Program (RSVP) provides opportunities for people 55 and over to make a difference in their community through volunteer service. RSVP volunteers contribute anywhere from a few to over forty hours a week, serving though schools, day care centers, police departments, hospitals and other nonprofit and public organizations to help meet critical community needs. RSVP offers maximum flexibility and choice to its volunteers. RSVP matches the personal interests and skills to older Americans with opportunities to help solve community problems and offer supplemental insurance while on duty, on-the-job training from the agency or organization where volunteers are placed.

1982 **RSVP KnoHo**
2004 Campus Drive
Mount Vernon, OH 43050   740-393-3633
                                 Fax: 740-397-3306

The Retired and Senior Volunteer Program (RSVP) provides opportunities for people 55 and over to make a difference in their community through volunteer service. RSVP volunteers contribute anywhere from a few to over forty hours a week, serving though schools, day care centers, police departments, hospitals and other nonprofit and public organizations to help meet critical community needs. RSVP offers maximum flexibility and choice to its volunteers. RSVP matches the personal interests and skills to older Americans with opportunities to help solve community problems and offer supplemental insurance while on duty, on-the-job training from the agency or organization where volunteers are placed.

1983 **RSVP Lake County**
25 Public Square
Willoughby, OH 44094-7863   440-269-3015
                                 Fax: 440-975-3741

The Retired and Senior Volunteer Program (RSVP) provides opportunities for people 55 and over to make a difference in their community through volunteer service. RSVP volunteers contribute anywhere from a few to over forty hours a week, serving though schools, day care centers, police departments, hospitals and other nonprofit and public organizations to help meet critical community needs. RSVP offers maximum flexibility and choice to its volunteers. RSVP matches the personal interests and skills to older Americans with opportunities to help solve community problems and offer supplemental insurance while on duty, on-the-job training from the agency or organization where volunteers are placed.

1984 **RSVP Lorain County**
320 Gateway Boulevard N
Elyria, OH 44035-4955   440-329-5114
                                 Fax: 440-326-4828

State Organizations & Government Agencies/Ohio

The Retired and Senior Volunteer Program (RSVP) provides opportunities for people 55 and over to make a difference in their community through volunteer service. RSVP volunteers contribute anywhere from a few to over forty hours a week, serving thourgh schools, day care centers, police departments, hospitals and other nonprofit and public organizations to help meet critical community needs. RSVP offers maximum flexibility and choice to its volunteers. RSVP matches the personal interests and skills to older Americans with opportunities to help solve community problems and offer supplemental insurance while on duty, on-the-job training from the agency or organization where volunteers are placed.

1985 RSVP Mahoning County
5500 Market Street
Youngstown, OH 44512-2601   330-782-6171
                                      330-782-5001
Virginia Leskanic, Executive Director

The Retired and Senior Volunteer Program (RSVP) provides opportunities for people 55 and over to make a difference in their community through volunteer service. RSVP volunteers contribute anywhere from a few to over forty hours a week, serving thourgh schools, day care centers, police departments, hospitals and other nonprofit and public organizations to help meet critical community needs. RSVP offers maximum flexibility and choice to its volunteers. RSVP matches the personal interests and skills to older Americans with opportunities to help solve community problems and offer supplemental insurance while on duty, on-the-job training from the agency or organization where volunteers are placed.

1986 RSVP Maimi Valley
116 E 3rd Street
Greenville, OH 45331-1950   937-548-8002
                                 Fax: 937-548-2664
Jeff Vaughn, Executive Director

The Retired and Senior Volunteer Program (RSVP) provides opportunities for people 55 and over to make a difference in their community through volunteer service. RSVP volunteers contribute anywhere from a few to over forty hours a week, serving thourgh schools, day care centers, police departments, hospitals and other nonprofit and public organizations to help meet critical community needs. RSVP offers maximum flexibility and choice to its volunteers. RSVP matches the personal interests and skills to older Americans with opportunities to help solve community problems and offer supplemental insurance while on duty, on-the-job training from the agency or organization where volunteers are placed.

1987 RSVP Marion-Crawford Counties
605 South Market Street
Galion, OH 44833   740-387-0175
                                      800-854-4020
                                 Fax: 740-387-1652
                           e-mail: rsvpwap@gte.net
Brenda L Tharp, Contact

Provides opportunities for people 55 and over to make a difference in their community through volunteer service. RSVP volunteers contribute anywhere from a few to over forty hours a week, serving through schools, day care centers, police departments, hospitals and other nonprofit and public organizations to help meet critical community needs. RSVP matches the personal interests and skills of older Americans with opportunities to help solve community problems and offers supplemental insurance while on duty, and on-the-job training from the agency or organization where volunteers are placed.

1988 RSVP Meigs
112 E Memorial Drive
Pomeroy, OH 45769-9569   740-992-3722
                                 Fax: 740-992-7886
Nancy Broderick, Executive Director

The Retired and Senior Volunteer Program (RSVP) provides opportunities for people 55 and over to make a difference in their community through volunteer service. RSVP volunteers contribute anywhere from a few to over forty hours a week, serving thourgh schools, day care centers, police departments, hospitals and other nonprofit and public organizations to help meet critical community needs. RSVP offers maximum flexibility and choice to its volunteers. RSVP matches the personal interests and skills to older Americans with opportunities to help solve community problems and offer supplemental insurance while on duty, on-the-job training from the agency or organization where volunteers are placed.

1989 RSVP Montgomery County
122 Salem Avenue
Dayton, OH 45406-5805   937-223-8246
                                 Fax: 937-223-6078
Sharon Minturn, Owner

The Retired and Senior Volunteer Program (RSVP) provides opportunities for people 55 and over to make a difference in their community through volunteer service. RSVP volunteers contribute anywhere from a few to over forty hours a week, serving thourgh schools, day care centers, police departments, hospitals and other nonprofit and public organizations to help meet critical community needs. RSVP offers maximum flexibility and choice to its volunteers. RSVP matches the personal interests and skills to older Americans with opportunities to help solve community problems and offer supplemental insurance while on duty, on-the-job training from the agency or organization where volunteers are placed.

1990 RSVP Perry County
526 Rear Mill Street
PO Box 605
New Lexington, OH 43764-0605   740-342-2149
                                 Fax: 740-342-5121
Rita Bartimus, Contact

Provides opportunities for people 55 and over to make a difference in their community through volunteer service. RSVP volunteers contribute anywhere from a few to over forty hours a week, serving through schools, day care centers, police departments, hospitals and other nonprofit and public organizations to help meet critical community needs. RSVP matches the personal interests and skills of older Americans with opportunities to help solve community problems and offers supplemental insurance while on duty, on-the-job training from the agency or organization where volunteers are placed.

1991 RSVP Richland County
35 Park Street N
Mansfield, OH 44902-1722   419-525-2816
                                 Fax: 419-524-3467
Skip Allman, Executive Director

The Retired and Senior Volunteer Program (RSVP) provides opportunities for people 55 and over to make a difference in their community through volunteer service. RSVP volunteers contribute anywhere from a few to over forty hours a week, serving thourgh schools, day care centers, police departments, hospitals and other nonprofit and public organizations to help meet critical community needs. RSVP offers maximum flexibility and choice to its volunteers. RSVP matches the personal interests and skills to older Americans with opportunities to help solve community problems and offer supplemental insurance while on duty, on-the-job training from the agency or organization where volunteers are placed.

1992 RSVP Scioto County
221 Court Street
Portsmouth, OH 45662-3907   740-354-3137
                                 Fax: 740-353-4965
Vicki Daily, Executive Director

State Organizations & Government Agencies/Oklahoma

The Retired and Senior Volunteer Program (RSVP) provides opportunities for people 55 and over to make a difference in their community through volunteer service. RSVP volunteers contribute anywhere from a few to over forty hours a week, serving thourgh schools, day care centers, police departments, hospitals and other nonprofit and public organizations to help meet critical community needs. RSVP offers maximum flexibility and choice to its volunteers. RSVP matches the personal interests and skills to older Americans with opportunities to help solve community problems and offer supplemental insurance while on duty, on-the-job training from the agency or organization where volunteers are placed.

1993 RSVP Warren County
570 N State Route 741
Lebanon, OH 45036-8839
513-695-2252
Fax: 513-695-2277
e-mail: dolceeh@wccsinc.org
Dolcee Hoffman, RSVP Director

The Retired and Senior Volunteer Program (RSVP) provides opportunities for people 55 and over to make a difference in their community through volunteer service. RSVP volunteers contribute anywhere from a few to over forty hours a week, serving thourgh schools, day care centers, police departments, hospitals and other nonprofit and public organizations to help meet critical community needs. RSVP offers maximum flexibility and choice to its volunteers. RSVP matches the personal interests and skills to older Americans with opportunities to help solve community problems and offer supplemental insurance while on duty, on-the-job training from the agency or organization where volunteers are placed.

1994 RSVP Washington County
333 4th Street
Marietta, OH 45750-2002
740-373-3107
Fax: 740-373-7251
e-mail: rsvpwashingtoncounty@yahoo.com
Judith Grize, Director

Volunteer program for individuals 55 years of age or older. Finds volunteer opportunities for our members, matching life skills and experience with organizations.

1995 Railroad Retirement Board: Cincinnati Office
36 E 7th Street
Cincinnati, OH 45202-4434
513-684-3188
Fax: 513-684-3182
Jeffrey F Szabo, Representative

The Railroad Retirement Board (RRB) is an independent agency in the executive branch of the Federal Government. The RRB's primary function is to administer comprehensive retirement-survivor and unemployment-sickness benefit programs for the nation's railroad workers and their families, under the Railroad Retirement and Railroad Unemployment Insurance Acts.

1996 Railroad Retirement Board: Cleveland District Office
AJC Federal Building, Room 907
1240 East 9th Street
Cleveland, OH 44199-2093
216-522-4053
800-808-0772
Fax: 216-522-2320
http://www.rrb.gov/field/do_clev
Kevin B McCrone, Representative

The Railroad Retirement Board (RRB) is an independent agency in the executive branch of the Federal Government. The RRB's primary function is to administer comprehensive retirement-survivor and umemployment-sickenss benefit programs for the nation's railroad workers and their families, under the Railroad Retirement and Railroad Unemployment Insurance Acts.

1997 Region Nine Area: Agency on Aging
60788 Southgate Road
Byesville, OH 43723-9533
740-439-4478
800-945-4250
Fax: 740-432-1060
Shirley Blackledge, Director

Cambridge, Holmes County, Coshocton County, Muskingum County, Tuscarawas County, Guernsey County, Carroll County, Harrison County, Belmont County, Jefferson County.

1998 Retired Teachers Association
8050 N High Street
#190
Columbus, OH 43235-6488
614-431-7002
Fax: 614-431-7003
http://www.oata.org
Ann Hanning, Executive Director

Represents members' interests;at STRS. Provides programs and networking opportunities for retirees.

1999 Senior Center of Sidney Shelby County
PO Box 4362
Sidney, OH 45365-4362
937-492-5266
e-mail: srcenter@bright.net

2000 Serving Our Seniors
620 E Water Street
Sandusky, OH 44870-2874
419-624-1856
Fax: 419-624-8176
e-mail: Mail@servingourseniors.org
http://www.ServingOurSeniors.org
Sue Daugherty, Director
Chris Ferguson, Manager

Mission is to create a full spectrum of quality services for adults, 60 years and older, who live in Erie county, Ohio, that will assist them in maintaing their independence, and enable them to live full, active healthy lives in their own residence.

2001 Western Reserve Area: Agency on Aging
1030 Euclid Avenue
Suite 318
Cleveland, OH 44115-1509
216-621-8010
Fax: 216-621-9262
Ron Hill, Director

Cleveland, Lorain County, Cuyahoga County, Medina County, Lake County, Geauga County.

Oklahoma

2002 Aging Services Division
2401 NW 23rd Street
Suite 40a
Oklahoma City, OK 73107-2422
405-691-0339
Fax: 405-521-2086
Marcie Cunnyngham, Manager

2003 Areawide Aging Agency
3200 NW 48th Street
Suite 104
Oklahoma City, OK 73112-5911
405-943-4344
Fax: 405-942-8535
Don Hudman, Director

Oklahoma City, Logan County, Canadian County, Oklahoma County, Cleveland County.

2004 Bryan County Retired and Senior Volunteer Program
101 N 16th Avenue
Durant, OK 74701-3609
580-924-3659
Fax: 580-924-7821
e-mail: bcrsvp@redriverok.com
Sheila Risner, Contact

People aged 55 or more in Bryan County, OK who participate and assist in various community programs.

State Organizations & Government Agencies/Oklahoma

2005 Central Oklahoma Economic Development District: Area Agency on Aging (COEDD)
PO Box 3398
Shawnee, OK 74802-3398
405-273-6410
Fax: 405-273-3213
e-mail: jshea@sbcglobal.net
TDD 405-273-6410
John Shea, Director Aging Services
Laura Waukechon, Information/Assistance
Wayne Manley, Executive Director

Administers OAA programs in seven county rural area to Oklahomans 60 and older.

2006 Disability Determination Division
3535 NW 58th Street
Suite 500
Oklahoma City, OK 73112-4824
405-951-3400
Fax: 405-951-3529
TDD 405-951-3400
Linda S Parker, Executive Director

2007 Eastern Oklahoma Development District Area: Agency on Aging (EODD)
PO Box 1367
Muskogee, OK 74402-1367
918-682-7891
Fax: 918-682-5444
TDD 918-684-5300
Ken Recoy, Director
Karen Sedberry, I&A
Bruce Mahaffey, Executive Director

2008 Grand Gateway Area: Agency on Aging
333 South Oak Street
PO Drawer B
Big Cabin, OK 74332-0502
918-783-5793
800-482-4594
Fax: 918-783-5786
http://www.ggeda.com
Kay Carter, Director

2009 KEDDO Area: Agency on Aging
PO Box 638
Wilburton, OK 74578
918-465-2367
Fax: 918-465-3873
e-mail: kimrose@eosc.edu
http://keddo.org
Kim Rose, Director
Chester Dennis, Executive Director

Serving senior citizens 60 and older in a seven county area in Oklahoma.

2010 KI BOIS Retired Senior Volunteer Program
PO Box E
Poteau, OK 74953-1505
918-647-3267
Fax: 918-647-3268
e-mail: maryland.frizzell@kibois.org
http://www.kibois.org
Maryland Frizzell, Project Director
Lavone Coyle, Manager

2011 NODA Area: Agency on Aging
1216 W Willow Road
Suite A
Enid, OK 73703-2532
580-237-2236
800-749-1149
Fax: 580-237-8230
Rick Billings, Director
Judy Rupp, Manager

2012 OKDHS Aging Services Division
2401 NW 23rd Street
Suite 40
Oklahoma City, OK 73107-2442
405-521-2327
Fax: 405-521-2086
http://www.okdhs.org/aging

2013 Oklahoma Association Area: Agencies onAging
3200 NW 48th Street
Suite 104
Oklahoma City, OK 73112-5911
405-942-8500
Fax: 405-942-8535

2014 Oklahoma Association of Homes and Services for the Aging
906 N Boulevard Street
Edmond, OK 73034-3655
405-341-0810
Fax: 405-341-0976
Richard Pruett, Manager

2015 Oklahoma Client Assistance Program
4300 N Lincoln Boulevard
Oklahoma City, OK 73105-5107
405-521-3756
Fax: 405-943-7550
Helene Kutz, Director
Steve Stokes, Executive Director

2016 Oklahoma Department of Aging
PO Box 25352
Oklahoma City, OK 73125
405-521-2327
Fax: 405-521-2086
Roy Keen, Director

2017 Oklahoma Department of Veterans Affairs
2311 N Central Avenue
Oklahoma City, OK 73105-3200
405-521-3684
Fax: 405-521-6533
e-mail: sclymer@odva.state.ok.us
http://www.odva.state.ok.us/
Phillip Driskill, Executive Director

2018 Oklahoma Developmental Disability Council
2401 NW 23rd Street
Suite 74
Oklahoma City, OK 73107-2431
405-521-4984
800-836-4470
Fax: 405-521-4910
e-mail: staff@okddc.ok.gov
http://www.ok.ddc.ok.gov
Ann Trudgeon, Director

The mission of the Oklahoma Developmental Disabilities Council is to promote services and programs which enable persons with developmental disabilities to fully realize their maximum potential through increased independence and productivity, as well as through integration and inclusion in the community.

2019 Oklahoma Protection & Advocacy Agecny
Oklahoma Disability Law Center
2915 Classen Boulevard
Suite 300
Oklahoma City, OK 73106
405-525-7755
800-880-7755
Fax: 405-525-7759
e-mail: odlcokc@flash.net
http://www.oklahomadisabilitylaw.org
Kayla Bower, Executive Director

The mission of the Oklahoma Disability Law Center is to protect, promote and expand the rights of people with disabilities. The ODLC mission reflects a belief that people with disabilities are entitled to be treated with dignity and respect; to be free from abuse, neglect, exploitation and discrimination. The ODLC mission also reflects the belief that people with disabilites are entitled to equal rights and to equally effective access to the same opportunities as are afforded to other members of society.

2020 Oklahoma Tax Commission
2501 N Lincoln Boulevard
Oklahoma City, OK 73194-1001
405-521-3160
http://www.oktax.state.ok.us
Larry Wilson, Executive Director

The mission is to serve the people of Oklahoma by promoting tax compliance through quality service and fair administration.

State Organizations & Government Agencies/Oklahoma

2021 RSBP Altus
PO Box 1088
Altus, OK 73522-1088   580-482-4141
                               Fax: 580-482-5433
Teresa Williams, Executive Director

The Retired and Senior Volunteer Program (RSVP) provides opportunities for people 55 and over to make a difference in their community through volunteer service. RSVP volunteers contribute anywhere from a few to over forty hours a week, serving thourgh schools, day care centers, police departments, hospitals and other nonprofit and public organizations to help meet critical community needs. RSVP offers maximum flexibility and choice to its volunteers. RSVP matches the personal interests and skills to older Americans with opportunities to help solve community problems and offer supplemental insurance while on duty, on-the-job training from the agency or organization where volunteers are placed.

2022 RSVP Atoka
210 N Main Street
Coalgate, OK 74538-2872   580-927-2369
                               Fax: 580-927-3783
Sandra Riley, Manager

The Retired and Senior Volunteer Program (RSVP) provides opportunities for people 55 and over to make a difference in their community through volunteer service. RSVP volunteers contribute anywhere from a few to over forty hours a week, serving thourgh schools, day care centers, police departments, hospitals and other nonprofit and public organizations to help meet critical community needs. RSVP offers maximum flexibility and choice to its volunteers. RSVP matches the personal interests and skills to older Americans with opportunities to help solve community problems and offer supplemental insurance while on duty, on-the-job training from the agency or organization where volunteers are placed.

2023 RSVP Cleveland-McClain Counties
1125 E Main Street
Norman, OK 73071   405-701-2132
                               Fax: 405-701-2119
Carla Fry, RSVP Program Manager

Provides opportunities for people 55 and over to make a difference in their community through volunteer service. RSVP volunteers contribute anywhere from a few to over forty hours a week, serving through schools, day care centers, police departments, hospitals and other nonprofit and public organizations to help meet critical community needs. RSVP matches the personal interests and skills of older Americans with opportunities to help solve community problems and offers supplemental insurance while on duty, on-the-job training from the agency or organization where volunteers are placed.

2024 RSVP Enid
602 S Van Buren Street
Enid, OK 73703-6931   580-233-5914
                              405-233-5914
                              TDD 405-233-5937
Bennie Mullins, Executive Director

The Retired and Senior Volunteer Program (RSVP) provides opportunities for people 55 and over to make a difference in their community through volunteer service. RSVP volunteers contribute anywhere from a few to over forty hours a week, serving thourgh schools, day care centers, police departments, hospitals and other nonprofit and public organizations to help meet critical community needs. RSVP offers maximum flexibility and choice to its volunteers. RSVP matches the personal interests and skills to older Americans with opportunities to help solve community problems and offer supplemental insurance while on duty, on-the-job training from the agency or organization where volunteers are placed.

2025 RSVP Inca
PO Box 1232
Sulphur, OK 73086-8232   580-622-5700
                               Fax: 580-622-5720
Nadine Tinker, Manager

The Retired and Senior Volunteer Program (RSVP) provides opportunities for people 55 and over to make a difference in their community through volunteer service. RSVP volunteers contribute anywhere from a few to over forty hours a week, serving thourgh schools, day care centers, police departments, hospitals and other nonprofit and public organizations to help meet critical community needs. RSVP offers maximum flexibility and choice to its volunteers. RSVP matches the personal interests and skills to older Americans with opportunities to help solve community problems and offer supplemental insurance while on duty, on-the-job training from the agency or organization where volunteers are placed.

2026 RSVP Lawton
1405 SW 11th Street
Lawton, OK 73501-7304   580-581-3400
                               Fax: 580-581-3437
http://www.cityof.lawton.ok.us/parksnrec/rsvp
Margaret A Perry, RSVP Director

The RSVP Program encourages seniors aged 55 and older to volunteer in their community at nonprofit organizations. By volunteering in the community, the seniors utilize their talents and skills. The volunteers get to share their experience of a lifetime with others. The RSVP Program has special recognitions for the seniors and provides several other benefits for them..

2027 RSVP Little Dixie
502 W Duke Street
Hugo, OK 74743-3216   580-326-5165
                               Fax: 580-326-0556

The Retired and Senior Volunteer Program (RSVP) provides opportunities for people 55 and over to make a difference in their community through volunteer service. RSVP volunteers contribute anywhere from a few to over forty hours a week, serving thourgh schools, day care centers, police departments, hospitals and other nonprofit and public organizations to help meet critical community needs. RSVP offers maximum flexibility and choice to its volunteers. RSVP matches the personal interests and skills to older Americans with opportunities to help solve community problems and offer supplemental insurance while on duty, on-the-job training from the agency or organization where volunteers are placed.

2028 RSVP Love & Marshall Counties
910 West Main Street
PO Box 286
Marietta, OK 73448-0286   580-276-5122
                               Fax: 580-276-4675
                               e-mail: big5hs@brightok.net
Pat Eggleston, Director

Provides opportunities for people 55 and over to make a difference in their community through volunteer service. RSVP volunteers contribute anywhere from a few to over forty hours a week, serving through schools, day care centers, police departments, hospitals and other nonprofit and public organizations to help meet critical community needs. RSVP matches the personal interests and skills of older Americans with opportunities to help solve community problems and offers supplemental insurance while on duty, and on-the-job training from the agency or organization where volunteers are placed.

2029 RSVP Muskogee
502 Boston Street
Muskogee, OK 74401-7517   918-683-1578
                               Fax: 918-683-4068
Etta Nuttingham, Manager

State Organizations & Government Agencies/Oklahoma

The Retired and Senior Volunteer Program (RSVP) provides opportunities for people 55 and over to make a difference in their community through volunteer service. RSVP volunteers contribute anywhere from a few to over forty hours a week, serving though schools, day care centers, police departments, hospitals and other nonprofit and public organizations to help meet critical community needs. RSVP offers maximum flexibility and choice to its volunteers. RSVP matches the personal interests and skills to older Americans with opportunities to help solve community problems and offer supplemental insurance while on duty, on-the-job training from the agency or organization where volunteers are placed.

2030 RSVP Ponca City and Kay County
119 W Grand Avenue
Ponca City, OK 74601-5118
580-762-9412
Fax: 580-762-9413
e-mail: rsvp@cableone.net

Marie Trenary, Program Director

The Retired and Senior Volunteer Program (RSVP) provides opportunities for people 55 and over to make a difference in their community through volunteer service. RSVP volunteers contribute anywhere from a few to over forty hours a week, serving though schools, day care centers, police departments, hospitals and other nonprofit and public organizations to help meet critical community needs. RSVP offers maximum flexibility and choice to its volunteers. RSVP matches the personal interests and skills to older Americans with opportunities to help solve community problems and offer supplemental insurance while on duty, on-the-job training from the agency or organization where volunteers are placed.

2031 RSVP Pottawatomie-Seminole Counties
401 North Bell
Shawnee, OK 74801
405-275-7910
Fax: 405-275-9442
e-mail: cmeiser@cocaa.org

Patty Heer, RSVP Program Manager

Provides opportunities for people 55 and over to make a difference in their community through volunteer service. RSVP volunteers contribute anywhere from a few to over forty hours a week, serving through schools, day care centers, police departments, hospitals and other nonprofit and public organizations to help meet critical community needs. RSVP matches the personal interests and skills of older Americans with opportunities to help solve community problems and offers supplemental insurance while on duty, on-the-job training from the agency or organization where volunteers are placed.

2032 RSVP Seven County
117 E 1st Street
Watonga, OK 73772-3817
580-623-7283
Fax: 580-623-7290
e-mail: rsvp@opportunities-inc.org

Vickie Summerall, Director
Georgie Forthum, Executive Director

Works with senior citizens age 55 and over who volunteer to work in their communities services such as hospital auxiliaries, tutoring/mentoring and literacy programs with schools, assisting in nursing homes, clinics, libraries, museums, county offices, legal programs, senior centers and other related facilities.

2033 RSVP Tulsa
5756 E 31st Street
Tulsa, OK 74135-5103
918-280-8656
Fax: 918-280-8659
e-mail: rsvp@rsvptulsa.org
http://www.rsvptulsa.org

Claudia Meiling, Executive Director

Matches the talents and interests of volunteers 55 and over with meaningful efforts that enhance the quality of our community.

2034 Service Corps of Retired Executives of Tulsa
107n S Detroit Avenue
Suite 1012
Tulsa, OK 74120-4215
918-581-7462
Fax: 918-581-6908
e-mail: consult@tulsascore.org
http://www.tulsascore.org

Richard Crow, Chairperson
Bill Mount, Manager

Volunteer program through which active and retired businesspeople provide free management assistance to people who are considering starting a small business, encountering problems with their business, or expanding their business.

2035 South Western Oklahoma Development Authority Area Agency on Aging
Clinton-Sherman Industrial Airpark
Building 420, Sooner Drive
PO Box 569
Burns Flat, OK 73624
800-627-4882
Fax: 580-562-4880
e-mail: info@swoda.org
http://www.swoda.org

James Boyd, Director
Christi Christian, Ombudsman Supervisor
Chris Hamilton, Ombudsman Supervisor

Our mission is to strengthen local governments by providing services and technical assistance; promote orderly growth and development through job creation and the preservation of environmental integrity, and improve the quality of life by maximizing economic and social opportunities for the region and its population.

2036 Southern Oklahoma Development Association Area: Agency on Aging (SODA)
422 Cessna
PO Box 709
Durant, OK 74702
580-920-1391
800-211-2116
Fax: 580-920-1391
e-mail: aaa@nomail.com
http://www.soda-aaa.org
TDD 405-226-2250

Kathy Weiner, Director

The Southern Oklahoma Development Association Area Agency on Aging strives to improve the quality of life of older Oklahomans by serving as their advocate; encourages older Oklahomans to fully and equally exercise their rights and benefits as citizens of this state and nation. The SODA/Area Agency on Aging administers programs providing nutrition services, outreach and information services, transportation, legal aid, ombudsman services, education/training, and other supportive services.

2037 Southwest Society on Aging
Company of Environmental Science
Ches
125
Stillwater, OK 74078
Fax: 405-744-6843

2038 Tulsa Area: Agency on Aging
111 S Greenwood Avenue
Suite 200
Tulsa, OK 74120-1410
918-596-7688
Fax: 918-596-7653
e-mail: taaa@ci.tulsa.ok.us
http://www.cityoftulsa.org
TDD 918-582-8911

Cindy Johnson, Director
Clark Miller, Executive Director

2039 Worker's Compensation Enforcement Division
4001 N Lincoln Boulevard
Oklahoma City, OK 73105-5206
405-528-1500
888-269-5353
Fax: 405-528-5751

Brenda Reneau, Manager

State Organizations & Government Agencies/Oregon

This division ensures that all employers comply with the Oklahoma Workers' Compensation Act by provising appropriate coverage for their employees.

Oregon

2040 Access Technologies
3070 Lancaster Drive NE
Salem, OR 97305-1396
503-361-1201
800-677-7512
Fax: 503-370-4530
e-mail: ati@oregonvos.net

Joy Rostson, Contact
Laurie Brooks, Manager

A not-for-profit organization whose mission is to assure that persons with disabilities in Oregon will be able to secure and effectively use assistive technologies.

2041 Berks County Senior Citizens Council
40 N 9th Street
Reading, PA 19601-3657
610-374-3195
Fax: 610-374-3483

Lu Ann Oatman, Executive Director

Provides activities and services for the health and welfare of senior citizens including audio-visual, craft, dance, dining, exercise, needlework, and orchestra programs. Offers consumer services, volunteer opportunities, and workshops. Operates two multi-purpose activity centers.

2042 Bureau of Naval Personnel: Oregon Retired Activities Office
6735 N Basin Avenue
Portland, OR 97217-3929
503-285-4566
Fax: 503-735-1788

Edward Hall, Manager

2043 Central Oregon Council on Aging
2303 SE 1st Street
Redmond, OR 97756-9608
541-548-8817
Fax: 541-548-3826

Veronica C Zecchini, Director
Carol Bro, Executive Director

2044 Clackamas County Social Services Area: Agency on Aging
PO Box 2950
Oregon City, OR 97045-0295
503-655-8640
Fax: 503-650-5722
http://www.co.clackamas.or.us
TDD 503-650-5637

John Mullin, Director

Clackamas County Aging and Disability Services (an Area Agency on Aging) is a partner in the County's Social Services Division, joining the Community Action Agency in a shared mission to work for the well being of vulnerable citizens.

2045 Columbia County Council Area: Agency onAging
Columbia County Courthouse
Saint Helens, OR 97051
503-397-3682

Don Fields, Director

2046 Community Connection of Northeast Oregon
104 Elm Street
La Grande, OR 97850-2621
541-963-3186
Fax: 541-963-3187

Margaret Davidson, Executive Director

2047 Disability Determination Services
3150 Lancaster Drive NE
Salem, OR 97305-1350
800-452-2147
Fax: 866-432-9178
http://www.oregon.gov/dhs

People with disabilities may be able to qualify for one of two federal disability programs; Social Security Disability Insurance (SSDI) or Supplemental Security Income (SSI). These programs are governed by the federal Social Security Administration (SSA).

2048 Douglas County Health & Disabilities Services AAA (Area Agency on Aging) of Douglas County
621 West Madrone
Suite 160
Roseburg, OR 97470
541-957-3005
Fax: 541-464-3901
e-mail: vlnunenk@co.douglas.or.us

Vicki Nunenkamp PhD, Director
Bill Poulter, SS Program Supervisor
Merry Larsen, SPD & DSO Program Manager

The AAA of Douglas County provides Older American Act and Medicaid services to those eligible among our county's 24,000 residents age 60 and older (23% of the total population) through its main office in Roseburg and eight community facilities throughout the County. We are committed to working together with our community partners to assist seniors and people with disabilities to enjoy independence, dignity, choice and quality of life.

2049 Douglas County Senior Services Division
621 W Madrone Street
Roseburg, OR 97470-3090
541-440-3500
Fax: 541-440-3599
TDD 503-440-3548

G John DeGroot, Director
Peggy Kennerly, Manager

2050 Gray Panthers of Portland
1020 SW Taylor Street
Suite 610
Portland, OR 97205-2506
503-224-1585
Fax: 202-737-1160
e-mail: davisjasr@aol.com
http://www.graypanthers.org

Jim Davis, Director

2051 Harney County Senior Center
PO Box 728
Burns, OR 97720-728
541-573-6024
Fax: 541-573-6025

Theresa Williams, Executive Director

2052 Klamath Basin Senior Citizens' Council
PO Box JE
Klamath Falls, OR 97602-1205
541-883-7171
Fax: 541-883-7175
e-mail: mob41@juno.com

Mike O'Brien, Executive Director
Allen R Cate, Programs Manager

2053 Lane Council of Governments: Senior and Disabled Services Division
1025 Willamette Street
Suite 200
Eugene, OR 97401-2490
541-682-4283
Fax: 541-682-3959
TDD 800-526-0661

Ted Stevens, Director
George Kloeppel, Executive Director

State Organizations & Government Agencies/Oregon

2054 Mid-Columbia Senior and Disabled Services
700 Union Street
Suite 214
The Dalles, OR 97058-1858
541-298-4114
800-452-2333
Fax: 541-298-1251

Sally Zuck, Director
Carol Mauser, Manager

2055 Multnomah County Aging Services Division
421 SW 5th Avenue
3rd Floor
Portland, OR 97204-2205
503-988-3801
Fax: 503-248-3656
TDD 503-248-3683

James McConnell, Director
Cate Connell, Manager

2056 Oregon Advocacy Center
620 SW 5th Avenue
5th Floor
Portland, OR 97204-1428
503-243-2081
800-452-1694
Fax: 503-243-1738
TTY 503-323-9161

Bob Joondeph, Executive Director
Rosemary DiSiervi, CAP Advocate
Barbara Printemps Herget, Director Operations

2057 Oregon Alliance of Senior & Health Services
7340 SW Hunziker Street
Suite 207
Tigard, OR 97223-2304
503-684-3788
Fax: 503-624-0870
e-mail: info@oashs.org
http://www.oashs.org

Ruth Gulyas, Executive Director

2058 Oregon Cascades West Senior Services
1400 Queen Avenue SE
Suite 206
Albany, OR 97322-7092
541-967-8720
Fax: 541-967-6423

Bill Wagner, Executive Director

2059 Oregon Commission on Disabilities
1257 Ferry Street SE
Salem, OR 97310
503-378-3142
800-358-3117
Fax: 503-378-3599

Danielle Knight, Executive Director

2060 Oregon Council on Developmental Disabilities
540 24th Place NE
Salem, OR 97301-4517
503-945-9941
800-292-4154
Fax: 503-945-9947
e-mail: ocdd@ocdd.org
http://www.ocdd.org

Bill Lynch, Executive Director
Barrie Brewer, Communications Coordinator
Terry Butler, Project Coordinator

Our mission is to join with Oregonians with developmental disabilities and their families to promote change, through self-determination, leading to a more accessible, inclusive and culturally responsive world.

2061 Oregon Department of Aging
313 Public Service Building
Salem, OR 97310
503-304-3400
Fax: 503-304-3434

James Wilson, Administrator
Barry Donenfeld, Executive Director

2062 Oregon Department of Human Services: Division of Senior & Disabled Services
500 Summer Street NE
Salem, OR 97301-1063
503-945-5944
800-282-8096
Fax: 503-373-7823
e-mail: SDSD.info@state.or.us
http://www.sdsd.hr.state.or.us

Bruce Goldberg, Executive Director

2063 Oregon Department of Revenue
955 Center Street
Salem, OR 97310
503-378-4988
800-356-4222
http://www.state.nv.us/taxation

Elizabeth Harchenko, Executive Director

2064 Oregon Department of Veterans Affairs
700 Summer Street NE
Salem, OR 97310
503-945-5944
800-633-6826

Bruce Goldberg, Executive Director

2065 Oregon Hearing Society
PO Box 30404
Portland, OR 97294-3404
503-256-4233
866-OHS-HEAR
Fax: 503-256-5367
http://www.oregonhearingsociety.org

Dan King MBA, President
Chris Gustafson, Vice President
Scott DeRieux, Public Relations

Representing and promoting the interests of hearing and professionals and the hearing aid consumers of the state of Oregon.

2066 Oregon Protection & Advocacy for Persons with Disabilities
310 SW 4th Avenue
Suite 625
Portland, OR 97204-2345
503-243-2081
Fax: 503-243-1738

Robert Joondeph, Executive Director

2067 Oregon Public Employees Retirement System
PO Box 23700
Tigard, OR 97281-3700
503-598-7377
Fax: 503-598-0561

Paul Cleary, CEO

2068 Oregon Senior Services
500 Summer Street NE
Salem, OR 97310
503-945-5811
Fax: 503-373-7823

James Toews, Executive Director

2069 Pilot Rock Senior Center
235 W Main Street
Pilot Rock, OR 97868
541-443-2993
541-443-2253

Carol Elliott, Manager

2070 RSVP Columbia County
2194 Columbia Boulevard
Saint Helens, OR 97051-1739
503-397-5655
Fax: 503-397-3198
e-mail: rsvp@crpud.net

Nancy Harwood, Contact

State Organizations & Government Agencies/Oregon

The Retired and Senior Volunteer Program (RSVP) provides opportunities for people 55 and over to make a difference in their community through volunteer service. RSVP volunteers contribute anywhere from a few to over forty hours a week, serving though schools, day care centers, police departments, hospitals and other nonprofit and public organizations to help meet critical community needs. RSVP offers maximum flexibility and choice to its volunteers. RSVP matches the personal interests and skills to older Americans with opportunities to help solve community problems and offer supplemental insurance while on duty, on-the-job training from the agency or organization where volunteers are placed.

2071 RSVP Coos County
2110 Newmark Avenue
Room 220
Coos Bay, OR 97420
541-888-7332
Fax: 541-888-7120
e-mail: rsvp@socc.edu

Tonya Schoonmaker, Director
Helen Thomsen, RSVP Assistant
Chere Kifer, Senior Program Coordinator

The Retired and Senior Volunteer Program (RSVP) provides opportunities for people 55 and over to make a difference in their community through volunteer service. RSVP volunteers contribute anywhere from a few to over forty hours a week, serving though schools, day care centers, police departments, hospitals and other nonprofit and public organizations to help meet critical community needs. RSVP offers maximum flexibility and choice to its volunteers. RSVP matches the personal interests and skills to older Americans with opportunities to help solve community problems and offer supplemental insurance while on duty, on-the-job training from the agency or organization where volunteers are placed.

2072 RSVP Curry County
PO Box 746
Gold Beach, OR 97444
541-247-3280
Fax: 541-247-2705
e-mail: mathers @co.curry.or.us

Sharon Mather, Director

The Retired and Senior Volunteer Program (RSVP) provides opportunities for people 55 and over to make a difference in their community through volunteer service. RSVP volunteers contribute anywhere from a few to over forty hours a week, serving though schools, day care centers, police departments, hospitals and other nonprofit and public organizations to help meet critical community needs. RSVP offers maximum flexibility and choice to its volunteers. RSVP matches the personal interests and skills to older Americans with opportunities to help solve community problems and offer supplemental insurance while on duty, on-the-job training from the agency or organization where volunteers are placed.

2073 RSVP Deschutes County
2500 NE Neff Road
Bend, OR 97701-6015
541-388-7746
Fax: 541-385-6345

The Retired and Senior Volunteer Program (RSVP) provides opportunities for people 55 and over to make a difference in their community through volunteer service. RSVP volunteers contribute anywhere from a few to over forty hours a week, serving though schools, day care centers, police departments, hospitals and other nonprofit and public organizations to help meet critical community needs. RSVP offers maximum flexibility and choice to its volunteers. RSVP matches the personal interests and skills to older Americans with opportunities to help solve community problems and offer supplemental insurance while on duty, on-the-job training from the agency or organization where volunteers are placed.

2074 RSVP Jackson County
1045 Ellendale Drive
Medford, OR 97504-8706
541-779-5257
TDD 541-779-4883

2075 RSVP Josephine County
233 NE C Street
Grants Pass, OR 97526-2153
541-955-5547
Fax: 541-955-5549

Kelly Wessels, Executive Director

The Retired and Senior Volunteer Program (RSVP) provides opportunities for people 55 and over to make a difference in their community through volunteer service. RSVP volunteers contribute anywhere from a few to over forty hours a week, serving though schools, day care centers, police departments, hospitals and other nonprofit and public organizations to help meet critical community needs. RSVP offers maximum flexibility and choice to its volunteers. RSVP matches the personal interests and skills to older Americans with opportunities to help solve community problems and offer supplemental insurance while on duty, on-the-job training from the agency or organization where volunteers are placed.

2076 RSVP Lincoln County
308 SW Coast Highway
PO Box 1276
Newport, OR 97365
541-574-2684
Fax: 541-265-3689
e-mail: worke@oregonpacific.redcross.org

Elli Work, Contact

Provides opportunities for people 55 and over to make a difference in their community through volunteer service. RSVP volunteers contribute anywhere from a few to over forty hours a week, serving through schools, day care centers, police departments, hospitals and other nonprofit and public organizations to help meet critical community needs. RSVP matches the personal interests and skills of older Americans with opportunities to help solve community problems and offers supplemental insurance while on duty, on-the-job training from the agency and organization where volunteers are placed.

2077 RSVP Linn Benton County
630 NW 7th Street
Corvallis, OR 97330-6312
541-753-9197
Fax: 541-757-9537
e-mail: foxb@linnbenton.edu
http://http://linnbenton.edu/rsvp

Beth Fox, Director

The Retired and Senior Volunteer Program (RSVP) provides opportunities for people 55 and over to make a difference in their community through volunteer service. RSVP volunteers contribute anywhere from a few to over forty hours a week, serving though schools, day care centers, police departments, hospitals and other nonprofit and public organizations to help meet critical community needs. RSVP offers maximum flexibility and choice to its volunteers. RSVP matches the personal interests and skills to older Americans with opportunities to help solve community problems and offer supplemental insurance while on duty, on-the-job training from the agency or organization where volunteers are placed.

2078 RSVP Marion County
270 Montgomery Street
Woodburn, OR 97071-4730
503-982-5255
Fax: 503-982-5244

State Organizations & Government Agencies/Oregon

The Retired and Senior Volunteer Program (RSVP) provides opportunities for people 55 and over to make a difference in their community through volunteer service. RSVP volunteers contribute anywhere from a few to over forty hours a week, serving though schools, day care centers, police departments, hospitals and other nonprofit and public organizations to help meet critical community needs. RSVP offers maximum flexibility and choice to its volunteers. RSVP matches the personal interests and skills to older Americans with opportunities to help solve community problems and offer supplemental insurance while on duty, on-the-job training from the agency or organization where volunteers are placed.

2079   RSVP Multonamah County
2145 NW Overton Street
Portland, OR 97210-2924
503-413-7787
Fax: 503-413-7671

Andy Nelson, Executive Director

The Retired and Senior Volunteer Program (RSVP) provides opportunities for people 55 and over to make a difference in their community through volunteer service. RSVP volunteers contribute anywhere from a few to over forty hours a week, serving though schools, day care centers, police departments, hospitals and other nonprofit and public organizations to help meet critical community needs. RSVP offers maximum flexibility and choice to its volunteers. RSVP matches the personal interests and skills to older Americans with opportunities to help solve community problems and offer supplemental insurance while on duty, on-the-job training from the agency or organization where volunteers are placed.

2080   RSVP Roseburgburg
621 W Madrone Street
Roseburg, OR 97470-3090
541-440-3640
Fax: 541-440-3564

The Retired and Senior Volunteer Program (RSVP) provides opportunities for people 55 and over to make a difference in their community through volunteer service. RSVP volunteers contribute anywhere from a few to over forty hours a week, serving though schools, day care centers, police departments, hospitals and other nonprofit and public organizations to help meet critical community needs. RSVP offers maximum flexibility and choice to its volunteers. RSVP matches the personal interests and skills to older Americans with opportunities to help solve community problems and offer supplemental insurance while on duty, on-the-job training from the agency or organization where volunteers are placed.

2081   RSVP Roseburg-Douglas
621 W Madrone Street
Suite 132
Roseburg, OR 97470-3090
541-440-3500
Fax: 541-440-3564
e-mail: sramsey@co.douglas.or.us

Vicki Cloud, Director
Peggy Kennerly, Manager

Serves as a clearinghouse for retired persons 55 yrs and older who are interested in performing community volunteer work.

2082   RSVP Washington County
15405 SW 116th Avenue
Suite 108A
King City, OR 97224
503-639-5620
Fax: 503-431-2057

Art Ellickson, Contact

2083   Railroad Retirement Board: -Oregon District Office
1220 SW 3rd Avenue
Portland, OR 97204-2825
503-326-2143
Fax: 503-215-9339

Judy Oxborrow, Representative

2084   Rogue Valley Council of Governments: Senior and Disability Services Division
PO Box 3275
Central Point, OR 97502
541-664-6674
Fax: 541-664-7927

Donald Bruland, Director

2085   RsVP Clackamas County
603 12th Street
Oregon City, OR 97045-1630
503-655-8862
Fax: 503-650-3513
http://www.co.clackamas.or.us

Pam Vick, Director

The Retired and Senior Volunteer Program (RSVP) provides opportunities for people 55 and over to make a difference in their community through volunteer service. RSVP volunteers contribute anywhere from a few to over forty hours a week, serving though schools, day care centers, police departments, hospitals and other nonprofit and public organizations to help meet critical community needs. RSVP offers maximum flexibility and choice to its volunteers. RSVP matches the personal interests and skills to older Americans with opportunities to help solve community problems and offer supplemental insurance while on duty, on-the-job training from the agency or organization where volunteers are placed.

2086   Salem Deaf Fellowship
4455 Silverton Road N
Salem, OR 97305-2061
503-585-6793

Douglas Slama, DVM

Provides programs and services to benefit the deaf in Salem, OR.

2087   South Salem Seniors
6450 Fairway Avenue SE
Salem, OR 97306-1443
503-588-0748

Alice Wells, President

2088   Vocational Rehabilitation Division
500 Summer Street NE
E15
Salem, OR 97301-1063
503-945-5880
Fax: 503-378-2897

Stephanie Taylor, Administrator

2089   Washington County Area Agency on Aging
Washington County Deptartment of Aging Services
155 North First Avenue
Suite 300
Hillsboro, OR 97124
503-640-3489
Fax: 503-693-6127
http://www.co.washington.or.us

Rod Branyan, Director
Jeff Hill, Supervisor

The mission is to create options for older persons to enable them to live independently in the appropriate care setting for as long as possible. This involves assessing need planning and coordinating services, developing services, advocating for their needs, and delivering and monitoring social and health services.

2090   Washington County Department of Aging Services
133 SE 2nd Avenue
Hillsboro, OR 97123-4026
503-640-3489
Fax: 503-640-6167
TDD 503-640-6398

Mary Lou Ritter, Director

State Organizations & Government Agencies/Pennsylvania

Pennsylvania

2091 Active Aging
1034 Park Avenue
Meadville, PA 16335-4325
814-336-1792
800-321-7705
Fax: 814-336-1705
TDD 814-333-3691

Pauline Mooney, Director

2092 Adams County Office for Aging
220 Baltimore Street
Gettysburg, PA 17325-2314
717-337-9833
800-548-3240
Fax: 717-334-4715

Steven D Niebler, Director
Theresa Adamik, Manager

2093 Aging Services
PO Box 519
Indiana, PA 15701
724-349-4500
800-442-8016
Fax: 724-349-9535

Carole A Ling, Executive Director
James McQuown, Executive Director

2094 Allegheny County Department of Aging
441 Smithfield Street
2nd Floor
Pittsburgh, PA 15222-2227
412-350-5460
800-344-4319
Fax: 412-350-3091
e-mail: SeniorLine@dhs.county.allegheny.pa.us
http://county.allegheny.pa.us/dhs/AAA/aaa.html
TDD 412-350-2727

Mildren Morrisson, Administrator

2095 Area Agency on Aging for Tioga, Bradford, Sullivan and Susquehanna Counties
220 Main Street
Unit 2
Towanda, PA 18848-1822
570-265-6121
Fax: 570-265-5680
e-mail: bfarley@bsstaaa.org

William Farley, Director

2096 Area Agency on Aging of Somerset County
1338 S Edgewood Avenue
Somerset, PA 15501-2678
814-443-1218
800-452-0825
Fax: 814-445-4398

Kathy Gibbs, Administrative Assistant
Debbie Baker, Executive Director

2097 Armstrong Area: Agency on Aging
125 Queen Street
Kittanning, PA 16201-1313
724-548-3290
800-368-1066
Fax: 724-548-3296
e-mail: armstrongaging@welo-unwired.net

Janet D Talerico, Director

2098 Beaver County Office on Aging
1020 8th Avenue
Beaver Falls, PA 15010-4506
724-847-2262
Fax: 724-847-3490
e-mail: Aging@BCOA.US
http://www.co.beaver.pa.us

Beverly Sullivan, Administrator

2099 Blair Senior Services
1320 12th Avenue
Altoona, PA 16601-3308
814-946-1235
800-245-3282
Fax: 814-949-4857
TDD 814-949-4856

David M Slat, Director

2100 Bucks County Area: Agency on Aging
30 E Oakland Avenue
Doylestown, PA 18901-4681
215-348-0510
Fax: 215-348-3146
e-mail: Aging@co.bucks.pa.us
http://www.buckscounty.org/AAA.htm
TDD 800-243-3767

Charles A Kane, Director

Services for older adults aged 60+.

2101 Butler County Area: Agency on Aging
111 Sunnyview Circle
Suite 101
Butler, PA 16001-3537
724-282-3008
888-367-2434
Fax: 724-282-1466

Lisa M Monday, Director

A wide range of senior services is available to Butler County residents over the age of 60. Most services are available on a donation basis.

2102 Butler Township Senior Citizens
RR 3
Box 796
Drums, PA 18222
570-788-4881

Betty Cunfer, Secretary
Charlotte Freerick, Manager

Individuals over 55 years of age. Provides opportunities for senior citizens in northeastern Pennsylvania to stay active by interacting with one another, creating crafts, and pursuing hobbies. Provides entertainment.

2103 Carbon County Area: Agency on Aging
401 Delaware Avenue
3rd Floor
Palmerton, PA 18071-1908
610-824-7830
800-441-1315
Fax: 610-824-7836
e-mail: ccaging1@ptd.net

Stephanie Cawley, Administrator

2104 Carmichaels Senior Citizens
100 Nemacolin Road
Carmichaels, PA 15320-1036
724-966-2290

Mary Bokat, Manager

2105 Centre County Office on Aging
420 Holmes Street
Bellefonte, PA 16823-1401
814-355-6716
800-643-5432
Fax: 814-355-6757
e-mail: jgtaylor@co.centre.pa.us
TDD 814-355-6711

Jane G Taylor, Director

Area agency on aging offering information and referral, senior center services, care management, and protective services and placement information. Also provides Health Insurance Counseling Program.

2106 Clarion County Area: Agency on Aging
12 Grant Street
Clarion, PA 16214-1006
814-226-4640
800-672-7116
Fax: 814-226-6744

Stephanie Wilshire, Director

State Organizations & Government Agencies/Pennsylvania

2107 Clearfield County Area: Agency on Aging
PO Box 550
Clearfield, PA 16830
814-765-2696
800-225-8571
Fax: 814-765-2760

John Kordish, Executive Director

2108 Colonial Meals on Wheels
107 E 4th Avenue
Conshohocken, PA 19428-1931
610-825-4254
Fax: 610-825-3117

Jean R Smith, Director

Provides meals and visitors to homebound and/or disabled people in the Conshohocken, Plymouth, and Whitemarsh area.

2109 Columbia-Montour-Area: Agency on Aging
15 Perry Avenue
Bloomsburg, PA 17815-8401
570-784-9272
800-598-5001
Fax: 570-784-3678

Kathleen Lynn, Director

2110 Community Action Senior Corps
105 Grace Way
Punxsutawney, PA 15767-1209
814-223-9988
800-648-3381
Fax: 814-938-7596
e-mail: mgatesman@jccap.org
http://www.jccap.org

Maria Gatesman, Senior Corps Director
Janeen Love, Senior Corps Recruitment
Karla Moses, Manager

The organization in the Jefferson, Clarion, and Indiana Counties of Pennsylvania responsible for solving community by utilizing the skills of persons ages 55 and older.

2111 Connellsville Area Senior Tigers
100 E Fayette Street
Connellsville, PA 15425-3334
724-626-1515
Fax: 724-628-4701

Patricia L Pritts, Executive Director

Senior citizens united for social interaction.

2112 Cumberland County Office of Aging
16 W High Street
Carlisle, PA 17013-2919
717-240-6110
Fax: 717-240-6118
e-mail: aging@ccpa.net
http://www.ccpa.net/aging

Terry Barley, Director
Jennifer Manoich, Information/Referral Coordinator

Provides coordinated services to county residents that are 60 years of age or older. Goal is to provide programs and services that allow the older adult to maintain their health, welfare and independence.

2113 Experience Area: Agency on Aging
905 4th Avenue
Warren, PA 16365-1802
814-723-3763
Fax: 814-723-6433

Allen R Roberts, Director
Peter Carnovale, Executive Director

2114 Franklin County Area: Agency on Aging
425 Franklin Farm Lane
Chambersburg, PA 17201-3064
717-263-1900
800-528-3240
Fax: 717-261-3198

Kimberly Murdaugh, Director
Doug Amsley, Executive Director

2115 Golden Slipper Center for Seniors
1901 Conshohocken Avenue
Philadelphia, PA 19131-5430
215-877-6667

Marsha Garrell, Executive Director

2116 Gray Panthers of Pittsburgh
Pittsburgh, PA 15512
412-433-0755
Fax: 202-737-1160

2117 Greater Erie Community Action Committee (GECAC)
18 W 9th Street
Erie, PA 16501-1343
814-459-4581
Fax: 814-456-0161

Carolyn Chester, Director

2118 Greensburg Bureau of Disability Determination
351 Harvery Avenue
Greensburg, PA 15605
724-836-5100
Fax: 724-832-5284

Stuart Louchheim, Administrator

2119 Harrisburg Bureau of Disability Determination
1171 S Cameron Street
Room 200
Harrisburg, PA 17104-2594
717-783-3620
800-932-0701
Fax: 717-783-3016

Determines the nonfinancial eligibility of claimants for federal Social Security disability benefits. The bureau follows the guidelines established by the federal government.

2120 Huntington-Bedford-Fulton Area: Agency on Aging
PO Box 46
Bedford, PA 15522
814-623-8148
Fax: 814-623-5929

Alan Smith, Director

2121 Jefferson County Area: Agency on Aging
PO Box 47
Brookville, PA 15825
814-849-3096
800-852-8036
Fax: 814-849-4655

Laura Mae Baker, Director
Randy Davis, Executive Director

2122 Korean Senior Citizens Association of Greater Philadelphia
230 E Tabor Road
Philadelphia, PA 19120-3025
215-457-6310

2123 Lackawanna County Area: Agency on Aging
200 Adams Avenue
Suite 300
Scranton, PA 18503-1607
570-963-6740
Fax: 570-963-6401
TDD 717-299-7981

Kevin Russin, Director

2124 Lancaster County Office of Aging
PO Box 3480
Lancaster, PA 17608-3480
717-299-7979
Fax: 717-293-7234
TDD 717-299-7981

Patricia H Mann, Executive Director
Jacqueline Birch, Manager

State Organizations & Government Agencies/Pennsylvania

2125 Lawrence County Area Agency on Aging
Shenley Square
2706 Mercer Road
New Castle, PA 16105-1422 724-658-3729
Fax: 724-658-7532
e-mail: lawcoage@ccpph.com
http://www.ccpgh.org/challenges
Roberta M Taylor, Director

Offers a wide range in programs and services for older persons ranging from job training and employment opportunities to in-home services for those who are seeking alternatives to nursing home care. Many social and recreational activities are available at community centers and satellite centers throughout Lawrence County. All services seek to enhance independence and to maintain the highest quality of life possible.

2126 Lebanon County Area: Agency on Aging
710 Maple Street
Lebanon, PA 17046-3537 717-273-9262
Fax: 717-274-3882
e-mail: lebcoaaa@lebcnty.org
Michael G Kristovensky, Director
Mary Miller, Information & Referral

Provide services to senior residents of Lebanon county.

2127 Life Insurance for Veterans: Veterans Benefits Administration
US Department of Veterans Affairs
PO Box 8079
Philadelphia, PA 19101-8079 215-842-2000
800-669-8477
Fax: 215-381-3084
http://www.va.gov

Our insurance programs were developed to provide insurance benefits for veterans and service members who may not be able to get insurance from private companies because of the extra risks involved in military service, or a service connected disability.

2128 Lock Haven Golden Age Club
Ymcagrove & Water Streets
Lock Haven, PA 17745 724-662-6222
800-570-6222
Fax: 724-662-0611
Helen E Mayes, President
Senior citizens.

2129 Luzerne-Wyoming Bureau for the Aging
111 N Pennsylvania Avenue
Wilkes Barre, PA 18701-3508 570-822-1158
800-252-1512
Fax: 570-823-9129
Charles J Lewis, Director
Linda Kohut, Executive Director

2130 Lycoming-Clinton Office of Aging
PO Box 770
Lock Haven, PA 17745 570-748-8665
Fax: 570-893-8141
Patricia Essip, Director
Darlla Conway, Executive Director

2131 Mercer County Area: Agency on Aging
404 Mercer County Courthouse
Mercer, PA 16137 724-662-6222
Fax: 724-662-0611
Ann Marie Spiardi, Executive Director

2132 Mifflin-Juniata Area: Agency on Aging
PO Box 750
Lewistown, PA 17044 717-242-0315
800-348-2277
Fax: 717-242-1448
e-mail: mjaaa@acsworld.net
Carlene S Hack, Director

2133 Monroe County Area: Agency on Aging
724 Phillips Street
Suite B
Stroudsburg, PA 18360-2244 570-420-3735
Fax: 570-420-3734
e-mail: monroeaging@co.monroe.pa.us
http://www.co.monroe.pa.us
Dorothy Kaufman, Executive Director

2134 Montgomery County Office on Aging and Adult Services
Human Services Center
1430 Dekalb Street
Norristown, PA 19401-3406 610-278-3601
Fax: 610-278-3769
http://www.montcopa.org/mcaas
Jeanne Kline, Director

The Montgomery County Office of Aging and Adult Services is the agency responsible for planning, coordinating, and monitoring services for county residents, age 60 and older. As the area agency on aging, AAS is part of a state and national network of agencies established by the older persons through a wide range of service options.

2135 Northampton County Area: Agency on Aging
45 N 2nd Street
Easton, PA 18042-3699 610-559-3245
Fax: 610-559-3297
e-mail: jmehler@northamptoncounty.org
http://www.northamptoncounty.org
John R Mehler, Director

Maintains and enhances the independence and dignity of older adults while providing protection as necessary.

2136 Northumberland County Area: Agency onAging
2154 Trevorton Road
Coal Township, PA 17866-9406 570-644-4447
800-479-2626
Fax: 570-644-4457
e-mail: rum@ptd.net
Jackie Klemick, Executive Director

2137 Office of Human Services
PO Box A
Ridgway, PA 15853 814-776-2191
800-672-7145
Fax: 814-776-2194
Bill Orzechowski, Director

2138 Pennsylvania Association of Area Agencies on Aging Directors
1540 N Progress Avenue
Suite 101
Harrisburg, PA 17110-9637 717-541-4214
Fax: 717-541-4217
http://www.p4a.org
M Crystal Lowe, Executive Director

2139 Pennsylvania Association of Non-Profit Homes for the Aging
Executive Park W Old Gettysburg
Suite 4094720
Mechanicsburg, PA 17055 717-763-5727
Fax: 717-763-1057
e-mail: info@panpha.org
http://www.panpha.org
Ronald L Barth, Executive Director

Nursing homes, assisted living facilities, elderly housing, retirement communities.

2140 Pennsylvania Client Assistance Program
1650 Arch Street
Suite 2310
Philadelphia, PA 19103-2029 215-557-7112
Fax: 610-555-7602
Stephen Pennington, Executive Director

State Organizations & Government Agencies/Pennsylvania

2141 Pennsylvania Department of Revenue
11 Strawberry Square
Harrisburg, PA 17101-1800
717-236-3610
Fax: 717-783-4447
http://www.revenue.state.pa.us
Alfred Baker, President

2142 Pennsylvania Department on Aging
555 Walnut Street
5th Floor
Harrisburg, PA 17101-1925
717-783-3126
800-225-7223
Fax: 717-783-6842
Lori Gerhard, Acting Secretary
Ivonne Bucher, Deputy Secretary
Nora Dowdeisenhower, Manager

2143 Pennsylvania Developmental Disabilities Council
Room 569 Forum Building
Commonwealth Avenue
Harrisburg, PA 17120
717-787-6057
Fax: 717-772-0738
e-mail: paddpc@aol.com
http://www.paddc.org
Graham Mulholland, Executive Director

The Council engages in advocacy, systems change and capacity building for people with disabilities and their families in order to: Support people with disabilities in taking control of their own lives; Ensure access to goods, services, and supports; Build inclusive communities; Pursue a cross-disability agenda; Change negative societal attitudes towards people with disabilities.

2144 Pennsylvania Protection & Advocacy for Persons with Disabilities
116 Pine Street
Harrisburg, PA 17101-1244
717-236-8110
800-692-7443
Fax: 717-236-0192
Ilene Shane, Executive Director

Provide advocacy, information and referral for persons with disabilities and mental illness issues.

2145 Pennsylvania Public School Employees' Retirement System
PO Box 125
Harrisburg, PA 17108
717-787-8540
888-773-7748
Fax: 717-783-9424
Jeffrey Clay, Executive Director

2146 Pennsylvania Society of Directors of Volunteer Services
PO Box 8600
Harrisburg, PA 17105-8600
717-564-9200
Fax: 717-561-5216
Mercedes Piesco, President
Carolyn Scanlan, CEO

2147 Pennsylvania Workers Compensation Board
1171 S Cameron Street
Room 103
Harrisburg, PA 17104-2510
717-783-5421
Fax: 717-772-0342
John Kupchinsky, Manager

2148 Perry County Office for Aging
PO Box 596
New Bloomfield, PA 17068
717-582-2131
Fax: 717-582-5160
Joan L Brodisch, Director

2149 Philadelphia Corporation for Aging
642 N Broad Street
Philadelphia, PA 19130-3499
215-765-9000
Fax: 215-765-9066
e-mail: sspencer@pcaphl.org
http://www.pcaphl.org
TDD 215-765-9041
Rodney D Williams, Director

2150 Pike County Area: Agency on Aging
150 Pike County Boulevard
Hawley, PA 18428-9107
570-775-5550
Fax: 570-296-5939
e-mail: rlodolce@ptd.net
http://www.pikeaaa.org
Robin Lodolce, Executive Director

2151 Plum Enterprises
PO Box 85
Valley Forge, PA 19481
610-783-7377
800-321-PLUM
Fax: 610-783-7577
http://www.plument.com

Patented Protective Wear made with material engineered specifically to absorb the energy of a fall. We exquisitley design each garment around its protective core with exacting detail and unmatched standards of quality.

2152 Potter County Area: Agency on Aging
PO Box 241
Roulette, PA 16746-241
814-544-7315
Fax: 814-544-9062
e-mail: shoffman@pottercountyhumansvcs.org
http://www.pottercountyhumansvcs.org
Sherry Hoffman, Aging Director
Jame Kockler, Administrator

Provides assessment, care management and services to eligible older adults, age 60 years and older.

2153 RSVP Allegheny County
225 Boulevard of the Allies
Pittsburgh, PA 15222
412-263-3179
Fax: 412-263-5268
Linda Soldressen, Project Director
Helen Harrison, Field Coordinator

RSVP helps people 55 years of age and older put their skills and life experience to assist others in their communities and to increase their own personal satisfaction and enrichment.

2154 RSVP Allegheny County-Pittsburgh
225 Boulevard of the Allies
Pittsburgh, PA 15222-1615
412-263-3184
Fax: 412-263-5268
e-mail: gueldnerm@usa.redcross.org
Linda Soldressen, Contact

The Retired and Senior Volunteer Program (RSVP) provides opportunities for people 55 and over to make a difference in their community through volunteer service. RSVP volunteers contribute anywhere from a few to over forty hours a week, serving though schools, day care centers, police departments, hospitals and other nonprofit and public organizations to help meet critical community needs. RSVP offers maximum flexibility and choice to its volunteers. RSVP matches the personal interests and skills to older Americans with opportunities to help solve community problems and offer supplemental insurance while on duty, on-the-job training from the agency or organization where volunteers are placed.

2155 RSVP Beaver County
124 Franklin Avenue
Aliquippa, PA 15001-3728
724-378-2882
Fax: 724-378-9809
e-mail: chaney@aaud.org
Colleen Haney, Contact
Timothy J Morton, Executive Director

State Organizations & Government Agencies/Pennsylvania

The Retired and Senior Volunteer Program (RSVP) provides opportunities for people 55 and over to make a difference in their community through volunteer service. RSVP volunteers contribute anywhere from a few to over forty hours a week, serving though schools, day care centers, police departments, hospitals and other nonprofit and public organizations to help meet critical community needs. RSVP offers maximum flexibility and choice to its volunteers. RSVP matches the personal interests and skills to older Americans with opportunities to help solve community problems and offer supplemental insurance while on duty, on-the-job training from the agency or organization where volunteers are placed.

2156 RSVP Bedford-Cambria County
550 Main Street
Johnstown, PA 15901-2011
814-539-4511
Fax: 814-535-8637

The Retired and Senior Volunteer Program (RSVP) provides opportunities for people 55 and over to make a difference in their community through volunteer service. RSVP volunteers contribute anywhere from a few to over forty hours a week, serving though schools, day care centers, police departments, hospitals and other nonprofit and public organizations to help meet critical community needs. RSVP offers maximum flexibility and choice to its volunteers. RSVP matches the personal interests and skills to older Americans with opportunities to help solve community problems and offer supplemental insurance while on duty, on-the-job training from the agency or organization where volunteers are placed.

2157 RSVP Blair County
1320 12th Avenue
Altoona, PA 16601-3308
814-946-1235
Fax: 814-949-4857

David Slat, President

The Retired and Senior Volunteer Program (RSVP) provides opportunities for people 55 and over to make a difference in their community through volunteer service. RSVP volunteers contribute anywhere from a few to over forty hours a week, serving though schools, day care centers, police departments, hospitals and other nonprofit and public organizations to help meet critical community needs. RSVP offers maximum flexibility and choice to its volunteers. RSVP matches the personal interests and skills to older Americans with opportunities to help solve community problems and offer supplemental insurance while on duty, on-the-job training from the agency or organization where volunteers are placed.

2158 RSVP Buck County
10 E Oakland Avenue
Doylestown, PA 18901-4609
215-340-1210
Fax: 215-348-0356

Joanne Kozak, Executive Director

The Retired and Senior Volunteer Program (RSVP) provides opportunities for people 55 and over to make a difference in their community through volunteer service. RSVP volunteers contribute anywhere from a few to over forty hours a week, serving though schools, day care centers, police departments, hospitals and other nonprofit and public organizations to help meet critical community needs. RSVP offers maximum flexibility and choice to its volunteers. RSVP matches the personal interests and skills to older Americans with opportunities to help solve community problems and offer supplemental insurance while on duty, on-the-job training from the agency or organization where volunteers are placed.

2159 RSVP Capitol Region
5301 Jonestown Road
Harrisburg, PA 17112-2967
717-541-9521
Fax: 717-541-8466
e-mail: rsvp@paontine.com

Carol A Oman, Executive Director
Judy Bentz, Perry County Coordinator
Anne Meek, Dauphin County Coordinator

Volunteer recruitment and placement in Cumberland, Dauphin, Franklin and Perry counties.

2160 RSVP Centre County
420 Holmes Street
Room 253
Bellefonte, PA 16823
814-355-6816
Fax: 814-355-6757

Bonnie Wick Everett, Director
Shelley R Miller, Special Projects Coordinator
Brenda L Reeve, Secretary

RSVP of Centre County helps individuals age 55 and older out their skills and life experiences to use through volunteering in our communities. The staff assists each person in choosing the right opportunity based on the volunteer's interests, abilities and schedule. RSVP receives requests for volunteer help from more than 100 community agencies and organizations.

2161 RSVP Chester County
310 N Matlack Street
West Chester, PA 19380-2620
610-696-4900
Fax: 610-696-4476

Leslie Stauffer, Manager

The Retired and Senior Volunteer Program (RSVP) provides opportunities for people 55 and over to make a difference in their community through volunteer service. RSVP volunteers contribute anywhere from a few to over forty hours a week, serving though schools, day care centers, police departments, hospitals and other nonprofit and public organizations to help meet critical community needs. RSVP offers maximum flexibility and choice to its volunteers. RSVP matches the personal interests and skills to older Americans with opportunities to help solve community problems and offer supplemental insurance while on duty, on-the-job training from the agency or organization where volunteers are placed.

2162 RSVP Clearfield County
103 N Front Street
Clearfield, PA 16830-2512
814-765-2226
Fax: 814-765-1730

Donna English, Executive Director

The Retired and Senior Volunteer Program (RSVP) provides opportunities for people 55 and over to make a difference in their community through volunteer service. RSVP volunteers contribute anywhere from a few to over forty hours a week, serving though schools, day care centers, police departments, hospitals and other nonprofit and public organizations to help meet critical community needs. RSVP offers maximum flexibility and choice to its volunteers. RSVP matches the personal interests and skills to older Americans with opportunities to help solve community problems and offer supplemental insurance while on duty, on-the-job training from the agency or organization where volunteers are placed.

2163 RSVP Crawford County
956 S Main Street
Meadville, PA 16335-3242
814-336-6111
Fax: 814-336-6521

Sally Kennerknecht, Executive Director

The Retired and Senior Volunteer Program (RSVP) provides opportunities for people 55 and over to make a difference in their community through volunteer service. RSVP volunteers contribute anywhere from a few to over forty hours a week, serving though schools, day care centers, police departments, hospitals and other nonprofit and public organizations to help meet critical community needs. RSVP offers maximum flexibility and choice to its volunteers. RSVP matches the personal interests and skills to older Americans with opportunities to help solve community problems and offer supplemental insurance while on duty, on-the-job training from the agency or organization where volunteers are placed.

2164 RSVP Delaware County
149 W Baltimore Avenue
Media, PA 19063-2686
610-565-5563
Fax: 610-565-5176

Norma Testa, Executive Officer

State Organizations & Government Agencies/Pennsylvania

Provides volunteer assignments for persons age 55 or over with nonprofit public service agencies in Delaware County, PA. Volunteer oppurtuities are based on community need and are encouraged in areas where there is impact on the community.

2165 RSVP Elk-Cameron Counties
118 Center Street
Ridgway, PA 15853-1702
814-776-2191
Fax: 814-776-2193
e-mail: rsvpohs@alltel.net
Janet Beck, Project Director
William Orzenchowski, Executive Director

The Retired and Senior Volunteer Program (RSVP) provides opportunities for people 55 and over to make a difference in their community through volunteer service. RSVP volunteers contribute anywhere from a few to over forty hours a week, serving thourgh schools, day care centers, police departments, hospitals and other nonprofit and public organizations to help meet critical community needs. RSVP offers maximum flexibility and choice to its volunteers. RSVP matches the personal interests and skills to older Americans with opportunities to help solve community problems and offer supplemental insurance while on duty, on-the-job training from the agency or organization where volunteers are placed.

2166 RSVP Greater Erie Community Action
18 W 9th Street
Erie, PA 16501-1343
814-459-4581
Fax: 814-456-0161

The Retired and Senior Volunteer Program (RSVP) provides opportunities for people 55 and over to make a difference in their community through volunteer service. RSVP volunteers contribute anywhere from a few to over forty hours a week, serving thourgh schools, day care centers, police departments, hospitals and other nonprofit and public organizations to help meet critical community needs. RSVP offers maximum flexibility and choice to its volunteers. RSVP matches the personal interests and skills to older Americans with opportunities to help solve community problems and offer supplemental insurance while on duty, on-the-job training from the agency or organization where volunteers are placed.

2167 RSVP Greene County
1070 Old National Pike
Fredericktown, PA 15333-2114
724-632-6801
Fax: 724-632-6312
e-mail: msnee@centervilleclinics.com
Carolyn Capozza, Contact
James Quinn, Administrator

The Retired and Senior Volunteer Program (RSVP) provides opportunities for people 55 and over to make a difference in their community through volunteer service. RSVP volunteers contribute anywhere from a few to over forty hours a week, serving thourgh schools, day care centers, police departments, hospitals and other nonprofit and public organizations to help meet critical community needs. RSVP offers maximum flexibility and choice to its volunteers. RSVP matches the personal interests and skills to older Americans with opportunities to help solve community problems and offer supplemental insurance while on duty, on-the-job training from the agency or organization where volunteers are placed.

2168 RSVP Lackawanna County
538 Spruce Street
Suite 420
Scranton, PA 18503-1816
570-346-3630
Fax: 570-341-5816
Nancy Post, Executive Director

The Retired and Senior Volunteer Program (RSVP) provides opportunities for people 55 and over to make a difference in their community through volunteer service. RSVP volunteers contribute anywhere from a few to over forty hours a week, serving thourgh schools, day care centers, police departments, hospitals and other nonprofit and public organizations to help meet critical community needs. RSVP offers maximum flexibility and choice to its volunteers. RSVP matches the personal interests and skills to older Americans with opportunities to help solve community problems and offer supplemental insurance while on duty, on-the-job training from the agency or organization where volunteers are placed.

2169 RSVP Lebanon-Lancaster Counties
430 W Orange Street
Lancaster, PA 17603-3752
717-299-5561
Fax: 717-299-9225
Kathy Panza, Manager

The Retired and Senior Volunteer Program (RSVP) provides opportunities for people 55 and over to make a difference in their community through volunteer service. RSVP volunteers contribute anywhere from a few to over forty hours a week, serving thourgh schools, day care centers, police departments, hospitals and other nonprofit and public organizations to help meet critical community needs. RSVP offers maximum flexibility and choice to its volunteers. RSVP matches the personal interests and skills to older Americans with opportunities to help solve community problems and offer supplemental insurance while on duty, on-the-job training from the agency or organization where volunteers are placed.

2170 RSVP Lehigh County
800 Hausman Road
Allentown, PA 18104-9393
610-391-8211
Fax: 610-391-8495

The Retired and Senior Volunteer Program (RSVP) provides opportunities for people 55 and over to make a difference in their community through volunteer service. RSVP volunteers contribute anywhere from a few to over forty hours a week, serving thourgh schools, day care centers, police departments, hospitals and other nonprofit and public organizations to help meet critical community needs. RSVP offers maximum flexibility and choice to its volunteers. RSVP matches the personal interests and skills to older Americans with opportunities to help solve community problems and offer supplemental insurance while on duty, on-the-job training from the agency or organization where volunteers are placed.

2171 RSVP Luzerne-Wyoming Counties
93 N State Street
Wilkes Barre, PA 18701-3105
570-822-1159
Fax: 570-970-9250

The Retired and Senior Volunteer Program (RSVP) provides opportunities for people 55 and over to make a difference in their community through volunteer service. RSVP volunteers contribute anywhere from a few to over forty hours a week, serving thourgh schools, day care centers, police departments, hospitals and other nonprofit and public organizations to help meet critical community needs. RSVP offers maximum flexibility and choice to its volunteers. RSVP matches the personal interests and skills to older Americans with opportunities to help solve community problems and offer supplemental insurance while on duty, on-the-job training from the agency or organization where volunteers are placed.

2172 RSVP McKean County
Old Sena Kean Manor
Smethport, PA 16749
814-887-5683
Fax: 814-887-5691
Barb Rider, Manager

State Organizations & Government Agencies/Pennsylvania

The Retired and Senior Volunteer Program (RSVP) provides opportunities for people 55 and over to make a difference in their community through volunteer service. RSVP volunteers contribute anywhere from a few to over forty hours a week, serving though schools, day care centers, police departments, hospitals and other nonprofit and public organizations to help meet critical community needs. RSVP offers maximum flexibility and choice to its volunteers. RSVP matches the personal interests and skills to older Americans with opportunities to help solve community problems and offer supplemental insurance while on duty, on-the-job training from the agency or organization where volunteers are placed.

2173 RSVP Monroe County
411 Main Street
Stroudsburg, PA 18360-2499
570-420-3747
Fax: 570-420-3732
Norma Fagan, Executive Director

The Retired and Senior Volunteer Program (RSVP) provides opportunities for people 55 and over to make a difference in their community through volunteer service. RSVP volunteers contribute anywhere from a few to over forty hours a week, serving though schools, day care centers, police departments, hospitals and other nonprofit and public organizations to help meet critical community needs. RSVP offers maximum flexibility and choice to its volunteers. RSVP matches the personal interests and skills to older Americans with opportunities to help solve community problems and offer supplemental insurance while on duty, on-the-job training from the agency or organization where volunteers are placed.

2174 RSVP Montgomery County
531 Plymouth Road
Plymouth Meeting, PA 19462-1642
610-834-1040
Fax: 610-834-1087

The Retired and Senior Volunteer Program (RSVP) provides opportunities for people 55 and over to make a difference in their community through volunteer service. RSVP volunteers contribute anywhere from a few to over forty hours a week, serving though schools, day care centers, police departments, hospitals and other nonprofit and public organizations to help meet critical community needs. RSVP offers maximum flexibility and choice to its volunteers. RSVP matches the personal interests and skills to older Americans with opportunities to help solve community problems and offer supplemental insurance while on duty, on-the-job training from the agency or organization where volunteers are placed.

2175 RSVP Philadelphia East
10100 Jamison Avenue
208
Philadelphia, PA 19116-3832
215-331-7787
Fax: 215-599-6494
e-mail: rsvpeast@libertynet.org
Marcia Gross, Project Director

Provides opportunities for people 55 and over to make a difference in their community through volunteer service. RSVP volunteers contribute anywhere from a few to over forty hours a week, serving through schools, day care centers, police departments, hospitals and other nonprofit and public organizations to help meet critical community needs. RSVP matches the personal interests and skills of older Americans with opportunities to help solve community problems and offers supplemental insurance while on duty, on-the-job training from the agency or organization where volunteers are placed.

2176 RSVP Philadelphia West
227 N 18th Street
Philadelphia, PA 19103-1212
215-854-7077
Fax: 215-854-7100

2177 RSVP Schuylkill County
110 E Laurel Boulevard
Pottsville, PA 17901
717-622-3103
Fax: 717-622-1732
e-mail: cjb@co.schuylkill.pa.us
Carol J Bowen, Director

Provides opportunities for people 55 and over to make a difference in their community through volunteer service. RSVP volunteers contribute anywhere from a few to over forty hours a week, serving through schools, day care centers, police departments, hospitals and other nonprofit and public organizations to help meet critical community needs. RSVP matches the personal interests and skills of older Americans with opportunities to help solve community problems and offers supplemental insurance while on duty, on-the-job training from the agecny or organization where volunteers are placed.

2178 RSVP Somerset County
1338 S Edgewood Avenue
Somerset, PA 15501-2678
814-443-2681
Fax: 814-445-4398
Arthur Di Loreto, Executive Director

The Retired and Senior Volunteer Program (RSVP) provides opportunities for people 55 and over to make a difference in their community through volunteer service. RSVP volunteers contribute anywhere from a few to over forty hours a week, serving though schools, day care centers, police departments, hospitals and other nonprofit and public organizations to help meet critical community needs. RSVP offers maximum flexibility and choice to its volunteers. RSVP matches the personal interests and skills to older Americans with opportunities to help solve community problems and offer supplemental insurance while on duty, on-the-job training from the agency or organization where volunteers are placed.

2179 RSVP Venango County
1283 Liberty Street
Franklin, PA 16323-1333
814-432-9723
Fax: 814-432-9759
Anna Claire Chacknes, Executive Director

The Retired and Senior Volunteer Program (RSVP) provides opportunities for people 55 and over to make a difference in their community through volunteer service. RSVP volunteers contribute anywhere from a few to over forty hours a week, serving though schools, day care centers, police departments, hospitals and other nonprofit and public organizations to help meet critical community needs. RSVP offers maximum flexibility and choice to its volunteers. RSVP matches the personal interests and skills to older Americans with opportunities to help solve community problems and offer supplemental insurance while on duty, on-the-job training from the agency or organization where volunteers are placed.

2180 RSVP Warren-Forest Counties
100 Fourth Avenue
Warren, PA 16365
814-723-7551
Fax: 814-723-9690
Susan Himes, Director

State Organizations & Government Agencies/Pennsylvania

The Retired and Senior Volunteer Program (RSVP) provides opportunities for people 55 and over to make a difference in their community through volunteer service. RSVP volunteers contribute anywhere from a few to over forty hours a week, serving though schools, day care centers, police departments, hospitals and other nonprofit and public organizations to help meet critical community needs. RSVP offers maximum flexibility and choice to its volunteers. RSVP matches the personal interests and skills to older Americans with opportunities to help solve community problems and offer supplemental insurance while on duty, on-the-job training from the agency or organization where volunteers are placed.

2181 RSVP Westmoreland County
Armbrust Road
Youngwood, PA 15697   724-925-4213
                        Fax: 724-925-1150

The Retired and Senior Volunteer Program (RSVP) provides opportunities for people 55 and over to make a difference in their community through volunteer service. RSVP volunteers contribute anywhere from a few to over forty hours a week, serving though schools, day care centers, police departments, hospitals and other nonprofit and public organizations to help meet critical community needs. RSVP offers maximum flexibility and choice to its volunteers. RSVP matches the personal interests and skills to older Americans with opportunities to help solve community problems and offer supplemental insurance while on duty, on-the-job training from the agency or organization where volunteers are placed.

2182 Railroad Retirement Board: Altoona Pennslvania District Office
PO Box 990
Altoona, PA 16603   814-946-3601
                        Fax: 814-946-3620

William Lambert, Representative

2183 Railroad Retirement Board: Harrisburg Pennsylvania Branch Office
PO Box 11697
Harrisburg, PA 17108-1697   717-221-4490
                        Fax: 717-221-3464
                e-mail: harrisburg@rrb.gov

Karen E Keefer, Branch Manager

2184 Railroad Retirement Board: Philadelphia Pennsylvania District Office
Nix Federal
Building 900
Philadelphia, PA 19107   215-597-2674
                        Fax: 215-597-2794
                e-mail: philadelphia@rrb.gov

Edward M Chochek, Representative

2185 Railroad Retirement Board: Pittsburgh Pennsylvania District Office
1000 Liberty Avenue
Pittsburgh, PA 15222-4004   412-395-4634
                        Fax: 412-395-4711

Michael L Bauer, Representative

2186 Railroad Retirement Board: Scranton Pennsylvania District Office
717 Scranton Carbondale Highway
Scranton, PA 18508-1164   570-346-5774
                        Fax: 570-346-6042
                e-mail: scranton@rrb.gov

Robert C Ralston, Representative

2187 Schuylkill County Area: Agency on Aging
110 E Laurel Boulevard
Pottsville, PA 17901   570-622-3103
                             800-832-3313
                        Fax: 717-622-1732
                e-mail: seniorsvcs@hotmail.com
                        http://www.p4a.org

Crystal Lowe, Executive Director
Janet R Neidig, Training Coordinator

Pennsylvania Association of Area Agencies on Aging's mission is a statement of its commitment to act as an advocate for the aging - promoting the continued physical, social, and economic self-sufficiency of Pennsylvania's seniors. It pursues elders' right to choice and dignity in daily living, and strives to furnish its members with the essential informational/educational resources to deliver quality service toward this end.

2188 Scottdale Community Senior Citizens Club
102 Parker Avenue
Scottdale, PA 15683-1031   724-887-7299

Wilbert Deer, President

Provides recreational activities for citizens in Scottsdale, PA.

2189 Senior Adult Activities Center of Montgomery County
536 George Street
Norristown, PA 19401-4638   610-275-1960
                        Fax: 610-275-0878

Thomas Armstrong, Executive Director

Senior centers of Norristown, Ambler and Glenside, PA. Provides adult day care. Conducts educational, health, and recreational services for seniors at centers. Provides Meals on Wheels and congregate meals. Adult Day Care at Norristown site, as well. Publishes newsletter at no charge.

8 pages Frequency: Monthly

2190 Senior Centers of Bethlehem
720 Old York Road
Bethlehem, PA 18015-1613   610-867-4233
                        Fax: 610-865-5100

Vicki Jackson, Executive Director

Senior citizens in Lehigh and Northampton counties, PA. Promotes voluntarism. Operates multi-purpose center providing congregate meals, life skills education, and physical fitness, recreation, and socialization programs.

2191 Social Security for Public Employees
Pennsylvania Department of Labor & Industry
715 L&I Building
7th & Forster Streets
Harrisburg, PA 17120   717-783-8860
                        Fax: 717-783-4716
                        http://www.dli.state.pa.us

Stephen M Schmerin, Secretary

Our mission is to improve the quality of life and economic security for Pennsylvania workers and businesses, encourage labor-management cooperation, and prepare the Commonwealth's workforce for the jobs of the future.

2192 Southwestern Pennsylvania Area Agency on Aging
Eastgate 8
Monessen, PA 15062   724-684-9000
                        Fax: 724-489-1116
                        TDD 412-684-8032

Robert Willison, Director

2193 Southwestern Pennsylvania Partnership for Aging
201 Smith Drive
Suite D2
Cranberry Township, PA 16066-4130   412-772-8340
                        Fax: 412-779-2131
                e-mail: swppa@zoominternet.net
                        http://www.swppa.org

Brandon James, President
Mary Anne Kelly, Executive Director
Heather Mayger, Operations Manager

State Organizations & Government Agencies/Rhode Island

The Southwestern Pennsylvania Partnership for Aging (SWPPA) is a regional coalition of individuals and groups who are committed to the well being of an aging population. Our mission is to serve as a catalyst to promote policies, programs and system change which will improve the quality of life of older adults.

Number of Members: 398

2194 Union-Snyder Area: Agency on Aging
116 N 2nd Street
Lewisburg, PA 17837-1565
570-524-2100
Fax: 570-524-5999
e-mail: usaaa@prolog.net

Fraida Zaid, Manager

2195 Voluntary Action Center of Northeastern Pennsylvania
538 Spruce Street
Scranton, PA 18503-1845
717-347-5616
Fax: 570-341-5816
e-mail: volunteer@vacnepa.org
http://www.vacnepa.org

Ellen Stevens, Executive Director

2196 Volunteer Center of Centre County
139 S Pugh Street
8
State College, PA 16801-4745
814-234-8222
Fax: 814-235-1896
e-mail: tamgentzel@aol.com

Tammy Gentzel, Executive Director
Bill McConnel, Program Coordinator

Individuals and organizations. Provides volunteer recruitment and referral center to coordinate volunteer activities. Sponsors transportation corps.

2197 Wayne County Area: Agency on Aging
323 10th Street
Honesdale, PA 18431-1918
570-253-4262
Fax: 570-253-9115
e-mail: awhyte@co.wayne.pa.us
http://www.waynecountyhsa.org

Andrea C Whyte, Director

2198 Westmoreland County Area: Agency on Aging
200 S Main Street
Greensburg, PA 15601-3100
724-337-6660
Fax: 724-830-4513
e-mail: mhelinsk@co.westmoreland.pa.us
http://www.co.westmoreland.pa.us/aaa/aoaa.shtml
TDD 412-830-4444

Ray Ducoeur, Manager

2199 Wilkes Barre Bureau of Disability Determination
PO Box R
Wilkes Barre, PA 18703
570-824-8971
Fax: 570-826-2043

Diane Vaccaro, Manager

2200 York County Area: Agency on Aging
141 West Market Street
York, PA 17401
800-632-9073
Fax: 717-771-9044
e-mail: aging@york-county.org
http://www.york-county.org/services
TDD 717-771-9045

Dianna Benaknin, Director

The York County Area Agency on Aging promotes the independence of older adults through education, advocacy, and coordination of community based services. Our primary commitment is to deliver quality services to older adults with the greatest social or economic needs; as resources allow we may serve others with similar characteristics.

Rhode Island

2201 Bureau of Naval Personnel: Rhode Island Retired Activities Office
Fleet and Family Support Center
Naval Education and Training Center
1260 Peary Street
Newport, RI 02841-1629
401-841-4089
Fax: 401-841-1586

The RAO serves as a link between local retired military and the active-duty community which provides assistance to retired military. It provides installation commanders with a means of providing more effective services and improving communication for the local retired community. The RAO is staffed and operated by volunteer retired military who assist other retired members, their families and survivors to receive entitled services and benefits. Through newsletters, seminars and appreciation days, the RAO supports quality of life issues throughout the retirement years to their fellow service members.

2202 Department of Mental Health, Retardation and Hospitals of Rhode Island
14 Harrington Road
Cranston, RI 02920-3080
401-462-3201
Fax: 401-462-3204
http://www.mhrh.state.ri.us/
TDD 401-462-6087

Kathleen M Spangler, Manager

2203 Disability Determination Services
40 Fountain Street
Providence, RI 02903-1830
401-222-3182
Fax: 401-222-3868

John Microulis, Executive Director

2204 Gray Panthers of Rhode Island
32 E Avenue
Pawtucket, RI 02860
401-725-1122
Fax: 401-725-1020
e-mail: grayppanthersri@hotmail.com
http://www.graypanthersri.com

Kathy J Kushair, Director
Richard Bidwell, Executive Director

The mission of the Gray Panthers of Rhode Island is to identify and expose the oppressive conditions under which many seniors live; to empower seniors, their families and allies to exercise their democratic right to correct these injustices; and although we work with all ages and have members of all ages, we focus primarily to insure the right of all elders to live with dignity, justice and peace of mind.

2205 Narragansett Senior Citizens Association
53 Mumford Road
Narragansett, RI 02882-3211
401-782-0675

Barbara E Wright, Coordinator

Serves Senior citizens. To help senior citizens fulfill and enjoy their leisure years with weekly group activities. Sponsors day trips, extended trips, chorus and senior stretch.

2206 RSVP Blackstone Valley
12 Goff Avenue
Pawtucket, RI 02860-2928
401-723-4520
Fax: 401-725-6550

Shannon Kramarski, RSVP Director
Vincent Cegile, Executive Director

BVCAP RSVP (Blackstone Valley Community Action Program - Retired Senior Volunteer Program) provides the opportunity for people 55 and over to become involved in their communities through volunteer service.

State Organizations & Government Agencies/Rhode Island

2207 **RSVP Capital Region**
55 Bradford Street
Suite 202
Providence, RI 02903-1677
401-421-7472
Fax: 401-272-1655
Susan Contrass

The Retired and Senior Volunteer Program (RSVP) provides opportunities for people 55 and over to make a difference in their community through volunteer service. RSVP volunteers contribute anywhere from a few to over forty hours a week, serving though schools, day care centers, police departments, hospitals and other nonprofit and public organizations to help meet critical community needs. RSVP offers maximum flexibility and choice to its volunteers. RSVP matches the personal interests and skills to older Americans with opportunities to help solve community problems and offer supplemental insurance while on duty, on-the-job training from the agency or organization where volunteers are placed.

2208 **RSVP Cranston**
1070 Cranston Street
Cranston, RI 02920-7344
401-461-1000
Fax: 401-946-5909

The Retired and Senior Volunteer Program (RSVP) provides opportunities for people 55 and over to make a difference in their community through volunteer service. RSVP volunteers contribute anywhere from a few to over forty hours a week, serving though schools, day care centers, police departments, hospitals and other nonprofit and public organizations to help meet critical community needs. RSVP offers maximum flexibility and choice to its volunteers. RSVP matches the personal interests and skills to older Americans with opportunities to help solve community problems and offer supplemental insurance while on duty, on-the-job training from the agency or organization where volunteers are placed.

2209 **RSVP East Bay**
110 Waterman Avenue
East Providence, RI 02914-2427
401-435-7876
Fax: 401-435-7597
e-mail: ebayrsvp@selfhelp.com
Audrey Field, Director
Joanne Tavares, Coordinator

The Retired and Senior Volunteer Program (RSVP) provides opportunities for people 55 and over to make a difference in their community through volunteer service. RSVP volunteers contribute anywhere from a few to over forty hours a week, serving though schools, day care centers, police departments, hospitals and other nonprofit and public organizations to help meet critical community needs. RSVP offers maximum flexibility and choice to its volunteers. RSVP matches the personal interests and skills to older Americans with opportunities to help solve community problems and offer supplemental insurance while on duty, on-the-job training from the agency or organization where volunteers are placed.

2210 **RSVP Northern Rhode Island**
84 Social Street
Woonsocket, RI 02895-3152
401-766-2300
Fax: 401-769-6792
Charles B Ryan, Executive Director

The Retired and Senior Volunteer Program (RSVP) provides opportunities for people 55 and over to make a difference in their community through volunteer service. RSVP volunteers contribute anywhere from a few to over forty hours a week, serving though schools, day care centers, police departments, hospitals and other nonprofit and public organizations to help meet critical community needs. RSVP offers maximum flexibility and choice to its volunteers. RSVP matches the personal interests and skills to older Americans with opportunities to help solve community problems and offer supplemental insurance while on duty, on-the-job training from the agency or organization where volunteers are placed.

2211 **RSVP West Bay**
105 Buttonwoods Avenue
Warwick, RI 02886-7506
401-732-4660
Fax: 401-739-2761
Jean Gattengo, President

The Retired and Senior Volunteer Program (RSVP) provides opportunities for people 55 and over to make a difference in their community through volunteer service. RSVP volunteers contribute anywhere from a few to over forty hours a week, serving though schools, day care centers, police departments, hospitals and other nonprofit and public organizations to help meet critical community needs. RSVP offers maximum flexibility and choice to its volunteers. RSVP matches the personal interests and skills to older Americans with opportunities to help solve community problems and offer supplemental insurance while on duty, on-the-job training from the agency or organization where volunteers are placed.

2212 **Rhode Island Client Assistance Program**
349 Eddy Street
Providence, RI 02903-4204
401-831-3150
Fax: 401-274-5568
Raymond Bandusky, Executive Director

Rehabilitation programs as well as other assistance.

2213 **Rhode Island Department of Elderly Affairs**
35 Howard Avenue
Cranston, RI 02920-3001
401-462-3000
http://www.dea.state.ri.us
Corrine Russo, Manager

2214 **Rhode Island Department of Human Services: Veterans Affairs**
600 New London Avenue
Cranston, RI 02920-3041
401-462-0350
Fax: 401-462-6339

2215 **Rhode Island Department of Human Services**
006 Elmwood Avenue
Providence, RI 02907-1474
401-222-7000
Fax: 401-521-4875
http://www.dhs.state.ri.us

Offers services for the blind and visually impaired.

2216 **Rhode Island Department of Treasury: Retirement Office**
102 State House
Providence, RI 02903
401-222-2203
Fax: 401-222-2430
Joann E Flaminio, Executive Director

2217 **Rhode Island Developmental Disabilities Council**
400 Bald Hill Road
Suite 515
Warwick, RI 02886-1692
401-732-3240
Fax: 401-737-3395
e-mail: riddc@riddc.org
http://www.riddc.org
TDD 401-737-1238
Marie V Citrone, Executive Director
Christine Singleton, Chairperson
Don Ouelette, Manager

The Rhode Island Developmental Disabilities Council works to make Rhode Island a better place for people with developmental disabilities to live, work, go to school and be part of their communities.

2218 **Rhode Island Division of Taxation**
1 Capitol Hill
Providence, RI 02908-5816
401-222-1040
Fax: 401-222-6006
http://www.doa.state.ri.is/tax
R Gary Clark, Administrator

197

State Organizations & Government Agencies/South Carolina

2219 **Rhode Island Governor's Committee on the Disabled**
115 State House
Suite 115
Providence, RI 02903-1121
401-222-6905
Fax: 401-222-8096
Stephen Tocco, Manager

2220 **Rhode Island Organizing Project**
134 Mathewson Street
Providence, RI 02903-1807
401-351-5577
Fax: 401-453-2545
Duane Clinker, Contact
Luke Hill, Manager

2221 **Rhode Island Protection & Advocacy for Persons with Disabilities**
Rhode Island Disability Law Center
349 Eddy Street
Providence, RI 02903-4204
401-831-3150
Fax: 401-274-5568
Raymond Bandusky, Director

2222 **Seniors Helping Others Volunteer Program of Washington County**
25 Saint Dominic Road
Wakefield, RI 02879-1878
401-789-2362
Fax: 401-789-1138
e-mail: seniors-rsvp@netsense.net
http://www.sho-ri.tripod.com
Fred Vanley, Volunteer Coordinator
Debra Tanner, Executive Director

South Carolina

2223 **Aiken Area Council on Aging**
PO Box 235
Aiken, SC 29802
803-648-5447
800-603-5627
Fax: 803-649-1005
e-mail: aacoa@csra.net
Scott K Murphy, Executive Director

Interested persons aged 60 and older. Provides focal point for information, advocacy, and other services for senior citizens. Promotes independence and quality of life.

2224 **Catawba Area: Agency on Aging**
2225 Ebenezer Road
Suite 0
Rock Hill, SC 29732-9288
803-329-9670
Fax: 803-329-6537
e-mail: catawbaAAA@catawba-aging.com
http://www.catawba-aging.com
Sherron Marshall, Director
Barbara Robinson, Executive Director

2225 **Disability Determination Division**
PO Box 60
West Columbia, SC 29171
803-896-6700
Fax: 803-896-6426
Thomas Paige, Executive Director

2226 **Good Faith**
921 Holland Avenue
Cayce, SC 29033-3629
803-791-9278
Schhrl B Amos, Executive Secretary-Treasurer
Rebecca Mercado CPA, Owner

Raises funds to cover the cost of dental plates for elderly and handicapped persons.

2227 **Lancaster County Council on Aging**
PO Box 1809
Lancaster, SC 29721-1809
803-416-9306
Fax: 803-285-3361
http://lancastercountysc.net
Lisa Robinson, Manager

Provides services for the elderly.

2228 **Low Country Area: Agency on Aging**
Interstate 95, US Highway 17
Yemassee, SC 29945
843-726-5536
Fax: 843-726-5165
Corona Harrigan, Director
Chris Bickley, Executive Director

2229 **Lower Savannah Area: Agency on Aging**
PO Box 850
Aiken, SC 29802
803-649-7981
Fax: 803-649-2248
Linda H Holmes, Director
Wayne Rogers, Executive Director

2230 **Protection & Advocacy for People with Disabilities**
3710 Landmark Drive
Suite 208
Columbia, SC 29204-4034
803-782-0639
800-922-5225
Fax: 803-790-1946
e-mail: scpa0639@aol.com
Gloria Prevost, Executive Director

2231 **RSVP Aiken County**
PO Box 2066
Aiken, SC 29802-2066
803-648-6836
Fax: 803-649-1588
George Anderson, Executive Director

The Retired and Senior Volunteer Program (RSVP) provides opportunities for people 55 and over to make a difference in their community through volunteer service. RSVP volunteers contribute anywhere from a few to over forty hours a week, serving though schools, day care centers, police departments, hospitals and other nonprofit and public organizations to help meet critical community needs. RSVP offers maximum flexibility and choice to its volunteers. RSVP matches the personal interests and skills to older Americans with opportunities to help solve community problems and offer supplemental insurance while on duty, on-the-job training from the agency or organization where volunteers are placed.

2232 **RSVP Carolina Low Country**
8085 Rivers Avenue
Suite F
North Charleston, SC 29406
843-764-2323
Fax: 843-764-2318
e-mail: dillonp@usa.redcross.org
http://www.lowcountryredcross.org
Pam Dillon, Director
Marlene Williamon, Area Coordintor

Engages persons 55 and older in volunteer service to meet critical community needs; and to provide a high quality experience that will enrich the lives of volunteers,

2233 **RSVP Florence County**
2685 S Irby Street
Florence, SC 29505-3440
843-669-6761
Fax: 843-665-2266

State Organizations & Government Agencies/South Carolina

The Retired and Senior Volunteer Program (RSVP) provides opportunities for people 55 and over to make a difference in their community through volunteer service. RSVP volunteers contribute anywhere from a few to over forty hours a week, serving though schools, day care centers, police departments, hospitals and other nonprofit and public organizations to help meet critical community needs. RSVP offers maximum flexibility and choice to its volunteers. RSVP matches the personal interests and skills to older Americans with opportunities to help solve community problems and offer supplemental insurance while on duty, on-the-job training from the agency or organization where volunteers are placed.

2234 RSVP Greenville
102 E McBee Avenue
Greenville, SC 29601-2935
864-467-3660
Fax: 864-467-3668

Cynthia Schaffer, Executive Director

The Retired and Senior Volunteer Program (RSVP) provides opportunities for people 55 and over to make a difference in their community through volunteer service. RSVP volunteers contribute anywhere from a few to over forty hours a week, serving though schools, day care centers, police departments, hospitals and other nonprofit and public organizations to help meet critical community needs. RSVP offers maximum flexibility and choice to its volunteers. RSVP matches the personal interests and skills to older Americans with opportunities to help solve community problems and offer supplemental insurance while on duty, on-the-job training from the agency or organization where volunteers are placed.

2235 RSVP McCormick
1300 S Main Street
Mc Cormick, SC 29835-7927
864-465-2822
Fax: 864-465-3446

Becky McDade, Executive Director

The Retired and Senior Volunteer Program (RSVP) provides opportunities for people 55 and over to make a difference in their community through volunteer service. RSVP volunteers contribute anywhere from a few to over forty hours a week, serving though schools, day care centers, police departments, hospitals and other nonprofit and public organizations to help meet critical community needs. RSVP offers maximum flexibility and choice to its volunteers. RSVP matches the personal interests and skills to older Americans with opportunities to help solve community problems and offer supplemental insurance while on duty, on-the-job training from the agency or organization where volunteers are placed.

2236 RSVP Newberry County
1300 Hunt Street
Newberry, SC 29108-3036
803-276-8266
Fax: 803-276-6312

Lynn M Stockman, Executive Director

The Retired and Senior Volunteer Program (RSVP) provides opportunities for people 55 and over to make a difference in their community through volunteer service. RSVP volunteers contribute anywhere from a few to over forty hours a week, serving though schools, day care centers, police departments, hospitals and other nonprofit and public organizations to help meet critical community needs. RSVP offers maximum flexibility and choice to its volunteers. RSVP matches the personal interests and skills to older Americans with opportunities to help solve community problems and offer supplemental insurance while on duty, on-the-job training from the agency or organization where volunteers are placed.

2237 RSVP Richland
1817 Millwood Avenue
Columbia, SC 29205-1261
803-252-7734
Fax: 803-649-1588

Robin McCartha, Executive Director

The Retired and Senior Volunteer Program (RSVP) provides opportunities for people 55 and over to make a difference in their community through volunteer service. RSVP volunteers contribute anywhere from a few to over forty hours a week, serving though schools, day care centers, police departments, hospitals and other nonprofit and public organizations to help meet critical community needs. RSVP offers maximum flexibility and choice to its volunteers. RSVP matches the personal interests and skills to older Americans with opportunities to help solve community problems and offer supplemental insurance while on duty, on-the-job training from the agency or organization where volunteers are placed.

2238 RSVP Spartanburg
142 S Dean Street
Spartanburg, SC 29302-1937
864-596-3910
Fax: 864-596-2970

Nancy K Ogle, Executive Director

The Retired and Senior Volunteer Program (RSVP) provides opportunities for people 55 and over to make a difference in their community through volunteer service. RSVP volunteers contribute anywhere from a few to over forty hours a week, serving though schools, day care centers, police departments, hospitals and other nonprofit and public organizations to help meet critical community needs. RSVP offers maximum flexibility and choice to its volunteers. RSVP matches the personal interests and skills to older Americans with opportunities to help solve community problems and offer supplemental insurance while on duty, on-the-job training from the agency or organization where volunteers are placed.

2239 RSVP Sumter County
120 E Liberty Street
Sumter, SC 29150-5239
803-773-5508
Fax: 803-773-3294

Shirley Baker, Executive Director

The Retired and Senior Volunteer Program (RSVP) provides opportunities for people 55 and over to make a difference in their community through volunteer service. RSVP volunteers contribute anywhere from a few to over forty hours a week, serving though schools, day care centers, police departments, hospitals and other nonprofit and public organizations to help meet critical community needs. RSVP offers maximum flexibility and choice to its volunteers. RSVP matches the personal interests and skills to older Americans with opportunities to help solve community problems and offer supplemental insurance while on duty, on-the-job training from the agency or organization where volunteers are placed.

2240 RSVP York County
150 Johnston Street
Rock Hill, SC 29730-4506
803-327-6649
Fax: 803-327-5210

The Retired and Senior Volunteer Program (RSVP) provides opportunities for people 55 and over to make a difference in their community through volunteer service. RSVP volunteers contribute anywhere from a few to over forty hours a week, serving though schools, day care centers, police departments, hospitals and other nonprofit and public organizations to help meet critical community needs. RSVP offers maximum flexibility and choice to its volunteers. RSVP matches the personal interests and skills to older Americans with opportunities to help solve community problems and offer supplemental insurance while on duty, on-the-job training from the agency or organization where volunteers are placed.

2241 Santee-Lynches Council of Governments Area Agency on Aging
PO Box 1837
Sumter, SC 29151-1837
803-775-7381
Fax: 803-773-6902

Connie D Munn, Director
James Darby, Executive Director

State Organizations & Government Agencies/South Carolina

2242 **Social Security: West Columbia Disability Determination**
SC Vocational Rehabilitation Department
1410 Boston Avenue
PO Box 15
West Columbia, SC 29171
803-896-6500
800-832-7526
Fax: 803-896-6553
e-mail: info@scvrd.state.sc.us

Larry C Bryant, SCRVD Commissioner/Secretary

The South Carolina Vocational Rehabilitation Department's Disability Determination Services processes Social Security and Supplemental Security Income claims under the provisions of the Social Security Act.

2243 **South Carolina Assistive Technology Projects**
USC School of Medicine
Columbia, SC 29208
803-256-6457
Fax: 803-935-5342
e-mail: youngs@cdd.sc.edu
http://www.sc.edu/scatp
TDD 803-935-5263

Evelyn Evans, Director

A statewide program promoting assistive technology devices and services for persons of all ages with all disabilities.

2244 **South Carolina Association Area: Agencies on Aging**
236 Stoneridge Drive
Columbia, SC 29210-8010
803-376-5390
Fax: 803-376-5394

Norman Whitaker, Executive Director

2245 **South Carolina Association of Nonprofit Homes for the Aging**
2711 Middleburg Drive Ste309-12
Columbia, SC 29204
803-988-0005
Fax: 803-988-1017
e-mail: scanpha@scanpha.org
http://www.scanpha.org

Vickie L Moody, President

Our mission is to represent and to promote the common interests of its members through leadership, advocacy, education, and other services in order to enhance its members' ability to serve their constituencies.

2246 **South Carolina Budget and Control Board: Retirement System Division**
PO Box 11960
Columbia, SC 29211-1960
803-737-6800
800-868-9002
Fax: 803-737-7594

Peggy Boykin, Manager

2247 **South Carolina Client Assistance Program Office of the Governor of South Carolina**
1205 Pendleton Street
Columbia, SC 29201-3756
803-734-0285
800-868-0040
Fax: 803-734-0546
e-mail: lbarker@govpoepp.state.sc.us
http://www.govpoepp.state.sc.us
TDD 803-734-1147

Larry Barker, PhD, Director
Marjorie Butler, MRC, Program Administrator

The Client Assistance Program (CAP) helps citizens of the State by acting as advocates regarding services provided by the Vocational Rehabilitation Department (VR), Commission for the Blind, and all Independent Living programs and projects funded under the Rehabilitation Act of 1973. As advocates, CAP staff can investigate, negotiate, mediate, and pursue administrative, and other remedies to ensure that clients rights are protected.

2248 **South Carolina Commission on Aging**
PO Box 8206
Columbia, SC 29202-8206
803-898-2850
Fax: 803-737-7501

2249 **South Carolina Department of Aging**
#B-500, 400 Arbor Lake Drive
Columbia, SC 29223
803-741-0826

Ruth Seigler, Director

2250 **South Carolina Department of Veterans Affairs**
1205 Pendleton Street
Columbia, SC 29201-3756
803-734-0200
Fax: 803-734-0197

Jimmie Ruff, Executive Director

2251 **South Carolina Developmental Disability Council**
1205 Pendleton Street
Suite 372
Columbia, SC 29201-3751
803-734-0660
Fax: 803-734-0241
http://www.scddc.state.sc.us/

Sherry Copeland, Manager

2252 **South Carolina Services Information System**
University of South Carolina
School of Medicine
Columbia, SC 29208
803-935-5231
800-922-1107
Fax: 803-935-5250
e-mail: deniser@cdd.sc.edu

Denise Rivers, Program Director
Donald Wuori MD

SCSIS provides information on aging and disability services in the state of South Carolina. Also, has a used equipment referral exchange where buyers and sellers are matched.

2253 **South Carolina Workers Compensation Commission**
PO Box 1715
Columbia, SC 29202-1715
803-737-5700
Fax: 803-737-5768
http://www.state.sc.usa/wcc

Gary Thibault, Manager

2254 **Trident Area Agency on Aging**
ElderLink
1360 Truxton Avenue
Suite 210
North Charleston, SC 29405-8538
843-554-2790
Fax: 843-745-1718

Angela Edwards, Director

Trident Area Agency on Aging plan, coordinate and offer services that help older adults remain in their home - if that is their preference - aided by services such as Meals-on-Wheels, homemaker assistance and whatever else it may take to make independent living a viable option.

2255 **Upper Savannah Council of Government Area: Agency on Aging**
222 Phoenix Avenue
Greenwood, SC 29648
864-941-8050
800-922-7729

Patricia Hartung, Executive Director

2256 **Vantage Point: Division of Caresouth Carolina**
PO Box 238
Hartsville, SC 29551
843-383-8632
800-922-1641
Fax: 843-383-8754

Earlene Mark, Director
Shelia Capps, Executive Director

South Dakota

2257 Division of Developmental Disabilies
E Highway 34, C/O 500 E Capitol
Pierre, SD 57501
605-773-3438
Fax: 605-773-5483
http://www.state.nd.us/dhs
Wanda Seiler, Executive Director

2258 Glacial Lakes Retired & Senior Volunteer Program
711 W 1st Street
Webster, SD 57274-1361
605-345-3741
Fax: 605-345-1333
e-mail: mkilber.rsvp@midconetwork.com
http://www.seniorservice.org/glaciallakes_rsvp
Marge Kilber, Director

Serving Codington, Day, Deuel, Grant and Robert's counties.

2259 RSVP Brown County
1303 7th Avenue SE
Aberdeen, SD 57401-4935
605-626-3332
Fax: 605-626-3330

The Retired and Senior Volunteer Program (RSVP) provides opportunities for people 55 and over to make a difference in their community through volunteer service. RSVP volunteers contribute anywhere from a few to over forty hours a week, serving though schools, day care centers, police departments, hospitals and other nonprofit and public organizations to help meet critical community needs. RSVP offers maximum flexibility and choice to its volunteers. RSVP matches the personal interests and skills to older Americans with opportunities to help solve community problems and offer supplemental insurance while on duty, on-the-job training from the agency or organization where volunteers are placed.

2260 RSVP East Central South Dakota
290 7th Street SW
Huron, SD 57350-2759
605-353-8586
Fax: 605-353-9585
e-mail: rsvp@basec.net
Dar French, RSVP Director

Approximately 630 retired individuals in the East Central South Dakota Area volunteer 116,000 hours in their communities covering a 5300 square mile area we feel they cover most of the community needs. Is a community service organization.

2261 RSVP Northern Black Hills
1200 University Street
Unit 9089
Spearfish, SD 57799-9089
605-642-5198
Fax: 605-642-7668
e-mail: rsvp@bhsu.edu
Kathleen Schneider, Contact

The Retired and Senior Volunteer Program (RSVP) provides opportunities for people 55 and over to make a difference in their community through volunteer service. RSVP volunteers contribute anywhere from a few to over forty hours a week, serving though schools, day care centers, police departments, hospitals and other nonprofit and public organizations to help meet critical community needs. RSVP offers maximum flexibility and choice to its volunteers. RSVP matches the personal interests and skills to older Americans with opportunities to help solve community problems and offer supplemental insurance while on duty, on-the-job training from the agency or organization where volunteers are placed.

2262 RSVP Rapdi City Area
333 6th Street
Rapid City, SD 57701-5025
605-394-2507
Fax: 605-394-2508
Angelique Weeks, Executive Director

The Retired and Senior Volunteer Program (RSVP) provides opportunities for people 55 and over to make a difference in their community through volunteer service. RSVP volunteers contribute anywhere from a few to over forty hours a week, serving though schools, day care centers, police departments, hospitals and other nonprofit and public organizations to help meet critical community needs. RSVP offers maximum flexibility and choice to its volunteers. RSVP matches the personal interests and skills to older Americans with opportunities to help solve community problems and offer supplemental insurance while on duty, on-the-job training from the agency or organization where volunteers are placed.

2263 RSVP Siouxland
1000 N West Avenue
Suite 260
Sioux Falls, SD 57104-1367
605-367-7274
Fax: 605-367-7106
e-mail: sosdakota1013@gwest.net
Sandra Hansen, Project Director

RSVP is a national nonprofit organization that provides meaningful volunteer experiences for individuals 55+ within their local communities. Locally, the SIOUXLAND RSVP utilizes the time and talents of 600 volunteers in 200 local nonprofit organizations, health related facilities and public agencies in Minnehaha, Lincoln, and Union Counties in southeastern South Dakota.

2264 South Dakota Association of Homes for the Aging
3708 W Brooks Place
Sioux Falls, SD 57106-4207
605-361-2281
Fax: 605-361-5175
Ken Senger, Executive Director
Dave Hewett, President

Non-profit nursing home administrators. Promotes quality long-term health care for the elderly through educational sessions and input in regulatory issues.

2265 South Dakota Client Assistance Program
221 S Central Avenue
Pierre, SD 57501-2479
605-224-8294
Fax: 605-224-5125
e-mail: sdas@iw.net
Nancy Chadd, Director
Robert Kean, Executive Director

2266 South Dakota Department of Aging
700 Governors Drive
Pierre, SD 57501-2291
605-773-3656
Fax: 605-773-6834
http://www.state.sd.us/social/asp/
Gail Ferris, Administrator

2267 South Dakota Department of Military and Veterans Services
425 E Capitol Avenue
Pierre, SD 57501-3100
605-773-3361
Fax: 605-773-5380
Doneen Hollingsworth, Manager

2268 South Dakota Department of Revenue
445 E Capitol Avenue
Pierre, SD 57501-3185
605-773-3361
800-829-9188
Fax: 605-773-5129
http://www.state.sd.us/executive/revenue
Doneen Hollingsworth, Manager

2269 South Dakota Department of Social Services: Adult Services and Aging
700 Governors Drive
Pierre, SD 57501-2291
605-773-3656
Fax: 605-773-6834
Gail Ferris, Manager

State Organizations & Government Agencies/Tennessee

2270 South Dakota Disability Determination Sevices
811 E 10th Street
Department 24
Sioux Falls, SD 57103-1650
605-367-5499
800-658-2272
Fax: 605-367-5485
e-mail: Dave.Tschetter@ssa.gov
David Tschetter, Manager

The DARS Division for Disability Determination Services (DDS), funded entirely through the Social Security Administration (SSA), makes disability determinations for persons with severe disabilities who apply for Social Security Disability Insurance and/or Supplemental Security Income.

2271 South Dakota Division of Rehabilitation
E Highway 34, C/O 500 E Capitol
Pierre, SD 57501
605-773-3195
Fax: 605-773-5483
http://www.state.nd.us/dhs
Grady Kickul, Division Director

Provides individualized services to assist people with significant disabilities to get and keep jobs that are compatible with their disability. Services can consist of: vocational rehabilitation counseling, assessment and diagnostic, work skills training, job site accommodations, job placement, and employer services.

2272 South Dakota Office of Adult Services
70 Governors Drive
Pierre, SD 57501
605-773-3656
Fax: 605-773-6834
Gail Ferris, Manager

2273 South Dakota Protection Advocacy Services
221 S Central Avenue
Pierre, SD 57501-2479
605-773-3181
Fax: 605-224-5125
e-mail: sdas@sdadvocacy.com
http://www.sdadvocacy.com
Darlys Baum, Executive Director

2274 South Dakota Workers Compensation Board
700 Governors Drive
Pierre, SD 57501-2291
605-773-3681
Fax: 605-773-4211
e-mail: jamesm@dol_pp.state.sd.us
James Marsh, Director
Pam Roberts, Manager

Tennessee

2275 Disability Determinations
PO Box 775
Nashville, TN 37202
615-313-5464
800-342-1117
Fax: 800-208-9973

2276 East Tennessee Area Agencies on Aging
9111 Cross Park Drive
Suite D100
Knoxville, TN 37923-4517
865-691-2551
Fax: 865-531-7216
http://www.ethra.org
Aaron Bradley, Administrator
Gordan A Acuff, Executive Director

2277 McMinn County Senior Citizens
PO Box 41
Athens, TN 37371
423-745-6830
Fax: 423-745-6803
e-mail: mcminnsenior@wmconnect.com
Holly Henderson, Executive Director

Extends senior citizen's quality of life by involving children and community in providing educational, physical, nutritional, intergenerational, recreational, and social programs including volunteer service opportunities. Serves ages 55+.

2278 Midsouth Area: Agency on Aging
2670 Union Avenue Extension
Suite 1000
Memphis, TN 38112
901-324-6333
Fax: 901-327-7755
e-mail: kspears@agingcommission.org
http://www.agingcommision.org
Kathleen Spears, PhD, Director

The Agency on Aging serves as the local point for aging services. The Agency on Aging also acts as the uniting link between senior citizens and agencies and programs that serve them.

2279 Northwest Tennessee Area Agency on Aging and Disability
Northwest Tennessee Development District
124 Weldon Drive
PO Box 963
Martin, TN 38237-0963
731-587-4213
Fax: 731-588-5833
e-mail: shill@charterbn.com
http://www.setaaad.org
Susan Hill, Director

Northwest Tennessee Area Agency on Aging strives to secure, promote and provide essential services to enhance the quality of life in a diverse and changing society. We meet this challenge through advocacy, coordination, building alliances, and promoting public awareness, guided by integrity, vision, and sustained commitment.

2280 RSVP Clarksville County
PO Box 487
Clarksville, TN 37041
931-648-5774
Fax: 931-648-5784
Joel Riddle, Executive Director

The Retired and Senior Volunteer Program (RSVP) provides opportunities for people 55 and over to make a difference in their community through volunteer service. RSVP volunteers contribute anywhere from a few to over forty hours a week, serving thourgh schools, day care centers, police departments, hospitals and other nonprofit and public organizations to help meet critical community needs. RSVP offers maximum flexibility and choice to its volunteers. RSVP matches the personal interests and skills to older Americans with opportunities to help solve community problems and offer supplemental insurance while on duty, on-the-job training from the agency or organization where volunteers are placed.

2281 RSVP Dyer County
710 Highway 51 By Pass
Dyersburg, TN 38024
901-286-7828
Fax: 731-286-6886

The Retired and Senior Volunteer Program (RSVP) provides opportunities for people 55 and over to make a difference in their community through volunteer service. RSVP volunteers contribute anywhere from a few to over forty hours a week, serving thourgh schools, day care centers, police departments, hospitals and other nonprofit and public organizations to help meet critical community needs. RSVP offers maximum flexibility and choice to its volunteers. RSVP matches the personal interests and skills to older Americans with opportunities to help solve community problems and offer supplemental insurance while on duty, on-the-job training from the agency or organization where volunteers are placed.

2282 RSVP East Central Tennessee
240 Carlen Avenue
Cookeville, TN 38501-3622
931-528-6488
Fax: 615-528-6488
e-mail: fgprsvp@frontiernet.net
Sandra Wilson, Contact

State Organizations & Government Agencies/Tennessee

The Retired and Senior Volunteer Program (RSVP) provides opportunities for people 55 and over to make a difference in their community through volunteer service. RSVP volunteers contribute anywhere from a few to over forty hours a week, serving though schools, day care centers, police departments, hospitals and other nonprofit and public organizations to help meet critical community needs. RSVP offers maximum flexibility and choice to its volunteers. RSVP matches the personal interests and skills to older Americans with opportunities to help solve community problems and offer supplemental insurance while on duty, on-the-job training from the agency or organization where volunteers are placed.

2283 RSVP Fayettevill Area
PO Box 638
Fayetteville, TN 37334   931-433-7182
                                913-438-0074
Roy Tipps, Executive Director

The Retired and Senior Volunteer Program (RSVP) provides opportunities for people 55 and over to make a difference in their community through volunteer service. RSVP volunteers contribute anywhere from a few to over forty hours a week, serving though schools, day care centers, police departments, hospitals and other nonprofit and public organizations to help meet critical community needs. RSVP offers maximum flexibility and choice to its volunteers. RSVP matches the personal interests and skills to older Americans with opportunities to help solve community problems and offer supplemental insurance while on duty, on-the-job training from the agency or organization where volunteers are placed.

2284 RSVP Knoxville-Knox County
1247 Western Avenue
Knoxville, TN 37921-5756   865-637-6244
                           Fax: 865-546-0832
Beth Shamir, Manager

The Retired and Senior Volunteer Program (RSVP) provides opportunities for people 55 and over to make a difference in their community through volunteer service. RSVP volunteers contribute anywhere from a few to over forty hours a week, serving though schools, day care centers, police departments, hospitals and other nonprofit and public organizations to help meet critical community needs. RSVP offers maximum flexibility and choice to its volunteers. RSVP matches the personal interests and skills to older Americans with opportunities to help solve community problems and offer supplemental insurance while on duty, on-the-job training from the agency or organization where volunteers are placed.

2285 RSVP Lexington-Henderson Counties
145 South Main Street
Lexington, TN 38351   901-968-7548
                           Fax: 901-968-4559
                      e-mail: hotdog@ncol.net
Evelyn M Parker, Director

Several of our senior volunteers provide highway cleanup/beautification; others help with the Community Center Gardens.

2286 RSVP McMinnville
203 W Main Street
McMinnville, TN 37111   931-473-5367
                           Fax: 931-473-5637
                    e-mail: rsvp@blomand.net
Sue Jones, Contact

RSVP volunteers provide hundreds of community services while volunteering around the community. Individuals age 55 and older put their skills and life experiences to work for the community. Each senior adult volunteer chooses how, when and how many hours they want to serve.

2287 RSVP Rutherford
126 E Prince Street
Gallatin, TN 37066-2854   615-452-8521
                           Fax: 615-452-8521
Linda Moncrief, Executive Director

The Retired and Senior Volunteer Program (RSVP) provides opportunities for people 55 and over to make a difference in their community through volunteer service. RSVP volunteers contribute anywhere from a few to over forty hours a week, serving though schools, day care centers, police departments, hospitals and other nonprofit and public organizations to help meet critical community needs. RSVP offers maximum flexibility and choice to its volunteers. RSVP matches the personal interests and skills to older Americans with opportunities to help solve community problems and offer supplemental insurance while on duty, on-the-job training from the agency or organization where volunteers are placed.

2288 RSVP Shelby County
110 Vance Avenue
Memphis, TN 38126-2911   901-527-0208
                           Fax: 901-527-3202
Margaret Craddock, Executive Director

The Retired and Senior Volunteer Program (RSVP) provides opportunities for people 55 and over to make a difference in their community through volunteer service. RSVP volunteers contribute anywhere from a few to over forty hours a week, serving though schools, day care centers, police departments, hospitals and other nonprofit and public organizations to help meet critical community needs. RSVP offers maximum flexibility and choice to its volunteers. RSVP matches the personal interests and skills to older Americans with opportunities to help solve community problems and offer supplemental insurance while on duty, on-the-job training from the agency or organization where volunteers are placed.

2289 Railroad Retirement Board: Tennessee District Office
233 Cumberland Bnd
Suite 206
Nashville, TN 37228-1808   615-736-5131
                           Fax: 615-736-7071
Suzanna Givan, Representative

2290 Senior Citizens
174 Rains Avenue
Nashville, TN 37203-5319   615-743-3400
                           Fax: 615-743-3480
                          e-mail: info@scitn.org
                              http://www.scitn.org
Nancy Northern, Contact

Senior Citizens offers six activity centers in Davidson and Williamson counties for persons 55 and older. Aside from extraordinary volunteer opportunities including work with children, there are travel, trips and excursions events. We also offer care management, respite care, adult day care, Meals on Wheels, Victory Over Crime, conservatorship, and much more.

2291 Southwest Tennessee Area: Agency on Aging
27 Conrad Drive
Suite 150
Jackson, TN 38305-2844   731-668-7112
                           Fax: 731-668-6421
                      http://www.swtdd.org/aaa.htm
Wanda C Simmons, Director
Everlyn Robertson Jr, Owner

2292 Tennessee Association of Homes and Services for the Aging
500 Interstate Boulevard
Nashville, TN 37210-4634   615-256-1800
                           Fax: 615-726-3082
                    e-mail: jvandiver@tha.com
                      http://www.tha.com/tnahsa
James Vandiver, President

2293 Tennessee Client Assistance Program
PO Box 121257
Nashville, TN 37212-1257   615-298-1080
                           Fax: 615-298-2046
Shirley Shea, Executive Director

State Organizations & Government Agencies/Texas

2294 **Tennessee Commission on Aging**
706 Church Street
Suite 201
Nashville, TN 37243
615-741-2056
Fax: 615-741-3309

2295 **Tennessee Council on Developmental Disabilities**
Andrew Jackson Building
404 James Robertson Pkwy
Suite 1310
Nashville, TN 37243-0228
615-532-6615
Fax: 615-532-6964
e-mail: tnddc@state.tn.us
http://www.state.tn.us/cdd
TTY 615-741-4562

Wanda Willis, Executive Director
Errol Elshtain, Planning Coordinator

The Tennessee Council of Developmental Disabilities is a State office that promotes public policies to increase and support the inclusion of individuals with developmental disabilities in their communities. The Council works with public and private groups across the State to find necessary supports for individuals with disabilities and their families, so that they may have equal access to public education, employment, housing, health care, and all other aspects of community life.

2296 **Tennessee Department of Aging**
706 Church Street
Suite 201
Nashville, TN 37203-3586
615-741-2056
Fax: 615-741-3309

Emily Wiseman, Executive Director

2297 **Tennessee Department of Revenue**
500 Deaderick Street
Nashville, TN 37242
615-741-2330
800-342-1003
http://www.state.tn.us/revenue

Ruth S Letson, Manager

2298 **Tennessee Department of Veterans Affairs**
215 8th Avenue N
Nashville, TN 37243
615-741-2931
Fax: 615-741-4785

John Keys, Manager

2299 **Tennessee Division of Rehabilitation Services**
State Vocational Rehabilitation Agency
400 Deaderick Street
15th Floor
Nashville, TN 37248
615-313-4714
Fax: 615-741-4165
e-mail: carlbrown@mail.state.tn.us
http://www.state.tn.us/humanserv

Gina Lodge, Commissioner
Andrea Cooper, Assistant Commissioner

The Division of Vocational Rehabilitation is the state's public program that helps people with physical and mental disabilities obtain or retain employment. Its mission is to provide opportunities and resources to eligible individuals with disabilities, leading to success in employment and independent living.

2300 **Tennessee Technology Access Project**
Citizens Plaza State Office Building
14th Floor
400 Deaderick Street
Nashville, TN 37248
615-313-5183
800-732-5059
Fax: 615-532-4685
e-mail: tn.ttap@state.tn.us
http://www.state.tn.us
TTY 615-313-5695

Kevin White, Program Director

The Tennessee Technology Access Project (TTAP) is a statewide program designed to increase access to, and acquisition of, assistive technology devices and services.

2301 **Upper Cumberland Area: Agency on Aging**
1225 S Willow Avenue
Cookeville, TN 38506-4158
931-432-4111
Fax: 931-432-6010
http://www.ucdd.org

Nancy Peace, Director
Wendy Askins, Executive Director

2302 **Workers Compensation Division**
710 James Robertson Parkway
Nashville, TN 37243-1219
615-741-2395
Fax: 615-532-1468

Texas

2303 **AARP Southwest Regional Office**
AARP
8144 Walnut Hill Lane
Suite 700lb-39
Dallas, TX 75231-4388
214-265-4060
Fax: 404-888-0902
http://www.aarp.org
TTY 916-446-2680

A resource for AARP members in the states of Arizona, Arkansas, Colorado, Kansas, Louisiana, Missouri, New Mexico, Oklahoma, Texas and Utah. Hours are 9-5 Monday through Friday.

2304 **Alamo Area: Agency on Aging**
8700 Tesoro Drive
Suite 700
San Antonio, TX 78217-6228
210-362-5291
Fax: 210-225-5937
e-mail: mail@aacog.com

2305 **Area Agency on Aging of Southeast Texas**
2210 Eastex Freeway
Beaumont, TX 77703
409-899-8444
800-395-5465
Fax: 409-899-4829
e-mail: aaa@setrpc.org
http://www.setaaa.org
TDD 409-347-2769

Roxanne Smith Parks, Director

The Area Agency on Aging of Southeast Texas (AAASET) assists older individuals and their families in finding appropriate resources to further the independence and dignity of an older adult residing in Hardin, Jefferson or Orange County.

2306 **Area Agency on Aging of the Capital Area**
2512 Interstate Highway 35 S
Suite 100
Austin, TX 78704
512-916-6062
Fax: 512-916-6042
e-mail: aaaca@capco.state.tx.us
http://www.aaacap.org

Glenda Rogers, Director

Services for 60+ individuals.

2307 **Area Agency on Aging of the Concho Valley**
4850 Knickerbocker Road
San Angelo, TX 76904
325-223-5704
Fax: 325-223-8233
e-mail: aging@cvcog.org
http://www.cvcog.org/aging

Betty Ford, Director
Rosie Quintela, Operations Manager
Terry Lockhart, Local Managing Ombudsman

Our mission is to be the visible advocate and leader in the Concho Valley in providing for a comprehensive and coordinated continuum of services and opportunities so that older people can lead dignified, independent, and productive lives.

State Organizations & Government Agencies/Texas

2308 **Ark-Tex Council of Governments Area Agency on Aging**
PO Box 5307
Texarkana, TX 75505-5307
903-832-8636
800-372-4464
Fax: 903-832-3441
e-mail: msmith@atcog.org
Maratha Hall Smith, Manager
Judy Mattson, Manager

2309 **Austin Disability Determination Services**
Department of Assistive and Rehabilitative Svcs
PO Box 149198
Austin, TX 78714-9198
512-437-8000
800-252-7009
http://www.dars.state.tx.us
Terrell I Murphy, DARS Commissioner
Mary Elder, Deputy Commissioner
Alvin Miller, Chief Operating Officer

The DARS Division for Disability Determination Services (DDS), funded entirely through the Social Security Administration (SSA), makes disability determinations for Texans with severe disabilities who apply for benefits at their local Social Security Office and their applications are forwarded to DDS for a disability determination; however, SSA is responsbile for making final decisions as to whether or not a person is eligible to receive benefits.

2310 **Austin State School Volunteer Council**
2203 W 35th Street
Austin, TX 78703-1203
512-454-4731
Fax: 512-374-6068
http://www.austinstateschoolcouncil.org
Ray Wells, Administrator

Nonprofit advocacy group working for the benefit of residents of Austin State School.

2311 **Bexar County Area: Agency on Aging**
8700 Tesoro Drive
Suite 700
San Antonio, TX 78217-6228
210-362-5200
Fax: 210-225-5937
e-mail: mail@aacog.com
Tina Smith, Executive Director

2312 **Bureau of Naval Personnel: Houston Retired Activities Office**
1902 Old Spanish Trail
Houston, TX 77054-2025
713-795-4109
Fax: 713-795-5733

The RAO serves as a link between local retired military and the active-duty community which provides assistance to retired military. It provides installation commanders with a means of providing more effective services and improving communicatin for the local retired community. The RAO is staffed and operated by volunteer retired military who assist other retired members, their families and survivors to receive entitled services and benefits.Through newsletters, seminars and appreciation days, the RAO supports quality of life issues throughout the retirement years to their fellow service members.

2313 **Bureau of Naval Personnel: Kingsville Retired Activities Office**
Fleet and Family Support Center
NAS Kingsville-NFSC
746 Rosendahl Street
Kingsville, TX 78363-5110
361-516-6105
Fax: 361-516-6927
http://www.navyfamily.com

The RAO serves as a link between local retired military and the active-duty community which provides assistance to retired military. It provides installation commanders with a means of providing more effective services and improving communication for the local retired community. The RAO is staffed and operated by volunteer retired military who assist other retired members, their families and survivors to receive entitled services and benefits. Through newsletters, seminars and appreciation days, the RAO supports quality of life issues throughout the retirement years to their fellow service members.

2314 **Bureau of Naval Personnel: San Antonio Retired Activities Center**
3837 Binz Engleman Road
San Antonio, TX 78219-2219
210-225-2997
Fax: 210-225-3082

The RAO serves as a link between local retired military and the active-duty which provides assistant to retired military, It provides installation commanders with a means of providing more effective services and improving communication for the local retired community. The RAO is staffed and operated by volunteer retired military who assist other retired members, their families and survivors to receive entitled services and benefits. Throughnewsletters, seminars and appreciation days, the RAO supports quality of life issues throughout the retirement years to their fellow service members.

2315 **Bureau of Naval Personnel: Texas Retired Activities Office**
Fleet and Family Support Center
Naval Air Station Corpus Christi
11001 D Street, Suite 143
Corpus Christi, TX 78419-5021
361-961-2811
Fax: 361-961-3797
http://www.nascc.cnatra.navy.mil
Timothy E Coolidge, Commanding Officer

To support the mission of Naval Air Station Corpus Christi, effectively provide professional customer-focused services, counseling/guidance, and education to help enhance the foundation of support for both the individual and family unit improving the quality of life and ultimately integrating the Navy lifestyle within the community.

2316 **Center for Lifelong Learning**
University Of Texas-El Paso
Miner's Hall
Room 209
El Paso, TX 79968
915-747-6280
Fax: 915-747-5538
e-mail: cll@utep.edu
http://www.admin.utep.edu/cll
Peter A Rivera, Coordinator

Institute for learning in retirement.

2317 **Center for Professional Development**
East Texas State University at Texarkana
Texas A&M University & Techno
Texarkana, TX 75505
903-792-7515
Fax: 903-832-8890
George R Hunter MD

2318 **Coastal Bend Area: Agency on Aging**
PO Box 9909
Corpus Christi, TX 78469-9909
361-883-5743
800-421-4636
Fax: 361-883-5749
Betty Lamb, Director
John Buckner, Executive Director

2319 **Dallas Association of Directors of Volunteers**
4009 Elm Street
Dallas, TX 75226-1221
214-826-8330
Fax: 214-826-8579
Mary Brown, President
Yesenia Reyes, Administrator

State Organizations & Government Agencies/Texas

2320 East Texas Area: Agency on Aging
3800 Stone Road
Kilgore, TX 75662-6927
903-984-8641
800-442-8845
Fax: 903-983-1440

Claude I Andrews, Director
Wendell Holcombe, Executive Director

2321 Golden Crescent Area: Agency on Aging
PO Box 2028
Victoria, TX 77902-2028
361-578-1587
Fax: 361-578-8865
TDD 512-820-1262

Cindy Cornish, Director
Jov Brannon, Executive Director

2322 Gray Panthers of Austin
PO Box 15
Austin, TX 78767
512-458-3738
Fax: 512-458-9727
e-mail: gp-austin@ev1.net
http://www.graypanthersofaustin.org

Charlotte Flynn, Director
Jeanette Payne, Staff

Promotes universal access to health care. Provides education on aging.

2323 Greater Lakewood Shepherd's Center
6306 Kenwood Avenue
Dallas, TX 75214-3018
214-823-2583

Jean Heft, Administrator

2324 Heart of Texas Council of Governments Area: Agency on Aging
300 Franklin Avenue
Waco, TX 76701-2297
254-756-7822
Fax: 817-756-0102

John McCue, Director
Kenneth Simons, CEO

2325 Hill Country Community Action Association
2905 West Wallace Street
San Saba, TX 76877-3840
915-372-5167
Fax: 915-372-3526
e-mail: rault@hccaa.com

Ronnie Ault, Contact

2326 Houston Harris County Area: Agency on Aging
8000 N Stadium Drive
8th Floor
Houston, TX 77054-1823
713-794-9001
Fax: 713-794-9464

Charlene Hunter James, Director

2327 Houston-Galveston Area: Agency on Aging
PO Box 22777
Houston, TX 77227-2777
713-627-3200
800-437-7396
Fax: 713-993-4578
http://www.hgac.cog.tx.us/aging

Curtis Cooper, Director

2328 Kings Manor Methodist Retirement System
400 Ranger Street
Hereford, TX 79045-2812
806-364-0661

Jerry Jasper, Administrator

2329 Lower Rio Grande Valley Area: Agency onAging
4900 N 23rd Street
McAllen, TX 78504-4011
956-682-1109
800-365-6131
Fax: 512-631-4670

Jose L Gonzalez, Director
Kenneth Jones, Manager

2330 Middle Rio Grande Area: Agency on Aging
PO Box 1199
Carrizo Springs, TX 78834-7199
830-876-3533
Fax: 830-876-9415

Hector Flores, Director
Leo Dor Martinez, Executive Director

2331 North Central Texas Area: Agency on Aging
PO Box 5888
Arlington, TX 76005-5888
817-640-3300
800-272-3921
Fax: 817-695-9274

Michael Eastland, Executive Director

2332 Panhandle Area: Agency on Aging
PO Box 9257
Amarillo, TX 79105-9257
806-372-3381
800-642-6008

Gary Pitner, Manager

2333 Permian Basin Area: Agency on Aging
PO Box 60660
Midland, TX 79711
432-563-1061
800-491-4636
Fax: 432-563-1728

Sue Fielder, Manager

2334 RSVP Bexar County
1405 N Main Avenue
San Antonio, TX 78212-4665
210-222-0301
Fax: 210-222-9983

Les Herrera, Manager

The Retired and Senior Volunteer Program (RSVP) provides opportunities for people 55 and over to make a difference in their community through volunteer service. RSVP volunteers contribute anywhere from a few to over forty hours a week, serving though schools, day care centers, police departments, hospitals and other nonprofit and public organizations to help meet critical community needs. RSVP offers maximum flexibility and choice to its volunteers. RSVP matches the personal interests and skills to older Americans with opportunities to help solve community problems and offer supplemental insurance while on duty, on-the-job training from the agency or organization where volunteers are placed.

2335 RSVP Big Country
4601 Hartford Street
Abilene, TX 79605-4603
325-793-3520
Fax: 325-793-3580
e-mail: btrojcak@wtrc.com

Brenda Trojcak, Contact

The Retired and Senior Volunteer Program (RSVP) provides opportunities for people 55 and over to make a difference in their community through volunteer service. RSVP volunteers contribute anywhere from a few to over forty hours a week, serving though schools, day care centers, police departments, hospitals and other nonprofit and public organizations to help meet critical community needs. RSVP offers maximum flexibility and choice to its volunteers. RSVP matches the personal interests and skills to older Americans with opportunities to help solve community problems and offer supplemental insurance while on duty, on-the-job training from the agency or organization where volunteers are placed.

State Organizations & Government Agencies/Texas

2336 RSVP Big Spring
501 Runnels Street
Big Spring, TX 79720-2732
432-264-2397
Fax: 432-264-2534
e-mail: njones@crcom.net
Nancy J Jones, Project Director

Provides opportunities for people 55 and over to make a difference in their community through volunteer service. RSVP volunteers contribute anywhere from a few to over forty hours a week, serving through schools, day care centers, police departments, hospitals and other nonprofit and public organizations to help meet critical community needs. RSVP matches the personal interests and skills of older Americans with opportunities to help solve community problems and offers supplemental insurance while on duty, on-the-job training from the agency or organization where volunteers are placed.

2337 RSVP Brazos Valley
PO Box 4128
Bryan, TX 77805-4128
979-595-2800
e-mail: ckraus@bvcog.org
Carolyn Kraus, Project Director
Paul Turney, Vice President

The Retired and Senior Volunteer Program (RSVP) provides opportunities for people 55 and over to make a difference in their community through volunteer service. RSVP volunteers contribute anywhere from a few to over forty hours a week, serving though schools, day care centers, police departments, hospitals and other nonprofit and public organizations to help meet critical community needs. RSVP offers maximum flexibility and choice to its volunteers. RSVP matches the personal interests and skills to older Americans with opportunities to help solve community problems and offer supplemental insurance while on duty, on-the-job training from the agency or organization where volunteers are placed.

2338 RSVP Chisholm Trail County
1400 Crescent Street
Denton, TX 76201-2757
940-383-1508
Fax: 940-387-0862
Diana Corona, Executive Director

The Retired and Senior Volunteer Program (RSVP) provides opportunities for people 55 and over to make a difference in their community through volunteer service. RSVP volunteers contribute anywhere from a few to over forty hours a week, serving though schools, day care centers, police departments, hospitals and other nonprofit and public organizations to help meet critical community needs. RSVP offers maximum flexibility and choice to its volunteers. RSVP matches the personal interests and skills to older Americans with opportunities to help solve community problems and offer supplemental insurance while on duty, on-the-job training from the agency or organization where volunteers are placed.

2339 RSVP Concho Valley
6185 Chadbourne
San Angelo, TX 76903
325-655-5888
Fax: 325-655-6294
e-mail: dschwertner@wtrc.com
Dolores A Schwertner, Director
Greg Bowman, President

The Retired and Senior Volunteer Program (RSVP) provides opportunities for people 55 and over to make a difference in their community through volunteer service. RSVP volunteers contribute anywhere from a few to over forty hours a week, serving though schools, day care centers, police departments, hospitals and other nonprofit and public organizations to help meet critical community needs. RSVP offers maximum flexibility and choice to its volunteers. RSVP matches the personal interests and skills to older Americans with opportunities to help solve community problems and offer supplemental insurance while on duty, on-the-job training from the agency or organization where volunteers are placed.

2340 RSVP Concho Valley Texas
618 S Chadbourne Street
San Angelo, TX 76903-6930
325-223-6388
Fax: 325-655-6294
e-mail: dschwertner@wtrc.com
Dolores A Schwertner, Contact

The Retired and Senior Volunteer Program (RSVP) provides opportunities for people 55 and over to make a difference in their community through volunteer service. RSVP volunteers contribute anywhere from a few to over forty hours a week, serving though schools, day care centers, police departments, hospitals and other nonprofit and public organizations to help meet critical community needs. RSVP offers maximum flexibility and choice to its volunteers. RSVP matches the personal interests and skills to older Americans with opportunities to help solve community problems and offer supplemental insurance while on duty, on-the-job training from the agency or organization where volunteers are placed.

2341 RSVP Corpus Christi
1201 Leopard Street
Corpus Christi, TX 78401-2120
361-880-3199
Fax: 361-880-3151

The Retired and Senior Volunteer Program (RSVP) provides opportunities for people 55 and over to make a difference in their community through volunteer service. RSVP volunteers contribute anywhere from a few to over forty hours a week, serving though schools, day care centers, police departments, hospitals and other nonprofit and public organizations to help meet critical community needs. RSVP offers maximum flexibility and choice to its volunteers. RSVP matches the personal interests and skills to older Americans with opportunities to help solve community problems and offer supplemental insurance while on duty, on-the-job training from the agency or organization where volunteers are placed.

2342 RSVP Dallas
1215 Skiles Street
Dallas, TX 75204-6019
214-823-5700
Fax: 214-826-2441

The Retired and Senior Volunteer Program (RSVP) provides opportunities for people 55 and over to make a difference in their community through volunteer service. RSVP volunteers contribute anywhere from a few to over forty hours a week, serving though schools, day care centers, police departments, hospitals and other nonprofit and public organizations to help meet critical community needs. RSVP offers maximum flexibility and choice to its volunteers. RSVP matches the personal interests and skills to older Americans with opportunities to help solve community problems and offer supplemental insurance while on duty, on-the-job training from the agency or organization where volunteers are placed.

2343 RSVP Deep East Texas
PO Box 1423
Lufkin, TX 75902-1423
936-634-2247
Fax: 936-634-2869
e-mail: mwittmann@detcog.org
Marilyn J Wittmann, Contact

The Retired and Senior Volunteer Program (RSVP) provides opportunities for people 55 and over to make a difference in their community through volunteer service. RSVP volunteers contribute anywhere from a few to over forty hours a week, serving though schools, day care centers, police departments, hospitals and other nonprofit and public organizations to help meet critical community needs. RSVP offers maximum flexibility and choice to its volunteers. RSVP matches the personal interests and skills to older Americans with opportunities to help solve community problems and offer supplemental insurance while on duty, on-the-job training from the agency or organization where volunteers are placed.

2344 RSVP El Paso City
2 Civic Center Plaza
El Paso, TX 79901-1153
915-541-4374
Fax: 817-877-5807
Norma Carona, Executive Director

State Organizations & Government Agencies/Texas

The Retired and Senior Volunteer Program (RSVP) provides opportunities for people 55 and over to make a difference in their community through volunteer service. RSVP volunteers contribute anywhere from a few to over forty hours a week, serving though schools, day care centers, police departments, hospitals and other nonprofit and public organizations to help meet critical community needs. RSVP offers maximum flexibility and choice to its volunteers. RSVP matches the personal interests and skills to older Americans with opportunities to help solve community problems and offer supplemental insurance while on duty, on-the-job training from the agency or organization where volunteers are placed.

2345 RSVP Galveston County
301 University Boulevard
Galveston, TX 77555
409-772-5361
Fax: 409-747-2119

The Retired and Senior Volunteer Program (RSVP) provides opportunities for people 55 and over to make a difference in their community through volunteer service. RSVP volunteers contribute anywhere from a few to over forty hours a week, serving though schools, day care centers, police departments, hospitals and other nonprofit and public organizations to help meet critical community needs. RSVP offers maximum flexibility and choice to its volunteers. RSVP matches the personal interests and skills to older Americans with opportunities to help solve community problems and offer supplemental insurance while on duty, on-the-job training from the agency or organization where volunteers are placed.

2346 RSVP Golden Triangle
2210 Eastex Fairway
Beaumont, TX 77703-4929
409-899-8444
Fax: 409-892-0560
e-mail: challiburton@setrpc.org
Colleen Halliburton, Contact

The Retired and Senior Volunteer Program (RSVP) provides opportunities for people 55 and over to make a difference in their community through volunteer service. RSVP volunteers contribute anywhere from a few to over forty hours a week, serving though schools, day care centers, police departments, hospitals and other nonprofit and public organizations to help meet critical community needs. RSVP offers maximum flexibility and choice to its volunteers. RSVP matches the personal interests and skills to older Americans with opportunities to help solve community problems and offer supplemental insurance while on duty, on-the-job training from the agency or organization where volunteers are placed.

2347 RSVP Heart of Texas
1400 College Drive
Waco, TX 76708-1402
254-299-8577
Fax: 254-299-8578
Susan Copeland, Executive Director

The Retired and Senior Volunteer Program (RSVP) provides opportunities for people 55 and over to make a difference in their community through volunteer service. RSVP volunteers contribute anywhere from a few to over forty hours a week, serving though schools, day care centers, police departments, hospitals and other nonprofit and public organizations to help meet critical community needs. RSVP offers maximum flexibility and choice to its volunteers. RSVP matches the personal interests and skills to older Americans with opportunities to help solve community problems and offer supplemental insurance while on duty, on-the-job training from the agency or organization where volunteers are placed.

2348 RSVP Hockley County
1202 Houston Street
Levelland, TX 79336-3524
806-894-7642
Fax: 806-894-2220

The Retired and Senior Volunteer Program (RSVP) provides opportunities for people 55 and over to make a difference in their community through volunteer service. RSVP volunteers contribute anywhere from a few to over forty hours a week, serving though schools, day care centers, police departments, hospitals and other nonprofit and public organizations to help meet critical community needs. RSVP offers maximum flexibility and choice to its volunteers. RSVP matches the personal interests and skills to older Americans with opportunities to help solve community problems and offer supplemental insurance while on duty, on-the-job training from the agency or organization where volunteers are placed.

2349 RSVP Houston County
5601 S Braeswood Boulevard
Houston, TX 77096-3907
713-729-3200
Fax: 713-551-7223
Jerry Wische, Manager

The Retired and Senior Volunteer Program (RSVP) provides opportunities for people 55 and over to make a difference in their community through volunteer service. RSVP volunteers contribute anywhere from a few to over forty hours a week, serving though schools, day care centers, police departments, hospitals and other nonprofit and public organizations to help meet critical community needs. RSVP offers maximum flexibility and choice to its volunteers. RSVP matches the personal interests and skills to older Americans with opportunities to help solve community problems and offer supplemental insurance while on duty, on-the-job training from the agency or organization where volunteers are placed.

2350 RSVP Laredo
1901 Corpus Christi Street
Laredo, TX 78043-3308
956-722-7271
Fax: 956-722-2670
Jose A Valdez, Regional Coordinator
Roxanna Guerra, Executive Director

RSVP matches the talents and interests of volunteers 55 and over with meaningful efforts that enhance the quality of our community.

2351 RSVP Lubbock
PO Box 41162
Lubbock, TX 79409-1162
806-742-2423
Fax: 806-742-1639
Bonne Phillips, Executive Director

The Retired and Senior Volunteer Program (RSVP) provides opportunities for people 55 and over to make a difference in their community through volunteer service. RSVP volunteers contribute anywhere from a few to over forty hours a week, serving though schools, day care centers, police departments, hospitals and other nonprofit and public organizations to help meet critical community needs. RSVP offers maximum flexibility and choice to its volunteers. RSVP matches the personal interests and skills to older Americans with opportunities to help solve community problems and offer supplemental insurance while on duty, on-the-job training from the agency or organization where volunteers are placed.

2352 RSVP Metro Tarrant
1000 Macon Street
Fort Worth, TX 76102-4527
817-338-4433
Fax: 817-877-5807
e-mail: devansyoung@scstc.org
Deborah Evans-Young, Project Director
Carlton Lancaster, Executive Director

State Organizations & Government Agencies/Texas

The Retired and Senior Volunteer Program (RSVP) provides opportunities for people 55 and over to make a difference in their community through volunteer service. RSVP volunteers contribute anywhere from a few to over forty hours a week, serving though schools, day care centers, police departments, hospitals and other nonprofit and public organizations to help meet critical community needs. RSVP offers maximum flexibility and choice to its volunteers. RSVP matches the personal interests and skills to older Americans with opportunities to help solve community problems and offer supplemental insurance while on duty, on-the-job training from the agency or organization where volunteers are placed.

2353 RSVP Metro Tarrant County
1000 Macon Street
Fort Worth, TX 76102-4527
817-338-4433
Fax: 817-877-5807

Carlton Lancaster, Executive Director

The Retired and Senior Volunteer Program (RSVP) provides opportunities for people 55 and over to make a difference in their community through volunteer service. RSVP volunteers contribute anywhere from a few to over forty hours a week, serving though schools, day care centers, police departments, hospitals and other nonprofit and public organizations to help meet critical community needs. RSVP offers maximum flexibility and choice to its volunteers. RSVP matches the personal interests and skills to older Americans with opportunities to help solve community problems and offer supplemental insurance while on duty, on-the-job training from the agency or organization where volunteers are placed.

2354 RSVP Midland
1301 Sinclair Avenue
Midland, TX 79707-6620
432-689-6693
Fax: 432-689-6699
e-mail: rsvpsaul@cssmidland.org
http://www.cssmidland.org/rsvp

Saul Herrera, RSVP Director
Kelly Ives, Executive Director

The Retired and Senior Volunteer Program (RSVP) provides opportunities for people 55 and over to make a difference in their community through volunteer service. RSVP volunteers contribute anywhere from a few to over forty hours a week, serving though schools, day care centers, police departments, hospitals and other nonprofit and public organizations to help meet critical community needs. RSVP offers maximum flexibility and choice to its volunteers. RSVP matches the personal interests and skills to older Americans with opportunities to help solve community problems and offer supplemental insurance while on duty, on-the-job training from the agency or organization where volunteers are placed.

2355 RSVP North Texas
PO Box 5144
Wichita Falls, TX 76307-5144
940-322-5281
Fax: 940-322-6743
e-mail: dbooker@texasconnection.org

DeeAnna Booker, Program Director
Dennis Wilde, Manager

The Retired and Senior Volunteer Program (RSVP) provides opportunities for people 55 and over to make a difference in their community through volunteer service. RSVP volunteers contribute anywhere from a few to over forty hours a week, serving though schools, day care centers, police departments, hospitals and other nonprofit and public organizations to help meet critical community needs. RSVP offers maximum flexibility and choice to its volunteers. RSVP matches the personal interests and skills to older Americans with opportunities to help solve community problems and offer supplemental insurance while on duty, on-the-job training from the agency or organization where volunteers are placed.

2356 RSVP Outer Houston
6437 High Star Drive
Houston, TX 77074-5005
713-271-5683
Fax: 713-271-0587
e-mail: jcuret@bbbshouston.org

Jodi Curet, Contact

The Retired and Senior Volunteer Program (RSVP) provides opportunities for people 55 and over to make a difference in their community through volunteer service. RSVP volunteers contribute anywhere from a few to over forty hours a week, serving though schools, day care centers, police departments, hospitals and other nonprofit and public organizations to help meet critical community needs. RSVP offers maximum flexibility and choice to its volunteers. RSVP matches the personal interests and skills to older Americans with opportunities to help solve community problems and offer supplemental insurance while on duty, on-the-job training from the agency or organization where volunteers are placed.

2357 RSVP Red River Valley
2400 Clarksville Street
Paris, TX 75460-6258
903-782-0441
Fax: 903-782-0443

Susan Kahn, Manager

The Retired and Senior Volunteer Program (RSVP) provides opportunities for people 55 and over to make a difference in their community through volunteer service. RSVP volunteers contribute anywhere from a few to over forty hours a week, serving though schools, day care centers, police departments, hospitals and other nonprofit and public organizations to help meet critical community needs. RSVP offers maximum flexibility and choice to its volunteers. RSVP matches the personal interests and skills to older Americans with opportunities to help solve community problems and offer supplemental insurance while on duty, on-the-job training from the agency or organization where volunteers are placed.

2358 RSVP Rio Grande Valley
PO Box 204
Edinburg, TX 78540
956-316-2005
Fax: 956-380-4324

The Retired and Senior Volunteer Program (RSVP) provides opportunities for people 55 and over to make a difference in their community through volunteer service. RSVP volunteers contribute anywhere from a few to over forty hours a week, serving though schools, day care centers, police departments, hospitals and other nonprofit and public organizations to help meet critical community needs. RSVP offers maximum flexibility and choice to its volunteers. RSVP matches the personal interests and skills to older Americans with opportunities to help solve community problems and offer supplemental insurance while on duty, on-the-job training from the agency or organization where volunteers are placed.

2359 RSVP Runningwater Draw
1900 W 7th Street
Plainview, TX 79072-6900
806-291-1895
Fax: 806-291-1979
e-mail: rsvp@texasonline.net

Linda Milner, Contact

The Retired and Senior Volunteer Program (RSVP) provides opportunities for people 55 and over to make a difference in their community through volunteer service. RSVP volunteers contribute anywhere from a few to over forty hours a week, serving though schools, day care centers, police departments, hospitals and other nonprofit and public organizations to help meet critical community needs. RSVP offers maximum flexibility and choice to its volunteers. RSVP matches the personal interests and skills to older Americans with opportunities to help solve community problems and offer supplemental insurance while on duty, on-the-job training from the agency or organization where volunteers are placed.

State Organizations & Government Agencies/Texas

2360 RSVP Swisher County
321 SW 2nd Street
Tulia, TX 79088-2743
806-995-2104
Fax: 806-995-1404
Cynthia Zolman, Executive Director

The Retired and Senior Volunteer Program (RSVP) provides opportunities for people 55 and over to make a difference in their community through volunteer service. RSVP volunteers contribute anywhere from a few to over forty hours a week, serving though schools, day care centers, police departments, hospitals and other nonprofit and public organizations to help meet critical community needs. RSVP offers maximum flexibility and choice to its volunteers. RSVP matches the personal interests and skills to older Americans with opportunities to help solve community problems and offer supplemental insurance while on duty, on-the-job training from the agency or organization where volunteers are placed.

2361 RSVP Texas Panhandle
121 W 7th Avenue
Amarillo, TX 79101-2207
806-373-8389
Fax: 806-373-8380
Ginger Robertson, Manager

The Retired and Senior Volunteer Program (RSVP) provides opportunities for people 55 and over to make a difference in their community through volunteer service. RSVP volunteers contribute anywhere from a few to over forty hours a week, serving though schools, day care centers, police departments, hospitals and other nonprofit and public organizations to help meet critical community needs. RSVP offers maximum flexibility and choice to its volunteers. RSVP matches the personal interests and skills to older Americans with opportunities to help solve community problems and offer supplemental insurance while on duty, on-the-job training from the agency or organization where volunteers are placed.

2362 RSVP Texoma
1117 Gallagher Drive
Suite 200
Sherman, TX 75090-3107
903-813-3587
Fax: 903-813-3515
e-mail: jfullylove@texoma.cog.tx.us
Judy Fullylove, RSVP Director

Provides opportunities for people 55 and over to make a difference in their community through volunteer service. RSVP volunteers contribute anywhere form a few to over forty hours a week, serving through schools, day care centers, police departments, hospitals and other nonprofit and public organizations to help meet critical community needs. RSVP matches the personal interests and skills of older Americans with opportunities to help solve community problems and offers supplemental insurance while on duty, on-the-job trainng from the agency or organization where volunteers are placed.

2363 RSVP Travis County
PO Box 1748
Austin, TX 78767-1748
512-854-7787
Fax: 512-854-4131
e-mail: fred.lugo@co.travis.tx.us
Fred Lugo, Contact

The Retired and Senior Volunteer Program (RSVP) provides opportunities for people 55 and over to make a difference in their community through volunteer service. RSVP volunteers contribute anywhere from a few to over forty hours a week, serving thourgh schools, day care centers, police departments, hospitals and other nonprofit and public organizations to help meet critical community needs. RSVP offers maximum flexibility and choice to its volunteers. RSVP matches the personal interests and skills to older Americans with opportunities to help solve community problems and offer supplemental insurance while on duty, on-the-job training from the agency or organization where volunteers are placed.

2364 Railroad Retirement Board: Fort Worth, Texas District Office
PO Box 17420
Fort Worth, TX 76102
817-978-2638
Fax: 817-978-2740
e-mail: fortworth@rrb.gov
Barbara Gettman, Representative

2365 Railroad Retirement Board: Houston, Texas District Office
1919 Smith Street
Suite 845
Houston, TX 77002-8098
713-209-3045
Fax: 713-759-0349
e-mail: houston@rrb.com
Margie M Grimes, Representative

2366 Region 6: Administration on Aging (AoA)
US Department of Health & Human Services
1301 Young Street
Room 736
Dallas, TX 75201
214-767-2971
Fax: 214-767-2951
http://www.aoa.gov
Larry Brewster, Regional Administrator
Josefina G Carbonell ASA, Assistant Secretary
Edwin Walker PDASA, Deputy Assistant Secretary

Region includes Arkansas, Louisiana, New Mexico, Oklahoma, and Texas.

2367 Rio Grande Area: Agency on Aging
1014 N Stanton Street
Suite 100
El Paso, TX 79902-4109
915-533-0998
800-333-7082
Fax: 915-532-9385
Andrea G Capprillo, Director
Jake Brisben, Executive Director

2368 Round Rock Volunteer Center
1009e N Georgetown Street
Round Rock, TX 78664-3289
512-388-4575
Fax: 512-388-2755
e-mail: volrock@volrock.org
http://www.volrock.org
Pat Patterson, Executive Director

Connecting volunteers to nonprofit agencies.

2369 Senior Citizens of Earth: Springlake Area
PO Box 192
Earth, TX 79031
806-285-7769
Charles A Miranda, President

2370 Shallowater Senior Citizens
PO Box 526
Shallowater, TX 79363
806-832-4365
Bud Teague, Manager

2371 South Plains Association of GovernmentsArea: Agency on Aging
PO Box 3730
Lubbock, TX 79452-3730
806-762-8721
800-858-1809
Fax: 806-765-9544
e-mail: plara@spag.org
http://www.spag.org
TDD 806-762-8721
Peter H Lara, Director Aging Programs
OB Brooks, Administrative Assistant
Jerry Casstevens, Executive Director

State Organizations & Government Agencies/Texas

2372 South Texas Area: Agency on Aging
PO Box 2187
Laredo, TX 78044-2187
956-722-3995
800-292-5426
Fax: 512-722-3998

Andy Smith Jr, Director
Alberto Rivera Jr, Manager

2373 Texaco Retirees Club of Houston
7506 Prestwick Street
Houston, TX 77025-2322
713-453-2893

2374 Texas Association of Area Agencies on Aging
Heart of Texas Area Agency on Aging
100 Franklin Avenue
Waco, TX 76701-2244
254-756-7822
Fax: 254-756-0102
http://www.aaahot.org

Gary Luft, Executive Director

Carries out a program of advocacy and education for area agencies on aging.

2375 Texas Association of Directors of Volunteer Services
PO Box 15587
Austin, TX 78761-5587
512-465-1000
800-252-9403
Fax: 512-465-1090
http://www.healthshare-tha.com/tadvs

Judith Latimer, Executive Officer
Richard Bettis, President

Directors of volunteer services in hospitals and other health care settings.

2376 Texas Association of Homes and Services for the Aging
2205 Hancock Drive
Austin, TX 78756-2508
512-467-2242
Fax: 512-467-2275
e-mail: jblanchard@tahsa.org
http://www.tahsa.org

Jessica Blanchard, Member Services Coordinator
George Linial, President

Association of non profit honest seniors for the aging in Texas.

2377 Texas Comptroller of Public Accountants
111 E 17th Street
Austin, TX 78774-1440
512-463-4000
888-4FI-LING
http://www.window.state.tx.us

Carole Strayhorn, Manager

2378 Texas Department of Aging and Disability Services
PO Box 149030
Austin, TX 78751
512-438-3011
Fax: 512-438-4747
e-mail: mail@dads.state.tx.us
http://www.dads.state.tx.us

Adelaide Horn, Commissioner
Jon Weizenbaum, Deputy Commissioner
Lawrence Parker, Chief Operating Officer

The Texas Department of Aging and Disability Services (DADS) mission is to provide a comprehensive array of aging and disability services, supports, and opportunities that are easily accessed in local communities.

2379 Texas Department on Aging
PO Box 12786
Austin, TX 78711-2786
512-438-3200
Fax: 512-438-4374
e-mail: mail@tdoa.state.tx.us
http://www.tdoa.state.tx.us

James Hine, Manager

The Texas Department on Aging is the state's visable advocate for a full range of services and opportunities that allow older Texans to live healthy, dignified, and independent and steward lives.

2380 Texas Developmental Disability Council
6201 E Oltorf Street
Suite 600
Austin, TX 78741-7509
512-437-5432
800-262-0334
Fax: 512-437-5434
e-mail: TXDDC@txddc.state.tx.us
http://www.txddc.state.tx.us
TDD 512-437-5431

Roger Webb, Executive Director
Lucy Walker, Public Information Specialist

Works to create change so all people are fully included in their own communities and excersise control over their own lives.

2381 Texas Employees' Retirement System
PO Box 13207
Austin, TX 78711-3207
512-476-6431
800-252-3645
Fax: 512-867-3441

Sheila Wilson-Beckett, CEO

2382 Texas Geriatrics Society
401 W 15th Street
Austin, TX 78701-1670
512-370-1503

Represents members' interests; conducts lobbying activities. Provides assistance programs for retirees.

2383 Texas Governor's Committee for People With Disabilities
PO Box 12428
Austin, TX 78711-2428
512-463-5739
Fax: 512-463-5745
http://http://www.governor.state.tx.us
TDD 512-463-5764

Pat Pound, Executive Director

The Govenor's Committee on People with Disabilities envisions a state where people with disabilities have the opportunity to enjoy full and equal access to lives of independence, productivity and self determination.

2384 Texas Planning Council for Developmental Disabilities
4900 N Lamar Boulevard
Austin, TX 78751-2316
512-424-4080
Fax: 512-424-4097

Roger Webb, Executive Director

2385 Texas Protection & Advocacy Services for Disabled Perosns
Advocacy
7800 Shoal Creek Boulevard
Austin, TX 78757-1098
512-454-4816
800-252-9108
Fax: 512-323-0902

James Contos-Galon, Director
Jonas Schwartz, Manager

2386 Texas Veterans Commission
PO Box 12277
Austin, TX 78711-2277
512-463-5538
Fax: 512-475-2395
e-mail: info@tvc.state.tx.us
http://www.tvc.state.tx.us

James E Nier, Manager

To assist veterans by informing them of their rights.

2387 Texas Workers Compensation Commission
7551 Metro Center Drive
Austin, TX 78744-1625
512-804-4000
Fax: 512-804-4101
http://www.twcc.state.tx.us/index.html

Robert Shipe, Executive Director

State Organizations & Government Agencies/Utah

2388 **Texoma Area: Agency on Aging**
1117 Gallagher Drive
Sherman, TX 75090-1797
903-813-3574
800-677-8264
Fax: 903-813-3511
http://www.texoma.cog.tx.us/Aging/Aging.htm

2389 **The Chandler Senior Center**
137 W French Place
San Antonio, TX 78212-5804
210-737-5195
Fax: 210-737-5157
e-mail: dawna@morningsidemin.org

Dawn Alexander, Director Community Relations
Irma Rodriguez, Community Program Coordinator
Kathy Miller, Administrator

Membership includes newsletter, day trips, exercise, travelogues, arts and crafts, game days, special luncheons and parties.

2390 **West Central Texas Council of Governments-Area Agency on Aging**
PO Box 3195
Abilene, TX 79604-3195
325-672-8544
800-928-2262
Fax: 325-675-5214

Gail Kaiser, Director
Jim Compton, Executive Director

Utah

2391 **Bear River Area: Agency on Aging**
170 N Main Street
Logan, UT 84321-4567
435-752-7242
Fax: 435-752-6962
http://www.brag.dst.ut.us/aging.html

Michelle Benson, Director

2392 **Cache County Retired And Senior Volunteer Program (RSVP)**
240 N 100 E
Logan, UT 84321-4002
435-755-1720
Fax: 435-752-9513
e-mail: marylou.schroeder@cachecounty.org

Tom Hogan, Executive Director
Mary Lou Schroeder, RSVP Director

The Retired and Senior Volunteer Program (RSVP) provides opportunities for people 55 and over to make a difference in their community through volunteer service. RSVP volunteers contribute anywhere from a few to over forty hours a week, serving thourgh schools, day care centers, police departments, hospitals and other nonprofit and public organizations to help meet critical community needs. RSVP offers maximum flexibility and choice to its volunteers. RSVP matches the personal interests and skills to older Americans with opportunities to help solve community problems and offer supplemental insurance while on duty, on-the-job training from the agency or organization where volunteers are placed.

2393 **Disability Determinations Services**
555 E 500 S
Salt Lake City, UT 84102
801-321-6500
Fax: 801-321-6594

2394 **Five County Area: Agency on Aging**
906 N 1400 W
St George, UT 84770-4989
435-673-3548
Fax: 435-673-3540

Bob Rasmussen, Director
John S Williams, Executive Director

2395 **Five County Retired Senior Volunteer Program**
1070 W 1600 S
Building B
Saint George, UT 84770-5573
435-674-5757
Fax: 435-674-9105

Linda Sappington, Executive Director

2396 **RSVP Carbon County**
30 E 200 S
Price, UT 84501-3048
435-637-9118
Fax: 435-637-7787
e-mail: rsvp@co.carbon.ut.us

Rebecca Mason, Contact

The Retired and Senior Volunteer Program (RSVP) provides opportunities for people 55 and over to make a difference in their community through volunteer service. RSVP volunteers contribute anywhere from a few to over forty hours a week, serving thourgh schools, day care centers, police departments, hospitals and other nonprofit and public organizations to help meet critical community needs. RSVP offers maximum flexibility and choice to its volunteers. RSVP matches the personal interests and skills to older Americans with opportunities to help solve community problems and offer supplemental insurance while on duty, on-the-job training from the agency or organization where volunteers are placed.

2397 **RSVP Davis County**
140 Center Street
Clearfield, UT 84015-1053
801-779-1287
Fax: 801-779-1370

Debbie De Vries, Manager

The Retired and Senior Volunteer Program (RSVP) provides opportunities for people 55 and over to make a difference in their community through volunteer service. RSVP volunteers contribute anywhere from a few to over forty hours a week, serving thourgh schools, day care centers, police departments, hospitals and other nonprofit and public organizations to help meet critical community needs. RSVP offers maximum flexibility and choice to its volunteers. RSVP matches the personal interests and skills to older Americans with opportunities to help solve community problems and offer supplemental insurance while on duty, on-the-job training from the agency or organization where volunteers are placed.

2398 **RSVP Emery**
140 Center Street
Clearfield, UT 84015-1053
801-779-1287
Fax: 801-779-1370

Debbie De Vries, Manager

The Retired and Senior Volunteer Program (RSVP) provides opportunities for people 55 and over to make a difference in their community through volunteer service. RSVP volunteers contribute anywhere from a few to over forty hours a week, serving thourgh schools, day care centers, police departments, hospitals and other nonprofit and public organizations to help meet critical community needs. RSVP offers maximum flexibility and choice to its volunteers. RSVP matches the personal interests and skills to older Americans with opportunities to help solve community problems and offer supplemental insurance while on duty, on-the-job training from the agency or organization where volunteers are placed.

2399 **RSVP Grand County**
100 N 450 E
Moab, UT 84532
435-259-1302
Fax: 435-259-2601

Kate Thompson, Manager

State Organizations & Government Agencies/Utah

The Retired and Senior Volunteer Program (RSVP) provides opportunities for people 55 and over to make a difference in their community through volunteer service. RSVP volunteers contribute anywhere from a few to over forty hours a week, serving thorough schools, day care centers, police departments, hospitals and other nonprofit and public organizations to help meet critical community needs. RSVP offers maximum flexibility and choice to its volunteers. RSVP matches the personal interests and skills to older Americans with opportunities to help solve community problems and offer supplemental insurance while on duty, on-the-job training from the agency or organization where volunteers are placed.

2400   RSVP Mountainland
586 E 800 N
Orem, UT 84097-4146   801-229-3810
                        Fax: 801-229-3671

Gayla Muir, Manager

The Retired and Senior Volunteer Program (RSVP) provides opportunities for people 55 and over to make a difference in their community through volunteer service. RSVP volunteers contribute anywhere from a few to over forty hours a week, serving thorough schools, day care centers, police departments, hospitals and other nonprofit and public organizations to help meet critical community needs. RSVP offers maximum flexibility and choice to its volunteers. RSVP matches the personal interests and skills to older Americans with opportunities to help solve community problems and offer supplemental insurance while on duty, on-the-job training from the agency or organization where volunteers are placed.

2401   RSVP Salt Lake County
2001 S 1500
Salt Lake City, UT 84190-2300   801-468-2191
                             Fax: 801-468-2989

The Retired and Senior Volunteer Program (RSVP) provides opportunities for people 55 and over to make a difference in their community through volunteer service. RSVP volunteers contribute anywhere from a few to over forty hours a week, serving thorough schools, day care centers, police departments, hospitals and other nonprofit and public organizations to help meet critical community needs. RSVP offers maximum flexibility and choice to its volunteers. RSVP matches the personal interests and skills to older Americans with opportunities to help solve community problems and offer supplemental insurance while on duty, on-the-job training from the agency or organization where volunteers are placed.

2402   RSVP Six County
250 N Main Street
Suite 5
Richfield, UT 84701-2158   435-896-9222
                           Fax: 435-896-6951
              e-mail: kerickso@sixaog.stat.ut.us

Russell Cowley, Executive Director

The Retired and Senior Volunteer Program (RSVP) provides opportunities for people 55 and over to make a difference in their community through volunteer service. RSVP volunteers contribute anywhere from a few to over forty hours a week, serving thorough schools, day care centers, police departments, hospitals and other nonprofit and public organizations to help meet critical community needs. RSVP offers maximum flexibility and choice to its volunteers. RSVP matches the personal interests and skills to older Americans with opportunities to help solve community problems and offer supplemental insurance while on duty, on-the-job training from the agency or organization where volunteers are placed.

2403   Railroad Retirement Board
125 S State Street
Suite 1205
Salt Lake City, UT 84138-1137   801-524-5725
                             Fax: 801-524-4313
                  e-mail: saltlakecity@rrb.gov

Frank Kurek, Representative

2404   Salt Lake County Aging Services
2001 S State Street
Salt Lake City, UT 84190-2300   801-468-2556
                             Fax: 801-468-2852
                             TDD 801-468-2480

Shauna O'Neil, Director
Sharon Pierce, Manager

2405   San Juan Area: Agency on Aging
PO Box 9
Monticello, UT 84535   435-587-3225
                         Fax: 435-587-2447

Frank Morrill, Director
Rick Bailey, Administrator

2406   Six County Area: Agency on Aging
PO Box 820
Richfield, UT 84701   435-896-9222
                         Fax: 435-896-6951

Ross Bumgardner, Director
Russell Cowley, Executive Director

2407   Southeastern Utah Area: Agency on Aging
PO Box 1106
Price, UT 84501-1106   435-637-1959
                         Fax: 435-637-5448

Maughan Guymon, Director
Bill Howell, Executive Director

2408   Tooele County Division of Aging and Adult Services
59 E Vine Street
Tooele, UT 84074   435-882-2870
                         Fax: 435-882-6971
              e-mail: bdymocke@co.tooele.ut.us
                    http://ww.co.tooele.ut.us

Butch Dymock, Director

The mission of the Division of Aging and Adult Services is to provide leadership and advocacy in addressing issues that impact older Utahans, and serve elder and disabled adults needing protection from abuse, neglect or exploitation.

2409   Uintah Basin Area: Agency on Aging
120 S 100 E
43-4
Roosevelt, UT 84066-2921   435-722-3952
                            Fax: 435-722-4890

Anna Maria Whitmore, Director
Jolene Daniels, Executive Director

2410   Uintah County Area Agency on Aging
155 S 100 E
Vernal, UT 84078-2613   435-789-2169
                          Fax: 435-789-2171

Joan Janes, Director
Louise Martin, Manager

2411   Utah Assistive Technology Projects
6588 Old Main Hill
Logan, UT 84322   435-797-3811

Marvin Fifield, Director
Marilyn Hammond, Manager

A statewide program promoting assistive technology devices and services for persons of all ages with all disabilities.

2412   Utah Client Assistance Program
455 E 400 S
Suite 201
Salt Lake City, UT 84111-3008   801-532-3657
                             Fax: 801-363-1437

Nancy Firel, Director
Roi Stone, Owner

State Organizations & Government Agencies/Vermont

2413 Utah Department of Aging
120 N 200 W
Salt Lake City, UT 84103-1550
801-538-3910
Fax: 801-538-4395

Percy Devine III, Director

2414 Utah Department of Health Division of Community Health Services
Bureau of HIV
288 N 1460 W
Salt Lake City, UT 84116-3231
801-538-6096
Fax: 801-538-6036

Craig Nichols MPA, Director
Teresa Garrett, Executive Director

Secures and distributes funds for AIDS prevention services, provides educational programs and counseling to the general public, AIDS service organizations, health workers and groups at risk.

2415 Utah Department of Human Services for People with Disabilities
PO Box 45500
Salt Lake City, UT 84145
801-538-4200
Fax: 801-538-4279

George Kelner, Executive Director

2416 Utah Department of Human Services: Aging
PO Box 45500
Salt Lake City, UT 84145
801-538-3910
Fax: 801-538-4395

2417 Utah Division of Services for the Disabled
309 E 1st S
Salt Lake City, UT 84111-1701
801-538-4200

Wayne Noble, Director
George Kelner, Executive Director

Offers services for the totally blind, legally blind, visually impaired, mentally retarded blind and more with health, counseling, educational, recreational, rehabilitation, computer training and professional training services.

2418 Utah Governor's Council for People with Disabilities
155 S 300 W
Suite 100
Salt Lake City, UT 84101-1288
801-533-4636
800-333-8824
Fax: 801-533-3968
http://www.gcpd.org

Mark Smith, Manager

2419 Utah Office of Social Services: Department of Human Services
120 N 200 W
Room 324
Salt Lake City, UT 84103-1550
801-538-4001
Fax: 801-538-4016

Steve Wrigley, Director
Lisa-Michel Church, Executive Director

Information and referrals offering many different office locations for various counties in the state of Utah.

2420 Utah Protection & Advocacy Services for Perosns with Disabilities
Legal Center for People with Disabilities
455 E 400 S
Suite 201
Salt Lake City, UT 84111-3008
801-532-3657
Fax: 801-363-1437

Roi Stone, Owner

2421 Utah Retirement Board
540 E 2nd S
Salt Lake City, UT 84102-2099
801-366-7700
800-753-7834

Bob Newman, Executive Director

2422 Utah State Association of Area Agencies on Aging
170 N Main Street
Logan, UT 84321-4567
435-752-7242
Fax: 435-752-6962
http://www.brag.dst.ut.us/aging.html

Michelle Benson, Director

2423 Utah State Tax Commission
210 N 1950 W
Salt Lake City, UT 84134
801-297-3800
800-662-4335
e-mail: taxmaster@utah.gov
http://www.txdm01.tax.ex.state.ut.us

Pam Hendrickson, Manager

2424 Utah Workers Compensation Board
PO Box 146610
Salt Lake City, UT 84114-6610
801-530-6800
Fax: 801-530-6804

R Lee Ellertson, Manager

2425 Weber-Morgan Area: Agency on Aging
237 26th Street
320
Ogden, UT 84401-3105
801-625-3700
Fax: 801-778-6830
e-mail: kellyv@weberhs.org
TDD 801-625-3638

Kelly VanNoy, Associate Director
Harold Morrill, CEO

Vermont

2426 Central Vermont Council on Aging (CVCOA)
18 S Main Street
Barre, VT 05641-4826
802-479-0531
Fax: 802-479-4235

Charles Castle, Executive Director

2427 Champlain Valley Area: Agency on Aging
1 Mill Street
Burlington, VT 05401-1530
802-865-0360
Fax: 802-865-0363
e-mail: info@cvaa.org
http://www.cvaa.org
TDD 802-865-0360

John Barbour, Executive Director
Kim Gural, Director Communications

A private, nonprofit United Way organization. We support people 60 and older in their efforts to remain active, healthy, financially, secure, and in control of their own lives. CVAA connects older people and the services they need to live independently for as long as possible.

2428 Disability Determination Services
93 Pilgrim Park Road
Suite 6
Waterbury, VT 05676
802-241-2463
800-734-2463
Fax: 802-241-2492
e-mail: Trudy.Lyon-Hart@ssa.gov
http://www.dcf.state.vt.us

Trudy Lyon-Hart, Director

State Organizations & Government Agencies/Vermont

The Office of Disability Determination Services (DDS) serves Vermonters who apply for disability benefits under Social Security, Supplemental Security Income (SSI), and Medicaid programs. The mission of DDS is to provide applicants with accurate decisions as quickly as possible, as governed by Social Security federal statutes, regulations, and policy, with full and fair consideration of each applicant's situation and respect and concern for the individual's well-being and legal rights.

2429 Northeastern Vermont Area: Agency on Aging
1161 Portland Street
St Johnsbury, VT 05819-2064
802-748-5182
800-640-5119
Fax: 802-748-6622
e-mail: info@nevaaa.org

Kenneth E Gordon, MSW

2430 RSVP Addison County
39 E Center Street
Rutland, VT 05701-4134
802-775-8220
Fax: 802-775-8221

Nan Hart, Executive Director

The Retired and Senior Volunteer Program (RSVP) provides opportunities for people 55 and over to make a difference in their community through volunteer service. RSVP volunteers contribute anywhere from a few to over forty hours a week, serving though schools, day care centers, police departments, hospitals and other nonprofit and public organizations to help meet critical community needs. RSVP offers maximum flexibility and choice to its volunteers. RSVP matches the personal interests and skills to older Americans with opportunities to help solve community problems and offer supplemental insurance while on duty, on-the-job training from the agency or organization where volunteers are placed.

2431 RSVP Bennington County
215 Pleasant Street
Bennington, VT 05201-2527
802-447-1545
Fax: 802-447-2550

Pat Palencsar, Executive Director

The Retired and Senior Volunteer Program (RSVP) provides opportunities for people 55 and over to make a difference in their community through volunteer service. RSVP volunteers contribute anywhere from a few to over forty hours a week, serving though schools, day care centers, police departments, hospitals and other nonprofit and public organizations to help meet critical community needs. RSVP offers maximum flexibility and choice to its volunteers. RSVP matches the personal interests and skills to older Americans with opportunities to help solve community problems and offer supplemental insurance while on duty, on-the-job training from the agency or organization where volunteers are placed.

2432 RSVP Central Vermont
PO Box 433
Barre, VT 05641
802-828-4770
Fax: 802-828-5476

J Guy Isabelle, Manager

The Retired and Senior Volunteer Program (RSVP) provides opportunities for people 55 and over to make a difference in their community through volunteer service. RSVP volunteers contribute anywhere from a few to over forty hours a week, serving though schools, day care centers, police departments, hospitals and other nonprofit and public organizations to help meet critical community needs. RSVP offers maximum flexibility and choice to its volunteers. RSVP matches the personal interests and skills to older Americans with opportunities to help solve community problems and offer supplemental insurance while on duty, on-the-job training from the agency or organization where volunteers are placed.

2433 RSVP Chittenden County
95 Saint Paul Street
Suite 200
Burlington, VT 05401-4486
802-860-1677
Fax: 802-864-7401

Holly Reed, Executive Director

The Retired and Senior Volunteer Program (RSVP) provides opportunities for people 55 and over to make a difference in their community through volunteer service. RSVP volunteers contribute anywhere from a few to over forty hours a week, serving though schools, day care centers, police departments, hospitals and other nonprofit and public organizations to help meet critical community needs. RSVP offers maximum flexibility and choice to its volunteers. RSVP matches the personal interests and skills to older Americans with opportunities to help solve community problems and offer supplemental insurance while on duty, on-the-job training from the agency or organization where volunteers are placed.

2434 RSVP Windham County
230 Main Street
Suite 304
Brattleboro, VT 05301-2880
802-254-7515
Fax: 802-254-7519
e-mail: rsvp@sover.net

Virginia A Milkey, Director

RSVP is part of a nationwide program that offers people fifty-five and older the opportunity to have a positive impact on the quality of life in their communities, and on their own lives, by sharing their experience, abilities and skills through volunteer service.

2435 Southwestern Vermont Council on Aging
1085 US Route 4 E
Suite 2b
Rutland, VT 05701-8007
802-786-5991
Fax: 802-786-5994
e-mail: svcoa@svcoa.com
http://www.svcoa.org

Diane M Novak, Executive Director

2436 Vermont Assistive Technology Projects
103 South Main Street
Weeks Building
Waterbury, VT 05676-2305
802-241-2620
800-750-6355
Fax: 802-241-2174
e-mail: atinfo@dail.state.vt.us
http://atinfo@dail.state.vt.us
TTY 802-241-1464

Julie L Tucker, Project Director

Our mission is to increase awareness and change policies to ensure assistive technology (AT) is available to all Vermonters with disabilities.

2437 Vermont Client Assistance Program
264 N Winooski Avenue
Burlington, VT 05401-3621
802-863-5620
Fax: 802-863-7152

Eric Azildsen, Executive Director

2438 Vermont Council on Aging
18 S Main Street
Barre, VT 05641-4826
802-479-0531
Fax: 802-479-4235

2439 Vermont Department of Disabilities, Aging and Independent Living
Aging and Disabilities
103 S Main Street
Waterbury, VT 05671-1601
802-241-2400
Fax: 802-241-2325
http://www.dcd.state.ct.us

Patrick Flood, Commissioner

2440 Vermont Department of Taxes
109 State Street
Montpelier, VT 05609-1401
802-828-2821
866-828-2865
http://www.state.vt.us/tax
TDD 800-253-0191

Brenda Vovakes, Executive Director

State Organizations & Government Agencies/Virginia

2441 Vermont Developmental Disabilities Council
Agency of Human Services
103 South Main Street
Waterbury, VT 05671-0204
802-241-2612
Fax: 802-241-2989
e-mail: vtddc@wpgate1.ahs.state.vt.us
http://www.ahs.state.vt.us

Tom Pombar, Director

The mission of the VTDDC is to facilitate connections and to promote supports that bring people with developmental disabilities into the heart of Vermont communities.

2442 Vermont Protection & Advocacy for Persons with Disabilities
12 North Street
Burlington, VT 05401-5103
802-863-2881
Fax: 802-863-7152

Judy Dickson, Director

2443 Vermont Protection and Advocacy Agency
Disability Law Project
57 North Main Street
Rutland, VT 05701
802-775-0021
800-769-7459
Fax: 802-863-7152
e-mail: nbreiden@vtlegalaid.org
http://www.vtlegalaid.org
TTY 800-769-7459

Nancy Breiden, Director

Legal services (protection and advocacy) for people with disabilities on legal issues arising from disability. Statewide. Adults and children. Employment, education, discrimination, housing, public benefits, health care.

2444 Vermont State Retirement Board
133 State Street
Montpelier, VT 05602-2701
802-828-2301
Fax: 802-828-5182

James H Douglas, Manager

2445 Vermont Veterans Affairs
118 State Street
Montpelier, VT 05620-4401
802-828-3379
Fax: 802-828-5932

Clayton Clark, Manager

2446 Workers Compensation Board Vermont
State Office Building
Montpelier, VT 05602
802-828-2286
Fax: 802-828-2195

Laura Collins, Manager

Virginia

2447 Alexandria Office of Aging and Adult Services
2525 Mount Vernon Avenue
Unit 5
Alexandria, VA 22301-1159
703-838-0920
Fax: 703-838-0886
e-mail: maryann.griffin@alexandriava.gov
http://www.ci.alexandria.va.us/dhs
TDD 703-836-1493

Maryann Griffin, Director

Offers information, referral, outreach, home assessment, and assistance to Alexandria residents 60 years of age or older and their families.

2448 Alexandria Volunteer Bureau
1210 Mt Vernon Avenue
Alexandria, VA 22301-1361
703-836-2176
Fax: 703-683-1793
e-mail: mail@alexandriavolunteers.org
http://www.alexandriavolunteers.org

Bill North-Rudlin, Executive Director
Marion Brunken, Operations Manager

2449 American Association for Active Lifestyle & Fitness
1900 Association Drive
Reston, VA 20191-1502
703-476-3400
Fax: 703-476-9527
e-mail: aaalf@aahperd.org
http://www.aaalf.org

Janet A Seaman, Executive Director
Rosalie Barretta, Program Administrator
Michael Davis, Manager

Committed to promoting active lifestyles and fitness for all individuals by facilitating the application of diverse professional interests through knowledge expansion, information, dissemination, and collaborative efforts.

2450 Arlington Area Agency on Aging
3033 Wilson Boulevard
Suite 700B
Arlington, VA 22201
703-228-1700
Fax: 703-228-1148
e-mail: arlaaa@arlingtonva.us
http://www.co.arlington.va.us
TDD 703-228-4612
TTY 703-228-1788

Terri Lynch, Director

The Arlington Agency on Aging serves Arlington residents aged 60 and older by providing to them and their families, friends and caregivers information on, assistance in accessing, and referrals to services and resources available for older residents of Arlington County.

2451 Bureau of Naval Personnel: Virginia Retired Activities Center
Fleet and Family Support Center
7928 14th Street
Suite 202
Norfolk, VA 23505-1219
757-332-9113
800-372-5463
Fax: 757-445-5328
e-mail: raonorfolk@ffscrnorva.navy.mil
http://www.ffscrnorva.navy.mil/rao

Our mission is to provide assistance to retirees, surviving spouses, active duty personnel contemplating retirement and family members. We extend our offer of assistance to Navy/Marine Corps retirees and their families as well as those from all other branches of the military including retired reserves.

2452 Crater District: Area Agency on Aging
23 Seyler Drive
Petersburg, VA 23805-9243
804-732-7020
Fax: 804-732-7232

David Sadowski, Director

2453 Disability Determination Services
Department of Rehabilitative Services
Northern Regional Office
11150 Main Street, Suite 200
Fairfax, VA 22030
703-934-7400
800-379-9548
Fax: 703-934-7410
http://www.vadrs.org

Sharon Gottovi, Regional Director
Sandy Boo, Professional Relations Officer

The Disability Determination Services (DDS), is a division within DRS, processes disability claims for benefits under the Social Security Disability Insurance and Supplemental Security Income Disability Programs. DDS is committed to making accurate, prompt decisions on disability claims under the Disability Insurance Benefits and Supplemental Security Income (SSI) Programs.

State Organizations & Government Agencies/Virginia

2454 **Disability Determination Services: Roanoke**
111 Franklin Road SE
Suite 250
Roanoke, VA 24011-2111 540-857-7748
Fax: 540-857-7128
Betsy Stone, Manager

2455 **District Three Governmental Cooperative**
4453 Lee Highway
Marion, VA 24354-2999 276-783-8157
800-541-0933
Fax: 276-783-3003
e-mail: district-three@smyth.net
http://www.district-three.org
Michael Guy, Executive Director

We are dedicated to improving the quality of life for our citizens, especially those who are elderly and those who need assistance with transportation. Our services are designed to help our citizens to live independently and productively as long as possible. We promote self-sufficiency and family care-giving.

2456 **Eastern Shore Area: Agency on Aging, Community Action Agency**
PO Box 415
Belle Haven, VA 23306
800-452-5977
Fax: 757-442-9303
George V Podelco, Executive Director

Community action agency serving the elderly, poor, and disabled citizens of Accomack and Northampton counties, VA. Utilizes the community's resources to reduce the effects of poverty and alleviate the problems of aging.

2457 **Fairfax Area: Agency on Aging**
12011 Government Center Parkway
Suite 708
Fairfax, VA 22035-1100 703-324-5411
Fax: 703-449-8689
http://www.fairfaxcounty.gov/service/aaa
TDD 703-803-7914
Grace Starbird, Director

2458 **Falls Church Senior Center**
223 Little Falls Street
Falls Church, VA 22046-4304 703-248-5020
Fax: 703-536-8150
http://www.fallschurchva.gov
Tracy Browand, Senior Center Coordinator

Senior citizens in Arlington and Fairfax counties, and cities of Falls Church and Alexandria, VA. Provides health, education, recreation, and information services to area senior citizens. Sponsors lectures, classes, activities, and parties.

2459 **Lake County Area: Agency on Aging**
1105 W Danville Street
South Hill, VA 23970-3501 434-447-7661
800-252-4464
Fax: 434-447-4074
Gay S Currie, Director
Joseph E Taylor, Executive Director

2460 **League of Older Americans**
PO Box 14205
Roanoke, VA 24038-4205 540-345-0451
Fax: 703-981-1487
Susan Williams, Director

2461 **Loudoun County Area: Agency on Aging**
751 Miller Drive SE
Suite D2
Leesburg, VA 20175-8993 703-777-4534
800-552-4464
Fax: 703-771-5161
Anne H Edwards, Director

2462 **Mercy Medical Airlift**
PO Box 1940
Manassas, VA 20108 703-361-1191
800-296-1191
Fax: 703-257-1642
e-mail: mercymedicalops@erols.com
http://www.mercymedical.org

2463 **Mountain Empire Older Citizens**
PO Box 888
Big Stone Gap, VA 24219 276-523-4202
800-252-6362
Fax: 276-523-4208
e-mail: meoc@mounet.com
Marilyn Pace Maxwell, Executive Director

MEOC is the designated area agency on aging and public transit provider, and serves older citizens, disabled citizens, family caregivers, and the general public.

2464 **Norfolk Senior Center & Adult Day Health Care**
924 W 21st Street
Norfolk, VA 23517-1516 757-625-5857
Fax: 757-625-5858
e-mail: nsc.executive@whru.net
http://http://sites.communitylink.org/senior
Barbara Q Lifland, Executive Director
Candace N Skinner, Adult Day Services Director
Cynthia Morrill, Coordinator

Individuals aged 50 years and over. Promotes quality of life for older persons through meeting of social, emotional, intellectual and physical needs. Promotes community awareness of the needs of older individuals; operates licensed adult day-health care. Newsletter (Prime Time) is published monthly.

2465 **Northern Neck Middle Penninsula Area: Agency on Aging**
Urbanna Professional Center
PO Box 610
Urbanna, VA 23175 804-758-2386
Fax: 804-758-5773
Allyn W Gemerek, Director

2466 **Nutrition Services Incentive Program (NSIP)**
National Food Distribution Division Office
3101 Park Center Drive
Room 504
Alexandria, VA 22302-1500 703-305-2680
Fax: 703-305-2420
http://www.fns.usda.gov
Beth Beville, Program Administrator

To improve diets of those people age 60 and older and their spouses (regardless of age) or disabled and handicapped persons, not yet 60, who reside in housing facilities occupied primarily by the elderly and at which congregate meals service for the elderly is provided. Also to increase the market for domestically produced foods acquired under surplus removal or price support operations.

2467 **Piedmont Senior Resources Area: Agency on Aging**
PO Box 398
Burkeville, VA 23922 434-767-5588
Fax: 434-767-2529
Ronald Dunn, Director

2468 **Prince William Area: Agency on Aging**
7987 Ashton Avenue
Suite 204
Manassas, VA 20109-8212 703-792-6400
Fax: 703-792-4734
TDD 703-792-6444
Lin D Wagener, Director

State Organizations & Government Agencies/Virginia

2469 RSVP Alexandria
418 S Washington Street
Alexandria, VA 22314-3630
703-549-1607
Fax: 703-549-2097
e-mail: rsvpcamp@aol.com
http://www.campagnacenter.org

Leslie Herzog, Director
Linda Dienno, Manager

The Retired and Senior Volunteer Program (RSVP) provides opportunities for people 55 and over to make a difference in their community through volunteer service. RSVP volunteers contribute anywhere from a few to over forty hours a week, serving though schools, day care centers, police departments, hospitals and other nonprofit and public organizations to help meet critical community needs. RSVP offers maximum flexibility and choice to its volunteers. RSVP matches the personal interests and skills to older Americans with opportunities to help solve community problems and offer supplemental insurance while on duty, on-the-job training from the agency or organization where volunteers are placed.

2470 RSVP Campbell County
PO Box 369
Rustburg, VA 24588-0369
804-592-9572
Fax: 804-332-9617
e-mail: tmblair@co.campbell.va.us

Tammy M Blair, Contact

Provides opportunities for people 55 and over to make a difference in their community through volunteer service. RSVP volunteers contribute anywhere from a few to over forty hours a week, serving through schools, day care centers, police departments, hospitals and other nonprofit and public organizations to help meet critical community needs. RSVP matches the personal interests and skills of older Americans with opportunities to help solve community problems and offers supplemental insurance while on duty, on-the-job training from the agency or organization where volunteers are placed.

2471 RSVP Chesapeake Bay
279 North Main Street
PO Box 827
Kilmarnock, VA 22482-0827
804-435-4047
Fax: 804-435-3180
e-mail: rsvpbay@crosslink.net

Richard J Donovan, Contact

Provides opportunities for people 55 and over to make a difference in their community through volunteer service. RSVP volunteers contribute anywhere from a few to over forty hours a week, serving through schools, day care centers, police departments, hospitals and other nonprofit and public organizations to help meet critical community needs. RSVP matches the personal interests and skills of older Americans with opportunities to help solve community problems and offers supplemental insurance while on duty, on-the-job training from the agency or organization where volunteers are placed.

2472 RSVP Clinch Valley
PO Box 188
North Tazewell, VA 24630
276-988-5583
Fax: 276-988-4041
e-mail: e_shrader@hotmail.com

Elizabeth Shrader, Contact
Chris Thompson, Executive Director

The Retired and Senior Volunteer Program (RSVP) provides opportunities for people 55 and over to make a difference in their community through volunteer service. RSVP volunteers contribute anywhere from a few to over forty hours a week, serving though schools, day care centers, police departments, hospitals and other nonprofit and public organizations to help meet critical community needs. RSVP offers maximum flexibility and choice to its volunteers. RSVP matches the personal interests and skills to older Americans with opportunities to help solve community problems and offer supplemental insurance while on duty, on-the-job training from the agency or organization where volunteers are placed.

2473 RSVP East Shore
PO Box 415
Belle Haven, VA 23306
757-442-9652
Fax: 757-442-9303
e-mail: esowp@visi.net

Ann Preston, Director
Julia Spickofsky, RSVP Coordinator
Diane Musso, CEO

The Retired and Senior Volunteer Program (RSVP) provides opportunities for people 55 and over to make a difference in their community through volunteer service. RSVP volunteers contribute anywhere from a few to over forty hours a week, serving though schools, day care centers, police departments, hospitals and other nonprofit and public organizations to help meet critical community needs. RSVP offers maximum flexibility and choice to its volunteers. RSVP matches the personal interests and skills to older Americans with opportunities to help solve community problems and offer supplemental insurance while on duty, on-the-job training from the agency or organization where volunteers are placed.

2474 RSVP Floyd County
323 Floyd Highway S
Floyd, VA 24091-3083
540-745-2105
Fax: 540-745-2106
e-mail: judyw@nrcaa.org

Judy Wietzenfeld, Co Director

Provides opportunities for persons age 55 or over to participate more fully in the life of their community through significant volunteer service.

2475 RSVP Jefferson Area
674 Hillsdale Drive
Suite 9
Charlottesville, VA 22901-1799
434-817-5245
Fax: 434-817-5230
e-mail: kcrosier@jabacares.org

Kathy Crosier, Contact

The Retired and Senior Volunteer Program (RSVP) provides opportunities for people 55 and over to make a difference in their community through volunteer service. RSVP volunteers contribute anywhere from a few to over forty hours a week, serving though schools, day care centers, police departments, hospitals and other nonprofit and public organizations to help meet critical community needs. RSVP offers maximum flexibility and choice to its volunteers. RSVP matches the personal interests and skills to older Americans with opportunities to help solve community problems and offer supplemental insurance while on duty, on-the-job training from the agency or organization where volunteers are placed.

2476 RSVP Lee Scott Wise Norton
PO Box 888
Big Stone Gap, VA 24219
540-523-4202
Fax: 540-523-4208
e-mail: lstuart@mcoc.org

Wanda Tatum, Contact

Provides opportunities for people 55 and over to make a difference in their community through volunteer service. RSVP volunteers contribute anywhere from a few to over forty hours a week, serving though schools, day care centers, police departments, hospitals and other nonprofit and public organizations to help meet critical community needs. RSVP matches the personal interests and skills of older Americans with opportunities to help solve community problems and offers supplemental insurance while on duty, on-the-job training from the agency or organization where volunteers are placed.

2477 RSVP Loudoun
102 Heritage Way NE
Leesburg, VA 20176-4544
703-777-0505
Fax: 703-771-5161

State Organizations & Government Agencies/Virginia

The Retired and Senior Volunteer Program (RSVP) provides opportunities for people 55 and over to make a difference in their community through volunteer service. RSVP volunteers contribute anywhere from a few to over forty hours a week, serving though schools, day care centers, police departments, hospitals and other nonprofit and public organizations to help meet critical community needs. RSVP offers maximum flexibility and choice to its volunteers. RSVP matches the personal interests and skills to older Americans with opportunities to help solve community problems and offer supplemental insurance while on duty, on-the-job training from the agency or organization where volunteers are placed.

2478 RSVP Montgomery County
210 Pepper Street S
Christiansburg, VA 24073-3522   540-382-5775
Fax: 540-381-6856
Angela Little, Manager

The Retired and Senior Volunteer Program (RSVP) provides opportunities for people 55 and over to make a difference in their community through volunteer service. RSVP volunteers contribute anywhere from a few to over forty hours a week, serving though schools, day care centers, police departments, hospitals and other nonprofit and public organizations to help meet critical community needs. RSVP offers maximum flexibility and choice to its volunteers. RSVP matches the personal interests and skills to older Americans with opportunities to help solve community problems and offer supplemental insurance while on duty, on-the-job training from the agency or organization where volunteers are placed.

2479 RSVP Portsmouth
1300 Centre Avenue
Portsmouth, VA 23704-6909   757-393-9333
Fax: 757-399-5174

The Retired and Senior Volunteer Program (RSVP) provides opportunities for people 55 and over to make a difference in their community through volunteer service. RSVP volunteers contribute anywhere from a few to over forty hours a week, serving though schools, day care centers, police departments, hospitals and other nonprofit and public organizations to help meet critical community needs. RSVP offers maximum flexibility and choice to its volunteers. RSVP matches the personal interests and skills to older Americans with opportunities to help solve community problems and offer supplemental insurance while on duty, on-the-job training from the agency or organization where volunteers are placed.

2480 RSVP Prince William
9248 Center Street
Manassas, VA 20110-5537   703-369-5292
Fax: 703-369-5671
e-mail: dragghianti@volunteerprincewilliam.org
http://www.volunteerprincewilliam.org
Dana M Ragghianti, RSVP Project Director
Brigitte Winkie, RSVP Volunteer Liaison

Federally funded program designed to promote volunteerism in citizens 55 years of age and older. Program benefits included mileage reimbursment/cab service, supplemental accident insurance, volunteer training luncheons, volunteer get togethers, advisory board leadership roles, shirt and tote bags and more. Volunteer choose their volunteer site and set their own schedule.

2481 RSVP Pulaski County
106 N Washington Avenue
Pulaski, VA 24301   540-994-0300
e-mail: rsvp@usit.net
Amanda Quesenberry, Director

Provides opportunities for people 55 and over to make a difference in their community through volunteer service. RSVP volunteers contribute anywhere form a few to over forty hours a week, serving through schools, day care centers, police departments, hospitals and other nonprofit and public organizations to help meet critical community needs. RSVP matches the personal interests and skills of older Americans with opportunities to help solve community problems and offers supplemental insurance while on duty, on-the-job training from a agency or organization where volunteers are placed.

2482 RSVP Rappahannock-Rapidan
PO Box 1568
Culpeper, VA 22701-6568   540-825-3100
Fax: 540-825-6245

The Retired and Senior Volunteer Program (RSVP) provides opportunities for people 55 and over to make a difference in their community through volunteer service. RSVP volunteers contribute anywhere from a few to over forty hours a week, serving though schools, day care centers, police departments, hospitals and other nonprofit and public organizations to help meet critical community needs. RSVP offers maximum flexibility and choice to its volunteers. RSVP matches the personal interests and skills to older Americans with opportunities to help solve community problems and offer supplemental insurance while on duty, on-the-job training from the agency or organization where volunteers are placed.

2483 RSVP Richmond
24 E Cary Street
Richmond, VA 23219-3733   804-343-3050
Fax: 804-649-2258

The Retired and Senior Volunteer Program (RSVP) provides opportunities for people 55 and over to make a difference in their community through volunteer service. RSVP volunteers contribute anywhere from a few to over forty hours a week, serving though schools, day care centers, police departments, hospitals and other nonprofit and public organizations to help meet critical community needs. RSVP offers maximum flexibility and choice to its volunteers. RSVP matches the personal interests and skills to older Americans with opportunities to help solve community problems and offer supplemental insurance while on duty, on-the-job training from the agency or organization where volunteers are placed.

2484 RSVP Shenandoah Area
207 Mosby Lane
Front Royal, VA 22630-3029   540-635-7141
Fax: 540-636-7810

The Retired and Senior Volunteer Program (RSVP) provides opportunities for people 55 and over to make a difference in their community through volunteer service. RSVP volunteers contribute anywhere from a few to over forty hours a week, serving though schools, day care centers, police departments, hospitals and other nonprofit and public organizations to help meet critical community needs. RSVP offers maximum flexibility and choice to its volunteers. RSVP matches the personal interests and skills to older Americans with opportunities to help solve community problems and offer supplemental insurance while on duty, on-the-job training from the agency or organization where volunteers are placed.

2485 RSVP Southside
23 Seyler Drive
Petersburg, VA 23805-9243   804-861-1767
Fax: 804-732-7232
Patricia Hale, Manager

State Organizations & Government Agencies/Virginia

The Retired and Senior Volunteer Program (RSVP) provides opportunities for people 55 and over to make a difference in their community through volunteer service. RSVP volunteers contribute anywhere from a few to over forty hours a week, serving though schools, day care centers, police departments, hospitals and other nonprofit and public organizations to help meet critical community needs. RSVP offers maximum flexibility and choice to its volunteers. RSVP matches the personal interests and skills to older Americans with opportunities to help solve community problems and offer supplemental insurance while on duty, on-the-job training from the agency or organization where volunteers are placed.

2486 Railroad Retirement Board: Richmond, Virginia District Office
400 N 8th Street
Richmond, VA 23240-1005
804-771-2997
Fax: 804-771-8481
e-mail: richmond@rrb.gov

David P Griffith, Representative

2487 Railroad Retirement Board: Roanoke, Virginia District Office
PO Box 270
Roanoke, VA 24002
540-857-2335
Fax: 540-857-2769
e-mail: roanoke@rrb.gov

Fred E Way, Representative

2488 Rappahannock Area: Agency on Aging
171 Warrenton Road
Fredericksburg, VA 22405-1343
540-371-3375
800-262-4012
Fax: 540-371-3384
e-mail: raaa@infionline.net
http://http://raaa.home.infionline.net

James Schaefer, Executive Director

2489 Rappahannock-Rapidan Community Services Board and Area Agency on Aging
PO Box 1568
Culpeper, VA 22701-6568
540-825-3100
Fax: 540-825-6245
e-mail: rrcsb@rrcsb.org
TDD 540-825-7391

Brian D Duncan, Executive Director

2490 Senior Connections The Capital Area: Agency
24 E Cary Street
Richmond, VA 23219-3733
804-343-3000
800-989-2286
Fax: 804-649-2258

Beverly S Beck, Director
Thelma B Watson, Executive Director

Serves persons age 60 and over in the City of Richmond and surrounding counties: Services provided: congregate meals, home-delivered meals, long-term care ombudsman, newsletter, volunteer program, foster grandparents, short-term home care, volunteer money management, partners in guardianship, Virginia insurance counseling and assistance project, senior employment, resource coordination, home equity conversion mortgage loan counseling, fan care.

2491 Virginia Association of Area Agencies on Aging
316 E Clay Street
Richmond, VA 23219-1404
804-343-3000
Fax: 804-649-2258

Betty Reams, Director
Thelma Watson, Executive Director

2492 Virginia Association of Nonprofit Homes for the Aging
4201 Dominion Boulevard
Suite 100
Glen Allen, VA 23060-6743
804-965-5500
Fax: 804-965-9089
e-mail: vanha@vanha.org
http://www.vanha.org

Sandra Levin, President

2493 Virginia Board for People with Disabilities
PO Box 613
Richmond, VA 23218
804-786-0016
800-846-4464
Fax: 804-783-1118
e-mail: parsonbs@vbpd.state.va.us

Sandy K Reen, Director
Brian S Parsons, Contact
Heidi Lawyer, Manager

2494 Virginia Client Assistance Program
1910 Byrd Avenue
Suite 5
Richmond, VA 23230-3034
804-225-2042
Fax: 804-662-7057
http://www.vopa.state.va.us

V Coleen Miller, Executive Director

2495 Virginia Department for the Aging
1610 Forest Avenue
Suite 100
Richmond, VA 23229
804-662-9333
800-552-3402
Fax: 804-662-9354
e-mail: aging@vda.virginia.gov
http://www.aging.state.va.us

Julie Christopher, Commissioner
Janet D Brown, Esq, Guardianship/Legal Svcs Coord
Faye Cates MSSW, Program Coordinator

The Department's objective is to help Virginians find the information and services they need to lead healthy and independent lives as they grow older. Our mission is to foster the dignity, independence, and security of older Virginians by promoting partnerships with families and communities.

2496 Virginia Department of Health and Human Resources: Department of Aging
700 E Franklin Street
10th Floor
Richmond, VA 23219-2328
804-662-9333
800-552-3402
Fax: 804-662-9354

Julie Christopher, Manager

2497 Virginia Department of Taxation
PO Box 1115
Richmond, VA 23218-1115
804-367-8031
http://www.state.va.us/tax

Kenneth W Thorson, Manager

2498 Virginia Developmental Disability Council
202 N 9th Street
9th Floor
Richmond, VA 23219-3426
804-786-0016
800-846-4464
Fax: 804-786-1118
http://www.vaboard.org

Melissa Edmonds, Chairman
Heidi L Lawyer, Director

2499 Virginia Office for Protection and Advocacy
1910 Byrd Avenue
Suite 5
Richmond, VA 23230-3034
804-225-2042
Fax: 804-662-7057
http://www.vopa.state.va.us

V Colleen Miller, Executive Director

Helps with disability-related problems like abuse, neglect and discrimination. Helps people with disabilities obtain services and treatment. Individuals with problems targeted in program priorities may receive advocacy services and/or legal representation.

2500 Virginia Protection & Advocacy for Persons with Disabilities
101 N 14th Street
Floor 17
Richmond, VA 23219-3684
804-225-2042
Fax: 804-225-3221

V Colleen Miller, Executive Director

Washington

2501 AARP West Regional Office
AARP
1750 3rd Avenue NE
Suite 400
Seattle, WA 98115-2029
206-526-7918
Fax: 206-523-8138
http://www.aarp.org
TTY 916-446-2680

A resource for AARP members in the states of Alaska, California, Hawaii, Idaho, Montana, Nevada, Oregon, Washington, and Wyoming, as well as Guam. Hours are 9-5 Monday through Friday.

2502 Abused Deaf Women's Advocacy Services
4738 11th Avenue NE
Seattle, WA 98105-4610
206-726-0093
Fax: 206-726-0017
e-mail: adwas@adwas.org
http://www.adwas.org

Marilyn J Smith, Executive Director
Kay Amos, Office Manager
Sheli Barber, Therapist/Direct Services Coord.

Advocacy group for deaf and deaf-blind women who have been mentally, physically, or sexually abused.

2503 Aging and Long Term Care of Eastern Washington
1222 N Post Street
Spokane, WA 99201-2518
509-458-2509
Fax: 509-458-2003
e-mail: Rossjn@dshs.wa.gov
http://www.altcew.org

Nick Beamer, Director
Judith Ross, Public Information Manager
Mike Hilborn, Planner/Resource Development

One of 13 area agencies on aging in Washington state. An administrative agency that funds programs and services that promote independence and keep older persons and individuals needing long term care living in their own homes for as long as possible.

2504 Bureau of Naval Personnel: Bremerton Retired Affairs
Navy Fleet and Family Support Center
Naval Base Kitsap - NBK
120 S Dewey Street, Building 864
Bremerton, WA 98314-5020
360-476-5113
800-572-4341
Fax: 360-476-8874
e-mail: Brem-FFSC@navy.mil

Captain Reid Tanaka, Commander

The Fleet and Family Support throughout Navy Region Northwest is an on-base social service organization whose goal is to improve the quality of life for the Navy member and family through Counseling and Advocacy Prevention Services (CAPS) and Life Skills Programs.

2505 Bureau of Naval Personnel: Washington Retired Activities Office
Fleet and Family Support Center
NSB Bangor, Programs Code N4761
2901 Barbel Street
Silverdale, WA 98315-2905
360-396-4115
800-562-3301
Fax: 360-396-6310
e-mail: marie.walmsley@subase.nsb.navy.mil

Marie Walmsley, Contact

The Fleet and Family Support Program throughout Navy Region Northwest is an on-base social service organization whose goal is to improve the quality of life for the Navy member and family through Counseling and Advocacy Prevention Services (CAPS) and Life Skills Programs.

2506 Bureau of Naval Personnel: Whidbey Island Retired Activities Office
Fleet & Family Support Center
Naval Air Station Whidbey Island
3675 W Lexington Street, Building 2256
Oak Harbor, WA 98278
360-257-8054
Fax: 360-257-8061

The Fleet and Family Support Program throughout Navy Region Northwest is an on-base social service organization whose goal is to improve the quality of life for the Navy member and family through Counseling and Advocacy Prevention Services (CAPS) and Life Skills Programs.

2507 Columbia River Area: Agency on Aging
50 Simon Street SE
East Wenatchee, WA 98802-7734
509-886-0700
800-572-4459
Fax: 509-884-6943

Bruce Buckles, Director

2508 Colville Indian Area: Agency on Aging
PO Box 150
Nespelem, WA 99155
509-634-2758
Fax: 509-634-2793

Tommy Waters, Director

2509 Division of Disability Determination Services
PO Box 9303
Olympia, WA 98507-9303
360-664-7356
Fax: 360-586-0851
e-mail: John.Peters@ssa.gov

John Peters, Medical Relations Manager

2510 Gray Panthers of Seattle
5625 12th Avenue NE
Seattle, WA 98105-2603
206-675-8859
Fax: 202-737-1160
e-mail: jadcoc@mac.com
http://www.graypanthers.org

Cynthia Adcock, Director

2511 Kitsap County Area: Agency on Aging
614 Division Street
Ms 5
Port Orchard, WA 98366-4614
360-337-7129
Fax: 360-337-5746

Ade Ariwoola, Manager

2512 Olympic Area: Agency on Aging
11700 Rhody Drive
Port Hadlock, WA 98339-9773
360-385-2552
Fax: 360-379-4400

Roy B Walker, Director

State Organizations & Government Agencies/Washington

2513 RSVP Benton-Franklin Counties
303 Columbia Center
Kennewick, WA 99336-1163
509-735-6772
Fax: 509-735-7884
e-mail: rsvp@bfvc.org
http://www.bfvc.org
Diane Hart, RSVP Director

The Retired and Senior Volunteer Program (RSVP) provides opportunities for people 55 and over to make a difference in their community through volunteer service. RSVP volunteers contribute anywhere from a few to over forty hours a week, serving though schools, day care centers, police departments, hospitals and other nonprofit and public organizations to help meet critical community needs. RSVP offers maximum flexibility and choice to its volunteers. RSVP matches the personal interests and skills to older Americans with opportunities to help solve community problems and offer supplemental insurance while on duty, on-the-job training from the agency or organization where volunteers are placed.

2514 RSVP Clallam Jefferson County
181 Quincy Street
Suite 201
Port Townsend, WA 98368-5762
360-457-1771
Fax: 360-385-4290

The Retired and Senior Volunteer Program (RSVP) provides opportunities for people 55 and over to make a difference in their community through volunteer service. RSVP volunteers contribute anywhere from a few to over forty hours a week, serving though schools, day care centers, police departments, hospitals and other nonprofit and public organizations to help meet critical community needs. RSVP offers maximum flexibility and choice to its volunteers. RSVP matches the personal interests and skills to older Americans with opportunities to help solve community problems and offer supplemental insurance while on duty, on-the-job training from the agency or organization where volunteers are placed.

2515 RSVP Clark County
PO Box 1995
Vancouver, WA 98668-1995
360-750-7514
Fax: 360-759-4424
e-mail: rsvp@ci.vancouver.wa.us
Bobbi Casanova, Program Director
Jeanne Phipps, Senior Office Assistant

Recruits volunteers 55 and older and matches their skills, talents and time availability with the right volunteerposition at one of 200 private and public non profit organizations. Volunteers choose what, where and how much time they give. Volunteers have the opportunity to keep skills active, learn new ones and make new friends. Provides supplemental insurance, limited mileage reimbursment and recognition.

2516 RSVP Grays Harbor Pacific County
117 E 3rd Street
Aberdeen, WA 98520-4002
360-532-4900
Fax: 360-532-4623
e-mail: roxie@coastalcap.org
Roxanna Jackson, Program Manager

The Retired and Senior Volunteer Program (RSVP) provides opportunities for people 55 and over to make a difference in their community through volunteer service. RSVP volunteers contribute anywhere from a few to over forty hours a week, serving though schools, day care centers, police departments, hospitals and other nonprofit and public organizations to help meet critical community needs. RSVP offers maximum flexibility and choice to its volunteers. RSVP matches the personal interests and skills to older Americans with opportunities to help solve community problems and offer supplemental insurance while on duty, on-the-job training from the agency or organization where volunteers are placed.

2517 RSVP King County
1501 N 45th Street
Seattle, WA 98103-6708
206-694-6790
Fax: 206-694-6795
Chris Marx, Manager

The Retired and Senior Volunteer Program (RSVP) provides opportunities for people 55 and over to make a difference in their community through volunteer service. RSVP volunteers contribute anywhere from a few to over forty hours a week, serving though schools, day care centers, police departments, hospitals and other nonprofit and public organizations to help meet critical community needs. RSVP offers maximum flexibility and choice to its volunteers. RSVP matches the personal interests and skills to older Americans with opportunities to help solve community problems and offer supplemental insurance while on duty, on-the-job training from the agency or organization where volunteers are placed.

2518 RSVP Kitsap County
830 Pacific Avenue
Suite 101
Bremerton, WA 98337-1934
360-377-5511
Fax: 360-377-3548
e-mail: ktanno@lcsnw.org
Kay Tanno, Director
Jennifer Smith, Volunteer Coordinator

The Retired and Senior Volunteer Program (RSVP) provides opportunities for people 55 and over to make a difference in their community through volunteer service. RSVP volunteers contribute anywhere from a few to over forty hours a week, serving though schools, day care centers, police departments, hospitals and other nonprofit and public organizations to help meet critical community needs. RSVP offers maximum flexibility and choice to its volunteers. RSVP matches the personal interests and skills to older Americans with opportunities to help solve community problems and offer supplemental insurance while on duty, on-the-job training from the agency or organization where volunteers are placed.

2519 RSVP Kittitas County
207 N Pearl Street
Ellensburg, WA 98926-4010
509-962-4311
Fax: 509-925-1730

The Retired and Senior Volunteer Program (RSVP) provides opportunities for people 55 and over to make a difference in their community through volunteer service. RSVP volunteers contribute anywhere from a few to over forty hours a week, serving though schools, day care centers, police departments, hospitals and other nonprofit and public organizations to help meet critical community needs. RSVP offers maximum flexibility and choice to its volunteers. RSVP matches the personal interests and skills to older Americans with opportunities to help solve community problems and offer supplemental insurance while on duty, on-the-job training from the agency or organization where volunteers are placed.

2520 RSVP Pierce County
1235 South Tacoma Way
Tacoma, WA 98409
253-474-1700
Fax: 253-473-4843
e-mail: rsvp@rainier-redcross.org
http://www.rainier-redcross.org
Alison Leiman, RSVP Project Director
Nicolin Langlow, RSVP Project Coordinator

The Retired and Senior Volunteer Program (RSVP) provides opportunities for people 55 and over to make a difference in their community through volunteer service. RSVP volunteers contribute anywhere from a few to over forty hours a week, serving though schools, day care centers, police departments, hospitals and other nonprofit and public organizations to help meet critical community needs. RSVP offers maximum flexibility and choice to its volunteers. RSVP matches the personal interests and skills to older Americans with opportunities to help solve community problems and offer supplemental insurance while on duty, on-the-job training from the agency or organization where volunteers are placed.

2521 RSVP Skagit County
315 S 3rd Street
Mount Vernon, WA 98273-3855
360-336-9315
Fax: 360-336-9310
Donna Sitts, Executive Director

State Organizations & Government Agencies/Washington

The Retired and Senior Volunteer Program (RSVP) provides opportunities for people 55 and over to make a difference in their community through volunteer service. RSVP volunteers contribute anywhere from a few to over forty hours a week, serving though schools, day care centers, police departments, hospitals and other nonprofit and public organizations to help meet critical community needs. RSVP offers maximum flexibility and choice to its volunteers. RSVP matches the personal interests and skills to older Americans with opportunities to help solve community problems and offer supplemental insurance while on duty, on-the-job training from the agency or organization where volunteers are placed.

2522 RSVP Snohomish County
1918 Everett Avenue
Everett, WA 98201-3607
509-735-6772
Fax: 509-735-7884

The Retired and Senior Volunteer Program (RSVP) provides opportunities for people 55 and over to make a difference in their community through volunteer service. RSVP volunteers contribute anywhere from a few to over forty hours a week, serving though schools, day care centers, police departments, hospitals and other nonprofit and public organizations to help meet critical community needs. RSVP offers maximum flexibility and choice to its volunteers. RSVP matches the personal interests and skills to older Americans with opportunities to help solve community problems and offer supplemental insurance while on duty, on-the-job training from the agency or organization where volunteers are placed.

2523 RSVP Spokane County
PO Box 208
Spokane, WA 99210
509-344-7787
Fax: 509-343-4096
e-mail: rsvp@mcaspokane.org

Michael Holland, Director
Angee Friedrich, Volunteer Coordinator
Clint Kruiswyk, Exectuve Director

The Retired and Senior Volunteer Program (RSVP) provides opportunities for people 55 and over to make a difference in their community through volunteer service. RSVP volunteers contribute anywhere from a few to over forty hours a week, serving though schools, day care centers, police departments, hospitals and other nonprofit and public organizations to help meet critical community needs. RSVP offers maximum flexibility and choice to its volunteers. RSVP matches the personal interests and skills to older Americans with opportunities to help solve community problems and offer supplemental insurance while on duty, on-the-job training from the agency or organization where volunteers are placed.

2524 RSVP Walla Walla CountySenior Citizen Center
PO Box 1595
Walla Walla, WA 99362
509-527-3775
Fax: 509-527-3776

Susan Stewart, Manager

The Retired and Senior Volunteer Program (RSVP) provides opportunities for people 55 and over to make a difference in their community through volunteer service. RSVP volunteers contribute anywhere from a few to over forty hours a week, serving though schools, day care centers, police departments, hospitals and other nonprofit and public organizations to help meet critical community needs. RSVP offers maximum flexibility and choice to its volunteers. RSVP matches the personal interests and skills to older Americans with opportunities to help solve community problems and offer supplemental insurance while on duty, on-the-job training from the agency or organization where volunteers are placed.

2525 RSVP Yakima County
PO Box 22520
Yakima, WA 98907-2520
509-574-6858
Fax: 509-574-6874
e-mail: dwilson@yvcc.edu
http://www.rsvpyakima.org

Deborah F Wilson, Director
Pam Kelley, RSVP Volunteer Coordinator

A nonprofit dedicated to activating seniors 55 and over to volunteer in schools, nonprofits and government agencies throughout Yakima County.

2526 Railroad Retirement Board: Bellevue, Washington District Office
Pacific First Plaza 155 108th
Suite 201
Bellevue, WA 98004
206-553-5483
Fax: 206-553-0179
e-mail: bellevue@rrb.gov

Virgie Seaton, Representative

2527 Railroad Retirement Board: Spokane, Washington District Office
920 W Riverside Avenue
Spokane, WA 99201-1081
509-353-2795
Fax: 509-353-2741

Nancy M Hand, Representative

2528 Region 10: Administration on Aging (AoA)
US Department of Health & Human Services
2201 6th Avenue
Suite 600
Seattle, WA 98121-1853
206-615-2298
Fax: 206-553-6790
http://www.aoa.gov

Region includes Alaska, Idaho, Oregon, and Washington.

2529 Seattle King County Division on Aging
618 2nd Avenue
Suite 1020
Seattle, WA 98104-2248
206-684-0660
800-972-9990
Fax: 206-684-0689
TDD 206-684-0702

Frank Jose, Director
Pamela Piering, Executive Director

2530 Shoreline Lake Forest Park Senior Center
18560 1st Avenue NE
Suite 1
Shoreline, WA 98155-2148
206-417-4645
Fax: 206-364-8930

2531 Washington Association of Area Agencies on Aging
2401 Bristol Court SW
Olympia, WA 98502-6003
360-754-2136
Fax: 360-754-4240

Richard Dorsett, Executive Director

2532 Washington Association of Houses and Services for the Aging
1570 Wilmington Drive
Suite 220
DuPont, WA 98327
253-964-8870
Fax: 253-964-8876
http://www.wahsa.com

WAHSA is the state association of not-for-profit organizations and other affiliated members dedicated to providing quality housing, health, community and related services to the elderly.

2533 Washington Client Assistance Program
2531 Rainier Avenue S
5
Seattle, WA 98144-5328
206-721-5999
800-544-2121
Fax: 206-721-4537

Jerry Johnsen, Director

Advocacy and information assistance for persons of disability seeking services through Vocational Rehabilitation or other program under the 1973 Rehabilitation Act as commented. We provide counseling.

State Organizations & Government Agencies/West Virginia

2534 **Washington Department of Retirement Systems**
1025 E Union Capital Plaza
Olympia, WA 98504-2511
360-236-4018
800-547-6657
Fax: 360-753-3166
Maxine Hayes MD

2535 **Washington Department of Revenue**
PO Box 47450
Olympia, WA 98507
360-236-4018
800-647-7706
http://www.wa.gov/dor
Maxine Hayes MD

2536 **Washington Department of Social and Health Services Aging and Adult Services**
PO Box 45010
Olympia, WA 98504-5100
360-236-4018
800-422-3263
Maxine Hayes MD

2537 **Washington Department of Veterans Affairs**
PO Box 41150
Olympia, WA 98504-1150
360-753-5586
John Lee, Executive Director

2538 **Washington Governor's Committee on Disability Issues & Employment**
PO Box 9046
Olympia, WA 98507-9046
360-753-6780
Fax: 360-438-3208
Tom Fitzsimmons, Manager

2539 **Washington Protection & Advocacy for Persons with Disabilities**
315 5th Avenue S
Suite 850
Seattle, WA 98104-2691
206-324-1521
Fax: 206-957-0729
http://www.wpas-rights.org
Mark Stroh, Executive Director

2540 **Washington State Aging & Disability Services Administration**
640 Woodland Square Loop
Lacey, WA 98503
360-725-2300
800-422-3263
Fax: 360-407-0369
http://www.aasa.dshs.wa.gov
TDD 800-737-7931
Kathy Leitch, Assistant Secretary

The Aging and Disability Services Administration assists children and adults with developmental delays or disabilities, cognitive impairment, chronic illness and related functional disabilities to gain access to needed services and supports by managing a system of long-term care and supportive services that are high quality, cost effective, and responsive to individual needs and preferences.

2541 **Washington State Department of Services**
521 Legion Way SE
Olympia, WA 98501-1422
360-586-1224
800-552-7103
Fax: 360-586-7627
Shirley Smith, Director
Luoana Durand, Executive Director

Offers diagnostic, medical and surgical treatment and referral services for the disabled.

2542 **Washington State Developmental Disabilities Council**
2600 Martin Way, Suite F
PO Box 48314
Olympia, WA 98501-8314
425-753-3908
800-634-4473
Fax: 360-586-6502
http://www.wa.gov/ddc
Ed Holen, Executive Director
Eva Rocks, Program Coordinator

The Washington State Developmental Disabilities Council is appointed by the Governor to promote a comprehensive system of services, and serve as an advocate and a planning body for Washington State's citizens with developmental disabilities.

2543 **Washington Workers Compensation Board**
Department of Labor and Industries
PO Box 4400
Olympia, WA 98504-4000
360-586-0441
800-547-8367
Fax: 360-902-5798
http://www.lni.wa.gov
Gary Weeks, Director
Vickie Kennedy, Special Assistant to Director
Judy Schurke, Deputy Director Operations

Protecting workers wages and working conditions.

2544 **Yakama Nation Area Agency on Aging**
PO Box 151
Toppenish, WA 98948
509-865-5121
Fax: 509-865-2098
e-mail: mmiller@yakama.com
Marie Miller, Director
Carol Castellano, Office Assistant
William Yallup, Manager

West Virginia

2545 **Appalachian Area: Agency on Aging**
PO Box 1432
Princeton, WV 24740-1432
304-425-1147
Fax: 304-487-3767
Ramona McNeely-Stanley, Director

2546 **Charleston Disability Determination Services**
500 Quarrier Street
Suite 500
Charleston, WV 25301
304-343-5055
Fax: 304-353-4212
http://www.wvdrs.org
Jane Johnstone, Assistant Director

Under contract with the US Social Security Administration, the Disability Determination Services Section determines eligibility for Social Security Disability Insurance and Supplemental Security Income benefits.

2547 **Clarksburg Disability Determination Services**
Federal Center
320 West Pike Street, Suite 120
Clarksburg, WV 26301
304-624-0200
Fax: 304-624-0252
http://www.wvdrs.org
Janice A Holland, Interim Director

Under contract with the US Social Security Administration, the Disability Determination Services Section determines eligibility for Social Security Disability Insurance and Supplemental Security Income benefits.

2548 **Communication Workers of America Retirees Club of Local 2011**
270 E Main Street
Clarksburg, WV 26301-2170
304-622-2011

Represents members' interests; conducts lobbying activities. Provides assistance programs for retirees.

State Organizations & Government Agencies/West Virginia

2549 Disability Determination Section
500 Quarrier Street
Suite 500
Charleston, WV 25301-2198
304-343-5055
Fax: 304-353-4257
Rae A Burdette, Professional Relations
Jane Johnstone, Manager

2550 Northwestern Area: Agency on Aging
PO Box 2086
Wheeling, WV 26003
304-242-1800
Fax: 304-242-2437
e-mail: lwilliams@belomar.org
http://www.belomar.org
Lynn Williams DiPasquada, Director
Joyce Farmer, Assistant Director
William Phipps, Manager

The NWAAA maintains Older Americans Act programs through subgrants and contracts with senior centers within its 16 county PSA.

2551 RSVP Case
115 Morrison Drive
Princeton, WV 24740-2322
304-425-1911
Fax: 304-425-2089

The Retired and Senior Volunteer Program (RSVP) provides opportunities for people 55 and over to make a difference in their community through volunteer service. RSVP volunteers contribute anywhere from a few to over forty hours a week, serving though schools, day care centers, police departments, hospitals and other nonprofit and public organizations to help meet critical community needs. RSVP offers maximum flexibility and choice to its volunteers. RSVP matches the personal interests and skills to older Americans with opportunities to help solve community problems and offer supplemental insurance while on duty, on-the-job training from the agency or organization where volunteers are placed.

2552 RSVP Mercer Summer Monroe Counties
701 Mercer Street
Suite 304
Princeton, WV 24740-3113
304-425-1911
Fax: 304-425-2089
Brenda Miller, Contact

Retirees in Mercer, Monroe, and Summers counties, WV. Volunteer service program.

2553 RSVP Mid-Ohio Valley
531 Market Street
Parkersburg, WV 26101-5143
304-422-4993
Fax: 304-422-1025
Jim Mylott, Executive Director

The Retired and Senior Volunteer Program (RSVP) provides opportunities for people 55 and over to make a difference in their community through volunteer service. RSVP volunteers contribute anywhere from a few to over forty hours a week, serving though schools, day care centers, police departments, hospitals and other nonprofit and public organizations to help meet critical community needs. RSVP offers maximum flexibility and choice to its volunteers. RSVP matches the personal interests and skills to older Americans with opportunities to help solve community problems and offer supplemental insurance while on duty, on-the-job training from the agency or organization where volunteers are placed.

2554 RSVP Morgantown
1837 Listravia Avenue
Morgantown, WV 26505-6317
304-296-7454
Fax: 304-296-7361

The Retired and Senior Volunteer Program (RSVP) provides opportunities for people 55 and over to make a difference in their community through volunteer service. RSVP volunteers contribute anywhere from a few to over forty hours a week, serving though schools, day care centers, police departments, hospitals and other nonprofit and public organizations to help meet critical community needs. RSVP offers maximum flexibility and choice to its volunteers. RSVP matches the personal interests and skills to older Americans with opportunities to help solve community problems and offer supplemental insurance while on duty, on-the-job training from the agency or organization where volunteers are placed.

2555 RSVP Panhandle
404 S Green Street
Berkeley Springs, WV 25411-1416
304-258-3069
Fax: 304-258-3190

The Retired and Senior Volunteer Program (RSVP) provides opportunities for people 55 and over to make a difference in their community through volunteer service. RSVP volunteers contribute anywhere from a few to over forty hours a week, serving though schools, day care centers, police departments, hospitals and other nonprofit and public organizations to help meet critical community needs. RSVP offers maximum flexibility and choice to its volunteers. RSVP matches the personal interests and skills to older Americans with opportunities to help solve community problems and offer supplemental insurance while on duty, on-the-job training from the agency or organization where volunteers are placed.

2556 Railroad Retirement Board: West Virginia District Office
New Federal Building 310w
Huntington, WV 25721
304-529-5561
Fax: 304-529-5546
William M Stevens, Representative

2557 Upper Potomac Area Agency on Aging
Airport Road
PO Box 869
Petersburg, WV 26847
304-257-1221
877-833-5084
Fax: 304-257-4958
e-mail: upaaa@regioneight.org
http://www.upaaa.net/index
Scott Gossard, Executive Director
Carl Faller, Fiscal Officer
Patti Bennett, Administrative Assistant

Our mission is one of service, with emphasis on providing assistance to older West Virginians, with dignity and a caring spirit. The UPAAA believes its goal is to provide technical assistance, training, and counseling to county providers with the intent of enhancing the hapiness and standard of living of older West Virginians. In this way, we feel, elderly West Virginians will be able to retain their dignity and independence while remaining in their own households.

2558 West Virginia Advocates
1207 Quarrier Street
Charleston, WV 25301-1826
304-346-0847
800-950-5250
Fax: 304-346-0867
http://www.wvadvocates.org
TDD 304-346-0847
Clarice Hausch, Executive Director

2559 West Virginia Department of Aging
Holly Grove State Capitol
Charleston, WV 25305
304-558-3317
Fax: 304-558-0004
e-mail: hollygrove@juno.com
Patricia Bedford, Director

State Organizations & Government Agencies/Wisconsin

2560 West Virginia Department of Health
1900 Capital Complex
Building 3
Charleston, WV 25305
304-558-0549
Fax: 304-558-1008
Taunja Willis-Miller, Secretary
Sarah Hamrick, Executive Director

2561 West Virginia Department of Health and Human Services: Human Services Bureau Commission on Aging
1900 Kanawha Boulevard E
Charleston, WV 25305
304-558-0549
Fax: 304-558-0004
Sarah Hamrick, Executive Director

2562 West Virginia Developmental Disability Plan Council
1601 Kanawha Boulevard W
Suite 200
Charleston, WV 25312-2500
304-204-2091
Fax: 304-558-0941
Gary Sims, Owner

2563 West Virginia Directors of Senior and Community Services
PO Box 10
Kingwood, WV 26537
304-555-3317

2564 West Virginia Division of Tax and Revenue
PO Box 3784
Charleston, WV 25337-3784
304-558-0211
800-982-8297
http://www.satte.wv.us/taxrev
Urita Lanham, Executive Director

2565 West Virginia Protection & Advocacy for Persons with Disabilities
1524 Kanawha Boulevard E
Charleston, WV 25311-2413
304-346-0847
Fax: 304-346-0867
Clarice Hausch, Executive Director

2566 West Virginia State University Metro Area Agency on Aging
Sullivan Hall
PO Box 518
Institute, WV 25112
304-766-3374
Fax: 304-766-4126
James D Recco, Director

2567 West Virginia Workers Compensation Board of Review
PO Box 2628
Charleston, WV 25329-2628
304-558-5230
Fax: 304-558-1322
http://www.wvinsurance.gov/boardofreview
Robert G Wolpert, Chair
W Jack Stevens, Member
Rita Hedrick-Helmick, Member

The Board of Review shall reverse, vacate or modify the order or decision of the administrative law judge if the substantial rights of the petitioner or petitioners have been prejudiced because the administrative law judge's findings.

Wisconsin

2568 AgeAdvantAge Area: Agency on Aging Western Office
2427 N Hillcrest Parkway
Suite 205
Altoona, WI 54720-2589
715-836-4105
Fax: 715-836-5810
e-mail: dmrhein@discover-net.net
http://http://discover.discover-net.net
Dianne Rhein, Regional Planner

2569 Area Agency on Aging of Dane County
2322 South Park Street
Madison, WI 53713
608-261-9930
Fax: 608-261-9787
e-mail: aaa@co.dane.wi.us
http://www.co.dane.wi.us
TTY 608-261-9905
Barb Thoni, Director
Janie Riebe, Aging Program Specialist

The mission of the Dane County Commission on Aging is to advocate for older people in order to enable them to maintain their full potential and enhance their quality of life.

2570 Bay Area Managers of Volunteer Services
131 S Madison Street
Green Bay, WI 54301-4501
414-435-1101
Fax: 920-492-5965
James Radey, President

Managers or coordinators of volunteer programs and volunteer supervisors in northeastern Wisconsin.

2571 Bureau of Naval Personnel: Wisconsin Retired Activities Office
Navy and Marine Corps Reserve Center
2401 South Lincoln Memorial Drive
Milwaukee, WI 53207-1999
414-744-9766
Fax: 414-744-2258

The mission of Retired Activities Branch at Navy Personnel Command (NPC) is to keep the retired community apprised of their benefits and provide customer services to our retirees and their families.

2572 Coalition of Wisconsin Aging Groups
2850 Dairy Drive
Suite 100
Madison, WI 53718-6742
608-224-0606
800-366-2990
Fax: 608-224-0607
e-mail: cwag@cwag.org
http://www.cwag.org
Thomas L Frazier, Executive Director

2573 Disability Determination Bureau
PO Box 7886
Madison, WI 53707-7886
608-266-1565
Fax: 608-266-8297
e-mail: kathleen.lane@ssa.gov
Kathleen M Lane, Professional Relations
Judy Fryback, Manager

2574 Douglas County Activity Association
1800 New York Avenue
Superior, WI 54880-2008
715-394-5591
Fax: 715-394-5098
Patsy Zimmerman, President
Jill Kennedy, Administrator

Activity directors of long-term care facilities and senior centers. Provides educational and social opportunities. Conducts charitable activities.

State Organizations & Government Agencies/Wisconsin

2575 Friends of Seniors
1318 Hamilton Avenue
Racine, WI 53403-3175   262-632-1939
Charles Clark, President

2576 Governor's Committee for People with Disabilities
1 West Wilson Street, Room 1150
PO Box 7851
Madison, WI 53707-7851   608-266-7974
Fax: 608-266-3386
http://www.dhfs.wisconsin.gov
TTY 608-267-9880
A Governor's Committee was established with one goal: to improve employment opportunities for people with disabilities. The group's mission was broadened to cover many aspects of disability in Wisconsin, and the group became the Governor's Committee for People with Disabilites (GCPD).

2577 Milwaukee County Department on Aging
235 West Galena Street
Suite 180
Milwaukee, WI 53212-3948   414-289-5950
866-229-9695
Fax: 414-289-8590
http://www.co.milwaukee.wi.us
TDD 414-289-5951
Stephanie Stein, Director

The mission of the Milwaukee County Department on Aging is to affirm the dignity and value of older adults of Milwaukee County by supporting their choices for living in, and giving to, our community.

2578 Northern Area: Agency on Aging
PO Box 1028
Rhinelander, WI 54501-1028   715-365-2525
Fax: 715-365-2534
Richard Sicchio, Executive Director

2579 RSVP Advacapcap
181 En Water Street
Neenah, WI 54956   920-725-2791
Fax: 920-725-6337
e-mail: karak@advocap.org
Kara Klein, RSVP Director
Terri Stern, Manager

The Retired and Senior Volunteer Program (RSVP) provides opportunities for people 55 and over to make a difference in their community through volunteer service. RSVP volunteers contribute anywhere from a few to over forty hours a week, serving though schools, day care centers, police departments, hospitals and other nonprofit and public organizations to help meet critical community needs. RSVP offers maximum flexibility and choice to its volunteers. RSVP matches the personal interests and skills to older Americans with opportunities to help solve community problems and offer supplemental insurance while on duty, on-the-job training from the agency or organization where volunteers are placed.

2580 RSVP Brown County
984 9th Street
Green Bay, WI 54304-3441   920-429-9445
Fax: 920-429-9449
Christine Danielson, Executive Director

The Retired and Senior Volunteer Program (RSVP) provides opportunities for people 55 and over to make a difference in their community through volunteer service. RSVP volunteers contribute anywhere from a few to over forty hours a week, serving though schools, day care centers, police departments, hospitals and other nonprofit and public organizations to help meet critical community needs. RSVP offers maximum flexibility and choice to its volunteers. RSVP matches the personal interests and skills to older Americans with opportunities to help solve community problems and offer supplemental insurance while on duty, on-the-job training from the agency or organization where volunteers are placed.

2581 RSVP Coulee Region
1025 South Avenue
La Crosse, WI 54601-4289   608-785-0500
Fax: 608-785-2573
Lynnetta Kopp, Manager

The Retired and Senior Volunteer Program (RSVP) provides opportunities for people 55 and over to make a difference in their community through volunteer service. RSVP volunteers contribute anywhere from a few to over forty hours a week, serving though schools, day care centers, police departments, hospitals and other nonprofit and public organizations to help meet critical community needs. RSVP offers maximum flexibility and choice to its volunteers. RSVP matches the personal interests and skills to older Americans with opportunities to help solve community problems and offer supplemental insurance while on duty, on-the-job training from the agency or organization where volunteers are placed.

2582 RSVP Dane County
517 N Segoe Road
Suite 300
Madison, WI 53705-3172   608-238-7787
Fax: 608-238-7931
e-mail: info@rsvpdane.org
http://www.rsvpdane.org
David Tetzlaff, Executive Director

The Retired and Senior Volunteer Program (RSVP) provides opportunities for people 55 and over to make a difference in their community through volunteer service. RSVP volunteers contribute anywhere from a few to over forty hours a week, serving though schools, day care centers, police departments, hospitals and other nonprofit and public organizations to help meet critical community needs. RSVP offers maximum flexibility and choice to its volunteers. RSVP matches the personal interests and skills to older Americans with opportunities to help solve community problems and offer supplemental insurance while on duty, on-the-job training from the agency or organization where volunteers are placed.

2583 RSVP Kenosha CountySponsored By Kenosha Area Family And Aging Services, Inc.
7730 Sheridan Road
Kenosha, WI 53143-1518   262-658-1892
Fax: 262-658-2263
e-mail: rsvp@kafasi.org
http://www.kafasi.org
Darleen Coleman, RSVP Director
Rose Cerda Perez, Program Assistant

RSVP(The Retired and Senior Volunteer Program) provides adults 55+ with a wide variety of fulfilling and fun volunteer opportunities throughout Kenosha County. RSVP offers volunteers choice, flexibility, and the chance to make a difference.

2584 RSVP Manitowoc County
2 N 8th Street
Suite 211
Manitowoc, WI 54220-4639   920-683-4504
Fax: 920-686-7640
e-mail: vc@hfmhealth.org
Susan M Vocke, Contact

The Retired and Senior Volunteer Program (RSVP) provides opportunities for people 55 and over to make a difference in their community through volunteer service. RSVP volunteers contribute anywhere from a few to over forty hours a week, serving though schools, day care centers, police departments, hospitals and other nonprofit and public organizations to help meet critical community needs. RSVP offers maximum flexibility and choice to its volunteers. RSVP matches the personal interests and skills to older Americans with opportunities to help solve community problems and offer supplemental insurance while on duty, on-the-job training from the agency or organization where volunteers are placed.

2585 RSVP Milwaukee
600 W Virginia Street
Milwaukee, WI 53204-1500   414-291-7500
Fax: 414-291-7510

State Organizations & Government Agencies/Wisconsin

The Retired and Senior Volunteer Program (RSVP) provides opportunities for people 55 and over to make a difference in their community through volunteer service. RSVP volunteers contribute anywhere from a few to over forty hours a week, serving though schools, day care centers, police departments, hospitals and other nonprofit and public organizations to help meet critical community needs. RSVP offers maximum flexibility and choice to its volunteers. RSVP matches the personal interests and skills to older Americans with opportunities to help solve community problems and offer supplemental insurance while on duty, on-the-job training from the agency or organization where volunteers are placed.

2586 RSVP Northwest
400 Chapple Avenue
Ashland, WI 54806-1477
715-682-6502
Fax: 715-682-2062
e-mail: washrsvp@ncis.net

Jan Washnieski, RSVP Director

National and statewide program which involves people 55 and over in significant volunteer service to their community, utilizing their many skills and talents to postively impact their community.

2587 RSVP Outagamie County
2616 S Oneida Street
Appleton, WI 54915-2101
920-832-9360
Fax: 920-832-9317
e-mail: rsvp@volunteercenter.net

Julia Drobeck, Executive Director

The Retired and Senior Volunteer Program (RSVP) provides opportunities for people 55 and over to make a difference in their community through volunteer service. RSVP volunteers contribute anywhere from a few to over forty hours a week, serving though schools, day care centers, police departments, hospitals and other nonprofit and public organizations to help meet critical community needs. RSVP offers maximum flexibility and choice to its volunteers. RSVP matches the personal interests and skills to older Americans with opportunities to help solve community problems and offer supplemental insurance while on duty, on-the-job training from the agency or organization where volunteers are placed.

2588 RSVP Portage County
1519 Water Street
Stevens Point, WI 54481-3548
715-346-1401
Fax: 715-346-1418

Kathy Fandre, Manager

The Retired and Senior Volunteer Program (RSVP) provides opportunities for people 55 and over to make a difference in their community through volunteer service. RSVP volunteers contribute anywhere from a few to over forty hours a week, serving though schools, day care centers, police departments, hospitals and other nonprofit and public organizations to help meet critical community needs. RSVP offers maximum flexibility and choice to its volunteers. RSVP matches the personal interests and skills to older Americans with opportunities to help solve community problems and offer supplemental insurance while on duty, on-the-job training from the agency or organization where volunteers are placed.

2589 RSVP Rock County
81 Beloit Mall
Beloit, WI 53511-3550
608-362-9593
Fax: 608-362-9820

Robert W Harlow, Executive Director

The Retired and Senior Volunteer Program (RSVP) provides opportunities for people 55 and over to make a difference in their community through volunteer service. RSVP volunteers contribute anywhere from a few to over forty hours a week, serving though schools, day care centers, police departments, hospitals and other nonprofit and public organizations to help meet critical community needs. RSVP offers maximum flexibility and choice to its volunteers. RSVP matches the personal interests and skills to older Americans with opportunities to help solve community problems and offer supplemental insurance while on duty, on-the-job training from the agency or organization where volunteers are placed.

2590 RSVP Superior-Douglas
1416 Cumming Avenue
Suite 2B
Superior, WI 54880-3757
715-394-4425
Fax: 715-394-5951
e-mail: rsvpdoug@pressenter.com
http://www.ccbsuperior.org

Kendra-Sue Rohde, Director

RSVP develops and supports volunteer opportunities for adults 55 and over to share their talents and expertise in areas where needs are expressed in the community.

2591 RSVP Walworth County
162 W Main Street
Suite H
Whitewater, WI 53190-1995
262-472-9632
Fax: 262-472-9636
e-mail: arcrsvp@genevaenline.com

Patti O'Brien, Area Driector
Pat Gogin, Program Coordinator

The Retired and Senior Volunteer Program (RSVP) provides opportunities for people 55 and over to make a difference in their community through volunteer service. RSVP volunteers contribute anywhere from a few to over forty hours a week, serving though schools, day care centers, police departments, hospitals and other nonprofit and public organizations to help meet critical community needs. RSVP offers maximum flexibility and choice to its volunteers. RSVP matches the personal interests and skills to older Americans with opportunities to help solve community problems and offer supplemental insurance while on duty, on-the-job training from the agency or organization where volunteers are placed.

2592 RSVP Waukeesha County
310 South Street
Waukesha, WI 53186-4710
262-544-9559
Fax: 262-544-5307
e-mail: dpinkalla@rsvpwaukesha.org

Diane Pinkalla, Contact

The Retired and Senior Volunteer Program (RSVP) provides opportunities for people 55 and over to make a difference in their community through volunteer service. RSVP volunteers contribute anywhere from a few to over forty hours a week, serving though schools, day care centers, police departments, hospitals and other nonprofit and public organizations to help meet critical community needs. RSVP offers maximum flexibility and choice to its volunteers. RSVP matches the personal interests and skills to older Americans with opportunities to help solve community problems and offer supplemental insurance while on duty, on-the-job training from the agency or organization where volunteers are placed.

2593 Railroad Retirement Board: Wisconsin District Office
310 W Wisconsin Avenue
Suite 1300
Milwaukee, WI 53203-2219
414-297-3961
Fax: 414-297-3833

Thomas P Hammersley, Representative

State Organizations & Government Agencies/Wisconsin

2594 Retired Senior Volunteer Program of Western Dairyland
23122 Whitehall Road
Independence, WI 54747
715-985-2391
Fax: 715-985-3239

James Schwartz, Manager

2595 Southeastern Wisconsin Area: Agency on Aging
125 N Executive Drive
Suite 102
Brookfield, WI 53005-6035
262-821-4440
Fax: 262-821-4445

Helen A Ramon, Director

2596 United Electric Workers Retirees
939 S 2nd Street
Milwaukee, WI 53204-1824
414-645-2769

Bob Rudick, President

2597 Volunteer Center of Racine County
12169 Washington Avenue
Suite G
Racine, WI 53406
262-886-9612
Fax: 262-886-9632
e-mail: volunteer@rootcom.net

Marilyn Pelky, Executive Director

2598 Volunteer Services of Barron County
PO Box 673
Rice Lake, WI 54868
715-236-2184

Rita Vanek, Manager

2599 WisTech Assistive Technology Program
Office of Independent and Employment
1 West Wilson Street, Room 1151
PO Box 7851
Madison, WI 53707-7851
608-266-8905
Fax: 608-266-3386
e-mail: lauxhm@dhfs.state.wi.us
http://www.dhfs.wisconsin.gov
TTY 608-267-9880

Holly Laux O'Higgins, Director

A statewide program promoting assistive technology devices and services for persons of all ages with all disabilities.

2600 Wisconsin Aging and Long Term Care Board
1402 Pankratz Street
Suite 111
Madison, WI 53704-4046
608-246-7013
800-242-1060
Fax: 608-246-7001
e-mail: BOALTC@ltc.state.wi.us

George Potaracke, Manager

2601 Wisconsin Association of Area Agencies on Aging
Southeastern Wisconsin Area Agency on Aging
125 N Executive Drive
Suite 102
Brookfield, WI 53005-6035
262-821-4444
Fax: 262-821-4445

Helen Ramon, Director

2602 Wisconsin Association of Homes and Services for the Aging
204 S Hamilton Street
Madison, WI 53703-3212
608-255-7060
Fax: 608-255-7064

John Sauer, Executive Director

2603 Wisconsin Client Assistance Program
PO Box 8911
Madison, WI 53708-8911
608-224-5070
800-362-1290
Fax: 608-224-5069

2604 Wisconsin Coalition for Advocacy
16 N Carroll Street
Suite 400
Madison, WI 53703-2762
608-267-0214
800-928-8778
Fax: 608-267-0368

Kim Hogan, Intake Specialist
Lynn Breedlove, Director

The protection and advocacy agency for people with disabilities in Wisconsin. WCA provides guidance, advice, investigation, negotiation, and in some cases legal representation to people with disabilities and their families. Local and state level systems advocacy and training are also provided.

2605 Wisconsin Council of Senior Citizens
1611 West Oklahoma Avenue
Milwaukee, WI 53215
414-385-9779
Fax: 414-385-9807
e-mail: wcsc@execpc.com

Grant Waldo, Contact

Retired people. Represents members' interests.

2606 Wisconsin Council on Developmental Disabilities
201 West Washington Avenue
Suite 110
Madison, WI 53703
608-266-7826
888-332-1677
Fax: 608-267-3906
e-mail: help@wcdd.org
http://www.wcdd.org
TDD 608-266-6660
TTY 608-266-6660

Jennifer Ondrejka, Executive Director
Helen Hartman, Office Manager

The Wisconsin Council on Developmental Disabilities was established to advocate on behalf of individuals with developmental disabilities, foster welcoming and inclusive communities, and improve the disability service system. The Council's mission is to help people with developmental disabilities become independent, productive, and included in all facets of community life.

2607 Wisconsin Department of Aging & Long-Term Care Resources
PO Box 7851
Madison, WI 53707-7851
608-266-2536
Fax: 608-267-3203

Donna McDowell, Director

2608 Wisconsin Department of Revenue
PO Box 8906
Madison, WI 53708-8906
608-266-2772
Fax: 608-267-0834
http://www.dor.state.wi.us

Michael Morgan, Manager

2609 Wisconsin Department of Veterans Affairs
PO Box 7843
Madison, WI 53707-7843
608-266-1018
Fax: 608-264-7616
e-mail: wdvaweb@dva.state.wi.us
http://http://dva.state.wi.us

Andy Schuster, Public Affairs Director
Mary Burke, Manager

Offers an array of benefits and services to eligible Wisconsin veterans and their families.

2610 Wisconsin Retired Educators Association
2564 Branch Street
Middleton, WI 53562-2858
608-831-5115
Fax: 608-831-1694
e-mail: wrea@wrea.net
http://www.wrea.net

Jane Elmer, Executive Director

The voice and choice of retired educators since 1951.

State Organizations & Government Agencies/Wyoming

2611 **Wisconsin Workers Compensation Board**
PO Box 7901
Madison, WI 53707-7901
608-266-1340
Fax: 608-267-0394

Frances Huntley-Cooper, Administrator

Wyoming

2612 **Disability Determination Services**
821 W Pershing Boulevard
Cheyenne, WY 82002
307-777-7341
Fax: 307-637-0247
e-mail: gabriel.barajas@ssa.gov

Gabriel Barajas, Disability Hearing Officer
Jeff Graham, Manager

2613 **RSVP Central Wyoming**
1831 E 4th Street
Casper, WY 82601-3052
307-265-4678
Fax: 307-265-2481

Wayne Clemments, Executive Director

The Retired and Senior Volunteer Program (RSVP) provides opportunities for people 55 and over to make a difference in their community through volunteer service. RSVP volunteers contribute anywhere from a few to over forty hours a week, serving though schools, day care centers, police departments, hospitals and other nonprofit and public organizations to help meet critical community needs. RSVP offers maximum flexibility and choice to its volunteers. RSVP matches the personal interests and skills to older Americans with opportunities to help solve community problems and offer supplemental insurance while on duty, on-the-job training from the agency or organization where volunteers are placed.

2614 **RSVP Southeastern Wyoming**
3304 Sheridan Street
Cheyenne, WY 82009-5366
307-693-4778
Fax: 307-637-4663

The Retired and Senior Volunteer Program (RSVP) provides opportunities for people 55 and over to make a difference in their community through volunteer service. RSVP volunteers contribute anywhere from a few to over forty hours a week, serving though schools, day care centers, police departments, hospitals and other nonprofit and public organizations to help meet critical community needs. RSVP offers maximum flexibility and choice to its volunteers. RSVP matches the personal interests and skills to older Americans with opportunities to help solve community problems and offer supplemental insurance while on duty, on-the-job training from the agency or organization where volunteers are placed.

2615 **Wyoming Client Assistance Program**
2424 Pioneer Avenue
Suite 101
Cheyenne, WY 82001-3064
307-638-7668
Fax: 307-777-5340

Kristen Smith, Director

2616 **Wyoming Department of Aging**
6101 N Yellowstone Avenue
Room 259b
Cheyenne, WY 82002
307-777-7986
Fax: 307-777-5340

Morris Gardner, Administrator
Beverly Morrow, Manager

2617 **Wyoming Department of Health: Aging Division**
Hathaway Building
Room 139
Cheyenne, WY 82002
307-777-7986
Fax: 307-777-5340

Beverly Morrow, Manager

2618 **Wyoming Department of Revenue**
122 W 25th Street
Cheyenne, WY 82002
307-777-7961
http://www.revenue.state.wy.us

2619 **Wyoming Developmental Disability Council**
122 W 25th Street
Cheyenne, WY 82001-3004
307-777-7230
Fax: 307-777-5690

Lynn Achter, Director
Brenda Oswalk, Manager

2620 **Wyoming Division of Rehabilitation**
122 W 25th Street
Cheyenne, WY 82002
307-777-8650
Fax: 307-777-5857
http://www.wyomingworkforce.org

Offers diagnostic, medical and surgical treatment, counseling, social work, professional training, employment services and computer training services for the disabled.

2621 **Wyoming Protection & Advocacy for Persons with Disabilities**
2424 Pioneer Avenue
Suite 101
Cheyenne, WY 82001-3064
307-638-7668
Fax: 307-777-5340

Kris Smith, Executive Director

2622 **Wyoming Workers Safety & Compensation Division**
1510 E Pershing Boulevard
Cheyenne, WY 82002
307-777-7159
Fax: 307-777-5946

Awards, Honors & Prizes/National

National

2623 Clark Tibbitts Award
Association for Gerontology in Higher Education
1220 L Street NW
Suite 901
Washington, DC 20005-1527
202-289-9806
Fax: 202-289-9824
e-mail: ctompkins@aghe.org
http://www.aghe.org

Derek Stepp, Manager

For recognition of significant contributions to the advancement of gerontology as a field of study in institutions of higher learning. Selection is by nomination. A certificate is awarded each year at the annual meeting and the awardee presents a lecture at a plenary session. Established in 1980. Re-named in 1987 to honor Clark Tibbitts, a pioneer in the field of gerontological education who founded the US Administration on Aging and authored over 100 publications.

2624 Claude Pepper Award
Claude Pepper Foundation
636 West Call Street
Tallahassee, FL 32306-1122
850-644-9309
Fax: 850-644-9301
e-mail: info@claudepepperfoundation.org
http://www.claudepepperfoundation.org

A not-for-profit corporation, established by Claude Pepper in 1986. Provides the resources to properly preserve, store, conserve, and make availiable the collection and to develop the curricula and public activities that would maximize its educational potential. Since its founding, the Foundation has not only fullfilled that purpose but developed programs to further the objectives of Senator Pepper.

2625 Community Awards Program (CAP)
Retirement Research Foundation
8765 W Higgins Road
Suite 430
Chicago, IL 60631-4170
773-714-8080
Fax: 773-714-8089
e-mail: info@rrf.org
http://www.fdncenter.org

Marilyn Hennessy, President

To recognize outstanding community efforts to serve the elderly and to encourage replication of these efforts in other parts of the Chicago metropolitan area. Social service, religious congregations, health organizations, hospitals, nursing homes, educational organizations, and community organizations in Cook, Lake, and DuPage counties, IL are eligible. Up to four monetary prizes of $25,000, in addition six prizes of $5,000 each are awarded annually. Established in 1987.

2626 Community Outreach Awards
Self Help for Hard of Hearing People
7910 Woodmont Avenue
Suite 1200
Bethesda, MD 20814-7022
301-657-2248
Fax: 301-913-9413
http://www.hearingloss.org

Anne Pope, President

To recognize chapters, groups, or individuals who have been involved in a project(s) which had a positive influence in the community on making hearing loss an issue of national concern. The recipients of these awards will have planted a seed of hope for hard of hearing people, followed through on the project, and have had the opportunity to watch the project grow to fruition. Any publicity generated by this activity will have had a positive impact on the goals of SHHH, as well as on the lives of hearing impaired persons in the community. Chapters, groups, or individual SHHH members may submit nominations of members for these awards by completing an application for nomination. Members of the Executive Committee of the Board of Directors will select the recipients of the awards. The deadline for nominations is March 1. Awards are presented in two categories: Community Awareness; and Community Access. A plaque is awarded.

2627 Deaf/Hard of Hearing Entrepreneur of the Year
Deaf and Hard of Hearing Entrepreneurs Council
4405 East West Hwy,
Ste. 502
Bethesda, MD 20814-4536
301-587-8596
Fax: 301-587-5997

Louis J Schwarts, Contact

For recognition of excellence in: being an entrepreneur in a deaf/hard of hearing community; helping in deaf/hard of hearing worthy causes; and providing good mentorship to others. Qualified deaf/hard of hearing entrepreneurs with at least five years in business are eligible. A plaque is awarded each year at the Annual Gala/Auction (late winter/early spring, usually in Metro Washington, DC). Established in 1992.

2628 Distinguished Mentorship in Gerontology Award
Gerontological Society of America
1220 L Street NW
Suite 901
Washington, DC 20005-1526
202-842-1275
Fax: 202-842-1150
e-mail: geron@geron.org
http://www.geron.org

Linda Krogh Harootyan, Interim Executive Director
Carol Ann Schutz, Advisor
Laurie Johnson, Office Manager

To recognize individuals who have fostered excellence and who have had a major impact on the field of gerontology by virtue of their mentoring, and whose inspiration is sought by students and colleagues. Membership in the BSS section is required.

2629 Distinguished Service in Aging Award
American Assn. of Homes & Services for the Aging
2519 Connecticut Avenue NW
Washington, DC 20008-1520
202-783-2242
Fax: 202-783-2255
e-mail: info@aahsa.org
http://www.aahsa.org

William L. Minnix Jr., President/CEO
Katrinka Smith Sloan, VP Member Services/COO
Tom Slemmer, AAHSA Board Chair

To recognize a public figure who has performed extraordinary service to the aging that has had or could have an impact on the total field of care and service to the aging.

2630 Donald P. Kent Award
Gerontological Society of America
1220 L Street NW
Suite 901
Washington, DC 20005-1526
202-842-1275
Fax: 202-842-1150
e-mail: geron@geron.org
http://www.geron.org

Linda Krogh Harootyan, Interim Executive Director
Carol Ann Schultz, Advisor
Laurie Johnson, Office Manager

Awards, Honors & Prizes/National

To recognize a member who exemplifies the highest standard of professional leadership through teaching, service, and the interpretation of gerontology to the larger society. Nominees must be fellows of the Society. The deadline for nominations is May 8. The award requires a lecture at the time of the annual scientific meeting. Established in 1973 to honor Donald P. Kent, a pioneer in the field of gerontology.

2631 Durward K. McDaniel Ambassador Award
American Council of the Blind
1155 15th Street NW
Suite 1004
Washington, DC 20005-2706
202-467-5081
800-424-8666
Fax: 202-467-5085
e-mail: info@acb.org
http://www.acb.org

Melanie Brusons, Executive Director

To recognize a blind or visually impaired person who has performed distinguished service to the community or in the state where he or she resides. A certificate is awarded annually at the Council's national convention. Established in 1964.

2632 Edward Henderson Memorial Student Award
American Geriatrics Society
350 Fifth Aveune
Suite 801
New York, NY 10118
212-308-1414
Fax: 212-832-8646
e-mail: info@americangeriatrics.org
http://www.americangeriatrics.org

Linda Hiddemen Barondess, Executive Vice President
Ellen Baumritter, PT Administrative Assistant
Shirley Burnett, Membership Assistant

For medical students demonstrating excellence and initiative in geriatrics.

2633 Employment Awards
Self Help for Hard of Hearing People
7910 Woodmont Avenue
Suite 1200
Bethesda, MD 20814-7022
301-657-2248
Fax: 301-913-9413
http://www.hearingloss.org

Anne Pope, President

To recognize affiliates that have taken specific steps to initiate programs to provide support for senior, hard of hearing members.

2634 Excellence in Practice Award
American Assn. of Homes & Services for the Aging
2519 Connecticut Avenue NW
Washington, DC 20008-1520
202-783-2242
Fax: 202-783-2255
e-mail: info@aahsa.org
http://www.aahsa.org

William L. Minnix Jr., President/CEO
Katrinka Smith Sloan, VP/Member Services/COO
Tom Slemmer, AAHSA Board Chair

To recognize standards of excellence through programs that address some of the most complex challenges in the field of housing, care and services for the aging. By honoring benchmark, best practices in AAHSA-member organizations, this award seeks to showcase programs that demonstrate superior achievement throughout the continuum of aging services. An organization's total program of services or an individual program may be nominated. Criteria for inclusion: demonstrates an overall level of excellence that far exceeds what would be considered a merely good or even commendable standard of care and service; emphasizes quality of life for the individuals served, including the demonstrated capacity for change in response to their needs and desires; provides tangible, quantifiable benefits to persons being served; and in operation at least two years and ongoing. Each receives a plaque.

2635 Geneva Mathiasen Award
National Council on the Aging
1901 L Street NW
4th Floor
Washington, DC 20036
202-479-1200
800-867-2755
Fax: 202-479-0735
e-mail: info@ncoa.org
http://www.ncoa.org
TDD 202-479-6674

James P Firman, President/CEO
Howard Bedlin, VP Public Policy & Advocacy
Donald L Davis, VP Workforce Development

To recognize an individual for major contributions to NCOA and its programs. Awarded annually. Established to honor Geneva Mathiasen, an NCOA founder and Executive Director from 1950 until 1969.

2636 George Card Award
American Council of the Blind
1155 15th Street NW
Suite 1004
Washington, DC 20005-2706
202-467-5081
800-424-8666
Fax: 202-467-5085
e-mail: info@acb.org
http://www.acb.org

Melanie Brunson, Executive Director

To honor an outstanding blind or visually impaired person who has made noteworthy contributions to the welfare of his fellow blind. A certificate is awarded occasionally. Established in 1968.

2637 Geriatric Oral Health Care Award
American Dental Association
211 East Chicago Avenue
Chicago, IL 60611-2678
312-440-2500
Fax: 312-440-4640
e-mail: mcginley@ada.org
http://www.ada.org

Dr. Robert M Brandjord, President

To recognize and reward those individuals and organizations who have improved the oral health care of the elderly through innovative health care delivery projects. The award is open to any individual or organization responsible for developing research or projects that further the understanding of dental caries, periodontal disease, denture stomatitis, or other oral diseases in older Americans. The entry deadline is May 15. The first prize consists of a monetary award of $2,500 and a plaque. A meritorious award of $500 and a plaque may also be awarded. Awarded annually at the ADA annual session. The award is administered by the ADA.

2638 Glen Bollinger Humanitarian Award
HEAR Center
301 E Del Mar Boulevard
Pasadena, CA 91101-2714
626-796-2016
Fax: 626-796-2320
e-mail: info@hearcenter.org
http://www.hearcenter.org

Josephine Wilson, Executive Director

To honor civic and service minded individuals for their efforts in behalf of hearing and speech impaired individuals, and for their loyalty and support of the HEAR Center. A plaque and/or trophy are awarded periodically. Established in 1979 for Glen H Bollinger, co-founder of HEAR (and founder of Sparkletts Drinking Water Corporation, Los Angeles) in memory of his generous contributions to the welfare of others.

2639 Glenn Foundation Award
Gerontological Society of America
1220l Street NW
Suite 901
Washington, DC 20005-1526
202-842-1275
Fax: 202-842-1150
e-mail: geron@geron.org
http://www.geron.org

Linda Krogh Harootyan, Interim Executive Director
Carol Ann Schutz, Advisor
Laurie Johnson, Office Manager

Awards, Honors & Prizes/National

For recognition of a significant research contribution in the biology of aging. Any scientist may be nominated for original research. A monetary prize of $2,500 is awarded annually at the annual meeting.

2640 Group Development Awards
Self Help for Hard of Hearing People
7910 Woodmont Avenue
Suite 1200
Bethesda, MD 20814-7022
301-657-2248
Fax: 301-913-9413
http://www.hearingloss.org

Anne Pope, President

To honor SHHH groups that are developing successfully at a steady pace with a goal to prepare themselves to petition for chapter charter.

2641 Harold W. McGraw, Jr. Prize in Education
McGraw-Hill
1221 Avenue of the Americas
15th Floor
New York, NY 10020-1001
212-512-4100
Fax: 212-512-4769
http://www.mcgraw-hill.com

Joseph L Dionne, CEO

To recognize individuals who have made significant contributions to the advancement of knowledge through education. The prize honors individuals whose accomplishments are making a difference today, and whose programs and ideas can serve as effective models for the education of future generations of Americans. Only individuals who are presently committed to the cause of education are eligible. Institutions, boards, organizations and other groups are not. Nominees need not be professional educators, nor is eligibility limited to traditional educational achievement. Individuals may be nominated in the areas of teaching, administration, policy planning, business, government, publishing and adult education. Each year, a Nominating Committee, consisting of leaders in the educational community across the country, submit nominations to the Board of Judges. In addition, the Board of Judges considers nominations received directly, if they meet eligibility requirements, and include references from the educational community.

2642 Hobart Jackson Social Responsibility Award
American Assn. of Homes & Services for the Aging
2519 Connecticut Avenue NW
Washington, DC 20008-1520
202-783-2242
Fax: 202-783-2255
e-mail: info@aahsa.org
http://www.aahsa.org

William L Minnix Jr, President/CEO
Katrinka Smith Sloan, VP Member Services/COO
Tom Slemmer, AAHSA Board Chair

To recognize significant commitment to affirmative action goals. The nominees must show commitment to social justice and equal opportunity for minorities. Members, an agency of AAHSA, and/or individuals associated with an AAHSA agency are eligible.

2643 Innovation of the Year Awards
American Assn. of Homes & Services for the Aging
2519 Connecticut Avenue NW
Washington, DC 20008-1520
202-783-2242
Fax: 202-783-2255
http://www.aahsa.org

William L Minnix Jr., President/CEO
Katrinka Smith Sloan, VP Member Services/COO
Tom Slemmer, AAHSA Board Chair

To recognize creative problem solving within the AAHSA membership, to encourage professionals to document, display, and share their successes in the spirit of mutual helpfulness, and to motivate others to a higher level of development and professional practice. Three AAHSA members whose innovations in their own facilities have proven beneficial receive this award each year. An abstract of an innovation may be submitted in any of the following categories: care and services to residents or clients, management operations, and community or public relations. Recognition by AAHSA and peers at the annual meeting, publication of selected innovations, and presentation of selected papers at an education session during the annual meeting are awarded.

2644 Irving Diener Award
Blinded Veterans Association
477 H Street NW
Washington, DC 20001-2617
202-371-8880
800-669-7079
Fax: 202-371-8258
e-mail: bva@bva.org
http://www.bva.org

Dr. Norman Jones, National President
Dr. Sindney Ordway, Vice President
Thomas H Miller, Executive Director

To recognize veterans for outstanding service to a regional group of the Association. Blinded veterans who are members or associate members are eligible for nomination. A scroll and a $50 stipend are awarded annually. Established in 1962 in honor of the late Irving Diener, a former member of the BVA National Advisory Committee.

2645 Irving S Wright Award of Distinction
American Federation for Aging Research
55 West 39th Street
16th Floor
New York, NY 10018-2619
212-703-9977
888-582-2327
Fax: 212-997-0330
e-mail: info@afar.org
http://www.afar.org

Terrie T Wetle PhD, President
Diane A Nixon, Vice Chair
John B Rhodes MBA, Treasurer

To recognize exceptional accomplishments and contributions to the field of aging research. Nominations are by invitation only. A monetary award of $500 and a plaque are awarded annually. Established in 1981 to honor Dr Irving S Wright, founder of AFAR.

2646 Jack Weinberg Memorial Award for Geriatric Psychiatry
American Psychiatric Association
1000 Wilson Boulevard
Suite 1825
Arlington, VA 22209
703-907-7300
888-357-7924
Fax: 703-907-1085
e-mail: apa@psych.org
http://www.psych.org

James Scully, Manager

For demonstrating leadership and exemplary work in geriatric psychiatry.

2647 Jacobus TenBroek Award
National Federation of the Blind
1800 Johnson Street
Baltimore, MD 21230-4914
410-659-9314
Fax: 410-685-5653
e-mail: nfb@nfb.org
http://www.nfb.org

Marc Maurer, President

To honor the member of the Federation who has made an outstanding contribution to the welfare of the blind. A brass plate mounted on a walnut plaque is awarded as merited. Established in 1955.

Awards, Honors & Prizes/National

2648 **Jean Camper Cahn Award**
National Caucus and Center on Black Aged
1424 K Street NW
Suite 500
Washington, DC 20005-2410
202-637-8400
Fax: 202-347-0895
e-mail: info@ncba-aged.org
http://www.erols.com

Karyne Jones, President/CEO
Elias Hussein, Executive Vice President
Angela Hughes, Director

To recognize increasing minority participation in programs and services for the aging.

2649 **John H. McAulay Award**
Association for Education and Rehabilitation
1703 N. Beauregard Street
Suite 440
Alexandria, VA 22331
703-671-4500
877-492-2708
Fax: 703-671-6391
e-mail: aernet@laser.net
http://http://aerbvi.org

Jim Gandorf CAE, Executive Director
Angela Booker, Associate For Executive Support
Ginger Croce, Director Membership & Marketing

For recognition of outstanding achievement in the placement of blind persons. Nominations must be accompanied by biographical material. Awarded biennially.

2650 **Keystone Award**
Self Help for Hard of Hearing People
7910 Woodmont Avenue
Suite 1200
Bethesda, MD 20814-7022
301-657-2248
Fax: 301-913-9413
http://www.hearingloss.org

Anne Pope, President

To recognize individuals whose contributions to the formation and development of SHHH have been outstanding.

2651 **Louise B Gerrard Award**
National Association of State Units on Aging
1201 15th Street NW
Suite 350
Washington, DC 20005-2842
202-898-2578
Fax: 202-898-2583
e-mail: info@nasua.org
http://www.nasua.org

Theresa Lambert, Executive Director

To recognize the meritorious contributions of individuals committed to enhancing the quality of life of rural older Americans through improvements in policy, planning, advocacy or services. Practitioners, researchers, educators, service providers, administrators or public officials at the Federal, state or local levels whose exemplary efforts reflect improvement in the lives of the rural elderly are eligible.uise B. Gerrard, former Executive Director for the West Virginia Commission on Aging, whose pioneering efforts in the development of the Aging Network have impacted the lives of millions of older Americans, especially rural older persons.

2652 **Major General Melvin J. Maas Achievement Award**
Blinded Veterans Association
477 H Street NW
Washington, DC 20001-2617
202-371-8880
800-669-7079
Fax: 202-371-8258
e-mail: bva@bva.org

Dr. Norman Jones, President
Dr. Sidney Ordway, Vice President
Thomas H Miller, Executive Director

To recognize the achievement of outstanding service-connected blinded veterans in their adjustment to blindness, participation in community affairs, and employment. From the beginning, presentation of this award has contributed to the enhancement of a positive image of blind people and to the elimination of the concept of helplessness. A monetary award and a scroll are awarded annually. Established in 1945 and renamed in 1973 to honor General Maas, a former president of BVA, Congressman, and Chairman of the President's Committee on the Handicapped.

2653 **Marie Haug Student Award in Gerontology**
University Center on Aging and Health
10900 Euclid Avenue
Cleveland, OH 44106
216-368-4945
Fax: 216-368-6389
e-mail: mhw4@po.cwru.edu
http://http://fpb.case.edu/cfa

May L Wykle PhD RN, Director
Diana L Morris, Associate Director
Elizabeth E O'Toole, Associate Director

To recognize excellence in aging studies. Awarded annually with a monetary prize and plaque. Established in 1990.

2654 **Meritorious Service Award**
American Assn. of Homes & Services for the Aging
2519 Connecticut Avenue NW
Washington, DC 20008-1520
202-783-2242
Fax: 202-783-2255
e-mail: info@aahsa.org
http://www.aahsa.org

William L Minnix Jr., President/CEO
Katrinka Smith Sloan, VP Member Services COO
Tom Slemmer, AAHSA Board Chair

To recognize significant contributions to the field of long-term care, services, and housing for the elderly. Awarded to individuals whose organizations are full members of the association, or organizations that are full members. The nominee's accomplishments must show excellence, must have provided recognizable leadership in the aging services field, and must demonstrate a commitment to the nonprofit philosophy. The nominee's contribution must be of national importance.

2655 **Migel Medal for Outstanding Service to Blind Persons**
American Foundation for the Blind
11 Penn Plaza
Suite 300
New York, NY 10001-2006
212-502-7600
800-232-5463
Fax: 212-502-7777
e-mail: afbinfo@afb.net
http://www.afb.org

Carl Augusto, President

To honor professionals and volunteers whose dedication and achievements have significantly improved the lives of blind and visually-impaired people. Two medals are awarded annually: one to a professional; and one to a lay person. Presently it is awarded on Foundation Day, the fourth Thursday in October, following the annual meeting of the Board of Trustees. Established in 1937.

2656 **Mildred M. Seltzer Distinguished Service Recognition**
Association for Gerontology in Higher Education
1220I Street NW
Suite 901
Washington, DC 20005-4018
202-289-9806
Fax: 202-289-9824
e-mail: ctompkins@aghe.org
http://www.aghe.org

Derek Stepp, Manager

For recognition and thanks to colleagues who are retired or near retirement and who have given significant service to the Association. A certificate of recognition and a lifetime subscription to the Association's newsletter, the AGHExchange, are awarded. Established in 1994, and renamed in 1995 to honor Mildred M. Seltzer, a nationally known gerontologist and senior faculty member at Miami's Scripps Gerontology Center.

Awards, Honors & Prizes/National

2657 Milo D. Leavitt Memorial Lecture Award
American Geriatrics Society
350 Fifth Avenue
Suite 801
New York, NY 10021-8165
212-308-1414
Fax: 212-832-8646
e-mail: info@americangeriatrics.org
http://www.americangeriatrics.org

Linda Hiddemen Baroness, Executive Vice President
Ellen Baumritter, PT Administrative Assistant
Shirley Burnett, Membership Assistant

Recognizing a distinguished educator in the geriatric field.

2658 NCSC Community Service Award/Certificate of Merit
National Council of Senior Citizens
8403 Colesville Road
Suite 1200
Silver Spring, MD 20910-6322
301-578-8923
Fax: 301-578-8859

Tony Sarmento, Executive Director

2659 NUCEA Divisional Awards
National University Continuing Education Assoc.
1 Dupont Circle NW
Suite 615
Washington, DC 20036-1134
202-659-3130
Fax: 202-785-0374

Richard Novak, President

To recognize individuals for outstanding contributions to the field of continuing education. Awards are presented in the following divisions: Division of Business, Industry, and Labor; Division of Community Development and Services Programs; Division of Conferences and Institutes; Division of Continuing Education for the Professions; Division of Humanities, Arts, and Sciences; Division of Independent Study; Division of Marketing and Promotion; Division of Programs for Military; Division of Programs for Women; Division of Rural Continuing Education; Division of Certificate and Non-Traditional Degree Programs; Division of Futures Study and Educational Change; Division of Research; Division of Summer Evening and Off-Campus Credit Programs; and Division of Career Counseling, Advising, and Adult Student Services. In addition, NUCEA presents Regional Awards.

2660 Nathan Shock New Investigator Award
Gerontological Society of America
1220 L Street NW
Suite 901
Washington, DC 20005-1526
202-842-1275
Fax: 202-842-1150
e-mail: geron@geron.org
http://www.geron.org

Linda Krogh Harootyan, Interim Executive Director
Carol Ann Schutz, Advisor
Laurie Johnson, Office Manager

To recognize outstanding original research in the field of gerontology. The deadline is May 8. A monetary award of $1,500 and a certificate are presented at the Biological Sciences Section annual business meeting at the Society's annual meeting. Established in 1986 by the Biological Sciences Section.

2661 National Federation of the Blind Scholarship Program
National Federation of the Blind
1800 Johnson Street
Baltimore, MD 21230-4998
410-659-9314
Fax: 410-685-5653
e-mail: info@nfb.org
http://www.nfb.org

Marc Maurer, President

To recognize outstanding achievement by blind scholars. Applicants must be legally blind and be pursuing or planning to pursue a full-time post secondary course of study. Awarded on the basis of academic achievement, service to the community, and financial need. The deadline for applications is March 31.

2662 National Media Owl Awards
Retirement Research Foundation
8765 W Higgins Road
Suite 401
Chicago, IL 60631-4022
773-714-8080
Fax: 773-714-8089
e-mail: info@rrf.org
http://www.fdncenter.org

Marilyn Hennessy, President
Sharon Markham, Associate Vice President
Downey R Varey, Treasurer

For recognition of outstanding production in the media on the subject of aging. Entrants are judged on the basis of: Technical Quality, Presentation, and Potential Utility. Entries are accepted in four categories: Training Films or Videotapes - films or videotapes produced specifically for the purpose of training professionals and paraprofessionals working with aging or aged people; Independent Films or Videotapes - films or videotapes produced for the general public on issues related to aging. To be considered independent, a film or videotape must be the creative work of a film or video producer(s) who has control over its production and content; and Television Non-Fiction - news, public affairs, special reports, or documentary programs produced for television or cable stations or networks on issues related to aging. A Community Video Award of $2,000 is presented in this category. Films, videotapes, and television programs produced in the United States, and released or initially broadcast or cablecast during the preceding year are eligible. Films, videotapes, and television programs must deal primarily with concerns that are of spe$5,000 and a bronze carved Owl statuette are presented to the producers of the film, videotape, or television program judged to be the best in each category. Second prizes of $2,000 and up to two honorable mention awards of $1,000 are presented.

2663 National Support Awards
Self Help for Hard of Hearing People
7910 Woodmont Avenue
Suite 1200
Bethesda, MD 20814-7022
301-657-2248
Fax: 301-913-9413
http://www.hearingloss.org

Anne Pope, President

To recognize the chapter or group that has made significant contributions to SHHH National by undertaking special projects or events that advance SHHH National programs. Chapters or groups may apply. A plaque is awarded. Formerly known as the Founders' Day Project Award.

2664 Ned E. Freeman Excellence in Writing Award
American Council of the Blind
1155 15th Street NW
Suite 1004
Washington, DC 20005-2706
202-467-5081
800-424-8666
Fax: 202-467-5085
e-mail: info@acb.org
http://www.acb.org

Melanie Brunson, Executive Director

To recognize the author of the best article written specifically for the Braille Forum. A monetary prize and a certificate are awarded annually at the Council's national convention. Established in 1971.

2665 Nelson Cruikshank Award
National Council of Senior Citizens
8403 Colesville Road
Suite 1200
Silver Spring, MD 20910-6322
301-578-8800
Fax: 301-578-8859

Anthony Sarmiento, Executive Director

Awards, Honors & Prizes/National

2666 New Investigator Awards
American Geriatrics Society
350 Fifth Avenue
Suite 801
New York, NY 10118
212-308-1414
Fax: 212-832-8646
e-mail: info@americangeriatrics.org
http://www.americangeriatrics.org

Linda Hiddemen Barondess, Executive Vice President
Ellen Baumritter, Pt Administrative Assistant
Shirley Burnett, Membership Assistant

Awarded for innovative research in geriatrics.

2667 Newel Perry Award
National Federation of the Blind
1800 Johnson Street
Baltimore, MD 21230-4914
410-659-9314
Fax: 410-685-5653
e-mail: info@nfb.org
http://www.nfb.org

Marc Maurer, President

To honor an individual who has made an outstanding contribution to the welfare of the blind. Members of the Federation are not eligible. A brass plate mounted on a walnut plaque is awarded as merited. Established in 1973.

2668 Ollie A. Randall Award
National Council on the Aging
1901 L Street NW
4th Floor
Washington, DC 20036
202-479-1200
800-867-2755
Fax: 202-479-0735
http://www.ncoa.org

To recognize an individual who has made singular and outstanding contributions toward advancing the cause of the aging in accordance with the Council's philosophy of enabling the older person to live a dignified, healthy, and productive life. A Steuben glass trophy is awarded annually. Established in 1964 to honor Ollie A. Randall, an NCOA founder.

2669 Outstanding Continuing Education Student Awards
National University Continuing Education Assoc.
1 Dupont Circle NW
Suite 615
Washington, DC 20036-1134
202-659-3130
Fax: 202-785-0374

Kay J Kohl, Executive Director

To recognize adult students over the age of 25 for their noteworthy achievements in the pursuit of excellence in continuing education. Two awards are presented.

2670 Outstanding Newsletter Recognitions
Self Help for Hard of Hearing People
7910 Woodmont Avenue
Suite 1200
Bethesda, MD 20814-7022
301-657-2248
Fax: 301-913-9413
http://www.hearingloss.org

Anne Pope, President

To recognize an outstanding editor of a chapter newsletter. Chapters publishing a regular newsletter are eligible for recognition. Recognizing that a newsletter is an excellent educational tool as well as a vehicle for basic information, judges look for the following: that the publication keeps members informed of Chapter activities; that it educates its readers about issues of concern that the data are accurate; that the product is neat and easy to read; the size of its circulation; and how often it is issued. A plaque is awarded.

2671 Outstanding Service Medallion
AAACE
10111 Martin Luther King Jr Highway
Suite 200C
Bowie, MD 20720
301-459-6261
Fax: 301-459-6241
e-mail: aaace10@aol.com
http://www.aaace.org

Cle Anderson, Association Manager
Amy Rose Ed.D., President

To recognize a person who has an outstanding record of service to the profession of adult and continuing education at the state, national, or international level. The nominator and nominee must be AAACE members.

2672 Paul B Beeson Career Development Awardsin Aging Research Program
American Federation for Aging Research
55 West 39th Street
16th Floor
New York, NY 10018
212-703-9977
888-582-2327
Fax: 212-997-0330
e-mail: info@afar.org
http://www.afar.org/beeson

Terrie T Wetle PhD, President
Diane A Nixon, Vice Chair
John B Rhodes, Treasurer

For outstanding research in the geriatric field.

2673 Peter J. Salmon Award - Blind Worker of the Year
National Industries for the Blind
1310 Braddock Place
Alexandria, VA 22314-1691
703-310-0500
Fax: 703-671-9053
e-mail: services@nib.org
http://www.nib.org

Jamie Classen, Public Relations Specialist

To recognize an outstanding blind worker employed in an NIB Workshop below the administrative level. Each local Workshop selects a Blind Worker of the Year and the NIB selects the national winner for the Peter J. Salmon Award. A plaque is awarded at the Annual Meeting of the General Council of Workshops for the Blind. Established in 1968 in memory of Dr. Peter J. Salmon, who was instrumental in the establishment of NIB.

2674 Pfizer/AGS Postdoctoral Research Awards
American Geriatrics Society
3540 Fifth Avenue
Suite 801
New York, NY 10018
212-308-1414
Fax: 212-832-8646
e-mail: info@americangeriatrics.org
http://www.americangeriatrics.org

Linda Hiddemen Barondess, Executive Vice President
Ellen Baumritter, PT Administrative Assistant
Shirley Burnett, Membership Assistant

Provides physicians interested in geriatrics with research and clinical training opportunities

2675 President's Award for Exceptional andInnovative Leadership in Adult and Continuing Education
AAACE
4380 Forbes Boulevard
Lanham, MD 20706-4863
301-918-1913
Fax: 301-918-1846
http://www.aaace.org

To recognize exceptional leadership to, or in support of, adult and continuing education.need not be employed directly in the field of adult or continuing education.

2676 Professional Advisory Support Award
Self Help for Hard of Hearing People
7910 Woodmont Avenue
Suite 1200
Bethesda, MD 20814-7022
301-657-2248
Fax: 301-913-9413
http://www.hearingloss.org

Anne Pope, President

To honor professionals in appreciation for what they are doing or have done to support the self help movement. To acknowledge how helpful these people can be with publicity, awareness, involvment in special events and in referring people with hearing loss to SHHH. The nominees must be current SHHH National members. Established in 1996.

Awards, Honors & Prizes/National

2677 Purpose Prize
Civic Ventures
114 Sansome Street
Suite 850
Sanfrancisco, CA 94101
415-222-7487
Fax: 415-430-0144
e-mail: jemerman@civicventures.org
http://www.purposeprize.org

Jim Emerman, Director
Stefanie Weiss, VP Communications

Presented to people over 60 who are taking on society's biggest challenges. It's for those with the passion and experience to discover new opportunities, create new programs, and make lasting change.

2678 Rebuilding Together
Honeywell
131 Madison Avenue
Morristown, NJ 07960
973-971-0100
800-707-4555
Fax: 973-971-0826
http://www.rebuildingtogether.org

Angela Beddoe, Chairman

Nonprofit organization dedicated to revitalizing communities by refurbishing homes and community buildings. Honeywell is a leading national sponsor of Rebuilding Together and by combining the hard work of Honeywell volunteers, we are helping make life better for low-income homeowners — including elderly and disabled people and single-parent families in our hometowns all around the country.

2679 Richard Kalish Innovative Publication Award
Gerontological Society of America
1220 L Street NW
Washington, DC 20005-1526
202-842-1275
Fax: 202-842-1150
e-mail: geron@geron.org
http://www.geron.org

Linda Krogh Harootyan, Interim Executive Director
Carol Ann Schutz, Advisor
Laurie Johnson, Office Manager

To recognize insightful and innovative publications on aging and life course development in the behavioral and social sciences. Publications published in the past three years and written in English are eligible. A monetary prize of $500 is awarded annually at the annual meeting. Established in honor of Dr. Richard Kalish.

2680 Robert B. Irwin Award
National Industries for the Blind
1310 Braddock Place
Suite 200
Alexandria, VA 22311-1705
703-310-0500
Fax: 703-671-9053
e-mail: services@nib.org
http://www.nib.org

John C Peoples, Chairman
Dr. James A Kutsch Jr., Vice Chairman
William B Johnson CPA, Treasurer

To recognize an individual for significant contributions to an area related to sheltered workshop employment for blind persons. A plaque is awarded annually at the National Sales Meeting of The General Council of Workshops for the Blind. Established in 1953 in memory of Dr. Robert B. Irwin, who pioneered and led the way for creating employment opportunities for the blind.

2681 Robert S. Bray Award
American Council of the Blind
1155 15th Street NW
Suite 1004
Washington, DC 20005-2706
202-467-5081
800-424-8666
Fax: 202-467-5085
e-mail: info@acb.org
http://www.acb.org

Melanie Brunson, Executive Director

To recognize outstanding achievement in extending library service, access to published materials, or the improvement of communication devices and techniques for the blind. Awarded occasionally. Established in 1975.

2682 Robert W. Kleemeier Award
Gerontological Society of America
1220 L Street NW
Washington, DC 20005-1526
202-842-1275
Fax: 202-842-1150
e-mail: geron@geron.org
http://www.geron.org

Linda Krogh Harootyan, Interim Executive Director
Carol Ann Scutz, Advisor
Laurie Johnson, Office Manager

To recognize a member for outstanding research in the field of gerontology. Nominees must be fellows of the Society. The award requires a lecture at the time of the annual scientific meeting. Established in 1965 in memory of Robert W. Kleemeier, the Society's twenty-first president.

2683 Rubens-Alcais Challenge
International Committee of Sports for the Deaf
528 Trail Avenue
Frederick, MD 21701
Fax: 301-620-2990
e-mail: info@ciss.org
http://www.ciss.org

To recognize countries that have promoted exceptionally well sports for the deaf. Member countries of the CISS are eligible. Awarded biennially. Established in 1967.

2684 Special Friend of Hearing Impaired People Award
Self Help for Hard of Hearing People
7910 Woodmont Avenue
Suite 1200
Bethesda, MD 20814-7022
301-657-2248
Fax: 301-913-9413
http://www.hearingloss.org

Anne Pope, President

To recognize individuals who have worked diligently over a long period of time to improve the lives and circumstances of hearing-impaired people. Recipients are usually hearing people.

2685 Spirit of SHHH Award
Self Help for Hard of Hearing People
7910 Woodmont Avenue
Suite 1200
Bethesda, MD 20814-7022
301-657-2248
Fax: 301-913-9413
http://www.hearingloss.org

Anne Pope, President

To recognize individuals whose continued selfless dedication to the development of SHHH has contributed to the success of the organization.

2686 State Public Official Award for Significant Legislative Achievement
AARP
601 E Street NW
Washington, DC 20049
202-434-2277
888-687-2277
Fax: 202-434-3443
e-mail: member@aarp.org
http://www.aarp.org

William D Novelli, CEO

To recognize a public official, active or former, who has made a significant contribution, via legislative or administrative action, to the older citizens of the state and/or the field of aging. The award is based on the recipient's efforts on a specific issue. It is not given on a partisan basis or to imply, in any manner, AARP's endorsement of the candidacy of the recipients. The award is not issued during the election season. The award bears the logo of AARP and is presented by the State Legislative Committee.

Awards, Honors & Prizes/National

2687 Trustee of the Year Award
American Assn. of Homes & Services for the Aging
2519 Connecticut Avenue NW
Washington, DC 20008-1520
202-783-2242
Fax: 202-783-2255
e-mail: info@aahsa.org
http://www.aahsa.org

William L Minnix Jr., President/CEO
Katrinka Smith Sloan, VP Member Services/COO
Tom Slemmer, AAHSA Board Chair

To recognize the outstanding achievements that a volunteer trustee or director has made to an AAHA member facility during his or her tenure on the member organization's board. The nominee must demonstrate a significant contribution to the well-being of the elderly and others the organization serves, must have displayed a personal commitment to the life of the organization, must have provided outstanding leadership to the organization and the community at large, and must have fostered growth and change through understanding the environment and the need for a continuum of care for the elderly. Primary consideration is given to notable acts or unusual commitment to service. service. Each recipient will receive a plaque, one night's lodging to attend the annual meeting in New Orleans and complimentary registration to the annual meeting's Governance Assembly. Established in 1985.

2688 Vernon Henley Media Award
American Council of the Blind
1155 15th Street NW
Suite 1004
Washington, DC 20005-2706
202-467-5081
800-424-8666
Fax: 202-467-5085
e-mail: info@acb.org
http://www.acb.org

Melanie Brunson, Executive Director

To recognize an individual, either sighted or blind, who has created a radio, television, or print media product conveying positive and useful information concerning blind people in general and the American Council of the Blind in particular. Nominations must be submitted by May 1. A plaque is awarded annually. Established in 1989 by the ACB Board of Publications to honor Vernon Henley.

2689 Walter T. Ridder Award
Self Help for Hard of Hearing People
7910 Woodmont Avenue
Suite 1200
Bethesda, MD 20814-7022
301-657-2248
Fax: 301-913-9413
http://www.hearingloss.org

Anne Pope, President

To recognize an individual, an organization, or a corporation that has provided outstanding support (moral, financial, or both) to SHHH, enabling the organization to achieve goals that might otherwise not have been attained. Nominations of members are made by the SHHH Executive Committee, which includes the Executive Director, the group most familiar with the overall support given on the National level. Final selection of the recipient will be made by the Executive Commitee, or by a ballot among all members of the SHHH National Board of Directors. The deadline is March 1. A plaque is awarded.

2690 Widowed Persons Service Award
AARP
601 E Street NW
Washington, DC 20049
202-434-2277
800-424-3410
Fax: 202-434-3443
e-mail: member@aarp.org
http://www.aarp.org

William Novelli, CEO

To recognize Widowed Persons Service programs completing five years of successful operation. The Program Department presents a certificate.

Continuing Education/Alabama

This chapter is arranged by state, and includes both institutions of higher learning that offer specific course programs for older Americans, as well as specific learning centers dedicated to specific interests and needs of older Americans. Due to the combined efforts of many agencies, listings in the following chapters may also address Continuing Education: State Organizations & Government Agencies; Libraries & Information Centers; Independent Living Centers.

Alabama

2691 AARP: Alabama-Huntsville OfficeInformation Center
2200 Drake Avenue
Huntsville, AL 35805
256-885-2277
Fax: 256-885-0882
e-mail: alaarp@aarp.org
http://www.aarp.org/states/al
Ray Warren, AARP Alabama State President
Joan Carter, AARP Alabama State Director
Erik Olsen, AARP President Corporate Office

Resources for online classes, training and more. Topics include Computers/Technology, Health/Wellbeing, Personal Finance. AARP Membership open to individuals age 50+, benefits include access to insurance services, travel discounts, advice on healthy living, financial planning, consumer protection. AARP represents members on issues like Medicare, Social Security, and consumer safety. Publications include the AARP Magazine and AARP Bulletin.

2692 AARP: Alabama-Mobile OfficeInformation Center
1717 Dauphin Street
Mobile, AL 36604
251-470-5235
Fax: 251-478-3357
e-mail: alaarp@aarp.org
http://www.aarp.org/states/al
Ray Warren, AARP Alabama State President
Joan Carter, AARP Alabama State Director
Erik Olsen, AARP President Corporate Office

Resources for online classes, training and more. Topics include Computers/Technology, Health/Wellbeing, Personal Finance. AARP Membership open to individuals age 50+, benefits include access to insurance services, travel discounts, advice on healthy living, financial planning, consumer protection. AARP represents members on issues like Medicare, Social Security, and consumer safety. Publications include the AARP Magazine and AARP Bulletin.

2693 AARP: Alabama-Montgomery Office
201 Monroe Street
Suite 1880, RSA Tower
Montgomery, AL 36104
866-542-8167
Fax: 334-954-3050
e-mail: alaarp@aarp.org
http://www.aarp.org/states/al
Ray Warren, AARP Alabama State President
Joan Carter, AARP Alabama State Director
Erik Olsen, AARP President Corporate Office

Resources for online classes, training and more. Topics include Computers/Technology, Health/Wellbeing, Personal Finance. AARP Membership open to individuals age 50+, benefits include access to insurance services, travel discounts, advice on healthy living, financial planning, consumer protection. AARP represents members on issues like Medicare, Social Security, and consumer safety. Publications include the AARP Magazine and AARP Bulletin.

2694 Shepherd's Center Southside
PO Box 550058
Birmingham, AL 35255
205-933-1273
Fax: 205-933-7774
e-mail: shepherdscenter@bellsouth.net
http://www.shepherdcenters.org
Scott Cullen, Director
Nancy Whitson, Chair
Sam Matthews, Executive Director/Corporate

Individual centers partner with all faiths representing the diversity of their communities. The mission is to empower older adults to use their wisdom and skills for the good of their communities. Providing health enhancement, cultural enrichment and lifelong learning opportunities.

2695 Shepherd's Center of Bluff Park
733 Valley Street
Birmingham, AL 35226
205-822-0910
Fax: 205-824-0228
e-mail: info@shepherdscenter.org
http://www.shepherdscenter.org
Peggy Crowley, Chair
Sam Matthews, Executive Director/Corporate
Harry B Underwood, President Board of Directors

Individual centers partner with all faiths representing the diversity of their communities. The mission is to empower older adults to use their wisdom and skills for the good of their communities. Providing health enhancement, cultural enrichment and lifelong learning opportunities.

Alaska

2696 AARP: Alaska-Anchorage Branch Office Information Center
3101 Penland Parkway
Northway Mall
Anchorage, AK 99508
907-272-1444
888-805-1540
Fax: 907-272-1114
e-mail: aarpic@acsalaska.net
http://www.aarp.org/states/ak
Ken Osterkamp, AARP Alaska State Director
Erik Olsen, AARP President Corporate Office
Bill Novelli, AARP CEO Corporate Office

Resources for online classes, training and more. Topics include Computers/Technology, Health/Wellbeing, Personal Finance. AARP Membership open to individuals age 50+, benefits include access to insurance services, travel discounts, advice on healthy living, financial planning, consumer protection. AARP represents members on issues like Medicare, Social Security, and consumer safety. Publications include the AARP Magazine and AARP Bulletin.

2697 AARP: Alaska-Anchorage Main Office
3601 C Street
Suite 1420
Anchorage, AK 99503
866-227-7447
Fax: 907-341-2270
e-mail: ak@aarp.org
http://www.aarp.org/states/ak
Ken Osterkamp, AARP Alaska State Director
Erik Olsen, AARP President Corporate Office
Bill Novelli, AARP CEO Corporate Office

Resources for online classes, training and more. Topics include Computers/Technology, Health/Wellbeing, Personal Finance. AARP Membership open to individuals age 50+, benefits include access to insurance services, travel discounts, advice on healthy living, financial planning, consumer protection. AARP represents members on issues like Medicare, Social Security, and consumer safety. Publications include the AARP Magazine and AARP Bulletin.

Continuing Education/Arizona

2698 University of Alaska Southeast Campus: Adult Education Program
The Learning Center
1332 Seward Avenue
Sitka, AK 99835
907-747-7716
Fax: 907-747-7737
e-mail: student.info@uas.alaska.edu
http://www.uas.alaska.edu/sitka/learning_center
Jeff Johnston, Campus Director
Kathie Etulain, Assistant Campus Director
Bonnie Elsensohn, Media Specialist/Web

Full range of adult education services is available for all adults in Sitka at no charge through a contract with the Alaska Department of Labor and the Southeast Regional Resource Center.

Arizona

2699 AARP: Arizona-Phoenix Office
Collier Center
201 E Washington Street, Suite 1795
Phoenix, AZ 85004-2428
866-389-5649
Fax: 602-256-2928
e-mail: azaarp@aarp.org
http://www.aarp.org/states/az
Leonard Kirschner, AARP Arizona State President
Cynthia J Fagyas, AARP Arizona Media Relations
Erik Olsen, AARP President Corporate Office

Resources for online classes, training and more. Topics include Computers/Technology, Health/Wellbeing, Personal Finance. AARP Membership open to individuals age 50+, benefits include access to insurance services, travel discounts, advice on healthy living, financial planning, consumer protection. AARP represents members on issues like Medicare, Social Security, and consumer safety. Publications include the AARP Magazine and AARP Bulletin.

2700 AARP: Arizona-Tucson Information Center
6700 N Oracle Road
Suite 331
Tucson, AZ 85704
520-571-9884
Fax: 520-571-9832
e-mail: azaarp@aarp.org
http://www.aarp.org/states/az
Leonard Kirschner, AARP Arizona State President
Cynthia J Fagyas, AARP Arizona Media Relations
Erik Olsen, AARP President Corporate Office

Resources for online classes, training and more. Topics include Computers/Technology, Health/Wellbeing, Personal Finance. AARP Membership open to individuals age 50+, benefits include access to insurance services, travel discounts, advice on healthy living, financial planning, consumer protection. AARP represents members on issues like Medicare, Social Security, and consumer safety. Publications include the AARP Magazine and AARP Bulletin.

2701 Custom Training and Education: LifelongLearning Program
Phoenix College
640 N 1 Avenue 1st Floor
Phoenix, AZ 85003
602-223-4053
Fax: 602-223-4040
e-mail: anna.lopez@pcmail.maricopa.edu
http://www.pc.maricopa.edu/cte/continuing.htm
Anna Lopez, Director
Don Jensen Bobadilla, Administrative Assistant
Alfredo Herndanez, Marketing Assistant

Formerly known as by the Senior Adult Program, promoting learning across the lifespan and adults of all ages. Courses are designed to provide informational and enriching learning opportunities without the pressure of tests and grades. Some classes are offered free of charge, while others are provided for minimal fees. Other features of the program include informal discussions with an emphasis on friendship and sharing.

2702 Lifelong Learning Program
Glendale Community College
Center for Learning
6000 W Olive Avenue
Glendale, AZ 85302
623-845-3812
Fax: 623-845-3818
e-mail: GCC@info@gcmail.maricopa.edu
http://www.gccaz.edu/cfl/
Velvie Green, President
Dawn Meyer, Department Secretary/Reading-Eng
Carmela Arnoldt, Department Chair/Reading-Eng

Helps adults looking to improve their reading skills.

2703 OASIS of Tucson
c/o Macy's
3435 E Broadway
Tucson, AZ 85716-5410
520-795-3950
Fax: 520-323-7984
e-mail: jgiglesias@cox.net
http://www.oasisnet.org/tucson/index.htm
George Iglesias, Interim Director
Stacey Moore, Assistant Director
L'Don Sawyer, Person-to-Person Coordinator

OASIS is a national nonprofit educational organization designed to enhance the quality of life for mature adults. Offering challenging programs in the arts, humanities, wellness, technology and volunteer service, OASIS creates opportunities for older adults to continue their personal growth and provide meaningful service to the community. OASIS is nationally sponsored by Macy's Foundation.

Number of Members: 16,000

2704 Pima Community College: Adult EducationPrograms
Pima Community College
Lindsey Center
1602 S Third Avenue
Tucson, AZ 85705-7427
520-884-8628
Fax: 520-884-8614
e-mail: pcae@pima.edu
http://www.pima.edu/pcae/
Roy Flores, Chancellor
Cynthia Meier, Division Dean Adult Education
Jana Kooi, President Community Campus

Offering classes to adults for basic reading, writing and math, GED high-school equivalency preparation, English for speakers of other languages and citizenship preparation.

2705 Rio Salado Community College: Adult Basic Education Program
Rio Salado Community College
2323 W 14th Street
Tempe, AZ 85281-6948
480-517-8110
800-729-1197
Fax: 480-517-8030
http://www.riosalado.edu/ci/programs/abe.shtml
Dr Linda Thor, President
Blair Liddicoat M.Ed, Associate Dean Adult Basic Ed
Sylvia Hantla M.A., Dean Student Enrollment Services

Provides free instruction in basic skills, in the subjects required for the GED, English for speakers of other languages, and in citizenship, to students 16 years of age and older. Classes are offered at sites throughout Maricopa County, and meet during convenient daytime and evening hours. Books and materials are provided for students to use in the classroom.

2706 Senior Adult Educational Program
Scottsdale Community College
Senior Adult Office
9000 E Chaparral Road
Scottsdale, AZ 85256
480-423-6560
Fax: 480-423-6695
e-mail: john.thaxton@sccmail.maricopa.edu
http://www.scottsdalecc.edu/senior
John T Thaxton, Program Coordinator
Art DeCabooter PhD, Chancellor
Denise Kronsteiner, Public Relations & Marketing

Continuing Education/Arkansas

Providing courses and lecture series to adults; such as Health and Wellness, Language and Communications, Politics, History, Religion and Philosophy, and Arts and Humanities, Cinema.

2707 **YMCA Older Adult Programs**
60 W Alameda Street
Tucson, AZ 85702
520-623-5511
Fax: 520-624-1518
e-mail: info@ywcatucson.org
http://www.tucsonymca.org/

Dane Woll, Executive Director
Helen Schaefer, Chief Volunteer Officer
Dan McDonald, YMCA Activate Tucson Chair

Programs for older adults include health and fitness, swimming classes, trips and programs, social clubs, and senior centers in addition to volunteer and service learning.

Arkansas

2708 **AARP: Arkansas State Office**
1701 Centerview Drive
Suite 205
Little Rock, AR 72211
866-554-5379
Fax: 501-227-7710
e-mail: araarp@aarp.org
http://www.aarp.org/states/ar/

Billie Ann Myers, AARP Arkansas State President
Pat Jones, AARP Arkansas Media Relations
Erik Olsen, AARP President Corporate Office

Resources for online classes, training and more. Topics include Computers/Technology, Health/Wellbeing, Personal Finance. AARP Membership open to individuals age 50+, benefits include access to insurance services, travel discounts, advice on healthy living, financial planning, consumer protection. AARP represents members on issues like Medicare, Social Security, and consumer safety. Publications include the AARP Magazine and AARP Bulletin.

2709 **LifeQuest of Arkansas**
3805 W 12th
Little Rock, AR 72004
501-225-6073
Fax: 501-379-1599
e-mail: info@LifeQuestOfArkansas.org
http://www.lifequestofarkansas.org/

Jan L Zelnick, Executive Director
Leanna D Wall, Development Director
Jo Ann McQuade, Services Coordinator

Volunteer based, nonprofit established by and for active adults. We are dedicated to enhancing life's journey through the middle and later years through life long learning and meaningful volunteerism within a community of peers.

2710 **Shepherd's Center of Beebe**
302 N Main Street
PO Box 247
Beebe, AR 72012
501-882-0243
Fax: 501-882-0243
e-mail: bbshepherds@sbcglobal.net
http://www.shepherdcenters.org

Paul Ramsey, Director
Dorothy Hatfield, Chair

Individual centers partner with all faiths representing the diversity of their communities. The mission is to empower older adults to use their wisdom and skills for the good of their communities. Providing health enhancement, cultural enrichment and lifelong learning opportunities.

2711 **Shepherd's Center of Hot Springs**
3819 Central Avenue
Hot Springs, AR 71913
501-525-9001
Fax: 501-525-5750
e-mail: shepherdscenterofhotsprings@yahoo.com
http://www.shepherdcenters.org

Deborah Wright, Director
Roger Carter, Chair

Individual centers partner with all faiths representing the diversity of their communities. The mission is to empower older adults to use their wisdom and skills for the good of their communities. Providing health enhancement, cultural enrichment and lifelong learning opportunities.

2712 **Shepherd's Center of North Little Rock**
4314 Idlewild Avenue
PO Box 94783
North Little Rock, AR 72190
501-771-0774
e-mail: shepherdnlr@aristotle.net
http://www.shepherdcenters.org

Sheila Whitfield, Director
Bettina Steele, Chair

Individual centers partner with all faiths representing the diversity of their communities. The mission is to empower older adults to use their wisdom and skills for the good of their communities. Providing health enhancement, cultural enrichment and lifelong learning opportunities.

2713 **Shepherd's Center of SW Litte Rock**
6401 W 32nd Street
Little Rock, AR 72204-5909
501-562-5998
http://www.shepherdcenters.org

Betty Rhodes, Director
Darrell Way, Chair

Individual centers partner with all faiths representing the diversity of their communities. The mission is to empower older adults to use their wisdom and skills for the good of their communities. Providing health enhancement, cultural enrichment and lifelong learning opportunities.

California

2714 **AARP: California-Pasadena Office**
200 S Los Robles Avenue
Suite 400
Pasadena, CA 91101-2422
866-448-3615
Fax: 626-583-8500
e-mail: calosangeles@aarp.org
http://www.aarp.org/states/ca

Jeannine English, AARP California State President
Thomas A Porter, AARP California State Director
Erik Olsen, AARP President Corporate Office

Resources for online classes, training and more. Topics include Computers/Technology, Health/Wellbeing, Personal Finance. AARP Membership open to individuals age 50+, benefits include access to insurance services, travel discounts, advice on healthy living, financial planning, consumer protection. AARP represents members on issues like Medicare, Social Security, and consumer safety. Publications include the AARP Magazine and AARP Bulletin.

2715 **AARP: California-Sacramento Office**
1415 L Street
Suite 960
Sacramento, CA 95814
916-556-3065
866-448-3615
Fax: 916-446-2223
e-mail: calosangeles@aarp.org OR mbeach@aarp.org
http://www.aarp.org/states/ca

Jeannine English, AARP California State President
Mark Beach, AARP California Media Relations
Erik Olsen, AARP President Corporate Office

Continuing Education/California

Resources for online classes, training and more. Topics include Computers/Technology, Health/Wellbeing, Personal Finance. AARP Membership open to individuals age 50+, benefits include access to insurance services, travel discounts, advice on healthy living, financial planning, consumer protection. AARP represents members on issues like Medicare, Social Security, and consumer safety. Publications include the AARP Magazine and AARP Bulletin.

2716 California State University at Fullerton University Extended Education
College Park
2600 Nutwood Avenue
Suite 100
Fullerton, CA 92834-6870
714-278-2611
Fax: 714-278-2088
e-mail: uceinfo@fullerton.edu
http://www.csufextension.org/
Carol Creighton, Director of Extension Programs
Christine Pircher Barnes, Asst Director Student Services
Dennis Robinson, Director Online Distance Ed

University Extended Education provides quality learning experiences that extend access to the university into the community and around the globe. We offer a wide selection of educational programs that are accessible (online or in the classroom) and scheduled at convenient times. We have programs for working professionals and businesses, international students and groups, Open University and Intersession students, retirees and youth.

2717 College Avenue Adult Centers College Avenue Baptist Church Adult Ministries (CABC)
4747 College Avenue
San Diego, CA 92115-3906
619-582-7222
Fax: 619-582-5346
e-mail: suzannelederer@cabc.org
http://http://cabc.org/weconnect/adult.php
Cliff Anderson, Senior Adults Pastor
Mike Bradbury, Facilities Manager
Bruce Robertson, Business Administrator

The best place to begin forming relationships with others at CABC is in our varied communities. There are Sunday Communities and Mid-Week Communities, please check what is best for your schedule.

2718 Community Service Program of Van Nuys
Los Angeles Valley College
5800 Fulton Avenue
Valley Glen, CA 91401-4062
818-947-2600
Fax: 818-947-2930
e-mail: webmaster@lavc.edu.
http://www.lavc.cc.ca.us/Calendar.html
Tyree Wieder Ed.D, President

Educational and recreational programs for children to senior adults, not for academic credit. Designed for those seeking enrichment, new skills. Also have extensive summer camps, sports oriented.

2719 Continuing Education Center at RB
16769 Bernardo Center Drive
Professional Building, Suite K-14
San Diego, CA 92128-2558
858-487-2640
Fax: 858-487-3740
e-mail: learning@rbernardo.com
http://www.rbernardo.com/index.html
Barbara Crouch, President Board of Directors
Jo Driscoll, VP/Secretary Board of Directors
Jim Reading, Treasurer Board of Directors

Continuing Education Center is a program of learning and sharing for adults in the North County area.

2720 Learning in Retirement Program (LIR)
University of California at Berkeley
Berkeley Retirement Center
1925 Walnut Street, #1550
Berkeley, CA 94720-1550
510-642-5461
Fax: 510-643-1460
e-mail: ucbrc@berkeley.edu
http://http://thecenter.berkeley.edu/box.html
Shelley Glazer, Executive Director
Andre Porter, Program Manager
Linda Dayce, Administrative Assistant

The University of California/UC Berkeley Retirement Center is dedicated to developing programs and services that contribute to the well being and creativity of retired faculty, staff and their families and that support the UC community.

2721 Modesto Institute for Continued Learning
Modesto Junior College
435 College Avenue
Modesto, CA 95350
209-575-6550
Fax: 209-575-6859
e-mail: mjcadmissions@mjc.edu
http://www.mjc.edu/commed/micl.html
Odessa Johnson, Dean Community Education
Eileen Hibbard, Program Coordinator
Kris Digiacomo, Executive Director

MICL is an institute for mature learners, offering lectures, workshops, study and discussion groups, as well as trips and social events. All classes are not-for-credit and most have no tests, attendance requirements, homework or books to buy. They are a way to keep our brains exercised and stimulated as we age.

2722 OASIS Los Angeles
c/o Macy's
4005 Crenshaw Boulevard
Los Angeles, CA 90008
323-298-3414
e-mail: crobinson@oasisnet.org
http://www.oasisnet.org/losangeles/index.htm
Connie Robinson, Director
Kay Wallick, Executive Director Corporate

OASIS is a national nonprofit educational organization designed to enhance the quality of life for mature adults. Offering challenging programs in the arts, humanities, wellness, technology and volunteer service, OASIS creates opportunities for older adults to continue their personal growth and provide meaningful service to the community. OASIS is nationally sponsored by Macy's Foundation.

2723 OASIS San Diego
c/o Macy's
1702 Camino del Rio N
Third Floor
San Diego, CA 92108
619-574-0674
Fax: 619-574-0156
e-mail: oasissd@yahoo.com
http://www.oasisnet.org/sandiego/index.htm
Harry Matheny, Director
Shawna P Yaley, Marketing & Program Coordinator
Kay Wallick, Executive Director Corporate

OASIS is a national nonprofit educational organization designed to enhance the quality of life for mature adults. Offering challenging programs in the arts, humanities, wellness, technology and volunteer service, OASIS creates opportunities for older adults to continue their personal growth and provide meaningful service to the community. OASIS is nationally sponsored by Macy's Foundation.

2724 OASIS of Escondido
c/o Macy's
280 E Via Rancho Parkway
Escondido, CA 92025
760-432-0635
Fax: 760-739-0675
e-mail: dtoasis@cox.net
http://www.oasisnet.org/escondido/index.htm
Donna Toro, Director
Kay Wallick, Executive Director Corporate

Continuing Education/California

OASIS is a national nonprofit educational organization designed to enhance the quality of life for mature adults. Offering challenging programs in the arts, humanities, wellness, technology and volunteer service, OASIS creates opportunities for older adults to continue their personal growth and provide meaningful service to the community. OASIS is nationally sponsored by Macy's Foundation.

2725 Older Adult Program
Monterey Peninsula College
980 Fremont Street
Office/Administration Building
Monterey, CA 93940
831-646-4058
Fax: 831-655-2627
e-mail: kkress@mpc.edu
http://www.mpc.edu/academics/olderadultprogram
Kathryn Kress, Older Adult Program Coordinator
Richard Monton, Public Information Coordinator
Steve Morgan, Facilities Director

The Older Adult Program, popularly know as the Learning is Living Program, offers special interest classes without charge to older adults at a variety of locations throughout the Monterey Peninsula. These non-credit courses meet at convenient senior citizen centers and other easily accessible places. A wide range of courses has been specially created to meet current growth patterns of senior citizens' education requirements.

2726 Osher Lifelong Learning InstituteCollege of Extended Studies
San Diego State University
5250 Campanile Drive
Suite 2503
San Diego, CA 92182
619-594-2863
Fax: 619-594-5152
e-mail: extended.std@sdsu.edu
http://www.ces.sdsu.edu/osher/
Stanley M Faer, President Board of Directors
Dave Fish, Vice President Programs
Pat Fleming, Public Relations/Marketing

Join us in an atmosphere of meaningful intellectual and social engagement without the burden of career preparation or emphasis on grades; students are given the opportunity to take academically rich courses that delve into topics that encourage discussion and intellectual stimulation.

2727 Peninsula Shepherd Senior Centers
3740 Sports Arena Boulevard
Suite 2
San Diego, CA 92110-5132
619-223-1640
Fax: 619-223-8944
e-mail: psscenter@gmail.com
http://www.shepherdcenters.org/
Jean Durgan, Director
Sam Matthews, Executive Director Corporate
Cathy Wilson, Chair Corporate Office

Our mission is to build and support a nationwide network of interfaith community-based centers that provide meaning and purpose for adults throughout their mature years.

2728 Plato Society of UCLA
University of California at Los Angeles
1083 Gayley Avenue
Los Angeles, CA 90024-3401
310-794-0231
Fax: 310-794-0672
e-mail: jcripe@uncx.ucla.org
http://www.uclaextension.edu/plato/
Jim Adler, President Executive Council
Bill Rohrer, Vice President Executive Council
Elsie Parker, Secretary/Historian Exec Council

PLATO is a dynamic community of about 400 adults who have the time and commitment to continue a lifelong pursuit of knowledge. Each member researches, participates in - and periodically leads - weekly small group discussions of topics they've chosen. PLATO is not a passive experience. Like our namesake, we learn and teach through interactive dialogue - an educational opportunity like no other.

2729 Renaissance SocietyCenter for Learning in Retirement
California State University, Sacramento
Adams Building, Room 210
6000 J Street
Sacramento, CA 95819-6074
916-278-7834
e-mail: renaissa@csus.edu
http://www.csus.edu/ORG/RENSOC/
Harriette Work, President Executive Committee
Mike Sands, VP Executive Committee
Coby Bonner, Secretary Executive Committee

The Renaissance Society is a participatory Center for Learning in Retirement in which members choose to study topics proposed by their peers who coordinate the seminar. These subjects constantly evolve from the interests of the members. The goals of the Society are to provide opportunities for continued learning and to foster creative expression for members.

2730 Sage Society
Roland Tseng College of Extended Learning
California State University Northridge
18111 Nordhoff Street
Northridge, CA 91330
818-831-5064
e-mail: elders@csun.edu
http://http://exlweb.csun.edu/sage/senior.html
Al Ross, President
Reuben Allen, Webmaster
Morrie Cutler, SAGE Founder

The SAGE Society is a learning-in-retirement organization for retired and semi-retired seniors interested in intellectual and cultural stimulation. SAGE offers a dynamic program for individuals who desire to share learning with like-minded people. SAGE operates under the auspices of the Roland Tseng College of Extended Learning at California State University Northridge.

2731 San Diego Community College District(SDCCD)
3375 Camino Del Rio S
San Diego, CA 92108-3807
619-388-6500
619-388-6913
http://www.sdccd.edu
Lynn Neault, VC Student Services
Richard Dittbenner, Government/Public Relations
John Nunes, Assistant Director Information

Earn college credit online with courses developed and taught by professors from City, Mesa and Miramar colleges. SDCCD Online offers student support services designed to make your registration, educational planning and learning as efficient and user-friendly as possible.

2732 Sixty Plus Club
California State University of Bakersfield
9001 Stockdale Highway
Bakersfield, CA 93311-1022
661-664-2011
Fax: 661-664-3324
e-mail: jloveless@csub.edu
http://www.csub.edu/
Gigi Nordquist, Academic Special Sessions Drtr
Jaclyn Loveless, Retirement Seminar Coordinator

The Sixty-Plus Club (60+) at California State University, Bakersfield, offers a variety of seminars - past topics have included Retirement Planning, Positive Planning, Sex After 60, and Positive Psychology.

2733 UC San Diego Extension
University of California, San Diego
9500 Gilman Drive
La Jolla, CA 92093-5004
858-534-2230
Fax: 858-534-7385
e-mail: olli@ucsd.edu
http://http://extension.ucsd.edu/programs/osher
Francesca Ringland, Exec Director Extension Program
Dale Bonifield, Marketing/Public Relations
Barbara Strumsky, Exec Director Finance

UC San Diego Extension was an early pioneer in the national movement of learning in retirement. Originally named the Institute for Continued Learning, the program began in 1974 in response to ideas offered by a group of retirees from New York who wished to replicate the learning in retirement program they had participated in at the New School for Social Research.

Continuing Education/Colorado

2734 **University of San Francisco: Fromm Institute for Lifelong Learning**
2130 Fulton Street
San Francisco, CA 94117-1080
415-422-6805
Fax: 415-422-6535
http://www.usfca.edu/fromm/fromm_institute.html
Robert Fordham, Program Director
Hanna Fromm, Executive Director
Derek Leighnor, Assistant Program Director

Educational program for retired persons at the University of San Fransisco. Program offers day-time, non-credit, college-level courses in a wide range of academic subjects taught by retired professors. Three eight-week sessions per year: fall, winter and spring. Call to be placed on our mailing list.

Colorado

2735 **AARP: Colorado-Denver Office**
1301 Pennsylvania Street
Suite 200
Denver, CO 80203
866-554-5376
Fax: 303-764-5999
e-mail: coaarp@aarp.org
http://www.aarp.org/states/co
Jim Dolbier, AARP Colorado State President
Jon Looney, AARP Colorado State Director
Erik Olsen, AARP President Corporate Office

Resources for online classes, training and more. Topics include Computers/Technology, Health/Wellbeing, Personal Finance. AARP Membership open to individuals age 50+, benefits include access to insurance services, travel discounts, advice on healthy living, financial planning, consumer protection. AARP represents members on issues like Medicare, Social Security, and consumer safety. Publications include the AARP Magazine and AARP Bulletin.

2736 **AARP: Colorado-Pueblo Information Center**
1117 S Prairie Avenue
Pueblo, CO 81005
719-543-8876
Fax: 719-543-8846
e-mail: coaarp@aarp.org OR mpiercesmile@aarp.org
http://www.aarp.org/states/co
Jim Dolbier, AARP Colorado State President
Morie Pierce Smile, AARP Colorado Media Relations
Erik Olsen, AARP President Corporate Office

Resources for online classes, training and more. Topics include Computers/Technology, Health/Wellbeing, Personal Finance. AARP Membership open to individuals age 50+, benefits include access to insurance services, travel discounts, advice on healthy living, financial planning, consumer protection. AARP represents members on issues like Medicare, Social Security, and consumer safety. Publications include the AARP Magazine and AARP Bulletin.

2737 **Front Range Community College**
3645 W 112th Avenue
Westminster, CO 80031-2199
303-404-5550
Fax: 303-466-1623
http://www.frontrange.edu/
Karen Reinertson, President
Erin Hoag, Dean of Student Services

Located near the crossroads of Adams, Boulder, Broomfield, and Jefferson counties at the start of the U.S. 36 technology corridor, FRCC-Westminster blends up-to-date technology with an old-fashioned commitment to personal attention and small class size.

2738 **OASIS Denver**
c/o Macy's
8501 W Bowles Avenue
Denver, CO 80123
303-922-5178
Fax: 303-899-5134
e-mail: jclover@oasisnet.org
http://www.oasisnet.org/denver/index.htm
Jan Clover, Director
Kay Wallick, Executive Director Corporate

OASIS is a national nonprofit educational organization designed to enhance the quality of life for mature adults. Offering challenging programs in the arts, humanities, wellness, technology and volunteer service, OASIS creates opportunities for older adults to continue their personal growth and provide meaningful service to the community. OASIS is nationally sponsored by Macy's Foundation.

Connecticut

2739 **AARP: Connecticut State Office**
Capitol Place
21 Oak Street, Suite 104
Hartford, CT 06106-8003
866-295-7279
Fax: 860-249-7707
e-mail: ctaarp@aarp.org
http://www.aarp.org/states/ct
Susan Bibisi, AARP Connecticut Media Relations
Erik Olsen, AARP President Corporate Office
Bill Novelli, AARP CEO Corporate Office

Resources for online classes, training and more. Topics include Computers/Technology, Health/Wellbeing, Personal Finance. AARP Membership open to individuals age 50+, benefits include access to insurance services, travel discounts, advice on healthy living, financial planning, consumer protection. AARP represents members on issues like Medicare, Social Security, and consumer safety. Publications include the AARP Magazine and AARP Bulletin.

2740 **Hartford Consortium for Higher Education Adult Learning Program**
950 Main Street
Suite 314
Hartford, CT 06103-1207
860-906-5016
Fax: 860-906-5118
http://www.hartnet.org/hche
Rosanne Druckman, Executive Director
Peg Johnson, Assistant to Executive Director
Eileen Peltier, Program Manager

Founded in 1972, the Consortium is a vehicle for the development of joint programs that serve faculty, students and the wider community. Its programs and initiatives include Career Beginnings, Consortium Grant Program, Cross-registration, Fifth Graders Go To College and Regional Roundtables.

2741 **Institute for Retired Professionals**
Fairfield University
1073 N Benson Road
Fairfield, CT 06430
203-254-4170
Fax: 203-254-4261
http://www.fairfield.edu/x7827.html
Elizabeth Hastings, Institute Seminar Coordinator
Nancy Habetz, Media Relations Director
Joan Grant, Publicist

The Institute for Retired Professionals is open to all retired and semi-retired people over 55 and the only requirement for joining is an intellectual curiosity. Members of The Institute may audit one undergraduate course during the fall and spring semesters as well as attend monthly symposia by distinguished Fairfield University faculty members.

Continuing Education/Delaware

2742 Taconic Learning Center (TLC)
PO Box 1752
Lakeville, CT 06039-1752   860-435-2922
http://www.taconiclearningcenter.org/index2.php
Marion Haeberle, Manager

Non-credit, tuition-free, college-level courses in a wide ariety of disciplines - art, literature, music, opera, the sciences, history, mathematics, current events, foreign affairs, economics, the law, government, religion, foreign languages, health and welfare, and more!

2743 University of the Third Age of Asnuntuck
Asnuntuck Community College
PO Box 68
Enfield, CT 06083   860-253-3000
                          800-501-3967
                    Fax: 860-253-3007
http://acc.commnet.edu/schooltocareer/UTA.htm
Mary Duffy, Membership Coordinator
Molly DiSalvo, Trip Coordinator

Programs are held at Asnuntuck Community College - past events have included trips to Radio City Christmas, Platzel Brauhaus Oktoberfest, and a Victorian Festival.

Delaware

2744 AARP: Delaware State Office
1100 N Market Street
Suite 1201
Wilmington, DE 19801
         866-227-7441
    Fax: 302-571-1984
e-mail: destate@aarp.org
http://www.aarp.org/states/de
Rita Landgraf, AARP Delaware State President
Lucretia Young, AARP Delaware State Director
Erik Olsen, AARP President Corporate Office

Resources for online classes, training and more. Topics include Computers/Technology, Health/Wellbeing, Personal Finance. AARP Membership open to individuals age 50+, benefits include access to insurance services, travel discounts, advice on healthy living, financial planning, consumer protection. AARP represents members on issues like Medicare, Social Security, and consumer safety. Publications include the AARP Magazine and AARP Bulletin.

2745 Academy of Lifelong Learning
University of Delaware
2700 Pennsylvania Avenue
115 Arsht Hall
Wilmington, DE 19806-1154   302-573-4417
                             Fax: 302-573-4505
e-mail: academy-ll@udel.edu
http://www.academy.udel.edu/index.html
Ruth M Flexman, Coordinator
Basil Maas, University Coordinator
James Broomall, Asisant Provost

The Academy of Lifelong Learning provides opportunities for intellectual and cultural exploration and development for men and women of retirement age. It utilizes the members' wealth of experience and talent in planning and implementing college-level educational experiences.

District of Columbia

2746 AARP: District of Columbia State OfficeCorporate Headquarters
601 E Street NW
Suite A1-200
Washington, DC 20049   202-434-7700
                        Fax: 202-434-7710
e-mail: dcaarp@aarp.org
http://www.aarp.org/states/dc
Erik Olsen, AARP President Corporate Office
Bill Novelli, AARP CEO Corporate Office
Grier Mendel, AARP Corporate Media Relations

Resources for online classes, training and more. Topics include Computers/Technology, Health/Wellbeing, Personal Finance. AARP Membership open to individuals age 50+, benefits include access to insurance services, travel discounts, advice on healthy living, financial planning, consumer protection. AARP represents members on issues like Medicare, Social Security, and consumer safety. Publications include the AARP Magazine and AARP Bulletin.

2747 Division of Continuing Education
University of the District of Columbia
410 8th Street NW, Room 609
Washington, DC 20004   202-274-6686
e-mail: mhailstock@udc.edu
http://www.udc.edu/ce/non_credit.htm
Lucious Anderson, Acting Director
Peggy Edler Mack, Training & Development Manager
Marshelle Hailstock, Systems Administrator

The Division of Continuing Education extends the resources of the University of the District of Columbia to the community by providing learning experiences in the form of short, non-credit activities, designed to provide opportunities for DC area residents to enrich and revitalize professional skills, expand career advancement opportunities, and promote personal growth and development.

2748 Osher Lifelong Learning Institute
American University
4400 Massachusetts Avenue NW
Washington, DC 20016-8143   202-895-4860
                             Fax: 202-895-4865
e-mail: OLLI@american.edu
http://www.olli-dc.org/contactus.html
Anne N Wallace, Executive Director
Lena Frumin, Program Coodinator

The Osher Lifelong Learning Institute is an association of, by, and for people who wish to continue to study and learn. OLLI is dedicated to the proposition that learning is a lifelong process, and curiosity never retires.

Florida

2749 AARP: Florida-Miramar Office
3350 SW 148th Avenue
Suite 120
Miramar, FL 33027
         866-595-7678
    Fax: 954-438-7871
e-mail: flaarp@aarp.org OR kmarma@aarp.org
http://www.aarp.org/states/fl
Lori Parham, AARP Florida State Director
Kathy Marma, AARP Florida Media Relations
Erik Olsen, AARP President Corporate Office

Resources for online classes, training and more. Topics include Computers/Technology, Health/Wellbeing, Personal Finance. AARP Membership open to individuals age 50+, benefits include access to insurance services, travel discounts, advice on healthy living, financial planning, consumer protection. AARP represents members on issues like Medicare, Social Security, and consumer safety. Publications include the AARP Magazine and AARP Bulletin.

Continuing Education/Florida

2750 AARP: Florida-St Petersburg Office
400 Carillon Parkway
Suite 100
St. Petersburg, FL 33716
866-595-7678
Fax: 727-571-2278
e-mail: flaarp@aarp.org
http://www.aarp.org/states/fl
TTY 727-561-9544

Lori Parham, AARP Florida State Director
Odette Bragg, AARP Florida State Operations
Erik Olsen, AARP President Corporate Office

Resources for online classes, training and more. Topics include Computers/Technology, Health/Wellbeing, Personal Finance. AARP Membership open to individuals age 50+, benefits include access to insurance services, travel discounts, advice on healthy living, financial planning, consumer protection. AARP represents members on issues like Medicare, Social Security, and consumer safety. Publications include the AARP Magazine and AARP Bulletin.

2751 AARP: Florida-Tallahassee Office
200 W College Avenue
Suite 305
Tallahassee, FL 32301
866-595-7678
Fax: 850-222-8968
e-mail: flaarp@aarp.org OR kmarma@aarp.org
http://www.aarp.org/states/fl

Lori Parham, AARP Florida State Director
Kathy Marma, AARP Florida Media Relations
Erik Olsen, AARP President Corporate Office

Resources for online classes, training and more. Topics include Computers/Technology, Health/Wellbeing, Personal Finance. AARP Membership open to individuals age 50+, benefits include access to insurance services, travel discounts, advice on healthy living, financial planning, consumer protection. AARP represents members on issues like Medicare, Social Security, and consumer safety. Publications include the AARP Magazine and AARP Bulletin.

2752 Academy of Senior Professionals of Eckerd (ASPEC)
Eckerd College
4200 54th Avenue S
St Petersburg, FL 33711-4744
727-864-8834
800-456-9009
Fax: 727-864-2964
http://www.eckerd.edu/aspec/

Richard Hallin PhD, Dean Emeritus of Admissions
Donald R Eastman III, President
Susan Harrison, Associate Dean of Faculty

From the Visual arts to the Culinary Arts, Philosophy to Bicycling, Religions and Faiths to Science and Society, Literature to Laughing Matters, ASPEC Study Groups enrich the minds, hearts and souls of its 300 plus members. Weekly Social Hours at Lewis House and monthly events at local restaurants provide ASPEC members with the opportunity to socialize with each other and strengthen the ASPEC community.

2753 Center for New Perspectivese
200 SW Prima Vista Boulevard
Port St Lucie, FL 34983-1963
561-879-4199
Fax: 561-462-4692

2754 Institute for Retired Professionals
University of Miami
5915 Ponce De Leon Boulevard
Suite 29
Coral Gables, FL 33146-2435
305-284-5072
Fax: 305-284-5851
e-mail: nfrye@maimi.edu
http://www.education.miami.edu/irp

Noreen Frye, Director

Provides intellectual and social opportunities for adults over 50 within the cultural environment of the university. Open to anyone looking to keep their mind active and stimulated in their retirement years.

2755 Institute of New Dimensions
Palm Beach Junior College
4200 Congress Avenue
Lake Worth, FL 33461-4705
561-967-7222
Fax: 561-868-3379

Dennis Gallon, Owner

2756 Life Center
819 Park Street
Jacksonville, FL 32204-3322
904-356-1423

William Finn, Religious Leader

2757 Life Enrichment Center
9704 N Boulevard
Tampa, FL 33612-7846
813-932-0241
Fax: 813-933-2256
e-mail: staff@lifeenrichmenttampa.org
http://www.lifeenrichmenttampa.org

Ronna J Metcalf, Executive Director

2758 Pensacola Junior College Seniors Club
1000 College Boulevard
Pensacola, FL 32504-8998
850-484-2002
888-897-3605

Barbara Bedell, Manager

2759 Senior Summer School
PO Box 4424
Deerfield Beach, FL 33442-4424
800-847-2466
http://www.seniorsummerschool.com

Offers adventurous senior citizens an affordable opportunity to enhance their summer through education, leisure, and discovery, at campus locations across the US and Canada.

2760 Shepherd's Center of Gainesville
4000 NW 53rd Avenue
Gainesville, FL 32653
352-376-6615
Fax: 352-332-0400
e-mail: kwallick@shepherdcenters.org
http://www.shepherdcenters.org/gainesville.aspx

Jean Wiley, Director
Kay Wallick, Executive Director Corporate

Individual centers partner with all faiths representing the diversity of their communities. The mission is to empower older adults to use their wisdom and skills for the good of their communities. Providing health enhancement, cultural enrichment and lifelong learning opportunities.

2761 Shepherd's Center of Orange Park
2105 Park Avenue
Suite 1
Orange Park, FL 32073
904-269-5315
Fax: 904-269-5315
e-mail: scoop@clearwire.net
http://www.shepherdcenters.org/orangepark.aspx

Cindy Stewart, Director
Keith Clark, Chair
Kay Wallick, Executive Director Corporate

Individual centers partner with all faiths representing the diversity of their communities. The mission is to empower older adults to use their wisdom and skills for the good of their communities. Providing health enhancement, cultural enrichment and lifelong learning opportunities.

Continuing Education/Georgia

Georgia

2762 AARP: Georgia State Office
999 Peachtree Street NE
Suite 1110
Atlanta, GA 30309
866-295-7281
Fax: 404-881-6997
e-mail: gaaarp@aarp.org
http://www.aarp.org/states/ga
Kenneth A Mitchell, AARP Georgia State Director
Matthew McWilliams, AARP Georgia Media Relations
Erik Olsen, AARP President Corporate Office

Resources for online classes, training and more. Topics include Computers/Technology, Health/Wellbeing, Personal Finance. AARP Membership open to individuals age 50+, benefits include access to insurance services, travel discounts, advice on healthy living, financial planning, consumer protection. AARP represents members on issues like Medicare, Social Security, and consumer safety. Publications include the AARP Magazine and AARP Bulletin.

2763 Life Enrichment Services
1340 McConnell Drive
Decatur, GA 30033-3516
404-321-6960
Fax: 404-321-3095

2764 North Atlanta Senior Services
3003 Howell Mill Road NW
Atlanta, GA 30327-1601
404-237-7307
Fax: 404-237-6080
Sister Kathleen Pursor GNSH, Director
Laura Stokes, Executive Director

Programs and services for older adults to improve their quality of life: educational programs, adult day care, friendly visitors, telephone reassurance, medium escort transportation and handyman services.

2765 Northside Shepherd's Center
425 10th Street NW
Atlanta, GA 30318-5711
404-352-9303
Bob Wiseman, Executive Director

2766 PACE II
Arthritis Foundation
PO Box 7669
Atlanta, GA 30357
770-451-3084
800-283-7800
Fax: 404-872-0457
http://www.arthritis.org
Sergio Pace, President

2767 Perimeter Adult Learning and Services
1548 Mount Vernon Road
Dunwoody, GA 30338-4119
770-698-0801
Fax: 770-617-7761
http://www.palsonline.org
Tom Stelson, President
Susan Stevens, Vice President
Jan Ewing, Treasurer

A nonprofit, interfaith organization for persons 50 and older in Dunwoody, Sandy Springs, Norcross and neighboring areas Metropolitan Atlanta. PALS is a volunteer organization sponsored by religious and civic groups, and by businesses. At present PALS' primary offerings are the quarterly sessions of the Lunch n' Learn program.

2768 Quality Living Services
PO Box 311045
Atlanta, GA 31131-1045
404-699-1686
Fax: 404-505-5788
Irene Richardson, Executive Director

2769 Senior Citizens Council of Cobb County: Enrichment of Life Movement
32 N Fairground Street
Marietta, GA 30060-2160
770-528-5355
Fax: 770-528-5378
Richard Meeks, Executive Director

2770 Senior University
Emory University
Atlanta, GA 30322
404-727-6000
Fax: 404-727-6001

Hawaii

2771 AARP: Hawaii-Big Island Information Center
PO Box 390148
Keahou, HI 96739-0148
808-334-4894
Fax: 808-329-4894
e-mail: hiaarp@aarp.org OR hikona@aloha.net
http://www.aarp.org/states/hi
Stuart T K Ho, AARP HI Interim State President
Bruce Bottorff, AARP HI Media Relations
Erik Olsen, AARP President Corporate Office

Resources for online classes, training and more. Topics include Computers/Technology, Health/Wellbeing, Personal Finance. AARP Membership open to individuals age 50+, benefits include access to insurance services, travel discounts, advice on healthy living, financial planning, consumer protection. AARP represents members on issues like Medicare, Social Security, and consumer safety. Publications include the AARP Magazine and AARP Bulletin.

2772 AARP: Hawaii-Honolulu Office
1132 Bishop Street
Suite 1920
Honolulu, HI 96813
888-227-7669
Fax: 808-537-2288
e-mail: hiaarp@aarp.org
http://www.aarp.org/states/hi
Stuart T K Ho, AARP HI Interim State President
Barbara Kim Stanton, AARP HI State Director
Erik Olsen, AARP President Corporate Office

Resources for online classes, training and more. Topics include Computers/Technology, Health/Wellbeing, Personal Finance. AARP Membership open to individuals age 50+, benefits include access to insurance services, travel discounts, advice on healthy living, financial planning, consumer protection. AARP represents members on issues like Medicare, Social Security, and consumer safety. Publications include the AARP Magazine and AARP Bulletin.

2773 AARP: Hawaii-Kauai Information Center
4212-A Rice Street
Lihue, HI 96766
808-246-4500
Fax: 808-245-6172
e-mail: kauaia001@hawaii.rr.com OR bbottorff@aarp.org
http://www.aarp.org/states/hi
Stuart T K Ho, AARP HI Interim State President
Bruce Bottorff, AARP HI Media Relations
Erik Olsen, AARP President Corporate Office

Resources for online classes, training and more. Topics include Computers/Technology, Health/Wellbeing, Personal Finance. AARP Membership open to individuals age 50+, benefits include access to insurance services, travel discounts, advice on healthy living, financial planning, consumer protection. AARP represents members on issues like Medicare, Social Security, and consumer safety. Publications include the AARP Magazine and AARP Bulletin.

Continuing Education/Idaho

2774 AARP: Hawaii-Oahu Information Center
1199 Dillingham Boulevard
Suite A-106
Honolulu, HI 96817
808-843-1906
Fax: 808-843-1908
e-mail: oahuaarp@hawaii.rr.com OR bbottorff@aarp.org
http://www.aarp.org/states/hi

Stuart T K Ho, AARP HI Interim State President
Bruce Bottorff, AARP HI Media Relations
Erik Olsen, AARP President Corporate Office

Resources for online classes, training and more. Topics include Computers/Technology, Health/Wellbeing, Personal Finance. AARP Membership open to individuals age 50+, benefits include access to insurance services, travel discounts, advice on healthy living, financial planning, consumer protection. AARP represents members on issues like Medicare, Social Security, and consumer safety. Publications include the AARP Magazine and AARP Bulletin.

2775 Emeritus College
74 Dillingham Boulevard
Honolulu, HI 96817
808-845-9211
Fax: 808-845-3767

Ramsey Pedersen, Principal

Idaho

2776 AARP: Idaho State Office
3080 E Gentry Way
Suite 100
Meridian, ID 83642
866-295-7284
Fax: 202-288-4424
e-mail: aarpid@aarp.org
http://www.aarp.org/states/idaho/

Janice Stover, AARP Idaho State President
Jim Wordelman, AARP Idaho State Director
Erik Olsen, AARP President Corporate Office

Resources for online classes, training and more. Topics include Computers/Technology, Health/Wellbeing, Personal Finance. AARP Membership open to individuals age 50+, benefits include access to insurance services, travel discounts, advice on healthy living, financial planning, consumer protection. AARP represents members on issues like Medicare, Social Security, and consumer safety. Publications include the AARP Magazine and AARP Bulletin.

Illinois

2777 AARP: Illinois State Office
222 N LaSalle Street
Suite 710
Chicago, IL 60601
866-448-3613
Fax: 312-372-2204
e-mail: aarpil@aarp.org
http://www.aarp.org/states/il

Evelyn Gooden, AARP Illinois State President
David Irwin, AARP Illinois Media Relations
Erik Olsen, AARP President Corporate Office

Resources for online classes, training and more. Topics include Computers/Technology, Health/Wellbeing, Personal Finance. AARP Membership open to individuals age 50+, benefits include access to insurance services, travel discounts, advice on healthy living, financial planning, consumer protection. AARP represents members on issues like Medicare, Social Security, and consumer safety. Publications include the AARP Magazine and AARP Bulletin.

2778 Lifelong Learning Institute
Parkland College
2400 W Bradley Avenue
Champaign, IL 61821-1806
217-403-1429
Fax: 217-356-7067
e-mail: mreed@parkland.edu

Marica Reed, Coordinator

Educational enrichment programs for retirees or those nearly retired. Travelogues, lectures, classes in the arts, history, crafts, gardening, and a wide array of other topics.

2779 Older Adult Institute
College of Du Page
425 Fawell Boulevard
Glen Ellyn, IL 60137-6599
630-942-2800
Fax: 630-858-3614
http://www.cod.edu/conted/oai

Marget Hamilton, Manager
Sunil Chand, President

Offers mature adults an opportunity to engage in intellectual discovery through lifelong learning.

2780 Quality Care Conference
Alzheimer's Association
919 N Michigan Avenue
Suite 1000
Chicago, IL 60611-1696
312-335-8700
800-272-3900
Fax: 312-335-1110
e-mail: info@alz.org
http://www.alz.org

Gary Bieting, President

Selected educational sessions from the conference discussing topics such as special care units, drug therapies, behavior management, and care strategies.

Frequency: Audiotapes

Indiana

2781 AARP: Indiana State Office
1 N Capitol Avenue
Suite 1275
Indianapolis, IN 46204-2025
866-448-3618
Fax: 317-423-2211
e-mail: inaarp@aarp.org
http://www.aarp.org/states/in

June Lyle, AARP Indiana Interim Director
Anita Price, AARP Indiana Volunteer President
Erik Olsen, AARP President Corporate Office

Resources for online classes, training and more. Topics include Computers/Technology, Health/Wellbeing, Personal Finance. AARP Membership open to individuals age 50+, benefits include access to insurance services, travel discounts, advice on healthy living, financial planning, consumer protection. AARP represents members on issues like Medicare, Social Security, and consumer safety. Publications include the AARP Magazine and AARP Bulletin.

2782 Forever Learning Institute
54191 Ironwood Road
South Bend, IN 46635
574-282-1901
Fax: 574-282-1901
e-mail: jloranger2@netzero.net
http://www.foreverlearninginstitute.org

Joan Loranger, Executive Director
John Chapleau, Office Manager

Forever Learning Institute's mission is to improve the quality and dignity of senior adult life through continuing intellectual challenge, spiritual reflection, and social interaction.

Continuing Education/Iowa

2783 High Street UMC Older Adult Ministry
219 S High Street
Muncie, IN 47305-1622 765-747-8500
Fax: 765-741-5282
Charlotte B Overmyer, Reverand, Director Older Adult Ministries
Jack Hartman, Religious Leader

High Street Methodist Church has an intention ministry by, for and with the older adults. Programs open to the community include Thursday Luncheon, Update Learning (continuing education), Senior Health Insurance Program, Elder-law Counseling, and various interest groups. High Street UMC is recognized as an advocate for the elderly in the community.

2784 Shepherd's Center Indianapolis
3808 N Meridian Street
Indianapolis, IN 46208-4019 317-924-0959
Fax: 317-924-5161
e-mail: mnscenter@aol.com
http://www.mnscenter.org
Mary Dickerson, Director
Anita Gibson, Chair

Individual centers partner with all faiths representing the diversity of their communities. The mission is to empower older adults to use their wisdom and skills for the good of their communities. Providing health enhancement, cultural enrichment and lifelong learning opportunities.

2785 Shepherd's Center Westfield
318 N Union Street
Westfield, IN 46074 317-833-2418
Fax: 317-726-0569
e-mail: schedirector@sbcglobal.net
http://www.shepherdcenters.org
Mary Ann Graybrook, Chair
Kay Wallick, Executive Director Corporate

Individual centers partner with all faiths representing the diversity of their communities. The mission is to empower older adults to use their wisdom and skills for the good of their communities. Providing health enhancement, cultural enrichment and lifelong learning opportunities.

Iowa

2786 AARP: Iowa State Office
600 E Court Avenue
Suite C
Des Moines, IA 50309
866-554-5378
Fax: 515-244-7767
e-mail: iaaarp@aarp.org
http://www.aarp.org/states/ia
Bruce Koeppl, AARP Iowa State Director
Ann Black, AARP Iowa State Media Relations
Erik Olsen, AARP President Corporate Office

Resources for online classes, training and more. Topics include Computers/Technology, Health/Wellbeing, Personal Finance. AARP Membership open to individuals age 50+, benefits include access to insurance services, travel discounts, advice on healthy living, financial planning, consumer protection. AARP represents members on issues like Medicare, Social Security, and consumer safety. Publications include the AARP Magazine and AARP Bulletin.

2787 Chautauqua Program for Senior Adults
Cornell College
Mount Vernon, IA 52314 319-895-4000
Fax: 319-895-5237

Kansas

2788 AARP: Kansas State Office
555 S Kansas
Suite 201
Topeka, KS 66603
866-448-3619
Fax: 785-232-8259
e-mail: ksaarp@aarp.org
http://www.aarp.org/states/ks
Maren Turner, AARP Kansas State Director
David Wilson, AARP Kansas Volunteer President
Erik Olsen, AARP President Corporate Office

Resources for online classes, training and more. Topics include Computers/Technology, Health/Wellbeing, Personal Finance. AARP Membership open to individuals age 50+, benefits include access to insurance services, travel discounts, advice on healthy living, financial planning, consumer protection. AARP represents members on issues like Medicare, Social Security, and consumer safety. Publications include the AARP Magazine and AARP Bulletin.

2789 Cowley County Community College
125 S 2nd Street
Arkansas City, KS 67005-2662 620-442-0430
Fax: 620-441-5350
Pat McAtee, President

2790 DVS Senior Shepherd's Center
1013 W 1st Avenue
Hutchinson, KS 67501-5139 620-662-0111
Earline Polk, Executive Director

2791 Kansas Cosmosphere and Space Center
1100 N Plum Street
Hutchinson, KS 67501-1499 620-662-2305
Fax: 620-662-3693
http://www.cosmo.org
Trish Oakley, Marketing Director

The Kansas Cosmosphere and Space Center is home to one of the world's premier space museums, with a space artifact collection second only to the Smithsonian's National Air and Space Museum. The Cosmosphere's collections include such notable artifacts as the restored Apollo 13 command module 'Odyssey' and the largest collection of Russian space artifacts outside of Moscow. There is a week-long Elderhostel Astronaut Training Program for people 55+Space Museum, the Cosmosphere has an IMAX Dome Theater, a planetarium and Dr. Goddard's Lab, a live rocket science program. The Cosmosphere is also home to the Future Astronaut Training Program for students entering 7-10 and Space Camp for Seniors - The Elderhostel Astronaut Training Program for people 55 and older.

2792 Kansas Geriatric Education Center (KS-GEC)
Center on Aging
Kansas City, KS 66160-7177 913-588-1549
Fax: 913-588-1201
http://www.kumc.edu/gec

KS-GEC provides information and support for developing community-based, long-term care for rural older people.

2793 Learning Resources Network (LERN)
PO Box 1448
Manhattan, KS 66505-1448 785-539-5376
Fax: 785-539-7766
http://www.lern.org
Rebel Rush, Executive Director

Aids in the development and growth of adult learning programs. Provides speakers, technical assistance and publications.
1974

249

Continuing Education/Kentucky

2794　Life Enrichment Program of El Dorado
Butler County Community College
901 S Haverhill Road
El Dorado, KS 67042-3225
316-322-3193
Fax: 316-322-3109
e-mail: prussell@butler.buccc.cc.ks.us
Pat Russell, Director Community Education

The Life Enrichment Service is an educational, entertaining and cultural program for citizens 60 years of age and above.

2795　Life Enrichment Program of North Newton
Bethel College
300 E 27th Street
North Newton, KS 67117
316-283-2500
Fax: 316-284-5286
J Harold Moyer, Life Enrichment Secretary

Educational weekly programs for adults age 60 and over.

2796　Shepherd's Center of Kansas City
21 N 12th Street
Suite 330
Kansas City, KS 66102
913-281-8908
Fax: 913-281-8910
e-mail: karenh@shepherdcenterkck.org
http://www.shepherdcenters.org
Karen Hostetler, Director
Diane Clark, Chair
Kate Wallick, Executive Director Corporate

Individual centers partner with all faiths representing the diversity of their communities. The mission is to empower older adults to use their wisdom and skills for the good of their communities. Providing health enhancement, cultural enrichment and lifelong learning opportunities.

2797　Tabor College
400 S Jefferson Street
Hillsboro, KS 67063-1758
620-947-3121
Fax: 620-947-2607
http://www.tabor.edu
Larry Nikkel, President

2798　Washburn Walkers
University of Topeka
1700 SW College Avenue
Topeka, KS 66621-1101
785-231-1124
Amanda Martin-Hamon, Executive Director

Kentucky

2799　AARP: Kentucky State Office
10401 Linn Station Road
Suite 121
Louisville, KY 40223
866-295-7275
Fax: 502-394-9918
e-mail: kyaarp@aarp.org
http://www.aarp.org/states/ky
Laurel True, AARP Kentucky Advocacy Rep
Fred Smith, AARP Kentucky Community Service
Erik Olsen, AARP President Corporate Office

Resources for online classes, training and more. Topics include Computers/Technology, Health/Wellbeing, Personal Finance. AARP Membership open to individuals age 50+, benefits include access to insurance services, travel discounts, advice on healthy living, financial planning, consumer protection. AARP represents members on issues like Medicare, Social Security, and consumer safety. Publications include the AARP Magazine and AARP Bulletin.

2800　Donovan Scholars Program
University of Kentucky
Lexington, KY 40506
859-257-2656
Fax: 859-323-4940
e-mail: jhensel@uky.edu
http://www.research.uky.edu/aging
Judy Henselman, Registar
Arleen Johnson, Director

Free education for seniors aged 65 and older.

2801　United Crescent Hill Ministries
1860 Frankfort Avenue
Louisville, KY 40206-3146
502-893-0346
Fax: 502-893-0352
Sue Gentry, Executive Director

Louisiana

2802　AARP: Louisiana State Office
301 Main Street
Suite 1012
Baton Rouge, LA 70825
866-448-3620
Fax: 225-387-3400
e-mail: la@aarp.org
http://www.aarp.org/states/la
Earl White, AARP Louisiana State President
Nancy McPherson, AARP Louisiana State Director
Erik Olsen, AARP President Corporate Office

Resources for online classes, training and more. Topics include Computers/Technology, Health/Wellbeing, Personal Finance. AARP Membership open to individuals age 50+, benefits include access to insurance services, travel discounts, advice on healthy living, financial planning, consumer protection. AARP represents members on issues like Medicare, Social Security, and consumer safety. Publications include the AARP Magazine and AARP Bulletin.

2803　Centenary College of Louisiana
PO Box 4188
Shreveport, LA 71134
318-869-5011
Fax: 318-869-5795
Kenneth Schwab, President

Maine

2804　AARP: Maine State Office
1685 Congress Street
Portland, ME 04102
866-554-5380
Fax: 207-775-5727
e-mail: me@aarp.org
http://www.aarp.org/states/me
Cheryl Miller, AARP Maine Executive Council Rep
Phyllis Cohn, AARP Maine Media Relations Rep
Erik Olsen, AARP President Corporate Office

Resources for online classes, training and more. Topics include Computers/Technology, Health/Wellbeing, Personal Finance. AARP Membership open to individuals age 50+, benefits include access to insurance services, travel discounts, advice on healthy living, financial planning, consumer protection. AARP represents members on issues like Medicare, Social Security, and consumer safety. Publications include the AARP Magazine and AARP Bulletin.

2805　Senior Adult Growth Exchange
University of Southern Maine
68 High Street
Portland, ME 04101-3813
207-780-5900
Fax: 207-780-5954
Stacy Calderwood, Executive Director

Continuing Education/Maryland

Maryland

2806 AARP: Maryland State Office
200 Saint Paul Place
Suite 2510
Baltimore, MD 21202
866-542-8163
Fax: 410-837-0269
e-mail: mdaarp@aarp.org
http://www.aarp.org/states/md

Erwin M Sekulow, AARP Maryland State President
Tiffany Lundquist, AARP Maryland Media Relations
Erik Olsen, AARP President Corporate Office

Resources for online classes, training and more. Topics include Computers/Technology, Health/Wellbeing, Personal Finance. AARP Membership open to individuals age 50+, benefits include access to insurance services, travel discounts, advice on healthy living, financial planning, consumer protection. AARP represents members on issues like Medicare, Social Security, and consumer safety. Publications include the AARP Magazine and AARP Bulletin.

2807 Evergreen Society
Johns Hopkins University
4545 N Charles Street
Baltimore, MD 21210-2693
410-516-0341
Fax: 410-516-0864

Robert Saarnio, Executive Director

2808 Institute for Retired Persons
Salisbury University
1101 Camden Avenue
Salisbury, MD 21801-6837
410-543-6150
888-543-0148
Fax: 410-543-6000
e-mail: jmmaise@salisbury.edu
http://www.salisbury.edu/irp

Darrell Mullins, President
Elizabeth Curtin, Vice President

The IRP offers continuing education designed for adults aged 50 and above. The IRP offers programs to enlighten, educate and offer better understanding of our world.

2809 Learning is for Everyone
Anne Arundel Community College
101 College Parkway
Arnold, MD 21012-1895
410-647-7100
Fax: 410-777-2822

Martha Smith, President

2810 OASIS Hyattsville
c/o Macy's
3500 East-West Highway
Hyattsville, MD 20782-1916
301-559-6575
Fax: 301-559-2976
e-mail: kholk@oasisnet.org
http://www.oasisnet.org/hyattsville/index.htm

Karen Holk, Director
Kay Wallick, Executive Director Corporate

OASIS is a national nonprofit educational organization designed to enhance the quality of life for mature adults. Offering challenging programs in the arts, humanities, wellness, technology and volunteer service, OASIS creates opportunities for older adults to continue their personal growth and provide meaningful service to the community. OASIS is nationally sponsored by Macy's Foundation.

2811 OASIS Montgomery County
c/o Macy's
7125 Democracy Boulevard
Bethesda, MD 20817
301-469-6800
Fax: 301-926-0475
e-mail: mdroz@oasisnet.org
http://www.oasisnet.org/montgomery/index.htm

Marcy Drozdowicz, Co-Director
Jane Silberman, Co-Director
Kay Wallick, Executive Director Corporate

OASIS is a national nonprofit educational organization designed to enhance the quality of life for mature adults. Offering challenging programs in the arts, humanities, wellness, technology and volunteer service, OASIS creates opportunities for older adults to continue their personal growth and provide meaningful service to the community. OASIS is nationally sponsored by Macy's Foundation.

2812 Prince George's Community College
301 Largo Road
Largo, MD 20774-2199
301-336-6000
Fax: 301-386-7502
e-mail: crawfoca@pg.cc.md.us
http://www.pg.cc.md.us

Camille Crawford, Director
Ronald A Williams, President

Educational programs designed for Maryland residents, age 60 and older. Explore art, music, health, history, and more in 13-15 week sessions. $50.00 yearly for unlimited classes.

2813 Renaissance Institue
College of Notre Dame of Maryland
4701 N Charles Street
Baltimore, MD 21210-2404
410-532-5351
Fax: 410-435-5937

Massachusetts

2814 AARP: Massachusetts State Office
1 Beacon Street
Suite 2301
Boston, MA 02108
866-448-3621
Fax: 617-723-4224
e-mail: ma@aarp.org
http://www.aarp.org/states/ma

Charles Desmond, AARP Massachusetts President
James J Callahan Jr, AARP Massachusetts Advocacy Rep
Erik Olsen, AARP President Corporate Office

Resources for online classes, training and more. Topics include Computers/Technology, Health/Wellbeing, Personal Finance. AARP Membership open to individuals age 50+, benefits include access to insurance services, travel discounts, advice on healthy living, financial planning, consumer protection. AARP represents members on issues like Medicare, Social Security, and consumer safety. Publications include the AARP Magazine and AARP Bulletin.

2815 Academy for Lifelong Learning and Community Center for Successful Aging
2240 Iyannough Road
West Barnstable, MA 02668-1532
508-362-2131
Fax: 508-362-3988

Kathleen Schatzberg, President

2816 Five College Learning in Retirement
Smith College
Northampton, MA 01063
413-584-2700

Carol T Christ, President

2817 Institute for Learning in Retirement
Harvard University
51 Brattle Street
Cambridge, MA 02138-3701
617-495-4072
Fax: 617-495-9176
http://www.dce.harvard.edu/hilr/

2818 Learning in Later Life
263 Alden Street
Springfield, MA 01109-3707
413-748-3089
Fax: 413-748-3787
e-mail: cgorman@spfldcol.edu

Tina Gorman, Director

Continuing Education/Michigan

2819 Lifetime Learning Program
492 Waltham Street
West Newton, MA 02465-1920
617-969-5906
Fax: 617-964-3975

William Garr, Executive Director

2820 Seniors for Lifelong Learning
Curry College
1071 Blue Hill Avenue
Milton, MA 02186-2302
617-333-0500
Fax: 617-333-6860

2821 World Education
44 Farnsworth Street
Boston, MA 02210-1209
617-482-9485
Fax: 617-482-0617
e-mail: Wei@worlded.com
http://www.worlded.com

Joel Lamstein, Owner

Assists in the development of adult education programs. Topics include literacy, health, nutrition, agriculture, income and family planning.

1951

Michigan

2822 AARP: Michigan-Detroit Information Cntr
4750 Woodward Avenue
Suite 404
Detroit, MI 48201
313-832-6846
Fax: 313-832-6847
e-mail: midetroit@aol.com OR sschlinker@aarp.org
http://www.aarp.org/states/mi

Eric Schneidewind, AARP Michigan State President
Stepheni Schlinker, AARP Michigan Media Relations
Erik Olsen, AARP President Corporate Office

Resources for online classes, training and more. Topics include Computers/Technology, Health/Wellbeing, Personal Finance. AARP Membership open to individuals age 50+, benefits include access to insurance services, travel discounts, advice on healthy living, financial planning, consumer protection. AARP represents members on issues like Medicare, Social Security, and consumer safety. Publications include the AARP Magazine and AARP Bulletin.

2823 AARP: Michigan-Lansing Office
309 N Washington Square
Suite 110
Lansing, MI 48933
866-227-7448
Fax: 517-482-2794
e-mail: miaarp@aarp.org
http://www.aarp.org/states/mi
TTY 877-434-7598

Eric Schneidewind, AARP Michigan State President
Stepheni Schlinker, AARP Michigan Media Relations
Erik Olsen, AARP President Corporate Office

Resources for online classes, training and more. Topics include Computers/Technology, Health/Wellbeing, Personal Finance. AARP Membership open to individuals age 50+, benefits include access to insurance services, travel discounts, advice on healthy living, financial planning, consumer protection. AARP represents members on issues like Medicare, Social Security, and consumer safety. Publications include the AARP Magazine and AARP Bulletin.

2824 Emeritus College
Aquinas College
1607 Robinson Road SE
Grand Rapids, MI 49506-1741
616-732-4466
Fax: 616-732-4480

2825 University of Michigan: Learning inRetirement
2401 Plymouth Road
Suite C
Ann Arbor, MI 48105-2193
734-998-9353
Fax: 734-998-9340
e-mail: crcwhite@umich.edu
http://www.mcd.umich.edu/geriatrics

Carolyn White, Center Coordinator

Minnesota

2826 AARP: Minnesota-BloomingtonInformation Center
Mall of America
228 West Market
Bloomington, MN 55425
952-858-9040
Fax: 952-858-9131
e-mail: aarpmn@aarp.org
http://www.aarp.org/states/mn

Skip Humphrey, AARP Minnesota State President
Amy Gromer McDonough, AARP Minnesota Media Relations
Erik Olsen, AARP President Corporate Office

Resources for online classes, training and more. Topics include Computers/Technology, Health/Wellbeing, Personal Finance. AARP Membership open to individuals age 50+, benefits include access to insurance services, travel discounts, advice on healthy living, financial planning, consumer protection. AARP represents members on issues like Medicare, Social Security, and consumer safety. Publications include the AARP Magazine and AARP Bulletin.

2827 AARP: Minnesota-St Paul Office
30 E Seventh Street
Suite 1200
St. Paul, MN 55101
866-554-5381
Fax: 651-221-2636
e-mail: aarpmn@aarp.org
http://www.aarp.org/states/mn

Skip Humphrey, AARP Minnesota State President
Amy Gromer McDonough, AARP Minnesota Media Relations
Erik Olsen, AARP President Corporate Office

Resources for online classes, training and more. Topics include Computers/Technology, Health/Wellbeing, Personal Finance. AARP Membership open to individuals age 50+, benefits include access to insurance services, travel discounts, advice on healthy living, financial planning, consumer protection. AARP represents members on issues like Medicare, Social Security, and consumer safety. Publications include the AARP Magazine and AARP Bulletin.

2828 University for Seniors: Continuing Education and Extension Program
10 University Drive
Duluth, MN 55812-2403
218-726-6347
Fax: 218-726-6336

Mississippi

2829 AARP: Mississippi State Office
6360 I-55 N
Suite 160
Jackson, MS 39211
866-554-5382
Fax: 601-991-3342
e-mail: msaarp@aarp.org
http://www.aarp.org/states/ms

Bruce Brice, AARP MS State Interim President
Sherri Davis Garner, AARP MS State Director
Erik Olsen, AARP President Corporate Office

Continuing Education/Missouri

Resources for online classes, training and more. Topics include Computers/Technology, Health/Wellbeing, Personal Finance. AARP Membership open to individuals age 50+, benefits include access to insurance services, travel discounts, advice on healthy living, financial planning, consumer protection. AARP represents members on issues like Medicare, Social Security, and consumer safety. Publications include the AARP Magazine and AARP Bulletin.

Missouri

2830 AARP: Missouri Information Center North
600 N Kingshighway
St Louis, MO 63108
314-361-0550
Fax: 314-361-0706
e-mail: moaarp@aarp.org OR aparran@aarp.org
http://www.aarp.org/states/mo
Rosetta Robins, AARP MO Volunteer President
Anit K Parran, AARP MO Media Relations Rep
Erik Olsen, AARP President Corporate Office

Resources for online classes, training and more. Topics include Computers/Technology, Health/Wellbeing, Personal Finance. AARP Membership open to individuals age 50+, benefits include access to insurance services, travel discounts, advice on healthy living, financial planning, consumer protection. AARP represents members on issues like Medicare, Social Security, and consumer safety. Publications include the AARP Magazine and AARP Bulletin.

2831 AARP: Missouri Information Center South
8059-A Watson Road
Webster Groves, MO 63119
314-918-7563
Fax: 314-918-7584
e-mail: moaarp@aarp.org OR aparran@aarp.org
http://www.aarp.org/states/mo
Rosetta Robins, AARP MO Volunteer President
Anit K Parran, AARP MO Media Relations Rep
Erik Olsen, AARP President Corporate Office

Resources for online classes, training and more. Topics include Computers/Technology, Health/Wellbeing, Personal Finance. AARP Membership open to individuals age 50+, benefits include access to insurance services, travel discounts, advice on healthy living, financial planning, consumer protection. AARP represents members on issues like Medicare, Social Security, and consumer safety. Publications include the AARP Magazine and AARP Bulletin.

2832 AARP: Missouri-Kansas City Office
700 W 47th Street
Suite 110
Kansas City, MO 64112-1805
866-389-5627
Fax: 816-561-3107
e-mail: moaarp@aarp.org
http://www.aarp.org/states/mo
Rosetta Robins, AARP MO Volunteer President
John McDonald, AARP MO State Director
Erik Olsen, AARP President Corporate Office

Resources for online classes, training and more. Topics include Computers/Technology, Health/Wellbeing, Personal Finance. AARP Membership open to individuals age 50+, benefits include access to insurance services, travel discounts, advice on healthy living, financial planning, consumer protection. AARP represents members on issues like Medicare, Social Security, and consumer safety. Publications include the AARP Magazine and AARP Bulletin.

2833 Learning is Fun Together
PO Box 3947
Springfield, MO 65808-3947
417-862-3598
Fax: 417-862-2129
e-mail: ccozarks@dialus.com
Connie Payne, Director
David Hockensmith, Executive Director

2834 Neighborhood Family Care
4601 Independence Avenue
Kansas City, MO 64124-2927
816-241-6334
Fax: 816-333-5466
Anne Maschger

2835 OASIS Institute
7710 Carondelet Avenue
Suite 125
Saint Louis, MO 63105-3319
314-862-2933
Fax: 314-862-2149
e-mail: mkerz@oasisnet.org
http://www.oasisnet.org/stlouis/index.htm
Marcia Kerz, President
Dawn Anderson, Finance Director
Janice Branham, Communications & Technology

OASIS is a national nonprofit educational organization designed to enhance the quality of life for mature adults. Offering challenging programs in the arts, humanities, wellness, technology and volunteer service, OASIS creates opportunities for older adults to continue their personal growth and provide meaningful service to the community.

2836 School of Metaphysics
Hc 1
Box 15
Windyville, MO 65783-9703
417-345-8411
Fax: 417-345-6668
e-mail: som@som.org
Dr. Barbara Condron, Chairperson
Pam Blosser, President

Conducts adult metaphysical education programs, sponsors social service, charity activities and children's services. Seeks to promote the creation of world peace and human spirituality.
1973

2837 Shepherd's Center of Grandview
PO Box 115
Grandview, MO 64030
816-765-7005
e-mail: staff@shepherdcenters.org
http://www.shepherdcenters.org/
June Leslie, Chair
Kay Wallick, Executive Director Corporate

Individual centers partner with all faiths representing the diversity of their communities. The mission is to empower older adults to use their wisdom and skills for the good of their communities. Providing health enhancement, cultural enrichment and lifelong learning opportunities.

2838 Shepherd's Center of Kansas City Central
5200 Oak Street
Kansas City, MO 64112
816-444-1121
800-547-7073
Fax: 916-444-1177
e-mail: jwurth@sccentral.org
http://www.sccentral.org
Bill Hembree, Chair
JoEllen Wurth, Director
Kay Wallick, Executive Director Corporate

Individual centers partner with all faiths representing the diversity of their communities. The mission is to empower older adults to use their wisdom and skills for the good of their communities. Providing health enhancement, cultural enrichment and lifelong learning opportunities.

2839 Shepherd's Center of Raytown
7900 Blue Ridge Boulevard
Raytown, MO 64138
816-356-9000
Fax: 816-356-6526
e-mail: shepherdscenterr@sbcglobal.net
http://www.shepherdscenterraytown.org
Iris Miller, Director
Ruthie Schweiterman, Chair
Kay Wallick, Executive Director Corporate

Continuing Education/Montana

Individual centers partner with all faiths representing the diversity of their communities. The mission is to empower older adults to use their wisdom and skills for the good of their communities. Providing health enhancement, cultural enrichment and lifelong learning opportunities.

Montana

2840 **AARP: Montana State Office**
30 W 14th Street
Suite 301
Helena, MT 59601
866-295-7278
Fax: 406-441-2230
e-mail: mtaarp@aarp.org
http://www.aarp.org/states/mt
Max Logan, AARP Montana Volunteer President
Bob Bartholomew, AARP Montana State Director
Erik Olsen, AARP President Corporate Office

Resources for online classes, training and more. Topics include Computers/Technology, Health/Wellbeing, Personal Finance. AARP Membership open to individuals age 50+, benefits include access to insurance services, travel discounts, advice on healthy living, financial planning, consumer protection. AARP represents members on issues like Medicare, Social Security, and consumer safety. Publications include the AARP Magazine and AARP Bulletin.

Nebraska

2841 **AARP: Nebraska-Lincoln Office**
301 S 13th Street
Suite 201
Lincoln, NE 68508
866-389-5651
Fax: 402-323-6908
e-mail: neaarp@aarp.org
http://www.aarp.org/states/ne
Connie Benjamin, AARP Nebraska State Director
Elena Guerra, AARP Nebraska Operations Rep
Erik Olsen, AARP President Corporate Office

Resources for online classes, training and more. Topics include Computers/Technology, Health/Wellbeing, Personal Finance. AARP Membership open to individuals age 50+, benefits include access to insurance services, travel discounts, advice on healthy living, financial planning, consumer protection. AARP represents members on issues like Medicare, Social Security, and consumer safety. Publications include the AARP Magazine and AARP Bulletin.

2842 **AARP: Nebraska-Omaha Information Center**
The Center
1941 S 42nd Street
Suite 220
Omaha, NE 68105
402-398-9568
Fax: 402-398-9587
e-mail: omnebraska@aol.com
http://www.aarp.org/states/ne
Connie Benjamin, AARP Nebraska State Director
Elena Guerra, AARP Nebraska Operations Rep
Erik Olsen, AARP President Corporate Office

Resources for online classes, training and more. Topics include Computers/Technology, Health/Wellbeing, Personal Finance. AARP Membership open to individuals age 50+, benefits include access to insurance services, travel discounts, advice on healthy living, financial planning, consumer protection. AARP represents members on issues like Medicare, Social Security, and consumer safety. Publications include the AARP Magazine and AARP Bulletin.

Nevada

2843 **AARP: Nevada State Office**
5820 S Eastern Avenue
Suite 190
Las Vegas, NV 89119
866-389-5652
Fax: 702-938-3225
e-mail: nvaarp@aarp.org
http://www.aarp.org/states/nv
Marlene Rengert, AARP Nevada State President
Carla Sloan, AARP Nevada State Director
Erik Olsen, AARP President Corporate Office

sources for online classes, training and more. Topics include Computers/Technology, Health/Wellbeing, Personal Finance. AARP Membership open to individuals age 50+, benefits include access to insurance services, travel discounts, advice on healthy living, financial planning, consumer protection. AARP represents members on issues like Medicare, Social Security, and consumer safety. Publications include the AARP Magazine and AARP Bulletin.

New Hampshire

2844 **AARP: New Hampshire-ConcordInformation Center**
118 N Main Street
Concord, NH 03301
603-224-6095
800-905-4730
Fax: 603-224-5029
e-mail: nh@aarp.org
http://www.aarp.org/states/nh
Ally McNair, AARP New Hampshire President
Kelly Clark, AARP New Hampshire Director
Erik Olsen, AARP President Corporate Office

Resources for online classes, training and more. Topics include Computers/Technology, Health/Wellbeing, Personal Finance. AARP Membership open to individuals age 50+, benefits include access to insurance services, travel discounts, advice on healthy living, financial planning, consumer protection. AARP represents members on issues like Medicare, Social Security, and consumer safety. Publications include the AARP Magazine and AARP Bulletin.

2845 **AARP: New Hampshire-Manchester Office**
900 Elm Street
Suite 702
Manchester, NH 03101
866-542-8168
Fax: 603-629-0066
e-mail: nh@aarp.org
http://www.aarp.org/states/nh
Ally McNair, AARP New Hampshire President
Kelly Clark, AARP New Hampshire Director
Erik Olsen, AARP President Corporate Office

Resources for online classes, training and more. Topics include Computers/Technology, Health/Wellbeing, Personal Finance. AARP Membership open to individuals age 50+, benefits include access to insurance services, travel discounts, advice on healthy living, financial planning, consumer protection. AARP represents members on issues like Medicare, Social Security, and consumer safety. Publications include the AARP Magazine and AARP Bulletin.

Continuing Education/New Jersey

New Jersey

2846 AARP: New Jersey State Office
Forrestal Village
101 Rockingham Row
Princeton, NJ 08540
866-542-8165
Fax: 609-987-4634
e-mail: njaarp@aarp.org
http://www.aarp.org/states/nj
Sy Larson, AARP New Jersey State President
Jim Dieterle, AARP New Jersey State Director
Erik Olsen, AARP President Corporate Office

Resources for online classes, training and more. Topics include Computers/Technology, Health/Wellbeing, Personal Finance. AARP Membership open to individuals age 50+, benefits include access to insurance services, travel discounts, advice on healthy living, financial planning, consumer protection. AARP represents members on issues like Medicare, Social Security, and consumer safety. Publications include the AARP Magazine and AARP Bulletin.

2847 Florham Institute for Lifelong Learning(FILL)
Farleigh Dickinson University
285 Madison Avenue
Madison, NJ 07940
973-443-8653
Fax: 973-443-8654
e-mail: cuccini@fdu.edu
http://www.fdu.edu
Neil Salzman, MD, Director
Geraldine Cucciniello, Assistant to Director

Program for people who are 62 years and older who wish to attend college for credit, credit towards a degree or simply audit, both Graduate and Undergraduate classes on available space for only $250 per class. We also offer Retired Persons Institute (RPI) classes, class day trips to museums, plays, parks, etc. We offer the program as many years as you want to participate.

2848 Older is Better Senior Adult Program
262 S Main Street
Lodi, NJ 07644-2117
201-559-6000
Fax: 201-559-6188

New Mexico

2849 AARP: New Mexico-AlbuquerqueInformation Center
11130 Lomas Boulevard
Albuquerque, NM 87121
505-830-3096
Fax: 505-872-0581
e-mail: nmaarp@aarp.org
http://www.aarp.org/states/nm
Louis Sarabia, AARP NM Volunteer President
Beth Velasquez, AARP NM Media Relations Rep
Erik Olsen, AARP President Corporate Office

Resources for online classes, training and more. Topics include Computers/Technology, Health/Wellbeing, Personal Finance. AARP Membership open to individuals age 50+, benefits include access to insurance services, travel discounts, advice on healthy living, financial planning, consumer protection. AARP represents members on issues like Medicare, Social Security, and consumer safety. Publications include the AARP Magazine and AARP Bulletin.

2850 AARP: New Mexico-Sante Fe Office
535 Cerrillos Road
Suite A
Santa Fe, NM 87501
866-389-5636
Fax: 505-820-2889
e-mail: nmaarp@aarp.org
http://www.aarp.org/states/nm
Louis Sarabia, AARP NM Volunteer President
Stan Cooper, AARP NM State Director
Erik Olsen, AARP President Corporate Office

Resources for online classes, training and more. Topics include Computers/Technology, Health/Wellbeing, Personal Finance. AARP Membership open to individuals age 50+, benefits include access to insurance services, travel discounts, advice on healthy living, financial planning, consumer protection. AARP represents members on issues like Medicare, Social Security, and consumer safety. Publications include the AARP Magazine and AARP Bulletin.

2851 Amigos del Valle
1116 N Conway Avenue
Mission, TX 78572-4103
956-581-9494
Fax: 956-581-2210
Isaias Aguayo, Executive Director

New York

2852 AARP: New York Albany State Office
1 Commerce Plaza
Suite 706
Albany, NY 12260
866-227-7442
Fax: 518-434-6949
e-mail: nyaarp@aarp.org
http://www.aarp.org/states/ny
Madeleine Moore, AARP New York State President
Lois Aronstein, AARP New York State Director
Erik Olsen, AARP President Corporate Office

Resources for online classes, training and more. Topics include Computers/Technology, Health/Wellbeing, Personal Finance. AARP Membership open to individuals age 50+, benefits include access to insurance services, travel discounts, advice on healthy living, financial planning, consumer protection. AARP represents members on issues like Medicare, Social Security, and consumer safety. Publications include the AARP Magazine and AARP Bulletin.

2853 AARP: New York City State Office
780 Third Avenue
33rd Floor
New York, NY 10017
866-227-7442
Fax: 212-644-6390
e-mail: nyaarp@aarp.org
http://www.aarp.org/states/ny
Madeleine Moore, AARP New York State President
Lois Aronstein, AARP New York State Director
Erik Olsen, AARP President Corporate Office

Resources for online classes, training and more. Topics include Computers/Technology, Health/Wellbeing, Personal Finance. AARP Membership open to individuals age 50+, benefits include access to insurance services, travel discounts, advice on healthy living, financial planning, consumer protection. AARP represents members on issues like Medicare, Social Security, and consumer safety. Publications include the AARP Magazine and AARP Bulletin.

2854 AIDS Treatment Data Network
611 Broadway
Room 613
New York, NY 10012-2608
212-253-7922
800-734-7104
Fax: 212-260-8869
Mark Harrington, Executive Director

Provides HIV treatment and research information, educational resources and training to professionals and the individuals which they serve.

Continuing Education/New York

2855 American ORT
817 Broadway
Floor 10
New York, NY 10003-4756
212-353-5800
800-364-9678
Fax: 212-353-5888
e-mail: info@aort.org
http://www.aort.org

Hope Kessler, Executive Director

Provides quality technical education and training to students in the international ORT network of schools in 60 countries around the world.

2856 College at Sixty
Fordham University at Lincoln Center
113 W 60th Street
Room 301
New York, NY 10023-7414
212-636-6372
Fax: 212-636-6375

Cira Vernazza, Director

For retired and pre-retirement men and women over 50 years of age, Fordham offers a variety of non-credit seminar courses, each of which meets two hours per week over a 13-week term. Subjects include fine and performing arts, literature, theology, psychology, history, philosophy, etc. Social events, topical lectures, and an annual trip to a destination of cultural or historical interest are also offered to College at Sixty students.

2857 Elder Craftsmen
307 7th Avenue
Suite 1401
New York, NY 10001-6046
212-319-8128
Fax: 212-319-8141
e-mail: info@eldercraftsmen.org
http://www.eldercraftsmen.org

Janet Langlois, Executive Director

Helps men and women 55 and older be creative, productive, and independent. Seeks broader recognition by the general public of the skills and capabilities of older people. Sponsors craft training workshops for representatives of Senior Centers. Sponsors community service projects with older adults making items for people in need. Sponsors art projects (and exhibits) for older adults.

1955

2858 Guest Scholar Program
Eddy Hall N
Garden City, NY 11550
516-877-3400
Fax: 516-877-3424

2859 Institute for Retired Professionals and Executives
2900 Bedford Boylan Hall
Room 3160
Brooklyn, NY 11210
718-951-5647

2860 Institute for Retired Professionals atSyracuse
Syracuse University
700 University Avenue
Room 407
Syracuse, NY 13244
315-443-4846
Fax: 315-443-4410
e-mail: cps@uc.syr.edu
http://www.succ.syr.edu/IRP

Sandra Barrett, Director
Alice DeCastro, Program Assistant

Twice each month, members meet to hear speakers and share views. Topics include political and social issues, fine arts, science, environment, community organizations. September through May. Annual membership fee of $25.00.

2861 Institute for Senior Education
145 College Road
Suffern, NY 10901-3620
845-574-4700
Fax: 845-574-4476

Mary A Gatterty, Director

2862 Lifelong Learners Program: Division of Special Programs
2970 Broadway
New York, NY 10027-6939
212-854-2020
Fax: 212-854-7400

2863 Lifelong Learning Center
Athenaeum Rochester Institute of Technology
30 Fairwood Drive
Rochester, NY 14623-4916
585-292-8989
Fax: 585-292-7697
e-mail: RMS85087@rit.edu
http://www.rit.edu

Rose Marie Sepos, Program Director
Sara Connor, Staff Assistant
Julie Blowers, Executive Director

Lifelong learning center for adults over 50.

2864 Mainstream Westchester Community College
75 Grasslands Road
Valhalla, NY 10595-1693
914-606-6600
Fax: 914-785-6526
http://www.sunywcc.edu/continuing_ed

Joseph N Hankin MD, President

Mainstream is an innovator in exciting educational programming and career change options for mature adults.

2865 My Turn Program
Kingsborough Community College
Oriental Boulevard Manhattan Beach
Brooklyn, NY 11235
718-368-5000

2866 National Council of Administrators of Adult Education (NCAAE)
Morton S Horowitz Oceanside Public Schools
145 Merle Avenue
Oceanside, NY 11572-2219
516-678-1200
Fax: 516-678-1224

Peggy Carlock, Coordinator
Dr Herb Brown, Manager

Supports involvement of local, state and national legislation in the development and improvement of adult and community educational programs.

1972

2867 OASIS Rochester
c/o Monroe Community Hospital
435 E Henrietta Road
Rochester, NY 14620-4629
585-760-5440
Fax: 585-760-5439
e-mail: prisminster@hotmail.com
http://www.oasisnet.org/rochester/index.htm

Priscilla Minster, Director
Kay Wallick, Executive Director Corporate

OASIS is a national nonprofit educational organization designed to enhance the quality of life for mature adults. Offering challenging programs in the arts, humanities, wellness, technology and volunteer service, OASIS creates opportunities for older adults to continue their personal growth and provide meaningful service to the community. OASIS is nationally sponsored by Macy's Foundation.

2868 Pace Adult Resource Center
Pace University
1 Pace Plaza
Room B3w
New York, NY 10038-1502
212-346-1200
800-874-PACE
http://www.pace.edu

David A Caputo, CEO

2869 Professionals and Executives in Retirement
Hofstra University
250 Hofstra University
Hempstead, NY 11549
516-463-6919
Fax: 516-463-4833

Continuing Education/North Carolina

2870 Round Table at the School of Professional Development
Social and Behavioral Sciences Building
Room S-109
Stony Brook, NY 11794
631-632-7063
Fax: 631-632-9046
e-mail: janetmclean@notes.cc.synysb.edu
http://www.stonybrook.edu/spd/roundtable
Janet McLean, Director
Laura West, Secretary

The Round Table, a program within the School of Professional Development, is open to all retired and semi-retired individuals who are interested in expanding their intellectual horizons in a university setting.

2871 School of Education and Human Development Lyceum
State University of New York
PO Box 6000
Binghamton, NY 13902-6000
607-777-4447
Fax: 607-777-6041
Allison Alden, Director R&D
Callie Demtrak, Coordinator Lyceum

Explore art, music, literature, science, history, current events, health, nature and more through lectures and slides, discussions, field trips and hands-on experience; all taught by volunteer course leaders from the Lyceum membership, the community, and current and retired faculty from Binghamton University and Broome Community College. Join with like-minded classmates to explore new areas without the pressure of assignments or exams. A wide variety of courses is offered each year with two terms in the Fall, a Winter term (Cabin Fever Break) and two in the Spring. Since its founding in 1988, Lyceum has grown to over 400 members. In lyceum's first ten years 650 courses were taught by more that 300 volunteer course leaders. Membership is open to all men and women over 50 years and older.

2872 Studies for Mature Adults
Skidmore College
Saratoga Springs, NY 12866
518-580-5590
Fax: 518-580-5749

2873 Union College Academy for Lifelong Learning
807 Union Street
Schenectady, NY 12308-3103
518-388-6000
888-843-6688
Roger Hull, President

North Carolina

2874 AARP: North Carolina State Office
225 Hillsborough Street
Suite 440
Raleigh, NC 27603
866-389-5650
Fax: 919-755-9684
e-mail: ncaarp@aarp.org
http://www.aarp.org/states/nc
TTY 919-508-0290
Diana D Hatch, AARP NC State President
Robert Jackson, AARP NC State Director
Erik Olsen, AARP President Corporate Office

Resources for online classes, training and more. Topics include Computers/Technology, Health/Wellbeing, Personal Finance. AARP Membership open to individuals age 50+, benefits include access to insurance services, travel discounts, advice on healthy living, financial planning, consumer protection. AARP represents members on issues like Medicare, Social Security, and consumer safety. Publications include the AARP Magazine and AARP Bulletin.

2875 Bennett College
900 E Washington Street
Greensboro, NC 27401-3298
336-273-4431
800-413-5323
Fax: 336-378-0511
http://www.bennett.edu
Johnnetta B Cole PhD, President

Bennett College is a small, private, historically Black liberal arts college for women. The College offers women and education conducive in excellence in scholarly pursuits; preparation for leadership roles in the workplace, society, and the world; and life-long learning in technologically advanced, complex global society.

2876 Caswell Parish
PO Box 967
Yanceyville, NC 27379
336-694-6428
Fax: 336-694-1405
e-mail: caswellparishnc@person.net
http://www.caswellparish.org
Kimberly Lafreniere, Religious Leader

2877 Institute for Senior Scholars
Appalachian State University
PO Box 32042
Boone, NC 28608-2042
828-262-6690
Fax: 828-262-4992
e-mail: blckbrnch@appstate.edu
Caroline Blackburn, Director ISS

Year-round programs/activities in a lifelong learning program.

2878 LIFE
Mars Hill College
Mars Hill, NC 28754
828-689-1167
Fax: 828-689-1290
e-mail: cep@mhc.edu

2879 North Carolina Center for CreativeRetirement
1 University Heights
Asheville, NC 28804-3251
828-251-6140
Fax: 828-251-6803
http://www.anca.edu/nccr/
Tina Schwartz, Secretary

Has the threefold purpose of promoting lifelong learning, leadership, and community service opportunities for individuals 50 and over.

2880 Orange County Department on Aging: Saturday School for Senior Citizens
Durham Tecnical Community College
1637 E Lawson Street
Durham, NC 27703-5023
919-686-3350
Fax: 919-686-3346

2881 Osherlifelong Learning Institutet
Duke University
PO Box 90704
Durham, NC 27708
919-684-2703
Fax: 919-681-8235
e-mail: caf14@duke.edu
http://www.learnmore.duke.edu/olli
Catherine Frank, Director
Mary Edwartz, Assitant Director

An educational program offering noncredit liberal arts courses.

2882 Shepherd's Center of Greater Winston Salem
1700 Ebert Street
Winston Salem, NC 27103-4809
336-748-0217
Fax: 336-724-6545
e-mail: shepcntr@bellsouth.net
http://www.shepherdscenter.org
Cathy Wilson, Chair
Sam Matthews, Director
Kay Wallick, Executive Director Corporate

Continuing Education/North Dakota

The Shepherd's Center of Greater Winston-Salem is an interfaith ministry whose mission is to support and promote successful aging through educational, service, volunteer and support opportunities for older adults.

2883 Shepherd's Center of Kernersville
PO Box 2044
Kernersville, NC 27285
336-996-6696
Fax: 336-996-7064
e-mail: rwoosley@shepherdscenterkville.com
http://www.shepherdscenterkville.com
Jum Waddell, Chair
Ruth Woosley, Director
Kay Wallick, Executive Director Corporate

Individual centers partner with all faiths representing the diversity of their communities. The mission is to empower older adults to use their wisdom and skills for the good of their communities. Providing health enhancement, cultural enrichment and lifelong learning opportunities.

North Dakota

2884 AARP: North Dakota State Office
107 W Main Avenue
Suite 125
Bismarck, ND 58501
866-554-5383
Fax: 701-255-2242
e-mail: ndaarp@aarp.org
http://www.aarp.org/states/nd
Betty Keegan, AARP ND State President
Lyle Halvorson, AARP ND State Media Relations
Erik Olsen, AARP President Corporate Office

Resources for online classes, training and more. Topics include Computers/Technology, Health/Wellbeing, Personal Finance. AARP Membership open to individuals age 50+, benefits include access to insurance services, travel discounts, advice on healthy living, financial planning, consumer protection. AARP represents members on issues like Medicare, Social Security, and consumer safety. Publications include the AARP Magazine and AARP Bulletin.

Ohio

2885 AARP: Ohio State Office
17 S High Street
Suite 800
Columbus, OH 43215-3467
866-389-5653
Fax: 614-224-9801
e-mail: ohaarp@aarp.org
http://www.aarp.org/states/oh
Joanne Limbach, AARP Ohio State President
Jane L Taylor, AARP Ohio State Director
Erik Olsen, AARP President Corporate Office

Resources for online classes, training and more. Topics include Computers/Technology, Health/Wellbeing, Personal Finance. AARP Membership open to individuals age 50+, benefits include access to insurance services, travel discounts, advice on healthy living, financial planning, consumer protection. AARP represents members on issues like Medicare, Social Security, and consumer safety. Publications include the AARP Magazine and AARP Bulletin.

2886 EHOVE Ghirst Adult Career Center
316 West Mason Road
Milan, OH 44846
419-499-4663
866-256-9707
Fax: 419-499-5391
http://www.ehove-jvs.k12.oh.us
Greg Edinger, Principal
John Brown, Director Adult Education

Individuals concerned w/public awareness and the quality of adult vocational education. Maintains an annual meeting, forums and publications.
1978

2887 OASIS Akron
c/o Franklin Elementary School
200 Takacs Drive
Wadsworth, OH 44281
330-335-1470
Fax: 330-335-1468
e-mail: rhavens@wadsworth.k12.oh.us
http://www.oasisnet.org
Roger Havens, Director
Kay Wallick, Executive Director Corporate

OASIS is a national nonprofit educational organization designed to enhance the quality of life for mature adults. Offering challenging programs in the arts, humanities, wellness, technology and volunteer service, OASIS creates opportunities for older adults to continue their personal growth and provide meaningful service to the community. OASIS is nationally sponsored by Macy's Foundation.

2888 OASIS Cleveland
c/o Macy's
8001 Ridgewood Drive
Parma, OH 44129
440-886-1157
Fax: 440-886-1194
e-mail: dsavage@oasisnet.org
http://www.oasisnet.org/cleveland/index.htm
Diane Savage, Director
Kay Wallick, Executive Director Corporate

OASIS is a national nonprofit educational organization designed to enhance the quality of life for mature adults. Offering challenging programs in the arts, humanities, wellness, technology and volunteer service, OASIS creates opportunities for older adults to continue their personal growth and provide meaningful service to the community. OASIS is nationally sponsored by Macy's Foundation.

2889 Program Sixty
Ohio State University
Mount Hall
1050 Carmack Road
Columbus, OH 43210
614-292-8860
Fax: 614-292-0492
http://www.continuinged.ohio.state.edu
Anthony Basil, PhD, Director
Trey-Tyler Harte, Assistant PR/Communications

The Ohio State University of Continuing Education (CEd) is committed to offering diverse, quality programs and services that create a desire for lifelong learning. One of those programs is Program 60, which is adminstered by CEd. Program 60 (P60) is a unique opportunity for Ohio's older citizens to take courses at the Ohio State University for free. Individuals are welcome to participate in P60 if they are residents of the state of Ohio and 60 years of age or older.

2890 Senior Adult Education Center for Applied Gerontology
4250 Richmond Road
Highland Hills, OH 44122-6104
216-987-2274
Fax: 216-987-2053

2891 Senior Scholars
Western Reserve University
10900 Euclid Avenue
Cleveland, OH 44106-1712
216-368-2090
Fax: 216-368-1861
Kathy Manos, Director

Academic program for men and women age 50 and older. The program is designed for those who seek college-level work and intellectual stimulation but do not want or need academic credit. Offers an intersession and three 11-week seminars each semester. All programs are faculty led. Members may participate in all or part of each semester's program.

Continuing Education/Oklahoma

2892 **Shepherd's Center of Fostoria**
900 Van Buren Street
Fostoria, OH 44830-1544
419-691-5815
Fax: 419-693-6612

Oklahoma

2893 **AARP: Oklahoma-Edmond Office**
126 N Bryant Avenue
Edmond, OK 73034
866-295-7277
Fax: 405-844-7772
e-mail: ok@aarp.org
http://www.aarp.org/states/ok

Robert Bristow, AARP OK Volunteer President
Nancy Coffer, AARP OK State Director
Erik Olsen, AARP President Corporate Office

Resources for online classes, training and more. Topics include Computers/Technology, Health/Wellbeing, Personal Finance. AARP Membership open to individuals age 50+, benefits include access to insurance services, travel discounts, advice on healthy living, financial planning, consumer protection. AARP represents members on issues like Medicare, Social Security, and consumer safety. Publications include the AARP Magazine and AARP Bulletin.

2894 **AARP: Oklahoma-Oklahoma CityInformation Center**
Crossroads Mall
7000 Crossroads Boulevard
Suite 2055
Oklahoma City, OK 73149
405-632-1945
Fax: 405-632-1955
e-mail: ok@aarp.org
http://www.aarp.org/states/ok

Robert Bristow, AARP OK Volunteer President
Nancy Coffer, AARP OK State Director
Erik Olsen, AARP President Corporate Office

Resources for online classes, training and more. Topics include Computers/Technology, Health/Wellbeing, Personal Finance. AARP Membership open to individuals age 50+, benefits include access to insurance services, travel discounts, advice on healthy living, financial planning, consumer protection. AARP represents members on issues like Medicare, Social Security, and consumer safety. Publications include the AARP Magazine and AARP Bulletin.

2895 **AARP: Oklahoma-Oklahoma City Office**
7000 Crossroads Boulevard
Oklahoma City, OK 73149
405-632-1945
Fax: 405-632-1955
e-mail: ok@aarp.org
http://www.aarp.org/states/ok

Robert Bristow, AARP OK Volunteer President
Nancy Coffer, AARP OK State Director
Erik Olsen, AARP President Corporate Office

Resources for online classes, training and more. Topics include Computers/Technology, Health/Wellbeing, Personal Finance. AARP Membership open to individuals age 50+, benefits include access to insurance services, travel discounts, advice on healthy living, financial planning, consumer protection. AARP represents members on issues like Medicare, Social Security, and consumer safety. Publications include the AARP Magazine and AARP Bulletin.

2896 **Oklahoma School for the Blind**
3300 Gibson Street
Muskogee, OK 74403
918-781-8200
877-229-7136
Fax: 918-781-8300
e-mail: osb@ok.azalea.net
http://www.osb.k12.ok.us

Stephen Kearney, Executive Officer

Our school's purpose is to meet the educational needs of blind and visually impaired students who are residents of the state by providing a program to help students reach their maximum potential.

Oregon

2897 **AARP: Oregon State Office**
9200 SE Sunnybrook Boulevard
Suite 410
Clackamas, OR 97015-5762
866-554-5360
Fax: 503-652-9933
e-mail: oraarp@aarp.org
http://www.aarp.org/states/or

Ray Miao, AARP Oregon State President
Sara Wurfel, AARP Oregon State Media Rep
Erik Olsen, AARP President Corporate Office

Resources for online classes, training and more. Topics include Computers/Technology, Health/Wellbeing, Personal Finance. AARP Membership open to individuals age 50+, benefits include access to insurance services, travel discounts, advice on healthy living, financial planning, consumer protection. AARP represents members on issues like Medicare, Social Security, and consumer safety. Publications include the AARP Magazine and AARP Bulletin.

2898 **OASIS Eugene**
c/o Macy's
100 Valley River Center
Eugene, OR 97401
541-342-6611
Fax: 541-342-5187
e-mail: eschmidt@peacehealth.org
http://www.oasisnet.org/eugene/index.htm

Elizabeth Scholze Schmidt, Director
Shirley Kirkpatrick, Volunteer Program Manager
Kay Wallick, Executive Director Corporate

OASIS is a national nonprofit educational organization designed to enhance the quality of life for mature adults. Offering challenging programs in the arts, humanities, wellness, technology and volunteer service, OASIS creates opportunities for older adults to continue their personal growth and provide meaningful service to the community. OASIS is nationally sponsored by Macy's Foundation.

2899 **OASIS Portland**
c/o Macy's
621 SW Fifth Avenue
Fourth Floor
Portland, OR 97204
503-241-3059
Fax: 503-241-3068
e-mail: rcostic@lhs.org.
http://www.oasisnet.org/portland/index.htm

Robin Costic, Director
Jane Griffin, Program Coordinator
Kay Wallick, Executive Director Corporate

OASIS is a national nonprofit educational organization designed to enhance the quality of life for mature adults. Offering challenging programs in the arts, humanities, wellness, technology and volunteer service, OASIS creates opportunities for older adults to continue their personal growth and provide meaningful service to the community. OASIS is nationally sponsored by Macy's Foundation.

2900 **Senior Adult Learning Center**
PO Box 751
Portland, OR 97207
503-725-4739
Fax: 503-725-5100
http://www.upa.pdr.edu/ioa/salc

Dr Arezu Movahed, Director

Tuition free University, class adult program for Oregon Seniors 65 and over and a member shiporganization for anyone who is 50 years or older.

Continuing Education/Pennsylvania

2901 **Senior Venture**
Southern Oregon University
1250 Siskiyou Boulevard
Ashland, OR 97520
541-552-6378
800-257-0577
Fax: 541-552-6285
e-mail: siskiyoucenter@sou.edu
http://www.sou.edu/siskiyoucenter/seniorventure

Elisabeth Zinser, President
Earl Potter, EVP/Provost

Senior Ventures is a program of educational adventures combining lively classess with recreation and travel for active, life-long learners.

Pennsylvania

2902 **AARP: Pennsylvania-Harrisburg Office**
30 N 3rd Street
Suite 750
Harrisburg, PA 17101
866-389-5654
Fax: 717-236-4078
e-mail: pa@aarp.org
http://www.aarp.org/states/pa

J Shane Creamer, AARP PA State President
Steve Gardner, AARP PA Harrisburg Media Rep
Erik Olsen, AARP President Corporate Office

Resources for online classes, training and more. Topics include Computers/Technology, Health/Wellbeing, Personal Finance. AARP Membership open to individuals age 50+, benefits include access to insurance services, travel discounts, advice on healthy living, financial planning, consumer protection. AARP represents members on issues like Medicare, Social Security, and consumer safety. Publications include the AARP Magazine and AARP Bulletin.

2903 **AARP: Pennsylvania-Philadelphia Office**
1650 Market Street
Suite 675
Philadelphia, PA 19103
866-389-5654
Fax: 215-665-8529
e-mail: pa@aarp.org
http://www.aarp.org/states/pa

J Shane Creamer, AARP PA State President
Angela Foreshaw, AARP PA Philadelphia Media Rep
Erik Olsen, AARP President Corporate Office

Resources for online classes, training and more. Topics include Computers/Technology, Health/Wellbeing, Personal Finance. AARP Membership open to individuals age 50+, benefits include access to insurance services, travel discounts, advice on healthy living, financial planning, consumer protection. AARP represents members on issues like Medicare, Social Security, and consumer safety. Publications include the AARP Magazine and AARP Bulletin.

2904 **Center for Learning in Retirement**
700 E Butler Avenue
Doylestown, PA 18901-2607
215-345-1500
Fax: 215-345-5277

Thomas Leamer, President

Wide variety of educational classes taught by peers, instructors, and guest speakers

2905 **Center for Lifelong Learning**
Cedar Crest College
100 College Drive
Allentown, PA 18104-6132
610-740-3770
800-360-1222
Fax: 610-740-3786
e-mail: lifelong@cedarcrest.edu
http://www.cedarcrest.edu

Nancy Hollinger, Director
Michael Yergey, Assistant Director/Admissions
Michele Potts, Admissions Representative

Basic educational courses for senior citizens

2906 **Community Scholars Program**
450 S Easton Road
Glenside, PA 19038-3215
215-572-2914
Fax: 215-881-8787

2907 **Institute for Retired Persons**
Wilson College
1015 Philadelphia Avenue
Chambersburg, PA 17201-1279
717-264-4141
Fax: 717-264-1578

Clifford J Miller, Director
Kathleen Murphy, Manager

College level course for senior citizens

2908 **Northampton County Area Community College**
3835 Green Pond Road
Bethlehem, PA 18020-7599
610-861-5300
Fax: 610-861-5070
http://www.northampton.edu

Art Scott EdD MEd, President
Tamara Tucker, Assistant to President

Northampton Community College strives to prepare members of its community with the knowledge and critical skills they need to adapt to challenges in life and employment.

2909 **OASIS Pittsburgh**
c/o Macy's
400 Fifth Avenue, 10th Floor
Pittsburgh, PA 15219-1713
412-232-2020
Fax: 412-566-0528
e-mail: gweisberg@oasisnet.org
http://oasisnet.org/pittsburgh/index.htm

Gail Weisberg, Director
Shirley Fisher, Health Stage Manager
Kay Wallick, Executive Director Corporate

OASIS is a national nonprofit educational organization designed to enhance the quality of life for mature adults. Offering challenging programs in the arts, humanities, wellness, technology and volunteer service, OASIS creates opportunities for older adults to continue their personal growth and provide meaningful service to the community. OASIS is nationally sponsored by Macy's Foundation.

2910 **School of Living**
215 Julian Woods Lane
Julian, PA 16844-8617
814-353-0130
Fax: 814-353-0130
e-mail: office@schoolofliving.org
http://www.schoolofliving.org

Ann Wilken, Office Manager

Provides philosophy based adult education, focusing on homesteading, permaculture, and community land trusts

1934

2911 **Temple Association for Retired Persons**
1616 Walnut Street
Suite 600
Philadelphia, PA 19103-5306
215-204-1505
Fax: 215-204-5813
e-mail: rquinno@astro.temple.edu
http://www.temple.edu

Monica Robinson, Secretary
Amelio Gighetti, President

TARP is a membership organization open to all retired men and women who want the challenge of intellectual learning without traditional academic requirements. Classes and all social activities are held during the day in the center of Philadelphia.toric sites.

Continuing Education/Rhode Island

Rhode Island

2912 AARP: Rhode Island State Office
10 Orms Street
Suite 200
Providence, RI 02904
866-542-8170
Fax: 401-272-0876
e-mail: ri@aarp.org
http://www.aarp.org/states/ri

Anthony J Regine, AARP RI Volunteer President
Kathleen S Connell, AARP RI State Director
Erik Olsen, AARP President Corporate Office

Resources for online classes, training and more. Topics include Computers/Technology, Health/Wellbeing, Personal Finance. AARP Membership open to individuals age 50+, benefits include access to insurance services, travel discounts, advice on healthy living, financial planning, consumer protection. AARP represents members on issues like Medicare, Social Security, and consumer safety. Publications include the AARP Magazine and AARP Bulletin.

2913 Brown Community for Learning in Retirement
Brown University
Alumnae Hall
Box 959
Providence, RI 02912
401-274-3990
Fax: 401-863-1121

Ted Brown, President

South Carolina

2914 AARP: South Carolina State Office
SouthTrust Tower
1201 Main Street, Suite 1280
Columbia, SC 29201
866-389-5655
Fax: 803-251-4374
e-mail: scaarp@aarp.org
http://www.aarp.org/states/sc

Charles A Johnson, AARP SC State President
Patrick Cobb, AARP SC Media Relations Rep
Erik Olsen, AARP President Corporate Office

Resources for online classes, training and more. Topics include Computers/Technology, Health/Wellbeing, Personal Finance. AARP Membership open to individuals age 50+, benefits include access to insurance services, travel discounts, advice on healthy living, financial planning, consumer protection. AARP represents members on issues like Medicare, Social Security, and consumer safety. Publications include the AARP Magazine and AARP Bulletin

2915 Shepherd's Center of Columbia
St. John's Episcopal Church
3401 Trenholm Road
Columbia, SC 29204-3336
803-779-4449
e-mail: shepherdscent626@bellsouth.net
http://www.shepherdcenters.org/columbia.aspx

Dottie Boatwright, Chair
Dorcas Giles, Director
Kay Wallick, Executive Director Corporate

Individual centers partner with all faiths representing the diversity of their communities. The mission is to empower older adults to use their wisdom and skills for the good of their communities. Providing health enhancement, cultural enrichment and lifelong learning opportunities.

2916 Shepherd's Center of Rock Hill
PO Box 3046
Rock Hill, SC 29732-5046
803-328-1343
Fax: 803-238-3281
e-mail: rhsc@comporium.net
http://www.shepherdscenterrh.org

Carol Butler, Director
Kay Wallick, Executive Director Corporate

Individual centers partner with all faiths representing the diversity of their communities. The mission is to empower older adults to use their wisdom and skills for the good of their communities. Providing health enhancement, cultural enrichment and lifelong learning opportunities.

2917 Shepherd's Center of Spartanburg
393 W Main Street
Spartanburg, SC 29302-1917
864-585-1999
Fax: 864-597-1711
e-mail: hurt106@bellsouth.net
http://www.shepherdcenters.org

Linda Hurteau, Director
Marc Wall, Chair
Kay Wallick, Executive Director Corporate

Individual centers partner with all faiths representing the diversity of their communities. The mission is to empower older adults to use their wisdom and skills for the good of their communities. Providing health enhancement, cultural enrichment and lifelong learning opportunities.

2918 Shepherd's Center of Sumter
PO Box 2301
Sumter, SC 29150-5110
803-773-1944
e-mail: staff@shepherdcenters.org
http://www.shepherdcenters.org

Rebecca Wetherby, Director
Maxine Taylor, Chair
Kay Wallick, Executive Director Corporate

Individual centers partner with all faiths representing the diversity of their communities. The mission is to empower older adults to use their wisdom and skills for the good of their communities. Providing health enhancement, cultural enrichment and lifelong learning opportunities.

South Dakota

2919 AARP: South Dakota-Rapid City Office
Rushmore Mall
2200 N Maple Avenue
Rapid City, SD 57701
605-394-7798
Fax: 605-394-7727
e-mail: sdaarp@aarp.org
http://www.aarp.org/states/sd

Patrick Gross, AARP SD State President
Sarah Jennings, AARP SD State Director
Erik Olsen, AARP President Corporate Office

Resources for online classes, training and more. Topics include Computers/Technology, Health/Wellbeing, Personal Finance. AARP Membership open to individuals age 50+, benefits include access to insurance services, travel discounts, advice on healthy living, financial planning, consumer protection. AARP represents members on issues like Medicare, Social Security, and consumer safety. Publications include the AARP Magazine and AARP Bulletin.

2920 AARP: South Dakota-Sioux Falls Office
5101 S Nevada Avenue
Suite 150
Sioux Falls, SD 57108
866-542-8172
Fax: 605-361-2323
e-mail: sdaarp@aarp.org
http://www.aarp.org/states/sd

Patrick Gross, AARP SD State President
Sarah Jennings, AARP SD State Director
Erik Olsen, AARP President Corporate Office

Continuing Education/Tennessee

Resources for online classes, training and more. Topics include Computers/Technology, Health/Wellbeing, Personal Finance. AARP Membership open to individuals, benefits include access to insurance services, travel discounts, advice on healthy living, financial planning, consumer protection. AARP represents members on issues like Medicare, Social Security, and consumer safety. Publications include the AARP Magazine and AARP Bulletin.

Tennessee

2921 **AARP: Tennessee State Office**
150 4th Avenue N
Suite 180
Nashville, TN 37219
866-295-7274
Fax: 615-313-8414
e-mail: tnaarp@aarp.org
http://www.aarp.org/states/tn
Margot Seay, AARP TN State President
Rebecca Kelly, AARP TN State Director
Erik Olsen, AARP President Corporate Office

Resources for online classes, training and more. Topics include Computers/Technology, Health/Wellbeing, Personal Finance. AARP Membership open to individuals age 50+, benefits include access to insurance services, travel discounts, advice on healthy living, financial planning, consumer protection. AARP represents members on issues like Medicare, Social Security, and consumer safety. Publications include the AARP Magazine and AARP Bulletin.

2922 **Shepherd's Center of Madison**
105 S Perkins Road
PO Box 1243
Madison, TN 37116
615-870-0770
e-mail: staff@shepherdcenters.org
http://www.shepherdcenters.orG
Barbara Hamishfeger, Director
Bitsey Riegle, Chair
Kay Wallick, Executive Director Corporate

Individual centers partner with all faiths representing the diversity of their communities. The mission is to empower older adults to use their wisdom and skills for the good of their communities. Providing health enhancement, cultural enrichment and lifelong learning opportunities.

Texas

2923 **AARP: Texas-Austin Office**
98 San Jacinto Boulevard
Suite 750
Austin, TX 78701
866-227-7443
Fax: 512-480-9799
e-mail: txaarp@aarp.org
http://www.aarp.org/states/tx
Gus Cardenas, AARP Texas Volunteer President
Bob Jackson, AARP Texas State Director
Erik Olsen, AARP President Corporate Office

Resources for online classes, training and more. Topics include Computers/Technology, Health/Wellbeing, Personal Finance. AARP Membership open to individuals age 50+, benefits include access to insurance services, travel discounts, advice on healthy living, financial planning, consumer protection. AARP represents members on issues like Medicare, Social Security, and consumer safety. Publications include the AARP Magazine and AARP Bulletin.

2924 **AARP: Texas-Dallas Office**
8144 Walnut Hill Lane
Suite 700
Dallas, TX 75231
214-265-4078
e-mail: txaarp@aarp.org
http://www.aarp.org/states/tx
Gus Cardenas, AARP Texas Volunteer President
Bob Jackson, AARP Texas State Director
Erik Olsen, AARP President Corporate Office

Resources for online classes, training and more. Topics include Computers/Technology, Health/Wellbeing, Personal Finance. AARP Membership open to individuals age 50+, benefits include access to insurance services, travel discounts, advice on healthy living, financial planning, consumer protection. AARP represents members on issues like Medicare, Social Security, and consumer safety. Publications include the AARP Magazine and AARP Bulletin.

2925 **AARP: Texas-Houston Office**
2323 S Shepherd
#1100
Houston, TX 77019
832-325-2205
Fax: 832-325-2213
e-mail: txaarp@aarp.org
http://www.aarp.org/states/tx
Gus Cardenas, AARP Texas Volunteer President
Bob Jackson, AARP Texas State Director
Erik Olsen, AARP President Corporate Office

Resources for online classes, training and more. Topics include Computers/Technology, Health/Wellbeing, Personal Finance. AARP Membership open to individuals age 50+, benefits include access to insurance services, travel discounts, advice on healthy living, financial planning, consumer protection. AARP represents members on issues like Medicare, Social Security, and consumer safety. Publications include the AARP Magazine and AARP Bulletin.

2926 **Learning Activities for Mature People**
University of Texas-Austin
One University Station
PO Box 7879
Austin, TX 78712-7879
512-471-3723
Fax: 512-471-1651
http://www.austin-utexas.edu

Learning Activities for Mature People offers 36 large group lectures, one study seminar, one member-presented lecture per each six-week term; there are three time per year (fall, winter and spring). Membership is limited to 500, and members may attend any or all of the presentations; each presentation lasts an hour.

2927 **OASIS Houston**
c/o Macy's
100 Northwest Mall, 2nd Floor
Houston, TX 77092-8533
713-957-2968
e-mail: mgmatz@sbcglobal.net
http://www.oasisnet.org/houston/index.htm
Marlene Matzner, Director
Jackie Brokenbourgh, Assistant
Kay Wallick, Executive Director Corporate.

OASIS is a national nonprofit educational organization designed to enhance the quality of life for mature adults. Offering challenging programs in the arts, humanities, wellness, technology and volunteer service, OASIS creates opportunities for older adults to continue their personal growth and provide meaningful service to the community. OASIS is nationally sponsored by Macy's Foundation.

2928 **OASIS San Antonio**
c/o Macy's
6161 NW Loop 410
San Antonio, TX 78238
210-647-2546
Fax: 210-647-2432
e-mail: bschmachtenberger@oasisnet.org
http://www.oasisnet.org/sanantonio/index.htm
Brenda Schmachtenberg, Director
Tracy Slate, Active for Life Coordinator
Kay Wallick, Executive Director Corporate

Continuing Education/Utah

OASIS is a national nonprofit educational organization designed to enhance the quality of life for mature adults. Offering challenging programs in the arts, humanities, wellness, technology and volunteer service, OASIS creates opportunities for older adults to continue their personal growth and provide meaningful service to the community. OASIS is nationally sponsored by Macy's Foundation.

2929 SAVE Senior Avocational/Vocational Education
Grayson County College
6101 Grayson Drive
Highway 691
Denison, TX 75020
903-463-8669
Fax: 903-463-8644
e-mail: rdecento@cwlgoc.org
http://www.cwlgoc.org

Alan Scheibmeir, President
Ron DeCento, Director Continuing Education
Shelle Cassell, Dir Marketing/Public Information

SAVE representatives will be on-hand to answer questions and collect ideas for additional courses that may have broad interest for the 50+ year old citizens of the area.

2930 Senior Citizens Educational Program
Del Mar College
101 Baldwin Boulevard
Corpus Christi, TX 78404
361-698-1298
Fax: 361-698-1092
http://www.delmar.edu/

Pam Pudelka, Coord Senior Citizens Program

The Senior Citizens Educational Program encourages lifetime learning for older adults. The Del Mar College offers courses to seniors 65 or older, tuition free.

Utah

2931 AARP: Utah State Office
6975 Union Park Center
Suite 320
Midvale, UT 84047
866-448-3616
Fax: 801-561-2209
e-mail: utaarp@aarp.org
http://www.aarp.org/states/ut

Pat Gamble Hovey, AARP Utah Volunteer President
Kate Fielder, AARP Utah Media Relations Rep
Erik Olsen, AARP President Corporate Office

Resources for online classes, training and more. Topics include Computers/Technology, Health/Wellbeing, Personal Finance. AARP Membership open to individuals age 50+, benefits include access to insurance services, travel discounts, advice on healthy living, financial planning, consumer protection. AARP represents members on issues like Medicare, Social Security, and consumer safety. Publications include the AARP Magazine and AARP Bulletin.

Vermont

2932 AARP: Vermont State Office
112 State Street
5th Floor
Montpelier, VT 05602
866-227-7451
Fax: 802-224-9057
e-mail: vtaarp@aarp.org
http://www.aarp.org/states/vt

Nancy Lang, AARP VT Volunteer President
Jennifer Wallace Brodeur, AARP VT Acting State Director
Erik Olsen, AARP President Corporate Office

Resources for online classes, training and more. Topics include Computers/Technology, Health/Wellbeing, Personal Finance. AARP Membership open to individuals age 50+, benefits include access to insurance services, travel discounts, advice on healthy living, financial planning, consumer protection. AARP represents members on issues like Medicare, Social Security, and consumer safety. Publications include the AARP Magazine and AARP Bulletin.

Virginia

2933 AARP: Virginia State Office
707 E Main Street
Suite 910
Richmond, VA 23219
866-542-8164
Fax: 804-819-1923
e-mail: vaaarp@aarp.org
http://www.aarp.org/states/va

Warren Stewart, AARP VA Volunteer President
Bill Kallio, AARP VA State Director
Erik Olsen, AARP President Corporate Office

Resources for online classes, training and more. Topics include Computers/Technology, Health/Wellbeing, Personal Finance. AARP Membership open to individuals age 50+, benefits include access to insurance services, travel discounts, advice on healthy living, financial planning, consumer protection. AARP represents members on issues like Medicare, Social Security, and consumer safety. Publications include the AARP Magazine and AARP Bulletin.

2934 Elderscholar
Roanoke College
221 College Lane
Salem, VA 24153-3747
540-375-2323
Fax: 540-375-2092
e-mail: esworthy@roanoke.edu

Stephen A Esworthy, Director

Elderscholar is a educational program designed for seniors to allow them the opportunity to commute to campus on a regular basis for challenging academic programs. Offerings include six-week lecture series programs and book review programs.

2935 Environmental Alliance for Senior Involvement
5615 26th Street N
Arlington, VA 22207-1407
540-788-3274
Fax: 703-538-5504
e-mail: easi@easi.org
http://www.easi.org

Thomas P Benjamin, President

Is the largest senior enviromental action network in the world used to coordinate seniors as volunteers within their own communities, for enviromental and other good works.
1991

2936 Free University for Senior Citizens: Tuition Waver Program
827 W Franklin Street
Richmond, VA 23284-9077
804-828-1831
Fax: 804-828-8172

Catherine Howard, Executive Director

2937 Lifelong Learning Society
12420 Warwick Boulevard
Bldg 6
Newport News, VA 23606-3001
757-594-7568
Fax: 757-594-8736

Learning in retirement, affiliate of the Elderhostel Institute Network.

Continuing Education/Washington

2938 Shepherd's Center of Richmond
4900 Augusta Avenue
Suite 102
Richmond, VA 23230-3611
804-355-7282
Fax: 804-355-9856
e-mail: frankl.sc@cavtel.net
http://www.richmondshepcntr.org

Linda Frank, Director
Betty Ann Dillon, Chair
Kay Wallick, Executive Director Corporate

Individual centers partner with all faiths representing the diversity of their communities. The mission is to empower older adults to use their wisdom and skills for the good of their communities. Providing health enhancement, cultural enrichment and lifelong learning opportunities.

Washington

2939 AARP: Washington State Office
9750 3rd Avenue NE
Suite 450
Seattle, WA 98115
866-227-7457
Fax: 206-517-9350
e-mail: wa@aarp.org
http://www.aarp.org/states/wa

Art Cruz, AARP WA State President
Doug Shadel, AARP WA State Director
Erik Olsen, AARP President Corporate Office

Resources for online classes, training and more. Topics include Computers/Technology, Health/Wellbeing, Personal Finance. AARP Membership open to individuals age 50+, benefits include access to insurance services, travel discounts, advice on healthy living, financial planning, consumer protection. AARP represents members on issues like Medicare, Social Security, and consumer safety. Publications include the AARP Magazine and AARP Bulletin.

2940 Center for Lifelong Learning
Central Washington University
400 E 8th Avenue
Ellensburg, WA 98926-7502
509-963-1504
800-752-4380
Fax: 509-963-1690

Marjorie Anderson, Director Senior Programs
Barbara Cook, Program Assistant
Kelly Lathrop, Office Assistant

Senior Ventures offers learning vacations at Central Washington University at the Ellensburg campus. Two 3-week sessions feature over 30 non-credit classes each session. One package price includes housing with private bath, meals, classes, field trips, and activities.

2941 Elderwise
611 17th Avenue E
Seattle, WA 98112-3919
206-325-0471
e-mail: sandy@elderwise.org
http://www.elderwise.org

Sandy Sabersky, President

Cultural and artistic enrichment program designed to promote healthy aging for seniors through a multi-faceted venue based on respect for the wisdom of elders. Aims to improve the quality of life of seniors in Seattle, helping to enhance and prolong the independence of this under-served population by providing healthy food, exercise, and intellectual and creative stimulation in a respectful, non-institutional environment.

2942 Focus on Mature Learning
Clark College
1800 E McLoughlin Boulevard
Vancouver, WA 98663-3509
360-992-2213
Fax: 360-992-2868

2943 Lifetime Learning Center of Seattle
160 John Street
Seattle, WA 98109-4922
206-985-3904

2944 Senior Adult Education
South Seattle Community College
6000 16th Avenue SW
Seattle, WA 98106-1401
206-764-5300
Fax: 206-764-5807

2945 Seniors Program Institute for Extended Learning
Spokane Falls Community College
3305 W Fort George Wright Drive
MS 3090
Spokane, WA 99224-5228
509-279-6003
800-845-3324
Fax: 509-533-3226
http://www.iel.spokane.edu

S James Perez PhD, Executive Vice President
Dixie L Simmons EdD, VP Learning
Adrienne J Taber, Dean of Students

The program offers a wide variety of non-credit courses designed specifically for seniors 55 years and older at senior centers, retirement housing, churches, other public locations, and community college campuses. Tuition ranges from $5 to $33 per course, depending on the total number of hours over the quarter (11 weeks). Explore art, history, w writing, computers, fitness, foreign language and more. Cost is $5 - $33 a quarter for courses.

West Virginia

2946 AARP: West Virginia State Office
300 Summers Street
Suite 400
Charleston, WV 25301
866-227-7458
Fax: 304-344-4633
e-mail: wvaarp@aarp.org
http://www.aarp.org/states/wv

Ruth Wagner, AARP WV Volunteer President
Frank Bellinetti, AARP WV State Director
Erik Olsen, AARP President Corporate Office

Resources for online classes, training and more. Topics include Computers/Technology, Health/Wellbeing, Personal Finance. AARP Membership open to individuals age 50+, benefits include access to insurance services, travel discounts, advice on healthy living, financial planning, consumer protection. AARP represents members on issues like Medicare, Social Security, and consumer safety. Publications include the AARP Magazine and AARP Bulletin.

2947 Shepherd's Center of Beekley
203 Kanawha Street
Beckley, WV 25801
304-252-6289
Fax: 304-252-5574

Bernard Hurtte, Director
Gladys Terry, Chair
Adrian Pratt, Religious Leader

Continuing Education/Wisconsin

Wisconsin

2948   AARP: Wisconsin State Office
222 W Washington Avenue
Suite 600
Madison, WI 53703

866-448-3611
Fax: 608-251-7612
e-mail: wistate@aarp.org
http://www.aarp.org/states/wi

Patricia Finder Stone, AARP WI Volunteer President
D'Anna Bowman, AARP WI State Director
Erik Olsen, AARP President Corporate Office

Resources for online classes, training and more. Topics include Computers/Technology, Health/Wellbeing, Personal Finance. AARP Membership open to individuals age 50+, benefits include access to insurance services, travel discounts, advice on healthy living, financial planning, consumer protection. AARP represents members on issues like Medicare, Social Security, and consumer safety. Publications include the AARP Magazine and AARP Bulletin.

2949   LaFarge Institute of Lifelong Learning
1501 S Layton Boulevard
Milwaukee, WI 53215-1924

414-383-2550
Fax: 414-385-6647

2950   University of Wisconsin Guild for Learning
University of Wisconsin-Milwaukee
PO Box 413
Milwaukee, WI 53201

414-229-1122
Fax: 414-227-3168

Wyoming

2951   AARP: Wyoming State Office
2020 Carey Avenue
Mezzanine
Cheyenne, WY 82001

866-663-3290
Fax: 307-634-3808
e-mail: wy@aarp.org
http://www.aarp.org/states/wy

Les Engelter, AARP WY Volunteer President
Rita Ingway, AARP WY State President
Erik Olsen, AARP President Corporate Office

Resources for online classes, training and more. Topics include Computers/Technology, Health/Wellbeing, Personal Finance. AARP Membership open to individuals age 50+, benefits include access to insurance services, travel discounts, advice on healthy living, financial planning, consumer protection. AARP represents members on issues like Medicare, Social Security, and consumer safety. Publications include the AARP Magazine and AARP Bulletin.

2952   Laramie Lyceum
University of Wyoming
PO Box 3972
Laramie, WY 82071-3972

307-766-6801
Fax: 307-766-3914

Disability Aids & Assistive Devices/Automobile

Automobile

2953 Adaptive Driving Conversions
156 E Commodore Boulevard
Jackson, NJ 08527-3018
908-928-2089
800-866-1529
Fax: 908-928-2449

Ted Jaeckrel
Ann Trainor

Vehicle modifications: automobile/vans/minibuses and driving aids for independent travel to include: hand controls, left gas pedals, foot pedals, wheelchair lifts and more. Serves New Jersey, New York, Pennsylvania and Delaware.

2954 Adaptive Vans for the Physically Challenged
Mobility Works
810 Moe Drive
Akron, OH 44310-2517
800-638-8267
Fax: 330-633-0330
e-mail: info@mobilityworks.com

Bill Koeblitz, President
Todd Slates, Sales Maanger
Frank Vitale, Client Advisor

Mobility Works builds adaptive vans for the disabled and their special needs. Adaptations include lowered floors, raised roofs, wheelchair lifts, custom interiors, custom exteriors, driving systems, power transfer seats, wheelchair tie downs, wheelchair ramps, remote entry systems, and rooftop wheelchair carriers for cars.

2955 Aeroquip Wheelchair Securement System
Kinedyne Corporation-Engineered Products Division
3701 Greenway Circle
Lawrence, KS 66046-5442
785-841-4000
800-848-6057
Fax: 785-841-3668
http://www.kinedyne.com

Hugh Lawrence, Plant Manager

Wheelchair users can have adaptable, safe, easily attached securement during transportation.

2956 Arcola Mobility
51 Kero Road
Carlstadt, NJ 07072-2604
201-507-8500
800-272-6521
Fax: 201-507-5372
e-mail: info@arcolasales.com
http://www.arcolamobility.com

Andrew Rolfe, President
John Akerlind, Controller

Arcola sells new and used accessible vehicles and adaptive driving equipment including hand controls, wheelchair lifts and securement systems. Daily, weekly and monthly vehicle rentals available. Stairway lift, porch elevators and ramps for the home sold and rented.

2957 Ball Bearing Spinner
Kroepke Kontrols
104 Hawkins Street
City Island
Bronx, NY 10464-1455
718-885-1100
Fax: 212-885-1110
e-mail: kkontrols@aol.com
http://www.kroepkekontrols.com

One lever fingertip control which is custom designed for each car but does not interfere with normal operation of your car and ball joints for perfect alignment.

2958 Blinker Buddy II Electronic Turn Signal
HARC Mercantile
1111 W Centre Avenue
Portage, MI 49024-5317
269-324-0301
800-445-9968
Fax: 269-324-2387
e-mail: home@hacofamerica.com
http://www.hacofamerica.com

Ronald Slager, President

Sounds a loud tone and flashes a light when the turn signal is on.

2959 Braun Mobility Products
PO Box 310
Winamac, IN 46996
800-843-5438
Fax: 800-946-6305
http://www.braunlift.com

Offers wheelchair lifts for vans and mobility products. The mission of The Braun Corporation is "providing access to the world." We believe we provide a valuable service to wheelchair users, scooter users, and others who need extra help to get around. By producing and supporting a wide range of automotive mobility products, we aim to fill the needs of customers with a broad spectrum of abilities and challenges.

2960 Care Concepts
3145 W Lewis Avenue
Phoenix, AZ 85009-1510
602-440-8272
800-322-1432
Fax: 602-272-5949
e-mail: minivans@care_concepts.com
http://www.care_concepts.com

Cheri R Sanchez, Sales Manager

Lowered floor, wheelchair accessible Chrysler or Ford Windstar minivans, featuring in-floor or fold-down ramp system, cable operated power door, electro-mechanical kneel and a wide range of adaptive equipment.

2961 Classic
Ricon
7900 Nelson Road
Panorama City, CA 91402-6090
818-267-3000
800-322-2884
Fax: 818-267-3001
e-mail: customerservice@riconcorp.com
http://www.riconcorp.com

William Baldwin, CEO

Ricon has 36 years of experience in the design manufacture and installation of wheelchair lifts and ramps for commercial paratransit, transit motorcoach and passenger rail vehicles. As a part of our strategic plan to meet the growing needs of the transit industry, Ricon is rapidly becoming a leading supplier of anti-graffiti transit windows. Operating from a modern 225,000 square foot facility located in LA, Ricon is the largest manufacturer of its kind in the world.

2962 Classic Coach Interiors
Classic Coach Interiors
1935 Burlington Avenue
Kewanee, IL 61443-8346
800-209-7225
Fax: 309-852-3463

George Giesenhagen, Manager

Offers van conversions with state-of-the-art equipment for the physically challenged.

2963 DW Auto & Home Mobility Specialties
1208 N Garth Avenue
Columbia, MO 65203-4056
573-449-3859
800-568-2271
Fax: 573-449-4187
e-mail: dwauto@dwauto.com
http://www.dwauto.com

Sheila Lynch, Business Manager
Darrell Whitmarsh, President
Shawn Bright, Owner

Disability Aids & Assistive Devices/Automobile

DW Auto is known throughout the industry as a leader in service and creativity. Darrell "DW" Whitmarsh's idea of catering to each individual person, and taking the time and extra effort to do so is what makes out company so successful.

2964 Drive-Master
37 Daniel Road
Fairfield, NJ 07004-2521
973-808-9709
Fax: 973-808-9713
e-mail: sales@drivemaster.net
http://www.drive-master.com

Peter B Ruprecht, President
Christina Ruprecht, Vice President
Shelby Wells, Sales Manager

Our team has over fifty years of experience desgning, installing, and servicing custom mobility solutions. Drive-Master has proven itself as an industry-leader in innovative solutions with unsurpassed quality. Our stat-of-the-art production facility allows us to quickly get you on the road. Drive-Master insalls and services all major brands of mobility products. We provide warranty repair, and tune-ups on all Drive-Master installed equipment.

2965 Dual Brake Control
Kroepke Kontrols
104 Hawkins Street
City Island
Bronx, NY 10464-1491
718-885-1100
Fax: 212-885-1110
e-mail: kkontrols@aol.com
http://www.kroepkekontrols.com

One lever fingertip brake controls, precision machines of the finest quality steel, are inconspicuous and do not take up lots of leg room.

2966 Dual Brakes Unit
Gresham Driving Aids
30800 Wixom Road
Wixom, MI 48393
248-624-1533
800-521-8930
Fax: 248-624-6358
e-mail: wixom@greshamdrivingaids.com
http://www.greshamdrivingaids.com

Bill Dillon, Owner

Manufacturers motor vehicle parts & accessories, manufactures industrial trucks & tractors and relays and industrial controls.

2967 EKA/ Health & Mobility Systems
9151 Hampton Overlook
Capitol Heights, MD 20743-3839
301-499-1000
800-835-2002
Fax: 301-499-5529

Denise Terribile, Sales

Mobility needs, van conversions, ramps and lifts, retail products, healthcare equipment and medical supplies, orthodontics and prosthetics, seating systems, augmentative communications, assistive technology, rehab and technical support services.

2968 Foot Steering
Drive Master Company
37 Daniel Road West
Fairfield, NJ 07004-3403
973-808-9709
Fax: 973-808-9713
e-mail: sales@drivemaster.net
http://www.drive-master.com

Peter B Ruprecht, President
Christina Ruprecht, Vice President
Shelby Wells, Sales Manager

For those customers without arms or the use of them, the foot steering system is usally combined with sensitzed steering and adaptations for other dash controls. Drive-Master understands that most items concerning foot controlled steering need to be customized according to individual needs.

2969 General Motors Mobility Program for Persons with Disabilities
GM Mobility Program
PO Box 5053
Troy, MI 48807
800-323-9935
http://www.gm.com/services/gm_mobility
TTY 800-833-9935

Percy N Barnevik, Chairman
Erskine B Bowles, President
John H Bryan, Chief Executive Officer

General Motors is committed to helping persons with disabilities equip their vehicles for easier and safer travel. Through the GM Mobility Reimbursement Program, new vehicle purchasers/lessors who install or reinstall eligible adaptive mobility equipment can receive a combination of financial assistance and the protection and convenience of OnStar. (Valid through 09/30/08)

2970 Gresham Driving Aids
30800 Wixom Road
Wixom, MI 48393
248-624-1533
800-521-8930
Fax: 248-624-6358
e-mail: wixom@greshamdrivingaids.com
http://www.greshamdrivingaids.com

Bill Dillon, Owner

Ofers a full-service package to physically challenged individuals including lowered floors, raised roofs and doors, and high-quad driver control systems. Dealer for Braun, Ricoh, Crow River and Bruno wheelchair lifts.

2971 Hand Brake Control Only
Kroepke Kontrols
104 Hawkins Street
City Island
Bronx, NY 10464-1455
718-885-1100
Fax: 718-885-1110
e-mail: kkontrols@aol.com
http://www.kroepkekontrols.com

One lever fingertip brake controls that are custom designed to fit each car, completely adjustable and offers positioning operation at your fingertips.

2972 Hand Gas & Brake Control
Kroepke Kontrols
104 Hawkins Street
City Island
Bronx, NY 10464-1455
718-885-1100
Fax: 718-885-1110
e-mail: kkontrols@aol.com
http://www.kroepkekontrols.com

Driving controls that are attached by a control level right on to the gas and brake pedals for easy maneuvering and convenience.

2973 Hand Parking Brake
Kroepke Kontrols
104 Hawkins Street
City Island
Bronx, NY 10464-1455
718-885-1100
Fax: 718-885-1110
e-mail: kkontrols@aol.com
http://www.kroepkekontrols.com

One lever fingertip brake controls for your car that offer easy instillment, complete adjustability, complete independence and more.

2974 Headlight Dimmer Switch
Kroepke Kontrols
104 Hawkins Street
City Island
Bronx, NY 10464-1455
718-885-1100
Fax: 718-885-1110
e-mail: kkontrols@aol.com
http://www.kroepkekontrols.com

One lever fingertip controls for the disabled driver.

Disability Aids & Assistive Devices/Automobile

2975 Horizontal Steering
Drive Master Company
37 Daniel Road W
Fairfield, NJ 07004-3403
973-808-9709
Fax: 973-808-9713
e-mail: sales@drivemaster.net
http://www.drivemaster.net

Peter Ruprecht, President
Christina Ruprecht, VP
Shelby Wells, Sales Manager

Horizontal steering system is customized to meet the needs of the high-level spinally injured and all others who experience limited arm strength and range of motion.

2976 Horn Control Switch
Kroepke Kontrols
104 Hawkins Street
City Island
Bronx, NY 10464-1455
718-885-1100
Fax: 212-885-1110
e-mail: kkontrols@aol.com
http://www.kroepkekontrols.com

One lever fingertip controls that do not interfere with the normal operation of your car.

2977 Institute for Driver Rehabilitation
494 West Country Line Road
Jackson, NJ 08527-3018
732-928-2088
800-866-1529
Fax: 732-928-2449

Debra Jackrel, President
Ted Jackrel, Program Director

Driver evaluation training for the physically/mentally challenged offering state certified driving instructors. Door-to-door pickup at home, work or rehab centers.

2978 Joystick Driving Control
Ahnafield Corporation
2444 Production Drive
Indianapolis, IN 46241
317-241-2444
800-636-8060
http://www.ahnafield.com

Jeff Ahnafield
Joe Kabat

Electronic microprocessor controlled hydraulic system specifically designed for persons with disabilities. It allows one-handed individuals and persons with impaired dexterity or limited and strength and range of motion to drive.

2979 Lazy Days RV Center
Lazy Days RV Center
6130 Lazy Days Boulevard
Seffner, FL 33584-2968
866-531-6820
800-500-5299
Fax: 866-246-4408
http://www.lazydays.com

Jack Graham, Contact
Don Wallace, President

Customized recreational vehicles for people with disabilities. Specializing in wheelchair accessible bathrooms.

2980 Left Foot Gas Pedal
Kroepke Kontrols
104 Hawkins Street
City Island
Bronx, NY 10464-1455
718-885-1100
Fax: 718-885-1110
e-mail: kkontrols@aol.com
http://www.kroepkekontrols.com

One lever fingertip controls that offer custom design, easy installment and complete freedom for the disabled driver.

2981 Low Effort and No Effort Braking
Drive Master Company
37 Daniel Road W
Fairfield, NJ 07004-3403
973-808-9709
Fax: 973-808-9713
e-mail: sales@drivemaster.com
http://www.drive-master.com

Peter B Ruprecht, President
Christina Ruprecht, Vice President
Shelby Wells, Sales Manager

Standard factory power breaks require 20 foot-pounds of pressure to operate. Drive-Master's low-effort modification reduces the required pressure to 11 foot-pounds. The no effort modification reduces the required pressure to 7 foot pounds (these statistics will vary slightly depending upon model of car or van.

2982 Low Effort and No Effort Steering
Drive Master Company
37 Daniel Road W
Fairfield, NJ 07004-3403
973-808-9709
Fax: 973-808-9713
e-mail: sales@drivemaster.com
http://www.drive-master.com

Peter B Ruprecht, President
Christina M Ruprecht, General Manager
J Shelby Wells, Sales Manager

Drive-Master's Reduced Effort Steering modification boxes and steering racks are availiable for all American vans and most cars with factory power steering. All factory power steering units sent to Drive-Master will be modified to low or no effort and return shipped within 24 hours. Standard factory power steering requires approximately 40 ounces of effort to operate. Drive-Master's steering modifications can reduce the effort to 20-24 ounces (low effort) or 6-8 ounces (no effort) These statistics will vary depending on model of car and tire size.

2983 Mac's Lift Gate
2715 Seaboard Lane
Long Beach, CA 90805-3751
562-634-5962
800-795-6227
Fax: 562-634-4291
e-mail: macslift@blvd.com
http://www.macsliftgate.com

Lawrence MacDonald, Owner
Richard MacDonald, President

Vertical home lifts for cars and vans, new vans, conversions, scooters, and scooter lifts.

2984 Mednet Ketronic Inc.
Mednet Ketronic Inc.
555 Industrial Park Drive
Battle Creek, MI 49015-1146
616-962-3800
Fax: 616-962-8841

Offers the ultimate van conversions with equipment that is easily installed and accessible for the physically challenged.

2985 Mini-Bus and Mini-Vans
Arcola Bus Sales
51 Kero Road
Carlstadt, NJ 07072-2601
201-507-8500
800-272-6521
Fax: 201-507-5372
e-mail: info@arcolasales.com
http://www.arcolamobility.com

Tony Perez, Mobility Vehicle Rep
Brian Pruiksma, Mobility Sales Rep
Andrew Rolfe, Owner

Offers a virtually unlimited choice of chassis size, body style, floor plan and optional features. We provide transporters for almost every use, including school buses, vans, mini-coaches, medium-duty buses and personalized vans for the disabled.

Disability Aids & Assistive Devices/Automobile

2986 Mini-Rider
Ricon
7900 Nelson Road
Panorama City, CA 91402-6090
818-267-3000
800-322-2884
Fax: 818-267-3001
e-mail: customerservice@riconcorp.com
http://www.riconcorp.com

William Baldwin, CEO

Ricon has 36 years of experience in the design manufacture and installation of wheelchair lifts and ramps for commercial paratransit, transit motorcoach and passenger rail vehicles.

2987 Monmouth Vans-Access and Mobility Equipment
5105 Route 33
34
Wall Township, NJ 07727-4003
732-919-1444
800-221-0034
Fax: 732-919-0256
e-mail: info@monmouthvans.com
http://www.monmouthvans.com

Eugene Morton, President
Raymond Morton, VP

Vehicle modifications for driving by and/or transport of people with disabilities. Access equipment for buildings, e.g. ramps, stair lifts, pool lifts automatic door openers, and patient transfer lifts. Authorized dealer for Pride Jazzy and Scooters.

2988 Mr. Escort Manual Wheelchair Carrier
Worldwide Mobility Products
720 N Golden Key St.
Suite B6
Gilbert, AZ 85233
480-497-4692
800-848-3433
e-mail: wwmoblift1@msn.com
http://www.worldwide-mobility.com

A wheelchair carrier which is fitted with a padlock feature for safety and security.

2989 Power Seat Base (6-Way)
Ricon
7900 Nelson Road
Panorama City, CA 91402-6090
818-267-3000
800-322-2884
Fax: 818-267-3001
e-mail: customerservice@riconcorp.com
http://www.riconcorp.com

William Baldwin, CEO

Facilitates a driver's self-transfer from a wheelchair to the driving seat and allows optimal driving positioning.

2990 Rampvan
Independent Mobility Systems
4100 W Piedras Street
Farmington, NM 87401-3653
505-326-4538
Fax: 505-326-4846
http://www.braunmobility.com

Greg Anesi, President

Accessible van offering automatic door and ramps.

2991 Rent-A-Van-Handicapped Driver Services
837 Liberty Hill Road NE
Marietta, GA 30066-5564
404-422-9674
877-437-8267
Fax: 404-425-9535
http://www.hdsvans.com

Handicapped Driver Services is a specialized team of adaptive equipment professionals. Our compassionate and committed workforce is dedicated to providing increased vehicular mobility and independence to individuals not fully served by the traditional automotive market. Our team provides innovative solutions and superior products to assist each client in obtaining the highest quality of life possible.

2992 Scooter Lift/Carrier
Dirico (Formerly RD Butler & Company)
157 Padelford
Berkley, MA 02779
508-823-7799
Fax: 508-823-1411

Diane Butler, Owner

Loading without lifting gives greater mobility for the physically challenged.

2993 Special Access Vans
Explorer Van Company
2749 N. Fox Farm Road
Warsaw, IN 46581
574-267-7666
Fax: 219-269-3628
e-mail: parts@explorervan.com
http://www.explorervan.com

Steve Kesler, President

Explorer Van Company is a leader in the van conversion business thanks to our very basic philosophy: "We deliver more, not less, than we promise."

2994 Superarm Lift
Handicaps, Inc.
4335 S Santa Fe Drive
Englewood, CO 80110-5417
303-782-2062
800-782-4335
Fax: 303-761-6811
e-mail: forest77@earthlink.net
http://www.handicapsinc.com

Made for vans and motorhomes. No platform is necessary and no doorways are blocked by lift that is simple and safe to use.

2995 Tim's Trim
25 Bermar Park
Rochester, NY 14624-1541
585-429-6270
888-468-6784
e-mail: timstriminc@yahoo.com
http://www.theoptionstore.com

Timothy Miller, President

Offers vehicle modifications, drop floors, raised tops/doors, driving equipment, touch pads, and lifts.

2996 Transportation Equipment for People with Disabilities
Drive Master Company
9 Spielman Road
Fairfield, NJ 07004-3403
973-808-9709
Fax: 973-808-9713
e-mail: sales@drivemaster.com

Peter B Ruprecht, President
Christina Ruprecht, Vice President
Shelby Wells, Sales Manager

Wheelchair lifts and ramps, hand and foot controls, steering and braking modifications, complete van conversions, home modifications, wheelchairs and scooters and wheelchair accessible van rentals.

2997 Ultra-Lite XL Hand Control
Drive Master Company
37 Daniel Road W
Fairfield, NJ 07004-3403
973-808-9709
Fax: 973-808-9713
e-mail: sales@drivemaster.net
http://www.drive-master,com

Peter B Ruprecht, President
Christina Ruprecht, Vice President
Shelby Wells, Sales Manager

Allows the driver to operate a gas and brake by hand - push for brake - pull for gas. Can be installed in nearly every vehicle.

2998 Wheeler's Accessible Van Rentals
6614 W Sweetwater Avenue
Glendale, AZ 85304-1040
623-776-8830
800-456-1371
Fax: 623-878-0501
http://www.wheelersvanrentals.com

Judy Jordan, Reservations Manager
Gery King, Operations Developer

Disability Aids & Assistive Devices/Bath

Offers customized van rentals to the disabled persons allowing them freedom and independence in their travel.

2999 Wright-Way
175 E. Interstate 30
Garland, TX 75043
972-240-8839
800-241-8839
Fax: 972-240-0412
e-mail: mobility@wrightwayinc.com
http://www.wrightwayinc.com

Tom Wright, President
Kathy Starnes, Inside Sales
Roy Jones, Operations Manager

Various automobile control systems that use hand, foot and steering aids for the disabled, including complete vehicle modifications.

Bath

3000 Adaptive Design Shop
12847 Point Pleasant Drive
Fairfax, VA 22033-3210
703-631-1585
800-351-2327
Fax: 775-256-2556
e-mail: info@adaptivedesignshop.com
http://www.adaptivedesignshop.com

Joe Rickerson, Owner

Offers various adjustable models of bath and shower chairs, as well as adjustable toilet and commodes supports for toddlers through adults. Call for a free brochure. Prices range from $200 to $800.

3001 Adjustable Raised Toilet Seat
Maxi Aids
42 Executive Boulevard
Farmingdale, NY 11735-4710
631-752-0521
800-522-6294
Fax: 631-752-0689
e-mail: sales@maxiaids.com
http://www.maxiaids.com
TTY 631-752-0738

Harold Zaretsky, President

Maxi-Aids has been an established special-needs provider for over two decades. In that time, we have evolved into the world's leading provider of adaptive products, products for independent living and products designed to enhance your lifestyle simply by making your every-day tasks easier.

3002 Adjustable Toilet Safety Rails
Cleo of New York
S Buckout Street
Irvington, NY 10533
914-591-4900
800-321-0595
Fax: 914-591-4083

Elliott Goldberg, President

Adjusts in width to fit around most toilet tanks. Rails may be raised off the floor for ease in cleaning.

3003 AirLift Toileting System from Mobility
5726 La Jolla Boulevard
Suite 104
La Jolla, CA 92037-7342
714-730-0982
866-456-8121
Fax: 858-456-8139
e-mail: info@mobilityinc.net
http://www.mobilityinc.net

Steve Winston, VP Sales
Eric Proffitt, VP Marketing

The Mobility AirLift toileting system makes it easy and painless to get on and off the toilet. With or without an assistant, the AirLift absorbs the user's weight, providing gentle lowering to a sitting position and smooth lifting to a standing position.

3004 BathEase
3815 Darston Street
Palm Harbor, FL 34685-3119
727-786-2604
Fax: 727-786-2604
e-mail: bathease@aol.com
http://www.bathease.com

Terry Stickler, Director/R&D
Gerry Grondin, Production Manager

Is the original standard size bathtub/shower, featuring ADOOR for easy access. More suitable for lifetime use an aid to daily living in privat homes, the door eliminates the barrier in convential unit. An award winning design, it is manufactured in high gloss acrylic.

3005 Bathtub Safety Rail
Arista Home Care
67 Lexington Avenue
New York, NY 10010-1898
212-679-3694
800-223-1984
Fax: 212-696-9046
e-mail: aristasurgical@juno.com

Stephen Howard, Manager

Made of stainless steel, this safety rail fits in any size bathtub and offers safety and independence at bathing time.

3006 Braun Corporation
PO Box 310
Winamac, IN 46996
574-946-6153
800-843-5438
Fax: 800-946-6305
http://www.braunlift.com

William Roth, President

Offers a variety of assistive devices for the bath and surrounding environment.

3007 Clarke Health Care Products
1003 International Drive
Oakdale, PA 15071-9226
724-695-2122
888-347-4537
Fax: 724-695-2922
e-mail: info@clarkehealthcare.com
http://www.clarkehealthcare.com

Gerard Clarke, Owner

Clarke Health Care Products is located in Oakdale, Pennsylvania, just seven miles west of Pittsburgh. Our location contains the corporate office and eastern warehouse. Our focus is to search the world for unique products to make your daily activities easier.

3008 Cleo Raised Toilet Seat
Cleo of New York
S Buckout Street
Irvington, NY 10533
914-591-4900
800-321-0595
Fax: 914-591-6900

Elliott Goldberg, President

Designed to fit securely standard and elongated bowls and includes a white enameled seat with liner.

3009 Commode Aluminum
Maxi Aids
42 Executive Boulevard
Farmingdale, NY 11735-4710
631-752-0521
800-522-6294
Fax: 631-752-0689
e-mail: sales@maxiaids.com
http://www.maxiaids.com
TTY 631-752-0738

Harold Zaretsky, President

Adjustable seat height for patient comfort.

Disability Aids & Assistive Devices/Bath

3010 Crane Plumbing/Fiat Products
1235 Hartrey Avenue
Evanston, IL 60202-1056
847-864-9777
Fax: 847-864-7652
http://www.craneplumbing.com
Carla Lindsey, Marketing Administrator
Reid L Beidler, CEO

Crane Plumbing LLC is one of the best-known manufacturers and distributors of plumbing fixtures and specialty plumbing products in North America. The Company offers various products and product lines that comprise all aspects of bathroom fixtures from a small porcelain sink to a luxury acrylic bath. Over 2,000 employees, many with decades of experience, distribute residential and commercial plumbing fixtures that blend modern design and efficiency with enduring beauty and style.

3011 Decorator Grab Bars
Cleo of New York
S Buckout Street
Irvington, NY 10533
914-591-4900
800-321-0595
Fax: 914-591-6900
Elliott Goldberg, President

Strong steel tubing coated with corrosion-resistant finish for bathrooms, entrance ways and more. Many sizes are available.

3012 Deluxe Bath Bench with Adjustable Legs
Maxi Aids
42 Executive Boulevard
Farmingdale, NY 11735-4710
631-752-0521
800-522-6294
Fax: 631-752-0689
e-mail: sales@maxiaids.com
http://www.maxiaids.com
TTY 631-752-0738
Harold Zaretsky, President

Features durable back support and adjustable legs with push-button adjustment that allows for wide range of height (18"x16.5")

3013 Driving Systems
16139 Runnymede Street
Van Nuys, CA 91406-2913
818-782-6793
Fax: 818-782-6485
e-mail: info@drivingsystems.com
http://www.drivingsystems.com
Greg Paquin, Marketing Manager
Rudolf Schinz, President
William Butt, VP

Designer grab bars with ergonomic grip. Available in colors and custom shapes. New fold down shower seat. Support grips extend out form the wall 24inches or 30 inches. Concealed fastener and modular components for many design possibilities. Price ranges from $30.00 to $280.00.

3014 Electric Leg Bag Emptier and Tub Slide Shower Chair
RD Equipment
230 Percival Drive
West Barnstable, MA 02668-1244
508-362-7498
Fax: 508-362-7498
e-mail: info@rdequipment.com
http://www.rdequipment.com
Richard J Dagostino, Inventor/President
Diana M Pontieri, Sales Manager

Designed for independence, this small, lightweight battery-operated valve attaches to the bottom of the leg bag. A simple flip of the switch empties the leg bag, allowing the user to take in unlimited amounts of fluids. Tub Slide Shower Chair is a complete bathroom care system, with no need of costly renovations.

3015 Great Big Safety Tub Mat
Maxi Aids
42 Executive Boulevard
Farmingdale, NY 11735-4710
631-752-0521
800-522-6294
Fax: 631-752-0689
e-mail: sales@maxiaids.com
http://www.maxiaids.com
TTY 631-752-0738
Harold Zaretsky, President

Tub mat provides security against falls in the bath and shower.

3016 Long Handled Bath Sponges
Therapro
225 Arlington Street
Framingham, MA 01702-8773
508-872-9494
800-257-5376
Fax: 508-875-2062
e-mail: info@theraproducts.com
http://www.theraproducts.com
Karen Conrad, Owner

Plastic-handled, 18-inch bath sponge. Handle may be heated and bent for easy reach.

3017 Magic Soaper
Cleo of New York
S Buckout Street
Irvington, NY 10533
914-591-4900
800-321-0595
Fax: 914-591-4900
Elliott Goldberg, President

Especially handy for one-hand use or limited range of motion.

3018 Modular Wall Grab Bars
Invacare
One Invacare Way
N Ridgeville, OH 44035-6263
440-329-6000
800-343-6059
Fax: 800-272-2822
e-mail: info@invacare.com
http://www.invacare.com
A Malachi Mixon III, Chairman Of The Board/CEO
Gerald B Blouch, President/COO
Dale LaPorte, Senior Vice President

Engineered for strength and beauty, these bars can be assembled in various combinations to fit any bath or shower.

3019 Padded Bathtub Transfer Bench
Cleo of New York
S Buckout Street
Irvington, NY 10533
914-591-4900
800-321-0595
Fax: 914-591-4083
Elliott Goldberg, President

Bench offers push button telescopic adjustments to change settings.

3020 Pik Stik
Mobilelectrics Company
4014 Bardstown Road
Louisville, KY 40218-2631
502-491-1943
800-876-6846
Fax: 502-495-2476

Provides reaching and grasping power with accuracy and ease.

3021 Quick Clamp Tub Grab Bar
Cleo of New York
S Buckout Street
Irvington, NY 10533
914-591-4900
800-321-0595
Fax: 914-591-4083
Elliott Goldberg, President

Easy, tool free installation grab bar for the bath.

Disability Aids & Assistive Devices/Bath

3022 Roll-In Shower
BraunAbility
627 West 11th Street
Box 310
Winamac, IN 46996
574-946-6153
800-843-5438
Fax: 800-946-6305
http://www.braunmobility.com

Designed for easy access by wheelchair users as well as elderly people.

3023 Snug Seat
Bath Products
12801 E. Independence Blvd.
Matthews, NC 28106-1739
704-882-0666
800-336-7684
Fax: 704-882-0751
e-mail: sales@snugseat.com
http://www.snugseat.com

Kirk Mackenzie, President
Steve Scribner, Vice President Sales
Greg Tilley, Controller

Offers a wide range of products to meet the transportation, mobility, seating and bath aid needs for people of all ages. From car seats and standers for children with special needs to versatile and wheelchairs that offer adults customized options and the freedom to go anywhere with confidence.

3024 Sure Safe Raised Toilet Seat
Cleo of New York
S Buckout Street
Irvington, NY 10533
914-591-4900
800-321-0595
Fax: 914-591-4083

Elliott Goldberg, President

All-plastic raised seat and clamp will not corrode or rust.

3025 Suregrip Bathtub Rail
Invacare
One Invacare Way
N Ridgeville, OH 44035-6263
440-329-6000
800-343-6059
Fax: 800-272-2822
e-mail: info@invacare.com
http://www.invacare.com

A Malachi Mixon III, Chairman of The Board/CEO
Gerald B Blouch, President/COO
Dale LaPorte, Senior Vice President

Compact and versatile, the bars have a soft-touch, contoured, white vinyl gripping area for added safety.

3026 Talking Bathroom Scale
Independent Living Aids
200 Robbins Lane
Jericho, NY 11753-2365
516-937-1848
800-537-2118
Fax: 516-937-3906
e-mail: techsupport@independentliving.com
http://www.independentliving.com

Marvin Sandler, President

Talking scale that will tell your weight.

3027 Terry-Wash Mitt
Therapro
225 Arlington Street
Framingham, MA 01702-8773
508-872-9494
800-257-5376
Fax: 508-875-2062
e-mail: info@theraproducts.com
http://www.theraproducts.com

Karen Conrad, Owner

Includes a thumb socket and a palm pocket to hold a bar of soap.

3028 Terry-Wash Mitt - Medium Size
Therapro
225 Arlington Street
Framingham, MA 01702-8773
508-872-9494
800-257-5376
Fax: 508-875-2062
e-mail: info@theraproducts.com
http://www.theraproducts.com

Karen Conrad, Owner

Includes a thumb socket and a palm pocket to hold a bar of soap.

3029 Toilet Guard Rail
Maxi Aids
42 Executive Boulevard
Farmingdale, NY 11735-4710
631-752-0521
800-522-6294
Fax: 631-752-0689
e-mail: sales@maxiaids.com
http://www.maxiaids.com
TTY 631-752-0738

Harold Zaretsky, President

Made of chrome-plated, heavy gauge steel. Fits securely to the toilet for maximum sturdiness.

3030 Transfer Tub Bench
Arista Surgical Supply Co
67 Lexington Avenue
New York, NY 10010-1833
212-679-3694
800-223-1984
Fax: 212-696-9046
e-mail: info@aristasurgicalcom.verizonsupersite.com
http://www.aristasurgical.com

Stephen Howard, Manager

Curved padded backrest for comfortable support. Backrest also assists patient during lateral transfer.

3031 Tri-Grip Bathtub Rail
Maxi Aids
42 Executive Boulevard
Farmingdale, NY 11735-4710
631-752-0521
800-522-6294
Fax: 631-752-0689
e-mail: sales@maxiaids.com
http://www.maxiaids.com
TTY 631-752-0738

Harold Zaretsky, President

Two gripping heights for easy bathtub entrance or exit.

3032 Tub Slide Shower Chair
RD Equipment
230 Percival Drive
West Barnstable, MA 02668-1244
508-362-7498
Fax: 508-362-7498
e-mail: info@rdequipment.com
http://www.rdequipment.com

Richard J Dagostino, Proprietor/Inventor
Diana M Pontieri, Sales Manager

The tub slide shower chair was designed for the elderly and disabled to make any bathroom (at home or when travelling) accessible with little or no renovations. Go from the bed, over the commode, and over the bathtub for a shower using one product. No transfers in the bathroom what so ever.

3033 White Bench
Access with Ease
PO Box 1150
Chino Valley, AZ 86323-1150
928-636-9469
800-531-9479
Fax: 928-636-0292

Karen Clymer, President/CEO

Safer, easier showering with this vinyl coated bench.

Disability Aids & Assistive Devices/Bed

Bed

3034 **Adjustable Bed**
Golden Technologies
401 Bridge Street
Old Forge, PA 18518-2323
570-451-7477
800-624-6374
Fax: 800-628-5165
e-mail: pobrien@goldentech.com
http://www.goldentech.com

Bob Golden, President

Trouble-free gear motor, safety features, dual massage variable speed timer and more, for the ultimate sleep experience.

3035 **Bye-Bye Decubiti Air Mattress Overlay**
Rand-Scot
401 Linden Center Drive
Fort Collins, CO 80524-2429
970-484-7967
800-467-7967
Fax: 970-484-3800
e-mail: info@randscot.com
http://www.easypivot.com

Joel Lerich, President

Originally designed for hospital beds, converts any bed into an exceptionally therapeutic flotation unit when used between the conventional mattress and pad. The complete overlay is comprised of five individually inflatable, 100 percent natural rubber, ventilated sections enclosed within separate pockets of a soft velour cover. This sectional conformation to any configuration of electric or manual beds.

3036 **DBC-1 DU-IT Bed Control**
APT Technology
236A North Main Street
Shreve, OH 44676
330-567-2001
888-549-2001
Fax: 330-567-3073
e-mail: sales@genesisone.net
http://www.apt-technology.com

Controls a powered hospital bed via a single switch or it can control the bed as an accessory to an environmental control system. Controls head up, head down, feet up, feet down to increase patient comfort and independence.

3037 **Foam Decubitus Bed Pads**
Profex Medical Products
PO Box 16043
Saint Louis, MO 63105
314-727-0196
800-325-0196
Fax: 314-727-1239
http://www.profexmed.com

Convoluted foam provides extra back support and comfort for wheelchair users.

3038 **Hard Manufacturing Company**
230 Grider Street
Buffalo, NY 14215-3797
716-893-1800
873-427-
Fax: 716-896-2579
e-mail: hardmfg@aol.com
http://www.hardmfg.com

Kevin Currier, Home Care Manager
William Godin, President

Manufactures metal cribs, hospital beds, mattresses and bedsprings and wood household furniture and furnishings.

3039 **Helping Handle**
Access with Ease
PO Box 1150
Chino Valley, AZ 86323-1150
928-636-9469
800-531-9479
Fax: 928-636-0292

Karen Clymer, President/CEO

Gives you a hand getting out of bed.

3040 **Priva Inc.**
PO Box 448
Champlain, NY 12919-0448
514-356-8881
800-761-8881
Fax: 514-356-0055
e-mail: piv@priva.inc.com
http://www.priva-inc.com

David Horowitz, President
Natasha Pietramala, Director, HHC Division

A leading manufacturer and distributor of branded and private label programs specialized in waterproof and absorbent textiles. Currently our channels of distribution are focused on Home Health Care, Home Furnishings, Infant & Juvenile, as well as the ever growing demand for environmentally safe multi-purpose reusable bags. These channels spread across North America into the UK, Spain & Australia.

3041 **Waterproof Sheet-Topper Mattress andChair Pad**
Pillow Talk
348 Pond Road
Freehold, NJ 07728-8343
732-780-9483
Fax: 732-708-0279
e-mail: info@pillowtalkusa.com
http://www.pillowtalkusa.com

Dorothy Fajerman, President
Dawn Fargione, Managing Vice President
Jack Fajerman, Director of Marketing

This soft pad lies on the top sheet, absorbing accidents from incontinence, pregnancy or medical problems. Waterproof barrier locks out moisture, soiling and stains and eliminates midnight linen changes and the resulting laundry. Available in bed sizes W/4 Anchor; twin; full; queen; king; and crib.

Chairs

3042 **Adjustable Rigid Chair**
Graham-Field Health Products
2935 Northeast Parkway
Atlanta, GA 30360
800-347-5678
Fax: 800-726-0601
e-mail: cs@grahamfield.com
http://www.grahamfield.com

Beatrice Scherer, President/CEO
Cherie Antoniazzi, Senior Vice President/HR
Alan Monahan, Chief Financial Officer

The Champion 3000 is a fully adjustable rigid frame chair weighing only 21 pounds with a new clamping system that adjusts seat height and angle without tools.

3043 **Better Back**
Orthopedic Products Corporation
4100 1/2 Glencoe Avenue
Marina Del Rey, CA 90292-5610
323-584-6977
Fax: 310-306-0177

An orthopedic multi-purpose seat.

3044 **Evac + Chair Emergency Wheelchair**
Evac + Chair Corporation
3000 Marcus Avenue
Lake Success, NY 11042-1012
516-502-4240
Fax: 516-327-8220
e-mail: sales@evac-chair.com
http://www.evac-chair.com

Gravity driven evaluation chair allows one non-disabled person to smoothly glide a seated passenger down fire stairs and across landings to exit on a combination of wheels and track belts. Pivots in own width for tight landing turns. Aluminum; weight 18 pounds. Compactly stores on wall mount, 38 by 20 by 9 inches. Maximum capacity 300 pounds. Self braking features. No installation, works on all fire exit stairs.

Disability Aids & Assistive Devices/Communication

3045 **Golden Power Lift Chair**
Golden Technologies
401 Bridge Street
Old Forge, PA 18518
570-824-1145
800-624-6374
Fax: 800-628-5165
e-mail: pobrien@goldentech.com
http://www.goldentech.com

Diane Golden, Owner

Comes in different heights and widths to comfortably lift the user to a standing position.

3046 **Lumex Recliner**
Graham-Field
2935 Northeast Parkway
Atlanta, GA 30360-2808
800-347-5678
Fax: 800-726-0601
e-mail: cs@grahamfield.com
http://www.grahamfield.com

Beatrice Scherer, President/CEO
Cherie Antoniazzi, Senior Vice President/HR
Alan Monahan, Chief Financial Officer

Combines therapeutic benefits of position change with attractive appearance.

3047 **Quality Lift Chair**
Mobilelectrics Company
4014 Bardstown Road
Louisville, KY 40218-2631
502-491-1943
800-876-6846
Fax: 502-495-2476

Come and go as you please, sit and stand when you want, without help from anyone.

3048 **Roll Chair**
Bailey Manufacturing Company
Po Box 130
Lodi, OH 44254-1056
330-948-1080
800-321-8372
Fax: 800-224-5390
e-mail: baileymfg@attmail.com
http://www.baileymfg.com

Larry Strimple, President

The padded roll helps maintain proper hip abduction and prevents scissoring of the legs.

3049 **Safari Tilt**
Convaid Products
PO Box 4209
Palos Verdes, CA 90274-9571
310-618-0111
888-266-8243
Fax: 310-618-8811
e-mail: custservice@convaid.com
http://www.convaid.com

Merv Watkins, President/Owner

A semi-contour seat provides positioning with 5-45 degree tilt adjustment. One step design folds compactly into a lightweight chair.

3050 **Spatial Tilt Custom Chair**
Redman Powerchair
1674 South Research Loop
Suite 402
Tucson, AZ 85710-6791
800-727-6684
Fax: 520-546-5530
http://www.redmanpowerchair.com

Custom chair designed for comfort with a solid seat and back with modifications available for seat depth, height or width.

3051 **Special Needs III**
Baby Jogger Company
8575 Magellan Parkway
Suite 1000
Richmond, VA 23227
800-241-1848
Fax: 804-262-6277
e-mail: customerservice@babyjogger.com
http://www.babyjogger.com

A baby jogger offering wheels that are designed for smooth rides on all terrains, even sand and snow. The aluminum frame supports weight up to 150 pounds.

3052 **Transfer Bench with Back**
Invacare
One Invacare Way
N Ridgeville, OH 44035-6263
440-329-6000
800-343-6059
Fax: 800-272-2822
e-mail: info@invacare.com
http://www.invacare.com

A Malachi Mixon III, Chairman/CEO
Gerald B Blouch, President/COO
Dale LaPorte, Senior Vice President

This bench with air-cushioned seat sections has a full, reversible backrest for safety and comfort.

Communication

3053 **3M Brailler**
Maxi Aids
42 Executive Boulevard
Farmingdale, NY 11735-4710
631-752-0521
800-522-6294
Fax: 631-752-0689
e-mail: sales@maxiaids.com
http://www.maxiaids.com
TTY 631-752-0738

Harold Zaretsky, President

For visually impaired, blind and sighted persons, produces braille on 3/8 and 1/2 inch vinyl tape. The dial has braille and regular characters.

3054 **3M Large Printed Labeler**
Maxi Aids
42 Executive Boulevard
Farmingdale, NY 11735-4710
631-752-0521
800-522-6294
Fax: 631-752-0689
e-mail: sales@maxiaids.com
http://www.maxiaids.com
TTY 631-752-0738

Harold Zaretsky, President

Ideal for persons with low vision. Can also be read tactually by blind persons with a knowledge of the print alphabet.

3055 **ABLEDATA**
8630 Fenton Street
Suite 930
Silver Spring, MD 20910-3820
301-608-8998
800-227-0216
Fax: 301-608-8958
e-mail: ABLEDATA@verizon.net
http://www.abledata.com
TTY 301-608-8912

Katherine Belknap, Project Director
David Johnson, Publications Director
Carolyn Johnson, Information Specialist

ABLEDATA is an electronic database of assistive technology and rehabilitation equipment products for children and adults with physical, cognitive and sensory disabilities. ABLEDATA staff can perform database searches or the database can be searched on the website.

Disability Aids & Assistive Devices/Communication

3056 ACS Wireless
10 Victor Square
Scotts Valley, CA 95066-3562
831-438-3883
800-995-5500
Fax: 831-438-2745
e-mail: sales@acs.com
http://www.acs.com

Phil Gattey, Chief Executive Officer
Gary Woerz, Chief Financial Officer
Beverly Robinson, Public Relations Contact

Maker of several different types of telephone headsets depending on individual needs.

3057 AIPHONE Intercom Systems
1700 130th Avenue NE
Bellevue, WA 98005-2262
425-455-0510
800-692-0200
Fax: 425-455-0071
e-mail: info@aiphone.com
http://www.aiphone.com

Tak Kanie, President

AIPHONE manufactures audio and video intercom systems for home or business to help the physically disabled answer doors and communicate through physical barriers, also ADA-compliant emergency call intercom stations for use in public facilities.

3058 APT Technology Switches
APT Technology
236A North Main Street
Shreve, OH 44676-9788
330-567-2001
Fax: 330-567-3073
e-mail: sales@genesisone.net
http://www.apt-technology.com

Manufacturers of single and dual switches, suitable for control of communication aids, ECU's, adaptive devices like page turners, toys, etc. BS-1 Single Body Switch (large push button $52), BS-2 is 2 BS-1 with a P-306 connector ($115), DPS-2 is a dual pneumatic switch ($295), TS-2C is a small movement tongue switch ($290).

3059 AT&T Portable Telephone Amplifier
Hear You Are
4 Musconetcong Avenue
Stanhope, NJ 07874-2936
973-347-7662
800-287-EARS
Fax: 973-691-0611
TTY 973-347-7662

Larry Cagno, Vice President
Eleanore Oudshoorn, Owner

Compact and lightweight portable amplifier that amplifies telephone conversation to a comfortable listening level with an adjustable volume control. The amplifier enables hearing aid users to use telephones that are not hearing aid compatible.

3060 Ability Research
PO Box 1721
Minnetonka, MN 55343
952-939-0121
Fax: 952-890-8393
e-mail: ability@skypoint.com
http://www.skypoint.com/~ability

John Severson, Manager

Manufacturers and marketers of assistive technology equipment.

3061 Able-Phone 100
Able-Phone
354 Chatfield Ave
Biggs, CA 95917
530-846-7466
800-456-4979
Fax: 530-846-7466
e-mail: ablephone@juno.com
http://www.ablephone.com

60 voice memories and enhanced voice recognition circuitry which provides accurate voice recognition. Able-phone is the only company that manufactures a fully adapted cordless phone. The Able-Phone Model 100 gives you complete freedom from wires.

3062 Able-Phone 1900
Able-Phone
354 Chatfield Ave
Biggs, CA 95917
530-846-7466
800-456-4979
Fax: 530-846-7466
e-mail: able-phone@juno.com
http://www.ablephone.com

Totally hands free. No manipulation or operation or other mechanical devices required for complete control of the Model 1900. The phone is operated by a puff or sip into the mouthpiece.

3063 Able-Switch SW-1
Able-Phone
354 Chatfield Avenue
Biggs, CA 95917
530-846-7466
800-456-4979
Fax: 530-846-7466
e-mail: able-phone@juno.com
http://www.ablephone.com

Touch switch.

3064 AbleNet
2808 Fairview Avenue North
Roseville, MN 55113-1308
651-294-2200
800-322-0956
Fax: 651-294-2259
e-mail: customerservice@ablenetinc.com
http://www.ablenetinc.com

Mary Kay Walch, Sales Specialist
Theresa I Curran, Marketing Support

Designs, manufactures and markets simple technology devices for people with disabilities along with digitalized voice output communication aids for beginning communicators. Switches, environmental control units and mounting systems that allow electrical and battery operated toys and appliances to be accessed through a single switch.

3065 Access USA
242 James Street
PO Drawer 160
Clayton, NY 13624-0160
800-263-2750
Fax: 800-563-1687
e-mail: info@access-usa.com
http://www.access-usa.com/usa

Deborah Webster, Contact

ACCESS USA provides all types of alternate media for people with blindness or visual impairments and/or hearing impairments. Documents (of all sizes) for transcription can be accepted as hard copy, disk copy or e-mail. Formats available include braille, large-type, simultaneous braille and print, audio recordings and electronic format. Video services include open and/or closed captioning and audio description. Specialties includes braille business cards, multipurpose braille labels and more.

3066 Adaptivation
2225 W 50th Street
Suite 100
Sioux Falls, SD 57105-6536
605-335-4445
800-723-2783
Fax: 605-335-4446
e-mail: info@adaptivation.com
http://www.adaptivation.com

Jonathan Eckrich, President

Manufacturers of environmental control switches, auditory paging systems, a mouse emulator program and communication devices.

3067 Adaptive Device Locator System
Academic Software
3504 Tates Creek Road
Lexington, KY 40517-2601
859-552-1020
Fax: 253-799-4012
e-mail: asistaff@acsw.com
http://www.acsw.com

Dr. Warren E Lacefield, President
Penelope D Ellis, COO/Sales & Marketing Director
Sylvia B Lacefield, Graphic Artist

Disability Aids & Assistive Devices/Communication

Academic Software, Inc. (ASI) is a small Kentucky-based educational research, development, and consulting firm completing its 21st year as a corporation headquartered in Lexington. ASI specializes in the field of assistive technology and computer access for children and adults with disabilities and for health professionals who work with people with disabilities.

3068 Akron Resources
20 La Porte Street
Arcadia, CA 91006-2827
626-254-9005
800-841-0884
Fax: 626-254-9266
http://www.arkon.com

Paul Brassard, Owner
Aaron Roth, VP, Marketing and Sales
Benjamin Arana, Sr. Account Manager

Arkon seeks to provide innovative consumer solutions designed to enhance the function and experience of complimentary products for the car and home.

3069 Ameriphone Hearing Assistance Telephone
Hear You Are
4 Musconetcong Avenue
Stanhope, NJ 07874-2936
800-287-EARS
Fax: 973-347-7662

Larry Cagno, Vice President
Eleanore Oudshoorn, Owner

A communication enhanced telephone with a large button and contrasting graphics for optimum visibility and dialing ease. Amplifies incoming voice by 30 db gain, and has a frequency screening feature that permits user to identify sound frequencies.

3070 Ameriphone-Wireless Notification System
HEAR You Are
4 Musconetcong Avenue
Stanhope, NJ 07874
973-347-7662
800-287-3277
Fax: 973-691-0611
e-mail: HEARYOUARE@aol.com

Larry Cagno, VP
Eleanor Oudshoorn, Owner

System alerts to activators in the home, telephone ringing, knock at the door, sounding of an alarm, motion detection sensor. The table top receiver has a digital clock and connectors for your notification lamp and/or bed vibrator.

3071 Amplified Handsets
HARC Mercantile
1111 W Centre Avenue
Portage, MI 49024-5317
269-324-0301
800-445-9968
Fax: 269-324-2387
e-mail: home@hacofamerica.com
http://www.hacofamerica.com

Ronald Slager, President

Choices of touch activated electronic control, rotary (thumb wheel) volume control, that can directly replace old handset, stocked in round and square styles. This also includes an electric transmitter with variable settings.

3072 Amplified Phones
HARC Mercantile
1111 W Centre Avenue
Portage, MI 49024-5317
269-324-0301
800-445-9968
Fax: 269-324-2387
e-mail: home@hacofamerica.com
http://www.hacofamerica.com

Ronald Slager, President

Low frequency ringer, indicator light, enhances or amplifies sound, some that automatically returns to normal dial tone when phone receiver is hung up, lighted easy to read dial pad and volume control boosts incoming sound.

3073 Amplified Portable Phone
HARC Mercantile
1111 W Centre Avenue
Portage, MI 49024-5317
269-324-0301
800-445-9968
Fax: 269-324-2387
e-mail: home@hacofamerica.com
http://www.hacofamerica.com

Ronald Slager, President

Portable amplified phones.

3074 Analog Switch Pad
Academic Software
3504 Tates Creek Road
Lexington, KY 40517-2601
859-552-1020
Fax: 253-799-4012
e-mail: asistaff@acsw.com
http://www.acsw.com

Dr. Warren E Lacefield, President
Penelope D Ellis, COO & Sales & Marketing Director
Sylvia B Lacefiled, Graphic Artist

Academic Software, Inc. (ASI) is a small Kentucky-based educational research, development, and consulting firm completing its 21st year as a corporation headquartered in Lexington. ASI specializes in the field of assistive technology and computer access for children and adults with disabilities and for health professionals who work with people with disabilities.

3075 Answerall 100
Able-Phone
354 Chatfield Avenue
Biggs, CA 95917
530-846-7466
800-456-4979
Fax: 530-477-7466
e-mail: ablephone@juno.com
http://www.ablephone.com

A Panasonic answering machine which has been modified to accept both voice and TDD phone calls for individuals who are deaf or hearing impaired.

3076 Arkenstone
Freedom Scientific
11800 31st Court North
St Petersburg, FL 33716-1805
727-803-8000
800-444-4443
Fax: 727-803-8001
http://www.freedomscientific.com

Jeff Bazer, Regional Sales Manager
Lee Hamilton, President/CEO

Offers various models of personal ready-to-read personal computers for the disabled.

3077 Arthwriter
Cleo of New York
S Buckout Street
Irvington, NY 10533
914-591-4900
800-321-0595
Fax: 914-591-4083

Elliott Goldberg, President

Writing aid for people who suffer from arthritis and other hand problems.

3078 Artificial Larynx
HARC Mercantile
1111 W Centre Avenue
Portage, MI 49024-5317
269-324-0301
800-445-9968
Fax: 269-324-2387
e-mail: home@hacofamerica.com
http://www.hacofamerica.com

Ronald Slager, President

For people unable to use their larynx, a hand held speaking aid that simulates the natural vibrations on voice.

Disability Aids & Assistive Devices/Communication

3079 Assistive Software Products
Innovation Management Group
21350 Nordhoff Street
Suite 112
Chatsworth, CA 91311
818-701-1579
800-889-0987
Fax: 818-701-1581
e-mail: cs@imgpresents.com
http://www.imgpresents.com

Jerry Hussong, VP Sales/Marketing
Kermit Komm, Owner

IMG is the publisher of The Magnifier a 2x-10x Area Magnifier software program with Cursor Tracker; My-T-Soft AT Onscreen Keyboard software program with progrmmable Macro Panels and Word prediction Completion; and Joystick-To-Mouse software that lets any gamepad or joystick run Windows just like a mouse.

3080 Assistive Technology
333 Elm Street
Dedham, MA 02026-4530
781-461-8200
800-793-9227
Fax: 617-461-8213
e-mail: customercare@assistivetech.com
http://www.assistivetech.com

James Lewis, President

A premiere developer of innovative technology solutions for people with physical and learning disabilities. Breakthrough products enable people of all ages and abilities to live and learn independently. Supportive material for teachers, clinicians, and those with disabilities.

3081 Augmentative Communication Systems (AAC)
ZYGO Industries
PO Box 1008
Portland, OR 97207-1008
503-684-6006
800-234-6006
Fax: 503-684-6011
e-mail: zygo@aygo-usa.com
http://www.zygo-usa.com

Lawrence Weiss, President

Full range of AAC systems and assistive technology including computer-based systems and computer access programs and devices.

3082 BESTspeech
Berkeley Speech Technologies
2246 Sixth Street
Berkeley, CA 94701
510-841-5083
Fax: 510-841-5093
e-mail: webmaster@bst.com
http://www.bestspeech.com

This text-to-speech facility is useful to persons who are blind or vision impaired and may be used by those with speech, hearing and learning difficulties.

3083 BIGmack Communication Aid
AbleNet
2808 Fairview Avenue North
Roseville, MN 55113-1308
651-294-2200
800-322-0956
Fax: 651-294-2259
e-mail: customerservice@ablenetinc.com
http://www.ablenetinc.com

Mary Kay Walch, Press Center

A single message communication aid, BIGmack has 20 seconds of memory and has a 5 inches diameter switch surface.

3084 Big Number Pocket Sized Calculator
Independent Living Aids
200 Robbins Lane
Jericho, NY 11753-2365
516-937-1848
800-537-2118
Fax: 516-937-3906
e-mail: techsupport@independentliving.com
http://www.independentliving.com

Marvin Sandler, President

A handy pocket size calculator with big numbers that fits easily into purse or pocket.

3085 Big Red Switch
AbleNet
2808 Fairview Avenue North
Roseville, MN 55113-1308
651-294-2200
800-322-0956
Fax: 651-294-2259
e-mail: customerservice@ablenetinc.com
http://www.ablenetinc.com

Mary Kay Walch, Press Center

Five inches across the top and activates no matter where on its surface it is touched. It is made of shatterproof plastic and contains a cord storage compartment. Also available in green, yellow and blue.

3086 Braille Blazer Printer
Freedom Scientific
11800 31st Court North
St Petersburg, FL 33716-1805
727-803-8000
800-444-4443
Fax: 727-803-8001
e-mail: listproc@blazie.com
http://www.blazie.com

Jeff Bazer, Regional Sales Manager
Lee Hamilton, President/CEO

The Braille Blazer by Blazie Engineering is a portable, durable, and inexpensive Brailee embosser. Simply connect Braille Blazer to any personal computer to quickly produce high quality Braille text and graphics. It's small size and sturdy design make it perfect for the office, in school or at home. The Braille Blazer also features a built in speech synthesizer. It's TWO machines for the price of ONE.

3087 Braille Compass
Maxi Aids
42 Executive Boulevard
Farmingdale, NY 11735-4710
631-752-0521
800-522-6294
Fax: 631-752-0689
e-mail: sales@maxiaids.com
http://www.maxiaids.com
TTY 631-752-0738

Harold Zaretsky, President

For the visually impaired to find directions. Graduations raised for touch orientation, north arrow, East, South and West, by Braille letters, and inter-cardinal points by dots.

3088 Braille N' Speak
Blazie Engineering
105 E Jarrettsville Road
Forest Hill, MD 21050-1611
410-893-9333
Fax: 410-893-5040
e-mail: david@blazie.com

A compact, portable talking device with a seven-key Braille keyboard, may be used as a talking computer terminal, a braille to print transcriber and a word processor.

3089 Braille Touch-Time Watches
Independent Living Aids
200 Robbins Lane
Jericho, NY 11753-2365
516-937-1848
800-537-2118
Fax: 516-937-3906
e-mail: techsupport@independentliving.com
http://www.independentliving.com

Marvin Sandler, President

White dial with black numerals and hands makes telling time possible quickly and easily for the visually impaired. $44.95-$59.95.

Disability Aids & Assistive Devices/Communication

3090 Braille/Print Protractor
American Printing House for the Blind
1839 Frankfort Avenue
PO Box 06085
Louisville, KY 40206-3148
502-895-2405
800-223-1839
Fax: 502-899-2274
e-mail: info@aph.org
http://www.aph.org

Tuck Tinsley, President
Bob Brasher, VP Advisory Services & Research
Gary Mudd, VP Public Affairs

This cleverly designed Braille/Print Protractor allows visually impaired users to measure angles up to 180 degrees. Bold large type numbers and braille dots mark the degrees along the half circle of the protractor. Two braille dots mark 10 degree increments, while a single braille dot marks the 5 degree increments.

3091 Braillemaster
Howtek
21 Park Avenue
Hudson, NH 03051-3985
603-882-5200
Fax: 603-880-3843

Kenneth M Ferry, CEO

A modified version of Howtek's Pixelmaster color ink jet printer, retains the functionality of Pixelmaster - a color printer capable of merging color graphics and images with crisp text on any standard paper at five to ten cents per page.

3092 CLOSE-UP 6.5
Norton-Lambert Corporation
PO Box 4085
Santa Barbara, CA 93140-4085
805-964-6767
e-mail: sales@norton-lambert.com
http://www.norton-lambert.com

Two-time winner of PC magazine Editor's Choice, Close-Up remotely controls PC's via modem. Telecommute from your home or laptop PC to your office PC, or give remote support with unmatched speed. Run applications, update spreadsheets, print documents remotely and access networks on remote PCs just as if you were there!

3093 Caleworthy
GW Micro
725 Airport North Office Park
Fort Wayne, IN 46825-6707
260-489-3671
Fax: 260-489-2608
e-mail: sales@gwmicro.com
http://www.gwmicro.com

Doug Geoffray, Vice President Development
Dan Weirich, VP Sales And Marketing
Lois Baich, Orders And Production

A pop-up calculator that may be activated anytime. It includes support for ten memories and review of 50 entries.

3094 Canon Communicator
Canon Communicator
1 Canon Plaza
New Hyde Park, NY 11042-1119
516-488-6700
Fax: 516-328-4369

Debra Piazza, Marketing Programs
George Shimazu, Marketing Director
Hase Gawa, VP

Designed for persons having difficulty in communicating through speech, sign language or handwriting.

3095 Canon Communicator M
Canon Communicator
1 Canon Plaza
New Hyde Park, NY 11042-1119
516-488-6700
Fax: 516-328-4369

Debra Piazza, Marketing Programs
George Shimazu, Marketing Director
Hase Gawa, VP

Designed for persons having difficulty in communicating through speech, sign language or handwriting.

3096 Captek/Science Products
PO Box 888
Southeastern, PA 19399
610-296-2111
800-888-7400
e-mail: info@captek.net
http://www.scienceproducts.org

Lee Benham, Owner

Offers a full line of better vision products for better living: low vision aids, magnifiers, large print, items that talk, conversation products.

3097 Circline Illuminated Magnifer
Dazor Manufacturing Corporation
11721 Dunlap Industrial Drive
Maryland Heights, MO 63043
314-652-2400
800-345-9103
Fax: 314-652-2069
e-mail: info@dazor.com
http://www.dazor.com

Richard Kupferer, Marketing Coordinator
Mark Hogrebe, President

Provides even, shadow free light under the magnifying lens with a 22-watt circline fluorescent. The magnifier is mounted on a 'floating arm' that allows you to position the light source and lens with the touch of a finger.

3098 Clarity
4289 Bonny Oaks Drive
Suite 106
Chattanooga, TN 37406-1600
423-622-7793
800-552-3368
Fax: 800-325-8871
e-mail: claritysales@plantronics.com
http://www.clarityproducts.com

Carsten Trads, President
Linda Owen, Director of Finance
Jamie Van Den Bergh, Director of Marketing

Leading supplier of amplified telephones, notification systems, assistive listening devices and other communications devices for the hearing loss and Deaf markets. Clarity Power patented technology truly and positively impacts people's lives with every product created.

3099 Compu-Lenz
Florida New Concepts Marketing
10825 Benbow Drive
Port Richey, FL 34673
727-842-3231
Fax: 727-845-7544
http://www.gulfside.com/compulenz

Compu-Lenz, a combination fresnel magnifier and glass glare filter in an adjustable hood. When placed on the front of a PC monitor it magnifies the character size, reduces glare and enhances contrast.

3100 Computer Paper for Brailling
Maxi Aids
42 Executive Boulevard
Farmingdale, NY 11735-4710
631-752-0521
800-522-6294
Fax: 631-752-0689
e-mail: sales@maxiaids.com
http://www.maxiaids.com
TTY 631-752-0738

Harold Zaretsky, President

Specially made paper for braille printing. 1,000 sheets/case, size 14 7/8 inches by 11 inches.

3101 Computer Switch Interface
AbleNet
2808 Fairview Avenue North
Roseville, MN 55113-1308
651-294-2200
800-322-0956
Fax: 651-294-2259
e-mail: customerservice@ablenetinc.com
http://www.ablenetinc.com

Mary Kay Walch, Press Center

Allows single switch access to an Apple computer.

Disability Aids & Assistive Devices/Communication

3102 Cordless Big Red Switch
AbleNet
2808 Fairview Avenue North
Roseville, MN 55113-1308
651-294-2200
800-322-0956
Fax: 651-294-2259
e-mail: customerservice@ablenetinc.com
http://www.ablenetinc.com
Mary Kay Walch, Press Center

The Cordless Big Red Switch, when used in conjunction with either the Cordless Receiver or the Small Appliance Receiver, gives you cordless control of toys, games, and appliances in your environment.

3103 Cornell Communications
7915 N 81st Street
Milwaukee, WI 53223-3830
414-351-4660
800-558-8957
Fax: 414-351-4657
e-mail: sales@cornell.com
http://www.cornell.com
Pauline Haack, Inside Sales
Jerel Johnson, President

Cornell's Rescue Systems allow personnel to request emergency assistance. Applications include life safety emergency evacuation, parking garages and elevators. Voice and visual only systems are available. Call for our free Americans with Disabilities Act Accessibility Guideline.

3104 Darci Too
WesTest Engineering Corporation
810 West Shepard Lane
Farmington, UT 84025-3846
801-451-9191
Fax: 801-451-9393
e-mail: webmail@westest.com
http://www.westest.com

A universal device which allows people with physical disabilities to replace the keyboard and mouse on a personal computer with a device that matches their physical capabilities. DARCI TOO works with almost any personal computer and provides access to all computer functions.

3105 DeltaTalker
Prentke Romich Company
1022 Heyl Road
Wooster, OH 44691-9786
330-262-1984
800-262-1990
Fax: 330-263-4829
e-mail: service@prentrom.com
http://www.prentrom.com
Dave Moffatt, President

A portable, electronic communication device that uses Minspeak so that symbols are used to represent words, sentences and phrases. The DT can be accessed by pressing keys scanning or optical pointing and can be configured with 8, 32 or 128 locations. It has both digitalized and synthesized speech. Optional infrared capabilities allow operation of remote controlled devices.

3106 Don Johnston
26799 W Commerce Drive
Volo, IL 60073-9675
847-740-0749
800-999-4660
Fax: 847-740-7326
e-mail: info@donjohnston.com
http://www.donjohnston.com
Ruth Ziolkowski, President

A provider of quality products and services that enable people with special needs to discover their potential and experience success. Products are developed for the areas of Physical Access, Augmentative Communication and for those who struggle with reading and writing.

3107 Door Flashing Announcment System
Hear You Are
4 Musconetcong Avenue
Stanhope, NJ 07874-2936
800-287-EARS
Fax: 973-347-7662

System provides audible and visual signals of doorbell actuation. Bell rings as long as pushbutton is depressed. Light continues to flash at a 100 flashes per minute rate after audible signal stops.

3108 Doorbell Signalers
HARC Mercantile
1111 W Centre Avenue
Portage, MI 49024-5317
269-324-0301
800-445-9968
Fax: 269-324-2387
e-mail: home@hacofamerica.com
http://www.hacofamerica.com
Ronald Slager, President

Doorbell signalers to alert with either louder chime or flashing light.

3109 Double Gong Indoor/Outdoor Ringer
HARC Mercantile
1111 W Centre Avenue
Portage, MI 49024-5317
269-324-0301
800-445-9968
Fax: 269-324-2387
e-mail: home@hacofamerica.com
http://www.hacofamerica.com
Ronald Slager, President

Loud outdoor ringer that attaches to the wall for outside applications.

3110 Duxbury Braille Translator
Duxbury Systems
270 Littleton Road
Unit 6
Westford, MA 01886-3523
978-692-3000
Fax: 978-692-7912
e-mail: info@duxsys.com
http://www.duxburysystems.com
Joe Sullivan, President
Peter Sullivan, VP of Software Development
Genevieve Sullivan, Treasurer

A complete line of braille easy to use word processing and translation software available for Windows (including NT), Macintosh, DOS, and UNIX. Applications for anyone wanting to produce or communicate with braille; signs, note cards, textbooks, business communications and forms, telephone bills, etc. Simple to use, FREE technical support. Free one year upgrades. DBT is for producing braille in English, Spanish, French, Portuguese, Italian, Latin

3111 Duxbury Systems
270 Littleton Road
Unit 6
Westford, MA 01886-3523
978-692-3000
Fax: 978-692-7912
e-mail: info@duxsys.com
http://www.duxburysystems.com
Joe Sullivan, President
Peter Sullivan, VP Software Development
Genevieve Sullivan, Treasurer

Software for the visually impaired.

3112 Enabling Technologies Company
1601 NE Braille Place
Jensen Beach, FL 34957-5345
772-225-3687
800-777-3687
Fax: 772-225-3299
e-mail: info@brailler.com
http://www.brailler.com
Greg Schenk, Marketing Executive

Disability Aids & Assistive Devices/Communication

Manufactures the most complete line of American made braille embossers, including desk top or portable models capable of producing high quality single sided or interpoint braille. Also carry a complete line of adaptive technology aids for the blind community at affordable prices.

3113 Environment Control System
Airphone Corporation
1700 130th Avenue NE
Bellevue, WA 98005-2203
425-455-0510
800-692-0200
Fax: 425-455-0071
e-mail: info@aiphone.com
http://www.aiphone.com

Chuck Watkins, Eastern Regional Sales Manager
Nancy McAlister, Western Regional Sales Manager
David McManamon, Owner

AIPHONE manufactures audio and video intercom systems for home or business to help the physically disabled answer doors and communicate through physical barriers; also ADA-compliant emergency call intercom stations for use in public facilities, and an Environmental Control System for persons with limited mobility.

3114 Extra Loud Alarm with Lighter Plug
HARC Mercantile
1111 W Centre Avenue
Portage, MI 49024-5317
269-324-0301
800-445-9968
Fax: 269-324-2387
e-mail: home@hacofamerica.com
http://www.hacofamerica.com

Ronald Slager, President

Battery operated, easy to read, digital clock with extra loud alarm.

3115 Eye Relief Word Processing Software
SkiSoft Publishing Corporation
1644 Massachusetts Avenue
Suite 79
Lexington, MA 02420-5311
781-863-1876
e-mail: info@skisoft.com
http://www.skisoft.com

Large-type word processing program for visually-impaired PC users.

3116 Eyegaze Computer System
LC Technologies
1483 Chain Bridge Road
Suite 104
McLean, VA 22031-4713
703-385-7133
800-393-4293
Fax: 703-385-7137
e-mail: info309@eyegaze.com
http://www.eyegaze.com

Dixon Cleveland, Co-Founder/Engineer
Arthur W Joyce, III, Ph.D., Senior Engineer
Peter Norloff, Senior Software Engineer

Enables people with physical disabilities to do many things with their eyes that they would otherwise do with their hands.

3117 Flashing Lamp Telephone Ring Alerter
Independent Living Aids
200 Robbins Lane
Jericho, NY 11753-2365
516-937-1848
800-537-2118
Fax: 516-937-3906
e-mail: techsupport@independentliving.com
http://www.independentliving.com

Marvin Sandler, President

Once your phone is plugged into the Telephone Ring Alerter, the lamp light will flash with each ring, alerting you that there is a phone call.

3118 Font-Tools BIGFONT
Worthington Data Solutions
623 Swift St.
Suite 220
Santa Cruz, CA 95060-5700
831-458-9938
800-345-4220
Fax: 831-458-9964
e-mail: wds@barcodehq.com
http://www.barcodehq.com

Steve Fent, Owner

Prints large text up to two inches tall on laser printers. It requires an IBM PC and runs from any MS-DOS language.

3119 GW Micro
725 Airport North Office Park
Fort Wayne, IN 46825-6707
260-489-3671
Fax: 260-489-2608
e-mail: support@gwmicro.com
http://www.gwmicro.com

Doug Geoffray, Vice President Development
Dan Weirich, VP Sales & Marketing
Louis Biach, Orders and Production

Computer hardware and software products for people with disabilities.

3120 Goals and Objectives
JE Stewart Teaching Tools
PO Box 15308
Seattle, WA 98115
206-367-1176
Fax: 206-262-9538

Donald E Gillis, Owner

Goals and Objectives software helps teachers make student plans including IEP's, IPP's and IHP's. The system provides curricula for all students and programs to develop and evaluate plans, print reports and make data forms. Systems are available for IBM's and compatibles, Macintosh and for networks. $19.00/disk.

3121 Headmaster Plus
Prentke Romich Company
1022 Heyl Road
Wooster, OH 44691-9786
330-262-1984
800-262-1984
Fax: 330-263-4829
e-mail: info@prentrom.com
http://www.prentrom.com

Dave Moffatt, President

A headpointing system that takes the place of a mouse, and allows individuals who cannot use their hands but have good head control access to the computer. A transmitting unit sits atop the monitor and sends signals to the user's headset. The user puffs into a tube connected to the headset to make selections. Typing can be done with optional on-screen keyboards.

3122 Ideal-Phone
IDEAMATICS
1364 Beverly Road
Suite 101
Mc Lean, VA 22101-3627
703-903-4972
800-247-4332
Fax: 703-903-8949
e-mail: ideamatics@ideamatics.net
http://www.mclean.va.us/~ideamatics

David L Danner, President/CEO
Mark Moore, Program Manager
Lia M Keston, Program Manager

Integrates the personal computer and the telephone into a single, efficient workstation. It is ideal for mobility-impaired persons and others who need a hands-free operation of the phone. The Ideal-Phone includes one PC Board, a Plantronics headset, software for access and logging and complete documentation. It can be integrated into programs, or pops-up over any application. MS-DOS based, version 3.0 or higher are available.

Disability Aids & Assistive Devices/Communication

3123 Jelly Bean Switch
AbleNet
2808 Fairview Avenue North
Roseville, MN 55113-1308
651-294-2200
800-322-0956
Fax: 651-294-2259
e-mail: customerservice@ablenetinc.com
http://www.ablenetinc.com

Mary Kay Walch, Press Center

A momentary touch switch made of shatterproof plastic, small and sensitive to 2-3 ounces of pressure, this switch is provided audible feedback when activated and is a compact version of the Big Red Switch.

3124 LPB
28 Bacton Hill Road
Frazer, PA 19355-1026
856-365-8080
Fax: 856-365-8999
e-mail: info@lpbinc.com
http://www.lpbinc.com

John Devecka, Sales Manager

Limited area AM and FM broadcast systems for hearing assistance and language translation manufacturing since 1960. Systems for small conference halls, churches and Olympic stadiums. Components or complete system.

3125 LT Switch
AbleNet
2808 Fairview Avenue North
Roseville, MN 55113-1308
651-294-2200
800-322-0956
Fax: 651-294-2259
e-mail: customerservice@ablenetinc.com
http://www.ablenetinc.com

Mary Kay Walch, Press Center

A light touch version of the Plate Switch, beneficial to users with minimal strength.

3126 Laptops/Word Processors
Perfect Solutions
10513 Versailles Blvd
Wellington, FL 33467
561-790-1070
800-726-7086
Fax: 561-790-0108
e-mail: perfect@gate.net
http://www.perfectsolutions.com

Andrew Kramer, President

A computer for every student! Wireless talking laptop computers starting at $290.00 are ideal for all ages.

3127 Large Button Speaker Phone
HARC Mercantile
1111 W Centre Avenue
Portage, MI 49024-5317
269-324-0301
800-445-9968
Fax: 269-324-2387
e-mail: home@hacofamerica.com
http://www.hacofamerica.com

Ronald Slager, President

Speakerphone with or without remote control.

3128 Large Print Telephone Dial
Maxi Aids
42 Executive Boulevard
Farmingdale, NY 11735-4710
631-752-0521
800-522-6294
Fax: 631-752-0689
e-mail: sales@maxiaids.com
http://www.maxiaids.com
TTY 631-752-0738

Harold Zaretsky, President

Pressure sensitive dial with numbers that are easy to see for the disabled.

3129 Large Print Touch-Telephone Overlays
Maxi Aids
42 Executive Boulevard
Farmingdale, NY 11735-4710
631-752-0521
800-522-6294
Fax: 631-752-0689
e-mail: sales@maxiaids.com
http://www.maxiaids.com
TTY 631-752-0738

Harold Zaretsky, President

Pressure-sensitive and easy to apply overlays that make everyday phones accessible.

3130 Large Print Typewriter
Typewriting Institute for the Handicapped
3102 W Augusta Avenue
Phoenix, AZ 85051-6530
602-939-5344

A reconditioned, converted IBM Model D electric typewriter with upper/lower case keys.

3131 Lighthouse Low Vision Products
111 E 59th Street
New York, NY 10022-1202
212-821-9200
800-829-0500
Fax: 212-821-9707
e-mail: info@lighthouse.org
http://www.lighthouse.org
TTY 212-821-9713

Tara A Cortes, RN, PhD, President/CEO
Noreen Brennan, VP, Childrens Services
Lisa Ferfoglia, VP Human Resources

Lighthouse International is the leading non-profit organization worldwide dedicated to preserving vision and to helping people of all ages overcome the challenges of vision loss.

3132 Line-A-Timers
Therapro
225 Arlington Street
Framingham, MA 01702-8773
508-872-9494
800-257-5376
Fax: 508-875-2062
e-mail: info@theraproducts.com
http://www.theraproducts.com

Karen Conrad, Owner

Four flexible, translucent yellow plastic strips make reading easier for everyone. Static electricity holds strips against most types of reading material.

3133 Location Finder
Maxi Aids
42 Executive Boulevard
Farmingdale, NY 11735-4710
631-752-0521
800-522-6294
Fax: 631-752-0689
e-mail: sales@maxiaids.com
http://www.maxiaids.com
TTY 631-752-0738

Harold Zaretsky, President

Helps find house, apartment, car or office. Just press the transmitter and sound will be emitted indicating the location.

3134 Luminaud
8688 Tyler Boulevard
Mentor, OH 44060-4348
440-255-9082
800-255-3408
Fax: 440-255-2250

Thomas Lennox, President
Dorothy Lennox, VP

Catalog offers a line of artificial larynx, personal voice amplifiers, special switches, stoma covers and other communication, health and safety items.

50 pages

Disability Aids & Assistive Devices/Communication

3135 Magni-Cam
Innoventions, Inc.
9593 Corsair Drive
Conifer, CO 80433-9317
303-797-6554
800-854-6554
Fax: 303-727-4940
e-mail: magnicam@magnicam.com
http://www.magnicam.com

Mark Freeman, President
Charleen Freeman, Vice President Marketing

Magni-Cam is a hand-held, light weight, inexpensive, auto-focus electronic magnification system designed to meet the reading and writing needs of those with low vision. The system presents the image in black and white or in color with three different view modes. Connects to any TV monitor in minutes. System reads any surface with no distortion. Two battery powered systems are availabe providing total portability and flexibility.

3136 Man's Low-Vision Quartz Watches
Independent Living Aids
200 Robbins Lane
Jericho, NY 11753-2365
516-937-1848
800-537-2118
Fax: 516-937-3906
e-mail: techsupport@independentliving.com
http://www.independentliving.com

Marvin Sandler, President

An inexpensive, easy-to-read watch with chrome case.

3137 MegaDots
Duxbury Systems
270 Littleton Road
Unit 6
Westford, MA 01886-3523
978-692-3000
Fax: 978-692-7912
e-mail: info@duxsys.com
http://www.duxburysystems.com

Joe Sullivan, President
Peter Sullivan, VP of Software Development
Genevieve Sullivan, Treasurer

A revolutionary new braille translator for the PC that lets you finish projects quickly and easily. Intelligent document importation recognizes what word processor your text is from and guesses that appropriate format for each paragraph, yielding high quality braille.

3138 Men's/Women's Low Vision Watches & Clocks
Maxi Aids
42 Executive Boulevard
Farmingdale, NY 11735-4710
631-752-0521
800-522-6294
Fax: 631-752-0689
e-mail: sales@maxiaids.com
http://www.maxiaids.com
TTY 631-752-0738

Harold Zaretsky, President

Choose from a wide range of watches from braille automatic to quartz pocket watches.

3139 MessageMate
Words+
42505 10th Street West
Lancaster, CA 93534-7059
661-723-6523
800-869-8521
Fax: 661-723-2114
e-mail: info@words-plus.com
http://www.words-plus.com

Walt Wolosz, Manager

Lightweight, hand-held communicator providing high-quality analog recording capability using either direct select keyboards or 1 to 2 switch access.

3140 Metropolitan Washington Ear
35 University Boulevard East
Silver Spring, MD 20901-2484
301-681-6636
Fax: 301-681-5227
e-mail: information@washear.org
http://www.washear.org

Neely Oplinger, Adminstrative Manager
Donna Hunsicker, Volunteer Manager
Debbie Fitch, Service Coordinator

This organization has pioneered audio description for blind audience members.

3141 Mini Teleloop
HARC Mercantile
1111 West Centre Avenue
Portage, MI 49024-5317
269-324-0301
800-445-9968
Fax: 269-324-2387
e-mail: home@hacofamerica.com
http://www.hacofamerica.com

Ronald Slager, President

Home induction loop amplifier for use with hearing aids equipped with T-Coil.

3142 Morse Code Equalizer
Words+
42505 10th Street West
Lancaster, CA 93534-7059
661-723-6523
800-869-8521
Fax: 661-723-2114
e-mail: info@words-plus.com
http://www.words-plus.com

Walt Wolosz, Manager

Provides complete word processing and voice output communications with single or dual switch Morse code inputs. Originally designed for a blind user with only eyelid movement. The system can be used by both sighted and visually impaired persons.

3143 Mouthsticks
Sammons Preston
1000 Remington Boulevard
Suite 210
Bolingbrook, IL 60440-5177
630-378-6000
800-323-5547
Fax: 630-378-6010
e-mail: customersupport@patterson-medical.com
http://www.sammonspreston.com

Wide offering of mouthsticks featuring various functions (BK 5380, 5381, 5383, 5385, 6002, or BK 5370 series).

3144 Multi-Scan Single Switch Activity Center
Academic Software
3504 Tates Creek Road
Lexington, KY 40517-2601
859-552-1020
Fax: 253-799-4012
e-mail: asistaff@acsw.com
http://www.acsw.com

Dr. Warren E Lacefield, President
Penelope D Ellis, COO & Sales & Marketing Director
Sylvia B. Lacefield, Graphic Artist

3145 Multiple Phone/Device Switch
HARC Mercantile
1111 W Centre Avenue
Portage, MI 49024-5317
269-324-0301
800-445-9968
Fax: 269-324-2387
e-mail: home@hacofamerica.com
http://www.hacofamerica.com

Ronald Slager, President

Used to switch phone lines between two devices.

3146 New Breakthroughs
89911 Greenwood Drive
Leaburg, OR 97489-9637
541-741-5070
Fax: 505-896-0123

Offers catalogs of communication products for the disabled.

Disability Aids & Assistive Devices/Communication

3147 Oticon Portable Telephone Amplifier
Hear You Are
4 Musconetcong Avenue
Stanhope, NJ 07874-2936
973-347-7662
800-287-EARS
Fax: 973-347-7662
TTY 973-347-7662

Attaches to any sound source, picks up sound, amplifies it and induces it onto hearing aid telecoils.

3148 Outdoor Loud Bell
Hear You Are
4 Musconetcong Avenue
Stanhope, NJ 07874-2936
800-297-EARS
Fax: 973-347-7662

This outdoor bell with a loud mechanical ringer features an easy plug-in installation to either a modular or hook-up.

3149 Personal FM Systems
HARC Mercantile
1111 West Centre Avenue
Portage, MI 49024-5317
269-324-0301
800-445-9968
Fax: 269-324-2387
e-mail: home@hacofamerica.com
http://www.hacofamerica.com

Ronald Slager, President

Wireless FM systems transmits sound via a radio carrier wave.

3150 Personal Infrared Listening System
HARC Mercantile
1111 West Centre Avenue
Portage, MI 49024-5317
269-324-0301
800-445-9968
Fax: 269-324-2387
e-mail: home@hacofamerica.com
http://www.hacofamerica.com

Ronald Slager, President

Wireless method if listening to TV and radio with individually controlled amplification.

3151 Phillip Roy
13064 Indian Rocks Road
Largo, FL 33774-2001
727-593-2700
800-255-9085
Fax: 727-595-2685
e-mail: info@philliproy.com
http://www.philliproy.com

Ruth Bralman PhD, President
Phillip Roy, Manager

Offers multimedia materials appropriate for use with individuals with disabilities. Programs range from preschool through the adult level. Many of the programs are high interest topics/low vocabulary, ideal for transition and employability skills. Materials are also available which focus on social and personal development. Call for a free catalog.

3152 Plantronics SP-04
Ablephone
354 Chatfield Ave.
Biggs, CA 95917
530-846-7466
800-456-4979
Fax: 530-846-7466
e-mail: able-phone@juno.com
http://www.ablephone.com

Headset telephone for people who have a hard time grasping the telephone.

3153 PortaPower Plus
Words+
42505 10th Street West
Lancaster, CA 93534-2902
661-723-6523
800-869-8521
Fax: 661-723-2114
e-mail: info@words-plus.com
http://www.words-plus.com

Walt Wolosz, Manager

Rechargeable battery pack designed to give longer life and remote usage time to laptop computers and other portable battery-operated devices and accessories. Requires a 12 volt auto adapter.

3154 Potomac Technology
1 Church Street
Suite 101
Rockville, MD 20850-4194
301-762-4005
800-433-2838
Fax: 301-762-1892

Patricia J Relihan, Manager

This catalog offers a variety of wake-up devices, alarm clocks, alerting systems, assistive listening devices, signalers, smoke detectors, TTY, telephones and telephone amplifiers.

24 pages

3155 Prentke Romich Company
1022 Heyl Road
Wooster, OH 44691-9744
330-262-1984
800-262-1933
Fax: 330-263-4829
e-mail: info@prentrom.com
http://www.prentrom.com

Barry Romich, Chairman
Joe Durbin, President
Dave Moffatt, President

The Prentke Romich Company is a full service company offering easy, yet powerful communication aids. The company believes in supporting customers before and after the sale by offering funding assistance, distance learning training, extended warranty, service assistance and much more. Visit our web-site to view our full-line catalogue, read about our success stories, and to sign up for our on-line newsletter.

3156 Prentke Romich Company Product Catalog
1022 Heyl Road
Wooster, OH 44691-9786
330-262-1984
800-262-1933
Fax: 330-263-4829

Larry Gigax, Contact
Dave Moffatt, President

A full-line product catalog containing information on speech-output communication devices, environmental controls and computer access products.

3157 Push to Talk Amplified Handset
HARC Mercantile
1111 W Centre Avenue
Portage, MI 49024-5317
269-324-0301
800-445-9968
Fax: 269-324-2387
e-mail: home@hacofamerica.com
http://www.hacofamerica.com

Ronald Slager, President

Replacement receiver which is hearing aid compatible and is designed for high noise conditions.

3158 Remote Control Speakerphone
Clarity Products
4289 Bonny Oaks Drive
Suite 106
Chattanooga, TN 37406-1600
423-622-7793
800-426-3738
Fax: 800-325-8871
e-mail: clarityes@plantronics.com
http://www.clarityproducts.com

Carsten Trads, President
Linda Owen, Director of Finance
Jamie Van Den Bergh, Director of Marketing

A multi-functional speaker phone specially designed to meet the needs of motion-impaired persons who are unable to use a conventional phone without assistance.

Disability Aids & Assistive Devices/Communication

3159 **Resource Directory of Special Education and Rehabilitation Computer Products**
Closing the Gap
PO Box 68
Henderson, MN 56044
507-248-3294
Fax: 507-248-3810
e-mail: info@closingthegap.com

Megan Turek, Editor
Dolores Hagen, President

About 300 suppliers of computer hardware and software designed for use by persons with disabilities. Entries include: Company or organization name, address, phone, description of products.

208 pages Frequency: Annual, Feb/Mar

3160 **Room Valet Visual-Tactile AlertingSystem**
HARC Mercantile
1111 W Centre Avenue
Portage, MI 49024-5317
269-324-0301
800-445-9968
Fax: 269-324-2387
e-mail: home@hacofamerica.com
http://www.hacofamerica.com

Ronald Slager, President

ADA compliant built-in visual-tactile alerting system. The Room Valet is fully supervised and has power failure back up. Alerts to in-room smoke, building alarm, door, phone and alarm clock. Designed for permanent installation.

3161 **Sound Induction Receiver**
HARC Mercantile
1111 W Centre Avenue
Portage, MI 49024-5317
269-324-0301
800-445-9968
Fax: 269-324-2387
e-mail: home@hacofamerica.com
http://www.hacofamerica.com

Ronald Slager, President

Sound induction receiver to be used with any loop system.

3162 **SpeakEasy Communication Aid**
AbleNet
2808 Fairview Avenue North
Roseville, MN 55113-1308
651-294-2200
800-322-0956
Fax: 651-294-2259
e-mail: customerservice@ablenetinc.com
http://www.ablenetinc.com

Mary Kay Walch, Press Center

SpeakEasy is a digitalized Voice Output Communication Aid that is ideal for anyone who is beginning to develop communication skills such as making choices and identifying symbols. It holds 12 messages totaling four minutes and 20 seconds of recording time. It measures 7 1/2 inches by 1 3/4 inches and weighs only one pound. Activate messages using the built in keyboard or via external switch.

3163 **Speech Discrimination Unit**
HARC Mercantile
1111 W Centre Avenue
Portage, MI 49024-5317
269-324-0301
800-445-9968
Fax: 269-324-2387
e-mail: home@hacofamerica.com
http://www.hacofamerica.com

Ronald Slager, President

Speech Adjust-A-Tone improves speech discrimination for use with telephone and/or TV and radio.

3164 **Speechmaker-Personal Speech Amplifier**
HARC Mercantile
1111 W Centre Avenue
Portage, MI 49024-5317
269-324-0301
800-445-9968
Fax: 269-324-2387
e-mail: home@hacofamerica.com
http://www.hacofamerica.com

Ronald Slager, President

Portable, body worn personal speech amplifier for people with a weak voice.

3165 **SpringBoard Plus**
Prentke Romich Company
1022 Heyl Road
Wooster, OH 44691
330-262-1984
800-262-1984
Fax: 330-263-4829
e-mail: info@prentrom.com
http://www.prentrom.com

Cherie Weaver, Marketing Coordinator

SpringBoard can be an excellent starting point for the child or adult just beginning the augmentative communication process. SpringBoard can also be the next step for someone who has demonstrated success with manual communication boards or static display devices with limited message capacity. SpringBoard is flexible, easy to customize and easy to support.

3166 **Step-by-Step Communicator**
AbleNet
2808 Fairview Avenue North
Roseville, MN 55113-1308
651-294-2200
800-322-0956
Fax: 651-294-2259
e-mail: customerservice@ablenetinc.com
http://www.ablenetinc.com

Mary Kay Walch, Press Center

The Step-by-Step Communicator allows you to record a series of messages (as many as you want up to the 75 second limit). It has a 2 1/2 inch diameter switch surface and is 3 inches at its tallest point. Angled switch surface makes it easy to see and access.

3167 **Stretch-View Wide-View Rectangular Illuminated Magnifier**
Dazor Manufacturing Corporation
11721 Dunlap Industrial Drive
Maryland Heights, MO 63043
314-652-2400
800-345-9103
Fax: 314-652-2069
e-mail: info@dazor.com
http://www.dazor.com

Richard Kupferer, Marketing Coordinator
Mark Hogrebe, President

Provides shadow-free illumination or a highlighting effect under the magnifying lens with an 18-watt compact fluorescent light source. The magnifier is mounted on a floating arm that allows you to position the light source and lens with the touch of a finger.

3168 **String Switch**
AbleNet
2808 Fairview Avenue North
Roseville, MN 55113-1308
651-294-2200
800-322-0956
Fax: 651-294-2259
e-mail: customerservice@ablenetinc.com
http://www.ablenetinc.com

Mary Kay Walch, Press Center

An activated switch beneficial for users with limited active movement or minimal strength.

3169 **Strobe Light Signalers**
HARC Mercantile
1111 W Centre Avenue
Portage, MI 49024-5317
269-324-0301
800-445-9968
Fax: 269-324-2387
e-mail: home@hacofamerica.com
http://www.hacofamerica.com

Ronald Slager, President

Strobe alerts. Plugs into receivers for signaling systems.

Disability Aids & Assistive Devices/Communication

3170 Symbi-Key Computer Switch Interface
AbleNet
2808 Fairview Avenue North
Roseville, MN 55113-1308
651-294-2200
800-322-0956
Fax: 651-294-2259
e-mail: customerservice@ablenetinc.com
http://www.ablenetinc.com
Mary Kay Walch, Press Center

The Symbi-Key can be programmed to simulate any key stroke or a series of keystrokes (up to 5 per key) for single switch access to software programs whether or not it was designed for switch access. Works well in DOS and all versions of Windows providing access to any IBM program.

3171 TAJ Braille Typewriter
Maxi Aids
42 Executive Boulevard
Farmingdale, NY 11735-4710
631-752-0521
800-522-6294
Fax: 631-752-0689
e-mail: sales@maxiaids.com
http://www.maxiaids.com
TTY 631-752-0738
Harold Zaretsky, President

Smooth edged, simple and sturdy construction. Creates braille on 8 1/2 x 11 paper.

3172 TALKBACK Wireless Doorbell Intercom
Rice International Corporation
7952 Pines Boulevard
Pembroke Pines, FL 33024-6918
954-983-6464
Fax: 305-895-7660
Donald Van Der Laan, General Manager
Suzanne Minnick, Advertising Manager

Wireless radio frequency combined with doorbell and intercom. Outside unit uses 9 volt battery and features hands free operation. This device automatically turns off after one minute.

3173 TTY's-Telephone Device for the Deaf
HARC Mercantile
1111 W Centre Avenue
Portage, MI 49024-5317
269-324-0301
800-445-9968
Fax: 269-324-2387
e-mail: home@hacofamerica.com
http://www.hacofamerica.com
Ronald Slager, President

With or without printer.

3174 TV & VCR Remote
AbleNet
2808 Fairview Avenue North
Roseville, MN 55113-1308
651-294-2200
800-322-0956
Fax: 651-294-2259
e-mail: customerservice@ablenetinc.com
http://www.ablenetinc.com
Mary Kay Walch, Press Center

The TV and VCR Remote will control a TV, a VCR, or a TV that is connected through a VCR tuner. It may be programmed to control functions such as on and off, channel up, preprogrammed TV channels and if desired, other TV functions such as mute and pause.

3175 Talking Clocks
HARC Mercantile
1111 W Centre Avenue
Portage, MI 49024-5317
269-324-0301
800-445-9968
Fax: 269-324-2387
e-mail: home@hacofamerica.com
http://www.hacofamerica.com
Ronald Slager, President

Talking clocks with loud alarms, high and low volume control, choices of sound effects, hourly report options. Other languages are available.

3176 Talking Desktop Calculators
Maxi Aids
42 Executive Boulevard
Farmingdale, NY 11735-4710
631-752-0521
800-522-6294
Fax: 631-752-0689
e-mail: sales@maxiaids.com
http://www.maxiaids.com
TTY 631-752-0738
Harold Zaretsky, President

Unique voice synthesizers call out numerals and functions as they are keyed in, or read out data stored in memory.

3177 Talking Watches
HARC Mercantile
1111 W Centre Avenue
Portage, MI 49024-5317
269-324-0301
800-445-9968
Fax: 269-324-2387
e-mail: home@hacofamerica.com
http://www.hacofamerica.com
Ronald Slager, President

Digital display, hourly reports, alarm with rooster crow, in English or Spanish.

3178 Telecaption Adapter
HARC Mercantile
1111 W Centre Avenue
Portage, MI 49024-5317
269-324-0301
800-445-9968
Fax: 269-324-2387
e-mail: home@hacofamerica.com
http://www.hacofamerica.com
Ronald Slager, President

Caption opens up the world of television to hearing impaired people. Viewers can read on the screen what they may not be able to hear. Closed captions are the dialogue and sound effects of a TV program or home video printed on the screen, similar to subtitles.

3179 Telephone Amplifier
Cleo of New York
S Buckout Street
Irvington, NY 10533
914-591-4900
800-321-0595
Fax: 914-591-4083
Elliott Goldberg, President

This telephone amplifier is easily activated by an on/off switch plate that is pressed once to activate. Amplifier also comes with a recording jack that can be used to connect the amplifier to a tape or cassette recorder.

3180 Timex Easy Reader
Independent Living Aids
200 Robbins Lane
Jericho, NY 11753-2365
516-937-1848
800-537-2118
Fax: 516-937-3906
e-mail: techsupport@independentliving.com
http://www.independentliving.com
Marvin Sandler, President

An easy-to-read large face watch that's water resistant.

3181 U-Control II
Words+
42505 10th Street West
Lancaster, CA 93534-2902
661-723-6523
800-869-8521
Fax: 661-723-2114
e-mail: info@words-plus.com
http://www.words-plus.com
Walt Wolosz, Manager

Disability Aids & Assistive Devices/Communication

Works with the Words+ system (EX Keys, Morse WSKE, Scanning WSKE, Talking Screen) to provide wireless, portable control of items which are already infrared-controlled such as a TV, VCR, CD player, etc.

3182 Ultratec-Auto Answer TTY
Hear You Are
4 Musconetcong Avenue
Stanhope, NJ 07874-2936
800-287-EARS
Fax: 973-347-7662

Full featured primitive TTY with auto answering features for business or emergency services. Has direct connect or acoustic coupling with turbo communications mode, equipped with auto ID and erelay Voice Announcer. Large memory buffer supports storing of conversation, memory message and directories.

3183 Unisex Low Vision Watch
Independent Living Aids
200 Robbins Lane
Jericho, NY 11753-2365
516-937-1848
800-537-2118
Fax: 516-937-3906
e-mail: techsupport@independentliving.com
http://www.independentliving.com

Marvin Sandler, President

Unisex watch with large numbers and wide hands. Gold-toned case with either expansion or leather band. $10.95 to $49.95.

3184 Unity/128
Prentke Romich Company
1022 Heyl Road
Wooster, OH 44691-9786
330-262-1984
800-262-1933
Fax: 330-263-4829
e-mail: info@prentrom.com
http://www.prentrom.com

Dave Moffatt, President

A Minspeak application program available for the Liberator and Delta Talker communication devices. Provides single word vocabulary to people of all ages at varying stages of language development, who may be either cognitively intact or challenged.

3185 Universal Switch Mounting System
AbleNet
2808 Fairview Avenue North
Roseville, MN 55113-1308
651-294-2200
800-322-0956
Fax: 651-294-2259
e-mail: customerservice@ablenetinc.com
http://www.ablenetinc.com

Mary Kay Walch, Press Center

Mounting system that allows switch placement in any position. A single lever locks all joints securely in place. Extends to 20 1/2 inches and holds up to five pounds. A mounting system for quick and easy positioning.

3186 Vantage Plus
Prentke Romich Company
1022 Heyl Road
Wooster, OH 44691
330-262-1984
800-262-1933
Fax: 330-263-4829
e-mail: info@prentrom.com
http://www.prentrom.com

Dave Moffat, President

Vantage is the dynamic choice for powerful language and portable design. The enhanced operating system makes Vantage easy to customize and support. Vantage includes 4,8 and 15 location display options, plus the 45 and 84 location Unity Enhanced vocabulary.

3187 Vibrotactile Personal Alerting System
HARC Mercantile
1111 W Centre Avenue
Portage, MI 49024-5317
269-324-0301
800-445-9968
Fax: 269-324-2387
e-mail: home@hacofamerica.com
http://www.hacofamerica.com

Ronald Slager, President

Composed of a small wireless personal device that receives coded signals and a group of transmitters that send them.

3188 Voice Amplified Handsets
HARC Mercantile
1111 W Centre Avenue
Portage, MI 49024-5317
269-324-0301
800-445-9968
Fax: 269-324-2387
e-mail: home@hacofamerica.com
http://www.hacofamerica.com

Ronald Slager, President

Designed for the person who has a weak speaking voice. Control increases the level of the user's voice and can increase as much as 30%.

3189 WINVISION
Artic Technologies
1000 John R. Road
Suite 108
Troy, MI 48083-2724
248-588-7370
Fax: 313-588-2650
http://www.artictech.com

The premier access system for blind users of IBM personal computers.

3190 Weitbrecht Communications
2656 29th Street
Suite 205
Santa Monica, CA 90405-2984
310-656-4924
800-233-9130
Fax: 310-450-9918
http://www.weitbrecht.com

Barbara Dreyfus, President

Catalog featuring a wide range of assistive devices for communication needs including telephones, amplifiers, signalers and more.

24 pages

3191 Whisper 2000
Ablephone
354 Chatfield Avenue
Biggs, CA 95917
530-846-7466
800-456-4979
Fax: 530-846-7466
e-mail: able-phone@juno.com
http://www.ablephone.com

Personal sound amplification system that features a transmitter, phone and relay system for the hard-of-hearing.

3192 WinSCAN-The Single Switch Interface forPCs with Windows
Academic Software
3504 Tates Creek Road
Lexington, KY 40517-2601
859-552-1020
Fax: 253-799-4012
e-mail: asistaff@acsw.com
http://www.acsw.com

Dr. Warren E Lacefield, President
Penelope D Ellis, COO & Sales & Marketing Director
Sylvia B Lacefield, Graphic Artist

3193 Words+ IST (Infrared, Sound, Touch)
Words+
42505 10th Street West
Lancaster, CA 93534-7059
661-723-6523
800-869-8521
Fax: 661-723-2114
e-mail: info@words-plus.com
http://www.words-plus.com

Walt Wolosz, Manager

Disability Aids & Assistive Devices/Cushions and Wedges

A unique switch that is activated by slight movement or faint sound. The switch provides user control when connected to a device driven by a single switch. Individuals are currently accessing a wide variety of communication and computer systems with movement using the IST switch.

Cushions and Wedges

3194 Action Products
954 Sweeny Drive
Hagerstown, MD 21740-4997
301-797-1414
800-228-7763
Fax: 301-733-2073
e-mail: service@actionproducts.com
http://www.actionproducts.com

Nancy Eddington, Customer Service Manager
Fred Nelson, Seating/Positioning Specialist
Troy McKnigh, President

Wheelchair pads, mattress pads, positioning cushions and insoles that aids in the prevention and cure of pressure sores by reducing pressure. All products are made of Akton viscoelastic polymer that doesnot leak, flow or bottom out. Manufacturer of the Xact line of positioning cushions for patients with high risk of skin breakdown.

3195 Back Machine
Kingstar International America
1443 N Dearborn Street
Chicago, IL 60610-1505
312-951-1115
800-336-6550
Fax: 312-943-1727
http://www.kingstar.com

Robin Morgenstern, President
Issa Alia, Manager

A nine position adjustable lumbar support that is compact and lightweight, portable and able to fit most chairs, adaptable for different body sizes, and will not lose its shape. The inner spring design will give the spinal column over-all support to compensate for stress, fatigue and improper posture.

3196 Back-Huggar Pillow
Bodyline Comfort Systems
3730 Kori Road
Jacksonville, FL 32257-6036
904-262-4068
800-874-7715
Fax: 800-323-2225
e-mail: info@bodyline.com
http://www.bodyline.com

Don Dodds, Office Manager
John Fiore, Owner

Exclusive design makes almost any seat more comfortable by exerting soothing pressure against back muscles and discs.

3197 Bye Bye Decubiti
Cleo of New York
S Buckout Street
Irvington, NY 10533
914-591-4900
800-321-0595
Fax: 914-591-4083

Elliott Goldberg, President

Inflatable rubber cushion that prevents decubitus ulcers. Three sizes available.

3198 Bye-Bye Decubiti (BBD)
Rand-Scot
401 Linden Center Drive
Fort Collins, CO 80524-2429
970-484-7967
800-467-7967
Fax: 970-484-3800
e-mail: info@randscot.com
http://www.randscot.com

Joel Lerich, President

The BBD therapeutic wheelchair cushions have been market-proven since 1951 - in the prevention and cure of pressure sores (decubiti). These natural rubber inflatable products have recently been expanded to include pediatric, sports and double-valve models. Moderately priced, they offer a viable and cost-effective alternative in the market. $84.00-$112.00

3199 Cervipillow Covers
Cleo of New York
S Buckout Street
Irvington, NY 10533
914-591-4900
800-321-0595
Fax: 914-591-4083

Elliott Goldberg, President

Washable, permanent press covers specifically designed for the Cervi pillow by the same manufacturer.

3200 Dynamic Systems
104 Morrow Branch
Leicester, NC 28748-5710
828-683-3523
Fax: 828-683-3511
e-mail: dsi@sunmatecashions.com
http://www.sunmatecushions.com

Charles A Yost, CEO

SunMate orthopedic foam sheets and cushions, pudgee pads for pressure relief and skin breakdown prevention, laminar wheelchair cushions, and Foam-in-Place Seating for custom molding seat inserts. Sample packs and literature available upon request.

3201 ENHANCER Cushion
ROHO
100 N Florida Avenue
Belleville, IL 62221-5429
618-277-9173
800-851-3449
Fax: 618-277-9561
e-mail: rohoinc@rohoinc.com
http://www.rohoinc.com

Julie Petry, Corporate Marketing

Uses AIR IN PLACE progressive positioning for enhanced midline channeling of the femurs, lateral stability and tissue protection.

3202 Econo-Float Water Flotation Cushion
Jefferson Industries
1985 Rutgers University Boulevard
Lakewood, NJ 08701-4537
732-905-9001
800-257-5145
Fax: 732-905-9899

Charles Landa, General Manager

An inexpensive, yet effective approach to the problem of pressure ulcers for patients confined to wheelchairs, geriatric chairs, etc.

3203 Econo-Float Water Flotation Mattress
Jefferson Industries
1985 Rutgers University Boulevard
Lakewood, NJ 08701-4537
732-905-9001
800-257-5145
Fax: 732-905-9899

Charles Landa, General Manager

Helps prevent and treat pressure ulcers by reducing and distributing pressure over the patient's bony prominences while supporting the body evenly over a greater surface area.

3204 Functional Forms
Consumer Care Products
1446 Pilgrim Road
Plymouth, WI 53073
920-459-8353
Fax: 920-459-9070
e-mail: ccpi@consumercareinc.com
http://www.consumercareinc.com

Terry Grall, President
Alice Maffongelli, Customer Service

Disability Aids & Assistive Devices/Cushions and Wedges

These blocks, wedges, rolls, cervical pillows, head and leg supports and barrel rolls in resilient high density foam covered with durable antibacterial, antistatic, flame resistant, non-absorbent vinyl are used to attain individualized support for the most difficult positioning needs for children and adults. Unique sizes allow fitting for almost any person. Use during exercise, feeding, therapy, recreation and rest at home, school and health carefacilities. Packages available.

3205 Gaymar
Gaymar Industries
10 Centre Drive
Orchard Park, NY 14127-2295
716-662-2551
800-828-7341
Fax: 716-662-0748
e-mail: websales@gaymar.com
http://www.gaymar.com

Frank Lumbar, CEO
Thomas P Stewart, President

Manufacturer of a complete line of support surfaces, including low-air-loss mattresses, specialty foam mattresses, turning mattresses, air overlays and fluid therapy beds. These products economically prevent and treat bedsores. Clinical and reimbursement support available.

3206 Geo-Matt for High Risk Patients
Span-America Medical Systems
70 Commerce Center
Greenville, SC 29615
864-288-8692
800-888-6752
Fax: 864-288-8692
http://www.spanamerica.com

James D Ferguson, CEO

For over 30 years, Span America Medical Systems has offered the industry's most comprehensive line of specialty solutions for pressure management and patient positioning. Recognized in medical facilities throughout North America.

3207 HIGH PROFILE Dual Compartment Cushion
ROHO
100 N Florida Avenue
Belleville, IL 62221-5429
618-277-9173
800-851-3449
Fax: 618-277-9561
e-mail: rohoinc@rohoinc.com
http://www.rohoinc.com

Julie Petry, Corporate Marketing

3208 HIGH PROFILE Single Compartment Cushion
ROHO
100 N Florida Avenue
Belleville, IL 62221-5429
618-277-9173
800-851-3449
Fax: 618-277-9561
e-mail: rohoinc@rohoinc.com
http://www.rohoinc.com

Julie Petry, Corporate Marketing

With 4 inch cells, the HIGH PROFILE is the cushion of choice for individuals who suffer from ischemic ulcers (pressure sores) or who have a history of tissue breakdown.

3209 Inflatable Invalid Ring
Cleo of New York
S Buckout Street
Irvington, NY 10533
914-591-4900
800-321-0595
Fax: 914-591-4083

Elliott Goldberg, President

Rubber ring with recessed valve gives support and comfort for the physically challenged.

3210 Jay Cushion
Jay Medical Ltd.
805 Walnut Street
Boulder, CO 80302-5034
303-442-5529
800-648-8282
Fax: 303-218-4690

Benefits the user by improving posture and preventing and healing pressure sores.

3211 LOW PROFILE Dual Compartment Cushion
ROHO
100 N Florida Avenue
Belleville, IL 62221-5429
618-227-9173
800-851-3449
Fax: 618-277-9561
e-mail: rohoinc@rohoinc.com
http://www.rohoinc.com

Julie Petry, Corporate Marketing

3212 LOW PROFILE Single Compartment Cushion
ROHO
100 N Florida Avenue
Belleville, IL 62221-5429
618-277-9173
800-851-3449
Fax: 618-277-9561
e-mail: rohoinc@rohoinc.com
http://www.rohoinc.com

Julie Petry, Corporate Marketing

Offers 2 inch cells for active users protection against skin breakdown.

3213 Lumbo-Posture Back Support
Rand-Scot
401 Linden Center Drive
Fort Collins, CO 80524-2429
970-484-7967
800-467-7967
Fax: 970-484-3800
e-mail: info@randscot.com
http://www.randscot.com

Joel Lerich, President

Rubber inflatable back support that offers therapeutic relief to all who must sit for lengthy periods of time, whether used in a wheelchair, auto or bed.

3214 Lumex's Cushions and Mattresses
Graham-Field
2935 Northeast Parkway
Atlanta, GA 30360-2808
800-347-5678
Fax: 800-726-0601
e-mail: cs@grahamfield.com
http://www.grahamfield.com

Beatrice Scherer, President/CEO
Cherie Antoniazzi, Senior VP, Human Resources
Alan Monahan, Chief Financial Officer

Line of cushions and pillows give comfort and independence to the physically challenged.

3215 Medpro Static Air Chair Cushion
Medpro
1950 Rutgers University Boulevard
Lakewood, NJ 08701-4537
732-905-9001
800-257-5145
Fax: 732-905-9899

Jody Gorran, President

Provides a protective layer of air beneath the patient helping prevent and treat pressure ulcers.

3216 Medpro Static Air Mattress Overlay
Medpro
1950 Rutgers University Boulevard
Lakewood, NJ 08701-4537
800-257-5145
Fax: 732-905-9899

Jody Gorran, President

Supports the patient on a cushioned network of air designed to redistribute the patient's weight reducing tissue interface pressure. Medpro's design incorporates a series of 65 air-breather vents that maintain air circulation. Medpro effectively reduces pressure and helps prevent and treat pressure ulcers.

Disability Aids & Assistive Devices/Cushions and Wedges

3217 Mini-Max Cushion
ROHO
100 N Florida Avenue
Belleville, IL 62221-5429
618-277-9173
800-851-3449
Fax: 618-277-9561
e-mail: rohoinc@rohoinc.com
http://www.rohoinc.com

Julie Petry, Corporate Marketing

Designed for the active individual with low risk of skin breakdown. The unique air cells of the MIN-MAX provide significant shock and impact absorption, skin protection and stability.

3218 NEXUS Wheelchair Cushioning System
ROHO
100 N Florida Avenue
Belleville, IL 62221-5429
618-227-9173
800-851-3449
Fax: 618-277-9561
e-mail: rohoinc@rohoinc.com
http://www.rohoinc.com

Julie Petry, Corporate Marketing

A unique modular cushion that mates a contoured polyurethane foam base with a DRY FLOTATION support pad. It is designed to give the user positioning and stability, while offering maximum protection to the ischia, sacrum and coccyx.

3219 Nek-Lo, Nek-Lo Hot and Cold, Pillow-Perfect, Body Buddy
Rinz-L-O Pillow Company
340 W Maplehurst Street
Ferndale, MI 48220-2712
248-548-3993
800-594-9093
Fax: 248-548-0447
e-mail: rinzlo@netzero.net

G Rick Rinz, President

Nek-Lo - a U-shaped cervical pillow; Nek-Lo Hot and Cold - U-shaped pillow with hot/cold pack; Pillow-Perfect - Uses your conventional pillow to insert cover that has cervical support form piece. Magne-Aid and Magne-Systems - Magnetic therapy braces.

3220 Performance Gel Cushions
Spenco Medical Corporation
PO Box 2501
Waco, TX 76702-2501
254-772-6000
800-877-3626
Fax: 817-751-5799
e-mail: info@spenco.com
http://www.spenco.com

Steven B Smith, Chairman/CEO

Spenco is an innovative healthcare company whose mission is to help people everywhere achieve more-more comfortably.

3221 Positioning Support Seats
Cleo of New York
S Buckout Street
Irvington, NY 10533
914-591-4900
800-321-0595
Fax: 914-591-4083

Elliott Goldberg, President

Brightly colored glossy foam seat for children and adolescents. Great for eating or relaxing. $105-$350.

3222 QUADTRO Cushion
ROHO
100 N Florida Avenue
Belleville, IL 62221-5429
618-277-9173
800-851-3449
Fax: 618-277-9561
e-mail: rohoinc@rohoinc.com
http://www.rohoinc.com

Julie Petry, Corporate Marketing

For individuals who require special positioning of the pelvis or thighs and are at risk of skin breakdown, the QUADTRO, with 4 inch cell height and AIR IN PLACE, progressive positioning is the cushion of choice.

3223 Silicone Padding
Spenco Medical Group
PO Box 2501
Waco, TX 76702-2501
817-772-6000
800-433-3334
Fax: 817-751-5799
http://www.spenco.com

Steven B Smith, Chairman/CEO
Patty Smith, Controller
Mark B Connors, VP Sales/Marketing

For the management of pressure sores, this padding provides a special support system which allows even distribution of pressure and cool, comfortable well-ventilated support.

3224 Soft-Touch Convertible Flotation Mattress
Medpro
275 Highway 18
East Brunswick, NJ 08816
732-905-9001
800-257-5145
Fax: 732-905-9899

Jody Gorran, President

Gives the patient the option to choose between water and gel flotation depending on the needs of the patient. The mattress helps prevent and treat pressure ulcers by spreading the patient's weight over a greater surface area. $164.95-$239.95.

3225 Soft-Touch Gel Flotation Cushion
Medpro
275 Highway 18
East Brunswick, NJ 08816
732-905-9001
800-257-5145
Fax: 732-905-9899

Jody Gorran, President

Acts like an additional layer of fatty tissue beneath the patient to help prevent and treat pressure sores.

3226 Spenco Medical Group
PO Box 2501
Waco, TX 76702-2501
254-772-6000
800-433-3334
Fax: 817-751-5799
e-mail: spenco@spenco.com
http://www.spenco.com

Mark B Connors, VP Sales/Marketing
Patty Smith, Controller
Steven B Smith, CEO

Wheel chair cushions, Silicore mattress pads, wound dressings, second skin blister and burn pads, Polysorb insoles, elbow, knee, wrist supports, walking shoes.

3227 Stop-Leak Gel Flotation Cushion
Jefferson Industries
1985 Rutgers University Boulevard
Lakewood, NJ 08701-4537
732-905-9001
800-257-5145
Fax: 732-905-9899

Charles Landa, General Manager

Helps protect against pressure ulcers by functioning as an extra protective layer of fat which helps reduce and distribute pressure.

3228 Stop-Leak Gel Flotation Mattress
Jefferson Industries
1985 Rutgers University Boulevard
Lakewood, NJ 08701-4537
732-905-9001
800-257-5145
Fax: 732-905-9899

Charles Landa, General Manager

Protects persons from messy leaks while it protects from pressure ulcers.

Disability Aids & Assistive Devices/Dressing Aids

3229 Sun-Mate Seat Cushions
Dynamic Systems
104 Morrow Branch
Leicester, NC 28748-5710
828-683-3523
Fax: 828-683-3511
e-mail: dsi@sunmatecushions.com
http://www.sunmatecushions.com

Charles A Yost, CEO
Ellie Brown, Operations Manager

Line of cushions, pads and accessory items for personal comfort of the disabled. SunMate Orthopedic foam cushions and sheets that contours slowly to give uniform pressure distribution and soft spring back. Liquid SunMate for Foam-in-Place Seating (FIPS) to make custom molded seat inserts.

3230 Synthetic Sheep-Skin Pads
Hallmark Orthopedic Company
414 Rolyn Place
Arcadia, CA 91066-1060
818-446-4882
Fax: 818-446-8668

William J Hall, Co-Owner

Made of 100% Kodel polyester pile fabric these synthetic, sheepskin pads are autoclavable, retain resilience, and act as an aid to prevent bed sores.

3231 Twin-Rest Seat Cushion & Glamour Pillow
Better Sleep
100 Readington Road
Suite 2
Branchburgh, NJ 08876
908-393-0120
Fax: 908-393-0126
e-mail: info@better-sleep.com
http://www.better-sleep.com

William H Emery, President

Makes any seat more comfortable because it is ingeniously designed to soothe sensitive areas while at work, in the car, or at home.

3232 Wal-Pil-O
Cleo of New York
S Buckout Street
Irvington, NY 10533
914-591-4900
800-321-0595
Fax: 914-591-4083

Elliott Goldberg, President

Uniquely designed pillow relieves discomforts of head, neck and shoulder pain.

3233 Wheelchair and Mattress Pads
Action Products
22 N Mulberry Street
Hagerstown, MD 21740-4910
301-797-1414
800-228-7763
Fax: 301-733-2073
e-mail: service@actionproducts.com
http://www.actionproducts.com

Troy McNight, President

Aids in the prevention and cure of pressure sores by reducing pressure.

Dressing Aids

3234 Button Aid
Maxi Aids
42 Executive Boulevard
Farmingdale, NY 11735-4710
631-752-0521
800-522-6294
Fax: 631-752-0689
e-mail: sales@maxiaids.com
http://www.maxiaids.com
TTY 631-752-0738

Harold Zaretsky, President

Makes buttoning possible with the use of only one hand.

3235 Crutch Pockets
Cleo of New York
S Buckout Street
Irvington, NY 10533
914-591-4900
800-321-0595
Fax: 914-591-4083

Elliott Goldberg, President

Snaps under the hand grips and tie to the adjustable bar. This washable, durable pouch is perfect for holding a wallet, glasses, keys, a drink or a book.

3236 Deluxe Sock and Stocking Aid
Therapro
225 Arlington Street
Framingham, MA 01702-8773
508-872-9494
800-257-5376
Fax: 508-875-2062
e-mail: info@theraproducts.com
http://www.theraproducts.com

Karen Conrad, Owner

Flexible plastic, lined with blue nylon to reduce friction and outside with beige terry cloth to hold sock firmly until it is on the foot.

3237 Dressing Stick
Maxi Aids
42 Executive Boulevard
Farmingdale, NY 11735-4710
631-752-0521
800-522-6294
Fax: 631-752-0689
e-mail: sales@maxiaids.com
http://www.maxiaids.com
TTY 631-752-0738

Harold Zaretsky, President

Helps put on coats, sweaters and garments even when arm and shoulder movement is limited.

3238 Elastic Shoelaces
Therapro
225 Arlington Street
Framingham, MA 01702-8773
508-872-9494
800-257-5376
Fax: 508-875-2062
e-mail: info@theraproducts.com
http://www.theraproducts.com

Karen Conrad, Owner

The elastic laces allow the wearer to slip tied shoes on and off.

3239 Featherweight Reachers
Therapro
225 Arlington Street
Framingham, MA 01702-8773
508-872-9494
800-257-5376
Fax: 508-875-2062
e-mail: info@theraproducts.com
http://www.theraproducts.com

Karen Conrad, Owner

Useful in dressing or retrieving objects.

3240 Folding Dressing Stick
Access with Ease
PO Box 1150
Chino Valley, AZ 86323-1150
928-636-9469
800-531-9479
Fax: 928-636-0292
e-mail: kmjc@northlink.com

Helps the physically-challenged user put on shirts, coats and jackets easily. This dressing stick folds for easy storage.

Disability Aids & Assistive Devices/Health Aids

3241 Mirror Go Lightly
AbleNet
2808 Fairview Avenue North
Roseville, MN 55113-1308
651-294-2200
800-322-0956
Fax: 651-294-2259
e-mail: customerservice@ablenetinc.com
http://www.ablenetinc.com

Mary Kay Walch, Press Center

Framed in plastic, the mirror can be tilted to provide either a normal or magnified image, or to direct its lights at, or away from, the user.

3242 Molded Sock and Stocking Aid
Therapro
225 Arlington Street
Framingham, MA 01702-8773
508-872-9494
800-257-5376
Fax: 508-875-2062
e-mail: info@theraproducts.com
http://www.theraproducts.com

Karen Conrad, Owner

Sock or stocking is pulled over the molded plastic and then can be put on more easily.

3243 No-Bows Shoe Lace Fasteners
Cleo of New York
S Buckout Street
Irvington, NY 10533
914-591-4900
800-321-0595
Fax: 914-591-4083

Elliott Goldberg, President

Small plastic device slides onto lace, firmly fastening the laces in place.

3244 Say What
Maxi Aids
42 Executive Boulevard
Farmingdale, NY 11735-4710
631-752-0521
800-522-6294
Fax: 631-752-0689
e-mail: sales@maxiaids.com
http://www.maxiaids.com
TTY 631-752-0738

Harold Zaretsky, President

Braille the tag with information that the wearer wants on the tag and place the tag on a hanger. The custom-identification program makes it easier for the user to remember and identify just the right clothes.

3245 Zipper Pull
Cleo of New York
S Buckout Street
Irvington, NY 10533
914-591-4900
800-321-0595
Fax: 914-591-4083

Elliott Goldberg, President

Hand-held hook makes using zippers trouble-free.

Health Aids

3246 AMI Aquamassage
PO Box 808
Groton, CT 06340
860-536-3735
800-248-4031
Fax: 860-536-4362
e-mail: sales@aquamassage.com
http://www.amiaqua.com

David Cote, President
Hilaire Cote, Sr. Vice President
Gerardo Aristi, Vice President of Operations

The Aqua PT's 36 computer controlled water jets provide the effects of accupressure massage on three sides of the body in either two directions (pain management) or one direction (edema reduction). Concentrate on the full body, one area, or one specific problem point. The client remains clothed and dry. Aqua PT has adjustable water pressure and pulsating frequency, an automatic frequency, travel speed control and is easy to operate. $20,000-$24,000

3247 American Medical Industries
330 E 3rd Street
Suite 2
Dell Rapids, SD 57022-1918
605-428-5501
Fax: 605-428-5502
e-mail: info@pillcrusherguys.com
http://www.pillcrusherguys.com

James Fiocchi, Sr., CEO
Dan Anderson, Vice President

EZ-Swallow, EZ-Health, WZ-Home Care, Kleen-Handz, Kleen-Scent, EZ-Irrigator, EZ-VU, Pureshark, Gobot, and AMI are all trademarks of American Medical Industries. Healthcare and Healthcare products made easy.

3248 Arm Volumeter Set
JA Preston Corporation
60 Page Road
Clifton, NJ 07012-1421
973-777-2700
800-631-7277

Provides a standard vessel with overflow design to use in evaluating edema and response to treatment.

3249 Blood Pressure Unit Auto Inflation
Cleo of New York
S Buckout Street
Irvington, NY 10533
914-591-4900
800-321-0595
Fax: 914-591-4083

Elliott Goldberg, President

Jumbo digital display, automatic air release valve, symbol key indicating errors make this blood pressure unit easy to use by the non-professional.

3250 Cleoplast Therapeutic Putty-2 oz.
Cleo of New York
S Buckout Street
Irvington, NY 10533
914-591-4900
800-321-0595
Fax: 914-591-4083

Elliott Goldberg, President

This nonirritating, nonsticking pliant silicon putty is excellent for rehabilitation exercise of the hand.

3251 Digi-Flex
Therapro
225 Arlington Street
Framingham, MA 01702-8773
508-872-9494
800-257-5376
Fax: 508-875-2062
e-mail: info@theraproducts.com
http://www.theraproducts.com

Karen Conrad, Owner

Disability Aids & Assistive Devices/Health Aids

This is a unique hand and finger exercise unit. Recommended for use of individuation of fingers, web space and general strengthening of work hands.

3252 Digital Battery Operated Blood Pressure
Cleo of New York
S Buckout Street
Irvington, NY 10533
914-591-4900
800-321-0595
Fax: 914-591-4083

Elliott Goldberg, President

Blood pressure and pulse measurement are taken from the left index finger and displayed on an LCD panel. For use by the professional as well as the layman.

3253 Digital and Audible Family Thermometer
Maxi Aids
42 Executive Boulevard
Farmingdale, NY 11735-4710
631-752-0521
800-522-6294
Fax: 631-752-0689
e-mail: sales@maxiaids.com
http://www.maxiaids.com
TTY 631-752-0738

Harold Zaretsky, President

Audible clinical thermometer.

3254 Drew Karol Industries
PO Box 1066
Greenville, MS 38702-1066
662-378-2188
Fax: 662-378-3188
e-mail: dki@techinfo.com

Andrew Hoszowski, President

Orally operated toothbrush and dental care system for persons with limited or complete loss of hand or arm use - wheelchair accessible.

3255 Duro-Med Industries
1788 West Cherry Street
Po Box 547
Jesup, GA 31598-0327
912-427-7358
800-526-4753
Fax: 800-479-7968
e-mail: cs@duromed.com
http://www.duro-med.com

John Hargrove, President
Carolina Dear, Owner

Manufacturers of a complete line of Home Health Care products. Featured products are patient gowns, back and seat cushions, pillows, and a complete line of aids for daily living.

3256 Electronic Stethoscopes
HARC Mercantile
1111 W Centre Avenue
Portage, MI 49024-5317
269-324-0301
800-445-9968
Fax: 269-324-2387
e-mail: home@hacofamerica.com
http://www.hacofamerica.com

Ronald Slager, President

High production fidelity with a number volume control wheel.

3257 Foot Inversion Tread
Bailey Manufacturing Company
Po Box 130
Lodi, OH 44254-1056
330-948-1080
800-321-8372
Fax: 800-224-5390
e-mail: baileymfg@attmail.com
http://www.baileymfg.com

Larry Strimple, President

Effective for correcting flat feet. These angled boards require the patient to walk on the outside of the foot instead of the arch.

3258 GA-SK
Telecommunications for the Deaf
8630 Fenton Street
Suite 604
Silver Spring, MD 20910-3822
301-589-3786
Fax: 301-589-3797
e-mail: info@tdi-online.org
http://www.tdi-online.org
TTY 301-589-3006

Claude Stout, Editor
James House, Managing Editor
ken glickman, Advertising manager

A quarterly publication focusing on telecommunications and media access for people who are deaf, late-deafened, hard of hearing and deaf-blind.

40 pages Frequency: Quarterly

3259 Hand/Nail Brush
Access with Ease
PO Box 1150
Chino Valley, AZ 86323-1150
928-636-9469
800-531-9479
Fax: 928-636-0292
e-mail: kmjc@northlink.com

Suction cups hold this special brush in place.

3260 Hygenics Direct Company
3968 194th Trail
Miami, FL 33160
610-397-0788
800-498-7051
Fax: 610-397-0790
e-mail: yourkleinerts@aol.com
http://www.hygienics.com

Michael Brier, President

Catalog offers a complete line of incontinence products and skin care products consisting of disposables and reuseables.

16 pages Frequency: BiAnnual

3261 International Deaf/Tek, Inc.
104 Catbriar Court
Summerville, SC 29485-8955
843-851-6444
Fax: 843-626-0270
e-mail: deaftek@deaftek.org
http://www.deaftek.org
TTY 843-851-6444

Brenda Monene RN, MEd, President

Provides the international electronic mail service, Deaftek, USA. This service is dedicated to communities that are deaf or hard of hearing; the service is used by individuals, organizations, agencies, schools, colleges and universities, service providers, and professionals in the field of deafness.

3262 Invacare Corporation
1 Invacare Way
Elyria, OH 44035-4196
440-329-6000
Fax: 440-329-6568
e-mail: susan.elder@invacare.com
http://www.invacare.com

Gerald B Blouch, President/COO
A Malachi Mixon III, CEO

The world's leading manufacturer and distributor of home health care products and mobility products for people with disabilities which are distributed worldwide through more than 10,000 provider locations in more than 80 countries.

3263 LS & S Products
PO Box 673
Northbrook, IL 60065
847-498-9777
800-468-4789
Fax: 847-498-1482
e-mail: info@lssproducts.com
http://www.lssproducts.com
TDD 866-317-8533

Melissa T Balbach, President
John K Bace, Executive VP

Disability Aids & Assistive Devices/Health Aids

LS&S has served the needs of the visually impaired and hard of hearing for over 20 years. We offer products that allow people to continue to live productive, independent lives. In order to find the right products, we constantly listen to customer feedback on products and ideas. In addition, we offer large print or cassette instructions for certain products upon request. Putting the customer first drives our mission at LS&S.

3264 MADAMIST 50/50 PSI Air Compressor
Mada Medical Products
625 Washington Ave
Carlstadt, NJ 07072-2503
201-460-0454
800-526-6370
Fax: 201-460-3509
http://www.madamedical.com

Jeffrey Adam, VP

The new compressor rated at 50 PSI is designed to drive humidifiers, nebulizers and mist tents, and ideal to administer pentamidine aerosol therapy.

3265 MedDev Corporation
730 N Pastoria Avenue
Sunnyvale, CA 94085-3522
408-730-9702
800-543-2789
Fax: 408-730-9732
e-mail: info@meddev-corp.com
http://www.meddev-corp.com

Suzanne Gray, Owner

Aids to rehabilitate hands following injury or illness, including patented complementary FingerHelper, ThumbHelper and Iso HandHelper models. Med Dev also manufactures Soft Touch foam exercisers and the FiddlLink exerciser for digital dexterity. New for 2000, the Ultimate Hand Helper, an Ergonomically designed hand excerciser curved to confirm to the shape of the hand.

3266 Medi-Grip
Therapro
225 Arlington Street
Framingham, MA 01702-8773
508-872-9494
800-257-5376
Fax: 508-875-2062
e-mail: info@theraproducts.com
http://www.theraproducts.com

Karen Conrad, Owner

Reasonably priced, non-skid material. This non-slip material is available in Marine Blue, Desert Sand and Burgundy, rolls 12 inches by 144 inches.

3267 Mini-Vibrator Stress Remover
Cleo of New York
S Buckout Street
Irvington, NY 10533
914-591-4900
800-321-0595
Fax: 914-591-4083

Elliott Goldberg, President

Small, handheld battery operated massager with three different rubber heads.

3268 Pill Splitter
Access with Ease
PO Box 1150
Chino Valley, AZ 86323-1150
928-636-9469
800-531-9479
Fax: 928-636-0292
e-mail: kmjc@northlink.com

A mechanical device for opening pill bottles.

3269 Plums Award Winning Protects Hip
Plum Enterprises
500 Freedom View Lane
Po Box 85
Valley Forge, PA 19481
610-783-7377
800-321-7586
Fax: 610-783-7577
e-mail: info@plument.com
http://www.plument.com

Lance S Wright III, VP Sales/Marketing

Is engineered for safety, designed for exquiste simplicity.

3270 Pocket Otoscope
HARC Mercantile
1111 W Centre Avenue
Portage, MI 49024-5317
269-324-0301
800-445-9968
Fax: 269-324-2387
e-mail: home@hacofamerica.com
http://www.hacofamerica.com

Ronald Slager, President

Simple, durable and dependable pocket otoscope uses standard replaceable parts.

3271 Protecta Capstet
Plum Enterprises
500 Freedom View Lane
PO Box 85
Valley Forge, PA 19481
610-783-7377
800-321-7586
Fax: 610-783-7577
e-mail: info@plument.com
http://www.plument.com

Lance S Wright III, VP Sales/Marketing

Fits and works better than custom made helmets, lightest safest most comfortable. Prescribed post brain surgery, drop seizures, autism, hemophilia.

3272 ProtectaCap+PLUS, ProtectaHip
Plum Enterprises
500 Freedom View Lane
Po Box 85
Valley Forge, PA 19481
610-783-7377
800-321-7586
Fax: 610-783-7577
e-mail: info@plument.com
http://www.plument.com

Lance S Wright III, VP Sales/Marketing

A distinctive dual core makes it the ultimate helmet for sports, hippo therapy and plagiocephaly.

3273 Talking Thermometers
Maxi Aids
42 Executive Boulevard
Farmingdale, NY 11735-4710
631-752-0521
800-522-6294
Fax: 631-752-0689
e-mail: sales@maxiaids.com
http://www.maxiaids.com
TTY 631-752-0738

Harold Zaretsky, President

Clearly announces temperature in Fahrenheit or Celcius.

3274 Therapy Putty
Therapro
225 Arlington Street
Framingham, MA 01702-8773
508-872-9494
800-257-5376
Fax: 508-875-2062
e-mail: info@theraproducts.com
http://www.theraproducts.com

Karen Conrad, Owner

Designed to exercise and strengthen hands, ranging from soft to firm for developing a stronger grasp. Available in two, four and six ounce sizes. In unique clear fist shaped container.

Disability Aids & Assistive Devices/Hearing Aids

Hearing Aids

3275 Battery Device Adapter
AbleNet
2808 Fairview Avenue North
Roseville, MN 55113-1308
651-294-2200
800-322-0956
Fax: 651-294-2259
e-mail: customerservice@ablenetinc.com
http://www.ablenetinc.com
Mary Kay Walch, Press Center

A cable which connects to and adapts battery-operated devices for external switch control. Two sizes are available to adapt devices with AA or C and D size batteries.

3276 Custom Earmolds
Lloyd Hearing Aid Corporation
4435 Manchester Drive
Rockford, IL 61104-1110
815-964-4191
800-323-4212
Fax: 815-964-8378
http://www.lloyohearingaid.com
Andrew Palmquist, President
Marv Palmquist, Founder

Hearing aid molds, custom built to the exact fit of the customer.

3277 Duracell & Rayovac Hearing Aid Batteries
Lloyd Hearing Aid Corporation
4435 Manchester Drive
Rockford, IL 61109
815-964-4191
800-323-4212
Fax: 815-964-8378
http://www.lloydhearingaid.com
Andrew Palmquist, President
Marv Palmquist, Founder

Batteries for hearing aids at discounted prices. As low as 70 cents each.

3278 HARC Mercantile-Division of HAC ofAmerica
1111 W Centre Avenue
Portage, MI 49024-5317
269-324-0301
800-445-9968
Fax: 269-324-2387
e-mail: home@hacofamerica.com
http://www.hacofamerica.com
Ron Slager, Owner

Specializes in products for the hard of hearing and deaf as required under ADA including visual alerting products for fire, phone, door, wake up, phone amplification, TTY, FM and infrared listening systems.

3279 Hearing Aid Batteries
HARC Mercantile
1111 W Centre Avenue
Portage, MI 49024-5317
269-324-0301
800-445-9968
Fax: 269-324-2387
e-mail: home@hacofamerica.com
http://www.hacofamerica.com
Ronald Slager, President

Hearing aid batteries in all popular sizes in mercury, zinc air, silver as well as Nicad and Varta, and batteries for electrolarynx and infrared systems.

3280 Hearing Aid Battery Testers
HARC Mercantile
1111 W Centre Avenue
Portage, MI 49024-5317
269-324-0301
800-445-9968
Fax: 269-324-2387
e-mail: home@hacofamerica.com
http://www.hacofamerica.com
Ronald Slager, President

From pocket size to professional type battery testers which test mercury, zinc air, silver, specialty and general usage batteries.

3281 Hearing Aid Dehumidifier
HARC Mercantile
1111 W Centre Avenue
Portage, MI 49024-5317
269-324-0301
800-445-9968
Fax: 269-324-2387
e-mail: home@hacofamerica.com
http://www.hacofamerica.com
Ronald Slager, President

Removes moisture from hearing aids and valuables. Contains desiccant pack and humidity guide, all in a rugged, vinyl case which provides protection and is water resistant.

3282 In the Ear Hearing Aid Battery Extractor
HARC Mercantile
1111 W Centre Avenue
Portage, MI 49024-5317
269-324-0301
800-445-9968
Fax: 269-324-2387
e-mail: home@hacofamerica.com
http://www.hacofamerica.com
Ronald Slager, President

Ideal tool to use when battery is stuck in battery compartment in ITE and canal hearing aids.

3283 Lloyd Hearing Aid Corporation
4435 Manchester Drive
Rockford, IL 61109
815-964-4191
800-323-4212
Fax: 815-964-8378
e-mail: info@lloydhearingaid.com
http://www.lloydhearingaid.com
Marv Palmquist, Founder
Andy Palmquist, President

Helps absorb any moisture that might damage the hearing aid.

3284 Mushroom Inserts
Lloyd Hearing Aid Corporation
4435 Manchester Drive
Rockford, IL 61109
815-964-4191
800-323-4212
Fax: 815-964-8378
http://www.lloydhearingaid.com
Andy Palmquist, President
Marv Palmquist, Founder

A universal earplug useful in wearing behind the ear type hearing instruments.

3285 Name Brand Hearing Aids
Lloyd Hearing Aid Corporation
4435 Manchester Drive
Rockford, IL 61109
815-964-4191
800-323-4212
Fax: 815-964-8378
http://www.lloydhearingaid.com
Andrew Palmquist, President
Marv Palmquist, Founder

Hearing aids at discounts of up to 60%. Most makes and models with service to/from anywhere in the United States with a 30-day home trial.

3286 Oval Window Audio
33 Wildflower Court
Nederland, CO 80466-9638
303-447-3607
Fax: 303-447-3607
e-mail: info@ovalwindowaudio.com
http://www.ovalwindowaudio.com
TDD 303-447-3607
Norman Lederman, Director/Research & Development
Paula Hendricks, Education Director

Manufacturer of induction loop hearing assistance technologies compatible with hearing aids already used by many hard of hearing people. Also multisensory sound systems for use in speech and music therapy and science classes.

Disability Aids & Assistive Devices/Hobbies and Sports

Hobbies and Sports

3287 **Adaptive Golf Car Model 4850**
Fairway Golf Cars
W220n507 Springfield Road
Waukesha, WI 53186
262-542-6060
888-320-4850
Fax: 262-542-4258

Robert Hanson, Director Sales
Cheryl Tesch, Executive Assistant
Cole Braun, President

Fairway believes that anyone should be able to enjoy the game of golf, regardless of physical challenge. The Spirit is designed to allow access to every aspect of the course - even greens and bunkers. The Spirit features an adjustable seat with flip up arms and pivots to each corner for optimal positioning of play and easy to use thumb controls. Design provides rider comfort as well as protection to areas on the course susceptible to damage.

3288 **Embroidery Hoop**
Cleo of New York
S Buckout Street
Irvington, NY 10533
914-591-4900
800-321-0595
Fax: 914-591-4083

Elliott Goldberg, President

Enables persons with use of only one hand to knit, crochet or embroider.

3289 **Hammatt Senior Products: Catalog for Activity Professionals**
PO Box 727
Mount Vernon, WA 98273
253-428-5850
Fax: 253-428-5760

Free 40 page catalog is offered of group and independent activities and games for the physically challenged and cognitively impaired.

3290 **Knitting Needle Holder**
Cleo of New York
S Buckout Street
Irvington, NY 10533
914-591-4900
800-321-0595
Fax: 914-591-4083

Elliott Goldberg, President

Clamps with quick-release device to chair arm or table. Snail clamp holds needle firm for one-handed use.

3291 **Score Card Set**
American Printing House for the Blind
1839 Frankfort Avenue
Po Box 6085
Louisville, KY 40206-0085
502-895-2405
800-223-1839
Fax: 502-899-2274
e-mail: info@aph.org
http://www.aph.org

Tuck Tinsley, President
Bob Brasher, VP Advisory Services & Research
Gary Mudd, VP Public Affairs

This handy card is made of durable plastic, has twenty buttons in two rows of ten and may be pushed up and down hundreds of times without wearing out. Can be used to keep count of the number of points scored by a sports team, or to count how many questions have been asked during '20 Questions.'

3292 **Spectrum Aquatics**
320 Industrial Drive
West Chicago, IL 60185
800-776-5309
Fax: 800-728-7143
e-mail: info@spectrumaquatics.com
http://www.specturmaquatics.com

David Murray, President
George Bowman, Sales/Marketing
Kelly Youbles, Marketing/Communications

Leading manufacturers of assisted access lifts, stainless steel hydrotherapy tanks for the swimming pool and medical therapy markets.

Home Aids

3293 **Abbey Home Healthcare**
2449 Larkin Street
San Francisco, CA 94109-1725
415-515-6734
800-233-0098
Fax: 702-441-2632

Ronald J Pion MD, Contact

Lifts, chairs, bathroom aids, bedroom aids, eating utensils and independent living aids for the physically challenged.

3294 **Analog Clock Model**
American Printing House for the Blind
1839 Frankfort Avenue
Po Box 6085
Louisville, KY 40206-0085
502-895-2405
800-223-1839
Fax: 502-899-2274
e-mail: info@aph.org
http://www.aph.org

Tuck Tinsley, President
Bob Brasher, VP/ Advisory Services & Research
Gary Mudd, VP Public Affairs

The Analog Clock Model has hour and minute hands which are geared together and minute hands which are geared together and synchronized just like the hands on a functional clock. The hour hand is textured, while the minute hand is smooth and thin.

3295 **BeOK Key Lever**
Sammons Preston Rolyan
Po Box 5071
Bolingbrook, IL 60440-4661
630-226-1300
800-323-5547
Fax: 800-547-4333
e-mail: customersupport@patterson-medical.com
http://www.sammonsprestonrolyan.com

Bonnie Polvinale CMP, Senior VP

Handy accessory helps position key to provide maximum leverage enabling the user to work the most stubborn lock.

3296 **Big Lamp Switch**
Maxi Aids
42 Executive Boulevard
Farmingdale, NY 11735-4710
631-752-0521
800-522-6294
Fax: 631-752-0689
e-mail: sales@maxiaids.com
http://www.maxiaids.com
TTY 631-752-0738

Harold Zaretsky, President

This big, three-spoked knob replaces small rotating knobs which are a problem for those with arthritis or other limitations of the fingers.

Disability Aids & Assistive Devices/Home Aids

3297 Cigarette Holder
Cleo of New York
S Buckout Street
Irvington, NY 10533
914-591-4900
800-321-0595
Fax: 914-591-4083

Elliott Goldberg, President

Holds cigarettes for the physically challenged.

3298 Cordless Receiver
AbleNet
2808 Fairview Avenue North
Roseville, MN 55113-1308
651-294-2200
800-322-0956
Fax: 651-294-2259
e-mail: customerservice@ablenetinc.com
http://www.ablenetinc.com

Mary Kay Walch, Press Center

The Cordless Receiver in conjunction with the Cordless Big Red Switch, can be used anywhere a switch is currently used to control battery- or electrically - operated toys, games or appliances; augmentative communication systems; computers (through a computer switch interface).

3299 Dazor Manufacturing Corporation
11721 Dunlap Industrial Drive
Maryland Heights, MO 63043
314-652-2400
800-345-9103
Fax: 314-652-2069
e-mail: info@dazor.com
http://www.dazor.com

Richard Kupferer, Marketing Coordinator
Morris Zuckerman, Inside Accounts Manager
Mark Hogrebe, President

Dazor is a US manufacturer of quality task lightning. Products include fluorescent, incandescent and halogen lighting fixtures to include illuminated magnifiers combine light and magnification to greatly enhance vision making activities such as reading as hobbies more enjoyable. All lamps come in a variety of mounting options to include desk bases, clamp on, floor stands and wall tracks. $95-$450.

3300 Dorma Architectural Hardware
Dorma Drive Drawer Ac
Reamstown, PA 17567
717-336-3881
800-523-8483
Fax: 717-336-2106
e-mail: archdw@dorma-usa.com
http://www.dorma-usa.com

Larry O'Toole, CEO
John Bergstrom, Director Sales

DORMA provides a complete line of door controls including barrier-free units that comply with the Americans with Disabilities Act. A wide variety of surface applied and concealed closers and exit devices are available to address these requirements.

3301 Dual Switch Latch and Timer
AbleNet
2808 Fairview Avenue North
Roseville, MN 55113-1308
651-294-2200
800-322-0956
Fax: 651-294-2259
e-mail: customerservice@ablenetinc.com
http://www.ablenetinc.com

Mary Kay Walch, Press Center

A Dual Switch Latch and Timer allows two users to activate two devices at a time in the latch, timed seconds or timed minutes mode of control.

3302 Electronic Keyless Entry System
Ahnafield Corporation
2444 Production Drive
Indianapolis, IN 46241
317-241-2444
800-636-8060
Fax: 317-636-8098
e-mail: joe@ahnafield.com
http://www.ahnafield.com

Jeff Ahnafield, President
Joe Kabat

A push button electronic combination lock that operates doors and wheelchair lifts in sequence.

3303 Everest & Jennings
Division of Graham Fields
3601 Rider Trail S
Earth City, MO 63045-1116
314-512-7000
800-235-4661
Fax: 800-542-3567

Manufactures more than 200 items for persons with physical disabilities, including wheelchairs, seat cushions, shower chairs, grab bars, and more.

3304 Folding Reacher
Accent Books & Products
PO Box 700
Bloomington, IL 61702
309-378-2961
800-787-8444
Fax: 309-378-4420

Lightweight, adjustable, foldable reacher allowing one-handed operation.

3305 Foot Placement Ladder
Bailey Manufacturing Company
Po Box 130
Lodi, OH 44254-1056
330-948-1080
800-321-8372
Fax: 800-224-5390
e-mail: baileymfg@attmail.com
http://www.baileymfg.com

Larry Strimple, President

Adjustable cross bars for different length steps. Reinforced metal crosses for easier climbing for the physically-disabled.

3306 Handy Reacher
Access with Ease
PO Box 1150
Chino Valley, AZ 86323-1150
928-636-9469
800-531-9479
Fax: 928-636-0292
e-mail: kmjc@northlink.com

Long handled reacher retrieves items off high shelves.

3307 Key Holder
Accent Books & Products
PO Box 700
Bloomington, IL 61702
309-378-2961
800-787-8444
Fax: 309-378-4420

Makes turning keys easier by offering a lever action. Holds two keys which fold back into the plastic holder when not in use.

3308 Knock Light
HARC Mercantile
1111 W Centre Avenue
Portage, MI 49024-5317
269-324-0301
800-445-9968
Fax: 269-324-2387
e-mail: home@hacofamerica.com
http://www.hacofamerica.com

Ronald Slager, President

Easily attaches to a door with velcro, portable.

Disability Aids & Assistive Devices/Kitchen and Eating Aids

3309 Lindustries
21 Shady Hill Road
Weston, MA 02493-1407 617-237-8177
William Lind, President
Louise Lind, Vice President

Open doors with an easy touch! LEVERON converts all standard doorknobs to lever action for people with hand, wrist, or visual impairment. Whether for temporary or long-term convenience while healing, LEVERON provides in-home assistance with ergonomic design, warmth of touch and ease of action even by elbow or palm of hand. At low-cost, one size fits left/right, inside/outside doorknobs and can be quickly installed without removing doorknob by any helping hand. Complying with ADA for schools/public buildings, LEVERON has been available since 1989 in medical catalogs, their websites and through Lindustries.

3310 Longreach Reacher
Therapro
225 Arlington Street
Framingham, MA 01702-8773 508-872-9494
 800-257-5376
 Fax: 508-875-2062
e-mail: info@theraproducts.com
http://www.theraproducts.com
Karen Conrad, Owner

Reacher is useful when reaching, sitting or when standing.

3311 Loop Scissors
Therapro
225 Arlington Street
Framingham, MA 01702-8773 508-872-9494
 800-257-5376
 Fax: 508-875-2062
e-mail: info@theraproducts.com
http://www.theraproducts.com
Karen Conrad, Owner

Pliable, plastic handles that allow for easy and controlled cutting.

3312 Magnifier Highlights
Independent Living Aids
200 Robbins Lane
Jericho, NY 11753-2365 516-937-1848
 800-537-2118
 Fax: 516-937-3906
e-mail: techsupport@independentliving.com
http://www.independentliving.com
Marvin Sandler, President

Carries a full line of magnifiers, ranging from high-powered vision aids to hoppy instruments and accessories.

3313 PowerLink 2 Control Unit
AbleNet
2808 Fairview Avenue North
Roseville, MN 55113-1308 651-294-2200
 800-322-0956
 Fax: 651-294-2259
e-mail: customerservice@ablenetinc.com
http://www.ablenetinc.com
Mary Kay Walch, Press Center

The PowerLink 2 Control Unit allows switch operation of electrical appliances. It can be used to activate 1 or 2 appliances (up to 1700 watts combined). If 2 appliances are used, they will activate simultaneously. There are four modes of control on the PowerLink 2; direct mode, timed (seconds) mode, timed (minutes) mode and latch mode.

3314 Small Appliance Receiver
AbleNet
2808 Fairview Avenue North
Roseville, MN 55113-1308 651-294-2200
 800-322-0956
 Fax: 651-294-2259
e-mail: customerservice@ablenetinc.com
http://www.ablenetinc.com
Mary Kay Walch, Press Center

The Small Appliance Receiver, in conjunction with the Cordless Big Red Switch, allows you to control small electrical appliances in the environment without a cord. It should only be used with low-wattage appliances (under 500 watts) which have two prong plugs (ie, radios, fans, lamps, blenders, etc.). It should not be used with heat generating appliances.

3315 Smoker's Robot
Cleo of New York
S Buckout Street
Irvington, NY 10533 914-591-4900
 800-321-0595
 Fax: 914-591-4083
Elliott Goldberg, President

Allows safe smoking of cigarettes in bed.

3316 Universal Knob Turner
Cleo of New York
S Buckout Street
Irvington, NY 10533 914-591-4900
 800-321-0595
 Fax: 914-591-4083
Elliott Goldberg, President

Lightweight handheld device makes turning knobs and handles really easy.

Kitchen and Eating Aids

3317 AIDS For Daily Living
ETAC USA
2325 Parklawn Drive
Suite J
Waukesha, WI 53186-2938 262-796-4600
 800-678-3722
 Fax: 414-796-4605
e-mail: etacusa@execpc.com

ETAC offers an entire line of products for people that have reduced or limited use of their hands. Cutlery goblets, knives, cutting board, fix preparation boards, plates, grooming aids, and a contoured pen are available.

3318 Adjustable Clear Acrylic Tray
Bailey Manufacturing Company
Po Box 130
Lodi, OH 44254-1056 330-948-1080
 800-321-8372
 Fax: 800-224-5390
e-mail: baileymfg@attmail.com
http://www.baileymfg.com
Larry Strimple, President

Adjusts for height and depth and is equipped with a spill rim for easy to clean edges.

3319 All-Purpose Openers
Enrichments
1000 Remington Blvd.
Bolingbrook, IL 60440-5117 603-378-6000
 800-323-5547
 Fax: 630-378-6010
e-mail: customersupport@sammonspreston.com
http://www.sammonspreston.com

Wall-mounted steel opener can pry-up edges or pop open a bottle with an opening as small as 1/2 or as large as 3 inch. Under cabinet model opens lid sizes 1/2 to 4 1/2 inches.

Disability Aids & Assistive Devices/Kitchen and Eating Aids

3320 Bagel Holder
Maxi Aids
42 Executive Boulevard
Farmingdale, NY 11735-4710
631-752-0521
800-522-6294
Fax: 631-752-0689
e-mail: sales@maxiaids.com
http://www.maxiaids.com
TTY 631-752-0738

Harold Zaretsky, President

Holds bagels in place for easy slicing.

3321 Big Bold Timer Low Vision
Maxi Aids
42 Executive Boulevard
Farmingdale, NY 11735-4710
631-752-0521
800-522-6294
Fax: 631-752-0689
e-mail: sales@maxiaids.com
http://www.maxiaids.com
TTY 631-752-0738

Harold Zaretsky, President

Sixty-minute mechanical timer with large, easy-to-read numbers for the vision impaired.

3322 Black & Decker Cordless Hand Blender
Enrichments
1000 Remington Blvd.
Bolingbrook, IL 60440-5117
603-378-6000
800-323-5547
Fax: 603-378-6010
e-mail: customersupport@patterson-medical.com
http://www.sammonspreston.com

This two-speed blender is both compact and lightweight, yet durable enough for daily food preparation.

3323 Box Top Opener
Enrichments
1000 Remington Blvd.
Bolingbrook, IL 60440-5117
603-378-6000
800-323-5547
Fax: 603-378-6010
e-mail: customersupport@patterson-medical.com
http://www.sammonspreston.com

This handy device exerts the pressure on those hard-to-open boxes of laundry/dishwasher soap, rice and prepared dinners.

3324 Capscrew
Access with Ease
PO Box 1150
Chino Valley, AZ 86323-1150
928-636-9469
800-531-9479
Fax: 928-636-0292
e-mail: kmjc@northlink.com

Remove lids and caps easily.

3325 Cheese Slicer
Cleo of New York
S Buckout Street
Irvington, NY 10533
914-591-4900
800-321-0595
Fax: 914-591-4083

Elliott Goldberg, President

A solid, angled handle makes cutting work easier for people with energy and movement impairment of the hand or arm.

3326 Cordless Receiver
AbleNet
2808 Fairview Avenue North
Roseville, MN 55113-1308
651-294-2200
800-322-0956
Fax: 651-294-2259
e-mail: customerservice@ablenetinc.com
http://www.ablenetinc.com

Mary Kay Walch, Press Center

The Cordless Receiver in conjunction with the Cordless Big Red Switch, can be used anywhere a switch is currently used to control battery- or electrically - operated toys, games or appliances; augmentative communication systems; computers (through a computer switch interface).

3327 Deluxe Long Ring Low Vision Timer Tactile
Maxi Aids
42 Executive Boulevard
Farmingdale, NY 11735-4710
631-752-0521
800-522-6294
Fax: 631-752-0689
e-mail: sales@maxiaids.com
http://www.maxiaids.com
TTY 631-752-0738

Harold Zaretsky, President

Bold black numerals on white background allows for easy reading at any distance.

3328 Deluxe Roller Knife
Enrichments
1000 Remington Blvd.
Bolingbrook, IL 60440-5117
603-378-6000
800-323-5547
Fax: 630-378-6010
e-mail: customersupport@patterson-medical.com
http://www.sammonspreston.com

Stainless steel blade rolls smoothly, cutting food cleanly.

3329 Dual Brush with Suction Base
Enrichments
1000 Remington Blvd.
Bolingbrook, IL 60440-5117
603-378-6000
800-323-5547
Fax: 603-378-6010
e-mail: customersupport@patterson-medical.com
http://www.sammonspreston.com

Two brushes clean the inside and outside of bottles and glasses at the same time using just one hand.

3330 Easy Pour Locking Lid Pot
Maxi Aids
42 Executive Boulevard
Farmingdale, NY 11735-4710
631-752-0521
800-522-6294
Fax: 631-752-0689
e-mail: sales@maxiaids.com
http://www.maxiaids.com
TTY 631-752-0738

Harold Zaretsky, President

Baked enamel and dishwasher safe, the pot comes with an easy lid that locks in place for extra safety.

3331 Electric Can Opener & Knife Sharpener
Maxi Aids
42 Executive Boulevard
Farmingdale, NY 11735-4710
631-752-0521
800-522-6294
Fax: 631-752-0689
e-mail: sales@maxiaids.com
http://www.maxiaids.com
TTY 631-752-0738

Harold Zaretsky, President

Disability Aids & Assistive Devices/Kitchen and Eating Aids

Features include a powerful magnet lid holder, the ability to open odd-shaped cans, and easy operation for the physically challenged.

3332 Evio Plastics
PO Box 2295
Sandusky, OH 44871-2295
419-621-1105
Fax: 419-626-2183

Doug Didion, Admininstrator Director
Danny Thomas, Owner

Handi Holder is a plastic holder for 1/2 gallon paper cartons of milk or juice. It is used to pour milk or juice without spills by using the handle.

3333 Food Markers/Magnets
Maxi Aids
42 Executive Boulevard
Farmingdale, NY 11735-4710
631-752-0521
800-522-6294
Fax: 631-752-0689
e-mail: sales@maxiaids.com
http://www.maxiaids.com
TTY 631-752-0738

Harold Zaretsky, President

These are durable plastic markers, easily identified by touch, texture, shape and form which help the visually impaired orient themselves to food location on the plate.

3334 Food Markers/Rubberbands
Maxi Aids
42 Executive Boulevard
Farmingdale, NY 11735-4710
631-752-0521
800-522-6294
Fax: 631-752-0689
e-mail: sales@maxiaids.com
http://www.maxiaids.com
TTY 631-752-0738

Harold Zaretsky, President

These are durable plastic markers, easily identified by touch, texture, shape and form which help the visually impaired orient themselves to food location on the plate.

3335 Good Grips Cutlery
Therapro
225 Arlington Street
Framingham, MA 01702-8773
508-872-9494
800-257-5376
Fax: 508-875-2062
e-mail: info@theraproducts.com
http://www.theraproducts.com

Karen Conrad, Owner

Stainless steel utensils have a special twist built into the metal to facilitate bending of a spoon or fork at any angle for right or left handed people.

3336 Guide A Knife
Maxi Aids
42 Executive Boulevard
Farmingdale, NY 11735-4710
631-752-0521
800-522-6294
Fax: 631-752-0689
e-mail: sales@maxiaids.com
http://www.maxiaids.com
TTY 631-752-0738

Harold Zaretsky, President

Adjustable food slicing system guides the knife for even, uniform slices while protecting the user.

3337 Handy-Helper Cutting Board
Maxi Aids
42 Executive Boulevard
Farmingdale, NY 11735-4710
631-752-0521
800-522-6294
Fax: 631-752-0689
e-mail: sales@maxiaids.com
http://www.maxiaids.com
TTY 631-752-0738

Harold Zaretsky, President

Laminated cutting board with unique features to hold food in place with corner ledge for cutting and spreading.

3338 Innerlip Plates
Therapro
225 Arlington Street
Framingham, MA 01702-8773
508-872-9494
800-257-5376
Fax: 508-875-2062
e-mail: info@theraproducts.com
http://www.theraproducts.com

Karen Conrad, Owner

Food maybe pushed to the side of the plate, then scooped up with a fork and spoon. Available in beige or blue.

3339 Long Oven Mitts
Enrichments
1000 Remington Blvd.
Bolingbrook, IL 60440-5117
603-378-6000
800-323-5547
Fax: 603-378-6010
e-mail: customersupport@patterson-medical.com
http://sammonspreston.com

Protect hands and forearms from heat, flames and oven grates with these practical mitts that allow a longer reach and less bending.

3340 Magnetic Card Reader
Maxi Aids
42 Executive Boulevard
Farmingdale, NY 11735-4710
631-752-0521
800-522-6294
Fax: 631-752-0689
e-mail: sales@maxiaids.com
http://www.maxiaids.com
TTY 631-752-0738

Harold Zaretsky, President

Produces audible labels so a recorded card could be taped on cans of food or a box of cake mix; even adding instructions for baking.

3341 Maxi Aid Braille Timer
Maxi Aids
42 Executive Boulevard
Farmingdale, NY 11735-4710
631-752-0521
800-522-6294
Fax: 631-752-0689
e-mail: sales@maxiaids.com
http://www.maxiaids.com
TTY 631-752-0738

Harold Zaretsky, President

Three raised dots at 15, 30 and 45, two raised dots at remaining five minute intervals and one raised dot at remaining two and a half minute intervals, offers ease of operation to make this a helpful aid for the visually impaired.

Disability Aids & Assistive Devices/Kitchen and Eating Aids

3342 Nosey Cup
Therapro
225 Arlington Street
Framingham, MA 01702-8773
508-872-9494
800-257-5376
Fax: 508-875-2062
e-mail: info@theraproducts.com
http://www.theraproducts.com

Karen Conrad, Owner

For those with a stiff neck, or persons who can't tip their head back while drinking.

3343 Paring Boards
Therapro
225 Arlington Street
Framingham, MA 01702-8773
508-872-9494
800-257-5376
Fax: 508-875-2062
e-mail: info@theraproducts.com
http://www.theraproducts.com

Karen Conrad, Owner

Suction feet stabilize board and stainless steel prongs hold food in place for easy one-handed cutting.

3344 PowerLink 2 Control Unit
AbleNet
2808 Fairview Avenue North
Roseville, MN 55113-1308
651-294-2200
800-322-0956
Fax: 651-294-2259
e-mail: customerservice@ablenetinc.com
http://www.ablenetinc.com

Mary Kay Walch, Press Center

The PowerLink 2 Control Unit allows switch operation of electrical appliances. It can be used to activate 1 or 2 appliances (up to 1700 watts combined). If 2 appliances are used, they will activate simultaneously. There are four modes of control on the PowerLink 2; direct mode, timed (seconds) mode, timed (minutes) mode and latch mode. Meets safety standards from Underwriters Laboratory (UL) and Canadian Standards Association (CSA) for electrical

3345 Rocking Knife
Cleo of New York
S Buckout Street
Irvington, NY 10533
914-591-4900
800-321-0595
Fax: 914-591-4083

Elliott Goldberg, President

The forged, stainless-steel blade is precisely curved to provide a rocker motion for ease in cutting.

3346 Slicing Aid
Snugseat
12801 E. Independence Blvd.
Matthews, NC 28106-1739
704-882-0668
800-336-7684
Fax: 704-882-0751
e-mail: sales@snugseat.com
http://www.snugseat.com

Krissy Natoli, Public Relations

The design of these knives allows a better working posture and makes optimal use of strength in the arms and hands.

3347 Small Appliance Receiver
AbleNet
2808 Fairview Avenue North
Roseville, MN 55113-1308
651-294-2200
800-322-0956
Fax: 651-294-2259
e-mail: customerservice@ablenetinc.com
http://www.ablenetinc.com

Mary Kay Walch, Press Center

The Small Appliance Receiver, in conjunction with the Cordless Big Red Switch, allows you to control small electrical appliances in the environment without a cord. It should only be used with low-wattage appliances (under 500 watts) which have two prong plugs (ie, radios, fans, lamps, blenders, etc.). It should not be used with heat generating appliances.

3348 Steel Food Guard
Maxi Aids
42 Executive Boulevard
Farmingdale, NY 11735-4710
631-752-0521
800-522-6294
Fax: 631-752-0689
e-mail: sales@maxiaids.com
http://www.maxiaids.com
TTY 631-752-0738

Harold Zaretsky, President

Provides stable area to push against while eating.

3349 Suction Grater
Cleo of New York
S Buckout Street
Irvington, NY 10533
914-591-4900
800-321-0595
Fax: 915-591-4083

Elliott Goldberg, President

3350 Thick-n-Easy
Therapro
225 Arlington Street
Framingham, MA 01702-8773
508-872-9494
800-257-5376
Fax: 508-875-2062
e-mail: info@theraproducts.com
http://www.theraproducts.com

Karen Conrad, Owner

Instant food thickener that sets in 30 seconds and will not become thicker even after refrigeration.

3351 Thumbs Up Cup
Therapro
225 Arlington Street
Framingham, MA 01702-8773
508-872-9494
800-257-5376
Fax: 508-875-2062
e-mail: info@theraproducts.com
http://www.theraproducts.com

Karen Conrad, Owner

This cup is designed for those with limited strength or coordination or arthritis. The two backward-tilt handles and thumb rests allow finger joint to be used to their greatest mechanical advantage.

3352 Undercounter Lid Opener
Enrichments
1000 Remington Blvd.
Bolingbrook, IL 60440-5117
603-378-6000
800-323-5547
Fax: 603-378-6010
e-mail: customersupport@patterson-medical.com
http://www.sammonspreston.com

The gripper of this unit which installs under the counter can help unscrew any cap.

3353 Uni-Turner
Enrichments
1000 Remington Blvd.
Bolingbrook, IL 60440-5117
603-378-6000
800-323-5547
Fax: 630-378-6010
e-mail: customersupport@patterson-medical.com
http://www.sammonspreston.com

Disability Aids & Assistive Devices/Lifts, Ramps, Elevators

Odd-shaped handles can be turned easily with one-handed L-shaped Uni-Turner.

3354 **Universal Hand Cuff**
Therapro
225 Arlington Street
Framingham, MA 01702-8773
508-872-9494
800-257-5376
Fax: 508-875-2062
e-mail: info@theraproducts.com
http://www.theraproducts.com

Karen Conrad, Owner

Comfortable cuff with Velcro strap holds utensils, toothbrushes, etc.

Lifts, Ramps, Elevators

3355 **Access Industries/ThyssenKrupp Access**
4001 E 138th Street
Grandview, MO 64030-2837
800-829-9760
Fax: 816-763-4467
http://www.accessind.com

Thomas Hance, President
Ray Demes, VP Field Office Consumer Care
Chuck Herling, CFO

Committed to improving the quality of life. We are the world's most trusted name in accessibility solutions. Offers a full line of sairway lifts, wheelchair lifts, and elevators. Our nationwide network of certifies dealers ensures you will recieve a prompt, courteous, knowledge service from professional in your area.

3356 **Accessibility Lift**
Inclinator Company of America
601 Gibson Blvd.
Po Box 1557
Harrisburg, PA 17104-1557
717-939-8420
800-343-9007
Fax: 717-939-8075
e-mail: sales@inclinator.com
http://www.inclinator.com

Paul R Krum, President

An economical lift for restricted usage that provides barrier-free access that can be used by churches, schools, lodging halls and meeting halls to meet compliance requirements, with the dignified convenience and freedom they deserve.

3357 **AlumiRamp**
855 E Chicago Road
Quincy, MI 49082-9450
800-800-3864
Fax: 800-753-7267
e-mail: sales@alumiramp.com
http://www.alumiramp.com

Linda Burke, President

Complete line of modular and portable ramps for both home and vehicle use. Welded construction and an wieght aluminum are featured on all our ramps.

3358 **Amigo Mobility International**
6693 Dixie Highway
Bridgeport, MI 48722-9375
989-777-2060
800-692-6446
Fax: 800-334-7274
e-mail: info@myamigo.com
http://www.myamigo.com

Beth Thieme, VP Commercial Sales
Alison Newkirk, West Region Account Manager
Sandy Roth, East Region Account Manager

An industry leader in power-operated vehicles/motorized scooters. we provide innovative, durable and customized mobility solutions to mobility challenges facing the disabled, injured and seniors worldwide.

3359 **Aquatic Access Pool Lifts for Pools andSpas**
417 Dorsey Way
Louisville, KY 40223-2833
502-425-5817
800-325-5438
Fax: 502-425-9607
e-mail: info@aquaticaccess.com
http://www.aquaticaccess.com

Linda Nolan, President
Liz Waters, Marketing
Ann Bryant, Sales

Aquatic Access manufactures a variety of water-powered lifts that provide access to in-ground and above-ground pools, spas, therapy tubs, boats and docks. ADA compliant models available.

3360 **Area Access**
8117 Ransell Road
Falls Church, VA 22042-1015
703-573-2111
800-333-2732
Fax: 703-207-0446
http://www.areaaccess.com

Scott Hobson, Owner

Serving the entire Mid-Atlantic with scooters, stairway lifts and elevators. Large inventory and fully stocked showrooms.

3361 **Barrier Free Lifts**
10505 Pineview Rd.
Manassas, VA 20110-5617
703-361-6531
800-582-8732
Fax: 703-361-7861
e-mail: bflinc@erols.com
http://www.bfl-inc.com

Deborah Hensley, VP/Operations
Teresa Kirk, Administrative Assistant
Robert Rocheford, Marketing and Sales

Barrier Free ceiling and floor model lift systems are available in many models. Ceiling lifts can be portable, fully motorized and state-of-the-art to provide truly barrier-free equipment for lifting and transferring patients. Floor models include the premier LEXA with motorized spreader bar for patient positioning and the RAISA with motorized, adjustable knee pads for standing patients up and gait training. Ceiling lifts available with AIR TUBE

3362 **Braille Plates for Elevator**
Maxi Aids
42 Executive Boulevard
Farmingdale, NY 11735-4710
631-752-0521
800-522-6294
Fax: 631-752-0689
e-mail: sales@maxiaids.com
http://www.maxiaids.com
TTY 631-752-0738

Harold Zaretsky, President

The plates have curing type pressure sensitive material applied for metal to metal bonding.

3363 **Bruno Independent Living Aids**
Bruno Independent Living Aids
1780 Executive Drive
Po Box 84
Oconomowoc, WI 53066
262-567-4990
800-882-8183
Fax: 262-953-5501
e-mail: service@bruno.com
http://www.bruno.com

Michael R Bruno II, President/CEO
Patrick Foy, National Sales Manager
Anne Tyler, Marketing

An ISO 9001 Certified Manufacturer of automotive lifts for scooter, wheelchairs, and powerchairs, three and four wheel scooters, and straight and custom curve stairlifts.

301

Disability Aids & Assistive Devices/Lifts, Ramps, Elevators

3364 Cheney's Liberty II
Handi-Lift
1051 Paulison Avenue
Clifton, NJ 07011-3628
845-429-0368
800-503-2003
Fax: 845-942-2016
e-mail: sales@handilift.com
http://www.handilift.com

Scott Darling, President

Economical lift for straight stairways.

3365 Classique
Handi-Lift
1051 Paulison Avenue
Clifton, NJ 07011-3628
845-429-0368
800-503-2003
Fax: 845-942-2016
e-mail: sales@handilift.com
http://www.handilift.com

Scott Darling, President

The Classique elevator answers access problems in churches, schools and small offices.

3366 Cub, SuperCub and Special EditionScooters
Bruno Independent Living Aids
1780 Executive Drive
Po Box 84
Oconomowoc, WI 53066
262-567-4990
800-882-8183
Fax: 262-953-5501
e-mail: service@bruno.com
http://www.bruno.com

Michael R Bruno II, President/CEO
Patrick Foy, National Sales Manager
Anne Tyler, Marketing

Bruno Independent Living Aids has over 12 different scooter models. Bruno Cub and SuperCub scooters, has front-or-rear wheel drive, in both 3-and-4 wheel versions and comes in four different colors plus a pediatric version. Each scooter can handle up to 300 pounds. Bruno Special Edition scooters resemble a fire engine, police car, Humvee and motorcycle.

3367 Custom Lift Residential Elevators
Waupaca Elevator Company
1726 N Ballard Road
Appleton, WI 54911-2444
920-991-9082
800-238-8739
Fax: 920-991-9087
e-mail: info@waupacaelevator.com
http://www.waupacaelevator.com

Kari C Stumpf, Administration/Dealer Referrals

Waupac Elevator is an industry leader in the manufacturing of residential elevators and dumbwaiters. Our residential elevators can readily accommodate several people, a motorized wheelchair or scooter, or a wheelchair with a caregiver. Consider Waupaca Elevator when you desire to add value, convenience, and reliability to today's homes.

3368 Deluxe Convertible Exercise Staircase
Sammons Preston
1000 Remington Blvd.
Suite 210
Bolingbrook, IL 60440-5117
630-378-6000
800-631-7277
Fax: 630-378-6010
e-mail: customersupport@patterson-medical.com
http://www.sammonspreston.com

Here's an exercise staircase to fit any department configuration. Just reposition a few nuts and bolts to change from a straight to a corner type staircase.

3369 EZ-Access Portable Ramps
Homecare Products
1704 B St NW Ste 110
Auburn, WA 98001-1650
253-631-4633
800-451-1903
Fax: 253-630-8196
e-mail: customerservice@exaccess.com
http://www.homecareproducts.com

Don Everard, VP Marketing
Deanne Sandvold, VP Sales

EZ-ACCESS Ramps bridge gaps over curbs and steps, allowing scooters and wheelchairs to continue on a smooth, safe course. Available in several different styles and sizes, ranging from a two-foot curb ramp to a 10-foot multi-purpose ramp. All ramps are made of anodized aluminum.

3370 Easy Pivot Transfer Machine
Rand-Scot
401 Linden Center Drive
Fort Collins, CO 80524-2429
970-484-7967
800-467-7967
Fax: 970-467-3800
e-mail: info@randscott.com
http://www.easypivot.com

Joel Lerich, President

The Easy Pivot Patient Lifting System allows for strain-free, one-caregiver transfers of the disabled individual.

3371 Easy Stand
Altimate Medica
PO Box 180
262 W 1st. St.
Morton, MN 56270
507-697-6393
800-342-8968
Fax: 507-697-6900
e-mail: info@easystand.com
http://www.easystand.com

Alan Tholkes, President/CEO

Designed to make standing fast and simple. The easy to operate hydraulic lift system provides a controlled lifting and lowering. With the convenience of simply transferring to the chair and reaching a standing position in seconds with no straps to hassle with.

3372 EcoTraction Surface
Bike Track
PO Box 235
Woodstock, VT 05091
802-457-3275
888-663-8537
Fax: 802-457-3704
e-mail: info@biketrack.com
http://www.biketrack.com

Nancy Hoblinest, Sales/Logistics
Barry McVey, President

EcoTrack panels maybe used for beach access, or bike/ped/wheelchair accessible pathways.

3373 Economical Liberty
Handi-Lift
730 Garden Street
Carlstadt, NJ 07072
201-933-0111
800-432-5438
Fax: 201-933-0050
http://www.handi-lift.com

Doug Boydston, President/Co-Founder

Installs quickly and easily on most straight stairways. It uses regular household current and mounts over the carpet or directly to the stairs without marring.

3374 Elevette 2100
Inclinator Company of America
601 Gibson Blvd.
Po Box 1557
Harrisburg, PA 17104-1557
717-939-8420
800-343-9007
Fax: 717-939-8075
e-mail: isales@inclinator.com
http://www.inclinator.com

Paul R Krum, President

Disability Aids & Assistive Devices/Lifts, Ramps, Elevators

A newly designed residential elevator which reduces weight dramatically and permits the use of lower power and less costly motors.

3375 Excel Stair Lift
Access Industries/ThyssenKrupp Access
4001 E 138th Street
Grandview, MO 64030-2837
800-925-3100
800-925-3100
Fax: 816-763-4467
e-mail: thomas.hance@tkaccess.com
http://www.accessind.com

Thomas Hance, President
Ray Demes, VP Field Office Consumer Care
Chuck Herling, CFO

Installs easily on either side of a straight stairway for independent, step-free living. The lift fastens securely to the stairs without marring walls and is adjustable to match any stairway slope with an incline angle up to 45 degrees. Available with battery back up.

3376 Ez International Inc./Ortho Kinetics
Po Box 1647
W220 N507 Springdale Road
Waukesha, WI 53187-1647
262-542-6060
800-558-7786
Fax: 262-542-4258
http://www.orthokinetics.com

William Grady, Sales Manager

Products to enhance people's lives through mobility. These electric three and four wheel vehicles are designed to surpass consumer expectations by providing total comfort, convenience and performance features found nowhere else. Ortho-Kinetics has a full line of vehicles for any application.

3377 Freedom Wheelchair Lifts
5032 Village Court
Haltom City, TX 76117-5561
817-431-9437
800-870-0629
Fax: 817-431-2292

Sandy Patterson, Contact

Complete vehicle modifications for the physically challenged.

3378 Gravity Down Platform Lift
Collins Mobile-Tech Corporation
15 Compound Drive
Hutchinson, KS 67502
620-663-5551
800-835-5007
Fax: 620-663-1630
http://www.collinsind.com

Powerlift with exciting features for the safe, convenient transportation of people with disabilities.

3379 Handi Home Lift
Handi-Lift
730 Garden Street
Carlstadt, NJ 07072-1635
201-933-0111
800-503-2003
Fax: 201-933-0050
e-mail: sales@handi-lift.com
http://www.handi-lift.com

Douglas Boydston, Owner

An outdoor lift designed to provide access over porch stairs or other steps that impede movement.

3380 Handi Prolift
Handi-Lift
730 Garden Street
Carlstadt, NJ 07072-1635
201-933-0111
800-503-2003
Fax: 201-933-0050
e-mail: sales@handi-lift.com
http://www.handi-lift.com

Douglas Boydston, Owner

Provides dependable vertical transportation for multi-level buildings.

3381 Handi-Ramp
Handi-Ramp
510 North Avenue
Libertyville, IL 60048
847-816-7525
800-876-7267
Fax: 847-816-7689
e-mail: info@handi-ramp.com
http://www.handi-ramp.com

Thom Disch, Contact
Ken Knapp, Contact

Provides a complete line of economical, ADA Compliant access ramping products. Line includes Van attachable and Wheelchair Tie Dows; Aluminum or Expanded Meal Folding Portables; aluminum channels; Portable, Sectional Ramp Systems; Semi-Permanent Ramps, Platforms and Systems. All ramp series are available in varied lengths and widths in combination with platforms and optional hand railing, single or double bar construction with return ends. Specia

3382 Homewaiter
Inclinator Company of America
601 Gibson Street
Po Box 1557
Harrisburg, PA 17104-1557
717-939-8420
800-313-9007
Fax: 717-939-8075
e-mail: isales@inclinator.com
http://www.inclinator.com

Paul R Krum, President

With its roller truck riding in a specially formed monorail, it is easy to install and highly adaptable to existing conditions. It can travel up to 35 feet, opening on any or all three sides at different stations, whether at counter level or floor level.

3383 Inclinette
Inclinator Company of America
601 Gibson Street
1557
Harrisburg, PA 17104-1557
717-939-8420
800-343-9007
Fax: 717-939-8075
e-mail: isales@inclinator.com
http://www.inclinator.com

Paul Krum, President

Inclinette provides comfort and convenience in providing multi-floor access to persons who have difficulty climbing stairs.

3384 Leg Elevation Board
Bailey Manufacturing Company
Po Box 130
Lodi, OH 44254-0130
330-948-1080
800-321-8372
Fax: 800-224-5390
http://www.baileymfg.com

Larry Strimple, President

Includes seven positions to a 30 degree incline, three pillows with Velcro, easy carry hand slot and a natural finish.

3385 Liberty LT
Handi-Lift
730 Garden Street
Carlstadt, NJ 07072
201-933-0111
800-432-5438
Fax: 201-933-0050
e-mail: sales@handi-lift.com
http://www.handi-lift.com

Douglas Boydston, President/Co-Founder

Stair lift with dual armrests that lock into position. The comfortable, contoured seat is designed to swivel and move forward at the bottom or top landings to facilitate transfer.

3386 Lizzie Lift
Handicap Helpers
604 W Main Street
Appalachia, VA 24216-1616
276-565-1889
Fax: 276-565-3623
e-mail: jay19482000@yahoo.com
http://www.hurtback.org

James W Blevins, President

Disability Aids & Assistive Devices/Lifts, Ramps, Elevators

A stable patient lift that provides independence for the disabled by allowing one caregiver to move them from bed to upright position more easily and effectively. The Lizzie Lift which can be used as a gurney bed, lounge chair, or wheelchair, not only decreases back injury for caregivers but also alleviates the fear of being moved. Can be used in hospitals, nursing homes, and homes. FDA listing, Patent pending. $7,000-$8,000.

3387 Minivator Residential Elevator
Access Industries/ThyssenKrupp Access
4001 E 138th Street
Grandview, MO 64030-2837
816-763-3100
800-925-3100
Fax: 816-763-4467
e-mail: thomas.hance@tkaccess.com
http://www.accessind.com

Evelyn Johnson, Marketing Supervisor
Tom Hance, President

The perfect choice for a person who is contemplating moving from their multi-storied home because they cannot get up and down the stairs. The low cost, compact Minivator elevator can help these people live independently. The Minivator can be installed in the corner of a room without a shaft or hoistway, so the elevator doesn't have to disfigure the structure. The Minivator elevator can take a person or persons between floors in less than a minute

3388 Pool Lifts for In-Ground Pools
Aquatic Access
417 Dorsey Way
Louisville, KY 40223-2833
502-425-5817
800-325-5438
Fax: 502-425-9607
e-mail: info@aquatic-access.com
http://www.aquatic-access.com

Kathy Nolan, Sales
Marie Worsham, Sales
Linda Nolan, President

Provide independent or assisted access to in-ground pools. Lifts are powered with water pressure from a garden hose, and are portable. Some lifts have a three-hundred pound lift capacity and others have a four-hundred pound capacity, perfect for commercial installations or home use. ADA compliant

3389 Porch-Lift Vertical Platform Lift
Access Industries/ThyssenKrupp Access
4001 E 138th Street
Grandview, MO 64030-2837
816-763-3100
800-925-3100
Fax: 816-763-4467
http://www.accessind.com

Thomas Hance, President
Ray Demes, VP Field Office Consumer Affairs
Chuck Herling, CFO

Provide stairway access indoor and out for people who use wheelchairs. Lifting heights range from 1 to 144 feet and are available for both commercial and residential applications. Easy to install and operate, the units are space and cost efficient solutions to ADA compliance.

3390 Porta Ramps
Division of Young Enterprises
5592 E La Palma Avenue
Anaheim, CA 92807-2108
800-654-7267
Fax: 714-970-6875

Lightweight, portable, and fiberglass ramps for wheelchair users.

3391 Porta-Ramp
Cleo of New York
S Buckout Street
Irvington, NY 10533
914-591-4900
800-321-0595
Fax: 914-591-4083

Elliott Goldberg, President

At last, a wheelchair ramp so light and portable it can be carried on the handles of the manual or motorized chair.

3392 RDL Supply
11240 Gemini Lane
Dallas, TX 75229-4710
214-630-3965
800-688-1758
Fax: 214-560-0326
e-mail: sales@rdlsupply.com
http://www.rdlsupply.com

Jim Goldthwaite, National Sales Manager
Sheri Martin, CEO

Power door, low energy door operators.

3393 Ricon Corporation
7900 Nelson Road
Panorama City, CA 91402-6090
818-267-3000
800-322-2884
Fax: 818-267-3001
e-mail: customerservice@riconcorp.com
http://www.riconcorp.com

William Baldwin, CEO

Ricon corporation is a world leader in the manufacture of lifts and other mobility products for people with disabilities. The Ricon product line features the Activan(R) a lowered floor minivan conversion, wheelchair lifts power seat base and automatic door openers.

3394 Scooter, Power Chair and WheelchairLifts
Bruno Independent Living Aids
1780 Executive Drive
Po Box 84
Oconomowoc, WI 53066
262-567-4990
800-882-8183
Fax: 262-953-5501
e-mail: service@bruno.com
http://www.bruno.com

Michael R Bruno II, President/CEO
Patrick Foy, National Sales Manager
Anne Tyler, Marketing

Over 18 different styles of automobile lifts for scooters, wheelchairs, and powerchairs for nearly any car, van, truck, or sport utility vehicle that can raise most scooters or wheelchairs under 200 pounds and powerchairs up to 300 pounds. All Bruno lifts are eligible for reimbursement of up to $1000.00 from GM, Saturn, Ford, and Chrysler under the terms of their Mobility Programs.

3395 Silver Glide Stairway Lift
Access Industries/Thyssenkrupp Access
4001 E 138th Street
Grandview, MO 64030-2837
816-763-3100
800-925-3100
Fax: 816-763-4467
e-mail: thomashance@tkaccess.com
http://www.accessind.com

Thomas Hance, President
Ray Demes, VP Field Office Consumer Care
Chuck Herling, CFO

The economical Silver-Glide easily installs on either side of a straight stairway. The seat, armrest and footrest can be folded to save stairway space when the unit is not in use. The unit plugs into an outlet at the top or bottom of the stairs and uses regular household current. Also available with battery operated system. Heavy duty steel cable drive system permits the rider to travel up to 20 feet.

3396 Sling Solutions
Arjo
50 Gary Avenue
Suite A
Roselle, IL 60172-1605
847-967-0360
800-323-1245
Fax: 847-967-0807
http://www.arjo.com

Takes all the effort out of lifting while protecting the caregiver from the risk of backstrain.

Disability Aids & Assistive Devices/Lifts, Ramps, Elevators

3397 Smart Leg
Invacare
1 Invacare Way
Elyria, OH 44035-4190
440-329-6000
800-333-6900
Fax: 440-329-6568
e-mail: info@invacare.com
http://www.invacare.com

A Malachi Mixon III, Chairman Of The Board/CEO
Gerald B Blouch, President/COO
Dale LaPorte, Senior Vice President

An ingenious elevating leg rest that automatically extends to correctly fit every outstretched leg.

3398 Smooth Mover
Dixie USA
Po Box 1969
Tomball, TX 77377
713-688-4993
800-233-3668
Fax: 800-688-2507
e-mail: info@dixieusa.com
http://www.dixieusa.com

Bob Beeley, Chairman

Patient mover is a board designed to transfer patients from bed to stretcher or table with one or two people.

3399 Stair & Glide Stairway Lift
Access Industries/ThyssenKrupp Access
4001 E 138th Street
Grandview, MO 64030-2837
816-763-3100
800-925-3100
Fax: 816-763-4467
e-mail: thomas.hance@tkaccess.com
http://www.tkaccess.com

Thomas Hanceon, President
Ray Demes, VP Field Office Consumer Care
Chuck Herling, CFO

Solves many multi-level accessibility problems in home. Lifts easily to install on straight or curved stairways. The rail attaches directly to steps without disturbing walls or staircase. The heavy duty drive mechanism means reliable, trouble-free operation. Public building and outdoor packages available.

3400 StairLIFT SC & SL
Inclinator Company of America
601 Gibson Blvd.
Po Box 1557
Harrisburg, PA 17104-1557
717-939-8420
800-343-9007
Fax: 717-939-8075
e-mail: isales@inclinator.com
http://www.inclinator.com

Paul R Krum, President

Simple, self-contained and efficient stair units.

3401 Stairway Elevators
Bruno Independent Living Aids
1780 Executive Drive
Po Box 84
Oconomowoc, WI 53066
262-567-4990
800-882-8183
Fax: 262-953-5501
e-mail: service@bruno.com
http://www.bruno.com

Michael R Bruno II, President/CEO
Patrick Foy, National Sales Manager
Anne Tyler, Marketing

Bruno offers a full line of stairway elevators, including the Electra-Ride II featuring access during power interruptions, convenient installation, comfort and a powerful drive system. The Electra-Ride which features battery-powered technology, a rail width of 25 inches and seat rotation for easy transfers. The Comfort-Ride AC stair lift which is battery operated, has a rail width of 7.25 inches and folded width of less than 14.5 inches.

3402 Stand Aid
Stand Aid of Iowa
1009 2nd Avenue
Po Box 386
Sheldon, IA 51201
712-324-2153
800-831-8580
Fax: 712-324-5210
e-mail: sales@stand-aid.com
http://www.stand-aid.com

Stand Aid can help you achieve independence and mobility safely and easily. Lifts you from a chair or bed with the flick of a switch, securing the user in an upright standing position.

3403 Straight and Custom Curved Stairlifts
Bruno Independent Living Aids
1780 Executive Drive
Po Box 84
Oconomowoc, WI 53066
262-567-4990
800-882-8183
Fax: 262-953-5501
e-mail: service@bruno.com
http://www.bruno.com

Michael R Bruno II, President/CEO
Patrick Foy, National Sales Manager
Anne Tyler, Marketing

Bruno stairlifts can fit almost any curve or straight rail application and requires little or no structural modification to the stairway. Normal rail position for a Bruno inside turn is 7 inches to 8 inches from the wall or obstruction which is the tightest radius of any stairlift manufacturing company in the world. The Bruno inside turn is ideal for bi-level homes or staircases with mid-level doors.

3404 Sure Hands International
982 Route 1
Pine Island, NY 10969-1205
845-258-6500
800-724-5305
Fax: 845-258-6634
e-mail: info@surehands.com
http://www.surehands.com

Thomas Herceg, President
Joyce Moraczewski, Marketing Coordinator

SureHands lift and care systems are available in permanent and portable styles for homes and workplaces. The patented, self-adjusting body support with curve-around cups assures gentle, easy and secure transfers without the use of a sling. In many cases, transfers can be made independently. SureHands systems offers independence as a self-transfer tool. They provide assistance in bathing, hygiene care, positioning, standing, ambulation, exercising, and they are the back-saver for caregivers.

3405 SureHands Lift & Care Systems
982 Route 1
Pine Island, NY 10969-1205
845-258-6500
800-724-5305
Fax: 845-258-6634
e-mail: info@surehands.com
http://www.surehands.com

Thomas Herceg, President
Joyce Moraczewski, Marketing Coordinator

SureHands Lift & Care Systems offer a unique, patented and exlusive range of lift and transfer systems to meet private and institutional needs of individuals with motor disabilties. Includes permanent and portable models for homes, workplaces and recreation. The SureHands Body Support offers safe, easy and secure transfers for user and the opportunity for independent transfers for some. They are a back-save for caregivers. All lifts are easily ma

3406 Swing-A-Way
The Braun Corporation
627 West 11th Street
Po Box 310
Winamac, IN 46996
574-946-6153
800-843-5438
Fax: 574-946-4670
http://www.braunmobility

305

Disability Aids & Assistive Devices/Scooters

A swing lift for transporting patients from bed to bath and more. It features a gravity-down operation made possible by a newly designed pump module package. The new, quieter module features a built-in hand pump and a plastic reservoir for easy fluid checking. This is a vehicle lift not bath lift.

3407 Tilt 'n Tote, Roamer Riding Chair
Wheelchair Carrier
203 Matzinger Road
Toledo, OH 43612
419-478-4423
800-541-3213
Fax: 419-478-4425
e-mail: admin@wheerchaircarrier.com
http://www.wheelchaircarrier.com

Christina Makulinski, Office Manager
Mike Siler, Engineering Manager
David Makulinski, Customer Service Assistance

Tilt 'n Tote is a wheelchair carrier that mounts to a Class 1 hitch on your vehicle. No lifting! Tilt the carrier to load your folding wheelchair. The Roamer Riding Chair is an electric powered mobility chair that folds to carry in trunk/ backseat. weight of chair is only 35lbs without the battery.

3408 Transfer Board
Cleo of New York
S Buckout Street
Irvington, NY 10533
914-591-4900
800-321-0595
Fax: 914-591-4083

Elliott Goldberg, President

This transfer board is tapered gradually at both ends to provide for easy transfer from wheelchair to bed, toilet to chair.

3409 VPL Series Vertical Wheelchair Lift
Access Industries/ThyssenKrupp Access
4001 E 138th Street
Grandview, MO 64030-2837
816-763-3100
800-925-3100
Fax: 816-763-4467
e-mail: thomas.hance@tkaccess.com
http://www.accessind.com

Thomas Hance, President
Ray Demes, VP Field Office Consumer Care
Chuck Herling, CFO

Provide stairway access indoors and out for people who use wheelchairs. Lifting heights from 1 to 144 feet for loads up to 750 pounds are available for both commercial and residential applications. Easy to install and operate, the units are space and cost efficient solutions to ADA access compliance. Attendant operation, toe-guard enclosure and restricted access hoistway enclosure options are available.

3410 Vangater, Vangater II, Mini-Vangater
Braun Corporation
627 West 11th Street
Po Box 310
Winamac, IN 46996
574-946-6153
800-843-5438
Fax: 574-946-0250
http://www.braunlift.com

Jerry Sirjord, General Manager

Tri-fold and fold-in-half lifts represent a major innovation in the field of adapted van transportation.

3411 Vertical Home Lift Sales
2715 Seaboard Lane
Long Beach, CA 90805-3751
562-634-5962
800-795-6227
Fax: 562-634-4291
e-mail: macslift@blvd.com
http://www.macsliftgate.com

Lawrence MacDonald, Owner

Sales and service of van and truck lifts. Sales and service of wheel chair lifts for vans and automobiles. Sales, installation and service of vertical home lifts, scooter lifts and pool lifts. Sales of scooters.

3412 Vertical Wheelchair Lift
Econol Stairway Lift Corporation
2513 Center Street
Cedar Falls, IA 50613-1055
319-277-4777
800-328-2560
Fax: 319-277-4778

Adrian L Martin, Sales
Sharon R Martin, President

Provides easy access for those where stairways of architectural barriers pose a problem.

3413 Wecolator Stairway Lift
Access Industries/ThyssenKrupp Access
4001 E 138th Street
Grandview, MO 64030-2837
816-763-3100
800-925-3100
Fax: 816-763-4467
http://www.accessind.com

Thomas Hance, President
Ray Demes, VP Field Office Consumer Care
Chuck Herling, CFO

Solves many multi-level accessibility problems in home. Lifts easily to install on straight or curved stairways. The rail attaches directly to steps without disturbing walls or staircase. The heavy duty drive mechanism means reliable, trouble-free operation. Public building and outdoor packages available.

3414 Wheelchair Carriers, Ramps, and Roamer Riding Chair
Wheelchair Carrier
203 Matzinger Road
Toledo, OH 43612
419-478-4423
800-541-3213
Fax: 419-478-4425
e-mail: admin@wheelchaircarrier.com
http://www.wheelchaircarrier.com

Christina Makukinski, Office Manager
Mike Siler, Engineering Manager
David Makulinski, Customer Service Assistance

Wheelchair carriers for hitch mount on vehicles, portable steel ramps, the Rider Roaming Chair, a lightweight, foldable electric mobility aid. Carriers $199-$999, ramps $189-429, the Roamer $1,995

3415 Ziggy Medi-Chair
Laszlo Corporation
1805 Scherer Parkway
St. Charles, MO 63303
636-447-1312
Fax: 636-447-1341

Les Suhayda, President

A motorized lift and transfer system that maximizes time and safety for disabled and bedridden patients. A multifunctional product that benefits patients with disabilities and caregivers in a home or institutional enviroment. A motorized system that lifts patients and saves caregivers from injury and workman's compensation claims.

Scooters

3416 Amigo Centra
Amigo Mobility International
6693 Dixie Highway
Bridgeport, MI 48722-9725
989-777-0910
800-692-6446
Fax: 800-334-7274
e-mail: info@myamigo.com
http://http://myamigo.com

Allan Thiem, CEO

Features an adjustable handle that bends, making steering comfortable and enjoyable. The rugged construction and variable speed make it the perfect choice for indoor/outdoor mobility.

Disability Aids & Assistive Devices/Scooters

3417 Amphibious ATV Distributors
Amphibious ATV Distributors
2760 Greendale Drive
Sarasota, FL 34232-3702
941-379-6186
800-843-2811
Fax: 941-377-8979

Clay Beach, Owner

A two and four passenger, all-terrain vehicle that can provide you with year round activities the whole family can enjoy. Accessible and drivable for the physically disabled. Used in hunting, fishing and outdoor activities on land and in the water. Many options and accessories available. Delivery anywhere in the US and worldwide. $5,000-$9,000.

3418 Bravo! + Three-Wheel Scooter
Ortho-Kinetics/EZ-International
3275 Intertech Drive
Suite 500
Brookfield, WI 53045
262-790-5200
800-824-1068
Fax: 262-790-5204
e-mail: info@ez-international.com
http://www.ex-international.com

Designed to increase your mobility indoors. The Bravo! plus has extendible rear wheels for outdoor use and comes with easy to use finger tip controls and a maintenance free gel-cell battery. Available in red, blue, green or light sand gray with an optional power seat lift. Call for complete line of 3 and 4-wheel electronic vehicles.

3419 Comb-O-Cycle
American Walker
4683 Schneider Drive
Oregon, WI 53575-2227
608-835-7523
800-765-3452

Combines 16 inch front wheels for stability outdoors, with swiveling rear wheels for maneuverability, even in the most confined spaces. The Comb-O-Cycle is a combination indoor-outdoor walking aid. The burgundy tubular steel frame is powder coated for a durable finish. The padded seat provides a comfortable resting place. Comb-O-Cycle folds flat and is made in USA.

3420 Cruiser Bus Buggy 4MB
Convaid Products
PO Box 4209
Palos Verdes, CA 90274-9571
310-618-0111
888-266-8243
Fax: 310-618-8811
e-mail: convaid@convaid.com
http://www.convaid.com

Merv Watkins, Owner

In sizes from infant through young adult, this positioning buggy is crash-tested.

3421 Explorer+ 4-Wheel Scooter
Ortho-Kinetics/EZ International
3275 Intertech Drive Suite 500
Brookfield, WI 53045
262-790-5200
800-824-1068
Fax: 262-790-5204
e-mail: info@ez-international.com
http://www.orthokinetics.com

William Grady, Sales Manager

A tough and rugged 4-wheel, rear-wheel drive, transaxle scooter designed to take you just about anywhere you want to go. Easy to use finger-tip controls and maintenance free gel-cell batteries and an extendible, take-apart frame, make the Explorer+ a perfect fit for people seeking greater mobility. Available in red, blue, green and gray, with an optional power seat lift.

3422 MVP+ 3-Wheel Scooter
Ortho-Kinetics-EZ-International Inc.
3275 Intertech Drive
Suite 500
Brookfield, WI 53045
262-790-5200
800-824-1068
Fax: 262-790-5204
e-mail: info@ez-international.com
http://www.ez-international.com

Thomas Dalums, Owner

The MVP+ is the rugged 3-wheel rear-wheel drive, tranaxle scooter with finger tip controls, and featuring an extendible, take-apart frame for a perfect fit. The MVP+ comes with maintenance free gel-cell batteries and is available in red, blue, green or light sand gray, with an optional power seat lift. $2,599-$3,099.

3423 Magni-Cam
American Printing House for the Blind
1839 Frankfort Avenue
Po Box 6085
Louisville, KY 40206-0085
502-895-2405
800-223-1839
Fax: 502-899-2274
e-mail: info@aph.org
http://www.aph.org

Tuck Tinsley, President
Bob Brasher, VP Advisory Services & Research
Gary Mudd, VP For Public Affairs

Magni-Cam is a light-weight, hand-held electronic magnifier that connects in minutes to any television set or computer monitor. It provides a crisp black and white image that enhances reading ability for people with low vision.

3424 Motorized Stander
Advanced Technology Corporation
115 Clemson Drive
Oak Ridge, TN 37830-7665
865-483-5756
Fax: 865-483-5860
e-mail: info@atc-ssm.com
http://www.atc-ssm.com

Fahmy Haggag, Owner

Occupant-operated motorized vehicle that offers independence, increased mobility and ease of movement to disabled people.

3425 Outdoor Independence
Palmer Industries
PO Box 5707
Endicott, NY 13763-5707
607-754-2957
800-847-1304
Fax: 607-754-1954
e-mail: palmer@palmerind.com
http://http://palmerind.com/company

Jack Palmer, President

The futuristic electric three-wheeler designed to take you almost anywhere.

3426 Pace Saver Plus II
Leisure-Lift
1800 Merriam Lane
Kansas City, KS 66106
800-255-0285
Fax: 913-722-2614
e-mail: leisure-lift@kc.rr.com
http://www.pacesaver.com

The scooter combines outdoor ruggedness with indoor maneuverability at a low price.

3427 Palmer Independence
Palmer Industries
PO Box 5707
Endicott, NY 13763
607-754-2957
800-847-1304
Fax: 607-754-1954
e-mail: palmer@palmerind.com
http://http://palmerind.com/company

William C Brunner, CEO

Futuristic electric three wheeler designed to take the rider almost anywhere.

3428 Palmer Twosome
Palmer Industries
PO Box 5707
Endicott, NY 13763-5707
607-754-2957
800-847-1304
Fax: 607-754-1954
e-mail: palmer@palmerind.com
http://http://palmerind.com/company

Jack Palmer, President

All electric two seat vehicle for those who can't pedal.

Disability Aids & Assistive Devices/Scooters

3429 Quickie 2
Sunrise Medical/Quickie Designs
2382 Faraday Avenue
Suite 200
Carlsbad, CA 92008-7220
760-930-1500
800-333-4000
Fax: 760-930-1575
http://www.sunrisemedical.com
Michael Hammes, CEO

This custom, ultralight, folding, everyday scooter offers portability and performance plus modular flexibility.

3430 Ranger
Ranger All Seasons
PO Box 132
George, IA 51237
712-475-2811
800-225-3811
Fax: 712-475-3320
e-mail: sales@rangerallseason.com
http://www.rangerallseason.com
Randy Rieeks, National Sales Manager
Larry Kruse, Owner

Makes 3 & 4 wheel electric scooters for physically challenged and elderly people. Ranger scooters feature two Patents. The first is for the easy disassembly of the scooter, which can be done in a matter of seconds. The second is for the easy to operate adjustable tiller. Ranger also manufactures an electric scooter and wheelchair lift for a car, van, pickup, or sport utility vehicle.

3431 Regal Scooters
Bruno Independent Living Aids
1780 Executive Drive
Po Box 84
Oconomowoc, WI 53066
262-567-4990
800-882-8183
Fax: 262-953-5501
e-mail: service@bruno.com
http://www.bruno.com
Michael R Bruno II, President/CEO
Patrick Foy, National Sales Manager
Anne Tyler, Marketing

This line includes the Regal Standard, the regal large Adult, the Regal Small Adult, the Regal Pediatric, The Regal Ten models 65 and 75, and The Regal Four. These scooters offer adjustable flip-up armrests, pneumatic tires front and rear, and more.

3432 Regent
Golden Technologies
401 Bridge Street
Old Forge, PA 18518-2323
574-517-477
800-624-6374
Fax: 800-628-5165
e-mail: pobrien@goldentech.com
http://www.goldentech.com

Top-rated performance scooter, with extra features and economically priced.

3433 Safari Scooter
Ranger All Seasons
PO Box 132
George, IA 51237
712-475-2811
800-225-3811
Fax: 712-475-3320
e-mail: sales@rangerallseason.com
http://www.rangerallseason.com
Randy Rieeks, Sales Manager
Larry Kruse, Owner

Safari is Ranger's most popular scooter. Available in either a 40 inch or 43 inch frame length with an ultra-quiet, totally enclosed transacle drive. The Safari has some of the same features as the SOLO, the user-friendly take-apart and tiller adjustment, color impregnated - not painted- ABS plastic body. The most versatile Ranger Scooter, the Safari is an excellent choice for indoor use, and can take the place of most front wheel drive scooters.

3434 Scoota Bug
Golden Technologies
401 Bridge Street
Old Forge, PA 18518-2323
570-451-7477
800-624-6374
Fax: 800-628-5165
e-mail: pobrien@goldentech.com
http://www.goldentech.com
Bob Golden, President

A lightweight, completely modular scooter, that disassembles and fits into most auto trunks.

3435 Shuttle
Mobilelectrics Company
4014 Bardstown Road
Louisville, KY 40218-2631
502-491-1943
800-876-6846
Fax: 502-495-2476

A three wheel scooter with safety features for ease of handling, comfort and maximum pleasure.

3436 Sidekick Scooter
Mobilelectrics Company
4014 Bardstown Road
Louisville, KY 40218-2631
502-491-1943
800-876-6846
Fax: 502-495-2476

The seat and foot space provides ample comfort for the average person and the length of the scooter gives it indoor maneuverability.

3437 Sierra 3000/4000
Ortho-Kinetics/EZ-International
3275 Intertechdrive
Suite 500
Brookfield, WI 53045
262-542-6060
800-558-7786
Fax: 262-542-4258
e-mail: info@ez-international.com
http://www.ez-international.com
William Grady, Sales Manager

Look to the Sierra 3000/4000 series vehicles for comfort, convenience and performance. Increased leg and foot room, adjustable seat height and arm width, as well as adjustable tiller angle provide maximum comfort. For convenience, the Sierra is equipped with integrated cargo and cup holders and thumb/finger controls with built in wrist rest. Advanced safety features such as stall and free-wheeling situation identification and correction, anti rol

3438 Solo Scooter
Ranger All Seasons
PO Box 132
George, IA 51237
712-475-2811
800-225-3811
Fax: 712-475-3320
e-mail: sales@rangerallseason.com
http://www.rangerallseason.com
Randy Rieeks, Sales Manager
Larry Kruse, Owner

The SOLO is Ranger's flagship model. Introduction of the SOLO 1991 set the standard for easy disassembly of a scooter. The SOLO has a long list of user friendly features including patented take-apart and tiller adjustment mechanisms, non-rusting aluminum frame, extra long, extra tall seats as standard, color impregnated-not painted-ABS plastic bodies, charger plug conveniently located on the Accelerator box and many more.

3439 Sterling
Golden Technologies
401 Bridge Street
Old Forge, PA 18518-2323
570-451-7477
800-624-6374
Fax: 800-628-5165
e-mail: pobrien@goldentech.com
http://www.goldentech.com
Bob Golden, President

Rear-wheel-drive vehicle that represents the best in powered mobility.

Disability Aids & Assistive Devices/Stationery

3440 Super Scout Three Wheeler
Burke
1800 Merriam Lane
Kansas City, KS 66106-4714
913-722-5658
800-255-0285
Fax: 913-722-2614
e-mail: leisure-lift@kc.rr.com
http://www.pacesaver.com

Duwayne Kramer, President

Be free to be as active as you like with this three wheel scooter.

3441 Systems 2000
BioMedical Life Systems
PO Box 1360
Vista, CA 92085-1360
760-727-5600
800-726-8367
Fax: 760-727-4220
e-mail: information@bmls.com
http://www.bmls.com

This five-mode TENS device has four adjustable modulations, plus conventional settings and comes with a five-year warranty.

3442 TERRA-JET: Utility Vehicle
TERRA-JET USA
PO Box 918
Innis, LA 70747
225-492-2249
800-864-5000
Fax: 225-492-2249

Larry Rabalais, President
Dora Rabalais, Secretary/Treasurer

TERRA-JET utility vehicles are unique in its ability to traverse many different types of terrain in remote areas otherwise inaccessible. It has a multitude of uses for industry, sportsmen or the whole family. Uniquely designed, industrial duty construction of low maintenance and low fuel consumption. $7,000-$9,000.

3443 Tri-Wheelers
The Braun Corporation
627 West 11th Street
Po Box 310
Winamac, IN 46996
574-946-6153
800-843-5438
Fax: 574-946-6305
http://www.braunlift.com

Provides convenience features, producing a high efficiency performance with ultra-smooth operation.

3444 Triumph 3000/4000
Ortho-Kinetics/EZ-International, Inc.
3275 Intertech Drive
Suite 500
Brookfield, WI 53045
262-790-5200
800-824-1068
Fax: 262-790-5204
e-mail: info@ez-international.com
http://www.ez-international.com

William Grady, Sales Manager

The Triumph 3000/4000 series vehicles provide unique comfort and convenience features found nowhere else. Digital Dash with soft touch keypad, deluxe seat with suspension and integral cargo and cup holders are just a few of these features. Equipped with TOPS 24 (Total Ortho Power System) ensures maximum power, performance and reliability. Luxurious options such as velour or allante seat fabrics, stylized wheels, metallic or pearl color options an

3445 Triumph Scooter
Ortho-Kinetics/EZ-International, Inc.
3275 Intertech Drive
Suite 500
Brookfield, WI 53045
262-790-5200
800-824-1068
Fax: 262-790-5204
e-mail: info@ez-international.com
http://www.ez-international.com

William Grady, Sales Manager

The sleek rugged three-wheel, rear-wheel drive, transaxle scooter with up-top controls, designed to help increase mobility and become more active. The Triumph is designed for both indoor and outdoor use. Available in red, blue, green or gray, with an optional power seat lift. $2,899-$3,399.

Stationery

3446 Address Book
The New Vision Store
919 Walnut Street
Philadelphia, PA 19107-5237
215-629-2990
http://www.thenewvisionstore.com

The big print address book is the first personal book to provide enlarged writing spaces, making it easier to write down and retrieve information.

3447 Audio Book Contractors
PO Box 40115
Washington, DC 20016-0115
202-363-3429
Fax: 202-363-3429
http://www.audiobookcontractors.com

Flo Gibson, President

Unabridged classic books on cassettes in sturdy vinyl covers with picture and spine windows.

3448 Audio Recordings
Access-USA
PO Box 160
242 James Street
Clayton, NY 13624
800-263-2750
Fax: 800-563-1687
e-mail: info@access-usa.com
http://www.access-usa.com

Deborah Haight, EOA

Access-USA produces auctio recordings for businesses, organizations and entrepreneurs. Information such as brochures, reports, documents, etc. can be made accessible. Other formats available include braille, large print, braille business cards and video services.

3449 Beyond Sight
5650 S Windermere Street
Littleton, CO 80120-1240
303-795-6455
Fax: 303-795-6425
e-mail: support@beyondsight.com
http://www.beyondsight.com

Jim Misener, President

Products for the blind and visually impaired including talking clocks, watches, and calculators. They also carry a large selection of Braille products, magnifiers, reading machines, and computer equipment.

3450 Big Print Address Book
Access with Ease
1755 S Johnson Lane
PO Box 1150
Chino Valley, AZ 86323
928-636-9469
800-531-9479
Fax: 928-636-0292

Karen Clymer, President

Oversized organizer makes locating information easier for those with limited vision.

3451 Bold Line Paper
The New Vision Store
919 Walnut Street
1st Floor
Philadelphia, PA 19107-5237
215-629-2990
http://www.thenewvisionstore.com

This pad consists of 100 sheets of paper with bold lines to help guide the writing of an individual with limited vision.

Disability Aids & Assistive Devices/Stationery

3452 Book Holder
Access with Ease
PO Box 1150
Chino Valley, AZ 86323-1150
928-636-9469
800-531-9479
Fax: 928-636-0292

This hands free reading book holder enables the user to read hands free.

3453 Bookholder: Roberts
Therapro
225 Arlington Street
Framingham, MA 01702-8723
508-872-9494
800-257-5376
Fax: 508-875-2062
e-mail: info@theraproducts.com
http://www.theraproducts.com

Karen Conrad, Owner

Gray plastic, ideal for hand free reading, adjusts to all sizes of books and prevents pages from flipping for the physically challenged.

3454 Braille Business Cards & More
Access USA
242 James Street
PO Drawer 160
Clayton, NY 13624
315-686-0065
800-263-2750
Fax: 800-563-1687
e-mail: info@access-usa.com
http://www.access-usa.com

Deborah Haight, EOA
Tim Baril, Owner

Braille on business cards, greeting cards, invitations, folders, plastic credit/ATM cards, advertising inserts, specialties and more.

3455 Braille Notebook
Maxi Aids
42 Executive Boulevard
Farmingdale, NY 11735-4710
631-752-0521
800-522-6294
Fax: 631-752-0689
e-mail: sales@maxiaids.com
http://www.maxiaids.com
TTY 631-752-0738

Harold Zaretsky, President

Made of heavy-duty board, covered with waterproof imitation leather and three rings for binding, including braille paper and titles.

3456 Brailled Desk Calendar
Maxi Aids
42 Executive Boulevard
Farmingdale, NY 11735-4710
631-752-0521
800-522-6294
Fax: 631-752-0689
e-mail: sales@maxiaids.com
http://www.maxiaids.com
TTY 631-752-0738

Harold Zaretsky, President

Schedule appointments, remember birthdays or write messages for a particular day.

3457 Bus and Taxi Sign
Maxi Aids
42 Executive Boulevard
Farmingdale, NY 11735-4710
631-752-0521
800-522-6294
Fax: 631-752-0689
e-mail: sales@maxiaids.com
http://www.maxiaids.com
TTY 631-752-0738

Harold Zaretsky, President

Signs that attract the attention of bus or taxi drivers.

3458 Calendars
American Printing House for the Blind
1839 Frankfort Avenue
PO Box 6085
Louisville, KY 40206-0085
502-895-2405
800-223-1839
Fax: 502-899-2274
e-mail: info@aph.org
http://www.aph.org

Tuck Tinsley, President
Bob Brasher, VP Advisory Services & Research
Gary Mudd, VP Public Affairs

The American Printing House for the Blind offers three different styles of large type/braille calendars for learning and daily living. The Classroom Calendar Kit, The Individual Calendar Kit and the APH InSights Art Calendar.

3459 Card Chart
American Printing House for the Blind
1839 Frankfort Avenue
Po Box 6085
Louisville, KY 40206-3148
502-895-2405
800-223-1839
Fax: 502-899-2274
e-mail: info@aph.org
http://www.aph.org

Tuck Tinsley, President
Bob Brasher, VP Advisory Services & Research
Gary Mudd, VP Public Affairs

The Card Chart is a handy device designed to hold the 3 1/2 x 2 inch braille/print cards sold by APH in a variety of products, such as the Expanded Dolch Word Cards.

3460 Deluxe Signature Guide
Maxi Aids
42 Executive Boulevard
Farmingdale, NY 11735-4710
631-752-0521
800-522-6294
Fax: 631-752-0689
e-mail: sales@maxiaids.com
http://www.maxiaids.com
TTY 631-752-0738

Harold Zaretsky, President

Rods supported by two rubber blocks facilitate writing.

3461 Finger Print Pen
Therapro
225 Arlington Street
Framingham, MA 01702-8773
508-872-9494
800-257-5376
Fax: 508-875-2062
e-mail: info@theraproducts.com
http://www.theraproducts.com

Karen Conrad, Owner

This pen was designed for those with limited digital mobility and decreased ability to grasp a conventional writing tool.

3462 Highlighter and Note Tape
Therapro
225 Arlington Street
Framingham, MA 01702-8773
508-872-9494
800-257-5376
Fax: 508-875-2062
e-mail: info@theraproducts.com
http://www.theraproducts.com

Karen Conrad, Owner

A great way to highlight and draw attention to words without damaging original. Price ranges from $4.00-$7.00.

Disability Aids & Assistive Devices/Walking Aids

3463 Letter Writing Guide
Independent Living Aids
200 Robbins Lane
Jericho, NY 11753-2365
516-937-1848
800-537-2118
Fax: 516-937-3906
e-mail: techsupport@independentliving.com
http://www.independentliving.com

Marvin Sandler, President

Sturdy plastic sheet with 13 apertures corresponding to standard line spacing.

3464 Lettering Guide Value Pack
Independent Living Aids
200 Robbins Lane
Jericho, NY 11753-2365
516-937-1848
800-537-2118
Fax: 516-937-3906
e-mail: techsupport@independentliving.com
http://www.independentliving.com

Marvin Sandler, President

Included in this useful pack are four durable plastic lettering and number guides for tracing letters when the individual is unable to write letters unassisted.

3465 Maxi Marks
Maxi Aids
42 Executive Boulevard
Farmingdale, NY 11735-4710
631-752-0521
800-522-6294
Fax: 631-752-0689
e-mail: sales@maxiaids.com
http://www.maxiaids.com
TTY 631-752-0738

Harold Zaretsky, President

Braille writing and identification products.

3466 Plastic Card Holder
Therapro
225 Arlington Street
Framingham, MA 01702-8773
508-872-9494
800-257-5376
Fax: 508-875-2062
e-mail: info@theraproducts.com
http://www.theraproducts.com

Karen Conrad, Owner

For those with reduced finger control.

3467 Raised Line Drawing Kit
Maxi Aids
42 Executive Boulevard
Farmingdale, NY 11735-4710
631-752-0521
800-522-6294
Fax: 631-752-0689
e-mail: sales@maxiaids.com
http://www.maxiaids.com
TTY 631-752-0738

Harold Zaretsky, President

For writing script or drawing graphs by the use of special plastic paper.

3468 Signature and Address Self-Inking Stamps
Independent Living Aids
200 Robbins Lane
Jericho, NY 11753-2365
516-937-1848
800-537-2118
Fax: 516-937-3906
e-mail: techsupport@independentliving.com
http://www.independentliving.com

Marvin Sandler, President

Gives thousands of impressions before requiring re-inking.

3469 Steady Write
Maxi Aids
42 Executive Boulevard
Farmingdale, NY 11735-4710
631-752-0521
800-522-6294
Fax: 631-752-0689
e-mail: sales@maxiaids.com
http://www.maxiaids.com
TTY 631-752-0738

Harold Zaretsky, President

Furnishes the writer with increased holding capacity and stabilizes the hand.

3470 Touch Page Turner
Cleo of New York
S Buckout Street
Irvington, NY 10533
914-591-4900
800-321-0595
Fax: 914-591-4083

Elliott Goldberg, President

Tabletop device supports books and magazines and turns pages — in either direction. Switch-operated, with big-target switches available.

3471 Weighted Holders
Therapro
225 Arlington Street
Framingham, MA 01702-8773
508-872-9494
800-257-5376
Fax: 508-875-2062
e-mail: info@theraproducts.com
http://www.theraproducts.com

Karen Conrad, Owner

These weighted holders allow for more control along with proprioceptive feedback to encourage better writing skills.

3472 Wings & Wheels Greeting Cards
Wings & Wheels
5 Cleveland Avenue
Dover, NJ 07801-5603
800-422-5309
Fax: 973-989-9072
http://www.wings-wheels.com

Nanette Courtine, Owner

Offer inclusive greeting cards. Depicts people with disabilities on the cards.

Walking Aids

3473 Adjustable Incline Board
Bailey Manufacturing Company
118 Lee Street
Po Box 130
Lodi, OH 44254-0130
330-948-1080
800-321-8372
Fax: 800-244-5390
e-mail: baileymfg@baileymfg.com
http://www.baileymfg.com

Larry Strimple, President

Incline board for the physically challenged with a foot board with non-slip tread.

3474 Aluminum Adjustable Support Canes for the Blind
Maxi Aids
42 Executive Boulevard
Farmingdale, NY 11735-4710
631-752-0521
800-522-6294
Fax: 631-752-0689
e-mail: sales@maxiaids.com
http://www.maxiaids.com
TTY 631-752-0738

Harold Zaretsky, President

Adjustable canes for the visually impaired.

Disability Aids & Assistive Devices/Walking Aids

3475 Aluminum Crutches
Arista Home Care
67 Lexington Avenue
New York, NY 10010-1833
212-679-3694
800-223-1984
Fax: 212-696-9046
e-mail: aristasurgical@juno.com

Stephen Howard, Manager

Lightweight aluminum crutches with wood underarms and handgrips.

3476 Aluminum Walking Canes
Maxi Aids
42 Executive Boulevard
Farmingdale, NY 11735-4710
631-752-0521
800-522-6294
Fax: 631-752-0689
e-mail: sales@maxiaids.com
http://www.maxiaids.com
TTY 631-752-0738

Harold Zaretsky, President

Lightweight but strong, these walking canes are made of a heavy gauge aluminum tube with safety locknuts and heavy-duty rubber tips.

3477 American Walker
4683 Schneider Drive
Oregon, WI 53575-1056
608-835-9255
800-828-6808
Fax: 608-835-5234

Luann Smith, President
Lu Burmeister, Production Manager

Full line of wheeled walkers, equipped with seats and locking handbrakes. Accessories such as baskets, oxygen cylinder molders, cane molders, and food and beverage trays, are available. Only line of wheeled walkers manufactured in the USA. All products are medicare reimbursable and will ship to anywhere in the US. Eliminates the tiresome lift and place motion of conventional walkers. $199.00-$579.00.

3478 CLEO Economy Folding Walker
Cleo of New York
S Buckout Street
Irvington, NY 10533
914-591-4900
800-321-0595
Fax: 914-591-4083

Elliott Goldberg, President

The geometric design of this folding, portable walker, eliminates side frame wobbling. Angled front legs and reinforced chrome-plated steel front enhances stability.

3479 Deluxe Standard Wood Cane
Arista Home Care
67 Lexington Avenue
New York, NY 10010-1833
212-679-3694
800-223-1984
Fax: 212-696-9046
e-mail: aristasurgical@juno.com

Stephen Howard, Manager

A standard old-fashioned wooden cane for the physically challenged.

3480 Dolomite Walkers
Clarke Health Care Products
1003 International Drive
Oakdale, PA 15071-9226
724-695-2122
888-347-4537
Fax: 724-695-2922
e-mail: info@clarkehealthcare.com
http://www.clarkehealthcare.com

Gerard Clarke, Owner

Dolomite walkers are available in 3 models and 8 sizes. All come with back supports, baskets, curb climbers.

3481 Easy Care Quad Canes
Cleo of New York
S Buckout Street
Irvington, NY 10533
914-591-4900
800-321-0595
Fax: 914-591-4083

Elliott Goldberg, President

Canes for patients 4 feet 10 inches to 6 feet 4 inches. Wide or narrow base available.

3482 Maxi Superior Cane
Maxi Aids
42 Executive Boulevard
Farmingdale, NY 11735-4710
631-752-0521
800-522-6294
Fax: 631-752-0689
e-mail: sales@maxiaids.com
http://www.maxiaids.com
TTY 631-752-0738

Harold Zaretsky, President

Convenient folding cane designed for optimum balance. Tapered joints provide rigidity when open, and are made of heavy gauge aluminum.

3483 Nova Walker
ETAC USA
2325 Parklawn Drive
Suite J
Waukesha, WI 53186-2938
414-796-4600
800-678-3822
Fax: 414-796-4605
e-mail: etac1usa@execpc.com
http://www.execpc.com

Elegant design that provides a comfortable, natural walking style. The seat offers security and stability wherever you go. Folds easily with one hand. Offers lifetime warranty on frame and brake straps for original user.

3484 Out-N-About American Walker
900 Market Street
Oregon, WI 53575-1056
608-835-9255
800-828-6808
Fax: 608-835-5234

Luann Smith, President
Lu Burmeister, Production Manager

The lightweight Out-N-About is easy to handle. The four wheel design provides greater support and stability than any other walking aids. Its large rubber tires move effortlessly over most surfaces, indoors and out. The small turning radius makes it ideal or getting through confined spaces and narrow doorways. The attractive, burgundy colored, tubular steel frame is extremely durable. The Out-N-About folds flat and stands alone for easy storage. M

3485 Prone Support Walker
Consumer Care Products
1446 Pilgrim Road
Plymouth, WI 53073
920-893-4614
Fax: 800-977-2256
e-mail: ccpi@consumercareinc.com
http://www.consumercareinc.com

Terry Grall, President
Alice Maffongelli, Customer Service

This walker, in five sizes for children to adults, facilitates semi-prone to full upright mobility and dynamic weight bearing. The walker requires the user to push off the floor teaching the user to work with the floor and achieving a more efficient gait. Options such as tray, back support, and hip pads allow adaptation to most needs. $750-$1,300.

Disability Aids & Assistive Devices/Wheelchairs

3486 Push-Button Quad Cane
Arista Home Care
67 Lexington Avenue
New York, NY 10010-1833
212-679-3694
800-223-1984
Fax: 212-696-9046
e-mail: aristasurgical@juno.com
Stephen Howard, Manager

A reliable walking cane offering independence to the physically challenged user.

3487 Rand-Scot
401 Linden Center Drive
Fort Collins, CO 80524-2429
970-484-7967
800-467-7967
Fax: 970-484-3800
e-mail: info@randscott.com
http://www.easypivot.com
Joel Lerich, President
Darcy Thor, Business Manager

Offers a line of patient lifts and standers for the disabled. Manufactures the EasyPivot patient lift for 1 person transfers. A video is available plus, no charge for potential users. $800.-$3,000.

3488 Rigid Aluminum Cane with Golf Grip
Maxi Aids
42 Executive Boulevard
Farmingdale, NY 11735-4710
631-752-0521
800-522-6294
Fax: 631-752-0689
e-mail: sales@maxiaids.com
http://www.maxiaids.com
TTY 631-752-0738
Harold Zaretsky, President

A straight, tubular, heavy gauge aluminum rigid cane for blind and visually impaired persons.

3489 Rollator Wheeled Walker
Cleo of New York
S Buckout Street
Irvington, NY 10533
914-591-4900
800-321-0595
Fax: 914-591-4083
Elliott Goldberg, President

Folds flat for storage, height adjusts from 20 inches to 39 inches with two large front wheels.

3490 StairClimber
Martin Technology
29 N Main Street
Gloversville, NY 12078-3006
518-725-1837
800-800-1410
Fax: 518-725-9522

A walker-capable person can climb and descend stairs with this walker-designed StairClimber.

3491 Standing Aid Frame with Rear Entry
Consumer Care Products
1446 Pilgrim Road
Plymouth, WI 53073
920-893-4614
Fax: 800-977-2256
e-mail: ccpi@consumercareinc.com
http://www.consumercareinc.com
Terry Grall, President
Alice Maffongelli, Customer Service

This rugged stander, made of natural hardwood in sizes for one to twelve year olds, allows weight bearing in an upright position. Table, upper trunk and/or head support, hip pads and casters allow individualized fitting. The new hinged rear entry option makes entry into this stander easy and quick for parents, teachers and therapists. $572-$1,800.

3492 Tri-Walker
American Walker
900 Market Street
Oregon, WI 53575-1056
608-835-9255
800-828-6808
Fax: 608-835-5234
Luann Smith, President
Lu Burmeister, Production Manager

The TRI-WALKER is designed for those who desire a lightweight, compact walking aid. The 7 inch diameter wheels roll easily while the three wheeled design offers maximum maneuverability in tight spaces. The handlebars adjust to most comfortable position. The handbrakes and basket offer added security and convenience. The TRI-WALKER is a high quality affordable walking aid made in the USA.

3493 WCIB Heavy-Duty Folding Cane
Maxi Aids
42 Executive Boulevard
Farmingdale, NY 11735-4710
631-752-0521
800-522-6294
Fax: 631-752-0689
e-mail: sales@maxiaids.com
http://www.maxiaids.com
TTY 631-752-0738
Harold Saretsky, President

A four section aluminum folding cane with a golf-type grip handle and flexible wrist loop. #1749015, 34-60"

3494 Walkane
Cleo of New York
S Buckout Street
Irvington, NY 10533
914-591-4900
800-321-0595
Fax: 914-591-4083
Elliott Goldberg, President

Lighter than a walker, more stable than a cane. Folds easily and securely with one hand. Adult and youth sizes are available.

3495 Walker Leg Support
Sammons Preston
1000 Remington Blvd
Suite 210
Bolingbrook, IL 60440-5177
630-378-6000
800-323-5547
Fax: 630-378-6010
e-mail: customersupport@patterson-medical.com
http://www.sammonspreston.com

For lower externity trauma. An alternative to crutches that allows safe, stable ambulation and frees hands and arms for daily tasks.

3496 Wire Walker Basket
Cleo of New York
S Buckout Street
Irvington, NY 10533
914-591-4900
800-321-0595
Fax: 914-591-4083
Elliott Goldberg, President

Steel-coated wire basket.

Wheelchairs

3497 Act Wheelchair
ETAC USA
2325 Parklawn Drive
Suite J
Waukesha, WI 53186-2938
262-796-4600
800-678-3822
Fax: 262-796-4605
e-mail: etaclusa@execpc.com
http://www.execpc.com/

Disability Aids & Assistive Devices/Wheelchairs

A carefully designed Swedish wheelchair made of lightweight titanium for active users. Seat frame and upholstery are adjustable to fit each individual. Available in frame widths from 15.5 to 18 inches and colors available are: black, red plum teal, blue and silver. Lifetime warranty on frame for original user.

3498 Bariatric Wheelchairs Regency
Gendron
520 Mulberry St.
Bryan, OH 43506
800-537-2521
Fax: 419-446-2631
e-mail: sales@gendroninc.com
http://www.gendroninc.com

Steven Cotter, President/CEO

Bariatric wheelchairs, for users weighing up to seven hundred pounds. Manual and power styles built to order for specific needs.

3499 Basic Wheelchair
ETAC USA
2325 Parklawn Drive
Suite J
Waukesha, WI 53186-2938
416-796-4600
800-678-3822
Fax: 262-796-4605

A carefully designed crossfolding wheelchair made from extruded aluminum, the Basic is designed with the caregiver in mind and easily folds for transportation or storage. Available in widths of 14 to 20 inches, has incontinence upholstery which is easily washable with mild soap and water. Swing away, detachable legrests and footrests are standard with fixed hub rear wheels. $1,000 - $2,000

3500 Big Bounder Power Wheelchair
21st Century Scientific
4915 Industrial Way
Coeur D Alene, ID 83814
208-667-8800
800-448-3680
Fax: 208-667-6600
e-mail: 21st@wheelchairs.com
http://www.wheelchairs.com

Ronald E Prior Ph.D., CEO
Susan Harris, CFO/Webmaster

Manufactured for the obese in virtually any dimension. Its powerful motors and rugged frame can accommodate users up to 1000 lb. 21st Century Scientific unique construction option can reduce the overall width of the chair by as much as 3 inches. This may make the difference between using normal doorways or remodeling a home. $10,695.

3501 Bil Jax Construction/Rental
Gendron
520 Mulberry St
Bryan, OH 43506
800-537-2521
Fax: 419-636-9261
e-mail: sales@gendroninc.com
http://www.gendroninc.com

Steven Cotter, President/CEO

Manufacturers of wheelchairs for a variety of other applications, specializing in obese patient products.

3502 Bounder Plus Power Wheelchair
21st Century Scientific
4915 Industrial Way
Coeur D Alene, ID 83814
208-667-8800
800-448-3680
Fax: 208-667-6600
e-mail: 21st@wheelchairs.com
http://www.21stcenturyscientific.com

Ronald E Prior Ph.D, CEO
Susan Harris, CFO/Webmaster

Available in widths of 16 to 20 feet for users up to 500 pounds with a 2 year warranty on the entire chair. It offers all the standard features of a BOUNDER, plus reinforced rear wheel mounts, reinforced caster barrels, and super duty upholstery (with double liner and web straps under every screw). The BOUNDER Plus also features tandem cross struts, middle vertical support strut, seat rails supported at five points, and back upholstery attached wwith machine screws.

3503 Bounder Power Wheelchair
21st Century Scientific
4915 Industrial Way
Coeur D Alene, ID 83814
208-667-8800
800-448-3680
Fax: 208-667-6600
e-mail: 21st@wheelchairs.com
http://www.21stcenturyscientific.com

Ronald E Prior Ph.D, CEO
Susan Harris, CFO/Webmaster

Available in a variety of widths from 16 to 18 feet for users up to 250 pounds. Its powerful 1/4 HP motors can achieve top speeds of over 10 mph. The rugged frame is constructed with steel tubing. The standard 12 position Adjustable Front Forks, made of 1/4 inch thick steel, provides impact dampening and seat tilt adjustment. A Dual Group 27 Sliding Battery Box provides extended range and easy battery maintenance.

3504 Breezy
Sunrise Medical/Quickie Designs
2382 Faraday Avenue
Suite 200
Carlsbad, CA 92008-7220
760-930-1500
Fax: 760-930-1585
http://www.sunrisemedical.com

Michael Hammes, CEO

This lightweight chair is durable, comfortable and flexible enough to meet the needs of a wide range of wheelchair users.

3505 Champion 1000
Kuschall of America/Graham Field Health Products
2935 Northeast Parkway
Atlanta, GA 30360
314-512-7000
800-347-5678
Fax: 800-726-0601
e-mail: cs@grahamfield.com
http://www.grahamfield.com

Ultralight wheelchair designed to improve mobility. $1,689

3506 Champion 2000
Kuschall of America/Graham Field Health Products
2935 Northeast Parkway
Atlanta, GA 30360
314-512-7000
800-347-5678
Fax: 800-726-0601
e-mail: cs@grahamfield.com
http://www.grahamfield.com

Rigid chair that folds side-to-side. $1,765

3507 Champion 3000
Kuschall of America/Graham Field Health Products
2935 Northeast Parkway
Atlanta, GA 30360
314-512-7000
800-347-5678
Fax: 800-726-0601
e-mail: cs@grahamfield.com
http://www.grahamfield.com

The high-performance chair built for perfectionists. $1,695

3508 Compax 12
Convaid Products
PO Box 4209
Palos Verdes, CA 90274-9571
310-618-0111
888-266-8243
Fax: 310-618-8811
e-mail: custservice@convaid.com
http://www.convaid.com

Merv Watkins, Owner

Disability Aids & Assistive Devices/Wheelchairs

This wheelchair folds to the size of a small golf bag and weighs 19 pounds.

3509 **Convaid Products**
PO Box 4209
Palos Verdes Peninsula, CA 90274-9571
310-618-0111
888-CON-VAID
Fax: 310-618-8811
http://www.convaid.com

Mervyn Watkins, Owner

Five different styles of wheelchairs. COnvaid's mission is to be sensitive to the broad needs of physically challenged children, and just as important, sensitive to the needs of the caregivers.

3510 **Cross Wheelchair**
ETAC USA
2325 Parklawn Drive
Suite J
Waukesha, WI 53186-2938
414-796-4600
800-678-3822
Fax: 262-796-4605

A carefully designed crossfolding Swedish wheelchair made of aluminum. The cross has a contouring back rest upholstery that can be adjusted as the user needs to change. Frame widths available from 14 to 20 inches. Seat frame and upholstery are adjustable to fit each individual. Lifetime warranty on frame for original user. $1,295 -$2,500

3511 **Custom Durable**
21279 Protecta Drive
Elkhart, IN 46516-9539
574-522-7199
800-933-0256
Fax: 219-293-0202

Dawn Slabach, President

Wheelchairs and accessories.

3512 **Damaco D90**
Damaco
20542 Plummer Street
Chatsworth, CA 91311-5109
818-709-4534
800-432-2434
Fax: 818-709-5282

Portable power unit that fits manual wheelchairs with large rear wheels. Weighing just 22 pounds, the power system can be removed and stored in a matter of seconds.

3513 **Eagle Sportschairs**
2351 Parkwood Road
Snellville, GA 30039-4003
770-972-0763
800-932-9380
Fax: 770-985-4885
e-mail: bewing@bellsouth.net
http://www.eaglesportschairs.com

Barry Ewing, Owner
Bernice Marston, Customer Service

The Eagle line of custom lightweight performance chairs includes a range of options to fit all racing and sport needs including; track, baseball, quad-rugby, tennis, field events and waterski. Also popular for daily use. We are able to customize any chair to accommodate size and disability, and all frames have a full five year warranty.

3514 **Evacu-Trac**
Garaventa Canada
PO Box L-1
Blaine, WA 98230
360-332-2231
866-824-8314
e-mail: productinfo@evacutrac.com
http://www.evacutrac.com

This emergency evacuation chair is designed for safety and fast operation.

3515 **F3 Wheelchair**
ETAC USA
2325 Parklawn Drive
Suite J
Waukesha, WI 53186-2938
414-796-4600
800-678-3822
Fax: 262-796-4605

A Swedish wheelchair designed to provide function, comfort and flexibility. Seat frame and upholstery are adjustable to fit each individual. Swing away, detachable footrests are standard. Available in frame widths from 14 to 18 inches and 20 inches. Numerous accessories are available in order to individualize each chair. Lifetime warranty on frame for original user.

3516 **Gadabout Wheelchairs**
Gadabout Wheelchairs
892 Ridge Road E
Rochester, NY 14621-1718
585-338-2110
800-828-4242
Fax: 585-388-2696

Michael Fonte, Owner

Enjoy independence with the wheelchair that is lightweight, portable, convenient, comfortable and sturdy.

3517 **Gem Wheelchair and Scooter Service**
176-39 Union Tpke
Flushing, NY 11366
718-969-8600
800-943-3578
Fax: 718-969-8300
http://www.wheelchairsusa.com

Jeff Bochner, President

GEM repairs and sells all makes and models of manual and motorized wheelchairs and power scooters. Clients are in all five New York City Boroughs and Nassau County. Workers Compensatation, Medicare and Medicaid accepted, pick-up and delivery and loaner equipment services available. Huge replacement parts inventory.

3518 **Gendron**
Lugbill Road
Archbold, OH 43502
419-445-6060
800-537-2521
Fax: 419-636-9261
e-mail: sales@gendroninc.com
http://www.gendroninc.com

Steven Cotter, President/CEO

Manufacturer of wheelchairs for a variety of other applications, specializing in bariatric mobility products.

3519 **Geronimo**
Redman Powerchair
1674 South Research Loop
Suite 402
Tucson, AZ 85710-6791
520-294-1466
800-727-6684
Fax: 520-546-5530
e-mail: info@redmanpowerchair.com
http://www.redmanpowerchair.com

Arnie Johnson, Owner
Don Redman, Founder

Wheelchair offering direct drive, two year electronic guarantee and micro controls.

3520 **HiRider**
Gaymar Industries
10 Centre Drive
Orchard Park, NY 14127-2280
716-662-2551
800-828-7341
Fax: 716-662-0748
e-mail: websalescontact@gaymar.com
http://www.gaymar.com

Frank Lumbar, CEO
Dr. Thomas P Stewart, President

A wheelchair that provides mobility in both sitting and standing positions.

Disability Aids & Assistive Devices/Wheelchairs

3521 Innovative Products Unlimited
2120 Industrial Drive
Niles, MI 49120
269-684-5050
800-833-2826
Fax: 888-757-4734
e-mail: ipu@ipu.com
http://www.ipu.com

Wheelchairs and accessories.

3522 Klassic-Plus
Kareco International
299 Route 22 East
Green Brook, NJ 08812-1714
732-752-9292
800-852-7326
Fax: 732-752-9636

Kevin O'Neil, Owner

Stainless steel lightweight wheelchair offers standard features.

3523 LEVO Standing Wheelchairs
LEVO USA Inc.
211 Fulton Court
Peachtree, GA 30290
770-486-0033
888-538-6872
Fax: 770-486-6096
e-mail: request@levousa.com
http://www.levousa.com

Daniel Johnson, CEO, Founder

LEVO will be the leader in stand-up wheelchairs. We will provide our clients with innovative solutions and products, delivering the greatest value, supported with exceptional service.

3524 Lightweight Breezy
Motion Design
2382 Faraday Avenue
Suite 200
Carlsbad, CA 92008-7220
760-930-1500
Fax: 760-930-1585

Michael N Hammes, CEO

A lightweight wheelchair.

3525 Permobil Max 90
Permobil USA
6961 Eastgate Blvd.
Lebanon, TN 37090
781-229-9748
800-736-0925
Fax: 800-231-3256
e-mail: info@permobilus.com
http://www.permobilusa.com

Larry Jackson, President
Tom Rolick, VP Business Development
John Coffay, Customer Support Manager

The power wheelchair for those needing an easily maneuverable and quiet indoor chair but who also need to use their chair outdoors.

3526 Permobil Super 90
Permobil
6961 Eastgate Blvd.
Lebanon, TN 37090
800-736-0925
Fax: 800-231-3256
e-mail: info@permobilus.com
http://www.permobilusa.com

Larry Jackson, President
Tom Rolick, VP Business Development
John Coffay, Customer Support Manager

The power wheelchair is designed for travel over uneven and hilly terrain outdoors and indoors.

3527 Posture-Glide Lounger
Graham-Field
2935 Northeast Parkway
Atlanta, GA 30360-2808
800-347-5678
Fax: 800-726-0601
e-mail: cs@grahamfield.com
http://www.grahamfield.com

Beatrice Scherer, President/CEO
Cherie Antoniazzi, Senior VP, Human Resources
Alan Monahan, CFO

Provides all day comfort and safe, independent mobilization with feet or hands. The ergonomically engineered seat back provides correct support.

3528 Power Chairs
Bruno Independent Living Aids
1780 Executive Drive
PO Box 84
Oconomowoc, WI 53066
262-567-4990
800-882-8183
Fax: 262-953-5501
e-mail: service@bruno.com
http://www.bruno.com

Michael R Bruno II, President/CEO
Patrick Foy, National Sales Manager
Anne Tyler, Merketing

Products available in front and rear wheel drive. Our power chairs have excellent directional stability, rock solid construction and durability.

3529 Power for Off-Pavement
Redman Powerchair
1674 South Research Loop
Suite 402
Tucson, AZ 85710-6791
800-727-6684
Fax: 520-546-5530
e-mail: info@redmanpowerchair.com
http://www.redmanpowerchair.com

Power-drive wheelchair has a solid seat and safely and securely handle knolls and off-pavement terrain.

3530 Redman Apache
Redman Powerchair
1674 South Research Loop
Suite 402
Tucson, AZ 85710-6791
800-727-6684
Fax: 520-546-5530
e-mail: info@redmanpowerchair.com
http://www.redmanpowerchair.com

These ultralight, active use wheelchairs offer quick release rear wheels, adjustable arm height and detachable arm swing-away.

3531 Redman Crow Line
Redman Powerchair
1674 South Research Loop
Suite 402
Tucson, AZ 85710-6791
800-727-6684
Fax: 520-546-5530
e-mail: info@redmanpowerchair.com
http://www.redmanpowerchair.com

Reclining wheelchair that reclines a full 90 degrees to flat and can be stopped anywhere on the axis.

3532 Roll-Aid
Stand Aid of Iowa
1009 2nd Ave
PO Box 386
Sheldon, IA 51201
712-324-2153
800-831-8580
Fax: 712-324-5210
e-mail: sales@stand-aid.com
http://www.stand-aid.com

Mike Kleinwolterink, Owner

Adapts to fit all standard collapsible wheelchairs. It is convenient, portable and provides electric rollator mobility instantly.

Disability Aids & Assistive Devices/Wheelchair Accessories

3533 Rolls 2000 Series
Invacare
One Invacare Way
Elyria, OH 44035-4190
440-329-6000
800-333-6900
Fax: 440-329-6568
e-mail: info@invacare.com
http://www.invacare.com

A Malachi Mixon III, Chairman/CEO
Gerald B Blouch, President/COO
Dale LaPorte, Senior Vice President

These wheelchairs are the first light-weight wheelchairs designed for rental use.

3534 Side-to-Side Folding Chair
Kuschall of America
3601 Rider Trail S
Earth City, MO 63045-1116
314-512-7000
800-654-4768
Fax: 800-542-3567

The Champion 2000 is a folding chair with the ride and feel of a rigid chair.

3535 Sidekick Walk & Ride Power Wheelchair
21st Century Scientific
4915 Industrial Way
Coeur D Alene, ID 83815-8931
208-667-8800
800-448-3680
Fax: 208-667-6600
e-mail: 21st@wheelchairs.com
http://www.21stcenturyscientific.com

Ronald E Prior Ph.D., CEO
Susan Harris, CFO/Webmaster

Manufactured for people up to 200 pounds with walking disabilities. It is lightweight, easy to use and transport, and competitively priced. The patent pending Walk and Ride feature allows the user to drive the SIDEKICK as a normal power wheelchair or walk behind it as a power walker using controls located on the push-handles.

3536 Sport Lite 4000
Gendron
PO Box 197
400 E. Lugbill Road
Archbold, OH 43502
419-445-6060
800-537-2521
Fax: 419-446-2631
e-mail: sales@gendroninc.com
http://www.gendroninc.com

Steven Cotter, VP Sales

Swing-away armrests made of durable stainless steel and detachable anti-tippers.

3537 Sportaid
2462 Centerville Rosebud Road
Loganville, GA 30052-2563
770-554-5130
800-743-7203
Fax: 770-554-5944
e-mail: stuff@sportaid.com
http://www.sportaid.com

Jimmy Green, Contact
Norma Carden, Office Manager

Offers an assortment of wheelchairs (everyday and racing), wheelchair sports equipment, replacement tires, hubs, spokes, pushrims, cushions and more. Call for free catalog.

3538 Steven Motor Chair
Steven Motor Chair Company
20580 Placer Hills Road
Colfax, CA 95713-9766
530-637-5915

Wesley Stephens, Managing Partner
Brian Stephens, Managing Partner
Penny Todd, President

Completely self-powered, easy to operate, attractive and rugged.

3539 Sting Wheelchair
ETAC USA
2325 Parklawn Drive
Suite J
Waukesha, WI 53186-2938
800-678-3822
Fax: 262-796-4605

A swedish wheelchair designed to adjust to meet the growing child's every need. Both the seat and the backrest are width, height, and angle adjustable. Footrest, adjustable in height, depth and angle and swings back under the seat. Numerous accessories available. Lifetime warranty on frame for the original user.

3540 Surf Chair
2052 S Peninsula Drive
Daytona Beach, FL 32118-5237
386-253-0986
800-841-6610
Fax: 386-253-7600

Wheelchairs and accessories.

3541 Swede Elite
ETAC USA
2325 Parklawn Drive
Suite J
Waukesha, WI 53186-2938
414-796-4600
800-678-3822
Fax: 262-796-4605

A carefully designed Swedish wheelchair made of lightweight titanium for the active user. Available in frame widths from 14-18 inches and colors available are: black, red, plus, teal-blue, and Silver. Custom colors available at additional cost and there is a lifetime warranty on the frame for original user. $1,740-$2,500

3542 Wizz-ard
Wheelchairs of Kansas
204 W 2nd St.
Ellis, KS 67637
785-726-4885
800-537-6454
Fax: 800-337-2447
e-mail: wokinfo@go2wok.com
http://www.wheelchairsofkansas.com

A large-frame wheelchair constructed of high quality, stress tested stainless steel to insure durability and peak performance.

3543 YM 9000 Ride-Lite Series
Invacare
1 Invacare Way
Elyria, OH 44035-4190
440-329-6000
800-333-6900
Fax: 440-329-6568
e-mail: info@invacare.com
http://www.invacare.com

A Malachi Mixon III, Chairman/CEO
Gerald B Blouch, President/COO
Dale LaPorte, Senior Vice President

This wheelchair has adjustable toggle wheel locks with brackets that bolt through the frame, composite pneumatic wheels and casters, and foam-padded back upholstery.

Wheelchair Accessories

3544 Air Liftunlimited
Air Lift Unlimited
1212 Kerr Gulch Road
Evergreen, CO 80439-6397
303-526-0132
800-776-6771
Fax: 303-526-4774
e-mail: info@airlift.com
http://www.airlift.com

Phyllis King, Sales Associate

Conveniently attaches liquid oxygen or cylinder unit to any size wheelchair or walker.

Disability Aids & Assistive Devices/Wheelchair Accessories

3545 Convert-Able Table
Rehab and Educational Aids for Living
187 S Main Street
Dolgeville, NY 13329-1455
315-429-3071
800-696-7041
Fax: 315-429-3071
http://www.realdesigninc.com

Specially designed for use with wheelchairs, this table has push button height adjustment and interchangeable tops so it can become a desk, art easel, etc.

3546 Curtis Instruments
200 Kisco Avenue
Mount Kisco, NY 10549-1400
914-666-2971
Fax: 914-666-2188
e-mail: curtis1@cloud9.net
http://www.curtisinst.com

Nancy A Korman, National Sales Manager
John Kenneally, Application Engineer
Stuart E Marwell, CEO

Provides a readable, accurate indication of battery, in easy to read type of display. Innovative, efficient motor speed controllers for single or dual PM motor vehicles.

3547 Deluxe Wheelchair Pushing Cuffs
Cleo of New York
S Buckout Street
Irvington, NY 10533
914-591-4900
800-321-0595
Fax: 914-591-4083

Elliott Goldberg, President

Highest quality soft suede leather cuffs provide extra traction while protecting the hands.

3548 EZBACK Recline Control
APT Technology
236a N Main Street
Shreve, OH 44676-9788
330-567-2001
Fax: 330-507-3073
e-mail: sales@apt-technology.com
http://www.apt-technology.com

A versatile, easy to install and operate motor controller intended to control power recline and similar machinery on a power wheelchair. Optional EDMA permits control of 2 motors via a single or dual switch. Accommodates limit switches, various configurations and is rugged and reliable.

3549 East Penn Manufacturing Company
East Penn Manufacturing Company
PO Box 147
Lyon Station, PA 19536
610-682-6361
Fax: 610-682-4781
e-mail: eastpenn@eastpenn-deka.com

Harold Eberly, VP Sales
Daniel R Langdon, President

Specially engineered for demanding deep-cycle applications Gelled electrolyte Deka Dominator Batteries provides maintenance-free operation, longer battery life and hours of reliable performance. Their excellent recharge characteristics provide quick turn-a-round time.

3550 Featherspring
712 N 34th Street
Seattle, WA 98103-8881
206-545-8585
Fax: 206-547-8589

Peter Rothschild, President

Foot supports for wheelchair users to prevent and treat cold feet, sore heels, swollen feet and weak ankles.

3551 George H. Snyder Enterprises
5809 NE 21st Avenue
Fort Lauderdale, FL 33308
954-491-2886
Fax: 954-491-2886

George Snyder, President

Attachments for wheelchairs.

3552 Latchloc Automatic Wheelchair Tiedown
Ahnafield Corporation
2444 Production Drive
Indianapolis, IN 46241
317-241-2444
800-636-8060
Fax: 317-636-8098
e-mail: jeff@ahnafield.com
http://www.ahnafield.com

Independent wheelchair tiedown system utilized primarily by individuals who drive from their wheelchairs.

3553 Lester Dual-Mode Battery Charger
Lester Electrical
625 W A Street
Lincoln, NE 68522-1706
402-477-8988
Fax: 402-474-1769
e-mail: sales@lesterelectrical.com
http://www.lesterelectrical.com

Edith Earnest, Sales Service Coordinator
James L Carrier, President

Replaceable electrolyte batteries require an entirely different charge cycle than do sealed batteries.

3554 Lestronic II
Lester Electrical
625 West A Street
Lincoln, NE 68522-1706
402-477-8988
Fax: 402-474-1769
e-mail: sales@lesterelectrical.com
http://www.lesterelectrical.com

James Carrier, President

Fully automatic battery charger.

3555 Lift and Carry Wheelchair Caddy
Cleo of New York
S Buckout Street
Irvington, NY 10533
914-591-4900
800-321-0595
Fax: 914-591-4083

Elliott Goldberg, President

Spring-assisted action raises the wheelchair and locks securely into place on the back of the car.

3556 Mat Factory
760 W 16th Street
Suite E
Costa Mesa, CA 92627-4319
949-645-3122
800-628-7626
Fax: 949-645-0966
e-mail: matfat@pop3.concentric.net
http://www.matfactoryinc.com

Roger Maloney, President
Peggy Maloney, Owner

The safety deck II is an interlocking grid system made from recycled rubber tires. The tiles are set directly on top of the ground and permit grass to grow through the holes and cover the surface. It provides barrier free access for wheelchairs.

3557 Pac-All Wheelchair Carrier
Pac-All Carriers
2321 Carolton Road
Maitland, FL 32751-3624
407-830-6604
Fax: 407-339-2847

LE Angel, Contact

No more lifting and no more pain wheelchair carrier. VA approved. Made in USA.

3558 Reclining Power Wheelchairs
LaBac Systems
4965 Kingston Street
Denver, CO 80239
303-914-9914
800-445-4402
Fax: 303-914-8101
http://www.labaconline.com

Josh Barnum, President

Disability Aids & Assistive Devices/Wheelchair Accessories

Power recline seating systems for wheelchairs, offering more comfort and dependability for the physically challenged.

3559 Skyway
Skyway Machine
4451 Caterpillar Road
Redding, CA 96003-1496
530-243-5151
800-332-3357
Fax: 530-243-5104
e-mail: sales@skywaywheels.com
http://www.skywaytuffwheels.com

Parrey Cremeans, Sales Manager
Tad Raudman, Sales/Customer Service
Ken Coster, President

For over 20 years Skyway has been the world leader in composite wheels. Supplying over 650 different wheel combinations for wheelchairs, lawn and garden products, bicycles, and a large assortment of wheeled devices. Wheel sizes range from 5 to 24 inch diameter.

3560 Torso Support
Grandmar
1311 63rd Street
Emeryville, CA 94608
650-428-0441
Fax: 510-428-1330

An aid for people who are unable to maintain an upright position in an automobile or a wheelchair.

3561 Ventura Enterprises
35 Lawton Avenue
Danville, IN 46122-1217
317-745-2989
Fax: 317-745-3179

Linda Plunkett, President

Manufacturer of everyday living mobility aids. Products include carrying aids for walkers and wheelchairs and also wheelchair cushions.

3562 Wheelchair Aide
Graham-Field
2935 Northeast Parkway
Atlanta, GA 30360-2808
800-347-5678
Fax: 800-726-0601

Beatrice Scherer, President/CEO
Cheri Antoniazzi, Senior VP, Human Resources
Alan Monahan, CFO

This is a heavy-duty wheelchair comfort tray which surrounds the wheelchair user and provides a large, smooth surface for dining, writing, hobbies or work. The heavy gauge plastic tray is easy to clean and attaches with two Velcro straps.

3563 Wheelchair Parts & Fasteners
Thomas Hardware
1001 Rockland Street
Reading, PA 19604-1520
610-921-2723
800-634-4293
Fax: 800-634-3099

Bob Ruhe, Marketing Manager
Bill Stambaugh, Manager

Wheelchair restraint kits.

3564 Wheelchair Work Table
Bailey Manufacturing Company
PO Box 130
Lodi, OH 44254-1056
330-948-1080
800-321-8372
Fax: 800-224-5390
e-mail: baileymfg@attmail.com
http://www.baileymfg.com

Larry Strimple, President

An adjustable height, functional, individual cut-out work table featuring a wood-grain laminate, scratch resistant top with chrome plated steel legs.

Aging / Associations & Organizations

Associations & Organizations

3565 **Advanced Temporary Services**
121 Congressional Lane
Research Court
Suite 450
Rockville, MD 20850
301-933-5554
Fax: 301-933-5005
e-mail: info@advancednursing.com
http://www.advancednursing.com

Provides nursing services, home support, dimentia support, and a variety of resources.

3566 **American Association for Geriatric Psychiatry**
7910 Woodmont Avenue
Suite 1050
Bethesda, MD 20814-3004
301-654-7850
Fax: 301-654-4137
e-mail: main@aagponline.org
http://www.aagpgpa.org

Christine de Vries, CEO
Belinda D'Agostino, Director

Psychiatrists interested in promoting better mental health care for the elderly. Maintains placement service and speakers' bureau.

3567 **American Association of Retired Persons**
601 E Street NW
Washington, DC 20049
202-434-2277
888-687-2277
Fax: 202-434-6483
e-mail: member@aarp.org
http://www.aarp.org

Marie Smith, President
William D Novelli, CEO
Richard Henry, Associate Executive Director

AARP is a nonprofit, nonpartisan association dedicated to shaping and enriching the experience of aging for their members and for all Americans. Founded in 1958 they are the national's largest organization of midlife and older persons, with more than 30 million members. AARP membership is open to anyone age 50 or older. AARP has four primary areas of expertise: information and education; community service; legislative; judicial and consumer advocacy; and member services.

3568 **American Disabled for Attendant Programs**
201 S Cherokee
Denver, CO 80223
303-733-9324
Fax: 303-733-6211
e-mail: adapt@adapt.org
http://www.adapt.org/

Mike Auberger, Contact
Marsha Katz, Contact

Supports federal services and funding for the disabled and elderly. Provides resources, educational material and evaluates need for attendents for the elderly in their home.

3569 **American Geriatrics Society**
350 Fifth Avenue
Suite 801
New York, NY 10118
212-308-1414
800-247-4779
Fax: 212-832-8646
e-mail: info@americangeriatrics.org
http://www.americangeriatrics.org

Linda Hiddemen Barondess, Executive VP
Jane F. Potter, MD, Chairman

The premier professional organization of healthcare providers dedicated to improving the health and well-being of older adults. With an active membership of over 6,000 health care professionals, the AGS has a long history of affecting change in the provision of healthcare in older adults. The AGS Foundation for Health in Aging (FHA) aims to build a bridge between the research and practice of geriatrics health care professionals and the public. The FHA advocates on behalf of older adults and their special needs through public education, clinical research and public policy.

3570 **American Health Assistance Foundation**
22512 Gateway Center Drive
Clarksburg, MD 20871-2005
301-948-3244
800-437-2423
Fax: 301-258-9454
e-mail: janthony@ahaf.org
http://www.ahaf.org

Jane Anthony, AFRP Coordinator
Kathy Honaker, Executive Director

Funds research programs for Alzheimer's disease, heart disease, glaucoma, and macular degeneration. Provides financial assistance through Alzheimer's Family Relief Program. Public education materials on programs, brochures, and applications are provided.

3571 **American Medical Directors Association (AMDA)**
10480 Little Patuxent Parkway
Suite 760
Columbia, MD 21044
410-740-9743
800-876-2632
Fax: 410-740-4572
e-mail: cmd@amda.com
http://www.amda.com

Lorraine Tarnove, Executive Director
Alva (Buzz) Baker, MD, CMD, President

Supports continuing education in the field of geriatrics while promoting improvement of long term care.
1975

3572 **American Podiatric Circulatory Society**
5704 18th Avenue
Brooklyn, NY 11204
718-236-7952
Fax: 718-236-7953

Stanley Goldstein DPM, President/Executive Director

Disseminates information on the Suffuse Osmotic Chemisorb Asphyxiation (SOCA) therapy, known as the Tereno Method, devised by Dr. Isaac Tereno for treatment of geriatric patients suffering from arterial blockage in their limbs. The Tereno Method uses vitamins to enrich the blood and enlarge subcutaneous capillaries and lymph vessels, thus creating an alternate circulatory network which bypasses blocked arteries. It is an alternative to major surgery and/or amputation in geriatric patients with poor circulation in their limbs. Conducts research; maintains speakers' bureau.

3573 **American Society on Aging**
833 Market Street
Suite 511
San Francisco, CA 94103
415-974-9600
800-537-9728
Fax: 415-974-0300
e-mail: info@asaging.org
http://www.asaging.org

John Feather, Executive Director
Dominick Albano, Vice President

Health care and social service professionals, educators, researchers, administrators, businesspersons, students, and senior citizens. Works to enhance the well-being of older individuals and to foster unity among those working with and for the elderly. Offers 25 continuing education programs for professionals in aging-related fields. Publishes 'Aging Today,' a bi-monthly newspaper, and 'Generations,' a quarterly journal.
1954

Aging/Associations & Organizations

3574 Arizona Center on Aging
1807 E Elm Street
Tucson, AZ 85719-4324
520-626-5800
Fax: 520-626-5811
e-mail: contact@aging.arizona.edu
http://www.aging.arizona.edu

Linda R Phillips PhD RN FAAN, Professor, Nursing
Kristine M. Bursac, MPA, Director of Community Developmen

Long-term care, retirement communities, minority elderly, health and long-term care policy, and aging. Conducts applied research in service delivery system development and provides technical assistance and research dissemination.

3575 Association for Adult Development and Aging
5999 Stevenson Avenue
Alexandria, VA 22304
703-823-9800
800-347-6647
Fax: 703-823-0252
http://www.aadaweb.org

Wendy Enochs, President
Richard Yep, Executive Director

A division of the American Counseling Association. Individuals holding a master's degree or its equivalent in adult counseling or a related field. Seeks to: improve the competence and skills of ACA and AADA members; expand professional work opportunities in adult development and aging counseling; promote the development of guidelines for professional preparation of counselors. Provides leadership and information to families, legislators, communitty service agencies, counselors, and other service providers in professions related to adult development and aging. Serves as forum for the discussion of ethical, social, and technical issues related to counseling adults across the life span.

3576 Brookdale Center for Healthy Aging and Longevity of Hunter College
Hunter College
425 E 25th Street
13th Floor N
New York, NY 10010-2590
212-481-3780
Fax: 212-481-3791
e-mail: info@brookdale.org
http://www.brookdale.org

Naz Mirza, Executive Assistant
Laura Traynor, Associate Executive Director

BOCA sponsors a variety of programs including the Institute on Law and Rights of Older Adults which fights for grandparents rights. See the Legal Resources chapter for specific state listings.

3577 Center for Positive Aging
607 Peachtree Street NE
Atlanta, GA 30308
404-872-9191
Fax: 404-872-1737
e-mail: seconomopoulos@gahsa.org
http://http://centerforpositiveaging.org

Suzanne Economopoulos, Director of Programs and Service
Walter Coffey, President

The Center for Positive Aging is a partnership of individuals, community organizations and congregations working together to provide health, educational and recreational opportunities for older persons and their families. Through our programs, services, and affiliations, we educate people of all ages and walks of life about living independent and creative lives. Programs and services availacle from the Center include: Computers Made Easy classes, Educational classes, Eldercare Forums, Exercise videos, 'Focus on Fitness' exercise classes, Health Care Information, Information and Referral, Meals on Wheels, Support Groups, Trips and Special Events, and Workshops for Exercise Leaders.
1982

3578 Center for Social Gerontology
2307 Shelby Avenue
Ann Arbor, MI 48103
734-665-1126
Fax: 734-665-2071
e-mail: tcsg@tcsg.org
http://www.tcsg.org

Penelope A Hommel, Treasurer
Clifford Douglas, President

Purpose is to advance the well-being of older people in the US through research, education, technical assistance, and training. Focuses primarily on legal rights, guardianship and alternative protective services, and delivery of legal services. Provides consulting services. Develops and researches standards for the provision of guardianship services for older people; works to improve the court processes for determining the need for guardianship through development and evaluation of a new model. Conducts periodic training on legal rights and legal resources, for legal advocates, nonlawyers who work with the elderly, and older consumers.
1972

3579 Christian Foundation for Children and Aging
1 Elmwood Avenue
Kansas City, KS 66103
913-384-6500
800-875-6564
Fax: 913-384-2211
e-mail: mail@cfcausa.org
http://www.cfcausa.org

Bob Hentzen, President
Charity Navigator, Executive Director

Seeks to advance the physical, mental, spiritual, and social welfare of the economically disadvantaged, especially children and aging persons in developing countries. US sponsors provide financial support and correspond with individuals in need; volunteers help provide social services, including medical, educational, and nutritional programs. Provides Christian education and guidance. Conducts orientation program for volunteers and Mission Awareness trips to Mexico and Central America.
1981

3580 Jewish Council for the Aging
11820 Parklawn Drive
Suite 200
Rockville, MD 20852
301-255-4200
Fax: 301-231-9360
e-mail: jcagw@jcagw.org
http://www.jcagw.org
TDD 301-881-5263

Ed Bonder, President
David Gamse, Executive Director

Seeks to assist the elderly of all faiths lead independent lives. Provides transportation, job search assistance, fitness training, computer training and information and referrals. Conducts educational programs and presents an annual productive aging award. Maintains speakers' bureau.
1973

3581 National Center for Vision and Aging
Lighthouse
111 E 59th Street
New York, NY 10022-1202
212-821-9495
Fax: 212-821-9705
TDD 212-821-9705

Provides support, information, and resources on vision impairment and blindness.

3582 National Voluntary Organizations for Independent Living for the Aging
409 3rd Street SW
Washington, DC 20024-3212
202-205-6770
Fax: 202-479-0735
http://www.ncoa.org

Stephanie Trapp, Program Manager

Aging / Books

Emphasizes the needs for in-home and community-based health care and social services designed to help older persons remain in or return to their homes and live independently, works to educate and assist voluntary organizations to help develop such services.

3583 Office for American Indian, Alaskan Native and Native Hawaiian Programs: Administration on Aging
US Department of Health & Human Services
Hubert H Humphrey Building
200 Independence Avenue SW
Washington, DC 20201
202-619-0257
877-696-6775
Fax: 202-690-5400
http://www.aoa.gov

Michael O Leavitt, Secretary
Robert O'Connell, Tri-Regional Administrator

The Office for American Indians, Alaskan Natives, and Native Hawaiians advises the Secretary, through the Assistant Secretary for Children and Families, on matters relating to Native Americans. It represents the concerns of Native Americans and serves as the focal point in the Department on the full range of developmental, social, and economic strategies that support Native American self-determination and self-sufficiency.

3584 UCSF Memory and Aging Center
350 Parnassus Avenue
Suite 706
San Francisco, CA 94143-1207
415-476-6880
Fax: 415-476-4800
http://www.memory.ucsf.edu

Bruce L. Miller MD, Director
Kathleen Drew, Administrator

The UCSF Memory and Aging Center provides the highest quality of care for individuals with cognitive problems, to conduct research for degenerative brain diseases, and to educate health professionals, patients, and their families. The Memory and Aging Center also publishes a biannual newsletter, as well as other publications.

3585 Virginia Center on Aging
Virginia Commonwealth University
1200 E. Broad St.
4th Floor, East Wing
Richmond, VA 23298
804-828-1525
Fax: 804-828-7905
e-mail: lhwaters@hsc.vcu.edu
http://www.vcu.edu/vcoa

Jason Rachel, Public Relations Specialist
Edward F Ansello, Director
Connie Coogle PhD, Director Research

Mental and physical health of the elderly, focusing on community-living and health-related factors of aging. Studies include: eldercare responsibilities of employed family caregivers, staffing requirements in residential care facilities, impact of aging of adults with developmental disabilities, minority healthcare utilization, caregiving of demented elders, research and documentation project on rural geropharmacy.

3586 Washington University Center for Aging
4488 Forest Park Avenue
Suite 130
Saint Louis, MO 63108
314-286-2441
Fax: 314-286-2763
e-mail: pestronka@neuro.wustl.edu
http://http://wucfa.wustl.edu

John C Morris, Director

Provides academic and administrative leadership by fostering research, education, sevices and community development the address issues related to productive aging. The goal for the center is to promote individual and societal conditionals that enhance productive aging, defined as the ability of older adults to remain healthy, empowered, active, contributing, and independent for as long as possible.

Books

3587 36 Hour Day: A Family Guide to Caring for Persons with Alzheimer Disease
Hachette Book Group USA
237 Park Avenue
New York, NY 10017
http://www.hachettebookgroupusa.com

Nancy L Mace, Author
Peter V Rabins, Author

The trusted bible for families affected by dementia disorders. Provides all the practical and specific advice you need to make care easier, improve quality of life, and lift the whole family's spirit. Features the latest medical research and news on current delivery of care, with new appendices including Web site and association listings.

512 pages

3588 A Memory Retention Course for the Aged
National Council on the Aging
409 3rd Street SW
Washington, DC 20024-3212
800-867-2755
Fax: 301-206-9789

A guide for persons working with older adults in group settings, to help them cope with memory lapses and normal memory loss.

24 pages

3589 A New Look at Community Based Respite Programs: Utilization, Satisfaction, and Development
Haworth Press
10 Alice Street
Binghamton, NY 13904-1503
607-722-5857
800-342-9678
Fax: 607-722-3487
e-mail: getinfo@haworthpressinc.com
http://www.haworthpressinc.com

William Cohen, Owner

Detailed analyses of a variety of support service systems from across the country, providing you valuable information you can use to duplicate the many successful ADDGS (Alzheimer's Disease Demonstration Grants to State) programs with your own clients.

180 pages

3590 A Resource Guide for Injury Control: Programs for Older Persons
National Council on the Aging
409 3rd Street SW
Washington, DC 20024-3212
202-479-1200
800-867-2755
Fax: 202-479-0735

James P Firman, CEO

Prepared to assist local aging and health service agencies in developing injury control programs for their clients.

29 pages

3591 ABA Community on Legal Problems of the Elderly
1800 M Street NW
Washington, DC 20036-5802
202-331-2297

Litigation and support center for the elderly.

3592 Abstracts in Social Gerontology: Current Literature on Aging
National Council on the Aging
600 Maryland Avenue SW
Washington, DC 20024-2520
202-479-1200
Fax: 202-479-0735

James P Firman, CEO

Detailed abstracts are provided for recent major journal articles, books, reports and other materials on many facets of aging, including: adult education, demography, family relations, institutional care and work attitudes.

Aging/Books

3593 Activities Keep Me Going & Going, Vol 1
Otterbein Homes Program Department
585 N Street
Route 741
Lebanon, OH 45036
513-932-7218
Fax: 513-932-5159

Charles W Peckham, Author/Educator

A progressive guidebook for activity professionals who plan, direct and evaluate activity programs for older adults in long-term care, assisted living and community settings. It includes practical techniques, examples, forms, checklists and resources.

476 pages Frequency: Paperback

3594 Activities Keep Me Going & Going, Vol 2
Otterbein Homes Program Department
585 N Street
Route 741
Lebanon, OH 45036
513-932-7218
Fax: 513-932-5159

Charles W Peckham, Author/Educator

A comparison to Volume 1, focuses on Activities and How To. Each chapter lists activities and has a grid to indicate in which activities a person with physical and/or cognitive impairment could potentially participate. Ideas, instructions, suggestions for adaptations and resources are provided in each chapter.

289 pages Frequency: Spiral Bound

3595 Activities for the Elderly: Volume 1-A Guide to Quality Programming
Idyll Arbor
PO Box 720
Ravensdale, WA 98051
425-432-3231
Fax: 425-432-3726
e-mail: sales@IdyllArbor.com
http://www.IdyllArbor.com

Sandra D Parker, Author
Carol Will, Author
Cheryl L Burke, Author

A collection of 75 practical activities and programs for therapists working with older adults. In addition to the instruction and helpful hints for each activity, the authors have also included the therapeutic benefits of each activity. Paperback.

171 pages

3596 Activities for the Elderly: Volume 2-Working with Residents with Significant Physical and Cognitive Diseases
Idyll Arbor
PO Box 720
Ravensdale, WA 98051
425-432-3231
Fax: 425-432-3726
e-mail: sales@IdyllArbor.com
http://www.IdyllArbor.com

A collection of 86 practical activities for residents who are very impaired because of dementia or other severe disabilities. This book provides the therapist with instructions and helpful hints, as well as the therapeutic benefits for each activity. Spiral bound.

135 pages

3597 Activities in Action
The Haworth Press
10 Alice Street
Binghamton, NY 13904-1503
607-722-5857
800-429-6784
Fax: 607-771-0012
e-mail: getinfo@haworthpressinc.com
http://www.haworthpressinc.com

Jackie Blakeslee, Advertising
William Cohen, Owner

An invaluable resource which serves as a catalyst for professional and personal growth and provides a national forum on geriatric and activity issues.

98 pages

3598 Activities with Developmentally Disabled Elderly and Older Adults
The Haworth Press
10 Alice Street
Binghamton, NY 13904-1503
607-722-5857
800-429-6784
Fax: 607-771-5857
e-mail: getinfo@haworthpressinc.com
http://www.haworthpressinc.com

Jackie Blakeslee, Advertising
William Cohen, Owner

Learn how to effectively plan and deliver activities for a growing number of older people with developmental disabilities. It aims to stimulate interest and continued support for recreation program development and implementation among developmental disability and aging service systems.

156 pages

3599 Adult Children & Aging Parents
American Counseling Association
5999 Stevenson Avenue
Alexandria, VA 22304-3304
703-823-9800
800-347-6647
Fax: 703-823-0252
http://www.counseling.org

Richard Yep, Executive Director

Provides effective intervention strategies and suggestions for counselors who work with older persons, individually and with the family. Offers information on many vital topics such as Alzheimer's Disease, retirement, elder abuse and suicide.

216 pages

3600 Advancing Gerontological Social Work Education
Haworth Press
10 Alice Street
Binghamton, NY 13904-1503
607-722-5857
800-342-9678
Fax: 607-722-3487
e-mail: getinfo@haworthpressinc.com
http://www.haworthpressinc.com

William Cohen, Owner

Examines the current status of geriatric/gerontological education; offers models for curriculum development within the classroom and the practice arena.

276 pages

3601 Ageing, Spirituality and Well-Being
Jessica Kingsley Publishers
400 Market Street
Suite 400
Philadelphia, PA 19106
215-922-1161
Fax: 215-922-1474
e-mail: orders@jkp.com
http://www.jkp.com

Albert Jewell, Editor

Explores how well-being is not about physical health alone (having purpose in life and continual spiritual growth are vital elements for older people) and guides as to how the particular needs of this age group can be addresses, and how meaningful care and support can be given.

224 pages Year Founded:

3602 Aging Children & Aging Parents
American Counseling Association
5999 Stevenson Avenue
Alexandria, VA 22304-3304
703-823-9800
800-347-6647
Fax: 703-823-0252
http://www.counseling.org

Richard Yep, Executive Director

Full of facts and statistics about aging, as well as emotional issues that face the elderly and their families.

216 pages

Aging/Books

3603 Aging Comes of Age
Westminster/John Knox Press
100 Witherspoon Street
Louisville, KY 40202-1396
800-227-2872
Fax: 800-541-5113

Following retirement, older people today are starting new businesses, returning to universities, becoming world travelers, and setting new patterns of divorce and remarriage. In this 'why to' book, eighty year old Frank Hutchison gives encouragement to mature persons who wish to have satisfying personal lives while contributing to society. He states that an expanded life can be yours if you become aware of it and if you genuinely want it.

120 pages Frequency: Paperback

3604 Aging in Stride: A Practical Guide forOlder Adults & Their Families
Caresource Healthcare Communications
426 Yale Avenue N
Seattle, WA 98109-5431
800-448-5213
Fax: 206-682-2901
e-mail: service@caresource.com
http://www.caresource.com

Diane Kenny, Contact

A guide to the full range of aging and caregiver issues, including arranging in home services, maintaining health and independence; selecting and moving to retirement housing; addressing legal and financial issues; and doing advance health care planning. Contains a variety of user friendly forms and checklists, an extensive glossary, links to other resources, and index.

368 pages

3605 Aging in the Designed Environment
The Haworth Press
10 Alice Street
Binghamton, NY 13904-1503
607-722-5857
800-429-6784
Fax: 607-771-0012
e-mail: getinfo@haworthpressinc.com
http://www.haworthpressinc.com

Jackie Blakeslee, Advertising
William Cohen, Owner

The key sourcebook for physical and occupational therapists developing and implementing environmental designs for the aging.

133 pages

3606 Aging, Physical Activity, and Health
Human Kinetics Publishers
PO Box 5076
Champaign, IL 61825-5076
217-351-5076
800-747-4457
Fax: 217-351-2674
e-mail: humank@hkusa.com
http://www.humankinetics.com

Reference for exercise scientists, gerontologists, geriatric medicine specialists, physiologists, and other professionals who work with older populations.

496 pages 1997

3607 Aging, Rights and Quality of Life: Prospects for Older People with Developmental Disabilities
Brookes Publishing
PO Box 10624
Baltimore, MD 21285
410-337-9580
800-638-3775
Fax: 410-337-8539
e-mail: custserv@pbrookes.com
http://www.pbrookes.com

Sandy Jensen, Customer Service Director
Melissa Behm, VP
Jessica Reghard, Marketing Director

In this groundbreaking new book, the leading authorities in the fields of aging and developmental disabilities provide you with an interdisciplinary analysis of the critical issues in the lives of older adults with developmental disabilities. Hardcover.

416 pages

3608 Beat the Nursing Home Trap: A Consumer's Guide to Assisted Living and Long Term Care
NOLO
950 Parker Street
Berkeley, CA 94710-2524
510-549-1976
800-955-4775
Fax: 510-548-5902
http://www.nolo.com

David Rothenberg, CEO
Susan McConnell, Director Sales
Natasha Kaluza, Sales Assistant

Don't guess. Use this book to figure out how to choose a nursing home, or find a viable alternative. Covers how to get the most out of Medicare and other benefit programs.

336 pages

3609 Caregiver Survival Series: Positive Caregiver Attitudes
National Stroke Association
9707 E Easter Lane
Centennial, CO 80112-3754
303-649-9299
800-787-6537
Fax: 303-649-1328

James Baranski, CEO

Down-to-earth strategies for developing positive attitudes toward care receivers, caregivers and life in general.

3610 Caregivers' Roller Coaster
Loyola University Press
3441 N Ashland Avenue
Chicago, IL 60657-1355
800-621-1008
Fax: 773-281-0555
http://www.layolapress.com

A simply written self-help guide for caregivers of the frail elderly. Offers support for men and women, not trained professionals, who find themselves caring for aging family members in their own homes. Offers practical advice and information on Alzheimer's, Medicare, insurance and community services for the elderly.

150 pages

3611 Caring for Those You Love: A Guide to Compassionate Care for the Aged
Horizon Publishers
50 S 500 W
Bountiful, UT 84010-8727
801-295-9451

Duane Crowther, Owner

This book is a practical guide to coping with special problems of the aged and infirm, and examines the many challenges of caring for the elderly on a personal and family level.

3612 Caring for Your Parents: The CompleteAARP Guide
Sterling Publishing Company
387 Park Avenue South
New York, NY 10016
212-532-7160
e-mail: custservice@sterlingpublishing.com
http://www.sterlingpublishing.com

Hugh Delehanty, Author
Elinor Ginzler, Author

Offers both sensitive counsel and a practical road map through the complex emotional terrain many of us face as our parents age. This eye-opening book guides readers through a new, creative approach to caregiving that turns familial duty into a journey of emotional development and resolution.

256 pages

3613 Caring for the Disabled Elderly
The Brookings Institution
1775 Massachusetts Avenue NW
Washington, DC 20036-2103
202-797-6000
Fax: 202-797-6004

Strobe Talbott, President

Financial information for the elderly.

318 pages Frequency: Paperback

Aging/Books

3614 Change for the Better
AARP
601 E Street NW
Washington, DC 20049
202-434-2277
800-424-3410
Fax: 202-434-3443
e-mail: member@aarp.org
http://www.aarp.org

William D Novelli, CEO

Overview of the ways in which older people can provide leadership and create environmental and housing changes that will make their communities better places to live.

3615 Communicating with Older Adults: A Guidefor Health Care & Senior Service Professionals & Staff
Caresource Healthcare Communications
426 Yale Avenue N
Seattle, WA 98109-5431
800-448-5213
Fax: 206-682-2901
e-mail: service@caresource.com
http://www.caresource.com

Diane Kenny, Contact

A handbook for health care senior care professionals and workers on how to communicate more effectively with older patients and consumers. This book reports on findings of research funded by the Retirement Research, SPRY, and Robert Wood Johnson Foundations. Contains research based recommendations for clinical care workers, senior living workers, and senior information and referral staff.

124 pages

3616 Community Recreation and People with Disabilities for Inclusion
Brookes Publishing
PO Box 10624
Baltimore, MD 21285-624
410-337-9580
800-638-3775
Fax: 410-337-8539
e-mail: custserv@pbrookes.com
http://www.pbrookes.com

Sandy Jensen, Customer Service Director
Melissa Behm, VP
Ginny Whitescarver, Marketing Director

Updates abound in the second edition of this respected manual for professionals designing community recreation programs to include people with disabilities. Paperback.

368 pages

3617 Community Supports for Aging Adults with Lifelong Disabilities
Brookes Publishing
PO Box 10624
Baltimore, MD 21285
410-337-9580
800-638-3775
Fax: 410-337-8539
e-mail: custserv@pbrookes.com
http://www.pbrookes.com

Sandy Jensen, Customer Service Director
Melissa Behm, VP
Ginny Whitescarver, Marketing Director

Drawing on field-tested experiences and situations that can be applied to almost any setting, this text gives you practical approaches to real-life challenges facing people with disabilities as they grow older. An essential resource for anyone working with older adults. Hardcover.

560 pages

3618 Consumer Health USA: Volume 2
ORYX Press
4041 N Central Avenue
Suite 700
Phoenix, AZ 85012-3330
602-265-2651
800-279-6798
Fax: 800-279-4663
e-mail: info@oryxpress.com
http://www.oryxpress.com

This highly regarded reference source features the full text of nearly 150 articles available from the National Cancer Institute, the Food and Drug Administration, the National Institute on Aging, the Leukemia Society of America, the National Parkinson's Foundation, and the Alzheimer's Association. Chapters on stroke and musculoskeletal and connective tissue diseases are also included. Also gives a helpful list of national toll-free numbers.

608 pages

3619 Cumulative Subject Index to Current Literature on Aging
National Council on the Aging
409 3rd Street SW
Suite 200
Washington, DC 20024-3212
202-479-1200
800-867-2755
Fax: 202-479-0735

James P Firman, CEO

References more than 6,000 articles and books under 2,400 subject headings in an easy-to-use format.

33 pages

3620 Cycling Past 50
Human Kinetics Publishers
PO Box 5076
Champaign, IL 61825-5076
217-351-5076
800-747-4457
Fax: 217-351-2674
e-mail: humank@hkusa.com
http://www.humankinetics.com

The author shows cyclists that with proper training and the right attitude, the years after 50 can be their best ever. Written for cyclists of all types this book provides basic and advanced training programs, racing strategies, and injury prevention tips for middle-aged cyclists.

264 pages 1998

3621 Developing Adult Day Care: An Approach to Maintaining Independence
National Council on the Aging
600 Maryland Avenue SW
Washington, DC 20024-2520
202-479-1200
800-867-2755
Fax: 202-479-0735

James P Firman, CEO

A guide for developing new day care programs for older persons or improving existing ones.

192 pages

3622 Devolution and Aging Policy
Haworth Press
10 Alice Street
Binghamton, NY 13904-1503
607-722-5857
800-342-9678
Fax: 607-722-3487
e-mail: getinfo@haworthpressinc.com
http://www.haworthpressinc.com

William Cohen, Owner

Helps you to understand devolution — the decentralizing of service provision — and the roles that state/local governemtn and private organizations now play in addressing the needs of our aging population.

288 pages

3623 Elder Care
Center for Public Representation
121 S Pinckney Street
Madison, WI 53703-3338
608-256-8391
800-369-0388
Fax: 606-251-1263

James Expeseth, Manager

A compendium of alternatives for providing and financing long-term care. This practical guide provides the most comprehensive and comforting information to help navigate a number of consumer mine fields.

224 pages

Aging/Books

3624 Elder Fit: A Health and Fitness Guide
American Alliance for Health, Phys Ed & Dance
1900 Association Drive
Reston, VA 20191-1502
703-476-3400
Fax: 703-476-9527
e-mail: aaalf@aahperd.org
http://www.aahperd.org

Michael Davis, Manager

Senior citizens need planned fitness activities! This book gives instructors a comprehensive exercise and fitness program designed for older adults.

3625 Exercise for Older Adults
Human Kinetics Publishers
PO Box 5076
Champaign, IL 61825-5076
217-351-5076
800-747-4457
Fax: 217-351-2674
e-mail: humank@hkusa.com
http://www.humankinetics.com

Reference for health and fitness instructors, strength and conditioning professionals, personal trainers, athletic trainers, physical therapists, and kinesiotherapists.

244 pages 1998

3626 Facilitating Self Care Practices in the Elderly
Haworth Press
10 Alice Street
Binghamton, NY 13904-1503
607-722-5857
800-342-9678
Fax: 607-722-1424
e-mail: getinfo@haworthpress.com
http://www.haworthpress.com

William Cohen, Owner

This up-to-date book is a synthesis of current knowledge from published sources and expert consultants relating to three commonly occurring problems in home health care practice: self-administration of medications, family caregiving issues, and teaching the elderly.

185 pages

3627 Falling in Old Age
Springer Publishing Company
536 Broadway
New York, NY 10012-3915
212-965-0690
Fax: 212-941-7842
e-mail: springer@springerpub.com
http://www.springerpub.com

Gianni Longo, Manager

Presented are practical techniques for the prevention of falls and for determining and correcting the causes.

3628 Family Carebook
CAREsource Program Development
505 Seattle Tower
Seattle, WA 98101
206-625-9128

Dennis Kenny, Owner

Guide to aging, the special needs of older adults, and the demands of providing care and support. Experts explain potential conflicts, planning opportunities and strategies for success.

475 pages

3629 Feel Nifty After 50: Top Tips to Help Women Grow Young
Golden Aspen Publishing
PO Box 370333
Denver, CO 80237
303-694-6555
800-639-9664
Fax: 303-694-0737
e-mail: GAPub@concentric.net

Jo Peddicord, Publisher

Publishes books on image and health tips for women over age 50. Does not accept unsolicited manuscripts. Reaches market through direct mail, trade sales, and wholesalers and distributors, including Ingram Book Co., Baker & Taylor Books, and Quality Books.

178 pages

3630 Feil Method, VALIDATION
4614 Prospect Avenue
Cleveland, OH 44103-4394
216-881-0040
Fax: 216-751-6434
e-mail: naomifeil@aol.com
http://www.vfvalidation.org

Edward R Feil, President

A method of communicating with very old people.

135 pages

3631 Financial Power of Attorney Workbook: Who Will Finance If You Can't?
NOLO
950 Parker Street
Berkeley, CA 94710-2524
510-549-1976
800-955-4775
Fax: 510-548-5902
http://www.nolo.com

David Rothenberg, CEO
Susan McConnell, Director Sales
Natasha Kaluza, Sales Assistant

To help people create their own durable power of attorney with step-by-step instructions.

160 pages

3632 Fitness for the Aged, Disabled and Industrial Worker
Human Kinetics Publishers
PO Box 5076
Champaign, IL 61825-5076
217-351-5076
800-747-4457
Fax: 217-351-2674
e-mail: humank@hkusa.com
http://www.humankinetics.com

Emily Holler, Publicity Manager
Ginny Davis, Publicity Manager

The proportion of elderly and disabled citizens in Western countries is on the rise. And industrial workers are increasingly exposed to various health risks. These two factors are resulting in health problems that cannot be ignored.

304 pages

3633 Functional Fitness Assessment for Adults
American Alliance for Health, Phys. Ed. & Dance
1900 Association Drive
Reston, VA 20191-1502
703-476-3400
800-321-0789
Fax: 703-746-9527

Michael Davis, Manager

This field test assesses the functional fitness of adults over 60 years of age. It is designed to serve the larger population through field based measurement techniques that can be used in a facility where older persons live and can be conducted by personnel not necessarily trained for clinical responsibilities.

24 pages

3634 Gerontology: Responding to an Aging Society
Jessica Kingsley Publishers
118 Pentonville Road
London, England, N1 9JB
071-833-2307
Fax: 071-837-2917

This book aims specifically to recent developments in gerontology, and includes expert contributions from the disciplines of geography, economics, sociology and social policy.

200 pages

3635 Grandparenting with Love and Logic
Alexander Graham Bell Association for the Deaf
1537 35th Street NW
Washington, DC 20007-2753
202-337-5220
Fax: 202-337-8270
http://www.agbell.org
TTY 202-337-5220

Todd Houston, Executive Director

This book offers easy-to-use techniques to show grandparents how to develop and nurture fulfilling relationships with both their children and grandchildren based on the love and logic philosophy.

Aging/Books

3636 Health Care of the Aged
The Haworth Press
10 Alice Street
Binghamton, NY 13904-1503
607-722-5857
800-429-6784
Fax: 607-771-0012
e-mail: getinfo@haworthpressinc.com
http://www.haworthpressinc.com

Jackie Blakeslee, Advertising
William Cohen, Owner

Focusing on the need for developing new service delivery models for the aged, this book examines fiscal, political, and social criteria influencing this challenge of the 1990's. The aged are caught in the sweeping changes currently occurring in the financing, organizing and delivery of human health care services.

183 pages

3637 Health Promotion and Aging: Strategies for Action
National Council on the Aging
409 3rd Street SW
Suite 200
Washington, DC 20024-3212
202-479-1200
800-867-2755
Fax: 202-479-0735

James P Firman, CEO

Valuable suggestions for action and background material describing both the aging and health networks.

69 pages

3638 Housing Choices and Well-Being of Older Adults: Proper Fit
Haworth Press
325 Chestnut Street
Suite 800
Philadelphia, PA 19106
215-625-8900
800-354-1420
Fax: 215-625-2940
e-mail: haworthpress@taylorandfrancis.com
http://www.haworthpress.com

Leon A Pastalan, Editor
Benyamin Schwarz, Editor

3639 Housing and Living Arrangement for the Elderly: A Selected Bibliography
National Council on the Aging
409 3rd Street SW
Suite 200
Washington, DC 20024-3212
202-479-1200
800-867-2755
Fax: 202-479-0735

James P Firman, CEO

Includes references published since 1979 on all aspects of senior housing including architecture and design, financing assistance and rural elderly housing.

40 pages

3640 Housing for Older Adults: Options and Answers
National Council on the Aging
409 3rd Street SW
Suite 200
Washington, DC 20024-3212
202-479-1200
800-867-2755
Fax: 202-479-0735

James P Firman, CEO

An overview of housing for older persons. Discusses public and private funding and senior housing management concerns.

111 pages

3641 Human Resource Management and the Americans with Disabilities Act
Greenwood Publishing Group
88 Post Road
5007
Westport, CT 06880-4208
203-226-3571
800-225-5800
Fax: 203-222-1502
e-mail: prices@greenwood.com
http://www.greenwood.com

John G Veres III, Editor
Ronald R Sims, Editor
Wayne Smith, President

Concrete advice for human resource professionals on how to cope with the vague, often obscure provisions of the Americans with Disabilities Act.

232 pages

3642 International Health Guide for Senior Citizen Travelers
Pilot Books
PO Box 2102
Greenport, NY 11944
631-477-1094
Fax: 631-661-4379

Covers essential pre-departure health planning; advice on specific health concerns; disease prevention and more.

3643 Issues for Aging America: Employees and Eldercare: A Briefing Book
National Council on the Aging
409 3rd Street SW
Suite 200
Washington, DC 20024-3212
202-479-1200
800-867-2755
Fax: 202-479-0735

James P Firman, CEO

The first comprehensive study to be published on emerging issues of eldercare.

46 pages

3644 Knowing Your Rights
AARP Fulfillment
601 E Street NW
Washington, DC 20049
202-434-2277
800-424-3410
Fax: 202-434-3443
e-mail: member@aarp.org
http://www.aarp.org

William D Novelli, CEO

Describes how changes in Medicare's reimbursement policies are designed to reduce health care costs and suggests steps that Medicare beneficiaries, their families and friends can take to assure that they continue to receive quality care under the Prospective Payment System.

19 pages

3645 Long-Term Care: How to Plan and Pay for It
Nolo
950 Parker Street
Berkeley, CA 94710-2524
800-728-3555
Fax: 800-645-0895
http://www.nolo.com

Jospeh L Matthews, Author

Allows you to evaluate long-term care insurance, arrange home care, explore options beyond nursing homes, choose a nursing facility, get the most out of Medicare, Medicaid and other benefit programs, protect your assets, and recognize and prevent elder fraud. Also contains a chapter on hospice care, and up-to-date benefit numbers, laws and taxes, as well as the latest resources and websites.

384 pages Year Founded:

Aging/Books

3646 Look Like a Winner After 50 with Care, Color & Style
Golden Aspen Publishing
PO Box 370333
Denver, CO 80237
303-694-6555
800-639-9664
Fax: 303-694-0737
e-mail: GAPub@concentric.net

Jo Peddicord, Publisher

Publishes books on image and health tips for women over age 50. Does not accept unsolicited manuscripts. Reaches market through direct mail, trade sales, and wholesalers and distributors, including Ingram Book Co., Baker & Taylor Books, and Quality Books.
190 pages

3647 Managing Aging and Human Services Agencies
Springer Publishing Company
536 Broadway
New York, NY 10012-3915
212-431-4370
Fax: 212-941-7842
e-mail: pringer@pringerpub.com
http://www.springerpub.com

Ursula Springer, President

Offers specialized information for the human resources professional who works with the elderly.
160 pages

3648 Memory Retention Course for the Aged
National Council on the Aging
409 3rd Street SW
Suite 200
Washington, DC 20024-3212
800-867-2755
Fax: 301-206-9789

A guide for persons working with older adults in group settings, to help them cope with memory lapses and normal memory loss.
24 pages

3649 Mental Health and Spirituality in Later Life
Haworth Press
10 Alice Street
Binghamton, NY 13904-1503
607-722-5857
800-342-9678
Fax: 607-722-3487
e-mail: getinfo@haworthpressinc.com
http://www.haworthpressinc.com

William Cohen, Owner

Explores the relationship between mental health, spirituality, and religion in later life, including the search for meaning, cultural issues, spiritual issues, depression, dementia, and issues of suicide in older people.
154 pages

3650 Mentally Impaired Elderly: Strategies and Interventions to Maintain Function
The Haworth Press
10 Alice Street
Binghamton, NY 13904-1503
607-722-5857
800-429-6784
Fax: 607-771-0012
e-mail: getinfo@haworthpressinc.com
http://www.haworthpressinc.com

Jackie Blakeslee, Advertising
William Cohen, Owner

Provides effective support and sensitive care for the most vulnerable segment of the elderly population, those with mental impairment.
171 pages

3651 New Medicine Man: A Different Kind of Health Care for Elders
National Council on the Aging
409 3rd Street SW
Suite 200
Washington, DC 20024-3212
202-479-1200
800-867-2755
Fax: 202-479-0735

James Firman, CEO

Offers many examples of working models of team-care that are already operating successfully, and concludes with an extensive bibliography of books related to all aspects of health care for elders.
219 pages

3652 Night Light: A Book of Nighttime Meditations
Hazelden
15251 Pleasant Valley Road
Center City, MN 55012-9640
651-257-4010
800-328-0094
Fax: 651-213-4426
http://www.hazelden.org

Ellen Breyer, President

366 meditations designed to help relax and encourage prayer. Reminds readers to look to their Higher Power for strength, reassurance, comfort and guidance.
400- pages

3653 Nolo's Guide to Social Security Disability: Getting and Keeping Your Benefits
NOLO
950 Parker Street
Berkeley, CA 94710-2524
510-549-1976
800-955-4775
Fax: 510-548-5902
http://www.nolo.com

David Rothenberg, CEO
Susan McConnell, Director Sales
Natasha Kaluza, Sales Assistant

Not many bureaucratic programs are as large- and as confusing- as Social Security disability. This book shows you the ins and outs of the system.
350 pages

3654 Nursing Home Information Services
925 15th Street NW
Washington, DC 20005-2305
202-347-8800

Lists acceptable nursing homes across the nation and provides information about their costs, admission requirements, standards and programs.

3655 Older & Wiser: A Workbook for Coping with Aging
New Harbinger Publications
5674 Shattuck Avenue
Oakland, CA 94609-1662
510-652-0215
Fax: 510-652-5472
e-mail: dorothy@newharbinger.com
http://www.newharbinger.com

Matthew McKay, Owner

This compassion guide teaches the practical skills and elicits personal insight necessary to meet the demands of aging in our society.
300 pages

3656 Older Americans, Vital Communities
Johns Hopkins University Press
2715 North Charles Street
Baltimore, MD 21218-6968
410-516-6900
Fax: 410-516-6998
http://www.press.jhu.edu

W Andrew Achenbaum, Author

This thought-provoking work grapples with the vast range of issues associated with the aging population and challenges people of all ages to think more boldly and more creatively about the relationship between older Americans and their communities.
224 pages

Aging/Books

3657 Older People and Their Caregivers Across the Spectrum of Care
Haworth Press
10 Alice Street
Binghamton, NY 13904-1503
607-722-5857
800-342-9678
Fax: 607-722-3487
e-mail: getinfo@haworthpressinc.com
http://www.haworthpressinc.com
William Cohen, Owner

Focuses on numerous relating to caregiving and social work assessment for improving quality of life for the elderly.

149 pages

3658 On Your Behalf
CAREsource Program Development
505 Seattle Tower
Seattle, WA 98101
206-625-9128
Dennis Kenny, Owner

This book takes the mystery out of very important sets of legal options. It gives lay people as well as advisors, service providers, and caregivers the information they need to understand their options and the importance of individual choice.

16 pages

3659 Part of the Community: Strategies for Including Everyone
Brookes Publishing
PO Box 10624
Baltimore, MD 21285
410-337-9580
800-638-3775
Fax: 410-337-8539
e-mail: custserv@pbrookes.com
http://www.pbrookes.com
Sandy Jensen, Customer Service Director
Melissa Behm, VP
Ginny Whitescarver, Marketing Director

Full of models and strategies on designing natural community supports rather than separate programs, this book shows you how to help individuals with disabilities achieve their goals and benefit from inclusion. Emphasizing inclusion as a lifelong process and offering creative problem-solving techniques, this cutting edge bookk enables you to improve the lives of individuals with disabilities in your community. Paperback.

288 pages

3660 Physical Environments and Aging: Critical Contributions of M Powell Lawton to Theory and Practice
Haworth Press
10 Alice Street
Binghamton, NY 13904-1503
607-722-5857
800-342-9678
Fax: 607-722-3487
e-mail: getinfo@haworthpressinc.com
http://www.haworthpressinc.com
William Cohen, Owner

Practical guide to the field, offering you tractable theory, useful methods and measures, and financial research overviews in the realms of everyday experience of older adults.

155 pages

3661 Power of Attorney for Health Care
Center for Public Representation
121 S Pinckney Street
Madison, WI 53703-3338
800-369-0388
Fax: 606-251-1263

Discusses Wisconsin law regarding medical decisions, the Cruzan case and ethical considerations in addition to legal implications and advantages of this document. Book tells how to create a personalized Power of Attorney document, including language for the 'Special Provisions' portion.

132 pages

3662 Practical Theology for Aging
Haworth Press
10 Alice Street
Binghamton, NY 13904-1503
607-722-5857
800-342-9678
Fax: 607-722-3487
e-mail: getinfo@haworthpressinc.com
http://www.haworthpressinc.com
William Cohen, Owner

Demonstrates the importance of spirituality to the overall health of seniors; lists several occasions and techniques for promoting religion to the elderly.

225 pages

3663 Preparing for an Aging Society: Changes and Challenges
National Council on the Aging
409 3rd Street SW
Suite 200
Washington, DC 20024-3212
202-479-1200
800-867-2755
Fax: 202-479-0735
James P Firman, CEO

This book contains a series of four solidly researched, eye-opening feature articles on issues of greatest importance to the elderly community.

62 pages

3664 Psychological Functioning of Older People
National Council on the Aging
409 3rd Street SW
Suite 200
Washington, DC 20024-3212
202-479-1200
800-867-2755
Fax: 202-479-0735
James P Firman, CEO

A basic text presenting psychological truths about aging and the aging experience.

108 pages

3665 Racial and Ethnic Differences in the Health of Older Americans
The National Academies Press
500 Fifth Street NW
Washington, DC 20055
202-334-3313
888-624-8373
Fax: 202-334-2451
http://www.nap.edu
Linda G Martin, Editor
Beth J Soldo, Editor

Examines trends in mortality rates and selected causes of disability (cardiovascular disease, dementia) for older people of different racial and ethnic groups.

312 pages

3666 Resource Guide for Injury Control Programs for Older Persons
National Council on the Aging
409 3rd Street SW
Suite 200
Washington, DC 20024-3212
202-479-1200
800-867-2755
Fax: 202-479-0735
James P Firman, CEO

Prepared to assist local aging and health service agencies in developing injury control programs for their clients.

29 pages

3667 Resources for Elders with Disabilities
Resources for Rehabilitation
22 Bonad Road
Winchester, MA 01890-1302
781-368-9094
Fax: 781-368-9096
Susan Greenblatt, Contact

Aging / Books

A large print resource directory that helps elders function independently, with information on hearing loss, arthritis, osteoporosis, diabetes, vision loss, stroke and Parkinson's Disease. Information on laws, environmental adaptations, and aids for everyday living.
174 pages

3668 Respite Resource Guide
National Council on the Aging
409 3rd Street SW
Suite 200
Washington, DC 20024-3212
202-479-1200
800-867-2755
Fax: 202-479-0735

James P Firman, CEO

An invaluable tool for program planners and administrators who want to start a respite program for caregivers of frail older people.
40 pages

3669 Running Past 50
Human Kinetics Publishers
PO Box 5076
Champaign, IL 61825-5076
217-351-5076
800-747-4457
Fax: 217-351-2674
e-mail: humank@hkusa.com
http://www.humankinetics.com

The author shows how to make adjustments to running programs so that training becomes more effective and satisfying. He also discusses physical adjustments and pacing in workouts, getting proper rest, and incorporating walking into workouts.
256 pages 1998

3670 Senior Centers and the At-Risk Older Person
National Council on the Aging
409 3rd Street SW
Suite 200
Washington, DC 20024-3212
202-479-1200
800-867-2755
Fax: 202-479-0735

James P Firman, CEO

Detailed report presents project overviews, seminar findings and recommendations for planning, practice, training and research on the at-risk older person.
230 pages

3671 Social Security, Medicare and Pensions
NOLO
950 Parker Street
Berkeley, CA 94710-2524
510-549-1976
800-955-4775
Fax: 510-548-5902
http://www.nolo.com

David Rothenberg, CEO
Susan McConnell, Director Sales
Natasha Kaluza, Sales Assistant

A plain-English guide explaining the ins and outs of the Social Security system: retirement, disability and benefits for dependents and survivors.
320 pages

3672 Statistical Handbook on Aging Americans
ORYX Press
4041 N Central Avenue
Suite 700
Phoenix, AZ 85012-3330
602-265-2651
800-279-6799
Fax: 800-279-4663
e-mail: info@oryxpress.com
http://www.oryxpress.com

A resource for economic, demographic, social, health, employment and financial statistics. More than 300 tables and illustrative charts are accompanied by concise and expert commentary.
360 pages

3673 Strength Training Past 50
Human Kinetics Publishers
PO Box 5076
Champaign, IL 61825-5076
217-351-5076
800-747-4457
Fax: 217-351-2674
e-mail: humank@hkusa.com
http://www.humankinetics.com

Provides research based guidelines and tools to help anyone over 50 develop and perform a sound, safe strength training program.
240 pages 1998

3674 Strength Training for Seniors
Human Kinetics Publishers
PO Box 5076
Champaign, IL 61825-5076
217-351-5076
800-747-4457
Fax: 217-351-2674
e-mail: humank@hkusa.com
http://www.humankinetics.com

Reference for health and fitness instructors, strength and conditioning professionals, personal trainers, athletic trainers, physical therapists, and kinesiotherapists.
232 pages 1999

3675 Successful Models of Community Long Term Care Services for the Elderly
The Haworth Press
10 Alice Street
Binghamton, NY 13904-1503
607-722-5857
800-429-6784
Fax: 607-771-0012
e-mail: getinfo@haworthpressinc.com
http://www.haworthpressinc.com

Jackie Blakeslee, Advertising
William Cohen, Owner

Experienced practitioners provide examples of successful community-based long term care service programs for the elderly.
174 pages

3676 Temple University Institute on Aging
1601 N Broad Street
Philadelphia, PA 19122-6099
215-204-6834
Fax: 215-204-6733
e-mail: v2226a@vm.temple.edu
http://www.temple.edu/aging

Kathy Segrist PhD, Director

Changes in adaptive capabilities during aging, anti-aging effects of dehydroepiandrosterone (DHEA), the influences of characteristics of elderly disabled clients on their experiences in case management, minority/ethnic aging research, and service management and services to the frail elderly.

3677 The Elder Care Sourcebook
McGraw-Hill
220 East Danieldale Road
DeSoto, TX 75115-2490
800-621-1918
Fax: 800-998-3103
e-mail: mmh_orderservices@mcgraw-hill.com
http://www.mhcontemporary.com

Joan Breitung, Author

Presents a wealth of information on concerns of elderly people, from nutrition to physical and mental health to sexuality to pharmaceuticals to bereavement and more. A comprehensive overview of the demographics of the aging population is also featured, along with actual case histories.
304 pages   Year Founded:

3678 Volunteerism in Action for the Aging: A Handbook
National Council on the Aging
409 3rd Street SW
Suite 200
Washington, DC 20024-3212
202-479-1200
800-867-2755
Fax: 202-479-0735

James P Firman, CEO

Aging/Directories

Designed to encourage and assist national voluntary organizations and their state and local affiliates in developing special program initiatives targeted to older adults.

80 pages

3679 What Are Old People For? How Elders Will Save the World
VanderWyk & Burnham
PO Box 2789-WS
Acton, MA 01720-6789
978-263-7595
Fax: 978-263-0696
e-mail: info@vandb.com
http://www.vandb.com

William H Thomas, Author

Nodding to popular culture, history, science, and literature, a passionate and persuasive case is made for removing our ageist blinders and seeing old age as a developmental stage of life.

370 pages Year Founded:

3680 Widows and Divorcees in Later Life: On Their Own Again
Haworth Press
10 Alice Street
Binghamton, NY 13904-1503
607-722-5857
800-342-9678
Fax: 607-722-3487
e-mail: getinfo@haworthpressinc.com
http://www.haworthpressinc.com

William Cohen, Owner

Examines new perspectives on the problems older women face adjusting to life whitout a spouse. Examines the transition from the togetherness of marriage to the solitude of being suddenly single, exploring how older widows and divorcees adapt.

202 pages

3681 Work Options for Older Americas
University of Notre Dame Press
310 Flanner Hall
Notre Dame, IN 46556
574-631-6346
Fax: 574-631-8148
e-mail: undpress.1@nd.edu
http://www3.undpress.nd.edu

Teresa Ghilarducci, Editor
John Turner, Editor

Brings together discussion of these issues by well-known economists and scholars in other fields, from the Government Accountability Office, the AARPÆPublic Policy Institute, the U.S. Department of Labor, and academia.

392 pages

3682 Work, Health and Income Among the Elderly
The Brookings Institution
1775 Massachusetts Avenue NW
Washington, DC 20036-2103
202-797-6000
Fax: 202-797-6004

Strobe Talbott, President

Employment, health and financial information for the elderly.

276 pages

Directories

3683 A Place to Live: Housing Alternatives for the Elderly in Arizona
Aging & Adult Admin\AZ Dept of Economic Security
1789 W Jefferson Street
Suite 950a
Phoenix, AZ 85007-3202
602-542-4446
Fax: 602-542-6575

Joe Slattery, Mailing Contact
Rex Critchfield, Manager

Alternative senior citizen housing in Arizona.

45 pages

3684 A Woman's Guide to Coping with Disability
Resources for Rehabilitation
33 Bedford Street
Suite 19a
Lexington, MA 02420-4330
781-862-6455
Fax: 781-861-7517
e-mail: orders@rfr.org

Lists of services, professional providers, organizations, associations, and publications related to diseases most often causing disability in women. Entries include: Name, address, phone. Principal content of publication is information on the causes and effects of disability in women.

3685 A World of Options: A Guide to International, Educational, Exchange, Community Service...for Persons with Disabilities
Mobility International USA
PO Box 10767
Eugene, OR 97440-2767
541-343-1284
Fax: 541-343-6812
e-mail: info@miusa.org
http://www.miusa.org

Christa Bucks, Editor
Cindy Lewis, Editor
Susan Sygall, Editor

Hundreds of educational programs, workcamps, transportation and travel advisory services for persons with disabilities. Entries include: Name, address, phone, geographical area served, financial data, eligibility requirements, descriptions of projects. Personal stories included. Paperback.ith TDD.

400 pages Frequency: Irregular

3686 AAAS Resource Directory of Scientists and Engineers with Disabilities
American Assoc for the Advancement of Science
1200 New York Avenue NW
Washington, DC 20005-3928
202-326-6721
Fax: 202-289-4950

Phil Blair, CEO
Virginia Stern, Editor
Diane E Lifton, Editor

Approximately 1,000 disabled scientists and engineers offering their services as consultants, speakers, role models, and peer reviewers. Entries include: Scientist's and engineer's name, address, degree(s), position, disability, age of onset, consulting interest.

158 pages Frequency: Irregular

3687 AHA Guide to the Health Care Field
American Hospital Association
1 N Franklin Street
Chicago, IL 60606-4425
312-895-2500
800-424-4301
Fax: 312-422-4506

Lachelle Curry, Mailing contact
Anthony Burke, CEO

Hospitals, networks, multi-health care systems, freestanding ambulatory surgery centers, psychiatric facilities, long-term care facilities, substance abuse programs, hospices, Health Maintenance Organizations (HMOs), and other health-related organizations. Entries include: For hospitals—Facility name, address, phone, administrator's name, number of beds, facilities and services, number of employees, expenses, other statistics. For other. organizations—Name, address, phone, fax, name and title of contact.

963 pages Frequency: Annual

3688 Abstracts in Social Gerontology: Current Literature on Aging
National Council on the Aging
600 Maryland Avenue SW
Washington, DC 20024-2520
202-479-1200
800-867-2755
Fax: 202-479-0735

James P Firman, CEO

331

Aging/Directories

Detailed abstracts are provided for recent major journal articles, books, reports and other materials on many facets of aging, including: adult education, demography, family relations, institutional care and work attitudes.

3689 Accent Buyers Guide Edition
Accent Books & Products
PO Box 700
Bloomington, IL 61702
309-378-2961
800-787-8444
Fax: 309-378-4420

Raymond C Cheever, Publisher
Betty Garee, Editor

Offers hundreds of new products and sources that can help the disabled do things faster and easier. This guide compares products and prices, listing hundreds of sources, addresses and phone numbers.

144 pages Frequency: Paperback

3690 Accent on Living: Buyer's Guide
Accent Special Publications, Cheever Publishing, Inc
PO Box 700
Bloomington, IL 61702
309-378-2961
800-787-8444
Fax: 309-378-4420
e-mail: acntvng@aol.com

Julie Starshak, Mailing Contact/Editor

Over 400 manufacturers and distributors of products for disabled persons, ranging from wheelchairs to bowling ball pushers to talking calculators. Entries include: Company name, address, phone number, e-mail address.

112 pages Frequency: Biennial

3691 Age Care Sourcebook: A Resource Guide for the Aging and Their Families
Simon & Schuster Consumer Group
1230 Avenue of the Americas
New York, NY 10020-1513
212-698-7000
800-223-1360
Fax: 212-767-2993

Jean Crichton, Editor
Jack Romanos, CEO

Publication includes: List of more than 600 state and local agencies that provide information or assistance for the care of the elderly. Entries include: Agency name, address, phone, branch office locations. Principal content is a resource guide for adult children having to care for their aging parents, including information on financial planning, retirement housing, medical care, and wills.

3692 American Association of Homes and Services for the Aging: Directory of Members
Amer Assoc of Homes and Services for the Aging
901 E Street NW
Suite 500
Washington, DC 20004-2037
202-661-5700
Fax: 202-783-2255
http://www.aahsa.org

Miriam Washington, Mailing Contact/Editor
Daniel Smith, Vice President

Over 5,200 nonprofit member homes and health facilities; over 800 business firm suppliers, individuals, and other associate members. Entries include: Name of home, address, phone, names of administrative staff, sponsorship, levels of care, services.

500 pages Frequency: Annual

3693 American Blue Book of Funeral Directors
Kates-Boylston Publications
100 Wood Avenue S
Iselin, NJ 08830-2727
732-767-9300
Fax: 732-767-9741
e-mail: bluebook@kates-boylston.com
http://www.kates-boylston.com

Adrian F Boylston, Editor

Listing of manufactures and suppliers of funeral equipment, as well as funeral homes primarily found in the USA and Canada.

908 pages Frequency: Annual

3694 Artificial Organs & Tissues Markets
Theta Reports
1775 Broadway
Suite 511
New York, NY 10019-1903
212-262-8230
800-257-5376
Fax: 212-262-8234
e-mail: pharmabk20@aol.com

Phyllis Klaben, Editor
Karen Deehy, Mailing Contact

Publication includes: Directory of manufacturers of artificial organs and soft tissues. Entries include: Company name, address, phone, key personnel, background information, description of products, annual sales, research and development efforts, distribution systems, five year projection. Principal content of publication is data and analysis of the artificial organs and tissues market.

Frequency: Irregular

3695 Assisted-Living Care Roster
Nebraska Health and Human Services
PO Box 94986
Lincoln, NE 68509-4986
402-471-0309
Fax: 402-471-0555
http://www.hhs.state.ne.us/crl/rosters.htm

Nancy L Brown, Program Manager
Helen Meeks, Credentialing Administrator

Approximately 260 assisted-living facilities in Nebraska. Entries include: Facility name, address, phone, name and title of contact, number of beds, type of operation, license number.

Frequency: Annual

3696 Association for Continuing Higher Education Directory
Association for Continuing Higher Education (ACHE)
PO Box 118067
Charleston, SC 29423-8067
843-574-6658
800-807-ACHE
Fax: 843-574-6470
e-mail: zpbarrineaui@al.trident.tec.su.us

Wayne L Whelan, Executive VP

Directory of institutions and individual professionals that assist in continuing education.

102 pages Frequency: Annual, March

3697 Bailey
PO Box 130
Lodi, OH 44254
330-948-2655
800-321-8372
Fax: 216-948-4439

Dave Bailey, Owner

Catalog of ambulation aids, balance aids, benches, chairs, exercise devices, tables, stools, rehabilitation and physical therapy equipment for the physically challenged.

51 pages

3698 Best 25 Catalog Resources for Making Life Easier
Making Life Easier
933 Chapel Hill Road
Madison, WI 53711-2405
608-274-4380
Fax: 608-274-6993
e-mail: help@makinglifeeasier.com
http://www.makinglifeeasier.com

Shelley Peterman Schwarz, Author

Unique reference guide to locate thousands of useful and hard-to-find adaptive devices to make dressing, eating, cooking, grooming, communicating, playing, exercising, etc. easier, safer and less frustrating for people of all ages and disabilities. A comprehensive reference for people with disabilities, caregivers and healthcare professionals.

30 pages

Aging/Directories

3699 CARF Directory of Organizations with Accredited Programs
CARF..The Rehabilitation Accreditation Commission
4891 E Grant Road
Tucson, AZ 85712-2704
520-325-1044
Fax: 520-318-1129
e-mail: postmaster@carf.org
Donald E Galvin, Mailing contact
Brian J Boon, CEO

About 2,500 organizations in 5,000 locations offering more than 11,000 medical rehabilitation, behavioral health, and employment and community support services that have been accredited by CARF. Entries include: Organization name, address, phone, name and title of chief executive, accredited programs offered, accreditation outcome.

358 pages Frequency: Annual

3700 Cardiac Rehabilitation Directory
infoUSA
PO Box 27347
Omaha, NE 68127
402-593-4600
800-555-6124
Fax: 402-331-5481
e-mail: internet@infousa.com
http://www.abii.com
Bill Hippen, Vice President

Listings of cardiac rehabilitation programs
Frequency: Annual

3701 Complete Directory for People withChronic Illness
Grey House Publishing
185 Millerton Road
Millerton, NY 12546
518-789-8700
800-562-2139
Fax: 518-789-0545
e-mail: books@greyhouse.com
http://www.greyhouse.com
Leslie Mackenzie, Publisher
Laura Mars-Proietti, Editoral Director

This widely hailed directory, updated for 2003/4, contains 10,000 entries and is structured around the 80 most prevalent chronic illnesses from asthma to cancer to Wilson's disease. Each chronic condition has its own chapter and contains a brief description of the illness in layman's language followed by the national and local organizations, state agencies, newsletters, research centers, hot lines, books and periodicals.

1137 pages

3702 Complete Directory for People with Disabilities
Grey House Publishing
185 Millerton Road
Millerton, NY 12546
518-789-8700
800-562-2139
Fax: 518-789-0545
e-mail: books@greyhouse.com
http://www.greyhouse.com
Leslie Mackenzie, Publisher
Laura Mars-Proietti, Editoral Director

A wealth of information, this ninth edition is the most comprehensive resource available for people with disabilities. Detailing independent living centers, rehabilitation facilities, state and federal agencies, associations and support groups this one-stop resource provides immediate access to the latest products and services for people with disabilities, such as periodicals, books, assistive devices, employment, education, camps and travel.

1138 pages

3703 Complete Directory of Large Print Books and Serials
RR Bowker
121 Chanlon Road
New Providence, NJ 07974-1541
908-464-6800
888-269-5372
Fax: 908-771-7704
e-mail: info@bowker.com
http://www.bowker.com
D Gravesande, Editor
R Crego, Editor

Publication includes: List of over 340 publishers and distributors of more than 12,000 books, 200 periodicals, and paperbacks printed in at least 14-point type. Entries include: For publishers—Company name, address. Principal content of publication is bibliography of large type books, newspapers, periodicals, and paperback bestsellers.

350 pages Frequency: Annual, January

3704 Complete Listing of Nursing Facilities and Home for the Aged Beds when Licensed as a Part of a Nursing Facility
North Carolina Dept of Human Resources
PO Box 29530
Raleigh, NC 27626
919-733-1604
Fax: 919-715-3073
Emile Swearingen, Mailing Contact

About 400 nursing facilities. Entries include: Name, address, phone, name of administrator, whether certified for Medicare and/or Medicaid, number of beds for nursing care.

25 pages Frequency: Monthly

3705 Complete Mental Health Directory
Grey House Publishing
185 Millerton Road
Millerton, NY 12546
518-789-8700
800-562-2139
Fax: 518-789-0545
e-mail: books@greyhouse.com
http://www.greyhouse.com
Leslie Mackenzie, Publisher
Laura Mars-Proietti, Editoral Director

The first comprehensive resource covering the field of behavioral health, with critical information for both the layman and the health professional. For the layman, this directory offers understandable descriptions of 24 mental health disorders as well as detailed information on associations, support groups and mental health facilities. For the professional, it offers information on managed care, government agencies and provider organizations.

750 pages

3706 Consumer Health Information Source Book
Onyx Press
4041 N Central Avenue
Suite 700
Phoenix, AZ 85012-3330
602-265-2651
800-279-6799
Fax: 800-279-4663
e-mail: info@onyxpress.com
Alan M Rees, Editor

240 pages Frequency: Irregular

3707 Consumer's Directory of Continuing Care Retirement Communities
American Association of Homes and Services
901 E Street NW
Suite 500
Washington, DC 20004-2037
202-661-5700
Fax: 202-783-2255
Daniel Smith, Vice President

500 retirement communities providing an integrated continuum of short-term and long-term care, including health care, housing, and home and community-based services. Entries include: Community name, address, phone, size fee, services, agreement and refund options.

610 pages

3708 Contemporary Long-Term Care: Sourcebook
Bill Communications
355 Park Avenue S
New York, NY 10010-1706
212-592-6505
800-266-4712
Fax: 212-592-6339
Elise Nakhnikian, Editor

Aging/Directories

Publication includes: Lists of over 900 manufacturers and suppliers of furnishings, products, equipment, and services for long-term patient care in nursing homes and retirement communities. Entries include: Company name, address, phone, fax.

Frequency: Annual, Nov.

3709 Continuing Care Retirement Community Directory
American Assn. of Homes & Services for the Aging
901 E Street NW
Suite 500
Washington, DC 20004-2037 202-661-5700
Fax: 301-206-9789
Daniel Smith, Vice President

A national consumer's directory of continuing care retirement communities. This directory is a vital tool for individuals searching and evaluating a community for themselves or a loved one.

3710 Council for Health and Human Service Ministries: Directory of Services
Council for Health and Human Service Ministries
700 Prospect Avenue E
Cleveland, OH 44115-1131 216-861-5000
Fax: 216-736-2251
Annette R Doster, Mailing Contact/Editor
La Verne H Council

About 300 social welfare agencies, retirement homes, children's residential homes, hospitals, and other health and human service facilities affiliated with the United Church of Christ. Entries include: Agency name, type of institution and summary of services offered, certifications and memberships, name of chief administrator, mailing address, phone, and conference assignment.

90 pages Frequency: Annual

3711 Data Resources in Gerontology: A Directory of Selected Information Vendors, Databases, and Archives
Gerontological Society of America
1030 15th Street NW
Suite 250
Washington, DC 20005-1526 202-842-1275
Fax: 202-842-1150
e-mail: geron@geron.org
http://www.geron.org
Linda Krogh Harootyan, Editor
Mohammed Reyazuddin, Deputy Director
Carol Schutz, Executive Director

Approximately 55 vendors of database access/information sources, bibliographic or reference databases, and data archives related to aging; regional census offices; state agencies, universities, libraries, and regional and local governments that provide census information. Entries include: For vendors—Company name, address, phone, description of product/service. For regional census offices—Name, address, phone, geographical area servedFor others—Name, address, phone, name and title of contact, geographical area served.

45 pages Frequency: Irregular

3712 Directory of Aging Resources
Business Publishers
8737 Colesville Road
Suite 1100
Silver Spring, MD 20910-3956 301-589-5103
800-274-6737
Fax: 301-587-4530
e-mail: bpinews@bpinews.com

Organizations, professionals, universities, and federal, state, and local government agencies in the US involved with aging issues. Entries include: Organization, company or agency name, names of programs or divisions, address, phone, fax, e-mail address, TTY/TTD numbers, names and titles of key personnel, number of members or constituents, mission or goals, jurisdiction, activities and services, publications, funding sources.

500 pages Frequency: Annual

3713 Directory of American Baptist Retirement Homes, Nursing Homes, Children's Homes & Special Services
American Baptist Homes & Hospitals Association
PO Box 851
Valley Forge, PA 19482 610-768-2411
Fax: 610-768-2453
http://www.abc-usa.org
Victoria Buff, Mailing Contact

125 member American Baptist related retirement, nursing, and children's homes and special services. Entries include: Institution name, address, phone, facilities available.

14 pages Frequency: Annual

3714 Directory of Community Care Facilities
California Department of Social Services
744 P Street
Ms 19-50
Sacramento, CA 95814-6413 916-324-4031
Fax: 916-323-8352
Kristine Heller, Mailing Contact/Editor

Adoption and home finding agencies, residential care facilities for adults and children, preschool care centers, and day care centers located in California and licensed by the California Department of Social Services. Health facilities are not listed. Entries include: Facility name, address, phone; name of director or administrator; capacity; license limitations (age, sex, hours of care, etc.).

2,400 pages Frequency: Quarterly

3715 Directory of Department of Veterans Affairs Facilities
Dept of Veterans Affairs\Reports & Info Services
810 Vermont Avenue NW
Washington, DC 20420 202-273-5803
Fax: 202-273-6891
Henry Caplan, Editor

About 345 facilities, including medical centers and regional offices with associated outpatient clinics, veterans outreach centers, and other offices; national cemeteries, and data processing centers. Entries include: Location (state, county, city), congressional district, congressional representative, station numbers, code for facility type.

40 pages Frequency: Biennial

3716 Directory of Health Education Programs for Elders
Center on Aging Studies\Univ Missouri-Kansas City
5100 Rockhill Road
Kansas City, MO 64110-2481 816-235-1747
Fax: 816-235-5193

Lists 36 health education programs for the elderly in rural areas. Entries include: Name, address, phone of program, bibliography and abstracts of relevant publications and reviews.

219 pages

3717 Directory of Health, Medical, and Disability Sites on the World Wide Web and Internet
Twin Peaks Press
PO Box 129
Vancouver, WA 98666 360-694-2462
800-637-2256
Fax: 360-696-3210
e-mail: twinpeak@pacifier.com
http://www.netm.com
Helen Hecker RN, Editor

Internet and World Wide Web sites related to health and disabilities in categories such as alternative medicine, disorders, genetics, nutrition, women's health, and many others. Entries include: Name, contact information.

Aging/Directories

3718 **Directory of Jewish Homes and Housing for the Aged in the United States and Canada**
Association of Jewish Aging Services
316 Pennsylvania Avenue SE
Suite 402
Washington, DC 20003-1172
202-543-7500
Fax: 202-543-4090
e-mail: ajas@ajas.org
http://www.ajas.org
Herbert Shore, Mailing Contact/Editor
Harvey Tillipman, Executive Director

Nonprofit Jewish homes and housing for the aged in the United States and Canada. Entries include: Facility name, address, number of beds or units, admission requirements and procedures, name of administrator and description of residents' characteristics, financial data, services offered.

300 pages Frequency: Biennial

3719 **Directory of Long Term Care Facilities**
Illinois Department of Public Health
525 W Jefferson Street
Springfield, IL 62761
217-782-5180
Fax: 217-785-4200
Wendy Fry, Editor

Long term care facilities licensed by the state, including skilled care, skilled intermediate care, sheltered community living facilities, and persons under age 22. Entries include: Facility name, address, phone, level of care, number of beds, type of ownership, approvals, provider association, name of administrator.

141 pages Frequency: Bi-annual

3720 **Directory of Plan Sponsors**
Nelson Information
PO Box 591
Port Chester, NY 10573
914-937-8400
800-333-6357
Fax: 914-937-8590
e-mail: info@nelnet.com

Sponsors of pension, foundations, and funds with assets over $10 million, including approximately 7,200 corporate sponsors, 1,300 unions, 900 public/government funds, 2,500 endowments and foundations, and 950 hospitals. Entries include: Name, address, phone, fax, names and titles of key personnel, current investment interest, level of risk, externally and internally managed funds, investment managers and consultants used.

4,000 pages Frequency: Annual

3721 **Directory of Retirement Facilities**
HCIA
300 E Lombard Street
Baltimore, MD 21202-3219
410-576-9600
800-568-3282
Fax: 410-752-6309
e-mail: pubs@hcia.com
Beth Christ, Editor

Over 18,000 assisted living, congregate care, independent living and continuing care facilities in the United States. Entries include: Facility name, address, phone, name of contact, types of services available, capacity, entrance requirements, fees, type of ownership; professional society, religious, and fraternal affiliations.

1,295 pages Frequency: Annual

3722 **Directory of Self-Help/Mutual Aid Support Groups for Older People**
Lighthouse
370 Starke Road
Carlstadt, NJ 07072-2108
800-334-5497

State-by-state listings of over 650 support groups for older people with impaired vision, plus listings of state commissions for the blind, self-help clearinghouses, vision rehabilitation agencies, and national resource organizations.

3723 **Directory of Service for Persons with Disabilities**
Info, Protection & Advocacy Cntr\Handicapped Indv.
514 10th Street NW
Floor 9
Washington, DC 20004-1424
202-966-8081
Fax: 202-966-6313

Approximately 175 services available in the Washington, DC metropolitan area for persons with disabilities. Entries include: Company or organization name, address, phone, fax, telex, names and titles of key personnel, biographical data, number of employees, geographical area served, financial data, subsidiary and branch names and locations, requirements for eligibility, description of services.

400 pages Frequency: Irregular

3724 **Directory of Services for the Widowed in the United States and Canada**
AARP Grief and Loss Program
601 E Street NW
Washington, DC 20049
202-434-2277
800-424-3410
Fax: 202-434-6474
e-mail: member@aarp.org
http://www.aarp.org
Susan Eckrich, Manager
William D Novelli, CEO

Forms of assistance as well as counseling offered for widows and widowers. Directory of nearly 500 associations, services and agencies nationwide.

65 pages Frequency: Biennial

3725 **Directory of State Services for People with Disabilities**
Illinois Department of Rehabilitation Services
PO Box 19429
Springfield, IL 62794-9429
217-782-2093
800-233-3425
Fax: 217-524-2471
M Skilbeck, Mailing Contact
Carol Adams, Executive Director

About 25 state government agencies and their local offices and institutions offering educational, medical, rehabilitation, counseling, and other services to people with disabilities in Illinois. Entries include: Agency or institution name, address, phone, services.

28 pages Frequency: Annual

3726 **Directory of Suicide Prevention/Crisis Intervention Agencies in the United States**
American Association of Suicidology
4201 Connecticut Avenue NW
Suite 408
Washington, DC 20008-1128
202-237-2280
Fax: 202-237-2282
e-mail: aikulc@ix.netcom.com
http://www.suicidology.org
Alan L Berman, Mailing Contact/Editor

About 600 suicide prevention and crisis intervention centers. Entries include: Center name, sponsoring organization name (if different), address, phone, emergency phone number, hours of service.

60 pages Frequency: Annual

3727 **Directory of Survivors of Suicide Support Groups**
American Association of Suicidology
4201 Connecticut Avenue NW
Suite 310
Washington, DC 20008-1158
202-237-2280
Fax: 202-237-2282
e-mail: amyjomc@ix.netcom.com
Alan L Berman, Mailing Contact/Editor

220 support groups in the US and Canada for family, friends, and other survivors of people who commit suicide. Entries include: Name, address, phone.

28 pages Frequency: Annual

Aging/Directories

3728 Directory of Texas Long Term Care Facilities
Texas Dept of Human Service\Long Term Care
PO Box 149030
Austin, TX 78714-9030
512-438-2633
Fax: 512-438-2723
http://www.dhs.state.tx.us

Over 2,000 nursing, personal care, adult day care, mental retardation care, and Alzheimer's care facilities in Texas. Each type printed separately. Entries include: Name of institution, address, phone, owner address and phone, and number of beds.

Frequency: Annual

3729 Directory of Travel Agencies for the Disabled
Twin Peaks Press
PO Box 129
Vancouver, WA 98666
360-694-2462
800-637-2256
Fax: 360-696-3210
e-mail: twinpeak@pacifier.com
http://www.netm.com

Helen Hecker, Editor

Number of listings: 370. Entries include: Company name, address, phone, fax, names and titles of key personnel, subsidiary and branch names and locations, description of services.

80 pages Frequency: Quarterly

3730 Elderhostel Catalog
Elderhostel
75 Federal Street
Boston, MA 02110-1913
617-426-7788
Fax: 617-426-8351
http://www.elderhostel.org

Michael Zoob, Editor
James Moses, CEO

Short-course educational, residential programs on about 1,900 campuses in North America, South America, Asia, and Europe which are available to persons 55 years of age or older and their adult companions. Programs include noncredit courses taught by regular faculty (and sometimes based on local resources or culture). Campus living accommodations and meals are provided. In United States and Canada cost is an average of $325.00 per week; Alaska, Hawaii, and overseas programs are more. Entries include: Institution name, location, description of setting, programs available, dates, brief travel information.

100 pages Frequency: 8x Yearly

3731 External Degrees in the Information Age
Onyx Press
4041 N Central Avenue
Suite 700
Phoenix, AZ 85012-3330
602-265-2651
800-279-6799
Fax: 800-279-4663
e-mail: info@onyxpress.com

Eugene Sullivan, Editor

Programs at college and University levels that offer external and alternative degree classes.

248 pages Frequency: Irregular

3732 Federal Benefits for Veterans and Dependents
US Department of Veterans Affairs
810 Vermont Avenue NW
Washington, DC 20420
202-273-6763
http://www.va.gov

Bonner Day, Mailing Contact/Editor
Joseph Thompson, Manager

Publication includes: List of VA offices, assistance centers, insurance claims offices, medical facilities, and national cemeteries. Entries include: For offices—Name, address, phone, type of office or facility. For cemeteries—Name, address, phone. Principal content of publication is description of veterans' benefits.

100 pages Frequency: Annual

3733 Financial Aid for Veterans, Military Personnel and Their Dependents
Reference Service Press
5000 Windplay Drive
Suite 4
El Dorado Hills, CA 95762-9319
916-939-9620
Fax: 916-939-9626
e-mail: findaid@aol.com

Gail Schlachter, Editor
R David Weber, Editor

Organizations that offer approximately 1,100 scholarships, fellowships, loans, grants, awards, and internships to veterans, military personnel, and their families. Entries include: Organization name, address, phone, financial data, requirements for eligibility, duration, special features and limitations, deadline, number of awards.

350 pages Frequency: Biennial

3734 Financial Aid for the Disabled and Their Families
Reference Service Press
5000 Windplay Drive
Suite 4
El Dorado Hills, CA 95762-9319
916-939-9620
Fax: 916-939-9626

Gail Ann Schlachter, Editor
R David Weber, Editor

Over 900 scholarships, fellowships, grants, loans, and awards to disabled persons or their family members. Entries include: Program name, sponsor name, address, phone, description of program including purpose, financial data, and eligibility requirements.

370 pages Frequency: Biennial

3735 Funding in Aging
Foundation Center
79 5th Avenue
New York, NY 10003-3034
212-620-4230
800-424-9836
Fax: 212-807-3677

Sara Engelhardt, President
Ruth Kovacs, Editor
Stan Olson, Editor

1,000 foundations and private organizations that offer funding for programs about aging. Entries include: For federal government agencies—Agency name, address, phone; regional office name, address, phone; description of program, types of assistance awarded, eligibility requirements, description of past programs funded by the agency, application procedure. For state government agencies—Agency name, address, phone. For private organizations—Organization name, address, phone, description of funding program, types of financial assistance available, description of publications. For foundations—Foundation name, address, phone, names of key personnel, description of program, assets, amount of money awarded, deadline date for application, description of publications.

294 pages Frequency: Irregular

3736 Golden Opportunities
Peterson's
PO Box 2123
Princeton, NJ 08543-2123
609-243-9111
800-338-3282
Fax: 609-243-9150

Andrew Carroll, Editor
Rick Pinto, Partner

Organizations that need and welcome senior volunteers. Principal content of publication is selecting the right volunteer activity.

384 pages

3737 Grants for Literacy, Reading & Adult/Continuing Education
Foundation Center
79 5th Avenue
New York, NY 10003-3034
212-714-0699
800-424-9836
Fax: 212-807-3677

Michael Seltver, President

Aging/Directories

In past years this organization has awarded grants to foundations that support reading, adult basic education, continuing education programs, and literacy. This directory contains the recipient foundations general information as well as the grant limitations, amount and spending patterns.

3738 Grants of Aging
Foundation Center
79 5th Avenue
New York, NY 10003-3034
212-714-0699
800-424-9836
Fax: 212-807-3677

Michael Slevter, President
114 pages

3739 Great Buys for People over 50
Penguin USA
375 Hudson Street
New York, NY 10014-3658
212-366-2000
800-526-0275
Fax: 212-366-2666

Sue Goldstein, Editor

Mail order firms, bargain retail outlets, and other sources of bargain apparel, food, appliances, home furnishings, crafts kits, and other items appropriate for persons over 50; firms offering discounted fees for their services; and special services. Entries include: Name, address, phone, description, credit cards accepted, price of catalog.

420 pages

3740 Greatest of Ease Company Catalog
2443 Fillmore Street
345
San Francisco, CA 94115-1814
415-441-6649
800-845-1208
Fax: 415-441-4319

Offers 127 products designed to enable and enhance your independence and make everyday tasks a little easier.

3741 Guide to the Nation's Hospices
National Hospice Organization
1901 N Moore Street
Suite 901
Arlington, VA 22209-1717
703-243-5400
800-658-8898
Fax: 703-525-5762
http://www.drsnho@cais.com

Audra Kelly, Editor

About 3,000 hospices, palliative care centers, and other programs serving terminally ill persons. Entries include: Name of hospice program, address, and phone, fax, e-mail address, website, name and title of principal executive, service area, scope of services, budget and patient size.

350 pages Frequency: Annual

3742 Guide to the Nursing Home Industry
HCIA
300 E Lombard Street
Baltimore, MD 21202-3219
410-576-9600
800-568-3282
Fax: 410-783-0575
e-mail: info@hcia.com

Consolidated aggregate financial and operating performance data for more than 10,000 nursing homes in the US. Entries include: Name, address, state-by-state median values for 19 key nursing home indicators, national nursing home performance medians by ownership and location, and more.

Frequency: Annual

3743 HEATH Resource Directory
HEATH Resource Center, National Clearinghouse on
1 Dupont Circle NW
Suite 800
Washington, DC 20036-1149
202-939-9300
800-544-3284
Fax: 202-833-4760
e-mail: heath@ace.nche.edu

Vickie M Barr, Mailing Contact/Editor
David Ward, President

Over 150 organizations that provide information and resources on topics relevant to postsecondary education and disability. Entries include: Organization name, topic, address, phone, fax, talking telephone (TT) availability.

35 pages Frequency: Biennial

3744 Handbook of Assistive Devices for the Handicapped Elderly
The Haworth Press
10 Alice Street
Binghamton, NY 13904-1503
607-722-5857
800-429-6784
Fax: 607-771-0012
e-mail: getinfo@haworthpressinc.com
http://www.haworthpressinc.com

Jackie Blakeslee, Advertising
William Cohen, Owner

Concise yet comprehensive reference of the latest and most assistive devices for handicapped elders.

77 pages

3745 Help: A Guide to Community Services for Older Citizens
Volunteer Center
115 E Jefferson Street
Suite 400
Syracuse, NY 13202-2537
315-474-7011
Fax: 315-479-6772

Sally Star, Mailing Contact/Editor

Agencies and organizations in Onondaga County, New York, that offer health, employment, leisure, and other services to senior citizens. Entries include: Organization name, address, phone, description of services.

Frequency: Irregular

3746 Here Comes the Sun: Directory of Summer Programs for Handicapping Conditions
Info. Protection & Advocacy Ctr for Handicapped
514 10th Street NW
Floor 9
Washington, DC 20004-1424
202-966-8081
Fax: 202-966-6313

Summer programs for youth and adults with disabilities. Entries include: Program name, address, phone, fax, telex, names and titles of key personnel, biographical data, number of staff, geographical area served, financial data, description of program and facilities.

20 pages Frequency: Annual, April

3747 Home Care Agencies, Hospices and Nursing Pools
NC Dept of Human Resources
PO Box 29530
Raleigh, NC 27626
919-733-1604
Fax: 919-733-3207

Nancy Joyce, Mailing Contact

Computer printout. Covers more than 725 home care agencies, nursing pools, and hospice programs in North Carolina. Entries include: Agency name, address, phone; agency director; Medicare/Medicaid certification.

131 pages

3748 Home Health Agency Report & Directory
SMG Marketing Group
875 N Michigan Avenue
Chicago, IL 60611-1803
312-587-3436
800-678-3026
Fax: 312-642-9729
e-mail: bdorfman@smg.com
http://www.smgusa.com

John A Anderson, Editor
Kristy Hum, Manager

Listing of corporations and home health agencies.

400 pages Frequency: Quarterly

Aging/Directories

3749 Home Health Service Directory
infoUSA
PO Box 27347
Omaha, NE 68127
402-593-4600
800-555-6124
Fax: 402-331-5481
e-mail: internet@infousa.com
http://www.abii.com

Bill Hippen, Vice President

A health care directory for patients restricted to thier homes.
Frequency: Annual

3750 Home Healthcare Agency Directory
SMG Marketing Group
875 N Michigan Avenue
Chicago, IL 60611-1803
312-642-3026
800-678-3026
Fax: 312-642-9729
e-mail: bdorfman@smg.com
http://www.smgusa.com

John A Henderson, Editor

350 pages Frequency: Annual, October

3751 Homes Nursing Directory
infoUSA
PO Box 27347
Omaha, NE 68127
402-593-4600
800-555-6124
Fax: 402-331-5481
e-mail: internet@infousa.com
http://www.abii.com

Bill Hippen, Vice President

Over 23,000 listings of programs related to home nursing care.
Frequency: Annual

3752 Hospices Directory
infoUSA
PO Box 27347
Omaha, NE 68127
402-593-4600
800-555-6124
Fax: 402-331-5481
e-mail: internet@infousa.com
http://www.abii.com

Bill Hippin, Vice President

Number of listings: 2,639. Entries include: Name, address, phone, size of advertisement, name of owner or manager, number of employees, year first in 'Yellow Pages.' Compiled from telephone company 'Yellow Pages,' nationwide.

3753 ILRU Directory of Centers, SILCs, and Related Organizations (Independent Living Research Utilization)
Independent Living Research Utilization Program
2323 S Shepherd Drive
Suite 1000
Houston, TX 77019-7031
713-520-0232
Fax: 713-520-5785
e-mail: ilru@ilru.org
http://www.ilru.org

Laurel Richards, Editor
Laurie Redd, Executive Director

List of independent living programs for disabled people.
80 pages Frequency: Annual, January

3754 In-Home Care Services Directory
infoUSA
PO Box 27347
Omaha, NE 68127
402-593-4600
800-555-6124
Fax: 402-331-5481
e-mail: internet@infousa.com
http://www.abli.com

Bill Hippen, Vice President

Directory of in-home care related listings.
Frequency: Annual

3755 Information & Referral Services Directory Nursing Home
infoUSA
PO Box 27347
Omaha, NE 68127
402-593-4600
800-555-6124
Fax: 402-331-5481
e-mail: internet@infousa.com
http://www.abii.com

Bill Hippen, Vice President

Directory with over 350 listings of nursing homes. Available online.
Frequency: Annual

3756 International Directory of Libraries for the Disabled
KG Saur/ A Division of RR Bowker
121 Chanlon Road
New Providence, NJ 07974-1541
212-337-6900
Fax: 908-665-6688

An essential resource for improving the quality and quantity of materials available to the print-handicapped audience. Featuring talking books, braille books, large print books as well as production centers for these materials.
257 pages

3757 International Directory of Research and Researchers in Comparative Gerontology
University of South Florida
140 7th Avenue
St Pete Beach, FL 33706-4314
727-553-1514
Fax: 727-553-1126

Charlotte Nusberg, Editor
Jay Sokolovsky, Editor

Over 300 research projects in comparative gerontology conducted since 1984; international coverage. Entries include: Project title; sponsoring institution, organization, or individual name, address, phone; biographical data for researchers, description of study.
380 pages Frequency: Quadrennial

3758 International Telephone Directory for TDD Users
Gallaudet Univ. Press c/o Chicago Distrib. Center
11030 S Langley Avenue
Chicago, IL 60628-3830
800-621-2736
Fax: 800-621-8476
http://www.gallaudet.edu
TTY 888-630-9347

Offers 12,000 TDD members and organizations serving deaf people.
190 pages

3759 Large Print Loan Library Catalog
National Association for Visually Handicapped
22 W 21st Street
Floor 6
New York, NY 10010-6943
212-889-3141
Fax: 212-727-2931
e-mail: staff@navh.org
http://www.navh.org

Ann Illuzzi, Manager

Listing of over 6500 commercially published and NAVH large print books avaiable through NAVH on a loan basis. Includes a limited selection of titles available for purchase.

3760 Legal Rights of Persons with Disabilities: An Analysis of Federal Law
LRP Publications
PO Box 980
Horsham, PA 19044
215-784-0941
800-341-7874
Fax: 215-784-9639
e-mail: custserve@lrp.com
http://www.lrp.com

Gary Bagin, Director Communications

Aging/Directories

A comprehensive analysis of the rights accorded individuals with disabilities under federal law covering such issues as: Definitions of individuals with disabilities, reasonable accomodations, architectural barriers, access to transportation and communication services, education, and newborns.

1536 pages

3761 Live Better/Live Longer Resourcebook
Alta Mira Press
1630 N Main Street
Walnut Creek, CA 94596-4609
925-938-7243
Fax: 925-933-9720

RA Herman, Editor
Mitch Allen, Publisher

Approximately 4,000 information sources, publications, support groups, associations, and other referrals 'available to improve and extend the lives of those of us who have reached our middle years and beyond.' Topics covered include health, nutrition, travel, recreation, finances, consumer protection, housing, legal aid, insurance, crime, etc. Entries include: Organization name, address, phone, description, publications, services.

704 pages Frequency: Biennial-spring

3762 Managed Home Care Sourcebook
Faulkner & Gray
11 Penn Plaza
Floor 17
New York, NY 10001-2006
212-967-7000
800-535-8403
Fax: 212-967-7180
e-mail: order@faulknergray.com
http://www.faulknergray.com

Advice and strategies for home care

3763 Meals on Wheels Assoiation of America Directory
Meals on Wheels Association of America
1414 Prince Street
Suite 202
Alexandria, VA 22314-2853
703-548-5558
Fax: 703-548-8024
e-mail: mowaa@mowaa.org
http://mowaa@mowaa.org

Enid Borden, CEO

Online Directory of companies and organizations serving the needs of the elderly. Meals on Wheels home-delivers food to older citizens who are homebound.

130 pages Frequency: Annual

3764 Meeting the Needs of Employees with Disabilities
Resources for Rehabilitation
233 Bedford Street
19a
Lexington, MA 02420-3413
781-862-6455
Fax: 781-861-7517
e-mail: info@rfr.org

Susan Greenblatt, Mailing Contact

Publication includes: Descriptions of organizations and products that assist those involved in the employment of people with disabilities. Entries include: Organization name, address, phone, requirements for membership, admission, or eligibility, description, prices of product. Principal content of publication is information and advice for employers and counselors who recruit and retain employees with disabilities, including coverage of government programs and laws, supported employment, environmental adaptations, mobility impairments, vision impairments, and communication impairments (hearing and speech). Chapters on assistive technology, environmental modification, transition from school to work, and older workers.

Frequency: Biennial

3765 Mental Retardation & Developmentally Disabled Services Directory
infoUSA
PO Box 27347
Omaha, NE 68127
402-593-4600
800-555-6124
Fax: 402-331-5481
e-mail: internet@infousa.com
http://www.abii.com

Bill Hippen, Vice President

Number of listings: 2,759. Entries include: Name, address, phone, size of advertisement, name of owner or manager, number of employees, year first in 'Yellow Pages.' Compiled from telephone company 'Yellow Pages,' nationwide.

3766 Mentally Disabled and the Law
William S Hein & Company
1285 Main Street
Buffalo, NY 14209-1911
716-882-2600
800-828-7571
Fax: 716-883-8100
e-mail: mail@wshein.com
http://www.wshein.com

Kevin Marmion, President

Offers information on treatment rights, the provider-patient relationship, and the rights of the mentally disabled persons in the community.

867 pages

3767 NARIC Guide to Disability and Rehabilitation Periodicals
National Rehabilitation Information Center
1010 Wayne Avenue
Suite 800
Silver Spring, MD 20910-5633
301-562-2400
800-346-2742
Fax: 301-562-2401
e-mail: naricinfo@kra.com
http://www.naric.com

Dan Wendling, Media Manager

Listing of more than 400 national, local and international rehabiliatation newsletters and journals.

170 pages Frequency: Irregular

3768 NIDRR Program Directory
National Institute on Disability
1010 Wayne Avenue
Suite 800
Silver Spring, MD 20910-5633
301-562-2400
800-346-2742
Fax: 301-562-2401
e-mail: naricinfo@kra.com
http://www.naric.com

Dan Wendling, Editor

A directory of NIDRR funded demonstrations and research projects.

318 pages Frequency: Annual

3769 NLADA Directory of Legal Aid and Defender Offices in the United States and Territories
National Legal Aid & Defender Association
1625 K Street NW
Suite 800
Washington, DC 20006-1604
202-452-0620
Fax: 202-872-1031
e-mail: linfo@nlada.org

Approximately 3,600 civil legal aid and indigent defense organizations in the United States; includes programs for specific groups such as prisoners, senior citizens, the disabled, etc. Entries include: Agency name, address, phone, director's name.

265 pages Frequency: Biennial-Spring

Aging/Directories

3770 National Directory for Eldercare Information and Referral
National Association of Area Agencies on Aging
927 15th Street NW
6th Floor
Washington, DC 20005-2304
202-296-8130
Fax: 202-296-8134

Angela Heath, Editor

Federal, state and area offices on aging; Native American aging organizations; major national aging associations. Entries include: Name, address, phone, name of director, fax, local information and referral services, instate toll-free phone.

190 pages Frequency: Biennial

3771 National Directory of Educational Programs in Gerontology and Geriatrics
Association for Gerontology in Higher Education
1030 15th Street NW
Suite 240
Washington, DC 20005-1527
202-289-9806
Fax: 202-289-9824
e-mail: ctompkins@aghe.org

Derek Stepp, Manager

Over 1,000 degree and certificate programs and concentrations in the field of gerontology available at 507 institutions of higher education. Entries include: Institution name, name and title of contact, address, phone, fax, e-mail address, overview of campus gerontology instruction/activity, description of gerontology programs(s), year program began, number of credit courses offered, number of faculty teaching aging, and special resources available.

3772 National Directory of Healthcare and Human Service Ministries
United Methodist Assoc Health\Welfare Ministries
601 W Riverview Avenue
Dayton, OH 45406-5543
937-227-9494
800-411-9901
Fax: 937-222-7364
e-mail: uma@umassociation.org

Dean N Pullian, President/CEO

95 hospitals, 62 child care facilities, 345 long-term care facilities, 67 annual conferences, and 115 community centers connected with a connectional unit of The United Methodist Church. Entries include: Institution name, address, phone, name of executive, list of services.

137 pages Frequency: Annual

3773 National Home Care and Hospice Directory
National Association for Home Care
228 7th Street SE
Washington, DC 20003-4306
202-547-7424
Fax: 202-547-3540
http://www.nahc.org

Approximately 17,000 home care and hospice providers in the US & Puerto Rico. Entries include: Agency name, address, phone, fax, director's name, product/service provided, area served.

960 pages Frequency: Annual, January

3774 National Housing Directory for People with Disabilities
Grey House Publishing
185 Millerton Road
Millerton, NY 12546
518-789-8799
800-562-2139
Fax: 518-789-0545
e-mail: books@greyhouse.com
http://www.greyhouse.com

Leslie Mackenzie, Editor

The national Housing Directory for People with Disabilities is your guide to special housing state by state. You'll find state government agencies; referall agencies; intensive and intermediate care facilities;licensed group homes; and independent living facilities.

1500 pages

3775 National Yellow Book of Funeral Directors
Nomis Publications
PO Box 5122
Youngstown, OH 44514
330-788-9608
800-321-7479
Fax: 330-788-1112
e-mail: info@yelobk.com
http://www.yelobk.com

20,000 United States and Canadian funeral homes; Veteran's Administration hospitals and regional offices; major hospitals; foreign consulates and branch offices; daily papers; mortuary colleges. Entries include: Name of home, address, phone, code for shipping points, city code for daily papers available for obituaries.

1,000 pages Frequency: Annual

3776 Nursing & Convalescent Homes Directory
infoUSA
PO Box 27347
Omaha, NE 68127
402-593-4600
800-555-6124
Fax: 402-331-5481
e-mail: internet@infousa.com
http://www.abii.com

Bill Hippen, Vice President

Number of listings: 20,736. Entries include: Name, address, phone (including area code), size of advertisement, year first in 'Yellow Pages,' name of owner or manager, number of employees. Compiled from telephone company 'Yellow Pages,' nationwide.

Frequency: Annual

3777 Nursing Home Chain Directory
SMG Marketing Group
875 N Michigan Avenue
Chicago, IL 60611-1803
312-642-3026
800-678-3026
Fax: 312-642-9729
e-mail: bdorfman@smg.com
http://www.smgusa.com

John A Henderson, Editor

Almost 400 for-profit and nonprofit corporate owners of nursing homes, each of whom owns two or more facilities. Entries include: Corporation name, address, phone, name of director; facilities owned, each includes nursing home name, address, phone, number of beds, total number of residents.

500 pages Frequency: Biennial

3778 Nursing Home Directory
SMG Marketing Group
875 N Michigan Avenue
Chicago, IL 60611-1803
312-642-3026
800-678-3026
Fax: 312-642-9729
http://www.smgusa.com

John A Henderson, Editor

More than 15,200 nursing homes in the United States. Entries include: Nursing home name, address, phone, number of skilled and unskilled beds, total number of residents.

500 pages Frequency: Biennial

3779 Options: A Directory of Child and Senior Services
Five Star Publications
PO Box 6698
Chandler, AZ 85246-6698
480-940-8182
800-545-7827
Fax: 480-940-8787
e-mail: infor@fivestarsupport.com
http://www.fivestarsupport.com

Linda F Radke, Editor

Over 350 care services for children and senior citizens; primary coverage of Arizona with some national listings. Entries include: Facility/service name, address, phone, hours and days of week open, year established, commission or regulatory agency granting the operating license, ownership, available discounts, available handicapped facilities/services, and a description of services written by the listee.

90 pages Frequency: Irregular

Aging/Directories

3780 Over 50 Directory & Handbook
Area 10 Agency on Aging
7500 W Reeves Road
Bloomington, IN 47404-9688
812-876-3383
800-844-1010
Fax: 812-876-9922
e-mail: area10@bloomington.in.us
http://www.area10.bloomington.in.us
Jewel Echelbarger, Exeuctive Director

A free guide of local services and business who support local seniors, offer quality merchandise and services and many offer a senior discount.

3781 Pension & Profit Sharing Plan Companies Directory
infoUSA
PO Box 27347
Omaha, NE 68127
402-593-4600
800-555-6124
Fax: 402-331-5481
e-mail: internet@infousa.com
http://www.abii.com
Bill Hippen, Vice President

Number of listings: 5,428. Entries include: Name, address, phone (including area code), size of advertisement, year first in 'Yellow Pages,' name of owner or manager, number of employees. Compiled from telephone company 'Yellow Pages,' nationwide.

Frequency: Annual

3782 Pensions & Investments: 1,000 Largest Retirement Funds
Crain Communications
740 N Rush Street
Chicago, IL 60611-2526
312-649-5200
Fax: 312-649-5360
e-mail: jmurphy@crain.com
http://www.pionline.com
Mike Clowes, Editor
Lisa Shidler, Manager

The nations largest retirement plans compiled into a directory.

Frequency: Annual, January

3783 Products for People With Disabilities
LS&S Group
PO Box 673
Northbrook, IL 60065
847-498-9777
800-468-4789
Fax: 847-498-1482
e-mail: info@lssproducts.com
http://www.lssproducts.com
TDD 866-317-8533
Melissa T Balbach, President
John K Bace, Executive VP

3784 Publicist's Guide to Senior Media
Promoworks
4165 E Thousand Oaks Boulevard
Suite 335
Westlake Village, CA 91362-3892
805-379-3910
Fax: 805-379-1029

Directory of newspapers, media and syndicated columnists that are senior oriented.

130 pages Frequency: Biennial

3785 Purple Directory: National Listing of African-American Funeral Firms
Shugar's Publishing
PO Box 38665
Detroit, MI 48238
313-836-8600
e-mail: purfuneral@aol.com
http://www.purpledirectory.com
Miriam E Pipes, Editor

Approximately 2,700 Afircan American funeral firms, in the US Entries include: Firm name, address, phone; some listings include fax and name and title of contact.

248 pages Frequency: Bi Annually

3786 Rehabilitation Services Directory
infoUSA
PO Box 27347
Omaha, NE 68127
402-593-4600
800-555-6124
Fax: 402-331-5481
e-mail: internet@infousa.com
http://www.abii.com
Bill Hippen, Vice President

Directory of rehabilitation programs.

Frequency: Annual

3787 Resources for Elders with Disabilities
Resources for Rehabilitation
33 Bedford Street
Suite 19a
Lexington, MA 02420-4330
781-862-7050
Fax: 781-861-7517
e-mail: info@rfr.org
Susan Greenblatt, Mailing Contact
Julie Ann Shapiro, Owner

Services, products, and publications that enable people with hearing loss, vision loss, diabetes, stroke, arthritis, Parkinson's disease, and osteoporosis function independently. Entries include: Name, address, phone, criteria for receiving services, membership fees, description of product/service, prices. Available only in large print.

336 pages Frequency: Biennial

3788 Resources for People with Disabilities and Chronic Conditions
Resources for Rehabilitation
33 Bedford Street
Suite 19a
Lexington, MA 02420-4330
781-862-6455
Fax: 781-861-7517
e-mail: info@rfr.org
Susan L Greenblatt, Mailing Contact

Lists and describes rehabilitation services and laws affecting people with disabilities, with chapters on diabetes, hearing and speech disorders, visual impairment, spinal cord injury, epilepsy, multiple sclerosis and low back pain. Entries include: Company name, address, phone, fax, e-mail addresses, websites, requirements for membership, admission, or eligibility, description of services provided, price.

288 pages Frequency: Biennial

3789 Resources for People with Disablities: A National Directory
Ferguson Publishing Company
200 W Madison Street
Suite 300
Chicago, IL 60606-3414
312-580-5480
Fax: 312-580-4948
Elizabeth Oakes, Editor
John Bradford, Editor
Patrick Giordano, Exeuctive Director

1,026 pages

3790 Retirement Communities & Homes Directory
American Business Directories
5711 S 86th Circle
Omaha, NE 68127-4146
402-593-4600
Fax: 402-331-5481
e-mail: directory@abii.com
http://www.abii.com
Bill Hippen, Vice President

Number of listings: 18,371. Entries include: Name, address, phone (including area code), size of advertisement, year first in 'Yellow Pages,' name of owner or manager, number of employees. Compiled from telephone company 'Yellow Pages,' nationwide.

Frequency: Annual

341

Aging/Directories

3791 Retirement Housing & Foodservice Who's Who
Information Central
PO Box 3900
Prescott, AZ 86302-3900
928-778-1513
Fax: 928-778-1513
e-mail: jgwoodman@hotmail.com
Julie Woodman, Editor

1,700 largest retirement housing facilities with food service. Entries include: Facility name, type of institution, address, phone, food service director, number and type of beds, number of residents, annual food purchases, number of meals served per day, types of food service offered, name of food management company, cooperative buying organization, multi-unit affiliation.
120 pages Frequency: Triennial

3792 Retirement Planning Service Directory
infoUSA
PO Box 27347
Omaha, NE 68127
402-593-4600
800-555-6124
Fax: 402-331-5481
e-mail: internet@infousa.com
http://www.abii.com
Bill Hippen, Vice President

Number of listings: 2,396. Entries include: Name, address, phone, size of advertisement, name of owner or manager, number of employees, year first in 'Yellow Pages.' Compiled from telephone company 'Yellow Pages,' nationwide.

3793 Roster: Boarding Homes, Licensed
Health & Human Services-Regulation & Licensure
301 Centennial Mall S
Lincoln, NE 68508-2529
402-471-4363
Fax: 402-471-0555
Joann Erickson, Mailing Contact
Helen Meeks, Editor

Approximately 13 licensed boarding homes in Nebraska. Entries include: Facility name, address, phone, name and title of contact, number of beds, type of operation, license number.
5 pages Frequency: Annual

3794 Senior Citizens Service Organizations Directory
infoUSA
PO Box 27347
Omaha, NE 68127
402-593-4600
800-555-6124
Fax: 402-331-5481
e-mail: internet@infousa.com
http://www.abii.com
Bill Hippen, Vice President

Number of listings: 7,212. Entries include: Name, address, phone (including area code), size of advertisement, year first in 'Yellow Pages,' name of owner or manager, number of employees. Compiled from telephone company 'Yellow Pages,' nationwide.
Frequency: Annual

3795 Senior Citizens Services
Gale Research
27500 Drake Road
Farmington Hills, MI 48331-3535
248-699-4253
800-877-GALE
Fax: 248-699-8069
e-mail: galeord@gale.com
Linda Hubbard, Mailing Contact
Allen Paschal, CEO

15,000 organizations from the private sector that provide senior services, 57 State Agencies on Aging, 670 Area Agencies on Aging. Separated into four volumes each available separately: Northeastern States, Southern and Mid-Atlantic States, Midwestern States, and Western States. Entries include: Contact information and description of services.
1,852 pages

3796 Senior Media Directory
Creative Ink
PO Box 22383
Eagan, MN 55122-0383
952-894-6720
Fax: 952-894-1066
e-mail: sales@creativeinkinc.com
http://www.seniormediadirectory.com
Pat Picard, Sales Manager

Approximately 1,250 radio and television programs, newspapers, periodicals, other publications, and marketing and mailing programs that have targeted the senior citizen audience. Entries include: Name, address, phone, fax, e-mail, website, names and titles, circulation, PR contacts, etc. Paperback.
200 pages Frequency: Annual, Februa.

3797 Special Edition for Disabled People
Lawrence Research Group
PO Box 31039
San Francisco, CA 94131
415-468-3805
Fax: 415-468-3912
Amy Levinson, Marketing

Catalog of sexual aids for the handicapped. Includes product and informational resources and quotes from the top professionals in this field.
32 pages

3798 State Vocational Rehabilitation Agencies
US Office Special Educ and Rehabilitative Serv.
330 C Street SW
Room 3042-Mes
Washington, DC 20202
202-205-8358
Fax: 202-205-9163
Joan Dickie, Editor

State government agencies responsible for vocational rehabilitation activities, including those for the blind. Entries include: Agency name, address, phone, name and title of director, federal Rehabilitation Services Administration region number.
11 pages Frequency: Triannually

3799 State and Federal Programs for the Aging
Illinois Department on Aging
421 E Capitol Avenue
Suite 100
Springfield, IL 62701-1738
217-785-2870
800-252-8966
Fax: 217-785-4477
e-mail: ilsenior@age084rl.state.il.us
Maralee I Lindley, Mailing Contact
Charles D Johnson, Executive Director

Programs, services, and agencies directly serving the elderly throughout Illinois. Entries include: Program/service name, phone, description, requirements for admission/eligibility, sponsoring governmental agency/department.
32 pages Frequency: Irregular

3800 Third Opinion: International Directory to Complementary Therapy Centers
Avery Publishing Group
120 Old Broadway
Garden City Park, NY 11040-5015
516-741-2155
800-548-5757
Fax: 516-742-1892
e-mail: info@averypublishing.com
John M Fink, Editor

Discusses over 300 alternative treatment cancer centers, educational centers, support groups and other research services.
320 pages

3801 Travelin' Talk Directory
Travelin' Talk
PO Box 3534
Clarksville, TN 37043-3534
931-552-6670
Fax: 931-552-1182
e-mail: trvllntlk@aol.com
Rick Crowder, Editor

Aging/Directories

Over 1,000 resources for travelers with disabilities; international coverage. Entries include: Company, organization, or personal name, address, phone, biographical data for individuals, geographical area served, descriptions of services, projects, etc. $35.00

550 pages Frequency: Irregular

3802 US Aging Policy Interest Groups
Greenwood Publishing Group
88 Post Road W
5007
Westport, CT 06880-4208
203-226-3571
800-225-5800
Fax: 203-226-6009
e-mail: prices@greenwood.com
http://www.greenwood.com

David Van Tassel, Editor
Elaine Meyer, Editor
Wayne Smith, President

83 organizations interested in aging and aging policies. Entries include: Organization name, address, phone, fax, purpose and background, funding, primary concerns, activities, publications.

288 pages

3803 USTA Adult and Senior National Championships Booklet
Florentine Press
160 Varick Street
Floor 6
New York, NY 10013-1220
212-633-1110
Fax: 212-633-8831

Anne Humes, Editor
Susan Shaffer, Editor
Steve Fromkes, President

Directory of associations that promote senior activities and over 250 listings of clubs and organizations that offer tennis for seniors.

65 pages

3804 United States Naval Academy Alumni Association: Register of Alumni
United States Naval Academy Alumni Association
247 King George Street
Annapolis, MD 21402-1306
410-263-4448
Fax: 410-269-0151
e-mail: bcollins@arctic.nadn.navy.mil

David E Church, Editor
Ronald F Marryott, President

About 88,000 graduates and former naval cadets and midshipmen, living and deceased. Entries include: Name, date of birth, state appointed from, address (including duty address, if still on active duty), decorations, date of resignation or retirement, date and place of death and widow's name, where applicable.

700 pages Frequency: Annual, Aug.

3805 University of Continuing Education Association: Membership Directory
University Continuing Education Association
1 Dupont Circle NW
Suite 615
Washington, DC 20036-1134
202-659-3130
Fax: 202-785-0374
http://www.nucea.edu

Cyrus Homayounpour, Director Membership
Susan Goewey, Director Publications
Kay Kohl, Executive Director

Almost 400 college and University departments which offer continuing educations programs

175 pages Frequency: Annual, Sept.

3806 Veterans & Military Organizations Directory
infoUSA
PO Box 27347
Omaha, NE 68127
402-593-4600
800-555-6124
Fax: 402-331-5481
e-mail: internet@infousa.com
http://www.abii.com

Bill Hippen, Vice President

Number of listings: 8,849. Entries include: Name, address, phone (including area code), size of advertisement, year first in 'Yellow Pages,' name of owner or manager, number of employees. Compiled from telephone company 'Yellow Pages,' nationwide.

Frequency: Annual

3807 Volunteer Center Directory
The Points of Light Foundation
1400 I Street NW
Washington, DC 20005-2208
202-729-8209
Fax: 202-729-8105
e-mail: voinet@pointsoflight.org
http://www.pointsoflight.org

List of volunteer centers.

87 pages Frequency: Annual, January

3808 Volunteer Vacations
Chicago Review Press
814 N Franklin Street
Chicago, IL 60610-3813
312-337-0747
800-888-4741
Fax: 312-337-5985

Bill McMillon, Editor
Curt Matthews, President

Directory of more than 280 foundations and organizations that sponsor volunteer expeditions in environmental and wild life preservation.

480 pages Frequency: Biennial, March

3809 Volunteer! The Comprehensive Guide to Voluntary Service in the US and Abroad
Publications Department
205 E 42nd Street
New York, NY 10017-5706
888-COU-NCIL
Fax: 212-822-2699
e-mail: info@ciee.org; info@councilexchanges.org

Richard Christiano, Editor

A list of volunteer service programs in the United States and over seas.

189 pages Frequency: Semiannual

3810 Warren H Green
8356 Olive Boulevard
Saint Louis, MO 63132-2892
314-997-1788
800-537-0655
Fax: 314-997-1788
e-mail: whgreen@inlink.com
http://www.whgreen.com

Joyce R Green, President/Editor in Chief
Lucy Knapp, Editor
Jonah Weiss, Marketing Director

Warren H Green is a publisher of medical and scientific books, for both health professionals and laypersons. Titles that may be of interest to older Americans include: The Best of Health; Research and Recipes on Dementia, Heart Disease, Osteoporosis and Cancer, Understanding Arthritis, Psychological Aspects of the Aging Process, and Management of the Frail Elderly by the Healthcare Team.

343

Aging / Journals, Magazines

3811 **Wheel Chairs & Scooters Directory**
infoUSA
PO Box 27347
Omaha, NE 68127
402-593-4600
800-555-6124
Fax: 402-331-5481
e-mail: internet@infousa.com
http://www.abii.com

Bill Hippen, Vice President

Number of listings: 3,857. Entries include: Name, address, phone (including area code), size of advertisement, year first in Yellow Pages, name of owner or manager, number of employees. Compiled from telephone company Yellow Pages, nationwide.

Frequency: Annual

3812 **Wheel Chairs Renting Directory**
infoUSA
PO Box 27347
Omaha, NE 68127
402-593-4600
800-555-6124
Fax: 402-331-5481
e-mail: internet@infousa.com
http://www.abii.com

Bill Hippen, Vice President

Number of listings: 594. Entries include: Name, address, phone, size of advertisement, name of owner or manager, number of employees, year first in Yellow Pages. Compiled from telephone company Yellow Pages, nationwide.

Frequency: on request

3813 **William S Hein & Company**
1285 Main Street
Buffalo, NY 14209-1987
716-882-2600
800-828-7571
Fax: 716-883-8100

Kevin Marmion, President

Offers a catalog of periodicals, publications and reprints, microforms and government publications on medical, handicapped and health law.

Journals, Magazines

3814 **A Better Tomorrow**
Thomas Nelson
5301 Wisconsin Avenue NW
Suite 620
Washington, DC 20015-2015
202-364-8000
Fax: 202-364-8910

Bruce Barbour, Publisher
Dale Hanson, Editor

Magazine focusing on issues and concerns of senior citizens.

Frequency: Quarterly

3815 **AAC: Augmentative and Alternative Communication**
Decker Publications
3302 Gaston Avenue
Room 610
Dallas, TX 75246-2013
214-828-8478
800-568-7281
Fax: 214-828-8286

Brain C Decker, Publisher
Terry Pitz, Sales Manager

Medical journal on speech and hearing issues. Sponsored by the International Society for Augmentative and Alternative Communication.

Frequency: Quarterly

3816 **ACE Fitness Matters**
American Council on Exercise
PO Box 910449
San Diego, CA 92191
858-535-8227
Fax: 858-535-8778
e-mail: pubs@acefitness.org

Richard Cotton, Editor-in-Chief

Consumer magazine covering health and fitness news.

Frequency: Bimonthly

3817 **AER Report**
AER
206 N Washington Street
Alexandria, VA 22314-2528
703-548-1884
Fax: 703-683-2926

Contains organizational news, conference dates and information concerning services to visually impaired people.

3818 **Abstracts in Social Gerontology: Current Literature on Aging**
National Council on the Aging
409 3rd Street SW
Suite 200
Washington, DC 20024-3212
202-479-1200
800-867-2755
Fax: 202-479-0735

James P Firman, CEO

Detailed abstracts are provided for recent major journal articles, books, reports and other materials on many facets of aging including adult education, economics, illnesses, family life, day care and more.

3819 **Accent on Living**
Cheever Publishing
PO Box 700
Bloomington, IL 61702
309-378-2961
800-787-8444
Fax: 309-378-4420
e-mail: cheeverpub@aol.com

Betty Garee, Editor
Raymond Cheever, Publisher

Magazine for people with physical disabilities, their families, and the professional and lay persons working with disabled people. Features motivational articles that emphasize success stories of handicapped people and contains new inventions and ideas for making daily living easier.

Frequency: Quarterly

3820 **Adapted Physical Activity Quarterly**
Human Kinetics Publishers
PO Box 5076
Champaign, IL 61825-5076
217-351-5076
800-747-4457
Fax: 217-351-2674
e-mail: humank@hkusa.com
http://www.humankinetics.com

Claudine Sherrill, Editor

Journal on the study of physical activity for special populations.

Frequency: Quarterly

3821 **Aging International**
Transaction Publishers
35 Berrue
New Brunswick, NJ 08901
732-445-2280
888-999-6778
Fax: 732-445-3138
e-mail: trans@transactionpub.com

Blossom Wigdor, Contact

Journal dedicated to the well-being of older persons worldwide. Explores productive aging, empowerment, life-long learning, health promotion, and services for the elderly, with an emphasis on sharing both common concerns and practical applications. Focuses on social and economic issues, public policies, and use of resources. Published in cooperation with the International Federation on Aging.

Frequency: Quarterly

3822 **Aging News Alert**
CD Publications
8204 Fenton Street
Silver Spring, MD 20910-4502
301-588-6380
Fax: 301-588-6385
e-mail: info@cdpublications.com
http://www.cdpublications.com

Michael Gerecht, President

Aging/Journals, Magazines

Twice-monthly newsletter reporting on senior programs, funding opportunities and federal actions affecting the elderly.

3823 Aging Research & Training News
Business Publishers
8737 Colesville Road
Suite 1100
Silver Spring, MD 20910-3956
800-274-6737
Fax: 301-587-4530
e-mail: bpinews@bpinews.com
http://www.bpinews.com

Leonard A Eiserer, Publisher
Nancy Aldrich, Editor
Katie Johnson, Marketing Manager

Compilation of studies of aging populations; reports on innovative programs with aging community; federal funding and laws.
8 pages

3824 Aging and Society
Cambridge University Press
40 W 20th Street
New York, NY 10011-4211
212-924-3900
800-221-4512
Fax: 212-691-3239
e-mail: info@cup.org

Ken Blakemore, Editor
Bill Bythwway, Editor
Richard Ziemacki, Executive Director

International journal publishing on topics which further the understanding of human aging. The journal of the Centre for policy on aging and the British Socie for Gerontology.
Frequency: Bimonthly

3825 American Guidance for Seniors
Uniformed Services Almanac, Inc
PO Box 4144
Falls Church, VA 22044
703-532-1631
Fax: 703-532-1635
e-mail: militaryalmanac@erois.com

Sol Gordon, Circulation Manager
Ron Hunter, President

Consumer magazine covering benefits and entitlements for seniors and caregivers.
Frequency: Annual

3826 American Journal of Speech-Language Pathology
American Speech-Language-Hearing Association
10801 Rockville Pike
Rockville, MD 20852-3226
301-897-5700
800-638-8255
Fax: 301-897-7355

Russell L Malone PhD, Editor
Arlene Pietranton, Executive Director

3827 American Legion Auxiliary's National News
American Legion Auxillary's National News
777 N Meridian Street
3rd Floor
Indianapolis, IN 46204-1420
317-635-6291
Fax: 317-636-5590
e-mail: alahq@iquest.net

Lauralyn T Mohr, Editor

Magazine for Auxiliary members.
Frequency: Bimonthly

3828 American Legion Magazine
American Legion National Headquarters
PO Box 1055
Indianapolis, IN 46206-1055
317-630-1207
Fax: 317-630-1369

Dick McNally, Publisher

General interest magazine for veterans.
Frequency: Monthly

3829 American Rehabilitation Services Administration (RSA)
C Street SW
Washington, DC 20202
202-205-8296
Fax: 202-205-9874
e-mail: frank_romano@ed.gov

Frank Romano, Publisher/Editor

Magazine on rehabilitation of the handicapped.
Frequency: Quarterly

3830 American Wanderer
American Volkssport Association (AVA)
1001 Pat Booker Road
Suite 101
Universal City, TX 78148-4147
210-659-2112
800-830-9255
Fax: 210-659-1212
http://www.avapr@aol.com

Rob Gale, Editor
Jacklyn Wilson, Advertising Manager

Consumer magazine covering sports and health news.
Frequency: Bimonthly

3831 Assistive Technology
RESNA
1700 N Moore Street
Suite 1540
Arlington, VA 22209-1911
703-524-6686
Fax: 202-524-6630
http://www.resna.org

Journal focusing on assistive technology for persons with disabilities.

3832 Audecibel
International Hearing Society
16880 Middlebelt Road
Suite 4
Livonia, MI 48154-3374
734-522-7200
800-521-5247
Fax: 734-522-0200

Cindy J Helms, Managing Editor/Mailing Contact

Magazine publishing technical articles and product announcements on hearing aids and hearing.
Frequency: Quarterly

3833 Augmentative and Alternative Communication
Int'l Society/Argumentative/Alternative Comm.
428 E Preston Street
Baltimore, MD 21202-3923
301-528-4000
800-222-3790
Fax: 410-528-4452

Scholarly journal publishing articles with direct application to the communication needs of persons with severe speech and language impairments.

3834 Buena Vida
Casiano Communications
1700 Avenue Fernandez Juncos
San Juan, PR 00909-2938
787-728-3000
800-468-8167
Fax: 787-728-7325

Annette Oliveras, Publisher
Manuel Casiano, Publisher

Health and fitness magazine.
Frequency: Monthly

3835 Challenge Magazine
Disabled Sports, USA
451 Hungerford Drive
Suite 100
Rockville, MD 20850-5102
301-217-0960
Fax: 301-217-0968
e-mail: dsusa@dsusa.org

Karen Rountree, Contact

Magazine providing information on sports for people with physical disabilities.

Aging / Journals, Magazines

Frequency: Quarterly

3836 Clinical Gerontologist
The Haworth Press
10 Alice Street
Binghamton, NY 13904-1503
607-722-5857
800-429-6784
Fax: 607-771-0012
e-mail: getinfo@haworthpressinc.com
TL Brink, Mailing Contact/Editor
Bill Cohen, Publisher

Contains practical information and research on assessment and intervention of mental health needs of aged patients.

Frequency: Quarterly

3837 Clinical Gerontologist: The Journal of Aging and Mental Health
Haworth Press
10 Alice Street
Binghamton, NY 13904-1503
607-722-5857
800-342-9678
Fax: 607-722-3487
e-mail: getinfo@haworthpressinc.com
http://www.haworthpressinc.com
William Cohen, Owner

Presents timely material relevant to the needs of mental health professionals and all practitioners who deal with the aged client.

Frequency: Quarterly

3838 Clinics in Geriatric Medicine
WB Saunders Company, Harcourt Brace & Company
The Curtis Center
Suite 300
Philadelphia, PA 19106
215-238-7800
800-654-2452
Fax: 215-238-7883
Karen Whitaker, Mailing Contact/Editor

Journal reviewing new diseases, drugs, and diagnostic and management techniques in geriatric medicine.

Frequency: Quarterly

3839 Closing the Gap
Closing the Gap
PO Box 68
Henderson, MN 56044
507-248-3294
Fax: 507-248-3810
e-mail: info@closingthegap.com
Jan Latzke, Mailing Contact
Dolores Hagen, President

Magazine exploring the use of microcomputers for people with disabilities.

3840 Communication Outlook: Artificial Language Laboratory
405 Computer Center E
Lansing, MI 48824
517-353-0870
Fax: 517-353-4766
e-mail: artlang@pilot.msu.edu

Magazine reporting on the newest developments in the application of technology for neurologically impaired persons.

Frequency: Quarterly

3841 Community Mental Health Journal
Nat'l Council of Community Mental Health Center
12300 Twinbrook Parkway
Suite 320
Rockville, MD 20852-1606
301-984-6200
Fax: 301-881-7159
Linda Rosenberg, CEO

Contains research oriented articles giving you the data you need to evaluate the effectiveness of innovative programs, service systems, and clinical work.

3842 Computer-Disability News
National Easter Seal Society Publications
230 W Monroe Street
Suite 1800
Chicago, IL 60606-4703
312-726-6200
800-221-6827
Fax: 312-726-1494

Magazine highlighting news for persons with disabilities.

Frequency: Quarterly

3843 Conscious Choice
Conscious Communications
920 N Franklin Street
Suite 202
Chicago, IL 60610-3473
312-440-4373
Fax: 312-751-3973
Ross Thompson, Managing Editor
Jim Slama, Publisher

Consumer magazine covering health, nutrition and environmental issues.

Frequency: Bimonthly

3844 Contemporary Gerontology
Springer Publishing Company
536 Broadway
New York, NY 10012-3915
212-431-4370
Fax: 212-941-7842
e-mail: springer@springerpub.com
http://www.springerpub.com
Rafael Ortiz, Advertising Manager
Cory Sklaire, Circulation Manager
Ursula Springer, President

Scholarly journal covering gerontology.

Frequency: Quarterly

3845 Cook's Illustrated
Boston Common Press
17 Station Street
Brookline, MA 02445-7995
617-232-1000
Fax: 617-232-1572
http://www.cooksillustrated.com
Pam Caporino, Marketing Director
Connie Forbes, Marketing Assistant
Chris Kimball, Owner

A unique cooking magazine known for near-obsessive kitchen testing in pursuit of the best techniques, tools, and recipes for the home cook. Advertising free.

Frequency: Bimonthly

3846 Diet & Fitness
Lifetime Periodicals
2131 Hollywood Boulevard
Hollywood, FL 33020-6759
954-925-5242
Fax: 954-925-5244
e-mail: lifetime@shadow.net
Donald Lessne, President

Consumer magazine covering health, diet, and fitness.

Frequency: Quarterly

3847 Disability Rag's Ragged Edge Magazine
Advocado Press
PO Box 145
Louisville, KY 40201
502-894-9492
Fax: 502-899-9562
Mary Johnson, Mailing Contact/Editor

Magazine of debate on disability rights issues. ISSN# 1095-3949

35 pages Frequency: Bimonthly

3848 Disability Rights Now
Disability Rights Education and Defense Fund
2212 6th Street
Berkeley, CA 94710-2219
510-644-2555
800-466-4232
Fax: 510-841-8645
Sue Henderson, Executive Director

Aging/Journals, Magazines

Free quarterly publication describing the activities of the Disability Rights Education and Defense Fund, available in alternative formats.

3849 Disability Statistics Report
Institute for Health & Aging
3333 California Street
Suite 340
San Francisco, CA 94118-1944
415-502-5210
Fax: 415-476-9485

Magazine providing statistical data on disability in the US as collected by the Disability Statistics Program.

Frequency: Irregular

3850 Disability Studies Quarterly
University of Hawaii at Manoa
1776 University Avenue
Ua4-6
Honolulu, HI 96822-2463
808-956-9202
Fax: 808-956-3162
e-mail: pfeiffer@hawaii.edu

David Pfeiffer, Editor

Scholarly journal containing articles on all aspects of disability.

Frequency: Quarterly

3851 Disabled American Veterans Magazines
Disabled American Veterans National Headquarters
PO Box 14301
Cincinnati, OH 45250
859-441-7300
Fax: 859-441-8056

Thomas K Keller, Editor
James Chaney, Mailing Contact

Veterans magazine on disability issues.

Frequency: Bimonthly

3852 Disabled People as Second Class Citizens
Springer Publishing Company
536 Broadway
New York, NY 10012-3915
212-431-4370
Fax: 212-941-7842
e-mail: springer@springerpub.com
http://www.springerpub.com

Ursula Springer, President

Disability and legal practice.

320 pages

3853 Domestic Mistreatment of the Elderly: Towards Prevention
AARP Fulfillment
601 E Street NW
Washington, DC 20049
202-434-2170
800-424-3410
Fax: 202-434-3443
e-mail: member@aarp.org
http://www.aarp.org

Jan May, Manager

This comprehensive publication addresses the problem of mistreatment or neglect in the home.

39 pages

3854 Duplex Planet
Duplex Planet
PO Box 1230
Saratoga Springs, NY 12866
518-692-7410
Fax: 518-692-8208
e-mail: duplanet@global2000.net

David Greenberger, Editor

Consumer journal covering issues of aging and popular culture.

Frequency: Bimonthly

3855 Eating Well Magazine
Eating Well
823a Ferry Road
Charlotte, VT 05445-9092
802-425-5700
800-344-3350
Fax: 802-425-3675
e-mail: ewelledit@aol.comewelledit@aol.com

Marcelle Langon DiFalco, Editor-in-Chief
James Lawrence, Publisher

Food magazine with emphasis on delicious low-fat cooking and sensible nutrition.

3856 Educational Gerontology
Taylor & Francis
325 Chestnut Street
Philadelphia, PA 19106-2614
215-625-8900
800-354-1420
Fax: 215-625-2940
e-mail: info@taylorandfrancis.com

D Barry Lumsden, Editor
Kevin Bradley, CEO

Journal publishing original research in the fields of gerontology, adult education, and the social and behavioral sciences.

3857 Elderly Health Services Letter
Health Resources
1913 Atlantic Avenue
Suite F4
Manasquan, NJ 08736-1029
732-292-1100
Fax: 732-292-1111
http://www.healthresourcesonline.com

Robert K Jenkins, Publisher

An essential tool for senior services professionals. Stays on top of the most current challenges facing senior services professionals, including financing and funding senior services, marketing, positioning senior services for managed care, getting administrative support and more.

3858 Experimental Aging Research
Taylor & Francis
325 Chestnut Street
Philadelphia, PA 19106-2614
215-625-8900
800-354-1420
Fax: 215-625-2940
e-mail: info@taylorandfrancis.com

Jeffrey Elias, Editor
Kevin Bradley, CEO

International journal devoted to the scientific study of the aging process.

Frequency: Quarterly

3859 Fifty Something Magazine
Media Trends Publications
8250 Tyler Boulevard
Mentor, OH 44060-4200
440-974-9594
Fax: 440-974-1004

Linda L Linbeman, Editor

Consumer magazine featuring articles for the fifty and above market.

Frequency: Bimonthly

3860 Fitness Diet and Exercise Guide
Family Circle
110 5th Avenue
New York, NY 10011-5614
212-463-1673
Fax: 212-463-1906

Barbara Winkler, Editor
John Hillock, Publisher

Magazine suggesting ways to eat healthier and exercise better.

Aging / Journals, Magazines

3861 Focus on Geriatric Care and Rehabilitation
Aspen Publishers
7201 McKinney Circle
Frederick, MD 21704-8356
301-698-7105
800-234-1660
Fax: 800-901-9075
http://www.aspenpub.com

Jackael Bruggeman, Publisher

Monthly journal written for nurses, occupational therapists and administrators in geriatric settings.

3862 Focus: Library Service to Older Adults; People with Disabilities
216 N Frederick Avenue
Daytona Beach, FL 32114-3408

Michael G Gunde, Publisher/Editor

News and advice for librarians providing services to older adults and people with disabilities.

2 pages

3863 For Patients Only
Dialysis
6324 Variel Avenue
Suite 308
Woodland Hills, CA 91367-2514
818-704-5555
Fax: 818-704-6500

Gordon Lore, Editor
Karen Glasser, National Sales Manager

Lifestyle magazine for dialysis and kidney transplantation patients.

Frequency: Bimonthly

3864 Generations
American Society on Aging
833 Market Street
Suite 511
San Francisco, CA 94103-1824
415-974-9600
800-537-9728
Fax: 415-974-0300
e-mail: info@asa.asaging.org
http://www.asaging.org

Susan Markey, Director Marketing
Gloria Cavanaugh, Executive Director

Peer-review quarterly journal featuring guest editor.

3865 Generations, Journal of the American Society on Aging
American Society on Aging
833 Market Street
Suite 511
San Francisco, CA 94103-1824
415-974-9600
800-537-9728
Fax: 415-974-0300
e-mail: info@asa.as

Mary Johnson, Editor
Gloria Cavanaugh, Executive Director

Magazine for health, social service, and other professionals who work with older people; presenting in-depth view of a specific topic in aging emphasizing research and practice.

Frequency: Quarterly

3866 Geriatrics
7500 Old Oak Boulevard
Cleveland, OH 44130-3343
440-891-2769
Fax: 440-891-2635
http://www.geri.com

Janice Radak, Editor in Chief

Peer-reviewed, clinical journal for physicians and laypersons relating to medical care of middle-aged and older adults.

Frequency: Monthly

3867 Gerontologist
Gerontological Society of America
1030 15th Street NW
Suite 250
Washington, DC 20005-1526
202-842-1275
Fax: 202-842-1150
e-mail: geron@geron.org
http://www.geron.org

Vernon L Greene, Editor
Betty Borgen, Advertising Director
Carol Schutz, Executive Director

Multidisciplinary peer-reviewed journal presenting new concepts, clinical ideas, and applied research in gerontology. Includes book and audiovisual reviews.

Frequency: Bimonthly

3868 Gerontology
S Karger Publshers
PO Box 529
Unionville, CT 06085
860-675-7834
Fax: 860-675-7302
e-mail: karger@karger.ch

W Meier-Rage, Managing Editor
Monica Brendel, President

Medical journal.

Frequency: Bimonthly

3869 Gerontology & Geriatrics Education
The Haworth Press
10 Alice Street
Binghamton, NY 13904-1503
607-722-5857
800-429-6784
Fax: 607-771-0012
e-mail: getinfo@haworthpressinc.com

Grace D Dawson, Editor
Bill Cohen, Publisher

Journal presenting practical curriculum information for educators, trainers, and supervisors in the aging field.

Frequency: Quarterly

3870 Get Up and Go
Liberty Media
11551 Forest Central Drive
Suite 305
Dallas, TX 75243-3920
214-341-9429
Fax: 214-341-9779

Shirley Schwaller, Publisher

Magazine (tabloid) for people age 50 and over.

Frequency: Monthly

3871 Golden Years Magazine
Golden Years Magazine
PO Box 537
Melbourne, FL 32902
321-725-4888
Fax: 321-724-0736

Carol B Hittner, Editor
Steve Hittner, Publisher

Magazine for adults aged 50-64.

Frequency: Bimonthly

3872 Health
Time Health
2 Embarcadero Center
Suite 600
San Francisco, CA 94111-3823
415-248-2700
Fax: 415-248-2779
e-mail: editor@health.com

Barbara Paulsen, Editor-in-Chief
Sheri Warrick, Contact

Consumer magazine covering medicine, health, and fitness issues.

Aging/Journals, Magazines

3873 **Health Naturally**
Health Naturally Publications
74 James Street, 3rd Floor, Box 580
Parry Sound, ON
Canada, P2A 1O8
705-746-7839
Fax: 704-746-7893
Lorrie Imbert, Editor

Consumer magazine covering alternative health and nutrition.
Frequency: Bimonthly

3874 **Health Watch**
Health Watch Magazine
455 S 4th Avenue
Suite 908
Louisville, KY 40202-2511
502-568-2546
Fax: 502-585-4881
Mollie Vento, Editor
Bobby Baker, Publisher

Magazine for health care consumers.
Frequency: Bimonthly

3875 **Health World**
Health World
PO Box 4228
Thousand Oaks, CA 91359-1228
805-497-1308
Fax: 805-381-0191

Magazine focusing on nutrition and health.
Frequency: Bimonthly

3876 **HealthQuest**
Levas
200 Highpoint Drive
Suite 215
Chalfont, PA 18914-3925
215-822-7935
Fax: 215-997-9582
Tamara Jeffries, Editor

Consumer health magazine for African Americans.
Frequency: Bimonthly

3877 **Herb Quarterly**
Long Mountain Press
PO Box 689
San Anselmo, CA 94979
415-455-9540
800-371-4372
Fax: 415-455-9541
Linda Sparrowe, Editor
James Keough, Publisher

Magazine on herb gardening, cooking, crafts, medicinal herbal research, and alternative health care.
Frequency: Quarterly

3878 **Hippocrates**
Hippocrates Partners
301 Howard Street
Suite 1800
San Francisco, CA 94105-6614
415-538-9331
Fax: 415-512-9600
Eric W Schrier, Editor
John Klingel, Advertising Manager
Carla Curtis, Manager

Professional magazine covering medicine, health, and fitness issues.
Frequency: Bimonthly

3879 **HomeCare Magazine Buyers' Guide**
Intertec Publishing Corporation
PO Box 8987
Malibu, CA 90265-8987
310-317-4522
800-543-4116
Fax: 310-317-9644
e-mail: janis@miramar.com
http://www.homecaremag.com
Marie Blakely, Editor

Service providers, distributors and manufactures of rehabilitation and home health care products.
Frequency: Annual, July

3880 **Impact!**
World Institute on Disability (WID)
510 16th Street
Suite 100
Oakland, CA 94612-1520
510-763-4100
Fax: 510-763-4109
e-mail: wid@wid.org
Joan Leon, Editor

Magazine reporting on the activities of the World Institute on Disability.
Frequency: Semiannual

3881 **Incare Of**
RCP Publishing
4689 Ponce De Leon Boulevard
300
Coral Gables, FL 33146-2133
305-442-0888
Fax: 305-666-2144
Yolanda Lorie, Publisher
Roberto Incera, Owner

Magazine.
Frequency: Quarterly

3882 **Independent Living Provider**
Equal Opportunity Publications
1160 E Jericho Turnpike
Suite 200
Huntington, NY 11743-5405
516-421-9421
Fax: 516-421-0359
e-mail: info@eop.com
Anne Kelly, Editor
John Miller, Publisher

Business magazine for home health care.
Frequency: Quarterly

3883 **Informer**
The Simon Foundation for Continence
PO Box 835
Wilmette, IL 60091
847-864-3913
Fax: 847-864-9758
Cheryle B Gartley, President

Magazine for persons with bladder or bowel incontinence.
Frequency: Quarterly

3884 **Innovations in Aging**
National Council on the Aging
409 3rd Street SW
2nd Floor
Washington, DC 20024-3212
202-479-1200
800-867-2755
Fax: 202-479-0735
Michael Reinemer, Editor
James P Firman, CEO

Magazine exploring significant developments in the field of aging.
Frequency: Quarterly

3885 **Inside MS**
National Multiple Sclerosis Society
733 3rd Avenue
New York, NY 10017-3204
212-986-3240
800-FIG-HTMS
Fax: 212-986-7981
e-mail: editor@nmss.org
http://www.nationalmscociety.org
Gary Sullivan, Managing Editor
Bill Rosen, Director Advertising
Joyce Nelson, CEO

Magazine for people with multiple sclerosis, their families, attending professionals, and interested donors. Provides information on coping, research, legislation, medical advances and disability rights advocacy.
80 pages Frequency: Quarterly

Aging / Journals, Magazines

3886 **International Journal of Aging and Human Development**
Baywood Publishing Company
PO Box 337
Amityville, NY 11701
631-691-1270
800-638-7816
Fax: 631-691-1770
e-mail: baywood@baywood.com

Bert Hayslip Jr, Editor
Stuart Cohen, Publisher

Adult development and aging featuring original research theory, critial reviews.

3887 **International Journal of Technology and Aging**
Human Sciences Press
233 Spring Street
New York, NY 10013-1522
212-620-8000
Fax: 212-463-0742
TDD 0 - -

Rudiger Gebauer, Owner

Designed to serve health-care professionals, researchers, academicians and industries concerned with the convergence of two recent trends, the dramatic advances in technology and the rapidly growing elderly population.

3888 **International Psychogeriatrics**
Springer Publishing Company
536 Broadway
New York, NY 10012-3915
212-431-4370
Fax: 212-941-7842
e-mail: springer@springerpub.com
http://www.springerpub.com

Robin Eastwood, Editor-in-Chief
Rafael Ortiz, Advertising Manager
Ursula Springer, President

Scholarly journal covering psychogeriatric practice, research, and education worldwide.

Frequency: Quarterly

3889 **International Rehabilitation Review**
Rehabilitation International
125 E 21st Street
New York, NY 10010-7402
212-420-1500
Fax: 212-505-0871

Barbara Duncan, Editor
Tomas Lagerwall, Manager

Magazine overviewing the activities programs in the disability and rehabilitation fields.

3890 **JADARA California**
JADARA
PO Box 6956
San Mateo, CA 94403-6956
650-372-0620
Fax: 650-372-0661
e-mail: adaraorgn@aol.com

Elizabeth Charlson, Contact

Journal focusing on original research, news, and resources on deafness and rehabilitation.

3891 **Johns Hopkins: Health After 50**
Medletter Associates
632 Broadway
New York, NY 10012-2614
212-634-1450

Rodney Friedman, Publisher

Health newsletter for people over 50.

3892 **Journal of AAA**
American Academy of Audiology
1735 N Lynn Street
Suite 950
Arlington, VA 22209-2013
703-524-1923
800-222-
Fax: 703-524-2303

James Jerger, Editor

3893 **Journal of Aging & Pharmacotherapy**
Haworth Press
10 Alice Street
Binghamton, NY 13904-1503
607-722-5857
800-342-9678
Fax: 607-722-3487
e-mail: getinfo@haworthpressinc.com
http://www.haworthpressinc.com

William Cohen, Owner

Devoted exclusively to drug therapy issues for the geriatric patient

Frequency: Quarterly

3894 **Journal of Aging & Social Policy**
Haworth Press
10 Alice Street
Binghamton, NY 13904-1503
607-722-5857
800-342-9678
Fax: 607-722-3487
e-mail: getinfo@haworthpressinc.com
http://www.haworthpressinc.com

William Cohen, Owner

Essential resource for advocating effective social policy for the elderly.

Frequency: Quarterly

3895 **Journal of Aging Studies**
JAI Press
100 Prospect Street
Stamford, CT 06901-1696
203-363-7105
Fax: 203-661-8586
e-mail: jaber@nervm.nercd.ufl.edu

Jaber F Gubrium, Editor
Charles W Grinnell, Owner

Journal of aging studies.

Frequency: Quarterly

3896 **Journal of Aging and Ethnicity**
Springer Publishing Company
536 Broadway
New York, NY 10012-3915
212-431-4370
Fax: 212-941-7842
e-mail: springer@springerpub.com
http://www.springerpub.com

Donald ER Gelfand, Editor
Ursula Springer, President

Scholarly journal for researchers and professionals in gerontology and geriatrics, emphasizing the ethnic population of North America.

3897 **Journal of Aging and Health**
Sage Publications
2455 Teller Road
Thousand Oaks, CA 91320-2218
805-499-0721
Fax: 805-499-0871
e-mail: linfo@sagepub.com

Kyriakos S Markides, Editor
C Anderson, Circulation Manager
Blaise R Simqu, CEO

Journal presenting research relative to the social and behavioral factors related to aging and health.

Frequency: Quarterly

3898 **Journal of Aging and Physical Activity**
Human Kinetics Publishers
PO Box 5076
Champaign, IL 61825-5076
217-351-5076
800-747-4457
Fax: 217-351-2674
e-mail: humank@hkusa.com
http://www.humankinetics.com

Wojtek Chodzko-Zajko, Editor

Journal examining the relationship between physical activity and the aging process.

Frequency: Quarterly

Aging / Journals, Magazines

3899 Journal of American Aging Association
American Aging Association
110 Chesley Drive
Media, PA 19063-1755
610-892-0300
Fax: 610-565-9747
e-mail: ameraging@aol.com
http://www.americanaging.org
George Roth, Executive Director
Micheal Fossel, Executive Director

3900 Journal of Developmental and Physical Disabilities
Kluwer Academic/Plenum Publishers
233 Spring Street
Floor 7
New York, NY 10013-1522
212-620-8000
Fax: 212-463-0742
e-mail: info@plenum.com
http://www.wkap.nl
Vincent B Hassett, Editor
V Hersen, Advertising Manager
Rudiger Gebauer, Owner

Professional journal.
Frequency: Quarterly

3901 Journal of Elder Abuse & Neglect: An International Journal
Haworth Press
10 Alice Street
Binghamton, NY 13904-1503
607-722-5857
800-342-9678
Fax: 607-722-3487
e-mail: getinfo@haworthpressinc.com
http://www.haworthpressinc.com
William Cohen, Owner

Develop effective prevention and treatment strategies with this critical journal.
Frequency: Quarterly

3902 Journal of Elder Abuse and Neglect
The Haworth Press
10 Alice Street
Binghamton, NY 13904-1503
607-722-5857
800-429-6784
Fax: 607-771-0012
e-mail: getinfo@haworthpressinc.com
Rosalie S Wolf, Editor
S McMurray, Advertising Manager
William Cohen, Owner

Study causes, treatment, effects and prevention of the mistreatment of older people.
Frequency: Quarterly

3903 Journal of Ethics, Law, and Aging
Springer Publishing Company
536 Broadway
New York, NY 10012-3915
212-431-4370
Fax: 212-941-7842
e-mail: springer@springerpub.com
http://www.springerpub.com
Marshall Kapp, Editor
Ursula Springer, President

Scholarly journal covering ethical and legal issues regarding aging for professionals who plan, administer, and provide and finance services to the elderly.
Frequency: Semiannual

3904 Journal of Gerontological Nursing
Slack
6900 Grove Road
Thorofare, NJ 08086-9447
856-848-1000
800-257-8290
Fax: 856-848-1000
e-mail: slackinc@slackinc.com
Frances R DeStefano, Editor
Peter N Slack, President

Gerontological nursing journal.
Frequency: Monthly

3905 Journal of Gerontological Social Work
The Haworth Press
10 Alice Street
Binghamton, NY 13904-1503
607-722-5857
Fax: 607-771-0012
e-mail: getinfo@haworthpressinc.com
Rose Dobrof, Editor
Bill Cohen, Publisher
Kerry Roberts, Mailing Contact

Journal addressing social work practice, theory, administration, and consultation in the field of aging.
Frequency: Quarterly

3906 Journal of Housing for the Elderly
The Haworth Press
10 Alice Street
Binghamton, NY 13904-1503
607-722-5857
800-429-6784
Fax: 607-771-0012
e-mail: getinfo@haworthpressinc.com
Leon A Pastalan, Editor
William Cohen, Owner

Magazine dealing with issues on housing for the elderly.
Frequency: Biennial

3907 Journal of Intergenerational Relationships: Programs, Policy, and Research
Haworth Press
10 Alice Street
Binghamton, NY 13904-1503
607-722-5857
800-342-9678
Fax: 607-722-3487
e-mail: getinfo@haworthpressinc.com
http://www.haworthpressinc.com
William Cohen, Owner

A one-of-a-kind resource that reflects the global impact of intergenerational strategies, programs and policies.
Frequency: Quarterly

3908 Journal of Mental Health and Aging
Springer Publishing Company
536 Broadway
New York, NY 10012-3915
212-431-4370
Fax: 212-941-7842
e-mail: springer@springerpub.com
http://www.springerpub.com
Donna Cohen, Editor
Rafael Ortiz, Advertising Manager
Ursula Springer, President

Scholarly journal covering aging population for mental health professionals.

3909 Journal of Nutrition for the Elderly
Haworth Press
10 Alice Street
Binghamton, NY 13904-1503
607-722-5857
800-342-9678
Fax: 607-722-3487
e-mail: getinfo@haworthpressinc.com
http://www.haworthpressinc.com
William Cohen, Owner
Annette B Natow, Editor

It comprehensively examines the role of nutrition in disease prevention and management, fuctional performance, and overall quality of life for the elderly.
Frequency: Quarterly

3910 Journal of Rehabilitation
National Rehabilitation Association
633 S Washington Street
Alexandria, VA 22314-4109
703-836-0850
Fax: 703-836-0848
Paul Leung, Editor
Ronald J Acquavita, Managing Editor
Linda Winslow, Executive Director

Rehabilitation journal.
Frequency: Quarterly

Aging / Journals, Magazines

3911 Journal of Religious Gerontology
National Council on the Aging
409 3rd Street SW
Suite 200
Washington, DC 20024-3212
202-479-1200
800-867-2755
Fax: 202-479-0735
James P Firman, CEO

Features articles, research reports and reviews of new books and audiovisual resources on religion and aging.

3912 Journal of Religious Gerontology: The Interdisciplinary Journal of Practice, Theory, and Applied Research
Haworth Press
10 Alice Street
Binghamton, NY 13904-1503
607-722-5857
800-342-9678
Fax: 607-722-3487
e-mail: getinfo@haworthpressinc.com
http://www.haworthpressinc.com
William Cohen, Owner

A much-needed voice for the merging fields of religion and gerontology.
Frequency: Quarterly

3913 Journal of Therapeutic Horticulture
American Horticultural Therapy Association
362a Christopher Avenue
Gaithersburg, MD 20879-3512
301-948-3010
Fax: 301-869-2397
Steven H Davis, Contact

Journal containing articles on the therapeutic aspects of gardening and agriculture for persons with disabilities.
Frequency: Annual

3914 Journal of Women and Aging
The Haworth Press
10 Alice Street
Binghamton, NY 13904-1503
607-722-5857
800-429-6784
Fax: 607-771-0012
e-mail: getinfo@haworthpressinc.com
J Garner, Editor
Dianne Cohen, Publisher
William Cohen, Owner

Journal for professionals concerned with the health and well-being of the aging woman.
Frequency: Quarterly

3915 Journal of the American Geriatrics Society
Williams & Wilkins
351 W Camden Street
Baltimore, MD 21201-7912
410-528-4000
800-222-3790
Fax: 410-528-4452
e-mail: internetwwbooks@access.digest.net
David H Solomon, Editor
David Baker, Advertising Director

Journal reporting developments in the clinical fields of geriatric medicine and gerontology.
Frequency: Monthly

3916 Journal of the Association for Persons with Severe Handicaps
TASH
29 W Susquehanna Avenue
Suite 210
Baltimore, MD 21204-5218
410-828-8274
800-482-TASH
Fax: 410-828-6706
e-mail: tash@tash.org
Lori Goetz, Editor
Rose Holsey, Mailing Contact

Special education journal presenting articles that report original research, authoritative and comprehensive reviews, and conceptual and practical position papers offering new directions for people with disabilities.
Frequency: Quarterly

3917 Kaleidoscope: Exploring the Expirence of Disability through Literature & Fine Arts
United Disability Services
701 S Main Street
Akron, OH 44311-1019
330-762-9755
Fax: 330-762-0912
e-mail: mshiplett@usdakron.org
http://www.udsakron.org
Darshan Perusek, Editor-in-Chief
Gail Willmott, Senior Editor
Phyllis Boerner, Publication Director

Magazine featuring articles on literature and the arts. Disabilitiy related.
64 pages Frequency: Bi-Annually

3918 Let's Live
Franklin Publications
320 N Larchmont Boulevard
Los Angeles, CA 90004-3037
310-472-7387
800-225-6473
Fax: 323-469-9597
e-mail: letslivebs@aol.com
Beth Salmon, Editor
Paul Wolff, Publisher
Franklin Lett, Owner

Publication focuses on natural, holistic health, fitness, sports nutrition, herbs and vitamins/minerals. Articles are mostly written by industry experts.
Frequency: Monthly

3919 Library Outreach Reporter
Library Outreach Reporter
148 Liberty Street
Fords, NJ 08863-2042
732-738-5183
Fax: 732-738-5183
Allan M Kleiman, Editor

Magazine for outreach and special services librarians in all types of libraries.
Frequency: Quarterly

3920 Longevity
General Media
277 Park Avenue
Floor 4
New York, NY 10172
212-702-6000
Fax: 212-702-6262
Susan Millar Perry, Editor

Health and lifestyle magazine.
Frequency: Monthly

3921 Macrobiotics Today
George Ohsawa Macrobiotic Foundation
1999 Myers Street
Oroville, CA 95966-5340
916-533-7702
Fax: 916-533-7908
e-mail: bkligon@idt.com
Bob Ligon, Mailing Contact/Editor
Carl Ferre, Publisher

Magazine covering macrobiotics, health, and nutrition.
Frequency: Bimonthly

3922 Magazines in Special Media for the Handicapped
Nat Lib Serv for the Blind/Physically Handicapped
1291 Taylor Street NW
Washington, DC 20542
202-707-5100
800-424-8567
Fax: 202-707-0712
e-mail: nls@loc.gov
http://www.loc.gov/nls
Frank Cylke, Executive Director

Publication includes: List of over 100 public and private organizations that publish magazines in Braille, on cassette, on disc and computer diskette, or in large print or moon type for visually impaired and physically disabled individuals. Entries include: Name of publisher, address, price. Principal content is a bibliography of periodicals, with brief description, frequency, format, and price of each.

Aging/Journals, Magazines

Frequency: Biennial

3923 Mainstream
Mainstream
PO Box 370598
San Diego, CA 92137
619-234-3138
Fax: 619-234-3155

National news and lifestyle magazine for persons with disabilities.

3924 Massage Therapy Journal
American Massage Therapy Association
500 Davis Street
Suite 900
Evanston, IL 60201-4695
847-864-0123
Fax: 847-864-1178

Theodore Berland, Editor
Liz Lucas, Executive Director

Magazine focusing on professional massage therapy benefits, techniques, research, news, and practitioners.

Frequency: Quarterly

3925 Mature Health
Haymarket Group
45 W 34th Street
Room 500
New York, NY 10001-3173
212-239-0855

Michael Schneider, President

Magazine featuring articles on health aspects of aging, as well as articles on recreation and leisure.

3926 Mature Lifestyles
Mature Lifestyles
PO Box 44327
Madison, WI 53744-4327
608-274-5200
Fax: 608-274-5492

Pat O'Gara, Publisher

Newspaper for 50's population.

3927 Mature Outlook
PO Box 10448
Des Moines, IA 50306
800-336-6330
Fax: 515-334-9247

Alison Poklop, Marketing Manager

Provides information and support for individuals over 50 years of age.

3928 Mature Years
United Methodist Publishing House
201 8th Avenue S
Nashville, TN 37203-3919
615-749-6000
Fax: 615-749-6079
e-mail: newscope_office@econet.org

Marvin W Cropsey, Editor
Neil Alexander, Publisher

Magazine promoting the physical and spiritual well-being of older adults.

Frequency: Quarterly

3929 Men's Health
Rodale Press
33 E Minor Street
Emmaus, PA 18098
610-967-5171
Fax: 610-967-7725
e-mail: alica.debus@rodale.com
http://www.menshealth.com

David Zinczenks, Editor In Cheif
Maryann Bekkadahl, Publisher
Alice Debus, Office Manager

Magazine offering health advice for men.

3930 Mental Health Report
Business Publishers
951 Pershing Drive
Silver Spring, MD 20910-4400
301-495-5570
800-274-6737
Fax: 301-589-8493
e-mail: bpinews@bpinews.com

Emanuel Mandel

Magazine reporting on legislation affecting the mentally ill and their families.

3931 Mental and Physical Disability LawDigest
American Bar Association
740 15th Street NW
Washington, DC 20005-1019
202-662-1570
Fax: 202-662-1032
e-mail: cmpdl@abanet.org
http://www.abanet.org/disability

Sarina Khan, Office Administrator
Amy Allbright, Managing Editor
John Parry, Executive Director

Loose-leaf periodical, updated every 6 months, providing concise, expert explanation of 22 disability law topics, complete with case and statutory citations and references to books and journal articles.

3932 Mental and Physical Disability Law Reporter
American Bar Association
740 15th Street NW
Washington, DC 20005-1019
202-662-1570
Fax: 202-662-1032
e-mail: cmpdl@abanet.org
http://www.abanet.org/disability

Sarina Khan, Office Administrator
Amy Allbright, Managing Editor
John Parry, Executive Director

Periodical covering timely summaries of reported legal developments in 22 subject areas.

150 pages Frequency: Bi-Monthly

3933 Modern Maturity
AARP Fulfillment
601 E Street NW
Washington, DC 20049
202-434-2277
800-424-3410
Fax: 202-434-3443
e-mail: member@aarp.org
http://www.aarp.org

William D Novelli, CEO

Offers news and information of concern to those 50 and older. Features articles on current events, health, recreation, housing, family life, legislation and other issues.

3934 National Easter Seal Communicator
National Easter Seal Society Publications
230 W Monroe Street
Suite 1800
Chicago, IL 60606-4703
312-726-6800
800-221-6827
Fax: 312-726-1494

James E Williams Jr, CEO

Magazine for persons with any type of disability.

3935 Natural Way Magazine
Natural Way Publications
1 Bridge Street
Suite 125
Irvington, NY 10533-1550
914-591-2011
800-697-2267
Fax: 914-591-2017
e-mail: natway@aol.com

Cathy Raymond, Editor-in-Chief
Warren Tabatch, Advertising Director

Consumer magazine covering alternative health news and views.

Frequency: Bimonthly

Aging / Journals, Magazines

3936 New Choices
Retirement Living Publishing Company
28 W 23rd Street
New York, NY 10010-5204
212-366-8000
Fax: 212-366-8899

J Tomback, Mailing Contact

Magazine.

Frequency: Monthly

3937 New Living
New Living
PO Box 1519
Stony Brook, NY 11790
631-751-8819
Fax: 631-751-8910
http://www.newliving.com

Christine Harvey, Editor-in-Chief

Features and articles about holistic health and fitness; herbal remedies, preventive medicine, nutrition, mind/body health, spirituality, fitness, recipes, book reviews and more!

Frequency: Monthly

3938 New Mobility
No Limits Communications
PO Box 220
Horsham, PA 19044
215-675-9133
Fax: 215-675-9376

Jeff Leonard, Owner

Magazine for persons with spinal injuries.

Frequency: Quarterly

3939 Nexus Magazine
Back Office
PO Box 61363
Denver, CO 80206-8363
303-333-5310
Fax: 303-333-5335

Duncan Roads, Editor

Contains news on alternative health, politics, science, and metaphysics.

Frequency: Semimonthly

3940 Nutrition Health Review
PO Box 406
Haverford, PA 19041
610-896-1853
Fax: 610-896-1857

Frank R Rifkin, Editor
Andrew Rifkin, Publisher

Health magazine (tabloid).

Frequency: Quarterly

3941 PN
Paralyzed Veterans of America
2111 E Highland Avenue
Suite 180
Phoenix, AZ 85016
602-224-0500
888-888-2201
Fax: 602-224-0507
e-mail: info@pnnews.cm
http://www.pn-magazine.com

Cliff Crase, Editor
Sherri Shea, Marketing Director

Magazine spotlighting independent living for paraplegics and quadriplegics.

Frequency: Monthly

3942 Perspective on Aging
National Council on the Aging
600 Maryland Avenue SW
Washington, DC 20024-2520
202-554-5981
800-867-2755
Fax: 202-479-0735

Explores significant developments in the field of aging, including disabilities, through opinion articles, profiles and book reviews.

3943 Physical & Occupational Therapy in Geriatrics
The Haworth Press
10 Alice Street
Binghamton, NY 13904-1503
607-722-5857
800-429-6784
Fax: 607-771-0012
e-mail: getinfo@haworthpressinc.com

Jane Corvell, Editor
Ellen Dunleavey, Editor
William Cohen, Owner

Journal for allied health professionals focusing on current practice and emerging issues in the health care of and rehabilitation of the older client.

Frequency: Quarterly

3944 Physical Disabilities—Education & Related Services
Council for Exceptional Children
1920 Association Drive
Reston, VA 20191-1500
703-620-3660
888-CEC-SPED
Fax: 703-264-1637

Barbara Kulik, Editor

Professional magazine covering research, instructional innovations and issues regarding education and physical disabilities.

Frequency: Semiannual

3945 Plus Magazine
Plus Magazie
793 Higuera Street
Suite 10
San Luis Obispo, CA 93401
805-544-8711
Fax: 805-544-4450

George Brand, Editor
Steve Owens, Publisher
Michael Ortiz, Ad Director

Magazine featuring topics of interest for seniors 4 color magazine.

56 pages

3946 Polio Network News
Gazette International Networking Institute
4207 Lindell Boulevard
Suite 110
Saint Louis, MO 63108-2930
314-534-0475
Fax: 314-534-5070
e-mail: gini_intl@msn.com
http://www.post-polio.org

Joan L Headley, Executive Director

Quarterly newsletter for polio survivors. Contains current information about the late efects of polio, encourages research and promotes networking among the post-polio community worldwide. Publish an annual Post-Polio Directory.

12 pages Frequency: Quarterly

3947 Post-Polio Health International
Gazette International Networking Institute
4207 Lindell Boulevard
Suite 110
Saint Louis, MO 63108-2930
314-534-0475
Fax: 314-534-5070
e-mail: info@post-polio.org
http://www.post-polio.org

Joan L Headley, Executive Director

International concerning independent living for persons who are survivors of polio and other disabilities. Newsletter is called "Post-Polio Health."

8 pages Frequency: Biannual

3948 Prevention
Rodale Press
33 E Minor Street
Emmaus, PA 18098
610-967-5171
Fax: 910-967-8963

Mark Bricklin, Editor
Ken Wallace, Publisher
Carol Petrako, Mailing Contact

Aging/Journals, Magazines

Magazine containing articles on wellness, preventive medicine, self-care, and fitness.

Frequency: Monthly

3949 Prime Health & Fitness
Weider Publications
21100 Erwin Street
Woodland Hills, CA 91367-3772
818-884-6800
800-423-5590
Fax: 818-704-5734

Peter McGough, Manager
David Kalmansohn, Editor
Mike Carlson, Editor

Consumer magazine covering health, fitness, and lifestyle for men over 35 years.

Frequency: Quarterly

3950 Reach Out Magazine
Reach Out Magazine
3090 Sheridan Street
Suite 207
Hollywood, FL 33021-3730
954-985-0319
Fax: 954-985-0483
e-mail: jim@reachoutmag.com
http://www.reachoutmag.com

Jim Jakubek, Publisher

Online magazine by and for people with disabilities. Features personal ads, human interest stories, articles, advice, support group listings, humor, chat, resources, members only E-mail list and more. Free by subscription.

3951 Remedy
RX Remedy
120 Post Road W
Westport, CT 06880-4206
203-341-7000
Fax: 203-221-4913

Joan Montgomery, Publisher

Consumer magazine covering health and wellness for individuals over 50 years in the US.

Frequency: Bimonthly

3952 Research on Aging
Sage Publications
2455 Teller Road
Thousand Oaks, CA 91320-2218
805-499-0721
Fax: 805-499-0871
e-mail: info@sagepub.com

Angela M O'Rand, Editor
Blaise R Simqu, CEO

Social gerontology journal.

Frequency: Bimonthly

3953 Retirement Community Business
Great River Publishing
4719 Spottswood Avenue
Memphis, TN 38117-4818
901-762-0329
Fax: 901-762-0718

Sherry Campbell, Editor

Magazine for operators and managers of retirement communities.

Frequency: Quarterly

3954 Retirement Life
National Association of Retired Federal Employees
1533 New Hampshire Avenue NW
Washington, DC 20036-1203
202-234-0832
Fax: 202-797-9698

Kathleen E Delaney, Mailing Contact/Editor

Magazine for federal civil service retirees and employees.

Frequency: Monthly

3955 SELF Magazine
Conde Nast Publications
350 Madison Avenue
New York, NY 10017-3700
212-286-2860
800-223-0780
Fax: 212-880-8248

Rochelle Udell, Editor-in-Chief
Larry Burstein, Publisher

Magazine serving as a health sourcebook for contemporary women.

Frequency: Monthly

3956 Sandwich Generation
Carol Abaya Associates
PO Box 132
Wickatunk, NJ 07765
732-536-6215

Carol Abaya, Publisher

Consumer magazine covering aging issues and all aspects of elder parent care.

Frequency: Quarterly

3957 Secure Retirement, The Newsmagazine for Mature Americans
Nat Committee To Preserve Social Security/Medicare
2000 K Street NW
Suite 800
Washington, DC 20006-1860
202-822-9459
Fax: 202-822-9612

Denise Fremeau, Editor
Jack McDavitt, Editor

Magazine for senior citizens and others interested in politics and government and how they affect senior concerns and issues.

3958 Senior Times Magazine
Senior Times Magazine
PO Box 7325
Winter Haven, FL 33883-7325
941-294-9376
Fax: 941-293-2505

Judy A Kahler, Editor
Bill Bowen, Mailing Contacy

Magazine devoted to educating senior citizens on recreational, political, health and financial issues.

Frequency: Monthly

3959 Serenity
Little Sisters of The Poor
601 Maiden Choice Lane
Baltimore, MD 21228-3630
410-744-9367
Fax: 410-788-5614

S R Marguerite, Publications Coordinator

Magazine making known the apostolate of Little Sisters of the Poor and providing a positive view of the elderly and the respect due them.

32 pages Frequency: Quarterly

3960 Sign Language Studies
Linstock Press
4020 Blackburn Lane
Burtonsville, MD 20866-1167
301-421-0268
800-475-4756
Fax: 303-759-0359
e-mail: signmedial@aol.com

Verden Ness, President

Magazine concerning the use of primary and alternative sign languages.

Frequency: Quarterly

3961 Specialty Cooking Magazine
Lifetime Periodicals
2131 Hollywood Boulevard
Hollywood, FL 33020-6759
954-925-5242
Fax: 954-925-5244
e-mail: lifetime@shadow.net

Donald Lessne, President

Consumer magazine covering cooking, health and fitness.

Frequency: Quarterly

Aging/Newspapers

3962 Spirit of Change Magazine
Spirit of Change Magazine
PO Box 405
Uxbridge, MA 01569
508-839-2228
Fax: 508-839-1173

Carol Bedrosian, Publisher/Editor
Sosie Sagjer, Advertising Manager

Consumer magazine covering holistic health and New Age issues.

Frequency: Bimonthly

3963 Total Health
Total Health
6001 Topanga Canyon Boulevard
Suite 300
Woodland Hills, CA 91367-3625
818-887-6484
Fax: 818-887-7960

Robert L Smith, Publisher/Editor
Jeff Ward, Advertising

Magazine devoted to fitness and preventive health.

Frequency: Bimonthly

3964 VANTAGE
Signature Group
200 N Martingale Road
Schaumburg, IL 60173-2040
847-605-4601
Fax: 847-605-4595

Paul Misniak, Publisher
Joanie Davies, Mailing Contact

Magazine for active consumers over 55 years of age.

Frequency: Bimonthly

3965 VFW Auxiliary
Ladies Auxiliary to the VFW
406 W 34th Street
Kansas City, MO 64111-2767
816-968-2792
Fax: 816-931-4753
e-mail: info@ladiesauxvfw.com

Marilyn Ebersole, Mailing Contact/Editor
Jim Lierz, President

VFW auxiliary patriotic services magazine.

3966 Vegetarian Journal
The Vegetarian Resource Group
PO Box 1463
Baltimore, MD 21203-1463
410-366-8343
Fax: 410-366-8804
e-mail: vrg@vrg.org
http://www.wrg.org

Debra Warserman, Editor

Recipes and news related to vegetarianism.

36 pages Frequency: Quarterly

3967 Vegetarian Times
Cowles Enthusiast Media
4 High Ridge Park
Stamford, CT 06905-1325
203-322-2400
Fax: 203-322-1966
e-mail: susant@cowles.com

Susan Tauster, Contact
Gerry Calahan, Manager

Magazine devoted to vegetarian food and related topics such as health, fitness, and the environment.

3968 Vegetarian Voice
North American Vegetarian Society
PO Box 72
Dolgeville, NY 13329
518-568-7970
Fax: 518-568-7979
e-mail: navs@telenet.net
http://www.navs-online.org

Maribeth Abrams, Managing Editor
Brian Graff, Executive Manager

Consumer magazine covering vegetarianism, health, cooking, environmental and animal protection issues.

40 pages Frequency: Quarterly

3969 Veggie Life
EGW Publishing Company
4075 Papazian Way
208
Fremont, CA 94538-4300
925-671-9852
Fax: 925-671-0692

Shanna Masters, Editor
Rickie Wilson, Advertising Manager

Consumer magazine covering health, nutrition, and vegetarian cooking.

68 pages Frequency: Quarterly

3970 Vim & Vigor Magazine
McMurray Publishing
8805 N 23rd Avenue
Suite 11
Phoenix, AZ 85021-4171
602-395-5850
800-282-5850
Fax: 602-395-5853

Fred Petrovsky, Editor
Preston McMurry, Publisher
Chris McMurry, CEO

Magazine offering articles on health, fitness, and medical research.

Frequency: Quarterly

3971 Walking
Reader's Digest Publications
28 W 23rd Street
New York, NY 10010-5204
212-366-8853
800-937-9241
Fax: 212-633-4699

Seth Bauer, Editor

Magazine for recreational and fitness walkers; includes articles on health, fitness, nutrition, travel, gear and equipment, and events.

Frequency: Bimonthly

3972 Whole Life
Whole Life Enterprises
PO Box 2058
New York, NY 10159-2058

Marc Medoff, Publisher/Editor

Magazine focusing on the mind-body-spirit connection, with emphasis on dietary awareness and personal health.

Frequency: Bimonthly

3973 Your Health
Meridian International
PO Box 10010
Ogden, UT 84409-1610
801-394-9446
Fax: 801-627-1453

Magazine profiling health care, fitness, and nutritional needs of senior citizens.

Frequency: Monthly

Newspapers

3974 AARP Bulletin
AARP
601 E Street NW
Washington, DC 20049
202-434-2277
800-424-3410
Fax: 202-434-3443
e-mail: member@aarp.org
http://www.aarp.org

Elliot Carlson, Editor
Martha Ramsey, Advertising Director
William Novelli, CEO

Newspaper for mature Americans.

Frequency: Monthly

Aging/Newspapers

3975 Aging Today
American Society on Aging
833 Market Street
Suite 511
San Francisco, CA 94103-1824
415-974-9600
800-537-9728
Fax: 415-974-0300
e-mail: info@asa.asaging.org
Gloria Cavanaugh, Executive Director
Newspaper (tabloid) for health, social service, and other professionals who work with older people.

3976 Alliance Newspaper
Alliance Newspaper
PO Box 5164
Bradford, MA 01835
508-373-3291
Fax: 508-373-3291
Focusing on health and human services for health care and human service professionals, their clients, and the general public.

3977 Black Health
Altier & Maynard Communications
53 Oakwood Drive
Madison, CT 06443-1823
Fax: 203-431-6454
Bonnie Maynard, Publisher
Carlos Maynard, Publisher
Frequency: Quarterly

3978 Bulletin
AARP Fulfillment
601 E Street NW
Washington, DC 20049
202-434-2277
800-424-3410
Fax: 202-434-3443
e-mail: member@aarp.org
http://www.aarp.org
William Novelli, CEO
Frequency: 11x/year

3979 Fifty Plus Advocate
131 Lincoln Street
Worcester, MA 01605-2408
508-752-3400
Fax: 508-752-9057
http://www.fiftyplusadvocates.com
Reva Capellan, Office Manager
Karen Higgins, Editor
Philip Davis, Publisher
Newspaper for senior citizens.

3980 Golden Times
Golden Times Piano Works Mall
349 W Commercial Street
Suite 1025
East Rochester, NY 14445-2419
585-586-1445
Fax: 585-586-2093
e-mail: news@goldentimes.com
http://www.goldentimes.com
Carmen Viglucci, President
John Viglucci, VP
Senior citizen newspaper.
Frequency: Bi-Monthly

3981 HEALTH & YOU
Health Ink Communications
1 Executive Drive
Moorestown, NJ 08057-4222
856-778-0011
Fax: 856-778-4422
e-mail: healthlink@healthlink.com
Lou Antosh, President
Craig Ammerman, Contact
Consumer-oriented health publications distributed by hospitals, corporations, and managed care companies.
Frequency: Quarterly

3982 Health Perspective
Clayton-Davis & Associates
8229 Maryland Avenue
Saint Louis, MO 63105-3643
314-862-7800
Fax: 314-721-5171
Ruth Sirko, Editor
Mary Brown, Advertising Manager
Jennifer Jermak, President
Consumer health tabloid.
Frequency: Monthly

3983 Jewish Veteran
Jewish Veteran
1811 R Street NW
Washington, DC 20009-1659
202-265-6280
Fax: 202-234-5662
e-mail: jwv@erols.com
Tim Clarke, Managing Editor
Larry Richardson, Manager

3984 Lovin' Life After 50
PO Box 750146
Las Vegas, NV 89136
702-367-6709
Fax: 702-367-6883
http://www.lovinlife.com
Debbie Close, Account Executive
Newspaper for senior citizens.
Frequency: Monthly

3985 Mature American
Alternative Publications
1123 N Water Street
Milwaukee, WI 53202-6637
414-276-2222
800-516-2220
Fax: 414-276-3312
Newspaper for senior citizens.

3986 McCall's Prime Time
Y&J USA Publishing
375 Lexington Avenue
New York, NY 10017-5644
212-499-2000
Fax: 212-499-1778
David Mevorah, Publisher
Publication featuring articles for over 50 readers.
Frequency: Bimonthly

3987 New York Times Large Type Weekly
New York Times Company
229 W 43rd Street
New York, NY 10036-3913
212-556-1234
e-mail: dame@nytimes.com
Robert H Eoff, President
Newspaper for persons with impaired vision.

3988 Prime Time
PrimeTime Media Newspaper
PO Box 475
Bend, OR 97709
541-267-6587
Fax: 541-267-6587
e-mail: crow@koalas.com
Senior citizens newspaper (tabloid).

3989 Prime Times
Prime Times
47 Route 25a
Setauket, NY 11733-2858
631-246-6478
Fax: 516-689-3077
Rachael Krier, Editor
Ailee Heyen, Advertising Directro
Lynn Allopenna, Manager
Consumer publication featuring articles of interest to adults 45 years of age or older.
Frequency: Monthly

Aging/Newsletters, Pamphlets

3990 Regular
Regular Veterans Association
PO Box 511
Del Valle, TX 78617   512-389-2288
                        Fax: 512-389-1444
Newspaper (tabloid) covering pay, compensation, and medical benefits for veterans and military.

3991 Senior Citizen News
Senior Citizen News
621 N Ferncreek Avenue
Orlando, FL 32803-4836
                        Fax: 407-898-4613
Newspaper for senior citizens.

3992 Senior Times
Senior Times
523 N Pines Road
Spokane Valley, WA 99206-5124   509-924-2440
                        Fax: 509-927-1154
Mike Huffman, Manager
Newspaper for 50 market.

3993 Senior World Newsmagazine
Kendall Communications
PO Box 1565E1
El Cajon, CA 92022   619-593-2900
                        Fax: 619-442-4043
Newspaper (tabloid) for active older adults.

Newsletters, Pamphlets

3994 A Lifetime of Freedom from Smoking
American Lung Association
1740 Broadway
New York, NY 10019-4315   212-315-8700
                        Fax: 212-315-8870
John Kirkwood, CEO
Companion manual helps persons stay quit once they have stopped smoking.
28 pages

3995 A Profile of Older Americans
AARP
601 E Street NW
Washington, DC 20049   202-434-2277
                              800-424-3410
                        Fax: 202-434-3443
                e-mail: member@aarp.org
                    http://www.aarp.org
William D Novelli, CEO
Offers information on aging, retirement, illnesses and more for the elderly population.

3996 AAHA Provider News
American Assn. of Homes & Services for the Aging
901 E Street NW
Suite 500
Washington, DC 20004-2037   202-661-5700
                              800-508-
                        Fax: 301-206-9789
Daniel Smith, Vice President
Keeps nonprofit aging service providers informed of new trends and developments in quality of care for older persons.

3997 AARP Newsletter
601 E Street NW
Washington, DC 20049   202-434-2277
                              800-424-3410
                        Fax: 202-434-6451
                    http://www.aarp.org
William D Novelli, CEO
4 pages Frequency: Bimonthly

3998 AARP Pharmacy Service
601 E Street NW
Washington, DC 20049   202-434-2277
                        Fax: 202-434-6483
                    http://www.aarp.org
William D Novelli, CEO
4 pages Frequency: Bimonthly

3999 ADARA Updated
ADARA
PO Box 251554
Little Rock, AR 72225-1554   501-868-8850
                        Fax: 501-868-8812
Nanncy Long PhD, Editor
Updates readers on events, resources, legislation, information of national interest, conferences, workshops and employment opportunities. Information from and about local chapters, special interest sections, and national organizations is included in this publication.

4000 AGHE Exchange Newsletter
Association for Gerontology in Higher Education
1030 15th Street NW
Suite 240
Washington, DC 20005-1527   202-289-9806
                        Fax: 202-289-9824
                e-mail: ctompkins@aghe.org
Kathleen A Segrist, Editor
Derek Stepp, Manager
16-20 pages Frequency: Quarterly

4001 ARC's Government Report
Association for Retarded Citizens
1522 K Street NW
Washington, DC 20005-1202   202-785-3388
                        Fax: 202-467-4179
Reports on government activities related to individuals with disabilities with a focus on persons with mental retardation.

4002 AUL Forum
Americans United for Life
343 S Dearborn Street
Apt 1804
Chicago, IL 60604-4472   312-756-9494
                        Fax: 312-786-2131
Mary Ann Reardon, Editor
Frequency: Quarterly

4003 Ability
George J DePontis
PO Box 370788
Miami, FL 33137   305-751-2525
                        Fax: 305-754-1111
Features articles on living, working, playing and entertainment for the disabled.

4004 Abstracts in Social Gerontology
Sage Publications
2455 Teller Road
Thousand Oaks, CA 91320-2218 805-499-0721
                        Fax: 805-499-0871
                e-mail: info@sagepub.com
Julie L Moore, Editor
Jane Saquet, Publisher
Blaise R Simqu, CEO
Annotated bibliography of books, journal articles, and documents relevant to social gerontology.
Frequency: Quarterly

4005 Aging Alert
115 W Allegan Street
Suite 210
Lansing, MI 48933-1783   517-483-4871
                        Fax: 517-482-6866
4 pages

Aging/Newsletters, Pamphlets

4006 Aging Network News
PO Box 2018
Merrifield, VA 22116-2018
703-289-4670
Fax: 703-289-4678
Bob Hansan, Owner

Publishes articles on all aspects of aging including legislation, innovative programs and services.

4007 Aging Research and Training News
Business Publishers
8737 Colesville Road
Suite 1100
Silver Spring, MD 20910-3956
301-589-5103
Fax: 301-587-4530
Nancy Aldrich, Editor

Reports on sources of government and private sector grant and contract opportunities.

10 pages Frequency: Monthly

4008 American Geriatrics Society Newsletter
American Geriatrics Society
770 Lexington Avenue
Suite 300
New York, NY 10021-8165
212-308-1414
Fax: 212-832-8646
e-mail: info.amger@americangeriatrics.org
Ann D Gross, Editor

16-20 pages Frequency: Quarterly

4009 American Health Care Association
1201 L Street NW
Washington, DC 20005-4046
202-842-4444
Fax: 202-842-3860
Dave Kyllo, Vice President

8 pages

4010 American Health Consultants
3525 Piedmont Road
Building 6
Atlanta, GA 30305
404-262-7436
800-688-2421
Fax: 404-262-7837
e-mail: custerv@ahcpub.com
Jeff MacDonald, EVP

16 pages Frequency: Monthly

4011 American Senior Newsletter
Butler County Department on Aging
510 E Augusta Avenue
Augusta, KS 67019
316-775-0500
800-279-3655
Fax: 316-775-0555
http://www.bucoks.com
Connie Rausch, Director
Brenda Louthan, Assistant Director/Program Mgr

Subscription is free, but donations to help offset postage are apprectiated.

4012 Americans with Disabilities Act Manual:State and Local Government Services
American Bar Association
740 15th Street NW
Washington, DC 20005-1019
202-662-1570
Fax: 202-662-1032
e-mail: cmpdl@abanet.org
http://www.abanet.org/disability
Sarina Khan, Office Administrator
Amy Allbright, Managing Editor
John Parry, Executive Director

An in-depth analysis of the legal and practical implications of the ADA using non-technical language.

4013 Americans with Disabilities Act Resource Manual
Arthritis Foundation
PO Box 7669
Atlanta, GA 30357
404-872-7100
800-283-7800
Fax: 404-872-0457
http://www.arthritis.org
John H Klippel, CEO

4014 Anti-Aging Press/So Young Catalog/So Young Newsletter
PO Box 1489
Coral Gables, FL 33114
305-662-3928
800-SOY-OUNG
Fax: 305-661-4123
e-mail: julia2@gate.net
http://www.anti-agingprss.com
Julia Busch, President

Publishes self-help materials. Also publishes So Young newsletter. Offers audio cassettes. Reaches market through commission representatives, direct mail, telephone sales, trade sales, and wholesalers and distributors, including Baker & Taylor Books. Researches marketplace for products that really work. From a natural facelift to natural hormone replacement, free consultation via telephone.

12 pages Frequency: Bi Monthly

4015 Audiology Express
American Academy of Audiology
1735 N Lynn Street
Suite 950
Arlington, VA 22209-2013
703-524-1923
800-222-
Fax: 703-524-2303

4016 Between Classes
Elderhostel
75 Federal Street
Boston, MA 02110-1913
617-426-7788
Fax: 617-426-8351
http://www.elderhostel.org
Cady Goldfield, Editor
James Moses, CEO

4017 Bulletin on Long-Term Care Law
Health Resources
1913 Atlantic Avenue
Suite F4
Manasquan, NJ 08736-1029
732-292-1100
Fax: 732-292-1111
http://www.healthresourcesonline.com
Robert K Jenkins, Publisher

Covers federal and state laws and regulations governing long-term care facilities, compliance problems, changes to the Medicare and Medicaid programs, litigation and coverage of news of importance to long-term care providers.

4018 Capsule Newsletter
Children of Aging Parents
1609 Woodbourne Road
Suite 302a
Levittown, PA 19057-1500
215-945-6900
800-227-7294
Fax: 215-945-8720
Thomas Humphrey, Editor

4-8 pages Frequency: Bimonthly

4019 Carbohydrate Counting
Chronimed Publishing
PO Box 59032
Minneapolis, MN 55459
612-513-6475
800-848-2793
Fax: 952-443-2806

Using sample meal plans and actual food labels, this booklet explains how carbohydrate counting can add flexibility to meal plans.

12 pages

Aging/Newsletters, Pamphlets

4020 Center for Aging Newsletter
University of Alabama at Birmingham
933 19th Street S
Room 201
Birmingham, AL 35294
205-934-3007
Fax: 205-975-5930

Robert M Centor, MD
8 pages Frequency: Monthly

4021 Cigarette Smoking
American Lung Association
1740 Broadway
New York, NY 10019-4315
212-315-8700
Fax: 212-315-8870

John Kirkwood, CEO

Leaflet presenting the facts about how cigarette smoke is related to lung disease.

4022 Consumer Information Catalog
Federal Consumer Information Center
Pueblo, CO 81009-0001
888-878-3256
Fax: 719-948-9724
e-mail: catalog.pueblo@gsa.gov
http://www.pueblo.gsa.gov

Judi Mahaney, Public Affairs

This catalog lists more than 200 free and low cost publications from federal agencies. Topics covered include federal benefits, food, health, housing, travel, cars and much more.

4023 Council for Disability Rights
20 N Wacker Drive
Suite 1540
Chicago, IL 60606-2903
312-444-9484
Fax: 312-444-1977
e-mail: cdrights@interaccess.com
http://www.disabilityrights.org

Josephine E Holzer, Executive Director/Editor
Dorie Stewart, Information Specialist

Promotes human rights of persons with disabilities and their families. Offers a job placement service, legal referrals, information services, a website and monthly newsletter (CDR Reports).

4024 Currents
Association of Homes and Services for the Aging
901 E Street NW
Suite 500
Washington, DC 20004-2037
202-661-5700
Fax: 202-783-2255

Marion M Dinitz, Editor
Daniel Smith, Vice President
20 pages

4025 Disability Compliance Bulletin
LRP Publications
747 Dresher Road
980
Horsham, PA 19044-2247
215-784-0941
800-341-7874
Fax: 215-784-9639
e-mail: custserve@lrp.com
http://www.lrp.com

Honora O'Connell, Product Group Manager

This biweekly newsletter gives you timely coverage and insightful analyses of the latest developments in disability law. You'll learn the most recent case law dealing with the Americans with Disabilities Act, the Family and Medical Leave Act, and more. Disability Compliance Bulletin will help you understand the laws' obligations and show you emerging legal trends.

24 pages Frequency: Biweekly

4026 Disability Notes
Social Security Admin Office of Disability
545 Altmeyer Building
Baltimore, MD 21235
410-965-3987
Fax: 410-965-6503

Newsletter focusing on disability programs offered by Social Security and other agencies.

Frequency: Quarterly

4027 Disability Rights Now
Disability Rights Education and Defense Fund
2212 6th Street
Berkeley, CA 94710-2219
510-644-2555
800-466-4232
Fax: 510-841-8645

Sue Henderson, Executive Director

Free quarterly publication describing the activities of the Disability Rights Education and Defense Fund, available in alternative formats.

Frequency: Quarterly

4028 Don't Let Your Dreams Go Up in Smoke
American Lung Association
1740 Broadway
New York, NY 10019-4315
212-315-8700
Fax: 212-315-8870

John Kirkwood, CEo

Photos, testimonials and clear language to deliver the message that everyone can and should stop smoking.

4029 Federal Laws of the Mentally Handicapped: Laws, Legislative Histories and Admin. Documents
William Hein & Company
1285 Main Street
Buffalo, NY 14209-1911
716-882-2600
800-828-7571
Fax: 716-883-8100
e-mail: mail@wshein.com
http://www.wshein.com

Kevin Marmion, President

Chronological compilation of all relevant federal laws dealing with the mentally handicapped along with supporting documentation necessary to create a complete legislative history.

Frequency: 42 Volumes

4030 Finance Over 50
Ron Jackson Company
22 Yankee Hill
Oakland, CA 94618-2332
510-704-9490
800-769-6310
Fax: 510-704-0177

Jeff Carter, Editor
8 pages Frequency: Monthly

4031 Five Good Food Habits for People with Diabetes
Chronimed Publishing
PO Box 59032
Minneapolis, MN 55459
612-513-6475
800-848-2793
Fax: 952-443-2806

Focuses on simple changes in eating behavior that can help control blood glucose levels and weight.

29 pages Frequency: Pack of 10

4032 Foot Care
Chronimed Publishing
PO Box 59032
Minneapolis, MN 55459
612-513-6475
800-848-2793
Fax: 952-443-2806

4033 Freedom From Smoking Flyer
American Lung Association
1740 Broadway
New York, NY 10019-4315
212-614-2800
Fax: 212-315-8870

Hugh Fordin, President

4 color flyer describing all FFS programs.

Aging/Newsletters, Pamphlets

4034 Geriatric Rehabilitation Preview
RTC on Aging
7600 Consuelo Street
Downey, CA 90242-4155   310-940-7402

Covers research and training activities of the Center and other issues pertaining to the rehabilitation of elderly persons with disabilities.

4035 Gerontology News
Gerontological Society of America
1030 15th Street NW
Suite 250
Washington, DC 20005-1526   202-842-1275
Fax: 202-842-1150
e-mail: geron@geron.org
http://www.geron.org

Shirley V Brown, Editor
L Harootyan, Mananging Editor
Carol Schutz, Executive Director
12 pages Frequency: Monthly

4036 Gerontology Special Interest Section Quarterly
American Occupational Therapy Association
PO Box 31220
Bethesda, MD 20824-1220   301-652-6611
800-877-1383
Fax: 301-652-7711
e-mail: ajotsis@asta.org
http://www.asta.org

Barbara Scanlon, Managing Editor

Quarterly newsletter for occupational therapy practitioners, focusing on issues relating to gerontology practice.

4 pages Frequency: Quarterly

4037 Have Fun! Figure Out the Smoking Puzzle
American Lung Association
1740 Broadway
New York, NY 10019-4315   212-315-8700
Fax: 212-315-8870

John Kirkwood, CEO

Crossword puzzles make stimulating points on the effects of smoking.

4038 Healing Choices
Healing Choices
144 Saint Johns Place
Brooklyn, NY 11217-3402   718-636-4433
Fax: 718-616-0186
e-mail: mail@ralphmoss.com
http://www.ralphmoss.com

A unique series of in-depth reports on nearly every cancer diagnosis. Choose the report that corresponds to the exact type of cancer you are concerned with, and within days you will receceive Dr. Moss's report on the most successful alternative and complementary treatment approaches relevant to the condition.

4039 Health After 50: Johns Hopkins Medical Letter
Medletter Associates
PO Box 420179
Palm Coast, FL 32142   386-446-4675
Fax: 386-447-2321

Health newsletter for people over 50.

10 pages Frequency: 12

4040 Health Legislation and Regulation
Faulkner & Gray
11 Penn Plaza
Floor 17
New York, NY 10001-2006   212-967-7000
800-535-8403
Fax: 212-967-7180
e-mail: order@faulknergray.com
http://www.faulknergray.com

Stephanie Stapleton, Editor
4-12 pages Frequency: Weekly

4041 Health Resources Publishing
Brinley Professional Plaza
PO Box 1442
Wall, NJ 07719-1442   732-681-1133
800-516-4343

8-10 pages Frequency: Monthly

4042 Home Health Line
United Communications Group
11300 Rockville Pike
Suite 1100
Rockville, MD 20852-3012   301-287-2700
800-929-4824
Fax: 301-287-2049

Jason Huffman, Editor
Todd Foreman, Partner
8-16 pages Frequency: Weekly

4043 Hospice Letter
Health Resources
1913 Atlantic Avenue
Suite F4
Manasquan, NJ 08736-1029   732-292-1100
Fax: 732-292-1111
http://www.healthresourcesonline.com

Robert K Jenkins, Publisher

4044 Hospital Home Health
American Health Consultants
3525 Pwidmont Road
Building 6
Atlanta, GA 30305   404-262-7436
800-688-2421
Fax: 404-262-7837
e-mail: custserv@ahcpub.com

Park Morgan, Editor
Jeff MacDonald, EVP
12-16 pages Frequency: Monthly

4045 Housing for Seniors Report
CD Publications
8204 Fenton Street
Silver Spring, MD 20910-4502   301-588-6380
Fax: 301-588-6385
e-mail: info@cdpublications.com
http://www.cdpublications.com

Michael Gerecht, President

Monthly newsletter with practical advice for senior housing managers on marketing, financing and management issues.

4046 How to Feel & Look Nifty After 50
Golden Aspen Publishing
PO Box 370333
Denver, CO 80237   303-694-6555
800-639-9664
Fax: 303-694-0737
e-mail: GAPub@concentric.net

Jo Peddicord, Publisher

Publishes books on image and health tips for women over age 50. Does not accept unsolicited manuscripts. Reaches market through direct mail, trade sales, and wholesalers and distributors, including Ingram Book Co., Baker & Taylor Books, and Quality Books.

178 pages

4047 IDF Patient and Family Handbook
Immune Deficiency Foundation
25 W Chesapeake Avenue
Suite 206
Towson, MD 21204-4841   410-321-6647
800-296-4433
Fax: 410-321-9165

Marcia Boyle, CEO

Aging / Newsletters, Pamphlets

4048 ILRU Insights
ILRU Research/Training Center Independent Living
2323 S Shepherd Drive
Suite 1000
Houston, TX 77019-7031
713-520-0232
Fax: 713-520-5785

Laurie Redd, Executive Director

The national newsletter for independent living offers the reader information on laws, social issues, medicine and more for the disabled person.

10 pages

4049 IRA Reporter
Universal Pensions
PO Box 979
Brainerd, MN 56401
218-829-4781
800-346-3860
Fax: 218-829-2106

Jennifer M Norquist, Editor

8 pages Frequency: Monthly

4050 Impotence Causes and Treatments
American Medical Systems
1101 Bren Road E
Minnetonka, MN 55343
952-933-4666

Offers information on what impotence is, physical and emotional causes, treatments, questions and answers.

4051 Informer
Simon Foundation for Incontinence
PO Box 815
Wilmette, IL 60091
847-864-3913
800-223-1360
Fax: 847-864-9768
http://www.simonfoundation.org

Cheryle B Gartley, President

Seeks to bring the topic of incontinence out of the closet and remove the associated stigma; provides information to patients, their families, and the health care professionals who provide patient care.

4052 International Ventilator Users Network (IVUN) News
Gazette International Networking Institute
4207 Lindell Boulevard
Suite 110
Saint Louis, MO 63108-2930
314-534-0475
Fax: 314-534-5070
e-mail: gini_intl@msn.com
http://www.post-polio.org/ivun.html

Joan L Headley, Executive Director

IVUN is a worldwide network of ventilator users and health professionals experienced in and committed to home care and long term mechanical ventilation. IVUN News, a quarterly newsletter, offers articles on family adjustments, equipment, techniques, travel, ethical issues, medical topics, and resources. ISSN# 1066-534x. We also publish the annual IVUN Resource Directory. ($5.00)

8 pages Frequency: Quarterly

4053 Intestinal Fortitude
Intestinal Disease Foundation
1 Station Square
0
Pittsburgh, PA 15219-1120
412-261-5888
Fax: 412-471-2722

Linda Schorr, Executive Director

Newsletter, brochures and books for Intestinal Disease Foundation members.

4054 Is There a Safe Tobacco?
American Lung Association
1740 Broadway
New York, NY 10019-4315
212-315-8700
Fax: 212-315-8870

John Kirkwood, CEO

Offers information on the health risks of cigarette smoking, pipes and cigars.

4055 Knowing Your Rights
AARP Fulfillment
601 E Street NW
Washington, DC 20049
202-434-2277
800-424-3410
Fax: 202-434-3443
e-mail: member@aarp.org
http://www.aarp.org

William D Novelli, CEO

Describes how changes in Medicare's reimbursement policies are designed to reduce health care costs and suggests steps that Medicare beneficiaries, their families and friends can take to assure that they continue to receive quality care under the Prospective Payment System.

19 pages

4056 Legal Action Center
236 Massachusetts Avenue NE
Suite 510
Washington, DC 20002-4972
202-544-5478
Fax: 202-544-5712
e-mail: 76726.2112@compuserve.com

Willery Murray, Manager

Provides technical assistance and education programs for employers and employees on ADA issues related to individuals with drug and alcohol abuse and HIV disease.

4057 Let's Solve the Smokeword Puzzle
American Lung Association
1740 Broadway
New York, NY 10019-4315
212-315-8700
Fax: 212-315-8870

John Kirkwood, CEO

Fifth graders will love getting an antismoking message through solving a crossword puzzle.

4058 Lifetime of Freedom from Smoking Maintenance Manual
American Lung Association
1740 Broadway
New York, NY 10019-4315
212-315-8700
Fax: 212-315-8870

John Kirkwood, CEO

Companion manual helps persons stay quit once they have stopped smoking.

28 pages

4059 Manisses Communications Group
Fraser A Lang
208 Governor Street
Providence, RI 02906-3246
401-831-6020
800-333-7771
Fax: 401-861-6370
e-mail: manissesls@manisses.com
http://www.manisses.com

Richard J Goldberg MD, Editor
Karienne Stovell, Senior Managing Editor
Fraser Lang, Owner

Publishes the Brown University Geriatric Psychopharmacy Update- updates on the use of psychotropic medications in geriatrics.

4060 Medical Utilization Management
Faulkner & Gray
11 Penn Plaza
Floor 17
New York, NY 10001-2006
212-967-7000
800-535-8403
Fax: 212-967-7180
e-mail: order@faulknergray.com
http://www.faulknergray.com

Kenneth Moss, Mailing Contact/Editor

8 pages Frequency: Semimonthly

Aging/Newsletters, Pamphlets

4061 My Activity Plan
Chronimed Publishing
PO Box 59032
Minneapolis, MN 55459
612-513-6475
800-848-2793
Fax: 952-443-2806

Teaches how to increase daily and weekly physical activity, evaluate progress, and set goals.

4062 My Food Plan
Chronimed Publishing
PO Box 59032
Minneapolis, MN 55459
612-513-6475
800-848-2793
Fax: 952-443-2806

Includes food lists, serving sizes, and a personal food plan form. Incorporates carbohydrate counting and ADA nutrition guidelines.

4063 My Personal Goals
Chronimed Publishing
PO Box 59032
Minneapolis, MN 55459
612-513-6475
800-848-2793
Fax: 952-443-2806

Guides patients in setting reasonable, individualized goals for better health and diabetes management.

4064 NAHC Report
National Association for Home Care
228 7th Street SE
Washington, DC 20003-4306
202-547-7424
Fax: 202-547-3540
e-mail: dcs@nahc.org
http://www.nahc.org

Dana Sacks, Managing Editor
6-16 pages Frequency: Weekly

4065 NARIC Quarterly
National Rehabilitation Information Center
8455 Colesville Road
Suite 935
Silver Spring, MD 20910-3315
301-588-9284
800-346-2742
Fax: 301-587-1967
http://www.naric.com/naric
TDD 301-495-5626

Dan Wendling, Managing Editor
Jessica Chalken, Media Specialist
18 pages Frequency: Quarterly

4066 NCD Bulletin
National Council on Disability
1331 F Street NW
Suite 1050
Washington, DC 20004-1162
202-272-2004
Fax: 202-272-2022

Mark S Wuigley, Editor
Ethel Briggs, Executive Director

Reports on the latest issues and news affecting people with disabilities.

2 pages Frequency: Monthly

4067 NCOA Networks
National Council on the Aging
409 3rd Streete SW
Suite 200
Washington, DC 20024-3212
202-479-1200
800-867-2755
Fax: 202-479-0735

James P Firman, CEO

Offers the opportunity to learn more about professional interests, important developments and research in aging. Policy issues and NCOA activities are also included.

4068 NHCoA Noticias of Hispanic Aging Issues & News
National Hispanic Council on Aging
2713 Ontario Road NW
Washington, DC 20009-2107
202-265-1288
Fax: 202-745-2522
e-mail: nhcoa@aol.com

Marta Sotomayor, Editor
6 pages Frequency: Quarterly

4069 NHIF Newsletter
National Head Injury Foundation
1776 Massachusetts Avenue NW
Washington, DC 20036-1904
202-296-6443
800-444-6443
Fax: 202-296-8850
http://www.biausa.org

George Zitnay, President

Contains news and articles for families and professionals concerned with head injury.

4070 NHO NewsLine
National Hospice Organization
1901 N Moore Street
Suite 901
Arlington, VA 22209-1717
703-243-5400
800-658-8898
Fax: 703-525-5762

Jennifer Morales, Editor
6-8 pages Frequency: Semimonthly

4071 NSCLC Washington Weekly
National Senior Citizens Law Center
1815 H Street NW
Suite 700
Washington, DC 20006-3601
202-289-7224
Fax: 202-887-2198
e-mail: nsclc@nsclc.org

Brendan McTaggart, Editor
4 pages

4072 National Veterans Legal Services Program Newsletter
2001 S Street NW
Suite 610
Washington, DC 20009-1157
202-265-8305
Fax: 202-328-0063
e-mail: nvlsp@cyberrealm.net
http://www.nvlsp.ORG

D Addlestone, Joint Executive Director

Non-profit veterans law firm. Recruits volunteer lawyers to handle cases before the US Court of Veterans Claims. Engages in many activities around Agent Orange and VA reform.

Frequency: Quarterly

4073 News from the Points of Light Foundation
Points of Light Foundation
1737 H Street NW
Washington, DC 20006-3905
202-223-9186
800-272-8306
Fax: 202-223-9256

Catherine Quilty, Editor
Frequency: Monthly

4074 Newsline
Sertoma Foundation
1912 E Meyer Boulevard
Kansas City, MO 64132-1141
816-333-8300
Fax: 816-333-4320

Steven Murphy, Executive Director

Reports on activities of the Sertoma Foundation in the field of speech and hearing impairments.

Aging / Newsletters, Pamphlets

4075 Nicotine Addiction and Cigarettes
American Lung Association
1740 Broadway
New York, NY 10019-4315
212-315-8700
Fax: 212-315-8870
John Kirkwood, CEO

Offers information on nicotine and cigarette smoking.

4076 No Smoking: Lungs at Work
American Lung Association
1740 Broadway
New York, NY 10019-4315
212-315-8700
Fax: 212-315-8870
John Kirkwood, CEO

Describes how lungs work and how they are affected by smoking.

4077 Nonprofit Housing and Care Options for Older People
American Assn. of Homes & Services for the Aging
901 E Street NW
Suite 500
Washington, DC 20004-2037
202-661-5700
Fax: 202-783-2255
Daniel Smith, VP

Offers information on continuing care facilities, retirement communities and more for the elderly and relatives caring for Alzheimer's patients.

4078 Now Where Did I Put My Keys?
AARP Fulfillment
601 E Street NW
Washington, DC 20049
202-434-2277
800-424-3410
Fax: 202-434-3443
e-mail: member@aarp.org
http://www.aarp.org
William Novelli, CEO

Your copies of this brochure won't last long on your information counter.

4079 Nursing Home Law Letter
National Senior Citizens Law Center
1815 Hi Street NW
Suite 700
Washington, DC 20006
202-289-7224
Fax: 202-887-2198
e-mail: nsclc@nsclc.org
Toby Edelman, Editor

6-10 pages Frequency: Quarterly

4080 Nutrition Action Healthletter
Center for Science in the Public Interest
1875 Connecticut Avenue NW
Suite 300
Washington, DC 20009-5728
202-332-9110
Fax: 202-265-4954
e-mail: cspi@cspinet.org
http://www.cspinet.org
Stephen Schmidt, Editor
Michael Jacobson, Executive Director

The nation's leading consumer group concerned with food and nutrition issues. Focuses on diseases that result from consuming too many calories, too much fat, sodium and sugar such as cancer and heart disease.

16 pages

4081 Older Americans Report
Business Publishers
951 Pershing Drive
Silver Spring, MD 20910-4400
301-598-5103
800-274-6737
Fax: 301-589-8493
e-mail: bpinews@bpinews.com
Nancy Aldrich, Editor

Handles issues like long term care, Social Security, nutrition, retirement and other programs that effect older Americans.

8-10 pages Frequency: Weekly

4082 Opus Communications
PO Box 1168
Marblehead, MA 01945-5168
781-639-1872
800-650-6787
Fax: 781-639-2982
e-mail: customer_service@opuscomm.com
Bruce Guzowski, CEO

12 pages Frequency: Monthly

4083 Pattern Control
Chronimed Publishing
PO Box 59032
Minneapolis, MN 55459
612-513-6475
800-848-2793
Fax: 952-443-2806

Instruction about recognizing and resolving the puzzle of consistent and repeated blood glucose highs or lows. Includes simple steps for identifying and adjusting the appropriate insulin dose.

4084 Perspective on Aging
National Council on the Aging
600 Maryland Avenue SW
Washington, DC 20024-2520
202-479-1200
800-867-2755
Fax: 202-479-0735
James P Firman, CEO

Explores significant developments in the field of aging, including disabilities, through opinion articles, profiles and book reviews.

4085 Plain Talk About Depression
Superintendent of Documents
PO Box 371954
Pittsburgh, PA 15250-7954
202-512-2250
Fax: 202-512-2250

A flyer discussing types of depression, major depression, symptoms and causes.

4086 Positive Living
APLA
1313 Vine Street
Los Angeles, CA 90028-8107
323-993-1362

4087 Positively Aware
Test Positive Aware Network
5537 N Broadway Street
Chicago, IL 60640-1405
773-271-1437
Fax: 773-989-9494
Rick Beljocec, Executive Director

Chicago area HIV related services directory, that includes HIV news items, events and clinical trials in the Chicago area.

4088 Program Booklet
Women for Sobriety
PO Box 618
Quakertown, PA 18951
215-536-8026
800-333-1606
Fax: 215-536-8026
e-mail: WFSobriety@aol.com
http://www.womenfor sobriety.org

Purse size booklet that explains the Thirteen Statements of Dr. Kirkpatrick's New Life program, statement by statement.

4089 Public Interest Center on Long Term Care
1507 21st Street
Suite E109
Sacramento, CA 95814-5220
916-446-5085
Fax: 916-446-3057

6-12 pages

Aging/Newsletters, Pamphlets

4090 Q&A About Smoking and Health
American Lung Association
1740 Broadway
New York, NY 10019-4315
212-315-8700
Fax: 212-315-8870

John Kirkwood, CEO

Gives fact-crammed answers to questions on smoking and health.

4091 Quality Care
National Association for Continence
PO Box 8310
Spartanburg, SC 29305-8310
864-579-7900
Fax: 864-579-7902
e-mail: losby@nafc.org
http://www.nafc.org

Liv Osby, Director Marketing

Committed to alleviating the social stigma associated with bladder control problems. A source of education, advocacy, and support to the public and to the health profession about the causes, prevention, diagnosis, treatments, and management alternatives for incontinence.

4092 Quality Care Advocate
Natl Citizens' Coalition for Nursing Home Reform
1424 16th Street NW
Suite 202
Washington, DC 20036-2236
202-332-2276
Fax: 202-332-2949
e-mail: dlenhoff@ncnhr.org
http://www.ncnhr.org

Diane Menio, President
Donna R Lenhoff Esq, Executive Director

News, views, and inspiration to help you be a better advocate. Covers Congressional action, regulatory developments, state and local advocacy campaigns, important research, and more.

8 pages Frequency: 8 issues

4093 RTC Connection
Research And Training Center
University of Wisconsin-Stout
Menomonie, WI 54751
715-232-2236
Fax: 715-232-2251
e-mail: menz@uwstout.edu
http://www.rtc.uwstout.edu
TDD 715-232-5025

Reports on disability and rehabilitation research and policy topics.

4094 Recognizing and Treating Low Blood Sugar(Hypoglycemia)
Chronimed Publishing
PO Box 59032
Minneapolis, MN 55459
612-513-6475
800-848-2793
Fax: 952-443-2806

The causes, symptoms, and treatment of low blood sugar are clearly presented in this booklet, including guidelines for using glucagon.

12 pages

4095 Record Book
Chronimed Publishing
PO Box 59032
Minneapolis, MN 55459
612-513-6475
800-848-2793
Fax: 952-443-2806

Handy 26-week booklet to record daily blood glucose levels and medication and/or insulin doses. Encourages comments about activities and reactions.

56 pages

4096 Report on Disability Programs
Business Publishers
951 Pershing Drive
Silver Spring, MD 20910-4400
301-587-6300
800-274-6737
Fax: 301-587-4530
e-mail: bpinews@bpinews.com
http://www.bpinews.com

Leonard A Eiserer, Publisher
Bob Grupe, Editor
Adam Goldstein, President

Follows all programs and funding sources in education, housing, job training, therapy, Social Security Supplemental Security Income, Medicare, Medicaid and more. Also covers the latest on the Americans with Disabilities Act.

Frequency: BiWeekly

4097 Residential Care Today
4019 Glenolive Court
Sacramento, CA 95821-3215
916-483-NEWS
800-313-5853
Fax: 916-483-6243

Doug Britton, Editor

Offers information on community living, community care, licensing, operations management and housing information for the elderly.

15 pages Frequency: Monthly

4098 Retired Enlisted Association: Voice
Retired Enlisted Association
1111 S Abilene Court
Aurora, CO 80012-4909
303-752-0660
800-338-9337
Fax: 303-752-0835

Connie Thomas, Editor
Sharon Rhatican, Executive Director

48 pages Frequency: Monthly

4099 Retiree Newsletter
US Coast Guard Commandant (G-OPN)
2100 2nd Street SW
Washington, DC 20593
202-267-0980
Fax: 202-267-4222

20 pages Frequency: Quarterly

4100 Retirement Letter
Phillips Publishing International
7811 Montrose Road
Potomac, MD 20854-3363
301-340-2100
Fax: 301-424-0245
e-mail: philandpete@phillips.com

Peter A Dickinson, Editor
Philip Springer, Editor
Kevin Donoghue, CEO

8 pages Frequency: Monthly

4101 SAGE Newsletter
Senior Action in A Gay Environment
305 Fashion Avenue
16th Floor
New York, NY 10001
212-741-2247
Fax: 212-366-1947

Martin Wendel, Contact
Terry Kaelber, Executive Director

4 pages Frequency: Monthly

4102 Secondhand Smoke
American Lung Association
1740 Broadway
New York, NY 10019-4315
212-315-8700
Fax: 212-315-8870

John Kirkwood, CEO

Documents the effects of tobacco smoke on nonsmokers.

Aging/Newsletters, Pamphlets

4103 Secretariat for Pro-Life Activities
National Conference of
3211 4th Street NE
Washington, DC 20017-1104
202-541-3005
Fax: 202-541-3054

Arthur Kennedy, Executive Director

Addresses euthanasia and other death and dying issues.

4 pages

4104 Selling to Seniors
CD Publications
8204 Fenton Street
Silver Spring, MD 20910-4502
301-588-6380
Fax: 301-588-6385
e-mail: info@cdpublications.com
http://www.cdpublications.com

Michael Gerecht, President

Monthly newsletter reporting on innovative ways businesses can better reach the over-50 market.

4105 Senior Media
6500 Wilshire Boulevard
Suite 1200
Los Angeles, CA 90048-4932
323-933-9228

40 pages Frequency: Monthly

4106 Senior News Monthly
Senior News Monthly Executive Offices
PO Box 229
Salem, OR 97308
503-399-8478
Fax: 503-399-1645

Periodical with four separate editions targeted at 50 consumer group in Oregon state. Reports on travel, finance, health, politics, retirement, local activities.

4107 SeniorNet
1 Kearny Street
Floor 3
San Francisco, CA 94108-5560
415-352-1210
Fax: 415-352-1260
e-mail: seniornet@seniornet.org

16 pages Frequency: Quarterly

4108 Should Tobacco Advertising and Promotion Be Banned
American Lung Association
1740 Broadway
New York, NY 10019-4315
212-431-7489
Fax: 212-315-8870

Steven Shield, Owner

Answers many questions about tobacco advertising and promotion, and explains how ads are targeted to vulnerable populations.

4109 Simon Foundation for Continence
PO Box 815
Wilmette, IL 60091
847-864-3913
800-237-4666
Fax: 847-864-9758

Cheryle B Gartley, President

Publishes items of interest to people with bladder or bowel incontinence, including medical articles, helpful devices, publications and a pen pal list.

4110 Sobering Thoughts
Women for Sobriety
PO Box 618
Quakertown, PA 18951
215-536-8026
800-333-1606
Fax: 215-536-8026
e-mail: NewLife@nni.comcom
http://www.womenforsobriety.org

Rebecca Fenner, Director

A monthly membership newsletter for women with an addiction problem who wish for recovery and start a new life.

16 pages

4111 Social Security Bulletin
US Social Security Administration
4301 Connecticut Avenue NW
Room 209
Washington, DC 20008-2304
202-282-7138
Fax: 202-282-7219

Reports on results of research and analysis pertinent to the Social Security and SSI programs.

Frequency: Monthly

4112 Sounding Board
Sanders-Brown Center on Aging
101 Sanders Brown Building
Lexington, KY 40536
859-323-6040
Fax: 859-323-2866

Deborah D Danner, Editor

8 pages Frequency: Semiannual

4113 Speech Pathology
2131 Hollywood Boulevard
Suite 305
Hollywood, FL 33020-6751
954-925-5242
Fax: 954-925-5244

4 pages

4114 Stop Smoking: A Guide to Your Options
American Lung Association
1740 Broadway
New York, NY 10019-4315
212-315-8700
Fax: 212-315-8870

John Kirkwood, CEO

Describes a variety of approaches to smoking cessation. Offers guidance on how to choose a program.

4115 Taking Care of Your Feet
Chronimed Publishing
PO Box 59032
Minneapolis, MN 55459
612-513-6475
800-848-2793
Fax: 952-443-2806

Simple steps for daily foot care and preventing foot problems.

4116 Telephone Pioneer
Telephone Pioneers of America
PO Box 13888
Denver, CO 80201-3888
303-571-1200
Fax: 303-572-0520

Marty Lee, President

4117 Topics in Geriatric Rehabilitation
Aspen Publishers
7201 McKinney Circle
Frederick, MD 21704-8356
301-698-7105
800-234-1660
Fax: 800-901-9075
http://www.aspenpub.com

Peer-review journal presenting clinical, basic and applied research as well as theoretical information.

Frequency: Quarterly

4118 United States Department of the Interior: National Park Service
PO Box 37127
Washington, DC 20013-7127
202-783-3238

James Ridenour, Director

Offers an informational packet containing books, guides and tours for the disabled and elderly.

4119 University Center on Aging and Health Newsletter
Case Western Reserve University
10900 Euclid Avenue
Cleveland, OH 44106-1712
216-368-2692
Fax: 216-368-6389
e-mail: mlw4@po.cwru.edu

May L Wykle, Director

16 pages Frequency: Semiannual

Aging/Videos, Audio Tapes

4120 Unpuffables Promotional Brochure
American Lung Association
1740 Broadway
New York, NY 10019-4315
212-315-8700
Fax: 212-265-4652

John Kirkwood, CEO

Describes the ALA Unpuffables program.

4121 VoRtechs
Center for Rehabilitation Technology
1410c Boston Avenue
Suite 15
West Columbia, SC 29170-2138
803-822-5362
Fax: 803-822-4301
e-mail: rerc-br@scsn.net

Neil Lown, Technical Services

Rehabilitation technology and assistive device newsletter. Available in alternate formats.

8 pages Frequency: Quarterly

4122 Volunteer Committees of Art Museums of Canada and the United States News
Council of the Virginia Museum of the Fine Arts
2800 Grove Avenue
Richmond, VA 23221-2466
804-340-1400
Fax: 804-340-1548

Suzanne Hamblin, Editor
Tom Allen, Executive Director

4-8 pages

4123 Volunteer Leader
American Hospital Publishing
737 N Michigan Avenue
Suite 700
Chicago, IL 60611-6662
312-440-6800
800-621-6902
Fax: 312-951-8491

Laurie Larson, Editor

16 pages Frequency: Quarterly

4124 Volunteers of America
110 S Union Street
Alexandria, VA 22314-3353
703-548-2288
800-899-0089
Fax: 703-684-1972
e-mail: ams@voa.org

24 pages

4125 WA & NEWS
Wheelchair Access
PO Box 12
Glenmoore, PA 19343
610-942-3266
Fax: 610-942-0282
e-mail: info@waccess.org
http://www.waccess.org

Frank Gomez, Publisher

Features wheelchair accessible houses and apartments for rent or for sale. Currently the newsletter includes ads from all states. Ads received from any State will be accepted free of charge. Featured also are ads of wheelchairs, vans, equipment, etc., for sale. Complete ad information and more is listed in the Web site. A free copy of WA & NEWS sent upon request.

20 pages Frequency: Monthly

4126 Walking Tomorrow
American Paralysis Association
500 Morris Avenue
Springfield, NJ 07081-1027
973-379-2690
800-292-0292
Fax: 973-912-9433

Kathy Lewis, CEO

A newsletter offering medical and technological updates for people with physical disabilities, including paralysis.

Frequency: Quarterly

4127 Washington Report
Association of Homes and Services for the Aging
901 E Street NW
Suite 500
Washington, DC 20004-2037
202-661-5700
Fax: 202-783-2255
e-mail: mdinitz@aahsa.org

Marion M Dinitz, Editor
Daniel Smith, Vise President

4 pages Frequency: Semimonthly

4128 Washington Watch
United Cerebral Palsy Associations
1660 L Street NW
Suite 700
Washington, DC 20036-5638
202-776-0406
800-USA-5UCP
Fax: 202-785-3508
TDD 202-973-7197

Susanna L Gorton, Editor
Stepehn Bennett, CEO

Dependable, timely information on national legislative and regulatory issues affecting people with disabilities and their families.

4 pages Frequency: Bi-weekly

4129 What's Your Cigarette Smoking IQ ?
American Lung Association
1740 Broadway
New York, NY 10019-4315
212-315-8700
Fax: 212-315-8870

John Kirkwood, CEO

Brief true-or-false quiz that tests a persons knowledge of the effects of smoking.

4130 Working Age
AARP
601 E Street NW
Washington, DC 20049
202-434-2277
800-424-3410
Fax: 202-434-3443
e-mail: member@aarp.org
http://www.aarp.org

Ronald B Allen, Editor
William Novelli, CEO

8 pages

Videos, Audio Tapes

4131 A Safer Place
Fanlight Productions
4196 Washington Street
Suite 2
Boston, MA 02131-1731
800-937-4113
Fax: 617-469-3379
e-mail: fanlight@fanlight.com
http://www.fanlight.com

Sandy St Louis, Distribution Director
Kelli English, Publicity Coordinator

Profiles two elderly adults who were helped by social service agencies to recognize and get help for the abusive situations they were living in. 20-minute video.

4132 Age Base
Brookdale Foundation Group
1941 Massachusetts Avenue
Englewood, FL 34224-5521
813-697-9711
Fax: 813-697-9711

Victor Biggs, Editor

Over 800 direct service programs for the elderly, including programs for the home-bound, health promotions, and senior citizen classes. Database includes: Program name, address, phone, contact, date established, description, group of elderly served, funding level and source.

Aging / Videos, Audio Tapes

Frequency: Continuous

4133 As Times Goes By
Fanlight Productions
4196 Washington Street
Suite 2
Boston, MA 02131-1731
800-937-4113
Fax: 617-469-3379
e-mail: fanlight@fanlight.com
http://www.fanlight.com

Canadian Broadcasting Corp., Contact

Humans are sexual until the very end. The seniors profiled in this video open share their experiences with love, romance and growing old. 23 minutes.

4134 Assistive Devices Information Network
University of Iowa
Iowa City, IA 52242
319-356-0768
800-331-3027
Fax: 319-384-9273

Provides information on assistive devices, the vendors who make them, and suggestions on how to order.

4135 Challenge of Choice
Chronimed Publishing
PO Box 59032
Minneapolis, MN 55459
612-513-6475
800-848-2793
Fax: 952-443-2806

Discusses nutritional recommendations; how to reduce fat, sugar, and salt in the diet; how to increase fiber; fad diets, supplements, and caffeine. 66 slides/cassette. Item No. 4153.

4136 Choice & Challenge: Caring for Aggressive Older Adults Across Levels of Care
Fanlight Productions
4196 Washington Street
Suite 2
Boston, MA 02131-1731
800-937-4113
Fax: 617-469-3379
e-mail: fanlight@fanlight.com
http://www.fanlight.com

Presents a series of real-life situations in which health care providersmust cope with behaviorally impaired and aggressive elders. 22-minute video.

4137 Combined Health Information Database
National Cancer Institute - BRS Online
Building 31
Bethesda, MD 20892
301-496-7406
Fax: 301-480-8105

Provides citations to and abstracts of journal articles, books, reports, pamphlets and hard-to-find information sources.

4138 DVS Guide
Descriptive Video Service
Wgbh125 Western Avenue
Boston, MA 02134
617-492-2777
800-333-1203
Fax: 617-783-8668
e-mail: vita-long@wgbh.org

Vita Long, Mailing Contact

Magazine listing updates and programs available from the Descriptive Video Service, a free national service that makes television programs, cable programming and movies accessible to blind or visually impaired individuals.

Frequency: Quarterly

4139 Depression in Older Adults
Fanlight Productions
4196 Washington Street
Suite 2
Boston, MA 02131-1731
800-937-4113
Fax: 617-469-3379
e-mail: fanlight@fanlight.com
http://www.fanlight.com

Depression in later life is common and very treatable. This video explores its causes and current approaches. 30-minute video.

4140 Elder Abuse: 5 Case Studies
Fanlight Productions
4196 Washington Street
Suite 2
Boston, MA 02131-1731
800-937-4113
Fax: 617-469-3379
e-mail: fanlight@fanlight.com
http://www.fanlight.com

Illuminates the fear and ambivalence experienced by elderly people abused by family members and their struggles to find help. 40-minute video.

4141 ElderNet
246 Walnut Street
Suite B
Newton, MA 02460-1639
617-244-1774
Fax: 617-558-5504
e-mail: Webmaster@ElderNet.com
http://www.eldernet.com

A seniors' guide to health, housing, legal, financial, retirement, lifestyles, news, and entertainment information on the World Wide Web. Click on the front door.

4142 Emergency Care for the Elderly
Alzheimer's Disease Education & Referral Center
PO Box 8250
Silver Spring, MD 20907-8250
800-438-4380
Fax: 301-495-3334

Designed to teach paramedics, EMTs and first responders to address issues presented by geriatric patients. One videotape, manual and two student booklets. Produced by University of Pittsburgh.

4143 Golden Years?
Fanlight Productions
4196 Washington Street
Suite 2
Boston, MA 02131-1731
800-937-4113
Fax: 617-469-3379
e-mail: fanlight@fanlight.com
http://www.fanlight.com

A graphic and disturbing look at the growing incidence of domestic abuse against those over sixty-five. 60-minute vide.

4144 Grandparents Raising Grandchildren
Fanlight Productions
4196 Washington Street
Suite 2
Boston, MA 02131-1731
800-937-4113
Fax: 617-469-3379
e-mail: fanlight@fanlight.com
http://www.fanlight.com

It was supposed to be their golden years, a time to relax and spoil the grandchildren. For nearly 4 million grandparents, a new reality is taking shape as they are taking on sole responsiblity for raising their children's children. This hard-hitting investigation explores some of the difficulties surrounding this growing phenomenon and explores the emotional and financial difficulties that these families face. 37-minute video.

Aging/Videos, Audio Tapes

4145 Guide to Helping Elderly Relatives Near and Far
National Stroke Association
96 Inverness Drive E
Suite I
Englewood, CO 80112-5311
303-649-9299
800-787-6537
Fax: 303-649-1328
e-mail: info@stroke.org
http://www.stroke.org

James Baranski, CEO

Suggestions on how to deal with the fear and frustration of coping with long-distance caregiving, family communication, care alternatives, and much more.

Frequency: 92 minutes

4146 I'm Pretty Old
Fanlight Productions
4196 Washington Street
Suite 2
Boston, MA 02131-1731
800-937-4113
Fax: 617-469-3379
e-mail: fanlight@fanlight.com
http://www.fanlight.com

An engaging look at several elderly men and woman as they adapt to the realities of living in a nursing home. 20-minute video.

4147 Label Reading and Shopping
American Diabetes Association/Conn. Affiliate
300 Research Parkway
Meriden, CT 06450-7137
203-639-0385
800-842-6323
Fax: 203-639-0292
http://www.diabetes.org/adact

Provides practical information on how to shop and what to look for on labels.

4148 Line Dancing Video
Center for Positive Aging
PO Box 55079
Atlanta, GA 30308-5079
404-872-9191
Fax: 404-872-1737
e-mail: positiveaging@mindspring.com
http://www.positiveaging.home.mindspring.com

Joyce Horsley, Director
Ricki Moss, Production Coordinator
Walter Coffey, Executive Director

A unique and exciting new line dancing video designed especially for adults over 50. Executed at a safe, easy pace that lets you learn the steps while achieving the mobility, timing, flexibility, stamina, and muscle control that helps insure lasting fitness. The 45-minute video features warm-up exercises (limbering movements and static stretches) designed to prepare you for the body movements used in each of the six dances. The dances include 'Th Boogie Down,' 'The Country Call,' 'The Good Luck,' 'Latin Stroll,' and 'Jazz Boogie.' The video finishes with a cool-down period of stretching exercises.

4149 Meal Planning with Exchange Lists
Chronimed Publishing
PO Box 59032
Minneapolis, MN 55459
612-338-1680
800-848-2793
Fax: 952-443-2806

Laura Mell, Owner

Presents the exchange lists and their practical application to meal planning as developed by the American Dietetic Association and the American Diabetes Association. 23 minutes. Item No. 004102. Also available as 80 slides/cassette (Item No. 4151, $85.00).

4150 Medical Management of Impotence
Impotence Resource Center
PO Box 1593
Augusta, GA 30903-1593
800-433-4215
e-mail: info@gdo.org
http://www.impotence.org

4151 My Mother, My Father
Fanlight Productions
4196 Washington Street
Suite 2
Boston, MA 02131-1731
800-937-4113
Fax: 617-469-3379
e-mail: fanlight@fanlight.com
http://www.fanlight.com

Portraits of four families caring for aging parents; their choices include care at home, use of a variety of support services, and nursing home placement. 33-minute video.

4152 My Mother, My Father: Seven Years Later
Fanlight Productions
4196 Washington Street
Suite 2
Boston, MA 02131-1731
800-937-4113
Fax: 617-469-3379
e-mail: fanlight@fanlight.com
http://www.fanlight.com

Revisits each family seven years later, to explore changes in family dynamics and the caregivers' thoughts about their own aging. 33-minute video.

4153 National Library of Medicine
8600 Rockville Pike
Bethesda, MD 20894
301-496-6308
Fax: 301-596-4450
http://www.nlm.nih.gov

Robert Mehnert, Manager

Offers an extensive collection of published medical information, for free. Go to PubMed, then click on free medline.

4154 Not My Home
Fanlight Productions
4196 Washington Street
Suite 2
Boston, MA 02131-1731
800-937-4113
Fax: 617-469-3379
e-mail: fanlight@fanlight.com
http://www.fanlight.com

Suzanne Babin, Author
Tynette Deveaux, Author
Bert Deveaux, Author

A compelling look at life inside a nursing home, as residents, families, and staff discuss their problems and rewards. 45-minute video.

4155 Personals
Fanlight Productions
4196 Washington Street
Suite 2
Boston, MA 02131-1731
800-937-4113
Fax: 617-469-337
e-mail: fanlight@fanlight.c
http://www.fanlight.c

A group of senior citizens reveal their longing for love an form it on stage with energy and laughter. 37-minute vi

Aging / Videos, Audio Tapes

4156 Quality Care Conference
Alzheimer's Association
919 N Michigan Avenue
Suite 1000
Chicago, IL 60611-1696
312-335-8700
800-272-3900
Fax: 312-335-1110
e-mail: info@alz.org
http://www.alz.org

Gary Bieting, President

Selected educational sessions from the conference discussing topics such as special care units, drug therapies, behavior management, and care strategies.

4157 Right to Decide
Fanlight Productions
4196 Washington Street
Suite 2
Boston, MA 02131-1731
800-937-4113
Fax: 617-469-3379
e-mail: fanlight@fanlight.com
http://www.fanlight.com

Informed by the Patient Self-Determination Act, these outstanding physician-patient interviews explore patients' hopes, fears, and golas regarding end-of-life care. 43-minute video.

4158 Secret to a Satisfied Life: The Way You Encounter Life Can Bring Happiness...
Hazelden
15251 Pleasant Valley Road
Center City, MN 55012-9640
651-213-4030
800-328-9000
Fax: 651-213-4426
http://www.hazelden.org

Video. 45 minutes

4159 Seniors Sites
5443 Stag Mountain Road
Weed, CA 96094-9363
530-938-3163
Fax: 530-938-3850
e-mail: writers@seniors-site.com
http://www.seniors-site.com

Walt Cheney, Owner/Webmaster

Dedicated to provide a unique, informative, interesting and entertaining internet website for: senior citizens 50+, their children, grandchildren and caregivers.

4160 Sexuality & Aging
Fanlight Productions
4196 Washington Street
Suite 2
Boston, MA 02131-1731
800-937-4113
Fax: 617-469-3379
e-mail: fanlight@fanlight.com
http://www.fanlight.com

Explores society's attitudes and myths about sexuality in later life, while several elders contribute their perspectives on the importance of continued intimacy. 60-minute video.

4161 Signs for Computing Terminology
National Association of the Deaf
814 Thayer Avenue
Silver Spring, MD 20910-4504
301-587-6282
Fax: 301-587-4873
e-mail: sales@nad.org
http://www.nad.org
TTY 301-587-1789

Three videotapes designed to accompany the text, Signs for Computing Terminology (separately listed). Videotape #1 covers prefixes, suffixes, and vocabulary A-D. Videotape #2 covers vocabulary E-O. Videotape #3 cover vocabulary P-W.

4162 Solution Starts with You
Simon Foundation for Incontinence
PO Box 815
Wilmette, IL 60091
847-864-3913
800-223-1360
Fax: 847-864-9768
http://www.simonfoundation.org

Cheryle B Gartley, President

A movie that seeks to bring the topic of incontinence out of the closet and remove the associated stigma; provides information to patients, their families, and the health care professionals who provide patient care.

4163 Stay Fit Video
Center for Positive Aging
PO Box 55079
Atlanta, GA 30308-5079
404-872-9191
Fax: 404-872-1737
e-mail: positiveaging@mindspring.com
http://www.positiveaging.home.mindspring.com

Joyce Horsley, Director
Ricki Moss, Production Coordinator
Walter Coffey, Executive Director

Designed especially for the older adults, STAY FIT FOR LIFE offers stretching exercises that are safe, effective and motivating with easy-to-follow routines. With this video, you can quickly acquire increased flexibility and muscle strength, and improve your posture, balance, and corrdination. This 45-minute video features ten minutes of limbering movements and static stretches while seated, 20 minutes of muscle-strengthening and free-standing floor moevments, 10 minutes of cool-down stretches, and five minutes of relaxation exercises. Also includes modifications for standing and sitting exercises for those with different levels of physical fitness.

4164 Tonight's the Night
Fanlight Productions
4196 Washington Street
Suite 2
Boston, MA 02131-1731
800-937-4113
Fax: 617-469-3379
e-mail: fanlight@fanlight.com
http://www.fanlight.com

Canadian Broadcasting Corp., Contact

Three senior couples describe the evolution of their sexual relationships, while experts stress the importance of more accepting social attitudes about sexuality and aging. 25-minute video.

4165 Way We Die
Fanlight Productions
4196 Washington Street
Suite 2
Boston, MA 02131-1731
800-937-4113
Fax: 617-469-3379
e-mail: fanlight@fanlight.com
http://www.fanlight.com

Intimately filmed interviews between caregivers and terminally ill patients encourage professionals to attend more closely to their patients' values, needs, and wishes. 24-minute video.

4166 We Will Remember
Compassion Books
477 Hannah Branch Road
Burnsville, NC 28714-7569
828-675-5909
Fax: 828-675-9687
http://www.compassionbooks.com

Bruce Greene, Vice President

A video meditation that uses the beauty of natural photography, soothing music and gentle words to give permission and encouragement in using the memories of the past for healing in the present.

Frequency: 10 Minutes

Aging/Websites

4167 Women's Perspective
Impotence Resource Center
PO Box 1593
Augusta, GA 30903-1593

800-433-4215
e-mail: info@gdo.org
http://www.impotence.org

Talking with your partner about impotence and choosing a treatment together.

Websites

4168 10 Questions to Help You Make Sense of Health Headlines

http://www.health-insight.harvard.edu

This website aims to help consumers take charge of health information.

4169 50+ Friends Club

http://www.jps.net

Website offering over 30 chat rooms and links for seniors.

4170 60 Plus Association

http://www.60plus.org

A non-partisan seniors advocacy group with a free enterprise, less government, less taxes approach to seniors issues.

4171 AARP

http://www.aarp.org

AARP is a nonprofit membership organization of persons 50 and older dedicated to addressing their needs and interests. AARP is dedicated to enhancing quality of life for all as we age. We lead positive social change and deliver value to members through information, advocacy and service.

4172 AARP-Consumer Protection

http://www.aarp.org/money

AARP is a nonprofit membership organization of persons 50 and older dedicated to addressing their needs and interests. AARP is dedicated to enhancing quality of life for all as we age. We lead positive social change and deliver value to members through information, advocacy and service.

4173 Administration on Aging

http://www.aoa.dhhs.gov/aoa/webres/craig.htm

Links you to other websites dealing with aging.

4174 Administration on Aging/Statistical Information

http://www.aoa.dhhs.gov/

Information designed for Older Americans and their families as well as those concerned about providing the opportunities and services to enrich the lives of older persons and support their independence.

4175 Advance Directive and Living Will Resources

http://www.adiwills.com/adiread.htm

Links to other sites relating to direct and living wills and other resources.

4176 Age of Reason

http://www.ageofreason.com

Over 5,000 Links to sites of interest to the over 50 age group.

4177 Alice B. Silver Size Clothing Designs for Senior Women

http://www.alicebfitsu.com/mainframe.html

On-line fashion revolution for women 55 and over.

4178 American Academy of Dermatology

http://www.aad.org

An organization of doctors who specialize in diagnosing and treating skin problems.

4179 American Academy of Otolaryngology-Head & Neck Surgery

http://www.entnet.org

Advance the art and science of otalaryngology-head and neck surgury through state-of-the-art education, research, and learning; and to unite, serve, and represent the interests of its members and their patients to the public.

4180 American Association of Homes and Services for the Aging

http://www.aahsa.org/

Organizations dedicated to providin high-quality health care, housing and services to the nation's elderly.

4181 American Association of Retired Persons(AARP)

http://www.aarp.org

AARP is the nation's leading organization for people age 50 and older. Information and education, advocacy, and community services provided by a network of local chapters and experienced volunteers throughout the country.

4182 American Lung Association

http://www.lungusa.org

A voluntary organization interested in the prevention and control of lung disease.

4183 American Prostate Society

http://www.ameripros.org

Organization dedicated exclusively to using existing medical capabilities to reduce death due to prostate cancer and to reduce unnecessary or ineffective prostate surgery.

4184 American Society of Colon and Rectal Surgeons

http://www.fascrs.org

Represents more than 1000 board certified colon and rectal surgeons and other surgeons dedicated to advancing and promoting the science and practice of the treatment of patients with diseases and disorders affecting the colon, rectum and anus.

4185 Auditory-Verbal International

http://www.auditory-verbal.org

Promotes the Auditory-Verbal Therapy approach, which is based on the belief that the overwhelming majority of these children can hear and talk by using their residual hearing and hearing aids.

4186 Caresource Healthcare Communications

http://www.SeniorClix.com

This web site is a free information and resource pool for senior services community. It includes a community bulletin board for coming events, a database of senior and caregiver opportunities, directories of services and service providers, and extensive forms library.

Aging / Websites

4187 Centers for Medicare and Medicaid Services (CMS)

http://www.cms.hhs.gov

CMS, part of the Federal Government, administers health insurance through Medicare and Medicaid. CMS regulates hospitals, nursing homes, and home health agencies.

4188 Consultation and Education Unlimited

http://www.staug.com

Complete catalog on line of items to help those in pain or with physical disabilities with tasks of daily living.

4189 Council of Better Business Bureau

http://www.bbbonline.org

BBBOnLine's mission is to promote trust and confidence on the Internet through the BBBOnLine Reliability and Privacy Seal Programs. BBBOnLine's web site seal programs allows companies with web sites to display the seals once they have been evaluated and confirmed to meet the program requirements.

4190 Dentists Concerned for Dentists

http://www.caries.dental.my.edu/wda/dcd.html

A nonprofit organization for chemically dependent Minnesota dentists and concerned others.

4191 ElderCare Advocates

http://www.eldercareadvocates.com

Provides long term care management to those elders and their families who are in need of assistance to stay in their homes for as long as possible.

4192 ElderConnect

http://www.extendedcare.com

Information of over 33,000 acute rehabilitation providers, retirement communities, and providers specializing in all levels of long-term nursing care as well as home health agencies.

4193 Eldercare Locator

http://www.eldercare.gov

Eldercare Locator links those who need assistance with state and local area agencies on aging and community-based organizations that serve older adults and their caregivers.

4194 Elderhostel

http://www.elderhostel.org

Elderhostel.

4195 Family Meds

http://www.familymeds.com

A site providing information on impotence and its various treatments, including over the counter, natural, and prescription medication choices.

4196 Federal Trade Commission

http://www.ftc.gov

The FTC site includes news and alerts, consumer protection and anti-trust information.

4197 Fidelco Guide Dog Foundation

http://www.fidelco.org

Fidelco breeds, raises, trains, and places German shepherd guide dogs with men and women who are visually impaired, primarily in the Northeast.

4198 Food Allergy Network

http://www.foodallergy.org

Information to help families living with food allergies, and to increase public awareness about food allergies and anaphylaxis.

4199 Friends-In-Art

http://www.acb.org

Offers consultation to program planners in establishing accessible art and museum exhibits and presents Performing Arts Showcases.

4200 General Fitness

http://www.coolware.com/health/medical_reporter

Important reasons why senior citizens should exercise regardless of age.

4201 Generations Online

http://www.generationsonline.com

4202 Gerontological Society of America

http://www.geron.org

Provides researchers, educators, practitioners, and policy makers with opportunities to understand, advance, integrate, and use basic and applied research on aging to improve the quality of life as one ages.

4203 Government Grants and Loans for Seniors

http://www.ns.net/~jdr/seniors.html

Insite on how to obtain grants and loans for the US federal government for senior citizens.

4204 Grand Times

http://www.grandtimes.com

A weekly Internet magazine foe seniors. Controversial, entertaining and informative, Grand Times celebrates life's opportunities and examines life's challanges.

4205 HMOs4seniors.com

http://www.hmos4seniors.com

Dedicated to assisting seniors and caregivers with making informed choices regarding Medicare and Choice options.

4206 Hazelden

http://www.hazelden.com

Organization dedicated to providing quality rehabilitation, education and professional services for chemical dependency and related addictive behaviors.

4207 Healing Well

http://www.healingwell.com

An online health resource guide to medical news, chat, information and articles, newsgroups and message boards, books, disease-related web sites, medical directories, and more for patients, friends, and family coping with disabling diseases, disorders, or chronic illnesses.

4208 Helios Health

http://www.helioshealth.com

The best onlines resource for your health information. Detailed information about specific health topics, access to expert advice from our Medical Advisory Board, and up-to-date health news.

Aging/Websites

4209 Immune Deficiency Foundation

http://www.primaryimmune.org
Offers information and referral services to immune deficient patients and their families.

4210 International Association of Eating Disorder Professionals

http://www.iaedp.com
Supplies printed information and sponsors meetings and other activities. Publishes a directory of speech instructors and maintains a list of sources for supplies for laryngectomee.

4211 Internet Health Coalition

http://www.ihealthcoalition.org
The mission of the Internet Healthcare Coalition is quality healthcare resources on the Internet.

4212 Leukemia Society of America

http://www.leukemia.org
A national voluntary health agency dedicated to curing leukemia, lymphoma, Hodgkin's disease and myeloma and to improving the quality of life of patients and their families.

4213 Living Will Form

http://www.easylegalforms.com/
These are easy-to-use law documents that you individually customize for your specific needs.

4214 Medical Library Association

http://www.mlanet.org
A nonprofit, educational organization of more than 1,100 institutions and 3,600 individual members in the health sciences information field, committed to educating health information professionals, supporting health information research, promoting access to the world's health sciences information, and working to ensure that the best health information is available to all.

4215 Medicare

http://www.medicare.gov
Official US Government website for people with Medicare.

4216 Mediconsult

http://www.mediconsult.com
Provides links to information on disease, illness, and disorders, including such content areas as conference highlights, educational material, journal articles, research, news, and support.

4217 MedlinePlus®

http://www.medlineplus.gov
MedlinePlus will direct you to information to help answer health questions. MedlinePlus brings together authoritative information from NLM, the National Institutes of Health (NIH), and other government agencies and health-related organizations.

4218 Merck & Company

http://www.merck.com
This site features several sections from the on-line version of the doctors' bible, the recently updated Merck Manual of Medical Information-Home Edition, the definitive guide to disease, diagnosis, prevention and treatment. Click on Publications.

4219 NIA Publishers

http://www.niapublications.org
Free publications online.

4220 National Academy on Aging

http://www.geron.org
Promotes the scientific study of aging.

4221 National Aging Information Center

http://www.aoa.dhhs.gov/naic/Notes/default.htm
Links to major web resources on selected topics and issues in Aging.

4222 National Association for Continence

http://www.nafc.org
Committed to alleviating the social stigma associated with bladder control problems. Information to consumers and health professionals and advocating on their behalf to increase public awareness about incontinence.

4223 National Association for Home Care and Hospice (NAHC)

http://www.nahc.org
Providers of home health care, hospice, and homemaker-home health aide services; interested individuals and organizations. Develops and promotes high standards of patient care in home care services. Seeks to affect legislative and regulatory processes concerning home care services; gathers and disseminates home care industry data; develops public relations strategies; works to increase political visibility of home care services. Interprets home care services to governmental and private sector bodies affecting the delivery and financing of such services. Provides legal and accounting consulting services; conducts market research and compiles statistics. Offers members insurance discounts. Sponsors educational programs for organizations and individuals concerned with home care services.

4224 National Association of Area Agencies onAging

http://www.n4a.org
N4A is the umbrella organization for the AoA-funded Area Agencies on Aging. The association administers the AoA sponsored Eldercare Locator.

4225 National Association of Professional Geriatric Care Managers (PGCM)

http://www.caremanager.org
Information resource for those interested in the field of geriatriccare while supporting quality care and services for the elderly.
1985

4226 National Association of State Units on Aging

http://www.nasua.org
Offers support, information and technical assistance to state units on aging.
1990

4227 National Center on Elder Abuse

http://www.elderabusecenter.org
A national resource for elder rights, law enforcement and legal professionals, public policy leaders, researchers, and the public. The Center's mission is to promote understanding, knowledge sharing, and action on elder abuse, neglect, and exploitation.

4228 National Crime Prevention Council

http://www.ncpc
This organization works to prevent crime and drug use in many ways, including developing materials for parents and children.

373

Aging/Websites

4229 National Domestic Violence Hotline

http://www.ndvh.org
At the National Domestic Violence Hotline (NDVH), we continue our commitment to answering this call for help by creating the NDVH Advisory Board, consisiting of eleven prominent national leaders who are committed to raising awareness and the resources necessary to ensure that the Hotline's lifesaving work continues.

4230 National Heart, Lung & Blood Institute

http://www.nhlbi.nih.gov
The mission is to improve meaning of one American people by supporting and understanding research to prevent, detect, diagnose and treat diseases of heart, lungs, blood vessels, and sleep disorders.

4231 National Institute of Dental and Craniofacial Research

http://www.nidcr.nih.gov
Our mission is to improve oral, dental and craniofacial health through research, research training, and the dissemination of health information.

4232 National Institute of Neurological Disorders and Stroke

http://www.ninds.nih.gov
Offers a brochure on stroke. The leading supporter of research on brain and nervous system disorders, including stroke.

4233 National Institute on Aging

http://www.nih.gov/nia
The NIA promotes healthy aging by conducting and supporting biomedical, social, and behavioral research and public education.

4234 National Institutes of Health

http://www.nih.gov
NIH is the steward of medical and behavioral resararch for the Nation. Its mission is science in pursuit of fundamental knowledge about the nature and behavior of living systems and the application of that knowledge to extend healthy life and reduce the burdens of illness and disability.

4235 National Meditation Center

http://www.nationalmeditation.org/
A humanitarian agency with volunteer camps to the Philippines. We need seniors for our volunteer projects overseas and here in America.

4236 National Organization for Victim Assistance

http://www.trynova.org
NOVA's mission is to promote rights and services for victims of crime and crisis everywhere.

4237 Office on Smoking and Health

http://www.cdc.gov
Offers reference services to researchers through the Technical Information Center. Publishes and distributes a number of titles in the field of smoking and health.

4238 Onhealth

http://www.onhealth.com
A search engine providing links to websites with information on illnesses, diseases, and disorders.

4239 Our Grandchild

http://www.ourgrandchild.com/cards
Free greeting cards especially geared towards grandparents keeping in touch with their grandchildren.

4240 Over 50 and a Skier?

http://www.skiersover50.com/
Over The Hill Gang, International offers unsurpassed camaraderie, outstanding discounts, and great trips if your age 50 or over.

4241 Partnership for Prescription Assistance

http://www.pparx.org
Our mission is to increase awareness of patient assistance programs and boost enrollment of those who are eligible. The Partnership for Prescription Assistance offers a single point of access to more than 475 public and private patient assistance programs, including more than 150 programs offered by pharmaceutical companies.

4242 Pensions

http://www.pensionplace.com/
Comprehensive, independent source of information on all types of retirement and pension plans.

4243 QuackWatch

http://www.quackwatch.org
A nonprofit corporation whose purpose is to combat health-related frauds, myths, fads, fallacies, and misconduct. Its primary focus is on quackery-related information that is difficult or impossible to get elsewhere.

4244 Randolph-Sheppard Vendors of America

http://www.acb.org
Protects the interests of blind vendors, seeks proper implementation of the Randolph-Sheppard Act and encourages facility locations in more visible and profitable areas.

4245 Retirement Planning

http://www.vanguard.com/
Helps you create a personal financial plan based on information you enter.

4246 Safe Homes

http://www.crisny.org
This national organization encourages parents to sign a contract stipulating that when parties are held in one another's homes they will adhere to a strict no-alcohol/no-drug-use rule.

4247 Senior Health

http://www.nihseniorhealth.gov
A website with health information designed specifically for older people. NIH SeniorHealth.gov makes aging-related health information easily accessible for family members and friends seeking reliable, easy to understand online health information. This site was developed by the National Institute on Aging (NIA), and the National Library of Medicine (NLM) both parts of the National Institutes of Health (NIH).

4248 Senior Housing Net

http://www.seniorhousing.net
Comprehensive guide to retirement communities, assisted living residences, Alzheimer's facilities, and nursing homes nationwide.

Aging/Research Centers

4249 Senior Job Bank

http://www.seniorjobbank.com

4250 Senior Law Home Page

http://www.seniorlaw.com
Information about Elder Law, Medicare, Medicaid, estate planning, trusts and the rights of the elderly and disabled.

4251 Senior Options Online Guide to Senior Services

http://www.senioroptions.com
Senior living facilities, adult day care centers, home health agencies, geriatric care managers, and Hospices, everywhere in the USA.

4252 Senior Summer School

http://www.seniorsummerschool.com
The Education Vacation for seniors. Visit college campuses across the US and Canada from 2 to 10 weeks during the summer.

4253 Senior Times

http://www.theseniortimes.com
By, for, and about exraordinary seniors.

4254 Senior Women's Travel

http://www.poshnosh.com
Senior Women's Travel brings a new dimension to senior travel and eliminates many of the annoyances of single travel. It's for 50+ women, with a large cultural appetite, who love to shop and eat.

4255 United Ostomy Association

http://www.uoa.org
Produces and distributes materials about ostomy care and management; through trained UOA members, offers practical assistance and emotional support to ostomy patients; sponsors annual youth rally and state and regional conferences for local affiliates; has 500 chapters to serve people locally.

4256 Webhelp

http://www.webhelp.com
Provides links to information, including research, treatment, prevention, support, and more.

4257 Women's Health

http://www.nytimes.com
Click on Web Specials-women's health to reach this site operated by *The New York Times*. Consult Resources for a guide to more than 100 women-related Web sites.

Research Centers

4258 Ackerman Institute for the Family
149 E 78th Street
New York, NY 10021-0405
212-879-4900
Fax: 212-744-0206
e-mail: ackerman@ackerman.org
http://www.ackerman.org

Lois Braverman MSW, President/CEO
Marcia Sheinberg LCSW, Director, Training/Clinical Svc.

Provides mental health care professionals with new skills, and brings innovative perspectives to community service agencies and other health care facilities.

4259 Aging Research Institute
217 SE 8th Avenue
Topeka, KS 66603-3906
785-233-0585
Fax: 785-233-9471
e-mail: jgrace@kahsa.org
http://www.kahsa.org

John R Grace, President

Managed care and nursing facilities staff recruitment and retention.

4260 Aging Research: National Institute on Aging, Public Health Service
US Department of Health and Human Services
9000 Rockville Pike
Room 5c15
Bethesda, MD 20892
301-496-4996
800-422-6237
Fax: 301-402-0010

To encourage biomedical, social, and behavioral research, and research training directed toward greater understanding of the aging process and the diseases, special problems, and needs of people as they age.

4261 Aging in America
1500 Pelham Parkway S
Bronx, NY 10461-1198
718-824-4004
Fax: 413-586-1121
e-mail: cemoylan@aol.com

Ralph Hall, President
Julie Dalton, VP

Research and services organization for professionals in gerontology. Objectives are: to produce, implement and share effective and affordable programs and services that improve the quality of life for the elderly community; to better prepare professionals and students interested in, or currently involved with, aging and the aged.

4262 Alliance for Aging Research
2021 K Street NW
Suite 305
Washington, DC 20006-1003
202-293-2856
800-497-0360
Fax: 202-785-8574
e-mail: info@agingresearch.org
http://www.agingresearch.org

Daniel Perry, Executive Director

Gerontologists and other medical professionals, executives and members of Congress are participants. Works to increase private and public research into aging. Supports policies concerning: productive aging; independence for older Americans; successful aging. Public and professional educational literature, newsletter web site.

4263 American Aging Association
110 Chesley Drive
Media, PA 19063-1755
610-892-0300
Fax: 610-565-9747
e-mail: ameraging@aol.com
http://www.americanaging.org

Norman Wolf DVM PhD, President
Micheal Fossel MD PhD, Executive Director

Laymen and scientists primarily in the biomedical field. Dedicated to helping people live better, longer by promoting biomedical aging studies directed toward slowing down the aging process, informing the public of the progress of aging research and of practical means of achieving a long and healthy life and increasing knowledge of gerontology among physicians and other health workers.

4264 American Federation for Aging Research
70 W 40th Street
11th Floor
New York, NY 10018
212-703-9977
888-582-2327
Fax: 212-997-0330
e-mail: info@afar.org
http://www.afar.org

Aging/Research Centers

4265 American Foundation for Aging Research
North Carolina State University
140 Polk Hall, Biochemistry Department
Raleigh, NC 27695
919-515-5679
Fax: 919-515-2047
e-mail: afar_office@ncsu.edu
http://www.agingresearchfoundation.org
Susie Petretich, Educational Program Coordinator

A nonprofit organization whose mission is to help improve and maintain the health and vitality of the American population. Accomplishes this goal by providing fellowships to innovative, young scientists who apply cutting edge techniques to the understanding of aging and age related diseases.

4266 Arthur M Fishberg Research Center in Neurobiology
Mt. Sinai Medical Center
PO Box 1065
New York, NY 10029
212-659-5992
Fax: 212-996-9785
e-mail: james_roberts@fishmailserver.mssm.edu
http://www.mssm.edu.neurobio/home-page.html

Neurobiological systems in humans and mammals, emphasizing aging research. Specific interests include the neuroendocrinology of stress, reproduction and metabolism, the molecular biology of Alzheimer's disease, schizophrenia, and other neurological/psychiatric diseases, and growth factors and growth factor receptor gene expression in the central nervous system.

4267 Augusta Biomedical Research Corporation
PO Box 3134
Augusta, GA 30914-3134
706-823-2238
Fax: 706-823-3949
Nancy M Parks, Executive Director
Earl Payne, Manager

Alzheimer's disease, strokes, cardiology, infectious diseases, gastroenterology, surgery, schizophrenia, neurology, post-traumatic stress disorder, tardive dyskinesia, mental health, and substance abuse.

4268 Baylor College of Medicine: Roy M and Phyllis Gough Center on Aging
1 Baylor Plaza
Houston, TX 77030-3498
713-798-6105
Fax: 713-798-6688
http://www.hcoa.org
Robert S Luchi MD, Contact
Mark M Udden MD

Internal unit of Baylor College representing research into the biology of aging.

4269 Baylor University Institute forGerontological Studies
PO Box 97320
Waco, TX 76798
254-710-3701
Fax: 254-710-6455
e-mail: Marilyn_Gusukuma@baylor.edu
http://www.baylor.edu/gerontology
Marilyn Gusukuma, Project Coordinator

Physical, emotional, social, and spiritual needs of older persons, including family solidarity in later life, geriatric dentistry, problems of the older offender, and life-long learning.

4270 Beth Israel Deaconess Medical Center
General Clinical Research Center
330 Brookline Avenue
Room Gz800
Boston, MA 02215-5491
617-667-5696
Fax: 617-667-1525
e-mail: kjordan@bidmc.harvard.edu
http://www.corelan.bih.harvard.edu/purpose
Diane Pliner, Manager

Biomedicine, cardiology, endocrinology, gastroenterology, gerontology, hematology, nephrology, neurology, nutrition, obstetrics, pulmonary physiology, psychiatry, and surgery.

4271 Boston University Gerontology Center
53 Bay State Road
Boston, MA 02215-2101
617-353-5045
Fax: 617-353-5047
e-mail: edelston@bu.edu
http://www.bu.edu/gerontology
Rebecca Sullivan, Director Gerontology/Geriatrics
Elizabeth Markson, Academic Director Gerontology
Rita Edelston, Educational Coordinator

Gerontology, including biological, psychological, social, medical, and humanistic concerns relating to aging and the elderly. Identifies socially relevant problems in the fields of gerontology and human development, socioeconomic factors impinging upon the lives and well-being of older adults, historical context in which values and attitudes toward the aging have been defined and redefined, and the medical and social services developed to serve the older person in American society.

4272 Brain Research Institute University ofCalifornia, Los Angeles
1506 Gonda Goldschmied Neuroscience and Genetics Research Center
Los Angeles, CA 90095-1761
310-825-5061
Fax: 310-206-5855
e-mail: lmaninger@mednet.ucla.edu
http://www.bri.ucla.edu
Christopher Evans, Director
Bernard Balleine, Associate Director for Research
Barbara Cross, Chief Administrative Officer

Brain and central nervous system, including interdisciplinary studies in developmental neurobiology, molecular neurobiology, neuroanatomy, neurobiophysics, neurochemistry, neurocytology, neuroendocrinology, neuroimaging, neuromuscular physiology, neuropathology, neuropharmacology, neurophysiology, behavior, neuroimmunology, and experimental epilepsy.

4273 Brandeis University Institute for Health Policy
Brandeis University
PO Box 549110
Waltham, MA 02254
781-736-3860
Fax: 781-736-3865
e-mail: wallack2@binah.cc.brandeis.edu
http://www.brandeis.edu/heller/ihp/ihp
Stuart Altman PhD, Dean

Health services research and policy analysis, focusing on the design, development, implementation, and evaluation of innovative financing and delivery systems. Specific areas of research include establishing and implementing national health care expenditure limits, all-payer payment systems, an Alcohol and Drug Services Survey, the changing trends of substance abuse, financing and reimbursement of drug abuse treatment programs, and long-term care for the elderly, including home care services for the disabled elderly and cost effective models and standards for assisted living. Operates the [Center for Substance Abuse Services Research], [Center for Drug Abuse Policy Analysis], [Center on Vulnerable Populations], and the [National Resource Center].

4274 Brandeis University Policy Center on Aging
Heller Graduate School 035
Waltham, MA 02254
781-736-3866
800-929-1995
Fax: 781-736-3865
e-mail: NATWONCTR@brandeis.edu
http://www.heller.brandeis.edu/national/

Retirement income adequacy and policy, long term care and health service delivery, aging and mental health, supportive service in senior housing and resource allocation for the elderly. Generates, synthesizes, and disseminates knowledge on policy alternatives affecting the economic security of the aging; analyzes the economic, legal, administrative, and political consequences and feasibility of alternative policies; participates in the formulation and implementation of policy; and trains professionals for careers focused in the area of policy analysis.

Aging/Research Centers

4275 Brown University Center for Gerontology and Health Care Research
2 Stimson Street
Providence, RI 02912-9042
401-863-3604
Fax: 401-863-3489
http://www.chcr.brown.edu
Richard Besdine, MD

Fundamental and applied research relating to aging, chronic disease, and long-term care with particular emphasis on the assessment of function and health status and its application to diagnosis, prognosis and monitoring of long-term care. Offers data collection and teaching and training services.

4276 Brown University Population Studies and Training Center
PO Box 1916
Providence, RI 02912-1916
401-274-2712
Fax: 401-863-3351
e-mail: Population_Studies@brown.edu
http://www.pstc3.pstc.brown.edu
Constance Brown, Owner

Family and household demography, health and fertility transitions in developing nations, infant mortality, child health, social and economic development, migration/immigration and population distribution, aging and health in developed societies and developing nations. Develops new methods for assessing the dynamics of population change, evaluates the causes and consequences of these changes assessment of policies to influence population change. Focuses on quantitative and qualitative methods in the collection and analysis of demographic data, uses econometric and biostatistical methods in demographic analysis. Promotes the knowledge of the patterns, factors, and consequences of population change, and makes this knowledge available for formulating and evaluating population policy.

4277 California State University: Bakersfield Applied Research Center
9001 Stockdale Highway
Bakersfield, CA 93311-1022
661-664-2173
Fax: 661-665-6927
e-mail: excellence@csub.edu
http://www.csubak.edu

Committed to providing high quality undergraduate and graduate programs.

4278 Case Western Reserve University Center for Biomedical Ethics
10900 Euclid Avenue
Cleveland, OH 44106-4976
216-368-3200
800-773-2633
Fax: 216-368-8713
e-mail: xx245@po.cwru.edu
http://www.cwru.edu/cwru/dept/med/bioethics/bio
Thomas Murray PhD, Director
Edward M Hundert, President

Bioethics, including human genetics, decisions to end life, aging, and reproductive alternatives.

1985 Frequency: 3X

4279 Case Western Reserve University Elderly Care Research Center
10900 Euclid Avenue
Cleveland, OH 44106-7124
216-368-3200
Fax: 216-368-8713
e-mail: exk@po.cwru.edu
http://www.socwww.cwru.edu
Edward Hundert, President

Aging, health, and mental health, including public policy issues, predictors of wellness and vulnerability, environmental and social influences on well-being of the elderly, cross-national and cross-cultural comparisons, and health and mental health outcomes of stress, coping, and adaptation.

4280 Case Western Reserve University School of Medicine
10900 Euclid Avenue
Cleveland, OH 44106-7288
216-368-3611
Fax: 216-368-0495
e-mail: pathology@case.edu
http://www.case.edu/med/pathology
John B Lowe MD, Chair Department of Pathology

Immunology, immunopathology, aging, cell biology, neurobiology, Alzheimer disease, oncology, and drug delivery.

1929

4281 Case Western Reserve University: University Center on Aging and Health
10900 Euclid Avenue
Cleveland, OH 44106-7131
216-368-3200
Fax: 216-368-6389
e-mail: dxf5@po.cwru.edu
May L Wykle PhD RN, Director
Edward M Hundert, President

Conducts, supports, and facilitates research at the University Center on Aging and Health, including the effects of stress and strains, and elderly physical health on persons over 65 years of age. Emphasizes prevention, diagnosis, treatment, management of illness or disability, and service utilization of care giver.

4282 Center for Clinical and Aging Services Research
3330 Geary Boulevard
2nd Floor
San Francisco, CA 94118-3347
415-750-4111
e-mail: mbrod@gioa.org
http://www.careguide.net/careguide.cgi/ccasr/cc
Glenn Dowling PhD, Contact
David Werdegar, President

Geriatrics and gerontology, including testing and improvement of medical and social interventions; drug efficacy studies and medication compliance in the elderly; outcomes of long-term care interventions in the areas of Alzheimer's disease, respite care, and home care; and ethical issues arising from the extended life cycle.

4283 Center for Clinical and Lifestyle Research
21 N Quinsigamond Avenue
Shrewsbury, MA 01545-2400
508-756-1228
Fax: 508-754-5098
e-mail: bporcaro@jamesrippe.com
http://www.jamesrippe.com
James M Rippe MD, Director

Aging, hypertension, ischemic heart disease, osteoarthritis, psychological well being, cholesterol control, weight management, children's health and fitness, health benefits of walking, women's health issues, hydration and temperature regulation, and evaluation of exercise and medical equipment.

1994

4284 Center for Human Services
7200 Wisconsin Avenue
Suite 600
Bethesda, MD 20814-4830
301-654-8338
Fax: 301-941-8427
e-mail: dnicholas@urc-chs.com
http://www.urc-chs.com
Dr. David Nicholas, Director
Melvyn Estrin, President

Quality healthcare research

1963

4285 Center for Neural Recovery and Rehabilitation Research
RR 9w
West Haverstraw, NY 10993
845-786-4859
Fax: 845-786-4875
http://www.helenhayeshospital.org/cnrrcnt.htm

Epilepsy, brain injury, and neuroendocrinology. Degenerative neurological disorders such as Huntington's and Alzheimer's diseases are also investigated.

Aging / Research Centers

4286 Center for Study of Aging
Int'l Association of Pysical Activity/Aging/Sports
706 Madison Avenue
Albany, NY 12208
518-465-6927
Fax: 518-462-1339
http://www.centerforthestudyofaging-albany.org

4287 Center for Understanding Aging
200 Executive Boulevard
Suite 201
Southington, CT 06489-1058
718-824-4004
Fax: 718-824-4242
e-mail: couper.natla@snet.net
Donna Couper, Director

Seeks to dispel myths about aging and old age, encourages communication among generations and works to create a social environment where people of all ages can live together. Also serves as a clearinghouse of information on issues of aging and intergenerational programs. Provides professional speakers and workshop leaders.

4288 Center for the Study of Aging
706 Madison Avenue
Albany, NY 12208-3695
518-462-1331
Fax: 518-462-1339
e-mail: iapaas@aol.com
http://www.members.aol.com/iapaas
Sarah Harris, Executive Director

Social and medical research on aging, including physical activity and aging, housing for the elderly, geriatric cardiology, nutrition, mental health, oral history, public policy, caregiving, prevention and respite care for the frail elderly.

4289 Center for the Study of Pharmacy and Therapeutics for the Elderly
Peter Lamy Center
515 W Lombard Street
Baltimore, MD 21201-1602
410-706-2434
877-706-2434
Fax: 410-706-1488
e-mail: lamycenter@rx.umaryland.edu
http://www.pharmacy.umaryland.edu
Nicole Brandt PharmD, Director
Bruce Stuart PhD, Professor/Executive Director
Reba Cornman MSW, Director Communication/Outreach

Provides educational programs, researches gerontology and geriatrics. Also compiles statistics and maintains a speaker's bureau.
1978

4290 Central Michigan University: Center for Adult Longitudinal Studies
108 E Smith Hall
Mt Pleasant, MI 48859
989-774-3686
Fax: 517-794-7406
e-mail: Lawrence.R.Lepisto@cmich.edu
http://www.cmich.edu/ACA-CIC
Lawrence R Lepisto, Contact
Stan Shingles, Executive Director

Measurement of psychological and consumer behavior dimensions of the aging process for adults over the entire lifespan.

4291 Cerebral Blood Flow Laboratories
Veterans Admin. Medical Center
2002 Holcombe Boulevard
Bldg 110
Houston, TX 77030-4211
713-795-5807
Fax: 713-794-7583
e-mail: jmeyer@bcm.tmc.edu
John Stirli Meyer MD

Measurement of CT morphological changes and cerebral blood flow; cerebrovascular disorders; aging, Alzheimer's and ischemic vascular dementias and responses to medical, surgical, pharmacological, and behavioral treatment; prevention, diagnosis, and treatment of stroke and migraine; cerebral blood flow control and cerebral metabolism; neuropharmacology and physiology; aging; dementia; transient ischemic attacks; and risk factors for stroke.
1981

4292 Children of Aging Parents
PO Box 167
Richboro, PA 18954
610-293-6960
800-227-7294
Fax: 215-945-8720
http://www.careguide.net
Mirca Liberti, Development Director
Louise Fradkin, Operations Director

A national clearinghouse for caregivers of the elderly. It provides information and referral, educational programs and materials and caregiver support groups. CAPS also produces a bi-monthly newsletter which is available through the organization. Individuals: $15.00. Professionals: $50.00. Corporations: $100.00.

4293 College of Maharishi Vedic Medicine Center for Health and Aging Studies
Db 1134
Fairfield, IA 52557-1134
641-472-1129
Fax: 641-472-1167
e-mail: rschneid@mum.edu
http://www.mum.edu/CHAS
Robert H Schneider MD, Director

Behavioral cardiology, minority health, preventive cardiology, behavioral and preventive gerontology, and traditional and alternative medicine. Conducts controlled clinical trials on cardiovascular disease treatment and prevention in community settings with behavioral methods; research into methods to slow or retard aging processes; research and development in traditional natural medicine; and programs with African American populations.

4294 Columbia University Irving Center for Clinical Research
Columbia University
622 W 168th Street
Ph 10
New York, NY 10032-3720
212-305-9362
Fax: 212-305-3213
e-mail: ginsberg@cudept.cis.columbia.edu
http://www.cpmcnet.columbia.edu/dept

Multidisciplinary studies of human disease and clinical pharmacology. Areas include arrhythmia control, heart failure, atherosclerosis, nutrition, metabolism, clinical pharmacology, dermatology, endocrinology, hypertension, immunology, mineral metabolism and skeletal disease, neuromuscular disease, physiology, pulmonary disease, pulmonary physiology, reproductive research studies, neurology (including dementia, stroke, and seizure disorders), oncology, AIDS/infectious disease, geriatrics, epidemiology, and substance abuse.

4295 Columbia University: Center for Geriatrics & Gerontology
100 Haven Avenue
New York, NY 10032-2645
212-795-0211
Fax: 212-305-3213
Dr. Barry Gurland, Director

Methodological, epidemiological, and clinical research in geriatrics/gerontology and long-term care. Specific studies are directed toward mental disorders, psychosocial problems, and functional impairments of the elderly. The Center has developed model projects using a comprehensive assessment instrument that has been refined for use in various settings. The Center is also active in cross-national research with a collaborating group in London.

4296 Coriell Institute for Medical Research
403 Haddon Avenue
Camden, NJ 08103-1505
856-966-7377
Fax: 856-964-0254
e-mail: webmaster@coriell.org
http://www.coriell.org
Joseph L Mintzer, Executive VP/COO
Josefina J Nash, Director Information Systems

Aging/Research Centers

Cell and molecular biology, microbiology, genetics, aging, cancer and cancer immunology, tumor virology, antibodies, genetic disorders, vascular disorders, infectious diseases and virus/chromosome relationships, environmental mutagenesis, and genetic probes. Studies utilization of cells grown in tissue culture for isolation and characterization of tumor cell antigens, viruses, genetic abnormalities, tumor viruses, and chromosomes.

4297 Creighton University Center for Health Policy and Ethics
2500 California Plaza
Omaha, NE 68178
402-280-5060
Fax: 402-280-5735
e-mail: rpurtilo@creighton.edu

Steven Friedriche, Manager

Cross-cultural ethics, ethical issues involving the elderly and neonates, health care reform, legal ethics, medical economics, nursing ethics, pharmacy ethics, racial and ethnic health concerns, religious ethics, rural health policy, and women's issues.

4298 Creighton University Center for Healthy Aging
42nd & Center Streets
Omaha, NE 68105
402-281-2017
Fax: 402-280-5735

David Haber PhD, Director

Focuses on human development, aging and health care for the elderly.

4299 Dartmouth College Center for Evaluative Clinical Sciences
7251 Strasenburghdartmout Medical
Hanover, NH 03755
603-643-4490
http://www.dartmouth.edu/dms/cecs

Jeff Robbins, Executive Director

Evaluative clinical science and health care delivery, including medical care epidemiology, health policy, health behavior, efficacy of medical procedures, quality of medical and surgical care, distribution of health care resources, medical interventions and consequences for patients, care at the end of life, distribution of health care resources across hospital market areas, geriatric health, and sociology of medical organizations.

4300 Duke University Center for the Study of Aging and Human Development
Duke University
PO Box 3003
Durham, NC 27710
919-477-9292
Fax: 919-684-8569
e-mail: ray00004@mc.duke.edu
http://www.geri.duke.edu

Harvey J Cohen MD, Director
Michael Duke, Owner

Human and animal physiology, immunology, neuroendocrinology, pharmacology, carcinogenesis, enzyme biochemistry, free radical effects, membrane and receptor function, bone metabolism and osteoporosis, central nervous system structure and function, Alzheimer's disease, dementia, cognitive processes, psychometrics, human personality and behavior, family structure and intergenerational relationships, social factors and illness, epidemiology of aging and chronic illness, stress and coping, cell growth and differentiation, signal transduction, and the demographics and economics of aging populations. The Aging Center coordinates research, training, and clinical services in aging for the University. The Division of Geriatrics focuses research on the basic and clinical aspects of aging, emphasizing neoplasia, bone and musculoskeletal disorders and rehabilitation involved, immunology, cardiovascular diseases, cerebrovascular disease/dementia, enzymatic and cellular basis for aging, and health services delivery for the aged.

4301 Duke University General Clinical Research Center
Duke University Medical Clinic
PO Box 3854
Durham, NC 27710
919-477-9292
Fax: 919-681-8829
e-mail: marke00l@mc.duke.edu
http://www.duke.edu/rankincru

M Louise Markert, Program Director
Michael Duke, Owner

Multidisciplinary, clinical research into the cause, progression, prevention, control, and cure of human disease. Sample projects have studied immunodeficiency diseases, Alzheimer's disease, food allergy, X-linked hypophosphatemic rickets, and cardiovascular disease.

4302 Economic and Social Research Institute
2100 M Street NW
Suite 605
Washington, DC 20037-1235
202-785-3669
Fax: 202-833-8932
http://www.esresearch.org

Elliot Wicks, Manager

4303 Edmund S. Muskie School of Public Service
University of Southern Maine
PO Box 9300
Portland, ME 04104-9300
207-780-4430
Fax: 207-780-4417
e-mail: andyc@usm.maine.edu
http://www.muskie.usm.maine.edu

Health, rehabilitation and special education, aging, mental health, developmental disabilities, children, youth, and families, and alcoholism. Projects include program evaluations, policy/planning analysis and research, training systems, training and curriculum materials, policy forums, and communication technologies.

4304 Edward and Esther Polisher Research Institute
5301 Old York Road
Philadelphia, PA 19141-2912
215-456-2000
Fax: 215-456-2017
e-mail: mlawton@thunder.OCIS.temple.edu

M Powell Lawton, Director

Social, cultural, psychological, medical, and biological aspects of aging and services to the aged. Conducts basic and applied research on caregivers of impaired elderly and treatments for depression. Also conducts studies of housing, ethnicity and aging, Alzheimer's disease, and biomarkers of depression.

4305 Ethel Percy Andrus Gerontology Center
University of Southern California
3715 McClintock Avenue
Los Angeles, CA 90089
213-740-6060
Fax: 213-740-8241
e-mail: ldsgero@usc.edu
http://http://www.usc.edu/gero

Gerontology, including interdisciplinary studies on biological, behavioral, social, and environmental aspects of aging process. Develops and evaluates curricula for training scientific and professional personnel specializing in study of aging processes and for improving associated personal, medical and social disorders, cognitive behavior, employment and retirement, state politics of aging, Alzheimer's disease, income maintenance and more.nd reproductive aspects of aging. Also responsible for coordination of graduate and postgraduate instruction and research training in gerontology conducted within academic disciplines of architecture, biology, economics, education, linguistics, pharmacy, political science, psychology, psychiatry, public administration, urban and regional planning, social work, and sociology at the University.

4306 Families and Work Institute
267 5th Avenue
Floor 2
New York, NY 10016-7503
212-465-2044
Fax: 212-465-8637
http://www.familiesandwork.org

Aging/Research Centers

Child care, elder care, family and work issues, men and families, diversity, flexibility, community planning, organizational change, and public policy.

4307 Florida Policy Exchange Center on Aging
4202 E Fowler Avenue
Tampa, FL 33620-9951
813-974-3466
Fax: 813-974-5766
e-mail: lpolivka@admin.usf.edu
http://www.usfweb.usf.edu/fpeca
Larry Polivka, Director

Aging and aging related issues and policies, particularly effective, innovative programs for elderly in other countries. Activities include studies on crime, housing, health care, aging, service delivery issues, and other issues regarding the elderly.

4308 Florida State University: Pepper Institute on Aging and Public Policy
203 Pepper Center
Tallahassee, FL 32306
850-644-2831
Fax: 850-644-2304
e-mail: mhardy@garnet.acns.fsu.edu
http://www.fsu.edu/pia
Melissa Hardy, Contact

Public policy issues affecting the elderly, including health care, income security, and social welfare. Research programs have included historical and comparative studies of income security programs for the elderly, the elderly in the work force, the elderly and the political system, gender and racial dimensions of poverty in old age, retirement decisions, elder abuse in Florida health care facilities, and alternatives to nursing home care and health care financing.

4309 Fordham University Third Age Center
441 E Fordham Road
Bronx, NY 10458-9993
718-817-4398
Fax: 718-817-4769
e-mail: lewis@murray.fordham.edu
http://www.fordham.edu

Concentrates on the intellectual, emotional, economic, spiritual, and cultural opportunities that confront the elderly. Programs include studies on the interface of informal and formal support systems, long-term care and service delivery, alternative forms of housing, older persons in families, neighborhood ethnography, life styles of the suburban elderly, employment and the older worker, religion and aging.

4310 Georgia Consortium on the Psychology of Aging
100 Candler Hall
Athens, GA 30602
706-542-3954
Fax: 706-542-4805
e-mail: lpoon@geron.uga.edu
http://www.geron.uga.edu
Leonard W Poon PhD, Director

Psychology of aging, including basic studies in cognition, and clinical diagnosis and treatment of behavioral dysfunctions most often found with the aged. The Consortium was formed to share training and research resources and to foster interaction between psychologists and other scientists.

4311 Georgia State University Center for Mature Consumer Studies
Broad Street
Atlanta, GA 30303
404-880-9595
Fax: 404-651-4198
e-mail: gmoschis@gsu.edu
http://www.gsu.edu/mkteer/cmcs
Jimmy George, Manager

Mature consumer marketing, with emphasis on industries of special importance to the older consumer, including financial services, health care, housing, leisure, insurance, technology, mass media, and telecommunications industries. Studies include analysis of older consumer needs, lifestyles, purchasing habits and consumption patterns. Serves as an information resource, assisting in strategy development for reaching the mature consumer market.

4312 Geriatrics Education and Research Institute
University of North Texas Health
3500 Camp Bowie Boulevard
Fort Worth, TX 76107-2644
817-735-5440
Fax: 817-735-2486
e-mail: tfairchi@hsc.unt.edu
http://www.hsc.unt.edu/research/aging

Biology of aging, including fundamental chemical and molecular biological changes that may cause aging; health promotion in older adults including health programs promoting physical, psychological, and social well being; geriatric care and practice including evaluation of new clinical programs, physical/mental functions, long term care system development focusing on case management, and in-home health screen/assessment of home-bound elderly.

4313 Gerontological Society of America
1030 15th Street NW
Suite 250
Washington, DC 20005-1526
202-842-1275
Fax: 202-842-1150
e-mail: geron@geron.org
http://www.geron.org
Carol Ann Schutz, Executive Director
Linda Krogh Harootyan, Deputy Director

The society was formed in 1945 to promote the scientific study of aging, to encourage exchanges among researchers and practitioners from the various disciplines related to gerontology and to foster the use of gerontological research in forming public policy. Publishes five scientific journals.

4314 Harbor-UCLA Research and Education Institute
1124 W Carson Street
Torrance, CA 90502-2006
310-222-2218
Fax: 310-320-6515
e-mail: steers@rei.humc.edu
http://www.rei.edu
Manny Manglit, Manager

Cardiology, reproductive endocrinology, neuroscience (psychiatry, neurology, neurosurgery, and radiology), pathology, respiratory physiology, oncology, rheumatology, medical genetics, perinatology, laser surgery, sleep disorders, Alzheimer's disease, immunizations, emergency medicine, and depression. Also studies infectious diseases, including AIDS. Conducts clinical research studies using volunteers to determine the effectiveness of new drugs and therapies, including vaccines.

4315 Harvard Brain Tissue Resource Center
115 Mill Street
Belmont, MA 02478-1041
800-272-4622
http://www.brainbank.mclean.org

Provides tissues to the neuroscience community for studies of movement disorders, major psychoses, and dementia.

4316 Harvard University Division of Health Policy Research and Education
180 Longwood Avenue
Boston, MA 02115-5821
617-432-1325
Fax: 617-432-3503
e-mail: newhouse@hcp.med.harvard.edu

Coordinates health policy resources throughout the University, including suggestion of new research initiatives, stimulation of educational activities, coordination of research and educational efforts, promotion of multidisciplinary analysis of complex health policy issues, and dissemination of health policy findings.

4317 Huffington Center on Aging
Baylor College of Medicine
1 Baylor Plaza
M-320
Houston, TX 77030-3411
713-798-5804
Fax: 713-798-6688
e-mail: jsmith@bcm.tmc.edu

Cell and molecular biology of aging, cardiovascular disease, and ethics in long-term care.

Aging / Research Centers

4318 Hunter College of City University of New York: Brookdale Center on Aging
1114 Avenue of the Americas
Floor 40
New York, NY 10036-7703
212-974-6856
Fax: 646-366-1041
e-mail: brookdale@shiva.hunter.cuny.edu
http://www.hunter.cuny.edu
Brian Hunter, Manager

Legal support program for social workers, paralegals, attorneys and other professionals engaged in providing advocacy assistance to the elderly poor.

4319 Indiana Family Institute
55 Monument Circle
Suite 322
Indianapolis, IN 46204-5910
317-423-9178
800-269-2959
Fax: 317-423-9421
http://www.hoosierfamily.org
Curt Smith, President

Family issues research.

4320 Indiana University Bloomington Center on Aging and Aged
2805 E 10th Street
Bloomington, IN 47408-2619
812-855-3403
Fax: 812-855-6194
http://www.indiana.edu/rugs/ctrdir/caa
Suzanne Thorin, Manager

Gerontology, including developmentally disabled, handicapped, minorities, rural-isolated, and mainstream aging populations.

4321 Indiana University Human Genetics Center
School of Medicine
975 W Walnut Street
Indianapolis, IN 46202-5181
317-274-5740
Fax: 317-274-2387
Joe C Christian MD, Chairman
Jo Lynn Bahr, Manager

4322 Indiana University: General Clinical Research Center
550 University Boulevard
Indianapolis, IN 46202-5149
317-274-8231
Fax: 317-274-7346
e-mail: mpeacock@iupui.edu
Dr. Munro Peacock, Director
Sharon Deem, Administrator

General health research
1971

4323 Indiana University: Purdue University at Indianapolis Hackney Dermatopathology Research Laboratory
975 W Walnut Street
Room 349
Indianapolis, IN 46202-5181
317-274-5555
e-mail: dspanda@iupui.edu
http://www.indiana.edu/rugs/ctrdir/hdrl
Daniel F Spandau, Director
Charles Bantz, Manager

Skin diseases, including skin cancer and psoriasis and the genetic changes that occur with these conditions. Wound healing and the aging of skin are also studied.

4324 Institute for Community Inclusion
100 Morrissey Boulevard
Dorchester, MA 02125-3300
617-287-4300
Fax: 617-287-4352
e-mail: ici@umb.edu
http://www.communityinclusion.org

Research in health issues and the community.

4325 Institute of Developmental Neuroscience and Aging
301 University Boulevard
Galveston, TX 77555
409-772-3667
Fax: 409-772-8028
e-mail: jperezpo@utmb.edu
Regino Perez-Polo PhD, President

Developmental neuroscience and aging, focusing on establishing neuroscience programs in developing and third world countries.

4326 International Center for the Disabled
340 E 24th Street
New York, NY 10010-4019
212-679-0100
Fax: 212-585-6161
e-mail: ccgodfrey@aol.com
Dr. Herbert Krauss, Director

Promising techniques designed to prevent, reduce, and control disabilities arising from persistent physical disorders. Studies focus on the control of deterioration and disability associated with recurring ear infections in children, symptom magnification in those with disabling conditions, and factors associated with gainful employment. Other projects examine the parameters of post-laryngectomy speech, nerve conduction patterns in overuse syndromes, relapse factors in alcoholism, and methods used in the management of individuals with Alzheimer's disease. Techniques that prove effective are transferred to ICD clinical programs and communicated to professionals nationally and internationally.

4327 Irvington Institute for ImmunologicalResearch
245 5th Avenue
Room 2101
New York, NY 10016-8728
212-576-1005
Fax: 212-576-1006
http://www.irvingtoninstitute.org
Kerry W Walsh, Executive Director

Studies and educates on subjects like cancer, AIDS, diabetes, organ rejection, allergies and other medical issues.

4328 Johns Hopkins University Health Services Research and Development Center
624 N Broadway
Room 482
Baltimore, MD 21205-1900
410-955-9725
e-mail: hsrdc.center@phnet.sph.jhu.edu
Norma Lee Barton, Manager

Conducts health services research, including studies on the following: determinants of health outcomes; the impacts of alternative health care systems on cost and quality; effective strategies for health promotion and disease prevention; and methods of meeting the needs of high risk populations such as the poor, elderly, mentally ill, disabled, and children. Research is conducted using experimental (randomized controlled trials) or nonexperimental methods, and relies to varying degrees on primary data sources obtained through interviews and observation and secondary data sources obtained from management information systems, financial reports, and existing regional and national data sources and surveys.

4329 Johns Hopkins University Institute for Policy Studies
3400 N Charles Street
Baltimore, MD 21218-2680
410-235-3435
Fax: 410-516-8233
e-mail: sjn@jhunix.hcf.jhu.edu
http://www.jhu.edu/ips
William R Brody, CEO

Economic development, at risk youth, economic structural change, problems of the elderly, future of the welfare state, the role of nonprofit organizations, youth employment, human resource investment, crime and delinquency, public finance, housing, regional capital flows.

Aging / Research Centers

4330 Johns Hopkins University: Center for Immunization Research
Johns Hopkins University School of Hygiene
624 N Broadway
Baltimore, MD 21205-1900
410-955-7894
Fax: 410-502-6898
e-mail: dburke@jhsph.edu
http://www.ih.jhsph.edu/cir

Dr. Donald Burke, Director

Research in vaccine immunization

4331 Kansas State University Galichia Center for Aging
203 Fairchild Hall
Manhattan, KS 66506-1113
785-532-5945
Fax: 785-532-5944
e-mail: gerontology@ksu.edu
http://www.oznet.ksu.edu/mhaging

Lyn Norris Baker, Director
Pam Evans, Administrative Officer

Coordinates and develops educational and training programs in aging, engages in aging research, coordinates outreach activities, and serves as a referral center for information on aging resources in Kansas. The center on aging faculty are committed to programs of education, training, outreach and research, which address general issues of aging and seek solutions to the challenges of aging in rural areas and smalltowns.g, adult education, and learning problems of the elderly.

4332 Kent State University Exercise Physiology Lab
162 Gym Anx
Kent, OH 44242
330-673-4000
Fax: 330-672-4106
e-mail: wsinning@kentvm.kent.edu

Wayne E Sinnig PhD, Contact
Mike Morrow, President

Exercise physiology, body composition, and physical fitness, including studies of protein metabolism and exercise, cardiovascular/respiratory responses during exercise in heat and cold, an neuromuscular integration/biomechanics, and psychosocial reactivity to behavioral stressors.

4333 Kent State University Gerontology Center
PO Box 5190
Kent, OH 44242
330-672-2857
Fax: 330-672-4106
e-mail: david@ccs.kent.edu
http://www.kent.edu/continuing-studies

All facets of aging and related issues. Works with the School of Family and Consumer Studies and the Northeastern Ohio Universities College of Medicine on a continual basis.

4334 Lehigh University Center for Social Research
516 Brodhead Avenue
520
Bethlehem, PA 18015-3008
610-758-4200
Fax: 610-758-6350

Diane T Hyland PhD, Director
Edward Shupp, Manager

Interdisciplinary studies in social and behavioral sciences, including health and human development, families and children, aging, and program evaluation, with particular emphasis on family dynamics and child rearing practices, family responses to perinatal loss, social influences on health, and evaluation of technology transfer and educational programs. Collaborates with local corporations and private and governmental agencies on some projects.

4335 Lion's Club International
300 W 22nd Street
Oak Brook, IL 60523-8806
630-571-5466
Fax: 630-571-8890
e-mail: lions@lionsclubs.org
http://www.lionsclubs.org

Gary Lapetina, CEO

International organization with over 1.4 million members dedicated to the largest blindness prevention program ('SightFirst').

4336 Los Amigos Research and Education Institute
PO Box 3500
Downey, CA 90242-3500
562-401-8111
Fax: 562-803-5569

Julia F LaPlount, Contact

Clinical medicine, including multidisciplinary study of severe chronic disabilities in pulmonary and respiratory functions, cardiology, spinal cord injury, orthopedic disabilities, environmental health, stroke, pathokinesiology, liver disease, neuromuscular stimulation and control, rehabilitation of severely disabled persons, cerebral palsy, problem amputations, arthritis, and diabetes. Treats effects of atmospheric pollutants on human lung function, investigates possible causes of Alzheimer's disease, and explores new methods and procedures for care and treatment of gerontology patients.

4337 Maharishi International University: Lab for Health & Aging Studies
1000 N 4th Street
Fairfield, IA 52557
641-472-1148
Fax: 641-472-1167

Robert H Schneider, Director

4338 Mankind Research Foundation
1315 Apple Avenue
Silver Spring, MD 20910-3307
301-587-8686
Fax: 301-587-8688
e-mail: uv@uvbi.com
http://www.uvbi.com

Dr. Carl Schneider, President
Nader A Dakak MD

General health research
1973

4339 Massachusetts Institute of Technology General Clinical Research Center
50 Ames Street
Room 445
Cambridge, MA 02142-1308
617-253-2871
Fax: 562-803-5569
e-mail: dick@mit.edu

Dr. Richard J Wartman, Program Director
Joe Graham, Manager

Normal human metabolism, physiology, and behavior, including studies on hormones (melatonin and sleep), fates of deuterated amino acids, behavioral and neuroendocrine effect of foods (carbohydrate, protein, and caffeine), effects of drugs on memory and other behaviors, and endocrine and metabolic effects on aging. Also studies human diseases such as obesity, Alzheimer's disease, brain injury, Parkinson's disease, seasonal depression, use of brain imaging techniques to follow metabolic events, and facilitation of smoking withdrawal by psychopharmacologic agents.

4340 Mayo Clinic and Foundation-General Clinical Research Center
St. Mary's Hospital
1216 2nd Street SW
Rochester, MN 55902-1906
507-255-5123
Fax: 507-255-7445
e-mail: andersen@mayo.edu
http://www.mayo.edu

Jeffrey Rome, Manager

Researches inpatient and outpatient sleep pattern, cardiac telemetry monitoring, endocrinology and many other medical issues.
1971

4341 Minneapolis Medical Research Foundation
914 S 8th Street
Minneapolis, MN 55404-1210
612-347-5099
Fax: 612-337-7189
http://www.mmrfweb.org

Philip Peterson MD, President

General health research
1952

Aging/Research Centers

4342 Mount Sinai School of Medicine of City University of New York
Department of Geriatrics & Adult Development
PO Box 1070
New York, NY 10029
212-241-6696
Fax: 212-360-6338

Robert N Butler, Director
Kelli Ann Bailey, Manager

Health, long-term care, and productive aging, emphasizing policy implications for future generations and institutions.

4343 National Institute on Aging
US Department of Health & Human Services
9000 Rockville Pike
Room 5c35
Bethesda, MD 20892
301-496-1993
800-422-6237
Fax: 301-496-2525

The Institute conducts and supports biomedical and behavioral research to increase the knowledge of the aging process and associated physical, psychological, and social factors resulting from advanced age. Incontinence, menopause, susceptibility to disease, and memory loss are among the areas of special concern.

4344 National Institute on Aging Gerontology Research Center
5600 Nathan Shock Drive
Baltimore, MD 21224-6825
410-558-8110
Fax: 410-558-8137
e-mail: longod@grc.nia.nih.gov

Dr. Dan Longo MD, Director

Gerontology research, including molecular genetics, human physiology, personality, behavioral research, and Alzheimer's disease studies.

4345 National Institute on Aging: Information Center
31 Center Drive
Room 5c27
Bethesda, MD 20892
301-496-1752
800-222-2225

Richard Hodes, Executive Director

Concerned with the health problems of older Americans. The Center offers free printed materials, including fact sheets about going to the hospital and about prostate problems.

4346 Neuropsychiatric Research Institute
700 1st Avenue S
Fargo, ND 58103-1802
701-293-1335
Fax: 701-293-3226
e-mail: rerickson@mail.med.UND.Nodak.edu
http://www.narifargo.com

James Mitchell, President

Basic and clinical studies of the central nervous system. Specific applications include eating disorders, studies of Alzheimer's disease, Parkinson's disease, Huntington's disease, and schizophrenia.

4347 New York State Institute for BasicResearch in Developmental Disabilities
1050 Forest Hill Road
Staten Island, NY 10314-6356
718-494-5333
Fax: 718-494-0833
http://www.omr.state.ny.us/

Dr Piotr B Kozlowski, Director
William T Brown MD

4348 Nisonger Center for Mental Retardation and Developmental Disabilities
Ohio State University
1581 Dodd Drive
Columbus, OH 43210-1257
614-292-8365
Fax: 614-292-3727
e-mail: reiss.7@osu.edu
http://www.osu.edu

Steven Reiss, Executive Director

Developmental disabilities, psychometric assessment, rehabilitation engineering, psychopathology, psychopharmacology, adults and aging, and family studies. Special attention given to applied research related to mental retardation and development and implementation of training programs to prepare professional personnel to work with the developmentally disabled. Provides early childhood classes for developmentally disabled preschoolers and offers information services to clients, students, staff, and faculty.

4349 Noll Physiological Research Center
Pennsylvania State University
119 Noll Laboratory Building
University Park, PA 16802
Fax: 760-434-5476
e-mail: paf4@psu.edu
http://www.noll.psu.edu

Metabolic adaptations to stress, biology of aging, and environmental and exercise physiology. Studies the effects of aging, physical activity, nutritional status, and heat, cold, and altitude stress on muscle metabolism and function, thermoregulation and cardiovascular control, immune function, and carbohydrate, insulin, and protein metabolism.

4350 Northwestern University: Buehler Center on Aging
750 N Lake Shore Drive
Room 601
Chicago, IL 60611-4403
312-503-3087
e-mail: j-webster@nwu.edu
http://www.nwu.edu/aging/index.htm

Dr. James R Webster, Director
Linda Emmanuel, Executive Director

Aging research
  1982

4351 Northwestern University: General Clinical Research Center
303 E Chicago Avenue
Chicago, IL 60611-3072
312-503-8649

Ennio C Rossi MD
  1961

4352 Ohio State University Neuroscience Program
333 W 10th Avenue
Columbus, OH 43210-1239
614-292-6192
Fax: 614-292-0490
e-mail: cole115@osu.edu
http://www.med.ohiostate.edu/

Gregory Cole, Contact
Eileen Mehl, Manager

Spinal cord injury, tumor biology, neuromuscular disease, epilepsy, Parkinson Disease, multiple sclerosis, stroke, neural development, regeneration, plasticity, regeneration, molecular neurobiology, and neuroimmunology.

4353 Olive View: UCLA Education and Researchnstitute
14445 Olive View Drive
Sylmar, CA 91342-1437
818-364-3566
Fax: 818-364-4584
e-mail: ovinfo@earthlink.net

Jeffrey Guterman, MD

Researches head injury, neurology, perinatal issues, genetic counseling and other health related studies.
  1986

4354 Oregon Research Institute
1715 Franklin Boulevard
Eugene, OR 97403-1983
541-484-2123
Fax: 541-484-1108
http://www.ori.org

Amy Greenwold, Manager

Aging / Research Centers

Behavioral sciences, including studies in tobacco prevention and cessation, compliance with diabetic regimens, children's social skills, personality structure, drug abuse prevention, depression and family interaction, special education technology, adolescent depression, and community child-rearing practices. Provides behavioral research and consultation services to other public and private agencies in fields of education, health, and mental health.

4355 Orentreich Foundation for the Advancement of Science
PO Box 375
Cold Spring, NY 10516
845-265-4206
Fax: 845-265-4210
e-mail: ofarms@juno.com

Norman Orentreich, President

Dermatology, aging, endocrinology, and serum markers for human diseases.

4356 Pennsylvania State University Center for Developmental and Health Genetics
101 Amy Gardner House
University Park, PA 16802
814-865-5471
Fax: 814-863-4768
e-mail: gm1@psu.edu

Gerald McCleam, Director
Randy Deike, Manager

Role of genetics in infant, child, and adolescent behavioral development, in aging, and in common drug and health problems. Also studies molecular, nutritional and immunological genetics. Uses human and animal model research projects to study personality, cognition, functional capacity, immune system functioning, and use and effects of alcohol and tobacco.

4357 Pennsylvania State University Gerontology Center
S-105 Henderson Building
University Park, PA 16802
814-865-1710
Fax: 814-863-9423
e-mail: arh1@psu.edu
http://www.hhdev.psu.edu/CENTERS

Broad interdisciplinary approach to questions on aging. Major areas of research are cognition in aging, developmental methodology, family and informal supports, and animal models of aging. Specific topics include reversing cognitive decline, human services for the elderly, caregiving, urinary incontinence, and the use of pharmaceutical products.

4358 Pennsylvania State University: Noll Physiological Research Center
129 Noll Laboratory Building
University Park, PA 16802
814-865-3453
Fax: 814-865-4602
e-mail: paf4@psu.edu
http://www.noll.psu.edu

Researches metabolic adaptations to stress, the effects of physical activities, nutritional status and other related topics.

1963

4359 Peter Lamy Center for Drug Therapy and Aging
University of Maryland School Pharmacy
515 West Lombard Street
Suite 166
Baltimore, MD 21201
410-706-2434
877-706-2434
Fax: 410-706-1488
e-mail: lamycenter@rx.umaryland.edu
http://www.pharmacy.umaryland.edu

Nicole Brandt, PharmD, Director
Bruce Stewart, PhD, Professor/Executive Director
Reba Cornman, MSW, Director Communication/Outreach

The Lamy Center is dedicated to improving drug therapy for aging adults through innovative research, education and clinical initiatives.

4360 Population Reference Bureau
1875 Connecticut Avenue NW
Suite 520
Washington, DC 20009-5738
202-462-2726
800-877-9881
Fax: 202-328-3937
e-mail: popref@prb.org
http://www.prb.org

Jim Scott, Manager

Demography, particularly national and international population trends as they relate to education, aging, employment, minority populations, health and welfare, and the environment.

4361 Portland State University Institute on Aging
PO Box 751
Portland, OR 97207
503-725-4891
Fax: 503-725-5100
e-mail: kutzae@psu4.pdx.edu
http://www.upa.pdx.edu/ioa

Alba Scholz, Manager

Adult development and aging, including health and social care systems, social and economic life maintenance, political behavior, age status, economic behavior, social and psychological phenomena, and communication.

4362 Purdue University: Center for Research on Aging
1365 Stone Hall
West Lafayette, IN 47907
765-494-4668
Fax: 765-494-3660

Dr. Sidney Stahl, Director

Social science research on aging, health and health care delivery.

4363 Rehabilitation Research and Training Center on Aging With a Disability
Rancho Los Amigos Medical Center
7601 Imperial Highway
Downey, CA 90242-3456
310-401-7402
Fax: 310-401-7011
http://www.agingwithdisability.org

Bryan Kemp PhD, Director

Aging research

4364 Research Institute of the Hebrew Home of Greater Washington
6121 Montrose Road
Rockville, MD 20852-4803
301-770-8449
Fax: 301-770-8455
e-mail: cohen-mansfield@hebrew-home.org

Jiska Cohen-Mansfield, Director

Gerontology, aging, and issues concerning the elderly, focusing on nursing home residents, their families, and staff. Areas include: agitated behaviors among the elderly; stress in families caring for elderly relatives; staff stress; back injuries among staff caretakers; the preferences of nursing home residents regarding life-sustaining treatments; standardized assessment procedures of the physical and emotional states of nursing home residents; sleep patterns of nursing home residents; the use of physical restraints in the nursing home; and the use of psychotropic medication in the nursing home.

4365 Retirement Research Foundation
8765 W Higgins Road
Suite 401
Chicago, IL 60631-4022
773-714-8080
Fax: 773-714-8089
e-mail: info@rrf.org
http://www.fdncenter.org/grantmaker/rrf/new

Marilyn Hennessy, President

Supports research to improve the well-being of elderly persons in the US Also provides support for model demonstration projects.

Aging / Research Centers

4366 Rockefeller University Laboratory of Neuroendocrinology
PO Box 165
New York, NY 10021
212-327-8909
Fax: 212-327-8634
e-mail: mcewen@rockvax.rockefeller.edu
Patricia Mackey, Manager

Seeks to locate brain sites and understand the mechanisms by which hormones promote neural plasticity and thereby alter endocrine function, behavior, neurological states, and mood. Also studies the influence of gonadal and adrenal hormones on aging in the brain.

4367 Rush University Neuroscience Institute
Rush-Presbyterian-St. Luke's Medical Center
1725 W Harrison Street
Chicago, IL 60612-3841
312-942-5555
Fax: 312-942-2380
e-mail: jfox@neuro.rush.edu
Dr. Jacob H Fox, Chairperson
Larry Goodman, CEO

Alzheimer's disease, Parkinson's disease, and stroke, including community-based studies, clinical investigations, and laboratory investigations using brain tissue and animal experimentation. Studies also focus on development of new drugs to improve symptoms of multiple sclerosis.

4368 Rush University: Rush Institute for Healthy Aging
1645 W Jackson Boulevard
Suite 675
Chicago, IL 60612-3276
312-421-8940
Fax: 312-942-2861
e-mail: devans2@rush.edu
Dennis A Evans PhD, Contact

Epidemiology of Alzheimer's disease, community-based studies of Alzheimer's disease and other common problems of older persons, physical functions among older persons, and statistical methods in aging research.

4369 Rutgers University Institute for Health, Health Care Policy: and Aging Research
30 College Avenue
New Brunswick, NJ 08901-1283
732-932-8413
Fax: 732-932-6872
e-mail: caboyer@rci.rutgers.edu
http://www.ihhcpar.rutgers.edu
Dr. David Mechanic, Director

Research divisions include and focus on the impact of stress on emotional states and health and risk behaviors and how these latter factors influence the immune system and morbidity and mortality; how stress and emotional states affect symptom appraisal and the decision to use health care; the health and cost outcomes of the current allocation of health and resources; the evolution of managed care and its impact on patient outcomes, medical professions and utilzation of services; trust relationships among consumers and physicians and managed care organizations; income inequality; chronic pain and poor self-assessments of health among the elderly; health care utilization and cost among patients with HIV illness; interdisciplinary research and training on mental health services and policy for persons with severe and persistant mental illness; and the human services and family support systems.

4370 San Jose State University Gerontology Education and Training Center
San Jose, CA 95192-0140
408-924-1000

Gerontology and the social aspects of aging, focusing on personal autonomy of elderly persons in long-term care and ethnogerontology.

4371 SeniorNet
900 Lafayette Street
Suite 604
San Francisco, CA 94105-3608
408-615-0699
800-747-6848
Fax: 408-615-0928
e-mail: seniornet@aol.com
http://www.seniornet.org

Interaction between computers and older individuals through online telecomputer system. Studies include psychological effects of the computer on the individual at the introduction, learning, and user levels.

4372 Southwest Foundation for Biomedical Research
PO Box 760549
San Antonio, TX 78245
210-674-1410
Fax: 210-670-3301
e-mail: fledford@sfbr.org
http://www.sfbr.org
Dr. Frank F Ledford Jr, President

Aging research
1941

4373 Syracuse University Biological Research Laboratories
Syracuse University
130 College Place
Syracuse, NY 13244
315-443-3186
Fax: 314-443-2012
e-mail: hrlevy@mailbox.syr.edu
http://www.web.syr.edu
H Richard Levy, Chairperson

Biochemistry, nucleic acids, and proteins; enzymology, including enzyme mechanisms and control of enzymatic activity; molecular, developmental, and population genetics; evolutionary biology; cell biology, including cell fine-structure, cell physiology, morphogenesis, particularly biochemical regulation of development; membrane physiology, including cell communication, membrane permeability, ion transport; microbial metabolism; community and population ecology; animal behavior; genetic control of development; proteasomes; bioenergetics; epigenetic regulation of cell fate decisions; chromatin structure; control of skeletal muscle growth and differentiation; intracellular signaling pathways; optimal strategies for animals to apportion energy to different tasks; functions of heat shock proteins; genetics and molecular biology of meiosis; molecular genetics of telomeres; conservation biology; ecosystem and plant ecology; the nature of reproductive competition; evolution of reproductive and life history traits; ecological genetics of microorganisms and insects; relationship between gene expression and cell function; genetics and molecular

4374 Syracuse University: Gerontology Center
426 Eggers Hall
Syracuse, NY 13244-1020
315-443-2703
Fax: 315-443-1081
e-mail: mbonney@maxwell.syr.edu
http://www.cpr.maxwell.syr.edu
Madonna Harrington Meyer, Director
Martha W Bonney, Assistant Director

Economics and demography of aging, income security policy, long-term care, gender and minority aging, and cross-national aging comparisons.

4375 Tampa Bay Research Institute
10900 Roosevelt Boulevard N
St Petersburg, FL 33716-2308
727-576-6675
Fax: 727-577-9862
Dr. Meihan Nonoyama, President
Akiko Tanaka, Manager

Aging / Research Centers

4376 Temple University: General Clinical Research Center
3401 N Broad Street
Philadelphia, PA 19140-5103
215-707-2000
Fax: 215-707-1560
e-mail: gcrc@vm.temple.edu
Guenther Boden MD, Program Director
Robin Deshield, Manager

4377 Thomas Jefferson University: Center for Research in Medical Education
Jefferson Medical College
1025 Walnut Street
Room 119
Philadelphia, PA 19107-5001
215-955-5492
Fax: 215-923-6939
Joseph Gonnella MD, Director

4378 Tulane University Occupational Lung Disease Center
School of Medicine
1700 Perdido Street
New Orleans, LA 70112-1290
504-588-5363
Fax: 504-588-5035
Dr. Hans Weill, Director
James V Talano MD

4379 USDA Human Nutrition Research Center on Aging
711 Washington Street
Boston, MA 02111-1524
617-542-8966
Fax: 617-556-3295
Irwin H Rosenberg MD, Director

Investigates the relationship of nutrition to aging, including research programs in nutrient metabolism, nutrient requirements, nutritional epidemiology, functional systems, and drug-nutrient interactions.

4380 University at Albany: State University of New York Ringel Institute of Gerontology
State University of New York
217135 Western Avenue
Albany, NY 12203
518-442-3568
Fax: 607-777-6041
e-mail: rwt68@cnsibm.albany.edu
Frank D Andraia, Executive Director

Applied research on aging, primarily in the social sciences, and services for the elderly, including studies on institutional and noninstitutional care of the elderly, nursing homes, day care, foster home care, the church as service provider, retirement and preretirement, and other social aspects of aging. Collaborates in the development of community programs and their evaluation.

4381 University of Akron Institute for LifeSpan Development and Gerontology
University of Akron
340 Arts and Sciences Building
Akron, OH 44325
330-972-7037
Fax: 330-972-5174
e-mail: hsterns@uakron.edu
http://www3.uakron.edu/ilsdg
Harvey L Sterns, Director

Improving older adult cognitive functioning, aging and work, mental retardation and aging, training and retraining adult older workers, gender identity, human development, health and aging, and family and aging. Programs concentrate on aging changes in perception, perceptual style, selective attention, and learning and memory. Other studies focus on performance appraisal and selection of older adult workers.

4382 University of California, San Francisco Center for Social and Behavioral Sciences
Department of Social and Behavioral Sciences
San Francisco, CA 94143
415-206-5820
Fax: 415-826-3381
Morris Schambelan, MD

Sponsors pre- and postdoctoral research and training activities in the areas of stress and illness, cognitive factors in health behavior, mental health and aging, adult development, gerontology, Alzheimer's Disease, and AIDS.

4383 University of California: Center for Health & Community
3333 California Street
Suite 465
San Francisco, CA 94118
415-476-7408
Fax: 415-502-1010
e-mail: chc@chc.ucsf.edu
http://www.chc.ucsf.edu
Nancy E Adler PhD, Director
Dina Dudum MPA, Manager

Facilitate multidisciplinary research that will provide comprehensive understanding of problems of health, illness and health care.
1984

4384 University of California: Los Angeles Center for Research on Aging Project
Harbor-UCLA Medical Center
PO Box 4981000
Torrance, CA 90509
510-642-6000
Fax: 310-320-3515
e-mail: ilesser@humc.edu

Neuroanatomic and neurophysiologic aspects of psychotic states of the elderly and ethnic differences in psychopharmacology in psychiatric patients. Conducts clinical evaluations of elderly psychiatric patients with neuroimaging techniques and performs comparisons of clinical course and blood levels of psychotropic drugs in Asian and Caucasian schizophrenic and depressed patients.

4385 University of California: San Diego Center for Population Research
06339500 Gilman Drive
La Jolla, CA 92093
858-534-3703
e-mail: repromed@ucsd.edu
http://www.repromed.ucsd.edu
Homer G Chin, Chief, Obstetrics & Gynecology
Steven C Plaxe, Chief, Gynecologic Oncology
Thomas R Moore, Director, Perinatal Medicine

Hypothalamic control of the pituitary and gonadal function in human and animal models, focusing on issues related to neuroendicrine metabolic dysfunction in the aging population.

4386 University of California: San Francisco Institute for Health and Aging
Laurel Hights Campus 3333
Suite 340
San Francisco, CA 94118
415-885-7464
Fax: 415-476-3915
e-mail: ihafoi@itsa.ucsf.edu
http://www.nurseweb.ucsf.edu/iha
Carroll L Estes PhD, Director
Lena Borodina, Manager

Aging health policy issues and policy alternatives; state discretionary policies in long-term care, social services, and income maintenance; private sector involvement in supporting health and social services for the elderly; effects of intergovernmental relations and state and federal fiscal conditions on services to the elderly; coordination between state and local aging programs and health planning, financing, and regulatory programs; specialhealth and social service needs of the low-income, isolated elderly; enrollment of the elderly in health maintenance and social/health organizations; gender issues; Alzheimers' disease resources and program evaluation; AIDS; international alcohol; health promotion and injury and disease prevention; disability statistics; and health status of the elderly, with special emphasis on selected acute and chronic health conditions.

Aging/Research Centers

4387 University of Chicago Brain Research Institute
5841 S Maryland Avenue
Chicago, IL 60637-1447　　　　　　　　　773-702-1865
　　　　　　　　　　　　　　　　Fax: 773-702-3518
　　　　　　e-mail: btorrey@surgery.bsd.uchicago.edu
Bryce Wier MD, Director
Sue Curtis, Manager

Alzheimer's disease, amyotrophic lateral sclerosis, myasthenia gravis, AIDS, sleep and sleep disorders, dyslexia, hyperkinesia, epilepsy and epileptoid disorders, mental retardation, mental illness, and brain and nervous system disorders such as multiple sclerosis, muscular dystrophy, cerebral palsy, encephalitis, Parkinson's disease, stroke, cerebral hemorrhage, aneurysm tumor, head injury, and intractable pain. Conducts basic research in neurophysiology, neuropharmacology, neuroanatomy, molecular biology, neuroimmunology, and virology.

4388 University of Chicago Committee on Human Development
5730 S Woodlawn Avenue
Chicago, IL 60637-1603　　　　　　　　　773-702-2150
　　　　　　　　　　　　　　　　Fax: 773-702-0320
Susan Cohen, Manager

Conducts research and graduate study in life course development (including child and adolescent development, adult development and aging, and philosophy of development), mental health research (including personality psychology), and cross-cultural studies (including psychological anthropology and cultural psychology). Seeks to provide education for innovative careers in research and teaching, and to contribute to the interdisciplinary understanding of human behavior.

4389 University of Colorado at Boulder Institute for Behavioral Genetics
1480 30th Street
Boulder, CO 80303-1010　　　　　　　　　303-492-6596
　　　　　　　　　　　　　　　　Fax: 303-492-8063
　　　　　　　　e-mail: info@ibg.colorado.edu
　　　　　　　　http://http://ibgwww.colorado.edu
Kathy Huckfeldt, Contact

Application of behavioral genetics to pharmacogenetics, learning disabilities, cognitive development, and vulnerability to drug abuse. Specific interests include genetics of aging, reading disability, genetic and neurobiological correlates of animal behavior, human alcohol studies, and genetic factors in personality and cognitive development of twins and adopted children.

4390 University of Connecticut Health Center: Biomolecular Structure Analysis Center
263 Farmington Avenue
Farmington, CT 06030　　　　　　　　　860-679-3267
　　　　　　　　　　　　　　　　Fax: 860-679-1989
　　　　　　　　e-mail: herbette@bsac.uchc.edu
Dr. Leo G Herbette, Director
Lee Ann Maximowicz, Administrator

Drug-membrane interaction, drug-receptor interaction, membrane drug design, pulmonary surfactant research, and collagen structure research as it relates to cardiology, alcoholism, Alzheimer's disease, CNS disorders, skeletal and smooth muscle disorders, and atherosclerosis.

4391 University of Connecticut: Center on Aging
Social and Behavioral Science Division
348 Mansfield Road
Storrs Mansfield, CT 06269-2058　　　　860-486-4721
　　　　　　　　　　　　　　　　Fax: 860-486-3452
　　　　　　e-mail: nancy.w.sheehane@UCONN.EDU
　　　　　　　http://www.familystudies.UCONN.EDU
Nancy W Sheehan PhD, Director

Geriatrics and gerontology, including: housing; improved linkage between the University, the community, and at-risk elderly; different aspects of retirement; public policy on aging; Alzheimer's disease and other health issues; death and bereavement; and coping with various lifestyle changes.

4392 University of Florida Brain Institute
JHMHC
PO Box 100015
Gainesville, FL 32610　　　　　　　　　352-392-0490
　　　　　　　　　　　　　　　　Fax: 352-846-0185
　　　　　　　e-mail: ufbi@cortex.health.ufl.edu
　　　　　　　http://www.ufbi.ufl.edu
William G Luttge PhD, Director

Peripheral Nerve Trauma Research Program, including biomaterials research, peripheral nerve regeneration, and mechanisms and control of pain associated with peripheral nerve trauma; Head Injury Research Program, including injury- and/or stroke-induced problems with memory, language, attention, emotion, motor skills, and epilepsy; molecular, cellular, and immunological mechanisms involved in nerve cell death and injury following stroke or closed head injury; Neurodegenerative Diseases Program, including molecular biologic studies of genetic bases of a variety of neurologic dysfunctions, including neurodegenerative movement disorders, cell biological studies on Batten's disease, and cell biological and MRI studies of laboratory animal models of multiple sclerosis. Additional studies include the underlying causes of Alzheimer's disease; the neurobiological consequences of alcohol and cocaine abuse in both adults and fetuses; and the molecular and cellular mechanisms and the behavioral and neurologic consequences of such viral-induced neurodegenerative diseases as AIDS, polio, and measles.

4393 University of Florida Health Policy and Epidemiology
PO Box 100177
Gainesville, FL 32610　　　　　　　　　352-265-8035
　　　　　　　　　　　　　　　　Fax: 352-265-8047
　　　　　　　http://www.hpe.ufl.edu
David Challoner, MD

Policy research and evaluations of long-term care and aging, hospital cost controls, regulatory and administrative methods in the health sector, health economics and financing, maternal and child health, HIV/AIDS, community epidemiology, outcomes research.

4394 University of Florida: Claude D Pepper Center for Research on Oral Health in Aging
PO Box 100416
Gainesville, FL 32610　　　　　　　　　352-392-1374
　　　　　　　　e-mail: mheft@dental.ufl.edu

Health services research and basic oral-health functions of the elderly, including the development of periodontal disease, the effects of medications on saliva production, and the effects of aging on the senses.

4395 University of Florida: Institute for Gerontology
PO Box 117335
Gainesville, FL 32611-7335　　　　　　　352-392-2116
　　　　　　　　e-mail: rwest@geron.ufl.edu
　　　　　　　http://www.gerou.ufl.edu
Robin Lea West, Contact

Faculty associates conduct interdisciplinary studies on family economic status, labor force participation and survivorship in life course perspective, alternative living environments for older people, political attitudes and policy issues in aging, preventive health self-care learning for intergenerational groups, nutritional status of elderly, memory fitness and intelligence in adulthood and old age, training needs of counselors and physician assistants, age-sensitive counseling and self-help resource development, geriatric dentistry, older driver fitness and transportation safety, ambulatory health care case mix management for older persons, caregiving, and demography.

4396 University of Georgia: Gerontology Center
100 Candler Hall
Athens, GA 30602　　　　　　　　　　　706-542-3954
　　　　　　　　　　　　　　　　Fax: 706-542-4805
　　　　　　　e-mail: lpoon@omega.geron.uga.edu
　　　　　　　http://www.geron.uga.edu
Leonard W Poon PhD, Director

Aging / Research Centers

Aging, focusing on applied gerontology, demography as it relates to the aged, mental and physical health of the oldest-old, Alzheimer's disease and other dementia in the aged, and cognitive aging, especially memory for pictures.

4397 University of Illinois Health Systems Research
College of Medicine
1601 Parkview Avenue
Rockford, IL 61107-1822
815-395-5639
800-854-4461
Fax: 815-395-5602
e-mail: joelc@uic.edu
http://www.rockford.uic.edu/hsr.htm
Joel B Cowen, Assistant Dean

Community health, including primary care, public health, geriatrics, substance abuse, evaluation of delivery of health services, survey research, focus groups, demographic studies, health care planning, program evaluation, and feasibility studies.

4398 University of Iowa Center for HealthServices Research
200 Hawkins Drive
Iowa City, IA 52242-1009
319-384-5120
Fax: 319-384-5125
http://www.public-health.uiowa.edu/hmp/

Delivery, organization, and financing of health care. Studies the health practices and needs of specific populations such as individuals in rural areas. Develops multidisciplinary research teams from the University's ten colleges and facilitates interaction between researchers, policy makers, and providers to address regional health care problems.

4399 University of Kansas Laboratory of Biological Anthropology
Department of Anthropology
622 Fraiser Hall
Lawrence, KS 66045-7542
785-864-4170
Fax: 785-864-5224
e-mail: crawford@ku.edu
http://www.ukans.edu
Michael H Crawford, Director

Cancer etiology, twin research, aging and longevity, genetic epidemiology, anthropological genetics in Saint Vincent, Hungary, Mexico, Siberia, Belize, rural and urban US ethnic enclaves, dental anthropology, forensic medicine, and skeletal identification.

4400 University of Kansas Neurobiology Research Laboratory
4801 E Linwood Boulevard
Kansas City, MO 64128-2226
816-861-4700
Fax: 816-922-3375
e-mail: bfestoff@kunc.edu
http://www.kumc.edu/kcbamc/research/nbrl
Barry W Festoff, Director
Kent Hill, Executive Director

Development, plasticity, and diseases of the nervous system. Studies focus on synaptic formation and metabolism; roles of serine proteases and inhibitors (serpins); regulation of amyloid precursor protein processing in Alzheimer's disease; and biological markers in head injuries.

4401 University of Kansas: Center on Aging
Kansas University Medical Center
3901 Rainbow Boulevard
Kansas City, KS 66160
913-588-1265
Fax: 913-588-1201
e-mail: sstudens@kumc.edu
http://www2.kumc.edu/coa
Stephanie A Studenski MD, Director

Provides support for interdisciplinary research on issues of age and aging.

4402 University of Kansas: Gerontology Center
4089 Dole Building
Lawrence, KS 66045
785-864-4130
Fax: 785-864-5063
e-mail: rhonda@dole.lsi.ukans.edu
Rhonda J V Montgomery PhD, Director

Aging and the problems of the aged, including applied and social gerontology, family caregiving, minority aging, service to the aging, cognitive aging, and housing options for elders.

4403 University of Kentucky: Sanders-Brown Center on Aging
800 S Limestone Street
Lexington, KY 40536
859-323-6040
Fax: 859-323-2866
e-mail: wmark0@uky.edu
http://www.mc.uky.edu/coa
William R Markesbery MD, Director

Biology of aging, including studies on the aging nervous systems, Alzheimer's disease, stroke, immunology.

4404 University of Louisville Center for Research in the Special Senses
Myers Hall
Louisville, KY 40292
502-852-5442
Fax: 502-852-8375
e-mail: snbarno1@ulkyum.louisville.edu
Anne Weimer, Manager

Sensory research, including deterioration through aging. Investigates the effects of chronic sinusitis, loss of balance, and diabetes on the senses.

4405 University of Maryland Division of Infectious Diseases
10 S Pine Street
Room 900
Baltimore, MD 21201-1116
800-492-5538

Infections in the elderly, including infection from urinary catheterization, epidemiology of nursing home patients, tests of antimicrobial agents, and pharmacokinetics and microbiology using animal models and clinical techniques.

4406 University of Maryland: Center for the Study of Pharmacy and Therapeutics for the Elderly
School of Pharmacy
20 N Pine Street
Baltimore, MD 21201-1142
410-706-2536
Fax: 410-706-1488
Misbah Khan, MD

Geriatrics and gerontology, focusing on drug use in the elderly and the development of artificial intelligence programs in support of optimal drug use. Also responsible for three elder care programs, the Parke-Davis Center for the Education of the Elderly, the Elder-Health Program, and the Maryland Caregiver Program.

4407 University of Maryland: Center on Aging
College Park, MD 20742
301-405-2469
Fax: 301-314-9167
e-mail: lw20@mail.umd.edu
http://www.inform.umd.edu/aging
Laura B Wilson, Contact

Gerontology, including senior service and volunteerism, long-term care financing, service credit banking, informal caregiving, aging and disabilities, productive aging, health care delivey systems and cost containment. Conducts health assessment and longitudinal data base projects on aging in the Interdisciplinary Health Research Laboratory.

Aging/Research Centers

4408 **University of Massachusetts at Boston: Gerontology Institute and Center**
100 Morrissey Boulevard
Dorchester, MA 02125-3300
617-287-7300
Fax: 617-287-7080
e-mail: geronto@umb.edu
http://www.geront.umb.edu
Robert P Gerary, Managing Editor

Aging Journal of Aging social policy, including health care, economics, security, long-term care, productive aging, systems delivery, older women's issues, and minority issues.

110 pages Frequency: Quarterly

4409 **University of Miami Center for Neurological Diseases**
PO Box 16960
Miami, FL 33101-6960
305-243-6732
800-707-5589
Fax: 305-243-4678
Noble David MD, Contact
Matilde Camjel, Manager

Neuroscience, including physiological, neurochemical, anatomical, metabolic, neuropharmacological and vascular mechanisms that account for normal brain function, and the changes in these which underlie neurological diseases such as stroke, senile dementia, epilepsy, Parkinson's syndrome, Alzheimer's disease, multiple sclerosis, amyotrophic lateral sclerosis (ALS), and other neurological dysfunctions.

4410 **University of Miami Touch Research Institute**
PO Box 16820
Miami, FL 33101-6820
305-585-5160
Fax: 305-243-6488
e-mail: tfield@mednet.med.miami.edu
http://www.miami.edu/touch-research
Tiffany M Field PhD, Contact
Noris Reyes, Manager

Sense of touch, including the biology of touch in health and development, and the role of touch therapy in medicine and the treatment of disease. Specific research areas include the use of massage in enhancing immune function in AIDS and cancer patients, massage effects on growth in premature infants, underlying mechanism responsible for the relationship between touch and physical growth and emotional development in infants and children, the role of massage in sports medicine and wound healing, the effects of touch therapy on addictive personalities, pain reduction during invasive medical procedures, and alleviation of skin disorders such as eczema and psoriasis. Studies the effects of touch on persons of all ages.

4411 **University of Miami: Center on Adult Development and Aging**
1425 NW 10th Avenue
Floor 2
Miami, FL 33136-1024
305-585-6746
Fax: 305-243-4414
Ronald Seigwald, Director

Biochemistry, neuropsychiatry, and clinical treatment of Alzheimer's disease and related disorders, including brain reactive antibodies and autoimmune responses. Also studies ethnicity and aging, human factors and aging, aging and developmental disabilities, biology of aging, osteoporosis, social and behavioral patterns of older persons and families, stress and aging, nutrition and aging, and demographics of elderly population in Florida and specific areas in Florida, including studies relating to the migration of elderly persons around the U.S., and the improvement of the quality of life for the elderly. Recently, awarded 11-year contract for the Women's Health Intiative, a 45-site national longitudinal clinical trial which follows the health of post-menopausal women.

4412 **University of Michigan Center for Human Growth and Development**
300 N Ingalls Street
Ann Arbor, MI 48109-2007
734-332-0295
Fax: 734-936-9288
e-mail: blozoff@umich.edu
http://www.umich.edu/tld/chgd
Betsy Lozoff PhD, Director

Human growth and development through childhood and adolescence, including interdisciplinary studies on normal and abnormal behavioral, physical, and mental development, focusing especially on the challenges to children who grow up in adverse conditions.

4413 **University of Michigan: Antiviral Laboratory**
4222 School of Dentistry
1011 N University Avenue
Ann Arbor, MI 48109-1012
734-763-5481
Fax: 734-764-7406
e-mail: jcdrach@umich.edu
http://www.umich.edu
Dr. John C Drach Hd, Contact

Antiviral research
1970

4414 **University of Michigan: Institute of Gerontology**
300 N Ingalls Street
Ann Arbor, MI 48109-2007
734-764-3493
Fax: 734-936-2116
e-mail: richard.c.adelman@uh.cc.uhich.edu
Joan A Faulkner PhD, Director

Gerontological research studies in the behavioral, biological, clinical, and social sciences and the humanities.

4415 **University of Minnesota: Center on Aging**
School of Public Health
PO Box 197
Minneapolis, MN 55440
734-764-5487
Fax: 734-764-3192
Aging.

4416 **University of Missouri Kansas City: Center for Aging Studies**
5100 Rockhill Road
Kansas City, MO 64110-2481
816-235-1000
e-mail: breytspraak@umkc.edu
http://www.iml.umkc.edu/cas
Stephen W Lehmkuhle, Manager

Caregiving to the elderly, health care systems and costs, health promotion/disease prevention, public perceptions of Social Security, voluntarism among the elderly, the care of Chinese elderly, and rural elderly. Rural studies include program assessment and testing in areas of health promotion/disease prevention, caregiving intergenerational relationships and the elderly, transportation, and housing.

4417 **University of North Dakota: UND Centerfor Rural Health**
PO Box 9037
Grand Forks, ND 58202
701-777-2011
Fax: 701-777-6779
e-mail: bgibbens@medicine.nodak.edu
http://http://medicine.nodak.edu/crh
Charles Kupchella, President

Rural health care delivery, especially in the areas of health professional shortage areas, the viability of rural health facilities, aging population, Native American health care, and uncompensated care. Collaborates with other research organizations throughout the nation.

Aging/Research Centers

4418 University of North Texas Health Science Center at Forth Worth: Geriatrics Education and Research Institute
3500 Camp Bowie Boulevard
Fort Worth, TX 76107-2644   817-735-5015
e-mail: tfairchi@hsc.unt.edu
http://www.hsc.unt.edu/research.aging.htm
Thomas J Fairchild PhD, Director
Arthur Eisenberg, Executive Director

Geriatric research.
1991

4419 University of North Texas: Center for Studies in Aging
Department of Applied Gerontology
PO Box 310919
Denton, TX 76203   940-565-2411
Fax: 940-565-4370
e-mail: lusky@scs.cmm.unt.edu
http://www.unt.edu/aging
Donald Grose, Manager

Social gerontology, including employee job performance in nursing homes, impact of leadership on culture of nursing homes and retirement communities, the Native American elderly, development of databases and models for community services planning, geriatric programs in community health centers, mediation and aging, and the low-income minority elderly. Conducts demographic, social-psychological, and evaluation studies and surveys for cities, labor unions, churches, and other client groups.

4420 University of Northern Iowa: Center forSocial and Behavioral Research
College of Social & Behaviora
Cedar Falls, IA 50614   319-273-2542
Fax: 319-273-3104
e-mail: GENE.LUTZ@UNI.EDU
http://www.csbs.csbs.uni.edu/college/centers/cs
Robert D Koob, CEO

Geography, history, home economics, political science, psychology, sociology, anthropology, criminology, social work, and public policy, including studies on adolescents, adult education, airline passengers, airports, educational needs assessment, elderly, environmental impact assessment, highways, human services needs assessment, outdoor recreation, radio listening habits, substance abuse, and television viewing habits. Performs feasbility studies on proposed projects such as sports complexes and auditoriums. Conducts special surveys for groups, organizations, localities, regions, and social aggregates.

4421 University of Pennsylvania Institute on Aging
3615 Chestnut Street
Philadelphia, PA 19104-2612   215-662-2746
Fax: 215-573-8684
e-mail: lavimour@mail.med.upenn
http://www.med.upenn.edu/aging
Risa Lovizzo-Mourey MD, Director
Laura Trean, Manager

Biomedical and social science research on aging, including cellular mechanisms of aging, Alzheimer's disease, sleep disturbances, arthritis, osteoporosis, population demographics of aging, nursing home quality, organization and structure of life care communities, social security, and social support systems for the aged.

4422 University of Pennsylvania: Center for Clinical Epidemiology and Biostatistics
School of Medicine
423 Guardian Drive
Philadelphia, PA 19104-4209   215-898-2368
Fax: 215-573-5315
e-mail: strom@cceb.upenn.edu
http://www.cceb.med.upenn.edu
Brian L Strom PhD, Director

Epidemiology of disease and risk factors of clinical importance, especially pharamacoepidemiology, molecular epidemiology, cancer, cardiovascular disease, renal disease, women's health, reproductive epidemiology, emergency medicine, injury, and aging.

4423 University of Pittsburgh University Center for Social and Urban Research
121 University Place
Pittsburgh, PA 15260-2600   412-624-4141
Fax: 412-624-4810
e-mail: ucsur@vms.cis.pitt.edu
http://www.pitt.edu/ucsur

Urban and regional analysis, child and family development, gerontology, intergenerational studies, and environmental policy. Conducts survey research, sampling, and data processing and analysis. Research findings are used for policy making at the international, national, regional, and local levels.

4424 University of South Dakota Social Science Research Institute
414 E Clark Street
Vermillion, SD 57069-2307   605-677-5306
Fax: 605-677-5583
http://www.usd.edu
Jim Abbott, President

Research includes studies on organizations, economic and social development, criminology, juvenile delinquency, child abuse, aged population, communications, social work and welfare, court administration, jury selection and community surveys for litigation, prison education, alcoholism, medical and educational problems on American Indian reservations, and follow-up on juvenile offenders. Conducts anthropological studies, including site preservation.

4425 University of Southern California: Institute for Health Promotion and Disease Prevention Research
1540 Alcazar Street
Los Angeles, CA 90033   213-342-2600
Fax: 213-342-2601
e-mail: carljohn@hsc.usc.edu
http://www.usc.edu/go/ipr
C Anderson Johnson PhD, Director

Disease prevention
1980

4426 University of Tennessee: Knoxville Society for the Study of Social Problems
906 McClung Tower
Knoxville, TN 37996   865-974-3620
Fax: 865-974-7013
e-mail: tomhood@utk.edu
http://www.it.utk.edu/sssp
Dr. Thomas C Hood, Executive Officer

Community research and development; crime and juvenile delinquency; drinking and drugs; racial and ethnic minorities; conflict, social action, and change; the family; poverty, class, and inequality; psychiatric sociology; social problems theory; sociology and social welfare; youth, aging, and the life course; educational problems; environment and technology; labor studies; sexual behavior; politics and communities; law and society; and health and health policy and services.

4427 University of Texas-Houston Health Science Center Mental Sciences Institute
University of Texas
1300 Moursund Street
Houston, TX 77030-3406   713-500-4472
e-mail: rguynn@msibb.msi.uth.tmc.edu
http://www.uth.tmc.edu/med/msi/index
James Willerson, President

Aging/Research Centers

Biochemical and behavioral aspects of psychiatric diseases, particularly physiopathology and pharmacology of alcohol and drug addiction, and affective and anxiety disorders. Performs basic and clinical studies in neuroendocrinology, metabolism, behavioral science, disorders, mental retardation, neurochemistry, psychophysiology, biochemistry, crime and delinquency, and gerontology.

4428 University of Utah Human Performance Research Laboratory
300 S 1850 E
Room 230c
Salt Lake City, UT 84112
801-581-7558
Fax: 801-585-3992

Effects of exercise and environment on muscular, cardiovascular, respiratory, nervous, and thermoregulatory systems of the human body. Programs are conducted on exercise and multiple sclerosis patients, women at risk for osteoporosis, exercise and functional abilities and health benefits.

4429 University of Utah: Gerontology Center
25 Medical Drive
Salt Lake City, UT 84112-1100
801-581-8199
e-mail: dale@nurfac.nurs.utah.edu
http://www.nurs.utah.edu/gorontology

Health and social sciences as they relate to the aged, including long-term care, gerontology curriculum and standards, bereavement of the elderly, in-home and respite care services, the family as a support system, family caregiving, and intergenerational families.

4430 University of Washington Northwest: Geriatric Education Center
1910 Fairview Avenue
Suite 203
Seattle, WA 98195
206-685-7478
Fax: 206-685-3436
e-mail: sgural@u.washington.edu

Provides education and training in geriatrics to health professionals, educators, and practitioners in Washington, Alaska, Montana, and Idaho.

4431 University of West Florida: Center on Aging
Department of Social Work
11000 University Parkway
Pensacola, FL 32514-5750
850-474-2000
e-mail: beechems@prodigy.net

John Cavanaugh, President

Gerontology, including rural elderly, housing, and death. Develops and evaluates training material for aging services.

4432 University of Wisconsin-Madison Neuropsychology Laboratory
600 Highland Avenue
Madison, WI 53792
608-262-1818
Fax: 608-263-6211

Clinical neuropsychology in neuropsychological correlates of epilepsy, cognitive and affective changes in aging, and differential diagnosis of dementia with a view toward cognitive and memory remediation.

4433 University of Wisconsin: Madison Institute on Aging
1300 University Avenue
Madison, WI 53706-1510
608-262-1818
Fax: 608-263-6211
e-mail: aging@ssc.wisc.edu
http://www.ssc.wisc.edu/aging

Carol Ruff, Director

Aging, including life course studies, biogerontology, social geroltology, and clinical geriatrics. Specific areas of study include, but are not limited to, Alzheimer's disease, caloric intake, coping with later life stress, demography, falls after hospital discharge, free radicals, housing and environment for older adults, muscle loss, osteoporosis, resilience in adulthood, primates, psychological well-being, swallowing disorders, and visual systems.

4434 University of Wisconsin: Milwaukee Institute on Aging and Environment
School of Architecture and Urban Planning
PO Box 413
Milwaukee, WI 53201
414-229-2991
Fax: 414-229-6976
e-mail: aging@csd.uwm.edu
http://www.uwm.edu/dept/iae

Uriel Cohen, Director

Interaction between the aged and the environment, with emphasis on environments for people with dementia. Specific issues include innovative environmental planning, programming, and design practice for enhancement of the quality of life of older persons; behavioral and social impacts of institutional settings; constraints of zoning in the creation of innovative forms of community housing; optimal thermal and luminous conditions for older persons; and the social history of the nursing home as a building type.

4435 Veterans Affairs Medical Center Research Service
1000 Locust Street
Reno, NV 89502-2597
775-328-1470

Alzheimer's disease, bone marrow transplantation, cancer, clinical trials of investigational drugs, diabetes, geriatric rehabilitation, in utero transplantation of blood-forming cells, stress in employment, health services, and surgery.

4436 Veterans Affairs Medical Center-Research Service
500 Foothill Drive
Salt Lake City, UT 84148
801-582-1565
e-mail: straight.richard_c@salt-lake.va.gov

Richard C Straight PhD, Contact
James Floyd, Executive Director

Diabetes, cancer, arthritis, aging and alcoholism, stroke and rehabilitation, dermatitis, neuroimmunological diseases, myasthenia gravis, tumors, dementia, laser medicine and surgery, herpes, genetics, cardiology, immunology, basic science, molecular biology, national cooperative drug studies, and rehabilitation research and development of artificial limbs, and clinical outcomes research.

4437 Veterans Affairs Medical Center: Geriatric Research, Education and Clinical Center
1601 SW Archer Road
Gainesville, FL 32608-1135
352-374-6051
Fax: 352-371-6142
e-mail: dlowenth@pharmacology.ufl.edu
http://www.med.ufl.edu/pharm/facdata/GRECC

Luann Cox, Manager

Geropharmacology, including mechanisms of drug action, pharmacokinetics, therapeutic uses, drug abuse, polypharmacy and drug compliance as it applies to geriatric patients. Clinical research is conducted in the areas of exercise in the healthy, frail, and elderly, cardiovascular function, and cognitive disorders in the elderly. Basic research is conducted in pharmacologic mechanisms of temperature regulation, obesity, febril response to infections, immunology, and muscle strength.

4438 Wayne State University Center for Health Research
5557 Cass Avenue
Detroit, MI 48202-3615
313-577-4082
Fax: 313-577-6949
e-mail: ajacox@cms.cc.wayne.edu
http://www.comm.wayne.edu/nursing

Janet Harden, Executive Director

Nursing, urban health, pain reduction in hospitalized children, adolescent health, teen pregnancy, aging, chronicity, health education and promotion (e.g. smoking cessation), community health, psychosocial oncology, health behavior, self care, stress and coping, parent/child health, family health, caregivers of aged individuals, drug use, violence and abuse, sleep patterns, risk-taking with respect to teen pregnancy and sexually transmitted diseases (including HIV), and transcultural nursing. Multidisciplinary studies involve health professionals and faculty members from disciplines such as nursing, psychology, sociology, anthropology, medicine, and epidemiology.

Aging / Research Centers

4439 Wayne State University: Institute of Gerontology
87 E Ferry Street
Detroit, MI 48202-3801
313-577-2840
Fax: 313-875-0127
e-mail: info@geroserver.iog.wayne.edu
http://www.iog.wayne.edu

Jeffrey W Dwyer, Director
Melinda Henderson, Executive Director

Gerontology, including studies on public policy, acute and long-term health care, service delivery, aging process, family relations, and work and retirement.

4440 Wichita State University: Gerontology Center
1845 Fairmount Street
Wichita, KS 67260
316-978-3490

Kevin Konda, Manager

Gerontology.

4441 Woodrow Wilson School of Public and International Affairs: Center for Health Care Strategies
Princeton University
353 Nassau Street
Princeton, NJ 08540-4623
609-258-3000
e-mail: mail@chcs.org
http://www.chcs.org

Christopher Eisgruber, CEO

Development and implementation of effective health and social policy for all Americans.

4442 Wright State University Fels Research Institute Division of Human Biology
School of Medicine
1005 Xenia Avenue
Yellow Springs, OH 45387-1600
937-767-1372
Fax: 937-775-3672
e-mail: rsiervog@desire.wright.edu
http://www.wright.edu/som/academic/divhum

Don Wright, Owner

Physical growth, body composition, and genetic epidemiology, including a long-term longitudinal study. Other projects are conducted in the areas of aging and nutritional assessment. Utilizes a population of over 1,100, most of whom have been studied since birth and many of whom had been studied prenatally. Studies groups from the community at large.

4443 Yeshiva University: Resnick Gerontology Center
Albert Einstein College of Medicine
1165 Morris Park Avenue
Bldg R
Bronx, NY 10461-1915
718-430-3850
Fax: 718-430-3870
e-mail: crystal@aecom.yu.edu

Dr Howard Crystal, Director
Lawrence Siegel, Principal

Alzheimer's disease and other dementia. Conducts the [Bronx Aging Study], a ten-year longitudinal study of the Bronx elderly. Also conducts a teaching nursing project, a biochemical research assessment program, and drug studies.

AIDS / Associations & Organizations

Associations & Organizations

4444 **AIDS Community Resources**
AIDS Task Force of Central New York
627 W Genesee Street
Syracuse, NY 13204
315-475-2437
800-343-AIDS
Fax: 315-472-6515
e-mail: information@aidscommunityresources.com
http://www.aidscommunityresources.com
Mary Doody, Director of Volunteer Services
Michael Crinnin, Executive Director

4445 **AIDSinfo**
PO Box 6303
Rockville, MD 20849-6303
301-519-0459
800-448-0440
Fax: 301-519-6616
e-mail: contactus@aidsinfo.nih.gov
http://www.aidsinfo.nih.gov
Florencia Nochetto, Manager
Sandra Lehrman, Manager

A call in service where trained staff offers quick access to federally approved HIV/AIDS treatment and prevention guidelines, clinical trials, and other research-related information.

4446 **Alabama Department of Public Health**
Division of Disease Control
434 Monroe Street
Montgomery, AL 36130-3017
334-206-5226
Fax: 334-206-5663
e-mail: jfree@adph.state.al.us
Sandra Langston, Information Director
Gary H Moody, Plant Manager

Offers health education and risk education activities, including compiling a state community resource directory.

4447 **Alaska Department of Health and Social Services-AIDS/STD Program**
Division of Public Health
350 Main Street, Room 404
PO Box 110601
Juneau, AK 99811-0601
907-465-3030
800-478-AIDS
Fax: 907-465-3068
e-mail: karleen.jackson@alaska.gov
Karleen K. Jackson, Commissioner
Sherry Hill, Assistant Commissioner

AIDS program offers education to providers and organizations serving those needing to modify behaviors pertaining to AIDS and HIV transmission statewide.

4448 **American Civil Liberties Union AIDS Project**
125 Broad Street
18th Floor
New York, NY 10004
212-944-9800
http://www.aclu.org
Nadine Strossen, President
Anthony D. Romero, Executive Director

Offers legislative and employment information, public awareness materials and support for persons with HIV/AIDS and their families.

4449 **American Federation of Teachers HIV/AIDS Education Project**
555 New Jersey Avenue NW
Washington, DC 20001
202-879-4400
Fax: 202-393-8648
e-mail: ccordovi@aft.org
http://www.aft.org/
Sandra Feldman, President

A group of education professionals whose main purpose is education and public awareness of HIV and AIDS.

4450 **Arizona Department of Health Services**
1740 W Adams Street
Phoenix, AZ 85007
602-542-1034
Fax: 602-542-1031
http://www.azdhs.gov
Karen Boswell, Administrator
Susan Gerard, Director

Provides HIV and AIDS seropositive surveillance, case investigation and analysis and AIDS health education and training for the public.

4451 **Arkansas Department of Health**
AIDS and STD Prevention Program
4815 W Markham Street
Slot H-37
Little Rock, AR 72205
501-661-2623
Fax: 501-661-2082
e-mail: Martin.Nutt@arkansas.gov
http://www.healthyarkansas.com
Martin Nutt, Certification Officer
Jeremy Rowe, Training Coordinator

Provides educational materials such as pamphlets and films, conducts HIV and AIDS research and operates a speakers bureau.

4452 **CDC National Prevention Information Network**
PO Box 6003
Rockville, MD 20849-6003
404-679-3860
800-458-5231
Fax: 888-282-7681
e-mail: info@cdcnpin.org
http://www.cdcnpin.org

CDCNPIN is the US reference, referral and distribution service for informtion on HIV/AIDS, STOs and TB.

4453 **California Collaborative Treatment Group**
University of California, San Diego
3900 Fifth Avenue
Suite 200
San Diego, CA 92103
619-543-5006
Fax: 619-298-1379
e-mail: rhaubrich@ucsd.edu
http://www.cctg.ucsd.edu
Richard Haubrich M.D., Professor of Medicine
Jill Kunkel, Manager

Develops treatment protocols and drug therapies and recruits research volunteers for AIDS studies and HIV related disorders.

4454 **California Department of Health Services Office of AIDS**
P.O. Box 15559
Sacramento, CA 95852-0559
916-445-4171
Fax: 916-323-4642
http://www.dhcs.ca.gov
Bryan Ballard, CEO

Works to develop strategies and implement programs for education and prevention, testing and counseling, supportive care and treatment and research to control the spread of HIV infection.

4455 **Chicago Department of Health**
4150 West 55th Street
Chicago, IL 60632
312-747-1020
Tonia Schaeffer, Program Director

Offers educational services, audiovisual materials, surveillance of HIV and AIDS, counseling, referrals.

4456 **Committee of Ten Thousand**
236 Massachusetts Avenue NE
Suite 609
Washington, DC 20002-4971
202-543-0988
800-488-COTT
Fax: 202-543-6720
http://www.cott1.org
Dave Cavenaugh, Manager

For and of people infected with HIV through blood and blood products.

AIDS / Associations & Organizations

4457 Connecticut Department of Health Services
AIDS Program
150 Washington Street
Hartford, CT 06106
203-566-4800
Fax: 860-509-7400
Beth Weinstein, Program Director
Bruce Douglas, Executive Director

Operates a speakers bureau, provides training, workshops, seminars and counseling services, conducts meetings and offers information and referral services.

4458 Delaware Department of Health and Social Services: Division of Public Health
3000 Newport Gap Pike
Building G
Wilmington, DE 19808
302-995-8635
Fax: 302-739-6617
http://www.dhss.delaware.gov/dhss
Ruth Ann Minner, Governor
John C. Carney, Jr, Lt. Governor

Provides HIV counseling and testing, prevention education and AIDS surveillance and studies.

4459 District of Columbia Public Service Commission
Office of AIDS Administration
1333 H Street NW
Suite 200, West Tower
Washington, DC 20005
202-626-5100
Fax: 202-626-9212
e-mail: ayates@psc.dc.gov
http://www.dcpsc.org
Agnes Alexan Yates, Chairman
Phylicia Fau Bowman, Ph.D., Executive Director

Coordinates the District's public response to the AIDS epidemic.

4460 Florida Department of Health & Rehabilitative Services: AIDS Program
1309 Winewood Boulevard
Suite 2
Tallahassee, FL 32399-6568
850-414-4615
Fax: 850-488-3480
John J Witte MD, Program Coordinator
Sandra Bell, Manager

Oversees four program activities: HIV education and prevention, counseling, testing and partner notification, patients care and surveillance.

4461 Georgia Department of Human Resources: Division of Public Health
AIDS Section
2 Peachtree Street NW
Suite 22-202
Atlanta, GA 30303-3109
404-657-2258
800-551-2728
http://http://dhr.georgia.gov
Zena Lewis, Information Specialist
Eva Patillo, Executive Director

Consists of seven projects: Planning, surveillance, special studies, laboratory, medical, health education and training, and clinical services.

4462 Hawaii Department of Health: Communicable Disease Division
AIDS/Sexually Transmitted Diseases Control Branch
1250 Punchbowl St.
Suite 305
Honolulu, HI 96813
808-586-4400
Fax: 808-586-4444
e-mail: janice.okubo@doh.hawaii.gov
http://http://hawaii.gov/health/about/org
Janice S Okubo, Communications Director and Admi
Jane Pang, Board of Health-Administrator

Offers research, education, surveillance and testing components. AIDS information and guidelines about the placement of infants, children and adolescents who test positive for HIV in nursery or school settings are also available.

4463 Health Education AIDS Liaison (HEAL)
PO Box 1103
New York, NY 10113
212-873-0780
800-410-HEAL
Fax: 212-873-0891
e-mail: HEALintl@aol.com
http://www.healtoronto.com
Sam Hilu, Owner

Alternative and holistic support groups and resources for people with HIV.

4464 Health Information Network for Women and AIDS
PO Box 30762
Seattle, WA 98103
206-784-5655

Offers information, public awareness and support for women with HIV/AIDS and the public in general.

4465 Houston Department of Health and Human Services: Bureau of HIV Prevention
8000 N Stadium Drive
Houston, TX 77054-1823
713-355-2939
Fax: 713-794-9464
e-mail: cabral@cityofhouston.net
http://www.houstontx.gov
Judy Gray Johnson, Director
Dennis Darling, Manager

Coordinates sexually transmitted disease surveillance, seroprevalence, contract tracing partner notification, public information, minority initiatives and health evaluation/risk reduction.

4466 Illinois Department of Public Health
Division of Infectious Diseases
100 W. Randolph St.
Suite 6-600
Chicago, IL 60601
312-793-3376
Fax: 312-793-2254
http://www.idph.state.il.us
Dr. Eric E. Whitaker, Director
Rod R. Blagojevich, Governor

Offers referrals for counseling and testing, education, seroprevalence, the Interagency Council and surveillance.

4467 Immune Deficiency Foundation
Immune Deficiency Foundation
25 W Chesapeake Avenue
Suite 206
Towson, MD 21204-4841
410-321-6647
800-296-4433
Fax: 410-321-9165
Marcia Boyle, CEO

The only national charitable organization aimed at fighting the primary immune deficiency diseases. The founders included parents of children with primary immune deficiency, immunologists who treat immune deficient patients and other individuals with an interest in helping others. The Foundation's main goal is to improve the care and treatment of adults and children with primary immune deficiency diseases and to promote public education and awaareness about the diseases.

4468 Kansas Department of Health & Environment
Curtis State Office Building
1000 SW Jackson
Topeka, KS 66612
785-296-1500
800-551-2728
Fax: 785-368-6368
e-mail: info@kdha.state.ks.us
http://www.kdheks.gov
Roderick L. Bremby, Secretary
Jimmy Woodcock, Executive Director

Provides surveillance of AIDS in Kansas, training for counselors, partial funding of counseling test sites and distribution of educational materials.

AIDS / Associations & Organizations

4469 **Life Force: Women Fighting AIDS**
175 Remsen Street,
Suite 1100
Brooklyn, NY 11201-4300 718-797-0937
Fax: 718-797-4011
e-mail: lfwfainc@aol.com
http://www.lifeforceinc.org
Gwen Carter, Executive Director
Thomasina Stallings, Director of Program Services

A support network offering legislative information, educational awareness and support for women with HIV/AIDS.

4470 **Los Angeles County Department of Health Services**
AIDS Programs
600 S Commonwealth Avenue
Floor 6
Los Angeles, CA 90005-4016 213-351-8000
Fax: 213-738-0825
e-mail: aids@ph.lacounty.org
http://www.lapublichealth.org/aids/
Peter Kurndt MD, Program Coordinator
David Jetton, Administrator

Responsible for planning, coordinating and implementing county wide HIV/AIDS efforts.

4471 **Louisiana Department of Health & Hospitals: Office of Public Health**
Louisiana AIDS Prevention/Surveillance Program
628 N. 4th Street,
P.O. Box 629
Baton Rouge, LA 70821-0629 225-342-9500
Fax: 225-342-5568
e-mail: webadmin@dhh.la.gov
http://www.dhh.louisiana.gov
Tapia Ruben, Immunization Program Director
Cambre Glenn, Public Health Executive Director

Provides 28 HIV-antibody testing and counseling sites throughout the state in addition to selected sites in targeted minority areas.

4472 **Maine Department of Human Services: Disease Control Division**
Office of AIDS
221 State Street
Augusta, ME 4333 207-287-3707
800-351-2437
Fax: 207-287-3005
http://www.maine.gov/dhhs
Brenda M. Harvey, Commissioner

Provides technical assistance to state agencies and private organizations regarding AIDS education and policy development.

4473 **Massachusetts Department of Public Health**
250 Washington Street
Boston, MA 02108-4619 617-624-6000
Fax: 617-727-6496
http://http://www.mass.gov/dph/
Deval L Patrick, Governor
John Auerbach, Commissioner

Provides case management, administration services, counseling services and medical services pertaining to HIV and AIDS prevention.

4474 **Michigan Department of Public Health: Bureau Infectious Disease Control**
HIV/AIDS Prevention & Intervention Section
3423 N Logan Martin Luther King Jr Boulevard
Lansing, MI 48909 517-373-3654
Fax: 517-335-8395
Randall S Pope, Chief
Bobbie Butler, Manager

Gives general public and high-risk education grants supporting educational materials, programs and a hotline.

4475 **Minnesota Department of Health: AIDS/STD Prvention Service**
717 Delaware Street SE
Minneapolis, MN 55414-2959 651-201-5414
Fax: 612-623-5743
http://www.health.state.mn.us
Michael E Moen, Program Director
Lisa Lange, Vice President

This division is to prevent death and disability from HIV and other sexually transmitted diseases by providing statewide leadership regarding the prevention of transmission, and the availability of health and supportive services for infected persons.

4476 **Mississippi Department of Public Health: AIDS/HIV Prevention Program**
2423 N State Street
Post Office Box 1700
Jackson, MS 39215-1700 601-321-6000
Fax: 601-960-7948
http://www.msdh.state.ms.us
F Edgar Thompson Jr, Health Officer
Robert Latham, Executive Director

Funds two statewide hotlines one for the general public and one for the gay community. Both offer health education, and risk reduction activities of the Program include baseline evaluation of public knowledge about AIDS through surveys.

4477 **Missouri Department of Health and Senior Services**
PO Box 570
930 Wildwood
Jefferson City, MO 65102-0570 573-751-6378
800-533-2437
Fax: 573-751-6447
e-mail: feedback@vitalrec.com
http://www.vitalrec.com/mo.html
Theodore N Northrup, Chief
Josh Campbell, Manager

Composed of activities directly relating to counseling and testing, health education and risk reduction, care coordination and surveillance programs.

4478 **NAMES Project Foundation**
AIDS Memorial Quilt
637 Hoke Street NW
Atlanta, GA 30318-4315 404-688-5500
Fax: 404-688-5552
e-mail: info@aidsquilt.org
http://www.aidsquilt.org
Darin Arrowood, Manager
Brad Gammell, Chapter Program Coordinator

To preserve, care for, and use the AIDS Memorial Quilt to foster healing, heighten awareness, and inspire action in the struggle against HIV and AIDS.

4479 **National Association on HIV Over Fifty**
23 Miner Street
Boston, MA 02215 617-233-7107
Fax: 617-262-5667
http://www.hivoverfifty.org
Jim Campbell, President
Paul Quinn, VP

NAHOF is a membership organization promoting the availability of a full range of education, prevention, service, and health care programs for people over age 50 and affected by HIV.

4480 **National Coalition on Immune System Disorders**
8730 Wilshire Blvd
Suite 305
Beverly Hills, CA 90211 310-657-1077
Fax: 310-657-1053
e-mail: immunsci@ix.netcom.com
http://www.immuno-sci-lab.com
Robert R Humphreys, Executive Director
Aristo Vojdani PhD., M.T, Vice President and Chief Executi

Professional and lay organizations with a primary interest in the immune system and its diseases.

AIDS/Associations & Organizations

4481 National Hospice Organization
1901 N Moore Street
Suite 901
Arlington, VA 22209-1717
703-243-5900
800-338-8619

The nation's only advocate for terminally ill children, patients and their families. Provides member programs, represents hospice care interests in Congress, regulatory agencies and the public.

4482 National Native American AIDS Prevention Center
720 S. Colorado Blvd
Suite 650-S
Denver, CO 80246
720-382-2244
800-288-2437
Fax: 720-382-2248
e-mail: information@nnaacp.org
http://www.nnaapc.org

Geoffrey Roth, President
Lurline McGregor, Vice President

Sole mission of this organization is to promote AIDS education, prevention and cures for Native Americans suffering from the illness.

4483 National Training Center for Professional AIDS Education
1800 Columbus Avenue
Roxbury, MA 02119-1042
617-442-7442
Fax: 617-442-1705

Geneva Woodruff PhD, Executive Director

Program training teachers, health care providers and other professionals who serve HIV-infected children and their families. Offers education, site workshops, technical assistance, regional conferences, printed materials and publication of articles in the media and professional journals. Training is designed for providers and administrators of early childhood/intervention programs, public school, preschool and special education programs.

4484 Nevada Department of Human Resources: Health Program Section
505 E King Street
Room 300
Carson City, NV 89701
702-687-4800
Fax: 702-687-4988

Yvonne Sylva, Program Director

Provides HIV counseling and testing, a speakers bureau, information and referrals, resource materials including AIDS video recordings and education.

4485 New Hampshire Department of Health and Human Services
Division of Public Health Services
6 Hazen Drive
Concord, NH 03301-6510
603-271-4477
800-752-AIDS
http://www.healthynh2010.org/

Joyce J Welch, Program Coordinator
Mary Ann Cooney, Executive Director

HIV/AIDS Program receives both state and Federal funding pertaining to AIDS education, risk reduction, testing and surveillance.

4486 New Jersey Department of Health: Division of AIDS Prevention & Control
363 W State Street
Trenton, NJ 08618-5705
609-292-2121
800-624-2377

Charles Dawson, Manager

Serves to coordinate and direct primary HIV activities within the Department, networking with other divisions and agencies to provide information and care programs to populations in need.

4487 New Jersey Women and AIDS Network
103 Bayard Street
3rd Floor
New Brunswick, NJ 8901
732-846-4462
Fax: 732-846-2674
e-mail: office@njwan.org
http://www.njwan.org

Monique Howard MPH, EdD, Executive Director
Christina Rodriguez, Secretary

Since 1988, New Jersey Women & AIDS Network has been a leader in identifying issues facing women with HIV/AIDS, educating service providers, advocating for appropriate policies and building a multicultural woman and HIV/AIDS movement.

4488 New Mexico Health Department: Public Health Division
HIV/AIDS/STD Prevention & Services Bureau
1170 N. Solano
Room S1100
Las Cruces, NM 88001
575-528-5001
800-545-AIDS
Fax: 575-528-6024
e-mail: jenny.liu@state.nm.us
http://www.health.state.nm.us/phd

Rebecca Watson, Bureau Chief
Anna Pentler, Executive Director

Provides training programs and HIV education to the general public and professionals, risk reduction information, AIDS school curriculums, classroom presentation information and an AIDS hotline.

4489 New York Department of Health: Office of Public Health, AIDS Institute
AIDS Institute
Empire State Plaza
Corning Tower
Albany, NY 12237
518-474-5370
Fax: 518-473-7286
http://www.health.state.ny.us

Nick Rango MD, Director

Awards grants and maintains relationships with regional AIDS service groups, crisis intervention, psychosocial counseling and legal, financial and housing assistance. The Institute also offers preventive education, risk reduction education, HIV counseling and testing and patient care.

4490 North Carolina Department of Health & Natural Resources: Communicable Disease Control Section
2501 Mail Service Center
Raleigh, NC 27699-2501
919-855-4100
Fax: 919-733-6608
e-mail: care.line@ncmail.net
http://www.dhhs.state.nc.us

Mark T. Benton, Director
William W. Lawrence, Jr., M.D., Senior Deputy Director

Oversee the AIDS surveillance program, HIV counseling, testing, partner notification, health education, risk reduction, and public information efforts in North Carolina.

4491 Ohio Department of Health: Division of Preventive Medicine
246 N High Street
8th Floor
Columbus, OH 43266-0118
614-466-3543
Fax: 614-644-1909
e-mail: OCISS@odh.ohio.gov
http://www.odh.ohio.gov

Alvin D. Jackson, Director
J. Nick Baird, Director

Consists of AIDS surveillance, seroprevalence programs, health care worker education, health education and risk reduction projects.

AIDS/Associations & Organizations

4492 Oklahoma Department of Health: HIV/STD Service
1000 NE 10th Street
Oklahoma City, OK 73117-1299   405-271-4636
Fax: 405-271-5149
e-mail: MichaelH@health.ok.gov
http://www.health.state.ok.us
Chang K Lee, Director
Michael G. Harmon, M.A., Chief

Provides prevention-related services and funding to the network of AIDS service delivery organizations, both public and private, in Oklahoma. The Division provides services and training and certification of AIDS educators, surveillance, and seroprevalence studies.

4493 Oregon Department of Human Resources
Health Division, HIV Program
800 NE Oregon Street
ste 850
Portland, OR 97232-2289   503-236-2147
800-777-AIDS
Fax: 503-731-4608
Claudia L Webster, HIV Coordinator
Desiree Paschall, Executive Director

HIV Program includes training workshops for AIDS trainers, curriculum development or revision, and an AIDS hotline through Cascade AIDS Project.

4494 Pennsylvania Department of Health: Bureau of HIV/AIDS
Health and Welfare Building
7th & Forster Streets
Harrisburg, PA 17120   877-724-3258
Fax: 717-772-4309
http://www.dsf.health.state.pa.us
Janice P Kopelman, Director
Alfred Baker, President

Offers various community health education presentations, counseling and testing sites. Also offers practical support services, counseling, HIV testing, a hotline and referrals.

4495 Philadelphia Department of Public Health: AIDS Program
1101 Market Street
Suite 840
Philadelphia, PA 19107   215-686-5000
Fax: 215-686-5398
http://www.phila.gov/health
Joseph C. Cronauer, Executive Deputy Commissioner
Carmen I Paris, Deputy Health Commissioner

Provides HIV prevention education and outreach targeting high risk populations including injecting drug users, their sexual partners and sex industry workers.

4496 Project Inform Hotline
205 13th Street
#2001
San Francisco, CA 94103   415-558-8669
Fax: 415-558-0684
e-mail: outreach@projectinform.org
http://www.projectinform.org
Dana Van Gorder, Executive Director
Martin Delaney, Founding Director

HIV/AIDS treatment information.

4497 Ramsey Foundation
444 Cedar Street
Suite 1250
Saint Paul, MN 55101   651-228-1770
Fax: 651-292-4040
http://www.ramseybar.org
Robert F Garland, President

AIDS research.

4498 Rhode Island Department of Health: Division of Disease Control
Office of AIDS/STD
3 Capitol Hill
Suite 105
Providence, RI 02908   401-222-2837
Fax: 401-222-6548
http://www.health.state.ri.us/
David R Gifford, MD, Director
Linda McMullen, Manager

Provides health education and risk reduction activities through its AIDS program. Services include professional conferences, providing assistance for in-service programs, presentation of two courses and organization of an AIDS minority program.

4499 South Carolina Department of Health & Environmental Control: Bureau of Preventive Health Services
2600 Bull Street
Columbia, SC 29201   803-898-3432
Fax: 843-724-5858
Jeff deBessonet, PE, Director
Bureau Chief, Administrator

A comprehensive statewide program of counseling and testing, partner notification, public health education and disease surveillance.

4500 Spellman Center for HIV Related Disease
St. Clare's Hospital
St. Clare's Hospital
New York, NY 10019-6301   212-586-1500
Fax: 212-459-8489
e-mail: gateway@nlm.nih.gov
http://http://gateway.nlm.nih.gov
Dr. Victoria Sharp, Executive Director
Len Walsh, CEO

4501 Tampa AIDS Network: Florida Women's AIDS Resource Movement
PO Box 8333
Tampa, FL 33574   813-237-6455

4502 Tennessee Department of Health: AIDS Program
Cordell Hull Building
425 5th Avenue North
Nashville, TN 37243   615-741-3111
Fax: 615-741-2491
e-mail: tn.health@state.tn.us
http://http://health.state.tn.us
Walter L. Stuart, Program Coordinator
Susan R. Cooper, Commissioner

Sponsors health education and risk reduction activities which include awarding grants for community education and risk reduction, education for employees in the state system and the private sector.

4503 Texas Department of Health: Bureau of HIV and STD Control
HIV Division
1100 W 49th Street
Austin, TX 78756   512-834-6757
800-299-2437
Fax: 512-719-0220
e-mail: kirk.wiles@tdh.state.tx.us
http://www.dshs.state.tx.us
Linda Sue Moore, M.S., R.N, Chief, HIV/STD Clinical Services
David L. Lakey, M.D, Commissioner

Establishes and maintains HIV health education and risk reduction programs, provides HIV counseling, testing and partner notification.

AIDS/Books

4504 URSA Institute
390 4th Street
Fl 1
San Francisco, CA 94107-1289
415-777-1922
Fax: 415-512-9625
e-mail: cmcgruder@usa.net

Ernest J Fazio Jr, Administration

Social policies, including AIDS prevention and education, crime and justice, aging, economic development, health care, housing, mental health, substance abuse, public education, public media, and public advertising.

4505 US National AIDS Hotlines and Resources
Public Health Service
Washington, DC 20210
718-378-7022
800-342-2437

Provides confidential information, referrals and educational materials free of charge to the public. Employees can call the Hotline for confidential information about HIV/AIDS transmission, prevention or risk reduction, testing, symptoms and other related issues.

4506 Vermont Department of Healt: HIV/AIDS Program
PO Box 70
Burlington, NJ 8016
609-386-8770
Fax: 802-863-7314
http://www.state.vt.us

Charles Granito, Sr., Contact

We provide riask reduction and health education services, Anonymous HIV counseling and testing sites through Vermont, HIV/AIDS educational materials.

4507 Virginia Department of Health: DivisionHIV/STD
PO Box 2448
Richmond, VA 23218-2448
804-864-7001
800-533-4148
Fax: 804-225-3517
e-mail: Questions@vdh.virginia.gov
http://www.vdh.state.va.us/std

Casey W Riley, Director
Preston Smith, Program Manager

The division provides a toll free hotline for HIV/STD and viral Hepatitis information, education, confidentiality and anoymous testing. Tghe division provides referrals for AIDS medication assistance and outpatient care services for income eligible persons with HIV.

4508 Washington Department of Health: Division of AIDS/HIV/STD
HIV/AIDS Program
101 Israel Road SE
Tumwater, WA 98504
360-236-4501
800-272-AIDS
http://www.doh.wa.gov

Mary Selecky, Secretary of Health
ill White, Deputy Secretary

Provides information and referrals to local, state and national resources relating to HIV/AIDS, provides informational and educational materials to individuals, agencies and organizations and actively works with print and broadcast media to promote HIV/AIDS education.

4509 West Virginia Department of Health & Human Resources
AIDS Program
State Capitol Complex
Building 3 Room 206
Charleston, WV 25305
304-558-0684
Fax: 304-558-1130
e-mail: wvdhhrsecretary@wvdhhr.org
http://www.wvdhhr.org/

Molly Jordan, Inspector General
Anita L Arnold, Secretary

Provides AIDS-related services in 15 public health HIV-counseling and testing centers which offer by appointment confidential or anonymous testing.

4510 Whitman-Walker Clinic: AIDS/Medical Services Programs
1407 S Street NW
Washington, DC 20009
202-797-3500
Fax: 202-797-3504
e-mail: wwcinfo@wwc.org
http://www.wwc.org

Paul J. Murphy, Vice-Chairman
Jannette Williams, Chair

4511 Wisconsin Department of Health and Social Services: Division of Health
AIDS/HIV Program
1 W. Wilson Street
Madison, WI 53703-3009
608-266-1865
Fax: 608-267-3696
e-mail: webmaster@dhfs.state.wi.us
http://dhfs.wisconsin.gov/contact.htm

Ivan E Imm, Program Director
Mary Burke, Manager

Coordinates counseling and testing sites activities and services to HIV-infected persons, produces a report that contains information and recommendations for health care workers, emergency medical technicians and food service workers.

4512 Women's AIDS Network
Women and Children's Service Program
10 United Nations Plaza
San Francisco, CA 94102-4911
415-487-3034
Fax: 415-487-3009
e-mail: feedback@sfaf.org
http://www.sfaf.org

Andrew Belschner, Chairman
LeRoy Blea, Director

4513 Wyoming Department of Health & Social Services: Medical Services Division
AIDS Prevention Program
3304 Sheridan Avenue
4th Floor
Cheyenne, WY 82009
307-777-5800
800-327-3577
e-mail: www.wdh.state.wy.us

Terrance L Foley, Director
Kim D. Maes, Director

100 percent federally funded and responsible for the solicitation, development and implementation of community core capacity to conduct AIDS prevention initiatives.

Books

4514 100 Questions and Answers About AIDS and HIV
Jones and Bartlett Publishers
40 Tall Pine Drive
Sudbury, MA 01776
978-443-5000
800-832-0034
Fax: 978-443-8000
e-mail: info@jbpub.com
http://www.jbpub.com

Joel E Gallant MD/MPH, Author

Provides answers to the most common questions asked by patients with HIV and AIDS, their partners, and their family members. An invaluable resource for people with HIV infection or for those who care about them. Also includes useful information on prevention and testing for HIV-negative readers.

209 pages Year Founded:

4515 AIDS Alert
American Health Consultants
PO Box 740056
Atlanta, GA 30374
404-351-4523
800-686-2421
Fax: 404-262-7837

Leslie Norins, Publisher

AIDS/Books

Covers risks, hazards, costs and prevention of AIDS and related conditions.

4516 AIDS Funding: A Guide to Giving by Foundations & Charitable Organizations
Foundation Center
79 5th Avenue
New York, NY 10003-3034
212-620-4230
800-424-9836
Fax: 212-691-1828
http://www.fdncenter.org

Sara Engelhardt, President

Includes current information on the grantmaking programs of foundations and corparate giving programs as well as public charities.

206 pages Frequency: 1997

4517 AIDS Reader
Branden Publishing Company
17 Station Street
Brookline, MA 02445-7995
617-734-2045
Fax: 617-734-2046
e-mail: branden@branden.com
http://www.branden.com

This anthology includes the best professional writing on AIDS by the world's foremost authorities.

4518 AIDS: A Communication Perspective
Lawrence Erlbaum Associates Publishers
10 Industrial Avenue
Suite 2
Mahwah, NJ 07430-2284
201-666-4110
Fax: 201-666-2394

4519 AIDS: Distinguishing Between Fact and Opinion
Greenhaven Press
PO Box 289009
San Diego, CA 92198-9009
858-485-7424
800-231-5163
Fax: 800-550-5480

Bruce Glassman, Owner

For beginning debaters, reports and classroom use this book offers three debates: Can AIDS be spread by casual contact? Should the Food and Drug Administration make AIDS drugs more available? Is AIDS a moral issue?.

4520 About AIDS
New Readers Press
PO Box 131
Syracuse, NY 13210
315-422-9121

Robert Wedgeworth, President

4521 An Annotated Bibliography of Recent Empirical Research in Methadone
National Clearinghouse for Alcohol and Drug Info.
PO Box 2345
Rockville, MD 20847-2345
301-468-2600
800-729-6686
Fax: 301-468-2600
e-mail: info@health.org
http://www.health.org

Provides guidelines and suggestions to investigators engaged in the demanding and essential task of followup research on intravenous drug users who have contracted AIDS.

97 pages

4522 Color of Light
Hazelden
15251 Pleasant Valley Road
Center City, MN 55012-9640
651-257-4010
800-328-9000
Fax: 651-213-4426
http://www.hazelden.org

Ellen Breyer, President

These 366 meditations speak to both the practical and spiritual journey of living with HIV/AIDS, and demonstrate how to integrate personal values with those offered in chemical dependency recovery and the Twelve Steps.

400 pages

4523 Guide to Living With HIV Infection
Johns Hopkins University Press
2715 N Charles Street
Baltimore, MD 21218-4319
410-516-6900
800-537-5487
Fax: 410-516-6998
http://www.jhu.edu/press/index.html

William Brody, President

This guidebook includes detailed discussions of new drugs; special considerations of the stages of infection; facts about opportunistic infection; and new information on prevention.

440 pages

4524 HIV/AIDS and Older Adults: Challenges for Individuals, Families, and Communities
Springer Publishing Company
11 West 42nd Street
15th Floor
New York, NY 10036
877-687-7476
e-mail: contactus@springerpub.com
http://www.springerpub.com

Charles A Emlet MSW/PhD, Editor

Focuses on the ways in which HIV/AIDS can affect older adults. The chapters in this book discuss the variety of HIV/AIDS problems that we face at the individual, family and community levels.

216 pages Year Founded:

4525 HIV: Third Edition
American College of Physicians
190 North Independence Mall West
Philadelphia, PA 19106-1572
215-351-2400
800-523-1546
http://www.acponline.org

Howard Libman MD, Editor
Harvey J Makadon MD, Editor

This comprehensively revised and updated new edition features all the practical guidance physicians need to care for HIV-infected patients. Details antiretroviral therapy; opportunistic infections, common clinical syndromes, long-term treatment complications; and the mangement of HIV in women, pregnant women, minorities, IV-drug users, and other special populations.

446 pages

4526 Learning AIDS
American Foundation for AIDS Research
120 Wall Street
Floor 13
New York, NY 10005-3908
212-806-1600
800-392-6327
Fax: 212-806-1601

Jerome Radwin, Manager

Lists organizations that distribute materials and information.

4527 Living Well with HIV and AIDS
Bull Publishing
PO Box 208
Palo Alto, CA 94302
650-322-2855
800-676-2855
Fax: 650-327-3300
e-mail: bullpublishing@msn.com
http://www.bullpub.com

Helps people overcome the day-to-day physical and emotional problems caused by the HIV disease, and encourages them to work with their medical team to make themselves as strong and healthy as possible.

292 pages

AIDS/Directories

4528 Longitudinal Studies of HIV Infection in Intravenous Drug Users
National Clearinghouse for Alcohol and Drug Info.
PO Box 2345
Rockville, MD 20847-2345
301-468-2600
800-729-6686
Fax: 301-468-2600
e-mail: info@health.org
http://www.health.org

This monograph is based upon papers and discussions from a NIDA technical review concerned with the methodological problems encountered in natural history studies of drug-related AIDS.

4529 Lving Well with HIV & AIDS
Bull Publishing Company
PO Box 1377
Boulder, CO 80306
800-676-2855
Fax: 303-545-6354
http://www.bullpub.com

Allen L Gifford MD, Author
Kate Lorig RN, Author
Diana Laurent MPH, Author

Offers the latest information based on the HIV care guidelines from the Department of Health & Human Services and the Center for Disease Control. Discusses a shift in treatments emphasis to the ways of managing side effects such as lypodystrophy, redistribution of body fat, cardiac risks, and concerns with vulnerability to other aliments called comorbidities.

4530 No Longer Immune: A Counselor's Guide to AIDS
American Counseling Association
5999 Stevenson Avenue
Alexandria, VA 22304-3304
703-823-9800
800-347-6647
Fax: 703-823-0252
http://www.counseling.org

Richard Yep, Executive Director

Covers a broad range of issues such as working with specific populations, handling pre- and posttesting situations, coping with fear, grief and survivor guilt, preventing caregiver burnout and dealing with countertransference.

295 pages

4531 Psychosocial Interventions in HIV Illness
Jason Aronson
PO Box 15100
York, PA 17405-7100
800-782-0015
Fax: 201-840-7242
http://www.aronson.com

240 pages

4532 The First Year: HIV: An Essential Guidefor the Newly Diagnosed
Perseus Books Group
387 Park Avenue South
12th Floor
New York, NY 10016
212-340-8100
http://www.perseusbooksgroup.com

Brett Grodeck

Guides readers through their first seven days following diagnosis, then the next three weeks of their first month, and finally the next eleven months of their first year-to provide answers and advice that will help everyone newly diagnosed with HIV come to terms with their condition and the lifestyle changes that accompany it.

Year Founded:

4533 The Guide to Living with HIV Infection
Johns Hopkins University Press
2715 North Charles Street
Baltimore, MD 21218-4363
410-516-6900
Fax: 410-516-6968

John G Bartlett MD, Author
Ann K Finkbeiner, Author

Developed at the Johns Hopkins AIDS Clinic is the most complete source of medical, emotional, social, and practical advice available for those infected with HIV and their loved ones. Provides essential information for making decisions about treatment and testing in a world transformed by new research and pharamcotherapy.

408 pages Year Founded:

Directories

4534 AIDS Action Bulletin
AIDS Action Baltimore
10 E Eager Street
Apartment 1
Baltimore, MD 21202-2546
410-837-2437

A directory of clinical research in AIDS for Baltimore and Washington.

4535 AIDS Crisis in America
ABC-CLIO
PO Box 1911
Santa Barbara, CA 93116-1911
805-968-1911
800-368-6868
Fax: 805-685-9685

Mary Ellen Hombs, Editor

Directory of organizations in the U.S that deal with AIDS issues.
268 pages

4536 AIDS Directory
LRP Publications
PO Box 980
Horsham, PA 19044
215-784-0941
800-341-7874
Fax: 215-784-0870

William Feldman, Editor

Directory of over 1,5000 educational, prevention, research and treatment organizations and government agencies working at national and state awareness.
808 pages

4537 AIDS and Deafness: Resource Directory
CDC National Aids Clearinghouse
PO Box 6003
Rockville, MD 20849-6003
800-458-5231
800-243-7012
Fax: 301-562-1050
e-mail: info@cdcnac.org
http://www.cdcnac.org

Computer printout. Lists national, state, and local organizations that offer AIDS (Acquired Immune Deficiency Syndrome)-related services to deaf and hard-of-hearing people; coverage includes Canada and the United Kingdom. Entries include: Organization name, address, phone, hotline numbers, hours of operation, access procedures, TTY/TDD numbers, names and titles of key personnel, geographic area served, description, product/service. Databasecompiled in cooperation with Gallaudet Research Institute at Gallaudet University.

4538 AIDS/HIV Treatment Directory
American Foundation for AIDS Research
120 Wall Street
Floor 13
New York, NY 10005-3908
212-806-1600
800-392-6327
Fax: 212-806-1601

Jerome Radwin, Manager

Directory has resources and assistance as well as lists active recruiting clinical tests on approved and experimental treatments for HIV, AIDS and opportunitistic infections.

Frequency: Biennial

AIDS/Journals, Magazines

4539 Local AIDS Services: The National Directory
US Conference of Mayors
1620 I Street NW
Washington, DC 20006-4005
202-293-7330
Fax: 202-293-2352

2,500 organizations that provide various information and services for AIDS coordinators and other health-related professionals.

4540 New York State Directory of AIDS/HIV Clinical Trials
Treatment Information Services - AmFAR
120 Wall Street
Floor 13
New York, NY 10005-3908
212-806-1600
Fax: 212-806-1601

Jerome Radwin, Manager

Provides the reader with easy to read, accurate information on clinical trials which are enrolling patients at sites throughout New York State and the surrounding area.

4541 Resources and Services Database
Centers for Disease Control
1600 Clifton Road NE
Atlanta, GA 30329-4018
404-639-3091
800-342-2437
Fax: 404-639-8910

Describes more than 16,000 organizations that provide HIV and AIDS prevention, education and social services. These include public health departments, community and social service organizations, hospitals and clinics.

4542 Worldwide AIDS Directory
Technology Management Group
PO Box 3260
New Haven, CT 06515
203-387-1430
Fax: 203-387-1470
e-mail: info@commtechsoftware.com

Manny Ratafia, Manager

A comprehensive text that spans all arenas for the AIDS industry.

545 pages Frequency: Irregular

Journals, Magazines

4543 Critical Path AIDS Project/AIDS Library
1233 Locust Street
5th Floor
Philadelphia, PA 19107-5453
215-985-9320
Fax: 215-985-4492

Julie Davids, Director

Articles and reprints on experimental treatments and alternative therapies, and a listing of Philadelphia-area resources.

Frequency: Monthly

Newsletters, Pamphlets

4544 AID Bulletin
Project AID Resource Center
PO Box 5190
Kent, OH 44242
330-672-2440
Fax: 330-672-4724

Alex Boros PhD, Director AID
J Sue Adams, Senior Counselor

Has the latest news on upcoming conferences, literature, developments in programs and/or services for disabled persons who are substance abusers. Offers articles on their experiences, ideas and questions of others in this field which includes providers and consumers.

4545 AIDS Health Pamphlets
Greenhaven Press
PO Box 289009
San Diego, CA 92198-9009
858-485-7424
800-231-5163
Fax: 800-550-5480

Bruce Glassman, Owner

Offers informational pamphlets on How serious is AIDS? Is AIDS a moral issue? Is AIDS testing effective? and How can the spread of AIDS be prevented?.

4546 AIDS Medicines in Development
Pharmaceutical Research & Manufacturers of America
1100 15th Street NW
Washington, DC 20005-1707
Fax: 202-835-3400

An annual chart of antivirals, as well as information on diagnostics and vaccines.

4547 AIDS News
Northern California Chapter of the NHF
7700 Edgewater Drive
Suite 710
Oakland, CA 94621-3023
510-568-6243
Fax: 510-568-2078

Robin Bias, Manager

Provides current information for people who need to cope mentally and physically with the issues of virus infection and transmission. Provides answers to questions about AIDS, ARC, HIV infection and transmission prevention.

4548 AIDS Policy and Law
Buraff Publications
1350 Connecticut Avenue NW
Washington, DC 20036-1722
800-333-

A report on AIDS policy and law developments from the courts, NIH, federal and state AIDS agencies and advocacy organizations.

4549 AIDS and Hemophilia: Protecting Yourself and Others
Northern California Chapter, NHF
Nhf 7700 Edgewater Drive
Suite 710
Oakland, CA 94621
510-568-6243
Fax: 510-568-2048

Robin Bias, Manager

Explains HIV transmission via sex, needle sticks and blood spills.

12 pages

4550 AIDS: What We Need to Know
March of Dimes Resource Center
1275 Mamaroneck Avenue
White Plains, NY 10605-5201
888-663-4637
Fax: 914-997-4763
e-mail: resourcecenter@modimes.org
http://www.modimes.org
TTY 914-997-4764

One to two page review and color brochure written for the general public.

4551 APLA Update
AIDS Project Los Angeles
6721 Romaine Street
Los Angeles, CA 90038-2425
323-962-1600

Elizabeth Starr, Owner

Presents news about AIDS and programs of AIDS Project Los Angeles to people affected by the disease.

20 pages

4552 Americans with Disabilities Act: What It Means for People with AIDS
American Civil Liberties Union AIDS Project
132 W 43rd Street
New York, NY 10036-6503
212-944-9800

AIDS/Newsletters, Pamphlets

4553 Basics of HIV Disease: Questions and Answers
National Hemophilia Foundation
116 W 32nd Street
Floor 11
New York, NY 10001-3212
888-463-6643
800-424-
Fax: 212-328-3777
http://www.infonhf.org
This publication contains basic information about hemophilia and HIV disease.
28 pages

4554 Be Smart About HIV
American Red Cross
1616 Fort Myer Drive
17th Floor
Arlington, VA 22209-3110
703-312-8724
Fax: 703-312-8738
Sandra L Mertz, Product Manager
This brochure offers very simple and informative information on the HIV virus. Half of this brochure is in English and the other half is in Spanish.

4555 Clinical Focus
Immune Deficiency Foundation
25 W Chesapeake Avenue
Suite 206
Towson, MD 21204-4841
410-321-6647
800-296-4433
Fax: 410-321-9165
e-mail: idf@primaryimmune.org
http://www.primaryimmune.org
Marcia Boyle, CEO
Bi-annual publication for medical professionals covering current issues and information regarding clinical approaches to primary immune deficiencies.

4556 Clinical Presentation of the Primary Immunodeficiency Diseases
Immune Deficiency Foundation
25 W Chesapeake Avenue
Suite 206
Towson, MD 21204-4841
410-321-6647
800-296-4433
Fax: 410-321-9165
Marcia Boyle, CEO
A primer for physicians.

4557 Clinical Update
Immune Deficiency Foundation
25 W Chesapeake Avenue
Suite 206
Towson, MD 21204-4841
410-321-6647
800-296-4433
Fax: 410-321-9165
Marcia Boyle, CEO

4558 Employee Attitudes About AIDS
National Leadership Coalition on AIDS
1730 M Street NW
Suite 905
Washington, DC 20036-4545
202-429-0930
Fax: 202-872-1977
A national survey of what working Americans think. Includes information on background surveys of AIDS in the workplace, key findings, conlusions, executive summaries and methodology.

4559 HIV Disease in People with Hemophilia: Your Questions Answered
National Hemophilia Foundation
116 W 32nd Street
Floor 11
New York, NY 10001-3212
888-463-6643
Fax: 212-328-3777
http://www.infonhf.org
Discusses hemophilia and HIV disease, AIDS, management of HIV disease, risks to sexual partners, and issues for children with hemophilia.

48 pages

4560 HIV Frontline
Center for AIDS Prevention Studies
74 New Montgomery Street
Suite 600
San Francisco, CA 94105-3411
415-597-9100
Fax: 415-597-9213
Dr. Leon McKusick, Contact
Cynthia Gomez, Manager
Monthly newsletter aimed at mental health and healthcare professionals who counsel people living with HIV/AIDS.

4561 HIV Infection and AIDS
NIAID Office of Communications and Public Liason
31 Center Drive MSC 2520
Building 31
Bethesda, MD 20892
301-496-5717
Fax: 301-402-0120
http://www.niaid.nih.gov
Offers information on transmission, treatment, early symptoms, diagnosis, prevention and research.

4562 HIV Treatment Information Exchange (HTIE)
National Hemophilia Foundation
116 W 32nd Street
Floor 11
New York, NY 10001-3212
888-463-6643
Fax: 212-328-3777
http://www.infonhf.org
Indexes and reprints articles from leading consumer-oriented HIV treatment newsletters. Areas covered include antiviral/retroviral treatments, opportunistic infections, immunotherapies, nutritional therapies, alternative therapies, and women's issues. Also highlights recent news stories involving HIV/AIDS treatments.

4563 Infections Linked to AIDS
NIAID Office of Communications and Public Liason
31 Center Drive MSC 2520
Building 31
Bethesda, MD 20892
301-496-5717
Fax: 301-402-0120
http://www.niaid.nih.gov
Offers information on infections related to HIV/AIDS and referral numbers of where to receive help.

4564 Managing Tuberculosis and HIV Infection in Today's General Workplace
National Leadership Coalition on AIDS
1730 M Street NW
Suite 905
Washington, DC 20036-4545
202-429-0930
Fax: 202-872-1977
Offers information on tuberculosis, HIV and AIDS in the workplace. How employers can protect themselves, special precautions to be taken, and the ADA and other legal information on this issue.

4565 NMAC Update
National Minority AIDS Council
1931 13th Street NW
Washington, DC 20009-4432
202-483-6622
Fax: 202-483-1135
A newsletter reporting on public policy issues and information on subjects in organizational management.

4566 Notes from the Underground
People with AIDS Working for Health
150 W 26th Street
Apt 201
New York, NY 10001-6813
212-255-0520
Current information on therapies and treatment strategies, concentrating on underground AIDS treatment access.

AIDS/Videos, Audio Tapes

4567 **Our Immune System**
Immune Deficiency Foundation
25 W Chesapeake Avenue
Suite 206
Towson, MD 21204-4841
410-321-6647
800-296-4433
Fax: 410-321-9165

Marcia Boyle, CEO

A booklet, in comic book form offering information and descriptions on the body's immune system.

22 pages

4568 **Primary Immune Deficiency Diseases: A Guide for Nurses**
Immune Deficiency Foundation
25 W Chesapeake Avenue
Suite 206
Towson, MD 21204-4841
410-321-6647
800-296-4433
Fax: 410-321-9165
e-mail: idf@primaryimmune.org

Marcia Boyle, CEO

Offers information on primary immune deficiency diseases to nurses working with patients suffering from these illnesses.

4569 **Report to Members**
National Leadership Coalition on AIDS
1730 M Street NW
Suite 905
Washington, DC 20036-4545
202-429-0930
Fax: 202-872-1977

Offers information on new medical research and breakthroughs, legal information and more to management personnel concerned with HIV/AIDS in the workplace.

4570 **Small Business and AIDS: How AIDS can Affect Your Business**
National Leadership Coalition on AIDS
1730 M Street NW
Suite 905
Washington, DC 20036-4545
202-289-0950

Tom Small, Manager

Offers the employer information on legal issues surrounding HIV in the workplace, educational programs, what employees need to know, health insurance and facts about AIDS.

4571 **Taking the HIV (AIDS) Test: How to Help Yourself**
NIAID Office of Communications and Public Liason
31 Center Drive MSC 2520
Building 31
Bethesda, MD 20892
301-496-5717
Fax: 301-402-0120
http://www.niaid.nih.gov

Offers information on the AIDS test, how it works, how it can help and should it be taken.

4572 **Testing Positive for HIV**
NIAID Office of Communications and Public Liason
31 Center Drive MSC 2520
Building 31
Bethesda, MD 20892
301-496-5717
Fax: 301-402-0120
http://www.niaid.nih.gov

Information on what a positive HIV test means, how not to spread the disease to others, and various health and dieting tips.

4573 **Testing for HIV Infection**
American Red Cross
1616 Fort Myer Drive
17th Floor
Arlington, VA 22209-3110
703-312-8724
Fax: 703-312-8738

Sandra L Mertz, Product Manager

4574 **Women, Sex and HIV**
American Red Cross
1616 Fort Myer Drive
17th Floor
Arlington, VA 22209-3110
703-312-8724
Fax: 703-312-8738

Sandra L Mertz, Product Manager

Videos, Audio Tapes

4575 **AIDS**
Rosen Publishing Group
29 E 21st Street
New York, NY 10010-6209
212-777-3017
800-237-9932
Fax: 888-436-4643
e-mail: rosenpub@tribeca.ios.com

Roger Rosen, President

This video presents moving portraits of people living with AIDS who generously share their experience with AIDS. Includes views on sex, condoms, and life.

4576 **Our Immune System**
Immune Deficiency Foundation
25 W Chesapeake Avenue
Suite 206
Towson, MD 21204-4841
410-321-6647
800-296-4433
Fax: 410-321-9165

Marcia Boyle, CEO

Slide set.

Websites

4577 **AIDS Info**

http://www.aidsinfo.nih.gov

A call in service where trained staff offers quick access to federally approved HIV/AIDS treatment and prevention guidelines, clinical trials, and other research-related information.

4578 **Arkansas Department of Health**

http://www.healthy.state.ar

Provides educational materials such as pamphlets and films, conducts HIV and AIDS research and operates a speakers bureau.

4579 **National AIDS Information Clearinghouse**

http://www.cdcnac.org

Provides information and materials for employers on national, state and local resources related to HIV/AIDS in the workplace.

4580 **Pennsylvania Department of Health: Bureau of HIV/AIDS**

http://www.state.pa.com

Offers various community health education presentations, counseling and testing sites. Also offers practical support services, counseling, HIV testing, a hotline and referrals.

4581 **Project Inform Hotline**

http://www.projectinform.org

HIV/AIDS treatment information.

AIDS / Research Centers

4582 Vermont Department of Healt: HIV/AIDS Program

http://www.state.vt.us

We provide riask reduction and health education services, Anonymous HIV counseling and testing sites through Vermont, HIV/AIDS educational materials.

4583 Virginia Department of Health: DivisionHIV/STD

http://www.vdh.state.va.us/std

The division provides a toll free hotline for HIV/STD and viral Hepatitis information, education, confidentiality and anonymous testing. Tghe division provides referrals for AIDS medication assistance and outpatient care services for income eligible persons with HIV.

Research Centers

4584 Aaron Diamond AIDS Research Center
455 1st Avenue
7th Floor
New York, NY 10016-9121
212-725-0018
Fax: 212-725-1126
http://www.adarc.org

David D Ho MD, Director

AIDS research.

4585 Agency for Health Care Research and Quality
301-594-6662
Fax: 301-594-2168
http://www.ahcpr.gov

Operated by a branch of the US Department of Health and Human Services, this site provides recommendations (in layman's lingo) on the prevention and treatment of common illnesses and conditions. Just click on Clinical Information, then on Clinical Practice Guidelines Online, then on Consumer's Guides.

4586 American Foundation for AIDS Research
120 Wall Street
Floor 13
New York, NY 10005-3908
212-806-1600
Fax: 212-806-1601
http://www.amfar.org

Jerome Radwin, Manager

Supports research in basic, clinical, prevention and public policy and publishes the AIDS/HIV Experimental Treatment Directory.

4587 Arizona State University: School of Health Administration & Policy
Tempe, AZ 85287
480-965-7778
Fax: 480-965-5539

Eugene S Schneller PhD, Director

Offers research into healthcare delivery issues in the US including program evaluation, rural health and swing beds, new systems and AIDS in managed care systems.

4588 Asian AIDS Project
730 Polk Street
Floor 4
San Francisco, CA 94109-7813
415-292-3400
Fax: 415-292-3404

John Manzon-Santos, Executive Director

Offers support and information for Asian Americans with HIV/AIDS.

4589 Cascade AIDS Project: Women's Phone Network
408 SW 2nd Avenue
414
Portland, OR 97204-3404
503-223-5907

Jean Ann Van Krevelen, Executive Director

4590 Center for Blood Research
800 Huntington Avenue
Boston, MA 02115-6399
617-731-6470
Fax: 617-278-3493
e-mail: lanner@cbr.med.harvard.edu

Michael Lanner, Executive VP
John Baldwin, CEO

Offers research into blood disorders including multidisciplinary studies on AIDS and hemophilia, cancer and diabetes research as well.

4591 Center for Disease Control
1600 Clifton Road NE
Stop E47
Atlanta, GA 30329-4018
404-639-3533
800-342-2437
Fax: 919-361-8425

Elizabeth R Unger PhD

Offers reprints, reports, public awareness and educational materials, research grants, and support for persons with HIV/AIDS.

4592 Center for Interdisciplinary Research in Immunology & Diseases at UCLA
12-262 Factor Building
Los Angeles, CA 90024
310-825-1510
Fax: 310-206-3865

JL Fahey MD, Director

Research into immunology and blood disorders with special focus on AIDS and HIV infections.

4593 City of Hope National Medical Center: Beckman Research
Virology & Infectious Diseases
1500 Duarte Road
Duarte, CA 91010-3000
626-359-8111
Fax: 626-301-8458
e-mail: jzaia@cityofhope.com
http://www.cityofhope.org

Dr. John A Zaia, Principal Investigator
Norio Azumi, MD

Developmental research into the treatment of AIDS.

4594 Clinical Research Center
Northwestern Center for Clinical Research
680 N Lake Shore Drive
Suite 1220
Chicago, IL 60611-8708
312-503-6227
http://www.ocrt@northwestern.edu

Dr. Tom Schnitzer, Program Director

Offers research into complications and effects of AIDS and HIV infection on the human body.

4595 Comprehensive AIDS Center
680 N Lake Shore Drive
Apt 1106
Chicago, IL 60611-4480
312-482-8484
Fax: 312-908-5820
e-mail: s-perez@nwu.edu

Dr. John P Phair, Director
Linda Hicks, Manager

AIDS research.

4596 Coulston Foundation: Primate Research Center
PO Box 1027
Alamogordo, NM 88311-1027
505-479-6101
Fax: 505-479-6101

Preston Marx PhD, Director

AIDS research.

4597 Dana-Farber Cancer Institute: National Drug Discovery Group for AIDS Treatment
44 Binney Street
Boston, MA 02115-6084
617-632-3000
Fax: 617-732-3113

Dr. William A Haseltine, Principal Investor
Edward Benz, President

AIDS / Research Centers

4598 **Developmental Evaluation Center**
Children's Hospital
300 Longwood Avenue
Boston, MA 02115-5724
617-355-6000
Fax: 617-735-7429
Allen C Crocker MD, Director
James Mandell, CEO

Studies developmental effects of infants at risk and development effects of congenital HIV infection.

4599 **Dwight David Eisenhower Army Medical Center**
Department of Clinical Investigation
Building 300
Fort Gordon, GA 30905
706-791-4273
Fax: 706-791-5216
e-mail: kentplowmn@aol.com
Col. Kent M Plowman MC, Chief

Focuses research on cardiac disorders, immune deficiencies and AIDS.

4600 **Emory University: National Cooperative Drug Discovery for AIDS Treatment**
Department of Pediatrics
2040 Ridgewood Drive NE
Atlanta, GA 30322-1028
404-727-5740
Fax: 404-728-7726
Dr. Raymond F Schanzi, Principal
Thomas Abshire, MD

4601 **Emory University: Yerkes Regional Primate Research Center**
954 Gatewood Road NE
Atlanta, GA 30322
404-349-7905
Fax: 404-727-0623
e-mail: insel@rmy.emory.edu
http://www.emory.edu
Dr. Thomas R Insel MD, Director
Thomas Emory, Owner

Immune research.

4602 **General Clinical Research Center**
100th Street & 5th Avenue
New York, NY 10029
212-241-6045
Dr. Robert Desnick, Director

Focuses on AIDS education and prevention.

4603 **George Washington National Cooperative Drug Discovery/AIDS Treatment**
2300 Eye Street NW
Washington, DC 20037-2337
202-994-2987
Fax: 202-994-2870
Monica Partch, Manager

Studies and researches natural products and synthetic anti-AIDS agents.

4604 **Hematology Research Laboratory: Universiy of Southern California**
2025 Zonal Avenue
Los Angeles, CA 90089-9102
213-224-6412
Fax: 213-224-6687
Alexandra Levine, Head

Research into AIDS and HIV infection, as well as sexually transmitted diseases.

4605 **Indiana University Bloomington: Rural Center for the Study and Promotion of AIDS/STD Prevention (RCAP)**
801 E 7th Street
Bloomington, IN 47405-3937
812-855-3403
Fax: 812-855-3717
e-mail: aids@indiana.edu
http://www.indiana.edu/~aids
William L Yarber, Director
Suzanne Thorin, Manager

AIDS research.

4606 **International Health Research Foundation**
3741 Lejune Road SW
Coconut Grove, FL 33146
305-663-9666
Fax: 305-663-9671
Dr. Caroline MacLeod, Chairperson

Focuses on issues of public health especially AIDS.

4607 **Johns Hopkins University: Center for Communication Problems**
111 Market Place
Suite 310
Baltimore, MD 21202-7112
410-659-6300
Fax: 410-659-6266
e-mail: ccp@jhuccp.org
http://www.jhuccp.org
Phyllis T Piotrow PhD, Director
Jane Bertrand, Executive Director

Health communications, family planning and AIDS prevention research.

4608 **Kaiser Foundation Research Institute**
3505 Broadway
Suite 112
Oakland, CA 94611-5714
510-450-2000
Fax: 510-873-5130
Paul Lairson MD, Director

4609 **Mariposa Education and Research Foundation**
3123 Schweitzer Drive
Topanga, CA 90290-4467
310-704-4812
Fax: 310-704-4830
Bruce Voeller PhD, President

Research involving the prevention of AIDS.

4610 **Maryland Medical Research Institute**
600 Wyndhurst Avenue
Baltimore, MD 21210-2489
410-435-4200
Fax: 410-323-8622
e-mail: postmaster@mmri.org
http://www.mmri.org
Dr. Michael Terrin, President
Genell Knatterud, Manager

Focuses on AIDS and HIV related research.

4611 **Medical University of South Carolina: Health Services Administration**
College of Health
Charleston, SC 29425
843-792-2118
Fax: 843-792-3327
David Ward PhD, Director

Devoted to public health policy and health care management including AIDS research.

4612 **National Hemophilia Foundation: Hemophillia and AIDS/HIV Network (HANDI)**
110 Greene Street
Suite 406
New York, NY 10012-3838
212-328-3700
Fax: 212-219-8180
Alan Kinniburgh, CEO

Dedicated to the treatment and the cure of hemophilia, AIDS and other blood related disorders. This foundation wishes to improve the quality of life of all those affected through promotion and support of research, education and other services.

4613 **National Prison Project: ACLU AIDS inPrison Project**
915 15th Street NW
Suite 700
Washington, DC 20005-2313
202-393-4930
Fax: 202-393-4931
Elizabeth Alexander, Executive Director

AIDS / Research Centers

4614 Northwestern Connecticut AIDS Project
100 Migeon Avenue
Torrington, CT 06790-4815
860-482-1596
Fax: 860-482-3606
e-mail: general@nwctaids.org
http://www.nwctaids.org
Debi Thibeault, Executive Director

A nonprofit organization offering support and a variety of services to people with AIDS and their loved ones. Provides education to all segments of the public about AIDS prevention and treatment.

4615 Philadelphia Biomedical Research Institute
100 Ross & Royal Road
King of Prussia, PA 19087
610-962-0615
Fax: 610-962-0614
e-mail: sttohnishi@aol.com
S Tsuyoshi Ohinishi PhD, Director

4616 SUNY at Buffalo: National Cooperative Drug Discovery Group for AIDS Treatment
Department of Biochemistry
304 Foster Hall
Buffalo, NY 14214-8031
716-831-3259
Fax: 716-831-3001
Dr. David M Rekosh, Principal Investor

4617 Sansum Diabetes Research Institute
2219 Bath Street
Santa Barbara, CA 93105-4321
805-682-7638
Fax: 805-682-3332
http://www.sansum.org
Lois Jovanovic MD, Director
Jeannine Glockler, Manager

4618 Stanford University: General Clinical Research Center
300 Pasteur Drive
Unit 1
Palo Alto, CA 94305-2200
650-723-6073
Fax: 650-725-6698
e-mail: mv.bis@forsythe.stanford.edu
http://www.leland.stanford.edu/dept/gcrc
Dr. David Stevenson, Director
Howard Sussman, MD

4619 Stanford University: National Cooperative Drug Discover /AIDS Group
Department of Pathology
800 Welch Road
Palo Alto, CA 94304-1607
650-723-6481
Fax: 650-725-0592
Dr. Edgar Engleman, Principal Investigator
Steven Foung, MD

4620 State University of New York: SUNY Stony Brook Drug Discovery Group
School of Medicine, Infectious Disease Division
T-15 80
Stony Brook, NY 11794
631-444-1660
Fax: 631-444-7518
Dr. Roy Steigbigel, Director
William H Greene, MD

Human immunodeficiency virus research.

4621 UCLA AIDS Clinical Research Center
10833 Le Conte Avenue
Los Angeles, CA 90024
310-206-6987
Fax: 310-206-3311
Ronald T Mitsuyana, Director
Ora Yadin, MD

4622 University of Alabama at Birmingham: National Cooperative Drug/AIDS
Department of Pediatrics
Children's Hospital
Suite 616
Birmingham, AL 35294
205-934-7714
Fax: 205-934-8559
Dr. Richard Whitley, Principal Investigator

4623 University of California/Davis: AIDS Virus Diagnostic Laboratory
Comparative Oncology
Old Davis Road
Davis, CA 95616
530-752-8242
Fax: 530-752-4816
e-mail: jcarlson@clb.ucdmc.ucdavis.edu
James R Carlson, Director

HIV production and purification of treatments, testing and vaccine development.

4624 University of California: Institute of Health Policy Studies
333 California Street
Suite 625
San Francisco, CA 94104-2600
415-476-4921
Fax: 415-476-0705
Philip R Lee, Director
Harold Luft, Executive Director

Health policy and AIDS research.

4625 University of California: Los Angeles Clinical AIDS Research & Education
10833 Le Conte Avenue
Room Bh-412
Los Angeles, CA 90095-1793
310-794-1456
Fax: 310-206-3311
e-mail: rmitsuya@med1.medsch.ucla.edu
http://www.med.ucla.edu/carectr/carehome.htm
Ronald T Mitsuyasu MD, Director

AIDS research
1983

4626 University of California: San Diego Center for AIDS Research
9500 Gilman Drive
La Jolla, CA 92093-5004
858-534-8805
Fax: 619-822-1934
e-mail: csussman@ucsd.edu
Flossie Wong-Staal PhD, Director
Gerry R Boss, MD

AIDS research
1994

4627 University of California: San Francisco Center for AIDS Prevention Studies
Prevention Science Group
74 New Montgomery Street
Suite 600
San Francisco, CA 94105-3411
415-885-7464
Fax: 415-597-9213
e-mail: fcoates@psg.ucsf.edu
http://www.caps.ucsf.edu/capsweb
Thomas J Coates PhD, Director
Lena Bordina, Manager

4628 University of Florida: Center for Health Policy Research
Jhmhc
Box J-177
Gainesville, FL 32610
352-392-2571
Fax: 352-392-3655
Prf. Michael Miller, Director

Studies into HIV infection and AIDS research.

AIDS / Research Centers

4629 University of Hawaii: Hawaii AIDS Clinical Research Program
3675 Kilauea Avenue
6th Floor
Honolulu, HI 96816-2333
808-737-2751
Fax: 808-735-7047
e-mail: shikuma@hawaii.edu
Cecilia M Shikuma MD, Director
William Walters, Manager
AIDS research
1990

4630 University of Maryland: Center for Research, Grants & Contracts
655 W Lombard Street
Baltimore, MD 21201-1512
410-328-3685
Fax: 410-321-8108
Dr. R Narker Bausell, Director
Focuses research on public and health policy laws, including AIDS research.

4631 University of Maryland: Division of Infectious Diseases
10 S Pine Street
Baltimore, MD 21201-1116
410-328-7560
Fax: 410-328-8700
John W Warren MD, Head
Focuses research on elderly studies including drug use, treatments and infectious diseases of the aged.

4632 University of Michigan: National Cooperative Drug/AIDS Group
School of Dentistry, Dept. of Biologic Sciences
1011 N University Avenue
Ann Arbor, MI 48109-1012
734-763-5579
Fax: 734-764-7406
John C Drach PhD, Director
Focuses on the design of new drugs to fight AIDS.

4633 University of North Carolina: General Clinical Research Center
Cb 7600
Chapel Hill, NC 27599
919-962-2211
Fax: 919-966-1576
Eugene P Orringer MD, Director
James Moeser, CEO
Focuses on public policy and health research pertaining to the AIDS community and sexually transmitted disease studies.

4634 University of San Francisco: AIDS Clinical Research Center
PO Box 0422
San Francisco, CA 94143
415-422-5555
Fax: 415-476-8919
e-mail: stom%suzi@ccmail.ucsf.edu
John S Greenspan, Director
John Lo Schiavo, CEO
AIDS research
1981

4635 University of South Florida: Center for HIV Education & Research
13301 Bruce B Downs Boulevard
Tampa, FL 33612-3807
813-974-4565
Fax: 831-974-6469
e-mail: hiventr@fmhi
http://www.fmni.usf.edu/hiv
Michael Knox PhD, Director
Treatment of persons affected and infected with HIV, provides current AIDS information to physicians and operates a resource center to provide educational materials as well as consultations.

4636 University of Vermont: Office of Health Promotion Research
1 S Prospect Street
Burlington, VT 05401-5505
802-656-4187
Fax: 802-656-8826
e-mail: rsektvw@zoo.uvm.edu
http://www.uvm.edu/~ohpr
Roger H Secker-Walker MD, Director
Research done into public policy and human health including AIDS information and evaluation.

4637 Utah Department of Health: Division of Community Health Services
288 N 1460 W
Salt Lake City, UT 84116-3231
801-538-6096
Fax: 801-538-6036
Craig Nichols MPA, Director
Teresa Garrett, Executive Director
Secures and distributes funds for AIDS prevention services, provides educational programs and counseling to the general public, AIDS service organizations, health workers and groups at risk.

4638 Wayne State University: Center for Health Research
College of Nursing
5557 Cass Avenue
Detroit, MI 48202-3615
313-577-4082
Fax: 313-577-5777
e-mail: ajacox@cms.cc.wayne.edu
http://www.comm.wayne.edu/nursing/nursing.html
Dr. Ada Jacox, Associate Dean
Janet Harden, Executive Director
AIDS and HIV infection research and studies.

4639 Whitehead Institute for Biomedical Research
9 Cambridge Center
Cambridge, MA 02142-1401
617-258-5000
Fax: 617-258-9872
e-mail: info@wi.mit.edu
http://www.wi.mit.edu/home.html
Dr. Gerald Fink, Director
David Page, Manager
AIDS information and research.

4640 Worcester Foundation for Biomedical Research: Biology/Drug Discovery/AIDS Group
University of Massachusetts Medical School
377 Plantation Street
Worcester, MA 01605-2300
508-856-1994
Fax: 508-856-8508
Dr. Paul C Zamecnik, Principal Investigator
Thoru Pederson, Executive Director
Developmental research on new advances and drug therapies for HIV infection and the prevention of AIDS.

Allergies/Associations & Organizations

Associations & Organizations

4641 AAN-MA's Toll-Free Hotline
National Allergy and Asthma Network
3529 Chain Bridge Rd.
Suite 200
Fairfax, VA 22030
703-385-4403
800-878-4403
e-mail: Marianne@Centrevillemooselodge2168.org
http://www.centrevillemooselodge2168.org
Marianne Beck, Social Quarters Manager

Offers answers to questions regarding allergies and asthma, provides referrals and support to assist the patient and their families.

4642 ASMA Hotline
American Academy of Allergy & Immunology
611 E Wells Street
Milwaukee, WI 53202
414-272-6071
800-822-2762
e-mail: info@aaaai.org
http://www.aaaai.org
Elaine Richheimer, President
Gaylene M Altman, Secretary

Referral line offering information on allergy and asthma treatments, referrals to an allergy/immunology specialist, lay organization or support groups across the country.

4643 Allergy and Asthma Network Mothers of Asthmatics
2751 Prosperity Avenue
Suite 150
Fairfax, VA 22031
703-641-9595
800-878-4403
Fax: 703-573-7794
http://www.aanma.org
Nancy Sander, President/Founder
Pamela Mason, Chairman

A nonprofit association dedicated to educating families with asthma and allergies. Facilitates communication of accurate information among patients, parents, physicians and industry. Provides an important communication link among the home, school, physician and pharmaceutical industry in an effort to help families create a management program for those with asthma and allergies.

4644 American Academy of Allergy and Immunology
555 East Wells Street
Suite 1100
Milwaukee, WI 53202-3823
414-272-6071
800-822-2762
Fax: 414-272-6070
e-mail: info@aaaai.org
http://www.aaaai.org
Kay Whalen, EVP
Thomas A.E. Platts-Mills, President

Strives to serve the public through information on asthma and allergies, as well as referrals to allergists. Also offers pollen and mold statistics from the Committee on Pollen & Molds.

4645 American Academy of Environmental Medicine
PO Box 1001-8001
New Hope, PA 18938
800-LET-HEAL

Offers names of Clinical Ecologists and Allergy Specialists in the United States.

4646 American Lung Association
61 Broadway
Floor 6
New York, NY 10006-2753
212-315-8700
800-586-4872
Fax: 212-315-8870
e-mail: info@lungusa.org
http://www.lungusa.org
John Kirkwood, President/CEO

A voluntary organization interested in the prevention and control of lung disease. Promotes and distributes public awareness information on a variety of lung disorders, including allergies.
1904

4647 An Overview of Allergy
American College of Allergy & Immunology
800 E Northwest Highway
Suite 1080
Palatine, IL 60067
847-427-1200
Fax: 847-427-1294
http://http://allergy.mcg.edu
James Slawny, Executive Director

Strengthen relationships with patients by providing them with the essential information they need.

4648 Asthma and Allergy Foundation of America
1233 20th Street, NW
Suite 402
Washington, DC 20036
202-466-7643
800-727-8462
Fax: 202-466-8940
e-mail: Info@aafa.org
http://www.aafa.org
William McLin, M.Ed., Executive Director
Yucynthia Jean-Louis, MPH, MBA, President

The Foundation was formed to alleviate suffering and loss from asthma and allergy disorders. The Foundation offers a nationwide network of chapters and support groups and provides education and emotional support for patients and their families.

4649 Food Allergy Anaphylaxis Network
11781 Lee Jackson Memorial Highway
Suite 160
Fairfax, VA 22033-3309
703-691-3179
800-929-4040
Fax: 703-691-2713
e-mail: faan@foodallergy.org
http://www.foodallergy.org
Anne Munoz-Furlong, Founder and Chief Executive Offi
Hugh A. Sampson, M.D., Medical Director

A nonprofit organization established to help families living with food allergies, and to increase public awareness about food allergies and anaphylaxis. Also provides emotional support and educational information.

4650 Immune Deficiency Foundation
25 W Chesapeake Avenue
Suite 206
Towson, MD 21204
410-321-6647
800-296-4433
Fax: 410-321-9165
e-mail: idf@primaryimmune.org
http://www.primaryimmune.org
Marcia Boyle, Chairman and President
Barbara Ballard, Secretary

Offers information and referral services to allergy patients and their families.

4651 National Eczema Association for Science and Education
4460 Redwood Hwy
Ste. 16-D
San Rafael, CA 94903-1953
415-499-3474
Fax: 415-472-5345
e-mail: info@nationaleczema.org
http://www.nationaleczema.org
Donald S. Young, JD -, Chairman
John [Jack] Crossen, PhD, CFO

Offers resources and information for allergy patients.

Books

4652 Allergies A to Z
Facts on File
11 Penn Plaza
Floor 15
New York, NY 10001-2006
212-967-8800
800-322-8755
Fax: 212-967-8107
e-mail: lmilberg@factsonfile.com

This vital resource for the one in five Americans who suffer from allercies provides reliable, up-to-date information on every aspect of this condition.
368 pages

4653 Allergy Plants That Cause Sneezing and Wheezing
Asthma and Allergy Foundation of America
1233 20th Street NW
Suite 402
Washington, DC 20036-2330
202-466-7643
800-727-8462
Fax: 202-466-8940
http://www.aafa.org

Bill McLin, Executive Director

Destined to be displayed on coffee tables, the spectacular photographs in this book actually show allergy sufferers what causes their sneezing and wheezing.
64 pages

4654 Allergy-Free Garening: The Revolutionary Guide to Healthy Landscaping
Ten Speed Press
PO Box 7123
Berkely, CA 94707
510-559-1600
800-841-2665
Fax: 510-599-1629
http://www.tenspeed.com

Thomas Leo Ogren, Author

This extensively researched, comprehensive, plant-by-plant reference alerts gardeners and helps them make landscaping choices that can drastically reduce their exposure to harmful allergens.
256 pages

4655 Best Guide to Allergy
Humana Press
999 Riverview Drive
Suite 208
Totowa, NJ 07512-1165
973-256-1699
Fax: 973-256-8341
e-mail: humana@humanapr.com
http://www.humanapress.com

Thomas Lanigan, Owner

Practical everyday approaches to your allergy and asthma problems, including food allergies, environmental control, skin conditions, allergy testing and shots, and more.
232 pages

4656 Essential Allergy
Blackwell Science
350 Main Street
Malden, MA 02148-5089
781-388-8250
800-215-1000
Fax: 781-388-8255
e-mail: csbooks@blacksci.com
http://www.blackwellscience.com

Gordan Tibbitts III, President

4657 Food Allergies for Dummies
For Dummies
10475 Crosspoint Boulevard
Indianpolis, IN 46256
877-762-2974
Fax: 800-597-3299
http://www.dummies.com

Robert A Wood MD, Author

This concise guide shows you how to identify and avoid food that triggers reactions. Covers how to care for a child with food allergies, such as getting involved with his/her school's allergy policies, packing safe lunches, and empowering him/her to take responsibility for his allergy.
384 pages

4658 Food Allergy: A Primer for People
Asthma and Allergy Foundation of America
1233 20th Street NW
Suite 402
Washington, DC 20036-2330
202-466-7643
800-727-8462
Fax: 202-466-8940
http://www.aafa.org

Bill McLin, Executive Director

Food allergies demystified.
66 pages

4659 Indoor Allergens: Assessing & Controlling Adverse Health Effects
National Academy Press
PO Box 285
Washington, DC 20055
202-334-3313
888-624-8373
Fax: 202-334-2793
e-mail: zjones@nas.edu
http://www.nap.edu

This unique volume summarizes what is known about indoor allergens and how they affect human health and how they can be controlled.
320 pages 1993

4660 Manual of Allergy & Immunology
Little Brown & Company
34 Beacon Street
Boston, MA 02108-1415
617-367-0520
Fax: 617-227-4633

Felice Mendell, Executive Director

4661 Sinus Survival: A Self-Help Guide for Allergies, Bronchitis, Colds & Sinusitis
JP Tarcher
5858 Wilshire Boulevard
Suite 200
Los Angeles, CA 90036-4523
323-935-9980
Fax: 323-935-9986

221 pages

4662 Taming Asthma and Allergy by Controlling Your Environment
Allergy Control Products
PO Box 793
Ridgefield, CT 06877
203-438-9580
Fax: 203-431-8963
http://www.allergycontrol.com

Edward Steube, President

Tells how to avoid allergens in simple, straight forward directions and also explains the reasons through interesting case examples.
170 pages

Directories

4663 Allergy Products Directory: Allergy/Asthma, Finding Help (Volume Three)
Allergy Publications
1259 El Camino Real
254
Menlo Park, CA 94025-4208
650-858-0363
Fax: 916-939-9626

Carol Rudoff, Pres. Amer. Allergy Association

Allergies/Newsletters, Pamphlets

A wealth of helpful resources including organizations, resource centers, health and hot lines, information lines, libraries, asthma camps, clearinghouses, self-help groups, agencies, support and education programs, databases, on-line information, newsletters, insurance information, patient aids and more.

942 pages Frequency: Irregular

Newsletters, Pamphlets

4664 **Advice From Your Allergist**
American College of Allergy & Immunology
800 E Northwest Highway
Suite 1080
Palatine, IL 60074-6580
847-359-2800
Fax: 847-427-1294

Offers information on the effects, triggers and causes of allergies including house dust, pets, hay fever, hives and exercise.

4665 **Allergies and You**
American Lung Association
1740 Broadway
New York, NY 10019-4315
212-315-8700
Fax: 212-315-8870

John Kirkwood, CEO

Answers basic questions about allergy, particularly as it relates to asthma.

4666 **FAN Flashbacks**
Food Allergy Network
10400 Eaton Place
Suite 107
Fairfax, VA 22030-2208
703-691-3179
800-929-4040
Fax: 703-691-2713
e-mail: fan@worldweb.net
http://www.foodallergy.org

Anne Munoz-Furlong, President

Series of reprints on specific topics of Food Allergy News. Specific pamphlets offer information on wheat, milk, soy, peanuts and special occasion tips.

4667 **Food Allergy News**
Food Allergy Network
11781 Lee Jackson Memorial Highway
Suite 160
Fairfax, VA 22033-3309
703-691-3179
800-929-4040
Fax: 703-691-2713
e-mail: fan@worldweb.net
http://www.foodallergy.org

Anne Munoz-Furlong, President

Contains allergy-free recipes, practical tips such as birthday party, trick-or-treating and travel tips, a dietitian's column, medical information and product information.

8 pages

4668 **Food Allergy and Atopic Dermatitis**
Food Allergy Network
10400 Eaton Place
Suite 107
Fairfax, VA 22030-2208
703-691-3179
800-929-4040
Fax: 703-691-2713
e-mail: fan@worldweb.net
http://www.foodallergy.org

Anne Munoz-Furlong, President

The purpose of this booklet is to provide tips and other sources of information to help parents raise a child who is afflicted with Atopic Dermatitis.

12 pages

4669 **Just One Little Bite Can Hurt! Important Facts About Anaphylaxis**
Food Allergy Network
10400 Eaton Place
Suite 107
Fairfax, VA 22030-2208
703-691-3179
800-929-4040
Fax: 703-691-2713
e-mail: fan@worldweb.net
http://www.foodallergy.org

Anne Munoz-Furlong, President

Offers information on what Anaphylaxis is, what the patient should do if they have a reaction and important medical safety tips regarding the illness.

8 pages

4670 **MA Report**
Allergy and Asthma Network/Mothers of Asthmatics
2751 Prosperity Avenue
Suite 150
Fairfax, VA 22031-4343
703-573-7782
800-878-4403
Fax: 703-573-7794
http://www.aanma.org

Monthly newsletter providing members with insider information on medical research, new products, practical how-to tips and helpful hints, updates on legislation, product recalls, prevention and coping techniques and much more.

Frequency: 12

4671 **Nutrition Guide to Food Allergies**
Food Allergy Network
10400 Eaton Place
Suite 107
Fairfax, VA 22030-2208
703-691-3179
800-929-4040
Fax: 703-691-2713
e-mail: fan@worldweb.net
http://www.foodallergy.org

Anne Munoz-Furlong, President

Offers answers to the most commonly asked questions about food allergies, common allergy-causing foods and resources for the patient.

24 pages

4672 **Something in the Air: Airborne Allergens**
National Institute of Allergy & Infectious Disease
9000 Rockville Pike
Bethesda, MD 20892
301-496-5717
Fax: 301-402-0120

Offers information on the symptoms to airborne substances, pollen, mold, dust, animal, chemical allergies and treatments for them.

4673 **Tips to Remember**
American Academy of Allergy & Immunology
611 E Wells Street
Suite 4a
Milwaukee, WI 53202-3816
414-272-6071
800-822-2762
Fax: 414-272-6070

Kay Whalen, Executive Vice President

A set of 23 informational pamphlets offering information on various aspects of allergies and asthma from allergies in the elderly to what is an allergic reaction.

Websites

4674 **Allergy and Asthma Network Mothers ofAsthmatics**

http://www.aanma.org

Allergies/Research Centers

A nonprofit association dedicated to educating families with asthma and allergies. Facilitates communication of accurate information among patients, parents, physicians and industry. Provides an important communication link among the home, school, physician and pharmaceutical industry in an effort to help families create a management program for those with asthma and allergies.

4675 American Academy of Allergy and Immunology

http://www.aaaai.org

Strives to serve the public through information on asthma and allergies, as well as referrals to allergists. Also offers pollen and mold statistics from the Committee on Pollen & Molds.

4676 American Lung Association

http://www.lungusa.org

A voluntary organization interested in the prevention and control of lung disease. Promotes and distributes public awareness information on a variety of lung disorders, including allergies.
1904

4677 Asthma and Allergy Foundation of America

http://www.aafa.org

Voluntary health organization dedicated to improving the quality of life for people with asthma and allergies and their caregivers through education, research and advocacy. The network of affiliated chapters and educational support groups.

4678 Food Allergy Anaphylaxis Network

http://www.foodallergy.org

A nonprofit organization established to help families living with food allergies, and to increase public awareness about food allergies and anaphylaxis. Also provides emotional support and educational information.

Research Centers

4679 Allergy Research Foundation
11620 Wilshire Boulevard
Bldg 210
Los Angeles, CA 90025-1706
310-312-5050
Fax: 310-575-9292
e-mail: joncorren@hotmail.com
Billy Loftus, Manager

Non-profit, independent organization that deals with allergy related issues.
1988

4680 American College of Allergy and Immunology
1645 Oakton Place
Des Plaines, IL 60018-2002
847-427-1200
800-842-7777
James Slawny, Executive Director

This association focuses its attention on research and public awareness of allergies. Distributes informational brochures and pamphlets, offers referrals and counseling services, as well as patient care.

4681 Brigham and Women's Hospital: Asthma & Allergic Diseases Research Center
1 Jimmy Fund Way
Boston, MA 02115-6085
617-525-1300
Fax: 617-525-1310
K Frank Austen, Contact

Directed to improve the prevention, treatment, research and diagnosis of asthma and other related issues.
1971

4682 John Hopkins Asthma & Allergy Center
5501 Hopkins Bayview Circle
Baltimore, MD 21224
410-550-2101
Fax: 410-550-1733
e-mail: jhuellergy@jhmi.edu
http://www.hopkinsmedicine.org/allergy
Bruce S Bochner MD, Director
Peter S Creticos MD, Clinical Director

Treatment of allergies, asthma and other lung disorders.
1976

4683 Johns Hopkins University: Asthma and Allergy Center
5501 Hopkins Bayview Circle
Baltimore, MD 21224-6821
410-550-0545
Fax: 410-550-1733
http://www.med.jhu.edu/allergy
Dr. Lawrence M Lichtenstein, Director

Research in areas including allergic, inflammation and pulmonary diseases.
1971

4684 La Jolla Institute for Allergy andImmunology
10355 Science Center Drive
San Diego, CA 92121-1118
858-558-3500
Fax: 858-558-3525
http://www.liai.org
Howard Grey, President

A nonprofit public benefit corporation dedicated to basic biomedical research and training. The essential purpose of the Institute is to use innovative approaches to advance our knowledge of how the immune system works, to study the regulatory mechanisms involved in the onset and maintenance of immune response, and to develop new, more sophisticated and precise strategies and/or therapies for managing various immunological and allergic disorders.

4685 Max Samter Institute of Allergy and Clinical Immunology
550 W Webster Avenue
Chicago, IL 60614-3965
773-883-3655
Hoeard J Zeitz, Director

4686 Mayo Clinic and Foundation: Allergy Disease Research Laboratory
200 1st Street SW
Rochester, MN 55905
507-284-8305
Fax: 801-581-6484
e-mail: gleich@mayo.edu
Gerald J Gleich MD, Director
Julie E Hammack, MD

Provides a focus for research into the causes, prevention and management of allergic diseases.

4687 National Institute of Allergy and Infectious Diseases
B-31 Room 7A50
Bethesda, MD 20892
301-496-2263
Fax: 301-402-0120

Conducts and supports research on allergies; focused on understanding what happens to the body during the allergic process. Educates patients and health care workers in controlling allergic disease; offers various research centers that conduct and evaluate educational programs focused on methods to control allergic diseases.

4688 National Jewish Center for Medical and Research Center
1400 Jackson Street
Denver, CO 80206-2762
303-388-4461
800-222-5864
Fax: 303-290-2165
e-mail: toussigi@nic.org
http://www.njrc.org
Lynn W Taussig MD, President

Basic and clinical research into the causes and treatments of asthmatic disorders.

Allergies/Research Centers

4689 Northwestern University: Ernest S Bazley Asthma and Allergic Disease Center
Northwestern Medical Center
303 E Chicago Avenue
Chicago, IL 60611-3072
312-503-8186
Fax: 312-908-0205
e-mail: rpatterson@nwu.edu

Lewis Landsberg, Administrator

Studies the mechanisms, etiology, diagnosis and treatment of allergic diseases.
1972

4690 Research Institute of Palo Alto Medical Foundation
860 Bryant Street
Palo Alto, CA 94301-2707
650-326-8120
Fax: 650-329-9114

Dr. Allen Cooper, Director
Haya Rubin, Manager

Clinical and general medical sciences research including allergy and immunology disorders.

4691 Scripps Clinic and Research Foundation: Autoimmune Disease Center
4275 Campus Point Court
Cp10
San Diego, CA 92121-1513
858-678-6340
Fax: 858-678-6900
http://www.scrippsclinic.com

John Engle, President

Immunologic studies on the development of allergic disorders.

4692 State University of New York Health Science Center at Stony Brook: Asthma and Allergic Diseases Center
HSC Level T16-040
State University of New York
Stony Brook, NY 11794-8161
631-444-8364
Fax: 631-444-3475

Allen P Kaplan, Director
David Volkman, MD

Allergy research.
1979

4693 Tufts University School of Medicine: Immunology Section
1700 Perdido Street
3rd Floor
New Orleans, LA 70112-1290
504-588-5578
Fax: 504-584-3686
e-mail: malopex@mailhost.tcs.tulane.edu

Prof. Manuel Lopez MD, Director

Allergy research.
1974

4694 Tufts University: Asthma and Allergic Diseases Cooperative Research Center
School of Medicine
750 Washington Street
Boston, MA 02111-1526
617-636-6678
Fax: 617-636-4843

Dr. John Ohman, Director
Nancy Arbree, Owner

Allergy research.

4695 University of Alabama at Birmingham: Asthma, Allergic and Immunologic Diseases Cooperative Research Center
378 Wallace Tumor Institute
Birmingham, AL 35294
205-934-3370
Fax: 205-934-1875

Max D Cooper, Director
Carolyn Strahan, Manager

Allergy research.
1986

4696 University of Colorado: Immunology Center
4200 E 9th Avenue B164
Denver, CO 80262
303-315-7601
Fax: 303-315-7642

Dr. Brian L Kotzin, Director
Sara Higgins, Manager

Allergy research.

4697 University of Florida: General Clinical Research Center
PO Box 100322
Gainesville, FL 32610
352-265-0761
Fax: 352-338-9843
e-mail: stacpool@gcrc.ufl.edu
http://www.acrc.ufl.edu

Peter W Stacpoole MD, Program Director
Edward M Copeland III, MD

Studies on allergies and immunology.

4698 University of Michigan: Montgomery Allergy Research Laboratory
6621 Kresge Medical Research Building
Ann Arbor, MI 48109
734-764-0227
Fax: 734-936-8898

William R Solomon MD, Director

4699 University of Texas: Southwestern Medical Center
5323 Harry Hines Boulevard
Dallas, TX 75390-8570
214-648-3067
Fax: 214-688-8275

Paul R Bergstresser, Program Director
Patricia Bergen, MD

Immunodermatology department researching allergies and immune disorders.

4700 University of Wisconsin: Allergy/Asthma Clinical Research Unit
Medical School, H6/367 CSC
600 Highland Avenue
Madison, WI 53792
608-263-6180
Fax: 608-265-9890
e-mail: mjb@medicine.wisc.edu
http://www.medicine.wisc.edu/sections/allergy

Dr William Busse, Director
Kathy Bell, Manager

Allergy research.
1972

Alzheimer's Disease/Associations & Organizations

Associations & Organizations

4701 Alzheimer Association: Boise/Treasure Valley Chapter
4696 Overland Road
Suite 482
Boise, ID 83705-2845
208-384-1788
Fax: 208-385-7191

Nancy Severance, President
Suzette Albers-Tunnell, Manager

Families of Alzheimer's disease patients; professionals. To act as a support group, educate the public and fund research.

4702 Alzheimer Association: Greater Idaho Region
1111 S Orchard Street
Suite 200
Boise, ID 83705
208-384-1788
800-574-1787
Fax: 208-385-7191
e-mail: suzette.albers-tunnell@alz.org
http://www.alz.org

Jake Plummer, Alzheimer's Benefit
Suzette Albers-Tunnell, Executive Director

The Alzheimer's Association Greater Idaho serves the citizens of Idaho and South Eastern Oregon. We are a part of the National Alzheimer's Association. Our mission is to eliminate Alzheimer's disease through the advancement of research; to provide and enhance care and support for all affected, and to reduce the risk of dementia through the promotion of brain health.

4703 Alzheimer's Alliance: Northeast Texas
3613 S Broadway Avenue
Suite 401
Tyler, TX 75701-8732
903-509-8323
Fax: 903-509-8373
e-mail: glenda.lauter@netxalz.org
http://www.alz.org

Glenda Lauter, Executive Director
Jana Humphrey, Manager

4704 Alzheimer's Assocation: South Central Michigan Chapter
107 Aprill Drive
Suite 1
Ann Arbor, MI 48103
734-677-3081
800-337-3827
Fax: 734-677-3091
e-mail: info@alz.org
http://www.alz.org

Elizabeth Longley, CEO
Tricia Bridgham, Communications Director

4705 Alzheimer's Association
8430 Bryn Mawr
Suite 800
Chicago, IL 60631
847-933-2413
800-272-3900
Fax: 312-335-1110
e-mail: info@alz.org
http://www.alz.org

Erna Colborn, President and Chief Executive Di
Lisa Lee, Vice president

Family members of sufferers of Alzheimer's disease. Combats Alzheimer's disease and related disorders. (Alzheimer's disease is a progressive, degenerative brain disease in which changes occur in the central nervous system and outer region of the brain causing memory loss and other changes in thought, personality, and behavior. It is the fourth leading cause of death in adults in the US) Promotes research to find the cause, treatment, and cure for the disease; provides educational programs for the public, media, and health care and medical professionals; represents the continuing care needs of the affected population before government and social service agencies. Seeks to destroy the myth that what were once called 'senile behaviors' are a natural part of aging. Works to develop family support systems for relatives of victims of the disease. Sponsors educational forums; operates speakers' bureau. Compiles statistics.

4706 Alzheimer's Association Autopsy Assistance Network
919 N Michigan Avenue
Suite 1000
Chicago, IL 60611-1696
312-335-8700
800-272-3900
Fax: 312-335-1110
e-mail: info@alz.org
http://www.alz.org

Gary Bieting, President

Provides families with information regarding autopsy, assists in obtaining a confirmed diagnosis, provides tissue for Alzheimer's disease research and establishes diagnosis for the purpose of clinical and epidemiological studies.

4707 Alzheimer's Association Greater Baton Rouge Chapter
3717 Government Street
Suite 7
Alexandria, LA 71302
318-619-8383
800-548-1211
e-mail: louisianainfo@alz.org
http://www.alz.org

Robert Stephen, Executive Director
Katie Sivil, Chairman

4708 Alzheimer's Association Greater RichmondChapter
4600 Cox Road
Suite 130
Glen Allen, VA 23060
804-967-2580
Fax: 804-967-2588
e-mail: sherry.peterson@alz.org
http://www.alz.org

Sherry E Peterson, MSW, CEO
Fran Foster, Office Manager

The Chapter provides educational and support services to individuals with Alzheimer's disease, their families, and caregivers. Services include a telephone helpline, support groups, educational programs, case manager services, a respite scholarship program, a lending library, the National Safe Return Program, and a quarterly newsletter with caregiving tips. In addition, the Chapter offers in-service training to professional caregivers.

4709 Alzheimer's Association Greater Youngstown Chapter
3695B Boardman-Canfield Rd
Suite 301
Canfield, OH 44406
330-533-3300
800-441-3322
Fax: 330-533-3307
e-mail: gcachl@alz.org
http://www.alz.org

Pam Schuellerman, Executive Director
Liz Mulroy, Education Director Development D

4710 Alzheimer's Association Hotline
Alzheimer's Association
919 N Michigan Avenue
Suite 1000
Chicago, IL 60611-1696
800-272-3900
e-mail: info@alz.org
http://www.alz.org

A 24-hour telephone information line offering information on Alzheimer's and local chapters across the country to Alzheimer's patients, families and caregivers.

Alzheimer's Disease/Associations & Organizations

4711 Alzheimer's Association Middle Tennessee Chapter
4205 Hillsboro Pike
Suite 216
Nashville, TN 37215
615-292-4938
Fax: 615-386-9768
e-mail: diane.gramann@alz.org
http://www.alz.org

Linda Blanding, Ph.D, President
Lynn Cooper, Vice President
William Youree, Executive Director

4712 Alzheimer's Association NW Florida Chapter
119 Hollywood Boulevard NW
Suite 103
Fort Walton Beach, FL 32548-4758
850-863-1244
800-302-0581

Ashley Brown, Office Manager
Susan McDonald, Manager

4713 Alzheimer's Association North Alabama Regional Office
3322 S. Memorial Pkwy
Suite 16
Huntsville, AL 35801
256-880-1575
Fax: 256-880-8696
e-mail: karen.motz@alz.org~~
http://www.alz.org

Marylou Kraatz, Program Director
Linda Blanding, President

4714 Alzheimer's Association of Ashland
400 Chapple Avenue
Ashland, WI 54806
715-682-3974
800-272-3900
Fax: 715-682-3974
e-mail: jfritz@alz.org
http://www.alz.org/gwwi/

Dianne Jacobson, President
Linda Negratti, Vice President

Serving Ashland, Iron and Bayfield Counties.

4715 Alzheimer's Association of GreaterWisconsin-Wausau Regional Office
PO Box 1469
Wausau, WI 54402-1469
715-848-1221
Fax: 715-845-6305
http://www.alzgw.org

4716 Alzheimer's Association of Greater Wisconsin: Eau Claire
1227 B Menomonie Street
Eau Claire, WI 54703
715-835-7050
800-272-3900
Fax: 715-835-0597
e-mail: jfritz@alz.org
http://www.alzgw.org

Dianne Jacobson, President
Linda Negratti, Vice President

4717 Alzheimer's Association of Greater Wisconsin: Fox Valley
Fox Valley Outreach Office
1535 Lyon Drive
Neenah, WI 54956
920-727-5555
800-272-3900
Fax: 920-727-5552
e-mail: info@alz.org
http://www.alzgw.org

Marty Anderson, Director
Dianne Jacobson, President

4718 Alzheimer's Association of Hayward Wisconsin
15856-5th Street
P.O. Box 1109
Hayward, WI 54843
715-934-2222
800-272-3900
Fax: 715-934-6561
e-mail: jfritz@alz.org
http://www.alz.org/gwwi/

Dianne Jacobson, President
Linda Negratti, Vice President

4719 Alzheimer's Association of Southern Minnesota Chapter
1001 14th Street NW
1001 - 14th Street NW
Rochester, MN 55901
507-289-3950
800-232-0851
Fax: 507-289-4666
e-mail: gerise.thompson@alz.org
http://www.alzmndak.org

Gerise Thompson, Director Southern MN Center
Stephanie Dix, Development and Administrative A

Our mission is to improve the lives of all individuals, families and care partners throughout their journey with Alzheimer's and related diseases by providing leadership, support, education, advocacy and research.

4720 Alzheimer's Association of Superior
2002 West Superior Street
Suite 10
Duluth, MN 55806
218-733-2560
800-272-3900
Fax: 218-733-2565
http://www.alzmndak.org

Esther Gieschen, Director

Serving Douglas, Burnett and Washington Counties.

4721 Alzheimer's Association:Hudson Valley/Rockland/Westchester, NY Chapter
2 Jefferson Plaza
Suite 203
Poughkeepsie, NY 12601-4060
845-471-2655
866-882-5772
Fax: 845-471-8960
http://www.alzhudsonvalley.org

Elaine Sproat, CEO

4722 Alzheimer's Association: Alaska Chapter
240 E Tudor Road
Suite 110
Anchorage, AK 99503-7244
907-561-3313
800-478-1080
Fax: 907-561-3313
e-mail: careplan@arctic.net
http://www.alz.org

Dulce Nobre, Executive Director
Dixie Amidon, Manager

4723 Alzheimer's Association: Aloha Chapter
1050 Ala Moana Boulevard
Ste. 2610
Honolulu, HI 96814
808-591-2771
Fax: 808-591-9071
http://www.alz.org

Thomas P. Brehm, Chairman
Bret Flynn, M.D., MPH, Vice Chair

4724 Alzheimer's Association: Augusta Chapter
1899 Central Avenue
Augusta Regional Office
Augusta, GA 30904-5755
706-731-9060
Fax: 706-731-9099
e-mail: kim.franklin@alz.org
http://www.alz.org/georgia/

Bennett Watts, Chairman
Peter Armstrong, Chair-Elect

Alzheimer's Disease/Associations & Organizations

4725 Alzheimer's Association: California Central Coast Chapter
1339 Del Norte Road
Camarillo, CA 93010
805-485-5597
800-272-3900
Fax: 805-485-4767
e-mail: info@centralcoastalz.org
http://www.alz.org

Loretta Redd, Ph.D., Executive Director
Sharon Kennedy, Chairman

Stands by people with Alzheimer's disease and their families through the following programs and services: Telephone Helpline, Support Groups, Respite Grants, Safe Return, Chapter Newsletter, Lending Library, Educational Programs for family and professional caregivers.

4726 Alzheimer's Association: California Southland Chapter
5900 Wilshire Boulevard
Suite 1100
Los Angeles, CA 90036
323-938-3379
800-272-3900
Fax: 323-938-1036
http://www.alzla.org

Suzanne Middelburg, Director
Peter Braun, President and Chief Executive Of
Debra L Cherry, PhD, Associate Executive Director

To eliminate Alzheimer's disease through the advancement of research; to provide and enhance care and support for all affected; and to reduce the risk of dementia through the promotion of brain health.

4727 Alzheimer's Association: Carolina Piemont Chapter
3800 Shamrock Drive
Charlotte, NC 28215-3220
704-532-7392
800-888-6671
Fax: 704-532-5421
e-mail: info@alz.org
http://www.alz-nc.org

Jackie E. Rivers, Executive Director
Molly Bristol, President

Dedicated to improving life for those with Alzheimer's and related disorders and their families and caregivers. Provides patient and family services designed to support an estimated 77,000 persons with the disease in North Carolina's 49 western counties. Services include a 24-hour toll-free helpline, family support groups, and a national Safe Return Program, as well as family, caregiver, professional and community education.

4728 Alzheimer's Association: Central GeorgiaChapter
277 Martin Luther King Jr Boulevard
Suite 201
Macon, GA 31201-3498
478-746-7050
Fax: 478-746-6679
e-mail: info@alz.org
http://www.alz-rochesterny.org/

Jackie Lenderman, Chairman
Kay Hricik, Development Chair

4729 Alzheimer's Association: Central Illinois Chapter
606 W Glen Avenue
Peoria, IL 61614
309-681-1100
800-681-1181
Fax: 309-681-1101
e-mail: nikki.vulgaris@alz.org
http://www.alz.org

Nikki Vulgaris, Executive Director
Dan Hinkley, Public Relations Director

To help optimize the quality of life for people with Alzheimer's Disease and their families through advocacy, education, suport and service delivery, while actively promoting research to eliminate the disease.

4730 Alzheimer's Association: Central Indiana Chapter
9135 N Meridian Street
Suite B4
Indianapolis, IN 46260
317-575-9620
Fax: 317-582-0669
e-mail: information@alzindiana.org
http://www.alz.org

Heather Allen Hershberger, Executive Director
Sarah Whiteman, Director of Development

4731 Alzheimer's Association: Central Maryland Chapter
1850 York Road
Suite D
Timonium, MD 21093-5122
410-561-9099
800-443-2273
Fax: 410-561-3433
e-mail: info.maryland@alz.org
http://www.alz.org/maryland/

Cass Naugle, Executive Director
Renee Wooding, President

4732 Alzheimer's Association: Central New York Chapter
441 W Kirkpatrick Street
Syracuse, NY 13204-1361
315-472-4201
800-339-4177
e-mail: alzcny@alzcny.org
http://www.alz.org

Catherine James, Chief Executive Officer
Tricia Bannister, Northern Regional Director

4733 Alzheimer's Association: Central Ohio Chapter
3380 Tremont Road
Columbus, OH 43221
614-457-6003
800-735-6751
Fax: 614-457-6634
e-mail: jeff.watson@alz.org
http://www.alz.org

Judith G D'Orsi, Executive Director
James Flynn, President

4734 Alzheimer's Association: Central Virginia Chapter
674 Hillsdale Drive
Suite 1
Charlottesville, VA 22901
434-973-6122
Fax: 434-845-8378
http://http://www.alz.org/cwva/

Susan B Friedman, President & CEO
E. Williams Pelton II, Vice Chair

4735 Alzheimer's Association: Central and North Florida Chapter
988 Woodcock Road
Suite 200
Orlando, FL 32803
407-228-4299
800-272-3900
Fax: 407-228-4201
e-mail: info@alzflorida.org
http://www.alz.org

Tish Sheesley, Chief Executive Officer
Erin Jones, Communications and Development C
Sharon Melton, Director Programs

The Central and North Florida Chapter provides services and programs in 31 counties. Our mission is to eliminate Alzheimer's disease through the advancement of research, to provide and enhance care and support for individuals, their families and caregivers.

4736 Alzheimer's Association: Central and Western Kansas
347 South Laura
Wichita, KS 67211
316-267-7333
877-267-7333
Fax: 316-267-6369
e-mail: marsha.hills@alz.org
http://www.alz.org

Marsha Hills, Executive Director
Evan Thompson, chairman

Alzheimer's Disease/Associations & Organizations

Program and services for those dealing with Alzheimer's disease in fourty nine Kansas counties

4737 Alzheimer's Association: CharlestonOffice
1941 Savage Road
Suite 400D~
Charleston, SC 29407-4704
843-571-2641
800-860-1444
Fax: 843-571-6020
e-mail: info@alz.org
http://www.alz.org

Van Matthews, Chairman
John Absher, Director

4738 Alzheimer's Association: Charlotte/DeSoto Counties Chapter
PO Box 510042
Punta Gorda, FL 33951
941-639-4717
Fax: 941-639-4717

Leon Ford, President

4739 Alzheimer's Association: Clark-Champaign-Logan Chapter
2634 Lexington Avenue
Springfield, OH 45505-2620
937-323-4001
800-441-3322
Fax: 937-323-9259
e-mail: info@alz.org
http://www.alz.org

Glenna Coleman, Executive Director

4740 Alzheimer's Association: Cleveland Area Chapter
12200 Fairhill Road
Cleveland, OH 44120
216-721-8457
800-441-3322
Fax: 216-721-1629
e-mail: helpline@alzclv.org
http://www.alz.org

Nancy B. Udelson, Executive Director
Christine B. Stevens, President

4741 Alzheimer's Association: Coastal Bend Chapter
3440 Bell St.
Suite 320, PMB 240
Amarillo, TX 79109
512-854-3887
800-460-3887
e-mail: ken.branum@alz.org
http://www.alz.org

Matt W. Spahn, Chair
Mitch Moss, Vice Chairman

4742 Alzheimer's Association: Colorado Chapter
455 Sherman Street
Suite 500
Denver, CO 80203
303-813-1669
800-272-3900
Fax: 303-813-1670
e-mail: cheryl.dunaway@alz.org
http://www.alz.org

Susan Barnhill, Chairman
Cheryl Dunaway, LCSW, VP Programs
Robyn Moore, VP Development

The primary provider of local information services to Alzheimer patients and families in Colorado, the leading funder of AD research and the leading voice representing those dealing with dementia on public policy issues.

4743 Alzheimer's Association: Connecticut Chapter
10 Wall Street
Norwalk, CT 06850
203-899-1805
Fax: 203-853-9246
http://www.alz.org

Eric Rennie, Vice-Chairman
Christine I. Andrew, Directors

4744 Alzheimer's Association: Corn Belt Chapter
Bromenn Life Care Center
303 N. Hershey
Ste 2A
Bloomington, IL 61704
309-662-8392
Fax: 309-827-0734
e-mail: GI.Chapter@alz.org
http://www.alz.org

Stephen C. Mack, Chairman
Bryan Selander, Vice Chair and Secretary

4745 Alzheimer's Association: Dallas Chapter
Vidalia House
4144 N. Central Expwy
Ste 750
Dallas, TX 75204-5935
214-827-0062
800-515-8201
e-mail: Helpline@alzdallas.org
http://www.alz.org/greaterdallas

Michel Webb, President
Steve Folsom, Vice President

4746 Alzheimer's Association: Delaware Valley
2306 Kirkwood Highway
Wilmington, DE 19805-4927
302-633-4420
800-219-7666
Fax: 302-633-4494
e-mail: info@alz.org
http://www.alz.org

Wendy L. Campbell, President
Edna Ellett, Executive Director

4747 Alzheimer's Association: Desert Southwest Chapter
1028 E McDowell Road
Phoenix, AZ 85006
602-528-0545
800-392-0022
Fax: 602-528-0546
e-mail: deborah.schaus@alz.org
http://www.alzdsw.org

Deborah Schaus, Executive Director
Dan Lawler, Director of Development

Serves the state of Arizona and Southern Nevada.

4748 Alzheimer's Association: Detroit Area Chapter
20300 Civic Center
Suite 100
Southfield, MI 48076-2114
248-351-0280
Fax: 248-351-0417
http://www.alzgmc.org/

Dian Wilkins, Executive Director

4749 Alzheimer's Association: Dubuque BranchMississippi Valley Chapter
5900 Saratoga Plaza
Suite 11
Dubuque, IA 52002
563-589-0030
800-272-3900
Fax: 563-588-4523
e-mail: Carol.Sipfle@alz.org
http://www.alz.org/greateriowa

Craig Miller, President
Nancy Carrick, Program Specialist
Sally Weber, Community Relations Coordinator

Serves persons with Alzheimer's disease and their caregivers. Provides educational programs and a forum for the alleviation of stress. Operates resource center.

4750 Alzheimer's Association: Dubuque Branch, Mississippi Valley Chapter
5900 Saratoga Plaza
Suite 11
Dubuque, IA 52002
563-589-0030
800-448-3650
Fax: 563-588-4523
e-mail: Carol.Sipfle@alz.org
http://www.alz.org

Carol Sipfle, Executive Director
Sally Weber, Community Relations Coordinator

Alzheimer's Disease/Associations & Organizations

Serves persons with Alzheimer's disease and their caregivers. Provides educational programs and a forum for the alleviation of stress. Operates resource center.

4751 Alzheimer's Association: East Central Iowa Chapter
1570 42nd St. NE
Cedar Rapids, IA 52402-3076
319-294-9699
Fax: 319-294-0068
e-mail: kelly.hauer@alz.org

4752 Alzheimer's Association: East Central Florida Chapter
140 South Beach Street
Suite 204
Daytona Beach, FL 32114
386-238-0066
Fax: 386-238-8293
e-mail: info@alzflorida.org
http://www.alz.org

Stu Gaines, Chairman
Susan Leger-Krall, Secretary

4753 Alzheimer's Association: East Central Michigan Chapter
G3287 Beecher Road
Flint, MI 48532
810-720-2791
Fax: 810-720-3040
http://www.alzgmc.org

Marlana Geha, Chairman
Dian Wilkins, President

4754 Alzheimer's Association: East Central Ohio Chapter
3380 Tremont Road
Columbus, OH 43015
614-457-6003
800-441-3322
Fax: 740-345-5099
e-mail: jeff.watson@alz.org
http://www.alz.org

James Flynn, President
Kirk Stalter, Vice president

4755 Alzheimer's Association: Eastern North Carolina Chapter
400 Oberlin Road
Suite 220
Raleigh, NC 27605
919-832-3732
800-228-8738
Fax: 919-832-7989
e-mail: awatkins@alznc.org
http://www.alznc.org

Alice Watkins, Executive Director
Rita Bhan, Development Director

4756 Alzheimer's Association: Eastern Shore Region
Eastern Shore Regional Office
209C Milford Street
Salisbury, MD 21804
410-543-1163
Fax: 410-546-0184
e-mail: info@alz.org
http://www.alzgmd.org

RaeAnn Butle, Director
Renee Wooding, President

The regional office is dedicated to enhancing care and support for people with Alzheimer's disease. Serves Eastern shore counties of Caroline, Dorchester, Kent, Queen Anne's, Somerset, Talbot, Wicomico and Worcester.

4757 Alzheimer's Association: Eastern Tennessee Chapter
2200 Sutherland Ave
Suite H102
Knoxville, TN 37919
865-544-6288
Fax: 865-544-6249
e-mail: info@alz.org
http://www.tnalz.org

Janice Wade, Executive Director
Judy Clabough, Development Director

4758 Alzheimer's Association: Eastern Washington Chapter
910 W. 5th Ave
Suite 256
Spokane, WA 99204
509-473-3390
800-256-6659
Fax: 509-483-6067
e-mail: InlandNW@alz.org
http://www.alz.org

Joel Loiacono, Executive Director
Sandra Druffel, Development Director

4759 Alzheimer's Association: El Paso Chapter
4400 N Mesa Street
Suite 9
El Paso, TX 79902-1147
915-544-2199
800-544-2199
e-mail: febe.leyva@alz.org
http://www.alz.org

Denese Watkins, Executive Director
Matt W Spahn, Chairman

4760 Alzheimer's Association: Florida Gulf Coast Chapter
9365 US Highway 19 N
Suite B
Pinellas Park, FL 33782-5400
727-578-2558
Fax: 727-578-2286
http://www.alzflgulf.org

Gloria Smith, Chief Executive Officer

Serving 17 Florida Counties. Care Consultations, 24/7 Helpline, Support Groups, Caregiver Education, Library, Information and Referral.

4761 Alzheimer's Association: Four Rivers Chapter
401 N Wall Street
Suite 103
Kankakee, IL 60901
815-936-0464
800-332-4495
http://www.alz.org

Sherry Johnson, Executive Director
Rachel Ferro, Manager

4762 Alzheimer's Association: Georgia Chapter
1925 Century Blvd
Suite 10
Atlanta, GA 30345
404-728-1181
Fax: 404-636-9768
e-mail: kim.franklin@alz.org
http://www.alz.org/georgia/

Bennett Watts, Chairman
Peter Armstrong, Chair-Elect

4763 Alzheimer's Association: Great Plains Area Chapter
5601 S 27th Street
Suite 201
Lincoln, NE 68512
402-420-2540
800-487-9668
Fax: 402-420-2541
e-mail: info@alzgreatplains.org
http://www.alz.org

Karen Noel, President and Chief Executive Di
Irene Hartwig, Finance and Operations Director

Serves persons with Alzheimer's disease and their families in 80 counties across Nebraska and the entire state of Wyoming. The mission is to enhance the quality of life for all persons affected by Alzheimer's disease and related disorders through comprehensive educational programs, compassionate services, access to resources and support for research.

4764 Alzheimer's Association: Greater Cincinnati Chapter
644 Linn Street
Suite 1026
Cincinnati, OH 45203~
513-721-4284
Fax: 513-345-8446
e-mail: clarissa.rentz@alz.org
http://www.alz.org/grtrcinc

Clarissa Rentz, Executive Director
Brigid Mercer, Development Director

Alzheimer's Disease/Associations & Organizations

4765 Alzheimer's Association: Greater Austin Chapter
3429 Executive Center Drive
Suite 100
Austin, TX 78731
512-241-0420
800-367-2132
Fax: 512-241-0430
http://www.alz-austin.org
Clint P. Hackney, Chairman

4766 Alzheimer's Association: Greater Billings Area Chapter
3010 11TH AVENUE NORTH
Billings, MT 59101
406-252-3053
Fax: 406-252-2933
e-mail: mtchapaabelser@bresnan.net
http://www.alz-mt.org
Ann Groff, President
Suzanne Belser, Executive Director

4767 Alzheimer's Association: Greater Columbus Chapter
5900 River Road
Suite 301
Columbus, GA 31904
706-327-6838
800-565-8421
Fax: 706-494-0533
e-mail: leslie.tripp@alz.org
http://www.alz.org
Bennett Watts, Chairman
Peter Armstrong, Chair-Elect

4768 Alzheimer's Association: Greater Eastern Ohio Chapter
4815 Munson St., NW
Suite 100
Canton, OH 44718
330-966-7343
800-441-3322
Fax: 330-966-7757
e-mail: geachl@alz.org
http://www.alz.org
Pam Schuellerman, Executive Director
Julie Falter, Family Service Director

4769 Alzheimer's Association: Greater East Texas Chapter
4400 N. Mesa
Suite 9
El Paso, TX 79902
915-544-1799
800-246-7888
http://http://www.alz.org/txstar/
Matt W Spahn, Chair
Mitch Moss, Vice Chair

4770 Alzheimer's Association: Greater Eastern Ohio Area Chapter
1815 W. Market Street
Suite 301
Akron, OH 44313
330-864-5646
800-441-3322
Fax: 330-864-7336
e-mail: geachl@alz.org
http://www.alz.org/akroncantonyoungstown/
Pam Schuellerman, Executive Director
Joan Sillasen, CPA - Finance Director

4771 Alzheimer's Association: Greater Idaho Chapter
1111 S. Orchard St
Suite 200
Boise, ID 83705
208-384-1788
800-574-1787
Fax: 208-385-7191
e-mail: suzette.albers-tunnell@alz.org
http://www.alz.org
Evan Thompson, Chairman
Samuel E. Coleman, Vice Chairman

4772 Alzheimer's Association: Greater Illinios Chapter
8430 Bryn Mawr
Suite 800
Chicago, IL 60631
847-933-2413
Fax: 847-933-2417
e-mail: GI.Chapter@alz.org
http://www.alz.org
Kent Barnheiser, President and Chief Executive Di
Erna Colborn, President and Chief Executive Of

A national voluntary health agency dedicated to researching the prevention, cure and treatment of Alzheimer's disease and related disorders and to providing support and assistance to individuals with alzheimer's disease, their families and caregivers.

4773 Alzheimer's Association: Greater Maryland Chapter Western Maryland Region
108 Byte Drive
Suite 103
Frederick, MD 21702
301-696-0315
800-696-6830
Fax: 301-696-9061
e-mail: info.maryland@alz.org
http://www.alz.org
Renee Wooding, President
Cass Naugle, Executive Director

The Alzheimer's Association provides a wide range of support, education and advocacy services for individuals with memory disorders, their families and care-providers, including support groups, newsletters, conferences, wanderers identification programs and others.

4774 Alzheimer's Association: Greater Miami Chapter
1175 NE 125th Street
Suite 600
North Miami, FL 33161
305-891-6228
Fax: 305-892-0355
e-mail: reni.rizzo@alz.org
http://www.alz.org
Samuel J. Ferreri, Chairman
Dr. Ruth Tappen, First Vice Chair

Provides information, support and referral assistance to Alzheimer families in Dade and Monroe Counties. Offers support groups, respite, education, training, telephone reassurance, and a newsletter.

4775 Alzheimer's Association: Greater NewJersey Chapter
400 Morris Avenue
Suite 251
Denville, NJ 7834
973-586-4300
800-883-1180
Fax: 973-586-4342
http://www.alznj.org
Patricia A Lombreglia, President/CEO
Bert Bruce, Director

The Alzheimer's Association Greater New Jersey Chapter provides programs and services to individuals with Alzheimer's disease, their families and caregivers who live in the New Jersey counties of Bergen, Essex, Hudson, Hunterdon, Mercer, Middlesex, Monmouth, Morris, Ocean, Passaic, Somerset, Sussex, Union and Warren. Programs and services include education and training, support groups, respite assistance and a 24-hour toll free phone helpline.

4776 Alzheimer's Association: Greater New Hampshire Chapter
One Bedford Farms Drive
Suite 105
Bedford, NH 3110
603-606-6590
800-750-3848
Fax: 603-225-8126
e-mail: info@alz.org
http://www.alz.org/nh/
Liz McConnell, Contact
Gail Tapply, Manager

Alzheimer's Disease/Associations & Organizations

4777 Alzheimer's Association: Greater North Valley Chapter
2105 Forest Avenue
Suite 130
Chico, CA 95928
530-895-9661
Fax: 530-872-7470
e-mail: info@alznorcal.org
http://www.alz.org

T. William Melis, President
Herb Williams, Vice President

4778 Alzheimer's Association: Greater OrlandoArea Chapter
988 Woodcock Road
Suite 200
Orlando, FL 32803-3715
407-228-4299
Fax: 407-228-4201
http://www.alzorlando.org

4779 Alzheimer's Association: Greater PalmBeach Chapter
4700 North Congress Avenue
Suite 101
West Palm Beach, FL 33407
800-861-7826
800-861-7826
Fax: 561-842-8336
http://www.alz.org

Ellen Brown, Chief Executive Officer
Dottie Carson, Director of Development

4780 Alzheimer's Association: Greater Pennsylvania Chapter
1128 State Street
Suite 301
Erie, PA 16501
814-456-9200
800-850-4402
Fax: 814-454-0414
e-mail: brad.etchberger@alz.org
http://www.alzpa.org

Angela Grimm, Regional Director
Brad Etchberger, Vice President of Finance

4781 Alzheimer's Association: Greater Pittsburgh Chapter
1100 Liberty Avenue
Suite E-201
Pittsburgh, PA 15222
412-261-5040
800-652-3370
Fax: 412-325-1684
e-mail: angela.grimm@alz.org
http://www.alz.org

Erica Hood, Vice President of Programs and S
Alyssa Rahner, Special Events Manager

4782 Alzheimer's Association: Greater Sacramento Chapter
Greater Sacramento Area Office
Suite A
Sacramento, CA 95814
916-930-9080
800-660-1993
e-mail: info@alznorcal.org
http://www.alz.org

Clifta Atlas, Director
T. William Melis, President

4783 Alzheimer's Association: Greater Texarkana Chapter
4144 N. Central Expwy
Ste 750
Dallas, TX 75204
214-827-0062
877-312-8536
Fax: 214-827-2064
e-mail: Helpline@alzdallas.org
http://www.alz.org

Beverly Huds Schneider, Executive Director
Lisa Brodsky, Director of Programs and Service

4784 Alzheimer's Association: Greater Wisconsin Chapter
3400 Ministry Parkway
B-0041
Wausau, WI 54476
715-393-3950
800-272-3900
Fax: 715-845-6305
e-mail: jfritz@alz.org
http://www.alz.org

Marty Anderson, Director
Brad Beckman, Director

4785 Alzheimer's Association: Grover Chapter
1528 Chapala Street
Suite 204
Santa Barbara, CA 93101
805-892-4259
800-272-3900
Fax: 805-481-9439
e-mail: info@centralcoastalz.org
http://http://alz.org/cacentralcoast/

Judy Miller, Area Coordinator
Diana Vandervoort, Office Manager

Stands by people with Alzheimer's disease and their families through the following programs and services: Telephone Helpline, Support Groups, Respite Grants, Safe Return, Chapter Newsletter, Lending Library, Educational Programs for family and professional caregivers.

4786 Alzheimer's Association: Hampton Roads Chapter
6315 North Center Drive
Suite 233
Norfolk, VA 23502
757-459-2405
800-755-1129
Fax: 757-461-7902
e-mail: info@alz.org
http://www.alz.org

Gino V Colombara, Executive Director
John H. Kellam, President

The Hampton Roads Chapter of the Alzheimer's Association is a not-for-profit voluntary organization which supports the care and dignity of persons with dementia caused by Alzheimer's disease and related disorders, their families, and other caregivers through quality programs of community-based support; information and referral; public awareness, education, education and training, research and advocacy.

4787 Alzheimer's Association: HarrisonburgRegion
250 East Market Street
Suite C
Harrisonburg, VA 22801
540-437-7444
866-568-6454
Fax: 540-568-6409
e-mail: annie.peterson@alz.org
http://www.alz.org

Susan B. Friedman, President and Chief Executive Di
Ann Anderson, Director

4788 Alzheimer's Association: Heart ofAmerica Chapter
3846 W 75th Street
Prairie Village, KS 66208
913-831-3888
800-733-1981
Fax: 913-831-1916
e-mail: kerry.mees@alz.org
http://www.alz.org

Debra R Brook, Executive Director
Nicole Clifford, Development Director

4789 Alzheimer's Association: Heart of Iowa Chapter
1730 28th Street
Suite 3
West Des Moines, IA 50266
515-440-2722
800-407-5840
Fax: 515-440-6385
e-mail: Carol.Sipfle@alz.org
http://www.alz.org

Carol Sipfle, Executive Director
Ann Riesenberg, Program Director

Alzheimer's Disease/Associations & Organizations

4790 Alzheimer's Association: Highland Rim Chapter
201 W. Lincoln St.
Tullahoma, TN 37388
931-455-3345
Fax: 931-455-5396
e-mail: tiffany.maicke@alz.org
http://www.alz.org

Linda Blanding, Ph.D, President
Lynn Cooper, Vice President

4791 Alzheimer's Association: Houston & Southeast Texas Chapter Area Chapter
Best Years Center
440 N. 18th,
Ste. 7
Beaumont, TX 77707
409-833-1613
Fax: 409-833-9758
e-mail: brozak@alz.org
http://www.alztex.org

Richard Elbein, Chief Executive Officer
Diana Valverde, Chief Financial Officer

Alzheimer's Association of Houston and Southeast Texas consits or families, caregivers, scientists, health professionals, and concerned citizens commited to finding a cure for Alzheimer's disease and to easing the burden of Alzheimer's and related disorders on patients and their familes and loved ones.

4792 Alzheimer's Association: Houston andSoutheast Texas Chapter
2242 W. Holcombe Blvd
Houston, TX 77030-2008
713-266-6400
Fax: 713-266-6487
e-mail: Melanie.Gehman@alz.org
http://www.alztex.org

Richard Elbein, CEO
Jan Johnson, President Elect, Board Developme
Wilma Eakins, Programs Officer

Regional nonprofit social services agency dedicated to providing support and assistance to the Alzheimer's and dementia community. Main foucus is to eliminate Alzheimer's disease through the advancement of research while enhancing care and support for individuals and their families and caregivers.

4793 Alzheimer's Association: Hudson Valley/Rockland/Westchester NY Chapter
Hudson Valley/Rockland/Westchester, NY - 2 Jefferson Plaza
Suite 203
Poughkeepsie, NY 12601-4060
800-872-0994
Fax: 845-471-8960
e-mail: info@alzhudsonvalley.org
http://www.alz.org/hudsonvalley/

Elaine Sproat, President/CEO
Meg Boyce, Director of Programs & Services

Provides information, assistance and support to individuals with Alzheimer's disease and related disorders, their families, and caregivers. Raises money for support of AD research and coordinates advocacy efforts on behalf of persons with AD and their families.

4794 Alzheimer's Association: Indianhead Chapter
1227b Menomonie Street
Eau Claire, WI 54703-5996
715-835-7050
800-499-7050
Fax: 715-835-0597

Margaret Hagaman, Executive Director
Karren Gunderlach, Manager

4795 Alzheimer's Association: Iowa Golden Chapter
Iowa Lutheran Hospital
1730 28th Street
West Des Moines, IA 50266
515-440-2722
800-738-8071
Fax: 515-440-6385
http://www.alz.org

Carol Sipfle, Executive Director
Ann Riesenberg, Program Director

4796 Alzheimer's Association: Lake Superior Chapter
Ashland Outreach
400 Chapple Avenue
Ashland, WI 54806-1660
715-682-3974
800-682-6478
Fax: 715-682-6561
e-mail: mary.bouche@alz.org
http://www.alz.org

Mary Bouche, Executive Director
Dianne Jacobson, President

4797 Alzheimer's Association: Laurel Mountains Chapter
1100 Liberty Avenue
Suite E-201
Pittsburgh, PA 15222
412-261-5040
800-327-4800
Fax: 412-325-1684
http://www.alzpa.org

Angela Grimm, Regional Director
Paula Cunningham, Administrative Assistant

Patient and family support groups, literature and other services

4798 Alzheimer's Association: Lexington/Bluegrass Chapter
1065 Dove Run Road
Suite 2
Lexington, KY 40502
859-266-5283
800-288-2323
Fax: 859-268-4764
e-mail: infoky-in@alz.org
http://www.alz.org

Linda Blair, Director
Tom Bodkin, Chairman

4799 Alzheimer's Association: Long IslandChapter
3281 Veterans Memorial Highway
Suite E13
Ronkonkoma, NY 11779
631-580-5100
Fax: 631-580-3100
e-mail: Info@alzheimersli.org
http://www.alz.org

Mary Ann Malack-Ragona, Executive Director
Nicholas Materdomini, Director of Development

4800 Alzheimer's Association: Los Angeles Chapter
5900 Wilshire Boulevard
Suite 1710
Los Angeles, CA 90036-5013
323-938-3370
800-660-1993

Peter Braun, Executive Director

4801 Alzheimer's Association: Louisville Chapter
3703 Taylorsville Road
Suite 102
Louisville, KY 40220
502-451-4266
800-221-1277
Fax: 502-456-2701
e-mail: infoky-in@alz.org
http://www.alz.org

Linda Blair, Director
Tom Bodkin, chairman

4802 Alzheimer's Association: Maine Chapter
170 US Route 1
Suite 250
Falmouth, ME 4105
207-772-0115
800-660-2871
Fax: 207-781-3312
e-mail: srohling@alz.org
http://www.alz.org/maine/

Mary Brant, Executive Director
Liz Weaver, Program Director

Alzheimer's Disease/Associations & Organizations

4803 Alzheimer's Association: Manatee/Sarasota Counties Chapter
1230 South Tuttle
Sarasota, FL 34239
941-365-8883
Fax: 941-351-4997
e-mail: services@alz-tbc.org
http://www.alz-tbc.org

Gloria J.T. Smith, President and Chief Executive Di
Chuck Albrecht, Vice President

4804 Alzheimer's Association: Marin Chapter
4340 Redwood Highway
Suite D314
San Rafael, CA 94903
415-472-4340
800-660-1993
Fax: 415-472-4350
e-mail: info@alznorcal.org
http://www.alz.org

T. William Melis, President
Herb Williams, Vice President

4805 Alzheimer's Association: Marquette/Alger Chapter
710 Chippewa Square
Suite 201
Marquette, MI 49855
906-228-3910
Fax: 906-228-2455
e-mail: alzgmc.upregion@az.org
http://www.alzgmc.org

Beverly Bartlett, Regional Director
Janet Yoder, Program Coordinator

The Chapter's mission is to enhance the quality of life for all persons affected by Alzheimer's disease and related disorders through comprehensive educational programs, compassionate services, access to resources and support for research.

4806 Alzheimer's Association: Mary's Peak Chapter
Oregon - 1311 N.W.
21st Avenue,
Portland, OR 97209
503-413-7114
e-mail: info@alz.org
http://www.alz.org/oregon/

Judy McKeller, Executive Director
Mary Edmeades, President

4807 Alzheimer's Association: MassachusettsChapter
36 Cameron Avenue
Cambridge, MA 02140
617-868-6718
800-548-2111
Fax: 617-868-6720
e-mail: communications@alzmass.org
http://www.alz.org

Mary Ann Marino, Chairman
Jeffrey Berry, Vice chairman

Nonprofit organization whose mission is to support people with dementia and their caregivers through education, advocacy, training and counseling. The association works to ensure quality dementia care and family support, and to promote research efforts to prevent, treat and cure dementing illness.

4808 Alzheimer's Association: Massachusetts Chapter
311 Arsenal Street
Watertown, MA 02472
617-868-6718
Fax: 617-868-6720
http://www.alz.org

Mary Ann Marino, Chairman
Jeffrey Berry, Vice Chairman

4809 Alzheimer's Association: Memphis Chapter
326 Ellsworth Street
Memphis, TN 38111
901-565-0011
Fax: 901-565-9550
e-mail: tammy.deniro@alz.org
http://www.alz.org

Sheryl Ludeke-Smith, Regional Director
Linda Blanding, President

4810 Alzheimer's Association: Miami Valley Chapter
3797 Summit Glen Road
Suite G100
Dayton, OH 45449
937-291-3332
800-441-3322
Fax: 937-291-0463
e-mail: eric.vanvlymen@alz.org
http://www.alz.org

Judy Turner, Executive Director

4811 Alzheimer's Association: Mid Missouri Chapter
2400 Bluff Creek Drive
Columbia, MO 65201
573-443-8665
800-693-8665
Fax: 573-499-9701
e-mail: linda.newkirk@alz.org
http://www.alz.org

Linda Newkirk, Executive Director
Joetta Coen, Program Director

4812 Alzheimer's Association: Mid-MichiganChapter
4604 N Saginaw Road
Suite F
Midland, MI 48640
989-839-9910
800-337-3827
Fax: 989-839-5910
http://www.alzgmc.org

Sue King, Regional Director
Dian Wilkins, President

4813 Alzheimer's Association: Mid-Ohio ValleyRegional Office
1111 Lee Street, East
Charleston, WV 25301
304-343-2717
800-441-3322
Fax: 304-343-2723
http://www.alz.org

Jane Marks, Executive Director
Susan Graves, Finance and Technology Director

4814 Alzheimer's Association: Mid-State South Carolina Chapter
4124 Clemson Blvd
Suite L
Anderson, SC 29621
864-224-3045
800-636-3346
Fax: 803-772-3349
http://http://www.alz.org/sc/

Van Matthews, Chair
Carroll A Campbell, Vice-Chair

4815 Alzheimer's Association: Middle Mississippi Chapter
1900 Dunbarton Dr.
Suite H
Jackson, MS 39216
601-987-0020
800-497-2121
Fax: 601-987-9020
e-mail: info@msalz.org
http://www.alz.org

Evan Thompson, Chairman
Samuel E. Coleman, Vice Chairman

4816 Alzheimer's Association: Midstate Wiconsin Chapter
2900 Curry Lane
Suite A
Green Bay, WI 54311
920-469-2110
Fax: 715-387-5727
e-mail: jfritz@alz.org
http://www.alz.org

Dianne Jacobson, President
Linda Negratti, Vice President

Alzheimer's Disease/Associations & Organizations

4817 Alzheimer's Association: Minnesota Lakes Chapter
4570 W 77th Street
Suite 200
Minneapolis, MN 55435
952-830-0512
800-232-0851
Fax: 952-830-0513
http://www.alzmndak.org
Michelle Barclay, Vice President
Mary Birchard, Executive Director

4818 Alzheimer's Association: Mississippi Valley Chapter
736 Federal Street
Suite 2318
Davenport, IA 52803
563-324-1022
800-448-5620
Fax: 563-324-6267
e-mail: Carol.Sipfle@alz.org
http://www.alz.org
Carol Sipfle, Executive Director
Marjean O'Brien, Program Specialist

4819 Alzheimer's Association: Mohawk Valley Chapter
360 Lexington Ave.,
4th Floor
New York, NY 10017
646-744-2900
Fax: 212-490-6037
http://www.alznyc.org/aboutus/
Lou-Ellen Barkan, President and Chief Executive Of
Jed A Levine, Executive Vice President

4820 Alzheimer's Association: Monroe RegionalCenter
513 Walnut Street
Monroe, LA 71201-3248
318-322-2828
800-459-3528
Fax: 318-998-7360
e-mail: info@alz.org
http://www.alz.org
Ellen Emfinger, Regional Director
Robert Stephens, Executive Director

4821 Alzheimer's Association: Monterey CountyChapter
182 El Dorado Street
Monterey, CA 93940-3118
831-647-9890
800-660-1993
Fax: 831-655-9241
e-mail: info@alznorcal.org
http://www.alz.org/norcal/
T. William Melis, President
Herb Williams, Vice President

4822 Alzheimer's Association: NationalCapital Area Chapter
11240 Waples Mill Road
Fairfax, VA 22030-6078
703-359-4440
800-259-0042
Fax: 703-359-4441
http://www.alz-nca.org
Anthony Sudler, CEO

4823 Alzheimer's Association: New Mexico Chapter
9500 Montgomery N. E.
Ste., 209
Albuquerque, NM 87111
505-266-4473
800-777-8155
e-mail: maralie.waterman@alz.org
http://www.alz.org
Maralie Waterman, Executive Director
Betty Kuehne, Program Director

4824 Alzheimer's Association: New York City Chapter
360 Lexington Avenue
4th Fl.
New York, NY 10017
646-744-2900
Fax: 212-490-6037
e-mail: helpline@alznyc.org
http://www.alznyc.org
John Jager, Executive Director
Princess Yas Aga Khan, Chairperson

4825 Alzheimer's Association: North Central Texas Chapter
301 South Pioneer
Suite 105
Abilene, TX 79605
325-672-2907
888-511-4132
Fax: 325-674-6804
e-mail: nctexas@alz.org
http://www.alz.org
Theresa Hocker, Executive Director
Lyn Downing, Director of Development

4826 Alzheimer's Association: North Central West Virginia Chapter
1111 Lee Street, East
Charleston, WV 25301
304-343-2717
Fax: 304-291-2577
http://http://www.alz.org/wv/
Edward C Martin, President
Gaylene Miller, Vice-President

4827 Alzheimer's Association: North Dakota Chapter
4550 West 77th Street
Suite 200
Minneapolis, MN 55435
952-830-0512
Fax: 952-830-0513
http://http://www.alzmndak.org/
Mary Birchard, Executive Director
Michelle Barclay, Vice President

4828 Alzheimer's Association: North New Jersey Chapter
400 Morris Ave
Ste. 251
Denville, NJ 7834
973-586-4300
Fax: 973-586-4342
e-mail: alzgnjhr@alz.org
http://www.alznj.org
Marcia Mohl, Executive Director
Andrew L. Hunt, Chair

4829 Alzheimer's Association: Northeast Michigan Chapter
100 Woods Circle
Suite 300
Alpena, MI 49707
989-356-4087
800-337-3827
Fax: 989-354-7879
http://www.alzgmc.org
Joel Bauer, Northeastern Member
Dawn Jacobs, Chair

4830 Alzheimer's Association: Northeast Pennsylvania Chapter
Kirby Health Center
57 North Franklin Street
Wilkes Barre, PA 18701
570-822-9915
800-773-6677
Fax: 570-822-5141
Brad Etchberger, Vice President of Finance
Estella Parker-Killian, Regional Director

4831 Alzheimer's Association: Northeast Tennessee Chapter
4205 Hillsboro Pike
Suite 216
Nashville, TN 37215
423-928-4080
Fax: 423-928-5209
e-mail: info@alz-nc.org
http://www.alz.org
Linda Blanding, President
Lynn Cooper, Vice President

4832 Alzheimer's Association: Northeast Texas Chapter
3613 S Broadway Avenue
Suite 401
Tyler, TX 75701-8732
903-509-8323
Fax: 903-509-8373
http://www.alz.org
Glenda Lauter, Executive Director
Jana Humphrey, Manager

Alzheimer's Disease/Associations & Organizations

4833 **Alzheimer's Association: Northeast Wisconsin Chapter**
2900 Curry Lane
Suite A
Green Bay, WI 54311
920-469-2110
800-360-2110
Fax: 920-469-2131
e-mail: jfritz@alz.org
http://www.alz.org/gwwi/

Mary Bouche, Executive Director
Dianne Jacobson, President

4834 **Alzheimer's Association: NorthernArizona**
1028 E McDowell
B
Phoenix, AZ 85006
602-528-0545
Fax: 602-528-0546
e-mail: info@alz.org
http://www.alz.org

Deborah Schaus, Executive Director
David Pile, Chairman

4835 **Alzheimer's Association: Northern Alabama Chapter**
3322 S. Memorial Pkwy
16
Huntsville, AL 35801
256-880-1575
Fax: 256-880-8596
e-mail: karen.motz@alz.org~~
http://www.alz.org

Linda Blanding, President
Marylou Kraatz, Program Director

4836 **Alzheimer's Association: Northern Connecticut Chapter**
279 New Britain Rd
Suite 5
Kensington, CT 06037
860-828-2828
800-356-5502
Fax: 860-828-2417
http://www.alz.org

Eric Rennie, Vice-Chairman
Christine I. Andrew, Director

4837 **Alzheimer's Association: Northern Idaho Resource Center**
2003 Lincolnway
McGrane Center
Coeur D Alene, ID 83814
208-666-2996
800-438-0641
Fax: 208-666-2945
e-mail: ~joel.loiacono@alz.org
http://www.alz.org

P.J. Christo, Outreach Coordinator
Joel Loiacono, Executive Director

Educating and supporting individuals, families and community affested by Alzheimer's disease and realted disorders.

4838 **Alzheimer's Association: Northern Indiana Chapter**
6324 Constitution Drive
Suite 1
Fort Wayne, IN 46804
260-420-5547
Fax: 219-232-4235
e-mail: information@alzindiana.org
http://www.alz.org

Curt Fankhauser, President
Stephen Adair, Director

4839 **Alzheimer's Association: Northern Nevada Chapter**
1060 La Avenida
Mountain View, CA 94043
650-962-8111
Fax: 775-786-1920
http://http://www.alz.org/norcal/

T. William Melis, President
Herb Williams, Vice President

4840 **Alzheimer's Association: Northern Virginia Chapter**
11240 Waples Mill Road
Suite 402
Fairfax, VA 22030-6078
703-359-4440
800-259-0042
Fax: 703-359-4441
http://www.alz.org

Gerry Sampson, Chairman
Jack Shankman, Vice Chair, Programs

4841 **Alzheimer's Association: Northwest Florida Chapter**
140 South Beach Street
Suite 204
Daytona Beach, FL 32114
386-238-0066
800-302-0581
Fax: 386-238-8293
e-mail: info@alzflorida.org
http://www.alz.org

Stu Gaines, Chairman
Susan Leger-Krall, Secretary

4842 **Alzheimer's Association: Northwest Lousiana Chapter**
3717 Government Street
Suite 7
Alexandria, LA 71302
318-619-8383
800-640-2072
Fax: 318-322-2851
e-mail: louisianainfo@alz.org
http://www.alz.org

Robert Stephens, Executive Director
Tammy Reardon, Development Director

4843 **Alzheimer's Association: Northwest Missouri Chapter**
10th and Faraon
Saint Joseph, MO 64501
816-364-4467
Fax: 816-364-2553
e-mail: brenda.gregg@alz.org
http://www.alz.org

Debra R. Brook, Executive Director
Michelle Niedens, LSCSW, Education Director

4844 **Alzheimer's Association: Northwest Ohio**
1 Marion Avenue
Suite 308
Mansfield, OH 44903
419-522-5050
800-441-3322
Fax: 419-522-5318
e-mail: alzheimers@nwoalz.org
http://www.nwoalz.org

Cheryl Conley, M.A, Program Director
Ann Bishop, Coordinator
Dolores Dove, Manager

Mission is to enhance quality Of life of all persons affected by Alzheimer's disease and related memory loss disorders.

4845 **Alzheimer's Association: Oklahoma Chapter**
6465 S Yale Avenue
Suite 312
Tulsa, OK 74136-7810
918-481-7741
800-493-1411
e-mail: admin@alzokar.org
http://www.alz.org

Judi Ver Hoef, President and Chief Executive Di

4846 **Alzheimer's Association: Oklahoma and Arkansas Chapter**
411 S. Victory
Suite 202
Little Rock, AR 72201
501-265-0027
800-689-6090
Fax: 501-227-6303
e-mail: admin@alzokar.org
http://www.alz.org

Phyllis Watkins, Executive Director

Alzheimer's Disease/Associations & Organizations

4847 Alzheimer's Association: Omaha/Eastern Nebraska Chapter
1941 South 42nd Street
Suite 205
Omaha, NE 68105
402-502-4301
800-309-2112
Fax: 402-502-7001
e-mail: bonnie.lingard@alz.org
http://www.alz.org

Duane Gross, President and Chief Executive Di
Clayton Freeman, Program Director
Tia schoenfeld, Program Coordinator

Information/referral line, educational presentations, brochures/information, lending library for chapter members.

4848 Alzheimer's Association: Orange County Chapter
17771 Cowan, Ste. 200
Orange, CA 92614
949-955-9000
800-660-1993
Fax: 714-283-1240
e-mail: helpoc@alz.org
http://www.alz.org/oc/

Paul Wexler, Chairman
Barry C. Cosgrove, Treasurer

4849 Alzheimer's Association: Oregon Chapter
1238 Lincoln Street
Eugene, OR 97401
541-345-8392
800-347-4457
http://www.alz.org

Mary Edmeades, President
Mark Donham, Vice President

4850 Alzheimer's Association: Oregon-Trail Chapter
1311 NW 21st Avenue
Portland, OR 97209
503-413-7114
800-733-0402
Fax: 503-413-6909
http://www.alz.org

Mary Edmeades, President
Mark Donham, Vice President

4851 Alzheimer's Association: Panhandle Area Chapter
3440 Bell St.
Suite 320, PMB 240
Amarillo, TX 79109
915-544-1799
800-687-8693
Fax: 915-544-8746
e-mail: ken.branum@alz.org
http://www.alz.org

Matt W. Spahn, Chairman
Mitch Moss, Vice Chair

4852 Alzheimer's Association: Piedmont Triad North Carolina Chapter
Western Carolina
3800 Shamrock Drive
Charlotte, NC 28215-3220
704-532-7392
800-228-9794
e-mail: info@alz-nc.org
http://www.alz.org/northcarolina/

Jackie E. Rivers, Executive Director
Molly Bristol, President

4853 Alzheimer's Association: Putnam County Chapter
453 Route 211 East
Suite 301
Middletown, NY 10940-2206
845-342-2247
e-mail: info@alzhudsonvalley.org
http://www.alz.org

Andrew Blazek, Directors
Bret Jacobowitz, Chairman

4854 Alzheimer's Association: Rhode Island Chapter
245 Waterman Street
Suite 306
Providence, RI 02906
401-421-0008
800-244-1428
Fax: 401-421-0115
e-mail: Elizabeth.Morancy@alz.org
http://www.alz-ri.org

Elizabeth Morancy, Executive Director
Camilla Farrell, Development director

The mission is to help support Alzheimers families in Rhode Island.

4855 Alzheimer's Association: Riverland Chapter
1022 Caledonia Street
Suite 421
La Crosse, WI 54603
608-784-5011
800-797-1656
Fax: 608-784-4428
e-mail: jfritz@alz.org
http://www.alz.org

Dianne Jacobson, President
Linda Negratti, Vice President

4856 Alzheimer's Association: Riverside/SanBernardino Counties Chapter
5900 Wilshire Boulevard
Suite 1100
Los Angeles, CA 90036-5036
323-938-3379
800-660-1993
Fax: 323-938-1036
http://www.alzla.org

Peter Braun, Executive Director

4857 Alzheimer's Association: Rochester Chapter
Rochester - 435 East Henrietta Road
Suite 401, Box 71
Rochester, NY 14620
585-760-5400
800-724-0587
Fax: 585-442-5675
e-mail: info@alz.org
http://www.alz-rochesterny.org/

James Burton, Director
Stewart C Putnam, Chair

4858 Alzheimer's Association: Rocky Mountain Chapter
455 Sherman Street
Suite 500
Denver, CO 80203
303-813-1669
800-864-4404
Fax: 303-813-1670

Susan Barnhill, Chairman
Linda Mitchell, President

4859 Alzheimer's Association: STAR Chapter
7400 Louis Pasteur Drive
Suite 200
San Antonio, TX 78229-4542
210-822-6449
Fax: 210-824-8069
e-mail: cara.palmieri@alz.org
http://www.alz.org

Ginny Funk, Communications Director
Denese Watkins, Executive Director

Chapter provides programs and services to the estimated millions of families who have a relative diagnosed with Alzheimer's or a related disease that causes irreversible dementia.

4860 Alzheimer's Association: STAR Chapter
3440 Bell St
Suite 320, PMB 240
Amarillo, TX 79109
915-544-1799
800-509-9590
Fax: 915-544-8746
e-mail: febe.leyva@alz.org
http://www.alz.org

Matt W. Spahn, Chairman
Mitch Moss, Vice Chairman

Alzheimer's Disease/Associations & Organizations

4861 Alzheimer's Association: Salem Regional Office
1311 N.W. 21st Avenue
Portland, OR 97209
503-413-7114
Fax: 503-371-9842
e-mail: midwilliamette@alz.org
http://www.alz.org

Mary Edmeades, President
Mark Donham, Vice President

Alzheimer's information and resources.

4862 Alzheimer's Association: San Diego Chapter
4950 Murphy Canyon Rd
Ste 250
San Diego, CA 92123
858-492-4400
800-660-1993
Fax: 858-492-4406
e-mail: info@sanalz.org
http://www.alz.org

Merle Brodie, President and Chief Executive Di
Lisa Bruner, Interim President and Chief Exec

4863 Alzheimer's Association: San Francisco Bay Chapter
1060 La Avenida
Suite A
Mountain View, CA 94043
650-962-8111
800-660-1993
Fax: 650-962-9644
e-mail: info@alznorcal.org

William H Fisher, Chief Executive Officer
T. William Melis, President

4864 Alzheimer's Association: Santa Barbara Chapter
2024 De La Vina Street
Suite A
Santa Barbara, CA 93105-3814
805-563-0020
800-660-1993
Fax: 805-682-1811

David Troxel, Executive Director

4865 Alzheimer's Association: Santa Barbara Chapter
1528 Chapala Street
Suite 204
Santa Barbara, CA 93101
805-892-4259
800-272-3900
Fax: 805-682-1811
e-mail: lredd@centralcoastalz.org
http://http://alz.org

Sharon Kennedy, Chairman
Loretta Redd, Executive Director

Stands by people with Alzheimer's disease and their families through the following programs and services: Telephone Helpline, Support Groups, Respite Grants, Safe Return, Chapter Newsletter, Lending Library, Educational Programs for family and professional caregivers.

4866 Alzheimer's Association: Santa CruzLocal Office
1777a Capitola Road
Santa Cruz, CA 95062-3024
831-464-9982
Fax: 831-464-8930
e-mail: info@alznorcal.org
http://www.alz.org/norcal/

T. William Melis, President
Herb Williams, Vice President

4867 Alzheimer's Association: Siouxland
420 Chambers St
P.O. Box 3716
Sioux City, IA 51101
712-279-5802
800-426-6512
Fax: 712-277-8076
http://http://www.alz.org/siouxland/

Nancy Wenell, Director
Patrick Gill, Chair

4868 Alzheimer's Association: Siouxland Chapter
1000 N West Avenue
Suite 250
Sioux Falls, SD 57104-6908
605-339-4543
800-615-4543
Fax: 605-335-6989
e-mail: jane.aspaas@alz.org
http://www.alz.org

Randy Maas, Executive Director
Jane Aspaas, Manager

4869 Alzheimer's Association: South Central Michigan Chapter
107 Aprill Dr # 1
Suite 1
Ann Arbor, MI 48103-5047
734-677-3081
800-782-6110
Fax: 734-677-3091
e-mail: info@alz.org
http://www.alz.org

Denise Rabidoux, Chairman
Olivia Samuels, 1st Vice Chairman

4870 Alzheimer's Association: South Central Wisconsin Chapter
517 N Segoe Road
Suite 301
Madison, WI 53705
608-232-3400
800-428-9280
Fax: 608-232-3407
e-mail: scwisc.support@alz.org
http://www.alz.org

Paul Rusk, Executive Director
Miriam Boegel, Director of Development

4871 Alzheimer's Association: South Dakota Office
1000 N West Avenue
Suite 250
Sioux Falls, SD 57104
605-339-4543
e-mail: jane.aspaas@alz.org
http://www.alz.org

Randy W Maas, Executive Director
Jane Aspaas, Contact

4872 Alzheimer's Association: South Jersey Chapter
3 Eves Drive
Suite 310
Marlton, NJ 08053-3431
856-797-1212
800-706-2112
e-mail: Wendy.Campbell@alz.org
http://www.alz.org

Edna Ellett, Executive Director
Wendy L. Campbell, President

4873 Alzheimer's Association: South Plains Chapter
Texas Technical University, Health Sciences
3601 4th Street
3a116
Lubbock, TX 79430
806-743-2786
http://www.alz.org

Patti Elkins, Executive Director

4874 Alzheimer's Association: SoutheastWisconsin Chapter
6130 W National Avenue
Suite 200
Milwaukee, WI 53214
414-479-8800
800-922-2413
Fax: 414-479-8819
e-mail: tom.hlavacek@alz.org

Lisa Ligocki, Manager
Tom Hlavacek, Executive Director

Alzheimer's Disease/Associations & Organizations

4875 Alzheimer's Association: Southeast Florida Chapter
4700 N. Congress Ave
#101
West Palm Beach, FL 33407
800-861-7826
Fax: 561-842-8336
http://www.alz.org

Ellen Brown, Chief Executive Officer
Dottie Carson, Director of Development

4876 Alzheimer's Association: Southeast Georgia Chapter
201 Television Circle
Savannah, GA 31406
912-920-2231
Fax: 912-921-7960
e-mail: kim.franklin@alz.org
http://www.alz.org

Bennett Watts, Chairman
Peter Armstrong, Chair-Elect

4877 Alzheimer's Association: Southeast Pennsylvania Chapter
399 Market Street
Suite 102
Philadelphia, PA 19106-2611
21- 56- 291
800-559-0404
Fax: 215-925-6154
http://www.alz.org

Andrew L Hunt, Chair
Deborah Haugh, Vice Chairman

Offers care giving services, support groups and training for care givers.

4878 Alzheimer's Association: Southeast Tennssee Chapter
4205 Hillsboro Pike
Suite 216
Nashville, TN 37215
615-292-4938
800-616-1922
Fax: 423-265-3611
e-mail: diane.gramann@alz.org
http://www.alz.org

Linda Blanding, President
Lynn Cooper, Vice President

4879 Alzheimer's Association: Southern Arizona
1028 E McDowell Rd
Phoenix, AZ 85006
602-528-0545
Fax: 602-528-0546
e-mail: deborah.schaus@alz.org
http://www.alzdsw.org

Deborah Schaus, Executive Director
David Pile, chairman

4880 Alzheimer's Association: Southern Illinois Chapter
303 N. Hershey
Ste 2A
Bloomington, IL 61704
309-662-8392
800-532-0177
e-mail: GI.Chapter@alz.org
http://www.alz.org

Erna Colborn, President and Chief Executive Di
Janet Devlin, Vice President

4881 Alzheimer's Association: Southern Nevada Chapter
5190 S Valley View Blvd
Suite 101
Las Vegas, NV 89118
702-248-2770
Fax: 702-248-2771
e-mail: luis.carrillo@alz.org
http://www.alzdsw.org

Susan Hirsch, Regional Director
David Pile, chairman

4882 Alzheimer's Association: Southern Tier Chapter
401 Hayes Avenue
Endicott, NY 13760
607-785-7852
Fax: 607-785-4004
e-mail: alzcny@alzcny.org
http://www.alz.org

Lynn Augenstern, Administrative Assistant
L. Jane Hudreck, Regional Director

4883 Alzheimer's Association: Southside Virginia Chpater
120 South Hill Avenue
P.O. Box 310
South Hill, VA 23970
434-447-3963
800-758-8318
Fax: 434-447-9024
e-mail: rusty.barton@alz.org
http://www.alz.org

Marcie McMillin, VP
Gino V. Colombara, Executive Director

4884 Alzheimer's Association: SouthwestMissouri Chapter
1500 South Glenstone
Springfield, MO 65804
417-886-2199
Fax: 417-886-0337
e-mail: rebecca.argilagos@alz.org
http://www.alz.org

Rebecca Argilagos, President and Chief Executive Di
Annette West, Development Director
Madelynn Innes, Development Director

4885 Alzheimer's Association: Southwest Georgia Chapter
1925 Century Boulevard
Suite 10
Atlanta, GA 30345
404-728-1181
800-236-0691
Fax: 229-888-2620
http://http://www.alz.org/georgia/

Bennett Watts, Chair
Peter Armstrong, Chair-Elect

4886 Alzheimer's Association: Southwest Montana Chapter
3010 11th Avenue North
721
Billings, MT 59101
406-252-3053
Fax: 406-252-2933
e-mail: alzbelser@bresnan.net
http://www.alz.org

Ann Groff, President
Kelly Donovan, Director

4887 Alzheimer's Association: SpringfieldRegional Office
2921 Greenbriar Dr
Ste C
Springfield, IL 62704
217-726-5184
Fax: 217-726-5185
e-mail: GI.Chapter@alz.org
http://www.alz.org

Erna Colborn, President and Chief Executive Di
Janet Devlin, Vice President, Finance and Oper

4888 Alzheimer's Association: St Louis Chapter
9374 Olive Boulevard
Saint Louis, MO 63132-3214
314-432-3422
800-980-9080
Fax: 314-432-3824
e-mail: Helpline@alzstl.org
http://www.alzstl.org

Jan Kraemer, Chairman
John J Inkley, Secretary

Alzheimer's Disease/Associations & Organizations

4889 Alzheimer's Association: Star Chapter West Texas Region
4400 N Big Spring Street
Suite C-32
Midland, TX 79705
915-570-9191
800-682-1174
Fax: 915-683-2345
e-mail: janet.cross@alz.org
http://www.alz.org

Janet Cross, Program Coordinator
Matt W Spahn, Chairman

4890 Alzheimer's Association: Staten Island Chapter
360 Lexington Avenue
4th Fl
New York, NY 10017
646-744-2900
Fax: 212-490-6037
e-mail: helpline@alznyc.org
http://www.alznyc.org

Princess Yas Aga Khan, Chairman
Andrew W. Albstein, Director

Provides information, diagnostic referral, counseling, helpline, and support groups. Conducts in-service seminars and educational forums. Offers services by trained volunteers.

4891 Alzheimer's Association: Sullivan/Delaware Chapter
2 Jefferson Plaza
Suite 103
Poughkeepsie, NY 12601
800-872-0994
http://http://www.alz.org/hudsonvalley/

Bret Jacobowitz, Chair
Charlotte Ostman, First Vice Chair

4892 Alzheimer's Association: Tarrant County Chapter
101 Summit Avenue
Suite 300
Fort Worth, TX 76102
817-336-4949
800-471-4422
Fax: 817-336-7966
e-mail: nctexas@alz.org
http://www.alz.org

Theresa Hocker, Executive Director
Libby Connally, Director

The Alzheimer's Association North Central Texas Chapter is commited to assistingthose afflicted with Alzheimer's Disease, their familes and professional caregivers by offering a wide range of support programs, comprehansive education, public awareness, advocacy and funding for research in a 40 county area.

4893 Alzheimer's Association: Topeka Regional Office Heart of America Chapter
4125 SW Gage Center Drive
Suite LL-15
Topeka, KS 66604
785-271-1844
Fax: 785-271-1804
e-mail: cindy.miller@alz.org
http://www.alz.org

Michelle Niedens, LSCSW, Education Director
Debra R. Brook, Executive Director

Information, resources and services for patients and families. Education and Training fro family and professional caregivers. Directed Training for medical emergency and law enforcement personnel. Public awareness, Advocacy and Public Policy.

4894 Alzheimer's Association: Traverse CityRegional
1040 Walnut Street
Traverse City, MI 49686
231-929-3804
800-337-3827
Fax: 231-929-2766
e-mail: Lorraine.Kremer@alz.org
http://www.alzgmc.org

Lorraine Kremer, Manager

4895 Alzheimer's Association: Upstate South Carolina Chapter
4124 Clemson Blvd
Suite L
Anderson, SC 29621
864-224-3045
800-273-2555
Fax: 864-225-1387
e-mail: cindy.alewine@alz.org
http://www.alz.org

Cindy Alewine, President and Chief Executive Di
Velma Haggan, Vice President of Finance and Op

Non-profit organization, affiliate of the National Alzheimer's Association. Serves to families and professionals.

4896 Alzheimer's Association: Utah Chapter
855 East 4800 South
Suite 100
Salt Lake City, UT 84107
801-274-1944
800-371-6694
Fax: 801-274-1226
e-mail: utah.chapter@alz.org
http://www.alz.org

Linda Blonsley, Executive Director
Nick Zullo, Program Director

4897 Alzheimer's Association: Vermont Chapter
172 North Main Street
Barre, VT 5641
802-477-7000
800-698-1022
Fax: 802-229-5231
e-mail: pam.smith@alz.org
http://www.alz.org

Pamela Smith, Executive Director
Randy Brock, President and Chair
Pam Smith, Administrative Director

The Alzheimer's Association is the only voluntary health organization dedicated to research aimed at the prevention, care, and treatment of Alzheimer's disease and related disorders, while providing support and assistance to those affected with the disease and their families.

4898 Alzheimer's Association: Volusia/Flagler Counties Chapter
140 South Beach Street
Suite 204
Daytona Beach, FL 32114
386-238-0066
Fax: 386-238-8293
e-mail: info@alzflorida.org
http://www.alz.org

Stu Gaines, Chair
Tish Sheesley, Chief Executive Officer

4899 Alzheimer's Association: West Central Florida Chapter
9365 US Highway 19 N
Suite B
Pinellas Park, FL 33782
727-578-2558
800-841-6669
Fax: 813-849-6124
http://www.alz-tbc.org

Dominick Depetrillo, Executive Director

4900 Alzheimer's Association: West Central Minnesota Chapter
4550 W 77th Street
Suite 200
Minneapolis, MN 55435
952-830-0512
Fax: 952-830-0513
e-mail: mary.birchard@alz.org
http://www.alzmndak.org

Mary Birchard, Executive Director
Lori Happel-Jarratt, Chief Operating Officer

Alzheimer's Disease/Associations & Organizations

4901 **Alzheimer's Association: West Hawaii Chapter**
1050 Ala Moana Blvd
Suite 2610
Honolulu, HI 96814
808-591-2771
Fax: 808-322-0008
http://http://www.alz.org/hawaii/
Tricia Medeiros, Executive Director
Michael Buck, Director

4902 **Alzheimer's Association: West Michigan Chapter**
20300 Civic Center
Suite 100
Southfield, MI 48076
248-351-028
800-893-8365
Fax: 248-351-0417

4903 **Alzheimer's Association: West Shore Chapter**
1060 W. Norton
Suite 2
Muskegon, MI 49441
231-780-1922
Fax: 616-726-6645
http://www.alz.org/mglc/in_my_community_about.a
Denise Rabidoux, Chairman
Olivia Samuels, 1st Vice Chairman

4904 **Alzheimer's Association: West South Dakota Chapter**
1000 N West Avenue
Suite 250
Sioux Falls, SD 57104
605-339-4543
Fax: 605-335-6989
e-mail: jane.aspaas@alz.org
http://www.alz.org
Evan Thompson, Executive Committee Chairman
Samuel E. Gandy, Vice Chairman

4905 **Alzheimer's Association: West VirginaChapter**
1111 Lee Street E
Charleston, WV 25301
304-343-2717
Fax: 304-343-2723
http://www.alz.org
Melissa Gandee, LSW, Program Director
Jane Marks, Executive Director

4906 **Alzheimer's Association: Western & Central Washington Chapter**
12721 - 30th Avenue NE
Suite 101
Seattle, WA 98125
206-363-5500
800-848-7097
Fax: 206-363-5700
e-mail: rowena.rye@alz.org
http://www.alz.org
Nancy Dapper, Executive Director
Rowena Rye, HelpLine Director

4907 **Alzheimer's Association: Western Massachusetts Chapter**
311 Arsenal Street
Watertown, MA 02472
617-868-6718
Fax: 617-868-6720
e-mail: communications@alzmass.org
http://www.alz.org
Mary Ann Marino, Chairman
Jeffrey Berry, PhD, Vice Chair

4908 **Alzheimer's Association: Western New York Chapter**
Western New York
2805 Wehrle Drive, Suite 6
Williamsville, NV 14221
716-626-0600
800-273-6737
Fax: 716-626-2255
e-mail: info@alz.org
http://www.alz.org
Marilyn Albert, Executive Director
Sue Murphy, Vice Chairman

4909 **Alzheimer's Association: Western North Carolina Chapter**
31 College Place
Suite D320
Asheville, NC 28801-2644
828-254-7363
800-522-2451
http://www.alz.org
Jackie E. Rivers, Executive Director
Molly Bristol, President

4910 **Alzheimer's Association: Western Slope**
2232 N. 7th St
Suite B1
Grand Junction, CO 81501
970-256-1274
Fax: 970-243-6924
http://www.alzrockymtn.org
Annie Smyth, Regional Director
Laurie Frasier, Memory Walk Coordinator

4911 **Alzheimer's Association: Wichita FallsRegional Office**
901 Indiana
Suite 350
Wichita Falls, TX 76301
940-767-8800
877-322-6259
Fax: 940-322-6259
e-mail: beverly.diekhoff@alz.org
http://www.alz.org/northcentraltexas
Beverly Diekhoff, Director

4912 **Alzheimer's Association: Wyoming Chapter**
5601 S. 27th Street
Suite 201
Lincoln, NE 68512
402-420-2540
Fax: 402-420-2541
Karen Noel, President and Chief Executive Di
Teresa Stitc Fritz, Program Director

4913 **Alzheimer's Association:-Michigan Great Lakes Chapter Southwest Region**
2300 Portage Street
Suite
Kalamazoo, MI 49001
269-342-1482
Fax: 616-372-4387
e-mail: info@alz.org
http://www.alz.org
Denise Rabidoux, Chairman
Rachel Yu, Secretary

4914 **Alzheimer's Disease & Related DisordersAssociation, Greater Iowa Chapter**
1730 28th Street
West Des Moines, IA 50266
515-440-2722
800-272-3900
Fax: 515-440-6385
http://www.alz.org
Carol Sipfle, Executive Director
Ann Riesenberg, Program Director

Provides vital services and support to individuals, families, and care partners in their communities. The Greater Iowa Chapter is committed to its mission to eliminate Alzheimer's disease through the advancement of research, while enhancing care and support services for individuals and families.

4915 **Alzheimer's Disease Center**
University of Washington
12721 - 30th Avenue NE
Suite 101
Seattle, WA 98125
206-363-5500
Fax: 206-363-5700
e-mail: rowena.rye@alz.org
http://www.alzwa.org/
Nora Gibson, President
Mark Davidson, Vice President

Researchers work to translate advances into improved care and diagnosis for Alzheimer's patients.

Alzheimer's Disease/Associations & Organizations

4916 Alzheimer's Disease Education and Referral (ADEAR) Center
11240 Waples Mill Road
Suite 402
Fairfax, VA 22030
703-359-4440
800-438-4380
Fax: 301-495-3334
e-mail: adear@alzheimers.org
http://http://www.alz.org/nca/
Gerry Sampson, Chair
Matthew Aaron, Vice Chair, Operations

A service of the National Institute on Aging, the ADEAR Center distributes information on Alzheimer's disease, on current research activities and on services available to patients and family members. Offers free publications. List available upon request.

4917 Alzheimer's Disease Support Group Janesville Chapter
1930 S River Road
Janesville, WI 53546-9066
608-756-8144
Myra Kobs, Administrator

4918 Alzheimer's Disease Support Group: Janesville Chapter
South Central Wisconsin Chapter
517 N. Segoe Rd. Suite
Madison, WI 53705
608-232-3400
e-mail: info@alz.org
http://www.alz.org
Sue Abitz, Director
Greg Allen, Director

Individuals united to provide support, social activities, education, information, and referral to those caring for someone with a chronic illness..

4919 Alzheimer's Disease and Related Disorders Association
8430 Bryn Mawr
Suite 800
Chicago, IL 60631
847-933-2413
800-272-3900
Fax: 312-335-1110
e-mail: GI.Chapter@alz.org
http://www.alz.org
TDD 312-335-8882
Claire Altschuler, Communication Director
Erna Colborn, President and Chief Executive Of
Gary Bieting, President

Dedicated to research for the prevention, cure and treatment of Alzheimer's disease and related disorders and to providing support and assistance to the afflicted patients and their families.

4920 Alzheimer's Foundation of America
360 Lexington Ave
4th Floor
New York, NY 10017
646-744-2900
Fax: 212-490-6037
http://www.alznyc.org
Lou-Ellen Barkan, CEO
Jed A Levine, Executive VP

4921 Alzheimer's Foundation of Staten Island
460 Brielle Ave
Staten Island, NY 10314-6427
718-667-7110
Fax: 718-667-8431
e-mail: alzheimersfound@aol.com
http://www.sialzheimers.com
Michael A DiMauro, President
Dr. Stephen McGee, First Vice President
Gladys Schweiger, Executive Director

Provides information, diagnostic referral, counseling, helpline, respite services and support groups. Conducts in-service seminars and educational forums. Offers services by trained volunteers.

4922 Alzheimer's Foundation of the South & Mississippi Division
1900 Dunbarton Dr
Suite H
Jackson, MS 39216
601-987-0020
800-950-6251
Fax: 601-987-9020
e-mail: info@msalz.org
http://www.alz.org
Evan Thompson, Executive Committee Chairman
Samuel E. Gandy, Vice Chairman

Non-profit charity

4923 Alzheimer's Resource Center
1506 Lake Highland Drive
Suite 2
Orlando, FL 32803
407-843-1910
Fax: 407-381-4155
e-mail: info@AlzheimerResourceCenter.org
http://www.alzheimerresourcecenter.org
Sandra O'Dowd, Marketing Director

Provides support groups, newsletters, caregiver workshops, books, videos, pamphlets and speakers.

4924 Alzheimer's Resource Center Orlando
988 Woodcock Road
Suite 200
Orlando, FL 32803
407-228-4299
800-330-1910
Fax: 407-228-4201
e-mail: info@alzflorida.org
http://www.alz.org
Nancy Wolt, Operations Director
Stu Gaines, Chairman

A non profit organization, has been athe forerunner in Central Florida bringing Alzheimer specific education and support to family caregivers as well as professional care providers.

4925 Alzheimer's Support Groups for Family and Friends
Rochester - 435 East Henrietta Road
Suite 401, Box 71
Rochester, NY 14620
585-760-5400
Fax: 585-442-5675
e-mail: info@alz.org
http://www.alz-rochesterny.org/
Melva Brown, Ph.D., Director
Stewart C Putnam, Chair

4926 Alzheimer's Wyoming
900 Werner Court Room 226
Po Box 1493
Casper, WY 82602
307-265-7960
888-276-9602
Fax: 307-265-7960
e-mail: alzawy@tribcsp.com
http://www.alzheimerswyoming.com
Mary Hein, Executive Director

4927 Alzheimers Aid Society of Northern California
PO Box 1824
Sacramento, CA 95812
916-448-7001
800-540-3340
e-mail: info@alzheimersaidsociety.org
http://www.alzheimersaidsociety.org
Goerge G. Glenner, President and Chief Executive Di

Family support: provide needed support and advice for victims and their families. Counseling and emotional support are a major need. Education and information for lay and professional people. To aid and support research into the causes, treatment, prevention and cure for Alzheimer's disease. To advocate the social needs of the afflicted population, provide information to increase public awareness. Bimonthly newsletters and a multitude of direct services, including distribution of free information packets, in-service training, workshops, home visits and 24-hour one-on-on phone call availability are supported through donations.

Number of Members: 15,000

Alzheimer's Disease/Associations & Organizations

4928 Alzheimers of Central Alabama
PO Box 2273
Birmingham, AL 35201
205-871-7970
Fax: 205-871-7355
e-mail: aca@alzca.org
http://www.alzca.org

Miller Piggott, MSW, Executive Director

Alzheimer's of Central Alabama is a nonprofit or volunteer organization and resource center serving Alzheimer's patients, caregivers and professionals. The goal of ACA is to support, education, caregiver services and research. The following counties are served: Bibb, Blount, Calhoun, Cleburne, Chilton, Clay, Coosa, Etowah, Fayette, Greene, Hale, Jefferson, Lamar, Pickens, Randolph, Shelby, St. Clair, Talladega, Tallapoosa, Tuscaloosa, and Walker.

4929 Alzhimer's Association of Greater Wisconsin
2900 Curry Lane
Suite A
Green Bay, WI 54311
920-469-2110
800-272-3900
Fax: 920-469-2131
http://www.alz.org/gwwi/

Dianne Jacobson, President
Linda Negratti, Vice President

To eliminate Alzheimer's disease through the advancement of research; to provide and enhance care and support for all affected, and to reduce the risk of dementia through the promotion of brain health.

4930 American Academy of Neurology
1080 Montreal Avenue
Saint Paul, MN 55116-2386
651-695-1940
800-879-1960
Fax: 651-695-2791
e-mail: memberservices@aan.com
http://www.aan.com

Sandra F Olson MD, President
Mark Hallett MD, VP
Catherine M Rydell, Executive Director

Professional society of medical doctors specializing in brain and nervous system diseases. Maintains placement service. Sponsors research and educational programs. Compiles statistics. Publishes scientific journal.

4931 American Board of Psychiatry and Neurology
500 Lake Cook Road
Suite 335
Deerfield, IL 60015-5249
847-945-7900
Fax: 847-945-1146
http://www.abpn.com

Stephen C Scheiber, Executive VP

Physicians with specialized training in psychiatry, neurology, child neurology, child adolescent psychiatry, clinical neurophysiology, and geriatric psychiatry. Determines eligibility requirements, administers examinations, and certifies physicians.

4932 American Health Assistance Foundation
22512 Gateway Center Drive
Clarksburg, MD 20871
301-948-3244
800-437-2423
Fax: 301-258-9454
e-mail: iquiroz@ahaf.org
http://www.ahaf.org

Brian K. Regan, Ph.D, AFRP Manager
Kathleen Honaker, Executive Director

Funds research programs for heart disease, glaucoma, and Alzheimer's disease. Provides financial assistance through Alzheimer's Family Relief Program. Public education materials on programs, brochures, and applications are provided. Hours: 9am to 5pm Monday-Friday.

4933 American Homes for the Aging: Eastern & Northeastern Regional Offices
170 Homestead Avenue
Albany, NY 12203-1926
518-437-9232
Fax: 518-437-9233

Regional office of the national association of more than 4,000 nonprofit nursing homes, retirement communities, independent living centers and community service providers.

4934 Clayton County Alzheimer's SupportServices
1512-1 Gillionville Rd
Riverdale, GA 31707
229-888-7676
Fax: 229-888-2620
e-mail: kim.franklin@alz.org
http://www.alz.org

Bennett Watts, Chairman
Iola Snow, Secretary

Provides assistance to people with Alzheimer's disease and their families.

4935 Clayton County Alzheimer's Support Services
6701 Highway 85
Riverdale, GA 30274-2316
770-603-4090
Fax: 770-603-4092
http://www.co.clayton.ga.us/alzheimers

Janice Coye, Executive Director

Our mission is to provide or cause to be provided, the highest quality of services to families dealing with Alzheimer's Disease and related disorders.

4936 French Alzheimer Foundation
11620 Wilshire Boulevard
Suite 270
Los Angeles, CA 90025
310-445-4650
800-477-
Fax: 310-479-0516
http://www.jdfaf.org

Michael M. Minchin, Jr., President
David Werthe, Director of Operations

Funds scientific and medical research into the cause, cure and prevention of Alzheimer's disease.

4937 Long Island Alzheimer's Foundation
3281 Veterans Memorial Highway
Suite E-13
Ronkonkoma, NY 11779
631-580-5100
e-mail: Info@alzheimersli.org

Mary Ann Malack-Ragona, Executive Director
Nicholas Materdomini, Director of Development

Provides information and referral services, materials, adult daycare program, support groups and caregiver conferences.

4938 Maine Alzheimer's Care Center
154 Dresden Avenue
Gardiner, ME 04345-2600
207-626-1770

Joyce Hemon, Administrator

4939 Oklahoma & Arkansas Alzheimer's Associaton
Western Arkansas Regional Center
320 N Greenwood Avenue
Fort Smith, AR 72901
479-783-2022
800-272-3900
Fax: 479-782-3185
e-mail: admin@alzokar.org
http://www.alz.org

Cheryl Bledsaw, Manager

The Oklahoma/Arkansas Alzheimer's Association is here to provide you with all the information you need to know about Alzheimer's, how to care for a person with Alzheimer's, and the research that is being done to eliminate the disease.

Alzheimer's Disease/Books

4940 Oklahoma Department of Health and Human Services: Alzheimer's Research Advisory Council
PO Box 25352
Oklahoma City, OK 73125
405-521-3646
Fax: 405-521-6684
http://www.okdhs.org

Larry Harmon, Chief Administrative Officer
George Earl Johnson, Director

The mission of the Oklahoma Department of Human Services is to help individuals and families in need help themselves lead safer, healthier, more independent and productive lives

4941 Olympic Alzheimers Foundation
3025 14th Avenue NW
Gig Harbor, WA 98335
253-851-5306
Fax: 253-858-2512

Denise Macartea, Contact

Individuals in the Tacoma, WA area suffering from alzheimers disease; their families and friends. Provides support and other services.

4942 Tender Social Day Center for Older Adults and Alzheimer's Group Respite Program
16 E Main Street
Moorestown, NJ 8057
856-234-5999
Fax: 856-234-9074
e-mail: barbara@thetender.org
http://www.help4caregivers.org

Barbara Fetty, Executive Director

A safe, structured, home-like setting in which seniors and those with Alzheimer's disease can receive peer support and participate in games, music, garden and pet therapy.

4943 Vallejo Alzheimers Support Group
1620 Fern Place
Vallejo, CA 94590-4406
707-643-7333

Virl M Swan, Executive Officer

Support group for Alzheimer's patients and their friends and families. Offers charitable services.

Books

4944 36-Hour Day
Alzheimer's Association
919 N Michigan Avenue
Suite 1000
Chicago, IL 60611-1696
773-342-4722
800-272-3900
Fax: 312-335-1110
e-mail: info@alz.org
http://www.alz.org

Steve Hier, Owner

A family guide to caring for persons with Alzheimer's disease, related dementing illnesses, and memory loss later in life. Spanish version available.

422 pages

4945 A Handbook of Activities for Persons With Dementia
Johns Hopkins University Press
2715 N Charles Street
Baltimore, MD 21218-4319
301-338-6900
Fax: 301-338-6998
http://www.jhu.edu/oress.index.html

192 pages

4946 ABC's of Dementia
Canyonlands Publishing
10320 W Indian School Road
Phoenix, AZ 85037-5822
602-224-9796
Fax: 623-877-9887

Jim Moritz, Owner

Provides basic information about the syndrome of Alzheimer's dementia. The topics include definition of the dementia syndrome, general characteristics, diagnosis, informational resources and treatment.

4947 Activity Programming for Persons with Dementia: A Sourcebook
Alzheimer's Association
919 N Michigan Avenue
Suite 1000
Chicago, IL 60611-1696
312-335-8700
800-272-3900
Fax: 312-335-1110
e-mail: info@alz.org
http://www.alz.org

Gary Bieting, President

Provides direction and suggestions for designing activities for people with Alzheimer's disease and other related dementias. Each activity is described and illustrated. Includes a list of reference materials and organizations.

138 pages

4948 Alzheimer's Disease Orientation Kit
Alzheimer's Association
919 N Michigan Avenue
Suite 1000
Chicago, IL 60611-1696
312-335-8700
800-272-3900
Fax: 312-335-1110
e-mail: info@alz.org
http://www.alz.org

Gary Bieting, President

A collection of materials developed to familiarize the audience with Alzheimer's disease and its effects on the patient and family. Includes the Orientation to Alzheimer's Disease videotape, Learning Guide and Caregiver Packet.

4949 Alzheimer's Disease Treatment and Family Stress: Directions for Research
Superintendent of Documents
PO Box 371954
Pittsburgh, PA 15250-7954
202-512-2250
Fax: 202-512-2250

Presents a collection of papers giving current information on research investigations that increase the understanding of the nature and consequences of family caregiving.

486 pages

4950 Alzheimer's Disease: A Guide to Federal Programs
Alzheimer's Disease Education & Referral Center
PO Box 8250
Silver Spring, MD 20907-8250
800-438-4380
Fax: 301-495-3334

Directory of Alzheimer's disease programs sponsored by federal agencies. Listed agency by agency, it provides locations and telephone numbers for multi-site activities and demonstration programs, and lists information resources.

113 pages

4951 Alzheimer's Disease: A Handbook for Caregivers
Mosby-Year Book
11830 Westline Industrial Drive
Saint Louis, MO 63146-3313
314-872-8370
800-426-4545
Fax: 432-432-1380
http://www.mosby.com

For nurses and caregivers without nursing degrees. Discusses the structure and functioning of the human brain, clinical aspects of Alzheimer's, management of dementia, issues of ethics, law, stress and abuse of elders, community support, and optimistic research areas.

451 pages

Alzheimer's Disease/Books

4952 Alzheimer's Disease: Activity-Focused Care
Butterworth-Heinemann
225 Wildwood Avenue
Woburn, MA 01801-2025
781-904-2500
800-366-2665
Fax: 800-446-6520
http://www.bh.com

Information for professional and family caregivers on activity-focused care for Alzheimer's patients.

436 pages

4953 Alzheimer's Handbook
Branden Publishing Company
17 Station Street
Box 843
Brookline, MA 02445-7995
617-734-2045
Fax: 617-734-2046
http://www.branden.com

4954 Alzheimer's, Stroke and 29 Other Neurological Disorders Sourcebook
Omnigraphics
615 Griswold Street
Suite 1400
Detroit, MI 48226-3993
313-961-1340
800-234-1340
Fax: 800-875-1340
http://www.omnigraphics.com

Georgiann Lavginiger, Customer Service Manager
Peter E Ruffner, President

Provides vital information for the nontechnical reader focusing on Alzheimer's Disease, stroke and various neurological disorders. Answers thousands of questions related to afflications of the central nervous system with each chapter reviewing a particular disorder and offers in-depth discussions.

4955 Alzheimer's: The Answers You Need
Elder Books
PO Box 490
Forest Knolls, CA 94933
415-488-9002
800-909-2673
Fax: 415-488-4720
e-mail: info@elderbooks.com
http://www.elderbooks.com

Designed for people in the early stages of Alzheimer's. Question-and-answer format provides information about the nature and causes of AD.

138 pages

4956 Complete Guide to Alzheimer's Proofing Your Home
Purdue University Press
1207 S Campus Courts E
West Lafayette, IN 47907
800-247-6553
Fax: 765-496-2442
http://www.thepress.purdue.edu/

Guide to modify homes of Alzheimer's patients to facilitate caregiving.

496 pages

4957 Confronting Alzheimer's Disease
American Assn. of Homes & Services for the Aging
901 E Street NW
Suite 500
Washington, DC 20004-2037
202-661-5700
Fax: 202-783-2255

Daniel Smith, Vice President

A resource for administrators, professional caregivers and families dealing with Alzheimer's Disease and related disorders.

225 pages

4958 Coping and Caring: Living with Alzheimer's Disease
AARP Fulfillment
601 E Street NW
Washington, DC 20049
202-434-2277
800-424-3410
Fax: 202-434-3443
e-mail: member@aarp.org
http://www.aarp.org

William D Novelli, CEO

Addresses the questions: What is Alzheimer's? How does the disease progress? How long does it last? How can families cope?.

24 pages

4959 Designing for Alzheimer's Disease: Strategies for Creating Better Care Environment
John Wiley & Sons
111 River Street
Hoboken, NJ 07030-5774
201-748-6000
Fax: 201-748-6088
e-mail: info@wiley.com
http://www.wiley.com

Elizabeth C Brawley, Author

A practical, thorough approach to the development of therapeutic special care settings. Equips designers and care providers with the information they need to plan environments that can greatly enhance the lives of those with alzheimer's.

340 pages

4960 From Theory to Therapy: The Development of Drugs for Alzheimer's Disease
Alzheimer's Association
919 N Michigan Avenue
Suite 1000
Chicago, IL 60611-1696
312-335-8700
800-272-3900
Fax: 312-335-1110
e-mail: info@alz.org
http://www.alz.org

Gary Bieting, President

Provides a layman's explanation of how experimental drugs are being developed and tested for Alzheimer's disease, and information about patient participation in clinical drug trials.

44+ pages

4961 Guidelines for Dignity
Alzheimer's Association
919 N Michigan Avenue
Suite 1000
Chicago, IL 60611-1696
312-335-8700
800-272-3900
Fax: 312-335-1110
e-mail: info@alz.org
http://www.alz.org

Gary Bieting, President

A resource for providers who are offerng Alzheimer/dementia care in residential settings. Eight goals target specific issues to be addressed and present practical ideas and advice. This resource for facility professionals corresponds to the Family Guide for Alzheimer Care in Residential Settings, which can be used as a companion resource.

40 pages

4962 Handbook of Activities for Persons with Dementia
Johns Hopkins University Press
2715 N Charles Street
Baltimore, MD 21218-4319
410-516-6900
800-537-5487
Fax: 410-516-6998
http://www.jhu.edu/press/index.html

William Brody, President

192 pages

Alzheimer's Disease/Books

4963 Hospice Care for Patients with Advanced Progressive Dementia
Springer Publishing Company
536 Broadway
New York, NY 10012-3915
212-431-4370
Fax: 212-941-7842
e-mail: springer@springerpub.com
http://www.springerpub.com

Ursula Springer, President

Discusses adpating hospice care for terminally ill patients with dementia. Topics include infections, eating difficulties, and providing palliative care.

305 pages

4964 Interventions for Alzheimer's Disease: A Caregiver's Complete Reference
Health Professions Press
PO Box 10624
Baltimore, MD 21285
410-337-9585
888-337-8808
Fax: 410-337-8539

Melissa Behm, President

For professionals who plan, administer or provide services to Alzheimer's patients.

239 pages

4965 Just the Facts & More Kit
Alzheimer's Association
919 N Michigan Avenue
Suite 1000
Chicago, IL 60611-1696
312-335-8700
800-272-3900
Fax: 312-335-1110
e-mail: info@alz.org
http://www.alz.org

Gary Bieting, President

Two-sided, easy-to-read fact sheets on a variety of topics of interest to caregivers of Alzheimer's patients.

4966 Key Elements of Dementia Care
Alzheimer's Association
919 N Michigan Avenue
Suite 1000
Chicago, IL 60611-1696
312-335-8700
800-272-3900
Fax: 312-335-1110
e-mail: info@alz.org
http://www.alz.org

Gary Bieting, President

Defines, describes, and illustrates dementia-capable care throughout the range of residential care settings.

90 pages

4967 Learning to Speak Alzheimer's A Groundbreaking Approach for Everyone Dealing with the Disease
Houghton Mifflin
222 Berkeley Street
Boston, MA 02116
617-351-5000
http://www.houghtonmifflinfbooks.com

Joanne Koenig Coste, Author

Offers a practical approach to the emotional well-being of both patients and caregivers that emphasizes relating to patients in their own reality.

256 pages

4968 Living in the Labyrinth: A Personal Journey Through the Maze of Alzheimers
Dell Publishing
1540 Broadway
New York, NY 10036-4039
212-782-9000
800-726-0600
Fax: 800-659-2436
http://www.randomhouse.com

Peter Olsen, CEO

4969 Safe Return Home: An Inspirational Book for Caregivers of Alzheimer's
Andrews McMeel Publishing Company
PO Box 419263
Kansas City, MO 64193
816-932-6700
800-826-4216
Fax: 800-437-8683
e-mail: www.shop.ucxpress.com
http://www.uclick.com

Kathleen W Andrews, CEO

Impact of Alzheimer's on patients and their families by using the Crankshaft cartoon and personal reminiscences.

112 pages

4970 Speaking Our Minds: Personal Reflections from Individuals with Alzheimer's
WH Freeman and Company
41 Madison Avenue
New York, NY 10010-2202
212-576-9400
Fax: 212-689-2383

Elizabeth Widdicombe, President

Personal reflections of people with Alzheimer's disease.

161 pages

4971 Therapeutic Activity for Persons with Alzheimer
Pro-Ed
8700 Shoal Creek Boulevard
Austin, TX 78757-6816
800-397-7633
Fax: 800-897-3202

A program of functional skills for activities of daily living. Hardcover.

256 pages

4972 Understanding Alzheimer's Disease
University Press of Mississippi
3825 Ridgewood Road
Jackson, MS 39211-6497
601-432-6205
Fax: 601-432-6217
e-mail: press@ihl.state.ms.us
http://www.upress.state.ms.us

Seetha Srinivasan, Executive Director

A guide to understanding a devastating illness that affects a significant segment of the elderly population.

150 pages

4973 Useful Information on Alzheimer's Disease
National Clearinghouse for Alcohol and Drug Abuse
PO Box 2345
Rockville, MD 20847-2345
301-468-2600
800-729-6686
Fax: 301-468-2600
e-mail: info@health.org
http://www.health.org

24 pages

4974 When Memory Fails: Helping the Alzheimer's& Dementia Patient
Plenum Press
233 Spring Street
Floor 7
New York, NY 10013-1522
212-620-8000
Fax: 212-463-0742
e-mail: info@plenum.com

Rudiger Gebauer, Owner

296 pages

Alzheimer's Disease/Directories

Directories

4975 **Alzheimer's Disease**
Franklin Watts
PO Box 1796
Danbury, CT 06816-1796
800-621-1115
Fax: 800-374-4329
http://www.publishing.grolier.com
Elaine Landau, Editor

Support organizations for family members of Alzheimer's patients. Entries include: Organization name, address, phone. Principal content of publication is true stories of patients, treatments currently used, and research concerning the cause of the illness.

4976 **Alzheimer's Disease: A Guide for Families**
Addison-Wesley Publishing Company
Jacob Way
Reading, MA 01867
617-944-3700
800-552-2259
Fax: 617-942-1117
Katie Courtice, Contact
Lenore S Powell, Contact

Publication includes: List of about 60 chapters of the Alzheimer's Disease and Related Disorders Association. Entries include: Chapter name, address, phone, name of contact person.
Frequency: Irregular

Journals, Magazines

4977 **Early Stage Alzheimer's Care: A Guide for Community Based Programs**
Springer Publishing Company
536 Broadway
New York, NY 10012-3915
212-431-4370
Fax: 212-941-7842
e-mail: springer@springerpub.com
http://www.springerpub.com
Ursula Springer, President

4978 **Research & Practice**
Alzheimer's Association
919 N Michigan Avenue
Suite 1000
Chicago, IL 60611-1696
312-335-8700
800-272-3900
Fax: 312-335-1110
e-mail: info@alz.org
http://www.alz.org
Gary Bieting, President

Provides practical information for healthcare professionals on the current status of prominent areas of Alzheimer research.

Newsletters, Pamphlets

4979 **Advances**
Alzheimer's Association
919 N Michigan Avenue
Suite 1000
Chicago, IL 60611-1696
312-335-8700
800-272-3900
Fax: 312-335-1110
e-mail: info@alz.org
http://www.alz.org
Gary Bieting, President

Provides information related to research and caregiving.

4980 **Alzheimer Disease and Associated Disorders**
Lippincott-Raven Publishers
PO Box 1600
Hagerstown, MD 21741-1600
301-714-2300
800-638-
Fax: 301-824-7390
e-mail: lrorders@phl.lrpub.com
http://www.lrpub.com

A leading international forum for reports of new research findings and new approaches to diagnosis and treatment.

4981 **Alzheimer's Advocates Handbook**
Alzheimer's Association
919 N Michigan Avenue
Suite 1000
Chicago, IL 60611-1696
312-335-8700
800-272-3900
Fax: 312-335-1110
e-mail: info@alz.org
http://www.alz.org
Gary Bieting, President

Guide for the individual advocate, offering tips in letter writing, meeting with public officials and getting results.
20 pages

4982 **Alzheimer's Association National Brochure**
Alzheimer's Association
919 N Michigan Avenue
Suite 1000
Chicago, IL 60611-1696
312-335-8700
800-272-3900
Fax: 312-335-1110
e-mail: info@alz.org
http://www.alz.org
Gary Bieting, President

Describes the Alzheimer's Association and its services.

4983 **Alzheimer's Association Newsletter**
Lexington\Bluegrass Chapter
801 S Limestone
Suite E
Lexington, KY 40508-3222
859-266-5283
Fax: 859-268-4764
Pat McCray, Editor
Marcey Ansley, Executive Director
8 pages Frequency: Quarterly

4984 **Alzheimer's Association Tarrant County Chapter**
PO Box 9709
Fort Worth, TX 76147-2709
817-336-4949
800-471-
Fax: 817-336-4966
e-mail: theresa.hocker@alz.org
http://www.alz.org
Theresa Hocker, Executive Director

Newsletter for those afflicted with Alzheimer's Disease. Includes education, support groups, case management, telephone helpline, and referral to services (i.e. long-term care, adult daycare, medical assistance, legal assistance, etc.).
8 pages

4985 **Alzheimer's Disease: A Guide to Federal Programs**
Alzheimer's Disease Education & Referral Center
PO Box 8250
Silver Spring, MD 20907-8250
800-438-4380
Fax: 301-495-3334

Directory of Alzheimer's disease programs sponsored by federal agencies. Listed agency by agency, it provides locations and telephone numbers for multi-site activities and demonstration programs, and lists information resources.
113 pages

Alzheimer's Disease/Newsletters, Pamphlets

4986 Alzheimer's Disease: An Overview
Alzheimer's Association
919 N Michigan Avenue
Suite 1000
Chicago, IL 60611-1696
312-335-8700
800-272-3900
Fax: 312-335-1110
e-mail: info@alz.org
http://www.alz.org

Gary Bieting, President

Basic facts on Alzheimer's disease, including a glossary.

4987 Alzheimer's Disease: Services You May Need
Alzheimer's Association
919 N Michigan Avenue
Suite 1000
Chicago, IL 60611-1696
312-335-8700
800-272-3900
Fax: 312-335-1110
e-mail: info@alz.org
http://www.alz.org

Gary Bieting, President

Guide to services available to Alzheimer's disease caregivers.

4988 Alzheimer's Disease: Statistics
Alzheimer's Association
919 N Michigan Avenue
Suite 1000
Chicago, IL 60611-1696
312-335-8700
800-272-3900
Fax: 312-335-1110
e-mail: info@alz.org
http://www.alz.org

Gary Bieting, President

Indicates basic information on incidence, prevalence, cost of care, etc.

4989 Alzheimer's Research Review
American Health Assistance Foundation
15825 Shady Grove Road
Suite 140
Rockville, MD 20850-4015
301-948-3244
800-437-2423
Fax: 301-258-9451

Kathy Honaker, Executive Director
4-6 pages

4990 Care for Advanced Alzheimer's Disease
Alzheimer's Association
919 N Michigan Avenue
Suite 1200
Chicago, IL 60611-1694
312-335-8700
800-272-3900
Fax: 312-335-1110
e-mail: info@alz.org
http://www.alz.org

Gary Bieting, President

Suggestions for coping with caregiving problems that commonly occur late in the progression of Alzheimer's disease.

4991 Caregiver Stress: Signs to Watch for... Steps to Take
Alzheimer's Association
919 N Michigan Avenue
Suite 1200
Chicago, IL 60611-1694
312-335-8700
800-272-3900
Fax: 312-335-1110
e-mail: info@alz.org
http://www.alz.org

Gary Bieting, President

Learn to recognize the warning signs and discover techniques for reducing stress.

4992 Caregiving at Home
Alzheimer's Association
919 N Michigan Avenue
Suite 1000
Chicago, IL 60611-1696
312-335-8700
800-272-3900
Fax: 312-335-1110
e-mail: info@alz.org
http://www.alz.org

Gary Bieting, President

Suggestions for considering and planning home care for the person with dementia.

4993 Caring for Alzheimer's Patients
Perseus Books
233 Spring Street
New York, NY 10013-1522
212-368-0770
800-221-8002
Fax: 800-324-3791

Ross Carnegie, Owner

This handbook is designed for families, friends, and health-care professionals coping with the myriad of problems encountered by those afflicted with Alzheimer's disease.

308 pages

4994 Charitable Trusts
Alzheimer's Association
919 N Michigan Avenue
Suite 1000
Chicago, IL 60611-1696
312-335-8700
800-272-3900
Fax: 312-335-1110
e-mail: info@alz.org
http://www.alz.org

Gary Bieting, President

Explains the benefits of several types of charitable trusts, including Unitrusts, Charitable Remainder Annuity Trusts, and Charitable Lead Trusts.

4995 Drug Fact Sheets
Alzheimer's Association
919 N Michigan Avenue
Suite 1000
Chicago, IL 60611-1696
312-335-8700
800-272-3900
Fax: 312-335-1110
e-mail: info@alz.org
http://www.alz.org

Gary Bieting, President

Concerns experimental drugs currently being tested.

4996 Especially for the Alzheimer Caregiver
Alzheimer's Association
919 N Michigan Avenue
Suite 1000
Chicago, IL 60611-1696
312-335-8700
800-272-3900
Fax: 312-335-1110
e-mail: info@alz.org
http://www.alz.org

Gary Bieting, President

Offers suggestions for the Alzheimer caregiver on how to cope with caregiving.

4997 Ethical Considerations: Issues in Diagnostic Disclosure
Alzheimer's Association
919 N Michigan Avenue
Suite 1000
Chicago, IL 60611-1696
312-335-8700
800-272-3900
Fax: 312-335-1110
e-mail: info@alz.org
http://www.alz.org

Gary Bieting, President

Discusses the individual's right to know the Alzheimer's diagnosis. Provides tips on disclosing the diagnosis and communicating with family members.

Alzheimer's Disease/Newsletters, Pamphlets

4998 Exploring Care Options for a Relative with Alzheimer's Disease
American Assn. of Homes & Services for the Aging
901 E Street NW
Suite 500
Washington, DC 20004-2037
202-661-5700
800-508-

Daniel Smith, Vice President

2 pages

4999 Family Guide for Alzheimer's Care in Residential Settings
Alzheimer's Association
919 N Michigan Avenue
Suite 1000
Chicago, IL 60611-1696
312-335-8700
800-272-3900
Fax: 312-335-1110
e-mail: info@alz.org
http://www.alz.org

Gary Bieting, President

This guide for families corresponds to Guidelines for Dignity which can be used as a companion resource. It provides 50 checkpoints for families to consider as they plan for long-term residential care for their Alzheimer/dementia patient. A checklist to use in evaluating residential settings is included.

40 pages

5000 Guidelines for Dignity
Alzheimer's Association
919 N Michigan Avenue
Suite 1000
Chicago, IL 60611-1696
312-335-8700
800-272-3900
Fax: 312-335-1110
e-mail: info@alz.org
http://www.alz.org

Gary Bieting, President

A resource for providers who are offerring Alzheimer/dementia care in residential settings. Eight goals target specific issues to be addressed and present practical ideas and advice.

40 pages

5001 Home Safety for the Alzheimer's Patient
Alzheimer's Disease Education & Referral Center
PO Box 8250
Silver Spring, MD 20907-8250
800-438-4380
Fax: 301-495-3334

Practical guide for those who provide in-home care to people with Alzheimer's disease or related disorders. Designed to improve home safety and identify problems and solutions to prevent increase accicents. Increases the patient's security and freedom.

32 pages

5002 If You Have Alzheimer's Disease: What You Should Know, What You Can Do
Alzheimer's Association
919 N Michigan Avenue
Suite 1000
Chicago, IL 60611-1696
312-335-8700
800-272-3900
Fax: 312-335-1110
e-mail: info@alz.org
http://www.alz.org

Gary Bieting, President

Guide for the person with Alzheimer's disease. Includes suggestions of things to do that will help the person cope.

5003 Is it Alzheimer's? Warning Signs You Should Know
Alzheimer's Association
919 N Michigan Avenue
Suite 1000
Chicago, IL 60611-1696
312-335-8700
800-272-3900
Fax: 312-335-1110
e-mail: info@alz.org
http://www.alz.org

Gary Bieting, President

Contains a list of symptoms and answers to the most frequently asked questions.

5004 Memory and Aging
Alzheimer's Association
919 N Michigan Avenue
Suite 1000
Chicago, IL 60611-1696
312-335-8700
800-272-3900
Fax: 312-335-1110
e-mail: info@alz.org
http://www.alz.org

Gary Bieting, President

Compares age-associated memory impairment with disease-caused memory impairment.

5005 National Public Policy Program to Conquer Alzheimer's Disease
Alzheimer's Association
919 N Michigan Avenue
Suite 1000
Chicago, IL 60611-1696
312-335-8700
800-272-3900
Fax: 312-335-1110
e-mail: info@alz.org
http://www.alz.org

Gary Bieting, President

Summary of the Association's public policy goals, objectives and policies.

12 pages

5006 Private Long-Term Care Insurance: To Buy or Not to Buy?
Alzheimer's Association
919 N Michigan Avenue
Suite 1000
Chicago, IL 60611-1696
773-298-9988
800-272-3900
Fax: 312-335-1110
e-mail: info@alz.org
http://www.alz.org

Chai Leung, Owner

Consumer guide to making decisions about purchasing a long-term care insurance policy, including affordability, key points to look for, and alternatives to long-term care insurance.

4 pages

5007 Respite Care Guide: How to Find What's Right for You
Alzheimer's Association
919 N Michigan Avenue
Suite 1000
Chicago, IL 60611-1696
312-335-8700
800-272-3900
Fax: 312-335-1110
e-mail: info@alz.org
http://www.alz.org

Gary Bieting, President

Designed to help caregivers and persons with dementia recognize the benefits of respite care as well as identify which respite care services will best meet their needs.

18 pages

Alzheimer's Disease/Newsletters, Pamphlets

5008 Ronald & Nancy Reagan Research Institute: To Treat and Prevent Alzheimer's Disease
Alzheimer's Association
919 N Michigan Avenue
Suite 1000
Chicago, IL 60611-1696
312-335-8700
800-272-3900
Fax: 312-335-1110
e-mail: info@alz.org
http://www.alz.org

Gary Bieting, President

Describes the goals of the Alzheimer's Association Ronald & Nancy Reagan Research Institute.

5009 Safe Return Brochure
Alzheimer's Association
919 N Michigan Avenue
Suite 1000
Chicago, IL 60611-1696
312-335-8700
800-272-3900
Fax: 312-335-1110
e-mail: info@alz.org
http://www.alz.org

Gary Bieting, Presidnet

General information on the Safe Return program. Includes the registration form.

5010 Standing By You: Family Support Groups
Alzheimer's Association
919 N Michigan Avenue
Suite 1000
Chicago, IL 60611-1696
312-335-8700
800-272-3900
Fax: 312-335-1110
e-mail: info@alz.org
http://www.alz.org

Gary Bieting, President

Explains how family members, particularly the caregiver of the person with Alzheimer's, can benefit from family support groups.

5011 Steps to Enhancing Communication
Alzheimer's Association
919 N Michigan Avenue
Suite 1000
Chicago, IL 60611-1696
312-335-8700
800-272-3900
Fax: 312-335-1110
e-mail: info@alz.org
http://www.alz.org

Gary Bieting, President

Offers caregivers techniques for improving their approach to listening to and communication with the individual with Alzheimer's disease.

12 pages

5012 Steps to Enhancing Your Home: Modifying the Environment
Alzheimer's Association
919 N Michigan Avenue
Suite 1000
Chicago, IL 60611-1696
312-335-8700
800-272-3900
Fax: 312-335-1110
e-mail: info@alz.org
http://www.alz.org

Gary Bieting, President

Offers caregivers tips for reducing accidents in the home and creating an environment that supports the changing needs of the individual with Alzheimer's disease.

12 pages

5013 Steps to Finding Home Health Care
Alzheimer's Association
919 N Michigan Avenue
Suite 1000
Chicago, IL 60611-1696
312-335-8700
800-272-3900
Fax: 312-335-1110
e-mail: info@alz.org
http://www.alz.org

Gary Bieting, President

Provides practical strategies for finding in-home care for the person with Alzheimer's disease.

15 pages

5014 Steps to Getting a Diagnosis: Finding Out if It's Alzheimer's Disease
Alzheimer's Association
919 N Michigan Avenue
Suite 1000
Chicago, IL 60611-1696
312-335-8700
800-272-3900
Fax: 312-335-1110
e-mail: info@alz.org
http://www.alz.org

Gary Bieting, President

Educates individuals and their families on the importance of seeking a diagnosis, and the various test completed to obtain an accurate diagnosis.

12 pages

5015 Steps to Planning Activities: Structuring the Day at Home
Alzheimer's Association
919 N Michigan Avenue
Suite 1000
Chicago, IL 60611-1696
312-335-8700
800-272-3900
Fax: 312-335-1110
e-mail: info@alz.org
http://www.alz.org

Gary Bieting, President

Guides the caregiver in planning meaningful activities for the person with Alzheimer's disease.

12 pages

5016 Steps to Understanding Challenging Behaviors
Alzheimer's Association
919 N Michigan Avenue
Suite 1000
Chicago, IL 60611-1696
312-335-8700
800-272-3900
Fax: 312-335-1110
e-mail: info@alz.org
http://www.alz.org

Gary Bieting, President

Offers caregivers ways to respond to the changing behaviors, including anxiety, agitation, and aggression that the individual with Alzheimer's disease is experiencing.

12 pages

5017 Steps to Understanding Legal Issues: Planning for the Future
Alzheimer's Association
919 N Michigan Avenue
Suite 1000
Chicago, IL 60611-1696
312-335-8700
800-272-3900
Fax: 312-335-1110
e-mail: info@alz.org
http://www.alz.org

Gary Bieting, President

Provides information on legal issues such as legal capacity, powers of attorney, wills and living wills, and guardianship.

12 pages

Alzheimer's Disease/Videos, Audio Tapes

5018 Taxes and Alzheimer's Disease
Alzheimer's Association
919 N Michigan Avenue
Suite 1000
Chicago, IL 60611-1696
312-335-8700
800-272-3900
Fax: 312-335-1110
e-mail: info@alz.org
http://www.alz.org

Gary Bieting, President

A series of three consumer education brochures about tax issues that may affect people with Alzheimer's and their families. Address the household and dependent care credit, federal employment texes, and the itemized deduction for medical expenses. Also includes a preliminary explanation of the medical deduction for long-term care expenses clarified by the Kassebaum-Kennedy health insurance law.

5019 Terms & Tips: An Alzheimer Care Handbook
Alzheimer's Association
919 N Michigan Avenue
Suite 1000
Chicago, IL 60611-1696
312-335-8700
800-272-3900
Fax: 312-335-1110
e-mail: info@alz.org
http://www.alz.org

Gary Bieting, President

Offers an explanation for over 250 terms and offers practical caregiver ideas and tips. Primarily for people with dementia and their caregivers, family members, and all providers of hands-on assistance.

84 pages

5020 Time Out!
Alzheimer's Association
919 N Michigan Avenue
Suite 1000
Chicago, IL 60611-1696
312-335-8700
800-272-3900
Fax: 312-335-1110
e-mail: info@alz.org
http://www.alz.org

Gary Bieting, President

Details the Association's position supporting a national respite care policy and recommends actions for federal and state policy makers.

14 pages

5021 Understanding Medicaid Long Term Care: A Primer for Alzheimer Advocates
Alzheimer's Association
919 N Michigan Avenue
Suite 1000
Chicago, IL 60611-1696
312-335-8700
800-272-3900
Fax: 312-335-1110
e-mail: info@alz.org
http://www.alz.org

Gary Bieting, President

Provides current information about the Medicaid program, including eligibility rules.

30 pages

5022 Wills and Bequests
Alzheimer's Association
919 N Michigan Avenue
Suite 1000
Chicago, IL 60611-1696
773-651-1369
800-272-3900
Fax: 312-335-1110
e-mail: info@alz.org
http://www.alz.org

Bill Walls, Owner

How to make a bequest to fight Alzheimer's disease through a will.

5023 World Without Alzheimer's: A Dream Within Reach
Alzheimer's Association
919 N Michigan Avenue
Suite 1000
Chicago, IL 60611-1696
312-335-8700
800-272-3900
Fax: 312-335-1110
e-mail: info@alz.org
http://www.alz.org

Gary Bieting, President

Covers the major trends and promising developments in conquering Alzheimer's disease.

10 pages

5024 You Can Make a Difference: 10 Ways to Help an Alzheimer Family
Alzheimer's Association
919 N Michigan Avenue
Suite 1000
Chicago, IL 60611-1696
773-777-4567
800-272-3900
Fax: 312-335-1110
e-mail: info@alz.org
http://www.alz.org

Kwang Yoo, Owner

Information specifically for friends, explaining how Alzheimer's disease affects the entire family and suggesting practical ways to assist.

Videos, Audio Tapes

5025 A Thousand Tomorrows
Fanlight Productions
4196 Washington Street
Suite 2
Boston, MA 02131-1731
800-937-4113
Fax: 617-469-3379
e-mail: fanlight@fanlight.com
http://www.fanlight.com

Spouses of people with Alzheimer's talk candidly about the impact of the illness on intimacy and sexuality. 30-minute video.

5026 Agitation... It's a Sign
Fanlight Productions
4196 Washington Street
Suite 2
Boston, MA 02131-1731
800-937-4113
Fax: 617-469-3379
e-mail: fanlight@fanlight.com
http://www.fanlight.com

A variety of caregivers share their experiences and thoughts on providing for residents with Alzheimer's while providing vivid examples of the techniques and concepts that have worked in their facilities. 14-minute videotape.

5027 Alzheimer's Disease
Fanlight Productions
4196 Washington Street
Suite 2
Boston, MA 02131-1731
800-937-4113
Fax: 617-469-3379
e-mail: fanlight@fanlight.com
http://www.fanlight.com

Dartmouth Hitchcock Medical, Center

From 'The Dr. Is In' series. The stories of three families offer caregivers thechance to share experiences and learn practical strategies for keeping people with Alzheimer's engaged in life. 29-minute videotape.

Alzheimer's Disease/Websites

5028 Alzheimer's Disease: an Educational Training Program for Social Workers
Alzheimer's Disease Education & Referral Center
PO Box 8250
Silver Spring, MD 20907-8250
800-438-4380
Fax: 301-495-3334
For training social workers who are not familiar working with Alzheimer's patients and families. Four videotapes and one manual. Produced by the University of Pittsburgh.

5029 Another Home for Mom
Fanlight Productions
4196 Washington Street
Suite 2
Boston, MA 02131-1731
800-937-4113
Fax: 617-469-3379
e-mail: fanlight@fanlight.com
http://www.fanlight.com
A couple confront the difficult decision of whether to place the husband's mother, who has Alzheimer's Disease, in a nursing home. 28-minute video.

5030 Caring... Sharing: The Alzheimer's Caregiver
Fanlight Productions
4196 Washington Street
Suite 2
Boston, MA 02131-1731
800-937-4113
Fax: 617-469-3379
e-mail: fanlight@fanlight.com
http://www.fanlight.com
Explores the frustrations, fears, loneliness, anger and guilt - as well as moment of joy - experienced by those who care for lvoed ones with Alzheimer's Disease. 38-minute video

5031 In and Out of Time
Fanlight Productions
4196 Washington Street
Suite 2
Boston, MA 02131-1731
800-937-4113
Fax: 617-469-3379
e-mail: fanlight@fanlight.com
http://www.fanlight.com
A tender personal chronicle of the filmmaker's grandmother's loss of memory due to Alzheimer's disease. 14-minute video.

5032 Memories of Love: Caring for the Caregiver
Alzheimer's Disease Education & Referral Center
PO Box 8250
Silver Spring, MD 20907-8250
800-438-4380
Fax: 301-495-3334
Produced by the University of Pittsburgh, this video features African-American members of a lay support group sharing personal perspectives of Alzheimer's and coping strategies.

5033 Resisting Care... Putting Yourself in Their Shoes
Fanlight Productions
4196 Washington Street
Suite 2
Boston, MA 02131-1731
800-937-4113
Fax: 617-469-3379
e-mail: fanlight@fanlight.com
http://www.fanlight.com

Assisted Living Federation of, America

A variety of caregivers share their experiences and thoughtso n providing for residents with Alzheimer's while providing vivid examples of the techniques and concepts that have worked in their facilities. 14-minute video.

5034 Something Should be Done About Grandma Ruthie
Fanlight Productions
4196 Washington Street
Suite 2
Boston, MA 02131-1731
800-937-4113
Fax: 617-469-3379
e-mail: fanlight@fanlight.com
http://www.fanlight.com
A moving and unsettling portrait of the filmmaker's family as they struggle to deal with her grandmother's deteriorating mental condition. 54-minute video.

5035 Speaking for Them: Identifying Psychiatric Complications in Alzheimer's Patients
Alzheimer's Disease Education & Referral Center
PO Box 8250
Silver Spring, MD 20907-8250
800-438-4380
Fax: 301-495-3334
Shows nursing staff in long-term care facilities to differentiate and describe psychiatric complications of Alzheimer's disease. Includes one video and syllabus. Produced by the University of California.

5036 Wandering: It Is a Problem?
Fanlight Productions
4196 Washington Street
Suite 2
Boston, MA 02131-1731
800-937-4113
Fax: 617-469-3379
e-mail: fanlight@fanlight.com
http://www.fanlight.com

Assisted Living Federation of, America

A variety of caretivers share their experiences and thoughts on providing for residents with Alzheimer's while providing vivid examples of the techniques and concepts that have worked in their facilities. 14-minute video.

5037 Waves of Stone
Alzheimer's Association
919 N Michigan Avenue
Suite 1000
Chicago, IL 60611-1696
312-335-8700
800-272-3900
Fax: 312-335-1110
e-mail: info@alz.org
http://www.alz.org

Gary Bieting, President

PBS documentary on Alzheimer's disease that discusses both scientific research and caregiver issues.
Frequency: 56 minutes

Websites

5038 Alzheimer Research Forum
http://www.alzforum.org
Dedicated to understanding Alzheimer's disease and related disorders.

5039 Alzheimer Support
http://www.alzheimersupport.com
Serves Alzheimer's sufferers and their loved ones by reporting the latest news in research and treatment, making hard-to-find, recommended nutritional supplements available at manufacturer-direct low prices, and, most importantly, donating profits from each purchase to fund Alzheimer's medical research.

Alzheimer's Disease / Research Centers

5040 **Alzheimer's Association Hotline**

http://www.alz.org

A 24-hour telephone information line offering information on Alzheimer's and local chapters across the country to Alzheimer's patients, families and caregivers.

5041 **Alzheimer's Association, STAR Chapter**

http://www.alztexas.org

Chapter provides programs and services to the estimated millions of families who have a relative diagnosed with Alzheimer's or a related disease that causes irreversible dementia.

5042 **Alzheimer's Disease Center**

http://www.depts.washington.edu/adrcweb

Researchers work to translate advances into improved care and diagnosis for Alzheimer's patients.

5043 **Alzheimer's Disease International**

http://www.alz.co.uk

We aim to help establish and strengthen Alzheimer associations throughout the world, and to raise global awareness about Alzheimer's disease and all other causes of dementia.

5044 **Alzheimer's Foundation of America**

http://www.alzfdn.org

5045 **American Academy of Neurology**

http://www.aan.com

Professional society of medical doctors specializing in brain and nervous system diseases. Maintains placement service. Sponsors research and educational programs. Compiles statistics. Publishes scientific journal.

5046 **American Board of Psychiatry and Neurology**

http://www.abpn.com

Physicians with specialized training in psychiatry, neurology, child neurology, child adolescent psychiatry, clinical neurophysiology, and geriatric psychiatry. Determines eligibility requirements, administers examinations, and certifies physicians.

5047 **American Health Assistance Foundation**

http://www.ahaf.org

Funds research programs for heart disease, glaucoma, and Alzheimer's disease. Provides financial assistance through Alzheimer's Family Relief Program. Public education materials on programs, brochures, and applications are provided. Hours: 9am to 5pm Monday-Friday.

5048 **Steps for Caregivers: Caring for Persons with Alzheimer's Disease**

http://www.alz.org

Provides guidance and support for caregivers of those with Alzheimer's.

Research Centers

5049 **Arthur M Fishberg Research Center in Neurobiology**
Mt. Sinai Medical Center
1 Gustave L Levy Place
New York, NY 10029-6500　　　212-241-5916
Fax: 212-996-9785

James L Roberts PhD, Co-Director
Steven Fishberger, MD

Studies and research done in neurobiological systems and the molecular biology of Alzheimer's disease, schizophrenia and growth factors.

5050 **Baylor College of Medicine Center for Allergy & Immunological Disorders**
1 Baylor Plaza
Houston, TX 77030-3498　　　713-798-6105
Fax: 713-770-1260
e-mail: wshearer@bcm.tmc.edu

William T Shearer MD, PhD, Director
Mark M Udden, MD

5051 **Center for Senility Studies: Alzheimer's Disease Treatment Research**
161 N Dithridge Street
Pittsburgh, PA 15213-2646　　　412-621-4132

Arthur C Walsh MD, President
Cathy Painter, Manager

Nonprofit organization dealing in research of Alzheimer's disease, senility and elderly/aging disorders.

5052 **Columbia University Alzheimer's Disease Research Center**
Department of Pathology
630 W 168th Street
New York, NY 10032-3725　　　212-305-6553
Fax: 212-365-4614
e-mail: MLS7@columbia.edu
http://www.156.111.205.100/Ahome.html

Michael L Shelanski, Director

Alzheimer's disease and elderly care. Serves as a resource for tissue, cells, and DNA from Alzheimer's disease and control patients. Areas of research include epidemiology, cell biology, molecular biology, and care-giving.

5053 **Duke University General Clinical Research Center**
Medical Center
PO Box 3854
Durham, NC 27710　　　919-477-9292
Fax: 252-684-5041
e-mail: marke001@mc.duke.edu
http://www.duke.edu/rankincru

Dr. M Louis Markert, Program Director
Michael Duke, Owner

Multidisciplinary, clinical research into the cause and prevention of human diseases such as Alzheimer's.

5054 **Georgetown University: International Center for Interdiciplinary Studies of Immunology**
3800 Reservoir Road NW
Washington, DC 20007-2113　　　202-687-8227
Fax: 202-784-3597
e-mail: bellantij@gunet.georgetown.edu

Joseph A Bellanti MD, Director

Studies of immunology and allergic disorders.

5055 **Gerontology Research Institute**
4940 Eastern Avenue
Baltimore, MD 21224-2735　　　410-558-8185

Dr. George Martin, Director

Nonprofit organization focusing on gerontology research including Alzheimer's disease studies.

Alzheimer's Disease/Research Centers

5056 Indiana University-Purdue University at Indianapolis: Center for Alzheimer's Disease & Related Neuropsychiatric Disorder
Cg 265
Indianapolis, IN 46202   317-274-4333
    http://www.indiana.edu/   rugs/ctrdir/cadrnd
Robby Smith, Manager

Alzheimer's Disease and related neuropsychiatric disorders characterized by memory loss and mood disorders in the elderly.

5057 Institute of the Neurosciences Research Program
Smith Hall Annex
1230 York Avenue
New York, NY 10021-6307   212-570-8975
                    Fax: 212-570-7628
Gerald M Edelman, Director

Nonprofit organization focusing on Alzheimer's and related disorders.

5058 Johns Hopkins University: Alzheimer's Disease Research Center
720 Rutland Avenue
Baltimore, MD 21205-2109   410-955-5000
                    Fax: 410-955-9777
        e-mail: adrc@welchlink.welch.jhu.edu
Dr. Donald L Price, Director
Lisa Bach, Manager

Alzheimer's disease, including basic and applied studies of symptoms and psychiatric problems.

5059 Massachusetts Alzheimer's Disease Research Center
15 Parkman Street
Suite 830
Boston, MA 02114-3117   617-726-1728
                    Fax: 617-726-7718
        e-mail: growdon@helix.mgh.edu
    http://www.neuro.www3mgh.harvard.edu/ADRC/main
John H Growdon MD, Director
Alireza Atri, MD

Coordinates research on Alzheimer's disease, including memory loss, dementia, neuropathology, neuropsychology, neurochemistry, and investigational drug studies. Projects focus on biochemical studies on the abnormal proteins that accumulate in the brains of Alzheimer's patients, possible genetic markers or familial traits, anatomical and neurotransmitter abnormalities, and clinical studies of behavior and neuropharmacology.

5060 Mount Sinai School of Medicine of City University of New York: Alzheimer's Disease Research Center
University of New York
1425 Madison Avenue
New York, NY 10029-6514   212-659-9268
                    Fax: 212-860-3945
        e-mail: kenneth.davis@mssm.edu
Dr. Kenneth L Davis, Chairman
Donnie Sauls, Manager

Etiology, diagnosis, and treatment of Alzheimer's disease and related dementias. Clinical studies include trials of new drugs and biological markers and longitudinal follow-up studies. An active autopsy network obtains brain material from Alzheimer patients.

5061 NHI Clinical Center
6100 Executive Boulevard
Suite 3C01
Bethesda, MD 20892   301-496-2563
                    Fax: 301-402-2984
                http://www.cc.nih.gov

Established in 1953 as the research hospital of the National Institutes of Health. Designed so that patient care facilities are close to research laboratories so new findings of basic and clinical scientists can be quickly applied to the treatment of patients. Upon referral by physicians or self-referral, qualifying patients are admitted to NIH clinical studies.

5062 Nathan Kline Institute for Psychiatric Research: Center for Alzheimer's Disease
140 Old Orangeburg Road
Orangeburg, NY 10962-1157   845-398-5595
                    Fax: 914-398-5422
            e-mail: nixon@nki.rfmh.org
Ralph Nixon PhD, Director
Leslie Citrome, MD

Molecular neuroscience and aging, including molecular neurobiology of proteases, signal transduction, neurodegenerative disease, protein/peptide analytical techniques, molecular genetics, vesicle biology, transgenic modeling.

5063 Ohio State University Neuroscience Program
333 W 10th Avenue
Columbus, OH 43210-1239   614-292-6192
                    Fax: 614-292-1544
Dr. James S King, Co-Director
Eileen Mehl, Manager

Specializes in brain disorders such as Alzheimer's disease.

5064 Rockefeller University: Zachary and Elizabeth M Fisher Center for Research on Alzheimer's Disease
1230 York Avenue
New York, NY 10021-6399   212-327-8000
        http://www.rockefeller.edu/graduate/cenzach
Prof. Paul Greengard, Director
Paul Nurse, President

Alzheimer's disease, including how brain cells process the amyloid precursor phosphoprotein (APP) leading to the production of b-amlyoid, a major component of the plaques that are a hallmark of Alzheimer's disease.

5065 Rush University Alzheimer's Disease Center
710 S Paulina Street
Chicago, IL 60612-3808   312-942-4463
                    Fax: 312-942-4154
            e-mail: jfox@nuro.rush.edu
                http://www.rush.edu
Dr. Jacob H Fox, Co-Director

Alzheimer's disease, including causes, treatment, and cure. Conducts clinical trials of new drug treatments and analyzes potential risk factors in the development of Alzheimer's disease.

5066 Sonoma County Alzheimers Task Force
PO Box 4900
Santa Rosa, CA 95402-4900   707-528-8712
                    Fax: 707-575-4910
Michele Osmon, Manager

Promotes research into the cause, treatment, and cure of Alzheimers disease.

5067 State University College at Plattsburgh: Biochemisrty/Biophysics Program
Plattsburgh, NY 12901   518-564-3159
Dr. Roger L Heintz, Chairman

Offers research services into genetic engineering relating to physiology and molecular aspects of Alzheimer's Disease.

5068 State University of New York at Stony Brook: Cognitive and Behavioral Neuroscience
Nicholis Road
Stony Brook, NY 11794-2575   631-420-1530
                    Fax: 516-632-9487
Mary Ann Short, Department Administrator

Alzheimer's disease research.
    1993

Alzheimer's Disease/Research Centers

5069 Sun Health Research Institute: Alzheimers Center
PO Box 1278
Sun City, AZ 85372-1278 623-876-5328
Fax: 623-876-5461
http://www.sunhealth.org
Dr Joseph Rogers, President

Alzheimer's disease, Parkinson's disease, rheumatoid arthritis, and other age-related diseases. Research focuses on molecular genetics molecular/cell biology, protein chemistry, and immunology of degenerative disorders affecting the elderly.

5070 University of California, Los AngelesAlzheimer's Disease Center
710 Westwood Plaza
Los Angeles, CA 90095-8353 310-825-7692
Fax: 310-206-5287
e-mail: jcummings@mednet.ucla.edu
http://www.neurology.medsch.ucla.edu
Dr. Jeffrey L Cummings, Director
Edward Wiessmeir, MD

Diagnosis, pathophysiology, and treatment of dementing illnesses such as Alzheimer's disease.

5071 University of California: San Diego Alzheimer's Disease Research Center
9500 Gilman Drive
La Jolla, CA 92093-5004 858-534-8805
Fax: 619-622-1017
e-mail: lthal@ucsd.edu
Gerry R Boss, MD

Longitudinal research on the clinical and cognitive changes associated with Alzheimer's disease and other dementing illnesses by obtaining epidemiological data, medical histories, analysis of blood and sera, administration of batteries of neuropsychological tests, and neurological examinations of patients. Performs clinical drug trials, research on electrophysiology and neuroimaging studies, evaluations of the effects of caregiving stress on thecaregivers, studies of memory and language dysfunction, and the possibility of a genetic or metabolic basis for Alzheimer's disease. Also conducts olfaction studies.

5072 University of Chicago: Brain Research Institute
Department of Neurology
5841 S Maryland Avenue
Chicago, IL 60637-1447 773-702-1865
Barry GW Arnason MD, Director
Sue Curtis, Manager

Studies brain disorders including Alzheimer's disease.

5073 University of Iowa: Alzheimer's Disease Research Center
College of Medicine
200 Hawkins Drive
Iowa City, IA 52242-1009 319-356-4296
800-854-4461
Fax: 319-356-4505
e-mail: antoniodamasio@uiowa.edu
Antoniogory Damasio, Director

Alzheimer's disease and related conditions. Departments with participating specialists include anatomy, radiology, pathology, ophthalmology, psychology.

5074 University of Kentucky: Alzheimer's Disease Research Center
800 S Limestone
Lexington, KY 40536 859-323-6042
Fax: 859-323-2866
e-mail: wmarkesbery@aging.coa.uky.edu
http://www.coa.uky.edu
William R Markesberg MD, Director

Alzheimer's disease, focusing on the cause, treatment, and eventual cure.

5075 University of Miami: Center for Neurological Diseases
1501 NW 9th Avenue
Miami, FL 33136-1407 305-547-6946
Noble David MD, Vice Chairperson

Focuses on aged disorders such as Alzheimer's research.

5076 University of Michigan: Alzheimer's Disease Research Center
Department of Neurology
PO Box 489
Ann Arbor, MI 48106 734-764-2190
Fax: 734-936-8967
e-mail: sgilman@umich.edu
http://www.med.umich.edu/madrc/madrc
Sid Gilman MD, Chairman

Alzheimer's disease and other neurodegenerative diseases associated with dementia, including Parkinson's disease, multiple system atrophy, progressive supranuclear palsy, and olivopontocerebellar atrophy. Studies involve positron emission tomography (PET) scanning of patients with neurological disorders, neuropathological studies of patients with neurodegenerative illnesses, animal models, and a statewide public opinion survey on Alzheimer's disease.

5077 University of Texas Southwestern Medical Center at Dallas: Alzheimer's Disease Center
Department of Psychiatry
5323 Harry Hines Boulevard
Dallas, TX 75390-8898 214-648-3067
Fax: 214-648-2450
e-mail: mcullu@mednet.swmed.edu
Dr Munro Cullum, Director
Patricia Bergen, MD

Alzheimer's diseaese and aging in the brain, focusing on loss of cognitive functions and test measurements including IQ, problem solving, abstract thinking, spatial and dexterity skills, attention and concentration, language function, and memory.

5078 University of Washington: Alzheimer's Disease Research Center
4225 Roosevelt Way NE
Suite 301
Seattle, WA 98105-6099 206-764-2069
http://www.depts.washington.edu/adrcweb/
Marie Walters, Administration

Basic mechanisms underlying the development of adult dementing disorders, with particular attention to heritable susceptibility factors underlying Alzheimer's disease.

5079 Winifred Masterson Burke Medical Research Institute
Cornell University
785 Mamaroneck Avenue
White Plains, NY 10605-2523 914-597-2332
Fax: 914-946-1722
e-mail: jpblass@mail.med.cosnell.edu

Clinical and basic studies in metabolic and nutritional aspects of degenerative diseases of the nervous system, especially Alzheimer's disease.

5080 Yeshiva University: Resnick Gerontology Center
Albert Einstein College of Medicine
1300 Morris Park Avenue
Bronx, NY 10461-1900 718-430-2000
Fax: 718-430-3870
Dr. Miriam Aronson, Director

Alzheimer's disease and other dementia studies.

Arthritis/Associations & Organizations

Associations & Organizations

5081 Alabama Chapter of the Arthritis Foundation
Alabama Chapter Office
2700 Hwy 280 E
Ste. 180
Birmingham, AL 35223
205-979-5700
800-879-7896
Fax: 205-979-4172
e-mail: info.al@arthritis.org
http://www.arthritis.org

Jan Bell, President
Jim Toomey, Vice President and Business Oper

Founded in 1948, this chapter affects thousands of lives through programs, services, information and referrals, public and professional education and more for residents of Alabama. Research is a great priority of the chapter which supports the advancements that are made by local researchers at the University of Alabama at Birmingham. In addition to research, the Alabama Chapter seeks to improve the quality of life for those affected by arthritiis.

5082 American Orthopaedic Association
6300 N River Road
Suite 505
Rosemont, IL 60018
847-318-7330
Fax: 847-318-7339
e-mail: info@aoassn.org
http://www.aoassn.org

Thomas E Stautzenbach, Executive Director
Peter J. Stern, President

Professional society of bone and joint surgeons. Seeks to further knowledge in the diagnosis and treatment of crippling diseases.

5083 Arkansas Chapter of the Arthritis Foundation
6213 Father Tribou St.
Little Rock, AR 72205-3002
501-664-7242
800-482-8858
Fax: 501-664-6588
e-mail: info.ar@arthritis.org
http://www.arthritis.org

Drew Ramey, Director of Development
Tracey Meyer Chesser, President

5084 Arthritis Consulting Services
2787 East Oakland Park Blvd
Suite 204
Ft Lauderdale, FL 33306
954-739-3202
Fax: 954-337-2887
e-mail: acs@stoparthritis.com
http://www.stoparthritis.com

Donna Pinorsky RN, Administrator

Provides information on holistic approaches to the treatment of arthritis.

5085 Arthritis Foundation
PO Box 7669
Atlanta, GA 30357
404-872-7100
800-568-4045
Fax: 404-872-0457
http://www.arthritis.org

John H Klippel, CEO

A nonprofit organization that depends on volunteers to provide services to help people with arthritis. Supports research to find ways to cure and prevent arthritis and provides services to improve the quality of life for those affected by arthritis. Provides help through information, referrals, speakers bureaus, forums, self-help courses, and various support groups and programs nationwide.

5086 Arthritis Foundation Information Line
2970 Peachtree Road NW
Suite 200
Atlanta, GA 30305
404-237-8771
800-283-7800
Fax: 404-872-0457
e-mail: info.ga@arthritis.org
http://www.arthritis.org

John H Klippel, CEO

Answers general questions on arthritis and services of the foundation; provides physician referrals and addresses of local chapters. Bimonthly magazine for sale; free brochures and literature available. Hours: 9:00 a.m. to 7:00p.m. Monday-Friday.

5087 Arthritis Foundation Mississippi Chapter
401 Fontaine Place
Suite 102
Ridgeland, MS 39157
601-206-7726
800-844-8400
Fax: 601-206-8868
e-mail: wmcbride@arthritis.org
http://www.arthritis.org

Peggy Wall, President
Barry McBride, Director of Community Developmen

Over 6,800 Mississippians volunteer their services to help the chapter with fund raising and program support. Programs include land and water based exercise classes, and support groups, direct assistance to needy individuals to purchase arthritis medications and special equipment.

5088 Arthritis Foundation Mississippi Gulf Coast Chapter
4387 Leisure Time Drive
Diamondhead, MS 39525
228-586-1351
800-844-8400
Fax: 228-586-1358
http://www.arthritis.org

TJ McSparrin, President

Over 6,800 Mississippians volunteer their services to help the chapter with fund raising and program support. Programs include land and water based exercise classes, and support groups, direct assistance to needy individuals to purchase arthritis medications and special equipment.

5089 Arthritis Foundation North Central Chapter
1902 Minnehaha Avenue W
Saint Paul, MN 55104-1029
651-644-4108
800-333-1380
Fax: 651-644-4219
e-mail: info.mn.arthritis.org
http://www.arthritis.org

Deborah Sales Maysack, President/CEO
Deb Cassidy, Assistant to the President
Paulette Olsen, Director Development

Nonprofit organization providing programs and services North Dakota and South Dakota areas, to anyone affected by arthritis in the Minnesota area. Offers aquatic programs, support groups, juvenile arthritis support groups, research, grants program and information and referrals.

5090 Arthritis Foundation Oregon Chapter
9700 SW Capitol Highway
Suite 160
Portland, OR 97219
503-245-5695
800-283-3004
Fax: 503-245-5691
e-mail: tzuchl@arthritis.org
http://www.arthritis.org

Cindy Elliott, National Director
John H Klippel, CEO

Offers public education, information and referrals, self-help courses, exercise programs, fund raising activities and more for the residents of Oregon and Clark County, Washington, that are managing with arthritis.

Arthritis/Associations & Organizations

5091 Arthritis Foundation, SouthernCalifornia Chapter
4311 Wilshire Boulevard
Suite 530
Los Angeles, CA 90010
323-954-5750
800-954-CURE
Fax: 323-954-5790
e-mail: info.sca@arthritis.org
http://www.arthritis.org
Manuel Loya, President
Carolyn Adams, Vice President, Patient and Comm

5092 Arthritis Foundation: Pool Exercise Program
PO Box 1327
Fortson, GA 30023-6996
770-442-8633
800-207-8633
Fax: 770-442-9742
e-mail: julie.katz@pbd.com
http://www.arthritis.org
John H. Klippel, M.D, President and Chief Executive Di
L. Brunson White, Vice President and Chief Informa

This video features water exercises that will help you increase and maintain joint flexibility, strengthen and tone muscles, and increase endurance. All exercises are performed in water at chest level. No swimming skills are necessary.

5093 Arthritis Health Professionals Association
60 Executive Park S
Suite 150
Atlanta, GA 30329
404-633-3777
Fax: 404-633-1870
http://www.rheumatology.org
David Haag, Executive Director
Mark Andrejeski, EVP

Nurses, occupational and physical therapists, social workers, psychologists, vocational counselors, physicians, pharmacists, and other health professionals concerned with the practice, education, and research of rheumatic diseases. Seeks to establish a scientific base of knowledge to improve the quality and provision of health services to individuals with rheumatic diseases. Disseminates information regarding the study and treatment of rheumaticdiseases. Develops and implements medical and scientific programs in the field of rheumatology. A section of the Arthritis Foundation.

5094 Carolinas Chapter of the Arthritis Foundatiob
4530 Park Road
Suite 230
Charlotte, NC 28209
704-529-5166
800-883-8806
Fax: 704-529-0626
e-mail: info.car@arthritis.org
http://www.arthritis.org
Cassie Umberger, Community Development Coordinato
Gail Norman, President

5095 Central New York Chapter of the Arthritis Foundation
5858 E Molloy Road
Suite 123
Syracuse, NY 13211
315-455-8553
Fax: 315-455-8714
e-mail: info.cny@arthritis.org
http://http://arthritisinsight.com/resources/or
Linda B Coddington, President
Sharon Conklin, Manager

5096 Central Ohio Chapter of the Arthritis Foundation
3740 Ridge Mill Drive
Hilliard, OH 43026
614-876-8200
Fax: 614-876-8363
e-mail: info.coh@arthritis.org
http://www.arthritis.org
Irene Baird, President
Linda Reynolds, Director of Programs and Service

Offers information and referral services, self-help courses, aquatics program, equipment loans, clinics, home assessment and continuing education to help more than 300,000 people in Central Ohio, including over 5,000 children affected with the 100 types of arthritis.

5097 Central Pennsylvania Chapter of the Arthritis Foundation
3544 North Progress Avenue
Suite 204
Harrisburg, PA 17110
717-763-0900
Fax: 717-763-0903
e-mail: info.cpa@arthritis.org
http://www.arthritis.org
Joan McCabe, Community Development Administra
Kelly Kulp, Senior Community Development Dir

Serves 28 counties in the central Pennsylvania area. More than 441,233 persons in the chapter area are affected with one of the forms of arthritis seriously enough to require medical care. The chapter offers research services, professional education and training, parent and community services and public health education.

5098 Chapter of the Arthritis Foundation: Greater Southwest
1313 E. Osborn Road
Ste. 200
Phoenix, AZ 85014-2831
602-264-7679
800-477-7679
Fax: 602-264-0563
e-mail: info.caz@arthritis.org
http://www.arthritis.org
Donald Goldman, Chairman
John H. Klippel, President and Chief Executive Of

A nonprofit health agency serving the needs of Arizona, New Mexico and El Paso residents with arthritis. This chapter provides arthritis self-help courses, aquatic programs, a juvenile arthritis parent group, exercise programs and informational brochures.

5099 Delaware Chapter of the Arthritis Foundation
1019 S. Governor's Avenue
Suite 1105
Dover, DE 19904
302-730-9000
800-292-9599
Fax: 302-777-1841
e-mail: info.de@arthritis.org
http://www.arthritis.org/communities/chapters/
John A. Gilpin, Chairman
John H Klippel, MD, President and Chief Executive Of

Offers services to residents in Delaware who are affected by arthritis and related diseases. Also raises funds for research toward the national effort to seek a cure.

5100 Eastern Missouri Chapter of the Arthritis Foundation
9433 Olive Boulevard
Suite 100
Saint Louis, MO 63132
314-991-9333
Fax: 314-991-4020
e-mail: info.emo@arthritis.org
http://www.arthritis.org
Linda Sherwin, President
Ann Mangelsdorf, Director of Services

5101 Georgia Chapter of the Arthritis Foundaton
2970 Peachtree Road NW
Suite 200
Atlanta, GA 30305
404-237-8771
Fax: 404-872-9559
e-mail: info.ga@arthritis.org
http://www.arthritis.org
John H Klippel, CEO
L. Brunson White, Chair

Offers people with arthritis and their families information and support, as well as activities designed to help manage the disease, improve daily functioning and lead to independence.

Arthritis/Associations & Organizations

5102 Greater Chicago Chapter of the Arthritis Foundation
29 East Madison
Suite 500
Chicago, IL 60602
312-372-2080
Fax: 773-616-9281
e-mail: info.gc@arthritis.org
http://www.arthritis.org
Tom File, President
Michele Pfeilschifter, Vice President of Health Promoti

Offers self-help courses, wellness workshops, educational seminars, aquatic programs, brochures and publications for persons with arthritis in the state of Illinois.

5103 Greater Illinois Chapter of the Arthritis Foundation
2621 N Knoxville Avenue
Peoria, IL 61604
309-682-6600
Fax: 309-682-6732
e-mail: greaterillinois@arthritis.org
http://www.arthritis.org
Gary M Dutro, President
Vickie Fogel, Contact

5104 Greater Kansas City Chapter of the Arthritis Foundation
1900 West 75th Street
Suite 200
Prairie Village, KS 66208
913-262-2233
Fax: 913-262-2288
e-mail: info.wmo@arthritis.org
http://www.arthritis.org
Brad Ziegler, President
Sherri Hayes, Director of Operations

The only organization in the area representing the National Office in support of its international research program and in providing services throughout the bi-state area. Offers a wide range of services and programs to deal with the needs of persons with arthritis and their family members such as speakers bureaus, aquatic programs, self-help courses, physician referrals and the American Juvenile Arthritis Organization.

5105 Gulfcoast Branch: Florida Chapter of the Arthritis Foundation
263 13th Avenue South
Suite 210
St Petersburg, FL 33701
727-824-5301
Fax: 727-579-0628
http://http://sero.nmfs.noaa.gov
Roy E. Crabtree, Administrator
Frederick C. Sutter III, Deputy Regional Administrator

Dedicated to improving the quality of life for those in the seven county area of Pinellas, Pasco, Citrus, Levy, Hillsborough, Hernando and Polk, who have one or more of over 100 conditions that comprise the disease known as arthritis. Provides patient education and service programs to the community, funds vital research and offers up-to-date information about arthritis.

5106 Hawaii Chapter of the Arthritis Foundation
45-1144 Kamehameha Highway
Suite 500
Kaneohe, HI 96744
808-235-3636
Fax: 808-235-0120
http://www.arthritis.org
Carol Applebaum, President

5107 Hudson Valley Branch of the Arthritis Foundation
785 Mamaroneck Avenue
White Plains, NY 10605-2523
914-683-0842
Fax: 914-683-8462
e-mail: info.ntx@arthritis.org
http://www.arthritis.org
John H. Klippel, President and Chief Executive Of
Eric Dahler, Executive Director

5108 Indiana Chapter of the Arthritis Foundation
615 N. Alabama
Suite 430
Indianapolis, IN 46240
317-879-0321
Fax: 317-876-5608
e-mail: info.in@arthritis.org
http://www.arthritis.org
Edward Wills Jr., President
Denise Wagner, Director of Development

Offers programs and services for the arthritis community of Indiana.

5109 Indiana University: Multipurpose Arthritis Center
School of Medicine, Rheumatology Division
1110 West Michigan Street
Room 492
Indianapolis, IN 46202-5233
317-274-4225
Fax: 317-274-7792
http://http://research.iu.edu/centers/mamdc.htm
Dr. Kenneth Brandt, Contact
Deborah Jenkins, Manager

Integral unit of the Division of Rheumatology, this department researches the causes and treatment of arthritis. Offers programs for health care providers and promotes cost-efficient care methods through community demonstration projects.

5110 Iowa Chapter of the Arthritis Foundation
2600 72nd Street
Suite D
Des Moines, IA 50322
515-278-0636
Fax: 515-278-2603
e-mail: info.ia@arthritis.org
http://www.arthritis.org
Melissa Marchant, Senior Development Director
Doyle Monsma, President and Chief Executive Of

5111 James P Mills Arthritis Resource Center
Virginia Chapter of the Arthritis Foundation
565 Southlake Boulevard
Richmond, VA 23236-3076
804-378-6766
800-456-4687

Provides free information, services and counseling to the public. Services include assistance in locating and accessing government and other health care programs for persons with arthritis, referral to doctors specializing in the treatment of arthritis, free literature about the different types of arthritis and counseling for people with arthritis and their families.

5112 Kansas Chapter of the Arthritis Foundation
1999 N. Amidon Avenue
Suite 105
Wichita, KS 67203-2122
316-263-0116
800-362-1108
Fax: 316-263-3260
e-mail: info.ks@arthritis.org
http://www.arthritis.org
Dennis H. Bender, President
Patty Dick, Executive Director

Serves 103 counties and is governed by the Volunteer Board of Directors elected from throughout the state. Services offered include water exercise classes, arthritis clubs, children's summer camp, loan closet of hospital equipment and self-help aids, group education classes and planned giving seminars.

5113 Kentucky Chapter of the Arthritis Foundation
2908 Brownsboro Road
Suite 100
Louisville, KY 40206
502-585-1866
800-633-5335
Fax: 502-585-1657
e-mail: myoung@arthritis.org
http://www.arthritis.org
Tracy Jodrey, Vice President Development
Barbara Perez, President and Chief Executive Of

Active with ongoing support and exercise programs, educational programs, and special events for individuals with arthritis or a related disease, and others interested in finding out more about arthritis and helping to find a cure.

Arthritis/Associations & Organizations

5114 Kuzell Institute for Arthritis and Infectious Diseases
2200 Webster Street
Suite 305
San Francisco, CA 94115
415-561-1734
Fax: 415-441-8548
e-mail: luizb@cooper.cpmc.org
Lowell S Young, MD, Director

One of seven units comprising the Medical Research Institute of San Francisco that offers basic and applied research in arthritis and related diseases.

5115 Long Island Chapter of the Arthritis Foundation
501 Walt Whitman Road
Melville, NY 11747
631-427-8272
Fax: 516-427-3546
e-mail: info.li@arthritis.org
http://www.arthritis.org
Patrick T McAsey, President
Patricia Brasley, Executive Vice President

5116 Louisiana Chapter of the Arthritis Foundation
1330 W Peachtree St., NW,
Ste 100
Atlanta, GA 30309
404-965-7888
800-673-7508
Fax: 225-275-1172
e-mail: help@arthritis.org
http://www.arthritis.org
Debbie Goss, President

Develops funds for medical research programs, enhances public awareness of arthritis, and provides service programs for those with arthritis.

5117 M C P Hahnemann Orthopedic Institute
221 N Broad Street
1st Floor
Philadelphia, PA 19107
215-762-7300
Fax: 215-564-2825
Dr. Arnold Berman, Director
Susan Hoch, MD

5118 Maryland Chapter of the Arthritis Foundation
9505 Reisterstown Road
Suite 1 North
Owings Mills, MD 21117
410-654-6570
800-365-3811
Fax: 410-654-9270
e-mail: info.md@arthritis.org
http://www.arthritis.org
Jan Thompson, President
Sarah Karantonis, Development Director
Anna Hipsley, Information Specialist

This chapter supports research both locally and nationally to help find causes, better treatments and ways to prevent the many forms of arthritis. Offers various educational booklets and brochures, a physician referral service a speakers bureau, self-help courses land and water excersises and activities for children.

5119 Massachusetts Chapter of the Arthritis Foundation
29 Crafts Street
Suite 450
Newton, MA 02458-1287
617-244-1800
800-766-9449
Fax: 617-558-7686
e-mail: info.ma@arthritis.org
http://www.arthritis.org
Bill Turner, President and Chief Executive Di
Mary Halpin, Vice President of Development

Offers essential information, research programs and services for the close-to-one-million Massachusetts residents with arthritis.

5120 Metropolitan Washington Chapter of the Arthritis Foundation
2011 Pennsylvania Avenue
NW, 6th Floor
Washington, DC 2006
202-537-6800
Fax: 202-537-6859
e-mail: info.mwa@arthritis.org
http://www.arthritis.org/chapters/metropolitan-
Jack Klippel, President
Christina Thomas, Director of Community Developmen

5121 Michigan Chapter of the Arthritis Foundation
1050 Wilshire Drive
Suite 302
Troy, MI 48084-1564
248-649-2891
800-968-3030
Fax: 248-424-9005
e-mail: info.mi@arthritis.org
http://www.arthritis.org
Michelle RB Glazier, President and Chief Executive Di
Dawn Hafeli, Vice President, Programs

Offers information and referral services, catalog of publications, physician referral list, speakers bureau, public forums and more for the arthritis community of Michigan.

5122 Nebraska Chapter of the Arthritis Foundation
600 North 93rd Street
Suite 206
Omaha, NE 68114
402-330-6130
Fax: 402-330-6167
e-mail: mpuccioni@arthritis.org
http://www.arthritis.org
Marzia Pucci Shields, Executive Director
Julie Hancock, Business Manager

For close to 40 years the Arthritis Foundation has been the source for help and hope to the 253,000 Nebraskans and residents of Pottawattamie County, Iowa, with arthritis. Provides a wide variety of services designed to help people better cope with arthritis and live happier, fuller lives.

5123 New Jersey Chapter of the Arthritis Foundation
200 Middlesex Tpke
Iselin, NJ 8830
732-283-4300
Fax: 732-283-4633
e-mail: info.nj@arthritis.org
http://www.arthritis.org
Lorna Krkich, President
Peggy Lotkowicz, Vice President, Mission Delivery

Offers various programs for the residents of New Jersey including support groups, self-help courses, water exercise and arthritis fitness classes and informational public forums.

5124 New Mexico Chapter of the Arthritis Foundation
P.O. Box 30846
Albuquerque, NM 87190
505-867-7430
800-999-8022
Fax: 505-867-4418
e-mail: info.caz@arthritis.org
http://www.arthritis.org
Vikki Scarafiotti, President
Thomas Avery, Executive Vice President of Admi

Offers public education information, referrals, educational materials, chapter lending library, professional education resources and support groups for the residents of New Mexico.

5125 New York Chapter of the Arthritis Foundaion
122 E 42nd Street
Floor 18
New York, NY 10168-1898
212-984-8700
Fax: 212-878-5960
e-mail: info.ny@arthritis.org
http://www.arthritis.org
Michael Friedman, President
Joe Moore, Vice President for Development

Arthritis/Associations & Organizations

Offers land exercise programs, warm water resources and programs, self-help groups and courses, events and activities, video clinics, peer support and a lending library to arthritis sufferers in the New York area.

5126 North Texas Chapter of the Arthritis Foundation
4300 MacArthur,
Suite 245
Dallas, TX 75209-6524
214-826-4361
800-442-6653
Fax: 214-824-5842
e-mail: info.ntx@arthritis.org
http://www.arthritis.org

Karen Stern, President and Chief Executive Di
Kim Jessup, Executive Director

Aims to improve lives in Northern Texas through leadership in the prevention, control, and cure of arthritis and related diseases.

5127 Northeast California Chapter of the Arthritis Foundation
2560 E. Sunset Rd., #106
Suite 108
Las Vegas, NV 89120
702-367-1626
Fax: 702-364-6381
e-mail: edahler@arthritis.org
http://www.arthritis.org

Eric Dahler, Executive Director
Hollie Henderson, Community Development Director

Offers information and referral services, hotlines, resources, booklets, physician referral lists and more for the Nevada arthritis community.

5128 Northeastern Ohio Chapter of the Arthritis Foundation
Chagrin Plaza East
4630 Richmond Road
Suite 210
Cleveland, OH 44128
216-831-7000
800-245-2275
Fax: 216-360-4382
e-mail: info.neoh@arthritis.org
http://www.arthritis.org

John T. Petures, President
Mary Kudasick, Executive Vice President

5129 Northern California Chapter of the Arthritis Foundation
657 Mission Street
Suite 603
San Francisco, CA 94105-4120
415-356-1230
800-464-6240
e-mail: info.nca@arthritis.org
http://www.arthritis.org

PJ Handeland, President
Deborah Jackson, Vice President of Programs

Offers research into the causes of arthritis and more effective treatments; serves people in California with arthritis through information and referral services, exercise programs, self-help courses, education and other activities.

5130 Northern New England Chapter of the Arthritis Foundation
257 S UNION ST
Burlington, VT 05401-4513
802-656-4177
800-639-2113
Fax: 802-864-5339

Bruce Erwin, Director

Programs and services offered by this chapter include: information and referral brochures and lists of medical personnel specializing in arthritis in the area, a speakers bureau, arthritis self-help courses, aquatic and exercise programs and support groups.

5131 Northwestern Ohio Chapter of the Arthritis Foundation
309 N Reynolds Road
Suite F
Toledo, OH 43615
419-537-0888
Fax: 419-537-6553
e-mail: info.nwoh@arthritis.org
http://www.arthritis.org

John H Klippel, President and Chief Executive Di
L. Brunson White, Chair

5132 Ohio River Valley Chapter of the Arthritis Foundation
7124 Miami Avenue
Cincinnati, OH 45243
513-271-4545
Fax: 513-271-4703
e-mail: info.orv@arthritis.org
http://www.arthritis.org

Barbara Perez, President
Carol Campbell, Executive Coordinator

5133 Oklahoma Chapter of the Arthritis Foundation
3232 W. Britton Rd
Ste. 200
Oklahoma City, OK 73120
405-936-3366
Fax: 405-521-0070
e-mail: apadilla@arthritis.org
http://www.arthritis.org

Amy Padilla, Manager
Suzi Clowers, President

5134 Patient Services Resource Center
New York Chapter of the Arthritis Foundation
122 E 42nd Street
Floor 18
New York, NY 10168-1899
212-984-8700
Fax: 212-878-5960

Ross Alfieri, President

A special place for people with arthritis, their families and all those with an interest in the rheumatic diseases to come for information about how to live every day to its fullest, even when affected by a chronic disease.

5135 Rockland/Orange Unit of the Arthritis Foundation
122 East 42nd Street
18th Floor
New York, NY 10168-1898
212-984-8700
Fax: 845-429-9602
e-mail: info.ny@arthritis.com
http://www.arthritis.com

Michael Friedman, President
Ayana Woods, Program Manager

5136 Rocky Mountain Chapter of the Arthritis Foundation
2280 S Albion Street
Denver, CO 80222-4906
303-756-8622
800-475-6447
Fax: 303-759-0359
e-mail: info.rm@arthritis.org
http://www.arthritis.org

Pat Gottfried, President
Laura Campbe Rosseisen, V.P. Development

Serves Colorado and Wyoming and is dedicated to finding solutions to over 100 forms of arthritis which affect millions of people nationwide.

5137 San Diego Area Chapter of the Arthritis Foundation
9089 Clairemont Mesa Boulevard
Suite 104
San Diego, CA 92123-1288
858-492-1090
800-422-8885
Fax: 858-492-9248
e-mail: info.sd@arthritis.org
http://www.arthritis.org

Veronica Braun, President
David Schultz, Chairman

Arthritis/Books

Offers various programs and services including professional seminars, a speakers bureau, public forums, exercise classes, patient and family support groups, arthritis self-help courses and medical research to the residents of the San Diego area living with arthritis.

5138 Southern Arizona Chapter of the Arthritis Foundation
434 S. Williams Blvd.
Suite 200
Tucson, AZ 85711
520-917-7070
800-444-5426
Fax: 520-917-7099
e-mail: info.caz@arthritis.org
http://www.arthritis.org

Sandra Moomey, Director
Carol J Willson, President
Sandy Moomey, Manager

Offers information and referral hotlines, support groups, public forums, summer camps, speakers bureau, self-help courses, self-help devices, aquatics programs and a lending library for persons living with arthritis.

5139 Southern New England Chapter of the Arthritis Foundation
39 Narragansett Ave
Providence, RI 02907
401-467-8600
800-541-8350
Fax: 401-434-5779

Lori N DiPersio, President

Offers programs and services for persons in the Rhode Island area that are living with arthritis.

5140 Tennessee Chapter of the Arthritis Foundation
421 Great Circle Road
Suite 104
Nashville, TN 37228
615-254-6795
Fax: 615-320-7399
e-mail: info.tn@arthritis.org
http://www.arthritis.org

Len Smith, President
Jean Schmidt, Chair

This chapter serves the residents of Tennessee by offering research and fellowship grants, self-help courses, aquatics program, educational programs, pharmacy services, loan closet, information and referrals, public forums and seminars, support groups and a telethon for persons living with arthritis.

5141 Utah Chapter of the Arthritis Foundation
448 E 400 S
Suite 103
Salt Lake City, UT 84111
801-536-0990
Fax: 801-536-0991
e-mail: info.utid@arthritis.org
http://www.arthritis.org

Leslie Nelson, Program Director
Lisa B. Fall, President

A nonprofit organization serving the arthritis community in the state of Utah by providing invaluable services, programs and activities.

5142 Virginia Chapter of the Arthritis Foundation
3805 Cutshaw Avenue
Suite 200
Richmond, VA 23230
804-359-1700
800-456-4687
Fax: 804-359-4900
e-mail: info.va@arthritis.org
http://www.arthritis.org

C Annie Magnant, President
Judy Altman, VP Programs/Services

Serves as a source of health and hope to the over 1 million Virginians living with arthritis. Provides the opportunity to learn about self-care through services such as land and aquatic exercise programs. Committed to information and education services, community programs, research support and fundraising.

5143 Warren Grant Magnuson Clinical Center
6100 Executive Boulevard
Suite 3c01
Bethesda, MD 20892-7511
301-496-2563
Fax: 301-402-2984
e-mail: prpl@mail.cc.nih.gov
http://www.cc.nih.gov

John I. Gallin, Clinical Center Director
Maureen Gormley, Chief Operating Officer

Established in 1953 as the research hospital of the National Institutes of Health. Designed so that patient care facilities are close to research laboratories so new findings of basic and clinical scientists can be quickly applied to the treatment of patients. Upon referral by physicians, patients are admitted to NIH clinical studies.

5144 Washington State Chapter of the Arthritis Foundation
5701 Sixth Avenue South
Suite 213
Seattle, WA 98108
206-762-4313
Fax: 206-762-8328
e-mail: communications@asidwa.org
http://www.asidwa.org

Linda Coan, President
Loraine Rogers, Manager

Offers arthritis helplines and information lines for residents of Washington state. Provides self-help courses, arthritis aquatic programs and resources for persons living with various forms of arthritis.

5145 Wisconsin State Chapter of the ArthritisFoundation
1650 S 108th Street
West Allis, WI 53214-4021
414-321-3933
Fax: 414-321-0365
e-mail: info.wi@arthritis.org
http://www.arthritis.org

Karen Sawicki, Health Promotion Coordinator
Kim Wilbur, Administrator

Programs offered include aquatics and land exercise programs, self-help courses, professional public education and information and refferal.

Books

5146 250 Tips for Making Life with Arthritis Easier
Professional Book Distributing
PO Box 6996
Alpharetta, GA 30023-6996
770-442-8633
800-207-8633
Fax: 770-442-9742
e-mail: julie.katz@pbd.com
http://www.arthritis.org

Scott A Dockter, CEO

What do aerosol cooking spray and snow-shoveling have in common? Learn the answer to this question, and other clever and handy tips to make your life with-or without-arthritis easier. Plus learn about helpful serviced you didn't know were available through you bank, post office, phone company, grocery store, and other businesses you frequent.

88 pages

5147 Arthritic's Cookbook
Zebra Books
475 Park Avenue S
New York, NY 10016-6901
212-407-1500

Steven Zacharius, President

5148 Arthritis Helpbook: A Tested Self-Management Program for Coping
Addison-Wesley
Rr 128
Reading, MA 01867
781-944-3700
800-552-2259
Fax: 781-944-9338

Arthritis/Books

288 pages

5149 Arthritis Rx: A Cutting-Edge Program for a Pain-Free Life
American Book Company
11130 Kingston Pike
Suite 1-183
Knoxville, TN 37922
865-966-7454
Fax: 865-675-0557
http://www.americanbookco.com

Nutrition and other supplements for managing arthritis; The Arthritis RX diet, including an anti-inflammatory nutrition plan and a sample week of meals, recipes, and exercises; The Arthritis RX exercises: three step-by-step exercise series, ranging from a gentle motion regimen to a strenuous core body workout, all demonstrated through over 100 precise photographs.

5150 Arthritis Self-Help Book
Addison-Wesley
Rr 128
Reading, MA 01867
781-944-3700
800-552-2259
Fax: 781-944-9338

A useful and informative book used in conjunction with the Arthritis Foundation's Self-Help Course.

5151 Arthritis Sourcebook: Everything You Need to Know
Lowell House
220 Avenue of the Stars
Suite 300
Los Angeles, CA 90067
310-552-7555
800-323-
Fax: 310-552-7573

252 pages

5152 Arthritis and Common Sense
1230 Avenue of the Americas
New York, NY 10020
212-698-7000
Fax: 212-698-7099
http://www.simonsays.com

The arthritis sufferer will find a simple dietary plan that may help to alleviate the pains and symptoms of this disease, without the use of drugs of any kind.

5153 Arthritis, What Exercises Work: Breakthrough Even after Drugs & Surgery Have Failed
MacMillan
175 Fifth Avenue
New York, NY 10010
646-307-5151
http://us.macmillan.com

Arthritis/exercise therapy.

5154 Arthritis: A Comprehensive Guide
Addison-Wesley
Rr 128
Reading, MA 01867
781-944-3700
800-552-2259
Fax: 781-944-9338

Reviews types of arthritis, different aspects of treatment including exercise, medications, surgery, the role of diet and an extensive section on challenges of daily living.

5155 Arthritis: Taking Care of Yourself Health Guide for Understanding Your Arthritis
Addison-Wesley
Rr 128
Reading, MA 01867
781-944-3700
800-552-2259
Fax: 781-944-9338

5156 Away with Arthritis
Vantage Press
516 W 34th Street
6th Floor
New York, NY 10001-1311
212-736-1767
Fax: 212-736-2273

Martin Kleinwald, President

5157 Bone Up on Arthritis
Arthritis Foundation
PO Box 7669
Atlanta, GA 30357
404-872-7100
800-283-7800
Fax: 404-872-0457
http://www.arthritis.org

John H Klippel, CEO

A self-help education packet designed for home-study use, this program can improve your pain and function levels by teaching proven self-help techniques.

5158 Clinical Care in the Rheumatic Disease
Professional Book Distributing
PO Box 6996
Alpharetta, GA 30023-6996
770-442-8633
800-207-8633
Fax: 770-442-9742
e-mail: julie.katz@pbd.com
http://www.arthritis.org

Scott A Dockter, CEO

This book was written for all health professionals caring for people with rheumatic diseases and for students in these disciplines.

224 pages

5159 Exercise Beats Arthritis
Bull Publishing
PO Box 208
Palo Alto, CA 94302
650-322-2855
800-676-2855
Fax: 650-327-3300
e-mail: bullpublishing@msn.com
http://www.bullpub.com

Easy-to-follow program will help arthritis sufferers of all ages manage the problems of living with this condition. In depth look at minimizing the pain and limitations of arthritis, keep their joints mobile, increase muscle strength, strengthen bones and ligaments, perform daily tasks more easily.

144 pages

5160 In Control
Arthritis Foundation
PO Box 7669
Atlanta, GA 30357
404-872-7100
800-283-7800
Fax: 404-872-0457
http://www.arthritis.org

John H Klippel, CEO

An excellent at-home program which includes video, audio cassettes and the Arthritis Helpbook. Provides tools to help meet the challenges of arthritis.

5161 Living With Rheumatoid Arthritis
Johns Hopkins University Press
2715 N Charles Street
Baltimore, MD 21218-4319
410-516-6900
800-537-5487
Fax: 410-516-6998
http://www.jhu.edu/press/index.html

William Brody, President

This book offers practical and usable answers to the questions of everyday life. The authors provide clear explanations of the causes, diagnosis, and treatment of the disease, and why medication, joint protection, physical activity, and good nutrition are essential components of care.

280 pages

Arthritis/Directories

5162 Preventing & Reversing Arthritis Naturally
Bear & Company
One Park Street
Rochester, VT 05767
800-246-8648
Fax: 802-767-3726
e-mail: info@innertraditions.com
http://www.inntertraditions.com
A comprehensive self-help program designed to prevent and reverse degenerative inflammatory diseases without drugs and their unwelcome side effects.
272 pages 1995

5163 Toward Healthy Living - A Wellness Journal, Arthritis Foundation Distribution Center
Professional Book Distributing
PO Box 6996
Alpharetta, GA 30023-6996
770-442-8633
800-207-8633
Fax: 770-442-9742
e-mail: julie.katz@pbd.com
http://www.arthritis.org
Scott A Dockter, CEO

This spiral-bound journal has ample pages where you can unleash you thoughts, plus scales to monitor your mook and pain. Throught the book you will also find wisdom from a variety of famous and ordinary people - those who live with chronic ilness, and those whose life lessons can help you gain a more positive outlook on daily living.
144 pages

5164 Yoga for Arthritis: The Complete Guide
WW Norton & Company
500 Fifth Avenue
New York, NY 10110
212-354-5500
Fax: 212-869-0856
http://www.wwnorton.com
A comprehensive, user-friendly medical yoga program designed for management and prevention of arthritis, with over 400 illustrations..

Directories

5165 Aids for Arthritis
35 Wakefield Drive
Medford, NJ 08055-3204
609-654-6918
800-654-0707
Fax: 609-654-8631
http://www.aidsforarthritis.com
Offers hundreds of arthritis self-help devices at low costs. Shop on website or call for catalog.

5166 Maxi Aids
42 Executive Boulevard
Farmingdale, NY 11735-4710
631-752-0521
800-522-6294
Fax: 631-752-0689
e-mail: sales@maxiaids.com
http://www.maxiaids.com
Catalog of aids and appliances for the arthritic, visually impaired, hearing impaired, physically challenged, mature adult and for the needs of home health care.
131 pages

Journals, Magazines

5167 Arthritis Today
Arthritis Foundation
1330 W Peachtree Street NW
Atlanta, GA 30309-2922
404-872-7100
800-933-7800
Fax: 404-872-9559
John H Klippel, CEO

The authoritative and respected source of information for persons with arthritis, their families and health professionals who manage their care. As the official magazine of the Arthritis Foundation, it is backed by the Foundation's experience of 44 years and leadership in the fight against arthritis. This magazine gives its readers the advice, information and inspiration they need to live better with arthritis.

Newsletters, Pamphlets

5168 Alerter
San Diego Area Chapter of the Arthritis Foundation
9089 Clairemont Mesa Boulevard
Suite 300
San Diego, CA 92123-1225
858-492-1090
800-422-
Fax: 619-492-9248
Veronica Braun, President

Offers chapter updates, information on activities and events, resources and medical research for members.

5169 Ankylosing Spondylitis
Arthritis Foundation
PO Box 7669
Atlanta, GA 30357
404-872-7100
800-283-7800
Fax: 404-872-0457
http://www.arthritis.org
John H Klippel, CEO

5170 Arthritis Accent
Arthritis Foundation Southern N.E. Chapter
35 Cold Spring Road
Suite 411
Rocky Hill, CT 06067-3164
860-563-1177
800-541-8350
Fax: 860-563-6018
http://www.arthritis.org
Stephen Evangelista, President

Newsletter that contains information on chapter events and activities.

5171 Arthritis Answers: Basic Information About Arthritis
Arthritis Foundation
PO Box 7669
Atlanta, GA 30357
404-872-7100
800-283-7800
Fax: 404-872-0457
http://www.arthritis.org
John H Klippel, CEO

5172 Arthritis Arizona Southwest
Chapter - Arthritis Foundation Greater Southwest
777 E Missouri Avenue
Suite 119
Phoenix, AZ 85014-2831
602-264-7679
800-477-7679
Fax: 602-264-0563
e-mail: info.caz@arthritis.org
http://www.arthritis.org
Michele Gama, Editor
Vikki Scarafiotti, President

A chapter newsletter offering updated information and resources pertaining to persons affected by arthritis.

5173 Arthritis Foundation Services
Arthritis Foundation
PO Box 7669
Atlanta, GA 30357
404-872-7100
800-283-7800
Fax: 404-872-0457
http://www.arthritis.org
John H Klippel, CEO

Arthritis/Newsletters, Pamphlets

5174 Arthritis Information: Advocacy and Government Affairs
Arthritis Foundation
PO Box 7669
Atlanta, GA 30357
404-872-7100
800-283-7800
Fax: 404-872-0457
http://www.arthritis.org

John H Klippel, CEO

5175 Arthritis News
Wisconsin Chapter of the Arthritis Foundation
1650 S 108th Street
West Allis, WI 53214-4021
414-321-3933
Fax: 414-321-0365
http://www.arthritis.org

Maureen Blattner, Health Promotion Coordinator
Kim Wilbur, Administrator

Offers information on activities, events, medical research, information and referrals to persons living in the Wisconsin area that are afflicted with arthritis.

5176 Arthritis Observer
Rocky Mountain Chapter of the Arthritis Foundation
2280 S Albion Street
Denver, CO 80222-4906
303-756-8622
800-475-6447
Fax: 303-759-0359

James Goddard, President

Offers chapter information and updates on fund-raising events and activities, resources and publications and medical updates for the arthritis community.

5177 Arthritis Reporter
New York Chapter of the Arthritis Foundation
122 E 42nd Street
Floor 18
New York, NY 10168-1899
212-984-8700
Fax: 212-878-5960

Ross Alfieri, President

Chapter newsletter offering information on upcoming events, activities and groups for the arthritis community.

5178 Arthritis Update of Rhode Island
Southern NE Chapter of the Arthritis Foundation
37 N Blossom Street
East Providence, RI 02914-2728
401-434-5792
Fax: 401-434-5779

Offers information, activities, events and updates on the chapter.

5179 Arthritis Volunteer
Tennessee Chapter of the Arthritis Foundation
1719 W End Avenue
Suite 303w
Nashville, TN 37203-5123
615-320-7626
Fax: 615-329-3982

Keeps members up-to-date on arthritis developments and on programs, services and special events in Tennessee.

5180 Arthritis and Diet
NAMSIC, National Institutes of Health
1 Ams Circle
Bethesda, MD 20892
301-495-4484
Fax: 301-587-4352
http://www.nih.gov/niams/
TTY 301-565-2966

Kelly Collins, Manager

Offers information on nutrition and diet pertaining to the arthritis community.

16 pages

5181 Arthritis and Employment: You Can Get the Job You Want
Arthritis Foundation
PO Box 7669
Atlanta, GA 30357
404-872-7100
800-283-7800
Fax: 404-872-0457
http://www.arthritis.org

John H Klippel, CEO

5182 Arthritis and Inflammatory Bowel Disease
Arthritis Foundation
PO Box 7669
Atlanta, GA 30357
404-872-7100
800-283-7800
Fax: 404-872-0457
http://www.arthritis.org

John H Klippel, CEO

5183 Arthritis and Vocational Rehabilitation
Arthritis Foundation
PO Box 7669
Atlanta, GA 30357
404-872-7100
800-283-7800
Fax: 404-872-0457
http://www.arthritis.org

John H Klippel, CEO

5184 Arthritis on the Job: You Can Work With It
Arthritis Foundation
PO Box 7669
Atlanta, GA 30357
404-872-7100
800-283-7800
Fax: 404-872-0457
http://www.arthritis.org

John H Klippel, CEO

5185 Arthritis, Rheumatic Diseases and Related Disorders
Nat'l Arthritis/Skin Diseases Info. Clearinghouse
9000 Rockville Pike
Bethesda, MD 20892
301-495-4484
Fax: 301-587-4352

Kelly Collins, Manager

This pamphlet offers information, technical articles and research on arthritis and related disorders. Also included are referral organizations to help patients uncover more information.

5186 Arthritis: Do You Know?
Arthritis Foundation
PO Box 7669
Atlanta, GA 30357
404-872-7100
800-283-7800
Fax: 404-872-0457
http://www.arthritis.org

John H Klippel, CEO

A brief overview of arthritis and the services of the Arthritis Foundation.

5187 Aspirin and Other Nonsteroidal Anti-Inflammatory Drugs
Arthritis Foundation
PO Box 7669
Atlanta, GA 30357
404-872-7100
800-283-7800
Fax: 404-872-0457
http://www.arthritis.org

John H Klippel, CEO

5188 Back Pain
Arthritis Foundation
PO Box 7669
Atlanta, GA 30357
404-872-7100
800-283-7800
Fax: 404-872-0457
http://www.arthritis.org

John Klippel, CEO

Arthritis/Newsletters, Pamphlets

5189 Behcet's Disease
Arthritis Foundation
PO Box 7669
Atlanta, GA 30357
404-872-7100
800-283-7800
Fax: 404-872-0457
http://www.arthritis.org

John H Klippel, CEO

5190 Bursitis, Tendonitis and other Soft Tissue
Arthritis Foundation
PO Box 7669
Atlanta, GA 30357
404-872-7100
800-283-7800
Fax: 404-872-0457
http://www.arthritis.org

John H Klippel, CEO

5191 CPPD Crystal Deposition Disease
Arthritis Foundation
PO Box 7669
Atlanta, GA 30357
404-872-7100
800-283-7800
Fax: 404-872-0457
http://www.arthritis.org

John H Klippel, CEO

5192 Carpal Tunnel Syndrome
Arthritis Foundation
PO Box 7669
Atlanta, GA 30357
404-872-7100
800-283-7800
Fax: 404-872-0457
http://www.arthritis.org

John H Klippel, CEO

Offers an introduction to Carpal Tunnel, causes, symptoms, diagnosis and resources.

5193 Corticosteriod Medications
Arthritis Foundation
PO Box 7669
Atlanta, GA 30357
404-872-7100
800-283-7800
Fax: 404-872-0457
http://www.arthritis.org

John Klippel, CEO

5194 Diet and Arthritis
Arthritis Foundation
PO Box 7669
Atlanta, GA 30357
404-872-7100
800-283-7800
Fax: 404-872-0457
http://www.arthritis.org

John H Klippel, CEO

5195 Ehlers-Danlos Syndrome
Arthritis Foundation
PO Box 7669
Atlanta, GA 30357
404-872-7100
800-283-7800
Fax: 404-872-0457
http://www.arthritis.org

John H Klippel, CEO

5196 Exercise and Your Arthritis
Arthritis Foundation
PO Box 7669
Atlanta, GA 30357
404-872-7100
800-283-7800
Fax: 404-872-0457
http://www.arthritis.org

John H Klippel, CEO

Types of exercise for people with arthritis and how to do them.

5197 Factor Fax
NE California Chapter - Arthritis Foundation
3040 Explorer Drive
Suite 1
Sacramento, CA 95827-2729
916-368-5599
Fax: 916-368-5596
e-mail: info.neda@arthritis.org
http://www.arthritis.org

Mark Warren, President

Offers information on all of the chapter's activites, events and resources for the arthritis community of central California.

5198 Family
Arthritis Foundation
PO Box 7669
Atlanta, GA 30357
404-872-7100
800-283-7800
Fax: 404-872-0457
http://www.arthritis.org

John H Klippel, CEO

Effects of arthritis on family life and ways to cope.

5199 Family: Making the Difference
Arthritis Foundation
PO Box 7669
Atlanta, GA 30357
404-872-7100
800-283-7800
Fax: 404-872-0457
http://www.arthritis.org

John H Klippel, CEO

5200 Gold Treatment
Arthritis Foundation
PO Box 7669
Atlanta, GA 30357
404-872-7100
800-283-7800
Fax: 404-872-0457
http://www.arthritis.org

John H Klippel, CEO

5201 Gout
Arthritis Foundation
PO Box 7669
Atlanta, GA 30357
404-872-7100
800-283-7800
Fax: 404-872-0457
http://www.arthritis.org

John H Klippel, CEO

5202 Guide to Effective Volunteer Lobbying
Arthritis Foundation
PO Box 7669
Atlanta, GA 30357
404-872-7100
800-283-7800
Fax: 404-872-0457
http://www.arthritis.org

John H Klippel, CEO

5203 Health, Life and Disability Insurance for People with Arthritis
Arthritis Foundation
PO Box 7669
Atlanta, GA 30357
404-872-7100
800-283-7800
Fax: 404-872-0457
http://www.arthritis.org

John H Klippel, CEO

Information about these three types of insurance.

5204 Hydroxychloroquine
Arthritis Foundation
PO Box 7669
Atlanta, GA 30357
404-872-7100
800-283-7800
Fax: 404-872-0457
http://www.arthritis.org

John H Klippel, CEO

Arthritis/Newsletters, Pamphlets

5205 Living and Loving: Information About Sexuality and Intimacy
Arthritis Foundation
PO Box 7669
Atlanta, GA 30357
404-872-7100
800-283-7800
Fax: 404-872-0457
http://www.arthritis.org

John H Klippel, CEO

5206 Managing Your Activities
Arthritis Foundation
PO Box 7669
Atlanta, GA 30357
404-872-7100
800-283-7800
Fax: 404-872-0457
http://www.arthritis.org

John H Klippel, CEO

5207 Managing Your Fatigue
Arthritis Foundation
PO Box 7669
Atlanta, GA 30357
404-872-7100
800-283-7800
Fax: 404-872-0457
http://www.arthritis.org

John H Klippel, CEO

5208 Managing Your Health Care
Arthritis Foundation
PO Box 7669
Atlanta, GA 30357
404-872-7100
800-283-7800
Fax: 404-872-0457
http://www.arthritis.org

John H Klippel, CEO

5209 Managing Your Pain
Arthritis Foundation
PO Box 7669
Atlanta, GA 30357
404-872-7100
800-283-7800
Fax: 404-872-0457
http://www.arthritis.org

John H Klippel, CEO

5210 Managing Your Stress
Arthritis Foundation
PO Box 7669
Atlanta, GA 30357
404-872-7100
800-283-7800
Fax: 404-872-0457
http://www.arthritis.org

John H Klippel, CEO

5211 Methotrexate
Arthritis Foundation
PO Box 7669
Atlanta, GA 30357
404-872-7100
800-283-7800
Fax: 404-872-0457
http://www.arthritis.org

John Klippel, CEO

5212 Myositis
Arthritis Foundation
PO Box 7669
Atlanta, GA 30357
404-872-7100
800-283-7800
Fax: 404-872-0457
http://www.arthritis.org

John H Klippel, CEO

5213 Newsletter of the Central Pennsylvania Chapter
Arthritis Foundation
17 S 19th Street
Camp Hill, PA 17011-5459
717-763-0900
Fax: 717-763-0903

Cathrine Penrod, President

Offers information on activities and events of the Chapter.

5214 Newsletter of the Kansas Chapter of the Arthritis Foundation
1602 E Waterman Street
Wichita, KS 67211-1828
316-263-0116
Fax: 316-263-3260

Dennis Bender, President

Contains information on research, medications, different types of arthritis and features on outstanding volunteers.

5215 Osteoarthritis
Arthritis Foundation
PO Box 7669
Atlanta, GA 30357
404-872-7100
800-283-7800
Fax: 404-872-0457
http://www.arthritis.org

John H Klippel, CEO

Offers introductions, examples, explanations and research pertaining to this type of arthritis.

5216 Osteonecrosis
Arthritis Foundation
PO Box 7669
Atlanta, GA 30357
404-872-7100
800-283-7800
Fax: 404-872-0457
http://www.arthritis.org

John H Klippel, CEO

5217 Overcoming Rheumatoid Arthritis
Michigan Chapter of the Arthritis Foundation
23999 Northwestern Highway
210
Southfield, MI 48075-2528
810-350-3030

Provides extensive information about the disease and treatment, with an emphasis on what you can do for yourself.

5218 Penicillamine
Arthritis Foundation
PO Box 7669
Atlanta, GA 30357
404-872-7100
800-283-7800
Fax: 404-872-0457
http://www.arthritis.org

John H Klippel, CEO

5219 Polyarteritis Nodosa and Wegener's Granulomatosis
Arthritis Foundation
PO Box 7669
Atlanta, GA 30357
404-872-7100
800-283-7800
Fax: 404-872-0457
http://www.arthritis.org

John H Klippel, CEO

5220 Polymyalgia Rheumatica and Giant Cell Arthritis
Arthritis Foundation
PO Box 7669
Atlanta, GA 30357
404-872-7100
800-283-7800
Fax: 404-872-0457
http://www.arthritis.org

John H Klippel, CEO

5221 Pseudoxanthoma Elasticum Fact Sheet
Arthritis Foundation
PO Box 7669
Atlanta, GA 30357
404-872-7100
800-283-7800
Fax: 404-872-0457
http://www.arthritis.org

John H Klippel, CEO

Arthritis/Videos, Audio Tapes

5222 Psoriatic Arthritis
NAMSIC, National Institutes of Health
1 Ams Circle
Bethesda, MD 20892
301-495-4484
Fax: 301-587-4352
http://www.nih.gov/niams/
TTY 301-565-2966

Kelly Collins, Manager

5223 Raynaud's Phenomenon
Arthritis Foundation
PO Box 7669
Atlanta, GA 30357
404-872-7100
800-283-7800
Fax: 404-872-0457
http://www.arthritis.org

John Klippel, CEO

5224 Reflex Sympathetic Dystrophy Syndrome Fact Sheet
Arthritis Foundation
PO Box 7669
Atlanta, GA 30357
404-872-7100
800-283-7800
Fax: 404-872-0457
http://www.arthritis.org

John H Klippel, CEO

5225 Reiter's Syndrome
Arthritis Foundation
PO Box 7669
Atlanta, GA 30357
404-872-7100
800-283-7800
Fax: 404-872-0457
http://www.arthritis.org

John H Klippel, CEO

5226 Rheumatoid Arthritis
NAMSIC, National Institutes of Health
1 Ams Circle
Bethesda, MD 20892
301-495-4484
Fax: 301-587-4352
http://www.nih.gov/niams
TTY 301-565-2966

Kelly Collins, Manager

Offers an introduction and definition of Rheumatoid Arthritis, treatments, causes, objectives, daily living, resources and medical information.

5227 Southern Arizona Chapter of the Arthritis Foundation Newsletter
616 N Country Club Road
Tucson, AZ 85716-4543
520-917-7070
Fax: 520-917-7099

Richard M Brown EdD, CFRE, President
Sandy Moomey, Manager

Offers updated information and news on chapter activities and events for persons with arthritis.

5228 Spectrum
Michigan Chapter of the Arthritis Foundation
17117 W 9 Mile Road
Suite 950
Southfield, MI 48075-4602
248-424-9001

Anthony Zambraus, Owner

Promotes various activities and programs and provides current information about arthritis.

5229 Surgery: Information to Consider
Arthritis Foundation
PO Box 7669
Atlanta, GA 30357
404-872-7100
800-283-7800
Fax: 404-872-0457
http://www.arthritis.org

John H Klippel, CEO

5230 Volunteer Voice
Kentucky Chapter of the Arthritis Foundation
410 W Chestnut Street
Suite 750
Louisville, KY 40202-2368
800-633-5335

Newsletter offering information and updates on chapter activities, events, camps, juvenile programs and government/legislative information.

Videos, Audio Tapes

5231 Arthritis Foundation DistributionCenter: Pool Exercise Program
PO Box 6996
Alpharetta, GA 30023-6996
770-442-8633
800-207-8633
Fax: 770-442-9742
e-mail: julie.katz@pbd.com
http://www.arthritis.org

Scott A Dockter, CEO

This video features water exercises that will help you increase and maintain joint flexibility, strengthen and tone muscles, and increase endurance. All exercises are performed in water at chest level. No swimming skills are necessary.

5232 FIT Video
Arthritis Foundation
PO Box 6996
Alpharetta, GA 30023-6996
800-207-8633
Fax: 770-442-9742

Research Centers

5233 Arthritis, Musculoskeletal & Skin Diseases Research: Public Health Service
US Department of Health and Human Services
9000 Rockville Pike
Room 4c32
Bethesda, MD 20892
301-496-4000
800-422-6237

To extramurally support basic laboratory research and clinical investigations, and to provide post-doctoral biomedical research training for individuals interested in careers in health sciences and fields related to these programs.

5234 Boston University: Arthritis Center
Conte Building
5th Floor
Boston, MA 02118
617-638-8000
Fax: 617-534-3573

Dr. Joseph Korn MD, Director
Syed S Ahmed, MD

5235 Boston University: Robert Dawson Evans Memorial Department of Clinical Research
75 E Newton Street
Boston, MA 02118-2657
617-638-7250
Fax: 617-638-7931

Dr. Joseph Loscalzo, Director
Jack Ansel, MD

Integral unit of the University Hospital specializing in arthritis and connective tissue studies.

Arthritis/Research Centers

5236 **Brigham and Women's Hospital: Robert B Brigham Arthritis Center**
75 Francis Street
Boston, MA 02115-6106
617-732-6816
Fax: 617-732-5766
Dr. Matthew Liang, Director
Judith Kennedy, Manager

Research studies into arthritis and rheumatic diseases.

5237 **Bucknell University Immunobiology Research Laboratory**
Department of Biology
Lewisburg, PA 17837
570-577-3757
Dr. David Pearson, Director

Studies into autoimmune diseases, particularly the causes of rheumatoid arthritis.

5238 **Harrington Arthritis Research Center**
300 N 18th Street
Phoenix, AZ 85006-4103
602-254-0377
Fax: 602-253-4817
http://www.arde.com/arde
Robert Case, President

Research into the various areas of arthritis, including assistive devices, joint repair and replacement, medical treatment and early detection and prevention.

5239 **Medical University of South Carolina: Arthritis Clinical Research Center**
171 Ashley Avenue
Charleston, SC 29425
843-792-8999
Fax: 843-792-7121
E Carwile LeRoy, Director
Fred Crawford, Manager

Offers basic and clinical research on various types of arthritis.

5240 **Multipurpose Arthritis & Musculoskeletal Center**
The University of Alabama At
Birmingham, AL 35294
205-934-5306
Fax: 205-934-1564
http://www.info.dom.uab.edu/rheum/centers
Robert Kimberly MD, Director

Arthritis and related rheumatic disorders are studied.

5241 **Multipurpose Arthritis and Musculoskeletal Disease Center**
University of California, San Diego
9500 Gilman Drive
La Jolla, CA 92093-5004
858-552-7439
Fax: 858-534-5475
Dr. Dennis Carson, Co-Director

Causes and treatment of arthritis.

5242 **National Arthritis and Musculoskeletal and Skin Diseases Information Clearinghouse**
1 Ams Circle
Bethesda, MD 20892
301-495-4484
Fax: 301-587-4352
http://www.nih.gov/niams
Kelly Collins

Supports and provides clinical and public information and research to increase understanding of the many rheumatic diseases and related disorders. Also provides lists and order forms for their resources and materials.

5243 **National Institute of Arthritis and Musculoskeletal and Skin Disease**
1 Ams Circle
Bethesda, MD 20892
301-495-4484
800-422-6237
Fax: 301-718-6366
http://www.niams.nih.gov
Kelly Collins, Manager

The Institute is a public service that provides health information and information sources. Supports research into the causes, treatment and prevention of arthritis and musculokeletal and skin diseases, the training of basic and clinical scientists to carry out this research, and dissemination of information on research progress in these diseases. Provides health information and resources.

5244 **Northwestern University: Multipurpose Arhritis & Musculoskeletal Center**
303 E Chicago Avenue
Chicago, IL 60611-3072
312-503-8186
Fax: 312-503-0994
Dr. Richard Pope, Head Master
Lewis Landsberg, Administrator

Conducts biomedical, educational and health services research into musculoskeletal diseases.

5245 **Oklahoma Medical Research Foundation**
825 NE 13th Street
Oklahoma City, OK 73104-5097
405-271-6673
Fax: 405-271-3980
J Donald Capra MD, President

Focuses on arthritis and muscoloskeletal disease research.

5246 **Oklahoma Medical Research Foundation: Arthritis Immunology Research**
825 NE 13th Street
Oklahoma City, OK 73104-5097
405-271-6673
Fax: 405-271-3980
J Donald Capra, CEO

5247 **Pearlman Biomedical Research Institute**
Mt. Sinani Medical Center
4300 Alton Road
Miami Beach, FL 33140-2800
305-674-2121
Fax: 305-674-2198
Dr. William Abraham, Director
Steven D Sonenreich, CEO

Pulmonary medicine, arthritis, sleep disorders and gynecology departments of research.

5248 **Rehabilitation Institute of Chicago**
345 E Superior Street
Chicago, IL 60611-4805
312-238-1000
Fax: 312-908-1197
Dr. W Zev Rymer, Director Research
Wayne Lerner, CEO

5249 **Rosalind Russell Medical Research Center for Arthritis**
350 Parnassus Avenue
Suite 600
San Francisco, CA 94143
415-476-1192
Fax: 415-476-3526
e-mail: ephraim@itsa.ucst.edu
http://www.medicine.ucsf.edu/divisions/rheum
Ephraim P Engelman MD, Director

Arthritis research and its probable causes.

5250 **University of Michigan: Orthopaedic Research Laboratories**
400 N Ingalls Street
Ann Arbor, MI 48109-2003
734-763-6784
Fax: 734-747-0003
Dr. SA Goldstein, Director
Ann De Mare, Executive Director

Develops and studies the causes and treatments for arthritis including new devices and assistive aids.

5251 **University of Missouri: Columbia Arthritis Center**
MA427 Health Sciences Center
1 Hospital Drive
Columbia, MO 65212
573-882-4677
Fax: 573-884-3996
Gordon C Sharp MD, Director

Arthritis/Research Centers

Research into arthritis and rheumatic diseases.

Cancer/Associations & Organizations

Associations & Organizations

5252 AMC Cancer Information and Counseling Line
AMC Cancer Research Center
1600 Pierce Street
Lakewood, CO 80214-1433
303-239-3422
800-525-3777
Fax: 303-233-1863

David Silberberg, President

Provides information on the prevention, detection, diagnosis, treatment, and rehabilitation of cancer. Offers professional counseling and support group referrals. Free literature is available. Hours: 8:30 a.m. to 4:45 p.m. Monday-Friday.

5253 AMC: Cancer Information and Counseling Line
1600 Pierce Street
Denver, CO 80214
303-233-6501
800-525-3777
Fax: 303-233-1863
e-mail: draperc@amc.org
http://www.amc.org

Bob Silberberg, President
Jean Schleski, Contact

5254 Alliance for Lung Cancer Advocacy Support and Education
1747 Pennsylvania Ave, NW
Ste 1150
Washington, DC 20006
202-463-2080
800-696-2436
Fax: 202-463-2038
e-mail: info@alcase.org
http://www.alcase.org

Laurie Fento Ambrose, President and Chief Executive Di
Rear Admiral Coady, Chairman

Non-profit organization solely dedicated to help people with lung cancer improve their quality of life through increased advocacy, support and education.

5255 American Bone Marrow Donor Registry:New England Donor Registry
University of Massachusetts
55 Lake Avenue N
Worcester, MA 01655
508-334-8969
800-726-2824
Fax: 508-334-8972
e-mail: info@crir.org
http://www.crir.org

June White, Coordinator
Thomas Wiegand, General Manager

Aims to educate and recruit an adequate, viable source of well-informed potential marrow donors and to effectively maintain the donor records. coordinates and processes patient search requests, and provides assistance to patient and physician throughout the search process.

5256 American Cancer Soceity: Monroe
1010 Kennedy Drive
Suite 303
Key West, FL 33040
305-292-2333
800-ACS-2345
Fax: 305-294-3964
http://www.cancer.org

Carolyn D. Runowicz, President
Elmer Huerta, First Vice President

Nationwide, community-based voluntary health organization dedicated to eliminating cancer as a major health problem by preventing cancer, saving lives, and diminishing suffering from cancer through research, education, advocacy, and service.

5257 American Cancer Society
South Atlantic Division
Williams Street
Suite 840
Atlanta, GA 30303
404-315-1123
800-ACS-2345
Fax: 843-842-9898
http://www.cancer.org

Richard C. Wender, President
Elmer Huerta, First Vice President
Sandy Ray, Manager

The American Cancer Society is the nationwide community-based voluntary health organization dedicated to eliminating cancer as a major health problem by preventing cancer, saving lives, and diminishing suffering from cancer, through research, education, advocacy and service.

5258 American Cancer Society: Aberdeen
525 5th Street SE
Suite 4
Watertown, SD 57201
605-882-2957
800-ACS-2345
Fax: 605-882-1701
http://www.cancer.org

Peg Schultz, Income Development manger
Elmer Huerta, First Vice President

Nationwide, community-based voluntary health organization dedicated to eliminating cancer as a major health problem by preventing cancer, saving lives, and diminishing suffering from cancer through research, education, advocacy, and service.

5259 American Cancer Society: Abescon
626 N Shore Road
Absecon, NJ 8201
609-645-7272
800-ACS-2345
Fax: 609-641-9469
http://www.cancer.org

Richard C. Wender, President
Elmer Huerta, First Vice President

Nationwide, community-based voluntary health organization dedicated to eliminating cancer as a major health problem by preventing cancer, saving lives, and diminishing suffering from cancer through research, education, advocacy, and service.

5260 American Cancer Society: Abingdon
230 Charwood Drive NE
Suite 23
Abingdon, VA 24210
276-739-7780
800-ACS-2345
Fax: 276-739-7781
http://www.cancer.org

Richard C. Wender, President
Elmer Huerta, First Vice President

Nationwide, community-based voluntary health organization dedicated to eliminating cancer as a major health problem by preventing cancer, saving lives, and diminishing suffering from cancer through research, education, advocacy, and service.

5261 American Cancer Society: Adams
PO Box 3535
Gettysburg, PA 17325
888-227-5445
800-ACS-2345
Fax: 717-334-3974
e-mail: jennifer.clarke@cancer.org
http://www.cancer.org

Richard C. Wender, President
Elmer Huerta, First Vice President

Nationwide, community-based voluntary health organization dedicated to eliminating cancer as a major health problem by preventing cancer, saving lives, and diminishing suffering from cancer through research, education, advocacy, and service.

Cancer/Associations & Organizations

5262 American Cancer Society: Aiea
98-029 Hekaha Street
Bldg 5 Unit #6
Aiea, HI 96701
808-486-8420
800-ACS-2345
Fax: 808-487-5247
http://www.cancer.org

Richard C. Wender, President
Elmer Huerta, First Vice President

Nationwide, community-based voluntary health organization dedicated to eliminating cancer as a major health problem by preventing cancer, saving lives, and diminishing suffering from cancer through research, education, advocacy, and service.

5263 American Cancer Society: Aiken
128 Stonemark Lane
Columbia, SC 29210-3841
803-750-1693
800-ACS-2345
Fax: 803-648-5094
http://www.cancer.org

Lisa Hartzog, Manager

Nationwide, community-based voluntary health organization dedicated to eliminating cancer as a major health problem by preventing cancer, saving lives, and diminishing suffering from cancer through research, education, advocacy, and service.

5264 American Cancer Society: Alachua High Five Unit
2119 SW 16th Street
Gainesville, FL 32608
352-376-6866
800-ACS-2345
Fax: 352-336-3861
http://www.cancer.org

Richard C. Wender, President
Elmer Huerta, First Vice President

Nationwide, community-based voluntary health organization dedicated to eliminating cancer as a major health problem by preventing cancer, saving lives, and diminishing suffering from cancer through research, education, advocacy, and service.

5265 American Cancer Society: Albany
Williams Street
Albany, GA 30303
404-315-1123
800-ACS-2345
Fax: 404-315-9348
http://www.cancer.org

Richard C. Wender, President
Elmer Huerta, First Vice President

Nationwide, community-based voluntary health organization dedicated to eliminating cancer as a major health problem by preventing cancer, saving lives, and diminishing suffering from cancer through research, education, advocacy, and service.

5266 American Cancer Society: Albuquerque
10501 Montgomery Boulevard NE
Suite 300
Albuquerque, NM 87111-3875
505-260-2105
800-ACS-2345
Fax: 505-266-9513
http://www.cancer.org

Richard C. Wender, President
Elmer Huerta, First Vice President

Nationwide, community-based voluntary health organization dedicated to eliminating cancer as a major health problem by preventing cancer, saving lives, and diminishing suffering from cancer through research, education, advocacy, and service.

5267 American Cancer Society: Alexandria
1450 Peterman Drive
B
Alexandria, LA 71301
318-445-4190
800-ACS-2345
Fax: 318-445-5008
http://www.cancer.org

Richard C. Wender, President
Elmer Huerta, First Vice President

Nationwide, community-based voluntary health organization dedicated to eliminating cancer as a major health problem by preventing cancer, saving lives, and diminishing suffering from cancer through research, education, advocacy, and service.

5268 American Cancer Society: Amador County
1765 Challenge Way
Suite 115
Sacramento, CA 95815
916-446-7933
800-ACS-2345
Fax: 916-325-2351
http://www.cancer.org

Richard C. Wender, President
Elmer Huerta, First Vice President

Nationwide, community-based voluntary health organization dedicated to eliminating cancer as a major health problem by preventing cancer, saving lives, and diminishing suffering from cancer through research, education, advocacy, and service.

5269 American Cancer Society: Amarillo
3915 Bell Street
Amarillo, TX 79109
806-353-4306
800-ACS-2345
Fax: 806-354-0668
http://www.cancer.org

Richard C. Wender, President
Elmer Huerta, First Vice President

Nationwide, community-based voluntary health organization dedicated to eliminating cancer as a major health problem by preventing cancer, saving lives, and diminishing suffering from cancer through research, education, advocacy, and service.

5270 American Cancer Society: Anchorage
1057 W Fireweed Lane
Suite 204
Anchorage, AK 99503-1760
907-277-8696
800-ACS-2345
Fax: 907-263-2073
http://www.cancer.org

Richard C. Wender, President
Elmer Huerta, First Vice President

Nationwide, community-based voluntary health organization dedicated to eliminating cancer as a major health problem by preventing cancer, saving lives, and diminishing suffering from cancer through research, education, advocacy, and service.

5271 American Cancer Society: Anderson
1220 Meridian Street
Anderson, IN 46016
765-642-6603
800-ACS-2345
Fax: 765-642-6711
http://www.cancer.org

Richard C. Wender, President
Elmer Huerta, First Vice President

Nationwide, community-based voluntary health organization dedicated to eliminating cancer as a major health problem by preventing cancer, saving lives, and diminishing suffering from cancer through research, education, advocacy, and service.

5272 American Cancer Society: Antelope Valley Eastern Sierra Unit
1043 W Avenue M4
Suite B
Palmdale, CA 93551-1439
661-945-7585
800-ACS-2345
Fax: 661-945-9039
http://www.cancer.org

Richard C. Wender, President
Elmer Huerta, First Vice President

Nationwide, community-based voluntary health organization dedicated to eliminating cancer as a major health problem by preventing cancer, saving lives, and diminishing suffering from cancer through research, education, advocacy, and service.

Cancer/Associations & Organizations

5273 American Cancer Society: Asheville Administrative Resource Center
120 Executive Park
Bldg 1
Asheville, NC 28801-2426
828-254-6931
800-ACS-2345
Fax: 828-252-8890
http://www.cancer.org

Richard C. Wender, President
Elmer Huerta, First Vice President

Nationwide, community-based voluntary health organization dedicated to eliminating cancer as a major health problem by preventing cancer, saving lives, and diminishing suffering from cancer through research, education, advocacy, and service.

5274 American Cancer Society: Ashland
4324 13th Street
Ashland, KY 41102
606-324-1819
800-ACS-2345
Fax: 606-327-1744
http://www.cancer.org

Richard C. Wender, President
Elmer Huerta, First Vice President

Nationwide, community-based voluntary health organization dedicated to eliminating cancer as a major health problem by preventing cancer, saving lives, and diminishing suffering from cancer through research, education, advocacy, and service.

5275 American Cancer Society: Athens
1684 Barnett Shoals Road
Athens, GA 30605
706-549-4893
800-ACS-2345
Fax: 706-549-2314
http://www.cancer.org

Richard C. Wender, President
Elmer Huerta, First Vice President

Nationwide, community-based voluntary health organization dedicated to eliminating cancer as a major health problem by preventing cancer, saving lives, and diminishing suffering from cancer through research, education, advocacy, and service.

5276 American Cancer Society: Atlanta
Williams Street
Suite 840
Atlanta, GA 30303
404-315-1123
800-ACS-2345
Fax: 404-315-9348
http://www.cancer.org

Richard C. Wender, President
Elmer Huerta, First Vice President

Nationwide, community-based voluntary health organization dedicated to eliminating cancer as a major health problem by preventing cancer, saving lives, and diminishing suffering from cancer through research, education, advocacy, and service.

5277 American Cancer Society: Augusta
2607 Commons Blvd
Bldg F # 104
Augusta, GA 30909
706-731-9900
800-ACS-2345
Fax: 706-731-0979
http://www.cancer.org

Richard C. Wender, President
Elmer Huerta, First Vice President

Nationwide, community-based voluntary health organization dedicated to eliminating cancer as a major health problem by preventing cancer, saving lives, and diminishing suffering from cancer through research, education, advocacy, and service.

5278 American Cancer Society: Austin
2433 Ridgepoint Drive
Suite B
Austin, TX 78754
512-919-1800
800-ACS-2345
Fax: 512-919-1846
http://www.cancer.org

Richard C. Wender, President
Elmer Huerta, First Vice President

Nationwide, community-based voluntary health organization dedicated to eliminating cancer as a major health problem by preventing cancer, saving lives, and diminishing suffering from cancer through research, education, advocacy, and service.

5279 American Cancer Society: Baker Clay Unit
1732 Kingsley Avenue
Suite 123
Orange Park, FL 32073
904-264-6039
800-ACS-2345
Fax: 904-264-6272
http://www.cancer.org

Richard C. Wender, President
Elmer Huerta, First Vice President

Nationwide, community-based voluntary health organization dedicated to eliminating cancer as a major health problem by preventing cancer, saving lives, and diminishing suffering from cancer through research, education, advocacy, and service.

5280 American Cancer Society: Bakersfield
1523 California Avenue
Bakersfield, CA 93304
661-327-2424
800-ACS-2345
Fax: 661-327-2921
http://www.cancer.org

Richard C. Wender, President
Elmer Huerta, First Vice President

Nationwide, community-based voluntary health organization dedicated to eliminating cancer as a major health problem by preventing cancer, saving lives, and diminishing suffering from cancer through research, education, advocacy, and service.

5281 American Cancer Society: Baldwin County
19059 Greeno Rd
Suite A
Fairhope, AL 36532
251-621-7996
800-ACS-2345
Fax: 251-929-3474
http://www.cancer.org

Richard C. Wender, President
Elmer Huerta, First Vice President

Nationwide, community-based voluntary health organization dedicated to eliminating cancer as a major health problem by preventing cancer, saving lives, and diminishing suffering from cancer through research, education, advocacy, and service.

5282 American Cancer Society: Barry County
129 Jefferson Avenue SE
Grand Rapids, MI 49503
616-364-6121
800-ACS-2345
Fax: 616-364-6451
e-mail: bonnie.nawara@cancer.org
http://www.cancer.org

Richard C. Wender, President
Elmer Huerta, First Vice President

Nationwide, community-based voluntary health organization dedicated to eliminating cancer as a major health problem by preventing cancer, saving lives, and diminishing suffering from cancer through research, education, advocacy, and service.

5283 American Cancer Society: Bartow West Polk Unit
809 S Florida Avenue
Lakeland, FL 33801
863-688-2326
800-ACS-2345
Fax: 863-687-6939
http://www.cancer.org

Richard C. Wender, President
Elmer Huerta, First Vice President

Cancer/Associations & Organizations

Nationwide, community-based voluntary health organization dedicated to eliminating cancer as a major health problem by preventing cancer, saving lives, and diminishing suffering from cancer through research, education, advocacy, and service.

5284 American Cancer Society: Batavia Fox Valley
11 E Wilson Street
Batavia, IL 60510-2656
630-879-9009
800-ACS-2345
Fax: 630-879-9047
http://www.cancer.org

Richard C. Wender, President
Elmer Huerta, First Vice President

Nationwide, community-based voluntary health organization dedicated to eliminating cancer as a major health problem by preventing cancer, saving lives, and diminishing suffering from cancer through research, education, advocacy, and service.

5285 American Cancer Society: Baton Rouge
10528 Kentshire Court
Suite 104
Baton Rouge, LA 70810
225-927-0782
800-ACS-2345
Fax: 225-767-1374
http://www.cancer.org

Richard C. Wender, President
Elmer Huerta, First Vice President

Nationwide, community-based voluntary health organization dedicated to eliminating cancer as a major health problem by preventing cancer, saving lives, and diminishing suffering from cancer through research, education, advocacy, and service.

5286 American Cancer Society: Bay Area
1480 W Center Road
Suite 1
Essexville, MI 48732
989-895-1730
800-ACS-2345
Fax: 989-895-1745
http://www.cancer.org

Richard C. Wender, President
Elmer Huerta, First Vice President

Nationwide, community-based voluntary health organization dedicated to eliminating cancer as a major health problem by preventing cancer, saving lives, and diminishing suffering from cancer through research, education, advocacy, and service.

5287 American Cancer Society: Bemidji
3721 23rd Street S
Suite 102
Saint Cloud, MN 56301
320-255-0220
800-ACS-2345
Fax: 320-255-5517
http://www.cancer.org

Richard C. Wender, President
Elmer Huerta, First Vice President

Nationwide, community-based voluntary health organization dedicated to eliminating cancer as a major health problem by preventing cancer, saving lives, and diminishing suffering from cancer through research, education, advocacy, and service.

5288 American Cancer Society: Billings
550 N 31st Street
Suite 103
Billings, MT 59101
406-256-7150
800-ACS-2345
Fax: 406-256-7170
http://www.cancer.org

Richard C. Wender, President
Elmer Huerta, First Vice President

Nationwide, community-based voluntary health organization dedicated to eliminating cancer as a major health problem by preventing cancer, saving lives, and diminishing suffering from cancer through research, education, advocacy, and service.

5289 American Cancer Society: Birmingham
1100 Ireland Way
Suite 201
Birmingham, AL 35205-7013
205-879-2242
800-ACS-2345
Fax: 205-930-8895
http://www.cancer.org

Richard C. Wender, President
Elmer Huerta, First Vice President

Nationwide, community-based voluntary health organization dedicated to eliminating cancer as a major health problem by preventing cancer, saving lives, and diminishing suffering from cancer through research, education, advocacy, and service.

5290 American Cancer Society: Bismark
2401 46th Avenue Southeast
Suite 102
Mandan, ND 58554
701-224-9954
800-ACS-2345
Fax: 701-250-9145
http://www.cancer.org

Richard C. Wender, President
Elmer Huerta, First Vice President

Nationwide, community-based voluntary health organization dedicated to eliminating cancer as a major health problem by preventing cancer, saving lives, and diminishing suffering from cancer through research, education, advocacy, and service.

5291 American Cancer Society: Blackfoot
2676 Vista Avenue
Boise, ID 83705
208-345-2164
800-ACS-2345
Fax: 208-343-9922
http://www.cancer.org

Richard C. Wender, President
Elmer Huerta, First Vice President

Nationwide, community-based voluntary health organization dedicated to eliminating cancer as a major health problem by preventing cancer, saving lives, and diminishing suffering from cancer through research, education, advocacy, and service.

5292 American Cancer Society: Bluefield
1816 Jefferson Street
Bluefield, WV 24701
304-327-8770
800-ACS-2345
Fax: 304-323-3161
http://www.cancer.org

Richard C. Wender, President
Elmer Huerta, First Vice President

Nationwide, community-based voluntary health organization dedicated to eliminating cancer as a major health problem by preventing cancer, saving lives, and diminishing suffering from cancer through research, education, advocacy, and service.

5293 American Cancer Society: Bowling Green
Greenwood Courtyard, 2425 Scottsville Rd
Suite 123
Bowling Green, KY 42104
270-782-3654
800-ACS-2345
Fax: 270-846-0202
http://www.cancer.org

Richard C. Wender, President
Elmer Huerta, First Vice President

Nationwide, community-based voluntary health organization dedicated to eliminating cancer as a major health problem by preventing cancer, saving lives, and diminishing suffering from cancer through research, education, advocacy, and service.

5294 American Cancer Society: Bradenton
4955 St. Road 64 E
Suite 136
Bradenton, FL 34208
941-745-1214
800-ACS-2345
Fax: 941-745-1760
http://www.cancer.org

Richard C. Wender, President
Elmer Huerta, First Vice President

Cancer/Associations & Organizations

Nationwide, community-based voluntary health organization dedicated to eliminating cancer as a major health problem by preventing cancer, saving lives, and diminishing suffering from cancer through research, education, advocacy, and service.

5295 American Cancer Society: Brainerd
3721 23rd Street S
Suite 102
Saint Cloud, MN 56301
320-255-0220
800-ACS-2345
Fax: 320-255-5517
http://www.cancer.org

Richard C. Wender, President
Elmer Huerta, First Vice President

Nationwide, community-based voluntary health organization dedicated to eliminating cancer as a major health problem by preventing cancer, saving lives, and diminishing suffering from cancer through research, education, advocacy, and service.

5296 American Cancer Society: Brawley
Pioneers Memorial Hospital
400 S Eighth Street
El Centro, CA 92243
760-352-6656
800-ACS-2345
Fax: 760-352-0316
http://www.cancer.org

Richard C. Wender, President
Elmer Huerta, First Vice President

Nationwide, community-based voluntary health organization dedicated to eliminating cancer as a major health problem by preventing cancer, saving lives, and diminishing suffering from cancer through research, education, advocacy, and service.

5297 American Cancer Society: Brevard
1260 Us Highway 1
Suite 201
Rockledge, FL 32955-2728
321-433-3109
800-ACS-2345
Fax: 321-631-8015
http://www.cancer.org

Richard C. Wender, President
Elmer Huerta, First Vice President

Nationwide, community-based voluntary health organization dedicated to eliminating cancer as a major health problem by preventing cancer, saving lives, and diminishing suffering from cancer through research, education, advocacy, and service.

5298 American Cancer Society: Brooklyn
31 Washington Street
Brooklyn, NY 11201
718-237-7850
800-ACS-2345
Fax: 718-852-9422
http://www.cancer.org

Richard C. Wender, President
Elmer Huerta, First Vice President

Nationwide, community-based voluntary health organization dedicated to eliminating cancer as a major health problem by preventing cancer, saving lives, and diminishing suffering from cancer through research, education, advocacy, and service.

5299 American Cancer Society: Broward
3407 NW 9th Avenue
Suite 100
Fort Lauderdale, FL 33309
954-564-0880
800-ACS-2345
Fax: 954-561-8072
http://www.cancer.org

Richard C. Wender, President
Elmer Huerta, First Vice President

Nationwide, community-based voluntary health organization dedicated to eliminating cancer as a major health problem by preventing cancer, saving lives, and diminishing suffering from cancer through research, education, advocacy, and service.

5300 American Cancer Society: Brunswick
3011 Hampton Avenue
Suite 361
Brunswick, GA 31520
912-265-7117
800-ACS-2345
Fax: 912-262-0773
http://www.cancer.org

Richard C. Wender, President
Elmer Huerta, First Vice President

Nationwide, community-based voluntary health organization dedicated to eliminating cancer as a major health problem by preventing cancer, saving lives, and diminishing suffering from cancer through research, education, advocacy, and service.

5301 American Cancer Society: Burlington
1223 S Gear Avenue
Suite 9
West Burlington, IA 52655-1683
319-752-4008
800-ACS-2345
Fax: 319-752-6750
http://www.cancer.org

Richard C. Wender, President
Elmer Huerta, First Vice President

Nationwide, community-based voluntary health organization dedicated to eliminating cancer as a major health problem by preventing cancer, saving lives, and diminishing suffering from cancer through research, education, advocacy, and service.

5302 American Cancer Society: Byfield
9 Riverside Rd
Suite 209
Weston, MA 02493
781-894-6633
800-ACS-2345
Fax: 781-314-2699
http://www.cancer.org

Richard C. Wender, President
Elmer Huerta, First Vice President

Nationwide, community-based voluntary health organization dedicated to eliminating cancer as a major health problem by preventing cancer, saving lives, and diminishing suffering from cancer through research, education, advocacy, and service.

5303 American Cancer Society: Cape Cod
1115 W Chestnut St
Brockton, MA 02301
508-584-9600
Fax: 508-584-9699
http://www.cancer.org

Richard C. Wender, President
Elmer Huerta, First Vice President

Nationwide, community-based voluntary health organization dedicated to eliminating cancer as a major health problem by preventing cancer, saving lives, and diminishing suffering from cancer through research, education, advocacy, and service.

5304 American Cancer Society: Cape Girardeau
106 Farrar Drive
Suite 104
Cape Girardeau, MO 63701
573-334-9197
800-ACS-2345
Fax: 573-334-5115
http://www.cancer.org

Richard C. Wender, President
Elmer Huerta, First Vice President

Nationwide, community-based voluntary health organization dedicated to eliminating cancer as a major health problem by preventing cancer, saving lives, and diminishing suffering from cancer through research, education, advocacy, and service.

5305 American Cancer Society: Carroll
905 E Hwy 30
Carroll, IA 51401
712-794-0100
800-ACS-2345
Fax: 712-794-0101
e-mail: Wymore@cancer.org
http://www.cancer.org

Richard C. Wender, President
Elmer Huerta, First Vice President

Cancer/Associations & Organizations

Nationwide, community-based voluntary health organization dedicated to eliminating cancer as a major health problem by preventing cancer, saving lives, and diminishing suffering from cancer through research, education, advocacy, and service.

5306 American Cancer Society: Casper
907 N Poplar Ave
Ste 185
Casper, WY 82601
307-577-4892
800-ACS-2345
Fax: 307-234-0926
http://www.cancer.org

Richard C. Wender, President
Elmer Huerta, First Vice President

Nationwide, community-based voluntary health organization dedicated to eliminating cancer as a major health problem by preventing cancer, saving lives, and diminishing suffering from cancer through research, education, advocacy, and service.

5307 American Cancer Society: Cedar Rapids
4080 1st Avenue NE
Ste #101
Cedar Rapids, IA 52402
319-365-5241
800-ACS-2345
Fax: 319-365-1739
http://www.cancer.org

Richard C. Wender, President
Elmer Huerta, First Vice President

Nationwide, community-based voluntary health organization dedicated to eliminating cancer as a major health problem by preventing cancer, saving lives, and diminishing suffering from cancer through research, education, advocacy, and service.

5308 American Cancer Society: Champaign
2003 N. Dunlap Ave.
Savoy, IL 61874
217-356-9076
800-ACS-2345
Fax: 217-356-7721
http://www.cancer.org

Richard C. Wender, President
Elmer Huerta, First Vice President

Nationwide, community-based voluntary health organization dedicated to eliminating cancer as a major health problem by preventing cancer, saving lives, and diminishing suffering from cancer through research, education, advocacy, and service.

5309 American Cancer Society: Charlotte
992 Tamiami Trl
Unit C2
Port Charlotte, FL 33953
941-627-3000
800-ACS-2345
Fax: 941-627-5229
http://www.cancer.org

Richard C. Wender, President
Elmer Huerta, First Vice President

Nationwide, community-based voluntary health organization dedicated to eliminating cancer as a major health problem by preventing cancer, saving lives, and diminishing suffering from cancer through research, education, advocacy, and service.

5310 American Cancer Society: Chattanooga
850 Fortwood Street
Chattanooga, TN 37403
423-267-8613
800-ACS-2345
Fax: 423-266-8494
http://www.cancer.org

Richard C. Wender, President
Elmer Huerta, First Vice President

Nationwide, community-based voluntary health organization dedicated to eliminating cancer as a major health problem by preventing cancer, saving lives, and diminishing suffering from cancer through research, education, advocacy, and service.

5311 American Cancer Society: Cheyenne
1020 9th Avenue
Greeley, CO 80631-4014
970-356-9727
800-ACS-2345
Fax: 307-638-1199
http://www.cancer.org

Richard C. Wender, President
Elmer Huerta, First Vice President

Nationwide, community-based voluntary health organization dedicated to eliminating cancer as a major health problem by preventing cancer, saving lives, and diminishing suffering from cancer through research, education, advocacy, and service.

5312 American Cancer Society: Chicago
225 N Michigan Ave
Ste 1210
Chicago, IL 60601
312-372-0471
800-ACS-2345
Fax: 312-372-0910
http://www.cancer.org

Richard C. Wender, President
Elmer Huerta, First Vice President

Nationwide, community-based voluntary health organization dedicated to eliminating cancer as a major health problem by preventing cancer, saving lives, and diminishing suffering from cancer through research, education, advocacy, and service.

5313 American Cancer Society: Citrus
21756 State Road 54
Suite 101
Lutz, FL 33549
813-949-0291
800-ACS-2345
Fax: 813-909-4843
http://www.cancer.org

Richard C. Wender, President
Elmer Huerta, First Vice President

Nationwide, community-based voluntary health organization dedicated to eliminating cancer as a major health problem by preventing cancer, saving lives, and diminishing suffering from cancer through research, education, advocacy, and service.

5314 American Cancer Society: Clark/Miami
1130 Vester Avenue
Suite G
Springfield, OH 45503-7302
937-399-0809
800-ACS-2345
Fax: 937-399-2060
http://www.cancer.org

Richard C. Wender, President
Elmer Huerta, First Vice President
Amaria Hough, Cancel Central Director

Nationwide, community-based voluntary health organization dedicated to eliminating cancer as a major health problem by preventing cancer, saving lives, and diminishing suffering from cancer through research, education, advocacy, and service.

5315 American Cancer Society: Collier
990 1st Avenue S
Suite 200
Naples, FL 34102
239-261-0337
800-ACS-2345
Fax: 239-649-5571
http://www.cancer.org

Richard C. Wender, President
Elmer Huerta, First Vice President

The American Cancer Society is the nationwide, community-based voluntary health organization dedicated to eliminating cancer as a major health problem by preventing cancer, saving lives, and diminishing suffering from cancer through research, education, advocacy, and service.

Cancer/Associations & Organizations

5316 American Cancer Society: Collinsville
5 Schiber Court
Bldg. A
Maryville, IL 62062
618-288-2320
800-ACS-2345
Fax: 618-288-2054
http://www.cancer.org

Richard C. Wender, President
Elmer Huerta, First Vice President

Nationwide, community-based voluntary health organization dedicated to eliminating cancer as a major health problem by preventing cancer, saving lives, and diminishing suffering from cancer through research, education, advocacy, and service.

5317 American Cancer Society: Colorado Springs
1445 N Union Boulevard
Suite B-100
Colorado Springs, CO 80909
719-636-5101
800-ACS-2345
Fax: 719-636-1480
http://www.cancer.org

Richard C. Wender, President
Elmer Huerta, First Vice President

Nationwide, community-based voluntary health organization dedicated to eliminating cancer as a major health problem by preventing cancer, saving lives, and diminishing suffering from cancer through research, education, advocacy, and service.

5318 American Cancer Society: Columbia
128 Stonemark Lane
Columbia, SC 29210-3855
803-750-1693
800-ACS-2345
Fax: 803-750-4000
http://www.cancer.org

Richard C. Wender, President
Elmer Huerta, First Vice President

Nationwide, community-based voluntary health organization dedicated to eliminating cancer as a major health problem by preventing cancer, saving lives, and diminishing suffering from cancer through research, education, advocacy, and service.

5319 American Cancer Society: Columbus
233 12th Street
Suite 710
Columbus, GA 31901
706-324-4573
800-ACS-2345
Fax: 706-324-4749
http://www.cancer.org

Richard C. Wender, President
Elmer Huerta, First Vice President

Nationwide, community-based voluntary health organization dedicated to eliminating cancer as a major health problem by preventing cancer, saving lives, and diminishing suffering from cancer through research, education, advocacy, and service.

5320 American Cancer Society: Contra Costa
1885 Oak Park Boulevard
Pleasant Hill, CA 94523
925-934-7640
800-ACS-2345
Fax: 925-934-5372
http://www.cancer.org

Richard C. Wender, President
Elmer Huerta, First Vice President

Nationwide, community-based voluntary health organization dedicated to eliminating cancer as a major health problem by preventing cancer, saving lives, and diminishing suffering from cancer through research, education, advocacy, and service.

5321 American Cancer Society: Corpus Christi
4101 S Alameda Street
Corpus Christi, TX 78411
361-857-0134
800-ACS-2345
Fax: 361-854-3260
http://www.cancer.org

Richard C. Wender, President
Elmer Huerta, First Vice President

Nationwide, community-based voluntary health organization dedicated to eliminating cancer as a major health problem by preventing cancer, saving lives, and diminishing suffering from cancer through research, education, advocacy, and service.

5322 American Cancer Society: Council Bluffs
905 E Hwy 30
Carroll, IA 51401
712-794-0100
800-ACS-2345
Fax: 712-794-0101
http://www.cancer.org

Richard C. Wender, President
Elmer Huerta, First Vice President

Nationwide, community-based voluntary health organization dedicated to eliminating cancer as a major health problem by preventing cancer, saving lives, and diminishing suffering from cancer through research, education, advocacy, and service.

5323 American Cancer Society: Covina
339 E Rowland Street
3
Covina, CA 91723
626-966-9994
Fax: 626-966-8664
e-mail: jmiele@cancer.org
http://www.cancer.org

Richard C. Wender, President
Elmer Huerta, First Vice President

Nationwide, community-based voluntary health organization dedicated to eliminating cancer as a major health problem by preventing cancer, saving lives, and diminishing suffering from cancer through research, education, advocacy and service.

5324 American Cancer Society: Culver City
5731 W Slauson Avenue
Suite 200
Culver City, CA 90230
310-348-0356
800-ACS-2345
Fax: 310-348-2328
http://www.cancer.org

Richard C. Wender, President
Elmer Huerta, First Vice President

Nationwide, community-based voluntary health organization dedicated to eliminating cancer as a major health problem by preventing cancer, saving lives, and diminishing suffering from cancer through research, education, advocacy, and service.

5325 American Cancer Society: Cumberland
182 N Mechanic Street
Cumberland, MD 21502
301-722-2145
800-ACS-2345
Fax: 301-724-6179
http://www.cancer.org

Richard C. Wender, President
Elmer Huerta, First Vice President

Nationwide, community-based voluntary health organization dedicated to eliminating cancer as a major health problem by preventing cancer, saving lives, and diminishing suffering from cancer through research, education, advocacy, and service.

5326 American Cancer Society: Cuyahoga County
10501 Euclid Avenue
Cleveland, OH 44106-2204
888-227-6446
800-ACS-2345
Fax: 877-227-2838
http://www.cancer.org

Richard C. Wender, President
Elmer Huerta, First Vice President

Nationwide, community-based voluntary health organization dedicated to eliminating cancer as a major health problem by preventing cancer, saving lives, and diminishing suffering from cancer through research, education, advocacy, and service.

Cancer/Associations & Organizations

5327 American Cancer Society: Dade/Miami Beach
3901 NW 79th Avenue
Suite 224
Miami, FL 33166
305-594-4363
800-ACS-2345
Fax: 305-592-5140
http://www.cancer.org

Richard C. Wender, President
Elmer Huerta, First Vice President

Nationwide, community-based voluntary health organization dedicated to eliminating cancer as a major health problem by preventing cancer, saving lives, and diminishing suffering from cancer through research, education, advocacy, and service.

5328 American Cancer Society: Dallas
8900 Carpenter Fwy
Dallas, TX 75247
214-819-1200
800-ACS-2345
Fax: 214-631-3869
http://www.cancer.org

Maria Clark, Executive Director
Elmer Huerta, First Vice President

Nationwide, community-based voluntary health organization dedicated to eliminating cancer as a major health problem by preventing cancer, saving lives, and diminishing suffering from cancer through research, education, advocacy, and service.

5329 American Cancer Society: Dalton
300 W Emery Street
Suite 106
Dalton, GA 30720
706-278-1960
800-ACS-2345
Fax: 706-226-7531
http://www.cancer.org

Richard C. Wender, President
Elmer Huerta, First Vice President

Nationwide, community-based voluntary health organization dedicated to eliminating cancer as a major health problem by preventing cancer, saving lives, and diminishing suffering from cancer through research, education, advocacy, and service.

5330 American Cancer Society: Davenport
8364 Hickman
Suite D
Des Moines, IA 50325
515-253-0147
800-ACS-2345
Fax: 515-253-0806
http://www.cancer.org

Richard C. Wender, President
Elmer Huerta, First Vice President

Nationwide, community-based voluntary health organization dedicated to eliminating cancer as a major health problem by preventing cancer, saving lives, and diminishing suffering from cancer through research, education, advocacy, and service.

5331 American Cancer Society: DeSoto
2801 Fruitville Road
Suite 250, Pen West Park
Sarasota, FL 34237
941-365-2858
800-ACS-2345
Fax: 941-365-2858
http://www.cancer.org

Richard C. Wender, President
Elmer Huerta, First Vice President

Nationwide, community-based voluntary health organization dedicated to eliminating cancer as a major health problem by preventing cancer, saving lives, and diminishing suffering from cancer through research, education, advocacy, and service.

5332 American Cancer Society: Denver
2255 S Oneida Street
Denver, CO 80224
303-758-2030
800-ACS-2345
Fax: 303-759-1615
http://www.cancer.org

Richard C. Wender, President
Elmer Huerta, First Vice President

Nationwide, community-based voluntary health organization dedicated to eliminating cancer as a major health problem by preventing cancer, saving lives, and diminishing suffering from cancer through research, education, advocacy, and service.

5333 American Cancer Society: Des Moines
8364 Hickman Road
Suite D
Des Moines, IA 50325
515-253-0147
800-ACS-2345
Fax: 515-253-0806
http://www.cancer.org

Richard C. Wender, President
Elmer Huerta, First Vice President

Nationwide, community-based voluntary health organization dedicated to eliminating cancer as a major health problem by preventing cancer, saving lives, and diminishing suffering from cancer through research, education, advocacy, and service.

5334 American Cancer Society: Dothan
2346 W Main Street
Suite 3
Dothan, AL 36301
334-793-1012
800-ACS-2345
Fax: 334-792-7278
http://www.cancer.org

Richard C. Wender, President
Elmer Huerta, First Vice President

Nationwide, community-based voluntary health organization dedicated to eliminating cancer as a major health problem by preventing cancer, saving lives, and diminishing suffering from cancer through research, education, advocacy, and service.

5335 American Cancer Society: Downey
9901 Paramount Boulevard
Suite 245
Downey, CA 90240
562-776-0201
800-ACS-2345
Fax: 562-776-0373
http://www.cancer.org

Richard C. Wender, President
Elmer Huerta, First Vice President

Nationwide, community-based voluntary health organization dedicated to eliminating cancer as a major health problem by preventing cancer, saving lives, and diminishing suffering from cancer through research, education, advocacy, and service.

5336 American Cancer Society: Dubuque
2774 University Avenue
Suite D
Dubuque, IA 52001
563-583-8249
800-ACS-2345
Fax: 563-583-8240
http://www.cancer.org

Richard C. Wender, President
Elmer Huerta, First Vice President

Nationwide, community-based voluntary health organization dedicated to eliminating cancer as a major health problem by preventing cancer, saving lives, and diminishing suffering from cancer through research, education, advocacy, and service.

5337 American Cancer Society: Duluth
Ll2 Suite 200
130 W Superior St
Duluth, MN 55802
218-727-7439
800-ACS-2345
Fax: 218-727-8069
http://www.cancer.org

Richard C. Wender, President
Elmer Huerta, First Vice President

Nationwide, community-based voluntary health organization dedicated to eliminating cancer as a major health problem by preventing cancer, saving lives, and diminishing suffering from cancer through research, education, advocacy, and service.

Cancer/Associations & Organizations

5338 **American Cancer Society: East Lansing**
3100 West Road, Building B
Suite 110
East Lansing, MI 48823
517-332-3300
800-ACS-2345
Fax: 517-641-1496
http://www.cancer.org

Richard C. Wender, President
Elmer Huerta, First Vice President

Nationwide, community-based voluntary health organization dedicated to eliminating cancer as a major health problem by preventing cancer, saving lives, and diminishing suffering from cancer through research, education, advocacy, and service.

5339 **American Cancer Society: East Syracuse**
PO Box 7
6725 Lyons St
East Syracuse, NY 13057
315-437-7025
800-ACS-2345
Fax: 315-437-8233
e-mail: Lynne.Jones@cancer.org
http://www.cancer.org

Richard C. Wender, President
Elmer Huerta, First Vice President

Nationwide, community-based voluntary health organization dedicated to eliminating cancer as a major health problem by preventing cancer, saving lives, and diminishing suffering from cancer through research, education, advocacy, and service.

5340 **American Cancer Society: Eastern Indiana**
1401 Chester Boulevard
Richmond, IN 47374
765-962-4180
800-ACS-2345
Fax: 765-966-8023
http://www.cancer.org

Richard C. Wender, President
Elmer Huerta, First Vice President

Nationwide, community-based voluntary health organization dedicated to eliminating cancer as a major health problem by preventing cancer, saving lives, and diminishing suffering from cancer through research, education, advocacy, and service.

5341 **American Cancer Society: Eau Claire**
2427 N Hillcrest Parkway
Suite 7
Altoona, WI 54720
715-832-0181
800-ACS-2345
Fax: 715-832-8570
http://www.cancer.org

Richard C. Wender, President
Elmer Huerta, First Vice President

Nationwide, community-based voluntary health organization dedicated to eliminating cancer as a major health problem by preventing cancer, saving lives, and diminishing suffering from cancer through research, education, advocacy, and service.

5342 **American Cancer Society: El Dorado**
1765 Challenge Way
Suite 115
Sacramento, CA 95815
916-446-7933
800-ACS-2345
Fax: 916-325-2351
http://www.cancer.org

Richard C. Wender, President
Elmer Huerta, First Vice President

Nationwide, community-based voluntary health organization dedicated to eliminating cancer as a major health problem by preventing cancer, saving lives, and diminishing suffering from cancer through research, education, advocacy, and service.

5343 **American Cancer Society: El Paso**
909 E San Antonio Avenue
El Paso, TX 79901
915-544-4425
800-ACS-2345
Fax: 915-532-3748
http://www.cancer.org

Richard C. Wender, President
Elmer Huerta, First Vice President

Nationwide, community-based voluntary health organization dedicated to eliminating cancer as a major health problem by preventing cancer, saving lives, and diminishing suffering from cancer through research, education, advocacy, and service.

5344 **American Cancer Society: Eldersburg**
1393 Progress Way
Suite 908
Eldersburg, MD 21784
410-781-4316
800-ACS-2345
Fax: 410-781-4317
http://www.cancer.org

Richard C. Wender, President
Elmer Huerta, First Vice President

Nationwide, community-based voluntary health organization dedicated to eliminating cancer as a major health problem by preventing cancer, saving lives, and diminishing suffering from cancer through research, education, advocacy, and service.

5345 **American Cancer Society: Elizabeth**
507 Westminster Avenue
Elizabeth, NJ 7208
908-354-7373
800-ACS-2345
Fax: 908-354-0284
http://www.cancer.org

Richard C. Wender, President
Elmer Huerta, First Vice President

Nationwide, community-based voluntary health organization dedicated to eliminating cancer as a major health problem by preventing cancer, saving lives, and diminishing suffering from cancer through research, education, advocacy, and service.

5346 **American Cancer Society: Elmira**
1316 College Ave
Elmira, NY 14901
607-734-1552
800-ACS-2345
Fax: 607-734-2435
http://www.cancer.org

Richard C. Wender, President
Elmer Huerta, First Vice President

Nationwide, community-based voluntary health organization dedicated to eliminating cancer as a major health problem by preventing cancer, saving lives, and diminishing suffering from cancer through research, education, advocacy, and service.

5347 **American Cancer Society: Erie**
2115 W 38th Street
Erie, PA 16508
888-227-5445
800-ACS-2345
Fax: 814-866-3890
http://www.cancer.org

Richard C. Wender, President
Elmer Huerta, First Vice President

Nationwide, community-based voluntary health organization dedicated to eliminating cancer as a major health problem by preventing cancer, saving lives, and diminishing suffering from cancer through research, education, advocacy, and service.

5348 **American Cancer Society: Eugene**
2350 Oakmont Way
Suite 200
Eugene, OR 97401
541-484-2212
800-ACS-2345
Fax: 541-687-9624
http://www.cancer.org

Richard C. Wender, President
Elmer Huerta, First Vice President

Nationwide, community-based voluntary health organization dedicated to eliminating cancer as a major health problem by preventing cancer, saving lives, and diminishing suffering from cancer through research, education, advocacy, and service.

Cancer/Associations & Organizations

5349 American Cancer Society: Eureka
2942 F Street
Eureka, CA 95501
707-442-1436
800-ACS-2345
Fax: 707-442-6427
http://www.cancer.org

Richard C. Wender, President
Elmer Huerta, First Vice President

Nationwide, community-based voluntary health organization dedicated to eliminating cancer as a major health problem by preventing cancer, saving lives, and diminishing suffering from cancer through research, education, advocacy, and service.

5350 American Cancer Society: Everett
728 134th Street SW
Suite 101
Everett, WA 98204
425-741-8949
800-ACS-2345
Fax: 425-741-9638
http://www.cancer.org

Richard C. Wender, President
Elmer Huerta, First Vice President

Nationwide, community-based voluntary health organization dedicated to eliminating cancer as a major health problem by preventing cancer, saving lives, and diminishing suffering from cancer through research, education, advocacy, and service.

5351 American Cancer Society: Fargo
4646 Amber Valley Parkway
Fargo, ND 58104
701-232-1385
800-ACS-2345
Fax: 701-232-1109
http://www.cancer.org

Richard C. Wender, President
Elmer Huerta, First Vice President

Nationwide, community-based voluntary health organization dedicated to eliminating cancer as a major health problem by preventing cancer, saving lives, and diminishing suffering from cancer through research, education, advocacy, and service.

5352 American Cancer Society: Fayetteville
301 Kelly Drive
Suite 3
Peachtree City, GA 30269
770-631-0625
800-ACS-2345
Fax: 770-631-8917
http://www.cancer.org

Richard C. Wender, President
Elmer Huerta, First Vice President

Nationwide, community-based voluntary health organization dedicated to eliminating cancer as a major health problem by preventing cancer, saving lives, and diminishing suffering from cancer through research, education, advocacy, and service.

5353 American Cancer Society: Flagler
LakeSide North Executive Center, 1737
North Clyde Morris Blvd., Suite 140
Daytona Beach, FL 32117
386-274-3274
800-ACS-2345
Fax: 386-274-5582
http://www.cancer.org

Richard C. Wender, President
Elmer Huerta, First Vice President

Nationwide, community-based voluntary health organization dedicated to eliminating cancer as a major health problem by preventing cancer, saving lives, and diminishing suffering from cancer through research, education, advocacy, and service.

5354 American Cancer Society: Flint
2413 S. Linden
Suite A
Flint, MI 48532
810-733-3702
800-ACS-2345
Fax: 810-733-1480
http://www.cancer.org

Richard C. Wender, President
Elmer Huerta, First Vice President

Nationwide, community-based voluntary health organization dedicated to eliminating cancer as a major health problem by preventing cancer, saving lives, and diminishing suffering from cancer through research, education, advocacy, and service.

5355 American Cancer Society: Florence
104 S Poplar Street
Florence, AL 35630-5712
256-767-0823
800-ACS-2345
Fax: 256-767-0894
http://www.cancer.org

Richard C. Wender, President
Elmer Huerta, First Vice President

Nationwide, community-based voluntary health organization dedicated to eliminating cancer as a major health problem by preventing cancer, saving lives, and diminishing suffering from cancer through research, education, advocacy, and service.

5356 American Cancer Society: Flushing
41-60 Main St
Ste 307
Flushing, NY 11355
718-886-8890
800-ACS-2345
Fax: 718-886-8981
http://www.cancer.org

Richard C. Wender, President
Elmer Huerta, First Vice President

Nationwide, community-based voluntary health organization dedicated to eliminating cancer as a major health problem by preventing cancer, saving lives, and diminishing suffering from cancer through research, education, advocacy, and service.

5357 American Cancer Society: Fords
2600 US Hwy 1
North Brunswick, NJ 8902
732-951-6308
800-ACS-2345
Fax: 732-225-8589
http://www.cancer.org

Richard C. Wender, President
Elmer Huerta, First Vice President

Nationwide, community-based voluntary health organization dedicated to eliminating cancer as a major health problem by preventing cancer, saving lives, and diminishing suffering from cancer through research, education, advocacy, and service.

5358 American Cancer Society: Fort Dodge
905 E Hwy 30
Suite 21
Carroll, IA 51401
712-794-0100
800-ACS-2345
Fax: 712-794-0101
http://www.cancer.org

Richard C. Wender, President
Elmer Huerta, First Vice President

Nationwide, community-based voluntary health organization dedicated to eliminating cancer as a major health problem by preventing cancer, saving lives, and diminishing suffering from cancer through research, education, advocacy, and service.

5359 American Cancer Society: Fort Myers
4575 Via Royale
Suite 110
Fort Myers, FL 33919
239-936-1113
800-ACS-2345
Fax: 239-936-3763
http://www.cancer.org

Richard C. Wender, President
Elmer Huerta, First Vice President

Nationwide, community-based voluntary health organization dedicated to eliminating cancer as a major health problem by preventing cancer, saving lives, and diminishing suffering from cancer through research, education, advocacy, and service.

Cancer/Associations & Organizations

5360 **American Cancer Society: Fort Walton Beach**
339 Racetrack Road
Suite 24
Fort Walton Beach, FL 32547
850-244-3813
800-ACS-2345
Fax: 850-664-5366
http://www.cancer.org

Richard C. Wender, President
Elmer Huerta, First Vice President

Nationwide, community-based voluntary health organization dedicated to eliminating cancer as a major health problem by preventing cancer, saving lives, and diminishing suffering from cancer through research, education, advocacy, and service.

5361 **American Cancer Society: Fort Worth**
3301 West Fwy
Fort Worth, TX 76107
817-737-9990
800-ACS-2345
Fax: 817-737-9977
http://www.cancer.org

Richard C. Wender, President
Elmer Huerta, First Vice President

Nationwide, community-based voluntary health organization dedicated to eliminating cancer as a major health problem by preventing cancer, saving lives, and diminishing suffering from cancer through research, education, advocacy, and service.

5362 **American Cancer Society: Franklin County**
870 Michigan Avenue
Columbus, OH 43215
888-227-6446
800-ACS-2345
Fax: 877-227-2838
http://www.cancer.org

Richard C. Wender, President
Elmer Huerta, First Vice President

Nationwide, community-based voluntary health organization dedicated to eliminating cancer as a major health problem by preventing cancer, saving lives, and diminishing suffering from cancer through research, education, advocacy, and service.

5363 **American Cancer Society: Fremont**
39235 Liberty Street
Suite D-0
Fremont, CA 94538
510-797-0600
800-ACS-2345
Fax: 510-797-0698
http://www.cancer.org

Richard C. Wender, President
Elmer Huerta, First Vice President

Nationwide, community-based voluntary health organization dedicated to eliminating cancer as a major health problem by preventing cancer, saving lives, and diminishing suffering from cancer through research, education, advocacy, and service.

5364 **American Cancer Society: Fresno**
2222 W Shaw Avenue
Suite 201
Fresno, CA 93711
559-451-0722
800-ACS-2345
Fax: 559-451-0744
http://www.cancer.org

Richard C. Wender, President
Elmer Huerta, First Vice President

Nationwide, community-based voluntary health organization dedicated to eliminating cancer as a major health problem by preventing cancer, saving lives, and diminishing suffering from cancer through research, education, advocacy, and service.

5365 **American Cancer Society: Gainesville**
2565 Thompson Bridge Road
Suite 114
Gainesville, GA 30501
770-297-1176
800-ACS-2345
Fax: 770-297-7418
http://www.cancer.org

Richard C. Wender, President
Elmer Huerta, First Vice President

Nationwide, community-based voluntary health organization dedicated to eliminating cancer as a major health problem by preventing cancer, saving lives, and diminishing suffering from cancer through research, education, advocacy, and service.

5366 **American Cancer Society: Gambrills**
1041 State Route 3 N
Bldg A
Gambrills, MD 21054-1734
410-721-4304
800-ACS-2345
Fax: 410-721-4307
http://www.cancer.org

Richard C. Wender, President
Elmer Huerta, First Vice President

Nationwide, community-based voluntary health organization dedicated to eliminating cancer as a major health problem by preventing cancer, saving lives, and diminishing suffering from cancer through research, education, advocacy, and service.

5367 **American Cancer Society: Gladwin County**
1480 West Center Road
Essexville, MI 48732
989-895-1730
800-ACS-2345
Fax: 989-435-1745
http://www.cancer.org

Richard C. Wender, President
Elmer Huerta, First Vice President

Nationwide, community-based voluntary health organization dedicated to eliminating cancer as a major health problem by preventing cancer, saving lives, and diminishing suffering from cancer through research, education, advocacy, and service.

5368 **American Cancer Society: Glen Allen**
4240 Park Place Court
Glen Allen, VA 23060
804-527-3700
800-ACS-2345
Fax: 804-527-3797
http://www.cancer.org

Richard C. Wender, President
Elmer Huerta, First Vice President

Nationwide, community-based voluntary health organization dedicated to eliminating cancer as a major health problem by preventing cancer, saving lives, and diminishing suffering from cancer through research, education, advocacy, and service.

5369 **American Cancer Society: Glen Ellyn**
1801 Meyers Rd
Ste 100
Oak Brook Terrace, IL 60181
630-932-1141
800-ACS-2345
Fax: 630-932-1171
http://www.cancer.org

Richard C. Wender, President
Elmer Huerta, First Vice President

Nationwide, community-based voluntary health organization dedicated to eliminating cancer as a major health problem by preventing cancer, saving lives, and diminishing suffering from cancer through research, education, advocacy, and service.

5370 **American Cancer Society: Grand Forks**
4646 Amber Valley Parkway
Fargo, ND 58104
701-232-1385
800-ACS-2345
Fax: 701-232-1109
e-mail: chardyl@cancer.org
http://www.cancer.org

Richard C. Wender, President
Elmer Huerta, First Vice President

Nationwide, community-based voluntary health organization dedicated to eliminating cancer as a major health problem by preventing cancer, saving lives, and diminishing suffering from cancer through research, education, advocacy, and service.

Cancer/Associations & Organizations

5371 American Cancer Society: Grand Junction
2754 Compass Drive
Suite 328
Grand Junction, CO 81506
970-242-9593
800-ACS-2345
Fax: 970-242-2283
http://www.cancer.org

Richard C. Wender, President
Elmer Huerta, First Vice President

Nationwide, community-based voluntary health organization dedicated to eliminating cancer as a major health problem by preventing cancer, saving lives, and diminishing suffering from cancer through research, education, advocacy, and service.

5372 American Cancer Society: Grand Rapids
Grand Rapids Community Cancer Center
130 W Superior Street
LL2 Suite 200
Duluth, MN 55802
218-727-7439
800-ACS-2345
Fax: 218-727-8069
http://www.cancer.org

Richard C. Wender, President
Elmer Huerta, First Vice President

Nationwide, community-based voluntary health organization dedicated to eliminating cancer as a major health problem by preventing cancer, saving lives, and diminishing suffering from cancer through research, education, advocacy, and service.

5373 American Cancer Society: Greater Tampa
1001 S MacDill Avenue
Tampa, FL 33629-5299
813-254-3630
800-ACS-2345
Fax: 813-349-4431
http://www.cancer.org

Richard C. Wender, President
Elmer Huerta, First Vice President

Nationwide, community-based voluntary health organization dedicated to eliminating cancer as a major health problem by preventing cancer, saving lives, and diminishing suffering from cancer through research, education, advocacy, and service.

5374 American Cancer Society: Greater Ventura
250 Citrus Grove Ln
Suite 200
Oxnard, CA 93036
805-983-8864
800-ACS-2345
Fax: 805-983-3751
http://www.cancer.org

Richard C. Wender, President
Elmer Huerta, First Vice President

Nationwide, community-based voluntary health organization dedicated to eliminating cancer as a major health problem by preventing cancer, saving lives, and diminishing suffering from cancer through research, education, advocacy, and service.

5375 American Cancer Society: Green Bay
3311 S Packerland Drive
De Pere, WI 54115
920-338-1541
800-ACS-2345
Fax: 920-338-1545
http://www.cancer.org

Richard C. Wender, President
Elmer Huerta, First Vice President

Nationwide, community-based voluntary health organization dedicated to eliminating cancer as a major health problem by preventing cancer, saving lives, and diminishing suffering from cancer through research, education, advocacy, and service.

5376 American Cancer Society: Green River
941 East 3300 South
Suite 3
Salt Lake City, UT 84106
801-483-1500
800-ACS-2345
Fax: 801-483-1558
http://www.cancer.org

Richard C. Wender, President
Elmer Huerta, First Vice President

Nationwide, community-based voluntary health organization dedicated to eliminating cancer as a major health problem by preventing cancer, saving lives, and diminishing suffering from cancer through research, education, advocacy, and service.

5377 American Cancer Society: Greenville
154 Milestone Way
Greenville, SC 29615
864-627-1903
800-ACS-2345
Fax: 864-458-8454
http://www.cancer.org

Richard C. Wender, President
Elmer Huerta, First Vice President

Nationwide, community-based voluntary health organization dedicated to eliminating cancer as a major health problem by preventing cancer, saving lives, and diminishing suffering from cancer through research, education, advocacy, and service.

5378 American Cancer Society: Greenwood
231 Hampton Ave
Suite 3
Greenwood, SC 29648
864-229-7373
800-ACS-2345
Fax: 864-229-7653
http://www.cancer.org

Richard C. Wender, President
Elmer Huerta, First Vice President

Nationwide, community-based voluntary health organization dedicated to eliminating cancer as a major health problem by preventing cancer, saving lives, and diminishing suffering from cancer through research, education, advocacy, and service.

5379 American Cancer Society: Gulfport
417 Security Square
Gulfport, MS 39507
228-896-7024
800-ACS-2345
Fax: 228-896-8620
http://www.cancer.org

Richard C. Wender, President
Elmer Huerta, First Vice President

Nationwide, community-based voluntary health organization dedicated to eliminating cancer as a major health problem by preventing cancer, saving lives, and diminishing suffering from cancer through research, education, advocacy, and service.

5380 American Cancer Society: Gwinnett
6500 Sugarloaf Parkway
Suite 260
Duluth, GA 30097
770-814-0123
800-ACS-2345
Fax: 770-814-9517
http://www.cancer.org

Richard C. Wender, President
Elmer Huerta, First Vice President

Nationwide, community-based voluntary health organization dedicated to eliminating cancer as a major health problem by preventing cancer, saving lives, and diminishing suffering from cancer through research, education, advocacy, and service.

5381 American Cancer Society: Hagerstown
1037 Haven Road
Hagerstown, MD 21742-3190
301-733-8272
800-ACS-2345
Fax: 301-733-0285
http://www.cancer.org

Richard C. Wender, President
Elmer Huerta, First Vice President

Nationwide, community-based voluntary health organization dedicated to eliminating cancer as a major health problem by preventing cancer, saving lives, and diminishing suffering from cancer through research, education, advocacy, and service.

Cancer/Associations & Organizations

5382 **American Cancer Society: Hamilton County**
2808 Reading Rd
Cincinnati, OH 45206   888-227-6446
                          800-ACS-2345
                     Fax: 877-227-2838
                    http://www.cancer.org

Richard C. Wender, President
Elmer Huerta, First Vice President

Nationwide, community-based voluntary health organization dedicated to eliminating cancer as a major health problem by preventing cancer, saving lives, and diminishing suffering from cancer through research, education, advocacy, and service.

5383 **American Cancer Society: Hanford**
1443 W 7th Street
Hanford, CA 93230   559-584-6691
                          800-ACS-2345
                     Fax: 559-584-2815
                    http://www.cancer.org

Richard C. Wender, President
Elmer Huerta, First Vice President

Nationwide, community-based voluntary health organization dedicated to eliminating cancer as a major health problem by preventing cancer, saving lives, and diminishing suffering from cancer through research, education, advocacy, and service.

5384 **American Cancer Society: Hannibal**
2910 Saint Marys Avenue
Suite 1
Hannibal, MO 63401   573-221-4660
                          800-ACS-2345
                     Fax: 573-221-3326
                    http://www.cancer.org

Richard C. Wender, President
Elmer Huerta, First Vice President

Nationwide, community-based voluntary health organization dedicated to eliminating cancer as a major health problem by preventing cancer, saving lives, and diminishing suffering from cancer through research, education, advocacy, and service.

5385 **American Cancer Society: Hattiesburg**
6652 US Hwy 98
Suite 4
Hattiesburg, MS 39402   601-271-7129
                          800-ACS-2345
                     Fax: 601-271-7994
                    http://www.cancer.org

Richard C. Wender, President
Elmer Huerta, First Vice President

Nationwide, community-based voluntary health organization dedicated to eliminating cancer as a major health problem by preventing cancer, saving lives, and diminishing suffering from cancer through research, education, advocacy, and service.

5386 **American Cancer Society: Helena**
3550 Mullan Road
Ste 105
Missoula, MT 59808   406-542-2191
                     Fax: 406-327-0146
                    http://www.cancer.org

Richard C. Wender, President
Elmer Huerta, First Vice President

5387 **American Cancer Society: Hilo**
614 Kilauea Avenue
Suite 2
Hilo, HI 96720-4272   808-935-9763
                          800-ACS-2345
                     Fax: 808-935-9780
                    http://www.cancer.org

Richard C. Wender, President
Elmer Huerta, First Vice President

Nationwide, community-based voluntary health organization dedicated to eliminating cancer as a major health problem by preventing cancer, saving lives, and diminishing suffering from cancer through research, education, advocacy, and service.

5388 **American Cancer Society: Hilton Head**
59 Pope Avenue
Suite 101
Hilton Head, SC 29928   843-842-5188
                          800-ACS-2345
                     Fax: 843-842-9898
                    http://www.cancer.org

Richard C. Wender, President
Elmer Huerta, First Vice President

Nationwide, community-based voluntary health organization dedicated to eliminating cancer as a major health problem by preventing cancer, saving lives, and diminishing suffering from cancer through research, education, advocacy, and service.

5389 **American Cancer Society: Honolulu**
2370 Nuuanu Avenue
Honolulu, HI 96817   808-595-7544
                          800-ACS-2345
                     Fax: 808-595-7545
                    http://www.cancer.org

Richard C. Wender, President
Elmer Huerta, First Vice President

Nationwide, community-based voluntary health organization dedicated to eliminating cancer as a major health problem by preventing cancer, saving lives, and diminishing suffering from cancer through research, education, advocacy, and service.

5390 **American Cancer Society: Houma**
614 Barrow Street
Houma, LA 70360   985-851-7776
                          800-ACS-2345
                     Fax: 985-851-5939
                    http://www.cancer.org

Richard C. Wender, President
Elmer Huerta, First Vice President

Nationwide, community-based voluntary health organization dedicated to eliminating cancer as a major health problem by preventing cancer, saving lives, and diminishing suffering from cancer through research, education, advocacy, and service.

5391 **American Cancer Society: Houston**
6301 Richmond Avenue
Houston, TX 77057   713-266-2877
                          800-ACS-2345
                     Fax: 713-266-4159
                    http://www.cancer.org

Richard C. Wender, President
Elmer Huerta, First Vice President

Nationwide, community-based voluntary health organization dedicated to eliminating cancer as a major health problem by preventing cancer, saving lives, and diminishing suffering from cancer through research, education, advocacy, and service.

5392 **American Cancer Society: Hudson Valley**
Vassar Brother's Hospital
45 Reade Place
Poughkeepsie, NY 12601   845-452-2635
                          800-ACS-2345
                     Fax: 845-452-8067
                    http://www.cancer.org

Richard C. Wender, President
Elmer Huerta, First Vice President

Nationwide, community-based voluntary health organization dedicated to eliminating cancer as a major health problem by preventing cancer, saving lives, and diminishing suffering from cancer through research, education, advocacy, and service.

5393 **American Cancer Society: Huntington**
611 7th Avenue
101
Huntington, WV 25701   304-523-7989
                          800-ACS-2345
                     Fax: 304-523-7996
                    http://www.cancer.org

Richard C. Wender, President
Elmer Huerta, First Vice President

Cancer/Associations & Organizations

Nationwide, community-based voluntary health organization dedicated to eliminating cancer as a major health problem by preventing cancer, saving lives, and diminishing suffering from cancer through research, education, advocacy, and service.

5394 American Cancer Society: Huntsville
2515-B Memorial Pkwy SW
Huntsville, AL 35801
256-536-1855
800-ACS-2345
Fax: 256-534-0843
http://www.cancer.org

Richard C. Wender, President
Elmer Huerta, First Vice President

Nationwide, community-based voluntary health organization dedicated to eliminating cancer as a major health problem by preventing cancer, saving lives, and diminishing suffering from cancer through research, education, advocacy, and service.

5395 American Cancer Society: Huron Valley
2010 Hogback Road
Suite 4
Ann Arbor, MI 48105
734-971-4300
800-ACS-2345
Fax: 734-971-2818
http://www.cancer.org

Richard C. Wender, President
Elmer Huerta, First Vice President

Nationwide, community-based voluntary health organization dedicated to eliminating cancer as a major health problem by preventing cancer, saving lives, and diminishing suffering from cancer through research, education, advocacy, and service.

5396 American Cancer Society: Indian River
3375 20th Street
Suite 100
Vero Beach, FL 32960
772-562-2272
772-ACS-2345
Fax: 772-562-2666
http://www.cancer.org

Richard C. Wender, President
Elmer Huerta, First Vice President

Nationwide, community-based voluntary health organization dedicated to eliminating cancer as a major health problem by preventing cancer, saving lives, and diminishing suffering from cancer through research, education, advocacy, and service.

5397 American Cancer Society: Indianapolis
6030 W 62nd Street
Indianapolis, IN 46278
317-347-6670
800-ACS-2345
Fax: 317-347-6679
http://www.cancer.org

Richard C. Wender, President
Elmer Huerta, First Vice President

Nationwide, community-based voluntary health organization dedicated to eliminating cancer as a major health problem by preventing cancer, saving lives, and diminishing suffering from cancer through research, education, advocacy, and service.

5398 American Cancer Society: Ionia
PO Box 45
Ionia, MI 48846
616-527-1730
800-ACS-2345
http://www.cancer.org

Carolyn D. Runowicz, President
Elmer Huerta, First Vice President

Nationwide, community-based voluntary health organization dedicated to eliminating cancer as a major health problem by preventing cancer, saving lives, and diminishing suffering from cancer through research, education, advocacy, and service.

5399 American Cancer Society: Iowa City
4080 First Ave NE
Ste #101
Cedar Rapids, IA 52402
319-365-5241
800-ACS-2345
Fax: 319-365-1739
http://www.cancer.org

Richard C. Wender, President
Elmer Huerta, First Vice President

Nationwide, community-based voluntary health organization dedicated to eliminating cancer as a major health problem by preventing cancer, saving lives, and diminishing suffering from cancer through research, education, advocacy, and service.

5400 American Cancer Society: Jackson
1380 Livingston Lane
Jackson, MS 39213
601-362-8874
800-ACS-2345
Fax: 601-362-8876
http://www.cancer.org

Buddy Graves, Director
Elmer Huerta, First Vice President

Nationwide, community-based voluntary health organization dedicated to eliminating cancer as a major health problem by preventing cancer, saving lives, and diminishing suffering from cancer through research, education, advocacy, and service.

5401 American Cancer Society: Jacksonville
1430 Prudential Dr
Jacksonville, FL 32207
904-398-0537
800-ACS-2345
Fax: 904-396-0240
http://www.cancer.org

Richard C. Wender, President
Elmer Huerta, First Vice President

Nationwide, community-based voluntary health organization dedicated to eliminating cancer as a major health problem by preventing cancer, saving lives, and diminishing suffering from cancer through research, education, advocacy, and service.

5402 American Cancer Society: Jacksonville Beach
2850 Isabella Boulevard
Suite 20
Jacksonville Beach, FL 32250
904-249-0022
800-ACS-2345
Fax: 904-270-0976
http://www.cancer.org

Richard C. Wender, President
Elmer Huerta, First Vice President

Nationwide, community-based voluntary health organization dedicated to eliminating cancer as a major health problem by preventing cancer, saving lives, and diminishing suffering from cancer through research, education, advocacy, and service.

5403 American Cancer Society: Jasper
1500 S Meridian Road
Jasper, IN 47546
812-482-7545
800-ACS-2345
Fax: 812-482-6962
http://www.cancer.org

Richard C. Wender, President
Elmer Huerta, First Vice President

Nationwide, community-based voluntary health organization dedicated to eliminating cancer as a major health problem by preventing cancer, saving lives, and diminishing suffering from cancer through research, education, advocacy, and service.

5404 American Cancer Society: Jefferson City
2413 Hyde Park Road
Jefferson City, MO 65109
573-635-4821
800-ACS-2345
Fax: 573-635-7821
http://www.cancer.org

Richard C. Wender, President
Elmer Huerta, First Vice President

Cancer/Associations & Organizations

Nationwide, community-based voluntary health organization dedicated to eliminating cancer as a major health problem by preventing cancer, saving lives, and diminishing suffering from cancer through research, education, advocacy, and service.

5405 American Cancer Society: Jersey Shore
801 Broad Street
Shrewsbury, NJ 7702
732-758-8220
800-ACS-2345
Fax: 732-758-8225
http://www.cancer.org

Richard C. Wender, President
Elmer Huerta, First Vice President

Nationwide, community-based voluntary health organization dedicated to eliminating cancer as a major health problem by preventing cancer, saving lives, and diminishing suffering from cancer through research, education, advocacy, and service.

5406 American Cancer Society: Johnson City
508 Princeton Road
Suite 102
Johnson City, TN 37601
423-926-2921
800-ACS-2345
Fax: 423-283-7112
http://www.cancer.org

Richard C. Wender, President
Elmer Huerta, First Vice President

Nationwide, community-based voluntary health organization dedicated to eliminating cancer as a major health problem by preventing cancer, saving lives, and diminishing suffering from cancer through research, education, advocacy, and service.

5407 American Cancer Society: Joplin
2700 McClelland Boulevard Bldg A
Suite 110
Joplin, MO 64804
417-627-7500
800-ACS-2345
Fax: 417-782-2348
http://www.cancer.org

Richard C. Wender, President
Elmer Huerta, First Vice President

Nationwide, community-based voluntary health organization dedicated to eliminating cancer as a major health problem by preventing cancer, saving lives, and diminishing suffering from cancer through research, education, advocacy, and service.

5408 American Cancer Society: Kaunakakai
95 Mahalani St
Wailuku, HI 96793
808-244-5553
800-ACS-2345
Fax: 808-244-6195
http://www.cancer.org

Richard C. Wender, President
Elmer Huerta, First Vice President

Nationwide, community-based voluntary health organization dedicated to eliminating cancer as a major health problem by preventing cancer, saving lives, and diminishing suffering from cancer through research, education, advocacy, and service.

5409 American Cancer Society: Kearney
3808 28th Avenue
Suite E
Kearney, NE 68845
308-237-7481
800-ACS-2345
Fax: 308-236-2016
http://www.cancer.org

Richard C. Wender, President
Elmer Huerta, First Vice President

Nationwide, community-based voluntary health organization dedicated to eliminating cancer as a major health problem by preventing cancer, saving lives, and diminishing suffering from cancer through research, education, advocacy, and service.

5410 American Cancer Society: Kennesaw
1825 Barrett Lakes Boulevard NW
Suite 280
Kennesaw, GA 30144
770-429-0089
800-ACS-2345
Fax: 770-429-9824
http://www.cancer.org

Richard C. Wender, President
Elmer Huerta, First Vice President

Nationwide, community-based voluntary health organization dedicated to eliminating cancer as a major health problem by preventing cancer, saving lives, and diminishing suffering from cancer through research, education, advocacy, and service.

5411 American Cancer Society: Kennewick
7325 W Deschutes Avenue
Suite A
Kennewick, WA 99336
509-783-5108
800-ACS-2345
Fax: 509-737-9702
http://www.cancer.org

Richard C. Wender, President
Elmer Huerta, First Vice President

Nationwide, community-based voluntary health organization dedicated to eliminating cancer as a major health problem by preventing cancer, saving lives, and diminishing suffering from cancer through research, education, advocacy, and service.

5412 American Cancer Society: Knoxville
871 N Weisgarber Road
Knoxville, TN 37909
865-584-1668
800-ACS-2345
Fax: 865-584-1673
http://www.cancer.org

Richard C. Wender, President
Elmer Huerta, First Vice President

Nationwide, community-based voluntary health organization dedicated to eliminating cancer as a major health problem by preventing cancer, saving lives, and diminishing suffering from cancer through research, education, advocacy, and service.

5413 American Cancer Society: Kokomo
2723 South Albright Rd
Kokomo, IN 46902
765-455-9905
800-ACS-2345
Fax: 765-455-9975
http://www.cancer.org

Richard C. Wender, President
Elmer Huerta, First Vice President

Nationwide, community-based voluntary health organization dedicated to eliminating cancer as a major health problem by preventing cancer, saving lives, and diminishing suffering from cancer through research, education, advocacy, and service.

5414 American Cancer Society: Lafayette
1604 W Pinhook Road
Suite 182
Lafayette, LA 70508
337-237-3736
800-ACS-2345
Fax: 337-237-6907
http://www.cancer.org

Richard C. Wender, President
Elmer Huerta, First Vice President

Nationwide, community-based voluntary health organization dedicated to eliminating cancer as a major health problem by preventing cancer, saving lives, and diminishing suffering from cancer through research, education, advocacy, and service.

5415 American Cancer Society: Lake Charles
1 Lakeshore Drive
Ste 1510
Lake Charles, LA 70629
337-433-5131
800-ACS-2345
Fax: 337-439-9620
http://www.cancer.org

Richard C. Wender, President
Elmer Huerta, First Vice President

Cancer/Associations & Organizations

5416 American Cancer Society: Lake County
100 Tri State International
Suite 125
Lincolnshire, IL 60069
847-317-0025
800-ACS-2345
Fax: 847-317-0366
http://www.cancer.org

Richard C. Wender, President
Elmer Huerta, First Vice President

Nationwide, community-based voluntary health organization dedicated to eliminating cancer as a major health problem by preventing cancer, saving lives, and diminishing suffering from cancer through research, education, advocacy, and service.

5417 American Cancer Society: Lakeland
809 S Florida Avenue
Lakeland, FL 33801-5234
863-294-0661
800-ACS-2345
Fax: 863-293-3906
http://www.cancer.org

Eunice Hutto, Executive Director

Nationwide, community-based voluntary health organization dedicated to eliminating cancer as a major health problem by preventing cancer, saving lives, and diminishing suffering from cancer through research, education, advocacy, and service.

5418 American Cancer Society: Lakes Region
1400 Winton Road N
Rochester, NY 14609
585-288-1950
800-ACS-2345
Fax: 585-288-6467
e-mail: vgroenen@cancer.org
http://www.cancer.org

Richard C. Wender, President
Elmer Huerta, First Vice President

Nationwide, community-based voluntary health organization dedicated to eliminating cancer as a major health problem by preventing cancer, saving lives, and diminishing suffering from cancer through research, education, advocacy, and service.

5419 American Cancer Society: Lakeshore
12723 N Bellwood
STE 20
Holland, MI 49424
616-396-5576
800-ACS-2345
Fax: 616-396-2673
http://www.cancer.org

Richard C. Wender, President
Elmer Huerta, First Vice President

Nationwide, community-based voluntary health organization dedicated to eliminating cancer as a major health problem by preventing cancer, saving lives, and diminishing suffering from cancer through research, education, advocacy, and service.

5420 American Cancer Society: Lancaster
314 Good Drive
Lancaster, PA 17603
888-227-5445
800-ACS-2345
Fax: 717-397-1526
http://www.cancer.org

Richard C. Wender, President
Elmer Huerta, First Vice President

Nationwide, community-based voluntary health organization dedicated to eliminating cancer as a major health problem by preventing cancer, saving lives, and diminishing suffering from cancer through research, education, advocacy, and service.

5421 American Cancer Society: Larimer County
6857 Paiute Avenue
Niwot, CO 80503
303-776-2689
800-ACS-2345
Fax: 303-776-2875
http://www.cancer.org

Richard C. Wender, President
Elmer Huerta, First Vice President

Nationwide, community-based voluntary health organization dedicated to eliminating cancer as a major health problem by preventing cancer, saving lives, and diminishing suffering from cancer through research, education, advocacy, and service.

5422 American Cancer Society: Las Vegas
6165 South Rainbow Blvd
Las Vegas, NV 89118
702-798-6877
800-ACS-2345
Fax: 702-798-0530
http://www.cancer.org

Richard C. Wender, President
Elmer Huerta, First Vice President

Nationwide, community-based voluntary health organization dedicated to eliminating cancer as a major health problem by preventing cancer, saving lives, and diminishing suffering from cancer through research, education, advocacy, and service.

5423 American Cancer Society: Lathrup Village
20450 Civic Center Drive
Southfield, MI 48076
248-663-3400
800-ACS-2345
Fax: 248-663-3409
http://www.cancer.org

Richard C. Wender, President
Elmer Huerta, First Vice President

Nationwide, community-based voluntary health organization dedicated to eliminating cancer as a major health problem by preventing cancer, saving lives, and diminishing suffering from cancer through research, education, advocacy, and service.

5424 American Cancer Society: Lawton
1320 NW Homestead Drive
Suite D
Lawton, OK 73505
580-353-8145
800-ACS-2345
Fax: 580-353-8146
http://www.cancer.org

Richard C. Wender, President
Elmer Huerta, First Vice President

Nationwide, community-based voluntary health organization dedicated to eliminating cancer as a major health problem by preventing cancer, saving lives, and diminishing suffering from cancer through research, education, advocacy, and service.

5425 American Cancer Society: Leesburg
3261 US Hwy 441/27
Suite B2
Fruitland Park, FL 34731
352-326-9599
800-ACS-2345
Fax: 352-326-3855
http://www.cancer.org

Richard C. Wender, President
Elmer Huerta, First Vice President

Nationwide, community-based voluntary health organization dedicated to eliminating cancer as a major health problem by preventing cancer, saving lives, and diminishing suffering from cancer through research, education, advocacy, and service.

5426 American Cancer Society: Lewistown
342 S Logan Blvd
Burnham, PA 17009
717-248-1421
800-ACS-2345
Fax: 717-248-8015
http://www.cancer.org

Richard C. Wender, President
Elmer Huerta, First Vice President

Cancer/Associations & Organizations

Nationwide, community-based voluntary health organization dedicated to eliminating cancer as a major health problem by preventing cancer, saving lives, and diminishing suffering from cancer through research, education, advocacy, and service.

5427 American Cancer Society: Lexington
1504 College Way
Suite 201
Lexington, KY 40502
859-276-3223
800-ACS-2345
Fax: 859-260-8299
http://www.cancer.org

Richard C. Wender, President
Elmer Huerta, First Vice President

Nationwide, community-based voluntary health organization dedicated to eliminating cancer as a major health problem by preventing cancer, saving lives, and diminishing suffering from cancer through research, education, advocacy, and service.

5428 American Cancer Society: Lihue
4371-C Puaole Suite
Lihue, HI 96766
808-245-2942
800-ACS-2345
Fax: 808-245-2302
http://www.cancer.org

Richard C. Wender, President
Elmer Huerta, First Vice President

Nationwide, community-based voluntary health organization dedicated to eliminating cancer as a major health problem by preventing cancer, saving lives, and diminishing suffering from cancer through research, education, advocacy, and service.

5429 American Cancer Society: Lincoln
5733 S 34th Street
Suite 500
Lincoln, NE 68516
402-423-4888
800-ACS-2345
Fax: 402-423-4915
http://www.cancer.org

Richard C. Wender, President
Elmer Huerta, First Vice President

Nationwide, community-based voluntary health organization dedicated to eliminating cancer as a major health problem by preventing cancer, saving lives, and diminishing suffering from cancer through research, education, advocacy, and service.

5430 American Cancer Society: Little Rock
901 N University Avenue
Little Rock, AR 72207
501-664-3480
800-ACS-2345
Fax: 501-666-0068
http://www.cancer.org

Richard C. Wender, President
Elmer Huerta, First Vice President

Nationwide, community-based voluntary health organization dedicated to eliminating cancer as a major health problem by preventing cancer, saving lives, and diminishing suffering from cancer through research, education, advocacy, and service.

5431 American Cancer Society: Livingston
2010 Hogback Rd
STE 4
Ann Arbor, MI 48105
734-971-4300
800-ACS-2345
Fax: 734-971-2818
http://www.cancer.org

Richard C. Wender, President
Elmer Huerta, First Vice President

Nationwide, community-based voluntary health organization dedicated to eliminating cancer as a major health problem by preventing cancer, saving lives, and diminishing suffering from cancer through research, education, advocacy, and service.

5432 American Cancer Society: Lompoc Valley
604 E Ocean Avenue
Lompoc, CA 93436
805-736-2610
800-ACS-2345
Fax: 805-736-9413
http://www.cancer.org

Richard C. Wender, President
Elmer Huerta, First Vice President

Nationwide, community-based voluntary health organization dedicated to eliminating cancer as a major health problem by preventing cancer, saving lives, and diminishing suffering from cancer through research, education, advocacy, and service.

5433 American Cancer Society: Long Beach
936 Pine Avenue
Long Beach, CA 90813
562-437-0791
800-ACS-2345
Fax: 562-495-1782
http://www.cancer.org

Richard C. Wender, President
Elmer Huerta, First Vice President

Nationwide, community-based voluntary health organization dedicated to eliminating cancer as a major health problem by preventing cancer, saving lives, and diminishing suffering from cancer through research, education, advocacy, and service.

5434 American Cancer Society: Longmont
6857 Paiute Avenue
Unit A
Niwot, CO 80503
303-776-2689
800-ACS-2345
Fax: 303-776-2875
http://www.cancer.org

Richard C. Wender, President
Elmer Huerta, First Vice President

Nationwide, community-based voluntary health organization dedicated to eliminating cancer as a major health problem by preventing cancer, saving lives, and diminishing suffering from cancer through research, education, advocacy, and service.

5435 American Cancer Society: Los Angeles
3333 Wilshire Boulevard
Suite 900
Los Angeles, CA 90010
213-386-6102
800-ACS-2345
Fax: 213-480-0806
http://www.cancer.org

Richard C. Wender, President
Elmer Huerta, First Vice President

Nationwide, community-based voluntary health organization dedicated to eliminating cancer as a major health problem by preventing cancer, saving lives, and diminishing suffering from cancer through research, education, advocacy, and service.

5436 American Cancer Society: Loudonville
260 Osborne Road
Loudonville, NY 12211
518-438-7841
800-ACS-2345
Fax: 518-438-9608
http://www.cancer.org

Richard C. Wender, President
Elmer Huerta, First Vice President

Nationwide, community-based voluntary health organization dedicated to eliminating cancer as a major health problem by preventing cancer, saving lives, and diminishing suffering from cancer through research, education, advocacy, and service.

5437 American Cancer Society: Louisville
701 W Muhammad Ali Boulevard
Louisville, KY 40203
502-584-6782
800-ACS-2345
Fax: 502-584-6767
http://www.cancer.org

Richard C. Wender, President
Elmer Huerta, First Vice President

Cancer/Associations & Organizations

Nationwide, community-based voluntary health organization dedicated to eliminating cancer as a major health problem by preventing cancer, saving lives, and diminishing suffering from cancer through research, education, advocacy, and service.

5438 American Cancer Society: Lynchburg
2316 Atherholt Road
Suite 108
Lynchburg, VA 24501
434-845-0973
800-ACS-2345
Fax: 434-845-8719
http://www.cancer.org

Richard C. Wender, President
Elmer Huerta, First Vice President

Nationwide, community-based voluntary health organization dedicated to eliminating cancer as a major health problem by preventing cancer, saving lives, and diminishing suffering from cancer through research, education, advocacy, and service.

5439 American Cancer Society: Macon
804 Cherry Street
Suite A
Macon, GA 31201
478-743-6391
800-ACS-2345
Fax: 478-741-5905
http://www.cancer.org

Richard C. Wender, President
Elmer Huerta, First Vice President

Nationwide, community-based voluntary health organization dedicated to eliminating cancer as a major health problem by preventing cancer, saving lives, and diminishing suffering from cancer through research, education, advocacy, and service.

5440 American Cancer Society: Madison
8317 Elderberry Road
Madison, WI 53717
608-833-4555
800-ACS-2345
Fax: 608-833-1195
http://www.cancer.org

Richard C. Wender, President
Elmer Huerta, First Vice President

Nationwide, community-based voluntary health organization dedicated to eliminating cancer as a major health problem by preventing cancer, saving lives, and diminishing suffering from cancer through research, education, advocacy, and service.

5441 American Cancer Society: Manhattan
1315 SW Arrowhead Rd
Apt 80
Topeka, KS 66604
785-273-4422
800-ACS-2345
Fax: 785-273-1503
http://www.cancer.org

Richard C. Wender, President
Elmer Huerta, First Vice President

Nationwide, community-based voluntary health organization dedicated to eliminating cancer as a major health problem by preventing cancer, saving lives, and diminishing suffering from cancer through research, education, advocacy, and service.

5442 American Cancer Society: Mankato
882 7th St NW
Rochester, MN 55901
507-287-2044
800-ACS-2345
Fax: 507-287-2178
http://www.cancer.org

Richard C. Wender, President
Elmer Huerta, First Vice President

Nationwide, community-based voluntary health organization dedicated to eliminating cancer as a major health problem by preventing cancer, saving lives, and diminishing suffering from cancer through research, education, advocacy, and service.

5443 American Cancer Society: Marco Island
917 N Collier Boulevard
Marco Island, FL 34145
239-642-8800
Fax: 239-642-0027
http://www.cancer.org

Richard C. Wender, President
Elmer Huerta, First Vice President

Nationwide, community-based voluntary health organization dedicated to eliminating cancer as a major health problem by preventing cancer, saving lives, and diminishing suffering from cancer through research, education, advocacy, and service.

5444 American Cancer Society: Marin County
750 Lindaro St.,
Suite 120
San Rafael, CA 94901
415-454-8464
800-ACS-2345
Fax: 415-456-1477
http://www.cancer.org

Richard C. Wender, President
Elmer Huerta, First Vice President

Nationwide, community-based voluntary health organization dedicated to eliminating cancer as a major health problem by preventing cancer, saving lives, and diminishing suffering from cancer through research, education, advocacy, and service.

5445 American Cancer Society: Marion
2201 SE 30th Avenue
Suite 301
Ocala, FL 34471
352-629-4727
800-ACS-2345
Fax: 352-629-5107
http://www.cancer.org

Richard C. Wender, President
Elmer Huerta, First Vice President

Nationwide, community-based voluntary health organization dedicated to eliminating cancer as a major health problem by preventing cancer, saving lives, and diminishing suffering from cancer through research, education, advocacy, and service.

5446 American Cancer Society: Marshall
2520 Pilot Knob Road
Suite 150
Mendota Heights, MN 55120
651-255-8100
800-ACS-2345
Fax: 651-255-8133
http://www.cancer.org

Richard C. Wender, President
Elmer Huerta, First Vice President

Nationwide, community-based voluntary health organization dedicated to eliminating cancer as a major health problem by preventing cancer, saving lives, and diminishing suffering from cancer through research, education, advocacy, and service.

5447 American Cancer Society: Martin
865 SE Monterey Commons Boulevard
Stuart, FL 34996
772-287-7467
800-ACS-2345
Fax: 772-287-7925
http://www.cancer.org

Richard C. Wender, President
Elmer Huerta, First Vice President

Nationwide, community-based voluntary health organization dedicated to eliminating cancer as a major health problem by preventing cancer, saving lives, and diminishing suffering from cancer through research, education, advocacy, and service.

5448 American Cancer Society: Marysville
618 5th Street
Marysville, CA 95901
530-741-1366
800-ACS-2345
Fax: 530-741-1383
http://www.cancer.org

Richard C. Wender, President
Elmer Huerta, First Vice President

Cancer/Associations & Organizations

Nationwide, community-based voluntary health organization dedicated to eliminating cancer as a major health problem by preventing cancer, saving lives, and diminishing suffering from cancer through research, education, advocacy, and service.

5449 **American Cancer Society: Mason City**
130 4th Street SW
Mason City, IA 50401-3807
641-422-9055
800-ACS-2345
Fax: 641-422-9091
http://www.cancer.org

Richard C. Wender, President
Elmer Huerta, First Vice President

Nationwide, community-based voluntary health organization dedicated to eliminating cancer as a major health problem by preventing cancer, saving lives, and diminishing suffering from cancer through research, education, advocacy, and service.

5450 **American Cancer Society: Medford**
31 W 6th Street
Medford, OR 97501
541-779-6091
800-ACS-2345
Fax: 541-779-1470
http://www.cancer.org

Richard C. Wender, President
Elmer Huerta, First Vice President

Nationwide, community-based voluntary health organization dedicated to eliminating cancer as a major health problem by preventing cancer, saving lives, and diminishing suffering from cancer through research, education, advocacy, and service.

5451 **American Cancer Society: Memphis**
1378 Union Avenue
Memphis, TN 38104
901-278-2000
800-ACS-2345
Fax: 901-278-2020
http://www.cancer.org

Richard C. Wender, President
Elmer Huerta, First Vice President

Nationwide, community-based voluntary health organization dedicated to eliminating cancer as a major health problem by preventing cancer, saving lives, and diminishing suffering from cancer through research, education, advocacy, and service.

5452 **American Cancer Society: Merced**
301 W 18th Street
Suite 101
Merced, CA 95340
209-722-3341
800-ACS-2345
Fax: 209-722-6628
http://www.cancer.org

Richard C. Wender, President
Elmer Huerta, First Vice President

Nationwide, community-based voluntary health organization dedicated to eliminating cancer as a major health problem by preventing cancer, saving lives, and diminishing suffering from cancer through research, education, advocacy, and service.

5453 **American Cancer Society: Mercer**
3208 Wilmington Rd
Suite 1
New Castle, PA 16105
888-227-5445
800-ACS-2345
Fax: 412-919-1101
http://www.cancer.org

Richard C. Wender, President
Elmer Huerta, First Vice President

Nationwide, community-based voluntary health organization dedicated to eliminating cancer as a major health problem by preventing cancer, saving lives, and diminishing suffering from cancer through research, education, advocacy, and service.

5454 **American Cancer Society: Meridian**
4927 Poplar Springs Drive
Meridian, MS 39305
601-481-1712
800-ACS-2345
Fax: 601-482-0258
http://www.cancer.org

Richard C. Wender, President
Elmer Huerta, First Vice President

Nationwide, community-based voluntary health organization dedicated to eliminating cancer as a major health problem by preventing cancer, saving lives, and diminishing suffering from cancer through research, education, advocacy, and service.

5455 **American Cancer Society: Minot**
2401 46th Avenue Southeast
Suite 102
Mandan, ND 58554
701-224-9954
800-ACS-2345
Fax: 701-250-9145
http://www.cancer.org

Richard C. Wender, President
Elmer Huerta, First Vice President
Jason Rohrer, Manager

Nationwide, community-based voluntary health organization dedicated to eliminating cancer as a major health problem by preventing cancer, saving lives, and diminishing suffering from cancer through research, education, advocacy, and service.

5456 **American Cancer Society: Missoula**
3550 Mullan Road
Suite 105
Missoula, MT 59808
406-542-2191
800-ACS-2345
Fax: 406-327-0146
http://www.cancer.org

Richard C. Wender, President
Elmer Huerta, First Vice President

Nationwide, community-based voluntary health organization dedicated to eliminating cancer as a major health problem by preventing cancer, saving lives, and diminishing suffering from cancer through research, education, advocacy, and service.

5457 **American Cancer Society: Mitchell**
4904 S Technopolis Dr
Sioux Falls, SD 57106
605-361-8277
800-ACS-2345
Fax: 605-361-8537
http://www.cancer.org

Richard C. Wender, President
Elmer Huerta, First Vice President

Nationwide, community-based voluntary health organization dedicated to eliminating cancer as a major health problem by preventing cancer, saving lives, and diminishing suffering from cancer through research, education, advocacy, and service.

5458 **American Cancer Society: Mobile**
900 Western America Circle
Suite 101
Mobile, AL 36609
251-344-9856
800-ACS-2345
Fax: 251-344-9882
http://www.cancer.org

Richard C. Wender, President
Elmer Huerta, First Vice President

Nationwide, community-based voluntary health organization dedicated to eliminating cancer as a major health problem by preventing cancer, saving lives, and diminishing suffering from cancer through research, education, advocacy, and service.

Cancer/Associations & Organizations

5459 American Cancer Society: Modesto
1604 Ford Avenue
Suite 8
Modesto, CA 95350
209-524-7242
800-ACS-2345
Fax: 209-524-7454
http://www.cancer.org

Richard C. Wender, President
Elmer Huerta, First Vice President

Nationwide, community-based voluntary health organization dedicated to eliminating cancer as a major health problem by preventing cancer, saving lives, and diminishing suffering from cancer through research, education, advocacy, and service.

5460 American Cancer Society: Monroe
1761 N 19th Street
Monroe, LA 71201
318-398-7248
800-ACS-2345
Fax: 318-361-0718
http://www.cancer.org

Richard C. Wender, President
Elmer Huerta, First Vice President

Nationwide, community-based voluntary health organization dedicated to eliminating cancer as a major health problem by preventing cancer, saving lives, and diminishing suffering from cancer through research, education, advocacy, and service.

5461 American Cancer Society: Montgomery
3054c McGehee Road
Montgomery, AL 36111
334-288-3432
800-ACS-2345
Fax: 334-612-8181
http://www.cancer.org

Richard C. Wender, President
Elmer Huerta, First Vice President

Nationwide, community-based voluntary health organization dedicated to eliminating cancer as a major health problem by preventing cancer, saving lives, and diminishing suffering from cancer through research, education, advocacy, and service.

5462 American Cancer Society: Moorhead
3721 23rd St S
Ste 102
Saint Cloud, MN 56301
320-255-0220
800-ACS-2345
Fax: 320-255-5517
http://www.cancer.org

Richard C. Wender, President
Elmer Huerta, First Vice President

Nationwide, community-based voluntary health organization dedicated to eliminating cancer as a major health problem by preventing cancer, saving lives, and diminishing suffering from cancer through research, education, advocacy, and service.

5463 American Cancer Society: Morgantown
122 South High Street
Morgantown, WV 26501
304-296-8155
800-ACS-2345
Fax: 304-296-6172
http://www.cancer.org

Richard C. Wender, President
Elmer Huerta, First Vice President

Nationwide, community-based voluntary health organization dedicated to eliminating cancer as a major health problem by preventing cancer, saving lives, and diminishing suffering from cancer through research, education, advocacy, and service.

5464 American Cancer Society: Morongo Basin
73-161 Fred Waring Dr
Ste 100
Palm Desert, CA 92260
760-568-2691
800-ACS-2345
Fax: 760-341-8783
http://www.cancer.org

Richard C. Wender, President
Elmer Huerta, First Vice President

Nationwide, community-based voluntary health organization dedicated to eliminating cancer as a major health problem by preventing cancer, saving lives, and diminishing suffering from cancer through research, education, advocacy, and service.

5465 American Cancer Society: Mountain Valley
754 Mangrove Avenue
Chico, CA 95926
530-342-4567
800-ACS-2345
Fax: 530-345-5871
http://www.cancer.org

Richard C. Wender, President
Elmer Huerta, First Vice President

Nationwide, community-based voluntary health organization dedicated to eliminating cancer as a major health problem by preventing cancer, saving lives, and diminishing suffering from cancer through research, education, advocacy, and service.

5466 American Cancer Society: Muncie
1220 Meridian Street
Anderson, IN 46016-1715
765-642-6603
800-ACS-2345
Fax: 765-642-6711
http://www.cancer.org

Richard C. Wender, President
Elmer Huerta, First Vice President

Nationwide, community-based voluntary health organization dedicated to eliminating cancer as a major health problem by preventing cancer, saving lives, and diminishing suffering from cancer through research, education, advocacy, and service.

5467 American Cancer Society: Muskegon
12723 N Bellwood
STE 20
Holland, MI 49424
616-396-5576
800-ACS-2345
Fax: 616-396-2673
http://www.cancer.org

Richard C. Wender, President
Elmer Huerta, First Vice President

Nationwide, community-based voluntary health organization dedicated to eliminating cancer as a major health problem by preventing cancer, saving lives, and diminishing suffering from cancer through research, education, advocacy, and service.

5468 American Cancer Society: Myrtle Beach
950 48th Avenue N
Myrtle Beach, SC 29577
843-213-0333
800-ACS-2345
Fax: 843-213-0055
http://www.cancer.org

Richard C. Wender, President
Elmer Huerta, First Vice President

Nationwide, community-based voluntary health organization dedicated to eliminating cancer as a major health problem by preventing cancer, saving lives, and diminishing suffering from cancer through research, education, advocacy, and service.

5469 American Cancer Society: Napa
1031 Jefferson Street
Napa, CA 94559-2418
707-255-5911
800-ACS-2345
Fax: 707-255-3823
http://www.cancer.org

Richard C. Wender, President
Elmer Huerta, First Vice President

Nationwide, community-based voluntary health organization dedicated to eliminating cancer as a major health problem by preventing cancer, saving lives, and diminishing suffering from cancer through research, education, advocacy, and service.

Cancer/Associations & Organizations

5470 **American Cancer Society: Nashville**
2000 Charlotte Avenue
Nashville, TN 37203
615-327-0991
800-ACS-2345
Fax: 615-341-7335
http://www.cancer.org

Richard C. Wender, President
Elmer Huerta, First Vice President

Nationwide, community-based voluntary health organization dedicated to eliminating cancer as a major health problem by preventing cancer, saving lives, and diminishing suffering from cancer through research, education, advocacy, and service.

5471 **American Cancer Society: Nassau Region**
41-60 Main St Ste 307
Flushing, NY 11355
718-886-8890
800-ACS-2345
Fax: 718-886-8981
http://www.cancer.org

Richard C. Wender, President
Elmer Huerta, First Vice President

Nationwide, community-based voluntary health organization dedicated to eliminating cancer as a major health problem by preventing cancer, saving lives, and diminishing suffering from cancer through research, education, advocacy, and service.

5472 **American Cancer Society: Natick**
9 Riverside Rd
Weston, MA 02493
781-894-6633
800-ACS-2345
Fax: 781-314-2699
http://www.cancer.org

Richard C. Wender, President
Elmer Huerta, First Vice President

Nationwide, community-based voluntary health organization dedicated to eliminating cancer as a major health problem by preventing cancer, saving lives, and diminishing suffering from cancer through research, education, advocacy, and service.

5473 **American Cancer Society: New Castle**
92 Reads Way
Suite 205
New Castle, DE 19720
302-324-4227
800-ACS-2345
Fax: 302-324-4233
http://www.cancer.org

Richard C. Wender, President
Elmer Huerta, First Vice President

Nationwide, community-based voluntary health organization dedicated to eliminating cancer as a major health problem by preventing cancer, saving lives, and diminishing suffering from cancer through research, education, advocacy, and service.

5474 **American Cancer Society: New England Div**
9 Riverside Rd
Weston, MA 02493
781-894-6633
800-ACS-2345
Fax: 781-314-2699
http://www.cancer.org

Richard C. Wender, President
Elmer Huerta, First Vice President

Nationwide, community-based voluntary health organization dedicated to eliminating cancer as a major health problem by preventing cancer, saving lives, and diminishing suffering from cancer through research, education, advocacy, and service.

5475 **American Cancer Society: New Jersey**
669 Littleton Road
Parsippany, NJ 7054
973-331-9300
800-ACS-2345
Fax: 973-331-9444
http://www.cancer.org

Richard C. Wender, President
Elmer Huerta, First Vice President

Nationwide, community-based voluntary health organization dedicated to eliminating cancer as a major health problem by preventing cancer, saving lives, and diminishing suffering from cancer through research, education, advocacy, and service.

5476 **American Cancer Society: New Orleans**
2605 River Rd
New Orleans, LA 70121
504-469-0021
800-ACS-2345
Fax: 504-219-2290
http://www.cancer.org

Richard C. Wender, President
Elmer Huerta, First Vice President

Nationwide, community-based voluntary health organization dedicated to eliminating cancer as a major health problem by preventing cancer, saving lives, and diminishing suffering from cancer through research, education, advocacy, and service.

5477 **American Cancer Society: Norfolk**
4416 Expressway Dr
Virginia Beach, VA 23452
757-493-7940
800-ACS-2345
Fax: 757-493-9450
http://www.cancer.org

Richard C. Wender, President
Elmer Huerta, First Vice President

Nationwide, community-based voluntary health organization dedicated to eliminating cancer as a major health problem by preventing cancer, saving lives, and diminishing suffering from cancer through research, education, advocacy, and service.

5478 **American Cancer Society: Norman**
6525 N Meridian Avenue
Suite 110
Oklahoma City, OK 73116
405-843-9888
800-ACS-2345
Fax: 405-848-0795
http://www.cancer.org

Richard C. Wender, President
Elmer Huerta, First Vice President

Nationwide, community-based voluntary health organization dedicated to eliminating cancer as a major health problem by preventing cancer, saving lives, and diminishing suffering from cancer through research, education, advocacy, and service.

5479 **American Cancer Society: North Central Indiana**
601 W. Edison
Suite 6
Mishawaka, IN 46545
866-522-2111
800-ACS-2345
Fax: 574-257-9790
http://www.cancer.org

Richard C. Wender, President
Elmer Huerta, First Vice President

Nationwide, community-based voluntary health organization dedicated to eliminating cancer as a major health problem by preventing cancer, saving lives, and diminishing suffering from cancer through research, education, advocacy, and service.

5480 **American Cancer Society: North Charleston**
5900 Core Avenue
Suite 504
North Charleston, SC 29406
843-744-1922
800-ACS-2345
Fax: 843-747-2761
http://www.cancer.org

Richard C. Wender, President
Elmer Huerta, First Vice President

Nationwide, community-based voluntary health organization dedicated to eliminating cancer as a major health problem by preventing cancer, saving lives, and diminishing suffering from cancer through research, education, advocacy, and service.

Cancer/Associations & Organizations

5481　American Cancer Society: North Coast Border
1301 Northcrest Drive
Crescent City, CA 95531-2332
707-464-8277
800-ACS-2345
Fax: 707-465-6710
http://www.cancer.org

Richard C. Wender, President
Elmer Huerta, First Vice President

Nationwide, community-based voluntary health organization dedicated to eliminating cancer as a major health problem by preventing cancer, saving lives, and diminishing suffering from cancer through research, education, advocacy, and service.

5482　American Cancer Society: North Shore
820 Davis Street
Ste. 400
Evanston, IL 60201
847-328-5147
800-ACS-2345
Fax: 847-570-6043
http://www.cancer.org

Richard C. Wender, President
Elmer Huerta, First Vice President

Nationwide, community-based voluntary health organization dedicated to eliminating cancer as a major health problem by preventing cancer, saving lives, and diminishing suffering from cancer through research, education, advocacy, and service.

5483　American Cancer Society: North Valley Region
1765 Challenge Way
Suite 115
Sacramento, CA 95815-5097
916-446-7933
800-ACS-2345
Fax: 916-325-4955
http://www.ca.cancer.org

Nationwide, community-based voluntary health organization dedicated to eliminating cancer as a major health problem by preventing cancer, saving lives, and diminishing suffering from cancer through research, education, advocacy, and service.

5484　American Cancer Society: Northeast Indiana
111 E Ludwig Road
Suite 105
Fort Wayne, IN 46825-4240
260-471-3911
800-ACS-2345
Fax: 260-483-5344
http://www.cancer.org

Richard C. Wender, President
Elmer Huerta, First Vice President

Nationwide, community-based voluntary health organization dedicated to eliminating cancer as a major health problem by preventing cancer, saving lives, and diminishing suffering from cancer through research, education, advocacy, and service.

5485　American Cancer Society: Northeast New England
1 Bowdoin Mill Island
Suite 300
Topsham, ME 4086
207-373-3700
800-ACS-2345
Fax: 207-725-6680
http://www.cancer.org

Richard C. Wender, President
Elmer Huerta, First Vice President

Nationwide, community-based voluntary health organization dedicated to eliminating cancer as a major health problem by preventing cancer, saving lives, and diminishing suffering from cancer through research, education, advocacy, and service.

5486　American Cancer Society: Northern Arizona
2724 E Lakin
Suite 9
Flagstaff, AZ 86004
928-526-3800
800-ACS-2345
Fax: 928-526-5870
http://www.cancer.org

Richard C. Wender, President
Elmer Huerta, First Vice President

Nationwide, community-based voluntary health organization dedicated to eliminating cancer as a major health problem by preventing cancer, saving lives, and diminishing suffering from cancer through research, education, advocacy, and service.

5487　American Cancer Society: Northern California
39235 Liberty St
Ste D-0
Fremont, CA 94538
510-797-0600
800-ACS-2345
Fax: 510-797-0698
http://www.cancer.org

Richard C. Wender, President
Elmer Huerta, First Vice President

Nationwide, community-based voluntary health organization dedicated to eliminating cancer as a major health problem by preventing cancer, saving lives, and diminishing suffering from cancer through research, education, advocacy, and service.

5488　American Cancer Society: Northern Idaho
920 N Washington St
Ste 200
Spokane, WA 99201
509-455-3440
800-ACS-2345
Fax: 509-455-3990
http://www.cancer.org

Richard C. Wender, President
Elmer Huerta, First Vice President

Nationwide, community-based voluntary health organization dedicated to eliminating cancer as a major health problem by preventing cancer, saving lives, and diminishing suffering from cancer through research, education, advocacy, and service.

5489　American Cancer Society: Northern Kentucky
297 Buttermilk Pk
Fort Mitchell, KY 41017
859-647-2200
800-ACS-2345
Fax: 859-647-2246
http://www.cancer.org

Richard C. Wender, President
Elmer Huerta, MD, MPH, First Vice President

Nationwide, community-based voluntary health organization dedicated to eliminating cancer as a major health problem by preventing cancer, saving lives, and diminishing suffering from cancer through research, education, advocacy, and service.

5490　American Cancer Society: Northern Michigan
525 W 14th Street
Unit 5
Traverse City, MI 49684
231-947-0860
800-ACS-2345
Fax: 231-947-0830
http://www.cancer.org

Richard C. Wender, President
Elmer Huerta, First Vice President

Nationwide, community-based voluntary health organization dedicated to eliminating cancer as a major health problem by preventing cancer, saving lives, and diminishing suffering from cancer through research, education, advocacy, and service.

5491　American Cancer Society: Northern Nevada
6490 S McCarran Boulevard
Suite 40
Reno, NV 89509
775-329-0609
800-ACS-2345
Fax: 775-329-8592
http://www.cancer.org

Richard C. Wender, President
Elmer Huerta, First Vice President

Nationwide, community-based voluntary health organization dedicated to eliminating cancer as a major health problem by preventing cancer, saving lives, and diminishing suffering from cancer through research, education, advocacy, and service.

Cancer/Associations & Organizations

5492 **American Cancer Society: Northern New Jersey**
669 Littleton Rd
Suite 6
Parsippany, NJ 7054
973-334-2249
800-ACS-2345
Fax: 973-331-5944
http://www.cancer.org

Richard C. Wender, President
Elmer Huerta, First Vice President

Nationwide, community-based voluntary health organization dedicated to eliminating cancer as a major health problem by preventing cancer, saving lives, and diminishing suffering from cancer through research, education, advocacy, and service.

5493 **American Cancer Society: Northern New Mexico**
10501 Montgomery Blvd NE
Ste 300
Albuquerque, NM 87111
505-260-2105
800-ACS-2345
Fax: 505-266-9513
http://www.cancer.org

Richard C. Wender, President
Elmer Huerta, First Vice President

Nationwide, community-based voluntary health organization dedicated to eliminating cancer as a major health problem by preventing cancer, saving lives, and diminishing suffering from cancer through research, education, advocacy, and service.

5494 **American Cancer Society: Northwest Illinois**
3727 Blackhawk Road
Rock Island, IL 61201
309-794-0601
800-ACS-2345
Fax: 309-793-3251
http://www.cancer.org

Richard C. Wender, President
Elmer Huerta, First Vice President

Nationwide, community-based voluntary health organization dedicated to eliminating cancer as a major health problem by preventing cancer, saving lives, and diminishing suffering from cancer through research, education, advocacy, and service.

5495 **American Cancer Society: Northwest Indiana**
1551 E 85th Avenue
Merrillville, IN 46410
219-793-1030
800-ACS-2345
Fax: 219-793-1033
http://www.cancer.org

Richard C. Wender, President
Elmer Huerta, First Vice President

Nationwide, community-based voluntary health organization dedicated to eliminating cancer as a major health problem by preventing cancer, saving lives, and diminishing suffering from cancer through research, education, advocacy, and service.

5496 **American Cancer Society: Northwest New England**
13 Loomis Street
Montpelier, VT 05602-3021
802-223-2348
800-ACS-2345
Fax: 802-223-4818
http://www.cancer.org

Richard C. Wender, President
Elmer Huerta, First Vice President

Nationwide, community-based voluntary health organization dedicated to eliminating cancer as a major health problem by preventing cancer, saving lives, and diminishing suffering from cancer through research, education, advocacy, and service.

5497 **American Cancer Society: Northwest New Jersey**
669 Littleton Rd
Parsippany, NJ 7054
973-331-9300
800-ACS-2345
Fax: 973-331-9444
http://www.cancer.org

Richard C. Wender, President
Elmer Huerta, First Vice President

Nationwide, community-based voluntary health organization dedicated to eliminating cancer as a major health problem by preventing cancer, saving lives, and diminishing suffering from cancer through research, education, advocacy, and service.

5498 **American Cancer Society: Northwest Suburban Illinois**
100 W Palatine Road
Suite 150
Palatine, IL 60067-5146
847-358-3965
800-ACS-2345
Fax: 847-358-9218
http://www.cancer.org

Richard C. Wender, President
Elmer Huerta, First Vice President

Nationwide, community-based voluntary health organization dedicated to eliminating cancer as a major health problem by preventing cancer, saving lives, and diminishing suffering from cancer through research, education, advocacy, and service.

5499 **American Cancer Society: Northwest Valley**
4550 East Bell Road
Suite 126
Phoenix, AZ 85032
602-224-0524
800-ACS-2345
Fax: 602-381-3096
http://www.cancer.org

Richard C. Wender, President
Elmer Huerta, First Vice President

Nationwide, community-based voluntary health organization dedicated to eliminating cancer as a major health problem by preventing cancer, saving lives, and diminishing suffering from cancer through research, education, advocacy, and service.

5500 **American Cancer Society: Northwest Wyoming**
907 N Poplar Ave
Ste 185
Casper, WY 82601
307-577-4892
800-ACS-2345
Fax: 307-234-0926
e-mail: dslider@cancer.org
http://www.cancer.org

Richard C. Wender, President
Elmer Huerta, First Vice President

Nationwide, community-based voluntary health organization dedicated to eliminating cancer as a major health problem by preventing cancer, saving lives, and diminishing suffering from cancer through research, education, advocacy, and service.

5501 **American Cancer Society: O'Fallon**
4207 Lindell Blvd
Saint Louis, MO 63108
314-286-8100
800-ACS-2345
Fax: 314-286-8160
http://www.cancer.org

Richard C. Wender, President
Elmer Huerta, First Vice President

Nationwide, community-based voluntary health organization dedicated to eliminating cancer as a major health problem by preventing cancer, saving lives, and diminishing suffering from cancer through research, education, advocacy, and service.

5502 **American Cancer Society: Oakland**
1700 Webster Street
Oakland, CA 94612
510-832-7012
800-ACS-2345
Fax: 510-763-8826
http://www.cancer.org

Richard C. Wender, President
Elmer Huerta, First Vice President

Nationwide, community-based voluntary health organization dedicated to eliminating cancer as a major health problem by preventing cancer, saving lives, and diminishing suffering from cancer through research, education, advocacy, and service.

Cancer/Associations & Organizations

5503 **American Cancer Society: Ogden**
941 E 3300 S
Salt Lake City, UT 84106-2100
801-483-1500
800-ACS-2345
Fax: 801-393-2260
http://www.cancer.org

Rose Defa, Executive Director

Nationwide, community-based voluntary health organization dedicated to eliminating cancer as a major health problem by preventing cancer, saving lives, and diminishing suffering from cancer through research, education, advocacy, and service.

5504 **American Cancer Society: Oklahoma City**
6525 N Meridian
Suite 110
Oklahoma City, OK 73116
405-843-9888
800-ACS-2345
Fax: 405-848-0795
http://www.cancer.org

Richard C. Wender, President
Elmer Huerta, First Vice President

Nationwide, community-based voluntary health organization dedicated to eliminating cancer as a major health problem by preventing cancer, saving lives, and diminishing suffering from cancer through research, education, advocacy, and service.

5505 **American Cancer Society: Omaha**
9850 Nicholas Street
Suite 200
Omaha, NE 68114
402-393-5800
800-ACS-2345
Fax: 402-393-7790
http://www.cancer.org

Richard C. Wender, President
Elmer Huerta, First Vice President

Nationwide, community-based voluntary health organization dedicated to eliminating cancer as a major health problem by preventing cancer, saving lives, and diminishing suffering from cancer through research, education, advocacy, and service.

5506 **American Cancer Society: Orange County Region**
1940 E Deere Avenue
Suite 100
Santa Ana, CA 92705
949-261-9446
800-ACS-2345
Fax: 949-261-9419
http://www.cancer.org

Richard C. Wender, President
Elmer Huerta, First Vice President

Nationwide, community-based voluntary health organization dedicated to eliminating cancer as a major health problem by preventing cancer, saving lives, and diminishing suffering from cancer through research, education, advocacy, and service.

5507 **American Cancer Society: Orlando Metro**
1601 W Colonial Drive
Orlando, FL 32804
407-843-8680
800-ACS-2345
Fax: 407-423-2383
http://www.cancer.org

Richard C. Wender, President
Elmer Huerta, First Vice President

Nationwide, community-based voluntary health organization dedicated to eliminating cancer as a major health problem by preventing cancer, saving lives, and diminishing suffering from cancer through research, education, advocacy, and service.

5508 **American Cancer Society: Osage Beach**
3322 S Campbell Ave
Suite P
Springfield, MO 65807
417-881-4668
800-ACS-2345
Fax: 417-881-7955
http://www.cancer.org

Richard C. Wender, President
Elmer Huerta, First Vice President

Nationwide, community-based voluntary health organization dedicated to eliminating cancer as a major health problem by preventing cancer, saving lives, and diminishing suffering from cancer through research, education, advocacy, and service.

5509 **American Cancer Society: Overland Park**
6700 Antioch Road
Suite 100
Merriam, KS 66204
913-432-3277
800-ACS-2345
Fax: 913-432-1732
http://www.cancer.org

Richard C. Wender, President
Elmer Huerta, First Vice President

Nationwide, community-based voluntary health organization dedicated to eliminating cancer as a major health problem by preventing cancer, saving lives, and diminishing suffering from cancer through research, education, advocacy, and service.

5510 **American Cancer Society: Owensboro**
1302 Fredrica St
Owensboro, KY 42301
270-683-0425
800-ACS-2345
Fax: 270-683-1471
http://www.cancer.org

Richard C. Wender, President
Elmer Huerta, First Vice President

Nationwide, community-based voluntary health organization dedicated to eliminating cancer as a major health problem by preventing cancer, saving lives, and diminishing suffering from cancer through research, education, advocacy, and service.

5511 **American Cancer Society: Oxnard**
250 Citrus Grove Lane
Suite 200
Oxnard, CA 93036
805-983-8864
800-ACS-2345
Fax: 805-983-3751
http://www.cancer.org

Richard C. Wender, President
Elmer Huerta, First Vice President

Nationwide, community-based voluntary health organization dedicated to eliminating cancer as a major health problem by preventing cancer, saving lives, and diminishing suffering from cancer through research, education, advocacy, and service.

5512 **American Cancer Society: Paducah**
3140 Parisa Drive
Paducah, KY 42003
270-444-0375
800-ACS-2345
Fax: 270-444-0380
http://www.cancer.org

Richard C. Wender, President
Elmer Huerta, First Vice President

Nationwide, community-based voluntary health organization dedicated to eliminating cancer as a major health problem by preventing cancer, saving lives, and diminishing suffering from cancer through research, education, advocacy, and service.

5513 **American Cancer Society: Palm Beach**
3350 NW Boca Raton Boulevard
Suite A-34
Boca Raton, FL 33431
561-394-7751
800-ACS-2345
Fax: 516-394-7909
http://www.cancer.org

Richard C. Wender, President
Elmer Huerta, First Vice President

Nationwide, community-based voluntary health organization dedicated to eliminating cancer as a major health problem by preventing cancer, saving lives, and diminishing suffering from cancer through research, education, advocacy, and service.

Cancer/Associations & Organizations

5514 **American Cancer Society: Palm Beach Benefit**
235 S County Road
Suite 20
Palm Beach, FL 33480   561-655-3449
                              800-ACS-2345
                              Fax: 561-655-3686
                              http://www.cancer.org

Richard C. Wender, President
Elmer Huerta, First Vice President

Nationwide, community-based voluntary health organization dedicated to eliminating cancer as a major health problem by preventing cancer, saving lives, and diminishing suffering from cancer through research, education, advocacy, and service.

5515 **American Cancer Society: Palm Desert**
73-161 Fred Waring Dr
Ste 100
Palm Desert, CA 92260   760-568-2691
                              800-ACS-2345
                              Fax: 760-341-8783
                              http://www.cancer.org

Richard C. Wender, President
Elmer Huerta, First Vice President

Nationwide, community-based voluntary health organization dedicated to eliminating cancer as a major health problem by preventing cancer, saving lives, and diminishing suffering from cancer through research, education, advocacy, and service.

5516 **American Cancer Society: Panama City**
2012-A-Lisenby Avenue
Panama City, FL 32405   850-785-9205
                              800-ACS-2345
                              Fax: 850-872-9431
                              http://www.cancer.org

Richard C. Wender, President
Elmer Huerta, First Vice President

Nationwide, community-based voluntary health organization dedicated to eliminating cancer as a major health problem by preventing cancer, saving lives, and diminishing suffering from cancer through research, education, advocacy, and service.

5517 **American Cancer Society: Parkersburg**
PO Box 4451
3901 Briscoe Road
Parkersburg, WV 26104   304-422-1472
                              800-ACS-2345
                              Fax: 304-422-9569
                              e-mail: brent.chambers@cancer.org
                              http://www.cancer.org

Richard C. Wender, President
Elmer Huerta, First Vice President

Nationwide, community-based voluntary health organization dedicated to eliminating cancer as a major health problem by preventing cancer, saving lives, and diminishing suffering from cancer through research, education, advocacy, and service.

5518 **American Cancer Society: Pasco**
21756 State Road 54
Suite 101
Lutz, FL 33549   813-949-0291
                              800-ACS-2345
                              Fax: 813-909-4843
                              http://www.cancer.org

Richard C. Wender, President
Elmer Huerta, First Vice President

Nationwide, community-based voluntary health organization dedicated to eliminating cancer as a major health problem by preventing cancer, saving lives, and diminishing suffering from cancer through research, education, advocacy, and service.

5519 **American Cancer Society: Peninsula**
11835 Canon Boulevard
Suite A102
Newport News, VA 23606-2570   757-591-8330
                              800-ACS-2345
                              Fax: 757-591-8328
                              http://www.cancer.org

Richard C. Wender, President
Elmer Huerta, First Vice President

Nationwide, community-based voluntary health organization dedicated to eliminating cancer as a major health problem by preventing cancer, saving lives, and diminishing suffering from cancer through research, education, advocacy, and service.

5520 **American Cancer Society: Pensacola**
5401 Corporate Woods Drive
Suite 100
Pensacola, FL 32504   850-475-0850
                              800-ACS-2345
                              Fax: 850-475-5044
                              http://www.cancer.org

Richard C. Wender, President
Elmer Huerta, First Vice President

Nationwide, community-based voluntary health organization dedicated to eliminating cancer as a major health problem by preventing cancer, saving lives, and diminishing suffering from cancer through research, education, advocacy, and service.

5521 **American Cancer Society: Petaluma**
1451 Guerneville Rd
Ste 220
Santa Rosa, CA 95403   707-545-6720
                              800-ACS-2345
                              Fax: 707-543-3179
                              http://www.cancer.org

Richard C. Wender, President
Elmer Huerta, First Vice President

Nationwide, community-based voluntary health organization dedicated to eliminating cancer as a major health problem by preventing cancer, saving lives, and diminishing suffering from cancer through research, education, advocacy, and service.

5522 **American Cancer Society: Pewaukee**
N19w24350 Riverwood Drive
Waukesha, WI 53188   262-523-5500
                              800-ACS-2345
                              Fax: 262-523-5533
                              http://www.cancer.org

Richard C. Wender, President
Elmer Huerta, First Vice President

Nationwide, community-based voluntary health organization dedicated to eliminating cancer as a major health problem by preventing cancer, saving lives, and diminishing suffering from cancer through research, education, advocacy, and service.

5523 **American Cancer Society: Phoenix**
4550 East Bell Road
Suite 126
Phoenix, AZ 85032   602-224-0524
                              800-ACS-2345
                              Fax: 602-381-3096
                              http://www.cancer.org

Richard C. Wender, President
Elmer Huerta, First Vice President

Nationwide, community-based voluntary health organization dedicated to eliminating cancer as a major health problem by preventing cancer, saving lives, and diminishing suffering from cancer through research, education, advocacy, and service.

5524 **American Cancer Society: Pierre**
221 S Central Avenue
Pierre, SD 57501   605-224-7836
                              800-ACS-2345
                              Fax: 605-224-7847
                              http://www.cancer.org

Richard C. Wender, President
Elmer Huerta, First Vice President

Cancer/Associations & Organizations

Nationwide, community-based voluntary health organization dedicated to eliminating cancer as a major health problem by preventing cancer, saving lives, and diminishing suffering from cancer through research, education, advocacy, and service.

5525 American Cancer Society: Pinellas
4801 86th Avenue North
Pinellas Park, FL 33782
727-546-9822
800-ACS-2345
Fax: 727-545-3753
http://www.cancer.org

Richard C. Wender, President
Elmer Huerta, First Vice President

Nationwide, community-based voluntary health organization dedicated to eliminating cancer as a major health problem by preventing cancer, saving lives, and diminishing suffering from cancer through research, education, advocacy, and service.

5526 American Cancer Society: Pittsfield
59 Bobala Rd
2nd Floor
Holyoke, MA 01040
413-734-6000
800-ACS-2345
Fax: 413-493-2199
http://www.cancer.org

Richard C. Wender, President
Elmer Huerta, First Vice President

Nationwide, community-based voluntary health organization dedicated to eliminating cancer as a major health problem by preventing cancer, saving lives, and diminishing suffering from cancer through research, education, advocacy, and service.

5527 American Cancer Society: Pleasant Hill
1885 Oak Park Boulevard
Pleasant Hill, CA 94523-4413
925-934-5372
800-ACS-2345
Fax: 925-934-5372
http://www.cancer.org

Nationwide, community-based voluntary health organization dedicated to eliminating cancer as a major health problem by preventing cancer, saving lives, and diminishing suffering from cancer through research, education, advocacy, and service.

5528 American Cancer Society: Porter
1551 E 85th Avenue
Merrillville, IN 46410-8901
219-793-1030
800-ACS-2345
Fax: 219-465-1044
http://www.cancer.org

Jim Puente, Executive Director

Nationwide, community-based voluntary health organization dedicated to eliminating cancer as a major health problem by preventing cancer, saving lives, and diminishing suffering from cancer through research, education, advocacy, and service.

5529 American Cancer Society: Portland
0330 SW Curry Street
Portland, OR 97201
503-795-3946
800-ACS-2345
Fax: 503-228-1062
http://www.cancer.org

Richard C. Wender, President
Elmer Huerta, First Vice President

Nationwide, community-based voluntary health organization dedicated to eliminating cancer as a major health problem by preventing cancer, saving lives, and diminishing suffering from cancer through research, education, advocacy, and service.

5530 American Cancer Society: Prairie Land
17060 Oak Park Avenue
Tinley Park, IL 60477
708-633-7770
800-ACS-2345
Fax: 708-633-7773
http://www.cancer.org

Richard C. Wender, President
Elmer Huerta, First Vice President

Nationwide, community-based voluntary health organization dedicated to eliminating cancer as a major health problem by preventing cancer, saving lives, and diminishing suffering from cancer through research, education, advocacy, and service.

5531 American Cancer Society: Provo
941 East 3300 South
Suite A
Salt Lake City, UT 84106
801-483-1500
800-ACS-2345
Fax: 801-483-1558
http://www.cancer.org

Richard C. Wender, President
Elmer Huerta, First Vice President

Nationwide, community-based voluntary health organization dedicated to eliminating cancer as a major health problem by preventing cancer, saving lives, and diminishing suffering from cancer through research, education, advocacy, and service.

5532 American Cancer Society: Pueblo
1445 N Union Boulevard
Suite 100
Colorado Springs, CO 80909-2881
719-636-5101
800-ACS-2345
Fax: 719-543-2877
http://www.cancer.org

Trish St John, Executive Director

Nationwide, community-based voluntary health organization dedicated to eliminating cancer as a major health problem by preventing cancer, saving lives, and diminishing suffering from cancer through research, education, advocacy, and service.

5533 American Cancer Society: Putnam
600 Zeagler Drive
Palatka, FL 32177
386-328-6224
800-ACS-2345
Fax: 904-325-8086
http://www.cancer.org

Richard C. Wender, President
Elmer Huerta, First Vice President

Nationwide, community-based voluntary health organization dedicated to eliminating cancer as a major health problem by preventing cancer, saving lives, and diminishing suffering from cancer through research, education, advocacy, and service.

5534 American Cancer Society: Queens Region
41-60 Main St Ste 307
Suite 1110
Flushing, NY 11355
718-886-8890
800-ACS-2345
Fax: 718-886-8981
http://www.cancer.org

Richard C. Wender, President
Elmer Huerta, First Vice President

Nationwide, community-based voluntary health organization dedicated to eliminating cancer as a major health problem by preventing cancer, saving lives, and diminishing suffering from cancer through research, education, advocacy, and service.

5535 American Cancer Society: Raleigh
11 S Boylan Avenue
Suite 221
Raleigh, NC 27603-1850
919-834-8463
800-ACS-2345
Fax: 919-839-0551
http://www.cancer.org

Richard C. Wender, President
Elmer Huerta, First Vice President

Nationwide, community-based voluntary health organization dedicated to eliminating cancer as a major health problem by preventing cancer, saving lives, and diminishing suffering from cancer through research, education, advocacy, and service.

Cancer/Associations & Organizations

5536 American Cancer Society: Rancho Cucamonga
1240 Palmyrita Ave
Ste A
Riverside, CA 92507
951-683-6415
800-ACS-2345
Fax: 951-682-6804
http://www.cancer.org

Richard C. Wender, President
Elmer Huerta, First Vice President

Nationwide, community-based voluntary health organization dedicated to eliminating cancer as a major health problem by preventing cancer, saving lives, and diminishing suffering from cancer through research, education, advocacy, and service.

5537 American Cancer Society: Rapid City
2465 W Chicago Street
Rapid City, SD 57702
605-342-7740
800-ACS-2345
Fax: 605-399-2062
http://www.cancer.org

Richard C. Wender, President
Elmer Huerta, First Vice President

Nationwide, community-based voluntary health organization dedicated to eliminating cancer as a major health problem by preventing cancer, saving lives, and diminishing suffering from cancer through research, education, advocacy, and service.

5538 American Cancer Society: Redding
3290 Bechelli Lane
Redding, CA 96002
530-222-1058
800-ACS-2345
Fax: 530-222-1409
http://www.cancer.org

Richard C. Wender, President
Elmer Huerta, First Vice President

Nationwide, community-based voluntary health organization dedicated to eliminating cancer as a major health problem by preventing cancer, saving lives, and diminishing suffering from cancer through research, education, advocacy, and service.

5539 American Cancer Society: Region VI Washington
1875 Connecticut Avenue NW
Suite 730
Washington, DC 20009
202-483-2600
800-ACS-2345
Fax: 202-483-1174
http://www.cancer.org

Richard C. Wender, President
Elmer Huerta, First Vice President

Nationwide, community-based voluntary health organization dedicated to eliminating cancer as a major health problem by preventing cancer, saving lives, and diminishing suffering from cancer through research, education, advocacy, and service.

5540 American Cancer Society: Rhode Island
931 Jefferson Boulevard
Suite 3004
Warwick, RI 02886
401-722-8480
800-ACS-2345
Fax: 401-421-0535
http://www.cancer.org

Richard C. Wender, President
Elmer Huerta, First Vice President

Nationwide, community-based voluntary health organization dedicated to eliminating cancer as a major health problem by preventing cancer, saving lives, and diminishing suffering from cancer through research, education, advocacy, and service.

5541 American Cancer Society: Rhode Island &Eastern Connecticut
106 Route 32
Franklin Commons
Franklin, CT 06254
860-887-2547
800-ACS-2345
Fax: 860-885-0820
http://www.cancer.org

Richard C. Wender, President
Elmer Huerta, First Vice President

Nationwide, community-based voluntary health organization dedicated to eliminating cancer as a major health problem by preventing cancer, saving lives, and diminishing suffering from cancer through research, education, advocacy, and service.

5542 American Cancer Society: Ridgecrest
1043 West Ave M-4
Ste B
Palmdale, CA 93551
661-945-7585
800-ACS-2345
Fax: 661-945-9039
http://www.cancer.org

Richard C. Wender, President
Elmer Huerta, First Vice President

Nationwide, community-based voluntary health organization dedicated to eliminating cancer as a major health problem by preventing cancer, saving lives, and diminishing suffering from cancer through research, education, advocacy, and service.

5543 American Cancer Society: Riverside
1240 Palmyrita Avenue
Suite A
Riverside, CA 92507-1728
951-320-2351
800-ACS-2345
Fax: 909-682-6804
http://www.ca.cancer.org

Richard C. Wender, President
Elmer Huerta, First Vice President

Nationwide, community-based voluntary health organization dedicated to eliminating cancer as a major health problem by preventing cancer, saving lives, and diminishing suffering from cancer through research, education, advocacy, and service.

5544 American Cancer Society: Roanoke
2840 Electric Road
Suite 106A
Roanoke, VA 24018
540-774-2716
800-ACS-2345
Fax: 540-774-9629
http://www.cancer.org

Richard C. Wender, President
Elmer Huerta, First Vice President

Nationwide, community-based voluntary health organization dedicated to eliminating cancer as a major health problem by preventing cancer, saving lives, and diminishing suffering from cancer through research, education, advocacy, and service.

5545 American Cancer Society: Rochester
882 7th Street NW
Rochester, MN 55901
507-287-2044
800-ACS-2345
Fax: 507-287-2178
http://www.cancer.org

Richard C. Wender, President
Elmer Huerta, First Vice President

Nationwide, community-based voluntary health organization dedicated to eliminating cancer as a major health problem by preventing cancer, saving lives, and diminishing suffering from cancer through research, education, advocacy, and service.

Cancer/Associations & Organizations

5546 American Cancer Society: Rockford
4312 E State Street
Rockford, IL 61108
815-229-1287
800-ACS-2345
Fax: 815-229-1363
http://www.cancer.org

Richard C. Wender, President
Elmer Huerta, First Vice President

Nationwide, community-based voluntary health organization dedicated to eliminating cancer as a major health problem by preventing cancer, saving lives, and diminishing suffering from cancer through research, education, advocacy, and service.

5547 American Cancer Society: Roseville
1765 Challenge Way
Suite 115
Sacramento, CA 95815
916-446-7933
800-ACS-2345
Fax: 916-325-2351
http://www.cancer.org

Richard C. Wender, President
Elmer Huerta, First Vice President

Nationwide, community-based voluntary health organization dedicated to eliminating cancer as a major health problem by preventing cancer, saving lives, and diminishing suffering from cancer through research, education, advocacy, and service.

5548 American Cancer Society: Rupert
2676 Vista Avenue
Boise, ID 83705
208-345-2164
800-ACS-2345
Fax: 208-343-9922
http://www.cancer.org

Richard C. Wender, President
Elmer Huerta, First Vice President

Nationwide, community-based voluntary health organization dedicated to eliminating cancer as a major health problem by preventing cancer, saving lives, and diminishing suffering from cancer through research, education, advocacy, and service.

5549 American Cancer Society: Rutland
734-9 US Route 4 East
9
Rutland, VT 5701
802-775-7557
800-ACS-2345
Fax: 802-773-8359
e-mail: sarah.green@cancer.org
http://www.cancer.org

Richard C. Wender, President
Elmer Huerta, First Vice President

Nationwide, community-based voluntary health organization dedicated to eliminating cancer as a major health problem by preventing cancer, saving lives, and diminishing suffering from cancer through research, education, advocacy, and service.

5550 American Cancer Society: Saint Cloud
3721 23rd Street S
Suite 102
Saint Cloud, MN 56301
320-255-0220
800-ACS-2345
Fax: 320-255-5517
http://www.cancer.org

Richard C. Wender, President
Elmer Huerta, First Vice President

Nationwide, community-based voluntary health organization dedicated to eliminating cancer as a major health problem by preventing cancer, saving lives, and diminishing suffering from cancer through research, education, advocacy, and service.

5551 American Cancer Society: Saint George
941 East 3300 South
Salt Lake City, UT 84106
801-483-1500
800-ACS-2345
Fax: 801-483-1558
http://www.cancer.org

Richard C. Wender, President
Elmer Huerta, First Vice President

Nationwide, community-based voluntary health organization dedicated to eliminating cancer as a major health problem by preventing cancer, saving lives, and diminishing suffering from cancer through research, education, advocacy, and service.

5552 American Cancer Society: Saint Joseph
6700 Antioch
Suite 100
Merriam, KS 66204
913-432-3277
800-ACS-2345
Fax: 913-432-1732
http://www.cancer.org

Richard C. Wender, President
Elmer Huerta, First Vice President

Nationwide, community-based voluntary health organization dedicated to eliminating cancer as a major health problem by preventing cancer, saving lives, and diminishing suffering from cancer through research, education, advocacy, and service.

5553 American Cancer Society: Saint Louis
4207 Lindell Boulevard
Saint Louis, MO 63108
314-286-8100
800-ACS-2345
Fax: 314-286-8160
http://www.cancer.org

Richard C. Wender, President
Elmer Huerta, First Vice President

Nationwide, community-based voluntary health organization dedicated to eliminating cancer as a major health problem by preventing cancer, saving lives, and diminishing suffering from cancer through research, education, advocacy, and service.

5554 American Cancer Society: Saint Paul
2520 Pilot Knob Road
Suite 150
Mendota Heights, MN 55120
651-255-8100
800-ACS-2345
Fax: 651-255-8133
http://www.cancer.org

Richard C. Wender, President
Elmer Huerta, First Vice President

Nationwide, community-based voluntary health organization dedicated to eliminating cancer as a major health problem by preventing cancer, saving lives, and diminishing suffering from cancer through research, education, advocacy, and service.

5555 American Cancer Society: Salinas
945 S Main St Ste 201
Suite 1
Salinas, CA 93901
831-442-2992
800-ACS-2345
Fax: 831-772-0959
http://www.cancer.org

Richard C. Wender, President
Elmer Huerta, First Vice President

Nationwide, community-based voluntary health organization dedicated to eliminating cancer as a major health problem by preventing cancer, saving lives, and diminishing suffering from cancer through research, education, advocacy, and service.

5556 American Cancer Society: Salisbury
1138 Parsons Road
Salisbury, MD 21801-8425
410-749-1624
800-ACS-2345
Fax: 410-860-0832
http://www.cancer.org

Richard C. Wender, President
Elmer Huerta, First Vice President

Nationwide, community-based voluntary health organization dedicated to eliminating cancer as a major health problem by preventing cancer, saving lives, and diminishing suffering from cancer through research, education, advocacy, and service.

Cancer/Associations & Organizations

5557 American Cancer Society: Salt Lake City
941 E 3300 S
Salt Lake City, UT 84106
801-483-1500
800-ACS-2345
Fax: 801-483-1558
http://www.cancer.org

Rose Defa, Executive Director
Elmer Huerta, First Vice President

Nationwide, community-based voluntary health organization dedicated to eliminating cancer as a major health problem by preventing cancer, saving lives, and diminishing suffering from cancer through research, education, advocacy, and service.

5558 American Cancer Society: San Antonio
8115 Datapoint Drive
San Antonio, TX 78229
210-614-4211
800-ACS-2345
Fax: 210-615-7724
http://www.cancer.org

Richard C. Wender, President
Elmer Huerta, First Vice President

Nationwide, community-based voluntary health organization dedicated to eliminating cancer as a major health problem by preventing cancer, saving lives, and diminishing suffering from cancer through research, education, advocacy, and service.

5559 American Cancer Society: San Diego
2655 Camino Del Rio N
Suite 100
San Diego, CA 92108
619-299-4200
800-ACS-2345
Fax: 619-296-0928
http://www.cancer.org

Richard C. Wender, President
Elmer Huerta, First Vice President

Nationwide, community-based voluntary health organization dedicated to eliminating cancer as a major health problem by preventing cancer, saving lives, and diminishing suffering from cancer through research, education, advocacy, and service.

5560 American Cancer Society: San Fernando Valley
4940 Van Nuys Boulevard
Suite 301
Sherman Oaks, CA 91403
818-905-7766
800-ACS-2345
Fax: 818-905-9058
http://www.cancer.org

Richard C. Wender, President
Elmer Huerta, First Vice President

Nationwide, community-based voluntary health organization dedicated to eliminating cancer as a major health problem by preventing cancer, saving lives, and diminishing suffering from cancer through research, education, advocacy, and service.

5561 American Cancer Society: San Jose
747 Camden Ave
Suite B
Campbell, CA 95008
408-871-1062
Fax: 408-871-2993
http://www.cancer.org

Richard C. Wender, President
Elmer Huerta, First Vice President

5562 American Cancer Society: San Luis Obispo
1428 Phillips Lane
Suite 201
San Luis Obispo, CA 93401
805-543-1481
800-ACS-2345
Fax: 805-543-1515
http://www.cancer.org

Richard C. Wender, President
Elmer Huerta, First Vice President

Nationwide, community-based voluntary health organization dedicated to eliminating cancer as a major health problem by preventing cancer, saving lives, and diminishing suffering from cancer through research, education, advocacy, and service.

5563 American Cancer Society: San Mateo County
1650 S Amphlett Boulevard
Suite 110
San Mateo, CA 94402
650-578-9902
800-ACS-2345
Fax: 650-578-9940
http://www.cancer.org

Richard C. Wender, President
Elmer Huerta, First Vice President

Nationwide, community-based voluntary health organization dedicated to eliminating cancer as a major health problem by preventing cancer, saving lives, and diminishing suffering from cancer through research, education, advocacy, and service.

5564 American Cancer Society: Santa Barbara
1432 Chapala Street
Santa Barbara, CA 93101
805-963-1576
800-ACS-2345
Fax: 805-963-6093
http://www.cancer.org

Richard C. Wender, President
Elmer Huerta, First Vice President

Nationwide, community-based voluntary health organization dedicated to eliminating cancer as a major health problem by preventing cancer, saving lives, and diminishing suffering from cancer through research, education, advocacy, and service.

5565 American Cancer Society: Santa Clara County
747 Camden Ave
Ste B
Campbell, CA 95008
408-871-1062
800-ACS-2345
Fax: 408-871-2993
http://www.cancer.org

Richard C. Wender, President
Elmer Huerta, First Vice President

Nationwide, community-based voluntary health organization dedicated to eliminating cancer as a major health problem by preventing cancer, saving lives, and diminishing suffering from cancer through research, education, advocacy, and service.

5566 American Cancer Society: Santa Clarita Valley
25020 W Avenue
Stanford Unit 170
Valencia, CA 91355
661-298-0886
800-ACS-2345
Fax: 661-775-9853
http://www.cancer.org

Richard C. Wender, President
Elmer Huerta, First Vice President

Nationwide, community-based voluntary health organization dedicated to eliminating cancer as a major health problem by preventing cancer, saving lives, and diminishing suffering from cancer through research, education, advocacy, and service.

5567 American Cancer Society: Santa Cruz County
Dominican Hospital Educaction Center
945 S Main St
Ste 201
Salinas, CA 93901
831-442-2992
800-ACS-2345
Fax: 831-772-0959
http://www.cancer.org

Richard C. Wender, President
Elmer Huerta, First Vice President

Nationwide, community-based voluntary health organization dedicated to eliminating cancer as a major health problem by preventing cancer, saving lives, and diminishing suffering from cancer through research, education, advocacy, and service.

Cancer/Associations & Organizations

5568 American Cancer Society: Santa Maria
426 Barcellus Avenue
Ste 305
Santa Maria, CA 93454
805-922-2354
800-ACS-2345
Fax: 805-925-1424
http://www.cancer.org

Richard C. Wender, President
Elmer Huerta, First Vice President

Nationwide, community-based voluntary health organization dedicated to eliminating cancer as a major health problem by preventing cancer, saving lives, and diminishing suffering from cancer through research, education, advocacy, and service.

5569 American Cancer Society: Santa Maria Valley
426 E Barcellus
Suite 305
Santa Maria, CA 93454
805-922-2354
800-ACS-2345
Fax: 805-925-1424
http://www.cancer.org

Richard C. Wender, President
Elmer Huerta, First Vice President

Nationwide, community-based voluntary health organization dedicated to eliminating cancer as a major health problem by preventing cancer, saving lives, and diminishing suffering from cancer through research, education, advocacy, and service.

5570 American Cancer Society: Santa Rosa
1451 Guerneville Road
Suite 220
Santa Rosa, CA 95403
707-545-6720
800-ACS-2345
Fax: 707-545-3179
http://www.cancer.org

Richard C. Wender, President
Elmer Huerta, First Vice President

Nationwide, community-based voluntary health organization dedicated to eliminating cancer as a major health problem by preventing cancer, saving lives, and diminishing suffering from cancer through research, education, advocacy, and service.

5571 American Cancer Society: Sarasota
2801 Fruitville Road
Suite 250, Pen West Park
Sarasota, FL 34237
941-365-3256
800-ACS-2345
Fax: 941-365-3256
http://www.cancer.org

Richard C. Wender, President
Elmer Huerta, First Vice President

Nationwide, community-based voluntary health organization dedicated to eliminating cancer as a major health problem by preventing cancer, saving lives, and diminishing suffering from cancer through research, education, advocacy, and service.

5572 American Cancer Society: Savannah
6600 Abercorn Street
Suite 206
Savannah, GA 31405
912-355-5196
800-ACS-2345
Fax: 912-355-0955
http://www.cancer.org

Richard C. Wender, President
Elmer Huerta, First Vice President

Nationwide, community-based voluntary health organization dedicated to eliminating cancer as a major health problem by preventing cancer, saving lives, and diminishing suffering from cancer through research, education, advocacy, and service.

5573 American Cancer Society: Seattle
728 134th St SW
Suite 101
Everett, WA 98204
425-741-8949
800-ACS-2345
Fax: 425-741-9638
http://www.cancer.org

Richard C. Wender, President
Elmer Huerta, First Vice President

Nationwide, community-based voluntary health organization dedicated to eliminating cancer as a major health problem by preventing cancer, saving lives, and diminishing suffering from cancer through research, education, advocacy, and service.

5574 American Cancer Society: Sheboygan
3311 S Packerland Drive
De Pere, WI 54115
920-338-1541
800-ACS-2345
Fax: 920-338-1545
http://www.cancer.org

Richard C. Wender, President
Elmer Huerta, First Vice President

Nationwide, community-based voluntary health organization dedicated to eliminating cancer as a major health problem by preventing cancer, saving lives, and diminishing suffering from cancer through research, education, advocacy, and service.

5575 American Cancer Society: Shreveport
920 Pierremont Road
Suite 300
Shreveport, LA 71106
318-227-8901
800-ACS-2345
Fax: 318-865-4831
http://www.cancer.org

Richard C. Wender, President
Elmer Huerta, First Vice President

Nationwide, community-based voluntary health organization dedicated to eliminating cancer as a major health problem by preventing cancer, saving lives, and diminishing suffering from cancer through research, education, advocacy, and service.

5576 American Cancer Society: Sierra View
300 N Willis
Visalia, CA 93291
559-734-1391
800-ACS-2345
Fax: 559-734-0429
http://www.cancer.org

Richard C. Wender, President
Elmer Huerta, First Vice President

Nationwide, community-based voluntary health organization dedicated to eliminating cancer as a major health problem by preventing cancer, saving lives, and diminishing suffering from cancer through research, education, advocacy, and service.

5577 American Cancer Society: Sikeston
201 N New Madrid
Sikeston, MO 63801
573-471-1823
800-ACS-2345
Fax: 573-471-1372
http://www.cancer.org

Richard C. Wender, President
Elmer Huerta, First Vice President

Nationwide, community-based voluntary health organization dedicated to eliminating cancer as a major health problem by preventing cancer, saving lives, and diminishing suffering from cancer through research, education, advocacy, and service.

5578 American Cancer Society: Silicon Valley
1715 S Bascom Avenue
Suite 100
Campbell, CA 95008
408-879-1032
Fax: 408-879-1030
http://www.ca.cancer.org

Rose Simmons, VP

Cancer/Associations & Organizations

Nationwide, community-based voluntary health organization dedicated to eliminating cancer as a major health problem by preventing cancer, saving lives, and diminishing suffering from cancer through research, education, advocacy and service.

5579 American Cancer Society: Silver Spring
11331 Amherst Avenue
Silver Spring, MD 20902-4656
301-933-9350
800-ACS-2345
Fax: 301-929-8243
http://www.cancer.org

Richard C. Wender, President
Elmer Huerta, First Vice President

Nationwide, community-based voluntary health organization dedicated to eliminating cancer as a major health problem by preventing cancer, saving lives, and diminishing suffering from cancer through research, education, advocacy, and service.

5580 American Cancer Society: Simi Valley
301 Science Dr
Ste 220
Moorpark, CA 93021
805-527-5360
800-ACS-2345
Fax: 805-529-2536
http://www.cancer.org

Richard C. Wender, President
Elmer Huerta, First Vice President

Nationwide, community-based voluntary health organization dedicated to eliminating cancer as a major health problem by preventing cancer, saving lives, and diminishing suffering from cancer through research, education, advocacy, and service.

5581 American Cancer Society: Sioux City
600 4th Street
Ste 229
Sioux City, IA 51101
712-233-1148
800-ACS-2345
Fax: 712-233-1507
http://www.cancer.org

Richard C. Wender, President
Elmer Huerta, First Vice President

Nationwide, community-based voluntary health organization dedicated to eliminating cancer as a major health problem by preventing cancer, saving lives, and diminishing suffering from cancer through research, education, advocacy, and service.

5582 American Cancer Society: Sioux Falls
4904 S Technopolis Dr
Sioux Falls, SD 57106
605-361-8277
800-ACS-2345
Fax: 605-361-8537
http://www.cancer.org

Richard C. Wender, President
Elmer Huerta, First Vice President

Nationwide, community-based voluntary health organization dedicated to eliminating cancer as a major health problem by preventing cancer, saving lives, and diminishing suffering from cancer through research, education, advocacy, and service.

5583 American Cancer Society: Solano County
744 Empire St
Ste 206
Fairfield, CA 94533
707-425-5006
800-ACS-2345
Fax: 707-425-5639
http://www.cancer.org

Richard C. Wender, President
Elmer Huerta, First Vice President

Nationwide, community-based voluntary health organization dedicated to eliminating cancer as a major health problem by preventing cancer, saving lives, and diminishing suffering from cancer through research, education, advocacy, and service.

5584 American Cancer Society: Somerset
402 Coomer Street
Somerset, KY 42503
606-679-6143
800-ACS-2345
Fax: 606-677-1943
http://www.cancer.org

Richard C. Wender, President
Elmer Huerta, First Vice President

Nationwide, community-based voluntary health organization dedicated to eliminating cancer as a major health problem by preventing cancer, saving lives, and diminishing suffering from cancer through research, education, advocacy, and service.

5585 American Cancer Society: South Bay
5731 W Slauson Ave
Ste 200
Culver City, CA 90230
310-348-0356
800-ACS-2345
Fax: 310-348-2328
http://www.cancer.org

Richard C. Wender, President
Elmer Huerta, First Vice President

Nationwide, community-based voluntary health organization dedicated to eliminating cancer as a major health problem by preventing cancer, saving lives, and diminishing suffering from cancer through research, education, advocacy, and service.

5586 American Cancer Society: South Burlington
121 Connor Way
Ste 240
Williston, VT 5495
802-872-6300
800-ACS-2345
Fax: 802-872-6399
http://www.cancer.org

Richard C. Wender, President
Elmer Huerta, First Vice President

Nationwide, community-based voluntary health organization dedicated to eliminating cancer as a major health problem by preventing cancer, saving lives, and diminishing suffering from cancer through research, education, advocacy, and service.

5587 American Cancer Society: South Central Indiana
2201 W Sudbury Drive
Suite C
Bloomington, IN 47403
812-336-8423
800-ACS-2345
Fax: 812-339-9213
e-mail: tbock@cancer.org
http://www.cancer.org

Richard C. Wender, President
Elmer Huerta, First Vice President

Nationwide, community-based voluntary health organization dedicated to eliminating cancer as a major health problem by preventing cancer, saving lives, and diminishing suffering from cancer through research, education, advocacy, and service.

5588 American Cancer Society: South Central Los Angeles
1875 W Redondo Beach Blvd
Gardena, CA 90247
310-768-2017
800-ACS-2345
Fax: 310-768-2016
http://www.cancer.org

Richard C. Wender, President
Elmer Huerta, First Vice President

Nationwide, community-based voluntary health organization dedicated to eliminating cancer as a major health problem by preventing cancer, saving lives, and diminishing suffering from cancer through research, education, advocacy, and service.

5589 American Cancer Society: Southeast Indiana
2201 W Sudbury Drive
C
Bloomington, IN 47403-3737
812-336-8423
800-ACS-2345
Fax: 812-282-5334
http://www.cancer.org

Sukie Decker, Manager

Cancer/Associations & Organizations

Nationwide, community-based voluntary health organization dedicated to eliminating cancer as a major health problem by preventing cancer, saving lives, and diminishing suffering from cancer through research, education, advocacy, and service.

5590   American Cancer Society: Southeast New England
1115 W Chestnut Street
Suite 301
Brockton, MA 02301-7501
508-584-9600
800-ACS-2345
Fax: 508-584-9699
http://www.cancer.org

Richard C. Wender, President
Elmer Huerta, First Vice President

Nationwide, community-based voluntary health organization dedicated to eliminating cancer as a major health problem by preventing cancer, saving lives, and diminishing suffering from cancer through research, education, advocacy, and service.

5591   American Cancer Society: Southeastern Arizona
1636 N Swan Road
Suite 151
Tucson, AZ 85712
520-321-7989
800-ACS-2345
Fax: 520-321-7988
http://www.cancer.org

Richard C. Wender, President
Elmer Huerta, First Vice President

Nationwide, community-based voluntary health organization dedicated to eliminating cancer as a major health problem by preventing cancer, saving lives, and diminishing suffering from cancer through research, education, advocacy, and service.

5592   American Cancer Society: Southern Illinois
4503 W DeYoung St
Suite200 C
Marion, IL 62959
618-998-9898
800-ACS-2345
Fax: 618-997-8456
http://www.cancer.org

Richard C. Wender, President
Elmer Huerta, First Vice President

Nationwide, community-based voluntary health organization dedicated to eliminating cancer as a major health problem by preventing cancer, saving lives, and diminishing suffering from cancer through research, education, advocacy, and service.

5593   American Cancer Society: Southern New England
538 Preston Avenue
Meriden, CT 06450
203-379-4700
800-ACS-2345
Fax: 203-379-5060
http://www.cancer.org

Richard C. Wender, President
Elmer Huerta, First Vice President

Nationwide, community-based voluntary health organization dedicated to eliminating cancer as a major health problem by preventing cancer, saving lives, and diminishing suffering from cancer through research, education, advocacy, and service.

5594   American Cancer Society: Southwest Colorado
1800 E 3rd Ave
Suite 101
Durango, CO 81301
970-247-0278
800-ACS-2345
Fax: 970-247-4200
http://www.cancer.org

Richard C. Wender, President
Elmer Huerta, First Vice President

Nationwide, community-based voluntary health organization dedicated to eliminating cancer as a major health problem by preventing cancer, saving lives, and diminishing suffering from cancer through research, education, advocacy, and service.

5595   American Cancer Society: Southwest Kansas
818 N Emporia
Suite 100
Great Bend, KS 67214
316-265-3400
800-ACS-2345
Fax: 316-265-3490
http://www.cancer.org

Richard C. Wender, President
Elmer Huerta, First Vice President

Nationwide, community-based voluntary health organization dedicated to eliminating cancer as a major health problem by preventing cancer, saving lives, and diminishing suffering from cancer through research, education, advocacy, and service.

5596   American Cancer Society: Southwest Michigan
5110 S Sprinkle Road
Portage, MI 49002
269-349-8719
800-ACS-2345
Fax: 269-349-0846
http://www.cancer.org

Richard C. Wender, President
Elmer Huerta, First Vice President

Nationwide, community-based voluntary health organization dedicated to eliminating cancer as a major health problem by preventing cancer, saving lives, and diminishing suffering from cancer through research, education, advocacy, and service.

5597   American Cancer Society: Southwest New England
372 Danbury Road
Wilton, CT 06897
203-563-0740
800-ACS-2345
Fax: 203-563-0738
http://www.cancer.org

Richard C. Wender, President
Elmer Huerta, First Vice President

Nationwide, community-based voluntary health organization dedicated to eliminating cancer as a major health problem by preventing cancer, saving lives, and diminishing suffering from cancer through research, education, advocacy, and service.

5598   American Cancer Society: Southwest Ohio
2808 Reading Rd
Cincinnati, OH 45206
888-227-6446
800-ACS-2345
Fax: 877-227-2838
http://www.cancer.org

Jill Raleigh, regional vice president
Elmer Huerta, First Vice President

Nationwide, community-based voluntary health organization dedicated to eliminating cancer as a major health problem by preventing cancer, saving lives, and diminishing suffering from cancer through research, education, advocacy, and service.

5599   American Cancer Society: Southwest Pennsylvania
320 Bilmar Drive
Pittsburgh, PA 15205
888-227-5445
800-ACS-2345
Fax: 412-919-1101
http://www.cancer.org

Richard C. Wender, President
Elmer Huerta, First Vice President

Nationwide, community-based voluntary health organization dedicated to eliminating cancer as a major health problem by preventing cancer, saving lives, and diminishing suffering from cancer through research, education, advocacy, and service.

5600   American Cancer Society: Southwestern Indiana
6301 Old Boonville Hwy
Ste B
Evansville, IN 47715
800-543-5245
800-ACS-2345
Fax: 812-476-3567
http://www.cancer.org

Richard C. Wender, President
Elmer Huerta, First Vice President

Cancer/Associations & Organizations

Nationwide, community-based voluntary health organization dedicated to eliminating cancer as a major health problem by preventing cancer, saving lives, and diminishing suffering from cancer through research, education, advocacy, and service.

5601 American Cancer Society: Spokane
920 N Washington St
Ste 200
Spokane, WA 99201
509-455-3440
800-ACS-2345
Fax: 509-455-3990
http://www.cancer.org

Richard C. Wender, President
Elmer Huerta, First Vice President

Nationwide, community-based voluntary health organization dedicated to eliminating cancer as a major health problem by preventing cancer, saving lives, and diminishing suffering from cancer through research, education, advocacy, and service.

5602 American Cancer Society: Springfield
1305 Wabash Avenue
Springfield, IL 62704-4970
217-546-7586
800-ACS-2345
Fax: 217-546-7631
http://www.cancer.org

Richard C. Wender, President
Elmer Huerta, First Vice President

Nationwide, community-based voluntary health organization dedicated to eliminating cancer as a major health problem by preventing cancer, saving lives, and diminishing suffering from cancer through research, education, advocacy, and service.

5603 American Cancer Society: Stark Area
925 S Main Street
Canfield, OH 44406
888-227-6446
800-ACS-2345
Fax: 877-227-2838
http://www.cancer.org

Richard C. Wender, President
Elmer Huerta, First Vice President

Nationwide, community-based voluntary health organization dedicated to eliminating cancer as a major health problem by preventing cancer, saving lives, and diminishing suffering from cancer through research, education, advocacy, and service.

5604 American Cancer Society: State College
123 S Sparks Street
State College, PA 16801-3915
888-227-5445
800-ACS-2345
Fax: 814-238-3236
http://www.cancer.org

Richard C. Wender, President
Elmer Huerta, First Vice President

Nationwide, community-based voluntary health organization dedicated to eliminating cancer as a major health problem by preventing cancer, saving lives, and diminishing suffering from cancer through research, education, advocacy, and service.

5605 American Cancer Society: Staten Island
173 Old Town Rd
Staten Island, NY 10305
718-987-8871
800-ACS-2345
Fax: 718-351-0361
http://www.cancer.org

Alberta Brescia, VP
Elmer Huerta, First Vice President

Nationwide, community-based voluntary health organization dedicated to eliminating cancer as a major health problem by preventing cancer, saving lives, and diminishing suffering from cancer through research, education, advocacy, and service.

5606 American Cancer Society: Statesboro
515 Denmark Street
Suite 500
Statesboro, GA 30458
912-764-7410
800-ACS-2345
Fax: 912-764-3089
http://www.cancer.org

Richard C. Wender, President
Elmer Huerta, First Vice President

Nationwide, community-based voluntary health organization dedicated to eliminating cancer as a major health problem by preventing cancer, saving lives, and diminishing suffering from cancer through research, education, advocacy, and service.

5607 American Cancer Society: Sterling
941 East 3300 South
Salt Lake City, UT 84106
801-483-1500
800-ACS-2345
Fax: 801-483-1558
http://www.cancer.org

Richard C. Wender, President
Elmer Huerta, First Vice President

Nationwide, community-based voluntary health organization dedicated to eliminating cancer as a major health problem by preventing cancer, saving lives, and diminishing suffering from cancer through research, education, advocacy, and service.

5608 American Cancer Society: Stockton
207 E Alpine Avenue
Stockton, CA 95204
209-941-2676
800-ACS-2345
Fax: 209-941-2824
http://www.cancer.org

Richard C. Wender, President
Elmer Huerta, First Vice President

Nationwide, community-based voluntary health organization dedicated to eliminating cancer as a major health problem by preventing cancer, saving lives, and diminishing suffering from cancer through research, education, advocacy, and service.

5609 American Cancer Society: Storm Lake
600 4th St Ste 229
Sioux City, IA 51101
712-233-1148
800-ACS-2345
Fax: 712-233-1507
http://www.cancer.org

Richard C. Wender, President
Elmer Huerta, First Vice President

Nationwide, community-based voluntary health organization dedicated to eliminating cancer as a major health problem by preventing cancer, saving lives, and diminishing suffering from cancer through research, education, advocacy, and service.

5610 American Cancer Society: Suburban Hillsborough
1462 Oakfield Drive
Brandon, FL 33511
813-685-0670
800-ACS-2345
Fax: 813-689-1320
http://www.cancer.org

Richard C. Wender, President
Elmer Huerta, First Vice President

Nationwide, community-based voluntary health organization dedicated to eliminating cancer as a major health problem by preventing cancer, saving lives, and diminishing suffering from cancer through research, education, advocacy, and service.

5611 American Cancer Society: Suffolk Region
75 Davids Drive
Hauppauge, NY 11788
631-436-7070
800-ACS-2345
Fax: 631-436-5380
http://www.cancer.org

Richard C. Wender, President
Elmer Huerta, First Vice President

Cancer/Associations & Organizations

Nationwide, community-based voluntary health organization dedicated to eliminating cancer as a major health problem by preventing cancer, saving lives, and diminishing suffering from cancer through research, education, advocacy, and service.

5612 American Cancer Society: Summit Area
525 N Broad Street
Canfield, OH 44406
888-227-6446
800-ACS-2345
Fax: 877-227-2838
http://www.cancer.org

Richard C. Wender, President
Elmer Huerta, First Vice President

Nationwide, community-based voluntary health organization dedicated to eliminating cancer as a major health problem by preventing cancer, saving lives, and diminishing suffering from cancer through research, education, advocacy, and service.

5613 American Cancer Society: Tacoma
1313 Broadway
#100
Tacoma, WA 98402
253-272-5767
800-ACS-2345
Fax: 253-272-4485
http://www.cancer.org

Richard C. Wender, President
Elmer Huerta, First Vice President

Nationwide, community-based voluntary health organization dedicated to eliminating cancer as a major health problem by preventing cancer, saving lives, and diminishing suffering from cancer through research, education, advocacy, and service.

5614 American Cancer Society: Tallahassee
2619 Centennial Blvd.,
Suite 101
Tallahassee, FL 32308
850-297-0588
800-ACS-2345
Fax: 850-297-0592
http://www.cancer.org

Richard C. Wender, President
Elmer Huerta, First Vice President

Nationwide, community-based voluntary health organization dedicated to eliminating cancer as a major health problem by preventing cancer, saving lives, and diminishing suffering from cancer through research, education, advocacy, and service.

5615 American Cancer Society: Templeton
1310 Las Tablas
Suite 203
Templeton, CA 93465
805-238-9657
800-ACS-2345
Fax: 805-434-3947
http://www.cancer.org

Richard C. Wender, President
Elmer Huerta, First Vice President

Nationwide, community-based voluntary health organization dedicated to eliminating cancer as a major health problem by preventing cancer, saving lives, and diminishing suffering from cancer through research, education, advocacy, and service.

5616 American Cancer Society: Tequesta
621 Clearwater Park Road
Suite 33e
West Palm Beach, FL 33401
561-744-2275
800-ACS-2345
Fax: 561-659-2316
http://www.cancer.org

Richard C. Wender, President
Elmer Huerta, First Vice President

Nationwide, community-based voluntary health organization dedicated to eliminating cancer as a major health problem by preventing cancer, saving lives, and diminishing suffering from cancer through research, education, advocacy, and service.

5617 American Cancer Society: Texas City
6301 Richmond Ave
Houston, TX 77057
713-266-2877
800-ACS-2345
Fax: 713-266-4159
http://www.cancer.org

Richard C. Wender, President
Elmer Huerta, First Vice President

Nationwide, community-based voluntary health organization dedicated to eliminating cancer as a major health problem by preventing cancer, saving lives, and diminishing suffering from cancer through research, education, advocacy, and service.

5618 American Cancer Society: Thousand Oaks
301 Science Dr
Ste 220
Moorpark, CA 93021
805-497-0114
800-ACS-2345
Fax: 805-529-2536
http://www.cancer.org

Richard C. Wender, President
Elmer Huerta, First Vice President

Nationwide, community-based voluntary health organization dedicated to eliminating cancer as a major health problem by preventing cancer, saving lives, and diminishing suffering from cancer through research, education, advocacy, and service.

5619 American Cancer Society: Topeka
1315 SW Arrowhead Road
Topeka, KS 66604-4056
785-273-4422
800-ACS-2345
Fax: 785-273-1503
http://www.cancer.org

Richard C. Wender, President
Elmer Huerta, First Vice President

Nationwide, community-based voluntary health organization dedicated to eliminating cancer as a major health problem by preventing cancer, saving lives, and diminishing suffering from cancer through research, education, advocacy, and service.

5620 American Cancer Society: Treasure Valley
2676 Vista Avenue
Boise, ID 83705
208-345-2164
800-ACS-2345
Fax: 208-343-9922
http://www.cancer.org

Richard C. Wender, President
Elmer Huerta, First Vice President

Nationwide, community-based voluntary health organization dedicated to eliminating cancer as a major health problem by preventing cancer, saving lives, and diminishing suffering from cancer through research, education, advocacy, and service.

5621 American Cancer Society: Trenton
2881 Grand Drive
Suite B
Chillicothe, MO 64601
660-707-0547
800-ACS-2345
Fax: 660-646-5238
e-mail: dave.hatfield@cancer.org
http://www.cancer.org

Richard C. Wender, President
Elmer Huerta, First Vice President

Nationwide, community-based voluntary health organization dedicated to eliminating cancer as a major health problem by preventing cancer, saving lives, and diminishing suffering from cancer through research, education, advocacy, and service.

5622 American Cancer Society: Tri-Valley
7000 Village Pkwy
Suite E
Dublin, CA 94568
925-833-2784
800-ACS-2345
Fax: 925-833-9137
http://www.cancer.org

Richard C. Wender, President
Elmer Huerta, First Vice President

Cancer/Associations & Organizations

Nationwide, community-based voluntary health organization dedicated to eliminating cancer as a major health problem by preventing cancer, saving lives, and diminishing suffering from cancer through research, education, advocacy, and service.

5623 American Cancer Society: Tulare County
300 N Willis
Visalia, CA 93291
559-734-1391
800-ACS-2345
Fax: 559-734-0429
http://www.cancer.org

Richard C. Wender, President
Elmer Huerta, First Vice President

Nationwide, community-based voluntary health organization dedicated to eliminating cancer as a major health problem by preventing cancer, saving lives, and diminishing suffering from cancer through research, education, advocacy, and service.

5624 American Cancer Society: Tulsa
4110 S 100th E Ave, Grant Building
Suite 101
Tulsa, OK 74146
918-743-6767
800-ACS-2345
Fax: 918-743-9655
http://www.cancer.org

Richard C. Wender, President
Elmer Huerta, First Vice President

Nationwide, community-based voluntary health organization dedicated to eliminating cancer as a major health problem by preventing cancer, saving lives, and diminishing suffering from cancer through research, education, advocacy, and service.

5625 American Cancer Society: Tuscaloosa
2132 McFarland Boulevard E
Suite C
Tuscaloosa, AL 35404
205-758-0700
800-ACS-2345
Fax: 205-758-0116
http://www.cancer.org

Richard C. Wender, President
Elmer Huerta, First Vice President

Nationwide, community-based voluntary health organization dedicated to eliminating cancer as a major health problem by preventing cancer, saving lives, and diminishing suffering from cancer through research, education, advocacy, and service.

5626 American Cancer Society: Ukiah
115 E Smith
Ukiah, CA 95482
707-462-7642
800-ACS-2345
Fax: 707-462-2317
http://www.cancer.org

Richard C. Wender, President
Elmer Huerta, First Vice President

Nationwide, community-based voluntary health organization dedicated to eliminating cancer as a major health problem by preventing cancer, saving lives, and diminishing suffering from cancer through research, education, advocacy, and service.

5627 American Cancer Society: Upper Peninsula
1075 Woodward Avenue
Suite C
Kingsford, MI 49802
906-776-2150
800-ACS-2345
Fax: 906-776-2155
http://www.cancer.org

Richard C. Wender, President
Elmer Huerta, First Vice President

Nationwide, community-based voluntary health organization dedicated to eliminating cancer as a major health problem by preventing cancer, saving lives, and diminishing suffering from cancer through research, education, advocacy, and service.

5628 American Cancer Society: Upper Valley Texas
5413 S McColl Road
Edinburg, TX 78539
956-682-8320
800-ACS-2345
Fax: 956-682-8410
http://www.cancer.org

Richard C. Wender, President
Elmer Huerta, First Vice President

Nationwide, community-based voluntary health organization dedicated to eliminating cancer as a major health problem by preventing cancer, saving lives, and diminishing suffering from cancer through research, education, advocacy, and service.

5629 American Cancer Society: Victorville
1240 Palmyrita Ave
Ste A
Riverside, CA 92507
951-683-6415
800-ACS-2345
Fax: 951-682-6804
http://www.cancer.org

Richard C. Wender, President
Elmer Huerta, First Vice President

Nationwide, community-based voluntary health organization dedicated to eliminating cancer as a major health problem by preventing cancer, saving lives, and diminishing suffering from cancer through research, education, advocacy, and service.

5630 American Cancer Society: Vincennes
318 Main Street
Vincennes, IN 47591
812-886-9007
800-ACS-2345
Fax: 812-886-9008
http://www.cancer.org

Richard C. Wender, President
Elmer Huerta, First Vice President

Nationwide, community-based voluntary health organization dedicated to eliminating cancer as a major health problem by preventing cancer, saving lives, and diminishing suffering from cancer through research, education, advocacy, and service.

5631 American Cancer Society: Volusia East
LakeSide North Executive Center, 1737
North Clyde Morris Blvd., Suite 140
Daytona Beach, FL 32117
386-274-3274
800-ACS-2345
Fax: 386-274-5582
http://www.cancer.org

Richard C. Wender, President
Elmer Huerta, First Vice President

Nationwide, community-based voluntary health organization dedicated to eliminating cancer as a major health problem by preventing cancer, saving lives, and diminishing suffering from cancer through research, education, advocacy, and service.

5632 American Cancer Society: Volusia West
1737 North Clyde Morris Boulevard
Suite 140
Daytona Beach, FL 32117
386-760-6078
800-ACS-2345
Fax: 386-322-3631
http://www.cancer.org

Richard C. Wender, President
Elmer Huerta, First Vice President

Nationwide, community-based voluntary health organization dedicated to eliminating cancer as a major health problem by preventing cancer, saving lives, and diminishing suffering from cancer through research, education, advocacy, and service.

5633 American Cancer Society: Wabash Valley
705 Putnam Street
Terre Haute, IN 47802
812-232-2679
800-ACS-2345
Fax: 812-232-2741
http://www.cancer.org

Richard C. Wender, President
Elmer Huerta, First Vice President

Cancer/Associations & Organizations

Nationwide, community-based voluntary health organization dedicated to eliminating cancer as a major health problem by preventing cancer, saving lives, and diminishing suffering from cancer through research, education, advocacy, and service.

5634　American Cancer Society: Waco
1311 N New Road
Waco, TX 76710-4899
254-753-0806
800-ACS-2345
Fax: 254-753-0544
http://www.cancer.org

Richard C. Wender, President
Elmer Huerta, First Vice President

Nationwide, community-based voluntary health organization dedicated to eliminating cancer as a major health problem by preventing cancer, saving lives, and diminishing suffering from cancer through research, education, advocacy, and service.

5635　American Cancer Society: Wailuku
95 Mahalani Street
Wailuku, HI 96793
808-244-5553
800-ACS-2345
Fax: 808-244-6195
http://www.cancer.org

Richard C. Wender, President
Elmer Huerta, First Vice President

Nationwide, community-based voluntary health organization dedicated to eliminating cancer as a major health problem by preventing cancer, saving lives, and diminishing suffering from cancer through research, education, advocacy, and service.

5636　American Cancer Society: Waterloo
2101 Kimball Ave
Suite 130
Waterloo, IA 50702
319-272-2880
800-ACS-2345
Fax: 319-272-2881
http://www.cancer.org

Richard C. Wender, President
Elmer Huerta, First Vice President

Nationwide, community-based voluntary health organization dedicated to eliminating cancer as a major health problem by preventing cancer, saving lives, and diminishing suffering from cancer through research, education, advocacy, and service.

5637　American Cancer Society: Watertown
525 5th Street SE
Suite 4
Watertown, SD 57201-4974
605-882-2957
800-ACS-2345
Fax: 605-882-1701
http://www.cancer.org

Peg Schultz, Manager

Nationwide, community-based voluntary health organization dedicated to eliminating cancer as a major health problem by preventing cancer, saving lives, and diminishing suffering from cancer through research, education, advocacy, and service.

5638　American Cancer Society: Waycross
3011 Hampton Ave
Suite 361
Brunswick, GA 31520
912-265-7117
800-ACS-2345
Fax: 912-262-0773
http://www.cancer.org

Richard C. Wender, President
Elmer Huerta, First Vice President

Nationwide, community-based voluntary health organization dedicated to eliminating cancer as a major health problem by preventing cancer, saving lives, and diminishing suffering from cancer through research, education, advocacy, and service.

5639　American Cancer Society: Weld County
1020 9th Avenue
Greeley, CO 80631-4014
970-356-9727
900-ACS-2345
Fax: 970-356-9238
http://www.cancer.org

Nationwide, community-based voluntary health organization dedicated to eliminating cancer as a major health problem by preventing cancer, saving lives, and diminishing suffering from cancer through research, education, advocacy, and service.

5640　American Cancer Society: West Bay Region San Francisco County Unit
201 Mission Street
Suite 720
San Francisco, CA 94105
415-394-7100
800-ACS-2345
Fax: 415-495-1877
http://www.ca.cancer.org

Richard C. Wender, President
Elmer Huerta, First Vice President

Nationwide, community-based voluntary health organization dedicated to eliminating cancer as a major health problem by preventing cancer, saving lives, and diminishing suffering from cancer through research, education, advocacy, and service.

5641　American Cancer Society: West Central Illinois
4234 N Knoxville Avenue
Suite B
Peoria, IL 61614
309-688-3488
800-ACS-2345
Fax: 309-688-9493
http://www.cancer.org

Richard C. Wender, President
Elmer Huerta, First Vice President

Nationwide, community-based voluntary health organization dedicated to eliminating cancer as a major health problem by preventing cancer, saving lives, and diminishing suffering from cancer through research, education, advocacy, and service.

5642　American Cancer Society: West Contra Costa County
1885 Oak Park Blvd
Suite 4
Pleasant Hill, CA 94523
925-934-7640
800-ACS-2345
Fax: 925-934-5372
http://www.cancer.org

Richard C. Wender, President
Elmer Huerta, First Vice President

Nationwide, community-based voluntary health organization dedicated to eliminating cancer as a major health problem by preventing cancer, saving lives, and diminishing suffering from cancer through research, education, advocacy, and service.

5643　American Cancer Society: West Hawaii
75-5995 Kuakini Highway
Suite 443
Kailua Kona, HI 96740
808-334-0442
800-ACS-2345
Fax: 808-334-0443
http://www.cancer.org

Richard C. Wender, President
Elmer Huerta, First Vice President

Nationwide, community-based voluntary health organization dedicated to eliminating cancer as a major health problem by preventing cancer, saving lives, and diminishing suffering from cancer through research, education, advocacy, and service.

5644　American Cancer Society: West Michigan
129 Jefferson Avenue SE
Suite 202
Grand Rapids, MI 49503
616-364-6121
800-ACS-2345
Fax: 616-364-6451
http://www.cancer.org

Richard C. Wender, President
Elmer Huerta, First Vice President

Cancer/Associations & Organizations

Nationwide, community-based voluntary health organization dedicated to eliminating cancer as a major health problem by preventing cancer, saving lives, and diminishing suffering from cancer through research, education, advocacy, and service.

5645 American Cancer Society: West Palm Beach
621 Clearwater Park Rd
Suite 110
West Palm Beach, FL 33401
561-366-0013
800-ACS-2345
Fax: 561-659-2316
http://www.cancer.org

Richard C. Wender, President
Elmer Huerta, First Vice President

Nationwide, community-based voluntary health organization dedicated to eliminating cancer as a major health problem by preventing cancer, saving lives, and diminishing suffering from cancer through research, education, advocacy, and service.

5646 American Cancer Society: Westchester Region
2 Lyon Place
White Plains, NY 10601
914-949-4800
800-ACS-2345
Fax: 914-397-8851
http://www.cancer.org

Richard C. Wender, President
Elmer Huerta, First Vice President

Nationwide, community-based voluntary health organization dedicated to eliminating cancer as a major health problem by preventing cancer, saving lives, and diminishing suffering from cancer through research, education, advocacy, and service.

5647 American Cancer Society: Western New England
59 Bobala Rd
Holyoke, MA 01040
413-734-6000
800-ACS-2345
Fax: 413-493-2199
http://www.cancer.org

Richard C. Wender, President
Elmer Huerta, First Vice President

Nationwide, community-based voluntary health organization dedicated to eliminating cancer as a major health problem by preventing cancer, saving lives, and diminishing suffering from cancer through research, education, advocacy, and service.

5648 American Cancer Society: Western New York
101 John James Audubon Pkwy
Amherst, NY 14228
716-689-6981
800-ACS-2345
Fax: 716-689-4923
http://www.cancer.org

Richard C. Wender, President
Elmer Huerta, First Vice President

Nationwide, community-based voluntary health organization dedicated to eliminating cancer as a major health problem by preventing cancer, saving lives, and diminishing suffering from cancer through research, education, advocacy, and service.

5649 American Cancer Society: Western Yavapai
2724 E Lakin
Ste 9
Flagstaff, AZ 86004
928-526-3800
800-ACS-2345
Fax: 928-526-5870
e-mail: tracy.cooke@cancer.org
http://www.cancer.org

Richard C. Wender, President
Elmer Huerta, First Vice President

Nationwide, community-based voluntary health organization dedicated to eliminating cancer as a major health problem by preventing cancer, saving lives, and diminishing suffering from cancer through research, education, advocacy, and service.

5650 American Cancer Society: White Marsh
8219 Town Center Drive
Baltimore, MD 21236
410-931-6850
800-ACS-2345
Fax: 410-931-6875
http://www.cancer.org

Richard C. Wender, President
Elmer Huerta, First Vice President

Nationwide, community-based voluntary health organization dedicated to eliminating cancer as a major health problem by preventing cancer, saving lives, and diminishing suffering from cancer through research, education, advocacy, and service.

5651 American Cancer Society: Wichita
818 N Emporia
Suite 100
Wichita, KS 67214
316-265-3400
800-ACS-234
Fax: 316-265-3490
http://www.cancer.org

Richard C. Wender, President
Elmer Huerta, First Vice President

Nationwide, community-based voluntary health organization dedicated to eliminating cancer as a major health problem by preventing cancer, saving lives, and diminishing suffering from cancer through research, education, advocacy, and service.

5652 American Cancer Society: Willmar
3721 23rd Street S
Suite 102
Saint Cloud, MN 56301
320-255-0220
800-ACS-2345
Fax: 320-255-5517
http://www.cancer.org

Richard C. Wender, President
Elmer Huerta, First Vice President

Nationwide, community-based voluntary health organization dedicated to eliminating cancer as a major health problem by preventing cancer, saving lives, and diminishing suffering from cancer through research, education, advocacy, and service.

5653 American Cancer Society: Windward
130 Kailua Road
Suite 102b
Kailua, HI 96734-3420
808-262-5124
800-ACS-2345
Fax: 808-262-4212
http://www.cancer.org

Richard C. Wender, President
Elmer Huerta, First Vice President

Nationwide, community-based voluntary health organization dedicated to eliminating cancer as a major health problem by preventing cancer, saving lives, and diminishing suffering from cancer through research, education, advocacy, and service.

5654 American Cancer Society: Wood Area
740 Commerce Drive
Suite B
Perrysburg, OH 43551
888-227-6446
800-ACS-2345
Fax: 877-227-2838
http://www.cancer.org

Richard C. Wender, President
Elmer Huerta, First Vice President

Nationwide, community-based voluntary health organization dedicated to eliminating cancer as a major health problem by preventing cancer, saving lives, and diminishing suffering from cancer through research, education, advocacy, and service.

5655 American Cancer Society: York
924 N Colonial Ave
York, PA 17403
888-227-5445
800-ACS-2345
Fax: 717-852-0919
http://www.cancer.org

Richard C. Wender, President
Elmer Huerta, First Vice President

Cancer/Associations & Organizations

Nationwide, community-based voluntary health organization dedicated to eliminating cancer as a major health problem by preventing cancer, saving lives, and diminishing suffering from cancer through research, education, advocacy, and service.

5656 American Cancer Socity: Imperial Central
400 S 8th Street
El Centro, CA 92243
760-352-6656
800-ACS-2345
Fax: 760-652-0316
http://www.cancer.org

Richard C. Wender, President
Elmer Huerta, First Vice President

Nationwide, community-based voluntary health organization dedicated to eliminating cancer as a major health problem by preventing cancer, saving lives, and diminishing suffering from cancer through research, education, advocacy, and service.

5657 American Foundation for Urologic Disease: Us Too Line
1000 Corporate Boulevard
410
Linthicum, MD 21090
410-689-3700
800-828-7866
Fax: 410-689-3800
e-mail: auafoundation@auafoundation.org
http://www.auafoundation.org

Sandra Vassos, Executive Director
Paul F. Schellhammer, MD, President

Provides patient education information and referrals for family members, victims and other individuals concerned with urologic disease.

5658 American Lung Association
61 Broadway
Floor 6
New York, NY 10006
212-315-8700
800-586-4872
Fax: 212-315-8870
e-mail: info@lungusa.org
http://www.lungusa.org

Irwin Martin Berlin, Director
Ross P Lanzafame, Director

A voluntary organization interested in the prevention and control of lung disease. Promotes and distributes public awareness information on a variety of lung disorders, including allergies.
1904

5659 American Prostate Society
1340 Charwood Road
Hanover, MD 21076-3117
410-859-3735
Fax: 410-850-0818
http://www.ameripros.org

Claude Gerard, President

Formed approximately 4 years ago, it is the only organization dedicated exclusively to using existing medical capabilities to reduce death due to prostate cancer and to reduce unnecessary or ineffective prostate surgery.

5660 Association for the Cure of Cancer of the Prostate
1250 4th Street
Suite 360
Santa Monica, CA 90401
310-570-4700
800-757-CURE
Fax: 310-570-4701
e-mail: info@prostatecancerfoundation.org
http://www.prostatecancerfoundation.org/

Mike Milken, Founder and Chairman
Jonathan W. Simons, MD, President and Chief Executive Of

5661 Association of Community Cancer Centers
11600 Nebel Street
Suite 201
Rockville, MD 20852
301-984-9496
Fax: 301-770-1949
e-mail: mmilburne@accc-cancer.org
http://www.assoc-cancer-ctrs.org

Lee E Mortenson, Executive Director

Institutions (517), individuals (300), and 14 state oncology societies involved in the provision of community cancer care. Fosters communication among providers of community cancer care; seeks to improve the quality of care available to cancer patients in community settings; encourages clinical research utilizing the community as a setting.

5662 Baton Rouge Regional Tumor Registry
4950 Essen Lane
Baton Rouge, LA 70809
225-767-0430
Fax: 225-766-0218
e-mail: humanresources@marybird.com
http://www.marybird.org/

Lori McCallum, Executive Director
Steven Todd, President and Chief Executive Of

5663 Burger King Cancer Caring Center
4117 Liberty Avenue (Bloomfield)
Pittsburgh, PA 15224
412-622-1212
Fax: 412-622-1216
e-mail: info@cancercaring.org
http://www.cancercaring.org

Rebecca Whitlinger, Executive Director
Josette Janczak, President

Provides a wide variety of support services to cancer patients, their families and friends, including support groups, education classes, personal counseling, telephone helpline.

5664 CanHelp
3111 Paradise Bay Road
Port Ludlow, WA 98365
360-437-2291
Fax: 360-437-2272
e-mail: canhelp@cablespeed.com
http://www.canhelp.com

Patrick M McGrady Jr, Founder
Madeleen Herreshoff, Director

Offers reports for cancer patients on orthodox and alternative therapies.

5665 Cancer Care
Public Information Associates
275 Seventh Ave
Floor 22
New York, NY 10001
212-712-8400
Fax: 212-712-8495
e-mail: info@cancercare.org
http://www.cancercare.org

Diane S. Blum, Executive Director
Ellen Coleman, MSSA, Associate Executive Director

Voluntary social service agency that functions as the service arm of the National Cancer Care Foundation. Provides professional social work counseling and guidance to help patients and families cope with the emotional, psychological, and financial consequences of cancer. In conjunction with professional counseling and where appropriate to the individual casework plan, supplementary financial aid may be given to self-supporting families to share the cost of home care services such as nursing care, home health aides, housekeepers, child care, and transportation. Sponsors symposia.

5666 Cancer Control Society and Cancer Book House
2043 N Berendo Street
Los Angeles, CA 90027
323-663-7801
Fax: 323-663-7757
http://www.cancercontrolsociety.com/

Lorraine Rosenthal, Co-Founder
Frank Cousineau, President

An informational organization offering books, films, videos, clinic tours and lists of patients with cancer.

Cancer/Associations & Organizations

5667 Cancer Counseling Center of Ohio
1515 Lake Martin Drive
Kent, OH 44240-6257   330-922-1855
                                   Fax: 330-626-3115

Offers counseling treatments for persons with Cancer, MS, and other chronic or life-threatening illness. Focus is on will to recover, stress factors, inner healing, spiritual issues, interpersonal relationships. Mind-body techniques especially important, with strong support from family and/or others is sought. Individual sessions at the Center, home or hospital; local or long-distance.

5668 Cancer Federation
PO Box 1298
Banning, CA 92220   951-849-4325
                                   Fax: 951-849-0156
                          e-mail: info@cancerfed.org
                          http://www.cancerfed.com

John Steinbacher, Executive Director
Jules Vautrot, President

Offers a quarterly magazine, holds free meetings, counsels cancer patients and their families, maintains a lending library of materials on cancer and more.

5669 Cancer Information Service (CIS)
National Cancer Institute
900 Rockville Pike
Building 31
Bethesda, MD 20892   301-933-9350
                                        800-525-3777

Provides information on cancer causes, prevention, detection, diagnosis, and rehabilitation. Offers referrals to doctors, cancer centers, and support groups. Free information packet available. Hours: 9:00 to 10:00 p.m. Monday-Friday.

5670 Cancer Institute of Brooklyn
927 49th Street
Borough Park, NY 11219-2923   718-972-5816
                                   Fax: 718-972-8693

Jo-Ann Hertz, Executive Director

5671 Cancer Victors and Friends National Headquarters
7740 W Manchester Avenue
Suite 203
Playa Del Rey, CA 90293-6401   310-822-5032
                                        888-613-6733
                                   Fax: 310-822-4193
                          e-mail: iacvfbroward@juno.com
                          http://www.cancervictors.com

Ann Cinguina, Executive Secretary

Offers referrals to recovered patients and provides information packets.

5672 Cancer and Leukemia Group B
230 West Monroe
Suite 2050
Chicago, IL 60606   773-702-9171
                                   Fax: 773-345-0117
                          e-mail: marciak@uchicago.edu
                          http://www.calgb.org

Richard L Schilsky MD, Chairman
Marcia Kelly, Administrative Coordinator

Cancer research.
        1955

5673 Cancervive
11636 Chayote Street
Los Angeles, CA 90049   310-203-9232
                                        800-4TO-CURE
                                   Fax: 310-471-4618
                          e-mail: cancerviver@aol.com
                          http://www.cancervive.org

Susan Nessim, Founder and President

This nonprofit organization that helps cancer survivors deal with the challenges of life after cancer. They offer support groups in some states, insurance information and assistance, and patient advocacy.

5674 Chemocare
231 N Avenue W
Westfield, NY 07090-1428   908-233-1103
                                        800-55C-HEMO
                                   Fax: 908-233-0228
                          e-mail: chemocare@aol.com

CHEMOcare is a telephone support network for chemotherapy and/or radiation patients. They have a newsletter, a tollfree information line, and offer peer counseling and advocacy.

5675 Chemotherapy Foundation
183 Madison Avenue
Suite 403
New York, NY 10016   212-213-9292
                                   Fax: 212-213-3831
                          e-mail: scox@chemotherapyfoundation.org
                          http://www.chemotherapyfoundation.org

Shirley Cox, Executive Director
Barry Richter, President

The Chemotherapy Foundation is dedicated to developing more effective methods of treatment for the control and cure of cancer. They procvide ecucational materials and provide funds for innovative chemotherapy research, and sponsor professional and public educational symposia.

5676 Collaborative Medicine Center
1341 S Eliseo Drive
Suite 350
Greenbrae, CA 94904-2000   415-925-8600

Martin L Rossman MD, director

Not specifically a cancer treatment center but works with cancer patients by using a variety of supportive modalities. The emphasis at the center is on helping people learn to support and activate their own healing processes.

5677 Commonwealth Cancer Help Program
451 Mesa Raod
Bolinas, CA 94924   415-868-0970
                                   Fax: 415-868-2230
                          http://www.commonweal.org/programs/cancer-help.

Waz Thomas, Program Coordinator
Michael Lerner, President

An educational program designed to help participants reduce the stress of cancer, explore health habits, be with others experiencing the same difficulties and consider information on established and complementary therapeutic options.

5678 Corporate Angel Network
Westchester County Airport
Westchester County Airport
One Loop Road
White Plains, NY 10604-1215   914-328-1313
                                   Fax: 914-328-3938
                          e-mail: info@corpangelnetwork.org
                          http://www.corpangelnetwork.org

Bonnie Le Var, President
Paul P Bollinger, Jr, Director

A service which fills available space on corporate airplanes with cancer patients in need of transportation to treatment centers.

5679 Duke University Comprehensive Cancer Center
Medical Center
2424 Erwin Road
Hock Plaza Suite 601
Durham, NC 27705   919-684-3377
                                   Fax: 919-684-5653
                          e-mail: michael.colvin@duke.edu
                          http://www.cancer.duke.edu

Karen Cochran, Executive Director
George Barth Geller, Director

Cancer/Associations & Organizations

5680 **Exceptional Cancer Patients**
522 Jackson Park Drive
Middletown, CT 16335
203-865-8392
Fax: 814-337-0699
e-mail: keb@touchstarpro.com
http://www.ecap-online.org
Barry Bittman, MD, Chief Executive Officer and Medi
Bernie Siegel, Founder

Support groups for those suffering from cancer.

5681 **Foundation for Advancement in Cancer Therapy**
PO Box 1242
Old Chelsea Station
New York, NY 10113-1242
212-741-2790
http://www.fact-ltd.org
Ruth Sackman, President and Co-Founder

Distributes information on cancer prevention and nontoxic therapies for cancer.

5682 **Gilda's Club**
195 W Houston Street
New York, NY 10014
212-647-9700
Fax: 212-647-1151
http://www.jesthealth.com/art19jnj.html
Richard N Gould, Owner

5683 **Gilda's Club: Metro Detroit**
3517 Rochester Road,
Suite 200
Royal Oak, MI 48073
248-577-0800
Fax: 248-577-0898
e-mail: jperry@gildasclubdetroit.org
http://www.gildasclubdetroit.org
Joe Perry, Senior Director
Laura Ortiz, Director of Marketing and Commun

5684 **Gilda's Club: Quad Cities**
1234 East River Drive
100
Davenport, IA 52803
563-326-7504
Fax: 563-326-1658
e-mail: gildasclub@qconline
http://www.gildasclubqc.org/
Claudia Robinson, Chief Executive Officer
Melissa Wright, Program Director

Free, non-residential, social and emotional support community for men, women and children living with all types of cancer and for their families and friends.

5685 **Gilda's Club: South Florida**
119 Rose Drive
Fort Lauderdale, FL 33316
954-763-6776
Fax: 954-763-6761
e-mail: info@gildasclubsouthflorida.org
http://www.artistsvue.com/
Armond Leighton, Jr, Chairman
Dennis Giordano, VICE CHAIR

Free, non-residential, social and emotional support community for men, women and children living with all types of cancer and for their families and friends.

5686 **Healing Light Center Church**
261 E Alegria Avenue
Apt 12
Sierra Madre, CA 91024
626-306-2170
Fax: 626-355-0996
http://www.rosalynlbruyere.org
Rosalyn L Bruyere, Founder/Director

5687 **Health Resource**
933 Faulkner Street
Conway, AR 72034
501-329-5272
Fax: 501-329-9489
e-mail: research@thehealthresource.com
http://www.thehealthresource.com/
Jan Guthrie, Contact
Deby Wood, Contact

A medical information service which provides clients with an individualized, in-depth research report on his or her specific health problem and type of cancer.

5688 **International Holistic Center**
5515 N 7th Street
Suite 5-129
Phoenix, AZ 85014-2573
602-287-0605
Fax: 602-287-8972
e-mail: ihcinc@holisticresources.org
http://www.holisticresources.org/
Stan Kalson, Director

Provides information and referrals concerning holistic health care in Arizona and beyond.

5689 **Leukemia & Lymphoma Society**
1311 Mamaroneck Avenue
Suite 130
White Plains, NY 10605
914-949-5213
800-955-4572
Fax: 914-949-6691
e-mail: Infocenter@leukemia.org
http://www.leukemia-lymphoma.org
Dwayne Howell, President
Dennis P Chillemi, Executive Director

A national voluntary health agency dedicated to curing leukemia, lymphoma, Hodgkin lymphoma and myeloma and to improving the quality of life of patients and their families.

5690 **Leukemia & Lymphoma Society: Alabama Chapter**
100 Chase Park South
Suite 220
Birmingham, AL 35244-1851
205-989-0098
Fax: 251-989-0099
e-mail: noralyn.hamilton@lls.org
http://www.leukemia-lymphoma.org
Noralyn Hamilton, Executive Director
Darlene Dean, General Contact

Dedicated to finding cures for leukemia and related cancers and to improving the quality of life for patients and their families.

5691 **Leukemia & Lymphoma Society: Austin Office**
9211 Waterford Centre Boulevard
Suite 275
Austin, TX 78758
512-491-6610
Fax: 512-491-5052
e-mail: laura.wallace@lls.org
http://www.leukemia-lymphoma.org
Gracie Guajardo, Patient Services Manager
Larcombe Teichgraeber, Manager

Dedicated to find a cure for leukemia and lymphoma, and to improve the quality of life for patients and their families.

5692 **Leukemia & Lymphoma Society: Central Florida Chapter**
3319 Maguire Boulevard
Suite 101
Orlando, FL 32803
407-898-0733
800-955-4572
Fax: 407-896-8645
e-mail: Maria.avenancio@lls.org
http://www.leukemia.org
Carroll Franklin, Executive Director
Linda Gurian, Operations Director and Patient

Dedicated to finding cures for leukemia and related cancers and to improving the quality of life for patients and their families.

Cancer/Associations & Organizations

5693 Leukemia & Lymphoma Society: Central New York Chapter
401 N. Salina Street, Learbury Centre
Suite 304
Syracuse, NY 13203
315-471-1050
800-690-8944
Fax: 315-471-6434
e-mail: chip.lockwood@lls.org
http://www.leukemia-lymphoma.org
Chip Lockwood, Executive Director
Kristen Duggleby, Campaign Director

Dedicated to finding cures for leukemia and related cancers and to improving the quality of life for patients and their families.

5694 Leukemia & Lymphoma Society: Central Ohio Chapter
2225 Citygate Drive
Suite E
Columbus, OH 43219
614-476-7194
800-686-CURE
Fax: 614-476-7189
http://www.leukemia-lymphoma.org
Phil Tanner, Executive Director
Mike Uscio, Patient Services Manager

Dedicated to finding cures for leukemia and related cancers and to improving the quality of life for patients and their families.

5695 Leukemia & Lymphoma Society: Central Pennsylvania Chapter
800 Corporate Circle
Suite 100
Harrisburg, PA 17110
717-652-6520
800-822-2873
Fax: 717-652-8614
e-mail: Cathy.Chisholm@LLS.org
http://www.leukemia-lymphoma.org
Cathy Chisholm, Executive Director
Danielle Renteria-Bubnis, LSW, Patient Services Manager

Dedicated to finding cures for leukemia and blood related illnesses and improving the quality of life for patients and their families.

5696 Leukemia & Lymphoma Society: Central Valley Branch
470 E Henderson Avenue
Suite 102
Fresno, CA 93720
559-435-1482
Fax: 559-435-4873
http://www.leukemia-lymphoma.org
Vicki Weiland, Executive Director
Dave Kyle, President

5697 Leukemia & Lymphoma Society: Connecticut Chapter
300 Research Parkway
Suite 310
Meriden, CT 06450
203-379-0445
800-955-4572
Fax: 203-379-0451
e-mail: john.clark@lls.org
http://www.leukemia.org
James Kimball, Executive Director
John Clark, Executive Director

Dedicated to finding cures for leukemia and related cancers and to improving the quality of life for patients and their families. Serves residents of the counties: Hartford, Litchfield, Middlesex, New Haven, Tolland, and Windham.

5698 Leukemia & Lymphoma Society: Desert Mountain States Chapter
3877 N. 7th St
Suite 300
Phoenix, AZ 85014
602-788-8622
800-568-1372
Fax: 602-788-3455
e-mail: PalmenbergJ@lls.org
http://www.leukemia-lymphoma.org
Rebecca Villicana, Executive Director
Jessica Drury, Manager

Serves New Mexico and the Greater El Paso, TX area - dedicated to finding cures for leukemia and related cancers and to improving the quality of life for patients and their families.

5699 Leukemia & Lymphoma Society: Eastern Iowa Satellite Office
8033 University Blvd
Suite A
Des Moines, IA 50325
515-270-6169
Fax: 515-270-5392
e-mail: brownm@ia.leukemia-lymphoma.org
http://www.leukemia.org
Janna LaCook, Executive Director
Melanie Brown, Campaign Manager Iowa

Dedicated to finding a cure for leukemia and related cancers and to improving the quality of life for patients and their families.

5700 Leukemia & Lymphoma Society: Eastern Philadelphia Chapter
2 International Plaza
Suite 245
Philadelphia, PA 19113
610-521-8274
Fax: 610-521-6132
e-mail: singletonk@lls.org
http://www.leukemia-lymphoma.org
Kenneth Singleton, Executive Director
Julie W. Hyland, Deputy Executive Director

Dedicated to finding cures for leukemia and related cancers and to improving the quality of life for patients and their families.

5701 Leukemia & Lymphoma Society: Gateway Chapter
77 Westport Plaza
Suite 101
Saint Louis, MO 63146
314-878-0780
800-264-CURE
Fax: 314-878-4050
http://www.leukemia.org
Judith Swiecicki, Executive Director

Dedicated to finding cures for leukemia, lymphoma, Hodgkin's disease and myeloma and to improving the quality of life for patients and thier families.

5702 Leukemia & Lymphoma Society: Georgia Chapter
3715 Northside Parkway, 400 Northcreek
Suite 300
Atlanta, GA 30327
678-279-2001
800-399-7312
Fax: 678-279-2060
http://www.leukemia.org
Dick Brown, Executive Director

Dedicated to finding cures for leukemia and related cancers and to improving the quality of life for patients and their families.

5703 Leukemia & Lymphoma Society: Greater Los Angeles Chapter
6033 West Century Blvd
Suite 300
Los Angeles, CA 90045
310-216-7600
Fax: 310-216-1500
e-mail: Tricia.Jarmer@lls.org
http://www.leukemia.org
Lance Slaughter, Executive Director
Tricia Jarmer, Patient Services Manager
Christy Ward, Campaign Development Director

Dedicated to finding cures for leukemia and related cancers and to improving the quality of life for patients and their families.

5704 Leukemia & Lymphoma Society: Greater Sacramento Area
4604 Roseville Road
Suite 100
North Highlands, CA 95660
916-348-1793
Fax: 916-348-7864
e-mail: tracy.newman@lls.org
http://www.lls.org
Tracy F. Newman, Executive Director
Lonnie Biehl, TNT Director

Cancer/Associations & Organizations

Dedicated to finding cures for leukemia and related cancers and to improving the quality of life for patients and their families.

5705 Leukemia & Lymphoma Society: Idaho Branch Office
921 S. Orchard Street
Suite I
Boise, ID 83705
208-658-6662
800-955-4572
Fax: 208-658-6708
e-mail: gerstenk@ks.leukemia-lymphoma.org
http://www.leukemia.org
Sean McParland, Divisional Director
Kelly Gerstenkorn, Managing Director

Dedicated to finding cures for leukemia and related cancers, and to improving the quality of life for patients and their families.

5706 Leukemia & Lymphoma Society: Illinois Chapter
651 W Washington Boulevard
Suite 400
Chicago, IL 60661
312-651-7350
800-955-4572
Fax: 312-463-0980
e-mail: nancy.mcinroy@lls.org
http://www.leukemia.org
Nancy McInroy, Executive Director
Jill Kulbok, TNT Director

Dedicated to finding cures for leukemia and related cancers and to improving the quality of life for patients and their families.

5707 Leukemia & Lymphoma Society: Indiana Chapter
941 E 86th Street
Suite 100
Indianapolis, IN 46240
317-726-2270
800-846-7764
Fax: 317-726-2280
e-mail: amy.kwas@lls.org
http://www.leukemia-lymphoma.org
Amy Kwas, Executive Director
Julie Creech, Office Manager

Cure leukemia, lymphoma, Hodgkin's disease and myeloma, and improve the quality of life of patients and their families.

5708 Leukemia & Lymphoma Society: Iowa Branch Office
8033 University Blvd
Suite A
Des Moines, IA 50325
515-270-6169
800-347-1074
Fax: 515-270-5392
e-mail: janna@crn.org
http://www.leukemia-lymphoma.org
Kristen Johnson, Executive Director
Victoria Blume, Deputy Executive Director

Dedicated to finding cures for leukemia, lymphoma, and related cancers, and to improving the quality of life for patients and thier families.

5709 Leukemia & Lymphoma Society: Kansas Chapter
555 N Woodlawn Street
Bldg. 1, Suite 113
Wichita, KS 67208
316-687-2222
800-779-2417
Fax: 316-687-1122
e-mail: kansas@ks.leukemia-lymphoma.org
http://www.leukemia.org
Kelly Gerstenkorn, Managing Director
Sean McParland, Divisional Director
Anna Maria Gentile, Manager

Dedicated to finding cures for leukemia and related cancers and to improving the quality of life for patients and their families.

5710 Leukemia & Lymphoma Society: Kentucky Chapter
710 West Main Street
Suite 201
Louisville, KY 40202
502-584-8490
800-955-2566
Fax: 502-589-5316
e-mail: marybeth.oreilly@lls.org
http://www.leukemia.org
Mary Beth O'Reilly, Executive Director
Leanne Dockter, Office Manager

Serves Kentucky and Southern Indiana residents touched by leukemia, lymphoma, Hodgkin's disease and myeloma.

5711 Leukemia & Lymphoma Society: Las Vegas Office
6280 S.Valley View Blvd
Suite 342
Las Vegas, NV 89118
702-436-4220
Fax: 702-436-2396
e-mail: mitchelle@lls.org
http://www.leukemia.org
Duffy Gold, Campaign Manager
Judith Mitchell, Executive Director

Dedicated to finding cures for leukemia, lymphoma, Hodgkin's disease, and myeloma and to improving the quality of life for patients and thier families.

5712 Leukemia & Lymphoma Society: Lehigh Valley Office
2 International Plaza
Suite 245
Philadelphia, PA 19113
610-521-8274
Fax: 610-521-6132
http://www.leukemia-lymphoma.org
Kenneth Singleton, Executive Director
Julie W. Hyland, Deputy Executive Director

Dedicated to finding cures for leukemia, lymphoma, Hodgkin's disease, and myeloma and to improving the quality of life for patients and their families.

5713 Leukemia & Lymphoma Society: Long Island Chapter
Leukemia Society of America
555 Broadhollow Road
Suite 403
Melville, NY 11747
631-752-8500
Fax: 631-752-9066
e-mail: tammy.philie@lls.org
http://www.leukemia-lymphoma.org
Tammy Philie, Executive Director
Karen DeMairo, Patient Services Manager

Established to serve Long Islanders with leukemia, lymphoma, Hodgkin's disease and myeloma, their families and friends.

5714 Leukemia & Lymphoma Society: Louisiana Chapter
3636 S i 10 Service Road W
Suite 304
Metairie, LA 70001
504-837-0945
888-290-0945
Fax: 504-837-9193
e-mail: devaughnm@lls.org
http://www.leukemia.org
John Walter, Chief Operating Officer
Dwayne Howell, President

Dedicated to finding cures for leukemia and related cancers and to improving the quality of life for patients and their families.

5715 Leukemia & Lymphoma Society: Maryland Chapter
8600 LaSalle Road, Chester Building
Suite 314
Baltimore, MD 21286-2011
410-825-2500
800-955-4572
Fax: 410-825-2515
e-mail: sharon.yateman@LLS.org
http://www.mdleukemia.org
Sharon E. Yateman, Executive Director

Dedicated to finding cures for leukemia and related cancers and to improving the quality of life for patients and their families.

Cancer/Associations & Organizations

5716 Leukemia & Lymphoma Society: Massachusetts Chapter
495 Old Connecticut Path
Suite 220
Framingham, MA 01701-4567 508-879-5083
Fax: 508-879-8163
http://www.leukemia.org

Iris Gleason, Executive Director

Serves residents of Massachusetts, Maine and New Hampshier who are dealing with leukemia, lymphoma, Hodgkin's disease and myeloma.

5717 Leukemia & Lymphoma Society: Michigan Chapter
1421 E 12 Mile Road
Bldg A
Madison Heights, MI 48071 248-582-2900
800-456-5413
Fax: 248-582-2925
e-mail: peggy.shriver@lls.org
http://www.leukemia.org

Peggy Shriver, Executive Director
Tami Duquette, TNT Director

Serving the state of Michigan.

5718 Leukemia & Lymphoma Society: Mid-America Chapter
6811 W. 63rd Street, Cloverleaf Building 1
Suite 202
Shawnee Mission, KS 66202 913-262-1515
800-256-1075
Fax: 913-262-2167
e-mail: janna.lacock@lls.org
http://www.leukemia.org

Janna LaCock, Executive Director
Amy Michale, Office Manager
Angela Reinhardt, Bookeeper

Dedicated to finding cures for leukemia and related cancers and to improving the quality of life for patients and their families.

5719 Leukemia & Lymphoma Society: Minnesota Chapter
5217 Wayzata Boulevard
Suite 221
St Louis Park, MN 55416 952-545-3309
800-955-4572
Fax: 952-545-5926
e-mail: Murray.Schmidt@lls.org
http://www.leukemia.org

Murray Schmidt, Executive Director
Vickie Shaw, Deputy Executive Director

Serves Minnesota, North Dakota and South Dakota patients affected with leukemia and realted cancers.

5720 Leukemia & Lymphoma Society: Mississippi Chapter
408 Fontaine Place
Suite 104
Ridgeland, MS 39157 601-956-7447
Fax: 601-956-6957
http://www.leukemia-lymphoma.org/all_page?item_

Sharon Dischner, Manager
Frances Mobley, Patient Services Manager

Dedicated to finding a cure for leukemia, lymhpoma, and realted diseases, and to improving the quality of life for patients and thier families.

5721 Leukemia & Lymphoma Society: Nebraska Chapter
10832 Old Mill Road
200
Omaha, NE 68154 402-344-2242
888-847-4974
Fax: 402-344-2422
e-mail: pattie.gorham@lls.org
http://www.leukemia.org

Pattie Gorham, Executive Director
Tonya Schroeder, Patient Services Manager

Serves patients throughout Nebraska and western Iowa who are touched by leukemia, lymphoma, Hodgkin's disease and myeloma.

5722 Leukemia & Lymphoma Society: New Mexico Office
3411 Candelaria Road NE
Suite M
Albuquerque, NM 87107 505-872-0141
888-286-7846
Fax: 505-872-2480
e-mail: ankiewiczc@nm.leukemia-lymphoma.org

Deberah Hoffman, Executive Director
Marcie Summerlin, Patient Aid Coordinator and Admi

Dedicated to finding cures for leukemia and related cancers and to improving the quality of life for patients and their families. Serves New Mexico and the Greater El Paso, TX area.

5723 Leukemia & Lymphoma Society: New York City Chapter
475 Park Avenue S
8th Floor
New York, NY 10016 212-448-9206
Fax: 212-448-9214
e-mail: info@nyc.leukemia-lymphoma.org
http://www.leukemia-lymphoma.org

Michael Osso, Executive Director
Sara Lipsky, Deputy Executive Director
Ellen Yoshiuchi MPS, Patient Services Manager

Dedicated to finding cures for leukemia and related cancers and to improving the quality of life for patients and their families. Educational materials, support services and financial aid available. Volunteer opportunities.

5724 Leukemia & Lymphoma Society: North Carolina Chapter
5950 Fairview Road
Suite 250
Charlotte, NC 28210 704-998-5012
800-888-9934
Fax: 704-998-5010
e-mail: jane.weaver@lls.org
http://www.leukemia-lymphoma.org

Jane Weaver, Executive Director
Kelly Drometer, TNT Director

Dedicated to finding cures for leukemia and related cancers and to improving the quality of life for patients and their families.

5725 Leukemia & Lymphoma Society: North Texas Chapter
8111 Lyndon B Johnson Fwy
Suite 425
Dallas, TX 75251 972-239-0959
800-800-6702
Fax: 972-239-0892
e-mail: garciat@lls.org
http://www.leukemia-lymphoma.org

Tina May-Garcia, Executive Director
Kim Brown, Patient Services Manager
Farida Shipchandler, Patient Services

The world's largest private organization concerned solely with finding cures for leukemia, lymphoma and other blood related cancers, and improving the quality of life of patients and their families.

5726 Leukemia & Lymphoma Society: Northern California Chapter
1390 Market Street
Suite 1200
San Francisco, CA 94102 415-625-1100
Fax: 415-625-1155
e-mail: Shirley.McGrath@LLS.org
http://www.leukemia-lymphoma.org

Shirley McGrath, Patient Services Manager

Dedicated to finding cures for leukemia, lymphoma, Hodgkin's disease and myeloma and to improving the quality of life for patients and thier families.

Cancer/Associations & Organizations

5727 Leukemia & Lymphoma Society: Northern Florida Chapter
7077 Bonneval Road
Suite 610
Jacksonville, FL 32216
904-332-6414
800-868-0072
Fax: 904-332-6422
e-mail: jill.tager@lls.org
http://www.leukemia.org

Jill Tager, Executive Director
Michelle Long, Office Manager

Dedicated to finding cures for all blood-related cancers.

5728 Leukemia & Lymphoma Society: Northern New Jersey Chapter
116 S Euclid Avenue
Westfield, NJ 7090
908-654-9445
Fax: 908-654-9496
e-mail: Stacey.boman@lls.org
http://www.leukemia.org

Stacey Boman, Executive Director
Joyce Warner, Director of Operations

Dedicated to finding cures for leukemia and related cancers and to improving the quality of life for patients and their families.

5729 Leukemia & Lymphoma Society: Northern Ohio Chapter
902 Westpoint Parkway
Suite 300
Cleveland, OH 44122
440-617-2873
Fax: 440-617-2879
e-mail: littmanb@lls.org
http://www.leukemia.org

Elizabeth A Littman, Executive Director
Nancy Toghill, Office Manager~

Dedicated to finding cures for leukemia and related cancers and to improving the quality of life for patients and their families.

5730 Leukemia & Lymphoma Society: Oklahoma Chapter
500 N Broadway Avenue
Suite 250
Oklahoma City, OK 73102
405-943-8888
Fax: 405-945-8355
e-mail: martins@ok.leukemia-lymphoma.org
http://www.lls.org

Sherry Martin, Patient Services Manager
Jill Hull, Campaign Director

Dedicated to finding cures for leukemia and related cancers and to improving the quality of life for patients and their families.

5731 Leukemia & Lymphoma Society: Oregon Chapter
9320 SW Barbur Boulevard
Suite 140
Portland, OR 97219-5404
503-245-9866
Fax: 503-245-9865
http://www.leukemia.org

Craig Nichols, Director
Sue Sumpter RN, MS, Patient Services Manager
Becky Nahlum, President

Dedicated to finding cures for leukemia,lymphoma and myeloma quality of life for patients and their families.

5732 Leukemia & Lymphoma Society: Palm Beach Chapter
4360 Northlake Boulevard
Suite 109
Palm Beach Gardens, FL 33410
561-775-9954
888-478-8550
Fax: 561-775-0930
e-mail: McDonald@FL-wpb.leukemia.org
http://www.leukemia.org

Julie Healey, Chairman
Elizabeth M. Fago, Chairman Emeritus
Renee Lodes, President

Dedicated to finding cures for leukemia and related cancers and to improving the quality of life for patients and their families.

5733 Leukemia & Lymphoma Society: Raleigh Office
401 Harrison Oaks Boulevard
Suite 200
Cary, NC 27513
919-677-3993
Fax: 919-677-3992
e-mail: margaret.valyou@lls.org
http://www.leukemia-lymphoma.org

Margaret Valyou, TNT Director
Tiffany Armstrong, Deputy Executive Director

Dedicaetd to finding a cure for leukemia, lymphoma, and related cancers, and to improving the quality of life for patients and their families.

5734 Leukemia & Lymphoma Society: Rhode Island Chapter
1150 Pontiac Avenue
1
Cranston, RI 02920
401-943-8888
Fax: 401-943-1377
e-mail: koconisb@lls.org
http://www.leukemia-lymphoma.org

Lynn Aaronson, National Director
Bill Koconis, Executive Director

Serves patients and their families touched by leukemia, lymphoma, Hodkin's disease and myeloma.

5735 Leukemia & Lymphoma Society: Rocky Mountain Chapter
5353 W.Dartmouth Ave
Suite 400
Denver, CO 80227
303-984-2110
800-955-4572
Fax: 303-984-2352
http://www.leukemia.org

John Quinette, Executive Director

Dedicated to finding cures for Leukemia, and related cancers, and to improving the quality of life for patients and their families.

5736 Leukemia & Lymphoma Society: San Diego & Hawaii Chapter
4715 Viewridge Avenue
Suite 110
San Diego, CA 92123
858-277-1800
800-215-1098
Fax: 858-277-1748
e-mail: SotoLevyL@lls.org
http://www.leukemia.org

Joseph V. Raffa, Ed.D, Director
Januario E. Castro, M.D, Assistant Clinical Professor

Dedicated to finding cures for leukemia and related cancers and to improving the quality of life for patients and their families.

5737 Leukemia & Lymphoma Society: South Carolina Chapter
107 Westpark Boulevard
Suite 150
Columbia, SC 29210
803-731-4060
Fax: 803-731-4066
e-mail: paul.jeter@lls.org
http://www.leukemia-lymphoma.org

Paul Jeter, Executive Director
Amy Harmon, Campaign Director

Serves patients diagnosed with leukemia and related illnesses. Supports research, education, and patient-aid programs.

5738 Leukemia & Lymphoma Society: Southern Florida Chapter
Two Oakwood Blvd
Suite 200
Hollywood, FL 33020
954-744-5300
800-955-4572
Fax: 954-744-5301
e-mail: silvermanb@FL-so.leukemia-lymphoma.org
http://www.leukemia.org

Barbara Silverman, Execitive Director
Susan Hutchinson, Patient Services Director
Carmen Maria Herrera, Patient Aid Coordinator

Cancer/Associations & Organizations

Dedicated to finding cures for leukemia, lymphoma, Hodgkin's disease and myeloma and to improving the quality of life for patients and their families.

5739 Leukemia & Lymphoma Society: Southern New Jersey Shore Region Chapter
216 Haddon Avenue
Suite 328
Westmont, NJ 8108
856-869-0200
Fax: 856-869-7383
e-mail: Natalie.Abernathy@lls.org
http://www.leukemia-lymphoma.org
Karen Zatzariny, Executive Director

Dedicated to finding cures for leukemia and blood related cancers and to improving the quality of life for patients and their families.

5740 Leukemia & Lymphoma Society: Southern Ohio Chapter
105 W 4th Street
Suite 900
Cincinnati, OH 45202
513-361-2100
Fax: 513-361-2109
e-mail: doug.ventura@lls.org
http://www.leukemia-lymphoma.org
Jay Van Winkle, Executive Director
Doug Ventura, Executive Director

Dedicated to finding cures for leukemia and related cancers and to improving the quality of life for patients and their families. This chapter serves a 22-county geographic area that includes Adams, Brown, Butler, Clermont, Clinton, Darke, Gallia, Greene, Hamilton, Highland, Jackson, Lawrence, Meigs, Miami, Montgomery, Pike, Preble, Scioto and Warren counties in Ohio and Boone, Campbell and Kenton counties in Kentucky.

5741 Leukemia & Lymphoma Society: Southwest Missouri Satellite Office
305 E Walnut Street
Suite 210/Box 23
Springfield, MO 65806
417-864-6360
Fax: 417-864-4959
e-mail: lacockj@lls.org
http://www.leukemia.org
Janna LaCook, Executive Director
Dee Gavin, Campaign Manager

Dedicated to finding a cure for leukemia and realted cancers and to improving to quality of life for patients and their families.

5742 Leukemia & Lymphoma Society: Southwest Texas Chapter
950 Isom Road
Suite 104
San Antonio, TX 78216
210-377-1775
800-683-2458
Fax: 210-344-3717
http://www.leukemia-lymphoma.org
Kathy Griesenbeck, Contact

Dedicated to finding cures for leukemia and related cancers and to improving the quality of life for patients and their families.

5743 Leukemia & Lymphoma Society: Suncoast Chapter
13907 N Dale Mabry Highway
Suite 101
Tampa, FL 33618
813-963-6461
Fax: 813-963-1306
http://www.leukemia.org
Annette M Knowles, MSW, Patient Services Manager
Kathy Whitney, Executive Director

Serves patients with leukemia, lymphoma, multiple myeloma, and Hodgekin's disease in Charlotte, Citrus, Collier, DeSoto, Hardee, Hernando, Hillsborough, Lee, Manatee, Pasco, Pinellas and Sarasota Counties.

5744 Leukemia & Lymphoma Society: Tennessee Chapter
446 Metroplex Drive
Suite 200a
Nashville, TN 37211-3139
615-331-2980
800-332-2980
Fax: 615-331-2941
e-mail: winslowm@tn.leukemia-lymphoma.org
http://www.leukemia-lymphoma.org
Colleen Grady, Executive Director
Leslie Allen, TNT Campaign Coordinator

Offers contribution-funded community services, family support groups, free educational materials and financial assistance for those affected by leukemia, lymphoma, myeloma, and Hodgkin's disease.

5745 Leukemia & Lymphoma Society: Texas Gulf Coast
5005 Mitchelldale
Suite 115
Houston, TX 77092
713-680-8088
Fax: 713-683-9504
e-mail: BillieSue.Parris@lls.org
http://www.leukemia-lymphoma.org
Billie Sue Parris, Executive Director
Cherry Evans, Patient Services Manager

Dedicated to finding cures for leukemia and related cancers and to improving the quality of life for patients and their families.

5746 Leukemia & Lymphoma Society: Tri-County Chapter
1744 W Katella Avenue
Suite 8
Orange, CA 92867
714-633-6858
800-955-4572
Fax: 714-633-6182
e-mail: quintero@ca-tri.leukemia.org
http://www.leukemia.org
Sam Thomas, Executive Director

Dedicated to finding cures for leukemia and related cancers and to improving the quality of life for patients and their families.

5747 Leukemia & Lymphoma Society: Upstate New York Chapter
6 Automation Lane
Albany, NY 12205
518-438-3583
Fax: 518-438-6431
e-mail: Maureen.Thornton@lls.org
http://www.leukemia-lymphoma.org
Maureen O'Brien-Thornton, Executive Director
Raechel Hunt, Patient Services Manager

Dedicated to finding cures for leukemia and related cancers and to improving the quality of life for patients and their families.

5748 Leukemia & Lymphoma Society: Utah Office
180 South 300 West
Suite 260
Salt Lake City, UT 84101
801-519-6600
Fax: 801-519-6606
http://www.leukemia.org
Jessica Drury, Patient Services Manager
Meg King, Campaign Manager

Dedicated to finding a cure for leukemia, lymphoma, and realted diseases, and to improving the quality of life for patients and their families.

5749 Leukemia & Lymphoma Society: Virginia Chapter
2101 Executive Drive
Tower Box 21
Hampton, VA 23666
757-838-9351
800-866-4483
Fax: 757-827-7337
e-mail: Danielle.Smith@lls.org
http://www.leukemia-lymphoma.org
Diane Hagemann, Executive Director
Rosalee Baker, Manager

Dedicated to finding a cure for leukemia and related cancers and to improving the quality of life for patients and thier families.

Cancer/Associations & Organizations

5750 Leukemia & Lymphoma Society: Washington & Alaska Chapter
530 Dexter Avenue North
Suite 300
Seattle, WA 98109
206-628-0777
888-345-4572
Fax: 206-292-9791
e-mail: norman.schwamberg@lls.org
http://www.leukemia-lymphoma.org
Norman Schwamberg, Executive Director
Kimberly Conn, Deputy Executive Director

Dedicated to finding cures for leukemia and related cancers and to improving the quality of life for patients and their families.

5751 Leukemia & Lymphoma Society: West Virginia Branch
River Walk Corporate Center, 333 E. Carson Street
Suite 441
Pittsburgh, PA 15219
412-395-2873
800-827-1443
Fax: 412-95-888
http://www.leukemia-lymphoma.org
George J Omiros, Executive Director
Tricia Jarmer, Patient Services Manager

Dedicated to finding a cure for leukemia and related illnesses and to improving the quality of life for patients and thier families.

5752 Leukemia & Lymphoma Society: Western New York & Finger Lakes Chapter
4053 Maple Road
Suite 110
Amherst, NY 14226
716-834-2578
Fax: 716-837-0335
e-mail: nancy.hails@lls.org
http://www.leukemia.org
Nancy Hails, Executive Director
Luann Burgio, Deputy Executive Director

Dedicated to finding cures for leukemia and related cancers and to improving the quality of life for patients and their families.

5753 Leukemia & Lymphoma Society: Western Pennsylvania/West Virginia Chapter
Downtown Pittsburgh, 2 Gateway Center, 4 North
Suite 13n
Pittsburgh, PA 15222
412-395-2873
800-726-2873
Fax: 412-395-2888
http://www.leukemia-lymphoma.org
George J Omiros, Executive Director

Dedicated to finding cures for leukemia and realted cancers and to improving the quality of life for patients and thier families.

5754 Leukemia & Lymphoma Society: Wisconsin Chapter
1126 S 70th Street
Suite N405A
Milwaukee, WI 53214
414-256-4020
800-261-7399
Fax: 414-256-4025
e-mail: wakefielp@wi.leukemia-lymphoma.org
http://www.leukemia-lymphoma.org
Bede Barth, Executive Director
Rhonda Deaver, Office Manager

Founded in 1963 to serve Wisconsites touched by leukemia, lymphoma, Hodgkin's disease and myeloma.

5755 Leukemia Society of America
25 3rd Street
4th Floor
Stamford, CT 06905
203-967-8326
Fax: 203-325-8559
e-mail: MontanoJ@lls.org
http://www.leukemia.org
Jean Montano, Executive Director
Rob Gerowe, Campaign Director
Jean Montano, Manager

Dedicated to finding cures for leukemia and related cancers and to improving the quality of life for patients and their families.

5756 Leukemia Society of America: Delaware Chapter
100 W 10th Street
Suite 209
Wilmington, DE 19801
302-661-7300
800-955-4572
Fax: 302-661-0363
http://www.leukemia.org
Sharon Schuh, Executive Director
Michelle Sobczyk, Patient Services Manager

Dedicated to finding cures for leukemia and related cancers and to improving the quality of life for patients and their families.

5757 Leukemia Society of America: National Capitol Area Chapter
5845 Richmond Highway
Suite 800
Alexandria, VA 22303
703-960-1100
800-955-4572
Fax: 703-960-0920
http://www.leukemia.org
Donna McKelvey, Executive Director

Serves the greater Washington DC metropolitan area, including Northern Virginia, Prince George's and Montgomery counties.

5758 Leukemia Society of America: Northern Nevada Office
8175 S VIRGINIA ST
STE 850-326
Reno, NV 89511
775-852-1241
Fax: 775-852-1239
Kelly Anderson, Manager

Dedicated to finding cures for leukemia, lymphoma, Hodgkin's disease and myeloma and to improving the quality of life for patients and thier families.

5759 Look Good... Feel Better
American Cancer Society
Williams Street
Suite 950
Atlanta, GA 30303
404-315-1123
800-ACS-2345
Fax: 404-315-9348
http://www.cancer.org
Carolyn D. Runowicz, President
Elmer Huerta, First Vice President

Program developed with the help of the Cosmetic, Toiletry and Fragrance Association Foundation in cooperation with the American Cancer Society. Focuses on techniques that can help people undergoing cancer treatment.

5760 Make Today Count
1235 E Cherokee Street
Springfield, MO 65804-2203
417-885-3324
800-432-2273
Fax: 417-885-2584
Connie Zimmerman, Director

An organization that helps patients and their families cope with cancer and other serious diseases and improve their quality of life.

5761 National Alliance of Breast Cancer Organizations
9 East 37th Street
Suite 1600
New York, NY 10016
212-889-0606
800-719-9154
Fax: 212-689-1213
e-mail: nabcoinfo@aol.com
http://www.nabco.org

A network of breast cancer organizations that provides information, assistance and referral to anyone with questions about breast cancer and acts as a voice for the interests and concerns of breast cancer survivors and women at risk.

Cancer/Associations & Organizations

5762 **National Chronic Pain Outreach Association**
P.O. Box 274
Millboro, VA 24460
540-862-9437
Fax: 540-862-9485
e-mail: ncpoa@cfw.com
http://www.chronicpain.org
Michael Troyer, Executive Director

NCPOA is an information and referral service for patients dealing with chronic pain due to cancer. They offer numerous educational materials, support groups, heath professional referrals, and a newsletter.

5763 **National Coalition for Cancer Survivorship**
1010 Wayne Avenue
7th Floor
Silver Spring, MD 20910
301-650-9127
877-622-7937
Fax: 301-565-9670
e-mail: info@canceradvocacy.org
http://www.canceradvocacy.org
Ellen Stovall, President and Chief Executive Di
Robert Sachs, J.D., Chairman

Founded in 1986 by and for people with cancer and those who care for them, the National Coalition for Cancer Survivorship (NCCS) is the only patient-led organization advocating on behalf of survivors of all types of cancer. NCCS's mission is to ensure quality cancer care for all americans by leading and strenghtening the survivorship movement, empowering cancer survivors and advocating on issues that affect cancer survivors' quality of life.

5764 **National Foundation for Cancer Research Hotline**
4600 E West Highway
Suite 525
Bethesda, MD 20814
301-654-1250
Fax: 301-654-5824
e-mail: info@nfcr.org
http://www.nfcr.org
Mark Baran, Vice President
Kevin Connolly, Chairman

5765 **National Health Federation**
P.O. Box 688
Monrovia, CA 91017
626-357-2181
Fax: 626-303-0642
e-mail: contact-us@thenhf.com
http://www.thenhf.com
Scott Tips, President
Dr. James R. Privitera, M.D.,, Vice-President

5766 **National Hospice Helpline**
1901 N Moore Street
Suite 901
Arlington, VA 22209-1717
703-243-5900
800-658-8898

Offers more information on hospice in general and offers referrals to a hospice program in your area.

5767 **National Hospice Organization**
1901 N Moore Street
Suite 901
Arlington, VA 22209-1717
703-243-5900
Fax: 703-525-5762

The nation's only advocate for terminally ill patients and their families. Founded in 1978, the NHO is the only organization devoted to hospice in the US. Support is included from 46 state hospice organizations, patients, families, communities, provider program members and professional/volunteer members. Represents hospice care interests to Congress, regulatory agencies, courts, voluntary organizations and the public.

5768 **Norris Cotton Cancer Center**
Dartmouth-Hitchcock Medical Center
1 Medical Center Drive
Lebanon, NH 3756
603-653-9000
Fax: 603-653-9003
e-mail: cancerhelp@dartmouth.edu
http://www.cancer.dartmouth.edu
Mark A. Israel, MD, Director
Burton L. Eisenberg, MD, Deputy Director

Norris Cotton Cancer Center is dedicated to reducing the burden of cancer among the people of New England, and playing a significant part in the world effort to eliminate cancer.

5769 **Northern California Cancer Center**
32960 Alvarado Niles Road
Suite 600
Union City, CA 94587
510-429-2500
Fax: 510-429-2550
e-mail: education@nccc.org
http://www.nccc.org
Esther John, Director of Epidemiology
Dee West, Chief Scientific Officer

The Northern California Canter Center is dedicated to understanding the causes, prevention and detection of cancer and to improving the quality of life for individuals living with cancer.

5770 **Nutrition Education Association**
3647 Glen Haven Boulevard
Houston, TX 77025-1307
713-665-2946
Ruth Yale Long PhD, Nutritionist

Offers nutrition information and education through books for cancer patients.

5771 **Oncology Nursing Society**
125 Enterprise Drive
Pittsburgh, PA 15275
412-859-6100
Fax: 412-859-6162
e-mail: customer.service@ons.org
http://www.ons.org
Pearl B Moore, Chief Executive Officer
Georgia M. Decker, President

Registered nurses interested in oncology. Seeks to: promote high professional standards in oncology nursing; provide a network for the exchange of information, resources, and peer support; encourage nurses to specialize in oncology; promote and develop educational programs in oncology nursing extending through the graduate level; identify, encourage, and foster nursing research in improving the quality of patient care. Conducts instructional andabstract sessions. Compiles statistics.

5772 **Patient Advocates for Advanced Cancer Treatments**
1143 Parmelee Avenue NW
Grand Rapids, MI 49504-3844
616-453-1477
Fax: 616-453-1846
e-mail: paact@paactusa.org
http://www.paactusa.org
Richard H Profit Jr, Director
Janet E. Ney, President and Chairperson

Offers state-of-the-art detection, diagnostics, evaluations and treatments for all stages of prostate cancer and related problems.

5773 **People Against Cancer**
PO Box 10
604 East Street
Otho, IA 50569
515-972-4444
Fax: 515-972-4415
e-mail: info@PeopleAgainstCancer.net
http://www.peopleagainstcancer.net
Frank D Wiewel, Founder

Cancer/Associations & Organizations

5774 Physicians Committee for Responsible Medicine
5100 Wisconsin Avenue NW
Suite 400
Washington, DC 20016
202-686-2210
800-875-4837
Fax: 202-686-2216
e-mail: pcrm@pcrm.org
http://www.pcrm.org

Neil Barnard, President
Russell Bunai, Director

Literatire and factsheets on good nutrition and preventive medicine is avilable, as well as PCRM's quarterly magazine Good Medicine. Hours are 9:00 a.m. to 5:30 p.m. Monday-Friday.

Frequency: Quaterly

5775 Private Cancer Clinic Tours
PO Box 530218
San Diego, CA 92153-0218
619-475-3834
Fax: 619-475-0753
e-mail: getwell@healthtours.com
http://www.healthtours.com

Peggy Pousson, Owner/Tour Guide

Tours offered by private automobile of alternative cancer clinics in or near Tijuana. Clinics and therapies are discussed on the way down to the border with free doctor appointments.

5776 Prostate Cancer Resource Network
2803 Fruitville Road
Sarasota, FL 34237-5344
727-847-1619
800-915-1001
Fax: 727-848-2494
http://www.pcrn.org

Don Kaltenbach, President

Provides information, counsel and support to patients and their families.

5777 Reach to Recovery
American Cancer Society
2200 Century Parkway NE
Suite 950
Atlanta, GA 30345-3118
404-816-4994
800-ACS-2345
Fax: 404-315-9348
http://www.cancer.org

A rehabilitation program for women who have or have had breast cancer. The program helps breast cancer patients meet the physical, emotional and cosmetic needs related to their disease and its treatment.

5778 Regional Cancer Foundation
1200 Gough Street
Suite 500
San Francisco, CA 94109
415-775-9956
Fax: 415-346-8652
e-mail: mail@thesecondopinion.org
http://http://thesecondopinion.org

Michael Stoll, Executive Director
Wells Whitney, President

This foundation offers, at no charge, a second opinion consultation to individuals diagnosed with cancer. The patient and a family member or friend meet with an interdisciplinary panel of local cancer specialists with expertise in radiation therapy, chemotherapy, surgery, radiology, and pathology.

5779 Rose Kushner Breast Cancer Advisory Center
PO Box 224
Kensington, MD 20895
Fax: 301-897-3444

Provides a mail service offering referrals to health professionals, as well as information about detection, diagnosis, treatment and physical and psychological rehabilitation for patients with breast cancer.

5780 Salick Health Care
8201 Beverly Boulevard
Los Angeles, CA 90048
323-966-3400
Fax: 213-966-3458
e-mail: info@aptiumoncology.com
http://www.aptiumoncology.com

Peter Jessup, President and Chief Executive Di
John S. Macdonald, Chief Medical Officer

Provider of diagnostic and therapeutic services to patients with catastrophic illnesses requiring sophisticated long-term care, principally in the areas of cancer, kidney disease, organ transplantation and immunodeficiency diseases.

5781 Stanford University: Oncology Day Care Clinic
300 Pasteur Drive
Stanford, CA 94305
650-725-6452
Fax: 650-725-1420
e-mail: brandy@stanford.edu
http://http://med.stanford.edu/

Charlotte Jacobs MD, Professor
Ronald Levy, Professor

Consultation, diagnosis and treatment for patients with all types of malignant disease, including administration of chemotherapy, homornal therapy, biologic modifiers, and patient education and counseling. Combined modality approach to cancer, including chemotherapy, radiotherapy and surgery, is emphasized. Patients receive comprehensive care and can participate in clinical trials.

5782 Support for People with Oral and Head and Neck Cancer
PO Box 53
Locust Valley, NY 11560-0053
516-759-5333
800-377-0928
Fax: 516-671-8794
e-mail: info@spohnc.org
http://www.spohnc.org

Nancy E Leupold, President and founder

Non-profit organization founded in 1991 to address the broad emotional, physical and humanistic needs of oral and head and neck cancer patients.

5783 Sylvester Comprehensive Cancer Center
University of Miami Medical School
1475 NW 12th Avenue
Miami, FL 33136
305-243-1000
Fax: 305-243-9161
http://www.sylvester.org/

Glen N. Barber, Ph.D., Associate Director
W. Jarrard Goodwin, M.D., Director

5784 Tour of Cancer Clinics
PO Box 4651
Modesto, CA 95352
209-529-4697

Tour of various alternative therapy clinics nationwide sponsored by the Cancer Control Society and Life Support.

5785 United Ostomy Association
P.O. Box 66
Fairview, TN 37062-0066
949-660-8624
800-826-0826
Fax: 949-660-9262
e-mail: kenaukett@uoaa.org
http://www.uoaa.org

Ken Aukett, President
Linda Aukett, Advocacy Chairman

Produces and distributes materials about ostomy care and management; through trained UOA members, offers practical assistance and emotional support to ostomy patients; sponsors annual youth rally and state and regional conferences for local affiliates; and 650 chapters serve people locally.

Cancer/Books

5786 University of Hawaii: Clinical & Community Outrech Program
Cancer Research Center of Hawaii
1236 Lauhala Street
Honolulu, HI 96813-2424
808-586-3010
Fax: 808-548-8418
e-mail: webmaster@crch.hawaii.edu
http://www.crch.org/CenHistoryandLocation.htm#1
Carl-Wilhelm Vogel, Center Director
Laurence Kolonel, Center Deputy Director

5787 Y-Me National Organization for Breast Cancer Information & Support
212 W. Van Buren
Suite 1000
Chicago, IL 60607-3903
312-986-8338
800-221-2141
Fax: 312-294-8597
http://www.y-me.org
Karen Alber, Director
Pat Harris, President

Trained staff and volunteers who have experienced breast cancer provide information, referral, and emotional support to individuals concerned about or diagnosed with breast cancer. Also conducts support meetings and educational workshops. A wig and prosthesis bank is available for those in need. Free literature is available. 24 hour hotline in English and Spanish.

Books

5788 3rd Opinion: International Directory to Complementary Therapy Centers
Avery Publishing Group
120 Old Broadway
New Hyde Park, NY 11040-5015
516-741-2155
800-548-5757
Fax: 516-742-1892

Discusses over 300 alternative treatment cancer centers, educational centers, support groups and other research services.

5789 Alternative Medicine Magazine's Definitive Guide to Cancer
Ten Speed Press
PO Box 7123
Berkeley, CA 94707
515-559-1600
800-841-2665
Fax: 510-559-1629
http://www.tenspeed.com

Comprehensive guide to cancer helps patients and their caregivers learn about causes and prevention of cancer; offset the side effects of conventional medicine; evaluate effective alternative treatments; utilize natural therapies involving diet, lifestyle, and nutritional supplements; and achieve deep healing through a mind-body-spirit approach.

5790 Ask the Doctor: Breast Cancer
Andrews McMeel Publishing
PO Box 419263
Kansas City, MO 64193
816-932-6700
800-826-4216
Fax: 800-437-8683
e-mail: www.shop.uexpress.com
http://www.uclick.com
Kathleen W Andrews, CEO
128 pages

5791 Cancer Dictionary
Facts on File
11 Penn Plaza
Floor 15
New York, NY 10001-2006
212-766-9152
800-322-8755
Fax: 212-967-8107
e-mail: lmilberg@factsonfile.com
Maggie Kok, Owner

352 pages

5792 Cancer Facts and Figures
American Cancer Society
1599 Clifton Road NE
Atlanta, GA 30329-4250
404-320-3333
800-ACS-2345
John Seffrin PhD, CEO

Publishes over 57 treatment centers.

5793 Cancer Rates and Risks
National Cancer Institute
6116 Executive Boulevard
Suite 3036a
Bethesda, MD 20892
301-929-1779

This book is a compact guide to statistics, risk factors, and risks for major cancer sites.
136 pages

5794 Cancer Sourcebook
Omnigraphics
Penobscot Building
Detroit, MI 48226
313-961-1340
800-234-
Fax: 800-875-1340
Peter E Ruffner, President

Offers basic information on cancer types, symptoms, diagnostic methods, and treatments. Includes statistics on cancer occurrences worldwide and the risks associated with known carcinogens and activities.

5795 Cancer Therapy: The Independant Consumer's Guide to Non-Toxic Treatment & Prevention
Equinox Press
144 Saint Johns Place
Brooklyn, NY 11217-3402
718-636-4433
Fax: 718-636-0186
e-mail: mail@ralphmoss.com
http://www.ralphmoss.com

A must for cancer patients and their families who want: Practical information on the most promising non-toxic treatments; Scientific evidence in readable language; Well-documented resource lists and medical references.
528 pages

5796 Cancer-Free: Your Guide to Gentle
AuthorHouse
1663 Liberty Drive
Suite 200
Bloomington, IN 47403
888-519-5121
http://www.authorhouse.com

This book tells you how to work with the medical system anywhere in the world to save the life of those you care about.

5797 Cancervive
11636 Chayote Street
Los Angeles, CA 90049-3308
310-203-9232
800-4TO-CURE
Fax: 310-471-4618
http://www.cancervive.org
Susan Nessim, Manager

This nonprofit organization that helps cancer survivors deal with the challenges of life after cancer. They offer support groups in some states, insurance information and assistance, and patient advocacy. They also publish a coloring book (kids age 3-6), a story/activity book (age 7-11), and a guide for teachers of children with cancer.

5798 Everyone's Guide To Cancer Therapy
Andrews McMeel Publishing
PO Box 419263
Kansas City, MO 64193
816-932-6700
800-826-4216
Fax: 800-437-8683
Kathleen W Andrews, CEO

505

Cancer / Journals, Magazines

5799 Everyone's Guide to Cancer Therapy
Andrews McMeel Publishing LLC
100 Front Street
Riverside, NJ 08075
800-943-9839
Fax: 800-943-9831
http://www.andrewsmcmeel.com

848 pages

Inside Everyone's Guide to Cancer, the world's top cancer specialists-141 to be exact-provide the latest medical breakthroughs, treatments, and accessible information on the more than 200 forms of cancer, highlighting the 54 most common types of the disease.

5800 Home Care Guide for Cancer
Johns Hopkins University Press
2715 N Charles Street
Baltimore, MD 21218-4319
410-516-6900
800-537-5487
Fax: 410-516-6998
http://www.jhu.edu/press/index.html

William Brody, President

This easy to use workbook was designed for home cargivers, patients, support groups, and education programs; it features easy to read type, and index for quick reference, and advice on twenty common cancer caregiving problems.

260 pages

5801 No Less a Woman
Simon & Schuster
1819 L Street NW
Washington, DC 20036-3807
202-293-0202
Fax: 202-293-0202

Offers intimate interviews that explore the major issues of coping and surviving breast cancer, from diagnosis and treatment to physical and psychological recovery. In their own words, ten women describe how they successfully adjusted to the changes in their bodies and their feelings about themselves.

288 pages

5802 Older Than My Mother: A Nurse's Life & Triumph
Ananse Press
PO Box 22565
Seattle, WA 98122-0565
206-325-8205

This book describes childhood as a young African-American woman in the rural Louisiana, struggles to become a nurse, and the development of a strong self-advocacy that has led to her longevity as a breast cancer survivor..

5803 Prostate Cancer: A Survivor's Guide
Prostate Cancer Resource Network
PO Box 966
New Port Richey, FL 34656
727-847-1619
800-915-
Fax: 727-848-2494
http://www.pcrn.org

Written with the aid of leading prostate cancer specialists, this book clearly explains tests, the latest statistics and how to interpret them.

5804 Teratologies: A Cultural Study of Cancer
Routledge
29 W 35th Street
Floor 10
New York, NY 10001-2299
212-244-3336
800-634-7064
Fax: 212-248-4724
http://www.routledge.com

A distinctively feminist look at how cancer is perceived, experienced and theorized in contemprary society. Beginning with powerful personal accounts of her own illness, as well as self-help manuals and patients' personal stories, Jackie Stacey explores changing beliefs about the causes and treatments of cancer in both biomedicine and its increasingly popular alternative counterparts.

5805 What to Eat if you Have Cancer
McGraw-Hill Companies
7500 Chavenelle Road
Dubuque, IA 52002
877-833-5524
Fax: 614-759-3749
e-mail: pbg.ecommerce_custserv@mcgraw-hill.com
http://www.mhprofessional.com

Improved dietary habits can support cancer treatment programs; yet too few cancer guides provide much information on just what kind of diet should be followed. Enter this title, written by two licensed nutritionists and focusing on foods which reduce toxicity from chemotherapy and increase the body's recovery process. From supplement dos and don'ts to insights on natural foods, this covers many topics.

Journals, Magazines

5806 Coping: Living with Cancer
Media America
PO Box 682268
Franklin, TN 37068-2268
615-790-2400
Fax: 615-794-0179

Kay Thomas, Editor
Michael Holt, Publisher
P Chadwell, Advertising Manager

Consumer magazine for people whose lives have been touched by cancer.

Frequency: Bimonthly

5807 Diseases of the Colon and Rectum
American Society of Colon and Rectal Surgeons
85 W Algonquin Road
Suite 550
Arlington Heights, IL 60005-4460
847-290-9184
Fax: 847-290-9273
e-mail: ascrs@fascrs.org
http://www.fascrs.org

Information for professionals specializing in the diagnosis and treatment of colorectal disorders.

5808 Journal of Cancer Education
Hanley & Belfus
210 S 13th Street
Philadelphia, PA 19107-5467
215-546-4995
800-962-
Fax: 215-790-9330

A peer-reviewed quarterly journal that addresses varied aspects of cancer education for physicians, dentists, nurses, students, social workers, and other allied health professionals. Articles include reports of original results of educational research and discussions of current problems and techniques in cancer education.

5809 Skin Cancer Foundation Journal
Skin Cancer Foundation
245 5th Avenue
Room 2402
New York, NY 10016-8728
212-725-5176
Fax: 212-725-5751
http://www.skincancer.org

Mitzi Moulds, Executive Director

A collection of articles by physicians, scientists and lay writers on the subject.

Frequency: Once a year

Newsletters, Pamphlets

5810 Advanced Cancer: Living Each Day
National Cancer Institute
Building 31
Bethesda, MD 20892
301-496-7406
Fax: 301-480-8105

Cancer/Newsletters, Pamphlets

Booklet delving into all aspects of everyday living with cancer. Offers information on coping, how children react, facing the unknown, living wills, additional resources and making treatment decisions.

30 pages

5811 Breast Cancer: Understanding Treatment Options
National Cancer Institute
Building 31
Bethesda, MD 20892   301-496-7406
                           Fax: 301-480-8105

Summarizes the biopsy procedure and examines the pros and cons of various types of breast surgery. It discusses lumpectomy and radiation therapy as primary treatment.

19 pages

5812 Cancer of the Bladder: Research Report
National Cancer Institute
Building 31
Bethesda, MD 20892   301-496-7406
                           Fax: 301-480-8105

Offers information on the types of bladder cancer, mortality rates, diagnosis, symptoms, therapies, rehabilitation, clinical trials, and selected references.

5813 Cancer of the Colon and Rectum: Research Report
National Cancer Institute
Building 31
Bethesda, MD 20892   301-496-7406
                           Fax: 301-480-8105

Informative pamphlet offering factual statistics on causes and prevention, detection, diagnosis, staging, treatment, followup, clinical trials and selected references.

5814 Cancer of the Ovary: Research Report
National Cancer Institute
Building 31
Bethesda, MD 20892   301-496-7406
                           Fax: 301-480-8105

5815 Cancer of the Pancreas: Research Report
National Cancer Institute
Building 31
Bethesda, MD 20892   301-496-7406
                           Fax: 301-480-8105

Offers information on the various types of pancreatic cancer, treatments, surgical procedures, chemotherapy, biological therapy, hormone therapy, clinical trials and selected references.

5816 Cancer of the Uterus: Research Report
National Cancer Institute
Building 31
Bethesda, MD 20892   301-496-7406
                           Fax: 301-480-8105

5817 Chemotherapy and You: A Guide to Self-Help During Treatment
National Cancer Institute
Building 31
Bethesda, MD 20892   301-496-7406
                           Fax: 301-480-8105

Explains chemotherapy and addresses problems and concerns of patients undergoing this treatment.

5818 Clearing the Air: A Guide to Quitting Smoking
National Cancer Institute
Building 31
Bethesda, MD 20892   301-496-7406
                           Fax: 301-480-8105

Offers hints on quitting smoking and cancer prevention.

24 pages

5819 Diet, Nutrition and Cancer Prevention: A Guide to Food Choices
National Cancer Institute
Building 31
Bethesda, MD 20892   301-496-7406
                           Fax: 301-480-8105

Describes what is known about diet, nutrition and cancer prevention. Provides information about foods that contain components like fiber, fat and vitamins that may affect a person's risk of getting certain cancers.

5820 Diet, Nutrition and Cancer Prevention: The Good News
National Cancer Institute
Building 31
Bethesda, MD 20892   301-496-7406
                           Fax: 301-480-8105

Provides an overview of dietary guidelines that may assist individuals in reducing their risks for some cancers.

16 pages

5821 Do the Right Thing: Get a Mammogram
National Cancer Institute
Building 31
Bethesda, MD 20892   301-496-7406
                           Fax: 301-480-8105

Targets black women age 40 and older. Describes the importance of regular mammograms in the early detection of breast cancer.

5822 Eating Hints: Recipes and Tips for Better Nutrition During Cancer Treatment
National Cancer Institute
Building 31
Bethesda, MD 20892   301-496-7406
                           Fax: 301-480-8105

Provides recipes that help patients meet their needs for good nutrition during treatment.

5823 Facing Forward: A Guide for Cancer Survivors
National Cancer Institute
Building 31
Bethesda, MD 20892   301-496-7406
                           Fax: 301-480-8105

Presents a concise overview of important survivor issues, including ongoing health needs, psychosocial concerns, insurance and employment.

43 pages

5824 Facts About Lung Cancer
American Lung Association
1740 Broadway
New York, NY 10019-4315   212-315-8700
                           Fax: 212-315-8870

John Kirkwodd, CEO

5825 How to Interpret Your Biopsy and other Lab Reports
Prostate Cancer Resource Network
PO Box 966
New Port Richey, FL 34656 727-847-1619
                           Fax: 727-848-2494
                           http://www.pcrn.org

Describes the most commonly used diagnostic tests for prostate cancer, what they are, how and why they are performed and what information each test provides.

5826 Immune System: How it Works
National Cancer Institute
Building 31
Bethesda, MD 20892   301-496-7406
                           Fax: 301-480-8105

Written for the high school level, this booklet explains the human immune system for the general public. It describes the sophistication of the body's immune responses, the impact of immune disorders and the relation of the immune system to cancer therapies.

28 pages

5827 Mastectomy: A Treatment for Breast Cancer
National Cancer Institute
Building 31
Bethesda, MD 20892   301-496-7406
                           Fax: 301-480-8105

Cancer/Newsletters, Pamphlets

Presents information about the different types of breast surgery, explains what to expect at the hospital and during the recovery period.

25 pages

5828 **Melanoma Newsletter**
Skin Cancer Foundation
245 5th Avenue
Room 2402
New York, NY 10016-8728
212-725-5176
Fax: 212-725-5751
http://www.skincancer.org

Mitzi Moulds, Executive Director

For medical investigators and practitioners.

Frequency: Quarterly

5829 **Melanoma: Research Report**
National Cancer Institute
Building 31
Bethesda, MD 20892
301-496-7406
Fax: 301-480-8105

Offers information on types of skin cancer, detection, diagnosis, staging, treatment, clinical trials, selected references and additional information for patients with skin cancer.

5830 **NABCO Breast Cancer Resource List**
National Alliance of Breast Cancer Organizations
9 E 37th Street
Floor 10
New York, NY 10016-2822
212-889-0606
Fax: 212-689-1213
e-mail: nabcoinfo@aol.com
http://www.nabco.org

A comprehensive breast cancer and breast care resource guide with more than 2,000 listed publications and services, many at free or low cost.

5831 **NABCO News**
National Alliance of Breast Cancer Organizations
9 E 37th Street
Floor 10
New York, NY 10016-2822
212-889-0606
Fax: 212-689-1213
e-mail: nabcoinfo@aol.com
http://www.nabco.org

Newsletter on developments in breast cancer.

5832 **Nutrition for Patients Receiving Chemotherapy/Radiation Treatment**
National Cancer Institute
Building 31
Bethesda, MD 20892
301-496-7406
Fax: 301-480-8105

Describes the importance of maintaining nutritional intake while receiving chemotherapy and radiation.

5833 **Once a Year for a Lifetime**
National Cancer Institute
Building 31
Bethesda, MD 20892
301-496-7406
Fax: 301-480-8105

Targets all women age 40 and older describing the importance of regular mammograms in the early detection of breast cancer.

5834 **Oral Cancers: Research Report**
National Cancer Institute
Building 31
Bethesda, MD 20892
301-496-7406
Fax: 301-480-8105

Describes types of oral cancer, causes and risk factors, symptoms, prevention, detection, diagnosis, treatment, staging, methods of treatments, followup care, clinical trials and selected references for more information.

5835 **Pap Test: It Can Save Your Life**
National Cancer Institute
Building 31
Bethesda, MD 20892
301-496-7406
Fax: 301-480-8105

Easy-to-read pamphlet tells women of the importance of getting a Pap test, how often to get it done and where to go to get it.

5836 **Questions and Answers About Breast Lumps**
National Cancer Institute
Building 31
Bethesda, MD 20892
301-496-7406
Fax: 301-480-8105

Describes some of the most common noncancerous breast lumps and what can be done about them.

22 pages

5837 **Questions and Answers About Choosing a Mammography Facility**
National Cancer Institute
Building 31
Bethesda, MD 20892
301-496-7406
Fax: 301-480-8105

Lists questions to ask in selecting a quality mammography facility.

5838 **Questions and Answers About Metastatic Cancer**
National Cancer Institute
Building 31
Bethesda, MD 20892
301-496-7406
Fax: 301-480-8105

Presents information on detection, treatment methods and common areas of reoccurrence.

5839 **Questions and Answers About Pain Control**
National Cancer Institute
Building 31
Bethesda, MD 20892
301-496-7406
Fax: 301-480-8105

Discusses pain control using both medical and nonmedical methods.

5840 **Radiation Therapy and You: A Guide To Self-Help During Treatment**
National Cancer Institute
BUILDING 31
Bethesda, MD 20892
301-496-7406
Fax: 301-480-8105

Explains radiation therapy and addresses concerns of patients receiving radiation treatment.

5841 **Recurrence: What Do I Do Now?**
Prostate Cancer Resource Network
PO Box 966
New Port Richey, FL 34656
727-847-1619
Fax: 727-848-2494
http://www.pcrn.org

Learn what methods doctors use to monitor patients after treatment and how likely it is that your cancer will recur.

5842 **Research Report: Adult Kidney Cancer and Wilms' Tumor**
National Cancer Institute
Building 31
Bethesda, MD 20892
301-496-7406
Fax: 301-480-8105

5843 **Skin Cancer: Preventable and Curable**
Skin Cancer Foundation
245 5th Avenue
Suite 2402
New York, NY 10016-8728
212-725-5176
Fax: 212-725-5751
http://www.skincancer.org

Mitzi Moulds, Executive Director

Brochure on preventing and curing skin cancer

5844 **Skin Cancers: Basal Cell and Squamous Cell Carcinomas: Research Report**
National Cancer Institute
Building 31
Bethesda, MD 20892
301-496-7406
Fax: 301-480-8105

Cancer/Newsletters, Pamphlets

Offers information on types of skin cancer, incidence and mortality, risk factors, prevention, symptoms, detection, diagnosis, staging, treatment, followup care and clinical trials.

5845 Students with Cancer: A Resource for the Educator
National Cancer Institute
Building 31
Bethesda, MD 20892
301-496-7406
Fax: 301-480-8105
Designed for teachers who have students with cancer in their classrooms or schools.
22 pages

5846 Sun and Skin News
Skin Cancer Foundation
245 5th Avenue
Room 2402
New York, NY 10016-8728
212-725-5176
Fax: 212-725-5751
http://www.skincancer.org
Mitzi Moulds, Executive Director
Deals with skin cancer and related subjects in non-technical terms.

5847 Sunlight, Ultraviolet Radiation and the Skin
National Cancer Institute
Building 31
Bethesda, MD 20892
301-496-7406
Fax: 301-480-8105

5848 Support for People with Oral, Head and Neck Cancer
PO Box 53
Locust Valley, NY 11560
516-759-5333
Nancy Leupold, Owner
This a patient-run support program. Other services include patient networking oportunities, a national newsletter, a resource library, and insurance information and assistance.

5849 Taking Time: Support for People with Cancer & People Who Care for Them
National Cancer Institute
Building 31
Bethesda, MD 20892
301-496-7406
Fax: 301-480-8105
Discusses the emotional sides of cancer, how to deal with the disease and learn to talk with friends, family members and others about cancer.

5850 Testicular Cancer: Research Report
National Cancer Institute
Building 31
Bethesda, MD 20892
301-496-7406
Fax: 301-480-8105

5851 Testicular Self-Examination
National Cancer Institute
Building 31
Bethesda, MD 20892
301-496-7406
Fax: 301-480-8105
Contains information about risks and symptoms of testicular cancer and provides instructions on how to perform testicular self-examination.

5852 What Are Clinical Trials All About?
National Cancer Institute
Building 31
Bethesda, MD 20892
301-496-7406
Fax: 301-480-8105
Explains clinical trials (studies of new cancer treatments) to help patients decide if they want to take part in a trial.

5853 What Every Man Should Know About Seeding
Prostate Cancer Resource Network
PO Box 966
New Port Richey, FL 34656
727-847-1619
800-915-
Fax: 727-848-2494
http://www.pcrn.org
Describes interstitial implantation therapy commonly known as seeding. Includes a question and answer section based on questions commonly asked by patients and a glossary.

5854 What You Need to Know About Bladder Cancer
National Cancer Institute
Building 31
Bethesda, MD 20892
301-496-7406
Fax: 301-480-8105
Offers information on the history, symptoms, diagnosis, treatment, followup care, support groups, medical terms and resources for more information.

5855 What You Need to Know About Cancer
National Cancer Institute
Building 31
Bethesda, MD 20892
301-496-7406
Fax: 301-480-8105
Offers information on signs and symptoms, diagnosis, treatment, early detection and advances in medical technology.

5856 What You Need to Know About Cancer of the Colon and Rectum
National Cancer Institute
Building 31
Bethesda, MD 20892
301-496-7406
Fax: 301-480-8105
Offers information on symptoms, diagnosis, treatments, and support for cancer patients.

5857 What You Need to Know About Cervical Cancer
National Cancer Institute
Building 31
Bethesda, MD 20892
301-496-7406
Fax: 301-480-8140
Areas covered include early detection, symptoms, treatments, diagnosis, followup care, support, medical terms and resources.

5858 What You Need to Know About Esophagus Cancer
National Cancer Institute
Building 31
Bethesda, MD 20892
301-496-7406
Fax: 301-480-8105
Offers information on symptoms, causes, preventions, diagnosis, support, medical terms and available resources.

5859 What You Need to Know About Kidney Cancer
National Cancer Institute
Building 31
Bethesda, MD 20892
301-496-7406
Fax: 301-480-8105
Offers factual information on diagnosis, symptoms, prevention, treatment and referral sources.

5860 What You Need to Know About Larynx Cancer
National Cancer Institute
Building 31
Bethesda, MD 20892
301-496-7406
Fax: 301-480-8105
Offers information on what cancer is, symptoms, diagnosis, treatment options, side effects of medication, rehabilitation, learning to speak again, living with cancer, causes and preventions, medical terms and resources.

5861 What You Need to Know About Lung Cancer
National Cancer Institute
Building 31
Bethesda, MD 20892
301-496-7406
Fax: 301-480-8105
Offers information on types of lung cancer, symptoms, diagnosis, treatments, support, medical terms and resources.

Cancer/Videos, Audio Tapes

5862 What You Need to Know About Oral Cancers
National Cancer Institute
Building 31
Bethesda, MD 20892
301-496-7406
Fax: 301-480-8105

Offers information on symptoms, diagnosis, treatments, rehabilitation, followup care, support, medical terms and resources for cancer patients.

5863 What You Need to Know About Ovarian Cancer
National Cancer Institute
Building 31
Bethesda, MD 20892
301-496-7406
Fax: 301-480-8105

Early detection, symptoms, diagnosis, treatments, medical terms and resources for further information.

5864 What You Need to Know About Pancreatic Cancer
National Cancer Institute
Building 31
Bethesda, MD 20892
301-496-7406
Fax: 301-480-8105

Offers information on symptoms, diagnosis, treatment, support, medical terms and resources.

5865 What You Need to Know About Prostate Cancer
National Cancer Institute
Building 31
Bethesda, MD 20892
301-496-7406
Fax: 301-480-8105

Offers information on symptoms, diagnosis, treatment options, side effects of medications, followup care, living with cancer and support resources for patients.

5866 What You Need to Know About Skin Cancer
National Cancer Institute
Building 31
Bethesda, MD 20892
301-496-7406
Fax: 301-480-8105

Offers information on types of skin cancer, symptoms, causes, prevention, treatment planning, treating skin cancer, research and medical terms.

5867 What You Need to Know About Testicular Cancer
National Cancer Institute
Building 31
Bethesda, MD 20892
301-496-7406
Fax: 301-480-8105

Offers information on the symptoms, diagnosing of testicular cancer, side effects of treatments, followup care, support for patients, cancer research, medical terms and resources.

5868 What You Need to Know About Uterine Cancer
National Cancer Institute
Building 31
Bethesda, MD 20892
301-496-7406
Fax: 301-480-8105

Offers information on symptoms, diagnosing cancer of the uterus, treatments, followup care, support for patients, medical terms and resources.

5869 What You Need to Know About...
National Cancer Institute
Building 31
Bethesda, MD 20892
301-496-7406
Fax: 301-480-8105

This is a series of booklets, broken down in this directory. Each provides information about a specific type of cancer. These booklets discuss emotional issues, treatment, diagnosis, symptoms and questions to ask the doctor about cancer.

5870 When Cancer Recurs: Meeting the Challenge Again
National Cancer Institute
Building 31
Bethesda, MD 20892
301-496-7406
Fax: 301-480-8105

Offers information on why cancer can recur, where cancers can recur, diagnosing recurrent cancer, treatment methods and resources that offer more help.

5871 When Someone in Your Family Has Cancer
National Cancer Institute
Building 31
Bethesda, MD 20892
301-496-7406
Fax: 301-480-8105

Written for young people whose parent or sibling has cancer.
28 pages

5872 Who Is This Person Who Helped Save My Life?
Bone Marrow Foundation
981 1st Avenue
Suite 129
New York, NY 10022-5102
212-838-3029
Fax: 212-223-0081
e-mail: thebmf@aol.com
http://www.bonemarrow.org

Discusses the wide range of emotions for a patient in the process of searching for and identifying a donor.

5873 Why Do You Smoke?
National Cancer Institute
Building 31
Bethesda, MD 20892
301-496-7406
Fax: 301-480-8105

Contains a self-test to determine why people smoke and suggest alternatives that can help them stop and prevent cancer.

Videos, Audio Tapes

5874 Living with Ovarian Cancer
National Ovarian Cancer Coalition
1451 W Cypress Creek Road
Suite 300
Fort Lauderdale, FL 33309-1953
954-351-9555
800-343-
Fax: 954-351-7655
e-mail: nocc@ovarian.org
http://www.ovarian.org

Videotape for women who have been recently diagnosed with ovarian cancer. Created to orient and inform patients and their families; describes the experiences of individuals intimately connected with the disease.

Websites

5875 American Cancer Society

http://www.cancer.org
Provides free printed materials, offers a range of services to patients and their families.

5876 Association for the Cure of Cancer of the Prostate

http://www.capcure.org

5877 Bone Marrow Foundation

http://www.bonemarrow.org

5878 National Alliance of Breast Cancer Organizations

http://www.nabco.org
A network of breast cancer organizations that provides information, assistance and referral to anyone with questions about breast cancer and acts as a voice for the interests and concerns of breast cancer survivors and women at risk.

5879 National Ovarian Cancer Coalition

http://www.ovarian.org

Cancer/Research Centers

Research Centers

5880 AMC Cancer Research Center
1600 Pierce Street
Lakewood, CO 80214-1897
303-239-3422
Fax: 303-233-9562

David Silberberg, President

Offers research activities, publications, meetings, educational activities, public services, testing services, community-based cancer control programs and knowledge of cancer mortality rates.

5881 Albany Medical College: Joint Center for Cancer and Blood Disorders
A-167
Albany, NY 12208
518-262-5623
Fax: 518-445-5011

Gregory R Harper, Acting Head
James J Barba, CEO

Offers research in the fields of cancer and blood disorders, focusing on radiotherapy, pathology and surgery.

5882 American Institute for Cancer Research
1759 R Street NW
Washington, DC 20009-2585
202-328-7744
800-843-8114
Fax: 202-328-7744
e-mail: aicrweb@aicr.org

Marilyn Gentry, President

Fosters research on diet, nutrition and cancer. Call toll free to request educational materials, information on specific cancers, and personalized answers to your nutrition questions.

5883 Arizona State University: Cancer Research Institute
University Drive
Tempe, AZ 85287
480-965-3351

George R Pettit, Director

Offers research into new cancer drugs and treatments.

5884 Baylor University: Bone Marrow Transplantation Research Center
3409 Worth Street
Suite 410
Dallas, TX 75246-2053
214-820-3361
Fax: 214-820-6890

Joseph W Fay MD, Director
Rebecca Robbins, Manager

Offers bone marrow transplantation research in leukemia studies.

5885 Bone Marrow Foundation
981 1st Avenue
Suite 129
New York, NY 10022-5102
212-838-3029
Fax: 212-223-0081
e-mail: thebmf@aol.com
http://www.bonemarrow.org

5886 Boston University Cancer Research Center
80 E Concord Street
Boston, MA 02118-2307
617-638-8000
Fax: 617-638-4176

Douglas V Faller, Director
Glenn St Marie, Manager

5887 Brigham Young University: Cancer Research Center
S125 Esc
Provo, UT 84602
801-378-4636

Daniel L Simmons, Director
Kim L O'Neill, Associate Director
Merrill J Bateman, President

5888 Brown University: Division of Biology and Medicine
PO Box G-B
Providence, RI 02912
401-274-3990
Fax: 401-863-2660

Dr. Pierre Gallleti, VP
Ted Brown, President

Interdisciplinary studies in biological and medical sciences including studies in health care problems and fields of research such as cancer and diabetes.

5889 Cancer Center of Wake Forest University: Bowman Gray School of Medicine
300 S Hawthorne Road
Winston Salem, NC 27157
336-758-5000
Fax: 336-758-4324

William C Gordon, CEO

5890 Cancer Research Center
3501 Berrywood Drive
Columbia, MO 65201-6570
573-875-2255

Dr. Abraham Eisenstark, Director
Marnie Tutt, Executive Director

5891 Cancer Research Center: Albert Einstein College of Medicine
1300 Morris Park Avenue
Bronx, NY 10461-1900
718-430-2302
Fax: 718-822-6538
e-mail: aecc@aecom.yu.edu
http://www.aecom.yu.edu/cancer/staging/

5892 Cancer Research Foundation of America
1600 Duke Street
Alexandria, VA 22314-3466
703-836-4412
Fax: 703-836-4413
e-mail: mmcleod@crfa.org
http://www.preventcancer.or

Merle Goldblatt Cohen, President
Carolyn Aldige, Manager

5893 Cancer Research Institute
New England Deaconess Hospital
185 Pilgrim Road
Boston, MA 02215-5324
800-223-7874
Fax: 212-832-9376

J Richard Gaintner, President

5894 Cancer Research Institute of New York
681 5th Avenue
New York, NY 10022-4209
212-688-7515
Fax: 212-832-9376
e-mail: info@cancerresearch.org
http://www.cancerresearch.org

James E Siegel, Executive Director
Jill Tormey, Manager

5895 Cancer Therapy and Research Center
4450 Medical Drive
San Antonio, TX 78229-3779
210-616-5500
Fax: 210-692-9823

Dr. Charles Coltman, Director

5896 City of Hope Clinical Cancer Research Center
1450 E Duarte Road
Duarte, CA 91010
626-359-8111
Fax: 626-301-8111

Paul A Chervenick, Director
Argelia J Sandoval, MD

Cancer/Research Centers

5897 College of Physicians & Surgeons: Columbia University Cancer Center
College of Physicians and Surgeons
630 W 168th Street
New York, NY 10032-3795   212-305-2575

William L Young, MD

5898 Colorado Cancer Research Program
Presbyterian-St. Luke's Medical Center
1719 E 19th Avenue
Denver, CO 80218-1235   303-839-6000
Fax: 303-839-7294

Ester Hayden, Executive Director
Mimi Roberson, CEO

5899 Colorectal Center at St Elizabeth's Medical Center of Boston
736 Cambridge Street
5th Floor
Boston, MA 02135-2907   617-789-3000
Fax: 617-789-3204
http://www.semc.org

Robert Haddad, CEO

Multidisplinary service for the diagnosis and management of medical and surgical disorders of the colon and rectum.

5900 Columbia University Comprehensive Cancer Center
701 W 168th Street
New York, NY 10032-2704   212-305-6921
Fax: 212-305-6889

I Bernard Weinstein, Director

5901 Dana-Farber Institute: Division of Biostistics & Epidemiology
44 Binney Street
Boston, MA 02115-6013   617-632-3000
Fax: 617-737-8614

Dr. Marvin Zelen, Chief
Edward Benz, President

Integral unit of the Institute organized into laboratories of biostatistics, computing and epidemiology.

5902 Eastern Cooperative Oncology Group
420 N Charter Street
Room 4765
Madison, WI 53706   608-263-6650
Fax: 608-262-4403

Dr. Tormey, Chairperson

Studies into cancer, including biological response modifiers and cancer studies.

5903 Emory University: Georgia Center for Cancer Statistics
1599 Clifton Road NE
Atlanta, GA 30329-4250   404-778-5472
Fax: 404-727-8737

Raymond S Greenberg MD, PhD, Director
William T Branch Jr, MD

Serves as a cancer registry for five counties of metropolitan Atlanta and ten rural counties of central Georgia.

5904 Emory University: Winship Cancer Center
1327 Clifton Road NE
Atlanta, GA 30322-1013   404-349-7905
Fax: 404-248-5016

Kenneth W Sell MD, Director
Thomas Emory, Owner

A clinical cancer center coordinating basic and clinical cancer research.

5905 Fox Chase Cancer Center: Institute for Cancer Research
7701 Burholme Avenue
Philadelphia, PA 19111-2497   215-214-1421
Fax: 215-728-3574

Minhhuyen Nguyen, MD

Comprehensive cancer center

5906 Fred Hutchinson Cancer Research Center
1100 Fairview Avenue N
Seattle, WA 98109-4433   206-288-1024

Lee Hartwell, CEO

5907 Georgetown University: Vincent T Lombardi Cancer Research Center
3800 Reservoir Road NW
Washington, DC 20007-2113   202-342-2400
Fax: 202-687-6402

Marc Lippman MD, Director
Joy Drass, CEO

5908 Geraldine Brush Cancer Research Institute
Medical Research Institute
2330 Clay Street
San Francisco, CA 94115-1932   415-561-1728
Fax: 415-561-1390

Dr. Helene S Smith, Director

5909 Goodwin Institute for Cancer Research
1850 NW 69th Avenue
Plantation, FL 33313-4569   954-587-9020
Fax: 954-587-6378

Claire Thuning-Robinson, Director
Richard Dix, Executive Director

5910 Heimlich University
2368 Victory Parkway
Suite 410
Cincinnati, OH 45206-2810   513-221-0002
Fax: 513-221-0003

Henry J Heimlich MD, President

Malaria therapy for cancer and Lyme Disease.

5911 Henry Vogt Cancer Research Institute
James Graham Brown Cancer Center
529 S Jackson Street
Louisville, KY 40292   502-562-0082
Fax: 502-588-7799

Roger H Herzig MD, Director

5912 Hereditary Cancer Institute
Creighton University
Omaha, NE 68178   402-280-2700
Fax: 402-280-1734

Henry T Lynch MD, President

Offers research into hereditary cancer including studies of its incidence and patterns.

5913 Hipple Cancer Research Center
601 W Riverview Avenue
Dayton, OH 45406-5543   937-293-8508
Fax: 937-293-7652

Dr. Martin Murphy Jr, President

Nonprofit organization focusing research activities primarily on cancer, studies on human tumor cloning, hormone purification and human tumor marker identification.

5914 Howard University Cancer Center
2041 Georgia Avenue NW
Washington, DC 20060   202-865-6711
Fax: 202-667-1686

Dr. Alfred Goldson, Interim Director
Sandra Holt, Administrator

Cancer/Research Centers

5915 Illinois Cancer Center
200 S Michigan Avenue
Chicago, IL 60604-2402
312-739-0600
Fax: 312-986-0404

Shirley Lansky MD, President

Serves as a consortium cancer research center for the state of Illinois in National Cancer Institute's nationwide program for coordinating basic and clinical cancer research.

5916 Illinois Oncology Research Association
900 Main Street
Suite 780
Peoria, IL 61602-1067
309-672-5681

Robert Cooper, Director
James Knost, MD

Research into cancer treatments.

5917 Indiana University Laboratory for Experimental Oncology
School of Medicine
702 Barnhill Drive
Indianapolis, IN 46202-5128
317-274-7921
Fax: 317-274-3939

Prof. George Weber MD, Director

5918 Institute for Cancer and Blood Research
150 N Robertson Boulevard
Beverly Hills, CA 90211-2142
310-657-4706
Fax: 310-657-2185

Dr. Howard Bierman, Scientific Director
Susan Kane, Administrator

5919 Iowa Oncology Research Association
1044 Seventh Street
Des Moines, IA 50314
515-244-7586
Fax: 515-244-7757

Roscoe F Morton MD, Principal Investigator
Sherri Rickabaugh, Administrator

Clinical cancer studies and research.

5920 Ireland Cancer Center at Case Western Reserve University
2074 Abington Road
Cleveland, OH 44106
216-844-5432
Fax: 216-844-1129

Patty Balas, Manager

5921 JL and Helen Kellogg Cancer Care Center
Evanston Hospital
2650 Ridge Avenue
Evanston, IL 60201-1718
847-570-2000
Fax: 847-570-2918

Dr. JD Khandekar, Director
Raymond Grady, CEO

Integral unit of the Evanston Hospital, this center researches treatment and diagnosis of cancer, including phase 1 and phase 2 studies.

5922 John P Caulfield Technology Extension Center for Cancer Treatment
1 Bruce Street
Newark, NJ 07103-2709
973-456-4600
Fax: 973-456-7047

David M Goldenberg, Director

Develops and provides new and more effective technologies for the early detection, diagnosis and treatment of cancer.

5923 Johns Hopkins Oncology Center
600 N Wolfe Street
Room B156
Baltimore, MD 21287
410-955-5089

Edward Chambers, Administrator

5924 Jonsson Comprehensive Cancer Center
University of California at Los Angeles
100 Ucla Medical Plaza
Suite 255
Los Angeles, CA 90024-6900
310-443-8999
800-825-2631
Fax: 310-825-5268

Robert Mohr DPM, Owner

5925 Kansas State University: Center for Basic Cancer Research
Division of Biology
Ackert Hall
Manhattan, KS 66506
785-532-6705
Fax: 785-532-6707
http://www.kso.edu/cancer.center

Terry C Johnson, Director
Janis Clare Galitzer, Administrative Assistant

5926 Kaplan Cancer Center
New York University Medical Center
550 1st Avenue
New York, NY 10016-6402
212-964-1800
Fax: 212-263-2150

Mitchell Kaplan CPA, Owner

The mission of NYU Cancer Institute is to decrease and eliminate cancer as a significant helth problem throughout New York, the nation, and the world, by developing and maintaining excellent programs in patient care, research, education and prevention.

5927 Kentucky Cancer Program
800 Rose Street
Lexington, KY 40536
859-219-0772
Fax: 859-258-1902

Gilbert H Friedell, Director
Candace Robbinnette, Manager

5928 La Jolla Cancer Research Foundation
10901 N Torrey Pines Road
La Jolla, CA 92037-1005
858-646-3100
Fax: 858-455-0181

Erkki Rudslahti MD, President

5929 Leukemia Research Foundation
4761 W Touhy Avenue
Suite 211
Lincolnwood, IL 60712-1622
312-982-1480
Fax: 312-982-1485
e-mail: leukresear@aol.com

Janie Weisenberg, Executive Director

Founded to conquer leukemia by funding research into the causes and cures of the disease and to enrich the quality of life by those touched by leukemia.

5930 Mary Imogene Bassett Medical Research Institute
1 Atwell Road
Cooperstown, NY 13326-1394
607-547-3390
Fax: 607-547-3061

Thomas A Pearson MD, Director
Alan Kozak, MD

5931 Mary Margaret Walther Center
Walther Cancer Institute
3202 N Meridian Street
Indianapolis, IN 46208-4646
317-921-2040
Fax: 317-924-4688

Dorothy Weber, Director
Fred Haslam, Executive Director

Focuses research on all types of cancer studies.

Cancer/Research Centers

5932 Massachusetts Institute of Technology: Center for Cancer Research
77 Massachusetts Avenue
Cambridge, MA 02139-4307
617-253-1000
Fax: 617-253-8728

Dr. Richard Hynes, Director

5933 Mayo Comprehensive Cancer Center
200 First Street SW
Rochester, MN 55902
507-284-2511
http://www.mayo.edu

Denis Cortese, President

5934 Medical College of Toledo: Cancer Research Division
Department of Pathology
3000 Arlington Avenue
Toledo, OH 43614-2595
419-383-3742
Fax: 419-381-3002

Dr. Gary Stoner, Director
Varsha Moudgal, MD

Researches into all aspects of cancer.

5935 Medical Foundation of Buffalo
73 High Street
Buffalo, NY 14203-1149
716-856-9600
Fax: 716-852-4846

Herbert A Hauptman PhD, President

Nonprofit organization devoted to cancer research.

5936 Melanoma Research Foundation
23704-5 El Toro Road
Suite 206
Lake Forest, CA 92630
800-MRF-1290
Fax: 800-MRF-1290
e-mail: mrf@dna.rockefeller

Founded in October 1996 by melanoma patients and their families to support research which will lead to a cure for melanoma. Strictly a volunteer organization - not one person will receive compensation for his or her efforts.

5937 Michigan Cancer Foundation
110 E Warren Avenue
Detroit, MI 48201-1379
313-831-4035
Fax: 313-831-8714

Mary Mulligan, Contact

5938 Natalie Warren Bryant Cancer Center
St. Francis Hospital
5151 S Yale Avenue
Tulsa, OK 74135-7404
918-494-2273
Fax: 918-494-1886

Dr. Alan M Keller, Principal Investor

5939 National Cancer Institute
US Department of Health & Human Services
9000 Rockville Pike
Bethesda, MD 20892
301-496-2481
800-422-6237
Fax: 301-402-2594
http://www.nci.nih.gov

Sallie Baird, Manager

NCI grants and contracts support cancer research in most of the Nation's university medical centers and many other non-Federal institutions. NCI also coordinates the cancer research programs of Federal and private institutions in accordance with a constantly updated National Cancer Program, which encompasses the lines of research effort considered to be most important in solving the major problems of cancer.

5940 New England Deaconess Hospital: Laboratory of Cancer Biology
50 Binney Street
Boston, MA 02115-6013
617-732-9875
Fax: 617-738-9188

Peter Thomas PhD, Research Director

5941 New Hope Institute
500 Main Street
El Segundo, CA 90245-3005
213-640-6605
Fax: 310-322-5546

Barbara O'Hara, Contact

The Institute uses visualization and hypnosis to enhance other therapies and to improve the psychological condition of the patient.

5942 New York University: Kaplan Comprehensive Cancer Center
550 1st Avenue
New York, NY 10016-6402
212-263-5349
Fax: 212-263-8211
e-mail: ira.goodman@atmccmsf.med.nyu.edu
http://www.nyu.edu/kccc/homepage.html

Franco Muggia MD, Director

5943 Northwestern University Cancer Center
303 E Chicago Avenue
Chicago, IL 60611-3072
312-503-8186
Fax: 312-908-1372

Steven T Rosen, Director
Lewis Landsberg, Administrator

5944 Ohio State University Comprehensive Cancer Center
Arthur G James Cancer Hospital
410 W 10th Avenue
Columbus, OH 43210-1240
614-293-3810
800-638-6996

Peter Geier, CEO

5945 Ohio State University: Clinical Research Center
410 W 10th Avenue
Columbus, OH 43210-1240
614-293-2096

Manuel Tzagournis, Principal Investigator

Provides facilities and financial support for inpatient and outpatient cancer research.

5946 Oklahoma Medical Research Foundation: Immunology & Cancer Research
825 NE 13th Street
Oklahoma City, OK 73104-5097
405-271-6673

William G Thurman MD, President
J Donald Capra, CEO

5947 Pacific Health Research Institute
Straub Pacific Health Foundation
846 S Hotel Street
Suite 303
Honolulu, HI 96813-2583
808-524-4411
Fax: 808-531-0123

Dr. Fred Gilbert Jr, Medical Director
Wally Izumigawa, Administrator

5948 Peralta Cancer Research Institute
1933 Davis Street
Suite 310
San Leandro, CA 94577-1259
510-729-0399
Fax: 510-729-0383

Dr. Adeline Hackett, Director

Cancer/Research Centers

5949 Pohl Cancer Research Laboratory
Georgia College CBX 082
Department of Chemistry & Phy
Milledgeville, GA 31061
478-453-4565
Fax: 478-453-5271

Prf. Douglas Pohl, Director

5950 Purdue University Cancer Center
Life Sciences Research Buildi
West Lafayette, IN 47907
765-494-9129
Fax: 765-494-9193

William M Baird, Director

5951 Radiation Oncology Research & Development Center
4201 Street Antoine
Detroit, MI 48201
313-745-9207
Fax: 313-745-2314

Arthur T Porter MD, President

Radiation therapy and cancer treatment and research.

5952 Roger Williams Cancer Research
Roger Williams General Hospital
825 Chalkstone Avenue
Providence, RI 02908-4735
401-456-2433
Fax: 401-456-6793

Elaine Mysliwiec, Manager

5953 Roswell Park Cancer Institute
Elm and Carlton Streets
Buffalo, NY 14263
716-845-2300
800-ROS-WELL

David C Hohn, CEO

5954 Salk Institute for Biological Studies Library
PO Box 85800
San Diego, CA 92186-5800
858-453-4100
Fax: 858-452-7472
e-mail: library@salk.edu

Kimberlee K Antrimco, Librarian

Basic science research in the areas of molecular biology, genetics, neuroscience, AIDS, Alzheimer's disease, biochemistry, cancer, neurobiology, plant biology, structural biology, virology.

5955 Samuel Roberts Noble Foundation: Biomedical Division
PO Box 2180
Ardmore, OK 73402-2180
580-223-5810
Fax: 580-221-7362

Dr. MK Patterson Jr, Director
Michael Cawley, CEO

5956 San Antonio Cancer Institute
7979 Wurzbach Road
San Antonio, TX 78229-4427
210-616-5590
Fax: 210-616-5981
http://www.ccc.saci.org

5957 Santa Barbara Breast Cancer Institute
5333 Hollister Avenue
Santa Barbara, CA 93111-2341
805-681-6459
Fax: 805-681-7341

Dr. Otto Sartorius, Director
Rob Manchester, Manager

5958 Skin Cancer Foundation
245 5th Avenue
Suite 2402
New York, NY 10016-8728
212-725-5176
Fax: 212-725-5751

Mitzi Moulds, Executive Director

Conducts public and medical education programs to help reduce skin cancer. Major goals are to increase public awareness of the importance of taking protective measures against the damaging rays of the sun and to teach people how to recognize the early signs of skin cancer.

5959 Southwest Biomedical Research Institute
6401 E Thomas Road
Scottsdale, AZ 85251-6078
480-945-4363
Fax: 480-947-8220

Charles Atkinson, President

5960 Susan G Komen Cancer Foundation
PO Box 97100
Dallas, TX 75397
800-462-9273

Provides education on breast care issues such as prevention and cancer. Educational pamphlets on request. 8:00 a.m. to 5:00 p.m. Monday-Friday.

5961 Temple University FELS Institute for Cancer Research
School of Medicine
3420 N Broad Street
Room 700
Philadelphia, PA 19140-5104
215-221-4300
Fax: 215-221-4318

Sally Carre, Senior Administrator

5962 University of Alabama at Birmingham: Comprehensive Cancer Center
1918 University Boulevard
Birmingham, AL 35294
205-934-7161
Fax: 205-975-7428

Maryann B Pass, MD

5963 University of Arizona Cancer Center
1501 N Campbell Avenue
Tucson, AZ 85724
520-626-6236
Fax: 520-626-2032

Craig Comiter, MD

5964 University of California: Berkeley Cancer Research Laboratories
447 Life Science Addition
Berkeley, CA 94720-2751
510-642-0460
Fax: 510-643-6791

Dr. James Allison, Director

Research with a special emphasis on mammary and hepatic cancers.

5965 University of California: Irvine Cancer Research Institute
Department of Molecular Biology and Biochemistry
Irvine, CA 92717
949-856-5886
Fax: 714-886-4023

Dr. Hung Fan, Director

5966 University of California: Los Angeles Bone Marrow Transplantation Program
Center For Health Sciences
Los Angeles, CA 90024
310-825-4321
Fax: 310-206-5511

David W Golde MD, Director

Treatment of leukemia and anemia.

5967 University of California: San Diego Cancer Center
La Jolla, CA 92093
858-534-7600
Fax: 858-534-7628

Georgia Robbins Sadler, Associate Director

Cancer/Research Centers

5968 University of California: San Francisco Cancer Research Institute
Moffit Hospital
505 Parnassus Avenue
Room 1282
San Francisco, CA 94143-2204   415-502-8633
Dr. Marvin Sleisenger, Acting Director
Harold S Bernstein, MD

5969 University of Chicago: Cancer Research Center
5841 S Maryland Avenue
Chicago, IL 60637-1447   773-702-1865
                                    Fax: 773-702-0666
Sue Curtis, Manager

5970 University of Chicago: Clinical Nutrition Research Unit
5841 S Maryland Avenue
Box 223
Chicago, IL 60637-1447   773-702-1865
Michael D Sitrin MD, Director
Sue Curtis, Manager

5971 University of Colorado Cancer Center
PO Box B188
Denver, CO 80262   303-315-3007

5972 University of Iowa Cancer Center
20 Medical Laboratories
Iowa City, IA 52242   319-335-7905
Richard L DeGowin, Director

5973 University of Kansas Cancer Center
Medical Center
39th & Rainbow Boulevard
Kansas City, KS 66103   913-588-4700
                                    Fax: 913-588-4701
Stephen W Russell DVM, Director

5974 University of Kentucky: Lucille Parker Markey Cancer Center
800 Rose Street
Lexington, KY 40536   859-323-5861
                                    Fax: 859-323-2074
James F Glenn, Executive Director
A Byron Young, MD

5975 University of Michigan Cancer Center
Cancer Research Committee
PO Box 0752
Ann Arbor, MI 48109   734-936-4000
                                    Fax: 734-936-9582
Dr. Irwin J Goldstein, Chairperson

5976 University of Michigan: Stimpson Memorial Institute for Medical Research
102 Observatory Street
Ann Arbor, MI 48109-2000   734-936-1831
                                    Fax: 734-764-2566
Max S Wicha MD, Director
Focuses on leukemia research and cancer studies.

5977 University of Minnesota: Coordinating Centers for Biometric Research
Division of Biostatistics
2221 University Avenue SE
Suite 200
Minneapolis, MN 55414-3075   612-626-8887
                                    Fax: 612-626-9054
                                    e-mail: biostat@gopher.ccbr.umn.edu
                                    http://www.biostat.umn.edu
Thomas A Louis, Division Head
Cancer research
1972

5978 University of Minnesota: Masonic Cancer Center
Division of Oncology
PO Box 286
Minneapolis, MN 55440   612-624-9611
                                    Fax: 612-625-8966
BJ Kennedy MD, Contact

5979 University of Nebraska at Omaha: Eppley Institute for Research in Cancer
600 S 42nd Street
Omaha, NE 68198-1023   402-559-4656
                                    Fax: 402-559-4651
Raymond Ruddon MD, Director
Ed Raspott, Manager
Focuses on the causes, prevention and early detection of cancer.

5980 University of Nevada Reno: Natural Products Lab
Department of Biochemistry
Reno, NV 89557   702-784-6031
                                    Fax: 702-784-6096
Dr. Ronald Pardini, Director
Cancer research.

5981 University of New Mexico Cancer Center
900 Camino De Salud NE
Albuquerque, NM 87131   505-272-4946
                                    Fax: 505-277-2841
James A Neidhart MD, Director

5982 University of New Mexico: Center for Non-Invasive Diagnosis
1201 Yale NE
Albuquerque, NM 87131   505-272-1734
Dr. Nicholas Matwiyoff, Director
Cardiology and cancer research.

5983 University of North Carolina: UNC Lineberger Comprehensive Cancer Center
Cb 7295
Chapel Hill, NC 27599   919-962-2211
                                    Fax: 919-966-3015
Dr. Joseph Pagano, Director
James Moeser, CEO

5984 University of Pennsylvania Cancer Center
3400 Spruce Street
Philadelphia, PA 19104-4274   215-662-2862
                                    Fax: 215-349-8299
                                    http://www.health.upenn
David Porter, MD

5985 University of Pennsylvania: Comparative Leukemia Unit
New Bolton Center
382 W Street Road
Kennett Square, PA 19348-1691   610-444-5800
                                    Fax: 610-925-8123
                                    e-mail: jfferrer@nbc.upenn.edu
Jorge Ferrer MD, Director
Korinne Sweeney, Administrator

5986 University of Southern California's Hematology, Hematologic Malignancy and Retroviral Research Program
1441 Eastlake Avenue
Los Angeles, CA 90033   323-865-3950
                                    Fax: 323-865-0060
                                    e-mail: horner@hsc.usc.edu
                                    http://ccnt.hsc.usc.edu/hamatology/index.html
Alexandra Levine MD, Head Master
Ilene C Weitz, MD
Cancer research.

Cancer/Research Centers

5987 **University of Southern California: Comprehensive Cancer Center**
1441 Eastlake Avenue
Los Angeles, CA 90033 323-865-3950
Brian Henderson MD, Director
Ilene C Weitz, MD

5988 **University of Southern California: Kenneth T Norris Jr Comprehensive Cancer Center**
1441 Eastlake Avenue
Los Angeles, CA 90033 323-865-3950
800-USC-CARE
Ilene C Weitz, MD

5989 **University of Tennessee: Memphis Cancer Center**
N327 Van Vleet
Building 3n
Memphis, TN 38163 901-448-5757
Fax: 901-528-5033
Alvin M Mauer MD, Director
Latasha Williams, Manager

5990 **University of Texas: MD Anderson Cancer Center**
1515 Holcombe Boulevard
Houston, TX 77030-4009 713-792-2121
Leon J Leach, CEO

5991 **University of Texas: Medical Branch at Galveston Cancer Center**
106 Basic Science Boulevard
Galveston, TX 77550 409-772-1011
Fax: 409-772-4865
Courtney M Townsend Jr, Interim Director
Abdul Osman, MD

5992 **University of Utah: Rocky Mountain Cancer Data System**
420 Chipeta Way
Suite 120
Salt Lake City, UT 84108-1256 801-583-2500
Fax: 801-581-5704
Lawrence Derrick, Assistant Director
Ross Vranken, Executive Director

Consucts cancer research and provides data to participating hospitals and state registries.

5993 **University of Vermont Cancer Center**
1 S Prospect Street
Burlington, VT 05401-3456 802-656-4414
Fax: 802-656-8788
David W Yandell, Director
Barbara Higgins, Administrator

5994 **University of Wisconsin: Comprehensive Cancer Center**
600 Highland Avenue
Madison, WI 53792 608-263-1416

5995 **Utah Cancer Center**
University of Utah School of Medicine
50 N Medical Drive
Salt Lake City, UT 84132 801-581-7201
Fax: 801-585-2300

5996 **Veterans Administration Medical Center: Research & Development**
700 19th Street S
Birmingham, AL 35233-1996 205-939-2159
Jerry G Spenney MD, Associate Chief

5997 **Virginia Commonwealth University: Massey Cancer Center**
PO Box 37
Richmond, VA 23218 804-828-0488
I David Goldman MD, Director

Gene regulation and prevention of cancer.

5998 **Wainwright House Cancer Support Programs**
260 Stuyvesant Avenue
Rye, NY 10580-3115 914-967-6080
Richard Grossman, Program Director
Jessica Seal, Administrator

Weeklong residential retreats offered four times a year to cancer patients. Retreats are devoted to cancer patient education, health promotion and stress management.

5999 **Warren Grant Magnuson Clinical Center**
6100 Executive Boulevard
Suite 3c01
Bethesda, MD 20892 301-496-2563
Fax: 301-402-2984
http://www.cc.nih.gov

Established in 1953 as the research hospital of the National Institutes of Health. Designed so that patient care facilities are close to research laboratories so new findings of basic and clinical scientists can be quickly applied to the treatment of patients. Upon referral by physicians, patients are admitted to NIH clinical studies.

6000 **Wayne State University Center for Molecular Biology**
5047 Gullen Mall
Detroit, MI 48202-3917 313-577-2116
Fax: 313-577-6200
Robert H Rownd PhD, Director
Denise Torres, Executive Director

Research focusing on human conditions such as cancer and neuromuscular disorders.

6001 **West Virginia University: Mary Babb Randolph Cencer Center**
Health Sciences Center
Morgantown, WV 26506 304-293-3528
Fax: 304-293-4667
Dr. Fred Butcher, Director

6002 **Women's Suffrage for Prostate Cancer Awareness**
743 Caribou Court
Sunnyvale, CA 94087-4229
800-776-2262
e-mail: info@pcawomen.org
http://www.pcawomen.org

Women banded together to help people cope with the effects of prostate cancer on their lives and educate others about it. Members understand problems of patients and families and strive to support and educate.

6003 **Worcester Foundation for Biomedical Research Biology, Cancer Center**
University of Massachusetts Medical School
377 Plantation Street
Worcester, MA 01605-2300 508-856-1994
Fax: 508-856-8508
Thoru Pederson PhD, Co-Director

6004 **Yale University: Comprehensive Cancer Center**
333 Cedar Street
New Haven, CT 06510-3206 203-785-4184
Denise Krause, Manager

Death & Bereavement/Associations & Organizations

Associations & Organizations

6005 Compassion Books
7036 State Highway 80 S
Burnsville, NC 28714
828-675-5909
Fax: 828-675-9687
e-mail: orders@compassionbooks.com
http://www.compassionbooks.com
Bruce Greene, VP

A resource organization providing networking, training and resources related to loss and grief, death and dying, comfort and hope. The organization's primary concern is to help people of all ages transform the despair and hopelessness that often accompanies death and loss into healing awareness and a deeper spiritual connectedness to all life.

6006 Compassion in Dying Federation
PO Box 61369
Seattle, WA 98141-6369
206-256-1636
877-222-2816
Fax: 206-256-1640
e-mail: wa@compassionandchoices.org
http://www.candcofwa.org
Robb Miller, Executive Director
Van Zandt Williams, Chairman

Provides information, counseling, and emotional support to terminally ill patients who are deciding how life should come to an end. This includes counseling patients and families about intensive pain management, comfort or hospice care, and safe, effective methods for hastening death.

6007 Compassionate Friends
PO Box 3696
Oak Brook, IL 60522-3696
630-990-0010
Fax: 630-990-0246
e-mail: nationaloffice@compassionatefriends.org
http://www.compassionatefriends.org
Patricia Loder, Executive Director
Kitty Edler, President

A national organization that offers 470 local chapters that give support to people who have experienced the death of a child. Offers monthly support meetings to get through the difficult times and learn how to cope.

6008 Grief and Loss Program
AARP
601 E Street NW
Washington, DC 20049
202-434-2260
Fax: 202-434-6474
e-mail: jgibala@aarp.org
http://www.aarp.org/griefandloss
Marie Smith, President
Bill Novelli, CEO

Offers information and resources pertaining to grief and loss. Assists communities in coping and bereavement programs.

6009 Gundersen Lutheran Medical Center Bereavement Services
1900 S Avenue, Alex
La Crosse, WI 54601
608-775-4747
800-362-9567
Fax: 608-775-5137
e-mail: info@bereavementservices.org
http://www.bereavementservices.org
Jeff Thompson, CEO

Seeks to promote bereavement care by developing and continually improving bereavement training and support materials and by providing respectful, compassionate care for those experiencing a loss.
1981

6010 Hospice Association of America
228 7th Street SE
Washington, DC 20003
202-546-4759
Fax: 202-547-9559
http://www.hospice-america.org
Janet E Neigh, Executive Director

Promotes the concepts of hospice, a philosophy of health care which is expressed through the provision of a variety of medical and nonmedical services to terminally ill patients and their families.

6011 International Cemetery and Funeral Association
107 Carpenter Drive
Suite 100
Sterling, VA 20164
703-391-8400
800-645-7700
Fax: 703-391-8416
e-mail: rfells@icfa.org
http://www.icfa.org
Robert Fells, External COO/General Counsel
Joseph W Budzinski, Internal COO

Serves the needs of the cemetery, funeral service, cremation and memorialization professions with a number of services and products.

6012 International Task Force on Euthanasia and Assisted Suicide
PO Box 760
Steubenville, OH 43952
740-282-3810
Fax: 740-282-0769
http://www.iaetf.org
Rita Marker, Executive Director

Addressing the issues of euthanasia, assisted suicide, advance directives, assisted suicide proposals, right-to-die cases, euthanasia practices, disability rights, pain control and much more.

6013 National Hospice Organization
1700 Diagonal Road
Suite 625
Alexandria, VA 22314
703-837-1500
Fax: 703-837-1233
e-mail: info@nhpco.org
http://www.nho.org
J. Donald Schumacher, President/CEO
Galen Miller, PhD, Executive Vice President

The nation's only advocate for terminally ill patients and their families. Founded in 1978, the NHO is the only organization devoted to hospice in the United States. Support is included from 48 state hospice organizations, patients, families, communities, provider program members and professional/volunteer members. Represents hospice care interests to Congress, regulatory agencies, courts, voluntary organizations and the public.

6014 National Institute for Jewish Hospice (NIJH)
8723 Alden Drive
Suite 219
Los Angeles, CA 90048
310-854-3036
800-446-4448
Fax: 619-322-3817
LeVana Lev, Executive Director

Serves as a resource center that seeks to help terminal patients and their families deal with their grief by providing information on traditional Jewish views on death, dying and managing the loss of a loved one.
1985

6015 Rainbows for All God's Children
2100 Golf Road
Suite 370
Rolling Meadows, IL 60008
847-952-1770
Fax: 847-952-1774
e-mail: info@rainbows.org
http://www.rainbows.org
Mary Lou Lowry, Executive Director
Suzy Yehl Marta, President

Death & Bereavement/Books

A support program operating in 7 countries for individuals who have suffered a significant loss in their lives due to death, divorce or any other painful transition.

6016 Right to Life League of Southern California
1028 N Lake Avenue
Suite 207
Pasadena, CA 91104
626-398-6100
Fax: 626-398-6101
e-mail: info@rtllsc.org
http://www.rtllsc.org

Connie Martin, Manager
Sherry Smith, RN, Education Director

The Right to Life League of Southern California is an education and service organization dedicated to the support and protection of innocent human life from conception to natural death. We exist to defend the God-given gift of life. We are dedicated to exerting every effort to produce a universal change of heart, resulting in the cessation of the deliberate termination of innocent human life.

Books

6017 Anatomy of Bereavement
Jason Aronson Publishers
400 Keystone Industrial Park
Dunmore, PA 18512-1507
800-782-0015
Fax: 201-840-7242
http://www.aronson.com

In this comprehensive book, Dr. Raphael describes all the stages of mourning and healing.

454 pages Frequency: Softcover

6018 Compassion Book Service
Mail Order Division
477 Hannah Branch Road
Burnsville, NC 28714-7569
828-675-5909
Fax: 828-675-9687

Bruce Greene, Vice President

The country's largest mail-order collection of carefully selected books, audios and videos on death and dying, bereavement and change, comfort, healing and hope, collected from hundreds of publishers in the United States.

6019 Death: The Final Stage of Growth
Simon & Schuster
1819 L Street NW
Washington, DC 20036-3807
202-293-0202
Fax: 202-293-0202

6020 Grief Dreams: How They Help Us Heal After the Death of a Loved One
Jossey Bass Inc
989 Market Street
Suite 5
San Francisco, CA 94103-1741
415-433-0135

This book is designed to help mourners reclaim some measure of power in navigating the most difficult journey of their lives.

6021 Grief, Dying and Death
Research Press
PO Box 9177
Champaign, IL 61826-9177
217-352-3273
800-519-2707
Fax: 217-352-1221
e-mail: rp@researchpress.com
http://www.researchpress.com

Russell Pence, President

A comprehensive manual providing theoretical background and practical treatment interventions necessary for working with those who are bereaved or dying.

488 pages Frequency: Paperback

6022 Hospice Alternative
Harper Collins Publishers/Basic Books
10 E 53rd Street
New York, NY 10022-5244
212-207-7057
800-242-7737
Fax: 212-207-7203

An account of the hospice experience. An innovative and humane way of caring for the terminally ill.

256 pages

6023 Love You Forever
Compassion Books
477 Hannah Branch Road
Burnsville, NC 28714-7569
828-675-5950
Fax: 828-675-9687
http://www.compassionbooks.com

This endearing and heart-warming story shows how love can survive death and is passed down for generations to come.

Frequency: Paperback

6024 On Death and Dying
MacMillan
175 Fifth Avenue
New York, NY 10010
646-307-5151
http://us.macmillan.com

A wonderful book offering information on how to deal and cope with death and dying.

Frequency: Paperback

6025 Recovery from Bereavement
Jason Aronson Publishers
400 Keystone Industrial Park
Dunmore, PA 18512-1507
800-782-0015
Fax: 201-840-7242
http://www.aronson.com

Outstanding authorities on loss and bereavement discuss the factors that play a role in successful recovery.

344 pages Frequency: Softcover

6026 So Many of My Friends Have Moved Away or Died
AARP Fulfillment
601 E Street NW
Washington, DC 20049
202-434-2277
800-424-3410
Fax: 202-434-3443
e-mail: member@aarp.org
http://www.aarp.org

Willilam D Novelli, CEO

A typical problem faced by older persons, discussion focuses on coping with the loss of old friends and finding new ones.

6027 Talking About Death
Beacon Press
25 Beacon Street
Boston, MA 02108-2824
617-742-2110
Fax: 617-723-3097

Helen Atwan, Executive Director

6028 The Tender Scar: Life After the Death of a Spouse
Kregel Publications
PO Box 2607
Grand Rapids, MI 49501-2607
616-451-4775
Fax: 616-451-9330
http://www.kregel.gospelcom.net

Written by a former physician and recent widower, this warmly practical book guides the bereaved through the grief process and explains how to live after the death of a spouse.

6029 The Wisdom of Death: Six Paths to Understanding Loss and Grief
AuthorHouse
1663 Liberty Drive
Suite 200
Bloomington, IN 47403
888-519-5121
http://www.authorhouse.com

Death & Bereavement/Directories

6030 **Treatment of Complicated Mourning**
Research Press
PO Box 9177
Champaign, IL 61826-9177
217-352-3273
800-519-2707
Fax: 217-352-1221
e-mail: rp@researchpress.com
http://www.researchpress.com

Russell Pence, President

The first book to specifically focus on complicated mourning, often referred to as unresolved or abnormal grief. It provides caregivers with practical therapeutic strategies that are necessary when traditional grief counseling is insufficient.

768 pages Frequency: Hardcover

6031 **Understanding Dying, Death and Bereavement**
Cengage Learning
10 Davis Drive
Belmont, CA 94002
650-595-2350
http://academic.cengage.com

Coverage encompasses the study of death and dying, the American experience, growing up with death, cultural perspectives including life after death, the dying process, and living with a terminal illness.

6032 **What Helped Me When My Loved One Died**
Beacon Press
25 Beacon Street
Boston, MA 02108-2824
617-742-2110
Fax: 617-723-3097

Helen Atwan, Executive Director

Directories

6033 **National Directory of Bereavement Support Groups and Services**
ADM Publishing
PO Box 608606
Orlando, FL 32860-8606
407-774-5260
800-299-7716
Fax: 407-774-5260
e-mail: admpub@aol.com
http://www.admpublishing.com

Mary M Wong, Editor

More than 2,500 bereavement support groups and resources in 12 categories: AIDS, death of a child, death of an infant, general bereavement, grieving children, homicide/murder, organ/tissue donation, pet loss, suicide, vehicular homicide, the widowed, 24-hour crisis hotlines. Entries include: Name, address, phone, fax, geographical area served, requirements for eligibility, description of services offered.

130 pages Frequency: Biennial, June

Newsletters, Pamphlets

6034 **Death and Dying Health Pamphlets**
Greenhaven Press
PO Box 289009
San Diego, CA 92198-9009
858-485-7424
800-231-5163
Fax: 800-550-5480

Bruce Glassman, Owner

Offers various pamphlets such as: What is the best treatment for the terminally ill?; How can dying patients control the decision for end treatment?; How should one cope with grief?; and Is there life after death?.

Research Centers

6035 **Center for Thanatology Research**
391 Atlantic Avenue
Brooklyn, NY 11217-1701
718-858-3026
Fax: 718-858-3026
e-mail: rhalporn@pipeline.com
http://www.thanatology.org

Roberta Halporn, Director

Aging, dying, death, bereavement, and gravestone studies.

6036 **University of Minnesota: Center for Bioethics**
410 Church Street SE
Suite N504
Minneapolis, MN 55455
612-624-9440
Fax: 612-624-9108
e-mail: kahnx009@gdd.tc.umn.edu
http://www.med.umn.edu/bioethics

Jeffrey Kahn, Executive Director

Biomedical ethics and ethical issues in health care and health policy, including the use of fetal tissue in medicine, human genetics and genetic counseling, ethical issues in long-term care, humane care of dying people, ethics and cost-containment, health care reform, and ethics of managed care. Sets up task forces on related issues.

Depression/Mental Health/Associations & Organizations

Associations & Organizations

6037 American Board of Psychiatry and Neurology
2150 E Lake Cook Road
Suite 900
Buffalo Grove, IL 60089
847-229-6500
Fax: 847-229-6600
e-mail: rcallen@abpn.com
http://www.abpn.com
Stephen C Scheiber, Executive VP
Robin Callen, Director, Finance and Office Ope

Physicians with specialized training in psychiatry, neurology, child neurology, child adolescent psychiatry, clinical neurophysiology, and geriatric psychiatry. Determines eligibility requirements, administers examinations, and certifies physicians.

6038 Anxiety Disorders Association of America
8730 Georgia Avenue
Suite 600
Silver Spring, MD 20910
240-485-1001
Fax: 240-485-1035
http://www.adaa.org
Alies Muskin, Chief Operating Officer
J. Teichroew, Director

Offers help, support and information for persons with anxiety disorders, manic and depressive disorders and mental illness.

6039 Lithium Information Center
Dean Foundation
7617 Mineral Point Road
Suite 300
Madison, WI 53717
608-827-2470
Fax: 608-827-2479
e-mail: mim@miminc.org
http://www.miminc.org
John H. Greist, Founder
James W. Jefferson, Founder

Offers information on the drug lithium, and its effect on manic and depressive episodes.

6040 Louis de la Parte Florida Mental Health Institute
University of South Florida
13301 Bruce B Downs Boulevard
Tampa, FL 33612-3899
813-974-4602
Fax: 813-974-1968
e-mail: mhlpinfo@fmhi.usf.edu
http://www.fmhi.usf.edu/
Bruce Lubots Levin, DrPH, Editor-in-Chief
Kevin D. Hennessy, PhD, Associate Editor

Mental health care, including aging and mental health, child and family studies, community mental health, and mental health law and policy.

6041 Louisiana Division of Mental Health
Bienville Building
628 North 4th Street
Baton Rouge, LA 70802
225-342-2540
Fax: 225-342-5066
http://www.dhh.la.gov/offices/?ID=62
Darlene W. Smith, State Registrar and Center Direc
Robert Starszak, State Center for Health Statisti

6042 Maine Department of Mental Health & Mental Retardation
221 State Street
Augusta, ME 4333
207-287-3707
Fax: 207-287-3005
e-mail: gary.r.sawyer@state.me.us.web
http://www.maine.gov/dhhs
Susan A. Gendron, Commissioner
Brenda M. Harvey, Health and Human Services Commis

6043 Maryland Department of Health and Mental Hygiene
201 West Preston Street
Baltimore, MD 21201
410-767-6500
877-463-3464
Fax: 410-767-6489
e-mail: healthmd@dhmh.state.md.us
http://www.dhmh.state.md.us
TDD 800-735-2258
Marlin O'Malley, Governor
John M. Colmers, Secretary
Van T Mitchell, Principal Deputy Secretary

The mission of the Department of Health and Mental Hygiene is to protect, promote and improve the health and well being of all Maryland citizens in a fiscally responsible way.

6044 Massachusetts Department of Mental Health
25 Staniford Street
Boston, MA 02114
617-626-8000
Fax: 617-727-4350
Barbara Leadholm, Commissioner
Steve Gangemi, Manager

6045 National Anxiety Foundation
3135 Custer Drive
Lexington, KY 40517
859-272-7166
Stephen Michael Cox, M.D, President and Medical Director

Offers information and help to persons with panic disorders, manic and depressive disorders and mental illness.

6046 National Depressive and Manic Depressive Association
730 N Franklin Street
Suite 501
Chicago, IL 60610-7224
312-642-0049
800-826-8008
Fax: 312-642-7243
e-mail: info@dbsalliance.org
http://www.dbsalliance.org
Christy B Beckmann, Directors
Renice Rodriguez, Secretary

Consists of 250 patient groups providing support and direct services to persons with clinical depression.

6047 National Foundation for Depressive Illness
PO Box 40395
Glen Oaks, NY 11004
718-470-4007
800-239-1265
Fax: 718-343-7739
http://www.depression.org
T.J. Arneson, President
David S. Chowes, Chairman

Provides information concerning correct diagnosis and treatment, and the availability of qualified doctors and support groups.

6048 National Mental Health Association
1021 Prince Street
Alexandria, VA 22314
703-684-7722
Fax: 703-684-5968
e-mail: infoctr@nmha.org
http://www.nmha.org
David L. Shern, Ph.D., President and Chief Executive Di
Sergio Aguilar-Gaxiola, M.D.,, Chair

Serves over 700 affiliates nationally providing information, publications and other services.

6049 North Carolina Division of Mental Health, Developmental Disabilities and Substance Abuse Services
NC Department of Health and Human Services
3001 Mail Service Center
Raleigh, NC 27699-3001
919-733-7011
Fax: 919-508-0951
e-mail: contactdmh@ncmail.net
http://www.dhhs.state.nc.us
Michael Moseley, Director
Leza Wainwright, Deputy Director

Depression/Mental Health/Associations & Organizations

Community-based mental health, developmental disabilities and substance abuse services are managed through a network of local management entities that cover the state's 100 counties. These programs oversee and manage local services.

6050 North Dakota Department of Mental Health
600 E. Boulevard Ave
Suite 1d
Bismarck, ND 58505-0200
701-328-8989
800-755-2719
Fax: 701-328-8969
http://www.health.state.nd.us/DoH/Overview/
Sam Ismir, Director

6051 Ohio Department of Mental Health
30 E Broad Street
8th Floor
Columbus, OH 43215-3430
614-466-9989
Fax: 614-466-1571
e-mail: baileyd@mh.state.oh.us
http://www.mh.state.oh.us/
Donald C. Anderson, Acting Director
Ted Strickland, Governor

6052 Oklahoma Department of Mental Health
1200 NE 13th Street
53277
Oklahoma City, OK 73117-1022
405-522-3908
800-522-3908
Fax: 405-522-3650
Sharon Boehler, Commissioner
David V Statton, Manager

6053 Oregon Department of Mental Health
500 Summer St. NE
E86
Salem, OR 97301
503-945-5763
Fax: 503-378-8467
e-mail: omhas.web@state.or.us
http://www.oregon.gov/DHS/mentalhealth/
Stan Mazur-Hart, Ph.D, Director
Gina Firman, Executive Director

6054 Rhode Island Department of Mental Health
14 Harrington Road
Cranston, RI 02920
401-462-3201
Fax: 401-462-3204
http://www.mhrh.state.ri.us/
TDD 401-462-6087
Patricia M. Leddy, Chief of Staff
Ellen R. Nelson, PhD, Director

6055 South Carolina Commission for the Blind
PO Box 2467
Columbia, SC 29202
803-898-8731
800-922-2222
Fax: 803-898-8800
e-mail: publicinfo@sccb.sc.gov
http://www.sccb.state.sc.us/
James Kirby, Commissioner
Charlene Grice, Board Member

Offers services for the totally blind, legally blind, visually impaired, mentally retarded blind and more with health, counseling, educational, recreational, rehabilitation, computer training and professional training services.

6056 South Carolina Department of Mental Health
2414 Bull Street
Columbia, SC 29202
803-898-8581
http://www.state.sc.us/dmh/
John H. Magill, Director
Brenda Hart, Deputy Director

6057 South Dakota Department of Mental Health
700 Governors Drive
Pierre, SD 57501-2291
605-773-3134
Fax: 605-773-6139
e-mail: diane.lowery@state.sd.us
http://http://doe.sd.gov
Amy Arbach, Business Official
Dorothy Liegl, Director

6058 Tennessee Department of Mental Health & Developmental Disabilities
Cordell Hull Building
425 5th Avenue North
Nashville, TN 37243
615- 53- 650
Fax: 615-532-6719
e-mail: opic.tdmhdd@state.tn.us
http://www.state.tn.us
Virginia Trotter Betts, Commissioner
Jan Thompson, Director

The Department is the state's mental health and developmental disabilities authority and is responsible for system planning, setting policy and quality standards, system monitoring and evaluation, disseminating public information and advocating for persons of all ages who have mental illness, serious emotional disturbance or developmental disability.

6059 Texas Department of Mental Health & Mental Retardation
PO Box 12668
Austin, TX 78711-2668
512-206-4516
Fax: 512-206-4560
Don Gilbert, commissioner
Ann K. Utley, Chairman

Offers information and referrals.

6060 Utah Department of Mental Health
120 N 200 W
Salt Lake City, UT 84190
801-965-4574
Fax: 801-538-9892
Dave Dangerfield, Director
Shirlene Bingham, Manager

6061 Vermont Department of Developmental and Mental Health Services
108 Cherry Street
P.O. Box 70
Burlington, VT 05402-0070
802-652-2000
Fax: 802-652-2005
http://http://healthvermont.gov/mh/
Michael Hartman, Commissioner
Dr. Bill McMains, Medical Director of the Vermont
Theresa Wood, Director Developmental Services

6062 Virginia Department of Mental Health Mental Retardation and Substance Abuse Services
PO Box 1797
Richmond, VA 23218-1797
804-786-3921
800-451-5544
Fax: 804-371-6638
http://www.dmhmrsas.virginia.gov
James Reinhard, Commissioner
Deborah Whitten-Williams, Co-Executive Director

6063 Washington Department of Mental Health
8805 Steilacoom Blvd. SW
Tacoma, WA 98498-4771
253-756-2504
888-713-6010
Fax: 253-756-3911
e-mail: RosexAM@dshs.wa.gov
http://www1.dshs.wa.gov
April Rose, Chief Executive Officer
Jane Brazell, Administrative Secretary

Depression/Mental Health/Books

6064 Wisconsin Department of Mental Health
PO Box 7851
Madison, WI 53707-7851
608-267-7792
Fax: 608-267-7793

Joyce Allen, Executive Director

6065 Wyoming Department of Mental Health
6101 North Yellowstone Road
Room 220
Cheyenne, WY 82002 81
307-777-7094
Fax: 307-777-5580
e-mail: wdh@health.wyo.gov
http://wdh.state.wy.us

Mary Flanderka, Administrator
Barb Metcalf, Fiscal Admin

The Mental Health Division of the Wyoming Department of Health exists to be a leader in providing high-quality behavioral services that anticipate and respond to the changing needs of persons served. Our strategic plan is to advocate for and participate in the development and maintenance of a comprehensive system of mental health services and supports throughout Wyoming, which stresses independence, dignity, security, and recovery.

Books

6066 Anxiety & Depression in Adults & Children
Sage Publications
2455 Teller Road
Thousand Oaks, CA 91320-2218
805-499-0721
Fax: 805-499-0871

Blaise R Simqu, CEO
304 pages

6067 Depression & Antidepressants: A Guide
Lithium Information Center
7617 Mineral Point Road
Suite 300
Madison, WI 53717-1623
608-827-2470
Fax: 608-827-2479
e-mail: mim.miminc.org
http://www.miminc.org

Margaret Baudhuin, Manager
48 pages 1999

6068 Depression Sourcebook
Lowell House Press
220 Avenue of the Stars
Suite 300
Los Angeles, CA 90067
310-552-7555
800-323-
Fax: 310-552-7573

Everything anyone afflicted with a depressive disorder - or the people who care about them - need to know about unipolar and bipolar depression.
266 pages

6069 Depression and Its Treatment
Warner Books
1271 Avenue of the Americas
New York, NY 10020-1300
212-522-7200

Laurence J Kirshbaum, CEO

A layman's guide to help one understand and cope with America's #1 mental health problem.
157 pages

6070 Depression for Dummies
John Wiley & Sons
111 River Street
Hoboken, NJ 07030-5774
201-748-6000
Fax: 201-748-6088
e-mail: info@wiley.com
http://www.wiley.com

Depression For Dummies is to present you with the facts on depression and explain the options for dealing with it..

6071 Depression, the Mood Disease
Johns Hopkins University Press
2715 N Charles Street
Baltimore, MD 21218-4319
410-516-6900
800-537-5487
Fax: 410-516-6998
http://www.jhu.edu/press/index.html

William Brody, President

This book explores the many faces of an illness that will affect as many as 36 million Americans at some point in their lives. Updated to reflect state-of-the-art treatment.
240 pages

6072 Depressive Illnesses: Treatments Bring New Hope
Superintendent of Documents
PO Box 371954
Pittsburgh, PA 15250-7954
202-512-2250
Fax: 202-512-2250

Offers the general public an overview of the various depressive illnesses. Topics include causes, symptoms and types of depression, clinical evaluation and treatment, helpful suggestions for family and friends, and other sources of information.
28 pages

6073 Listening to Depression: How Understanding Your Pain Can Heal Your Life
New Harbinger
5674 Shattuck Avenue
Oakland, CA 94609
800-748-6273
Fax: 510-652-5472
http://www.newharbinger.com

Depression For Dummies is to present you with the facts on depression and explain the options for dealing with it..

6074 Mood Apart
Basic Books
10 E 53rd Street
New York, NY 10022-5244
212-832-5550
Fax: 212-207-7203

C Propopulon, Owner

An overview of the depression and manic depression and the available treatments for them.
363 pages

6075 Overcoming Depression
Harper & Row
10 E 53rd Street
New York, NY 10022-5244
212-207-7000
Fax: 212-207-7203

Jane Friedman, CEO
318 pages

6076 Questions & Answers About Depression & Its Treatment
Charles Press Publishers
PO Box 15715
Philadelphia, PA 19103
215-496-9616
Fax: 215-496-9637

Lauren Meltzer, Owner

All the questions you'd like to ask, asked and answered.
136 pages

6077 The Mindful Way through Depression: Freeing Yourself from Chronic Unhappiness
Guilford Press
72 Spring Street
New York, NY 10012
800-365-7006
Fax: 212-966-6708
e-mail: info@guilford.com
http://www.guilford.com

The Mindful Way through Depression draws on the collective wisdom of four internationally renowned mindfulness experts, including bestselling author Jon Kabat-Zinn, to provide effective relief from the most prevalent psychological disorder.

Depression/Mental Health/Directories

6078 **Yoga for Depression**
Random House
1745 Broadway
New York, NY 10019
212-782-9000
http://www.randomhouse.com
Comprehensive guide to the art and science of Yoga..

Directories

6079 **Depression in the Elderly: a Multimedia Sourcebook**
Greenwood Publishing Group
88 Post Road W
5007
Westport, CT 06880-4208
203-226-3571
800-225-5800
Fax: 203-226-6009
e-mail: prices@greenwood.com
http://www.greenwood.com

John J Miletich, Editor
Wayne Smith, President

Information providers, associations, and television programs related to depression in the elderly. Entries include: Contact information. Principal content of publication is annotated entries for a variety of alternate formats covering material from 1970-96.

6080 **Encyclopedia of Depression**
Facts on File
11 Penn Plaza
Floor 15
New York, NY 10001-2006
212-967-8800
800-322-8755
Fax: 212-967-8107
e-mail: lmilberg@factsonfile.com

This volume defines and explains all terms and topics relating to depression.

170 pages

Journals, Magazines

6081 **Journal of Mental Health and Aging**
Springer Publishing Company
536 Broadway
New York, NY 10012-3915
212-431-4370
Fax: 212-941-7842
e-mail: springer@springerpub.com
http://www.springerpub.com

Donna Cohen, Editor
Rafael Ortiz, Advertising Manager
Ursula Springer, President

Scholarly journal covering aging population for mental health professionals.

6082 **Journal of the American Psychoanalytic Association**
American Psychoanalytic Association
309 E 49th Street
New York, NY 10017-1601
212-752-0450
Fax: 212-593-0571
e-mail: central.office@apsa.org
http://www.apsa.org

Dean K Stine, Executive Director
Dottie Jeffries, Director Public Affairs
Steven T Levy, Editor

Quarterly journal.

250 pages 1911Frequency: 4

6083 **Journals of Gerontology; Psychological Sciences & Social Sciences**
Gerontological Society of America
1030 15th Street NW
Suite 250
Washington, DC 20005-1526
202-842-1275
Fax: 202-842-1150
e-mail: geron@geron.org
http://www.geron.org

Elizabeth Borgen, Contact
Carol Schutz, Executive Director

Two journals under one cover presenting scientific articles and research in the fields of biology and medicine, as they relate to aging.

Frequency: Bimonthly

6084 **Rehabilitation Counseling Bulletin**
American Counseling Association
5999 Stevenson Avenue
Alexandria, VA 22304-3304
703-823-9800
800-347-6647
Fax: 703-823-0252
http://www.counseling.org

Stephren Brooks, Editor
Richard Yep, Executive Director

Journal including new information on the rehabilitation field, career development, and job placement of persons with special needs.

Frequency: Quarterly

Newsletters, Pamphlets

6085 **Adjustment, Adaptation and Accomodation: Psychological Approaches**
National Parkinson Foundation
1501 NW 9th Avenue
Miami, FL 33136-1407
305-547-6666
800-327-4545
Fax: 305-548-4403
http://www.parkinson.org

Jose Garcia-Pedrosa, Executive Director

Coping strategies for Parkinson's disease.

6086 **Bell**
National Mental Health Association
1021 Prince Street
Alexandria, VA 22314-2979
703-684-7722
Fax: 703-684-5968
e-mail: nmhainfo@aol.com
http://www.nmha.org
TDD 800-433-5959

Sandy Alexander, Publications Manager
Patrick Cody, Senior Director Media Relations
Micheal Faenze, CEO

Targets public and private mental health organizations as well as interested corporations, agencies and individuals. The Bell contains information about a variety of issues pertaining to mental health, including: the effects of managed care on mental health care; the implications of Congressional decisions for mental health; prevention efforts on the local, state and national levels; national anti-stigma efforts and national public education camppaigns.

Frequency: Monthly

6087 **Depression and Recovery From Chemical Dependency**
Hazelden
15251 Pleasant Valley Road
Center City, MN 55012-9640
651-257-4010
800-328-9000
Fax: 651-213-4426
http://www.hazelden.org

Ellen Breyer, President

Outlines depression's warning signs.

Depression/Mental Health/Newsletters, Pamphlets

6088 If You're Over 65 and Feeling Depressed...
National Institutes on Mental Health
5600 Fishers Lane
Room 7c-02
Rockville, MD 20857
301-443-3706
Fax: 301-443-6349

Many older people believe that their age alone is responsible for feelings of exhaustion, helplessness and worthlessness. This brochure discusses the causes of depression in the older years, symptoms, types of treatment and where to go for help.

12 pages

6089 Let's Talk About Depression
Superintendent of Documents
PO Box 371954
Pittsburgh, PA 15250-7954
202-512-2250
Fax: 202-512-2250

Targeted especially for inner-city youth. The colorful design will capture attention and focus on depression in a way that young people will understand and identify with.

6090 Lifespan
Nat'l Council of Community Mental Health Center
12300 Twinbrook Parkway
Suite 320
Rockville, MD 20852-1606
301-984-6200
Fax: 301-881-7159

Linda Rosenberg, CEO

Information on tax tips, insurance, medical care, law and legislation for people with mental disabilities.

Frequency: Monthly

6091 Lithium and Manic Depression
Lithium Info. Center-Dean Foundation for Health
7617 Mineral Point Road
Suite 3000
Madison, WI 53717-1623
608-827-2470
Fax: 608-827-2479

Margaret Baudhuin, Manager

A guidebook about lithium and its effects on bipolar affective disorders and manic depression.

32 pages

6092 Mental Health Law News
Interwood Publications
3 Interwood Place
20241
Cincinnati, OH 45220-1821
513-221-3715

Mental health case law summaries — malpractice, patient rights, discrimination, alcoholism, guardianship, negligence, professional liability, commitment, drug dependency and conservatorship.

6 pages Frequency: Monthly

6093 Mental Health Law Reporter
Business Publishers
951 Pershing Drive
Silver Spring, MD 20910-4400
301-587-6300
800-274-6737
Fax: 301-584-4530
e-mail: bpinews@bpinews.com
http://www.bpinews.com

Leonard A Eiserer, Publisher
Bonnie Becker, Editor
Adam Goldstein, President

Brings you the most timely, focused and thorough information on the legal issues that concern mental health practitioners in mental health litigation. Topics include: malpractice litigation, patient-therapist confidentiality, sexual victimization of patients, the insanity defense, social security administrative case law and much more.

8 pages Frequency: newsletter

6094 Mental and Physical Disability Law Reporter
American Bar Association
740 15th Street NW
Washington, DC 20005-1019
202-662-1570
Fax: 202-662-1032
e-mail: cmpdl@abanet.org
http://www.abanet.org/disability

John Parry, Executive Director

Covers case law, legislative and regulatory developments that affect persons with mental or physical disabilities.

6095 NFDI Newsletter
National Foundation for Depressive Illness
PO Box 2257
New York, NY 10116-2257
212-268-4260
800-248-4344
Fax: 212-268-4434
e-mail: pross@att.net
http://www.depression.org

Amy C Russell, Administrator

To correct the myths and misconceptions surrounding the illness and help reverse the devastating effects depression has on the individual and our society and to inform the public, primary health care providers, other healthcare professionals and corporations about depression and manic depression and to provide the information about correct diagnosis and treatment and the availability of qualified doctors and support groups.

4 pages

6096 National Council News
Nat'l Council of Community Mental Health Center
12300 Twinbrook Parkway
Suite 320
Rockville, MD 20852-1606
301-984-6200
Fax: 301-881-7159

Linda Rosenberg, CEO

Gives you news about legislative and regulatory developments, public policy and mental health issues, editorials, perspectives, new publications and seminars.

6097 National Institute of Mental Health
6001 Executive Boulevard
Room 8184
N Bethesda, MD 20852-3831
301-443-4513
866-615-6464
Fax: 301-443-4279
e-mail: nimhinfo@nih.gov
http://www.nimh.nih.gov

Jac Cramer, Project Director

A variety of publications is available from this Federal research Institute that conducts and supports research that focuses on the causes, diagnosis, prevention and treatment of severe mental illnesses. The Institute Office of Communications provides a public inquiries line that is staffed with trained information specialists who respond to information requests from the lay public, clinicians, and the scientific community.

6098 Panic Disorder
National Institutes of Health
5600 Fishers Lane
Room 7c-02
Rockville, MD 20857
301-443-3706
Fax: 301-443-6349

Written for the lay public, this pamphlet contains a description of panic disorder, gives the symptoms, describes treatment methods, and encourages the person who has the symptoms to seek treatment.

6099 Public Policy Report
National Council of Community Mental
Health Center 12300 Twinbrook Parkway
Suite 320
Rockville, MD 20852
301-984-6200
Fax: 301-881-7159

Linda Rosenberg, CEO

Information on promoting advocacy, action and association for people with mental disabilities.

Depression/Mental Health/Research Centers

Frequency: Monthly

6100 Understanding Panic Disorder
National Institutes of Health
5600 Fishers Lane
Room 7c-02
Rockville, MD 20857
301-443-3706
Fax: 301-443-6349

Offers information on what an panic disorder is, symptoms, causes, treatment, medications and therapy.

6101 Useful Information on Phobias and Panic
Superintendent of Documents
PO Box 371954
Pittsburgh, PA 15250-7954
202-512-2250
Fax: 202-512-2250

This booklet provides information on both phobias and panic. Symptoms, causes and treatments of these disorders are referred to. If you know someone who is excessively fearful, this booklet will be of great help to them in understanding their problem.

40 pages

Research Centers

6102 National Alliance for Research on Schizophrenia and Depression
60 Cuttermill Road
Suite 404
Great Neck, NY 11021-3104
516-829-0091
Fax: 516-487-6930
e-mail: info@narsad.org

Steve Doochin, Executive Director

Raises and distributes funds for scientific research into the causes, cures and treatments, and prevention of severe mental illness, primarily schizophrenia and depression.

6103 St. Louis University: Department of Psychiatry
1221 S Grand Boulevard
Saint Louis, MO 63104-1016
314-577-8742
Fax: 314-664-7248
e-mail: waldmans@wpogate.slu.edu
http://www.slucare.edu/clinical/psychiatry

Adult and child psychiatry, geriatric psychiatry, psychopharmacology, psychology, and behavioral medicine, including psychophysiologic reactions in pyschotherapeutic relationships, personality profiles in a general hospital population, emotional response to cardiovascular surgery, emotional responses of children to chronic illness, factors influencing career choice in medicine, and impact of direct entry into psychiatric training on residents and their training programs.

6104 University of Michigan: Tecumster Mental Health Study
Department of Epidemiology
Ann Arbor, MI 48109
734-764-5435
Fax: 734-764-3192

George Caplan PhD, Chairman

6105 University of Minnesota: Division of Health Services Research and Policy
420 Delaware Street SE
Minneapolis, MN 55455
612-624-6151
Fax: 612-624-2196
e-mail: krale001@maroon.tc.umn.edu
http://www.hsr.umn.edu

Long-term care, health insurance, managed health care, patient care outcomes, rural health services, and health policy analysis.

6106 University of Pennsylvania: Depression Research Unit
School of Medicine, Department of Psychiatry
3600 Spruce Street
Philadelphia, PA 19104-4211
215-662-3462
Fax: 215-662-6443

Jay D Amsterdam MD, Director
Maryanne Giampapa, Manager

Focuses on mental health and depression.

6107 University of Pittsburgh Medical Center: Clinic Western Psychiatric Institute and Clinic
3811 Ohara Street
Pittsburgh, PA 15213-2593
412-624-9167
http://www.wpic.pitt.edu

Oscar G Bukstein MD

Advancement of basic and clinical knowledge in psychological, biological, environmental, and social interactions related to mental health and psychiatric care. Conducts research on psychiatric disorders, including depression, schizophrenia, anorexia nervosa, Alzheimer's disease, autism, anxiety, obsessive-compulsive disorders, and borderline disorders.adolescent and young adult disorders, affective disorders, psychogeriatrics, schizophrenia, and children's services. Clinical laboratory investigations include studies in clinical pharmacology, neuroendocrinology, psychophysiology, neuropharmacology, neurophysics, molecular neurobiology and genetics, and EEG sleep. Also researches health habits and precursors of medical disease states such as hypertension, diabetes, obesity, effects of drug abuse, and epidemiology of psychiatric disorders.

6108 Yale University: Behavioral Medicine Clinic
Yale School of Medicine
333 Cedar Street
New Haven, CT 06510-3206
203-785-4095

Hoyle Leigh MD, Director
Margaret Wylie, Manager

Focuses on mental disorders including schizophrenia and depression.

6109 Yale University: Ribicoff Research Facilities
34 Park Street
New Haven, CT 06510
203-432-0828
Fax: 203-562-7079

George Heninger MD, Director
Terri Boustad, Administrator

Clinical research in the areas of schizophrenia, depression and mental disorders.

Diabetes/Associations & Organizations

Associations & Organizations

6110 American Association of Diabetes Educators
200 W. Madison Street
Suite 800
Chicago, IL 60606
312-424-2426
800-338-3633
Fax: 312-424-2427
e-mail: communications@aadenet.org
http://www.diabeteseducator.org
Amparo Gonzalez, RN, BSN, CDE, President
Deborah S. Fillman, RD, LD, MS, C, TREASURER

An independent, multidisciplinary organization of health professionals involved in teaching persons with diabetes. The mission is to enhance the competence of health professionals who teach persons with diabetes, advance the specialty practice of diabetes education, and to improve the quality of diabetes education and care for all those affected by diabetes.

6111 American Diabetes Association
380 SE Spokane
#110
Portland, OR 97202
503-736-2770
Fax: 503-736-2774
e-mail: AskADA@diabetes.org
http://www.diabetes.org
Toni L Sutton, Area Director

Offers a network of 52 affiliates with over 55,000 volunteers, including a professional membership of more than 10,000 physicians, social workers, nutritionists, educators and nurses.

6112 American Diabetes Association Southern: New Jersey District Office
1060 Kings Highway N
Ste 309
Cherry Hill, NJ 8034
856-482-9047
Fax: 856-667-8631
http://www.diabetes.org
Susan Yannessa, Executive Director

6113 American Diabetes Association: Oklahoma City District Office
3000 United Founders Boulevard
Suite 108
Oklahoma City, OK 73112
405-840-3881
Fax: 405-840-3899
e-mail: AskADA@diabetes.org
http://www.diabetes.org
R. Stewart Perry, Chairman
John B. Buse, MD, PhD, President

6114 American Diabetes Association: Alaska Area Office
801 W Fireweed Lane
Suite 103
Anchorage, AK 99503
907-272-1424
Fax: 907-272-1428
http://www.diabetes.org
Michelle Cassano, Executive Director

6115 American Diabetes Association: Arizona Area Office
8125 N. 23rd Avenue
Suite 222
Phoenix, AZ 85021
602-861-4731
Fax: 602-995-1344
http://www.diabetes.org
Robert A. Rizza, President
Alexandria , Chief Executive Officer

6116 American Diabetes Association: Arkansas
320 Executive Court
Suite 104
Little Rock, AR 72205
501-221-7444
Fax: 501-221-3138
e-mail: nperkins@diabetes.org
http://www.diabetes.org
Lynn Nicholas, FACHE, Chief Executive Officer
Lawrence T. Smith, Chairman

6117 American Diabetes Association: Atlanta Metro Area Office, Georgia
17 Executive Park Dr., N.E
Suite 115
Atlanta, GA 30329
404-320-7100
Fax: 404-320-0025
e-mail: dmcdonald@diabetes.org
http://www.diabetes.org
Diana McDonald, Market Manager
John B. Buse, MD, President

6118 American Diabetes Association: Baton Rouge District Office
2644 S Sherwood Forest Blvd
Suite 122
Baton Rouge, LA 70816
225-216-3980
Fax: 225-295-7005
e-mail: AskADA@diabetes.org
http://www.diabetes.org
R. Stewart Perry, Chairman
John B. Buse, MD, PhD, President

6119 American Diabetes Association: Border Area Office
333 W Ft. Lowell Road
Suite 123
Tucson, AZ 85705
520-795-3711
Fax: 520-795-1179
http://www.diabetes.org
Robert A. Rizza, President
Alexandria , Chief Executive Officer

6120 American Diabetes Association: Bowling Green District Office
161 St. Matthews Avenue
Suite 3
Louisville, KY 40207
502-452-6072
Fax: 502-893-2698
http://www.diabetes.org
Robert A. Rizza, President
Alexandria , Chief Executive Officer

6121 American Diabetes Association: California
2720 Gateway Oaks Drive
Suite 110
Sacramento, CA 95833
916-924-3232
Fax: 916-924-0529
http://www.diabetes.org
Robert A. Rizza, President
Alexandria , Chief Executive Officer

6122 American Diabetes Association: Cedar Rapids District Office
St. Lukes Resource Center
Box RC15
Cedar Rapids, IA 52406
319-247-5124
Fax: 319-247-5125
http://www.diabetes.org
Kathy E. Eno, DIRECTOR

Diabetes/Associations & Organizations

6123 American Diabetes Association: Central Ohio Area Office
471 E Broad Street
Suite 1630
Columbus, OH 43215
614-436-1917
Fax: 614-436-0348
e-mail: AskADA@diabetes.org
http://www.diabetes.org

R. Stewart Perry, Chairman
John B Buse, President, Medicine and Science

6124 American Diabetes Association: Central Pennsylvania Area
3544 North Progress Avenue
Suite 101
Harrisburg, PA 17110
717-657-4310
Fax: 717-657-4320
http://www.diabetes.org

Robert A. Rizza, President
Alexandria, Chief Executive Officer

6125 American Diabetes Association: Columbus District Office
17 Executive Park
Suite 115
Atlanta, GA 30329
404-320-7100
Fax: 404-320-0025
http://www.diabetes.org

Robert A. Rizza, President
Alexandria, Chief Executive Officer

6126 American Diabetes Association: Connecticut
306 Industrial Park Road
Suite 105
Middletown, CT 06457
203-639-0385
Fax: 860-632-5098
http://www.diabetes.org

Lynn Nicholas, FACHE, Chief Executive Officer
Lawrence T. Smith, Chair

6127 American Diabetes Association: Delaware/Eastern Shore Area Office
Community Service Building
100 W 10th Street
Suite 1002
Wilmington, DE 19801-1652
302-656-0030
Fax: 302-656-7331
e-mail: AskADA@diabetes.org
http://www.diabetes.org

Greg Elfers, Chief Development Officer
Debbie Johnson, Executive Vice President, Chief

6128 American Diabetes Association: Districtof Columbia
1025 Connecticut Avenue NW
Suite 1005
Washington, DC 20036
202-331-8303
Fax: 202-331-1402
e-mail: AskADA@diabetes.org
http://www.diabetes.org

R. Stewart Perry, Chairman
John B. Buse, MD, PhD, President

6129 American Diabetes Association: East Washington/North Idaho District Office
3117 E. Chaser Lane
#201
Spokane, WA 99223
509-624-7478
Fax: 509-624-7212
e-mail: AskADA@diabetes.org
http://www.diabetes.org

R. Stewart Perry, Chairman
John B Buse, President, Medicine and Science

6130 American Diabetes Association: Eastern Regional Office
7 Washington Square
Albany, NY 12205
518-218-1755
Fax: 518-218-0114
http://www.diabetes.org

Robert A. Rizza, President
Alexandria, Chief Executive Officer

6131 American Diabetes Association: Eugene Branch Office
2350 Oakmont Way
Suite 208
Eugene, OR 97401
541-343-0735
Fax: 541-342-1491
e-mail: AskADA@diabetes.org
http://www.diabetes.org

R. Stewart Perry, Chairman
John B Buse, President, Medicine and Science

6132 American Diabetes Association: Great Lakes and Heartland Regional Office, Wisconsin
2323 N Mayfair Road
Suite 502
Wauwatosa, WI 53226
414-778-5500
Fax: 414-778-5511
http://www.diabetes.org

Robert A. Rizza, President
Alexandria, Chief Executive Officer

6133 American Diabetes Association: Greater Hampton Roads Area Office
870 Greenbrier Circle, Greenbrier Tower II
Suite 404
Chesapeake, VA 23320
757-424-6662
Fax: 757-420-0490
http://www.diabetes.org

Robert A. Rizza, President
Alexandria, Chief Executive Officer

6134 American Diabetes Association: Hawaii Area Office
1500 S Beretania Street
Suite 111
Honolulu, HI 96826
808-947-5979
Fax: 808-947-5978
e-mail: AskADA@diabetes.org
http://www.diabetes.org

R. Stewart Perry, Chairman
John B Buse, President, Medicine and Science

6135 American Diabetes Association: Huntsville District Office
117c Longwood Drive SE
Huntsville, AL 35801
256-539-4404
Fax: 256-539-8285
e-mail: AskADA@diabetes.org
http://www.diabetes.org

Daniel Perry, Executive Director
John M. Taylor, Executive Vice President

6136 American Diabetes Association: Iowa Area Office
2600 72nd Street
Suite O
Urbandale, IA 50322
515-276-2237
Fax: 515-251-5831
http://www.diabetes.org

Robert A. Rizza, President
Alexandria, Chief Executive Officer

6137 American Diabetes Association: Kansas Area Office
837 S. Hillside
Wichita, KS 67211
316-684-6091
Fax: 316-684-5675
e-mail: askADA@diabetes.org
http://www.diabetes.org

Lynn Nicholas, FACHE, Chief Executive Officer
Lawrence T. Smith, Chair

Diabetes/Associations & Organizations

6138 **American Diabetes Association: Kentucky Area Office**
161 Saint Matthews Avenue
Suite 3
Louisville, KY 40207
502-452-6072
Fax: 502-893-2698
e-mail: AskADA@diabetes.org
http://www.diabetes.org

R. Stewart Perry, Chairman
John B Buse, President, Medicine and Science

6139 **American Diabetes Association: Madison District Office**
6400 Gisholt Drive
Suite 213
Monona, WI 53713
608-222-7785
Fax: 608-222-7795
e-mail: AskADA@diabetes.org
http://www.diabetes.org

R. Stewart Perry, Chairman
John B. Buse, MD, PhD, President

6140 **American Diabetes Association: Maryland Area Office**
800 Wyman Park Drive
Suite 110
Baltimore, MD 21211
410-265-0075
Fax: 410-235-4048
e-mail: AskADA@diabetes.org
http://www.diabetes.org

R. Stewart Perry, Chairman
John B Buse, President, Medicine and Science

6141 **American Diabetes Association: Memphis District Office**
5583 Murray Road
Suite 200A
Memphis, TN 38119
901-682-8232
Fax: 901-682-8170
http://www.diabetes.org

Robert A. Rizza, President
Alexandria, Chief Executive Officer

6142 **American Diabetes Association: Mid-America Regional Office**
1944 E Sunshine Street
Suite A
Springfield, MO 65804-1510
417-624-8455
Fax: 573-875-2152

Renee Paulsell, Executive Director

6143 **American Diabetes Association: Minnesota Area Office**
5100 Gamble Drive
Suite 394
St. Louis Park, MN 55416
763-593-5333
Fax: 763-593-1520
http://www.diabetes.org

Robert A. Rizza, President
Alexandria, Chief Executive Officer

6144 **American Diabetes Association: Mississippi Area Office**
200 Office Park Drive
Suite 303
Birmingham, AL 35223
205-870-5172
Fax: 205-879-2903
http://www.diabetes.org

Robert A. Rizza, President
Alexandria, Chief Executive Officer

6145 **American Diabetes Association: Missoula District Office**
3203 3rd Avenue North
Suite 203
Billings, MT 59101
406-256-0616
Fax: 406-896-0289
http://www.diabetes.org

Robert A. Rizza, President
Alexandria, Chief Executive Officer

6146 **American Diabetes Association: Missouri Area Office**
1944 E Sunshine Street
Suite A
Springfield, MO 65804
417-890-8400
Fax: 417-890-8484
http://www.diabetes.org

Robert A. Rizza, President
Alexandria, Chief Executive Officer

6147 **American Diabetes Association: Montana**
3203 3rd Avenue North
Suite 203
Billings, MT 59101
406-256-0616
Fax: 406-256-0616
e-mail: AskADA@diabetes.org
http://www.diabetes.org

R. Stewart Perry, Chairman
John B Buse, President, Medicine and Science

6148 **American Diabetes Association: Mountain States & Pacific/Northwest Regional Office**
2480 W 26th Avenue
Suite 120b
Denver, CO 80211
720-855-1102
Fax: 720-855-1302
http://www.diabetes.org

Robert A. Rizza, President
Alexandria, Chief Executive Officer

6149 **American Diabetes Association: Nebraska/South Dakota Area Office**
14216 Dayton Circle
Suite 6
Omaha, NE 68137
402-571-1101
Fax: 402-572-8141
e-mail: AskADA@diabetes.org
http://www.diabetes.org

R. Stewart Perry, Chairman
John B Buse, President, Medicine and Science

6150 **American Diabetes Association: Nevada**
2785 East Desert Inn Road
Suite 140
Las Vegas, NV 89121
702-369-9995
Fax: 702-369-3717
http://www.diabetes.org

Robert A. Rizza, President
Alexandria, Chief Executive Officer

6151 **American Diabetes Association: New Mexico Area Office**
2625 Pennsylvania NE
Suite 225
Albuquerque, NM 87110
505-266-5716
Fax: 505-268-4533
http://www.diabetes.org

Robert A. Rizza, President
Alexandria, Chief Executive Officer

Non profit organization gives out literature on prevention and to newly diagnosed diabetics.

6152 **American Diabetes Association: New Orleans District Office, Louisiana**
2644 S Sherwood Forest Blvd.
Suite 122
Baton Rouge, LA 70816
225-216-3980
Fax: 225-295-7005
http://www.diabetes.org

Robert A. Rizza, President
Alexandria, Chief Executive Officer

Diabetes/Associations & Organizations

6153 American Diabetes Association: New York City Area Office
7 Washington Square
Albany, NY 12205
518-218-1755
Fax: 518-218-0114
http://www.diabetes.org

Robert A. Rizza, President
Alexandria, Chief Executive Officer

6154 American Diabetes Association: North Dakota
1323 23rd Street South
Suite C
Fargo, ND 58103
701-234-0123
Fax: 701-235-3080
http://www.diabetes.org

Lynn Nicholas, FACHE, Chief Executive Officer
Lawrence T. Smith, Chair

6155 American Diabetes Association: Northeast Texas/North Louisiana Area Office
4100 Alpha Road
Suite 100
Dallas, TX 75244
972-392-1181
Fax: 972-392-1366
e-mail: AskADA@diabetes.org
http://www.diabetes.org

Quincy Neal, EVP

6156 American Diabetes Association: Northern Ohio/Cleveland Area Office
4500 Rockside Road
Suite 440
Independence, OH 44131
216-328-9989
888-342-2383
Fax: 216-328-0007
e-mail: AskADA@diabetes.org
http://www.diabetes.org

R. Stewart Perry, Chairman
John B Buse, President, Medicine and Science

6157 American Diabetes Association: Oklahoma Area Office
6600 South Yale Avenue
Suite 1310
Tulsa, OK 74136
918-492-3839
Fax: 918-492-4262
http://www.diabetes.org

Robert A. Rizza, President
Alexandria Roberson, Chief Executive Officer
Janice Curtis, Area Associate

Diabetes information & research

6158 American Diabetes Association: Oregon Area Office
380 SE Spokane Street
Suite 110
Portland, OR 97202
503-736-2770
Fax: 503-736-2774
http://www.diabetes.org

Robert A. Rizza, President
Alexandria, Chief Executive Officer

6159 American Diabetes Association: Rhode Island/Massachusetts Area Office
222 Richmond St
Suite 204
Providence, RI 02903
401-351-0498
Fax: 401-351-1674
http://www.diabetes.org

Bruce Davis, Executive Director
R. Stewart Perry, Chair

6160 American Diabetes Association: Seattle Area Office
1730 Minor Avenue
Suite 130
Seattle, WA 98101
206-282-4616
Fax: 206-282-4729
http://www.diabetes.org

Robert A. Rizza, President
Alexandria, Chief Executive Officer

6161 American Diabetes Association: Sioux Fallls District Office
14216 Dayton Circle
Suite 6
Sioux Falls, SD 68137
402-571-1101
Fax: 402-572-8141
http://www.diabetes.org

Lawrence T. Smith, Chairman
Lynn Nicholas, FACHE, Chief Executive Officer

6162 American Diabetes Association: South Central Regional Office
4100 Alpha Road
Suite 100
Dallas, TX 75244
972-392-1181
800-252-
Fax: 972-392-1366
e-mail: AskADA@diabetes.org
http://www.diabetes.org

R. Stewart Perry, Chairman
John B Buse, President, Medicine and Science

6163 American Diabetes Association: South Coastal Regional Office, Central Florida Area
1101 N Lake Destiny Road
Suite 415
Maitland, FL 32751
407-660-1926
Fax: 407-660-1080
http://www.diabetes.org

Lawrence T. Smith, Chairman
Lynn Nicholas, FACHE, Chief Executive Officer

6164 American Diabetes Association: Southeast Michigan Area Office
30200 Telegraph Road
Suite 105
Bingham Farms, MI 48025
248-433-3830
Fax: 248-433-1095
http://www.diabetes.org

Lynn Nicholas, FACHE, Chief Executive Officer
Lawrence T. Smith, Chair

6165 American Diabetes Association: Southern Regional Office, Eastern North Carolina
2418 Blue Ridge Road
Suite 206
Raleigh, NC 27607
919-743-5400
Fax: 919-783-7838
http://www.diabetes.org

Robert A. Rizza, President
Alexandria, Chief Executive Officer

6166 American Diabetes Association: Tennessee Area Office
4205 Hillsboro Pike
Suite 200
Nashville, TN 37215
615-298-3066
Fax: 615-292-5357
e-mail: AskADA@diabetes.org
http://www.diabetes.org

R. Stewart Perry, Chairman
John B Buse, President, Medicine and Science

Diabetes/Books

6167 American Diabetes Association: Upstate Alabama Area Office
200 Office Park Drive
Suite 303
Birmingham, AL 35223
205-870-5172
Fax: 205-879-2903
http://www.diabetes.org

Robert A. Rizza, President
Alexandria, Chief Executive Officer

6168 American Diabetes Association: Utah Area Office
182 S 600 E Suite 100
Suite 30
Salt Lake City, UT 84102
801-363-3024
Fax: 801-363-3031
e-mail: AskADA@diabetes.org
http://www.diabetes.org

Laura Landon, Executive Director

6169 American Diabetes Association: Virginia Area Office
530 E. Main Street
Suite 200
Richmond, VA 23219
804-225-8038
Fax: 804-225-8211
e-mail: AskADA@diabetes.org
http://www.diabetes.org

R. Stewart Perry, Chairman
John B. Buse, MD, PhD, President

6170 American Diabetes Association: West Virginia/Southern Ohio
PO Box 238
Hurricane, WV 25526
304-768-2596
Fax: 304-562-1887
e-mail: AskADA@diabetes.org
http://www.diabetes.org

Lynn Monday, Manager

6171 American Diabetes Association: Western Pennsylvania Area Office
300 Penn Center Boulevard
Suite 602
Pittsburgh, PA 15235
412-824-1181
Fax: 412-824-2191
http://www.diabetes.org

Robert A. Rizza, President
Alexandria, Chief Executive Officer

6172 American Diabetes Association: Wyoming District Office
2480 W. 26th Avenue
Suite 120B
Denver, CO 80211
720-855-1102
Fax: 720-855-1302
http://www.diabetes.org

Robert A. Rizza, President
Alexandria, Chief Executive Officer

6173 American Dietetic Association
120 South Riverside Plaza
Suite 2000
Chicago, IL 60606-6995
312-899-0040
800-877-1600
Fax: 312-899-4817
e-mail: cade@eatright.org
http://www.eatright.org

Connie B. Diekman, MEd., President
Susan C. Finn, PhD, Chair

Offers information and support to those with special diet needs due to a variety of health issues, includiung diabetes and allergies.

6174 American Gastroenterological Association
4930 Del Ray Avenue
Suite 700
Bethesda, MD 20814
301-654-2055
Fax: 301-654-5920
e-mail: member@gastro.org
http://www.gastro.org

Nicholas F. LaRusso, MD, AGAF, President
Gail A. Hecht, MD, MS, AGAF, VP

Physicians of internal medicine certified in gastroenterology; radiologists, pathologists, surgeons, and physiologists with special interest and competency in gastroenterology. Studies normal and abnormal conditions of the digestive organs and problems connected with their metabolism; conducts scientific research; offers placement services.

6175 Black Experience
306 Industrial Park Road
Suite 105
Middletown, CT 06457
203-639-0385
Fax: 860-632-5098
e-mail: AskADA@diabetes.org
http://www.diabetes.org

Beatriz Gomez, Market Director/Programs
John Buse, President

Designed to increase awareness of diabetes in the black community.

6176 National Certification Board for Diabetes Educators
435 N Michigan Avenue
Suite 1717
Chicago, IL 60611-4066
312-644-0828
Fax: 312-644-8557

The Board for Diabetes Educators is dedicated to promoting excellence in the field of diabetes education through the development, maintenance, and protection of the certified Diabetes Educator credential and the certification process.

6177 National Diabetes Action Network for the Blind
National Federation of the Blind
1800 Johnson Street
Baltimore, MD 21230-4914
410-659-9314
Fax: 410-685-5653

Marc Maurer, President

Leading support and information organization of persons losing vision due to diabetes. Provides personal contact and resource information with other blind diabetics about non-visual techniques of independently managing diabetes, monitoring glucose levels, measuring insulin and other matters concerning diabetes. Publishes 'Voice of the Diabetic,' the leading publication about diabetes and blindness.

6178 National Diabetes Information Clearinghouse
1 Information Way
Bethesda, MD 20892-2560
301-654-3327
800-860-8747
Fax: 703-738-4929
e-mail: ndic@info.niddk.nih.gov
http://www.niddk.nih.gov

Griffin P Rodgers, M.D, Director
Judith Fradkin, MD, Executive Editor

Offers various materials, resources, books, pamphlets and more for persons and families in the area of diabetes.

Books

6179 101 Tips for Improving Your Blood Sugar
American Diabetes Association
1701 N Beauregard Street
Alexandria, VA 22311-1742
800-232-3472
Fax: 703-549-6995
http://www.diabetes.org

Lee Barona, National Call Center Director
Jacqueline Amaya, Operations Manager

Diabetes/Books

Tips for 101 common situations and questions to reduce the risk of complications from blood sugar at the wrong level.

122 pages

6180 50 Secrets of the Longest Living People with Diabetes
Perseus Books Group
387 Park Avenue South
New York, NY 10016   212-340-8100
http://www.perseusbooksgroup.com
Sheri R Colberg MD, Author
Steven V Edelman MD, Author

From interviews with more than fifty people who have thrived with the condition for as many as 84 years, the authors distill their lifelong habits into fifty user-friendly, easy-to-adopt secrets.

6181 Balance Your Act: A Book for Adults with Diabetes
Pritchett & Hull
3440 Oakcliff Road
Suite 110
Atlanta, GA 30340-3006   770-451-0602
                            800-241-4925
Betty Westmoreland, President
96 pages

6182 Caring for the Diabetic Soul
American Diabetes Association
1660 Duke Street
Suite 100
Alexandria, VA 22314-3427
                 800-232-3472
            Fax: 703-549-6995
            http://www.diabetes.org

Restoring emotional balance for yourself and your family.

213 pages

6183 Clinical Practice Recommendations
American Diabetes Association
1660 Duke Street
Suite 100
Alexandria, VA 22314-3427
                 800-232-3472
            Fax: 703-549-6995
            http://www.diabetes.org

Features all current position and consensus statements of the American Diabetes Association.

6184 Control Diabetes the Easy Way
Random House Trade Books
400 Hahn Road
Westminster, MD 21157-4627
                 800-733-
            Fax: 800-659-2436

6185 Diabetes 101
Chronimed Publishing
PO Box 59032
Minneapolis, MN 55459   612-513-6475
                           800-848-2793
                      Fax: 952-443-2806

Revised and expanded second edition. A layman's guide to everything you need to know to live healthfully with diabetes.

175 pages

6186 Diabetes A to Z
American Diabetes Association
1660 Duke Street
Alexandria, VA 22314-3473
                 800-232-3472
            Fax: 703-549-6995
            http://www.diabetes.org

Dictionary-style guidebook discussing basic terms and issues concerning diabetes. Third edition.

202 pages

6187 Diabetes Annual Vol. 8
Elsevier Scientific Publishing Company
655 Avenue of the Americas
New York, NY 10010-5107   212-989-5800
                       Fax: 212-633-3965

504 pages

6188 Diabetes Burnout: What To Do When You Can't Take It Anymore
American Diabetes Association
1701 North Beauregard Street
Alexandria, VA 22311
                 800-342-2383
            http://www.diabetes.org
William H Polonsky PhD/CDE, Author

Provides the tools you need to keep from being overwhelmed, addressing such issues as dealing with friends and family, and how you can better handle the stress for better health.

348 pages

6189 Diabetes Care Made Easy
Chronimed Publishing
PO Box 59032
Minneapolis, MN 55459   612-513-6475
                           800-848-2793
                      Fax: 952-443-2806

Written and designed for both adults and for children with limited reading skills, this easy-to-read book explains how to exercise and eat for better health, prevent foot problems, test blood sugar, cope with emotions, take insulin, and more. Also available in Spanish.

180 pages

6190 Diabetes Education Goals
American Diabetes Association
1660 Duke Street
Suite 100
Alexandria, VA 22314-3427
                 800-232-3472
            Fax: 703-549-6995
            http://www.diabetes.org

Features advice on how to assess, plan, and evaluate patient education and counseling programs. Covers both short-term and in-depth goals. Focuses on the education process and assessing the unique needs of each patient.

64 pages

6191 Diabetes Medical Nutrition Therapy
American Diabetes Association
1660 Duke Street
Suite 100
Alexandria, VA 22314-3427
                 800-232-3472
            Fax: 703-549-6995
            http://www.diabetes.org

A professional guide to management and nutrition education resources. Provides in-depth coverage of nutrition assessment, goal setting, intervention, and outcome evaluation. Information is provided on specific resources and case studies are cited for practical examples.

6192 Diabetes Mellitus: A Practical Handbook
Bull Publishing
PO Box 208
Palo Alto, CA 94302   650-322-2855
                         800-676-2855
                    Fax: 650-327-3300
           e-mail: bullpublishing@msn.com
                http://www.bullpub.com

Helpful and user-friendly, the guide teaches readers how to balance diet, medication, and exercise for optimal health, 7th edition.

212 pages

Diabetes/Books

6193 Diabetes Self-Management
RA Rapaport Publishing
150 W 22nd Street
Suite 800
New York, NY 10011-2421
212-989-0200
800-234-0923
Fax: 212-989-4786
e-mail: editor@diabetes-self-mgmt.com
http://www.diabetesselfmanagement.com
Ingrid Strauch, Managing Editor

Publishes practical, how-to information, focusing on the day-to-day and long-term aspects of diabetes in a positive and upbeat style. Gives subscribers up-to-date news, facts, and advice to help them maintain their wellness and make informed decisions regarding their health.
56 pages

6194 Diabetes Sourcebook - Vol. 3
Omnigraphics
Penobscot Building
Detroit, MI 48226
313-961-1340
Fax: 800-875-1340
Peter E Ruffner, President

6195 Diabetes Teaching Guide for People Who Use Insulin
Joslin Diabetes Center
1 Joslin Place
Boston, MA 02215-5306
617-732-2400
Fax: 617-732-2487

Discusses the causes of diabetes, the role of diet and exercise, meal planning and complications. Also provide information on drawing blood, mixing and injecting insulin.

6196 Diabetes for Dummies
For Dummies
111 River Street
Hoboken, NJ 07030-5774
201-748-6000
Fax: 201-748-6088
http://www.dummies.com
Alan L Rubin MD, Author

Provides the most up-to-date information about the disease, covering everything from new medications to recent studies on ethnic groups and children.
408 pages

6197 Diabetes in Old Age
John Wiley & Sons
605 3rd Avenue
6th Floor
New York, NY 10158-180
212-850-6000
Fax: 212-850-6088

Designed to provide clinicians with basic practical information on the problems, care and management associated with this disease.
302 pages

6198 Diabetes: A Guide to Living Well
Chronimed Publishing
PO Box 59032
Minneapolis, MN 55459
612-513-6475
800-848-2793
Fax: 952-443-2806

Offers a guide to helping the person with diabetes design a program of individualized self-care and gain the willingness to follow it. Also tells how to deal with diet, exercise, stress, emotions, negative beliefs, and self-image.
450 pages

6199 Diabetes: Your Complete Exercise Guide
Human Kinetics Publishers
PO Box 5076
Champaign, IL 61825-5076
217-351-5076
800-747-4457
Fax: 217-351-2674
e-mail: humank@hkusa.com
http://www.humankinetics.com

Part of the Cooper Clinic and Research Institute Fitness Series providing exercise rehabilitation for persons with diabetes.
144 pages

6200 Diabetic Low-Fat & No-Fat Meals in Minutes
Chronimed Publishing
PO Box 59032
Minneapolis, MN 55459
612-513-6475
800-848-2793
Fax: 952-443-2806

Includes more than 250 recipes, 60 days of diabetic menus, and 16 pages of full-color photographs. Each recipe features a complete nutrition analysis, including diabetic exchanges.
335 pages

6201 Diabetic's Guide to Health and Fitness
Human Kinetics Publishers
PO Box 5076
Champaign, IL 61825-5076
217-351-5076
800-747-4457
Fax: 217-351-2674
e-mail: humank@hkusa.com
http://www.humankinetics.com

Information about achieving and maintaining physical fitness and proper health living with diabetes.
272 pages

6202 Diabetic's Innovative Cookbook
Henry Holt & Company
115 W 18th Street
New York, NY 10011-4113
212-886-9200
Fax: 212-633-0748
John Sterling, CEO

6203 Dr. Bernstein's Diabetes Solution
Chronimed Publishing
PO Box 59032
Minneapolis, MN 55459
612-513-6475
800-848-2793
Fax: 952-443-2806

A complete guide to achieving normal blood sugars with strong emphasis on diet and up-to-date information on products, insulins, and oral agents.
416 pages

6204 Fitness Book: For People with Diabetes
American Diabetes Association
1660 Duke Street
Suite 100
Alexandria, VA 22314-3427
800-232-3472
Fax: 703-549-6995
http://www.diabetes.org

Advice on learning to exercise to lose weight, exercise safely, increase your competitive edge, get your mind and body ready to exercise, and more.
149 pages

6205 How To Cook for People with Diabetes
American Diabetes Association
1660 Duke Street
Suite 100
Alexandria, VA 22314-3427
800-232-3472
Fax: 703-549-6995
http://www.diabetes.org

150 recipes featuring unusual techniques.
205 pages

6206 Intensive Diabetes Management
American Diabetes Association
1660 Duke Street
Suite 100
Alexandria, VA 22314-3427
800-232-3472
Fax: 703-549-6995
http://www.diabetes.org

Diabetes/Books

Delivers practical advice on how to help your patients achieve better glucose control through intensified management.

128 pages

6207 Learning to Live Well with Diabetes
Chronimed Publishing
PO Box 59032
Minneapolis, MN 55459
612-513-6475
800-848-2793
Fax: 952-443-2806

Updated and revised edition reflects the latest medical advances, technologies, and research. In straight-forward language, it explains how to take charge of your diabetes and live an active, healthy life.

525 pages

6208 Managing Type II Diabetes
Chronimed Publishing
PO Box 59032
Minneapolis, MN 55459
612-513-6475
800-848-2793
Fax: 952-443-2806

Revised and updated guide for people with Type II diabetes. Offers the latest medical advances and practical advice. Includes tips on dealing with emotions, finding motivation to manage diabetes, preventing and treating complications, monitoring blood glucose, and more.

192 pages

6209 Managing Your Gestational Diabetes
Chronimed Publishing
PO Box 59032
Minneapolis, MN 55459
612-513-6475
800-848-2793
Fax: 952-443-2806

Gives answers to questions on weight gain, injecting insulin, and preventing complications.

128 pages

6210 Maximizing the Role of Nutrition in Diabetes Management
American Diabetes Association
1660 Duke Street
Suite 100
Alexandria, VA 22314-3427
800-232-3472
Fax: 703-549-6995
http://www.diabetes.org

Integrates medical, nutritional, and behavioral sciences and recognizes the importance of each in total diabetes care.

64 pages

6211 Medical Management of Type II Diabetes
American Diabetes Association
1660 Duke Street
Suite 100
Alexandria, VA 22314-3427
800-232-3472
Fax: 703-549-6995
http://www.diabetes.org

Complete overview of Type II diabetes, including diagnosis and classification, pathogenesis, and prevention/treatment of complications.

112 pages

6212 Outsmarting Diabetes
Chronimed Publishing
PO Box 59032
Minneapolis, MN 55459
612-513-6475
800-848-2793
Fax: 952-443-2806

Shows how intensive control can dramatically reduce the effects of insulin-dependent diabetes and the risk of long-term complications.

256 pages

6213 Prediabetes: What You Need to Know to Keep Diabetes Away
Perseus Books Group
387 Park Avenue South
12th Floor
New York, NY 10016
212-340-8100
http://www.perseusbooksgroup.com

Gretchen Becker, Author

This first-ever practical guide offers fifty essential, informative ideas and simple steps to help this vast and rapidly growing constituency manager their condition and thereby reduce their chances of developing full-blown diabetes.

6214 Pumping Insulin
Chronimed Publishing
PO Box 59032
Minneapolis, MN 55459
612-513-6475
800-848-2793
Fax: 952-443-2806

Features information for achieving excellent blood sugar control, correcting pump problems quickly, and lowering risks for complications.

166 pages

6215 Reversing Diabetes: Reduce or Even Eliminate Your Dependence on Insulin or Oral Drugs
Hachette Book Group USA
237 Park Avenue
New York, NY 10017
http://www.hachettebookgroupusa.com

Julian M Whitaker MD, Author

Thoroughly revides and updated with new material, this classic guide wil show you how to reduce, or even eliminate, your dependence on insulin or oral drugs-while losing weight and lowering your cholesterol levels, blood pressure, and risk of heart attack.

448 pages

6216 Stop Prediabetes Now: The Ultimate Planto Lose Weight and Prevent Diabetes
Wiley
10475 Crosspoint Boulevard
Indianapolis, IN 46256
877-762-2974
Fax: 800-597-3299
http://www.wiley.com

Jack Challem, Author
Ron Hunninghake MD, Author

Offers a practical step-by-step program for improving eating habots and using nutritional supplements to reverse prediabetes and related weight problems. Also includes shopping instructions, meal plans, and easy-to-prepare recipes.

304 pages

6217 Stop the Rollercoaster
Chronimed Publishing
PO Box 59032
Minneapolis, MN 55459
612-513-6475
800-848-2793
Fax: 952-443-2806

How to take charge of your blood sugars in diabetes. Information on feeling better, improving your health, and achieving peace of mind.

240 pages

6218 The First Year: Type 2 Diabetes: An Essential Guide for the Newly Diagnosed
Perseus Books Group
387 Park Avenue South
12th Floor
New York, NY 10016
212-340-8100

Gretchen Becker, Author

Uniquely guides you step-by-step through your first year with diabetes, walking you through everything you need to learn and do each day of your first week after diagnosis, each subsequent week of the first month, and each subsequent month of the crucial first year.

Diabetes/Directories

6219 **The New Glucose Revolution for Diabetes**
Perseus Books Group
387 Park Avenue South
12th Floor
New York, NY 10016
212-340-8100
http://www.perseusbooksgroup.com
The first comprehensive guide to using the glycemic index to control type 1 diabetes, type 2 diabetes, and more. Includes GI-based recipes and menus for type 1, type 2, prediabetes, gestational diabetes, and juvenile diabetes, as well as related conditions like obesity and celiac disease, plus practical dietary guidance on sugar, sweeteners, alcohol, snacking, and eating out.

6220 **The Official Pocket Guide for Diabetic Exchanges**
American Diabetes Association
1701 North Beauregard Street
Alexandria, VA 22311
800-342-2383
http://www.diabetes.org
Newly updated with expanded food lists and carbohydrate for every food. ADA's official guide that goes anywhere you go-to the grocery store, out to eat, on vacation. Use it to be sure you are chosing the right foods and portion sizes.
64 pages

6221 **Therapy for Diabetes Mellitus and Related Disorders**
American Diabetes Association
1660 Duke Street
Suite 100
Alexandria, VA 22314-3427
800-232-3472
Fax: 703-549-6995
http://www.diabetes.org
Guides through the treatment of specific problems of persons with diabetes. Represents the views and experience of leading clinicians in a concise, practical approach to treatment.
384 pages

6222 **Touch of Diabetes**
Chronimed Publishing
PO Box 59032
Minneapolis, MN 55459
612-513-6475
800-848-2793
Fax: 952-443-2806
Information for newly-diagnosed non-insulin-dependent diabetics, from curbing potential complications to counting calories. Shows how to control diabetes and improve quality of life.
192 pages

6223 **Type 2 Diabetes: Your Healthy Living Guide**
American Diabetes Association
1660 Duke Street
Suite 100
Alexandria, VA 22314-3427
800-232-3472
Fax: 703-549-6995
http://www.diabetes.org
A thorough guide to staying healthy with Type 2. Includes everything from choosing a health care team and eating and exercising properly to self-monitoring, insulin, dealing with complications, and keep mentally fit.
180 pages

6224 **Voice of the Diabetic**
1412 170 Srive SW
Suite C
Columbia, MO 15203
573-875-8911
Fax: 573-875-8902
Personal stories and practical guidelines by blind diabetics and medical professionals, medical news, resource column and a recipe corner.
28 pages Frequency: Quarterly

6225 **When Diabetes Complicates Your Life**
Chronimed Publishing
PO Box 59032
Minneapolis, MN 55459
612-513-6475
800-848-2793
Fax: 952-443-2806
Directly addresses the subject of diabetic complications. This revised edition includes chapters on nerves and circulation, kidneys, and eyes. Enhancements to the new edition include a chapter on vitamins, herbs, and supplements, and reference to the latest research.
208 pages

Directories

6226 **Buyer's Guide**
American Diabetes Association
1660 Duke Street
Suite 100
Alexandria, VA 22314-3427
800-232-3472
Fax: 703-549-6995
http://www.diabetes.org
A catalog listing all manufacturers of insulin, syringes, pumps, test strips, monitors and more.

6227 **Diabetes Dictionary**
National Diabetes Information Clearinghouse
1 Information Way
Bethesda, MD 20892
301-654-3327
Fax: 301-907-8906
e-mail: ndic@aeric.com
http://www.niddk.nih.gov
Illustrated glossary of more than 300 deabetes-related terms.
64 pages

Journals, Magazines

6228 **Diabetes**
American Diabetes Association
1660 Duke Street
Suite 100
Alexandria, VA 22314-3427
800-232-3472
Fax: 703-549-6995
http://www.diabetes.org
A peer-reviewed journal focusing on laboratory research.

6229 **Diabetes Care**
American Diabetes Association
1660 Duke Street
Suite 100
Alexandria, VA 22314-3427
800-232-3472
Fax: 703-549-6995
http://www.diabetes.org
A peer-reviewed journal emphasizing reviews, commentaries and original research on topics of interest to clinicians.

6230 **Diabetes Forecast**
American Diabetes Association
1660 Duke Street
Alexandria, VA 22314-3473
800-232-3472
Fax: 703-549-6995
http://www.diabetes.org
The monthly lifestyle magazine for people with diabetes, featuring complete, in-depth coverage of all aspects of living with diabetes.

Diabetes/Newsletters, Pamphlets

6231 Diabetes Reviews
American Diabetes Association
1701 N Beauregard Street
Alexandria, VA 22311-1742
703-549-1500
800-232-3472
Fax: 703-549-6995
http://www.diabetes.org

Lynn Nichols, CEO

A peer-reviewed journal providing comprehensive literature reviews of both basic science and clinical issues in diabetes.

Frequency: Quarterly

6232 Diabetes Spectrum: From Research to Practice
American Diabetes Association
1701 N Beauregard Street
Alexandria, VA 22311-1742
703-549-1500
800-232-3472
Fax: 703-549-6995
http://www.diabetes.org

Lynn Nichols, CEO

A journal translating research into practice and focusing on diabetes education and counseling.

6233 Diabetes in the News
Miles
1201 N Clark Street
Chicago, IL 60610-2270
312-664-9782
Fax: 312-664-9770

Morton B Stone, Publisher/Editor

Diabetes news magazine.

Frequency: Bimonthly

6234 Diabetes: A Positive Approach
American Diabetes Association/Conn. Affiliate
1701 N Beauregard Street
Alexandria, VA 22311-1742
703-549-1500
800-232-3472
Fax: 703-549-6995
http://www.diabetes.org/adact

Lynn Nichols, CEO

Combines education and humor, this video will motivate and inspire individuals to take better care of themselves. Touches on fitness, insulin adjustment, oral medication and more to the viewer.

6235 Voice of the Diabetic
National Federation of the Blind
1800 Johnson Street
Suite 2
Baltimore, MD 21230-4914
410-659-9314
Fax: 410-685-5653

Marc Maurer, President

The leading publication in the diabetes field. Each issue addresses the problems and concerns of diabetes, with a special emphasis for those who have lost vision due to diabetes. Available in print and on cassette.

Newsletters, Pamphlets

6236 Clinical Diabetes
American Diabetes Association
1660 Duke Street
Suite 100
Alexandria, VA 22314-3427
800-232-3472
Fax: 703-549-6995
http://www.diabetes.org

A bi-monthly newsletter providing practical treatment information for primary care physicians.

6237 Dental Tips for Diabetics
National Diabetes Information Clearinghouse
1 Information Way
Bethesda, MD 20892
301-654-3327
Fax: 301-907-8906
e-mail: ndic@aeric.com
http://www.niddk.nih.gov

Discusses the relationship between diabetes and periodontal disease. Describes the symptoms of periodontal problems and preventive measures.

6238 Diabetes Advisor
American Diabetes Association
1660 Duke Street
Suite 100
Alexandria, VA 22314-3427
703-549-1500
800-232-3472
Fax: 703-549-6995
http://www.diabetes.org

Lynn Nicholas, CEO

Offers informative articles and research in the area of diabetes for professionals and patients. Offers facts and research on diagnosis, symptoms, technology and the newest devices for persons with diabetes, as well as referral and hotline numbers.

6239 Diabetes Dateline
National Diabetes Information Clearinghouse
1 Information Way
Bethesda, MD 20892
301-654-3327
Fax: 301-907-8906
e-mail: ndic@aeric.com
http://www.niddk.nih.gov

This bulletin features news about current issues in diabetes research and control, special events, patient and professional meeting, and new publications available from NDIC and other organizations.

6240 Diabetes Educator
American Association of Diabetes Educators
444 N Michigan Avenue
Suite 1240
Chicago, IL 60611-3903
312-644-2233
Fax: 312-644-4411

James J Balija, Executive Director

Offers information to health professionals working with persons with diabetes.

6241 Diabetes Self-Management
RA Rapaport Publishing
150 W 22nd Street
Suite 800
New York, NY 10011-2421
212-989-0200
800-989-0200
Fax: 212-989-4786

James Hazlett, Editor
Melissa Glim, Associate Editor
Jim Moorehead, Manager

Publishes practical, how-to information, focusing on the day-to-day and long-term aspects of diabetes in a positive and upbeat style. Gives subscribers up-to-date news, facts, and advice to help them maintain their wellness and make informed decisions regarding their health.

56 pages Frequency: BiMonthly

6242 Diabetes and Brief Illness
Chronimed Publishing
PO Box 59032
Minneapolis, MN 55459
612-513-6475
800-848-2793
Fax: 952-443-2806

This booklet gives self-care instructions and eating suggestions to prevent development of ketoacidosis during brief illness that disrupts normal eating.

12 pages

Diabetes/Videos, Audio Tapes

6243 Diabetes and Exercise
Chronimed Publishing
PO Box 59032
Minneapolis, MN 55459
612-513-6475
800-848-2793
Fax: 952-443-2806

Exercise and weight loss tips and precautions for those with both insulin and non-insulin-dependent diabetes.

36 pages

6244 Diabetes, Vision Impairment and Blindness
American Foundation for the Blind
11 Penn Plaza
Suite 300
New York, NY 10001-2006
212-502-7600
800-232-5463
Fax: 212-502-7777

Carl Augusto, President

A presentation of how chronic diabetes affects vision and how diabetes can be managed at home by blind and visually impaired individuals.

32 pages

6245 Diabetic Foot Care
American Diabetes Association
1660 Duke Street
Suite 100
Alexandria, VA 22314-3427
800-232-3472
Fax: 703-549-6995
http://www.diabetes.org

Booklet discussing early detection and prompt treatment of diabetic foot problems.

12 pages

6246 Diabetic Traveler
1701 N Beauregard Street
Alexandria, VA 22311-1742
800-342-2383

Maury E Rosenbaum, Contact

Provides information to assist individuals with diabetes to plan safe travel. Includes information like adjusting insulin doses on air flights, reviews of storage cases for insulin and diabetes supplies, emergency medical contacts in designated destinations, information on carrying medical history. Written by a diabetic and reviewed by a medical advisory panel of experts.

6 pages Frequency: Quarterly

6247 Do Your Level Best: Start Controlling Your Blood Sugar Today
National Diabetes Information Clearinghouse
1 Information Way
Bethesda, MD 20892
301-654-3327
Fax: 301-907-8906
e-mail: ndic@aerie.com
http://www.niddk.nih.gov

Provides comprehensive information in an easy to read format for people with Type I and Type II diabetes.

6248 End-Stage Renal Disease: Choosing A Treatment That's Right for You
National Diabetes Information Clearinghouse
1 Information Way
Bethesda, MD 20892
301-654-3327
Fax: 301-907-8906
e-mail: ndic@aerie.com
http://www.niddk.nih.gov

Patient education booklet reviews three main treatment modalities for end-stage renal disease.

6249 Healthy Food Choices
American Diabetes Association
1660 Duke Street
Suite 100
Alexandria, VA 22314-3427
800-232-3472
Fax: 703-549-6995
http://www.diabetes.org

Pamphlet containing the basics of good nutrition.

6250 Low Blood Sugar
Chronimed Publishing
PO Box 59032
Minneapolis, MN 55459
612-513-6475
800-848-2793
Fax: 952-443-2806

6251 Staying Healthy with Type 2 Diabetes
Chronimed Publishing
PO Box 59032
Minneapolis, MN 55459
612-513-6475
800-848-2793
Fax: 952-443-2806

A simple, clear explanation of the symptoms and management of Type 2 diabetes. Available in Spanish.

6252 Taking Care of Gestational Diabetes
Chronimed Publishing
PO Box 59032
Minneapolis, MN 55459
612-513-6475
800-848-2793
Fax: 952-443-2806

Available in Spanish.

6253 Type II Diabetes
Chronimed Publishing
PO Box 59032
Minneapolis, MN 55459
612-513-6475
800-848-2793
Fax: 952-443-2806

Explains the basics of what diabetes is and how it is treated.

6254 Type II Diabetes Prevention Pyramids
Chronimed Publishing
PO Box 59032
Minneapolis, MN 55459
612-513-6475
800-848-2793
Fax: 952-443-2806

Teaches ways to decrease risks by improving nutrition, increasing physical activity, and balancing stress.

21 pages

6255 Understanding Gestational Diabetes
National Diabetes Information Clearinghouse
1 Information Way
Bethesda, MD 20892
301-654-3327
Fax: 301-907-8906
e-mail: ndic@aerie.com
http://www.niddk.nih.gov

A guide for women who develop diabetes during pregnancy. It discusses symptoms and diagnosis of gestational diabetes, risk factors, tests during pregnancy and daily management including the use of insulin and blood glucose monitoring.

44 pages

Videos, Audio Tapes

6256 ADA Clinical Education Series on CD-Rom
American Diabetes Association
1660 Duke Street
Suite 100
Alexandria, VA 22314-3427
800-232-3472
Fax: 703-549-6995
http://www.diabetes.org

Features complete texts of Medical Management of Type 1 Diabetes, Medical Management of Type 2 Diabetes, Therapy for Diabetes Mellitus and Related Disorders, 2nd Ed., and Medical Management of Pregnancy Complicated by Diabetes, 2nd Ed.

Diabetes/Research Centers

6257 **Black Experience**
American Diabetes Association/Conn. Affiliate
300 Research Parkway
Meriden, CT 06450-7137
203-639-0385
800-842-6323
Fax: 203-639-0292
http://www.diabetes.org/adact
Designed to increase awareness of diabetes in the black community.

6258 **Diabetes & Exercise Video**
American Diabetes Association
1701 N Beauregard Street
Alexandria, VA 22311-1742
703-549-1500
800-232-3472
Fax: 703-549-6995
http://www.diabetes.org
Lynn Nichols, CEO

A video offering information on how to maintain good health and exercise in controlling diabetes.

6259 **Diabetes Update - Glucose Toxicity: The Need for 24-Hour Control**
American Diabetes Association/Conn. Affiliate
300 Research Parkway
Meriden, CT 06450-7137
203-639-0385
800-842-6323
Fax: 203-639-0292
http://www.diabetes.org/adact
Explores the two new issues in understanding Type II Diabetes: the important role of hepatic glucose overproduction and the concept of glucose toxicity.
Frequency: Videotape

6260 **Diabetes and You**
American Diabetes Association/Conn. Affiliate
300 Research Parkway
Meriden, CT 06450-7137
203-639-0385
800-842-6323
Fax: 203-639-0292
http://www.diabetes.org/adact
A 4-part series that emphasizes the important role patients play in their diabetes management.
Frequency: Videotape

6261 **Diabetes: What You Need to Know**
American Diabetes Association/Conn. Affiliate
300 Research Parkway
Meriden, CT 06450-7137
203-639-0385
800-842-6323
Fax: 203-639-0292
http://www.diabetes.org/adact
Created to increase patient awareness of the classic signs of diabetes and emphasizes the importance to reduce risks of serious complications.
Frequency: Videotape

6262 **Diabetic Foot**
American Diabetes Association/Conn. Affiliate
300 Research Parkway
Meriden, CT 06450-7137
203-639-0385
800-842-6323
Fax: 203-639-0292
http://www.diabetes.org/adact
Explains what to look for and what to do when a problem is suspected or detected in the diabetic foot.
Frequency: Videotape

6263 **Guidelines for Managing Diabetes During Brief Illness**
Chronimed Publishing
PO Box 59032
Minneapolis, MN 55459
612-513-6475
800-848-2793
Fax: 612-443-2806
Offers instructions and food suggestions to help prevent the development of ketoacidosis in persons with diabetes during common brief illnesses that interrupt regular food intake. 50 slides/cassette. Item No. 4101.

6264 **How to Measure and Inject Insulin**
Chronimed Publishing
PO Box 59032
Minneapolis, MN 55459
612-513-6475
800-848-2793
Fax: 952-443-2806
Provides step-by-step instructions on how to draw up, measure, and inject insulin. Also reviews types of insulin and syringes, storage of insulin, and injection sites. 12 minutes. Item No. 4125. Also available as 62 slides/cassette (Item No. 4150).
Frequency: VHS Video

6265 **Living Well with Diabetes**
American Diabetes Association/Conn. Affiliate
300 Research Parkway
Meriden, CT 06450-7137
203-639-0385
800-842-6323
Fax: 203-639-0292
http://www.diabetes.org/adact
Presents two patient role models who are successfully following a treatment plan for noninsulin dependent diabetes.

6266 **On Top of My Game: Living with Diabetes**
American Diabetes Association/Conn. Affiliate
300 Research Parkway
Meriden, CT 06450-7137
203-639-0385
800-842-6323
Fax: 203-639-0292
http://www.diabetes.org/adact
Six patients and their families share their day-to-day frustrations and successes in managing diabetes.
Frequency: Videotape

Research Centers

6267 **Center for Endocrinology, Metabolism & Nutrition**
303 E Chicago Avenue
Chicago, IL 60611-3093
312-908-8023
Fax: 312-908-9032
Dr. Lewis Landsberg, Director
Bonnie C Weston, MD

Nonprofit organization focusing research activities on endocrinology, metabolism, nutrition and specializing in diabetes.

6268 **Diabetes Education and Research Center**
Franklin Medical Building
829 Spruce Street
Suite 302
Philadelphia, PA 19107-5752
215-925-1481
Fax: 215-928-9150
e-mail: dcabetes@libertynet.org
http://www.libertynet.org/~diabetes
Ronald Morgan, Manager

6269 **Diabetes Research Center**
University of Virginia Diabetes Center
423 Health System
Charlottesville, VA 22908
434-295-1551
Fax: 434-982-3796
e-mail: jts@virginia.edu
Eugene J Barrett, Director
Richard De Butts, Owner

The mission of this center is to improve the quality and quanity of health care available to persons with diabetes in Virginia through the provision of professional education, assistance in program planning and development, and of educational resources realting to diabetes

Diabetes/Research Centers

6270 Diabetes Research and Training Center: University of Alabama at Birmingham
Department of Medicine
University Station
Birmingham, AL 35294
205-934-4116
Fax: 205-934-4389

Dr. Jeffrey Kudlow, Director

6271 Endocrinology Research Laboratory
Cabrini Medical Center
247 3rd Avenue
New York, NY 10010-7457
212-995-6000

Dr. Leonid Poretsky, Director
Robert Chaloner, CEO

Focuses on the effects of insulin and insulin-like growth factors on human body functions.

6272 Indiana University: Diabetes Research and Training Center
1001 W 10th Street
Indianapolis, IN 46202-2859
317-278-0907
Fax: 317-278-0000
http://www.iudrtc.com

Dr. Charles Clark Jr, Director

6273 Indiana University: Northwest Center for Medical Education
3400 Broadway
Gary, IN 46408-1101
219-980-6500
Fax: 219-980-6556

Panayotis Iatridis MD, Director
Marilyn Vasquez, Administrator

6274 Indiana University: Pharmacology Research Laboratory
635 Barnhill Drive
Indianapolis, IN 46223
317-274-7844
Fax: 317-274-7714

Dr. Henry Besch Jr, Chairman

6275 Institute for Metabolic Research
3508 Market Street
Suite 420
Philadelphia, PA 19104-3311
215-222-1818
Fax: 215-222-5325

Margo P Cohen MD, Director

6276 International Diabetes Center: Institute for Research & Education Health System
3800 Park Nicollet Boulevard
Minneapolis, MN 55416-2533
952-993-3393
Fax: 952-993-1302
e-mail: fruchs@found.hsmnet.com

Kathy Reynolds, Manager

Research center which improves the quality of life of individuals with diabetes and those at rick of developing diabetes by undertaking ckinical car, education, research, and outreach activities that stimulate and support health.

6277 Joslin Diabetes Center
1 Joslin Place
Boston, MA 02215-5394
617-732-2400
800-JOS-LIN1
Fax: 617-732-2487

Kenneth E Quickle Jr, MD, President

Offers research into diabetes mellitus, including investigations on chemical composition.

6278 Multiple District 22: Lions Vision Research Foundation
PO Box 1714
Baltimore, MD 21203-1714
410-955-1883
Fax: 410-955-1883

Heather Mays, Administrative Manager

Promotes eye research in eye diseases of all types, particularly those related to diabetes, such as diabetic retinopathy, cataracts, glaucoma, and low vision impairment. Works directly with the Wilmer Eye Institute of the Johns Hopkins Medical Institutes, Baltimore, MD in support of its research into eye diseases and cures. Sponsors Lions Vision Days each October. Currently running Lions Vision 2000 campaign to raise a 4 million dollar endowmentfor the Low Vision department at Wilmer.

6279 National Institute of Diabetes & Digestive & Kidney Disease
US Department of Health and Human Services
9000 Rockville Pike
Bldg 31
Bethesda, MD 20892
301-496-3583
800-422-6237
Fax: 301-496-7422

Elizabeth Singer, Executive Director

The Institute conducts, fosters, and supports basic and clinical research into the causes, prevention, diagnosis, and treatment of the various metabolic and digestive diseases. It covers the broad areas of diabetes, blood, endocrine, and metabolic diseases; digestive diseases and nutrition; and kidney and urologic diseases.

6280 Omaha Department of Veteran Affairs Medical Center Research Service
4101 Woolworth Avenue
Omaha, NE 68105-1850
402-346-8800
Fax: 402-449-0604

Lynell W Klassen MD, Associate Chief

6281 University of California, Irvine: UCI Diabetes Research Program
Department of Medicine, Med Sci I C264
Irvine, CA 92717
949-824-5011

M Arthur Charles MD, PhD, Head Master

Basic and clinical diabetes research.

6282 University of Chicago: Diabetes Research & Training Center
5841 S Maryland Avenue
Chicago, IL 60637-1473
773-702-1865
Fax: 773-702-4427

Dr. Arthur Rubenstein, Director
Sue Curtis, Manager

6283 University of Iowa: Diabetes Control and Complications Trial
Department of Internal Medicine
General Hospital
Iowa City, IA 52242
319-356-4879
Fax: 319-356-3564

Rodney Zeitler MD, Director

Clinical trial to determine whether control of certain blood factors can prevent diabetes complications.

6284 University of Iowa: Diabetes Research Center
3e19 Va Hospital
Iowa City, IA 52240
319-338-0581
Fax: 319-339-7025

Robert S Bar MD, Director
Kimberly Ephgrave, MD

6285 University of Kansas: Regional Diabetes Center
Kansas City, KS 66103
913-588-6326
Fax: 913-588-6319

Wayne V Moore MD, Executive Director
James Casey, MD

Diabetes/Research Centers

6286 University of Massachusetts: Diabetes Endocrinology Research Center
Medical School, Department of Biochemistry
55 Lake Avenue N
Worcester, MA 01655
617-856-3047
Fax: 617-856-6231

Dr. William Chick, Director

6287 University of Miami: Diabetes Research Institute
1450 NW 10th Avenue
Miami, FL 33136-1011
305-243-6504
Fax: 305-243-4404

Daniel H Mintz MD, Scientific Director

6288 University of Missouri: Columbia Cosmopolitan Diabetes Center
Columbia, MO 65212
573-882-3818
Fax: 573-884-4609

Dr. Thomas Burns, Director

6289 University of New Mexico: General Clinical Research Center
221 Lomas Boulevard NE
Albuquerque, NM 87106
505-277-0111
Fax: 505-277-6686

Dr. Philip Zager, Contact
Louis Caldera, CEO

Diabetes research.

6290 University of Pennsylvania: Diabetes Research Center
501 Medical Education Walk
Building 36th
Philadelphia, PA 19104
215-898-4365
Fax: 215-898-2178

Franz M Matschinsky MD, Director

6291 University of Pittsburgh: Nutrition and Biochemistry Laboratory
Graduate School of Public Health
505 Parran Hall
Pittsburgh, PA 15261
412-624-4141
Fax: 412-624-7397
e-mail: rwe2@pitt.edu

Rhobert Evans MD, Director

Focuses on, diabetes and obesity research. AIDS, cardiovascular disease, wide range of analytical techniques to analyse cytokines, hormones, vitamins and fatty acids.

6292 University of Texas: General Clinical Research Center
7703 Floyd Curl Drive
San Antonio, TX 78229-3901
210-567-8400
Fax: 210-567-6693

Gregory Mundy MD, Program Director

Focuses on diabetes and infectious disease research.

6293 University of Washington: Diabetes Endocrinology Research Center
1660 S Columbian Way
Seattle, WA 98108-1532
206-764-2222
Fax: 206-764-2598

Daniel Porte Jr, Director
Jodie K Haselkorn, MD

6294 Vanderbilt University: Diabetes Research and Training Center
B3307 Medical Center N
Nashville, TN 37232
615-322-2571
Fax: 615-322-2198

Dr. Oscar B Crofford, Director
Rhonda Venable, PhD

6295 Veterans Affairs Medical Center: Research Service
500 Foothill Drive
Salt Lake City, UT 84148
801-582-1565
Fax: 801-583-9624

Andrew Deiss MD, Associate Chief
James Floyd, Executive Director

Diabetes and cancer research.

6296 Virginia Mason Research Center
1000 Seneca Street
Seattle, WA 98101-2744
206-583-6525
Fax: 206-223-7543

Dwight Sutton PhD, Director
Jerry Nepom, Executive Director

Immunology and diabetes research.

6297 Warren Grant Magnuson Clinical Center
6100 Executive Boulevard
Suite 3c01
Bethesda, MD 20892
301-496-2563
Fax: 301-402-2984
http://www.cc.nih.gov

Established in 1953 as the research hospital of the National Institutes of Health. Designed so that patient care facilities are close to research laboratories so new findings of basic and clinical scientists can be quickly applied to the treatment of patients. Upon referral by physicians, patients are admitted to NIH clinical studies.

6298 Washington University: Diabetes Research and Training Center
660 S Euclid Avenue
Saint Louis, MO 63110-1093
314-362-7080
Fax: 314-454-6225

Julio V Santiago MD, Director
Paul Schoening, Executive Director

6299 Whittier Institute for Diabetes & Endocrinology
9894 Genesee Avenue
La Jolla, CA 92037-1205
858-626-5672
Fax: 858-535-0894

Roy H Norris, Director
Alisa Minear, Manager

Research into employment for handicapped adults.

Hearing Impaired/Associations & Organizations

Associations & Organizations

6300 ADARA
PO Box 6956
San Mateo, CA 94403
650-372-0620
Fax: 650-372-0661
e-mail: ADARAorgn@aol.com
http://www.adara.org
TTY 501-868-8850

David Tout, President
Tim Beatty, President-Elect

Professional networking for excellence in service delivery with individuals who are deaf or hard of hearing. A partnership of national organizations, local affiliates, professional sections, and individual members working together to support social services and rehabilitation delivery for deaf and hard of hearing people.

6301 Abledata
8630 Fenton Street
Suite 930
Silver Spring, MD 20910
800-227-0216
800-227-0216
Fax: 301-608-8958
e-mail: abledata@verizon.net
http://www.abledata.com

Lynn Halverson, Director
Katherine Belknap, Project Director

An information and referral project that maintains a database of 20,000-plus assistive technology products. The project also produces fact sheets on types of devices and other aspects of assistive technology.

6302 Abused Deaf Women's Advocacy Services
8623 Roosevelt Way NE
Seattle, WA 98115
206-726-0093
Fax: 206-726-0017
e-mail: adwas@adwas.org
http://www.adwas.org

Marilyn J Smith, Executive Director
Kay Amos, Office Manager
Cathy Hoog, Coordinator Advocacy Services

Advocacy group for deaf and deaf-blind women who have been mentally, physically, or sexually abused.

6303 Academy of Dispensing Audiologists
1796 Paysphere Circle
Chicago, IL 60674
312-644-0575
Fax: 803-765-0860
e-mail: info@audiologist.org
http://www.audiologist.org

Kevin Hacke, Executive Director
David Berkey, Au.D., President

Encourages audiology training programs to include pertinent aspects of hearing aid dispensing in their curriculum.

6304 Academy of Rehabilitative Audiology
PO Box 26532
Minneapolis, MN 55426
952-920-0484
Fax: 952-920-6098
e-mail: ara@incnet.com
http://www.audrehab.org

Charlotte Avery, Coordinator
Francis X. Blair, Director

Provides professional education, research, and interest in programs for hearing handicapped persons.

6305 Alexander Graham Bell Association for the Deaf: Kentucky Chapter
3417 Volta Place, NW
Washington, DC 20007
202-337-5220
Fax: 202-337-8314
e-mail: info@agbell.org
http://www.agbell.org

Karen Youdelman, Ed.D. (OH), President
John R. Jay Wyant (OH), President-Elect and Treasurer

The Alexander Graham Bell Association for the Deaf and Hard of Hearing (AG Bell) is a lifelong resource, support network and advocate for listening, learning, talking and living independently with hearing loss. Through publications, advocacy, training, scholarships and financial aid, AG Bell promotes the use of spoken language and hearing technology.

6306 Alexander Graham Bell Association for the Deaf and Hard of Hearing
3417 Volta Place NW
Washington, DC 20007
202-337-5220
800-255-4817
Fax: 202-337-8314
e-mail: info@agbell.org
http://www.agbell.org
TTY 202-337-5221

Todd Houston, Executive Director
Inez Janger, President
Rebecca Rarlakain, Director Member Services

Emphasizes the use of technology, speech, speechreading, residual hearing, and written and spoken language for people with hearing loss. Publishes books and brochures on the subject of hearing loss, auditory approaches in education, advocacy, employment, and advances in hearing technology. Offers resource/referral services to individuals with questions about hearing loss and auditory approaches.

6307 Alexander Graham Bell Association for the Deaf
3417 Volta Place NW
Washington, DC 20007-2737
202-337-5220
Fax: 202-337-8314
e-mail: agbell2@aol.com
TDD 202-337-5220

Susan Cofffman, Meeting Coordinator
Todd Houston, Executive Director

Nonprofit membership organization that exists to: encourage children with hearing loss to communicate by developing maximum use of residual hearing, speech-reading and speech and language skills; promotes better understanding of hearing loss in children and adults; promotes detection of hearing loss in early infancy; informs, encourages and helps adults who are deaf or hard of hearing; collaborates on research; works for better educational opport

6308 American Academy of Audiology
11730 Plaza America Drive
Suite 300
Reston, VA 20190
703-790-8466
800-222-2336
Fax: 703-790-8631
e-mail: info@audiology.org
http://www.audiology.org
TTY 703-610-9022

Barry Freeman, President
J Bruce Wardle, Director

A professional organization of individuals dedicated to providing high quality hearing care to the public. Provides professional development, education and research and provides increased public awareness of hearing disorders and audiologic services.

Hearing Impaired/Associations & Organizations

6309 American Academy of Otolaryngology-Head and Neck Surgery
1 Prince Street
Alexandria, VA 22314-3357
703-836-4444
Fax: 703-683-5100
e-mail: international@entnet.org
http://www.entnet.org
Robert L Ferris, MD, PhD, FACS, President
Tom Kryzer, MD, Vice President

Promotes the art and science of medicine related to otolaryngology-head and neck surgery, including providing continuing medical education courses and publications.

6310 American Academy of Otolaryngology:Head and Neck Surgery
1 Prince Street
Alexandria, VA 22314-3357
703-836-4444
Fax: 703-683-5100
e-mail: info@entnet.org
http://www.entnet.org
Jerome C Goldstein, Executive VP
Tom Harlow, Finance Executive

Professional society of medical doctors specializing in otolaryngology (diseases of the ear, nose and throat) and head and neck surgery. Represents otolaryngology in governmental and socio-economic areas and provides high-quality medical education for otolaryngologists. Coordinates Combined Otolaryngological Spring Meetings for ten national otolaryngological societies. Operates job information exchange service and museum.

6311 American Association of the Deaf-Blind
8630 Fenton Street
Suite 121
Silver Spring, MD 20910-3803
301-588-8705
Fax: 301-588-8705
Joy Larson, Program Manager

Promotes better opportunities and services for deaf-blind people. The mission is to assure that a comprehensive, coordinated system of services is accessible to all deaf-blind adults.

6312 American Athletic Association for the Deaf
3607 Washington Boulevard
Suite 4
Ogden, UT 84403-1737
801-393-8710
Fax: 801-393-2263
e-mail: aaadeaf@aol.com
TTY 801-393-7916
Shirley Platt, Executive Director

To recognize outstanding athletic accomplishments by coaches and leaders who have given their time unselfishly and without compensation, and to honor those who have contributed over the years in the field of sports writing covering events for the deaf.

6313 American Auditory Society
352 Sundial Ridge Circle
Dammeron Valley, UT 84783
435-574-0062
Fax: 435-574-0063
e-mail: amaudsoc@aol.com
http://www.amauditorysoc.org
Michael Gorga, President
Wayne Staab, Executive Director

6314 American Neurotology Society
3096 Riverdale Road
Suite 102
The Villages, FL 32162
352-751-0932
Fax: 352-751-0696
e-mail: segossard@aol.com
http://www.americanneurotologysociety.com
Dr. D. Bradl Welling, President
Barb Koltrs, Manager

Physicians and audiologists interested in the diagnosis and treatment of hearing and balance disorders. Promotes education and research in the field of neurotology.

6315 American Society of Deaf Social Workers
11300 Us Highway 19 N
Clearwater, FL 33764-7451
727-541-2646
Fax: 727-541-4402
e-mail: inquiry2006@windmoor-healthcare.com
C William Brett, President

6316 American Speech-Language-Hearing Association
10801 Rockville Pike
Rockville, MD 20852
301-897-5700
800-638-8255
Fax: 301-468-9742
e-mail: pgardner@asha.org
http://www.asha.org
Arlene A. Pietranton, Executive Director
Patricia M Gardner, Contact

A professional and scientific organization for speech-language pathologists; audiologists and speech, language and hearing scientists concerned with commutation disabilities. Provides information and referral and a toll-free HELPLINE number for consumers to inquire about speech, language or hearing disabilities.

6317 American Tinnitus Association
65 SW Yamhill St
Suite 200
Portland, OR 97204
503-248-9985
Fax: 503-248-0024
e-mail: tinnitus@ata.org
http://www.ata.org
Scott C Mitchell, Chairman
Cheryl McGinnis, Executive Director

Membership organization that carries out and supports research and education on tinnitus. Provides resources to both professionals and patients about seeking help and information. Publishes quarterly journal, Tinnitus Today. $25 annual membership includes subscription to Tinnitus Today.

6318 Arizona Commission for the Deaf & Hard of Hearing
1400 W Washington Street
Room 126
Phoenix, AZ 85007
602-542-3323
800-352-8161
Fax: 602-542-3380
e-mail: info@acdhh.az.gov
http://www.acdhh.org
TTY 602-364-0990
Sherri L Collins, Executive Director
Carmen M Green, Deputy Director

The purpose of the Arizona Commission for the Deaf and the Hard of Hearing is to ensure, in partnership with the public and private sector, accessibility for the Deaf and the Hard of Hearing to improve the quality of life.

6319 Auditory-Verbal International
2121 Eisenhower Ave.
Ste. 402
Alexandria, VA 22314
703-739-1049
Fax: 703-739-0395
e-mail: avi@auditory-verbal.org
http://www.auditory-verbal.org
TDD 703-739-0874
Steven Rech, J.D., President
Sara Blair Lake, Executive Director
Mary Benson, Executive Assistant

Dedicated to helping children who have hearing losses learn to listen and speak.

6320 Aurora of Central New York
518 James Street
Syracuse, NY 13203-2282
315-422-7263
Fax: 315-422-9746
e-mail: auroracny@aol.com
TDD 315-422-4792
Debra Chaiken, Executive Director

Professional counseling services helps to assist individuals and their families deal with the trauma of hearing or vision loss.

Hearing Impaired/Associations & Organizations

6321 Berks Deaf and Hard of Hearing Service
201 West Wyomissing Blvd.,
West Lawn, PA 19609
610-685-4520
Fax: 610-685-4526
e-mail: bdhhs@bdhhs.org
http://www.bdhhs.org
Kandy Reyes, Executive Director
Denise A. Colvin, President

Deaf and hard of hearing individuals, their families, and interested individuals. Advocates for services for the deaf and hard of hearing. Provides lending library, interpretation service, screening tests, and sign language classes. Lends assistive devices.

6322 Better Hearing Institute
1444 I Street, NW
Suite 700
Washington, DC 20005
202-449-1100
Fax: 202-216-9646
e-mail: mail@betterhearing.org
http://www.betterhearing.org
TDD 800-327-9355
Sergei Kochkin, Executive Director
Aaron Kelstone, Artistic Manager

A nonprofit educational organization that implements national public information programs on hearing loss and available medical, surgical, hearing aid and rehabilitation assistance for millions with uncorrected hearing problems. Its award-winning series of television, radio and print media public service messages include many celebrities who overcame hearing loss. BHI maintains a toll-free Hearing HelpLine telephone service that provides informat

6323 Betty and Leonard Phillips Deaf Action Center
601 Jordan Street
Shreveport, LA 71101
318-425-7781
Fax: 318-226-1299
e-mail: david@deafactioncenter.org
http://www.deafactioncenter.org
Steve Carby, 2nd Vice-President
Patty Warmack, President
David W Hylan, Jr, Executive Director

The center provides comprehensive services through one central agency 'to bridge the gap' between the hearing and deaf worlds. Since its inception, the Center has made every effort to identify those deaf individuals who have specific needs and to provide adequate services for them.

6324 California Latino Council of the Deaf and Hard of Hearing
422 Baskin Avenue
La Puente, CA 91744-4603
626-336-5199
Fax: 253-423-1835
http://www.deafvision.net/clc/

6325 Canine Assistance for the Disabled
CADI
3160 Francis Road
Alpharetta, GA 30004
770-664-7178
Fax: 770-664-7820
e-mail: info@canineassistants.com
http://www.canineassistants.com
Jennifer Arnold, Executive Director

Provides individuals with physical or hearing impairments with a dog trained to assist in meeting daily needs. Offers Service Dogs for the physically disabled that can open doors, turn off and on lights, pull wheelchairs up ramps, etc. Signal Dogs for the deaf and hard of hearing person become 'ears' for their masters and Social Dogs that help disabled persons build their self-esteem and confidence.

6326 Caption Center
WGBH Educational Foundation
125 Western Avenue
Boston, MA 02134
617-300-3600
Fax: 617-300-1020
e-mail: access@wgbh.org
http://http://main.wgbh.org/
Tom Apone, Director of Operations
Mary Alice Holmes, Director of Finance and Marketin

A nonprofit service of the WGBH Educational Foundation with offices in Boston, New York and Los Angeles. Produces captions for every segment of the entertainment and advertising industries and offers clients an array of services including off-line captions, real-time captions, and open captions.

6327 Captioned Media Program
1447 E Main Street
Spartanburg, SC 29307
864-585-1778
800-237-6213
Fax: 800-538-5636
e-mail: info@dcmp.org
http://www.cfv.org
TDD 800-237-6819
Bill Stark, Director

Distributes open-captiones media on a free loan basis to deaf and hard of hearing individuals, schools and organizations serving deaf and hard of hearing person, families of deaf and hard of hearing children and other qualified individuals. Thousands of titles to choose from. Funded by the US Department of Education

6328 Center for Community and Professional Services of the PA School for the Deaf
100 W School House Lane
Philadelphia, PA 19144
215-951-4700
Fax: 215-951-4708
e-mail: info@psd.org
http://www.psd.org
Dr. Jay J Basch, President
Joseph E Fischgrund, Headmaster

Classes and assistance for the deaf and hard of hearing. Involved in operation of George W. Nevil Home for aged and infirm deaf and blind-deaf persons. Operates camping facility. Bestows awards.

6329 Central Institute for the Deaf
825 South Taylor Avenue
Saint Louis, MO 63110
314-977-0132
Fax: 314-977-0023
e-mail: bf@cidmac.wustl.edu
http://www.cid.edu
TTY 314-997-0001
Robin M. Feder, Executive Director
Bree DeGraw, Annual Giving Coordinator

Central Institute for the Deaf is a private, nonprofit institute composed of research laboratories in which scientists study the normal aspects as well as the disorders of hearing, language, and speech; a school for children who have hearing impairments; speech, language, and hearing clinics; and professionals with hearing impairment, and communication sciences.

6330 Central Minnesota Self-Help for Hard of Hearing
1527 Northway Drive
Room E
Saint Cloud, MN 56303-1221
320-654-8353
Herbert Cantrell, MD

6331 City University of New York: Center for Research in Speech & Hearing
535 East 80th Street
33 West 42nd Street (17th Floor)
New York, NY 10075
212-794-5555
Fax: 212-642-2379
http://http://portal.cuny.edu
Richard P Alvarez, University Director of Admission
Howard Apsan, University Director of Environme

Hearing Impaired/Associations & Organizations

Programmable research of digital and auditory hearing aids and sensory aids for the speech and hearing impaired person.

6332 Cleveland Hearing and Speech Center
11206 Euclid Avenue
Cleveland, OH 44106-1798
216-231-8787
Fax: 216-231-7141
e-mail: bambuske@chsc.org
http://www.chsc.org

Bernard P Henri, Executive Director
Michelle Burnett, Director of Clinical Services

Offers research and studies into speech, language and hearing disorders.

6333 Cleveland West Chapter: Self-Help for Hard of Hearing People
689 Olde Orchard Court
Columbus, OH 43213-3409
614-861-7956
e-mail: cohear@aol.com

Eugene Buzzelli, President

Hearing impaired individuals, their families, medical professionals, and interested individuals in the western suburbs of Cleveland, OH. Provides education, self-help techniques, mutual support, and advocacy for hard of hearing individuals; makes available assistive listening devices.

6334 Cochlear Implant Association
Hearing Loss Association of America
PO Box 464
Buffalo, NY 14223-0464
716-838-4662
Fax: 716-838-4662
e-mail: 76207.3114@compuserve.com
TDD 716-838-4662

Bev Fish, President
Craig G Carpenter, Executive Director

Not-for-profit voluntary organization dedicated to serving implant users, candidates, their families and professional supporters. Purposes are to promote opportunities afforded by the use of cochlear implants through mutual sharing of ideas and personal experiences; enhance community awareness of hearing impairment and to promote better understanding of implants; and to promote improved financial support. Publishes educational materials including

6335 Committee for Purchase from People who are Blind or Severely Disabled
1421 Jefferson Davis Highway
Jefferson Plaza 2, Suite 10800
Arlington, VA 22202-3259
703-603-7740
Fax: 703-603-0655
e-mail: info@abilityone.gov
http://www.abilityone.gov

Patrick Rowe, Executive Director
LaWanda York, Public Affairs
Robert M Hartt, Program Analyst

A federal agency that administers the Javits-Wagner-O'Day Program, directing federal agencies to purchase products and services from nonprofit agencies that employ people who are blind or have other severe disabilities. Provides a wide range of vocational options to individuals with severe disabilities.

6336 Communication Service for the Deaf
102 N Krohn Place
Sioux Falls, SD 57103
605-367-5760
Fax: 605-367-5958
http://www.c-s-d.org
TDD 608-367-5760

Dr. Benjamin Soukup, CEO
Dr. Bobbie Beth, Chief Operations Officer

Offers peer counseling, information and referrals and advocacy services.

6337 Communications Services for the Deaf and Hard of Hearing
122 North Elm Street
Suite M-2
Greensboro, NC 27401
336-274-1461
Fax: 336-273-0015
e-mail: info@csdhh.org
http://www.csdhh.org

Sheeyl Williamson, Director

Provides services to the deaf and hearing impaired.

6338 Conference of Educational Administrators Serving the Deaf
PO Box 1778
St Augustine, FL 32085-1778
904-810-5200
Fax: 904-810-5525
e-mail: NationalOffice@ccasd.org
http://www.ccasd.org

James E. Tucker, President
Claire Bugen, President

Focuses on improvements in the education of deaf and hard of hearing people through research, personnel development, advocacy and training.

6339 Connecticut Commission on Deaf and Hearing Impaired
67 Prospect Avenue
3rd Floor
Hartford, CT 06106-2980
860-231-8756
Fax: 860-231-8746
e-mail: CDHI@ct.gov
http://www.state.ct.us/CDHI/index.htm

Stacie J. Mawson, Executive Director
Carmen Ragland, Executive Secretary

6340 Convention of American Instructors of the Deaf
Membership Services Office
PO Box 377
Bedford, TX 76095-0377
817-354-8414
Fax: 585-475-6500
e-mail: caid@swbell.net
http://www.caid.org

Helen Lovato, CAID Office Manager
Kathy Obenhaus, President

The professional organization for teachers, administrators, educational interpreters, residential personnel, and other professionals involved in education of the deaf. CAID provides biennial conventions, networking of professionals with shared interests through Special Interest Groups, and advocacy for national and state legislation concerning the deaf.

6341 Council on Education of the Deaf
Deaf Studies Department, California State Univ.
18111 Nordhoff Street
Northridge, CA 91330-8265
801-629-4750
Fax: 801-629-4896
e-mail: carmely@usdb.org
http://www.deafed.net
TTY 818-667-2335

Dr. Carmel C Yarger, President
Dr. Karen Dilka, Executive Director

Offers information and referral services to the hearing impaired.

6342 Davis Center for Hearing, Speech and Learning: Hearing Therapy
98 Us Highway 46
Budd Lake, NJ 07828-1818
973-691-8220
Fax: 973-691-0611
e-mail: info@daviscenter.net
http://www.daviscenter.net

Dorinne S Davis, Director

This center offers hearing therapy to people with hypersensitive hearing, ADD, and Central Auditory Processing Problems. Therapies include: Auditory Integration Training, Tomatis Method, Fast Forward, and Earobics.

Hearing Impaired/Associations & Organizations

6343 Deaf Action Center of Central Louisiana
338 Main Street
Pineville, LA 71360-6961   318-487-4322
                                  Fax: 318-484-3640
Frances M Blair, Executive Officer

Supports and promotes the non-hearing population of Central Louisiana.

6344 Deaf Adults Education Access Program
300 W Washington Street
Suite 1200
Chicago, IL 60606   312-802-3566
                                 Fax: 312-580-7175
                                 http://www.dhs.state.il.us
                                 TTY 847-925-6602
Carol L. Adams, Ph.D.,, Secretary
Teyonda Wertz, Chief of Staff

DAEAP offers classes in ASL, basic English, and citizenship preparation for Deaf and Hard of Hearing Immigrants in the Chicagoland area.

6345 Deaf Artists of America
302 N Goodman Street
Suite 205
Rochester, NY 14607   716-244-3460
                                 800-421-1220
                                 Fax: 585-244-3690
Tom Willard, Executive Director
Richard Duff, Administrator

Deaf and hard-of-hearing artists and other interested individuals organized to support and recognize hearing-impaired artists. Primary goal is to make the arts more accessible to America's deaf and hard-of-hearing citizens. Serves as a clearinghouse for information about deaf people and the arts. Operates speakers' bureau. Conducts workshops; sponsors competitions; bestows awards. Plans to provide financial support for deaf artists and sponsor art classes.

6346 Deaf REACH
3521 12th Street NE
Washington, DC 20017   202-832-6681
                                 Fax: 202-832-8454
                                 e-mail: Lweinstock@deaf-reach.org
                                 http://www.deaf-reach.org
Sarah Brown, Executive Director
Brandon Arthur, President

Offers referral, education, advocacy, counseling, and housing services for deaf mentally ill, multihandicapped and/or low income deaf people in the metro District of Columbia area.

6347 Deaf and Hard of Hearing Entrepreneurs Council
814 Thayer Avenue
Suite 150
Silver Spring, MD 20910-4500   301-587-1788
                                 Fax: 301-587-1789
Louis Schwartz, President

A nonprofit association of business owners who are deaf or hard of hearing. Purpose is to encourage, recognize and promote entrepreneurship by deaf and hard of hearing people through educational information, fostering fellowship, creating a forum for discussion of problems and solutions and influencing others within the larger business community.

6348 Deaf and Hard of Hearing Services Center
5340 N. Fresno Street
Fresno, CA 93710   559-225-3382
                                 Fax: 559-221-8224
                                 http://www.dhhsc.org
Danielle Thompson, Executive Director
Susan Coulter, Program Manager

6349 Deafness and Communicative Disorders Branch
Rehabilitation Services Administration
330 C Street, S.W
Room 3228
Washington, DC 20202-2736   202-205-9152
                                 Fax: 202-205-9340
Annette Reichman, Branch Chief

Promotes improved and expanded rehabilitation services for deaf and hard of hearing people, individuals with speech or language impairments, and individuals who are deaf-blind.

6350 Deafpride
800 Florida Avenue NE
Washington, DC 20002-3600   202-675-6700
                                 Fax: 202-547-0547
Al Slmnenstrahl, Director
Irving King Jordan, President

Works for the human rights of deaf people and their families. Assists groups to organize and work together for change in the District of Columbia and throughout the United States.

6351 Dogs for the Deaf
10175 Wheeler Road
Central Point, OR 97502   541-826-9220
                                 Fax: 541-826-6696
                                 e-mail: info@dogsforthedeaf.org
                                 http://www.dogsforthedeaf.org
Robin Dickson, President/CEO
Pam Slater, Development Director

Trains hearing dogs to alert deaf persons to certain sounds. Dogs are chosen from pet adoption shelters and assigned on the basis of a prioritized waiting list. Four to five months of training teaches them to alert their masters to the sounds of alarm clocks, smoke alarms, doorbells, oven timers, telephones, etc.

6352 EAR Foundation
PO Box 330867
Nashville, TN 37206   615-627-2724
                                 Fax: 615-627-2728
                                 e-mail: info@earfoundation.org
                                 http://www.earfoundation.org
Suzanne Wyatt, Executive Director
Steve Masie, Chairman

A national, nonprofit organization dedicated to integrating the hearing and balance impaired person into the mainstream of society through public awareness and special education. Programs include the Meniere's Network, the Minnie Pearl Scholarship Fund and Young EARS Program, newsletter.

10 pages

6353 Eaton-Peabody Laboratory of Auditory Physiology
243 Charles Street
Boston, MA 02114   617-523-7900
                                 Fax: 617-523-5498
                                 http://www.meei.harvard.edu/
Dr. Joseph Bayes, Director
John Fernandez, President

Auditory system and auditory information processing, including ear-brain interactions in normal and pathologic hearing.

6354 Episcopal Conference of the Deaf
PO Box 27069
Philadelphia, PA 19118   215-247-1059
                                 Fax: 215-247-1059
                                 TTY 215-247-6454
Rev. Roger Pickering, President
Marianne D Stephens, Religious Leader

Promotes ministry for deaf people throughout the Episcopal Church.

Hearing Impaired/Associations & Organizations

6355 Farthest North Club of the Deaf
475 Hall Street
Fairbanks, AK 99701
907-456-5913
800-847-0939
Fax: 907-456-2604
e-mail: dcs@polarnet.com
http://www.arthritis.org

Doug Cluff, Executive Director
Cecelia Davis, Program Manager

Supports the rights of the deaf. Promotes deaf social activities.

6356 Florida Dog Guides for the Deaf
PO Box 20662
Bradenton, FL 34203
941-748-8245
800-520-4589
Fax: 941-747-0969
e-mail: adogs@floridadogguidesftd.org
http://www.floridadogguidesftd.org

Arlene Dickinson, Executive Officer
Gary Johnson, CEO

Deaf and hard of hearing individuals interested in working with and providing trained certified hearing dogs for the deaf. Sponsors state-wide dog shows and canine good citizen testing. Provides deaf awareness and advocacy.

6357 Florida Language, Speech and Hearing Association
335 Beard Street
Tallahassee, FL 32301
850-222-6000
Fax: 850-681-2890
e-mail: mark@hmgnet.com

Corey Matthews, Executive Director

6358 Forsyth Center for the Deaf and Hard of Hearing
1006 S. Marshall Street
Suite 107
Winston Salem, NC 27101
336-759-2900
Fax: 336-759-3248
e-mail: ablevins@fcdhh.org

Angela Blevins, Coordinator
Richard O'Donnell

Deaf and hard of hearing persons and their families. Provides a variety of services such as: interpreting; counseling/referrals; information/referral; technical assistance; advocacy; sign language; in-service training; consultation/public relations; consumer education; family support; personal assistance; networking with other agencies. Seeks to identify educational needs of deaf population. Acts as a clearinghouse for resource information. Works to meet special needs of hearing impaired senior citizens. Encourages the development of leadership skills.

6359 Gallaudet University
Office of Financial Aid
800 Florida Avenue NE
Washington, DC 20002
202-651-5000
Fax: 202-651-5880
e-mail: meloyde.batten-mickens@gallaudet.edu
http://www.gallaudet.edu

Robert R Davila, President
MJ Bienvenu, Chairman

A comprehensive multipurpose educational institution serving deaf and hard of hearing individuals through education, research and public service. Disseminates information through such units as the Gallaudet University Press; Research Institute; Pre-College Outreach; College for Continuing Education; Media Distribution Center and the National Information Center on Deafness.

6360 Greater St. Louis Association of the Deaf
PO Box 14444
Saint Louis, MO 63178-4444
314-963-7817
Fax: 314-963-7850

6361 HEAR Center
301 E Del Mar Boulevard
Pasadena, CA 91101
626-796-2016
Fax: 626-796-2320
e-mail: info@hearcenter.org
http://www.hearcenter.org

Josephine Wilson, Executive Director
Lawrence L. Wilson, President

Auditory and verbal program designed to help hearing impaired children, infants and adults lead normal and productive lives. Seeks to develop auditory techniques to aid people who have communication problems due to deafness. Offers diagnostic evaluations for hearing. And hearing aid dispensing. Aural rehabilitation program.

6362 Hands Organization for the Deaf and Hard of Hearing
2501 W 103rd Street
Chicago, IL 60655-1003
773-239-6662
Fax: 773-239-2565
e-mail: ridgeadmissions@aol.com
http://www.ridgeacademy.org

Kate Kubey, Executive Director

A nonprofit organization of both deaf and hearing persons working together to address the needs and concerns of the deaf community. The organization is working to raise the consciousness of the hearing world to the realities of deafness, and to bridge the gap between services already in place for the deaf and the large number of deaf people who have never been reached by those services.

6363 Hear Now
9745 E Hampden Avenue
Suite 300
Denver, CO 80231-4923
303-695-7797
Fax: 303-695-7789
e-mail: hearnow@charitiesusa.org
http://www.leisurelan.com/~hearnow
TDD 800-648-4327

Dr. Bernice Dinner, President
MaryAnn Fleet, Executive Director

Voluntary not-for-profit health organization dedicated to helping those who cannot afford assistance for hearing and cochlear disorders. Provides applications for medical assistance to those affected by hearing disorders. Publishes a newsletter, Hear Now.

6364 Hearing Aid Helpline
International Hearing Society
20361 Middlebelt Road
Livonia, MI 48152
248-478-4520
800-521-5247
Fax: 810-478-4520

Robin C lowes IHS, Executive Director

A hearing specialist is ready to answer questions of the consumer about hearing aids, hearing loss and treatments.

6365 Hearing Dog Resource Center (HDRC)
PO Box 1080
Renton, WA 98057-1080
800-869-6898
800-869-6898
Fax: 541-341-5927

Provides information on hearing dogs. Free information packet is available; publications for sale. Hours: 8:30 a.m. to 5:00 p.m. Monday-Friday.

6366 Hearing Education and Awareness for Rockers
1405 Lyon Street
San Francisco, CA 94115
415-409-3277
Fax: 415-409-LOUD
e-mail: hear@hearnet.com
http://www.hearnet.com
TTY 415-476-7600

Kathy Peck, Executive Director
Douglas L. Beck Au.D, Director

Educates the public about the real dangers of hearing loss resulting from repeated exposure to excessive noise levels.

Hearing Impaired/Associations & Organizations

6367 **Hearing Impaired Persons of Charlotte County Florida**
24901 Sandhill Boulevard
Unit 8
Pt Charlotte, FL 33983-5207
941-743-8347
Fax: 941-743-9236

Carol Moyer, Executive Director

6368 **Hearing Impaired Persons of Charlotte County Florida**
24901 Sandhill Boulevard
Unit 8
Pt Charlotte, FL 33983
941-743-8347
888-878-8477
Fax: 941-743-9236
http://www.hearingimpairedpersons.com
TTY 941-743-9286

Albert Pimentel, President
Bonnie Holbach, Vice President
Kim Gaut, Executive Director

6369 **Hearing Industries Association**
1444 I Street, NW
Suite 700
Washington, DC 20005
202-409-1090
Fax: 202-216-9646
e-mail: mspangler@bostrom.com
http://www.hearing.org

Carole M Rogin, President

The association for hearing aid manufacturers and suppliers of component parts.

6370 **Hearing Loss Association of America**
Laguna Woods Village at Laguna Woods
Clubhouse 3, Dining Room 2
Laguna Woods, CA 92653
949-859-4088
Fax: 949-699-2931
e-mail: woodjr@teambase.com
http://www.hearinglossca.org

Woodley O Butler Jr, President
George Henson, VP/Director Special Activities

It is an international, non-sectarian, educational organization of people with hearing loss, their relatives and friends. It is devoted to the welfare and interests of those who cannot hear well, but are committed to participating in the hearing world.

6371 **Hearling Loss Association of America**
7910 Woodmont Avenue
Suite 1200
Bethesda, MD 20814
301-657-2248
Fax: 301-913-9413
e-mail: national@shhh.org
http://www.hearingloss.org
TDD 301-657-2249

Anne T. Pope, President
Victor M. Matsui, Vice-president
Terry Portis, Executive Director

A nonprofit, educational organization that is dedicated to the well-being of people of all ages and communication styles who do not hear well. SHHH is the largest international consumer organization of its kind.

6372 **Helen Keller National Center for Deaf: North Central Region**
Helen Keller National Center
485 Avenue of the Cities
Suite 5
East Moline, IL 61244-4040
309-755-0018
Fax: 309-755-0025
e-mail: HKNC5LJT@aol.com
http://www.hknc.org
TTY 309-755-0018

Laura J Thomas, Regional Representative
Catherine Papish, Administrative Assistant

Provides rehabilitation services to persons who are deaf-blind. The phone number is a TTY, if you are a hearing caller, please dial 309-755-0018, extension 711.

6373 **Hispanic Deaf Teacher Training Program**
PO Box 10076
Beaumont, TX 77710
409-880-8174
Fax: 409-880-2265

6374 **House Ear Institute**
2100 W 3rd Street
Los Angeles, CA 90057-1922
213-483-2642
Fax: 213-483-8789
e-mail: info@hei.org
http://www.hei.org
TDD 213-484-2642

John W. House, President
James Boswell, Chief Executive Officer

Studies the causes of hearing impairments and trains professionals in diagnosis, treatment and rehabilitation.

6375 **Independent Living Services for Older Individuals who are Blind**
US Department of Education OSERS
400 Maryland Avenue, SW
Room 5057 PCP
Washington, DC 20202
202-245-7454
800-437-0833
Fax: 202-245-7588
http://www.ed.gov

Suzanne Mitchell, Project Director

To provide independent living services to older blind individuals, i.e., individuals aged 55 or older, whose severe visual impairments make gainful employment extremely difficult to attain but for whom independent living in their own homes and communities is feasible.

6376 **Indiana Hearing Aid Specialists Association**
3165 E Center Street
Warsaw, IN 46582
574-269-6236
Fax: 574-269-6236

Donna H Heckters, President

Custom style hearing aids.

6377 **International Catholic Deaf Association**
7202 Buchanan Street
Landover Hills, NV 20784-2236
301-429-0697
Fax: 301-429-0698
e-mail: homeoffice@icda-us.org
http://www.icda-us.org
TTY 708-887-9472

Peter UN, President
Brian Swatek, Vice President

Promotes ministry for Catholic deaf people with chapters encouraging to arrange Sunday masses for deaf people in their local areas with the liturgy presented in sign language.

6378 **International Hearing Dog**
5901 E 89th Avenue
Henderson, CO 80640
303-287-3277
Fax: 303-287-3425
e-mail: ihdi@aol.com
http://www.ihdi.org

Martha A Foss, President and Director
Valerie Foss-Brugger, President and Executive Director

Trains dogs to 'hear' for deaf persons - telephones, doorbells, babies, etc.

6379 **International Hearing Society**
16880 Middlebelt Road
Ste. 4
Livonia, MI 48154
734-522-7200
Fax: 734-522-0200
e-mail: rclowers@ishinfo.org
http://www.ihsinfo.org

Cindy Helms, Executive Director
Phyllis Wilson, Associate Director
Cindy Helms, Manager

Hearing Impaired/Associations & Organizations

The society recognizes the need for promoting and maintaining the highest possible standards for its members in the best interest of the consumer. As the membership organization for thousands of independent specialists, IHS conducts programs in competency accreditation, education and training, and promotes specialty-level certification for its members.

1951

6380 **International Hearing Society: Hearing Aid Helpline**
16880 Middlebelt Rd.,
Ste.4
Livonia, MI 48154
734-522-7200
800-521-5247
Fax: 734-522-0200
http://http://ihsinfo.org/

Cindy Helms, Executive Director
James Ogurek, President
Phyllis V Wilson, Associate Director

Provides information on hearing aids and hearing loss and offers referrals to hearing-aid specialists in the caller's area. Free information packetis available. Hours: 8:30 a.m. to 4:00 p.m., Monday-Friday.

6381 **International Kaf/Tek**
104 Catbriar Court
Summerville, SC 29485
843-851-6444
Fax: 617-626-0270
e-mail: deaftek@deaftek.org
http://www.deaftek.org
TTY 508-620-1777

Brenda Monene RN, MEd, President

Provides the international electronic mail service, Deaftek, USA. This service is dedicated to communities that are deaf or hard of hearing; the service is used by individuals, organizations, agencies, schools, colleges and universities, service providers, and professionals in the field of deafness.

6382 **International Lutheran Deaf Association**
1333 S Kirkwood Road
Saint Louis, MO 63122-7295
314-965-9917
http://www.lcmsdeaf.org/ilda/

Greg Desrosiers, President
Jeff Padon, President-elect

Promotes ministry for deaf people throughout the Lutheran Church-Missouri.

6383 **International Organization for the Education of the Hearing Impaired**
3417 Volta Place NW
Washington, DC 20007-2737
202-337-5220
Fax: 202-337-8314

Elizabeth Wilkes PhD, Chairperson
Elizabeth Quigley, IOEHI Liaison
Todd Houston, Executive Director

IOEHI promotes excellence in education for children and adults who are deaf or hard of hearing, encourages scientific study of the educational and communicative processes and stimulates the exchange of information among educators through seminars.

6384 **Iowa Hearing Association**
1001 Office Park Road
Suite 105
West Des Moines, IA 50265
515-440-6057
Fax: 515-440-6055
e-mail: apmsthomas@aol.com
http://www.iowahearingassociation.org

Peggy Stephens, President
Steve Sword, President-Elect
Bev Thomas, Executive Director

Our mission is to promote and encourage an effective program of public education as to the benefits of the use of hearing aids.

6385 **Kansas Commission for the Deaf and Hard of Hearing**
3640 SW Topeka Boulevard
Suite 150
Topeka, KS 66611-2373
785-267-6100
800-432-0698
Fax: 785-267-0655
e-mail: Rebecca.Rosenthal@srs.ks.gov
http://www.srskansas.org

Rebecca Rosenthal, Executive Director
Don Jordan, Secretary

Provides interpreter, coordination advocacy for individuals who are deaf and hard of hearing, information and refferal.

6386 **Kansas Hearing Aid Association**
1200 SW College Avenue
Topeka, KS 66611-2052
785-266-4833
Fax: 785-266-4833

M Day Kaufmann, Executive Director

Professional society of licensed audiologists and hearing instrument specialists dispensers. Promotes the welfare of hearing impaired persons. Works to improve professional standards of hearing aid dispensers. Seeks better methods of dispensing, fitting, and using hearing aids. Promotes goodwill and cooperation among disciplines in the hearing industry. Sponsors educational seminars.

6387 **Kansas Hearing Society**
3200 SW College Avenue
Topeka, KS 66611
785-266-4833
Fax: 785-266-4833
e-mail: mdayk@scbglobal.net
http://www.kansashearingsociety.com/

M Day Kaufmann, Executive Director
Haris Zafar, PRESIDENT

Professional society of licensed hearing aid dispensers. Promotes the welfare of hearing impaired persons. Works to improve professional standards of hearing aid dispensers. Seeks better methods of dispensing, fitting, and using hearing aids. Promotes goodwill and cooperation among hearing aid examiners. Sponsors educational seminars.

6388 **Kentucky Chapter: Alexander Graham Bell Association for the Deaf**
3417 Volta Place, NW
Washington, DC 20007
202-337-5220
Fax: 202-337-8314
e-mail: info@agbell.org
http://www.agbell.org

Karen Youdelman, Ed.D, President
John R. ""Ja Wyant, President-Elect and Treasurer

Educators, professionals, parents of deaf and hard of hearing children, as well as deaf and hard of hearing adults. Promotes speech and auditory skills training and services for the deaf population. Worked to acquire TDDs and volume control telephones for area airport. Provides networking and communication between agencies and individuals. Conducts letterwriting campaigns. Participates in health fairs. Disseminates information from the National A.G. Bell Association; provides workshops on topics related to deafness.

6389 **Kentucky State Affliate of American Academy of Audiology**
1707 Cumberland Falls Highway
Suite U-7
Corbin, KY 40701
606-528-9993
Fax: 606-528-5553
e-mail: angela@sekyaudiology.com
http://www.kyaudiology.org

Angela M Morris AuD, President
Austin C Black, AuD, Vice President
Pam Ison, AuD, Administrator

The KKA promotes quality hearing and balance care by advancing the profession of Audiology through leadership, advocacy, education, public awareness and support of research.

Hearing Impaired/Associations & Organizations

6390 Lexington School for the Deaf
30th Avenue & 75th Street
Jackson Heights, NY 11370
718-350-3300
Fax: 718-899-9846
http://www.lexnyc.com

Regina Carroll, Ph.D., Superintendent and Chief Executi
Gerard J. Buckley, Ed.D., President

Offers a comprehensive range of services to deaf, hard of hearing and speech impaired persons from infancy to elderly through its affiliate agencies: The Center for Mental Health Services; The Lexington Hearing and Speech Center, Lexington Vocational Services, and the Lexington School for the Deaf. The Lexington Center also provides services through its research division which houses the only federally funded Rehabilitation Engineering Center.

6391 Maryland Chapter: Alexander Graham Bell Association for the Deaf
7113 Pheasant Cross Drive
Baltimore, MD 21209-1023
410-486-3385
Fax: 410-602-1634

Benjamin J Dubin, President

Promotes verbal communication including speech, speech-read, and use of residual hearing by people with hearing impairments and their families.

6392 Media & Captioning for Individuals with Disabilities
US Department of Education
Office of Special Education & Rehabilitative Services
400 Maryland Avenue SW, Room 4070
Washington, DC 20202-2550
202-245-7366
800-USA-LEAR
Fax: 202-401-0689
e-mail: ernest.hairston@ed.gov
http://www.ed.gov
TTY 800-437-0833

Ernest Hairston, Contact

To maintain a free loan service of captioned films for the deaf and instructional media for the educational, cultural, and vocational enrichment of the disabled. Provide for acquisition and distribution of media materials and equipment; provide contracts and grants for research into the use of media and technology; and train teachers, parents, and others in the media and technology utilization.

6393 Michigan Association for the DeafHearing and Speech Services
2929 Covington Court
Unit 200
Lansing, MI 48912-4942
517-487-0066
800-YOU-HEAR
Fax: 517-487-2586
e-mail: yourear@pilot.msu.edu
http://www.miserybay.com/madhs
TDD 517-487-0202

Nancy Asher, Executive Director
Pat Walton, Office Manager

Substance Abuse Prevention for the deaf and hard of hearing students (alcohol, marijuana, inhalents) acted in sign language, voicing, and captioning. HIV/AIDS Prevention and Information for the deaf and hard of hearing. Lending Library books, videos and audio tapes. Accessibility in Courts video and information. TTY distribution Program. TRACKMAN-Youth Substance Abuse Video and Education Series.

6394 Michigan Association for the Deaf: Hearing and Speech Services
2929 Covington Court
Suite 200
Lansing, MI 48912-4939
517-487-0066
Fax: 517-487-2586
e-mail: yourear@MADHH.org
http://www.madhs.org
TDD 517-487-0202

Nancy Asher, Executive Director
Pat Walton, Office Manager

Substance Abuse Prevention for the deaf and hard of hearing students (alcohol, marijuana, inhalants) acted in sign language, voicing, and captioning. AIV/AIDS Prevention and Information for the deaf and hard of hearing. Lending Library books, videos and audio tapes.

6395 Michigan Speech Language Hearing Association
790 W Lk Lansing Road
Suite 500-A
East Lansing, MI 48823-8465
517-332-5691
Fax: 517-332-5870
e-mail: mainoffice@michiganspeechhearing.org
http://www.michiganspeechhearing.org

Sandra Glista, President
Judy Lytwynec, President-Elect
Elaine Deroover, VP Public Relations

Speech pathologists, audiologists, and teachers of the hearing-impaired. Promotes professional development among those working in the speech, language, and hearing field.

6396 Michigan Speech, Language & Hearing Association
790 W Lake Lansing Road
Suite 500-A
East Lansing, MI 48823
517-332-5691
Fax: 517-332-5870
e-mail: msha@att.net
http://www.michiganspeechhearing.org

Sherry Dean, Secretary
Mary Peterson, President
Kim Wesoloski, Manager

Speech pathologists, audiologists, and teachers of the hearing-impaired. Promotes professional development among those working in the speech, language, and hearing field.

6397 Minnesota Chapter No. 1 SHHH - Self Help for Hard of Hearing People
PO Box 8037
Minneapolis, MN 55408-0037
952-941-2087
e-mail: jlobrien1103@yahoo.com

Joe O'Brien, President
Merrilee Knoll, Co-Vice Presidents

Promotes participation in recreational activities by the hard of hearing. Promotes coping skills, self esteem building, and assertiveness.

6398 Mount Vernon Center for Community Mental Health: Deaf Services
8119 Holland Road
Alexandria, VA 22306
703-360-6910
Fax: 703-360-0899

Ken Disselkoen, Contact
Gary Lupton, Executive Director

Offers deaf persons in the Mt. Vernon area counseling, education and advocacy.

6399 Nashville Chapter Black Deaf Advocates
PO Box 40064
Nashville, TN 37204-0064
615-333-6175
Fax: 615-333-6175
e-mail: joycec258@aol.com

Dorothy A Nelson, President
Nellie Hudson, Vice President

Promotes participation in recreational activities by the deaf. Promotes the well-being and empowerment of African Americans who are deaf or hard of hearing.

6400 National Association for Hearing and Speech Action
2200 Research Boulevard
#450
Rockville, MD 20850
301-296-8705
800-638-8255
Fax: 301-571-0457
e-mail: nsslha@asha.org
http://www.nsslha.org

Carlin F. Hageman, PhD, CCC-SLP, Executive Director
Dawn D. Dickerson, Director of Operations

Hearing Impaired/Associations & Organizations

Professional membership association for speech pathologists and audiologists. Offers referrals to doctors. Free information packets are available.

6401 National Association of the Deaf
8630 Fenton Street
Suite 820
Silver Spring, MD 20910-3819
301-587-1788
Fax: 301-587-4873
e-mail: nadinfo@nad.org
http://www.nad.org
TDD 301-587-1789

Nancy J Bloch, Executive Director

Nation's largest organization safeguarding the accessability and civil rights of 28 million deaf and hard of hearing Americans in eduction, employment, health care, and telecommunications. Focuses on grassroots advocate and empowermet, captioned media deafness-related information and publications, legal assistance, and policy development.

6402 National Association of the Deaf Law Center
National Association of the Deaf
8630 Fenton Street
Suite 820
Silver Spring, MD 20910
301-587-1788
Fax: 301-587-1791
http://www.nad.org
TTY 301-587-1789

Rosaline H. Crawford, Director
Nancy J. Bloch, Chief Executive Officer

Represents deaf and hard of hearing individuals in cases of discrimination on the basis of deafness under federal laws such as the ADA, IDEA and the Rehabilitation Act. Provides legal information about how these laws affect deaf people in jobs, education, the courts, public access and government services.

6403 National Black Deaf Advocates
P.O. Box 1126
Asheville, NC 28802
585-475-2411
Fax: 585-475-6500
e-mail: secretary@nbda.org
http://www.nbda.org

Fred Michael Beam, President
Benro Ogunyipe, Vice President

Promotes leadership, deaf awareness and active participation in the political, educational and economic processes that affect the lives of black deaf citizens.

6404 National Captioning Institute
1900 Gallows Road
Vienna, VA 22182-4012
703-917-7600
Fax: 703-917-9853
e-mail: mail@ncicap.org
http://www.ncicap.org
TDD 703-917-7600

Gene Chao, President
Betty Hallman, VP Marketing

Formed in 1979, the nonprofit National Captioning Institute is the global captioning leader, supplying the highest quality closed-captioning services to the television, cable, and home video industries.

6405 National Catholic Office of the Deaf
7202 Buchanan Street
Landover Hills, MD 20784-2299
301-577-4184
Fax: 301-577-1684
e-mail: info@ncod.org
http://www.ncod.org
TTY 301-585-5084

Consuelo Martinez Wild, Executive Director
William F Murphy, Episcopal Representative

Assists in the coordination of the efforts of people and organizations involved in the church's ministry with deaf and hard of hearing people; serves as a resource center for information concerning spirtual needs and religious educational materials; and assists bishops and pastors with their pastoral duties to people who are deaf or hard of hearing.

6406 National Center for Accessible Media
WGBH Educational Foundation
125 Western Avenue
Boston, MA 02134
617-300-3400
Fax: 617-300-1035
e-mail: access.wgbh.org
http://http://main.wgbh.org/

Larry Goldberg, Director
Tom Apone, Director of Operations

6407 National Center for Voice and Speech
University of Iowa
The University of Iowa, 330 Wjshc
Iowa City, IA 52242
319-335-6600
Fax: 319-335-8851
e-mail: titze@shc.uiowa.edu
http://www.ncvs.org

Ingo R Titze PhD, Director
Doug Montequin, PhD, Clinic Director

This is a consortium of institutions focusing on voice and speech disorders. The members of this consortium are the University of Iowa, the Denver Center for Performing Arts, the University of Wisconsin-Madison, and the University of Utah. NCVS trains scientists interested in careers in voice and spech research, provides continuing education for professionals, and conducts research on voice and speech production.

6408 National Center on Deafness
California State University
18111 Nordhoff Street
Northridge, CA 91330-8267
818-677-2054
Fax: 818-677-7192
e-mail: ncod@csun.edu
http://www.csun.edu/ncod/
TDD 818-677-2611

Roz Rosen, Director
Tom McCarron, Executive Director

Taking full advantage of the educational, social, and cultural opportunities a large public university has to offer poses a challenge to the most gifted student. For students who are deaf or hard of hearing, the obstacles are multiplied.
1962

6409 National Center on Employment for the Deaf
NTID at College of Rochester Technology
52 Lomb Memorial Drive
Rochester, NY 14623
585-475-6700
Fax: 585-475-6500
e-mail: thnktank@rit.edu
http://www.rit.edu/ntid

Stephen Aldersley, Conference Chairperson
T. Alan Hurwitz, Chief Executive Officer

Operated by the National Technical Institute for the Deaf at Rochester Institute of Technology, the National Center was established to promote successful employment of RIT's deaf graduates. NCED offers training and consultations to employers and professionals working with deaf persons.

6410 National Congress of Jewish Deaf
33 South Landing Road
Rochester, NY 14610
585-387-0762

Produced a book on Jewish signs, publishes a quarterly newsletter and holds a conference every two years. The group has a listing of deaf synagogues and deaf Jewish groups in major metropolitan areas around the country.

6411 National Cued Speech Association
Nazareth College-Speech & Language Department
4245 East Avenue
Rochester, NY 14618-3703
585-389-2525

Mary Elsie Daisey, Executive Director

Provides instruction, support services and information pertaining to deafness and the application of Cued Speech. The center provides classes and workshops in Cued Speech, maintains a speakers bureau and provides counseling and support for hearing-impaired adults and their families.

Hearing Impaired/Associations & Organizations

6412 National Family Association for Deaf-Blind
141 Middle Neck Road
Sands Point, NY 11050
800-255-0411
800-225-0411
Fax: 516-883-9060
e-mail: NFADB@aol.com
http://www.nfadb.org
TTY 516-944-8637

Linda Syler, President
Pearl Veesart, Vice President

NFADB advocates for all persons who are deaf-blind of any chronological age and cognitive ability, supports national policy to benifit people who are deaf-blind, encourages the founding and strengthening of family organizations in each state, shares information related to deaf-blindness, provides resources and referrals, collaborates with professionals, and assists in the develpment of materials and training seminars which benefit family members.

6413 National Fraternal Society of the Deaf
1118 S 6th Street
Springfield, IL 62703
217-789-7429
Fax: 217-789-7489
e-mail: thefrat@nfsd.com
http://www.nfsd.com

Al Van Nevel, Grand President

This organization is comprised of over 80 divisions across the country that work in the area of life insurance and advocacy for deaf people.

6414 National Information Center on Deafness
Gallaudet University Bookstore
800 Florida Avenue NE
Washington, DC 20002-3600
202-651-5000
Fax: 202-651-5054
e-mail: nicd@gallux.gallaudet.edu
http://www.gallaudet.edu
TDD 202-651-5051

Loraine DiPietro, Director
Erving King Jordan, President

Located on the Gallaudet University campus, this center is a centralized source of accurate, up-to-date information on topics dealing with deafness and hearing loss. Responds to questions from the general public and deaf and hard of hearing people, families and professionals who work with them. Collects, develops and disseminates information on deafness, hearing loss, services and programs related to people with hearing loss.

6415 National Organization for Hearing Research
225 Haverford Avenue
Suite 1
Narberth, PA 19072
610-664-3135
Fax: 610-668-1428
e-mail: smsnohr@worldnet.att.net
http://https://secure.dca.net
TTY 610-664-3135

Geraldine Dietz Fox, President

This organization is a nonprofit private foundation seeking to fund exceptional researchers with $5,000 seed money grants.

6416 National Organization for the Advancement of the Deaf
Lamar University Station
PO Box 10076
Beaumont, TX 77710
409-880-8921
Fax: 409-880-2265
http://www.mbeany.aol.com

Michael Bienenstock, President
Juan Zabala, Executive Director

This organization is dedicated to facilitation communication on issues related to the deaf and providing technical assistance for professionals and parents working with deaf and hard-of-hearing children, adolescents, and adults.

6417 National Rehabilitation Information Center
8455 Colesville Road
Suite 935
Silver Spring, MD 20910-3315
301-588-9284

Mark Odum, Director

6418 National Technical Institute for the Deaf
52 Lomb Memorial Drive
Rochester, NY 14623-5604
585-475-6426
Fax: 585-475-6500
e-mail: ntidmc@rit.edu
http://www.rit.edu/ntid
TDD 716-475-6906

Admissions Department, Contact

Provides technological postsecondary education to deaf and hard-of-hearing students. One of seven colleges of Rochester Institute of Technology.

6419 National Theatre of the Deaf
139 North Main Street
West Hartford, CT 06107
860-236-4193
Fax: 860-236-4163
e-mail: ntd-info@ntd.org
http://www.ntd.org
TTY 860-526-0066

Harvey J. Corson, Chairman
Aaron Kubey, Executive Director and President

Concentrates on artistic and theatrical professional development of deaf actors.

6420 Nebraska Commission for the Deaf & Hard of Hearing
4600 Valley Road
Lincoln, NE 68510-4855
402-471-3593
Fax: 402-471-3067
http://www.nol.org/home

Tanya Wendel, Executive Director

6421 New Jersey Academy of Audiology
77 Schanck Rd.,
Suite A-6
Freehold, NJ 7728
908-232-2900
Fax: 908-232-3583
e-mail: 74072.733@compuserve.com

Robert M Di Sogra, Owner and Director
Robert Woods, Contact

Promotes audiology to consumers, physicians, and schools through outreach and continuing educational programs.

6422 New York Society for the Deaf
817 Broadway
7th Floor
New York, NY 10003
212-777-3900
Fax: 212-777-5470

6423 North Carolina Department of Human Resources: Deaf & Hard of Hearing Division
101 Blair Drive
Adams Building
Raleigh, NC 27699-2001
919-733-6976
Fax: 919-715-0094
e-mail: Diana.Simmons@ncmail.net
http://www.dhhs.state.nc.us

Mark T. Benton, Director
William W. Lawrence, Jr., M.D, Senior Deputy Director

6424 Northern Virginia Resource Center for Deaf and Hard of Hearing Persons
3951 Pender Drive
Suit 130
Fairfax, VA 22030
703-352-9055
Fax: 703-352-9058
e-mail: info@nvrc.org
http://www.nvrc.org

Cheryl A Heppner, Executive Director
Melody Hotek, Director of Operations

Provides services designed to empower persons who are deaf and hard of hearing in the metropolitan areas of Northern Virginia, including the cities of Alexandria, Fairfax, Leesburg, Manassas, Manassas Park, and Falls Church, and the counties of Fairfax, Arlington, Loudoun, and Prince William.

Hearing Impaired/Associations & Organizations

6425 Occupation Hearing Services
PO Box 1880
Media, PA 19063-8880
610-544-7700
800-222-EARS
Fax: 610-543-2802
George Biddle, Executive Director

Hearing help information center. Provides local phone number for Dial-a-Hearing Screening Test and hearing information.

6426 Occupational Hearing Service
PO Box 1880
Media, PA 19063
610-544-7700
800-222-3277
Fax: 610-543-2802
e-mail: dahst@aol.com
http://www.dialatest.com
George Biddle, Executive Director

A national telephone resource providing information about hearing impairments and deafness. Gives referrals to local hearing health care professionals and offers hearing screenings over the telephone at no extra charge.

6427 Ohio School for the Deaf Alumni Association
901 S Sunbury Road
Westerville, OH 43081
614-890-5533
Fax: 614-890-5534
e-mail: osdaa@aol.com
Richard Huebner, President

Provides services to the elderly deaf, deaf-blind, and multi-handicapped persons. Advocates on behalf of the disabled; conducts charitable programs; sponsors festival.

6428 Okada Specialty Guide Dogs
7509 E. Saviors Path
Floral City, FL 34436
352-344-2212
Fax: 352-344-0210
e-mail: okada@okadadogs.com
http://www.okadadogs.com
Patti Putnam, Founder

Trains dogs to aid deaf, hearing-impaired, Alzheimer's, seizure, amnesia and residential companion guide dogs.

6429 Pennsylvania Hearing Aid Alliance
100 S 21st Street
Harrisburg, PA 17104
717-233-6844
Fax: 717-238-2799
e-mail: paletter@paonline.com
http://www.phaa.net
Bob Stewart, Executive Director
Dorothy Kardos, President

6430 Pennsylvania Society for the Advancement of the Deaf and Hearing Impaired
3028 W Liberty Street
Allentown, PA 18104-4713
610-435-6123
Fax: 610-432-7107
e-mail: psadpresident@juno.com
http://www.psadweb.org
Rachel Alburger, Vice President
Gene McGowan, President

Deaf and hearing impaired persons seeking to serve the deaf and promote their special needs in legislation, education, communication, health, research, taxes, rehabilitation, family and community life, and in fighting discrimination and public misconceptions in insurance and employment. Provides governmental representation. Sponsors Leadership Training Program, Miss Deaf Pennsylvania Pageant, Political Action Network, political rallies, and workshops. Involved in operation of George W. Nevil Home for aged and infirm deaf and blind-deaf persons. Operates camping facility. Bestows awards.

6431 Philadelphia 1 Chapter-Self Help for Hard of Hearing People
362 Mallard Road
Feasterville Trevose, PA 19053-5924
Marianne C Grabania, Contact

6432 Pittsburgh Hearing Speech and Deaf Services
1945 5th Avenue
Pittsburgh, PA 15219-5547
412-281-1375
Fax: 412-281-6564
Thomas Bellucci, President/CEO

Provides diagnostic, rehabilitative, and support services for persons who are deaf, hard of hearing, or speech impaired. Offers hearing tests, hearing aid sales and repair, and assistive listening/signaling devices. Offers speech/language evaluation and therapy; provides sign language interpreting, psychological, mental health counseling and social rehabilitation services.

6433 Pittsburgh Hearing, Speech and Deaf Services
1945 5th Avenue
Pittsburgh, PA 15219-5543
412-281-1375
Fax: 412-281-6564
http://www.hdscenter.org
Amy Hart, President and Chief Executive Di
Craig Weber, Director, Financial Services

Provides diagnostic, rehabilitative, and support services for persons who are deaf, hard of hearing, or speech impaired. Offers hearing tests, hearing aid sales and repair, and assistive listening/signaling devices. Offers speech/language evaluation and therapy; provides sign language interpreting, psychological, mental health counseling and social rehabilitation services.

6434 Prevent Blindness Texas Central Regional
P.O. Box 6157
Austin, TX 78762
512-972-4465
Fax: 512-972-4475
e-mail: pbtaustin@yahoo.com
http://www.preventblindness.org/TX/
Vicki Weston, Executive Director
Jim B. Hubbard, President and Chief Executive Of

Individuals interested in preventing blindness and preserving sight through research and education programs.

6435 Providence Speech and Hearing Center
1301 Providence Avenue
Orange, CA 92868
714-639-4990
Fax: 714-744-3841
e-mail: pshc@pshc.org
http://www.pshc.org
Linda Smith, Chief Executive Officer
Raul Lopez, COO/Director of Finance

Providence speech and hearing center's mission is to provide the highest quality services available in the identification, diagnosis, treatment and prevention of speech, language and hearing disorders for persons of all ages.

6436 RRTC on Mental Health/Late Deaf & HOH
California School of Professional Psychology
6160 Cornerstone Court E
San Diego, CA 92121-3720
858-623-2777
Fax: 858- 64- 026
e-mail: rrtc@mail.cspp.edu
http://www.hearinghealth.org
Raymond J Trybus, Director

6437 Regional Resource Center on Deafness
Western Oregon University
345 North Monmouth Avenue
Monmouth, OR 97361
503-838-8444
Fax: 503-838-8228
e-mail: rrcd@wou.edu
http://www.wou.edu
Cheryl Davis PhD, Director

The mission is to prepare professionals in the Northwest who are qualified to serve the unique communication, rehabilitation, and educational needs of deaf and hard of hearing children and adults. The center offers graduate and undergraduate degree programs for professionals entering various fields that serve this population, continuing education opportunities for currently particing professionals; and consultation and community service activities designed to enhance the quality of life for all citizens who are hard of hearing or deaf.

Hearing Impaired/Associations & Organizations

6438 **Registry of Interpreters for the Deaf**
333 Commerce Street
Suite 324
Alexandria, VA 22314
703-838-0030
Fax: 703-838-0454
e-mail: 72620.3143@compuserve.
http://www.rid.org
Clay Nettles, Executive Director
Cheryl Moose, President

A membership organization with over 7,000 members, including professional interpreters and translators, individuals who are deaf or hard of hearing, and professionals in related fields.

6439 **Research and Training Center for Persons Who are Deaf or Hard of Hearing**
26 Corporate Hill Drive
Little Rock, AR 72205
501-686-9691
Fax: 501-686-9698
e-mail: rehabres@cavern.uark.edu
http://www.uark.edu/depts/rehabres/
Dr. Douglas Watson, Director
Steven E. Boone, Director

Rehabilitation of the deaf and hearing impaired.

6440 **Rochester Institute of Technology: National Technical Institute for the Deaf**
Lyndon Baines Johnson Building
52 Lomb Memorial Drive
Rochester, NY 14623
585-475-6400
Fax: 585-475-5978
e-mail: ntidmc@rit.edu
http://www.ntid.rit.edu
T. Alan Hurwitz, Chief Executive Officer
Albert J Simone, President

Provides technical and professional education and training for deaf students.

6441 **Rochester Regional Service Center for Hearing Impaired People**
2116 Campus Drive SE
Suite 32
Rochester, MN 55904
507-285-7295
Jeff Erickson, Executive Officer

Sponsors services to the deaf and hard of hearing. Provides interpreter referral, message relay, vocational rehabilitation, assistance in dealing with agencies, and loans of materials.

6442 **Self-Help for Hard of Hearing People, Cleveland West Chapter**
689 Olde Orchard Ct
Columbus, OH 43213-3409
614-861-7956
e-mail: cohcar@aol.com
http://www.hearingloss.org
Anne Pope, President
Toni Barrient, Director

Hearing impaired individuals, their families, medical professionals, and interested individuals in the western suburbs of Cleveland, OH. Provides education, selfhelp techniques, mutual support, and advocacy for hard of hearing individuals; makes available assistive listening devices.

6443 **Self-Help for Hard of Hearing People: Rochester Chapter**
145 Regatta Drive
Webster, NY 14580-9017
585-266-7890
e-mail: Mail@hlaa-rochester-ny.org
http://www.hlaa-rochester-ny.org
Hal Hood, Treasurer
Doris McWilliams, Corresponding Secretary

Provides support, education, and advocacy for hard of hearing people. Serves as a catalyst that makes mainstream society accessible to hard of hearing people. Conducts charitable activities and participates in area health fairs. Operates letterwriting campaign and professional advisory committee. Holds monthly general and board meetings and annual dinner.

6444 **Self-Help for Hard of Hearing People: South Nassau Chapter**
PO Box 533
Oceanside, NY 11572
516-763-7444
e-mail: myraorfred@aol.com
Myra Sonnenfeld, President

Hard of hearing people, their families, and interested individuals in Nassau County, NY. Devoted to the welfare of hard of hearing individuals. Provides support programs, education, and advocacy.

6445 **Sensor Hearing Aids**
300 S Chester Road
Swarthmore, PA 19081
610-544-2700
800-622-3277
Fax: 610-543-2802
George Biddle, President

Provides information on hearing loss and hearing aids. Offers referrals to audiologists in caller's local area. Free brochure is available. Hours: 9:00 a.m. to 5:00 p.m. Monday-Friday.

6446 **Society of Hearing Impaired Physicians**
1999 Mowry Ave
Suite L
Fremont, CA 94538-1622
510-797-2939
Fax: 510-797-0168
e-mail: fphochship@aol.com
Frank MD, Founder, Managing Director
Ann Hochman, Manager

This Society aids and assists physicians, medical students and prospective medical students whose hearing impairment may necessitate different tools and/or approaches to medical practice and training.

6447 **South Carolina Association of the Deaf**
437 Center Street
West Columbia, SC 29169
803-794-3175
Fax: 803-794-4420
e-mail: info@scadservices.org
http://www.scadservices.org
Clara Gantes, Executive Director
Lee Anne Glover, Administrative Assistant

Advocates for hearing impaired persons. Acts as an information clearinghouse. Provides interpreter information, does statewide interpreter assessments, sells assistive devices for the deaf and hard of hearing.

6448 **Speech Simulation Research Foundation**
600 WATER ST SW 6 11
Box 824
Washington, DC 20024-2471
757-442-2755
Monte Penney, Director

Focuses on hearing and speech disorders.

6449 **Tele-Consumer Hotline**
901 15th Street NW
Suite 230
Washington, DC 20005-2347
202-347-7208
800-332-1124
Fax: 202-408-1134
Sylvia Rosenthal, Executive Director

6450 **Telecommunications for the Deaf**
8630 Fenton Street
Suite 604
Silver Spring, MD 20910
301-589-3786
Fax: 301-589-3797
e-mail: info@tdi-online.org
http://www.tdi-online.org
TDD 301-589-3006
Claud L Stout, Executive Director
Roy Miller, President

553

Hearing Impaired/Associations & Organizations

Dedicated to promoting full visual access to information and telecommunications through consumer educaiton and involvement; technical assistance and consulting; application of existing and emerging technologies; networking and collaboration; uniformity of standards; and national policy development and advocacy. The organization serves people who are deaf, hear of hearing, deaf/blind and/or speech impaired. Provides a comprehensive overview of dea

6451 Texas Association of 504 Coordinators and Hearing Officers
9801 Anderson Mill Road
Suite 230
Austin, TX 78750
512-918-0051
Fax: 512-918-3013
http://www.504idea.org
David M. Richards, Administrator

6452 Texas Commission for the Deaf
4800 N. Lamar Blvd.
Austin, TX 785756
800-628-5115
Fax: 512-451-9316
http://www.dars.state.tx.us/dhhs
David Myers, Director

6453 Travis County Services for the Deaf
2201 Post Road
Suite 100
Austin, TX 78704-4300
512-854-9205
Fax: 512-473-9289
Nancy Riley, Program Manager
Deborah Drummond, Manager

Promotes participation in recreational activities by the deaf. Provides social services, advocacy, and communications access by people who are deaf. Makes available interpreter services to facilitate communication between deaf people and agencies and corporations.

6454 Travis County Services for the Deaf and Hard of Hearing
2201 Post Road
Suite 100
Austin, TX 78704
512-854-9205
Fax: 512-854-9289
e-mail: doug.rollins@co.travis.tx.us
http://www.austindeafservices.com
TTY 512-854-9210
Stacy Landry, Program Manager
Doug Rollins, Manager

Promotes participation in recreational activities by the deaf. Provides social services, advocacy, and communications access by people who are deaf. Makes available interpreter services to facilitate communication between deaf people and agencies and corporations.

6455 Treasure Valley Association of the Hearing Impaired
2712 S Zola Avenue
Boise, ID 83705-3872
208-377-9699
Jackie Baxter, Executive Officer
Sherry Clark, Owner

Hearing impaired individuals, interpreters, parents of hearing impaired, and educators in Boise, ID. To educate the community about the hearing impaired; to teach the hearing impaired to be community leaders. Offers workshops, referral services, and information and referral on deafness, and sign language classes.

6456 Treasure Valley Hearing and Balance Clinics
1084 North Cole Road
Boise, ID 83704
208-377-0019
800-726-1019
Fax: 208-377-0313
e-mail: info@treasurevalleyhearing.com
http://www.treasurevalleyhearing.com
Jacquie Elcox, Chief Executive Officer
Jacquelyn Wolf, Vice President

Hearing impaired individuals, interpreters, parents of hearing impaired, and educators in Boise, ID. To educate the community about the hearing impaired; to teach the hearing impaired to be community leaders. Offers workshops, referral services, and information and referral on deafness, and sign language classes.

6457 Tripod Captioned Filys
1727 W Burbank Boulevard
Burbank, CA 91506
818-972-2080
Fax: 818-972-2090
e-mail: info@tripod.org
http://www.tripod.org
Christopher Opie, Executive Director

Provides first feature filys in movie theatres throughout the United States. Filys are open captioned and no special equipment is needed by either the theatre or audience.

6458 USA Deaf Sports Federation
102 N Krohn Place
Sioux Falls, SD 57103-1800
605-367-5760
Fax: 605-977-6625
e-mail: HomeOffice@usdeafsports.org
http://www.usadsf.org
Dr. Lawrence Fleischer, President
Valarie Kinney, Administrator

Governing body for all deaf sports and recreation in the United States. Seventeen different sports organizations and 200 member clubs are affiliates. Publishes a newsletter three times a year and an annual magazine.

6459 Vermont Agency of Human Services Commission for the Deaf and Hearing Impaired
103 S Main Street
Waterbury, VT 05676-1201
802-241-2800
Fax: 802-241-2830
http://www.dsw.state.vt.us
Diane Dalmasse, Director
Joseph Patrissi, Deputy Commissioner

6460 Virginia Department of Deaf and Hard of Hearing
1602 Rolling Hills Drive
Suite 203
Richmond, VA 23229-5012
804-662-9502
800-552-7917
Fax: 804-662-9718
e-mail: frontdsk@vddhh.virginia.gov
http://www.vddhh.org
Ronald L Lanier, Director
Clayton E Bowen, Business Manager
Elaine S Ziehl, Executive Director

Works to reduce the communication barriers between persons who are deaf or hard of hearing and their families and the professionals who serve them. Operates with the full understanding that communication is the most critical issue facing persons who are deaf or hard of hearing.

6461 Washington Hearing and Speech Center
Sibley Memorial Hospital
5255 Loughboro Road NW
Washington, DC 20016
202-537-4010
Edward J Miller, Chairman
Robert L Sloan, President and Chief Executive Of

Offers individuals with hearing or speech impairments, in the DC area, speech reading classes, audiological services and new aids.

6462 West Virginia Bureau of Human Resources: Commission for the Hearing Impaired
Room 702
350 Capitol Street
Charleston, WV 25301
304-558-2971
Fax: 304-558-1035
http://www.wvdhhr.org
James A. Kaplan, M.D., Chief Medical Examiner
Dwayne O. Combs M.S., M.L.S, Director of Administration

Hearing Impaired/Books

6463 **Wisconsin Alliance of Hearing Professionals**
30 W Mifflin Street
Suite 301
Madison, WI 53703
608-267-1799
Fax: 608-257-8755
e-mail: veterans.museum@dva.state.wi.us
http://http://museum.dva.state.wi.us/

Dr. Richard Zeitlin, Director
Lynne Wolfe, Operations Manager

Hearing instrument specialists and audiologists. Disseminates information on hearing health care to the public and on the use and care of hearing instruments to the hearing impaired.

Books

6464 **Advanced Sign Language Vocabulary**
Charles C Thomas Publisher
2600 S 1st Street
Springfield, IL 62704-4730
217-789-8980
Fax: 217-789-9130
e-mail: books@ccthomas.com
http://www.ccthomas.com

Michael P Thomas, President

A resource text for educators, interpreters, parents and sign language instructors.

202 pages

6465 **American Deaf Culture**
Gallaudet Univ. Press c/o Chicago Distrib. Center
11030 S Langley Avenue
Chicago, IL 60628-3830
800-621-2736
Fax: 800-621-8476
http://www.gallaudet.edu
TTY 888-630-9347

This book presents a collection of classic articles which have been selected to provide a variety of perspectives on language and culture of deaf people in America.

132 pages

6466 **American Deaf Culture: An Anthology**
Sign Media
4020 Blackburn Lane
Burtonsville, MD 20866-1167
301-421-0268
800-475-6447
Fax: 303-759-0359
http://www.signmedia.com
TTY 301-421-4460

Barbara Olmert, Director Marketing
Sherman Wilcox, Editor
Verden Ness, President

Features Deaf and hearing authors offering their experience and perspectives on cultural values, ASL, social interaction in the Deaf community, education, folklore, and more.

6467 **American Sign Language Phrase Book**
TJ Publishers
817 Silver Spring Avenue
Suite 206
Silver Spring, MD 20910-4617
301-585-4440
Fax: 301-585-5930
e-mail: TJPubinc@aol.com

Angela K Thames, President
Jerald A Murphy, VP

The author provides interesting, realistic and meaningful situations. Sign language is learned through novel remarks cleverly organized around everyday topics.

362 pages

6468 **American Sign Language: A Beginning Course**
National Association of the Deaf
814 Thayer Avenue
Silver Spring, MD 20910-4504
301-587-6282
Fax: 301-587-4873
e-mail: sales@nad.org
http://www.nad.org
TTY 301-587-1789

An interactive approach to teaching and learning American Sign Language, with 700 sign illustrations, each accompanied by an object drawing.

199 pages

6469 **An Invisible Condition: the Human Side of Hearing Loss**
SHHH Publications
7800 Wisconsin Avenue
Bethesda, MD 20814-3524
301-657-2248
Fax: 301-913-9413

Terry Portis, Executive Director

Offers editorials from the SHHH Journal that have shaped the past decade of self help with their focus on the plight and hopes and the aspirations of hard of hearing people everywhere.

6470 **Basic Course in American Sign Language**
TJ Publishers
817 Silver Spring Avenue
Suite 206
Silver Spring, MD 20910-4617
301-585-4440
Fax: 301-585-5930
e-mail: TJPubinc@aol.com
TDD 301-585-4440

Angela K Thames, President
Jerald A Murphy, VP

Accompanying videotapes and textbooks include voice translations. Hearing students can analyze sound for initial instruction, or opt to turn off the sound to sharpen visual acuity. Package includes the Basic Course in American Sign Language text, Student Study Guide, the original four 1-hour videotapes plus the ABCASI Vocabulary videotape.

6471 **Basic Course in Manual Communication**
Gallaudet University Bookstore
11030 S Langley Avenue
Chicago, IL 60628-3830
312-644-8300
800-451-1073
Fax: 202-651-5489
TTY 301-587-1789

Angelo Bosco, Owner

Teach your students manual communication - that living, changing, growing language of signs.

158 pages

6472 **Basic Sign Communication: Vocabulary**
National Association of the Deaf
814 Thayer Avenue
Silver Spring, MD 20910-4504
301-587-6282
Fax: 301-587-4873
e-mail: sales@nad.org
http://www.nad.org
TTY 301-587-1789

Features sections on Sign Vocabulary, Numbers, and Classifiers. Contains 1000 illustrated signs, organized alphabetically by gloss for quick reference.

162 pages

6473 **Between Friends**
Beltone Electronics Corporation
4201 W Victoria Street
Chicago, IL 60646-6718
773-583-3600
Fax: 773-583-2027

Renee Rockoff, Editor

For hearing aid wearers: quizzes, jokes, health, recipes and financial items.

6 pages

Hearing Impaired/Books

6474 Black and Deaf in America
TJ Publishers
817 Silver Spring Avenue
Suite 206
Silver Spring, MD 20910-4617
301-585-4440
Fax: 301-585-5930

Angela K Thames, President
Jerald A Murphy, VP

An in-depth look at some of the problems of the Black Deaf community, including undereducation and underemployment. This book includes an important chapter on signs used in the black community and presents interviews with prominent Black Deaf individuals who share their joys, fears and hope for the future.

6475 Book of Name Signs
Gallaudet University Bookstore
11030 S Langley Avenue
Chicago, IL 60628-3830
202-651-5488
800-451-1073
Fax: 202-651-5489
TTY 888-630-9347

Discusses the rules for American Sign Language name sign formation and their appropriate use.

112 pages

6476 Bridges Beyond Sound
Brookes Publishing
PO Box 10624
Baltimore, MD 21285-624
410-337-9580
800-638-3775
Fax: 410-337-8539
e-mail: custserv@pbrookes.com
http://www.pbrookes.com

Paul Brooks, Owner

An instructional workbook on understanding and including students with a hearing loss. Supplement to the Bridges Beyond Sound videotape. Besides the videotape script, background information on hearing loss, discussion questions, activities, and reproducible worksheets are included.

176 pages

6477 Changing the Rules
TJ Publishers
817 Silver Spring Avenue
Suite 206
Silver Spring, MD 20910-4617
301-585-4440
Fax: 301-585-5930
e-mail: TJPubinc@aol.com

Angela K Thames, President
Jerald A Murphy, VP

Like many deaf adults, Frank Bowe was mainstreamed in the small Pennsylvania town where he was raised. This is a humorous and poignant account of the obstacles that shaped this leading disability rights activist. Bowe's account of coming of age and personal growth, the discovery of signed language and an insider's view of the equal rights movement is a compelling record of one man's struggle with the challenges of profound deafness.

6478 Chelsea: The Story of a Signal Dog
Gallaudet University Bookstore
800 Florida Avenue NE
Washington, DC 20002-3600
202-651-5000
800-451-1073
Fax: 202-651-5489
TTY 888-630-9347

Erving King Jordan, President

This is a story of a young deaf couple and their Belgian sheepdog, who acts as their 'ears'. It explains how these dogs are trained and paired with their new owners.

169 pages

6479 Choices in Deafness
Woodbine House
6510 Bells Mill Road
Bethesda, MD 20817-1636
301-897-3570
800-843-7323
Fax: 301-897-5838
e-mail: info@woodbinehouse.com
http://www.woodbinehouse.com

Irv Shapell, Owner

A useful aid in choosing the appropriate communication option for a child with a hearing loss. Experts present the following communication options: Auditory-Verbal Approach, Bilingual-Bicultural Approach, Cued Speech, Oral Approach, and Total Communication. This new edition explains medical causes of hearing loss, the diagnostic process, audiological assessment, and cochlear implants. Children and parents also offer their personal experiences.

275 pages

6480 Cognition, Education and Deafness
Gallaudet University Press
800 Florida Avenue NE
Washington, DC 20002-3600
202-651-5488
800-621-2736
Fax: 202-651-5489
TDD 888-630-9347

The work of 54 authors is gathered in this definitive collection of current research on deafness and cognition. The articles are grouped into seven sections: cognition, problem solving, thinking processes, language development, reading methodologies, measurement of potential, and intervention programs.

260 pages

6481 Come Sign with Us
Gallaudet Univ. Press c/o Chicago Distrib. Center
11030 S Langley Avenue
Chicago, IL 60628-3830
800-621-2736
Fax: 800-621-8476
http://www.gallaudet.edu
TTY 888-630-9347

Lessons including fingerspelling and signing are overviewed.

6482 Communicating with Deaf People: An Introduction
Gallaudet University Bookstore
800 Florida Avenue NE
Washington, DC 20002-3600
202-651-5000
800-451-1073
Fax: 202-651-5489

Erving King Jordan, President

This illustrated publication introduces the various ways deaf people can communicate, including gesture and facial expression, speech-reading, fingerspelling and other manual communication systems.

20 pages

6483 Communication Access for Persons with Hearing Loss
Alexander Graham Bell Association for the Deaf
1537 35th Street NW
Washington, DC 20007-2753
202-337-5220
Fax: 202-337-8270
http://www.agbell.org
TTY 202-337-5220

Todd Houston, Executive Director

Filled with information about available technologies, this book explores equipment and options available uner the ADA. The book stresses that technology is a tool, not a solution, for combination hearing loss and for improving communication.

306 pages

6484 Communication Disorders in Aging
Gallaudet University Press
800 Florida Avenue NE
Washington, DC 20002-3600
202-651-5488
800-621-2736
Fax: 202-651-5489
TDD 888-630-9347

Hearing Impaired/Books

This text presents contemporary practices in the medical and clinical assessment of the aged, reviews clinical evaluation techniques, and provides a comprehensive discussion of neurological imaging techniques.

528 pages

6485 **Communication Issues Among Deaf People**
Gallaudet Univ. Press c/o Chicago Distrib. Center
11030 S Langley Avenue
Chicago, IL 60628-3830
800-621-2736
Fax: 800-621-8476
http://www.gallaudet.edu
TTY 888-630-9347

Monograph discussing important aspects of communication including total communication and the value of ASL.

138 pages

6486 **Communication Issues Among Deaf People - Eyes, Hands, and Voices**
National Association of the Deaf
814 Thayer Avenue
Silver Spring, MD 20910-4504
301-587-6282
Fax: 301-587-4873
e-mail: sales@nad.org
http://www.nad.org
TTY 301-587-1789

Includes over thirty relevant articles reflecting a wide range of perceptions and attitudes on communication among deaf people.

145 pages

6487 **Communication Issues Related to Hearing Loss**
Self Help for Hard of Hearing People
7910 Woodmont Avenue
Suite 1200
Bethesda, MD 20814-7022
301-657-2248
Fax: 301-913-9413
e-mail: national@shhh.org
http://www.shhh.org
TTY 301-657-2249

Terry Portis, Executive Director

An overview of causes and effects of hearing loss on those who experience it - both people with hearing loss and their families. Helpful also to professionals who provide services to people with hearing loss.

6488 **Communication Therapy for Hearing Impaired Adults**
Alexander Graham Bell Association for the Deaf
1537 35th Street NW
Washington, DC 20007-2753
202-337-5220
Fax: 202-337-8270
http://www.agbell.org
TTY 202-337-5220

Todd Houston, Executive Director

A conversation-based aural habilitation approach offers assessment materials and relevant therapy procedures for hearing impaired adults in daily conversation.

228 pages

6489 **Communication and Adult Hearing Loss**
Alexander Graham Bell Association for the Deaf
1537 35th Street NW
Washington, DC 20007-2753
202-337-5220
Fax: 202-337-8270
http://www.agbell.org
TTY 202-337-5220

Todd Houston, Executive Director

This informative book was written for anyone who wants to communicate more effectively with a person with adult hearing loss.

136 pages

6490 **Communication-Based Learning Communities**
Alexander Graham Bell Association for the Deaf
1537 35th Street NW
Washington, DC 20007-2753
202-337-5220
Fax: 202-337-8270
http://www.agbell.org
TTY 202-337-5220

Trinka Messenheimer-Young, Editor
Kathleena Whitesell, Editor
Todd Houston, Executive Director

This 1995 monograph of The Volta Review examines how teachers work with students who are deaf or hard of hearing to construct knowledge rather than to transmit information to students and to create meaningful context.

169 pages

6491 **Comprehensive Reference Manual for Signers and Interpreters 4th Edition**
Charles C Thomas Publisher
2600 S 1st Street
Springfield, IL 62704-4730
217-789-8980
800-258-8980
Fax: 217-789-9130
e-mail: books@ccthomas.com
http://www.ccthomas.com

Michael P Thomas, President

Manual for signers. Paperback only.

314 pages 1994

6492 **Comprehensive Signed English Dictionary**
Harris Communications
15155 Technology Drive
Eden Prairie, MN 55344-2273
952-906-1180
800-825-6758
Fax: 952-906-1099
e-mail: mail@harriscomm.com
http://www.harriscomm.com

Karen L Saulnier, Author
Lillian B Hamilton, Author
Bill Williams, National Sales Manager

Complete dictionary offers 3,100 signs, including signs reflecting contemporary vocabulary.

457 pages

6493 **Conversational Sign Language II**
Harris Communications
15155 Technology Drive
Eden Prairie, MN 55344-2273
952-906-1180
800-825-6758
Fax: 952-906-1099
e-mail: mail@harriscomm.com
http://www.harriscomm.com

Bill Williams, National Sales Manager
Robert Harris, Owner

This book presents English words and their American Sign Language equivalents.

218 pages

6494 **Coping with the Multi-Handicapped Hearing Impaired: A Practical Approach**
Charles C Thomas Publisher
2600 S 1st Street
Springfield, IL 62704-4730
217-789-8980
800-258-8980
Fax: 217-789-9130
e-mail: books@ccthomas.com
http://www.ccthomas.com

Michael P Thomas, President

Professional text offers suggestions on how to deal with the multi-handicapped deaf person. Available in cloth, paperback and hardcover.

90 pages

Hearing Impaired/Books

6495 **Dancing Without Music**
Gallaudet Univ. Press c/o Chicago Distrib. Center
11030 S Langley Avenue
Chicago, IL 60628-3830
800-621-2736
Fax: 800-621-8476
http://www.gallaudet.edu
TTY 888-630-9347

Investigates being deaf and its ramifications in society.
320 pages

6496 **Deaf in America: Voices from a Culture**
TJ Publishers
817 Silver Spring Avenue
Suite 206
Silver Spring, MD 20910-4617
301-585-4440
Fax: 301-585-5930
e-mail: TJPubinc@aol.com

Angela K Thames, President
Jerald A Murphy, VP

Now available in paperback, this book opens deaf culture to outsiders, inviting readers to imagine and understand a world of silence. This book shares the joy and satisfaction many people have with their lives and shows that deafness may not be the handicap most hearing people think.

6497 **Deafness 1993-2013**
National Association of the Deaf
814 Thayer Avenue
Silver Spring, MD 20910-4504
301-587-1788
Fax: 301-587-4873
TTY 301-587-1789

Over 30 articles cover such topics as magnet schools, deaf identity, technology, multicultural education, communication, leadership, and sign language research.

6498 **Discovering Sign Language**
Gallaudet University Press
800 Florida Avenue NE
Washington, DC 20002-3600
202-651-5488
800-621-2736
Fax: 202-651-5489
TDD 888-630-9347
TTY 888-630-9347

Here is a book of information about deaf people and sign communication.
104 pages

6499 **Do You Hear Me?**
Alexander Graham Bell Association for the Deaf
1537 35th Street NW
Washington, DC 20007-2753
202-337-5220
Fax: 202-337-8270
http://www.agbell.org
TTY 202-337-5220

Todd Houston, Executive Director

This little book is a collection of all the jokes and cartoons that help the author cope with his hearing impairment. He believes strongly that family members and friends who offer encouragement and understanding play an extremely important role in whether people with hearing losses decide to seek professional help to overcome the problems that their hearing loss causes.
138 pages

6500 **Ear Book**
Gallaudet Univ. Press c/o Chicago Distrib. Center
11030 S Langley Avenue
Chicago, IL 60628-3830
800-621-2736
Fax: 800-621-8476
http://www.gallaudet.edu
TTY 888-630-9347

A how-to book on obtaining and using an otoscope, recognizing and managing common ear disorders, when to call the doctor and when your child needs ear tubes.
136 pages

6501 **Educating the Deaf: Psychology, Principles and Practices**
Gallaudet Univ. Press c/o Chicago Distrib. Center
11030 S Langley Avenue
Chicago, IL 60628-3830
800-621-2736
Fax: 800-621-8476
http://www.gallaudet.edu
TTY 888-630-9347

Offers extensive coverage of the background and history of the education of the deaf, as well as specific information on working with multihandicapped students.
383 pages

6502 **Encyclopedia of Deafness and Hearing Disorders**
Gallaudet University Bookstore
800 Florida Avenue NE
Washington, DC 20002-3600
202-651-5000
800-451-1073
Fax: 202-651-5489

Erving King Jordan, President

Presents the most current information on deafness and hearing disorders in an authoritative A-to-Z compendium.
278 pages

6503 **FM Auditory Training Systems**
Alexander Graham Bell Association for the Deaf
1537 35th Street NW
Washington, DC 20007-2753
202-337-5220
Fax: 202-337-8270
http://www.agbell.org
TTY 202-337-5220

Todd Houston, Executive Director

This brand new text is a collection of papers written by notable experts in the field of FM auditory training systems and speech development.
254 pages

6504 **GA and SK Etiquette**
Gallaudet University Bookstore
800 Florida Avenue NE
Washington, DC 20002-3600
202-651-5000
800-451-1073
Fax: 202-651-5489
TTY 888-630-9347

Erving King Jordan, President

This booklet presents guidelines for proper usage of the TDD. It includes everything you wanted to know about sending and receiving TDD calls.
53 pages

6505 **Gallaudet Encyclopedia of Deaf People and Deafness**
Gallaudet Univ. Press c/o Chicago Distrib. Center
11030 S Langley Avenue
Chicago, IL 60628-3830
800-621-2736
Fax: 800-621-8476
http://www.gallaudet.edu
TTY 888-630-9347

Three-volume set of research and information on deaf people and deafness.
1400 pages

6506 **HEAR: Solutions, Skills, and Sources for People with Hearing Loss**
DK Publishing
375 Hudson Street
New York, NY 10014
806-318-571
Fax: 201-256-0000
TDD 2 - -

Hearing Impaired/Books

6507 **Hear: Solutions, Skills, and Sources for People with Hearing Loss**
Alexander Graham Bell Association for the Deaf
1537 35th Street NW
Washington, DC 20007-2753
202-408-7901
Fax: 202-337-8270
http://www.agbell.org
TTY 202-337-5220

Michael J Hoare, President

This practical, well-designed self-help guide is a valuable resource for people who are hard of hearing and their families and friends. HEAR features real-life case studies and interviews with people who have become hard of hearing. The reader will learn about sound and how we hear; tips for making changes, finding self-help groups, and knowing your rights; about types of hearing loss and hearing tests.ing loss, from hearing aids to cochlear implant.

128 pages Frequency: Hardbound

6508 **Hearing Rehabilitation for Deafened Adults: A Psychosocial Approach**
Wiley
10475 Crosspoint Boulevard
Indianapolis, IN 46256
877-762-2974
Fax: 800-597-3299
http://www.wiley.com

Anthony Hogan, Author

Provides the reader with a psycho-social framework for understanding practice, while offering a range of practical strategies,tools and counseling ideas for use in the clinic.

200 pages

6509 **Hearing in Aging**
Alexander Graham Bell Association for the Deaf
1537 35th Street NW
Washington, DC 20007-2753
202-337-5220
Fax: 202-337-8270
http://www.agbell.org
TTY 202-337-5220

Todd Houston, Executive Director

A useful title for hearing professionals that discusses rehabilitative services and delivery for adults with age-related hearing loss.

302 pages

6510 **How to Survive a Hearing Loss**
Gallaudet Univ. Press c/o Chicago Distrib. Center
11030 S Langley Avenue
Chicago, IL 60628-3830
800-621-2736
Fax: 800-621-8476
http://www.gallaudet.edu
TTY 888-630-9347

This book presents the results of the author's intensive research about hearing and the ear.

241 pages

6511 **I Didn't Hear the Dragon Roar**
Gallaudet Univ. Press c/o Chicago Distrib. Center
11030 S Langley Avenue
Chicago, IL 60628-3830
800-621-2736
Fax: 800-621-8476
http://www.gallaudet.edu
TTY 888-630-9347

The remarkable true story of a deaf woman's journey from Hong Kong to Katmandu.

251 pages

6512 **I Think I Have a Hearing Problem! What Should I Do?**
Self Help for Hard of Hearing People
7910 Woodmont Avenue
Suite 1200
Bethesda, MD 20814-7022
301-657-2248
Fax: 301-913-9413
e-mail: national@shhh.org
http://www.shhh.org
TTY 301-657-2249

Terry Portis, Executive Director

A basic introduction to hearing loss and where to go for help.

6513 **In All Our Affairs: Making Crises Work for You**
Al-Anon Family Group Headquarters
1600 Corporate Landing Parkway
Virginia Beach, VA 23454-5617
757-563-1600
800-356-9996
Fax: 757-563-1655
e-mail: wso@al-anon.alateen.org
http://www.al-anon.alateen.org

Shatters the silence surrounding crises that go hand in hand with alcoholism.

256 pages

6514 **Intermediate Conversational SignLanguage**
TJ Publishers
817 Silver Spring Avenue
Suite 206
Silver Spring, MD 20910-4617
301-585-4440
Fax: 301-585-5930
e-mail: TJPubinc@aol.com

Angela K Thames, President
Jerald A Murphy, VP

Unique approach to using American Sign Language and English in a bilingual setting. Each of the 25 lessons includes an introductory paragraph, glossed vocabulary review, translation exercises, grammatical notes, substitution drills and activities.

6515 **Interpretation: A Sociolinguistic Model**
Gallaudet University Bookstore
800 Florida Avenue NE
Washington, DC 20002-3600
202-651-5000
800-451-1073
Fax: 202-651-5489

Erving King Jordan, President

This text presents a sociolinguistically sensitive model of the interpretation process. The model applies to interpretation in any two languages although this one focuses on ASL and English.

199 pages

6516 **Introduction to Communication**
Gallaudet Univ. Press c/o Chicago Distrib. Center
11030 S Langley Avenue
Chicago, IL 60628-3830
800-621-2736
Fax: 800-621-8476
http://www.gallaudet.edu
TTY 888-630-9347

Curriculum materials exploring the areas of sound, hearing and interpersonal communication.

100 pages

6517 **Invisible Condition: The Human Side of Hearing Loss**
Self Help for Hard of Hearing People
7910 Woodmont Avenue
Suite 1200
Bethesda, MD 20814-7022
301-657-2248
Fax: 301-913-9413
e-mail: national@shhh.org
http://www.shhh.org
TTY 301-657-2249

Terry Portis, Executive Director

A collection of 14 years of editorials by the author from the SHHH Journal.

Hearing Impaired/Books

6518 Journey Into the DEAF-WORLD
DawnSignPress
6130 Nancy Ridge Drive
San Diego, CA 92121-3223
858-625-0600
800-549-5350
Fax: 858-625-2336
e-mail: dps@dawnsign.com
http://www.dawnsign.com

Barry Howland, Marketing Director
Joe Dannis, President

Provides explanation about the nature and meaning of the DEAF-WORLD. Comprehensive work discusses latest findings and theories for Deaf Studies students and professionals working with Deaf people.

528 pages

6519 Journey Into the World of the Deaf
TJ Publishers
817 Silver Spring Avenue
Suite 206
Silver Spring, MD 20910-4617
301-585-4440
Fax: 301-585-5930
e-mail: TJPubinc@aol.com

Angela K Thames, President
Jerald A Murphy, VP

Well known for his exploration of how people respond to neurological impairments, Dr Sacks explores the world of the deaf and discovers how deaf people respond to their loss of hearing and how they develop language. A highly readable introduction to deaf people, deaf culture and American Sign Language.

6520 Joy of Listening: An Auditory Training Program
Alexander Graham Bell Association for the Deaf
1537 35th Street NW
Washington, DC 20007-2753
202-337-5220
Fax: 202-337-8270
http://www.agbell.org
TTY 202-337-5220

Todd Houston, Executive Director

This manual contains lessons to improve listening skills, auditory discrimination, attention span, memory, and sequencing in children with hearing losses. The lessons can be used when working with children alone, or in small groups.

160 pages

6521 Joy of Signing
Gallaudet University Bookstore
800 Florida Avenue NE
Washington, DC 20002-3600
202-651-5000
800-451-1073
Fax: 202-651-5489

Erving King Jordan, President

This manual on signing includes illustrations, information on sign origins, practice sentences, and step-by-step descriptions of hand positions and movements.

336 pages

6522 Keys to Living with Hearing Loss
Self Help for Hard of Hearing People
7910 Woodmont Avenue
Suite 1200
Bethesda, MD 20814-7022
301-657-2248
Fax: 301-913-9413
e-mail: national@shhh.org
http://www.shhh.org
TTY 301-657-2249

Terry Portis, Executive Director

Guidebook that provides helpful advice on a wide range of topics, from living alone with a hearing loss, to going to the hospital, to legal rights.

6523 Learning To Hear Again
Alexander Graham Bell Association for the Deaf
1537 35th Street NW
Washington, DC 20007-2753
202-337-5220
Fax: 202-337-8270
http://www.agbell.org
TTY 202-337-5220

Todd Houston, Executive Director

This audiologic rehabilitation curriculum guide is designed to help audiologists and speech language pathologist provide rehabilitation and education for adults with hearing losses. The authors are practicing audiologists and have used these methods successfully in individual and group sessions. This comprehensive manual comprises lesson plans, activities, and materials ready to be duplicated and distributed to clients. Three-ring binder.

224 pages

6524 Learning to See: American Sign Language as a Second Language
Gallaudet Univ. Press c/o Chicago Distrib. Center
11030 S Langley Avenue
Chicago, IL 60628-3830
800-621-2736
Fax: 800-621-8476
http://www.gallaudet.edu
TTY 888-630-9347

Provides a comprehensive introduction to the history and structure of ASL to the deaf community.

134 pages

6525 Legal Rights of Hearing-Impaired People
Gallaudet Univ. Press c/o Chicago Distrib. Center
11030 S Langley Avenue
Chicago, IL 60628-3830
800-621-2736
Fax: 800-621-8476
http://www.gallaudet.edu
TTY 888-630-9347

Includes updated interpretations of legislation affecting hearing-impaired people, including chapters dealing with the ADA.

297 pages

6526 Lessons in Laughter: The Autobiography of a Deaf Actor
Gallaudet Univ. Press c/o Chicago Distrib. Center
11030 S Langley Avenue
Chicago, IL 60628-3830
800-621-2736
Fax: 800-621-8476
http://www.gallaudet.edu
TTY 888-630-9347

Born deaf of deaf parents, Bernard Bragg dreamed of using sign language to act. This book recounts how he starred in his own television show.

237 pages

6527 Linguistics of American Sign Language
McFarland & Company
PO Box 611
Jefferson, NC 28640
336-246-4460
800-253-2187
Fax: 336-246-5018

How signers communicate thoughts, ideas and feelings through a gesturing/seeing medium instead of a speaking/hearing process. Also explored in this book is the grammatical structure and technical aspects of the language.

268 pages

6528 Lipreading Made Easy Book and Video Tape
Alexander Graham Bell Association for the Deaf
1537 35th Street NW
Washington, DC 20007-2753
202-337-5220
Fax: 202-331-8314
http://www.agbell.org

Elizabeth Quigley, Director Publications
Todd Houston, Executive Director

Hearing Impaired/Books

This photo primer was written to satisfy the need for easy practice-at-home material for people who want to learn the basics of lipreading. 120 minute videotape that gives one hour lessons.
32 pages

6529 Lisa and Her Soundless World
Resources for Rehabilitation
22 Bonad Road
Winchester, MA 01890-1302
781-368-9094
Fax: 781-368-9096

Describes the impact deafness has on communication and functioning in a hearing world. Lisa, born with a severe hearing loss, was not diagnosed as hearing impaired until her parents were worried about her lack of speech and other children had rejected her.
30 pages

6530 Look Now, Hear This: Combined Auditory Training and Speechreading Instruction
Charles C Thomas Publisher
2600 S 1st Street
Springfield, IL 62704-4730
217-789-8980
800-258-8980
Fax: 217-789-9130
e-mail: books@ccthomas.com
http://www.ccthomas.com

Michael P Thomas, President
230 pages

6531 Looking Back: A Reader on the History of Deaf Communities & Sign Language
Gallaudet Univ. Press c/o Chicago Distrib. Center
11030 S Langley Avenue
Chicago, IL 60628-3830
800-621-2736
Fax: 800-621-8476
http://www.gallaudet.edu
TTY 888-630-9347

Renowned researchers from around the world present provocative findings in six areas relating to the deaf culture.
558 pages

6532 Meeting Halfway in ASL
PO Box 23380
Rochester, NY 14692-3380
585-442-6370
Fax: 585-442-6371
e-mail: Books@deaflife.com
http://www.deaflife.com
TTY 716-442-6370

Matthew Moore, Publisher

Illustrated photographic sign-language book containing 1,300 photos.

6533 Mental Health Services for Deaf People
Gallaudet Univ. Press c/o Chicago Distrib. Center
11030 S Langley Avenue
Chicago, IL 60628-3830
800-621-2736
Fax: 800-621-8476
http://www.gallaudet.edu
TTY 888-630-9347

Contains information on over 350 mental health programs and services for deaf people across the United States.
210 pages

6534 Missing Words: The Family Handbook on Adult Hearing Loss
Gallaudet Univ. Press c/o Chicago Distrib. Center
11030 S Langley Avenue
Chicago, IL 60628-3830
800-621-2736
Fax: 800-621-8476
http://www.gallaudet.edu
TTY 888-630-9347

Written by a mother who lost her hearing and her daughter, learning to cope.
304 pages

6535 NAD Deaf Awareness Kit
National Association of the Deaf
814 Thayer Avenue
Silver Spring, MD 20910-4504
301-587-1788
Fax: 301-587-4873
TTY 301-587-1789

Includes information that can be used both during Deaf Awareness Week and year-round to recognize the accomplishments and heritage of the deaf community.

6536 On My Own
Gallaudet Univ. Press c/o Chicago Distrib. Center
11030 S Langley Avenue
Chicago, IL 60628-3830
800-621-2736
Fax: 800-621-8476
http://www.gallaudet.edu
TTY 888-630-9347

Book examining doorbell devices, alarm clocks, telephone amplifiers and other assistive devices for the deaf.
50 pages

6537 Other Side of Silence
Gallaudet Univ. Press c/o Chicago Distrib. Center
11030 S Langley Avenue
Chicago, IL 60628-3830
800-621-2736
Fax: 800-621-8476
http://www.gallaudet.edu
TTY 888-630-9347

Explores the deaf community through interviews from across the country.
256 pages

6538 Outsiders in a Hearing World
Gallaudet University Bookstore
800 Florida Avenue NE
Washington, DC 20002-3600
202-651-5000
800-451-1073
Fax: 202-651-5489
TTY 888-630-9347

Erving King Jordan, President

An introduction to the social world of deaf people. The author gives a sociologists view of what it's like to be deaf.
240 pages

6539 Place of Their Own: Creating the DeafCommunity in America
TJ Publishers
817 Silver Spring Avenue
Suite 206
Silver Spring, MD 20910-4617
301-585-4440
Fax: 301-585-5930
e-mail: TJPubinc@aol.com
TTY 888-630-9347

Angela K Thames, President
Jerald A Murphy, VP

Traces development of American deaf society to show how deaf people developed a common language and sense of community. Views deafness as the distinguishing characteristic of a distinct culture.

6540 Senior Citizen Program Packet
Self Help for Hard of Hearing People
7910 Woodmont Avenue
Suite 1200
Bethesda, MD 20814-7022
301-657-2248
Fax: 301-913-9413
e-mail: national@shhh.org
http://www.shhh.org
TTY 301-657-2249

Terry Portis, Executive Director

Information and ideas for anyone working with groups of older adults with hearing loss. Materials include a model program of one senior center, information on communication access and assistive devices, coping strategies, publications, programs, and resources.

Hearing Impaired/Books

6541 Signing Exact English
Modern Signs Press
PO Box 1181
Los Alamitos, CA 90720-1181
562-596-8548
800-572-7332
Fax: 562-795-6614
TTY 310-493-4168

Esther Zawolkow, President

A reference manual containing manual signs representing nearly 4,000 words, plus signs for letters, numbers, prefixes and suffixes.

479 pages

6542 Signing Illustrated
Gallaudet Univ. Press c/o Chicago Distrib. Center
11030 S Langley Avenue
Chicago, IL 60628-3830
800-621-2736
Fax: 800-621-8476
http://www.gallaudet.edu
TTY 888-630-9347

A guide presenting illustrations of over 1,350 signs.

85 pages

6543 Signing: How to Speak with Your Hands
TJ Publishers
817 Silver Spring Avenue
Suite 206
Silver Spring, MD 20910-4617
301-585-4440
Fax: 301-585-5930
e-mail: TJPubinc@aol.com

Angela K Thames, President
Jerald A Murphy, VP

Presents 1,200 basic signs with clear illustrations in logical topical groupings. Linguistic principles are described at the beginning of each chapter, giving insight into the rules which govern American Sign Language.

6544 Signs Across America
TJ Publishers
817 Silver Spring Avenue
Suite 206
Silver Spring, MD 20910-4617
301-585-4440
Fax: 301-585-5930
e-mail: TJPubinc@aol.com

Angela K Thames, President
Jerald A Murphy, VP

A look at regional variations in ASL. Signs for selected words collected from 25 different states. More than 1,200 signs illustrated in the text.

285 pages

6545 Signs for Computing Terminology
Gallaudet University Bookstore
11030 S Langley Avenue
Chicago, IL 60628-3830
202-651-5488
800-451-1073
Fax: 202-651-5489
TTY 301-587-1789

This sign reference will facilitate communication among deaf persons involved with computers by providing a significant vocabulary base for the computing field of today and tomorrow.

182 pages

6546 Silent Alarm: On the Edge with a Deaf EMT
Gallaudet Univ. Press c/o Chicago Distrib. Center
11030 S Langley Avenue
Chicago, IL 60628-3830
800-621-2736
Fax: 800-621-8476
http://www.gallaudet.edu
TTY 888-630-9347

Silent Alarm tells the gripping story of survival and the good that the author did as a topnotch EMT.

160 pages

6547 Software to Go
Gallaudet Univ. Press c/o Chicago Distrib. Center
11030 S Langley Avenue
Chicago, IL 60628-3830
800-621-2736
Fax: 800-621-8476
http://www.gallaudet.edu
TTY 888-630-9347

Lists and describes commercial software that may be borrowed by educators of hearing impaired students.

100 pages

6548 Speak Out! Tips on Speaking in Public for Individuals with a Hearing Loss
Self Help for Hard of Hearing People
7910 Woodmont Avenue
Suite 1200
Bethesda, MD 20814-7022
301-657-2248
Fax: 301-913-9413
e-mail: national@shhh.org
http://www.shhh.org
TTY 301-657-2249

Terry Portis, Executive Director

Learn how to be an effective speaker.

6549 Speech & Lip Reading
Charles C Thomas Publisher
2600 S 1st Street
Springfield, IL 62704-4730
217-789-8980
800-258-8980
Fax: 217-789-9130
e-mail: books@ccthomas.com
http://www.ccthomas.com

Michael P Thomas, President

6550 Understanding Deafness Socially
Charles C Thomas Publisher
2600 S 1st Street
Springfield, IL 62704-4730
217-789-8980
800-258-8980
Fax: 217-789-9130
e-mail: books@ccthomas.com
http://www.ccthomas.com
TTY 888-630-9347

Michael P Thomas, President

A look at the social difficulties of being hearing impaired in a 'hearing' society.

168 pages

6551 VISION
National Catholic Office for the Deaf
7202 Buchanan Street
Landover Hills, MD 20784-2236
301-577-1684
Fax: 301-577-1690
e-mail: ncod@erols.com
http://www.ncod.org

Arvilla Rank, Executive Director/Editor

Published as a pastoral service for the deaf and hard of hearing.

16 pages Frequency: Quarterly

6552 When the Mind Hears
Gallaudet University Bookstore
800 Florida Avenue NE
Washington, DC 20002-3600
202-651-5000
800-451-1073
Fax: 202-651-5489
TTY 888-630-9347

Erving King Jordan, President

Comprehensive history of the deaf and their relationship with hearing academic communities.

414 pages

Hearing Impaired/Directories

6553 Working With Deaf People: Accessibility and Accommodation in the Workplace
Charles C Thomas Publisher
2600 S 1st Street
Springfield, IL 62704-4730
217-789-8980
800-258-8980
Fax: 217-789-9130
e-mail: books@ccthomas.com
http://www.ccthomas.com

Michael P Thomas, President

Reveals the kinds of patterns of work adjustment problems that can surface among deaf employees, including the points of view of both supervisors and deaf people.

250 pages

Directories

6554 AIDS and Deafness: Resource Directory
CDC National Aids Clearinghouse
PO Box 6003
Rockville, MD 20849-6003
800-458-5231
800-243-7012
Fax: 301-562-1050
e-mail: info@cdcnac.org
http://www.cdcnac.org

Computer printout. Lists national, state, and local organizations that offer AIDS (Acquired Immune Deficiency Syndrome)-related services to deaf and hard-of-hearing people; coverage includes Canada and the United Kingdom. Entries include: Organization name, address, phone, hotline numbers, hours of operation, access procedures, TTY/TDD numbers, names and titles of key personnel, geographic area served, description, product/service. Database compiled in cooperation with Gallaudet Research Institute at Gallaudet University.

6555 Academy of Dispensing Audiologists Membership Directory
Academy of Dispensing Audiologists
1796 Paysphere Circle
Chicago, IL 60674
803-252-5646
Fax: 803-765-0860

Carol Davis, Executive Director

Encourages audiology training programs to include pertinent aspects of hearing aid dispensing in their curriculum.

Frequency: annual

6556 American Annals of the Deaf: Reference Issue
Conf of Educational Admin Serving Deaf
800 Florida Avenue NE
Washington, DC 20002-3600
202-651-5340
800-526-9105
Fax: 202-651-5708

Donald F Moores, Editor

Publication includes: Lists of educational programs and services, supportive and rehabilitation programs and services, and research and information programs and services focusing on the deaf and aurally handicapped. Entries include: Generally, name of sponsoring organization, address, and description of programs offered. School listings include staff and enrollment data.

208 pages Frequency: Annual

6557 Assistive Devices Demonstration Centers
National Information Center on Deafness
800 Florida Avenue NE
Washington, DC 20002-3600
202-651-5051
Fax: 202-651-5054
TTY 202-651-5052

A resource list identifying demonstration centers across the United States.

6558 Audiologists Directory
InfoUSA
PO Box 27347
Omaha, NE 68127
402-593-4600
800-555-6124
Fax: 402-331-5481
e-mail: internet@infousa.com
http://www.abii.com

Bill Hippin, Vice President

Number of listings: 3,617. Entries include: Name, address, phone (including area code), size of advertisement, year first in 'Yellow Pages,' name of owner or manager, number of employees. Compiled from telephone company 'Yellow Pages,' nationwide.

6559 Deaf Artists of America: Artists Directory
Deaf Artists of America
302 N Goodman Street
Suite 205
Rochester, NY 14607-1148
585-244-3460
800-421-1220
Fax: 585-244-3690
e-mail: deafartist@aol.com
TTY 716-244-3460

Tom Willard, Mailing Contact/Editor
Giovanni Lopassio, Owner

About 200 hearing-impaired visual and performing artists, writers, and performing arts groups. Entries include: Name, address, phone, biographical data, type of artwork produced, exhibitions or workshops, availability and fees (where applicable).

100 pages Frequency: Biennial

6560 Directory of Auditory-Oral Programs
Alexander Graham Bell Association for the Deaf
1537 35th Street NW
Washington, DC 20007-2753
202-337-5220
Fax: 202-337-8270
http://www.agbell.org
TTY 202-337-5220

Todd Houston, Executive Director

This directory lists auditory-oral programs in public and private schools, auditory-oral programs in speech and hearing centers, and therapists who offer private tutoring and auditory-oral therapy.

204 pages

6561 Directory of Interpreters for Persons who are Deaf, Hard of Hearing or Deaf-Blind
Illinois Office of Rehabilitation Services
623 E Adams Street
Springfield, IL 62701-1614
217-785-9304
800-ASK-DORS
Fax: 217-785-7798
e-mail: imays@dors.state.il.us
TDD 217-785-7749

Leesa Mays, Editor

Approximately 175 interpreters of sign language for the hearing impaired in Illinois. Entries include: Personal name, address, phone, whether phone is equipped with a TTY/TDD teletypewriter, professional certification level, availability, geographic area served, whether qualified to interpret for deaf-blind individuals.

37 pages Frequency: Irregular

6562 Directory of National Organizations of and for Deaf and Hard of Hearing People
National Information Center on Deafness
800 Florida Avenue NE
Washington, DC 20002-3600
202-651-5051
Fax: 202-651-5054
e-mail: nicd.infotogo@gallaudet.edu
http://www.gallaudet.edu

Loraine DiPietro, Mailing Contact/Editor

National focus and nonprofit organizations who serve the deaf and hard of hearing. Entries include: Name, address, phone, names and titles of key personnel, name and title of contact, publications and description of available services.

8 pages Frequency: Annual

Hearing Impaired/Journals, Magazines

6563 **Encyclopedia of Deafness and Hearing Disorders**
Facts on File
11 Penn Plaza
Floor 15
New York, NY 10001-2006
212-967-8800
800-322-8755
Fax: 212-967-8107
e-mail: lmilberg@factsonfile.com

Carol Turkington, Editor

Publication includes: In appendixes, community services and associations, sources of devices and equipment, federal programs, general organizations and resources, genetic and deafness information sources, homes and housing for the aged deaf, performance groups, periodicals, religious organizations, summer camps, Hearing Ear Dogs training centers, and communications skills programs serving deaf and hearing impaired persons and their families. Entries include: Name, address, phone. Principal content of publication is an encyclopedia of clinical and anatomical terms, devices and equipment, organizations, and hearing specialists and famous deaf persons.

6564 **GLAD Directory of Resources Available to Deaf and Hard-of-Hearing Persons**
Greater Los Angeles Council on Deafness
2222 Laverna Avenue
Los Angeles, CA 90041-2625
323-478-8000
Fax: 323-550-4205

Jill Dohy, Editor
Patty Hughes, CEO

About 1,200 agencies and resources in the Los Angeles area serving the deaf and hard of hearing. Entries include: Generally, name, address, phone, telecommunications device for the deaf number (TDD), description of service, name of contact. Some listings also include hours of operation and restrictions such as age group served.

190 pages Frequency: Semiannual

6565 **Hear You Are**
125 Main Street
Netcong, NJ 07857-1326
973-347-7662
800-278-EARS
Fax: 973-691-0611
e-mail: hearyoua@aol.com
TDD 973-691-0663

Dorinne S Davis MA CCC-A, President
Larry Cagno, VP

A large catalog of various assistive and communication devices for people who are hearing impaired.

42 pages

6566 **Leading National Publications of and for Deaf People**
National Information Center on Deafness
800 Florida Avenue NE
Washington, DC 20002-3600
202-651-5051
Fax: 202-651-5054
TTY 202-651-5052

Identifies publications with national circulations to deaf audiences.

6567 **National Directory of Hearing Assistance Technology Assistive Device Demo Centers**
Self Help for Hard of Hearing People
7910 Woodmont Avenue
Suite 1200
Bethesda, MD 20814-7022
301-657-2248
Fax: 301-913-9413
e-mail: national@shhh.org
http://www.shhh.org
TTY 301-657-2249

Terry Portis, Executive Director

Journals, Magazines

6568 **ASHA**
American Speech-Language-Hearing Association
10801 Rockville Pike
Rockville, MD 20852-3226
301-897-5700
800-638-8255
Fax: 301-897-7355

Joanne Jessen, Managing Editor
Pamela Leppin, Advertising Manager
Arlene Pietranton, Executive Director

Magazine on hearing, language, and speech.

Frequency: Quarterly

6569 **ASHA Magazine: ASHA Leader**
American Speech-Language-Hearing Association
10801 Rockville Pike
Rockville, MD 20852-3226
301-897-5700
800-638-8255
Fax: 301-897-7355

Joanne K Jessen, ASHA Leader, Managing Editor-in-Chief
Arlene Pietranton, Executive Director

Association publication containing news, notices of events and activities and information for members on issues facing the profession.

16 pages

6570 **American Annals of the Deaf**
Convention of American Instructors of the Deaf
800 Florida Avenue NE
Washington, DC 20002-3600
202-651-5530
Fax: 202-651-5860
http://www.gallaudet.edu
TTY 202-651-5530

Donald Moores, Editor

Scholarly journal at the forefront of research related to the education of deaf people. Annual reference Issue identifies programs and services for deaf people nationwide.

6571 **American Journal of Audiology**
American Speech-Language-Hearing Association
10801 Rockville Pike
Rockville, MD 20852-3226
301-897-5700
800-638-8255
Fax: 301-897-7355

Russell L Malone PhD, Editor
Arlene Pietranton, Executive Director

6572 **Audiology Today**
1735 N Lynn Street
Suite 950
Arlington, VA 22209-2013
703-524-1923
Fax: 703-524-2303

Jerry Northern PhD, Editor

6573 **Auricle**
Auditory-Verbal International
2121 Eisenhower Avenue
Suite 402
Alexandria, VA 22314-4688
703-739-1049
Fax: 703-739-0395
e-mail: audioverb@aol.com
http://www.auditory-verbal.org
TTY 703-739-0874

Sra Lake, Executive Director/CEO

To provide the choice of listening and speaking as the way of life for children and adults who are deaf on hard of hearing.

6574 **Between Friends**
Beltone Electronics Corporation
4201 W Victoria Street
Chicago, IL 60646-6718
800-621-1275
Fax: 773-583-4681

Renee Rockoff, Editor

Hearing Impaired/Journals, Magazines

For hearing aid wearers: quizzes, jokes, health, recipes and financial items.
6 pages

6575 Deaf Life
PO Box 23380
Rochester, NY 14692-3380
585-442-6370
Fax: 585-442-6371
http://www.deaflife.com

Matthew Moore, Publisher

This magazine focuses on profiles, news, controversial issues, cultural topics and more relating to the Deaf community.
50 pages

6576 Deaf Sports Review
American Athletic Association of the Deaf
3607 Washington Boulevard
Suite 4
Ogden, UT 84403-1761
801-393-8710
Fax: 801-393-2263
TTY 801-393-7916

Shirley Platt, Editor

A magazine that describes deaf athletes and past and upcoming events.

6577 Deaf USA
Eye Festival Communications
6917b Woodley Avenue
Van Nuys, CA 91406-4844
Fax: 818-902-9840

David Rosenbaum, Editor

Provides news coverage on all activities and issues of interest to deaf and hard of hearing readers as well as professionals and associates within this specialized market.

6578 Deaf-Blind American
American Association of the Deaf-Blind
8630 Fenton Street
Suite 121
Silver Spring, MD 20910-3803
Fax: 301-588-8705
e-mail: aadb@erols.com
TTY 301-588-6545

Jamie McNamara, Editor

A journal of the American Association of the Deaf-Blind with articles on new technology, legislation news affecting deaf-blind Americans, success storeis on deaf-blind, conference news, and many other topics of interest to deaf-blind people.

6579 Hearing Health
PO Box V
Ingleside, TX 78362
361-884-8388
Fax: 361-884-3314

Paula Bartone-Bonillas, Editor

A publication for deaf and hard-of-hearing people, as well as hearing health care professionals, libraries, agencies, schools and organizations.

6580 Hearing Journal
Williams & Wilkins
351 W Camden Street
Baltimore, MD 21201-7912
410-528-4000
800-222-3790
Fax: 410-528-4452
e-mail: internetwwbooks@access.digest.net

David H Kirkwood, Editor-in-Chief
Jerry Laux, Publisher

Magazine on hearing, health care, and technology.
Frequency: Monthly

6581 Interpreter Views
Registry of the Interpreters for the Deaf
8630 Fenton Street
Suite 324
Silver Spring, MD 20910-3816
301-608-0050
Fax: 301-608-0508

Information on the deaf and hard of hearing.

6582 Journal of Speech and Hearing Disorders
American Speech-Language-Hearing Association
10801 Rockville Pike
Rockville, MD 20852-3226
301-897-5700
800-638-8255
Fax: 301-897-7355

Arlene Pietranton, Executive Director

Articles cover case histories, clinical techniques, position papers and literature surveys.

6583 Journal of Speech and Hearing Research
American Speech-Language-Hearing Association
10801 Rockville Pike
Rockville, MD 20852-3226
301-897-5700
800-638-8255
Fax: 301-897-7355

Pam Leppin, Advertising Manager
Joanne Jessen, Director
Arlene Pietranton, Executive Director

Journal covering research in communication science.
Frequency: Bimonthly

6584 Journal of Speech-Language-Hearing Research
American Speech-Language-Hearing Association
10801 Rockville Pike
Rockville, MD 20852-3226
301-897-5700
800-638-8255
Fax: 301-897-7355

Russell L Malone PhD, Editor
Arlene Pietranton, Executive Director

6585 Journal of the Academy of Rehabilitation Audiology
Academy of Rehabilitative Audiology
PO Box 26532
Minneapolis, MN 55426
952-920-0484
Fax: 952-920-6098
e-mail: ara@incnet.com
http://www.audreb.org

Frances Laven MS, Executive Director

Professional journal providing a forum for the exchange of ideas on, knowledge of and experience with habilitative and rehabilitative aspects of audiology.

6586 National Association of the Deaf
8630 Fenton Street
Suite 820
Silver Spring, MD 20910-3819
301-587-1788
Fax: 301-587-4873
e-mail: nadinfo@nud.org
http://www.nad.org
TDD Y 3-158-1789

Nation's largest organization safeguarding the accessibilty and civil rights of 28 million deaf and hard of hearing Americans in education, employment, health care, and telecommunications. Focuses on grassroots advocacy and empowerment, captioned media, deafness-related information and publications, legal assistance, policy development and research, public awareness, and youth leadership development.

6587 Paws for Silence
International Hearing Dog (IHDI)
5901 E 890th Avenue
Henderson, CO 80640
303-287-3277
Fax: 303-287-3425
e-mail: ihdi@aol.com

Martha A Foss, Mailing Contact
Valerie Foss-Brugger, President

Hearing Impaired/Newspapers

Magazine covering news of the International Hearing Dog.
Frequency: Quarterly

6588 **Perspectives in Education and Deafness**
Gallaudet Univ. Press c/o Chicago Distrib. Center
11030 S Langley Avenue
Chicago, IL 60628-3830
800-621-2736
Fax: 800-621-8476
http://www.gallaudet.edu
TTY 888-630-9347

Mary Abrams Perica, Editor

A practical, reader-friendly magazine, offering help and advice in and beyond the classroom, tuned to the needs of today's students, teachers, and families.

6589 **SHHH Journal**
Self Help For Hard of Hearing People
7910 Woodmont Avenue
Suite 1200
Bethesda, MD 20814-7022
301-657-2248
Fax: 301-913-9413
TTY 301-657-2249

Barbara G Harris, Editor
Terry Portis, Executive Director

An educational journal about hearing loss for hard-of-hearing people.

6590 **Teaching English to the Deaf as a Second Language**
Department of English, Gallaudet University
Washington, DC 20002
202-651-5580
Fax: 202-651-5599
e-mail: @department@gallua.gallaudet.edu

Barbara Bodner Johnson, Chair

Publishes articles of practical interest to classroom teachers of hearing impaired and second language students.

6591 **Tinnitus Today**
American Tinnitus Association
PO Box 5
Portland, OR 97207
503-248-9985
Fax: 503-248-0024
http://www.teleport.com

Patricia Daggett, Information/Research
Barbara Tabachnick-Sanders, Editor
Cheryl McGinnis, Executive Director

Information, hearing professional referrals, support group contacts, and a bibliography service are available as well as this quarterly magazine.
28 pages

6592 **USA Deaf Sports Federation**
3607 Washington Boulevard
Suite 4
Ogden, UT 84403-1761
801-393-8710
Fax: 801-393-2263
e-mail: homeoffice@usadsf.org
http://www.usadsf.org
TTY 801-393-7916

Dr. Joseph J Innes III, Editor

A glossy magazine called Deaf Sports Review featuring articles on all deaf sports and recreation.

6593 **Volta Voices**
Alexander Graham Bell Association for the Deaf
1537 35th Street NW
Washington, DC 20007-2753
202-337-5220
Fax: 202-337-8314
http://www.agbell.org
TTY 202-337-5220

Lisa Speckhardt, Managing Editor
Todd Houston, Executive Director

Contains Association news and educates readers on the abilities and needs of children and adults who are deaf or hard of hearing. Includes subscription to The Valta Review, published five times a year.

Newspapers

6594 **NAD Broadcaster**
National Association of the Deaf
814 Thayer Avenue
Silver Spring, MD 20910-4504
301-587-1788
Fax: 310-587-1791

Newspaper for deaf and hard of hearing people, and their parents and educators.

6595 **Tinnitus Today**
American Tinnitus Association
PO Box 5
Portland, OR 97207
503-248-9985
Fax: 503-248-0024

Gloria E Reich PhD, Director
Cheryl McGinnis, Executive Director

Newsletters, Pamphlets

6596 **AAAD Bulletin**
American Athletic Association of the Deaf
3607 Washington Boulevard
Suite 4
Ogden, UT 84403-1761
801-393-8710
Fax: 801-393-2263
TTY 801-393-7916

Shirley Platt, Editor

A newsletter describing deaf athletes and upcoming events.

6597 **ADA & the Consumer Who is Deaf or Hard of Hearing**
Alexander Graham Bell Association for the Deaf
1537 35th Street NW
Washington, DC 20007-2753
202-337-5220
Fax: 202-337-8270
http://www.agbell.org
TTY 202-337-5220

Todd Houston, Executive Director

This brochure describes how the ADA prohibits discrimination against persons with disabilities in four main domains: employment settings, public services from state and local government agencies, public accomodations, and telecommunications.

6598 **ADA and Hearing-Impaired Consumers**
Alexander Graham Bell Association for the Deaf
1537 35th Street NW
Washington, DC 20007-2753
202-337-5220
Fax: 202-337-8270
http://www.agbell.org
TTY 202-337-5220

Todd Houston, Executive Director

This brochure describes how the ADA prohibits discrimination against people based on impairments in their employment, state and local governments, and public accommodations.

6599 **ATA Newsletter**
American Tinnitus Association
PO Box 5
Portland, OR 97207
503-248-9985
Fax: 503-248-0024
http://www.teleport.com

Patricia Daggett, Executive Assistant
Barbara Tabachnick, Client Services
Cheryl McGinnis, Executive Director

Hearing Impaired/Newsletters, Pamphlets

Information, hearing professional referrals, support group contacts, and a bibliography service are available in this quarterly magazine.

28 pages Frequency: Quarterly

6600 Adult Bible Lessons for the Deaf
LifeWay
127 9th Avenue N
Nashville, TN 37203
615-251-2500
800-458-2772
Fax: 615-251-5017
http://www.lifeway.com

Matt Jaggers, Manager

Bible study quarterly that relates to the needs of deaf and hearing impaired persons.

6601 Advocacy & Access
Self Help for Hard of Hearing People
7910 Woodmont Avenue
Suite 1200
Bethesda, MD 20814-7022
301-654-7850
Fax: 301-913-9413
e-mail: national@shhh.org
http://www.shhh.org
TTY 301-657-2249

Christine DeVries, Manager

6602 Aging and Hearing Loss: Some Commonly Asked Questions
National Information Center on Deafness
800 Florida Avenue NE
Washington, DC 20002-3600
202-651-5051
Fax: 202-651-5054
TTY 202-651-5052

Discusses the hearing evaluation, tests used to determine type and extent of hearing loss and what an audiogram tells us.

6603 Alerting and Communication Devices for Deaf & Hard of Hearing People
National Information Center on Deafness
800 Florida Avenue NE
Washington, DC 20002-3600
202-651-5051
Fax: 202-651-5054
TTY 202-651-5052

Describes general communication in everyday life.

6604 All About the New Generation of Hearing Aids
National Information Center on Deafness
800 Florida Avenue NE
Washington, DC 20002-3600
202-651-5051
Fax: 202-651-5054
TTY 202-651-5052

Explains the terms digital hearing aid, and digitally controlled hearing aid.

6605 American Hearing Research Foundation
8 S Michigan Avenue
Suite 814
Chicago, IL 60603-3461
312-726-9670
Fax: 312-726-9695

William L Lederer, Executive Director

The purposes of the Foundation are to promote, conduct and furnish financial assistance for medical research into the cause, prevention and cure of deafness, impaired hearing and balance disorders; encourage the collaboration of clinical and laboratory research; encourage and improve teaching in the medical aspects of hearing problems; and disseminate the most reliable scientific knowledge to physicians, hearing professionals and the public.

6606 American Hearing Research Foundation Newsletter
American Hearing Research Foundation
55 E Washington Street
Suite 2022
Chicago, IL 60602-2341
312-726-9670
Fax: 312-726-9695

William L Lederer, Editor

Concerned with hearing research and education.

8 pages

6607 Americans with Disabilities Act: Selected Resources for Deaf
Gallaudet University Bookstore
800 Florida Avenue NE
Washington, DC 20002-3600
773-568-1550
800-451-1073
Fax: 202-651-5489
http://www.gallaudet.edu
TDD 888-630-9347

This resource identifies programs and publications specific to the ADA and deafness and also lists ADA materials and programs for people with any disability.

6608 Assistive Devices Demonstration Centers
National Information Center on Deafness
800 Florida Avenue NE
Washington, DC 20002-3600
202-651-5051
Fax: 202-651-5054
TTY 202-651-5052

A resource list identifying demonstration centers across the United States.

6609 Audio Induction Loops
Self Help for Hard of Hearing People
7910 Woodmont Avenue
Suite 1200
Bethesda, MD 20814-7022
301-657-2248
Fax: 301-913-9413
e-mail: national@shhh.org
http://www.shhh.org
TTY 301-657-2249

Terry Portis, Executive Director

6610 Be in the Know: Communication Access Terms
Self Help for Hard of Hearing People
7910 Woodmont Avenue
Suite 1200
Bethesda, MD 20814-7022
301-657-2248
Fax: 301-913-9413
e-mail: national@shhh.org
http://www.shhh.org
TTY 301-657-2249

Terry Portis, Executive Director

6611 Better Hearing News
Better Hearing Institute
5021b Backlick Road
Annandale, VA 22003-6043
703-642-0580
800-327-
Fax: 703-750-9302

Jerry J Rizzo, Executive Director

6612 Between Friends
Beltone Electronics Corporation
4201 W Victoria Street
Chicago, IL 60646-6718
773-583-3600
Fax: 773-583-4681

Renee Rockoff, Editor

For hearing aid wearers: quizzes, jokes, health, recipes and financial items.

6 pages

6613 Between Two Worlds of Hearing and Not Hearing
Self Help for Hard of Hearing People
7910 Woodmont Avenue
Suite 1200
Bethesda, MD 20814-7022
301-657-2248
Fax: 301-913-9413
e-mail: national@shhh.org
http://www.shhh.org
TTY 301-657-2249

Terry Portis, Executive Director

Hearing Impaired/Newsletters, Pamphlets

6614 Breaking the Chain of Substance Abuse and Hearing Loss
Self Help for Hard of Hearing People
7910 Woodmont Avenue
Suite 1200
Bethesda, MD 20814-7022
301-657-2248
Fax: 301-913-9413
e-mail: national@shhh.org
http://www.shhh.org
TTY 301-657-2249

Terry Portis, Executive Director

6615 CICI's Contact
Cochlear Implant Club Association
5335 Wisconsin Avenue NW
Suite 440
Washington, DC 20015-2054
202-895-2781
Fax: 202-895-2782
e-mail: pwms.cici@worldnet.att.net
http://www.cici.org

Peg Williams, Executive Director
52 pages

6616 Canine Listener
Dogs for the Deaf
10175 Wheeler Road
Central Point, OR 97502-9360
541-826-9220
Fax: 541-826-6696

Robin Dickson, Executive Director

Offers information on various dogs for the deaf that are available, hotlines, support groups and articles on the newest technology for the hard of hearing person.

6617 Caption Center News
Caption Center
125 Western Avenue
Boston, MA 02134-1008
617-927-9225
Fax: 617-562-0590

Reports developments in closed captioning for persons with hearing impairments.

6618 Care of the Ears and Hearing for Health
American Hearing Research Foundation
55 E Washington Street
Chicago, IL 60602-2103
312-726-9670
Fax: 312-726-9670

Offers information on ear infections relating to chronic progressive deafness.

6619 Cellular Phones - Hearing Aid Wearers Can Use Them
Self Help for Hard of Hearing People
7910 Woodmont Avenue
Suite 1200
Bethesda, MD 20814-7022
301-657-2248
Fax: 301-913-9413
e-mail: national@shhh.org
http://www.shhh.org
TTY 301-657-2249

Terry Portis, Executive Director

6620 Cochlear Impants
Alexander Graham Bell Association for the Deaf
1537 35th Street NW
Washington, DC 20007-2753
202-337-5220
Fax: 202-337-8270
http://www.agbell.org
TTY 202-337-5220

Todd Houston, Executive Director

This brochure discusses how adult consumers benefit from a cochlear implant and follows the entire process of evaluation, surgery and follow-up visits.

6621 Cochlear Implants: Comprehensive Overview
Self Help for Hard of Hearing People
7910 Woodmont Avenue
Suite 1200
Bethesda, MD 20814-7022
301-657-2248
Fax: 301-913-9413
e-mail: national@shhh.org
http://www.shhh.org
TTY 301-657-2249

Terry Portis, Executive Director

6622 Common Mis-Information About Hearing Loss and Hearing Aid Use
Self Help for Hard of Hearing People
7910 Woodmont Avenue
Suite 1200
Bethesda, MD 20814-7022
301-657-2248
Fax: 301-913-9413
e-mail: national@shhh.org
http://www.shhh.org
TTY 301-657-2249

Terry Portis, Executive Director

6623 Communicating with People Who Have a Hearing Loss
Alexander Graham Bell Association for the Deaf
1537 35th Street NW
Washington, DC 20007-2753
202-337-5220
Fax: 202-337-8270
http://www.agbell.org
TTY 202-337-5220

Todd Houston, Executive Director

This brochure describes ways to communicate more effectively with people who have hearing losses.

6624 Communication Access in Houses of Worship
Self Help for Hard of Hearing People
7910 Woodmont Avenue
Suite 1200
Bethesda, MD 20814-7022
301-657-2248
Fax: 301-913-9413
e-mail: national@shhh.org
http://www.shhh.org
TTY 301-657-2249

Terry Portis, Executive Director

6625 Communication Access in Medical Facilities
Self Help for Hard of Hearing People
7910 Woodmont Avenue
Suite 1200
Bethesda, MD 20814-7022
301-657-2248
Fax: 301-913-9413
e-mail: national@shhh.org
http://www.shhh.org
TTY 301-657-2249

Terry Portis, Executive Director

6626 Communication Tips to Go (Movies, Restaurants, Planes, Car...)
Self Help for Hard of Hearing People
7910 Woodmont Avenue
Suite 1200
Bethesda, MD 20814-7022
301-657-2248
Fax: 301-913-9413
e-mail: national@shhh.org
http://www.shhh.org
TTY 301-657-2249

Terry Portis, Executive Director

Hearing Impaired/Newsletters, Pamphlets

6627 Computer-Assisted Notetaking
Self Help for Hard of Hearing People
7910 Woodmont Avenue
Suite 1200
Bethesda, MD 20814-7022
301-657-2248
Fax: 301-913-9413
e-mail: national@shhh.org
http://www.shhh.org
TTY 301-657-2249

Terry Portis, Executive Director

How-to guide and consumer's guide to real-time notetaking.

6628 Consumer's Guide for Purchasing a Hearing Aid
Self Help for Hard of Hearing People
7910 Woodmont Avenue
Suite 1200
Bethesda, MD 20814-7022
301-657-2248
Fax: 301-913-9413
e-mail: national@shhh.org
http://www.shhh.org
TTY 301-657-2249

Terry Portis, Executive Director

6629 Cued Speech
Self Help for Hard of Hearing People
7910 Woodmont Avenue
Suite 1200
Bethesda, MD 20814-7022
301-657-2248
Fax: 301-913-9413
e-mail: national@shhh.org
http://www.shhh.org
TTY 301-657-2249

Terry Portis, Executive Director

6630 Deaf American
National Association of the Deaf
814 Thayer Avenue
Silver Spring, MD 20910-4504
301-587-1788
Fax: 301-587-4873

Discusses current issues of importance to the deaf community.

6631 Deaf Artists of America
302 Goodman Street N
Suite 205
Rochester, NY 14607-1148
585-271-4548
Fax: 585-244-3690
TTY 716-244-3460

Tom Willard, Editor
Richard Duff, Administrator

6632 Deaf Culture Videotapes
National Information Center on Deafness
800 Florida Avenue NE
Washington, DC 20002-3600
202-388-1448
Fax: 202-651-5054
TTY 202-651-5052

Oumi Diouf, Owner

This list identifies deaf culture and deaf history videotapes available from the Historic Film Collection of the National Association of the Deaf.

6633 Deaf Culture: Suggested Readings
National Information Center on Deafness
800 Florida Avenue NE
Washington, DC 20002-3600
202-388-1448
Fax: 202-651-5054
TTY 202-651-5052

Oumi Diouf, Owner

A selected reading list providing annotations for 62 books highlighting the community, and history of deaf people.

6634 Deaf Episcopalian
Episcopal Conference of the Deaf
PO Box 27459
Philadelphia, PA 19118
215-247-1059
Fax: 215-247-1059

Rev. Virginia Nagel, Editor
Marainne D Stephens, Religious Leader

6635 Deafness: A Fact Sheet
National Information Center on Deafness
800 Florida Avenue NE
Washington, DC 20002-3600
202-651-5051
Fax: 202-651-5054
TTY 202-651-5052

6636 Deafpride Advocate
Deafpride
1350 Potomac Avenue SE
Washington, DC 20003
202-675-6700
Fax: 202-547-0547

6637 Dealing with Anger and Echoes of a Common Fate
Self Help for Hard of Hearing People
7910 Woodmont Avenue
Suite 1200
Bethesda, MD 20814-7022
301-657-2248
Fax: 301-913-9413
e-mail: national@shhh.org
http://www.shhh.org
TTY 301-657-2249

Terry Portis, Executive Director

6638 Developing an Identity for People with Hearing Loss
Self Help for Hard of Hearing People
7910 Woodmont Avenue
Suite 1200
Bethesda, MD 20814-7022
301-657-2248
Fax: 301-913-9413
e-mail: national@shhh.org
http://www.shhh.org
TTY 301-657-2249

Terry Portis, Executive Director

6639 Developments in Technology
Self Help for Hard of Hearing People
7910 Woodmont Avenue
Suite 1200
Bethesda, MD 20814-7022
301-657-2248
Fax: 301-913-9413
e-mail: national@shhh.org
http://www.shhh.org
TTY 301-657-2249

Terry Portis, Executive Director

Hearing aids and assistive devices.

6640 Digital Hearing Aids: An Update
Self Help for Hard of Hearing People
7910 Woodmont Avenue
Suite 1200
Bethesda, MD 20814-7022
301-657-2248
Fax: 301-913-9413
e-mail: national@shhh.org
http://www.shhh.org
TTY 301-657-2249

Terry Portis, Executive Director

6641 Ear and Hearing
National Information Center on Deafness
800 Florida Avenue NE
Washington, DC 20002-3600
202-651-5051
Fax: 202-651-5054
TTY 202-651-5052

An illustrated publication of the ear and what can go wrong with it.

Hearing Impaired/Newsletters, Pamphlets

6642 Early/Mild Hearing Loss
Self Help for Hard of Hearing People
7910 Woodmont Avenue
Suite 1200
Bethesda, MD 20814-7022
301-657-2248
Fax: 301-913-9413
e-mail: national@shhh.org
http://www.shhh.org
TTY 301-657-2249

Terry Portis, Executive Director

6643 Educational Perspective
Self Help for Hard of Hearing People
7910 Woodmont Avenue
Suite 1200
Bethesda, MD 20814-7022
301-657-2248
Fax: 301-913-9413
e-mail: national@shhh.org
http://www.shhh.org
TTY 301-657-2249

Terry Portis, Executive Director

6644 Employers of Individuals Who are Deaf and Hard of Hearing & the ADA
Alexander Graham Bell Association for the Deaf
1537 35th Street NW
Washington, DC 20007-2753
202-337-5220
Fax: 202-337-8270
http://www.agbell.org
TTY 202-337-5220

Todd Houston, Executive Director

Written for employers, this brochure discusses workplace accommodations that are required under the ADA. Most of the suggestions listed in this brochure are simple and, for the most part, relatively inexpensive to implement.

6645 Employers of Individuals with Hearing Impairments & the ADA
Alexander Graham Bell Association for the Deaf
1537 35th Street NW
Washington, DC 20007-2753
202-337-5220
Fax: 202-337-8270
http://www.agbell.org
TTY 202-337-5220

Todd Houston, Executive Director

For employers, this brochure discusses workplace accommodations required by the ADA for employees with hearing impairments; communication options, procedural alterations and technologies.

6646 Employment Discrimination: How to Recognize it and What to Do About it
Self Help for Hard of Hearing People
7910 Woodmont Avenue
Suite 1200
Bethesda, MD 20814-7022
301-657-2248
Fax: 301-913-9413
e-mail: national@shhh.org
http://www.shhh.org
TTY 301-657-2249

Terry Portis, Executive Director

6647 Endeavor
American Society for Deaf Children
PO Box 3355
Gettysburg, PA 17325
717-334-7922
Fax: 717-334-8808

Linda Cumbran, Operations Manager
Alicia Notarianni, Editor

Newsletter for parents of deaf children.

6648 Facts About Hearing Aids
Alexander Graham Bell Association for the Deaf
1537 35th Street NW
Washington, DC 20007-2753
202-337-5220
Fax: 202-337-8270
http://www.agbell.org
TTY 202-337-5220

Todd Houston, Executive Director

This brochure describes defferent types of hearing aids, factors to consider when choosing a hearing aid, the best way to go about purchasing a hearing aid. It also addresses cost and provides information on hearing conservation.

6649 Facts and Fancies About Hearing Aids
American Hearing Research Foundation
55 E Washington Street
Chicago, IL 60602-2103
312-641-3522
Fax: 312-726-9695

Pierre Massih, Owner

Offers information on types of hearing aids and hearing aid evaluations.

6650 Financial Help for Hearing Aids
Self Help for Hard of Hearing People
7910 Woodmont Avenue
Suite 1200
Bethesda, MD 20814-7022
301-657-2248
Fax: 301-913-9413
e-mail: national@shhh.org
http://www.shhh.org
TTY 301-657-2249

Terry Portis, Executive Director

6651 Finding the Right Aural Rehabilitation Program
Self Help for Hard of Hearing People
7910 Woodmont Avenue
Suite 1200
Bethesda, MD 20814-7022
301-657-2248
Fax: 301-913-9413
e-mail: national@shhh.org
http://www.shhh.org
TTY 301-657-2249

Terry Portis, Executive Director

6652 Forgotten Family
Self Help for Hard of Hearing People
7910 Woodmont Avenue
Suite 1200
Bethesda, MD 20814-7022
301-657-2248
Fax: 301-913-9413
e-mail: national@shhh.org
http://www.shhh.org
TTY 301-657-2249

Terry Portis, Executive Director

6653 Frat
National Fraternal Society of the Deaf
1300 W Northwest Highway
Mt Prospect, IL 60056-2217
847-392-9282
Fax: 847-392-9298
TTY 708-392-1409

Wayne D Shook, Editor

Offers fraternal insurance information and news about members.

6654 GASK Newsletter
Telecommunications for the Deaf
8630 Fenton Street
Suite 604
Silver Spring, MD 20910-3822
301-589-3786
Fax: 301-589-3797
e-mail: kglickmn@aol.com
http://www.tdi-online.org

Claude Stout, Managing Editor
Kenneth Samson, Contact

Hearing Impaired/Newsletters, Pamphlets

32 pages Frequency: Quarterly

6655 Gallaudet Today
Gallaudet University
800 Florida Avenue NE
Washington, DC 20002-3676
202-651-5220
Fax: 202-651-5670

Vickie Walter, Editor

A university publication with both general and special issues on deafness-related topics.

6656 Genetics and Deafness
National Information Center on Deafness
800 Florida Avenue NE
Washington, DC 20002-3600
202-651-5051
Fax: 202-651-5054
TTY 202-651-5052

Written for deaf people and their families who wish to learn more about the relationship between heredity and deafness.

6657 Genetics and Hearing Loss
Self Help for Hard of Hearing People
7910 Woodmont Avenue
Suite 1200
Bethesda, MD 20814-7022
301-657-2248
Fax: 301-913-9413
e-mail: national@shhh.org
http://www.shhh.org
TTY 301-657-2249

Terry Portis, Executive Director

6658 Getting Beyond Hearing Loss: A Guide for Families
Self Help for Hard of Hearing People
7910 Woodmont Avenue
Suite 1200
Bethesda, MD 20814-7022
301-657-2248
Fax: 301-913-9413
e-mail: national@shhh.org
http://www.shhh.org
TTY 301-657-2249

Terry Portis, Executive Director

6659 Getting Help with a Job: Exploring Vocational Rehabilitation
Self Help for Hard of Hearing People
7910 Woodmont Avenue
Suite 1200
Bethesda, MD 20814-7022
301-657-2248
Fax: 301-913-9413
e-mail: national@shhh.org
http://www.shhh.org
TTY 301-657-2249

Terry Portis, Executive Director

6660 Growing Up Hearing: A Sister's Memoir
Self Help for Hard of Hearing People
7910 Woodmont Avenue
Suite 1200
Bethesda, MD 20814-7022
301-657-2248
Fax: 301-913-9413
e-mail: national@shhh.org
http://www.shhh.org
TTY 301-657-2249

Terry Portis, Executive Director

6661 Guide for Students with Hearing Loss
Self Help for Hard of Hearing People
7910 Woodmont Avenue
Suite 1200
Bethesda, MD 20814-7022
301-657-2248
Fax: 301-913-9413
e-mail: national@shhh.org
http://www.shhh.org
TTY 301-657-2249

Terry Portis, Executive Director

Resources for college-bound students.

6662 Guidelines for Helping Deaf-Blind Persons
Helen Keller National Center
111 Middle Neck Road
Sands Point, NY 11050-1218
516-944-8900
Fax: 312-726-3503

Joseph McNulty, Executive Director

Pamphlet offering information on how persons should interact with deaf-blind individuals. Includes drawings of the one hand manual alphabet.

6663 Hair Cell Regeneration
Self Help for Hard of Hearing People
7910 Woodmont Avenue
Suite 1200
Bethesda, MD 20814-7022
301-657-2248
Fax: 301-913-9413
e-mail: national@shhh.org
http://www.shhh.org
TTY 301-657-2249

Terry Portis, Executive Director

6664 Hearing Aids and the Consumer: Current Wisdom
Self Help for Hard of Hearing People
7910 Woodmont Avenue
Suite 1200
Bethesda, MD 20814-7022
301-657-2248
Fax: 301-913-9413
e-mail: national@shhh.org
http://www.shhh.org
TTY 301-657-2249

Terry Portis, Executive Director

6665 Hearing Alert! Informational Brochures
Alexander Graham Bell Association for the Deaf
1537 35th St NW
Washington, DC 20007-2753
202-337-5220
Fax: 202-337-8270
http://www.agbell.org
TTY 202-337-5220

Todd Houston, Executive Director

These brochures encourage early detection of hearing loss in young children. For medical facilities, speech and hearing clinics, and schools.

6666 Hearing Dogs in Public
Self Help for Hard of Hearing People
7910 Woodmont Avenue
Suite 1200
Bethesda, MD 20814-7022
301-657-2248
Fax: 301-913-9413
e-mail: national@shhh.org
http://www.shhh.org
TTY 301-657-2249

Terry Portis, Executive Director

6667 Hearing Healthcare Team
Self Help for Hard of Hearing People
7910 Woodmont Avenue
Suite 1200
Bethesda, MD 20814-7022
301-657-2248
Fax: 301-913-9413
e-mail: national@shhh.org
http://www.shhh.org
TTY 301-657-2249

Terry Portis, Executive Director

6668 Hearing Instruments
Harcourt Brace Jovanovich Publications
7500 Old Oak Boulevard
Cleveland, OH 44130-3343
440-243-8100

Contains short feature articles by and for professionals.

Frequency: Monthly

Hearing Impaired/Newsletters, Pamphlets

6669 Hearing Loss and Staying Connected: Personal Accounts
Self Help for Hard of Hearing People
7910 Woodmont Avenue
Suite 1200
Bethesda, MD 20814-7022
301-657-2248
Fax: 301-913-9413
e-mail: national@shhh.org
http://www.shhh.org
TTY 301-657-2249

Terry Portis, Executive Director

6670 Hearing Loss: How to Get Help-A Guide for Consumers by Consumers
Self Help for Hard of Hearing People
7910 Woodmont Avenue
Suite 1200
Bethesda, MD 20814-7022
301-657-2248
Fax: 301-913-9413
e-mail: national@shhh.org
http://www.shhh.org
TTY 301-657-2249

Terry Portis, Executive Director

Information on getting tested for deafness and practical advice on the next steps.

6671 Hearing Loss: Information for Professionals in the Aging Network
National Information Center on Deafness
800 Florida Avenue NE
Washington, DC 20002-3600
202-399-5906
Fax: 202-651-5054
TTY 202-651-5052

Fred T Herring

Introduces professionals in the aging network to the realities of hearing loss.

6672 Hearing Loss: Personal and Social Considerations
Self Help for Hard of Hearing People
7910 Woodmont Avenue
Suite 1200
Bethesda, MD 20814-7022
301-657-2248
Fax: 301-913-9413
e-mail: national@shhh.org
http://www.shhh.org
TTY 301-657-2249

Terry Portis, Executive Director

6673 Hearing, Speech & Deafness Center(HSDC) Newsletter
1625 19th Avenue
Seattle, WA 98122-2848
206-323-5770
Fax: 206-328-6871
e-mail: adminathsdc.org
http://www.hsdc.org

Susie Burdick, Executive Director

Bi-annual news and clinical material for members and the community.
8 pages

6674 Houston Ear Research Foundation
7737 SW Fwy
Suite 630
Houston, TX 77074-1867
713-771-9966
800-843-0706
Fax: 713-771-0546

Jan Gilden, Executive Director
Frequency: Annual

6675 How to Get the Most Out of Your Hearing Aid
Alexander Graham Bell Association for the Deaf
1537 35th Street NW
Washington, DC 20007-2753
202-337-5220
Fax: 202-337-8270
http://www.agbell.org
TTY 202-337-5220

Todd Houston, Executive Director

This informative booklet for hearing aid users tells how to wear and adapt to your hearing aid, and provides helpful hints on care, and troubleshooting.

6676 Inheriting Hearing Loss
Self Help for Hard of Hearing People
7910 Woodmont Avenue
Suite 1200
Bethesda, MD 20814-7022
301-657-2248
Fax: 301-913-9413
e-mail: national@shhh.org
http://www.shhh.org
TTY 301-657-2249

Terry Portis, Executive Director

A personal narrative by SHHH Executive Director Donna Sorkin.

6677 Interpreter Views
Registry of the Interpreters for the Deaf
8719 Colesville Road
Suite 310
Silver Spring, MD 20910-3919
301-588-2406
Fax: 301-608-0508

Information on the deaf and hard of hearing.
Frequency: Monthly

6678 Introduction to Cochlear Implants
Alexander Graham Bell Association for the Deaf
1537 35th Street NW
Washington, DC 20007-2753
202-337-5220
Fax: 202-337-8270
http://www.agbell.org
TTY 202-337-5220

Todd Houston, Executive Director

This brochure, designed for parents, explores how children can benefit from a cochlear implant. It explains candidacy, surgery, rehabilitation, educational emplications, and costs.

6679 It's Our Hearing Loss: What Families Need to Know and Do
Self Help for Hard of Hearing People
7910 Woodmont Avenue
Suite 1200
Bethesda, MD 20814-7022
301-657-2248
Fax: 301-913-9413
e-mail: national@shhh.org
http://www.shhh.org
TTY 301-657-2249

Terry Portis, Executive Director

6680 Large-Room Listening Systems for Hard of Hearing People
Self Help for Hard of Hearing People
7910 Woodmont Avenue
Suite 1200
Bethesda, MD 20814-7022
301-657-2248
Fax: 301-913-9413
e-mail: national@shhh.org
http://www.shhh.org
TTY 301-657-2249

Terry Portis, Executive Director

6681 Late-Deafened Adults: A Selected Annotated Bibliography
National Information Center on Deafness
800 Florida Avenue NE
Washington, DC 20002-3600
202-651-5051
Fax: 202-651-5054
TTY 202-651-5052

A selected reading list of books and articles for late-deafened people and their families.

Hearing Impaired/Newsletters, Pamphlets

6682 **Leading National Publications of and for Deaf People**
National Information Center on Deafness
800 Florida Avenue NE
Washington, DC 20002-3600
202-651-5051
Fax: 202-651-5054
TTY 202-651-5052

Identifies publications with national circulations to deaf audiences.

6683 **League for the Hard of Hearing**
50 Broadway
5
New York, NY 10004-1607
917-305-7700
Fax: 212-255-4413

Nancy Nadler, Executive Director
4 pages

6684 **Listener**
HEAR Center
301 E Del Mar Boulevard
Pasadena, CA 91101-2714
626-796-2016
Fax: 626-796-2320

Beverly Biber, Editor
Josephine Wilson, Executive Director
4 pages Frequency: Bimonthly

6685 **Listening**
National Catholic Office for the Deaf
7202 Buchanan Street
Landover Hills, MD 20784-2236
301-577-1684
Fax: 301-577-1690
e-mail: ncod@erols.com
http://www.ncod.org

Arvilla Rank, Executive Director/Editor

Published as a pastoral service for the deaf and hard of hearing. Provides information to members and others working in ministry. Prepares an annual gathering called Pastoral Week meeting in January.

6686 **Living Alone with a Hearing Loss**
Self Help for Hard of Hearing People
7910 Woodmont Avenue
Suite 1200
Bethesda, MD 20814-7022
301-657-2248
Fax: 301-913-9413
e-mail: national@shhh.org
http://www.shhh.org
TTY 301-657-2249

Terry Portis, Executive Director

6687 **Living with Hearing Loss: Focus Group Results**
Self Help for Hard of Hearing People
7910 Woodmont Avenue
Suite 1200
Bethesda, MD 20814-7022
301-657-2248
Fax: 301-913-9413
e-mail: national@shhh.org
http://www.shhh.org
TTY 301-657-2249

Terry Portis, Executive Director

6688 **Making New Friends**
National Information Center on Deafness
800 Florida Avenue NE
Washington, DC 20002-3600
202-651-5051
Fax: 202-651-5054
TTY 202-651-5052

Identifies resources that offer opportunities for deaf people.

6689 **Meniere's Disease**
Self Help for Hard of Hearing People
7910 Woodmont Avenue
Suite 1200
Bethesda, MD 20814-7022
301-657-2248
Fax: 301-913-9413
e-mail: national@shhh.org
http://www.shhh.org
TTY 301-657-2249

Terry Portis, Executive Director

6690 **Meniere's Disease: Hearing Loss & Inner Ear Blood Flow**
Self Help for Hard of Hearing People
7910 Woodmont Avenue
Suite 1200
Bethesda, MD 20814-7022
301-657-2248
Fax: 301-913-9413
e-mail: national@shhh.org
http://www.shhh.org
TTY 301-657-2249

Terry Portis, Executive Director

Plus a personal narrative.

6691 **NAD Broadcaster**
National Association of the Deaf
814 Thayer Avenue
Silver Spring, MD 20910-4504
301-587-1788
Fax: 301-587-4873
TTY 301-587-1789

Nancy Creighton, Senior Editor

Association publication that provides coverage of issues, accomplishments, activities and events of importance to deaf and hard-of-hearing people, their families, and professionals.

6692 **National Information Center on Deafness Brochure**
National Information Center on Deafness
800 Florida Avenue NE
Washington, DC 20002-3600
202-884-8200
Fax: 202-651-5054
TTY 202-651-5052

Susan Ripley, Manager

A description of services offered by NICD.

6693 **Older Adults with Hearing Loss**
Self Help for Hard of Hearing People
7910 Woodmont Avenue
Suite 1200
Bethesda, MD 20814-7022
301-657-2248
Fax: 301-913-9413
e-mail: national@shhh.org
http://www.shhh.org
TTY 301-657-2249

Terry Portis, Executive Director

6694 **Oral Interpreters: A Communication Option**
Self Help for Hard of Hearing People
7910 Woodmont Avenue
Suite 1200
Bethesda, MD 20814-7022
301-657-2248
Fax: 301-913-9413
e-mail: national@shhh.org
http://www.shhh.org
TTY 301-657-2249

Terry Portis, Executive Director

6695 **Oral Interpreters: Facts for Consumers**
Alexander Graham Bell Association for the Deaf
1537 35th Street NW
Washington, DC 20007-2753
202-337-5220
Fax: 202-337-8270
http://www.agbell.org
TTY 202-337-5220

Todd Houston, Executive Director

Hearing Impaired/Newsletters, Pamphlets

This handy brochure for consumers or anyone who works with oral interpreters will answer frequently asked questions about many aspects of oral interpreting, including locating, using, and paying for an oral interpreter.

11 pages

6696 Otosclerosis
Self Help for Hard of Hearing People
7910 Woodmont Avenue
Suite 1200
Bethesda, MD 20814-7022
301-657-2248
Fax: 301-913-9413
e-mail: national@shhh.org
http://www.shhh.org
TTY 301-657-2249

Terry Portis, Executive Director

6697 Ototoxic Medications: What You Should Know
Self Help for Hard of Hearing People
7910 Woodmont Avenue
Suite 1200
Bethesda, MD 20814-7022
301-657-2248
Fax: 301-913-9413
e-mail: national@shhh.org
http://www.shhh.org
TTY 301-657-2249

Terry Portis, Executive Director

6698 Persuading Your Spouse/Relative/Friend to Acknowledge a Hearing Loss and Seek Help
Self Help for Hard of Hearing People
7910 Woodmont Avenue
Suite 1200
Bethesda, MD 20814-7022
301-657-2248
Fax: 301-913-9413
e-mail: national@shhh.org
http://www.shhh.org
TTY 301-657-2249

Terry Portis, Executive Director

6699 Physician Answers Your Questions About Hearing Health Care
Self Help for Hard of Hearing People
7910 Woodmont Avenue
Suite 1200
Bethesda, MD 20814-7022
301-657-2248
Fax: 301-913-9413
e-mail: national@shhh.org
http://www.shhh.org
TTY 301-657-2249

Terry Portis, Executive Director

6700 Psychological Stress and Hearing Loss
Self Help for Hard of Hearing People
7910 Woodmont Avenue
Suite 1200
Bethesda, MD 20814-7022
301-657-2248
Fax: 301-913-9413
e-mail: national@shhh.org
http://www.shhh.org
TTY 301-657-2249

Terry Portis, Executive Director

6701 Publications from the National Information Center on Deafness
National Information Center on Deafness
800 Florida Avenue NE
Washington, DC 20002-3600
202-651-5051
Fax: 202-651-5054
TTY 202-651-5052

Order form and explanations of NICD publications.

6702 Putting You in the Successful Employment Picture
Self Help for Hard of Hearing People
7910 Woodmont Avenue
Suite 1200
Bethesda, MD 20814-7022
301-657-2248
Fax: 301-913-9413
e-mail: national@shhh.org
http://www.shhh.org
TTY 301-657-2249

Terry Portis, Executive Director

6703 Questions and Answers About Employment of Deaf People
National Information Center on Deafness
800 Florida Avenue NE
Washington, DC 20002-3600
202-651-5051
Fax: 202-651-5054
TTY 202-651-5052

6704 Questions and Answers on Hearing Loss
Self Help for Hard of Hearing People
7910 Woodmont Avenue
Suite 1200
Bethesda, MD 20814-7022
301-657-2248
Fax: 301-913-9413
e-mail: national@shhh.org
http://www.shhh.org
TTY 301-657-2249

Terry Portis, Executive Director

6705 Review
House Ear Institute
2100 W 3rd Street
5th Floor
Los Angeles, CA 90057-1922
213-483-4431
Fax: 213-483-8789

Dilys J Jones, Editor
Jim Boswell, CEO

8 pages

6706 SHHH News
Self Help for Hard of Hearing People
7910 Woodmont Avenue
Suite 1200
Bethesda, MD 20814-7022
301-657-2248
Fax: 301-913-9413
e-mail: national@shhh.org
http://www.shhh.org
TTY 301-657-2249

Terry Portis, Executive Director

Information about SHHH affiliates.

6707 Sensorineural Hearing Loss
Self Help for Hard of Hearing People
7910 Woodmont Avenue
Suite 1200
Bethesda, MD 20814-7022
301-657-2248
Fax: 301-913-9413
e-mail: national@shhh.org
http://www.shhh.org
TTY 301-657-2249

Terry Portis, Executive Director

6708 Set-Ups for Speeches
Self Help for Hard of Hearing People
7910 Woodmont Avenue
Suite 1200
Bethesda, MD 20814-7022
301-657-2248
Fax: 301-913-9413
e-mail: national@shhh.org
http://www.shhh.org
TTY 301-657-2249

Terry Portis, Executive Director

Hearing Impaired/Newsletters, Pamphlets

6709 Signaling and Assistive Listening Devices for Hearing-Impaired People
Alexander Graham Bell Association for the Deaf
1537 35th Street NW
Washington, DC 20007-2753
202-337-5220
Fax: 202-337-8270
http://www.agbell.org
TTY 202-337-5220

Todd Houston, Executive Director

This illustrated pamphlet for consumers describes alarms, signalers and telephone/doorbell devices.

6710 Situation is Serious But Not Hopeless: The Psychological Benefits of Hearing Loss
Self Help for Hard of Hearing People
7910 Woodmont Avenue
Suite 1200
Bethesda, MD 20814-7022
301-657-2248
Fax: 301-913-9413
e-mail: national@shhh.org
http://www.shhh.org
TTY 301-657-2249

Terry Portis, Executive Director

6711 So You Have Had an Ear Operation...What Next?
American Hearing Research Foundation
55 E Washington Street
Chicago, IL 60602-2103
312-726-9670
Fax: 312-726-9695

William L Lederer, Executive Director

Offers information on ear infections and surgery.

6712 Speech and Deafness Newsletter
Hearing, Speech
1620 18th Avenue
Seattle, WA 98122-7001
206-323-5770
Fax: 206-328-6871

Patty Tumberg, Editor
Susie Burdick, Executive Director

Agency newsletter for membership and community.
   8 pages

6713 Speechreading for Better Communication
Alexander Graham Bell Association for the Deaf
1537 35th Street NW
Washington, DC 20007-2753
202-337-5220
Fax: 202-337-8270
http://www.agbell.org
TTY 202-337-5220

Todd Houston, Executive Director

This brochure describes speechreading, discusses its importance to many people with hearing losses, and lists additional resources for consumers.

6714 Speechreading: Methods and Materials
Self Help for Hard of Hearing People
7910 Woodmont Avenue
Suite 1200
Bethesda, MD 20814-7022
301-657-2248
Fax: 301-913-9413
e-mail: national@shhh.org
http://www.shhh.org
TTY 301-657-2249

Terry Portis, Executive Director

6715 Statewide Services for Deaf and Hard of Hearing People
National Information Center on Deafness
800 Florida Avenue NE
Washington, DC 20002-3600
202-651-5051
Fax: 202-651-5054
TTY 202-651-5052

A resource list of states that have established commissions and other offices to serve deaf people.

6716 Stress Management
Self Help for Hard of Hearing People
7910 Woodmont Avenue
Suite 1200
Bethesda, MD 20814-7022
301-951-3505
Fax: 301-913-9413
e-mail: national@shhh.org
http://www.shhh.org
TTY 301-657-2249

Patricia Silver, Owner

6717 Technical Assistance Resource Guide
Self Help for Hard of Hearing People
7910 Woodmont Avenue
Suite 1200
Bethesda, MD 20814-7022
301-657-2248
Fax: 301-913-9413
e-mail: national@shhh.org
http://www.shhh.org
TTY 301-657-2249

Terry Portis, Executive Director

Includes technical assistance centers and sources of communication access products.

6718 Telecommunications Access Updates
Self Help for Hard of Hearing People
7910 Woodmont Avenue
Suite 1200
Bethesda, MD 20814-7022
301-657-2248
Fax: 301-913-9413
e-mail: national@shhh.org
http://www.shhh.org
TTY 301-657-2249

Terry Portis, Executive Director

6719 Tinnitus
Self Help for Hard of Hearing People
7910 Woodmont Avenue
Suite 1200
Bethesda, MD 20814-7022
301-657-2248
Fax: 301-913-9413
e-mail: national@shhh.org
http://www.shhh.org
TTY 301-657-2249

Terry Portis, Executive Director

6720 To Our Family Members Who Are Hard of Hearing
Self Help for Hard of Hearing People
7910 Woodmont Avenue
Suite 1200
Bethesda, MD 20814-7022
301-657-2248
Fax: 301-913-9413
e-mail: national@shhh.org
http://www.shhh.org
TTY 301-657-2249

Terry Portis, Executive Director

6721 Total Access Courtroom
Self Help for Hard of Hearing People
7910 Woodmont Avenue
Suite 1200
Bethesda, MD 20814-7022
301-657-2248
Fax: 301-913-9413
e-mail: national@shhh.org
http://www.shhh.org
TTY 301-657-2249

Terry Portis, Executive Director

6722 Travel Resources for Deaf and Hard of Hearing People
National Information Center on Deafness
800 Florida Ave NE
Washington, DC 20002-3600
202-651-5051
Fax: 202-651-5054
TTY 202-651-5052

Hearing Impaired/Newsletters, Pamphlets

A publication list of travel industry resources for deaf and hard of hearing people.

6723 Troubleshooting Your Hearing Aid
Self Help for Hard of Hearing People
7910 Woodmont Avenue
Suite 1200
Bethesda, MD 20814-7022
301-657-2248
Fax: 301-913-9413
e-mail: national@shhh.org
http://www.shhh.org
TTY 301-657-2249

Terry Portis, Executive Director

6724 Understanding Our Needs: Results of the SHHH Member Survey
Self Help for Hard of Hearing People
7910 Woodmont Avenue
Suite 1200
Bethesda, MD 20814-7022
301-657-2248
Fax: 301-913-9413
e-mail: national@shhh.org
http://www.shhh.org
TTY 301-657-2249

Terry Portis, Executive Director

6725 Update on Captioning
Self Help for Hard of Hearing People
7910 Woodmont Avenue
Suite 1200
Bethesda, MD 20814-7022
301-657-2248
Fax: 301-913-9413
e-mail: national@shhh.org
http://www.shhh.org
TTY 301-657-2249

Terry Portis, Executive Director

6726 Update: Hearing and Vision Loss
Self Help for Hard of Hearing People
7910 Woodmont Avenue
Suite 1200
Bethesda, MD 20814-7022
301-657-2248
Fax: 301-913-9413
e-mail: national@shhh.org
http://www.shhh.org
TTY 301-657-2249

Terry Portis, Executive Director

6727 Using Assistive Listening Devices
Self Help for Hard of Hearing People
7910 Woodmont Avenue
Suite 1200
Bethesda, MD 20814-7022
301-657-2248
Fax: 301-913-9413
e-mail: national@shhh.org
http://www.shhh.org
TTY 301-657-2249

Terry Portis, Executive Director

6728 Using Telecommunications Relay Service
Self Help for Hard of Hearing People
7910 Woodmont Avenue
Suite 1200
Bethesda, MD 20814-7022
301-657-2248
Fax: 301-913-9413
e-mail: national@shhh.org
http://www.shhh.org
TTY 301-657-2249

Terry Portis, Executive Director

6729 Vestibular Disorders
Self Help for Hard of Hearing People
7910 Woodmont Avenue
Suite 1200
Bethesda, MD 20814-7022
301-657-2248
Fax: 301-913-9413
e-mail: national@shhh.org
http://www.shhh.org
TTY 301-657-2249

Terry Portis, Executive Director

6730 Volta Voices
Alexander Graham Bell Association for the Deaf
1537 35th Street NW
Washington, DC 20007-2753
202-337-5220
Fax: 202-337-8314
http://www.agbell.org

Elizabeth Quigley, Director Publications
Todd Houston, Executive Director

Contains Association news and educates readers on the abilities and needs of children and adults who are deaf or hard of hearing. Includes subscription to 'The Valta Review,' published 5 times a year.

6731 What Are TTYs? TDDs? TTs?
National Information Center on Deafness
800 Florida Avenue NE
Washington, DC 20002-3600
202-651-5051
Fax: 202-651-5054
TTY 202-651-5052

Discusses text telephones used by deaf people.

6732 What Do I Do with My Old Decoder?
Self Help for Hard of Hearing People
7910 Woodmont Avenue
Suite 1200
Bethesda, MD 20814-7022
301-657-2248
Fax: 301-913-9413
e-mail: national@shhh.org
http://www.shhh.org
TTY 301-657-2249

Terry Portis, Executive Director

6733 What Employers Want to Know About Assistive Technology in the Workplace
Self Help for Hard of Hearing People
7910 Woodmont Avenue
Suite 1200
Bethesda, MD 20814-7022
301-657-2248
Fax: 301-913-9413
e-mail: national@shhh.org
http://www.shhh.org
TTY 301-657-2249

Terry Portis, Executive Director

6734 What You Should Know About Cochlear Implants in Adults
Alexander Graham Bell Association for the Deaf
1537 35th Street NW
Washington, DC 20007-2753
202-337-5220
Fax: 202-337-8270
http://www.agbell.org
TTY 202-337-5220

Todd Houston, Executive Director

This informative brochure for adults considering a cochlear implant discusses evaluation, decisionmaking, surgery, follow-up visits, and typical costs for a cochlear implant.

Hearing Impaired/Videos, Audio Tapes

6735 **Why People Don't Acquire and/or Wear Hearing Aids**
Self Help for Hard of Hearing People
7910 Woodmont Avenue
Suite 1200
Bethesda, MD 20814-7022
301-657-2248
Fax: 301-913-9413
e-mail: national@shhh.org
http://www.shhh.org
TTY 301-657-2249

Terry Portis, Executive Director

6736 **Wireless Phones: Don't Mix Them Up**
Self Help for Hard of Hearing People
7910 Woodmont Avenue
Suite 1200
Bethesda, MD 20814-7022
301-657-2248
Fax: 301-913-9413
e-mail: national@shhh.org
http://www.shhh.org
TTY 301-657-2249

Terry Portis, Executive Director

6737 **Without Sight and Sound**
Helen Keller National Center
111 Middle Neck Road
Sands Point, NY 11050-1218
516-944-8900
Fax: 312-726-3503

Joseph McNulty, Executive Director

Pamphlet offering facts, causes, types and descriptions of deaf-blindness.

6738 **World of Sound**
International Hearing Society
16880 Middlebelt Road
Livonia, MI 48154-3336
313-478-2610
800-521-5247
Fax: 313-478-4520

The purpose of this booklet is to provide basic information for those with questions about hearing loss, hearing aids and Hearing Instrument Specialists.

6739 **You Don't Have to Hate Meetings: TryComputer-Assisted Notetaking Instead**
Self Help for Hard of Hearing People
7910 Woodmont Avenue
Suite 1200
Bethesda, MD 20814-7022
301-657-2248
Fax: 301-913-9413
e-mail: national@shhh.org
http://www.shhh.org
TTY 301-657-2249

Terry Portis, Executive Director

6740 **You've Done Something About It! Helpful Hints to the New Hearing Aid User**
Self Help for Hard of Hearing People
7910 Woodmont Avenue
Suite 1200
Bethesda, MD 20814-7022
301-657-2248
Fax: 301-913-9413
e-mail: national@shhh.org
http://www.shhh.org
TTY 301-657-2249

Terry Portis, Executive Director

6741 **You, Me and Hearing Loss Makes Three**
Self Help for Hard of Hearing People
7910 Woodmont Avenue
Suite 1200
Bethesda, MD 20814-7022
301-657-2248
Fax: 301-913-9413
e-mail: national@shhh.org
http://www.shhh.org
TTY 301-657-2249

Terry Portis, Executive Director

Videos, Audio Tapes

6742 **AFB Press**
American Foundation for the Blind
11 Penn Plaza
Suite 300
New York, NY 10001-2018
212-502-7600
800-232-5463
Fax: 212-502-7777
e-mail: afbpress@afb.net
http://www.afb.org

Natalie Hilzen, Editor-in-Chief
Sharon Baker Harris, Marketing Manager
Carl Augusto, President

Publication/Video orders. AFB Press publishes a variety of books and videos for blind and visually impaired people and their families, for students, professionals, researchers, and anyone involved in making the mainstream community accessible.

6743 **Assistive Devices: Doorways to Independence**
Alexander Graham Bell Association for the Deaf
1537 35th Street NW
Washington, DC 20007-2753
202-337-5220
Fax: 202-337-8270
http://www.agbell.org
TTY 202-337-5220

Todd Houston, Executive Director

This extensive videotape and handbook introduce auditory, visual, and vibro-tactile devices that help people with hearing losses.

67 pages

6744 **Basic Course in American Sign LanguageVideotape Package**
TJ Publishers
817 Silver Spring Avenue
Suite 206
Silver Spring, MD 20910-4617
301-585-4440
Fax: 301-585-5930
e-mail: TJPubinc@aol.com

Angela K Thames, President
Jerald A Murphy, VP

Includes four 1-hour videotapes, plus vocabulary videotapes and two texts.

6745 **Beginning Reading and Sign LanguageVideo**
TJ Publishers
817 Silver Spring Avenue
Suite 206
Silver Spring, MD 20910-4617
301-585-4440
Fax: 301-585-5930

Angela K Thames, President
Jerald A Murphy, VP

Learning Sign improves reading, motor skills and visual perception and increases language acquisition abilities. For kids from 2 to 12, this video picture book features deaf actress Susan Bressler signing over a hundred words at the zoo, at home, and around the community.

6746 **Deaf Culture Autobiographies**
Harris Communications
15155 Technology Drive
Eden Prairie, MN 55344-2273
952-906-1180
800-825-6758
Fax: 952-906-1099

Robert Harris, Owner

Inspiring videotapes offer encouragement and enlightenment to the hearing impaired. Total of eight videotapes.

6747 **Deaf Culture Series**
Harris Communications
15155 Technology Drive
Eden Prairie, MN 55344-2273
952-906-1180
800-825-6758
Fax: 952-906-1099

Robert Harris, Owner

Hearing Impaired/Videos, Audio Tapes

Each video in this 5-part series features a variety of Deaf talent. It is an excellent resource for Deaf studies programs, Interpreter Preparation programs and Sign Language programs.

6748 Deaf Mosaic Series
Harris Communications
15155 Technology Drive
Eden Prairie, MN 55344-2273
952-906-1180
800-825-6758
Fax: 952-906-1099

Robert Harris, Owner

A national magazine show produced monthly by Gallaudet University, this show has been awarded nine Emmys. As the only nation-wide program about the Deaf community, these videotapes are the best of the best from the shows programs.

6749 Diagnosis and Treatment of Unilateral Hearing Loss
American Academy of Otolaryngology
1 Prince Street
Alexandria, VA 22314-3354
703-836-4444
Fax: 703-683-5100
http://www.entnet.org

Tom Harlow, Finance Executive

This CD-ROM focuses on evaluation and treatment of unilateral hearing loss arising from skull base lesion.

6750 Do You Hear That?
Alexander Graham Bell Association for the Deaf
1537 35th Street NW
Washington, DC 20007-2753
202-337-5220
Fax: 202-337-8270
http://www.agbell.org
TTY 202-337-5220

Todd Houston, Executive Director

This video documents auditory-verbal therapy as it is practiced at North York General Hospital in Toronto, Canada.

Frequency: 35 minutes

6751 Getting Through Audiotape
Self Help for Hard of Hearing People
7910 Woodmont Avenue
Suite 1200
Bethesda, MD 20814-7022
301-657-2248
Fax: 301-913-9413
e-mail: national@shhh.org
http://www.shhh.org
TTY 301-657-2249

Terry Portis, Executive Director

Simulates hearing loss for better understanding of communication dificulties. The tape features an unfair hearing test.

6752 Getting the Most Out of Your Hearing Aids
Self Help for Hard of Hearing People
7910 Woodmont Avenue
Suite 1200
Bethesda, MD 20814-7022
301-657-2248
Fax: 301-913-9413
e-mail: national@shhh.org
http://www.shhh.org
TTY 301-657-2249

Terry Portis, Executive Director

Helps people new to hearing loss to accept and get the best use of their hearing aids. Open-captioned.

Frequency: 30 minutes

6753 Granny Good's Sign of Christmas
Gallaudet University Bookstore
800 Florida Avenue NE
Washington, DC 20002-3600
800-451-1073
Fax: 800-621-8476
http://www.gallaudet.edu
TTY 888-630-9347

Twas The Night Before Christmas told in American Sign Language.

6754 HEAR's to the ADA
Self Help for Hard of Hearing People
7910 Woodmont Avenue
Suite 1200
Bethesda, MD 20814-7022
301-657-2248
Fax: 301-913-9413
e-mail: national@shhh.org
http://www.shhh.org
TTY 301-657-2249

Terry Portis, Executive Director

A guide for consumers about communication access and the Americans with Disabilities Act. Open-captioned.

Frequency: 23 minutes

6755 Hearing Loss and Rehabilitation
American Academy of Otolaryngology
1 Prince Street
Alexandria, VA 22314-3354
703-836-4444
Fax: 703-683-5100
http://www.entnet.org

Tom Harlow, Finance Executive

Slides.

6756 I Can Hear!
Alexander Graham Bell Association for the Deaf
1537 35th Street NW
Washington, DC 20007-2753
202-337-5220
Fax: 202-337-8270
http://www.agbell.org
TTY 202-337-5220

Todd Houston, Executive Director

This inspirational video describes the auditory-verbal approach for developing speech and language for hearing impaired children and adults.

Frequency: 23 minutes

6757 I Can Hear-II
Alexander Graham Bell Association for the Deaf
1537 35th Street NW
Washington, DC 20007-2753
202-337-5220
Fax: 202-337-8270
http://www.agbell.org
TTY 202-337-5220

Todd Houston, Executive Director

An exciting videotape that gives more examples of auditory-verbal therapy and a variety of kids who have been taught to speak using this method.

6758 I Only Hear You When I See Your Face
Alexander Graham Bell Association for the Deaf
1537 35th Street NW
Washington, DC 20007-2753
202-337-5220
Fax: 202-337-8270
http://www.agbell.org
TTY 202-337-5220

Todd Houston, Executive Director

This video is for medical personnel providing tips on how to communicate more effectively with the hearing impaired patient.

Frequency: 11 minutes

6759 I See What You Say: Self Help Lipreading Program
Alexander Graham Bell Association for the Deaf
1537 35th Street NW
Washington, DC 20007-2753
202-337-5220
Fax: 202-337-8270
http://www.agbell.org
TTY 202-337-5220

Todd Houston, Executive Director

Easy-to-follow videotape and manual for consumers teaches visual recognition of speech sounds in single words and phrases.

Frequency: 54 minutes

Hearing Impaired/Videos, Audio Tapes

6760 Interview with Kirsten Gonzales
Alexander Graham Bell Association for the Deaf
1537 35th Street NW
Washington, DC 20007-2753
202-337-5220
Fax: 202-337-8270
http://www.agbell.org
TTY 202-337-5220

Todd Houston, Executive Director

Interviews a longtime user and trainer of oral interpreters who offers techniques in articulation and natural gestures.
Frequency: 20 minutes

6761 Joy of Signing
Gallaudet University Bookstore
800 Florida Avenue NE
Washington, DC 20002-3600
800-451-1073
Fax: 202-651-5489
http://www.gallaudet.edu
TDD 888-630-9347
TTY 888-630-9347

Three tapes full of useful information to help increase skill and comfort with sign.

6762 Lipreading Made Easy
Alexander Graham Bell Association for the Deaf
1537 35th Street NW
Washington, DC 20007-2753
202-337-5220
Fax: 202-337-8270
http://www.agbell.org
TTY 202-337-5220

Todd Houston, Executive Director

Uses actual photos of lips to teach the student to listen with their eyes.

6763 Models of Oral Interpreting
Alexander Graham Bell Association for the Deaf
1537 35th Street NW
Washington, DC 20007-2753
202-337-5220
Fax: 202-337-8270
http://www.agbell.org
TTY 202-337-5220

Todd Houston, Executive Director

Modeling effective techniques, three experienced oral interpreters interpret the same lectures featuring the handling of multiple speakers, phrasing, facial expressions, and articulation.
Frequency: 46 minutes

6764 National 4th Biennial Campvention of the Deaf
National Association of the Deaf
814 Thayer Avenue
Silver Spring, MD 20910-4504
301-587-1788
Fax: 301-587-4873
TTY 301-587-1789

Depicts the big event held at the Casa De Fruta in Hollister, CA.
Frequency: Videotape

6765 People vs. Noise
Better Hearing Institute
5021b Backlick Road
Annandale, VA 22003-6043
703-642-0580
Fax: 703-750-9302
http://www.betterhearing.org

6766 Read My Lips
Alexander Graham Bell Association for the Deaf
1537 35th Street NW
Washington, DC 20007-2753
202-546-2838
Fax: 202-337-8270
http://www.agbell.org
TTY 202-337-5220

David A Reed OD, Partner

A six videotape series that takes adults from lipreading to basic words to complex phrases and sentences in a variety of real life situations.

6767 Speaking Off the Cuff
Alexander Graham Bell Association for the Deaf
1537 35th Street NW
Washington, DC 20007-2753
202-337-5220
Fax: 202-337-8270
http://www.agbell.org
TTY 202-337-5220

Todd Houston, Executive Director

This videotape series features adults with hearing impairments speaking on different topics with varying degrees of speaking abilities.
Frequency: Tapes A-C

6768 Teaching Strategies for the Developmentof Auditory Verbal Communication
Alexander Graham Bell Association for the Deaf
1537 35th Street NW
Washington, DC 20007-2753
202-337-5220
Fax: 202-337-8270
http://www.agbell.org
TTY 202-337-5220

Todd Houston, Executive Director

This educational series of five-hour videotapes demonstrates teaching strategies for developing auditory-verbal communication in young children with severe to profound hearing loss.

6769 Telecoil: Plugging into Sound
Self Help for Hard of Hearing People
7910 Woodmont Avenue
Suite 1200
Bethesda, MD 20814-7022
301-657-2248
Fax: 301-913-9413
e-mail: national@shhh.org
http://www.shhh.org
TTY 301-657-2249

Terry Portis, Executive Director

Guide for consumers explaining a telecoil in their hearing aid. SHHH members are featured, talking about their experiences. Includes 50 brochures. Open-captioned.
Frequency: 10 minutes

6770 Telecoils in Hearing Aids
Self Help for Hard of Hearing People
7910 Woodmont Avenue
Suite 1200
Bethesda, MD 20814-7022
301-657-2248
Fax: 301-913-9413
e-mail: national@shhh.org
http://www.shhh.org
TTY 301-657-2249

Terry Portis, Executive Director

6771 Telling Stories
Harris Communications
15155 Technology Drive
Eden Prairie, MN 55344-2273
952-906-1180
800-825-6758
Fax: 952-906-1099

Robert Harris, Owner

This international, award winning play, now on video, uses the symbols and myths drawn from the struggles between the world of the deaf and the world of the hearing.

6772 You Shared the World with Me Video
Alexander Graham Bell Association for the Deaf
3417 Volta Place NW
Washington, DC 20007-2737
202-337-5220
Fax: 202-337-8270
TTY 202-337-5220

Todd Houston, Executive Director

Johnny Whitaker hosts this inspiring video about having a hearing impairment and working with the hearing impaired.
Frequency: 16 minutes

Hearing Impaired/Websites

Websites

6773 ACB Government Employees

http://www.acb.org
Concerns of the organization include recruitment, placement and advancement of blind and visually impaired employees.

6774 ACB Radio Amateurs

http://www.acb.org
A radio amateur network of blind, visually impaired and sighted members who gather and share common problems and solutions to help members improve radio amateurs in getting started, provides access to educational materials in special media and publishes a directory for the visually impaired.

6775 ACB Social Service Providers

http://www.acb.org
Information on blind and visually impaired social workers, social service professionals, students pursuing careers in social work, and other interested persons.

6776 Alexander Graham Bell Association for the Deaf and Hard of Hearing

http://www.agbell.org
Information on pediatric hearing loss, and educational issues for hearing impaired children, promotes better public understanding of hearing loss in children and adults, provides scholarships and financial aid to families of children with hearing loss, and promotes early detection of hearing loss in infants.

6777 American Academy of Audiology

http://www.audiology.org
Provides professional development, education and research and provides increased public awareness of hearing disorders and audiologic services.

6778 American Tinnitus Association

http://www.teleport.com/~ata
Provides information about tinnitus and referrals to local contacts/support groups nationwide.

6779 Better Hearing Institute

http://www.betterhearing.org
Information programs on hearing loss and available medical, surgical, hearing aid, and rehabilitation assistance for millions with uncorrected hearing problems.

6780 CAPCOM

http://www.capcom1.com
Presents workshops on law and the deaf and on promoting productive working relationships for the hearing impaired employees of agencies and corporations.

6781 Council on Education of the Deaf

http://www.monster.educ.kent.edu/deaf
Offers information and referral services to the hearing impaired.

6782 Deafness Research Foundation

http://www.idt.net
Committed to public awareness and support for basic and clinical research into deafness and hearing disabilities.

6783 EAR Foundation

http://www.theearfound.com
The Meniere's Network is a national network of patient organized self-help groups which allow the exchange of experiences and coping strategies associated with Meniere's Disease.

6784 Hear Now

http://www.leisurelan.com/~hearnow
Committed to making technology accessible to deaf and hard of hearing individuals throughout the United States. Also raises funds to provide hearing aids, cochlear implants and related services to children and adults who have hearing losses but do not have financial resources to purchase their own devices.

6785 Hearing Education and Awareness for Elders

http://www.hearnet.com/
Educates the public about the real dangers of hearing loss resulting from repeated exposure to excessive noise levels.

6786 House Ear Institute

http://www.hei.org

6787 National Association of the Deaf

http://www.nad.org
Focus on advocacy, captioned media, deafness-related information/publications, legal assistance and more.

6788 National Association of the Deaf Law

http://www.nad.org
Provides legal information about how these laws affect deaf people in jobs, education, the courts, public access and government services.

6789 National Information Center on Deafness

http://www.gallaudet.edu
Provides information or referrals on questions about deafness, including general information, education, research, legislation, assistive devices and more. Offers a bibliography of readings available on 30 topics relating to deafness.

6790 National Institute on Deafness and Other Communication Disorders Clearinghouse

http://www.nidcd.nih.gov
Our mission is to uncover new knowledge that will lead to better health for everyone.

6791 Registry of Interpreters for the Deaf

http://www.RID.org
Professional interpreters and translators, persons with deafness or hearing impairments and professionals in related fields.

6792 Self-Help for Hard of Hearing People

http://www.shhh.org/
Promotes awareness and information about hearing loss, communication, assistive devices, and alternative communication skills through publications, exhibits and presentations.

6793 USA Deaf Sports Federation

http://www.usadsf.org
A governing body for all deaf sports and recreation in the United States.

Hearing Impaired/Research Centers

Research Centers

6794 **American Hearing Research Foundation**
8 S Michigan Avenue
Suite 814
Chicago, IL 60603-3461
312-726-9670
Fax: 312-726-9695
http://www.@american-hearing.org

William L Lederer, Executive Director

Supports medical resarch and education into the causes, prevention, and cures of deafness, hearing losses, and balance disorders. Also keeps physicians and the public informed of the latest developments in hearing research and education.

6795 **Arkansas Rehabilitation Research and Training Center for Deaf Persons**
4601 W Markham Street
Little Rock, AR 72205-3822
501-686-6219
Fax: 501-686-9698

Douglas Watson PhD, Director
Victoria Akins, MD

Focuses on issues affecting the employability of deaf and hard-of-hearing rehabilitation clients.

6796 **Bill Wilkerson Center**
1114 19th Avenue S
Nashville, TN 37212-2110
615-936-5000
Fax: 615-343-7705

Dr. Fred H Bess, Director

Community-operated research and treatment center focusing studies on hearing sciences.

6797 **Brooklyn College of City University of New York: Speech & Hearing Center**
Boylan Hall
Room 4400
Brooklyn, NY 11210
718-780-5186

Dr. Oliver Bloodstein, Director

Research activities include normal communications and communication disorders, studies relating to language, hearing and speech disorders.

6798 **CAPCOM**
5010 Wisconsin Avenue NW
Washington, DC 20016-4114
202-331-5771
Fax: 202-331-5788
TTY 703-749-1876

Katherine Blauer, Executive Director

Conducts research on the special needs of the hearing impaired, including senior citizens. Presents workshops on law and the deaf and on promoting productive working relationships for the hearing impaired employees of agencies and corporations. Maintains speakers' bureau and file of publications from organizations serving the deaf.

6799 **David T Siegel Institute for Communicative Disorders**
Humana Hospital-Michael Reese
3033 S Cottage Grove Avenue
Chicago, IL 60616-3346
312-276-6868
Fax: 773-791-4014

Edward Applebaum, Chief Service

Conducts behavioral research on language development and sign language for the deaf.

6800 **Deafness Research Foundation**
9 E 38th Street
New York, NY 10016
212-599-0027
Fax: 212-599-0039
e-mail: drf1@village.iof.com
http://www.drf.org

Jane Fortune, Chairperson

The nation's largest voluntary health organization, providing grants for fellowship, symposia, and research into causes, treatment, and prevention of all ear disorders.

6801 **Duke University: RERC on Communication Enhancement Duke University**
DUMC Box 3887
Durham, NC 27710
919-684-3859
http://www.aac-rerc.com

Franklin DeRuyler, PhD, Chief, Division of Pathology
Kevin Caves, ME, ATP, RET, Director

Conducts a comprehensive program of research, development, training and dissemination activities that address the NIDRR priorities and seek to improve technologies for individuals who rely on augmentative and alternative communication (AAC) technologies.

6802 **Houston Ear Research Foundation**
7737 SW Fwy
Suite 630
Houston, TX 77074-1867
713-771-9966
Fax: 713-771-0546

Kathleen Stallworth, Program Administrator
Jan Gilden, Executive Director

Aims to improve health care and education for deaf and hearing-impaired children.

6803 **International Center for Hearing & Speech Research**
1 Lomb Memorial Drive
Rochester, NY 14623-5603
585-475-6403
Fax: 585-475-6677

Dr. Robert Firisina Sr, Director

Focuses on prevention, early detection and treatment of hearing impaired people.

6804 **League for the Hard of Hearing**
50 Broadway
Floor 6
New York, NY 10004-3810
917-305-7700
Fax: 917-305-7888
e-mail: postmaster@lhh.org
http://www.lhh.org

Nancy Nadler, Executive Officer
Amy Boyle, Assistant Director

The mission of this non profit agency is to improve the quality of life for people with all degrees of hearing loss and to offer comprehensive services regardless of age or mode of communication.

6805 **Memphis State University: Center for the Communicatively Impaired**
807 Jefferson Avenue
Memphis, TN 38105-5042
901-678-2009
Fax: 901-525-1282

Maurice I Mendel, Director

Offers research into hearing loss and deafness as well as speech impairments.

6806 **Minnesota Academy of Audiology**
PO Box 20499
Bloomington, MN 55420
612-885-0095
800-347-8165
Fax: 612-625-8901
http://www.minnesotaaudiology.org

Charles R Stone, AuD, President
Joscelyn R K Martin, AuD, President-Elect

The Minnesota Academy of Audiology is organized for the purpose of promoting the public good by fostering the growth, development, recognition, and status of the profession of Audiology and its members. We are dedicated to providing quality hearing and balance care to our patients by enhancing our members to achieve practice objectives through education, legislation, and increased public awareness of hearing and balance disorders.

Hearing Impaired/Research Centers

6807 **National Institute on Deafness & Other Communication Disorders**
US Department of Health & Human Services
9000 Rockville Pike
Bldg 31
Bethesda, MD 20892
301-496-1993
800-422-6237
Fax: 301-402-0018
TDD 301-402-6596

James Snow MD, Director
Martin Allen, Contact

Conducts and supports research and training with respect to disorders of hearing and other communication processes, including diseases affecting hearing, balance, voice, speech, language, touch, taste and smell through research performed in its own laboratories; a program of research grants; individual and institutional research training awards, career development awards, center grants, and contracts to public and private research institutions.

6808 **New York Foundation for Otologic Research**
920 Park Avenue
New York, NY 10028
212-980-3100

Dr. Alan Austin Scheer, Director
Geza J Marx, Owner

Unsolved hearing problems and deafness research.

6809 **Northern Illinois University: Research and Training Center**
1425 W Lincoln Highway
Dekalb, IL 60115-2825
815-753-1000
Fax: 815-753-1545
TTY 815-753-6520

Sue E Ouellette PhD, Project Director
John Peters, President

Conducts research, resource development, and training/technical assistance projects geared toward enhancing the employment, independent living, and quality of life outcomes for traditionally underserved people who are deaf.

6810 **Ohio State University: Otological Research Laboratories**
456 W 10th Avenue
Columbus, OH 43210-1240
614-293-8100
Fax: 614-293-5506

Dr. Thomas DeMaria, Acting Director

Clinical and basic research in otology.

6811 **Ohio University: School of Hearing and Speech Science**
Lindley Hall
Room 201
Athens, OH 45701
740-593-1407

Dr. Edwin Leach, Director

Focuses on hearing and speech impairments.

6812 **Oregon Health Sciences University: Oregon Hearing Research Center**
3181 SW Sam Jackson Park Road
Portland, OR 97239-3079
503-494-3460
Fax: 503-494-5656

Jack A Vernon PhD, Director
James Morgan, Executive Director

Hearing problems, including clinical and basic research into the field of hearing disorders.

6813 **Princeton University: Cutaneous Communication Laboratory**
Psychology Department, Green Hall
Princeton, NJ 08544
609-258-5277
Fax: 609-258-1113

Dr. Roger Cholewiak, Contact

6814 **State University College at Fredonia: Youngman Center**
Thompson Hall
Fredonia, NY 14063
716-673-3553

Dr. Robert Manzella, Director
Patricia Feraldi, Executive Director

Studies communications disorders including hearing and speech.

6815 **State University College at Plattsburgh: Auditory Research Laboratory**
107 Beaumont
Plattsburgh, NY 12901
518-564-7701

Dr. Roger Hamernik, Director

6816 **Syracuse University: Institute for Sensory Research**
Merrill Lane
Syracuse, NY 13244
315-443-4164
Fax: 315-443-1184

Dr. Ronald Verrillo, Director

Sensory processing and hearing disorders.

6817 **Temple University: Section of Auditory Research**
3440 Kruege N Broad Street
Philadelphia, PA 19140
215-221-3661

William Hal Martin, Director

6818 **Temple University: Speech and Hearing Science Laboratories**
13th & Cecil B Moore Avenues
Philadelphia, PA 19122
215-787-7543

Dr. Aquilles Iglesias, Director

Speech and hearing studies.

6819 **Texas Tech University: Speech-Language-Hearing Clinic**
Lubbock, TX 79409
806-742-3907

Sherry Sancribian, Director

6820 **Trace Center**
University of Wisconsin-Madison
1500 Highland Avenue
Room S-151
Madison, WI 53705-2274
608-263-9339
Fax: 608-262-8848

Peter Borden, Communication Director
Gregg Vanderheiden, Center Director

Research and development center working with communication, control, and computer access technologies for people with disabilities.

6821 **University of Alabama: Speech and Hearing Center**
PO Box 870242
Tuscaloosa, AL 35487
205-348-7628
Fax: 205-934-8559

Dr Eugene Cooper, Director
James Phifer, Manager

6822 **University of Chicago: Temporal Bone Laboratory for Ear Research**
PO Box 412
Chicago, IL 60690
773-702-6152
Fax: 773-702-6809

Dr. Raul Hinojasa, Director
Gail Vijuk, Manager

Focuses on hearing impairments and deafness research.

6823 **University of Colorado: Boulder Communication Disorders Clinic**
Boulder, CO 80309
303-492-5375

Susan M Moore, Director

Hearing Impaired/Research Centers

Focuses on communication disorders including speech and hearing impairments.

6824 University of Michigan: Communicative Disorders Clinic
1111 Catherine Street
Ann Arbor, MI 48109-2054
734-764-8440
Fax: 734-747-2489

Dr. Holly Craig, Director

Focuses on communicative disorders including hearing impairments and speech disorders.

6825 University of Michigan: Kresge Hearing Research Institute
1301 E Ann Street
Room 5032
Ann Arbor, MI 48109
734-763-9600
Fax: 734-764-0014

Josef M Miller, Director
Allen Lichter, Administrator

Focuses on hearing and auditory disorders.

6826 University of Nebraska: Lincoln Barkley Memorial Center
Barkley Center 301
Lincoln, NE 68583
402-472-6707
Fax: 402-472-7697

John Bernthal, Director

Focuses on hearing impairments and deaf research.

6827 University of Nevada: Speech and Language Pathology Department
Reno, NV 89557
702-784-4887
Fax: 702-784-4889

Dr. Stephen McFarlane, Chairman

Communication disorders research pertaining to hearing and speech impairments.

6828 University of North Carolina at Chapel Hill: Divsion of Speech & Hearing
Medical School, Wing D
Cb 7190
Chapel Hill, NC 27599
919-966-1006
Fax: 617-856-6231

Dr. Thomas Layton, Director

6829 University of Oklahoma: Speech & Hearing Center
PO Box 26901
Oklahoma City, OK 73190
405-271-4214

Dr. Glenda Ochaner, Director
Stephan Painton, Manager

6830 University of Texas Health Science Center at Houston: Speech & Hearing
1343 Moursund Street
Houston, TX 77030-3405
713-500-2550
Fax: 713-792-4513

Louise Kent-Udolf, Director
Mary Battaglia, Manager

Provides rehabilitation services for children and adults with hearing and speech disorders.

6831 University of Texas at Dallas: Callier Center for Communication Disorders
1966 Inwood Road
Dallas, TX 75235-7205
972-883-3165
Fax: 214-905-3022

Dr. Ross J Roeser, Director
Allen Clayton, Manager

Focuses on communication and behavioral disorders including hearing impairments and deafness research.

6832 University of Virginia: Communication Disorders Program
132 Emmet Street
Charlottesville, VA 22906
434-924-3377
Fax: 434-924-0747

Dr. Richard Talbott, Director

6833 University of Washington: Department of Speech & Hearing Sciences
1417 NE 42nd Street
Seattle, WA 98195
206-543-2100
Fax: 206-543-1093

Dr. Wesley Wilson, Chairman
Mark A Emmert, CEO

Communication sciences and disorders.

6834 University of Washington: Speech & Hearing Clinic
4131 15th Avenue NE
Seattle, WA 98195
206-543-5440

Robert Carpenter PhD, Director
Nancy Alarcon, Executive Director

Normal speech, language and hearing processes, development and disorders research.

6835 University of Wisconsin: Auditory Physiology Center
273 Medical Sciences Building
Madison, WI 53706
608-262-0818

Dr. John Brugge, Director

Activities include studies in hearing loss and deafness.

6836 Utah Chapter: Alexander Graham Bell Association for the Deaf
PO Box 27461
Salt Lake City, UT 84127
801-969-8353

Janeal M McOmie, Executive Officer

Promotes research on deafness. Provides assistance to parents of children with hearing impairments.

6837 Yeshiva University: Institute of Communication Disorders
Montefiore Medical Center
111 E 210th Street
Bronx, NY 10467-2401
718-920-4321
Fax: 718-405-9014

Robert Ruben MD, Chairman
Spencer Foreman, CEO

Studies on communicative disorders including speech and hearing.

Heart Disease/Associations & Organizations

Associations & Organizations

6838 **American Heart Association**
7272 Greenville Avenue
Dallas, TX 75231
214-373-6300
800-AHA-USA1
Fax: 214-987-9361
e-mail: Kevin.Turner@heart.org
http://www.americanheart.org

M Cass Wheeler, CEO
Robert Eckel, President

Physicians, scientists, and laypersons. Supports research, education, and community service programs with the objective of reducing premature death and disability from cardiovascular diseases and stroke; coordinates the efforts of physicians, nurses, health professionals, and others engaged in the fight against heart and circulatory disease. Financed entirely by voluntary contributions of the public, principally during the Heart Campaign held in. February.

6839 **Arizona Heart Institute**
2632 N 20th Street
Phoenix, AZ 85006
602-266-2200
Fax: 602-264-5332
e-mail: escott@azheart.com
http://www.azheart.com/

Edward B. Diethrich, MD, Medical Director and Founder
Kenneth G. Howell, President and Chief Executive Of

6840 **Congenital Heart Disease Anomalies Support Education and Resources**
2112 Wilkins Road
Swanton, OH 43558
419-825-5575
Fax: 419-825-2880
e-mail: myer106w@wonder.em.cdc.gov
http://www.csun.edu/~hfmth006/chaser/

Anita Myers, Contact

An organization established to meet the emotional and educational needs of parents and professionals who deal with congenital heart disease in children. Offers resource materials and support for parent to parent networking.

6841 **Council on Geriatric Cardiology**
777 W Putnam Avenue
Greenwich, CT 06830-5091
203-531-0916
Fax: 203-531-0450

Sarah Howell, Executive Director

Geriatric cardiologists and physicians in related fields are members; medical practitioners certified in specialties other than geriatrics or cardiologists are fellows; other individuals with an interest in geriatric cardiology are nonphysician members. Works to improve the clinical and therapeutic management of older individuals with cardiovascular disease; encourages use of preventive measures to avert the onset of cardiovascular aging and disease. Promotes more effective public policy and education regarding cardiac health. Conducts educational programs for physicians, other health care professionals, and the public. Supports research into cardiovascular aging and diseases relevant to older people. Serves as a clearinghouse on geriatric cardiology. Sponsors competitions.

6842 **National Heart, Lung and Blood Institute**
National Institutes of Health
31 Center Drive MSC 2486
Building 31, Room 5A48
Bethesda, MD 20892
301-592-8573
Fax: 240-629-3246
e-mail: nhlbiinfo@nhlbi.nih.gov
http://www.nhlbi.nih.gov

Elizabeth G. Nabel M.D.,, Director

Primary responsibility of this organization is the scientific investigation of heart, blood vessel, lung and blood disorders. Oversees research, demonstration, prevention, education, control and training activities in these fields and emphasizes the prevention and control of heart diseases.

6843 **Philadelphia Heart Institute: Geriatrics Practice**
39th & Market Streets
Philadelphia, PA 19104
215-472-8520
Fax: 215-349-5648
http://www.pennhealth.com/

Bernard Segal, Director

6844 **San Francisco Heart Institute**
1900 Sullivan Avenue
Daly City, CA 94015
650-991-6601
Fax: 650-755-7315
http://www.sfhi.com

Colman J. Ryan, MD, Executive Medical Director
Louis Manila, Manager of Research and Operatio

6845 **Sodium Information Hotline**
PO Box 2506
Stuart, FL 34995-2506
800-622-3274
Fax: 800-333-0005

Provides low-sodium recipies and sodium content information on 10,000 foods. Registered dieticians are available to answer questions. Free publications are available. Sponsored by Mrs. Dash salt substitute products.

6846 **Texas Heart Institute**
PO Box 20345
Houston, TX 77225-0345
832-355-4011
Fax: 713-791-3089
http://www.texasheartinstitute.org

James Cuthbertson, President
Mark Mattson, CEO

6847 **University of Tennessee: Division of Cardiovascular Diseases**
1414 Cumberland Avenue
M303 Walters Life Sciences Bldg
Knoxville, TN 37996
865-974-6841
Fax: 865-974-4057
e-mail: rakin1@utk.edu
http://www.bio.utk.edu/division/

Dr. John Koontz, Director

Cardiovasular system disorders including heart disease prevention and treatment.

Books

6848 **Adult Congenital Heart Disease: A Practical Guide**
Wiley Publishing
10475 Crosspoint Boulevard
Indianapolis, IN 46256
877-762-2974
Fax: 800-597-3299
http://www.wiley.com

Michael A Gatzoulis, Author
Lorna Swan, Author
Judith Therrien, Author

This practical guide with its straighforward a,b,c approach is written for those professionals.

288 pages

Heart Disease/Journals, Magazines

6849 **Advances in Cardiac and Pulmonary Rehabilitation**
Haworth Press
10 Alice Street
Binghamton, NY 13904-1503
607-722-5857
800-342-9678
Fax: 607-722-1424
e-mail: getinfo@haworthpress.com
http://www.haworthpress.com

William Cohen, Owner

Enhance your rehabilitation program with this authoritative volume.

74 pages

6850 **American Medical Association Guide to Preventing and Treating Heart Disease**
American Medical Association
515 N State Street
Chicago, IL 60610
800-621-8335
http://www.ama-assn.org

Martin S Lipsky MD, Author
Marla Mendelson MD, Author
Stephen Havas MD, Author

Offers essential tools and timely information on the prevention and treatment of heart disease. Also features practical strategies for lifestyle changes, advice about warning signs to report to a doctor, guidance on heart-health ways to exercise, and a section on the unique risks ans symptons for women.

312 pages

6851 **Diet & Heart Disease: It's Not What You Think**
Whitman Publications
400 Oak Hill Drive
Winona Lake, IN 46590
574-267-3941
800-421-2401
e-mail: books@whitman.com
http://www.whitman.com

Stephen Byrnes, Author

96 pages

6852 **Heart Smart: A Cardiologists 5-Step Plan for Detecting, Preventing and Even Reversing Heart Disease**
Wiley Publishing
10475 Crosspoint Boulevard
Indianapolis, IN 46256
877-762-2974
Fax: 800-597-3299
http://www.wiley.com

Matthew S DeVane, Author

Provides the latest cutting-edge methods to treat, detect, and prevent heart disease, which is the number 1 killer in North America, Europe, and many other regions of the world. Helps readers identify their current health status through interactive quizzes and then recommends specific diagnostic procedures and lifestyle changes.

272 pages

6853 **Heart to Heart: A Guide to the Psychological Aspects of the Disease**
Health Press
PO Box 1388
Santa Fe, NM 87504-1388
505-982-9373
Fax: 505-983-1383

130 pages Frequency: Paperback

6854 **Outliving Heart Disease**
Newmarket Press
18 East 48th Street
New York, NY 10017
212-832-3575
Fax: 212-832-3629
http://www.newmarketpress.com

Dr Richard A Stein, Author

Explains vascular changes that take place as you age- and how they affect your heart. The specific risk factors affecting women, African-Americans, and other group. The latest on research on statins-those miracle drugs that have revolutionized the prevention and treatment of heart disease. How to create a heart-healthy diet and cardiovascular exercise program. How depression, anxiety, and stress can impact the heart, and what you can do about it.

286 pages

6855 **Prevent and Reverse Heart Disease: The Revolutionary, Scientifically Proven, Nutrition-Based Care**
Penguin Group USA
375 Hudson Street
New York, NY 10014-3657
212-366-2000
http://us.penguingroup.com

Caldwell B Esselstyn, Author

320 pages

Journals, Magazines

6856 **Heart Beat**
Healthteam Interactive Communications
274 Madison Avenue
Floor 19
New York, NY 10016
212-265-9166
Fax: 212-779-2094

John Nittoli, Editor
Paul Sisia, Publisher

Magazine for cardiology patients.

Frequency: Quarterly

Newsletters, Pamphlets

6857 **Cholesterol and Your Heart**
American Heart Association
7272 Greenville Avenue
Dallas, TX 75231-5129
214-373-6300
800-553-6321
Fax: 214-696-5211

M Cass Wheeler, CEO

Offers information on lowering blood cholesterol levels.

6858 **Easy Food Tips for Heart Healthy Eating**
American Heart Association
7272 Greenville Avenue
Dallas, TX 75231-5129
214-373-6300
800-553-6321
Fax: 214-696-5211

M Cass Wheeler, CEO

Offers food selection hints for fat-controlled meals.

6859 **Exercise and Your Heart**
American Heart Association
7272 Greenville Avenue
Dallas, TX 75231-5129
214-373-6300
800-553-6321
Fax: 214-696-5211

M Cass Wheeler, CEO

Offers information on how to get enough exercise from daily activities, what the benefits of exercise are and what the risks of exercising are.

Heart Disease/Research Centers

Research Centers

6860 American Health Assistance Foundation
22512 Gateway Center Drive
Clarksburg, MD 20871-2005
301-948-3244
800-437-2423
Kathy Honaker, Executive Director

Funds research programs for heart disease, glaucoma, and Alzheimer's disease. Provides financial assistance through Alzheimer's Family Relief Program. Public education materials on programs, brochures, and applications are provided.

6861 Baylor College of Medicine: DeBakey Heart Center
Texas Medical Center
1 Baylor Plaza
Houston, TX 77030-3498
713-798-6105
Fax: 713-793-1192
Dr. Michael DeBakey, Director
Mark M Udden, MD

Research activities have an emphasis on therapeutic intervention and prevention of heart diseases.

6862 Bees-Stealy Research Foundation
2001 4th Avenue
San Diego, CA 92101-2303
619-446-1560
Fax: 619-234-8190
HD Peabody Jr, Director
Alex Layson, Manager

Basic cardiac research.

6863 Bockus Research Institute
Graduate Hospital
415 S 19th Street
Philadelphia, PA 19146-1464
215-893-2000
Fax: 215-893-4178
Dr. Robert Cox, Director
Brian Finestein, CEO

Cardiovascular physiology with specific emphasis on excitation-contraction coupling in smooth and cardiac muscle. Activities include signal transduction mechanisims involving inositol lipids; regulation of contraction in intact and skinned preparations; laser photolysis of caged compounds; whole cell and patch clamp electrophysiological studies of ion channels in cardiac and vascular muscle; and studies of regulation of cytoplasmic calcium usingratiometric fluorescence probes. Applications of these studies include the areas of hypertension, atherosclerosis, and aging. Research also includes studies of gene therapy and cell biology of coronary restenosis following coronary angioplasty.

6864 Boston University: General Clinical Research Center
Boston Medical Center
Boston, MA 02118
617-638-4620
Fax: 617-414-1969
e-mail: jkopp@bu.edu
http://www.bumc.bu.edu/
Janice Kopp, Contact
Ilga Wohlrab, Manager

Biomedical clinical research

6865 Boston University: Whitaker Cardiovascular Institute
80 E Concord Street
Boston, MA 02118-2307
617-638-8000
Fax: 617-638-5258
Aram V Chobanian MD, Director
Glenn St Marie, Manager

Offers basic and clinical care research relating to cardiovascular diseases.

6866 Cardiovascular Research and Training Center: University of Alabama
Tht
Room 311
Birmingham, AL 35294
205-934-3624
Fax: 205-934-5596
Gerald Prohost MD, Director

6867 Cleveland Clinic Foundation Research Institute
9500 Euclid Avenue
Cleveland, OH 44195
216-444-2200
Fax: 216-444-3279
Amiya K Banerjee PhD, Acting Chairperson
Floyd D Loop, CEO

Research institute focusing on diseases of the cardiovascular system.

6868 Columbia University Irving Center for Clinical Research
Presbyterian Hospital
622 W 168th Street
New York, NY 10032-3720
212-305-2071
Fax: 212-305-3213
Robert E Canfield MD, Program Director

Research center focusing on pulmonary diseases.

6869 Creighton University Cardiac Center
601 N 30th Street
Omaha, NE 68131-2137
402-449-4560
Fax: 402-280-5735
Dr. Michael Sketch, Medical Director

Research into the clinical aspects of cardiology and heart disease.

6870 Framingham Heart Study
5 Thurber Street
Framingham, MA 01702-6334
508-872-6556
Dr. William Castelli, Director

6871 General Clinical Research Center at Beth Israel Hospital
330 Brookline Avenue
Boston, MA 02215-5400
617-667-3351
Fax: 617-667-1525
Lewis Landsberg MD, Program Director

Studies into cardiology, pulmonary disorders and heart disease.

6872 General Clinical Research Center: University of California at Los Angeles
Center for Health Sciences
27-066b
Los Angeles, CA 90024
310-825-7177
Fax: 310-206-5012
Isidro Salusky MD, Program Director

Cardiovascular and heart disease disorders and illness research.

6873 Georgetown University: Research Resources Facility
3900 Reservoir Road NW
Room G05
Washington, DC 20007-2126
202-687-1154
Stephen P Schiffer, Director

Studies of medical sciences with particular emphasis on heart disease.

6874 Harvard Thorndike Laboratory
Harvard Medical Center
330 Brookline Avenue
Boston, MA 02215-5400
617-667-4387
Fax: 617-735-4833
Dr. James Morgan, Director

Heart Disease/Research Centers

6875 **Heart Disease Research Foundation**
50 Court Street
Brooklyn, NY 11201-4859   718-649-6210
Robert A 18ters, CEO
2

6876 **Heart Research Foundation of Sacramento**
3900 J Street
Sacramento, CA 95819-3625   916-456-3365
                                  Fax: 916-452-5579
Patti Gantenbein, Executive Director

6877 **Heart and Vascular Institute**
2799 W Grand Boulevard
Detroit, MI 48202-2608   313-876-2737
                                  Fax: 313-916-3014
Dr. Norman Silverman, Codirector

6878 **Hope Heart Institute**
528 18th Avenue
Seattle, WA 98122-5720   206-328-8600
                                  Fax: 206-328-0355
Dr. Lester Sauvage MD, Director
Heart and blood vessel research.

6879 **Jackson Foundation for Medical Research & Education**
345 W Washington Avenue
Madison, WI 53703-2701   608-266-7482
                                  Fax: 608-258-2296
Dorothy Adams, Executive Director
Celia Jackson, Manager

6880 **John L McClellan Memorial Veterans' Hospital Research Office**
4300 W 7th Street
Little Rock, AR 72205-5446   501-580-3346
                                  Fax: 501-671-2510
Karl David Straub MD, PhD, Chief of Staff
J D McClellan, Owner

6881 **Krannert Institute of Cardiology**
1111 W 10th Street
Indianapolis, IN 46202-4800   317-274-5000
                                  Fax: 317-274-9697
Dr. David Hathaway, Director
Ali Sonel, MD

6882 **Mallory Institute of Pathology Foundation**
784 Massachusetts Avenue
Boston, MA 02118-2317   617-414-5309
                                  Fax: 617-424-5315
Dr. Leonard Gottlieb, Director
Focuses research on cardiac disorders and heart disease.

6883 **Miami Heart Institute**
4701 N Meridian Avenue
Miami Beach, FL 33140-2997   305-674-3004
                                  Fax: 305-674-3009
David J Crutchley, Research Director
Allison Grabin, Manager
General cardiovascular research.

6884 **Oklahoma Medical Research Foundation: Cardiovascular Research Program**
825 NE 13th Street
Oklahoma City, OK 73104-5097   405-271-6673
William G Thurman, President
J Donald Capra, CEO

6885 **Pennsylvania State University: Artificial Heart Research Project**
500 University Drive
Hershey, PA 17033-2360   717-531-8407
                                  Fax: 717-531-5011
William S Pierce MD, Director

6886 **Preventive Medicine Research Institute**
1001 Bridgeway
Suite 305
Sausalito, CA 94965-2104   415-332-2525
                                  Fax: 415-332-5730
Dean Ornish MD, President
Alice Pierce, Manager
Nonprofit organization focusing on prevention and treatment of heart disease through modification of diet, exercise and relaxation techniques.

6887 **Purdue University: William A Hillenbrand Biomedical Engineering Center**
AA Potter Engineering Center
Room 204
West Lafayette, IN 47907   765-494-2995
                                  Fax: 765-494-0811
WA Tacker Jr, Acting Director
Cardiology and heart disease research.

6888 **Research and Education Institute**
Harbor-UCLA Medical Center
1124 W Carson Street
Torrance, CA 90502-2006   310-222-1860
                                  Fax: 310-320-6515
Frank De Santis CAE, President
Alan Jobe, MD

6889 **Rockefeller University: Laboratory of Cardiac Physiology**
1230 York Avenue
New York, NY 10021-6399   212-327-8000
                                  Fax: 212-570-8996
Paul F Cranefield, Head Master
Paul Nurse, President
Causes of cardiac arrhythmias and prevention of heart disease.

6890 **Rocky Mountain Heart Research Institute**
1955 Pennsylvania Street
Suite 205
Denver, CO 80203-1334   303-286-7651
Ann Fenton, Executive Director
Chris Remetes, Owner
Clinical heart and cardiovascular research.

6891 **Specialized Center of Research in Ischemic Heart Disease**
University Station
Birmingham, AL 35294   205-934-3624
                                  Fax: 205-975-5150
Gerald Pohost MD, Program Director
Coronary artery disease.

6892 **University of Alabama at Birmingham: Congenital Heart Disease Center**
Department of Surgery
University Station
Birmingham, AL 35294   205-934-7161
                                  Fax: 205-934-7514
Dr. Albert Pacifico, Director
Maryann B Pass, MD

Heart Disease/Research Centers

6893 University of California: San Francisco General Clinical Research Center
1202 Moffitt Hospital
San Francisco, CA 94143
415-476-1016
Fax: 415-476-0986
e-mail: tierneyc@gcrc.ucsf.edu
Joel Palefsky MD, Program Director

Heart disease research
1962

6894 University of California: Cardiovascular Research Laboratory
Center for Health Sciences
Ucla Medical Center
Los Angeles, CA 90024
310-825-6824
Fax: 310-206-5777
Dr. Glenn Langer, Director

Cellular and subcellular cardiac conditions.

6895 University of California: San Diego General Clinical Research Center
UCSD Medical Center, 8203
225 Dickinson Street
San Diego, CA 92103-1910
619-543-3793
Fax: 619-543-5536
Orville G Kolterman, Director

Cardiovasular and heart disease research.

6896 University of California: San Francisco Cardiovascular Research Institute
San Francisco, CA 94143
415-476-1241
Fax: 415-476-0986
Richard J Havel MD, Director

Cardiovascular and heart disease research.

6897 University of Cincinnati: Department of Pathology & Laboratory Medicine
231 Bethesda Avenue
Cincinnati, OH 45267-2827
513-558-4361
Fax: 513-558-2289
C Fenoglio Preiser, Director
Kevin P Yakuboff, MD

6898 University of Iowa: Iowa Cardiovascular Center
College of Medicine
616 Mrc
Iowa City, IA 52242
319-335-8588
800-854-4461
Fax: 319-335-6969
Francois M Abboud, Director

6899 University of Missouri: Columbia Division of Cardiothoracic Surgery
School of Medicine
1 Hospital Drive
Columbia, MO 65212
573-882-2011
Dr. Jack Curtis, Contact

Cardiac surgery research.

6900 University of Rochester: Clinical Research Center
601 Elmwood Avenue
Med
Rochester, NY 14642
585-275-4711
Fax: 585-442-9176
John M Amatruda MD, Director

Studies of normal tissue functions pertaining to heart diseases.

6901 University of Southern California: Coronary Care Research
1200 N State Street
305
Los Angeles, CA 90033-1029
323-442-5215
Dr. L Julian Haywood, Director

6902 University of Texas: Southwestern Medical Center at Dallas
5323 Harry Hines Boulevard
Dallas, TX 75390-8570
214-648-3067
Dr. Joseph Sambrook, Principal Investigator
Patricia Bergen, MD

Cardiology department research.

6903 University of Utah: Artificial Heart Research Laboratory
803 N 300 W
Salt Lake City, UT 84103-1414
801-581-6991
Fax: 801-581-4044
Dr. Don B Olsen, Director

Cardiac and blood vessel research.

6904 University of Utah: Cardiovascular Genetic Research Clinic
50 N Medical Center Drive
Salt Lake City, UT 84132
801-581-5873
Fax: 801-581-7735
Dr. Roger Williams, Director
Harry Hill, MD

Cardiovascular genetics research.

6905 Urban Cardiology Research Center
2300 Garrison Boulevard
Suite 150
Baltimore, MD 21216-2316
410-945-8600
Dr. Arthur White, Director

Causes, diagnosis and treatment of cardiovascular diseases.

6906 Warren Grant Magnuson Clinical Center
6100 Executive Boulevard
Suite 3c01
Bethesda, MD 20892
301-496-2563
Fax: 301-402-2984
http://www.cc.nih.gov

Established in 1953 as the research hospital of the National Institutes of Health. Designed so that patient care facilities are close to research laboratories so new findings of basic and clinical scientists can be quickly applied to the treatment of patients. Upon referral by physicians, patients are admitted to NIH clinical studies.

Hypertension/Associations & Organizations

Associations & Organizations

6907 **American Society of Hypertension**
515 Madison Avenue
Suite 1212
New York, NY 10022-5403
212-644-0650
Fax: 212-644-0658
e-mail: ash@pipeline.com
http://www.ash-us.org

Kathleen Sheridan, Manager

To organize and conduct educational seminars, materials, and products in all aspects of hypertension and other cardiovascular diseases.

6908 **Hypertension Center**
Bowman Gray School of Medicine
Wake Forest University Medica
5th Floor
Winston Salem, NC 27157
919-716-2011

This center works towards developing a comprehensive collection of basic science and clinical research in the field of hypertension.

6909 **National Hypertension Association**
324 E 30th Street
New York, NY 10016-8329
212-889-3557
http://www.nathypertension.org/

Dr. William Manger MD, PhD, Chairman
F Rowley, Director Special Projects
Alla Krayro, Office Manager

Produces professional education seminars, public information sessions, publishes annual news reports.

Books

6910 **Answers to 100 Questions About Hypertension**
National Hypertension Association
324 E 30th Street
New York, NY 10016-8329
212-889-3557
http://www.nathypertension.com

Francine Rowley, Executive Director

Book describing hypertension in layman's terms.

6911 **Conquering Hypertension: An Illustrated Guide to Understanding Treatment**
Login Publishers Consortium
1436 W Randolph Street
Chicago, IL 60607-1414
312-733-8228
Fax: 312-666-2680

168 pages

6912 **Hypertension: An Integrated, Clinical Approach**
Carolina Academic Division
387 Park Avenue S
Floor 5
New York, NY 10016-8810
212-779-1822
Fax: 212-779-1834

400 pages

6913 **Management of Hypertension**
EMIS Medical Publishers
PO Box 1607
Durant, OK 74702-1607
580-924-0643
Fax: 580-924-9414

6914 **Manual of Hypertension**
Blackwell Science
350 Main Street
Malden, MA 02148-5089
781-388-8250
Fax: 781-388-8255

Gordan Tibbitts III, President

6915 **Reversing Hypertension: A Vital New Program to Prevent, Treat, and Reduce High Blood Pressure**
Hachette Book Group USA
237 Park Avenue
New York, NY 10017
http://www.hachettebookgroupusa.com

Julian M Whitaker MD, Author

Provides what causes blood pressure to rise and how to bring it down to normal levels. The natural therapy, light-on drugs, healthly lifestyle way to safely reduce blood pressure.

336 pages

Newsletters, Pamphlets

6916 **About High Blood Pressure**
American Heart Association
7272 Greenville Avenue
Dallas, TX 75231-5129
214-373-6300
800-553-6321
Fax: 214-696-5211

M Cass Wheeler, CEO

Offers information on what blood pressure is, risk factors and at risk persons.

6917 **News Report**
National Hypertension Association
324 E 30th Street
New York, NY 10016-8329
212-889-3557
Fax: 212-447-7032

Francine Rowley, Executive Director

Offers information and medical updates regarding hypertension.

Research Centers

6918 **Alton Ochsner Medical Foundation**
1516 Jefferson Highway
New Orleans, LA 70121-2429
504-842-3000
Fax: 504-838-4047

Richard N Re MD, Director
Patrick J Quinlan, CEO

Nonprofit organization for scientific research and medical education concentrating on cardiovascular research.

6919 **Charles R Drew Hypertension Research Center**
1621 E 20th Street
Los Angeles, CA 90011-1317
323-563-4800

Clarence E Grim MD, Director

6920 **Creighton University: Midwest Hypertension Research Center**
601 N 30th Street
Suite 6730
Omaha, NE 68131-2137
402-449-4000
Fax: 402-280-4101

Dr. William Pettinger, Director
Linda Ollis, CEO

6921 **Hahnemann University: Division of Surgical Research**
Broad & Vine Streets
Philadelphia, PA 19102
215-762-7960

Teuro Matsumoto PhD, Director

Studies hypertension and management of stress ulcers.

Hypertension/Research Centers

6922 Henry Ford Hospital: Hypertension and Vascular Research Division
2799 W Grand Boulevard
Detroit, MI 48202-2689
313-916-1860
Fax: 313-876-1479

Dr. Oscar Carretero, Division Head
B Martuziewicz, Manager

6923 Indiana University: Hypertension Research Center
541 Clinical Drive
Indianapolis, IN 46223
317-274-8153
Fax: 317-278-0673

Dr. Myron Weinberger, Director

6924 New York University: General Clinical Research Center
NYU Medical Center
550 1st Avenue
Room 36
New York, NY 10016-6402
212-263-5072
Fax: 212-263-8501
e-mail: rom01@mcgc16.med.nyu.edu
http://www.med.nyu.edu/gcrc/homepage.html

Dr William Rom MPH, Director
Susan Firestone, Manager

Focuses in the areas of hypertension and studies into endocrinology.

6925 University of Michigan: Division of Hypertension
3918 Taubman Center
Ann Arbor, MI 48109
734-764-6443

Dr S Julius, Director
Pat Blackmar, Administrator

6926 University of Minnesota: Hypertensive Research Group
611 Beacon Street SE
Minneapolis, MN 55455
612-624-1438

Jack Stoulil, Study Coordinator

Research pertaining to hypertension and stress disorders.

6927 University of Southern California: Division of Nephrology
2025 Zonal Avenue
Los Angeles, CA 90033
323-669-2303
Fax: 213-226-3958

Dr Shaul G Massry, Head Master
Roberta G Williams, Manager

Research into hypertension and sleep disorders.

6928 University of Virginia: Hypertension and Atherosclerosis Unit
PO Box 146
Charlottesville, VA 22908
434-924-8470
Fax: 434-924-2581

Dr. Carlos Ayers, Director

6929 Vanderbilt University: Specialized Center of Research in Hypertension
Garland Avenue
Nashville, TN 37232
615-322-2571
Fax: 615-322-4349

Dr. Tadashi Inagami, Director
Rhonda Venable, PhD

6930 Wake Forest University: Arteriosclerosis Research Center
Department of Comparative Medicine
300 S Hawthorne Road
Winston Salem, NC 27103-2732
336-764-3600
Fax: 336-764-5818

Thomas Clarkson DVM, Director

Hypertension research.

Impotence/Associations & Organizations

Associations & Organizations

6931 Impotence Information Center
PO Box 9
Minneapolis, MN 55440
800-843-4315

6932 Impotence World Association
PO Box 410
Bowie, MD 20718-0410
301-262-2400
e-mail: iwabowie@aol.com
http://www.impotence.com

Informs and educates the public on the subject of impotence and its causes and treatments. Serving the impotence industry since 1983 by bringing total care to the treatment of impotence.

6933 Impotents Anonymous
8630 Fenton Street
Suite 218
Silver Spring, MD 20910
301-588-5777
Fax: 301-588-6220

Bruce MacKenzie, Founder
Connie Morina, Manager

Serves as an educational organization providing concerned individuals with information regarding impotence.

6934 Male Sexual Dysfunction Center
357 Genesee St Ste 1
Oneida, NY 13421-2611
315-363-8862
Fax: 315-363-5477
http://www.cnymsdc.com

6935 Male Sexual Medicine Clinic
404 N Commerical Street
Harrisburg, IL 62946-3307
618-252-7424

Han M Hanafy MD, Contact

Office procedures include no scalpel vasectomy, vasectomy reversals, laser surgery for warts and impotence evaluation and treatment.

6936 National Kidney and Urologic Diseases Information Clearinghouse
3 Information Way
Bethesda, MD 20892-3580
301-654-4415
Fax: 703-738-4929
e-mail: nkudic@info.niddk.nih.gov
http://http://kidney.niddk.nih.gov/

Phillip Gorden, Director
Griffin P. Rodgers, M.D, Director

Provides information about diseases of the kidneys and urologic system to people with such afflictions and to their families, health care professionals, and the public. Answers inquiries; develops, reviews, and distributes publications; and works closely with professional and patient organizations and government agencies to coordinate research.

Books

6937 Impotence: How to Overcome It
HealthProlnk Publishing
562 Wind Drift Lane
Spring Lake, MI 49456-2168
810-355-3686

6938 Overcoming Impotence: A Leading Urologist Tells You Everything You Need to Know
Prometheus Books
59 John Glenn Drive
Amherst, NY 14228-2197
716-691-0133
800-421-0351
Fax: 716-691-0137
e-mail: marketing@prometheusbooks.com
http://www.prometheusbooks.com

J Stephen Jones MD, Author

A user-friendly, emotionally supportive, and extremely informative that addresses the serious questions that men or their significant others may have about an increasingly common condition.

318 pages

Websites

6939 Impotence Resource Center
http://www.impotence.org

6940 Impotence World Association
http://www.impotence.com

Informs and educates the public on the subject of impotence and its causes and treatments. Serving the impotence industry since 1983 by bringing total care to the treatment of impotence.

6941 International Journal of Impotence Research
http://www.nature.com

Offers the latest research on men's and women's sexual function incuding important research related to cardiovascular disease, diabetes, menopause and vascular deficits.

6942 International Society for Sexual Medicine
http://www.issm.info

Promotes research and exchange of knowledge for the clinical entity impotence throughout the internatioanl scientific community.

Research Centers

6943 Sexual Function Health Council
American Foundation for Urologic Disease
300 W Pratt Street
Suite 401
Baltimore, MD 21201-6504
410-727-2908
800-242-2383
Fax: 410-468-1808

Incontinence/Associations & Organizations

Associations & Organizations

6944 **American Urological Association**
1000 Corporate Boulevard
Linthicum, MD 21090
410-689-3700
866-746-4282
Fax: 410-689-3800
e-mail: aua@auanet.org
http://www.auanet.org
Barry A. Kogan, M.D, President
James W.L. Wilson, M.D, President-Elect
Michael T Sheppard CPA, Executive Director

Professional society of physicians specializing in urology. Provides placement service. Conducts educational programs; maintains museum.

1902 Number of Members: 15,000

6945 **Help for Incontinent People: National Association for Continence**
P.O. Box 1019
Charleston, SC 29402
843-377-0900
Fax: 843-377-0905
e-mail: nmuller@nafc.org
http://www.nafc.org
Nancy Muller, Executive Director
Rachel Levkowicz

A leading source of education, advocacy and support to the public and to the health profession about the causes, prevention, diagnosis, treatments and management alternatives for incontinence.

6946 **International Foundation for Bowel Dysfunction**
PO Box 17864
Milwaukee, WI 53217
414-964-1799
Nancu Norton, President

Provides support and educational information for people affected by the various forms of functional bowel disorders, including irritable bowel syndrome, constipation, diarrhea, pain and incontinence.

6947 **Intestinal Disease Foundation**
1323 Forbes Avenue
Suite 200
Pittsburgh, PA 15219
412-261-5888
877-587-9606
Fax: 412-471-2722
e-mail: intdis@stargate.net
http://www.intestinalfoundation.org
Linda Schorr, Executive Director
Harriet Gibbs, Client Services Manager

Mission is to improve the quality of life of adults and children affected by chronic digestive illness through information, guidance and support.

6948 **National Association for Continence**
PO Box 1019
Charleston, SC 29402-1019
864-579-7900
800-252-3337
Fax: 864-579-7902
e-mail: memberservices@nafc.org
http://www.nafc.org
Nancy Muller, Executive Director
Katherine F Jeter, EdD Founder

Founded in 1982 as Help for Incontinent People, NAFC, with 130,000 members. Committed to alleviating the social stigma associated with bladder control problems. A leading source of education, advocacy, and support to the public and to the health professionals.

6949 **Simon Foundation for Continence**
Post Office Box 815
Wilmette, IL 60091
847-864-3913
800-237-4666
Fax: 847-864-9758
e-mail: cbgartley@simonfoundation.org
http://www.simonfoundation.org
Cheryle B Gartley, President
Anita Saltmarche, Vice-President

Helps thousands of people to find cures and management techniques for incontinence. The mission of this Foundation is to bring the topic out of the closet, remove the stigma and educate both medical professionals and sufferers about cure, treatment and management techniques. The Foundation also operates a Helpline at the above numbers.

6950 **Wound, Ostomy and Continence Nurses Society**
15000 Commerce Parkway
Suite C
Mt. Laurel, NJ 8054
888-224-9626
Fax: 866-615-8560
e-mail: info@wocn.org
http://www.wocn.org
Nicolette Zuecca, Executive Director
Margaret T. Goldberg, MSN RN, President

The WOCN Society is a professional nursing society which supports its members by promoting educational, clinical and research opportunities to advance the practice and guide the delivery of expert health care to individuals with wounds, ostomies and incontinence.

1968

Books

6951 **Female Urinary Incontinence**
International Specialized Book Services
5602 NE Hassalo Street
Portland, OR 97213-3640
503-287-3093
Rod Walker, Manager
156 pages

6952 **Managing Incontinence: A Guide to Living with Loss of Bladder Control**
Simon Foundation for Incontinence
PO Box 815
Wilmette, IL 60091
847-864-3913
800-223-1360
Fax: 847-864-9768
http://www.simonfoundation.org
Cheryle B Gartley, President

Seeks to bring the topic of incontinence out of the closet and remove the associated stigma; provides information to patients, their families, and the health care professionals who provide patient care.

80+ pages

Directories

6953 **The Official Patient's Sourcebook on Female Urinary Incontinence**
ICON Group International
7404 Trade Street
San Diego, CA 92121
Fax: 858-635-9414
e-mail: orders@icongrouponline.com
http://www.icongrouponline.com
James N Parker MD, Editor
Philip M Parker PhD, Editor

A comprehensive manual for anyone interested in self-directed research on fully referenced with ample Internet listings and glossary. This book has ben created for patients who have decided to make education and research an integral part of the treatment process.
112 pages

Parkinson's Disease/Associations & Organizations

Associations & Organizations

6954 **American Parkinson's Disease Association**
135 Parkinson Avenue
Suite 4b
Staten Island, NY 10305
718-981-8001
800-223-2732
Fax: 718-981-4399
e-mail: apda@apdaparkinson.org
http://www.apdaparkinson.org/

Vincent N. Gattullo, President
Joel Gerstel, Executive Director

Works to find the cure for Parkinson's disease and to alleviate the suffering of its victims by subsidizing information and referral centers and providing funds for research. Offers counseling services to patients and their families. Maintains 43 information and referral centers. Conducts symposia.

6955 **Greater Philadelphia Parkinson's Disease and Other Movement Disorders Council**
1501 N.W. 9th Avenue
Bob Hope Road
Miami, NV 33136-1494
305-243-6666
Fax: 305-243-5595
e-mail: contact@parkinson.org
http://www.parkinson.org

Amy Colcher, MD

Affiliate of the National Parkinson Foundation.

6956 **National Parkinson Foundation**
1501 NW 9th Avenue Bob Hope Road
Miami, FL 33136-1494
305-547-6666
800-433-7022
Fax: 305-243-5595
e-mail: contact@parkinson.org
http://www.parkinson.org

Paul F. Oreffice, Chairman
Daniel Arty, Vice Chairman

A nonprofit organization dedicated to research, diagnosis, treatment and care for men and women suffering from Parkinson's and other related neurological diseases. The Foundation also supports the Bob Hope research and rehabilitation center, which is the leading institute of its kind in the world, donating their time to Parkinson's research.

6957 **National Parkinson Foundation Adult Day Care Center**
1501 NW 9th Avenue
Miami, FL 33136-1407
305-547-6666
800-327-4545
Fax: 305-243-4403
http://www.parkinson.org

Jose Garcia-Pedrosa, Executive Director

A specialized program for Parkinsonians offering adult day care, transportation and support groups.

6958 **National Parkinson Foundation Hotline**
National Parkinson Foundation
1501 NW 9th Avenue Bob Hope Road
Miami, FL 33136
305-547-6666
800-327-4545
Fax: 305-243-4403
http://www.parkinson.org

Jose Garcia-Pedrosa, Executive Director

Offers support and emergency information for persons with Parkinson's and their families.

6959 **PROPATH**
525 Middlefield Road
Suite 250
Menlo Park, CA 94025
888-447-9584
800-447-7672

The first program designed to help Parkinson's patients take control of their disease. The program analyzes personal conditions, medical treatments and lifestyles to create a specific program to help the patient take more control of their condition and their lives.

6960 **Parkinson Association of Arizona**
2033 E. Speedway Blvd
Suite 203
Tucson, AZ 85719
520-326-5400
Fax: 520-326-8591
e-mail: info@azapda.org
http://www.azapda.org

Ila Stadie, Director of Development and Fina
David Richter, President of the Board of Direct

Affiliate chapter of the National Parkinson Foundation.

6961 **Parkinson Association of Davenport**
3450 Maple Glen Drive
Bettendorf, IA 52722-2899
563-322-5071

Affiliate of the National Parkinson Foundation.

6962 **Parkinson Association of Florida West Coast**
1888 Hillview Street
Sarasota, FL 34239-3605
239-948-0229

Affiliate of the National Parkinson Foundation.

6963 **Parkinson Association of Greater Kansas City**
7808 Foster Street
Overland Park, KS 66204-2955
913-341-8828
Fax: 885-341-8885
e-mail: meg@parkinsonheartland.org

Meg Duggan, Executive Director

Affiliate of the National Parkinson Foundation.

6964 **Parkinson Association of Hawaii**
347 N Kuakini Street HPM-9
Honolulu, HI 96817
808-528-0935
e-mail: info.hpa@gmail.com
http://www.hawaiiparkinson.org

Linda Ann S. Tom, President
Chuck Lyden, Vice-President

Affiliate of the National Parkinson Foundation.

6965 **Parkinson Association of Michigan**
Michigan Parkinson Foundation
30400 Telegraph Road
Suite 150
Bingham Farms, MI 48025
248-433-1011
800-852-9781
Fax: 248-433-1150
e-mail: mpfdir@aol.com
http://www.parkinsonsmi.org

Deborah M. Orloff, R.N., M.P.H., Chief Executive Officer
Leonard S. Borman, Chairman

6966 **Parkinson Association of Minnesota**
6701 Country Club Drive
Golden Valley, MN 55427
952-993-5495
http://www.parkinsonmn.org

Jackie Hunt Christensen, Vice President
Kris Maser, President

Parkinson Association of Minnesota is a nonprofit, voluntary alliance, dedicated to improving the lives of those affected by Parkinson's Disease, through fundraising, community building, advocacy, and increasing public awareness. This chapter sponsors research and treatment centers around the world.

Parkinson's Disease/Associations & Organizations

6967 Parkinson Association of New York
1359 Broadway
Suite 1509
New York, NY 10018
212-923-4700
Fax: 212-923-4778
e-mail: info@pdf.org
http://www.pdf.org
Page Morton Black, Chairman
Lewis P. Rowland, M.D., President

6968 Parkinson Association of Orange County
9940 Talbert Ave.
#204
Fountain Valley, CA 92708
877-610-2732
Fax: 714-378-5061
e-mail: information@apdaoc.org
http://www.apdaoc.org
Debbie Baires, BA,, Coordinator
Affiliate of the National Parkinson Foundation.

6969 Parkinson Association of South Dakota
Phyllis Newstrom c/o Sioux Valley Hospital
1025 Vermont Ave, NW
Suite 1120
Washington, DC 20005
202-638-4101
Fax: 202-638-7257
e-mail: info@parkinsonsaction.org
http://www.parkinsonsaction.org
Hayley Carpenter, Program Manager
Amy L. Comstock, Executive Director
Affiliate of the National Parkinson Foundation.

6970 Parkinson Association of South West Florida
6226 Tamiami Trail N.
Naples, FL 34108
239-254-7791
Fax: 239-254-9421
e-mail: pasfi@aol.com
http://www.pasfi.org
Marlene Huff, Coordinator
Jacque Urso, Executive Director

The Parkinson Association og Southwest Flordia is a non for profit organization. The mission is to promote quiality of life for persons with Pakinson's Disease and their care partners. This is accomplished by providing educational, physical and social programs. The organization also provides education for the community regarding Parkinson's Disease and its effects.

6971 Parkinson Association of Wisconsin
945 N 12th Street
Suite 4602
Milwaukee, WI 53233
414-219-7061
800-972-5455
Fax: 414-219-6564
e-mail: jackie.hoeft@aurora.org
http://www.wiparkinson.org
Keith Brewer, President
Vicki Conte, Coordinator

The Wisconsin Parkinson Association is a regional nonprofit organization assisting people who are affected by Parkinson's disease. As a Center of aExcellence with the National Parkinson Foundation, the Regional Parkinson Center is a part of a nationwide effort to provide information and resources about Parkinson's Disease, to enhance public education and awarenessof the disease and to support research for a cure.

6972 Parkinson Association of the Sacramento Valley
900 Fulton Avenue
Suite 100-5
Sacramento, CA 95825-4516
916-489-0226
Fax: 916-489-0241
e-mail: parkanc@sbcglobal.net
http://www.parkinsonsacramento.org
Chris Hopson, President
Julie Bianucci, Executive Director
Affiliate of The National Parkinson Foundation.

6973 Parkinson Association of Greater Daytona
1501 N.W. 9th Avenue / Bob Hope Road
Miami, FL 33136-1494
305-243-6666
Fax: 305-243-5595
e-mail: contact@parkinson.org
http://www.parkinson.org
Pamela Olmo, Director of Finance and Administ
Paul F. Oreffice, Oreffice
Affiliate of the National Parkinson Foundation.

6974 Parkinson Network of Mt Diablo
PO Box 3127
Walnut Creek, CA 94598-0127
925-939-4210
Fax: 925-939-4210
e-mail: mmhansell@hotmail.com
Margaret M Hansell, President of Chapter
Claudia Boyars, VP
Affiliated Chapter of the National Parkinson Foundation.

6975 Parkinson Rehabilitation Center
2500 Harbor Boulevard
Port Charlotte, FL 33952
941-766-4122
Fax: 941-766-4287
e-mail: bevin.gallo@prrmc.hma-corp.com
http://www.peaceriverregional.com
J. David McCormack, Chief Executive Officer
Affiliate of the National Parkinson Foundation.

6976 Parkinson's Support Group of Upstate New York
PO Box 23204
Rochester, NY 14692
585-234-5355
e-mail: info@psguny.org
http://www.psguny.org
Harvey Berson, President
Dennis Whitney, Vice President

This chapter will work in partnership with the National Parkinson's Foundation to provide patient and educational services, raise funds for research and create public awareness of the disease. Group Meetings will often include guest speakers representing specialists in the Parkinson's community to discuss important issues such as current research initiatives, new treatments and therapies.

6977 Parkinsons Action Network
1025 Vermont Ave, NW
Suite 1120
Washington, DC 20005
202-638-4101
Fax: 202-638-7257
e-mail: info@parkinsonsaction.org
http://www.parkinsonsaction.org
Robin Anthon Elliott, Executive Director
Anne Udall, Ph.D.,, Chair/Founding Chair
Joan Samuelson, President

A unified advocacy voice of The Parkinson's community, fighting for a cure within 5 years.

6978 United Parkinson Foundation
833 W Washington Boulevard
Chicago, IL 60607
312-733-1893
Fax: 312-733-1896
e-mail: info@pdf.org
http://www.pdf.org
Jeanne Rosner, Director
Robin Anthon Elliott, Executive Director

Patients, family members, medical personnel and other interested persons. Assembles and publishes reliable information about symptoms, medications and therapy helpful to sufferers of Parkinson's disease and related illnesses. Fosters and supports scientific research on the disease. Assists patients and their families with medical referrals, education and other means.

Parkinson's Disease/Books

Books

6979 100 Questions & Answers About Parkinson's Disease
Jones and Bartlett Publishers
40 Tall Pine Drive
Sudbury, MA 01776
978-443-5000
800-832-0034
Fax: 978-443-8000
http://www.jbpub.com

Abraham Lieberman, Author
Marcia McCall, Author

The only text to provide the doctor and patient view, gives you authoraitative, practical answers to your questions about treatment options, quality of life, sources of support, and more.
238 pages

6980 Coping with Parkinson's Disease
American Parkinson Disease Association
1250 Hylan Boulevard
Suite 4b
Staten Island, NY 10305-1945
800-223-2732
Fax: 718-981-4399

88 pages

6981 Living with Parkinson's Disease
Demos Vermande
386 Park Avenue S
Suite 201
New York, NY 10016-8804
212-683-0072
800-532-8663
Fax: 212-683-0118

Phyllis Gold, Owner

Written specifically for anyone who has been diagnosed with Parkinson's disease, as well as family members and friends.
150 pages

6982 Parkinson's Disease & Movement Disorders
Williams & Wilkins
351 W Camden Street
Baltimore, MD 21201-7912
301-528-4000
800-222-3790
Fax: 410-528-4452

640 pages

6983 Parkinson's Disease Handbook
National Parkinson Foundation
1501 NW 9th Avenue
Miami, FL 33136-1407
305-547-6666
800-327-4545
Fax: 305-548-4403
http://www.parkinson.org

Jose Garcia-Pedrosa, Executive Director

A guide for patients and their families regarding the illness of Parkinson's.

6984 Parkinson's Disease for Dummies
For Dummies
1475 Crosspoint Boulevard
Indianapolis, IN 46256
877-762-2974
Fax: 800-597-3299
http://www.dummies.com

Michele Tagliati MD, Author
Gary Guten MD, Author
Jo Horne, Author

Discover how to keep a positive attitude and lead an active, productive life as this user-friendly, guide pilots you through the important steps toward taking charge of your condition. Provides proven coping skills, first-hand advice, and practical tools, such as worksheets to assess care options, questions to ask doctors, and current listing of care providers.
384 pages

6985 Parkinson's Disease: 300 Tips for Making Life Easier
Demos Medical Publishing
386 Park Avenue South
Suite 301
New York, NY 10016
212-683-0072
e-mail: info@demosmedpub.com
http://www.demosmedpub.com

Shelley Peterman Schwartz, Author

Helps readers lead a remarkably unlimited life. Filled with tips, techniques, and shortcuts readers will learn basic lessons for conserving time and energy, enabling them to do more of the things they want to do.
128 pages

6986 Parkinson's Disease: A Complete Guide for Patients and Families
Johns Hopkins University Press
2715 North Charles Street
Balitmore, MD 21218-4363
410-516-6900
Fax: 410-516-6968
http://www.press.jhu.edu

William J Weiner MD, Author
Lisa M Shulman MD, Author
Anthony E Lang MD, Author

Provides crucial information for managing this complex condition, including details on the use of medication, diet, exercise, complementary therapies an d surgery.
296 pages

6987 The First Year: Parkinson's Disease: AnEssential Guide for the Newly Diagnosed
Perseus Books Group
387 Park Avenue South
12th Floor
New York, NY 10016
212-340-8100

Jackie Christensen, Author

Provides guidance for the newly diagnosed step by step through their first year with Parkinson's. Also provides crucial information about the nature of the disease, treatment options, diet, exercise, charts and tables, social concerns, emotional issues, networking with others, and more.

6988 Understanding Parkinson's Disease: A Personal and Professional View
Greenwood Publishing Group
88 Post Road West
Westport, CT 06881
203-226-3571
http://www.greenwood.com

Richard B Rosenbaum, Author

Topics covered include challenges of correct diagnosis, variations in prognosis, investigations of causes including exciting progress in possible toxins and genetic factors that play a role, and different treatment options including natural remedies as well as new drugs for symptom treatment.
364 pages

Newsletters, Pamphlets

6989 Akathisia in Parkinson's Disease
United Parkinson Foundation
833 W Washington Boulevard
Chicago, IL 60607-2331
312-733-1893
Fax: 312-733-1896
e-mail: pdfchicago@enteract.com

Jeanne Rosner, Executive Director

6990 American Parkinson Disease Association Newsletter
1250 Hylan Boulevard
Suite 4b
Staten Island, NY 10305-1945
718-981-8001
800-223-2732
Fax: 718-981-4399

Joel Gerstel, Executive Director

Parkinson's Disease/Newsletters, Pamphlets

Offers information on the association activities and events, convention and legislative information, medical updates and research reports for the Parkinson's patient and their families.

6991 Autonomic Failure and Parkinson's Disease
United Parkinson Foundation
833 W Washington Boulevard
Chicago, IL 60607-2331
312-733-1893
Fax: 312-733-1896
e-mail: psfchicago@enteract.
Jeanne Rosner, Executive Director

6992 Balance Disturbances and Parkinson's Disease
United Parkinson Foundation
833 W Washington Boulevard
Chicago, IL 60607-2331
312-733-1893
Fax: 312-733-1896
Jeanne Rosner, Executive Director

6993 Basic Information About Parkinson's Disease
American Parkinson Disease Association
1250 Hylan Boulevard
Suite 4b
Staten Island, NY 10305-1945
718-273-4046
800-223-2732
Fax: 718-981-4399
John Bosco

Offers information on the illness, incidence, treatments, education and support for both patients and professionals.

6994 Dental Care for the Patient with Parkinson's Disease
United Parkinson Foundation
833 W Washington Boulevard
Chicago, IL 60607-2331
312-733-1893
Fax: 312-733-1896
Jeanne Rosner, Executive Director

6995 Depression and Dementia in Parkinson's Disease
United Parkinson Foundation
833 W Washington Boulevard
Chicago, IL 60607-2331
312-733-1893
Fax: 312-733-1896
Jeanne Rosner, Executive Director

6996 Depression and Dementia in Parkinson's Disease
United Parkinson Foundation
833 W Washington Boulevard
Chicago, IL 60607-2331
312-733-1893
Fax: 312-733-1896
Jeanne Rosner, Executive Director

6997 Dietary Considerations for Parkinson's Disease Patients
United Parkinson Foundation
833 W Washington Boulevard
Chicago, IL 60607-2331
312-733-1893
Fax: 312-733-1896
Jeanne Rosner, Executive Director

6998 Differential Diagnosis of Parkinsonism
United Parkinson Foundation
833 W Washington Boulevard
Chicago, IL 60607-2331
312-733-1893
Fax: 312-733-1896
Jeanne Rosner, Executive Director

6999 Driving and the Parkinson's Disease Patient: Some Considerations
United Parkinson Foundation
833 W Washington Boulevard
Chicago, IL 60607-2331
312-733-1893
Fax: 312-733-1896
Jeanne Rosner, Executive Director

7000 Efficacy of Antiparkinson Medications
United Parkinson Foundation
833 W Washington Boulevard
Chicago, IL 60607-2331
312-733-1893
Fax: 312-733-1896
Jeanne Rosner, Executive Director

7001 Equipment and Suggestions for Persons with Parkinson's Disease
American Parkinson Disease Association
1250 Hylan Boulevard
Suite 4b
Staten Island, NY 10305-1945
800-223-2732
Fax: 718-981-4399

19 pages

7002 Eyes and Parkinson's Disease
United Parkinson Foundation
833 W Washington Boulevard
Chicago, IL 60607-2331
312-733-1893
Fax: 312-733-1896
Jeanne Rosner, Executive Director

7003 Fighting Back Against PD: One Women's Story
National Parkinson Foundation
1501 NW 9th Avenue
Miami, FL 33136-1407
305-547-6666
800-327-4545
Fax: 305-548-4403
http://www.parkinson.org
Jose Garcia-Pedros, Executive Director

One woman's battle against Parkinson's disease.

7004 Good Nutrition in Parkinson's Disease
American Parkinson Disease Association
60 Bay Street
Suite 401
Staten Island, NY 10301-2514
800-223-2732
Fax: 718-981-4399

Offers information on diet, nutrients, proteins and recipes for people with Parkinson's disease.

7005 How to Start a Parkinson's Disease Support Group
American Parkinson Disease Association
1250 Hylan Boulevard
Suite 4b
Staten Island, NY 10305-1945
800-223-2732
Fax: 718-981-4399

42 pages

7006 MR Imaging in Parkinson's Disease
United Parkinson Foundation
833 W Washington Boulevard
Chicago, IL 60607-2331
312-733-1893
Fax: 312-733-1896
Jeanne Rosner, Executive Director

7007 Micrographia
United Parkinson Foundation
833 W Washington Boulevard
Chicago, IL 60607-2331
312-733-1893
Fax: 312-733-1896
Jeanne Rosner, Executive Director

7008 Neuropsychology and Parkinson's Disease
United Parkinson Foundation
833 W Washington Boulevard
Chicago, IL 60607-2331
312-733-1893
Fax: 312-733-1896
Jeanne Rosner, Executive Director

Parkinson's Disease/Newsletters, Pamphlets

7009 Neurotrophic Factors in Parkinson's Disease
United Parkinson Foundation
833 W Washington Boulevard
Chicago, IL 60607-2331
312-733-1893
Fax: 312-733-1896
Jeanne Rosner, Executive Director

7010 One Step at a Time Brochure
United Parkinson Foundation
833 W Washington Boulevard
Chicago, IL 60607-2331
312-733-1893
Fax: 312-733-1896
Jeanne Rosner, Executive Director

An exercise manual for the Parkinsonian patient.

7011 Pain Syndromes and Parkinson's Disease
United Parkinson Foundation
833 W Washington Boulevard
Chicago, IL 60607-2331
312-733-1893
Fax: 312-733-1896
Jeanne Rosner, Executive Director

7012 Parkinson Handbook: A Guide for Patients and Their Families
National Parkinson Foundation
1501 NW 9th Avenue
Miami, FL 33136-1407
305-547-6666
800-327-4545
Fax: 305-548-4403
http://www.parkinson.org
Jose Garcia-Pedrosa, Executive Director

Offers informative, up-to-date information on exercises, hobbies, treatments, speech impairments and psychological aspects.

7013 Parkinson Report
National Parkinson Foundation
1501 NW 9th Avenue
Miami, FL 33136-1407
305-547-6666
800-327-4545
Fax: 305-548-4403
http://www.parkinson.org
Jose Garcia-Pedrosa, Executive Director

Offers association news and events, conference and symposia news, legislative and medical updates, research reports and more for the Parkinson's patient, their families and the general public.

7014 Parkinson's Disease Foundation Newsletter
Parkinson's Disease Foundation
1359 Broadway
Room 1510
New York, NY 10018-7867
212-923-4700
Robin Elliott, Executive Director

Provides information on Parkinson's Disease Foundation events, news stories of research findings, and technical advances in the field of patient care.

7015 Parkinson's Disease Handbook
American Parkinson Disease Association
1250 Hylan Boulevard
Suite 4b
Staten Island, NY 10305-1945
718-981-8001
800-223-2732
Fax: 718-981-4399
Joel Gerstel, Executive Director
40 pages

7016 Parkinson's Disease: The Patient Experiance
United Parkinson Foundation
833 W Washington Boulevard
Chicago, IL 60607-2331
312-733-1893
Fax: 312-733-1896
Jeanne Rosner, Executive Director

Booklet designed for patients with Parkinson's disease and their families to explain medical terminology and offer suggestions on how to deal with the disease more easily.

7017 Parkinson's Patient: What You and Your Family Should Know
National Parkinson Foundation
1501 NW 9th Avenue
Miami, FL 33136-1407
305-547-6666
800-327-4545
Fax: 305-548-4403
http://www.parkinson.org
Jose Garcia-Pedrosa, Executive Director

Offers a brief overview of Parkinson's Disease causes, symptoms and treatments as well as offering an insight into statistical information on the illness.

7018 Parkinsons Report
National Parkinson Foundation
1501 NW 9th Avenue
Miami, FL 33136-1407
305-547-6666
800-327-4545
Fax: 305-243-4403
Julian Pearson, Administrator
Jose Garcia-Pedrosa, Executive Director

Articles, reports and news on Parkinson's disease and the activities of the National Parkinson Foundation.
32 pages Frequency: Qarterly

7019 Patient Perspectives on Parkinson's
National Parkinson Foundation
1501 NW 9th Avenue
Miami, FL 33136-1407
305-547-6666
800-327-4545
Fax: 305-548-4403
http://www.parkinson.org
Jose Garcia-Pedrosa, Executive Director

Offers a brief overview of Parkinson's disease, the onset of the illness, depression, sexuality, exercise, sleep and nutrition information for daily living.
45 pages

7020 Perioperative Management of Parkinson's Disease
United Parkinson Foundation
833 W Washington Boulevard
Chicago, IL 60607-2331
312-733-1893
Fax: 312-733-1896
Jeanne Rosner, Executive Director

7021 Pet Scans: A New Look at Parkinson's Disease
United Parkinson Foundation
833 W Washington Boulevard
Chicago, IL 60607-2331
312-733-1893
Fax: 312-733-1896
Jeanne Rosner, Executive Director

7022 Podiatry and Parkinson's Disease
United Parkinson Foundation
833 W Washington Boulevard
Chicago, IL 60607-2331
312-733-1893
Fax: 312-733-1896
Jeanne Rosner, Executive Director

7023 Postural Hypotension
United Parkinson Foundation
833 W Washington Boulevard
Chicago, IL 60607-2331
312-733-1893
Fax: 312-733-1896
Jeanne Rosner, Executive Director

7024 Practical Pointers for Parkinson Patients
National Parkinson Foundation
1501 NW 9th Avenue
Miami, FL 33136-1407
305-547-6666
800-327-4545
Fax: 305-548-4403
http://www.parkinson.org
Jose Garcia-Pedrosa, Executive Director

Parkinson's Disease/Research Centers

7025 **Role of Physical Therapy in Parkinson's Disease**
United Parkinson Foundation
833 W Washington Boulevard
Chicago, IL 60607-2331
312-733-1893
Fax: 312-733-1896
Jeanne Rosner, Executive Director

7026 **Sexual and Bladder Difficulties in Parkinson's Disease**
United Parkinson Foundation
833 W Washington Boulevard
Chicago, IL 60607-2331
312-733-1893
Fax: 312-733-1896
Jeanne Rosner, Executive Director

7027 **Sleep Problems with Parkinson's Disease**
United Parkinson Foundation
833 W Washington Boulevard
Chicago, IL 60607-2331
312-733-1893
Fax: 312-733-1896
Jeanne Rosner, Executive Director

7028 **Speech & Swallowing Problems for Parkinsonians**
National Parkinson Foundation
1501 NW 9th Avenue
Miami, FL 33136-1407
305-547-6666
800-327-4545
Fax: 305-548-4403
http://www.parkinson.org
Jose Garcia-Pedrosa, Executive Director

7029 **Speech Problems & Swallowing Problems In Parkinson's Disease**
American Parkinson Disease Association
60 Bay Street
Suite 401
Staten Island, NY 10301-2514
800-223-2732
Fax: 718-981-4399
Offers information on speech problems, swallowing problems, hearing impairments and facial mobility for the person with Parkinson's.

7030 **Speech and Voice Impairment**
United Parkinson Foundation
833 W Washington Boulevard
Chicago, IL 60607-2331
312-733-1893
Fax: 312-733-1896
Jeanne Rosner, Executive Director

7031 **Stages of Parkinson's Disease**
United Parkinson Foundation
833 W Washington Boulevard
Chicago, IL 60607-2331
312-733-1893
Fax: 312-733-1896
Jeanne Rosner, Executive Director

7032 **Suggested Exercise Program for People with Parkinson's Disease**
American Parkinson Disease Association
60 Bay Street
Suite 401
Staten Island, NY 10301-2514
800-223-2732
Fax: 718-981-4399
Exercise program pamphlet with full illustrations explaining each exercise.
23 pages

7033 **Treatment of Parkinson's Disease with Carbidopa-Levodopa**
National Parkinson Foundation
1501 NW 9th Avenue
Miami, FL 33136-1407
305-547-6666
800-327-4545
Fax: 305-548-4403
http://www.parkinson.org
Jose Garcia-Pedrosa, Executive Director
Offers information on treating Parkinson's Disease.

7034 **UPF Newsletters**
United Parkinson Foundation
833 W Washington Boulevard
Chicago, IL 60607-2331
312-733-1893
Fax: 312-733-1896
Jeanne Rosner, Executive Director
Offers information on association activities, support group services, research reports, book reviews and medical updates.
Frequency: Quarterly

Research Centers

7035 **California Institute for Medical Research**
2260 Clove Drive
San Jose, CA 95128-2637
408-998-4554
Fax: 408-998-2723
Robert O'Reiley, President
Medical research, including infectious diseases, stroke and cancer specializing in Parkinson's Disease related studies.

7036 **Mulligan Foundation**
Mulligan Foundation
10663 Nine Mile Road
Whitmore Lake, MI 48189-9130
734-449-8442
Fax: 734-449-4931
e-mail: mulligan@frostbyte.com
http://www.frostbyte.com/mulligan

7037 **National Institute of Neurological Disorders & Stroke**
PO Box 5801
Bethesda, MD 20824-5801
301-496-5751
800-352-9424
Fax: 301-402-2186
http://www.ninds.nih.gov
Audrey Penn, Executive Director
Offers a brochure on Parkinson's disease and America's focal point for support of research on brain and nervous system disorders

7038 **New York College of Osteopathic Medicine**
512-626-6114
Information and referral research center for Parkinson's disease patients and their families.

7039 **Oregon Health Sciences University**
3181 SW Sam Jackson Park Road
Portland, OR 97239-3079
503-494-3460
James Morgan, Executive Director
Information and referral research center for Parkinson's disease patients and their families.

7040 **Parkinson's Disease Foundation**
Presbyterian Medical Center
710 W 168th Street
New York, NY 10032-3726
212-923-4700
800-457-6676
Fax: 212-923-4778
Robin Elliott, Executive Director
Raises funds for support of scientific research into causes, prevention, and cure of Parkinson's disease. Supports its own laboratories for research in Parkinsonism. Prepares and distributes information on patient care and rehabilitation including list of clinics where treatment is available, and a list of patient selfhelp groups. Supports a brain bank to permit anatomical and chemical studies. Sponsors scientific symposia. Offers patient and family counseling and advocacy services. Maintains research advisory board. Sponsors summer fellowship program for medical students and undergraduate.

Parkinson's Disease/Research Centers

7041 Peninsula Hospital of Far Rockway
5115 Beach Channel Drive
Far Rockaway, NY 11691-1074   718-734-2000
                                  Fax: 718-734-2993
Robert Levine, CEO

Information and referral research center for Parkinson's disease patients and their families.

7042 Presbyterian Hospital of Dallas
8200 Walnut Hill Lane
Dallas, TX 75231-4426   214-345-6789
                                  Fax: 214-345-2019
                      e-mail: lindagoelzer@texashealth.org
                             http://www.texashealth.org
Linda Goelzer, Manager Public Realtions
Mark Merrill, President

Information and referral research center for Parkinson's disease patients and their families.

7043 Robert Wood Johnson University Hospital
1 Robert Wood Johnson Place
New Brunswick, NJ 08901-1966   732-828-3000
Harvey Holzberg, President

Information and referral research center for Parkinson's disease patients and their families.

7044 San Diego Information & Referral Center
8555 Aero Drive
Suite 205
San Diego, CA 92123-1745   858-453-3842
                                  Fax: 858-535-9390
                              e-mail: sdpc@sd-pc.com
Dee Silver MD, Medical Director

Information and referral research center for Parkinson's disease patients and their families.

7045 St. John's Episcopal Hospital
327 Beach 19th Street
Far Rockaway, NY 11691-4423   718-869-7000
                                  Fax: 718-869-8532
Louis A Hernandez, CEO

Information and referral research center for Parkinson's disease patients and their families.

7046 Texas Tech University: Tarbox Parkinson's Disease Institute
3601 4th Street
Lubbock, TX 79430   806-743-2391
Joseph Green, Chairperson
Josie Handarlite, Manager

7047 University of Alabama at Birmingham: Parkinson's Disease Center
Jefferson Tower
Room 1218c
Birmingham, AL 35294   205-934-7714
                                  Fax: 205-934-8559
James Halsey, Director

7048 University of Texas HSC at San Antonio
7703 Floyd Curl Drive
San Antonio, TX 78229-3901   210-567-8400
W A J Van Heuven, MD

Information and referral research center for Parkinson's disease patients and their families.

7049 Washington University Medical Center
2300 Eye Street NW
Washington, DC 20037-2336   202-994-2715
                                  Fax: 202-994-0465
Information and referral research center for Parkinson's disease patients and their families.

7050 William T Gossett Parkinson's Disease Center
Henry Ford Hospital Department of Neurology
2799 W Grand Boulevard
Detroit, MI 48202-2608   313-972-1693
Jay M Gorell MD, Director

Stroke/Associations & Organizations

Associations & Organizations

7051 American Academy of Neurology
1080 Montreal Avenue
Saint Paul, MN 55116
651-695-2717
800-879-1960
Fax: 651-695-2791
e-mail: memberservices@aan.com
http://www.aan.com
Stephen M. Sergay, MB BCh, FAAN, President
Michael L. Goldstein, MD, FAAN, VP
Catherine M Rydell, Executive Director

Professional society of medical doctors specializing in brain and nervous system diseases. Maintains placement service. Sponsors research and educational programs. Compiles statistics. Publishes scientific journal.

7052 NIH/National Institute of Neurological Disorders and Stroke
31 Center Drive MSC 2540
Building 31
Bethesda, MD 20892
301-496-1333
800-352-9424
Fax: 301-402-2186
Jay H Hoffnagle, MD

Offers advice on treatments and care of individual patients with neurological disorders and stroke.

7053 National Rehabilitation Information Center
8201 Corporate Drive
Suite 600
Landover, MD 20785
800-346-2742
800-346-2742
Fax: 301-459-4263
e-mail: naricinfo@heitechservices.com
http://www.naric.com
Mark Odum, Director
Steven Tingus, Director

Offers information about coping with stroke, rehabilitation research and disability programs.

7054 National Stroke Association
9707 E Easter Lane Building B
Centennial, CO 80112
303-649-9299
800-STR-OKES
Fax: 303-649-1328
e-mail: info@stroke.org
http://www.stroke.org
Diane Mulligan-Fairfield, Vice President of Communications
James Baranski, CEO

A national organization whose sole purpose is to reduce the incidence and impact of stroke by changing the way stroke is viewed and treated. NSA offers public, patient, and professional education.

7055 Neurology Institute
P.O. Box 5801
Building 31
Bethesda, MD 20824
301-496-5751
Fax: 301-402-2186
http://www.ninds.nih.gov/
Audrey Penn, Special Advisor to the Director
Story C Landis, Director

Offers information, support and resources for persons with neurological disorders, heart disease and stroke victims.

7056 Stroke Research and Treatment Center
Medical Center
Department of Neurology, 1813 6th Avenue South
RWUH-M226
Birmingham, AL 35294
205-975-8569
Fax: 205-975-6785
http://www.main.uab.edu
Prof. James Halsey, Director
Andrei V. Alexandrov, Director and Professor

Books

7057 Adaptive Resources Guide
National Stroke Association
9707 E Easter Lane
Centennial, CO 80112-3754
303-649-9299
800-787-6537
Fax: 303-649-1328
James Baranski, CEO

A guide for stroke survivors listing adaptive resources, products, equipment, manufacturers, clothing, books and tapes.

7058 After a Stroke: 300 Tips to Making LifeEasier
Demos Medical Publishing
386 Park Avenue S
Suite 301
New York, NY 10016
212-683-0072
e-mail: info@demosmedpub.com
http://www.demosmedpub.com
Phyllis D Gold, President/CEO

Stroke survivor and nurse Hutton gives practical tips for going through the recovery process as patient or caregiver.

7059 Can You Hear the Clapping of One Hand? Learning to Live with a Stroke
Jason Aronson
PO Box 15100
York, PA 17405-7100
800-782-0015
Fax: 201-840-7242
http://www.aronson.com

120 pages

7060 Clinical Program for Evaluating and Managing Stroke-at-Risk Patients
National Stroke Association
96 Inverness Drive E
Suite 1
Englewood, CO 80112-5311
303-754-0921
800-787-6537
Fax: 303-649-1328

Includes stroke appraisal forms and instructions for selecting patients for appraisal, evaluating stroke risk, counseling patients and motivating and reinforcing positive behavior.

7061 Discovery Circles
National Stroke Association
9707 E Easter Lane
Centennial, CO 80112-3754
303-649-9299
800-787-6537
Fax: 303-649-1328
James Baranski, CEO

NSA's guide to organizing and facilitating stroke support groups. This detailed manual describes the support group structure and the facilitator's role.

213 pages

7062 Helpmates
National Stroke Association
9707 E Easter Lane
Centennial, CO 80112-3754
303-649-9299
800-787-6537
Fax: 303-649-1328
James Baranski, CEO

Stroke/Books

Offers advice, guidance and support for survivors and caregivers.
167 pages

7063 Introduction to Stroke
Idyll Arbor
PO Box 720
Ravensdale, WA 98051
425-432-3231
Fax: 425-432-3726
e-mail: sales@IdyllArbor.com
http://www.IdyllArbor.com

This book contains the basic information about patients with strokes that a professional needs to provide good, quality services. It is especially appropriate for someone who is just starting to work with patients who have had a stroke or for orienting interns. Three-ring binder.
945 pages

7064 Invaluable Guide to Life After Stroke: An Owner's Manual
National Stroke Association
96 Inverness Drive E
Suite I
Englewood, CO 80112-5311
303-754-0921
800-787-6537
Fax: 303-649-1328

Practical advice and medical information to fight stroke's devastating effects.
152 pages

7065 Life After Stroke: The Guide to Recovering
Johns Hopkins University Press
2715 North Charles Street
Baltimore, MD 21218-4363
410-516-6900
Fax: 410-516-6968
http://www.press.jhu.edu

Practical advice on treatment, rehabilitation, and lifestyle changes to help prevent another stroke.

7066 Living with Stroke: A Guide for Families
Delmar Learning
PO Box 8007
Clifton Park, NY 12065-8007
800-487-8488
Fax: 800-451-3661

7067 November Days
National Stroke Association
9707 E Easter Lane
Centennial, CO 80112-3754
303-649-9299
800-787-6537
Fax: 303-649-1328

James Baranski, CEO

A caregiver's story of her struggle with a loved one's stroke.
225 pages

7068 Pathways: Moving Beyond Stroke and Aphasis
National Stroke Association
9707 E Easter Lane
Centennial, CO 80112-3754
303-649-9299
800-787-6537
Fax: 303-649-1328

James Baranski, CEO

A guide for those coping with issues caused by stroke and aphasia.
195 pages

7069 Road Ahead: A Stroke Recovery Guide
National Stroke Association
9707 E Easter Lane
Centennial, CO 80112-3754
303-649-9299
800-787-6537
Fax: 303-649-1328

James Baranski, CEO

This book offers comprehensive descriptions of stroke impairments and practical suggestions for coping, common concerns of caregivers, goal setting procedures, glossary terms and appendices.
153 pages

7070 Stroke - A Clinical Approach
Butterworth-Heinemann
225 Wildwood Avenue
Woburn, MA 01801-2025
781-904-2500
800-366-2665
Fax: 800-446-6520
http://www.bh.com

584 pages

7071 Stroke Book
Throndike Publishing
295 Kennedy Drive
Waterville, ME 04901
800-223-1244
Fax: 800-558-4676

7072 Stroke Therapy
Butterworth-Heinemann
225 Wildwood Avenue
Woburn, MA 01801-2025
781-904-2500
800-366-2665
Fax: 800-446-6520
http://www.bh.com

7073 Stroke and the Family: A New Guide
Harvard University Press
79 Garden Street
Cambridge, MA 02138
800-405-1619
http://www.hup.harvard.edu

To make sense of the confusing variety of diagnoses and treatment options, and goes on to explore challenges the recovering stroke patient and the recovering family will face during a long recuperation with an uncertain outcome.

7074 Stroke for Dummies
Wiley Publishing
10475 Crosspoint Boulevard
Indianapolis, IN 46256
877-762-2974
Fax: 800-597-3299
http://www.wiley.com

Get the latest on the symptoms, diagnosis, and treatment of stroke.
354 pages

7075 Stroke: Putting the Pieces Back Together
National Stroke Association
96 Inverness Drive E
Suite I
Englewood, CO 80112-5311
303-754-0921
800-787-6537
Fax: 303-649-1328

A training program designed for LTC facilities that includes audio and video tapes, student handout materials and an instructor's guide.

7076 Stroke: Your Complete Exercise Guide
Human Kinetics Publishers
PO Box 5076
Champaign, IL 61825-5076
217-351-5076
800-747-4457
Fax: 217-351-2674
e-mail: humank@hkusa.com
http://www.humankinetics.com

Part of the Cooper Clinic and Research Institute Fitness Series providing exercise rehabilitation for persons suffering from strokes.
126 pages

Stroke/Directories

7077 **Winning Over Stroke**
National Stroke Association
96 Inverness Drive E
Suite I
Englewood, CO 80112-5311
303-754-0921
800-787-6537
Fax: 303-649-1328

An honest and inspiring depiction of the trials and successes of a stroke survivor. Encourages others to never give up hope on road to recovery.
110 pages

Directories

7078 **US Stroke Club Listing**
National Stroke Association
9707 E Easter Lane
Centennial, CO 80112-3754
303-649-9299
800-787-6537
Fax: 303-649-1328
e-mail: info@stroke.org
http://www.stroke.org

Victoria Schelling-Armstrong, Mailing Contact
James Baranski, CEO

About 1500 state stroke clubs and support groups that assist stroke survivors and their families. Entries include: Organization name, address, coordinator name, sponsor name. Lists of clubs and support groups covering a single state are available.
Frequency: Irregular

Journals, Magazines

7079 **Journal of Stroke and Cerebrovascular Diseases**
National Stroke Association
9707 E Easter Lane
Centennial, CO 80112-3754
303-649-9299
800-787-6537
Fax: 303-649-1328

James Baranski, CEO

A multidisciplinary quarterly clinical journal devoted to all aspects of stroke.

Newsletters, Pamphlets

7080 **African-Americans and Stroke**
National Stroke Association
9707 E Easter Lane
Centennial, CO 80112-3754
303-649-9299
800-787-6537
Fax: 303-649-1328

James Baranski, CEO

7081 **Aneurysm Answers**
National Stroke Association
9707 E Easter Lane
Centennial, CO 80112-3754
303-649-9299
800-787-6537
Fax: 303-649-1328

James Baranski, CEO

7082 **Atrial Fibrillation and Stroke**
National Stroke Association
9707 E Easter Lane
Centennial, CO 80112-3754
303-649-9299
800-787-6537
Fax: 303-649-1328

James Baranski, CEO

7083 **Be Stroke Smart**
National Stroke Association
9707 E Easter Lane
Centennial, CO 80112-3754
303-649-9299
800-787-6537
Fax: 303-649-1328

Lisa Gibson, Editor
James Baranski, CEO

A monthly newsletter with information on stroke, prevention, treatment, rehabilitation, resources and support for stroke survivors and caregivers.

7084 **Be Stroke Smart - Communication**
National Stroke Association
96 Inverness Drive E
Suite I
Englewood, CO 80112-5311
303-754-0921
800-787-6537
Fax: 303-649-1328

Groups of articles from the Be Stroke Smart series.

7085 **Be Stroke Smart - Emotional Aspects**
National Stroke Association
9707 E Easter Lane
Centennial, CO 80112-3754
303-649-9299
800-787-6537
Fax: 303-649-1328

James Baranski, CEO

A group of 5 articles from the Be Stroke Smart series.

7086 **Be Stroke Smart - Home and Work Adaptation**
National Stroke Association
96 Inverness Drive E
Suite I
Englewood, CO 80112-5311
303-754-0921
800-787-6537
Fax: 303-649-1328

Mini-packet of articles from the Be Stroke Smart series.

7087 **Be Stroke Smart - Prevention and Warning Signs**
National Stroke Association
9707 E Easter Lane
Centennial, CO 80112-3754
303-649-9299
800-787-6537
Fax: 303-649-1328

James Baranski, CEO

Mini-packet of articles from the Be Stroke Smart series.

7088 **Be Stroke Smart - Rehabilitation Guidelines and Resources**
National Stroke Association
96 Inverness Drive E
Suite I
Englewood, CO 80112-5311
303-754-0921
800-787-6537
Fax: 303-649-1328

Mini-packet of articles from the Be Stroke Smart series.

7089 **Be Stroke Smart Series**
National Stroke Association
9707 E Easter Lane
Centennial, CO 80112-3754
303-649-9299
800-787-6537
Fax: 303-649-1328

James Baranski, CEO

Series of 24 articles in response to the most asked about questions about stroke.

7090 **Brain at Risk: Understanding and Preventing Stroke**
National Stroke Association
96 Inverness Drive E
Suite I
Englewood, CO 80112-5311
303-889-0022
800-787-6537
Fax: 303-649-1328

Dan O'Brien, Owner

Stroke / Newsletters, Pamphlets

7091 Clinical Trials Participation
National Stroke Association
9707 E Easter Lane
Centennial, CO 80112-3754
303-649-9299
800-787-6537
Fax: 303-649-1328

James Baranski, CEO

Explains what acute stroke treatment clinical trials are and how patients can participate.

7092 Disability Workbook for Social Security Applicants
National Stroke Association
96 Inverness Drive E
Suite I
Englewood, CO 80112-5311
303-649-9299
800-787-6537
Fax: 303-649-1328
e-mail: info@stroke.org
http://www.stroke.org

James Baranski, CEO
120 pages

7093 Guide to Understanding Stroke
National Stroke Association
96 Inverness Drive E
Suite I
Englewood, CO 80112-5311
720-875-0551
800-787-6537
Fax: 303-649-1328

R K Gadi, MD

Detailed color illustrations on stroke and its action for physicians to present to patients.

7094 Heart and Stroke Facts
American Heart Association
7272 Greenville Avenue
Dallas, TX 75231-5129
214-373-6300
800-553-6321
Fax: 214-706-1341

M Cass Wheeler, CEO

7095 Heart and Stroke Risk Factors
American Heart Association
7272 Greenville Avenue
Dallas, TX 75231-5129
214-373-6300
800-553-6321
Fax: 214-706-1341

M Cass Wheeler, CEO

7096 High Blood Pressure and Stroke
National Stroke Association
9707 E Easter Lane
Centennial, CO 80112-3754
303-649-9299
800-787-6537
Fax: 303-649-1328

James Baranski, CEO

7097 Home Exercises for Stroke Survivors
National Stroke Association
96 Inverness Drive E
Suite I
Englewood, CO 80112-5311
303-754-0921
800-787-6537
Fax: 303-649-1328

7098 Living at Home After a Stroke
National Stroke Association
9707 E Easter Lane
Centennial, CO 80112-3754
303-649-9299
800-787-6537
Fax: 303-649-1328

James Baranski, CEO

7099 NSA's Guide to Stroke
National Stroke Association
9707 E Easter Lane
Centennial, CO 80112-3754
303-649-9299
800-787-6537
Fax: 303-649-1328

James Baranski, CEO

7100 Recovery After a Stroke
National Stroke Association
9707 E Easter Lane
Centennial, CO 80112-3754
303-649-9299
800-787-6537
Fax: 303-649-1328

James Baranski, CEO

7101 Recurrent Stroke
National Stroke Association
9707 E Easter Lane
Centennial, CO 80112-3754
303-649-9299
800-787-6537
Fax: 303-649-1328

James Baranski, CEO

7102 Reducing Risk and Recognizing Symptoms
National Stroke Association
9707 E Easter Lane
Centennial, CO 80112-3754
303-649-9299
800-787-6537
Fax: 303-649-1328

James Baranski, CEO

7103 Stroke Connection
American Heart Association
7272 Greenville Avenue
Dallas, TX 75231-5129
214-373-6300
800-553-6321
Fax: 214-696-5211

M Cass Wheeler, CEO

A forum for stroke survivors and their families to share information about coping with stroke. Provides information and referral and carriers stroke related books, videos and literature available for purchase.
Frequency: BiMonthly

7104 Stroke Treatment and Recovery
National Stroke Association
9707 E Easter Lane
Centennial, CO 80112-3754
303-649-9299
800-787-6537
Fax: 303-649-1328

James Baranski, CEO

7105 Stroke is a Brain Attack!
National Stroke Association
9707 E Easter Lane
Centennial, CO 80112-3754
303-649-9299
800-787-6537
Fax: 303-649-1328

James Baranski, CEO

7106 Stroke: Clinical Updates
National Stroke Association
9707 E Easter Lane
Centennial, CO 80112-3754
303-649-9299
800-787-6537
Fax: 303-649-1328

James Baranski, CEO

Offers the lates medical advances and technology news for the health care professional.

Stroke/Videos, Audio Tapes

7107 **Stroke: Questions & Answers**
National Stroke Association
96 Inverness Drive E
Suite I
Englewood, CO 80112-5311
303-754-0921
800-787-6537
Fax: 303-649-1328

7108 **Stroke: Reducing Your Risk (Spanish)**
National Stroke Association
9707 E Easter Lane
Centennial, CO 80112-3754
303-649-9299
800-787-6537
Fax: 303-649-1328

James Baranski, CEO

This brochure helps persons learn what stroke is, how to recognize warning signs, what factors affect stroke risk and how to reduce stroke risks. Available in Spanish only.

7109 **Understanding Speech and Language Problems After Stroke**
National Stroke Association
96 Inverness Drive E
Suite I
Englewood, CO 80112-5311
303-754-0921
800-787-6537
Fax: 303-649-1328

7110 **What Every Family Should Know About Stroke**
National Stroke Association
9707 E Easter Lane
Centennial, CO 80112-3754
303-649-9299
800-787-6537
Fax: 303-649-1328

James Baranski, CEO

Videos, Audio Tapes

7111 **Brain at Risk: Understanding and Preventing Stroke**
National Stroke Association
96 Inverness Drive E
Suite I
Englewood, CO 80112-5311
303-889-0022
800-787-6537
Fax: 303-649-1328

Dan O'Brien, Owner

Explains strokes, describes symptoms, and instructs individuals on how to reduce their risk of stroke. Available in an opened caption version for people with hearing impairments.

7112 **NSA Audio Tape Series**
National Stroke Association
9707 E Easter Lane
Centennial, CO 80112-3754
303-649-9299
800-787-6537
Fax: 303-649-1328
e-mail: info@stroke.org
http://www.stroke.org

James Baranski, CEO

Jackie Mayer Townsend, Miss America 1963 and a stroke survivor, shares her story and provides hope, motivation, and inspiration.

Frequency: 30 minutes

Research Centers

7113 **Cerebral Blood Flow Laboratories**
Veterans Administration Medical Center
2002 Holcombe Boulevard
Houston, TX 77030-4211
713-795-5807
Fax: 713-795-7501

John S Meyer MD, Director

Offers research in cerebrovascular disorders and risk factors for stroke.

7114 **Comprehensive Stroke Center of Oregon**
University of Oregon Health Sciences Center
3181 SW Sam Jackson Park Road
Portland, OR 97239-3011
503-494-7225
Fax: 503-494-7556

Bruce Coull MD, Professor
Wayne M Clark, MD

7115 **Cornell University Medical College: Departments of Neurology and Neuroscience**
PO Box 130
New York, NY 10021
212-746-2631
Fax: 212-746-8214
e-mail: nbannett@med.cornell.edu

Peter Kam, Associate Administrator
Rick Hostnik, Administrator

7116 **Departments of Neurology & Neurosurgery: University of California**
505 Parnassus Avenue
San Francisco, CA 94143-2204
415-476-3428
Fax: 415-476-1487
e-mail: hauser@itsa.ucsf.edu

Stephen Hauser MD, Chairman
Ralph Christy, Director Administration
Kelly Bolen, Executive Assistant

7117 **Duke University Medical Center**
PO Box 3209
Durham, NC 27710
919-477-9292
Fax: 919-684-4431

Victor Nadler PhD, Professor
Michael Duke, Owner

7118 **Hospital of the University of Pennsylvania**
36th & Hamilton Walk
Philadelphia, PA 19104
215-662-4000
Fax: 215-349-5165
http://www.uphs.upenn.edu

Francisco Gonzalez-Scarano, Professor
Ralph Muller, CEO

7119 **Massachusetts General Departments of Neurology and Neurosurgery**
Fruit Street
Boston, MA 02114
617-726-8442
Fax: 617-726-2547

Michael A Moskowitz MD, Professor

7120 **New York University Medical Rehabilitation Research and Training Center**
550 1st Avenue
New York, NY 10016-6402
212-263-6427
Fax: 212-263-5923

Orrin Devinsky MD, Professor
Mary Zupanc MD, Associate Professor
Jerome Block MD, Clinical Professor

Rehabilitation for brain trauma and stroke victims.

7121 **University of California: Los Angeles Department of Medicine**
Los Angeles, CA 90024
213-825-8858

William Partridge MD, Professor

7122 **University of Iowa College of Medicine**
E-318-1 Gh
Iowa City, IA 52242
319-335-9650
Fax: 319-335-7155

Donald D Heistad MD, Professor
David Johnsen, Manager

Stroke / Research Centers

7123 University of Miami School of Medicine: Department of Neurology
1150 NW 14th Street
Suite 701
Miami, FL 33136-2118
305-243-7100
Fax: 305-243-7525
e-mail: Wbradley@mednet.med.miami.edu
http://www.miami.edu

Minor Anderson, Vice President
Cyril Ramlakan, Manager Billing
Walter G Bradley DM, Professor

7124 Wake Forest University: CerebrovascularResearch Center
Department of Neurology
300 S Hawthorne Road
Winston Salem, NC 27103-2732
336-748-2338
Fax: 336-748-5477

Dr. James Toole, Director

Cerebrovascular research.

7125 Washington University School of Medicine
660 S Euclid Avenue
Saint Louis, MO 63110-1093
314-362-8681
Fax: 314-362-4658
e-mail: wumscoa@msnotes.wustl.edu

Marcus Raichle MD, Contact
Janet B McGill, MD

Substance Abuse/Associations & Organizations

Associations & Organizations

7126 Al-Anon Family Group Headquarters
Family Group Headquarters
1600 Corporate Landing Parkway
Virginia Beach, VA 23454-5617
757-563-1600
Fax: 757-563-1655
e-mail: wso@al-anon.org
http://www.al-anon.alateen.org
Claire Riccuasser, Associate Director Public Outrea

A fellowship of relatives and friends of alcoholics whose lives have been affected by someone else's drinking and a self-help recovery program based on the 12 steps of Alcoholics Anonymous. The single purpose of this organization is to help families and friends of alcoholics, whether the alcoholic is still drinking or not.

7127 Alabama Division of Mental Illness and Substance Abuse Community Programs
100 N Union Street
Post Office Box 301410
Montgomery, AL 36130-1410
334-242-3454
Fax: 334-242-0725
e-mail: dmhmr@mh.alabama.gov
http://www.mh.alabama.gov
John Davis, Manager
John Houston, Commissioner

The Division of Substance Abuse Services has the resposibility for development, coordination, and management of a comprehensive system of trearment and prevention services for alcoholism/drug addiction and abuse.

7128 Alcohol & Drug Abuse Services Administration
Department of Health and Human Services
1300 1st Street NE
Suite 300
Washington, DC 20002-3335
202-727-9393
Fax: 202-487-2239
Herbert Tilman, Manager

7129 Alcohol Rehabilitation for the Elderly
PO Box 267
Hopedale, IL 61747-0267
800-344-0824
800-344-0824
e-mail: mfrossi@trianglenet.net
http://www.hmc.net

Provides information anf also makes refferals to treatment programs for people aged 50 and older. A residential treatment center.

7130 Alcohol Research Group: Public Health Institute
6475 Christie Avenue
Suite 400
Emeryville, CA 94608-1010
510-597-3440
Fax: 510-985-6459
e-mail: alcresgp@arg.org
http://www.arg.org
Debbie Gill, Manager
Debbie Rich, Administrative Assistant
Dominique Lampert, Research Program Administrator

One of ten national research centers funded by the National Institute on Alcohol Abuse and Alcoholism. Its alcoholism library carries 5,500 books, 130 journals, 150 newsletters and 60,000 other materials.

7131 Alcohol-Drug Treatment Referral
1316 S Coast Hwy
Laguna Beach, CA 92651
949-499-1311
Fax: 949-499-7582
e-mail: info@southcoastmedcenter.com
http://www.nationalhotline.org
Bruce Christian, President

National Help and Referral Network, a nonprofit organization available 24 hours a day to assist people troubled by drug or alcohol abuse. Here to provide information on addiction treatment and support services and to help save lives and mend broken dreams.

7132 Alcoholics Anonymous
General Service Office/Grand Central Station
PO Box 459
New York, NY 10163
212-870-3400
Fax: 212-870-3003
e-mail: literature@aa.org
http://www.aa.org
Valerie O'Neill, Regional Forums Coordinator
Greg H. Muth, coordinador

Founded in 1935, Alcoholics Anonymous is a world-wide fellowship of men and women who have found solutions to their drinking problems. The only requirement for A.A. membership is a desire to stop drinking. There are no dues or fees: A.A. is supported by voluntary contributions of its members and groups.

7133 American Council for Drug Education
164 W 74th Street
New York, NY 10023
800-488-DRUG
Fax: 212-595-2553
e-mail: acde@phoenixhouse.org
http://www.acde.org
Robert Balster, Ph.D., Professor and Advisor
Robert C. Petersen, Ph.D., Research Psychologist - ADVISOR

This organization provides information on drug use, develops media campaigns, reviews scientific findings, publishes books and offers films and curriculum materials for preteens.

7134 American Council on Alcohol Problems
3426 Bridgeland Drive
Bridgeton, MO 65044
314-739-5944
Fax: 314-739-0848
Sharon Bartlett, VP

Provides the forum and the mechanism through which concerned people can find common ground on alcohol and other drug problems and address these issues with a united voice. Members of the organization include 36 state temperance organizations, 22 national Christian denominations and other fraternal organizations which support the ACAP's philosophy of abstinence.

7135 American Council on Alcoholism
1000 E Indian School Road
Phoenix, AZ 85014
602-264-7897
800-527-5344
Fax: 602-264-7403
e-mail: info@aca-usa.org
http://www.aca-usa.org
Lloyd Vacovsky, Executive Director
Yvonne Theodore, Secretary

AcA's mission is to increase public awareness and undersatnding of the nature of the disease alcoholism and related issues. To provide a national information network of resources on prevention, treatment, research, education, and rehabilitation of alcoholism. To emphasize the critical importance of early detection of alcoholism thjrough education in schools, businesses, and communities.

7136 Arizona Alcoholism and Drug Abuse
Department of Health Services
150 N. 18th Avenue
Phoenix, AZ 85007
602-542-1001
Fax: 602-542-0883
e-mail: cdyc@hs.state.az.us
http://www.hs.state.az.us
Cathy Eden, Director
Cheryl A. Smith, President

Substance Abuse/Associations & Organizations

7137 Arizona Bureau of Alcohol and Drug Abuse
4313 West Markham, Third Floor Administration
3
Little Rock, AR 72205-4023
501-686-9871
Fax: 501-686-9035
e-mail: Joe.Hill@arkansas.gov
Joe M. Hill, Director

7138 Arizona Office of Substance Abuse & General Mental Health
2122 E Highland Avenue
Phoenix, AZ 85016-4739
602-381-8999
Fax: 602-553-9143
http://www.aaafts.org

7139 Arkansas Division of Alcoholism & Drug Abuse
Department of Health and Social Services
240 Main Street
Suite 701
Juneau, AK 99811-0607
907-465-2071
Fax: 907-465-2185
e-mail: Gary.Kostenko@alaska.gov
http://www.hss.state.ak.us/dbh
Melissa Witz Stone, Director
Stacy Toner, Deputy Director

7140 Arkansas Office of Alcoholism and Substance Abuse
Department of Health & Social Services
PO Box 110601
350 Main Street, Room 404
Juneau, AK 99811
907-465-3030
800-478-2072
Fax: 907-465-3068
e-mail: webmaster@health.state.ak.us
http://www.hss.state.ak.us
Loren Jones, Executive Director

The Division of Alcoholism and Drug Abuse exists to promote the health, safety and well-being of Alaska's citizens by preventing and treating alcohol, other drug, and inhalant abuse. Its primary method of implementing comprehensive prevention and treatment services is through the award of grants to local government and nonprofit agencies to support a variety of community based substance abuse services.

7141 Associate Administrator for Alcohol Prevention & Treatment Policy
Substance Abuse & Mental Health Services Offices
5600 Fishers Lane
Room 13C-05
Rockville, MD 20857
301-443-8956
Fax: 301-443-9050
e-mail: dgoodman@samhsa.hhs.gov
http://www.samhsa.gov
Deborah Goodman, Editor
Charles G Curie, Administrator

Promotes, monitors, evaluates and coordinates programs for the prevention and treatment of alcoholism and alcohol abuse.

7142 Association of Halfway House Alcoholism: Programs of North America
786 7th Street E
Saint Paul, MN 55106-5027
651-771-0933

Acts as a clearinghouse of the latest literature on alcoholism, assists chemical dependency counselors in placing post treatment individuals in halfway houses and helps in setting up halfway houses.

7143 California Women's Commission on Alcohol and Drug Dependencies
14622 Victory Boulevard
#100
Van Nuys, CA 91411
818-376-0470
Fax: 818-376-1307
e-mail: kathie@cwcadd.org
http://www.cwcadd.org
Kathie Mathis, Contact

Dedicated to improving the quality and increasing the quantity of services to women with alcohol-related problems.

7144 Center for Substance Abuse Prevention
Substance Abuse & Mental Health Services Offices
5600 Fishers Lane
Room 16-105
Rockville, MD 20857
301-443-8956
Fax: 301-443-9847
http://www.samhsa.gov
Mark Weber, Manager

This organization's goal is to connect people and resources with innovative ideas, strategies and programs designed to encourage creative and effective efforts aimed at reducing and eliminating alcohol, tobacco and other drug problems in our society.

7145 Cocaine Anonymous
3740 Overland Avenue
Suite C
Los Angeles, CA 90034
310-216-4444
800-347-8988
Fax: 310-559-2554
e-mail: cawso@ca.org
http://www.ca.org
Robin Long, Manager
Patty Flanagan, Director of Operations

A fellowship of men and women whose primary purpose is to stay free from all other mind. Altering substances and to help others achieve the same freedom.

7146 Community Service Project
Just Say No International
7200 Fair Oaks Boulevard
Carmichael, CA 95608-6454
916-971-7022
Fax: 916-971-7767
e-mail: kward@sanjuan.edu
Michael Koerner, Administrator

Promotes personal and social responsibility through community-service/service-learning projects.

7147 Connecticut Department of Mental Health and Addiction Services
410 Capitol Avenue
P.O. Box 341431
Hartford, CT 06134
860-418-7000
Fax: 860-418-6691
e-mail: samuel.segal@po.state.ct.us
Tom Kirk, Commissioner
Samuel R. Segal, LPC, LADC, Senior Clinical Officer and Addi

7148 Cornerstone
Medical Arts Center Hospital
57 W 57th Street
New York, NY 10019
212-755-0200
Fax: 212-755-4670
http://www.cornerstoneny.com
Michael Richards, Data Processing Executive

Offers a complete integrated program for alcohol assessment, alcohol and drug rehabilitation, continuing care, community education and comprehensive family recovery.

7149 Cornerstone of Eagle Hill
32 Alberts Hill Road
Sandy Hook, CT 06482
203-426-8085
800-334-4744
Fax: 203-426-2821
e-mail: cma1-2@mail.idt.net
http://www.cornerstone-treatment.com

Offers alcohol and drug detox assessment, alcohol and drug rehabilitation, continuing care, comprehensive family recovery and community education programs.

Substance Abuse/Associations & Organizations

7150 Delaware Division of Alcoholism, Drug Abuse & Mental Health
1901 N Du Pont Highway
Main Bldg
New Castle, DE 19720
302-255-9399
Fax: 302-255-4427
e-mail: dhssinfo@state.de.us
http://www.dhss.delaware.gov/dhss/main
Renata J Henry, Director
Michael Kelleher, Deputy Director

The mission is to improve the quality of life for Delaware's citizens by promoting health and well-being, fostering self-sufficiency, and protecting vulnerable populations.

7151 Delaware Drug Abuse & Mental Health
Division of Alcohol
1901 N Dupont Highway
Main Bldg
New Castle, DE 19720
302-255-9040
Fax: 302-255-4429
http://www.dhss.delaware.gov/dhss
Jim Lafferty, Executive Director
Renata Henry, Director

7152 Dentists Concerned for Dentists
400 Robert Street N
Suite 270
Saint Paul, MN 55101-2015
651-224-2787
Fax: 732-821-1082
Peter N Cannon, DDS

A nonprofit organization for chemically dependent Minnesota dentists and concerned others.

7153 Do It Now Foundation
PO Box 27568
Tempe, AZ 85285-7568
480-736-0599
Fax: 480-736-0771
e-mail: info@doitknow.org
http://www.doitnow.org
James Parker, Executive Director

An information clearinghouse for service providers that publishes well-written pamphlets, booklets, and materials on chemical dependency amd recovery.

7154 Drug Abuse Resistance Education of America
9800 S La Cienega Boulevard
Suite 401
Inglewood, CA 90301
310-215-0575
800-223-3273
Fax: 310-215-0180
e-mail: webmaster@dare.com
http://www.dare.com
Charlie J. Parsons, President and Chief Executive Di

7155 Drug-Free Workplace Hotline
National Clearinghouse for Alcohol and Drug Info.
PO Box 2345
Rockville, MD 20847-2345
301-468-2600
800-729-6686
Fax: 301-468-2600
e-mail: info@health.org
http://www.health.org

A hotline for businesses to obtain information on a wide range of drug abuse related problems, issues and services.

7156 Drugs Anonymous
PO Box 9999
Van Nuys, CA 91409
818-773-9999
Fax: 818-700-0700
e-mail: fsmail@na.org
http://www.na.org
Anthony Edmondson, Executive Director
Bob Stewart, Marketing and Public Relations M

A twelve-step program that holds more than 30 meetings for drug addicts in the Greater New York Area including several in hospitals and institutions.

7157 Families Anonymous
PO Box 3475
Culver City, CA 90231-3475
310-815-8010
Fax: 310-815-9682
e-mail: famanon@FamiliesAnonymous.org
http://www.familiesanonymous.org

Addresses the needs of families who are concerned about a relative with a drug problem and with related behavioral problems. Offers informational packets, meetings and support networks for these families.

7158 Fighting Back
National Program Office
2553 the Vanderbilt Clinic
Nashville, TN 37232
615-936-0678
Fax: 615-936-0676
e-mail: info@fightingback.org
http://www.fightingback.org
David Rosenbloom, Director
Ronda Zakocs, Research Director

7159 Florida Department of Health & Rehabilitative Services
4052 Bald Cypress Way
Bldg B
Tallahassee, FL 32399-6570
850-245-4147
Fax: 850-487-4574
Sandra Bell, Manager

7160 Friday Night Live
Department of Drug and Alcohol Programs
PO Box 5091
2637 W. Burrel
Visalia, CA 93278-5091
559-733-6496
Fax: 559-737-4231
e-mail: croman@tcoe.org
http://www.fridaynightlive.org
Jim Kooler, Administrator
Carol Hodson, Operations Manager

These groups, located in California, are all run by students with a faculty adviser. They arrange local alcohol and drug free events, from dances and movies to visiting hospitalized children. Students not only have fun but they learn to have fun sober.

7161 Georgia Division of Mental Health and Substance Abuse
2 Peachtree Street NE
4th Floor, Suite 130
Atlanta, GA 30303-3142
404-657-2252
Fax: 404-657-5681

7162 Governor's Policy Council on Drug & Alcohol Abuse
1700 K Street
5th Floor, Executive Office
Sacramento, CA 95811
916-445-1943
Fax: 916-323-5873
http://www.adp.ca.gov

7163 Harvard Cocaine Recovery Project
Cambridge Hospital
1493 Cambridge Street
Cambridge, MA 02139-1047
617-498-1000
Fax: 617-864-2658
Dr. William McAuliffe, Principal Investigator

Six-year study of relapse and recovery in cocaine addicts.

7164 Hawaii Alcohol and Drug Abuse Division
Department of Health
601 Kamokila Blvd.
Suite 305
Kapolei, HI 96707
808-692-7506
Fax: 808-586-4016
http://http://hawaii.gov/health
Chiyome Fukino, M.D., Director
Susan Jackson, Deputy Director

Substance Abuse/Associations & Organizations

7165 **Hazelden Foundation**
CO3, PO Box 11
Center City, MN 55012-0011
651-213-4200
800-257-7810
Fax: 651-213-4411
e-mail: info@hazelden.org
http://www.hazelden.com
Jim Steinhagen, Executive Director
Brenda J. Iliff, Clinical Director

A nonprofit organization dedicated to providing quality rehabilitation, education and professional services for chemical dependency and related addictive behaviors. Services offered include assessment and rehabilitation, family services, community prevention and professional education, counselor and clergy training and educational materials.

7166 **Idaho Department of Alcoholism & Substance Abuse**
450 W State Street
5th Floor
Boise, ID 83720
208-334-5935
Fax: 208-334-6669

7167 **Illinois Church Action on Alcohol Problems**
PO Box 2437
1132 West Jefferson Street
Springfield, IL 62702
217-546-6871
Fax: 217-546-2814
e-mail: ilcaaap@ilcaaap.org
http://www.ilcaaap.org
Anita Bedell, Executive Director

An interdenominational Christian agency representing church groups in Illinois. Works to prevent alcohol and other drug-related problems through education, legislative action and public awareness.

7168 **Illinois Department of Alcoholism and Substance Abuse**
100 W Randolph Street
Suite 5-600
Chicago, IL 60601
312-814-3840
Fax: 312-814-2419
Tom Green, Acting Administrator of Communic
Jim Long, Director

7169 **Illinois Family & Social Services**
Division of Mental Health
402 W Washington Street
Room W-386
Indianapolis, IN 46207-7083
317-232-2429
Fax: 317-232-7948
e-mail: mgreer@fssa.state.in.us
Maureen Greer, Assistant Deputy Director

7170 **Indian Health Service**
801 Thompson Avenue
Suite 120
Rockville, MD 20852-1627
301-443-1083
Fax: 301-594-6213
e-mail: Ramona.Williams@ihs.gov
http://www.ihs.gov
Michael Trujillo, Executive Director
Don Kashevaroff, President and Chairman

The Indian Health Service an agency within the Department of Health Services, is responsible for providing federal health services to American indians and Alaska natives.

7171 **Indiana Division of Addiction Services**
Department of Mental Health
117 E Washington Street
Indianapolis, IN 46204-3614
317-232-7824
Fax: 317-233-3472

7172 **Institute on Black Chemical Abuse**
2616 Nicollet Avenue
Minneapolis, MN 55408
612-871-7878
Fax: 612-871-2811
http://www.aafs.net/ibca/ibca.htm
Raymond Harp, Chairperson
Julie Jones, Manager

This institute provides training and technical assistance to programs that want to serve African-American/black clients and others of color more effectively.

7173 **International Lawyers in Alcoholics Anonymous**
455 Cayuga Rd
Suite 600
Buffalo, NY 14225
716-204-1055
Fax: 716-204-1080
e-mail: cbeinhauer@pbmlawyers.com
http://www.ilaa.org
Ian Aikenhead, Q.C., Chairman
Charles W. Beinhauer, Trustees

Provides 40 independent local groups.

7174 **Iowa Division of Substance Abuse & Health Promotion**
Lucas State Office Building
1211 Vine Street
Suite 2230
West Des Moines, IA 50265
515-223-6211
Fax: 515-309-3317
e-mail: julie@isapda.org
http://http://www.isapda.org/

7175 **Kansas Alcohol and Drug Abuse Services**
Department of Social and Rehabilitation Services
300 SW Oakley Avenue
Topeka, KS 66606-1861
913-296-3925
Fax: 785-296-0494

7176 **Kentucky Division of Substance Abuse**
Department of Mental Health and Mental Retardation
100 Fair Oaks Lane, 4E-D
KY 40621
Frankfort, KY 40621
502-564-2880
Fax: 502-564-7152
Michael Townsend, Director
Karyn Hascal, Assistant Director

7177 **Louisiana Office of Alcohol & Drug Abuse**
Department of Health and Hospitals
PO Box 2790
628 N. 4th Street
Baton Rouge, LA 70821-2790
225-342-6717
Fax: 225-342-3875
e-mail: jbordeln@dhh.la.gov

7178 **Marin Institute**
24 Belvedere Street
2nd Floor
San Rafael, CA 94901
415-455-1676
Fax: 415-455-1683
http://www.marininstitute.org/
Bruce Lee Livingston, M.P.P., Executive Director
Michael Scippa, Advocacy Director

The mission of this Institute is to reduce the toll of alcohol and other drug problems on Marin County and society in general. The Institute fulfills this mission by developing, implementing, evaluating and disseminating innovative approaches to prevention locally, nationally and internationally.

7179 **Maryland Center for Abuse Prevention**
Center for Substance Abuse Prevention
PO Box 2345
Rockville, MD 20847-2345
301-468-2600
800-729-6686
Fax: 301-468-2600
e-mail: info@health.org
http://www.health.org

This program is designed to support alcohol and other drug abuse prevention efforts in the States.

Substance Abuse/Associations & Organizations

7180 Massachusetts Bureau of Substance Abuse Services
Department of Public Health
250 Washington Street
3rd Floor
Boston, MA 02108-4603
617-624-5159
Fax: 617-624-5185
e-mail: questions.bsas@state.ma.us
http://www.mass.gov/dph/bsas/bsas.htm
Michael Botticelli, Executive Director
John Auerbach, Commissioner

7181 Media Center on Alcohol Issues
1717 Kettner Boulevard
Suite 200
San Diego, CA 92101-2533
619-645-7744

7182 Michigan Center for Substance Abuse Services
PO Box 30195
3423 N. Martin Luther King Jr Boulevard
Lansing, MI 48909
517-335-9483
Fax: 517-335-8294
e-mail: lauberc@michigan.gov
http://www.michigan.gov
Cheryl Lauber, State FAS Coordinator

7183 Minnesota Chemical Dependency Program
Department of Human Services
444 Lafayette Road N
Saint Paul, MN 55101
612-296-4610
Fax: 651-297-1862
http://www.dhs.state.mn.us/contcare/chemicalhea

7184 Mississippi Division of Alcohol and Drug Abuse
Department of Mental Health
239 N Lamar Street
1101 Robert E. Lee Building
Jackson, MS 39201-1328
601-359-1288
Fax: 601-359-6295
Herb Loving, Executive Director

7185 Montana Division of Addictive & Mental Disorders
Department of Public Health and Human Services
PO Box 202951
1400 Broadway, Room C118
Helena, MT 59620-2951
406-444-3969
Fax: 406-444-4435
e-mail: daanderson@state.mt.us
Dan Anderson, Administrator

7186 National Association for Addiction Professionals
901 N Washington Street
Suite 600
Alexandria, VA 22314-1535
703-741-7686
800-548-0497
Fax: 800-377-1136
e-mail: naadac@naadac.org
http://www.naadac.org
Cynthia Moreno Tuohy, Executive Director
Shirley Beckett Mikell, Director

This organization is comprised of addiction focused professionals who enhance the health and recovery of individuals, families and communities. NAADAC's mission is to lead, unify and empower addiction focused professionals to achieve excellence through education, advocacy, knowledge, standards of practice, ethics, professional development and research.

7187 National Association of Addiction Treatment Providers
313 W. Liberty Street
Suite 129
Lancaster, PA 17063-2748
717-392-8480
Fax: 717-392-8481
e-mail: rhunsicker@naatp.org
Kenneth S Ramsey, Chairman
Cathy Palm, Secretary

7188 National Association on Drug Abuse Problems
355 Lexington Avenue
New York, NY 10017
212-986-1170
Fax: 212-697-2939
e-mail: giving@nadap.org
http://www.nadap.com
John A Darin, President
Lawrence Singer, Chairman

Provides skills evaluation, job training and job placement to recovering drug addicts in the metropolitan New York area.

7189 National Clearinghouse for Alcohol and Drug Information
PO Box 2345
Rockville, MD 20847-2345
240-221-4019
800-729-6686
Fax: 240-221-4292
e-mail: info@health.org
http://www.health.org
Duiona Baker, M.P.H., Public Health Advisor
Jacqueline M Bowens, Clinical Coordinator

A resource for alcohol and other drug information. It carries a wide variety of publications dealing with alcohol and other drug abuse.

7190 National Council on Alcoholism and Drug Dependence
12 West 21st Street
New York, NY 10010
212-269-7797
Fax: 212-269-7510
e-mail: national@ncadd.org
http://www.ncadd.org
Robert Lindsey, President
Leah Brock, Director of Affiliate Relations

Provides education, information, help and hope in the fight against addictions. Founded in 1944, NCADD, with its nationwide network of affiliates, advocates prevention, intervention and treatment, is committed to ridding the disease of its stigma and its sufferers of their denial and shame.

7191 National Crime Prevention Council
1000 Connecticut Avenue NW
13th Floor
Washington, DC 20036
202-466-6272
Fax: 202-296-1356
http://www.ncpc.org
Alfonso E Lenhardt, President and Chief Executive Di
U. J Brualdi, Jr, Executive Committee Chairman

This organization works to prevent crime and drug use in many ways, including developing materials for parents and children.

7192 National Families in Action
2957 Clairmont Road NE
Suite 150
Atlanta, GA 30329
404-248-9676
Fax: 404-248-1312
e-mail: nfia@nationalfamilies.org
http://www.nationalfamilies.org
Sue Rusche, Chairman, President and Chief Ex
Paula Kemp, executive vice president

Offers news and information for persons interested in drug abuse prevention. Operates the Parent Corps in 9 states. Operates tch Addiction Studies Progerem for journalists and state legislatures with several University Medical Schools.

7193 National Institute on Drug Abuse
6001 Executive Boulevard
Room 5213
Bethesda, MD 20892
301-443-6245
800-662-4357
Fax: 301-443-7397
e-mail: mmuth@nida.nih.gov
http://www.nih.gov
Beverly Jackson, Contact
Nora D Volkow, Directors

Substance Abuse/Associations & Organizations

NIDA's mission is to lead the Nation in bringing the power of science to bear drug abuse and addiction. The Institute operate's a toll-free hotline at the above number, with drug information and a nationwide alcohol and drug abuse treatmanet referral line.

7194 National Prevention Resource Center
Center for Substance Abuse Prevention
PO Box 2345
Rockville, MD 20847-2345
301-468-2600
800-729-6686
Fax: 301-468-2600
e-mail: info@health.org
http://www.health.org

Supports an array of prevention program evaluation approaches, including individual grantee evaluations, program evaluations and a National Evaluation Project. Also offers a National Data Base to provide information on programs for prevention of substance abuse.

7195 National Volunteer Training Center for Substance Abuse Prevention
Center for Substance Abuse Prevention
PO Box 2345
Rockville, MD 20847-2345
301-468-2600
800-729-6686
Fax: 301-468-2600
e-mail: info@health.org
http://www.health.org

Volunteers are always on hand to provide answers, information, referrals and resources pertaining to alcohol, drugs and substance abuse.

7196 Nebraska Division of Alcoholism and Drug Abuse
Department of Public Institutions
PO Box 94728
Lincoln, NE 68509-4728
402-471-2851
Fax: 402-479-5162
http://www.hhs.state.ne.us

Kent E Dodson, DDS

7197 Nevada Bureau of Alcohol and Drug Abuse
4150 Technology Way,
Suite 300
Carson City, NV 89119-7514
775-684-4200
Fax: 702-486-8253
http://http://health2K.state.nv.us

Dr. Jade Miller, Chairman
Kevin Kennedy, Nevada Diabetes Council-CHAIRMAN

Mission is to reduce the impact of substance abuse in Nevada.

7198 New Jersey Department of Health & Senior Services
Department of Health Division of Addiction Service
120 S Stockton Street
PO Box 367
Trenton, NJ 08625-0367
609-292-7837
Fax: 609-292-3816
http://www.nj.gov/health/

Susan Evans, Ed.D., Autism Program Specialist
Heather Howard, J.D.,, Commissioner

Provides information and support for prevention and treatment services for alcohol, tobacco and other drugs in New Jersey.

7199 New Mexico Behavioral Health Services
PO Box 2348
Room 3200n
Santa Fe, NM 87504-2348
505-827-6250
800-962-8963
Fax: 505-827-0097
e-mail: deborah.fickling@state.nm.us
http://www.bhd.state.nm.us

Karen Meador, Manager
Betina McCracken, Director of Communications

7200 New York Center on Alcohol and Substance Abuse
Columbia University
633 Third Avenue
19th Floor
New York, NY 10017-6706
212-841-5200
Fax: 212-305-3213
http://www.casacolumbia.org

Nora D. Volkow, MD,, Director
Terry Cline, PhD,, Administrator

7201 New York State OASIS
1450 Western Avenue
Albany, NY 12203
518-473-3460
Fax: 518-485-6014
e-mail: communications@oasas.state.ny.us
http://www.oasas.state.ny.us

Gail LaMora, Manager
Eliot Spitzer, Governor

7202 New York State Office of Alcoholism & Substance Abuse Services
1450 Western Avenue
Albany, NY 12203-3526
518-457-2061
Fax: 518-457-5474
http://www.oasas.state.ny.us

7203 North Carolina Division of Mental Health, Developmental Disabilities and Abuse Services
Department of Human Resources
325 N Salisbury Street
3005 Mail Service Center
Raleigh, NC 27699-3005
919-733-7011
Fax: 919-733-9455
e-mail: NV
http://www.ncspfsig.org

Michael Eisen, State EUDL Coordinator

7204 North Dakota Mental Health & Substance Abuse
1237 West Divide Avenue
Suite 1C
Bismark, ND 58501-1208
701-328-8920
800-642-6042
Fax: 701-328-8969
e-mail: dhsmhsas@nd.gov
http://www.nd.gov

Joanne Hoesel, Director

7205 Odyssey Institute Corporation
5 Hedley Farms Road
Westport, CT 06880
203-255-4198
Fax: 203-255-3006

Promotes the development of PACT (Protect Americas Children Today) chapters nationwide to help communities safeguard children.

7206 Office of Women's Services
Substance Abuse & Mental Health Services Offices
5600 Fishers Lane
Room 16-105
Rockville, MD 20857
301-443-0525
Fax: 301-443-9847
http://www.samhsa.gov

Provides leadership and guidance in creating and maintaining an agency-wide focus for addressing the substance abuse and mental health needs of women.

7207 Office on Smoking and Health
National Center for Chronic Disease Prevention
4770 Buford Highway
Atlanta, GA 30341-3717
770-488-5705
800-CDC-1311
Fax: 888-232-3299
e-mail: tobaccoinfo@cdc.gov
http://www.cdc.gov

David Satcher MD, PhD, Surgeon General
Linda Bailey JD, MHS, Executive Secretary

Substance Abuse/Associations & Organizations

Offers reference services to researchers through the Technical Information Center. Publishes and distributes a number of titles in the field of smoking and health.

7208 Ohio Bureau on Alcohol Abuse and Recovery
Ohio Department of Health
614 W. Superior
Suite 300
Cleveland, OH 44113
216-348-4830
Fax: 614-644-1909
e-mail: kayer@adasbcc.org
http://www.adasbcc.org
Russell S. Kaye, Ph.D., MBA,, Executive Director
Frances Mills, Deputy Director

7209 Oklahoma Department of Mental Health and Substance Abuse Services
1200 NE 13th Street
PO Box 53277
Oklahoma City, OK 73152-3277
405-522-3908
Fax: 405-522-3650
e-mail: aharrison@odmhsas.org
http://www.odmhsas.org
Rand Baker, Commissioner

7210 Oregon Office of Alcohol and Drug Abuse Programs
1178 Chemeketa Street NE
102
Salem, OR 97310
503-378-2163
Fax: 503-378-2140

7211 Parkside Medical Services Corporation
205 W Touhy Avenue
Park Ridge
Park Ridge, IL 60068-4201
708-698-4700
Fax: 847-698-6875
http://www.ParksideAssociates.com
This establishment offers treatment and hope for the alcoholic/substance abuser. A resource center that provides information, books and resources pertaining to substance abuse and offers treatment facilities in various states across the country.

7212 Partnership for a Drug-Free America
405 Lexington Avenue
Room 1601
New York, NY 10174
212-922-1560
Fax: 212-922-1570
http://www.drugfree.org
Stephen J Pasierb, President and Chief Executive Di
Roy J. Bostock, Chairman

7213 Pennsylvania Drug and Alcohol Programs
Department of Health
17 N. Front Street
Harrisburg, PA 17101
717-232-7554
Fax: 717-232-2162
http://www.pacdaa.org
Joanne Corte Grossi, Deputy Secretary
Michele Denk, Executive Director

7214 Prevention Resource Center
PO Box 4210
Helena, MT 59604
406-444-3484
800-252-8951
Fax: 406-444-1970
Vicki Turner, Director
Steve Tielking, Program Specialist
Operates two lending libraries with materials on alcoholism and drug addiction. Provides free prevention booklets, pamphlets and brochures and posters to Illinois residents and offers prevention training to parents and family groups, educators, helping professionals and community organizations.

7215 Pride Institute
14400 Martin Drive
Eden Prairie, MN 55344
952-934-7554
Fax: 952-934-8764
e-mail: james.stolz@pride-institute.com
http://www.pride-institute.com
Marty Perry, National Business Development Di
Jim Stolz, Chief Executive Officer

An inpatient treatment center run by and for gay men and lesbians with addition problems. The program lasts one month and has a Twelve-Step orientation.

7216 RADAR Network
National Clearinghouse for Alcohol and Drug Info.
PO Box 2345
Rockville, MD 20847-2345
301-468-2600
800-729-6686
Fax: 301-468-2600
e-mail: info@health.org
http://www.health.org
Consists of state clearinghouses, specialized information centers of national organizations, and the Department of Education Regional Training Centers. Each RADAR member can offer the public a variety of information services.

7217 Rhode Island Division of Substance Abuse
14 Harrington Road
Cranston, RI 02920
401-462-4680
Fax: 401-462-6078
http://www.mhrh.state.ri.us
Craig Stenning, Executive Director
Ellen R. Nelson, PhD, Director

7218 Rutgers University: Center of Alcohol Studies
Busch Campus
Dept. Environmental & Community Medicine
675 Hoes Lane
Piscataway, NJ 8854
732-463-5041
Fax: 732-932-5944
http://http://alcoholstudies.rutgers.edu
Barbara McCrady PhD, program director

Studies the causes and effective treatment of alcoholism. Also operates a controlled drug-delivery research center.

7219 South Carolina Department of Alcohol & Other Drug Abuse Services
3700 Forest Drive
Suite 300
Columbia, SC 29204-4082
803-734-9520
Fax: 803-734-9663
e-mail: BHarrison@daodas.state.sc.us
http://www.daodas.state.sc.us
Bettye Harrison, Coordinator of Adult Services

7220 State University of New York at Buffalo Toxicology Research Center
102 Farber Hall
Buffalo, NY 14214-8001
716-829-2800
Fax: 716-829-2801
e-mail: harison@acsu.buffalo.edu
Paul J Kostyniak PhD, Director
Ronald P. Rubin, Ph.D.,, Chairman

Toxicology-related research and services, including the development of tests to evaluate toxins, chemicals and drugs.

7221 Tennessee Bureau of Alcohol & Drug Abuse
425 5th Avenue, North
Nashville, TN 37219
615-741-1921
Fax: 615-532-2419
e-mail: tn.health@state.tn.us
http://http://health.state.tn.us
Susan R. Cooper, Commissioner

Substance Abuse/Books

7222 Texas Commission on Alcohol and Drug Abuse
909 West 45th Street
Austin, TX 78758
512-206-5000
Fax: 512-474-6675
e-mail: contact@tcada.state.tx.us
http://www.tcada.state.tx.us
John P Keppler, Clinical Director
Clifton Mitchell, Project Officer

7223 Utah Division of Substance Abuse
120 N 200 W
Room 209
Salt Lake City, UT 84103
801-538-3939
Fax: 801-538-9892
e-mail: dsamhwebmaster@utah.gov
http://www.dsamh.utah.gov
Dr. Michael Crookston, Chairman
Paula Bell, Vice-Chair

7224 Vermont Office of Alcohol & Drug Abuse Programs: Agency of Human Services
130 S Main Street
Waterbury, VT 05671
802-241-2170
Fax: 802-241-3095

7225 Virginia Division of Substance Abuse Services
Department of Mental Health and Mental Retardation
PO Box 1797
Richmond, VA 23218-1797
804-786-3921
Fax: 804-371-6638
http://www.dmhmrsas.virginia.gov

7226 WFS' New Life Program
Women for Sobriety
PO Box 618
Quakertown, PA 18951-0618
215-536-8026
800-333-1606
Fax: 215-538-9026
http://www.womenforsobriety.org
Dr. Jean Kirkpatrick, Executive Director
Rebecca Fenner, Assistant Director

A self-help program for women that can be used independent from AA or with AA. Groups are in many states in the United States.

7227 Washington Division of Alcoholism & Substance Abuse
PO Box 45330
612 Woodland Sq Loop SE, Bldg C
Olympia, WA 98504-5330
206-722-3700
Fax: 360-438-8078
http://http://www1.dshs.wa.gov/dasa/default.sht

7228 West Virginia Division of Alcohol and Drug Abuse
1900 Kanawha Boulevard E
Charleston, WV 25305
304-558-0549
Fax: 304-558-1008
Sarah Hamrick, Executive Director

7229 Wisconsin Bureau of Substance Abuse Services
PO Box 7851
1 West Wilson Street
Madison, WI 53707-7851
608-266-2717
Fax: 608-266-1533
e-mail: meierca@dhfs.state.wi.us
Philip McCullough, Director

7230 Woman to Woman
Association of Junior Leagues
660 1st Avenue
New York, NY 10016-3295
212-263-0060
Susan Danish, Executive Director

Programs that target health issues relevant to all woman who drink.

7231 Women for Sobriety
PO Box 618
Quakertown, PA 18951
215-536-8026
800-333-1606
Fax: 215-536-8026
http://www.womenforsobriety.org
Dr. Jean Kirkpatrick, Executive Director
Rebecca Fenner, Assistant Director

A national organization with local units that address the specific needs of women with alcohol-related problems.

7232 Workplace Program
Center for Substance Abuse Prevention
PO Box 2345
Rockville, MD 20847-2345
301-468-2600
800-729-6686
Fax: 301-468-2600
e-mail: info@health.org
http://www.health.org

This program sets standards for drug testing in workplace settings.

7233 Wyoming Division of Behavioral Health
Substance Abuse Program
2300 Capitol Avenue
Hathaway Building, 2nd Floor
Cheyenne, WY 82002-0050
307-777-7690
Fax: 307-777-6234
e-mail: supt@educ.state.wy.us
http://www.k12.wy.us/
Dr. Jim McBride, Public Instruction

Books

7234 A Resource Guide for Drug Management for Older Persons
National Council on the Aging
409 3rd Street W
Washington, DC 20024-3212
202-479-1200
800-867-2755
Fax: 202-479-0735
James P Firman, CEO

A resource to assist in developing a drug management program for older men and women. This guide consists of five sections that include an introduction to drug and the elderly, community involvement, strategies for using community resources and more.

45 pages

7235 Addiction and Responsibility
Crossroad Publishing Company
370 Lexington Avenue
New York, NY 10017-6503
212-532-3650
800-395-
Fax: 212-532-4922

Anyone who has wrestled with such basic questions about addiction such as: Is drug addiction a behavior disorder or a character flaw? Is it genetic or learned? What is it like to be addicted? will find welcome answers in this groundbreaking philosophical inquiry into the addictive mind. The author helps readers understand addiction.

192 pages

7236 Addictions Counseling
Crossroad Publishing Company
370 Lexington Avenue
New York, NY 10017-6503
212-532-3650
800-395-
Fax: 212-532-4922

A practical guide to counseling people with chemical and other addictions.

144 pages

Substance Abuse/Books

7237 Addictive Personality
Hazelden
15251 Pleasant Valley Road
Center City, MN 55012-9640
651-257-4010
800-328-9000
Fax: 651-213-4426
http://www.hazelden.org

Ellen Breyer, President

Understanding how an individual becomes an addict through examination of addiction's causes, stages of development, and consequences. Second edition further refines these ideas and includes the most recent information on the addictive process, cultural influences on addictive behaviors, recovery, genetic factors in addiction, mental health issues, and new research findings.

130 pages

7238 Addictive Thinking Understanding Self-Deception
Hazelden
15251 Pleasant Valley Road
Center City, MN 55012-9640
651-257-4010
800-328-9000
Fax: 651-213-4426
http://www.hazelden.org

Ellen Breyer, President

Illustrates the irrational perspective and complicated, contradictory thinking patterns of addictive thinking, and demonstrates how they lead to low self-esteem, addiction, and relapse. Revised edition includes expanded information on depression and affective disorders, the relationship between addictive thinking and relapse, and the new research related to the origins of addictive thinking.

140 pages

7239 Al-Anon Family Groups - Classic Edition
Al-Anon Family Group Headquarters
1600 Corporate Landing Parkway
Virginia Beach, VA 23454-5617
757-427-0680
Fax: 757-563-1655
e-mail: wso@alanon.org
http://www.al-anon.alateen.org

Basic book that explains the purpose of fellowship, how it works and how it is held in unity. Includes real life stories by husbands, wives, parents and children of those who suffer from alcoholism.

177 pages

7240 Alcoholics Anonymous, The Big Book
Hazelden
15251 Pleasant Valley Road
Center City, MN 55012-9640
651-257-4010
800-328-9000
Fax: 651-213-4426
http://www.hazelden.org

Ellen Breyer, President

Classic text that guides Alcoholics Anonymous programs and describes how millions of men and women have recovered from alcoholism.

575 pages

7241 Blueprint for Progress: Al-Anon's Fourth Step Inventory
Al-Anon Family Group Headquarters
1600 Corporate Landing Parkway
Virginia Beach, VA 23454-5617
757-563-1600
800-356-9996
Fax: 757-563-1655
e-mail: wso@al-anon.org
http://www.al-anon.alateen.org

A practical guide in taking the Fourth Step. Shows the way toward becoming self-nurturing while making a fearless moral search of ourselves.

64 pages

7242 Body, Mind and Spirit
Hazelden
15251 Pleasant Valley Road
Center City, MN 55012-9640
651-257-4010
800-328-9000
Fax: 651-213-4426
http://www.hazelden.org

Ellen Breyer, President

Addressing such issues as self-esteem, fear, anger, and spirituality, these 366 daily meditations and affirmations integrate the physical, mental, and spiritual aspects of healing from addiction.

410 pages

7243 Came to Believe
Alcoholics Anonymous
PO Box 459
New York, NY 10163
212-870-3400
Fax: 212-870-3137

Greg Muth, Manager

A collection of stories by AA members who write about what the phrase spiritual awakening means to them.

120 pages

7244 Concepts of Chemical Dependency, Third Edition
Brooks/Cole Publishing Company
511 Forest Lodge Road
Pacific Grove, CA 93950-5040
408-373-0728
Fax: 408-375-6414
e-mail: bc-info@brookscole.com
http://www.brookscole.com

A useful introduction to the basics of chemical dependency focusing on one substance at a time as it presents the facts about the most common chemicals of abuse and their effects.

473 pages

7245 Day at a Time Daily Reflections for Recovering People
Hazelden
15251 Pleasant Valley Road
Center City, MN 55012-9640
651-257-4010
800-328-9000
Fax: 651-213-4426
http://www.hazelden.org

Ellen Breyer, President

Offers inspiration and hope for people recovering from chemical dependency or other addictions. Each daily passage reinforces the message of Twelve Step recovery.

384 pages

7246 Day by Day
Hazelden
15251 Pleasant Valley Road
Center City, MN 55012-9640
651-257-4010
800-328-9000
Fax: 651-213-4426
http://www.hazelden.org

Ellen Breyer, President

A book of daily meditations for recovering addicts that reinforce Narcotics Anonymous principles and objectives.

400 pages

7247 Dual Disorders Recovery Book
Hazelden
15251 Pleasant Valley Road
Center City, MN 55012-9640
651-257-4010
800-328-0094
Fax: 651-213-4426
http://www.hazelden.org

Ellen Breyer, President

Helps individuals with dual disorders develop a plan for daily living through a specially designed Twelve-Step program.

242- pages

Substance Abuse/Books

7248 Each Day a New Beginning
Hazelden
15251 Pleasant Valley Road
Center City, MN 55012-9640
651-257-4010
800-328-9000
Fax: 651-213-4426
http://www.hazelden.org

Ellen Breyer, President

Promotes the development of a significant spiritual core for recovery that can be enhanced throughout the rest of the victims lives.

400 pages

7249 Eye Opener
Hazelden
15251 Pleasant Valley Road
Center City, MN 55012-9640
651-257-4010
800-328-9000
Fax: 651-213-4426
http://www.hazelden.org

Ellen Breyer, President

Daily meditations about understanding the Alcoholics Anonymous program, written by a favorite early AA member and author.

380 pages

7250 Gentle Path Through the Twelve Steps
Hazelden
15251 Pleasant Valley Road
Center City, MN 55012-9640
651-257-4010
800-328-0094
Fax: 651-213-4426
http://www.hazelden.org

Ellen Breyer, President

This workbook provides a unique set of structured forms and exercises to help recovering people integrate the Twelve Steps into all aspects of their lives.

224- pages

7251 Getting Started in AA
Hazelden
15251 Pleasant Valley Road
Center City, MN 55012-9640
651-257-4010
800-328-0094
Fax: 651-213-4426
http://www.hazelden.org

Ellen Breyer, President

Practical suggestions for staying sober, summaries of AA principles, concepts and slogans, and a historical overview to help the reader understand the spirit of the program.

211- pages

7252 God Grant Me the Laughter: A Treasury of Twelve Step Humor
Hazelden
15251 Pleasant Valley Road
Center City, MN 55012-9640
651-257-4010
800-328-0094
Fax: 651-213-4426
http://www.hazelden.org

Ellen Breyer, President

Hearty cartoons and humorous anecdotes clearly demonstrate how readers' lives today contrast with their drinking and drug using in the past.

200- pages

7253 Good First Step
Hazelden
15251 Pleasant Valley Road
Center City, MN 55012-9640
651-257-4010
800-328-0094
Fax: 651-213-4426
http://www.hazelden.org

Ellen Breyer, President

Features a structured format and emphasis on the meaning of the First Step to help build a solid foundation for recovery.

60 - pages

7254 Grateful to Have Been There
Hazelden
15251 Pleasant Valley Road
Center City, MN 55012-9640
651-257-4010
800-328-0094
Fax: 651-213-4426
http://www.hazelden.org

Ellen Breyer, President

Aide and executive secretary to AA's co-founder, Bill W. for 20 years, Wing shares her memories and impressions of 42 years of involvement with the Fellowship.

150 pages

7255 How Al-Anon Works for Families & Friends of Alcoholics
Al-Anon Family Group Headquarters
1600 Corporate Landing Parkway
Virginia Beach, VA 23454-5617
757-427-0680
800-356-9996
Fax: 757-563-1655
e-mail: wso@al-anon.org
http://www.al-anon.alateen.org

Everything you wanted to know about Al-Anon and more. This is the one book that has it all.

400 pages

7256 I'm Black and I'm Sober
Hazelden
15251 Pleasant Valley Road
Center City, MN 55012-9640
651-257-4010
800-328-9000
Fax: 651-213-4426
http://www.hazelden.org

Ellen Breyer, President

An autobiography written by a recovering African American woman who discusses the impact of discrimination and the obstacles faced through the journey back to sobriety.

279 pages

7257 In God's Care
Hazelden
15251 Pleasant Valley Road
Center City, MN 55012-9640
651-257-4010
800-328-0094
Fax: 651-213-4426
http://www.hazelden.org

Ellen Breyer, President

Excellent relaxation and education tool for clients working on their Second and Third Steps.

400- pages

7258 Keep It Simple
Hazelden
15251 Pleasant Valley Road
Center City, MN 55012-9640
651-257-4010
800-328-0094
Fax: 651-213-4426
http://www.hazelden.org

Ellen Breyer, President

Daily prayers that help clients learn to ask for help and to turn their self-will over to a Higher Power.

400- pages

7259 Keep Quit
Hazelden
15251 Pleasant Valley Road
Center City, MN 55012-9640
651-257-4010
800-328-9000
Fax: 651-213-4426
http://www.hazelden.org

Ellen Breyer, President

Daily motivational guide to help the new nonsmoker understand the craving for nicotine and learn how to break the rituals and patterns associated with relapse.

300 pages

Substance Abuse/Books

7260 Life of My Own: Daily Meditations on Hope and Acceptance
Hazelden
15251 Pleasant Valley Road
Center City, MN 55012-9640
651-257-4010
800-328-0094
Fax: 651-213-4426
http://www.hazelden.org

Ellen Breyer, President

Offers daily access to strength, serenity and insight in our relationships with chemically dependent people.

400- pages

7261 Little Red Book
Hazelden
15251 Pleasant Valley Road
Center City, MN 55012-9640
651-257-4010
800-328-9000
Fax: 651-213-4426
http://www.hazelden.org

Ellen Breyer, President

A primer for members of Alcoholics Anonymous. Each page acts as a study guide to the Big Book and its teachings.

164 pages

7262 Living Sober
Hazelden
15251 Pleasant Valley Road
Center City, MN 55012-9640
651-257-4010
800-328-9000
Fax: 651-213-4426
http://www.hazelden.org

Ellen Breyer, President

Offers clients sound advice about how to stay sober.

88 pages

7263 Lois Remembers
Al-Anon Family Group Headquarters
1600 Corporate Landing Parkway
Virginia Beach, VA 23454-5617
757-563-1600
800-356-9996
Fax: 757-563-1655
e-mail: wso@al-anon.org
http://www.al-anon.alateen.org

The memoirs of a co-founder of Al-Anon. Lois tells her personal story and recalls the eventful years before and after the funding of AA and Al-Anon.

204 pages

7264 My Mind is Out to Get Me: Humor and Wisdom in Recovery
Hazelden
15251 Pleasant Valley Road
Center City, MN 55012-9640
651-257-4010
800-328-9000
Fax: 651-213-4426
http://www.hazelden.org

Ellen Breyer, President

500 inspirational sayings and slogans that reflect both the lighter side of living a sober life and the profound wisdom offered in recovery. Each quote has been drawn from the wisdom of Alcoholics Anonymous.

180 pages

7265 Narcotics Anonymous
Hazelden
15251 Pleasant Valley Road
Center City, MN 55012-9640
651-257-4010
800-328-9000
Fax: 651-213-4426
http://www.hazelden.org

Ellen Breyer, President

Men and women describe the N.A. program and how it works.

289 pages

7266 One Day at a Time in Al-Anon
Al-Anon Family Group Headquarters
1600 Corporate Landing Parkway
Virginia Beach, VA 23454-5617
757-427-0680
800-356-9996
Fax: 757-563-1655
e-mail: wso@al-anon.org
http://www.al-anon.alateen.org

Inspirational daily readings cover various aspects of the Al-Anon philosophy and relate it to everyday situations. Large print.

376 pages

7267 Passages Through Recovery
Hazelden
15251 Pleasant Valley Road
Center City, MN 55012-9640
651-257-4010
800-328-0094
Fax: 651-213-4426
http://www.hazelden.org

Ellen Breyer, President

Guides clients through the six stages of recovery.

130- pages

7268 Program for You
Hazelden
15251 Pleasant Valley Road
Center City, MN 55012-9640
651-257-4010
800-328-9000
Fax: 651-213-4426
http://www.hazelden.org

Ellen Breyer, President

Study guide interpreting the original AA program as described in Alcoholics Anonymous and helps apply the wisdom to everyday life.

183 pages

7269 Quit & Stay Quit: A Personal Program to Stop Smoking
Hazelden
15251 Pleasant Valley Road
Center City, MN 55012-9640
651-257-4010
800-328-9000
Fax: 651-213-4426
http://www.hazelden.org

Ellen Breyer, President

Guide to nicotine recovery offerring an effective long-term program to quit by showing readers how smoking has subtly shaped their values, attitudes, and lives.

196 pages

7270 Quit Smoking Manual
American Lung Association
1740 Broadway
New York, NY 10019-4315
212-315-8700
Fax: 212-315-8870

John Kirkwood, CEO

Original self-help smoking cessation manual showing the public how to quit smoking in 20 days.

64 pages

7271 Recovery Journal for Exploring Who I Am
Hazelden
15251 Pleasant Valley Road
Center City, MN 55012-9640
651-257-4010
800-328-9000
Fax: 651-213-4426
http://www.hazelden.org

Ellen Breyer, President

Introduces clients to journal writing as an effective therapeutic adjunct for addiction recovery.

48 pages

Substance Abuse/Directories

7272 Resource Guide for Drug Management for Older Persons
National Council on the Aging
409 3rd Street W
Suite 200
Washington, DC 20024-3212
202-479-1200
800-867-2755
Fax: 202-479-0735

James P Firman, CEO

A resource to assist in developing a drug management program for older men and women. This guide consists of five sections that include an introduction to drug and the elderly, community involvement, strategies for using community resources and more.

45 pages

7273 Shame Faced
Hazelden
15251 Pleasant Valley Road
Center City, MN 55012-9640
651-257-4010
800-328-0094
Fax: 651-213-4426
http://www.hazelden.org

Ellen Breyer, President

Discusses the relationship between shame and chemical dependency.

28 - pages

7274 Skeptic's Guide to the Twelve Steps
Hazelden
15251 Pleasant Valley Road
Center City, MN 55012-9640
651-257-4010
800-328-0094
Fax: 651-213-4426
http://www.hazelden.org

Ellen Breyer, President

Investigates each of the Twelve Steps to gain a deeper understanding of a Higher Power.

241- pages

7275 Sober But Stuck
Hazelden
15251 Pleasant Valley Road
Center City, MN 55012-9640
651-257-4010
800-328-9000
Fax: 651-213-4426
http://www.hazelden.org

Ellen Breyer, President

Collection of personal stories by men and women who are long-time members of Alcoholics Anonymous. Each story shows the antidotes and resources which helped members break through the barriers that limited their enjoyment of a sober life.

215 pages

7276 Social Policy Prevention Handbook
African American Family Services
2616 Nicollet Avenue
Minneapolis, MN 55408-1628
612-871-7878
Fax: 612-871-2567
e-mail: bernice@aafs.net
http://www.aafs.net

Bernice Mack, Contact
Julie Jones, Manager

A manual that details IBCA's community based approach to the development of alcohol and drug abuse prevention strategies.

24 pages

7277 Substance Abuse Intervention, Prevention, Rehabilitation and Systems Change
Columbia University Press
136 S Broadway
Irvington, NY 10533
800-944-8648
Fax: 800-944-1844
http://www.cup.columbia.edu

Approach of social work practice with substance-abusing clients, bridging clinical, community, and social policy approaches in order to place individual addiction in its sociopolitical context.

7278 Substance Abuse and Physical Disability
Haworth Press
10 Alice Street
Binghamton, NY 13904-1503
607-722-5857
800-342-9678
Fax: 607-722-1424
e-mail: gctinfo@haworthpress.com
http://www.haworthpress.com

William Cohen, Owner

This book offers information on alcohol and drug abuse being a contributing factor in traumatic and disabling injuries.

289 pages

7279 Turnabout
Women for Sobriety
PO Box 618
Quakertown, PA 18951
215-536-8026
800-333-1606
Fax: 215-536-8026
e-mail: WFSobriety@aol.com
http://www.womenforsobriety.org

This is the story of the founder of Women for Sobriety and her struggle to quit drinking.

183 pages

Directories

7280 Alcoholism Information and Treatment Directory
infoUSA
PO Box 27347
Omaha, NE 68127
402-593-4600
800-555-6124
Fax: 402-331-5481
e-mail: internet@infousa.com
http://www.abii.com

Bill Hippen, Vice President

Contains 14,355 entries with specific information regarding all aspects of alcoholism and the recovery process.

Frequency: Annual

7281 Drug Abuse and Addiction Information/Treatment Programs
American Business Directories
5711 S 86th Circle
Omaha, NE 68127-4146
402-593-4600
Fax: 402-331-1505

Bill Hippen, Vice President

Number of entries is 9,425.

7282 National Conference on Drug Abuse Research & Practice
National Clearinghouse for Alcohol and Drug Info.
PO Box 2345
Rockville, MD 20847-2345
301-468-2600
800-729-6686
Fax: 301-468-2600
e-mail: info@health.org
http://www.health.org

Offers summaries of workshops, forums, dinner speeches and sessions presented at the National Conference on Drug Abuse Research and Practice.

275 pages

7283 National Directory of Drug and Alcohol Abuse Treatment and Programs
Office of Applied Studies
5600 Fishers Lane
Room 16-105
Rockville, MD 20857
301-443-0525
Fax: 301-443-9847
http://www.findtreatment.samhsa.gov

Deborah Trunzo, DASIS Team Leader
Gerri Scott-Pinkney, DASIS Team

11,000 listings of substance abuse treatment facilities across the nation.

Substance Abuse/Journals, Magazines

550 pages Frequency: Annual

Journals, Magazines

7284 **ACAP Recap**
American Council on Alcohol Problems
3426 Bridgeland Drive
Bridgeton, MO 63044-2603
314-739-5944
Fax: 314-739-0848
Offers information on organization activities and events, updates on resources and publications and legislative information for affiliate executives.

7285 **American Issue**
American Council on Alcohol Problems
3426 Bridgeland Drive
Bridgeton, MO 63044-2603
314-739-5944
Fax: 314-739-0848
Offered to contributors of the organization.

7286 **Drug Abuse Update**
2296 Henderson Mill Road NE
Suite 204
Atlanta, GA 30345-2739
770-934-6364
Fax: 404-248-1312
A journal of news and information for persons interested in drug prevention.

Newsletters, Pamphlets

7287 **AA Member - Medications and Other Drugs**
Alcoholics Anonymous
PO Box 459
New York, NY 10163
212-870-3400
Fax: 212-870-3137
Greg Muth, Manager
Report from a group of doctors in Alcoholics Anonymous.

7288 **AA Service Manual/Twelve Concepts for World Service**
Alcoholics Anonymous
PO Box 459
New York, NY 10163
212-870-3400
Fax: 212-870-3137
Gret Muth, Manager
This manual opens with a history of AA services.

7289 **AA and the Armed Services**
Alcoholics Anonymous
PO Box 459
New York, NY 10163
212-870-3400
Fax: 212-870-3137
Greg Muth, Manager
Personal stories tell how men and women in the military can beat a drinking problem.

7290 **AA and the Gay/Lesbian Alcoholic**
Alcoholics Anonymous
PO Box 459
New York, NY 10163
212-870-3400
Fax: 212-870-3137
Greg Muth, Manager
Excerpts from experience, strength and hope of sober gay and lesbian alcoholics.

7291 **AA as a Resource for Health Care Professionals**
Alcoholics Anonymous
PO Box 459
New York, NY 10163
212-870-3400
Fax: 212-870-3137
Greg Muth, Manager
Information about the Fellowship and describes some approaches that health care professionals use in referring problem drinkers to AA.

7292 **AA for the Native North American**
Alcoholics Anonymous
PO Box 459
New York, NY 10163
212-870-3400
Fax: 212-870-3137
Greg Muth, Manager
Addressed to and contains stories by Native American AA members.

7293 **AA for the Woman**
Alcoholics Anonymous
PO Box 459
New York, NY 10163
212-870-3400
Fax: 212-870-3137
Greg Muth, Manager
Relates the experiences of alcoholic women, all ages and from all walks of life.

7294 **AA in Correctional Facilities**
Alcoholics Anonymous
PO Box 459
New York, NY 10163
212-870-3400
Fax: 212-870-3137
Greg Muth, Manager
Experience based on the functioning of AA groups in prisons, with institutional opinions recommending AA as a helpful ally.

7295 **AA in Treatment Facilities**
Alcoholics Anonymous
PO Box 459
New York, NY 10163
212-870-3400
Fax: 212-870-3137
Greg Muth, Manager
Shares experiences of treatment facility administrators and of AA's who have carried the message into these facilities.

7296 **Al-Anon Fact File**
Al-Anon Family Group Headquarters
1600 Corporate Landing Parkway
Virginia Beach, VA 23454-5617
757-427-0680
800-356-9996
Fax: 757-563-1655
e-mail: wso@al-anon.org
http://www.al-anon.alateen.org
Factual information for the general public, media, professional community and those working in the field of alcohol treatment.
16 pages

7297 **Al-Anon Focus**
Al-Anon Family Group Headquarters
1600 Corporate Landing Parkway
Virginia Beach, VA 23454-5617
757-427-0680
800-356-9996
Fax: 757-563-1655
e-mail: wso@al-anon.org
http://www.al-anon.alateen.org
Recovering alcoholics find help in Al-Anon.
6 pages

Substance Abuse/Newsletters, Pamphlets

7298 **Al-Anon Is for Men**
Al-Anon Family Group Headquarters
1600 Corporate Landing Parkway
Virginia Beach, VA 23454-5617
757-427-0680
800-356-9996
Fax: 757-563-1655
e-mail: wso@al-anon.org
http://www.al-anon.alateen.org
Straightforward questions to help men identify their reactions to alcoholism in another person.
6 pages

7299 **Al-Anon Newcomer Packet**
Al-Anon Family Group Headquarters
1600 Corporate Landing Parkway
Virginia Beach, VA 23454-5617
757-427-0680
800-356-9996
Fax: 757-563-1655
e-mail: wso@al-anon.org
http://www.al-anon.alateen.org
Material specifically for the newcomer to Al-Anon packed in a handsome sleeve. Members can add local meeting information and literature of special interest.
8 pages

7300 **Al-Anon Spoken Here**
Al-Anon Family Group Headquarters
1600 Corporate Landing Parkway
Virginia Beach, VA 23454-5617
757-427-0680
800-356-9996
Fax: 757-563-1655
e-mail: wso@al-anon.org
http://www.al-anon.alateen.org
Why are Al-Anon meetings the way they are? Questions and answers that lead to a better understanding of the importance of keeping Al-Anon.
8 pages

7301 **Al-Anon and Professionals**
Al-Anon Family Group Headquarters
1600 Corporate Landing Parkway
Virginia Beach, VA 23454-5617
757-427-0680
800-356-9996
Fax: 757-563-1655
e-mail: wso@al-anon.org
http://www.al-anon.alateen.org
Questions and answers to help members and professionals learn how Al-Anon cooperates with the professional community.

7302 **Al-Anon, Newcomer's Packet**
Al-Anon Family Group Headquarters
1600 Corporate Landing Parkway
Virginia Beach, VA 23454-5617
757-427-0680
800-356-9996
Fax: 757-563-1655
e-mail: wso@al-anon.org
http://www.al-anon.alateen.org
Material specifically for the newcomer to Al-Anon packed in a handsome sleeve.

7303 **Al-Anon, You, and the Alcoholic**
Al-Anon Family Group Headquarters
1600 Corporate Landing Parkway
Virginia Beach, VA 23454-5617
757-427-0680
800-356-9996
Fax: 757-563-1655
e-mail: wso@al-anon.org
http://www.al-anon.alateen.org
Answers the most frequently asked questions about Al-Anon and how it helps families deal with problems brought about by alcoholism.
12 pages

7304 **Alateen Talks Back on Higher Power**
Al-Anon Family Group Headquarters
1600 Corporate Landing Parkway
Virginia Beach, VA 23454-5617
757-563-1600
800-356-9996
Fax: 757-563-1655
e-mail: wso@al-anon.org
http://www.al-anon.alateen.org
Members express views on the God of their understanding.
32 pages

7305 **Alcohol Alert #11: Estimating the Cost of Alcohol Abuse**
National Clearinghouse for Alcohol and Drug Info.
PO Box 2345
Rockville, MD 20847-2345
301-468-2600
800-729-6686
Fax: 301-468-2600
e-mail: info@health.org
http://www.health.org
Discusses the various problems of estimating the cost of alcohol abuse.

7306 **Alcohol Alert #15: Alcohol and AIDS**
National Clearinghouse for Alcohol and Drug Info.
PO Box 2345
Rockville, MD 20847-2345
301-468-2600
800-729-6686
Fax: 301-468-2600
e-mail: info@health.org
http://www.health.org
Discusses the relationship between alcohol consumption and HIV infection and AIDS.

7307 **Alcohol Alert #16: Moderate Drinking**
National Clearinghouse for Alcohol and Drug Info.
PO Box 2345
Rockville, MD 20847-2345
301-468-2600
800-729-6686
Fax: 301-468-2600
e-mail: info@health.org
http://www.health.org
Defines moderate drinking and explores the benefits and risks associated with moderate drinking.

7308 **Alcohol Alert #17: Treatment Outcome Research**
National Clearinghouse for Alcohol and Drug Info.
PO Box 2345
Rockville, MD 20847-2345
301-468-2600
800-729-6686
Fax: 301-468-2600
e-mail: info@health.org
http://www.health.org
Discusses purpose, methodology, randomization, blinding, followup and what treatment outcome research reveals.

7309 **Alcohol Alert #18: The Genetics of Alcoholism**
National Clearinghouse for Alcohol and Drug Info.
PO Box 2345
Rockville, MD 20847-2345
301-468-2600
800-729-6686
Fax: 301-468-2600
e-mail: info@health.org
http://www.health.org
Presents the results of studies that investigate the role of genes and the environment in the development of alcoholism.

7310 **Alcohol Alert #21: Alcohol and Cancer**
National Clearinghouse for Alcohol and Drug Info.
PO Box 2345
Rockville, MD 20847-2345
301-468-2600
800-729-6686
Fax: 301-468-2600
e-mail: info@health.org
http://www.health.org

Substance Abuse/Newsletters, Pamphlets

7311 Alcohol Alert #23: Alcohol and Minorities
National Clearinghouse for Alcohol and Drug Info.
PO Box 2354
Rockville, MD 20847-2354
301-468-2600
800-729-6686
Fax: 301-468-2600
e-mail: info@health.org
http://www.health.org

7312 Alcohol Alert #24: Animal Models in Alcohol Research
National Clearinghouse for Alcohol and Drug Info.
PO Box 2345
Rockville, MD 20847-2345
301-468-2600
800-729-6686
Fax: 301-468-2600
e-mail: info@health.org
http://www.health.org

7313 Alcohol Alert #25: Alcohol-Related Impairment
National Clearinghouse for Alcohol and Drug Info.
PO Box 2345
Rockville, MD 20847-2345
301-468-2600
800-729-6686
Fax: 301-468-2600
e-mail: info@health.org
http://www.health.org

7314 Alcohol Alert #26: Alcohol and Hormones
National Clearinghouse for Alcohol and Drug Info.
PO Box 2345
Rockville, MD 20847-2345
301-468-2600
800-729-6686
Fax: 301-468-2600
e-mail: info@health.org
http://www.health.org

7315 Alcohol Alert #27: Alcohol Medication Interactions
National Clearinghouse for Alcohol and Drug Info.
PO Box 2345
Rockville, MD 20847-2345
301-468-2600
800-729-6686
Fax: 301-468-2600
e-mail: info@health.org
http://www.health.org

7316 Alcohol and Drug Abuse in Black America: A Guide for Community Action
African American Family Services
2616 Nicollet Avenue
Minneapolis, MN 55408-1628
612-871-7878
Fax: 612-871-2567
e-mail: bernice@aafs.net
http://www.aafs.net

Bernice Mack, Contact
Julie Jones, Manager

A booklet giving a description of the history and the current manifestations of alcohol and drug problems in Black America with a discussion of strategies for fundamental change.
24 pages

7317 Alcoholics Anonymous and Employee Assistance Program
Alcoholics Anonymous
PO Box 459
New York, NY 10163
212-870-3400
Fax: 212-870-3137

Greg Muth, Manager

Of interest to management and union officials, this pamphlet gives concise descriptions of the help AA can offer to the alcoholic employee.

7318 Alcoholism Tends to Run in Families
National Clearinghouse for Alcohol and Drug Info.
PO Box 2345
Rockville, MD 20847-2345
301-468-2600
800-729-6686
Fax: 301-468-2600
e-mail: info@health.org
http://www.health.org

Provides answers and questions about how to help children of alcoholics and where to find resources for additional information.

7319 Alcoholism, a Merry-Go-Round Named Denial
Al-Anon Family Group Headquarters
1600 Corporate Landing Parkway
Virginia Beach, VA 23454-5617
757-563-1600
800-356-9996
Fax: 757-563-1655
e-mail: wso@al-anon.org
http://www.al-anon.alateen.org

Dramatic explanations that help family members and friends see the roles they play in the problems of alcoholism.
18 pages

7320 Alcoholism: The Family Disease
Al-Anon Family Group Headquarters
1600 Corporate Landing Parkway
Virginia Beach, VA 23454-5617
757-563-1600
800-356-9996
Fax: 757-563-1655
e-mail: wso@al-anon.org
http://www.al-anon.alateen.org

A treasury of information and inspiration, purpose of the Al-Anon program, actual stories for people who found serenity in Al-Anon.

7321 Anonymity
Al-Anon Family Group Headquarters
1600 Corporate Landing Parkway
Virginia Beach, VA 23454-5617
757-563-1600
800-356-9996
Fax: 757-563-1655
e-mail: wso@al-anon.org
http://www.al-anon.alateen.org

Offers information on Al-Anon and Alateen traditions and what a big factor anonymity plays for members.
6 pages

7322 Basic Al-Anon Program Card
Al-Anon Family Group Headquarters
1600 Corporate Landing Parkway
Virginia Beach, VA 23454-5617
757-427-0680
800-356-9996
Fax: 757-563-1655
e-mail: wso@al-anon.org
http://www.al-anon.alateen.org

Wallet card with the Preamble, Twelve Steps, Twelve Traditions and Serenity Prayer.

7323 Breaking the Chain of Substance Abuse and Hearing Loss
Self Help for Hard of Hearing People
7910 Woodmont Avenue
Suite 1200
Bethesda, MD 20814-7022
301-657-2248
Fax: 301-913-9413
e-mail: national@shhh.org
http://www.shhh.org
TTY 301-657-2249

Terry Portis, Executive Director

7324 Chemical Dependency Pamphlets
Greenhaven Press
PO Box 289009
San Diego, CA 92198-9009
858-485-7424
800-231-5163
Fax: 800-550-5480

Bruce Glassman, Owner

Pamphlet titles included in this set are: What are the causes of chemical dependency?; Is smoking harmful?; How harmful is alcohol?; Should drug laws be reformed?; Should pregnant women be prosecuted for drug abuse?; and How can chemical dependency be reduced?.

7325 Chemical Dependency and the African American
Hazelden
15251 Pleasant Valley Road
Center City, MN 55012-9640
651-257-4010
800-328-9000
Fax: 651-213-4426
http://www.hazelden.org

Ellen Breyer, President

Substance Abuse/Newsletters, Pamphlets

Reviews the impact alcohol and other drug abuse has on African American communities.

66 pages

7326 Chemical Dependency: An Acceptable Disease
Hazelden
15251 Pleasant Valley Road
Center City, MN 55012-9640
651-257-4010
800-328-9000
Fax: 651-213-4426
http://www.hazelden.org

Ellen Breyer, President

Help persons identify and acknowledge their chemical dependency.

14 pages

7327 Concepts: Al-Anon's Best Kept Secret?
Al-Anon Family Group Headquarters
1600 Corporate Landing Parkway
Virginia Beach, VA 23454-5617
757-427-0680
800-356-9996
Fax: 757-563-1655
e-mail: wso@al-anon.org
http://www.al-anon.alateen.org

An illustrated introduction to Al-Anon's third legacy - service. The Concepts are the Twelve Steps and Traditions expanded to the business level.

16 pages

7328 Cooperating with the Professional
1600 Corporate Landing Parkway
Virginia Beach, VA 23454-5617
757-563-1600
800-356-9996
Fax: 757-563-1655
e-mail: wso@al-anon.org
http://www.al-anon.alateen.org

All the information you need to get started in Al-Anon CPC service.

Frequency: 46 pieces

7329 Crack Cocaine - The Big Lie
National Clearinghouse for Alcohol and Drug Info.
PO Box 2345
Rockville, MD 20847-2345
301-468-2600
800-729-6686
Fax: 301-468-2600
e-mail: info@health.org
http://www.health.org

Offers information on what crack and cocaine are, how strong the addictions are from these drugs, how they affect the body and other risks in taking cocaine and crack.

7330 Crossing the Line Between Social Drinking and Alcoholism
Hazelden
15251 Pleasant Valley Road
Center City, MN 55012-9640
651-257-4010
800-328-9000
Fax: 651-213-4426
http://www.hazelden.org

Ellen Breyer, President

20 pages

7331 Denial
Hazelden
15251 Pleasant Valley Road
Center City, MN 55012-9640
651-257-4010
800-328-9000
Fax: 651-213-4426
http://www.hazelden.org

Ellen Breyer, President

Describes denial and its role in the five-stage acceptance process.

7332 Depression and Recovery From Chemical Dependency
Hazelden
15251 Pleasant Valley Road
Center City, MN 55012-9640
651-257-4010
800-328-9000
Fax: 651-213-4426
http://www.hazelden.org

Ellen Breyer, President

Outlines depression's warning signs.

7333 Detaching with Love
Hazelden
15251 Pleasant Valley Road
Center City, MN 55012-9640
651-257-4010
800-328-9000
Fax: 651-213-4426
http://www.hazelden.org

Ellen Breyer, President

Addresses the essential recovery tools clients need to cope with addiction and detach from the problem.

7334 Detachment
Al-Anon Family Group Headquarters
1600 Corporate Landing Parkway
Virginia Beach, VA 23454-5617
757-563-1600
800-356-9996
Fax: 757-563-1655
e-mail: wso@al-anon.org
http://www.al-anon.alateen.org

Everything you always wanted to know about detachment in an easy-to-use leaflet.

7335 Did You Grow Up with a Problem Drinker?
Al-Anon Family Group Headquarters
1600 Corporate Landing Parkway
Virginia Beach, VA 23454-5617
757-563-1600
800-356-9996
Fax: 757-563-1655
e-mail: wso@al-anon.org
http://www.al-anon.alateen.org

20 personal questions help individuals decide if they can benefit from Al-Anon.

7336 Do You Think You're Different?
Alcoholics Anonymous
PO Box 459
New York, NY 10163
212-870-3400
Fax: 212-870-3137

Greg Muth, Manager

Speaks to newcomers who may wonder how AA can work for someone different.

7337 Does She Drink Too Much?
Al-Anon Family Group Headquarters
1600 Corporate Landing Parkway
Virginia Beach, VA 23454-5617
757-563-1600
800-356-9996
Fax: 757-563-1655
e-mail: wso@al-anon.org
http://www.al-anon.alateen.org

Does a woman in your life drink too much? Men who found answers in Al-Anon share what has helped them.

12 pages

7338 Don't Lose a Friend to Drugs
National Crime Prevention Council
1000 Connecticut Avenue NW
Washington, DC 20036-5302
202-466-6272
Fax: 202-296-1356

Offers practical advice to teenagers on how to say no to drugs, how to help a friend who uses drugs and how to initiate community efforts to prevent drug use.

Substance Abuse/Newsletters, Pamphlets

7339 Drug Abuse Health Pamphlets
Greenhaven Press
PO Box 289009
San Diego, CA 92198-9009
858-485-7424
800-231-5163
Fax: 800-550-5480

Bruce Glassman, Owner

Offers informational pamphlets such as: How should the war on drugs be waged?; Are international drug campaigns effective?; Should drug testing be used?; What should be done about the drug problem in sports? and How should drugs be legally prescribed?.

7340 Drug Free Zones: A Manual
African American Family Services
2616 Nicollet Avenue
Minneapolis, MN 55408-1628
612-871-7878
Fax: 612-871-2567
e-mail: bernice@aafs.net
http://www.aafs.net

Bernice Mack, Contact
Julie Jones, Manager

This booklet describes a variety of strategies concerned citizens are using to reclaim their neighborhoods from rampant drug abuse and dealing.

24 pages

7341 Employer's Guide to Dealing with Substance Abuse
National Clearinghouse for Alcohol and Drug Info.
PO Box 2345
Rockville, MD 20847-2345
301-468-2600
800-729-6686
Fax: 301-468-2600
e-mail: info@health.org
http://www.health.org

Instructs employers in setting up comprehensive alcohol and other drug programs in the workplace.

18 pages

7342 Enabling
Hazelden
15251 Pleasant Valley Road
Center City, MN 55012-9640
651-257-4010
800-328-9000
Fax: 651-213-4426
http://www.hazelden.org

Ellen Breyer, President

Describes problems families encounter when they focus their lives on their chemically dependent family member.

7343 Facts About Alcohol Abuse
Medical Arts Center Hospital
57 W 57th Street
New York, NY 10019-2802
212-838-2169
Fax: 212-755-0200

Michael Richards, Data Processing Executive

A question and answer pamphlet that offers information on alcohol abuse and the effects the abuse has on the family unit.

7344 Family Denial
Hazelden
15251 Pleasant Valley Road
Center City, MN 55012-9640
651-257-4010
800-328-9000
Fax: 651-213-4426
http://www.hazelden.org

Ellen Breyer, President

Describes ways for families to recognize denial, examine common fears that cause denial and develop methods for overcoming it.

7345 Free to Care
Hazelden
15251 Pleasant Valley Road
Center City, MN 55012-9640
651-257-4010
800-328-9000
Fax: 651-213-4426
http://www.hazelden.org

Ellen Breyer, President

Explores today's definition of family and new attitudes about gender, technology, single-parents, relatives and friends.

7346 Freedom From Despair
Al-Anon Family Group Headquarters
1600 Corporate Landing Parkway
Virginia Beach, VA 23454-5617
757-563-1600
800-356-9996
Fax: 757-563-1655
e-mail: wso@alanon.org

A message of hope for those faced with a problem they can't solve alone.

4 pages

7347 Grieving
Hazelden
15251 Pleasant Valley Road
Center City, MN 55012-9640
651-257-4010
800-328-9000
Fax: 651-213-4426
http://www.hazelden.org

Ellen Breyer, President

Outlines the five-phase grieving process for clients and the significance of each.

7348 Guidance on Our Journeys
Hazelden
15251 Pleasant Valley Road
Center City, MN 55012-9640
800-328-9000
Fax: 651-213-4426
http://www.hazelden.org

Examines the relationship between the recovering person and his or her sponsor.

7349 Guide for the Family of the Alcoholic
Al-Anon Family Group Headquarters
1600 Corporate Landing Parkway
Virginia Beach, VA 23454-5617
757-563-1600
800-356-9996
Fax: 757-563-1655
e-mail: wso@al-anon.org
http://www.al-anon.alateen.org

A clear and realistic look at alcoholism, problems encountered by those close to the alcoholic and choices available to the family.

16 pages

7350 Homeward Bound
Al-Anon Family Group Headquarters
1600 Corporate Landing Parkway
Virginia Beach, VA 23454-5617
757-563-1600
800-356-9996
Fax: 757-563-1655
e-mail: wso@al-anon.org
http://www.al-anon.alateen.org

A booklet designed to help beginners make the transition from the family treatment setting to Al-Anon. Contains forty members' personal sharings, a basic glossary of Al-Anon terms, brief explanations of Al-Anon slogans and helpful suggestions for newcomers.

48 pages

Substance Abuse/Newsletters, Pamphlets

7351 How Drug Abuse Takes Profit Out of Buisness
National Clearinghouse for Alcohol and Drug Info.
PO Box 2345
Rockville, MD 20847-2345
301-468-2600
800-729-6686
Fax: 301-468-2600
e-mail: info@health.org
http://www.health.org

Answers employers questions about substance abuse in the workplace.

7352 How to Get the Most Out of Group Therapy
Hazelden
15251 Pleasant Valley Road
Center City, MN 55012-9640
651-257-4010
800-328-9000
Fax: 651-213-4426
http://www.hazelden.org

Ellen Breyer, President

Answers clients' questions about going to and getting help from group therapy.

7353 I Can't Be Addicted Because...
Hazelden
15251 Pleasant Valley Road
Center City, MN 55012-9640
651-257-4010
800-328-9000
Fax: 651-213-4426
http://www.hazelden.org

Ellen Breyer, President

Focuses on denial and elaborates on its most common forms.

7354 Ice Storm
Hazelden
15251 Pleasant Valley Road
Center City, MN 55012-9640
651-257-4010
800-328-9000
Fax: 651-213-4426
http://www.hazelden.org

Ellen Breyer, President

Prepares treatment professionals for the complications of one of the most recently synthesized drugs - ice.

7355 If Someone Close to You Has a Problem with Alcohol or Other Drugs
National Clearinghouse for Alcohol and Drug Info.
PO Box 2345
Rockville, MD 20847-2345
301-468-2600
800-729-6686
Fax: 301-468-2600
e-mail: info@health.org
http://www.health.org

This booklet is aimed at the general public and gives support and suggestions on coping with someone close who has an alcohol or drug problem.

7356 If You Are a Professional, AA Wants to Work with You
Alcoholics Anonymous
PO Box 459
New York, NY 10163
212-870-3400
Fax: 212-870-3137

Greg Muth, Manager

Directed at professionals of all types who deal with alcoholics.

7357 If Your Parents Drink Too Much
Al-Anon Family Group Headquarters
1600 Corporate Landing Parkway
Virginia Beach, VA 23454-5617
757-563-1600
800-356-9996
Fax: 757-563-1655
e-mail: wso@al-anon.org
http://www.al-anon.alateen.org

Alateen's cartoon booklet.

24 pages

7358 Index to Alcoholics Anonymous
Hazelden
15251 Pleasant Valley Road
Center City, MN 55012-9640
651-257-4010
800-328-9000
Fax: 651-213-4426

Ellen Breyer, President

Features page and line references to the topics discussed in Alcoholics Anonymous, the Big Book.

7359 Institutions Discount Package
Al-Anon Family Group Headquarters
1600 Corporate Landing Parkway
Virginia Beach, VA 23454-5617
757-563-1600
800-356-9996
Fax: 757-563-1655
e-mail: wso@al-anon.org
http://www.al-anon.alateen.org

A sampling of literature for Institutions groups and service projects.

7360 Institutions Service Kit
Al-Anon Family Group Headquarters
1600 Corporate Landing Parkway
Virginia Beach, VA 23454-5617
757-563-1600
800-356-9996
Fax: 757-563-1655
e-mail: wso@al-anon.org
http://www.al-anon.alateen.org

All the information needed to get started in Al-Anon Institutions service.

7361 Is AA for Me?
Alcoholics Anonymous
PO Box 459
New York, NY 10163
212-870-3400
Fax: 212-870-3137

Greg Muth, Manager

An illustrated easy to read version of the 12 questions in Is AA for You? pamphlet.

32 pages

7362 Is AA for You?
Alcoholics Anonymous
PO Box 459
New York, NY 10163
212-870-3400
Fax: 212-870-3137

Greg Muth, Manager

Symptoms of alcoholism are summed up in 12 questions most AA's had answered to identify themselves as alcoholics.

7363 Is There an Alcoholic in Your Life?
Alcoholics Anonymous
PO Box 459
New York, NY 10163
212-870-3400
Fax: 212-870-3137

Greg Muth, Manager

Explains the AA program as it affects anyone close to an alcoholic.

7364 It Happened to Alice
Alcoholics Anonymous
PO Box 459
New York, NY 10163
212-870-3400
Fax: 212-870-3137

Greg Muth, Manager

Easy to read comic-book style format for women alcoholics.

Substance Abuse/Newsletters, Pamphlets

7365 It Sure Beats Sitting in a Cell
Alcoholics Anonymous
PO Box 459
New York, NY 10163   212-870-3400
                            Fax: 212-870-3137
Greg Muth, Manager

An illustrated pamphlet which presents the experience of seven inmates who found AA while in prison. It also offers suggested dos and don'ts for staying sober after release.

7366 Let's Talk
Hazelden
15251 Pleasant Valley Road
Center City, MN 55012-9640   651-257-4010
                               800-328-9000
                            Fax: 651-213-4426
                         http://www.hazelden.org
Ellen Breyer, President

Offers 12 guidelines to promote effective communication between parent and child.

7367 Letter to a Woman Alcoholic
Alcoholics Anonymous
PO Box 459
New York, NY 10163   212-870-3400
                            Fax: 212-870-3137
Greg Muth, Manager

Describes with sensitive understanding the problem of the alcoholic woman.

7368 Letting Go of the Need to Control
Hazelden
15251 Pleasant Valley Road
Center City, MN 55012-9640   651-257-4010
                               800-328-9000
                            Fax: 651-213-4426
                         http://www.hazelden.org
Ellen Breyer, President

Discusses how control issues are common among chemically dependent people.

7369 Little More About Alcohol
Alcohol Research Information Service
1120 E Oakland Avenue
Lansing, MI 48906-5513   517-485-9900
Robert Hammond, Manager

A cartoon character explains the facts about alcohol and its effects on the body.

7370 Living Sober
Alcoholics Anonymous
PO Box 459
New York, NY 10163   212-870-3400
                            Fax: 212-870-3137
Greg Muth, Manager

Practical book demonstrating through simple examples, how AA members throughout the world live and stay sober one day at a time.
88 pages

7371 Living in a Shelter
Al-Anon Family Group Headquarters
1600 Corporate Landing Parkway
Virginia Beach, VA 23454-5617   757-563-1600
                                800-356-9996
                            Fax: 757-563-1655
                         e-mail: wso@al-anon.org
                         http://www.al-anon.alateen.org

7372 Living with Sobriety: Another Beginning
Al-Anon Family Group Headquarters
1600 Corporate Landing Parkway
Virginia Beach, VA 23454-5617   757-563-1600
                                800-356-9996
                            Fax: 757-563-1655
                         e-mail: wso@al-anon.org
                         http://www.al-anon.alateen.org

This book is for everyone who is trying to accept change, let go of guilt and resentment, deal with disappointments, improve communication and learn to be happy.
48 pages

7373 Look at Cross-Addiction
Hazelden
15251 Pleasant Valley Road
Center City, MN 55012-9640   651-257-4010
                               800-328-9000
                            Fax: 651-213-4426
Ellen Breyer, President

Discusses cross-addiction, denial, coping skills and avoidance.

7374 Look at Relapse
Hazelden
15251 Pleasant Valley Road
Center City, MN 55012-9640   651-257-4010
                               800-328-9000
                            Fax: 651-213-4426
Ellen Breyer, President

Addresses emotional consequences of relapse, such as decreased feelings of self-esteem and self-confidence.

7375 Managing Cocaine Cravings
Hazelden
15251 Pleasant Valley Road
Center City, MN 55012-9640   651-257-4010
                               800-328-9000
                            Fax: 651-213-4426
                         http://www.hazelden.org
Ellen Breyer, President

Offers clients hands-on plan to help them stay away from cocaine.

7376 Marijuana
Hazelden
15251 Pleasant Valley Road
Center City, MN 55012-9640   651-257-4010
                               800-328-9000
                            Fax: 651-213-4426
                         http://www.hazelden.org
Ellen Breyer, President

Outlines the physical and psychological effects of marijuana unique to episodic and chronic use.
65 pages

7377 Media Kit
Al-Anon Family Group Headquarters
1600 Corporate Landing Parkway
Virginia Beach, VA 23454-5617   757-563-1600
                                800-356-9996
                            Fax: 757-563-1655
                         e-mail: wso@al-anon.org
                         http://www.al-anon.alateen.org

An attractive silver folder containing information necessary to work with radio and TV stations.

7378 Member's Eye View of Alcoholics Anonymous
Alcoholics Anonymous
PO Box 459
New York, NY 10163   212-870-3400
                            Fax: 212-870-3137
Greg Muth, Manager

Designed to explain to people in the helping professionals how AA works.

Substance Abuse/Newsletters, Pamphlets

30 pages

7379 Members of the Clergy Ask About Alcoholics Anonymous
Alcoholics Anonymous
PO Box 459
New York, NY 10163
212-870-3400
Fax: 212-870-3137
Greg Muth, Manager

Introduction to AA for members of the clergy unfamiliar with the Fellowship.

7380 Memo to an Inmate Who May Be an Alcoholic
Alcoholics Anonymous
PO Box 459
New York, NY 10163
212-870-3400
Fax: 212-870-3137
Greg Muth, Manager

A message from AA's who have themselves been inmates. Their personal stories offer a new outlook to inmate alcoholics who want to know who AA can help.

7381 Men: Newcomer's Packet
Al-Anon Family Group Headquarters
1600 Corporate Landing Parkway
Virginia Beach, VA 23454-5617
757-563-1600
800-356-9996
Fax: 757-563-1655
e-mail: wso@al-anon.org
http://www.al-anon.alateen.org

For men who are not sure Al-Anon is for them, this collection offers a realistic look at alcoholism and straightforward answers to frequently asked questions.

7382 Message to Correctional Facilities Administrators
Alcoholics Anonymous
PO Box 459
New York, NY 10163
212-870-3400
Fax: 212-870-3137
Greg Muth, Manager

Information about what AA is and can do, and how groups function in correctional facilities.

7383 Military Packet
Al-Anon Family Group Headquarters
1600 Corporate Landing Parkway
Virginia Beach, VA 23454-5617
757-563-1600
800-356-9996
Fax: 757-563-1655
e-mail: wso@al-anon.org
http://www.al-anon.alateen.org

For those in the armed services with loved ones or colleagues who are alcoholic, here's a collection that says, Al-Anon can help.

7384 Moment to Reflect on Codependency
Hazelden
15251 Pleasant Valley Road
Center City, MN 55012-9640
651-257-4010
800-328-9000
Fax: 651-213-4426
Ellen Breyer, President

A collection of four booklets offering meditations that emphasize and reinforce self-esteem for young people recovering from addiction.

7385 Moment to Reflect on Self-Esteem
Hazelden
15251 Pleasant Valley Road
Center City, MN 55012-9640
651-257-4010
800-328-9000
Fax: 651-213-4426
http://www.hazelden.org
Ellen Breyer, President

Focuses on the fundamental recovery issue of self-esteem.

7386 NIDA Capsules
National Clearinghouse for Alcohol and Drug Info.
PO Box 2345
Rockville, MD 20847-2345
301-468-2600
800-729-6686
Fax: 301-468-2600
e-mail: info@health.org
http://www.health.org

7387 Newcomer Asks
Alcoholics Anonymous
PO Box 459
New York, NY 10163
212-870-3400
Fax: 212-870-3137
Greg Muth, Manager

Gives straightforward answers on 15 points that once puzzled many of us.

7388 Nonprescription Drugs: Modern Medicines for Mature Americans
National Council on the Aging
409 3rd Street SW
Suite 200
Washington, DC 20024-3212
202-479-1200
800-867-2755
Fax: 202-479-0735
James P Firman, CEO

Offers information on nonprescription drugs and medications for the elderly.

7389 Now What Do I Do for Fun?
Hazelden
15251 Pleasant Valley Road
Center City, MN 55012-9640
651-257-4010
800-328-9000
Fax: 651-213-4426
http://www.hazelden.org
Ellen Breyer, President

Explores the dilemma of finding new interests in recovery after completing treatment.

7390 Older Adults After Treatment
Hazelden
15251 Pleasant Valley Road
Center City, MN 55012-9640
651-257-4010
800-328-9000
Fax: 651-213-4426
http://www.hazelden.org
Ellen Breyer, President

Discusses aftercare issues, such as family relations, health, medication and relapse.

7391 Older Adults in Treatment
Hazelden
15251 Pleasant Valley Road
Center City, MN 55012-9640
651-257-4010
800-328-9000
Fax: 651-213-4426
http://www.hazelden.org
Ellen Breyer, President

Examines past beliefs about addiction and defines chemical dependency as a disease.

Substance Abuse/Newsletters, Pamphlets

7392 Our World Service Office
Al-Anon Family Group Headquarters
1600 Corporate Landing Parkway
Virginia Beach, VA 23454-5617
757-563-1600
800-356-9996
Fax: 757-563-1655
e-mail: wso@al-anon.org
http://www.al-anon.alateen.org
Briefly describes the function and services of Al-Anon's international clearinghouse, the World Service Office.
8 pages

7393 Preventing Relapse
Hazelden
15251 Pleasant Valley Road
Center City, MN 55012-9640
651-257-4010
800-328-9000
Fax: 651-213-4426
http://www.hazelden.org

Ellen Breyer, President

Offers practical information and personal stories to help clients better understand the relapse process.
28 pages

7394 Purpose and Suggestions
Al-Anon Family Group Headquarters
1600 Corporate Landing Parkway
Virginia Beach, VA 23454-5617
757-563-1600
800-356-9996
Fax: 757-563-1655
e-mail: wso@al-anon.org
http://www.al-anon.alateen.org
A brief introduction to Al-Anon with down-to-earth suggestions for making improvements.
6 pages

7395 Put on the Brakes Bulletin: Take a Look at College Drinking
National Clearinghouse for Alcohol and Drug Info.
PO Box 2345
Rockville, MD 20847-2345
301-468-2600
800-729-6686
Fax: 301-468-2600
e-mail: info@health.org
http://www.health.org
This second edition continues CSAP's campaign to raise awareness about the problems of college drinking.

7396 Quick List to Build Pride in Your Communities
National Clearinghouse for Alcohol and Drug Info.
PO Box 2345
Rockville, MD 20847-2345
301-468-2600
800-729-6686
Fax: 301-468-2600
e-mail: info@health.org
http://www.health.org
This parent guide is an adaptation of CSAP's Be Smart! Quick List: 10 Steps to Help Your Child Say No.

7397 Relapse and the Addict
Hazelden
15251 Pleasant Valley Road
Center City, MN 55012-9640
651-257-4010
800-328-9000
Fax: 651-213-4426
http://www.hazelden.org

Ellen Breyer, President

Identifies specific stages and triggers of relapse.

7398 Releasing Anger
Hazelden
15251 Pleasant Valley Road
Center City, MN 55012-9640
651-257-4010
800-328-9000
Fax: 651-213-4426
http://www.hazelden.org

Ellen Breyer, President

Discusses anger as a normal feeling and how anger can endanger recovery.

7399 Research on Drugs and the Workplace
National Clearinghouse for Alcohol and Drug Info.
PO Box 2345
Rockville, MD 20847-2345
301-468-2600
800-729-6686
Fax: 301-468-2600
e-mail: info@health.org
http://www.health.org
Discusses prevalence and costs to society of drug use in the workplace, along with information on employee assistance programs, drug testing, grants and additional resources.

7400 Sexual Intimacy and the Alcoholic Relationship
Al-Anon Family Group Headquarters
1600 Corporate Landing Parkway
Virginia Beach, VA 23454-5617
757-563-1600
800-356-9996
Fax: 757-563-1655
e-mail: wso@al-anon.org
http://www.al-anon.alateen.org
Sex and alcohol? Al-Anon members face this personal problem when they apply to the Al-Anon program indexed.
48 pages

7401 So You Love an Alcoholic
Al-Anon Family Group Headquarters
1600 Corporate Landing Parkway
Virginia Beach, VA 23454-5617
757-563-1600
800-356-9996
Fax: 757-563-1655
e-mail: wso@al-anon.org
http://www.al-anon.alateen.org
First steps to a changed attitude toward the alcoholic.
6 pages

7402 Sponsorship: What It's All About
Al-Anon Family Group Headquarters
1600 Corporate Landing Parkway
Virginia Beach, VA 23454-5617
757-563-1600
800-356-9996
Fax: 757-563-1655
e-mail: wso@al-anon.org
http://www.al-anon.alateen.org
An important part of getting the program and then giving it away is sponsorship.
12 pages

7403 Stress in Recovery
Hazelden
15251 Pleasant Valley Road
Center City, MN 55012-9640
651-257-4010
800-328-9000
Fax: 651-213-4426
http://www.hazelden.org

Ellen Breyer, President

Outlines methods for clients to overcome stress in their daily lives.

7404 Substance Abuse Funding News
CD Publications
8204 Fenton Street
Silver Spring, MD 20910-4502
301-588-6380
Fax: 301-588-6385
e-mail: info@cdpublications.com
http://www.cdpublications.com

Michael Gerecht, President

Detailed coverage of private and federal funding opportunities for alcohol, tobacco and drug abuse programs. Plus advice on successful grantseeking strategies and news affecting your programs.

7405 This Is AA
Alcoholics Anonymous
PO Box 459
New York, NY 10163
212-870-3400
Fax: 212-870-3137

Greg Muth, Manager

Substance Abuse/Newsletters, Pamphlets

A pamphlet offering an introduction to the AA recovery program.

7406 This Is Al-Anon
Al-Anon Family Group Headquarters
1600 Corporate Landing Parkway
Virginia Beach, VA 23454-5617
757-563-1600
800-356-9996
Fax: 757-563-1655
e-mail: wso@al-anon.org
http://www.al-anon.alateen.org

Explains Al-Anon through the Opening/Welcome, Preamble, Serenity Prayer, Twelve Steps and Traditions.

16 pages

7407 Three Talks to Medical Societies
Alcoholics Anonymous
PO Box 459
New York, NY 10163
212-870-3400
Fax: 212-870-3137

Greg Muth, Manager

Contains Bill Wilson's, the co-founder of AA, principles borrowed from medicine and religion and a summary of AA's first 23 years.

7408 Three Views of Al-Anon
Al-Anon Family Group Headquarters
1600 Corporate Landing Parkway
Virginia Beach, VA 23454
757-427-0680
800-356-9996
Fax: 757-563-1655
e-mail: wso@al-anon.org
http://www.al-anon.alateen.org

AA members tell how Al-Anon and AA cooperate to help alcoholics and their families.

8 pages

7409 Time to Start Living
Alcoholics Anonymous
PO Box 459
New York, NY 10163
212-870-3400
Fax: 212-870-3137

Greg Muth, Manager

Addresses the older alcoholic, with nine stories of men and women who came to AA after the age of 60 (large print edition is also available).

7410 Twelve Steps Illustrated
Alcoholics Anonymous
PO Box 459
New York, NY 10163
212-870-3400
Fax: 212-870-3137

Greg Muth, Manager

An easy-to-read version of AA's twelve steps.

7411 Twelve Steps and Traditions
Al-Anon Family Group Headquarters
1600 Corporate Landing Parkway
Virginia Beach, VA 23454-5617
757-563-1600
800-356-9996
Fax: 757-563-1655
e-mail: wso@al-anon.org
http://www.al-anon.alateen.org

Handy guide to understanding and using Al-Anon's Steps and Traditions in our daily lives.

32 pages

7412 Twelve Steps for Tobacco Users
Hazelden
15251 Pleasant Valley Road
Center City, MN 55012-9640
651-257-4010
800-328-9000
Fax: 651-213-4426
http://www.hazelden.org

Ellen Breyer, President

Presents the Surgeon General's findings that classify nicotine as an addictive substance.

25 pages

7413 Understanding Depression and Addiction
Hazelden
15251 Pleasant Valley Road
Center City, MN 55012-9640
651-257-4010
800-328-9000
Fax: 651-213-4426
http://www.hazelden.org

Ellen Breyer, President

29 pages

7414 Understanding Major Anxiety Disorders and and Addiction
Hazelden
15251 Pleasant Valley Road
Center City, MN 55012-9640
800-328-9000
Fax: 651-213-4426
http://www.hazelden.org

36 pages

7415 Understanding Ourselves and Alcoholism
Al-Anon Family Group Headquarters
1600 Corporate Landing Parkway
Virginia Beach, VA 23454-5617
757-563-1600
800-356-9996
Fax: 757-563-1655
e-mail: wso@al-anon.org
http://www.al-anon.alateen.org

Explains how compulsion, obsession and denial affect those close to an alcoholic as well as the alcoholic.

6 pages

7416 Understanding Personality Problems and Addiction
Hazelden
15251 Pleasant Valley Road
Center City, MN 55012-9640
651-257-4010
800-328-9000
Fax: 651-213-4426
http://www.hazelden.org

Ellen Breyer, President

Describes common features of personality problems, such as self-centeredness and setting boundaries.

28 pages

7417 Understanding Post-Traumatic Stress Disorder and Addiction
Hazelden
15251 Pleasant Valley Road
Center City, MN 55012-9640
651-257-4010
800-328-9000
Fax: 651-213-4426
http://www.hazelden.org

Ellen Breyer, President

17 pages

7418 Up Front Drug Information
5701 Biscayne Boulevard
Apt 602
Miami, FL 33137-2696
786-242-8222

Carlos Zaldivar, Administrator

Provides information on drugs and drug referrals.

Substance Abuse/Videos, Audio Tapes

7419 What Are the Signs of Alcoholism?
Hazelden
15251 Pleasant Valley Road
Center City, MN 55012-9640
651-257-4010
800-328-9000
Fax: 651-213-4426
http://www.hazelden.org

Ellen Breyer, President

Self-test for clients to review the role of alcohol in their lives.

7420 What Do You Do About the Alcoholics' Drinking?
Al-Anon Family Group Headquarters
1600 Corporate Landing Parkway
Virginia Beach, VA 23454-5617
757-563-1600
800-356-9996
Fax: 757-563-1655
e-mail: wso@al-anon.org
http://www.al-anon.alateen.org

Shows errors most people make in trying to cope with the problem of alcoholism before Al-Anon.

8 pages

7421 What Happened to Joe?
Alcoholics Anonymous
PO Box 459
New York, NY 10163
212-870-3400
Fax: 212-870-3137

Greg Muth, Manager

Dramatic story of a young construction worker and his drinking problem, told in brightly colored comic book style.

7422 What Is AA ?
Hazelden
15251 Pleasant Valley Road
Center City, MN 55012-9640
651-257-4010
800-328-9000
Fax: 651-213-4426
http://www.hazelden.org

Ellen Breyer, President

Answers the basic questions about Alcoholics Anonymous.

7423 What Is NA ?
Hazelden
15251 Pleasant Valley Road
Center City, MN 55012-9640
651-257-4010
800-328-9000
Fax: 651-213-4426
http://www.hazelden.org

Ellen Breyer, President

Helps clients evaluate their addiction to narcotics and answers their questions about N.A.

7424 When I Got Busy, I Got Better
Al-Anon Family Group Headquarters
1600 Corporate Landing Parkway
Virginia Beach, VA 23454-5617
757-563-1600
800-356-9996
Fax: 757-563-1655
e-mail: wso@al-anon.org
http://www.al-anon.alateen.org

Tried and true methods of building self-esteem and confidence while getting rid of anxiety and guilt.

64 pages

7425 When You Go Back to Work
Hazelden
15251 Pleasant Valley Road
Center City, MN 55012-9640
651-257-4010
800-328-9000
Fax: 651-213-4426
http://www.hazelden.org

Ellen Breyer, President

Stories demonstrating co-workers' attitudes clients may face upon their return to work.

7426 Where Do I Go From Here?
Alcoholics Anonymous
PO Box 459
New York, NY 10163
212-870-3400
Fax: 212-870-3137

Greg Muth, Manager

For people leaving treatment facilities, single-sheet flyer tells of continuing help offered by outside AAs.

7427 Why Is Al-Anon Anonymous?
Al-Anon Family Group Headquarters
1600 Corporate Landing Parkway
Virginia Beach, VA 23454-5617
757-563-1600
800-356-9996
Fax: 757-563-1655
e-mail: wso@al-anon.org
http://www.al-anon.alateen.org

Stresses the importance of preserving anonymity of Al-Anon and AA members.

8 pages

7428 Workers at Risk: Drugs and Alcohol onthe Job
National Clearinghouse for Alcohol and Drug Info.
PO Box 2345
Rockville, MD 20847-2345
301-468-2600
800-729-6686
Fax: 301-468-2600
e-mail: info@health.org
http://www.health.org

Gives facts about drugs in the workplace and suggests appropriate behavior for employees who are confronted with a coworker's use of alcohol or other drugs.

7429 You Can Help Your Community Get Rid of Drugs
National Clearinghouse for Alcohol and Drug Info.
PO Box 2345
Rockville, MD 20847-2345
301-468-2600
800-729-6686
Fax: 301-468-2600
e-mail: info@health.org
http://www.health.org

Supports drug abuse treatment and explains how drug use can create problems for your community.

7430 Your Job and HIV: Are There Risks?
American Red Cross
1616 Fort Myer Drive
17th Floor
Arlington, VA 22209-3110
703-312-8724
Fax: 703-312-8738

Sandra L Mertz, Product Manager

Videos, Audio Tapes

7431 Alcoholics Anonymous: An Inside View
Alcoholics Anonymous
PO Box 459
New York, NY 10163
212-870-3400
Fax: 212-870-3137

Greg Muth, Manager

Depicts alcoholics, recovering in A.A., going about their daily lives, attending A.A. meetings, and other gatherings.

Frequency: 28 minutes

7432 Art of Living with Change: Turning Your Good Intentions Into Progress...
Hazelden
15251 Pleasant Valley Road
Center City, MN 55012-9640
651-257-4010
800-328-0094
Fax: 651-213-4426
http://www.hazelden.org

Ellen Breyer, President

Video. 45 minutes

Substance Abuse/Websites

7433 Bill Discusses the Twelve Traditions
Alcoholics Anonymous
PO Box 459
New York, NY 10163
212-870-3400
Fax: 212-870-3137

Greg Muth, Manager

Bill W. tells how the principles safe-guarding A.A. unity developed.
Frequency: 60 minutes

7434 Bill's Own Story
Alcoholics Anonymous
PO Box 459
New York, NY 10163
212-369-7070
Fax: 212-870-3137

Leonard Biel Jr, MD

Co-founder Bill W. tells of his drinking and recovery.
Frequency: 60 minutes

7435 Caring for Ourselves: Hope for Healthy Relationships
Hazelden
15251 Pleasant Valley Road
Center City, MN 55012-9640
651-257-4010
800-328-9000
Fax: 651-213-4426
http://www.hazelden.org

Ellen Breyer, President

Video. 50 minutes

7436 Hope: Alcoholics Anonymous
Alcoholics Anonymous
PO Box 459
New York, NY 10163
212-870-3400
Fax: 212-870-3137

Greg Muth, Manager

Explains the principles of AA: what it is, steps, traditions, sponsorship, and basic recovery tools.
Frequency: 15 minutes

7437 Markings on the Journey
Alcoholics Anonymous
PO Box 459
New York, NY 10163
212-870-3400
Fax: 212-870-3137

Greg Muth, Manager

Videocassette depicts 45 years of AA history, using rare materials from our archives.

Websites

7438 Al-Anon

http://www.al-anon.alateen.org
The single purpose of this organization is to help families and friends of alcoholics, whether the alcoholic is still drinking or not.

7439 American Council for Drug Education

http://www.acdc.org
This organization provides information on drug use, develops media campaigns, reviews scientific findings, publishes books and offers films and curriculum materials for prevention.

7440 CSAP State Liason Program

http://www.samhsa.gov
This program is designed to support alcohol and other drug abuse prevention efforts in the States.

7441 Center for Substance Abuse Prevention

http://www.samhsa.gov
This organization's goal is to connect people and resources with innovative ideas, strategies and programs designed to encourage creative and effective efforts aimed at reducing and eliminating alcohol, tobacco and other drug problems in our society.

7442 Cocaine Anonymous

http://www.ca.org
A support group based on the twelve steps of Alcoholics Anonymous that focuses specifically on problems of cocaine addiction.

7443 Food and Drug Administration

http://www.fda.gov
The FDS is responsible for protecting the public health by assuring the safety, efficacy, and security of human and veterinary drugs, biological products, medical devices, our nation's food supply, cosmetics, and products that emit emit radiation.

7444 Health Answers

http://www.healthanswers.com
Information on substance abuse, including articles and resources.

7445 Healthlink USA

http://www.healthlinkusa.com
Excellent health information concerning treatment, cures, prevention, diagnosis, risk factors, research, support groups, email lists, personal stories and much more. Updated regularly.

7446 Indian Health Service

http://www.tuscon.ihs.gov
Charged with providing a comprehensive program of alcoholism and substance abuse prevention and treatment for Native Americans and Alaskan natives.

7447 National Clearinghouse for Alcohol and Drug Information

http://www.health.org

7448 National Council on Alcoholism and Drug Dependence

http://www.ncadd.org
Provides education, information, help and hope in the fight against addictions. Nationwide network of affiliates, advocates prevention, intervention and treatment, and is committed to ridding the disease of its stigma and its sufferers of their denial and shame.

7449 Peter Lamy Center for Drug Therapy and Aging

http://www.pharmacy.umaryland.edu
The Lamy Center is dedicated to improving drug therapy for aging adults through innovative research, education and clinical initiatives.

7450 Substance Abuse and Mental Health Services Administration

http://www.samhsa.gov
The goal of this organization is to reduce incidence and prevalence of mental disorders and substance abuse and improve treatment outcomes for persons suffering from addictive and mental health problems and disorders.

Substance Abuse/Research Centers

Research Centers

7451 American Academy of Addiction Psychiatry
7301 Mission Road
Suite 252
Prairie Village, KS 66208-3033
913-262-6161
Fax: 913-262-4311
e-mail: info@aaap.org
http://www.aaap.org

Becky Stein, Executive Director

Psychiatrists and other health care and mental health professionals treating people with addictions. Promotes excellence in the treatment of addictions; seeks to insure availability of addiction treatment programs; encourages improvement in the training of health and mental health care providers treating people with addictions.nsulting services to public policy makers. Serves as a clearinghouse on addictions and their treatment; provides support and assistance to addictions research.

7452 Boston University Laboratory of Neuropsychology
Department of Behavioral Neuroscience
80 E Concord Street
M-9
Boston, MA 02118-2307
617-638-4803
Fax: 617-638-4806

Marlene Oscar Berman PhD, Chief

Offers research and studies into the effects of Alcoholism pertaining to aphasia, apraxia, dementia, memory disorders and various other neurological malfunctions.

7453 Center for Alcohol & Addiction Studies
Brown University
PO Box G-B
Providence, RI 02912
401-444-1818
Fax: 401-444-1850
e-mail: denise_bayles@brown.edu
http://http://center.butler.brown.edu

Phyllis Joan Kuhn PhD, Director
David C Lewis, MD

The Center for Alcohol and Addiction Studies, through its affiliation with the Brown Medical School, occupies a unique position within the University. The Center brings together more that 90 faculty and professional staff members, from 11 University departments and eight affiliated hospitals, to promote the identification, prevention, and effective treatment of alcohol and other substance abuse.

7454 Center for Applied Prevention Research
4760 Walnut Street
Suite 106
Boulder, CO 80301-2561
303-443-5696
Fax: 303-443-4373

Bob D'Alessandro, Executive Director

Prevention of alcohol and drug abuse is the main focus of the research studies.

7455 Dorothea Dix Hospital: Clinical Research Unit
S Boylan Avenuenue
Raleigh, NC 27611
919-733-5540
Fax: 919-733-5351

James C Garbutt MD, Director
Walter Stelle, CEO

Researches the biological risk factors of alcoholism using young adults without the disease but with a history of familial alcoholism.

7456 Ernest Gallo Clinic and Research Center
San Francisco General Hospital
5858 Horton Street
Suite 200
Emeryville, CA 94608-2007
510-985-3100
Fax: 510-985-3101

Dr. Ivan Diamond, Contact

Alcoholism studies with a special emphasis on genetics.

7457 Friends Medical Science Research Center
2330 W Joppa Road
Suite 103
Lutherville, MD 21093-4605
410-747-0243
Fax: 410-744-8344

Meta P Barton, President

Studies narcotic addictions.

7458 Hahnemann University Laboratory of Human Pharmacology
Department of Pharmacology
Broad & Vine Streets
Philadelphia, PA 19102
215-762-8618
Fax: 215-448-3722

Benjamin Calesnick MD, Director

7459 Hamot Medical Center: Research Department
201 State Street
Erie, PA 16550
814-877-6000
Fax: 814-877-7590
http://www.hamot.org

Phyllis Joan Kuhn PhD, Director
John Malone, CEO

Drug evaluations and medical products.

7460 Hazeldon Foundation: Library and Information Resources
PO Box 11
Center City, MN 55012-0011
651-213-4200
800-257-7810
Fax: 651-213-4411
e-mail: info@hazelden.org
http://www.hazeldon.org

Barbara S Weiner, MLS. Ref. Cons.
Richard Kling, Chairman

Since its 1949 founding in a rural Minnesota lakeside farmhouse, Hazelden has grown into one of the world's largest, most respected, and best-known private alcohol and drug rehabilitation centers in the world. Thousands of people from all 50 states and 42 foreign countries have turned to Hazelden to find expertise, quality care, and leading authorities on addiction and recovery issues. Our mission today remains the same as our early founders had dreamed - to help alcoholics and addicts who need help.
1966

7461 Interdisciplinary Program in Cell and Molecular Pharmacology
Medical University of South Carolina
173 Ashley Avenue
Charleston, SC 29425
843-792-2476
Fax: 843-792-2475

Dr. Harry Margolis, Chariman

Research into pharmacology and toxicology.

7462 Johns Hopkins Behavioral Pharmacology Research Unit
School of Medicine
4940 Eastern Avenue
Baltimore, MD 21224-2735
410-550-0616
Fax: 410-550-0030

George E Bigelow PhD, Scientific Director
Patty King, Manager

7463 Maine State Office of Substance Abuse: Information and Resource Center
11 State House Station
Augusta, ME 04333-0011
207-287-2595
Fax: 207-287-4334
e-mail: osa.ircosa@maine.gov
http://www.maine.gov/dhhs/osa/about/index.htm
TTY 800-606-0215

Richard Hayward, Director Information Systems
Jo McCaslin, Librarian
Kimberly Johnson, Director

Substance Abuse/Research Centers

The Maine Office of Substance Abuse is the single state administrative authority responsible for the planning, development, implementation, regulation, and evaluation of substance abuse services. The Office provides leadership in substance abuse prevention, intervention, and treatment. Its goal is to enhance the health and safety of Maine citizens through the reduction of the overall impact of substance use, abuse, and dependency.
1979

7464 Narcotic and Drug Research
11 Beach Street
New York, NY 10013-2429
212-966-8700
Fax: 212-334-8058

Douglas S Lipton PhD, Director
Arthur Liu, CEO

Nonprofit organization that is devoted to drug abuse education, treatment and prevention.

7465 National Association of Perinatal Addiction Research and Education
11 E Hubbard Street
Suite 200
Chicago, IL 60611-5631
312-629-4321
800-638-BABY

The mission of NAPARE is to offer leadership in the development of multidisciplinary programs for the prevention and treatment of alchohol and other drug use in pregnancy. A goal of NAPARE is to provide a national network among professionals for the exchange of ideas regarding prevention and intervention.

7466 National Clearinghouse for Alcohol and Drug Information Library (NCADI)
11420 Rockville Pike
PO Box 2345
Rockville, MD 20847-2345
301-468-2600
800-729-6686
Fax: 301-468-2600
e-mail: info@health.org
http://www.health.org/research/

John Fay, Librarian

National Clearinghouse for Alcohol and Drug Information (NCADI) is the Nation's one-stop resource for information about substance abuse prevention and addiction treatment. We staff both English- and Spanish-speaking information specialists who are skilled at recommending appropriate publications, posters, and videocassettes; conducting customized searches; providing grant and funding information; and referring people to appropriate organizations. The NCADI library has hundreds of journals, newspapers, magazines, and reference books, plus equipment for reviewing audiotapes and videotapes.
1987

7467 National Development and Research Institutes: Library/Resource Center
71 West 23rd Street
8th Floor
New York, NY 10048-1698
212-845-4400
Fax: 212-438-0894
e-mail: bernard.arons@ndri.org
http://http://www.ndri.org/

Bernard S Arons MD, Executive Director/CEO
John A Dale, President
John G Nolan, Treasurer
1976

7468 National Institute on Drug Abuse Addiction Research Center Library (NIDA)
6001 Executive Boulevard
Room 5213
Bethesda, MD 20892-9561
410-550-1488
Fax: 410-550-1438
e-mail: mpfeiffe@intra.nida.nih.gov
http://www.nida.nih.gov/

Mary Pfieffer, Librarian

NIDA's mission is to lead the Nation in bringing the power of science to bear on drug abuse and addiction. Recent scientific advances have revolutionized our understanding of drug abuse and addiction. The majority of these advances, which have dramatic implications for how to best prevent and treat addiction, have been supported by the National Institute on Drug Abuse (NIDA). NIDA supports over 85 percent of the world's research on the health aspects of drug abuse and addiction. NIDA supported science addresses the most fundamental and essential questions about drug abuse, ranging from the molecule to managed care, and from DNA to community outreach research.

7469 Office of Applied Studies
Substance Abuse & Mental Health Services Offices
5600 Fishers Lane
Room 16-105
Rockville, MD 20857
301-443-8956
Fax: 301-443-9847
http://www.samhsa.gov

Mark Weber, Manager

Provides the leadership needed for collecting data on mental illness and substance abuse, including incidence and prevalence studies.

7470 Ohio Department of Drug and Alcohol Addiction Services: Ohio Prevention and Education Resource Center
280 North High Street
12th Floor
Cincinnati, OH 43215
614-466-3445
800-788-7254
Fax: 614-752-8645
e-mail: INFO@ada.state.oh.us
http://www.uc.edu/www/operc/

Carolyn Givens, Director

The Division of Prevention Services is committed to meeting the prevention needs of all individuals, families and communities in Ohio through the further development of an evidence-based prevention system. The Division is dedicated to working with local partners to assist them in increasing their capacity to implement evidence based practices, programs and strategies.

7471 Ohio State University: Division of Clinical Trials
333 W 10th Avenue
Columbus, OH 43210-1239
614-292-8600
800-854-4461
Fax: 614-292-7232
http://www.ohio-state.edu

Wolfgang Sadee, Professor/Chairman
Glen Apseloff MD, Clinical Trials

Clinical studies and clinical pharmacology research.

7472 Research Institute on Alcoholism
1021 Main Street
Buffalo, NY 14203-1014
716-887-2387
Fax: 716-887-2252
e-mail: webmaster@ria.buffalo.edu
http://www.ria.buffalo.edu

Kathleen M Weavers, Director Public Communications
Gerard Connors, Executive Director

Research center within the University at Buffalo. The State University of New York.

7473 Rockefeller University Laboratory of Biology
1230 York Avenue
New York, NY 10021-6399
212-327-8000
Fax: 212-570-7974

Vincent P Doyle, Head Master
Paul Nurse, President

7474 Ruth E Golding Clinical Pharmacokinetics Laboratory
College of Pharmacy
PO Box 210207
Tucson, AZ 85721
520-626-2823
Fax: 520-626-2466
e-mail: gandolfi@pharmacy.arizona.edu
http://www.pharmacy.arizona.edu

Michael Mayersohn, Head Master

Substance Abuse/Research Centers

Conducts studies of drugs in humans and animals.

7475 Southern California Research Institute
11912 W Washington Boulevard
Los Angeles, CA 90066-5816
213-427-3200
Fax: 310-398-6651
Dr. M Burns, Director
Dirk Stoehr, Manager

Effects of alcohol and drugs on behavior studies.

7476 Stanford Center for Research in Disease Prevention
Stanford University School of Medicine
211 Quarry Road
Palo Alto, CA 94304-1416
650-723-6963
Fax: 650-725-6906
John W Farquhar MD, Director
Jackie Keeling, Manager

Prevention and control of alcohol and drug abuse related disorders.

7477 Substance Abuse and Mental Health Services Administration
Office of Communications
5600 Fishers Lane
Rockville, MD 20857
301-443-8956
Fax: 301-443-9050
http://www.samhsa.gov
Mark Weber, Manager

The goal of this organization is to reduce incidence and prevalence of mental disorders and substance abuse and improve treatment outcomes for persons suffering from addictive and mental health problems and disorders.

7478 University of Alabama: Center for Alcohol and Addiction Studies
3211 Providence Drive
Anchorage, AK 99508-4614
907-786-1805
Fax: 907-786-4866
Dennis Fisher, Director

Basic, applied and evaluative research into alcohol and substance abuse.

7479 University of California: Los Angeles Alcohol Research Center
760 Westwood Plaza
Los Angeles, CA 90095-8353
310-825-7692
Fax: 310-206-7309
Dr. Ernest Noble, Director
Edward Wiesmeir, MD

Causes of alcoholism, including genetics.

7480 University of Delaware: Center for Drug and Alcohol Studies
Department of Social & Criminal Justice
77 E Main Street
Newark, DE 19711-5000
302-831-8828
Fax: 302-831-3307
e-mail: butzin@udel.edu
http://www.udel.edu/butzin/cdas.html
Dr. Clifford Butzin, Contact

Substance abuse research
1991

7481 University of Michigan Alcohol Research Center
400 E Eisenhower Parkway
Suite 2a
Ann Arbor, MI 48108-3308
734-615-6060
Fax: 734-615-6085
e-mail: zuckerra@umich.edu
http://www.med.umich.edu

Alcohol abuse among the elderly, including the relationship of alcohol and aging on the central nervous system. Also does general research pertaining to the effects of alcoholism and drug abuse.

7482 University of Minnesota: Program on Alcohol/Drug Control
321 Church Street SE
Minneapolis, MN 55455
612-625-9997
Fax: 612-625-8408
Horace H Loh PhD, Head Pharmacology
James Burak, Assistant Head Pharmacology
Ramona Schwasinger, Executive Assistant

Alcohol, tobacco and drug research.

7483 University of Missouri: Kansas City Drug Information Service
2411 Holmes Street
Suite Mg-2000
Kansas City, MO 64108-2741
816-235-1800
e-mail: richardsona@umkc.edu
Patrick J Bryant PharmD, Director
Antoine D Richardson PharmD, Assistant Director
Cydney E McQueen PharmD, Assistant Director

Literature research and evaluation of clinical drug problems and questions.

7484 University of Tennessee Drug Information Center
877 Madison Avenue
Suite 210
Memphis, TN 38163
901-448-6312
Fax: 901-524-4545
Dr. Peter A Chyka, Director

7485 University of Texas at Austin: Drug Synamics Institute
College of Pharmacy
Austin, TX 78712
512-499-4200
Fax: 512-471-8762
Dr. Thomas Gerding, Director
Mark Yudof, CEO

Pharmaceutical and drug research.

7486 University of Texas: Health Science Center Neurophysiology Research Center
Speech & Hearing Institute
1343 Moursund Street
Room 102
Houston, TX 77030-3405
713-500-2550
Fax: 713-792-4513
Malcolm Skolnick PhD, Director
Mary Battaglia, Manager

Conducts clinical and animal studies aimed at combatting alcohol, drug and tobacco dependence.

7487 University of Utah: Center for Human Toxicology
417 Wakara Way
Room 290
Salt Lake City, UT 84108-1436
801-581-5611
Fax: 801-581-5034
Douglas Rollins MD, Director

Clinical, forensic and toxicology research.

7488 University of Washington: Alcohol & Drug Abuse Institute Library
1107 Northeast 45th Street, Suite 120
Box 354805
Seattle, WA 98105-4631
206-543-0937
Fax: 206-543-5473
e-mail: adai@u.washington.edu
http://lib.adai.washington.edu/
Nancy Sutherland, Library Director
Pamela Miles, Librarian
Meg Wood, Librarian

The ADAI Library collection represents the spectrum of research and scientific literature on alcohol and other drug use from all relevant disciplines, including medicine, nursing, social work, criminal justice, sociology and psychology.
1975

Substance Abuse/Research Centers

7489 **University of Wisconsin: Milwaukee Medicinal Chemistry Group**
PO Box 413
Milwaukee, WI 53201   414-229-1122
Prf. James Cook, Director
Research on drugs, including studies of valium receptors.

7490 **Veterans Administration Medical Center: Research Service**
1900 E Main Street
Danville, IL 61832-5100   217-442-8000
                                Fax: 217-431-6523
Mukund 9278hudesai MD, R&D Coordinator
Alcoholism and rehabilitation research.

Visually Impaired/Associations & Organizations

Associations & Organizations

7491 1-800-BRAILLE
Braille Institute
741 N Vermont Avenue
Los Angeles, CA 90029-3514
323-660-3880
800-BRA-ILLE
Fax: 323-663-0867

Leslie Stocker, President

A toll free information and referral service where callers can obtain information about community programs and referrals to organizations serving the blind in their local areas.

7492 611 Washington Ear
35 University Boulevard E
Silver Spring, MD 20901
301-681-6636
Fax: 301-681-5227
e-mail: information@washear.org
http://www.washear.org

Nancy Knauss, Administrative Director
Margaret Pfanstiehl, President

A nonprofit organization providing reading and information services for the blind, visually impaired and physically disabled persons who cannot effectively read print, see plays, watch television programs or view museum exhibits. This organization provides radio reading services, dial-in telephone newspaper service, National Symphony Orchestra program notes on audio cassette and raised line and large print atlases and books.

7493 ACB Government Employees
American Council of the Blind
1155 15th Street NW
Suite 1004
Washington, DC 20005-2706
202-467-5081
800-424-8666
Fax: 202-467-5085
e-mail: info@acb.org
http://www.acb.org

Catherine Skivers, President
Mitch Pomerantz, Chairman

Members are present, former and retired employees of federal, state and local government agencies. Concerns of the organization include recruitment, placement and advancement of blind and visually impaired employees.

7494 ACB Radio Amateurs
American Council of the Blind
1155 15th Street NW
Suite 1004
Washington, DC 20005-2706
202-467-5081
800-424-8666
Fax: 202-467-5085
e-mail: info@acb.org
http://www.acb.org

John Glass, President
Mike Duke, Chairman

A radio amateur network of blind, visually impaired and sighted members who gather and share common problems and solutions to help members improve radio amateurs in getting started, provides access to educational materials in special media and publishes a directory for the visually impaired.

7495 ACB Social Service Providers
American Council of the Blind
1155 15th Street NW
Suite 1004
Washington, DC 20005-2706
202-467-5081
800-424-8666
Fax: 202-467-5085
e-mail: info@acb.org
http://www.acb.org

Mitch Pomerantz, President
Kim Charlson, First Vice President

Blind and visually impaired social workers, social service professionals, students pursuing careers in social work, and other interested persons are members of this organization. ACBSSP works to promote full participation by visually impaired social services professionals in the field of social welfare.

7496 AFB Toll-Free Hotline
American Foundation for the Blind
11 Penn Plaza
Suite 300
New York, NY 10001-2018
212-502-7600
800-232-5463
Fax: 212-502-7777

Carl Augusto, President

Supplies information on visual impairment and blindness, answers queries regarding AFB services, products, publications, technology, the Careers and Technology Information Bank (a national data bank) and much more.

7497 Achromatopsia Network
PO Box 214
Berkeley, CA 94701-0214
510-540-4700
Fax: 510-540-4767
e-mail: futterman@achormat.org
http://www.achromat.org

Frances Futterman, President

The Achromatopsia Network is a nonprofit organization for individuals concerned with achromatopsia. It is committed to sharing informaiton about achromatopsia and providing resources to meet the special needs of those affected by this eye condition; helping individuals and families concerned with achromatopsia to connect with one another; and promoting awareness and educating with a special emphasis on accomplishing this goal among those who prov

7498 Akron Blind Center and Workshop
325 E Market Street
Akron, OH 44304-1340
330-253-2555
Fax: 330-996-4089
http://www.societyoftheblind.org

Kristen Baysinger, Executive Director

7499 Alabama Industries for the Blind
1209 Ft. Lashley Ave.
Talladega, AL 35160
256-761-3512
Fax: 256-761-3505

Billy J Sparkman, Executive Director
Charles Roden, Plant Manager

7500 Alliance on Aging and Vision Loss
American Council of the Blind
1155 15th Street NW
Suite 1004
Washington, DC 20005-2706
202-467-5081
800-424-8666
Fax: 202-467-5085
e-mail: info@acb.org
http://www.acb.org

Carl E. Foley, President
Michael Richman, Chairman

This group advocates, challenges, educates, enlightens, informs, provokes, and welcomes anyone who is interested in the causes and problems of vision loss and aging.

7501 American Academy of Ophthalmology
Public Education Program
PO Box 7424
San Francisco, CA 94120-7424
415-561-8500
Fax: 415-561-8533
e-mail: aaoe@aao.org
http://www.aao.org

H. Dunbar Hoskins Jr, EVP
David W. Parke II, President

Sponsors National Eye Care Project that gives free eye care to the elderly.

Visually Impaired/Associations & Organizations

7502 American Action Fund for Blind Children and Adults
18440 Oxnard Street
Tarzana, CA 91356
818-343-3219
e-mail: actionfund@actionfund.org
http://www.actionfund.org

Jean Dyon Norris, Director Operations
Lucille Abbazia, Librarian

Offers charitable and educational fund, braille assistive devices and a library for the visually impaired.

7503 American Association of the Deaf-Blind
8630 Fenton Street
Suite 121
Silver Spring, MD 20910-3803
301-495-4403
Fax: 301-495-4404
e-mail: AADB-Info@aadb.org
http://www.aadb.org

Arthur ""Art Roehrig, President
Vincent ""Le Clark, Vice President

The American Association of the Deaf-Blind is a nonprofit, beneficial society of persons with deaf-blindness and other concerned individuals. It was organized for the purpose of advancing the economic, educational, and social welfare of individuals with deaf-blindness and improving moral among persons with deaf-blindness.

7504 American Blind Lawyers Association
American Council of the Blind
1155 15th Street NW
Suite 1004
Washington, DC 20005-2706
202-467-5081
800-424-8666
Fax: 202-467-5085
e-mail: info@acb.org
http://www.acb.org

Steve Speicher, President
Pshon Barrett, Chairman

Membership includes licensed attorneys, judges, law professors, students and other interested people concerned with law school admission tests and bar exams, private sector and government employment relations and specialized work techniques for the blind and visually impaired.

7505 American Council of Blind Lions
American Council of the Blind
148 Vernon Ave.
Suite 1004
Louisville, KY 40206
502-897-1472
800-424-8666
Fax: 502-721-9929
e-mail: adam148@bellsouth.net
http://www.acb.org

Alan Beatty, Contact
Adam Ruschival, President

Educates Lions Club members about the needs and capabilities of blind people, exchanges information concerning Club activities in the field of work for the blind and encourages blind people to join Lions Clubs and other civic activities.

7506 American Foundation for the Blind
11 Penn Plaza
Suite 300
New York, NY 10001
212-502-7600
800-232-5463
Fax: 212-502-7777
e-mail: afbinfo@afb.net
http://www.afb.org

Carl R Augusto, President and Chief Executive Of
Jeanette Bonzani, Director of Human Resources

The American Foundation for the Blind, the organization to which Helen Keller devoted over 40 years of her life, is a national, nonprofit organization whose mission is to enable people who are blind or visually impaired to achieve quality of access and opportunity that will ensure freedom of choice in their lives. AFB is headquartered in New York City and maintains offices in Atlanta, Chicago, Dallas, San Francisco, and Washington, DC.

7507 American Foundation for the Blind Southwest
11030 Ables Lane
Dallas, TX 75229
214-352-7222
Fax: 214-352-3214
e-mail: dallas@afb.net
http://www.afb.org

Judy Scott, Director
Carl R. Augusto, President and Chief Executive Of

Provide public education about the capabilities of people who are blind and resource information related to blindness.

7508 American Foundation for the Blind: National Literacy Center
100 Peachtree Street
Suite 620
Atlanta, GA 30303-1909
404-525-2303
Fax: 404-659-6957
e-mail: literacy@arb.org
http://www.afb.org/afb

Ike Presley, Executive Director

The AFB National Literacy Center (NLC) in Atlanta, GA, develops and promotes a wide variety of initiatives to address the alarmingly low literacy rate among people who are blind or who have low vision. The NLC leads the blindness field in developing teacher training curriculum, providing up-to-date resources and workshops for professionals, and providing resources on braille, assistive technology, and low vision. NLC programs benefit teachers who work with blind and visually impaired children, rehabilitation specialists who work with adults and seniors, school administrators, parents, and family members of people who are blind or visually impaired.

7509 American Foundation for the Blind: Atlanta
100 Peachtree Street
Suite 620
Atlanta, GA 30303
404-525-2303
Fax: 404-659-6957
e-mail: literacy@afb.net
http://www.afb.org

Carl R Augusto, President and Chief Executive Of
Pearl Van Zandt, Executive Director

Information or referral services; provides training for service providers related to literacy issues.

7510 American Foundation for the Blind: Chigago
11 Penn Plaza
Suite 300
New York, IL 10001
212-502-7600
Fax: 312-245-9965
e-mail: afbinfo@afb.net
http://www.afb.org

Carl R Augusto, President and Chief Executive Of
Richard J. O'Brien, Chair

Provides information, referrals, advocacy groups and public education programs for the midwest region of the United States.

7511 American Foundation for the Blind: Midwest
101 N Michigan Avenue
Suite 308
Chicago, IL 60611
312-245-9961
Fax: 312-527-4660
e-mail: chicago@afb.org
http://www.afb.org

Carl R. Augusto, President and Chief Executive Of
Jeanette Bonzani, Director of Human Resources

AFB's efforts on behalf of people who are blind or visually impaired in the eleven states that make up the Midwest region: Illinois, Indiana, Iowa, Kentucky, Michigan, Minnesota, Missouri, North Dakota, Ohio, South Dakota, Wisconsin.

Visually Impaired/Associations & Organizations

7512 American Foundation for the Blind: San Francisco
111 Pine Street
Suite 725
San Francisco, CA 94111
415-392-4845
Fax: 415-392-0383
e-mail: sanfran@afb.org
http://www.afb.org

Gil L Johnson, Director of Professional Develop
Jeanette Bonzani, Director of Human Resources

Provides information and referral assistance relating to vision loss.

7513 American Foundation for the Blind: Washington DC
1155 Vermont Avenue NW
Suite 720
Washington, DC 20005
202-467-5081
800-424-8666
Fax: 202-467-5085
e-mail: preeder@acb.org
http://www.afb.org

Melanie Brunson, Executive Director
Penny Reeder, Contact

Provides information on blindness to individuals, institutions, and organizations. Offers programs, lobbying and advocacy information and referral services to blind and visually impaired persons. Free and low-cost literature is available.

7514 American Optometric Association
243 N Lindbergh Boulevard
Saint Louis, MO 63141
314-991-4100
Fax: 314-991-4101
e-mail: Geriatrics@aoa.org
http://www.aoa.org

Jeffrey L Weaver OD, Director Clinical Care Group
Renee A. Brauns, Associate Director
Michael Jones, Executive Director

Eye and vision care.

7515 American Printing House for the Blind
PO Box 6085
Louisville, KY 40206-0085
502-895-2405
Fax: 502-899-2274
e-mail: info@aph.org
http://www.aph.org

Fred Gissoni, Customer Support Specialist
Tuck Tinsley, President

The world's largest company devoted solely to producing products for people who are visually impaired. We manufacture books and magazines in braille, large type, recorded and computer disk form. We also make a wide range of educational and daily living aids, such as braille paper and styluses, talking book equipment, and synthetic speech computer products. APH also offers CARL ET AL, an electronic database that lists accessible books in all fo

7516 American Society of Contemporary Medicine Surgery & Ophthalmology
820 N Orleans Street
Suite 208
Chicago, IL 60610
312-440-0699
800-621-4002
Fax: 312-440-0580
e-mail: iaos@aol.com
http://www.ascmso.com

Randall T Bellows MD, President

Ophthalmologists interested in promoting clinical investigative advances in ophthalmology. Offers continuing medical education courses approved by the American Council for Continuing Medical Education (ACCME) on new opthalmic developments in medical, therapeutic, diagnostic, and surgical procedures.

7517 American Society of Ophthalmic Registered Nurses
655 Beach Street
San Francisco, CA 94119
415-561-8513
Fax: 415-561-8575
e-mail: asorn@aao.org
http://www.aao.org

Dan B Jones, President
Lisa L Brown, Administrator

Registered nurses specializing in the field of ophthalmology. Promotes excellence in ophthalmic nursing for the best and safest care of patients with eye disorders or injuries. Facilitates continuing education through the study, discussion, and exchange of knowledge, experience, and ideas in the field. Represents members' interests before governmental agencies, hospitals, industries, research organizations, technical societies, universities, andother professional associations. Conducts educational programs.

7518 Arizona Center for the Blind and Visually Impaired
3100 E Roosevelt Street
Phoenix, AZ 85008
602-273-7411
Fax: 602-273-7410
e-mail: jlamay@acbvi.org
http://www.acbvi.org

Jim LaMay, Executive Director
Diana Miladin, Director Communications and Deve

Provides services for individuals to 'enhance the quality of life of people who are blind or otherwise visually impaired.' Services are available to adults who are either legally blind or visually impaired, as well as those who have a degenerative eye condition which may eventually become a visual impairment.

7519 Arizona Industries for the Blind
3013 W Lincoln Street
Phoenix, AZ 85009-5797
602-269-5131
Fax: 602-269-9462

Richard Monaco, Manager

7520 Arizona Industries for the Blind
3013 W Lincoln Street
Phoenix, AZ 85009
602-269-5131
Fax: 602-269-9462
e-mail: JOLeary@azdes.gov
http://https://www.azdes.gov/aib

John O'Leary, Account Manager
Tim Adams, Unit Manager

7521 Arizona Rehabilitation State Services for the Blind and Visually Impaired
1789 West Jefferson 2, NW
Phoenix, AZ 85007-3202
602-542-3332
800-563-6049
Fax: 602-542-3778
e-mail: azrsa@cirs.org
http://www.de.state.az.us/rsa/
TDD 602-542-3778

Kenneth House, State Manager
Craig Warren, Administrator

Offers clients a conservation program, eye examinations, treatments, counseling, social work, psychological testing and evaluation, professional training, computer training and more for the visually impaired. The staff includes 56 full time employees.

7522 Arkansas Lighthouse for the Blind
6818 Murray St
Little Rock, AR 72209
501-562-2222
Fax: 501-568-5275
e-mail: info@arkansaslighthouse.org
http://www.arkansaslighthouse.org

Bill Johnson, EVP

Visually Impaired/Associations & Organizations

7523 Associated Blind
315 5th Avenue
Suite 807
New York, NY 10016
212-683-4950
Fax: 212-645-1638
e-mail: hq@tabinc.org
http://www.tabinc.org
Nancy O'Connell, Executive Director
Herbert R. Brinberg, Chairman

Organization dedicated to fostering economic and social independence among individuals who are blind or visually impaired. Services include adaptive computer education, information and referral and life enrichment programs.

7524 Associated Services for the Blind and Visually Impaired
919 Walnut Street
Philadelphia, PA 19107
215-627-0600
Fax: 215-922-0692
e-mail: asbinfo@asb.org
http://www.asb.org
Patricia C Johnson, President
Dolores Ferrara-Godzieba, Director

Rehabilitation services; computer training; books and magazines in braille/large print/tape; radio reading service; Philadelphia Lighthouse of the Blind.

7525 Association for Macular Diseases
210 E 64th Street
8th Floor
New York, NY 10021
212-605-3719
Fax: 212-605-3795
e-mail: association@retinal-research.org
http://www.macula.org
Lawrence A. Yannuzzi, M.D., President
Yale L. Fisher, M.D., VP

A nonprofit corporation to promote education and research in this scarcely-explored field. A nationwide support group for individuals and their families to adjust to the restrictions and changes brought about by macular disease. This Association counsels those who are afflicted, issue updates on medical advances as they occur, and keeps members advised on the newest developments in low-vision aids.

7526 Association for the Blind & Visually Impaired of Greater Rochester
422 S Clinton Avenue
Rochester, NY 14620-1198
585-232-1111
800-646-8166
Fax: 716-232-6707

To advance the independence of people who are visually impaired and to promote the prevention of blindness.

7527 Association for the Blind and Visually Impaired
456 Cherry Street SE
Grand Rapids, MI 49503
616-458-1187
Fax: 616-458-7113
e-mail: abvi@abvimichigan.org
http://www.abvimichigan.org
Richard A. Stevens, Executive Director
George Kremer, Director of Rehabilitation Servi

To advance the independence of people who are visually impaired and to promote the prevention of blindness.

7528 Association for the Blind of South Carolina
1071 Morrison Dr
Charleston, SC 29403
843-723-6915
Fax: 843-577-4312
e-mail: aftb@associationfortheblindsc.org
http://www.associationfortheblindsc.org
Cornelia Pelzer, Executive Director
Nicole Harvey, Marketing and Program Director

7529 Aurora of Central New York
518 James Street
Suite 100
Syracuse, NY 13203
315-422-7263
Fax: 315-422-9746
e-mail: auroracny@auroraofcny.org
http://www.auroraofcny.org
TDD 315-422-4792
Debra Chaiken, Executive Director
Earleen Foulk, President

Professional counseling services to assist individuals and their families deal with the trauma of hearing or vision loss.

7530 BESB Industries
184 Windsor Avenue
Suite B
Windsor, CT 06095
860-602-4000
800-842-4510
Fax: 860-602-4220
e-mail: besb@po.state.ct.us
http://www.ct.gov/besb
Brian S. Sigman, Executive Director

7531 Bay State Council of the Blind
57 Grandview Avenue
Watertown, MA 02472
617-923-4519
Fax: 617-923-0004
e-mail: bhachey@comcast.net
http://www.acb.org/baystate
Bob Hachey, President
Jerry Berrier, Editor

The Council strives to improve the well-being of all blind and visually impaired people by serving as a representative national organization of blind people; improving educational and rehabilitation facilities and opportunities; cooperating with the public and private institutions and organizations concerned with blind services; encouraging and assisting all blind persons to develop their abilities and conducting a public education program to promote greater understanding of blindness and the capabilities of blind people.

7532 Beaver County Association for the Blind
616 4th Street
Beaver Falls, PA 15010-4704
724-843-1111
Fax: 724-943-8886
e-mail: bcab@bcblind.org
http://www.bcblind.org
Fay Lentz, Executive Director
Linda Borghi, Controller and Business Manager

Blind and visually impaired persons. Promotes the interests of the blind and visually impaired and works for blindness prevention.

7533 Bestwork Industries for the Blind
801 East Clements Bridge Road
Runnemede, NJ 8078
856-939-5220
Fax: 856-939-5022
e-mail: bestwork@bestworkindustries.org
http://www.bestworkindustries.org
Belinda Moore, President

7534 Blair County Association for the Blind and Visually Handicapped
300 5th Avenue
Altoona, PA 16602-2730
814-944-2021
e-mail: Bcab@pennswoods.net
Marty Sekerak, Executive Director

Individuals interested in helping to meet the needs of the visually impaired. Promotes blindness prevention. Sponsors errand, life skills training, radio reading, and transportation services. Provides public education information.

Visually Impaired/Associations & Organizations

7535 **Blind Association of Western New York**
1170 Main Street
Buffalo, NY 14209
716-882-1025
Fax: 716-882-5577
e-mail: cdecker@olmstedcenter.org
http://www.olmstedcenter.org

Ronald S Maier, President
Michael Cropp, Chairman

Sponsors rehabilitation, education, vocation, employment services, housing, adult day health care, and programs for the blind and visually impaired.

7536 **Blind Enterprises of Oregon**
6540 SE Foster Road
Portland, OR 97206-4662
503-774-6387
Fax: 503-774-0585
e-mail: blindent@aol.com
http://www.blindenterprises.com

Tami Foss, Executive Director
Jennifer Williams, Operations Manager

7537 **Blind Industries and Services of Maryland**
3345 Washington Boulevard
Halethorpe, MD 21227-1602
410-737-2600
Fax: 410-233-0544

Fred Puente, President

7538 **Blind Service Association**
22 W Monroe Street
11th Floor
Chicago, IL 60603
312-236-0808
Fax: 312-236-8679
e-mail: blindsrvc@aol.com

Anna N Perlberg, Executive Director
Louis E Bellande Jr, Partner

Individuals who promote the welfare of blind and partially blind persons through voluntary service or financial support. Through its service program, the association maintains reading rooms for daily oral readings of textbooks and work-related material primarily to blind students, senior citizens, and business and professional people; records textbooks on cassette tapes for blind people's home, study, work and leisure needs; supplies visual aids, field trips, and other assistance to blind and visually handicapped children in Chicago, IL schools; helps maintain eye clinics in hospitals; helps support recreational programs for visually impaired minors and workshop program for the blind retarded; sponsors cultural activities for blind adults and provides tickets for some events; provides emergency relief for blind in need of assistance and cooperates with other charitable agencies in referral cases.

7539 **Blind Veterans Rehabilitation Centers and Clinics**
Veterans Health Administration
Washington, DC 20420
202-535-7637
800-669-8477
Fax: 215-381-3524

To provide personal and social adjustment programs and medical or health-related services for eligible blind veterans at selected VA Medical Centers maintaining blind rehabilitation centers.

7540 **Blind Work Association**
174 Court Street
Binghamton, NY 13901-3514
607-724-2428
Fax: 607-771-8045

Robert K Hanye, President and Chief Executive Di
Ken Fernald, Vice President of Operations

To assist people who are blind or visually impaired attain or maintain economic and personal independence

7541 **Blinded Veterans Association**
477 H Street NW
Northwest Washington, DC 20001-2694
202-371-8880
800-669-7079
Fax: 202-371-8258
e-mail: bva@bva.org
http://www.bva.org

Thomas H Miller, Executive Director
Norman Jones, Jr., National President

Offers two main service programs without cost to blinded veterans. Field service program provides counseling to veterans and families, and information on benefits and rehabilitation.

7542 **Bosma Industries for the Blind**
8020 Zionsville Road
Indianapolis, IN 46268
317-684-0600
Fax: 317-684-1946
e-mail: info@bosma.org
http://www.bosma.org

Lou Moneymaker, President and Chief Executive Of
Connie F. Campbell, CPA, J.D, Executive Vice President, Chief

7543 **Braille Institute Desert Center**
70-251 Ramon Road
Rancho Mirage, CA 92270-5203
760-321-1111
Fax: 760-321-9715
e-mail: dc@brailleinstitute.org
http://www.brailleinstitute.org

Penny R. Miller, Regional Director
Lars Hansen, Assistant Regional Director

Dedicated to providing blind and visually impaired men, women and children with the training, programs and services they need to enjoy productive lives. Services offered include child development, youth programs, library services and adult education.

7544 **Braille Institute Sight Center**
741 N Vermont Avenue
Los Angeles, CA 90029-3594
323-663-1111
Fax: 323-663-0867
e-mail: la@brailleinstitute.org
http://www.brailleinstitute.org

Dr. Henry Chang, Librarian
Leslie Stocker, President

Offers help, programs, services and information to the blind and visually impaired children and adults.

7545 **Braille Institute of America**
741 North Vermont Avenue
Los Angeles, CA 90029
323-663-1111
800-BRA-ILLE
Fax: 323-663-0867
e-mail: la@brailleinstitute.org
http://www.brailleinstitute.org

James H. Jackson, Chairman
Leslie E Stocker, President

7546 **Braille Institute of America**
741 N Vermont Avenue
Los Angeles, CA 90029-3594
323-660-3880
800-BRA-ILLE
Fax: 323-663-0867
http://www.brailleinstitute.org

Leslie E Stocker, President

Provides educational training and services to blind and visually impaired persons in the Southern California area. Operates speakers' bureau and local community and outreach programs. Offers tours; provides child development services also braille publishing. All services are free.

Visually Impaired/Associations & Organizations

7547 Braille Institute of America Library
741 N Vermont Avenue
Los Angeles, CA 90029
323-663-1111
Fax: 323-663-0867
e-mail: la@brailleinstitute.org
http://www.brailleinstitute.org
James H. Jackson, Chairman
Leslie E. Stocker, President

Discs, cassettes, braille, Optacon, home visits, braille writer, reference materials on blindness and other handicaps. Closed-circuit TV, Optacon, braille writer, and large print copier also available. Home visits and cassette books are part of special services offered.

7548 Braille Institute: Orange County Center
527 N Dale Avenue
Anaheim, CA 92801
714-821-5000
Fax: 714-527-7621
e-mail: oc@brailleinstitute.org
Sheila F Daily, Regional Director
Gene Mathiowetz, Assistant Regional Director

Offers services, publications, information and programs to blind and visually impaired persons.

7549 Braille Institute: Santa Barbara Center
2031 De La Vina Street
Santa Barbara, CA 93105
805-682-6222
Fax: 805-687-6141
e-mail: sb@brailleinstitute.org
http://www.brailleinstitute.org
Michael Larzarovits, Regional Director
Angela Nowlin, Assistant Regional Director

Offers programs, services and information for persons with visual impairments.

7550 Braille Materials Production Center
National Braille Association
3 Townline Circle
Rochester, NY 14623-2537
585-427-8260
Fax: 585-427-0263
http://www.nationalbraille.org
David Shaffer, Executive Director

Certified braillists fill requests for college textbooks and other technical works through this service of the National Braille Association.

7551 Braille Revival League
American Council of the Blind
1102 W. International Airport Road
Suite 1004
Anchorage, AK 99518
202-467-5081
800-424-8666
Fax: 202-467-5085
e-mail: aiblink@ak.net
http://www.acb.org
Lynne Koral, President

Encourages blind people to read and write in braille, advocates for mandatory braille instruction in educational facilities for the blind, strives to make available a supply of braille materials from libraries and printing houses and more.

7552 Brevard Association for Advancement of the Blind
674 S Patrick Drive
Satellite Beach, FL 32937-3873
321-773-7222
Joyner Judity, Contact

Volunteers providing educational services to the blind and visually impaired. Transfers books and magazines to audio tapes. Offers independent living programs.

7553 Brevard Association for the Advancement of the Blind
674 S Patrick Drive
Satellite Beach, FL 32937-3873
407-773-7222
Fax: 407-773-7222
Judith Joyner, President

Volunteers providing educational services to the blind and visually impaired. Transfers books and magazines to audio tapes. Offers independent living programs.

7554 Canine Companions for Independence
National Offices
PO Box 446
Santa Rosa, CA 95402-0446
707-528-0830
800-767-BARK
http://www.caninecompanions.org
Kathy Pierson, Executive Director
Daniel Harris, Director of Development

A nonprofit organization that provides loyal canine partners for people with disabilities, helping them to achieve greater independence and live happier and more fulfilling lives.

7555 Canine Helpers for the Handicapped
5699 Ridge Road
5705
Lockport, NY 14094
716-433-4035
Fax: 716-439-0822
e-mail: chhdogs@aol.com
http://http://caninehelpers.netfirms.com
Beverly Underwood, Executive Director
Jeanne Schmidt, Director

7556 Carroll Center for the Blind
770 Centre Street
Newton, MA 02458
617-969-6200
800-852-3131
Fax: 617-969-6204
http://www.carroll.org
Mrs. Rachel Rosenbaum, President
Brian Charlson, Vice President

Assists blind and visually impaired adults and adolescents to adjust to loss of vision. The goal of this dynamic program is to help the person become more independent, to restore self-confidence, prepare for employment and improve the quality of life. Programs of individual counseling are offered as part of the program.

7557 Catholic Guild for the Blind
Catholic Charities of the Archdiocese of New York
1011 1st Avenue
New York, NY 10022-4112
212-371-1000
Fax: 212-826-8377
e-mail: TSnyder@archny.org
Edward Cardi Egan, Religious Leader

A nonprofit organization under the sponsorship of the Catholic Charities of the Archdiocese of New York. Daily living skills, orientation and mobility training, communication skills and bilingual preparation for high school equivalency diplomas are among the programs designed to help visually impaired people maintain their independence.

7558 Center for the Blind and Visually Impaired
100 W 15th Street
Chester, PA 19013
610-874-1476
Fax: 610-874-6454
e-mail: bob.nelson@cbvi.net
http://www.cbvi.net
Bob Nelson, Executive Director
Rosemary Keefe, Marketing and Communications Coo

Multiservice agency with specialized services for people who have lost or are losing vision.

7559 Central Association for the Blind and Visually Impaired
507 Kent Street
Utica, NY 13501
315-797-2233
Fax: 315-797-2244
http://www.cabvi.org
Donald Loguidice, President and Chief Executive Di

Visually Impaired/Associations & Organizations

7560 Chester County Branch Pennsylvania Association for Blind
11 S 1st Avenue
Coatesville, PA 19320-3461
610-384-2767
Fax: 610-384-8005
Anita Cavuto, Executive Director

Blind and visually impaired individuals. Works toward the prevention of blindness. Sponsors employment workshop and Visiting and Prevention and Counseling Program.

7561 Chester County Branch, Pennsylvania Association for Blind
71 S 1st Avenue
Coatesville, PA 19320-3461
610-384-2767
Fax: 610-384-8005
Anita Cavuto, Executive Director

Blind and visually impaired individuals. Works toward the prevention of blindness. Sponsors employment workshop and Visiting and Prevention and Counseling Program.

7562 Chicago Lighthouse for People who areBlind or Visually Impaired
1850 W Roosevelt Road
Chicago, IL 60608-1298
312-666-1331
Fax: 312-243-8539
e-mail: sheila.perkins@chicagolighthouse.org
http://www.thechicagolighthouse.org
James Kesteloot, President and Executive Director
Sheila Perkins, Contact

An organization offering progressive programs for the blind, visually impaired, deaf-blind and multi-disabled children and adults, including vocational programs, computer and office skills training, job placement, independent living skills, orientation and mobility training, counseling, and low vision adaptation.es Store on premises.

7563 Christian Record Services
4444 South 52nd Street
Lincoln, NE 68516-1302
402-488-0981
Fax: 402-488-7582
e-mail: info@christianrecord.org
http://www.christianrecord.org
Bert Williams, Director Reading Services
Larry Pitcher, President

Organization that provides interdenominational services to the visually impaired. Produces materials in large print, braille and on cassette. Membership includes access to lending library and information about summer camps for the blind upon request.

7564 Cincinnati Association for the Blind
2045 Gilbert Avenue
Cincinnati, OH 45202
513-221-8558
Fax: 513-221-2995
e-mail: info@cincyblind.org
http://www.cincyblind.org/
John Mitchell, Executive Director
Mary L. Rust, Vice President and Secretary

7565 Clearinghouse for Specialized Media and Technology
California Department of Education
1430 N Street
Suite 3207
Sacramento, CA 95814
916-445-5103
Fax: 916-323-9732
e-mail: rbrawley@cde.ca.gov
http://www.cde.ca.gov
Rod Brawley, Manager
Kenneth Noonan, President

Assists schools and students in the identification and acquisition of textbooks, reference books and study materials in aural media, braille, large print and electronic media access technology.

7566 Cleveland Sight Center
1909 E 101st Street
PO Box 1988
Cleveland, OH 44106-8696
216-791-8118
Fax: 216-791-1101
e-mail: kmassey@clevelandsightcenter.org
http://www.clevelandsightcenter.org
Michael E. Grady, Executive Director
James P. Sacher, Chairman

Mission is to enable people with vision impairment to reach their full potential and assure that adequate services are available for a 'normal' life.

7567 Cleveland Skilled Industries
2239 E. 55th St.
Cleveland, OH 44103-4451
216-431-8085
Fax: 216-431-5123

7568 Clovernook Center: Opportunities for the Blind
7000 Hamilton Avenue
Cincinnati, OH 45231-5240
513-522-3860
Fax: 513-728-6229
e-mail: cincinnati@clovernook.org.
http://www.clovernook.org

Jacqueline L Conner, Vice President, Multi-State Cent

Offers various library services, information and resources for the blind and visually impaired.

7569 Collier County Association for the Blind
392 Goodlette Road S
Naples, FL 34102-6456
239-434-6222
Peter Carroll, President

A nonprofit organization dedicated to providing independent-living education; computer, Braille and mobility programs; peer support and fellowship; recreation and entertainment; and personal enrichment opportunities for individuals in Collier County who are visually impaired or blind.

7570 Columbia Lighthouse for the Blind
1120 20th Street, NW
Suite 750
Washington, DC 20036
202-454-6400
Fax: 202-454-6401
e-mail: info@clb.org
http://www.clb.org
Anthony J. Cancelosi, President and Chief Executive Di
Sherrie L. Borden, Vice President of Corporate Comm
Matt Ater, Assoc. Dir. Assistive Tech.

Offers persons who are blind and visually impaired in the areas of DC, Maryland and Virginia, training in assistive technology, career development and rehabilitation and offers services such as braille production, speakers bureau, visionaries store, volunteer assistance, low-vision clinics and Columbia Extension recreational activities.

7571 Connecticut Braille Association
Braille Division
107 Vanderbilt Avenue
West Hartford, CT 06110
860-953-9692
Yolanda Rossi, Chairperson
Eileen Akers, President

Produce braille and large tape text books and other materials.

7572 Connecticut Braille Association
44 Imperial Avenue
Westport, CT 06880
203-227-5243
Fax: 203-227-5243
Eileen Akers, President
Peggy Smith, Chairperson

Serves the visually handicapped, with special emphasis on aid for children and young adults in school.

Visually Impaired/Associations & Organizations

7573 Dallas Lighthouse for the Blind
4245 Office Parkway
Dallas, TX 75204
214-821-2375
Fax: 214-824-4612
e-mail: bonnie.glazer@dallaslighthouse.org
http://www.dallaslighthouse.org
Micheal H Orfinik, President
Bonnie Glazer, Director of Events
Steve VanderPoel, VP HR Development

Serves adults and senior citizens with vision disabilities. Programs include vocational rehabilitation, independent living rehabilitation and employment. Services include orientation and mobility skills training, information and referral, case work services, personal and social adjustment counseling, employment readiness training, on-the-job training, job placement assistance, technology training, adult basic education, Braille instruction.

7574 Delaware Association for the Blind
800 West Street
Wilmington, DE 19801
302-655-2111
Fax: 302-655-1442
e-mail: contact@dabdel.org
http://www.dabdel.org
Linda S Lauria, Executive Director

Provides recreational and counseling services not provided by the government to the blind and visually impaired.

7575 Delaware Association for the Blind
800 N West Street
Wilmington, DE 19801-1526
302-655-2111
Fax: 302-655-1442
http://www.dabdel.org
Linda S Lauria, Executive Director

Provides recreational and counseling services not provided by the government to the blind and visually impaired.

7576 Delaware Division for the Visually Impaired
1901 N Dupont Highway
Biggs Building
New Castle, DE 19720
302-577-3333
Fax: 302-577-4758
http://www.dati.org
Beth Mineo, Director
David P. Roselle, President

State agency serving the visually impaired persons from birth, with or without other handicaps. Services offered include educational, computer training, employment and pre-vocational training.

7577 Delta Society National Service
875 124th Ave NE
Suite 101
Bellevue, WA 98005-2531
425-679-5500
Fax: 425-679-5539
e-mail: info@deltasociety.org
http://www.deltasociety.org
TTY 800-809-2714
Karen Miller, Director of Training
Lawrence J Norvell, CEO

A service of the Delta Society, provides information about the selection, training, stewardship, and roles of service dogs; referral to service dog training programs and related resources; education to businesses, health care professionals, and the general public regarding service dog issues; research assistance athrough a resource library and network of professional esperts; and advocacy on behalf of people with service dogs.

7578 Department of Blind Rehabilitation
Western Michigan University
1903 W Michigan Ave
Kalamazoo, MI 49008-5218
269-387-3455
Fax: 269-387-3567
http://www.wmich.edu
Jim Leja BS, MS, RhD, Professor/Chairman
Gayla Dennis, Office Coordinator

Rehabilitation teachers offer adults who are blind or visually impaired information and resources they need to lead successful, productive lives. By offering instruction in specialized methods and adaptive techniques required for independent living and communication, the rehabilitation teacher helps people to achieve independent lifestyles.

7579 Duluth Lighthouse for the Blind
4505 W Superior Street
Duluth, MN 55807
218-624-4828
Fax: 218-624-4479
e-mail: info@lighthousefortheblind-duluth.org
http://www.lighthousefortheblind-duluth.org
Helga Wallner, President
Hamilton Smith, Vice President

7580 East Central Region: Helen Keller National Center
4351 Garden City Drive
Suite 645
Hyattsville, MD 20785-2204
301-459-5474
Fax: 301-459-5070
TDD 301-459-5433

7581 Ed Lindsey Industries of the Blind
4110 Charlotte Avenue
Nashville, TN 37209-3706
615-627-4012
Fax: 615-741-5024
Edward Lindsey, Chairman

7582 El Paso Lighthouse for the Blind
200 Washington Street
El Paso, TX 79905
915-532-4495
Fax: 915-532-6338
http://www.whc.net/lighthouse
Harry Tyler, President

El Paso Lighthouse for the Blind provides employment, vocational counseling, and life skills training to the blind and visually impaired.

7583 Elizabeth Pierce Olmsted Center for the Visually Impaired
1160 Main Street
Buffalo, NY 14209
716-882-5690
Fax: 716-882-5490
e-mail: dpotocki@statlercenter.org
http://www.olmstedcenter.org
Carlton Sprague, President
Heather Telford, Vice President of Rehabilitation
Michael Jackson, Operations Manager

Sponsors rehabilitation, education, vocation, employment services, housing, adult day health care, and programs for the blind and visually impaired.

7584 Evansville Association for the Blind
PO Box 6445
500 2nd Avenue
Evansville, IN 47719-6445
812-422-1181
Fax: 812-424-3154
e-mail: eabcdc@evansville.net
http://www.eab.evansville.edu
Fred Dormeier, President
C Kenneth Fischer, MD, FACS, Vice President
Karla Horrell, Executive Director

The low vision support group is open to all ages with a wide range of vision problems. Members recieve a monthly calendar and newsletter to inform participants on the social, entertainment, and informational events at the Association. Low vision aids are available at the Low Vision Center

Visually Impaired/Associations & Organizations

7585 Extensions for Independence
555 Saturn Boulevard
#B-368
San Diego, CA 92154
619-618-2154
866-632-7149
Fax: 619-423-7709
e-mail: info@mouthstick.net
http://http://mouthstick.net
Arthur Heyer, President

Develops, manufactures and markets vocational equipment for the visually handicapped. Promotes improvements in design, materials, production and quality of products while maintaining affordable prices.

7586 Eye Bank Association of America
1015 Eighteenth Street NW
Suite 1010
Washington, DC 20036
202-775-4999
Fax: 202-429-6036
e-mail: info@restoresight.org
http://www.restoresight.org
Patricia Acken-O'Neil, President
Edward J. Holland, MD, Chairman

Not-for-profit organization dedicate to the restoration of sight through the promortion and advancement of eye banking. Promotes research and professional education with a newsletter, brochures and pamphlets.

7587 Ferguson Industries for the Blind
11 Highland Avenue
Malden, MA 02148
781-324-0800
Fax: 781-324-3111
e-mail: David.Jansen@state.ma.us
http://www.mass.gov
Susan Lavin, Director
David Jansen, Contact

7588 Fidelco Guide Dog Foundation
103 Old Iron Ore Road
Bloomfield, CT 06002
860-243-5200
Fax: 860-769-0567
e-mail: info@fidelco.org
http://www.fidelco.org
Roberta C. Kaman, Chairman
Nancy R Levin, Vice President

Purpose is to breed, train and place Fidelco German shepherd guide dogs with blind persons throughout the Northeast. Provides training services to blind persons, reviews performance of the guide dog teams to see that satisfactory level of achievement is maintained, utilizes genetic processes and clinical methods to improve and refine the breed and maintains an ongoing program for development and improvement of training methods.

7589 Fight for Sight
381 Park Avenue S
Room 809
New York, NY 10016
212-679-6060
Fax: 212-679-4466
e-mail: info@fightforsight.com
http://http://fightforsight.com
Mary Prudden, Executive Director
Kenneth R. Barasch, President

Voluntary health organization that works to conquer defective sight and blindness. Provides grants to accredited medical colleges and institutions to help supply equipment, technical assistance and materials for research projects and a limited number of clinical service projects.

7590 Foundation Fighting Blindness
11435 Cronhill Drive
Owings Mills, MD 21117-2220
410-568-0150
800-683-5555
Fax: 410-771-9470
e-mail: info@FightBlindness.org
http://www.blindness.org
TTY 800-683-551
Edward H. Gollob, President
Gordon Gund, Chairman

Provides information and referral services and support networks for individuals with retinitis pigmentosa and their families. The main focus of the Foundation is to fund research on the causes, cures, and prevention of retinites pigmentosa, Usher syndrome, and related reetinal degenerations.

7591 Friends for Sight
661 S 200 E
Salt Lake City, UT 84111-3834
801-524-2020
800-675-LOOK
Fax: 801-322-3647
e-mail: 2020@for-sight.com,
http://www.for-sight.com
Colleen Malouf, President/CEO
John A. Adams, Director and Officer

Individuals wishing to prevent loss of eyesight. Works to preserve sight and prevent blindness through comprehensive eye screening programs. Offers educational programs and self-help support groups. Makes available free glaucoma and amblyopia, visual acuity, screening; operates speakers' bureau.

7592 Friends of Tennessee School of the Blind
115 Stewarts Ferry Pike
Nashville, TN 37214
615-231-7300
Fax: 615-231-7307
e-mail: rabrewer@comcast.net
http://www.friendsoftsb.org/
Jim Oldham, Superintendent
Ralph Brewer, President

7593 Friends-In-Art
American Council of the Blind
1155 15th Street NW
Suite 1004
Washington, DC 20005-2706
202-467-5081
800-424-8666
Fax: 202-467-5085
e-mail: info@acb.org
http://www.acb.org
Mike Mandel, President
Nancy Pendegraph, Chairman

Aims to enlarge the art experience of blind people, encourages blind people to visit museums, galleries, concerts, the theater, etc., offers consultation to program planners in establishing accessible art and museum exhibits and presents Performing Arts Showcases.

7594 Georgia Industries for the Blind
PO Box 218
700 Faceville Highway
Bainbridge, GA 39818
229-248-2666
Fax: 229-248-2669
http://www.vocrehabga.org/gib
James Hughes, Executive Director

7595 Glaucoma Support Network
Glaucoma Research Foundation
251 Post Street
Suite 600
San Francisco, CA 94108
415-986-3162
800-826-6693
Fax: 415-986-3763
e-mail: question@glaucoma.org
http://www.glaucoma.org
June Behrendt, Executive Director
Thomas M. Brunner, President and Chief Executive Of

A peer support service for glaucoma patients and their families. The Network provides meaningful, helpful answers to questions from individuals concerned about vision and glaucoma.

Visually Impaired/Associations & Organizations

7596 Great Plains Region Helen Keller National Center
4330 Shawnee Mission Parkway
Suite 108
Shawnee Mission, KS 66205-2538
913-677-4562
Fax: 913-677-1544
e-mail: Hknc7bj@aol.com
http://www.HKNC.org

Beth Jordan, Regional Representative

Serving deaf-blind youth and adults.

7597 Greater Detroit Agency F/T Blind and Visually Impaired
16625 Grand River Avenue
Detroit, MI 48227
313-272-3900
Fax: 313-272-6893
e-mail: gen_info@gdabvi.org
http://www.gdavi.org

Fred Simpson, Chairman
Gail McEntee, President and Chief Executive Of

We provide rehabilitation and daily living skills training to blind and visually impaired senior citizens.

7598 Guide Dog Foundation for the Blind
371 E Jericho Turnpike
Smithtown, NY 11787-2976
631-930-9000
800-548-4337
Fax: 631-930-9009
e-mail: info@guidedog.org
http://www.guidedog.org

Barrie Madasu, Consumer Services Manager
Wells B. Jones, Chief Executive Officer

Provides guide dogs for the blind. All programs, including training with instructor and guide dog, transportation to and from the foundation, and aftercare are free.

7599 Guide Dog Users
American Council of the Blind
1155 15th Street NW
Suite 1004
Washington, DC 20005-2706
202-467-5081
800-424-8666
Fax: 202-467-5085
e-mail: info@acb.org
http://www.acb.org

Debbie Grubb, President
Sheila Styron, Chairman

Promotes the acceptance of blind people and their dogs, works for enforcement and expansion of laws admitting guide dogs into public places, advocates for quality training and follow-up services.

7600 Guide Dogs for the Blind
350 Los Ranchitos Road
San Rafael, CA 94903
415-499-4000
800-295-4050
Fax: 415-499-4035
e-mail: Information@guidedogs.com
http://www.guidedogs.com

Sue Sullivan, Admissions Manager
Robert L Phillips, President

Offers educational materials, transportation, seminars and newsletters for the blind, providing 2 field offices.

7601 Guiding Eyes for the Blind
611 Granite Springs Road
Yorktown Heights, NY 10598
914-245-4024
Fax: 914-245-1609
e-mail: info@guidingeyes.org
http://www.guidingeyes.org

William D Badger, President/CEO
Bev Klayman, Admission Manager

Provides the means for blind and visually impaired individuals to achieve mobility, independence and companionship through the use of our professionally bred and trained guide dogs. Each month Guiding Eyes graduates approximately 12 guide dog/student teams. The guide dogs, 26 day residential training program, special needs program and home training programs are free of charge.

7602 Helen Keller International
57 Willoughby Street
Brooklyn, NY 11201
718-522-2122
Fax: 718-935-9463
e-mail: info@helenkeller.org
http://www.helenkeller.org

Fred W. McPhilliamy, President
John P. Lynch, Executive Director

Nonprofit organization for the blind.

7603 Helen Keller National Center
141 Middle Neck Road
Sands Point, NY 11050
516-944-8900
Fax: 516-944-7302
e-mail: hkncinfo@rcn.com
http://www.hknc.org

Joseph J McNulty, Executive Director
Matthew Campo, Director of Development
Paige Berry, Older Adult Specialist

Provides diagnostic, evaluation, short term comprehensive rehabilitation and personal adjustment training. A technical assistance center is offered providing assistance to public and private agencies and to parent groups who work towards community integration and the enhancement of the quality of life. A national parent network is also provided that develops and shares information about advocacy, legislation, new services and achievements.

7604 Helen Keller National Center: North Central Region
485 42nd Avenue
Suite 5
East Moline, IL 61244
309-755-0018
Fax: 309-755-0025
e-mail: HKNCSJT@aol.com
http://www.helenkeller.org
TDD 309-755-0021

Thomas J Edwards, Chairman
John P. Lynch, Executive Director

7605 Helen Keller National Center: NorthwestRegion
1620 18th Avenue
Suite 201
Seattle, WA 98122
206-720-4642
Fax: 206-324-9159
e-mail: nwhknc@juno.com
http://www.hknc.org

Dorothy Walt, Regional Representative

Our Regional Representative provides information on local services and referrals, on site assessment, consultation, training and suggestions for accommodating the Deaf-Blind individual at home, in the workplace, at school, etc. They will also provide assistance for the application process if the Deaf-Blind Individual wants to attend the HKNC Headquarters in New York.

7606 Helping Hands for the Blind
20734-C Devonshire Street
Chatsworth, CA 91311
818-341-8217
Fax: 818-341-8217
e-mail: boacosta@pacbell.net
http://www.helpinghands4theblind.com/

Robert ""Bob Acosta, President

7607 Ho'opono Services for the Blind
1901 Bachelot Street
Honolulu, HI 96817-2485
808-586-5269
Fax: 808-586-5288
e-mail: develand@dhs.hawaii.gov
http://www.rrhi.com/hooponoblindservices/

Jon Koki, Community Services Coordinator
Dave Eveland, Administrator

Provides services to blind and visually impaired persons in Adjustment to Blindness, Vocational Rehabilitation, Low Vision evaluation and assistance. Work Assessment and Vending training.

Visually Impaired/Associations & Organizations

7608 **Ho'opono Workshop for the Blind**
1901 Bachelot Street
Honolulu, HI 96817-2485
808-586-5269
Fax: 808-586-4144

Dave Eveland, Administrator

7609 **Horizons for the Blind**
2 N Williams Street
Crystal Lake, IL 60014-4401
815-444-8800
800-318-2000
Fax: 815-444-8830
e-mail: mail@horizons-blind.org
http://www.horizons-blind.org

Camille Caffarelli, Executive Director
Camille Caffarelli, Chairperson

Braille and large print books on recipes, crafts, healthy living and poetry; monthly magazine and tactile pictures. Call for a free catalog.

7610 **IN-SIGHT**
750 Narragansett Park Drive
East providence, RI 02916
401-434-1211
Fax: 401-434-1218
e-mail: jgunn@in-sight.org

Christopher Butler, Executive Director
Richard Gaffney, President

7611 **Idaho Commission for the Blind**
341 W Washington Street
P.O. Box 83720
Boise, ID 83702
208-334-3220
Fax: 208-334-2963
e-mail: dard@icbvi.idaho.gov
http://www.icbvi.state.id.us

Nancy Wise, Coordinator
Angela Roan, Administrator

Independent living services for individual over 55 years of age. Orientation and mobility, adaptive technology, cooking, braills, money management, advocacy, and related services. Peer support group services available.

7612 **Illinois Society for the Prevention of Blindness**
211 West Wacker Drive
Suite 1700
Chicago, IL 60606
312-922-8710
800-433-4772
Fax: 312-922-8713
e-mail: visionary@eyehealthillinois.org
http://www.eyehealthillinois.org

Leslee Williams, President
Wesley E Bass, Jr, Vice President
James A McKechnie, Jr, Executive Director

To prevent the tragedy of needless blindness. Dedicated to the care, protection, and preservation of sight, ISPB programs stress education, eye safety, information and research.

7613 **Independent Visually Impaired Enterprisers**
American Council of the Blind
1155 15th Street NW
Suite 1004
Washington, DC 20005-2706
202-467-5081
800-424-8666
Fax: 202-467-5085
e-mail: info@acb.org
http://www.acb.org

Carla Hayes, Chairman

Strives to broaden vocational opportunities in business for the visually impaired. Works to improve rehabilitation facilities for all types of business enterprises and publicizes the capabilities of blind and visually impaired business persons.

7614 **Indiana County Association for the Blind**
31 S 10th Street
Indiana, PA 15701
724-465-5549
Fax: 724-465-7683

Mariann McGee, Executive Director

7615 **Industries for the Blind and Visually Impaired of Louisiana**
PO Box 366
Delhi, LA 71232
318-878-8171

7616 **Information Access Project: National Federation of the Blind**
1800 Johnson Street
Baltimore, MD 21230
410-659-9314
Fax: 410-685-5653
e-mail: nfb@nfb.org
http://www.nfb.org

Marc Maurer, President
Patricia A. Maurer, Director of Reference

Assists entities covered by the ADA in finding methods for converting visually displayed information, such as flyers, brochures and pamphlets, to formats accessible to individuals who are visually impaired.

7617 **Insight**
43 Jefferson Boulevard
Warwick, RI 02888
401-941-3322
Fax: 401-941-3356
e-mail: info@in-sight.org
http://www.in-sight.org

David Vito, OD, President
Alan Jacobs, Vice president

Sponsors rehabilitation and vocational programs for blind and visually impaired individuals in Rhode Island and southeastern Massachusetts. Seeks to enable blind and visually impaired persons to become more active, independent, and productive.

7618 **International Braille Research Center**
1800 Johnson Street
Baltimore, MD 21230
410-659-9314
Fax: 410-685-5653
e-mail: yoshi@nfbcal.org
http://www.braille.org

Michael Gosse, President
Darlene Bogart, Vice President

Conducted a definitive research study which validates the efficacy of the new Unified Braille Code. The new system establishes one English Braille code in palce of many seperate ones. A single Braille code is easier to teach, to learn, and to use. Provides expertise and guidance to both public and private entities who wish to make Braille more widely available to blind persons.

1994

7619 **International Braille and Technology Center for the Blind**
National Federation of the Blind
1800 Johnson Street
Baltimore, MD 21230
410-659-9314
Fax: 410-685-5653
e-mail: nfb@nfb.org
http://www.nfb.org

Marc Maurer, President
Patricia A. Maurer, Director of Reference

World's largest and most complete evaluation and demonstration center of all assistive technology used by the blind from around the world. Includes all Braille, synthetic speech, print-to-speech scanning, internet and portable devices and programs. Available for tours by appointment to blind persons, employers, technology manufacturers, teachers, parents and those working in the assistive technology field.

7620 **International Communication Service for the Blind**
34-57 60th St. 2nd floor
Woodside, NY 11377
718-803-3200
Fax: 718-803-3200
e-mail: info@icsb.net
http://www.icsb.net

Yo Kano, Board member
Leonard Suchanek, Board member

Visually Impaired/Associations & Organizations

7621 Iowa Regional Library for the Blind & Physically Handicapped
524 4th Street
Des Moines, IA 50309-2364
515-281-1333
800-362-2587
Fax: 515-281-1263
e-mail: information@blind.state.ia.us
http://www.blind.state.ia.us

Karen Keninger, Library Director
Dan Bakke, Circulation Supervisor

Offers services to blind and visually-impaired individuals; provides counseling, educational, recreational, rehabilitation, home visits, computer training, and professional training services. Access to Braillewriters, magnifiers, closed-circuit TV, large print photocopiers, cassette, Braille, large print books, cassette magazines, descriptive videos, and other reference materials on blindness and handicaps.

7622 Jewish Braille Institute of America
110 E 30th Street
New York, NY 10016
212-889-2525
Fax: 212-689-3692
e-mail: admin@jbilibrary.org
http://www.jbilibrary.org

Israel A. Taub, Vice President and Chief Financi
Pearl Lam, Director Library Operations

Supplies books and reading material of Jewish interest in braille, on audio cassette and in large print. Provides various services free of charge to those in more than 50 countries.

7623 Job Opportunities for the Blind
National Federation of the Blind
1800 Johnson Street
Baltimore, MD 21230
410-659-9314
Fax: 410-685-5653
e-mail: nfb@nfb.org
http://www.nfb.org

Marc Maurer, President
Patricia A. Maurer, Director of Reference

A specialized service that provides free support, resources and information to blind persons seeking employment and to employers interested in hiring the blind. A partnership program with the US Department of Labor, this is the most successful program of it's kind in helping blind persons find competitive work.

7624 Kansas Association for the Blind and Visually Impaired
603 SW Topeka Boulevard
Suite 303
Topeka, KS 66612
785-235-8990
800-799-1499
e-mail: byington@cox.net
http://www.kabvi.org

Michael Byington, President
David Schwinn, Vice President

KABVI strives to increase the independence, opportunity, and quality of life for all the blind and visually impaired Kansans, and to assist them in taking their rightful place as equals among their sighted peers.

7625 Kansas Association for the Blind and Visually Impaired
2536 McBride Pkwy
Great Bend, KS 67530
316-793-5645
http://www.kabvi.org

Paul Berscheidt, President

7626 Kansas City Association for the Blind
7501 Prospect Avenue
Kansas City, MO 64132-2103
816-421-5848
Fax: 816-237-2019
e-mail: sliptak@alphapointe.org
http://www.alphapointe.org

Reinhard Mabry, President and Chief Executive Of
Judi Moritz, Director of Marketing

7627 Kansas Division of Services for the Blind
2601 SW East Circle Drive North, (1st and MacVicar)
Kanza Business and Technology Park
Topeka, KS 66606-1703
785-296-3311
Fax: 785-267-0263
http://www.srskansas.org/rehab
TTY 785-267-0352

Don Jordan, Secretary
Laura Howard, Assistant Secretary

Offers services for the totally blind, legally blind, visually impaired, mentally retarded blind and more with health, counseling, educational, recreational, rehabilitation, computer training and professional training services.

7628 Kentucky Department for the Blind
209 St. Clair Street
4th Floor
Frankfort, KY 40601
502-564-4754
800-321-6661
Fax: 502-564-2951
e-mail: dbohannon@state.ky.us.dfblind
http://http://workforce.ky.gov
TDD 502-564-2929

Stephen Johnson, Executive Director
Barbara Miller, Director

Provides career services and assistance to adults with severe visual handicaps who want to become productive in the home or work force. Also provides the Client Assistance Program established to provide advice, assistance and information available from rehabilitation programs to persons with handicaps.

7629 Kentucky Division: Prevent Blindness America
13000 Equity Place
Suite 100
Louisville, KY 40223
502-254-4973
800-828-1179
Fax: 502-253-6889
e-mail: lrepperson@aol.com
http://www.preventblindness.org

Michael Daley, President and Chief Operating Of
John D. O'Neill, Jr, Chairman

Prevent Blindness America is the nation's volunteer eye health and safety organization dedicated to fighting blindness and saving sight. Focused on promoting a continuum of vision care, Prevent Blindness America touches the lives of millions of people each year.

7630 Lancaster County Association for the Blind
244 N Queen Street
Lancaster, PA 17603
717-291-5951
Fax: 717-291-9183
e-mail: gfeldman@sabvi.com
http://www.sabvi.com/

Gary Feldman, Product Development Manager
Stephen Patterson, President

7631 Library Users of America
American Council of the Blind
1155 15th Street NW
Suite 1004
Washington, DC 20005-2706
202-467-5081
800-424-8666
Fax: 202-467-5085
e-mail: info@acb.org
http://www.acb.org

Sharon Strzalkowski, President
Winifred Downing, Chairman

Provides for chapters in states through the US to encourage the development, acquisition and use of technology which enables blind and visually impaired persons to use printed material independently in library settings and elsewhere.

Visually Impaired/Associations & Organizations

7632 Lighthouse
The Sol and Lillian Goldman Building
111 East 59th Street
New York, NY 10022-1202
212-821-9200
800-334-5497
Fax: 212-821-9707
e-mail: info@lighthouse.org
http://www.lighthouse.org

Tara A Cortes, RN, PhD, President and Chief Executive Di
Roger O. Goldman, Chairman

Works to build confidence, independence, opportunity, quality of life and hope for people with impaired vision. Provides information and resources to individuals and professionals. Operates the Lighthouse National Center for Vision and Aging and the Lighthouse National Center for Vision and Child Development; conducts continuing education programs for eye care providers; provides educational and advocacy services; offers training and employment t individuals with impaired vision; conducts laboratory research and studies on the consequences of vision impairment in everyday life.

7633 Lighthouse National Center for Vision and Aging (LNCVA)
The Sol & Lillian Goldman Building
111 E 59th Street
New York, NY 10022-1202
212-821-9200
800-829-0500
Fax: 212-821-9707
e-mail: info@lighthouse.org
http://www.lighthouse.org

Tara A Cortes RN PhD, President/CEO
A. James Forbes, Executive VP/CFO

LNCVA provides advocacy, support, information, and resources on vision impairment and blindness.

7634 Lighthouse for the Blind of Houston
PO Box 130435
Houston, TX 77219
713-527-9561
Fax: 713-284-8451
e-mail: houstonlighthouse@houstonlighthouse.org
http://www.lighthouse.org

Gibson DuTerroil, President

7635 Lighthouse for the Blind of Miami
601 SW 8th Ave
Miami, FL 33130
305-856-2288
Fax: 305-285-6967
e-mail: info@miamilighthouse.org
http://www.miamilighthouse.org

Virginia A. Jacko, President/CEO
Joseph A Fernandez, Treasurer
Sheldon Roy, Deputy Director/CDO

Miami Lighthouse for the Blind and Visually Impaired is the oldest and largest private agency in Florida to serve people of all ages who are blind or visually impaired.

7636 Lighthouse for the Blind of Washington
2501 South Plum Street
Seattle, WA 98114
206-322-4200
Fax: 206-329-3397
e-mail: sales@seattlelh.org
http://www.seattlelighthouse.org

Robert S. Johnson, Vice President
Kirk Adams, Executive Vice-President

7637 Lighthouse of Oakland
46156 Woodward Avenue
Pontiac, MI 48342
510-444-6422
800-334-5497
http://www.lighthouseoakland.com

John Ziraldo, Chief Executive Officer and Pres
Judith W. Robinson, Executive Director

7638 Louisiana Center for the Blind
101 South Trenton Street
Ruston, LA 71270
318-251-2891
800-234-4166
Fax: 318-251-0109
e-mail: pallen@lcb-ruston.com
http://www.lcb-ruston.com

Eric Guillory, Director of Youth Services
Pam Allen, Executive Director

Provides adult rehabilitation training for the blind. Conducts summer children's programs. Sponsors seminars.

7639 Maine Center for the Blind and Visually Impaired
189 Park Avenue
Portland, ME 4102
207-774-6273
Fax: 207-774-0679
e-mail: info@theiris.org
http://www.theiris.org

James E. Phipps, President and Chief Executive Di
Dr. David J. Stuchiner, Chairman

7640 Maine Division for the Blind & Visually Impaired Services
Bureau of Rehabilitation Services
2 Anthony Avenue
73 State House Station
Augusta, ME 04333-0073
207-624-5120
800-760-1573
Fax: 207-624-5133
e-mail: harold.j.lewis@state.me.us
http://www.state.me.us/rehab/dvr/dvr_vr.htm
TTY 207-624-5314

Harold Lewis, Director

Comprehensive services for visually impaired and blind individuals of all ages.

7641 Maryland Blind Industries and Services
3345 Washington Boulevard
Baltimore, MD 21227
410-737-2600
Fax: 410-737-2665
http://http://bism.org

Fred Puente, President
Don Morris, Chairperson

7642 Maryland Society for Sight
1313 W Old Cold Spring Lane
Baltimore, MD 21209-4989
410-243-2020
800-677-3937
Fax: 410-889-2505
e-mail: info@mdsocietyforsight.org
http://www.mdsocietyforsight.org

Drew Rock, President
Kathleen M. Curtin, Executive Director

To preserve sight by providing early detection of conditions that can lead to blindness and through public education on the causes of blindness. Quarterly newsletter, Eye Openers.

7643 Massachusetts Association for the Blind
200 Ivy Street
Brookline, MA 02446
617-738-5110
800-682-9200
Fax: 617-738-1247
e-mail: ccanham@mabcommunity.org
http://www.mabcommunity.org

Barbara Salisbury, Chief Executive Officer
J. Lawrence Guihan, President

Provides services to the blind, visually impaired, multihandicapped, or individuals with traumatic brain injury. Promotes self-reliance, equal opportunities, and community participation. Specializes in: recruiting and matching volunteers with consumers; braille, recording, and assistance supplies for the visually impaired; education for multi-handicapped children (visual impairment not required or adolescents with traumatic brain injury); information and referrals; residential and work services for adults with mental retardation.

Visually Impaired/Associations & Organizations

7644 Massachusetts Commission for the Blind
48 Boylston Street
Boston, MA 02116-4718
617-727-5550
800-392-6450
Fax: 617-626-7685
http://www.mass.gov/?pageID=eohhs2agencylanding
TDD 800-392-6556

Dave Govostes, Manager

Provides services to blind citizens of Massachusetts, enabling them to lead more fulfilling and independent lives. Offers vocational rehabilitation, independent living social services, home care and respite assistance, radio reading programs, resource information, community systems advocacy and residential and day services.

7645 Media Access Group
125 Western Avenue
Boston, MA 02134
617-300-3600
Fax: 617-300-1020
e-mail: access@wgbh.org
http://http://main.wgbh.org/

Amanda Moment, Manager
Mary Watkins, Director of Outreach

Media Access Group at WGBH has been pioneering and delivering accessible media to disabled adults, students, and their families, teachers, and friends for over 30 years and is made up of the Caption Center, Descriptive Video Service, and National Center for Accessible Media. Founded in 1993, NCAM is a research, development, and advocacy entity that works to make existing and emerging technologies more accessible to all audiences.

7646 Miami Lighthouse for the Blind
601 SW 8th Avenue
Miami, FL 33130-3200
305-856-2288
Fax: 305-285-6967
e-mail: miamilighthouse@the-directory.com
http://www.the-directory.com/miamilighthous

Vernon Metcalf, Executive Director
Virginia Jacko, Executive Director

Provides training and other services for persons blind or visually impaired. Serves as clearinghouse for information relating to blind and visually handicapped persons. Holds quarterly board meetings.

7647 Michigan Council of the Blind and Visually Impaired (MCBVI)
517 S. 13th Street
Escanaba, MI 49829
888-95-2284
888-956-2284
Fax: 313-381-7844
e-mail: mcbvi@sbcglobal.net

Michael Geno, President
John Mc Mahon, Treasurer

Michigan Council of the Blind and Visually Impaired (MCBVI) offer the united support of others who are blind and visually impaired. MCBVI provides social activities, community awareness and advocacy.

7648 Minnesota State Services for the Blind
2200 University Avenue W
Suite 240
Saint Paul, MN 55114-1840
651-642-0512
800-652-9000
Fax: 651-649-5927
e-mail: chuk.hamilton@state.mn.us
http://www.mnssb.org

Bonnie Elsey, Assistant Commissioner
Chuck Hamilton, Director
David Andrews, Director Communication Center

State agency serving blind and visually impaired persons with rehabilitation, information access, assistive technology, training, and job placement services. Extensive older blind program.

7649 Mississippi Industries for the Blind
PO Box 4417
2501 North West Street
Jackson, MS 39296-4417
601-984-3200
Fax: 601-987-3892
e-mail: dhey@msblind.org
http://www.msblind.org

Joe Carballo, Executive Director
Dee Hey, Marketing Manager

The missions is to provide viable work opputunities for Mississippians who are blind or visually impaired.

7650 Missouri Council of the Blind
5453 Chippewa
A
Saint Louis, MO 63109
314-832-7172
Fax: 314-832-7796
http://www.missouricounciloftheblind.org

Steve Schnelle, Director
Beverly Kaskadden, Director

Blind and visually impaired individuals united to improve conditions for the blind in the areas of employment, cultural opportunities, companionship, financial assistance, rehabilitation, and housing. Conducts legislative advocacy.

7651 Missouri Rehabilitation Services for the Blind
PO Box 2320
Jefferson City, MO 65102-2320
573-751-4249
Fax: 573-751-4984
TDD 800-735-2966

Mike Festor, Director

Offers services for the totally blind, legally blind, visually impaired, mentally retarded blind and more with health, counseling, educational, recreational, rehabilitation, computer training and professional training services.

7652 Mobile Association for the Blind
2440 Gordon Smith Drive
Mobile, AL 36617
251-473-3585
Fax: 251-470-8622
http://www.mobileblind.org

Mahlon McCracken, Executive Director
Jim Bullock, Contact

Offers work adjustment training, job placement, activities of daily living, mobility, communication skills and sheltered employment for adults who are visually impaired and for persons with other disabilities.

7653 National Alliance of Blind Students
American Council of the Blind
1155 15th Street NW
Suite 1004
Washington, DC 20005-2706
202-467-5081
800-424-8666
Fax: 202-467-5085
e-mail: info@acb.org
http://www.acb.org

Jonathan Simeone, President
Enjie Wu, Chairman

Works to facilitate progress toward full accessibility of college programs and facilities, provides opportunities for discussion of issues important to students and assists with National Student Seminars.

7654 National Association for Parents of the Visually Impaired (NAPVI)
National Office
PO Box 317
Watertown, MA 02471
617-972-7441
Fax: 617-972-7444
e-mail: napvi@perkins.org
http://www.spedex.com

Susan LaVenture, Executive Director
Mary Zabelski, President
Lars Anderson, VP

Visually Impaired/Associations & Organizations

A partnership organization with the National Eye Health Education Program and the National Agenda for the Education of Children and Youths with Visual Impairments including those with multiple disabilities.

7655 National Association for Visually Handicapped (NAVH)
22 W 21st Street
Floor 6
New York, NY 10010
212-889-3141
Fax: 212-727-2931
e-mail: navh@navh.org
http://www.navh.org

Lorraine Marchi, Founder and Chief Executive Offi

Serves the partially seeing (not totally blind) with informational literature, newsletters for adults and children, educational outreach, referrals, counsel and guidance. Works with eye care professionals and the business community regarding abilities for the partially seeing.

7656 National Association of Blind Educators
National Federation of the Blind
2214 Emerson Avenue South
Apartment 4
Minneapolis, MN 55405
612-977-9110
Fax: 410-685-5653
e-mail: shekoenig@comcast.net
http://www.nfb.org

Sheila Koenig, President
Priscilla McKinley, Vice-President

Membership organization of blind teachers, professors and instructors in all levels of education. Provides support and information regarding professional responsibilities, classroom techniques, national testing methods and career obstacles. Publishes The Blind Educator, national magazine specifically for blind educators.

7657 National Association of Blind Lawyers
National Federation of the Blind
1660 South Albion Street
Suite 918
Denver, CO 80222
303-504-5979
Fax: 303-757-3640
e-mail: slabarre@labarrelaw.com
http://www.blindlawyer.org

Scott C. LaBarre, President
Charles Brown, First Vice President

Membership organization of blind attorneys, law students, judges and others in the law field. Provides support and information regarding employment, techniques used by the blind, advocacy, laws affecting the blind, current information about the American Bar Association and other issues for blind lawyers.

7658 National Association of Blind Secretaries and Transcribers
National Federation of the Blind
7001 Hamilton Avenue
Unit 2
Cincinnati, OH 45231
513-931-7070
Fax: 410-685-5653
e-mail: Lhall007@cinci.rr.com
http://www.zeli.net/nabop.html

Lisa Hall, President
Mary Donahue, Vice-President

Membership organization of blind secretaries and transcribers at all levels, including medical and paralegal transcription, office workers, customer-service personnel and many other similar fields. Addresses issues such as technology, accomodation, career planning and job training.

7659 National Association of Blind Teachers
American Council of the Blind
1155 15th Street NW
Suite 1004
Washington, DC 20005-2706
202-467-5081
800-424-8666
Fax: 202-467-5085
e-mail: info@acb.org
http://www.acb.org

Granger Ricks, President
Carla Hayes, Chairman

Works to advance the teaching profession for blind and visually impaired people, protects the interest of teachers, presents discussions and solutions for special problems encountered by blind teachers and publishes a directory of blind teachers in the US.

7660 National Association of Guide Dog Users
National Federation of the Blind
55 Delaware Avenue
Somerset, MA 02726
508-673-0218
Fax: 410-685-5653
e-mail: nfbmass@verizon.net
http://www.nfb-nagdu.org

Priscilla Ferris, President
Marion Gwizdala, Vice-President

Provides information and support for guide dog users and works to secure high standards in guide dog training. Addresses issues of discrimination of guide dog users and offers public education about guide dog use.

7661 National Association to Promote the Use of Braille
National Federation of the Blind
5805 Kellogg Avenue
Edina, MN 55424
952-927-7694
Fax: 410-685-5653
e-mail: nadine.jacobson@visi.com
http://www.nfb.org

Nadine Jacobson, President
Robert S. Jaquiss, First Vice President

Dedicated to securing improved Braille instruction, increasing the number of Braille materials available to the blind and providing information about the importance of Braille in securing independence, education and employment for the blind.

7662 National Braille Association
3 Townline Circle
Rochester, NY 14623-2513
585-427-8260
Fax: 585-427-0263
e-mail: NBAoffice@nationalbraille.org
http://www.nationalbraille.org

David W. Shaffer, Executive Director
Diane Spence, President

The National Braille Association provides continuing education to those who prepare braille by sponsoring workshops and publishing manuals for the production of technical and nontechnical materials. Direct services to the blind include a print-to-braille transcription service and duplication of braille materials from our collection of textbooks, music, technical tables, and general interest materials.

7663 National Braille Press
88 Saint Stephen Street
Boston, MA 02115-4302
617-266-6160
800-548-7323
Fax: 617-437-0456
e-mail: orders@nbp.org
http://www.nbp.org

Jason Griffiths, Customer Service Representative
Paul V. McLaughlin, Chairman

Offers support and informational groups.

Visually Impaired/Associations & Organizations

7664 National Captioning Institute
1900 Gallows Road
Suite 3000
Vienna, VA 22182
703-917-7600
Fax: 703-917-9853
e-mail: mail@ncicap.org
http://www.ncicap.org
TDD 800-321-8337
Gene Chao, Chairman, President and Chief Ex
Mary Presswood, Corporate Secretary

NCI provides closed-captioning technology and related services to the broadcast, cable and home video industries for the benefit of people who are deaf and hard of hearing and others who can benefit from the service. In addition, NCI provides access to televised and recorded video programming for people who are blind or have low vision.

7665 National Center for Sight
Prevent Blindness America
500 E Remington Road
Schaumburg, IL 60173-5624
847-843-2020
Fax: 847-843-8458
e-mail: info@preventblindness.org
http://www.preventblindness.org

A toll-free line offering information on a broad range of vision, eye health and safety topics including sports eye safety, lazy eye, diabetic retinopathy, glaucoma, cataracts, children's eye disorders and more.

7666 National Center for Vision and Aging
Lighthouse International
111 E 59th Street
New York, NY 10022-1202
800-829-0500
Fax: 212-821-9702
http://www.lighthouse.org

Promotes an understanding of the vision problems of older Americans. Answers questions and provides referrals to older people, their families, and vision professionals. Brochures available.

7667 National Diabetes Action Network for the Blind
National Federation of the Blind
1800 Johnson Street
Baltimore, MD 21230-4914
410-659-9314
Fax: 410-685-5653
e-mail: pmaurer@nfb.org
http://www.nfb.org
Marc Maurer, President
Mark A. Riccobono, Executive Director

Leading support and information organization of persons losing vision due to diabetes. Provides personal contact and resource information with other blind diabetics about non-visual techniques of independently managing diabetes, monitoring glucose levels, measuring insulin and other matters concerning diabetes. Publishes 'Voice of the Diabetic,' the leading publication about diabetes and blindness.

7668 National Eye Care Project
PO Box 429098
San Francisco, CA 94142-9098
877-887-6327
800-222-3937
Fax: 415-561-8567
e-mail: gmyman-york@aao.org
http://www.aao.org
Betty Lucas, Director

Ophthalmologists dedicated to ensuring eye care for the elderly, particularly those who are economically disadvantaged. Provides medical and surgical eye care to individuals 65 and over who normally would not have access or the means to consult an ophthalmologist. Disseminates information on participating physicians and eye diseases of the aging. Offers referral services. A project of the Foundation of the American Academy of Ophthalmology.

7669 National Eye Care Project (NECP)
PO Box 429098
San Francisco, CA 94142-9098
800-222-3937

Provides information on eligibility guidelines for the eye care project, a program designed for the disadvantaged elderly, age 65 or older. The program does not include eye-glasses or hospitalization. Offers referrals to local participating opthalmologists. Free information packet is available. Hours: 8:00a.m. to 4:00 p.m. Monday-Friday.

7670 National Eye Health Education Program
2020 Vision Place
Bethesda, MD 20892-3655
301-496-5248
Fax: 301-402-1065
http://www.nei.nih.gov/nehep/
Paul A. Sieving, M.D., Ph.D., Director

Offers information and support for persons with vision disorders, including Retinitis Pigmentosa.

7671 National Federation of the Blind
1800 Johnson Street
Baltimore, MD 21230
410-659-9314
Fax: 410-685-5653
e-mail: nfb@access.digex.net
http://www.nfb.org
Marc Maurer, President

The largest membership organization of blind people in the nation, with chapters in every state and approximately 50,000 individual members. It seeks to integrate the blind into society on the basis of equality with the sighted so that the blind are seen as normal, participating citizens. 50,000 members and 700 local chapters.

80 pages

7672 National Federation of the Blind in Computer Science
Naional Federation of the Blind
3000 Grand Avenue
Apartment 810
Des Moines, IA 50312
515-277-1288
Fax: 410-685-5653
e-mail: curtischong@earthlink.net
http://www.nfb.org
Curtis Chong, President

National organization of blind persons knowledgeable in the computer science and technology fields. Works to develop new technologies, to secure access to current technology and to develop new ways of using current or new technologies by the blind.

7673 National Federation of the Blind of California: Santa Barbara County Chapter
5530 Corbin Avenue
Suite 313
Tarzana, CA 91356
818-342-6524
Fax: 818-344-7930
e-mail: nfbcal@sbcglobal.net
http://www.nfbcal.org
Robert Stigile, President
Jim Willows, First Vice-President

To serve the visually impaired. Offers scholarships.

7674 National Federation of the Blind of Kansas
11405 West Grant Street
Wichita, KS 67209
913-339-9341
800-542-3053
e-mail: Donna.Wood@khrc.ststc.ks.us
http://www.nfbks.org
Ms Donna J. Wood, President
Susan L. Stanzel, First Vice President

Works for complete equality and integration of the blind in society. Provides support and information services.

7675 National Federation of the Blind of New Jersey
69 Prospect Place
Bloomfield, NJ 7003
973-743-0075
Fax: 866-632-1940
e-mail: center@webspan.net
http://www.nfbnj.org
Joe Ruffalo, President
Peggy Elliott, second vice president

Visually Impaired/Associations & Organizations

7676 National Federation of the Blind of South Dakota
1800 Johnson Street
Baltimore, MD 21230
410-659-9314
800-558-1843
Fax: 410-685-5653
http://www.nfb.org

Karen S Mayry, President
Jerry Lazarus, Director

Blind persons and interested sighted people. Promotes continuing public education on visual impairments and the circumstances of the visually impaired. Works towards the attainment of equality, security, and opportunity for all blind persons. Provides speakers.

7677 National Federation of the Blind of Texas: Austin Chapter
314 East Highland Mall Blvd
Suite 253
Austin, TX 78752
512-323-5444
Fax: 512-420-8160
e-mail: austin@nfb-texas.org
http://www.nfb-texas.org

Tommy Craig, President
James Gashel, Director of Governmental Affairs

Individuals interested in preventing blindness and preserving sight through research and education programs. Promotes equality, opportunity, and security for the visually impaired.

7678 National Federation of the Blind: Blind Merchants Division
National Federation of the Blind
1800 Johnson Street
Baltimore, MD 21230-4998
410-659-9314
Fax: 410-685-5653

Marc Maurer, President

Membership organization of blind persons employed in either self-employment work or the Randolph-Sheppard vending program. Provides information regarding rehabilitation, social security, tax and other issues which directly affect blind merchants. Serves as advocacy and support group.

7679 National Federation of the Blind: Blind Industrial Workers of America
National Federation of the Blind
1800 Johnson Street
Baltimore, MD 21230-4998
410-659-9314
Fax: 410-685-5653

Marc Maurer, President

Membership organization of blind persons employed in industrial and manufacturing work or in government job programs for the blind. Dedicated to protecting the rights of blind workers in salary, job stability, advancement and labor issues.

7680 National Federation of the Blind: Human Services Division
National Federation of the Blind
1026 East 36th Street
Baltimore, MD 21218
410-235-3073
Fax: 410-685-5653
e-mail: marieco@uwalumni.com
http://www.nfb.org

Melissa Riccobono, President

Membership organization of blind persons working in counseling, personnel, psychology, social work, psychiatry, rehabilitation and other social science and human resource fields. Dedicated to improving employment opportunities and advancement for blind persons and provides resources regarding blindness-related techniques and methods used in these fields.

7681 National Federation of the Blind: Job Opportunities for the Blind
1800 Johnson Street
Baltimore, MD 21230-4998
410-659-9314
800-638-7518

Marc Maurer, President

Provides information, services, and free materials to legally blind US citizens seeking work in the US, employers interested in hiring blind persons, and anyone assisting the blind. National reference and referral services include introduction to blind peers and national job seminars. Hours: 8:00 a.m. to 5:00 p.m. Monday-Friday.

7682 National Federation of the Blind: Masonic Square Club
National Federation of the Blind
3110 Wisteria Avenue
Baltimore, MD 21214
410-598-0155
Fax: 410-685-5653
http://www.nfb.org

Fred Flowers, President

Blind individuals committed to sharing of Masonic experiences, goals and history.

7683 National Federation of the Blind: Music Division
National Federation of the Blind
1737 Tamarack Lane
Janesville, WI 53545-0951
608-752-8749
Fax: 410-685-5653
http://www.nfb.org

Linda Mentink, President

Blind persons dedicated to advancing employment and entertainment opportunities in various music fields. Offers support and information regarding copyright, publishing, promotion and other career details.

7684 National Federation of the Blind: Public Employees Division
National Federation of the Blind
4301 Clogston Avenue NE
Bremerton, WA 98310
360-782-9575
Fax: 410-685-5653
e-mail: IEWeich@comcast.net
http://www.nfb.org

Ivan Weich, President

Organization of blind persons holding local, state or federal jobs. Focuses on issues such as changes in governmental hiring and retention practices, new job skills needed for the future, government employment downsizing, electronic means of finding public sector jobs, self-advocacy, career planning strategies.

7685 National Federation of the Blind: Science and Engineering Division
National Federation of the Blind
10955 Deering Street
San Diego, CA 92126
858-527-1727
Fax: 410-685-5653
e-mail: JMiller@ccpu.com
http://www.nfb.org

John Miller, President

Blind persons with expertise and experience in fields such as genetics, telecommunications, biology, chemistry, physics and nuclear physics or mechanical, electronic and chemical engineering. This is a strong support group to encourage blind persons in pursuit of these careers, many of which have been considered not possible for the blind in the past.

7686 National Federation of the Blind: Sligo Creek Chapter
11923 Parklawn Drive
Rockville, MD 20852
301-881-1892
Fax: 410-558-0739
e-mail: mgosse@nfb.org
http://www.nfbmd.org

Michael Gosse, President
Deborah Brown, First Vice President

Blind persons in Montgomery and Prince George's counties, MD. Promotes the complete integration of blind people into society, through employment, public education, and legislation.

Visually Impaired/Associations & Organizations

7687 National Federation of the Blind: Writers Division
National Federation of the Blind
504 South 57th Street
Omaha, NE 68106-1202
402-556-3216
Fax: 410-685-5653
e-mail: newmanrl@cox.net
http://www.nfb.org
Robert L. Newman, President

Blind writers in all styles, including poetry, short story, fiction, non-fiction, magazine writing and theatrical work offer encouragement and support to blind writers and authors. Issues cover various aspects of this business, including selling your work, publishing, technology, motivation and discovering writing and publishing resources.

7688 National Industries for the Blind
PO Box 969
Wayne, NJ 07474
973-595-9200
Fax: 973-595-9122

A nonprofit organization that represents over 100 associated industries serving people who are blind in thirty-six states. These agencies serve people who are blind or visually impaired and help them to reach their full potential. Services include job and family counseling, job skills training, instruction in Braille and other communication skills, children's programs and more.

7689 National Library Service for the Blind and Physically Handicapped
Library of Congress
1291 Taylor Street NW
Washington, DC 20011
202-707-5100
800-424-8567
Fax: 202-707-0712
e-mail: nls@loc.gov
http://www.loc.gov/nls
TDD 202-707-0744
Frank Kurt Cylke, Director
Carolyn Sung, NLS Network Division chief

Administers a national library service that provides braille and recorded books and magazines on free loan to anyone who cannot read standard print because of visual or physical disabilities.

7690 National Organization of the Senior Blind
National Federation of the Blind
3404 Indian School Road, Northeast, Apartment #C
Albuquerque, NE 87106-1154
505-268-3895
Fax: 410-685-5653
e-mail: nfb@iamdigex.net
http://www.nfb.org
Christine Hall, President

Membership organization of elderly blind persons providing support and information to other blind seniors. Issues include concerns such as remaining active in community and social life, maintaining private homes or living in retirement communities or nursing homes, learning the techniques used by the blind, independently caring for oneself and maintaining a positive approach to vision loss.

7691 National Retinitis Pigmentosa Foundation Helpline
11350 McCormick Rd
#800
Hunt Valley, 21031-1002
800-638-2300

Provides information and referral services to persons suffering from Retinitis Pigmentosa.

7692 National Society to Prevent Blindness
500 E Remington Road
Schaumburg, IL 60173-5624
847-843-2020
Fax: 847-843-8458
e-mail: info@preventblindness.org
http://www.preventblindness.org

Information and referral services provided on specific eye disorders. Publishes literature and supports community screening and testing programs.

7693 Nebraska Commission for the Blind & Visually Impaired
4600 Valley Road
Suite 100
Lincoln, NE 68510-4844
402-471-2891
Fax: 402-471-3009
e-mail: pearl.vanzandt@ncbvi.ne.gov
http://www.ncbvi.ne.gov
Pearl Van Zandt, Ph.D, Executive Director
Bill Brown, Business Manager

Rehabilitation agency for the blind and visually impaired

7694 Nevada's Bureau of Services to the Blind and Visually Impaired
NV Dept of Employment, Training & Rehabilitation
1370 South Curry Street
Carson City, NV 89701
775-684-0400
Fax: 775-684-0361
e-mail: detrbsb@nvdetr.org
http://www.detr.state.nv.us
Terry Johnson, Director

Offers services for the totally blind, legally blind, visually impaired, mentally retarded blind and more with health, counseling, educational, recreational, rehabilitation, computer training and professional training services.

7695 New England Region: Helen Keller National Center
PO Box 266
Lincoln, MA 01773
718-259-7100
Fax: 781-259-4014
http://www.hknc.org
Mary Ellen Barbiasz, Regional Rep
Julie Sahli, Administrative Assistant

7696 New Eyes for the Needy
PO Box 332
549 Millburn Avenue
Short Hills, NJ 7078
973-376-4903
Fax: 973-376-3807
http://www.neweyesfortheneedy.org
Pamela DePompo, Executive Director
Clelia Biamonti, President

Provides new glasses for those with low vision who may not be able to afford them.

7697 New Hampshire Association for the Blind
25 Walker Street
Concord, NH 3301
603-224-4039
800-464-3075
Fax: 603-224-4378
e-mail: services@sightcenter.com
http://www.sightcenter.com
George F Theriault, President/CEO
Shelley M. Proulx, M.B.A., Vice President for Development

Provides rehabilitation services to blind and visually impaired New Hampshire residents in their homes, workplaces, and communities. Maintains Access Center, which produces large print, braille and audio tape materials for corporations and individuals.

7698 New Hampshire Association for the Blind
25 Walker Street
Concord, NH 03301-4592
603-224-4039
800-464-3075
Fax: 603-224-4378
http://www.peekaboo.net.nhab
George F Theriault, President/CEO

Provides rehabilitation services to blind and visually impaired NH residents in their homes, workplaces, and communities. Maintains Access Center, which produces large print, braille and audio tape materials for corporations and individuals.

7699 New Jersey Blind Citizens Association
18 Burlington Avenue
Leonardo, NJ 07737-1615
732-291-0878
Fax: 732-297-0878
J Douglas Scott, Executive Director

Visually Impaired/Associations & Organizations

Legally blind and some sighted individuals. To promote social, economical, physical, vocational, mental, moral, and education welfare of blind men and women. Conducts charitable activities.

7700　New Jersey Blind Citizens' Association
18 Burlington Avenue
Leonardo, NJ 7737
732-291-0878
Fax: 732-291-0878
e-mail: newjerseyblind@aol.com
http://www.njbca.org

Phyllis Bass, Director
J Douglas Scott, Executive Director

Organization dedicated to improving the lives of the blind. Services available to blind men, women, and couples age 18 and over who are legally blind and residents of New Jersey. Summer vacation program and day camp program. Both programs inlcude: mobility training, Braille lessons, social and recreational activities.

7701　New Jersey Commission for the Blind and Visually Impaired
153 Halsey Street
Newark, NJ 7101
973-648-3126
Fax: 973-648-3389
TDD 201-648-4559

Jamie C Hilton, President

Offers services for the totally blind, legally blind, visually impaired, deaf blind and more with eye health, counseling, educational, recreational, rehabilitation, computer training and vocational services.

7702　New Mexico Commission for the Blind
2905 RODEO PARK DR. EAST, BLDG. 4
SUITE 100
Santa Fe, NM 87505
505-476-4479
888-513-7968
Fax: 505-476-4475

Greg D Trapp, Executive Director
SANDY SANDOVAL, Deputy Director

Offers services for the totally blind, legally blind, visually impaired, mentally retarded blind and more with health, counseling, educational, recreational, rehabilitation, computer training and professional training services.

7703　New Vision Enterprises
2200 Brownsboro Road
Louisville, KY 40206-2141
502-893-0211
800-405-9135
Fax: 502-893-3885
http://http://www.nvces.com/

Provides assistance to Kentucky residents with vision problems.

7704　North Carolina Society to Prevent Blindness
4011 WestChase Blvd
Suite 225
Raleigh, NC 27607-2972
919-755-5044
Fax: 203-598-0584
e-mail: jtalbot@pbnc.org
http://www.preventblindness.org

Jennifer Talbot, Chief Executive Officer
Dan Bernstein, Chairman

Volunteers working to prevent blindness and preserve maximum vision. Conducts glaucoma and preschool vision screenings and eye safety campaigns. Issues publications. Certification of vision screeners.

7705　North Central Regional Training Center: Canine Companions for Independence
4989 State Route 37 E
Delaware, OH 43015
740-548-4447
Fax: 740-363-0555
http://www.cci.org/northcentral/

Jim Cunningham, Director
Cheryl Lesko, Executive Director

7706　North Central Sight Services
PO Box 3292
2121 Reach Road
Williamsport, PA 17701
570-323-9401
800-326-9370
Fax: 570-323-8194
e-mail: ncss@ncsight.org
http://www.ncsight.org

Robert Garrett, President
Jeffrey Rauff, Chairman

7707　North Country Association for the Visually Impaired
PO Box 1338
2693 Main Street
Lake Placid, NY 12946-5338
518-523-1950
Fax: 518-523-2337
e-mail: NCAVI2001@yahoo.com
http://www.ncavi.org

Karen Mergenthaler, Executive Director
Donna Abair, Director

7708　Northeast Regional Training Center: Canine Companions for Independence
SUNY Farmingdale
PO Box 205
SUNY Farmingdale Farm Complex, Melville Road
Farmingdale, NY 11735-0205
631-694-6938
http://www.caninecompanions.org

Paul Mundell, Director
Ronald A Knell, Executive Director

7709　Northeastern Association of the Blind at Albany
301 Washington Avenue
Albany, NY 12206
518-463-1211
Fax: 518-436-4194
http://www.naba-vision.org

Tom Robertson, Executive Director
Anthony S. Esposito, President
Thomas A Robertson, Executive Director

Commited to helping blind or visually impaired individuals remain independent by providing individualized rehabilitation, low vision equipment, adaptive technology, vocational assessment, and job placement services.

7710　Northwest Regional Training Center: Canine Companions for Independence
PO Box 446
Santa Rosa, CA 95402
707-546-2265
TDD 707-577-1756

Katherine Davis, Director
Virginia Gustin, Manager

7711　Oklahoma League for the Blind
501 N. Douglas Ave
Oklahoma City, OK 73106
405-232-4644
Fax: 405-236-5438
e-mail: info@olb.org
http://www.olb.org

Lauren White, President
Joe Crouch, Executive Vice President

7712　Oklahoma State Office of Rehabilitation Services: Visually Impaired
2409 N Kelley Avenue
Oklahoma City, OK 73111
405-522-5818
Fax: 405-525-7759
http://www.ok.gov

Kayla Bauer, Director

Offers services for the totally blind, legally blind, visually impaired, mentally retarded blind and more with health, counseling, educational, recreational, rehabilitation, computer training and professional training services.

Visually Impaired/Associations & Organizations

7713 Oregon Commission for the Blind
535 SE 12th Avenue
Suite 405
Portland, OR 97214
971-673-1588
Fax: 971-673-1570
e-mail: ocb.mail@state.or.us
http://www.cfb.state.or.us
Don Dartt, Representative of Blind Oregonia
Joyce Green, Representative of The National F

State agency that provides vocational and independent living services to the blind and visually impaired Oregonans.

7714 Oregon State Commission for the Blind
535 SE 12th Avenue
Portland, OR 97214-2408
503-731-3221
Charles Young, Administrator
Peter MacDonald, Executive Director

Offers services for the totally blind, legally blind, visually impaired, mentally retarded blind and more with health, counseling, educational, recreational, rehabilitation, computer training and professional training services.

7715 Pasadena Braille Club
386 S Los Robles Avenue
Pasadena, CA 91101-3216
626-793-7636
Felix Fresquez, Administrator

Blind and visually impaired persons in the Pasadena, CA area. Provides assistance to blind persons by offering educational, rehabilitation, and social activities. Teaches braille, mobility, and independent living skills.

7716 Pasadena Braille Club
386 S Los Robles Avenue
Pasadena, CA 91101
626-793-7636
Fax: 626-449-2586
http://www.pasadenasocialservices.com
Felix Fresquez, Administrator

Blind and visually impaired persons in the Pasadena, CA area. Provides assistance to blind persons by offering educational, rehabilitation, and social activities. Teaches braille, mobility, and independent living skills.

7717 Pennsylvania Bureau of Blindness and Visual Services
Harrisburg District Office
1521 North 6th Street
Harrisburg, PA 17102
717-787-6176
800-622-2842
http://www.dli.state.pa.us
Stephen M Schmerin, Secretary
Edward G. Rendell, Governor

Provides services to Pennsylvanians who are blind and visually impaired to promote economic and social independence in their daily life activities. Services include vocational rehabilitation to help working age Pennsylvanians gain employment; older blind independent living services (age 55 and up); children's services (birth to age 17); services to adults with multiple disabilities.

7718 Pittsburgh Branch of the Pennsylvania Association for the Blind
300 S Craig Street
Pittsburgh, PA 15213-3707
412-255-2398
Judy Hill, Manager

7719 Pittsburgh Vision Service
1800 West Street
Homestead, PA 15233
412-368-4400
Fax: 412-368-4090
e-mail: info&ref@pghvis.org
http://www.pghvis.org/
Stephen S. Barrett, M. Ed.,, President
James Baumgartner, Vice President of Finance and Ad

7720 Pony Express Association for the Blind
11695 SW Rogers Road
Stewartsville, MO 64490
816-364-4447
e-mail: phylaron@webtv.net
Phyllis Zirkle, President

Visually impaired persons; interested others. Promotes the interests of the visually impaired; monitors legal activity affecting the blind; conducts social activities. Meets at the Joyce Raye Patterson Senior Center.

7721 Pony Express Association of the Blind
3643 Gene Field Road
Apt F40
Saint Joseph, MO 64506-4839
816-232-9761
800-342-632
e-mail: csa3099@ccp.com
Carolyn Anderson, Executive Officer

Visually impaired persons; interested others. Promotes the interests of the visually impaired; monitors legal activity effecting the blind; conducts social activities.

7722 Prevent Blindness America
211 W. Wacker Dr
Suite 1700
Chicago, IL 60606
847-843-2020
Fax: 847-843-8458
e-mail: info@preventblindness.org
http://www.preventblindness.org
Joanne Angle, Executive Director
Kevin Buehler, Senior Vice President

Dedicated to fighting blindness and saving sight. Nationwide affiliates, divisions, and chapters serves millions of people each year through public and professional education, community and patient service programs, and research. The organization produces educational materials including brochures. Limited materials available in Spanish.

7723 Prevent Blindness Connecticut
984 Southford Road
Middlebury, CT 06762-3234
203-598-0529
800-850-2020
Fax: 860-347-0613
e-mail: 104706.1100@compuserve.com
Paul L Blawie, President/CEO

Preserves and enhances visual health through eye screenings, education, safety activities and support of research. Places special emphasis on preschool children, the elderly, and individuals at risk for eye injuries throughout Connecticut.

7724 Prevent Blindness Iowa
1111 9th Street
Suite 250
Des Moines, IA 50314-2585
515-244-4341
800-329-8782
Fax: 515-244-4718
e-mail: pbiowa@netins.net
http://www.preventblindness.org/Iowa
Jeanne Burmeister, Executive Director
Amy G O'Brien, Assistant Director

To prevent blindness, preserve sight and enhance and extend the quality of vision for all Iowans.

7725 Prevent Blindness Nebraska
6818 Grover Street
Suite 102
Omaha, NE 68106
402-505-6119
Fax: 402-505-6242
e-mail: pbn@mb3.net
http://www.preventblindness.org/ne
Kim Shillito, Executive Director
Sherri Peterson, Assistant Executive Director

Visually Impaired/Associations & Organizations

Volunteers and service organizations. Seeks to improve eye health awareness and prevent unnecessary blindness through education, health training, and mass screenings. Provides information and referral services. Conducts public awareness campaign on eye health and safety topics; operates speakers' bureau; audio-visual lending library; participates in health fairs, LifeSight programs, and Wise Owl Club safety incentive program. Holds charity golf tournament and Most Beautiful Eyes contest. Offers vision screenings for children and adults.

7726 Prevent Blindness Northern California
1388 Sutter Street
Suite 408
San Francisco, CA 94109
415-567-7500
800-338-3041
Fax: 415-567-7600
e-mail: g@eyeinfo.org
http://www.eyeinfo.org
Peter Jangochian, Executive Director
Debora Babe RN, Program Director
Gus Gunn, Director Operations

Individuals interested in preventing blindness and preserving sight through research and education programs. Provides preschool vision and adult vision screening services and eye safety programs. Large print guidebook, Coping With Sight Loss in Northern California, available also in audio cassette, Braile, or on disk. Single copies free.

7727 Prevent Blindness Ohio
1500 W 3rd Avenue
Suite 200
Columbus, OH 43212
614-464-2020
800-301-2020
Fax: 614-481-9670
e-mail: info@pbohio.org
http://www.preventblindness.org/Ohio/
Sherill K. Williams, President and Chief Executive Di
Tricia Cunningham, Director Development

Volunteers. Works to preserve sight and prevent blindness. Conducts charitable activities.

7728 Prevent Blindness Oklahoma
6 NE 63rd Street
Suite 150
Oklahoma City, OK 73105
405-848-7123
Fax: 405-848-6935
e-mail: brenda-pbo@coxinet.net
http://www.preventblindnessok.org/
Dianna Bonfiglio, President and Chief Executive Di
Becky Cunningham, Director of Programs

Individuals interested in preventing blindness and preserving sight through research and education programs.

7729 Prevent Blindness Tennessee
95 White Bridge Road
Suite 513
Nashville, TN 37205
615-352-0450
800-335-0450
Fax: 615-352-5750
e-mail: foryereyes@aol.com
http://www.preventblindness.org/tn
Alice Orr, Executive Director
Jeane McCullough, Coordinator

Individuals interested in preventing blindness and preserving sight through research, education programs, and community service. Conducts charitable activities.

7730 Prevent Blindness Texas
PO Box 5325
Midland, TX 79701
432-620-8228
Fax: 432-620-8448
e-mail: pbtvickey@sbcglobal.net
http://www.preventblindness.org/TX/
Vickey Banks, Executive Director
Irma Ochoa, Program Director

7731 Prevent Blindness Tri-State
984 Southford Road
Middlebury, CT 06762
800-850-2020
800-850-2020
Fax: 203-598-0584
e-mail: info@preventblindnessct.org
http://www.preventblindnessct.org
Kathryn Garre-Ayars, President/CEO
James Belcher, Chairman
Richard Taft, Treasurer

Our mission is to save sight and prevent vision loss from illness or accident through vision information, education, advocacy, and screening services, touching lives with a clear vision for the future.

7732 Prevent Blindness Virginia
11618 Busy Street
Richmond, VA 23236
804-423-2020
888-790-2020
Fax: 804-423-5409
http://www.pbv.org
Timothy L Gresham, President/CEO
Robin Mead, Director of Development

Individuals working to prevent blindness. Provides children's and adult vision screening and eye health programs to the public.

7733 Prevention of Blindness Society of Metropolitan Washington
1775 Church Street NW
Washington, DC 20036
202-234-1010
Fax: 202-234-1020
e-mail: mhartlove@youreyes.org
http://www.youreyes.org
Michele D Hartlove, MA, Executive Director
Meredith Larkin, Assistant to Executive Director

Organization provides comprehensive information on vision problems, macular degeneration, glaucoma, diabetic retinopathy, eyeglasses, other vision correction, and a directory of professional members. Provides services in the entire Metropolitan Area, including Northern Virginia, surburan Maryland, and Washington, DC.

7734 RP Foundation Fighting Blindness (RPFFB)
1401 W Mt Royal Avenue
4th Floor
Baltimore, MD 21217
410-255-9400
800-638-5555
Fax: 410-225-9409

Provides information and referral for interested individuals regarding inherited retinal degenerations such as Retinitis Pigmentosa.

7735 Recorded Periodicals
Associated Services for the Blind
919 Walnut Street
Philadelphia, PA 19107-5237
215-627-4230
Fax: 215-922-0692
Patricia C Johnson, CEO

A subscription service of Associated Services for the Blind, these periodicals provide 21 magazines through this subscription service. A magazine list can be sent, in both large print and on audio cassette.

7736 Recording Service for Visually Handicapped
PO Box 610
Falls Church, VA 22040
703-533-7413
Jane Gailey, Executive Secretary

Individuals and organizations united to make available to the blind, and other visually or perceptually impaired, at no cost, tape-recordings of printed materials.

Visually Impaired/Associations & Organizations

7737 Recording for the Blind & Dyslexic
20 Roszel Road
Princeton, NJ 8540
609-452-0606
Fax: 609-987-8116
e-mail: info@rfbd.org
http://www.rfbd.org

MIKE DAVIS, Executive Director
John Kelly, President and Chief Executive Of

Provides recorded and computerized textbooks, library services and other educational resources to people who cannot effectively read standard print because of a visual impairment, learning disability or other physical disability. RFB&D also provides bibliographic reference services and acts as a recording service for additional titles. RFB&D has two membership programs—individual and institutional (school).

7738 Recording for the Blind Helpline
20 Roszel Road
Princeton, NJ 08540-6294
609-452-0606
800-221-4792

John Kelly, CEO

7739 Research to Prevent Blindness
645 Madison Ave
Floor 21
New York, NY 10022-1010
212-752-4333
800-621-0026
e-mail: inforequest@rpbusa.org
http://www.rpbusa.org/rpb

Diane S. Swift, President
James Romano, Chief Operating Officer

National voluntary health foundation supported by foundations, corporations, and voluntary gifts and bequests from individuals. Established to stimulate basic and applied research into the causes, prevention and treatment of blinding eye diseases.

7740 Rhode Island Department of Human Services for the Blind
40 Fountain Steet
Providence, RI 02903
401-222-2300
Fax: 401-222-1328
http://www.dhs.state.ri.us

Tina Janik, Administrator
Gary Alexander, Director

7741 Rhode Island Services for the Blind and Visually Impaired
40 Fountain Street
Providence, RI 02903
401-421-7005
Fax: 401-222-3574
http://www.ors.state.ri.us/
TDD 401-421-7016

Raymond A Carroll, Administrator
Stephen Brunero, Acting Administrator

Offers services for the totally blind, legally blind, visually impaired, mentally retarded blind and more with health, counseling, educational, recreational, rehabilitation, computer training and professional training services.

7742 Seeing Eye
PO Box 375
Morristown, NJ 7963
973-539-4425
Fax: 973-539-0922
e-mail: info@seeingeye.org
http://www.seeingeye.org

Kenneth Rosenthal, President
Doug Roberts, Director of Programs

A training school for dogs to guide qualified blind persons.

7743 Sight-Loss Support Group of Central Pennsylvania
111 Sowers Street
Suite 310
State College, PA 16801
814-238-0132
e-mail: slsg@papower.net
http://www.slsg.org

Rana Arnold, contact
Judy Williams, Contact

Persons with any degree of sight loss. Provides information on talking book records and large print libraries. Offers self-help and information referral services. Maintains optical and non-optical aids exhibit, and speakers panel.

7744 South Central Region: Helen Keller National Center
141 Middle Neck Road
Suite 340
Sands Point, NY
516-944-8900
Fax: 516-944-7302
e-mail: HKNCinfo@hknc.org
http://www.helenkeller.org

Fred W McPhilliamy, President
John P. Lynch, Executive Director

7745 South Dakota Association of the Blind
PO Box 1622
Sioux Falls, SD 57101-1622
605-367-5322
Fax: 605-367-5485
http://www.sd-sdab.org

Virginia Miller, Vice President
Dawn Brush, Vice President

7746 South Texas Lighthouse for the Blind
4421 Agnes Street
Corpus Christi, TX 78405
361-883-6553

Regis Barber, President
Nicky Ooi, Vice President Mfg. and New Busi

7747 Southeast Regional Center: Canine Companions for Independence
PO Box 547511
Orlando, FL 32854-7511
407-834-2555
Fax: 407-830-9996
http://www.caninecompanions.org

Ted Rogahn, President
Anne Gittinger, Vice President

7748 Southeastern Region: Helen Keller National Center
1003 Virginia Avenue
Suite 104
Atlanta, GA 30354
404-766-9625
Fax: 404-766-3447
e-mail: rebecca.sills@dol.state.ga.us
http://www.hknc.org
TDD 404-766-2820

Rebecca Sills, Contact
Barbara Chandler, Regional Representative

7749 Southern Tier Association for the Visually Impaired
719 Lake Street
Elmira, NY 14901-2538
607-734-1554
Fax: 607-734-9467
e-mail: info@st-avi.org
http://http://st-avi.org/

Timothy Hertlein, Executive Director
Gail Cordes, president

Visually Impaired/Associations & Organizations

7750 **Southwest Regional Training Center: Canine Companions for Independence**
124 Rancho del Oro Drive
PO Box 4568
Oceanside, CA 92052
760-901-4300
800-572-2275
Fax: 760-901-4350
http://www.cci.org
TDD 760-901-4326

Rhonda Carpenter, Director
Ted Rogahn, President

Assistance dogs for people with disabilities.

7751 **Southwestern Region: Helen Keller National Center**
6160 Cornerstone Court E
San Diego, CA 92121-3720
858-623-2777
Fax: 858-642-0266
e-mail: hkncinfo@hknc.org
http://www.hknc.org

Joe McNulty, executive director
Art Roehrig,, president

7752 **St. Louis Society for the Blind**
8770 Manchester Road
Saint Louis, MO 63144
314-968-9000
Fax: 314-968-9003
e-mail: socserv@slsbvi.org
http://www.slsbli.org

David Ekin, President

Offers rehabilitation services for blind and visually impaired adults in St. Louis area. Contracts with local schools for services to school age students.

7753 **Tampa Lighthouse for the Blind**
1106 W Platt Street
Tampa, FL 33606-2142
813-251-2407
Fax: 813-254-4305
e-mail: TLH@tampalighthouse.org
http://www.tampalighthouse.org

Lucien Lue, Assistant Project Manager
Mercy Ransom, Project Manager
Cliff Olstrom, Executive Director

Provides employment opportunites and maximize independence for persons who are blind or visually impaired.

7754 **Taping for the Blind**
3935 Essex Lane
Houston, TX 77027
713-622-2767
Fax: 713-622-2772
http://www.tapingfortheblind.org

Randy de la Garza, President
Michael Garrett, Director

Records reading material on audiotape, copied onto cassettes, for use by blind and physically handicapped persons. Promotes increased interest in and use of, free audio materials. Books, textbooks and technical manuals are recorded and sent to the Library of Congress for duplication and distribution on cassette tapes to 50 regional libraries.

7755 **Tarrant County Association for the Blind**
912 West Broadway
Fort Worth, TX 76104
817-332-3341
Fax: 817-332-3456
e-mail: bob@lighthousefw.org
http://lighthousefw.org

Robert W Mosteller, President
Michele Hahnfeld, Chairman

7756 **Telephone Pioneers of America**
930 15th Street
12th Floor
Denver, CO 80201-3888
303-571-1200
800-872-5995
Fax: 303-572-0520
e-mail: johnmccullouch@bellsouth.net
http://www.telecompioneers.org

John M. McCullouch, Chairman
Marty Lee, President

7757 **Tennessee Council of the Blind**
313 Overridge Cove
Hermitage, TN 37076
615-874-1223
e-mail: brendan0@bellsouth.net
http://www.acb.org

Brenda Dillon, President

7758 **Texas Association of Retinitis Pigmentosa**
PO Box 8388
Corpus Christi, TX 78468-8388
361-852-8515
Fax: 361-852-8515
e-mail: tarpmail@homebiz101.com
http://www.geocities.com

Dorothy H Stiefel AAS, Executive Director

A nonprofit organization based in Texas serving as a national information-sharing center to provide human services to persons with progressive vision loss from retinitis pigmentosa and other retinal degenerative disorders.

7759 **Texas Commission for the Blind**
4800 N Lamar Boulevard
Austin, TX 78756
512-377-0300
800-252-5204
Fax: 512-377-0432
http://www.dars.state.tx.us/dbs/ccrc/

Ed Kunz, Center Director

Offers services for the totally blind, legally blind, and visually impaired, with counseling, educational, recreational, rehabilitation, computer training and professional training services.

7760 **Texas Society to Prevent Blindness**
2202 Waugh Drive
Houston, TX 77006
713-526-2559
888-98S-1GHT
Fax: 713-529-8310
e-mail: hubbardjim@msn.com
http://www.preventblindness.org/TX/chronology.h

Jim B. Hubbard, President/CEO
Joanie Wentz, Executive Director

Provides programs and services geared toward the prevention of blindness. Conducts workshops.

7761 **Tower Club of the Blind**
2628 Hope
Maplewood, MO 63143
314-646-8272

Marie Kelley, President

Visually impaired persons in Missouri united to improve their quality of life through social, educational, and moral programs. Makes available disability benefit program. Issues publications.

7762 **Travis Association for the Blind**
PO Box 3297
Austin, TX 78764-3297
512-442-2329
Fax: 512-442-5498
e-mail: info@austinlighthouse.org
http://www.austinlighthouse.org

Jerry A. Mayfield, Executive Director
Benny Galloway, Chief Financial Officer

7763 **Tri-State Blind Society**
3333 Asbury Road
Dubuque, IA 52002-2802
563-556-8746
Fax: 563-556-3592

Donald Gagne, Director

Visually Impaired/Associations & Organizations

Blind and visually impaired persons in Iowa, Wisconsin, and Illinois. Provides education, training, referral, and low vision services to visually impaired citizens and their families. Services include braille and cooking classes, cane travel, emergency transportation to and from activities, and training classes.

7764 Tri-State Independent Blind Society
3333 Asbury Road
Dubuque, IA 52002
563-556-8746
Fax: 563-556-3592
Donald Gagne, Executive Director

Blind and visually impaired persons in Iowa, Wisconsin, and Illinois. Provides education, training, referral, and low vision services to visually impaired citizens and their families. Services include braille and cooking classes, cane travel, emergency transportation to and from activities, and training classes.

7765 United States Association for Blind Athletes
33 North Institute Street
Colorado Springs, CO 80903
719-630-0422
Fax: 719-630-0616
e-mail: usaba@usa.net
http://www.usaba.org
Mark Lucas, Executive Director
Carolina Bayon, Communications Director

Athletic association for blind athletes, this association is the national governing body for the United States visually impaired athletes.

7766 Utah Industries for the Blind
3495 S West Temple
Salt Lake City, UT 84115-4338
801-269-0314
Fax: 801-975-0279
Jan Quinn, Executive Director
Shirlene Bingham, Manager

Job placement for blind and visually impaired.

7767 Vermont Association for the Blind and Visually Impaired
37 Elmwood Avenue
Burlington, VT 5401
802-863-1358
Fax: 802-863-1481
e-mail: general@vabvi.org
http://www.vabvi.org/main/
Steven Pouliot, Executive Director
Ayeshah Raftery, Director of Development and Publ

Information and referral services.

7768 Vermont Division for the Blind and Visually Impaired
103 S Main Street
Weeks Building
Waterbury, VT 05671-2304
802-241-2210
Fax: 802-241-3359
e-mail: Fred.Jones@ahs.state.vt.us
http://www.dad.state.vt.us
Fred Jones, Director
Loreen Guyette, Administrative Assistant

Offers services for the totally blind, legally blind, visually impaired, mentally retarded blind and more with health, counseling, educational, recreational, rehabilitation, computer training and professional training services.

7769 Virginia Association for Education & Rehabilitation of the Blind & Visually Impaired
1703 N. Beauregard Street
Suite 440
Alexandria, VA 22311
703-671-4500
Fax: 703-671-6391
e-mail: jgandorf@aerbvi.org
http://http://aerbvi.org
Jim Gandorf, Executive Director
Ginger Croce, Director, Membership and Marketi

The only professional membership organization dedicated to the advancement of education and rehabilitation of blind and visually impaired children and adults.

7770 Virginia Department for the Blind & Vision Impaired
397 Azalea Avenue
Richmond, VA 23227
804-371-3140
Fax: 804-371-3351
e-mail: Joe.Bowman@dbvi.virginia.gov
http://www.vdbvi.org
Joesph A Bowman, Commissioner
Jane B Ward-Solomon, Program Director

Offers services for the totally blind, legally blind, visually impaired, mentally retarded blind and more with health, counseling, educational, recreational, rehabilitation, computer training and professional training services.

7771 Virginia Industries for the Blind
1535 High Street
Richmond, VA 23220
804-786-2057
http://www.vdbvi.org/vib
Richard C Bohrer, Plant Manager

7772 Vision Community Services
818 Mount Auburn Street
Watertown, MA 02472-1567
781-926-4232
Fax: 781-926-1412
Barbara R Kibler, Executive Director

Resource information service for the blind, newly blind and visually impaired. Self-help support groups, networks and telephone buddy systems within Massachusetts. Additionally, rehabilitation teachers will visit senior citizens and persons with AIDS-related vision loss. Community volunteers work with individuals at home and in the community as readers, shoppers, friendly visitors. Also: braille transcribing, recording studio, assistive devices.

7773 Vision Foundation
818 Mount Auburn Street
Watertown, MA 02472-1567
781-926-4232
Fax: 781-926-1412
Barbara Kibler, Executive Director

Offers peer counseling, support groups, seminars, information and referral and services for persons with vision loss, AIDS project, rehabilitation services for elders with vision loss.

7774 Vision Use in Employment (VUE)
Carroll Center for the Blind
770 Centre Street
Newton, MA 02458-2530
617-969-6200
800-852-3131
Fax: 617-969-6204
Rachel E Rosenbaum, President

Provides engineering solutions plus training to help people keep jobs despite their vision loss.

7775 Vision World Wide
5707 Brockton Drive
Ste. 302
Indianapolis, IN 46220-5481
317-254-1332
Fax: 317-251-6588
e-mail: info@visionww,org
http://www.visionww.org
Patricia L Price, Editor-In-Chief
William Corbin, Chairman

Believing there is hope when vision fails, Vision World wide disseminates relevant information on a variety of topics through its Information and referral Helpline, Website, E-Mail Announce List, Information Packets, and Journal, all designed to encourage and support individuals with vision loss, family members, and professionals who serve them. Its aims to enhance everyday living as to maintain an independent lifestyle. Also serves as a consumer

Visually Impaired/Associations & Organizations

7776 Visual Impairment and Blindness Services of Northampton County
260 E. Broad Street
Bethlehem, PA 18018
610-866-8049
Fax: 610-866-8730
e-mail: viabl@viablservices.org

Judi Pobuda, Executive Director
David A. Pike, President

Blind and visually impaired persons. Promotes independence for blind and visually impaired persons. Seeks to educate public on importance of eye safety. Sponsors life skills programs, training, rehabilitation teaching, and low vision clinic. Free and low cost eye care for needy individuals.

7777 Visually Impaired Center
1422 W Court Street
Flint, MI 48503
810-235-2544
Fax: 810-235-2597
e-mail: info@vicflint.org
http://www.vicflint.org

Sharon Reigle, Executive Director
Jared Whittey, President

7778 Visually Impaired Data Processors International
American Council of the Blind
1155 15th Street NW
Suite 1004
Washington, DC 20005
202-467-5081
800-424-8666
Fax: 202-467-5085
e-mail: info@acb.org
http://www.acb.org

Robert Rogers, President
Frank Welte, Chairman

Advocates for higher standards in the training of qualified blind students, creates a healthy environment for more employment opportunities in government, provides for the exchange of work technique ideas and works with agencies to increase the availability of braille and recorded materials.

7779 Visually Impaired Veterans of America
American Council of the Blind
1075 N. Rancho Ave.
Suite 1004
Colton, CA 92324
909-825-3067
800-424-8666
Fax: 202-467-5085
e-mail: bj2kiowa@worldnet.att.net
http://www.acb.org/viva

John A. Fleming, President

Directs members to resources, promotes the rights of visually impaired veterans to receive all benefits, encourages research and development of new products for blind people.

7780 Volunteers for the Visually Handicapped
8720 Georgia Avenue
Suite 210
Silver Spring, MD 20910-3614
301-589-0894
Fax: 301-589-7281

Ann Thompson Cook, Executive Director

Offers services for the totally blind, legally blind, visually impaired, mentally retarded blind and more with counseling, educational, recreational, rehabilitation and professional training services. Sells adaptive products; provides readers and shoppers; teaches braille and independent travel skills. Braille transcription services for businesses.

7781 Washington Department of Services for the Blind
PO Box 40933
4565 7th Avenue SE, Lacey
Olympia, WA 98504-0933
360-725-3830
800-552-7103
Fax: 360-407-0679
e-mail: information@dsb.wa.gov
http://www.dsb.wa.gov

Bill Palmer, Executive Director

7782 Washington Ear
35 University Boulevard E
Silver Spring, MD 20901-2484
301-681-6636
Fax: 301-681-5227
e-mail: washear@his.com

Nancy Knauss, Executive Director

A nonprofit organization providing reading and information services for the blind, visually impaired and physically disabled persons who cannot effectively read print, see plays, watch television programs or view museum exhibits. This organization provides radio reading services, dial-in telephone newspaper service, National Symphony Orchestra program notes on audio cassette and raised line and large print atlases and books.

7783 Washington-Greene County Branch of the Pennsylvania Association for Blind
566 E Maiden Street
Washington, PA 15301-3720
724-222-7010
Fax: 724-228-6617

Dennis Charlton, Executive Director

7784 West Tennessee Lions Blind Industries
PO Box 2175
346 St. Paul Avenue
Memphis, TN 38101
901-543-7874
Fax: 901-529-0640

7785 West Texas Lighthouse for the Blind
2001 Austin Street
San Angelo, TX 76903
325-653-4231
Fax: 915-657-9367
e-mail: wtlb@wcc.net
http://www.lighthousefortheblind.org

Robert Porter, Contact

West Texas Lighthouse for the Blind provides employment for the blind and visually impaired.

7786 Winston-Salem Industries for the Blind
7730 North Point Drive
Winston Salem, NC 27106-3310
336-759-0551
800-242-7726
Fax: 336-759-0990
e-mail: info@wsifb.com
http://www.wsifb.com

Daniel J Boucher, President
David Horton, Executive Director

7787 Wiscraft: Wisconsin Enterprises for theBlind
445 S. Curtis Rd
West Allis, WI 53214
414-778-3040
Fax: 414-778-3041
e-mail: customerservice@ibmilw.com
http://www.ibmilw.com

Charles Lange, President

The mission is to provide employment.

7788 York Industries for the Blind: A Division of York County Blind Center
1380 Spahn Avenue
York, PA 17403
717-848-1690
Fax: 717-848-3889
http://www.forsight.org

William H Rhinesmith, President

7789 Youngstown Radio Reading Service
2747 Belmont Avenue
Youngstown, OH 44505-1819
330-759-0100
800-452-2525
Fax: 330-759-0678
http://www.ohioradioreadingservices.org

Mike Bosela, Radio Reading Coordinator
Michael Muder, Chief Broadcast Technician

Visually Impaired/Books

Provides vocational development, employment, personal adjustment, and supportive services to the visually handicapped, severely disabled, and persons otherwise handicapped in Mahoning, Trumbull, Columbiana, and Ashtabula counties, OH. Sponsors Radio Reading Service.

7790 Michigan Commission for the Blind
201 N Washington Square
2nd Floor, P.O. Box 30652
Lansing, MI 48909
517-373-2062
Fax: 517-335-5140

Patrick D. Cannon, Director
Jo Ann Pilarski,, MCB Commission Chair

The Commission for the Blind serves as the vocational rehabilitation agency for the blind. The Commission also operates a residential training center in Kalamazoo, provides independent living services for Michigan's older blind population, low-vision services for the state's youth, a deaf/blind program, and entrepreneurial opportunities for blind persons through its Business Enterprise Program.

Books

7791 A Guide to Independence for the Visually Impaired and Their Families
Demos Vermande
386 Park Avenue S
Suite 201
New York, NY 10016-8804
212-683-0072
800-532-8663
Fax: 212-683-0118

Phyllis Gold, Owner

This first comprehensive, hands-on book for the newly visually impaired and their families presents detailed instructions to deal with emotional reactions and fioght depression; contact organizations and get information; obtain federal and other types of financial aid; use the other senses more effectively; adapt their homes and do household chores; handle paperwork and become socially active.

248 pages

7792 A Picture is Worth a Thousand Words for Blind and Visually Impaired Persons Too!
American Foundation for the Blind/AFB Press
PO Box 1020
Sewickley, PA 15143
412-741-1142
232-304-
Fax: 412-741-0609
e-mail: afborders@abdintl.com
http://www.afb.org

Audiodescription - the art of describing in words for visually impaired viewers the visual aspects seen in television, film, etc. - is highlighted in this book for the blind and visually impaired person.

32 pages

7793 A Step-By-Step Guide to Personal Management for Blind Persons
American Foundation for the Blind/AFB Press
PO Box 1020
Sewickley, PA 15143
412-741-1142
232-304-
Fax: 412-741-0609
e-mail: afborders@abdintl.com
http://www.afb.org

A manual of techniques in the areas of hygiene, grooming, clothing, shopping and child care.

136 pages

7794 AFB Directory of Services for Blind and Visually Impaired Persons in the US
American Foundation for the Blind
11 Penn Plaza
Suite 300
New York, NY 10001-2018
212-502-7600
800-232-5463
Fax: 212-502-7777

Carl Augusto, President

Information concentrates on over 1,500 government and national voluntary agencies, as well as other organizations which serve blind and visually impaired persons.

664 pages

7795 APH Catalog of Accessible Books for People who are Visually Impaired
American Printing House for the Blind
1839 Frankfort Avenue
Louisville, KY 40206-3148
502-895-2405
Fax: 502-895-1509
e-mail: info@aph.org

Tuck Tinsley, President

Offers thousands of selections and publishers of large type and braille books for persons with visual impairments.

7796 Access to Art: A Museum Directory for the Blind and Visually Impaired People
American Foundation for the Blind
11 Penn Plaza
Suite 300
New York, NY 10001-2006
212-502-7600
800-232-5463
Fax: 212-502-7777

Carl Augusto, President

Details the access facilities of over 300 museums, galleries and exhibits in the United States. Also included are organizations offering art-related resources such as, art classes, competitions and traveling exhibits.

144 pages

7797 Age-Related Macular Degeneration
National Association for Visually Handicapped
22 W 21st Street
Floor 6
New York, NY 10010-6943
212-889-3141
Fax: 212-727-2931
e-mail: staff@navh.org
http://www.navh.org

Ann Illuzzi, Manager

A large booklet offering information, with illustrations and up-to-date research, on macular degeneration. Also available in Russian. Revised in 1999.

7798 Aging Eye and Low Vision
Lighthouse International
111 E 59th Street
New York, NY 10022-1202
800-829-0500
Fax: 212-821-9702
http://www.lighthouse.org

A free study guide for physicians on common age-related vision disorders.

7799 Art and Science of Teaching Orientation and Mobility to Persons with Visual Impairments
American Foundation for the Blind/AFB Press
PO Box 1020
Sewickley, PA 15143
412-741-1142
232-304-
Fax: 412-741-0609
e-mail: afborders@abdintl.com
http://www.afb.org

Comprehensive decription of the techniques of teaching orientation and mobility, presented along with considerations and strategies for sensitive and effective teaching. Hardcover. Paperback also available.

200 pages

Visually Impaired/Books

7800 Being in Touch
Gallaudet Univ. Press c/o Chicago Distrib. Center
11030 S Langley Avenue
Chicago, IL 60628-3830
773-248-0387
800-621-2736
Fax: 800-621-8476
http://www.gallaudet.edu
TTY 888-630-9347

Geoff Benge, Owner

Provides information on hearing and vision loss.

80 pages

7801 Berthold Lowenfeld on Blindness and Blind People
American Foundation for the Blind/AFB Press
PO Box 1020
Sewickley, PA 15143
412-741-1142
232-304-
Fax: 412-741-0609
e-mail: afborders@abdintl.com
http://www.afb.org

These writings of the pioneering educator, author and advocate range over a forty-year period include various ground-breaking papers for the blind educator, a rememberance of Helen Keller and other essays on education, sociology and history.

254 pages

7802 Blindness: What it is, What it Does and How to Live with it
American Foundation for the Blind/AFB Press
PO Box 1020
Sewickley, PA 15143
412-741-1142
232-304-
Fax: 412-741-0609
e-mail: afborders@abdintl.com
http://www.afb.org

A classic work on how blindness affects self-perception and social interaction and what can be done to restore basic skills, mobility, daily living and an appreciation of life's pleasures.

396 pages

7803 Burns Braille Transcription Dictionary
American Foundation for the Blind/AFB Press
PO Box 1020
Sewickley, PA 15143
412-741-1142
232-304-
Fax: 412-741-0609
e-mail: afborders@abdintl.com
http://www.afb.org

A handy, portable guide that is a quick reference for anyone who needs to check print-to-braille and braille-to-print meanings and symbols. Paperback.

96 pages

7804 Career Perspectives: Interviews with Blind and Visually Impaired Professionals
American Foundation for the Blind/AFB Press
PO Box 1020
Sewickley, PA 15143
412-741-1142
232-304-
Fax: 412-741-0609
e-mail: afborders@abdintl.com
http://www.afb.org

Profiles of 20 successful archivers who describe in their own words what it takes to pursue and attain professional success in a sighted world. Available in large print, cassette and braille.

96 pages

7805 Cataracts
National Association for Visually Handicapped
22 W 21st Street
Floor 6
New York, NY 10010-6943
212-889-3141
Fax: 212-727-2931
e-mail: staff@navh.org
http://www.navh.org

Ann Illuzzi, Manager

A booklet offering information about Cataracts, diagnosis and treatment of this common condition.

7806 Comprehensive Examination of Barriers to Employment Among Persons who are Blind or Impaired
Mississippi State University
PO Box 6189
Mississippi State, MS 39762-6189
662-325-2001
800-675-7782
Fax: 662-325-8989
e-mail: rrtc@ra.state.edu
http://www.blind.msstate.edu
TDD 601-325-8693

J Elton Moore, Author
Kelly Shaefer, Dissemination Specialist

A multi-phase research project designed to: identify barriers to employment; identify and develop innovative successful strategies to overcome these barriers; develop methods for others to utilize these strategies; disseminate this information to rehabilitation providers; replicate the use of selected strategies in other settings.

90 pages

7807 Contrasting Characteristics of Blind and Visually Impaired Clients
Rehab/Training Center on Blindness and Low-Vision
PO Box 6189
Mississippi State, MS 39762-6189
601-325-2001
675-778-
Fax: 662-325-8989
e-mail: rrtc@ra.msstate.edu
http://www.blind.msstate.edu

Kelly Schaefer, Publications Manager

This report examines cases in the National Blindness and Low Vision Employment Database to identify and profile environmental and personal characteristics of clients who are blind or visually impaired and who were achieving successful and unsuccessful retention of competitive jobs. A total of 787 cases were analyzed.

44 pages

7808 Coping with Vision Loss: Maximizing What You See & Do
Hunter House Publishers
PO Box 2914
Alameda, CA 94501
510-865-5282
800-266-5592
Fax: 510-865-4295
e-mail: ordering@hunterhouse.com
http://www.hunterhouse.com

Christina Sverdrup, Customer Service Manager
Bill Chapman EdD, Author

Helps readers with severe vision loss maximize the use of their remaning visual perception.

304 pages Frequency: Paperback

7809 Data on Blindness and Visual Impairment in the US: A Resource Manual
American Foundation for the Blind
15 W 16th Street
New York, NY 10011-6301
212-502-7600
800-232-5463
Fax: 212-502-7777

Carl Augusto, President

Provides facts and figures for long-range planning, preparing grant proposals and legislative services.

412 pages

7810 Eye and Your Vision
National Association for Visually Handicapped
22 W 21st Street
Floor 6
New York, NY 10010-6943
212-889-3141
Fax: 212-727-2931
e-mail: staff@navh.org
http://www.navh.org

Ann Illuzzi, Manager

A large booklet offering information, with illustrations, on the eye. Includes information on protection of eyesight, how the eye works and vision disorders. Available in Russian and Spanish also.

Visually Impaired/Books

7811 Finding Wheels: A Curriculum for Nondrivers with Visual Impairments for Gaining Control
AFB Press
PO Box 1020
Sewickley, PA 15143-1020
412-741-1398
800-232-3044
http://www.afb.org

It is designed to be used by teachers, child-care workers, houseparents or others who are responsible for helping students to develop daily living skills. It is a set of suggested goals and objectives.

7812 Foundations of Rehabilitation Counseling with Persons who are Blind
American Foundation for the Blind/AFB Press
PO Box 1020
Sewickley, PA 15143
412-741-1142
800-232-3044
Fax: 412-741-0609
e-mail: afborders@abdintl.com
http://www.afb.org

Rehabilitation professionals have long recognized that the needs of people who are blind or visually impaired are unique and require a special knowledge and expertise to provide and coordinate rehabilitation services.

477 pages

7813 Guide to Independence for the Visually Impaired and Their Families
Demos Vermande
386 Park Avenue S
Suite 201
New York, NY 10016-8804
212-683-0072
800-532-8663
Fax: 212-683-0118

Phyllis Gold, Owner

Comprehensive guide for the newly visually impaired and their families that provides concise, practical information on learning to live with the second major cause of disability in the US.

248 pages

7814 If Blindness Comes
National Federation of the Blind
1800 Johnson Street
Baltimore, MD 21230-4914
410-659-9314
Fax: 410-685-5653
e-mail: nfb@iamdigex.net
http://www.nfb.org

Marc Maurer, President

An introduction to issues relating to vision loss and provides a positive, supportive philosophy about blindness. It is a general information book which includes answers to many common questions about blindness, information about services and programs for the blind and resource listings. Contact the Materials Center.

7815 If Blindness Strikes; Don't Strike Out
Charles C Thomas Publisher
2600 S 1st Street
Springfield, IL 62704-4730
217-789-8980
800-258-8980
Fax: 217-789-9130
e-mail: books@ccthomas.com
http://www.ccthomas.com

Michael P Thomas, President

This book is a storehouse of information on daily life for the visually impaired and those around them. From opticons and laser canes to housekeeping to travel, the author describes how to successfully cope with the problems posed by visual impairment and blindness.

316 pages

7816 Intervention Practices in the Retention of Competitive Employment Among Individuals who are Blind
Mississippi State University
PO Box 6189
Mississippi State, MS 39762-6189
662-325-2001
800-675-7782
Fax: 662-325-8989
e-mail: rrtc@ra.state.edu
http://www.blind.msstate.edu
TDD 601-325-8693

Kelly Schaefer, Dissemination Specialist
Elton Moore, Executive Director

This study investigated the methods by which an individual can retain competitive employment after the onset of a significant vision loss. Interviews were conducted with 89 rehabilitation counselors across the US. Strategies that contribute to successful job retention were identified as well as best rehabilitation practices in job retention.

60 pages

7817 Issues in Aging and Vision: A Curriculum for University Programs and In-Service Training
American Foundation for the Blind
11 Penn Plaza
Suite 300
New York, NY 10001-2006
212-502-7600
Fax: 212-502-7771

Carl Augusto, President

Provides information involving university programs in gerontology, training programs and related areas.

224 pages

7818 Large Print Loan Library
National Association for Visually Handicapped
22 W 21st Street
New York, NY 10010-6904
212-889-3141
Fax: 212-727-2931

Ann Illuzzi, Manager

A huge large print catalog of all the publications, fiction and non-fiction, cassette tapes, books-on-tape and videos available for the visually impaired from the loan library of the National Association for the Visually Handicapped.

100 pages

7819 Library Resources for the Blind and Physically Handicapped
National Library Service for the Blind
1291 Taylor Street NW
Washington, DC 20542
202-707-5100
800-424-8567
Fax: 202-707-0712
http://www.loc.gov/nls

Frank Cylke, Executive Director

7820 Life of My Own Daily Meditations on Hope and Acceptance
Hazelden
15251 Pleasant Valley Road
Center City, MN 55012-9640
651-257-4010
800-328-9000
Fax: 651-213-4426
http://www.hazelden.org

Ellen Breyer, President

Offers daily access to strength, serenity, and insight in our relationships with chemically dependent people.

400 pages

7821 Lifestyles of Employed Legally Blind People
Rehab Research & Training Center on Blindness
PO Box 6189
Mississippi State, MS 39762-6189
601-325-2001
Fax: 662-325-8989
e-mail: rrtc@ra.state.edudu
http://www.blind.msstate.edu
TDD 601-325-8693

Lynn W McBroom PhD, Senior Research Scientist

Visually Impaired/Books

Results from a telephone survey show that visually impaired respondents are involved in a wide variety of activities with little restrictions on their range of activities. Sighted respondents tended to spend more time in child care, obtaining goods and services, attending to self-care activities, and engaging in social activities, while visually impaired respondents spent more time in education and passive activities. This report is a study of ex

193 pages

7822 Living with Low Vision: A Resource Guide for People with Sight Loss
Resources for Rehabilitation
22 Bonad Road
Winchester, MA 01890-1302
781-368-9094
Fax: 781-368-9096

Susan Greenblatt, Contact

A large print resource directory that helps people with sight loss locate the services and products that they need to keep reading, working and enjoying life.

272 pages

7823 Low Vision: Reflections of the Past, Issues for the Future
American Foundation for the Blind/AFB Press
PO Box 1020
Sewickley, PA 15143
412-741-1142
Fax: 412-741-0609
e-mail: afborders@abdintl.com
http://www.afb.org

Background papers and a strategies section are used to identify the shifting needs of visually impaired persons and the resources that may be needed to address them. Paperback.

7824 Making Life More Livable
American Foundation for the Blind/AFB Press
11 Penn Plaza
Suite 300
New York, NY 10001-2006
212-502-7600
Fax: 212-502-7774
e-mail: afborder@abdintl.com
http://www.afb.org

Sharon Baker Harris, Sales/Marketing Manager
Carl Augusto, President

Shows how simple adaptations in the home and environment can make a big difference in the lives of blind and visually impaired older persons. The suggestions offered are numerous and specific, ranging from how to mark food cans for greater visibility to how to get out of the shower safley. Large print.

132 pages

7825 Perigee Visual Dictionary of Signing
Harris Communications
15155 Technology Drive
Eden Prairie, MN 55344-2273
952-906-1180
800-825-6758
Fax: 952-906-1099
e-mail: mail@harriscomm.com
http://www.harriscomm.com

Bill Williams, National Sales Manager
Robert Harris, Owner

An A-to-Z guide to American Sign Language vocabulary.

450 pages

7826 Picture is Worth a Thousand Words for Blind and Visually Impaired Persons
American Foundation for the Blind
11 Penn Plaza
Suite 300
New York, NY 10001-2006
212-946-2738
800-232-5463
Fax: 212-502-7777

Larry Nipon, Owner

Audiodescription - the art of describing in words for visually impaired viewers the visual aspects seen in television, film, etc. - is highlighted in this book for the blind and visually impaired person.

32 pages

7827 Prescriptions for Independence
American Foundation for the Blind/AFB Press
PO Box 1020
Sewickley, PA 15143
412-741-1142
Fax: 412-741-0609
e-mail: afborders@abdintl.com
http://www.afb.org

Easy-to-read manual on how older visually impaired persons can pursue their interests and activities in community residences, senior centers, long-term care facilities and other community settings. Paperback.

7828 Providing Services for People with Vision Loss: Multidisciplinary Perspective
Resources For Rehabilitation
22 Bonad Road
Winchester, MA 01890-1302
781-368-9094
Fax: 781-368-9096

A collection of articles by ophthalmologists and rehabilitation professionals, including chapters on operating a low vision service, starting self-help programs, mental health services, aids and techniques that help people with vision loss.

136 pages

7829 Referring Blind and Low Vision Patients for Rehabilitation Services
American Foundation for the Blind
15 W 16th Street
New York, NY 10011-6301
212-620-2155
800-232-5463
Fax: 212-620-2105

Clear information on such basic topics as the objectives of low vision services, what's covered in the examinations, what rehabilitation services do and how to locate these services.

7830 Rehabilitation Resource Manual: Vision
Resources for Rehabilitation
33 Bedford Street
Suite 19a
Lexington, MA 02420-4330
781-862-6455
Fax: 781-861-7517
e-mail: orders@rfr.org

Susan Greenblatt, Mailing Contact

Publication includes: Descriptions of information sources, products, and publications in North America for people who are visually impaired or blind. Entries include: Company or organization name, address, phone, fax, description, prices of product or publication.

Frequency: Biennial

7831 Smith Kettlewell Rehabilitation Engineering Research Center
Smith-Kettlewell Eye Research Institute
2318 Fillmore Street
San Francisco, CA 94115-1813
415-345-2000
Fax: 615-345-8655
e-mail: rerc@ski.org
http://www.ski.org

Henry Metz, President

Reports on technology and devices for persons with visual impairments.

7832 Unseen Minority: A Social History of Blindness in the United States
American Foundation for the Blind/AFB Press
PO Box 1020
Sewickley, PA 15143
412-741-1142
Fax: 412-741-0609
e-mail: afborders@abdintl.com
http://www.afb.org

A lively narrative, peppered with anecdotes, recounts how the blind overcame discrimination to gain full participation in the social, educational, economic and legislative spheres. Hardcover.

573 pages

Visually Impaired/Directories

7833 Vision and Aging: Crossroads for Service Delivery
American Foundation for the Blind
11 Penn Plaza
Suite 300
New York, NY 10001-2006
212-502-7600
800-232-5463
Fax: 212-502-7777

Carl Augusto, President

An overview of the service delivery systems in the aging and blindness fields that covers the essential issues concerning vision loss among older persons in this country, the growth of visual impairments in the elderly, and the policy and service questions.

392 pages

7834 Vision and Aging: Issues in Social Work Practice
Haworth Press
10 Alice Street
Binghamton, NY 13904-1503
607-722-5857
800-429-6784
Fax: 607-771-0012
e-mail: getinfo@haworthpressinc.com
http://www.haworthpressinc.com

Jackie Blakeslee, Advertising
William Cohen, Owner

Responds to the needs of the growing population of blind or severely disabled elderly.

196 pages

7835 Visual Impairment: An Overview
American Foundation for the Blind/AFB Press
PO Box 1020
Sewickley, PA 15143
412-741-1142
Fax: 412-741-0609
e-mail: afborders@abdintl.com
http://www.afb.org

An overall look at the most common forms of vision loss and their impact on the individual. Includes drawings as well as photographs that stimulate how people with vision loss see. Paperback.

56 pages

7836 Visually Impaired Seniors as Senior Companions: A Reference Guide
American Foundation for the Blind/AFB Press
PO Box 1020
Sewickley, PA 15143
412-741-1142
Fax: 412-741-0609
e-mail: afborders@abdintl.com
http://www.afb.org

This useful guide describes the Senior Companion Program that is intended to broaden opportunities for older persons with disabilities. Appendix includes training materials, evaluation forms, recruitment and public relations information.

108 pages

Directories

7837 AFB Directory of Services for Blind and Visually Impaired Persons in the US
American Foundation for the Blind
15 W 16th Street
New York, NY 10011-6301
212-620-2155
800-232-5463
Fax: 212-620-2105

Information concentrates on over 1,500 government and national voluntary agencies, as well as other organizations which serve blind and visually impaired persons.

664 pages Frequency: CD-ROM

7838 APH Catalog of Accessible Books for People Who Are Visually Impaired
American Printing House for the Blind
1839 Frankfort Avenue
Louisville, KY 40206-3148
502-895-2405
Fax: 502-899-2274
e-mail: info@aph.org

Tuck Tinsley, President

Offers thousands of selections and publishers of large type and braille books for persons with visual impairments.

7839 Access Travel: Airports
Airport Council International - North America
1775 K Street NW
Suite 500
Washington, DC 20006-1529
202-293-8500
Fax: 202-331-1362

Gregory Principato, President

About 553 airports worldwide; dot matrix tabulation. Entries include: Airport name, location, TDD and toll free numbers of hotels and rental cars, indication of presence or absence of about 60 facilities and services of special importance to persons in wheelchairs and to blind, deaf, and elderly persons.

50 pages Frequency: Irregular

7840 Access to Art: A Museum Directory for Blind & Visually Impaired People
American Foundation for the Blind
15 W 16th Street
New York, NY 10011-6301
212-620-2155
800-232-5463
Fax: 212-620-2105

Details the access facilities of over 300 museums, galleries and exhibits in the United States. Also included are organizations offering art-related resources such as, art classes, competitions and traveling exhibits.

144 pages Frequency: Large Print

7841 Address List: Regional and Subregional Libraries for the Blind and Physically Handicapped
Nat Lib Serv for the Blind/Physically Handicapped
1291 Taylor Street NW
Washington, DC 20542
202-707-5100
800-424-8567
Fax: 202-707-0712
e-mail: nls@loc.gov
http://www.loc.gov

Frank Cylke, Executive Director

143 state and local libraries that serve blind and physically handicapped persons as part of the Library of Congress cooperating network. Entries include: Name, address, contact name, phone.

25 pages Frequency: Semiannual

7842 Blindness and Visual Impairments: National Organizations
Nat Lib Svc for the Blind & Physically Handicapped
1291 Taylor Street NW
Washington, DC 20542
202-707-5100
800-424-8567
Fax: 202-707-0712
e-mail: nls@loc.gov

Frank Cylke, Executive Director

Organizations providing services and publications listing sources of products and information for blind and visually-impaired individuals; state-level agencies that administer public programs providing special education and rehabilitation services. Entries include: Organization or agency name, address, phone, descriptions of services and publications.

33 pages Frequency: last pub 12/96

7843 Braille Catalog of General InterestItems
National Braille Association
3 Townline Circle
Rochester, NY 14623
585-427-8260
Fax: 585-427-0263
http://www.nationalbraille.org

Lists hundreds of titles of fiction and non-fiction books offered in large print, braille or on cassette to visually impaired readers.

Visually Impaired/Journals, Magazines

7844 **Carolyn's Low Vision Solutions**
1415 57th Avenue W
Bradenton, FL 34207-3646
941-739-5555
800-648-2266
Fax: 941-739-5503
e-mail: carolynscatalog.com
http://www.carolynscatalog.com

Carolyn Tojek, President
John Colton, Owner

Free mail-order catalog of items for visually impaired people.

7845 **Directory of Interpreters for Persons who are Deaf, Hard of Hearing or Deaf-Blind**
Illinois Office of Rehabilitation Services
623 E Adams Street
Springfield, IL 62701-1614
217-785-9304
800-ASK-DORS
Fax: 217-785-7798
e-mail: imays@dors.state.il.us
TDD 217-785-7749

Leesa Mays, Editor

Approximately 175 interpreters of sign language for the hearing impaired in Illinois. Entries include: Personal name, address, phone, whether phone is equipped with a TTY/TDD teletypewriter, professional certification level, availability, geographic area served, whether qualified to interpret for deaf-blind individuals.

37 pages Frequency: Irregular

7846 **Directory of Radio Reading Services**
National Association of Radio Reading Services
2100 Wharton Street
Suite 140
Pittsburgh, PA 15203-1942
412-488-3944
800-280-5325
Fax: 412-488-3953
e-mail: risdavid@aol.com

David Noble, Mailing Contact
Laurie Anderson, Executive Director

Approximately 150 radio reading service worldwide, as well as association members and associate members. Entries include: Service name, address, phone, fax, names and titles of key personnel, e-mail addresses.

Frequency: Annual

7847 **Directory of Resources for the Blind & Visually Impaired**
John Milton Society for the Blind
475 Riverside Drive
Suite 455
New York, NY 10115
212-870-3335
Fax: 212-870-3229
e-mail: order@jmsblind.org
http://www.jmsblind.org

Darcy Quigley, Mailing Contact/Editor

Over 100 church and secular publications available in Braille, large type, and on cassette for the visually impaired; transcription services, organizations who provide camps and other associations assisting the visually impaired. Entries include: Organization name, address, phone, financial data, description of product/service.

125 pages Frequency: Irregular

7848 **Library Resources for the Blind and Physically Handicapped**
Nat Lib Serv for the Blind/Physically Handicapped
1291 Taylor Street NW
Washington, DC 20542
202-707-5100
800-424-8567
Fax: 202-707-0712
e-mail: nls@loc.gov
http://www.loc.gov/nls

Frank Cylke, Executive Director

57 regional and 85 subregional libraries, and 4 machine-lending agencies in the United States, Puerto Rico, the US Virgin Islands, and Guam that provide a free library service of Braille and recorded books and magazines to visually and physically handicapped persons; other agencies distributing Braille materials and talking book machines are also indicated. Entries include: Name of library, address, phone, fax, in-WATS number, e-mail address, TDD number (for the deaf), name of librarian, name of contact for machines (if any), hours of operation, list of book collections (includes disc, cassette, Braille, large type), list of special collections (films, foreign language cassettes), list of special services.

91 pages Frequency: Annual

7849 **Living with Low Vision: A Resource Guide for People with Sight Loss**
Resources for Rehabilitation
33 Bedford Street
Suite 19a
Lexington, MA 02420-4330
781-862-6455
Fax: 781-861-7517
e-mail: info@rfr.org

Susan Greenblatt, Mailing Contact

Resources and services for people with vision loss, including national organizations, publications, distributors of large print publications, reading services, technological aids, and organizations and publications for groups such as the elderly, adolescents, veterans, and those with hearing loss as well. Entries include: Company or organization name, address, phone, fax, e-mail address and web sites, description, price of product or publication. Printed in large print.

288 pages Frequency: Biennial

7850 **New Vision Store**
919 Walnut Street
Philadelphia, PA 19107-5237
215-629-2990
http://www.thenewvisionstore.com

Store and catalog for individuals with visual impairments, listing visual aids, magnifiers, large print books and more.

30 pages

7851 **Visual Aids and Informational Material**
National Association for Visually Handicapped
22 W 21st Street
Floor 6
New York, NY 10010-6943
212-889-3141
Fax: 212-727-2931
e-mail: staff@navh.org
http://www.navh.org

Ann Illuzzi, Manager

A complete listing of the visual aids NAVH carries such as magnifiers, talking clocks, large print playing cards, etc.

65 pages

Journals, Magazines

7852 **Access Review**
Sensory Access Foundation
1142 W Evelyn Avenue
Sunnyvale, CA 94086-5742
408-245-7330
Fax: 408-245-3762

Kenneth Fras, Publisher
Diana Drews, Manager

Magazine outlining new technology for people with vision impairments.

Frequency: Quarterly

7853 **Aging & Vision News**
Lighthouse International
111 E 59th Street
New York, NY 10022-1202
800-829-0500
Fax: 212-821-9702
http://www.lighthouse.org

665

Visually Impaired/Journals, Magazines

Intended for professionals engaged in research, education or service delivery in the field of vision and aging.

7854 Aging and Vision: Declarations of Independence
American Foundation for the Blind/AFB Press
PO Box 1020
Sewickley, PA 15143
412-741-1142
Fax: 412-741-0609
e-mail: afborders@abdintl.com
http://www.afb.org

A very personal look at five older people who have successfully coped with visual impairment and continue to lead active, satisfying lives. Their stories are not only inspirational, but also provide practical, down-to-earth suggestions for adapting to vision loss later in life. 18 minute video tape. Also available in PAL, $52.95, 0-89128-276-9.

7855 American Printing House for the Blind
1839 Frankfort Avenue
6085
Louisville, KY 40206-3152
502-895-2405
223-183-
Fax: 502-899-2274
e-mail: info@aph.org
http://www.aph.org

Fred Gissoni, Customer Support
Tuck Tinsley, President

The world's largest company devoted solely to producing products for people who are visually impaired. We manufacture books and magazines in braille, large type and recorded form from over 200 vendors across the US. We also make a wide range of educational and daily living aids, such as braille paper and styluses, talking book equipment, and synthetic speech computer products. APH also offers LOUIS, an electronic database that lists accessible b

7856 Blind Educator
National Federation of the Blind
1800 Johnson Street
Baltimore, MD 21230-4914
410-659-9314
Fax: 410-685-5653
e-mail: nfb@iamdigex.net
http://www.nfb.org

Marc Maurer, President

Magazine specifically for blind educators.

7857 Blindness, A Family Matter
American Foundation for the Blind/AFB Press
PO Box 1020
Sewickley, PA 15143
412-741-1142
Fax: 412-741-0609
e-mail: afborders@abdintl.com
http://www.afb.org

A frank exploration of the effects of an individual's visual impairment on other members of the family and how those family members can play a positive role in the rehabilitation process. Features interviews with three families whose 'success stories' provide advice and encouragement, as well as interviews with newly blinded adults currently involved in a rehabilitation program. 23 minute video tape. Also available in PAL, $49.95, 0-89128-271-8.

7858 Braille Book Review
National Library Service for the Blind
1291 Taylor Street NW
Washington, DC 20542
202-707-5100
800-424-8567
Fax: 202-707-0712
http://www.loc.gov/nls

Frank Cylke, Executive Director

New braille books and product news.

7859 Braille Forum
American Council of the Blind
1155 15th Street NW
Suite 1004
Washington, DC 20005-2706
202-467-5081
800-424-8666
Fax: 202-467-5085
e-mail: info@acb.org
http://www.acb.org

Penny Reeder, Editor
Melanie Brunson, Executive Director

Offered in print, braille, cassette, IBM computer disk, and e-mail. $25 per format per year for companes and non-US residents.

48 pages

7860 Braille Mirror
Braille Institute Press
741 N Vermont Avenue
Los Angeles, CA 90029-3514
323-660-3880
800-BRA-ILLE
Fax: 323-663-0867

Douglas Menville, Editor
Leslie Stocker, President

General interest magazine (Braille).

7861 Braille Monitor
National Federation of the Blind
1800 Johnson Street
Baltimore, MD 21230-4914
410-837-6763
Fax: 410-685-5653

The leading publication in the blindness field, with a circulation of 30,000, this publication addresses issues of concern to the blind and the philosophy and activities of the National Federation of the Blind.

7862 Braille Star Theosophist
Theosophical Book Association for the Blind
54 Krotona Street
Ojai, CA 93023-3901
805-646-2121
Fax: 805-646-2121
e-mail: tbab@compuserve.com

Magazine dealing with the Theosophical Book Association for the Blind.

Frequency: Irregular

7863 Bulletin
National Association for Visually Handicapped
22 W 21st Street
New York, NY 10010-6904
212-889-3141
Fax: 212-727-2931

Ann Illuzzi, Manager

Annual report offering information on Association activities and events, conferences, vision aids and resources for the visually impaired.

7864 Choice Magazine Listening
85 Channel Drive
Port Washington, NY 11050-2278
516-883-8280
888-724-6423
Fax: 516-944-6849
e-mail: choicemag@aol.com
http://www.choicemagazinelisting.org

Sondra Mochson, Editor
Lois Miller, Manager

A free audio anthology available to visually impaired/physically disabled or dyslexic persons nationwide. Playable on the special free 4-track cassette playback equipment which is provided by the Library of Congress through the National Library Service. Each issue free to keep; bimonthly — six times yearly.

Visually Impaired/Journals, Magazines

7865 Dialogue
Blindskills
PO Box 5181
Salem, OR 97304-0181
503-581-4224
800-860-4224
Fax: 503-581-0178
e-mail: info@blindskills.com
http://www.blindskills.com

Karen Lynn Thomas, Editor
Tisha Herring, Administrative Assistant
Carol M McCarl, Executive Director

Bimonthly magazine written by and for visually impaired people, available in large print, audio cassette, Braille, disk and via e-mail. It features articles on adapting to life with low vision, techniques of daily living, careers, education, sports and recreation, technology tips and reviews, and descriptions of new products and services designed for visually impaired people.

Frequency: Bimonthly

7866 Gleams Newsletter
Glaucoma Research Foundation
200 Pine Street
Suite 200
San Francisco, CA 94104-2704
415-986-3162
800-826-6693
Fax: 415-986-3763
http://www.glaucoma.org

Tom Brunner, CEO

Offers updated and medical information on vision loss and glaucoma. Included are legislative information, professional articles and book reviews.

7867 Guideway
Guide Dog Foundation for the Blind
371 E Jericho Turnpike
Smithtown, NY 11787-2906
631-265-2121
800-548-4337
Fax: 631-361-5192
e-mail: info@guidedog.org
http://www.guidedog.org

Cathy McDougall, Office Manager
Michelle Lavitt, Communications Coordinator
Wells Jones, Executive Director

Offers updates and information on the foundation's activities and guide dog programs. In print form but is also available on cassette.

Frequency: Quarterly

7868 Hub
SPOKES Unlimited
PO Box 7896
Klamath Falls, OR 97602
541-883-7547

Meg Graf, Resource Librarian
Wendy Howard, Executive Director

Newsletter on rehabilitation, peer counseling, blindness, visual impairments, information and referral.

7869 Illinois Braille Messenger
Illinois Council For The Blind
PO Box 1336
Springfield, IL 62705-1336
217-512-4967

Clyde Forth, Editor

7870 Information Access Project
National Federation of the Blind
1800 Johnson Street
Baltimore, MD 21230-4914
410-837-6763
Fax: 410-685-5653
e-mail: nfb@iamdigex.net
http://www.nfb.org

Marc Maurer, President

Assists entities covered by the ADA in finding methods for converting visually displayed information, such as flyers, brochures and pamphlets, to formats accessible to individuals who are visually impaired.

7871 Insight
US Association of Blind Athletes
33 N Institute Street
Colorado Springs, CO 80903-3508
719-630-0422
Fax: 719-630-0616
e-mail: usaba@usa.net

Mark Lucas, Executive Director

Magazine reporting on news and activities of the US Association of Blind Athletes.

Frequency: Quarterly

7872 Jewish Braille Review
Jewish Braille Institute Of America
110 E 30th Street
New York, NY 10016-7375
212-889-2525
800-433-1531
Fax: 212-689-3692
e-mail: admin@jewishbraille.org

Jacob Freid, Editor
Ellen Isler, President

Magazine for the blind. Printed in braille.

7873 John Milton Magazine
John Milton Society for the Blind
475 Riverside Drive
Suite 455
New York, NY 10115
212-870-3335
Fax: 212-870-3229

Darcy Quigley, Contact
Ingrid Peck, Contact

Large print digest covering inspirational articles from religious periodicals.

Frequency: Quarterly

7874 Journal of Vision Rehabilitation
Media Productions & Marketing
2440 O Street
Suite 202
Lincoln, NE 68510-1125
402-474-2676

Multidisciplinary journal containing articles and papers dealing with low vision, its evaluation, instrumentation and rehabilitation.

7875 Journal of Visual Impairment and Blindness
American Foundation for the Blind
15 W 16th Street
New York, NY 10011-6301
212-502-7600
800-232-5463

Carl Augusto, President

The peer reviewed, interdisciplinary, scholarly journal for special educators, rehabilitators, mobility instructors, low vision specialists, technologists and others who care about new possibilities who are blind and visually impaired; the impact of public policy on services and people; new approaches to working with students and clients; new directions in service delivery world-wide and the latest news on products and programs, technology and activities around the world.

Frequency: Monthly

7876 Journal of Visual Impairments and Blindness
Sheridan Press
PO Box 465
Hanover, PA 17331
717-632-3535
Fax: 717-633-8929
e-mail: pubsvc@tsp.sheridan.com
http://www.sheridanreprints.com

Sharon Shively, Managing Editor
Jane Erin, Editor-in-Chief
Joan Davidson, President

Published in braille, regular print and on ASC II disk and cassette, this journal contains a wide variety of subjects including rehabilitation, psychology, education, legislation, medicine, technology, employment, sensory aids and childhood development as they relate to visual impairments. $90 Annual individual subscription, $125 Annual institutional subscription.

64 pages

Visually Impaired/Journals, Magazines

7877 **Lifeglow**
Christian Record Service
PO Box 6097
Lincoln, NE 68506
402-488-0981
Fax: 402-488-7582
e-mail: crsnet@compuserve.net

Gaylena Gibson, Editor
Lawrence Pitcher, President

Magazine for the blind. Printed in braille and large print.
Frequency: Bimonthly

7878 **Lion's Club Headquarters**
300 W 22nd Street
Oak Brook, IL 60523-8842
630-571-5466
Fax: 630-571-8890
http://www.lionsclubs.org

Gary Lapetina, CEO

Publications for the blind from this large international organization dedicated to the largest blindness prevention program ('SightFirst').

7879 **Long Cane News**
American Foundation for the Blind/AFB Press
PO Box 1020
Sewickley, PA 15143
412-741-1142
232-304-
Fax: 412-741-0609
e-mail: afborders@abdintl.com
http://www.afb.org

Liz Greco, Contact

7880 **Low Vision Questions and Answers: Definitions, Devices, Services**
American Foundation for the Blind/AFB Press
PO Box 1020
Sewickley, PA 15143
412-741-1142
232-304-
Fax: 412-741-0609
e-mail: afborders@abdintl.com
http://www.afb.org

What does low vision mean? What do low vision services cost? What diseases cause low vision? Answers to these and other questions are presented in a comprehensive format with accompanying photographs. $50.00/pack of 25.
21 pages

7881 **Magazines in Special Media**
National Library Service for the Blind/Phys. Hand.
1291 Taylor Street NW
Washington, DC 20542
202-707-5100
800-424-8567
Fax: 202-707-0712
e-mail: nls@loc.gov
http://www.loc.gov/nls

Frank Cylke, Executive Director
Frequency: Biennial

7882 **Matilda Ziegler Magazine for the Blind**
Matilda Ziegler Magazine for the Blind
80 8th Avenue
Suite 1304
New York, NY 10011-7161
212-242-0263
Fax: 212-633-1601

Michael Mellor, Editor
Gregory Evanina, Owner

Publication presenting general interest articles, humor, fiction, and poetry from newspapers, magazines, and books. Also includes news and information of special interest to people with vision problems.
Frequency: Monthly

7883 **Musical Mainstream**
National Library Service for the Blind
1291 Taylor Street NW
Washington, DC 20542
202-707-5100
800-424-8567
Fax: 202-707-0712

Frank Cylke, Executive Director

Articles selected from print music magazines.

7884 **NLS News**
National Library Service for the Blind
1291 Taylor Street NW
Washington, DC 20542
202-707-5100
800-424-8567
Fax: 202-707-0712

Frank Cylke, Executive Director

Newsletter on current program developments.

7885 **NLS Update**
National Library Service for the Blind
1291 Taylor Street NW
Washington, DC 20542
202-707-5100
800-424-8567
Fax: 202-707-0712

Frank Cylke, Executive Director

Newsletter on the services volunteer activities.

7886 **Newsline for the Blind**
National Federation of the Blind
1800 Johnson Street
Baltimore, MD 21230-4914
410-659-9314
Fax: 410-685-5653
e-mail: nfb@iamdigex.net
http://www.nfb.org

Peggy Chong, Contact
Marc Maurer, President

Nation's only digital talking newspaper service for the blind. Allows the blind to read the full text of leading national and local newspapers by using a touch-tone telephone. Service is free of charge and available 24 hours a day, 7 days per week.

7887 **Not Without Sight**
American Foundation for the Blind/AFB Press
PO Box 1020
Sewickley, PA 15143
412-741-1142
232-304-
Fax: 412-741-0609
e-mail: afborders@abdintl.com
http://www.afb.org

This video describes the major types of visual impairment and their causes and effects on vision, while camera simulations approximate what people with each impairment actually see. Also demonstrates how people with low vision make the best use of the vision they have. 20 minute video tape. Also available in PAL, $52.95, 0-89128-272-6.

7888 **Opportunity**
National Industries For The Blind
PO Box 969
Wayne, NJ 07474
973-595-9200
Fax: 973-595-9122

George J Mertz, President/CEO

Offers information and articles on the newest technology, equipment, services and programs for blind and visually impaired persons.

7889 **Our Special**
National Braille Press
88 Saint Stephen Street
Boston, MA 02115-4302
617-266-6160
800-548-7323
Fax: 617-437-0456
e-mail: orders@nbp.org

Jeanne Neale, Editor
Diane Croft, Mailing Contact
William Kilimanjaro, President

General interest Braille magazine for blind women.

Visually Impaired/Journals, Magazines

7890 Out of Left Field
American Foundation for the Blind/AFB Press
PO Box 1020
Sewickley, PA 15143
724-846-7200
232-304-
Fax: 412-741-0609
e-mail: afborders@abdintl.com
http://www.afb.org

Stephen M Otto, Owner

Illustrates how youngsters who are blind or visually impaired integrated with their sighted peers in a variety of recreational and athletic activities. 17 minute video tape. Also available in PAL, $33.95, 0-89128-270-X.

7891 Personal Reader Update
Personal Reader Department
9 Centennial Drive
Peabody, MA 01960-7906
978-977-2000
Fax: 978-977-2437

Offers information on new services, assistive devices and technology for the blind.

7892 Quarterly Update
National Association for Visually Handicapped
22 W 21st Street
Floor 6
New York, NY 10010-6943
212-889-3141
Fax: 212-727-2931
e-mail: staff@navh.org
http://www.navh.org

Ann Illuzzi, Manager

Quarterly newsletter offering information on new products for the visually impaired, advances in medical treatments, new books available in the NAVH large print loan library and any new/updated booklets. Free.

7893 Recorded Periodicals
Associated Services for the Blind
919 Walnut Street
Philadelphia, PA 19107-5237
215-627-4230
Fax: 215-922-0692

Vincent McVeigh, Executive Director
John Corrigan, Manager

A subscription service of Associated Services for the Blind, these periodicals provide 21 magazines through this subscription service. A magazine list can be sent, in both large print and on audio cassette.

7894 Recording for the Blind News
Recording for the Blind
20 Roszel Road
Princeton, NJ 08540-6294
609-452-0606
Fax: 609-987-8116

John Kelly, CEO

7895 Seeing Clearly
National Association for Visually Handicapped
22 W 21st Street
Floor 6
New York, NY 10010-6943
212-889-3141
Fax: 212-727-2931
e-mail: staff@navh.org
http://www.navh.org

Ann Illuzzi, Manager

This newsletter offers short stories, news, medical updates, assistive device information, poems, resources, crossword puzzles and more for the visually impaired.

7896 Seeing Eye Guide
Seeing Eye
PO Box 375
Morristown, NJ 07963
973-539-4425
Fax: 973-539-0922
e-mail: semaster@seeingeye.org
http://www.seeingeye.org

Kenneth Rosenthal, President

Newsletter.

8 pages Frequency: 4

7897 Smith-Kettlewell Technical File
Smith-Kettlewell Eye Research Institute
2232 Webster Street
San Francisco, CA 94115-1897
415-345-2000
Fax: 415-561-1610

William Gerrey, Mailing Contact
Henry Metz, President

Magazine reporting on technology and devices for visually impaired persons.

7898 Tactic
Clovernook Home And School For The Blind
7000 Hamilton Avenue
Cincinnati, OH 45231-5240
513-522-3860

7899 Talking Book Topics
National Library Service for the Blind
1291 Taylor Street NW
Washington, DC 20542
202-707-5100
800-424-8567
Fax: 202-707-0712

Frank Cylke, Executive Director

Offers hundreds of listings of books, fiction and nonfiction, for adults and children on cassette. Also offers listings on foreign language books on cassette, talking magazines and reviews.

7900 Tract Messenger
Lutheran Braille Evangelism Association
1740 Eugene Street
White Bear Lake, MN 55110-3312
651-426-0469
e-mail: lbeassoc@aol.com

Dennis Hawkinson, Contact

Religious magazine in Braille.

Frequency: Monthly

7901 USABA Newsletter
United States Association for Blind Athletes
33 N Institute Brown Hall
Colorado Springs, CO 80903
719-333-4195
Fax: 719-630-0616

Covers news, announcements and activities of the Association.

7902 Update (Library of Congress)
National Library Services Blind & Physically Hand.
1291 Taylor Street NW
Washington, DC 20542
202-707-5100
800-424-8567
Fax: 202-707-0712
e-mail: nls@loc.gov

Frank Cylke, Executive Director

Magazine reporting on current information on library services for disabled individuals.

Frequency: Quarterly

7903 Vision
National Catholic Office for the Deaf
7202 Buchanan Street
Landover Hills, MD 20784-2236
301-577-1684
Fax: 301-577-1690
e-mail: ncod@erols.com
http://www.ncod.org

Arvilla Rank, Executive Director/Editor

Published as a pastoral service for the deaf and hard of hearing.

16 pages

Visually Impaired/Newspapers

7904 **Vision Enhancement, Journal**
Vision World Wide
5707 Brockton Drive
Apt 302
Indianapolis, IN 46220-5481　　　　317-254-1332
800-431-1739
Fax: 317-251-6588
e-mail: info@visionww.org
http://www.visionww.org

Patricia Price, President/Managing Editor

Provides information through helplines, a website, internet lists, information packets, and comprehensive quarterly journal, Vision Enhancement (available in large print, audiocassette, and computer disk) - all designed to inform, encourage, and support individuals with vision loss, family members, and professionals who serve them. Aim is to enhance everyday living so as to make it possible to maintain an independent lifestyle.

68-75 pages Frequency: 4

7905 **Visions**
National Easter Seal Society Publications
230 W Monroe Street
Suite 1800
Chicago, IL 60606-4703　　　　312-726-6200
800-221-6827
Fax: 312-726-1494

Magazine concerning the National Easter Seal Society's activities.

Frequency: Quarterly

7906 **Viva Vital News**
5016 Silk Oak Drive
Sarasota, FL 34232-5410

Membership service organization offering information for veterans and is an affiliate of the American Council of the Blind.

7907 **Voice of Vision**
GW Micro
725 Airport North Office Park
Fort Wayne, IN 46825-6707　　　　260-489-3671
Fax: 260-489-2608
e-mail: sales@gwmicro.com
http://www.gwmicro.com

Doug Geoffray, Vice President Development
Dan Weirich, VP Sales And Marketing
Lois Baich, Orders And Production

Offers product reviews, product announcements, tips for making systems or applications more accessible, or explanations of concepts of interest to any computer user or would-be computer user. This association newsletter is available in braille, in large print, on audio cassette and on 3.5 or 5.25 IBM format diskette.

7908 **We Can Do It Together!**
American Foundation for the Blind/AFB Press
PO Box 1020
Sewickley, PA 15143　　　　412-741-1142
232-304-
Fax: 412-741-0609
e-mail: afborders@abdintl.com
http://www.afb.org

This video illustrates a transdisciplinaty team orientation and mobility program for students with severe visual and multiple impairments, covering both adapted communication systems used to teach mobility skills and basic indoor mobility in the school. For mobility instructors, administrators, teachers of the visually and severely handicapped, occupational, physical and speech therapists and parents. Discussion guide included. 10 minute video t

Newspapers

7909 **Newsline for the Blind**
National Federation of the Blind
1800 Johnson Street
Baltimore, MD 21230-4914　　　　410-659-9314
Fax: 410-685-5653

Marc Maurer, President

Nation's only digital talking newspaper service for the blind. Allows the blind to read the full text of leading national and local newspapers by using a touch-tone telephone. Service is free of charge and available 24 hours a day, 7 days per week.

Newsletters, Pamphlets

7910 **A Patient's Guide to Visual Aids and Illumination**
National Association for Visually Handicapped
22 W 21st Street
New York, NY 10010-6904　　　　212-889-3141
Fax: 212-727-2931

Ann Illuzzi, Manager

A reference booklet offering information on aids for the visually impaired.

7911 **ACB Reports**
American Council of the Blind
1155 15th Street NW
Suite 1004
Washington, DC 20005-2706　　　　202-467-5081
800-424-8666
Fax: 202-467-5085
e-mail: info@acb.org
http://www.acb.org

Melanie Brunson, Executive Director

Radio news feature program for radio information services.

7912 **AER Report**
AER
206 N Washington Street
Alexandria, VA 22314-2528　　　　703-823-9690
Fax: 703-823-9695

Contains organizational news, conference dates and information concerning services to visually impaired people.

7913 **AFB News**
American Foundation for the Blind
11 Penn Plaza
Suite 300
New York, NY 10001-2018　　　　212-502-7600
800-232-5463
Fax: 212-502-7777

Carl Augusto, President

National newsletter for general readership about blindness and visual impairments featuring people, programs, services and activities.

12 pages

7914 **ALDA News**
Association of Late-Deafened Adults
10310 Main Street
274
Fairfax, VA 22030-2410
Fax: 815-899-3040
TTY 815-899-3040

Marilyn Howe, Publisher

7915 **Age-Related Macular Degeneration**
National Eye Institute, Information Office
Building 31
Bethesda, MD 20892　　　　301-496-5248
Fax: 301-402-1065
http://www.nei.nih.gov

Visually Impaired/Newsletters, Pamphlets

7916 **Aging and Vision**
American Foundation for the Blind
15 W 16th Street
New York, NY 10011-6301
212-502-7600
800-232-5463
Fax: 212-502-7777

Carl Augusto, President

Booklet offering information on the causes of vision loss with aging, cataracts, macular degeneration, lighting, vision aids and more for the elderly persons.

7917 **Aging and Vision News**
National Center for Vision and Aging
800 2nd Avenue
New York, NY 10017-4709
212-808-0077

Sang Park, Owner

7918 **American Heart Association Diet**
American Heart Association
7272 Greenville Avenue
Dallas, TX 75231-4596
214-373-6300
800-553-6321
Fax: 214-696-5211

M Cass Wheeler, CEO

An eating plan for healthy americans.

7919 **Annual Report/Newsletter**
National Accreditation Council for Agencies/Blind
15 E 40th Street
Room 1004
New York, NY 10016
212-481-7130
Fax: 212-683-4475

Ruth Westman, Executive Director

Provides standards and a program of accreditation for schools and organizations which serve children and adults who are blind or vision impaired.

7920 **BVA Bulletin**
Blinded Veterans Association
477 H Street NW
Washington, DC 20001-2617
202-371-8880
800-669-7079
Fax: 202-371-8258

Thomas H Miller, Executive Director

7921 **Books are Fun for Everyone**
National Library Service for the Blind
1291 Taylor Street NW
Washington, DC 20542
202-707-5100
800-424-8567
Fax: 202-707-0712

Frank Cylke, Executive Director

7922 **Braille Book Review**
National Library Service for the Blind
1291 Taylor Street NW
Washington, DC 20542
202-707-5100
800-424-8567
Fax: 202-707-0712
http://www.loc.gov/nls

Frank Cylke, Executive Director

New braille books and product news.

7923 **Braille: An Extraordinary Volunteer Opportunity**
National Library Service for the Blind
1291 Taylor Street NW
Washington, DC 20542
202-707-5100
800-424-8567
Fax: 202-707-0712

Frank Cylke, Executive Director

7924 **Bulletin**
National Association for Visually Handicapped
22 W 21st Street
New York, NY 10010-6904
212-889-3141
Fax: 212-727-2931

Ann Illuzzi, Manager

Annual report offering information on Association activities and events, conferences, vision aids and resources for the visually impaired.

7925 **Cataracts**
National Eye Institute, Information Office
Building 31
Bethesda, MD 20892
301-496-5248
Fax: 301-402-1065
http://www.nei.nih.gov

Provides information about this common condition and its treatment.

7926 **Classification of Impaired Vision**
National Association for Visually Handicapped
22 W 21st Street
Floor 6
New York, NY 10010-6943
212-889-3141
Fax: 212-727-2931
e-mail: staff@navh.org
http://www.navh.org

Ann Illuzzi, Manager

Describes various degrees of impaired vision.

7927 **Communicating with People Who Have Trouble Hearing & Seeing: A Primer**
National Association for Visually Handicapped
22 W 21st Street
Floor 6
New York, NY 10010-6943
212-889-3141
Fax: 212-727-2931
e-mail: staff@navh.org
http://www.navh.org

Ann Illuzzi, Manager

Line drawings that depict problems for those with both deficiencies.

7928 **D.V.H. Quarterly**
University of Arkansas At Little Rock
2801 S University Avenue
Little Rock, AR 72204-1000
Fax: 501-663-3536

Bob Brasher, Editor

Offers information on upcoming events, conferences and workshops on and for visual disabilities. Book reviews, information on the newest resources and technology, educational programs, want ads and more.

7929 **Department for the Blind & Physically Handicapped**
South Carolina Library
1430 Senate Street
Columbia, SC 29201-3710
803-734-4611
800-922-7818
Fax: 803-734-4610
TDD 813-734-7298

James B Johnson Jr, Executive Director

4 pages Frequency: Quarterly

7930 **Diabetes, Vision Impairment and Blindness**
American Foundation for the Blind
11 Penn Plaza
Suite 300
New York, NY 10001-2006
212-502-7600
800-232-5463
Fax: 212-502-7777

Carl Augusto, President

A presentation of how chronic diabetes affects vision and how diabetes can be managed at home by blind and visually impaired individuals.

32 pages

Visually Impaired/Newsletters, Pamphlets

7931 **Diabetic Retinopathy**
National Association for Visually Handicapped
22 W 21st Street
Floor 6
New York, NY 10010-6943
212-889-3141
Fax: 212-727-2931
e-mail: staff@navh.org
http://www.navh.org

Ann Illuzzi, Manager

Describes types of this disease and methods of treatment.

7932 **Directory of Services for Blind and Visually Impaired Persons in the United States and Canada**
American Foundation for the Blind
11 Penn Plaza
Suite 300
New York, NY 10001-2006
212-502-7600
800-232-3044
Fax: 212-502-7774
e-mail: newyork@afb.net
http://www.afb.org/afb

Natalie Hiltzen, Editor
Carl Augusto, President

624 pages Frequency: irregular

7933 **Diseases of the Macula**
National Association for Visually Handicapped
22 W 21st Street
Floor 6
New York, NY 10010-6943
212-889-3141
Fax: 212-727-2931
e-mail: staff@navh.org
http://www.navh.org

Ann Illuzzi, Manager

Describes various conditions which affect the macular area and hot to best maximize the use of residual peripheral vision.

7934 **Dog Sponsorship Program**
Guide Dog Foundation for the Blind
371 E Jericho Tpke
Smithtown, NY 11787-2906
631-265-2121
800-548-4337
Fax: 631-361-5192
e-mail: info@guidedog.org
http://www.guidedog.org

Wells Jones, Executive Director

Offers information to an individual or an organization that wishes to sponsor a guide dog.

7935 **Don't Lose Sight of Age-Related Macular Degeneration**
National Eye Institute, Information Office
Building 31
Bethesda, MD 20892
301-496-5248
Fax: 301-402-1065
http://www.nei.nih.gov

7936 **Don't Lose Sight of Cataracts**
National Eye Institute, Information Office
Building 31
Bethesda, MD 20892
301-496-5248
Fax: 301-402-1065
http://www.nei.nih.gov

7937 **Don't Lose Sight of Glaucoma**
National Eye Institute, Information Office
Building 31
Bethesda, MD 20892
301-496-5248
Fax: 301-402-1065
http://www.nei.nih.gov

7938 **Eye-Q Test**
National Association for Visually Handicapped
22 W 21st Street
Floor 6
New York, NY 10010-6943
212-889-3141
Fax: 212-727-2931
e-mail: staff@navh.org
http://www.navh.org

Ann Illuzzi, Manager

Five questions and answers to assist in knowing more about vision.

7939 **Facts: Books for Blind and Physically Handicapped Individuals**
National Library Service for the Blind
1291 Taylor Street NW
Washington, DC 20542
202-707-5100
800-424-8567
Fax: 202-707-0712

Frank Cylke, Executive Director

7940 **Facts: Music for Blind and Physically Handicapped Individuals**
National Library Service for the Blind
1291 Taylor Street NW
Washington, DC 20542
202-707-5100
800-424-8567
Fax: 202-707-0712

Frank Cylke, Executive Director

7941 **Facts: Playback Machines and Accessories Provided On Free Loan**
National Library Service for the Blind
1291 Taylor Street NW
Washington, DC 20542
202-707-5100
800-424-8567
Fax: 202-707-0712

Frank Cylke, Executive Director

7942 **Facts: Sources for Purchase of Cassette & Disc Players From NLS**
National Library Service for the Blind
1291 Taylor Street NW
Washington, DC 20542
202-707-5100
800-424-8567
Fax: 202-707-0712

Frank Cylke, Executive Director

7943 **Family Guide - Growth & Development of the Partially Seeing Child**
National Association for Visually Handicapped
22 W 21st Street
Floor 6
New York, NY 10010-6943
212-889-3141
Fax: 212-727-2931
e-mail: staff@navh.org
http://www.navh.org

Ann Illuzzi, Manager

Offers information for parents and guidelines in raising a partially seeing child.

7944 **Fighting Blindness News**
RP Foundation Fighting Blindness
1401 W Mount Royal Avenue
Suite 4
Baltimore, MD 21217-4245
410-785-1414
800-683-
Fax: 410-771-9470
TDD 410-225-9409

Offers information on medical updates, donor programs, assistive devices, resources and clinical trial information for persons with visual impairments, blindness and retinal degenerative diseases.

Visually Impaired/Newsletters, Pamphlets

7945 General Facts and Figures on Blindness
Prevent Blindness America
500 E Remington Road
Schaumburg, IL 60173-5624
847-843-2020
Fax: 847-843-8458
e-mail: info@preventblindness.org
http://www.preventblindness.org

7946 Gift of Sight
RP Foundation Fighting Blindness
1401 W Mount Royal Avenue
Baltimore, MD 21217-4245
410-225-9409
800-683-
Fax: 410-771-9470

A pamphlet offering information on the Retina Donor Program, which studies diseased, human retinal tissue in their search for a cure of retinal degenerative diseases.

7947 Glaucoma
Foundation for Glaucoma Research
200 Pine Street
Suite 200
San Francisco, CA 94104-2704
415-986-3162
Fax: 415-986-3763

Offers information on what glaucoma is, the causes, treatments, types of glaucoma, eye exams and prevention.

7948 Glaucoma - the Sneak Thief of Sight
National Association for Visually Handicapped
22 W 21st Street
Floor 6
New York, NY 10010-6943
212-889-3141
Fax: 212-727-2931
e-mail: staff@navh.org
http://www.navh.org

Ann Illuzzi, Manager

A pamphlet describing the disease, treatment and medications.

7949 Guide Dog Foundation Flyer
Guide Dog Foundation for the Blind
371 E Jericho Tpke
Smithtown, NY 11787-2976
631-265-2121
800-548-4337
Fax: 631-361-5192
e-mail: info@guidedog.org
http://www.guidedog.org

Wells Jones, Executive Director

Offers information on the programs and services provided by the Foundation.

7950 Guidelines for Comprehensive Low Vision Care
National Association for Visually Handicapped
22 W 21st Street
Floor 6
New York, NY 10010-6943
212-889-3141
Fax: 212-727-2931
e-mail: staff@navh.org
http://www.navh.org

Ann Illuzzi, Manager

A description of the proper method to conduct a low vision evaluation.

7951 Guild Briefs
Guild for the Blind
180 N Michigan Avenue
Suite 1700
Chicago, IL 60601-7479
312-236-8569
Fax: 312-236-8128

David Tabak, Executive Director

8-16 pages Frequency: Monthly

7952 Heartbreak of Being A Little Bit Blind
National Association for Visually Handicapped
22 W 21st Street
Floor 6
New York, NY 10010-6943
212-889-3141
Fax: 212-727-2931
e-mail: staff@navh.org
http://www.navh.org

Ann Illuzzi, Manager

Summary of what it means to have impaired vision with illustrations. Free for members; 50 cents for non-members.

7953 History and Use of Braille
American Council of the Blind
1155 15th Street NW
Suite 1004
Washington, DC 20005-2706
202-467-5081
800-424-8666
Fax: 202-467-5085
e-mail: info@acb.org
http://www.acb.org

Melanie Brunson, Executive Director

7954 How Does a Blind Person Get Around?
American Foundation for the Blind
15 W 16th Street
New York, NY 10011-6301
212-502-7600
800-232-5463
Fax: 212-502-7777

Carl Augusto, President

Offers information on daily living as a blind person.

7955 How to Develop a Self-Help Group for Elders Losing Eyesight
National Association for Visually Handicapped
22 W 21st Street
Floor 6
New York, NY 10010-6943
212-889-3141
Fax: 212-727-2931
e-mail: staff@navh.org
http://www.navh.org

Ann Illuzzi, Manager

The pioneer for development of self-help groups, using the NAVH model, this publication is designed to help start and facilitate self-help groups.

7956 How to Use Your Low Vision Glasses
National Association for Visually Handicapped
22 W 21st Street
Floor 6
New York, NY 10010-6943
212-889-3141
Fax: 212-727-2931
e-mail: staff@navh.org
http://www.navh.org

Ann Illuzzi, Manager

A line drawing showing the correct way to benefit from low vision glasses.

7957 In Focus
National Association for Visually Handicapped
22 W 21st Street
Floor 6
New York, NY 10010-6943
212-889-3141
Fax: 212-727-2931
e-mail: staff@navh.org
http://www.navh.org

Ann Illuzzi, Manager

Offers information on new items for the partially seeing, advances made in treatments and medical science, stories and poems from readers, humor and crossword puzzles for young adults.

Visually Impaired/Newsletters, Pamphlets

7958 **InSight**
Prevent Blindness America
500 E Remington Road
Schaumburg, IL 60173-5624
847-843-2020
Fax: 847-843-8458
e-mail: info@preventblindness.org
http://www.preventblindness.org

7959 **Information on Glaucoma**
Glaucoma Research Foundation
200 Pine Street
Suite 200
San Francisco, CA 94104-2704
415-986-3162
800-826-6693
Fax: 415-986-3763
http://www.glaucoma.org

7960 **Information on Macular Degeneration**
American Council of the Blind
1155 15th Street NW
Suite 1004
Washington, DC 20005-2706
202-467-5081
800-424-8666
Fax: 202-467-5085
e-mail: info@acb.org
http://www.acb.org

Melanie Brunson, Executive Director

7961 **It's All Right to Be Angry**
National Association for Visually Handicapped
22 W 21st Street
Floor 6
New York, NY 10010-6943
212-889-3141
Fax: 212-727-2931
e-mail: staff@navh.org
http://www.navh.org

Ann Illuzzi, Manager

A helpful pamphlet describing reactions to learning to live with vision impairment.

7962 **JBI Points**
Jewish Braille Institute of America
110 E 30th Street
New York, NY 10016-7393
212-889-2525
800-433-1531
Fax: 212-689-3692
e-mail: admin@jewishbraille.org

Ellen Isler, President

8 pages Frequency: Periodic

7963 **Jewish Guild for the Blind Newsletter**
Jewish Guild for the Blind
15 W 65th Street
New York, NY 10023-6601
212-769-6200
Fax: 212-769-6266

Pete Williamson, Editor
Alan Morse, Manager

8-12 pages Frequency: Quarterly

7964 **Know Your Eye**
American Council of the Blind
1155 15th Street NW
Suite 1004
Washington, DC 20005-2706
202-467-5081
800-424-8666
Fax: 202-467-5085
e-mail: info@acb.org
http://www.acb.org

Melanie Brunson, Executive Director

7965 **Large Print Loan Library Catalog**
National Association for Visually Handicapped
22 W 21st Street
Floor 6
New York, NY 10010-6943
212-889-3141
Fax: 212-727-2931
e-mail: staff@navh.org
http://www.navh.org

Ann Illuzzi, Manager

Listing of over 7,000 commercially published and NAVH large print books available through NAVH on a loan basis. Includes a limited selection of titles available for purchase.

7966 **Long Cane News**
American Foundation for the Blind
15 W 16th Street
New York, NY 10011-6301
212-502-7600
800-232-5463
Fax: 212-502-7777

Carl Augusto, President

7967 **Low Vision Questions and Answers**
American Foundation for the Blind
11 Penn Plaza
Suite 300
New York, NY 10001-2006
212-502-7600
800-232-5463
Fax: 212-620-2105

Carl Augusto, President

What does low vision mean? What do low vision services cost? What diseases cause low vision? Answers to these and other questions are presented in a comprehensive format with accompanying photographs.

21 pages

7968 **Lutheran Braille Evangelism Association**
1740 Eugene Street
White Bear Lake, MN 55110-3312
651-426-0469
e-mail: lbeassoc@aol.com

Dennis Hawkinson, Executive Director

2 pages Frequency: Quarterly

7969 **Magnifier Highlights**
Independent Living Aids
200 Robbins Lane
Jericho, NY 11753-2365
516-937-1848
800-537-2118
Fax: 516-937-3906
e-mail: techsupport@independentliving.com
http://www.independentliving.com

Marvin Sandler, President

Full line of magnifiers, ranging from high-powered vision aids to hoppy instruments and accessories

7970 **Music Is for Everyone**
National Library Service for the Blind
1291 Taylor Street NW
Washington, DC 20542
202-707-5100
800-424-8567
Fax: 202-707-0712

Frank Cylke, Executive Director

7971 **Musical Mainstream**
National Library Service for the Blind
1291 Taylor Street NW
Washington, DC 20542
202-707-5100
800-424-8567
Fax: 202-707-0712

Frank Cylke, Executive Director

Articles selected from print music magazines.

7972 **NLS News**
National Library Service for the Blind
1291 Taylor Street NW
Washington, DC 20542
202-707-5100
800-424-8567
Fax: 202-707-0712

Frank Cylke, Executive Director

Newsletter on current program developments.

Visually Impaired/Newsletters, Pamphlets

7973 NLS Update
National Library Service for the Blind
1291 Taylor Street NW
Washington, DC 20542
202-707-5100
800-424-8567
Fax: 202-707-0712
e-mail: nls@loc.gov
http://www.loc.gov/nls

Frank Cylke, Executive Director

Newsletter on the services volunteer activities.
Frequency: Quarterly

7974 Newsline for the Blind
National Federation of the Blind
1800 Johnson Street
Suite 2
Baltimore, MD 21230-4914
410-659-9314
Fax: 410-685-5653

Marc Maurer, President

Nation's only digital talking newspaper service for the blind. Allows the blind to read the full text of leading national and local newspapers by using a touch-tone telephone. Service is free of charge and available 24 hours a day, 7 days per week.

7975 Opportunity
National Industries for the Blind
PO Box 969
Wayne, NJ 07474
973-595-9200

George J Mertz, President/CEO

Offers information and articles on the newest technology, equipment, services and programs for blind and visually impaired persons.
Frequency: Quarterly

7976 Patient's Guide to Visual Aids and Illumination
National Association for Visually Handicapped
22 W 21st Street
New York, NY 10010-6904
212-889-3141
Fax: 212-727-2931

Ann Illuzzi, Manager

A reference booklet offering information on aids for the visually impaired.

7977 Personal Reader Update
Personal Reader Department
9 Centennial Drive
Peabody, MA 01960-7906
978-977-2000
Fax: 978-977-2437

Offers information on new services, assistive devices and technology for the blind.

7978 Prevent Blindness News
Prevent Blindness America
500 E Remington Road
Schaumburg, IL 60173-5624
847-843-2020
Fax: 847-843-8458
e-mail: info@preventblindness.org
http://www.preventblindness.org

Offers information and articles on eye safety, programs and services of the Society, conferences and seminars on safety in the workplace, sports eye safety information and more.
12-14 pages Frequency: Three

7979 Puppy Walker Brochure
Guide Dog Foundation for the Blind
371 E Jericho Tpke
Smithtown, NY 11787-2906
631-265-2121
800-548-4337
Fax: 631-361-5192
e-mail: info@guidedog.org
http://www.guidedog.org

Wells Jones, Executive Director

Offers information on being a volunteer Puppy Walker family.

7980 RP Messenger
Texas Association of Retinitis Pigmentosa
PO Box 8388
Corpus Christi, TX 78468-8388
361-852-8515

A bi-annual newsletter offering information on Retinitis Pigmentosa.

7981 Reading Is for Everyone
National Library Service for the Blind
1291 Taylor Street NW
Washington, DC 20542
202-707-5100
800-424-8567
Fax: 202-707-0712

Frank Cylke, Executive Director

7982 Reading with Low Vision
National Library Service for the Blind
1291 Taylor Street NW
Washington, DC 20542
202-707-5100
800-424-8567
Fax: 202-707-0712

Frank Cylke, Executive Director

7983 Recording for the Blind News
Recording for the Blind
20 Roszel Road
Princeton, NJ 08540-6294
609-452-0606
Fax: 609-987-8116

John Kelly, CEO

7984 Reference and Information Services from NLS
National Library Service for the Blind
1291 Taylor Street NW
Washington, DC 20542
202-707-5100
800-424-8567
Fax: 202-707-0712

Frank Cylke, Executive Director

7985 Referring Blind and Low Vision Patients for Rehabilitation Services
American Foundation for the Blind
15 W 16th Street
New York, NY 10011-6301
212-620-2155
800-232-5463
Fax: 212-620-2105

Clear information on such basic topics as the objectives of low vision services, what's covered in the examinations, what rehabilitation services do and how to locate these services.

7986 Resource List for Persons with Low Vision
American Council of the Blind
1155 15th Street NW
Suite 1004
Washington, DC 20005-2706
202-467-5081
800-424-8666
Fax: 202-467-5085
e-mail: info@acb.org
http://www.acb.org

Melanie Brunson, Executive Director

7987 Seeing
National Association for Visually Handicapped
22 W 21st Street
Floor 6
New York, NY 10010-6943
212-889-3141
Fax: 212-727-2931
e-mail: staff@navh.org
http://www.navh.org

Ann Illuzzi, Manager

This newsletter offers short stories, news, medical updates, assistive device information, poems, resources, crossword puzzles and more for the visually impaired.
Frequency: BiAnnually

Visually Impaired/Videos, Audio Tapes

7988 Seeing Clearly
National Association for Visually Handicapped
22 W 21st Street
Floor 6
New York, NY 10010-6943
212-889-3141
Fax: 212-727-2931
e-mail: staff@navh.org
http://www.navh.org

Ann Illuzzi, Manager

This newsletter for adults offers information on new items, advances in medical treatments and science, stories, crosswords, poems, humor and more.

7989 Sharing Solutions: A Newsletter forSupport Groups
Lighthouse International
111 E 59th Street
New York, NY 10022-1202
800-829-0500
Fax: 212-821-9702
http://www.lighthouse.org

A newsletter for members and leaders of support groups for older adults with impaired vision. The letter provides a forum for support groups members to network and share information, printed in a very large type format.

7990 Smith-Kettlewell Technical File
Smith-Kettlewell Eye Research Foundation
2232 Webster Street
San Francisco, CA 94115-1897
415-345-2000
Fax: 415-561-1610

Henry Metz, President

7991 Talking Book Topics
National Library Service for the Blind
1291 Taylor Street NW
Washington, DC 20542
202-707-5100
800-424-8567
Fax: 202-707-0712

Frank Cylke, Executive Director

Offers hundreds of listings of books, fiction and nonfiction, for adults and children on cassette. Also offers listings on foreign language books on cassette, talking magazines and reviews.

7992 Talking Books for Senior Adults
National Library Service for the Blind
1291 Taylor Street NW
Washington, DC 20542
202-707-5100
800-424-8567
Fax: 202-707-0712

Frank Cylke, Executive Director

7993 Vision Over 50
American Optometric Association
243 N Lindbergh Boulevard
Floor 1
Saint Louis, MO 63141-7851
314-991-4100
Fax: 314-991-4101
e-mail: slthomas@aoa.org
http://www.aoa.org

Susan Thomas, PR Manager
Julie Mahoney, PR Specialist
Michael Jones, Executive Director

Offers information among adults over 50, medicare coverage, eye examinations, and tips for better seeing.

7994 Vision Resource Update
Vision Foundation
818 Mount Auburn Street
Watertown, MA 02472-1567
781-926-4232
800-852-3029
Fax: 781-926-1423

Fran Weisse, Editor
8-10 pages

7995 Visions World Wide
5707 Brockton Drive
Apt 302
Indianapolis, IN 46220-5481
317-254-1332
800-431-1739
Fax: 317-251-6588
e-mail: 71756.216@compuserve.com

62-78 pages Frequency: Quarterly

7996 Voice of Vision
GW Micro
725 Airport North Office Park
Fort Wayne, IN 46825-6707
260-489-3671
Fax: 260-489-2608
e-mail: sales@gwmicro.com
http://www.gwmicro.com

Doug Geoffray, Vice President Development
Dan Weirich, VP Sales And Marketing
Lois Baich, Orders And Production

Offers product reviews, product announcements, tips for making systems or applications more accessible, or explanations of concepts of interest to any computer user or would-be computer user. This association newsletter is available in braille, in large print, on audio cassette and on 3.5 or 5.25 IBM format diskette.

7997 Volunteer at Your Braille and Talking Book Library
National Library Service for the Blind
1291 Taylor Street NW
Washington, DC 20542
202-707-5100
800-424-8567
Fax: 202-707-0712
e-mail: nls@loc.gov
http://www.loc.gov/nls

Frank Cylke, Executive Director

7998 Wings for the Future
American Printing House for the Blind
1839 Frankfort Avenue
Louisville, KY 40206-3148
502-895-2405
800-223-
Fax: 502-895-1509
e-mail: info@ahp.org

Tuck Tinsley, President

This booklet offers an introduction to the American Printing House For The Blind's programs, services, tools, aids and more.
13 pages

7999 Without Sight and Sound
Helen Keller National Center
111 Middle Neck Road
Sands Point, NY 11050-1218
516-944-8900
Fax: 312-726-3503

Joseph McNulty, Executive Director

Pamphlet offering facts, causes, types and descriptions of deaf-blindness.

Videos, Audio Tapes

8000 Making Life More Livable
American Foundation for the Blind/AFB Press
11 Penn Plaza
Suite 300
New York, NY 10001-2006
212-502-7600
232-546-
Fax: 212-502-7774
e-mail: afborder@abdintl.com
http://www.afb.org

Sharon Baker Harris, Sales & Marketing Manager
Carl Augusto, President

Shows how simple adaptations in the home and environment can make a big difference in the lives of blind and visually impaired older persons. The suggestions offered are numerous and specific, ranging from how to mark food cans for greater visibility to how to get out of the shower safley. Large print.
132 pages

Visually Impaired/Websites

8001 **Visions**
Visions/Services for the Blind & Visually Impaired
500 Greenwich Street
Floor 3
New York, NY 10013-1354   212-625-1616
                         Fax: 212-425-7114
Albert Widman, Associate Executive Director
Anisio Correia, Executive Director/Programs
Nancy D Miller, Executive Director

Offers rehabilitation services for older blind persons in New York City; self study kits on audio cassette for blind and visually impaired persons in the areas of personal management, mobility training, and sensory development.

Websites

8002 **ACB Government Employees**

http://www.acb.org

Concerns of the organization include recruitment, placement and advancement of blind and visually impaired employees.

8003 **ACB Radio Amateurs**

http://www.acb.org

A radio amateur network of blind, visually impaired and sighted members who gather and share common problems and solutions to help members improve radio amateurs in getting started, provides access to educational materials in special media and publishes a directory for the visually impaired.

8004 **ACB Social Service Providers**

http://www.acb.org

Information on blind and visually impaired social workers, social service professionals, students pursuing careers in social work, and other interested persons.

8005 **American Blind Lawyers Association**

http://www.acb.org

Information on law school admission tests and bar exams, private sector and government employment relations and specialized work techniques for the blind and visually impaired.

8006 **American Council of Blind Lions**

http://www.acb.org

Information concerning Club activities in the field of work for the blind and encourages blind people to join Lions Clubs and other civic activities.

8007 **American Printing House for the Blind**

http://www.aph.org

This organization promotes the independence of blind persons by providing special media, tools and materials needed for education and life.

8008 **Blinded Veterans Association**

http://www.bva.org

Offers two main service programs without cost to blinded veterans. Field service program provides counseling to veterans and families, and information on benefits and rehabilitation.

8009 **Braille Revival League**

http://www.acb.org

Information for people to read and write in braille, advocates for mandatory braille instruction in educational facilities for the blind, strives to make available a supply of braille materials from libraries and printing houses and more.

8010 **Guide Dog Foundation for the Blind**

http://www.guidedog.org

Furnishes guide dogs, free of charge, to qualified people who seek independence, mobility and companionship.

8011 **Guide Dog Users**

http://www.acb.org

Promotes the acceptance of blind people and their dogs, works for enforcement and expansion of laws admitting guide dogs into public places, advocates for quality training and follow-up services.

8012 **Independent Visually Impaired Enterprisers**

http://www.acb.org

Information on rehabilitation facilities for all types of business enterprises and publicizes the capabilities of blind and visually impaired business persons.

8013 **Lighthouse International**

http://www.lighthouse.org

Offers information about vision impairment and vision rehabilitation, and provides referrals to services and support groups nationwide.

8014 **National Association for Visually Handicapped**

http://www.navh.org

Serves the partially seeing (not totally blind) with informational literature, newsletters for adults and children, educational outreach, referrals, counsel and guidance.

8015 **National Association of Blind Educators**

http://www.nfb.org

Provides support and information regarding professional responsibilities, classroom techniques, national testing methods and career obstacles. Publishes The Blind Educator, national magazine specifically for blind educators.

8016 **National Association of Blind Lawyers**

http://www.nfb.org

Provides support and information regarding employment, techniques used by the blind, advocacy, laws affecting the blind, current information about the American Bar Association and other issues for blind lawyers.

8017 **National Association of Blind Secretaries and Transcribers**

http://www.nfb.org

Addresses issues such as technology, accomodation, career planning and job training.

8018 **National Association of Guide Dog Users**

http://www.nfb.org

Provides information and support for guide dog users and works to secure high standards in guide dog training. Addresses issues of discrimination of guide dog users and offers public education about guide dog use.

8019 **National Association to Promote the Use of Braille**

http://www.nfb.org

Visually Impaired/Research Centers

Provides information about the importance of Braille in securing independence, education and employment for the blind.

8020 National Braille Association

http://www.members.aol.com

Provides transcription service for, and maintains a depository of, braille books.

8021 National Captioning Institute

http://www.ncicap.org

Advocates captioned television for people who want to see, as well as hear, the dialogue of a television program. It not only enables deaf and hard-of-hearing people to understand all of a program's content, but it is also beneficial for new Americans learning English as a second language, as well as children learning to read.

8022 National Federation of the Blind Merchants Division

http://www.nfb.org

Provides information regarding rehabilitation, social security, tax and other issues which directly affect blind merchants. Serves as advocacy and support group.

8023 National Federation of the Blind in Computer Science

http://www.nfb.org

New technologies, to secure access to current technology and to develop new ways of using current or new technologies by the blind.

8024 National Federation of the Blind: BlindIndustrial Workers of America

http://www.nfb.org

Membership organization of blind persons employed in industrial and manufacturing work or in government job programs for the blind. Dedicated to protecting the rights of blind workers in salary, job stability, advancement and labor issues.

8025 National Federation of the Blind: HumanServices Division

http://www.nfb.org

Organization of blind persons working in counseling, personnel, psychology, social work, psychiatry, rehabilitation and other social science and human resource fields. Provides resources regarding blindness-related techniques and methods used in these fields.

8026 National Federation of the Blind: Masonic Square Club

http://www.nfb.org

Blind individuals committed to sharing of Masonic experiences, goals and history.

8027 National Federation of the Blind: MusicDivision

http://www.nfb.org

Offers support and information regarding copyright, publishing, promotion and other career details.

8028 National Federation of the Blind: Public Employees Division

http://www.nfb.org

Focuses on issues such as changes in governmental hiring and retention practices, new job skills needed for the future, government employment downsizing, new electronic means of finding public sector jobs, self-advocacy and career planning strategies.

8029 National Federation of the Blind: Science and Engineering Division

http://www.nfb.org

This is a strong support group to encourage blind persons in pursuit of these careers, many of which have been considered not possible for the blind in the past.

8030 National Federation of the Blind: Writers Division

http://www.nfb.org

Covers various aspects of this business, including selling your work, publishing, technology, motivation and discovering writing and publishing resources.

8031 National Library Service for the Blind and Physically Handicapped

http://www.loc.gov/nls

Administers a national library service that provides braille and recorded books and magazines on free loan to anyone who cannot read standard print because of visual or physical disabilities who are eligible residents of the United States or American citizens living abroad.

8032 National Organization of the Senior Blind

http://www.nfb.org

Provides support and information to other blind seniors. Issues include concerns such as remaining active in community and social life, maintaining private homes or living in retirement communities or nursing homes, learning the techniques used by the blind, independently caring for oneself and maintaining a positive approach to vision loss.

8033 Vision World Wide

http://www.visionww.org

Aims is to enhance everyday living so as to maintain an independent lifestyle. It also serves as a consumer protection against misrepresentation and fraud.

8034 Visually Impaired Data Processors International

http://www.acb.org

Provides for the exchange of work technique ideas and works with agencies to increase the availability of braille and recorded materials.

8035 Visually Impaired Veterans of America

http://www.acb.org

Promotes the rights of visually impaired veterans to receive all benefits, encourages research and development of new products for blind people.

Research Centers

8036 Baylor College of Medicine: Cullen Eye Institute
6501 Fannin Street
Houston, TX 77030-2703
713-798-7259
Fax: 713-798-4364

Dan B Jones MD, Chairperson

Research activities focus on restoring vision and preventing blindness through a better understanding of the disease.

8037 Berman-Gund Laboratory for the Study of Retinal Degenerations
243 Charles Street
Boston, MA 02114-3002
617-573-5520
Fax: 617-573-3444

Visually Impaired/Research Centers

8038 Dean A McGee Eye Institute
608 Stanton L Young Boulevard
Oklahoma City, OK 73104-5065
405-271-6060
Fax: 405-271-4442

David W Parke II, MD, President
Selina McGee, OD

Basic and clinical investigations in visual sciences.

8039 Emory University Laboratory for Ophthalmic Research
1327 Clifton Road NE
Room 37045
Atlanta, GA 30322-1013
404-349-7905
Fax: 404-778-5128

Henry F Edelhauser, Director
Thomas Emory, Owner

Various studies into the aspects of blindness.

8040 Florida Ophthalmic Institute
7106 NW 11th Place
Gainesville, FL 32605-3157
352-331-2020
Fax: 352-331-2019

Norman S Levy MD, Director

Nonprofit organization that understands and treats ocular diseases including glaucoma.

8041 Glaucoma Foundation
310 E 14th Street
New York, NY 10003-4201
212-387-9240
800-832-3926
Fax: 212-260-1002

Hotline provides answers to questions and makes referrals. The Foundation supports research into the causes and treatment of glaucoma. Publishes free copies of About Glaucoma and Glaucoma Medications-Purpose and Side Effects.

8042 Glaucoma Research Foundation
251 Post Street
Suite 600
San Francisco, CA 94108-5017
415-986-3162
800-826-6693
Fax: 415-986-3763
e-mail: info@glaucoma.org
http://www.glaucoma.org

Robert C Nevins, Chairman
Seth Cunningham, Vice Chairman
Tom Brunner, CEO

A national organization dedicated to protecting the sight of people with glaucoma through research and education. The Foundation conducts and supports research that contributes to improved patient care and a better understanding of the disease process. Provides education, advocacy and emotional support to patients and their families.

8043 Harvard University: Howe Laboratory of Ophthalmology
243 Charles Street
Boston, MA 02114-3002
617-573-3621
Fax: 617-573-3444

Eliot L Berson MD

Development ophthalmology and eye research.

8044 Johns Hopkins University: Dana Center for Preventive Ophthalmology
601 N Broadway
Baltimore, MD 21205-2104
410-955-6100
Fax: 410-955-9777

Harry A Quigley, Director
Cindy Difernando, Manager

8045 Macular Degeneration Foundation
PO Box 515
Northampton, MA 01061
413-268-7660

8046 Medical College of Wisconsin Eye Institute
8700 W Wisconsin Avenue
Milwaukee, WI 53226-3512
414-805-5440

Richard Schultz MD, Director
Arlen D Denny, MD

Research vision loss including ophthalmology.

8047 National Eye Institute
National Institutes of Health
Bldg 31
Bethesda, MD 20892
301-496-0417

Mission is to discover safe and effective methods to prevent, diagnose and treat diseases and disorders of the visual system. In this way the Institute helps to prevent, reduce and possibly eliminate blindness and visual impairment.

8048 National Eye Research Foundation
910 Skokie Boulevard
Suite 207a
Northbrook, IL 60062-4033
847-205-0002
800-621-2258
Fax: 847-564-0807

Elliot S Silber, Owner

Provides information on orthokeratology (a non-surgical procedure for myopia). Offers a patient pamphlet and doctor list. Offers referrals to otherorganizations. Hours: 9:00 a.m. to 5:00 p.m. Monday-Friday.

8049 National Glaucoma Research
American Health Assistance Foundation
22512 Gateway Center Drive
Clarksburg, MD 20871-2005
301-948-3244
800-437-2423
Fax: 301-258-9454
e-mail: jwilson@ahaf.org
http://www.ahaf.org

Jarmel Wilson, AFRP Manager
Kathy Honaker, Executive Director

Offers up to date information on research, treatments, and publications. Also provides a free newsletter, National Glaucoma Research Report.

8050 Ophthalmic Research Laboratory Eye Institute
747 Summit Avenue E
Seattle, WA 98102-5914
206-386-6000
Fax: 206-386-2625

Dr. Brian Godell, Director
Richard Peterson, CEO

Color vision physiology, vision disorders and blindness research.

8051 Pennsylvania College of Optometry Eye Institute
13th & Spencer Streets
Philadelphia, PA 19141
215-276-6200
Fax: 215-276-6082

Dr. Eugene Wayne, Director

8052 Schepens Eye Research Institute
20 Staniford Street
Boston, MA 02114-2508
617-912-0100
Fax: 617-523-3463
e-mail: geninfo@@vision.eri.harvard.edu

Michael Gilmore, President

Prominent center for research on eye, vision, and blinding diseases; dedicated to research that improves the understanding, management, and prevention of eye diseases and visual deficiencies; fosters collaboration among its faculty members; trains young scientists and clinicians from around the world; promotes communication with scientists in allied fields; leader in the worldwide dispersion of basic scientific knowledge of vision.

Visually Impaired/Research Centers

8053 Smith-Ketterwell Eye Research Institute
2232 Webster Street
San Francisco, CA 94115-1821
415-561-1620
Fax: 415-561-1610

GT Gamble, President
Bernard Petrie Esq, VP

Dedicated to research on human vision. The Institute was founded to encourage a productive collaboration between the medical clinic and scientific laboratory. Research is conducted with clinical studies which relate directly to the diagnosis and treatment of eye diseases, the development of devices and vocational programs to aid the partially sighted and basic research to understand how the eye and brain work for both the clinical and rehabilittation programs.

8054 Society of Geriatric Ophthalmology
63 2nd Street
South Orange, NJ 07079-1855
973-763-1381
Fax: 973-762-9449

John Norris, Executive Director

Ophthalmologists interested in the vision problems of the elderly. Works to disseminate information regarding the problems of geriatric patients and to stimulate research. Provides speakers and programs dealing with the needs of the elderly.

8055 University of California: Los Angeles Jules Stein Eye Institute
100 Stein Plaza
Los Angeles, CA 90095-7000
310-825-5053
Fax: 310-206-7488
e-mail: mondino@jsei.ucla.edu
http://www.medsch.ucla.edu/som/jsei

Bartly J Mondino MD, Director

Visual impairment research.

8056 University of Illinois at Chicago: Lions of Illinios Eye Research Institute
UIC Eye Center
1905 W Taylor Street
Chicago, IL 60612-3731
312-996-8937
Fax: 312-996-7770

Prf. John W Chandler, Head Master
Jingtao J Guo, MD

Visual impairments and blindness research, including glaucoma studies.
288 pages

8057 University of Miami: Bascom Palmer Eye Institute
Department of Ophthalmalogy
1638 NW 10th Avenue
Miami, FL 33136-1015
305-326-6031
Fax: 305-326-6306

John G Clarkson MD, Chairman

Clinical and basic research into blindness and visual impairments.

8058 University of North Texas: Health Science Center at Fort Worth
3500 Camp Bowie Boulevard
Fort Worth, TX 76107-2644
817-735-5015
Fax: 817-735-2610
e-mail: jturner@molly.hsc.unt.edu
http://www.hsc.unt.edu/research/eye

James E Turner PhD, Director
Arthur Eisenberg, Executive Director

Eye diseases, including studies on the retina, RPE cells, trophic factors, ocular diabetes, autoimmune diseases, optic nerve regeneration, glaucoma, corneal wound healing, cell death, and aging.

8059 Warren Grant Magnuson Clinical Center
6100 Executive Boulevard
Suite 3c01
Bethesda, MD 20892
301-496-2563
Fax: 301-402-2984
http://www.cc.nih.gov

Established in 1953 as the research hospital of the National Institutes of Health. Designed so that patient care facilities are close to research laboratories so new findings of basic and clinical scientists can be quickly applied to the treatment of patients. Upon referral by physicians, patients are admitted to NIH clinical studies.

8060 Yale University: Vision Research Center
330 Cedar Street
New Haven, CT 06510-3218
203-785-2020
Fax: 203-785-6123

Marvin Sears, Prin/Investigator
Pam Burkheiser, Manager

Vision including studies on growth and development.

Assisted Living Facilities/Alabama

This chapter is arranged by state. Due to the nature of Assisted Living Facilities and the combined efforts of certain state agencies, be sure to review both State Organizations & Government Agencies and Independent Living Facilities for a comprehensive list of resources.

Alabama

8061 Azalea Manor
1304 Pounder and Sims Road
Haleyville, AL 35565
205-485-9343
Fax: 205-485-9652
http://www.azaleamanor.net

Wanda Nutter, Admnistrator

8062 Fair Haven Retirement Community
1424 Montclair Road
Birmingham, AL 35210-2208
205-956-4150
Fax: 205-951-7681
http://methodisthomes.org

Ernestine Thompson, Administrator

Offers quality assisted living services. We provide 70 assisted living units.

8063 Gardens of Clanton
850 Scott Drive
Clanton, AL 35045-8725
205-280-0084
Fax: 205-280-0449

O Neal Green, Owner

Offers quality assisted living services.

8064 Gordon Oaks Assisted Living
3151 Knollwood Drive
Mobile, AL 36693-2753
251-661-7600
Fax: 334-602-9146
http://www.gordonoaks.com/assisted.html

Gordon Oaks provides for the residents' wide variety of daily needs from within the community.

8065 Homestead Village of Fairhope
924 Plantation Boulevard
Fairhope, AL 36532-2952
251-929-0252
800-395-3864
Fax: 251-929-0259
e-mail: info@hvfairhope.com
http://www.fairhope.com

Barbara Ladnier, Director Marketing

Located on a 17-acre campus community proiding a variety of residential options for seniors. An array of services and amenities are offered to promote each resident's sence of security while promoting healthy and fulfilling lifestyles. Residents can easily maintain their individual lifestyles while enjoying the comfort of knowing assistance is close at hand.

8066 Kirkwood by the River
3605 Ratliff Road
Birmingham, AL 35210-4512
205-956-2184
Fax: 205-956-0990
http://www.kirkwoodbytheriver.com

Paula Foust, Director Marketing

Kirkwood by the River is a non profit continuing care retirement community located on 120 beautiful wooded acres in the foothills of the Appalachians. Incorporated as a Presbyterian Homes of Birmingham and sponsored by Independent Presbyterian Church, it is open to all people regardless of church affiliation. An applicant or spouse must be at least sixty-two to move into kirkwood.

8067 Knowlwood Assisted Living
4804 Highway 25
Montevallo, AL 35115
205-665-5955
Fax: 205-665-2855
e-mail: Kathykno@knowlwood.com
http://www.knowlwood.com

Kathy Turner, Owner

We are a state licensed facility, providing 24 hour care to senior citizens needing assistance.

8068 Liveoak Village
300 Village Square
Foley, AL 36535
251-971-1940
877-231-6981
Fax: 251-971-1944
e-mail: info@liveoakvillage.com
http://www.liveoakvillage.com

Richard Denham, Manager

Our goal is to create a community that ofers our families fredom to live the retirement lifestyle they have always wanted.

8069 Mitchell Hollingsworth Annex
PO Box 818
Florence, AL 35631
256-740-5400
Fax: 256-740-5495

Thomas Whetstone, Contact
Brian Scheri, Administrator

8070 Morningside of Decatur
Five Star Quality Care
2115 Point Mallard Drive SE
Decatur, AL 35601-6765
256-350-0089
Fax: 256-350-1530
http://www.morningsideassistedliving.com

Lanette Arnold, Executive Director

We are uniquely designed to provide different levels of assisted living.

8071 Mount Royal Towers
300 Royal Tower Drive
Birmingham, AL 35209-6865
205-870-5666
Fax: 205-871-3111
http://www.healthcaregrp.com/mountRoyal/index

Renee Barnard, CEO

Mount Royal Towers Retirement Community has a full contnuum of health care on site including Independent Living, Independent Plus, Skilled Nursing and ActivCare Residential Alzheimer's Care. Whether you require personal assistance or full fursing care, you'll find courteous and caring staff and a safe, secure enviroment.

8072 Murray House
1257 Government Street
Mobile, AL 36604-2410
251-432-2272
Fax: 251-432-1935

Posey Cook, Executive Director

Offers quality assisted living services.

8073 North Mobile Retirement Center
300 Baker Road
Satsuma, AL 36572-2446
251-679-9192
Fax: 334-679-9868

Elizabeth Frye, Administrator

Assisted Living Facilities/Alaska

8074 **Plantation Manor Assisted Living I**
6450 Old Tuscaloosa Highway
McCalla, AL 35111-3606   205-477-6161
Gary Ball, Administrator

8075 **Saint Martins in the Pines**
4949 Montevallo Road
Birmingham, AL 35210   205-956-9440
Fax: 205-956-9124
http://www.stmartins.ws
Terry Rogers, CEO
To serve God through a ministry that provides a continuum of care and quality of life to aging individuals and their families.

8076 **Somerby at Jones Farm**
2815 Carl T Jones Drive SE
Huntsville, AL 35802-1258   256-881-6111
Fax: 256-881-8748
The Apartment Homes are designed for those who still enjoy an independent lifestyle and want to be an integral part of a state of the art, service-oriented community. The homes offer comfort and convenience in an ideal setting with a variety of plans to accommodate different needs and desires.

8077 **Somerset Assited Living Facility**
815 John D Odom Road
Dothan, AL 36303-9347   334-671-1176
Fax: 334-793-9104
Kim Pritchett, Manager
Provides assisted living residential services. This includes assistance with medication, bathing, dressing, meal preparation, laundry, recreational activities and supervision.

8078 **Village at Cook Springs**
Noland Health Services
415 Cooks Spring Road
Cook Springs, AL 35052   205-338-2221
Fax: 205-814-3189
e-mail: cookspring@nolandhealth.com
http://www.villageatcooksprings.com
Assisted Living residents enjoy the independence of their own suite, while knowing they have special assistance from a caring staff when needed.

8079 **Westminster Village**
500 Spanish Fort Boulevard
Spanish Fort, AL 36527-5018   251-626-2900
Fax: 334-626-8529
http://www.westminstervillageal.com
Bobby Fortenberry, Chairman

Alaska

8080 **Amazing Grace Family Living**
200 West 34th Avenue
PMB 392
Anchorage, AK 99503-3969   907-522-7644
Fax: 907-522-7646
Marilyn Rabb RN, Administrator
Don Rabb, Co-Owner
Provides assistance with all adults for an in home setting for those needing assistance.

8081 **Anchorage Pioneers' Home**
923 W 11th Avenue
Anchorage, AK 99501-4306   907-276-3414
Fax: 907-343-7291
e-mail: david_frain@health.state.ak.us
http://www.state.ak.us
David Frain, Administrator
Assisted living home for Alaskans age 65 and over including Alzheimer's and related dementia care.

8082 **Arctic Hearth Assisted Living Homes**
109 E 5th Street
North Pole, AK 99705   907-488-9159
Fax: 907-488-7979
e-mail: montafaye@gci.net
Monta Lane, Owner/Administrator
James Lane, Assistant Administrator
Brenda Ratzlaff, Resident Manager
Both Homes serve Ladies and Gentlemen. We are committed to helping our frail elders age in place. They live with love and dignity and choices. We honor them, home and community and basic service's are available. Food and personal care is the best of the best.

8083 **Bear Mountain Manor**
17214 Meadow Creek Drive
Eagle River, AK 99577-8180   907-694-9005
Fax: 907-694-9004
Shelia Wolfe, Administrator

8084 **Chugiak Senior Center**
22424 North Birchwood Loop
Chugiak, AK 99567-6476   907-688-2677
Fax: 907-688-1319
e-mail: csc@mtaonline.net
http://www.chugiak-seniors.org
Linda Hendrickson, Executive Director
Providing senior community congregate senior housing 62 units and assisted living 20 units meals on wheels dining, activities for seniors. Adult day care, wellness clinics.

8085 **Dignified Home Life Care**
3330 Creekside Drive
Anchorage, AK 99504-4027   907-333-2968
Fax: 907-333-2968
Candice Dryton III, Administrator
Offers quality assisted living services.

8086 **Downtown Care**
110 2nd Avenue
Fairbanks, AK 99701-4809   907-452-7946
Fax: 907-452-7942
Cathy Westling, Administrator
Les Westling, Owner
Offers quality assisted living services.

8087 **Easy Living AFC**
7710 Maryland Avenue
Anchorage, AK 99504-1916   907-333-1846
Fax: 907-333-3562
e-mail: mertis@gci.net
Mertis Johnson, Administrator
Offers quality assisted living services.

8088 **Graceful Living Assisted Living Home**
1100 Friendly Lane
Anchorage, AK 99504-2024   907-338-3135
Fax: 907-388-3012
e-mail: olohigie@aol.com
Christiana Ulofoshio LPN, Administrator
Offers quality assisted living services.

8089 **Health Care Bridges**
2521 Tradewind Drive
Anchorage, AK 99516-3404   907-345-0496
Fax: 907-348-0355
e-mail: hcb@gci.net
Sheri Bruce, Administrator
Assisted Living and Palliative care.

Assisted Living Facilities/Alaska

8090 **Hidden Heights Assisted Living Home**
3536 E 17th Avenue
PO Box 149024
Anchorage, AK 99508-3361   907-242-9531
Fax: 907-677-8594
e-mail: eereeves@gci.net
Ernest Reeves, Administrator
Offers quality assisted living services.

8091 **Holy Family Adult Foster Home**
8600 Witherspoon Circle
Anchorage, AK 99504-4227   907-338-7570
Fax: 907-338-7520
e-mail: cva2917903@aol.com
Carol Valdez RN, Administrator
Ilumianda Flores, Manager
Offers quality assisted living services.

8092 **Holy Family Assisted Living Home**
8600 Witherspoon Circle
Anchorage, AK 99504-4227   907-338-7570
Fax: 907-338-6590
Carol Valdez RN, Administrator
Lolita Matienzo-Johnson, Caregiver
Provides personal care to the elderly and assist in ADL and medication mangement.

8093 **Immaculate Conception Home, II**
7110 Miranda Drivea Drive
Anchorage, AK 99507   907-522-5671
Fax: 907-868-3937
Florence Cuanan RN, Administrator
We are uniquely designed to provide different levels of assisted living.

8094 **Juneau Pioneers Home**
4675 Glacier Highway
Juneau, AK 99801-9518   907-780-6422
Fax: 907-780-4765
e-mail: rosemary_gute-gruening@admin.state.ak.us
Jill Sandelben, Administrator

8095 **Kat's Eldercare**
53030 Aurora Avenue
Kasilof, AK 99610   907-262-0496
Fax: 907-260-3340
e-mail: katseldercare@yahoo.com
Kathy Walsh, Administrator/Manager
Karla Hudson, Assistant Administrator
Assisted Living Home, State Licensed to care for 8 residents.

8096 **Marlow Manor/Manor Management**
2030 Muldoon Road
Anchorage, AK 99504-3611   907-338-8708
Fax: 907-338-8627
e-mail: Theresa@marlowmanor.com
http://www.marlowmanor.com
Theresa A Brisky, Executive Director
Diana Matukonis, Director Marketing
Darlene Cudia, Facility Manager
Forty eight assisted living community for seniors. Four of the apartments are designated for dementia care on a secured floor.

8097 **Palmer Pioneers' Home**
250 E Fireweed Avenue
Palmer, AK 99645-6699   907-745-4241
Fax: 907-745-0230
Mary Ann Harmon, Administrator

8098 **Respect Your Elders Tender Loving AdultCare**
PO Box 2422
2301 Colleen Street
Palmer, AK 99645-2422   907-745-3687
Fax: 907-746-3687
e-mail: jldavis@mtaonline.net
Donna Davis, Administrator/Director/Owner
"TLC" Adult Day Services, est. 1996, for frail adults with Alzheimer's or other physical or mental limitations. "ALL THE COMFORTS OF HOME" in a Safe Supervised Small Group Setting. One on One Care, Dedicated and Qualified Staff. Services: Transportation, Nutritional Meals, Exercise, Health Monitoring, Games, Crafts, Music, Parties, State Licensed, Medicaid, Choice Waiver, Private Pay. Mon-Fri 8am-4pm(Extended Hours by Special Arrangement)COME JOIN THE FUN!!!FIRST VISIT NO CHARGE!!!

8099 **Saint Augustine Assisted Living Home**
3750 West 74 Avenue
Anchorage, AK 99518   907-522-4635
Fax: 907-522-4635
e-mail: corralalh@acsalaska.net
Teresita Corral, Administrator
Offers quality assisted living services.

8100 **Saint Augustine Assisted Living Home II**
8801 Greenbelt Drive
Anchorage, AK 99502   907-345-9690
Fax: 907-345-4369
Patricia Perez, Administrator
We are uniquely designed to provide different levels of assisted living services.

8101 **Scott Manor**
18242 Tonsina Court
Eagle River, AK 99577-8258   907-694-7555
Fax: 907-694-7555
Lydia Guerrero, Administrator
Offers quality assisted living services.

8102 **Shirley's Assisted Living Home**
16221 Bridgeview Drive
Anchorage, AK 99516   907-248-1598
Fax: 907-248-1598
Shirley Agcaoili, Administrator/Owner
Shirley's A.L.H.

8103 **Summer Shades Residential Care**
319 6th Avenue
Fairbanks, AK 99701-5029   907-456-5909
Fax: 907-456-2652
Thelma Pierce, Administrator
Offers quality assisted living services.

8104 **Thania's Assisted Living Home**
1747 Wickersham Drive
Anchorage, AK 99507-1349   907-563-6028
Fax: 907-562-9749
e-mail: flacacdk41@aol.com
Thania Alfaro, Administrator
Offers quality assisted living services, including Dementia care, cancer care, and diabetic care.

8105 **Tranquility Manor**
1205 N Tranquility Lane
Palmer, AK 99645-8624   907-746-4220
Fax: 907-746-4207
Catherine Korman, Administrator
Bruce Korman, Manager
Offers quality assisted living services.

Assisted Living Facilities/Arkansas

8106 Turnagain Adult Foster Home
2812 W 29th Avenue
Anchorage, AK 99517-1701
907-243-4115
Fax: 907-243-4115

Mila Jennings, Administrator

Arkansas

8107 Baxter Retirement Village
550 West 6th Street
Mountain Home, AR 72653
870-424-3599
Fax: 870-424-6808

Annette Thrasher, Contact

An assisted living community dedicated to the independence, dignity and purpose of every resident.

8108 Outlook Pointe at Mountain Home
715 West 6th Street
Mountain Home, AR 72653
870-425-6868
Fax: 870-425-7310
e-mail: outlook@mtnhome.com

Diane West, Contact
Erica Warmoth, Contact

An assisted living community dedicated to the independence, dignity and purpose of every residence. Outlook Pointe offers truly worry-free assisted living.

8109 West Shores Retirement Community
2607 Albert Pike Road
Hot Springs, AR 71913-4501
501-767-1200
800-818-1201
Fax: 501-767-2083
http://www.westshores.org

Nina Alter, Executive Director

Offers a lifestyle that is genuinely inviting with a combination of comfort and freedom. In addition to luxurious surrounding and friendly people, we offer the special accomodations and considerations that allow your retirement to be worry free.

Arizona

8110 ALC Copper Hills House
12234 E N Frontage Road
Yuma, AZ 85364
928-305-0892
Fax: 928-342-1768

Mary Ward, Executive Director

Offers quality assisted living services.

8111 Autumn Leaves Adult Care
2416 W Orangewood Avenue
Phoenix, AZ 85021-7629
602-864-1044
Fax: 602-864-3356

8112 Bee Hive Homes of Yuma
1839 W 25th Street
Yuma, AZ 85364-6910
928-317-3086
Fax: 928-317-3091

Connie Morris, Owner

8113 Bethesda Gardens
13825 N Cave Creek Road
Phoenix, AZ 85022-6178
602-765-4000
Fax: 602-765-4001

Dennis Smith, Administrator

8114 Broadway Proper
115 I West Esperanza
Green Valley, AZ 85614
520-625-4850
Fax: 520-625-4857
http://www.leisurecare.com

Features apartment homes in a fun and active retirement community.

8115 C& C Adult Care Home
2144 W Manor Street
Chandler, AZ 85224-8365
480-786-3412
Fax: 480-899-4027

Arne Lopez, Owner

8116 Capable Hands Adult Care Home
9912 N 87th Avenue
Peoria, AZ 85345-8314
623-486-1584
Fax: 623-486-2572

Phil Gallinaro, Owner

8117 Care with Love
813 E Belmont Avenue
Phoenix, AZ 85020-4102
602-216-0291
Fax: 602-216-0291

Lana Akhenblit, Contact

An alternative, state licensed, care facility capable of handling residents at a skilled care level.

8118 Cypress Court at Tucson
3701 N Swan Road
Tucson, AZ 85718-6968
520-299-7755
Fax: 520-299-7827
e-mail: judy.silverman@cypresscourt.com
http://www.cypresscourttucson.com

Judy Silverman, Director of Marketing and Sales
Teresa Warren, Executive Director

We are uniquely designed to provide different levels of assisted living services.

8119 Desert Point-La Reserve
10701 North La Reserve Drive
Oro Valley, AZ 85737
520-498-1111
http://www.leisurecare.com

Located in the foothills of the Santa Catalina Mountain Range in Oro Valley, and offers luxurious apartment homes.

8120 Emerald Springs Retirement & Assisted Living Community
1475 S 46th Avenue
Yuma, AZ 85364-4010
928-329-7707
Fax: 928-329-7717
http://www.EmeraldSpringsALF.com

Lupita Garranza, Administrator

Our apartments are fully carpeted with individual climate control and emergency call systems. At Emerald Springs, you will enjoy the privacy of your own individual apartment within a community of care and support.

8121 Forum at Tucson
2500 N Rosemont Boulevard
Tucson, AZ 85712-2167
520-320-6532
Fax: 520-319-4076

Kay Warren, Administrator

Offers quality assisted living services.

8122 La Casa Asperanza Assisted Living
6161 E Fairmount Street
Tucson, AZ 85712-4342
520-885-9439
Fax: 520-577-3445

John Haines, Owner

We provide different levels of assisted living services.

Assisted Living Facilities/California

8123 La Posada
350 E Morningside Road
Green Valley, AZ 85614
520-648-8131
Fax: 520-648-8397
http://www.laposadagv.com

Lisa Israel, President/CEO
Joni Condit, COO
Tim Carmichael, VP of Marketing

Maximizes the well being and care of seniors.

8124 La Siena
909 East Northern Avenue
Phoenix, AZ 85020
602-870-5500
http://www.leisurecare.com

Retirement living center.

8125 McDowell Village
8300 East McDowell Road
Scottsdale, AZ 85257
480-970-6400
http://www.leisurecare.com

Designed to offer a full complement of services for independent seniors who want to spend their time having fun.

8126 Springhouse Assisted Living
3701 N Swan Road
Tucson, AZ 85718-6968
520-299-7755
Fax: 520-229-7827

Teresa Warren, Executive Director

8127 Sunquest Village of Yuma
265 E 24th Street
Yuma, AZ 85364
928-344-8680
Fax: 928-344-4985

Linda Gwinn, Administrator

Offers quality assisted living services.

8128 Villa Hermosa
6300 East Speedway Blvd
Tucson, AZ 85710
520-298-6400
http://www.leisurecare.com

Retirement living center.

8129 Westown Adult Care Home
3044 W Corrine Drive
Phoenix, AZ 85029-1315
602-564-9528
Fax: 602-564-1431

California

8130 Aegis Escondido
3012 Bear Valley Parkway S
Escondido, CA 92025
760-735-8084
Fax: 760-735-8182
http://www.aegisliving.com

Dee Wieringa, Executive Director

Offers a range of lifestyle options including retirement living and assisted living.

8131 Aegis Gardens
36281 Fremont Boulevard
Fremont, CA 94536
510-739-0909
Fax: 510-739-0946
http://www.aegisliving.com

Emily Poon, Executive Director

A unique retirement community offering assisted living and Alzheimer's care and is dedicated to the Asian culture. Located close to shopping, medical centers and our sister community, Aegis of Fermont. Those who call Aegis Gardens Home will feel enveloped in the Asian culture through the interiors, landscaping and authentic Asian cusine.

8132 Aegis at Shadowridge
1440 S Melrose Drive
Oceanside, CA 92056
760-806-3600
Fax: 760-806-9508
http://www.aegisliving.com

Renato Alesiani, Executive Director

Located centrally to Carlsbad, Oceanside and Vista and is the beneficiary of the warm California Climate. Aegis at Shadowridge is committed to being an active part of the North Country community by providing education and leadership on senior issues, and helping wherever we can promote quality of life for the elderly and their families.

8133 Aegis of Aptos
125 Heather Terrace
Aptos, CA 95003
831-684-2700
Fax: 831-684-2719
http://www.aegisliving.com

Diana Savard, Executive Director

Assisted living with separate wings for Alzheimer's and dementia care.

8134 Aegis of Carmichael
4050 Walnut Avenue
Carmichael, CA 95608
916-972-1313
Fax: 916-972-1060
http://www.aegisliving.com

Terry Ervin, Executive Director

Situation in a quite residential neighborhood where there are 48 assisted living apartments which are a mix of one bedrooms and spacious studios, plus 27 apartments for residents with alzheimer's disease or other dementia.

8135 Aegis of Chino Hills
14837 Peyton Drive
Chino Hills, CA 91709
909-606-3010
Fax: 909-597-3383
http://www.aegisliving.com

Aziz Amiri, Executive Director

Choose from different apartments. Some offering spacious kitchens and fireplaces, garages and carports.

8136 Aegis of Concord
4756 Clayton Road
Concord, CA 94521
925-692-5838
Fax: 925-692-0071
http://www.aegisliving.com

Gerry Vadnais, Executive Director

Offers seven different floor plans all featuring nine foot ceilings with crown molding and private balconies.

8137 Aegis of Corte Madera
5555 Paradise Drive
Corte Madera, CA 94925
415-927-4200
Fax: 415-927-4244
http://www.aegisliving.com

Renee Hamilton, Executive Director

Located in a quiet residential neighborhood convenient to great shopping, bay trails and beautiful view of Mt. Tamalpais. Here we feature services for independent living and Alzheimer's care.

8138 Aegis of Dana Point
26922 Camino De Estrella
Dana Point, CA 92624-1603
949-488-2650
Fax: 949-488-2669
http://www.aegisliving.com

Sondra Brakeville, Executive Director

Knows the importance of recognizing, celebrating, and honoring people's lives.

Assisted Living Facilities/California

8139 Aegis of Fremont
3850 Walnut Avenue
Fremont, CA 94538
510-739-1515
Fax: 510-739-1559
http://www.aegisliving.com
Dianne Pederson, Executive Director

Assisted living services and dedicated care for individuals living with Alzheimer's or dementia.

8140 Aegis of Granada Hills
10801 Lindley Avenue
Granada Hills, CA 91344
818-363-3373
Fax: 818-363-1933
http://www.aegisliving.com
Terry Records, Executive Director

Provides assisted living services and dedicated care especially designed for residents with Alzheimer's or other dementia.

8141 Aegis of Laguna Niguel
32170 Niguel Road
Laguna Niguel, CA 92677
949-496-8080
Fax: 949-496-8181
http://www.aegisliving.com
Pamela Kerr, Executive Director

Aegis of Laguna Niguel is nestled in the beautiful and residential Beacon Hill area. Located in a special place and surrounded by some of the finest senior housing anywhere, it has become the preferred choice for those who seek the best in assisted living services and also for those residents with Alzheimer's disease or other dementia. The quality of care there is rated with the very best.

8142 Aegis of Moraga
950 Country Club Drive
Moraga, CA 94556
925-377-7900
Fax: 925-377-7929
http://www.aegisliving.com
Steven Mattingly, Executive Director

Located close to shopping, banking, and walking trails. Temperatures are typically warm and moderate in this part of California so it allows residents to enjoy an exceptional climate in a lovely part of the country.

8143 Aegis of Napa
2100 Redwood Road
Napa, CA 94558
707-251-1409
Fax: 707-251-1410
http://www.aegisliving.com
Bill Keck, Executive Director

Enhance resident care, promote independence, and celebrate residents' lives.

8144 Aegis of Pleasant Hill
1660 Oak Park Boulevard
Pleasant Hill, CA 94523
925-939-2700
Fax: 925-939-2785
http://www.aegisliving.com
Kurt Knauer, Executive Director

Situated in a quite residential neighborhood, there are 50 assisted living apartments, a mix of one bedrooms and spacious studios, plus 29 apartments for residents with Alzheimer's or dementia.

8145 Aegis of San Francisco
2280 Gellert Boulevard
San Francisco, CA 94080
650-952-6100
Fax: 650-952-5186
http://www.aegisliving.com
Tricia Palermo, Executive Director

Provides different levels of assisted living services.

8146 Aegis of San Rafael
111 Merrydale Road
San Rafael, CA 94903
715-472-6530
Fax: 415-472-3969
http://www.aegisliving.com
Bill Keck, Executive Director

Assisted living services specifically designed to meet your individual needs.

8147 Aegis of Ventura
4964 Telegraph Road
Ventura, CA 93003-8181
805-650-1114
Fax: 805-650-6283
http://www.aegisliving.com
Reggie Mullis, Executive Director

Offers assisted living services and specially designed care for those living with Alzheimer's or other dementia.

8148 Alhambra Retirement Community
2400 S Fremont Avenue
Alhambra, CA 91803
626-289-6211
Fax: 626-570-5254
http://www.frontporch.net/alhambra
Bob Moses, Manager

Residents receive assistance as needed with medication management and the activities of daily living.

8149 Alpine View Lodge
973 Arnold Way
Alpine, CA 91901
619-445-5291
Fax: 619-659-0617
e-mail: alpineviewlodge@cox.net
Linda Cioffi, Administrator

8150 Atherton Baptist Homes
214 South Atlantic Boulevard
Alhambra, CA 91801
626-289-4178
Fax: 626-576-0857
http://www.abh.org
Dennis McFadden, President/CEO
Jackie Pascual, CFO

Offers residents freedom from the day-to-day chores necessary to run a home but still offers the benefits of an fulfilling lifestyle.

8151 Belmont Village Cardiff by the Sea
3535 Manchester Avenue
Cardiff By The Sea, CA 92007
760-436-8900
http://www.belmontvillage.com

Location is convenient to worship and is less than two miles south of the El Camino Real retail corridor.

8152 Belmont Village Crown Cove
3901 E Coast Highway
Corona del Mar, CA 92625
949-760-2800
http://www.belmontvillage.com

Located in the seaside village of Corona del Mar, overlooking the Pacific Ocean.

8153 Belmont Village Westwood
10475 Wilshire Blvd
Los Angeles, CA 90024
310-475-7501
http://www.belmontvillage.com

Located along Wilshire Boulevard's Golden Mile, and adjacent to the Westwood United Methodist Church.

8154 Belmont Village at Sabre Springs
13075 Evening Creek Drive
San Diego, CA 92128
858-486-5020
Fax: 858-486-3540
http://www.belmontvillage.com
Inan Linton, Community Manager

Offers residents a more dignified, independent life in a comfortable residential neighborhood setting.

Assisted Living Facilities/California

8155 Belmont Village of Burbank
455 E Angeleno Avenue
Burbank, CA 91501
818-972-2405
Fax: 323-874-4123
http://www.belmontvillage.com
Jane Hirsch, Manager
Offers residents a more dignified, independent life in a comfortable residential neighborhood setting.

8156 Belmont Village of Encino
15451 Ventura Blvd
Sherman Oaks, CA 91403
818-788-8870
http://www.belmontvillage.com
Located on the prime residential areas of Encino and Sherman Oaks in the San Fernando Valley.

8157 Belmont Village of Hollywood Hills
2051 N Highland Avenue
Los Angeles, CA 90068
323-874-7711
Fax: 323-874-4123
http://www.belmontvillage.com
Offers residents a more dignified, independent life in a comfortable residential neighborhood setting.

8158 Belmont Village of Rancho Palos Verdes
5701 Crestridge Road
Rancho Palos Verdes, CA 90275
310-377-9977
http://www.belmontvillage.com
Located in a beautiful Palos Verdes peninsula residential neighborhood, overlooking the ocean and Greater Los Angeles basin.

8159 Belmont Village of San Jose
500 S Winchester Boulevard
San Jose, CA 95128
408-984-4767
http://www.belmontvillage.com
Offers residents a more dignified, independent life in a comfortable residential neighborhood setting.

8160 Belmont Village of Sunnyvale
1039 E El Camino Real
Sunnyvale, CA 94087
408-720-8498
http://www.belmontvillage.com
Offers residents a more dignified, independent life in a comfortable residential neighborhood setting.

8161 British Home in California
647 Manzanita Avenue
Sierra Madre, CA 91024
626-355-7240
Fax: 626-355-7267
e-mail: info@britishhome-ca.us
http://www.britishhome-ca.us
We are uniquely designed to provide different levels of assisted living services from minimum daily supervision to 24 hour care.

8162 Broadview Residential Care Center
535 W Broadway
Glendale, CA 91204
818-246-4951
Fax: 818-243-0437
http://www.thebroadview.net
Marcia Spears Cihon, Administrator
Specialize in caring for elderly with mild dementia who need a helping hand with their daily routine. Also able to help seniors recovering from sugery.

8163 Californian Retirement Residence
1224 Cottonwood Street
Woodland, CA 95695
530-666-2433
Fax: 530-666-2458
e-mail: info@thecalifornian.net
http://www.thecalifornian.net
Offers expanded assisted living area; nonambulatory residents; secured Alzhimer's special care,

8164 Campbell Adult Center
1 W Campbell Avenue
C-33
Campbell, CA 95008
408-866-2146
Fax: 408-374-6965
http://www.cityofcampbell.com
For individuals over 50 years of age. Provides programs and services to assist older adults in remaining independent and improve their quality of life.

8165 Chancellor Health Care
3554 Round Barn Blvd
Suite 302
Santa Rosa, CA 95403
707-573-3008
Fax: 707-573-1929
e-mail: amy.c@chancellorhealthcare.com
http://www.chancellorhealthcare.com
Danit Cave, Administration
The goal is to provide exceptional care for residents and to be recognized as the premier provider in the senior housing and care industry.

8166 Chancellor Place of Chino Hills
6500 Butterfield Ranch Road
Chino Hills, CA 91709-6379
909-606-2553
Fax: 707-573-1929
http://www.chancellorhealthcare.com
Allan Slight, Administrator
We provide different levels of assisted living services. Our goal is to provide exceptional care for residents, and to be recognized as the provider in the long term care industry.

8167 Chancellor Place of Lodi
2220 West Kettlemen Lane
Lodi, CA 95242
209-367-8870
http://www.chancellorhealthcare.com

8168 Chancellor Place of Murrieta
24350 Jackson Avenue
Murrieta, CA 92562
909-696-5753
http://www.chancellorhealthcare.com

8169 Chancellor Place of Pasadena
990 East Del Mar Blvd
Pasadena, CA 91106
626-577-0215
http://www.chancellorhealthcare.com

8170 Chancellor Place of Windsor
907 Adele Drive
Windsor, CA 95492
707-837-8785
http://www.chancellorhealthcare.com

8171 Citrus Heights Terrace
7952 Old Auburn Road
Citrus Heights, CA 95610
916-727-4400
Fax: 916-727-4232
http://www.ciminocare.com
Mark Cimino, Owner
An array of programs designed with the individual's capabilities in mind.

8172 Cordia Senior Living
5161 Foothills Boulevard
Roseville, CA 95747-6546
916-780-3330
Fax: 916-780-3331
http://www.cordia.biz
Karen Anderson, President/CEO
Comitted to creating opportunities for seniors to continue to lead meaningful lives.

8173 Country Villa Terrace Assisted Living
6050 W Pico Boulevard
Los Angeles, CA 90035
323-653-5565
Fax: 323-782-9516

Assisted Living Facilities/California

Country Villa Terrace Assisted Living Center provides supportive individualized care and is conveniently located in the museum row area. We offer religious services and feature Kosher menus. The residence is fully accessible to wheelchair and walker residents. Three levels of assisted care are provided. A companion facility, Country Villa Terrace Nursing Center, is adjacent and accessible by walkway.

8174 Country Villa West Assisted Living Center
10955 Washington Boulevard
Culver City, CA 90232-4045
310-558-0635
Fax: 310-838-5826

Linda Monaco, Administrator

8175 Country Village Senior Services
10241 Country Club Drive
Suite H
Mira Loma, CA 91752-1329
951-681-5718
Fax: 951-681-5773

Pat Shivers, Manager

Afternoons by appointment and scheduled meetings, information and assistance for residents of this retirement community, linkage with Social Security, DPSS, Public Health, Mental Health, Legal Services, Office on Aging, Nutrition Counseling, planning with Doctors Discharge Planners for homecare, extensive use of volunteers for meal delivery, telephone reassurance, transportation, roster of available homemakers, support group for caregivers, educational lectures and videos. Must be 55+ and resident.

8176 Courtyards at Pine Creek
1081 Mohr Lane
Concord, CA 94518
925-798-3900
Fax: 925-798-0773
http://www.courtyardsatpinecreek.com

An assisted living community committed to assisting our residents through the natural aging process with grace, a little humor, and the utmost dignity. The delicate balance of enriching their independence while maintaining their safety is our ongoing challenge.

8177 Crown Cove
3901 E Pacific Coast Highway
Corona Del Mar, CA 92625
949-760-2800
Fax: 949-760-2888

Vicki Kaiser, Manager

Assisted living program is designed for residents who need help with the activities of daily living, but do not require intensive nursing intervention.

8178 Cypress Court Escondido
1255 N Broadway
Escondido, CA 92026-2863
760-747-1940
Fax: 760-747-3723
e-mail: cypresscourt@kiscosl.com

Stuart Ostseld, Manager

Cypress Court caters to residents who value their freedom and independence, yet need an occasional helping hand. Here you'll find all the comforts of home designed expressly to meet the needs and interests of independent seniors.

8179 Eskaton Cameron Park Lodge
3421 Palmer Drive
Cameron Park, CA 95682
530-672-8900
Fax: 530-672-0390
http://www.eskaton.org

Our philosophy is to blend up-to-the-minute health technology with a home-like environment to enhance the independence and quality of life for each resident in the comfort of his or her own home.

8180 Eskaton Gold River Lodge
11390 Coloma Road
Gold River, CA 95670
916-852-7900
http://www.eskaton.org

We blend up-to-the-minute health technology with a home-like environment to enhance the independence and quality of life of each resident in the comfort of his or her own home. Our community includes cozy touches like fireplaces and warm-water spas. Each resident room is personally identified with a customized shadow box just outside his or her door. Our grounds are carefully manicured and feature walkways and courtyards.

8181 Fairwinds-Ivey Ranch
4490 Mesa Drive
Oceanside, CA 92056
760-439-8090
http://www.leisurecare.com

Our community's inviting atmosphere is complemented by regularly scheduled social and recreational activities designed to fit a variety of lifestyles. Residents are free to enjoy life at their pace, participating in activities, or spending time with a friend. Peace of mind can also be enjoyed knowing that our staff is available 24 hours a day to answer questions and that every apartment is equipped with an emergency communication system.

8182 Fairwinds-West Hills
8138 Woodlake Avenue
West Hills, CA 91304
818-713-0900
http://www.leisurecare.com

Offers luxurious studio, one-and two-bedroom apartment homes in a fun and active retirement community.

8183 Fairwinds-Woodward Park
9525 North Fort Washington Rd
Fresno, CA 93720
559-434-6444
http://www.leisurecare.com

Offers luxurious studio, one-and two-bedroom apartment homes in a fun and active retirement community.

8184 Fountaingrove Lodge
1401 Fountaingrove Parkway
Santa Rosa, CA 95403
707-526-1226
http://www.aegisliving.com

Offers a choice of individual cottages, apartments, or flats.

8185 Fountains at Sea Bluffs
25411 Sea Bluffs Drive
Dana Point, CA 92629
949-443-9543
800-846-4440
Fax: 949-443-0290
http://www.sunriseseniorliving.com

Emphasize proactive wellness through prevention, education and socialization.

8186 Garden of Palms
1025 N Fairfax Avenue
Los Angeles, CA 90046
323-656-7900
Fax: 323-656-9321
e-mail: director@gardenofpalms.com
http://www.gardenofpalms.com

Every aspect of living at Garden of Palms has been planned to ensure maximum enjoyment and comfort_ nurturing the spirit, emotional and physical well being of our residents while providing support to their families. Our residents with Alzheimer's live in The Gardens where they benefit from a specially designed program for individuals with memory loss.

8187 Gardens at Hillsborough Village
11918 Central Avenue
Chino, CA 91710-1914
909-517-1769

Heather Thomas, Administrator

Daily activities which encourage and promote socialization, independence and dignity.

Assisted Living Facilities/California

8188 **Gardens at Park Balboa**
7046 Kester Avenue
Van Nuys, CA 91405
818-787-0462
Fax: 818-787-7472
http://www.parkbalboa.com

Garrett Loube, President
Maru Cohen, Executive Director

In addition to independent living, we offer our residents assisted living services and Safe Haven, a secure environment for those facing Alzheimer's Disease and dementia.

8189 **Gardens of Santa Monica**
851 Second Street
Santa Monica, CA 90403
310-393-2260
Fax: 310-394-5002
e-mail: glacbs@assisted.com
http://www.brookdaleliving.com

Gary Lachs, Director of Marketing

The Gardens of Santa Monica (formerly Pacific Gardens) is the perfect place to enjoy the best in retirement living, offering Independent and Assisted Living tailored to suit your unique needs. Located a few blocks from beaches, restaurants, the Santa Monica Pier and the Promenade. The Gardens provides an exceptional retirement lifestyle.

8190 **Grossmont Gardens**
5480 Marengo Avenue
La Mesa, CA 91942
619-463-0281
Fax: 619-461-7736
http://www.healthcaregrp.com

Grossmont Gardens offers a retirement lifestyle on a nine-acre garden community that will inspire you to enjoy the various daily activities. You will also feel assured knowing that there is qualified, professional staff on campus to provide multilevel health care services.

8191 **Hacienda**
5790 Fleet Street
Suite 300
Carlsbad, CA 92008-4703
559-486-3000
Fax: 559-233-2758
e-mail: Hacienda@kiscosl.com

Offers a continuum of care, senior apartments, independent and assisted living.

8192 **Heritage Estates**
900 E Stanley Blvd
Livermore, CA 94550
925-373-3636
http://www.leisurecare.com

Offers luxurious apartment homes in a fun and active retirement community.

8193 **Heritage Estates Senior Apartments**
800 E Stanley Blvd
Livermore, CA 94550
925-371-2300
http://www.leisurecare.com

Offers luxurious apartment homes in a fun and active retirement community.

8194 **Heritage Pointe**
27356 Bellogente
Mission Viejo, CA 92691-6341
949-364-9685
Fax: 949-582-8957

Bernadette Reily, Manager

8195 **Hollenbeck Palms**
573 S Boyle Avenue
Los Angeles, CA 90033-3897
323-263-6195
Fax: 323-264-6955
e-mail: holpalms@aol.com
http://www.hollenbeckpalms.com

William G Heideman, Executive Director

To accommodate our members' changing needs, three levels of continuing care are available: Independent Residential Living, Assisted Residential Living and Skilled Nursing Care. Transition from one level of care to another may be temporary or longer term. The goal of our entire staff is to ensure that our members lives as independently and comfortably as possibly.

8196 **Integrated Care Communities**
14315 Davis Street
Moreno Valley, CA 92557-6316
951-243-3837
866-391-8820
Fax: 909-485-2642
http://www.icarecommunities.com

Carl Rowe, Executive Director

Guests include high care, frail-elderly and those suffering from memory impairment, Alzheimer's and related dementias.

8197 **Las Villas De Carlsbad**
1088 Laguna Drive
Carlsbad, CA 92008-1896
760-434-7116
Fax: 760-434-9261

Rudy Littlefield, Administrator

Las Villas de Carlsbad is a multi-level retirement community that offers independent residential living apartments catering to active seniors who desire the comfort of home. Residential assisted living is available for those who may require additional services in the privacy of their own apartment. The Health Center is available for those who require more care featuring 24-hour nursing care.

8198 **Las Villas Del Norte**
1325 Las Villas Way
Escondido, CA 92026-1946
760-741-1047
Fax: 760-741-0221

Sharyl Ronan, Executive Director

As a resident of Las Villas del Norte, you'll enjoy an active lifestyle, comfortable apartment living and the shared pride of living in a community of caring neighbors and staff members. You'll also feel secure knowing that optional health care services are available, should the need arise.

8199 **Linda Valley Care Center**
25383 Cole Street
Loma Linda, CA 92354
909-796-0235
http://www.chancellorhealthcare.com

8200 **Linda Valley Villa**
11075 Benton Street
Loma Linda, CA 92354
909-796-7501
http://www.chancellorhealthcare.com

8201 **Malash Gardens**
3106 Sombreado
San Clemente, CA 92673-3232
949-369-0446
Fax: 949-369-0446
e-mail: malahsalah@aol.com

Salah Malash, Administrator

Provides a professional and quality home care environment. Our goal is to enhance dignity and encourage independence.

8202 **Matilda Brown Home**
360 Forty Second Street
Oakland, CA 94609
510-658-5565
Fax: 510-653-4129

Kim Marsh, Administrator

Our staff, experienced in geriatric care, takes pride in helping residents to maintain independence and dignity.

8203 **Mountview Retirement Community**
2640 Honolulu Avenue
Montrose, CA 91020-1707
818-248-6737
Fax: 818-248-3072

Lorretta Thompson, Administrator

Assisted Living Facilities/California

Full-service retirement and assisted living features planned activities, housekeeping and linen services, conveniently scheduled transportation.

8204 Newport Beach Plaza
1455 Superior Avenue
Newport Beach, CA 92663
949-645-6833
http://www.leisurecare.com
Offers luxurious apartment homes in a fun and active retirement community.

8205 O'Connor Woods
3400 Wagner Heights Road
Stockton, CA 95209-4843
209-956-3400
800-249-6637
Fax: 209-952-6201
e-mail: info@oconnorwoods.org
http://www.oconnorwoods.org
Scot Sinclair, Administrator

O'Connor Woods is a multi-level retirement community designed for active seniors. O'Connor Woods offers residents the services and amenities to match their personal interests.

8206 Pacific Gardens Tarzana
18700 Burbank Boulevard
Tarzana, CA 91356-3367
818-342-0003
Fax: 818-342-0298
e-mail: pgtmarket@asl.cc
http://www.pacificgardensonline.com
Sarah S Laloyan, Executive Director

8207 Palo Alto Commons
4075 El Camino Way
Palo Alto, CA 94306-4005
650-494-0760
Fax: 650-494-0942
e-mail: vschnitzer@paloaltocommons.com
http://www.paloaltocommons.com
Sue Jordan, Executive Director

A unique concept in senior living offering personalized care in a gracious residential setting, located in Northern California. It's where our lovely home-like environment, cozy private apartments and supportive personal care services provide a positive and affordable alternative.

8208 Paragon Gardens
27783 Center Drive
Mission Viejo, CA 92692-3603
949-364-6210
Fax: 949-364-6270
Mac Tamayo, Administrator
Russell Milnes, Executive Director

Focused on providing the comfort, security and personal assistance essential for getting the very most out of life.

8209 Prestige Assisted Living
3120 W Caldwell Avenue
Visalia, CA 93277-7003
559-735-0828
Fax: 559-735-8352
e-mail: ctran@prestigecare.com
http://www.prestigecare.com
Helen Hurley, Manager

This community offers an enhanced service package that is not offered by direct competitors. Autumn Wind is licensed to provide the highest level of care (Level III) allowed in Idaho outside the nursing home setting.

8210 Prestige Assisted Living at Yorba Linda
4792 Lakeview Avenue
Yorba Linda, CA 92886-2464
714-693-5368
Fax: 714-777-6105
http://www.prestigecare.com
Mary Jane Rodriguez, Executive Director

8211 Rancho Vista
760 E Bobier Drive
Vista, CA 92084-3899
760-941-1480
Fax: 760-941-5981
Jeremy Liu, Executive Director

Offers a comfortable atmosphere and friendly, caring staff.

8212 Regency Park-El Molino
245 S El Molino Avenue
Pasadena, CA 91101-2996
626-578-0460
Fax: 626-568-8216
Virginia Garcia, Administrator

8213 Regency Place
8190 Arroyo Vista Drive
Sacramento, CA 95823-5956
916-681-7800
Fax: 916-681-7844
Brenda Chappell, Administrator

Eskaton's service continuum encompasses retirement communities, affordable senior apartment communities, independent living with services, assisted living, memory care, rehabilitation and skilled nursing care, home care services, adult day health care, information and assistance, telephone reassurance and home visitors, and senior care coordination.

8214 Rehman Retirement Resorts-Poway
14548 Garden Road
Poway, CA 92064-5126
858-679-1587
Fax: 858-780-0222
Jamal Khalid, CEO

8215 Renaissance at the Gables
201 E Foothill Boulevard
Monrovia, CA 91016-5500
626-301-0204
Fax: 626-303-8655
Susan Forythe, Executive Director

In addition to independent living, we are proud to offer residents our Heritage Personal Care Program. Heritage is designed for those who require additional care to meet their daily living needs.

8216 Rio Las Palmas
877 E March Lane
Stockton, CA 95207-5800
209-957-4711
Fax: 209-957-1407
Sam Ogden, Manager

8217 San Clemente Villas by the Sea
660 Camino De Los Mares
San Clemente, CA 92673-1800
949-489-3400
Fax: 949-234-0081
Aileen Brazeau, Owner

Free to spend quality time with family and friends. Providing a full social calendar of culturally enriching social activities, special events, physical fitness in our Fitness room and swimming in our beautifully designed pool and Jacuzzi, arts and crafts and socializing with friendly neighbors and caring staff.

8218 Springfield Place
101 Ely Boulevard S
Petaluma, CA 94954
707-769-3300
Fax: 707-766-9233
http://www.leisurecare.com
Our Assisted Living staff provides personalized services to those who may need special care and support with their daily activities of living.

8219 St. Paul's Senior Homes & Services
328 Maple Street
San Diego, CA 92103-6522
619-232-2996
Fax: 619-239-1256
John Scholte, Director of Marketing

Assisted Living Facilities/California

St. Paul's Senior Homes & Services provides affordable, innovative and comprehensive programs in a secure, interdenominational environment with great value placed on optimal independence at all stages of life.

8220 St. Regis
23950 Mission Boulevard
Hayward, CA 94544-1052
510-881-7888
Fax: 510-582-0812

Gene Rapp, Manager

Full service assisted living residence, centrally located in Hayward on 5 acres with a park like setting.

8221 Summerville at Garden Manor
10200 Chapman Avenue
Garden Grove, CA 92840-2858
714-636-6453
Fax: 714-636-0978

Monica Negrete, Manager

We are passionately commited to providing care and services of the highest quality and value in a safe, supportive, residential environment, promoting the health, independence and social interaction of seniors.

8222 Summerville at Main Place
2025 N Bush Street
Santa Ana, CA 92706-2817
714-541-3357
Fax: 714-541-5441
http://www.summervilleseniorliving.com

Eve Iten, Manager

Located at the end of a cul-de-sac, Summerville at Main Place serves the needs of independent seniors, those needing assisted living and residents with memory impairment. Summerville's assisted living and SummerBrook(sm) programs offer help with bathing, dressing, grooming, medication management and other activities of daily living.

8223 Summerville at Orange
142 S Prospect Street
Orange, CA 92869-3842
714-639-3590
Fax: 714-639-0833
http://www.summervilleseniorliving.com

Berneice Holmes, Administrator

Private and semi-private apartments complement the homey atmosphere of the beautifully decorated common areas. Residents of Summerville at Orange enjoy three delicious meals a day, snacks, social activities and easy access to medical care. For those needing an extra hand, Summerville's assisted living program offers help with bathing, dressing, grooming and other activities of daily living.

8224 Summerville at Valley View
5900 Chapman Avenue
Garden Grove, CA 92845-1604
714-898-3524
Fax: 714-891-3052
http://www.summervilleseniorliving.com

Lori Loucks, Executive Director

We are committed to providing care and services of the highest quality and value in a safe supportive, residential enviroment, promoting the health, independence and social interaction of seniors.

8225 Summerville at Victorian Court
1031 N Euclid Avenue
Ontario, CA 91762-1920
909-391-2622
Fax: 909-391-8587
http://www.summervilleseniorliving.com

Kim Weidman, Executive Director

Should you ever need extra support, we're a fully licensed assisted living community, so we can give you personalized services.

8226 Summerville at Villa De Anza
5881 El Palomino Drive
Riverside, CA 92509-7006
951-685-3333
Fax: 909-685-8453
http://www.summervilleseniorliving.com

Lori McCracken, Executive Director

In addition to numerous social activities, residents of Summerville at Villa de Anza benefit from easy access to shopping, movie theatres and golf courses. Each private apartment features high ceilings and air conditioning. For those needing extra care, Summerville's assisted living program offers help with bathing, dressing, grooming and other activities of daily living.

8227 Sunny View Manor
22445 Cupertino Road
Cupertino, CA 95014-1097
408-253-4300
Fax: 408-255-6015

Sally Plank, Executive Director

Our special care unit is designed exclusively for individuals with Alzhimer's disease or with related memory impairment disorders.

8228 Sunshine Care Mountain Vistas
12738 Monte Vista Road
Poway, CA 92064-2524
858-674-1255
800-811-9595
Fax: 858-674-1282
e-mail: inquiries@sunshinecare.com
http://www.suneshinecare.com

Adrienne Lake French, Director Community Relations

Offers one-on-one individual care. Bright, airy rooms and individualized care programs by our specially trained staff, cater to our residents.

8229 Trinity House
911 N Studebaker Road
Suite 100
Long Beach, CA 90815-4980
916-446-4806
Fax: 916-446-9947

8230 Varenna at Fountaingrove
1401 Fountaingrove Parkway
Santa Rosa, CA 95403
707-526-1226
http://www.aegisliving.com

Sam Faye, Executive Director

Assisted living and dementia care services, housed in a separate building, are available to you on a priority basis, offering peace of mind for the future.

8231 Villa Capri
1397 Fountaingrove Parkway
Santa Rosa, CA 95403
707-526-9090
Fax: 707-526-9099
http://www.aegisliving.com

Sam Faye, Executive Director

Provides care, but more importantly they provide respect and friendship.

8232 Villa Santa Barbara
227 E Anapamu Street
Santa Barbara, CA 93101-2098
805-963-4428
Fax: 805-963-2357

Mary Gensler, Executive Director

8233 Wellington Court
601 Sunset Blvd
Arcadia, CA 91007
626-447-0106
http://www.leisurecare.com

Offers private apartment homes in a fun and active retirement community.

Assisted Living Facilities/Colorado

Colorado

8234 Anam Chara Homes
1795 Quince Avenue
Boulder, CO 80304   303-442-4484
http://www.anamchara.org

Anam Chara operates two homes for elders who are unable to live alone. The homes are in residential neighborhoods, and the focus is on family and community. The approach to care is holistic, with self-reliance being held as long as possible.

8235 Apple Ridge Assisted Living Apartments
1640 South Quebec Way
Denver, CO 80231   302-283-0400
e-mail: marketing@appleridgeassistedliving.com
http://www.appleridgeassistedliving.com

We offer private studios as well as 1 and 2 bedroom apartments. All units have kitchenettes and private bathrooms. Our facility offers 24 hour standby assistance, meals, numerous amenities including on-site beauty salon, library, cozy living room with fireplace and activities.

8236 Argyle Square
4115 West 38th Street
Denver, CO 80212   303-455-9513
Fax: 303-433-7127
e-mail: info@theargyle.org
http://www.TheArgyle.org

Gina Berg, Executive Director

The Argyle Square provides delightful apartment-style living for the individual who needs some assistance, but does not require ongoing medical care. Our facility has 109 stuido apartments.

8237 Atria Inn at Lakewood
555 South Pierce Street
Lakewood, CO 80226-3470   303-742-4800
http://www.atriaassistedliving.com

We are dedicated to being the senior living community of choice where residents have all the conveniences and comforts of home, and the right amount of assistance with activities of daily living.

8238 Beatrice Hover Assisted Living
1380 Charles Drive
Longmont, CO 80503   303-772-8102
Fax: 303-651-7279
e-mail: hover@hovercommunity.org
http://www.hovercommunity.org

Jon Schuttinga, Administrator

Dedicated to providing retirement living with dignity in every aspect of life. The private suites in the Beatrice Hover Assisted Living Residence vary in size, floor plan and monthly rates. All are combination living room/bedroom suites with full private baths.

8239 Broadmoor Court
Bethesda Adult Community
2045 Roanoke Street
Colorado Springs, CO 80906   719-471-2285
http://www.bethesdaadultcommunities.com

Cindy Batey, Executive Director

Broadmoor Court is a assisted-living community with a wide variety of services, which makes this community an easy choice for those who need the added advantages of assisted living.

8240 Collinwood
Bethesda Adult Community
5055 South Lemay Avenue
Fort Collins, CO   970-223-3552
http://www.bethesdaadultcommunities.com

Kristen Jacoby, Executive Director

Provides both independent and assisted living services. Collinwood offers six apartment styles to choose from for a total of 87 units.

8241 Golden Pond
1270 North Ford Street
Golden, CO 80403   303-271-0430
Fax: 303-278-0623
e-mail: info@goldenpondliving.com
http://www.goldenpondliving.com

The goal is to ensure and preserve each resident's privacy, dignity, independence and well-being.

8242 Grand Villa
Bethesda Adult Community
1501 Patterson Road
Grand Junction, CO 81506   970-241-9706
http://www.bethesdaadultcommunities.com

Judith Shue, Executive Director

An assisted living community of 45 apartment units in two styles. The assisted living community is dedicated to promoting independence and nuturing each resident by offering many features and services.

8243 Granville Assisted Living Center
1325 Vance Street
Lakewood, CO 80214   303-274-4400
Fax: 303-274-4100
e-mail: vennita@thegranvilleassisted.com
http://www.thegranvilleassisted.com

Vennita Jenkins, Administrator
Myra Aceves, Resident Services Director
Susan Rose, Activities Director

The Granville Assisted Living Center provides a residential setting for elderly individuals and couples who need supportive services to maintain their independence.

8244 Harvard Square
10200 East Harvard Avenue
Denver, CO 80231   303-696-0622
http://www.leisurecare.com

Offers apartment homes in a fun and active retirement community.

8245 MacKenzie Place: Colorado Springs
1605 Elm Creek View
Colorado Springs, CO 80907   719-633-8181
http://www.leisurecare.com

Retirement living community.

8246 MacKenzie Place: Fort Collins
4750 Pleasant Oak Drive
Fort Collins, CO 80525   970-207-1939
http://www.leisurecare.com

Retirement living community.

8247 Nightingale Suites at Springwood
12825 W 65th Way
Arvada, CO 80004-2298   303-424-6550
Fax: 303-778-0299
http://www.SpringwoodRetirement.com

Pat Gallinger, Executive Director
Mary Kay Vezina, RN, Nightingale Suites Director

The Suites are comfortable, with many built-in features. Each opens onto a cheerful common area where residents may gather to work on projects, talk and develop friendships. Residents can also take advantage of the award-winning food services along with an excellent activity program.

8248 Sterling House of Arvada
7720 Allison Street
Arvada, CO 80005-5024   303-423-8100
http://www.brookdaleliving.com

Mark Schulte, Co-CEO
Mark W Ohlendorf, Co-President
John P Rijos, Co-President

Our assisted living programs and communities provide housing, care and services to older adults who want to retain their independence while receiving daily support, but don't require the skilled care provided in nursing homes.

Assisted Living Facilities/Connecticut

8249 **Sunrise of Boulder**
3955 28th Street
Boulder, CO 80304　　　　　　　　　　720-406-1000
　　　　　　　　　　　　　　　　Fax: 720-406-1003
　　　　　　http://www.sunriseseniorliving.com
Paul J Klaassen, Founder/Chairman/CEO
Teresa M Klaassen, Founder/Chief Cultural Officer
Thomas B Newell, President

Sunrise's assisted living options offer personalized assistance, supportive services and compassionate care in a professionally managed, carefully designed, community setting. It's the perfect alternative for seniors who can no longer live on their own at home, yet don't need 24-hour, complex medical supervision.

8250 **View Pointe**
Bethesda Adult Community
555 South Rockrimmon Boulevard
Colorado Springs, CO 80919　　　　　719-528-8000
　　　　　http://www.bethesdaadultcommunities.com
Leslie Eldridge, Executive Director

Provides both independent and assisted living services. View Pointe offers 21 assisted living apartments.

8251 **Winslow Court**
3920 East San Miguel
Colorado Springs, CO 80909　　　　　719-597-1700
　　　　　　　　　　http://www.leisurecare.com

Offers comfortable studio, and one-and tow-bedroom apartment homes in a fun and active retirement community.

Connecticut

8252 **Academy Point at Mystic**
20 Academy Lane
Mystic, CT 06355-2557　　　　　　　860-536-1133
　　　　　　　　　　　　　　　　Fax: 860-536-2245
Bollie Pollard Johnson, Executive Director

Academy Point at Mystic offers senior families the rental of an apartment, personal care services, 3 meals served daily in an elegant dining room, housekeeping and linen service and security in a homelike environment.

8253 **Arbors at Hop Brook**
403 W Center Street
Manchester, CT 06040-4700　　　　　860-647-9343
Chante Drasdis, Director
Paul T Lisstro, Manager

Arbors offers a stress free lifestyle with security, companionship, services and access to long term and rehabilitative health care.

8254 **Arden Courts Alzheimer's Assisted Living**
45 South Road
Farmington, CT 06032-2022　　　　　860-674-8580
　　　　　　　　　　　　　　　　Fax: 860-677-2795
Ron Bowen, Executive Director

8255 **Atria Crossroads Place**
161 Boston Post Road
Waterford, CT 06385-2831　　　　　　860-444-6700
　　　　　　　　　　　　　　　　Fax: 860-443-6880
Kathy Ryan, Executive Director

Offer elegant rental apartments, personal care assistance, and a full continuum of care should health needs change, including a special, secure memory impaired neighborhood.

8256 **Atria at Stratford**
6911 Main Street
Stratford, CT 06614-1360　　　　　　203-380-0006
　　　　　　　　　　　　　　　　Fax: 203-380-0007
David Vail, Executive Director

At Atria Stratford we encourage each and every resident to take the time to do the things they enjoy. And if that requires a little extra assistance at times, then we're always there to help. Because the safety of our residents and the peace of mind of their family members come first and foremost at Atria.

8257 **Bellmarie**
122 E Main Street
Plainville, CT 06062-1902　　　　　　860-747-4759
　　　　　　　　　　　　　　　　Fax: 860-747-5185
Marie Belanger, Owner

Assisted living services include 24 hr. supervision, nursing and personal care services, planned activities, and meals.

8258 **Bridges at Lake Whitney**
1450 Whitney Avenue
Hamden, CT 06517-2451　　　　　　　203-248-8880
　　　　　　　　　　　　　　　　Fax: 203-248-8833
Mark Barwise, Executive Director

Offers the privacy of your own spacious rental apartment enhanced with security, services and friends that make life a carefree pleasure and the availability of services 24 hours a day gives you the peace of mind you need to fully enjoy your lifestyle.

8259 **Bridges at the Green**
1 Elizabeth Court
Rocky Hill, CT 06067-1187　　　　　　860-257-0000
　　　　　　　　　　　　　　　　Fax: 860-257-0075

Offers privacy of your own spacious rental apartment enhanced with security, services and friends that make life a carefree pleasure and the availability of services 24 hours a day gives you the peace of mind you need to fully enjoy your lifestyle.

8260 **Chancellor Gardens of Southington**
58 Mulberry Street
Plantsville, CT 06479-1704　　　　　　860-276-1020
　　　　　　　　　　　　　　　　Fax: 860-628-5340
Perry Phillips, Executive Director

8261 **Chester Village West**
317 W Main Street
Chester, CT 06412-1057　　　　　　　860-526-6800
　　　　　　　　　　　　　　　　Fax: 860-526-6018
　　　　　　e-mail: info.@chestervillagewest.com
　　　　　　http://www.chestervillagewest.com
David Allen, Administrator

When it comes to your health care, Chester Village West offers you flexibility. You can select from a variety of health care services, including completely independent living, personal assistance services, or in-home health care.

8262 **Cold Springs Commons**
60 Cold Spring Road
Rocky Hill, CT 06067-3175　　　　　　860-257-3820
　　　　　　　　　　　　　　　　Fax: 860-258-4803
Gery Alexader, Executive Director

8263 **Crescent Point at Niantic**
East Lyme, CT

8264 **Curtis Home**
380 Crown Street
Meriden, CT 06450-6497　　　　　　　203-237-4338
　　　　　　　　　　　　　　　　Fax: 203-630-1127
Paul Sprague, Executive Director

8265 **East Hill Woods**
611 E Hill Road
Southbury, CT 06488-1386　　　　　　203-262-6868
　　　　　　　　　　　　　　　　Fax: 203-264-6311
　　　　　　e-mail: marketing@easthillwoods.com
Joseph Vannucci, Executive Director

Assisted Living Facilities/Connecticut

All under one roof, you'll find services to make your life easier, amenities to make it more vibrant, and quality health care services for complete peace of mind.

8266 Edgehill Health Center
122 Palmers Hill Road
Stamford, CT 06902-2134
203-323-2323
Fax: 203-323-6437

Robert Newcomer, Administrator

8267 Elim Park Baptist Home
140 Cook Hill Road
Cheshire, CT 06410
203-272-3547

8268 Essex Meadows
30 Bokum Road
Essex, CT 06426-1509
860-767-7201
888-377-3972
Fax: 860-767-0014
e-mail: info@essexmeadowsct.com
http://www.essexmeadows.com

Jennifer Rannestad, Administrator

Our large selection of 188 apartment homes gives you choices about the way you will reflect your individuality and sense of style. The services and amenities have been chosen to serve your needs and desires: first-class dining, numerous and varied activities, meticulous housekeeping, 24-hour security, health care, and maintenance of grounds and buildings.

8269 Evergreen Woods
88 Notch Hill Road
N Branford, CT 06471-1846
203-488-8000
Fax: 203-488-9429
e-mail: info@evergreenwoods.com
http://www.evergreenwoods.com

Jeannie Kinnard, Administrator

Our finely crafted lifestyle is a perfect balance of privacy and hospitality, freedom and security. It expertly complements who you are and the way you live. More importantly, our lifestyle inspires you to be yourself.

8270 Gables at Farmington
20 Devonwood Drive
Farmington, CT 06032-1486
860-677-1772
Fax: 860-676-2372

Jonathan Collins, Executive Director

Whether you're ready to simplify your life, eliminate the daily demands of home ownership or simply need a little assistance with day-to-day activities, The Gables at Farmington is the perfect solution.

8271 Gables at Guilford
201 Granite Road
Guilford, CT 06437-2313
203-458-3337

Deborah Dooley, Manager

8272 Gardenside Terrace
173 Alps Road
Branford, CT 06405-4742
203-483-7260
800-707-1354
Fax: 203-483-7752

Christian Shelton, Administrator

8273 Greens at the Greenwich
1155 King Street
Greenwich, CT 06831-3246
203-531-5500
Fax: 203-531-1224

Sherry Dey, Executive Director

8274 Hamilton Heights Place of West Hartford
1 Hamilton Heights Drive
West Hartford, CT 06119-6320
860-523-9333
Fax: 860-523-9337

Warren Strong, Executive Director

Apartments are not differentiated as either independent or assisted, so residents can stay in familiar surroundings if their needs increase. Also, couples with different needs can still be together.

8275 Heights at Avery Heights
705 New Britain Avenue
Hartford, CT 06106-4039
860-527-9126
Fax: 860-525-2090
e-mail: mmiller@churchhomes.org
http://www.AveryHeights.org

Mary C Miller, Director Admissions/Marketing
Patrick Gilland, CEO

Offering a full continum of care, seniors at lifestyle options for older adults including Independent and assisted living; subacute care, comprehensive medical care and rehabilitation for seniors.

8276 Laurel Gardens at Milford
77 Plains Road
Milford, CT 06461-2583
203-874-4408
Fax: 203-874-4655
e-mail: jsponauer@athenacommunities.com
http://www.laurelgardens.net

Bonnie Pollard, Executive Director

Offer elegant rental apartments, personal care assistance, and a full continuum of care should health needs change over time.

8277 Laurel Gardens of Avon
101 Bickford Ext
Avon, CT 06001-3741
860-677-2155
Fax: 860-677-1412
e-mail: jsponauer@athenacommunities.com
http://www.laurelgardens.net

Jennie Eisenhaure, Executive Director

Elegant rental apartments, personal care assistance, and a full continuum of care should health needs change, including a special, secure memory impaired neighborhood.

8278 Laurel Gardens of Hamden
335 Hamden Hills Drive
Hamden, CT 06518
203-248-1864
Fax: 203-248-1875
e-mail: ed.hamden@laurelgardens.net

Neal David, Executive Director

Offer elegant rental apartments, personal care assistance, and a full continuum of care shoudl health needs change over time.

8279 Laurel Gardens of Orange
245 Indian River Road
Orange, CT 06477-3634
203-795-3117
Fax: 203-795-3118
e-mail: admin@laurelestatesalf.com
http://www.laurelestatesalf.com

Louis Iannuccilli, Administrator
Lakisha Langley, Community Relations Coordinator

Offer elegant rental apartments, personal care assistance, and a full continuum of care should health needs change over time.

8280 Laurel Gardens of Woodbridge
21 Bradley Road
Woodbridge, CT 06525-2248
203-397-7544
Fax: 203-397-7543

Joseph Dellapuca, Executive Director

Offer elegant rental apartments, personal care assistance, and a full continuum of care should health needs change, including a special, secure memory impaired neighborhood.

8281 Lockwood Lodge at Ashlar of Newtown
139 Toddy Hill Road
Sandy Hook, CT 06482-1362
203-364-3179
Fax: 203-364-3299

Assisted Living Facilities/Connecticut

8282 Marriott's Brighton Gardens of Stamford
59 Roxbury Road
Stamford, CT 06902-1283
203-322-2100
Fax: 203-322-4300
Paul Klaassen, Founder/Chairman/CEO
Louis Iannuccilli, Executive Director

8283 McAuley
275 Steele Road
West Hartford, CT 06117-2716
860-920-6300
Fax: 860-232-4077
http://www.themcauleyct.com
Steven Suprenant, Executive Director

Continuing care retirement community provides for care needs of older adults starting with independent living and continuing to long term health care if needed. Skilled nursing care is offered at Saint Mary Home, on the same campus as McAuley, or at another skilled nursing facility of the resident's choice.

8284 Middlewoods of Farmington
509 Middle Road
Farmington, CT 06032-2046
860-284-5700
Fax: 860-232-4077
http://www.umh.org
Eileen Oconnor-Kamins, Executive Director

Provides meaningful options built upon a foundation of spirituality that allow people to maintain their independence for as long as possible, to rehabilitate from sickness or injury, and to be vital members of their community.

8285 Middlewoods of Newington
2125 Main Street
Newington, CT 06111-4020
860-667-1336
Fax: 860-594-0734
http://www.umh.org
Kathy Braga, Director
Assisted living.

8286 Miller Memorial Community
360 Broad Street
Meriden, CT 06450
203-237-8815
Fax: 203-630-3714
e-mail: cahamel@emmci.org
http://www.millercommunity.org
Cindy Hamel, Director Marketing
Nancy Luddy, Director Admissions
Brandon Munson, Administrator

8287 Orchards at Southington
34 Hobart Street
Southington, CT 06489-3322
888-340-2775
888-340-2775
Fax: 860-628-5311
Audrey Vinci, Executive Director

The Orchards at Southington offers a service-rich environment which allows seniors the freedom to do the things they enjoy most without all the worry of upkeep, security, or unexpected financial burdens of owning their own home. In addition, The Orchards offers residents and their families peace of mind in knowing that assisted living is available within the community should the need arise.

8288 Pomperaug Woods
80 Heritage Road
Southbury, CT 06488-3851
203-262-6555
Fax: 203-264-2155
e-mail: mwhpwoods@aol.com
http://www.pomperaugwoods.com
Nancy Hughan, Marketing Director
Kevin Moshier, Administrator
Continuing care retirement community.

8289 Rosedale of Glastonbury
1177 Hebron Avenue
Glastonbury, CT 06033-5008
860-652-3444
Fax: 860-659-2273
Robin Russotto, Executive Director

Offer elegant rental apartments, personal care assistance, and a full continuum of care should health needs change, including a special, secure memory impaired neighborhood.

8290 Rosedale of Trumbull Assisted Living Community
2750 Reservoir Avenue
Trumbull, CT 06611-5715
203-268-2400
Fax: 203-268-7034
e-mail: marketing@rosedaletrumball.com
http://www.rosedaleoftrumbull.com
Judy Begley, Executive Director
Gary Benzel, Director Marketing
Gail Bromer, Director Community Relations

Offer elegant rental apartments, personal care assistance, and a full continuum of care should health needs change, including a special, secure memory impaired neighborhood.

8291 Shady Oaks Assisted Living
344 Stevens Street
Bristol, CT 06010-2769
860-583-1526
Fax: 860-583-1297
Kay Belanger, Owner

8292 Spring Meadows at Trumbull
6949 Main Street
Trumbull, CT 06611-6304
203-261-0006
Fax: 203-452-0549
Mindy Stollman, Manager

Today's seniors are bringing a new attitude to retirement living — they want to live where they can enjoy not just services and security but also independence, wellness, and lifelong opportunities for growth and learning. We are dedicated to helping our residents make the most out of retirement.

8293 Stony Brook Court
50 Ledge Road
Darien, CT 06820-4439
203-662-1090
888-640-1090
Fax: 203-655-2892
Wendy Winnick, Executive Director

provides a beautifully appointed apartment and a full complement of services, from gourmet meals to housekeeping. Extensive community areas offer such amenities as an elegant dining room, library, sundry shop/ice cream parlor, and a wellness and fitness center.

8294 Suffield by the River
7 Canal Road
Suffield, CT 06078-1970
860-668-6672
Fax: 860-668-4770
Celia Moffie, Owner

8295 Summerville at Litchfield Hills
376 Goshen Road
Torrington, CT 06790-2722
860-489-8022
Fax: 860-489-5200
Greg Dempsey, Executive Director

8296 Summerville at South Windsor
1715 Ellington Road
South Windsor, CT 06074-2707
860-644-4408
Fax: 860-644-4485

Seniors enjoy three delightful meals a day, snacks, social activities and accessibility to all the best South Windsor has to offer. For those needing extra care, Summerville's assisted living program offers help with bathing, dressing, grooming and other activities of daily living.

695

Assisted Living Facilities/Delaware

8297 Sunrise Assisted Living of Stamford
251 Turn of River Road
Stamford, CT 06905-1320
203-968-8393
Fax: 203-968-8348

Jenifer Salamino, Executive Director

Sunrise is built on a commitment to our residents and their families. We believe no two people are alike, so the services and attention we provide should never be exactly the same. That's also why we offer a variety of lifestyle, service and care options. By providing these choices, we not only offer solutions for today, but we provide the security of knowing that there are options for tomorrow.

8298 Sunrise Assisted Living of Wilton
96 Danbury Road
Wilton, CT 06897-4409
203-761-8999
Fax: 203-761-6663

Jean Madden, Executive Director

8299 Tower One Tower East
18 Tower Lane
New Haven, CT 06519-1764
203-772-1816
Fax: 203-785-8280
http://www.seniorhousing.net

Karen Stoudmire, Executive Assistant
Dorothy Giannini-Meyer, President

Tower One/Tower East strives to create and maintain a compassionate and supportive community is an atmosphere of dignity, respect and cooperation enabling and assisting elders to preserve their independence in the privacy of their own homes. tower One/Tower East is not-for-profit and non-denominational.

8300 Village Gate
88 Scott Swamp Road
Farmington, CT 06032-2978
860-678-8016
Fax: 860-651-1247

Carolyn Urso, Owner

8301 Village at Brookfield Common
246a Federal Road
Brookfield, CT 06804-2652
203-775-8696
Fax: 203-775-1786

Diane Vaseturo, Executive Director

8302 Village at Buckland Court
432 Buckland Road
South Windsor, CT 06074-3741
860-644-7366
Fax: 860-644-7360

Tom Sebula, Administrator

Our unique, maintenance-free catered living options allow you to pursue your interests, form lasting friendships and experience the retirement lifestyle of your dreams. Enjoy the peace of mind that comes from our full range of services supporting the health and wellness of all our residents.

8303 Village at East Farms
180 Scott Road
Waterbury, CT 06705-3284
203-757-7660
Fax: 203-754-4331

Perry Phillips, Manager

Our unique, maintenance-free catered living options allow you to pursue your interests, form lasting friendships and experience the retirement lifestyle of your dreams. Enjoy the peace of mind that comes from our full range of services supporting the health and wellness of all our residents.

8304 Village at South Farms
645 Saybrook Road
Middletown, CT 06457-4746
860-344-8788
Fax: 860-346-6225

Richard Damarjian, Administrator

Our unique, maintenance-free catered living options allow you to pursue your interests, form lasting friendships and experience the retirement lifestyle of your dreams. Enjoy the peace of mind that comes from our full range of services supporting the health and wellness of all our residents.

Delaware

8305 Arden Courts Manorcare Health Services
700 Foulk Road
Wilmington, DE 19803-3708
302-762-7800
Fax: 302-762-8200

Kim Roman, Executive Director

8306 Bebee Medical Center/Peach Tree Acres
424 Savannah Road
Lewes, DE 19958-1462
302-645-3300
Fax: 302-645-3405

Jeffrey Fried, President

Beebe is a full-service facility providing comprehensive inpatient, outpatient, emergency, and home care in medical-surgical, obstetrics, pediatrics, oncology, and critical care medicine. Outpatient services include an Outpatient Surgical Center, Diagnostic Imaging Centers, and Rehabilitation.

8307 Brandywine Assisted Living at Seaside
100 Seaside Boulevard
Rehoboth Beach, DE 19971-1189
302-226-8750
Fax: 302-226-8751

Georgann Diest, Manager

Brandywine Assisted Living at Seaside Pointe is a premier assisted living residence designed to provide an affordable, yet exhilarating environment for older adults who desire an alternative to the daily worries and expense of maintaining a home. Our personalized service is designed for older adults who desire the finer things in life and who may require some degree of personal assistance with daily routines.

8308 Captain's Deck
7807 Governor Printz Boulevard
Claymont, DE 19703-2623
302-798-3500
Fax: 302-798-7662

Brenda Cuart, Executive Director

8309 Elder Wood Village of Dover
21 N State Street
Dover, DE 19901-3802
302-674-2144
http://www.elderwood.com

Marijane Copes, Administrator

8310 Forwood Manor Assisted Living
1912 Marsh Road
Wilmington, DE 19810-3954
302-529-1600
Fax: 302-529-1250

Gail Deerdorff, Contact

8311 Foulk Manor North
1212 Foulk Road
Wilmington, DE 19803-2797
302-478-4296
Fax: 302-478-2956

Virginia Grey, Executive Director

We pride ourselves in our ability to offer freedom of choice to our residents. Beginning with various apartment selections, and including fine dining and activities, all areas of our service and hospitality are delivered according to our residents' unique needs and preferences.

Assisted Living Facilities/Florida

8312 **Foulk Manor South**
407 Foulk Road
Wilmington, DE 19803-3899
302-655-6249
Fax: 302-655-5451

Gregory Artis, Executive Director

We pride ourselves in our long-standing reputation for excellent care, as one of the friendliest retirement communities in North Wilmington. Our residents and their families especially appreciate our delicious meals, the cleanliness of our community and the creativity of our activity programming.

8313 **Gardens at White Chapel**
200 E Village Road
Newark, DE 19713-3845
302-366-8100
Fax: 302-368-5660

Phillip Santoro, Executive Director

8314 **Green Meadows at Dover**
150 Saulsbury Road
Dover, DE 19904-2776
302-674-4407
Fax: 302-674-3341

Marijames Copes, Contact
Donna Winegar, Executive Director

8315 **Heritage at Milford**
500 S Dupont Highway
Milford, DE 19963-1758
302-422-8700
Fax: 302-422-8744

Eileen Hanhauser, Executive Director

8316 **Lorelton**
2200 W 4th Street
Wilmington, DE 19805-3362
302-573-3580
Fax: 302-573-3590

Richard Stat, Owner

8317 **Methodist Country House**
4830 Kennett Pike
Wilmington, DE 19807-1899
302-654-5101
Fax: 302-426-8108

Mary Ann Stanley, Administrator

Senior citizen retirement and long term care facility offering: food, medical care, skilled nursing, activities, & housekeeping.

8318 **Methodist Manor House**
1001 Middleford Road
Seaford, DE 19973-3697
302-629-4593
Fax: 302-628-5638
e-mail: epetrucci@pumh.org
http://www.pumh.org

Provides medical treatment, special supplies, inpatient therapy, occupational therapy for senior citizen residents.

8319 **Millcroft Assisted Living**
255 Possum Park Road
Newark, DE 19711-3877
302-366-0160
Fax: 302-366-7634

Steve Rovner, Contact
Annie Cantylmagli, Executive Director

8320 **Pioneer House**
413 Salem Church Road
Newark, DE 19702-1452
302-286-0892
Fax: 302-286-0893

Joseph Hargis, Manager

8321 **Rockland Place**
1519 Rockland Road
Wilmington, DE 19803-3611
302-777-3099
Fax: 302-777-3166

Paula Susaro, Executive Director

8322 **Seaford Center Assisted Living**
1100 Norman Eskridge Highway
Seaford, DE 19973-1724
302-629-3575
Fax: 302-629-0561

Lon Kieffer, Administrator

8323 **Shipley Manor Assisted Living**
2723 Shipley Road
Wilmington, DE 19810-3251
302-479-0111
Fax: 302-479-5880

Kathy Scott, Contact
Lynn Weiser, Executive Director

8324 **Somerford House**
501 S Harmony Road
Newark, DE 19713-3338
302-266-9255
Fax: 302-266-9250

Joyce Medkeff, Executive Director

8325 **Somerford Place**
4175 Ogletown Road
Newark, DE 19713
302-283-0540
Fax: 302-283-0543
http://www.somerford.com

8326 **Stockley Center**
2651 Patriots Way
Georgetown, DE 19947
302-934-8031
Fax: 302-934-7875

Adele Wemlinger, Executive Director

8327 **Village at Green Valley**
231 S Washington Street
Millsboro, DE 19966-1236
302-934-7300
Fax: 302-934-9399

Roger Connell, Administrator

8328 **Westminster Village**
1175 McKee Road
Dover, DE 19904-2268
302-744-3600
Fax: 302-674-8650

Robert Kratz, Executive Director

Florida

8329 **Abbey Delray Health Center**
2000 Lowson Boulevard
Delray Beach, FL 33445-6095
561-454-2000
800-936-7397
e-mail: info@AbbeyDelray.com
http://www.abbeydelray.com

Tim Smith, Owner

We've gone to great lengths to create a community that lets you take a permanent vacation from everyday worries. Living at Abbey Delray means giving up the worrisome responsibilities of maintaining a house. Instead you can spend more of your time the way you want. Socializing and pursuing the activities you enjoy. From housekeeping and maintenance services to scheduled transportation and delicious dining.

8330 **Albany Avenue Adult Congregate Living Facility**
211 North Albany Avenue
Tampa, FL 33606
813-253-0034
Fax: 813-258-3400

Peter Manescala, Owner
Jackie Manescala, Owner

Assisted Living Facilities/Florida

8331 Alderman Oaks Retirement Center
727 Hudson Avenue
Sarasota, FL 34236-7785
941-955-9099
Fax: 941-316-7878
http://www.aldermanoaks.com
Rusty Blix, Administrator
Linda Foster, Director Of Marketing

Both residents and their family find it comforting to know that help, if needed, is only seconds away. Most of the time residents feel better because they eat regular, healthy, and delicious meals. Transportation often helps residents to be more active than they have been for years, and it's nice to have energy to do things you enjoy.

8332 Alterra Clare Bridge of Bradenton
6101 Pointe West Boulevard
Bradenton, FL 34209-5534
941-795-5533
Fax: 941-795-8317
Janice Kenny, Community Sales Representative
Sandy Wells, Residence Director
Carol Crawford RN, Health Care Coordinator

Memory care residence for those with cognitive loss or memory impairment.

8333 Alterra Sterling House of Jacksonville
10050 Old St Augustine Road
Jacksonville, FL 32257
904-288-8700
Debra Wilce, Administrator

8334 Alterra Sterling House of Punta Gorda
250 Bal Harbor Boulevard
Punta Gorda, FL 33950-5294
941-575-9900
Fax: 941-575-9285
Beth Kohl, Executive Director

8335 Alterra Sterling House of Tavares
2232 Dora Avenue
Tavares, FL 32778-5708
352-343-2500
Fax: 352-343-2971
Debbie Flaherty, Executive Director

8336 Alterra Sterling House of Venice
1200 Avenida Del Circle
Venice, FL 34285-4109
941-485-8885
Fax: 941-485-1939
Kathy Dodyns, Executive Director

8337 Alterra Wynwood of Boynton Beach East
1935 S Federal Highway
Boynton Beach, FL 33435-6967
561-736-2424
Fax: 561-738-1205
Andrea McNemar, Executive Director

8338 Alterra Wynwood of Dunedin
880 Patricia Avenue
Dunedin, FL 34698-6072
727-734-4696
Fax: 727-736-1897
Kathy Hummel, Executive Director

8339 Altria Windsor Woods
13707 Dallas Drive
Hudson, FL 34667-7179
727-869-3533
Fax: 727-869-1643
Jennifer Astuto, Executive Director

8340 Apollo Gardens Retirement Residence
2718 Johnson Street
Hollywood, FL 33020-3824
954-923-5553
Fax: 954-920-5358
Grace Ueberlauer, Owner

APOLLO GARDENS is an Assisted Living Facility that provides a friendly, cheerful, affordable homelike atmosphere for secure and comfortable living for you or a loved one.

8341 Arbor Village of North Tampa
13107 N 22nd Street
Tampa, FL 33612-3815
813-972-3616
Fax: 813-971-6890
Ester DeLeon, Manager

8342 Assisted Living Center at Azalea Trace
10100 Hillview Road
Pensacola, FL 32514-5436
850-478-5200
800-828-8274
Fax: 850-474-0558
Jeff Rock, Administrator

8343 Atria Wekiwa Springs
203 S Wekiwa Springs Road
Apopka, FL 32703-4778
407-889-7704
Fax: 407-889-3425
Mary Anne Corbett, Executive Director

Our Life Guidance neighborhood features protective security features and planned activities designed to enrich the lives of residents with Alzheimer's disease and other memory impairments and help them feel comfortable and connected to their environment.

8344 Autumn West
2801 N Branch Forbes Road
Plant City, FL 33565
813-752-1076
Fax: 813-764-8270
Bill Brown, Owner

8345 Avante Terrace at Boca Raton
1130 NW 15th Street
Boca Raton, FL 33486-1343
561-394-6282
Fax: 561-394-7492
Daniel Benson, Administrator

8346 Bahia Oaks Lodge
2186 Bahia Vista Street
Sarasota, FL 34239-2451
941-954-1911
Fax: 941-954-3892
e-mail: bahiaoaks@hom.com
Mary Jo Harper, Administrator

8347 Barrington Place
2341 W Norvell Bryant Highway
Lecanto, FL 34461-9438
352-746-2273
Fax: 352-746-4166
Pamela Campbell, Administrator

8348 Bay Breeze Nursing & Retirement Center
3387 Gulf Breeze Parkway
Gulf Breeze, FL 32563-3360
850-932-9257
Fax: 850-932-5989
Jamie Richardson, Administrator

8349 Bay Gardens Retirement Village
1415 E 124th Avenue
Tampa, FL 33612-5647
813-977-2369
Fax: 813-631-8849
Elsa Thomas, Administrator

8350 Bay Oaks Home for the Aged
435 NE 34th Street
Miami, FL 33137-4012
305-573-4337
Fax: 305-573-1346
Kathryn Kassner, Administrator

Assisted Living Facilities/Florida

8351 Bay Village of Sarasota
8400 Vamo Road
Sarasota, FL 34231-7807
941-918-0682
Fax: 941-966-4040
e-mail: fgrady@mindspring.com
http://www.bayvillage.org

Susan Richardson, Contact
Jack McClelland, Administrator

Bay Village of Sarasota, Inc., is a not-for-profit, accredited continuing care retirement community, which offers its residents a gracious home and a full array of services for senior living. It combines elegance and security with continuing healthcare provided by its Health Care Clinic, Home Health Services, Assisted Living Facility, and Licensed Skilled Nursing Center.

8352 Bayview Gardens
2855 Gulf To Bay Boulevard
Clearwater, FL 33759-4087
727-797-7400
Fax: 727-726-7357

Judy Cunningham, Administrator

8353 Beneva Park Club
743 S Beneva Road
Sarasota, FL 34232-2411
941-316-0151
Fax: 941-316-0218

Barry Landref, Executive Director

For our resident's convenience and well being, our caregivers are there to help with any need you may have at any hour of the day or night. Our cook specializes in providing 3 delicious meals served restaurant style in our grand dining room. Beneva Park Club offers special catering to meet all dietary needs. We also welcome small pets in our community, because we understand the importance of having your best friend with you.

19We

8354 Benton House
2000 Principal Lane
Fort Walton Beach, FL 32547-6636
850-243-7735
Fax: 850-315-2145

Elizabeth Barr, Executive Director

8355 Bon Secours Place at Healthpark
1121 Jacaranda Boulevard
Venice, FL 34292-4586
941-497-1117
Fax: 941-492-3455

We are committed to quality care and the neighborhood living concept, we also have one of the best staff-to-resident ratios of any assisted living facility in the Venice area. This will assure you of the care you need, no matter when you may need it. And, best of all, we have the Bon Secours Venice Healthcare continuum behind us in the event you should need to be hospitalized or require special service like rehabilitation, home health or therapy.

8356 Bon Secours Place at St Petersburg
10401 Roosevelt Boulevard N
St Petersburg, FL 33716-3836
727-563-9733
Fax: 727-563-9595

Linda Marshall, Administrator

8357 Brentwood Retirement Community
1900 W Alpha Court
Lecanto, FL 34461-7507
352-746-6611
Fax: 352-746-6662

Mary Alice Tillman, Executive Director

8358 Bridge Assisted Living at Life Care Center
3201 Rouse Road
Orlando, FL 32817-2117
407-384-5858
Fax: 407-384-8810

Jeff Thomas, Administrator

8359 Bridgewater at Waterman Village
500 Waterman Avenue
Mount Dora, FL 32757-9567
352-383-0051
800-654-7670
Fax: 352-383-0081

Dale Lind, CEO

8360 Brighton Gardens by Marriott of Maitland
1301 W Maitland Boulevard
Maitland, FL 32751-4338
407-645-3390
Fax: 407-645-3878

8361 Bristol Park of Coral Springs
2975 NW 99th Way
Coral Springs, FL 33065-5084
954-255-5557
Fax: 954-255-6821
http://www.bristol-park.com

Sheryl James, Administrator
Terri D'Alessandro, Assistant Administrator
Carolynn Alongi, Marketing

Assisted Living.

8362 Cabot Reserve on the Green
4450 8th Street
Sarasota, FL 34232-1702
941-377-3231
Fax: 941-342-0844
e-mail: cabotreserve@aol.com

Susan Morgan, Administrator

Residents will enjoy the serenity of country living within a few short. Outdoors recreation areas provide opportunities for regular excercise, gardening, or a leisurely stroll with family and friends through our beautifully landscaped grounds.

miles pages

8363 Carpenter's Creek by Encore Senior Living
5918 N Davis Highway
Pensacola, FL 32503-2050
850-477-8998
Fax: 850-477-8919
e-mail: nancy.platten@encoresl.com

Nancy Platten, Administrator

Promoting independence as well as caring for our residents will always be our primary focus. Nothing is more important to us than ensuring each resident had a happy, active life. Our residents can age in place and receive the special care and attention they need.

8364 Chambrel at Island Lake
160 Islander Court
Longwood, FL 32750-4925
407-767-6600
Fax: 407-767-5503

Thomas Gagnon, Contact
Debbie Michelet, Executive Director

8365 Clare Bridge of Leesburg
710 S Lake Street
Leesburg, FL 34748-7327
352-728-6661
http://www.brookdaleliving.com

8366 Clare Bridge of Tequesta
211 Village Boulevard
Tequesta, FL 33469-2317
561-743-2626

8367 Coral Landing Assisted Living Residences
2820 Old Moultrie Road
Saint Augustine, FL 32086-5454
904-794-2273
Fax: 904-794-2465

Janet Pierce, Administrator

Located in a natural setting that feels like home where you get assistance with dignity and compassion. All the services and amenities you expect and deserve such as transportation to events and outings as well as indoor activities and intresting events.

699

Assisted Living Facilities/Florida

8368 **Coral Plaza Retirement Residence**
5850 Margate Boulevard
Margate, FL 33063-3621
954-970-0053
Fax: 954-971-7961

Campbell Epes, Owner

8369 **Country Residence**
14327 69th Drive N
West Palm Beach, FL 33418-7240
561-302-9296
Fax: 561-575-5110

Clyde Lawman, Owner

8370 **Court at Plam Aire**
2701 N Course Drive
Pompano Beach, FL 33069-3089
954-975-8900
Fax: 954-979-6614

Leon Willingham, Administrator

8371 **Cross Key Manor**
1550 Lee Boulevard
Lehigh Acres, FL 33936-4888
239-369-2194
Fax: 941-369-8148

Edward Slampak, Administrator

8372 **Crown Pointe of Sebring**
5005 Sun N Lake Boulevard
Sebring, FL 33872-2175
863-386-1060
Fax: 863-386-4925

8373 **Cypress Village**
4600 Middleton Park Circle E
Jacksonville, FL 32224-6624
904-223-6100
800-228-6163
http://www.brookdaleliving.com

The campus has a wide variety of living accommodations, ranging from single family homes or apartments to a health center with skilled nursing care and assisted living. Most importantly, however, it is a community that encourages residents to pursue all kinds of activities, so the lifestyle is anything but retiring. This is a retirement community designed for people 55 years of age or older.

8374 **Donnelly Place-A Classic Residence by Hyatt**
2792 Donnelly Drive
Lantana, FL 33462-6431
561-963-3441
Fax: 561-963-2159

Donnelly Place offers assisted living, memory support/Alzheimer's care and skilled nursing care with the Hyatt Touchr on the campus of the award-winning Lakeside Village life care community.

8375 **East Ridge Retirement Village**
19301 SW 87th Avenue
Miami, FL 33157-8984
305-238-2623
800-605-7778
Fax: 305-256-3516
e-mail: info@eastridgerc.com

Ken Kremer, Executive Director

Our amenities and calendar of activities offer a wide variety of recreational, entertaining and educational opportunities. Conveniences such as a branch bank, sundries shop, beauty salon and barber shop, make it easier to accomplish the tasks and errands of everyday living.

8376 **Edwinola Retirement Community**
14235 Edwinola Way
Dade City, FL 33523-3763
352-567-6500
Fax: 352-567-0272

Mark Davis, Administrator

8377 **Epworth Village Retirement Community**
5300 W 16th Avenue
Hialeah, FL 33012-2104
305-556-3500
Fax: 305-556-0887

K C Cross, CEO

8378 **Florida Living Center**
3355 E Semoran Boulevard
Apopka, FL 32703-6062
407-862-6263
Fax: 407-862-4188

Jeannie De Prada, Administrator

8379 **Florida Lutheran Retirement Center**
450 N McDonald Avenue
Deland, FL 32724-3698
386-736-5800
Fax: 386-736-5858

Jon Conrad, Administrator

As a continuing care rental community, Florida Lutheran offers senior residential living cottages, apartments and villas (The Village), two levels of assisted living, and rehab and long-term care in The Health Center. No entry fee is required.

8380 **Forest Trace at Inverrary**
5500 NW 69th Avenue
Lauderhill, FL 33319-7266
954-572-1800
Fax: 954-572-4752
e-mail: ken@searchwizmarketing.com
http://www.foresttrace.com

Kenneth Kosakowski, Owner
Candy Rechtschaffer, Manager

Forest Trace is a luxury, resort-style retirement community in Fort Lauderdale, Florida, providing full-service housing, assisted living, nursing home and lifestyle services to senior adults.

8381 **Fountainview by Marriott**
101 Executive Center Drive
West Palm Beach, FL 33401-4801
561-697-5500
Fax: 561-697-5897

Carole Williams, Human Resources Executive

8382 **Freedom Inn at Tarpon Springs**
1651 S Pinellas Avenue
Tarpon Springs, FL 34689-1946
727-934-1000
888-891-7207
Fax: 727-945-9219

Steve Boisen, Manager

8383 **Ft Lauderdale Retirement Home**
420 SE 12th Court
Ft Lauderdale, FL 33316-1920
954-524-3312
Fax: 954-524-3314

Jackie Heath, Administrator

8384 **Gables of Lake Mary**
3655 W Lake Mary Boulevard
Lake Mary, FL 32746-3497
407-688-1660
Fax: 407-688-2550

Julie Fernandex, Administrator

8385 **Golden Cove Assisted Living Facility**
918 Egan Drive
Orlando, FL 32822-6018
407-281-1886
Fax: 407-281-7176

Yolette Precil, Owner

8386 **Gulf Coast Village Assisted Living**
1333 Santa Barbara Boulevard
Cape Coral, FL 33991-2803
239-772-1333
http://www.gulfcoastvillage.com

Richard Heath, Contact

Assisted Living Facilities/Florida

8387 Gulf Coast Village Retirement Community
1333 Santa Barbara Boulevard
Cape Coral, FL 33991-2803 239-772-1333
http://www.gulfcoastvillage.com
Richard Heath, Executive VP

Gulf Coast Village is a retirement community built around the idea of living life to the fullest. We want you to spend your time enjoying life instead of worrying about all the little details. Here you'll have plenty of time to enjoy yourself, and you'll be able to keep your mind on what's important, because we take care of everything else.

8388 Gulf Winds
2745 E Venice Avenue
Venice, FL 34292-2425 941-488-5970
Fax: 941-485-4187
Diana Cullen, Owner

8389 Hampton Court Independent & AssistedLiving
301 S 10th Street
Haines City, FL 33844-5601 863-421-9581
Fax: 863-422-9581
Charles Bowers, Admissions Director
Ken Wilder, Executive Director

8390 Hampton Manor Belleview
10590 SE 62nd Avenue Road
Belleview, FL 34420-3004 352-245-6201
Fax: 352-245-9188
http://www.hamptonmanor.net

8391 Harbor Place at Port St Lucie
3700 SE Jennings Road
Port St Lucie, FL 34952-7778 772-337-4330
Fax: 772-398-8689
e-mail: madeline_sottile@lcca.com
http://retirementresort.com
Sharon Wilford, Manager

8392 Henderson Village
5700 NW 27th Court
Bldg D
Lauderhill, FL 33313-2389 954-486-4005
Fax: 954-735-6717

8393 Heritage Oaks Senior Housing
4501 W Shannon Lakes Drive
Tallahassee, FL 32309-2221 850-668-4004
Fax: 850-668-4426
Karen Pinney, Manager

8394 Heron House
3221 Fruitville Road
Sarasota, FL 34237-6452 941-955-7575
Fax: 941-955-7576
Robin Jones, Executive Director

Heron House is an assisted living community you will be proud to call home. Our unique approach to assisted living is simply better by design. Heron House was built to provide affordable luxury and quality care in an environment that was created specifically with you in mind. From your residence to the countless in-house amenities, you'll find that Heron House has included the details that make the difference.

8395 Highland Terrace Assisted Living Community
700 Medical Court E
Inverness, FL 34452-4698 352-860-2525
Fax: 352-860-1133
e-mail: highland@caravita.com
Ellen Mallon, Executive Director

Friendly, caring, and specialty-trained staff members are here 24 hours a day to meet scheduled and unscheduled needs. Thanks to our building's design, our residents have the opportunity to stroll in a comfortable, secure setting while also taking advantage of specialty-designed activities throughout the building.

8396 Homewood Residence at Boca Raton
9591 Yamato Road
Boca Raton, FL 33434-5549 561-477-8808
877-259-6225
Fax: 561-477-1665
Paul Markowitz, Manager

Here, in a community of friendly neighbors and supportive staff, you'll discover for yourself just how much the ARC commitment will mean to you.

8397 Homewood Residence at Boynton Beach
2400 S Congress Avenue
Boynton Beach, FL 33426-7461 561-733-8444
877-259-6226
Fax: 561-733-0229
Chris Spencer, Administrator

8398 Homewood Residence at Delray Beach
8020 W Atlantic Avenue
Delray Beach, FL 33446-9713 561-498-0134
877-259-8068
Fax: 561-498-3161
Kim Welsch, Executive Director

As an American Retirement Corporation community, we are committed to offering you a living environment that maintains the highest standards while providing a personal touch.

8399 Homewood Residence at Freedom Plaza
3910 Galen Court
Sun City Center, FL 33573-6817 813-633-4340
Fax: 813-634-1548
Sally Nichols, Contact
Trenna Russ, Manager

8400 Indian River Estates-East
2250 Indian Creek Boulevard W
Vero Beach, FL 32966-1395 772-770-0058
Fax: 561-778-7747
Joyce Keeler, Administrator
Charles Coxson, Executive Director

You'll find the security of our Advantage Lifecare program provides a lifestyle of independence, activity and companionship - with the all-important assurance of a worry-free future. Should your health care needs ever change, the best of care is available... and your monthly rate will not change as a result of a need for a higher level of care, including assisted living or skilled nursing.

8401 Inn at Cypress Village
4600 Middleton Park Circle E
Jacksonville, FL 32224-6624 904-223-6100
Fax: 904-223-6186
David Watkins, CEO

8402 Inn at University Village
12401 N 22nd Street
Tampa, FL 33612-4670 813-975-5009
Fax: 813-975-5141
Tim Parker, Executive Director

8403 John Knox Village of Central Florida
698 Monastery Road
Orange City, FL 32763-6220 386-775-3840
800-344-4504
Fax: 386-775-6064
e-mail: info@johnknox.com
http://www.johnknox.com
Lester Barker, Contact

Assisted Living Facilities/Florida

Our residents enjoy a wide selection of social, recreational and cultural activities, the security of life-care and the fellowship of good friends.

8404 John Knox Village of Florida
651 SW 6th Street
Pompano Beach, FL 33060-3700
954-783-4000
Fax: 954-783-4011
http://www.johnknoxvillage.com
Robert R Rigel, RHPF

8405 John Knox Village of Tampa Bay
4100 E Fletcher Avenue
Tampa, FL 33613-4864
813-971-7038
Fax: 813-632-2446
http://www.johnknoxvillage.com
Dennis Norton, Contact
Suresh Pai, Executive Director

8406 Just Like Home at Orange City
202 Strawberry Oaks Drive
Orange City, FL 32763-7444
386-775-3030
Fax: 386-775-3637
Tonilynn Ferris-Miller, Executive Director

8407 Kiva of Mount Dora
505 E 9th Avenue
Mount Dora, FL 32757-4937
352-383-5005
Fax: 352-735-1350
e-mail: info@kivaassistedliving.com
Julie Young, Administrator

8408 Kiva of Palatka
201 Zeagler Drive
Palatka, FL 32177-3818
386-325-0699
Fax: 386-325-0758
e-mail: kiva@msn.com
Dennis Childers, Contact
Cindy Lewis, Administrator

8409 Kobernick/Anchin
1959 N Honore Avenue
Sarasota, FL 34235-9117
941-379-3553
Fax: 941-377-1893
http://www.kobernickanchin.org
Kathy VanDusen, Director Marketing
Adine Kaufman, Administrator

Trade in the uncertainties of living alone and the responsibilities of maintaining a home for the affordable services and amenities that simplify life. We take the work and the worry out of your daily routine so you can enjoy life's pleasures - to come and go as you please and make the choices that suit you best.

8410 Kristianna's Assisted Living Facility
104 E Garland Court
Tampa, FL 33613-1826
813-961-6887
Fax: 813-961-6887
Ning Bonoan, Owner

8411 Lake Towers Retirement Community
101 Trinity Lakes Drive
Sun City Center, FL 33573-5755
813-634-3347
Fax: 813-641-1215
Laura Jean Goodsell, Contact
Ron Melner, Administrator

8412 Living Legends Retirement Center
4001 W Hillsboro Boulevard
Deerfield Beach, FL 33442-9492
954-426-9700
Fax: 954-429-8896
Janet Perez, Administrator

8413 Loving Care for the Elderly South
PO Box 279
Eustis, FL 32727
652-589-8944
Fax: 352-589-0794

8414 Mangrove Bay
110 E Mangrove Bay Way
Jupiter, FL 33477-6401
561-575-3123
Fax: 561-575-4341
Sarbeth Hanson, Executive Director

8415 Marriott's Brighton Garden of Port St Lucie
1699 SE Lyngate Drive
Port St Lucie, FL 34952-5016
772-335-9990
Fax: 772-335-9993
Lona Aiken, Administrator

8416 Marriott's Brighton Gardens of Boca Raton
6347 Congress Avenue
Boca Raton, FL 33487-2831
561-394-6385
Fax: 561-392-1587

8417 Marriott's Brighton Gardens of Boynton
1425 S Congress Avenue
Boynton Beach, FL 33426-6381
561-369-7919
Fax: 561-369-3413
Nichola Williams, Manager

8418 Marriott's Brighton Gardens of WPB
2090 N Congress Avenue
West Palm Beach, FL 33401-8210
561-686-5100
Fax: 561-686-9530
Cathy Davis, President

8419 Marriott's Park Summit
8500 Royal Palm Boulevard
Coral Springs, FL 33065-5715
954-752-9500
Fax: 954-755-9559
David Olson, Manager

8420 Masonic Home of Florida
3201 1st Street NE
St Petersburg, FL 33704-2299
727-822-3499
Fax: 727-821-6775
e-mail: masonichm@aol.com
Lois Clutter, Executive Director

The Masonic Home of Florida offers care on two levels: skilled nursing for residents who require round-the-clock care and assisted living for residents who need little or no supervision. More than 140 staff members, under the direction of career professionals in geriatric disciplines, join together to create a lifestyle through which residents can reach their full potential.

8421 Mayflower Assisted Living Facility
1620 Mayflower Court
Winter Park, FL 32792-2500
407-672-1620
800-228-6518
Fax: 407-671-6336
e-mail: info@themayflower.com
http://www.TheMayflower.com
David McGuffin, CEO

The Mayflower is structured to permit residents to enjoy their retirement years with grace, dignity, independence and security; to ensure that all residents are treated equally; to provide services which meet the physical, spiritual, social and psychological needs of the residents; to create an environment which will enrich the lives of people who live and work at the Mayflower.

8422 Mease Manor
700 Mease Plaza
Dunedin, FL 34698-6680
727-733-1161
http://www.measemanor.com
Jack Norton, Contact

Assisted Living Facilities/Georgia

8423 Merrill Gardens at Lutz
414 Chapman Road E
Lutz, FL 33549-5779
813-909-9679
Fax: 813-948-2878
http://www.merrillgardens.com
Cathy Bennick, Community Relations Director
Michael Cavallo, Manager

Merrill Gardens community living for seniors is a place where you're absolutely free to be yourself. You can enjoy the quiet comforts of independent living, participate in our active retirement community, or both. The choice is yours, and it's just one of the many choices you'll find all around you.

8424 Merrill Gardens at Orange City
500 Grand Plaza Drive
Orange City, FL 32763-7900
386-775-3561
Fax: 386-775-1997
Kim Smith, Administrator

Merrill Gardens community living for seniors is a place where you're absolutely free to be yourself. You can enjoy the quiet comforts of independent living, participate in our active retirement community, or both. The choice is yours, and it's just one of the many choices you'll find all around you.

8425 Moorings Park
120 Moorings Park Drive
Naples, FL 34105-2188
239-643-9111
http://www.mooringspark.org
Guenther Gosch, Executive Director

8426 Northpark-A Classic Residence by Hyatt
2480 N Park Road
Hollywood, FL 33021-3744
954-963-0200
800-989-9159
Fax: 954-961-1266
Nancy Bubick, Executive Director

In addition to apartments for independent living, NorthPark features an assisted living center, where trained professionals provide a helping hand with bathing, dressing, grooming and supervising medications. For residents with memory impairments such as Alzheimer's disease, NorthPark offers a memory support center.

8427 Orlando Lutheran Towers
300 E Church Street
Orlando, FL 32801-3551
407-422-4103
800-859-1033
e-mail: marketing@orlandolt.com
http://www.orlandolt.com
Richard Lewis, Executive Director

8428 Seasons: A Classic Residence by Hyatt
1371 S Ocean Boulevard
Pompano Beach, FL 33062-7130
954-943-1936
800-943-1936
Fax: 954-943-0504
Amy Matero, Administrator

Dedicated to understanding the needs and desires of older adults, and, through our valued employees, to providing our residents with high-quality services, distinctive amenities, enriching programs and compassionate care to complement their lifestyles and enhance their well-being.

8429 Stanford Centre
433 Orange Drive
Altamonte Springs, FL 32701-5377
407-260-2433
Fax: 407-260-0392
Karen Decker, Executive Director

8430 Sterling Aventura
2777 NE 183rd Street
Aventura, FL 33160-2165
305-918-0000
Fax: 305-918-0099
Charles Hatch, Executive Director

The Sterling Aventura offers the very finest available in independent and assisted living housing. Every aspect of our community has been meticulously planned to provide discriminating seniors the luxury and gracious lifestyle they expect and deserve.

8431 Sunrise Atrium of Boca Raton
1080 NW 15th Street
Boca Raton, FL 33486-1311
561-750-7555
Fax: 561-750-6746
Amy Stevenson, Administrator

8432 Victoria Villa Assisted Living
5151 SW 61st Avenue
Davie, FL 33314-5303
954-791-8881
Fax: 954-791-1157
Susan Eichler, Contact

8433 Westminster Towers
700 Lucerne Ter
Orlando, FL 32801-3730
407-841-1310
Fax: 407-849-0900
Joe Trainor, Manager

Georgia

8434 Belmont Village at Buckhead
5455 Glendridge Drive NE
Atlanta, GA 30342
404-252-6271
http://www.belmontvillage.com

Offers convenient access to healthcare, places of worship, shopping and restaurants.

8435 Belmont Village at Johns Creek
4315 Johns Creek Parkway
Suwanee, GA 30024
770-813-9505
http://www.belmontvillage.com

Offers easy access to shopping, dining, healthcare and places of worship.

8436 Mount Carmel Personal Care
3084 Mount Carmel Road
Hampton, GA 30228-2881
770-946-3376
Fax: 770-946-8214
Mouhad Khouri, Administrator

Provide a caring home where residents can live in a low stress and secured environment with dignity, comfort and the assurance that help is always available.

8437 Plantation South at Duluth
3450 Duluth Park Lane
Duluth, GA 30096-3257
770-623-0617
Fax: 770-497-8278
Margaret Lynn, Contact
Jan Boatright, Executive Director

Personalized care and supportive surroundings help create the ideal environment for meeting professional care needs. Friendly, caring, and specially trained staff members are here round the clock to provide the assistance necessary to deal with minor health matters, medications and more. Residents enjoy a home environment that nourishes their interests, satisfies their needs and maintains their independence.

8438 Plantation South at Dunwoody
4594 Barclay Drive
Dunwoody, GA 30338-5883
770-936-9857
Fax: 770-936-9614
Kristi Foster, Contact

Personalized care and supportive surroundings help create the ideal environment for meeting personal care needs.

Assisted Living Facilities/Idaho

8439 Remington House
1504 Renaissance Drive NE
Conyers, GA 30012-3895
770-761-4888
Fax: 770-761-4509
Joanne Elrod, Executive Director

8440 Savannah Court
886 Johnson Ferry Road
Marietta, GA 30068-4227
770-977-4420
Fax: 770-977-2240
Kathryn Chandler, Executive Director
Compassionate and highly trained staff provides assistance with the activities of daily living to ensure the highest quality of life. Residents enjoy safety, security and socialization with a quality-dining program, creative activities and personalized care program.

8441 Southern Plantation
580 Tommy Lee Fuller Drive
Loganville, GA 30052-3928
770-466-2273
Fax: 770-466-2220
Sherry King, Executive Director
This family owned and operated retirement community offers independent living in the cottages and villas, as well as assisted living in the manor house and alzheimer's care in the carriage house.

8442 Sweetwater Springs
1600 Lee Road
Lithia Springs, GA 30122-3057
770-819-6777
Fax: 770-819-0898
Paulett Brock, Administrator
In addition to the Basic Services, additional levels of Personal Assistance are available and tailored to meet each resident's specific needs. Residents will be assessed prior to move-in and regularly thereafter, to determine which level of care is needed.

8443 Tapestry House
2725 Holcomb Bridge Road
Alpharetta, GA 30022-6812
770-649-0808
Fax: 770-649-0807
Katherine Liabastre, Contact
Thomas Comte, President
Mission is to love, respect, and be caring.

8444 Winthrop at Buckhead
5455 Glenridge Drive NE
Atlanta, GA 30342-4968
404-252-6271
Fax: 404-252-6508
Charles William Jr, CEO/Management Services
Patricia Godfrey, Manager
Mission is to enhance physical and spiritual wellness through our Feel Good Program.

8445 Winthrop at Tucker
5844 Lawrenceville Highway
Tucker, GA 30084-1930
770-925-9170
Fax: 770-925-1258
Charles William Jr, CEO/ Management Services
Quinn Hopkins, Executive Director
Our mission is to enhance your physical and spiritual wellness through our Feel Good Program.

8446 Yellow Brick House
6903 Main Street
Lithonia, GA 30058-4441
770-482-4044
Fax: 770-482-4981
Dawn Stewart, Administrator
Offers a friendly helping hand to seniors in need of security, social opportunities and services. Family owned and operated with the help of a dependable and caring staff.

Idaho

8447 Aarenbrooke Place: Ashley Manor
9327 Cory Lane
Boise, ID 83704-6808
208-376-1300
888-376-7298
Fax: 208-376-3242
Vickie McCuistion, Administrator
Gary May, Manager
We provide clean, homelike living environments with loving, caring staff we truly strive to be a part of your family. Our dream has always been to provide the kind of care to our residents that will make a positive difference to them and their families.

8448 Adult Residential Care Home
830 N 23rd Street
Coeur D Alene, ID 83814-5909
208-667-1511
Fax: 208-667-7997
Bettie Atkission, Owner

8449 Alterra Wynwood at Riverplace
739 E Parkcenter Boulevard
Boise, ID 83706-6511
208-338-5600
Fax: 208-338-6553
Shannon Macham, Administrator

8450 Alterra Wynwood at Twin Falls
1367 Locust Street N
Twin Falls, ID 83301-3451
208-735-0700
Fax: 208-735-0900
Anita Burdick, Administrator

8451 Americare-Creekview
5685 Bannock Highway
Pocatello, ID 83204-3825
208-239-0480
Fax: 208-239-7586
J J Johnson, Manager

8452 Americare-Delphic
1590 Delphic Way
Pocatello, ID 83201-2285
208-238-9215
Fax: 208-238-7834

8453 Americare-Hiland
1919 Hiland Avenue
Burley, ID 83318-2714
208-677-5451
Fax: 208-677-1168
Rochelle Taylor, Contact
Lisa Junod, Administrator

8454 Americare-Lomax I
755 Lomax Street
Idaho Falls, ID 83401-2786
208-552-2860
Fax: 208-552-3131
Jessica Gepford, Manager

8455 Americare-Pendlebury
875 Pendlebury Lane
Blackfoot, ID 83221-3484
208-785-3627
Fax: 208-782-3528
Shawn Sharp, Manager

8456 Annabelle House
917 E Ustick Road
Caldwell, ID 83605-6357
208-455-2324
Fax: 208-442-3371
Shirley Farley, Administrator

Assisted Living Facilities/Idaho

8457 **Apple Valley Residential Care**
715 N Butte Avenue
Emmett, ID 83617-2724
208-365-1497
Fax: 208-365-2854

Viki McCuistion, Manager

8458 **Arrowhead Acres Estate**
3855 Flint Drive
Eagle, ID 83616-4539
208-939-3754
Fax: 208-939-3754

8459 **Ashley Manor Care Centers-Harmony**
2703 Harmony Avenue
Boise, ID 83706-5025
208-331-9228
Fax: 208-377-8310

Priscilla Landeros, Manager

8460 **Ashley Manor Care Centers-Highmont**
11099 W Highmont Drive
Boise, ID 83709-7702
208-377-4107
Fax: 208-377-4107

8461 **Ashley Manor Care Centers-Nampa**
69 S Midland Boulevard
Nampa, ID 83651-2422
208-463-0259
Fax: 208-463-0259

Christina Williams, Manager

8462 **Ashley Manor-Beverly Hills**
861 Beverly Hills Drive
Payette, ID 83661-3065
208-642-1711
Fax: 208-642-1711

8463 **Aspen Grove Assisted Living-Bellevue**
3214 S 7th
Bellevue, ID 83313
208-788-9698
Fax: 208-788-9698

Amanda Olson, Administrator

8464 **Aspen Grove Assisted Living-Gooding**
745 California Street
Gooding, ID 83330-1525
208-934-5506
Fax: 208-934-9781

Kim Milloy, Administrator

8465 **Aspen Grove Assisted Living-Idaho Falls**
2705 E 17th Street
Ammon, ID 83406-6601
208-522-4044
Fax: 208-522-4046

Laurie Field, Administrator

8466 **Aspen Grove Assisted Living-Lava Hot Sprrings**
580 W Elm Street
Lava Hot Springs, ID 83246
208-776-5899
Fax: 208-776-5899

Sally Nichols, Administrator

8467 **Aspen Springs Pioneer Home**
3254 Spirit Lake Cut Off Road
Spirit Lake, ID 83869-9376
208-263-2314
Fax: 208-265-4055

Marcy Larsen, Owner

8468 **Assisted Living on Shamrock**
2716 Shamrock Avenue
Nampa, ID 83686-8552
208-465-5923
Fax: 208-377-2550

Trysta Moore, Contact
Debra Landeros, Manager

8469 **Autumn Haven I**
264 W Hilgren Avenue
Hayden, ID 83835-9644
208-772-5728
Fax: 208-772-1471

Helen Reynolds, Owner

8470 **Autumn Haven II**
9886 N Reed Road
Hayden, ID 83835-9708
208-772-6160
Fax: 208-772-1471

8471 **Bannock Street Place**
1819 W Bannock Street
Boise, ID 83702-5109
208-338-1661
Fax: 208-387-1910

8472 **Beehive Homes of Grangeville**
709 W North 2nd Street
Grangeville, ID 83530-1174
208-983-3793
Fax: 208-983-3762

Gary Ghramm, Owner
Linda Ghramm, Owner
Diane Walker, President

The mission of Bee Hive Homes is to provide assistance with the activities of daily living in a respectful, dignified manner in a home like setting to the frail elderly who choose to retain their independence and dignity to the fullest measure possible.

8473 **Beehive Homes of Idaho I**
1081 Fairwood Court
Meridian, ID 83646-1443
208-888-4791
Fax: 208-888-4791
e-mail: ccastagneto@beehivehomes.com

Cory Castagneto, Owner
Linda Palmer, Owner
Dawn Lindsay, Owner

The mission of Bee Hive Homes is to provide assistance with the activities of daily living in a respectful, dignified manner in a home like setting to the frail elderly who choose to retain their independence and dignity to the fullest measure possible.

8474 **Beehive Homes of Idaho II**
2321 Kenmere Drive
Meridian, ID 83646-1675
208-888-3699
Fax: 208-888-3699
e-mail: ccastagneto@beehivehomes.com

Cory Castagneto, Owner
Linda Palmer, Owner
Tanya Ripley, Manager

The mission of Bee Hive Homes is to provide assistance with the activities of daily living in a respectful, dignified manner in a home like setting to the frail elderly who choose to retain their independence and dignity to the fullest measure possible.

8475 **Beehive Homes of Idaho VI**
652 S Main Street
Star, ID 83669-5253
208-286-7783
Fax: 208-286-7783
e-mail: ccastagneto@beehivehomes.com

Cory Castagneto, Owner
Linda Palmer, Owner
Diana Rushin, Manager

The mission of Bee Hive Homes is to provide assistance with the activities of daily living in a respectful, dignified manner in a home like setting to the frail elderly who choose to retain their independence and dignity to the fullest measure possible.

8476 **Beehive Homes of North Idaho**
632 N 21st Street
Coeur D Alene, ID 83814-5500
208-765-8364
Fax: 208-765-3396

Gary Ghramm, Owner

Assisted Living Facilities/Idaho

8477 **Beehive Homes of Rigby**
290 N 4064 E
Rigby, ID 83442-5710
208-520-3214
Fax: 208-745-7315
The mission of Bee Hive Homes is to provide assistance with the activities of daily living in a respectful, dignified manner in a home like setting to the frail elderly who choose to retain their independence and dignity to the fullest measure possible.

8478 **Beehive Homes-Mountain Home**
940 W 8th S
Mountain Home, ID 83647-3681
208-587-1308
Fax: 208-587-1316

8479 **Birch Avenue Residential Care**
910 E Birch Avenue
Coeur D Alene, ID 83814-4431
208-664-6547
Fax: 208-664-3307
Vern Johnson, Owner

8480 **Birchwood Retirement Estate**
641 Rimview Drive
Twin Falls, ID 83301-4447
208-734-4445
Fax: 208-734-4445
Ramona Farnsworth, Administrator

8481 **Bridgeview Estates**
1828 Bridgeview Boulevard
Twin Falls, ID 83301-3051
208-736-3933
Fax: 208-736-3941
Lori Bentzler, Executive Director

8482 **Brookside Landing**
431 Johnson Avenue
Orofino, ID 83544-9516
208-476-2000
Fax: 208-476-7748
Jill Tyler, Administrator

8483 **Burley Care Assisted Living**
1729 Miller Avenue
Burley, ID 83318-2338
208-678-9474
Fax: 208-678-3727
Renee Mai, Contact
Carol Gonzales, Administrator

8484 **Capital City Assisted Living-Spaulding**
PO Box 5394
Boise, ID 83705
208-384-1393
Fax: 208-333-0636

8485 **Carousel Homes I**
3535 N 3000 E
Twin Falls, ID 83301
208-732-8102
Fax: 208-735-8969

8486 **Carousel Homes II**
1210 Harmony Road
Twin Falls, ID 83301-7719
208-737-4655
Fax: 208-735-8969

8487 **Cascade Assisted Living**
507 S Highway 55
Cascade, ID 83611
208-382-6000
Fax: 208-382-6000

8488 **Cedar Crest Residential Care**
1200 E 6th S
Mountain Home, ID 83647-3241
208-587-9073
Fax: 208-587-9074
Charlene Humphreys, Contact
Robert Decker, Administrator

8489 **Cedar Draw Living Center**
4094 N 2100 E
Filer, ID 83328-5042
208-326-3342
Fax: 208-326-6571
Robin York, Administrator

8490 **Cenoma House**
1930 Heyburn Avenue E
Twin Falls, ID 83301-4921
208-736-7471
Fax: 208-736-7471
Linda Biain, Owner

8491 **Clark House**
1401 N Polk Ext
Moscow, ID 83843-9003
208-882-3438
Fax: 208-882-3369
Kiley Stueve, Administrator

8492 **Clearwater House Assisted Living Concept**
715 W Comstock Avenue
Nampa, ID 83651-8406
208-463-1732
Fax: 208-463-9381
Stacey Stallings, Executive Director

8493 **Coeur D'Alene Home**
704 W Walnut Avenue
Coeur D Alene, ID 83814-2361
208-664-8119
Fax: 208-666-0749
e-mail: coeurdalenehomes@hotmail.com
http://www.cdahomes.org
Mike Grabenstein, Administrator
Our ecumenical mission is to provide a not-for-profit housing campus, offering Christian care without discrimination, for our elderly and disadvantaged residents.

8494 **Community Restorium**
540 Kanisku
Bonners Ferry, ID 83805
208-267-2453
Fax: 208-267-7564
Mary Ann Tritt, Administrator

8495 **Cotttages of Emmett**
411 E 12th Street
Emmett, ID 83617-3628
208-365-9490
Fax: 208-323-5593
Garold Maxwell, Owner

8496 **Country Care Homes**
779 S Tennyson Way
Boise, ID 83709-7738
208-375-3555
Fax: 208-672-9010
Caroline White, Manager

8497 **Country Care at Cottonwood**
601 Blaine Avenue
Nampa, ID 83651-2457
208-461-0216
Fax: 208-467-2376
Duke Van Campen, Owner

8498 **Country Inn**
18938 Midland Boulevard
Nampa, ID 83687-8032
208-466-2164
Fax: 208-466-2164
Angie Soesbe, Administrator

8499 **Country Meadows**
912 W Greenhurst Road
Nampa, ID 83686-2918
208-442-7250
Fax: 208-442-7251

Assisted Living Facilities/Idaho

8500 **Creekside Care Center**
222 6th Avenue W
Jerome, ID 83338-1834
208-324-4912
Fax: 208-324-8536
Diane Holly, Contact
Dorothy Butler, Executive Director

8501 **Desano Place Residential Care**
PO Box 147
Shoshone, ID 83352
208-886-7665
Fax: 208-886-2737
e-mail: terri@pendleton.myrf.net
Terri Pendleton RN, Owner/Administrator
9-bed residential care.

8502 **Discovery Care Centre of Salmon**
600 Shanafelt Street
Salmon, ID 83467-4261
208-756-8391
Fax: 208-756-8398
George Boodgett, Owner

8503 **Elite Care**
3265 E Saint James Avenue
Hayden, ID 83835-7548
208-772-7540
Fax: 208-762-8857
Patti Newell, Administrator

8504 **Evergreen Idaho Health Care Sandpoint**
624 S Division Avenue
Sandpoint, ID 83864-1749
208-265-2354
Fax: 208-263-8787
Kiley Turner, Administrator

8505 **Fairwinds-Coeur d'Alene**
2340 West Seltice Way
Coeur d'Alene, ID 83814
208-765-5505
http://www.leisurecare.com
Offers luxurious apartment homes in a fun and active retirement community.

8506 **Fairwinds-Sand Creek**
3310 Valencia Drive
Idaho Falls, ID 83404
208-542-6200
http://www.leisurecare.com
Offers luxurious apartment homes in a fun and active retirement community.

8507 **Hayden Country Guest Home**
705 S 9th Avenue
Spirit Lake, ID 83869
208-623-6154
Fax: 208-623-5020

8508 **Hayden Country Guest Home III**
PO Box 177
Hayden, ID 83835
208-762-9292
Fax: 208-762-8481
Dawn Hayden-Gates, Contact

8509 **Heritage Parkview**
616 16th Avenue N
Nampa, ID 83687-3540
208-466-9209
Fax: 208-466-4508

8510 **Heritage Retirement Center-Boise**
1777 S Curtis Road
Boise, ID 83705-2708
208-376-4191
Fax: 208-376-9512
Cathy Lynch, Administrator

8511 **Heritage Retirement Center-Twin Falls**
622 Filer Avenue W
Twin Falls, ID 83301-4533
208-733-9064
Fax: 208-733-0343
Cathy Lynch, Contact

8512 **Hettinger Living Center**
217 Ruby Street
Boise, ID 83705-5939
208-345-8017
Fax: 208-343-5683

8513 **Highland Estates**
2050 Hiland Avenue
Burley, ID 83318-2761
208-678-4411
Fax: 208-678-4470
Bill Hines, Owner

8514 **Highland Hills**
1501 Baldy Avenue
Pocatello, ID 83201-7117
208-237-6866
Fax: 208-237-3889
Robyn Smith, Administrator

8515 **Hillcrest**
1093 S Hilton Street
Boise, ID 83705-1971
208-345-4460
Fax: 208-345-0178
Eric Bultez, Manager

8516 **Huckleberry Retirement Homes II**
1408 Ponderosa Drive
Sandpoint, ID 83864-8270
208-255-7248
Fax: 208-265-7284

8517 **Huckleberry Retirement Homes III**
1412 4th Street
Priest River, ID 83856-6603
208-448-4231
Fax: 208-265-7284
Lynn Hyuck, Owner

8518 **Huckleberry Retirement Homes IV**
1513 Hemlock Court
Sandpoint, ID 83864-8279
208-255-5999
Fax: 208-265-7284

8519 **Imperial Care Center**
1135 Imperial Street
Twin Falls, ID 83301-3133
208-734-7977
Fax: 208-734-9678

8520 **Indianhead Estates**
590 W Indianhead Road
Weiser, ID 83672-1512
208-549-3455
Fax: 208-549-3483
Patricia Caroll, Contact
Renee Edwards, Owner

8521 **Joyce's Orchard Residential Care Home**
615 Cedar Avenue
Lewiston, ID 83501-5121
208-746-5695
Fax: 208-798-4667
Joy Dunlap, Manager

8522 **Karcher Estates**
1127 Caldwell Boulevard
Nampa, ID 83651-1719
208-465-4935
Fax: 208-465-4953
Donna Lant, Administrator

Assisted Living Facilities/Idaho

Experience is a fundamental benefit when choosing a Frontier Management, LLC community. Our team has the expertise in retirement living and assisted living to meet your needs. Our entire company is dedicated to those who have selected one of our communities as "home" for themselves or their loved ones.

8523 Larkspur Land Residential & Assisted Living Center
214 Larkspur Lane
Lewiston, ID 83501-9600
208-743-0460
Fax: 208-758-9048

8524 Legends Park Assisted Living Community
1820 W Golf Course Road
Coeur D Alene, ID 83815-1627
208-666-9900
Fax: 208-765-6587

Trudie Chamberlain, Manager

8525 Lilly Home
840 1st Street
Idaho Falls, ID 83401-4065
208-522-1221
Fax: 208-529-4063

Jerry Mitchell, Owner

8526 Lincoln Court
850 Lincoln Drive
Idaho Falls, ID 83401
208-529-3456
http://www.leisurecare.com

Offers a luxurious studio, and one-and two-bedroom apartment homes in a fun and active retirement community.

8527 Lincoln Court Retirement Community
850 Lincoln Drive
Idaho Falls, ID 83401-4922
208-529-3456
Fax: 208-529-0641

Tom Sass, Manager

8528 Living Springs
1605 N Catherine Street
Post Falls, ID 83854-7237
208-773-6145
Fax: 208-773-1138

Alice Thibault, Administrator
Jennifer Trefz, Administrator
Gary Trefz, Owner

Assisted Living.

8529 Loyaton of Coeur d'Alene
205 E Anton Avenue
Coeur D Alene, ID 83815-3721
208-667-6490
Fax: 208-765-4352

Tambra Maple, Contact
Jodie Lynch, Administrator

ttractive apartment homes. Delicious, restaurant-style dining. Housekeeping and laundry services. Personal care and assistance, if needed, from skilled caregivers and licensed specialists. A daily offering of fun and enlightening activities. You'll find all these things, and more, in Emeritus communities.

8530 Magic Valley Manor Assisted Living
210 N Idaho Street
Wendell, ID 83355-5036
208-536-6623
Fax: 208-536-6799

Kim Milloy, Adminstrator

8531 Mallory House
3400 S 5th W
Idaho Falls, ID 83402-7309
208-528-6599
Fax: 208-529-2916

Mariann Yancey, Executive Director

8532 Markham Residential Care
11525 W 3rd Street
Star, ID 83669-5511
208-286-7873
Fax: 208-286-0576

Dana Jasper, Manager

8533 Meadowlark Home of Grangeville
701 W North 2nd Street
Grangeville, ID 83530-1174
208-983-3793
Fax: 208-983-3762

Diane Walker, President

8534 Meyer Manor II
3610 Lamont Road
Meridian, ID 83642-6430
208-888-4111
Fax: 208-888-4201

Shirley Meyer, Owner

8535 New Horizon Care Center
1140 Science Center Drive
Idaho Falls, ID 83402-1506
208-542-6856
Fax: 208-542-6028

Ron Hedelius, Owner

8536 New Life Living Center
2206 E 3700 N
Filer, ID 83328-5608
208-326-3203
Fax: 208-326-3201

Robin L York, Contact

8537 Odd Fellows Home of Idaho
720 N 16th Avenue
Caldwell, ID 83605-3499
208-459-7601
Fax: 208-459-0139

8538 Paramount Parks at Boise
10250 W Smoke Ranch Drive
Boise, ID 83709-1467
208-322-2900
Fax: 208-322-2345

D Curry, Manager

8539 Parkwood Meadows Assisted Living Community
1885 Parkwood Street
Idaho Falls, ID 83401-6135
208-523-7800
Fax: 208-523-2240

Winnie Welker, Administrator

8540 Parma Living Center
401 N 8th Street
Parma, ID 83660-5907
208-722-5496
Fax: 208-337-4892

Rick Holloway, Owner

8541 Philos House
525 16th Avenue E
Jerome, ID 83338-1500
208-324-3020
Fax: 208-324-8536

Coral Holley, Owner

8542 Pine Brook Assisted Living Center
4020 E 300 N
Rigby, ID 83442-5502
208-745-0100
Fax: 208-745-8364

Fawn Hedelius, Manager

8543 Plantation Place Retirement & Assisted Living
3921 N Kessinger Lane
Garden City, ID 83703-3003
208-853-7300
Fax: 208-853-9328

Linda Simon, Administrator

Assisted Living Facilities/Idaho

8544 Pleasant Valley Shelter Home
1911 17th Avenue
Lewiston, ID 83501-4039
208-743-0026
Fax: 208-798-4667

Joy Dunlap, Owner

8545 Pocatello Assisted Living Center
520 Willard Avenue
Pocatello, ID 83201-4537
208-232-2610
Fax: 208-234-1900

Gary Davis, Administrator

8546 Prestige Assisted Living at Autumn Wind
200 W Beech Street
Caldwell, ID 83605-5692
208-459-3335
Fax: 208-459-3300

Steve Matthews, Manager

8547 Prestige Living Northwest Residential
11950 N Thames Court
Hayden, ID 83835-7553
208-772-8297
Fax: 208-772-8282

8548 Quail Ridge Assisted Living
797 Hospital Way
Pocatello, ID 83201-2760
208-233-8875
Fax: 208-233-8797

Jodi Thomas, Manager

8549 Ridge Wind Assisted Living
4080 Hawthorne Road
Pocatello, ID 83202-2746
208-237-3000
Fax: 208-237-6024

Sandy Guidinger, Administrator

8550 Riverview Assisted Center
679 Troy Avenue
Idaho Falls, ID 83402-2901
208-523-5773
Fax: 208-342-4149

Corinne Schneider, Owner

8551 Riviera
924 Riviera Drive
Boise, ID 83703-5731
208-333-8050
Fax: 208-342-4149

8552 Rockhaven Retirement Home
PO Box 29
Oakley, ID 83346
208-862-3486
Fax: 208-862-3875
e-mail: poultons@pmt.org

Lynne Poulton, Administrator/Owner
James C Poulton, Owner

Assisted Living/8 bed facility, Level 2.

8553 Roosevelt Avenue Shelter Home
103 20th Avenue S
Nampa, ID 83651-4816
208-465-7299
Fax: 208-465-7299

8554 Rosewind House
5815 W Coffey Street
Garden City, ID 83714-1300
208-377-9980
Fax: 208-373-0684

Tambra Hunter, Administrator

8555 Royal Villa
1713 Center Avenue
Payette, ID 83661-2614
208-642-9808
Fax: 208-642-9821

Barbara Little, Contact

8556 Seasons Residential Care Living Center
730a Warner Avenue
Lewiston, ID 83501-4916
208-746-8080
Fax: 208-743-7421

8557 Snake River Living Center
820 Sprague Avenue
Buhl, ID 83316-1827
208-543-6401
Fax: 208-543-4221

Donna Robinson, Administrator

8558 South Shores Dignified Living
7612 W Emerald Street
Boise, ID 83704-9017
208-331-4173
Fax: 208-321-0933

8559 Spring Creek Manor Assisted Living
653 N Eagle Road
Eagle, ID 83616-5007
208-938-5578
Fax: 208-938-1589
e-mail: eagle@scmanor.com
http://www.scmanor.com

Rita Corella, Administrator

8560 Spring Creek Manor-American Falls
605 Hillcrest Avenue
American Falls, ID 83211-1365
208-226-1856
Fax: 208-226-1842

Liana Gutierrez, Administrator

8561 Spring Creek Manor-Montpelier
855 Boise Street
Montpelier, ID 83254-1070
208-847-2400
Fax: 208-847-1776

Bonnie Duncan, Administrator

8562 Spring Creek Manor-Soda Springs
425 S Spring Creek Drive
Soda Springs, ID 83276-1628
208-547-0257
Fax: 208-547-4027

Malynda Seiler, Administrator

8563 Spring Hills
326 N State Street
Shelley, ID 83274-1141
208-357-3162
Fax: 208-357-2015

8564 Stoney Creek Living Center
2538h E 3800 N
Twin Falls, ID 83301
208-736-5705
Fax: 208-736-3848

Charles Hansen, Administrator

8565 Summer Wind
5955 Castle Drive
Boise, ID 83703-3215
208-331-1300
Fax: 208-331-0483

Carol Foster, Manager

8566 Sunbridge Care
201 Eisman
McCall, ID 83638
208-634-2112
Fax: 208-634-3605

Bobette Steffler, Administrator

8567 Sunbridge Living Center-Meridian
1111 W Pine Avenue
Meridian, ID 83642-2062
208-888-7049
Fax: 208-888-7246

Jeff Turnbow, Administrator

Assisted Living Facilities/Illinois

8568 **Sunbridge Retirement**
2609 Sunnybrook Drive
Nampa, ID 83686-6399
208-467-7298
Fax: 208-463-0901

David Chinchurreta, Executive Director

8569 **Sylvan House**
660 W Honeysuckle Avenue
Hayden, ID 83835-9759
208-762-4097
Fax: 208-772-9335

Tanya Wilson, Manager

8570 **Turtle & Crane Assisted Living**
1950 1st Street
Idaho Falls, ID 83401-4342
208-529-8112
Fax: 208-529-4063

Sumiko Mitchell, Manager

8571 **Valley View Assisted Living**
1130 Allumbaugh Street
Boise, ID 83704-8700
208-322-0311
Fax: 208-327-1050

Peggy McMillen, Administrator

8572 **Viewpoint Residential Care**
725 N Robinson Boulevard
Nampa, ID 83687-8619
208-466-8156
Fax: 208-375-2564

8573 **Warren House**
1301 Bennett Avenue
Burley, ID 83318-2675
208-677-8212
Fax: 208-677-9022

Jim Serve, Administrator

8574 **Wedgewood Terrace**
2114 Vineyard Avenue
Lewiston, ID 83501-6374
208-743-4545
Fax: 208-743-2268
e-mail: wedgwoodter@cableone.net

Melissa Lichti, Executive Director

8575 **Willow Park Assisted Living**
2600 N Milwaukee Street
Boise, ID 83704-5784
208-373-1234
Fax: 208-375-1316
e-mail: willowpark2@rgnt.com

Bryan Elliott, Manager

Personal care assistance around the clock, medication assistance, weekly housekeeping, and apartment maintenance are only some of the amenities and services included in your basic monthly rent at Willow Park. From Tai Chi to painting, residents are having fun while improving their flexibility, mobility and emotional well-being.

8576 **Willowbrook Assisted Living**
1871 Julie Lane
Twin Falls, ID 83301-3525
208-736-3727
Fax: 208-732-6047

Melody B Gambrel, Owner

8577 **Willows**
898 S Meridian Street
Blackfoot, ID 83221-2660
208-782-1478
Fax: 208-785-0090
e-mail: willows5@TrueYellow.net

Bill Hines, CEO

8578 **Woodstone Retirement Center**
491 Caswell Avenue W
Twin Falls, ID 83301-3743
208-734-6062
Fax: 208-734-9046

LaVone Jones, Contact
Cathy Lynch, Administrator

Illinois

8579 **Addolorata Villa**
555 McHenry Road
Wheeling, IL 60090-3899
847-537-2900
Fax: 847-215-5805
e-mail: mturk@franciscancommunities.com
http://www.franciscommunities.com

Maggie Turk, Contact
Larry Carlson, Executive Officer

Offers elegant living accommodations, amenities and a positive environment to enjoy life to the fullest.

8580 **Belmont Village at Geneva Road**
545 Belmont Lane
Carol Stream, IL 60188
630-510-1515
Fax: 630-510-0633
http://www.belmontvillage.com

Offers residents a more dignified, independent life in a comfortable residential neighborhood setting.

8581 **Belmont Village of Buffalo Grove**
500 McHenry Road
Buffalo Grove, IL 60089
847-537-5000
Fax: 847-537-7260
http://www.belmontvillage.com

Seniors community that sets a new standard in Assisted Living. Offers residents a more dignified, independent life in a comfortable residential neighborhood setting.

8582 **Belmont Village of Glenview**
2200 Golf Road
Glenview, IL 60025
847-657-7100
Fax: 847-657-7171
http://www.belmontvillage.com

Offers residents a more dignified, independent life in a comfortable residential neighborhood setting.

8583 **Belmont Village of Oak Park**
1035 Madison Street
Oak Park, IL 60302
708-848-7200
http://www.belmontvillage.com

Convenient to shops, galleries and museums.

8584 **Bethesda Home and Retirement Center**
2833 N Nordica Avenue
Chicago, IL 60634-4794
773-622-6144
Fax: 773-622-8261

Julie Boggess, Administrator

Offering continuum of care, this facility is located in an attractive and quiet residential neighborhood with access to shopping, local churches and civic activites.

8585 **Bethlehem Woods Retirement Community**
1571 W Ogden Avenue
La Grange Park, IL 60526-1723
708-579-3663
Fax: 708-579-7159

Nick Papp, Administrator

Located on 42 wooded acres we offer elegant independent living residentces, while enhanced supportive living services are also provided. We are dedicated to assuring you wellness, independence, security and spiritual comfort.

Assisted Living Facilities/Illinois

8586 Concord Place Retirement & Assisted Living Community
401 W Lake Street
Northlake, IL 60164-2436
708-562-9000
Fax: 708-409-2750
Cheryl Cohen, Manager

Assisted living at the most affordable rental prices combined with quality support services.

8587 Cordia Senior Residence
865 N Cass Avenue
Westmont, IL 60559
630-887-7000
866-430-2890
Fax: 630-887-7577
http://www.cordia.biz
Teresa Rogala, Acting Executive Director

Through our staff, programming and residential environment, we encourage residents to live their lives to their fullest potential.

8588 Devonshire of Hoffman Estates
1515 Barrington Road
Hoffman Estates, IL 60169-5021
847-490-5800
Fax: 847-490-5830
Jennifer Gamache, Manager

Our approach to senior living, which combines a variety of services ranging from independent living to personal assistance, enables us to accommodate the changing needs of our residents. In the event that needs change, we can arrange services to accommodate every situation.

8589 Fountains at Crystal Lake-The Inn
965 N Brighton Circle
Crystal Lake, IL 60012-2036
815-455-8400
800-382-1308
Fax: 815-477-6502
Michael Ross, Executive Director

The Inn offers a lovely, amenity-rich environment in which residents can enjoy privacy, independence and freedom of choice while receiving all the care and support they need.

8590 Hearthstone of Arlington Heights
800 W Oakton Street
Arlington Heights, IL 60004-4602
847-368-7400
Fax: 847-368-3702
Vicki Schlomann, Executive Director

Offers the independent senior peace of mind. Apartments in a wide choice of floor plans are accented with beautiful sitting areas, porches and a fine dining room.

8591 Holland Home Assisted Living
16300 Louis Avenue
South Holland, IL 60473-2281
708-596-3050
Fax: 708-596-3067
Wayne Rost, Administrator

Program serves those people needing help with daily tasks such as dressing, bathing, and medication supervision.

8592 Kenwood of Lake View
3121 N Sheridan Road
Chicago, IL 60657-4945
773-404-9800
Fax: 773-404-7898
Anna Anderson, Owner

Our approach to senior living, which combines a variety of services ranging from independent living to personal assistance, enables us to accommodate the changing needs of our residents. In the event that needs change, we can arrange services to accommodate every situation.

8593 Lake Barrington Woods
22320 Classic Court
Lake Barrington, IL 60010-5903
847-842-8900
888-223-9663
Fax: 847-381-7253
e-mail: lbw@parkside-sr.com
http://www.parksidesenior.com
Cheryl Black, Executive Director

Offers independent living and assisted living. Whatever your interests, you'll find endless opportunities for exceptional retirement living at Lake Barrington Woods.

8594 Marian Village
555 McHenry Road
Wheeling, IL 60090-3856
847-537-2900
Fax: 847-215-5805
Larry Carlson, Executive Director

At Marian Village, whether you are an active senior looking for just the right place to enjoy your retirement or a person needing a little assistance, our comprehensive range of supportive services are designed to fit your individual needs.

8595 Moorings of Arlington Heights
811 E Central Road
Arlington Heights, IL 60005-3244
847-956-4027
800-445-8431
Fax: 847-956-4451
Pat Walsh, Executive Director

Residents are able to receive light assistance in a residential setting. Private rooms as well as two room suites are available.

8596 North Shore Retirement Hotel
1611 Chicago Avenue
Evanston, IL 60201-6019
847-864-6400
Fax: 847-864-0947
Margaret Gergen, Manager

Each resident has a lovely, fully-furnished private apartment with daily maid service and three delicious meals a day.

8597 Norwood Park Home
6016 N Nina Avenue
20
Chicago, IL 60631-2498
773-631-4856
Fax: 773-631-4850
Marcia R Hagopian, Executive Director

Not-for-profit residence for seniors, offering private suites in assisted living with emergency call system in a clean, family atmosphere. Provides continuum of care, including skilled nursing in addition to hospice and respite services.

8598 Provena Fox Knoll Retirement Community
421 N Lake Street
Aurora, IL 60506-4180
630-844-0380
Fax: 630-844-0702
Patricia Beebee, Director of Admissions/Marketing
Carol Ricken, Administrator

A senior retirement community offering Independent Living, Assisted Living, Residential Memory Loss Floor, Adult Day Care and Respite (short term) Care. Spacious apartments, private studio apartments, all with private bathrooms.

8599 Saint Andrew Life Center
7000 N Newark Avenue
Niles, IL 60714-4577
847-647-8332
Fax: 708-647-7073
Jean Kennedy, Contact
Nikki Curth, Administrator

Provides independent living, assisted living, or 24-hour nursing care with an intermediate care facility and a wellness center.

8600 Spring Meadows Libertyville
901 Florsheim Drive
Libertyville, IL 60048-5200
847-816-9990
Fax: 847-816-6633
Mary Jester, Executive Director

Assisted Living Facilities/Illinois

8601 **St. James Villas**
1251 E Richton Road
Crete, IL 60417-1623
708-672-6700
800-524-6126
Fax: 708-672-4939

Tina Strimbu, Executive Director

Offer 60 one-story apartment-like units for residents needing a certain level of personal care and supervision.

8602 **Summit Square of Park Ridge**
10 N Summit Avenue
Park Ridge, IL 60068-3310
847-825-1161
Fax: 847-823-5741

Audrey Yohanna, Owner

We know that often just a little help with daily activities can make a major difference in the quality of life for seniors, we offer the Wellness and Assistance Program. It's a great help for seniors who were once totally independent, but who now may need some personalized care to make life easier. The Program is a comfort to families who may not have to face the prospect of placing a family member in a nursing home.

8603 **Sunrise Assisted Living of Naperville**
960 E Chicago Avenue
Naperville, IL 60540
630-579-1400
Fax: 630-579-1772
e-mail: naperville.dcr@sunriseseniorliving.com
http://www.sunriseseniorliving.com

Mark Blau, Executive Director
Laura Wolst, Director Community Relations
Julie Gimpel, Director Community Relations

Sunrise is built on a commitment to our residents and their families. We believe no two people are alike, so the services and attention we provide should never be exactly the same. That's also why we offer a variety of lifestyle, service and care options. By providing these choices, we not only offer solutions for today, but we provide the security of tomorrow.

8604 **Sunrise of Bloomingdale**
129 E Lake Street
Bloomingdale, IL 60108-1104
630-295-8600
Fax: 639-295-8498

For residents with memory impairment, Sunrise offers an innovative program called Reminiscence.

8605 **Sunrise of Buffalo Grove**
180 W Half Day Road
Buffalo Grove, IL 60089-6552
847-478-8484
Fax: 847-478-2039

Joann Guarneri, Executive Director

Sunrise is built on a commitment to our residents and their families. We believe no two people are alike, so the services and attention we provide should never be exactly the same. That's also why we offer a variety of lifestyle, service and care options. By providing these choices, we not only offer solutions for today, but we provide the security of knowing that there are options for tomorrow.

8606 **Sunrise of Crystal Lake**
751 E Terra Cotta Avenue
Crystal Lake, IL 60014-3604
815-444-6600
Fax: 815-444-6600

Beth Johnston, Executive Director

Sunrise is built on a commitment to our residents and their families. We believe no two people are alike, so the services and attention we provide should never be exactly the same. That's also why we offer a variety of lifestyle, service and care options. By providing these choices, we not only offer solutions for today, but we provide the security of knowing that there are options for tomorrow.

8607 **Sunrise of Flossmoor**
19715 Governors Highway
Flossmoor, IL 60422-1794
708-798-1600
Fax: 708-798-3406

John Brimm, Executive Director

8608 **Sunrise of Glen Ellyn**
95 Carleton Avenue
Glen Ellyn, IL 60137-5500
630-469-5555
Fax: 630-469-0922

Christi Oliver, Manager

Sunrise is built on a commitment to our residents and their families. We believe no two people are alike, so the services and attention we provide should never be exactly the same. That's also why we offer a variety of lifestyle, service and care options. By providing these choices, we not only offer solutions for today, but we provide the security of knowing that there are options for tomorrow.

8609 **Sunrise of Gurnee**
500 N Hunt Club Road
Gurnee, IL 60031-2416
847-856-8100
Fax: 847-856-8188

Rita Jedkins, Executive Director

Sunrise is built on a commitment to our residents and their families. We believe no two people are alike, so the services and attention we provide should never be exactly the same. That's also why we offer a variety of lifestyle, service and care options. By providing these choices, we not only offer solutions for today, but we provide the security of knowing that there are options for tomorrow.

8610 **Sunrise of Naperville-North**
535 W Ogden Avenue
Naperville, IL 60563-3286
630-305-9400
Fax: 630-305-9444

Georgean Sweiss, Executive Director

Sunrise is built on a commitment to our residents and their families. We believe no two people are alike, so the services and attention we provide should never be exactly the same. That's also why we offer a variety of lifestyle, service and care options. By providing these choices, we not only offer solutions for today, but we provide the security of knowing that there are options for tomorrow.

8611 **Sunrise of Palos Park**
12828 S La Grange Road
Palos Park, IL 60464-2247
708-361-3577
Fax: 708-361-3889

Kathleen Roloff, Executive Director

8612 **Sunrise of Park Ridge**
1725 Ballard Road
Park Ridge, IL 60068-1005
847-824-1724
Fax: 847-824-9864

Denny Zook, Executive Director

Sunrise is built on a commitment to our residents and their families. We believe no two people are alike, so the services and attention we provide should never be exactly the same. That's also why we offer a variety of lifestyle, service and care options. By providing these choices, we not only offer solutions for today, but we provide the security of knowing that there are options for tomorrow.

8613 **Sunrise of Schaumburg**
790 N Plum Grove Road
Schaumburg, IL 60173-4764
847-517-9700
Fax: 847-517-8701

Desma Thrist, Executive Director

Assisted Living Facilities/Indiana

Sunrise is built on a commitment to our residents and their families. We believe no two people are alike, so the services and attention we provide should never be exactly the same. That's also why we offer a variety of lifestyle, service and care options. By providing these choices, we not only offer solutions for today, but we provide the security of knowing that there are options for tomorrow.

8614 Sunrise of Willowbrook
6300 Clarendon Hills Road
Willowbrook, IL 60527-2133   630-734-9954
                                   Fax: 630-734-9956

Sunrise is built on a commitment to our residents and their families. We believe no two people are alike, so the services and attention we provide should never be exactly the same. That's also why we offer a variety of lifestyle, service and care options. By providing these choices, we not only offer solutions for today, but we provide the security of knowing that there are options for tomorrow.

8615 The Park at Vernon Hills
145 N Milwaukee Avenue
Vernon Hills, IL 60061-4170   847-793-2470
                                   Fax: 847-793-2471

8616 Victorian Inn at Victorian Village
12600 Renaissance Circle
Lockport, IL 60491-5891   708-301-0800
                                   Fax: 708-301-2493

Mike Venzon, Administrator

Provides convenient and comfortable living arrangements with choice of studio, one bedroom or shared suite settings.

8617 Village Woods
2681 Route 394
Crete, IL 60417-4353   708-672-6111
                                   Fax: 708-672-8914

Tom Travato, Manager

8618 Westbridge Assisted Living
500 Wyndemere Circle
Wheaton, IL 60187-2451
                                        866-933-4797
                                   Fax: 630-690-2362
                   http://www.wyndemereseniorliving.com
Shirley Pollard, Executive Director

Residents at this premier assisted living facility receive a helping hand with daily tasks and enjoy a variety of activities, amenities and services.

Indiana

8619 Atria Eastlake Terrace
3109 E Bristol Street
Elkhart, IN 46514-4372   574-266-4508
                       http://www.atriaassistedliving.com

Come to Atria Eastlake Terrace's traditionally designed, one-story building offering an active, carefree lifestyle for today's seniors. Assisted living care plans are designed to promote independence and enhance the quality of life of our residents.

8620 Bethesda Gardens at the Crossings
Bethesda Adult Community
1450 E Crossing Boulevard
Terre Haute, IN 47802-5316   812-298-8209
                                   Fax: 812-298-9190
                     http://www.bethesdaadultcommunities.com
Gaynell McKenzie, Executive Director

This 70-unit apartment complex has five assisted living apartment styles.

8621 Meridan Oaks
1251 West 96th Street
Indianapolis, IN 46260   317-575-9200
                                        877-771-8285
                                   Fax: 317-575-8209
                              http://www.emeritus.com
Daniel R Baty, Chairman/CEO
Raymond B Brandstrom, Vice Chairman/VP Finance
Gary Becker, SVP Operations

Meridan Oaks' commitment to our residents is to provide a nuturing environment that preserves dignity, fosters independence, encourages freedom of choice, promotes emotional well being and includes family and friends.

8622 Shamrock Gardens
17650 Generations Drive
South Bend, IN 46635   574-271-1151
                       http://www.shamrockgardens.net
Richard Herath, Administrator
Joan Ross, LPN, Director Nursing
Kelly Buwa, Activities Director

A licensed residential care (Assisted Living) facility offering a supportive environment while maximizing independence.

8623 Sunrise of Carmel
301 Executive Drive
Carmel, IN 46032   317-580-0389
                                   Fax: 317-843-9790
                       http://www.sunriseseniorliving.com
Paul J Klaassen, Founder/Chairman/CEO
Teresa M Klaassen, Founder/Chief Cultural Officer
Thomas B Newell, President

Our care is designed to meet the individualized needs of each of our residents.

8624 Towne Centre
7250 Arthur Boulevard
Merrillville, IN 46410-3766   219-736-2900
                                   Fax: 219-736-2209
Michael D Moore, Executive Vice President
Nitsa Foundos, Contact

Iowa

8625 3801 Grand
3801 Grand Avenue
Des Moines, IA 50312-2800   515-255-3499
                                   Fax: 515-255-9344
Mary Ann Larsen, Manager

You want to remain in charge of your life, and needing help with activities of daily living should not change that. Our certified facility offers a supportive environment that empowers tenants to remain as independent and autonomous as possible. You and your family can relax, knowing that professional staff is available to meet scheduled and unscheduled needs.

8626 AASE Hougen Assisted Living
4 Ohio Street
Decorah, IA 52101-1516   563-382-3603
                                   Fax: 563-382-3606

Sue Bjelland, Administrator

8627 Afton Oaks Assisted Living
405 9th Street
Elma, IA 50628-8217   641-393-2125
                                   Fax: 641-393-2004

713

Assisted Living Facilities/Iowa

We offer the option of independent living with the reassurance that assistance is just a phone call away. We will manage the day-to-day functions, while directing the dietary, housekeeping, and maintenance staff to meet the needs of our residents. This is the affordable answer to secure, elegant, senior living. Afton Oaks is dedicated to the care and well being of adults and their families who are seeking peace of mind.

8628 Alison Health Care Center
902 7th Street
Allison, IA 50602-9440
319-267-2791
Fax: 319-267-2422

Kathy Meyer-Allbee, Administrator

8629 Allen House
1406 E 19th Street
Atlantic, IA 50022-2897
712-243-3820
Fax: 712-243-6707

8630 Amber Ridge
107 E 2nd Street
De Witt, IA 52742-2140
563-659-1678
Fax: 563-659-1678

Cathy Morel, Executive Director

8631 Amelia House
57 W Ferndale Drive
Council Bluffs, IA 51503-4889
712-325-4400
Fax: 712-323-1436

Mary Johnson, Administrator

8632 Arbor Heights at University
233 University Avenue
Des Moines, IA 50314-3124
515-284-1280
Fax: 515-284-0127

Ron Osby, Administrator

8633 Arbor Place
1140 K Avenue NW
Cedar Rapids, IA 52405-2430
319-363-2402
Fax: 319-363-5312

8634 Arlin Flack Assisted Living
911 Ridgewood Drive
Decorah, IA 52101-2354
563-387-3777
Fax: 563-382-8788

Karl Jacobsen, Administrator

8635 Arlington Place of Grundy Center
95 D Avenue
Grundy Center, IA 50638-1950
319-824-5674
Fax: 319-824-5676

Teri Hook, Administrator

8636 Arlington Place of Red Oak
800 E Ratliff Road
Red Oak, IA 51566-5102
712-623-1999
Fax: 712-623-2007

8637 Avoca Lodge Assisted Living
610 E York Road
Avoca, IA 51521-2052
712-343-6398
Fax: 712-343-2207
e-mail: Avoca@careinitiatives.org

Kellie Jimerson, Administrator

Our residents enjoy a beautiful area for dining and relaxing and many activities scheduled throughout the day to keep our seniors active and independent for as long as possible. Our continuum of long term care with our assisted living and nursing facility provide a wide range of specialized services.

8638 Ballard Creek Community
908 N Highway 69
Huxley, IA 50124-9764
515-597-2555
Fax: 515-597-3877

Angie Gurius, Administrator

8639 Beehive Home Assisted Living
2116 1st Avenue E
Spencer, IA 51301-2313
712-262-1430
Fax: 712-262-1454
e-mail: ltingle@beehivehomes.com

Dave Tingle, Owner
Lisa Tingle, Owner
Candi Gilani, Manager

The mission of the Bee Hive Homes is to provide assistance with the activities of daily living in a respectful, dignified manner in a home like setting to the frail elderly who choose to retain their independence and dignity to the fullest measure possible.

8640 Beehive Home Assisted Living-Hawarden
1126 Oakhill Drive
Hawarden, IA 51023-1355
712-551-4284
Fax: 712-551-4283
e-mail: ltingle@beehivehomes.com

Dave Tingle, Owner
Lisa Tingle, Owner
Trish Warner, Manager

The mission of the Bee Hive Homes is to provide assistance with the activities of daily living in a respectful, dignified manner in a home like setting to the frail elderly who choose to retain their independence and dignity to the fullest measure possible.

8641 Bickford Cottage-Davenport
4040 E 55th Street
Davenport, IA 52807-2905
563-322-0000
Fax: 319-441-0758

Laura Brock, Executive Director

8642 Bickford Cottage-Marshalltown
101 New Castle Road
Marshalltown, IA 50158-5241
641-753-5700
Fax: 641-753-0829

Patricia Hayes, Manager

8643 Bickford Cottage-Muscatine
2807 Cedar Street
Muscatine, IA 52761-2276
563-263-6600
Fax: 563-263-3508

Bobbe Kreiger, Executive Director

8644 Briarcliff Retirement Center
3734 8th Street SW
Altoona, IA 50009-1013
515-967-4511
Fax: 515-967-3672

Connie Clark, Contact

8645 Brickford Cottage
5101 University Avenue
Cedar Falls, IA 50613-6246
319-266-6800
Fax: 319-277-1294

Jill Knipp, Executive Director

8646 Brickford Cottage II
4022 Indian Hills Drive
Sioux City, IA 51108-1418
712-239-6851
Fax: 712-239-0848

Shari Dorsey, Executive Director

Assisted Living Facilities/Iowa

8647 Brickford Cottage-Ames
2418 Kent Avenue
Ames, IA 50010-7119
515-233-6000
Fax: 515-268-9817

Susan Doran, Contact
Kelley Loenser, Manager

8648 Brickford Cottage-Burlington
3301 Sterling Driveive
Burlington, IA 52601-8660
319-754-7500
Fax: 319-754-0447

Christa Poggemiller, Director

8649 Brickford Cottage-Clinton
1150 13th Avenue N
Clinton, IA 52732-3490
563-242-2400
Fax: 319-242-7620

Kim Schaffer, Director

8650 Brickford Cottage-Des Moines
5915 Sutton Place
Des Moines, IA 50322-1877
515-331-3000
Fax: 515-270-1781

Stacey Alexander, Manager

8651 Brickford Cottage-Fort Dodge
1536 20th Avenue N
Fort Dodge, IA 50501-7134
515-573-3300
Fax: 515-576-1593

Laura Moen, Contact
Nicole Lacina, Manager

8652 Brickford Cottage-Iowa City
3500 Lower West Branch Road
Iowa City, IA 52245-4106
319-351-3200
Fax: 319-351-6861

Barbara Faust, Executive Director

8653 Brickford Cottage-West Des Moines
5050 Hawthorne Drive
W Des Moines, IA 50265-5353
515-327-9400
Fax: 515-223-0151

Jenny Knust, Contact
Kris Lange, Manager

8654 Calvin Community Assisted Living Service
4210 Hickman Road
Des Moines, IA 50310-3333
515-277-6141
Fax: 515-271-0933
http://www.calvincommunity.org

Debra Peterson, Administrator

Our mission is to provide, on a nonprofit basis, services to older adults in a caring, Christian community designed to meet their physical, social, spiritual and psychological needs and contribute to their health, security and happiness. We offer a full range of living options to give you just the right amount of assistance when you need it.

8655 Cardinal Grove
1355 Division Street
Garner, IA 50438-1968
641-923-2114
Fax: 641-923-0074

8656 Char-Mac Assisted Living
200 E Char Mac Drive
Lawton, IA 51030-8171
712-944-4893
Fax: 712-944-4853

Jeanine Chartier, Owner

8657 Clearview Estates Assisted Living
500 W Columbus Street
Mount Ayr, IA 50854-1100
641-464-0651
Fax: 641-464-0655

Joe Routh, Administrator

8658 Clover Ridge
205 Ehlers Lane
Maquoketa, IA 52060-9615
563-652-2125
Fax: 563-625-0147

Nancy Miller, Contact
Lynne Popp, Manager

8659 Cornerstone Assisted Living
302 2nd Street NE
Mason City, IA 50401-3412
641-424-1740
Fax: 641-424-4260

Diane Horning, CEO

8660 Cottage Grove Place
2115 1st Avenue SE
Cedar Rapids, IA 52402-6358
319-363-2420
Fax: 319-297-5555

Tom Knoepke, Administrator

8661 Country House
900 W 46th Street
Davenport, IA 52806-4362
563-391-1111
Fax: 319-391-6267

Tammy Humphreys, Contact

8662 Courtyard
401 W 10th Avenue N
Clear Lake, IA 50428-4202
641-357-1648
Fax: 641-357-7154

8663 Crown Pointe
1400 7th Avenue SE
Sioux Center, IA 51250-1199
712-722-8260
Fax: 712-722-8708

Kathy Gerdes, Executive Director

8664 Davenport Lutheran Assisted Living
1130 W 53rd Street
Davenport, IA 52806-2401
563-386-6933
Fax: 563-386-1056

Shelley Hopp, Administrator

8665 Dora Barns Residential Home
305 W Washington Street
Centerville, IA 52544-1415
641-437-1290
Fax: 641-437-1290
http://www.dorabarnes.com

Wallace M Carter, Administrator
Sandra Lilley, Residential Home Manager
Roxanne Roger, In Home Care Manager

Provider of assited living care.

8666 Eagle Ridge Assisted Living
6000 Harding Road
Elgin, IA 52141-9696
563-423-7365
Fax: 563-423-7365

John Chapman, Owner

8667 Eiler House
920 W Garfield Street
Clarinda, IA 51632-2072
712-542-5508
Fax: 712-542-2587

Joy Cox, Manager

Assisted Living Facilities/Iowa

8668 Elm Crest Retirement Community
2104 12th Street
Harlan, IA 51537-2025
712-755-5174
Fax: 712-755-5654

Mike Jarrell, Administrator

8669 Elm Heights Assisted Living
1203 S Elm Street
Shenandoah, IA 51601-2221
712-246-4627
Fax: 712-246-3109

Carolyn Hamblin, Administrator

8670 Fieldcrest Assisted Living
2501 E 6th Street
Sheldon, IA 51201-1763
712-324-2338
Fax: 712-324-5331

Tony Haning, Executive Director

8671 Fleur Heights Care Center
4911 SW 19th Street
Des Moines, IA 50315-4484
515-285-2559
Fax: 515-285-6487

John Beaudette, Administrator

8672 Floyd House
403 C Street
Sergeant Bluff, IA 51054
712-943-7171
Fax: 712-943-7172

Geane Figg, Administrator

8673 Forest Plaza Assisted Living
635 Highway 9 E
Forest City, IA 50436
641-585-1555
Fax: 641-585-2522

Lonny Smith, Owner

8674 Franken Manor
527 S Main Avenue
Sioux Center, IA 51250-1450
712-722-8263
Fax: 712-722-0787

Franken Manor is an affordable senior living community that promotes independence, security, and well-being. With service attitudes grounded in Christian values, Franken Manor is a community owned senior apartment complex offering independent and assisted living services.

8675 Garnett Place
202 35th Street Drive SE
Cedar Rapids, IA 52403-1353
319-362-3630
Fax: 319-365-7936

Justine Omar, Contact
Melissa Reed, Manager

8676 Glenwood Place
2907 S 6th Street
Marshalltown, IA 50158-4687
641-752-8410
Fax: 641-752-8515

Patt Holder, Contact
Amy Edmonson, Manager

8677 Greenfield Manor Assisted Living
615 SE Kent Street
Greenfield, IA 50849-9499
641-743-6131
Fax: 641-343-7090

Suzie Morgan, Administrator

8678 Hallmark Care Center
215 Highway 30 SW
Mount Vernon, IA 52314-1579
319-895-8891
Fax: 319-895-6730

Peggy Chensvold, Manager

8679 Hawthorne Inn at Windmill
1500 1st Avenue
Coralville, IA 52241-1192
319-337-6320
Fax: 319-337-3099

Bernie Daly, Manager

8680 Heartland Care Center Assisted Living
604 E Fenton Street
Marcus, IA 51035-7170
712-376-2500
Fax: 712-376-2512

Luanne Rogge, Administrator

8681 Heartwood Heights
409 9th Avenue
Sibley, IA 51249
712-754-3009
Fax: 712-754-3782

Theresa Riley, Manager

It is the mission of Heartwood Heights to provide a comfortable, secure living environment that promotes independence and personal care with a sense of community.

8682 Heritage Court
1499 Office Park Road
W Des Moines, IA 50265-6500
515-223-1224
Fax: 515-223-1392

Gary Tiemeyer, Administrator

8683 Heritage House
1200 Brookridge Circle
Atlantic, IA 50022-2346
712-243-1850
Fax: 712-243-3418

Damon Buskohl, Administrator
Bob Johannsen, Executive Director

8684 Holy Spirit
1701 W 25th Street
Sioux City, IA 51103-1705
712-252-2726
Fax: 712-252-2728

Patrick Tomscha, Administrator

8685 Homestead Acres
2306 State Street
Guthrie Center, IA 50115-8896
641-332-2204
Fax: 515-747-8717

Nancy Wells, Social Worker
Barbara Howell, Administrator
Maradith Janssen, Manager

The assisted living offered by Homesteaad Acres provides a community for older adults who want to live an independent lifestyle but need some assistance with life's daily tasks. You will have the security of knowing that certified staff is available 24 hours a day to meet your needs.

We ar pages

8686 Jersey Ridge
5605 Jersey Ridge Road
Davenport, IA 52807-3132
563-355-2027
Fax: 563-441-9227

Karen McCoy, Contact

8687 Jewish Senior Life Center
900 Polk Boulevard
Des Moines, IA 50312-2225
515-255-5433
Fax: 515-255-1920

Stephen Blend, Executive Director

8688 Kensington
2210 Avenue H
Fort Madison, IA 52627-4000
319-372-4233
Fax: 319-372-7940

Linda Larkin, Executive Director

Assisted Living Facilities/Iowa

8689 Keystone Senior Suites
250 5th Street
Keystone, IA 52249-9521
319-442-3234
Fax: 319-442-3550

Sue Meyer, Administrator

8690 Kosgrove Estates Assisted Living
4155 Us 75 Avenue
Sioux Center, IA 51250-7522
712-722-4972
Fax: 712-722-3294

Kay Kosters, President

8691 Lakeview Lodge
312 Southbrooke Drive
Waterloo, IA 50702-5804
319-291-1300
Fax: 319-291-1360

Kathy Martin, Executive Director

8692 Lakeview Village
3012 F Drive
Amana, IA 52203-8224
319-622-6500
Fax: 319-622-6458

Rod Buch, CEO

8693 Landsmeer Ridge Retirement Community
400 Central Avenue NW
Orange City, IA 51041-1342
712-737-4984
Fax: 712-737-8934

Landsmeer Ridge is a unique retirement community for those age 62 and above, offering a relaxed, carefree living environment featuring both independent and assisted living apartments. We offer the peace and serenity of country living and the convenience of shopping, medical and other community services just minutes away.

8694 Lincolnwood Assisted Living
302 W Lincoln Street
Edgewood, IA 52042-8722
563-928-6461
Fax: 319-928-6462

Melissa Kann, Administrator

8695 Linden Place Assisted Living
1922 5th Avenue NW
Waverly, IA 50677-1903
319-352-4540
Fax: 319-352-2161

Deb Schroeder, Manager

Linden Place residents receive health care services and personal support while living in the privacy of their own apartment, with their own bathroom and kitchenette. It's an approach that makes the transition from independent living much easier to accept.

8696 Longview Retirement Apartments
1010 Longview Road
Missouri Valley, IA 51555-1227
712-642-2309
Fax: 712-642-2578

John Sherer, Owner

We realize that each resident is a unique individual with differing care needs. In order to meet these needs, we provide a diversified offering of services which include skilled nursing facility, alzheimers unit, assisted living appartments, and independent living appartments.

8697 Lutheran Home Apartments
1413 2nd Avenue
Vinton, IA 52349-1695
319-472-2092
Fax: 319-472-3070

Kim Emerick, Administrator

8698 MICA Hill Estates
2121 Avenue L
Hawarden, IA 51023-1361
712-551-1075
Fax: 712-551-2393

Melody Wilkens, Administrator

8699 Madison Square Assisted Living
209 W Jefferson Street
Winterset, IA 50273-1676
515-462-5087
Fax: 515-462-5151

Elecia Henke, Manager

8700 Maple Manor Village
345 Parrott Street
Aplington, IA 50604-1014
319-347-2309
Fax: 319-347-6347

Sharon Quail, Administrator

8701 Maple Ridge Assisted Living
1500 Highway 2 E
Mount Ayr, IA 50854
641-464-3204
Fax: 641-464-3723

Robert Hinz, Administrator

8702 Martina Place
5815 Winwood Drive
Johnston, IA 50131-1666
515-251-7999
Fax: 515-331-8860

Sharon Brown, Executive Director

8703 Mason City Homestead
2501 W State Street
Mason City, IA 50401-8916
641-423-4809
Fax: 641-423-0441

Mary Montgomery, Executive Director

8704 Mayflower Assisted Living
927 1st Avenue
Grinnell, IA 50112-2480
641-236-6151
Fax: 641-236-6153

Sharon Mathis, Manager

8705 Meadows
200 McCarren Drive
Manchester, IA 52057-1874
563-927-6467
Fax: 563-927-8437

Elaine Seaman, Operator
Leslie Nussle, Manager

8706 Meadows Assisted Living
528 N Kelly Street
Shell Rock, IA 50670-1006
319-885-4341
Fax: 319-885-6596

Betty Oren, Administrator

8707 Meth-Wick Community
1224 13th Street NW
Cedar Rapids, IA 52405-2499
319-365-9171
Fax: 319-363-5312

Robin Mixdorf, President

8708 Mill Pond Assisted Living
1201 SE Mill Pond Court
Ankeny, IA 50021-6534
515-964-2273
Fax: 515-965-3100

8709 Monticello Nursing and Rehab Center
500 Pinehaven Drive
Monticello, IA 52310-2049
319-465-5415
Fax: 319-524-3001

Dave Chensvold, Administrator

8710 Mulberry Place
11 Deborah Drive
Bloomfield, IA 52537-1174
641-664-2523
Fax: 515-664-2929

Beth Owens, Administrator

Assisted Living Facilities/Iowa

8711 Northern Hills
4002 Teton Tree
Sioux City, IA 51104-4387
712-239-9402
Fax: 712-255-9799

Gary Troth, Executive Director

8712 Oak Estates
511 E Center Street
Conrad, IA 50621-2013
641-922-7100
Fax: 641-922-7110

Dorothy McHone, Administrator

8713 Oakland Heights
904 N Scenic Drive
Oakland, IA 51560-4070
712-482-3566
Fax: 712-482-3003

Judy Pleak, Assistant Administrator
Charles Pleak, Administrator

8714 Oaknoll Assisted Living
701 Oaknoll Drive
Iowa City, IA 52246-5168
319-351-1720
Fax: 319-351-6772
http://www.oaknoll.com

Patricia Heiden-Ringham, Executive Director

Our Assisted Living area provides services and programs that support residents who may need additional assistance in their daily lives. With the option of assisted living, our residents will maintain their independence and dignity while living in their own apartment.

8715 Oakwood Place Assisted Living at Ridgecrest Village
4130 Northwest Boulevard
Davenport, IA 52806-4243
563-391-3430
Fax: 563-388-3287
http://www.ridgecrestvillage.org

Shelley H Wicks, Administrator
Bert Vigen, Executive Director

Life Care is a unique concept that truly benefits Ridgecrest residents. There is a wonderful peace of mind knowing that although you may not ever need nursing care services, you have immediate access to excellent care...just in case. And you are insulated from escalating private pay charges in a nursing home.

8716 Park Place Estates
900 Lincoln Street NE
Le Mars, IA 51031-3345
712-546-6793
Fax: 712-578-5214
e-mail: ppe@floydvalleyhospital.org
http://www.parkplaceestates.org

Judith Roddy, Executive Director

We offer affordable assisted living options for adult seniors who do not require skilled nursing care. Our residents appreciate a secure, comfortable environment with maintenance-free living and the camaraderie of a friendly community.

8717 Perry Lutheran Home Assisted Living
2323 Willis Avenue
Perry, IA 50220-2148
515-465-5342
Fax: 515-465-5344

Doug Wood, Contact

8718 Pioneer Place Assisted Living
501 E Pioneer Road
Lone Tree, IA 52755-7721
319-629-4255
Fax: 319-629-5300

8719 Port Charles Assisted Living
801 Blunt Parkway
Apt 39
Charles City, IA 50616-2207
641-257-3003
Fax: 641-257-3038
e-mail: pcal@fiai.net
http://www.pcalcc.com

Dennis Sanvig, Owner

Join our residents in having an active independent lifestyle with all of the comforts of your home in a safe setting. Your total well being is our number one priority. We are committed to ensuring quality in all aspects of our residents' lives from fine dining to tender loving care. Our supportive staff assists residents in enhancing one of life's retirement pleasures.

8720 Praire View Inn
610 N Eastern Street
Sanborn, IA 51248-1089
712-729-3228
Fax: 712-729-3036

8721 Premier Estates
1510 S Carroll Street
Rock Rapids, IA 51246-2099
712-472-4100
Fax: 712-472-4231

Gary Durbin, Administrator

8722 Premier Suites
701 E Mapleleaf Drive
Mount Pleasant, IA 52641-1402
319-385-1400
Fax: 319-385-2385

Jennifer Wirt, Administrator

8723 Promise House
405 N 15th Avenue
Hiawatha, IA 52233-2347
319-743-9812
Fax: 319-378-8598

Kent Walton, Owner

8724 Ramsey Home
1611 27th Street
Des Moines, IA 50310-5499
515-274-3612
Fax: 515-274-6541

Karen Broman, Administrator

8725 Reed House
2506 3rd Avenue N
Denison, IA 51442-1730
712-263-8657
Fax: 712-263-2371

Colleen Alesch, Administrator

8726 Ridgeway Place
155 E Ridgeway Avenue
Waterloo, IA 50702-5000
319-272-2622
Fax: 319-272-2633

Colleen O'Connell, Manager

8727 River Hills Village
10 Village Circle
Keokuk, IA 52632-2059
319-524-5772
Fax: 319-524-3001

Cindy Shriver, Administrator

8728 Riverview Terrace
1301 Saint Luke Drive
Spencer, IA 51301-6043
712-262-5932
Fax: 712-262-4743

Nancy Ketcham, Executive Director

8729 Rosebush Gardens
4925 West Avenue
Burlington, IA 52601-9469
319-752-1200
Fax: 319-752-5800

Kirk Erickson, Administrator

8730 Senior Suites
4700 84th Street
Urbandale, IA 50322-7352
515-270-9700
Fax: 515-270-9582

Demaris Luttengger, Administrator

Assisted Living Facilities/Iowa

8731 **Silvercrest Ames Assisted Living**
1325 Coconino Road
Suite 300
Ames, IA 50014-7842
515-292-2858
Fax: 515-296-2134

Karen Eubank, Executive Director

Independent Living with Assistance:24 Hour Certified Staffing, Restaurant Style Dining, Schedule Transportation, Weekly Housekeeping, Planned Activities and Outings, Secure Enclosed Courtyard, Beauty and Barber Shop, RN Monitoring and Assessment

Spaci pages 1924

8732 **Silvercrest Assisted Living: Garner Farms**
1575 W 53rd Street
Davenport, IA 52806-2448
563-386-9196
Fax: 563-445-7397

Pat Day, Owner

We tailor our residents' care plans to provide just the right amount of assistance for a comfortable lifestyle. Services are based on assessment at admission and varying intervals. Type of services include assistance with bathing, dressing, medication, orientation, continence managment and reassurance.

8733 **Silvercrest Legacy Pointe**
1020 S Scott Boulevard
Iowa City, IA 52240-2944
319-341-0911
Fax: 402-493-8069

David Burkhart, Manager

Silvercrest Legacy Pointe Assisted Living is thoughtfully designed with an environment of ease with high-standard services and beautiful furnishings. An array of carefully chosen amenities are available to enhance day-to-day living along with social activity and convenient personal services. Our residents can expect to enjoy a quality home-like lifestyle, which recognizes individuality, privacy, choice, and dignity.

8734 **Sister Center for Helpful Living**
1013 S Iowa Avenue
Washington, IA 52353-1100
319-653-7264
Fax: 319-653-8383

Stecy Kiser-Willey, Administrator

8735 **Skiff Medical Center Assisted Living**
204 N 4th Avenue E
Newton, IA 50208-3135
641-792-1273
Fax: 641-792-4603

Patti Hayes, Director
Eric Lothe, CEO

8736 **Spring Valley Senior Assisted Living**
501 12th Street
Perry, IA 50220-1913
515-465-7501
Fax: 515-465-7509

Heidi Thompson, Contact

8737 **Summit Heights**
8 S Summit Avenue
Nora Springs, IA 50458-8638
641-749-2411
Fax: 641-749-5331

Mary Grauerholz, Manager

8738 **Sunnybrook Assisted Living**
2199 S 32nd Street
Fairfield, IA 52556-4736
641-469-5778
Fax: 641-469-5578

Betty D Howell, Administrator

8739 **Sunrise Villa**
1201 Park Street
Bellevue, IA 52031-1911
563-872-5521
Fax: 319-872-5609

Lyman Bailey, Manager

8740 **Sunset Park Place**
3730 Pennsylvania Avenue
Dubuque, IA 52002-3701
563-583-7939
Fax: 563-365-2982

Janet Marxen, Contact
Jerry Bell, Manager

8741 **Swan House**
1024 E 12th Street
Carroll, IA 51401-3913
712-792-6974
Fax: 712-792-9811

Nancy Snyder, Administrator

8742 **Sylvan Woods**
2 Pennsylvania Place
Ottumwa, IA 52501-2188
641-684-4000
Fax: 641-684-4079

Lisa Heinrichs, Manager

8743 **Terrace Park Senior Living**
203 SW Lorraine Street
Leon, IA 50144-1176
641-446-4165
Fax: 641-446-4443

Diane Hill, Administrator

8744 **The Villages at Marion**
365 Marion Boulevard
Marion, IA 52302-3139
319-377-9808
Fax: 319-377-9821
e-mail: spage@marionvillages.com
http://www.marionvillages.com

Sharlynn Page, Marketing Coordinator
Cindy Dason, Executive Director

The Villages at Marion provides senior independent housing (Village Place) and assisted living including Memory Care and Respite care (Village Ridge).

8745 **Valley Lodge Assisted Living**
1118 Highway 20
Correctionville, IA 51016-8056
712-372-4466
Fax: 712-372-4251

Loretta Frahm, Manager

8746 **Valley View Manor Assisted Living**
2421 Lutheran Drive
Muscatine, IA 52761-9382
563-263-1241
Fax: 563-263-5180

Sheryl Wieskamp, Contact
Eric Thomas, Administrator

8747 **Villa Cottages**
925 Martin Luther King Drive
Fort Dodge, IA 50501-2866
515-576-7525
Fax: 515-955-7528

Debra Koenig, Administrator

8748 **Waukon Living Center**
209 2nd Avenue SW
Waukon, IA 52172-1900
563-568-2915
Fax: 319-245-1684

Diane Erickson, Owner

8749 **Wel-Life at Alta**
705 W 7th Street
Alta, IA 51002-1525
712-200-2620
Fax: 712-286-2620

Sheila Thomson, Manager

We are a family-oriented health care provider, dedicated to excellence, whose mission is to enhance the lives of those we serve by providing quality care with respect, dignity and kindness.

Assisted Living Facilities/Kansas

8750 **Wel-Life at Spirit Lake**
1819 23rd Street
Spirit Lake, IA 51360-7096
712-336-3553
Fax: 712-336-4478
Kim Ingwersen, Manager

8751 **Wesley Acres Memorial Loss Center**
3520 Grand Avenue
Des Moines, IA 50312-4359
515-271-6500
Fax: 515-271-6898
Rick Meyer, Manager
Janet Simpson, Administrator

8752 **West Libery Assisted Living Residences**
1000 N Miller Street
West Liberty, IA 52776-1102
319-627-4775
Fax: 563-627-4738
Shelley Wick, Administrator

8753 **Western Home Assisted Living**
420 E 11th Street
Cedar Falls, IA 50613-3364
319-277-2141
Fax: 319-277-5158
Jerry Harris, President

8754 **Willow Pointe**
17396 Kingbird Avenue
Mason City, IA 50401-9251
641-423-7722
Fax: 641-421-8078
Rick Burke, Contact

8755 **Willows**
324 SW 6th Street
Stuart, IA 50250-2169
515-523-1693
Fax: 641-523-9123
Sue Forcht, Manager

Kansas

8756 **Alterra Sterling House of Abilene**
1100 N Vine Street
Abilene, KS 67410-4009
785-263-7400
Fax: 785-263-3044
Alterra Sterling House is an assisted living residence that provides housing and assistance to older adults who want to retain their independence while receiving the daily support they need. The intimate setting for those with limited mobility, as well as specialized programming, help residents maximize independence and quality of life.

8757 **Alterra Sterling House of Abilene II**
1102 N Vine Street
Abilene, KS 67410-4015
785-263-7800
Fax: 785-263-2455
Alterra Sterling House is an assisted living residence that provides housing and assistance to older adults who want to retain their independence while receiving the daily support they need. The intimate setting for those with limited mobility, as well as specialized programming, help residents maximize independence and quality of life.

8758 **Alterra Sterling House of Arkansas**
402 E Windsor Road
Arkansas City, KS 67005-3894
620-442-4400
Fax: 620-442-1230
Janice Thomas, Exeuctive Director

Alterra Sterling House is an assisted living residence that provides housing and assistance to older adults who want to retain their independence while receiving the daily support they need. The intimate setting for those with limited mobility, as well as specialized programming, help residents maximize independence and quality of life.

8759 **Alterra Sterling House of Augusta**
1611 Fairway Drive
Augusta, KS 67010-2246
316-775-1000
Fax: 316-775-6309
Debra Mullen, Executive Director

8760 **Alterra Sterling House of Derby**
6708 S Rock Road
Derby, KS 67037-9047
316-788-6100
Fax: 316-788-1239
Bruce Monrue, Executive Director
Alterra Sterling House is an assisted living residence that provides housing and assistance to older adults who want to retain their independence while receiving the daily support they need. The intimate setting for those with limited mobility, as well as specialized programming, help residents maximize independence and quality of life.

8761 **Alterra Sterling House of Dodge City**
2400 N 14th Avenue
Dodge City, KS 67801-2370
620-225-7555
Fax: 620-225-6714
Connie Watkins, Executive Director
Alterra Sterling House is an assisted living residence that provides housing and assistance to older adults who want to retain their independence while receiving the daily support they need. The intimate setting for those with limited mobility, as well as specialized programming, help residents maximize independence and quality of life.

8762 **Alterra Sterling House of Emporia**
1200 W 12th Avenue
Emporia, KS 66801-2557
620-342-1000
Fax: 620-342-2762
Lori Wisdom, Executive Director
Alterra Sterling House is an assisted living residence that provides housing and assistance to older adults who want to retain their independence while receiving the daily support they need. The intimate setting for those with limited mobility, as well as specialized programming, help residents maximize independence and quality of life.

8763 **Alterra Sterling House of Fairdale**
2251 E Crawford Street
Salina, KS 67401-1317
785-823-8600
Fax: 785-825-8284
Ben Schmitz, Executive Director

8764 **Alterra Sterling House of Great Bend**
1206 Patton Road
Great Bend, KS 67530-3190
620-792-7000
Fax: 620-792-5955
Jim Herman, Executive Director
Alterra Sterling House is an assisted living residence that provides housing and assistance to older adults who want to retain their independence while receiving the daily support they need. The intimate setting for those with limited mobility, as well as specialized programming, help residents maximize independence and quality of life.

8765 **Alterra Sterling House of Hays**
1801 E 27th Street
Hays, KS 67601-2136
785-628-1111
Fax: 785-628-0830
Lisa Leiker, Executive Director

Assisted Living Facilities/Kansas

Alterra Sterling House is an assisted living residence that provides housing and assistance to older adults who want to retain their independence while receiving the daily support they need. The intimate setting for those with limited mobility, as well as specialized programming, help residents maximize independence and quality of life.

8766 Alterra Sterling House of Junction
1022 Caroline Avenue
Junction City, KS 66441-5230
785-762-3123
Fax: 785-762-6222

Joye Gfeller, Manager

Alterra Sterling House is an assisted living residence that provides housing and assistance to older adults who want to retain their independence while receiving the daily support they need. The intimate setting for those with limited mobility, as well as specialized programming, help residents maximize independence and quality of life.

8767 Alterra Sterling House of Lawrence
3220 Peterson Road
Lawrence, KS 66049-1963
785-832-9900
Fax: 785-832-9167

Amy Homer, Manager

8768 Alterra Sterling House of Leawood
12724 State Line Road
Leawood, KS 66209-1619
913-663-3351
Fax: 913-663-2357

Shannon Newson, Executive Director

Alterra Sterling House is an assisted living residence that provides housing and assistance to older adults who want to retain their independence while receiving the daily support they need. The intimate setting for those with limited mobility, as well as specialized programming, help residents maximize independence and quality of life.

8769 Alterra Sterling House of Lenexa I
8710 Caenen Lake Road
Lenexa, KS 66215-2069
913-894-6979
Fax: 913-894-0901

D J Brown, Executive Director

8770 Alterra Sterling House of Lenexa II
8740 Caenen Lake Road
Lenexa, KS 66215-2069
913-894-0014
Fax: 913-894-9147

Deb Hatlestad, Executive Director

8771 Alterra Sterling House of McPherson
1460 N Main Street
McPherson, KS 67460-1902
620-241-6600
Fax: 620-241-7406

Joan Diehl, Executive Diretor

Alterra Sterling House is an assisted living residence that provides housing and assistance to older adults who want to retain their independence while receiving the daily support they need. The intimate setting for those with limited mobility, as well as specialized programming, help residents maximize independence and quality of life.

8772 Alterra Sterling House of Olathe
751 N Somerset Ter
Olathe, KS 66062-5450
913-829-4663
Fax: 913-829-6495

Jeri Willson, Executive Director

Alterra Sterling House is an assisted living residence that provides housing and assistance to older adults who want to retain their independence while receiving the daily support they need. The intimate setting for those with limited mobility, as well as specialized programming, help residents maximize independence and quality of life.

8773 Alterra Sterling House of Olathe II
791 N Somerset Ter
Olathe, KS 66062-5450
913-829-1403
Fax: 913-829-6182

Jeri Willson, Administrator

8774 Alterra Sterling House of Salina
1200 E Kirwin Avenue
Salina, KS 67401-6333
785-825-8200
Fax: 785-825-8284

Christen Robinson, Manager

Alterra Sterling House is an assisted living residence that provides housing and assistance to older adults who want to retain their independence while receiving the daily support they need. The intimate setting for those with limited mobility, as well as specialized programming, help residents maximize independence and quality of life.

8775 Alterra Sterling House of Topeka
5800 SW Drury Lane
Topeka, KS 66604-2262
785-272-2200
Fax: 785-272-3862

Susan Bullock, Executive Director

Alterra Sterling House is an assisted living residence that provides housing and assistance to older adults who want to retain their independence while receiving the daily support they need. The intimate setting for those with limited mobility, as well as specialized programming, help residents maximize independence and quality of life.

8776 Alterra Sterling House of Wichita
8600 E 21st Street N
Wichita, KS 67206-2939
316-684-3100
Fax: 316-684-6612

Michael Agpoon, Executive Director

Alterra Sterling House is an assisted living residence that provides housing and assistance to older adults who want to retain their independence while receiving the daily support they need. The intimate setting for those with limited mobility, as well as specialized programming, help residents maximize independence and quality of life.

8777 Alterra Sterling House of Woodland
1500 Terrace Avenue
Liberal, KS 67901-5708
620-624-8000
Fax: 620-624-9513

Gail Gordon, Executive Director

8778 Andover Court Assisted Living
721 W 21st Street
Andover, KS 67002-8491
316-733-2662
Fax: 316-733-6754

Janet Garretson, General Manager

From around-the-clock nursing services to retirement living, Life Care Centers of America offers a full continuum of care for today's seniors. We also ease the challenges of the caregiver with specialty services such as home care, rehabilitation services and respite care.

8779 Assisted Lifestyles Of KS Inc.
625 N Lincoln Street
Olathe, KS 66061-2501
913-829-6920
Fax: 913-829-6993
http://www.assistedlifestyles.com

Diane Klemm, Contact/Executive Director
Gary Aull, Owner

43 bed assisted living.

8780 Assisted Living at Windsor Place
106 Tyler Boulevard
Coffeyville, KS 67337-2425
620-251-6538
Fax: 620-251-5345

Kalynn Showalter, Manager

Assisted Living Facilities/Kansas

8781 Atria Assisted & Retirement Living
3515 SW 6th Avenue
Topeka, KS 66606-1900
785-234-6225
Fax: 785-234-4002

Jared Holroyd, Executive Director

8782 Brookside Assisted Living
702 W 7th Street
Overbrook, KS 66524-9496
785-665-3246
Fax: 785-665-3247

Scott Averill, Executive Director

8783 Carriage House of Greensburg
723 S Elm Street
Greensburg, KS 67054-1910
620-723-3400
Fax: 620-723-3436

Steve Dawson, Administrator

8784 Cedar Lake Village
15325 S Lone Elm Road
Olathe, KS 66061-5416
913-780-9916
Fax: 913-768-8903

Joanna Randall, Executive Director

8785 Cedarview Assisted Living
2929 Sternberg Drive
Hays, KS 67601-2055
785-628-3200
Fax: 316-628-4833

Treva Benoit, Executive Director

8786 Chaucer Estates-Retirement
10550 E 21st Street N
Wichita, KS 67206-3509
316-630-8111
Fax: 316-630-6193

Don Schmidt, Owner

8787 Cherry Creek Village Retirement Center
8200 E Pawnee Street
Wichita, KS 67207-5447
316-684-0905
Fax: 316-691-2622

Elaine McDaniels, Administrator

8788 Cornerstone Assisted Living
1240 N Broadmoor Avenue
Wichita, KS 67206-3896
316-636-5101
Fax: 316-636-2576

Ellie Garrett, Executive Director

8789 Cornerstone Ridge Plaza
3636 N Ridge Road
Apt 400
Wichita, KS 67205-1221
316-462-3636
Fax: 316-462-3676

Monty Warren, Manager

8790 Elm Grove Estates
2416 Brentwood Street
Hutchinson, KS 67502-5000
620-669-5241
Fax: 620-663-6602

For seniors who want the convenience of retirement community living, for families caring for an aging adult, or for people with Alzheimer's, Elm Grove Estates offers a world of options - all designed to help residents maintain as much independence as possible. There are no hidden costs, buy-in fees or pre-paid leases; everything is included for one monthly fee.

8791 Evergreen Gardens of Garden City
531 Campus View Street
Garden City, KS 67846-7904
620-276-3200
Fax: 627-276-0740

8792 Fort Scott Presbyterian Village
2401 Horton Street
Fort Scott, KS 66701-3178
620-223-5550
Fax: 620-223-7800

Ginger Dierksen, Administrator

8793 Georgetown Village
1655 S Georgetown Street
Wichita, KS 67218-4140
316-685-0400
Fax: 316-685-0174
e-mail: Beth_Smith@via-christi.org

Beth Smith, Contact
Maggie Rader, Executive Director

8794 Gran Villas
410 Juniper Drive
Holton, KS 66436-1535
785-364-5051
Fax: 785-364-5010

Angela Hall, Manager

8795 Gran Villas-Atchison
1635 Riley Street
Atchison, KS 66002-1518
913-367-2077
Fax: 913-367-1755

Brenda Meudt, Manager

Offers personal and health care services to a residential environment, assisted living centers enable frail individuals to remain independent and to avoid institutionalization for as long as possible. Offering community living and minimal supervision, assisted living provides the solution for the active senior who should not be living alone.

8796 Gran Villas-Eureka
1820 E River Street
Eureka, KS 67045-2156
620-583-7473
Fax: 620-583-7574

Betty Cline, Manager

Offers personal and health care services to a residential environment, assisted living centers enable frail individuals to remain independent and to avoid institutionalization for as long as possible. Offering community living and minimal supervision, assisted living provides the solution for the active senior who should not be living alone.

8797 Gran Villas-Fredonia
2111 E Washington Street
Fredonia, KS 66736-1757
620-378-2329
Fax: 620-378-2792

Connie Evenson, Manager

Offers personal and health care services to a residential environment, assisted living centers enable frail individuals to remain independent and to avoid institutionalization for as long as possible. Offering community living and minimal supervision, assisted living provides the solution for the active senior who should not be living alone.

8798 Gran Villas-Hiawatha
400 Kansas Avenue
Hiawatha, KS 66434-1954
785-742-4566
Fax: 913-742-4573

Michelle Catrell, Manager

Offers personal and health care services to a residential environment, assisted living centers enable frail individuals to remain independent and to avoid institutionalization for as long as possible. Offering community living and minimal supervision, assisted living provides the solution for the active senior who should not be living alone.

8799 Gran Villas-Neodesha
400 Fir Street
Neodesha, KS 66757-1298
620-325-2244
Fax: 620-325-2762

Terri Greaves, Manager

Assisted Living Facilities/Kansas

Offers personal and health care services to a residential environment, assisted living centers enable frail individuals to remain independent and to avoid institutionalization for as long as possible. Offering community living and minimal supervision, assisted living provides the solution for the active senior who should not be living alone.

8800 Gran Villas-Osage City
1403 E Laing Street
Osage City, KS 66523-9203
785-528-5095
Fax: 785-528-4263

Betsy Elkinton, Manager

Offers personal and health care services to a residential environment, assisted living centers enable frail individuals to remain independent and to avoid institutionalization for as long as possible. Offering community living and minimal supervision, assisted living provides the solution for the active senior who should not be living alone.

8801 Gran Villas-Wamego
1607 4th Street
Wamego, KS 66547-1915
785-456-8997
Fax: 785-456-8796

Jan DeBord, Manager

Offers personal and health care services to a residential environment, assisted living centers enable frail individuals to remain independent and to avoid institutionalization for as long as possible. Offering community living and minimal supervision, assisted living provides the solution for the active senior who should not be living alone.

8802 Grand Court of Overland Park II
11909 Lamar Avenue
Overland Park, KS 66209-2706
913-345-9339
Fax: 913-345-9383

David Thompson, Executive Director

8803 Great Bend Homestead
3820 Broadway Avenue
Great Bend, KS 67530-3645
620-792-7017
Fax: 670-792-7117

Darlene Schulz, Executive Director

8804 Halstead Place
715 W 6th Street
Halstead, KS 67056-2173
316-830-0242
Fax: 316-835-2994

8805 Homestead of Garden City
2414 N Henderson Drive
Garden City, KS 67846-7600
620-272-9800
Fax: 620-272-0555

Gilbert Cruz, Executive Director

8806 Hutchinson Homestead
1700 E 23rd Avenue
Hutchinson, KS 67502-1159
620-662-4114
Fax: 620-662-9002
e-mail: crileyhutchh@ourtownusa.net

Darlean Schulz, Executive Director
Judy Wineland, Administrator

8807 Kansas Masonic Home
400 S Martinson Street
Wichita, KS 67213-3939
316-267-0271
Fax: 316-267-2199

8808 Leavenworth Homestead
5150 Hughes Road
Leavenworth, KS 66048-4973
913-727-9600
Fax: 913-727-9604

Vicky Walker, Executive Director

8809 Linwood Place I & II
1509 Linn Street
Valley Falls, KS 66088-1185
785-945-3634
Fax: 785-945-3684

Marilyn Zieg, Owner

8810 Manhattan Homestead Assisted
1923 Little Kitten Avenue
Manhattan, KS 66503-7583
785-776-1772
Fax: 785-565-6707

Joe Braun, Executive Director

8811 Marquis Place
205 W 21st Street
Concordia, KS 66901-5205
785-243-2255
Fax: 785-243-2409

8812 Meadows
1201 Martindale Street
Burlington, KS 66839-2400
620-364-8861
Fax: 620-364-5504

Elaine Seamen, Manager

8813 Overland Park Place
6555 W 75th Street
Overland Park, KS 66204-3019
913-383-9876
Fax: 913-383-9875

Jennifer Evers, Administrator

8814 Park View Assisted Living
750 N Missouri Street
Ulysses, KS 67880-1868
620-424-2000
Fax: 620-424-3699

Billie Upshaw, Administrator

8815 Parkwood Village
401 Rochester Street
Pratt, KS 67124-2990
620-672-5541
Fax: 620-672-2123

Kelly Thomas, Executive Director

8816 Peterson Assisted Living
629 Holliday Street
Osage City, KS 66523-1137
785-528-3301
Fax: 785-528-3501

Crystal May, Administrator

8817 Redbud Plaza
205 W 9th Street
Onaga, KS 66521-9625
785-889-4142
Fax: 785-889-4172

Linda Werren, Executive Director

Redbud Plaza Assisted Living Center is a unique home away from home. It's a warm friendly place with all the comforts of home without worries. Our personal caregivers believe in providing our residents with the very best services. We take pride in giving you the assistance you need and the companionship you desire.

8818 Rolling Hills Assisted Living Apartments
2410 SW Urish Road
Topeka, KS 66614-4347
785-273-5001
Fax: 785-271-2496

Brian Falk, Administrator

Rolling Hills Assisted Living is home for a group of friendly, retired people who share a desire for independent living with the comfort of 24-hour health care. Residents have independence in their own apartments while enjoying the benefits of many support services.

Assisted Living Facilities/Kansas

8819 **Sealye House**
619 N 4th Avenue
Hill City, KS 67642-1509
785-421-2662
Fax: 785-421-2198

Jo McDermott, Owner

8820 **Shawnee Heartland Assisted Living**
16207 Midland Drive
Shawnee, KS 66217-9499
913-248-6600
Fax: 913-789-8989

Phyllis Hornbaker, Owner

8821 **St John's New Horizons**
2225 Canterbury Drive
Hays, KS 67601-2300
785-628-8742
Fax: 785-625-3793

Vicki Frohling, Operator
Theresa Thomas, Administrator

8822 **Twin Oaks Assisted Living**
657 W Eisenhower Road
Lansing, KS 66043-2204
913-727-6100
Fax: 913-727-1722

Debbie Eyerly, Executive Director

Superior care is continued at Twin Oaks Retirement Community with our exceptional Assisted Living facility. Medication assistance, nursing and social services are only some of the needs we assist our residents with every day. Our professional staff includes 24-hour nursing and home health care specialists ready to help each resident.

8823 **Valley Springs Assisted Living**
280 Valley Springs Drive
Auburn, KS 66402-9464
785-256-7100
Fax: 785-256-7902

Karen Conley, Manager

8824 **Village East**
PO Box 346
Nortonville, KS 66060
913-886-6400
Fax: 913-886-8695

Suzanne Mifenhelter, Administrator

8825 **Village of Ninnescah**
440 N 4th Street
Clearwater, KS 67026-9708
620-584-4257
Fax: 620-584-2277

Izena Monk, CEO

8826 **Vintage Park of Atchison**
1301 N 4th Street
Atchison, KS 66002-1207
913-367-2655
Fax: 913-367-0642

Cindy Weigman, Administrator

Vintage Park Assisted Living offers security, independence, comfort, beautiful surroundings and local worry-free living. Filled with your own furnishings, our home provides a family-oriented atmosphere and peace of mind to those who need some assistance with their activities of daily living.

19Fi

8827 **Vintage Park of Baldwin City**
321 Crimson Avenue
Baldwin City, KS 66006-4157
785-594-4255
Fax: 785-594-2280

Sue Brown, Administrator

Vintage Park Assisted Living offers security, independence, comfort, beautiful surroundings and local worry-free living. Filled with your own furnishings, our home provides a family-oriented atmosphere and peace of mind to those who need some assistance with their activities of daily living.

8828 **Vintage Park of Gardner**
869 S Juniper Ter
Gardner, KS 66030-1468
913-856-7643
Fax: 913-884-4582

Mitzie Terrell, Administrator
Marilyn McDonald, Manager

Vintage Park Assisted Living offers security, independence, comfort, beautiful surroundings and local worry-free living. Filled with your own furnishings, our home provides a family-oriented atmosphere and peace of mind to those who need some assistance with their activities of daily living.

8829 **Vintage Park of Louisburg**
202 S Rogers Road
Louisburg, KS 66053-4064
913-837-5133
Fax: 913-837-5169

Ava Purvis, Administrator

Vintage Park Assisted Living offers security, independence, comfort, beautiful surroundings and local worry-free living. Filled with your own furnishings, our home provides a family-oriented atmosphere and peace of mind to those who need some assistance with their activities of daily living.

8830 **Vintage Park of Paola**
601 N East Street
Paola, KS 66071-1183
913-557-0202
Fax: 913-294-5187

Tina Rhoades, Administrator

Vintage Park Assisted Living offers security, independence, comfort, beautiful surroundings and local worry-free living. Filled with your own furnishings, our home provides a family-oriented atmosphere and peace of mind to those who need some assistance with their activities of daily living.

8831 **Vintage Place of Derby**
1701 Walnut Grove Road
Derby, KS 67037-3528
316-788-9600
Fax: 316-788-9775

Lori Mouak, Executive Director

8832 **Vintage Place of Russell**
1070 E Wichita Avenue
Russell, KS 67665-2452
785-483-5882
Fax: 785-483-2797

Vicki Frohling, Administrator

8833 **Vintage Point of Pittsburg**
1004 E Centennial Drive
Pittsburg, KS 66762-6565
620-231-4554
Fax: 620-231-1156

Debbie Walker, Administrator

8834 **Vyne at Crestview**
600 N 127th Street E
Wichita, KS 67206-2830
316-733-8100
Fax: 316-733-8103

8835 **Vyne at Meadows Park**
1221 W Maple Street
Wichita, KS 67213-3915
316-729-2400
Fax: 316-729-2403

Shiela Landis, Executive Director

8836 **Waterfront Inn Assisted Living**
900 N Bayshore Drive
Wichita, KS 67212-4807
316-945-3344
Fax: 316-945-3344

Karen Loy, Manager

Assisted Living Facilities/Kentucky

8837 **Wheat Ridge Acres**
707 Wheat Ridge Circle
Goodland, KS 67735-2256
785-899-0100
Fax: 785-899-0277

Donna Swagger, Exective Director

8838 **Woodridge Estates**
329 Kay Lane
Parsons, KS 67357-3501
620-421-4700
Fax: 620-421-2666

Don Woodworth, Owner

Kentucky

8839 **Baptist Homes**
108 Boyles Drive
Russellville, KY 42276-8838
270-726-4187
Fax: 270-726-4188

James B Lewis, President
Amy Arnold, Manager

Our goal is to provide a continuum of quality care to all of our residents through caring, qualified professionals, state-of-the-art facilities and support services

8840 **Beehive of Danville**
5124 Shephard Lane
Lexington, KY 40515-8534
877-363-2757
Fax: 859-236-1553

8841 **Beehive of Shelbyville**
74 Mack Walters Road
Shelbyville, KY 40065-1738
502-633-1599
Fax: 502-633-6785

Charles Shontz, Owner

The mission of Bee Hive Homes is to provide assistance with the activities of daily living in a respectful, dignified manner in a home like setting to the frail elderly who choose to retain their independence and dignity to the fullest measure possible.

8842 **Belmont Village at St Matthews**
4600 Bowling Boulevard
Louisville, KY 40207-5155
502-721-7500
Fax: 502-896-8224
http://www.belmontvillage.com

Sheila Carter, Manager

Located in St. Matthews residential neighborhood of Louisville.

8843 **Four Courts Senior Center**
2100 Millvale Road
Louisville, KY 40205-1604
502-451-0990
Fax: 502-459-1018
e-mail: info@jhhs.org
http://www.jhhs.org

Deborah May, Executive Director

Provides the community's seniors with a continuum of care - from personal and intermediate to skilled nursing home care - along with a complete program of activities.

8844 **Frontier Nursing Service**
132 FNS Drive
Wendover, KY 41775-8921
606-672-2317
Fax: 606-672-3022
e-mail: fnstours@yahoo.com
http://www.frontiernursing.org

Barb Gibson, Director

Provides health care to persons in approximately 1000 square miles of eastern Kentucky using a 40-bed hospital, two primary care centers, three rural health clinics, and a home health agency.

8845 **Liberty Ridge**
2550 Liberty Road
Lexington, KY 40509-4461
859-543-9449
Fax: 859-543-0059

Dan Wilkerson, Executive Director

8846 **McCready Manor**
300 Stocker Drive
Richmond, KY 40475-4304
859-625-1400
Fax: 606-625-1623

Gil Shew, Administrator

8847 **McDowell Place of Danville**
1181 Ben Ali Drive
Danville, KY 40422-8939
859-239-4663
Fax: 859-238-0171

Susan Matherly, Administrator

Our community offers assistance with some daily activities as well as security for your peace of mind and that of your family. McDowell Place of Danville is spacious, comfortable, and finely appointed to make your stay, or that of a loved one, as pleasant as possible.

8848 **Morningside Paducah**
1700 Elmdale Road
Paducah, KY 42003-5517
270-534-9173
Fax: 270-554-7126
e-mail: jacksong@lifetrust.com
http://www.morningsideassistedliving.com

Gerry Jackson, Contact

8849 **Morningside of Bowling Green**
981 Campbell Lane
Bowling Green, KY 42104-4136
270-746-9600
Fax: 270-842-4104

Melissa Kincaid, Executive Director

8850 **River's Bend Retirement Community**
300 Beech Street
Kuttawa, KY 42055-6214
270-388-2868
Fax: 270-684-6283

Tammy Workman, Administrator

8851 **Stonecreek Lodge**
9251 Stonecrest Road
Louisville, KY 40272
502-935-5884
Fax: 502-935-5802

Jackie Hancock, Executive Director

8852 **Weley Manor**
5012 E Manslick Road
Louisville, KY 40219-5100
502-964-3959
Fax: 502-966-0819

Denise Garland, Contact

Louisiana

8853 **Arbor of Natchitoches**
1907 Highway 1 S
Natchitoches, LA 71457
318-356-0016
Fax: 318-323-0016

Angie Ingram, Manager

8854 **Arbor of Ruston**
4518 Highway 80
Ruston, LA 71270-8952
318-323-2115
Fax: 318-323-6281

Assisted Living Facilities/Louisiana

8855 Assisted Living Center at St James Place
333 Lee Drive
Baton Rouge, LA 70808-4980
225-215-4500
800-460-7007
Fax: 225-215-4515

Enjoy the freedom to travel, to discover new friendships, to pursue outside interests and personal growth. St. James Place provides a variety of services and amenities that encourage residents to maintain their zest for living active and interesting lives.

8856 Azalea Estates of Gonzales
2305 S Purpera Avenue
Gonzales, LA 70737-5416
225-644-1028
800-567-0650
Fax: 225-647-9520

Lorraine Lavigne, Manager

8857 Azalea Estates of Monroe
4380 Old Sterlington Road
Monroe, LA 71203-2359
318-343-1626
Fax: 318-345-4825

Bonnie Westmoreland, Executive Director

8858 Azalea Estates of New Iberia
1318 Andre Street
New Iberia, LA 70563-2148
337-364-1695
888-364-1695
Fax: 337-367-8280

Christine Thibodeaux, Executive Director

8859 Azalea Estates of Shreveport
516 E Flournoy Lucas Road
Shreveport, LA 71115-3856
318-797-2408
Fax: 317-797-8540

Cheryl Foster, Manager

8860 Bailey House
650 Pershing Avenue
Bunkie, LA 71322-2100
318-346-8400
Fax: 318-346-6206

Annette Lacombe, Manager

8861 Cornerstone Village
103 W Martial Avenue
Lafayette, LA 70508-6719
337-981-5335
Fax: 337-269-1255

Lance Linscombe, Administrator

8862 Cornerstone Village South
103 W Martial Avenue
Lafayette, LA 70508-6719
337-981-5335
Fax: 337-981-0775

Lance Linscombe, Administrator

8863 Grand Cove
1525 W McNeese Street
Lake Charles, LA 70605-4293
337-474-6000
Fax: 337-478-7522

Randy Stelly, Administrator

8864 Haven at Windermere
8225 Ymca Plaza Drive
Baton Rouge, LA 70810
225-769-9996
Fax: 225-819-1334

Annette Willis, Contact
Thomas Elkins, Owner

8865 Kingsley Place at Alexandria
351 Windermere Boulevard
Alexandria, LA 71303-2600
318-443-6770
Fax: 318-443-2366

Judy White, Executive Director

8866 Kingsley Place at Lafayette
215 W Farrel Road
Lafayette, LA 70508-7019
337-993-0077
Fax: 337-993-0071

Madeline Husband-Ardoin, Executive Director

8867 Kingsley Place at Shreveport
7110 University Drive
Shreveport, LA 71105-5034
318-524-2100
Fax: 318-524-2300

Bridget Lyman, Executive Director

If your loved one has difficulties with bathing, dressing, remembering medications or has memory impairment, a retirement community may not offer enough support, a nursing home may be too much care and home health may lack a sense of community or social interaction. Assisted Living often offers just the right amount of care in the right type of setting.

8868 Lakewood Quarters Retirement Community
8585 Summa Avenue
Baton Rouge, LA 70809
225-767-7877
Fax: 225-767-7807
e-mail: admis.lakewoodalf@chcmgc.com
http://www.cypresshealthcare.net

Regina McMakin, Admissions
Terri Achette, Executive Director

Lakewood Quarters is a retirement living community, especially designed to combine independence with individualized assistance. When residents begin relying on family or friends for added support for everyday activities, the homelike setting of Lakewood Quarters can provide a welcome alternative. Lakewood also offers a secure Alzheimer's wing to the retirement community.

8869 Landmark Retirement Community
714 N Avenue K
Crowley, LA 70526-3800
337-783-1144
Fax: 337-788-3877

8870 Live Oak Village of Slidell
2200 Gause Boulevard E
Slidell, LA 70461-4223
985-781-4545
Fax: 985-781-8786

Tara Picou, Administrator

Our Principles of Service are encouraging independence, enabling freedom of choice, preserving dignity, celebrating individuality, nurturing the spirit and involving family and friends. All Sunrise team members are trained to provide services and care in a manner that supports these principles and furthers Sunrise's mission.

8871 Maison Oaks Assisted Living
504 W 5th Street
La Place, LA 70068-3940
985-653-8858
Fax: 225-652-9583

Guy Birch, Administrator

8872 Malta Park: Willwoods II
1101 Aline Street
New Orleans, LA 70115-2453
504-894-6000
Fax: 504-894-6009

Charlie Dilapi, Manager

8873 Malta Square at Sacred Heart: Willwoods II
3222 Canal Street
New Orleans, LA 70119-6248
504-826-7600
Fax: 504-826-2698

Mary Quaid, Contact

Assisted Living Facilities/Louisiana

8874 **Merrill Gardens at Bossier**
2540 Beene Boulevard
Bossier City, LA 71111-5459
318-747-2114
Fax: 318-747-2164

Mark Terry, Manager

It's a place where you're absolutely free to be yourself. You can enjoy the quiet comforts of independent living, participate in our active retirement community, or both. The choice is yours, and it's just one of the many choices you'll find all around you. At Merrill Gardens, the door is always open for creating a lifestyle that's rich, rewarding and one of a kind, just like you.

8875 **Montclair Park Assisted Living**
9100 E Kings Highway
Shreveport, LA 71115-2766
318-797-1114
Fax: 318-797-1158

David Abdehou, Contact
Melanie Bond, Executive Director

8876 **Monte Carlo Outreach Facility**
1406 Reynes Street
New Orleans, LA 70117-4238
504-948-9659
Fax: 504-246-8171

Vaughn Green, Contact

8877 **Norman House Group Home**
5424 Nmiro Street
New Orleans, LA 70117
504-944-8166
Fax: 504-948-4493

8878 **Oakmont Estate**
204 Cocoville Road
Mansura, LA 71350-4266
318-240-7424
Fax: 877-280-0573

Joseph Loughman, Contact

8879 **Oakwood Village**
4400 McHugh Road
Zachary, LA 70791-5324
225-658-8888
Fax: 225-658-8211

Milton Ourso, Owner

Our mission is to serve older or infirm persons through loving, caring Christian communities, respinding to thier physical, social, emotional, intellectual and spiritual needs, and to encourage a sense of independence, individuality, dignity and worth throughout life.

8880 **Pratt-Stanton Manor**
1224 Saint Charles Avenue
New Orleans, LA 70130-4396
504-525-0895
Fax: 504-525-0895

Michael Calhoun, Executive Director

8881 **Regency Place**
14333 Old Hammond Highway
Baton Rouge, LA 70816-1146
225-272-1401
Fax: 225-527-2933

Heather Marsh, Marketing Executive

8882 **Retirement Center**
14686 Old Hammond Highway
Baton Rouge, LA 70816-1278
225-272-9339
Fax: 225-273-3008

8883 **Rosewood Retirement & Assisted Living Community**
203 Rue Fountaine
Lafayette, LA 70508-5775
337-981-0333
Fax: 337-988-1706

Nicol Hannie, Owner

8884 **Russ House**
165 Jefferson Avenue
Ruston, LA 71270-7067
318-251-9068
Fax: 318-251-9060

Claire Givens, Executive Director

8885 **Southside Gardens Assisted Living Center**
4536 Perkins Road
Baton Rouge, LA 70808-3057
225-928-1600
Fax: 225-922-9945

Becky Gammon, Executive Director

8886 **St Francis Villa Assisted Living**
10411 Jefferson Highway
New Orleans, LA 70123-1865
504-738-1060
Fax: 504-738-9870

Greg Deris, Owner

8887 **St Joesph Manor**
1201 Cardinal Drive
Thibodaux, LA 70301-4880
985-448-1154
Fax: 985-449-0047

Joel Landroy, Manager

8888 **Summerville at Kenner**
1600 Joe Yenni Boulevard
Kenner, LA 70065-1380
504-467-1000
Fax: 504-467-1017

Deeni Shannon, CEO

8889 **Sunrise Assisted Living**
5958 Saint Bernard Avenue
New Orleans, LA 70122-1324
504-288-7200
Fax: 504-288-5080

8890 **Sunrise Assisted Living of Baton Rouge**
8502 Jefferson Highway
Baton Rouge, LA 70809-2230
225-932-9400
Fax: 255-932-9409

Sally King, Executive Director

8891 **Tender Love & Company**
1559 Senate Street
61
New Orleans, LA 70122-1758
504-286-0365
Fax: 504-525-0895

8892 **Terrace of Shreveport**
8950 E Kings Highway
Shreveport, LA 71115-2704
318-323-2115
Fax: 318-323-6281

8893 **Terreboone House**
1163 Museum Drive
Houma, LA 70360-5910
985-580-0620
Fax: 985-873-6880

Jessica Ledt, Executive Director

8894 **Thompson House Group Home**
5432 N Tonti Street
New Orleans, LA 70117-3133
504-949-9566
Fax: 504-948-4493

8895 **Village in the Oaks**
75520 Highway 1081
Covington, LA 70435-2604
985-871-0111
Fax: 985-875-0009
e-mail: gnanse@cs.com
http://www.villageintheoaks.com

Gnanse Nelson, Director
Muril Ruppel, Manager

Independent and assisted living retirement community.

Assisted Living Facilities/Maryland

8896 Ville Ste Marie Senior Living Community
4112 Jefferson Highway
Jefferson, LA 70121-1500
504-834-3164
Fax: 504-849-0608
e-mail: vsmseniors@aol.com
http://www.VilleSteMarie.com
Aurora Alleman, Marketing/Community Relations
Barbara Eschete, General Manager
87 unit independent and assisted living complex.

8897 Willamsburg Senior Living Community
5445 Government Street
Baton Rouge, LA 70806-6000
225-929-8917
Fax: 225-928-3284
Mike Harvey, Manager

8898 Windsor Senior Living Community
1770 N Causeway Boulevard
Mandeville, LA 70471-3168
985-624-8040
Fax: 985-624-8822
Sondra Bellott, Administrator

8899 Wynhoven Living Center
1050a Medical Center Boulevard
Marrero, LA 70072-3144
504-347-0777
Fax: 504-341-7240
Jane Fockler, Administrative Executive

Maryland

8900 Abbeyville Assisted Living
1210 Downs Drive
Silver Spring, MD 20904-2034
301-622-6380
Fax: 301-384-8032

8901 Asbury Methodist Village
201 Russell Avenue
Gaithersburg, MD 20877-2801
301-216-4103
Fax: 301-216-4392
Edwin D Thomas III, CEO

8902 Ausburg Lutheran Home Maryland
6811 Campfield Road
Baltimore, MD 21207-4698
410-592-5310
Fax: 410-653-8744

8903 Blossom Place at Edenton
5901 Genesis Lane
Frederick, MD 21703-5104
301-694-7813
Fax: 301-694-0745
Rayann Butler, Administrator

8904 Brighton Gardens at Friendship Heights
5555 Friendship Boulevard
Chevy Chase, MD 20815-7243
301-656-1900
Fax: 301-656-5840
Jim Hackett, Executive Director

8905 Brighton Gardens of Columbia
7110 Minstrel Way
Columbia, MD 21045-5426
410-884-0773
Fax: 410-884-0776
Steve Gaylor, Manager

8906 Brighton Gardens of Pikesville
1840 Reisterstown Road
Baltimore, MD 21208-1305
410-580-0892
Fax: 410-580-0892
Bridget Babcock, Executive Director

8907 Buckinghams Choice
3200 Baker Circle
Adamstown, MD 21710-9653
301-874-5630
800-409-6111
Fax: 301-631-5491
e-mail: Fullerd@emaseniorcare.org
http://www.emaseniorcare.org
Donna M Fuller, Director Marketing
Collier Baird, Executive Director
Continuing care retirement community.

8908 Byron House
9210 Kentsdale Drive
Potomac, MD 20854-4529
301-469-9400
Fax: 301-765-8112
Stacey Guthrie, Manager

8909 Copper Ridge
710 Obrecht Road
Sykesville, MD 21784-7650
410-795-8808
Fax: 410-795-8893
e-mail: info@copperidge.org
http://www.copperidge.org
Cheryl Fisher, Director Addmissions
Marcie Koenig, Executive Director
Dedicated exclusively to care for persons with Alzheimer's disease and dementia.

8910 Eden Pines
310 Cameo Drive
Hagerstown, MD 21740-5854
301-766-9202
Fax: 301-766-7953

8911 Edenwald Retirement Community
800 Southerly Road
Towson, MD 21286-8403
410-339-6000
Fax: 410-823-1845
e-mail: marketing@edenwald.org
http://www.edenwald.org
Diana Fusting, Marketing Director
Sal Molite Jr, President
Anne Almirovdis, Marketing Assistant
Continuing care retirement community.

8912 General German Aged Peoples Home
800 Southerly Road
Towson, MD 21286-8403
410-339-6000
Fax: 410-583-8786
Sal Molite Jr, President

8913 Hausler
3722a Point of Rocks Road
Jefferson, MD 21755-7503
301-834-5500
Fax: 301-834-7308
Mae Hausler, President

8914 Heartfields Hall at Heartlands
3004 N Ridge Road
Ellicott City, MD 21043-3381
888-461-9494
Fax: 410-461-8233
Joyce Marier, Marketing Director
Nanci Target, Executive Director
Debbie Davis, Assistant Administrator
Heartlands Senior Living Village is a rental retirement community that offers full continuum of care, including independent living apartments, cottages and assisted living suites. Heartlands' features and amenities are bound to keep you vigorous with a great activities program, indoor swimming pool, onsite Wellness Center and the taste of delightful restaurant style dishes prepared by our experienced chefs.

Assisted Living Facilities/Massachusetts

8915 **Heartfields at Frederick**
1820 Latham Drive
Frederick, MD 21701-9395   301-663-8800
                              Fax: 301-663-8801

Heather Junta, Executive Director

8916 **Hearthhomes Resedence Bay Ridge I**
3023a Arundel on the Bay Road
Annapolis, MD 21403-4301   410-974-8208
                              Fax: 410-974-8210

Lakeshia Hooper, Administrator

8917 **Hearthhomes Residence Piney Orchard**
8735 Piney Orchard Parkway
Odenton, MD 21113-2245   410-695-0366
                              Fax: 410-695-0286

Jaime Weyaled, Owner

8918 **Hillhaven Assisted Living**
3210 Powder Mill Road
Adelphi, MD 20783-1029   301-937-2622
                              Fax: 301-937-8798

Joyce Milin, President

8919 **Homewood at Crumland Farms**
7407 Willow Road
Frederick, MD 21702-2500   301-694-7292
                              Fax: 301-293-6331
                              e-mail: cowright@hmud.org
                              http://www.homewood.com

Eric Nichols, Manager

8920 **Homewood of Williamsport**
16505 Virginia Avenue
Williamsport, MD 21795-1321   301-582-1472
                              Fax: 301-582-1805
                              http://www.homewood.com

Richard Lenehan, Executive Director
Anne Whitman, Director Marketing

Continuing care retirement community offering independent cottages and apartments, assisted living and nursing care.

8921 **Independence Court of Hyattsville**
5821 Queens Chapel Road
Hyattsville, MD 20782-3867   301-699-7900
                              Fax: 301-779-8723

Yveonne Coram, Administrator

8922 **Kensington Park Woodlands-Groves**
3616 Littledale Road
Kensington, MD 20895-3434   301-946-7700
                              Fax: 301-292-4000

George Oxx, Executive Director

8923 **Lifesprings Eldercare I**
4107 Buck Creek Road
Temple Hills, MD 20748-4930   301-894-4255
                              Fax: 301-449-0046

Faye Hutchinson, Owner

8924 **Miracle Assisted Living**
12113 Donnybrook Drive
Ft Washington, MD 20744-6055 301-203-7558
                              Fax: 301-203-8737

8925 **Oakcrest Village**
8800 Walther Boulevard
Parkville, MD 21234-9001   410-665-1000
                              Fax: 410-665-7481

Elmer J Klein

8926 **Providence Assisted Living**
15006 Dunleigh Drive
Bowie, MD 20721-3265   301-390-9484
                              Fax: 301-509-3050

8927 **Renaissance Gardens at Charlestown**
709 Maiden Choice Lane
Catonsville, MD 21228-3632   410-737-8922
                              Fax: 410-737-8817
                              http://www.thecareexperts.com

Taryn Toman, Health Care Counselor
Michael Conord, Manager

Features all private Assisted Living apartments and private and semi-private Long-Term Care rooms; full-time, on-site staff doctors with nurses on duty 24-hours a day. Short-Term Rehab (physical, speech and occupational therapy); dementia and Alzheimer's care also available. Renaissance Gardens, the choice you can feel good about.

8928 **Renaissance Gardens at Oak Crest**
8832 Walther Boulevard
Parkville, MD 21234-9020   410-882-3295
                              Fax: 410-657-3545
                              http://www.thecareexperts.com

Randi Bershak, Health Care Counselor
Mark Erickson, Executive Director

Features all private Assisted Living apartments and all private Long-Term Care rooms; full-time, on-site staff doctors with nurses on duty 24-hours a day. Short-Term Rehab (physical, speech and occupational therapy); dementia and Alzheimer's care also available. Renaissance Gardens, the choice you can feel good about.

8929 **Renaissance Gardens at Riderwood**
3160 Gracefield Road
Silver Spring, MD 20904-1986 301-572-8420
                              Fax: 301-572-8416
                              http://www.thecareexperts.com

Elena Price, Health Care Counselor
Timothy Sanna, Manager

Features all private Assisted Living apartments and all private Long-Term Care rooms; full-time, on-site staff doctors with nurses on duty 24-hours a day. Short-Time Rehab (physical, speech and occupational therapy); dementia and Alzheimer's care also available. Renaissance Gardens, the choice you can feel good about.

8930 **Ronald Park Place**
830 W 40th Street
Baltimore, MD 21211-2116   410-243-5800
                              Fax: 401-243-4929

Massachusetts

8931 **Alden Place**
391 Alden Road
Fairhaven, MA 02719-4405   508-994-9238
                              Fax: 508-994-9239

Susan Mosher, Executive Director

8932 **Allerton House at Central Park**
43 School House Road
Weymouth, MA 02188-4142   781-335-8666
                              Fax: 781-335-7666

Paul Casale Jr, Owner

8933 **Allerton House at Hancock Park**
164 Parkingway Street
Quincy, MA 02169-5020   617-471-2600
                              Fax: 617-773-1115

Richard Coughllin, Executive Director

Assisted Living Facilities/Massachusetts

8934 Allerton House at Harbor Park
15 Condito Road
Hingham, MA 02043-1753
781-749-3322
Fax: 781-749-3330

Tom Karnes, Executive Director

8935 Allerton House at the Village at Duxbury
290 Kingstown Way
Duxbury, MA 02332-4635
781-585-7136
Fax: 781-582-2274

8936 American Inn at Sawmill
802 College Highway
Southwick, MA 01077-9690
413-569-1215
Fax: 413-569-0945

Offer elegant independent cottages and apartments with private bath, 24 hour security, personal care assistance, and housekeeping/linen service.

8937 Arbors at Amherst
130 University Drive
Amherst, MA 01002-2296
413-548-6800
Fax: 413-548-6888

Carol Gianthetti, Executive Director

8938 Artia in Falmouth
339 Gifford Street
Falmouth, MA 02540-2913
508-540-1600
Fax: 508-548-2996

Joan Houlihan, Manager

8939 Atrium at Cardinal Drive
153 Cardinal Drive
Agawam, MA 01001-2182
413-821-9911
Fax: 413-821-9912

8940 Atrium at Drum Hill Alzheimer's DementiaAssisted Living
2 Technology Drive
N Chelmsford, MA 01863-2400
978-934-0000
Fax: 978-934-0022
http://www.the-atrium.net

Susan Antkowiak, Admissions Director
Avril Taylor, Admissions Coordinator
Joanne Thomas, Executive Director

The Atrium is a specifically designed assisted living facility exclusively for those with Alzheimer's Disease, dementia and related memory impairments. Within our safe and secure environment, Alzheimer specific activity programs promote resident's functional abilities, well-being and happiness. Our trained staff provide each resident with 24-hour assistance and supervision with daily living needs.

8941 Atrium at Faxon Woods
2003 Falls Boulevard
Quincy, MA 02169-8202
617-471-5595
Fax: 671-471-6335

Susan Loiurio, Manager

8942 Atrium at Veronica Drive
1 Veronica Drive
Danvers, MA 01923-5213
978-762-7625
Fax: 978-646-9393

Jan Chiampa, Executive Director

8943 Avery Crossing
110 West Street
Needham, MA 02494-1399
781-444-6655
Fax: 781-444-2794

Elayne Labrecque, Executive Director

8944 Bertram House of Swampscott
565 Humphrey Street
Swampscott, MA 01907-2600
781-595-1991
Fax: 781-595-1999

Walter Berdachowski, Executive Director

8945 Billerica Crossings
20 Charnstaff Lane
Billerica, MA 01821-6702
978-667-0898
Fax: 978-667-0890

Sarah Barber, Executive Direcctor

8946 Briarwood Continuing Care Retirement Community
70 Briarwood Circle
Worcester, MA 01606-1249
508-852-2670
Fax: 508-856-0309

Paul Bowler, CEO

8947 Brighton Gardens of Dedham
391 Common Street
Dedham, MA 02026-4055
781-407-7711
Fax: 781-407-7722

Karen Wheaton, Executive Director

8948 Brighton Gardens of North Shore by Marriott
220 Conant Street
Danvers, MA 01923-2586
978-777-5717
Fax: 978-777-1283

Lisa Orgettas, Executive Director

8949 Cadbury Commons at Cambridge
66 Sherman Street
Cambridge, MA 02140-3527
617-868-0575
Fax: 617-868-0023

Steve Elswig, Executive Director

8950 Cambridge Homes
360 Mount Auburn Street
Cambridge, MA 02138-5599
617-876-0369
Fax: 617-876-6432

Helene Quinn, Executive Director

8951 Cameron House
109 Housatonic Street
Lenox, MA 01240-2633
413-637-3100
Fax: 413-525-8153

Barbara Comalli, Executive Director

8952 Carmel Terrace
933 Central Street
Framingham, MA 01701-4813
508-788-8000
Fax: 508-626-1603

Sister Gustin, Executive Director

8953 Chelmsford Crossings
199 Chelmsford Street
Chelmsford, MA 01824-2306
978-250-8855
Fax: 978-250-2750

Margaret Palm, Executive Director

8954 Christopher Heights Assisted Living
20 Mary Scano Drive
Worcester, MA 01605-2892
508-792-1456
Fax: 508-792-3156

Wendi B Willette, Executive Director

8955 Christopher Heights of Webster
Thompson Road
Webster, MA 01570
508-949-0400
Fax: 508-792-3156

Thomas McMullen, Executive Director

Assisted Living Facilities/Massachusetts

8956 Cohen Florence Levine Estates
201 Captains Row
Chelsea, MA 02150-4068
617-887-0826
Fax: 617-889-8745

Tama Bello, Administrator

8957 Concord Park Assisted Living
68 Commonwealth Avenue
Concord, MA 01742-2967
978-369-4728
Fax: 978-369-5381

Nancy Crowley, Manager

8958 Country Club Heights
3 Rehabilitation Way
Woburn, MA 01801-6050
781-935-4094
800-533-0861
Fax: 781-938-5571

Daniella Guarracino, Manager

8959 Davis Manor
200 Harvard Road
Lancaster, MA 01523-2505
978-368-6590
Fax: 781-368-6590

Charles Conroy, Executive Director

8960 Decatur House
176 Main Street
Sandwich, MA 02563-2269
508-888-6404
Fax: 508-833-2781

Linda Austin, Executive Director

8961 Draper Place at Hopedale
25 Hopedale Street
Hopedale, MA 01747-1734
508-482-5995
800-854-0576
Fax: 508-482-0600

Brian Pillo, Manager

8962 Emmanuel House Residence
25 E Nilsson Street
Brockton, MA 02301-6604
508-588-5334
Fax: 508-588-8775

Sara Goverman, Executive Director

8963 Falls at Cordingly Dam
2300 Washington Street
Newton, MA 02462-1472
617-928-0007
Fax: 617-928-0697

Susan Cwieka, Executive Director

8964 Forge Hill Senior Living Community
4 Forge Hill Road
Franklin, MA 02038-3162
508-528-9200
Fax: 508-541-6591
http://www.forgehill.com

Carol O'Connor, Marketing Director
Arlene Lowney, Executive Director
Independent assisted living mamory impaired program.

8965 Gabriel House of Fall River
261 Oliver Street
Fall River, MA 02724-2917
508-678-9095
Fax: 508-677-2973

Dennis Etzkorn, Manager

8966 Goddard House in Brookline
165 Chestnut Street
Brookline, MA 02445-7573
617-731-8500
Fax: 617-731-5188

Nancy Shapiro, Executive Director

8967 Grace Morgan House
489 Prospect Street
Methuen, MA 01844-7511
978-682-4324
Fax: 978-682-4802

Scott Erickson, Owner

8968 Grey & Emil Eisenber Assisted Living Residence
631 Salisbury Street
Worcester, MA 01609-1120
508-757-0981
Fax: 508-757-7080

Vincent Librandi, Executive Director

8969 Grove Manor Estates Assisted Living
160 Grove Street
Braintree, MA 02184-7216
781-843-3700
Fax: 781-843-3744

Anthony Franchi Jr, Owner

8970 Harbor Point at Centerville
22 Richardson Road
Centerville, MA 02632-2453
508-778-2311
Fax: 508-862-9887

Jamie Matthews, Executive Director

8971 Harthstone at Laural Lake
610 Laurel Street
Lee, MA 01238-9181
413-243-2727
Fax: 413-243-5736

Debbie Richardson, Executive Director

8972 Haverhill Crossings
254 Amesbury Road
Haverhill, MA 01830-2348
978-556-1600
Fax: 978-556-1601

Shelli Hermance, Executive Director

8973 Hearthstone at New Horizons
400 Hemenway Street
Marlborough, MA 01752-6771
508-481-9898
Fax: 580-460-0270

Maureen Diana, Executive Director

8974 Heatherwood Assisted Living
100 Heatherwood
Yarmouth Port, MA 02675-1444
508-362-4400
800-852-0365
Fax: 508-375-0479

Bob La Crosse, Manager

8975 Henrietta Brewer House
11 Macs Lane
Vineyard Haven, MA 02568-5573
508-693-4500
Fax: 508-693-5754

Ellen Gerstmar, Owner

8976 Heritage Woods
462 Main Street
Agawam, MA 01001-1869
413-786-9704
Fax: 413-789-8366

Richard Cabral, Manager

8977 Heritage at Cleveland Circle
50 Sutherland Road
Brighton, MA 02135-7132
617-566-1700
Fax: 617-566-1752

Neil Tockman, President

731

Assisted Living Facilities/Massachusetts

8978 **Heritage at Danvers**
9 Summer Street
Danvers, MA 01923-1558
978-774-5959
Fax: 978-774-5454

Chris Sintros, Manager

8979 **Heritage at Dartmouth**
239 Cross Road
N Dartmouth, MA 02747-1992
508-992-8880
Fax: 508-992-8884

Lois Spirlet, Executive Director

8980 **Heritage at Falmouth**
140 Ter Heun Drive
Falmouth, MA 02540-2531
508-457-6400
Fax: 508-457-6437

Margret Corrideau, Manager

8981 **Heritage at Framingham**
747 Water Street
Framingham, MA 01701-3208
508-788-6050
Fax: 508-788-6601

Ellen Adam, Executive Director

8982 **Heritage at North Andover**
700 Chickering Road
Haverhill, MA 01832
978-683-1300
Fax: 978-683-0330

Steve Ostrander, Executive Director

8983 **Heritage at Vernon Court**
430 Centre Street
Newton, MA 02458-2036
617-965-9400
Fax: 617-965-9440

Kristen Bergeron, Manager

8984 **Herrick House**
89 Herrick Street
Beverly, MA 01915-2767
978-922-1999
Fax: 978-922-3402

Sandra Earl, Executive Director

8985 **Inn at Silver Lake**
21 Chipman Way
Kingston, MA 02364-1065
781-585-4100
Fax: 781-582-1884

Elinor Black, President

8986 **Landmark at Fall River**
400 Columbia Street
Fall River, MA 02721-1500
508-324-7960
Fax: 508-324-7961

Kathleen Cardenas, Executive Director

8987 **Landmark at Ocean View**
3 Essex Street
Beverly, MA 01915-4527
978-927-4227
Fax: 978-921-4885

Gayel Cote, Marketing Director
Steve Galante, Executive Director

8988 **Leominster Crossings**
1160 Main Street
Leominster, MA 01453-8709
978-537-2424
Fax: 978-537-2421

Thomas Burns, Executive Director

8989 **Longmeadow Place at Burlington**
42 Mall Road
Burlington, MA 01803-4568
781-270-9008
800-854-0576
Fax: 781-270-9009

Kellie McHugh, Executive Director

8990 **Longwood Place at Reading**
75 Pearl Street
Reading, MA 01867-2689
781-944-9200
Fax: 781-942-3833

Frank Petras, Executive Director

8991 **Manor on the Hill**
450 N Main Street
Leominster, MA 01453-5499
978-537-1661
Fax: 978-840-3341

8992 **Maplewood Place at Malden**
295 Broadway
Malden, MA 02148-4535
781-324-4999
800-854-0576
Fax: 781-324-5335

Sara Rizzari, Executive Director

8993 **Marina Place at Quincy**
4 Seaport Drive
North Quincy, MA 02171-1591
617-770-3264
800-854-0576
Fax: 617-770-3682

Maria Lastoria, Executive Director

8994 **Marland Place at Andover**
15 Stevens Street
Andover, MA 01810-3599
978-475-4225
800-854-0576
Fax: 978-475-5818

Marilyn Stasonis, Executive Director

8995 **Marriott Mapleridge of Plymouth**
97 Warren Avenue
Plymouth, MA 02360-2425
508-746-9733
Fax: 508-746-9683

Karen Foley, Executive Director

8996 **Mason Wright Retirement Community**
74 Walnut Street
Springfield, MA 01105-2179
413-733-1517
Fax: 413-747-8357

Lisa Walters Vucco, Manager

8997 **Mayflower Place**
579 Buck Island Road
W Yarmouth, MA 02673-3200
508-790-0200
Fax: 508-790-0004

Peg Holmes, Executive Director

8998 **Meadow Lodge at Drum Hill**
4 Technology Drive
N Chelmsford, MA 01863-2438
978-458-0099
Fax: 978-453-9143

Evelyn Whiteway, Executive Director

8999 **Melbourne Place**
140 Melbourne Road
Pittsfield, MA 01201-8533
413-499-1992
Fax: 413-443-8870

Diane Weinstein, Executive Director

Assisted Living Facilities/Massachusetts

9000 **Merrimack Place**
85 Storey Avenue
Newburyport, MA 01950-3571
978-462-7324
800-854-0576
Fax: 978-462-7325

Donna Byrnes, Executive Director

9001 **New Horizons at Choate**
21 Warren Avenue
Woburn, MA 01801-4981
781-932-8000
Fax: 781-938-8355

Rob Nigro, Executive Dirctor

9002 **New Horizons at Marlboro**
400 Hemenway Street
Marlborough, MA 01752-6771
508-460-5000
Fax: 508-460-7682

Robert O'Connor, Manager

9003 **New Pond Village**
180 Main Street
Walpole, MA 02081-4020
508-660-1555
Fax: 508-668-8893

Peter Welsh, President

9004 **Norumbega Point at Weston**
99 Norumbega Road
Weston, MA 02493-2482
781-899-5505
Fax: 781-899-3673

Betsy O'Brien, Executive Director

9005 **Orchard Hill At Sudbury**
761 Boston Post Road
Sudbury, MA 01776-3384
978-443-0080
Fax: 978-443-7277

Clifford T Hughes, Owner

9006 **Orchard Valley at Wilbraham**
2387 Boston Road
Wilbraham, MA 01095-1246
413-596-0006
Fax: 413-596-4181

Nancy Harper, Manager

9007 **Pinehill at Kimball Farms**
235 Walker Street
Lenox, MA 01240-2762
413-637-7000
Fax: 413-637-7277

Albert Ingegni, Executive Director

9008 **Pines of Tewksbury**
2580 Main Street
Tewksbury, MA 01876-3155
978-657-0800
Fax: 978-657-8087

Jennifer King, Executive Director

9009 **Plymouth Crossings**
157 South Street
Plymouth, MA 02360-7605
508-830-4744
Fax: 508-830-4748

Susan Lubke, Executive Director

9010 **Reeds Landing**
807 Wilbraham Road
Springfield, MA 01109-2067
413-782-1800
Fax: 413-782-8083

Matthew Leahey, Executive Director

9011 **Renaissance Gardens at Brooksby Village**
400 Brooksby Village Drive
Peabody, MA 01960-1447
978-536-7920
Fax: 978-536-7922
http://www.thecareexperts.com

Deb Laflamme, Health Care Counselor

Features all private Assisted Living apartments and all private Long-Term Care rooms; full-time, on-site staff doctors with nurses on duty 24-hours a day. Short-Time Rehab (physical, speech and occupational therapy); dementia and Alzheimer's care also available. Renaissance Gardens, the choice you can feel good about.

9012 **Ruth's House**
780 Converse Street
Longmeadow, MA 01106-1719
413-567-6212
Fax: 413-567-4380

Linda Donoghue, Manager

9013 **Salisbury Assisted Living Center**
19 Beach Road
Salisbury, MA 01952-2014
978-463-9809
Fax: 978-463-3009

Arthur Signorelli, President

9014 **Sarawood Retirement Home**
1 Loomis Avenue
Holyoke, MA 01040-2000
413-532-7879
Fax: 413-535-2015

William G Lyons, Owner

9015 **Scandinavian Living Center**
206 Waltham Street
Newton, MA 02465-1733
617-527-6566
Fax: 617-527-2078

Joseph Carella, Executive Director

9016 **Shrewsbury Crossing**
311 Main Street
Shrewsbury, MA 01545-2298
508-845-2100
Fax: 508-845-2101

Robert Moran, Executive Director

9017 **Southgate at Shrewsbury**
30 Julio Drive
Shrewsbury, MA 01545-3054
508-842-8331
Fax: 508-842-8331

Donald Flanagan, President

9018 **Springhouse Retirement Community**
46 Allandale Street
Boston, MA 02130-3466
617-522-0043
Fax: 617-522-0893
e-mail: sguhman@springhouse.info.org
http://www.springhouseinfo.org

Catherine Gouhman, Marketing Director
Kathy Sigman, Executive Director

9019 **Standish Village at Lower Mills**
1190 Adams Street
Dorchester Center, MA 02124-5772
617-298-5656
Fax: 617-298-2508

Kim Diaz, Executive Director

9020 **Sunrise Assisted Living at Gardner Park**
73 Margin Street
Peabody, MA 01960-1877
978-532-3200
Fax: 978-532-3211

Carol Styczo, Executive Director

Assisted Living Facilities/Michigan

9021 Sunrise Assisted Living of Cohasset
125 King Street
Cohasset, MA 02025-1364
781-383-6300
Fax: 781-383-2830

Denise Baxter, Executive Director

9022 Sunrise Assisted Living of Norwood
86 Saunders Road
Norwood, MA 02062-3249
781-762-1333
Fax: 781-255-7493

Patricia Blackburn, Executive Director

9023 Sunrise Assisted Living of Wayland
285 Commonwealth Road
Wayland, MA 01778-5042
508-652-6300
Fax: 508-655-6608

Eileen Mahoney, Executive Director

9024 Tatnuck Park at Worcester
340 May Street
Worcester, MA 01602-1800
508-755-7277
Fax: 508-755-6333

Lonna Greco, Executive Director

9025 Traditions of Wayland
10 Green Way
Wayland, MA 01778-2616
508-358-0700
Fax: 508-358-4726

Judy Huber, Executive Director

9026 Victorian of Chatham
389 Orleans Road
Chatham, MA 02633
508-945-1211
Fax: 508-945-2245

Ann Lavalle, Executive Director

9027 Village at Farm Pond
200 W Farm Pond Road
Framingham, MA 01702-6286
508-628-7700
Fax: 508-620-6580

Roald Rolfson, Executive Director

9028 Village at Willow Crossings
25 Cobb Street
Mansfield, MA 02048-2541
508-261-1333
Fax: 508-261-8844

Don Walsh, Executive Director

9029 Westfield Meadows
74 Old Holyoke Road
Westfield, MA 01085-1487
413-562-6940
Fax: 413-564-0175

Mary Ellen Morissette, Resident Manager
John Shannon, Owner

Westfield Meadows is an Assisted Living Residence, licensed by the Commonwealth of Massachsetts providing 24 hour service, three meals per day, laundry service and other needs to all Tenants which include Medicaid eligible individuals.

9030 Whitcomb House
245 West Street
Milford, MA 01757-2201
508-634-2440
Fax: 508-473-6366

Chris Dulaney, Owner

9031 Whitehall Estate
790 Falmouth Road
Hyannis, MA 02601-2397
508-790-7666
Fax: 508-790-7667

Patricia Herlihy, Executive Director

9032 Whitney Place at Natick
3 Vision Drive
Natick, MA 01760-2078
508-655-9767
800-372-3800
Fax: 508-655-1661

Donna Deleo, Manager

9033 Whitney Place at Northbridge
85 Beaumont Drive
Northbridge, MA 01534-1093
508-234-6481
Fax: 508-234-2635

9034 Woodbridge Assisted Living
240 Lynnfield Street
Peabody, MA 01960-5052
978-532-4411
Fax: 978-532-2407

Harriet Flashenberg, Executive Director

9035 Woods at Eddy Pond
667 Washington Street
Auburn, MA 01501-2722
508-832-2200
Fax: 508-832-8488

Steven Sacco, Executive Director

9036 Youville House Assisted Living Residence
1573 Cambridge Street
Cambridge, MA 02138-4377
617-491-1234
Fax: 617-491-8838

Joanne Parsons, Executive Director

9037 Youville Place
10 Pelham Road
Lexington, MA 02421-8400
781-861-3535
Fax: 781-862-4289

Joanne Scianna, Manager

Michigan

9038 Ann Arbor Center for Independent Living
2568 Packard Street
Ann Arbor, MI 48104-6852
734-971-0277
Fax: 734-971-0826
http://www.aacil.org

James K Magyar, President/CEO
Tom Hoatlin, Director Development

The Ann Arbor Center for Independent Living assists people with disabilities and their families in living full and productive lives. Our mission is to assure the equality of opportunity, full participation, independent living and economic self-sufficiency of people with disabilities in our community.

9039 Argentine Care Center
9051 Silver Lake Road
Linden, MI 48451-9730
810-735-9487
Fax: 810-735-9035

Emil Kovacs, Owner

9040 Arnold Home
485 Central Avenue NE
Cleveland, TN 37311-5541
313-531-4001
Fax: 313-531-1477

9041 Burcham Hills Retirement Center
2700 Burcham Drive
East Lansing, MI 48823-3898
517-351-8377
Fax: 517-351-1738

Pam Ditri, Executive Director

Assisted Living Facilities/Michigan

9042 CQC Stephenson Home
120 N Locust Street
Adrian, MI 49221-2855
517-265-8185
Fax: 517-265-8186

Theresa Chang, Administrator

9043 Cherrywood Nursing & Living Center
2372 Fiften Mile Road
Sterling Heights, MI 48310
586-978-2280
Fax: 810-978-8407

Greg Trombley, Administrator

9044 Clark Retirement Home
1551 Franklin Street SE
Grand Rapids, MI 49506-8203
616-452-1568
Fax: 616-452-0428

Robert Perl, Executive Director

9045 Countryside Care Center
2121 Robinson Road
Jackson, MI 49203-3680
517-787-4150
Fax: 517-782-2936

John Ganton, Owner

9046 Covenant Village of the Great Lakes
2520 Lake Michigan Drive NW
Grand Rapids, MI 49504-4696
616-735-4541
Fax: 616-735-4546
e-mail: dlmay@covenantretiremant.org
http://www.covenantretirement.com

Steven Karnes, Campus Administrator
Deborah May, Marketing Director

9047 Cumberland Manor
11535 Fulton Street E
Lowell, MI 49331-9121
616-897-8413
Fax: 616-897-4884

Melissa Chambers, Administrator

9048 Fairview Living Centre
441 E Main Street
Centreville, MI 49032-9626
269-467-9575
Fax: 616-467-7077

Vickie Cox, Executive Director

9049 Fountains at Franklin
28301 Franklin Road
Southfield, MI 48034-1672
248-353-2810
Fax: 248-368-1874

Cathy Lubanski, Executive Director

Offers different and better choices for extraordinary assisted living.

9050 Fraser Villa: A Mercy Living Center
33300 Utica Road
Fraser, MI 48026-2017
586-293-3300
Fax: 582-293-6949

Gail Fliwinski, Administrator

9051 Gilbert Residence
203 S Huron Street
Ypsilanti, MI 48197-5422
734-482-9498
Fax: 734-482-1848

Maryjo Gibbons, Administrator

9052 Glacier Hills Retirement Center
1200 Earhart Road
Ann Arbor, MI 48105-2768
734-663-5202
Fax: 734-769-0058

Julia Van De Car, Manager

9053 Hazel I Findlay Country Manor
1101 S Scott Road
Saint Johns, MI 48879-9039
989-224-8936
Fax: 989-224-9423

Mary Ann Bond, Administrator

9054 Heartland HCC-Crestview
625 36th Street SW
Wyoming, MI 49509-4004
616-531-0200
Fax: 616-531-1385

Deborah Gross, Administrator

9055 Hume Home of Muskegon
1244 W Southern Avenue
Muskegon, MI 49441-2271
231-755-1715
Fax: 231-755-1715

Barbara Betts, Administrator

9056 Ingham Regional Assisted Living
6429 Earlington Lane
Lansing, MI 48917-8279
517-321-3391
Fax: 517-321-3646

Lolaurie Shepard, Executive Director

9057 Jackson Friendly Home
435 W North Street
Jackson, MI 49202-3390
517-782-2616
Fax: 517-784-1235

Donna Luckadoo, Administrator

9058 John George Home
1501 E Ganson Street
Jackson, MI 49202-3593
517-783-4134
Fax: 517-783-0872

Karrie Good, Administrator

9059 Laurel Park West
38910 6 Mile Road
Livonia, MI 48152-2697
734-464-2772
Fax: 734-464-8154

Narain Raisinghani, Administrator

9060 Luther Village
2000 32nd Street SE
Grand Rapids, MI 49508-7910
616-452-6084
Fax: 616-452-0706

Sue Lemon, Executive Director

9061 Maple Village
6257 Telegraph Road
Bloomfield Hills, MI 48301-1622
248-723-6275
Fax: 248-593-5148

Forrest Graves, Executive Director

9062 McLaren Homewood Village
4444 W Court Street
Flint, MI 48532-4329
810-720-5184
Fax: 810-720-5187
http://www.arclp.com

Deanna Colby, Executive Director
Teresa McCulloch Stilson, Community Relations Coordinator
Tina Olshove, Wellness Director

Assisted Living and Alzheimer's/Dementia community.

9063 Meadows at Silver Maples
200 Silver Maples Drive
Chelsea, MI 48118-1192
734-475-4111
Fax: 734-475-4112

Jerry Wilcznski, CEO

Assisted Living Facilities/Michigan

9064 **Mercy Pavilion of Battle Creek**
80 N 20th Street
Battle Creek, MI 49015-1796
269-964-5400
Fax: 616-964-5559

Jackie Zimmerman, Administrator

9065 **Michigan Christian Home**
1845 Boston Street SE
Grand Rapids, MI 49506-4400
616-245-9179
Fax: 616-245-0572

Sue Vander Werf, Administrator

9066 **Michigan Department of Labor Commission for the Blind: Center for Independent Living Program for Elderly**
PO Box 30652
Lansing, MI 48909-8152
517-373-2062
Fax: 517-335-5140

Patrick Cannon, Executive Director

9067 **Northpointe Woods Assisted Living**
700 N Avenue G
Battle Creek, MI 49017
269-964-7625
Fax: 616-964-4973

Nancy Kruse, Executive Director

9068 **Park Village Pines**
2920 Crystal Lane
Kalamazoo, MI 49009-2195
269-372-1928
Fax: 616-372-0638

Wilson Haarsma, Executive Director

9069 **Pilgram Manor**
2000 Leonard Street NE
Grand Rapids, MI 49505-5894
616-458-1133
Fax: 616-458-8900

Karen Messick, Administrator

9070 **Plymouth Inn**
205 N Haggerty Road
Plymouth, MI 48170-6131
734-451-0700
Fax: 734-451-0727

William Gala, Manager

9071 **Porter Hills Presbyterian Village**
3600 E Fulton Street
Grand Rapids, MI 49546-1322
616-949-4971
Fax: 616-954-1795

Bette Morris, Executive Director

9072 **Presbyterian Village Redford**
17383 Garfield
Redford, MI 48240-2195
313-541-6000
Fax: 313-531-6820

9073 **Renaissance Gardens at Henry FordVillage**
15101 Ford Road
Dearborn, MI 48126-4611
313-584-1700
Fax: 313-846-7731
http://www.thecareexperts.com

Kristine Anderson, Health Care Counselor
Larry Vidovish, President

Features all private Assisted Living apartments and all private Long-Term Care rooms; full-time, on-site staff doctors with nurses on duty 24-hours a day. Short-Time Rehab (physical, speech and occupational therapy); dementia and Alzheimer's care also available. Renaissance Gardens, the choice you can feel good about.

9074 **Rest Haven Home**
1424 Union Avenue NE
Grand Rapids, MI 49505-5152
616-363-6819
Fax: 616-363-1658

Brian Wilson, Administrator

9075 **Riverview Manor**
55378 Wilbur Road
Three Rivers, MI 49093-8815
269-279-7441
Fax: 616-278-1222

Jennifer Beam, Administrator

9076 **Rose Garden Home**
3391 Prairie Street SW
Grandville, MI 49418-1992
616-538-1914
Fax: 616-831-2444

Sue Wedekind, Executive Director

9077 **Saginaw Geriatrics Home**
1413 Gratiot Avenue
Saginaw, MI 48602-2699
989-793-3471
Fax: 989-793-7090

George Pike, Administrator

9078 **St Ann's Home**
2161 Leonard Street NW
Grand Rapids, MI 49504-3891
616-453-7715
Fax: 616-453-7359

Steve Rolston, Administrator

9079 **St Anne's Mead Retirement Home**
16106 W 12 Mile Road
Southfield, MI 48076-2974
248-557-1221
Fax: 248-557-4744

Rick Mehrer, Administrator

9080 **St Joesph's Home for the Aged**
4800 Cadieux Road
Detroit, MI 48224-2293
313-882-3800
Fax: 313-882-6944

Carolyn Ford, Administrator

9081 **Sunrise Assisted Living at Farmington Hills**
29681 Middlebelt Road
Farmington Hills, MI 48334-2313
248-538-9200
Fax: 248-538-0411

Patricia Henning, Executive Director

9082 **Sunrise Assisted Living at Northville**
16100 N Haggerty Road
Plymouth, MI 48170-4857
734-420-4000
Fax: 734-420-5468

Tricia McTaggart, Manager

9083 **Sunrise Assisted Living of Ann Arbor**
2190 Ann Arbor Saline Road
Ann Arbor, MI 48103-9710
734-327-1350
Fax: 734-327-1351

9084 **Sunrise Assisted Living of Rochester**
500 E University Drive
Rochester, MI 48307-2110
248-601-9000
Fax: 248-601-9001

Karen Parrott, Executive Director

9085 **Sunrise Assisted Living of Troy**
6870 Crooks Road
Troy, MI 48098-1704
248-293-1200
Fax: 248-293-1201

Kathy Szajna, Executive Director

Assisted Living Facilities/Minnesota

9086 **Sunrise Assisted Living of WestBloomfield**
7005 Pontiac Trl
W Bloomfield, MI 48323-2181   248-738-8101
                                Fax: 248-738-8177
                http://www.sunriseseniorliving.com
Suzanne Withorn, Executive Director
Assisted living and memory care.

9087 **Thurston Woods Village: The Villa**
307 N Franks Avenue
Sturgis, MI 49091-1298   269-651-7841
                                Fax: 616-651-2050
Theo Omo, CEO

9088 **Waltonwood of Royal Oak**
2450 W 13 Mile Road
Royal Oak, MI 48073-3004   248-549-6400
                                Fax: 248-549-6426
Jean Brace, Administrator

9089 **Woodhaven Retirement Community**
29667 Wentworth Street
Livonia, MI 48154-6231   734-261-9000
                                Fax: 734-261-9003
Randy Gasser, Executive Director

9090 **Woodside at Friendship Village**
1390 N Drake Road
Kalamazoo, MI 49006-3940   269-381-8837
                                Fax: 616-381-7129
Stan Clouse, CEO
Assisted living is an ideal solution for people who wish to maintain their privacy and independence yet receive the help they need with daily life.

Minnesota

9091 **Agape Senior Homes**
15000 Orchard Drive
Burnsville, MN 55306-4913   952-435-6203
                                Fax: 952-435-6203

9092 **Alliance Assisted Living Services**
2204 E 117th Street
Burnsville, MN 55337-1265   952-882-1030
                                Fax: 952-882-1477

9093 **Almond House**
802 28th Street SE
Brainerd, MN 56401-6308   218-825-9255
                                Fax: 218-822-3068
Sue Johnson, Owner

9094 **Alterra Clare Bridge Cottage of West St Paul**
315 Thompson Avenue E
West Saint Paul, MN 55118-3239   651-453-1805
                                Fax: 651-453-1806
Gayle Sajewicz, Executive Director
Alterra Sterling House is an assisted living residence that provides housing and assistance to older adults who want to retain their independence while receiving the daily support they need. The intimate setting for those with limited mobility, as well as specialized programming, help residents maximize independence and quality of life.

9095 **Alterra Clare Bridge Cottage-Coon Rapids**
1770 113th Lane NW
Coon Rapids, MN 55433-3019   763-754-2800
                                Fax: 763-754-4800

9096 **Alterra Clare Bridge Cottage-Owatonna**
364 Cedardale Drive SE
Owatonna, MN 55060-4467   507-446-8600
                                Fax: 507-446-8601
Emily Shelstad, Executive Director
Alterra Sterling House is an assisted living residence that provides housing and assistance to older adults who want to retain their independence while receiving the daily support they need. The intimate setting for those with limited mobility, as well as specialized programming, help residents maximize independence and quality of life.

9097 **Alterra Clare Bridge of Eagan**
1365 Crestridge Lane
Eagan, MN 55123-1042   651-686-5557
                                Fax: 651-686-7778
Andrea Schroetke, Executive Director
Alterra Sterling House is an assisted living residence that provides housing and assistance to older adults who want to retain their independence while receiving the daily support they need. The intimate setting for those with limited mobility, as well as specialized programming, help residents maximize independence and quality of life.

9098 **Alterra Clare Bridge of North Oaks**
300 Village Center Drive
North Oaks, MN 55127-3021   651-482-8111
                                Fax: 651-482-8333
Alterra Sterling House is an assisted living residence that provides housing and assistance to older adults who want to retain their independence while receiving the daily support they need. The intimate setting for those with limited mobility, as well as specialized programming, help residents maximize independence and quality of life.

9099 **Alterra Clare Bridge of Plymouth**
15855 22nd Avenue N
Plymouth, MN 55447-6452   763-476-8200
                                Fax: 763-476-5900
Heather Roduenz, Executive Director
Alterra Sterling House is an assisted living residence that provides housing and assistance to older adults who want to retain their independence while receiving the daily support they need. The intimate setting for those with limited mobility, as well as specialized programming, help residents maximize independence and quality of life.

9100 **Alterra Sterling House of Apple Valley**
14625 Pennock Avenue
Apple Valley, MN 55124-3502   952-891-2711
                                Fax: 952-953-3132
Janis Rivers, Administrator

9101 **Alterra Sterling House of Blaine**
1005 Paul Parkway NE
Blaine, MN 55434-3926   763-755-2800
                                Fax: 763-755-6400
Joy Williams, Executive Director
Alterra Sterling House is an assisted living residence that provides housing and assistance to older adults who want to retain their independence while receiving the daily support they need. The intimate setting for those with limited mobility, as well as specialized programming, help residents maximize independence and quality of life.

9102 **Alterra Sterling House of Coon Rapids**
11372 Robinson Drive NW
Coon Rapids, MN 55433-3776   763-754-3500
                                Fax: 763-754-3700
Jennifer Frazer-John, Manager

Assisted Living Facilities/Minnesota

9103 Alterra Sterling House of Faribault
935 Spring Road
Faribault, MN 55021-6975
507-333-2559
Fax: 507-333-2557
Jeff Treml, Manager
Alterra Sterling House is an assisted living residence that provides housing and assistance to older adults who want to retain their independence while receiving the daily support they need. The intimate setting for those with limited mobility, as well as specialized programming, help residents maximize independence and quality of life.

9104 Alterra Sterling House of Inver Grove Heights
5891 Carmen Avenue
Inver Grove Heights, MN 55076-4414
651-306-0919
Fax: 651-306-1020
Jeannie Gatlin, Manager
Alterra Sterling House is an assisted living residence that provides housing and assistance to older adults who want to retain their independence while receiving the daily support they need. The intimate setting for those with limited mobility, as well as specialized programming, help residents maximize independence and quality of life.

9105 Alterra Sterling House of West St Paul
305 Thompson Avenue E
West Saint Paul, MN 55118-3239
651-453-1803
Fax: 651-453-1804
Mary Bryan-Day, Manager
Alterra Sterling House is an assisted living residence that provides housing and assistance to older adults who want to retain their independence while receiving the daily support they need. The intimate setting for those with limited mobility, as well as specialized programming, help residents maximize independence and quality of life.

9106 Alterra Sterling House-Brooklyn Center
6001 Earle Brown Drive
Brooklyn Center, MN 55430-2522
763-566-1495
Fax: 763-566-1625
Anne Nowatzki, Administrator

9107 Alterra Sterling House-Mankato
100 Teton Lane
Mankato, MN 56001-4827
507-386-1779
Fax: 507-386-1174
Shawn Soucek, Executive Director
Alterra Sterling House is an assisted living residence that provides housing and assistance to older adults who want to retain their independence while receiving the daily support they need. The intimate setting for those with limited mobility, as well as specialized programming, help residents maximize independence and quality of life.

9108 Alterra Sterling House-Sauk Rapids
1325 Summit Avenue N
Sauk Rapids, MN 56379-2545
320-203-8142
Fax: 320-203-8207
Amanda Chirsten, Manager
Alterra Sterling House is an assisted living residence that provides housing and assistance to older adults who want to retain their independence while receiving the daily support they need. The intimate setting for those with limited mobility, as well as specialized programming, help residents maximize independence and quality of life.

9109 Alterra Sterling House-Willmar
1501 19th Avenue SW
Willmar, MN 56201-4940
320-235-1024
Fax: 507-451-7083
Lois Isley
Alterra Sterling House is an assisted living residence that provides housing and assistance to older adults who want to retain their independence while receiving the daily support they need. The intimate setting for those with limited mobility, as well as specialized programming, help residents maximize independence and quality of life.

9110 Alterra Sterling House-Winona
835 E Belleview Street
Winona, MN 55987-4502
507-454-3090
Fax: 507-454-5466
Bernadette Merchlewitz, Manager
Alterra Sterling House is an assisted living residence that provides housing and assistance to older adults who want to retain their independence while receiving the daily support they need. The intimate setting for those with limited mobility, as well as specialized programming, help residents maximize independence and quality of life.

9111 Alterra Sterling-Owatonna
334 Cedardale Drive SE
Owatonna, MN 55060-4467
507-451-6914
Fax: 507-451-7083
Deidra Burke, Executive Director
Alterra Sterling House is an assisted living residence that provides housing and assistance to older adults who want to retain their independence while receiving the daily support they need. The intimate setting for those with limited mobility, as well as specialized programming, help residents maximize independence and quality of life.

9112 Alterra Wynwood of Rochester
3035 Salem Meadows Dr SW
Rochester, MN 55902-2847
507-252-5400
Fax: 507-252-5500
Cheryl Saballa, Executive Director

9113 Arlington Place
21 16th Avenue SE
Saint Joseph, MN 56374-9789
320-363-1313
Fax: 320-363-1313
Mary Hawkins, Executive Director

9114 Arrowhead Senior Living Community
601 Grant Avenue
Eveleth, MN 55734-1314
218-741-9800
Fax: 218-749-8929

9115 Assisted Living in Heritage Hall
11501 Masonic Home Drive
Minneapolis, MN 55437-3661
952-948-7000
Fax: 952-948-6210

9116 Assumption Court
615 N 1st Street
Shakopee, MN 55379
952-445-2123
Fax: 952-496-2013

9117 Assured Care
206 Mallard Drive
Shakopee, MN 55379-9375
952-445-2123
Fax: 952-496-2013

9118 Auburn Courts
501 Oak Street N
Chaska, MN 55318-2646
952-448-9303
Fax: 952-892-0305
Wayne Ward, Administrator

9119 Barrett Assisted Living Community
800 Spruce Avenue
Barrett, MN 56311-4505
320-528-2371
Fax: 320-528-2642
Vern Junker, Owner

Assisted Living Facilities/Minnesota

9120 Barross House
414 1st Avenue
Two Harbors, MN 55616-1614
218-834-6174
Fax: 218-834-6174

Mary Prestidge, Owner

9121 Brickford Cottage
4020 Indian Hills Drive
Saint Paul, MN 55108
712-239-2065
Fax: 712-239-3417

9122 Brookridge
180 Sunset Avenue NW
Cokato, MN 55321-9601
320-286-2158
Fax: 320-286-3163

Deb Loe, Manager
9500 pages

9123 Brooks of St Paul
2480 Saint Paul Road
Owatonna, MN 55060-2455
507-446-5855
Fax: 507-446-5858

Sue Doty, Manager

9124 Bryant House
5515 Bryant Street
Maple Plain, MN 55359-9446
763-479-3655
Fax: 763-479-3656

Kay Olson, Manager

9125 Burnsdale Extended Care
540 Southtown Plaza
Montevideo, MN 56265-2104
320-269-6640
Fax: 320-269-7789

Tami Dorenkamper, Manager

9126 Callista Court
1455 W Broadway Street
Winona, MN 55987-2392
507-457-0280
Fax: 507-494-5117

Sue Wilber, Manager

9127 Care Pointe
1995 Oakcrest Avenue
Roseville, MN 55113-2605
651-636-5633
Fax: 651-636-5655

9128 Care-Age Country Home
18846 Eagle Bend Road
Park Rapids, MN 56470-2073
218-732-3721
Fax: 218-732-1208

Chris Niemeyer, Owner

9129 Carefree Living America-Brainerd
2723 Oak Street
Brainerd, MN 56401-3818
218-829-8622
Fax: 218-829-4463

Angela Sandelin, Manager

9130 Carefree Living America-Burnsville
600 E Nicollet Boulevard
Burnsville, MN 55337-6739
952-892-5559
Fax: 952-892-1585

Tim McLain, Manager

9131 Carefree Living of America-St Cloud
1225 E Division Street
Saint Cloud, MN 56304
320-251-6483
Fax: 320-251-2714

Linda Corrigan, Manager

9132 Carric Manor
9530 Kingswood Drive
Chaska, MN 55318-9364
952-443-2308
Fax: 952-443-2002

9133 Cartens Harbour
436 6th Avenue SW
Cambridge, MN 55008-1815
763-552-1340
Fax: 763-689-5470

David Scofield, Owner

9134 Catholic Eldercare at Home
817 Main Street NE
Minneapolis, MN 55413-1900
612-379-1370
Fax: 612-362-2449

Paula Finn, Executive Director

9135 Cedar Crest Estate
225 Shady Ridge Road NW
Hutchinson, MN 55350-1407
320-587-7077
Fax: 320-587-4299

Roz Ewald, Owner

9136 Cedars of Austin
700 1st Drive NW
Austin, MN 55912-3095
507-437-3246
Fax: 507-437-3248

Clark Cipra, Manager

9137 Centennial Villa Assisted Living
660 Park Street E
Annandale, MN 55302-3057
320-274-5031
Fax: 320-274-3631

9138 Central Todd County Care Center
406 Highway 71 E
Clarissa, MN 56440-2000
218-756-3636
Fax: 218-756-3639

Margaret Taggart, Administrator

9139 Chandler Place
3701 Chandler Drive NE
Minneapolis, MN 55421-4413
612-788-7321
Fax: 612-913-5370

Mark Anderson, Administrator

9140 Chappys Golden Shore
604 Summit Avenue NE
Hill City, MN 55748-9616
218-697-2705
Fax: 218-697-8145

9141 Claddagh House
333 S 2nd Street
Ofc
La Crescent, MN 55947-1608
507-895-4134
Fax: 507-895-9239

9142 Clearwater Suites Assisted Living
1902 7th Avenue E
Alexandria, MN 56308-2364
320-759-2121
Fax: 320-759-2120

Doris Denal, Director Operations

9143 Commons on Marice
1380 Marice Drive
Eagan, MN 55121-9748
651-688-9999
Fax: 651-688-7888

Mary Yeager, Executive Director

739

Assisted Living Facilities/Minnesota

9144 Community Assisted Living
912 4th Street
Farmington, MN 55024-1523
651-460-6762
Fax: 651-460-2217

Chris Helgeson, Manager

9145 Copperfield Hill Phase II
4020 Lakeland Avenue N
Robbinsdale, MN 55422-5800
763-533-1268
Fax: 763-533-6146

Shae Rodger, Executive Director

9146 Country Care Homes
5384 Country Care Lane
Pequot Lakes, MN 56472-3360
218-568-7375
Fax: 218-568-5401

9147 Country Neighbors
206 3rd Avenue SE
Mapleton, MN 56065-9746
507-524-4990
Fax: 507-524-3239

Traci A Birr, Manager

9148 Country Neighbors-Lake Crystal
511 W Blue Earth Street
Lake Crystal, MN 56055-9401
507-726-6537
Fax: 507-726-2402

9149 Country Neighbors-Le Center
175 E Derrynane Street
Le Center, MN 56057-1603
507-357-4104
Fax: 651-766-4310

Anne Casper, Manager

9150 Country Oaks Elder Care
Rr 4
Pine City, MN 55063
320-629-1296
Fax: 320-629-1296

9151 Country Villa
7475 Country Club Drive
Minneapolis, MN 55427-4622
763-512-1579
Fax: 763-540-6899
e-mail: asamrock@extendicare.com
http://www.countryv.com

Arlene Samrock, Marketing Director
Ned Ammons, Manager
Assisted living community.

9152 Dignified Living
PO Box 273
Prior Lake, MN 55372
952-440-1563
Fax: 952-447-0422

Kathy Bolton-Iverson, Manager

9153 Dignified Living-Prior Lake
16728 Lyons Avenue SE
Prior Lake, MN 55372-2930
952-440-1563
Fax: 952-447-0422

Kathy Bolton-Iverson, Manager

9154 Edgewood Vista
4195 Westberg Road
Hermantown, MN 55811-3916
218-723-8905
Fax: 218-723-4051

Carolyn Fisher, Administrator

9155 Edgewood Vista-Virginia
705 17th Street N
Virginia, MN 55792-2176
218-741-7106
Fax: 218-741-7229

Julie Winans, Administrator

9156 Elder Haven Homes
367 4th Street SW
Forest Lake, MN 55025-1539
651-464-0899
Fax: 651-464-3861

Brenda Ward, Owner

9157 Emerald Care
13409 Lake Street Extension
Minnetonka, MN 55305-4905
952-908-2205
Fax: 952-936-0794

9158 English Rose Suites
7409 Gleason Road
Minneapolis, MN 55439-2557
952-983-0412
Fax: 952-938-2548

Jayne Clairmont, Owner

9159 Evergreen Knoll
1309 14th Street
Cloquet, MN 55720-2562
218-878-3302
Fax: 218-878-3340

Terri Langevin, Manager

9160 Evergreens of Moorhead
512 3rd Avenue S
Moorhead, MN 56560-2703
218-233-1535
Fax: 218-291-1162

Michelle Seibel, Manager

9161 Four Star
600 18th Avenue N
South St Paul, MN 55075-1533
651-739-1409
Fax: 651-731-5210

9162 Franciscan Assisted Living
1925 Norfolk Avenue
Saint Paul, MN 55116-2667
651-696-8411
Fax: 651-696-8404

9163 Garden Cottage Assisted Living
500 1st Avenue SE
Stewartville, MN 55976-1281
507-533-8990
Fax: 507-533-9220

Janice Carr, Owner

9164 Gianna Homes-Sursum Corda
4605 Fairhills Road E
Minnetonka, MN 55345-3502
952-988-0953
Fax: 952-988-6935

Anne Marie Hansen, Owner

9165 Golden Manor
21751 NW Pickerel Lake Road
Detroit Lakes, MN 56501-7522
218-847-3195
Fax: 218-847-2770

9166 Golden Oaks Residence
5072 Jennifer Circle
Hermantown, MN 55811-1467
218-729-5014
Fax: 218-729-0319

Laura Bromme, Owner

9167 Grace Manor
6825 Gleason Road
Minneapolis, MN 55439-1602
612-789-1122
Fax: 612-781-8147

Adell Petsolt, President

Assisted Living Facilities/Minnesota

9168   **Grace Place**
630 Cedar Avenue S
Suite B-1
Minneapolis, MN 55454-1259
612-332-3483
Fax: 612-342-1341

Yoonju Park, Executive Director

9169   **Granite Falls Senior Services**
640 Center Avenue
Granite Falls, MN 56241-1719
320-564-3308
Fax: 320-269-9451

Tammy Tammen, Manager

9170   **Guardian Angels Elem HomeCare**
400 Evans Avenue NW
Elk River, MN 55330-2699
763-241-0654
Fax: 763-241-0274

Linda Olson, President

9171   **Health East Residence of South St Paul**
744 19th Avenue N
South St Paul, MN 55075-1360
651-326-6500
Fax: 651-326-6550

9172   **Healtheast Care Center-Marian St Paul**
200 Earl Street
Saint Paul, MN 55106-6714
651-771-2914
Fax: 651-714-4509

Jeff Thorne, Administrator

9173   **Healtheast Residence on Humboldt**
514 Humboldt Avenue
Saint Paul, MN 55107-4013
651-220-1700
Fax: 651-220-1724

Peter Schuna, Administrator

9174   **Healtheast Residence-White Bear Lake**
4615 2nd Avenue
White Bear Lake, MN 55110-3375
651-232-1867
Fax: 651-232-1878

Trudy Fuller, Manager

9175   **Heritage Home**
1711 Delton Avenue NW
Bemidji, MN 56601-2536
218-444-3047
Fax: 218-444-9060

Sherry Denault, Manager

9176   **Heritage House Assisted Living Facility**
5825 Saint Croix Avenue N
Golden Valley, MN 55422-4419
763-544-1555
Fax: 763-544-8032

Lynette Clausen, Manager

9177   **Heritage House of Bemidji**
1700 36th Street
Bemidji, MN 56601
218-444-1745
Fax: 218-444-1744

Jim Birchem, Owner

9178   **Heritage Manor**
602 Fair Avenue
Park Rapids, MN 56470-1394
218-237-7275
Fax: 218-237-1210

Pat Burkman, Manager

9179   **Hillcrest Rehabilitation & Healthcare Center**
15409 Wayzata Boulevard
Wayzata, MN 55391-1402
952-473-5466
Fax: 952-473-6842

Lisa Harrell, Executive Director

9180   **Hillside Homes of Duluth**
404 N 8th Avenue E
Duluth, MN 55805-2031
218-720-5890
Fax: 218-720-6022

Diane Lindsey, Executive Director

9181   **Homestead Place**
901 Highway 71 NE
Willmar, MN 56201-2654
320-235-5897
Fax: 320-231-0633

Catherine Johnson, Administrator

9182   **Hub City Developmental**
Linden & Front Street
Slayton, MN 56172
507-836-1055
Fax: 507-836-1075

Cathy Kor, Manager

9183   **Hyza Home**
1310 21st Street
Cloquet, MN 55720-3126
218-345-6999
Fax: 218-345-6999

9184   **Interim Assisted Care**
2200 University Avenue W
Suite 160
Saint Paul, MN 55114-8769
651-917-3634
Fax: 651-917-3620

Grace Boatman, Manager

9185   **Interim Healthcare**
330 Canal Park Drive
Duluth, MN 55802-2316
218-722-0053
Fax: 218-722-0318

Gary Halgren, Manager

9186   **Interlachen Senior Suites**
5240 Interlachen Boulevard
Edina, MN 55436-1427
952-848-8765
Fax: 952-848-8765

9187   **Intrepid USA-Becklund**
8421 Wayzata Boulevard
Suite 100
Golden Valley, MN 55426-1353
763-544-0315
Fax: 763-544-9406

Bruny Fullerton, Administrator

9188   **Island View Manor**
700 N Highway
71
Willmar, MN 56201
320-235-2447
Fax: 320-235-4974

Laural Reickman, Owner

9189   **Jasper Sunrise Village**
100 Robert Avenue N
Jasper, MN 56144-1219
507-348-8620
Fax: 507-348-6100

Laurel Ykema, Administrator

9190   **Johnson Park Place**
1011 E Elm Street
Redwood Falls, MN 56283-1300
507-627-8121
Fax: 507-637-4446

Sandi Reck, Manager

9191   **Jones Harrison Residence Assisted Living**
3700 Cedar Lake Avenue
Minneapolis, MN 55416-4240
612-920-2030
Fax: 612-225-1190

Joanne Buytendorp, Administrator

Assisted Living Facilities/Minnesota

9192 Just Like Home
PO Box 770
Albert Lea, MN 56007
507-373-4060
Fax: 507-373-1961

Rollie Keyeski, Manager

9193 Kenwood Heritage Living
400 15th Avenue SW
Austin, MN 55912-3232
507-437-4594
Fax: 507-434-7201

James Ingersoll, Administrator

9194 Kenwood Retirement Community
825 Summit Avenue
Minneapolis, MN 55403-4141
612-374-8100
Fax: 612-377-3600

Jared Schei, Executive Director

9195 Keystone Bluffs
2528 Trinity Road
Duluth, MN 55811-3315
218-727-2800
Fax: 218-727-2850

9196 Kingsway Assisted Living
311 Columbus Avenue N
New Prague, MN 56071-1700
952-758-5264
Fax: 952-758-5384

9197 Kinyon Residence
3000 W Owasso Boulevard
Saint Paul, MN 55113-2161
507-451-9190
Fax: 507-455-1618

9198 Knutson Place Apartments
801 Luther Place
Albert Lea, MN 56007-1500
507-373-8226
Fax: 507-373-8226

Peggy Vandersnick, Manager

9199 LSS/Westwind
315 6th Street SW
Little Falls, MN 56345-1529
320-632-2996
Fax: 320-632-2997

Sherrie Otremba, Manager

9200 La Bonnie Vie
6443 Westchester Circle
Minneapolis, MN 55427-4966
763-544-0200
Fax: 763-544-0202

Tammy Tuntilla, Owner

9201 Lafayette Good Samartian Assisted Living
251 7th Street
Lafayette, MN 56054-9782
507-228-8238
Fax: 507-228-8389

Lori Bussler, Administrator

9202 Lake Ridge Manor at Ebenezer Covenant Home
310 Lake Blvoulevard
Buffalo, MN 55313-1456
763-682-1434
Fax: 763-682-2973

Joel Nyquist, Administrator

9203 Lakeside Manor
4831 London Road
Duluth, MN 55804-2499
218-525-2784
Fax: 218-525-3411

Tom Kolar, Owner

9204 Lakeview Ranch Adult Foster Care
69516 213th Street
Darwin, MN 55324-6602
320-275-4610
Fax: 320-275-4028

Judy Berry, CEO

9205 Lakeview Retirement Residence
611 Lake Street NE
Warroad, MN 56763-2311
218-386-1235
Fax: 218-386-3548

Rod Kutter, Administrator

9206 Lakewood Pine Senior Housing
1702 Airport Road
Staples, MN 56479-3345
218-894-4460
Fax: 218-894-4453

9207 Laurel Lodge Assisted Living Home
6870 Schultz Drive NE
Remer, MN 56672-3221
218-566-4722
Fax: 218-566-4723

Debra Engen, Manager

9208 Laurels Edge
77 Stadium Road
Mankato, MN 56001-6099
507-387-2133
Fax: 507-387-1135

Mary Milbrath, Executive Director

9209 Life Care Concepts
1302 Oak Street
Brainerd, MN 56401-3730
218-829-0901
800-434-7569

Bobbie Lee Debros, Owner

9210 Lindenwood
812 Linden Street N
Northfield, MN 55057-1340
507-645-4126
Fax: 507-645-4126

Joy Melby, Manager

9211 Little House on Prairie
823 Prairie Avenue SW
Faribault, MN 55021-6663
507-334-8845
Fax: 507-334-8845

9212 Loving Residence
1760 Perlich Avenue
Red Wing, MN 55066-2978
651-388-7442
Fax: 651-385-0776

Sandy McDonald, Manager

9213 Lutheran Home-Cedar Haven
630 and 640 Reed Street
Mankato, MN 56001
507-625-1512
Fax: 507-388-6428

Mary Ann Snyder, Administrator

9214 Lutheran Memorial Retirement Center
PO Box 480
Twin Valley, MN 56584
218-584-5181
Fax: 218-584-5304

Dwight Fulie, Executive Director

9215 Lutheran Memorial Retirement Center-Brainerd
1008 S 10th Street
Brainerd, MN 56401-4172
218-828-4823
Fax: 218-828-0676

Assisted Living Facilities/Minnesota

9216 Lutheran Social Services
316 Sunrise Lane N
Atwater, MN 56209-1062
320-974-8538
Fax: 320-974-8538

9217 Madison Avenue Apartments
700 N Madison Street
Minneota, MN 56264-9373
507-872-5312
Fax: 507-872-5359

Cody Morris, Manager

9218 Manor House
722 N Pokegama Avenue
Grand Rapids, MN 55744-2661
218-326-3469
Fax: 218-326-5339

Sheila Bullock, Manager

9219 Maranatha Place
5415 69th Avenue N
Minneapolis, MN 55429-4508
763-569-4500

9220 Margaret Place
1555 118th Lane NW
Coon Rapids, MN 55448-7579
763-754-2505
Fax: 763-754-0332

Mary Tjosvole, Owner

9221 Martin Luther Manor
1401 E 100th Street
Bloomington, MN 55425-2614
952-948-5154
Fax: 952-888-5465

Sally Peterson, Manager

9222 May Creek Lodge Assisted Living
303 10th Street S
Walker, MN 56484
218-547-4515
Fax: 218-547-4713

Ann Noland, Owner

9223 McCarthy Manor
2221 N Arlington Avenue
Duluth, MN 55811-2029
218-722-1501
Fax: 218-722-1501

John Hansen, Administrator

9224 Meadow Woods
1301 E 100th Street
Bloomington, MN 55425-2625
952-888-1010
Fax: 952-888-4323

Bev Heise, Executive Director

9225 Meadowland Elder Care Home
Rr 1
Box 44a
Tenstrike, MN 56683
218-586-2710
Fax: 218-586-3746

Donna Stevens, Owner

9226 Meadows
117 2nd Street SE
Grand Meadow, MN 55936-1402
507-754-4000
Fax: 507-754-5224

Paula Lewis, Administrator

9227 Meadows of Worthington
1801 Collegeway
Worthington, MN 56187-3075
507-372-7838
Fax: 507-372-7804

Patricia Hendersciedt, Executive Director

9228 Meadows on Main
611 S Main Street
Renville, MN 56284-1816
320-329-3788
Fax: 320-329-3678

Jane Dikken, Manager

9229 Moorhead Manor
1710 13th Avenue N
Moorhead, MN 56560-1898
218-236-6286
Fax: 218-236-1632

Susan Christianson, Executive Director

9230 Mother Lucille Leisure Living
58 Ivy Avenue NE
Richmond, MN 56368-4506
320-597-2129
Fax: 320-597-4371

Kathy Schultz, Owner

9231 Mother of Mercy Nursing & Retirement Center
230 Church Avenue
Albany, MN 56307
320-845-2195
Fax: 320-845-7092

Bob Wikan, Administrator

9232 New Perspective of Minnesota
113 E Avenue
Mahtomedi, MN 55115-2225
651-407-9076
Fax: 651-407-9084

Kathy Mason, Administrator

9233 Nicollet Place
311 S Nicollet Street
Blue Earth, MN 56013-1347
507-526-3237
Fax: 507-653-4379

Mary Beyer, Owner

9234 North Oaks on Emerson
2929 Emerson Avenue N
Minneapolis, MN 55411-1300
612-521-2929
Fax: 612-287-3505

Deanna Winge, Manager

9235 Northfield Parkview
910 Cannon Valley Drive
Northfield, MN 55057-3300
507-645-6007
Fax: 507-645-0117

Kyle Nordine, Executive Director

9236 Northside Retirement Home
2004 8th Avenue N
Moorhead, MN 56560-1806
218-233-1583
Fax: 218-233-6046

Jennifer Young, Owner

9237 Oak Hill Living Center Assisted Living
1314 8th North Street
New Ulm, MN 56073-1554
507-359-3100
Fax: 507-354-2751

9238 Oak Park Place
1575 Hoover Drive
North Mankato, MN 56003-2667
507-387-2037
Fax: 507-387-6282

Dennis Hood, Owner

Assisted Living Facilities/Minnesota

9239 Oak Park Place-Albert Lea
1615 Bridge Avenue
Albert Lea, MN 56007-2111
507-373-5600
Fax: 507-373-1121
e-mail: oakpark2@lakes.com
Jessica Richards, Director Housing
Stephanie Erdman RN, Director Resident Care Services
Joyce Nixon, Exeuctive Director

Assisted living community with memory are providing independence when you want it and assistance when you need it.

9240 Oak Ridge Assisted Living-Hastings
1128 Bahls Drive
Hastings, MN 55033-4500
651-438-0418
Fax: 651-438-0419
Diane Fiala, Administrator

9241 Oak Ridge Place
6060 Oxboro Avenue N
Stillwater, MN 55082-6123
651-439-8034
Fax: 651-439-8305
David Smith, Manager

9242 Oakenwald Terrace
218 Winona Street SE
Chatfield, MN 55923-1238
507-867-3806
Fax: 507-867-3806
Marion Lund, Owner

9243 Oaks
945 Century Avenue SW
Hutchinson, MN 55350-3788
320-234-9791
Fax: 320-234-6008
Joyce Aakre, Executive Director

9244 On Golden Pond
PO Box 245
Cohasset, MN 55721
218-328-5235
Fax: 218-328-5235

9245 Osseo Gardens
525 2nd Street SE
Osseo, MN 55369-1658
763-476-0152
Fax: 763-476-6794

9246 Our Circle of Friends
18 6th Street NW
Faribault, MN 55021-4236
507-332-9731
Fax: 507-333-9052
Cheryl Glende, Owner

9247 Our Home, Your Home
609 Front Street
Henning, MN 56551
218-583-4428
Fax: 218-583-2504
Jody Lohse, Owner

9248 Our House
204 14th Street NW
Austin, MN 55912-4645
507-437-2179
Fax: 507-437-2310
Shannon Pacholl, Manager

9249 Our House Board and Lodge
1017 7th Street NW
Faribault, MN 55021-4724
507-334-6853
Fax: 507-332-0447
Deb Sonnek, Owner

9250 Park Lane Estates
111 Fillmore Place SE
Preston, MN 55965-1140
507-765-9986
Fax: 507-765-9987
Helen Winslow, Manager

9251 Park Place Senior Congregate Assisted Living
125 E Park Street
Owatonna, MN 55060-4067
507-451-0808
Fax: 507-446-8116
Jennifer Redman, Manager

9252 Parker Oaks Assisted Living
211 6th Street NW
Winnebago, MN 56098-1067
507-893-3171
Fax: 507-893-3174
Deb Barnes, Administrator

9253 Parkwood Apartments
505 S 2nd Street
Belview, MN 56214-1003
507-938-3020
Fax: 507-938-4110
Paula Pohlen, Manager

9254 Pines
1508 North Highway
Jackson, MN 56143-1095
507-847-5762
Fax: 507-847-5763
Mary Lou Drahota, Manager

9255 Pines Senior Care
575 9th Street
Pine City, MN 55063-1638
320-629-4904
Fax: 320-629-1296
Mark Schwope, Owner

9256 Pioneer Estates of Minnesota
8751 Preserve Boulevard
Eden Prairie, MN 55344-5301
952-914-0934
Fax: 952-943-2563
Karen Banning, Owner

9257 Pioneer Senior Cottages
1327 S Mabelle Avenue
Fergus Falls, MN 56537-3758
218-998-9677
Fax: 218-998-9972

9258 Prairie Senior Cottages-Alexandria
812 McKay Avenue
Alexandria, MN 56308-2362
320-763-8244
Fax: 320-763-8255
Jenny Jones, Executive Director

9259 Prairie Senior Cottages-Hutchinson
1310 Bradford Street SE
Hutchinson, MN 55350-3302
320-587-5508
Fax: 320-587-7419

9260 Prairie Senior Cottages-Willmar
1705 19th Avenue SW
Willmar, MN 56201-4944
320-235-6022
Fax: 320-235-6029
Becky Holmgrem, Executive Director

9261 Presbyterian Assisted Living Homecare
1910 County Road D W
Saint Paul, MN 55112-3503
651-631-6200
Fax: 651-631-6094
Scott Welter, Administrator

Assisted Living Facilities/Minnesota

9262 **Primrose**
1360 Adams Street
Mankato, MN 56001-4298
507-388-9292
Fax: 507-388-9292

Brooke Britton, Manager

9263 **Rakhma Peace Home**
4953 Aldrich Avenue S
Minneapolis, MN 55419-5352
612-824-2345
Fax: 612-824-3165

Janelle Johnson, Manager

9264 **Regina Retirement Center**
1175 Nininger Road
Hastings, MN 55033-1056
651-480-4100
Fax: 651-480-4212

Mark Wilson, CEO

9265 **Rem Canby Senior Services**
110 St Olaf Avenue N
Canby, MN 56220-1372
507-223-5633
Fax: 507-223-5659

Laurie Driessen, Executive Director

9266 **Rem Montevideo Senior Services**
542 S 1st Street
Montevideo, MN 56265-2104
320-269-6104
Fax: 320-269-9451

9267 **Rem Southview**
310 Haarfager Avenue S
Canby, MN 56220-1425
507-223-5633
Fax: 507-223-5659

Laurie Driessen, Executive Director

9268 **Reminiscence Home**
34388 County Road 233
Grand Rapids, MN 55744-5324
218-327-4954
Fax: 218-327-4954

Linda Carraevu, Owner

9269 **Richfield Senior Suites**
6808 3rd Avenue S
Richfield, MN 55423-2418
612-866-3961
Fax: 612-866-9303

Lavonne Seeman, Owner

9270 **Ridgeway on German**
715 S German Street
New Ulm, MN 56073-4403
507-354-7400
Fax: 507-359-5711

Kyla Franta, Manager

9271 **River Birch Residence**
231 Washington Street
Holdingford, MN 56340-9513
320-746-2540
Fax: 320-255-5383

Mary Edens, Manager

9272 **Rivers Edge Villa**
1406 Highway 71
International Falls, MN 56649-2183
218-283-5740
Fax: 218-283-9497

9273 **Roseview Court Care Agency**
425 N Badger Street
Caledonia, MN 55921-1567
507-725-2380
Fax: 507-724-5142

Mary Schmitz, Manager

9274 **Rosewood Estate-Highland**
750 Mississippi River Boulevard S
Saint Paul, MN 55116-1006
651-698-1111
Fax: 651-698-8688

Scott Mixer, Manager

9275 **Rosewood Estate-Maplewood**
1200 Lakewood Drive N
Saint Paul, MN 55119-7601
651-770-1111
Fax: 561-773-7399

Wendy Traffie, Manager

9276 **Rosewood Estates-Roseville**
2750 Victoria Street N
Roseville, MN 55113-2094
651-486-4100
Fax: 651-482-0429

9277 **Ruth Homes**
1306 Lincoln Lane
Hastings, MN 55033-1068
651-437-8446
Fax: 651-437-0265

Jane Hausman, Owner

9278 **Salmi Homes**
5482 Meadow Lane
Aurora, MN 55705-8329
218-638-2990
Fax: 218-744-5907

9279 **Samaritan Bethany Terrace**
24 8th Street NW
Rochester, MN 55901-6817
507-289-4031
Fax: 507-289-6001

Sue Knutson, Administrator

9280 **Senior Suites of New Brighton**
805 6th Avenue NW
Saint Paul, MN 55112-2717
651-633-7200
Fax: 651-697-7377

Michael Chies, Administrator

9281 **September House**
2140 Woodland Avenue
Duluth, MN 55803-2252
218-728-9065
Fax: 218-728-4815

9282 **Shade Tree Retirement Center**
115 4th Avenue S
Brownton, MN 55312-6432
320-328-5949
Fax: 320-328-2301

Ron Beltz, Owner

9283 **Shepherds Inn**
46 1st Avenue SW
Wells, MN 56097-1932
507-553-6271
Fax: 507-553-6830

Joe Mueller, Manager

9284 **Sibley Manor Assisted Living**
718 Mound Avenue
Mankato, MN 56001-1626
507-345-4576
Fax: 507-345-7943

James Gatchel, Executive Director

9285 **Skylight Gardens**
501 1st Street N
Saint Cloud, MN 56303-4705
320-259-4584
Fax: 320-259-6159

Michael Pattee, Manager

Assisted Living Facilities/Minnesota

9286 Solbakken
7733 W 99th Street Circle
Minneapolis, MN 55438-2079
952-943-8485
Fax: 952-943-2941

9287 Southview on Main
445 Main Street
Revere, MN 56166
507-752-7467
Fax: 507-752-7082

9288 Spectrum Community Health
14505 Minnetonka Drive
Minnetonka, MN 55345-2210
952-988-0011
Fax: 952-988-0151

Todd Klein, Manager

9289 Spectrum Community Health-Minneapolis
2021 E Hennepin Avenue
Suite 300
Minneapolis, MN 55413-2500
612-627-9177
Fax: 612-627-9122

9290 Spring Valley Estates
815 Memorial Drive
Spring Valley, MN 55975-1014
507-346-7381
Fax: 507-346-7903

Penny Solberg, Administrator

9291 St Anns Residence
330 E 3rd Street
Duluth, MN 55805-1846
218-727-8831
Fax: 218-727-8833

David Kern, Administrator

9292 St Benedicts Senior Community
1810 Minnesota Boulevard
Saint Cloud, MN 56304-2436
320-252-0010
Fax: 320-654-2351

Linda Doerr, Executive Director

9293 St Paul Urban League
401 Selby Avenue
Saint Paul, MN 55102-1797
651-224-5771
Fax: 651-224-8009

Willie Mae Wilson, President

9294 St Williams Foster Care
122 N McCornell Avenue
Parkers Prairie, MN 56361-4959
218-338-4671
Fax: 218-338-5917

Paul Baer, Administrator

9295 Sterling Park Commons
35 1st Avenue N
Waite Park, MN 56387-1225
320-252-7224
Fax: 320-252-5629

Carla Brunn, Manager

9296 Sterling Park Ridgeview
1009 10th Avenue NE
Sauk Rapids, MN 56379-9448
320-251-5228
Fax: 320-259-8964

Tina Roering, Manager

9297 Stevens Residence
3704 Cardinal Road
Minnetonka, MN 55345-2204
952-930-9144
Fax: 952-930-9184

9298 Sunrise Assisted Living of Buffalo
201 1st Street NE
Buffalo, MN 55313-1550
763-682-5489
Fax: 763-682-6511

Cheryl Klinkhammer, Executive Director

9299 Sunrise Assisted Living of Edina
7128 France Avenue S
Edina, MN 55435-4301
952-927-8000
Fax: 952-927-6400

Renae Witschen, Executive Director

9300 Sunrise Assisted Living-Roseville
255 Snelling Avenue N
Saint Paul, MN 55104-5327
651-636-4800
Fax: 651-636-4809

Anneliese Soldner, Executive Director

9301 Sunrise Cottage of Mankato
300 Bunting Lane
Mankato, MN 56001-7020
507-345-8787
Fax: 507-345-8870

Kim Alinder, Executive Director

9302 Sunrise Cottages of Rochester
4220 55th Street NW
Rochester, MN 55901-8900
507-286-8528
Fax: 507-286-8527

Alicia Adams, Executive Director

9303 Sunrise Village
1125 9th Street SE
Willmar, MN 56201-4683
320-235-1602
Fax: 320-235-4517

Angie Gerhardson, Manager

9304 Terrace Heights
410 W Main Street
Osakis, MN 56360-8243
320-859-2111
Fax: 320-859-3288

John Pollard, Manager

9305 The Country Place
23110 347th Street SE
Erskine, MN 56535-9491
218-687-2288
Fax: 218-687-2047

Sharlene Knutson LSW, Manager
Assisted living.

9306 Thorne Crest Retirement Center
1201 Garfield Avenue
Albert Lea, MN 56007-3637
507-373-2311
Fax: 207-377-1216

Karolee Coppoc, Administrator

9307 Town Hall Estates
607 E Center Street
Rochester, MN 55904-4654
507-288-3615
Fax: 507-288-3616

9308 Tracy's House
4009 Roanoke Circle
Golden Valley, MN 55422-5313
763-381-0417
Fax: 952-924-9099

Cristina Kamla, Coordinator Resident Services
Senior residential care home.

9309 Transitional Senior Housing
1609 Piedmont Avenue
Duluth, MN 55811-5327
218-727-5080
Fax: 218-727-4330

Assisted Living Facilities/Missouri

9310 Tuff Village
301 County Road 6
Hills, MN 56138-1068
507-962-3500
Fax: 507-962-3277

Bonnie Hengeveld, Administrator

9311 Valley Country Care
569 State Street N
Eden Valley, MN 55329-1112
320-453-6747
Fax: 320-453-7256

Todd Nouis, Owner

9312 Valley View Estates
1104 4th Avenue NE
Long Prairie, MN 56347
320-732-3516
Fax: 320-732-7018

Chuck Lane, Owner

9313 Valleyview Board and Lodge
4061 W 173rd Street
Jordan, MN 55352-8318
952-492-6160
Fax: 952-492-6446

Grace Guemple, Administrator

9314 Viking Manor Nursing Home
317 1st Street NW
Ulen, MN 56585-4010
218-494-3404
Fax: 218-596-8894

Todd Kjos, Administrator

9315 Villa St Vincent
516 Walsh Street
Crookston, MN 56716-2757
218-281-3424
Fax: 218-281-4755

Michael Siekas, Administrator

9316 Volunteers of America of Minnesota
5905 Golden Valley Road
Suite 110
Minneapolis, MN 55422-4490
763-546-3242
Fax: 612-546-2774

Mike Weber, CEO

9317 Wellington
2235 Rockwood Avenue
Saint Paul, MN 55116-3175
651-699-2664
Fax: 651-699-9726

Kim Webster, Manager

9318 Wellstead of Rogers
20600 S Diamond Lake Road
Rogers, MN 55374-4515
763-428-1981
Fax: 763-428-3792

Tom Wiskow, Owner

9319 Wesley Residence
5601 Grand Avenue
Duluth, MN 55807-2545
218-628-2307
Fax: 218-628-9623

9320 Westview Estates
703 W Yellowstone Trl
Buffalo Lake, MN 55314-1042
320-833-5364
Fax: 320-833-5526

Mark Rust, Administrator

9321 Westwood Place
209 Jefferson Avenue SW
Watertown, MN 55388-8100
952-955-1399
Fax: 952-955-1399

Deanne Beito, Manager

9322 Whispering Pines Care Center
2153 7th Avenue
Anoka, MN 55303-1770
763-712-8363
Fax: 763-712-8363
e-mail: whisperingpinescc@msn.com

Kathy Floia, Nurse Manager
Jake Nelson, CEO

9323 Wild Acre Homes
4071 20th Street SW
Backus, MN 56435-2227
218-587-2429
Fax: 218-829-9619

9324 Wilder Assisted Living Programs
753 7th Street E
Saint Paul, MN 55106-5025
651-774-6574
Fax: 651-772-5227

Jane Vohs, Manager

9325 Wildflower Lodge
9251 Black Oaks Lane N
Maple Grove, MN 55311-5446
763-420-3768
Fax: 763-420-5728

F Farr, President

9326 Wilds of Sand Prairie
700 Knight Street
Saint Peter, MN 56082-1739
507-931-4375
Fax: 651-766-4477

Kristi Keller-Smith, Manager

9327 Wildwood Grove
412 E Main Street
Le Roy, MN 55951-6740
507-324-9515
Fax: 507-324-5355

Laurie Schwarck, Executive Director

9328 Woodland Good Samaritan Village Apartments
200 Buffalo Hills Lane
Brainerd, MN 56401-4555
218-829-1429
Fax: 218-829-4815

Michael Deuth, Religious Leader

9329 Woodland Manor
610 Summit Drive
Fairmont, MN 56031-2247
507-235-6606
Fax: 507-235-3995
e-mail: sur.owens@lumhsi.org
http://www.lumhsi.org

Sue Owens RN, Director
Robert Lake, Administrator

Missouri

9330 Autumn Ridge
300 Autumn Ridge Drive
Herculaneum, MO 63048
636-931-8400
877-231-1243
Fax: 636-933-3975
http://www.emeritus.com

Daniel R Baty, Chairman/CEO
Raymond R Brandstrom, Vice Chairman/VP Finance
Gary Becker, SVP Operations

Assisted living services are designed with a focus on wellness to help residents maintain or improve their health.

Assisted Living Facilities/Montana

9331 Autumn View Gardens
Bethesda Adult Community
16219 Autumn View Terrace
Ellisville, MO 63011
636-458-5225
http://www.bethesdaadultcommunities.com
Cathy Krege, Executive Director

Provides assisted living in a secure environment for individuals with Alzheimer's disease or related dementia.

9332 Fairwinds-River's Edge
600 River's Edge Drive
St. Charles, MO 63303
636-754-0100
http://www.leisurecare.com

Offers luxurious apartment homes in a fun and active retirement community.

9333 Gardens Assisted Living
Bethesda Adult Community
1302 West Sunset
Springfield, MO 65807
417-889-7600
800-274-7132
Fax: 417-889-7681
http://www.bethesdaadultcommunities.com
Brian Miller, Executive Director

Provides assisted living in a secure environment for individuals with Alzheimer's disease or related dementia.

9334 McKnight Place Assisted Living
Three McKnight Place
Saint Louis, MO 63124
314-997-5333
http://www.mpassistedliving.com
Christie Wolff, LNHA, Administrator
Patti Romeo, Admissions Coordinator/SS
Patrick Majors, MD, Medical Director

We provide complete assisted living services for seniors who want to remain independent, but need extra attention and care.

9335 Saint Louis Altenheim
5408 South Broadway
Saint Louis, MO 63111
314-353-7225
Fax: 314-353-7389
e-mail: knewell@stlouisaltenheim.com
http://www.altenheim-stlouis.com
Kathy Clark, Administrator
Kay Newell, Director Marketing
Sue Grace, Director Nursing

St. Louis Altenheim is an assisted and continuing care residence with style. We offer services to meet each resident's needs, while maintaining the highest level of privacy, respect and individuality. Our goal is to enhance the quality of life for each resident at every level of care.

9336 Sunrise Senior Living
2100 Swope Drive
Independence, MO 64057-2808
816-257-5100
Fax: 816-257-2442
http://www.sunriseseniorliving.com
Paul J Klaassen, Founder/Chairman/CEO
Teresa M Klaassen, Founder/Chief Cultural Officer
Thomas B Newell, President

The Fountains at Greenbriar offers extraordinary rental retirement living in a quaint, suburban setting that is ideally located to all the area has to offer. The Fountains at Greenbriar can be tailored to meet your needs and desires.

Montana

9337 Ashley Manor Medley I
2000 16th Avenue S
Great Falls, MT 59405-4911
406-453-2882
Fax: 406-268-1159
Aubrey Matoon, Administrator

9338 Aspen Meadows Retirement Community
3155 Avenue C
Billings, MT 59102-8109
406-656-8818
800-325-1774
Fax: 406-656-9552
Anne Gonzalez, Administrator

9339 Bee Hive Homes of Flathead County
645 Liberty Street
Kalispell, MT 59901-3058
406-755-4483
Fax: 405-755-4483
Ron Cattron, Owner
Claudia Cattron, Owner
Kathleen Jacobs, Administrator

The mission of Bee Hive Homes is to provide assistance with the activities of daily living in a respectful, dignified manner in a home like setting to the frail elderly who choose to retain their independence and dignity to the fullest measure possible.

9340 Bee Hive Homes of Helena
13 Bumble Bee Court
Helena, MT 59601-8612
406-457-0092
Fax: 406-495-9005
Aimee Shein, Owner

9341 Buffalo Hill Terrace
40 Claremont Street
Kalispell, MT 59901-3527
406-752-9624
Fax: 406-752-9609
Carol Cockrell, Manager

9342 Edgewood Vista
1011 Cardinal Drive
Belgrade, MT 59714-8373
406-388-9439
Fax: 406-388-7722
Glenda Elkins, Manager

9343 Grand Park Assisted Living Community
1221 28th Street W
Billings, MT 59102-3790
406-652-6989
Fax: 406-652-4879
Judy Annin, Manager

9344 Hamilton House
9430 Haggerty Lane
Bozeman, MT 59715-9263
406-586-9459
Fax: 406-586-9459
Don Hamilton, Owner

9345 Harmony House
230 4th Avenue W
Kalispell, MT 59901-4436
406-257-5991
Fax: 406-755-0364

9346 Hawthorne House
1811 S 7th Street W
Missoula, MT 59801-3399
406-543-4055
Fax: 406-327-0042
Diane Hopewell, Manager

9347 Heritage Acres Assisted Living
200 N Mitchell Avenue
Hardin, MT 59034-1696
406-665-2802
Fax: 406-665-3809
Paula Small-Plenty, Administrator

9348 Heritage Retirement Home
3815 S 7th Street W
Missoula, MT 59804-1915
406-728-8181
Fax: 406-829-1912
Jolynn Dennis, Owner

Assisted Living Facilities/North Carolina

9349 **Hillside Place**
4718 23rd Avenue
Missoula, MT 59803-1163
406-251-5912
Fax: 406-251-4278

9350 **Hunters Glen at Grizzly Peak**
3620 American Way
Missoula, MT 59808-1379
406-542-7009
Fax: 406-542-7094

Janice Barber, Executive Director

9351 **Kathy's Place**
466 Hidden Valley Road S
Florence, MT 59833-6949
406-273-6826
Fax: 406-273-6826

Kathy Porter, Owner

9352 **Lodge at Lone Tree Creek**
1015 7th Avenue SW
Sidney, MT 59270-4900
406-488-4682
Fax: 406-488-2260

Tawnya Gurney, Executive VP

9353 **Lodge at Mission River Manor**
1801 9th Street S
Great Falls, MT 59405-5608
406-771-7440
Fax: 406-771-7443

Mike Masters, Administrator

9354 **Loveland Acres**
4485 Thorning Loop
Darby, MT 59829-9743
406-821-3519
Fax: 406-821-3519

9355 **Magnolia Place**
3201 Rugby Drive
Billings, MT 59102
406-248-2853
Fax: 406-248-3626

Janelle Siems, Manager

9356 **Montana Masonic Home**
2010 Masonic Home Road
Helena, MT 59602-9514
406-458-5431
Fax: 406-458-9322

Gale Evans, Administrator

9357 **Next Best Place**
1025 E Center Street
Dillon, MT 59725-3215
406-683-2902
Fax: 406-683-4002

9358 **Prestige Assisted Living at Kalispell**
125 Glenwood Drive
Kalispell, MT 59901-6075
406-756-1818
Fax: 406-756-0583

Ginia Siebenaler, Manager

9359 **River Ridge**
1415 Yellowstone River Road
Billings, MT 59105-1834
406-245-9330
Fax: 406-245-4219

Loree Aman, Manager

9360 **Springmeadows**
3175 Graf Street
Bozeman, MT 59715-7160
406-587-4570
Fax: 406-582-0032

Penelope Watkins, Executive Director

9361 **Waterford on Elizabeth Warren**
3701 Elizabeth Warren Avenue
Butte, MT 59701-4367
406-494-4900
Fax: 406-494-6281

Patrick Holland, Manager

9362 **Waterford on Saddle Drive**
915 Saddle Drive
Helena, MT 59601-5754
406-449-4900
Fax: 406-449-4999

Steve Nistler, Executive Director

North Carolina

9363 **Abbotswood at Irving Park Assisted Living**
3504 Flint Street
Greensboro, NC 27405-3488
336-282-8870
Fax: 336-282-9148
e-mail: irvingpark@kiscosl.com
http://www.kiscosl.com

Julie Butel Grimmett LPC, Marketing Director
Grege Woodward, Executive Director

Our vision is to grow as a unique and enduring company dedicated to meeting the changing needs of our residents and their families. To create a collaborative environment where associates are appreciated and inspired to develop as individuals where strengths and abilities are nurtures and rewarded. A company of high quality retirement communitites and services delivered with a warm and friendly feeling.

9364 **Aberdeene Meadows**
8981 Tartan Road
Laurinburg, NC 28352-1415
910-276-8140
Fax: 910-276-8606

9365 **Abington Place of Gastonia**
1680 S New Hope Road
Gastonia, NC 28054-5854
704-864-0801
Fax: 704-886-4848

Patti Lineberger, Executive Director

9366 **Ahoskie House**
407 Loftin Lane S
Ahoskie, NC 27910-3447
252-862-4700
Fax: 252-862-4800

9367 **Alterra Clare Bridge Cottage of Raleigh**
1130 Falls River Avenue
Raleigh, NC 27614-7772
919-844-2499
Fax: 919-844-6995

9368 **Alterra Clare Bridge of Asheville**
4 Walden Ridge Drive
Asheville, NC 28803-8583
828-687-0155
Fax: 828-687-0511

Kevin Parries, Administrator
Susan Woofter, Executive Director

9369 **Alterra Clare Bridge of Cary**
7870 Chapel Hill Road
Cary, NC 27513-5428
919-852-1355
Fax: 919-852-0899

Chris Amspacher, Manager

9370 **Alterra Clare Bridge of Charlotte**
5326 Park Road
Charlotte, NC 28209-3648
704-544-7255
Fax: 704-544-6965

Assisted Living Facilities/North Carolina

9371 Alterra Clare Bridge of Greensboro
3896 N Elm Street
Greensboro, NC 27455-2596
336-286-1235
Fax: 336-286-1252

9372 Alterra Clare Bridge of South Park
5326 Park Road
Charlotte, NC 28209-3648
704-553-8700
Fax: 704-553-8922

Robert Nye, Executive Director

9373 Alterra Clare Bridge of Southern Pines
101 Brucewood Road
Southern Pines, NC 28387-5159
910-695-1277
Fax: 910-695-1278

9374 Alterra Clare Bridge of Wilmington
3501 Converse Drive
Wilmington, NC 28403-6179
910-790-8664
Fax: 910-790-5662

Esther Hynes, Manager

9375 Alterra Clare Bridge of Winston Salem
275 S Peace Haven Road
Winston Salem, NC 27104-4419
336-659-7797
Fax: 336-659-6474

Scott Steckey, Manager

9376 Alterra Sterling House of Goldsboro
1800 N Berkeley Boulevard
Goldsboro, NC 27534-3368
919-759-1900
Fax: 919-759-1927

Troy Smothers, Executive Director

9377 Alterra Sterling House of Greenville
2105 W Arlington Boulevard
Greenville, NC 27834-5744
252-758-9155
Fax: 252-758-3738

Troy Smothers, Executive Director

9378 Alterra Sterling House of Hickory
910 29th Avenue NE
Hickory, NC 28601-1135
828-328-6090
Fax: 828-328-6090

Sheila Madigan, Executive Director

9379 Alterra Sterling House of New Bern
1336 S Glenburnie Road
New Bern, NC 28562-2624
252-638-6660
Fax: 252-638-2063

Donna Le Blanc, Executive Director

9380 Alterra Sterling House of Raleigh
1110 Falls River Avenue
Raleigh, NC 27614-7800
919-844-9747
Fax: 919-844-6995

David Chamberlin, Executive Director

9381 Alterra Sterling House of Rocky Mount
650 Goldrock Road
Rocky Mount, NC 27804-8804
252-446-6005
Fax: 252-446-0974

Debra Warren, Administrator

9382 Alterra Sterling House of Shelby
1425 E Marion Street
Shelby, NC 28150-4979
704-481-0150
Fax: 704-471-9935

Elsie Carter, Executive Director

9383 Alterra Sterling House of Southern Pines
101 Brucewood Road
Southern Pines, NC 28387-5159
910-692-4928
Fax: 910-692-0899

Gary Smith, Owner

9384 Alterra Wynwood of Chapel Hill
2220 Farmington Drive
Chapel Hill, NC 27517-7843
919-933-1430
Fax: 919-933-1543

Agnes Mauro, Finance Executive

9385 Alterra Wynwood of Charlotte
11230 Ballantyne Trace Court
Charlotte, NC 28277-2791
704-544-7220
Fax: 704-544-7221

Connie Siekkinen, Manager

9386 Alterra Wynwood of Greensboro
3896 N Elm Street
Greensboro, NC 27455-2596
336-286-1235
Fax: 336-286-1252

9387 Arbor Care Assisted Living
510 Banner Avenue
Greensboro, NC 27401-4303
336-273-2380
Fax: 336-274-1690

9388 Arbor Terrace of Asheville
3199 Sweeten Creek Road
Asheville, NC 28803-2136
828-681-5533
888-214-6884
Fax: 828-681-5554
e-mail: spegg@arborcompany.com
http://www.arborterrace-asheville.com

Nancy Miller, Executive Director

Provides a warm, nurturing environment in gracious surroundings, encouraging individual responsibility and freedom of choice, and creates a home atmosphere where residents make decisions regarding their daily lives.

9389 Arbors at Carriage Club of Charlotte
5800 Old Providence Road
Charlotte, NC 28226-6872
704-366-4960
Fax: 704-366-4914

Jackie Pittman, Executive Director

9390 Ardenwoods
2400 Appalachian Boulevard
Arden, NC 28704-8327
828-684-0040
Fax: 828-684-7800
e-mail: info@ardenwoodsrc.com
http://www.ardenwoodsatsaveryscreek.com

The warmth of our intimate community is enhanced by our gracious, professional staff. Not only do they know you by name and take care of daily chores such as housekeeping, home maintenance and lawn care, but they also remember your special preferences. It's these thougtfull touches that make living at Ardenwoods so wonderful.

9391 Asheville Manor
308 Overlook Road
Arden, NC 28704
828-684-1982
Fax: 828-684-1917

Chris Szalony, Executive Director

9392 Ashland Healthcare
215 Badger Street
West Jefferson, NC 28694
336-246-2381
Fax: 336-246-2169

Assisted Living Facilities/North Carolina

9393 Ashwood Estates Retirement Center
1115 Carthage Street
Sanford, NC 27330-4162
919-774-3774
Fax: 919-774-7084

Nina Gibson, Administrator

9394 Atria Assisted Living-Merrywood South
7745 Little Avenue
Charlotte, NC 28226-8168
704-547-9333
Fax: 704-541-5358

9395 Atria Assisted Retirement LivingMerrywood
3600 Park Road
Charlotte, NC 28209-4102
704-523-4949
Fax: 704-527-8866
http://atriaassistedliving.com

Connie Brown, Executive Director

Retirement living at Atria MerryWood means enjoying a wonderful sense of independence, along with an active community life with social, recreational and cultural events available both within our community and in town. We also offer assisted living services.

9396 Autumn Manor
115 N Main Street
Rich Square, NC 27869
252-539-4145
Fax: 252-539-2479

Joan Garvey, Administrator

9397 Autumn Wind of Smithfield
4302 Nc Highway 210
Smithfield, NC 27577-7915
919-934-7050
Fax: 919-934-3584

Danette Rogers, Administrator

9398 Azalea Village
145 Dairy Road
Clayton, NC 27520-4965
919-553-6144
Fax: 919-553-8714

Bonnie Jones, Administrator

9399 Becky's Rest Home
316 Lower Brush Creek Road
Fletcher, NC 28732-8484
828-628-1943
Fax: 828-628-9931

Becky McIntosh, Owner

9400 Bell House
2400 Summit Avenue
Greensboro, NC 27405-5014
336-621-0938
Fax: 336-621-0947

Linda Gordon, Executive Director

9401 Bethany Retirement Center
909 N Salisbury Avenue
Spencer, NC 28159-1828
704-633-1985
Fax: 704-637-1146

Susan Morris, Administrator

9402 Blackwell's Rest Home
3782 Cherry Grove Road
Elon College, NC 27244-9484
336-421-9488
Fax: 336-421-5862

Melanie Meadors, Manager

9403 Blakey Hall Assisted Living
501 Manning Avenue
Elon College, NC 27244-9136
336-506-2300
Fax: 336-506-2455
e-mail: bhhamlet@netpath.net
http://www.bhhamlet.com

John Ketcham, Owner

Our purpose is to care for residents in an environment that encourages them to make the most of their abilities. We want them to feel they are engaged in meaningful activities and not merely passing time.

9404 Boger City Rest Home
1428 Little Valley Lane
Lincolnton, NC 28092
704-732-2220
Fax: 704-732-4757

9405 Bradford Village East
413 N Main Street
Kernersville, NC 27284-2643
336-993-4696
Fax: 336-993-8957

Mark Mitchel, Administrator

9406 Bradford Village West
602 Piney Grove Road
Kernersville, NC 27284-2333
336-993-8711
Fax: 336-993-8499

Mark Mitchell, Administrator

9407 Bridging the Gap of Care
56 W Vineyard Lane
Hayesville, NC 28904-5603
828-389-8350
Fax: 828-389-9064

Irene Penland, Owner

9408 Brighton Gardens by Marriott-Greensboro
1208 New Garden Road
Greensboro, NC 27410-2679
336-297-4700
Fax: 336-297-1244

Debbie Ankrom, Manager

9409 Brighton Gardens by Marriott-Raleigh
3101 Duraleigh Road
Raleigh, NC 27612-4189
919-571-1123
Fax: 919-571-9091

Greg Fox, Manager

9410 Brighton Gardens of Winston Salem
2601 Reynolda Road
Winston Salem, NC 27106-3863
336-722-2224
Fax: 336-722-7212
http://www.sunriseseniorliving.com

Mary Locicero, Executive Director

At Sunrise Senior Living we take living personally. That's why we offer our seniors a variety of living arrangements, amenities, services, meal plans, social activities and care. It's a broad range of options that help seniors enjoy a full life - all on their own terms.

9411 Britthaven of Kannapolis
1808 N Cannon Boulevard
Kannapolis, NC 28083-2670
704-932-5517
Fax: 704-932-1200

April Roberts, Administrator

9412 Britthaven of La Grange
PO Box 6159
La Grange, NC 28551
252-566-4112
Fax: 252-566-2267

Jean Hines, Administrator

9413 Brookstone Haven Residential Care
501 Pointe South Drive
Randleman, NC 27317-9503
336-495-2800
Fax: 336-495-4865

David Dean Wilson, Owner

Assisted Living Facilities/North Carolina

9414 Brookstone Rest Home & Retirement Center
2968 Old Salisbury Road
Lexington, NC 27295-7293
336-243-2500
Fax: 336-243-2910

Rebecca Garcia, Owner

9415 Brookstone Terrace
PO Box 1682
Clemmons, NC 27012-1682
336-766-5000
Fax: 336-766-5020

Sherry Dube, Administrator

9416 Burlington Manor
3615 S Mebane Street
Burlington, NC 27215-5221
336-584-9066
Fax: 336-584-9026

Tammy Conklin, Executive Director

9417 Cambridge Assisted Living Community
935 Page Drive
Mount Pleasant, NC 28124-9735
704-436-2923
Fax: 704-436-2338

Vanessa Chambers, Administrator

9418 Cambridge Hills of Raleigh
6200 Falls of Neuse Road
Suite 102
Raleigh, NC 27609-3563
919-781-6605
Fax: 919-781-5030

9419 Cardinal Care Center-Hendersonville
1000 W Allen Street
Hendersonville, NC 28739-4881
828-693-3388
Fax: 828-697-5461

Sandee Barnwell, Administrator

9420 Carillon Assisted Living of Asheboro
2925 Zoo Parkway
Asheboro, NC 27205-1410
336-633-7600
Fax: 336-633-7621

9421 Carillon Assisted Living of Cramer Mountain
500 Cramer Mountain Road
Cramerton, NC 28032-1663
704-823-0500
Fax: 704-823-0504
http://www.carillonassistedliving.com
Charlene Swilling, Marketing
Zerina Francum, Executive Director

Carillon facilities provide assistance with activities of daily living and a secure dementia care unit.

9422 Carillon Assisted Living of Newton
1088 Radio Station Road
Newton, NC 28658-9478
828-466-7474
Fax: 828-466-7477

9423 Carillon Assisted Living of Shelby
1550 Charles Road
Shelby, NC 28152-7036
704-471-2828
Fax: 704-471-2829

9424 Carillon of Salisbury
1915 Mooresville Road
Salisbury, NC 28147-8813
704-633-4666
Fax: 704-633-6400

Wendy Hooper, Executive Director

9425 Carmel Hills
2801 Carmel Road
Charlotte, NC 28226-6393
704-364-8302
Fax: 704-364-8819

Richard Todd, Administrator

9426 Carolina House of Asheboro
514 Vision Drive
Asheboro, NC 27203-3895
336-672-6600
Fax: 336-683-0073

Ellen Hill, Sales Director

9427 Carolina House of Cary
111 Macarthur Drive
Cary, NC 27513-8900
919-460-5959
Fax: 919-460-4505

Rhonda Quattlebaum, Sales Director
Matt Cross, Executive Director

9428 Carolina House of Durham
1001 Prologue Road
Durham, NC 27712-1313
919-479-9966
Fax: 919-479-9977

Allison Lee, Sales Director
Angela Wright, Manager

9429 Carolina House of Elizabeth City
401 Hastings Lane
Elizabeth City, NC 27909-3327
252-333-1171
Fax: 252-331-0334

Sharee Wilder, Executive Director

9430 Carolina House of Forest City
493 Piney Ridge Road
Forest City, NC 28043-9017
828-288-1171
Fax: 828-288-1178

Tina Rippy, Executive Director

9431 Carolina House of Greenville
2715 Dickinson Avenue
Greenville, NC 27834-5099
252-353-2400
Fax: 252-353-6577

Randy Jackson, Executive Director

9432 Carolina House of Lexington
161 Young Drive
Lexington, NC 27292-4435
336-238-1700
Fax: 336-224-1448

Cindy Smith, Executive Director

9433 Carolina House of Pinehurst
17 Regional Drive
Pinehurst, NC 28374-8650
910-235-0700
Fax: 910-235-0650

James Floyd, Executive Director

9434 Carolina House of Reidsville
2931 Vance Street Extension
Reidsville, NC 27320-9409
336-634-0002
Fax: 336-349-2240

Becky Vance, Executive Director

9435 Carolina House of Smithfield
830 Berkshire Road
Smithfield, NC 27577-4729
919-989-3100
Fax: 919-989-3032

Kathy Vidal, Executive Director

9436 Carolina House of Wake Forest
611 Brooks Street
Wake Forest, NC 27587-2978
919-562-8400
Fax: 919-562-4687

Greg Fox, Executive Director

Assisted Living Facilities/North Carolina

9437 **Carolina Inn at Village Green**
405 Forsythe Street
Fayetteville, NC 28303-5488
910-829-0100
Fax: 910-829-7100

Franklin Clark, Owner

9438 **Carolina Rest Home**
Old Halifax Road
Roanoke Rapids, NC 27870
252-537-2777
Fax: 252-537-1903

9439 **Carolina Village**
600 Carolina Village Road
Hendersonville, NC 28792-2845
828-692-6275
Fax: 828-692-7876
http://www.carolinavillage.com

Doley Bell, Administrator

A non profit, continuing care for the retired.

9440 **Carriage Club of Charlotte**
5800 Old Providence Road
Charlotte, NC 28226-6872
704-366-4960
Fax: 704-366-4270

Jackie Pittman, Executive Director

9441 **Cedar Cove at Wilmington**
Jasmine Cove Way
Wilmington, NC 28408
910-395-5220
Fax: 910-395-8218

Stacey Locklear, Executive Director

9442 **Cedar Manor Rest Home**
4288 Us 17 Hiway
Chocowinity, NC 27817
252-946-2604

Qucanda Spruill, Manager

9443 **Cedar Rock Assisted Living**
PO Box 1237
Mocksville, NC 27028-1237
336-751-1515
Fax: 336-751-1621

Sheila Simons, Owner

9444 **Central Care**
125 Apex Lane
Mount Airy, NC 27030-5595
336-320-2185
Fax: 336-320-2186

Billy Payne, Administrator

9445 **Champions at Porters Neck**
1007 Porters Neck Road
Wilmington, NC 28411-7383
910-686-6462
Fax: 918-686-8320

Jim Wood, Executive Director

9446 **Chancellor Gardens of Charlotte**
9120 Willow Ridge Road
Charlotte, NC 28210-8313
704-540-0098
Fax: 704-540-9020

9447 **Charlotte Square**
5820 Carmel Road
Charlotte, NC 28226-8106
704-544-4979
Fax: 704-540-7883

Alverita Peeples, Manager

9448 **Chatham Creek Rest Home**
809 W Chatham Street
Cary, NC 27511-3136
919-469-9309
Fax: 919-469-4565

Mary Hart, Administrator

9449 **Cherry Springs Village**
2222 N Main Street
Hendersonville, NC 28792-2438
828-698-6501
Fax: 828-698-6504
http://www.cherryspringsvillage.com

Angela White, Owner

Cherry Springs offers a wide range of social activites and special events designed to promot active involvement. Transportation is provided for medical appointments outside the facility.

9450 **Christian Care Center of New Bern**
PO Box 12383
New Bern, NC 28561-2383
252-633-3455
Fax: 252-633-3898

Kathie Holt, Manager

9451 **Christian Care of Smithfield**
303 Hospital Road
Smithfield, NC 27577-4101
919-934-7708
Fax: 919-989-6695

Nellie Adams, Administrator

9452 **Christian Care of Winston-Salem**
2900 Reynolds Park Road
Winston Salem, NC 27107-1699
336-785-0050
Fax: 336-789-6187

Dennis Reid, Administrator

9453 **Churchhill Assisted Living Residences**
140 Carriage Club Drive
Mooresville, NC 28117-9002
704-658-1200
Fax: 704-814-0350

9454 **Clare Bridge of Chapel Hill**
2230 Farmington Drive
Chapel Hill, NC 27517-7843
919-929-5850
Fax: 919-493-7123

Mary Casey, Executive Director

9455 **Clemmons Village**
6401 Holder Road
Clemmons, NC 27012-9207
336-766-2990
Fax: 336-766-2138

Kathy Edens, Owner

9456 **Cleveland Health Care Center**
1056 College Avenue
Shelby, NC 28152-9510
704-482-1056
Fax: 704-482-1056

9457 **Colonial Manor Rest Home**
160 Health Care Drive
Rutherfordton, NC 28139-8058
828-287-7353
Fax: 828-286-4890

James E Yelton, Owner

9458 **Community Care of Haywood**
67 Loving Way
Clyde, NC 28721-9471
828-452-3822
Fax: 828-452-3820
http://www.comcarenc.com

Mary Allen, Manager

Our facilities are licensed and monitored monhly by the state.

9459 **Concord Place**
2452 Rock Hill Church Road
Concord, NC 28027-8048
704-782-7594
Fax: 704-786-3173

Kellee Armsworthy, Executive Director
Beverly Register, Administrator

Assisted Living Facilities/North Carolina

9460 **Core Family Care Center**
217 Jonesboro Road
Dunn, NC 28334-6240
910-892-1711
Fax: 910-822-5343

Wallace Core, Owner

9461 **Country Club Prime Time Retirement Home**
2800 Kidd Road
Raleigh, NC 27610-1842
919-231-6271
Fax: 919-231-9788

Eddie Houchin, Manager

9462 **Country Meadow Rest Home**
108 Hazelton Drive
Hendersonville, NC 28739-5524
828-693-6170
Fax: 828-693-6398

Debbie Pratt, Owner

9463 **Country Oaks Manor**
Rr 2
Box 350
Hertford, NC 27944-9802
252-426-7464
Fax: 252-426-2044

Andrea Brown, Manager

9464 **Country Sunshine Rest Home**
148 Cox Avenue
Richlands, NC 28574-6163
910-324-1121
Fax: 910-324-5371

Debbie Moscow, Manager

9465 **Countryside Living**
5383 Us Highway 117 N
Pikeville, NC 27863-9443
919-242-6369
Fax: 919-242-9884
http://www.countyside-living.com

Marsha Sauls, Administrator

9466 **Countrytime Inn**
602 Brevard Street
Kings Mountain, NC 28086-8692
704-739-2760
Fax: 704-789-4775

Tahir Majeed, Executive Director

9467 **Creekside Manor**
6206 Reidsville Road
Kernersville, NC 27284-7609
336-595-4317
Fax: 336-595-9395

Mary Sauls, Manager

9468 **Crescent View Retirement Community**
2533 Hendersonville Road
Arden, NC 28704-8583
828-687-0068
Fax: 828-684-8929

Marget Abbott, Executive Director

9469 **Croasdaile Village**
2600 Croasdaile Farm Parkway
Durham, NC 27705-1397
919-384-2000
Fax: 919-384-2513

Howard Dewitt, Executive Director

9470 **Cross Road Retirement Community**
1302 Old Cox Road
Asheboro, NC 27205-9466
336-629-7811
Fax: 336-629-6264
e-mail: crrc@triad.rr.com
http://www.cross-road.org

Janet Harllee, Admissions/Marketing
Steve Rumbley, Administrator

Provides a safe and comfortable environment for seniors.

9471 **Crown Colony at Mooresville**
PO Box 598
Mooresville, NC 28115
704-663-7600
Fax: 704-663-2881

Thomas Taylor, Owner

9472 **Davie Place Residential Care**
337 Hospital Street
Mocksville, NC 27028-2060
336-751-2175
Fax: 336-751-0135

Suzanne Simpson, Administrator

9473 **Discovery Program at Burlington Manor**
3619 S Mebane Street
Burlington, NC 27215-5221
336-538-0367
Fax: 336-538-1724

Tammy Conklin, Office Manager
Marilyn Williams, Executive Director

9474 **Divine Country Manor**
312 Lynch Street
Apex, NC 27502-2028
919-362-6266
Fax: 919-362-6298

Berdie Briggs, Owner

9475 **Dogwood Forest Adult Care Home**
PO Box 2828
Burlington, NC 27216-2828
336-229-5165
Fax: 336-222-9068

9476 **Durham Manor Rest Home**
3218 Apex Highway
Durham, NC 27713
919-544-1390
Fax: 919-572-2539

9477 **Durham Village**
5010 S Alston Avenue
Durham, NC 27713-4425
919-544-0257
Fax: 919-361-0534

Kim Blackwell, Owner

9478 **Eden Estates**
314 W Kings Highway
Eden, NC 27288-5012
336-623-1901
Fax: 336-623-5144

Tammy Martin, Executive Director

9479 **Eden Gardens of Statesville**
2147 Davie Avenue
Statesville, NC 28625-9200
704-878-0123
Fax: 704-878-8689

Danny Boone, Manager

9480 **Edengardens of Concord**
15801 Zion Chuch Road E
Concord, NC 28085
704-782-1100
Fax: 704-721-3144

Chuck Pierce, Executive Director

9481 **Edengardens of Kings Mountain**
1001 Phifer Road
Kings Mountain, NC 28086-3748
704-739-6772
Fax: 704-739-6449

Kristi Anthony, Executive Director

9482 **Edengardens of Mooresville**
128 Brawley School Road
Mooresville, NC 28117-9102
704-799-2712
Fax: 704-704-7992

Lindsay Smith, CEO

Assisted Living Facilities/North Carolina

9483 Elms at Tanglewood
3750 Harper Road
Clemmons, NC 27012-8682
336-766-2131
Fax: 336-766-2160
http://www.elmsattanglewood.com
Charlotte Tullock, Administrator

Our mission is to provide quality, professional assisted care in a comfortable, nurturing, homelike environment, an atmosphere of respect and warmth and dignity, where our residents can feel a sense of purpose and community.

9484 Elon Village Home
PO Box 245
Elon, NC 27244
336-584-7930
Fax: 336-584-5266
Ronnie Moore, Owner

9485 Fountains at the Albemarle Inn
200 Trade Street
Tarboro, NC 27886-5055
252-823-2799
Fax: 252-823-6555
Christopher Casteel, Executive Director

We offer a lovely, amenity-rich environment in which residents can enjoy privacy, independence and freedom of choice while receiving all the care and support they need.

9486 Friendship Care
4501 Old Battleground Road
Greensboro, NC 27410-9352
336-282-2253
Fax: 336-282-1308
Avery Green, Administrator

9487 Gaston Manor
1717 Union Road
Gastonia, NC 28054-5583
704-864-9440
Fax: 704-865-1548
Diane Payne, Executive Director

9488 Gaston Place
1750 Robinwood Road
Gastonia, NC 28054-1664
704-864-2480
Fax: 704-864-4448
Hal Shoup, Executive Director

9489 Gastonia Village
850 Majestic Court
Gastonia, NC 28054-5131
704-864-4220
Fax: 704-853-2109
Suzanne Iaculli, Executive Director

9490 Greenbrier
703 S Walnut Street
Fairmont, NC 28340-1837
910-628-9021
Fax: 910-628-7441
Karen Hunt, Executive Director

9491 Greensboro Manor
5809 Old Oak Ridge Road
Greensboro, NC 27410-9265
336-297-9900
Fax: 336-856-1060
Carol Royals, Executive Director

9492 Greensboro Place on Lawndale
4400 Lawndale Drive
Greensboro, NC 27455-1819
336-286-3432
Fax: 336-286-3005
Jo Frazier, Sales Director
Patricia McCulloh, Executive Director

9493 Harbours Edge Retirement Center
143 Rosedale Drive
Elizabeth City, NC 27909-9810
252-331-2149
Fax: 252-331-1170
Barbara Jones, Administrator

9494 Haven Heights Rest Home
PO Box 456
Burnsville, NC 28714
828-682-3417
Fax: 828-678-9253
Ron Dodson, Owner

9495 Haven in the Village at Carolina Place
13150 Dorman Road
Pineville, NC 28134-9327
704-540-0155
Fax: 704-540-7769
Nancy Nye, Manager

9496 Haywood Lodge & Retirement Center
251 Shelton Street
Waynesville, NC 28786-3362
828-456-8365
888-238-0103
Fax: 828-456-6792
http://www.haywoodlodge.com
Aaron Crawford, Owner

Our mission is to provide the highest standard of care possible for our residents while maintaining a high quality of life, independence and self-esteem. Our dedicated staff works closely with outside health professionals to meet the specific needs of each resident.

9497 HeartFields Assisted Living at Cary
1050 Cresent Drive
Cary, NC 27511
919-852-5757
Fax: 919-852-2628
http://www.heartforseniors.com
Denise Alala, Executive Director

HeartFields provides seniors the perfect blend of comfort, care and choice. The heart of our program rests on providing just the right level of personalized services, while allowing residents to be as independent as possible.

9498 Heritage Place
325 N Cool Spring Street
Fayetteville, NC 28301-5197
910-323-4925
Fax: 910-678-8673
Shelia Sorkin, Executive Director

9499 Heritage Woods
3812 Forrestgate Drive
Winston Salem, NC 27103-3036
336-768-2011
Fax: 336-760-4258

9500 Hickory Manor
2530 16th Street NE
Hickory, NC 28601-7603
828-324-5400
Fax: 828-326-9770
BJ Fore, Sales Director
Jeff Dula, Executive Director

9501 High Point Manor
201 W Hartley Drive
High Point, NC 27265-2843
336-885-8600
Fax: 336-885-5817
Kimberly Hemric, Executive Director

9502 High Point Place
1568 Skeet Club Road
High Point, NC 27265-9530
336-869-0026
Fax: 336-869-0062
Gina Floyd, Executive Director
Trudy Snuggs, Manager

Assisted Living Facilities/North Carolina

9503 Homeplace of Burlington
823 N Elm Street
Greensboro, NC 27401-1510
336-227-2328
Fax: 336-227-2329

9504 Homeplace of Durham
823 N Elm Street
Suite 200
Greensboro, NC 27401-1510
919-484-8518
Fax: 919-484-8520

Homeplace of Durham, is an assisted living retirement community, and is committed to providing residents with a lifestyle of dignity as well as skillful, compassionate assistance in and at home environment.

9505 Homeplace of New Bern
823 N Elm Street
Greensboro, NC 27401-1510
336-272-7196
Fax: 336-378-9705

Steven D Bell, Owner

9506 Homestead Hills Assisted Living
2101 Homestead Hills Drive
Winston Salem, NC 27103-6445
336-659-0708
Fax: 336-659-8506

Phyllis Shore, Executive Director

9507 Inn at Quail Haven
155 Blake Boulevard
Pinehurst, NC 28374-8497
910-295-2294
Fax: 910-295-2379

Myron Dice, Administrator

The Inn provides respite care, skilled nursing, rehabilitative and restorative servivces. Residents recieve truly individualized service from a staff of caring, competent professionals in an atmosphere of genuine warmth and compassion.

9508 Kerner Ridge Assisted Living
250 Hopkins Road
Kernersville, NC 27284-9314
336-993-1881
Fax: 336-993-2592

Mary Spainhour, Administrator

9509 Knollwood Gardens Rest Home
PO Box 1932
Lillington, NC 27546-1932
910-893-2786
Fax: 910-814-2016

Crescent Mozingo, Administrator

9510 Laurels in Highland Creek
6101 Clarke Creek Parkway
Charlotte, NC 28269-6936
704-947-8050
Fax: 704-947-2363

Jennifer Davidson, Executive Director

9511 Laurels in the Village at Carolina Place
13180 Dorman Road
Pineville, NC 28134-9327
704-540-8007
Fax: 704-540-8088

Stacy Gatto, Executive Director

We offer licensed nursing professionals on-site 24 hours a day/7 days a week, alcove, companion, one and two bedroom apartments with kitchenettes, a personal emergency call system, individually controlled thermostats for comfort as well as home cooked meals, scheduled transportation, activities and housekeeping services.

9512 Lawndale Manor
601 Lakeside Drive
Garner, NC 27529-4216
919-662-0099
Fax: 919-662-1166

Ron Whaley, Administrator

9513 Lawyers Glen Retirement Living Center
10830 Lawyers Road
Charlotte, NC 28227
704-545-9555
Fax: 704-545-2075
e-mail: johnelliotte@lawyersglen.com
http://www.lawyersglen.com

The campus is dedicated to our philosophy: to enhance independence, productivity, security, and dignity while providing affordable healthcare to promote comfort, conveniences, companionship and place of mind and to provide for social, emotional, physical and spiritual well-being of our residents. To fulfill this mission, Lawyers Glen will cater to the desired lifestyle of its residents by proviging the highest quality and best services available.

9514 Lee's Living Center
9108 Reames Road
Charlotte, NC 28216-1824
704-597-7575
Fax: 704-596-2735

Tammy Barnes, Administrator

9515 Liberty Commons Assisted Living
3045 Henderson Drive
Jacksonville, NC 28546-5247
910-355-1996
Fax: 910-455-7665

Karen Kinarney, Administrator

9516 Little Flower Assisted Living Residence
8700 Lawyers Road
Charlotte, NC 28227-8740
704-545-7005
Fax: 704-545-7016

Doloris Brown, Administrator

9517 Manorhouse Assisted Living
190 Fox Holw
Pinehurst, NC 28374-8549
910-695-0011
Fax: 910-695-1147

Kim Obrine, Manager

9518 Manorhouse of Wilmington
2744 S 17th Street
Wilmington, NC 28412-6606
910-452-1114
Fax: 910-452-9379

Patricia Knox, Executive Director

9519 Marriotts Brighton Gardens of Charlotte
6000 Park South Drive
Charlotte, NC 28210-3298
704-643-1400
Fax: 704-643-9400

Lynne Napoli, Manager

9520 Mars Hill Retirement Community
170 S Main Street
Mars Hill, NC 28754-6622
828-689-7970
888-420-6983
Fax: 828-689-7972
e-mail: tammie.chandler@marshillretire.com
http://www.marshillretire.com

Tammie S Chandler, Marketing Director
Richard Pridgen, Administrator
Gail Blankenship, Office Manager

Mars Hill offers a cost-effective quality care that is personalized for the individuals needs, fosters independence for each resident, treats each resident with dignity and respect, promotes individuality of each resident, allows each resident choice of care and lifestyle, protects each resident's right to privacy, provides a safe residential environment, and makes the assisted living residence a valuable community asset.

Assisted Living Facilities/North Carolina

9521 Maryfield
1315 Greensboro Road
High Point, NC 27260-2611
336-886-2444
Fax: 336-886-4036

Sylvia Wunch, Staff Development
Lucy Hennessy, Manager

Provides assisted living accommodations to residents who need a little help to remain independent. Our assisted living wing provides residents with a higher level of independence and activity range. Residents enjoy privacy, independence and have many choices in their desired activites.

9522 Meadowbrook Terrance of Greensboro
1915 Boulevard Street
Greensboro, NC 27407-4513
336-299-9945
Fax: 336-299-9942

9523 Mount Olive Retirement Village
600 Smith Chapel Road
Mount Olive, NC 28365-2632
919-658-6501
Fax: 919-658-0086

Glen Kornegay, Owner

9524 North Carolina Assisted Living Association
1306 Annapolis Drive
Suite 120
Raleigh, NC 27608-2136
919-467-2486
Fax: 919-467-5132
e-mail: info@ncassistedliving.org
http://www.ncassistedliving.org

Jerry Cooper, Executive Director
Kathy Rodgers, Meeting/Membership Coordinator

9525 Oak Hill Living Center
PO Box 759
Angier, NC 27501
919-639-9000
Fax: 919-639-9435

Jackie Castlebury, Administrator

9526 Oakview Assisted Living Center
306 Oakview Road
High Point, NC 27265-2050
336-869-2911
Fax: 336-869-9048

Evelyn McCubbin, Owner

9527 Outlook Pointe at Northridge
600 Newton Road
Raleigh, NC 27615-6214
919-848-4906
Fax: 919-848-3664

Debbie Hart, Executive Director

9528 Parkway Retirement Home
201 W High Street
Cary, NC 27513-5737
919-460-8644
Fax: 919-463-0128

James Anderson, Administrator

9529 Piedmont Christian Home
1510 Deep River Road
High Point, NC 27265-3400
336-883-6023
Fax: 336-883-6024

Bonnie Smith, Owner

9530 Ridge Crest Retirement
100 Ridgecrest Drive
Mount Airy, NC 27030-9196
336-786-9100
Fax: 336-786-2899

Laney Johnson, Executive Director

9531 Rose Haven
3520 Crittenden Ceter
Apex, NC 27502
919-362-5883
Fax: 919-362-7697

Ruby Artis, Owner

9532 Rose Terrace of Wendell
4230 Wendell Boulevard
Wendell, NC 27591-8412
919-366-9737
Fax: 919-365-3394

Eddie Houchn, Administrator

9533 Salisbury Gardens
2201 Salisbury Boulevard
Salisbury, NC 28147
704-636-0588
Fax: 704-639-1146

Lou Cranford, Executive Director

9534 Samaritan Place Assisted Living
52 Lower Grassy Branch Road
Asheville, NC 28805-1639
828-298-7592
Fax: 828-298-2637

Tammy Wise, Manager

Our mission statement is to provide caring assistance in daily living with dignity and respect while promoting individual independence.

9535 Shallotte Assisted Living
520 Mulberry Street
Shallotte, NC 28470-4586
910-754-6621
Fax: 910-754-6621

Denise Kirby, Manager

9536 Shepherd House Assisted Living Community
405 Smith Level Road
Chapel Hill, NC 27516-9108
919-929-7859
Fax: 919-933-9413

Crystal Wilder, Administrator

9537 Somerset Court
915 W 4th Street
Winston Salem, NC 27101-2517
910-582-0082
Fax: 910-582-8567

9538 Somerset Court of Mocksville
150 Ken Dwiggins Drive
Mocksville, NC 27028-2439
336-751-1209
Fax: 336-751-0602

Martha Crouse, Administrator

9539 Somerset Court of Newport
915 W 4th Street
Winston Salem, NC 27101-2517
252-223-2600
Fax: 252-223-4754

9540 Spring Arbor of Apex
907 Spring Arbor Court
Apex, NC 27502-4951
919-303-9990
Fax: 919-303-0520

Sandy Gegax, Executive Director

9541 Spring Arbor of Herdersonville
1820 Pisgah Drive
Hendersonville, NC 28791-3759
828-692-6440
Fax: 828-692-8922

Jeffrey Marhafer, Executive Director

9542 Spring Arbor of Kinston
3207 Carey Road
Kinston, NC 28504-1205
252-523-3099
Fax: 252-523-8074

Cynthia Sparks, Administrator

Assisted Living Facilities/North Dakota

9543 **Spring Arbor of Raleigh**
1810 N New Hope Road
Raleigh, NC 27604-8305
919-250-0255
Fax: 919-250-0247

Pam Mayo, Executive Director

9544 **Spring Arbor of Rocky Mount**
1251 S Winstead Avenue
Rocky Mount, NC 27803-1557
252-443-3999
Fax: 252-443-3113

Rebecca Holoman, Administrator

9545 **Spring Arbor of Wilmington**
809 John D Barry Drive
Wilmington, NC 28412
910-799-4999
Fax: 910-799-8210

Loretta Evans, Administrator

9546 **Spring Arbor of Wilson**
2045 Ward Boulevard
Wilson, NC 27893-2873
252-234-2100
Fax: 252-234-0001

Eve Artis, Executive Director

Pur dedicated team nurtures our residents independence by promoting dignity and choice within a setting of professional, compassionate care. Assistance is always offered, never imposed and our full-service lifestyle offers our residents and their families the time to focus on opportunities, not challenges.

9547 **Statesville Place**
2806 Peachtree Road
Statesville, NC 28625-8204
704-872-1946
Fax: 704-872-1992

Karen Cline, Executive Director

9548 **Sunrise Assisted Living at Eastover**
3610 Randolph Road
Charlotte, NC 28211-1318
704-366-2550
Fax: 704-366-4041
http://www.sunriseseniorliving.com

Carrie Dellinger, Executive Director

At Sunrise Senior Living we take living personally. Thats why we offer our seniors a variety of living arrangements, amenities, services, meal plans, social activities and care. It's a broad range of options that help seniors a full life, all on their own terms.

9549 **Sunrise Assisted Living of Raleigh**
4801 Edwards Mill Road
Raleigh, NC 27612-4417
919-787-0777
Fax: 919-787-6105

Karen Sherman, Executive Director

9550 **Sunrise Assisted Living of South Charlotte**
5515 Rea Road
Charlotte, NC 28226-3446
704-544-2094
Fax: 704-544-6530
http://www.sunriseseniorliving.com

Rita Shew, Executive Director

At Sunrise Senior Living we take living personally. That's why we offer our seniors a variety of living arrangements, amenities, services, meal plans, social activities and care. It's a broad range of options that help seniors enjoy a full life, all on their own terms.

9551 **Sunrise of Providence**
5114 Providence Road
Charlotte, NC 28226-5852
704-365-5252
Fax: 704-365-4306
http://www.sunriseseniorliving.com

Nancy Myer, Manager

At Sunrise Senior Living we take living personally. That's why we offer our seniors a variety of living arrangements, amenities, services, meal plans, social activities and care. It's a broad range of options that help seniors enjoy a full life, all on their own terms.

9552 **Thompson Gardens of Garland**
500 W 3rd Street
Garland, NC 28441
910-529-9651
Fax: 910-529-1932

9553 **Trinity Oaks Retirement Community**
728 Klumac Road
Salisbury, NC 28144-5720
704-633-1002
Fax: 704-636-5038

Mike Walsh, Executive Director

North Dakota

9554 **Altera Sterling House of Fargo**
1401 W Gateway Circle S
Fargo, ND 58103-3529
701-239-4524
Fax: 701-298-2985

Deb Olson, Administrator

9555 **Baptist Home of Kenmare**
PO Box 787
Kenmare, ND 58746
701-385-4941
Fax: 701-385-4215
http://www.abhomes.net

Karen Schwartz, Asministrator

Attention to physical well-being is an important aspect of life at the Baptist Home with weekly exercise opportunities. Delicious, balanced meals are enjoyed daily by residents of the Baptist Home of Kenmare.

9556 **Bethany Homes**
201 University Drive S
Fargo, ND 58103-8299
701-239-3000
Fax: 701-239-3237
http://www.bethanyhomes.org

Ray Weisgarber, Executive Director

We dedicate outselves to making Bethany a place where residents can live in comfort and dignity in a communiyt that is shaped by Christian concern.

9557 **Bethel Four Acres**
1404 1st Avenue N
Jamestown, ND 58401-2379
701-252-6090
Fax: 701-252-6090

Dolores Bagan, Administrator

9558 **Bethel Lutheran Home**
1515 Second Avenue
Williston, ND 58801
701-572-6766
Fax: 701-572-7579
http://home.att.net/~bethel/

Kurt Stoner, Administrator

Our Mission at Bethel Lutheran is dedicated to serving the physical, emotional and spiritual needs of each aging person regardless of race, color, sex, religion, age, national origin or handicap by striving to provide the highest quality facilities, personal care and programs out of obedience to and love for christ in order to enhance the dignity, self worth and purpose of life for each individual who enters the sphere of Bethel's influence.

9559 **Chateau for Seniors Citizens**
1120 S 3rd Street
Bismarck, ND 58504-6300
701-223-9223
Fax: 701-223-9223

Assisted Living Facilities/North Dakota

9560 Devils Lake Good Samaritan
302 7th Avenue NE
Devils Lake, ND 58301-2516
701-662-6580
Fax: 701-662-6585

Karen Boulden, Administrator

9561 Edgewood Vista - Minot
1400 S Broadway
Minot, ND 58701-5933
701-852-1399
Fax: 701-383-0613

Becky Rotvedt, Administrator

Edgewood Vista exists to provide personalized care in settings designed specifically for Elderly, including those with Alzheimer's Disease or other forms of fementia. Our individualizes approach provides a high quality, safe, home-like setting to Seniors who choose to no longer reside alone, but who can live better in social settings. Through empathetic hearts we eill serve the needs of our residents 24 hours a day.

9562 Edgewood Vista of Bismark
3406 Dominion Street
Bismarck, ND 58503-5577
701-258-7489
Fax: 701-258-7491
http://www.edgewoodvista.com

Dale Klein, President

Edgewood Vista exists to provide personalized care in settings designed specifically for Seniors, including those with Alzheimer's Disease or other forms of dementia. Our individualized approach provides a high quality, safe, home-like setting to Seniros who choose to no longer redside alone, but who can live better in social residential settings. Through empathetic hearts we will serve the needs of our residents 24 hours a day.

9563 Edmore Memorial Rest Home
301 E 4th Street
Edmore, ND 58330
701-644-2202
Fax: 701-664-2698

Tammy Berg, Administrator

9564 Ellendale Evergreen Place
241 Main Street
Ellendale, ND 58436-7103
701-349-4550
Fax: 701-349-4656

Tony Hanson, Executive Director

9565 Golden Acres Manor
PO Box 261
Carrington, ND 58421
701-652-3117
Fax: 701-652-3118
e-mail: gamnh@daktel.com
http://www.goldenacresmanor.com

Allan Metzger, Administrator

This organization was formed to enhance the lives of residents of Golden Acres Manor by making possible the purchase of special needs equipment, furnishings, etc. which the nursing home would not otherwise be able to fund.

9566 Good Shepherd Home
709m 4th Avenue NE
Watford City, ND 58854-7628
701-444-2331
Fax: 701-842-4629

Kris Pacheco, Administrator

9567 Harolds Haaland Home
800 S Main Avenue
Rugby, ND 58368-2118
701-776-5261
Fax: 701-776-6688

Mark Weber, Manager

Our mission is to provide quality medical care, as reflected by the needs and demographics of north central North Dakota. Although we are determined to be self-supporting, our Christian dedication is primarliy to provide an array of quality services for patients and residents regardless of race, color, creed, or disability.

9568 Karrington Commons
114 N 3rd Street
Bismarck, ND 58501-3899
701-223-9505
Fax: 701-222-8808

Ardith Wahl, Administrator
Tina Kambeitz, Manager

9569 Karrington Cottages
2625 N 19th Street
Bismarck, ND 58503
701-258-5482
Fax: 701-258-5585

Char Schmidt, Administrator

9570 Luther Memorial Home
750 Main Street E
Mayville, ND 58257-1698
701-786-3401
Fax: 701-786-9022

Brett Ulrich, Administrator

9571 Maddock Memorial Home
301 Roosevelt Avenue
Maddock, ND 58348-7138
701-438-2641
Fax: 701-438-2641

Beth Olsen

9572 Manor St Joesph
404 4th Avenue
Edgeley, ND 58433-7417
701-493-2477
Fax: 701-493-2477
e-mail: stjoesph@drtel.net

Tammy Jangula, Administrator

9573 Marian Manor
604 E Ash Avenue
Glen Ullin, ND 58631-7138
701-348-3107
Fax: 701-348-3080

Rod Auer, Administrator

9574 Marillac Manor
1016 N 28th Street
Bismarck, ND 58501-3139
701-258-8702
Fax: 701-223-3127

Pheobe Schwartze, Admissions
Grant Wilz, Administrator

9575 Noonan Good Samaritan Center
PO Box 69
Noonan, ND 58765
701-925-5670
Fax: 701-925-5718
http://www.good-sam.com

Elaine Heide, Administrator

The mission of the Society is to share God's love in word and deed by providing shelter and supportive services to older persons and others in need.

9576 Old Fellows Home
1107 Walnut Street E
Devils Lake, ND 58301-3240
701-662-3330
Fax: 701-662-6672
e-mail: ndioof@gondtc.com

Mark Ulrich, Administrator

9577 Park River Good Samaritan
301 S Highway 12b
Park River, ND 58270-4134
701-284-7115
Fax: 701-284-7117
e-mail: gss6300@good-sam.com

David Carda, Administrator

Our center provides physical, occupational and speech therapy services; a full range of activities; delicious meals; an on-site chaplain; and the living care of a dedicated and comapssionate staff.

Assisted Living Facilities/Nebraska

9578 Prairie Home
705 3rd Street
Bowman, ND 58623
701-523-3214
Fax: 701-523-4139

Darrold Bertsch, CEO

9579 Primrose Retirement Center
1144 College Drive
Bismarck, ND 58501-1212
701-222-8183
Fax: 701-250-9719

Chuck Wolfgram, Manager

9580 Redwood Village
PO Box 339
Wilton, ND 58579
701-734-6410
Fax: 701-523-4139

Judy Pepple, Administrator

9581 Riverview Place
5300 12th Street S
Fargo, ND 58104-6427
701-237-4700
Fax: 701-235-5738

9582 Sheridan Memorial Home
610 S Main
McClusky, ND 58463
701-363-2203
Fax: 701-363-2703

Theresa Jorgenson, Administrator

9583 St Catherine's Living Center
1307 7th Street N
Wahpeton, ND 58075-3624
701-642-6667
Fax: 701-642-2485

Steve Williams, Manager

9584 St Francis Residence
Highway 281 N
Cando, ND 58324
701-968-4411
Fax: 701-968-2574

Les Wietstock, CEO

9585 Tri-County Retirement Home
930 Dakota Avenue
Hatton, ND 58240-4506
701-543-3102
Fax: 701-543-4059

Jason Carlson, Administrator

9586 Tufte Manor
3300 Cherry Street
Grand Forks, ND 58201-7699
701-775-2581
Fax: 701-775-2259

Mary Beth Martin, Manager

9587 Valley View Heights
2500 Valleyview Avenue
Bismarck, ND 58501-3090
701-221-3018
Fax: 701-223-2091

Cathy Schmidt, Manager

9588 Waterford at Hardwoodgroves
1200 Harwood Drive S
Fargo, ND 58104-6298
701-476-1200
Fax: 701-476-1201

Deb Magnuson, Manager

9589 Waterford on West Century
1000 W Century Avenue
Bismarck, ND 58503
701-323-7000
Fax: 701-221-2525

Arlene Farnsworth, Executive Director

9590 Wheatland Terrace
4006 24th Avenue S
Grand Forks, ND 58201-8871
701-787-7621
Fax: 701-787-7564
e-mail: nanadrews@valleymemorial.org
http://www.valleymemorial.org

Greg Hanson, CEO
Nancy Andrews, Administrator
Nancy Hartvikson, Director Personal Services

We are committed to providing quality care and services from a Christian perspective in an environment designed to enhance the dignity and independence of those we serve.

Nebraska

9591 Ambassabor Nebraska City Assisted Living
1800 14th Avenue
Nebraska City, NE 68410-1159
402-873-6650
Fax: 402-873-6621

Mike Brogman, Executive Director

9592 An Angels Touch
1113m N 85th Street
Omaha, NE 68114-2916
402-397-9597
Fax: 402-697-1311

Judy Allington, Owner

9593 Bell View Rehabilitation Center
1702 Hillcrest Drive
Bellevue, NE 68005-3652
402-291-8500
Fax: 402-291-8500

Jolene Robert, Owner

9594 Belle Aims Assisted Living Facility
715 S First Street
Fort Calhoun, NE 68023
402-468-4700
Fax: 402-756-4752

Duane Sprick, Owner

9595 Berverly Square Franklin
1006 N Street
Franklin, NE 68939
308-425-6262
Fax: 308-258-8200

Dan Stauffer, Executive Director

9596 Bethany Home
515 W 1st Street
Minden, NE 68959-1401
308-832-1594
Fax: 308-832-0662

James Dyck, Administrator

9597 Betty's House
3562 Jones Street
Omaha, NE 68105-1310
402-498-4454
Fax: 402-344-4780

Dennis Baty, Owner

9598 Betty's House-Maple Street
8001 Maple Street
Omaha, NE 68134-6554
402-393-4960
Fax: 402-393-7991

Mary Jo Wilson, Owner

9599 Beverly Health Oak Grove
4809 Redman Avenue
Omaha, NE 68104-1842
402-455-5025
Fax: 402-455-1819

David Bennett, Executive Director

Assisted Living Facilities/Nebraska

9600 **Beverly Healthcare Norfolk Chateau**
1824 Vicki Lane
Norfolk, NE 68701-4621
402-379-3118
Fax: 402-371-2376

Trich Montgomery, Manager

9601 **Beverly Square Cozad**
1006 M Street
Franklin, NE 68939-1119
308-784-3715
Fax: 308-784-3746

9602 **Beverly Square Fullerton**
202 N Esther Street
Fullerton, NE 68638-3029
308-536-2488
Fax: 308-536-3226

9603 **Beverly Square Nebraska City**
1420 N 10th Street
Nebraska City, NE 68410-1236
402-873-3304
Fax: 402-873-6307

Jim Nachtigal, Administrator

9604 **Beverly Square Scottsbluff**
111 W 36th Street
Scottsbluff, NE 69361-4623
308-635-2019
Fax: 308-635-2458

Jay Cooburn, Administrator

9605 **Blue Valley Riverside Apartments**
715 S 1st Street
Hebron, NE 68370-2006
402-768-6073
Fax: 402-768-6014

Michelle Plock, Manager

9606 **Brighton Gardens of Omaha**
9220 Western Avenue
Omaha, NE 68114-2297
402-393-7313
Fax: 402-393-7340

Diane Ross, Executive Director

9607 **Cambridge Court**
4107 Central Avenue
Kearney, NE 68847-2577
308-237-3773
Fax: 308-234-9932

Gayla Roberts, Administrator

9608 **Carter House**
1028 Joann Drive
Blair, NE 68008-2725
402-426-1977
Fax: 402-426-0322

Susan McDunn, Manager

9609 **Centennial Park Retirement Village**
510 Centennial Circle
North Platte, NE 69101-6520
308-534-7000
Fax: 308-534-8216

Bob Tank, Administrator

9610 **Chancellor Place at Aspen Park**
3700 W Philip Avenue
North Platte, NE 69101
308-534-8808
Fax: 308-534-8818

Anne Franklin, Administrator

9611 **Chapion Home of Hastings**
602 S Wabash Avenue 1Po Box 1197
Hastings, NE 68901-6152
402-463-6021
Fax: 402-463-7011
e-mail: ch602@inebraska.com

Vivian Sullivan, Administrator
Gary Barrera, Owner

Assisted living for adults with mental disabilities.

9612 **Chrisoma West Assisted Living**
1923 W 4th Avenue
Holdrege, NE 68949-3113
308-995-4493
Fax: 308-995-8702

Don Bakke, Administrator

9613 **Christian Homes Assisted Living Center**
1927 W 4th Avenue
Holdrege, NE 68949-3114
308-995-4493
Fax: 308-995-8702

Don Bakke, Administrator

9614 **Circus House**
1509 1st Avenue
Scottsbluff, NE 69361-3106
308-635-1488
Fax: 308-635-1271

Marcia Estrada, Manager

9615 **Clara-Ellen House**
PO Box 610
Fort Calhoun, NE 68023
402-468-4700
Fax: 402-468-4747

Duane Sprick, Owner

9616 **Clark Jeary Home**
1313 Eldon Drive
Lincoln, NE 68510-5024
402-489-0331
Fax: 402-489-0462

Kathleen Pearson, Administrator

9617 **Comfortcare Homes of Nebraska**
3618 N 114th Avenue
Omaha, NE 68164-2769
402-445-4474
Fax: 402-397-1114

Tom Ruffino, Owner

9618 **Community Memorial Health Center**
295 N 8th Street
Central City, NE 68826
308-364-4440
Fax: 308-364-5184

Our mission is to be the healthcenter of choice of selected health care services, through a commitment to preformance improvement. We act as the region's helth care resource, we partner with other health care providers and, we remain finanially viable.

9619 **Community Pride Care Center**
901 S 4th Street
Battle Creek, NE 68715-3035
402-675-2955
Fax: 402-675-2965

Steve Freese, Administrator

9620 **Cornor Cottage**
1820 N Street
Ord, NE 68862-1623
308-728-3967
Fax: 308-728-7958

Kathy Morrow, Administrator

9621 **Cottonwood House**
3271 29th Avenue
Columbus, NE 68601-3811
402-562-9136
Fax: 402-563-2097

Patti Stuthman, Administrator

9622 **Cottonwood Villa**
450 S Main Street
Ainsworth, NE 69210-1701
402-387-1000
Fax: 402-238-1015

Ann Fiala, Administrator

Assisted Living Facilities/Nebraska

9623 Countryside Home
703 N Main Street
Madison, NE 68748-6061
402-454-3373
Fax: 402-454-9021

Dolores Woodruff, Manager

9624 Crossroads Assisted Living
150 W 24th Street
Alliance, NE 69301-2156
308-762-1615
Fax: 308-762-1621

Felisha Hoagland, Administrator

9625 Crowell Memorial Home
245 S 22nd Street
Blair, NE 68008-1811
402-426-2177
Fax: 402-426-2577
e-mail: bwilliard@huntel.net

Pat Williby, Administrator

The home provides a compassionate care for seniros. We offer a full time physical, occupational, and speech therapies, that are available on site to help residents maintain the highest level of independence possible.

9626 Crown Villa
3030 S 80th Street
Omaha, NE 68124-3254
402-392-0892
Fax: 402-391-1033

Velinda El-Refaie, Manager

9627 Custer Care Center
346 N 16th Avenue
Broken Bow, NE 68822-1422
308-872-6303
Fax: 308-872-5236

Jeanette Denson, Executive Director

Our mission is to provide high quality and reliable services and to maintain the clients independence in their home or at the Center.

9628 East Park Villa
1704 L Street
Aurora, NE 68818-2100
402-694-2300
Fax: 402-694-2305

9629 Eastmont Towers
6315 O Street
Lincoln, NE 68510-2237
402-489-6591
Fax: 402-486-2331

9630 Edgewood Vista Columbus
3386 53rd Avenue
Columbus, NE 68601-1512
402-564-3785
Fax: 402-564-4157
http://www.edgewoodvista.com

Patty Voichoskie, Manager

We provide personalized care in settings designed sepcifically for the Elderly, including those with Alzheimer's Disease or other forms of dementia. Our individualized approach provides a high quality, safe, home-like setting to Seniors who choose to no longer reside alone, but who can live better in social residential settings.

9631 Edgewood Vista Grand Island
214 Piper Street
Grand Island, NE 68803-4027
308-384-0717
Fax: 308-384-0728
http://www.edgewoodvista.com

Faye Roebuck, Manager

We provide personalized care in settings designed specifically for the Elderly, including those with Alzheimer's Disease or other forms of dementia. Our individualized approach provides a high quality, safe, home like setting to Seniors who choose to on longer reside alone, but who can live better in social residential settings.

9632 Edgewood Vista Norfolk
1109 Oasewalk Avenue
Norfolk, NE 68701
402-371-0052
Fax: 402-371-0053
http://www.edgewoodvista.com

Ann Saegebarth, Manager

We provide personalized care in settings designed specigically for the Elderly, including those with Alzheimer's Disease or other forms of dementia. Our individualized approach provides a high quality, safe, home-like setting to Seniors who choose to no longer reside alone, but who can live better in social residential settings.

9633 Edgewood Vista of Fremont
2910 N Clarkson Street
Fremont, NE 68025-2399
402-753-8800
Fax: 402-753-8801
http://www.edgewoodvista.com

9634 Edgewood Vista of Hastings
2400 W 12th Street
Hastings, NE 68901-3501
402-462-4633
Fax: 402-462-6828

Tami Newbery, Manager

We provide personalized care in settings designed specifically for the Elderly, including those with Alzheimer's Disease or other forms of dementia. Our individualized approach provides a high quality, safe, home like setting to Seniors who choose to no longer reside alone, but who can live better in social residential settings.

9635 Edgewood Vista of Omaha
17620 Poppleton Avenue
Omaha, NE 68130-4614
402-333-5749
http://www.edgewoodvista.com

Marysue Pook, Manager

We provide personalized care in settings designed specifically for the Elderly, including those with Alzheimer's Disease or other forms of dementia. Our individualized approach provides a high quality, safe, home like setting to Seniors who choose to no longer reside alone, but who can live better in social residential settings.

9636 El Dorado Manor Nursing Home
Junction Highway 25 & 34
Trenton, NE 69044
308-334-5241

Sandra Brunkhorst, Administrator

9637 Emerald Court
315 W 33rd Street
Scottsbluff, NE 69361-4359
308-220-4007

Arlene Miller, Manager

9638 Florence Home Assisted Living
7915 N 30th Street
Omaha, NE 68112-2418
402-827-6000
Fax: 402-827-6005

Dr Greg Witte, Administrator
Timothy Malloy, Medical Director
Steve Hess, CEO

9639 Garden Square of Crete
1405 Hickory Avenue
Crete, NE 68333-1955
402-826-2241
Fax: 402-826-2775

Jane Boden, Administrator

9640 Gateway Manor
225 N 56th Street
Lincoln, NE 68504-3577
402-464-6371
Fax: 402-467-0299

Linda Tisdel, Executive Director

Assisted Living Facilities/Nebraska

9641 Gold Crest Retirement Center
200 Levi Lane
Adams, NE 68301-8830
402-988-7115
Fax: 402-988-2111

Heath Boddy, Executive Director

9642 Golden Manor Assisted Living
3853 Decatur Street
Omaha, NE 68111-4015
402-551-2484
Fax: 402-551-1114

Rachel Pinkerton, Executive Director

9643 Good Samaritan Towers
423 Boyd Avenue
Alliance, NE 69301-3668
308-762-8970
Fax: 308-762-7740
http://www.good-sam.com

Wayne McLaughlin, Manager

The mission of the Society is to share God's love in a word and deed by providing shelter and supportive services to older persons and others in need.

9644 Good Shepherd Lutheran Home
805 N 22nd Street
Blair, NE 68008-1192
402-426-4663

Lois Pfeiffer, Administrator

9645 Gordon Countryside Care
500 E 10th Street
Gordon, NE 69343-1160
308-282-0806
Fax: 308-282-0251

Krissa Rucker, Administrator

9646 Grabd Island Sterling House
3285 Woodridge Boulevard
Grand Island, NE 68801-7204
308-384-3800

Donell Hulse, Executive Director

9647 Gramercy Hill
600 a Street
Lincoln, NE 68502-1119
402-483-1010
Fax: 402-483-2197
http://www.gramercyhill.com

Carol Rafat, Manager

We are a community that offers you the opportunity to live to life you've always wanted.

9648 Grand Court Seward Retirement Community Assisted Living
500 Heartland Park Drive
Seward, NE 68434-1088
402-643-6500

Julie Pulec, Executive Director

9649 Grand Court Seward Retirment Community Assisted Living
500 Heartland Park Drive
Seward, NE 68434-1088
402-643-6500

Julie Pulex, Executive Director

9650 Grand Island Veterand Home
2300 W Capital Avenue
Grand Island, NE 68803-2097
308-385-6252
Fax: 308-385-6257

Allen M Thompkins, MD

9651 Greeley Assisted Living
301 E Oconnor Avenue
Greeley, NE 68842-4208
308-428-5145
Fax: 308-428-2013

Brenda Snodgrass, Administrator

9652 Greene House
600 Church Street
Seward, NE 68434-1099
402-643-9111
Fax: 402-643-9128

Terry Schoen, Manager

9653 Hastings Homestead
1116 Sycamore Avenue
Hastings, NE 68901-3380
402-461-3841
Fax: 402-461-4398

Tammy Price, Executive Director

9654 Haven Manor Assisted Living
PO Box 6125
Lincoln, NE 68506
402-434-2680
Fax: 402-434-2683

Gus Peach, Administrator

9655 Haven Manor College View
4848 S 48th Street
Lincoln, NE 68516-1290
402-434-2680
Fax: 402-434-2683

Gustavis Peach, Administrator

9656 Heather and Shamrock Apartments
2039 Q Street
Lincoln, NE 68503-3643
402-474-2121

Mary O'Shea, CEO

9657 Hester Memorial Home
407 Dakota Street
Benkelman, NE 69021
308-423-2179
Fax: 308-423-2177

Janice Edwards, Administrator

9658 Hickory Villa
7315 Hickory Street
Omaha, NE 68124-1678
402-392-0767
e-mail: hvinfo@bethesdalivingcenters.org

Monte McVey, Administrator

Hickory Villa has been providing assisted living services to the Omaha community since 1988. This community is also one of the most affordable homes, with rates tailored to a wide range of income.

9659 Hidden Pines Assisted Living Community
309 W 7th Street
McCook, NE 69001-3507
308-345-4600

Peggy Rogers, Administrator

9660 Highland House
PO Box 241
Spencer, NE 68777
402-589-0025

Pam Vanderwerf, Manager

9661 Homestead
4205 6th Avenue
Kearney, NE 68845-3470
308-234-5600
Fax: 308-236-6663

Tanya Stephens, Executive Director

9662 Hospice House
7415 Cedar Street
Omaha, NE 68124-2367
402-343-8600

Assisted Living Facilities/Nebraska

The in patient hospice facility is primarily designed to care for those who do not have a caregiver at home. We are also able to provide respite care for caregivers, five days at a time. For patients already in out home program who develop symptoms that cannot be managed adequatley at home, or for those caregivers who are unable to provide care anylonger at home, then Hospice is the place to be.

9663 Immanuel Lakeside Terrace
17475 Frances Street
Omaha, NE 68130-2344
402-932-9500
Tammy Sealer, Executive Director

9664 Immanuel Trinity Village
522 W Lincoln Street
Papillion, NE 68046-3121
402-614-5500
Cheri Mundt, Executive Director

9665 Imperial Manor Nursing Home
PO Box 757
Imperial, NE 69033
308-882-5333
Diane Cooper, Administrator

9666 Improved Living
114 S 9th Street
Norfolk, NE 68701-5165
402-371-3712
Donna Finkral, Manager

9667 Improved Living House II
203 N 9th Street
Norfolk, NE 68701-3913
402-371-4175
Kathy Pollard, Manager

9668 Improved Living II
203 N 9th Street
Norfolk, NE 68701-3913
402-371-4175
Kathy Pollard, Manager

9669 Kimball County Manor Nusing Home
810 E 7th Street
Kimball, NE 69145-1699
308-235-4693
Bev Schnell, Administrator

9670 Kirkwood House
514 E 6th Street
Wayne, NE 68787-2211
402-375-2515
Jeannia Bressler, Manager

9671 Lebensraum Retirement Residence
118 Ingalls Street
Grand Island, NE 68803-5725
308-382-9066
Fax: 308-395-8822
Nancy Prescott
David Prescott, Owner

Lebensraum Retirement Residence offers affordable Assisted Living with a charming peronal touch. Tucked away in a quiet neighborhood, residents recieve individual attention from direct care staff, with medications monitored by a registered nurse. Home cooked meals, housekeeping, laundry services and social activities are inculded in the daily rate.

9672 Legacy
5600 Pioneers Boulevard
Lincoln, NE 68506-5172
402-436-3000
Fax: 402-436-3013
Jay Bohlken, Executive Director

9673 Legacy Terrace
5700 Fremont Street
Lincoln, NE 68507-1674
402-464-5700
Fax: 402-464-5825
John Kopetzky, Administrator

9674 Longs Creek Village
418 Q Street
Auburn, NE 68305-1040
402-274-5511
Fax: 402-274-5050
Marilyn Swanson, Manager

9675 Madison House
1120 N 1st Street
Norfolk, NE 68701-2926
402-644-4567
Fax: 402-644-8111
Stephanie Hoff, Executive Director

9676 Madonna Assisted Living
2120 S 52nd Street
Lincoln, NE 68506-2028
402-486-8449
Fax: 402-486-8464

9677 Mahoney House
1810 E 12th Street
York, NE 68467-2241
402-362-5538
Fax: 402-362-5690
Kristi Roberts, Manager

9678 Meadows
500 S 18th Street
Norfolk, NE 68701-4543
402-371-1730
Fax: 402-644-4702
e-mail: meadows@cableone.net
Jan Nixon, Executive Director

9679 Merrick Manor Assisted Living
1415 16th Street
Central City, NE 68826-1836
308-946-2624
Fax: 308-946-5700
Gene Church, Manager

9680 Methodist Memorial Homes
1320 11th Avenue
Holdrege, NE 68949-1999
308-995-8631
Fax: 308-995-8636
Kevin Moriarty, Administrator

9681 Morton House
1500 14th Avenue
Nebraska City, NE 68410-1150
402-873-5551
Fax: 402-873-5994
Candy Herzog, Executive Director

9682 New Cassel Retirement Center
900 N 90th Street
Omaha, NE 68114-2704
402-393-2277
Fax: 402-393-3784
Joe Schulte, Religious Leader

9683 Norfolk Homestead
3614 Koenigstein Avenue
Norfolk, NE 68701-8010
402-379-9622
Fax: 402-379-4794
e-mail: info@norfolkhomestead.com
http://www.norfolkhomestead.com
Gayle Wright, Executive Director
Kim Summers, Assistant Executive Director
Char Brewer, Resident Care Coordinator

Assisted Living Facilities/Nebraska

Our mission is to create an environment in which residents can continue to enjoy thier individuality, their independence, and their dignity in a secure, supportive environment. The Homestead represents our proud achievement of this mission.

9684 Northridge Retirement Community
5410 17th Avenue
Kearney, NE 68845-8305
308-698-5410
Fax: 308-698-5157
e-mail: daynap@northridgeretirement.com
http://www.norhtridgeretirement.com

Deb Prange, Administrator

Our modern, well-appointed facility, beautiful spacious grounds and friendly capable staff provide our independent and assisted living residents freedom and piece of mind. From out comfortable apartments and suites to out very own Main Street, you will find that Northridge feels just like home.

9685 Nye Square Retirement Community
650 W 21st Street
Fremont, NE 68025-2589
402-721-9224
Fax: 402-721-1447

Russ Peterson, Manager

9686 Oakland Heights
207 S Engdahl Avenue
Oakland, NE 68045-1419
402-685-5683
Fax: 402-685-5684

Dee Bailey, Administrator

9687 Oaks Retirement Center
1500 Vintage Hill Drive
Wayne, NE 68787-1227
402-375-1500
Fax: 402-375-3579

Susan Wells, Administrator

9688 Orchard Park
3110 S 48th Street
Lincoln, NE 68506-3305
402-488-8191
Fax: 402-483-2931

Virgil Carner, Owner

9689 Our Homes
2445 R Street
Lincoln, NE 68503-3000
402-474-4922
Fax: 402-474-4923

Mary O'Shea, Owner

9690 Paddock Kensington
105 N 6th Street
Beatrice, NE 68310-3994
402-228-2000
Fax: 402-228-3287
e-mail: laurie@paddock-kensington.com
http://www.paddock-kensington.com

Diana Meyer, Executive Director
Laurie Leners, Resident Services

The Paddock-Kinsington strives to provide each of its residents with a healthy, safe, enjoyable place to live. Meeting your expectations and daily needs is out highest priority. The Paddock-Kensington strives to make the most of living each day, by encouraging as well as supporting — the way families do.

9691 Park Avenue Estates
1811 Ridgeway Drive
Lexington, NE 68850-1188
308-324-5490
Fax: 308-324-5181

Arletta Childress, Administrator

9692 Park Place
808 W Park Avenue
Norfolk, NE 68701-5122
402-370-4208
Fax: 402-370-3250

9693 Parkview Lodge Asssited Living
307 Conrad Street
Rushville, NE 69360
308-327-2248
Fax: 308-327-2066

Karen Edwards, Administrator

9694 Parsons House on Eagle Run
14325 Eagle Run Drive
Omaha, NE 68164-5435
402-498-9554
Fax: 402-498-0047
e-mail: info@parsonshouseoneaglerun.com
http://www.parsonshouseoneaglerun.com

Penny Coatman, Executive Director

At Parsons House, service is not simply limited to a laundry list of offerings. Its a philosophy that's put into action in all we do to make livinghere at first choice, not a last resort. That's why you will find that we not only provide these types of assistance, we also tailor how they are delievered to demonstrate that the resident is always at the center of our focus.

9695 Pathfinder House
3010 N Clarkson Street
Fremont, NE 68025-7709
402-721-7714
Fax: 402-727-4225

Linda Parker, Administrator

9696 Pawnee Hills
324 N Pine Street
Genoa, NE 68640-3037
402-993-2811
Fax: 402-993-9972

Joseph Hoffmeister Jr, Owner

9697 Pender Care Center
200 Valley View Drive
Pender, NE 68047-4443
402-385-3072
Fax: 402-385-2603

Pat Licthy, Administrator

9698 Pine Lane of Hartington
403 W Darlene Street
Hartington, NE 68739-4509
402-254-2500
Fax: 402-254-9020

Deena Solonen, Administrator

9699 Plum Creek Care Center
1505 N Adams Street
Lexington, NE 68850-1255
308-324-5531
Fax: 308-324-5630

Keith Sladky, Manager

Plum Creek Care Center is a cozy skilled nursing facility with a caring home environment. Rehabilitation services at plum creek focus on assisting patients in becoming as independent and safe as they can be in their everyday funcional activities. Plum Creek offers Physical Therapy, Occupational Therapy, and Speech-Language Pathology to Care Center Patients as well as outpatients.

9700 Ponderosa Villa
First & Passock
Crawford, NE 69339
308-665-1224
Fax: 308-665-2450

Barb Dreyer, Administrator

9701 Prairie Pines Lodge
900 W 7th Street
Chadron, NE 69337-2500
308-432-4305
Fax: 308-432-2737
http://www.chadronhospital.com

Tom Serres, Manager

Assisted Living Facilities/Nebraska

Prairie Pines is devoted to improving the choices for better housing alternatives for the retired citizens of the Chadron area. Prairie Pines offers both housing and services tailored to each individual's needs, with the best of retirement living: security, peach of mind, and the absence of worry and responsibility in a comforatble setting.

9702 Prairie View Gardens
1705 Prairie View Place
Kearney, NE 68845-8300
308-865-2650
866-337-6408
Fax: 308-865-2657
http://www.gshs.org

Rita Weber, Executive Director

We encourage residents to live life to the fullest as independently as possible while offering personalized assistance, with daily living needs. We also offer an innovative program of care called Reminiscience in separate, secure area for residents with Alzheimer's disease or other types of memory impairments.

9703 Prairie Village Retirement
3000 39th Avenue
Columbus, NE 68601-2250
402-563-4213
Fax: 402-563-9314

Rich Widga, Executive Director

9704 Prairie Winds
603 W 6th Street
Doniphan, NE 68832-9677
402-845-4500
Fax: 402-845-4501

Tammy Price, Manager

9705 Precious Time
103 S Kimball Street
109
Grand Island, NE 68801-7734
308-384-4590
Fax: 308-389-9015

Jeanie Cooper, Owner

9706 Premier Estates
2895 We Street
North Platte, NE 69101
308-534-1900
Fax: 308-537-6477

Ruth Sands Jerke, Administrator

9707 Premier Estates Senior Living Community
811 E 14th Street
Wayne, NE 68787-1216
402-375-1922
Fax: 402-975-1933

Cory Loft, Administrator

9708 Prescott Place
4603 Prescott Avenue
Lincoln, NE 68506-4963
402-483-4086
Fax: 402-483-4124

Brian Reiling, Owner

9709 Princess Anne Residential Care
2024 Binney Street
Omaha, NE 68110-2034
402-451-2242
Fax: 402-451-1907

Lanese Boss, Manager

9710 Quality Living
6409 N 70th Plaza
Omaha, NE 68104-1075
402-573-3700
Fax: 402-573-3792

Kim Hoogeveen, CEO

9711 Regency Square Care Center
3501 Dakota Avenue
South Sioux City, NE 68776-3699
402-494-4273
Fax: 402-494-7267

Greg Gregerson, Administrator

9712 Remington Heights Retirement Center
12606 W Dodge Road
Omaha, NE 68154-2349
402-493-5807
Fax: 402-493-3967

Amy Birkel, Executive Director

9713 Riverside Lodge Retirement Community
404 Woodland Drive
Grand Island, NE 68801-8813
308-382-1657
Fax: 308-381-1863

Jan Thayer, Owner

9714 Rosewood Court Assisted Living Center
4801 N 52nd Street
Omaha, NE 68104-2229
402-827-6060
Fax: 402-723-4520

Lois Siestima, Administrator

9715 Royale Oaks
4801 N 52nd Street
Omaha, NE 68104-2229
402-827-6060
Fax: 402-827-6065

Lois Siestima, Administrator

9716 Saunders House
1313 N Hackberry Street
Wahoo, NE 68066-1148
402-443-3333
Fax: 402-443-5578

Angi Streek, Administrator

9717 Seneca Sunrise
710 Grand Avenue
Ravenna, NE 68869-1100
308-452-4444
Fax: 308-452-4452

Linda Zinnell, Owner

9718 Senior Living Choices at Curtis
217 Crook Avenue
Curtis, NE 69025-9531
308-367-4259
Fax: 308-367-4387

Steve Krull, Owner

Senior Living Choices offers Assisted Living and Independent Cottages. Small facility with that homey atmosphere. Qualified staff 24-7, LPN part time. Medicaid waiver, Helping hands caring heart.

9719 Serenity Place
4520 N 56th Street
Lincoln, NE 68504-1713
402-466-2688
Fax: 402-466-2713

Travis Jacobs, Administrator

9720 Silvercrest Van Dorn Assisted Living
7208 Van Dorn Street
Lincoln, NE 68506-3651
402-486-0011
Fax: 402-484-9170

Tracy Hoffman, Manager

9721 Silvercrest at Fountain View
5728 S 108th Street
Omaha, NE 68137-3547
402-537-0544
Fax: 402-593-8010

Shelly Watson, Executive Director

Assisted Living Facilities/Nevada

9722 Silvercrest at Miracle Hills Assisted Living
11909 Miracle Hills Drive
Omaha, NE 68154-4408
402-431-0011
Fax: 402-431-9257

Pearl Guy, Executive Director

9723 Skyline Retirement Community
7300 Graceland Drive
Omaha, NE 68134-4358
402-572-5750
Fax: 402-572-5777
e-mail: info@skylinerc.com
http://www.skylinerc.com

Tim Smith, Executive Director

Our warm and inviting community encourages active independent seniros to flourish. We offer convenient services and amenities to make life a little easier and more enjoyable. We also offer day trips, group dinners at local restaurants and outings to the symphony, theaters and museums, all with the convenience of regularly scheduled transportation.

9724 Southview Heights Nursing Home
5110 S 49th Street
Omaha, NE 68117-2159
402-731-2118
Fax: 402-233-0782

Paul Randazzo, Administrator

9725 St Joseph Tower Assisted Living
2205 S 10th Street
Omaha, NE 68108-1155
402-952-5000
Fax: 402-952-5117

Tracy Lichti, Executive Director

9726 St Joseph's Retirement Community
320 E Decatur Street
West Point, NE 68788-1593
402-372-3477
Fax: 402-372-6600

Emy Beth Furrer, Administrator

9727 St Joseph's Villa
927 7th Street
David City, NE 68632-1398
402-367-3045
Fax: 402-367-3730
http://www.adorers.org/stjosephsvilla/page1

Joyce Stewart, Administrator

We are in existance to imitate the compassionate Jesus by creating a home for aging men and women where they feel secure, loved and respected. We enable residents to live thier lives to the fullest while preparing themselves for a new dimenstion-life after death. We also maintain a warm, friendly, clean, orderly, safe, and comfotable environment.

9728 St Josephs Nursing Home
401 N 18th Street
Norfolk, NE 68701-3686
402-644-7375
Fax: 402-379-4867

Bill Disch, Administrator

9729 St Luke's Countryside Villa
2300 E 32nd Street
Kearney, NE 68847-1910
308-236-9395
Fax: 308-237-3799
http://www.good-sam.com

Racy Bauer, Manager

Offers independent as assisted living for seniors on a budget.

9730 Sterling Assisted Living
4451 Old Cheney Road
Lincoln, NE 68516-2821
402-420-6058
Fax: 402-420-6073

Pamela Carlson, Manager

9731 Sterling House at Omaha
11308 Blondo Street
Omaha, NE 68164-3822
402-491-0400
Fax: 402-445-2412

Karen Sides, Executive Director

9732 Sterling House at Omaha II
7337 Hickory Street
Omaha, NE 68124-1677
402-391-3000
Fax: 402-391-0504

Jeanette Blackstone, Executive Director

9733 Sunset View Assited Living
Second & Jay Street
Bloomfield, NE 68718
402-373-4150
Fax: 402-373-4160

Mark Luger, Manager

Nevada

9735 Aegis of Las Vegas
9100 West Desert Inn Road
Las Vegas, NV 89117
702-240-3070
Fax: 702-240-3072
http://www.aegisliving.com

Debra Moore, Executive Director

Offers dedicated care to help make life more comfortable and secure. Our community has outdoor grounds with plenty of walking paths and sitting areas to enjoy the warm, sunny weather.

9736 Plaza at Sun Mountain
6031 W Cheyenne Avenue
Las Vegas, NV 89108-4200
http://www.adultcareconsultants.org/plaza

The Plaza at Sun Mountain Independent and Assistd Living offers affordable elegance and gracious living to fit your lifestyle. You will enjoy the riches of retirement with continuing privacy and independence with as much or as little assistance as you choose.

9737 Prestige Assisted Living
1050 E Lake Mead Parkway
Henderson, NV 89015-3200
702-564-1771
Fax: 702-567-1985
http://www.prestigecare.com

Sarah Delamarter, President

We are uniquely designed to provide different levels of assisted living, from minimum daily supervision to personal 24-hour care.

9738 Red Rock Independent & Assisted Living
5975 W Twain Avenue
Las Vegas, NV 89103-1243
702-368-7700

Michelle Kirtz, Administrator

9739 Rose Cottage
3985 S Pearl Street
Las Vegas, NV 89121-7205
702-436-6400

Brad Boman, Administrator

9740 Silver Rose Manor
1490 Grimes Street
Fallon, NV 89406-3103
775-423-4137
e-mail: manor@oasisol.com
http://www.silverrosemanor.com

Dell Williams, Owner

Assisted Living Facilities/New Jersey

Silver Rose Manor provides a home-like, family oriented atmosphere for adults in need of assistance. Visitors are always welcome and residents are free to come and go at will. Residents are provided with three healty, home-cookes meals a day. Everyone is encourages to participate in the exercise classes which meet three days a week. Additionally, transportation is provided for local doctor visites and all medication is supervised.

New Jersey

9741 Acorn Glen
775 Mount Lucas Road
Princeton, NJ 08540-1954
609-430-4000
Fax: 609-430-4001
http://www.assisted.com

Jack Occonor, Owner

We are one of the nation's leading providers of assisted living residences for the physically frail elderly and the nation's largest iperator of freestanding residences for individuals with Alzheimer's disease or other forms of memory loss. The companies mission has remained steadfast: to maximize the quality of life and dignity of older adults.

9742 Allendale Community for Mature Living
85 Harreton Road
Allendale, NJ 07401-1317
201-825-0660

Michael Giancarlo, Administrator

9743 Alterra Clare Bridge Cottage of Monroe
1648 S Black Horse Pike
Williamstown, NJ 08094-9247
856-740-9400

Alane Melendez, Executive Director

9744 Alterra Clare Bridge of Brick
1594 Route 88
Brick, NJ 08724-3036
732-785-3370

Nancy Snyder, Executive Director

9745 Alterra Clare Bridge of Galloway
42 W Jimmie Leeds Road
Galloway, NJ 08205-9401
609-404-1126
Fax: 694-041-174

9746 Alterra Clare Bridge of Hamilton
1645 Whitehorse
Trenton, NJ 08619
609-586-4000
http://www.assisted.com

Nicole Salvi, Executive Director

We are one of the nation's leading providers of assisted living residences for the physically frail elderly and the nation's largest operator of freestanding residences for individuals with Alzheimer's disease or other forms of memory loss. The company's mission has remained steadfast: to maximize the quality of life and dignity of older adults.

9747 Alterra Clare Bridge of Westhampton
480 Woodlane Road
Mount Holly, NJ 08060-3828
609-877-0555
http://www.assisted.com

Ted Hamilton, Manager

We are one of the nation's leading providers of assisted living residences for the physically frail elderly and the nation's largest operator of freestanding residences for individuals with Alzheimer's disease or other forms of memory loss. The company's mission has remained steadfast: to maximize the quality of life and dignity of older adults.

9748 Alterra Sterling House of Florence
901 Broad Street
Florence, NJ 08518-2813
609-499-6662
http://www.assisted.com

Joel Davey, Manager

We are one of the nation's leading providers of assisted living residences for the physically frail elderly and the nation's largest operator of freestanding residences for individuals with Alzheimer's disease or other forms of memory loss. The company's mission has remained steadfast: to maximize the quality of life and dignity of older adults.

9749 Alterra Wynwood of Emerson
590 Old Hook Road
Emerson, NJ 07630-1378
201-986-9009
http://www.assisted.com

Dana Smiles, Manager

We are one of the nation's leadng providers of assisted living residences for the physically frail elderly and the nation's largest operator of freestanding residences for individuals with Alzheimer's disease or other forms of memory loss. The company's mission has remaines steadfast: to maximize the quality of life and dignity of older adults.

9750 Alterra Wynwood of Galloway
820 Hamburg Tpke
Wayne, NJ 07470-2019
973-942-4800
http://www.assisted.com

Gilbert Santa, Executive Director

We are one of the nation's leading providers of assisted living residences for the physically frail elderly and the nation's largest operator of freestanding residences for individuals with Alzheimer's disease or other forms of memory loss. The company's mission has remained steadfast: to maximise the quality of life and dignity of older adults.

9751 Alterra Wynwood of Wayne
820 Hamburg Tpke
Wayne, NJ 07470-2019
973-942-4800
Fax: 973-942-3099

Gilbert Santa, Executive Director

9752 Arbor Glen
100 Monroe Street
Bridgewater, NJ 08807-5002
908-595-6500
Fax: 908-595-6515

Thomas Mondloch, CEO

9753 Arden Courts of Whippany
18 Eden Lane
Whippany, NJ 07981-1402
973-581-1800
Fax: 973-581-1979

Kathy Harrison, Executive Director

9754 Assisted Living Chancellor Park at theWindrows
1000 Windrow Drive
Princeton, NJ 08540-5007
609-514-9111
Fax: 609-419-1326

9755 Assisted Living at Spring Oak
1611 S Main Road
Vineland, NJ 08360-6513
856-507-1505
Fax: 856-507-1528
e-mail: alvineland@earthlink.net
http://www.springoak.net

Dawn Lavoir, Resident Relations Specialist
Dawn Watkins, Administrator
Trish Benfor, Administrative Assistant

Assisted Living

Assisted Living Facilities/New Jersey

9756 Atria Tinton Falls
44 Pine Street
Eatontown, NJ 07724
732-918-1960
Fax: 732-918-1952

Carolann Koerner, Executive Director

9757 Avalon at Bridgewater
Rr 28
Bridgewater, NJ 08807
908-707-8800
Fax: 908-707-9805

Julia Paima, Executive Director

9758 Bayside Manor
7 Laurel Avenue
Keansburg, NJ 07734-1122
732-471-1600
Fax: 732-471-1077

Joseph A Cappadona, Owner

9759 Behavior-Dementia Management
1427 Brace Road
Cherry Hill, NJ 08034-3524
856-795-3131
Fax: 856-795-7062

9760 Bey Lea Village
1351 Old Freehold Road
Toms River, NJ 08753-2795
732-240-0090
Fax: 732-244-8551
http://www.baycare.com

Michael Norbury, Administrator

Bey Lea Village is a skilled nursing center that offers quality long-term and subacute care and specializes in Alzheimer's and related dementia care throughout all states of the disease. Using the collaborative efforts of our interdisciplinary team, we provide a wide range of comprehensive care and services to meet the specific needs of each resident.

9761 Brandall Estates
432 Central Avenue
Linwood, NJ 08221-1372
609-926-4663
Fax: 609-926-5354

Eileen Bennett, Administrator

9762 Brandywine Assisted Living at Middlebrook Cross
2005 Route 22 W
Bridgewater, NJ 08807
732-868-8181
Fax: 732-868-8178

Richard Heaney, Executive Director

9763 Brandywine Assisted Living at Moorestown
1205 N Church Street
Moorestown, NJ 08057-1198
856-778-0600
Fax: 856-778-4544

9764 Brandywine Assisted Living at the Gables
515 Jack Martin Boulevard
Brick, NJ 08724-7744
732-836-1400
Fax: 732-836-9600

Ulla Meylan, President

9765 Brighton Gardens of Cherry Hill
1979 Route 70 E
Cherry Hill, NJ 08003-1833
856-424-7227
Fax: 856-424-7885

Elizabeth Eichfeld, Executive Director

9766 Brighton Gardens of Edison
1801 Oak Tree Road
Edison, NJ 08820-2772
732-767-1031
Fax: 732-767-0835

Sanford Mann, Executive Director

9767 Brighton Gardens of Florham Park
21 Ridgedale Avenue
Florham Park, NJ 07932-2336
973-966-8999
Fax: 973-966-8998

George Edson, Executive Director

9768 Brighton Gardens of Middletown
620 Highway 35
Middletown, NJ 07748-4224
732-275-0790
Fax: 732-275-0797
e-mail: middletown.dcr2@sunriseseniorliving.com
http://www.sunriseseniorliving.com

Patsy Distler, Director of Community Relations
Tom Kessler, Manager

Assisted Living and Alzheimer's Care.

9769 Brighton Gardens of Paramus
186 Paramus Road
Paramus, NJ 07652-1309
201-251-9600
Fax: 201-251-0776

Wilson Anhar, Executive Director

9770 Brighton Gardens of Saddle River
5 Boroline Road
Upper Saddle River, NJ 07458-2343
201-818-8680
Fax: 201-818-7875

Gail Spencer, Executive Director

9771 Brighton Gardens of West Orange
220 Pleasant Valley Way
West Orange, NJ 07052-2997
973-731-9840
Fax: 973-731-9170

Merri Buckstone, Executive Director

9772 Bristol Glen
200 Bristol Glen Drive
Newton, NJ 07860-2329
973-300-5788
Fax: 973-579-2351
e-mail: snorton@bristolglen.org
http://www.umh-nj.org/bristolglen

G Scott Norton, Executive Director
James W McCracken, Administrator
Jeffrey J Quinn, Marketing Director

9773 Cardinal Retirement Village
455 Hurffville Crosskeys Road
Sewell, NJ 08080-2328
856-582-5292
Fax: 856-582-5026
http://www.cardinalvillage.com

Skip Broomall, Owner

9774 Chancellor Park of Park Ridge
124 Noyes Drive
Park Ridge, NJ 07656-1296
201-782-0440
Fax: 201-782-0899

John Forrentino, Executive Director

9775 Chelsea at East Brunswick
606 Cranbury Road
E Brunswick, NJ 08816-5422
732-651-6100
Fax: 732-651-6446

Gloria Petro, Executive Director

9776 Chelsea at Fanwood
295 South Avenue
Fanwood, NJ 07023-1357
908-654-5200
Fax: 908-789-0451
http://www.chelseaal.com

Jennifer Ricci, Manager

Assisted Living Facilities/New Jersey

We the staff, will provide a comfortable, safe and secure home to our residents in a caring atmosphere of respect and dignity. Through individualized support and health care services, encouragement of maximum independence, emphasis on freedom of choice and protection of privacy, our residents will enjoy the greatest quality life possibel.

9777 Chelsea at Montville
165 Changebridge Road
Montville, NJ 07045-9563
973-882-0800
Fax: 973-402-4132
http://www.chelseaal.com

Chris Nichols, Manager

We, the staff, will provide a comfortable, safe, and secure home to our residents in a caring atmosphere of respect and dignity. Through individualized support and health care services, encouragement of maximum independence, emphasis on freedom of choice and protection of privacy, our residents will enjoy thr greatest quality of life.

9778 Chelsea at Tinton Falls
1 Hartford Drive
Tinton Falls, NJ 07701
732-933-4700
Fax: 732-933-0999
http://www.chelseaseniorliving.com

Eileen Weller, Community Relations Director

Assisted Living, Respite, Separate Memory Impaired Unit, near Jersey shore.

9779 Chestnut Hill Residence
338 Chestnut Street
Passaic, NJ 07055-3158
973-777-7800
Fax: 937-778-9013

Michael Mazzola, Administrator

9780 Collinswood Manor
460 Haddon Avenue
Collingswood, NJ 08108-1336
856-854-4331
Fax: 856-854-0879

Arlene Toussaint, Administrator

9781 Elms of Cranbury
61 Maplewood Avenue
Cranbury, NJ 08512-3237
609-395-0641
Fax: 609-395-8200
http://www.elmsofcranbury.com

Anita M Dietrick, Owner

We provide the highest levels of care in a warm, comfortable and personal environment.

9782 Father Hudson House
111 Dehart Place
Elizabeth, NJ 07202-1224
908-353-6060
Fax: 908-353-4504

Sally Sinclair, Manager

9783 Fountains at Cedar Parke
114 Hayes Mill Road
Atco, NJ 08004-2457
856-753-2000
Fax: 856-753-2333

Jennifer Kelley, Executive Director

9784 Francis Asbury Manor
70 Stockton Avenue
Ocean Grove, NJ 07756-1150
732-774-1316
Fax: 732-776-6313

Diane Scott, Executive Director

9785 Green Acres Manor
1931 Lakewood Road
Toms River, NJ 08755-1211
732-286-2323
Fax: 732-914-9095

Tejas Patel, Administrator

9786 Haven at Holiday Manor
1700 Route 37 W
Toms River, NJ 08757-2347
732-341-0880
Fax: 732-341-3506

Barbara Estabrook, Administrator

9787 Hearthside Commons at the Job HainesHome
250 Bloomfield Avenue
Bloomfield, NJ 07003-5689
973-743-0792
888-743-0794
Fax: 973-743-1135
e-mail: dplotnick@earthlink.net
http://www.job-haines.org

Donna Plotnick, Community/Resident Coordinator
Noreen Haveron, Executive Director

Has been committed to providing exeptional care at an affordable cost to seniors older than 65. To accommodate our emphasis on compassionate care, individual expression and freedom of choice. From the beginning, residents were encourages to make our residence thier home.

9788 Heritage Assisted Living at Hammonton
45 Route 206
Hammonton, NJ 08037-2722
609-561-8977
Fax: 609-564-1158

Diane Welke, Administrator

9789 House of the Good Shepherd
798 Willow Grove Street
Hackettstown, NJ 07840-1721
908-852-9956
Fax: 908-852-2615

Fred Heleine, Executive Director

9790 Independence Manor at Hunterdon
188 State Route 31
Flemington, NJ 08822-5764
908-788-4893
Fax: 908-788-3783

Gary Nagle, Owner

9791 Liberty Manor Assisted Living Residence
49 Lasatta Avenue
Englishtown, NJ 07726-1656
732-786-1000
Fax: 732-786-0689
http://www.libertymanor.com

Noreen Heller, Administration

We are dedicated to making your family member feel every bit a part of ours. Those who join our family recieve individualized attention, patient support, and warm companionship. And while we are there whenever we're needed, we are always carful to respect privacy and protect independence.

9792 Mill Gardens at Midland Park
36 Faner Road
Midland Park, NJ 07432-1719
201-493-7400
Fax: 201-493-7374

Nicholas Drivanos, Executive Director

9793 Newseasons of Cherry Hill
490 Cooper Landing Road
Cherry Hill, NJ 08002-2560
856-482-9300
Fax: 856-482-9330

Peggy O'Neill, Manager

9794 Newseasons of Voorhees
501 Laurel Oak Road
Voorhees, NJ 08043-4418
856-566-2340
Fax: 856-566-2341

Allyson Buscher, Administrator

Assisted Living Facilities/New Jersey

Assisted living offers all the attention you'd expect from traditional nursing home care, but in a beautiful, home-like setting. Assisted living communities emphasize a warm and comfortable physical environment through the style of dining areas and services, social and recreational activities, common areas for group or private socializing and ongoing accessibility to community resources and health professionals.

9795 Nottingham House Assited Living Residenc
94 Stevens Road
Toms River, NJ 08755-1237
732-286-5005
Fax: 732-286-4885

9796 Orchards at Bartley Assisted Living
100 N County Line Road
Jackson, NJ 08527-1264
732-730-1700
Fax: 732-730-1738

Phil Scalo, CEO

9797 Renaissance Gardens at Seabrook
3002 Essex Road
Tinton Falls, NJ 07753-7758
732-643-2060
Fax: 732-643-2081
http://www.thecareexperts.com

Steve Olsen, Health Care Counselor
Ben Unkle, Executive Director

Features all private Assisted Living apartments and all private Long-Term Care rooms; full-time, on-site staff doctors with nurses on duty 24-hours a day. Short-Time Rehab (physical, speech and occupational therapy); dementia and Alzheimer's care also available. Renaissance Gardens, the choice you can feel good about.

9798 Rose Hill Assisted Living
1150 Washington Boulevard
Trenton, NJ 08691-3154
609-371-7007
Fax: 609-371-7027

Georgeann Polito, Administrator

9799 Shores at Wesley Manor
22nd Bay Aveunenue
Ocean City, NJ 08226
609-399-8505
Fax: 609-391-8411

Sue Handron, Executive Director

9800 Somerset Manor North
473 Demott Lane
Somerset, NJ 08873-7700
732-873-4800
Fax: 732-873-5800

Erio Rosario, Executive Director

9801 Somerset Manor South
1135 Hamilton Street
Somerset, NJ 08873-3347
732-247-1460
Fax: 732-247-0930

9802 Spring Hills at Morristown
17 Spring Place
Morristown, NJ 07960-3947
973-539-3370
Fax: 973-539-9210

Tanya Massicot, Sales Executive

9803 Spring Meadows at Summit
41 Springfield Avenue
Summit, NJ 07901-4038
908-522-8852
Fax: 908-522-8862

Mary Majors, Executive Director

9804 St Marys Assisted Residence at Morris Hill
1 Bishops Drive
Lawrenceville, NJ 08648-2050
609-896-0006
Fax: 609-895-0242

Charles Brennan, CEO

9805 Summerville at Hillsborough
600 Auten Road
Somerville, NJ 08876
908-431-1403
Fax: 908-431-1304
http://www.sslusa.com

We provide care for residence with Alzheimer's disease and other forms of memory impairments. All Summerville communities are designed to provide a comfortable residential enviornoment for seniors, with a distinct hospitality feel. Summerville residents from independent to frail, enjoy services tailored to meet their individual needs and preferences.

9806 Summerville at Stafford
1275 Route 72 W
Manahawkin, NJ 08050-2473
609-597-2500
Fax: 609-597-9898

Shaun Lynch, Executive Director

9807 Summerville at Voorhees
1301 Laurel Oak Road
Voorhees, NJ 08043-4339
856-770-8209
Fax: 856-783-8484

Kevin Summerville, Vice President

9808 Sunnyside Manor
2501 Ramshorn Drive
Manasquan, NJ 08736-2133
732-528-9311
Fax: 732-528-9026

John Keane, Owner

9809 Sunrise Assisted Living East Brunswick
190 Summerhill Road
East Brunswick, NJ 08816-4908
732-613-1355
Fax: 732-613-1365

Sundeep Jeste, Executive Director

9810 Sunrise Assisted Living of Edgewater
351 River Road
Edgewater, NJ 07020-1028
201-941-6111
Fax: 201-941-6638

Edward Midgley, Executive Director

9811 Sunrise Assisted Living of Morris Plains
209 Littleton Road
Morris Plains, NJ 07950-2934
973-538-7878
Fax: 973-359-0994

9812 Sunrise Assisted Living of Mt Laurel
400 Fern Brook Lane
Mount Laurel, NJ 08054-9542
856-222-1213
Fax: 856-802-9749

Bruce Bosco, Executive Director

9813 Sunrise Assisted Living of Paramus
567 Paramus Road
Paramus, NJ 07652-1708
201-493-9889
Fax: 201-493-0888

Donna Zayat, Executive Director

9814 Sunrise Assisted Living of Wall
2600 Allaire Road
Wall Township, NJ 07719-9568
732-282-1700
Fax: 732-282-1720

David Woodward, Executive Director

9815 Sunrise Assisted Living of West Essex
47 Greenbrook Road
Fairfield, NJ 07004-3890
973-228-7890
Fax: 973-228-7918

Richard Caminiti, Executive Director

Assisted Living Facilities/New Mexico

9816 Sunrise Assisted Living of Westfield
240 Springfield Avenue
Westfield, NJ 07090-1023
908-317-3030
Fax: 908-789-5778
Andrew Harris, Executive Director

9817 Sunrise of Old Tappan
195 Old Tappan Road
Old Tappan, NJ 07675-7042
201-750-1110
Fax: 201-750-1191
Richard Lombardo, Executive Director

9818 Sunrise of Wayne
184 Berdan Avenue
Wayne, NJ 07470-3232
973-628-4900
Fax: 973-633-0680
Anna Marie Novak, Executive Director

9819 Sunrise of Woodbury Lake
752 Cooper Street
Deptford, NJ 08096-2521
856-848-8777
Fax: 856-848-3171
Anda Constina, Executive Director

9820 Surnise of Woodcliff Lake
430 Chestnut Ridge Road
Woodcliff Lake, NJ 07677-7604
201-782-1888
Fax: 201-782-1899
Gina Bizzarro, Executive Director

9821 Twin Cedars
1456 Glassboro Road
Wenonah, NJ 08090-1606
856-468-6824
Fax: 856-468-6318
Adeline Murphy, Owner

9822 Van Dyke Valley Assisted Living
197 Cahill Cross Road
West Milford, NJ 07480-1947
973-728-7945
Fax: 973-657-1657

9823 Victoria Mews Assisted Living
51 N Main Street
Boonton, NJ 07005-8740
973-263-3000
Fax: 973-263-3107
Anthony Bastardi, Owner

9824 Whispering Knoll Assisted Living
62 James Street
Edison, NJ 08820-3938
732-744-5541
Fax: 732-906-4908
Rose Chavez, Executive Director

We offer an alternative for people who are looking for that special place to call home. With a dedicated staff of professionals, assistance is always available, 24 hours a day, seven days a week. Our housekeeping staff can assist you with any or all of your needs, and out health care staff provides nursing assistance around the clock. There is also an emergency call and repsonse system installed in every suite.

9825 Willows at Holmdel Assisted Living Community
713 N Beers Street
Holmdel, NJ 07733-1503
732-335-4405
Fax: 732-962-7441
e-mail: pbrown@bchs.com
http://www.bchs.com
Patricia Brown LSW, CALA, Director Marketing
Cathy Movny, Administrator

Assisted living and a secure community for Alzheimer's care.

New Mexico

9826 Acantilado Vista
920 Riverview Drive SE
Rio Rancho, NM 87124
505-896-3000
http://www.leisurecare.com

Offers resort style living in an active retirement community.

New York

9827 Altria Plainview
150 Sunnyside Boulevard
Plainview, NY 11803-1504
516-576-3330
Fax: 516-576-1112
Mitch Sarpio, Executive Director

Offers personalized assisted living in a warm and caring environment supervised 24-hours a day.

9828 Anna Erika Home for Adults
110 Henderson Avenue
Staten Island, NY 10301-2196
718-727-8100
Fax: 718-981-9116
Daniel Stern, Administrator

9829 Atria Forest Hills
10825 Horace Harding Expy
Corona, NY 11368-4532
718-760-4600
Fax: 718-592-1808
Susan Koster, Executive Director

Offers a unique supportive living environment with all the comforts of home.

9830 Bellevue Manor Assisted Living Community
4330 Onondaga Boulevard
Syracuse, NY 13219-3030
315-468-5108
Fax: 315-468-5108
David Quirello, Administrator

9831 Birchwood Assisted Living and Physical Rehabilitation
423 Clay Pitts Road
East Northport, NY 11731-3801
631-368-5252
Fax: 631-368-3128
James Steffens, Owner

9832 Briarwood Manor
1001 Lincoln Avenue
Lockport, NY 14094-6195
716-433-1513
Fax: 716-433-8142
Salvatore Ferreri, Owner

9833 Bronxwood Home for the Aged
799 E Gun Hill Road
Bronx, NY 10467-6192
718-881-9100
Fax: 718-515-0150
Betty Bonta, Administrator

Socially active adults will find a myriad of supervised activities and services.

9834 Clark Meadows
1 Clark Mdws
Canandaigua, NY 14424-1754
585-393-4330
Fax: 585-393-0567
Dan Goldstein, Executive Director

Assisted Living Facilities/New York

9835 **Country House in Westchester**
2000 Baldwin Road
Yorktown Heights, NY 10598-4010
914-962-3625
800-362-1957
Fax: 914-962-4130
e-mail: astone@countryhouseretirement.com
http://www.countryhouseretirement.com
Anita R Stone, Administrator
Sherry Weber, Admissions Associate
Maureen Hildebrand, Case Manager

At the Country House, you can enjoy retiremet living in th comfort and privacy of your own charming studio or suite - with added security of knowing that our Health Services Department and other staff are available around the clock to serve you, should you need assistance.

9836 **Dosberg Manor Adult Home**
2680 N Forest Road
Getzville, NY 14068-1556
716-639-3311
Fax: 716-639-3309
David Dunkelman, President

9837 **Elm York Home for Adults**
10030 Ditmars Boulevard
East Elmhurst, NY 11369-1395
718-446-7900
Fax: 718-446-7938
Tibor Klein, Owner

9838 **Empire State Association of Assisted Living**
646 Plank Road
Suite 207
Clifton Park, NY 12065
518-371-2573
Fax: 518-371-3774
e-mail: nyasstliv@aol.com
http://www.ny-assisted-living.org
Jim Kane Jr, President
Jim Vitale, Executive Vice President
Lisa Newcomb, Executive Director

Dedicated to strengthening New York State's assisted living industry and promoting the best interests of providers and residents.
Number of Members: 20,000

9839 **Fountains at Millbrook**
79 Flint Road
Millbrook, NY 12545-6410
845-677-8550
Fax: 845-677-8630
Deborah Slocum, Administrator

Our continuum of care gives residents the ability to choose the service program that best suits their current lifestyle and to add more services as their needs change.

9840 **Golden Care Home for Adults**
35 Prospect Street
Spring Valley, NY 10977-7308
845-356-2440
Fax: 845-356-4158
Steven Schomburg, Administrator

9841 **Hillcrest Spring**
Upper Market Street
Amsterdam, NY 12010
518-843-3770
Fax: 518-843-3878
Catherin Sha, Administrator

9842 **Long Island Living Program Assisted Living**
431 Beach 20th Street
Far Rockaway, NY 11691
718-327-2700
Fax: 718-327-2223
e-mail: ahe1836@aol.com
http://www.livingcenteralp.com
Amram Shetrit, Administrator

The Long Island Living Center Adult Home has extended our services to include an Assisted Living Program. We offer personalized attentive care to the frail and elderly i n a homelike atmosphere. Our retirement home is non-sectarian and is designed to help meet the physical, emotional and social needs of the elderly. For those eligible, wh have a Medicard funded program. All rates include 3 delicious Kosher meals, recreation, synagogue on premises. Housekeeping, laundry, physical therapy and beauty salon services as well as 24 hour secured environment.

9843 **Madison York Home For Adults**
6180 Woodhaven Boulevard
Rego Park, NY 11374-2742
718-446-4300
Fax: 718-446-4758
Where your respect, dignity and human growth come first.

9844 **Maplewood Residence**
225 Bennett Road
Buffalo, NY 14227-1528
716-681-9480
Fax: 716-681-8762
Patrice Evans, Administrator

9845 **Marie Louise Heins Home for Adults**
Bradley Avenue
Mt Vernon, NY 10552
914-699-0800
Fax: 914-699-2158
Frank Tripodi, Administrator

9846 **New Central Manor Assisted Living Progra**
1509 Central Avenue
Far Rockaway, NY 11691-4001
718-471-7700
Fax: 718-471-7732
Alex Klein, Manager

9847 **Palm Beach Home for Adults**
2900 Bragg Street
Brooklyn, NY 11235-1199
718-891-8400
Fax: 718-769-1006
Shimon Lefkowitz, Executive Director

Offers you a luxurious lifestyle in a secure and caring environment.

9848 **Presbyterian Residential Community**
4310 Middle Settlement Road
New Hartford, NY 13413-5316
315-724-9300
Fax: 315-724-7470

9849 **Regency at Glen Cove**
94 School Street
Glen Cove, NY 11542-2513
516-674-3007
Fax: 516-674-4144
e-mail: Beth@theregencyatglencove.com
http://www.theregencyatglencove.com
Beth Dressler, Administrator

At the Regency, you can relax, while our exclusive MediComfort program, customized to provide for each resident's individual needs, ensures that you retain the level of independence that you are use to, all while preserving your dignity and privacy. From personal care assistance to health care monitoring and management, everything is taken care of. The Regency's devoted and caring staff go out of their way to enhance residents day to day living.

9850 **Savoy at Brooklyn**
385 McDonald Avenue
Brooklyn, NY 11218-2211
718-871-8600
Fax: 718-871-5503

9851 **Savoy at Little Neck Assusted Living Community**
5515 Little Neck Parkway
Little Neck, NY 11362-2244
718-423-7900
Fax: 718-423-5050
Joanna Laba, Executive Director

Assisted Living Facilities/Ohio

9852 **Scharome Manor Home for Adults**
631 Foster Avenue
Brooklyn, NY 11230-1398
718-859-2400
Fax: 718-859-4412

Leo Rosenson, Owner

9853 **Seneca Lake Terrace Adult ResidentialCommunity**
3670 Pre Emption Road
Geneva, NY 14456-9138
315-789-4162
Fax: 315-781-1494
e-mail: cjv2552@dreamscape.com
http://www.senecalaketerrace.com

Chris Vitale, Administrator

Our home provides quality care in a home-like supportive environment to ensure independence, dignity, privacy, and individuality.

9854 **Shire at Culverton Adult Home**
2515 Culver Road
Rochester, NY 14609-1751
585-467-4544
Fax: 585-338-2877

Tracy Vogl, Administrator

9855 **Tanglewood Manor**
560 Fairmount Avenue
Jamestown, NY 14701-2797
716-483-2876
Fax: 716-483-2832
http://www.tanglewoodmanor.com

Terri Ingersoll, Administrator

Tanglewood Manor was created to be a community that feels functious like family. Care programs offered include Assisted Living, Adult Day Care, Respite Care and Private Care.

9856 **Tappan Zee Manor**
51 Mountainview Avenue
Nyack, NY 10960-1709
845-353-6100
Fax: 845-353-1660

Michele Rothbuan, Manager

9857 **Vassar-Warner Home**
52 S Hamilton Street
Poughkeepsie, NY 12601-4198
845-454-3754
Fax: 845-454-6967

Karen Harvatin, Executive Director

Ohio

9858 **Alterra Sterling House of Alliance**
1277 S Sawburg Road
Alliance, OH 44601-5750
330-829-0180
Fax: 330-821-5587

Andrea Williams, Executive Director

9859 **Alterra Sterling House of Springfield**
3270 Middle Urbana Road
Springfield, OH 45502-7805
937-390-0432
Fax: 937-390-7805

Michael Campbell, Executive Director

9860 **Amanda House**
1070 Gloria Avenue
Lima, OH 45805-2900
419-224-6327
Fax: 419-224-5554

Jenny Connelly, Manager

9861 **Amherst Manor**
175 N Lake Street
Amherst, OH 44001-1332
440-988-4415
Fax: 440-988-5612

Kristen Root, Administrator

9862 **Anchor Lodge Retirement Village**
3756 W Erie Avenue
Lorain, OH 44053-1298
440-244-2019
Fax: 440-244-5612

Staci Lehmkuhl, Administrator

9863 **Anna Maria of Aurora**
889 N Aurora Road
Aurora, OH 44202-9503
330-562-6171
Fax: 330-562-3572

George Norton, Owner

9864 **Apostolic Christian Home**
10680 Steiner Road
Rittman, OH 44270-9714
330-927-1010
Fax: 330-937-1020

David Maletich, Administrator

9865 **Arbors at Clyde Assisted Living Center**
700 Helen Street
Clyde, OH 43410-2051
419-547-9595
Fax: 419-547-1605

Bonnie Stephanian, Administrator

9866 **Arbors at Dayton Residential Care**
320 Albany Street
Dayton, OH 45408-1402
937-496-6200
Fax: 937-496-1990

Ed Roberts, Administrator

9867 **Arbors at Fairlawn Residential Care**
575 Scleveland Massillon Road
Fairlawn, OH 44333
330-666-5866
Fax: 330-666-3215

Monica Herberth, Administrator

9868 **Arbors at Marietta Residential Care**
400 17th Street
Marietta, OH 45750
740-373-3597
Fax: 740-373-3597

9869 **Arden Courts of Parma**
9205 W Sprague Road
N Royalton, OH 44133-1208
440-886-5858
Fax: 440-886-5880

Meredith Pasco, Executive Director

9870 **Aspen Woodside Village**
19455 Rockside Road
Bedford, OH 44146-2000
440-439-8666
Fax: 440-439-7352
http://www.aspenretirement.com

Jill Risner, Administrator

9871 **Bayley Place**
990 Bayley Place Drive
Cincinnati, OH 45233-1655
513-347-5500
Fax: 513-347-5553
http://www.bayleyplace.org

Adrain Walsh, Administrator

Bayley PLace is a non profit ministry of the Sisters of Charity, that is a continuing care retirmenet community that offers a full spectrum of health and wellness lifestyle options. Bayley Place meets the changing needs of today's mature adults. Our beautiful campus includes maintenance free cottages, assisted living apartments, Alzheimer's and Dementia care, nursing care, Eldermont Adult Day Program, Community Outreach Services and more.

Assisted Living Facilities/Ohio

9872 Berea Lake Towers Retirement Community
4 Berea Commons
Berea, OH 44017-2524
440-243-9050
Fax: 440-243-3049
http://www.berealaketowers.com
Tammy Cummins, Administrator

Berea Lake Towers is committed to providing the highest quality and most cost effective services possible to its clients and residents community. Through our commitment, Berea Lake Towers will strive to enhance its position as a predominant provider of health care and management services.

9873 Berkley Square Retirement Community
100 Berkley Drive
Hamilton, OH 45013-1787
513-856-8600
Fax: 513-856-8324
James Mayer, Administrator

9874 Blossom Hill Care Center
12496 Princeton Road
Huntsburg, OH 44046-9792
440-635-5567
Fax: 440-338-7833
Donald Gray, Owner

9875 Breckenridge Village
36855 Ridge Road
Willoughby, OH 44094-4198
440-942-0093
Debbie Knokch, Manager

9876 Briarfield Manor Residential Care
461 S Canfield Niles Road
Youngstown, OH 44515-4089
330-270-3468
Fax: 330-270-3479
http://www.briarfield.net
Diane Reese, Administrator

Briarfield Health Care Centers are dedicated to offering a variety of health services that meet the rehabilitation, nursing, psychological, social and spiritual needs of the community we serve. We recognize the importance of meeting individual needs by offering our experience and knowledge in cooperation with clients and residents in setting realistic expecations for their outcomes and quality of life in an environment of comapssion and dignity.

9877 Briarwood
3700 Englewood Drive
Stow, OH 44224-3223
330-688-1828
Fax: 330-688-2071
Jonathan Trimble, President

9878 Brookhaven the Lifecare Community
804 Vinnie Connecticut
Brookville, OH 45309
937-833-2133
Fax: 937-297-6904
Mike McKinniss, Administrator

9879 Brookside Estates
15435 Bagley Road
Middleburg Heights, OH 44130-4827
440-887-1125
877-839-0591
Fax: 440-887-1126
Mary Kelly, Executive Director

We offer the perfect complement of housing, health care, support services, meals, activities and many extra amenities for seniors who can no longer live on their own, but want to maintain their independence. These are all provided in one customized Service Care Plan, all for one affordable monthly fee. Our community also has a licensed nurse on staff.

9880 Canton Christian Home
2550 Cleveland Ave NW
Canton, OH 44709-3371
330-456-0004
Fax: 330-452-9951
e-mail: info@cantonchristianhome.org
http://www.cantonchristianhome.org
Tom Strobl, Administrator

The mission of Canton Christian Home is to provide the highest level of quality care and services to older adults, compassionately meeting their needs in a Christian homelike environment, and promoting their health, security, happiness, and usefulness in longer living.

9881 Canton Regency Retirement Community
4515 22nd Street NW
Canton, OH 44708-1573
330-477-7664
Fax: 330-477-9634
Alan Gruber, Administrator

9882 Commons of Providence
5000 Providence Drive
Sandusky, OH 44870-1410
419-624-1171
Fax: 419-624-0302
e-mail: jwindisch@commonsatsandusky.org
http://www.commonsatsandusky.org
Jane E Windisch, Marketing Director
Rick Didomienico, Executive Director

9883 Commons of Providence: Specialized Assisted Living
4901 Providence Drive
Sandusky, OH 44870-1422
419-624-1171
Fax: 409-624-0302
Rick Didomienico, Executive Director

9884 Community's Hearth & Home
550 W Harding Road
Springfield, OH 45504-1709
937-399-8622
Fax: 937-399-8863
Kim Henry, Executive Director

9885 Community's Hearth & Home at El Camino
3185 El Camino Drive
Cincinnati, OH 45236
513-984-9400
Fax: 937-399-1781

9886 Cottingham Retirement Community
3995 Cottingham Drive
Cincinnati, OH 45241-1686
513-563-3600
Fax: 513-563-3601
e-mail: cotadmin@deaconessltc.org
Margie Berryman, Executive Director

We are committed to providing the highest quality of care to our residents and thier families. This care is to be provided with dediction to spiritual values, compassion, customer service and continuous improvement, public accountability, respect, teamwork and finanial strength. We are also dedicated to maximizing the abilities of our valued employees and to being a productive, responsible member of each community we serve.

9887 Country Club Retirement Center
55801 Conno Mara Drive
Bellaire, OH 43906-9698
740-676-2300
Fax: 740-676-1277
Joe Zvoick, Administrator

9888 Delaware Court
4 New Market Drive
Delaware, OH 43015-4282
740-369-6400
Fax: 740-369-6401
Ken Levering, Administrator

775

Assisted Living Facilities/Ohio

9889 **East Park Retirement Community**
6360 Elmdale Road
Brook Park, OH 44142-4075
216-267-7067
Fax: 216-267-0603
e-mail: info@sovereighcare.com
http://www.sovereignhealthcare.com/eprc
Pat Zingale, Executive Director

East Park Care Center is designed with the resident in mind. Accommodations include private and semi-private suites. A family/resident lounge encourages families and friends to enjoy private visits.

9890 **Elms Retirement Village**
136 S Main Street
Wellington, OH 44090-1344
440-647-2414
Fax: 440-647-9004
Monique Cech, Administrator

9891 **Emerald Ridge of Solon**
5625 Emerald Ridge
Solon, OH 44139-1860
440-498-3000
Fax: 440-498-8257
Will Grunspan, CEO

9892 **Genoa Retirement Village Assisted Living**
300a Cherry Street
Genoa, OH 43430-1823
419-855-7755
Fax: 419-855-4047
Phil Witker, Administrator

9893 **Good Shepherd Home**
725 Columbus Avenue
Fostoria, OH 44830-3255
419-435-1801
Fax: 419-435-1594
Chris Widman, Administrator

9894 **Greene Oaks Willow Place**
164 Office Park Drive
Xenia, OH 45385-1647
937-376-8217
Fax: 937-376-8214
Jeff Eyrich, Administrator

9895 **Homewood Residence-Richmond Heights**
2 Homewood Drive
Richmond Heights, OH 44143-2955
216-291-6140
Fax: 216-291-6149
Cheryl Walker, Manager

9896 **Homewood Residence-Rockefeller Gardens**
3151 Mayfield Road
Cleveland, OH 44118-1753
216-321-6331
Fax: 216-321-6651
Patrick Payne, Manager

9897 **Inn at Belden Village**
3927 38th Street NW
Canton, OH 44718-2900
330-493-0096
Fax: 330-493-9600
e-mail: information@theinnatbeldenvillage.com
http://www.innatbeldenvillage.com
Jo Ann Matyasi, Administrator
Phyllis Mussina, Marketing Director
Nannette Gammill, Executive Director

The Village was designed to give as mich assistance as one watns, while carefully preserving dignity. We believe every life deserves to be cherished, needs to be cared for, and longs to be needed. We know every person desires independence, the freedom to choose, a sense of dignity and self-esteem.

9898 **Inn at Chestnut Hill**
5055 Thompson Road
Columbus, OH 43230-6336
614-855-3700
Fax: 614-855-7020
http://www.innatchestnuthill.com
Donn E Alspach, President
Marion C Green, Executive Director
Dee Anderson, Marketing/Admissions

Our goal is to fulfill the living needs of our residenc, to give them an enriched lifestyle, a better quality of life and the opportunity to share new experiences and activities in new surroundings. We have provided a comfortable, "homey" environment for our residents and have included the elements of privacy, security, and convenience.

9899 **Inn at Lakeview**
4000 Lakeview Xing
Groveport, OH 43125-9059
614-836-5990
Fax: 614-836-5978
e-mail: admin@innatlakeview.com
http://www.innatlakeview.com
Kelly Wilson, Administrator

We provide a comfortable, "homey" environment for our residents. We provide a combination of housing, personalized health care, and assistance with daily living activities in an environment that includes privavy, security and convenience. We will strive to give our residents an enriched lifestyle, better quality of life, and the opportunity to share new experiences and activities.

9900 **Kendal at Oberlin**
600 Kendal Drive
Oberlin, OH 44074-1900
440-775-0094
Fax: 440-775-9820
e-mail: admissions@kao.kendal.org
http://www.kao.kendal.org
Barbara Thomas, Executive Director

Kendal at Oberlin offers independent living in spacious cottages and apartments.

9901 **Kingston Residence of Perrysburg**
333 E Boundary Street
Perrysburg, OH 43551-2861
419-872-6200
Fax: 419-872-6209
e-mail: krp@kingstonhealthcare.com
http://www.kingstonhealthcare.com

It has been our goal to create an environment that went well beyond making our residents feel welcome or comfortable. Our caring and attentive staff and you will realize this is a place that successfully balances the delacate requirements of independence and assistance.

9902 **Landing of Canton**
4550 Hills and Dales Road NW
Canton, OH 44708-1508
330-477-5727
Fax: 330-477-5327
e-mail: mail@thelandingofcanton.com
http://www.thelandingofcanton.com
Chanin McElroy, Executive Director
Darlene Fleming, Marketing Director
Colleen Gulling, Office Manager

Emertius Assisted Living operates the Landing of Canton. They provide cost-effective quality care that is personalized for individual needs, fosters independence for each resident, treats each resident with dignity and respect, promotes the individuality of each resident, allows each resident choice of care and lifestyle, protects each residents right to privacy, nurtures the spirit of each resident, and provides a safe, residential environment.

9903 **Laurel Lake Retirement Community**
200 Laurel Lake Drive
Hudson, OH 44236-2156
330-650-2100
Fax: 330-650-6725
http://www.laurellake.com
David Oster, President

Assisted Living Facilities/Ohio

Our community offers you a gracious and comfortable home, first class support services, and an active community life to fulfill your social recreational and spiritual needs. The following services and amenities will make your life at Laurel Lake more carefree and convenient.

9904 Liberty Arms Assisted Living Facility
1353 Churchill Hubbard Road
Youngstown, OH 44505-1380
330-759-2893
Fax: 330-758-9282

Krista Reese, Executive Director

9905 Life Center at Wesley Ridge
2225 State Route 256
Reynoldsburg, OH 43068-9538
614-759-0023
Fax: 614-860-4200

Elizabeth Vogt, President

At Life Center clients recieve and individualized plan of day time care in a well supervides environment. Clients are able to socialize in a comforatble yet, stimulating atmosphere which offers social and therapeutic activities based on individual interests and needs. Clients are helped to maintain maximun functioning, health and wellness through nursing care and rehabilitative services.

9906 Light of Hearts Villa
283 Union Street
Bedford, OH 44146-4578
440-232-1991
Fax: 440-232-1782
e-mail: information@lightofheartsvilla.org
http://www.lightofheartsvilla.org

Helen T Scasny, Administrator

We provide three meals per day, daily housekeeping, daily personal care, weekly laundry as needed, and medication monitoring.

9907 Lincoln Park Manor
694 Isaac Prugh Way
Kettering, OH 45429-3481
937-297-4300
Fax: 937-297-4199
http://www.lincolnparkseniors.com

Anita Theis, Manager

We offer the best in resident care that is provided by our professional staff. Individual needs, raging from advances in medical attention to a friendly helping hand are provided in warm, home-like surroundings.

9908 Lochaven Apartments
1640 Allentown Road
Lima, OH 45805-1875
419-227-5450
Fax: 419-224-2761

Mary Jo Horstman, Executive Director

9909 Lodge of Montgomery
12050 Montgomery Road
Cincinnati, OH 45249-2003
513-683-9966
Fax: 513-683-3709

Tawnya Hensely, Executive Director

9910 Lutheran Home at Toledo Assisted Living
2519 Seaman Street
Toledo, OH 43605-1509
419-693-0751
Fax: 419-693-1026

9911 Lutheran Village of Columbus
935 N Cassady Avenue
Columbus, OH 43219-2283
614-252-4987
Fax: 614-525-5952

Terri Martin, Administrator

9912 Mallard Crove Seniors Community
1410 Mallard Cove Drive
Cincinnati, OH 45246-3943
513-772-6655
Fax: 513-772-7908

Barb Lingby, Administrator

9913 Manor at Autumn Hills
2567 Niles Vienna Road
Niles, OH 44446-5401
330-652-6745
Fax: 330-652-9009

Carl Gillette, Owner

9914 Manor at the Meadows
301 W Western Reserve Road
Youngstown, OH 44514-3527
330-726-7110
Fax: 330-726-2517

9915 Maple Knoll Village-Beecher Place
11100 Springfield Pike
Cincinnati, OH 45246-4112
513-782-2400
Fax: 513-772-1056

9916 Marian Living Center
9800 Market Street
North Lima, OH 44452-9560
330-549-2434
Fax: 330-549-0701

Warren Harris, Administrator

9917 Marriott Maple Ridge of Willoughby
35300 Kaiser Court
Willoughby, OH 44094-6633
440-269-8600
Fax: 440-269-2398

Scott Peters, Manager

9918 Marymount Place
11960 McCracken Road
Garfield Heights, OH 44125-2952
216-587-8800
Fax: 216-587-8212
e-mail: info@marymountplace.org
http://www.marymountplace.com

Peggy Mathews, Administrator

Our mission is to offer older adults housing and supportive services enhancing the physical, social and spiritual needs of each individual while recognizing one's privacy, dignity, and personal choice.

9919 Mayfair Village Retirement Community
3011 Hayden Road
Columbus, OH 43235-7250
614-889-6202
Fax: 614-889-7532

Jamie Foley, Manager

9920 McKnight Terrace
3000 McGee Avenue
Middletown, OH 45044-4991
513-423-2322
Fax: 513-423-2323

Lisa Minera, Executive Director
Amy Newland, Marketing Director

We were created in the belief that people truly thirve when they can be active and maintain their independence. And everything we do is directed toward helping our residents achieve that goal. Its living at its best. Our residents are free from the everyday cares of living, so they can pursue life on ther terms and be as active as they want to be.

9921 Meadows at Friendship Village
6000 Riverside Drive
Dublin, OH 43017-1492
614-717-0000
Fax: 614-764-7466

Alyson Hoover, Executive Director

Assisted Living Facilities/Ohio

9922 Mennonite Memorial Home
410 W Elm Street
Bluffton, OH 45817-1199
419-358-1015
Fax: 419-358-1919

Lynn Thompson, Administrator

9923 Mount Royal Villa
13900 Bennett Road
N Royalton, OH 44133-3897
440-237-7966
Fax: 440-237-2558

Matt Haynes, Administrator

9924 Oakwood Village
1500 Villa Road
Springfield, OH 45503-1656
937-390-9000
Fax: 937-390-9333

9925 Ohio Assisted Living Association
1335 Dublin Road
Suite 221b
Columbus, OH 43215-7013
614-481-1950
Fax: 614-481-1954
e-mail: oala@ohioassistedliving.org
http://www.ohioassistedliving.org

Jean Thompson, Executive Director

9926 Ohio Masonic Home
2655 W National Road
Springfield, OH 45504-3617
937-325-1531
Fax: 937-325-5238
http://www.ohiomasonichome.org

David Bannerman, CEO

9927 Omni West
3259 Vestal Road
Youngstown, OH 44509-1000
330-793-4404
Fax: 330-793-6004

Melanie Thirion, Executive Director

9928 Orchard Grove
670 Flat Rock Road
Bellevue, OH 44811-9486
419-484-1111
Fax: 419-832-7020

Robert Tebeau, Administrator

9929 Otterbein Portage Valley
20311 Pemberville Road
Pemberville, OH 43450-9413
419-833-7000
Fax: 419-833-5763
http://www.otterbein.org

Joe Devore, Executive Director

9930 Outlook Pointe at Lima
2075 N Eastown Road
Lima, OH 45807-2021
419-331-2442
Fax: 419-331-9267
http://www.outlookpointe.com

Provides Senior Health Care that balances senior's desire for independence and their evolving health care needs. We incorporate a comprehensive regimen of preventive, restorative and theraputic care.

9931 Outlook Pointe at Medina
1046 N Jefferson Street
Medina, OH 44256-1102
330-764-3877
Fax: 330-723-0742
e-mail: mcmc@outlookpointe.com
http://www.outlookpointe.com

Jackie Mitchell, Community Director
Martin Gitlin, Marketing Coordinator
Ann Haltrich, Health Promotions Coordinator

Provides Senior Health Care that balacnes senior's desire for independence and their evolving health care needs. We incorporate a comprehensive regimen of preventive, restorative and theraputic care.

9932 Outlook Pointe at Ontario
2010 Walker Lake Road
Mansfield, OH 44906-1412
419-747-1119
Fax: 419-747-4887
http://www.outlookepointe.com

Cindy Smith, Manager

Provides Senior Health Care that balances senior's desire for independence and their evolving health care needs. We incorporate a comprehensive regimen of preventive, restorative and therapeutic care.

9933 Outlook Pointe at Ravenna
141 Chestnut Hill Drive
Ravenna, OH 44266-3916
330-296-4545
Fax: 330-296-5504

Chanin McElroy, Executive Director

9934 Outlook Pointe at Sagamore Hills
997 W Aurora Road
Sagamore Hills, OH 44067-1687
330-908-1166
Fax: 330-908-1156
http://www.outlookpoint.com

Provides Senior Health Care that balances seniors' desire for independence and thier evolving health care needs. We incorporate a comprehensive regimen of preventive, restorative and therapeutic care.

9935 Outlook Pointe at Xenia
60 Paceline Circle
Xenia, OH 45385-1281
937-372-1530
Fax: 937-291-1608
http://www.outlookpointe.com

Lynne Bailey, Executive Director

Provides Senior Health Care that balances seniors' desire for independenc and their evolving health care needs. We incorporate a comprehensive regimen of preventive, restorative and therapeutic care.

9936 Paisley House for Aged Women
1408 Mahoning Avenue
Youngstown, OH 44509-2595
330-799-9431
Fax: 330-799-8810

Audean Patterson, Executive Director

9937 Patriot Ridge Community
789 Stoneybrook Trail
Fairborn, OH 45324-6099
937-878-0262
Fax: 937-878-8407

Greg Nijak, Administrator

9938 Pebble Creek Senior Care Residence
670 Jarvis Road
Akron, OH 44319-2538
330-645-0200
Fax: 330-645-2010

Jim Egli, Manager

9939 Residence of Sterling Oaks
540 Great Oaks Trl
Wadsworth, OH 44281-8799
330-336-1141
Fax: 330-334-0647

9940 Ridgewood at Friendship Village
5675 Ponderosa Drive
Columbus, OH 43231-3137
614-890-8285
Fax: 614-891-6556

Mike Heys, Administrator

Assisted Living Facilities/Ohio

9941 **Rockmill Springs Assisted Living**
3682 Dolson Court
Carroll, OH 43112-9721   740-654-4529
Danielle Ashbaugh, Manager

9942 **Rutherford House**
805 S Buchanan Street
Fremont, OH 43420-4992   419-334-6962
                                Fax: 419-332-7346
Judy Rendon, Executive Director

9943 **Sara Moore Home**
26 N Union Street
Delaware, OH 43015-1922   740-362-9641
                                Fax: 740-369-2834
Lisa Graham, Manager

9944 **Shepherd of the Valley Howland**
4100 N River Road NE
Warren, OH 44484-1041   330-856-9232
                                Fax: 330-856-2571
Tamara Salvino, Administrator

9945 **Shepherd of the Valley Lutheran Retirmen**
1500 McKinley Avenue
Niles, OH 44446-3718   330-544-0771
                                Fax: 330-544-6840
Rick Mattix, Manager

9946 **St Augustine Health Campus**
7801 Detroit Avenue
Cleveland, OH 44102-2813   216-939-7600
                                Fax: 216-634-2717
Pat Gareua, Owner

9947 **St Joseph Assisted Residence**
1882 Knob Street
Louisville, OH 44641-8645   330-875-5562
                                Fax: 330-875-8947
Mary Welch, Administrator

9948 **Summerville at Mentor Assisted Living**
5700 Emerald Court
Mentor, OH 44060-1870   440-354-5499
                                Fax: 440-354-5422
http://www.summervilleseniorliving.com
Lisa Reed, Director of Community Relations
Valerie Hayden LNHA, Executive Director
Kathy Loy RN, Director of Resident Care

The community is known for its warmth and hospitality, with beautiful common areas including a parlor, library, and two courtyards. In addition, the community is complemented with both private and semi-private suites for residents to comfortably enjoy. Summerville provides an on-site healthcare professional 24 hours a day to assist those residents who may needs extra care with their activities of daily living.

9949 **Summerville at Middletown**
3851 Towne Boulevard
Franklin, OH 45005-5595   513-424-9999
                                Fax: 513-424-9988
Sean Hunt, Executive Director

9950 **Summerville of Singing Woods**
140 E Woodbury Drive
Dayton, OH 45415-2841   937-274-1400
                                Fax: 937-274-8759
Connie Harvey, Executive Director

9951 **Summit Villa Assisted Living**
330 Southwest Avenue
Tallmadge, OH 44278-2235   330-633-4723
                                Fax: 330-633-5012
e-mail: mkt@tandemhealthcare.com
http://www.tandemhealthcare.com
Doug Pearson, Executive Director

9952 **Sunrise Assisted Living**
216000 Detroit Road
Rocky River, OH 44116   440-356-9797
                                Fax: 440-356-9997
http://www.sunriseseniorliving.com
Rima Hansen, Executive Director

Our residents maintain their independence in a secure home like setting, with individualized service plans dedicated to their specific needs.

9953 **Sunrise Assisted Living at Bexley**
2600 E Main Street
Bexley, OH 43209-2446   614-235-3900
                                Fax: 614-235-1919
http://www.sunriseassistedliving.com
Stacie Cingle, Administrator

At sunrise we take living personally. That's why we offer our seniors a variety of living arrangements, amentities, services, meal plans, social activities, and care. It's a broad range of options that help seniors enjoy a full life - all on their own terms.

9954 **Sunrise Assisted Living at Finneytown**
9101 Winton Road
Cincinnati, OH 45231-3829   513-729-5233
                                Fax: 513-729-5234
http://www.sunriseseniorliving.com
Nancy Phillips, Executive Director

9955 **Sunrise Assisted Living of Bath**
101 N Cleveland Massillon Road
Akron, OH 44333-2422   330-666-7011
                                Fax: 330-665-1493
http://www.sunriseseniorliving.com

Our assisted living provides the ideal solution for seniors who need some help with daily activities.

9956 **Sunrise Assisted Living of Cuyahoga Falls**
1500 State Road
Cuyahoga Fls, OH 44223-1302   330-929-8500
                                Fax: 330-929-2090
http://www.sunriseseniorliving.com
Don Poteet, Manager

We pride ourselves in being an alternative to nursing home care by providing care and services with a "personalized touch" in an environment that looks and feels like home.

9957 **Sunrise Assisted Living of Englewood**
95 W Wenger Road
Englewood, OH 45322-2723   937-836-9617
                                Fax: 937-836-9616
http://www.sunriseseniorliving.com
Valerie Heine, Executive Director

9958 **Sunrise Assisted Living of Hamilton**
896 NW Washington Boulevard
Hamilton, OH 45013-1281   513-893-9000
                                Fax: 513-893-9001
http://www.sunriseseniorliving.com
Jamie Cianciolo, Executive Director

9959 **Sunrise Assisted Living of Kenwood**
9090 Montgomery Road
Cincinnati, OH 45242-7712   513-745-9292
                                Fax: 513-745-9666
http://www.sunriseseniorliving.com
John Eberle, Executive Director

Assisted Living Facilities/Oklahoma

We pride ourselves in our customer service and the outstanding quality of life we provide for our residents.

9960 Sunrise Assisted Living of Oakwood
1701 Far Hills Avenue
Dayton, OH 45419-2532
937-294-1772
Fax: 937-294-1134
http://www.sunriseseniorliving.com
Robert Burns, Executive Director

9961 Sunrise Assisted Living of Parma
7766 Broadview Road
Parma, OH 44134-6743
216-447-8909
Fax: 216-328-9272
http://www.sunriseseniorliving.com
Matt Lanzi, Executive Director

9962 Sunrise Assisted Living of Shaker Heights
16333 Chagrin Boulevard
Shaker Heights, OH 44120-3711
216-751-0930
Fax: 216-751-0980
http://www.sunriseseniorliving.com
Pamela Zivot, Executive Director

9963 Sunrise Assisted Living of Wooster
1615 Cleveland Road
Wooster, OH 44691-2335
330-262-1615
Fax: 330-264-1666
http://www.sunriseseniorliving.com
Ann Worley, Executive Director

We pride ourselves in our great reputation in the community for being the place to live if you need assistance.

9964 Sunrise at Tucker Creek
6525 N High Street
Worthington, OH 43085-4045
614-846-6500
Fax: 614-845-6654
http://www.sunriseseniorliving.com
Deb Iacoboni, Manager

9965 Sunrise of Gahanna
775 E Johnstown Road
Gahanna, OH 43230-2115
614-418-9775
Fax: 614-418-9799
http://www.sunriseseniorliving.com
Holly Franko, Executive Director

9966 Sunrise of Poland
335 W McKinley Way
Youngstown, OH 44514-1681
330-707-1313
Fax: 330-707-1411
http://www.sunriseseniorliving.com
Kerry Collins, Executive Director

9967 Sunrise on the Scioto
3500 Riverside Drive
Upper Arlington, OH 43221-1753
614-457-3500
Fax: 614-457-4300
http://www.sunriseseniorliving.com
Kim Lee, Executive Director

9968 Traditions at Bath Road
300 E Bath Road
Cuyahoga Fls, OH 44223-2510
330-929-6272
Fax: 330-945-3404
e-mail: bathinfo@ncrccd.org
TDD 800-925-8689
Bob Cameron, Administrator

9969 Traditions at Mill Run
3550 Fishinger Boulevard
Hilliard, OH 43026-9549
614-771-0100
Fax: 614-529-2584
Connie Mancuso, Administrator

9970 Traditions of Chillicothe
142 University Drive
Chillicothe, OH 45601-2198
740-773-8107
Fax: 740-772-5113
http://www.chillicotheohio.com
Our services are as simple as providing meals, flt linen and light housekeeping. Also, we help with dressing, personal hygiene, medication adminitration and many types of health care.

9971 Vancrest Assisted Living
10357 Van Wert Decatur Road
Van Wert, OH 45891-9209
419-238-4646
Fax: 419-238-5727
Mick Murphy, Administrator

9972 Villas at St Therese Assisted Living
25 Noe Bixby Road
Columbus, OH 43213-1411
614-864-3576
Fax: 614-864-3577
Sister Michaels, Administrator

9973 Washington County Home
Rr 10
Box 124
Marietta, OH 45750-9156
740-373-2028
Fax: 740-373-2094

9974 Wedgewood Estates of Mansfield
600 Timble Road
Mansfield, OH 44906
419-756-7400
Fax: 418-756-5891
William Casto, Owner

9975 Westlake Village
28550 Westlake Village Drive
Westlake, OH 44145-3880
440-892-4200
Fax: 440-892-4756
Sharon Essi, Administrator

9976 Whetstone Gardens
3710 Olentangy River Road
Columbus, OH 43214-3450
614-457-1100
Fax: 614-442-5139
Erin Hennesy, Executive Director

9977 Willow Knoll Retirement Community
4400 Vannest Avenue
Middletown, OH 45042-2770
513-422-5600
Fax: 513-422-6532

9978 Worthington Christian Village
165 Highbluffs Boulevard
Columbus, OH 43235-1400
614-846-6076
Fax: 614-842-9541
Brian Cooper, Administrator

Oklahoma

9979 Alterra Clare Bridge Cottage of Oklahoma City
10001 S May Avenue
Oklahoma City, OK 73159-6600
405-691-0409
Fax: 405-692-4229

9980 Alterra Clare Bridge Oklahoma City
12401 Dorset Drive
Oklahoma City, OK 73120-9190
405-752-4220
Fax: 405-752-2771
Anita Burkhaulter, Executive Director

Assisted Living Facilities/Oklahoma

9981 **Alterra Sterling House of Bartlesville**
3737 Camelot Drive
Bartlesville, OK 74006-7589
918-333-9400
Fax: 918-330-9503

Carrie Kruouac, Manager

9982 **Alterra Sterling House of Bethany**
4101 N Council Road
Bethany, OK 73008-3108
405-787-9200
Fax: 405-787-9208

Carrie Elmore, Executive Director

9983 **Alterra Sterling House of Broken Arrow**
4011 S Aspen Avenue
Broken Arrow, OK 74011-1431
918-451-1987
Fax: 918-451-2585

Kay Jenkins, Executive Director

9984 **Alterra Sterling House of Claremore**
1605 N Highway 88
Claremore, OK 74017-4874
918-343-3300
Fax: 918-343-9840

Norma Muller, Manager

9985 **Alterra Sterling House of Durant**
1500 N 19th Avenue
Durant, OK 74701-2152
580-931-0600
Fax: 580-931-8030
e-mail: wferguson@assisted.com
http://www.assisted.com

Willie Ferguson, Residence Director

Assisted living at its finest. We take care of memory care residents, incontinence, dementia, etc.

9986 **Alterra Sterling House of Edmond**
116 W Danforth Road
Edmond, OK 73003-5280
405-330-9100
Fax: 405-330-9102

Lynnette Streobele, Administrator

9987 **Alterra Sterling House of Enid**
4613 W Willow Road
Enid, OK 73703-2757
580-237-0700
Fax: 580-237-0767

Glenda Kouba, Executive Director

9988 **Alterra Sterling House of Lawton**
6302 SW Lee Boulevard
Lawton, OK 73505-9103
580-536-6800
Fax: 580-536-6924

Lynette Carter, Executive Director

Provides housing and assistance to older adults who want to reatin their independence while recieving the daily support they need.

9989 **Alterra Sterling House of Midwest City**
615 W Blueridge Drive
Midwest City, OK 73110-1241
405-741-2000
Fax: 405-741-2926

Kara Bolino, Executive Director

9990 **Alterra Sterling House of Muskogee**
3211 Chandler Road
Stillwater, OK 74075
405-624-1616
Fax: 405-624-1619

Misty Keeble, Executive Director

9991 **Alterra Sterling House of Norman**
1701 Alameda Street
Norman, OK 73071-3078
405-573-9200
Fax: 405-573-9298
http://www.assisted.com

Mary Stacey, Executive Director

9992 **Alterra Sterling House of Oklahoma City**
7535 W Hefner Road
Oklahoma City, OK 73162-4462
405-773-8300
Fax: 405-755-5631

Anita Burkhalter, Executive Director

9993 **Alterra Sterling House of Ponca City**
1500 Bradley Avenue
Ponca City, OK 74604-2524
580-765-9900
Fax: 580-762-1915

Tammie McWilliams, Executive Director

9994 **Alterra Sterling House of Shawnee**
3947 N Kickapoo Avenue
M
Shawnee, OK 74804-1708
405-275-7747
Fax: 405-275-7973

Bryan Hiel, Executive Director

9995 **Alterra Sterling House of Tulsa**
6022 E 71st Street
Tulsa, OK 74136-6742
918-494-4011
Fax: 918-494-4742

Chantelle Julian, Manager

9996 **Alterra Sterling House of Tulsa South**
8231 S Mingo Road
Tulsa, OK 74133-4549
918-461-1100
Fax: 918-459-9402

Shari Beguin, Executive Director

9997 **Alterra Sterling House of Weatherford**
800 Gartrell Place
Weatherford, OK 73096-2074
580-772-6600
Fax: 580-772-0484

Charlene Jantz, Manager

9998 **Alterra Sterling of ADA**
801 Stadium Driveive
Shawnee, OK 74801
405-275-7747
Fax: 405-275-7971

Bryan Hiel, Executive Director

9999 **Ambassadors Courtyards**
1380 E 61st Street
Tulsa, OK 74136-693
918-743-7887
Fax: 918-293-3050

Phoebe Blackwell, Administrator

10000 **Angel House Residential Assisted Living**
10018 E 29th Street
Tulsa, OK 74129-4409
918-664-1215
Fax: 918-664-2575

Rita Cook, Owner

10001 **Arbor House Assisted Living Center**
4501 W Main Street
Norman, OK 73072-4459
405-292-9200
Fax: 405-292-5672

Angie Nance, Administrator

Assisted Living Facilities/Oklahoma

10002 Ash Street Place
111 S Ash Street
Guthrie, OK 73044-4935
405-282-2000
Fax: 405-282-3782

Holly Chapell, Owner

10003 Brighton Gardens of Oklahoma City
12928 N May Avenue
Oklahoma City, OK 73120
405-748-6464
Fax: 405-748-6551

Luella Nabors, Executive Director

10004 Brighton Gardens of Tulsa
5211 S Lewis Avenue
Tulsa, OK 74105-6556
918-743-2700
Fax: 918-743-1343

Matt Hoskin, Manager

10005 Brookridge Retirement Community
7802 Quanah Parker Trailway
Lawton, OK 73505
580-536-9700
Fax: 580-536-7954

Ronnie Stringer, Administrator

10006 Country Wood Manor Living Center
1604 S 13th Street
Kingfisher, OK 73750-4619
405-375-5232
Fax: 405-375-5830

Vickie Trent, Manager

10007 Crystal Place Assisted Living Center
400 SW 79th Street
Oklahoma City, OK 73139-8120
405-616-1980
Fax: 405-616-2985

Natalie Jewel, Administrator

10008 Crystalwood Assisted Living Center
2610 Reardon Road
Woodward, OK 73801-5846
580-256-4001
Fax: 580-256-7289

Ginger Canico, Manager

10009 Davis Home
PO Box 205
Yale, OK 74085
918-387-2849
Fax: 918-387-4001

10010 Dogwood Creek Retirement Center
3230 E Shawnee Road
Muskogee, OK 74403-1813
918-683-5100
Fax: 918-683-5113

Kim McConnell, Administrator

10011 Elkwood Assisted Living
1000 Elkwood Boulevard
Elk City, OK 73644-9580
580-225-0506
Fax: 580-225-1458

Bobby McGuire, Manager

10012 Emerald Square Assisted Living Center
701 N Council Road
Oklahoma City, OK 73127-4980
405-787-4466
Fax: 405-789-8101
e-mail: info@emerald-square.com
http://www.emerald-square.com

Mary Harris, Administrator

Emerald Square provides assistance with bathing and dressing, medication administration, housekeeping, laundry and physician appointment transportation.

10013 Epworth Villa
14901 N Pennsylvania Avenue
Oklahoma City, OK 73134-6071
405-752-1200
800-579-8776
Fax: 405-755-4813
http://www.epworthvilla.com

Kendra Carlson, Public Relations Coordiantor
Mark Whitley, Director of Funds Development
Holley Izard, Director of Employee Services

10014 Forest Glade Retirement Center II
2500 N Glade Avenue
Bethany, OK 73008-7905
405-495-7100
Fax: 405-495-7458

Charlotte Fulbright, Administrator

10015 Forest Hills Health Care Center
4300 W Houston Street
Broken Arrow, OK 74012-4519
918-254-5000
Fax: 918-250-2538

Carla Jackson, Administrator

10016 Frances Strietel Villa
2300 W Broadway Street
Collinsville, OK 74021-1625
918-371-2545
Fax: 918-371-0564

Ron Hoffman, Administrator

10017 Gardens Assisted Living
1165 Brenner Road
Sapulpa, OK 74066-6141
918-224-0600
Fax: 918-224-6287

Jeanne Taylor, Administrator

10018 Gardens at Rivermont
750 Canadian Trails Drive
Norman, OK 73072-7639
405-360-6056
Fax: 405-360-0225

Eric Legleiter, Executive Director

10019 Golden Oaks Village
5801 N Oakwood Road
Enid, OK 73703-9344
580-234-2817
Fax: 580-233-3426

Wesley Kroeker, Owner

10020 Green County Village Assisted Living
1027 Swan Drive
Bartlesville, OK 74006-5048
918-335-2086
Fax: 918-335-3254

Wes Ramsey, Administrator

10021 Hearthstone at Quail Springs
14300 N Portland Avenue
Oklahoma City, OK 73134-4030
405-755-6469
Fax: 405-755-6474
http://www.hearthstoneassisted.com

Karen Lorimor, Manager

To provide quality and affordable assisted iving care and services that offer value and exceed the expectations of our residents and their families.

10022 Heartsworth House
821 N Foreman Street
Vinita, OK 74301-1434
918-256-7856
Fax: 918-256-3703

Pam Wolfe, Administrator

Assisted Living Facilities/Oklahoma

10023 Heathridge Assisted Living Comunity
2130 S 85th E Avenue
Tulsa, OK 74129
918-622-9191
Fax: 918-622-9205

Patsy Holland, Finance Executive

10024 Heritage Assisted Living Center
9025 NW Expressway Street
Yukon, OK 73099-8374
405-722-5552
Fax: 250-798-8842

Curtis Aduddell, Owner

10025 Heritage Place Assisted Living
1380 Heritage Lane
Tahlequah, OK 74464-2136
918-456-7117
Fax: 918-456-7960

Steve Cox, Owner

10026 Jefferson's Garden
15401 N Pennsylvania Avenue
Edmond, OK 73013-1514
405-715-1717
Fax: 405-715-9017

Carl Balaban, Director
Judith Wartman, Manager
Kay Coldiron, Social Services

Independent homes assisted living mamory care and fitness center for seniors.

10027 Manchester House
2333 Manchester Drive
Oklahoma City, OK 73120-3791
405-775-9009
Fax: 405-775-9292

Shelee Stewart, Manager

10028 Mansion at Waterford
6110 N Pennsylvania Avenue
Oklahoma City, OK 73112-7361
405-848-1817
Fax: 405-607-0006

10029 Mustang Manor Assisted Living
1017 W State Highway 152
Mustang, OK 73064-2310
405-376-5600
Fax: 405-376-3867

Sandra Killian, Administrator

10030 Oklahoma Methodist Manor
4134 E 31st Street
Tulsa, OK 74135-1599
918-743-2565
Fax: 918-743-1782

Steve Dickey, Administrator

10031 Parke Senior Living
7821 E 76th Street
Tulsa, OK 74133-3680
918-249-1262
Fax: 918-250-9666

10032 Plantation House-Okmulgee
1001 S Belmont Avenue
Okmulgee, OK 74447-6300
918-756-1253
Fax: 918-756-2764

Sherri Powell, Administrator

10033 Quail Ridge by Encore Senior Center
12401 Trail Oaks Drive
Oklahoma City, OK 73120-1701
405-755-5775
Fax: 405-749-9324

Barbara Hambtree, Manager

10034 Rambling Oaks Assisted Living Center
1060 Rambling Oaks Drive
Norman, OK 73072-4187
405-360-4755
Fax: 405-292-5191

Dirk O'Hara, Owner

10035 Renaissance of Ponca City
2616 Turner Street
Ponca City, OK 74604-2203
580-765-5900
Fax: 580-765-5916

George Rahme, Owner

10036 Renaissance of Stillwater Extended
1405 E McElroy
Stillwater, OK 74075
405-743-4900
Fax: 405-624-3639

Jinny Rahme, Owner

10037 Schallmo Assisted Living Center
101 Naylor Street
Okeene, OK 73763-9107
580-822-4437
Fax: 580-822-3010
e-mail: tuckeerm@pldi.net
http://www.okeenhospital/assistedliving.com

Mattie Tucker, Administrator

We provide meals, houskeeping, laundry and medication over site, and other amenities. Your loved one will feel secure with our state of the art security system. We encourage them to be involved in the social activities, their care and peronal needs.

10038 Smith Manor
1103 Birch Street
Perry, OK 73077-6269
580-336-1119
Fax: 580-336-2285

10039 Sommerset Assisted Living Residences
1601 SW 119th Street
Oklahoma City, OK 73170-4902
405-691-9221
Fax: 405-691-9253

Diana Hendrix, Administrator

10040 Sycamore Square Assisted Living
850 N Clear Springs Road
Mustang, OK 73064-1513
405-376-2872
Fax: 405-376-5868

Kathy Hankey, Executive Director

10041 Tamarack Retirement Center
1224 E Tamarack Road
Altus, OK 73521-1234
580-477-4848
Fax: 580-481-2345

Kay Stewart, Manager

We are dedicated to making your life easy and comforatble.

10042 Ten Oaks at Merrill Gardens Community
3610 SE Huntington Circle
Lawton, OK 73501-8444
580-353-1190
Fax: 580-353-1006

Tracy Cantwell, Executive Director

10043 Unlimited Care-Richmond Hills
7002 S Richmond Avenue
Tulsa, OK 74136-4603
918-499-1988
Fax: 918-499-1992

Tammry R Skalenda, Owner

10044 Victorian Estates
1129 Cameo Drive
Yukon, OK 73099-5152
405-350-1055
Fax: 405-354-2629

Joan Wolf, Administrator

Assisted Living Facilities/Oregon

10045 Village of Lee Retirement Center
6920 SW Lee Boulevard
Lawton, OK 73505-9104
580-536-4848
Fax: 580-536-0304

Connie Greb, Administrator

10046 Vyne at Cedar Ridge
14701 E 86th Street N
Owasso, OK 74055-8474
918-461-1955
Fax: 918-249-8829

Jackie Bell, Executive Director

10047 Welch Assisted Living Center
320 NE Saint Louis Avenue
Welch, OK 74369-9301
918-788-3377
Fax: 918-788-3379

Jayne McCarty, Administrator

10048 Windsor Manor Assisted Living
4825 NW 23rd Street
Oklahoma City, OK 73127-1800
405-945-0010
Fax: 405-947-6542

Judith Wartman, Administrator

10049 the Retirement Village at Copper Lake
1600 Lakeshore Drive
Edmond, OK 73013-3006
405-340-5121
Fax: 405-359-0202

Chris Kincaid, Executive Director

Oregon

10050 Adams House
121 Cordelia Drive
Myrtle Creek, OR 97457-7411
541-863-4444
Fax: 541-863-7978

Susan Lebengood, Executive Director

10051 Alderwood Assisted Living
131 Alder Street
Central Point, OR 97502-2225
541-664-3757
Fax: 541-664-8527
e-mail: alderwood@ccountry.net

Dee Lopez, Administrator

Now you can live in lovely surroundings while recieveing the extra help you might need to keep your independence without leaving your community.

10052 Alpine House Assisted Living
204 N Park Street
Joseph, OR 97846-8319
541-432-7402
Fax: 541-432-3301

Margo Peppers, Executive Director

10053 Alpine Springs Assisted Living and Cottages
3760 N Clarey Street
Eugene, OR 97402-8744
541-607-9525
Fax: 541-607-5838

Jill Krupoff, Administrator

10054 Alterra Wynwood of Albany
2445 Geary Street SE
Albany, OR 97322-6074
541-926-8200
Fax: 541-926-8300

Curt Moyes, Manager

10055 Alterra Wynwood of McMinnville
721 NE 27th Street
McMinnville, OR 97128-2147
503-435-0100
Fax: 503-435-0200

Wendy McIlnay, Community Sales Representative
Darlene Pallin, Executive Director

10056 Aspen Court
470 NE Oak Street
Madras, OR 97741-2201
541-475-6425
Fax: 541-475-6001

10057 Assisted Living at Summerplace
15727 NE Russell Street
Portland, OR 97230-8222
503-252-9361
Fax: 503-252-9405

Sharon Ogan, Manager

10058 Astor House
999 Klaskanine Avenue
Astoria, OR 97103-5131
503-325-6970
Fax: 503-325-9555

Debra Hart, Executive Director

10059 Avamere at Hillsboro
650 SE Oak Street
Hillsboro, OR 97123-4120
503-693-9944
Fax: 503-640-6654

Trudy Irwin, Administrator

10060 Avamere at Newberg
730 Foothills Drive
Newberg, OR 97132-6004
503-554-0767
Fax: 503-554-0436

Virginia Gaines, Administrator

10061 Avamere at Sandy
17727 SE Langensand Road
Sandy, OR 97055-6487
503-668-4199
Fax: 503-668-7758

Connie Easter, Manager

10062 Avamere at Sherwood
16500 SW Century Drive
Sherwood, OR 97140-6100
503-625-7333
Fax: 503-625-6565

Frankie Knighton, Administrator

10063 Awbrey House
2825 Neff Road
Bend, OR 97701-7914
541-317-8464
Fax: 541-317-4147

Suzanne Travis, Executive Director

10064 Beaverton Hills Assisted Living
4525 SW 99th Avenue
Beaverton, OR 97005-3342
503-520-1350
Fax: 503-671-0511

Lissa Guyton, Administrator

10065 Bridgewood Rivers
1901 NW Hughwood Avenue
Roseburg, OR 97470-9970
541-440-1914
Fax: 541-440-9009

Teresa Courtney, Manager

10066 Brookside House
3550 SW Canal Boulevard
Redmond, OR 97756-8947
541-923-2068
Fax: 541-923-7335

Barb Thompson, Administrator

Assisted Living Facilities/Oregon

10067 Cambridge Terrace Assisted Living
2800 14th Avenue SE
Albany, OR 97322-7079
541-928-9494
Fax: 541-812-9198
e-mail: administratorct@mtwestret.com
Kay Hayez-Rodiguez, Administrator

Provides the services you need, delicious meals, and a host of amenities in a gracious setting that has been designed with your comfort and security in mind.

10068 Canfield Place Retirement
14570 SW Hart Road
Beaverton, OR 97007-7000
503-626-5100
Fax: 503-526-3803
http://www.leisurecare.com

Offers a luxurious studio and one-and two bedroom apartment homes in a fun and active retirement community.

10069 Carman Oaks Assisted Living Facility
3800 Carman Drive
Lake Oswego, OR 97035-2575
503-636-3800
Fax: 503-636-9545
Gail Raymond, Executive Director

10070 Carriage House
150 SE Williamson Drive
Prineville, OR 97754-9115
541-416-0500
Fax: 541-416-1445
Kristy Spindler, Manager

10071 Cascadia Village Retirement Community
39495 Cascadia Village Drive
Sandy, OR 97055-6384
503-668-0300
Fax: 503-668-1154
http://www.mtwestvet.com
Jerry Ruark, Administrator
Rochelle Fischer, Office Manager
Dan Wolfe, Activity Director

Independent and Assisted Living.

10072 Cedar Sinai Park
6140 SW Boundary Street
Portland, OR 97221-1065
503-535-4300
Fax: 503-535-4334
http://www.cspark.com
David Fuks, Manager

Cedar Sinai Park is a comprehensive provider of housing and care services for elders and the infirm. We provide a full continuum of care on our 27 - acre campus in Sout West Portland. Our continuum includes: assisted living and independent housing provided at the Rose Schnitzer Manor and Skilled Intermediate and Residential care, provided at the Robinson Jewish Health Center.

10073 Cedar Village Assisted Living Community
4452 Lancaster Drive NE
Salem, OR 97305-1551
503-390-9600
Fax: 503-390-9152
Ryan Bethke, Administrator

10074 Cherry Wood Village
10610 SE Clay Street
Portland, OR 97216-3187
503-946-0225
Fax: 503-946-0207
e-mail: jnorris@cherrywoodvillage.tv
http://www.gebnerationclc.com
Jim Norris, Marketing Director
Tory Thompson, Marketing Associate
Traci Manley, President

Cherry Wood Village is convenienty locates in southeast Portland near the Adventist Medical Center and professional buildings. The nearby Gateway business district offers a wide variety of shopping opportunities. Cherry Wood Village is serves by Tri-Met buses and is locates near light rail trains, which literally put the city of Portland at your door step.

10075 Churchill Clubhouse Estates
1919 Bailey Hill Road
Eugene, OR 97405-1139
541-485-8320
Fax: 541-484-8405
Larry Boman, Administrator

10076 Clackamas Woods Assisted Living
14314 SE Webster Road
Milwaukie, OR 97267-1910
503-654-3413
Fax: 503-353-0225
Lisa Maynard, Manager

10077 Cornell Estates Living Center
1005 NE 17th Avenue
Hillsboro, OR 97124-2701
503-640-2884
Fax: 503-693-1037
Debbie Van Dynn, Administrator

10078 Courtyard Senior Living
6323 SE Division Street
Portland, OR 97206-1385
503-772-9795
Fax: 503-788-8711
Pam Urico, Administrator

10079 Dallas Retirement Assisted Living Facility
340 NW Brentwood Avenue
Dallas, OR 97338-1066
503-831-0214
Fax: 503-831-0278
David Parrett, Executive Director

10080 Davenport House
930 Oak Street
Silverton, OR 97381-1813
503-873-7162
Fax: 503-873-6672
Jama Plummer, Administrator

10081 Deer Meadow Assisted Living Community
1330 W Main Street
Sheridan, OR 97378-1012
503-843-7799
Fax: 503-843-7849
Raedeane Poff, Administrator

10082 Deerfield Village
5770 SE Kellogg Creek Drive
Milwaukie, OR 97222-2128
503-653-4064
Fax: 503-659-4525
Denise Cockreham, Manager

10083 Dorian Place
375 N Dorian Drive
Ontario, OR 97914-1805
541-889-8545
Fax: 541-889-7340
Ashley Holiday, Administrator

10084 Douglas House
1465 E Central Avenue
Sutherlin, OR 97479-9700
541-459-7505
Fax: 541-459-8619
Judy Cain, Manager

10085 Elliott Residence
390 Church Street
Sublimity, OR 97385
503-769-8444
Fax: 503-769-8318
April Donohue, Administrator

10086 Emerald Valley
4450 W Amazon Drive
Eugene, OR 97405-4558
541-345-9668
Fax: 541-345-1190
Elizabeth Moss, Manager

Assisted Living Facilities/Oregon

10087 Flagstone Retirement & Assisted Living
3325 Columbia View Drive
D
The Dalles, OR 97058-9740
541-298-5656
Fax: 541-298-2599
http://www.lifestylesllc.com

Alan Perry, Executive Director
Cindy Phillips, Administrator

Offers duplex cottags for independent Retirement Living plus Assisted Living apartments with a broad choive of personal support services. Besides delivious homestyle meals and a compassionate, dedicated staff, residents enjoy our convenient busopopular for appointments, shopping and social outings. Our Flagstone community is well respected and continues to be a desirable addition to the local area.

10088 Forest Grove Beehive
2122 Hawthorne Street
Forest Grove, OR 97116-1778
503-357-6409
Fax: 503-357-9046

Kathleen Leatham, Administrator

10089 Fountains at Town Center Village
8607 SE Causey Avenue
Happy Valley, OR 97086-7579
503-654-4500
Fax: 503-786-1232

Town Center Village offers a full range of housing and services designed for comfort, enjoyment and a sense of community. The complex contains a variety of housing units, fitness and health care facilities - to serve a wide range of interests and needs of retired adults. A highly trained staff is available to provide the level of services that best suit your lifestyle, from housekeeping and meal preparation to personal fitness training.

10090 Gibson Creek Retirement and Assisted Living
1615 Brush College Road NW
Salem, OR 97304-1400
503-361-8599
Fax: 503-371-1160

Laura Miller, Administrator

10091 Gilman Park
2205 Gilman Drive
Oregon City, OR 97045-1563
503-657-5700
Fax: 503-667-1183

Elaine Rust, Administrator

10092 Grace House
380 NW 6th Avenue
Estacada, OR 97023-7713
503-630-5341
Fax: 503-630-5348

Catherine Hammell, Administrator

10093 Grande Ronde Retirement Residence
1809 Gekeler Lane
La Grande, OR 97850-3375
541-963-4700
Fax: 541-963-6519
http://www.frontiermgmt.com

John Lamoreau, Administrator

Grande Ronde is more than a place to live - it's a community. You can enjoy our salon, our library, our gardens, and our recreational rooms and lounges. Grande Ronde is filled with live, family, friends, and a sense of pride.

10094 Greenridge Estates
4 Greenridge Drive
Lake Oswego, OR 97035-1400
503-635-8818
Fax: 503-635-6857

Marika Johnson, Manager

10095 Grove Assisted Living Community
2112 Oak Street
Forest Grove, OR 97116-2044
503-359-1002
800-652-0750
Fax: 503-359-0615

Sherry Ward, Manager

The Grove is a unique assisted living opportunity for those who value their independence, yet may need additional support with the details of daily living. We provide services designed to help people remain independent while living in their own apartments as long as possible.

10096 Harvest Homes
6921 N Roberts Avenue
Portland, OR 97203-6385
503-286-2423
Fax: 503-289-6473

Lynda Moyer, Owner

10097 Hearthstone of Beaverton
12520 SW Hart Road
Beaverton, OR 97008-5783
503-641-0911
Fax: 503-641-1118
http://www.hearthstonealc.com

Mike Magill, Business Manager
Suzie Reeb, Activities Director
Susan Magnuson, Administrator

Hearthstone of Beaverton is a privately owned non smoking assisted living community where seniors are served with love, respect and integrity. We endeavor to serve the whole person promoting physical mental, spiritual and emotional wellness.

10098 Heights Assisted Living
3000 SW 32nd Street
Redmond, OR 97756-8321
541-923-5452
Fax: 541-923-0280

Joyce Werner, Administrator

10099 Heritage Place Assisted Living
100 6th Avenue W
Bandon, OR 97411
541-347-7502
800-819-1001
Fax: 541-347-1412
e-mail: heritage5@ucinet.com

Betty Peper, Administrator

We have a professional staff that is knowledgeable, skilled, and compassionate to the needs of our residents. We combine the dignity and independence of a homelike environment with the quality and care that allows our residents to enjoy to richness of like and wonders of the surroundng area.

10100 Hermiston Terrace Assisted Living Facility
980 W Highland Avenue
Hermiston, OR 97838-2146
541-567-3141
Fax: 541-567-2282

Charotte King, Administrator

10101 Heron Pointe Retirement & Assisted Living
504 Gwinn Street E
Monmouth, OR 97361-1571
503-838-6850
Fax: 503-838-6443

John Kaiser, Administrator

10102 Hillside Communities
440 Hillside Park Way
McMinnville, OR 97128
503-472-9534
800-275-2384
Fax: 503-472-9306

Jacklyn Friedman, Manager

10103 Hillside House Assisted Living Center
1400 SE 19th Street
Lincoln City, OR 97367-2333
541-994-8028
Fax: 541-994-8331

Sandra Taylor, Manager

Assisted Living Facilities/Oregon

10104 Homewood Heights Assisted Living Facility
17999 SE River Road
Milwaukie, OR 97267-5885
503-659-6600
Fax: 503-659-8193

Eric Murk, Executive Director

10105 Huffman House
1307 N College Street
Newberg, OR 97132-7395
503-537-0422
Fax: 503-538-1584

Terry Hacker, Administrator

10106 Huntington Terrace Assisted Living
1410 NE Cleveland Avenue
Gresham, OR 97030-4283
503-465-1404
Fax: 503-669-8896
http://www.mtwestret.com

Kristina Carney, Administrator

Our community provides the services you need, delicious meals, and a host of amenities in a gracious setting that has been designed with your comfort and security in mind.

10107 Inland Point Assisted Living
2290 Inland Drive
North Bend, OR 97459-1240
541-756-0176
Fax: 541-756-8405
http://www.sunholdingscorp.com

Chris Cooney, Manager

We assist you with activities of daily living, such as dressing, grooming, and bathing, but will encourage you to do as much as you can for yourself. We will help you to remain as independent as possible.

10108 Jackson House
300 Suncrest Road
Talent, OR 97540-7601
541-512-9474
Fax: 541-512-9340

Ivy Olvera, Administrator

10109 Jennings McCall Center II
2221 Oak Street
Forest Grove, OR 97116-2048
503-357-4499
Fax: 503-359-4468
e-mail: rean@jenningsmccall.com

Doris Kinzle, Manager

10110 Johnson Assisted Living
10801 NE Weidler Street
Portland, OR 97220-3066
503-255-0685
Fax: 503-256-1140

Steve Williams, Administrator

10111 Johnson Assisted Living Center
10801 NE Weidler Street
Portland, OR 97220-3066
503-255-0685
Fax: 503-256-1140

Steve Williams, Administrator

10112 Junction City Retirement & Assisted Living Facility
500 E 6th Avenue
Junction City, OR 97448-1557
541-998-6060
Fax: 541-998-3747

Gary Heagy, Administrator

10113 Juniper House
301 SW 28th Drive
Pendleton, OR 97801-1871
541-278-0666
Fax: 541-278-1578

Toni Sims, Manager

10114 Kilchis House
4212 Marolf Place
Tillamook, OR 97141-3257
503-842-2204
Fax: 503-815-1694

Carol Helser, Manager

10115 Lakeside Assisted Living Community
2201 N 3rd Avenue
Stayton, OR 97383-1388
503-769-3200
Fax: 503-769-1286

John Buckley, Administrator

10116 Lakewood Pointe Assisted Living
524 N G Street
Lakeview, OR 97630-1400
541-947-2060
Fax: 541-947-4902

Lisa Powell, Manager

10117 Lancaster Assisted Living
4138 Market Street NE
Salem, OR 97301-2065
503-364-3383
Fax: 503-371-0498

Judy Belt, Manager

10118 Lancaster Village
4138 Market Street NE
Salem, OR 97301-2065
503-364-3383
Fax: 503-364-6433

Judy Belt, Manager

10119 Lancaster Woods
4398 Glencoe Street NE
Salem, OR 97301-2172
503-581-4239
Fax: 503-581-5052

Linda Fortune, Administrator

10120 Laurelhurst House Assisted Living Community
15 SE 55th Avenue
Portland, OR 97215-1288
503-234-5050
Fax: 503-234-5050

Ben Brendt, Administrator

10121 Lincolnshire Retirement & Assisted Living
2690 NE Yacht Avenue
Lincoln City, OR 97367-5143
541-994-7400
Fax: 541-994-4972

Debbie Smith, Administrator

10122 Linkville House
2437 Kane Street
Klamath Falls, OR 97603-6820
541-882-0440
Fax: 541-884-8576

Tracey Amaral, Executive Director

10123 Lone Oak Assisted Living
2615 Lone Oak Way
Eugene, OR 97404-2554
541-463-7700
Fax: 541-461-0539

Tricia Pruen, Administrator

10124 MacDonald Residence
605 NW Couch Street
Portland, OR 97209-3646
503-241-7374
Fax: 503-241-7375

David Berger, Manager

We provide in a caring environment which promotes good health, tolerance, and respect for the value of every individual. The Residence offers assisted livng for older adults with disabilities who want to retain their independence while receiving services they need.

Assisted Living Facilities/Oregon

10125 Macklyn House
755 Elk Drive
Brookings, OR 97415-9066
541-469-7182
Fax: 541-469-5672

Kathy McCourt, Executive Director

10126 Magnolia Gardens Assisted Living Facilities
1425 Daugherty Avenue
Cottage Grove, OR 97424-4837
541-942-0054
Fax: 541-942-3994

Carmen Dake, Owner

10127 Markham House
10606 SW Capitol Highway
Portland, OR 97219
503-244-9500
Fax: 503-244-1022
http://www.leisurecare.com

Offers luxurious apartment homes in a fun and active retirement community.

10128 Marquis Vintage Suites at Forest Grove
3336 19th Avenue
Forest Grove, OR 97116-1913
503-359-1129
Fax: 503-357-4449

Lynn Cole, Executive Director

10129 Mary's Woods at Marylhurst
17400 Holy Names Drive
Lake Oswego, OR 97034-5187
503-675-2004
Fax: 503-675-2015

Joan Hansen, Manager

This facility has been developed to help residents preserve their active lifestyles by offering assistance with activities of daily living.

10130 McAuley Terrace
3120 SE Stark Street
Portland, OR 97214-3091
503-535-4930
Fax: 503-535-4950
http://www.mtstjoseph.org

Residents enjoy our on site beauty/barber shop, our chapel and pastoral services provide spiritual meaning to staff, residents, and families. Our staff is experienced and committed to each resident's well-being, physically and emotionally.

10131 McKillop Residence Assisted Living Facility
500 SE Conifer Circle
Sublimity, OR 97385-9523
503-769-0900
Fax: 503-769-0950

Maurice Reece, Owner

10132 McLoughlin Place
1153 Molalla Avenue
Oregon City, OR 97045-4713
503-655-3337
Fax: 503-656-6939

Eva Steinbach, Executive Director
Linda Kipp, Owner

We offer a variety of Assisted Living apartments with a wide range of personal support services, plus The Atrium, a secured residence providing housing and care for individuals with memory loss or Alzheimer's disease. Meals are indcluding in the monthly rent and are served restaurant-style three times daily.

10133 Meadow Creek Village Assisted Living Residence
3988 12th Street SE
Salem, OR 97302
503-375-9732
Fax: 503-375-2144

Deborah Goodard, Manager

10134 Meadowbrook Place
4000 Cedar Street
Baker City, OR 97814-1649
541-523-6333
Fax: 541-523-9166

Gayle Gazley, Administrator

10135 Mt Saint Joseph
3060 SE Stark Street
Portland, OR 97214-3053
503-624-6300
Fax: 503-797-6702

Peter F Bechen, President

10136 Neawanna by the Sea
20 N Wahanna Road
Seaside, OR 97138-7862
503-738-5526
Fax: 503-738-0188

Debbie Brightmyer, Administrator
Tuula Reinoso, Nurse Director
Nell Stevens, Activities Director

10137 Northridge Center
3737 S Pacific Highway
Medford, OR 97501-8958
541-535-5497
Fax: 541-535-1221

Les Connell, Owner

10138 Oaks at Lebanon
621 W Oak Street
Lebanon, OR 97355-1725
541-258-7777
Fax: 541-258-7255
http://www.frontiermgmt.com

Mary Lail, Administrator

The Oaks was created to help you maintain your independence. We offer assisted living services which may include friendly reminders, assistance with bathing, dressing or personal hygiene, medication monitoring, personal laundry, plus much more.

10139 Ocean Crest Retirement & Assisted Living Facility
192 Norman Avenue
Coos Bay, OR 97420-4732
541-888-2255
Fax: 541-888-3598

Karla Dieterich, Administrator

10140 Park Place Assisted Living Residence
2595 NE Jack London Street
Corvallis, OR 97330-6915
541-754-5808
Fax: 541-752-8684

Debbie Stanley, Owner

10141 Parkhurst House
2450 May Street
Hood River, OR 97031-7747
541-387-4600
Fax: 541-387-4472

Tim Dufour, Executive Director

10142 Parkland Village Assisted Living Facility
3121 Three Mile Lane
McMinnville, OR 97128
503-435-1499
Fax: 503-435-2940

Sherry Kanger, Manager

10143 Pheasant Pointe Assisted Living
841 E Main Street
Molalla, OR 97038-9164
503-829-3777
Fax: 503-829-7392

Patricia Clark, Executive Director

10144 Powell Valley ASL & ALZ Care Community
4001 SE 182nd Avenue
Gresham, OR 97030-5063
503-665-2496
Fax: 503-661-9872

Karla Cheney, Administrator

Assisted Living Facilities/Oregon

10145 Prairie House Retirement & Assisted Community
51485 Morson Street
La Pine, OR 97739-9481
541-536-8559
Fax: 541-536-1373

Betty Musselman, Administrator

10146 Princeton Village
14370 SE Oregon Trail Drive
Clackamas, OR 97015-6290
503-558-1215
Fax: 503-558-8425

Cara Koenig, Administrator

10147 Providence Benedictine Orchard House
550 S Main Street
Mount Angel, OR 97362-9540
503-845-2544
Fax: 503-845-2560
http://www.providence.org

Deana Wentworth, Manager

Providence Benedictine Orchard House is state licenced as "assisted living" and offers different levels of personal care services. Residents have private apartments with full bathrooms (roll in showers), three daily meals, snacks, routine personal care services, weekly housekeeping and linen services, social activities and unlimited use of many of Orchard House's other amenities.

10148 Providence Brookside Manor
1550 Brookside Drive
Hood River, OR 97031-8553
541-387-6370
Fax: 541-387-2728
http://www.providence.org

Mary Delarue, Administrator

Providence Brookside Manor is an Assisted Living and Alzheimer's Dementia Residential Care Facility, located in scenic Hood River, Oregon - the heart of the Columbia River Gorge. Our facility is conveniently locates next to Down Manor Retirement Community and more.

10149 Quail Run Assisted Living at MennoniteVillage
2525 47th Avenue SE
Albany, OR 97322-8842
541-928-1122
Fax: 541-917-1393
http://www.mennonitevillage.org

Mary Ellen Lind, Administrator

We offer a community for seniros that is alive with activity, light, energy, and nature. We respect our seniors for their lifetime of accomplishments, their past and present talents, and the life lessions that have to share. We honor and nourish each individual's spiritual life.

10150 Rackleff House
655 SW 13th Avenue
Canby, OR 97013-4052
503-263-6123
Fax: 503-263-6502

Kim Lewis, Administrator

10151 Redwood Heights
4050 12th Street SE
Salem, OR 97302
503-540-0822
Fax: 503-540-8772

Gena Young, Administrator

10152 Redwood Terrace
3111 Canal Avenue
Grants Pass, OR 97527-6371
541-471-9543
Fax: 541-479-1928

Jim Thompson, Executive Director

10153 Regent at Regency Park Assisted Living
8300 SW Barnes Road
Portland, OR 97225-6300
503-292-8444
Fax: 503-292-8409

Susan Magnuson, Marketing Executive

We are committed to the highest quality of care. Our experienced and caring saff, enjoyable activity programs, and beautiful living environments combine the warmth of home with the safety of 24-hour care.

10154 Ridgeview Assisted Living
872 Golf View Drive
Medford, OR 97504-9651
541-779-2208
Fax: 541-779-2384

Dan Gregory, President

10155 River Road Assisted Living Residence
592 Bever Drive NE
Keizer, OR 97303-4991
503-463-4060
Fax: 503-304-3090

Carol Wassef, Administrator

10156 Riverwood Assisted Living
18321 SW Pacific Highway
Tualatin, OR 97062-8862
503-925-9310
Fax: 503-925-0211

Jeff Kaufman, Administrator

10157 Rose Arbor Assisted Living
540 NW 12th Street
Hermiston, OR 97838-9001
541-564-9070
Fax: 541-564-8178

Paula Oltman, President

Home-like apartment living for 32 seniors/disabled adults. personal services available according to level of need. Managed & operated by owners.

10158 Rose Valley Assisted Living Facility
33800 SE Frederick Street
Scappoose, OR 97056-3831
503-543-4646
Fax: 503-543-4648

Jamie Harwood, Administrator

10159 Rosewood Park
2405 SW 234th Avenue
Hillsboro, OR 97123-8294
503-642-2100
Fax: 503-642-1480

Lea Winslow, Executive Director

10160 Russellville Park
20 SE 103rd
Portland, OR 97216
503-254-5900
http://www.leisurecare.com

Offers luxurious apartment homes in a fun and active 55+ community.

10161 Sawyer House
1155 Darlene Lane
Eugene, OR 97401-1403
541-338-8780
Fax: 514-338-0387

Tris Legacy, Administrator

10162 Settler's Park Assisted Living & Memory Care
2895 17th Street
Baker City, OR 97814-1245
541-523-0200
Fax: 541-523-0268

Michael Shoemaker, Administrator

10163 Shore Pines Assisted Living
93975 Ocean Way
Gold Beach, OR 97444-8521
541-247-0333
Fax: 541-247-9213

Nancy Tiovannetti, Administrator

Assisted Living Facilities/Oregon

10164 Silver Creek Assisted Living
703 Evergreen Road
Woodburn, OR 97071-2909
503-981-4142
Fax: 503-982-0172

Wayne Buckles, Administrator

10165 Skylark Assisted Living
900 Skylark Place
Ashland, OR 97520-9640
541-552-1713
Fax: 541-552-1058

Bob Bolling, Administrator

10166 Southern Hills Assisted Living Community
4795 Skyline Road S
Salem, OR 97306-2404
503-378-7499
Fax: 503-378-1481
e-mail: administratorSH@mtwestret.com

Sue Robinson, Manager

Our community gives you the services you need in a gracious setting that has been designed with your comfort and security in mind.

10167 Spencer House
411 SE 35th Street
Newport, OR 97366-9700
541-867-7400
Fax: 541-867-7401

Susan Cain, Administrator

10168 Spring Meadows
36070 Pittsburg Road
Saint Helens, OR 97051-1169
503-397-0401
Fax: 503-397-2116

Ruth Chamberlain, Executive Director

10169 Spring Valley Assisted Living Residence
770 Harlow Road
Springfield, OR 97477-1132
541-744-2116
Fax: 541-744-0103

Kathy Neuberger, Manager

10170 Spring Village
1420 Redwood Circle
Grants Pass, OR 97527-5536
541-474-0200
Fax: 541-956-0190

Christina Liddycoat, Administrator

10171 Spruce Point
375 9th Street
Florence, OR 97439-9470
541-997-6111
Fax: 541-997-5747
e-mail: info@sprucepoint.com
http://www.spruce-point.com

Toni Underwood, Marketing Director
BJ Rollins, General Manger
Shirley Moore, Resident Care Coordiantor

Spruce Point offers a new resident-focused alternative - independent living supported by a wide range of personal services.

10172 St Anthony Village
3560 SE 79th Avenue
Portland, OR 97206-2372
503-775-4414
Fax: 503-771-9689

Melodi Kellenbeck, Administrator

10173 Summit Assisted Living
127 SE Wilson Avenue
Bend, OR 97702-1788
541-317-3544
Fax: 541-330-0121

Flora Meisner, Administrator

10174 Summit Springs Assisted Living Facility
133 S Church Street
Condon, OR 97823
541-384-2101
Fax: 541-384-2102

Persis Dyer, Administrator

10175 Sun Terrace Hermiston
1550 NW 11th Street
Hermiston, OR 97838-6692
541-564-2595
Fax: 541-564-3087

Laura Young, Administrator

10176 Suzanne Elise Assisted Living
101 Forest Drive
Seaside, OR 97138-7867
503-738-0307
Fax: 503-717-8102

Mike Maltman, Owner

10177 Tanner Spring
23000 Horizon Drive
West Linn, OR 97068-8247
503-655-4373
Fax: 503-655-4175

Wendell White, CEO

10178 Terwilliger Plaza
2425 SW Terwilliger Boulevard
Portland, OR 97201
503-226-4911
Fax: 503-299-4803

Dee Sellner, Executive Director

10179 Timberhill Place
989 NW Spruce Avenue
Corvallis, OR 97330-2182
541-753-1767
Fax: 541-757-3528

10180 Valley View Assisted Living
112 NW Valley View Drive
John Day, OR 97845-1286
541-575-3533
Fax: 541-575-2366

Barbara Weeks, Administrator

10181 Vintage Suites
1301 Parkdale Drive
Grants Pass, OR 97527-4990
541-955-9115
Fax: 541-471-7077

Catherine Jones, Manager

10182 Vintage Suites at Hope Village
1589 S Ivy Street
Canby, OR 97013-4341
503-266-2444
Fax: 503-266-6725

Jennifer Bay, Manager

10183 Well Springs Assisted Living Facility
2104 W Idaho Avenue
Ontario, OR 97914-1991
541-889-3020
Fax: 541-889-3020

Larry Chandler, Administrator

10184 Wiley Creek Community
4901 Highway 20
Sweet Home, OR 97386-3240
541-367-1800
Fax: 541-367-1700

Margaret Champion, Manager

Residents enjoy Wiley Creek's special services, including daytime excursions, delicious food, a respect for an individual's privacy, and friendly, professional staff. And your small pet is welcome at Wiley Creek.

Assisted Living Facilities/Pennsylvania

10185 Willamette Manor
176 W C Street
Lebanon, OR 97355-3193
541-258-8178
Fax: 541-258-8197

Jacine Vanatte, Administrator

10186 Willamette View
12705 SE River Road
Portland, OR 97222-8096
503-654-6581
800-446-0670
Fax: 503-652-6801
e-mail: info@willametteview.org
http://www.willametteview.org

James Mertz, CEO

A multi-licensed assisted living facility that offers skilled care.

10187 Willamette View Health Center
13145 SE River Road
Portland, OR 97222-8030
503-353-7000
Fax: 503-652-6255

Karen Stahlecker, Administrator

10188 Wilsonville
7600 SW Vlahos Drive
Wilsonville, OR 97070-5480
503-582-9414
Fax: 503-582-9236

Linda Swanson, Administrator

10189 Woodland Heights
9355 SW McDonald Street
Tigard, OR 97224-5906
503-684-9696
Fax: 503-684-9892

Jerry Crowe, Owner

10190 Woodside Assisted Living Community
4851 Main Street
Springfield, OR 97478-6057
541-747-1887
Fax: 541-747-0181

Grace Geil, Administrator

Pennsylvania

10191 Alterra Wynnwood of Northampton Manor
65 Newtown Richboro Road
Richboro, PA 18954-1726
215-357-6565
Fax: 215-953-6700

10192 Artman Lutheran Home
250 N Bethlehem Pike
Ambler, PA 19002-3597
215-643-6333
Fax: 215-643-6249
http://www.artmanhome.com

Luanne Fisher, CEO

Our care is designed to meet a wide variety of individual needs while providing peace of mind for our residents and their family members.

10193 D'Youville Manor
1750 Quarry Road
Yardley, PA 19067-3910
215-579-1750
Fax: 215-579-3054

Cecile Shocket, Administrator

Offers assisted living with personalized, loving care.

10194 Deer Meadows
8301 Roosevelt Boulevard
Philadelphia, PA 19152-2006
215-624-7575
Fax: 215-624-7020

Offer a supportive environment with a staff that is dedicated and responsive to each resident's needs.

10195 Fountains at Logan Square East
2 Franklin Towne Boulevard
Philadelphia, PA 19103-1238
215-563-1800
Fax: 215-563-7976

Thomas Clements, Manager

On-site continuum of care includes Alzheimer's residence, skilled nursing and rehabilitation, as well as retirement living.

10196 Grand Residence at Upper St. Clair
45 McMurray Road
Upper St Clair, PA 15241-1649
412-833-2500
Fax: 412-833-8826

Bill Polachek, Owner

Variety of programs and services aimed at fostering the strong sense of independence that has been developed over a lifetime.

10197 Luther Park Personal Assistance Community
3455 Davisville Road
Hatboro, PA 19040-4230
215-659-3900
Fax: 215-659-1461

Charla Holt, Administrator

Our caring staff supports the dignity and individuality of each guest while providing for physical, social and spiritual well-being.

10198 Masonic Retirement Community of Lafayette Hill
801 Ridge Pike
Lafayette Hill, PA 19444-1723
610-828-5760
Fax: 619-828-2803

Adrienne Staudenmayer, Administrator

10199 Residence
4004 Linglestown Road
Harrisburg, PA 17112-1017
717-549-9400
Fax: 717-441-8583

Residential independent and assisted living and respite care will be provided.

10200 Residence at Glen Riddle
263 Glen Riddle Road
Media, PA 19063-5810
610-358-9933
Fax: 619-358-5815
http://www.residenceatglenriddle.com

Lisa Grech, Executive Director

The Residence offers several types of accommodations within each of our retirement communities. We also provide the kind of exceptional amenities you would expect from the assisted living industry.

10201 Willow Lake
1120 York Road
Willow Grove, PA 19090-1334
215-830-0433
Fax: 215-830-0693

Renee Ackerman, President

Offers quality care with supportive service's designed to maintain a resident's independence.

Rhode Island

10202 Ashberry Manor
1081 Mineral Spring Avenue
North Providence, RI 02904-4101
401-728-8500
Fax: 401-728-7053

Rich Gesvauldi, Executive Director

10203 Bay Spring Village
147 Bay Spring Avenue
Barrington, RI 02806-1370
401-246-2500
Fax: 401-246-2145

Gerald Paulhus, Executive Director

Assisted Living Facilities/Rhode Island

10204 Better Days Residential
240 Central Avenue
Pawtucket, RI 02860-2319
401-728-2671
Fax: 401-726-0848

Sandra Greco, Owner

10205 Blackstone Valley Assisted Living
649 Broad Street
Central Falls, RI 02863-2803
401-725-7045
Fax: 401-725-0004

Concetta DiCenzo

10206 Blenheim Newport Residential Retirement Community
303 Valley Road
Middletown, RI 02842-5272
401-849-0031
Fax: 401-849-0199

Warren Strong, Executive Director

10207 Brick Manor Residential Care
29 9th Street
Providence, RI 02906-2926
401-331-6288
Fax: 401-861-3499

Agnes Wrzesien, Administrator

10208 Cortland Place
20 Austin Avenue
Greenville, RI 02828-1449
401-949-3880
Fax: 401-949-4170

Norman Audino, Owner

10209 Darlington Assisted Living Centers
123 Armistice Boulevard
Pawtucket, RI 02860-3207
401-725-2400
Fax: 401-722-3677

Margret Bubis, Administrator

Darlington is a small assisted living residence where residents enjoy a home-like environment and atmosphere with very personalized attention. Our primary goal is to create a carefree lifestyle for older individuals where all their daily needs are met.

10210 East Bay Manor
1440 Wampanoag Trl
Riverside, RI 02915-1050
401-433-5000
Fax: 401-433-4541

Christopher McGee, Administrator

10211 Edgelea
32 Braod Street
Warren, RI 02885
401-245-2626
Fax: 401-246-9630

10212 Elms Retirement Home
22 Elm Street
Westerly, RI 02891-2159
401-596-4630
Fax: 401-348-0113

Robert Elmer, Admiistrator

10213 Emerald Bay Manor
10 Old Diamond Hill Road
Cumberland, RI 02864-4611
401-333-3393
Fax: 401-333-6021

Richard Fishpaw, Executive Director

From independent living to assistedliving to the availability of skilled nursing care, Emerlad Bay Manor has it all. You have the option of selecting your private apartment from a variety of spacious and distinctive studios and one bedroom floor plans. Each feature has a full private bath, individual climate controls, spacious closets, emergency call systems and room for your furnishings.

10214 Ethan Place
85 Ethan Street
Warwick, RI 02888-3905
401-781-0172
Fax: 401-781-0479

Peggy Richard, Executive Director

10215 Evergreen Assisted Living Home
116 Greene Street
Woonsocket, RI 02895-4508
401-769-6869
Fax: 401-765-5906

Susan Cornell, Manager

10216 Forest Farm Assisted Living
191 Forest Avenue
Middletown, RI 02842-7415
401-849-9929
Fax: 401-849-9345

Nancy Nelson Caswell

10217 Greenwhich Bay Manor
945 Main Street
East Greenwich, RI 02818-3150
401-885-3334
877-716-3427
Fax: 401-885-1260

Jollen Melot, Executive Director

We offer a variety of spacious, private apartment syles in a cheerful atmosphere that promotes personal independence with every modern convenience. We also deliver the very finest assisted living services to help you live life to the fullest.

10218 Manchester Manor
12 Manchester Street
Pawtucket, RI 02860-2016
401-725-8390
Fax: 401-755-1559

Frances Goulet, Owner

10219 North Bay Manor
171 Pleasant View Avenue
Smithfield, RI 02917-1792
401-232-5577
800-367-8558
Fax: 401-232-0225

Raymond Maxwell, Administrator

At North Bay Manor, you'll take comfort in knowing that if your needs change, you're already in the perfect place. Our complete continuum of care includes the most cheerful independent living accommodations, assisted living services tailored to your personal needs, and the advanced care offered by a fully-licenced skilled nursing center.

10220 Pocasset Lodge Assisted Living
14 Old Pocasset Lane
Johnston, RI 02919-3143
401-272-0690
Fax: 401-272-2659

10221 Scandinavian Home
1811 Broad Street
Cranston, RI 02905-3533
401-461-1433
Fax: 401-461-4005
http://www.scandinavianhome.com

J Chris Woulfe, Executive Director
Linda Tucker, Administrator

Our mission is to provides a continuum of excellent health care to individuals through their stages of life in a warm homelike atmosphere. Resident dignity and quality of life are emphasized. Although Scandinavian traditions are recognized, admissions to our facility is open to all persons. A cooperative approach with resdients and their families is utilized to maximize the strengths of each resident.

Assisted Living Facilities/South Dakota

10222 Tockwotten Home
75 E Street
Providence, RI 02903-4499
401-272-5280
Fax: 401-421-0550
http://www.tockwotton.org
Kevin McKay, Administrator
Robert Martin, Assisted Living Administrator

Founded in 1856, Tockwotton Home provides skilled nursing and assisted living. Tockwotton Home is a 501 (c)(3) Non-Profit.

10223 United Methodist Retirement Center
40 Irving Avenue
E Providence, RI 02914-2301
401-438-4456
Fax: 401-431-9166
Karen Smith, Executive Director

10224 Victoria Court
55 Oaklawn Avenue
Cranston, RI 02920-9334
401-946-5522
Fax: 401-942-5582
Carolyn Delfino, Administrator

10225 Villa at St Antoine
400 Mendon Road
N Smithfield, RI 02896-6945
401-767-2574
Fax: 401-767-2581
Mary Ann Altruie, Executive Director

10226 Village at Elmhurst
700 Smith Street
Providence, RI 02908-3500
401-521-0090
Fax: 401-453-2514
http://www.villageretirement.com
Chris Stack, Executive Director

We provide residents exceptional access to medical resources. Our unique, maintenance-free catered living options allow you to pursue your interests, from lasting friends and experience the retirement lifestyle of your dreams. Our residents enjoy the peace of mind that comes from our full range of services supporting the health and wellness.

10227 Village at Hillsgrove
75 Minnesota Avenue
Warwick, RI 02888-6023
401-737-7222
Fax: 401-737-9702
http://www.villageretirement.com
Teri Le, Executive Director

The Village at Hillsgrove is a lively suburban hideaway, convenient to shop, amenities and the airport. Our unique, maintenance free catered living options allow you to pursue your interests, form lasting friendships and experience the retirement lifestyle of your dreams. Our residents enjoy the peace of mind that comes from our full range of services supporting the health and wellness.

10228 Warren Manor I
203 Greenville Avenue
Johnston, RI 02919-4107
401-232-1568
Fax: 401-232-9240
Ann Marie Coleman, Administrator

10229 West Bay Manor
2783 W Shore Road
Warwick, RI 02889-8659
401-739-7300
Fax: 401-738-3488
Cheryl Kingma, Administrator

10230 Whythebrook Terrace
1 Cherry Hill Road
Johnston, RI 02919-2647
401-233-2880
Fax: 401-233-2929
Treva Whalen, Manager

10231 Willows Assisted Living
47 Barker Avenue
Warren, RI 02885-2027
401-245-2323
Fax: 401-247-9030
Marey Beth Lefchuet, Owner

10232 Wyndemere Woods
1044 Mendon Road
Woonsocket, RI 02895-3997
401-762-4226
Fax: 401-766-5548
Jeffrey Roy, Owner

South Dakota

10233 Angela Hall Assisted Living Center
901 E Virgil Avenue
Milbank, SD 57252-2124
605-432-4538
Fax: 605-432-5412
Jeffrey Lang, Manager

10234 Avera Bormann Manor
501 N 4th Street
Parkston, SD 57366-2008
605-928-3384
Fax: 605-928-7368
Gail Walker, Administrator

10235 Avera Brady Assisted Living
1414 W Cedar Avenue
Mitchell, SD 57301-3868
605-996-7702
Fax: 605-996-0039
Veronica Smith, Administrator

10236 Avera Mother Joseph Manor Retirement Community
1002 N Jay Street
Aberdeen, SD 57401-2439
605-622-5850
Fax: 605-622-5851
Tom Snyder, Administrator

10237 Avera Prince of Peace Retirement Community
4504 S Prince of Peace Place
Sioux Falls, SD 57103-5865
605-322-5600
Fax: 605-332-5622
Lavonne Gaspar, Administrator

10238 Avera St Benedict Assisted Living
401 W Glynn Drive
Parkston, SD 57366-9605
605-928-3718
Fax: 605-928-7368
Gale Walker, CEO

10239 B and C Resthome
341 9th Street
Sturgis, SD 57785-1117
605-720-3659
Fax: 605-720-4384

10240 Belle Fourche Health Care Center
2200 13th Avenue
Belle Fourche, SD 57717-2299
605-892-3331
Fax: 605-723-0204
Laurie Posil, Administrator

10241 Bennett County Healthcare Center
PO Box 70D
Martin, SD 57551
605-685-6622
Fax: 605-685-1166
Marlene Christman, Administrator

Assisted Living Facilities/South Dakota

10242 Bethel Suites
911 S Egan Avenue
Madison, SD 57042-3315
605-256-4539
Fax: 605-256-4007

Jim Iverson, Administrator

10243 Bethesda Towne Square
1425 15th Avenue SE
Aberdeen, SD 57401-7726
605-225-7600
Fax: 605-225-7585

Gina Sommers, Manager

10244 Bowdle Hospital Assisted Living Center
8001 W 5th Street
PO Box 556
Bowdle, SD 57428
605-285-6146
Fax: 605-285-6410

10245 Carousel Living Center
PO Box 100
Faulkton, SD 57438
605-598-6262
Fax: 605-598-6260

Ken Barotholmew, Manager

10246 Castle View Assisted Living
108 W Main
Castlewood, SD 57223
605-793-2234
Fax: 605-793-2171

Tracy Laue, Manager

10247 Cedar View Assisted Living
225 14th Avenue NE
Watertown, SD 57201-1207
605-882-8419
Fax: 605-882-4961

Nancy Wittmeier, Manager

10248 Colton Assisted Living Center
706 E 1st Street
Colton, SD 57018-2137
605-446-3603
Fax: 605-446-3984

Chad Stroschein, Manager

10249 Cottages at Fairmont Grand
417 E Fairlane Drive
Rapid City, SD 57701-7207
605-348-1040
Fax: 605-399-1471

The Cottages at Fairmont Grand Manor are a unique part of Regional Senior Care Living Facilities. The Cottages specialize in the care of residential with Alzheimer's and other Dementia-realted disorders. We call this focused level of care Enhanced Care.

10250 Courtyard Villa Assisted Living Center
225 W 4th Street
Miller, SD 57362-1354
605-853-3611
Fax: 605-853-2831

Chip Rombough, Manager

10251 Dakota Sun Assisted Living
125 W 2nd Street
Volga, SD 57071-2023
605-627-9141
Fax: 605-627-9141

Lionel Torgrude, Administrator

10252 Deuel County Good Samaritan Center Assisted Living Center
913 Colonel Pete Street S
Clear Lake, SD 57226-2124
605-874-2159
Fax: 605-874-8449

Brenda Ferguson, Administrator

10253 Edgewood Vista of Sioux Falls
3401 W Ralph Rogers Road
Sioux Falls, SD 57108-2650
605-367-9570
Fax: 605-367-1432
http://www.edgewoodvista.com

Alyce Dobson, Manager

Edgewood Vista exists to provide personalized care in setting designed specifically for Elderly, including those with Alzheimer's Disease of other forms of dementia. Our individualized apporoach provides a high quality, safe, homelike setting to Seniors who choose to no longer reside alone, but who can live better in social residential settings.

10254 Estelline Nursing and Care Center
PO Box 130
Estelline, SD 57234
605-873-2278
Fax: 605-873-2989

Michael Ward

10255 Eureka Community Health Services: Assisted Living Center
PO Box 517
Eureka, SD 57437
605-284-2661
Fax: 605-284-2054

Robert Dockter, Administrator

10256 Evergreen Assisted Living
90 28th Avenue SE
Watertown, SD 57201-8400
605-882-8555
Fax: 605-882-8556

Terri Lynn M Becker, Administrator

10257 Evergreen Assisted Living Center
211 N Peterson Street
Viborg, SD 57070-2012
605-326-5503
Fax: 605-326-5511

Mary Herll, Manager

10258 Fairmont Grand Manor
417 E Fairlane Drive
Rapid City, SD 57701-7207
605-399-1551
Fax: 605-399-1471

Fay Kuhn, Manager

10259 Fay Wookey Memorial Assisted Living Center
700 N Smith Street
Clark, SD 57225-1120
605-532-5799
605-881-1663
Fax: 605-532-1320

Gail Wookey, Owner

10260 Foothills Assisted Living
1105 5th Street
Sturgis, SD 57785-1840
605-347-4460
Fax: 605-347-2333

10261 Fox Run Residences
301 Fox Run Drive
Rapid City, SD 57701-2313
605-342-4552
Fax: 605-343-3816

10262 Golden Prairie Manor
1145 Prairie Drive
Winner, SD 57580
605-842-0508
Fax: 605-842-0508

Shawna Kaiser, Manager

10263 Golden Ridge Retirement Community
200 Montana Avenue
Lead, SD 57754-1051
605-722-6380
Fax: 605-719-6389

Miranda Huddlesun, Manager

Assisted Living Facilities/South Dakota

10264 Good Samaritan Center
411 Calumet Avenue NW
De Smet, SD 57231-2114
605-854-3327
Fax: 605-853-3438

Melissa Tordoff, Administrator

10265 Greater Fall River Health Care Services
209 N 16th Street
Hot Springs, SD 57747-1374
605-745-3159
Fax: 605-745-3957

10266 Greenlead Assisted Living-Flandreau
800 S Wind Street
Flandreau, SD 57028-2008
605-997-2775
Fax: 605-997-3859

Peggy Taylor, Manager

10267 Greenleaf Assisted Living
2015 8th Street S
Brookings, SD 57006-3506
605-692-6311
Fax: 605-692-1979

Sue Oines, Administrator

10268 Greenleaf Assisted Living Center
700 S Main Street
Howard, SD 57349-8723
605-772-5885
Fax: 605-772-5886

Tiffany Stevens

10269 Greenleaf Assisted Living-Sisseton
308 Hillview Road
Sisseton, SD 57262-2300
605-698-3500
Fax: 605-698-3500

Carolyn Oetken, Manager

10270 Helping Hand Assisted Living
PO Box 916
Brandon, SD 57005
605-582-7939
Fax: 605-582-7958

Steve Dueas, Owner

10271 Heritage Senior Living
211 NW 1st Street
Madison, SD 57042-2884
605-256-1525
Fax: 605-256-1535

Jo Ann Cassanova, Manager

10272 Herreid Good Samaritan Center
PO Box 8
Herreid, SD 57632
605-437-2425
Fax: 605-437-2950

Mary Mitzel, Administrator

10273 Hiawatha Heights Assisted Living Facility
390 N Hiawatha Drive
Canton, SD 57013-5881
605-987-2731
Fax: 605-987-5631

Pat Halverson, Manager

10274 Hilda's Heritage Home
220 S Lincoln Street
Lennox, SD 57039-2306
605-647-5515
Fax: 605-647-5502

Edith Buseman, Owner

10275 Holy Infant Hospital Assisted Living Center
512 Main Street
Hoven, SD 57450
605-948-2262
Fax: 605-948-2379

Jay Duenwald, Administrator

10276 Homestead Assisted Living
300 W Hazel Avenue
Howard, SD 57349-8700
605-785-3310
Fax: 605-785-3310

10277 Howard Good Samaritan Center Assited Living Center
300 W Hazel Avenue
Howard, SD 57349-8700
605-772-4481
Fax: 605-772-4484

Kimberly Halverson, Manager

10278 Inn on Westport
4000 S Westport Avenue
Sioux Falls, SD 57106-2356
605-362-1210
Fax: 605-361-8866

Donna King, Administrator

10279 K-NOPF Assisted Living Center-Matthew Building
130 N Sycamore Avenue
Sioux Falls, SD 57110-1230
605-338-8495
Fax: 605-332-8598

Michael Knopf, President

10280 K-NOPF Assisted Living-John Building
146 N Sycamore Avenue
Sioux Falls, SD 57110-1230
605-338-8495
Fax: 605-332-0234

Michael Knopf, President

10281 K-NOPF Assisted Living-Luke Building
142 N Sycamore Avenue
Sioux Falls, SD 57110-1230
605-338-8495
Fax: 605-336-6925

Michael Knopf, President

10282 K-NOPF Assisted Living-Mark Building
138 N Sycamore Avenue
Sioux Falls, SD 57110-1230
605-338-8495
Fax: 605-339-0671

Michael Knopf, President

10283 Kelly's Retirement Home I
615 S Jefferson Avenue
Pierre, SD 57501-4118
605-224-5261
Fax: 605-224-0769

Brenda Stienblock, Administrator

10284 Kelly's Retirement Home II
1522 E Dakota Avenue
Pierre, SD 57501-3926
605-224-9811
Fax: 605-224-8067

Brenda Stienblock, Administrator

10285 Kirkwood Manor
Hc 73
Box 208
Deadwood, SD 57732
605-578-2058
Fax: 605-578-7789

10286 Lakeside Assisted Living Residence
1010 W 5th Street
Redfield, SD 57469-2026
605-472-2191
Fax: 605-472-2194

10287 Leisure Living
310 N Dakota Avenue
Apt 124
Corsica, SD 57328-2238
605-946-5229
Fax: 605-946-5229

Chris Fey, Manager

Assisted Living Facilities/South Dakota

10288 Marion Assisted Living Center
310 E State Street
Marion, SD 57043-2011
605-648-3611
Fax: 605-648-3363

Paul I Engbrecht, Administrator

10289 Marshall County Healthcare Center
413 9th Street
Britton, SD 57430-2274
605-448-2253
Fax: 605-448-2304

Stephanie Reasy, Administrator

10290 Morningside Manor Assisted Living
PO Box 500
Alcester, SD 57001
605-934-2011
Fax: 605-934-9923

Todd Willson, Administrator

10291 Morningside Manor Assisted Living II
101 Church Street
Alcester, SD 57001
605-934-1810
Fax: 605-934-9923

Desile Carlis, Administrator

10292 Morningstar Assisted Living
4120 Winfield Court
Rapid City, SD 57701-8306
605-348-2596
Fax: 605-341-5736

Linda Slezak, Administrator

10293 Orchard Hills
200 W 10th Street
Dell Rapids, SD 57022-1264
605-428-6200
Fax: 605-428-6201

Carmen Stoebner, Administrator

10294 Park Place Assisted Living
122 4th Street
Brookings, SD 57006-1914
605-692-9500
Fax: 605-692-5982

Diane Stroschein, Manager

10295 Parkview Apartments Assisted Living
PO Box 327
Wakonda, SD 57073
605-267-2081
Fax: 605-267-2690

Becky McManus, Administrator

10296 Pine Haven Heritage Home
23776 Pine Haven Drive
Rapid City, SD 57702-7407
605-348-2145
Fax: 605-341-1202

Paula DeMars, Owner

10297 Pine Lane West Assisted Living Center
2903 Douglas Avenue
Yankton, SD 57078-4888
605-668-2800
Fax: 605-668-2730

Marla Palmer, Administrator

10298 Platte Assisted Living
PO Box 307
Platte, SD 57369
605-337-3486
Fax: 605-337-3486

Bernice Wessling, Manager

10299 Prairie Crossings
901 14th Avenue NE
Suite A
Watertown, SD 57201-6820
605-882-2045
Fax: 605-229-6673

Glenda Soine, Manager

10300 Prairie Crossings-Brookings
817 Onaka Trl
Brookings, SD 57006-2925
605-692-6569
Fax: 605-692-1937

10301 Prairie Crossings-Huron
901 14th Avenue NE
Suite A
Watertown, SD 57201-6820
605-882-2045
Fax: 605-352-4873

Glenda Soine, Manager

10302 Prairie Crossings-Mitchell
2211 N Wisconsin Street
Mitchell, SD 57301-1074
605-996-2048
Fax: 605-996-2074

Donna Weiland, Manager

10303 Prairie Crossings-Sioux Falls
1806 S Dorothy Avenue
Sioux Falls, SD 57106-3826
605-361-0056
Fax: 605-361-0158

Mary Besson, Manager

10304 Prairie Crossings-Watertown
424 9th Street SE
Watertown, SD 57201-4554
605-882-9003
Fax: 605-882-9433

10305 Prairie Good Samaritan Center Assisted Living
421 E 4th Street
Miller, SD 57362-1599
605-853-2701
Fax: 605-583-5370

James Gisi, Administrator

10306 Prairie Homes Assisted Living
300 E 6th Street
Yankton, SD 57078-4000
605-665-1559
Fax: 605-260-6133

Carol Vendekop, Owner

10307 Prairie Sunset Village
PO Box 580
Mobridge, SD 57601
605-845-3692
Fax: 605-845-7905

Angie Svihovec, CEO

The facility is equipped with emergency responce buttons in each apartment and secured access after hours with 24-hour staff available to respond to the tenants needs.

10308 Prairie View Assisted Living Center
313 S Water Street
Kimball, SD 57355-2217
605-778-6711
Fax: 605-778-6718

Virginia Banek, Owner

10309 Primrose Assisted Living
224 E Minnesota Street
Rapid City, SD 57701-7734
605-342-6699
Fax: 605-342-1092

Lynn Ivey, Manager

Assisted Living Facilities/South Dakota

10310 Primrose Place
1801 3rd Avenue SE
Aberdeen, SD 57401-5049
605-226-1515
Fax: 605-226-1515

Deb Rice, Manager

10311 Riverview Health Services
611 E 2nd Avenue
Flandreau, SD 57028-1399
605-997-2481
Fax: 605-997-2488
http://www.riverviewhealth.com

Jo Ann Lind, Administrator

We provide skilled nursing home care, home health, independent living apartments, and an extensive rehabilitative therapy program (in and out patient).

10312 Riverview Retirement Home
PO Box 632
Chamberlain, SD 57325
605-734-5447
Fax: 605-734-5852

Dwain Blackwell, Owner

10313 Roetell Senior Housing
108 S Smith Street
Clark, SD 57225-1627
605-532-5430
Fax: 605-532-5430

Janet Roehrich, Manager

10314 Rosholt Care Center Assisted Living Center
PO Box 108
Rosholt, SD 57260
605-537-4272
Fax: 605-537-4335

Tina Muller, Administrator

10315 Salem Mennonite Home
106 W 7th Street
Freeman, SD 57029-2319
605-925-4994
Fax: 605-925-4764

Stewart Hofer, Administrator

10316 Sandstone Manor
2010 Windmill Drive
Spearfish, SD 57783-9475
605-642-4910
Fax: 605-642-4819

Nancy Barron, Owner

10317 Scotland Good Samaritan Center Assisted Living Center
130 6th Street
Scotland, SD 57059-2111
605-583-2216
Fax: 605-583-2256

10318 Shelby Good Samaritan Center Assisted Living
PO Box 299
Selby, SD 57472
605-649-7663

Jill Hoogeveen, Administrator

10319 Silver Threads Residence
210 E 12th Street
Gregory, SD 57533-1181
605-835-9717
Fax: 605-835-9719

Tami White, Manager

10320 Silverleaf
519 W Pine Street
Philip, SD 57567-3300
605-859-3434
Fax: 605-859-2948

10321 South Park Assisted Living
PO Box 247
Bryant, SD 57221
605-628-2155
Fax: 605-628-2773

Matt Heard, Administrator

10322 Springfield Assisted Living Center
701 Pine Street
Springfield, SD 57062-2129
605-369-5445
Fax: 605-369-2868

Charlene Tjeerdsma, Manager

10323 St Mary's Healthcare Center
606 E Garfield Avenue
Gettysburg, SD 57442-1325
605-765-2480
Fax: 605-765-2704

Mark Schmidt, Executive Director

10324 Stickney Manor
PO Box 305
Stickney, SD 57375
605-732-4224
Fax: 605-732-4285

10325 Stoneybrook Suites of Watertown
500 16th Avenue NE
Watertown, SD 57201-8642
605-882-0013
Fax: 605-884-1930

Beth Reynolds, Manager

10326 Sun Dial Manor
PO Box 337
Bristol, SD 57219
605-492-3615
Fax: 605-492-3616

Peggy Pierson, Administrator

10327 Sunpointe Senior Estates
2200 13th Avenue
Belle Fourche, SD 57717-2215
605-892-3333
Fax: 605-723-0204

10328 Sunset Court Assisted Living Center
1009 W 2nd Street
Redfield, SD 57469-1501
605-472-2994
Fax: 605-472-2661

Julinne Cass, Manager

10329 There's A Hart
2303 Michigan Avenue
Rapid City, SD 57701-5655
605-343-5563
Fax: 605-399-9651

Christa Uchytil, Director
Gina Schweitzer, Director

10330 Trail Ridge Retirement Community Assisted Living Center
3408 W Ralph Rogers Road
Sioux Falls, SD 57108-2683
605-339-9123
Fax: 605-373-0088

Allen Svennes, Administrator

10331 Trent Assisted Living Center
101 1st Avenue
Trent, SD 57065
605-428-4305
Fax: 605-428-4144

Clark Schmidtke, Administrator

10332 Victorian
1321 Columbus Street
Rapid City, SD 57701-2524
605-342-1913
Fax: 605-348-2078

Lavon Huneke, Manager

Assisted Living Facilities/Tennessee

10333 Walker's Assisted Living
1004 N 5th Street
Spearfish, SD 57783-2009
605-722-3911
Fax: 605-642-0248

10334 Waterford at All Saints
111 W 17th Street
Sioux Falls, SD 57104-4972
605-335-1117
Fax: 605-335-1100

Angi Rabon, Manager

10335 Wedgewood Assisted Living Facility
423 N 10th Street
Custer, SD 57730-1300
605-673-5588
Fax: 605-673-3586

Jason Petik

10336 Westhills South Assisted Living Facility
201 Anamaria Drive
Rapid City, SD 57701-7376
605-342-6821
Fax: 605-341-3605

Carol Christensen, Executive Director

10337 Westwood Assisted Living
PO Box 168
Roscoe, SD 57471
605-287-4200
Fax: 605-287-4201

Carol Thomas, Administrator

10338 White Pines Assisted Living Center
200 Patricks Avenue
White, SD 57276-2047
605-629-2881
Fax: 605-629-8871

Jessica Spencer, Plant Manager

Tennessee

10339 Adamsplace Assisted Living
1927 Memorial Boulevard
Murfreesboro, TN 37129-1545
615-904-2449
Fax: 615-867-5223

10340 Allen Morgan Health Center at Trezevant Manor
177 N Highland Street
Memphis, TN 38111-4747
901-325-4003
Fax: 901-325-4023

Charley Tirrell, Administrator

10341 Arbor Terrace
9051 Cross Park Drive
Knoxville, TN 37923-4602
865-670-4111
Fax: 865-670-4040

Joy Hall, Manager

10342 Asbury Acres
2648 Sevierville Road
Maryville, TN 37804-3643
865-984-1660
Fax: 865-982-1617

Bernie Bowman, CEO

10343 Atria Assisted Living Riverdale
6880 E Raines Road
Memphis, TN 38115-5404
901-794-7799
Fax: 901-794-0984

Bob Trantham, Administrator

10344 Atria Assisted Living-Cordova
1535 Appling Care Lane
Cordova, TN 38016-4933
901-377-7500
Fax: 901-794-0984

Rachel Whitfield, Executive Director

10345 Atria Weston Place
2900 Lake Brook Boulevard
Knoxville, TN 37909-1140
865-584-9857
Fax: 865-588-6223

Leigh Ann Garrett, Executive Director

10346 Baptist Assisted Living Center
700 Williams Ferry Road
Lenoir City, TN 37771-7375
865-986-3583
Fax: 865-986-1707

Fawn Mills, Manager

10347 Belmont Village of Green Hills
4206 Stammer Place
Nashville, TN 37215
615-279-9100
http://www.belmontvillage.com

10348 Belmont Village of Memphis
6605 Quail Hollow Road
Memphis, TN 38120
901-624-8820
http://www.belmontvillage.com

10349 Elder Day Eldereed Haus
124 John M Reed Road
Limestone, TN 37681-2681
423-257-6122
Fax: 423-257-6122

Jan Ford, Administrator

10350 Franklin Park
3393 Kirby Road
Memphis, TN 38115
901-366-6665
Fax: 901-366-4244
http://www.cordia.biz

Linda Messer, Senior Manager

Offers independent cottages surrounding the main building, and apartments on a rental basis.

10351 Hearthside at Castle Heights
215 Castle Heights Avenue
Lebanon, TN 37087-3418
615-443-1994
Fax: 614-443-7548

Sarah Johnston, Administrator

Dedicated to providing care and compassion to those who choose to make this place their home.

10352 Heritage Place
2990 Hickory Hill Road
Memphis, TN 38115
901-794-8857
Fax: 901-794-0162
http://www.cordia.biz

Barbara Martin, Senior Manager

Building amenities include a library, country store, craft area, exercise room, and beauty salon.

10353 Herrington Place
Rr 3
Box 64-2b
Cleveland, OK 74020-9551
731-584-7807
Fax: 731-584-5107

Assisted Living Facilities/Tennessee

10354 Homewood Residence at Brookmont Terrace Assisted Living and Alzheimer's Care Residence
6767 Brookmont Ter
Nashville, TN 37205-4636
615-353-1990
Fax: 615-353-1975
http://www.arclp.com

John Moore, Residence Manager
Jane Ann Sage, Community Relations Coordinator
Philip Schulz, Community Relations Coordinator

Our mission is to provide professional senior living services of the highest quality in order to: enhance the dignity ad quality of life for older Americans, to maintain the highest of professional and ethical standards, and to provide attractive rewards for our stakeholders.

10355 Homewood Residence at Deane Hill
401 Kathryn McAuley Way
Knoxville, TN 37923
865-690-4070
Fax: 865-690-4076

Monica Casey, Manager

10356 Jackson Park Christian Home
4107 Gallatin Pike
Nashville, TN 37216-2190
615-228-0356
Fax: 615-228-4592

Patricia Gammel, Administrator

10357 Kennington Pointe
6301 Village Grove Drive
Memphis, TN 38115
901-366-6200
Fax: 901-369-4564
http://www.cordia.biz

John Messer, Senior Manager

Appointed apartments, access to all the amenities offered in the common areas and a full complement of services.

10358 Knollwood Manor
405 Times Avenue
Lafayette, TN 37083-1247
615-666-3170
Fax: 615-666-9146

Linda Austin, Administrator

10359 Lakeshore Wedgewood
832 Wedgewood Avenue
Nashville, TN 37203-5499
615-383-4006
Fax: 615-383-1015

Gina Haley, Administrator

10360 Life Care Center of Sparta
508 Mose Drive
Sparta, TN 38583-1211
931-738-9430
Fax: 931-738-9455

Sabra York, Executive Director

10361 Lodge at Wood Village
520 Old Highway 68
Sweetwater, TN 37874-6258
423-351-1050
Fax: 423-213-4795

Richard Fields, Administrator

10362 Manorhouse Assisted Living
8501 S Northshore Drive
Knoxville, TN 37922-6006
865-670-0504
Fax: 864-670-2745

Bridgete Duver, Manager

10363 Martin Boyd Christian Home
6845 Standifer Gap Road
Chattanooga, TN 37421-1476
423-892-1020
Fax: 423-499-8734

Sandra Johnston, Administrator

10364 McMinnville Residential Care Center
114 Highland Drive
Mc Minnville, TN 37110-3245
931-473-2033
Fax: 931-473-2012

Cheryl Lecoru, Administrator

10365 Morningside of Gallatin
1085 Hartsville Pike
Gallatin, TN 37066-2501
615-230-5600
Fax: 615-230-4499

Sharon Spears, Executive Director

10366 NHC Place Farragut
122 Cavette Hill Lane
Knoxville, TN 37934-6674
865-777-9000
Fax: 865-777-4994
http://vakins@nhcfarragut.com

Karla Lane, Administrator
Vivian Akins, Admissions Director

10367 Oak Ridge Retirement Community
360 Laboratory Road
Oak Ridge, TN 37830-6911
865-483-1314
Fax: 865-483-3118

Toni Ladd, Administrator

10368 Oaks of Kingsport
2424 E Stone Drive
Kingsport, TN 37660-4739
423-378-3100
Fax: 423-378-5632

Sheilah Campbell, Administrator

10369 Outlook Pointe at Knoxville
8024 Gleason Drive
Knoxville, TN 37919-5405
865-690-3550
Fax: 865-390-7754

Pat Caron, Administrator

10370 Outlook Pointe at Morristown
2131 Walters Drive
Morristown, TN 37814-6903
423-585-0544
Fax: 423-585-0559

Phillip Moser, Executive Director

10371 Outlook Pointe at Oak Ridge
734 Emory Valley Road
Oak Ridge, TN 37830-7063
865-481-3900
Fax: 865-481-3988

Christina Trenthran, Administrator

10372 Park Place Retirement Community
31 Executive Park Drive
Hendersonville, TN 37075-3463
615-822-6002
Fax: 615-822-3765

Nancy Jenkins, Manager

10373 Place at Gallitan
400 Ahncock Street
Gallatin, TN 37066
615-451-1247
Fax: 615-451-7722

Nancy Mullen

10374 Place at Kingsport
2424 N John B Dennis Highway
Kingsport, TN 37660-5888
423-288-8600
Fax: 423-288-3221

Laura Smith, Administrator

Assisted Living Facilities/Texas

10375 Pointe at Kirby Gate
6518 Quince Road
Memphis, TN 38119-8211
901-753-3449
Fax: 901-753-3912

Ken Coleman, Administrator

10376 Regency House Assisted Living
2626 Walker Road
Chattanooga, TN 37421-1116
423-490-2282
Fax: 423-490-2161

Rhonda Donald, Manager

10377 Remington House Assisted Living
640 Rock Springs Road
Kingsport, TN 37664-5285
423-239-8803
Fax: 423-239-8599

Lisa Beedle, Executive Director

10378 Shelbyville Residential Care
895 Union Street
Shelbyville, TN 37160-2607
931-685-6900
Fax: 931-685-6950

Mary Ann Steelman, Administrator

10379 Southern Living Center of Lebanon
900 Coles Ferry Pike
Lebanon, TN 37087-5677
615-443-7929
Fax: 615-443-7502

Valerie Edwards, Executive Director

10380 Terrace at Bluegrass
674 E Main Street
Hendersonville, TN 37075-2680
615-824-4552
Fax: 615-824-4045

Karla Quinn, Executive Director

10381 Uplands Retirement Village
40 Heritage Circle
Pleasant Hill, TN 38578
931-277-3518
Fax: 931-277-5396

John Buck, Executive Director

10382 Waverly Gardens
6539 Knight Arnold Road Ext
Memphis, TN 38115
901-360-8785
Fax: 901-360-9044
http://www.waverlygardens.com

Patricia Bray, Administrator

Offers affordable rental apartments, restaurat style dining, housekeeping, planned social activities, and resident services.

10383 Wllington Place of Colonial Heights
400 Professional Park Pvt Drive
Kingsport, TN 37663-2234
423-239-0022
Fax: 423-239-9717

Joe Erwin, Executive Director

Texas

10384 Abundant Care
501 34th Street
Lubbock, TX 79404-2129
806-791-5851
Fax: 806-792-3558

Jill Rasberry, Owner

10385 Advent Residential Care
5601 Quail Lane
Arlington, TX 76016-3308
817-654-1763
Fax: 817-446-5601

10386 Affectionate Care
5615 Hickory Forest Drive
Houston, TX 77088-2807
281-999-0019
Fax: 281-999-2409

10387 Alterra Clare Bridge Cottage of Richland
7250 Glenview Drive
Richland Hills, TX 76180-8612
817-589-9688
Fax: 817-589-9689

Cleta Brock, Manager

10388 Alterra Clare Bridge of Richardson
410 Buckingham Road
Richardson, TX 75081-5704
972-235-1200
Fax: 972-235-1267

Michael Knight, Manager

10389 Alterra Sterling House of Cedar Hill
602 E Belt Line Road
Cedar Hill, TX 75104-2260
972-291-5000
Fax: 972-291-5046

Rodger Wells, Executive Director

10390 Alterra Sterling House of Desoto
700 W Pleasant Run Road
Desoto, TX 75115-3838
972-274-1700
Fax: 972-274-1488

Linda Martin, Manager

10391 Alterra Sterling House of Georgetown
2600 E University Avenue
Georgetown, TX 78626-6405
512-863-7700
Fax: 512-868-0182

Hilary Marshall, Executive Director

10392 Alterra Sterling House of Lancaster
2400 W Pleasant Run Road
Lancaster, TX 75146-1179
972-274-5000
Fax: 972-274-1855

Linda Horn, Executive Director

10393 Alterra Sterling House of Maltsberger
13303 Jones Maltsberger Road
San Antonio, TX 78247-4270
210-402-3807
Fax: 210-402-4047

Clay King, Manager

10394 Alterra Sterling House of Nacogdoches
14595 Nacogdoches Road
San Antonio, TX 78247-5712
210-653-6100
Fax: 210-653-2082

Linda Gieve, Executive Director

10395 Alterra Sterling House of Waxahachie
2250 Brown Street
Waxahachie, TX 75165-5128
972-937-2600
Fax: 972-938-1686

Brenda Scott, Manager

10396 Amber Oaks
4415 Rio D Oro
San Antonio, TX 78233-6748
210-653-3132
Fax: 210-653-9791

Stephanie Hawley, Executive Director

10397 Ameripark at Austin
1130 Camino La Costa
Austin, TX 78752-3333
512-454-0524
Fax: 512-454-5502

Janelle Parsons, Manager

Assisted Living Facilities/Texas

10398 Ameripark at Kerrville
135 Plaza Drive
Kerrville, TX 78028-2230
830-895-2626
Fax: 830-895-3927

Kay Trabinski, Executive Director

10399 Arden Courts Alzheimer's Assisted Living
11630 Four Iron Drive
Austin, TX 78750-3100
512-918-2800
Fax: 512-835-8814

10400 Arkansas House
1103 W Arkansas Lane
Arlington, TX 76013-7601
817-861-4644
Fax: 817-861-4645

Lynne Walraven, Executive Director

10401 Ashley Court at Turtle Creek
3611 Dickason Avenue
Dallas, TX 75219-4912
214-559-0140
Fax: 214-559-0171

Renee Barnard, Owner

10402 Ashwood Retirement & Assisted Living
12151 Hunters Chase Drive
Austin, TX 78729-7960
512-336-4100
Fax: 512-336-4100

Tommy Wood, Administrator

10403 Atria in Kingwood
2401 Green Oak Drive
Kingwood, TX 77339-2075
281-359-8959
Fax: 281-359-1237

Paula Brown, Executive Director

10404 Atria in West Chase
11424 Richmond Avenue
Houston, TX 77082-2507
281-759-6072
Fax: 281-370-4846

Kim Parnel, Executive Director

10405 Austin Elder Care Home
1612 Chasewood Drive
Austin, TX 78727-3304
512-339-8635
Fax: 512-989-1255

10406 Autumn Bridge at Amber Oaks
4415 Rio D Oro
San Antonio, TX 78233-6748
210-653-3132
Fax: 210-653-9791

Stephanie Hawley, Executive Director

10407 Barbee House
2210 Bainwood Trl
Arlington, TX 76015-3205
817-784-1931
Fax: 817-557-8583

Nicky Obawke, President

10408 Barton Hills Assisted Living
1606 Nash Avenue
Austin, TX 78704-3332
512-441-6000
Fax: 512-441-2205

Belinda Huerta, Administrator

10409 Barton Hills Guest House
1809 Ford Street
Austin, TX 78704-3343
512-444-6100
Fax: 512-441-2205

Belinda Huerta, Owner

10410 Barton House
3700 Adelphi Lane
Austin, TX 78727-5308
512-833-0114
Fax: 512-833-0060
e-mail: jennifers@thebartonhouse.com
http://www.thebartonhouse.com

Kim Greenwood, Administrator
Jennifer Scott, Manager
Joycelen Lankford, Activity Director

We tailor the care of each of our residents to his or her needs. This highly personlized program is made possible by our small size and unusually high staff ratio. Our philosophy of care is really quite simple. Focus on strengths, rather than weaknesses. Never stop communitcating, and be kind always.

10411 Barton House II
3706 Adelphi Lane
Austin, TX 78727-5308
512-833-0114
Fax: 512-833-0060

Jennifer Scott, Manager

10412 Barton House at First Colony
3060 Edgewater Boulevard
Sugar Land, TX 77478-4438
281-313-2500
Fax: 281-313-2505
e-mail: jrelton@thebartonhouse.com
http://www.thebartonhouse.com

Jane Relton, Administrator

We tailor the care of each of our residents to his or her needs. This highly personalized program is made possible by our small size and unusually high staff ratio. Our philosophy of care is really quite simple. Focus on the strengths rather than the weaknesses. Never stop communicating and be kind alays.

10413 Beacon House
8005 Chambers Road
San Antonio, TX 78229-2613
210-375-1441
Fax: 210-375-1445
e-mail: kb@thebeaconhouse.net
http://www.thebeaconhouse.net

Kevin Bumgarner, President

The Beacon House at Chambers provides the real alternative to nursing homes and many assisted living facilities in a beautiful residential setting. Our services encompass twenty-four hour assistance with all the activities of daily living. While so many senior care establishments strive to provide a 'home like atmosphere', The Beacon House at Chambers is a home to the residents and families we serve.

10414 Bellaire Lodge
10333 Harwin Drive
Houston, TX 77036-1545
713-272-9266
Fax: 713-776-1816

10415 Belmont Village at West University
2929 W Holcombe Boulevard
Houston, TX 77025
713-592-9200
Fax: 713-592-0274
http://www.belmontvillage.com

At Bellmont Village, we take great care to balance the independence our seniors desire with the support they need. Belmont Village programs and services have been designed to provide a sense of well-being for all residents, with a common support system that is thoughtful and sensitive to seniors at every turn.

10416 Bentley Manor
3344 Forest Lane
Dallas, TX 75234-7793
972-247-2266
Fax: 972-620-0514

Pat Bingaman, Manager

Assisted Living Facilities/Texas

10417 Bethesda Gardens of Fort Worth
5417 Altamesa Boulevard
Fort Worth, TX 76123-2804
817-292-8886
Fax: 817-292-3128
e-mail: delliott@blcmail.com
http://www.bethesdalivingcenters.com
Janet Mars, Administrator

We offer housekeeping services weekly, personal laundry and linen services, quality dining services and restaurant-style dining and much more.

10418 Braeswood Personal Care Homes
PO Box 20585
Houston, TX 77225
713-666-6545
Fax: 713-728-0322
Susan S Di Filippo, Administrator

The Braeswood Home is an assisted living facility that provides residential and personalized support services to older adults, the frail elderly, and those who need assistance with activities of daily living, but do not need skilled medical care.

10419 Brighton Gardens Marriot-San Antonio
855 E Basse Road
San Antonio, TX 78209-1890
210-930-1040
Fax: 210-930-1844
James Carter, Manager

10420 Broadway Plaza at Pecan Park
915 N Fielder Road
Arlington, TX 76012-3147
817-265-6900
888-550-9498
Fax: 817-265-6906
e-mail: mvwalker@arclp.com
http://www.arclp.com
Marlene Walker, Community Relations Coordinator
Mike Larson, Resident Manager
Rick Lee, Administrator

Broadway Plaza is committed to offering you a living environment that maintains the highest stadards while providing a personal touch. We stand behind this commitment with a solid track record of professionalism and quality, achieved through more than 20 years of experience exclusively in the Senior Living field.

10421 Broadway Plaza at Westover Hills
6201 Plaza Parkway
Fort Worth, TX 76116-2012
817-989-1174
888-339-7049
Fax: 817-989-1946
http://www.arclp.com
Candy Smith, Manager

Broadway Plaza Assisted Living prvides whatever extra help you mat need with your daily activites, while you maintain the privacy, dignity and independence that means so much to you. Our caring staff is the best in the industry.

10422 Brookwood Community
1752 Fm 1489 Road
Brookshire, TX 77423-8809
281-375-2100
Fax: 281-375-2160
Evonne Streit, Executive Director

10423 Brown-Karhan Health Care
3035 W Highway 290
Dripping Springs, TX 78620-3417
512-894-0801
Fax: 512-894-0701
Eric Makowski, President

10424 Buckner Retirement Services
600 N Pearl Street
Suite 2000
Dallas, TX 75201-2874
214-758-8000
Fax: 972-519-9765
e-mail: retirement@buckner.org
http://www.buckner.org
Kenneth Hall, President

We care for senior adlults, and care about them too. Rich in heritage and tradition, Buckner has provided care for senior adults for 100 years. That long history of caring for and about people has helped us create an atmosphere of warmth and friendship.

10425 Buckner Villas
1110 Tom Adams Drive
Austin, TX 78753
512-836-1515
Fax: 512-834-9763
Doyle Antle, Administrator

10426 Calimay Assisted Living Home
2715 Dawn Star Drive
Missouri City, TX 77489-5209
281-438-4530
Fax: 281-208-0408

10427 Cambridge Square Retirement Center
2700 Avenue N
Rosenberg, TX 77471-4507
281-344-8444
Fax: 281-344-8444
Tamara Scotch, Owner

10428 Carestone at Austin
7017 Manchaca Road
Austin, TX 78745-7800
512-916-4095
Fax: 512-916-9239
Julie Oberstar, Executive Director

10429 Caruth Haven Court
5585 Caruth Haven Lane
Dallas, TX 75225-8157
214-368-8545
Fax: 214-368-8998
Dick Blaylock, Owner

10430 Castle Rock Assisted Living
5519 S Collins Street
Arlington, TX 76018-1705
817-557-2221
Fax: 817-419-2590
Brenda Bernardo, Owner

10431 Champion Oaks by Marriot
17705 Red Oak Drive
Houston, TX 77090-7728
281-440-0966
Fax: 281-440-3636
Sandy Allie, Administrator

10432 Chandler Assisted Living
1510 Howard Street
San Antonio, TX 78212-3444
210-737-5200
Fax: 210-737-5221

10433 Collin Oaks Guest Home
4045 W 15th Street
Plano, TX 75093-5891
972-519-0480
Fax: 972-519-9765
Bill Helgesen, Manager

10434 Colonial Oaks at First Colony
13825 Lexington Boulevard
Sugar Land, TX 77478-5364
281-277-0900
Fax: 281-277-3674
Clarissa Woods, Executive Director

Assisted Living Facilities/Texas

10435 Courtyards at River Park
3201 River Park Drive
Fort Worth, TX 76116-9533
817-732-4436
Fax: 817-732-2667
http://www.elderlycareinc.com
Sherry Runion, Director Marketing
Vickie Pacek, Manager

10436 Covenant Place of Waxahachie
401 Solon Road
Waxahachie, TX 75165-1328
972-923-9911
Fax: 972-935-3289
http://www.covenantplacewaxahchie.com
Pam Fowler, Manager

All levels of assisted living are provided at Covenant Place of Waxahchie so you can be assured of quality care. A personalized assesment plan is used to determine your level of care as well as your monthly rent. Remember, at Covenant Place of Waxahachie we cater to you.

10437 Debbie's Sunshine Home
2211 Memorial Boulevard
Kerrville, TX 78028-5612
830-896-7987
Fax: 830-896-4766

10438 Derek Home
1752 Fm 1489 Road
Brookshire, TX 77423-8809
281-375-2100
Fax: 281-375-2160
Evonne Streit, Executive Director

10439 Duval Oaks
5310 Duval Road
Austin, TX 78727-6658
512-418-8228
Fax: 512-418-9211
Casey Litton, Administrator

10440 Eastman Estates
2920 N Eastman Road
Longview, TX 75605-5099
903-757-6020
Fax: 903-757-2491
Andy Bynum, Executive Director

10441 Eden Gardens
6155 Holiday Lane
North Richland Hills, TX 76180-9332
817-427-0275
Fax: 817-656-4227
Sabina Harlan, Executive Director

10442 Eden Home
631 Lakeview Boulevard
New Braunfels, TX 78130-4098
830-625-6291
Fax: 830-620-7786
Laurence Dahl, Executive Director

10443 Eden Terrace of Arlington
2517 Little Road
Arlington, TX 76016-1314
817-457-9710
Fax: 817-446-3264
Jane Roberts, Executive Director

10444 Edenbrook of Champions
14050 Cutten Road
Houston, TX 77069-2229
713-866-9898
Fax: 281-866-9933

10445 Edenbrook of the Woodlands
1730 Woodstead Court
The Woodlands, TX 77380-1411
281-681-9900
Fax: 281-681-9489

10446 Edenterrace of Kingwood
919 Rockmead Drive
Kingwood, TX 77339-2273
281-359-8800
Fax: 281-359-8812
John Googer, Executive Director

10447 Five Star Personal Care Homes
12610 Silver Spur
Austin, TX 78727-4345
512-388-5943
Fax: 512-454-5502
Terry Yates, Owner

10448 Gardens of Richardson
111 W Shore Drive
Richardson, TX 75080-4917
972-783-8000
Fax: 972-783-4267
Tammy Quickenbush, Manager

10449 Golden Manor
130 Spencer Lane
San Antonio, TX 78201-2163
210-736-4544
Fax: 210-732-4035
e-mail: letyv@goldenmanor.net
http://www.goldenmanor.net
Suzanne Huber, Administrator
Lety P Vargas, Executive Secretary

A jewish home for the aged.

10450 Good Place Assisted Living
7801 N Richland Boulevard
Fort Worth, TX 76180-6415
817-581-6310
Fax: 817-581-0608
Gilbert Gutierrez, Executive Director

10451 Grace House of Lake Travis
11825 Bee Caves Road
Bee Cave, TX 78738-5302
512-402-0968
Fax: 512-402-0950
Jud Wyatt, President

10452 Grand Court Greatwood
7001 Riverbrook Drive
Sugar Land, TX 77479-6508
281-343-8400
Fax: 281-343-8600
Lesha Vacarro, Executive Director

10453 Grand Court Round Rock
2700 Sunrise Road
Round Rock, TX 78664-9323
512-218-1175
Fax: 512-310-8884

10454 Hampton Assisted Living Residence at Pinegate
2121 Pinegate Drive
Houston, TX 77008-1388
713-861-9952
Fax: 713-861-9963
http://www.springstreet.com
Shannon Reny, Manager

The Hampton Assisted Living Residences provides extra help you may need with your daily activities, while you maintain the privacy, dignity, and independence that means so much to you.

10455 Hampton at Post Oaks
823 S Water Street
Apt 6a
Corpus Christi, TX 78401-3527
361-888-7711
Fax: 713-993-0169
http://www.springsteet.com
Jerry G Hampton CPA, Owner

Assisted Licing at The Hampton provides the extra help you may meed with your daily activities, while you maintain the privacy, dignity and independence that means so much to you.

803

Assisted Living Facilities/Texas

10456 Hampton at Spring Shadows
9889 Kempwood Drive
Houston, TX 77080-1111
713-934-8844
Fax: 713-934-7444
http://www.springstreet.com
Mary Beth Delehanty, Manager

The Hampton Assisted Living Residences provides extra help you may need with your daily activities, while you maintain the privacy, dignity, and independence that means so much to you.

10457 Harbourview Assisted Living of League City
300 Enterprise Avenue
League City, TX 77573-2936
281-334-4243
Fax: 281-334-4396
Leslie Burns, Administrator

10458 Harmony Elder Care
1801 Hermitage Drive
Round Rock, TX 78681-1919
512-250-1853
Fax: 512-671-9471

10459 Harvest Home Personal Care Facility
520 Baker Drive
Tomball, TX 77375-4121
281-357-5775
Fax: 281-351-4923
Annegret Shaw, Owner

10460 Hearthstone at Arlington
4101 W Arkansas Lane
Arlington, TX 76016-1496
817-469-7671
Fax: 817-469-1423
http://www.hearthstoneassisted.com
Lynda Gouker, Manager

Our mission is to provide quality and affordable assisted living care and services that offer value and exceed the expectations fo our residents and thier families.

10461 Hearthstone at Vista
400 Vista Road
Pasadena, TX 77504-1408
713-941-6025
Fax: 713-941-4666
http://www.hearthstoneassisted.com
Linda S Christopher, Executive Director

Our mission is to provide quality and affordable assisted living care and services that offer value and exceed the expectations of our residents and thier families.

10462 Hearthstone at Windcrest
6849 Crestway Drive
San Antonio, TX 78239-2321
210-946-4994
Fax: 210-946-5775
http://www.hearthstoneassisted.com
Pamela Wasieleski, Manager

Our mission is to provide quality and affordable assisted living care and services that offer value and exceed the expectations of our residents and their families.

10463 Heartland of Willowbrook
13631 Ardfield Drive
Houston, TX 77070-5837
281-955-9572
Fax: 281-955-1597
Freddie Green, Manager

10464 Heights Assisted Living
8307 Gault Lane
San Antonio, TX 78209-1028
210-828-9396
Fax: 210-822-3698
Beverly Moore, Manager

10465 Heritage at Gaines Ranch
4409 Gaines Ranch Loop
Austin, TX 78735-6555
512-721-3100
Fax: 512-899-1711
Linda Blyson, Administrator

10466 Heritage at Tomball
1221 Graham Drive
Tomball, TX 77375-6407
281-351-3912
Fax: 281-357-2280

10467 Hill Country Care Home
3106 Indian Mound Road
Georgetown, TX 78628-1200
512-930-1039
Fax: 512-428-0294
Lynda Conlee, Owner

10468 Homewood Residence at Air Force Village
4949 Ravenswood Drive
San Antonio, TX 78227-4314
210-675-0947
Fax: 210-675-1929
http://www.airforcevillages.com
Bonnie Moreno, Executive Director

Assisted living services are individually planned and tailored to residents' needs and desires at both branches of Homewood.

10469 Homewood Residence at Shavano Park
4096 De Zavala Road
San Antonio, TX 78249-2005
210-408-7411
Fax: 210-408-6411
http://www.arclp.com
Bonnie Moreno, Community Relations Coordinator
Jdy Hoover, Manager

Homewood Residence at Shavano Park provides whatever extra help you may need with your daily activities, while you maintain the privacy, dignity, and independence that means so much to you.

10470 IHS at Swan Manor
2508 Ward Road
Baytown, TX 77520-8103
281-422-9030
Fax: 281-420-0780
Virginia Walter, Administrator

10471 Ideal Personal Care Assisted Living
15526 Empanada Drive
Houston, TX 77083-4033
281-568-7927
Fax: 281-568-0182

10472 Incarnate Word Personal Care Facility
4707 Broadway Street
San Antonio, TX 78209-6215
210-829-7561
Fax: 210-828-0020
Tony Yezak, Administrator

10473 Independence Hill Assisted Living
20450 Huebner Road
San Antonio, TX 78258-3942
210-615-4000
Fax: 210-615-4289
Michelle Houriet, Manager

10474 Individual Care of Texas
1655 Private Road 2530
Quinlan, TX 75474-5459
903-356-4526
Fax: 903-356-4544
Velma Boyd, Executive Director

10475 Inn at Los Patios
8700 Post Oak Lane
San Antonio, TX 78217-5134
210-829-7357
Fax: 210-829-8238
Sandra Dietz, Manager

10476 Inn at Orchard Park
6410 Old Orchard Drive
Plano, TX 75023-4130
972-618-8100
Fax: 972-208-3631

Assisted Living Facilities/Texas

10477 Jefferson Place Assisted Living
911 S Jefferson Street
La Grange, TX 78945-3105
979-968-9161
Fax: 979-968-6962

Virginia Munoz, Administrator

10478 Kensington Cottages at Quail Creek
6811 Plum Creek Drive
Amarillo, TX 79124-1602
806-351-2271
Fax: 806-351-1310

Brenda Burns, Executive Director

10479 Kensington Cottages by Centex
2401 Fm 1460
Round Rock, TX 78664-3524
512-218-9757
Fax: 512-419-7926

Melissa Bower, Executive Director

10480 Kilroy House
1752 Fm 1489 Road
Brookshire, TX 77423-8809
281-375-2100
Fax: 281-375-2160

Evonne Streit, Executive Director

10481 Kings Manor Personal Care Home
400 Ranger Street
Hereford, TX 79045-2812
806-364-0661
Fax: 806-364-0675

Jerry Jasper, Administrator

10482 Kingsley Place at Oakwell
3360 Oakwell Court
San Antonio, TX 78218-3061
210-820-8744
Fax: 210-820-8233

10483 Kingsley Place at Stonebridge Ranch
1650 S Stonebridge Drive
McKinney, TX 75070-5612
972-542-9380
Fax: 972-542-9270

Crystal Webb, Executive Director

10484 Lakeridge Place
2649 Plaza Parkway
Wichita Falls, TX 76308-2913
940-696-1351
Fax: 940-696-1785

Lindsay Sanders, Executive Director

10485 Lakewood 24 Hour Personal Care
8416 Mesa Drive
Houston, TX 77028-2003
713-633-3609
Fax: 713-635-4871

Cheryl Waller, Administrator

10486 Lakewood Village: Cummings Assisted Living Apartments
5100 Randol Mill Road
Fort Worth, TX 76112-1553
817-451-8001
Fax: 817-654-1219

10487 Lexington Place
PO Box 832828
Richardson, TX 75083-2828
214-361-9488
Fax: 214-378-7754

10488 Lodge at Leon Springs
24137 Boerne Stage Road
San Antonio, TX 78255-9517
210-698-9365
Fax: 210-698-0353

Dana Tucker, Manager

10489 Magnolia Place
1216 Montezuma Street
Columbus, TX 78934-2117
979-732-3248
Fax: 979-732-3669

Janet Oldag, Manager

10490 Marbridge Ranch
2310 Bliss Spillar Road
Manchaca, TX 78652-4400
512-282-1144
Fax: 512-282-3723

Brian Haddock, Manager

10491 Meadow View Family Service
2815 Medlin Drive
Arlington, TX 76015-2329
817-465-9596
Fax: 817-465-4026

Judy Archer, Executive Director

10492 Memorial Oaks by Marriott
1414 Sandy Springs Road
Houston, TX 77042-1378
713-782-3355
Fax: 713-782-3398

Donna Methena, Executive Director

10493 Merrill Gardens at Denton, an AssistedLiving Community
2525 Lillian Miller Parkway
Denton, TX 76210-2945
940-320-1926
Fax: 940-566-1360
http://www.merrillgardens.com

Tiffany White, Executive Director

We are a lovely, active retirement community that mirrors the warmth and friendship of the city of Denton. We offer our residents enticing activities and meals. For independent seniors or those who need a little assistance, we offer an environment that's one of a kind.

10494 Merrill Gardens at North Richland Hills
8500 Emerald Hills Way
North Richland Hills, TX 76180-5662
817-577-3337
Fax: 817-427-1972
http://www.merrillgardens.com

Martha Mattison, Manager

Conveniently located in the heart of the Dallas/Fort Worth Metroplex, Merrill Gardens at North Richland Hills is near shopping, entertainment, churches and fantasite medical services.

10495 Merrill Gardens at Round
8005 Cornerwood Drive
Austin, TX 78717-4927
512-238-7200
Fax: 512-238-8593
http://www.merrillgardens.com

Sarah Boone, Manager

Our residents enjoy a wide variety of activities to accomodate an independent lifestyle. Our staff and friendly neighboring community make Round ROck an ideal place to retire.

10496 Merrill Gardens at San Antonio
9203 Cinnamon Hl
San Antonio, TX 78240-5450
210-641-5046
Fax: 210-641-5048
http://www.merrillgardens.com

Natalie Wright, Administrator

Our atmosphere encouraged independence, however Assisted living services are also available.

10497 Merrill Gardens at San Marcos
1720 Ranch Road 12
San Marcos, TX 78666-2597
512-392-7200
Fax: 512-396-3652
http://www.merrillgardens.com

Angie Smerz, Manager

Assisted Living Facilities/Texas

Offers independenct and assisted living services to meet your changing needs. Enjoy convenient month to month rental anytime dining, weekly housekeeping, schedules transportation and a variety of activities.

10498 Morningside Manor
602 Babcock Road
San Antonio, TX 78201-3158
210-731-1000
Fax: 210-731-1060

Bob Hultgren, Administrator

10499 New Life Outreach Boarding Home
2016 S High Street
Longview, TX 75602-3248
903-758-2866
Fax: 903-758-9153

10500 Nissi Care Homes
11107 Stroud Drive
Houston, TX 77072-3017
713-334-6061
Fax: 713-333-5722

Gloria Kauffman, Administrator
Joel A Nass, Owner

10501 Northwest Oaks
9505 Fredericksburg Road
San Antonio, TX 78240-4284
210-641-6257
Fax: 210-641-6922

Peaches Hall, Administrator

10502 Oak Park Retirement Center
4242 Bryant Irvin Road
Benbrook, TX 76109-4289
817-763-0088
Fax: 817-763-3841

Sarah Crouch, Executive Director

10503 Oak Shadows Allendale
4801 Allendale Road
Houston, TX 77017-5421
713-944-4030
Fax: 713-941-0173

Samuel Pinter, Owner

10504 Oak Wood Acres
27340 Blanco Road
San Antonio, TX 78258-5117
830-980-2584
Fax: 830-980-4985

10505 Oak Wood Place
603 Wood Street
Athens, TX 75751-4621
903-675-2002
Fax: 903-677-0659

David Daniels, Owner

10506 Oaktree Assisted Living
1750 Highway 46 W
New Braunfels, TX 78132-4750
830-608-9222
Fax: 830-608-0995

Karen Wolf, Administrator

10507 Pafford Place
615 Cr 430 A
Burnet, TX 78611
512-756-7854
Fax: 512-759-8088

Janie Pafford, Owner

10508 Park Place Retirement
11500 Fallbrook Drive
Houston, TX 77065-4280
281-970-6688
Fax: 281-970-6455

Sue Winder, Marketing Director
Ken Quiring, Administrator

10509 Park Place Retirement Residence of Friendswood
1310 S Friendswood Drive
Friendswood, TX 77546-4968
281-648-5454
Fax: 281-648-5455

Betty Martin, Administrator

10510 Park Place Retirement Residence of Stafford
11919 W Airport Boulevard
Stafford, TX 77477-2415
281-240-1707
Fax: 281-240-0140

Jim Hussey, Manager

10511 Park at Beckett Meadows
7709 Beckett Road
Austin, TX 78749-2955
512-891-9544
Fax: 512-899-2736

Brandon Erickson, Executive Director

10512 Parkwood Place
300 N Bynum Street
Lufkin, TX 75904-2722
936-637-7215
Fax: 936-637-2368

Terri Hutcherson, Administrator

10513 Pine Tree Cottage
5128 Pine Avenue
Pasadena, TX 77503-3765
281-487-3113
Fax: 281-487-5818
http://www.verandalving.net

Skip Comsia, President

Provides a secure and supportive residential environment designed specifically for persons with Alzheimer's and related dementias. Services are tailored around each individual's need.

10514 Pointe at Cedar Park
450 Discovery Boulevard
Cedar Park, TX 78613-2241
512-259-6525
Fax: 512-260-7365

Missi Dayringer, Executive Director

10515 Quality Personal Care Home
543 Dalewood Drive
Missouri City, TX 77489-2210
281-438-9231
Fax: 281-208-1627

Bertriche Ahamba, Manager

10516 Quality of Living Residential Home
2551 Mossglen Drive
Dallas, TX 75227-7844
972-285-5948
Fax: 214-388-8508

10517 Regal Estates Senior Living
500 Enterprise Avenue
League City, TX 77573-2924
281-538-5993
Fax: 281-538-9664
e-mail: asloan@hal-pc.org
http://www.regalestatesALF.com

Terri Lucas, Excutive Director
Ava Sloan, Marketing

Senior housing, assisted living and independent living.

10518 Regency of El Paso
221 Bartlett Drive
El Paso, TX 79912-1607
915-584-8438
Fax: 915-584-5115

Chris Christensen, Executive Director

10519 Regent at Hamilton House Assisted Living
5331 Hamilton Wolfe Road
San Antonio, TX 78229-4420
210-641-7200
Fax: 210-696-2911

Marta Maley, Executive Director

Assisted Living Facilities/Texas

10520 Regent at Parmer Woods Assisted Living
12429 Scofield Farms Drive
Austin, TX 78758-2640
512-835-9080
Fax: 512-835-1316

Joel Quade, Manager

10521 Remington Park
901 W Baker Road
Baytown, TX 77521-2398
281-427-4373
Fax: 281-420-9465

10522 Retirement Inn by Encore Senior Living
2920 Forest Lane
Dallas, TX 75234-7527
972-241-4100
Fax: 972-241-4464

Debbie Orr, Administrator

10523 Royal Estates of El Paso
435 S Mesa Hills Drive
El Paso, TX 79912-5447
915-833-3332
Fax: 915-833-3346

10524 Royal Estates of San Angelo
6101 Grand Court
San Angelo, TX 76901-4968
325-947-0043
Fax: 915-947-1992

Sandy Cole, Executive Director

10525 Sabine House
5301 Meeks Drive
Orange, TX 77632-1200
409-883-8248
Fax: 409-883-8302

Thelma Swearingen, Administrator

10526 Saddleridge Lodge
1808 W Loop 250 N
Midland, TX 79705-1500
432-687-0460
Fax: 915-687-0355

Kim Herring, Manager

10527 Serenity Gardens Personal Care
600 Leslie Drive
Kerrville, TX 78028-2518
830-792-6886
Fax: 830-792-6965

Linda Stewart, Administrator

10528 Signature Pointe on the Lake
14655 Preston Road
Dallas, TX 75254-7805
972-726-7575
Fax: 972-726-9742

Jody Carson, Executive Director

10529 Silverado Senior Living-Cypresswood
10225 Cypresswood Drive
Houston, TX 77070-3407
281-955-0880
Fax: 981-955-1270
http://www.silveradosenior.com

Travis Fogle, Administrator

At Silverado, we are committed to helping your loved one maintain the best health possible with no physical restraints and minimal use of medications. At Silverado Senior Living, we feel that no one should face this disease alone. That's why we take special care to offer support to the families of our assisted living residents. At Silverado, we do more than jyst welcome their residents, we welcome their families as well.

10530 Silverado Senior Living-Sugarland
1221 7th Street
Sugar Land, TX 77478-2774
281-277-1221
Fax: 281-277-1020
http://www.silveradosenior.com

Kendal Nelson, Administrator

At silverado we are committed to helping your loved one maintain the best health possible with no physical restraints and minimal use of medications. At Silverado Senior Living we feel that no one should face this disease alone. We at Silverado do more than just welcome its residents, we welcome their families as well.

10531 Southern Knights Assisted Living Center
27919 Johnson Road
Tomball, TX 77375-6427
281-351-8575
Fax: 281-351-1129

Elizabeth Howe, Owner

10532 St Joesph Haven
3620 Sunset Lane
Arlington, TX 76016-2416
817-548-7211
Fax: 817-548-7211

Paul Denning, President

10533 Sugar Land Oaks Guest Home
151 Commerce Green Boulevard
Sugar Land, TX 77478-3573
281-491-6257
Fax: 281-242-1833

Sue Moyniham, Executive Director

10534 Summer Ridge Assisted Living & Retirement Community
3020 Ridge Road
Rockwall, TX 75032-5805
972-771-2800
Fax: 972-771-0340

Marcela Wenzel, Executive Director

10535 Summit at Lakeway
1915 Lohmans Crossing Road
Lakeway, TX 78734-5269
512-261-7146
Fax: 512-261-7149
http://www.springstreet.com

Rose Vera, Manager

The Summit Assisted Living Residences provides extra help you may need with you daily activities, while you maintain the privacy, dignity and independence that means so much to you.

10536 Summit at Northwest Hills
5715 Mesa Drive
Austin, TX 78731-3773
512-454-5900
Fax: 512-419-1484

Annette McDonald, Manager

10537 Touch of Home
4301 Crestridge Drive
Round Rock, TX 78681-1406
512-218-0042
Fax: 512-218-0039

Sharon Scott, Co Owner
Theresa Scott, Co Owner

10538 Trinity Towers
2800 W Illinois Avenue
Midland, TX 79701-3133
915-694-1691
Fax: 915-699-0369

10539 Twelve Oaks Irving Assisted Living Center
820 N Britain Road
Irving, TX 75061-7675
972-721-1500
Fax: 972-438-4074

10540 Valley Ranch Retirement Center
38 Mockingbird Land Highway
Camp Wood, TX 78833
830-597-4123
Fax: 830-597-6337

Assisted Living Facilities/Virginia

10541 Village Oaks at Hollywood Park
16911 San Pedro
San Antonio, TX 78232-2244
210-495-9340
Fax: 210-495-3570

Kim Perez, Executive Director

10542 Vista Oaks of Lakeway
1604 Lohmans Crossing Road
Austin, TX 78734-5198
512-261-6653
Fax: 512-261-2699
e-mail: lshelton@asistacorp.com
http://www.vistaoaksal.com

Linda Shelton, Administrator

The mission of Vista Oaks is to provide personalized health care in a progresive, interdisciplinary model that strives to meet the needs of the whole person. Dedication to quality with a focus on customer satisfaction makes Vista Oaks the pregerred provider for long-term health-care services.

10543 Waterford Assisted Living
4018 Whiterock Trl
Garland, TX 75043-1951
817-265-3806
Fax: 817-303-9478

10544 Waterford at Plano
3401 Premier Drive
Plano, TX 75023-7087
972-423-7400
Fax: 972-423-8898

Valerie Wilds, Executive Director
Melissa Ouazzani, Director of Personal Care

Retirement/Assisted Living Community

10545 Weelington at Arapaho
600 W Arapaho Road
Richardson, TX 75080-4423
469-330-2800
888-880-8080
Fax: 469-330-2299

Susan Sergent, Executive Director

10546 Wesley Village
2800 Loy Lake Road
Denison, TX 75020-5648
903-465-6463
Fax: 903-465-6498

Brenda Kozikowski, Executive Director

10547 Westchase Gables
2865 Westminster Plaza Drive
Houston, TX 77082-2430
281-556-6020
Fax: 281-556-0136

Glenda Ray, President

10548 Whitley Place
800 Whitley Road
Keller, TX 76248-2519
817-379-0795
Fax: 817-337-1032

Dara Chapman, Administrator

10549 Wildflower House
706 Red Coat Drive
Temple, TX 76504-2200
254-742-1581
Fax: 254-742-0425

Melissa Collins, Administrator

10550 Windsor Court Assisted Living
2535 W Pleasant Run Road
Lancaster, TX 75146-1100
972-228-8059
Fax: 972-224-0887

Shawn Opinker, Administrator

Virginia

10551 Abingdon Manor for Adults
481 Bradley Street SW
Abingdon, VA 24210-3051
276-628-6631
Fax: 540-623-4276

Mac R Clifton, Administrator

10552 Asbury Center at Birdmont
990 Holston Road
Wytheville, VA 24382-4105
276-228-5595
Fax: 540-228-7343

Honor Chriscoe, Administrator

10553 CLC Tappahannock
1150 Marsh Street
Tappahannock, VA 22560
804-443-4308
Fax: 804-443-6425

Bruce McCorkle, Administrator

10554 Essex House
Rr 3
Tappahannock, VA 22560
804-443-5921
Fax: 804-449-4031

Debbie Morris, Manager

10555 Fairview Home
Hatcher Road
Dublin, VA 24084
540-674-5260
Fax: 540-674-9547

Reba Broyles, Administrator

10556 Gordon House
501 N Main Street
Gordonsville, VA 22942-9137
540-832-2286
Fax: 540-832-7571

Tom May, Administrator

10557 Grand Court
1 Liberty Place
Bristol, VA 24201-2360
276-669-1111
Fax: 540-669-8144

Theresa Taylor, Administrator

10558 Green Hill Home for Adults
2904 Double Cabin Road
Hillsville, VA 24343-4768
276-728-7094
Fax: 540-728-9997

10559 Magnolia Ridge Residential Care
1007 Amherst Street SW
Roanoke, VA 24015-2001
540-342-8861
Fax: 540-343-3184

Beverley Clarkson, Administrator

10560 Mayfair House
460 S Main Street
Kilmarnock, VA 22482-8500
804-435-9896
Fax: 804-435-1669

Andrea Freake, Administrator

10561 Mayflower
409 S Main Street
Lexington, VA 24450-2305
540-463-3161
Fax: 540-464-3214

Kim Hurt, Manager

Assisted Living Facilities/Washington

10562 Oak Hill Center
512 Houston Street
Staunton, VA 24401-3525
540-886-2335
Fax: 540-886-7459

Scott Overstreet, Administrator

10563 Orange County Home for Adults
120 Dogwood Lane
Orange, VA 22960-1058
540-672-2611
Fax: 540-672-3187

Vernon Baker, Administrator

10564 Presbyterian Group Home-Waynesboro
1035 Fairfax Avenue
Waynesboro, VA 22980-6026
540-949-8791
Fax: 540-949-4370

Beth Michael, Manager

10565 Pulaski Retirement Community
2421 Lee Hwyighway
Pulaski, VA 24301-2325
540-980-8535
Fax: 540-980-1876
http://www.rui.net

Janet Beahm, Executive Director
Kim Greene, Director Of Nursing

Independant and assisted living community

10566 Rappahannock Westminster-Canterbury
10 Lancaster Road
Irvington, VA 22480-2002
804-438-4000
Fax: 804-438-4027

Stuart Bunting, President

10567 Renaissance Gardens at Greenspring
7470 Spring Village Drive
Springfield, VA 22150-4487
703-923-4650
Fax: 703-923-4651
http://www.thecareexperts.com

Barbara Akst, Health Care Sales Manager

Features all private Assisted Living apartments and all private Long-Term Care rooms; full-time, on-site staff doctors with nurses on duty 24-hours a day. Short-Time Rehab (physical, speech and occupational therapy); dementia and Alzheimer's care also available. Renaissance Gardens, the choice you can feel good about.

10568 Shelby Manor Group Home
100 Abingdon Place
Abingdon, VA 24211-6122
704-482-0000
Fax: 704-487-0772

10569 Shenandoah Adult Care
601 Granville Avenue
Clifton Forge, VA 24422-1815
540-862-1614
Fax: 540-862-9282

10570 Shenandoah Valley Village
9137 N Congress Street
New Market, VA 22844-9543
540-740-8100
Fax: 540-740-9380

Tom Rice, Administrator

10571 St. Luke's Assisted Living
2359 Jefferson Hwy
Waynesboro, VA 22980-6540
540-943-9049
Fax: 540-943-9405
e-mail: vshifflet@stlukesinc.com
http://stlukesinc.com

Victor Shifflet, Owner
Pat Shifflet, Owner

10572 Stonewall Jackson Home for Adults
28 S Market Street
Staunton, VA 24401-4350
540-885-1581
Fax: 540-886-0875

10573 Virginian Manor
Rr 2
Tappahannock, VA 22560
804-443-1776
Fax: 804-443-1776

10574 Westwood Center
Westwood Medical Park
Bluefield, VA 24605
276-322-5439
Fax: 540-322-5442

Sandy Wright, Administrator

10575 Whatland Hills Retirement Center
7486 Lee Highway
Fairlawn, VA 24141-8579
540-639-2411
Fax: 540-639-9128

Barbara Holstein, Administrator

10576 Willows at Meadow Branch
1881 Harvest Drive
Winchester, VA 22601-6350
540-667-3000
Fax: 540-667-2174
e-mail: drs@thewillows-mb.com
http://www.thewillowsatmeadowbranch.com

Linda M Duvall, Administrator

Washington

10577 Aegis Lodge
12629 116th Avenue NE
Kirkland, WA 98034
425-814-2841
Fax: 425-823-2881
http://www.aegisliving.com

Rob Johnston, Executive Director

10578 Aegis Senior Living of Shoreline
14900 First Avenue NE
Shoreline, WA 98155
206-367-6700
Fax: 206-306-1064
http://www.aegisliving.com

Jarrett Houser, Executive Director

Offers assisted living services within a comfortable community and dedicated care for those living with Alzheimer's or dementia.

10579 Aegis at Northgate
11039 17th Avenue NE
Seattle, WA 98125
206-440-1700
Fax: 206-440-1613
http://www.aegisliving.com

Judy Adams, Executive Director

Offers assisted living services tailored to meet each individual's needs.

10580 Aegis of Bothell
10605 NE 185th Street
Bothell, WA 98011
425-487-3245
Fax: 425-481-9782
http://www.aegisliving.com

Karl Miller, Executive Director

Aegis of Bothell also provides dedicated care for individuals living with Alzheimer's or other dementia.

Assisted Living Facilities/Washington

10581 Aegis of Edmonds
21500 72nd Avenue W
Edmonds, WA 98026
425-776-3600
Fax: 425-776-3622
http://www.aegisliving.com
Wendy Mcilnay, Executive Director

10582 Aegis of Issaquah
780 NW Juniper Street
Issaquah, WA 98027
425-392-8100
Fax: 425-391-8804
http://www.aegisliving.com
Jim Cox, Executive Director
Offers assisted living services and dedicated care for those with Alzheimer's or other dementia.

10583 Aegis of Kent
10421 SE 248th Street
Kent, WA 98030
253-520-8400
Fax: 253-520-0360
http://www.aegisliving.com
Emma Cronin, Executive Director
Offers assisted living services and dedicated care for those with Alzheimer's or other dementia.

10584 Aegis of Kirkland
13000 Totem Lake Boulevard NE
Kirkland, WA 98034-2982
425-823-7272
Fax: 425-823-8227
http://www.aegisliving.com
Kathy Stewart, Executive Director
Aegis living is a national leader in independent and assisted living with a premier Alzheimer's and dementia care program. Assisted Living communities are newly constructed and specially designed for seniors who need a little help with assisted-living services or for those who need dementia care.

10585 Aegis of Lynnwood
18700 44th Avenue West
Lynnwood, WA 98037
425-712-9999
Fax: 425-744-1506
http://www.aegisliving.com
Larry Smith, Executive Director

10586 Aegis of Redmond
7480 West Lake Sammamish Parkway NE
Redmond, WA 98052
425-883-4000
Fax: 425-882-1823
http://www.aegisliving.com
Jason Porter, Executive Director
Offers programs for residents with Alxheimer's disease or other dementia.

10587 Aegis of Shoreline (Callahan House)
15100 First Avenue NE
Shoreline, WA 98155
206-417-9747
Fax: 206-417-9711
http://www.aegisliving.com
Jarrett Houser, Executive Director
Offers assisted living services within a comfortable community and dedicated care for those living with Alzheimer's or dementia.

10588 Brighton Court
6520-196th Street SW
Lynnwood, WA 98036
425-775-4440
http://www.leisurecare.com
Offers luxurious apartment homes in a fun and active retirement community.

10589 Brittany Park
17143 133rd Avenue NE
Woodinville, WA 98072
425-402-7100
http://www.leisurecare.com
Offers luxurious apartment homes in a fun and active retirement community.

10590 Eagle Meadows Assisted Living Community
550 East Whitman
College Place, WA 99324
509-526-7007
http://www.eaglemeadowsalf.com/assisted
Jen Zamora, Administrator
Our goal at Eagle Meadows is to meet each resident's individuals needs while maintaining the highest level of choice, dignity, privacy and respect - all in a homelike atmosphere. Assisted Living at Eagle Meadows is designed for senior adults who wish to maintain their independent lifestyle but may need some additional assistance to do so.

10591 Fairwinds-Redmond
9988 Avondale Rd NE
Redmond, WA 98052
425-558-4700
http://www.leisurecare.com
Offers luxurious apartment homes in a fun and active retirement community.

10592 Fairwinds-Spokane
520 East Holland Avenue
Spokane, WA 99218
509-468-1000
http://www.leisurecare.com
Offers spacious apartment homes in a fun and active retirement community.

10593 Farrington Court
516 Kenosia Avenue
Kent, WA 98030
253-852-2737
http://www.leisurecare.com
Offers luxurious apartment homes in a fun and active retirement community.

10594 Hawthorne Court
524 North Ely
Kennewick, WA 99336
509-783-8313
http://www.leisurecare.com
Offers luxurious apartment homes in a fun and active retirement community.

10595 Living Court Assisted Living Community
2229 Jensen Street
Enumclaw, WA 98022
360-825-0280
Fax: 360-825-6272
http://www.prestigecare.com
Sarah Delamarter, President
We are uniquely designed to provide different levels of assisted living, from minimum daily supervision to 24-hour care.

10596 Olympics West Retirement Inn
JEA Senior Living
929 Trosper Road
Tumwater, WA 98512
360-943-9900
800-254-9442
Fax: 360-956-0699
e-mail: info@jeacorp.com
http://www.jeaseniorliving.com
Jerry Erwin, Founder/CEO
Cody Erwin, Chief Operating Officer
JEA Senior Living offers personalized services that allow our residents to benefit from individualized care. Personalized assistance is provided in activities of daily living. We offer 89 beds for Assisted Living.

10597 Queen Anne Manor
100 Crockett Street
Seattle, WA 98109-2514
206-282-5001
Fax: 206-282-9064
http://www.qamanor.com
Carole Kelley, Executive Director
Sonja Bring, Resident Services Director
Patricia Del Von Nadon, Marketing Director

Assisted Living Facilities/Wisconsin

Offers a safe and comfortable assisted living community centrally located on Queen Anne hill in a beautiful turn of the century historic building.

10598 Regency Samaritan House
704 North 16th Avenue
Yakima, WA 98902
509-453-6357
Fax: 509-457-4438
e-mail: info@regencysamaritanhouse.com
http://www.regencysamaritanhouse.com
Samaritan House is an assisted living community that prides itself on personal care with a personal touch. Our community is small, allowing our staff to spend time with every resident.

10599 Regency on Whidbey
1040 Kimball Drive
Oak Harbor, WA 98277
360-279-0933
e-mail: annv@isomedia.com
http://www.regencywhidbey.com/assisted
Ann Votava, Administrator
Leta Benfield, RN, Residents Services Coordiantor
Heidi Kuzina, Activities Director

The individual and specific needs of each resident, determined by their personal assessment, are the foundation of our resident care plans, designed to meet these needs. We offer five levels of care to better serve a resident's special needs.

10600 Regent at Sterling Park Assisted Living
2956 152nd Avenue NE
Redmond, WA 98052-5356
425-883-0495
Fax: 425-881-5118
For those individuals interested in our Assisted Living community, we offer private studios, one and two bedroom apartments.

10601 Tapestry at Village Gate West
5129 Dundas Street West
Toronto ON, ZZ M9A 0B3
416-777-2911
http://www.leisurecare.com
Retirement living community.

10602 The Bellettini
1115 108th Avenue NE
Bellevue, WA 98004
425-450-0800
http://www.leisurecare.com
Retirement living community.

10603 Three Links Center
Washington Odd Fellows Home
534 Boyer Avenue
Walla Walla, WA 99362
509-525-6463
877-311-2786
Fax: 509-522-0578
e-mail: jwicklund@oddfellows.com
John Brigham, Administrator
Joani Wicklund, Director Admissions

A non-profit retirement facility offering three levels of care: independent apartments, assisted living, and skilled nursing.

10604 Van Mall
7808 NE 51st Street
Vancouver, WA 98662
360-896-9140
http://www.leisurecare.com
Offers luxurious apartment homes in a fun and active retirement community.

10605 Washington Oakes
1717 Rockefeller Avenue
Everett, WA 98201
425-339-3300
http://www.leisurecare.com
Retirement living community.

Wisconsin

10606 Ridgeview Heights Indepedent Living Corporation
2090 Ridgeview Drive
Reedsburg, WI 53959-2234
608-524-9088
Fax: 608-524-9745
Hal Keitel, Executive Director

Wyoming

10607 Aspen Wind Assisted Living
4010 N College Drive
Cheyenne, WY 82001-1960
307-778-9511
Fax: 307-772-0977
Maureen Walker, Administrator

10608 Bieske's Country Comfort Home Care
89 County Road 6 Route
Cody, WY 82414
307-587-5661
Fax: 307-527-7077

10609 Garden Square of Casper
1950 S Beverly Street
Casper, WY 82609-3348
307-472-1153
Fax: 307-472-1152
Heather Dronek, Executive Director

10610 Legacy Homes Assisted Living
2391 Muddy String County Road 117
Thayne, WY 83127
307-883-3800
Fax: 307-882-3801
Alan Merritt, Owner

10611 Meadow Wind Assisted Living
3955 E 12th Street
Casper, WY 82609-3114
307-577-3045
Fax: 307-266-3370
Josephine Ingram, Administrator

10612 New Horizons Assisted Living Facility
1111 Lane 12
Lovell, WY 82431-9537
307-548-5200
Fax: 307-548-2564
Mary Bair, Administrator

10613 Park Place
1930 E 12th Street
Casper, WY 82601-4075
307-265-2273
Fax: 307-265-5384
Kary Rate, Administrator

10614 Point Frontier Retirement Community
1406 Prairie Avenue
Cheyenne, WY 82009-4855
307-635-6953
Fax: 307-635-3566
Rich Pfeiffer, Manager

10615 Showboat Retirement Center
150 Wyoming Street
Lander, WY 82520-3993
307-332-6788
Fax: 307-332-2175
Ron Foote, Owner

10616 Sierra Hills
4606 N College Drive
Cheyenne, WY 82009-5456
307-638-7798
Fax: 307-638-7919
Brandy Camargo, Administrator

Assisted Living Facilities/Wyoming

10617 Spring Wind Assisted Living
1072 N 22nd Street
Laramie, WY 82072-5303
307-755-5811
Fax: 307-721-0478
e-mail: springwindadmin@springwindalf.com
http://www.springwindalf.com

Gary Gray, Administrator
James Oliver, Manager

10618 Sugarland Ridge
1551 Sugarland Drive
Sheridan, WY 82801-5721
307-674-5575
Fax: 307-674-8070

Lisa Garstad, Manager

10619 Veterans' Home of Wyoming
700 Veterans Lane
Buffalo, WY 82834-9402
307-684-5511
Fax: 307-648-7636

Jack Tarter, Administrator

10620 Wyoming Pioneer Home
141 Pioneer Home Drive
Thermopolis, WY 82443-2451
307-864-3151
Fax: 307-864-2934

Sharon Skiver, Manager

Independent Living Centers/Alabama

This chapter is arranged by state. Due to the nature of Independent Living Centers and the combined efforts of certain state agencies, be sure to review both State Organizations & Government Agencies and Assisted Living Facilities for a comprehensive list of resources.

Alabama

10621 Birmingham Independent Living Center
206 13th Street South
Birmingham, AL 35233-1317
205-251-2223
Fax: 205-251-0605
e-mail: bilc@bellsouth.net
http://www.ilrgb.org

Grahm Sisson, President
Phil Klebine, Vice President
Milton Moats, Treasurer

The Birmingham Independent Living Center encourages people with disabilities to support one another in reaching their own independent living goals. The Center also promotes equal access and disability rights through advocacy and public awareness activities. A majority of staff, decision-making staff, and board members are people with disabilities. Consumers, not professionals, set their own independent living goals. Consumers are offered the option of developing an independent living plan; however, consumers may elect to waive such a plan and receive services. Independent living is based upon peer relationships, and principles of integration, consumer control, cross-disability, and equal access. All services are community-based and non-residential in nature. At the core of independent living is advocacy. Equal access is promoted within the Center and in the community. Mission is to empower people with disabilities to fully participate in the community.

10622 Independent Living Center
5304-B Overlook Road
Mobile, AL 36618-2331
251-460-0301
Fax: 251-341-1267
e-mail: ilc@ilcmobil.org
http://www.ilcmobile.org
TTY 251-460-2872

Michael Davis, Executive Director
Ann Robertson, Assistant Director/Interpreter
Tobi Murphy, Program Manager YAAP

The Independent Living Center of Mobile/ILC, and its partner, the Birmingham Independent Living Center (BILC), offer choices of living options for people with disabilities and an array of services to help nursing home residents move to the community. Choosing where to live is a basic right of all Americans. But for people with disabilities who live in nursing homes, the opportunity to weigh community options is often limited. ILC strives to foster and promote programs which empower persons with disabilities to attain their maximum degree of independence. Services include independent living skills, peer support and advocacy, in addition to providing information and referral services.

10623 Independent Living Center-Jasper
300 Birmingham Ave.
Po Box 434
Jasper, AL 35502
205-387-0159
Fax: 205-387-1594
e-mail: ilcwalker@bellsouth.net
http://www.birminghamilc.org
TDD 205-387-0162

Grahm Sisson, President
Phil Klebine, Vice President
Milton Moats, Treasurer

The Birmingham Independent Living Center in Jasper encourages people with disabilities to support one another in reaching their own independent living goals. The Center also promotes equal access and disability rights through advocacy and public awareness activities. A majority of staff, decision-making staff, and board members are people with disabilities. Consumers, not professionals, set their own independent living goals. Consumers are offered the option of developing an independent living plan; however, consumers may elect to waive such a plan and receive services. Independent living is based upon peer relationships, and principles of integration, consumer control, cross-disability, and equal access. All services are community-based and non-residential in nature. At the core of independent living is advocacy. Equal access is promoted within the Center and in the community. Mission is to empower people with disabilities to fully participate in the community.

10624 Montgomery Independent Living Center
600 South Court Street
Montgomery, AL 36104
334-240-2520
Fax: 334-240-6869
e-mail: mcil@bellsouth.net
http://www.birminghamilc.org

Grahm Sisson, President
Phil Klebine, Vice President
Milton Moats, Treasurer

The Montgomery Independent Living center, a branch of the Birmingham Independent Living Center, encourages people with disabilities to support one another in reaching their own independent living goals. The Center also promotes equal access and disability rights through advocacy and public awareness activities. A majority of staff, decision-making staff, and board members are people with disabilities. Consumers, not professionals, set their own independent living goals. Consumers are offered the option of developing an independent living plan; however, consumers may elect to waive such a plan and receive services. Independent living is based upon peer relationships, and principles of integration, consumer control, cross-disability, and equal access. All services are community-based and non-residential in nature. At the core of independent living is advocacy. Equal access is promoted within the Center and in the community. Mission is to empower people with disabilities to fully participate in the community.

Alaska

10625 Access Alaska-Anchorage
121 West Fireweed Lane
Suite 105
Anchorage, AK 99503-2024
907-248-4777
800-770-4488
Fax: 907-248-0693
e-mail: info@accessalaska.org
http://www.accessalaska.org
TTY 907-248-8799

Serena Donling, Informations Referral Coord.
Jim Beck, Executive Director

Independent Living Centers/Alaska

Access Alaska is a private, non-profit, consumer-controlled organization that provides independent living services to people who experience a disability. As an Independent Living Center, our mission is to encourage & promote the total integration of people who experience a disability to live independently in the community of their choice. Through our assistance and support individuals with disabilities can identify and obtain needed services inan effort to maintain their independence as opposed to living in an institution. Access Alaska was formed in 1983 to serve the Anchorage area. Services were later expanded in 1984 and 1998 when offices were opened in Fairbanx and Matanuska-Susitna Valley.

10626 Access Alaska-Fairbanks
526 Gaffney Road
Suite 100
Fairbanks, AK 99709-4775
907-479-7940
800-770-7940
Fax: 907-474-4052
e-mail: info@accessalaska.net
http://www.accessalaska.org

Jim Beck, Executive Director

Access Alaska is a private, non-profit, consumer-controlled organization that provides independent living services to people who experience a disability. As an Independent Living Center, our mission is to encourage and promote the total integration of people who experience a disability to live independently in the community of their choice. Through our assistance and support individuals with disabilities can identify and obtain needed services inan effort to maintain their independence as opposed to living in an institution. Access Alaska was formed in 1983 to serve the Anchorage area. Services were later expanded in 1984 and 1998 when offices were opened in Fairbanks and the Matanuska-Susitna Valley.

10627 Kenai Peninsula Independent Living Center-Homer
3953 Bartlett Street
PO Box 2474
Homer, AK 99603-2474
907-235-7911
Fax: 907-235-6236
e-mail: ilc@xyz.net
http://www.peninsulailc.org
TTY 907-235-7911

Joyanna Geisler, Executive Director

The Kenai Peninsula Independent Living Center is a non-profit organization run by the persons with disabilities for persons with disabilities. Our primary goal is to assist persons with impairments to live as independently as possible in their own homes and in the communities of their choice. Independent Living Center offices are located in Homer, Soldotna, and Seward Alaska. We provide direct service to the entire Kenai Peninsula and outreach service to Kodiak Island and the Valdez-Cordova region. Contact any office for more information.

10628 Kenai Peninsula Independent Living-Central Peninsula
47255 Princeton Avenue, Suite 1
PO Box 1907
Soldotna, AK 99669-1907
907-262-6333
Fax: 907-260-4495
e-mail: ilc@xyz.net
http://www.peninsulailc.org
TTY 907-262-6333

Joyanna Geisler, Executive Director

The Keni Peninsula Independent Living Center is a non-profit organization run by persons with disabilities for persons with disaibilites. Our primary goal is to assist persons with impairments to live as independently as possible in their own homes and in the communities of their choice. Independent Living Center offices are located in Homer, Soldotna, and Seward Alaska. We provide direct service to the entire Keni Peninsula and outreach serviceto Kodiak Island and the Valdez-Cordova region. Contact any office for more information.

10629 Seward Independent Living Center
201 Third Avenue, Suite 1
PO Box 3523
Seward, AK 99664-3523
907-224-8711
Fax: 907-224-7793
e-mail: ilc@xyc.net
http://www.peninsulailc.org
TTY 907-224-8711

Joyanna Geisler, Executive Director

The Kenai Peninsula Independent Living Center is a non-profit organization run by persons with disabilities for persons with disabilities. Our primary goal is to assist persons with impairments to live as independently as possible in their own homes and in the communities of their choice. Independent Living Center offices are located in Homer, Soldotna, and Seward Alaska. We provide direct service to the entire Kenai Peninsula and outreach service to Kodiak Island and the Valdez-Cordova region. Contact any office for more information.

10630 Southeast Alaska Independent Living (SAIL)
602 Dock Street
Suite 107
Ketchikan, AK 99901-6072
907-225-4735
888-452-7245
Fax: 907-225-4753
e-mail: ketchikan@sailinc.org
http://www.sailinc.org
TTY 907-225-4735

Clark Gruening, President
Robert Purvis, Vice President
Elena Rath, Treasurer

Incorporated in 1992, SAIL is a private nonprofit organization that provides consumer-directed independent living services to people with disabilities throughout Southeast Alaska. SAIL offers an array of nonresidential disability related services and maintains three offices for your convenience, in the communities of Juneau, Sitka, and Ketchikan. The primary purpose of SAIL is to empower consumers with disabilities by providing services and information to support them in making choices that will positively affect their independence and productivity in society. SAIL serves all people with physical and mental disabilities regardless of race, ancestry, color, religion, age, marital status, sexual preference, gender and/or income.

10631 Southeast Alaska Independent Living Center (SAIL)
3225 Hospital Drive
Suite 300
Juneau, AK 99801-8080
907-586-4920
800-478-7245
Fax: 907-586-4980
e-mail: info@sailinc.org
http://www.sailinc.org
TTY 907-586-4920

Clark Gruening, President
Robert Purvis, Vice President
Elena Rath, Treasurer

Incorporated in 1992, SAIL is a private nonprofit organization that provides consumer-directed independent living services to people with disabilities throughout Southeast Alaska. SAIL offers an array of nonresidential disability related services and maintains three offices for your convenience, in the communities of Juneau, Sitka, and Ketchikan. The primary purpose of SAIL is to empower consumers with disabilities by providing services and information to support them in making choices that will positively affect their independence and productivity in society. SAIL serves all people with physical and mental disabilities regardless of race, ancestry, color, religion, age, marital status, sexual preference, gender and/or income.

Independent Living Centers/Arizona

10632 Southeast Alaska Living Center (SAIL)
514 Lake St.
Suite C
Sitka, AK 99835-7701
907-747-6859
800-500-7245
Fax: 907-747-6783
e-mail: sitka@sailinc.org
http://www.sailinc.org
TTY 907-747-6859

Clark Gruening, President
Robert Purvis, Vice President
Elena Rath, Treasurer

Incorporated in 1992, SAIL is a private nonprofit organization that provides consumer-directed independent living services to people with disabilities throughout Southeast Alaska. SAIL offers an array of nonresidential disability related services and maintains three offices for your convenience, in the communities of Juneau, Sitka, and Ketchikan. The primary purpose of SAIL is to empower consumers with disabilities by providing services and information to support them in making choices that will positively affect their independence and productivity in society. SAIL serves all people with physical and mental disabilities regardless of race, ancestry, color, religion, age, marital status, sexual preference, gender and/or income.

Arizona

10633 Arizona Bridge to Independent Living
1229 East Washington Street
Phoenix, AZ 85034-1101
602-256-2245
800-280-2245
Fax: 602-254-6407
e-mail: azbridge@abil.org
http://www.abil.org

Phil Pangrazio, Executive Director
Ann Pasco, Operations Director
Darrel Christenson, Director, Community Integration

Arizona Bridge to Independent Living (ABIL), offers and promotes programs designed to empower people with disabilities to take personal responsibility so they may achieve or continue independent lifestyles within the community. ABIL offers services to facilitate implementation of the Americans with Disabilities Act (ADA) throughout the state including ADA training, technical assistance and materials to businesses and persons with disabilities onthe requirements and options of the ADA. We offer advocacy services with the intent of facilitating cooperative compliance. ABIL provides ADA counseling on larger projects such as facilities surveys and job accommodations. In addition, ABIL offers a variety of opportunities for consumers to have input into the laws, policies and procedures that affect their lives. Through the use of self, one on one, systems, legislative and community Advocacy, cooking skills, self-advocacy, household management, communication skills and stress management. ABIL assists motivated consumers in developing self-determined goals to gain greater independence.ABIL's consumers participate in shaping the future of our community. ndependent Living is the freedom to direct one's own life. Each individual has the right to optimize their personal ability and fully integrate into the community. ABILis independent living skills instruction includes: use of community resources, budgeting, transportation skills,

10634 DIRECT Independent Living Center
1023 North Tyndall Avenue
Tucson, AZ 85719-4446
520-624-6452
800-342-1853
Fax: 520-792-1438
e-mail: direct@directilc.org
http://www.directilc.org

Ann Meyer, Executive Director
Alfred Zulli Jr., Acting President
Martha Schuetz, Secretary

DIRECT Center for Independence, Inc. is a consumer-directed, community-based advocacy organization, that promotes independent living and offers a variety of programs for all people with disabilities which encourages them to achieve their full potential and to participate in the community. Direct Center for Independence, Inc., came into existence as Metro Independent Living Center in 1980. It was the first agency of its kind in Arizona serving asa non-residential Independent Living Center operated by and for persons with disabilities. The Center became incorporated and got its 501(c)(3) status as an independent, non-profit agency in 1994. The Center has a variety of programs including independent living skills, information and referral, peer counseling services, mentoring services, personal care assistance, and the transit solutions program.

10635 New Horizons Independent Living Center - Prescott Valley
8085 East Manley Dr.
Prescott Valley, AZ 86314
928-772-1266
Fax: 928-772-3808
e-mail: nhilc@cableone.net
http://www.newhorizonsilc.org
TTY 927-772-8870

Kathleen Thompson, Board President
Mildred Adomeit, Vice President

New Horizons provides services and advocacy to empower and enable people with disabilities to self-determine the goals and activities of their lives in family, home, community and workplace. New Horizons provides the following services free to anyone with a disability: independent living skills; training-home management, cooking, cleaning, budgeting, etc.; Social Security benefits planning and work incentives assistance; information and referral; peer support and guidance in addition to community education public seminars and employment evaluation and training programs.

10636 Services Maximizing Independent Living and Empowerment (SMILE)
1929 South Arizona Avenue
Suite 12
Yuma, AZ 85364-4603
928-329-6681
Fax: 520-329-6715
e-mail: SMILE1929@adelphia.net
http://www.snap211.com/org/1482438.html
TDD 928-782-7458

Kathryn Robins, Executive Director
Laura Duval, Assistive Technology Specialist

SMILE's mission is to provide the catalyst for community change and life altering experiences and thereby empower individuals with significant disabilities, throughout Yuma and La Paz Counties: to function independently; to live safely, with dignity; and, to enjoy full access to one's communities. Services include independent living skills training; information and referral; peer support groups, and benefits planning, assistance and outreach.

10637 Statewide Independent Living Council (SILC)
2400 North Central Avenue
Suite 105
Phoenix, AZ 85004-1300
602-262-2900
Fax: 602-271-4100
e-mail: azsilc@qwest.net
http://www.azsilc.org
TDD 602-542-6049

Tony DiRienzi, Executive Director
Sharon Engelhardt, Exacutive Assistant

A non profit organization consisting of a council of advocates appointed by the governor of the state of Arizona. Their role is to advocate for the development of networks of programs, services, and options designed to empower Arizonans with disabilities to live independently in their community. The vision of the council is that all Arizonans with disabilities are treated equally and included fully in a society that embraces freedom of choice and integration so that people with disabilities can be responsible for the achievement of their potential. The goal of the independent living movement is integration and full inclusion of individuals with disabilities into the mainstream of society.

Independent Living Centers/Arkansas

Arkansas

10638 Arkansas Independent Living Council (AILC)
8500 West Markham Plaza
Suite 105
Little Rock, AR 72205-2455
501-372-0607
800-772-0607
Fax: 501-372-0598
e-mail: ailc@alltel.net
http://www.ar-ilc.org
TTY 501-372-0607

Angela Parker, Executive Director
Julie Finley, Office Manager
Kenneth Jackson, Chairman

The Arkansas Independent Living Council (AILC) is an education, advocacy and referral agency that works to provide information to consumers, families, and the public throughout the state about the Independent Living philosophy, civil rights, technology, and services. The AILC has a Board of Directors comprised of Governor-appointed Arkansans, the majority with disabilities. The mission of the AILC is to promote independence including freedom of choice and full inclusion into the mainstream of society for all Arkansans with disabilities. Services include information and referral; peer support; independent living skills training, and advocacy.

10639 Division of Aging and Adult Services - Elder Choices
Arkansas Department of Human Services
PO Box 1437
Slot S-530
Little Rock, AR 72203-1437
501-682-2441
Fax: 501-682-8155
e-mail: Herb.Sanderson@arkansas.gov
http://www.arkansas.gov/dhhs/aging

Herb Sanderson, Executive Director

ElderChoices is Arkansas' Medicaid home and community-based waiver designed for its elderly population. ElderChoices, implemented July 1, 1991, is designed for persons who due to physical, cognitive or medical reasons, require a level of assistance that would have to be provided in a nursing facility, if it were not for the services offered through this program. The program is designed to assist elderly persons reside in their own homes, or live with relatives or caregivers for as long as possible, if that is their choice. ElderChoices has provided services to more than 13,000 elderly Arkansans since 1991. There are currently 6,368 recipients participating in the program with a statewide total of 276 providers of service. In addition to ElderChoices services, waiver recipients may receive other Medicaid covered services such as physician visits, some prescription drugs, personal care and others.

10640 Mainstream Living
300 South Rodney Parham Road
Suite 5
Little Rock, AR 72205-4774
501-280-0012
Fax: 501-280-9267
e-mail: mainstreamlr@sbcglobal.net
http://www.mainstreamilrc.com
TDD 501-280-9262

Rita Byers, Executive Director

Mainstream is dedicated to the concept of consumer directed service delivery in that each consumer has control of his or her life, the services, support, and advocacy that they receive. The type of services a consumer receives are conducted within the framework of a written individual Independent Living Plan (ILP). These plans are developed by the consumer him/herself with the assistance of a qualified Mainstream staff member. The mission of Mainstream is to provide advocacy, peer support, and services which will enable people with severe disabilities to live independently in the community. The organization will work to achieve the integration of people with disabilities into the mainstream of society.

10641 Sources for Community Independent Living Services (SOURCES)
1918 North Birch Avenue
Fayetteville, AR 72703-3911
479-442-5600
888-284-7521
Fax: 479-442-5192
e-mail: jmather@arsources.org
http://www.arsources.org

Rene Boucher, President
Neill Williamson, Vice-President
Mike Tramill, Secretary

It is the mission of SOURCES to promote the independence of persons with disabilities by facilitating and supporting their full integration and participation in all aspects of community life. SOURCES will provide services, support, and advocacy for persons with disabilities, their families, and the community at large. SOURCES is dedicated to the Independent Living Philosophy and the concept of consumer-directed service delivery: each consumer has control of his or her own life. All services and activities reflect this concept. Services include information and referral; peer support; independent living skills training, and advocacy.

10642 Spa Area Independent Living Services (SAILS)
101 Archwood Street
Hot Springs, AR 71901
501-624-7710
Fax: 501-624-7510
e-mail: sails@hotsprings.net
http://www.arsails.org
TDD 501-624-7710

Brenda Stinebuck, Manager

This project aims to assist more people with disabilities in obtaining and maintaining employment. One objective is to work with consumers of VR services toward increased self-esteem, confidence and job seeking skills, making them more competitive in the job market. The program consists of a comprehensive two-week class focusing on the skills needed to obtain competitive employment. The course includes topics such as resume writing, job search, application process, ADA Title I training, mock interviews, etc. All of this is provided in a peer environment, facilitated by peers.

California

10643 CAPH Independent Living Center
3475 West Shaw Avenue
Suite 101
Fresno, CA 93711-3200
209-927-6777
Fax: 209-276-6778
e-mail: program_dir@earthlink.net
http://www.rehab.cahwnet.gov/ils/default.htm
TDD 209-927-6779

Fran Phillips, Executive Director

The Independent Living Section of the Department of Rehabilitation (DOR) is one part of California's independent living network, which includes 29 independent living centers (ILCs) and the State Independent Living Council (SILC). The network is dedicated to the ideal that communities become fully accessible and integrated so that all persons with disabilities can live, work, shop and play where they choose, without barriers. DOR administers the program in California and provides technical assistance and financial support for the independent living centersrogram in California and provides technical assistance and financial support for the independent living centers. The Independent Living Center provides numerous services including: peer couseling; indepedent living skills training; housing assistance; information and referral; individual advocacy; systems advocacy, and assistive technology. Independent living advocates direct their efforts toward the goal of freeing people with disabilities from institutional living, while educating the community in accessibility issues.

Independent Living Centers/California

10644 CCCIL-Central Coast Center for Independenet Living - Capitola
1395 41st Avenue
Suite B
Capitola, CA 95010-3930
831-462-8720
Fax: 831-462-8727
e-mail: ccciltcap@cccil.org
http://www.cccil.org
TDD 831-462-8729

Tink Miller, Executive Director

Services include advocacy, housing assistance, personal assistance, peer support, living skills, skills training, and community advocacy. Serves Santa Cruz, Monterey and San Benito counties.

10645 California Foundation for Independent Living Centers (CFILC)
1029 J Street
Suite 120
Sacramento, CA 95814-2494
916-325-1690
Fax: 916-325-1699
e-mail: CFILC@cfilc.org
http://www.cfilc.org
TTY 916-325-1695

Anna Guerra, Executive Director
Jo Black, Vice Chairperson-South
Dwight Baterman, Vice Chairperson-North

The California Foundation for Independent Living Centers, based in Sacramento, Calif., is a statewide, non-profit trade organization made up of 25 Independent Living Centers. Through unified action, CFILC envisions civil rights for all people with disabilities. CFILC'S mission is to support independent living centers in their local communities through advocating for systems change & promoting access & integration for people with disabilities.

10646 California State Independent Living Council (SILC)
1600 K Street
Suite 100
Sacramento, CA 95814-4020
916-445-0142
866-866-7452
Fax: 916-445-5973
e-mail: neal@calsilc.org
http://www.calsilc.org
TTY 916-445-5627

David Wilder, Chairman
Elizabeth Pazdral, Executive Director

In cooperation with the state Department of Rehabilitation, the SILC prepares a State Plan for Independent Living which sets the policy and funding levels for the state's network of Independent Living Centers (ILCs) and services. To help guide this policy, the SILC solicits continual public feedback on the effectiveness of independent living services and the changing needs of the community. In addition to preparing and updating the State Plan for Independent Living, the SILC monitors the implementation of it. The SILC also coordinates with similar agencies and councils at the state and federal levels to increase communication and help assure that services to people with disabilities are delivered effectively. SILC strongly supports a society where persons with disabilities have the choice to live without barriers and to fully participate in all aspects of the community that includes equal opportunity; equal access; self determination; self sufficiency and independence.

10647 Center for Independence of the Disabled (CID)
875 O'Neill Avenue
Belmont, CA 94002-3898
650-595-0783
Fax: 650-595-0261
e-mail: info@cidbelmont.org
http://www.cidbelmont.org
TDD 650-595-0743

Kent Mickelson, Executive Director
Terri Slaughter, Program Manager
Lynn Del Bene, Peer Counselor

The Center for Independence of the Disabled (CID) is a private, nonprofit Corporation located in Belmont, California. Incorporated in 1979 in the State of California, CID is a consumer-driven, community based, services and advocacy organization serving San Mateo County. By federal mandate, the majority of our Staff, Management Staff, and Board of Directors consist of people with significant disabilities. Annually CID helps more than 2,000 peoplewith disabilities in direct and indirect services. We also help more than 3,400 people with disabilities with individual and systems advocacy issues. CID's mission is to increase the social, educational, and economic participation of persons with disabilities in San Mateo County, and to encourage, support, and provide options for self-determination, equal access and freedom of choice.

10648 Center for Independence of the Disabled-North Branch
355 Gellert Boulevard
Suite 256
Daly City, CA 94015-2675
650-991-5124
Fax: 650-757-2075
e-mail: info@cidbelmont.org
http://www.cidbelmont.org
TTY 650-991-5182

Kent Mickelson, Executive Director
Terri Slaughter, Program Manager
Lynn Del Bene, Pper Counselor

The Center for Independence of the Disabled in Dale City is one of 29 Independent Living Centers in the State of California and 424 Independent Living Centers in the United States. We are affiliated with other ILCs through our membership and participation in the California Foundation of Independent Living Centers and the National Council of Independent Living. CID is affiliated with other nonprofit agencies through our membership in the California Association of Non-Profits. Annually CID helps more than 2,000 people with disabilities in direct and indirect services. We also help more than 3,400 people with disabilities with individual and systems advocacy issues. CID' s mission is to increase the social, educational, and economic participation of persons with disabilities, and to encourage, support, and provide options for self-determination, equal access and freedom of choice.

10649 Center for Independent Living (CIL)
2539 Telegraph Avenue
Berkeley, CA 94704-2997
510-841-4776
Fax: 510-841-6168
e-mail: info@cilberkeley.org
http://www.cilberkeley.org
TTY 510-848-3101

Jan Garrett, Executive Director
Carol Hirsch-Butler, President Of CIL Board Of Dir.
Chryl Pittman, Housing Counselor

The Center for Independent Living (CIL) is a national leader in supporting disabled people in their efforts to lead independent lives. As an organization founded by people with disabilities, CIL understands the challenges faced by their consumers. CIL strives toward the achievement of immediate and long-term solutions - be it assistance with finding housing or a job, equipping a home with assistive technologies, or enhancing independent living skills. CIL's consumer services give people with disabilities the tools and resources they need to achieve independence. All of these services are free and feature advocacy, counseling, education and referrals. Additionally, these services are offered in multiple languages.

10650 Center for Independent Living - Central Coast/Hollister (CCCIL)
1111 San Felipe Road
Suite 107
Hollister, CA 95023-3717
831-636-5196
Fax: 408-637-0478
e-mail: cccil@cccil.org
http://www.cccil.org
TDD 831-637-3265

Elsa Quezada, Executive Director
Georgina Alvarez, Contact

Independent Living Centers/California

Services include advocacy, education and support to all people with disabilities, their families and their community, such as independent living information, housing assistance, living and life skills training and technology support. Serves Santa Cruz, Monterey and San Benito counties.

10651 Center for Independent Living-Merced Outreach
710 W 18th Street
Suite 11
Merced, CA 95340
209-383-1683
Fax: 209-725-9153
http://www.cilfresno.org

Bob Hand, Executive Director
Jimmie Soto, Director Of Program Services
Tony Ko, Office Manager

The Center for Independent Living (CIL) is a national leader in supporting disabled people in their efforts to lead independent lives. As an organization founded by people with disabilities, CIL understands the challenges faced by their consumers. This motivates CIL to achieve immediate and long-term solutions - be it assistance with finding housing or a job, equipping a home with assistive technologies, or enhancing independent living skills. CIL's consumer services give people with disabilities the tools and resources they need to achieve independence. All of these services are free and feature advocacy, counseling, education and referrals. Additionally, these services are offered in multiple languages.

10652 Center for Independent Living-Oakland
610 16th Street
Suite 419
Oakland, CA 94612
510-763-9999
Fax: 510-763-4910
e-mail: info@cilberkeley.org
http://www.cilberkeley.org
TTY 510-444-1837

Jan Garrett, Executive Direrctor

The Center for Independent Living (CIL) is a national leader in supporting disabled people in their efforts to lead independent lives. As an organization founded by people with disabilities, CIL understands the challenges faced by their consumers. This motivates CIL to achieve immediate and long-term solutions - be it assistance with finding housing or a job, equipping a home with assistive technologies, or enhancing independent living skills. CIL's consumer services give people with disabilities the tools and resources they need to achieve independence. All of these services are free and feature advocacy, counseling, education and referrals. Additionally, these services are offered in multiple languages.

10653 Community Access Center
6848 Magnolia Avenue
Suite 150
Riverside, CA 92506-2858
951-274-0358
Fax: 951-274-0833
e-mail: execdir@ilcac.org
http://www.ilcac.org
TTY 951-274-0834

Mark Dyer, President
Janet Newcomer, Vice President
Perry Halterman, Secretary

The primary purpose of Community Access Center is to empower consumers with disabilities by providing services and information to support them in making choices that will positively affect their independence and productivity in society and in advocating to achieve complete social, economic, and political integration. The Community Access Center implements this vision by providing information, supportive services and independent living skills training.

10654 Community Resources for Independence (CRI) Napa
1040 Main Street
Suite 208
Napa, CA 94558
707-258-0270
Fax: 707-258-0275
http://www.cri-dove.org
TTY 707-258-0270

April Dawson, Independent Living Advocate
Matthew Schultz, Independent Living Advocate

Community Resources for Independence (CRI) is a non-profit corporation established in 1976 by a group of disabled and non-disabled individuals to advance the rights of persons with disabilities to equal justice, access, opportunity and participation in our communities. Persons with any type of disability, any age, and/or their familes, are eligible to receive services from CRI. Appointments are recommended and no fees are charged to consumers except for legal representation.

10655 Community Resources for Independence - CRI/Santa Rosa
980 Hopper Road
Santa Rosa, CA 95403-1649
707-528-2745
Fax: 707-528-9477
e-mail: cri@cri-dove.org
http://www.cri-dove.org
TTY 707-528-2151

Betsy Bridgman, Finance Assistant
Adam Brown Esq., Executive Director/Legal Srvs.
Sharon Dawson, Deaf Services Coordinator

Community Resources for Independence (CRI) is a non-profit corporation established in 1976 by a group of disabled and non-disabled individuals to advance the rights of persons with disabilities to equal justice, access, opportunity and participation in our communities. Persons with any type of disability, any age, and/or their familes are eligible to receive services from CRI. Appointments are recommended & no fees are charged to consumers exceptfor legal representation.

10656 Community Resources for Independent Living
439 A Street
Hayward, CA 94541-5013
510-881-5743
Fax: 510-881-1593
e-mail: info@cril-online.org
http://www.cril-online.org
TTY 510-881-0218

Chris Finn, President
Janet Jones, Vice President
Randy Dana, Treasurer/Secretary

Community Resources for Independent Living is founded on the principles of independent living philosophy. Independent living philosophy concentrates on inclusive communities, choice, equality, diversity, empowerment and independence. CRIL offers independent living services at no charge to persons with disabilities living in southern and eastern Alameda County. In order to become a CRIL consumer, an individual must have a disability and be pairedwith an Independent Living (IL) Coordinator.

10657 Dayle McIntosh Center for the Disabled
150 West Cerritos Avenue
Bldg 4
Anaheim, CA 92805-6546
714-772-8285
Fax: 714-772-8292
http://www.daylemc.org
TTY 714-772-8366

Bill Chrisner, Executive Director

The mission of the Dayle McIntosh Center (DMC) is to advance empowerment and inclusion of all persons with disabilities. Dayle McIntosh Center (DMC) was named in memory of a young woman with a severe physical disability who worked to found the Center in 1977. DMC is the largest Independent Living Center in California. Independent Living is a philosophy and a movement of people with disabilities who work for self-determination, equal opportunity,and self respect. A non-residential facility, DMC exists to succeed in every arena they desire.

Independent Living Centers/California

10658 Dayle McIntosh Center-Clubhouse
1832 North Glassell Street
Orange, CA 92665
714-921-9916
Fax: 714-921-1712
TTY 714-772-8366

Cathy Demello, Director

The mission of the Dayle McIntosh Center is to advance empowerment and inclusion of all persons with disabilities. Dayle McIntosh Center (DMC) was named in memory of a young woman with a severe physical disability who worked to found the Center in 1977. DMC is the largest Independent Living Center in California. Independent Living is a philosophy and a movement of people with disabilities who work for self-determination, equal opportunity, and self respect. A non-residential facility, DMC exists to succeed in every arena they desire.

10659 Dayle McIntosh-South County
24012 Calle de La Plata
Suite 210
Laguna Hills, CA 92653
949-460-7784
Fax: 949-855-8742
e-mail: dmc@daylemcintoshcenter.org
http://www.daylemc.org
TDD 714-643-7282
TTY 949-855-6749

Bill Chrisner, Executive Director

The mission of the Dayle McIntosh Center is to advance empowerment and inclusion of all persons with disabilities. Dayle McIntosh Center (DMC) was named in memory of a young woman with a severe physical disability who worked to found the Center in 1977. DMC is the largest Independent Living Center in California. Independent Living is a philosophy and a movement of people with disabilities who work for self-determination, equal opportunity, and self respect. A non-residential facility, DMC exists to succeed in every arena they desire.

10660 IL Resources of Contra Costa County-Fairfield
1545 Webster Street
Suite C
Fairfield, CA 94533-4917
707-435-8174
Fax: 707-435-8177
e-mail: info@ilrcoco-sol.org
http://http://ilrcoco.sol.org
TTY 510-794-5562

Eli Gelardin, Interim Executive Director
Claude Battaglia, Program Director
Susan Rotchy, Program Manager

Services include education, peer support and advocacy for social and politiacl integration.

10661 Independent Living Center of Kern County
1631 30th Street
Bakersfield, CA 93301
661-325-1063
800-529-9541
Fax: 661-325-6702
e-mail: pmcelwee@ilckc.org
http://www.ilcofkerncounty.org
TDD 661-325-3092
TTY 661-325-4143

Louis Lopez, Executive Director

A consumer-based, consumer-directed non-profit agency assisting persons with disabilities to live independently in their community. the ILCKC presently offers a wide range of services to a growing population of persons with disabilities. These services are designed to educate the community on disability issues as we provide persons with the information, support and opportunity to grow creatively, professionally, and personally. ILCKC empowers people by assisting people in developing options, making informed choices and controlling their own lives.

10662 Independent Living Center of SouthernCalifornia (ILCSC)
14407 Gilmore Street
Suite 101
Van Nuys, CA 91401-1481
818-785-6934
Fax: 818-785-0330
e-mail: ILCSC@ilcsc.org
http://www.ilcsc.org
TTY 818-785-7097

Norma Vescovo, Executive Director
Humberto Quintanar, Board-Directors President
Michael A Hansel, Board-Directors Vice President

A non-profit consumer-based, non-residential agency providing a wide range of services to a growing population of people with disabilities. ILCSC is dedicated to empowerin persons with disabilities to excercise independence, professionally, personally and creatively, while striving to educate the community on their needs.

10663 Independent Living Center-Lancaster
1505 West Avenue J
Suite 102
Lancaster, CA 93534
661-945-6602
Fax: 661-945-5690
e-mail: ilcsclanc@ilcsc.org
http://www.ilcsc.org
TTY 661-945-9624

Norma Vescovo, Executive Direcctor
Humberto Quintanar, Board-Directors President
Michael A Hansel, Board-Directors Vice President

A non-profit consumer-based, non-residential agency providing a wide range of services to a growing population of people with disabilities. ILCSC is dedicated to empowering persons with disabilities to excercise independence, professionally, personally, and creatively, while striving to educate the community on their needs.

10664 Independent Living Center-Santa Clarita
23560 Lyons Avenue
Suite 201
Santa Clarita, CA 91321-2521
661-290-2569
Fax: 661-290-2556
e-mail: ilcscsc@ilcsc.org
http://www.ilcsc.org
TTY 661-290-2420

Norma Vescovo, Executive Director
Humberto Quintanar, Board-Directors President
Michael A Hansel, Board-Directors Vice President

A non-profit, consumer-based, non-residential agency providing a wide range of services to a growing population of people with disabilities. ILCSC is dedicated to empowering persons with disabilities to excercise independence, professionally, personally, and creatively, while striving to educate the community on their needs.

10665 Independent Living Resource Center (ILRCSF)
649 Mission Street
3rd Floor
San Francisco, CA 94105-4128
415-543-6222
Fax: 415-543-6318
e-mail: info@ilrcsf.org
http://www.ilrcsf.org
TTY 415-543-6698

Katherine Martinez, President
Sandy O'Neill, Vice President
Sam Ruben, Secretary

Independent Living Centers/California

Independent Living Resource Center San Francisco (ILRCSF) is a disability rights advocacy and support organization. Our mission is to ensure that people with disabilities are full social and economic partners, within their families and within a fully accessible community. ILRCSF's mission is achieved by: systems change; community education; partnerships with business, community organizations and government; and consumer directed services. We work to empower individuals and community, so that all people with disabilities have as full, productive and independent lives as they so chose. ILRCSF programs and services include information and referrals, assistive technology education and support, peer counseling, system change advocacy, housing counseling, benefits and employment planning, and individual advocacy benefits eligibility.

10666 Independent Living Resource Contra Costa County-Antioch
310 West 10th Street
Unit 4
Antioch, CA 94509-1761
925-754-0539
e-mail: info@ilcilrcc.org
http://www.ilcilrcc.org
TTY 925-754-0539

Eli Gelardin, Interim Executive Director
Claude Battaglia, Program Director
Susan Rotchy, Program Manager

A non-profit organization, which promotes the full participation and inclusion of disabled persons in community life. Referred to as an Independent Living Center, the agency is part of a network of similar organizations throughout the nation. The mission of the agency is to empower people with disabilities to controll their own lives. Provide advocacy and support & create and accessable community free of physical & attitudinal barriers.

10667 Independent Living Resource of Contra Costa County
3200 Clayton Road
Concord, CA 94519-2819
925-363-7293
Fax: 925-363-7296
e-mail: info@ilrccc.org
http://www.ilrccc.org
TDD 925-363-7293
TTY 925-363-7293

Bryan M Balch, Executive Director

Services include advocacy and support for complete social and political integration, assistive technology training, information and referrals and peer support.

10668 Independent Living Resources Center-Santa Maria
327 East Plaza Drive
Suite 3A
Santa Maria, CA 93454-6930
805-925-0015
Fax: 805-349-2416
e-mail: jblack@ilrc-trico.org
http://www.ilrc-trico.org
TTY 805-925-0015

Laurie Colson-Young, Comm. Living Advocate-Benefits
Elizabeth Houston, Comm. Living Advocate-Deaf
Jennie Morales, Interpreter Advocate

The Independent Living Resource Center, Inc., is an organization of, by and for persons with disabilities who reside or work in our service area. Our purpose is to assist and encourage individuals to achieve their optimal level of self-sufficiency while eliminating the architectural, communication and attitudinal barriers which prevent them from full participation in the community. Services include that of independent living skills training, advocacy, assistive technology, information and referral, peer and benefits counseling, American Sign Language interpreter, and communications access assistance.

10669 Independent Living Resources Center-Santa Barbara
423 West Victoria Street
Santa Barbara, CA 93101-3619
805-963-0595
Fax: 805-963-1350
e-mail: jblack@ilrc-trico.org
http://www.ilrc-trico.org
TTY 805-963-0595

Josephine Black, Executive Director
Rebecca Gonzalez, Information and Referral
Petra Lowen, Community Living Advocate

The Independent Living Resource Center, Inc., is an organization of, by and for persons with disabilities who reside or work in our service area. Our purpose is to assist and encourage individuals to achieve their optimal level of self-sufficiency while eliminating the architectural, communication and attitudinal barriers which prevent them from full participation in the community. Services include that of independent living skills training, advocacy, assistive technology, benefits and peer counseling, American Sign Language interpreting, information and referral, and, communications access.

10670 Independent Living Resources Center-Ventura
1802 Eastman Avenue
Suite 112
Ventura, CA 93003-5759
805-650-5993
Fax: 805-650-9278
e-mail: jblack@ilrc-trico.org
http://www.ilrc-trico.org
TTY 805-650-0699

Josephine Black, Executive Director
Carol Baizer, Comm. Living Advocate-Benefits
Luz Diaz, Information & Referral Specialis

The Independent Living Resource Center, Inc., is an organization of, by and for persons with disabilities who reside or work in our service area. Our purpose is to assist and encourage individuals to achieve their optimal level of self-sufficiency while eliminating the architectural, communication and attitudinal barriers which prevent them from full participation in the community. Services include that of independent living skills training, advocacy, assistive technology, communications access assistance, American Sign Language interpreting, information and referrals, and peer and benefits counseling.

10671 Independent Living Services of Northern California
1161 East Avenue
Chico, CA 95926-1018
530-893-8527
800-464-8527
Fax: 530-893-8574
e-mail: info@ilsnc.org
http://www.ilsnc.org
TTY 830-593-8527

Sarah Bates, President
Brandi Zellers, Vice President
Eddie Evans, Secretary

Services include living skills training, peer counseling, housing assistance and a newsletter.

10672 Marin Center for Independent Living
710 4th Street
San Rafael, CA 94901-3213
415-459-6245
Fax: 415-459-7047
http://www.marincil.org
TTY 415-459-7027

Rocky Birdsey, Executive Director

Services include advocacy for people with disabilities in regard to health, acces, employment and education.

Independent Living Centers/California

10673 Placer Independent Resource Services/PIRS
11768 Atwood Road
Suite 29
Auburn, CA 95603-9074
530-885-6100
800-833-3453
Fax: 530-885-3032
e-mail: lbrewer@pirs.org
http://www.pirs.org
TTY 530-885-0326

Tim Cooper, President
Michael K. Flack, Vice President
Robert Hancock, Secretary

Placer Independent Resource Services (PIRS) advocates for the rights of people with disabilities, educates the community about disability issues, and provides services to persons with disabilities to live independent, productive lives. Any person with a disiability is eligible for our services. Services are free of charge.

10674 Resources for Independent Living
420 I Street
Suite 3
Sacramento, CA 95814-2319
916-446-3074
Fax: 916-446-2443
e-mail: francesg@ril-sacramento.org
http://www.ril-sacramento.org
TTY 916-446-3074

Frances Gracechild, Executive Director

Resources for Independent Living/ RIL supports and promotes the socio-economic independence of persons with disabilities by providing peer-supported, consumer-directed independent living services and advocacy. The majority of the policy-making board is comprised of individuals with disabilities thereby making the decision-making process both innovative and highly effective. RIL provides numerous services including that of information and referral, advocacy and legislative monitoring, peer counseling and assistive technology in addition to independent living skills training.

10675 Rolling Start
570 West 4th Street
Suite 107
San Bernardino, CA 92401-1438
909-884-2129
Fax: 909-386-7446
e-mail: rs.inc@verizon.net
http://www.rollingstart.com
TDD 909-884-7396

Mark Gomez, Assis. Technology Coordinator
Carol Ware, Helpline Coordinator

Rolling Start Center for Independent Living was incorporated in October of 1977. The center was established as a grassroots organization manned mostly by volunteers who were also persons with disabilities. The philosophy of the center has always been to empower individuals with all types of disabilities to be the best they can be. The driving force of the center is teaching people with disabilities to advocate for what they need to be productivemembers within the communities in which they live. The core services which Rolling Start currently provides are: independent living skills training; assistive technology; information and referral; systems and individual advocacy; peer counseling; personal assistant referral, and, housing information.

10676 Salinas-Central Coast Center for Independent Living
234 Capitol Street
Suites A&B
Salinas, CA 93901-2600
831-757-2968
Fax: 831-757-5549
e-mail: cccil@cccil.org
http://www.cccil.org
TDD 831-757-3949

Elsa Quezada, Executive Director

A non-profit organization founded in Santa Cruz County in 1984 as a grassroots organization dedicated to serving the unmet needs of people with disabilities. CCCIL moved its main office to Salinas in 1994.

10677 Service Center for Independent Living
109 Spring Street
PO Box 549
Claremont, CA 91711-1296
909-621-6722
800-491-6722
Fax: 909-445-0727
e-mail: carol@ilc-clar.org
http://www.ilc-clar.org
TTY 909-445-0726

Dr. Lee Nattress, Executive Director
Christie Mullikin-Jones, Finance Manager
Andrew Roundtree, Program Manager/Direct Srvs.

The Independent Living Center is dedicated to expanding access to information and resources to help increase independence and enhance the quality of life for the East San Gabriel Valley residents with disabilities. Independent Living is both a philosophy and a goal for people with disabilities, to make choices and exercise control over their own lives by eliminating the attitudinal, physical and communications barriers. The Independent Living Center serving the East San Gabriel Valley, formerly the Services Center for Independent Living (SCIL), was incorporated in 1980, by a number of Claremont residents with disabilities, their families and friends. The Independent Living Center shares the independent living philosophy of teaching, mentoring and preparing others to make informed choices, live independently and develop leaders of the future. Dedicated to expanding access to programs, services include that of independent living skills training; systems advocacy; assistive technology; advocacy; communications; housing assistance; information and referral, and, peer counseling.

10678 Service Center for Independent Living-Covina
963 West Badillo Street
Covina, CA 91722-4110
626-967-0995
Fax: 626-967-3132
e-mail: scilcovn@tstonramp.com
http://www.drcinc.org/ILC/ILC.htm
TDD 626-967-4401

Carol Lane, Executive Director
Andrew Rountree, Direct Services Manager
Michael Felten, Assistive Technology

The Independent Living Center is dedicated to expanding access to information and resources to help increase independence and enhance the quality of life for the East San Gabriel Valley residents with disabilities. Independent Living is both a philosophy and a goal for people with disabilities, to make choices and exercise control over their own lives by eliminating the attitudinal, physical and communications barriers. The Independent Living Center serving the East San Gabriel Valley, formerly the Services Center for Independent Living (SCIL), was incorporated in 1980, by a number of Claremont residents with disabilities, their families and friends. The Independent Living Center shares the independent living philosophy of teaching, mentoring and preparing others to make informed choices, live independently and develop leaders of the future. Dedicated to expanding access to programs, employment and housing, Independent Living Centers offer community outreach and education in addition to basic core services that include independent living skills training, assistive technology, information and referral, communication, housing assistance, advocacy, and peer counseling.

10679 Silicon Valley Independent Living Center
7800 Arroyo Circle
Suite A
Gilroy, CA 95020-7346
408-846-1480
Fax: 408-842-2321
e-mail: info@svilc.org
http://www.svilc.org
TTY 408-842-2591

Eleanor Sue, President
Gabe Lopez, Vice-President
Marie Lipari, Secretary

Independent Living Centers/Colorado

The mission of the Silicon Valley Independent Living Center (SVILC) is to empower people with disabilities by providing the advocacy, training, skill development, and services that enhance every individual's capabilities. SVILC strives to eliminate attitudinal, physical, and communication barriers faced by people with disabilities as they work towards independence and full integration in their communities. The programs and services available at SVILC meet a variety of independent living needs. In addition, SVILC offers classes, workshops, support groups, and recreational activities. Services include that of independent living skills training, information and referral, assistive technology, individual and systems advocacy, and peer counseling.

10680 Westside Center for Independent Living
12901 Venice Boulevard
Los Angeles, CA 90066-3509
310-390-3611
888-851-9245
Fax: 310-390-4906
e-mail: development@wcil.org
http://www.wcil.org
TTY 310-398-9204

Mary Ann Jones, Executive Director
Robin Hargrove, Development Director
Aliza Barzilay, Associate Director

The Westside Center for Independent Living was founded in 1976 as a non-residential, public-benefit corporation to enable people with disabilities and seniors in the Los Angeles community to live more independent, self supporting and satisfying lives. The mission of the Westside Center for Independent Living is to empower people with disabilities to reach their independent living goals through a variety of non-residential programs and services. WCIL advocates, educates and provides primarily peer-conducted services to its consumers and the community. WCIL is staffed primarily by people with disabilities. Through their guidance and support, consumers gain the confidence to take the first steps toward their own independence. WCIL has helped over 30,000 people achieve this goal by providing a wide range of services, including benefits and housing advocacy, peer counseling, personal assistance services, independent living skills training, job training and placement and information and referral.

Colorado

10681 Atlantis Community
201 South Cherokee Street
Denver, CO 80223
303-733-9324
Fax: 303-733-9324
e-mail: adaptbabs@atlantiscommunityinc.com
http://www.atlantiscommunity.net
TDD 303-733-0047

Tim Thorton, Executive Director
Babs Johnson, Assistant Director
Frank Krall, Administrative Assistant

The mission of Atlantis Community is to provide direct services, and to empower people with disabilities integrating, with full and equal rights, into all parts of society including employment, affordable, accessible, housing, transportation, recreation, communication, education, and public places while exercising and exerting choice and self determination.

10682 Center For People With Disabilities
1304 Berkley Avenue
Pueblo, CO 81003
719-546-1271
Fax: 719-546-1374
e-mail: ilcpueblo@yahoo.com
TTY 719-546-1867

Larry Williams, Executive Director

Private, non-profit corporation that provides services to maximize the independence of individuals with disabilities and the accessibility of the communities they live in.

10683 Center for Independence
740 Gunderson Avenue
Grand Junction, CO 81501-4647
970-241-0315
800-613-2271
Fax: 970-245-3341
http://www.cfigj.org/temp
TTY 970-245-3341

Tom Kenyon, President
Ken Stubler, Vice President
David Nelson, Secretary/Treasurer

A non-profit, non-residential, grassroots, State-of-Colorado certified independent living center, assisting people with disabilities since 1982. CFI is governed by people with disabilities and upholds the independent living philosophy that people with disabilities have the right to self-determination, and the right to live their lives independently and with dignity to their fullest potential.

10684 Colorado Springs Independence Center
21 East Las Animas Street
Colorado Springs, CO 80903-4139
719-471-8181
Fax: 719-471-7829
e-mail: vickicsic@aol.com
http://www.csicindliving.org
TTY 719-471-2076

Vicki Skoog, Founder/Executive Director

Services include independent living skills, advocacy, and assistive technology training. Our mission is to empower persons with disabilities to maximize their independence within the community and to remove barriers which impact their quality of life, while encouraging them to live independently in their community.

Connecticut

10685 Center for Disability Rights
Connecticut Tech Act Project
764 Campbell Avenue
Suite A
West Haven, CT 06516
203-934-7077
Fax: 203-934-7078
e-mail: cdr7077@aol.com
TTY 203-934-7079

Marc Gallucci, Executive Director

The Center for Disability Rights, in conjunction with the Connecticut Tech Art Project, provides information and guidance on the Americans with Disabilities Act, Section 508, and accessible information technology to individuals living in New England. In addition, the Center also provides information on the Assistive Technology Loan Program which is sponsored by the Connecticut Department of Social Services, Bureau of Rehabilitation Services in partnership with People's Bank. Assistive technology is any tool, device or equipment designed to help you develop, maintain or improve your ability to function daily. It could range from small, inexpensive kitchen gadgets that help you cook to a van adapted with special controls to help you drive independently. Hearing aids, motorized wheelchairs, computers controlled by voice or other special switch and augmentative alternative communication tools are included in a long list of assistive technology devices. The Peer Technology Counselors at the Center for Disability Rights can provide individuals with information about vendors who sell assistive technology and other funding sources.

10686 Center for Independent Living of Northwestern Connecticut
1183 New Haven Road
Suite 200
Naugatuck, CT 06770
203-729-3299
Fax: 203-729-2839
e-mail: indnw@aol.com
http://www.members.aol.com/indnw
TDD 203-729-1281

Eileen Healey, Executive Director
Scott M Robbins, Program Director
Luann Scarola, Administrative Assistant

Independent Living Centers/District of Columbia

Independence Northwest, is part of the nationwide network of Centers for Independent Living that grew out of the disability rights movement of the early 1970's. Centers for Independent Living are directed, managed and staffed to a substantial degree by qualified persons with severe disabilities. A majority of the staff and board of directors at Independence Northwest are persons with disabilities. Independence Northwest provides services in sucharcas as peer counseling, advocacy, independent living skills training and information and referral. In addition, we also provide services to the community in the form of disability awareness programs and technical assistance in such areas as architectural barrier removal and community organizing.

10687 Disability Resource Center of Fairfield County (DRCFC)
Connecticut Tech Art Project
80 Ferry Boulevard
Suite 210
Stratford, CT 06615
203-378-6977
Fax: 203-375-2748
e-mail: info@drcfc.org
http://www.drcfc.org
TDD 203-378-3248

Don F, President
Thomas S, Vice President
Rev. Bob K, Secretary

Disability Resource Center of Fairfield County (DRCFC) provides the means to put the values of Independent Living into action by providing individuals with empowerment and working for change in the attitudinal and physical barriers that face people with disabilities in the community. Services provided by DRCFC include that of information and referral, technical assistance and training, independent living skills training, disability awareness, peer support, systems advocacy and resource assistance.

10688 Independence Unlimited Inc.
151 New Park Avenue
Suite D
Hartford, CT 06106-2170
860-523-5021
Fax: 860-523-5603
e-mail: clow@independenceunlimited.org
TTY 860-523-2021

Candace Low, Executive Director

Independent Living is a philosophy that challenges the social attitudes and physical barriers that stigmatize and exclude people with disabilities from the community. Independence Unlimited is commited to increasing the independence of people with disabilities by assisting individuals in identifying and accessing services and supports, benefits, assistive technology, housing, personal assistance services, and other resources.

District of Columbia

10689 District of Columbia Center for Independent Living (DCCIL)
1400 Florida Avenue NE
Washington, DC 20002-5032
202-388-0033
Fax: 202-398-3018
e-mail: info@dccil.org
http://www.dccil.org
TTY 202-398-0277

Richard Simms, Executive Director

The D.C. Center for Independent Living Inc. (DCCIL) is a consumer controlled, cross disability, community based, private non-profit organization that promotes independent life styles for persons with significant disabilities in the District of Columbia. The District of Columbia Center for Independent Living (DCCIL) Inc. Was established to promote independent life styles for people with significant disabilities, to assist persons with significantdisabilities to meet their selectd independent living goals, and to mainstream people with disabilities to into society.

Delaware

10690 Carelink Community Support Services
100 W 10th Street
Suite 601
Wilmington, DE 19801-6604
302-429-6693
Fax: 302-429-8031
e-mail: development@carelink-svs.org
http://www.carelink-svs.org
TDD 302-429-8034

Eileen M Joseph, President/CEO
Bill Smith, Chief Financial Officer
Gary Woomer, Vice President Program Operation

CareLink provides a growing array of vocational, care management, residential, and day rehabilitation programs. Services are flexible and individually tailored to the interests, needs and goals of each person served. At CareLink, we encourage people to be active participants in their own recovery. By building upon strengths, residents can become more independent and effective in managing their own lives. A comprehensive assessment is completedwith the consumer. This leads to the development of an individualized personal plan that can include services such as monitoring living and vocational arrangements, skill training, financial stewardship, and providing crisis management services. Our rehabilitation services and professional staff provide the supports that people with serious mental illness, physical disabilities and other developmental challenges need to be active, productive members of their communities. Our mission is to serve individuals who need specialized supports to achieve recovery, wellness and self-determination.

10691 Independent Resources-Wilmington
6 Denny Road
Suite 101
Wilmington, DE 19809
302-765-0191
Fax: 302-765-0195
e-mail: lhenderson@iri-de.org
http://www.iri-de.org
TTY 302-765-0194

Larry D Henderson, Executive Director

The Independent Living (IL) Program is administered in Delaware by the DVR. However, eligibility for IL services is not dependent upon employment. Centers for independent living (CILs) are private, nonprofit corporations that provide services to maximize the independence of individuals with disabilities and the accessibility of the communities they live in. Services provided by the Independent Living Center include that of assistive technology, information and referral, advocacy, independent living skills training, and peer support.

10692 Sussex County Assistive Technology Resource Center
sussex coun
Delaware Assistive Technology Initiative (DATI)
20161 Office Circle
Suite C
Georgetown, DE 19947
302-856-7946
Fax: 302-856-6990
http://www.dati.org/aboutus/SussexSite
TDD 302-856-6714

Dan Fendler, Assistive Technology Specialist
Sandy Walls, Administrator

The Delaware Assistive Technology Initiative (DATI) connects Delawareans who have disabilities with the tools they need in order to learn, work, play and participate in community life safely and independently. (DATI) endeavors to improve access to assistive technology for all Delawareans with disabilities. DATI's services are available to all residents of Delaware. There are no eligibility limitations, other than Delaware residency. We address the needs of infants through older persons with all types of disabling conditions. With the exception of some training events, most DATI services are provided at no cost. DATI provides funding information, developes partnerships with state agencies and organizations and also publishes resource materials and event calendars all in the ongoing effort to promote the Assistive Technology Initiative that facilitates more independence in the lives of disabled individuals.

Independent Living Centers/Florida

Florida

10693 Caring and Sharing Center for Independent Living
12552 Belcher Road South
Largo, FL 33773
727-577-0065
866-539-7550
Fax: 727-539-7588
e-mail: cascil@cascil.org
http://www.cascil.org
TDD 727-577-0065

Jack Humburg, President
Dan McKenna, Vice President
Pat Bell, Treasurer

Caring & Sharing Center for Independent Living, Inc. (CASCIL) is a consumer controlled, community based, 501(c)(3), cross-disability organization that promotes the empowerment and self-determination of persons with disabilities through its services and advocacy. A majority of the staff and board of directors are persons with significant disabilities. The independent philosophy espouses the position that persons with disabilities, as well as society, benefit from living and functioning within the community as opposed to being maintained in an institutional setting. The mission of the Caring & Sharing Center for Independent Living, Inc. (CASCIL) is to assist persons with all types of disabilities and their families, to achieve the greatest degree of self-determination in accessibility, advocacy, education, employment, and place of residence in keeping with the consumer's freedom of choice.

10694 Center for Independent Living of North Central Florida-Ocala
3445 Northeast 24th Street
Ocala, FL 34470-3921
352-368-3788
Fax: 352-629-0098
e-mail: carol@cilncf.org
http://www.cilncf.org
TTY 352-368-2969

Ken Osfield, President
Claudia Munnis, Vice President
Alan West, Treasurer

A consumer driven, community based, non-residential private not-for-profit organization. The CILNCF serves 16 counties in the North Central Florida region from 4 locations. We are a consumer controlled organization and have at least 51 % people with disabilities comprising our governing board of directors as well as staff. Our center delivers the 4 core services of Advocacy, Information and Referral, Peer Support, and Independent Living Skills Education.

10695 Center for Independent Living of Broward
8857 West McNabb Road
Tamarac, FL 33321
954-722-6400
Fax: 954-722-9801
TTY 954-722-6400

Karen Dickerhoof, Executive Director
William Knight, Deputy Director
Terry Keter, Program Director

Services include advocacy, information and referrals, independent living skills and peer counseling.

10696 Center for Independent Living of Flordia-Lecanto
3774 West Gulf to Lake Highway
Lecanto, FL 34461
352-527-8399
877-232-8261
Fax: 352-527-9511
http://www.cilnwf.org
TTY 352-527-8399

Ken Osfield, President
Claudia Munnis, Vice President
Alan West, Treasurer

The CILNCF is a consumer driven, community based, non-residential private not-for-profit organization. The CILNCF serves 16 counties in the North Central Florida region from 4 locations. We are a conusmer controlled organization and have at least 51% people with disabilities comprising our governing board of directors as well as staff. Our center delivers the 4 core services of Advocacy, Information & referral, Peer Support & Independent living skills education.

10697 Center for Independent Living of Jacksonville
2709 Art Museum Drive
Jacksonville, FL 32207-5036
904-399-8484
Fax: 904-399-0448
e-mail: cilj@cilj.com
http://www.cilj.com
TTY 904-398-6322

John Trifiletti, President
Danny Powell, Vice-President
Mary Randall, Secretary

A consumer drivenm community based, non-residential, private not-for-profit organization. We serve as a resource agency serving people with disabilities in 5 counties throughout Northeast Florida. Founded in 1991, the ILRC is guided by its mission statement: "To empower all people with a disability (as defined in the American's With Disabilities act (ADA) or Rehab act of 1973), to live independent and self-empower lives."

10698 Center for Independent Living of North Central Florida
222 Southwest 36th Terrace
Gainesville, FL 32607-2863
352-378-7474
800-265-5724
Fax: 352-378-5582
http://www.cilnwf.org
TTY 352-372-3433

Ken Osfield, President
Claudia Munnis, Vice President
Alan West, Treasurer

The CILNCF is a consumer driven, community based, non-residential, not-for-profit organization. The CILNCF serves 16 counties in the North Central Florida region from 4 locations. We are a consumer-controlled organization and have at least 51% people with disabilities comprising our governing board of directors as well as staff. Our center delivers the 4 core services of Advocacy, Information & Referral, Peer Support, and Independent Living Skills Education.

10699 Center for Independent Living of Northern Florida / Ability 1st
1823 Buford Court
Tallahassee, FL 32308-1544
850-575-9621
Fax: 850-576-5740
e-mail: judithbarrett@ability1st.info
http://www.ability1st.info
TDD 850-575-5245

Judith Barrett, Executive Director
Steve Amnott, Director Of Finance & Admin.
Anne Leigh Keller, Office Manager

Offers advocacy, information and referrals, independent living skills and peer counseling. Mission is to empower persons with disabilities to live independently and participate actively in their community.

10700 Center for Independent Living of South Florida
6660 Biscayne Boulevard
Miami, FL 33138-6285
305-751-8025
Fax: 305-751-8944
e-mail: Info@soflacil.org
http://www.soflacil.org
TTY 305-751-8025

Kelly Greene, Executive Director

Independent Living Centers/Florida

The Center for Independent Living of South Florida (CIL) promotes and practices an independent living philosophy of consumer-control, peer role modeling, self-determination, equal access, and advocacy to maximize leadership, empowerment, independence, productivity, integration, and full inclusion of people with disabilities into the mainstream of society. CIL's mission is to assist anyone with a disability to achieve and maintain an independent and self-determined lifestyle to the maximum extent possible and to vigorously advocate for systems change that results in equality, dignity, and freedom of choice, and eliminates barriers that prevent people with disabilities from achieving their full potential. The foundation of the Center is based on the four core services of independent living skills training, information and referral, individual and systems advocacy, and, peer support.

10701 Center for Independent Living of Southwest Florida
2830 Winkler Avenue
Unit 201
Fort Myers, FL 33906
239-277-1447
888-343-6991
Fax: 239-277-1647
e-mail: lhendricks@cilfl.org
http://www.cilfl.org
TTY 239-277-3964

Linda Hendricks, Executive Director
Mary Davis, Coordinator
Gene Bruist, Fiscal Manager

At the Center for Independent Living Of Southwest Florida, we believe that independence and control of your life are personal and assertive decisions you are making. We will guide you, coach you, teach you, and advocate for you, but you must show the initiative to carry on by yourself once you have the skills and knowledge the Center is able to give you. We feel that being independent in your daily life, being free to help yourself, and being self-reliant are worthy and desirable goals. Don's let a disability become any more of a barrier than an inconvenience that can be overcome with a little help and confidence in your own abilities.

10702 Center for Independent Living-Central Florida
720 North Denning Drive
Winter Park, FL 32789-3095
407-623-1070
Fax: 407-623-1390
e-mail: info@cilorlando.org
http://www.cilorlando.org
TTY 407-623-1185

Elizabeth Howe, Executive Director
Rogue Gallart, Advocacy Director
Jan McCrea, Operations Director

The Center for Independent Living in Central Florida Inc. (CIL) is a private non-profit organization that was founded in 1976 by Central Floridians dedicated to helping people with disabilities achieve their self-determined goals for independent living. CIL is a consumer-driven organization whose philosophy is based on peer role models: people with disabilities empowering people with disabilities and their families on the road to independence.

10703 Center for Independent Living-Northwest Florida
3600 North Pace Boulevard
Pensacola, FL 32505-6625
850-595-5566
877-245-2457
Fax: 850-595-5560
e-mail: cilnwf@cilnwf.org
http://www.cilnwf.org
TDD 850-595-5566

Susan Patterson, President
Nancy Wise, Secretary
John Bouchard, Treasurer

The Center for Independent Living is a consumer-controlled, community-based cross-disibility, nonresidentail private non-profit agency that is designed and operated within a local community by individuals with disabilities and provides an array of independent living services. Our goal is to secure for all people with disabilities the opportunity to choose and realize their goals of where and how they live, learn, work and play. Also to assure that the consumer has optimal controll over all their services and options. You are not charged for our four core services.

10704 Coalition for Independent Living Options
6800 Forest Hill Boulevard
West Palm Beach, FL 33413
561-966-4288
800-683-7337
Fax: 561-641-6619
e-mail: cilo2000@bellsouth.net
http://www.cilo.org
TTY 561-641-6538

Shelley Gottsagen, Executive Director

The objectives of the Coalition for Independent Living Options (CILO) are: to increase advocacy efforts with public & private entities to promote independence for people with disabilities; to increase visibility & viability of CILO; to expand services in all geographic areas; to increase collaboration with other agencies; to diversify funding through resource development, and, to increase diversity in board, staff & consumers. Services provided by CILO include that of independent living skills training, information and referral, advocacy, and peer support.

10705 Florida Independent Living Council
1018 Thomasville Road
Suite 100A
Tallahassee, FL 32303
850-488-5624
877-822-1993
Fax: 850-488-5881
e-mail: filc@polaris.net
http://www.flailc.org
TTY 850-488-5624

Molly Gosline, Executive Director
Donald Dawkins, Advocacy Coordinator
Kristi Chapman, Consumer Advocacte

The Florida Independent Living Council is a statewide council established by federal mandate and Florida Statute. FILC's purpose is to promote independent living opportunities for persons with disabilities throughout the state of Florida. This includes the promotion of a direct service philosophy that is consumer controlled and directed. The Council also works to insure: that persons with disabilities have an opportunity for input into the development of a state plan for Independent Living Services; that the independent living needs of people with disabilities are identified and met; and that advocacy on behalf of independent living programs and consumers is initiated and carried out.

10706 Self-Reliance
8901 North Armenia Avenue
Tampa, FL 33604-1041
813-375-3965
Fax: 813-975-3970
e-mail: jdido@self-reliance.org
http://www.self-reliance.org
TTY 813-375-3972

Joseph DiDomenico, Executive Director

Self Reliance, Inc. Center for Independent Living is a nonprofit 501C3 organization established in 1978. Our mission is to promote independence through empowering persons with disabilities and improving the communities in which they live. We are a cross disability agency providing services to both children and adults with disabilities (regardless of age and type of disability) to identify and overcome barriers to independence in their lives. Services are provided free of charge. Self Reliance is one of 17 Centers for Independent Living statewide. Mandated by the Federal Government, Centers For Independent Living provide four core services to individuals with disabilities. The core services are Advocacy - giving aid to a cause; active verbal support for a cause or position. Peer Support & Mentoring - talking to a person with a disability who can understand and encourage you in your decicommunity independence.sion-making and quest for independence. Independent Living Skills Training - individual and group training in areas such as job readiness, home management, parenting, transportation, healthcare and other areas as needed. Information & Referral - learn about community resources and how to connect with valuable services to achieve your goals towards

Independent Living Centers/Georgia

10707 Space Coast Center for Independent Living
803 N, Fiske Blvd.
Suite B
Cocoa Beach, FL 32922
321-633-6011
Fax: 321-633-6472
e-mail: llfowler@bellsouth.net
http://http://esc.brevard.k12.fl.us/icb/scc
TTY 321-784-9008

Larry Fowler, Executive Director

Information & referral, independent living skills training, advocacy, peer support, social/recreational opportunities, low-cost wheelchair accessible transportation, sign language interpreter referral services, specialized telephones &Æequipment for people who are deaf, hard of hearing, deaf/blind or speech impaired, high school transitioning services, accessibility services, volunteer program, notary services.

10708 Suncoast Center for Independent Living
2989 Fruitville Road
Suite 101
Sarasota, FL 34237-5320
941-351-9545
Fax: 813-351-9875
e-mail: keith@scil4u.com
http://www.scil4u.org
TTY 941-351-9943

Keith Kitchens, Executive Director

Offers advocacy for the elimination of social and physical barriers for people with disabilities. Provides peer counseling, equipement and building of access ramps.

Georgia

10709 Access Center for Independent Living
430 Pryor Street
Suite 120
Gainesville, GA 30501
770-534-6656
706-891-6392
Fax: 770-534-6626
TTY 770-534-6656

Melissa Cartwright, Executive Director

Offers advocacy, information and referrals, independent living skills and peer support.

10710 Georgia Statewide Independent Living Council
755 Commerce Drive
Suite 415
Decatur, GA 30030-1852
770-270-6860
888-288-9780
Fax: 770-270-5957
e-mail: ppuckett@silcga.org
http://www.silcga.org
TTY 770-270-5671

Patricia Puckett, Executive Director
Colleen Caffrey, Business Manager
Sherita Robinson, Administrative Assistant

The SILC of Georgia is a nonprofit, non-governmental, consumer-controlled organization that plays the vital role of providing disability information, financial support, and technical assistance to a network of seven Centers for Independent Living (CILs) located throughout the state. Centers for Independent Living are non-residential, community-based organizations, governed and staffed by people with disabilities, that offer a wide variety of services to consumers with disabilities and their families. The foundation of these services is the peer-to-peer relationship, where people with disabilities act as mentors for other people with disabilities, showing them by example how to help themselves and to live independently. The core services that CILs provide are: Individual Advocacy and Systems Advocacy; Peer Counseling; Information and Referral; and Independent Living Skills Training. Whileo educate the public about our services and the unique needs of people with disabilities. We do this by conducting and publishing the results of public opinion polls, disseminating information on a variety of issues and advocating for social change. the SILC of Georgia is a private, non-profit organization, it is also a Governor-appointed body. Board members are composed of members from across the state who represent a broad range of disabilities and backgrounds, and who are knowledgeable about centers for independent living and independent living services. SILC of Georgia's purpose is also t

10711 Living Independence for Everyone (LIFE) Center for Independent Living
17 Travis Street
Savannah, GA 31406-5859
912-920-2314
Fax: 912-920-0007
e-mail: info@lifecil.com
http://www.lifecil.com
TTY 912-920-2419

Bart Brophy, Manager

Living Independence for Everyone (L.I.F.E) is a small nonprofit advocacy organization dedicated to empowering people with disabilities to achieve equal rights, equal opportunities and integration into the community. L.I.F.E. Inc. is operated by and for people with disabilities. Our organization embraces the independent living philosophy. This philosophy is based on the core of independent living concepts of consumer controll, self advocacy, community change, and cross-disability participation. One of the bases of the IL philosophy is that everyone, no matter what his or her disability, has the right to maker his or hew own informed decisions.

10712 Walton Options for Independent Living
948 Walton Way
Augusta, GA 30901
706-724-6262
Fax: 706-724-6729
e-mail: tjohnston@waltonoptions.org
http://www.waltonoptions.org
TTY 706-261-0206

Tiffany Johnston, Executive Director

Walton Options for Independent Living was established September of 1994 in Augusta, Georgia to serve 30 counties in north eastern Georgia and 10 counties in western South Carolina as a private, nonprofit, consumer-controlled (meaning that the organization is governed by a majority of people who have disabilities), nonresidential Center for Independent Living, as defined by the Rehabilitation Act of 1973, as amended. The mission of Walton Optionsis to empower persons of all ages with all types of disabilities to reach their highest level of independence, including community inclusion and employment. Over 70% of the Board and Staff at Walton Options are people with disabilities. The name of the organization came from George Walton, a native Augustan who was the youngest signer of the Declaration of Independence.

Independent Living Centers/Hawaii

Hawaii

10713 Center for Independent Living-East Hawaii
400 Hualani Street
Suite 16D
Hilo, HI 96820-4333
808-935-3777
Fax: 808-961-6737
TTY 808-935-3777

Laura Tobosa, Executive Director
Sabine Nagasawa, IL Specialist

Offers services and advocacy to address the needs of those with disabilities.

10714 Center for Independent Living-West Hawaii
81-6627 Mamalahoa Highway
Suite B-5
Kealakekua, HI 96750-8130
808-323-2221
Fax: 808-323-2383
e-mail: cilwh@ilhawaii.net
TDD 808-323-2383
TTY 808-323-2383

Merle Martin, Executive Director

Offers services and advocacy that addresses the needs of persons with disabilities.

10715 Hawaii Center for Independent Living
414 Kuwili Street
Suite 102
Honolulu, HI 96817-5362
808-522-5412
Fax: 808-522-5427
e-mail: mwhitecl@diverseabilities.com
http://www.hcil.org
TDD 808-522-5415
TTY 808-536-3739

Patricia Lockwood, Executive Director

Offers advocacy and services for those with disabilities.

10716 Regency at Hualalai
75-181 Hualalai Road
Kailua Kona, HI 96740-1787
808-329-7878
Fax: 808-329-7838
e-mail: Eileen@retirementhawaii.com
http://www.regencyhualalai.com

Eileen Lacerte, Coordinator
Claudia Burnett, Coordinator
Jean Nagle, Administrator

Regency at Hualalai's assisted living options offer personalized assistance, supportive services and compassionate care in a professionally managed, carefully designed, community setting. It's the perfect alternative for seniors who can no longer live on their own at home, yet don't need 24-hour, complex medical supervision. The Regency is a place where seniors can enjoy catered independent living, or various levels of assisted living, based on their individual needs. The setting of the Regency at Hualalai is within the comfortable atmosphere of a retirement community that is complemented by personal senior care services provided by a kind and helpful staff.

10717 Statewide Independent Living Council-Hawaii
Davies Pacific Center
841 Bishop Street, Suite 201
Honolulu, HI 96813
808-585-7452
Fax: 808-585-7453
e-mail: sikhi@lava.net
http://www.hisilc.org

Sandra Meehann, Chairwoman
Dara Fukuhara, Vice Chair
Nathan Say, Secretary

The Statewide Independent Living Council of Hawaii is made up of representatives from around the State, appointed by the Governor. The majority of our Council is represented by persons with disabilities. It is a not for profit, non-Governmental, consumer controlled organization, which develops, monitors and evaluates the federally-funded State Plan for Independent Living in the State of Hawaii. It promotes the independent living philosophy statewide and provides support and technical assistance to the Independent Living Center in Hawaii, which consists currently of five community based organizations run by and for people with disabilities. The mission of SILC-Hawaii is to promote independent living and the integration of persons with disabilities into the community and to aid individuals in achieving their goals and basic human rights.

Idaho

10718 Disability Action Center Northwest
East 124 3rd Street
Moscow, ID 83843-2906
208-883-0523
800-475-0070
Fax: 208-883-0524
e-mail: moscow@dacnw.org
http://www.dacnw.org
TTY 208-883-0523

Mark Leeper, Organization Director
David Wegeng, Web-Developer/IL Advocate
Mellowdee Brooks, FI Coordinator/ATP

Disability Action Center NW Inc. is a non-profit community partnership working to promote the independence and equality of all individuals with disabilities in all aspects of society. Utilizing our collective power, we provide information and referral services while fostering attitudes, policies, and environments of equality and freedom. DAC strives to create a compassionate and accessible place for people with disabilities. We encourage people with disabilities to take control of their lives and to live life to the fullest.

10719 IMPACT
2735 East Broadway
Alton, IL 62002-1859
618-462-1411
Fax: 618-474-5309
e-mail: contario@impactcil.org
http://www.incil.org

Cathy Contarino, Executive Director

The Illinois Network of Centers for Independent Living (INCIL) is a statewide organization made up of 24 Centers for Independent Living (CILs) in Illinois. INCIL coordinates the activities and efforts of all CILs, resulting in a stronger, more unified voice to promote the needs and priorities of the CILs and the people they serve. Operated by the executive directors of these CILs, this aggressive core of leadership advocates for and works to ensure that all people are treated with respect and given the same opportunities in life, regardless of their abilities.

10720 Living Independence Network (LINC)
2500 Kootenai
Boise, ID 83705-2408
208-336-3335
Fax: 208-384-5037
e-mail: info@lincidaho.org
http://www.lincidaho.org
TTY 208-336-3335

Roger Howard, Executive Director

Living Independence Network Corporation (LINC) is a non-profit organization empowering people with disabilities to achieve their desired level of independence. LINC promotes personal growth and freedom of choice through advocacy, networking, public awareness and modification of environments.

Independent Living Centers/Illinois

10721 Statewide Independent Living Council-Idaho
PO Box 83720
350 N. 9th Street Suite 102
Boise, ID 83720-9601
208-334-3800
800-487-4866
Fax: 208-334-3803
e-mail: kbucklan@silc.state.id.us
http://www.silc.idaho.gov
TDD 208-334-3800

Robbi Barrutia, Project Director
Jim Liddell, Development Specialist
Olivia Roberts, Administrative Assistant

The Idaho State Independent Living Council (SILC) whose service is provided to acquaint the disability community and service providers to our organization, which advocates for equal opportunity, equal access, self-determination, independence and choice for people with disabilities. The focus of the SILC is to maximize opportunity and to incorporate people with disabilities into all walks of life by empowering them. The Idaho SILC provides leadership development opportunities to empower grassroots advocates, who, in turn, will develop systemic changes in public policy to positively impact people with disabilities.

Illinois

10722 Access Living of Chicago
115 West Chicago Avenue
Chicago, IL 60610
312-640-2100
800-613-8549
Fax: 312-640-2101
e-mail: generalinfo@accessliving.org
http://www.accessliving.org
TTY 312-640-2102

Marca Bristo, President/CEO
Daisy Feidt, Executive Vice President
James Charlton, Special Projects Coordinator

Established in 1980, Access Living is a non-residential Center for Independent Living for people with all types of disabilities, providing services that promote the independence and the inclusion of people with disabilities in every aspect of community life. Access Living follows the independent living philosophy that calls for community-based, consumer-controlled service and advocacy programs that emphasize a cross-disability and self-help approach. All services are provided at no charge to our Consumers. Access Living is a cross-disability organization governed and staffed by a majority of people with disabilities. Access Living fosters the dignity, pride, and self-esteem of people with disabilities and enhances the options available to them so they may choose and maintain individualized and satisfying lifestyles. Access Living recognizes the innate rights, abilities, needs and diversity of people with disabilities, works toward their integration into community life and serves as an agent of social change.

10723 Center For Independent Living-Jacksonville
60 East Central Park Plaza
Jacksonville, IL 62650-2071
217-245-8371
888-317-3287
Fax: 217-245-1872
e-mail: info@jacil.org
http://www.jacil.org
TTY 217-245-8371

Becky McGinnis, Executive Director
Lori Shipley, Program Director
Steve Fristoe, Independent Living Specialist

The Jacksonville Area Center for Independent Living (JACIL) is organized to serve people with disabilities in Morgan, Scott, Cass and Mason counties. JACIL is committed to enabling persons with disabilities to gain effective control and direction of their lives in the home, in the workplace and in the community. The JACIL goal is to stimulate and promote a growing sense of personal dignity through individualized programs designed to provide the the tools necessary for maximum independence and community participation. Services provided by JACIL include that of information and referral, independent living skills training, individual and systems advocacy, and, peer counseling.

10724 Center for Comprehensive Services-Carbondale
306 West Mill Street
PO Box 2825
Carbondale, IL 62901
618-529-3060
800-203-5394
Fax: 618-457-5372
e-mail: abiinfo@thementornetwork.com
http://www.mentorabi.com

Sandy Gasaway, Executive Director

The Center for Comprehensive Services (CCS)-Carbondale was established in 1977 as the first dedicated after-hospital rehabilitation program in the country for persons with acquired brain injury. Located in Carbondale, Illinois, across from the campus of Southern Illinois University at Carbondale, our facilities provide a unique opportunity for collaborative research efforts, and for some, reintegration into post-secondary education.

10725 Central Illinois Center for Independent Living
614 West Glen Avenue
Peoria, IL 61614-8806
309-682-3500
877-501-9808
Fax: 309-682-3989
e-mail: hsalter2001@yahoo.com
http://www.cicil.org
TTY 309-682-3567

Henry Salter, President
Jim Huling, Vice President
Deb Penn, Treasurer

The Central Illinois Center for Independent Living (CICIL) is an organization managed by and for people with disabilities. We are dedicated to empowering persons with disabilities to achieve a higher quality of life through comprehensive programs that promote individual growth. To fulfill this mission, CICIL provides services combined with advocacy for social change to allow greater integration of persons with disabilities into the mainstream of community life. CICIL is a non-residential, community based organization, which provides resource and advocacy services to persons with disabilities. We serve residents in Peoria, Tazewell, Fulton, and Woodford counties. We differ from traditional service agencies because we are staffed and governed primarily by persons with disabilities. This brings a positive perspective based on personal experience with a disability and an understanding of barriers faced and the potential for success. CICIL services include that of independent living skills training, advocacy, information and referral, and, peer counseling.

10726 Dupage Center for Independent Living
739 Roosevelt Road Bldg 8
Suite 109
Glen Ellyn, IL 60137
630-469-2300
Fax: 630-469-2606
e-mail: ed_dupagecil@sbcglobal.net
http://www.incil.org/incil.asp
TTY 630-469-2492

Leigh Ann Heenan, Executive Director

Independent Living Centers/Illinois

Centers for Independent Living (CILs) exist to empower individuals with disabilities to take charge of their lives and make their own choices and decisions in order to be as self-sufficent as possible. CILs also lead efforts to break down barriers and prejudices within communities, replacing them with positive attitudes resulting in equal access to society for disabled persons. Run by people with disabilities who have successfully established independent lives of their own, the staff has a deep commitment to assisting other disabled people in achieving independence. The Illinois Network of Centers for Independent Living (INCIL) is a statewide organization made up of 24 Centers for Independent Living (CILs) in Illinois. INCIL coordinates the activities and efforts of all CILs, resulting in a stronger, more unified voice to promote the needs and priorities of the CILs and the people they seling.erve. Operated by the executive directors of these CILs, this aggressive core of leadership advocates for and works to ensure that all people are treated with respect and given the same opportunities in life, regardless of their abilities. Services include that of information and referral, independent living skills training, advocacy and peer couns

10727 Illinois-Iowa Center for Independent Living (IICIL)

3708 11th Street
Po Box 6156
Rock Island, IL 61204-6156

319-793-0090
877-541-2505
Fax: 309-283-0097
e-mail: iicil@iicil.com
http://www.iicil.com
TTY 309-793-0090

Liz Sherman, Executive Director
Shirley Holgersen, Staff Assistant
Hugh Pries, Board-Directors President

The mission of the IICIL is to create and maintain independence options for people with disabilities by advocating for civil rights, providing services, and promoting full participation of disabled individuals in all aspects of the community. IICIL provides a number of consumer directed services, including information and referral, advocacy, independent living skills training, and peer support, which are mandated by the Rehabilitation Act of 1973. In addition to these services, we also have a fully accessible computer lab, state of the art information and referral library, TTY/Amplified Phone acquisition, Low tech devices for people who have low vision or blind, Braille and transcription, Sign language and Spanish interpreters, Technical assistance on disability laws and policy, Disability Awareness Training, Accessibility audits, and a host of volunteer opportunities for consumers and other interested persons.

10728 LIFE Center for Independent Living

2201 Eastland Drive
Suite 1
Bloomington, IL 61704-7923

309-663-5433
888-543-3245
Fax: 309-663-7024
e-mail: lifecil@lifecil.org
http://www.lifecil.org
TTY 309-663-5433

Gail Kear, Executive Director
Marianne Cavanaugh-Wozniak, Admin. Services Coordinator
Dana Craig, Outreach Coordinator

LIFE Center for Independent Living advances equality and integration of all persons with disabilities. To achieve this mission, we: promote local, state and national advocacy; educate persons with disabilities about their rights and responsibilities; provide support services, and Raise community awareness about disability issues. LIFE Center for Independent Living serves persons of all ages with all kinds of disabilities in DeWitt, Ford, Livingston and McLean Counties in Illinois. We also provide community services that promote accessibility and break down attitudinal barriers. Services include that of information and referral, independent living skills training, advocacy, community reintegration, peer mentoring support, communication services and benefits counseling.

10729 Lake County Center for Independent Living (LCCIL)

377 North Seymour Avenue
Mundelein, IL 60060-2322

847-949-4440
Fax: 847-949-4445
e-mail: info@lccil.org
http://www.lccil.org/
TTY 847-949-4440

Anita Gorski, Executive Director
Donna Shalala, Community Integration Director

Lake County Center for Independent Living (LCCIL) is a disability rights organization governed and staffed by a majority of people with disabilities. Lake County Center for Independent Living offers services and advocacy that promote a fully accessible society, which expects participation by persons with disabilities. LCCIL's vision is that people with disabilities are involved in every aspect of society and have the freedom and opportunity to control their own lives. It is the belief of LCCIL that the quality of life is important for all people including people with disabilities. Services include that of information and referral, independent living skills training, advocacy, community reintegration, deaf services and peer counseling.

10730 Northwestern Illinois Center for Independent Living

229 1st Avenue
Suite 2
Rock Falls, IL 61071-5107

815-625-7860
888-886-4245
Fax: 815-625-7876
e-mail: kathy@nicil.com
http://www.incil.org/
TTY 815-625-7863

Kathy Fischer, Executive Director

Independent Living is a movement based on the philosophy that all persons with disabilities have the right and responsibility to determine the direction of their own lives, and to fully and meaningfully participate as equal members of society. It's about having the right to succeed, and the right to fail. It's about getting the opportunity to be an integral part of the community. The Northwestern Illinois Center for Independent Living is a community-based, non-residential, center for independent living dedicated to enhancing the options available to people with disabilities so they may choose and maintain individualized and satisfying lifestyles. To fulfill this mission, NICIL combines direct services to individuals with advocacy for social change to allow greater integration of persons with disabilities into the mainstream of life. Services include that of advocacy, peer counseling, information and referral, and independent living skills training.

10731 Opportunities for Access

4206 Williamson Place
Suite 3
Mount Vernon, IL 62864-2352

618-244-9212
Fax: 815-244-9310
e-mail: info@ofacil.org
http://www.ofacil.org/
TTY 618-244-9575

Michael Egbert, Executive Director

Opportunities for Access strives to empower persons with disabilities to increase their opportunities to access all aspects of community life, serving the counties of: Clinton, Edwards, Hamilton, Jefferson, Marion, Wabash, Washington; Wayne, and White. Services include that of peer advisory, system advocacy, information and referral, independent living skills training, interpreter referral, housing referral, community integration, and adaptive equipment selection.

10732 Options Center for Independent Living

22 Heritage Drive
Suite 107
Bourbonnais, IL 60914-2510

815-936-0100
Fax: 815-936-0117
e-mail: optionscil@optionscil.com
http://www.optionscil.com
TTY 815-936-0132

Carolyn Domont, President
Deborah Frooninckx, Secretary
Dale Gerretse, Treasurer

Independent Living Centers/Illinois

Options Center for Independent Living (CIL) is a non-residential, not-for-profit organization that promotes independent living for persons of all ages who have disabilities. Community-based, our service area encompasses Kankakee and Iroquois Counties. Options CIL is a consumer-based organization that is managed and controlled by persons who have disabilities. In fact, over 50 percent of our volunteer board of directors and staff are individuals with disabilities. Options Center for Independent Living (CIL) believes that persons with disabilities have the right to make choices about their own lives and to experience life as active participants in society. Services include that of independent living skills training, community integration, referrals for sign language interpreters, a TTY distribution and training center, peer support and advocacy, in addition to having an assistive technologcenter.

10733 Persons Assuming Control of their Environment (PACE)
1317 East Florida
Urbana, IL 61801-6043
217-344-5433
Fax: 217-344-2414
e-mail: info@pacecil.org
http://www.pacecil.org
TTY 217-344-5024

Nancy McClellan-Hickey, Executive Director

PACE provides services which assist people with disabilities in achieving or maintaining independence. People with disabilities direct our services in that our board and staff are mandated to be at least 51% people with disabilities. Services include that of access and advocacy, independent living counseling, information and referral, skills training, specialty services, interpreter referral, housing referral, and community intergration.

10734 Progress Center for Independent Living
7521 Madison Street
Forest Park, IL 60130-1407
708-209-1500
Fax: 708-209-1735
e-mail: info@progresscil.org
http://www.progresscil.org/
TDD 708-209-1826
TTY 708-209-1826

Diane Coleman, Executive Director
John Jansa, Program Director
Lucille Burns, Office Manager

Progress Center directly assists persons with disabilities to establish lives in the community, providng serves and support to people with disabilities of all ages to increase and maintain their independence, in addition to assisting families and communities. The Progress Center provides the services of independent living skills training, advocacy, information and referral, and peer counseling, in addition to community integration and housing referral.

10735 Regional Access & Mobilization Project (RAMP)
1022 West Lincoln Highway
Dekalb, IL 60115-9637
815-756-3202
Fax: 815-758-3556
http://www.rampcil.org
TTY 815-756-4263

Arles Hendershott Love, President
Harlan Knuth, Vice President
Sharon Opsahl, Secretary

Established in 1980, RAMP, Inc. is a non-profit, non-residential Cener for Independent Living (CIL). RAMP advocates for and serves people with disabilities and their communities in Boone, DeKalb, Stephenson and Winnebago Counties from offices in Belvidere, DeKalb, Freeport and Rockford. At no cost to the individual, we serve with the purpose of increasing the ability of people with disabilities to become productive, contributing and self-directing members of society. We also educate businesses, service providers and public entities on disability issues and help them to comply with the technical requirements of the Americans with Disabilities Act and other disability related laws and standards.

10736 Regional Access Mobilization Project (RAMP)
202 Market Street
Rockford, IL 61107-3954
815-968-7467
Fax: 815-968-7612
http://www.rampcil.org
TTY 815-968-2401

Arles Hendershott Love, President
Harlan Knuth, Vice President
Sharon Opsahl, Secretary

Established in 1980, RAMP Inc. is a non-profit, non-residential Center for Independent Living (CIL). RAMP advocates for and serves people with disabilities and their communities in Boone, DeKalb, Stephenson and Winnebago Counties from offices in Belvidire, DeKalb, Freeport and Rockford. At no cost to the individual, we serve with the purpose of increasing the ability of people with disabilities to become productive, contributing and self-directing members of society. We also educate businesses, service providers and public entities on disability issues and help them to comply with the technical requirements of the Americans with Disabilities Act and other disability related laws and standards.

10737 Southern Illinois Center for Independent Living
Po Box 627
2135 W. Ramada Lane
Carbondale, IL 62901-5326
618-457-3318
800-352-5691
Fax: 618-549-0132
e-mail: sicilccc@poofaccess.com
http://www.incil.org/
TTY 618-457-3318

Bonnie Vaughn, Executive Director

Centers for Independent Living (CILs) exist to empower individuals with disabilities to take charge of their lives and make their own choices and decisions in order to be as self-sufficent as possible. CILs also lead efforts to break down barriers and prejudices within communities, replacing them with positive attitudes resulting in equal access to society for disabled persons. Run by people with disabilities who have successfully established independent lives of their own, the staff has a deep commitment to assisting other disabled people in achieving independence. The Illinois Network of Centers for Independent Living (INCIL) is a statewide organization made up of 24 Centers for Independent Living (CILs) in Illinois. INCIL coordinates the activities and efforts of all CILs, resulting in a stronger, more unified voice to promote the needs and priorities of the CILs and the people they sety of services and support, CILs provide assistance for disabled persons in their transition to independenterve. Operated by the executive directors of these CILs, this aggressive core of leadership advocates for and works to ensure that all people are treated with respect and given the same opportunities in life, regardless of their abilities. CILs work to increase the involvement of people with disabilities in every aspect of life. Through a wide vari

10738 Soyland Access to Independent Living
2449 Federal Drive
Decatur, IL 62526-5924
217-876-8888
800-358-8080
Fax: 217-876-7245
e-mail: jwooters@decatursail.com
http://www.decatursail.com
TDD 217-876-8888
TTY 217-876-8888

Jeri Wooters, Executive Director
Rich Adams, Visual Servies Director
Laverla Carrington, Interpreter/Advocate for Blind

As an advocacy agency, Soylant Access to Independent Living (SAIL) is a community-based, non-residential Center for Independent Living (CIL). Its purpose is to promote and practice independent living for all people with disabilities. The organization strives to encourage and assist people with disabilities to gain effective control of their lives by participation in all aspects of society to their fullest extent possible, especially in performingroutine daily activities. The organization promotes personal dignity of people with disabilities and develops community awareness by providing training, direct services and information.

Independent Living Centers/Indiana

10739 Springfield Center for Independent Living (CIL)
330 S Grand Avenue W
Springfield, IL 62704-1318
217-523-2587
800-841-6167
Fax: 217-523-0427
e-mail: scil@sil.org
http://www.sil.org
TTY 217-523-6304

Pete Roberts, Executive Director
Susan Cooper, Program Director
Kathryn Cline, Business Manager

The Statewide Independent Living Council of Illinois (SILC), formed in 1993, is a not-for-profit statewide planning organization. The Federal Rehabilitation Act requires each state to create an autonomous Statewide Independent Living Council to develop a state plan for independent living services and Centers for Independent Living. The Statewide Independent Living Council of Illinois (SILC), formed in 1993, is a not-for-profit statewide planningorganization. The Federal Rehabilitation Act requires each state to create an autonomous Statewide Independent Living Council to develop a state plan for independent living services and Centers for Independent Living. Through the state plan, SILC works to expand existing Centers for Independent Living (CILs) and independent living services. SILC also supports the development of new programs where services are not currently available. The Councilworks to ensure that independent living services and CILs are accessible by all persons with disabilities.

10740 Stone-Hayes Center for Independent Living
39 North Prairie Street
Galesburg, IL 61401-4613
309-344-1306
888-347-4245
Fax: 309-344-1305
e-mail: catherineh@stone-hayes.org
http://www.incil.org
TTY 309-344-1269

Catherine Holland, Manager

The Illinois Network of Centers for Independent Living (INCIL) is a statewide organization made up of 24 Centers for Independent Living (CILs) in Illinois. INCIL coordinates the activities and efforts of all CILs, resulting in a stronger, more unified voice to promote the needs and priorities of the CILs and the people they serve. Operated by the executive directors of these CILs, this aggressive core of leadership advocates for and works to ensure that all people are treated with respect and given the same opportunities in life, regardless of their abilities. Centers for Independent Living (CILs) exist to empower individuals with disabilities to take charge of their lives and make their own choices and decisions in order to be as self-sufficent as possible. CILs also lead efforts to break down barriers and prejudices within communities, replacing them with positive attitudes resulting ireferral.n equal access to society for disabled persons. Run by people with disabilities who have successfully established independent lives of their own, the staff has a deep commitment to assisting other disabled people in achieving independence. Services include that of advocacy, peer counseling, independent livings skills training, and, information and

10741 West Central Illinois Center for Independent Living (WCICIL)
300 Maine St.
Suite 146
Quincy, IL 62301
217-223-0400
800-225-0407
Fax: 217-223-0479
e-mail: ciledgcy@adams.net
http://www.incil.org
TTY 217-223-0475

Glenda Farkas, Executive Director

WCICIL provides independent living services to people with disabilities to promote, increase and improve opportunities within the community needed by people with disabilities to live independently in and to actively participate in all aspects of society. WCICIL serves the counties of Adams, Pike, Brown, Hancock, Schuyler and McDonough counties. Independent living is a concept based on the premise that, regardless of disability, all persons have the right and responsibility to determine and control the direction of their lives to fully and meaningfully participate as equal members of society. Board and staff members with disabilities and parents of people with disabilities have personally experienced attitudinal, physical, communication and employment barriers. Services include that of information and referral, independent living skills training, advocacy and peer counseling.

10742 Will-Grundy Center for Independent Living
2415 West Jefferson Street
Joliet, IL 60435-6464
815-729-0162
Fax: 815-729-3697
e-mail: pamwgcil@smcglobal.net
http://www.will-grundycil.org
TTY 815-729-2085

Pam Heavens, Executive Director
Festus Fabilola, Program Manager
Carol Warunek, Office/Business Manager

As people with disabilities and their advocates, the Will-Grundy Center for Independent Living strives for equality and empowerment of persons with disabilities in the Will and Grundy County areas. As people with disabilities and their advocates, the Will-Grundy Center for Independent Living strives for equality and empowerment of persons with disabilities in the Will and Grundy County areas, inform persons with disabilities of their rights, educate them about their responsibilities, provide support services, promote advocacy, and raise community awareness about disability issues. Services include that of individual advocacy and systems advocacy, information referral, independent living skills training, peer support, deaf services and interpreter services.

Indiana

10743 Assistive Technology Training and Information Center
1721 Washington Avenue
Vincennes, IN 47591-2509
812-886-0575
877-962-8842
Fax: 812-886-1128
TTY 812-886-0575

Patricia Stewart, Executive Director

Offers services to persons with disabilities that include identifying personal goals, exploring options and gaining skills necessary to live as independently as they choose to.

10744 Cameron Woods
416 E Maumee Street
Angola, IN 46703-8808
260-665-2141
Fax: 260-665-2879
e-mail: info@cameronmch.com
http://www.cameronmch.com

Dennis L Knapp, CEO/Administrator

Cameron Woods is a spacious residential community, conveniently located in a natural setting just north of Angola, offering assisted living alternatives. Designed to provide a sense of security while helping residents maintain their independence, Cameron Woods offers a choice of apartment styles, care levels and financial options to suit the individual needs of each resident. A wide range of additional services is also available.

10745 Crown Point Senior Living-Anderson
2727 Crown Pointe Circle
Anderson, IN 46012
765-641-9995
Fax: 765-622-0340

Emily Carroll, Executive Director

Independent Living Centers/Iowa

Crownpointe can provide custom services individually designed for each person's lifestyle. Independent living services include a choice of apartments in studio, 1 bedroom or 2 bedroom styles, with all utilities included, three restaurant meals per day served to your table, cable tv, life enrichment activities, on site postal and copy services, 24 hour staff and security, weekly wellness clinic by staff registered nurse, emergency response pendant, apartment maintenance, trash removal and grounds keeping, housekeeping and linen service, in addition to the availibility of local transportation.

10746 Everybody Counts-Ruben Center for Independent Living
9111 Broadway
Suite A
Merrillville, IN 46410-3584
219-769-5055
Fax: 219-769-5325
e-mail: ecounts@netnitco.net
http://www.lakenetnwi.net/org/everybody_counts
TTY 219-756-3323

Teresa Torres, Executive Director

Everybody Counts provides assistance for individuals striving for independence, servicing all disabilities. Services include that of advocacy for support, information and referral, independent living skills training, peer support, orientation and mobility, and public education and development.

10747 Heritage Park Independent Living Apartments
2001 Hobson Road
Fort Wayne, IN 46805
260-484-9557
e-mail: kimily@netscape.net
http://http://americansrcommunities.com

Kim Hues, Manager

Senior Independent and Assisted Living Apartments are available in studio as well as one or two bedroom floor plans, furnished and decorated as you so desire, making a familiar and comfortable atmosphere where family members and friends can visit. Our residents enjoy the company of their neighbors while enjoying three meals a day offered in our unique, restaurant-style dining rooms. There are many opportunities to participate in a wide range of planned social activities, scheduled transportation to shopping, restaurants and appointments. We continue to add services designed to keep our residents as active as they desire while having the comfort and security of living in a senior community.

10748 Indianapolis Resource Center for Independent Living (IRCIL)
1426 West 29th Street
Suite 207
Indianapolis, IN 46208
317-926-1660
800-860-7181
Fax: 317-926-1687
e-mail: ircil@ircil.org
http://www.ircil.org
TTY 317-926-1660

Melissa Madill, Executive Director
India Anderson, Assistant Director
Carla Wuchner, Administrative Assistant

Since 1987, IRCIL has provided services, support and information to people with disabilities to help insure equal access to all aspects of community life. Additionally, IRCIL provides education and advocacy to all members of the community to help increase awareness and break down barriers that impede inclusion. IRCIL is a consumer-controlled organization. No less than 51% of our staff and governing board are persons with a disability to insure that the will and needs of people with disabilities are reflected in all we do. IRCIL was established to assist people with disabilities in developing the supports they need to assure full inclusion in community life. Services include that of information and referral, peer counseling, independent living skills training, individual and systems advocacy, services for people who are blind or visually impaired, braille reproduction, and benefits planning.

10749 Park Square Manor
6990 East County Road 100 North
Avon, IN 46123-9711
317-272-7300
Fax: 317-272-7400
e-mail: parksquare@retirementmanagement.net
http://www.retirementmanagement.net

Linda Jenks, Manager

Park Square Manor is an independent and asssited living community that provides numerous services including that of advocacy for support, information and referral, independent living skills training, peer support, orientation and mobility, and public education and development.

10750 Smith Farms Manor
406 Smith Drive
Auburn, IN 46706-3699
260-925-4800
Fax: 219-925-4801
e-mail: smithfarms@retirementmanagement.net
http://www.retirementmanagement.net

Freda Donley, Manager

Smith Farms Manor is an independent and assisted living community that provides numerous services including that of advocacy for support, information and referral, independent living skills training, peer support, orientation and mobility, and public education and development.

10751 Southern Indiana Center For IndependentLiving
651 X Street
Bedford, IN 47421-5282
812-277-9626
800-845-6914
Fax: 812-277-9628
e-mail: sicildir@msn.com
http://www.sicilindiana.org
TTY 812-277-9627

Al Tolbert, Executive Director

SICIL is a consumer controlled, community based, cross-disability, non-residential and not-for-profit organization that promotes and practices the philosophy of independent living: consumer control, peer support, self-help, self-determination, equal access, and individual and community advocacy.

10752 St Paul Hermitage
501 N 17th Avenue
Beech Grove, IN 46107
317-786-2261
Fax: 317-782-1411
http://www.stpaulhermitage.org

Sr. Sharon Bierman, Administrator

From the beginning, St. Paul Hermitage has been recognized as a leader in the area of healthcare for the aged and infirm. The Hermitage offers a truly Christian atmosphere.

Iowa

10753 Blackhawk Center for Independent Living
312 Jefferson Street
Waterloo, IA 50701-1322
319-291-7755
888-291-7754
Fax: 319-291-7781
e-mail: director@blackhawkcenter.org
http://www.blackhawkcenter.org/
TTY 319-232-3955

David Schumaker, Executive Director

Provides peer counseling and support, independent living skills training, information and referrals and advocacy.

10754 Central Iowa Center for Independent Living
655 Walnut Street
Suite 131
Des Moines, IA 50309
515-243-1742
Fax: 515-243-5385
http://www.centraliowacil.com
TTY 515-243-2177

Robert Jepson, Manager

Independent Living Centers/Kansas

The Central Iowa Center for Independent Living is a community based, non-residential program serving persons with disabilities. Our board of directors is composed of a majority of persons who have disabilities. CICIL is dedicated to assisting all persons, regardless of disability in making choices about their own lives and in experiencing success as active participants in society. CICIL serves people of all ages and disabilities. We also work with public officials, service providers and businesses that require technical assistance in responding to the needs of persons with disabilities. Services to individuals and families are provided free of charge or at a reduced rate.

10755 Evert Conner Rights & Resources Center for Independent Living
730 South Dubuque Street
Iowa City, IA 52240
319-338-3870
800-982-0272
Fax: 319-338-8385
e-mail: info@ownersvoices.com
http://www.ownersvoices.com
TTY 319-338-3870

Chris O'Hanlon, Executive Director

The Center provides advocacy to individuals in a direct effort to promote the idea that people with disabilities have the right to choice and are the experts regarding their own lives. The Center works to build advocacy on the individual level and also works to change attitudes of people running the system to change disability issues at the community level in addition to providing eduucation in promoting disability culture and inclusion. Other services include information and referral, independent living skills training, and peer counseling.

10756 SILC-Iowa Department for the Blind
524 4th Street
Des Moines, IA 50309-2364
515-281-1333
800-362-2587
Fax: 515-281-1263
e-mail: information@blind.state.ia.us
http://www.blind.state.ia.us/
TTY 515-281-1355

Allen C Harris, Director
Bruce Snethen, Deputy Director

The Iowa Department for the Blind provides programs that offer the specialized, integrated services that blind and severely visually impaired Iowans need to live independently and work competitively. It is the Department's belief that with the right training and opportunity, people who are blind can become full, contributing members of their communities. Services include a vocational rehabilitation program, an independent living program, assistive devices and technology services, in addition to a library for the blind and physically handicapped.

10757 Southwest Iowa Center for Independent Living
League of Human Dignity
1520 Avenue M
Council Bluffs, IA 51501
712-323-6863
Fax: 712-323-6811
e-mail: Cinfo@leagueofhumandignity.com
http://leagueofhumandignity.com/text/index.html

Mike Schafer, Executive Director

The League of Human Dignity is an organization of people concerned about the rights and quality of life for people with disabilities. League members collaborate to ensure social, economic, and political equality for persons with disabilities. We believe in emphasizing likeness not difference, ability not disability, normality not abnormality, and integration not segregation. We work toward independent living for people who have disabilities. League members are people from the citizenry, government, and the business community who recognize that human dignity comes only through equal opportunity for all citizens. We recognize that society as a whole benefits when all its members are enabled to contribute freely in accordance with their potential and without regard to their disabilities. The mission of the League of Human Dignity is to actively promote the full integration of individuals with disabilities into society. To this end, we will advocate their needs and rights, and provide quality services to involve these persons in becoming and remaining independent citizens. Services include that of information and referral, systems advocacy, individual advocacy, peer suport, and independent living skills training.

10758 Three Rivers Center for Independent Living
Gordon Recovery Center
800 5th Street
Stuie 131
Sioux City, IA 51101-1315
712-255-1065
Fax: 866-616-2526
e-mail: trilcbjd@aol.com
http://www.members.aol.com/trilc/

Becky Cadwell, President
Eleanor Luse, Vice President
Amanda Beller, Secretary/Treasurer

A non-profit, non residential, consumer driven organization committed to providing and increasing consumer designed services and community awareness regarding disabilities through the development of collaborations and partnerships.

Kansas

10759 Center for Independent Living for Southwest Kansas
1802 E Spruce Street
Po Box 2090
Garden City, KS 67846-5412
620-276-1900
800-736-9443
Fax: 316-271-0200
e-mail: info@cilswks.org
http://www.cilswks.org
TTY 620-276-1900

Troy Horton, Executive Director
Stacy Ritt, Office Coordinator
Q. Dea Kent, Chief Financial Officer

Center for Independent Living in Southwest Kansas is dedicated to helping people achieve full participation in society. Programs are consumer driven by individuals with disabilities, encompassing all ages, disabilities and ethnicity in all level of management and staff positions creating a unique environment. Staff relate and provide services to consumers from their own experiences with disabilities. We build services based on an individual's ability to choose and achieve a desired lifestyle. The center's emphasis is placed on establishing the consumers linkage with existing resources, stimulating the community to provide equal opportunities, an accessible environment and needed support services. We believe the strength of our programs resides with the individuals who has a disability as well as their families and friends.

10760 Center for Independent Living of Southwest Kansas
2601 Central Avenue
Dodge City, KS 67801-6211
620-227-6660
800-326-1366
Fax: 620-227-8185
e-mail: cilswks@gcnet.com
http://www.cilswks.org

Troy Horton, Executive Director
Stacy Ritt, Office Coordinator
Q. Dea Kent, Chief Financial Officer

Independent Living Centers/Kansas

Center for Independent Living in Southwest Kansas is dedicated to helping people achieve full participation in society. Programs are consumer driven by individuals with disabilities, encompassing all ages, disabilities and ethnicity in all level of management and staff positions creating a unique environment. Staff relate and provide services to consumers from their own experiences with disabilities. We build services based on an individual's ability to choose and achieve a desired lifestyle. The center's emphasis is placed on establishing the consumers linkage with existing resources, stimulating the community to provide equal opportunities, an accessible environment and needed support services. We believe the strength of our programs resides with the individuals who has a disability as well as their families and friends. Services include that of information and referral, individual and systems advocacy, indepedent living skills training, and peer support services.

10761 Hutchinson Independent Living Center
17 South Main Street
Hutchinson, KS 67501-5315
620-663-3989
888-715-6818
Fax: 620-663-4711
e-mail: info@pilr.org
http://www.pilr.org/
TTY 620-663-9920

Chris Owens, Executive Director
Roger Frischenmeyer, Independent Living Specialist
Christi Ireland, Administrative Assistant

The purpose of Prairie Independent Living Resource Center (PILR) is to achieve the full inclusion and acceptance of people with disabilities through education and advocacy. PILR is a non-profit organization.

10762 Independence, Inc.
2001 Haskell Avenue
Lawrence, KS 66046-3249
785-841-0333
888-824-7277
Fax: 785-841-1094
e-mail: tdorf@independenceinc.org
http://www.independenceinc.org
TDD 785-841-1046

Dorf Brunner, Executive Director
Tanya Coleman, Administrative Assistant
Faye Peterson, Assistant Director Of Operations

Independence, Inc. serves anyone with a physical or mental condition that limits one or more of life's major activities, or who is regarded as having such a disability. This includes individuals whose disability is controlled by medication or is in remission. We are located in Lawrence, Kansas and serve various portions of Northeast Kansas, depending on the specific service. Center staff and consumers are available to speak to civic groups, schools, churches and others to increase awareness of the needs of people with disabilities. The Center's monthly newsletter Ahead of the Times publicizes information on disability issues to consumers and other interested persons or organizations. Services include that of information and referral, advocacy, peer support, assistive technology, and independent living skills training.

10763 Independent Connection
1710 West Schilling Road
Po Box 1160
Salina, KS 67402-1160
785-827-9383
800-526-9731
Fax: 785-823-2015
e-mail: occk@occk.com
http://www.occk.com/icsection.htm
TTY 785-827-7051

Sheila Nelson Stout, Executive Director

Independent Connection is a Center for Independent Living (CIL). It is a non-residential, community-based organization that is staffed by people with disabilities. They operate under the philosophy of consumer control. CIL's, through their staff, address discrimination and barriers in the community. Independent Living Specialists at Independent Connection work not only with individuals of all ages and all disabilities, but also with their communities to locate services and eliminate physical and philosophical barriers so that living independently is a reality for all people. Staff provides information and support to businesses, schools, and government services as they develop communities accessible to everyone. Services include that of individual and systems advocacy, information and referral, and independent living skills training.

10764 Independent Living Resource Center
3033 West 2nd Street North
Wichita, KS 67203-5357
316-942-6300
800-479-6861
Fax: 316-942-2078
e-mail: jweigel@ilrcks.org
http://www.ilrcks.org
TTY 316-942-6300

Judy Weigel, Executive Director
La Rae Santiago, Independent Living Specialist
Sandy Evans, Public Relations

The mission of Independent Living Resource Center, Inc. (ILRC) is to empower people with disabilities to lead independent lives by providing advocacy, community education and direct services. ILRC is a consumer-focused, consumer-directed organization. Over half of the ILRC Board of Directors and staff have disabilities and they are committed to assisting others in choosing and achieving a desired level of independence in their daily lives. Consumers, board members and all ILRC employees work to improve the availability of affordable, accessible housing and transportation for people with disabilities, increase the accessibility of the community, and advocate for supports that assist people with disabilities to remain in the home setting of their choice. Services include that of information and referral, advocacy, independent living skills training, and peer support.

10765 Independent Living of Northeast Kansas
521 Commercial
Suite C
Atchison, KS 66002
913-367-1830
888-845-2879
Fax: 913-367-1430
e-mail: ilcnek@sbcglobal.net
http://www.ilcnek.org/

Ken Gifford, Executive Director

The Independent Living Center of Northeast Kansas is not-for-profit agency providing services within the State of Kansas. Funding for programs and services comes through grants from the Kansas Department of Social and Rehabilitation Services Division of Community Supports and Services, and also the Kansas Department of Rehabilitation Services. The mission of the Indepedent Living Center of Northeast Kansas is to assist people with disabilitiesto live an integrated, quality life with dignity, respect, and independence. Services include that of information and referral, peer support, independent living skills training, home and community based services, and vocational training.

10766 Living Independently in Northwest Kansas (LINK)
118 West Main Street
Suite 3
Osborne, KS 67473-2403
785-346-5865
800-569-5926
Fax: 785-346-5260
e-mail: judylink@ruraltel.net
http://www.linkinc.org
TTY 785-346-5865

Judy Droppleman, Manager

LINK promotes and supports the civil rights of people with disabilities and empowers them to achieve a life of indepedence and equality. Services include that of information and referral, independent living skills training, peer support, advocacy in addition to community based services and a newsletter.

Independent Living Centers/Kentucky

10767 Resource Center for Independent Living
1137 Laing Street
PO Box 257
Osage City, KS 66523-1013
785-528-3105
800-580-7245
Fax: 785-528-3665
e-mail: chad@rcilinc.org
http://www.rcilinc.org
TDD 913-528-3106

Chad Wilkins, Executive Director
Becky Brewer, Director Of Operations
Mike Pitts, Director Of Finance

RCIL, Inc. is committed to working with individuals, families, and communities to promote independent living and individual choice to persons with disabilities. Services include that of information and referral, advocacy, independent living skills training, peer support services and de-institutionalization. The purpose of the Resource Center for Independent Living is to enhance the capacity of persons with disabilities to the maximum extent possible to control their lives and live independently within their respective communities served by RCIL, Inc.

10768 Southeast Kansas Independent Living (SKIL)
1801 Main
PO Box 957
Parsons, KS 67357-1034
620-421-5502
800-688-5616
Fax: 620-421-3705
e-mail: skil@skilonline.com
http://www.skilonline.com
TDD 620-421-0983

Sheri Coatney, CEO

Southeast Kansas Independent Living, Inc. (SKIL) is a private, not-for-profit corporation devoted to meeting the needs of individuals with disabilities and to serving them, their families and communities. Services include that of independent livings skills, advocacy, peer counseling, assistive technology, in addition to home and community based services.

10769 Statewide Independent Living Council of Kansas
700 Southwest Jackson Street
Suite 212
Topeka, KS 66603-3777
785-234-6990
Fax: 785-234-6651
e-mail: shannon.jones@silck.org
http://www.silck.org
TDD 785-234-6990

Shannon Jones, Executive Director
Chris Owens, Board-Directors Chairman
Robert C Harder, Board-Directors Treasurer

The vision of the State Plan for Independent Living in Kansans (SILCK) s an inclusive community which would enable Kansans to live in the environment of their choice. Independent living demands consumer empowerment, control, equal access, and integration. The plan shall insure that there are civil rights in place for total integration. The mission of the SILCK is to: develop a state plan through external input, which ensures independent living for Kansans; advocate for the accomplishment of the state plan objectives; monitor, review, and evaluate the implementation of the plan; and to be a statewide catalyst for independent living.

10770 Three Rivers Independent Living
408 Lincoln Street
PO Box 408
Wamego, KS 66547-0408
785-456-9915
800-555-3994
Fax: 785-456-9923
e-mail: reception@threeriversinc.org
http://www.threeriversinc.org
TTY 785-456-9915

Audrey Schremmer Phillips, Executive Director
Cindy Diederich, Business Manager

The Center manages programs in independent living which offer an array of services for individuals requiring assistance with personal, nursing/medical, and social needs. These services allow individuals to remain in their own home as an alternative to costly institutional care and include independent living skills training, information and referral, advocacy and peer support.

10771 Three Rivers-Manhattan
200 Southwind Pl.
Suite 103
Manhattan, KS 66502-5058
785-537-8985
877-714-7272
Fax: 785-537-3435
e-mail: reception@threeriversinc.org
http://www.threeriversinc.org
TDD 785-537-8985

Audrey Schremmer Phillips, Executive Director

The Center manages programs in independent living which offer an array of services for individuals requiring assistance with personal, nursing/medical, and social needs. These services allow individuals to remain in their own home as an alternative to costly institutional care. Services include that of information and referral, advocacy, independent living skills training, and peer counseling.

10772 Topeka Independent Living Resource Center
501 Southwest Jackson Street
Suite 100
Topeka, KS 66603-3300
785-233-4572
Fax: 785-233-1561
e-mail: tilrc@tilrc.org
http://www.tilrc.org
TDD 785-233-4572
TTY 785-233-1815

Michael Oxford, Executive Director
Ami Hyten, Assistant Executive Director
Matt Laird, Human Resources Generalist

The Topeka Independent Living Resource Center is a civil and human rights organization. Our mission is to advocate for justice, equality and essential services for a fully integrated and accessible society for all people with disabilities. Services include that of information and referral, peer counseling, legal advocacy, independent living skills training and communications services.

Kentucky

10773 Center for Accessible Living
1051 North 16th Street
Suite C
Murray, KY 42071-1698
270-753-7676
888-261-6194
Fax: 270-753-7729
e-mail: murrayinfo@calky.org
http://www.calky.org
TDD 270-767-0549

Jeanne M Gallimore, Branch Director
Carissa Johnson, Employment Specialist
John Canter, Benefits Specialist

The Center for Accessible Living (CAL) is a disability resource center for people with disabilities, governed by people with disabilities. It operates on a cross disability basis, which means that individuals will be served regardless of type of disability. Experienced staff provides information, advocacy and services that create opportunities for people with disabilities to live as independently as possible. Independent living for people with disabilities means having the opportunity and responsibility to make decisions as well as to exercise their right to control their own lives. The Center for Accessible Living promotes equal access and the ultimate goal of equal and independent status for all people with disabilities by encouraging awareness, involvement, and support for the rights of all people with disabilities by the entire community. Services include that of independent living skills training, advocacy, information and referral, and peer counseling.

Independent Living Centers/Louisiana

10774 Center for Accessible Living-Louisville
305 West Broadway
Suite 200
Louisville, KY 40202
502-589-6620
888-813-8497
Fax: 502-589-3980
e-mail: murrayinfo@calky.org
http://www.calky.org
TTY 502-589-6690

Jan Day, CEO
David Allgood, Community Advocate
Kelly Peace, Interpreter Coordinator

The Center for Accessible Living (CAL) is a disability resource center for people with disabilities, governed by people with disabilities. It operates on a cross disability basis, which means that individuals will be served regardless of type of disability. Experienced staff provides information, advocacy and services that create opportunities for people with disabilities to live as independently as possible. Independent living for people with disabilities means having the opportunity and responsibility to make decisions as well as to exercise their right to control their own lives. The Center for Accessible Living promotes equal access and the ultimate goal of equal and independent status for all people with disabilities by encouraging awareness, involvement, and support for the rights of all people with disabilities by the entire community. Services include that of independent living skills training, advocacy, information and referral, and peer counseling.

10775 Disability Coalition of Northern Kentucky
525 West 5th Street
Suite 219
Covington, KY 41011
859-431-7668
800-648-6057
Fax: 859-431-7688
e-mail: dcnky@fuse.net
http://www.dcnky.org
TDD 800-648-6057
TTY 800-648-6057

Kit Heeg, Director
Linda Wermeling, Board-Directors President
Mary Campbell, Board-Directors Treasurer

Mission is empowering people with disabilities through education, networking, and positive attitudes.

10776 Independence Place
824 Euclid Avenue
Suite 101
Lexington, KY 40502
859-266-2807
877-266-2807
Fax: 859-335-0627
e-mail: info@indendenceplaceky.org
http://www.independenceplaceky.org

Pamela Roark Glisson, Executive Director
Barry Hamilton, Associate Director
Deshala Collier, Independent Living Coordinator

The philosophy of the Independent Living Center stresses the importance of all persons to be as responsible as possible for their own needs despite personal and external barriers. Also, to be free from over-dependence on others and on society as a whole. Independence Place aids individuals in attaining these goals by helping them make the necessary changes in themselves and their environment, thereby enhancing their integrity and maintaining control of their own life.

10777 Pathfinders for Independent Living
105 East Mound Street
Harlan, KY 40831
606-573-5777
Fax: 606-573-5739
e-mail: pathfinders@harlanonline.net
TTY 606-573-5777

Sandra Goodwyn, Executive Director

Works toward achieving equal participation in all communities for people with disabilities.

Louisiana

10778 New Horizons
9300 Mansfield Road
Suite 204
Shreveport, LA 71118
318-671-8131
877-219-7327
Fax: 318-688-7823
e-mail: nhilc@nhilc.org
http://www.nhilc.org
TTY 318-671-8131

Gale Dean, Executive Director
Joy Lennon, Office Manager
Kimberly Sisco, Administrative Assistant

New Horizons was established as an independent living center in 1984 and is an association of adults with disabilities working to improve the quality of life for all who have disabilities. New Horizons believes that the quality of life for persons with disabilities improves directly as they exert control over their lives through independent living. New Horizons is a non-residential independent living center that offers a variety of programs and services for persons with disabilities including that of information and referral, independent living skills training, advocacy and peer counseling. New Horizons is a consumer-driven organization, which means the consumer is in the driver's seat. The majority of both New Horizons staff and Board of Directors for New Horizons are people with disabilities themselves.

10779 Resources for Independent Living - Baton Rouge
11931 Industriplex Boulevard
Suite 200
Baton Rouge, LA 70809
225-753-4772
Fax: 225-753-4831
e-mail: contact@noril.org
http://www.noril.org
TTY 225-753-4831

Yavorika Archaga, Executive Director

Consumers have access to a variety of services provided by Resources for Independent Living/RIL within the southeast region of Louisiana. RIL provides quality services to individuals with disabilities to assist with living independently, including that of information and referral, advocacy, peer support and independent living skills training.

Maine

10780 ALPHA One
127 Main Street
South Portland, ME 04106-2639
207-767-2189
800-640-7200
Fax: 207-799-8346
e-mail: dfitzgibbons@alphaonenow.com
http://www.alphaonenow.com
TTY 207-767-5387

Dennis Fitzgibbons, Executive Director

Alpha One annually assists more than 4,000 people of all ages, including children and the elderly, with a range of disabilities: mobility impairments, traumatic brain injury, deafness, blindness, other vision and hearing impairments, developmental disabilities, mental illness, mental retardation, and AIDS. For more than two decades, Alpha One has been responsive to the needs of individuals with disabilities, initiating, advocating for, and implementing systems change to overcome the barriers that prevent people with disabilities from living independently. Alpha One offers a variety and depth of independent living services: information and referral, outreach, advocacy, one-to-one and group peer support, consumer-directed personal assistance services, assistive technology financing, access design, resume workshops, and independent living skills instruction. Alpha One's adapted driver assessment and education service enables people to learn to drive using adaptive equipment. Alpha One Medical, Alpha One's wholly-owned subsidiary, is a durable medical equipment sales and service company with locations in South Portland, and Lewiston, Maine.

Independent Living Centers/Maryland

10781 Maine Independent Living Services
150 State House Station
Augusta, ME 04330-0150
207-624-5950
800-698-4440
Fax: 207-287-5292
e-mail: bcas.webmaster@maine.gov
http://www.maine.gov/rchab/
TTY 888-755-0023

Penny Plourde, Director

The Independent Living Services (ILS) Program assists people who have significant disabilities to live more independently in their homes and communities. The program provides and arranges needed IL services subject to the availability of funds. The program is also an advocacy program for people with disabilities and their families. All ILS Program services are carried out through an Independent Living Plan that is mutually agreed upon by you andour IL counselor. The four core services that every Independent Living Center provides are: information and referral; individual independent living skills training; peer counseling; and individual and systems advocacy.

10782 Shalom House
400 Congress Street
Po Box 560
Portland, ME 04112-0560
207-874-1080
Fax: 207-874-1077
e-mail: generalmail@shalomhouseinc.org
http://www.shalomhouseinc.org
TDD 207-842-6888

Joseph Brannigan, Executive Director
David Bronson, Board-Directors President
Rebecca Eaton, Grant Writing/Marketing

Shalom House offers hope for adults living with severe mental illness by providing a choice of quality housing and support services that help people lead stable and fulfilling lives in the community. Shalom House helps hundreds of people with serious mental illness each year by providing affordable housing where people can escape the stress of homelessness, hunger, and isolation. Once basic housing needs have been met, peoples' lives can become more stable. Shalom House's mission is to help people address personal goals, receive services, take medication, and once again become a vital part of the community.

Maryland

10783 Deaf Independent Living Association
806 Snow Hill Road
Salisbury, MD 21804
410-742-5052
Fax: 410-543-4874
e-mail: dila@dila.org
http://www.dila.org

Jennifer Whitcomb, Executive Director
Murray Grimm, Program Director
Celeste Emerson, Independent Living Advisor

Deaf Independent Living Association, Inc. (DILA) was established in 1982. DILA offers a variety of services, including employment support, residential support, information and referral and communication resources, for Eastern Shore residents with hearing loss. Above all DILA strives to promote active, independent living among the people we serve. The mission is to promote access to the services and resources for the Eastern Shore residents who are deaf or hard of hearing and provide opportunities for full participation in all aspects of community life.

10784 Independence Now
1400 Spring Street
Suite 400
Silver Spring, MD 20910-4421
301-587-4162
Fax: 301-588-3951
e-mail: info@innow.org
http://www.innow.org

Nancy Diehl, Executive Director
Tonya Gilchrist, Associate Director/Dir. Advocacy
Bryan Abramson, Development Director

Established 1995, Independence Now (IN) is a nonprofit organization created by people with disabilities. Independence Now is a non-residential Center for Independent Living (CIL), one of more than 400 in the United States that provides an array of services to people with all types of disabilities who live in Montgomery and Prince George's Counties. The majority of our staff and Board of Directors have disabilities. Independence Now promotes the independent living philosophy and equal access for all people with disabilities. The mission of Independence Now (IN) is to facilitate independent thought and action by people with disabilities promoting the principle that each person has value. To this end, we provide the tools for individuals to develop and discover their power to control their interactions with the environment, their families and their communities.

10785 Resources for Independence
708 Fayette Street
Cumberland, MD 21502
301-784-1774
800-371-1986
Fax: 301-784-1776
e-mail: phcil@hereintown.net
http://www.rficil.org

Lori Magruder, Executive Director
John Michaels, Office Manager

Offers a strong consumer voice on a wide range of national, state and local issues for people with disabilities.

10786 Southern Maryland Center for LIFE
30265 Charlotte Hall
Suite 3
Charlotte Hall, MD 20622
301-884-4498
Fax: 301-884-6099
e-mail: cflife@comcast.net
TDD 800-735-2258

Eirgit Wilham, Director

Centers for independent living (CILs) are private, nonprofit organizations that provide services to maximize the independence of individuals with disabilities and the accessibility of the communities they live in. Southern Maryland Center for LIFE provides a variety of services for disabled individuals including the basic core services which are that of advocacy, information and referral, independent living skills training, and peer counseling.

Massachusetts

10787 AD LIB Incorporated
215 North Street
Pittsfield, MA 01201-4629
413-442-7047
800-232-7047
Fax: 413-443-4338
e-mail: adlib@adlibcil.org
http://www.adlibcil.org
TTY 413-442-7158

Joseph Castelani, Vice President
Lisa Sloane, Board-Directors President
Merle Ferber, Treasurer

Offers information and referrals, independent living skills training, advocacy and peer counseling for the residents of Berkshire County. A private non-profit, community based, consumer controlled, Independent Living Center. The Center provides independent living and specialized services for people with disabilities in Berkshire County. Adlib empowers people with disabilities to live more independently and have control of their own lives.

10788 Boston Center for Independent Living
60 Temple Place
Fifth Floor
Boston, MA 02111
617-338-6665
866-338-8085
Fax: 617-338-6661
e-mail: info@bostoncil.org
http://www.bostoncil.org
TTY 617-338-6662

William Henning, Executive Director
James Tierney, Deputy Director

Independent Living Centers/Massachusetts

The Boston Center for Independent Living is a frontline civil rights organization led by people with disabilities that advocates to eliminate discrimination, isolation and segregation by providing advocacy, information and referral, peer support, skills training, and PCA services in order to enhance the independence of people with disabilities.

10789 Cape Organization for Rights of the Disabled (CORD)
1019 Ivanough Road
Suite 4
Hyannis, MA 02601
508-775-8300
800-541-0282
Fax: 508-775-7022
e-mail: bhcord@cape.com
http://www.cordonline.org
TTY 508-775-8300

Pamela Burkley, Executive Director

The Cape Organization for Rights of the Disabled (CORD) has been aggressively working since 1984 to advance the independence, productivity, and integration of people with disabilities, including deaf and hard of hearing people, into mainstream society. CORD's Independent Living (IL) and Deaf and Hard of Hearing Independent Living (DHHILS) programs aim to empower the consumer. Services, which are consumer-controlled, include: information and referral, independent living skills training, advocacy, and peer counseling.

10790 Center for Living and Working
484 Main Street
Suite 345
Worcester, MA 01608-1824
508-363-0350
Fax: 508-797-4015
e-mail: centerlw@centerlw.org
http://www.centerlw.org

Terry Briggs, President
Bernard Bonsra, Treasurer
Rong-Rong Zhu, Secretary/Clerk

Center for Independent Living and Working is a non-profit Independent Living Center, incorporated in 1975, which takes its direction from persons with disabilities. We advocate to empower persons with disabilities to take active roles in their lives and in the community in which they live. We provide comprehensive and innovative programs and services in order to maximize individual independence and opportunities. We are driven by the belief thatpeople with disabilities must always be equal members of society with equal access.

10791 DEAF Inc.
215 Brighton Avenue
Allston, MA 02134-2000
617-254-4041
800-866-5195
Fax: 617-254-7091
e-mail: info@deafinconline.org
http://www.deafinconline.org
TTY 617-254-4041

Sharon Applegate, Executive Director
Karen Schwartzman, Board-Directors President
Elvira Belozvsky, Board-Directors Treasurer

D.E.A.F., Inc. encourages and empowers Deaf, Hard of Hearing, Deaf/Blind and Late-Deafened individuals to lead independent and productive lives. We offer a comprehensive package of programs and services in a supportive community environment that is linguistically and culturally accessible for Deaf, Hard of Hearing, Deaf/Blind and Late-Deafened individuals from diverse ethnic and cultural populations.

10792 Independent Living Center of the North Shore & Cape Ann
27 Congress Street
Suite 107
Salem, MA 01970-5577
978-741-0077
888-751-0077
Fax: 978-741-1133
e-mail: smeduff@ilcnsca.org
http://www.ilcnsca.org
TTY 978-741-1735

Mary M Moore, Executive Director
Kathy O'Brien, Associate Director
Shawn McDuff, Advocacy Director

The Independent Living Center of the North Shore and Cape Ann Inc. is a service and advocacy center run by and for people with disabilities. ILCNSCA supports the struggle of people who have all types of disabilities to live independently and participate fully in community life. ILCNSCA pursues this mission through a combination of self-advocacy services and community action. Self-advocacy services are designed to enable participants to develop the skills and knowledge necessary to achieve personal independence. ILCNSCA also organizes and supports collective action by people with disabilities aimed at positive social change, the elimination of discriminatory barriers, and the creation of a supportive and fully accessible community environment.

10793 Massachusetts Statewide Independent Living Council (MASILC)
280 Irving Street
Framingham, MA 01702
508-620-7452
866-662-7452
Fax: 508-620-7450
e-mail: info@masilc.org
http://www.masilc.org
TTY 508-620-7452

Pam Burkley, SILC Chair
Steve Higgins, SILC Coordinator

The Massachusetts Statewide Independent Living Council (MASILC) is a Governor appointed Council. Members include persons who are knowledgeable about centers for independent living and the services they provide. The Council was established by Executive Order No.373 of William F. Weld, Governor of the Commonwealth of Massachusetts on September 26, 1994. The Council includes representation of individuals with a range of physical and mental disabilities from the various geographic areas within the Commonwealth of Massachusetts. The Council along with the Designated State Units (Massachusetts Rehabilitation Commission and Massachusetts Commission for the Blind) Jointly develops and submits the State Plans required in section 704 of the Rehab Act. It is also charged with monitoring, reviewing, and evaluating the implementation of the State Plan for Independent Living as well as coordinatingnts of the Title VII of the Workforce Investment Act of 1998 and in accordance with Independent Living Philosophy.activities with the State Rehabilitation Advisory Council established under section 105 and other State Councils that address the needs of specific disability populations and issues under other federal laws. The goal of the Council is to insure provision of community-based, consumer-controlled, cross-disability services in compliance with requireme

10794 MetroWest Center for Independent Living
280 Irving Street
Framingham, MA 01702-7306
508-875-7853
Fax: 508-875-8359
http://www.mwcil.org
TTY 508-875-7853

Paul Spooner, Executive Director
Karen Murray, Director of Services
Rose Quinn, Executive Assistant

Independent Living Philosophy maintains that individuals with disabilities have the right to choose services that they want to receive and to make decisions about how they live their lives. Consistent with this philosophy, Metro West Center for Independent Living / MWCIL assists consumers in achieving the goals that they have set for themselves by providing training, information, and support. MWCIL's mission is twofold: to help individuals with disabilities become productive and contributing members of the community and to eliminate barriers within the community that impede this process.

10795 Northeast Independent Living Program
20 Ballard Road
Lawrence, MA 01843-1018
978-687-4288
Fax: 978-689-4488
e-mail: info@nilp.org
http://www.nilp.org
TTY 978-687-4288

Karen Bureau, Interim Executive Director
Jim Lyons, Director

Independent Living Centers/Michigan

The Northeast Independent Living Program, Inc. is a consumer controlled Independent Living Center providing Advocacy and Services to people with all disabilities in the greater Merrimack Valley who wish to live as independently as possible in the community. Services include that of information and referral, independent living skills training, advocacy, and peer counseling.

10796 Southeast Center for Independent Living
66 Troy Street Merrill Building
Suite 3
Fall River, MA 02720-3015
508-679-9210
Fax: 508-677-2377
e-mail: scil@secil.org
http://www.secil.org
TTY 508-679-9210

Lisa M. Pitta, Executive Director
Liz Harbison, Program Coordinator
Lisa Antonelli, Financial Manager

The Philosophy of Independent Living, maintains that individuals with disabilities have the right to choose services and make decisions for themselves. This belief is the foundation and guiding principle of all of SCIL's policies and operations. SCIL provides training, information and support to help consumers achieve individual goals, experience personal growth and participate fully in community life. Services include that of information referral, independent living skills training, advocacy, and peer counseling.

10797 Stavros Center for Independent Living
210 Old Farm Road
Amherst, MA 01002-3045
413-256-0473
800-804-1899
Fax: 413-256-0190
e-mail: jkruidenier@stavros.org
http://www.stavros.org
TTY 413-256-0473

James Kruidenier, Executive Director
Janet Shaw, Director Independent Living Svcs

Stavros Center for Independent Living was established in 1974 as a 501 c 3 not-for-profit organization. We are a grass-roots advocacy organization that works for justice and access for people with disabilities in western Massachusetts. It is our goal at Stavros to give people with disabilities the tools to take charge of their life choices, act on their own behalf, and overcome situations that reduce their potential for independence. Independent Living Services enable people with disabilities to live in an environment that encourages and supports the rights of people with disabilities to achieve and maintain a sense of autonomy in their lives. Our advocates accomplish this by providing counseling, skills training, general encouragement and support to people with disabilities in need of such assistance.

Michigan

10798 Ann Arbor Center for Independent Living
3941 Research Park Drive
Ann Arbor, MI 48108
734-971-0277
Fax: 734-971-0826
e-mail: cilstaff@aacil.org
http://www.aacil.org
TTY 734-971-0310

James Magyar, President/CEO
Tom Hoatlin, Development Director
Shirley Coombs, Chief Financial Officer

The Ann Arbor Center for Independent Living assists people with disabilities and their families in living full and productive lives. Our mission is to assure the equality of opportunity, full participation, independent living and economic self-sufficiency of people with disabilities in our community. The Ann Arbor Center for Independent Living utilizes the independent living model, a well-demonstrated and effective four-pronged advocacy and service delivery strategy. Fueled by a consumer-driven philosophy, we provide four core services required of all Centers for Independent Living along with several other services. The four core services are: information and referral, peer support, advocacy, and independent living skill development. The cornerstone of our approach requires that services are provided by people with disabilities for people with a full range of physical, cognitive, sensory (hearing and vision), and/or mental and emotional disabilities.

10799 Blue Water Center for Independent Living Center
310 Water Street
Port Huron, MI 48060-5431
810-987-9337
800-527-2167
Fax: 810-987-9548
e-mail: stclair@bwcil.org
http://www.bwcil.org
TTY 800-527-2167

Angela Hoff, Executive Director
Karen Massaro Mundt, Board-Directors President
Edward N. McGraw, Treasurer

The Blue Water Center for Independent Living is a consumer-based organization designed to serve persons with disabilities who have physical, psychiatric, sensory, cognitive, and multiple disabilities through the provision of advocacy, information and referral, service provision, and the promotion of needed services so to maximize the individual's optimal level of independence. The philosophy of the Blue Water Center for Independent Living is that every person has the right to control and self-direct his or her own life. Through the provision of advocacy, information and promotion of needed resources, people with disabilities can maximize their optimal level of ability.

10800 Capital Area Center for Independent Living
1048 Pierpont Drive
Suite 9-10
Lansing, MI 48911
517-241-0393
Fax: 517-241-0438
e-mail: cacil@cacil.org
http://www.cacil.org

Ellen Weaver, Executive Director
Al Swain, Associate Director
Marsha Moers, Community Advocacy

The Capital Area Center for Independent Living (CACIL) was established in 1976 to empower people with disabilities to take control of their lives. Independent Living is the principle that individuals with any disability, to the fullest extent possible, shall work, live in their own homes, raise families, and participate in the everyday activities of life. CACIL is one of nearly four hundred Independent Living Centers (CILs) around the country that were created under the Rehabilitation Act of 1973 and funded by the taxpayers of America. These centers can be easily distinguished from other service agencies by the extent of involvement of people with disabilities. CILs have a majority of people with disabilities on their governing boards, and they hire qualified people with disabilities to fill management and service delivery positions. Core services include information and referral, community awareness and advocacy, individual skills development, and peer support.

10801 Disability Advocates of Kent County
3600 Camelot Drive Southeast
Grand Rapids, MI 49546-8103
616-949-1100
Fax: 616-949-7865
e-mail: contact@dakc.us
http://www.disabilityadvocates.us
TTY 616-949-1100

David Bulkowski, Executive Director
Renee Thompson, Independent Living Specialist
Cindy L Watrous, Visual Communications Director

Independent Living Centers/Minnesota

Disability Advocates of Kent County advocate, assist, educate and inform on independent living options for people with disabilities and to create a barrier-free society for all. Core services provided include that of information and referral, independent living skills training, advocacy and peer counseling.

10802 Disability Network-Lakeshore Center for Independent Living
426 Century Lane
Holland, MI 49423-3079
616-396-5326
800-656-5245
Fax: 616-396-3220
e-mail: ruth@dnlakeshore.org
http://www.dnlakeshore.org/dnn
TTY 616-396-5326

Ruth Stegeman, Executive Director
Stacey Trowbridge, Mentoring Program Director
Kimberly Romero, Information/Referral Specialist

Disability Network/Lakeshore opened in Holland in 1992 under the name Lakeshore Center for Independent Living, as part of a state and national network serving people with disabilities. Our passionate and committed staff offer expertise on wide-ranging disability issues. Serving Allegan and Ottawa counties, Disability Network concentrates its efforts on building communities that work. Disability Network assists over 2,500 individuals with disabilities and their families on an annual basis, connecting them with supports and services as well as providing training and mentoring. Staff members are specialists in the areas of housing, employment, transportation, accessibility, education, transition, and long-term supports. We also provide general information and referral services.

10803 Disability Resource Center of Southwest Michigan
517 East Crosstown Parkway
Kalamazoo, MI 49001
269-345-1516
800-394-7450
Fax: 269-345-0229
e-mail: jcooper@drccil.org
http://www.drccil.org
TTY 269-345-5925

Joel Cooper, President/CEO
Karen Halsted, Assoicate Director
Sandra L Sullivan, Finance Director

Disability Resource Center of Southwest Michigan educates and empowers people with disabilities to create change in their own lives, and advocates for social change to create inclusive communities. Disability Resource Center provides services to people with a variety of disabilities, including physical, neurological, psychiatric, learning, cognitive, and sensory disabilities. Whether you were born with a disability or acquired a disability laterin life through accident, illness or through the aging process, you are welcome here. We are a resource for friends and family members of people with disabilities as well as community professionals and other human service providers.

10804 Midland Center for Independent Living
1160 James Savage Road
Suite C
Midland, MI 48640-6825
989-835-4041
800-782-4160
Fax: 989-835-8121
e-mail: info@cilmm.org
http://www.cilmm.org
TTY 989-835-4043

Sara Kristal-Brandon, Executive Director
Steven Locke, Associate Director
Terri Cady, Program Leader

The Center for Independent Living of Mid-Michigan (the CIL) exists to assist people with disabilities in learning skills and giving guidance in order for them to make choices and decisions for themselves. Established in 1990, the Center for Independent Living of Mid-Michigan (the CIL) is dedicated to its mission of promoting and encouraging independence for all people with disabilities. The CIL, a 501 (c) 3 organization, advocates for the removal of barriers to independence and full inclusion of people with disabilities throughout mid-Michigan. The CIL pledges to ensure its own compliance with the requirements of the ADA. Each year the CIL conducts a review of its architectural, environmental, attitudinal, employment communication, transportation and other barriers that might exist and prohibit full access to our services. The CIL pledges to ensure that its facilities and services are accessible to everyone.

10805 Oakland & Macomb Center for IndependentLiving
16645 15 Mile Road
Clinton Township, MI 48035
586-268-4160
800-284-2457
Fax: 586-285-9942
e-mail: kkwilson@omcil.org
http://www.omcil.org
TTY 800-649-3777

Kelley Wilson, Executive Director

The Oakland and Macomb Center for Independent Living is committed to assisting people with disabilities to achieve independence through participation, choice and self-determination working to establish a supportive and unified community inclusive of people with disabilities. The Oakland & Macomb Center for Independent Living (OMCIL) is a consumer driven, non-residential, community based organization helping people with disabilities live independently and become participating members of society. The Staff and Board, most of whom are people with disabilities, are strongly committed to supporting others in their efforts toward independence. Since its founding in 1987, OMCIL has been advocating for changes to make the community accessible to people with disabilities, and offering a core of services which include: peer support, independent living skills training, individual and systems advocacy, information and referral. This comprehensive package of services to people with all disabilities is offered in the belief that it is the most effective way to serve consumers who have complex needs.

Minnesota

10806 Freedom Resource Center for Independent Living
125 West Lincoln
Suite 17
Fergus Falls, MN 56537
218-998-1799
800-450-0459
Fax: 218-998-1798
e-mail: joycew@freedomrc.org
http://www.freedomrc.org
TTY 218-998-1799

Joyce Wolter, Executive Director

Provides a number of services for people with disabilities, their families and friends, service providers and interested community members. These services include information and referral, independent living skills, peer support, advocacy and support services, and personal care attendant programs. Each Center is an individual nonprofit agency and provides additional services.

10807 Metropolitan Center for Independent Living (MCIL)
1600 University Avenue West
Suite 16
Saint Paul, MN 55104-3834
651-646-8342
Fax: 651-603-2006
e-mail: mcil@mcil-mn.org
http://www.mcil-mn.org
TTY 651-603-2001

David Hancox, Executive Director

Independent Living Centers/Mississippi

MCIL is a Twin Cities metro-based, non-profit consumer-directed organization founded in 1981. MCIL is dedicated to the full promotion of the independent living (IL) philosophy by supporting individuals with disabilities in their personal efforts to pursue self-directed lives.

10808 Options Interstate Resource Center for Independent Living
318 3rd Street Northwest
East Grand Forks, MN 56721-1887
218-773-6100
800-726-3692
Fax: 218-773-7119
e-mail: options@myoptions.info
http://www.macil.org/options.html
TTY 218-773-6100

Randy Sorensen, Executive Director

Options provides people with disabilities advocacy, information, skills training and peer mentoring relationships to help them achieve their personal goals of how and where they live their lives. Options serves the eleven county region of Northwestern Minnesota and the eight county region of Northeastern North Dakota.

10809 Southeastern Minnesota Center for Independent Living
2720 North Broadway
Rochester, MN 55906
507-285-1815
888-460-1815
Fax: 507-288-8070
e-mail: semcil.uhhc@semcil.org
http://www.semcil.org
TTY 507-285-0616

Vicki Dalle Molle, Executive Director

The Southeastern Minnesota Center for Independent Living, Inc. which was founded in 1981, is a non profit organization that assists people with disabilities to become independent and productive community members. Our Independent Living and Personal Care Assistant Programs promote self-sufficiency and help assure that persons with a disability have the same opportunities as members of the general public. SEMCIL is located in Rochester, MN and has offices in Goodhue and Winona Counties. In 1980, a small group of community members - with the mission of creating or sustaining independence for all persons with disabilities-wrote a grant that got us started and formed our first Board of Directors. Their vision led to the establishment of the Rochester Center for Independent Living (RCIL) in 1981. SEMCIL offers numerous programs focused on living independently and becoming an active community member through various independent living programs. Services include that of information and referral, advocacy, peer counseling, assistive technology, and independent living skills training.

10810 Southern Minnesota IL Enterprises and Services (SMILES)
709 South Front Street
Suite 7
Mankato, MN 56001-3887
507-345-7139
888-676-6498
Fax: 507-345-8429
e-mail: smiles@smilescil.org
http://www.smilescil.org
TTY 507-345-7139

Alan Augustin, Executive Director
Doug Miller, Operations Manager
Howard Rosten, Information Referral

SMILES Center for Independent Living was established in 1988 to provide services for people with disabilities in the nine county region of South Central Minnesota. SMILESÆis a non-profit, non-residential center funded through private and public foundation grants, government and community grants, the United Way, fees for service, and public contributions. Since January 1990 hundreds have found asistance in their efforts to make positive life choices. Because consumers, parents, professionals, and community advocates saw a need for a support system that would empower people with disabilities to build independent, fulfilling lives, resulting in the birth of the center 15 years ago.

10811 Southwest Center for Independent Living
109 South 5th Street
Suite 700
Marshall, MN 56258-1298
507-532-2221
800-422-1485
Fax: 507-532-2222
e-mail: swcil@swcil.com
http://www.swcil.com/
TTY 507-532-2221

Steve Thovson, Executive Director

Since independent living is a dynamic process, SWCIL is dedicated to working with and responding to the ever changing needs of persons with disabilities in southwestern Minnesota. We strive to provide services, supports, and resources, as defined necessary by consumers, that will lead to the creation or enhancement of independent living options. We are committed to providing education and awareness to promote society acceptance, inclusion, andequal access for all persons with disabilities. Independent living programs offer a wide range of supportive services that are provided as a means to assist people with disabilities in obtaining and maintaining the greatest control over their lives. Independent living philosophy is based on the concept that persons with disabilities have the right to choose and live a lifestyle free from discrimination and segregation. Our services are designedsumer in establishing and achieving their independent living goals. Core services include that of information and referral, advocacy, independent living skills training, and peer support.to meet the specific needs of persons with all types of disabilities. Consumers are responsible to develop and control their own goal-oriented service plans. In addition, consumers are able to choose where their services are provided be it within the home, school or community Staff members provide assistance, support and encouragement to the con

Mississippi

10812 LIFE of North Mississippi
1914 University Avenue
Oxford, MS 38655-4114
662-234-7010
800-748-7471
TDD 800-748-7471

10813 LIFE of South Mississippi
1304 Vine Street
Jackson, MS 39202
601-969-4009
800-748-9398
Fax: 601-969-1662
e-mail: lifeofms@aol.com
http://www.lifeofms.com
TDD 800-748-9398
TTY 800-748-9398

Christi Dunaway, Executive Director
Augusta Smith, Assistant Director
Cindy Haslob, LIFE Regional Coordinator

The purpose of Living Independence For Everyone is to empower people with significant disabilities to be as independent and as fully involved in their communities as they can and want to be. The primary goal of LIFE is to assist in the independent living empowerment of people with significant disabilities by: Providing or coordinating the provision of devices, equipment, aids, modifications, or other services or forms of support that improve their capacity to live independently; Supplying information and referral services to allow sufficient access and utilization of available assistance; Furnishing peer counseling and guidance, encourage, establish, and maintain independent living attitudes and philosophies; Rendering advocacy support on and individual or systems-wide basis; Providing skills training instruction to improve specific independent living abilities and competencies; and, Contributing any other help that aids people with significant disabilities in acquiring, retaining, or enhancing their capacity to live independently.

Independent Living Centers/Missouri

Missouri

10814 Access II Independent Living Center
611 West Johnson
Gallatin, MO 64640-1489
660-663-2423
Fax: 660-663-2517
e-mail: access@accessii.org
http://www.accessii.org
TDD 660-663-2663

Debra Hawman, Executive Director
Vickie Tolen, Independent Living Specialist
Heidi Thorne, Independent Living Specialist

The Mission of Access II is to remove architectural and attitudinal barriers that limit the independence of persons with disabilities, promote a positive change in attitudes about disability and persons with disabilities, and encourage greater independence for persons with disabilities within our communities. As a Center for Independent Living, Access II is committed to the provision of a full range of independent living services. Core services include that of information and referral, independent living skills training, peer counseling, in addition to consumer and community advocacy.

10815 Bootheel Area Independent Living Services (BAILS)
719 Teaco Rd
Box 326
Kennett, MO 63857-0326
573-888-0002
888-449-0949
Fax: 573-888-0708
e-mail: tshaw@bails.org
http://www.bails.org
TTY 573-888-0002

Tim Shaw, Executive Director
Tommie Brown, Access/Assistive Technology
Sherry Dollins, Intake Specialist

Offers information and referrals, advocacy, independent living skills and peer counseling. BAILS goal is to foster an open, barrier free society for all people regardless of their disability. All persons regardless of disability, are entitles to and should have equal access to the rights and responsibilities that other citizens are provided; to be an active and productive member of society as they choose.

10816 Delta Center for Independent Living
5933 South Highway 94 South
Suite 107
St. Charles, MO 63304
636-926-8761
866-727-3245
Fax: 314-447-0341
e-mail: info@dcil.org
http://www.dcil.org
TTY 636-926-8761

Jennifer Mueller-Sparrow, President
Don Whalen, Vice-President
Mike Bender, Treasurer

Delta Center for Independent Living partners with people with disabilities and their communities to remove barriers and promote positive changes leading to greater independence for all. Delta Center is a consumer-controlled, not-for-profit agency that provides non-residential, community-based services for persons with all types of disabilities residing in the Missouri counties of St. Charles, Lincoln and Warren. Delta Center was formed in 1997 by a group of local citizens with disabilities and other persons concerned about disability issues. Helping those with physical and mental impairment, the Delta Center for Independent Living Services in St. Louis County, St. Charles County, Franklin County, Warren County, and Lincoln County can assist in maintaining and improve the ability to live independently. Core services include that of information and referral, peer support, advocacy, skillstraining for independent living, in addition to assistive technology.

10817 Disability Resource Association
420B South Truman Boulevard
Crystal City, MO 63019-1726
636-931-7696
Fax: 636-931-9400
e-mail: dra@disabilityresourceassociation.org
http://www.disabilityresourceassociation.org
TTY 636-937-9019

Craig Henning, Executive Director
Nancy Pope, Assistant Director
Suzan Weller, Director Of Programing

The independent living concept is based on the philosophy that people with all types of disabilities should have the same civil rights as those without disabilities. They have a right to control their lives based on options that minimize their reliance on others. Core services provided by Disability Resource Association (DRA) include that of information and referral, independent living skills, advocacy, and peer support. DRA is a member of the Missouri Statewide Independent Living Council, the purpose of which is to gather and disseminate information, conduct studies and analyses, develop model policies, conduct training on independent living issues, provide outreach to unserved and underserved populations, and work to expand and improve independent living services.

10818 Disabled Citizens Alliance for Independence-DCAI
8 Missouri Avenue
PO Box 675
Viburnum, MO 65566-0675
573-244-5402
Fax: 573-244-5609
e-mail: dcitizen@misn.com
TTY 573-244-3315

Richard Blakely, Executive Director

Disabled Citizens Alliance for Independence (DCIA) supports the vision that the independent living concept is based on the philosophy in which people with all types of disabilities should have the same civil rights as those without disabilities. They have a right to control their lives based on options that minimize their reliance on others. Core services provided by DCIA include that of information and referral, advocacy, independent living skills training, and peer support. DCAI is a member of the Missouri Statewide Independent Living Council, the mission of which is to gather and disseminate information, conduct studies and analyses, develop model policies, conduct training on independent living issues, provide outreach to unserved and underserved populations, and work to expand and improve independent living services.

10819 Independent Living Center
1001 East 32nd Street
Joplin, MO 64804-4313
417-659-8086
Fax: 417-659-8087
e-mail: jflowers@ilcenter.org
http://www.ilcenter.org
TTY 417-659-8702

Jeff Flowers, Executive Director

Offers information and referrals, advocacy, independent living skills training and peer support for individuals with disabilities. The mission of the Independent Living Center is to remove all barriers that limit the independence of persons with disabilities.

10820 Independent Living Resource Center
3620 West Truman Boulevard
PO Box 6787
Jefferson City, MO 65102-6787
573-556-0400
877-627-0400
Fax: 573-556-0402
e-mail: admin@ilrcjcmo.org
http://www.ilrcjcmo.org/
TTY 573-634-3876

Stephanie Cox, Executive Director
Lauren Tsutsumi, Administrative Assistant
Melinda Hayes, Program Manager

Independent Living Centers/Missouri

Independent Living Resource Center, Inc. (ILRC) is a consumer controlled, not-for-profit agency that provides community-based services for persons with all types of disabilities. ILRC was incorporated June 28, 1996 by a group of citizens with disabilities and others concerned about disability issues. All ILRC programs are consumer-controlled. Consumers make all decisions in individual and group activities and staff assists and/or advocates as requested. In minimizing reliance on others, consumers learn to manage their own lives and make key decisions, which increases their independence and move toward self-determination. People with disabilities know their needs best and have the right to make decisions regarding their daily lives. Independent Living Resource Center, Inc. promotes a barrier-free environment, free of both architectural and attitudinal barriers that place limits on the independence of persons with disabilities. ILRC encourages greater independence for persons with disabilities within our community. Core services include that of information and referral, advocacy, peer counseling, and independent living skills training, in addition to assistive technology.

10821 Living Independently for Everyone (LIFE)
725 E Karsch Blvd.
Po Box 967
Farmington, MO 63640-1125
573-756-4314
800-596-7273
Fax: 573-756-3507
e-mail: lifecenter@lifecilmo.org
http://www.lifecilmo.org
TTY 573-760-1402

Tim Azinger, Executive Director
Lucretia Katz, Assistant Director
Gary Copeland, Community Access Specialist

Independent Living is based on the concept that a person with a disability can lead a constructive life as a functioning member of his/her community. It affirms that ones worth as a vital human being is not diminished because of a disability. Building skills and confidence to live an independent lifestyle requires special programs - programs that provide peer support, assistance in purchasing needed equipment, hiring and managing a personal careattendant and a whole spectrum of services provided by professional persons. These programs and services are offered through Centers for Independent Living. L.I.F.E is the Independent Living Center serving St. Francois, Madison and St. Genevieve counties in southeast Missouri. Core services provided by L.I.F.E. include that of information and referral, advocacy, peer support, and independent living skills training.

10822 Midland Empire Resources for Independent Living (MERIL)
4420 South 40th Street
Saint Joseph, MO 64506
816-279-8558
800-242-9326
Fax: 816-279-1550
e-mail: meril@meril.org
http://www.meril.org
TTY 816-579-4943

Debbie Merritt, Director Of Programs
Marilyn Finney, Director Of ILS
Jim Pawlowski, Consumer Advocate

MERIL is a community-based, non-residential program, designed to promote independent living and to enhance the quality of life for persons with disabilities by empowering them to control and direct their lives and thus participate actively and independently in society. Our area is predominately rural and includes the nine-county area of Andrew, Atchison, Buchanan, Clinton, Holt, Nodaway, DeKalb, Gentry and Worth counties. Northwest Missouri has a high population of people with disabilities because of the extensive mental health services that exist here. MERIL also serves a large population of Deaf and hard of hearing persons and traumatic brain injury survivors. MERIL provides core services which include that of information and referral, advocacy, peer counseling and independent living skills training.

10823 NorthEast Independent Living Services (NEILS)
142 Jaycee Drive
Hannibal, MO 63401
573-221-8282
877-713-7900
Fax: 573-221-9445
e-mail: neils@neilscenter.org
http://www.neilscenter.org/
TTY 573-221-8282

Stephanie O'Bryan, Executive Director

NorthEast Independent Living Services (N.E.I.L.S) was incorporated on May 2, 1994. N.E.I.L.S. began as a group of people with diverse physical disabilities who started a grassroots effort to educate the community about disability related issues in the Northeast Missouri areas. In February, 1996, N.E.I.L.S. received funding and opened for services. N.E.I.L.S. offers a full range of programs for individuals with a disability and any family members, employers, and/or co-workers with disability concerns. Four core services provided by NorthEast Independent Living Services (N.E.I.L.S) include that of information and referral, advocacy, independent living skills training and peer counseling, in addition to assistive technology support.

10824 On My Own
111 North Elm Street
Nevada, MO 64772-2609
417-667-7007
800-362-8852
Fax: 417-667-6262
http://www.onmyowninc.com

Jennifer Gundy, Executive Director

A non-residential, Independent Living Center providing programs to persons with disabilities, core services of which include that of information and referral, advocacy, peer counseling, and independent living skills training. Advocacy works in partnership with consumers to resolve incidents of discrimination and denial of services through mediation with governments, business, and service providers. In addition, a clearing house of information concerning disabilities is available for access. Support in the form of one-on-one counseling and group counseling is available to assist individuals, families and groups with disability related problems and personal issues.

10825 Ozark Independent Living
109 Aid Avenue
West Plains, MO 65775
417-257-0038
888-440-7500
Fax: 417-257-2380
e-mail: ozark@townsqr.com
http://http://ozarkcil.com
TDD 417-256-8714

Jeanne McLaughlin, President

Independent Living supports people with disabilities in having the opportunity to make their own decisions about things that affect their lives. Independent Living also supports self determination, the right and opportunity to try a course of action, and the freedom to fail and learn from your mistakes. The Independent Living philosophy believes in consumer power, self reliance, political and economic rights. Services are provided by people withdisabilities. Ozark Independent Living (OIL) was created to provide independent living services to persons with disabilities who reside in the following counties in Missouri: Oregon, Ozark, Shannon, Wright, Howell, Texas, and Douglas. OIL is non-profit, non-residential supported by grants, donations, and volunteers in addition to being funded by a grant from the Dept. of Elementary and Secondary Education and Vocational Rehabilitation of Missouri. OIL provides the core services of information and referral, peer support, independent living skills, and advocacy.

10826 Paraquad
5240 Oakland Avenue
Saint Louis, MO 63110
314-289-4200
Fax: 314-289-4201
e-mail: contactus@paraquad.org
http://www.paraquad.org
TTY 314-289-4252

Robert Funk, Executive Director

Independent Living Centers/Missouri

Paraquad, Inc. is a private, not-for-profit community-based Center for Independent Living. Paraquad was founded in 1970 and is a St. Louis organization where professional independent living services are provided by staff members with disabilities. The fact that directors as well as staff members have disabilities enables us to establish keen insight into the ever-changing needs of individuals with all types of disabilities and to develop programs that respond to those needs. Paraquad's programs are created by staff, based on input from participants and have evolved and expanded along with the needs of the disability community. Paraquad exists for the sole purpose of offering services that assist people with disabilities to live independently in society. Our mission is fulfilled through direct and in-direct services as well as advocacy initiatives which shape our public policy agenda. Core services provided by Paraquad include that of information and referral, advocacy, peer counseling and independent living skills training.

10827 Rural Advocates for Independent Living (RAIL)
1100 South Jamison Street
Kirksville, MO 63501-3944
660-627-7245
888-295-6461
Fax: 660-665-9849
e-mail: center@cableone.net
http://www.nemr.net
TTY 660-627-0614

Jack E. Lambrecht, Executive Director
Terry K. Minnix, OutReach Coordinator
Carolyn Chambers, Independent Living Specialist

RAIL's Mission is to assist persons with disabilities to live as independently as they choose within the communities of their choice. RAIL supports people in accomplishing this through: Peer Support - The RAIL staff helps organize formal support groups throughout our service area; Advocacy - RAIL helps those with disablilites learn their rights and how to exercise them for themselves; Information and Referral - RAIL provides persons with disablitities with information on programs, services and products that can help them live more independently; Independent Living Skills Training - Independent Living Specialists (ILS) help persons with disabilities learn specific skills they need to live as independently as they wish. These could include: Rearranging their living environment, using assistive devices, and learning activities to increase their independence.

10828 SEMO Alliance for Disability Independence (SADI)
1913 Rusmar Avenue
Cape Girardeau, MO 63703
573-651-6464
800-898-7234
Fax: 573-651-6565
e-mail: miki@mail.sadi.org
http://www.sadi.org
TTY 573-651-6464

Mike Gudermuth, Executive Director

A community based, non-profit, nonresidential center for independent living. SADI is committed to providing services to persons with disabilities to enable them to remain in their own home and community, and not in an institution. Our service area is predominantly rural. Information and referral services are offered to anyone living in the Southeast Missouri counties of Bollinger, Cape Girardeau, Mississippi, Perry, Scott, and city of Sikeston

10829 Services for Independent Living
1401 Hathman Place
Columbia, MO 65201
573-874-1646
Fax: 573-874-3564
e-mail: sil@silcolumbia.org
http://www.silcolumbia.org
TTY 573-874-4121

Aimee Wehmeier, Executive Director
Jim Crane, Office Manager
Leslie Anderson, Program Manager

Services for Independent Living (SIL) is a not-for-profit center for independent living (CIL). As a CIL, 51 percent or more of the agency's Board of Directors and staff are persons with disabilities who have personally experienced the attitudinal and physical barriers associated with having a disability. SIL educates people with disabilities about the many opportunities available in their community, enabling them to make more informed choices. People with disabilities have control over their lives through informed choices. SIL empowers people with disabilities, encouraging them to become informed and thereby control their lives. Change occurs on an individual and systems level through information, education, and advocacy. The core services provided by SIL are that of information and referral, advocacy, peer counseling, and independent living skills training.

10830 Southwest Center for Independent Living (SCIL)
2864 South Nettleton Avenue
Springfield, MO 65807
417-886-1188
800-676-7245
Fax: 417-886-3619
e-mail: scil@swcil.org
http://www.swcil.org
TTY 417-886-1188

Reba Sims, President
Ray Sonnier, Vice President
Tim Landwehr, Secretary

The Southwest Center for Independent Living (SCIL) is a private, not-for-profit agency which was established in 1985 in Springfield, MO to provide services, advocacy, and resources for people with any disability in Southwest Missouri. SCIL is one of over 300 independent living centers around the country. People with disabilities serve on our board of directors and make up much of our staff. SCIL serves the counties of Christian, Dallas, Greene, Lawrence, Polk, Stone, Taney, and Webster. The mission of SCIL is to promote a barrier-free environment for all disabilities through public education and advocacy for social change, and to provide a full range of independent living services which will assist each in meeting his or her goals for independence. The basic consumer core services provided by SCIL include that of information and referral, advocacy, independent living skills training, and that of peer counseling, in addition to assistive technology support.

10831 Tri-County Center for Independent Living
1420 Hwy 72 East
Rolla, MO 65401-3638
573-368-5933
Fax: 573-368-5991
e-mail: vevans@fidnet.com
http://www.tricountycenter.com
TTY 573-368-5933

Victoria Evans, Executive Director

Independent Living is having the opportunity to make decisions that affect your life - limited only in the same manner as a person without a disability. Tri-County Center for Independent Living is a not-for-profit organization designed to assist persons with disabilities to achieve and maintain as much independence as they wish and in the setting of their choice. The Center provides services to people with disabilities to enable them to live independently in their own homes. Core services provided by the Center include that of information and referral, advocacy, peer support and independent living skills training.

10832 West Central Independent Living Solutions (WCILS)
710 N College Street
Suite D
Warrensburg, MO 64093
660-422-7883
Fax: 660-422-7895
e-mail: 7yman@w-ils.org
TTY 660-422-7894

Lyman Trachsler, Executive Director
Cathey Schrader, Program Coordinator
Anita Dabney, Independent Living Specialist

Independent Living Centers/Montana

Independent Living Centers (ILCs) help people with disabilities achieve or maintain more self-sufficient and productive lives in their communities. people with disabilities are assisted in exploring alternatives to institutionalization and are encouraged to make their own decisions about how they will live. ILCs directly provide or coordinate through referral those services, which assist people in increasing their abilities to exercise controlover their lives. Control over one's life means having a choice of acceptable options that minimize reliance on others in making decisions and performing every day activities. This includes managing one's own affairs, participating in day-to-day community life and fulfilling a range of social roles. West-Central Independent Living Solutions works to empower people with disabilities to become more independent by providing independent living skil ls training, peer support, information and referral and advocacy.

Montana

10833 Living Independently for Today & Tomorrow (LIFTT)
3333 2nd Avenue
Billings, MT 59101
406-259-5186
800-502-9700
Fax: 406-259-5259
e-mail: davess@liftt.org
http://www.liftt.org
TTY 406-259-5259

Bobbie Becker, Executive Director
Freda Mook, Administrative Assistant
Char Harasymczuk, Deaf Specialist

LIFTT's Independent living program works with people with disabilities so they can live independently and have access to the community. LIFTT staff, most of whom have disabilities, serve as mentors to people as they work to achieve the goals they have set for themselves. Core services provided by LIFTT include that of information and referral, advocacy, peer support and independent living skills training, in addition to guidance on accessibility and benefits counseling.

10834 Montana Independent Living Project
1820 11th Avenue
Helena, MT 59601-4768
406-442-5755
800-735-6457
Fax: 406-442-1612
e-mail: bmaffit@milp.us
http://www.milp.us
TTY 406-442-5756

Bob Maffit, Executive Director
Betty Bergstrom, Chief Financial Officer
Ken Christensen, Independent Living Specialist

The philosophy of independent living promotes consumer control, peer support, self-help, self-determination, equal access, and individual and systems advocacy in order to maximize the leadership, empowerment, independence, and productivity of individuals with disabilities. Full inclusion and integration of individuals with disabilities into the mainstream of American society is primary. This philosophy is implemented through the Montana Independent Living Council and the network of Montana centers for independent living. The four centers and their satellites provide statewide coverage with centers situated in Great Falls, Helena, Missoula, Billings, Glasgow, Miles City, Glendive, Kalispell, Ronan, and Hamilton. Services include information and referral, individual and systems advocacy, peer support and independent living skills training in addition to assistive technology support.

10835 North Central Independent Living Services
1120 25th Avenue Northeast
Black Eagle, MT 59414
406-452-9834
800-823-6245
Fax: 406-453-3940
e-mail: ncils.osborn@sofast.net
http://www.dphhs.mt.gov
TTY 406-452-9834

Tom Osborn, Director

The philosophy of independent living promotes consumer control, peer support, self-help, self-determination, equal access, and individual and systems advocacy in order to maximize the leadership, empowerment, independence, and productivity of individuals with disabilities. Full inclusion and integration of individuals with disabilities into the mainstream of American society is primary. This philosophy is implemented through the Montana Independent Living Council and the network of Montana centers for independent living. The four centers and their satellites provide statewide coverage with centers situated in Great Falls, Helena, Missoula, Billings, Glasgow, Miles City, Glendive, Kalispell, Ronan, and Hamilton. Services include that of information referral, advocacy, peer support and independent living skills training in addition to assistive technology support.

10836 Summit Independent Living Center-Kalispell
275 Corporate Drive
Suite 901
Kalispell, MT 59901-6020
406-257-0048
800-995-0029
Fax: 406-257-0634
e-mail: flokiewel~kalispell@summitlc.org
http://www.summitilc.org
TTY 406-257-0048

Flo Kiewel, Manager Kalispell Branch
Gab Skibsrub, Board-Directors Kalispell Branch

Summit Independent Living Center Inc. is a non-profit non-residential program serving people with mobility impairments, neurological disorders, hearing impairments, learning disabilities, visual impairments and other disabling conditions. Summit's mission is to promote community awareness, equal access, and the independence of people with disabilities through advocacy, education and the advancement of civil rights.

10837 Summit Independent Living Center-Missoula
700 Southwest Higgins Avenue
Suite 101
Missoula, MT 59803
406-728-1630
800-398-9002
Fax: 406-829-3309
e-mail: secretary~@summitlc.org
http://www.summitilc.org
TTY 406-728-1630

Mike Mayer, Executive Director

Summit Independent Living Cener, Inc. is a non-profit, non-residential program serving people with mobility impairments, neurological disorders, hearing impairments, learning disabilities, visual impairments, and other disabling conditions. Summit's mission is to promote community awareness, equal access, and the independence of people with disabilities through advocacy, education and the advancement of civil rights.

10838 Summit Independent Living Center-Ronan
111 Second Avenue Southwest
Ronan, MT 59864-2707
406-676-0190
866-230-6936
Fax: 406-676-0190
e-mail: garystevens~ronan@summitlc.org
http://www.summitilc.org/
TTY 406-676-0190

Gary Stevens, Director

Summit Independent Living Cener, Inc. is a non-profit, non-residential program serving people with mobility impairments, neurological disorders, hearing impairments, learning disabilities, visual impairments and other disabling conditions. Summit's mission is to promote community awareness, equal access, and the independence of people with disabilities through advocacy, education and the advancement of civil rights.

Independent Living Centers/North Carolina

North Carolina

10839 Disability Rights And Resources
5801 Executive Center Drive
Suite 101'
Charlotte, NC 28212-8870
704-537-0550
800-755-5749
Fax: 704-566-0507
http://www.disability-rights.org
TTY 704-537-0550

Julia Sain, Executive Director

PAL's mission and purpose is to guard the civil rights of people with disabilities as we empower ourselves and others to live as we choose. At least 51% of PAL's staff is living with a disability and serve a four-county service area including Mecklenburg, Cabarrus, Gaston and Union counties. Core services include that of information and referral, advocacy, peer support and independent living skills training.

10840 Pathways For the Future-Center For IndepEndent Living
525 Mineral Springs Drive
Sylva, NC 28779
828-631-1167
Fax: 828-631-1169
e-mail: bdavis@pathwayscil.org
http://www.pathwayscil.org
TTY 828-631-1167

Barbara Davis, Executive Director

Pathways is dedicated to increasing independence, changing attitudes, promoting equal access and building a peer support network in western north carolina through the use of community education, independent living services and advocacy

North Dakota

10841 Dakota Center for Independent Living
3111 East Broadway Avenue
Bismarck, ND 58501
701-222-3636
800-489-5013
Fax: 701-222-0511
e-mail: dcil@dakotacil.org
http://www.dakotacil.org/
TDD 701-222-3636

Royce Schultze, Executive Director
Mary Robinson, Program Manager
Gwen Beckler, Systems/Community Advocate

The Dakota Center for Independent Living advocates for community based services and training opportunities that assist people with disabilities to live more independently. Outreach services are provided in eighteen south west and south central N.D. counties, and on the Standing Rock and the southern part of the Fort Berthold Native American reservations. The Dakota Center for Independent Living believes in self-determination for people with disabilities and creates the environment in which it is achieved. Services include that of information and referral, advocacy, independent living skills training, and peer support.

10842 Freedom Resource Center for Independent Living
2701 Ninth Avenue Southwest
Fargo, ND 58103
701-478-0459
800-450-0459
Fax: 701-478-0510
e-mail: freedom@freedomrc.org
http://www.freedomrc.org
TTY 800-450-0459

Nate Aalgaard, Executive Director
Mikara Kverno, Information Specialist
Joyce Wolter, Independent Living Advocate

Freedom resource center is an independent non-profit organization, serving people of all ages and all disabilities. The mission of the Freedom Resource Center is to work toward equality and inclusion for people with disabilities through programs of empowerment, community education, and systems change.

10843 Independence
300 Third Avenue Southwest
Suite F
Minot, ND 58701-4308
701-839-4724
800-377-5114
Fax: 701-838-1677
e-mail: agency@independencecil.org
http://www.independencecil.org/
TDD 701-839-4724

Stephen Repnow, Executive Director

Independence, Inc is a private non-profit corporation devoted to meeting the needs of individuals with disabilities and serving them, their families and communities. The mission is to advocate for the freedom of choice for individuals with disabilities to live independently through the removal of barriers.

Nebraska

10844 Center for Independent Living of Central Nebraska
3204 College Street
Grand Island, NE 68803
308-382-9255
877-400-1004
Fax: 308-384-7832
e-mail: rnorris@cilne.org
http://www.cilne.org
TTY 308-382-9255

Ray Norris, Executive Director
Kaila Roeser, Resource Developer
Chuck Leach, Program Coordinator

The Center for Independent Living of Central Nebraska provides a comprehensive set of services designed to enable persons with disabilities to exercise control over their lives based on their choices of acceptable options that minimize their reliance on other people in making decisions and in performing everyday activities. This includes their managing their affairs, fulfilling the range of social roles, making decisions that lead to self-determination and minimizing their physical and psychological dependence on others. Our center will always strews that independence is not a matter of ability or limitation, but is instead a matter of making educated choices. Services include that of information and referral, advocacy, independent living skills training, and peer support.

10845 League of Human Dignity Independent Living Center
1701 P Street
Lincoln, NE 68508-1799
402-441-7871
Fax: 402-441-7650
e-mail: info@leagueofhumandignity.com
http://www.leagueofhumandignity.com
TTY 402-441-7871

Mike Schafer, CEO

The League of Human Dignity is an organization of people concerned about the rights and quality of life for people with disabilities. League members collaborate to ensure social, economic, and political equality for persons with disabilities. We believe in emphasizing likeness not difference, ability not disability, normality not abnormality, and integration not segregation. We work toward independent living for people who have disabilities. The mission of the League of Human Dignity is to actively promote the full integration of individuals with disabilities into society. To this end, we will advocate their needs and rights, and provide quality services to involve these persons in becoming and remaining independent citizens. Services include that of information and referral, systems advocacy, individual advocacy, independent living skills training, and peer support.

Independent Living Centers/Nevada

Nevada

10846 Northern Nevada Center for Independent Living
999 Pyramid Way
Sparks, NV 89431-4471
775-353-3599
Fax: 702-353-3588
e-mail: nncil7@sbcglobal.net
http://www.nncil.org/
TTY 775-353-3599

Lisa Erquiaga, Executive Director

The Northern Nevada Center for Independent Living is a consumer-controlled, community-based, cross-disability, nonresidential, private, nonprofit agency that is designed and operated within the local community by individuals with disabilities. The Center provides an array of independent living services including the core services of information and referral, independent living skills training, peer counseling, and individual and systems advocacy. The purpose of the independent living program is to maximize the leadership, empowerment, independence, and productivity of individuals with disabilities and to integrate these individuals into the mainstream of American society.

New Hampshire

10847 Granite State Independent Living Center
21 Chenell Drive
Concord, NH 03301
603-228-9680
800-826-3700
Fax: 603-225-3304
e-mail: clyde.terry@gsil.org
http://www.gsil.org
TTY 888-396-3459

Clyde Terry, Executive Director

AÆstatewide non-profit, service and advocacy organization that provides tools for living life on your own terms- so you can navigate your own live and participate as fully as you choose in your community, just like everyone else.

New Jersey

10848 Alliance for Disabled in Action
629 Amboy Avenue
Lower Level
Edison, NJ 08837
732-738-4388
Fax: 732-738-4416
e-mail: adacil@adacil.org
http://www.adacil.org
TTY 732-738-9644

Richard Ringhof, Executive Director

The Alliance for Disabled in Action, Inc. (ADA) is a private, not-for-profit center for independent living serving people in Middlesex, Somerset and Union Counties of New Jersey. Initially created in 1986 as an Independent Living Resource Center (as part of JFK Johnson Rehabilitation), the Alliance was incorporated as a separate, private nonprofit organization in 1991. The Alliance provides information & referral, peer support, advocacy and Independent Living Skill training to people with all disabilities of all ages to increase their independence in all aspects of integrated community life. We respond to their families, businesses, and governments to enable them to better meet the needs of people with disabilities. We educate and influence our community in pursuit of full inclusion. People with disabilities should be empowered to control the direction of their own lives. This means corts and promote self-reliance. CILs advocate for the inclusion and integration of people with disabilities in all aspects of community living.hoosing their goals, plotting their course and taking responsibility for their actions and results. People with disabilities have the right to make their own choices and decisions and the right to make mistakes and learn/benefit from those mistakes. Centers for Independent Living foster independence facilitate the development of networks and supp

10849 Camden City Independent Living Center (CCILC)
2600 Mount Ephriam Avenue
Suite 413
Camden, NJ 08104
856-966-0800
Fax: 856-966-0832
e-mail: lorrainecilc@aol.com
http://www.njsilc.org/city_camden.html
TTY 856-966-0830

Lorraine Culbertson, Executive Director

Centers for independent living (CILs) are private, nonprofit corporations that provide services to maximize the independence of individuals with disabilities and the accessibility of the communities they live in. Camden City Independent Living Center (CCILC) is designed and operated within a local community by individuals with disabilities, providing an array of independent living services, including the core services of information and referral, independent living skills training, peer counseling, and individual and systems advocacy. The purpose of the independent living programs is to maximize the leadership, empowerment, independence, and productivity of individuals with disabilities and to integrate these individuals into the mainstream of American society.

10850 Centers for Independent Living of South Jersey (CILSJ)
1150 Delsea Drive
Suite 1
Westville, NJ 08093
856-853-6490
Fax: 856-853-1466
e-mail: CILSJ@aol.com
TTY 856-853-7602

Hazel Lee-Briggs, Executive Director

Centers for independent living (CILs) are private, nonprofit corporations that provide services to maximize the independence of individuals with disabilities and the accessibility of the communities they live in. The Center for Independent Living of South Jersey (CILSJ) is designed and operated within the local community by individuals with disabilities providing an array of independent living services, including the core services of informationand referral, independent living skills training, peer counseling, and individual and systems advocacy. The purpose of the independent living programs is to maximize the leadership, empowerment, independence, and productivity of individuals with disabilities and to integrate these individuals into the mainstream of American society.

10851 Heightened Independence & Progress (HIP)
131 Main Street
Suite 120
Hackensack, NJ 07601-7182
201-996-9100
Fax: 201-996-9422
e-mail: bcr@hipcil.org
http://www.hipcil.org
TDD 201-996-9424

Eileen Goff, Executive Director

Centers for independent living (CILs) are private, nonprofit corporations that provide services to maximize the independence of individuals with disabilities and the accessibility of the communities they live in. Heightened Independence and Progress (HIP) is designed and operated within a local community by individuals with disabilities, providing an array of independent living services, including the core services of information and referral, independent living skills training, peer counseling, and individual and systems advocacy. The purpose of the independent living programs is to maximize the leadership, empowerment, independence, and productivity of individuals with disabilities and to integrate these individuals into the mainstream of American society.

10852 Heightened Independence & Progress-Hudson (HIP Hudson)
26 Journal Square
Suite 602
Jersey City, NJ 07306
201-533-4407
e-mail: hud@hipcil.org
http://www.hipcil.org
TDD 201-533-4409
TTY 201-533-4409

Kathy Wood, Executive Director

Independent Living Centers/New Mexico

Centers for independent living (CILs) are private, nonprofit corporations that provide services to maximize the independence of individuals with disabilities and the accessibility of the communities they live in. Heightened Independence and Progress (HIP Hudson) is designed and operated within a local community by individuals with disabilities, providing an array of independent living services, including the core services of information and referral, independent living skills training, peer counseling, and individual and systems advocacy. The purpose of the independent living programs is to maximize the leadership, empowerment, independence, and productivity of individuals with disabilities and to integrate these individuals into the mainstream of American society.

10853 Moceans Center for Independent Living
279 Broadway 2nd Floor
Suite 201
Long Branch, NJ 07740-6941
732-571-4884
Fax: 732-571-4003
e-mail: moceans@moceanscil.org
http://www.moceanscil.org
TDD 732-571-4878

Patricia McShane, Executive Director

Centers for independent living (CILs) are private, nonprofit corporations that provide services to maximize the independence of individuals with disabilities and the accessibility of the communities they live in. MOCEANS Center for Independent Living is designed and operated within a local community by individuals with disabilities, providing an array of independent living services, including the core services of information and referral, independent living skills training, peer counseling, and individual and systems advocacy. The purpose of the independent living programs is to maximize the leadership, empowerment, independence, and productivity of individuals with disabilities and to integrate these individuals into the mainstream of American society.

10854 Progressive Center for Independent Living (PCIL)
1262 Whitehorse Hamilton Road
Suite 102, Bldg A
Hamilton, NJ 08690
609-581-4500
877-917-4500
Fax: 609-581-4555
e-mail: info@pcil.org
http://www.pcil.org
TTY 609-581-4550

Scott Elliott, Executive Director

Centers for independent living (CILs) are private, nonprofit corporations that provide services to maximize the independence of individuals with disabilities and the accessibility of the communities they live in. Progressive Center for Independent Living (PCIL) is designed and operated within a local community by individuals with disabilities, providing an array of independent living services, including the core services of information and referral, independent living skills training, peer counseling, and individual and systems advocacy. The purpose of the independent living programs is to maximize the leadership, empowerment, independence, and productivity of individuals with disabilities and to integrate these individuals into the mainstream of American society.

10855 Total Living Center (TLC)
707 White Horse Pike
Suite B8
Absecon, NJ 08202
609-645-9547
Fax: 609-813-2318
e-mail: info@tlcenter.org
TDD 609-965-5390

Julia T. Bonelli, Executive Director

Centers for independent living (CILs) are private, nonprofit corporations that provide services to maximize the independence of individuals with disabilities and the accessibility of the communities they live in. Total Living Center (TLC) is designed and operated within a local community by individuals with disabilities, providing an array of independent living services, including the core services of information and referral, independent livingskills training, peer counseling, and individual and systems advocacy. The purpose of the independent living programs is to maximize the leadership, empowerment, independence, and productivity of individuals with disabilities and to integrate these individuals into the mainstream of American society.

New Mexico

10856 Ability Center for Independent Living
715 East Idaho Avenue
Bldg 3,
Las Cruces, NM 88001
505-526-5016
800-376-4372
Fax: 505-526-1202
e-mail: freedom@theabilitycenter.org
http://www.theabilitycenter.org
TTY 505-526-5016

Ruth D Rodriguez, President
Cesasr Rodriguez, Vice-President
Rev. C. Neil Gibbs, Treasurer

The Ability Center for Independent Living (TACIL) is a center for independent living (CIL), and is a private, nonresidential, nonprofit New Mexico corporation. The purpose of a CIL is to provide a variety of services to promote independence, self-reliance, and community integration. The Ability Center strives to enable persons with disabilities to gain effective control and direction of their own lives. The Ability Center attempts to stimulate and promote a growing sense of personal dignity and responsible community participation of persons with disabilities through training, community development, and direct services. The Ability Center seeks to meet the unserved needs of persons with disabilities living in the counties of Catron, Doña Ana, Grant, Hidalgo, Luna, Otero, and Sierra, New Mexico. Our Advocacy, Informational & Referral program provides the four core services of the Rehabilitation Act of 1992 to individuals of all ages and disabilities. These services are advocacy, information and referral, peer counseling, and life skills training.

10857 CHOICES Center for Independent Living
720 East College
Suite 15
Roswell, NM 88201-4670
505-627-6727
800-387-4572
Fax: 505-627-6754
e-mail: cbailey@ilchoices.com
http://www.ilchoices.com
TTY 505-627-6727

Charles Bailey, Executive Director
Jane Ann Oldrup, Advocacy & Public Policy
Fred McDonald, Board-Directors President

An Independent Living Center is a consumer-directed agency that works with individuals of all cultures with any disability. This is evident by the staff and board that operate our center. The staff is 88% individuals with disabilities and the Board of Director's has 87%. Community members from our service catchment area are always encouraged to volunteer their time and expertise to the community by serving on our Board of Directors. CHOICES mission is to promote a society in which persons with disabilities control their environment and destiny through informed choice and self-identified goals of independence. CHOICES provides a variety of services including that of information and referral, advocacy, independent living skills training, and peer support.

10858 New Vistas Independent Living Center
1205 Parkway Drive
Suite A
Santa Fe, NM 87507
505-471-1001
800-737-0330
Fax: 505-471-4427
e-mail: rgarcia@newvistas.org
http://www.newvistas.org
TTY 505-471-1001

Ron Garcia, Executive Director

Centers for independent living (CILs) are private, nonprofit corporations that provide services to maximize the independence of individuals with disabilities and the accessibility of the communities they live in. New Vistas Independent Living Center offers services for people with all types of disabilities. Independence and community integration are promoted by providing options in the following areas: information and referral, advocacy, independent livings skills training, and peer support services.

New York

10859 Access to Independence and Mobility (AIM
271 East 1st Street
Corning, NY 14830-2924
607-962-8225
Fax: 607-937-5125
e-mail: corning@aimcil.com
http://www.aimcil.com
TTY 607-962-8225

Diane DeMuth, Executive Director
Patricia Myers, Deputy Director

It is AIM's goal to enable the consumer to live an independent and comfortable lifestyle in the security of their home environment so they may feel dignity and pride in their achievements while controlling their own care. AIM is a human service agency with offices in Bath, Corning, Elmira and Hornell serving people whose lives have been affected by disability. AIM is a part of a national network of organizations called Independent Living Centers(ILC). An ILC is a nonresidential resource center run by and for people with a personal knowledge of disabilities. Our emphasis is on acknowledging consumers as unique individuals. Therefore, we often offer services and programs to meet specific requests. Our emphasis is on acknowledging consumers as unique individuals. Therefore, we often offer services and programs to meet specific requests. For instance, depending on a consumer's situation, wedent living skills such as money management, attendant care supervision and employment skills.may actively assist him or her in securing legal, civil, social or economic rights. Perhaps an individual's needs are more tangible - we can provide information on topics such as availability of accessing housing, sign language interpreters or TDDs. We can also help individual consumers access learning experiences and/or training to develop indepen

10860 Access to Independence and Mobility-Bath (AIM)
117 East Steuben Street
Bath, NY 14810
607-776-3838
Fax: 607-776-3838
e-mail: caim@aimcil.com
http://www.aimcil.com
TDD 607-776-3838

Diane Demuth, Executive Director
Patricia Myers, Deputy Director

It is AIM's goal to enable the consumer to live an independent and comfortable lifestyle in the security of their home environment so they may feel dignity and pride in their achievements while controlling their own care. AIM is a human service agency with offices in Bath, Corning, Elmira and Hornell serving people whose lives have been affected by disability. AIM is a part of a national network of organizations called Independent Living Centers(ILC). An ILC is a nonresidential resource center run by and for people with a personal knowledge of disabilities. Our emphasis is on acknowledging consumers as unique individuals. Therefore, we often offer services and programs to meet specific requests. For instance, depending on a consumer's situation, we may actively assist him or her in securing legal, civil, social or economic rights. Perhaps an individual's needs are more tangible - we can provide information on topics such as availability of accessing housing, sign language interpreters or TDDs. We can also help individual consumers access learning experiences and/or training to develop independent living skills such as money management, attendant care supervision and employment skills.

10861 Access to Independence of Cortland County
26 North Main Street
Cortland, NY 13045-2198
607-753-7363
Fax: 607-756-4884
e-mail: info@aticortland.org
http://www.cilcortland.org
TTY 600-753-7363

Mary E Ewing, Executive Director

Access to Independence of Cortland County's mission is to promote awareness of barriers, both structural and attitudinal, that affect the lives of people with disabilities. In carrying out its mission, the Center will: act as a resource for the provision of information and support services to individuals, groups and organizations; provide guidance and advocacy to individuals with disabilities in all areas that affect their ability to live independently; and advocate for an all-inclusive, barrier-free society.

10862 Action Toward Independence
33 Lakewood Avenue
Monticello, NY 12701
845-794-4228
Fax: 845-794-4475
e-mail: ati@in4web.com
http://actiontowardindependence.org

Andrea Putter, Mental Health Advocate

People with disabilities should be empowered to control the direction of their own lives. This means choosing their goals, plotting their course and taking responsibility for their actions and the results. People with disabilities have the right to make their own choices and decisions and the right to make mistakes and learn/benefit from those mistakes. Centers for Independent Living (CILs) foster independence, help disabled people to develop networks and supports, promote self-reliance, and advocate for the inclusion and integration of people with disabilities in all aspects of community life. Services include that of information and referral, advocacy, independent living skills training, and peer support.

10863 Auburn Options for Independence
75 Genesee Street
Auburn, NY 13021-3667
315-255-3447
800-496-9148
Fax: 315-255-0836
e-mail: options@optionsforindependence.org
http://www.optionsforindependence.org/
TTY 315-255-3447

Tracy Murphy, Executive Director
Nancy Wise, Chairperson
Judy Dove, First Vice-Chairperson

Independent Living Centers/New York

Options For Independence is an Independent Living Center which assists people with disabilities to gain opportunities, make their own decisions, pursue activities and become part of community life. We provide a variety of services to all people with disabilities, their family and friends in Cayuga and Seneca Counties. Services include that of information and referral, advocacy, independent living skills training, and peer support. Additionally, the Center also has a Resource Library in which we continually develop and collect information and subscribe to a variety of journals and disability related periodicals, including a magazine written in Braille for use. Options also has a selection of books on tape and the necessary equipment to use them from the Library of Congress Talking Book Program that may be borrowed by customers.

10864 Bronx Independent Living Services
3525 Decatur Avenue
Bronx, NY 10467-1720
718-515-2800
Fax: 718-515-2803
http://www.bils.org
TTY 718-515-2803

Susan Mendoza, Executive Director

Bronx Independent Living Services, Inc. (BILS) is a not-for-profit community agency serving people with all kinds of disabilities. Our mission is to empower people with disabilities toward living independent lives. We assist individuals by providing advocacy, peer counseling, housing information, and independent living training/counseling. We also work to educate and advocate for legislative and social change so that people who have disablities can live more independently. We educate people about their civil and human rights, and work on providing access to the tools and means necessary to insure those rights. A part of the international Independent Living movement, we are oriented towards self-help and control by those who are actually concerned.

10865 Brooklyn Center for Independence of the Disabled
2044 Ocean Avenue
Suite B-3
Brooklyn, NY 11230-7302
718-998-3000
Fax: 718-998-3743
e-mail: advocate@bcid.org
http://www.bcid.org
TTY 718-998-7406

Zainab Jama, Executive Director

The Brooklyn Center for Independence of the Disabled, Inc. (BCID) is a non-profit, grass roots organization operated by a majority of people with disabilities since 1956. We are dedicated to guaranteeing the civil rights of people with disabilities. We exist to improve the quality of life of Brooklyn residents with disabilities through programs that empower them to gain greater control of their lives and achieve full and equal integration into society. We accomplish this through our services, our advocacy for systems change to remove physical, attitudinal and communication barriers to people with disabilities, and through our education and awareness programs.

10866 Capital District Center for Independent Living
875 Central Avenue
South 4
Albany, NY 12206
518-459-6422
Fax: 518-459-7847
e-mail: info@cdciweb.com
http://www.cdciweb.com/index.html
TDD 518-459-6422

Laurel Kelley, Executive Director

Established in 1979, Capital District Center for Independence, Inc., one of 37 Independent Living Centers (ILC) in New York State, was initially known as Wheels to Independence. Upon incorporation in 1980, the name was officially changed to better reflect the wide range of services provided by the ILC. The Center is a non-residential, community based organization, which primarily serves Albany and Schenectady Counties; however some programs extend beyond these regions. By assisting people with disabilities to acquire self-advocacy skills and by teaching through example (peer advocacy), consumers achieve greater control over the direction of their lives. Staff and volunteers strive to educate community leaders and the general public in the areas of "inclusion" and universal access to enlist their support in the removal of attitudinal, economic and structural barriers, which prevent equalparticipation of people with disabilities in all aspects of community life.

10867 Catskill Center for Independence
6104 State Highway 23
Oneonta, NY 13820-5247
607-432-8000
Fax: 607-432-6907
e-mail: ccfi@ccfi.us
http://www.ccfi.us
TTY 607-432-8000

Chris Zachmeyer, Executive Director
Edward Lynch, Operations Manager
Charles Reichardt, Systems Advocate

Independent living centers are consumer driven What this means is that at least 50% of our governing board must be a person with a disability. Many of us who work at the Center are also people with disabilities. So independent living centers are run by people with disabilities for people with disabilities. We assist people with disabilities to achieve independence in everyday life. The Catskill Center for Independence is one of thirty-seven independent centers located throughout the state of New York. The Center provides a variety of services to individuals with disabilities who reside in Delaware, Otsego, or Schoharie County. The Center also provides information, training and other disability related assistance to family members and friends of people with disabilities, employers, landlords, government and other agencies and members of both the private and business sectors of our community.

10868 Center for Independence of Disabled in New York (CIDNY)
841 Broadway
Suite 301
New York, NY 10003
212-674-2300
Fax: 212-254-5953
e-mail: info@cidny.org
http://www.cidny.org
TTY 212-674-5619

Susan Dooha, Executive Director
Margi Trapani, Communications Director
Michael Fagan, Director Administration

The Center for Independence of the Disabled, New York's (CIDNY) goal is to ensure full integration, independence and equal opportunities for all people with disabilities by removing barriers to the social, economic, cultural and civic life of the community. CIDNY is a non-profit organization founded in 1979. We are part of the Independent Living Cenres movement- a national network of grassroots and community-based organizations that enhance opportunities for all people with disabilities to direct their own lives.

10869 East Orange County Center for Independent Living
5 Washington Ter
Newburgh, NY 12550-5338
845-565-1162
Fax: 845-565-0567

Doug Hovey, Executive Director

10870 Finger Lakes Independence Center
215 5th Street
Ithaca, NY 14850-3403
607-272-2433
Fax: 607-272-0902
e-mail: flic@clarityconntect.com
http://www.fliconline.org

Lenore Schwager, Executive Director

Independent Living Centers/New York

The Finger Lakes Independence Center assists all people with disabilities, their families and friends to promote independence and make informed decisions in pursuit of their goals. Our services are free of charge. We primarily serve residents of Tompkins, Cortland and Schuyler counties. We believe that a society which is inclusive of people with disabilities is beneficial to all of its members. Furthermore, we believe that individual and group attitudes toward people with disabilities often create closed social structures and architectural barriers which are detrimental to all members of society. The mission of the Finger Lakes Independence Center is to work toward the elimination of these obstacles, to empower people with disabilites, and thereby create an inclusive society.

10871 Harlem Independent Living Center
289 Saint Nicholas Avenue
Suite 21 Lower Level Between 124 & 125 Street
New York, NY 10027
212-222-7122
800-673-2371
Fax: 212-222-7199
e-mail: harlemilc@aol.com
http://www.hilc.org
TTY 212-222-7198

Christina Curry, Executive Director

The mission of the Harlem Independent Living Center is to create an accessible society where persons with disabilities realize their full potential throughout their lives. Services include information and referral, advocacy, independent living skills training, and peer support.

10872 Independent Center-Southern Tier
24 Prospect Avenue
Binghamton, NY 13901
607-724-2111
Fax: 607-722-3600
e-mail: stic@stic-cil.org
http://www.stic-cil.org
TTY 677-242-2111

Maria Dibble, Executive Director

In addition to providing services, the Southern Tier Independence Center is a gathering place for people and information. Our joint efforts in understanding the issues and concerns of people with disabilities can pave the way to this more accessible world. Services include that of information and referral, advocacy, independent living skills training, and peer support.

10873 Independent Living Center of Hudson Valley
802 Columbia Street
Hudson, NY 12534
518-828-4886
Fax: 518-828-2592
e-mail: jbachman@ilchv.org
http://www.ilchv.org
TTY 518-828-6293

Denise A Figueroa, Executive Director
Cliff Perez, Systems Advocate
Sally Baker, Benefits Planning

The Independent Living Center of the Hudson Valley is rooted in a philosophy of self reliance and self determination. We offer the following services to individuals with disabilities and their families: advocacy; peer counseling; benefits advisement; information and referral; housing information; consultation on architectural barriers; transportation; independent livings skills training; employment services; and personal assistance services.

10874 Independent Living of the Hudson Valley
49 Fourth Street
Troy, NY 12180
518-274-0701
Fax: 518-274-7944
e-mail: admin@ilchv.org
http://www.ilchv.org
TTY 518-274-0701

Denise Figueroa, Executive Director
Vincent Reiter, Personal Assistance Services
Lisa Dugan, Peer Advocate

The Independent Living Center of the Hudson Valley is rooted in a philosophy of self reliance and self determination. We offer the following services to individuals with disabilities and their families: advocacy; peer counseling; benefits advisement; information and referral; housing information; consultation on architectural barriers; transportation; living skills training; employment services, and personal assistance services.

10875 Long Island Center for Independent Living
3601 Hempstead Tpke
Suite 208 & 500
Levittown, NY 11756-1331
516-796-0144
Fax: 516-520-1247
e-mail: licil@aol.com
http://www.licil.net
TTY 516-796-0135

Patricia Moore, Executive Director

The Long Island Center for Independent Living, is committed to the empowerment of consumers with disabilities. LICIL staff functions as "ambassadors" to the belief that individuals with disabilities have a responsibility to take an active role in their own lives and a self-determined view of their futures. Services include that of information and referral, advocacy, independent living skills training, and peer support.

10876 Massena Independent Living Center
156 Center Street
Massena, NY 13662-1461
315-764-9442
Fax: 315-764-9464
e-mail: mindepli@twcny.rr.com
http://www.tlcil.org
TTY 315-764-9442

Jeff Reifensnyder, Executive Director

A Æprivate non-for-profit Organization that remains true to our mandate to be Consumer controlled and operated (by and for the people with disabilities). Incorporated in 1987, MILC has assisted thousands of North Country residents to increase their independence and access to community life. The MILC hs the important but unfulfilled Mission of working to ensure that we and our nation's more than 45 million fellow people experiencing disabilities are one day able to participate in, and be considered as equals in, all areas and aspects of the American way of life.

10877 New York State Independent Living Council
111 Washington Avenue
Suite 101
Albany, NY 12210-2280
518-427-1060
888-469-7452
Fax: 518-427-1139
e-mail: nysilc@nysilc.org
http://www.nysilc.org
TTY 518-842-7106

Brad Williams, Executive Director
Joseph Adler, Public Policy Coordinator
Richard Farruggio, Advocacy/Benefits Coordinator

The New York State Independent Living Council, Inc. is made up of representatives, a majority of whom have disabilities, from around the State, who are appointed by the Board of Regents. It is a not-for-profit, non-Governmental, consumer controlled organization which monitors the federally funded Independent Living Centers in New York State, promotes the independent living philosophy statewide, and provides support and technical assistance to the entire network of Independent Living Centers (ILC) in New York State.

10878 Niagara Frontier Center for Independent Living (NFCIL)
1522 Main Street
Niagara Falls, NY 14305-2522
716-284-2452
Fax: 716-284-0829
TDD 716-284-2454

Kathleen Pautler, Executive Director
Mike DeVinney, IL Services Coordinator

Sponsors a Adult & Youth Group, deaf services, &Æprovides education advocacy. Enhancement Center for students and people who want to learn computers. Call for further information.

Independent Living Centers/New York

10879 North Country Center for Independence
102 Sharron Avenue
Plattsburgh, NY 12901-3827
518-563-9058
Fax: 518-563-0292
e-mail: andrew@ncci-online.com
http://www.ncci-online.com
TTY 518-563-9058

Andrew Pulrang, Executive Director
J. Mike Gagnier, Assistant Director
Sandra Shampang, Community Work Coordinator

The Mission of the North Country Center for Independence is to empower people with disabilities to live more independent and productive lives, and to promote beneficial policies and community understanding of disability issues. All people have value, should be treated with respect, and have the right to make choices about their own lives. People with disabilities are limited mainly by the barriers they encounter in society. If they have the knowledge, tools and freedom they need, all pepople with disabilities can live independently, carry out the responsibilities of citizenship and reach their full potential.

10880 Northern Regional Center for Independent Living
210 Court Street
Suite 107
Watertown, NY 13601-4546
315-785-8703
800-583-8703
Fax: 315-785-8612
e-mail: brendac@nrcil.net
http://www.nrcil.net
TDD 315-785-8703
TTY 877-785-8704

Brenda Campany, Executive Director
Connie Blatz, Finance Director
Kim Smith, Independent Living Program

Northern Regional Center for Independent Living is a disability rights and resource center that promotes community efforts to end discrimination, segregation, and prejudice against people with disabilities. NRCIL serves people with disabilities and their families in Jefferson and Lewis counties. Services include that of information and referral, advocacy, independent living skills training, and peer counseling.

10881 Olean Center
512 West State Street
Olean, NY 14760-2544
716-373-4602
Fax: 716-373-1382
e-mail: oleanilc@yahoo.com
TTY 716-373-4602

Leonard Liguori, Executive Director

Directions in Independent Living can help people with disabilities learn to have more control over their own lives and to live more independently in their communities. Basic core services include that of information and referral, advocacy, independent living skills training, and peer support.

10882 Queens Independent Living Center (QILC)
23-35 Broadway
Astoria, NY 11106-3220
718-204-8693
Fax: 718-393-8575
e-mail: contact@qilc.org
http://www.qilc.org
TTY 718-658-4720

Daniel Aliberti, President
Lilian Modu, Executive Director
Caterina Curatolo, Treasurer

Queens Independent Living Center/QILC is an organization dedicated to freedom and full participation in society for people with disabilities through empowerment, universal access through education and advocacy. One of the ways we accomplish this is through providing information and referral to resources within the community. Persons with disabilities can use this information to achieve their social, vocational and personal goals.

10883 Regional Center for Independent Living
497 State Street
Rochester, NY 14608
585-442-6470
Fax: 585-271-8558
e-mail: rcil@rcil.org
http://www.rcil.org
TTY 585-442-6470

Bruce Darling, Executive Director
Michele Schwartz, Programs & Service Manager
Jane Chase, Independent Living Coordinator

The mission of the Regional Center for Independent Living is to empower people with disabilities to self-advocate, to live independently and to enhance the quality of community life. Our services and programs are primarily of an advocacy nature (both individual and systems). We seek to overcome the barriers faced by people with disabilities who choose to live independently. The independent living philosophy supports persons with disabilities having opportunities to make decisions that affect their lives just as their nondisabled counterparts do.

10884 Resource Center for Accessible Living
592 Ulster Avenue
Kingston, NY 12401
845-331-0541
Fax: 914-331-2076
e-mail: rcal@hvc.rr.com
http://www.rcal.org/
TTY 845-331-8680

Susan J Hoger, Executive Director
Suzanne De Beaumont, Assistant Executive Director
Dorothy Richards, Special Education Advocate

RCAL is a non-profit, community based service and advocacy organization run by and for people with any type of disability. Since 1983, RCAL has been dedicated to assisting and empowering individuals, of all ages, to live independently and participate in all aspects of community life. RCAL, as an Independent Living Center, has a long tradition of consumer controlled and directed service delivery. This approach, combined with OMRDD's newer PersonalCentered Planning ensures that participants will get the assistance in areas of their choice. It is the RCAL's philosophy that people with disabilities can and should make their own choices and decisions, and take control of all issues that affect their daily lives-education, employment, housing, healthcare, recreation, etc.

10885 Resource Center for Independent Living
409 Columbia Street
PO Box 210
Utica, NY 13503-0210
315-797-4642
Fax: 315-797-4747
e-mail: rcil@rcil.com
http://www.rcil.com
TDD 315-797-5837

Burton J Danovitz, Executive Director

RCIL is a civil rights organization offering a wide range of independent living and advocacy services for and — most importantly — with people with disabilities. To support these goals, RCIL helps individuals of all ages and types of disability obtain the community supports and services they need to live independently including that of information and referral, advocacy, independent living skills training, and peer support.

10886 Resource Center for Independent Living (RCIL)
347 West Main Street
Amsterdam, NY 12010-4614
518-842-3561
Fax: 518-842-0905
e-mail: rcil@link.net
http://www.rcil.com/
TTY 518-842-3593

Ramon Rodriguez, Executive Director

Resource Center for Independent Living (RCIL) is a civil rights organization offering a wide range of independent living and advocacy services for and — most importantly — with people with disabilities. To support these goals, RCIL helps individuals of all ages and types of disability obtain the community supports and services they need to live independently. Services include that of information and referral, advocacy, independent living skills training and peer support.

Independent Living Centers/New York

10887 Rockland Independent Living Center
75 W Route 59
Suite 2130
Nanuet, NY 10954
845-624-1366
Fax: 845-624-1369
e-mail: mail@rilc.org
http://www.rilc.org
TTY 845-426-1180

Miriam Cotto, Executive Director
William Cooperman, Independent Living Specialist
Gisele Gerard, Hatian Outreach Advocate

The Rockland Independent Living Center (RILC) is a not-for profit agency serving all individuals with disabilities. RILC is one of 37 Independent Living Centers in NY State helping to promote the philosophy of consumer empowerment and control. This includes all areas of life education, recreation, employment, housing, and community involvement. RILC opened its doors in October 1986 as a result of the hard work and perseverance of several individuals who were committed to removing architectural, attitudinal and legislative barriers to accessibility.

10888 Southern Adirondack Independent Living
71 Glenwood Avenue
Queensbury, NY 12804
518-792-3537
Fax: 518-792-0979
e-mail: kannthayer@aol.com
http://www.gfilc.com
TTY 518-792-0505

Karen Thayer, RRDS Manager
Anna Livingston, Assistant Director
Shirley Dumont, Advocate

Our focus at the Glens Falls Independent Living Center is to assist individuals with disabilities to become independent empowered self-advocates. We will work within our community to remove physical and attitudinal barriers that stand in the way of independence. The Center will promote the concepts of self-determination and person centered planning for work, leisure and life. Services include that of information and referral, advocacy, independent living and peer support.

10889 Staten Island Center for Independent Living
470 Castleton Avenue
Staten Island, NY 10301-2118
718-720-9016
Fax: 718-720-9664
e-mail: dorothy.doran@verizon.net
http://www.geocities.com/siciliving.com
TTY 718-720-9870

Dorothy M Doran, Executive Director
Paul Stallone, Community Housing
Richard Young, Benefits/Community Resources

The Staten Island Center for Independent Living (SICIL) mission is to provide all individuals with the information, life skills training, and facilitatitve assistance which contributes to independence, individuality, and integrationin the community and provides the skills and knowledge necessary to function in the least restrictive, personally fulfilling, most self reliant and productive manner. SICIL is committed to providing the support, information and resources necessary for people with disabilities to enjoy lives determined by their choices and preferences.

10890 Taconic Resources for Independence
82 Washington Street
Suite 214
Poughkeepsie, NY 12601-2305
914-452-3913
Fax: 914-485-3196
http://www.taconicresources.net
TTY 914-485-8110

Cynthia Fiore, Executive Director
Patrick Muller, MSW, Program Director

Taconic Resources for Independence, Inc. (TRI) is a center for independent living. TRI serves Dutchess County New York. Our services are familes, friends, and our community. TRI is one of over 38 centers for Independent Living (CIL's) in New York State. We are base-funded by the New York State Department of Education (VESID). We are mandated to be consumer-direct, and community oriented. Our goals are to assist people with disability to be as active, and independent as the desire, and educate, and involve our community in disability issues. TRI's staff is comprised of 75% persons with disabilities. Our Board of Directors is made up of 51% people with disabilities.

10891 Westchester Disabled on the Move
984 North Broadway
Suite L-1
Yonkers, NY 10701
914-968-4717
Fax: 914-968-6137
e-mail: info@wdom.org
http://www.wdom.org
TDD 914-968-4717
TTY 914-968-4717

Melvin Tanzman, Executive Director
Scott Smith, Program Director
Scott Barbar, Work Incentives Coordinator

Westchester Disabled on the Move is a notfor-profit community based organization. It is a non-residentail center for people with disabilities. WDOMI is part of a network of Independent Living Centers dedicated to independence and equal rights for individuals with disabilities. Westchester Disabled On the Move, Inc. is staffed and governed primarily by people with disabilities. The programs and services of WDOMI are free to consumers with disabilities and their families. WDOMI does not discriminate based on age, sex, disability, race or ethnicity, sexual orientation or religion.

10892 Westchester Independent Living Center
200 Hamilton Avenue
White Plains, NY 10601-1812
914-682-3926
Fax: 914-682-8518
http://www.wilc.org
TDD 914-682-0926

Joseph Bravo, Executive Director
Mildred Caballero Ho, Deputy Executive Director
Rick Romash, Fiscal Director

The Westchester Independent Living Center, Inc. (WILC) is a not-for-profit, community-based advocacy and resource center that serves people with all types of disabilities. It is part of a national network of centers that provide a wide spectrum of non-residential and non-medical services including that of information and referral, advocacy, independent living skills training, and peer support.

10893 Western New York Independent Living Project
3108 Main Street
Buffalo, NY 14214-1384
716-836-0822
Fax: 716-835-3967
e-mail: info@wnyilp.org
http://www.wnyilp.org
TDD 716-836-0822
TTY 713-836-0822

Douglas Usiak, President

The Western New York Independent Living Project, Inc. (WNYILP) a Family of Agencies is a multi-cultural, grassroots, peer directed, civil rights organization that provides a full range of assistance, programs and services to enhance the quality of life for all individuals with disabilities. The WNYILP Board of Directors, Native American Independent Living Services Council, Mental Health Peer Connection Council, staff and volunteers, comprised ofa majority of persons with disabilities, operate a professional and efficient organization creating opportunities for choice, independence and community participation. This is accomplished by eliminating physical and attitudinal barriers and facilitating transportation and communication access in our community. The WNYILP assists persons with disabilities to realize their life choices through information and referral, independent living skills,individual and systems advocacy, peer counseling, advocacy empowerment programs, self-help, leadership development, support to families and community education and partnerships.

Independent Living Centers/Ohio

Ohio

10894 Ability Center of Greater Toledo
5605 Monroe Street
Sylvania, OH 43560-2793
419-885-5733
866-885-5733
Fax: 419-882-4813
e-mail: tharrington@abilitycenter.org
http://www.abilitycenter.org
TTY 419-885-5733

Tim Harrington, Executive Director
Lisa Justice, Assistant To Executive Director
Dale Able, Director Of Program Development

The Ability Center is a non-profit independent living center in Northwest Ohio. The Center serves seven Ohio counties: Defiance, Fulton, Henry, Lucas, Ottawa, Williams and Wood; with satellite offices in Defiance and Ottawa counties. Our mission is to assist people with disabilities to live their lives as independently as possible. We do this by providing several core services including that of information and referral, advocacy, independent living skills training, and peer support.

10895 Access Center for Independent Living
35 South Jefferson Street
Dayton, OH 45402-2012
937-341-5202
Fax: 937-341-5217
e-mail: alan@acils.com
http://www.acils.com
TTY 937-341-5218

Alan Cochrun, Executive Director
Greg Kramer, Senior IL Specialist/Assist. Dir
Maria Matzik, Events Coordinator

The mission of the Access Center for Independent Living (ACIL) is to ensure that people with disabilities have full and complete access to the community in which they reside. The four core programs provided by the Center are that of advocacy, information and referral, independent living skills training, and peer support.

10896 Center for Independent Living Options (CILO)
632 Vine Street
Suite 305
Cincinnati, OH 45202
513-241-2600
Fax: 513-241-1707
e-mail: cilo@cilo.net
http://www.cilo.net
TTY 513-241-7170

Lin Laing, Executive Director
Kate Lyons, Advocacy Coordinator
Suzanne Hopkins, Program Director

The Center for Independent Living Options (CILO) is dedicated to helping individuals who have physical, sensory, cognitive, and/or psychological disabilities to maintain active, productive lives of their choosing. In fact, we are who we serve. We are governed, managed, and staffed by a majority of professionals with disabilities. This gives us personal insight into the issues that people with disabilities face. Our mission is to break down architectural and attitudinal barriers, build bridges to understanding, and create options and choices in the continuous process of empowerment of persons with disabilities.

10897 Services for Independent Living
25100 Euclid Avenue BraeBurn Building
Suite 105
Cleveland, OH 44117-2650
216-731-1529
Fax: 216-731-3083
e-mail: sil@sil-oh.org
http://www.sil-oh.org
TTY 216-731-1529

Lynn Hildebrand, Manager

Established in 1980, Services for Independent Living, Inc., is a nonprofit independent living center providing services and advocacy for persons with disabilities in Cuyahoga, Lake, Geauga and Lorain counties. The goal of SIL is to ensure that people with disabilities have the same opportunities and choices available to others in areas such as public access, education, employment, housing, transportation and recreation.

10898 Society for Equal Access Independent Living Center
1458 5th St. NW
New Philadelphia, OH 44663-1224
330-343-3668
888-213-4452
Fax: 330-343-3721
e-mail: drenicker@seailc.org
TDD 330-602-2557

Diane Renicker, Executive Director

The Society for Equal Access works with individuals with disabilities to help them become more independent. Our agency assists with Peer Support, Advocacy, Information and Referral and Independent Living Skills. Our goal is to move individuals with disabilties in the direction of independence and help them become active members within the community.

10899 Tri-County Independent Living Center
680 East Market Street
Suite 205
Akron, OH 44304-1640
330-762-0007
Fax: 330-762-7416
e-mail: rose@tcilc.org
http://www.tcilc.org
TTY 800-750-0750

Rose Juriga, Executive Director

Founded in 1985, Tri-County Independent Living Center, Inc. is a non-residential, non-profit 501(c)(3) organization whose Board of Directors and staff is comprised of a majority of persons with various disabilities. Tri-County's mission is to empower citizens with disabilities to be in charge of their lives and participate as members of their communities. Through our collective strength, we advocate for the elimination of societal barriers and strive to achieve community accessibility and acceptance. Services include that of information and referral, advocacy, independent living skills training, community education and technical assistance, and peer support.

Oklahoma

10900 Ability Resources
823 South Detroit Avenue
Suite 110
Tulsa, OK 74120-4223
918-592-1235
800-722-0886
Fax: 918-592-5651
e-mail: clawson@ability-resources.org
http://www.ability-resources.org

Carla Lawson, Executive Director
Debby Newman, Office Manager
Tita Talbot, Finance Manager

Ability Resources' mission is to assist people with disabilities in attaining and maintaining their personal independence. One way this can be achieved is in the creation of an environment in which people with disabilities can exercise their rights to control and direct their own lives. Services include that of information and referral, advocacy, independent living skills training, and peer support.

10901 Green County Independent Living Resource Center
4100 South East Adams Road
Suite C-105
Bartlesville, OK 74006-8438
918-335-1314
800-559-0567
Fax: 918-333-1814
e-mail: vhaws@bartnet.net
TTY 800-559-0567

Vicki Haws, Executive Director

The Green County Independent Living Center is a resource center that provides information and referral for disability needs, peer counseling, advocacy and independent living skills training.

10902 Oklahomans For Independent Living
601 East Carl Albert Parkway
McAlester, OK 74501-5410
918-426-6220
800-568-6821
Fax: 918-426-3245
e-mail: r-mike-ward@sbcglobal.net
TTY 918-426-6220

Mike Ward, Executive Director

Organization providing services to people with disabilities and education to te community on disability-related topics.

10903 Progressive Independence
121 N Porter Avenue
Norman, OK 73071-5834
405-321-3203
Fax: 405-321-7601
e-mail: jhughes@progind.org
http://www.progind.org
TTY 405-321-2942

Jeff Hughes, Executive Director

Offers information and referrals, advocacy, peer counseling and independent living skills training.

10904 Sandra Beasley Independent Living Center
705 S Oakwood Road
Suite B1
Enid, OK 73703-6276
580-237-8508
800-375-4358
Fax: 580-233-6403
e-mail: sbilcdirector@coxinet.net
http://http://members.tripod.com/%7ELew_3/index

Frieda Kliewer, Executive Director

The Center is designed to provide access to programs and services that enable people of all disabilities to realize the freedom to choose their personal, independent living styles. The Center assists people with all types of disabilities such as people with mobility impairments, people with hearing impairments and deaf-blindness, people with vision impairments and people with mental, cognitive or developmental disabilities.

Oregon

10905 Eastern Oregon Center for Independent Living
1021 SW 5th Avenue
Ontario, OR 97914
541-889-3119
866-248-8369
Fax: 541-889-4647
e-mail: eocil@eocil.org
http://www.eocil.org
TTY 541-889-3119

Kirt Toombs, Executive Director

Eastern Oregon Center for Independent Living (EOCIL) is a nonprofit community-based resource and advocacy center that promotes independent living and equal access for all persons with disabilities. Based in Ontario, Oregon, with a second office in Pendleton, it serves consumers in 10 eastern Oregon counties. EOCIL operates from a philosophy of consumer control, peer models and self-advocacy. The desired outcome of all EOCIL independent living services is to improve the individual's ability to function, continue functioning, or move toward functioning independently in his or her family or community.

10906 Independent Living Resources, Inc. (ILR)
2410 Southeast 11th Avenue
Portland, OR 97214
503-232-7411
Fax: 503-232-7480
e-mail: ilrpdx@qwest.net
http://www.ilr.org
TDD 503-232-8408
TTY 503-232-8408

Barry Quamee, Executive Director

Independent Living Resources (ILR) is a non-profit organization dedicated to helping people with disabilities. The agency provides services using both staff and volunteers. By offering the core services of Advocacy, Information and Referral, Peer Counseling, and Skills Training, ILR continues to help over 3000 people annually. Its mission is to promote the philosophy of Independent Living by creating opportunities, encouraging choices, advancingequal access, and furthering the level of independence for all people with disabilities.

10907 SPOKES Unlimited
415 Main Street
Klamath Falls, OR 97601-6003
541-883-7547
Fax: 541-885-2469
e-mail: info@spokesunlimited.org
http://www.spokesunlimited.org
TTY 541-883-7547

Wendy Howard, Executive Director

Offers information and referrals, advocacy, peer counseling and independent living skills training.

Pennsylvania

10908 Anthracite Region Center for Independent Living
8 West Broad Street
Suite 228
Hazleton, PA 18201-7801
570-455-9800
800-777-9906
Fax: 570-455-1731
e-mail: info@anthracitecil.org
http://www.anthracitecil.org
TDD 800-777-9906
TTY 570-455-9800

Carol Duda, Executive Director
Susan Kennedy, Program Director
Gail Barnhorst, PAS Manager

The mission of the Anthracite Region Center for Independent Living is to enable individuals with disabilities to attain their highest possible level of independence.

10909 Berks County Center for Independent Living
899 Penn Avenue
Suite 2
Sinking Spring, PA 19608
610-670-0734
800-732-6871
Fax: 610-670-0753

Offers informantion and referrals, advocacy, peer counseling and independent living skills training

10910 Center for Independent Living of Central Pennsylvania
207 House Avenue
Suite 107
Camp Hill, PA 17011-4908
717-731-1900
800-323-6060
Fax: 717-731-8150
e-mail: office@cilcp.org
TTY 717-737-1335

Theotis Braddy, Executive Director

The Center For Independent Living of Central Pennsylvania (CILCP)is a non-profit, nonresidential organization established for and by people with disabilities. To empower people with disabilities to fully participate in all aspects of society is the guiding principal of the CILCP. The mission of the Center is to advance the rights of persons with disabilities through the elimination and prevention of barriers that people with disabilities experience. Community participation is an integral part of the Center's activities.

Independent Living Centers/Pennsylvania

10911 Center for Independent Living of SouthCentral Pennsylvania
1630 9th Avenue
Altoona, PA 16602-2416
814-949-1905
800-237-9009
Fax: 814-949-1909
e-mail: cilspca@msn.com
http://www.cilspca.org
TTY 814-949-1905

Susan Estep, Executive Director

The mission of the Center for Independent Living Of South Central pennsylvanis is to empower people with disabilities to lead independent lives in their communities.

10912 Citizens for Independence and Access
150 Roosevelt Avenue
Suite 300
York, PA 17401-9311
717-840-9653
800-956-0099
Fax: 717-840-9748
e-mail: hhillary@verizon.net
TDD 717-840-9753

Hillary Hasson, Executive Director

10913 Community Resources for Independence
2222 Filmore Avenue
Erie, PA 16506-2943
814-838-7222
800-530-5541
Fax: 814-835-5104
http://www.crinet.org
TTY 814-838-8115

Timothy Finegan, Executive Director

Mission statement of the Community Resources for Independence, Inc. is that the we will strive, in partnership with others, to empower people with disabilities to become fully integrated into society.

10914 Freedom Valley Disability Enablement
3607 Chapel Road
Newtown Square, PA 19073-3602
610-353-6640
800-427-4754
Fax: 610-353-6753
e-mail: facopcfvdc@msn.com
TDD 610-353-6753
TTY 610-353-8900

Ann Cope, Executive Director

Offers information and referrals, advocacy, peer counseling, and independent living skills training.

10915 Lehigh Valley Center for Independent Living
435 Allentown Drive
Allentown, PA 18109
610-770-9781
800-495-8245
Fax: 610-770-9801
e-mail: info@lvcil.org
http://www.lvcil.org
TTY 610-770-9789

Amy Beck, Executive Director
Robert Graves, Assistant Director
Corrina Passaro, Development Coordinator

The Lehigh Valley Center for Independent Living, Inc. (LVCIL) is proud to be one of Pennsylvania's 18 centers for Independent Living. LVCIL is a private non-profit organization. We are both staffed and governed, at all times, by a majority of persons with disabilities. All Centers for Independent Living place the greatest emphasis on consumer self-determination, we are not here to make decisions for our consumers, but to provide information and resources to allow consumers to make independent decisions. We also work to increase inclusion in our community whether it is in housing, transportation, voting rights, employment, or many other ideas.

10916 Liberty Resources
714 Market Street
Suite 100
Philadelphia, PA 19106
215-634-2000
888-634-2155
Fax: 215-634-6628
e-mail: lrinc@libertyresources.org
http://www.libertyresources.org
TDD 215-634-6630

Thomas Earl, Owner

Liberty Resources, Inc. is a non-profit, Consumer driven organization that advocates and promotes Independent Living for persons with disabilities. More than 50 percent of our Board as well as 50 percent of our employees are persons with disabilities. Liberty Resources, Inc. is the Center for Idependent Living for the Philadelphia area, which advocates for and works with persons with disabilities to ensure their civil rights and equal access to all aspects of live in our community. It is our hope that the Center will be seen as the major point of entry into the community for people with disabilities, in Philadelphia and the surrounding area, a place where an individual can make contact and receive the services they need, or are referred to appropriate organizations in the community.

10917 Life and Independence for Today
503 E Arch Street
Saint Marys, PA 15857-1779
814-781-3050
800-341-5438
Fax: 814-781-1917
e-mail: lift@liftcil.org
http://www.liftcil.org

Kelly Valdez, Advocacy Specialist
Jill Rhoades, Independent Living Coordinator
Dawn Park, Information & Referral Spclist.

Life and Independence for Today (LIFT) is a non-profit organization developed by people with disabilities for people with disabilities. As a Center for Independent Living (CIL) LIFT offers services to enable people with disabilities to achieve new goals and broaded their horizons. It enables them to achieve and maintain self-sufficient and productive lives. Most services are provided free of charge and availiable to all age groups.

10918 Northeast Pennsylvania Center for Independent Living
431 Wyoming Avenue
Scranton, PA 18503-1228
570-344-7211
800-344-7211
Fax: 717-344-7218
e-mail: nepacilinfo@nepacil.org
http://www.nepacil.org
TTY 570-344-5275

Daniel Loftus, Executive Director

The Northeast Pennsylvania Center for Independent Living was established to assist in removing barriers and expanding independent living options availiable to people with disabilities in the counties of Bradford, Columbia, Lackawanna, Luzerne, Monroe, Pike, Sullivan, Susquehanna, Wayne and Wyoming. The individual controls and directs the services he or she receives to establish a more independent lifestyle.

10919 Three Rivers Center for Independent Living
900 Rebecca Avenue
Pittsburgh, PA 15221
412-371-7700
800-633-4588
Fax: 412-371-9430
http://www.trcil.org
TTY 412-371-6230

Stan Holbrook, Executive Director

The mission of the Three Rivers Center for Independent Living is to empower people with disabilities to enjoy self-directed, personally meaningful lives by providing outstanding consumer controlled services and by advocating for effective community change.

Independent Living Centers/Rhode Island

10920 Tri-County Partnership for Independent Living
69 E Beau Street
Washington, PA 15301-4711
724-223-5115
Fax: 724-223-5119
http://www.tripil.com
TTY 724-228-4028

Kathleen Kleinmann, Chief Executive Officer
Jeffry D. Woods, IT Director
Jorge Martich, Systems Administrator

The mission/purpose of TRPIL is to teach ourselves about the past, present, and future prospects of the Independent living movement as part of the disability and equal rights movement; to share ideas towards the building of a common vision for Independent Living in Pennsylvania; and to strengthen our sense of community and common purpose as part of the local, state, national, and international independent living movement.

Rhode Island

10921 Ocean State Center for Independent Living
1944 Warwick Avenue
Warwick, RI 02289
401-738-1013
866-857-1161
Fax: 401-738-1083
e-mail: info@oscil.org
http://www.oscil.org
TTY 401-738-1015

Lorna Ricci, Executive Director

Ocean State Center for Independent Living (OSCIL) is a consumer controlled, community based, nonprofit organization established to provide a range of independent living services to enhance, through self direction, the quality of life of Rhode Islanders with significant disability and to promote integration into the community.

10922 PARI Independent Living Center
500 Prospect Street
Pawtucket, RI 02860-6259
401-725-1966
Fax: 401-725-2104
e-mail: info@pari-ilc.org
http://www.pari-ilc.org
TDD 401-725-1966

Leo Canuel, Executive Director

PARI was incorporated in 1980 as a "consumer directed" Independent Living Center. Our staff works with people with any kind of disability to identify goals and provide training, equipment, advocacy, and counseling to help them to achieve their goals. Whether the consumer is seeking medical resources, new ways of performing activities of daily life, transportation, housing, or ways of becoming involved in the community, the PARI Independent Living Center is the individual's professional resource for reaching independence. The Independent Living Center is a unique concept in non-residential resources for the person with a disability. PARI is a private, not for profit, community based agency whose programs and policies are determined by people with disabilities.

Tennessee

10923 Center for Independent Living of Middle Tennessee
480 Craighead Street
Suite 200
Nashville, TN 37204-2343
615-292-5803
866-992-4568
Fax: 615-383-1176
e-mail: cilmt@tndisability.org
http://www.cil-mt.org
TTY 615-292-7790

Tom Hopton, Executive Director

A community-based non-residential program of services designed to assist persons with disabilities gain independence and to assist the community in eliminating barriers to independence.

10924 Jackson Center for Independent Living
191 Hollywood Drive
Jackson, TN 38305-2743
731-668-2211
Fax: 901-668-0406
e-mail: jcil05-spamguard@yahoo.com
http://www.j-cil.com
TTY 731-668-2211

Glen Barr, Executive Director

The Jackson Center for Independent Living (JCIL) is a nonprofit, tax deductible United Way agency. We work with people with significant disabilities and the Deaf Community in achieving their Independent Living goals while assisting the community in eliminating barriers to Independent Living.

10925 Memphis Center for Independent Living
1633 Madison Avenue
Memphis, TN 38104-2506
901-726-6404
Fax: 901-726-6521
e-mail: mcil@mcil.org
http://www.mcil.org

Deborah Cunningham, Executive Director
Sandi Klink, Assistant Director
Renee Ford, Office Manager

The Memphis Center for Independent Living works so that people with disabilities in the Memphis area may live independently. We believe that there is nothing more disabling then pity. People with disabilities are a powerful and significant part of the community, yet; as a group our social roles have been marginalized by bigotry, discrimination, poverty, isolation, dependency and pity. Americans with disabilities have not had access to transportation, housing and employment that other citizens have enjoyed; MCIL will change that.

Texas

10926 ABLE
3415 Brentwood
Odessa, TX 79761
432-580-3439
Fax: 432-580-0208
e-mail: info@ablecenterpb.org
http://http://ablecenterpb.org

Marylin Hancock M.Ed, Executive Director
Daniel Panter B.S., Transition/Relocation Specialist
Kathleen Story M.A., Independent Living Specialist

ABLE is dedicated to the idea that everyone should be living life to its fullest potential. We provide activities, education, and peer counseling for undividual desiring to soar above all expectations. ABLE is about focusing on abilities. ABLE teaches people to live independently, assists in providing support to promote independence.

10927 Center on Independent Living
2525 Ladd Street
Building 3850
Lackland AFB, TX 78236
210-671-7959
Fax: 210-671-7953
http://www.coil.org

Kim Biggs, Office Manager

Through evaluation and development of individual needs, COIL reaches out, encompassing many areas of physical disabilities. Over the years COIL has expanded to help not only those with congenital disabilites but also thouse with acquired disabilities. COIL passionately believes that all people should have the opportunity to beling and be accepted by a community. Living independently instead of being institutionalized can bring about many changes.

Independent Living Centers/Utah

10928 Coalition for Barrier Free Living: Houston Center for Independent Living
6201 Bonhomme Road
Suite 150 South
Houston, TX 77036
713-974-4621
Fax: 713-974-6927
e-mail: hcil@neosoft.com
http://www.coalitionforbarrierfreeliving.com
TTY 713-974-4621

Sandra Bookman, Executive Director
Tony Koosis, Director Programs/Services

Advocacy organization for people with disabilities. Mission is to promote the full inclusion, equal opportunity and participation of persons with disabilities in every aspect of community life. We believe that people with disabilities have the right to make choices affecting their lives, a right to take risks, a right to fail, and a right to succeed

10929 DARE
8929 Viscount Boulevard
Suite 101
El Paso, TX 79925-5823
915-591-0800
Fax: 915-591-3506
TDD 915-591-0800

Thomas Carter, Executive Director

10930 REACH of Dallas Resource Center on Independent Living
8625 King George Drive
Suite 210
Dallas, TX 75235-2275
214-630-4796
Fax: 214-630-6390
e-mail: reachdallas@reachcils.org
http://www.reachcils.org
TDD 214-630-5995

Charlotte Stewart, Executive Director
Susan Reukema, Assistant Director
Julie Espinoza, Skills Training Specialist

REACH is a nonprofit organization with the goal of advocating for and empowering people with disabilities to take charge of their lives and participate actively in community life. The centers are non-residential resource agencies which provide services for people with disabilities and education to the community on disability related topics. The Centers are governed and staffed by a majority of people with disabilities who bring a wide range of knowledge and experience to their work in assisting other people with disabilities.

10931 Reach Resource Center on Independent Living
1205 Lake Street
Fort Worth, TX 76102-4501
817-870-9082
Fax: 817-877-1622
e-mail: reachftw@reachcils.org
http://www.reachcils.org
TTY 817-870-9086

Charlotte Stewart, Executive Director
Robin Lassiter, Assistant Director
Karen Williams, Community Living Specialist

REACH is a nonprofit organization with the goal of advocating for and empowering people with disabilities to take charge of their lives and participate actively in community life. REACH centers are non-residential resource agencies which provide services for people with disabilities and education to the community on disability related topics. The Centers are governed and staffed by a majority of people with disabilities who bring a wide range of knowledge and experience to their work in assisting other people with disabilities.

10932 Reach of Denton Resource Center on Independent Living
405 S Elm Street
Suite 202
Denton, TX 76201-6068
940-383-1062
Fax: 817-383-2742
e-mail: reachden@reachcils.org
http://www.reachcils.org
TDD 817-383-1062

Charlotte Stewart, Executive Director
Missy Dickenson, Assistant Director
Murphy Hardinger, Independent Living Specialist

REACH Inc. is a nonprofit organization with the goal of advocating for and empowering people with disabilities to take charge of their lives and participate actively in community life. REACH Centers are non-residential resource agencies which provide services for people with disabilities and education to the community on disability related topics. The Centers are governed and staffed by a majority of people with disabilities who bring a wide range of knowledge and experience to their work in assisting other people with disabilities.

10933 SAILS
1028 S Alamo Street
San Antonio, TX 78210-1170
210-281-1878
800-474-0295
Fax: 210-281-1759
http://www.sailstx.org
TDD 210-281-1878

Kitty Britzke, Executive Director
Gloria Banik, Director Of Programs
Ricardo Rivas, Accountant

San Antonio Independent Living Center (SAILS) is a non-profit and federally designated Center for Independent Living aimed at those who reside in the Bexar county and 27 additional counties area. SAILS helps individuals with any disability: mental, physical, cognitive, or sensory, We can assist you or your family member by teaching independent living skills, providing up-to-date information and referrals, and training individuals on how to advocate for themselves.

Utah

10934 OPTIONS for Independence-Northern Utah Center For Independent Living
1095 N Main Street
Logan, UT 84341-2215
435-753-5353
Fax: 435-753-5390
e-mail: jbiggs@optionsind.org
http://www.optionsind.org
TTY 435-753-5353

Cheryl Atwood, Executive Director

OPTIONS for Independence (OPTIONS) is a nonresidential Independent Living Center where people with disabilities can learn skills to gain more control ovand independence over their lives. The mission of OPTIONS for Independence is to raise the vision and capability of the community at large to the point where people of all abilities will have equal access.

10935 Tri-County Independent Living Center
2726 Washington Blvd. (Rear)
Ogden, UT 84401
801-612-3215
866-734-5678
Fax: 801-612-3732
http://www.tri-county-ilc.com
TTY 801-612-3215

Andy Curry, Executive Director

The mission of the Tri-County Independent Living Council is to enhance independent living for all persons with disabilities.

Independent Living Centers/Virginia

10936 Utah Independent Living Center
3445 S Main Street
Salt Lake City, UT 84115-4453
801-466-5565
800-355-2195
Fax: 801-466-2363
e-mail: uilc@xmission.com
http://www.uilc.org
TDD 801-466-5565

Debra Mair, Executive Director
Patty Trent, Fiscal Manager
Debbie Lambrose, Secretary/Receptionist

The Utah Independent Living Center (UILC) is a private, non-profit, non-residential facility that teaches independent living skills to people with disabilities. The UILC was the first center in Utah and has been serving the community since 1982. The UILC is committed to providing services needed by people with disabilities to function more independently in their families and communities. In order to be eligible to receive UILC services, a person must have a physical of mental disability which impairs activities of daily living and a reasonable expectation exists that UILC services will increase independence.

10937 Utah Statewide Independent Living Council
1800 SW Temple
Suite 208
Salt Lake City, UT 84115-5817
801-463-1592
Fax: 801-463-1683
e-mail: byoung@usilc.org
http://www.usilc.org
TDD 801-463-1592

William Young, Executive Director
Cara Baldree, Office Manager

The Utah Statewide Independent Living Council is a private, nonprofit organization. The USILC mission is to promote full inclusion, independence and empowerment of people with disabilities through advocacy/system change, planning/organization, education, networking, resource development and independent living service enhancement.

Virginia

10938 Appalachian Independence Center
230 Charwood Drive
Abingdon, VA 24210-2566
276-628-2979
Fax: 540-628-4931
e-mail: aicadmin@ntelos.net
http://www.aicadvocates.org
TTY 276-676-0920

Greg Morrell, Executive Director
Scarlett Cox, Operations Director
Donna Buckland, Development Director

Appalachian Independence Center, Inc. (AIC) was founded in 1988 by a group of local citizens who had a desire to make sure services were availiable to people with disabilities and to help them learn about community services specific to their needs. AIC s a non-profit, non residential center for independent living which receives some of its funding from the State of Virginia and United Way. However, it is an independent organization governed by aboard of directors made up of local citizens, a majority of whom have disabilities themselves. This assures that AIC is in touch with the needs of people with disabilities in our community.

10939 Blue Ridge Independent Living Center
1502 Williamson Road NE
D
Roanoke, VA 24012-5100
540-342-1231
Fax: 540-342-9505
e-mail: sgarst@brilc.org
http://www.brilc.org
TTY 540-342-1231

Karen Michalski Karney, Executive Director
Wayne Anderson, Independent Living Coordinator
Lottie Diomedi, Independent Living Coordinator

The Blue Ridge Independent Living Center assists people with disabilities to live independently. The Center also serves the community at large by helping to create an environment that is accessible to all. The Center, established in 1989, is a private, non-profit community agency with non-residential programs. Support for service is received from state and federal sources and donations from regional business and individuals. The Center is governed by a Board of Directors with a majority of members having disabilities.

10940 Endependence Center
6300 E Virginia Beach Boulevard
Norfolk, VA 23502-2827
757-461-8007
Fax: 757-455-8223
e-mail: ecinorf@endependence.org
http://www.endependence.org
TDD 757-461-7527

Stephen Johnson, Executive Director

The Endependence Center, Incorporated (ECI) is a consumer controlled, community-based, cross-disability, non-residential, private, non-profit Center for Independent Living (CIL) operated by and for individuals with disabilities in South Hampton Roads, including the cities of Chesapeake, Norfolk, Portsmouth, Franklin, Suffolk, Virginia Beach and Isle of Wight County. ECI provides an array of independent living services to individuals with disabilities and to the community. The purposes of the ECI are 2 fold; to prepare individuals and to prepare the community for full integration of persons with disabilities into society.

10941 Endependence Center of Northern Virginia
3100 Clarendon Boulevard
Arlington, VA 22201-3001
703-525-3268
Fax: 703-525-3585
e-mail: info@ecnv.org
http://www.ecnv.org
TTY 703-525-3553

David Burds, Executive Director
Seville Allen, Peer Counselor
Sandra Bastidas, Personal Care Assistant

ENDependence Center of Northern Virginia (ECNV) is a community-based resource and advocacy center which is managed by and for people with disabilities. ECNV promotes independent living (IL) philosophy and equal access for all persons with disabilities and, like the nearly 400 centers for independent living across the country, ECNV grew from local disability rights and self help movements. We operate from a philosophy of consumer controll and peer-to-peer relationships to empower people with physical, mental, cognitive and sensory disabilities to direct their own lives.

10942 Independence Resource Center
815 Cherry Avenue
Charlottesville, VA 22903-3448
434-971-9629
Fax: 804-971-8242
e-mail: tvandever@ntelos.net
TTY 434-971-9629

Thomas Vandever, Executive Director

10943 Junction Center for Independent Living
PO Box 419
Big Stone Gap, VA 24219
540-523-1797
Fax: 540-523-2103
http://www.junctioncenter.org
TDD 540-523-1798

Dennis Horton, Executive Director

JCIL's mission is to assist people who have significant disabilities to live independently in the least restrictive and most integrated environment possible. The Junction Center for Independent Living is a non-profit, non-residential program which provides services to persons with disabilities, their families, and their community.

Independent Living Centers/Vermont

10944 Peninsula Center for Independent Living
2021-A Cunningham Drive
Suite 2
Hampton, VA 23666-3326
757-827-0275
Fax: 757-827-0655
e-mail: icpcil@iepcil.org
http://www.iepcil.org
TDD 757-827-8800

Ralph Shelman, CEO

The Centers Philosophy is that people with a disability should play a major role in deciding their future. A coalition of professionals working in the fields of education, Rehabilitation and community services can be instrumental in effecting true independence for people with a disabilitiy.

10945 Resources For Independent Living
4009 Fitzhugh Avenue
Suite 100
Richmond, VA 23230-3953
804-353-6503
Fax: 804-358-5606
e-mail: info@ril-va.org
http://www.ril-va.org
TDD 804-353-6583

Sandra Wagener, Executive Director

The Central Virginia Independent Living Center, Inc. (CVILC) was established in February, 1983. It is a community based, non-profit, non-residential program which provides services to persons with a disability, their family, and the community. In 2003, we changed our name to Resources for Independent Living to better reflect our mission. Our mission is assisting persons who are severely disabled to live independently in the community and to encourage necessary change within the community so independent living is a possiblitly.

Vermont

10946 Vermont Center for Independent Living
11 E State Street
Montpelier, VT 05602-3008
802-229-0501
800-639-1522
e-mail: vcil@vcil.org
http://www.vcil.org
TTY 802-229-0501

Deborah Lisi-Baker, Executive Director
Janet Dermody, Deputy Director
Nancy Dulac, Finance & Operations Officer

The Vermont Center for Independent Living (VCIL) works to promote the dignity, independence, and civil rights of Vermonters with disabilities. VCIL is committed to cross-disability services, the promotion of active citizenship, and working with others to create services that support self-determination and full participation in community life. Founded in 1979, VCIL is a statewide, nonprofit organization directed and staffed by individuals with disabilities. VCIL believes that individuals with disabilities have the right to live with dignity and with appropriate support in their own homes, fully participate in their communities, and to control and make decisions about their lives.

Washington

10947 Central Washington Disability Resources
422 N Pine Street
Ellensburg, WA 98926-3312
509-962-9620
800-240-5978
Fax: 509-933-1571
e-mail: marianne@cwdrinfo.org
http://www.cwdrinfo.org

Von Elison, Executive Director

Central Washington Disability Resources (CWDR) is committed to supporting opportunities, Locating resources, furthering self-advocacy for individuals with disabilities so that they may realize independence and full participation in all areas of life. Our goal is to enhance individual's abilities to live independently and to increase opportunities for full participation in the family & community. Independent living is the freedom to take risks andto make mistakes.

10948 Disability Resource Connection
607 SE Everett Mall Way
Suite 6C
Everett, WA 98208-3265
425-347-5768
800-315-3583
Fax: 206-710-0767
e-mail: drcservices@drconline.net
http://www.drconline.net

Sean Barrett, Manager

DRC is an organization run and controlled by persons with disabilities. As a community based center, people with disabilities receive assistance with a variety of daily living issues and learn the skills they need to take control of their lives, often assisted by people who have had similar experiences living with a disability.

10949 Independent Living Resource Southwest Washington
2700 NE Andersen Rd
Suite D5
Vancouver, WA 98662
360-694-6790
Fax: 360-882-1324
e-mail: disabilityresources@darsw.com
http://www.darsw.com
TTY 360-882-1324

Jim Baker, Executive Director

Disability Resources of Southwest Washington is a Center for Independent Living. In October of 2002 DARSW spun off of Independent Living Resources in Portland, Oregon to form a separate Independent Living Center, focusing on the specific needs in the southwest region of Washington. Our mission is empowering individuals with disabilities by creating opportunities, promoting choice, advancing equal access, educating, and furthering independent living.

West Virginia

10950 North Central West Virginia Center for Independent Living
601-603 E Brockway Avenue
Suite A26
Morgantown, WV 26505
304-296-6091
800-834-6408
http://www.nwvcil.org

Jan Derry, Executive Director

Northern West Virginia Center for Independent Living is an advocacy resource center for persons with disabilities and the communities in which they live, not a social service agency. We want our consumer to be independent, not dependent on us for their independence. We do all that is possible to ensure that consumers have the skills and information they need to make informed choices and assist communities to better meet the needs of their citizens with disabilities.

Wisconsin

10951 Access to Independence
2345 Atwood Ave.
Madison, WI 53704
608-242-8484
Fax: 608-242-0383
e-mail: info@accesstoind.org
http://www.accesstoind.org
TTY 608-242-8485

Bob Unkel, Executive Director

Independent Living Centers/Wisconsin

Access to independence promotes the integration of people with disabilities into communities, which have a wealth of opportunities. The mission of Access to Independence is to join with people with disabilities to create access to the community through education, action, and choice.

10952 Appalachian Center for Independent Living
4710 Chimney Drive
Charleston, WV 25302-4843
304-965-0376
800-642-3003
Fax: 304-965-0377
e-mail: acil@westco.net
TTY 304-965-0377

Larry E Paxton, Executive Director

10953 Center for Independent Living for Western Wisconsin
2920 Schneider Avenue East
Menomonie, WI 54751
715-233-1070
800-228-3287
Fax: 715-233-1083
e-mail: cilww@menomonie.com
http://www.cilww.com
TDD 715-233-1070

Tim Sheehan, Director
Kay Sommerfeld, Assistant Director
Tammy Grage, Fiscal & Human Resources Manager

The Center for Independent Living for Western Wisconsin (CILWW) advocates for the full participation in society of all persons with disabilities. Our goal is empowering individuals to exercise choices to maintain or increase their independence. Our strategy is providing consumer-driven services at no cost to persons with disabilities in Western Wisconsin.

10954 Independence First
600 W Virginia Street
4th Floor
Milwaukee, WI 53204-1516
414-291-7520
Fax: 414-291-7525
e-mail: lee@independencefirst.org
http://www.independencefirst.org
TTY 414-291-7520

Lee Schulz, Executive Director
Karen Avery, Associate Director
Scott Luber, Administrative Director

Independence First is a non-profit agency directed by, and for the benefit of, persons with disabilities, primarily serving the 4 country metropolitan Milwaukee area. Our agency mission is to effectively facilitate empowerment of individuals with disabilities through education, advocacy, independent living services, and coalition building. We promote diversity and multicultural participation in our operation and services.

10955 Independent Living Resources-La Crosse
4439 Mormon Coulee Road
La Crosse, WI 54601-8220
608-787-1111
888-474-5745
Fax: 608-787-1114
e-mail: advocacy@ilresources.org
http://www.ilresources.org
TTY 608-787-1148

Kathy Knoble-Iverson, Executive Director
Michelle Olson, Assistant Director
Steve Weiland, Finance Coordinator

Independent Living Resources is a non-profit agency operated by a skilled staff and board of directors composed primarily of people with disabilities. This firsthand experience with disabilities provides a unique base of expertise for effectively addressing and providing services to individuals with disabilities.

10956 Independent Living Resources-Richland
149 E Mill Street
Suite A
Richland Center, WI 53581-2261
608-647-8053
877-471-2095
Fax: 608-647-7783
e-mail: advocacy@ilresources.org
http://www.ilresources.org
TTY 608-647-8053

Kathie Knoble-Iverson, Executive Director
Michele Olson, Assistant Director
Steve Weiland, Finance Coordinator

Independent Living Resources is committed to community diversity through advocacy, choice and education resulting in empowerment for individuals with disabilities.

10957 Midstate Independent Living Consultants-Stevens Point
3262 Church Street
Stevens Point, WI 54481-5321
715-344-4210
800-382-8484
Fax: 715-344-4414
e-mail: milc@coredcs.com
http://www.milc-inc.org
TDD 715-344-4210

Jenny Fasula, Executive Director
Evelyn Buckles, Assistant Director
Laurie Lane, Program Manager

MILC is a private non-profit agency serving persons with disabilities of all ages. MILC is operated by staff and board composed primarily of people with disabilities. MILC services are consumer directed working together with staff to meet goals. You are eligible for services if you are a person with a disability and you reside in Adams, Florence, Forest, Langdale, Lincoln, Marathon, Oneida, Portage, Taylor, Vilas or Wood counties.

10958 Midstate Independent Living-Rhinelander
PO Box 369
Rhinelander, WI 54501
715-369-5040
800-311-5044
Fax: 715-369-5043
e-mail: milc@newnorth.net
http://www.milc-inc.org
TDD 715-369-5040

Jenny Fasula, Executive Director
Evelyn Buckles, Assistant Director
Laurie Lane, Program Manager

MILC is a private non-profit agency serving persons with disabilities of all ages. MILC is operated by staff and board composed primarily of people with disabilities. MILC services are consumer directed working together with staff to meet goals. You are eligible for services if you are a person with a disability and you reside in Adams, Florence, Forest, Langdale, Lincoln, Marathon, Oneida, Portage, Taylor, Vilas, or Wood counties.

10959 North County Independent Living-Ashland
422 3rd Street W
Suite 114
Ashland, WI 54806-1573
715-682-5676
800-499-5676
Fax: 715-682-3144
e-mail: ncilstew@charterinternet.com
http://www.northcountryil.com
TTY 715-682-5676

John Nedden-Durst, Disability Navigator
Stewart Holman, Independent Living Specialist

North Country Independent Living empowers people with disabilities. The mission is broad based, allowing North Country Independent Living to respond to a variety of needs. The philosophy promotes people with disabilities being active participants in daily living and being given the same opportunities and choices as others. This philosophy is promoted through consumer choice and control. People with disabilities are active participants within theagency. The majority of the Board of Directors and staff are people with disabilities.

Independent Living Centers/Wyoming

10960 North County Independent Living-Superior
2231 Catlin Avenue
Suite 16
Superior, WI 54880
715-392-9118
800-924-1220
Fax: 715-392-4636
e-mail: ncil@superior-nfp.org
http://www.northcountryil.com
TTY 715-392-9118

John Nousaine, Director
Dee Truhn, Assistant Director
Nickoel Anderson, Accountant

North Country Independent Living empowers people with disabilities. The mission is broad based, allowing North Country Independent Living to respond to a variety of needs. The philosophy promotes people with disabilities being active participants in daily living and being given the same opportunities and choices as others. This philosophy is promoted through consumer choice and control. People with disabilities are active participants within theagency. The majority of the Board of Directors and staff are people with disabilities.

10961 Options for Independent Living-Appleton
820 W College Avenue
Suite 5
Appleton, WI 54914-5275
920-997-9999
Fax: 920-997-9381
e-mail: info@optionsil.com
http://www.optionsil.com
TDD 920-997-9999

Thomas J Diedrick, Director
Kathryn C Barry, Assistant Director
Werner Burkat, Accessible Computers Technology

Options for Independent Living, Inc. is a non-profit organization committed to empowering people with disabilities to lead independent and productive lives in their community through advocacy, the provision of information, education, technology and related services. As part of the independent living philosophy of consumer directed services, Options staff will provide information so consumers can make informed choices and achieve their objectives. The direction and development of Options is determined by a Board of Directors comprised primarily of individuals with disabilities. Options is committed to hiring staff with disabilities.

10962 Options for Independent Living-Green Bay
555 Country Club Road
Po Box 11967
Green Bay, WI 54307-1967
920-490-0500
888-465-1515
Fax: 920-490-0700
e-mail: info@optionsil.com
http://www.optionsil.com
TTY 920-490-0600

Thomas J Diedrick, Director
Kathryn C Barry, Assistant Director
Werner Burkat, Accessible Computer Technology

Options for Independent Living, Inc. is a non-profit organization committed to empowering people with disabilities to lead independent and productive lives in their community through advocacy, the provision of information, education, technology and related services. As part of the independent living philosophy of consumer directed services, Options staff will provide information so consumers can make informed choices and achieve their objectives. The direction and development of Options is determined by a Board of Directors comprised primarily of individuals with disabilities. Options is committed to hiring staff with disabilities.

10963 Society's Assets-Elkhorn
615 E Geneva Street
Elkhorn, WI 53121-1738
262-723-8181
800-261-8181
Fax: 262-723-8184
http://www.sai-inc.org
TTY 262-723-8181

Bruce Nelsen, Executive Director

Society's Assets is an Independent Living Center, providing comprehensive services to assist people with living independently. Society's Assets provides assistants to seniors and people of all ages with disabilities. A skilled and experienced staff of consumers a broad range of services. Mission is to ensure the rights of all persons with disabilities to live and function as independently as possible in the community of their choice, through supporting individual's efforts to achieve control over their lives and become integrated into community life.

10964 Society's Assets-Kenosha
5727 6th Avenue
Kenosha, WI 53140-4103
262-657-3999
800-317-3999
Fax: 262-657-1672
http://www.sai-inc.org
TTY 262-657-3999

Bruce Nelsen, Executive Director

Society's Assets is an Independent Living Center, providing comprehensive services to assist people with living independently. Society's Assets provides assistance to seniors and people of all ages with disabilities. A skilled and experienced staff offer consumers a broad range of services. Mission is to ensure the rights of all persons with disabilities to live and function as independently as possible in the community of their choice, through supporting individual's efforts to achieve control over their lives and become integrated into community life.

10965 Society's Assets-Racine
5200 Washington Avenue
Suite 225
Racine, WI 53406-4238
262-637-9128
800-378-9128
Fax: 414-637-8646
http://www.sai-inc.org
TTY 262-637-9128

Bruce Nelsen, Executive Director

Society's Assets is an Independent Living Center, providing comprehensive services to assist people with living independently. Society's Assets provides assistance to seniors and people of all ages with disabilities. A skilled and experienced staff offer consumers a broad ranger of services. Mission is to ensure the rights of all persons with disabilities to live and function as independently as possible in the community of their choice, throughsupporting individual's efforts to achieve control over their lives and become integrated into community life.

10966 State Independent Living Council
Po Box 7851
Madison, WI 53707
608-261-8397
888-947-7452
Fax: 608-264-7742
e-mail: wisilc@hotmail.com
http://www.wisilc.org
TTY 608-261-8396

Scott Durin, Executive Director

The ILCW Inc. promotes self determination and full inclusion of people with disabilities in Wisconsin. We educate and advocate for policies, resources, practices, and attitudes that support independent living. We provide and support independent living philosophy and services to maximize the leadership, empowerment, and productivity of individuals with disabilities in order that each will live and participate in their community of choice.

Wyoming

10967 Wyoming Services For Independent Living
1156 South Second Street
Suite 10
Lander, WY 82520-3920
307-332-4889
800-266-3061
Fax: 307-332-2491
e-mail: wsil@wyoming.com
TTY 307-332-7582

Carol Fontaine, Executive Director

Legal Aid Resources/Alabama

This chapter is arranged by state, and includes contacts for legal protection and advocacy for both older and disabled Americans. You'll find information regarding health care, health insurance, Medicare, Medicaid, social security and other public benefits, in addition to who to contact about ethical guidelines in representing older Americans, guardianship issues, and Senior Citizens Referral Panels. See also State Organizations & Government Agencies for supplemental information.

Alabama

10968 Alabama Department of Senior Services
770 Washington Avenue
RSA Plaza, Suite 470
Montgomery, AL 36130
334-242-5743
877-425-2243
Fax: 334-242-5594
e-mail: ageline@adss.state.al.us
http://www.adss.state.al.us/
Irene B Collins, Executive Director

The Alabama Department of Senior Services received its primary funding under Title III of the Older Americans Act of 1965, as amended. Under the terms of that Legislation, the Alabama Department of Senior Services supports a network of agencies and programs throughout the State of Alabama for the following purposes: secure and maintain independence and dignity of older persons; remove social and individual barriers; assure the provision of a continuum of care for the vulnerable elderly; and develop comprehensive, coordinated systems for older persons.

10969 Alabama Disabilities Advocacy Program (ADAP)
Alabama Protection and Advocacy Agency
P O Box 870395
Tuscaloosa, AL 35487-0395
205-348-4928
800-826-1675
Fax: 205-348-3909
e-mail: adap@adap.ua.edu
http://www.adap.net
TDD 205-348-9484
Ellen Gillespie, Executive Director
James Tucker, Litigation Director
Tuwanna McGee, Senior Case Advocate

The Alabama Disabilities Advocacy Program (ADAP) is part of the nationwide federally mandated protection and advocacy (P&A) system. ADAP's mission is to provide quality, legally-based advocacy services to Alabamians with disabilities in order to protect, promote and expand their rights. ADAP's vision is one of a society where persons with disabilities are valued and exercise self-determination through meaningful choices, and have equality of opportunity.

10970 Alabama State Bar: Elder Law
415 Dexter Avenue
PO Box 671
Montgomery, AL 36014
334-269-1515
Fax: 334-261-6310
e-mail: ed.patterson@alabar.org
http://www.alabar.org
Keith B Norman, Executive Director

Formed in the early part of 1997 and the newest section of the Alabama State Bar, the Elder Law's mission is to develop, promote and enhance the quality of legal services for the elderly in Alabama.

10971 Jefferson County Office of Senior Citizens Services (OSCS)
2601 Highland Avenue
Birmingham, AL 35205
205-325-1416
Fax: 205-325-1429
http://jeffco.jccal.org/
Bettye Fine Collins, Commissioner
William M Voight, Executive Director
Lucy Lipp, Senior Aides Program Director

OSCS plans, coordinates and advocates for the development of a full array of services and programs on behalf of over 115,000 older adults currently residing in Jefferson County. Every four years OSCS prepares and implements an Area Plan to address the needs of older adults. Public Hearings are held receive information as to what the public sees as gaps in services, and suggestions for new services to meet the need. Our services are available to persons 60 years of age and older and their caregivers. Our Senior Employment Programs are available to persons 55 years of age of older. Although we do not charge a fee for our services, voluntary contributions are encouraged and are used to support and expand programs. We have no means test (no set income guidelines) for services. No one is denied service due to an inability to make a contribution. As mandated by our major funding source, the Older Americans Act, we give priority attention to serving older adults in the greatest social and /or economic need, especially minority older adults and those residing in rural areas.

10972 Legal Services for the Elderly: Area Agency on Aging
400 West Hamilton Street
Russellville, AL 35653
256-332-9173
800-232-4464
Fax: 256-381-0867
http://www.sarcoa.org/area_agencies.html
Lewis McCray, Executive Director
Pamela McDaniel, Area Agency Director

The Area Agency on Aging seeks to keep area seniors independent, active and healthy through the many available services including legal assistance, meals and transportation.

10973 West Alabama Regional Commission's Senior Programs: Legal Counsel for the Elderly (WARC)
4200 Highway 69 North
Suite 1
Northport, AL 35476
205-333-2990
e-mail: warc@adss.alabama.gov
http://www.warc.info/index.php
Robert B Lake, Executive Director
Mike McDaniel, Fiscal Officer

West Alabama Regional Commission's programs for senior citizens are broad and inclusive. Depending upon individual circumstances, a senior citizen in West Alabama can get advice on health insurance, legal counseling, a home-delivered meal, help with household chores, discounted prescription medicines, placement in a part-time job, and many other services. Legal Counsel for the Elderly provides assistance with a wide variety of issues including health care, public benefits, and protective services. The program is funded through West Alabama Regional Commission by Older Americans Act funds. No legal fees are charged, but contributions are welcomed.

Alaska

10974 Alaska Commission on Aging: Alaska Department of Health & Social Services
150 Third Street, Suite 103
PO Box 110693
Juneau, AK 99811-0693
907-465-3250
Fax: 907-465-1398
e-mail: denise_daniello@health.state.ak.us
http://www.alaskaaging.org/
Denise Daniello, Executive Director
Frank B Appel, Chairman
MaryAnn VandeCastle, H&SS Planner II

Legal Aid Resources/Arizona

The Alaska Commission on Aging (ACoA) advocates for state policy, public and private partnerships, state/federal projects and citizen involvement that assists each of us to age successfully in our homes, in our communities or as near as possible to our communities and families. Our work involves planning, advocacy, and interagency collaboration on issues and state and federal services affecting older Alaskans.

10975 Alaska Legal Services Corporation: Senior Legal Services Project
1016 West 6th Avenue
Suite 200
Anchorage, AK 99501
907-272-9431
Fax: 907-279-7417
e-mail: anchorage3@alsc-law.org
http://www.alsc-law.org

Greg Peters, Elder Law Attorney

Legal services are provided to residents 60 years old and over. Issues include income maintenance, health care, housing, consumer wills, family caregiver matters, and information and referral on other legal issues.

10976 Disability Law Center Of Alaska
3330 Arctic Boulevard
Suite 103
Anchorage, AK 99503
907-565-1002
Fax: 907-565-1000
e-mail: akpa@dlcak.org
http://www.dlcak.org
TDD 800-478-1234

Dave Fleurant, Executive Director
Cindy Hite, Business Manager
Penny Sorenson, Intake/Advocacy Specialist

Part of a nationwide system that provides protection and advocacy for the legal, civil and human rights of persons with disabilities.

10977 Elderlaw Project
1016 West 6th Avenue
Suite 200
Anchorage, AK 99501
907-272-9431
Fax: 907-279-7417
e-mail: anchorage3@alsc-law.org
http://www.alsc-law.org

Greg Peters, Attorney

This program has 9 offices located throughout Alaska - Anchorage, Bethel, Dillingham, Fairbanks, Juneau, Ketchikan, Kotzebue, and Nome. The program provides services to low income persons of all ages, with special attention given to seniorsan their family caregivers. Areas of interest include public benefits, wills, consumer issues, landlord/tenant, and caregiver issues.

Arizona

10978 Advocates for the Disabled
5060 North 19th Avenue
Suite 306
Phoenix, AZ 85015
602-212-2600
Fax: 602-212-2606
e-mail: afdagency@advocatesforthedisabled.org
http://www.cirs.org/homepage/advocates/

Roberto Armijo, Executive Director
Bill Austin, Chief Technology Officer
Greg Bullock, Business Services Director

Advocates services are establish the eligibility of individuals seeking benefits, manage benefits, educate the public how to obtain and use benefits, and to advoctae for the right to receive benefits. Providing social services. Provides a finding service.

10979 Arizona Center for Disability Law
3839 N 3rd Street
Suite 209
Phoenix, AZ 85012-2069
602-274-6287
Fax: 602-274-6779
e-mail: center@acdl.com
http://www.acdl.com

Judy Fox, Manager

A non profit law firm dedicated to protecting the rights of individuals with a wide range of disabilities.

10980 Arizona Department of Economic Security: Division of Aging and Community Services
Aging and Adult Administration
1789 W Jefferson
Site Code 950A
Phoenix, AZ 85007
602-542-4446
Fax: 602-542-6575
e-mail: rcritchfield@asdex.gov
http://www.de.state.az.us/aaa/

Rex Critchfield, Acting Assistant Director

The Aging and Adult Administration provides information and services to seniors within Arizona through Adult Protective Services, Benefits Counseling, Long Term Care Ombudsman Program, Legal Services Assistance, and the Home and Community Living Supports / Mature Workers Programs. Each of these services assists in accomplishing the administration's number one goal to provide opportunities for keeping vulnerable adults and older persons in their homes and communities.

10981 Arizona Elder Abuse and Fraud Taskforce Committee
Office of the Attorney General
Consumer Protection & Advocacy Section
1275 West Washington
Phoenix, AZ
602-542-2124
Fax: 602-542-4347
http://www.azag.gov/seniors/elder_abuse

Terry Goddard, Chief Legal Officer/Attrny Gnrl
Elvera Anselmo, Director Elder Affairs Program

Addresses the problems of elder abuse and exploitation. The direct services component uses in-house attorneys in areas such as licensing, nursing home regulation, adult protective services, civil rights, and criminal fraud.

10982 Arizona Protection and Advocacy Agency: Arizona Center for Disability Law
3839 North Third Street
Suite 209
Phoenix, AZ 85012
602-274-6287
800-927-2260
Fax: 602-274-6779
e-mail: hwatkins@azdisabilitylaw.org
http://www.azdisabilitylaw.org

Henry G Hawkins, Executive Director
Peri Jude Radecic, Public Advocacy Director
Kris Stocking, Finance & Admin. Director

The Arizona Center for Disability Law advocates for the legal rights of persons with disabilities to be free from abuse, neglect and discrimination and to have access to education, health care, housing and jobs, and other services in order to maximize independence and achieve equality. The Arizona Center for Disability Law (the Center) is a federally-designated Protection and Advocacy System for the State of Arizona. Protection and Advocacy Systems (P&As) throughout the United States assure that the human and civil rights of persons with disabilities are protected. In creating Protection and Advocacy Systems, Congress gave them unique authorities and responsibilities, including the power to investigate reports of abuse and neglect and violations of the rights of persons with disabilities. P&As are also authorized to pursue appropriate legal and administrative remedies on behalf of persons with disabilities to insure the enforcement of their constitutional and statutory rights.

Legal Aid Resources/Arkansas

10983 DNA People's Legal Services
PO Box 306
Window Rock, AZ 86515-0306
928-871-4151
800-789-7287
Fax: 928-871-5036
http://www.lawhelp.org/Program/
Levon Henry, Executive Director
Diana Shurley, Advocate/Office Manager
Philmer Bluhouse, Project Administrator

Offers legal assistance to Native Americans.

10984 Legal Advocate Program: Pinal-Gila Council for Senior Citizens
Area Agency on Aging
1895 North Trekell Road
Suite 2
Casa Grande, AZ 85222-1704
520-836-2758
800-293-9393
Fax: 520-421-2033
e-mail: info@pgcsc.org
http://www.pgcsc.org
Olivia Guerrero, President/CEO

10985 National Academy of Elder Law Attorneys
1604 North Country Club Road
Tucson, AZ 85716
520-881-4005
Fax: 520-325-7925
http://www.naela.com/
Susan McMahon, Executive Director
Debbie Barnett, Managing Director
Anabel Gray, Special Interest Projects

Provides legal advocacy, guidance and services to enhance the lives of older people with special needs.

10986 Southern Arizona Legal Aid (SALA)
64 East Broadway Boulevard
Tucson, AZ 85701
520-623-9465
800-231-5441
Fax: 520-620-0443
http://www.sazlegalaid.org/
Thomas J Berning, Executive Director
Doris Lee Butler, Chief Operations Officer
Rose Marie Castro, Chief Financial Officer

Offers workshops and representation for people with disabilities.

10987 William E Morris Institute for Justice
202 East McDowell Road
Suite 257
Phoenix, AZ 85001
602-252-3432
Fax: 602-257-8138
e-mail: ajinstitu@qwest.net
http://www.MorrisInstituteforJustice.org/
Ellen Katz, Director

Offers legal services for seniors in need.

Arkansas

10988 Arkansas Department of Health & Human Services: Division of Aging and Adult Services
PO Box 1437
Slot S-530
Little Rock, AR 72203
501-682-2441
Fax: 501-682-8155
e-mail: Herb.sanderson@arkansas.gov
http://www.arkansas.gov/dhhs/aging/
Herb Sanderson, Executive Director
Connie Parker, Assistant Director
Gloria Powell, Elder Programs Administrator

The Division of Aging and Adult Services serves as the focal point for all matters concerning older Arkansans; serves as an effective and visible advocate for the aging population; gives elderly citizens a choice of how and where they receive long term care services; plans, coordinates, funds and evaluates programs for senior adults.

10989 Arkansas Protection and Advocacy Agency: Disability Rights Center
1100 North University
Suite 201
Little Rock, AR 72207
501-296-1775
800-482-1174
Fax: 501-296-1779
e-mail: panda@arkdisabilityrights.org
http://www.arkdisabilityrights.org/
TDD 800-482-1174
Nan Ellen, Executive Director
Joyce Soularie, Chairperson
Kim Weser, Secretary

10990 Arkansas Volunteer Lawyers for the Elderly (AVLE)
2020 West 3rd Street
Suite 620
Little Rock, AR 72205-4467
501-376-9263
Fax: 501-376-9263
e-mail: avleprog@yahoo.com
http://www.arlegalservices.org/Home/
Catherine Edwards, Executive Director

Serves elderly in 67 Arkansas counties. Legal services and area agency on aging staff conduct initial intake and send cases to AVLE, where coordinator refers them to panel of 600 volunteer attorneys.

10991 Center for Arkansas Legal Services
303 West Capitol
Suite 200
Little Rock, AR 72201
501-376-3423
Fax: 501-376-3664
http://www.arlegalservices.org/Home/
Ron Lanoue, Executive Director
Vince Morris, Technology Advocate

10992 Legal Aid of Arkansas
714 South Main Street
Jonesboro, AR 72401
870-972-9224
Fax: 870-910-5562
http://www.arlegalservices.org/Home/
Ron Lanoue, Executive Director
Vince Morris, Technology Advocate

Legal Aid of Arkansas 501(c)3 is a nonprofit organization that provides free legal services to low-income Arkansans in non-criminal cases, ranging from family to consumer and housing to individual rights cases. LAA serves 31 counties within Arkansas. Their vision is to improve the lives of low-income Arkansans by championing equal access to justice for all regardless of economic or social circumstances.

California

10993 Amador Senior Services
Common Grounds
Area Agency on Aging
229 New York Ranch Road
Jackson, CA 95642
209-223-0442
Fax: 209-223-0471
e-mail: info@area12.org
http://www.area12.org/a12asp/aprograms
Elizabeth Thompson, Executive Director

Primary advocate and information center for elders and their caregivers. Provides educational, social and nutrition services to citizens of county. Provides volunteer opportunities as well as collaborating with other service providers.

10994 Bet Tzedek Legal Services
145 South Fairfax Avenue
Suite 200
Los Angeles, CA 90036
323-939-0506
http://www.bettzedek.org/
Mitchell A Kamin, Executive Director
Gus T May, Valley Bet Tzedek Director
Matt Scelza, Marketing/Development Director

Legal Aid Resources/California

Bet Tzedek is one of the nation's premier legal services organizations, providing free assistance to more than 10,000 people of every racial and religious background at its headquarters in the Fairfax area and its office in North Hollywood and at more than 30 senior centers throughout Los Angeles County. With a dedicated staff of over 55 and more than 400 active volunteers, Bet Tzedek makes a crucial difference in the lives of the most vulnerable members of the community.

10995 California Advocates for Nursing Home Reform
650 Harrison Street
2nd Floor
San Francisco, CA 94107
415-974-5171
Fax: 415-474-1116
e-mail: info@canhr.org
http://www.canhr.org/

Patricia L McGinnis, Executive Director
Terry Donnelly, Deputy Director
Prescott Cole, Staff Attorney

Provides pre placement counseling and information on all California nursing homes, advocates on behalf of long term care residents, and provides legal referrals in the areas of estate planning, protective services, residents' rights, personal injury, and medical malpractice in long term care facilities. Also produces consumer information on MediCal eligibility, residents' rights, family councils, and residential care.

10996 California Department of Aging
1300 National Drive
Suite 200
Sacramento, CA 95834
916-419-7500
Fax: 916-928-2268
e-mail: lconnoll@aging.ca.gov
http://www.aging.state.ca.us/
TDD 800-735-2929

Lora Connolly, Acting Director
Joyce Fukui, Deputy Director LTC/AS
Johanna Meyer, Senior Employment Program

The California Department of Aging serves as both a unifying force for services to seniors and adults with disabilities and as a focal point for federal, state and local agencies which serve the elderly and adults with disabilities in California. It fulfills the goals outlined in the Older Americans Act and also acts as an advocate for seniors and adults with disabilities by striving to develop an environment which respects and values the state's older residents and adults with disabilities. As the designated State Unit on Aging, the California Department of Aging is part of the California Health and Human Services Agency. The Department administers Older Americans Act programs for supportive services, in-home services, congregate and home-delivered meals and a system of multipurpose senior centers. It also administers the program for community service employment; programs for advocaivities, the Department works closely with private and public sector aging advocates.cy and protection; and programs which provide health insurance counseling, case management, Alzheimer's Day Care Resource Center and Adult Day Health Care services. Further, it performs a wide range of functions related to advocacy, planning, coordination, interagency linkages, information sharing, brokering, monitoring and evaluation. In its act

10997 California Protection and Advocacy Agency (PAI)
100 Howe Avenue
Suite 185N
Sacramento, CA 95825
916-488-9955
Fax: 916-488-9962
e-mail: catherine.blakemore@pai-ca.org
http://www.pai-ca.org

Catherine Blakemore, Executive Director

Protection & Advocacy, Inc. is a nonprofit disability rights advocacy organization dedicated to advancing the human and legal rights of people with disabilities. We strive to create a barrier free, inclusive society that values diversity and each individual. Protection & Advocacy Inc. serves Californians with a wide range of disabilities - including cognitive, mental, sensory, and physical disabilities - by guarding against abuse; advocating forbasic rights; and ensuring accountability in health care, education, employment, housing, transportation, and within the juvenile and criminal justice systems.

10998 California State Bar Committee on Legal Problems of Aging
555 Franklin Street
San Francisco, CA 94102
415-561-8200
Fax: 415-561-8305
http://www.calbar.ca.gov/calbar

Thomas G Stolpman, Executive Director

The Commission on Legal Problems of the Elderly (Commission) is an entity of the American Bar Association (ABA). Its goal is to examine and respond to law-related needs of older persons in the United States through policy development, education, and the provision of technical assistance. The Commission does not provide direct legal services or make referrals to private lawyers. The Commission can, however, help connect individuals with the freelegal services/legal aid programs serving older persons in the area in which they live.

10999 Central California Legal Services
1999 Tuolumne
Suite 700
Fresno, CA 93721-2011
559-441-1611
800-675-8001
e-mail: luisa@centralcallegal.org.
http://www.centralcallegal.org

Luisa Medina, Coordinator of Legal Services
Chris Schneider, Coordinator of Legal Services

11000 Council on Aging of Sonoma County
730 Bennett Valley Road
Santa Rosa, CA 95404-5514
707-525-0143
800-675-0143
Fax: 707-525-0454
e-mail: legalcoa@sonic.net
http://www.councilonaging.com

Barbara Swary, Attorney/Director
Carol Martin, Information/Referral
Shirlee Zane, CEO

The Council on Aging offers our senior clients timely legal services and advice to contribute to their sense of well being and support their independence and security. Those in social or financial need receive priority. To be eligible for our legal services you must be a Sonoma County resident 60 years of age or older. Our part-time Senior Legal Services staff includes an attorney, three paralegals, and an office manager.

11001 Disability Rights Education and Defense Fund
2212 6th Street
Berkeley, CA 94710
510-644-2555
800-348-4232
Fax: 510-841-8645
e-mail: dredf@dredf.org
http://www.dredf.org

Susan Henderson, Managing Director
Mary Lou Breslin, Senior Policy Advisor
Patrisha A Wright, Director Government Affairs

A national law and policy center dedicated to protecting and advancing civil rights of people with disabilities through legislation, litigation, formal and informal advocacy and education and training of people with disabilities, parents of children with disabilities, advocates and attorneys.

Legal Aid Resources/California

11002 Hawkins Center of Law and Services for the Disabled
101 Broadway Avenue
Suite 1
Richmond, CA 94804-1911   510-232-6611
e-mail: info@hawkinscenter.org
http://www.hawkinscenter.org/
Linda Mills, Contact

The Hawkins Center works to improve the health and financial stability of people with disabilities. In partnership with service organizations, The Hawkins Center provides high quality legal, social, and educational services, and advocates for changes in policy. In all its programs, the agency promotes dignity, respect, and fairness for people with disabilities.

11003 Inland Counties Legal Services for Seniors
715 North Arrowhead Avenue
Suite 113
San Bernardino, CA 92401   909-884-8615
                                 800-677-4257
http://www.inlandlegal.org/
Robert S Roddick, Managing Attorney

Inland Counties Legal Services provides free civil legal assistance to seniors who are 60 years or older who reside in Riverside and San Bernardino Counties. Elder law advocates travel to senior and community centers throughout both counties to give legal counsel and assistance. Priority is given to elder abuse cases, including matters involving financial, emotional and mental abuse as well as physical abuse, and help seniors with government andpublic benefits.

11004 Legal Assistance to the Elderly
100 McAllister Street
San Francisco, CA 94102   415-861-4444
                                Fax: 415-861-6458
Howard M Levy, Contact

Provides advice and representation to San Francisco residents age sixty and over experiencing problems with their housing, public benefits, health care or who are experiencing physical or financial abuse.

11005 Legal Center for the Elderly and Disabled
2862 Arden Way
Suite 215
Sacramento, CA 95825   916-486-2110
                                Fax: 916-486-2116
http://www.lcedlaw.org/index.html
Alice Ware, Executive Director

Free civil legal services for people over sixty and low income permanently disabled persons under sixty, specializing in social security, medical benefits, financial exploitation, long term care issues, disability rights and housing in North Central California.

11006 Legal Services for Seniors
21 West Laurel Avenue
Suite 83
Salinas, CA 93906   931-442-7700
http://www.legalservicesforseniors.org/
Michael Benoit, Executive Director
Paul Gallender, Development Director Legal Svcs
Robert Greathouse, Outreach Legal Advocate

11007 Los Angeles County Bar Association: Elderline Public Council
PO Box 55020
Los Angeles, CA 90055-2020   213-896-6590
                                312-988-5000
e-mail: abaelderly@abanet.org
http://www.abanet.org/aging/states/california06
Charles P Sabatino, Director ABA Law/Aging Cmmsn
Erica F Wood, Asst. Director ABA Law/Ag Csm
Holly Robinson, Associate Staff Director

Elderline is a Legal Referral for the Elderly Program. A phone counselor recieves calls and makes referrals for cases involving property, consumer problems, landlord-tenant problems, uninsured torts, uncontested probate, uncontested guardianship and conservatorship, grandparents rights, and tax.

11008 National Senior Citizens Law Center
1330 Broadway
Suite 525
Oakland, CA 94612   510-663-1055
                                Fax: 510-663-1051
                                http://www.nsclc.org
Edward C King, Executive Director
Rochelle Bobroff, Director Federal Rights Projecct
Jeanne Finberg, Directing Attorney

Advocates nationwide to promote the independence and well-being of low-income elderly individuals, as well as persons with disabilities, with particular emphasis on women and racial and ethnic minorities. Advocates through litigation, legistlative and agency representation and assistance to attorneys and paralegals in field programs.

11009 Senior Adults Legal Assistance (SALA)
160 East Virginia Street
Suite 260
San Jose, CA 95112   408-295-5991
                                Fax: 408-295-7401
                                e-mail: info@sala.org
                                http://www.sala.org/
Georgia Bacil, Contact

11010 Senior Citizens Legal Services
3675 Ruffin Road
Suite 315
San Diego, CA 92123   858-565-1392
http://www.seniorlaw-sd.org/metro.html
Carolyn L Reilly, Program Director
Jaime Levine, Staff Attorney

Senior Citizens Legal Services provides free legal services to San Diego County senior citizens age 60 or older.

11011 Senior Law Project
200B North Main Street
Lakeport, CA 95453   707-263-4703
                                800-260-4703
                                Fax: 707-263-0348
                                e-mail: andyr@pacific.net
                                http://www.co.lake.ca.us/
Andrew Rossoff, Executive Director

Lake County Community Action Agency through the Senior Law Project, provides seniors with assistance regarding Social Security, SSI, Medi-Cal, Medicare, Landlord/Tenant problems, Elder Abuse, Consumer Protection and planning for incapacity and long-term care.

11012 Senior Legal Center of Northern California
1647 Hartnell Avenue
Suite 6
Redding, CA 96002   530-225-6979
                                800-822-9687
                                Fax: 530-241-3565
                                http://www.lsnc.net
Thomas M Welsh, Contact

In Lassen, Modoc, Shasta, Siskiyou, and Trinity counties, the Senior Legal Hotline is available for legal advice or brief assistance by phone.

11013 Seniors' Law Center
615 California Avenue
Bakersfield, CA 93304   805-323-7881
                                800-285-2221
e-mail: abaaging@abanet.org
http://www.abanet.org/aging/statemap.html
                                TDD 312-988-5200
Charles P Sabatino, Director ABA Law/Aging Cmsn
Erica F Wood, Asst. Drctr ABA Law/Aging Cmsn
Holly Robinson, Associate Director

Senior's Law Center is an Area Agency on Aging-funded program that assists in the following areas: public benefits, Social Security, in-home support and institutional care, and subsidized housing. Services are free to Kern county residents 60+.

Legal Aid Resources/Colorado

11014 Volunteer Lawyers Project for the Elderly
2014 Tulare Street
Suite 200
Fresno, CA 93721
209-441-1611
800-675-8001
Fax: 209-441-7215
e-mail: ccls@gnis.net
http://www.abanet.org/aging/states/
Chris A Schnieder, Directing Attorney

Provides counseling on issues such as housing, consumer, domestic relations, simple wills, and tort defense litigation. Services are free to residents of Fresno County whose incomes are within Legal Services Croporation guidelines.

11015 Western Law Center for Disability Rights
919 South Albany Street
Los Angeles, CA 90015
213-736-1031
Fax: 213-736-1428
e-mail: DRLC@lls.edu
http://www.disabilityrightslegalcenter.org/
TTY 213-736-8310
Eve L Hill, Executive Director
Nicholas DeWitt, President of the Board

The Western Law Center for Disability Rights provides legal representation in accordance with the Americans With Disabilities Act of 1990 to people with a wide range of disabilities; provides information to people with cancer or with disabilities; advocates on behalf of disabled people through class-action lawsuits; and mediates disputes disabled people have with employers and others.

11016 Yuba-Sutter Legal Center for Seniors
725 D Street
Marysville, CA 95901
530-742-8289
530-742-2334
http://a4aa.com/html/yuba___sutter_county.html
Susan Townsend, Directing Attorney

Provides area seniors with free legal services to help them obtain benefits, safe homes and medical care so they can remain independent.

Colorado

11017 Boulder County Aging Services Division: Elder Rights Program
3482 North Broadway
PO Box 471
Boulder, CO 80306-0471
303-441-3570
Fax: 303-441-4550
e-mail: bcaaa@co.boulder.co.us
http://www.co.boulder.co.us/cs/ag/
Rosemary Williams MSW, Division Manager

The mission of Boulder County Aging Services Division is to promote the health and well-being of older adults by building on individual, family, and community strengths. Free and confidential services advocating for the rights of older adults in Boulder County are available.

11018 Colorado Department of Human Services: Division of Aging and Adult Services
1575 Sherman Street
10th Floor
Denver, CO 80203
303-866-2800
888-866-4243
Fax: 303-866-2696
e-mail: Jeanette.Hensley@state.co.us
http://www.cdhs.state.co.us/aas/
TTY 303-866-2850
Jeanette Hensley, Executive Director

The Division of Aging and Adult Services (AAS) will efficiently and effectively provide human services in support of independent living, self-sufficiency, safety and dignity goals. These goals are on behalf of adults who have disabilities or functional impairments or are otherwise at risk. The Division of Aging and Adult Services provides oversight for and coordination of programs that allow the elderly and adults with disabilities to live independently. These programs are administered through the County Departments of Social (Human) Services or through regional Area Agencies on Aging.

11019 Colorado Protection and Advocacy Agency: The Legal Center at Grand Junction
322 North 8th Street
Grand Junction, CO 81501-3406
970-241-6371
800-531-2105
Fax: 970-241-5324
e-mail: tlcmail@thelegalcenter.org
http://www.thelegalcenter.org
TTY 970-241-6371
Mary Anne Harvey, Executive Director

Works for systematic change that will improve the quality of life for seniors and those with disabilities.

11020 Larimer County Office on Aging (LCOA)
1501 Blue Spruce Drive
Fort Collins, CO 80524
970-498-6300
Fax: 970-498-6455
http://www.larimer.org/humanservices/seniors/
Karen A Wagner, Commissioner
Margaret Long, Executive Director

The Larimer County Office on Aging (LCOA), in the Larimer County Department of Human Services, is a comprehensive planning unit that advocates for the concerns of older adults and caregivers. LCOA will assist older adults, age 60 and over, in maintaining health, dignity, independence, and quality of life, by advocating, planning, coordinating, and delivering services and programs, with emphasis on meeting the needs of those who are socially and/or economically disadvantaged.

11021 Legal Center for People with Disabilities and Older People
455 Sherman Street
Suite 130
Denver, CO 80203-4403
303-722-0300
800-288-1376
Fax: 303-722-0720
e-mail: tlcmail@thelegalcenter.org
http://www.thelegalcenter.org/contact.html
Mary Anne Harvey, Executive Director

Provides legal representation to persons with disabilities, their advocates, including parents, guardians and family members concerned with the rights and responsibilities of persons with disabilities, when the disability is central to rather than incidental to the legal dispute; special knowledge of the disabling condition is required; and special knowledge of the applicable law is required.

Connecticut

11022 Center for Medicare Advocacy
PO Box 350
Willimantic, CT 06226-0350
860-456-7790
800-262-4414
Fax: 860-456-2614
e-mail: tlcmail@thelegalcenter.org
http://www.medicareadvocacy.org
Judith Stein, Executive Director/Attorney
Brad S Plebani, Deputy Director
Ellen Lang, Advocacy Coordinator

Legal Aid Resources/Connecticut

11023 **Connecticut Bar Association: Section on Legal Problems of the Elderly**
30 Bank Street
PO Box 350
New Britain, CT 06050-0350
860-223-4400
Fax: 860-223-4488
http://www1.ctbar.org/staff.aspx
Tim Hazen, Executive Director
Kate McEvoy, Chair
Hilary Stevens, Director External Affairs

The purpose of the Elder Law Section is to discuss and consider issues in elder law, promote the continuing education of CBA members and the general community, monitor and develop positions with respect to proposed legislation and regulatory action involving the elderly, and to foster relationships between attorneys and private, public, and governmental organizations dealing with the elderly.

11024 **Connecticut Department of Social Services: Elderly Services Division**
25 Sigourney Street
Hartford, CT 06106
860-424-5274
866-218-6631
Fax: 860-424-5301
e-mail: ctelderlyserv.dss@po.state.ct.us
http://www.ctelderlyservices.state.ct.us/
Pamela Giannini, Executive Director

Connecticut's Aging Services Division is committed to serving seniors by supporting and promoting programs that serve the growing needs of the aging community in all five regions of Connecticut. The Aging Services Division is the component within DSS which ensures that Connecticut's elders have access to the supportive services necessary to live with dignity, security and independence. The Division is responsible for planning, developing, and administering a comprehensive and integrated service delivery system for elderly persons in Connecticut. To accomplish this, the Division conducts needs assessments, surveys methods of service administration, evaluates and monitors such services, maintains information and referral services, and develops, coordinates, and/or collaborates with other appropriate agencies to provide outreach, social, housing, transportation, health, educational, cultural and nutritional programs that help Connecticut's elderly residents.

11025 **Connecticut Lawyers' Legal Aid to the Elderly Program (CLLAEP)**
Law and Regulatory Affairs
151 Farmington Avenue
RE4C
Hartford, CT 06156
860-273-3839
http://www.abanet.org/aging/states/
Charles P Sabatino, ABA Law/Aging Director
Erica F Wood, Assistant Director ABA Law/Aging
Holly Robinson, Staff Director ABA Law/Aging

Staffed by Hartford-area lawyers from corporate law departments and private law firms, the program offers free legal assistance to low-income elderly in the Greater-Hartford/Middletown areas.

11026 **Connecticut Protection and Advocacy Agency: Office of Protection and Advocacy for Persons with Disabilities**
60-B Weston Street
Hartford, CT 06120-1551
860-297-4300
800-842-7303
Fax: 860-566-8714
e-mail: james.mcgaughey@po.state.ct.us
http:///www.state.ct.us/opapd/
TTY 860-842-7303
James D McGaughey, Executive Director

The Office of Protection and Advocacy for Persons with Disabilities is an independent State agency created to safeguard and advance the civil and human rights of people with disabilities in Connecticut. Part of a nationwide network of protection and advocacy systems, we operate under both State and federal legislative mandates to provide information, referral, and advocacy services; pursue legal and administrative remedies on behalf of people with disabilities who experience disability-related discrimination; selectively investigate complaints from people with disabilities and into allegations of abuse and neglect with respect to adults who have mental retardation, and for people in psychiatric facilities; and, provide public education and training on disability issues and to inform policy makers about issues affecting people with disabilities.

11027 **Legal Assistance for Elders in Connecticut**
Connecticut Elder Law Program
62 Washington Street
Middletown, CT 06457
860-344-0447
Fax: 860-346-2938
http://www.ctelderlaw.org/
Marvin Farbman, Executive Director

Provides comprehensive, current information on elder law, government programs and legal assistance for residents of Connecticut age 60 and older. Services include free counseling and representation on many Elder Law issues such as Medicaid and other government programs, patients' rights, nursing home issues.

11028 **Legal Services Programs for Elders: Bridgeport**
211 State Street
Bridgeport, CT 06604
203-336-3861
800-809-4434
http://www.ctelderlaw.org/
Marvin Farbman, Executive Director

Provides comprehensive, current information on elder law, government programs and legal assistance for residents of Connecticut age 60 and older. Services include free counseling and representation on many Elder Law issues such as Medicaid and other government programs, patients' rights, nursing home issues.

11029 **Legal Services Programs for Elders: Hartford**
80 Jefferson Street
Hartford, CT 06106
860-541-5000
http://www.ctelderlaw.org/
Marvin Farbman, Executive Director

Provides comprehensive, current information on elder law, government programs and legal assistance for residents of Connecticut age 60 and older. Services include free counseling and representation on many Elder Law issues such as Medicaid and other government programs, patients' rights, nursing home issues.

11030 **Legal Services Programs for Elders: Waterbury**
85 Central Avenue
Waterbury, CT 06702
203-756-8074
800-413-7797
http://www.ctelderlaw.org/
Marvin Farbman, Executive Director

Provides comprehensive, current information on elder law, government programs and legal assistance for residents of Connecticut age 60 and older. Services include free counseling and representation on many Elder Law issues such as Medicaid and other government programs, patients' rights, nursing home issues.

11031 **Legal Services Programs for Elders: Willimantic**
872 Main Street
Willimantic, CT 06226
860-456-1761
800-413-7796
http://www.ctelderlaw.org/
Marvin Farbman, Executive Director

Legal Aid Resources/Delaware

Provides comprehensive, current information on elder law, government programs and legal assistance for residents of Connecticut age 60 and older. Services include free counseling and representation on many Elder Law issues such as Medicaid and other government programs, patients' rights, nursing home issues.

11032 New Haven Legal Assistance Association (LAA)
426 State Street
New Haven, CT 06112
203-946-4811
http://www.ctelderlaw.org/
Marvin Farbman, Executive Director

Provides comprehensive, current information on elder law, government programs and legal assistance for residents of Connecticut age 60 and older. Legal Services include free counseling and representation on many Elder Law issues such as Medicaid and other government programs, patients' rights, nursing home issues.

11033 No Longer Disabled: The Federal Courts
Greenwood Publishing Group
88 Post Road West
Westport, CT 06880
203-226-3571
800-225-5800
Fax: 203-222-1502
e-mail: prices@greenwood.com
http://www.greenwood.com/
Susan Gluck Mezey, Author
Ron Maas, VP Planning Greenwood Publishing

This book is a case study of judicial policy making. It focuses on the role of adjudication in the making and refining of federal policy.

208 pages

Delaware

11034 Community Legal Aid Society: Dover
840 Walker Road
Dover, DE 19904
302-674-8500
Fax: 302-674-8145
e-mail: cwhite@declasi.org
http://www.declasi.org
TDD 302-674-8500
TTY 302-674-8500
Christopher White, Esq., Executive Director
Wendeth W Kolb, Financial Director
Deborah I Gottschalk, Esq., Deputy Director/Program Director

Services provides by the Elder Law Program include that of powers of attorney and advance health care directives (formerly known as Living Wills); consumer problems such as debt collection and home repair cases; housing problems such as evictions, and, benefits issues such as Medicaid and Social Security. The Elder Law Program also conducts community legal education workshops for older people about legal problems that occur with advancing age.

11035 Community Legal Aid Society: Georgetown
144 East Market Street
Georgetown, DE 19947
302-856-0038
Fax: 302-856-6133
e-mail: cwhite@declasi.org
http://www.declasi.org
TDD 302-856-0038
TTY 302-856-0038
Christopher White, Esq., Executive Director
Wendeth W Kolb, Financial Director
Deborah Gottschalk, Esq., Deputy Director/Program Director

Services provides by the Elder Law Program include that of powers of attorney and advance health care directives (formerly known as Living Wills); consumer problems such as debt collection and home repair cases; housing problems such as evictions, and, benefits issues such as Medicaid and Social Security. The Elder Law Program also conducts community legal education workshops for older people about legal problems that occur with advancing age.

11036 Community Legal Aid Society: Wilmington
Community Service Building
100 West 10th Street
Suite 801
Wilmington, DE 19801
302-575-0660
Fax: 302-575-0840
e-mail: cwhite@declasi.org
http://www.declasi.org
TDD 302-575-0696
TTY 302-575-0696
Christopher White, Esq., Executive Director
William J Dunne Esq., Project Director
Wendeth Kolb, Financial Director

Services provides by the Elder Law Program include that of powers of attorney and advance health care directives (formerly known as Living Wills); consumer problems such as debt collection and home repair cases; housing problems such as evictions, and, benefits issues such as Medicaid and Social Security. The Elder Law Program also conducts community legal education workshops for older people about legal problems that occur with advancing age.

11037 Delaware Bar Association Committee on Law and the Elderly
301 North Market Street
Wilmington, DE 19801
302-658-5279
800-292-7869
Fax: 302-658-5212
http://www.dsba.org/SecComm/sections.htm
Rina Marks, Executive Director
Rebecca Baird, Publications/Communications
Alison Macindoe, Continuing Legal Education

The Committee produces a handbook for senior citizens, coordinates the publication of a bar journal on legal problems of the elderly, advises the bar on legislation affecting the elderly, sponsors two continuing legal education seminars, and sponsors three call-in nights for senior citizens.

11038 Delaware Division of Services for Aging and Adults with Physical Disabilities
Department of Health and Social Services
1901 North DuPont Highway
New Castle, DE 19720
302-255-9390
800-223-9074
Fax: 302-255-4445
e-mail: DSAAPDinfo@state.de.us
http://www.dhss.delaware.gov/dhss/dsaapd/
Allan Zaback, Executive Director

The Delaware Division of Services for Aging and Adults with Physical Disabilities (DSAAPD) carries out a broad range of activities to assist older persons and adults with physical disabilities. The Division operates a number of programs, including the Adult Protective Services Program, the Long Term Care Ombudsman Program, the Community Services Program, the Delaware Medicare Fraud Alert Program, the Delaware Money Management Program, and Joining Generations. In addition, the Division provides services such as information and assistance, caregiver support, and health promotion. The Division also contracts with agencies around the State to provide many home and community-based services. Finally, the Division advocates on behalf of older persons and adults with physical disabilities to create a broader awareness of the needs of these populations within Delaware.

District of Columbia

11039 AARP Legal Advocacy Group
601 E Street NW
Washington, DC 20049
202-434-2120
Fax: 202-434-6424
e-mail: tosborne@aarp.org
http://www.aarp.org/states/dc/dc-lce/

Wayne Moore, Director
Thomas Osborne, Senior Attorney
William Novelli, Chief Executive Officer

Operates a public interest litigation unit, provides technical assistance on legal hotlines, supports a discount legal services program for AARP membersand operates a national legal training program.

11040 Administrative Advocacy Clinic/Advocates for Older People
2136 Pennsylvania Avenue NW
Washington, DC 20052
202-676-3900
Fax: 202-676-5269
e-mail: susanjones@law.gwu.edu
http://www.gwu.edu/~ccommit/law.htm

Susan R Jones, Clinic Director

George Washington University Law students provide services for indigent and elderly Washington residents who are pursuing their entitlements to various government rights and benefits before local and federal agencies and courts. Services include free legal assistance, public benefits, wills, income tax return preparation and other legal problems for D.C. residents ages 55 and older.

11041 District of Columbia Bar: Individual Rights Section
1250 H Street NW, Sixth Floor
Washington, DC 20005-5937
202-737-4700
877-333-2227
Fax: 202-626-3471
e-mail: kmazzaferri@dcbar.org
http://www.abanet.org/irr/html or www.dcbar.org

Katherine A Mazzaferri, Executive Director
Al Wilcox, Director of Operations
Cynthia G Kuhn, Communications Director

Created in 1966, the Section of Individual Rights and Responsibilities provides leadership within the ABA and the legal profession in protecting and advancing human rights, civil liberties, and social justice. The Section fulfills this role by raising and addressing often complex and difficult civil rights and civil liberties issues in a changing and diverse society, and ensuring that protection of individual rights remains a focus of legal and policy decisions.

11042 District of Columbia Office on Aging
One Judciary Square
441 4th Street Northwest, Suite 900S
Washington, DC 20001
202-724-5622
Fax: 202-724-4979
e-mail: dcoa@dc.gov
http://http://dcoa.dc.gov/dcoa/site/default.asp
TDD 202-724-8925
TTY 202-724-8925

E. Veronica Pace, Executive Director

The mission of the District of Columbia Office on Aging is to advocate, plan, implement, and monitor programs in health, education, employment, and social services which promote longevity, independence, dignity, and choice for our senior citizens. The Office on Aging also funds a Senior Service Network comprising 20 community-based, nonprofit organizations that provide direct services to the District's elderly citizens. The 30 community-based, education, government, and private organizations that make up the Senior Service Network operate more than 40 programs for older persons. Crucial to the Network are five Lead Agencies that offer a broad range of legal, nutrition, social, and health services. The goal of these six agencies is to enhance the quality of life for older adults and their families throughout all eight wards of the District of Columbia. The agencies accomplish this goal through widespread distribution of information about the variety of services and programs offered seniors throughout the city and ways to access them.

11043 Equal Employment Advisory Council
1015 15th Street NW
Suite 1200
Washington, DC 20005
202-789-8650
Fax: 202-789-2291
e-mail: info@eeac.org
http://www.eeac.org/

Jeffrey A Norris, President
G John Tysse, Chief Operating Officer
Nick Kuriger, Director Information Technology

A nonprofit association for the purpose of monitoring federal equal employment litigation and filing amicus curiae briefs in precedent-setting cases. Also file comments on equal opportunity employment and affirmative action regulatory proposals and monitors judicial developments.

11044 Federal Bar Association
2215 M Street NW
Washington, DC 20037
202-785-1614
Fax: 202-785-1568
e-mail: fba@fedbar.org
http://www.fedbar.org/

Jack D Lockridge, Executive Director
James Estes, Financial Director
Stacy Bernstein, Publications Editor

Attorneys employed by the federal government as legislators, judges, lawyers, or members of quasi-judicial boards and commissions; those with previous government legal experience; and those with a substantive interest in federal law and who practice before a federal court or agency. Over 100 specialized committees, operating through 24 Sections and Divisions, provide various programs such as continuing legal education and professional and community service.

11045 Legal Counsel for the Elderly
601 East Street NW
Washington, DC 20049
202-434-2120
Fax: 202-434-6424
e-mail: tosborne@aarp.org
http://www.aarp.org/states/dc/dc-lce/

Thomas Osborne, Directing Attorney
William Novelli, Chief Executive Officer
Erik Olsen, President Board of Directors

Provides free legal services to Washington, DC residents aged 60 and older, with priority given to low income persons. Serves as the Long-Term Care Ombudsman for DC by advocating for residents of nursing homes and board and care homes.

11046 National Senior Citizens Law Center
1101 14th Street NW
Suite 400
Washington, DC 20005
202-289-6976
Fax: 202-289-7224
e-mail: nsclc@nsclc.org
http://www.nsclc.org

Edward C King, Executive Director
Rochelle Bobroff, Director Federal Rights Project
Simon Lazarus, Public Policy Counsel

Legal Aid Resources/Florida

Advocates nationwide to promote the independence and well-being of low-income elderly individuals, as well as persons with disabilities, with particular emphasis on women and racial and ethnic minorities. Advocates through litigation and agency representation and assistance to attorneys and paralegals in field programs.

11047 Paralyzed Veterans of America (PVA)
801 18th Street NW
Washington, DC 20006-3517
202-872-1300
800-424-8200
Fax: 202-785-4452
e-mail: info@pva.org
http://www.pva.org/

Randy Pleva, President
Thomas R Fjerstad, Senior Vice President
Craig Enenbach, Treasurer

The Paralyzed Veterans of America, a congressionally chartered veterans service organization founded in 1946, has developed a unique expertise on a wide variety of issues involving the special needs of our members- veterans of the armed forces who have experienced spinal cord injury or dysfunction.

11048 US Department of Labor
200 Constitution Avenue NW
Frances Perkins Building
Washington, DC 20210
202-693-6000
Fax: 202-219-7312
http://www.dol.gov/
TTY 877-889-5627

Elaine L Chao, Secretary of Labor
Paul T Conway, Chief of Staff
Ruth D Knouse, Executive Secretariat Director

The Department of Labor (DOL) fosters and promotes the welfare of the job seekers, wage earners, and retirees of the United States by improving their working conditions, advancing their opportunities for profitable employment, protecting their retirement and health care benefits, helping employers find workers, strengthening free collective bargaining, and tracking changes in employment, prices, and other national economic measurements. In carrying out this mission, the Department administers a variety of Federal labor laws including those that guarantee workers' rights to safe and healthful working conditions; a minimum hourly wage and overtime pay; freedom from employment discrimination; unemployment insurance; and other income support.

11049 Veterans' Advocate
2001 S Street NW
PO Box 65762
Washington, DC 20009-1157
202-265-8305
Fax: 202-328-0063
e-mail: info@nvlsp.org
http://www.nvlsp.org/

D Addlestone, Joint Executive Director
Barton F Stichman, Co-Director
Ronald B Abrams, Co-Director

Non-profit veterans law firm. Recruits volunteer lawyers to handle cases before the US Court of Veterans Claims. Engages in many activities around Agent Orange and VA reform. Publishes the only treatise on veteran's law.

11050 Washington D.C. Protection and Advocacy Agency
University Legal Services
220 I Street Northeast
Suite 130
Washington, DC 20002
202-547-0198
Fax: 205-547-2083
e-mail: jbrown@uls-dc
http://www.uls-dc.org

Jane M Brown Esq., Executive Director
Celeste Valente, Senior Advocate
Alicia Johns, Program Director

Provides litigation services and technical assistance for seniors and those with disabilities.

11051 Washington Watch
United Cerebral Palsy Association
1660 L Street NW
Suite 700
Washington, DC 20036-5638
202-776-0406
800-USA-5UCP
Fax: 202-776-0414
e-mail: info@ucp.org
http://www.ucp.org/
TDD 202-973-7197

Akua Kouyate, Contact

Provides information on national legislation and regulatory affairs, updates on disability and social service fields.
24-36 pages

Florida

11052 Bay Area Legal Services
829 West Dr. Martin Luther King Boulevard
2nd Floor
Tampa, FL 33603-3336
813-232-1343
Fax: 813-229-1403
e-mail: jreed@bals.org
http://www.bals.org/About%20Us

Richard C Woltmann, Executive Director
Judy Reed, Development Director Assistant

People served through this program receive legal advice over the phone and forms and informational materials by mail when needed. They are also referred for necessary social services and extended legal representation, when appropriate.

11053 Florida Bar Association: Lawyer Referral Service
651 East Jefferson Street
Tallahassee, FL 32399-2300
850-561-5600
800-342-8011
Fax: 850-561-5827
http://www.floridabar.org/

Mary Ellen Bateman, Interim Division Director
Kenneth L Marvin, Lawyer Regulation Director
John A Boggs, Consumer Assistance Program Dtr

The Florida Bar Lawyer Referral Service has established a reduced-fee panel for the elderly. The panel assists people over 60 years old who are not eligible for legal aid, but who have an annual income of $10,000 or less for a household of two or $13,000 or less for a household of four.

11054 Florida Legal Services: Tallahassee Office
2425 Torreya Drive
Tallahassee, FL 32303
850-385-7900
Fax: 850-385-9998
e-mail: kent@floridalegal.org
http://www.floridalegal.org/tallahas.htm

Kent Spuhler, Executive Director
Anne Swerlick, Deputy Director/Staff Attorney
Dorene Barker, Legislative Advocate

The Tallahassee office is the main office of Florida Legal Services (FLS) of which the staff advocates have expertise in all the major legal areas impacting the elderly and low income community in Florida. Policy advocacy, legislation and administration are major responsibilities for all of the advocates in the Tallahassee office. The staff is available for consultation with all those providing civil legal assistance to elderly, low income and disadvantaged persons in Florida. Statewide training and technical assistance is coordinated from the Tallahassee office.

Legal Aid Resources/Georgia

11055 South Florida Advocacy Center for Persons with Disabilities Florida's Protection and Advocacy Programs for Persons with Disab.
4411 Sheridan Street
Hollywood, FL 33021
954-967-1493
800-350-4566
Fax: 954-967-1496
e-mail: info@advocacycenter.org
http://www.advocacycenter.org
TDD 866-478-0640

Gary Weston, Executive Director
Doug Jones, Esq., Chairman

Provides advocacy for individuals with disabilities and works toward ensuring community inclusion with adequate support this population.

11056 Tallahassee Advocacy Center for Personswith Disabilities Florida's Protection and Advocacy Programs for Persons with Disab.
2671 Executive Center Circle West
Suite 100
Tallahassee, FL 32301-5024
850-488-9071
800-342-0823
Fax: 850-488-8640
e-mail: info@advocacycenter.org
http://www.advocacycenter.org
TDD 800-346-4127

Gary Weston, Executive Director
Doug Jones, Esq., Chairman
Elizabeth Holifield, Ph.D, Board Member

Provides advocacy and works towards assuring community inclusion with adequate support for all seniors and those with disabilities.

11057 Tampa Advocacy Center for Persons with Disabilities Florida's Protection and Advocacy Programs for Persons With Disab.
Times Building, Suite 513
100 N Ashley Drive
Tampa, FL 33602
813-233-2920
866-875-1794
Fax: 813-233-2917
e-mail: info@advocacycenter.org
http://www.advocacycenter.org
TDD 866-875-1837

Gary Weston, Executive Director
Doug Jones, Esq., Chairman
Susan McCulloch, Board Member Tampa Office

Provides advocacy and works toward ensuring community inclusion for all those with disabilities.

11058 University of South Florida Library: Special Collections Department
4202 East Fowler Avenue
Tampa, FL 33620-9951
813-974-2731
Fax: 813-396-9006
e-mail: tomkemp@lib.usf.edu
http://www.lib.usf.edu/spccoll/edu/spccoll

Thomas Jay Kemp, University Librarian
Paul Eugen Camp, University Librarian

The mission of the University of South Florida (USF) Library is to provide public services that focus on relevant collections and in addition facilitate the optimal use of resources, services, and facilities which support the university community's teaching, research and service initiatives. The Special Collections Department of the USF Libraries Digital Collections contain a wide range of digital content, including images, audio, video, full text, E-Journals, E-Books, articles, indexes, and collection guides. Many of the Tampa Library Special Collections Department collections may also contain a limited number of representative digital samples from the individual collections.

1962

Georgia

11059 Atlanta Council of Younger Lawyers: Committee on Legal Services to the Elderly
229 Peachtree Street
International Tower, Suite 400
Atlanta, GA 30303-1980
404-521-0781
Fax: 404-522-0269
e-mail: blomas@atlantabar.org
http://www.atlantabar.org/ABA/

Diane o'Steen, Executive Director
Nita Wilson, Financial Director
Byron Lomas, Administrator

The committee handles small consumer claims on a pro bono basis in the Atlanta area.

11060 Atlanta Legal Aid Society: Atlanta
151 Spring Street Northwest
Atlanta, GA 30303
404-524-5811
Fax: 404-525-5710
e-mail: pmckay_alas@yahoo.com
http://www.atlantalegalaid.org/

Rita A Sheffey, President Executive Committee
Stephen Krumm, Managing Attorney Law Project
Cheri Tipton, Managing Attorney Senior Hotline

Atlanta Legal Aid Society's primary function is to provide referrals and legal representation to people who otherwise cannot obtain access to the court system - the poor, minorities, the elderly, those disabled by mental illness or long term diseases, and recent immigrants. They come to us for help in meeting their basic needs, protecting their homes and safeguarding their families. In addition to the issues covered through special projects, we offer assistance with simple legal matters, such as drafting wills and seeking redress for substandard consumer goods. Staff attorneys are also available to speak publicly about legal issues.

11061 Atlanta Legal Aid Society: Decatur
246 Sycamore Street
Decatur, GA 30030-3434
404-377-0701
e-mail: pmckay_alas@yahoo.com
http://www.atlantalegalaid.org/

Rita A Sheffey, President Executive Committee
Stephen Krumm, Managing Attorney Law Project
Cheri Tipton, Managing Attorney Senior Hotline

Atlanta Legal Aid Society's primary function is to provide referrals and legal representation to people who otherwise cannot obtain access to the court system - the poor, minorities, the elderly, those disabled by mental illness or long term diseases, and recent immigrants. They come to us for help in meeting their basic needs, protecting their homes and safeguarding their families. In addition to the issues covered through special projects, we offer assistance with simple legal matters, such as drafting wills and seeking redress for substandard consumer goods. Staff attorneys are also available to speak publicly about legal issues.

11062 Atlanta Legal Aid Society: East Point
1514 East Cleveland Avenue
Suite 100
East Point, GA 30344
404-669-0233
e-mail: pmckay_alas@yahoo.com
http://www.atlantalegalaid.org/

Rita A Sheffey, President Executive Commitee
Stephen Krumm, Managing Attorney Law Project
Cheri Tipton, Managing Attorney Senior Hotline

Atlanta Legal Aid Society's primary function is to provide referrals and legal representation to people who otherwise cannot obtain access to the court system - the poor, minorities, the elderly, those disabled by mental illness or long term diseases, and recent immigrants. They come to us for help in meeting their basic needs, protecting their homes and safeguarding their families. In addition to the issues covered through special projects, we offer assistance with simple legal matters, such as drafting wills and seeking redress for substandard consumer goods. Staff attorneys are also available to speak publicly about legal issues.

Legal Aid Resources/Hawaii

11063 Atlanta Legal Aid Society: Lawrenceville
180 Camden Hill Road
Suite A
Lawrenceville, GA 30045
678-376-4545
e-mail: pmckay_alas@yahoo.com
http://www.atlantalegalaid.org/
Rita A Sheffey, President Executive Committee
Stephen Krumm, Managing Attorney Law Project
Cheri Tipton, Managing Attorney Senior Hotline

Atlanta Legal Aid Society's primary function is to provide referrals and legal representation to people who otherwise cannot obtain access to the court system - the poor, minorities, the elderly, those disabled by mental illness or long term diseases, and recent immigrants. They come to us for help in meeting their basic needs, protecting their homes and safeguarding their families. In addition to the issues covered through special projects, we offer assistance with simple legal matters, such as drafting wills and seeking redress for substandard consumer goods. Staff attorneys are also available to speak publicly about legal issues.

11064 Atlanta Legal Aid Society: Marietta
30 South Park Square
Marietta, GA 30090
770-528-2565
e-mail: pmckay_alas@yahoo.com
http://www.atlantalegalaid.org/
Rita A Sheffey, President Executive Committee
Stephen Krumm, Managing Attorney Law Project
Cheri Tipton, Managing Attorney

Atlanta Legal Aid Society's primary function is to provide referrals and legal representation to people who otherwise cannot obtain access to the court system - the poor, minorities, the elderly, those disabled by mental illness or long term diseases, and recent immigrants. They come to us for help in meeting their basic needs, protecting their homes and safeguarding their families. In addition to the issues covered through special projects, we offer assistance with simple legal matters, such as drafting wills and seeking redress for substandard consumer goods. Staff attorneys are also available to speak publicly about legal issues.

11065 Georgia Division for Aging Services
Two Peachtree Street Northwest
Suite 9385
Atlanta, GA 30303-3142
404-657-5258
Fax: 404-657-5285
e-mail: magreene@dhr.state.ga.us
http://http://aging.dhr.georgia.gov/portal/site
Maria Greene, Executive Director

The Georgia Department of Human Resources, Division of Aging Services (DAS) administers a statewide system of services for senior citizens, their families and caregivers, working with other aging agencies and organizations to effectively and efficiently respond to the needs of elderly Georgians. DAS meets the challenge of Georgia's growing older population through continued service improvement and innovation.

11066 Georgia Protection and Advocacy Agency
150 East Ponce de Leon Avenue
Suite 430
Decatur, GA 30030
404-885-1234
800-537-2329
Fax: 404-378-0031
e-mail: info@thegao.org
http://www.thegao.org/
TDD 404-885-1234
Ruby Moore, Executive Director
Denise Quigley, Director of Resource Advocacy
Naomi Walker, Program Director

Hawaii

11067 Hawaii Disability Rights Center: Honolulu Hawaii Protection and Advocacy Agency
900 Fort Street Mall
Suite 1040
Honolulu, HI 96813
808-949-2922
Fax: 808-949-2928
e-mail: info@hawaiidisabilityrights.org
http://www.HawaiiDisabilityRights.org
TDD 808-949-2922
Gary L Smith, Executive Director
Ann E Collins, Vice President
Kathleen E Delahanty, Director Client Services

Hawaii Disability Rights Center (HDRC is the designated Client Assistance Program (CAP) and Protection and Advocacy (P&A) System for Hawaii's estimated 180,000 residents with disabilities. We strive to serve as many individuals with disabilities with as many different legal rights issues as our resources will allow; and to achieve the following outcomes to advance the human, civil and legal rights of people with disabilities: freedom from abuse and neglect; accessible communities; independence, productivity, integration and inclusion, and, self determination.

11068 Legal Aid Society of Hawaii
305 Wailuku Drive
Hilo, HI 96720-2488
808-934-0678
Fax: 808-969-3983
http://www.legalaidhawaii.org/
David J Reber, Esq., President
Melissa Teves Pavlicek, Esq., Vice President
Sheri Bentley, Secretary/Treasurer

Serves older persons in Hawaii. Developed a long-term care planning presentation that discusses options for financing long-term care, living wills, powers of attorney, joint accounts, representative payees, due process in public benefits, and estate planning.

11069 Legal Aid Society of Hawaii: Hilo
305 Wailuku Drive
Hilo, HI 96720-2448
808-934-0678
Fax: 808-969-3983
http://www.legalaidhawaii.org/
David J Reber, Esq., President
Melissa Teves Pavlicek, Esq., Vice President
Sheri Bentley, Secretary/Treasurer

Serves older persons in Maui County. Provides ongoing outreach and community education programs regarding Medicaid, living wills, powers of attorney.

11070 Legal Aid Society of Hawaii: Honolulu
924 Bethel Street
Honolulu, HI 96813
808-536-4302
Fax: 808-527-8088
http://www.legalaidhawaii.org/
David J Reber, Esq., President
Melissa Teves Pavlicek, Esq., Vice President
Sheri Bentley, Secretary/Treasurer

Serves older persons in Maui County. Provides ongoing outreach and community education programs regarding Medicaid, living wills, powers of attorney.

11071 Legal Aid Society of Hawaii: Kaunakakai
19-23 Ala Malama Street
Kaunakakai, HI 96748
808-553-3251
Fax: 808-553-5809
http://www.legalaidhawaii.org/
David J Reber, Esq., President
Melissa Teves Pavlicek, Esq., Vice President
Sheri Bentley, Secretary/Treasurer

Serves older persons in Maui County. Provides ongoing outreach and community education programs regarding Medicaid, living wills, powers of attorney.

11072 Legal Aid Society of Hawaii: Lanai City
730 Lanai Avenue
Suite 129
Lanai City, HI 96763
808-565-6089
Fax: 808-565-6089
http://www.legalaidhawaii.org/
David J Reber, Esq., President
Melissa Teves Pavlicek, Esq., Vice President
Sheri Bentley, Secretary/Treasurer

Serves older persons in Maui County. Provides ongoing outreach and community education programs regarding Medicaid, living wills, powers of attorney.

11073 Legal Aid Society of Hawaii: Lihu'e
4334 Rice Street
#204A
Lihu'e, HI 96766
808-245-4728
Fax: 808-246-8824
http://www.legalaidhawaii.org/
David J Reber, Esq., President
Melissa Teves Pavlicek, Esq., Vice President
Sheri Bentley, Secretary/Treasurer

Serves older persons in Maui County. Provides ongoing outreach and community education programs regarding Medicaid, living wills, powers of attorney.

11074 Legal Aid Society of Hawaii: Maui
2287 Main Street
Wailuku, HI 96793-1655
808-242-0724
Fax: 808-244-5856
http://www.legalaidhawaii.org/
David J Reber, Esq., President
Melissa Teves Pavlicek, Esq., Vice President
Sheri Bentley, Secretary/Treasurer

Serves older persons in Maui County. Provides ongoing outreach and community education programs regarding Medicaid, living wills, powers of attorney.

11075 State of Hawaii: Department of Health & Executive Office on Aging
No. 1 Capitol District, Suite 406
250 South Hotel Street
Honolulu, HI 96813-2831
808-586-0100
Fax: 808-586-0185
e-mail: coa@doh.hawaii.gov
http://http://www4.hawaii.gov/eoa/index.html
Pat Sasaki, Executive Director

The mission of the Executive Office on Aging (EOA) is to assure the well-being of the State's 230,000+ adults, age 60 and older by: providing leadership in programs and policies for older adults; serving as a clearinghouse for information, and partnering with our Aging Network to provide home and community based care for frail, vulnerable seniors.

11076 University of Hawaii at Manoa: William S Richardson School of Law
2515 Dole Street
Honolulu, HI 96822-2328
808-956-6544
Fax: 808-956-9439
e-mail: uhelp@hawaii.edu
http://www.hawaii.edu/uhelp/UHELP_whatis.html
James H Pietsch, Executive Director

Operates an elder law clinic and an elder law unit that provide legal services to older persons. The Elder Law Clinic is a law school educational program with the primary responsibility of training law students in the Elder Law area.

Idaho

11077 Comprehensive Advocacy: Boise Idaho's Protection and Advocacy System
4477 Emerald
Suite B-100
Boise, ID 83706
208-336-5353
Fax: 208-336-5396
e-mail: coadinc@cableone.net
http://users.moscow.com/co-ad/
TDD 208-336-5353
James R Baugh, Executive Director

11078 Comprehensive Advocacy: Moscow Idaho's Protection and Advocacy System
428 West 3rd Street
Moscow, ID 83843
208-882-0962
Fax: 208-883-4241
e-mail: co-ad@moscow.com
http://http://users.moscow.com/co-ad/
TDD 208-882-0962
James R Baugh, Executive Director

11079 Comprehensive Advocacy: Pocatello Idaho's Protection and Advocacy System
845 West Center
Suite C107
Pocatello, ID 83204
208-232-0922
Fax: 208-232-0938
e-mail: coinc-tdd@qwest.net
http://users.moscow.com/co-ad/
TDD 208-232-0922
James R Baugh, Executive Director

11080 Idaho Commission on Aging
3380 Americana Terrace
Suite 120
Boise, ID 83706
208-334-3833
877-471-2777
Fax: 208-334-3033
e-mail: lbauer@aging.idaho.gov
http://www.idahoaging.com/
Lois Bauer, Administrator
Sarah Scott, Program Operations Unit Manager
Donna Denney, Public Information Officer

The Idaho Commission on Aging (ICOA) is the sole state agency designated under the Older Americans Act to administer programs and services for Idahoans 60 years of age and older. Located under the oversight of the Executive Office of the Governor, the ICOA plans and coordinates, funds, and monitors a statewide program of services to meet present and future needs of older Idahoans. Its second responsibility is to advocate for Idaho's elderly to secure existing rights, benefits and services under Federal, State and local law and to gain crucial new programs.

Illinois

11081 AIDS Legal Council of Chicago
180 North Michigan Avenue
Suite 2110
Chicago, IL 60601
312-427-8990
Fax: 312-427-8419
e-mail: info@aidslegal.com
http://www.aidslegal.com
Ann Hilton Fisher, Esq., Executive Director
Dale Green, Outreach Advocate
Mirta Woodall, Staff Attorney

Legal advice and services for persons who are HIV positive or have AIDS, and their companions, families, etc., regarding HIV-related legal matters.

Legal Aid Resources/Illinois

11082 Center for Medicare and Medicaid Services (CMS)
Chicago Region 5 Office
233 North Michigan Avenue
Suite 600
Chicago, IL 60601-5519
312-886-6432
Fax: 312-353-0252
http://www.CMS.gov

Jackie Garner, Regional Administrator
David Dupre, Deputy Regional Administrator

The Chicago Regional Office (Region 5) should be your initial point of contact on any Medicare, Medicaid, or State Child Health Insurance Program (SCHIP), issue in the following states: Illinois, Indiana, Michigan, Minnesota, Ohio and Wisconsin.

11083 Chicago Kent Law School Information Center Illinois Institute of Technology
565 West Adams Street
Chicago, IL 60661
312-906-5600
Fax: 312-906-5685
e-mail: kstivers@kentlaw.edu
http://http://library.kentlaw.edu/

Keith Stiverson, Director
Holly Lakatos, Public Services Director
Deborah Ginsberg, Electronic Resources Librarian

Information on federal and Illinois law, law and aging, international relations law, financial services law, business and management, environmental law.

11084 Chicago Lawyers' Committee For Civil Rights Under Law
100 North LaSalle Street
Suite 600
Chicago, IL 60602-2403
312-630-9744
Fax: 312-630-1127
e-mail: clccrul@aol.com
http://www.clccrul.org/index.html

Clyde Murphy, Executive Director
Susan Kaplan, Director Community Development
Elyssa Balingit Winslow, Director Fair Housing Project

Legal aid, including class action suits and impact cases concerning the rights of persons with disabilities and their families.

11085 Council for Disability Rights
30 East Adams
Suite 1130
Chicago, IL 60603
312-444-1967
Fax: 312-444-1977
e-mail: cdrights@interaccess.com
http://www.disabilityrights.org

Josephine E Holzer, Executive Director/Editor
Dorie Stewart, Information Specialist
Mary Beth Gahan, Disability Consultant

Promotes human rights of persons with disabilities and their families. Offers a job placement service, legal referrals, information services, a website and monthly newsletter (CDR Reports).

11086 Disabled Americans Rally for Equality
4752 South Kilpatrick Avenue
Chicago, IL 60632-4833
773-873-8703
Fax: 773-873-7818

Dennis Schreiber, Coordinator

Promotes awareness and lobbies for disabled persons rights.

11087 Equip for Equality: Chicago Advancing the Human & Civil Rights of People with Disabilities in IL
20 North Michigan Avenue
Suite 300
Chicago, IL 60602
312-341-0022
800-537-2632
Fax: 312-341-0295
e-mail: contactus@equipforequality.org
http://www.equipforequality.org
TTY 800-610-2779

Zena Naiditch, President/CEO
Carmelita Garcia-Kayes, Senior Advocate
Anne Orozco, Staff Interpreter

The mission of Equip for Equality is to advance the human and civil rights of children and adults with physical and mental disabilities in Illinois. It is the only statewide, cross-disability, comprehensive advocacy organization providing self-advocacy assistance, legal services, and disability rights education while also engaging in public policy and legislative advocacy and conducting abuse investigations and other oversight activities.

11088 Equip for Equality: Rock Island Advancing the Human & Civil Rights of People with Disabilities in IL
1612 Second Avenue
PO Box 276
Rock Island, IL 61204
309-786-6868
800-758-6869
Fax: 309-786-2393
e-mail: contactus@equipforequality.org
http://www.equipforequality.org
TTY 800-610-2779

Zena Naiditch, President/CEO
Janet M Cartwright, Senior Attorney

The mission of Equip for Equality is to advance the human and civil rights of children and adults with physical and mental disabilities in Illinois. It is the only statewide, cross-disability, comprehensive advocacy organization providing self-advocacy assistance, legal services, and disability rights education while also engaging in public policy and legislative advocacy and conducting abuse investigations and other oversight activities.

11089 Equip for Equality: Springfield Advancing the Human & Civil Rights of People with Disabilities in IL
235 South Fifth Street
PO Box 276
Springfield, IL 62705
217-544-0464
800-758-0464
Fax: 217-523-0720
e-mail: contactus@equipforequality.org
http://www.equipforequality.org
TTY 800-610-2779

Zena Naiditch, President/CEO
M H Bolden, Senior Advocate
Barry G Lowy, Senior Attorney

The mission of Equip for Equality is to advance the human and civil rights of children and adults with physical and mental disabilities in Illinois. It is the only statewide, cross-disability, comprehensive advocacy organization providing self-advocacy assistance, legal services, and disability rights education while also engaging in public policy and legislative advocacy and conducting abuse investigations and other oversight activities.

11090 Guardianship Services Associates
41A South Boulevard
Oak Park, IL 60302
708-386-5398
Fax: 708-386-5970
e-mail: GSAoakpark@aol.com

Robert R Wohlgemuth, Director

Information and counseling on guardianship issues. Can provide direct assistance in obtaining guardianship for disabled adults.

11091 Illinois Department on Aging
421 East Capitol Avenue
Suite 100
Springfield, IL 62701-1789
217-785-3356
800-252-8966
Fax: 217-785-4477
e-mail: ilsenior@aging.state.il.us
http://www.state.il.us/aging/
TTY 888-206-1327

Charles D Johnson, Executive Director
Ralph Cianchetti, Chair Council on Aging

The mission of the Illinois Department on Aging is to serve and advocate for older Illinoisans and their caregivers by administering programs and promoting partnerships that encourage independence, dignity, and quality of life.

Legal Aid Resources/Indiana

11092 Office of the Attorney General: Senior Citizens Advocacy Division
100 West Randolph Street
Chicago, IL 60601
312-814-3000
800-AGE-LESS
e-mail: webmaster@atg.state.il.us
http://www.illinoisattorneygeneral.gov/seniors/
TTY 312-814-3374
Lisa Madigan, Attorney General

Created in 1983, the Division assists senior citizens with the following: consumer protection, crime prevention, compensation and assistance for crime victims, nursing home resident advocacy, legislative proposals, speakers bureau, and Medigap insurance information.

11093 Pro Bono Center for Disability and Elder Law (CDEL): Lifelong Lawyers Project
Chicago Bar Association Senior Lawyers Committee
710 Lake Shore Drive
Chicago, IL 60611
312-908-4463
Fax: 312-908-0866
e-mail: bglaves@chicagobar.org
http://www.chicagobarfoundation.org/projects/
TTY 312-908-8705
Jann Dragovich-Stulberg, Executive Director
Robert Glaves, Foundation Liaison

The Pro Bono Center for Disability and Elder Law (CDEL) identifies, protects and advances the legal rights of persons with disabilities and the elderly by providing free, high quality legal services. CDEL bills itself as a pro bono law firm, and the spectrum of pro bono opportunities available is extensive and varied. Whether you choose direct legal services or community outreach activities, the staff will provide everything needed to accommodate individual schedule and service requirements.

11094 Senior Citizens' Wills Program: Chicago Bar Association
321 South Plymouth Court
Chicago, IL 60604
312-554-2001
e-mail: tmurphy@chicagobar.org
http://www.chicagobar.org/
Terrence M Murphy, Executive Director/President
Brenda Ott, Lawyer Referral Service

Provides senior citizens with access to low-cost wills and other important legal services.

11095 US Department of Health and Human Services: Office for Civil Rights
233 North Michigan Avenue
Suite 700
Chicago, IL 60603
312-353-5160
312-886-1709
Fax: 312-886-1718
e-mail: Donna.Weinstein@hhs.gov
http://www.state.il.us/agency/dhs/592ycrnp.html
Donna Morros Weinstein, Regional Chief Counsel

Enforces the Rehabilitation Act of 1973, prohibiting discrimination against handicapped persons by recipients of federal funding.

11096 US Department of Labor: Office of Federal Contract Compliance Programs
230 South Dearborn Street
Room 434
Chicago, IL 60604
312-596-7045
Fax: 312-596-7085
http://dol.gov/esa/contacts/ofccp/ofnation2htm
Margaret Kraak, Acting District Director

Investigates complaints brought under section 504 of the Rehabilitation Act of 1973 against federal contractors.

Indiana

11097 Aging and In Home Services of Northeast Indiana
Indiana Area Agency on Aging
2927 Lake Avenue
Fort Wayne, IN 76805-5414
260-745-1200
800-552-3662
Fax: 260-456-1066
e-mail: dshappell@agingihs.org
http://www.agingihs.org/
Diann McCormick, President

The Indiana Association of Area Agencies on Aging (IAAAA) advocates for quality programs and services for older adults and persons with disabilities. IAAAA believes in the individual's right to: choose among health care alternatives to maintain independence and dignity; practice healthy lifestyles to have a happier, healthier, and longer life; and, be educated about services and alternatives available.

11098 Indiana Division of Aging
Indiana Family & Social Services Administration
402 West Washington Street
PO Box 7083
Indianapolis, IN 46207-7083
317-232-7123
Fax: 317-232-7867
e-mail: Stephen.smith@fssa.in.gov
http://www.in.gov/fssa/elderly/aging/index.html
Stephen Smith, Executive Director
Dennis Rosebrough, Public Information Officer
Cindy Brown, Assistant Director

The Indiana Division of Aging (IDA) provides a broad range of in-home and community based services to older adults and persons of all ages with disabilities. Services provided focus on prevention, early intervention, protection and advocacy. The Division collaborates with communities, local organizations, and other units of government to provide services to individuals and their families.

11099 Indiana Legal Services: Senior Law Project
151 North Delaware Street
Suite 1800
Indianapolis, IN 46204-2504
317-631-9410
800-869-0212
Fax: 317-631-9775
http://www.indianajustice.org/Home/PublicWeb
Norman P Metzger, Executive Director

Provides free legal assistance to elderly residents. Assists older persons in living with choice, independence and dignity. Focuses on legal issues, including: long term care, advance directives, health, and income maintenance, among others. Also provides advice/referrals on issues of abuse, neglect, age discrimination, and protective services.

11100 Indiana Protection and Advocacy Agency
4701 North Keystone Avenue
Suite 222
Indianapolis, IN 46204
317-722-5555
800-622-4845
Fax: 317-722-5564
e-mail: tgallagher@ipas.state.in.us
http://www.IN.gov/ipas
TDD 317-722-5555
Tom Gallagher, Executive Director

IPAS was created in 1977 by state law (IC. 12-28-1-6 as amended) to protect and advocate the rights of people with disabilities and is Indiana's federally designated Protection and Advocacy (P&A) system and client assistance program.

11101 National Legal Center for the Medically Dependent and Disabled
1 South 6th Street
Terre Haute, IN 47807-3510
812-232-2434
Fax: 812-232-2434
e-mail: jboppjr@aol.com
http://www.vigo.lib.in.us/nonprofit/
James Bopp, President

Legal Aid Resources/Iowa

Service organization working to defend the legal rights of indigent older and disabled persons so that such people can obtain proper medical care. Provides lawyer referral services. Operates speakers' bureau. Provides analysis of pertinent legislation on request of legislators.

11102 Northwest Indiana Community Action Corp
Indiana Area Agency on Aging
5518 Calumet Avenue
Hammond, IN 46320
219-937-3500
800-826-7871
Fax: 219-932-0566
e-mail: golund@nwi-ca.org
http://www.nwi-ca.com
TTY 888-814-7597

Gary Olund, Executive Director
Jennifer Malone, Director Elderly Services

The Indiana Association of Area Agencies on Aging (IAAAA) advocates for quality programs and services for older adults and persons with disabilities. IAAAA believes in the individual's right to: choose among health care alternatives to maintain independence and dignity; practice healthy lifestyles to have a happier, healthier, and longer life; and, be educated about services and alternatives available.

11103 Resources For Enriching Adult Learning(REAL)
Indiana Area Agency on Aging
1151 South Michigan Street
PO Box 1835
South Bend, IN 46634-1835
574-233-8205
800-552-2916
Fax: 574-284-2642
http://www.realservicesinc.com

Lester Fox, President/CEO
Becky Zaseck, Executive Director

The Indiana Association of Area Agencies on Aging (IAAAA) advocates for quality programs and services for older adults and persons with disabilities. IAAAA believes in the individual's right to: choose among health care alternatives to maintain independence and dignity; practice healthy lifestyles to have a happier, healthier, and longer life; and, be educated about services and alternatives available.

11104 Southwestern Indiana Mental Health Center
415 Mulberry Street
Evansville, IN 47713-1298
812-436-4232
Fax: 812-422-7558
http://www.southwestern.org/

Tonee Brinkman, Contact

The mission of Southwestern shall be to provide quality mental health services to the citizens of Gibson, Posey, Vanderburgh and Warrick counties. The services provided shall be consistent with demonstrated community needs and prudent utilization of Southwestern's resources. The services shall be reasonably available and accessible to all citizens and shall be provided in an environment in which the rights of individual patients are recognized aNd respected.
1978

11105 Vincennes University: Byron R Lewis Historical Library
1002 North First Street
Vincennes, IN 47591
812-888-4330
Fax: 812-888-5471
e-mail: rking@vinu.edu
http://vinu.edu/AcademicResources/ShakeLibrary/

Richard King, Reference Librarian
Joseph Helms, Reference Librarian

The Byron R. Lewis Historical Collection Library is located on the main campus of Vincennes University. It is a comprehensive repository of historical documents, books and letters emphasizing the history of the former Indiana Territory, an area that once comprised the present states of Indiana, Michigan, Wisconsin, Illinois and a part of Minnesota.
1967

11106 Washington County Historical Society: Genealogy and Historical Library
307 East Market Street
Salem, IN 47167-2119
812-883-6495
e-mail: jhc@blueriver.net
http://www.blueriver.net/~jhc/

Martha Bowers, Librarian
Willie Harlen, President
Ann McRoden-Mensch, Historical Genealogist

Collections include materials relating to the history and genealogy of Washington County from 1800 to the present. Included are family histories, church records, obituaries, census records, marriage records, newspapers, state and county histories, war records, and photographs. Also maintains data and records from other states.

Iowa

11107 Area Agency on Aging: Senior Citizens Lawyer Referral Service
808 River Street
Decorah, IA 52101
563-382-2941
Fax: 563-382-6248
e-mail: mail@northlandaging.com
http://www.northlandaging.com

Bruce Butters, Executive Director

Reduced fee services to clients 60 years old or over.

11108 Elderbridge-Area Agency on Aging: Legal Referral Panel
22 North Georgia Avenue
Suite 216
Mason City, IA 50401
641-424-0678
800-243-0678
Fax: 641-424-2927
e-mail: elderbridge@jumpgate.net
http://www.elderbridge.org

Lahoma Counts, Executive Director

The Panel accepts cases in which the clients are not eligible for free legal services, yet cannot afford to retain a private attorney.

11109 Help Legal Assistance: Senior Citizens Law Project
Iowa Legal Aid
1111 9th Street
Suite 230
Des Moines, IA 50314
515-243-2980
Fax: 563-323-7345
http://www.iowalegalaid.org/hotline/

Dennis Groenenboom, Executive Director

The Legal Hotline is the first place to go to get information and advice about elder law issues. The Legal Hotline is a special project of Iowa Legal Aid that provides legal advice and other services to Iowans who are 60 or older. The Hotline's services are free and confidential. By getting legal advice when you need it, you can prevent and resolve legal problems, avoid being victimized, remain independent and make better life planning decisions.

11110 Iowa Department of Elder Affairs: Legal Assistance
Jesse M. Parker Building
510 East 12th Street
Suite 2
Des Moines, IA 50319-9025
515-725-3333
800-532-3213
Fax: 515-725-3300
e-mail: Deanna.Clingan@iowa.gov
http://www.state.ia.us/elderaffairs/advocacy/
TTY 515-725-3302

Mark Haverland, Executive Director
Deanna Clingan-Fischer, Legal Assistance Developer

Legal Aid Resources/Kansas

The Mission of the Iowa Department of Elder Affairs (DEA) is: to provide advocacy, educational, and prevention services to older Iowans so they can find Iowa a healthy, safe, productive, and enjoyable place to live and work. The DepEA serves a fast-growing segment of Iowa's population- people 60 years of age and older. As required under the Older Americans Act, the Department of Elder Affairs has a Legal Assistance Developer to develop & coordinate a legal assistance program & to secure and maintain the legal rights of older Iowans. The legal assistance program is implemented in collaboration with the thirteen area agencies on aging and legal providers across the state, including the Legal Hotline for Older Iowans.

11111 Iowa Protection and Advocacy Agency
950 Office Park Road
Suite 221
West Des Moines, IA 50265
515-278-2502
800-779-2502
Fax: 515-278-0539
e-mail: info@ipna.org
http://www.ipna.org
TDD 515-278-0571

Sylvia Piper, Executive Director

Iowa Protection and Advocacy Services, Inc., is a federally funded program that will protect and advocate for the human and legal rights that ensure individuals with disabilities and/or mental illness a free, appropriate public education, employment opportunities and residence or treatment in the least restrictive environment or method and for freedom from stigma. Iowa Protection and Advocacy Services will support people with disabilities to secucure their rights and full participation as citizens through a program of self-advocacy education, information and referral, non-legal advocacy and legal and systems advocacy.

11112 Iowa State Bar: Young Lawyer Section Committee on Delivery of Legal Services to the Elderly
801 Grand Street
Suite 3700
Des Moines, IA 50309-8004
515-246-5856
Fax: 515-246-5808
e-mail: miller.william@bradshawlaw.com
http://www.iowabar.org/YLD.nsf/

Wiliam J Miller, Committee Chair

The services to the elderly committee is a volunteer organization of lawyers who are interested in ensuring that the legal needs and rights of older iowans are met.

11113 Northwest Aging Association
Iowa Department of Elder Affairs
2 Grand Avenue
Spencer, IA 51301
712-262-1775
800-242-5033
Fax: 712-262-7520
e-mail: www.nwaging.org
http://www.nwaging.org

Cythina Beaumann, Director

Northwest Aging Association (NAA) serves as the gateway to programs and services that will assist older adults to maintain independence and quality of life. In addition, the NAA is a resource center that provides information regarding programs and services that will enable the elderly to remain independent in their own homes and preserve their dignity and quality of life.

11114 Seneca Area Agency on Aging
Iowa Department of Elder Affairs
117 North Cooper Street
Ottumwa, IA 52501
641-681-2270
800-642-6522
Fax: 641-682-2445
e-mail: seneca@seneca-aaa.org
http://www.seneca-aaa.org

Connie Holland, Director

Seneca Area Agency on Aging advocates for and provides assistance to older persons in a non-discriminatory manner, working toward fostering and maintaining independence while preserving the dignity of each individual and focusing on their quality of life.

11115 Siouxland Aging Services
Iowa Department of Elder Affairs
2301 Pierce Street
Sioux City, IA 51104
712-279-6900
800-798-6916
Fax: 712-233-3415
e-mail: siouxlandaging@siouxlandaging.org
http://www.SiouxlandAging.org

Ann DeBoom, Director

The mission of Siouxland Aging Services is to: secure and maintain maximum independence and dignity in a home environment for older individuals capable of self care with appropriate supportive services; remove individual and social barriers to economic and personal independence for older individuals; and, provide a continuum of care for the vulnerable elderly.

11116 Winifred Law Opportunity Center
Christian Opportunity Center
106 East 2nd Avenue
Indianola, IA 50125-2520
515-961-5341
Fax: 515-961-5002
http://www.christianopportunity.org/

Rod Braun, Executive Director
Bruce Kreuger, Records Center
Kristen Langstraat, Hubbell Project Archives

The Christian Opportunity Center sTrives to provide quality support to people with disabilities and is also committed to the Christian values of the founding fathers.

Kansas

11117 Kansas Department of Aging: Legal Assistance Services for Older Adults (KDOA)
Kansas Department on Aging
503 South Kansas Avenue
Topeka, KS 66603-3404
785-296-4986
Fax: 785-296-0256
e-mail: wwwmail@aging.state.ks.us
http://www.agingkansas.org/

Kathleen Sebelius, KDOA Governor
Kathy Greenlee, KDOA Acting Secretary

Legal assistance services provide access to the system of justice by offering advice and representation by a legal provider. This provider acts as an advocate for the social and economically needy older individual to ensure gaining access to essential services or financial resources, and protecting their rights to be autonomous and to retain their dignity.

11118 Kansas Protection and Advocacy Agency & Disability Rights Center of Kansas
635 Southwest Harrison
Suite 100
Topeka, KS 66603
785-273-9661
877-776-1541
Fax: 785-273-9414
e-mail: rocky@drckansas.org
http://www.drckansas.org
TDD 877-335-3725

Rocky Nichols, Executive Director
Timothy Voth, J.D., Advocacy Director
Debbie White, C.P.A., Fiscal Officer

The Disability Rights Center of Kansas (DRC), is a public interest legal advocacy agency empowered by federal law to advocate for the civil and legal rights of Kansans with disabilities. DRC is the Official Protection and Advocacy System for Kansas and is a part of the national network of federally mandated and funded protection and advocacy systems. As such, DRC advocates for the rights of Kansans with disabilities under state or federal laws (ADA, the Rehabilitation Act, Federal Medicaid Act, Kansas Act Against Discrimination, etc.).

Legal Aid Resources/Kentucky

Kentucky

11119 Kentucky Bar Association: Committee on Legal Concerns of Elderly Clients
514 West Main Street
Frankfort, KY 40601-1883
502-564-3795
Fax: 502-564-3225
e-mail: fburnette@kybar.org
http://www.kybar.org/

J Frank Burnette, Director
Charlene S Jones, Information Systems Manager
Peggy Morris, Administrator

Produces a handbook on eight broad law-related areas for the elderly, including information and referral sections, a reading list, and a resource guide.

11120 Kentucky Bar Association: Senior Lawyers Section
167 West Main Street
Suite 1004
Lexington, KY 40507
859-255-2313
e-mail: grabe@alltel.net
http://www.kybar.org/

George Rabe, Executive Director

The Senior Lawyers Section of the Kentucky Bar Association is comprised of lawyers 55 years old and older that includes senior practicing attorneys as well as retired and semi-retired lawyers. The section provides a common forum for exchanging ideas and promotes and provides continuing education for retired or semi-retired lawyers and fosters excellence and professionalism.

11121 Kentucky Division of Aging Services
Kentucky Cabinet for Health and Family Services
275 East Main Street 3W-F
Frankfort, KY 40621
502-564-6930
Fax: 502-564-4595
e-mail: bill.cooper@ky.gov
http://http://chfs.ky.gov/dhss/das/
TTY 888-642-1137

William Cooper, Executive Director
Donna Collins, Assistant Director
Phyllis Sosa, Branch Manager

The Division of Aging Services is the federally designated State Unit on Aging for Kentucky. It is empowered to provide services to help older Kentuckians and their families through a statewide network of local, private and public agencies. The Division of Aging Services develops community-based systems of care that foster independence, protect the quality of life, and ensure the efficient and effective integration of services for the aging population.

11122 Kentucky Legal Aid
1122 Jefferson Street
Paducah, KY 42001
270-442-5518
800-467-2218
http://www.klaid.org/

Jeffrey A Been, Executive Director/Attorney
Ronald E Marstin, Managing Attorney
S. Stewart Pope, Advocacy Director/Attorney

The mission of Kentucky Legal Aid (KLA) is to assist and to enable low-income families, as well as the elderly, disabled and other vulnerable individuals in South Central and Western Kentucky, to resolve legal problems that are barriers to self-sufficiency, and to provide these individuals an opportunity for an improved quality of life. KLA utilizes attorneys and other staff to provide direct legal assistance; coordinates referrals to volunteer (pro bono) attorneys; and also addresses these client needs through programs for Benefits Counseling and Domestic Violence Assistance.

11123 Kentucky Protection and Advocacy Agency
100 Fair Oaks Lane
3rd Floor
Frankfort, KY 40601
502-564-2967
Fax: 502-564-0848
e-mail: Maureen.Fitzgerald@ky.gov
http://www.kypa.net
TDD 800-372-2988

Maureen Fitzgerald, Executive Director

Protection and Advocacy (P&A) is an independent state agency that was designated by the Governor as the protection and advocacy agency for Kentucky. P&A's staff includes professional advocates and attorneys. Advocates work together with people who have disabilities to promote and protect their legal rights in addition to providing information and referral services regarding an individual's rights under disability laws.

Louisiana

11124 AIDSLAW of Louisiana
2515 Canal Street
Suite 401
New Orleans, LA 70119-6439
504-568-1631
Fax: 504-821-8326
e-mail: aidslaw@bellsouth.net
http://www.aidslaw.org/

Linton Carney, Executive Director

Second year of funding for new legal agency serving persons affected by HIV/AIDS.

11125 Acadiana Legal Service Corporation
1020 Surrey Street
Lafayette, LA 70501
337-237-4320
800-256-1175
Fax: 337-237-8839
e-mail: alsclaf@la-law.org
http://www.la-law.org/locations.html

Joseph R Oelkers, III, Executive Director
Clifton R Jackson, Administrative Director

Provides support and services to those with disabilities and the senior population.

11126 Baton Rouge Advocacy Center
2704 Wooddale Boulevard
Suite B
Baton Rouge, LA 70805
225-925-8884
800-711-1696
Fax: 225-925-9625
e-mail: lsimpson@advocacyla.org
http://www.advocacyla.org

Lois Simpson, Executive Director
Freddie Pincus, President
Denver D Nobles Jr, Advisory Council Co-Chair

The Advocacy Center believes in the dignity of every life, and in the freedom of all people to experience the highest degree of self-determination. Embracing this philosophy, the Advocacy Center protects and advocates for the human and legal rights of persons living in Louisiana who are elderly or disabled.

11127 Lafayette Advocacy Center
600 Jefferson Street
Suite 812
Lafayette, LA 70501
337-237-7380
800-822-0210
Fax: 337-237-0486
e-mail: advocacycenter@advocacyla.org
http://www.advocacyla.org

Lois Simpson, Executive Director
Freddie Incus, President
Denver D Nobles, Jr, Advisory Council Co-Chair

The Advocacy Center believes in the dignity of every life, and in the freedom of all people to experiencethe highest degree of self-determination. Embracing this philosophy, the Advocacy Center protects and advocates fo the human and legal rights of persons living in Louisianna who are elderly or disabled.

Legal Aid Resources/Maine

11128 Louisiana Governor's Office of Elderly Affairs
412 North 4th Street, 3rd Floor
PO Box 61
Baton Rouge, LA 70821-0061
225-342-7100
Fax: 225-342-7133
e-mail: elderlyaffairs@goea.state.la.us
http://www.state.la.us/
Godfrey P. White, Executive Director
Ron Blereau, Assistant Director
Paul Colomb, Legal Counsel

The Governor's Office of Elderly Affairs (GOEA) serves as a focal point for Louisiana's senior citizens and administers a broad range of home and community based services through a network of 37 Area Agencies on Aging. GOEA serves as the focal point for the development, implementation, and administration of the public policy for the state of Louisiana, and address the needs of the state's elderly citizens.

11129 New Orleans Advocacy Center
1010 Common Street
Suite 2600
New Orleans, LA 70112
504-522-2337
800-960-7705
Fax: 504-522-5507
e-mail: advocacycenter@advocacyla.org
http://www.advocacyla.org/
TTY 800-960-7705
Lois Simpson, Executive Director

The Advocacy Center serves individuals with disabilities and senior citizens as New Orleans and Louisiana struggle to rebuild.

11130 Shreveport Advocacy Center
2620 Centenary Boulevard
Building 2, Suite 248
Shreveport, LA 71104
318-227-6186
800-839-7688
Fax: 318-227-1841
e-mail: lsimpson@advocacyla.org
http://www.advocacyla.org
Lois Simpson, Executive Director
Freddie Pincus, President
Denver D Nobles Jr, Advisory Council Co-Chair

The Advocacy Center believes in the dignity of every life, and in the freedom of all people to experience the highest degree of self-determination. Embracing this philosophy, the Advocacy Center protects and advocates for the human and legal rights of persons living in Louisiana who are elderly or disabled.

Maine

11131 Advocates for Medicare Patients (AMP's)
9 Green Street
PO Box 2723
Augusta, ME 04338-2723
207-621-0374
800-750-5353
http://www.state.me.us/dhs/beas/resource/
Harold Hainke, Directing Attorney

This statewide program provides free representation to Medicare beneficiaries in claim denials and conducts training and community education on Medicare issues.

11132 Legal Services for the Elderly: Augusta
PO Box 2723
Augusta, ME 04338-2723
207-621-0087
800-750-5353
http://www.mainelse.org/
Jaye Martin, Executive Director
Stanley N Marshall Jr, Chairman
Patty Dugal, Finance Manager

Legal Services for the Elderly provides persons age 60 and over with free legal advice regarding health care, health insurance, medicare (including part d), MaineCare (medicaid), social security and other public benefits.

11133 Legal Services for the Elderly: Lewiston
8 Falcon Road
Lewiston, ME 04243
207-795-2709
800-750-5353
e-mail: advocate@drcme.org
http://www.mainelse.org/about/offices_lewiston
Kimberly Moody, Executive Director
Rick Langley, Advocacy Director
Leeann Mosley, Operations Director

The mission of the Disability Rights Center is to advance and enforce the rights of individuals with disabilities. In working with and on behalf of people with disabilities, we are committed to the principles that people with disabilities can make choices and that they are entitled to enjoy life's benefits as full and equal members of Maine's communities.

11134 Maine Office of Elder Affairs
442 Civic Center Drive
11 State House Station
Augusta, ME 04333-0011
207-287-9200
800-262-2232
Fax: 207-287-9229
e-mail: Diana.scully@maine.gov
http://www.maine.gov/dhhs/beas/services.htm
TTY 800-606-0215
Diana Scully, Executive Director
Mary Walsh, Community Services Director
Catherine Cobb, Resource Develpment

Services are supported primarily with federal Older Americans Act funds, provides home delivered meals, outreach, information and assistance, transportation, employment, volunteer, public education and legal services to 42,000 people annually through the five Area Agencies on Aging and Legal Services for the Elderly, Inc. Also includes federal demonstration grants for Alzheimer's services and health insurance counseling.

11135 Maine Protection & Advocacy AgencyDisability Rights Center: Bangor Office
450 Essex Street
Bangor, ME 04401
207-941-2280
800-750-5353
e-mail: advocate@drcme.org
http://www.mainelse.org/about/offices_bangor
Kimberly Moody, Executive Director
Julie Mallet, Managing Attorney
Eleanor Buchey, Legal Assistant

The mission of the Disability Rights Center is to advance and enforce the rights of individuals with disabilities. In working with and on behalf of people with disabilities, we are committed to the principles that people with disabilities can make choices and that they are entitled to enjoy life's benefits as full and equal members of Maine's communities.

11136 Maine Protection and Advocacy AgencyDisability Rights Center: Augusta Office
24 Stone Street
PO Box 2007
Augusta, ME 04338
207-626-2774
800-452-1948
Fax: 207-621-1419
e-mail: advocate@drcme.org
http://www.drcme.org
TDD 800-452-1948
Kimberly Moody, Executive Director
Rick Langley, Advocacy Director
Leeann Mosley, Operations Director

The mission of the Disability Rights Center is to advance and enforce the rights of individuals with disabilities. In working with and on behalf of people with disabilities, we are committed to the principles that people with disabilities can make choices and that they are entitled to enjoy life's benefits as full and equal members of Maine's communities.

Legal Aid Resources/Maryland

11137 Maine State Bar Association: Section on Elder Law
PO Box 788
Augusta, ME 04332
207-622-7523
Fax: 207-623-0083
e-mail: info@mainebar.org
http://www.mainebar.org/sections
Julie G Rowe, Executive Director
Angela P Weston, Deputy Executive Director
John Lovell, Communications Director

Projects include community education events for seniors, continuing legal education on elder law, legislation, formulation of ethical guidelines in representing older people, and a series of elder law techniques and management.

Maryland

11138 Maryland Department of Aging: Senior Legal Assistance
301 West Preston Street
Suite 1007
Baltimore, MD 21201
410-767-1100
800-243-3425
Fax: 410-333-7943
e-mail: jal@ooa.state.md.us
http://www.mdoa.state.md.us/srassist.html
Jean W Roesser, Secretary
Carol R Baker, Deputy Secretary

Senior Legal Assistance provides legal advice, counseling and representation to older Marylanders. Area Agencies on Aging contract with local attorneys for service and priority is given to issues involving income maintenance, disability benefits, health care, protective services, abuse, institutionalization, guardianship and housing.

11139 Maryland Disability Law Center
1800 North Charles Street
4th Floor
Baltimore, MD 21201
410-727-6389
Fax: 410-727-6387
http://www.mdlcbalto.org/
Laurence Eisenstein, Esq., Chairman
Virginia Knowlton, Executive Director
Lorraine Cheehan, Deputy Director Public Policy

11140 Maryland Legal Aid Bureau: Annapolis
229 Hanover Street
Annapolis, MD 21401
410-263-8330
410-269-0846
http://www.mdlab.org
Wilhelm H Joseph, Jr., Esq., Executive Director
Cheryl Hystad, Esq., Advocacy Director
Tricia L Trice, Esq., Development/Compliance Director

The Legal Aid Bureau has been providing free civil legal services in Maryland for low-income people, children and the elderly since 1911. Legal Aid handles civil, not criminal, cases. Priorities for general civil legal services are family/domestic, housing, income maintenance (public benefits), and consumer/finance.

11141 Maryland Legal Aid Bureau: Baltimore
500 East Lexington Street
Baltimore, MD 21202
410-951-7777
800-999-8904
Fax: 410-951-7818
http://www.mdlab.org
Wilhelm H Joseph Jr., Esq., Executive Director
Cheryl Hystad, Esq., Advocacy Director
Tricia L Trice, Program/Development Compliance

The Legal Aid Bureau has been providing free civil legal services in Maryland for low-income people, children and the elderly since 1911. Legal Aid determines financial eligibility for general legal services based on income and assets available to the household, using the Federal Poverty Income Guidelines (except for specialized services where eligibility conditions, such as age, are set by the terms of the grants). Legal Aid handles civil, not criminal, cases. Priorities for general civil legal services are family/domestic, housing, income maintenance (public benefits), and consumer/finance.

11142 Maryland State Bar Association of Legal Services
520 West Fayette Street
Baltimore, MD 21201
410-685-7878
800-492-1964
Fax: 410-685-1016
e-mail: president@msba.org
http://www.msba.org/about/service.htm
Paul V Carlin, Executive Director
Lawrence J Hicks, Information Technology Director
Richard Montgomery III, Legislative Relations Director

The Sixty Plus Program provides reduced fee wills, health care and financial powers of attorney, living wills, intra-family deeds, and small estate administration for financially eligible elderly persons.

Massachusetts

11143 Boston College Legal Assistance Bureau
24 Crescent Street
Suite 202
Waltham, MA 02453-4088
781-893-4793
Fax: 781-893-4799
e-mail: barenber@bc.edu
http://www.diversitycoalition.org/mass
TTY 781-736-9006
Alan Minuskin, Director
Lynn Barenberg, Assistant Director

Provides civil legal services primarily for low income and elderly Massachusetts residents. Elder Service area includes the towns of: Needham, Belmont, Brookline, Wellesley, Newton, Waltham, Watertown and Weston. Services include that of referrals and advice; wills; Homestead Act; landlord/tenant; powers of attorney; health care proxies, and real estate issues.'

11144 Bristol Elder Services
182 North Main Street
Fall River, MA 02720-2109
508-675-2105
800-462-4632
Fax: 508-679-0320
e-mail: info@bristolelder.org
http://www.bristolelder.org
TTY 508-646-9704
Melanie Minutelli-Ramos, Grants Manager/Planner
Margaret Pilkington, Program Director

Founded in 1973, Bristol Elder Services, Inc. (Bristol) is a not-for-profit corporation, designated as an Aging Services Access Point and Area Agency on Aging. Bristol recieves state and federal monies to assist elders in maintaining their independence in the community. Bristol serves as the entry point for elder services in southeastern Massachusetts. Additionally, through the federal Older Americans Act, Bristol coordinates and funds an array of community programs designed to bridge the gaps in services and promote independence for elders. Bristol offers many services for elders and their caregivers.

Legal Aid Resources/Michigan

11145 Commonwealth of Massachusetts ExecutiveOffice of Elder Affairs
One Ashburton Place
Fifth Floor
Boston, MA 02108
617-727-7750
800-243-4636
Fax: 617-727-9368
e-mail: elder.affairs@state.ma.us
http://www.mass.gov/
TTY 800-872-0166

Elana Margolis, Chief of Staff
Je'Lesia M. Jones, Communication Director
Jennifer Davis Carey, Secretary

The vision of the Executive Office of Elder Affairs is to ensure that elders in Massachusetts have the supports necessary to maintain their well being and dignity. In addition, the Office of Elder Affairs promotes the independence and well-being of elders and people needing medical and social supportive services by providing advocacy, leadership, and management expertise to maintain a continuum of services responsive to the needs of our constituents, their families, and caregivers.

11146 Disability Law Center (DLC)
11 Beacon Street
Suite 925
Boston, MA 02108
617-723-8455
800-872-9992
Fax: 617-723-9125
e-mail: mail@dlc-ma.org
http://www.dlc-ma.org/

Robert Whitney, President
Margaret Brown, Secretary

Provides support that allows those with disabilities to participate fully and equally in the social and economic life of Massachusetts.

11147 Greater Boston Legal Services: Elderly Ofice (GBLS)
197 Friend Street
Boston, MA 02114
617-371-1234
800-323-3205
Fax: 617-371-1222
http://www.gbls.org/legalhelp.htm
TDD 617-371-1228

Richard Marks, President
Robert Sable, Executive Director

GBLS represents individuals and families, assisting with individual client needs as well as systemic problems. We also represent community groups and provide community legal education. We give advice and represent people in court, before agencies, and before city councils and the state legislature.

11148 Housing Options for Massachusetts Elders(HOME)
25 West Street
Lobby 2
Boston, MA 02111-1213
617-451-0680
800-583-5337
Fax: 617-451-5838
http://www.home-ma.org/

Leonard Raymond, Executive Director

11149 Legal Assistance Corporation of Central Massachusetts: Senior Citizens Advocacy Program
405 Main Street
Worcester, MA 01608
508-752-3718
800-649-3718
Fax: 508-752-5918
http://www.mlac.org/mlac_grantees
TTY 508-755-3260

Robert Nasdor, Executive Director

Provides free legal assistance to elders on many issues including benefits, housing, civil matters, Medicaid/Medicare eligibility, and elder abuse and nursing home issues. Also conducts education programs and distributes literature on critical topics.

11150 Massachusetts Mutual Life Insurance Company Law Library
1295 State Street
Springfield, MA 01111-0001
413-788-8411
Fax: 413-744-6114
http://www.massmutual.com

Sally A Fortier-Murphy, Law Librarian
James R Birle, Chairman
Howard E Gunton, EVP/Chief Investment Officer

Law - insurance, taxation, securities, real estate, pensions; litigation.

11151 Mount Ida College: National Center for Death Education
777 Dedham Street
Newton Centre, MA 02459-3310
617-928-4500
Fax: 617-928-4713
e-mail: jharding@mountida.edu
http://www.mountida.edu/ncde

Judith Harding, Coordinator Resources/Director

The National Center for Death Education (NCDE) is an educational center dedicated to promoting knowledge and understanding in the field of Thanatology. NCDE aims to help people enhance their own awareness of death as well as provide them with the resources to support the dying and grieving of all ages. We provide ongoing learning opportunities for professional caregivers and others designed for acquiring and maintaining a current knowledge base, as well as developing creative and useful skills for providing care associated with end of life, bereavement and loss.

1984

11152 Sturgis Library
PO Box 606
Barnstable, MA 02630
508-362-6636
Fax: 508-362-5467
e-mail: info@sturgislibrary.org
http://www.sturgislibrary.org/

Lucy Loomis, Library Director
Steve Farrar, Archivist
Jen VanOlinda, Technical Services Librarian

Sturgis Library, a historic public library in the village of Barnstable, Massachusetts is dedicated to promoting the study of Cape Cod history and genealogy while serving the needs of a contemporary community.

1963

11153 Volunteer Lawyers Project of the Boston Bar Association
29 Temple Place
Boston, MA 02111-1340
617-423-0648
Fax: 617-423-0061

Mary M Connolly, Executive Director

Legal services for elgible clients.

Michigan

11154 Berrien County Legal Services: Senior Law Center
16 South 3rd Street
Niles, MI 49120
616-684-2920
888-418-1311
Fax: 616-983-1045
http://www.legalaidwestmich.org/

James C Boerigter, President
Preston Hopson Jr, Treasurer
Paul T Vlachos, Vice President

For more than 30 years, Legal Services Corporation funded agencies in Western Michigan have provided free legal assistance to low income persons and Seniors in non-criminal, non-fee generating matters. Legal Aid of Western Michigan currently serves people in 17 counties in the lower Western part of Michigan.

Legal Aid Resources/Minnesota

11155 Elder Law of Michigan: Legal Hotline for Michigan Seniors
3815 West Street
Suite C200
Lansing, MI 48917
517-485-9164
800-347-5297
Fax: 517-372-0792
e-mail: info@elderslaw.org
http://www.elderslaw.org/

Kate White, Executive Director
Talbott C Smith, Director
Forest Harper, Vice President

The Legal Hotline provides free basic legal advice and information to Michigan residents age 60 and older, over the telephone. Seniors can call Monday-Friday 9:00 am to 5:00 pm. An attorney will return their calls in 1-2 business days. All services are free but donations are appreciated. (Services are primarily for seniors who cannot afford advice from a private attorney).

11156 Michigan Office of Services to the Elderly
7109 West Saginaw, 1st Floor
PO Box 30676
Lansing, MI 48909-8176
517-373-8230
Fax: 517-373-4092
e-mail: OSADirector@michigan.gov
http://www.miseniors.net/

Sharon Gire, Executive Director
Peggy Brey, Deputy Director
Cherie Mollison, Research & Advocacy Development

The Michigan Office of Services to the Elderly maintains a Website, MiSeniors.net, which provides web-based information, online service referral, and assistance to senior citizens, and OSA staff provides information, help and professional guidance to support these resources. OSA takes its responsibility to advocate for Michigan's vulnerable aging population very seriously, and is committed to protecting and promoting the rights and independence of Michigan's older population.

11157 Michigan Protection & Advocacy Service: Livonia
29200 Vassar Boulevard
Suite 200
Livonia, MI 48152-2116
248-473-2990
800-414-3956
Fax: 248-473-4104
e-mail: ecerano@mpas.org
http://www.mpas.org/

Elmer Cerano, Director
Pamela Bellamy, Ph.D, Board of Directors/President
Donna DePalma, Board of Directors/Secretary

Michigan Protection and Advocacy Service strives to advance the dignity, equality, self-determination, and expressed choices of individuals. Michigan Protection and Advocacy Service, Inc. (MPAS) promotes, expands and protects the human and legal rights of people by providing them with information and advocacy.

11158 Michigan Protection and Advocacy Service: Lansing
4095 Legacy Parkway
Suite 500
Lansing, MI 48911
517-487-1755
800-288-5923
Fax: 517-487-0827
e-mail: ecerano@mpas.org
http://www.mpas.org/
TDD 517-487-1755

Elmer Cerano, Executive Director
Pamela Bellamy, Ph.D, Board of Directors/President
Donna DePalma, Board of Directors/Secretary

Michigan Protection and Advocacy Service strives to advance the dignity, equality, self-determination, and expressed choices of individuals. Michigan Protection and Advocacy Service, Inc. (MPAS) promotes, expands and protects the human and legal rights of people by providing them with information and advocacy.

11159 Sixty Plus Elderlaw Clinic
Thomas M. Cooley Law School
300 South Capitol Avenue
PO Box 13088
Lansing, MI 48901
517-344-5760
517-371-5140
Fax: 517-334-5761
http://www.cooley.edu/clinics/intro60.htm

James Peden, Coordinator
Terrence Cavanaugh, Professor Sixty Plus Clinic

Provides free legal assistance to elderly residents of Ingham, Eaton, and Clinton counties.

11160 State Bar of Michigan: Senior Justice Committee
Michael Franck Building
306 Townsend Street
Lansing, MI 48933-2083
517-346-6300
800-968-1442
Fax: 517-482-6248
http://http://www.michbar.org/programs/

Robert Fair Gillett, Chairman
Margaret A Costello, Vice Chair
Richard D McLellan, Co-Chair

Committee deals in pro bono, education of public and legal community, legislative activities, and long-range planning.

Minnesota

11161 Legal Aid Service of Northeastern Minnesota (LASNEM): Duluth Office
302 Ordean Building
424 West Superior Street
Duluth, MN 55802
218-726-4800
800-622-7266
Fax: 218-726-4804
http://www.lasnem.org/duluth.htm
TDD 218-726-4826

Michael Connolly, Executive Director
Dale Lucas, Sr Citizens Law Project Mgr
David Lund, Managing Attorney

The Duluth office of Legal Aid Service of Northeastern Minnesota (LASNEM) is a civil legal services office for residents of Carlton, Cook, Lake and Southern St. Louis Counties in the Arrowhead region of Northeastern Minnesota. The office includes a general legal services program and the Senior Citizens Law Project. The general legal services program provides legal services at no charge to eligible low income residents of our area whose legal issues fit within our priorities. The civil legal services we provide are geared to protect the basic needs of our clients: food, shelter, medical insurance, income protection and safety. The Senior Citizen Law Project, headquartered in the Duluth Legal Aid Service office, provides legal advice and assistance to persons 60 years of age or older in the seven county Arrowhead region. The counties of service include: St. Louis, Lake, Cook, Itasca, Carlton, Aitkin, and Koochiching.

11162 Minneapolis Age & Opportunity Center
1807 Nicollet Avenue South
Minneapolis, MN 55403
612-863-1000
Fax: 612-863-1451
http://www.abanet.org/aging/

Daphne H Krause, Exective Director

The Minneapolis Age and Opportunity Center offers and coordinates an impressive array of services for its homebound and disabled clients ranging from legal assistance to home-delivered meals, from skilled nursing to home maintenance.

Legal Aid Resources/Mississippi

11163 Minnesota Board on Aging
Elmer L Andersen Human Services Building
540 Cedar Street
St. Paul, MN 55164-0976
651-431-2500
Fax: 651-431-7543
e-mail: mba@state.mn.us
http://www.mnaging.org/
TTY 800-627-3529
Jim Varpness, Executive Director
Jeanette Metz, Chair

The Minnesota Board on Aging (MBA) is the gateway to services for seniors and their families. MBA listens to senior concerns, researches for solutions, and proposes policy to address senior needs. In addition, MBA administer funds from the Older Americans Act that provide a spectrum of services to seniors, including Senior LinkAge LineT, Insurance Counseling and more. First established in 1956, the MBA is one of the pioneers in the field of agingworks closely with its Area Agencies on Aging, which are located throughout the state, to provide services that seniors need.

11164 Minnesota State Bar Association: Elder Law Section
600 Nicollet Mall
Suite 380
Minneapolis, MN 55402
612-333-1183
800-882-6722
http://www2.mnbar.org/sections/elder-law/
Douglas J Debner, Chairman
Richard D Hawke, Treasurer

Fosters and enhances the special skills of Minnesota lawyers engaged in elder law practice.

Mississippi

11165 Mississippi Council on Aging
Division of Aging and Adult Services
750 North State Street
Jackson, MS 39205
601-359-4925
Fax: 601-359-4370
e-mail: Mdunn-tutor@mdhs.state.ms.us
http://www.mdhs.state.ms.us/aas.html
Marion Dunn Totor, Ph.D, Executive Director

The mission of the Division of Aging and Adult Services is to protect the right of older citizens while expanding their opportunities and access to quality services. Our vision is for each older citizen to live the best life possible. The Division of Aging and Adult Services plans, coordinates and advocates for, and ensures the provision of services to all older Mississippians.

11166 Mississippi Protection and Advocacy System
5305 Executive Place
Suite A
Jackson, MS 39206
601-981-8207
800-772-4057
Fax: 601-981-8313
e-mail: info@mspas.com
http://www.mspas.com
TDD 601-981-8207
Rebecca Floyd, Executive Director
Andy Agnew, Community Services Advocate
Pat Bruce, Chair

The mission of Mississippi Protection and Advocacy System, Inc. is to protect and advocate for the legal and human rights of all persons with disabilities and to assist them with full inclusion in home, community, education and employment.

11167 Mississippi State Bar Association: Young Lawyers on Legal Problems of Elderly & Handicapped
PO Box 1789
Jackson, MS 39215-1789
601-948-8000
Fax: 601-948-3000
e-mail: ajones@bradleyarant.com
http://www.msbar.org/young_lawyers_division.php
Amanda Jones, President
Rhea Tannehill, President-Elect
Will Manuel, Secretary

The Mississippi Bar Young Lawyers Division is governed by its Board of Directors and is active in many public service endeavors. The Young Lawyers Division is composed of all lawyers under the age of 37 and any lawyer over the age of 37 during their first three years of practice following their admission. The Young Lawyers Division utilizes committees that are responsible for planning and implementing many of its projects, including projects such as the Law-Related Education Programs.

11168 NMRLS - Northern Mississippi Rural LegalServices: Clarksdale Office
606 DeSoto Avenue
Clarksdale, MS 38614
662-627-4184
800-388-3163
Fax: 662-624-4009
http://www.nmrls.com/Elder.htm
Bryan J Petty, Managing Attorney
Lauren M Webb, Paralegal
Naomi Keaton, Administration

In 1985 NMRLS initiated its Elder Law Project, which has been ongoing for fifteen years. The project was developed to enhance the delivery of high quality legal services to the elderly population in the NMRLS service area. Through the project, NMRLS makes special efforts to overcome the access barriers which increase the difficulty older persons have in obtaining legal representation. Also, outreach is accomplished through community education activities and training on legal rights of older persons, which is provided each year to groups of older persons, advocates for older persons, and/or providers of social services for older persons.

11169 Northern Mississippi Rural Legal Services (NMRLS): Elder Law Project - Oxford (Administrative) Office
2134 West Jackson Avenue
PO Box 76
Oxford, MS 38655
662-234-8731
800-898-8731
Fax: 662-236-3263
http://www.nmrls.com/Elder.htm
Minnie P Howard, Managing Attorney
Nora Rasco, Hotline Unit Manager
Amanda Glover Evans, Staff Attorney

In 1985 NMRLS initiated its Elder Law Project, which has been ongoing for fifteen years. The project was developed to enhance the delivery of high quality legal services to the elderly population in the NMRLS service area. Through the project, NMRLS makes special efforts to overcome the access barriers which increase the difficulty older persons have in obtaining legal representation. Also, outreach is accomplished through community education action activities and training on legal rights of older persons, which is provided each year to groups of older persons, advocates for older persons, and/or providers of social services for older persons.

Legal Aid Resources/Missouri

Missouri

11170 Gateway Older Adult Legal Services
200 North Broadway
Suite 950
Saint Louis, MO 63102
314-534-0404
888-782-8380
Fax: 314-652-8308
http://www.gatewaylegal.org
Michael Ferry, Executive Director
Philip Senturia, Managing Attorney
Delores Kedley, Office Adminstrator

Screens cases and makes referrals to a small number of volunteer attorneys in St. Louis.

11171 Legal Aid of Western Missouri: Kansas City
1125 Grand Boulevard
Suite 1900
Kansas City, MO 64106
816-474-9868
e-mail: lawmo1@lawmo.org
http://www.lawmo.org/
Jerome T Wolf, Co-Chair
Jack Bangert, Co-Chair

Legal Aid of Western Missouri (LAWMo) has been providing essential legal services to low-income and elderly citizens since 1964. LAWMo staff attorneys, paralegals and volunteers assist over 20,000 people each year with problems that seriously affect their ability to provide for themselves and their families.

11172 Missouri Division of Senior & Disability Services
Michigan Department of Health & Senior Services
PO Box 570
Jefferson City, MO 65102-0570
573-526-3626
800-235-5503
Fax: 573-751-8687
e-mail: info@dhss.mo.gov
http://www.dhss.mo.gov/ProtectiveServices/
Brenda Campbell, Interim Division Director

The Missouri Department of Health and Senior Services (DHSS) provides Adult Protective Services (APS) to eligible adults living in the community with consideration to the following rights: self-determination; protection; confidentiality; obtaining assistance and participating in care planning; and refusal of services and/or medical treatment.

11173 Missouri Protection and Advocacy
925 South Country Club Drive
Jefferson City, MO 65109
573-893-3333
800-392-8667
Fax: 573-893-4231
e-mail: mopasjc@earthlink.net
http://www.moadvocacy.org
TDD 800-735-2966
Shawn Deloyola, Executive Director

Missouri Protection and Advocacy Agency (MO P&A) is a Federally mandated system in the state of Missouri which provides protection of the rights of persons with disabilities through legally based advocacy. MO P&A was established in 1977 to address public outcry in response to the abuse, neglect and lack of programming in institutions for persons with disabilities.

Montana

11174 Montana Advocacy Program
400 North Park
2nd Floor, PO Box 1681
Helena, MT 59624
406-449-2344
800-245-4743
Fax: 406-449-2418
e-mail: bernie@mtadv.org
http://www.mtadv.org/
TDD 406-449-2344
Bernadette Franks-Ongoy, Executive Director

11175 Montana Legal Services Association: Helena
616 Helena Avenue
Suite 100
Helena, MT 59601
406-442-9830
http://www.mtlsa.org/
Deborah Anspach, Project Director & Attorney

The Montana Legal Services Association (MLSA) is a federally and privately funded program that provides free legal assistance in civil cases to low-income people and the elderly.

11176 Montana Legal Services Developer Program & Office on Aging
111 North Sanders
PO Box 4210
Helena, MT 59604
406-444-5622
800-332-2272
Fax: 406-444-1910
http://www.dphhs.mt.gov
TTY 406-444-2590
Joan Miles, Director
John Chappuis, Deputy Director
Gayle Shirley, Public Information Officer

The Montana Legal Services Developer in the Office on Aging, provides elder law training and resources for seniors, family members and social outreach workers. The program also develops pro bono and local legal services referrals, training materials and telephone assistance to seniors on related matters.

Nebraska

11177 Division of Aging and Disability Services: Legal Services for Older Adults
Nebraska Department of Health & Human Services
Nebraska State Office Building
301 Centennial Mall South, 5t Floor
Lincoln, NE 68508
402-471-4623
800-942-7830
Fax: 402-471-4619
e-mail: joann.weis@hhss.ne.gov
http://www.hhs.state.ne.us/ags/agsindex.htm
Joann Weis, Executive Director
Bob Leopold, Interim Deputy Director
Joann Schaefer, M.D., Chief Medical Officer

Legal assistance is a service provided through Nebraska's eight Area Agencies on Aging. It is authorized by the federal Older Americans Act and helps older Nebraskans increase their financial and legal security. Legal assistance providers regularly visit senior centers around the state to share information. As needed, providers will visit with people in their home or in a nursing home, assisted living facility, or hospital. Common areas of assistance include wills, health care powers of attorney, durable powers of attorney, and other substitute decision-making forms. Each person's situation is unique and important to these providers.

11178 Nebraska Advocacy Services Center for Disability Rights, Law and Advocacy
134 South 13th Street
Suite 600
Lincoln, NE 68508
402-474-3183
800-422-6691
Fax: 402-474-3274
e-mail: nas@nas-pa.org
http://www.nebraskaadvocacyservices.org
TDD 402-474-3183
Timothy Shaw, Executive Director
Marlene Brondel, Chairperson

Provides services that focus of the independence, productivity, dignity, and participation of individuals with disabilities in their community.

Legal Aid Resources/Nevada

11179 Nebraska Bar Association: Elderlaw Committee
9910 North 48th Street
Suite 106
Omaha, NE 68112
402-451-1616
Fax: 402-457-6916
e-mail: jschoenike@nebar.com
http://http://www.nebar.com/
Jane L Schoenike, Executive Director
Sam Clinch, Associate Executive Director
Jean McNeil, Director Legal Services

Sponsors annual legal fairs around the state and continuing legal education sessions for Nebraska attorneys.

Nevada

11180 Nevada Department of Health & Human Services: Division for Aging Services
3416 Goni Road
Building D, Suite 132
Carson City, NV 89706
775-687-4210
Fax: 775-687-4264
e-mail: dasco@aging.nv.gov
http://http://aging.state.nv.us/index.htm
Carol Sala, Administrator
Tina Gerber-Winn, Deputy Administrator

The mission of the Division for Aging Services is to develop, coordinate and deliver a comprehensive support service system in order for Nevada's senior citizens to lead independent, meaningful and dignified lives. The Division for Aging Services in the State of Nevada, Department of Health and Human Services, represents Nevadans aged 60 years and older. We assist our seniors in every step of the service continuum from safeguarding their rights, fostering their self-sufficiency, providing counseling to advocating on their behalf.

11181 Nevada Disability Advocacy & Law CenterSparks Office/Northern Nevada
1311 North McCarran Boulevard
Suite 106
Sparks, NV 89431
775-333-7878
800-992-5715
Fax: 775-788-7825
e-mail: JMayes9524@aol.com
http://www.ndalc.org
TTY 775-788-7824
Jack Mayes, Executive Director
Norm Liwanag, Fiscal Director
Sheila King, President/Board of Directors

The Nevada Disability Advocacy & Law Center (NDALC) is a private, nonprofit organization and serves as Nevada's federally-mandated protection and advocacy system for the human, legal, and service rights of individuals with disabilities. NDALC was designated as Nevada's protection and advocacy system by the Governor in March 1995 and is funded by Federal grants and charitable, tax deductible contributions of private citizens. Services provided byNDALC include information and referral; education and training; negotiation or mediation; investigation of reported or suspected abuse or neglect; legal counsel, technical assistance, and litigation services; and technical assistance about policy, administration, and legislative developments.

11182 Nevada Disability Advocacy and Law Center (NDLAC)
6039 Eldora Avenue
Suite C, Box 3
Las Vegas, NV 89102
702-257-8150
Fax: 702-257-8170
e-mail: ndalc@earthlink.net
http://www.ndalc.org
TDD 702-257-8160
Jack Mayes, Executive Director
Norm Liwanag, Fiscal Director
Sheila King, President/Board of Directors

The Nevada Disability Advocacy & Law Center (NDALC) is a private, nonprofit organization and serves as Nevada's federally-mandated protection and advocacy system for the human, legal, and service rights of individuals with disabilities. NDALC was designated as Nevada's protection and advocacy system by the Governor in March 1995 and is funded by Federal grants and charitable, tax deductible contributions of private citizens. Services provided by NDALC include information and referral; education and training; negotiation or mediation; investigation of reported or suspected abuse or neglect; legal counsel, technical assistance, and litigation services; and technical assistance about policy, administration, and legislative developments.

11183 Senior Citizens Law Project
400 Stewart Avenue
Las Vegas, NV 89101-2927
702-229-6596
http://http://www.lasvegasnevada.gov/
Sheri Cane Vogel, Senior Citizen Project Director

The Senior Citizens Law Project provides free legal counsel and assistance to Clark County residents age 60 and older. Donations are accepted. Clients are responsible for applicable filing fees and other court costs. Services include legal advocacy/assistance in civil areas of law including simple wills, long-term health care planning issues, consumer disputes and small claims instructions, intervention in elder abuse, landlord/tenant and mobile home problems, homesteads, social security problems and other government benefits problems. Also helps with preparation of documents for handling medical/legal issues in the event that the client is unable to do so.

New Hampshire

11184 Bureau of Elderly & Adult Services
New Hampshire Division of Health & Human Services
129 Pleasant Street
Concord, NH 03301-3857
603-271-4394
Fax: 603-271-4643
e-mail: dmcnutt@dhhs.state.nh.us
http://www.dhhs.state.nh.us/DHHS/BEAS/
Doug McNutt, Bureau Chief

The Bureau of Elderly and Adult Services provides a variety of social and long-term supports to adults age 60 and older and to adults between the ages of 18 and 60 who have a chronic illness or disability. These services range from home care, meals on wheels, care management, transportation assistance and assisted living to nursing home care. Legal support services, advocacy for disabled adults, information and assistance regarding Medicare, and information about volunteer opportunities are also important support services provided in the community by BEAS. All services and supports are intended to assist people to live as independently as possible in safety and with dignity.

11185 New Hampshire Legal Assistance
1361 Elm Street
Suite 307
Manchester, NH 03101-1333
603-668-2900
800-562-3174
Fax: 603-625-1840
http://http://www.nhla.org/
John E Tobin, Executive Director
Velma McClure, Director
Judith Jones, Co-Director

New Hampshire Legal Assistance provides free legal help to low-income and elderly persons who cannot afford a private attorney. NH Legal Assistance handles legal matters involving health care, domestic violence, public and private housing issues, food stamps, welfare, unemployment compensation, utility shut-off and nursing home problems. Operates a senior citizens law project including a senior legal hotline.

Legal Aid Resources/New Jersey

11186 New Hampshire Legal Assistance: Senior Citizens Law Project
21 East Pearl Street
Suite 2
Nashua, NH 03060
603-598-3800
800-517-0577
http://www.nhla.org/Taxes.htm
Christine Wellington, Managing Attorney
Michael Perez, Staff Attorney
Velma McClure, Senior Citizens Project

The Senior Citizens Law Project is the program within New Hampshire Legal Assistance that provides free legal services to individuals who are at least 60 years old. In addition to operating the SCLP Advice Line, the SCLP lawyers provide eligible seniors with legal representation at hearings or in court. They are also available to meet with community groups to provide education and discuss legal issues affecting seniors.

11187 New Hampshire Protection and Advocacy Agency: Disabilities Rights Center
18 Low Avenue
Concord, NH 03302-4971
603-228-0432
800-834-1721
Fax: 603-225-2077
e-mail: advocacy@drcnh.org
http://www.drcnh.org
TDD 603-228-0432
Richard Cohen, Executive Director
Ronald K Lospennato, Esq., Legal Director
Katherine Davis, Advisory Council Chair

The Disabilities Rights Center (DRC) is New Hampshire's designated Protection and Advocacy agency and authorized by federal statute to pursue legal, administrative and other appropriate remedies on behalf of individuals with disabilities. The DRC is a statewide organization that is independent from state government or service providers. The Disabilities Rights Center is dedicated to eliminating barriers existing in New Hampshire to the full and equal enjoyment of civil and other legal rights by people with disabilities.ASL Version for Deaf/HH Community. The DRC provides information, referral, advice, and legal representation and advocacy to individuals with disabilities on a wide range of disability-related problems.

New Jersey

11188 Essex County Bar: Elder Law Committee
354 Eisenhower Parkway
Plaza II
Livingston, NJ 07039
973-622-6207
Fax: 973-533-6720
e-mail: info@essexbar.com
http://www.essexbar.com/
Brenda McElnea, Chairperson

Committee sponsors annual seminars on legal issues. Issues include rights of the elderly, living wills, and home equity and income.

11189 Legal Services of New Jersey: Atlantic City
26 South Pennsylvania Avenue
Suite 100, 1st Floor
Atlantic City, NJ 08401
609-348-4200
888-576-5529
http://www.lsnj.org/
Douglas E Gershuny, Deputy Director
Trinna Rodgers, Managing Attorney

11190 Legal Services of New Jersey: Edison
100 Metroplex Drive
Suite 402, PO Box 1357
Edison, NJ 08818-1357
732-572-9100
888-576-5529
e-mail: legalhelp@lsnj.org
http://www.lsnj.org/
Melville D Miller Jr, President/General Counsel

11191 New Jersey Division of Aging & Community Services: Office of the Public Guardian
Department of Health & Senior Services
PO Box 812
Trenton, NJ 08625-0812
609-943-3519
877-222-3737
Fax: 609-943-3464
e-mail: etetelman@doh.state.nj.us
http://state.nj.us/health/senior/sa_opg.shtml
Ed Tetelman, Acting Public Guardian

The Office of the Public Guardian is a State agency that makes legal, financial and healthcare decisions for individuals age 60 and older who have been determined by a Superior Court judge to be incapacitated. The office was created by State law in 1986 and administratively in the New Jersey Department of Health and Senior Services' Division of Aging and Community Services. It employs attorneys, investigators, care managers, accountants and support staff to assist its elderly clients. The mission of the Office of the Public Guardian for Elderly Adults is to provide guardianship and conservatorship services to vulnerable elderly adults who have no willing or responsible family member or friend to act in that capacity. In carrying out this mission, we will strive to preserve the autonomy, dignity and independence of the persons in our care, while ensuring that they are residing in a safe, and will make every effort to enlighten others regarding the effects of guardianship and to advocate for the use of less restrictive alternatives. We will serve as a clearinghouse for information concerning guardianship services.appropriate and caring environment. Where possible, we will ensure that the express or implied wishes of these individuals concerning living arrangements, medical care and other personal matters are respected. We will protect and preserve the estates of those in our care. We will endeavor to serve as many vulnerable elderly individuals as possible,

11192 New Jersey Protection and Advocacy Agency
210 South Broad Street
3rd Floor
Trenton, NJ 08608
609-292-9742
800-922-7233
Fax: 609-777-0187
e-mail: advocate@njpanda.org
http://www.njpanda.org
Sarah Wiggins-Mitchell, Executive Director
Richard West, Chair
Marilyn Goldstein, Vice Chair

Provides legal advocacy and representation for those with disabilities.

11193 New Jersey State Bar Association: Committee on the Elderly
One Constitution Square
New Brunswick, NJ 08901-1520
732-249-9500
Fax: 732-249-2815
e-mail: jbluriesq@aol.com
http://njsba.com/committees_sections/index.cfm
Janet B Lurie, Chair
Jerold E Rothkoff, Vice Chair
Robert F Brogan, Legislative Coordinator

The Committee operates a Senior Citizens Referral Panel in conjunction with the Office on Aging. Reviews and comments on issues of special concern to the elderly, their families and caregivers. Disseminates timely information on legal topics vitally important to the elderly.

11194 Office on Aging: Senior Citizens Referral Panel
Burlington County Bar Association
520 Stokes Road
PO Box 310
Mount Holly, NJ 08055
609-953-5600
http://abanet.org/aging/states/newjersey06.pdf
Joyce Miller, Contact

Approximately 50 attorneys work at a reduced fee for seniors. The committee operates a Senior Citizens Referral Panel in conjunction with the New Jersey Office on Aging. The committee has a public guardianship project, funded by the Office on Aging, to assist the New Jersey Mental Health Agency in adult guardianship proceedings.

New Mexico

11195 Native American Consortium Protection and Advocacy Agency
DNA-People's Legal Services
3535 East 30th Street
Suie 201
Farmington, NM 87402
505-566-5880
Fax: 505-566-5889
e-mail: tyanan@dnalegalservices.org
http://www.nativelegalnet.org
Therese Yanan, Executive Director
Leo Sheppard, Sr., Board of Directors/President
James E Padish, Secretary/Treasurer

DNA-People's Legal Services was founded in 1967 with a mission to strive for economic justice and human rights on behalf of Native people. Each year we provide thousands of rural poor with free legal assistance and the education needed to protect their legal rights. DNA's mission is to serve our client communities as advocates and teachers in order to address the causes and symptoms of poverty, foster individual independence and dignity, and protect and promote tribal sovereignty. Our services must help our clients develop the resources necessary to meet external challenges, and help off-reservation communities and businesses better understand our clients and respect their rights. We will focus our resources on the most vulnerable, and on those for whom we can achieve long-term benefits by breaking the cycle of poverty.

11196 New Mexico Aging & Long-Term Services Department: Elderly and Disability Services Division
Toney Anaya Building
2550 Cerillos Road
Santa Fe, NM 87505
505-476-4799
866-451-2901
e-mail: marise.mcfadden@state.nm.us
http://www.nmaging.state.nm.us/
Marise McFadden, Director
Doyle Smith, Deputy Director
Deborah Armstrong, Division Secretary

The Elderly and Disability Services Division has programs that provide support to enable older adults and individuals with disabilities to remain in their own homes and communities or to return to their homes from a nursing facility or institution. The Division also advocates for each consumer to live in the least restrictive environment, and provides education and training for consumers, case managers, and direct service providers.

11197 New Mexico Protection and Advocacy Agency
1720 Louisiana Boulevard, Northeast
Suite 204
Albuquerque, NM 87110
505-256-3100
800-432-4682
Fax: 505-256-3184
e-mail: nmpalonjose@yahoo.com
http://www.nmpanda.org
TDD 505-256-3100
Michael J Rourke, President
Tonia Ross, Vice President
Jonathan Toledo, Secretary/Treasurer

11198 Senior Citizens Law Office
4317 Lead Southeast
Albuquerque, NM 87108
505-265-2300
Fax: 505-265-3600
e-mail: info@sclo.net
http://www.sclo.net/
Patricia Steizner, Co-Director
Ellen Leitzer, Co-Director
David Monson, Finance Director

Provides civil legal assistance in areas of consumer rights, government benefits, and landlord-tenant issues, to people over age 60.

11199 State Bar of New Mexico: Elder Law Section
5121 Masthead Northeast
PO Box 92860
Albuquerque, NM 87019
505-797-6000
Fax: 505-828-3765
e-mail: sbnm@nmbar.org
http://nmbar.org/Template.cfm?Section=Elder_Law
Mary H Smith, Chair
Mary Ann Green, Finance Officer
M Dwight Hurst, Secretary

Advisory committee to the Lawyer Referral Project for the Elderly, their mission is to facilitate and improve the law and practice of law in areas of particular concern to the elderly, including preserving and enhancing the rights of physically and mentally challenged individuals with respect to care, housing and asset management and to lead, coordinate and serve as a coordinating agent and clearinghouse for the efforts of the various agencies involved in service to the elderly.

11200 State Bar of New Mexico: Lawyer Referral for the Elderly Program
5121 Masthead Northeast
PO Box 92860
Albuquerque, NM 87199-2860
505-797-6005
800-876-6657
Fax: 505-828-3760
e-mail: sbnm@nmbar.org
http://nmbar.org/Template.cfm?Section=Elder_Law
Mary H Smith, Chair
Mary Ann Green, Finance Officer
M Dwight Hurst, Secretary

Statewide referral project serving elderly in all 33 counties in New Mexico. Project is based in State Bar Complex in Albuquerque, with regional offices in Northern and Southern New Mexico.

New York

11201 Association of the Bar of the City of New York: Committee for Senior Volunteer Lawyers
42 West 44th Street
New York, NY 10036-6604
212-382-6600
Fax: 212-398-6634
e-mail: bopotowsky@nycbar.org
http://http://abcny.org/
Barry Kamins, President
Barbara Berger-Opotowsky, Executive Director
Jayce Bigelsen, Director Legislative Affairs

Provide services for senior lawyers; conduct programs for assistance to and of interest to senior lawyers; consider and promote programs for the benefit of the bar, law schools, law students, and the community, utilizing the services and experience of senior lawyers, both on a volunteer or compensated basis; and to act as the voice of senior lawyers within the Association of the Bar.

11202 Legal Services for the Elderly
130 W 42nd Street
17th Floor
New York, NY 10036-7902
212-391-0120
Fax: 212-719-1939
e-mail: dogtoyesky@juno.com
http://http://www.lsny.org/
Jonathan A Weiss, Executive Director

Lawyers who advise on and litigate cases concerning problems of the elderly. Funded through the Legal Services Corporation in New York City, attorney fees, grants, and the state of New York. Conducts research, litigation, and educational programs.

Legal Aid Resources/New York

11203 Legal Services for the Elderly, Disabled or Disadvantaged of Western New York
220 Delaware Avenue
Suite 409
Buffalo, NY 14202-2100
716-853-3087
Fax: 716-856-5317
http://www.lsed.org/index.php
Karen L Nicolson Esq., Executive Director
Thomas F Keefe Esq., President Board of Directors
David Chadwick Esq., Staff Attorney

It is the mission of Legal Services for the Elderly, Disabled or Disadvantaged of Western New York, Inc. (LSED) to improve the quality of life, primarily for elderly persons, but also disabled persons, in Western New York by providing free legal services in those areas which generally have a significant impact on their lives. These areas include health care, housing, income maintenance, family law and protective services. LSED's primary goal is to use the legal system to assure that older people in our community may live with dignity.

11204 National Organization of Social Security Claimants' Representatives
19 East Central Avenue
2nd Floor
Pearl River, NY 10965-2305
845-735-8812
800-431-2804
Fax: 845-735-8812
e-mail: sarahhbohr@aol.co
http://http://www.nosscr.org/
Sarah H Bohr, President
Lawrence D Rohlfing, Vice President
Gary R Parvin, Treasurer

Professional organization of attorneys who represent claimants before the Social Security Administration. The National Organization of Social Security Claimants' Representatives (NOSSCR) is committed to providing the highest quality representation and advocacy on behalf of persons who are seeking Social Security and Supplemental Security Income.

11205 New York Legal Aid Society
199 Water Street
New York, NY 10038
212-577-3300
888-218-6974
Fax: 212-509-8432
e-mail: webmaster@legal-aid.org
http://www.legal-aid.org/
Peter Z. Cobb, President
Steven Banks, Attorney-in-Chief
Christopher Conroy, Chief Financial Officer

The Legal Aid Society is the nation's oldest and largest provider of legal services to the indigent. Founded in 1876, the Society provides a full range of civil legal services, as well as criminal defense work, and juvenile representation in Family Court, ensuring that poverty is not a barrier to accessing the justice system. Our core service is to provide free legal assistance to New Yorkers who live at or below the poverty level and cannot afford to hire a lawyer when confronted with a legal problem. Through neighborhood and court-based offices in 18 facilities in the five boroughs of New York City, more than 800 lawyers working with approximately 600 paraprofessionals and other supporting staff, handle 300,000 cases annually. Legal Aid's fiscal budget is $140 million; 90% from public funding, principally for criminal defense work and representation of juveniles in child protective and delinquency matters. The remaining funding comes from the fund-raising activities of the organization, which include private donations from law firms, associates, corporations, foundations, individuals and special events. The largest source of current support is the New York legal community.

11206 New York State Bar Association: Elder Law Section
1 Elk Street
Albany, NY 12207
518-463-3200
Fax: 518-487-5517
e-mail: pbucklin@nysba.org
http://http://www.nysba.org/
Patricia K Bucklin, Esq., Executive Director
John A Williams Jr., Esq., Associate Executive Director
Lisa J Baitaille, Chief Section Liaison

The Elder Law Section provides services and opportunities for involvement on issues relating to Elder Law, for members of the New York State Bar Association. Among activities, the Section presents educational programs and publishes materials on practice, procedure and developments to enhance the competence and skill of lawyers who practice in this field and improve their ability to deliver the most efficient and highest quality services to theirclients; prepare studies, analyses and recommendations to seek improvement in the law and procedure relating to elder law; and undertake projects to increase the understanding of senior citizens, their families and the general pubic concerning legal issues affecting the elderly.

11207 New York State Commission On Quality ofCare and Advocacy for Persons with Disabilities
401 State Street
Schenectady, NY 12305-2303
518-388-2892
800-522-4369
Fax: 518-388-2890
e-mail: Gary.O'Brien@cqcad.state.ny.us
http://www.cqcapd.state.ny.us
TDD 800-624-4143
TTY 800-522-4369
Gary O'Brien, Executive Director

The New York State Commission on Quality of Care and Advocacy for Persons with Disabilities (CQCAPD) is an independent, New York State government agency charged with improving the quality of life for New Yorkers with disabilities and protecting their rights.

11208 New York State Office for the Aging
2 Empire State Plaza
Albany, NY 12223-1251
518-474-7012
800-342-9871
Fax: 518-474-1398
e-mail: Neal.lane@ofa.state.ny.us
http://http://aging.state.ny.us/
Neal Lane, Director

The New York State Office for the Aging is part of the Executive Department and is the designated State Unit on Aging under the Older Americans Act of 1965, as amended. It is the mission of the New York State Office for the Aging to help older New Yorkers to be as independent as possible for as long as possible through advocacy, development and delivery of cost-effective policies, programs and services which support and empower the elderly and their families, in partnership with the network of public and private organizations which serve them. The New York State Office for the Aging was created by Executive Order of the Governor in 1961 and was one of the first State Units on Aging in the Nation. In 1965 the Office was made an independent agency in the Executive Department and became the central State agency to plan and coordinate programs and services for the aging at all levels in both the public and private sectors.

11209 Samuel Sadin Institute on Law & Rights of Older Adults
425 East 25th Street
New York, NY 10010
212-481-3780
Fax: 212-481-3791
e-mail: brookdale@shiva.hunter.cuny.edu
http://http://www.brookdale.org/iol/index.html
Ellen P Rosenzweig, J.D., Director
Debra Studer Sacks, LPN/J.D., Senior Staff Attorney
Sara Meyers, J.D., Staff Attorney

The Sadin Institute on Law, Public Policy & Aging (The Law Institute) is a division of the Brookdale Center on Aging of Hunter College. We are a leader in providing services for professionals who assist older persons in securing their rights and public benefits. Since it's inception in 1977, the Law Institute's goal has been to ensure that impoverished older persons receive access to public benefits and entitlements. To this end, the Institute acts as a legal support program for social workers, paralegals, attorneys and other professionals engaged in providing advocacy assistance to the elderly poor.

Legal Aid Resources/North Carolina

North Carolina

11210 Cumberland County Coordinating Council for Older Adults: Elderly Law Unit
339 Devers Street
Fayetteville, NC 28303-4750
910-484-0111
Fax: 910-484-0627
http://www.dhhs.state.nc.us/aging/
Marshall Lanter, Executive Director

Refers cases to a panel of participating attorneys, on both a pro bono and reimbursement basis.

11211 Governor's Advisory Council for Personswith Disabilities (GACPD)
1314 Mail Service Center
Raleigh, NC 27699-1314
919-733-9250
800-821-6922
Fax: 919-733-9173
e-mail: allison.breedlove@ncmail.net
http://www.Gacpd.com
TDD 919-733-9250
Allison Breedlove, Acting Executive Director

The Governor's Advocacy Council for Persons with Disabilities (GACPD) Provides a statewide protection and advocacy program; investigate complaints; pursue legal remedies for protection; review and recommend changes in laws; aid and assist local advocacy programs; and advise and assist on employment issues. The Governor's Advocacy Council for Persons with Disabilities (GACPD) is part of a nationwide system of protection and advocacy agencies. It is a civil rights protection agency committed to serving citizens with disabilities in North Carolina. GACPD staff provide advocacy services to any citizen of North Carolina who has a physical or mental condition that substantially limits at least one major life activity and who falls within the agency's priorities and case selection criteria as set by the board each year.

11212 Legal Aid of North Carolina
224 South Dawson Street
Raleigh, NC 27601
919-856-2564
Fax: 919-856-2120
http://www.legalaidnc.org/
George R Hansen, Executive Director
Celia Pistolis, Advocacy/Compliance Asst. Drt.r
Christopher Marks, Finance/Administration

Legal Aid of North Carolina (LANC) is a statewide, nonprofit, 501(c)3 law firm that provides free legal services in civil matters to low-income people in order to ensure equal access to justice and to remove legal barriers to economic opportunity. Legal Aid of NC is committed to equal justice for all people. We help children, families, individuals and migrant workers solve problems that affect their basic needs, such as housing, safety from domesstic violence or abuse, health care (Medicare or Medicaid), subsistence income (SSI or SSDI), environmental safety and consumer loan problems.

11213 Legal Services for the Elderly
1431 Elizabeth Avenue
Charlotte, NC 28204
704-334-0400
e-mail: lseval@earthlink.net
http://www.dhhs.state.nc.us/aging/
Valerie Egzibher, Director

Provides legal assitance to those with disabilities.

11214 Mecklenburg County Bar: Volunteer Lawyers Program and Services for the Elderly
438 Queens Road
Charlotte, NC 28207-3330
704-375-8624
Fax: 704-333-6209
e-mail: jhowle@meckbar.org
http://www.meckbar.org
Nancy Roberson, Executive Director
Jennifer Howle, Volunteer Lawyers Coordinator
Sally Larsen, Lawyer Referral Coordinator

Coordinator screens and refers clients to panel of over 80 volunteer attorneys throughout Mecklenburg County who provide pro bono representation to elderly citizens over 60 years of age, and children through three programs. They are the Volunteer Lawyers Program (VLP), Legal Services for the Elderly (LSE), and The Children's Law Center (CLC). Opportunities available through pro bono service in Mecklenburg County encompass numerous areas of civillaw, including domestic or family law, real estate, bankruptcy, wills and estates, landlord-tenant, consumer, and social security disability law.

11215 North Carolina Division of Aging and Adult Services
2101 Mail Service Center
Raleigh, NC 27699-2101
919-733-3983
Fax: 919-733-0443
e-mail: dennis.streets@ncmail.net
http://www.dhhs.state.nc.us/aging/home.htm
Dennis Streets, Division Director
Debbie Brantley, Elder Rights Section Chief
Steve Freedman, Service Operations Chief

The mission of the North Carolina Division of Aging and Adult Services is to promote independence and enhance the dignity of North Carolina's older and disabled persons and their families through a community-based system of opportunities, services, benefits, and protections; to ready younger generations to enjoy their later years; and to help society and government plan and prepare for the changing demographics.

11216 Onslow Coordinating Council on Aging
4022 Richlands Highway
PO Box 982
Jacksonville, NC 28541-0982
910-455-2747
Fax: 910-455-0781
e-mail: Sheri_Slater@co.onslow.nc.us
http://co.onslow.nc.us/senior%5Fservices/
Sheri Slater, Director

The Onslow County Senior Services provides for the needs of the elderly population of Onslow County, keeping them active and involved in the community and preventing pre-mature institutionalization. The objective is to meet the needs of the older adult population of Onslow County through direct programs and services, advocacy, community involvement or referral to additional resources.

North Dakota

11217 Legal Services of North Dakota
PO Box 1893
Bismarck, ND 58502-1893
701-852-3870
800-634-5263
Fax: 701-222-2110
e-mail: lluchsinger@legalassist.org
http://www.legalassist.org/
Jim Fitzsimmons, Executive Director
Ricahrd R Lemay, Litigation Director
Lois Luchsinger, Intake Coordinator

Legal Services of North Dakota provides civil legal services for disadvantaged elderly or low-income North Dakotans who cannot afford an attorney.

11218 North Dakota Aging Services Division
North Department of Human Services
600 East Boulevard Avenue, Dept. 325
Bismarck, ND 58505-0250
701-328-4601
800-472-2622
Fax: 701-328-4061
e-mail: dhsaging@nd.gov
http://www.nd.gov/humanservices/services/
TTY 701-328-3480
Linda Wrigt, Director

Legal Aid Resources/Ohio

The Department of Human Services' Aging Services Division administers programs and services that help older adults and people with physical disabilities to live safely and productively in the least restrictive, appropriate setting. In addition, the Department of Human Services operates a Senior Information and Assistance Service funded under the Older Americans Act, called Senior Info-line that can link seniors, adult children, caregivers, professionals, and others up with information about important services that can help older adults and people with disabilities to live independently or meet their changing needs. This database of information is free and confidential.

11219 North Dakota Lawyer Referral and Information Service: Elder Law Panel
504 North Washington Street
PO Box 2136
Bismarck, ND 58502-2136
701-255-1406
800-932-8880
Fax: 701-224-1621
e-mail: bill@sband.org
http://http://www.sband.org/
Bill Neumann, Executive Director
MeDonna Fryer, Volunteer Lawyer Program
Justine Rowinski, Compliance Administrator

The State Bar Association of North Dakota offers a statewide pro bono and reduced fee panel for seniors emphasizing service to rural and low-income individuals. Legal Assistance refers clients to statewide panel of attorneys.

11220 North Dakota Protection and Advocacy Agency
400 East Broadway
Suite 409
Bismarck, ND 58501
701-328-2950
800-472-2670
Fax: 701-328-3934
e-mail: tlarsen@state.nd.us
http://www.ndpanda.org
TDD 800-366-6888
Teresa Larsen, Executive Director

The North Dakota Protection & Advocacy Project (P&A) is a state agency whose purpose is to advocate for, and protect the legal rights of, people with disabilities. The Protection & Advocacy Project is concerned with asserting the human, civil and legal rights of people with disabilities, especially those who are not able to protest deprivations on their own behalf. The Project operates in a manner which is consistent with the belief that people with disabilities have the same legal and constitutional rights and guarantees as every other American citizen. The Project believes that people with disabilities should be empowered to advocate on their own behalf to the extent possible. Services provided by the Project shall promote consumer control in decision-making and focus on the empowerment of people with disabilities in order to foster independence, productivity and integration into the community.

Ohio

11221 Office of the Ohio Attorney General: Health, Education & Human Services Section
30 East Broad Street
17th Floor
Columbus, OH 43215-3428
614-466-4320
Fax: 614-466-6090
http://www.ag.state.oh.us/
Sherry Maxfield, Senior Deputy Attorney General
Jim Petro, Attorney General
Melissa Vasil, Executive Assistant

The Health and Human Services Section specializes in health law by serving as general and trial counsel for more than 30 state departments and regulatory boards. This section handles defense challenges in the areas of provider reimbursement and health care delivery programs, enforcement litigation against individual and institutional providers for substandard care through Ohio's Patient Abuse and Neglect Law, and litigation relating to professional licensure for healthcare providers.

11222 Ohio Department of Aging
50 West Broad Street
9th Floor
Columbus, OH 43215-3363
614-466-5500
800-266-4363
Fax: 614-466-5741
e-mail: jsmith@age.state.oh.us
http://http://goldenbuckeye.com/about/
TTY 614-466-6191
Merle Grace Kearns, Director
Jason Smith, Chief of Staff
Roland Hornbostel, Deputy Director of Policy

The Ohio Department of Aging strives to help our citizens live active, healthy and independent lives. We accomplish this by providing services, information and supports to help older Ohioans remain engaged in their communities as long as possible. The Ohio Department of Aging works closely with statewide agencies, advocates and service providers to advocate for and serve older Ohioans.

11223 Ohio Protection and Advocacy Agency: Ohio Legal Rights Service (OLRS)
8 East Long Street
Suite 500
614-466-7264
800-282-9181
Fax: 614-644-1888
e-mail: CKnight@olrs.state.oh.us
http://www.state.oh.us/olrs/
TDD 614-466-7264
Carolyn S Knight, Executive Director
William Crum, Commission Chairman

The Ohio Legal Rights Service (OLRS) is an independent state agency and the federally and state designated Protection and Advocacy System for people with disabilities in the State of Ohio. The mission of the OLRS is to protect and guarantee the human, civil, and legal rights of Ohioans with disabilities.

11224 Pro Seniors
7162 Redding Road
Suite 1150
Cincinnati, OH 45237
513-345-4160
800-488-6070
Fax: 513-621-5613
http://www.proseniors.org/
Rhonda Y Moore, Executive Director
Frank J Pulsfort, Finance/Controller
Jane Winkler, Resource Development Manager

Oklahoma

11225 Legal Aid Services of Oklahoma
Oklahoma City Law Center
2901 North Classen Boulevard
Oklahoma City, OK 73106
405-521-1302
800-421-1641
Fax: 405-557-0023
http://www.lawhelp.org/
Jack L Brown, President
Richard Mitchell, Vice President
Lucille Logan, Secretary/Treasurer

Provides legal assistance to seniors regardless of income.

11226 Oklahoma Aging Services Division
Oklahoma Department of Human Services
2401 Northwest 23rd Street
Suite 40
Oklahoma City, OK 73107
405-521-2281
800-211-2116
Fax: 405-521-2086
e-mail: Carey.garland@okdhs.org
http:///www1.okdhs.org/en/whoweare/visd/asd/
Carey D Garland, Director
Robert E Adams, Support Services Unit Director
Stacy Gholson, Finance Director

Legal Aid Resources/Oregon

The Oklahoma Aging Services Division provides leadership in issues of concern to older Oklahomans, helps to develop community-based systems which support independence and protect the quality of life of older persons and helps to promote citizen involvement in planning and delivering those services.

11227 Oklahoma Department of Mental Health andSubstance Abuse Services (ODMHSAs)
1200 Northeast 13th Street
PO Box 53277
Oklahoma City, OK 73152-3277
405-522-3908
Fax: 405-552-3650
http://www.odmhsas.org/menthealth.htm
TDD 405-573-6683
Rand Baker, Deputy Commissioner
Peggy Jewell, Medical Director

The ODMHSAS was established through the Mental Health Law of 1953, although publicly supported services to Oklahomans with mental illness date back to early statehood. Today, ODMHSAS delivers services in the areas of mental health, substance abuse, and domestic violence and sexual assault. A governing board provides oversight regarding Department functions and activity related to the care, treatment, and recovery of persons suffering from mentalillness and substance abuse. The Board is responsible for appointing the Commissioner of Mental Health and Substance Abuse Services.
1950

11228 Oklahoma Disability Law Center: Oklahoma City
Oklahoma Protection and Advocacy Agency
2915 Classen Boulevard
Suite 300
Oklahoma City, OK 73106
405-525-7755
800-880-7755
Fax: 405-525-7759
e-mail: odlcokc@flash.net
http://www.oklahomadisabilitylaw.org
Kayla Bower, Program Director

The Mission of the Oklahoma Disability Law Center, Inc. is to protect, promote and expand the rights of people with disabilities. The ODLC mission reflects a belief that people with disabilities are entitled to be treated with dignity and respect; to be free from abuse, neglect, exploitation and discrimination. The ODLC mission also reflects the belief that people with disabilities are entitled to equal rights and to equally effective access to the same opportunities as are afforded to other members of society. Since 1977, ODLC has helped people with disabilities achieve equality, inclusion in society and personal independence without regard to disabling conditions. We are a system of protection and advocacy for people with disabilities in the State of Oklahoma. We are federally funded through the Administration for Children and Families, the Center for Mental Health Services of the Department of Health and Human Services, and the Department of Education. ODLC is a member of the National Disability Rights Network.

11229 Oklahoma Disability Law Center: Tulsa
Oklahoma Protection and Advocacy Agency
2828 East 51 Street
Suite 302
Tula, OK 74105
918-743-6220
800-226-5883
Fax: 918-743-7157
e-mail: odlcokc@flash.net
http://www.oklahomadisabilitylaw.org
TDD 800-226-5883
Kayla Bower, Program Director

The Mission of the Oklahoma Disability Law Center, Inc. is to protect, promote and expand the rights of people with disabilities. The ODLC mission reflects a belief that people with disabilities are entitled to be treated with dignity and respect; to be free from abuse, neglect, exploitation and discrimination. The ODLC mission also reflects the belief that people with disabilities are entitled to equal rights and to equally effective access to the same opportunities as are afforded to other members of society. Since 1977, ODLC has helped people with disabilities achieve equality, inclusion in society and personal independence without regard to disabling conditions. We are a system of protection and advocacy for people with disabilities in the State of Oklahoma. We are federally funded through the Administration for Children and Families, the Center for Mental Health Services of the Department of Health and Human Services, and the Department of Education. ODLC is a member of the National Disability Rights Network.

Oregon

11230 Governor's Commission on Senior Services (GCSS)
Department of Human Services
500 Summer Street Northeast, E02
Salem, OR 97301
503-945-6833
800-282-8096
Fax: 503-373-7823
e-mail: morgen.brodie@state.or.us
http://oregon.gov/DHS/spd/adv/gcss/home.shtml
TDD 503-945-6833
John C Helm, Chairman
Morgen Brody, Legislative Advocacy Manager
Becky Murphy, Administration

The Governor's Commission on Senior Services is dedicated to enhancing and protecting the quality of life for older Oregonians. Through cooperation with other organizations and advocacy, we work to ensure that seniors have access to services that provide choice, independence and dignity.

11231 Lane County Law and Advocacy Center: Senior Law Service
376 East 11th Avenue
Eugene, OR 97401
541-485-1017
800-575-9283
Fax: 541-342-5091
http://www.lanecountylegalservices.org/sls.htm
Laurence Hamblen, Regional Director
Ralph Saltus, Program Director
Jean Beachdel, Senior Law Service Director

Provides legal assistance for senior citizens.

11232 Legal Aid Services of Oregon: Senior LawProject
Multnomah County Office
921 Southwest Washington
Suite 500
Portland, OR 97205
503-224-4086
Fax: 503-220-2480
http://www.oregonlawhelp.org/OR/index.cfm
Lynn Spruill, CEO

The Senior Law Project (SLP) is a volunteer lawyer program that is operated by Legal Aid Services of Oregon. The SLP has provided legal assistance to seniors since 1978. Lawyers initially meet with clients for 30-minute appointments at nine senior centers in Multnomah County.

Legal Aid Resources/Pennsylvania

11233 Oregon Advocacy Center (OAC)
Oregon Protection and Advocacy Agency
620 Southwest Fifth Avenue
5th Floor
Portland, OR 97204-1428
503-243-2081
800-452-1694
Fax: 503-243-1738
e-mail: welcome@oradvocacy.org
http://www.oradvocacy.org
TDD 800-556-5351
TTY 503-323-9161

Robert Joondeph, Executive Director
Kathy Wilde, Litigation Director
Barbara Printemps Herget, Operations Director

Provides counseling on civil rights, special education, health care and rights to public and private services to people with disabilities.

11234 Oregon State Bar: Rights of Persons with Disabilities Section
5200 South Meadows Road
Lake Oswego, OR 97035-0889
503-620-0222
Fax: 503-684-1366
e-mail: nfo@osbar.org
http://www.osbar.org/index.html

Judith Baker, Administrator Legal Services
Jon Benson, Referral Services Administrator

Plays an active role in the passage of guardianship legislation.

Pennsylvania

11235 Allegheny County Area Agency on Aging
441 Smithfield Street
Pittsburgh, PA 15222-2219
412-350-5460
Fax: 412-350-3091
e-mail: SeniorLine@dhs.county.allegheny.pa.us
http://county.allegheny.pa.us/dhs/aaa/index.asp
TDD 412-350-2727
TTY 412-350-2727

Pat Sullivan, Chair

Our mission is to enhance the quality of life of all older Pennsylvanians by empowering diverse communities, the family and the individual. The Area Agency on Aging is an office of the Allegheny County Department of Human Services. Its purpose is to provide programs and services that enable the older adults of Allegheny County to maintain their independence, and to have safe, healthy lifestyles with the type of care that is needed.

11236 Bucks County Legal Aid Society: Social Security Referral Panel
1 Pond Street
Bristol, PA 19007-4814
215-781-0800
877-429-5994
http://http://www.lasp.org/

Carolyn Johnson, Executive Director

Provides legal assistance to those with disabilities and senior citizens.

11237 Chester County Services for Senior Citizens
14 East Biddle Street
West Chester, PA 19380-2616
215-431-6353
610-692-1889
Fax: 610-692-9546
e-mail: whoffman@chescobar.org
http://http://www.chescobar.org/public/probono/

Wendy C Hoffman, Executive Director

Reduced fee panel sponsored by the Chester County Bar Association and Services for Senior Citizens.

11238 Delaware County Legal Assistance Program: Senior Citizens Office
Legal Aid of Southeastern Pennsylvania
410 Welsh Street
Chester, PA 19013
215-874-8421
877-429-5994
Fax: 610-874-8547
e-mail: cfritsch@lasp.org
http://www.palegalservices.org/ or www.lasp.org

Elizabeth Wood Fritsch, Co-Executive Director

11239 Disabilities Law Project-Pennsylvania
1315 Walnut Street
Suite 400
Philadelphia, PA 19107-4798
215-238-8070
Fax: 215-772-3126
e-mail: dlp.phila@dlp-pa.org
http://http://www.ppainc.org/
TDD 215-789-2498

Mark Murphy, Executive Director
Carol Horowitz, Managing Attorney

The Disabilities Law Project (DLP) is a non profit statewide public interest law firm that provides legal assistance and other services to individuals with disabilities, their organizations, their families, and their advocates. DLP's main purpose is to advocate for the civil rights of persons with mental and physical disabilities, especially their right to live as integral parts of their communities. DLP works to ensure that people with disabilities have equal and unhindered access to employment, transportation, public accommodations, and government services; to enforce their rights to vocational, habilitative, post-secondary educational, health, and other services; and to protect them from abuse and neglect. DLP identifies systemic issues which are important to people with disabilities and seeks change and reform through litigation, administrative advocacy, and public education.

11240 Pennsylvania Bar Association: Elder LawSection
100 South Street
PO Box 186
Harrisburg, PA 17108-0186
717-238-6715
Fax: 717-238-1204
e-mail: info@pabar.org
http://http://www.pabar.org/

C Dale McClain, Chairman
Richard Thomas Murphy, Secretary
Katherine C Pearson, Treasurer

The Elder Law Section shall assist members of the legal community, the elderly population and those associated with the elderly community by developing educational programs focusing on advancements in elder law. The committee shall study, review and make recommendations concerning legislation affecting the elder community.

11241 Pennsylvania Department of Aging: LegalServices and Assistance
Commonwealth of Pennsylvania
555 Walnut Street
5th Floor
Harrisburg, PA 17101-1919
717-783-1550
Fax: 717-783-6842
e-mail: aging@state.pa.us
http://www.aging.state.pa.us/aging/cwp/

Nora Dowd-Eisenhower, Secretary of Aging
Gary Miller, Communications/Press Director
William Johnston-Walsh, Deputy Secretary

The mission of the Department of Aging/Legal Services and Assistance, is to enhance the quality of life of all older Pennsylvanians by empowering diverse communities, the family and the individual. Legal Assistance includes legal advice and representation by an attorney (and, to the extent feasible, counseling or other appropriate assistance by a paralegal or law student under the supervision of an attorney), as well as benefits and rights counseling or representation by a non-lawyer to older people with social or economic needs. These cases are only on non-fee generating (unless adequate representation is unavailable from private attorneys) and civil legal problems.

11242 Pennsylvania Protection and Advocacy Agency
1414 North Cameron Street
Suite C
Harrisburg, PA 17103
717-236-8110
800-692-7443
Fax: 717-236-0192
e-mail: ppa@ppainc.org
http://www.ppainc.org
TDD 717-236-8110

Ilene Shane, Chief Executive Officer
Linda Anthony, Policy Director
Bonnie Fronk, Finance/Administration Director

PPA works directly and though its legal subcontractors to make systemic changes that will remove barriers to people with disabilities and their ability to live and thrive in their communities.

11243 Public Interest Law Center of Philadelphia
125 South 9th Street
Suite 700
Philadelphia, PA 19107-5153
215-627-7100
Fax: 215-627-3183
e-mail: jclarke@pilcop.org
http://http://www.pilcop.org/

Jennifer Clarke, Executive Director
Michael Churchill, Co-Chief Counsel
Judith A Gran, Director Disabilities Rights

The Public Interest Law Center of Philadelphia is dedicated to advancing the Constitutional promise of equal citizenship to all persons irrespective of race, ethnicity, national origin, disability, gender or poverty. We use public education, continuing education of our clients and client organizations, research, negotiation and, when necessary, the courts to achieve systemic reforms that advance the central goals of self-advocacy, social justice and equal protection of the law for all members of society.

11244 Public Interest Law Center: Philadelphia
125 S 9th Street
Suite 700
Philadelphia, PA 19107-5153
215-627-7100
Fax: 215-627-3183

Mike Churchill, Director

11245 Senior Citizens Judicare Project
1101 Market Street
11th Floor
Philadelphia, PA 19107-2934
215-238-8943
Fax: 215-238-1159
http://http://www.scjudicare.org

Mary A Scherf, Executive Director
Angel Recchia, Manager
Karen Buck, Senior Law Center Director

Provides pro bono and reduced fee representation. For the past 20 years, the Senior Citizen Judicare Project has been dedicated to meeting the legal needs of the elderly living on limited incomes in Philadelphia. Judicare provides legal representation and counsel, community education, outreach and advocacy for Philadelphia's senior citizens, through the energies of its legal staff and panel of approximately 100 practitioners. Since its founding in 1978, Judicare has provided free legal services to more than 26,000 needy seniors, educated more than 65,000 seniors through community-based education, and assisted over 100,000 seniors by providing advice, information and referral services.

Rhode Island

11246 Legal Information and Referral Service for the Elderly
115 Cedar Street
Providence, RI 02903
401-521-5040
Fax: 401-521-2703
e-mail: santhony@ribar.com
http://http://www.ribar.com/public/elderly.asp
TDD 401-421-1666

Helen Desmond McDonald, Executive Director

The Legal Information and Referral Service for the Elderly is a public service program of the Rhode Island Bar Association designed to help persons 60 years of age and older obtain legal information and advice. Its purpose is to provide quality legal services to senior citizens in need of legal help.

11247 Rhode Island Department of Elderly Affairs
John O. Pastore Center
Benjamin Rush Building, No. 55
35 Howard Avenue
Cranston, RI 02920
401-462-0500
Fax: 401-462-0503
e-mail: crusso@dea.state.ri.us
http://www.dea.ri.gov/

Corrine Calisle-Russo, Director

The Department of Elderly Affairs (DEA) was established in 1977 (under RIGL 42-66-1) in response to the growing needs of elders in Rhode Island's older population. DEA is the state's primary agency devoted to the development, implementation and monitoring of a comprehensive system of community-based programs and services for seniors. The DEA is also designated as the state's single planning and services area agency on aging under the provisions of the Older Americans Act. DEA, through its community partners, serves the needs of 225,000 seniors and adults with disabilities constituents.

11248 Rhode Island Legal Service: Elderly Law Unit
56 Pine Street
4th Floor
Providence, RI 02903
401-274-2652
800-662-5034
Fax: 401-453-0310
e-mail: RBargeRi1s.org
http://www.rijustice.ri.gov/voca/VOCA/Legal.htm

Robert M Barge, Esq., Executive Director

Objectives are to ensure that low-income people have food, shelter, income, medical care, and freedom from domestic violence. To accomplish this, RILS provides a full range of legal assistance, including advice and brief service, investigation, negotiation, and litigation in all state and federal trial and appellate courts. RILS also provides community legal education services to its client community.

11249 Rhode Island Protection and Advocacy Agency: Rhode Island Disability Law Center
349 Eddy Street
Providence, RI 02903
401-831-3150
800-733-5332
Fax: 401-274-5568
e-mail: rbandusky@ridlc.org
http://www.ridlc.org
TDD 401-831-5335

Ray Bandusky, Executive Director

The mission of the Rhode Island Disability Law Center is to assist people with differing abilities in their efforts to achieve full inclusion in society and to exercise their civil and human rights through the provision of legal advocacy. Services include individual representation to protect rights or to secure benefits and services; self-help information; educational programs; and administrative and legislative advocacy.

South Carolina

11250 Senior Advocacy Program
American Red Cross - Carolina Low County Chapter
8085 Rivers Avenue
Suite F
North Charleston, SC 29406-6357
843-764-2323
Fax: 843-764-2318
e-mail: DillonP@usa.redcross.org
http://http://www.lowcountryredcross.org/

Pam Dillon, Retired/Senior Volunteer Program
Marlene Williamon, Area Coordinator
Cathy Quenga, Area Coordinator

Legal Aid Resources/South Dakota

An important additional source of volunteer power is generated through the Retired & Senior Volunteer Program (RSVP). This program is locally sponsored by the Carolina Lowcountry Chapter and is part of the Corporation for National Service. RSVP volunteers must be 55 years of age or older. They contribute their time and experience as they assist over 120 agencies to meet a variety of community needs. RSVP volunteers donate their time and skills inin dozens of different ways. Some examples are office help, school volunteers, guardian ad litems, hospital volunteers, meal delivery to the homebound, historical and garden tour guides, friendly visitation and much more. Open to volunteers 55 years of age or older.

11251 South Carolina Bar Association: Elder Law Committee
950 Taylor Street
Columbia, SC 29202
803-799-6653
Fax: 803-799-4118
e-mail: joan.brown@scbar.org
http://www.scbar.org/member/yld/default.asp
Joan Brown, Elder Law Committee Director
Robert Wells, Executive Director
Leigh Thomas, Public Relations Director

The Elder Law Committee provides education to members of the Bar and the public on issues affecting the elderly, monitors legislation and proposes statutory changes and publishes the South Carolina Senior Citizens Handbook.

11252 South Carolina Centers for Equal Justice (SCCEJ)
2109 Bull Street
Columbia, SC 29201
803-799-9668
888-799-9668
Fax: 803-799-9420
e-mail: andrealoney@sccej.org
http://www.sccej.org/locations.htm
Andrea Loney, Interim Executive Director

11253 South Carolina Lieutenant Governor's Office on Aging
1301 Gervais Street
Suite 200
Columbia, SC 29201
803-734-9900
Fax: 803-734-9887
e-mail: askus@aging.sc.gov
http://www.aging.sc.gov
Andre Bauer, Lieutenant Governor
William Gambrel, Medicaid Control Unit
Denny W Neilson, Legislative Committee Aging

The Lieutenant Governor's Office on Aging is the statewide leader for advocating, planning and developing resources in partnership with individuals and communities to meet the present and future needs of 660,000 older South Carolinians and their caregivers; to develop and coordinate a comprehensive continuum of care system; and to promote education, research and training in the field of gerontology. The Lieutenant Governor's Office on Aging works with a network of regional and local organizations to develop and manage programs and services to improve the quality of life of South Carolina's older citizens, and to help them remain independent in their homes and communities. The Lieutenant Governor's Office on Aging, through its administration of the Older Americans Act programs, aids 34,000 older adults who have the greatest social, economic, and health needs, and rural and low-income minority elders. Additionally, the Lieutenant Governor's Office on Aging works with many other state agencies, as well as with the private sector, to coordinate the needs and interests of older adults and to develop new resources.

South Dakota

11254 South Dakota Department of Social Services: Legal Services for the Elderly
700 Governors Drive
Pierre, SD 57501
605-773-3656
866-854-5465
Fax: 605-773-6834
e-mail: ASA@state.sd.us
http://http://dss.sd.gov/contactus/
Deborah K Bowman, Secretary
Kim Malsam-Rysdon, Deputy Secretary
Emily Currey, Communications Director

Adult Services and Aging (ASA) provides opportunities that enable disabled adults and older South Dakotans to live independent, meaningful and dignified lives while maintaining close family and community ties. Through various programs, ASA provides or purchases services for disabled adults and older persons who are determined eligible for the programs. ASA field staff directly provide assessment and case management services to evaluate the needsof the individual. Based on the assessment, appropriate services are authorized and an Individual Care Plan is developed with the needs of the individual specifically identified. Social workers may also work with community groups and organizations to identify needs of older citizens.

11255 South Dakota Protection and Advocacy Services
221 South Central Avenue
Pierre, SD 57501
605-224-8294
800-658-4782
Fax: 605-224-5125
e-mail: keanr@sdadvocacy.com
http://www.sdadvocacy.com
TDD 605-224-8294
Robert J Kean, Executive Director

South Dakota Advocacy Services is South Dakota's designated protection and advocacy (P&A) system. P&A systems are mandated under various federal statues to provide legal representation and other advocacy services to all eligible persons with disabilities. These services are provided through a variety of vehicles: individual representation, educating policy makers, advocacy for groups, information and referral services, rights education and self advocacy training. The fundamental mission of the P&A system is to respond to allegations of abuse, neglect and violations of the rights of persons with disabilities, including discrimination based on disability. P&As devote considerable resources to develop capacities of persons with disabilities, ensuring full access to inclusive educational programs, financial entitlement programs (e.g., Medicaid and Social Security), health care, accessible housing, and productive employment opportunities.

Tennessee

11256 Aging Services for the Upper Cumberlands
1225 South Willow Avenue
Cookeville, TN 38506-4194
931-432-4210
Fax: 931-432-6101
http://http://www.tba.org/LawBytes/T1_1002.html
Marie C Ferran, Executive Director

A not-for-profit law office that provides certain types of free legal help to people who cannot afford to pay a lawyer. Legal Aid does help with many civil law cases. They may be able to help you if you are having a problem with your landlord, food stamps, Families First (welfare), TennCare, Medicare; health care or family problems, especially domestic violence. Even if Legal Aid cannot represent you directly in a case, they may be able to tell you where to get help or give you advice that will help you handle the case yourself.

Legal Aid Resources/Texas

11257 Disability Law & Advocacy Center of Tennessee (DLAC)
2416 21st Avenue South
Nashville, TN 37212-1257
615-298-1080
800-342-1660
Fax: 615-298-2046
e-mail: GetHelp@DLACTN.org
http://www.dlactn.org/content.asp?contentID=10
TTY 888-852-2852

Nick Perenich, Esq., Chair
Charles West, Vice Chair
Barbara Simmons, Treasurer

Disability Law & Advocacy Center of Tennessee (DLAC) advocates for the rights of Tennesseans with disabilities to ensure they have an equal opportunity to be productive and respected members of our society.

11258 Legal Aid of East Tennessee (LAET)
502 South Gay Street
Suite 404
Knoxville, TN 37902
865-637-0484
Fax: 865-525-1162
e-mail: dyoder@laet.org
http://www.laet.org

Dave Yoder, Executive Director

The mission of Legal Aid of East Tennessee (LAET) is to ensure equal justice for elderly, abused, and low-income people, by providing a broad scope of legal assistance and advocacy. Legal Aid of East Tennessee, and our predecessor programs Legal Services of Upper East Tennessee and Knoxville Legal Aid Society, have been a part of the community fabric of Knoxville and surrounding areas for more than 40 years. Through the process of reconfiguration, LAET has come to serve 26 counties in East Tennessee. With a main office in the heart of downtown Knoxville and additional offices in Johnson City, Morristown, Maryville, Cleveland and Chattanooga, LAET staff provide civil legal representation to indigent clients in East Tennessee. For many, LAET is the only link to legal assistance when faced with seemingly insurmountable dilemmas in civil matters. LAET provides civil legal assistance to approximately 8,000 individuals each year. From gaining Orders of Protection for victims of domestic violence to preventing families from becoming homeless, the efforts of LAET have ensured that thousands of low-income families in our community have been given a chance.

11259 Memphis Area Legal Services: Pro Bono Panel for Senior Citizens
109 North Main Street
Claridge House, 2nd Floor
Memphis, TN 38103-2218
901-523-8822
Fax: 901-578-8566
e-mail: mais@maisi.org
http://http://www.malsi.org/

Harrison McIver, Executive Director

Approximately 225 lawyers volunteer their time to elderly clients who are 55 years of age or older, live in Shelby County, and meet the eligibility criteria of the Legal Services Corporation.

11260 Nashville Bar Association (NBA): Young Lawyers Division (YLD)
315 Union Street
Suite 800
Nashville, TN 37201
615-242-9272
Fax: 615-255-3026
e-mail: tgrindon@bakerdonelson.com
http://http://www.nashbar.org/yld/yld.htm

Tonya M Grindon, President YLD/Young Lawyers Dvn
Susan Wollar Sowards, NBA Executive Director

The Young Lawyers Division (YLD) of the NBA takes an active role in Bar programs and in other community activities. Some of their projects include programs for the elderly, the homeless, youth, and other groups with special needs. Honored in 1999, by Lexis for their outstanding work with the Tornado Hotline.

11261 Northwest Assistance for the Elderly Project
Northwest Tennessee Area Agency on Aging
124 Weldon Drive
PO Box 963
Martin, TN 38237-0963
731-587-4213
Fax: 731-588-5833
e-mail: shill@charterbn.com
http://www.state.tn.us/comaging/localarea.html

Susan Hill, Executive Director

The Northwest Assistance for the Elderly Project offers legal advice and education in these matters: food stamps, Social Security, SSI, Medicaid, TennCare, Medicare, nursing home care and access, boarding home care, federally subsidized housing, utilities, age discrimination, cases involving the immediate risk of loss of housing; adult abuse, neglect and exploitation; and medical collection actions threatening access to health care. Additionally, it offers advice, education and preparation of health care power of attorney and living will documents for elderly who are homebound, institutionalized or terminally ill. Representation is available in some cases that involve these areas of the law and to assist persons who wish to contest or defend against conservatorship actions. Also, project staff may serve as guardians-ad-litem in conservatorship actions. Legal representation in other matters is restricted due to limited staff availability.

11262 Tennessee Commission on Aging and Disability
500 Deaderick Street
8th Floor
Nashville, TN 37243-0860
615-741-2056
e-mail: nancy.peace@state.tn.us
http://www.state.tn.us/comaging/

Nancy Peace, Executive Director
Belina Bruns, Aging Program Planner
Louise Woodberry, Community Services

The Tennessee Commission on Aging and Disability is working for adults with disabilities and older Tennesseans by providing leadership and guidance for a system that promotes health, dignity, independence and security through an array of community and in-home services, the protection of rights and the implementation of best practices.

11263 Tennessee Justice Center
301 Charlotte Avenue
Nashville, TN 37201
615-255-0331
877-608-1009
Fax: 615-255-0354
e-mail: info@tnjustice.org
http://www.tnjustice.org/

Gordon Bonnyman, Executive Director

11264 West Tennessee Legal Services (WTLS)
210 West Main Street
PO Box 2066
Jackson, TN 38302
731-423-0616
800-372-8346
Fax: 731-423-2600
e-mail: wtls@wtls.org
http://www.wtls.org

Steven Xanthopoulos, Executive Director

Texas

11265 Dallas Young Lawyers Association: Committee on Legal Aid to the Elderly
2101 Ross Avenue
Dallas, TX 75201
214-969-7675
Fax: 214-220-7422
e-mail: chad@appeal.pro
http://http://www.dayl.com/

Chad Ruback, President
Cherie Harris, Executive Director

The Committee sponsors a speakers bureau in which attorneys talk with seniors in nursing homes, churches, nutrition sites, and senior centers concerning advance directives, guardianship, etc.

Legal Aid Resources/Utah

11266 Houston Bar Association: Judicare Program for the Elderly
1001 Fannin
Suite 1300
Houston, TX 77002
713-759-1133
Fax: 713-759-1710
http://http://www.hba.org/
Glenn A Ballard, Jr., President Board of Directors
Kay Sim, Executive Director
Rusty Bienvenue, Committees and Programs Director

Senior citizens have unique legal needs. Through this program, volunteer attorneys help income-eligible seniors with legal problems, including wills and medical directives. A free Elder Law Handbook is available in English, Spanish, Korean, and Mandarin Chinese to answer many legal questions facing the seniors and their caregivers.

11267 State Bar of Texas: Texas Young Lawyers Association
1414 Colorado
Suite 502
Austin, TX 78711-2487
512-427-1529
800-204-2222
Fax: 512-427-4117
e-mail: crump@mdjwlaw.com
http://http://www.tyla.org/
Karen Crump, President
Tracy Brown, Administrative Director
Denny Sheppard, Project Coordinator

Produces the booklet Rights and Needs of Senior Citizens in Texas.

11268 Texas Department of Aging and Disability Services (DAD)
John H. Winters Human Services Complex
701 West 51st Street
PO Box 149030
Austin, TX 78751
512-438-3011
Fax: 512-438-4747
e-mail: mail@dads.state.tx.us
http://www.dads.state.tx.us/
Adelaide Horn, Commissioner
Jon Weizenbaum, Deputy Commissioner
Lawrence Parker, Chief Operating Officer

The Texas Department of Aging and Disability Services (DADS) was established in September 2004 to support Older Texans and persons with disabilities through a comprehensive and cost-effective service delivery system that promotes and enhances individual well-being, dignity, and choice. The DADS mission is to provide a comprehensive array of aging and disability services, supports, and opportunities that are easily accessed in local communities.

11269 Texas Legal Services Center: Legal Hotline for Older Texans
815 Brazos Street
Suite 1100
Austin, TX 78701-2509
512-477-3950
800-622-2520
Fax: 512-477-6576
http://http://www.tlsc.org/hotline.html
Randall Chapman, Executive Director
Roger Curme, Hotline Managing Attorney

The Legal Hotline is a project of Texas Legal Services Center. The Hotline receives funding from the Texas Department on Aging, through the HICAP Program, coordinating services with the Texas Department on Aging and the Texas Department of Insurance for elderly clients needing benefits analysis and legal advice. We provide legal information and advice in obtaining benefits such as Medicaid for Qualified Medicare Beneficiaries, food stamps, elderly housing assistance, and SSI; we are also able to answer other legal questions. Common concerns include debt collection, advance planning and estate planning issues, powers of attorney, and housing and consumer problems. In addition, we are able to send informational publications to Texans age sixty (60) and older on a variety of topics such as alternatives to guardianship, wills and probate, public benefits, consumer and debtor rights, health care rights, and nursing homes.

11270 Texas Protection and Advocacy AgencyNorth Texas Regional Office: Dallas
1420 West Mockingbird Lane
Suite 450
Dallas, TX 75247-0450
214-630-0916
800-880-2884
Fax: 214-630-3472
e-mail: infoai@advocacyinc.org
http://www.advocacyinc.org/contact.htm
Betty Black, Executive Director

Advocacy, Inc. is a nonprofit corporation funded by the United States Congress to protect and advocate for the legal rights of people with disabilities in Texas. Program services include that of education, Medicaid issues, housing discrimination, community services, transportation, and accessible public accommodations.

Utah

11271 Utah Department of Human ServicesDivision of Aging and Adult Services
Legal Services for Older Adults in Utah
120 North 200 West
Room 325
Salt Lake City, UT 84103
801-538-3910
877-424-4640
Fax: 801-538-4395
e-mail: DAAS@utah.gov
http://www.hsdaas.utah.gov/index.htm
Alan Ormsbey, Executive Director

The Division administers the Adult Protective Services program to protect seniors and disabled adults from abuse, neglect, or exploitation. Trained staff within a statewide system of offices, working in cooperation with local law enforcement, investigate cases involving seniors and disabled adults. Adult Protective Services workers provide services designed to assist victims and prevent further abuse, neglect, and exploitation.

11272 Utah Protection and Advocacy Agency: Disability Law Center
The Community Legal Center
205 North 400 West
Salt Lake, UT 84103
801-363-1347
800-662-9080
Fax: 801-533-3968
e-mail: fnelson@disabilitylawcenter.org
http://www.disabilitylawcenter.org
TTY 801-924-3185
Fraser Nelson, Executive Director
Drew Hyde, President Advisory Council
Michael C Walch, Treasurer/Attorney

11273 Utah State Bar: Senior Legal Clinic Program Salt Lake County
645 South 200 East
Salt Lake City, UT 84101-1683
801-531-9077
Fax: 801-531-0660
e-mail: info@utahbar.org
http://utahbar.org/public/pro_bono_resources
Stephen M Jennings, Chairman

The Needs of the Elderly Committee of the Utah State Bar runs this program. Volunteer attorneys meet with senior citizens at senior citizen centers within Salt Lake County. Volunteers meet one-on-one with six clients for 20 minute consultations, over a two hour period. The goal is not to provide in-depth legal advice, but to determine whether the individual has a legal problem and then to identify potential legal services to address the problem.The volunteers do not need to have specialized knowledge of the legal issues affecting elderly persons.

11274 Utah State Bar: Young Lawyers Section
645 South 200 East
Salt Lake City, UT 84111
801-537-9077
801-532-1234
Fax: 801-531-0660
e-mail: dhall@parsonsbehle.com
http://www.utahbar.org/sections/yld/Welcome.htm

David R Hall, President
Stephanie Wilkins-Pugsley, President Elect
H Craig Hall Jr, Secretary

Produces the Utah Senior Citizens' Handbook: A Guide to Laws and Programs Affecting Senior Citizens. Includes sections on health care, financial assistance, estate planning, protective arragements and services, housing and landlord-tenant relations, rights and protection, and a resource directory. Also has a series of lectures at senior centers throughout the state focused on consumer fraud.

Vermont

11275 Funeral Consumers Alliance
1630 Clark Road
Montpelier, VT 05651
802-482-3437
800-765-0107
Fax: 802-482-5246
e-mail: ddgrundy@aol.com
http://www.funerals.org/vermont/

Dave Grundy, President

Mediates funeral complaints, monitors funeral industry practices and works to protect consumer rights. Local affiliates in most states.

11276 Senior Citizens Law Project of Vermont Legal Aid
264 North Winooski Street
PO Box 1367
Burlington, VT 05402
800-889-2047
http://http://www.vtlawhelp.org

Michael Benvenuto, Executive Director

Senior Citizens Law Project of Vermont, working in conjunction with the Administration on Aging, supports efforts to provide seniors with legal advice on topics such as wills, power of attorney and health care paperwork.

11277 State of Vermont Division of Disabilityand Aging Services
Agency of Human Services
103 South Main Street
Waterbury, CT 05671
802-241-2400
http://www.dad.state.vt.us/

Theresa Wood, Deputy Commissioner
June Bascom, Program Development
Karin Hammer Williamson, Residential Program Director

The Department of Disabilities, Aging and Independent Living is the center of the Agency of Human Services' program management and policy development with respect to older persons and persons with disabilities. The mission of the Department of Disabilities, Aging and Independent Living is to make Vermont the best state in which to grow old or to live with a disability - with dignity, respect and independence.

11278 Vermont Protection and Advocacy Agency
141 Main Street
Suite 7
Montpelier, VT 05602
802-229-1355
800-834-7890
Fax: 802-229-1359
e-mail: info@vtpa.org
http://www.vtpa.org

Ed Paquin, Executive Director
A.J. Ruben, Supervising Attorney
Tina Wood, Advocate/Paralegal

Vermont Protection and Advocacy is a statewide agency dedicated to advancing the rights of people with mental health and disabilities issues. Vermont Protection and Advocacy works towards a system that honors the dignity and needs of all people with disabilities.

Virginia

11279 AACD Legal Series
5999 Stevenson Avenue
Alexandria, VA 22304-3300
703-823-9800
800-347-6647
Fax: 800-472-2329
http://www.counseling.org
TDD 703-823-6862

Marie Wakefield, President
Richard Yep, Director

Offering three volumes: Preparing for Court Appearances; Documentation in Counseling Records; and The Counselor and The Law.

11280 Arlington County Bar Association: Legal Services of Northern Virginia
1425 North Courthouse Road
Suite 1800
Arlington, VA 22201
703-228-3390
Fax: 703-228-7360
e-mail: support@arlingtonbar.org
http://http://www.arlingtonbar.org/

Ronald L Hiss, President
Mary D Evans, Executive Director
Paul H Melnick, Secretary

Helps to plan the annual Arlington Law Day for the Elderly and co-sponsors education sessions for professionals and service providers on advance directives and the Patient Self Determination Act.

11281 National Center for State Courts
300 Newport Avenue
Williamsburg, VA 23185-4147
800-616-6164
Fax: 757-564-2022
e-mail: webmaster@ncsc,dni.us
http://http://www.ncsconline.org/D_KIS/

Mary Campbell McQueen, President/CEO
Thomas M Clarke, VP Research/Information Officer
Gwen W Williams, VP/CFO/Administration

Develops a national clearinghouse and resource center for local and state courts to focus on requirements and methods of compliances with ADA.

11282 National Right to Work Legal Defense and Education Foundation
8001 Braddock Road
Springfield, VA 22160
703-321-8510
800-336-3600
Fax: 703-321-9319
e-mail: info@nrtw.org
http://www.nrtw.org

Raymond J Lajeunesse Jr, VP / Legal Director
Richard J Clair, Corporate Counsel/Staff Attorney

Seeks to assist employees whose human civil rights are being violated.

11283 Virginia Department for the Aging
1610 Forest Avenue
Suite 100
Richmond, VA 23229
804-552-9333
800-552-3402
Fax: 804-662-9354
e-mail: aging@vda.virginia.gov
http://www.vda.virginia.gov

Julie Christopher, Commissioner
Janet D Brown, Esq., Guardianship & Legal Services
Faye Cates, M.S.S.W., Program Coordinator

Legal Aid Resources/Washington

The Virginia Department for the Aging (VDA) works with 25 local Area Agencies on Aging (AAAs) as well as various other public and private organizations to help older Virginians, their families and loved ones find the services and information they need to lead healthy and independent lives as they grow older. VDA's mission is to foster the dignity, independence, and security of older Virginians by promoting partnerships with families and communities. The Department for the Aging is designated by the federal government as the agency to oversee all state programs using funds provided by the federal Older Americans Act and the Virginia General Assembly. Area Agencies on Aging contract with the Department to provide services for older Virginians and their families in communities throughout Virginia.

11284 Virginia Protection and Advocacy Agency
1910 Byrd Avenue
Suite 5
Richmond, VA 23230
804-225-2042
800-552-3962
Fax: 804-662-7057
e-mail: generalvopa@dsa.state.va.gov
http://www.vopa.state.va.us
TDD 804-225-2042
Colleen Miller, Executive Director
Sherry Confer, Policy Director
Claunita Jones, Resource Advocate

The Virginia Office for Protection and Advocacy (VOPA) helps with disability-related problems like abuse, neglect, and discrimination in addition to assisting people with disabilities to obtain services and treatment. Through zealous and effective advocacy and legal representation, VOPA strives to protect and advance legal, human, and civil rights of persons with disabilities; combat and prevent abuse, neglect, and discrimination; and promote independence, choice, and self-determination for persons with disabilities.

11285 Virginia Protection and Advocacy Agency: Virginia Beach
287 Independence Boulevard
Suite 120
Virginia Beach, VA 23462
757-552-1148
800-552-3962
Fax: 757-552-1145
e-mail: general.vopa@vopa.virginia.gov
http://www.vopa.state.va.us
Faye Adams, Disbility Rights Advocate
Shannon Manning, Staff Attorney
Peter Widel, Investigator

The Virginia Office for Protection and Advocacy (VOPA) helps with disability-related problems like abuse, neglect, and discrimination in addition to assisting people with disabilities to obtain services and treatment. Through zealous and effective advocacy and legal representation, VOPA strives to protect and advance legal, human, and civil rights of persons with disabilities; combat and prevent abuse, neglect and discrimination; and promote independence, choice, and self-determination by persons with disabilities.

Washington

11286 Disabilities Law Project: Washington
Alliance of People With Disabilities
4649 Sunnyside Avenue North
Suite 100
Seattle, WA 98103-6900
206-284-9733
866-545-7055
Fax: 206-545-7059
e-mail: lonnie@wccd.org
http://http://www.disabilitypride.org/
TDD 206-633-6637
Lonnie Davis, Disabilities Law Program Manager
Jeanette Murphy, Executive Director
Gladys Springborn-Brannigan, Assistant Director

The Disabilities Law Project offers legal advice and representation in situations where an individual has been discriminated against because of his or her disability.

11287 Northwest Justice Project: Olympia
711 Capitol Way South
Suite 704
Olympia, WA 98501
360-753-3610
888-212-0380
Fax: 360-753-0174
e-mail: www.nwjustice.org
http://www.nwjustice.org/
Richard Harrison, Board of Directors Member
Roger Wynne, Board of Directors Member
Octavia Hathaway, Board of Directors Member

The Northwest Justice Project (NJP) is a not-for-profit statewide organization that provides free civil legal services to low-income people from ten offices and two satellite locations throughout the state of Washington. Each year, NJP assists more than 18,000 people in need of critical legal assistance. Clients in need of interpreter services in order to access legal services through NJP are entitled to those services. NJP strives to secure justice in a democratic society by working for equal access to the legal system by empowering low-income persons and communities through education about their legal rights and obligations, and by promoting respect for human dignity through legal advocacy.

11288 Northwest Justice Project: Seattle
401 Second Avenue S
Suite 407
Seattle, WA 98104
206-464-1519
888-201-1012
Fax: 206-624-7501
e-mail: njp@nwjustice.org
http://www.nwjustice.org
TDD 888-201-9737
Richard Harrison, Board of Directors Member
Roger Wynne, Board of Directors Member
Octavia Hathaway, Board of Directors Member

The Northwest Justice Project (NJP) is a not-for-profit statewide organization that provides free civil legal services to low-income people from ten offices and two satellite locations throughout the state of Washington. Each year, NJP assists more than 18,000 people in need of critical legal assistance. Clients in need of interpreter services in order to access legal services through NJP are entitled to those services. NJP strives to secure justice in a democratic society by working for equal access to the legal system by empowering low-income persons and communities through education about their legal rights and obligations, and by promoting respect for human dignity through legal advocacy.

11289 Northwest Justice Project: Vancouver
500 West 8th Avenue
Suite 275
Vancouver, WA 98660
360-693-6130
888-201-1020
Fax: 360-693-6352
e-mail: njp@nwjustice.org
http://www.nwjustice.org/
Richard Harrison, Board of Directors Member
Roger Wynne, Board of Directors Member
Octavia Hathaway, Board of Directors Member

The Northwest Justice Project (NJP) is a not-for-profit statewide organization that provides free civil legal services to low-income people from ten offices and two satellite locations throughout the state of Washington. Each year, NJP assists more than 18,000 people in need of critical legal assistance. Clients in need of interpreter services in order to access legal services through NJP are entitled to those services. NJP strives to secure justice in a democratic society by working for equal access to the legal system by empowering low-income persons and communities through education about their legal rights and obligations, and by promoting respect for human dignity through legal advocacy.

11290 Washington Aging and Disability Services
Washington State Department Social/Health Services
PO Box 45130
Olympia, WA 98504-5130
800-422-3263
Fax: 360-902-7848
e-mail: leitckj@dshs.wa.gov
http://www.aasa.dshs.wa.gov
TDD 800-737-7931

Kathy Leitch, Assistant Secretary

The Aging and Disability Services Administration assists seniors, adults, and children with developmental delays or disabilities, cognitive impairment, chronic illness and related functional disabilities to gain access to needed services and supports by managing a system of long-term care and supportive services that are high quality, cost effective, and responsive to individual needs and preferences.

11291 Washington Protection and Advocacy Agency
315 Fifth Avenue South
Suite 850
Seattle, WA 98104
206-324-1521
800-562-2702
Fax: 206-957-0729
e-mail: wpas@wpas-rights.org
http://www.wpas-rights.org
TTY 206-957-0728

Mark Stroh, Executive Director

West Virginia

11292 West Virginia Protection and Advocacy Agency
1207 Quarrier Street
Litton Building, 4th Floor
Charleston, WV 25301-1842
304-346-0847
800-950-5250
Fax: 304-356-0867
e-mail: wvainfo@wvadvocates.org
http://www.wvadvocates.org
TDD 304-346-0847

Clarice Hausch, Executive Director
Martha Barber, Staff Attorney
Ed West, Resource Development Specialist

West Virginia Advocates (WVA) protects and advocates for the human and legal rights of persons with disabilities. Services are based on the principles of equality, equity and fairness; meaningful choice and empowerment; individuality and independence; cultural competency; and, access and privacy.

11293 West Virginia Senior Legal Aid
235 High Street
Suite 519
Morgantown, WV 26505
304-296-0082
800-239-8819
Fax: 304-296-2746
e-mail: seniorlegalaid@yahoo.com
http://www.seniorlegalaid.org/

Cathy McConnell, Executive Director
Billie Jean Underwood, Staff Attorney
Robert Bastress, Esq., President Board of Directors

Wisconsin

11294 AgeAdvantAge Area Agency on Aging: Madison
2850 Dairy Drive
Suite 200
Madison, WI 53718
608-224-6300
Fax: 608-224-6306
e-mail: kellermanb@mailbag.com
http://www.discover-net.net/~ageadvan/

Robert Kellerman, Executive Director
Jayne F Mullins, Regional Program Planner
Carrie Kroetz, Program Assistant

11295 Elder Law Center: Coalition of Wisconsin Aging Groups
2850 Dairy Drive
Suite 200
Madison, WI 53718
608-224-0606
800-366-2990
Fax: 608-224-0607
e-mail: cwag@cwag.org
http://http://www.cwag.org/
TDD 888-758-6047

Tom Frazier, Executive Director Operations
Helen Marks Dicks, Elder Law Center Director
Kris Kawnowski, Development Director

Benefit specialists provide information, counseling, and representation to county citizens age 60 and older with problems of public benefits and health care financing. Trains AARP volunteers to provide information and counseling on Medicare and Medicaid. Also collaborates on publications with the Center for Public Representation.

11296 Milwaukee Young Lawyers Association: Committee on Legal Services to the Elderly
424 East Wells Street
Milwaukee, WI 53202
414-274-6760
Fax: 414-274-6765
e-mail: info@milwbar.org
http://http://www.milwbar.org/

Jane M R Mulcahy, Chair Elder Law Section

Operates a lawyer referral service in which seniors recieve half-hour consultations. Also provides a speakers bureau, on ongoing Senior Center Counseling Program at three senior centers, and a question and answer booklet on wills and probates.

11297 Wisconsin Bar Association: Elder Law
5302 Eastpark Boulevard
Madison, WI 53718-2101
608-257-3838
800-728-7788
Fax: 608-257-5502
e-mail: service@wisbar.org
http://http://www.wisbar.org/

George Brown, Executive Director
Gene Gosewehr, Director Information Services
Lynda Tanner, Finance/Administration Director

The Elder Law Section works to develop and improve the laws that affect the elderly, and promotes high standards of ethical performance and technical expertise for those who practice in the area. The section sponsors CLE programs at State Bar conventions, monitors proposed state legislation and publishes a newsletter.

11298 Wisconsin Coalition for Advocacy: Madison
16 North Carroll Street
Suite 400
Madison, WI 53703
608-267-0214
800-928-8777
Fax: 608-267-0368
e-mail: lynnb@w-c-a.org
http://www.w-c-a.org
TDD 608-267-0214
TTY 888-758-6049

Lynn Breedlove, Executive Director
Joan Karan, Assistant Director
Kim Hogan, Intake Specialist

Legal Aid Resources/Wyoming

The Wisconsin Coalition for Advocacy (WCA) is a private, non-profit agency chosen by Wisconsin's Governor to provide protection and advocacy for people with disabilities throughout the state. WCA is completely independent of state government and direct service providers. WCA works throughout the state with individual consumers, their families, human service and other professionals, and policymakers who make and implement decisions on disability rights. The skilled advocates, attorneys and consultants of WCA bring professional as well as personal experience in issues of disability rights to their work. The committed individuals who serve on the WCA Board of Directors include people with disabilities, family members and other community representatives. WCA is part of a national system of independent protection and advocacy agencies established by the United States Congress in the 1970s to safeguard the rights of people with disabilities. WCA receives funding from federal and state grants, training fees and private donations.

11299 Wisconsin Coalition for Advocacy: Milwaukee
6737 West Washington Street
Summit Place, Suite 3230
Milwaukee, WI 53214
414-773-4646
800-708-3034
http://www.w-c-a.org
TTY 800-708-3034
Palmer Bell, Office Director
Patrick Berigan, Supervising Attorney
Julie Dixon Seidl, Advocacy Project Coordinator

The Wisconsin Coalition for Advocacy (WCA) is a private, non-profit agency chosen by Wisconsin's Governor to provide protection and advocacy for people with disabilities throughout the state. WCA is completely independent of state government and direct service providers. WCA works throughout the state with individual consumers, their families, human service and other professionals, and policymakers who make and implement decisions on disability rights. The skilled advocates, attorneys and consultants of WCA bring professional as well as personal experience in issues of disability rights to their work. The committed individuals who serve on the WCA Board of Directors include people with disabilities, family members and other community representatives. WCA is part of a national system of independent protection and advocacy agencies established by the United States Congress in the 1970s to safeguard the rights of people with disabilities. WCA receives funding from federal and state grants, training fees and private donations.

11300 Wisconsin Coalition for Advocacy: Rice Lake
801 Hammond Avenue
Rice Lake, WI 54868
715-736-1232
877-338-3724
http://www.w-c-a.org
TTY 877-338-3724
Rick Pelishek, Office Director
Karen Lane, Advocacy Specialist

The Wisconsin Coalition for Advocacy (WCA) is a private, non-profit agency chosen by Wisconsin's Governor to provide protection and advocacy for people with disabilities throughout the state. WCA is completely independent of state government and direct service providers. WCA works throughout the state with individual consumers, their families, human service and other professionals, and policymakers who make and implement decisions on disability rights. The skilled advocates, attorneys and consultants of WCA bring professional as well as personal experience in issues of disability rights to their work. The committed individuals who serve on the WCA Board of Directors include people with disabilities, family members and other community representatives. WCA is part of a national system of independent protection and advocacy agencies established by the United States Congress in the 1970s to safeguard the rights of people with disabilities. WCA receives funding from federal and state grants, training fees and private donations.

11301 Wisconsin Department of Health and HumanServices: The State Bureau on Aging
201 East Washington Avenue
PO Box 7946
Madison, WI 53707-7946
608-266-3131
Fax: 606-266-1784
e-mail: dwdsec@dwd.state.wi.us
http://http://dhfs.wisconsin.gov/aging/
Roberta Gassman, Department Secretary
Micabil Diaz-Martinez, Deputy Secretary
Ellen Vogel, Chief Information Officer

County and tribal benefit specialists assist older persons who are having a problem with their private or government benefits. The benefits specialists are often called red tape cutters because they are experts at helping older persons with the extensive and complicated paperwork that is often required in benefit programs. They help older persons figure out what benefits they are entitled to and tell them what they must do to receive them. Benefit specialists receive ongoing training and are monitored by attorneys knowledgeable in elder law. The attorneys are also available to assist older persons in need of legal representation on benefit matters.

Wyoming

11302 State of Wyoming Aging Division
6101 Yellowstone Road
Room 259B
Cheyenne, WY 82002
307-777-7986
900-442-2766
e-mail: cnoon@state.wy.us
http://http://wdhfs.state.wy.us/aging/index.htm
Beverly Morrow, Administrator Aging Division
Marcia Harvey, Elder Rights Services Director
Liz Vigil, Grants Manager Aging Division

Allotments for vulnerable elder rights protection activities has several components: the Long Term Care Ombudsman advocates on behalf of older persons in institutions or receiving long term care in -home services and their families; the Legal Assistant Developer program provides, on a statewide basis, the protection of rights of vulnerable older persons; and,the Legal Services program provides legal assistance services to older Americans. To be eligible for these services a client must be over 60 years of age, a spouse of an individual over 60 years of age, or a disabled person living in senior housing attached to a congregate meals site.

11303 West Virginia Bureau of Senior Services
1900 Kanawha Boulevard East
Holly Grove, Building #10
Charleston, WV 25305-0160
304-558-3317
Fax: 304-558-0004
e-mail: svanin@boss.state.wv.us
http://www.state.wv.us/seniorservices/
Sandra Vanin, Commissioner
Janet H Frazier, Chairperson

The West Virginia Bureau of Senior Services is a cabinet-level agency within State Government and acts as the lead entity for programs serving older West Virginians. A Commissioner appointed by the Governor is the chief administrative officer and oversees all program and fiscal operations. In addition to agency staff members, the Bureau consists of a 15-member Advisory Council on Aging. The Bureau of Senior Services administers a wide range of programs available through the area agencies on aging and the providers operating on the local level.

11304 Wyoming Protection & Advocacy Agency: Evanston
350 City View Drive
Suite 207A
Evanston, WY 82930
307-789-3035
Fax: 307-789-8631
e-mail: wypanda@vcn.com
http://www.wypanda.vcn.com
Jeanne A Thobro, Executive Director
Mary Carson Barks, President Board of Directors

Legal Aid Resources/Wyoming

11305 Wyoming Protection and Advocacy Agency: Developmental Disabilities Protection and Advocacy Program
320 West 25th Street
2nd Floor
Cheyenne, WY 82001-3064
307-632-3496
800-624-7648
Fax: 307-638-0815
e-mail: wypanda@vcn.com
http://www.wypanda.vcn.com

Jeanne A Thobro, Executive Director
Mary Carson Barks, President Board of Trustees

Alabama

11306 Alabama Institute for Deaf and Blind
PO Box 698
205 South Street
Talladega, AL 35161-698
256-761-3331
Fax: 256-761-3337
e-mail: tlacy@aidb.state.al.us
http://www.aidb.org

Teresa Lacy, Librarian
Terry Graham, President

Book collection includes discs, cassettes, braille and large print. Also closed-circuit TV and magnifiers.

11307 Alabama Regional Library for the Blind and Physically Handicapped
Alabama Public Library Service
6030 Monticello Drive
Montgomery, AL 36130-6000
334-213-3900
800-723-8459
Fax: 334-213-3993
e-mail: fzaleski@apls.state.al.us
http://www.apls.state.al.us

Fara Zaleski, Executive Director

Special format material for US citizens unable to use standard print due to visual or physical impairment.

11308 Auburn University: Special Collections & Archives
231 Mell Street
Auburn University
Auburn, AL 36849-5606
334-884-4500
800-446-0387
Fax: 334-844-4424
e-mail: willily@auburn.edu
http://www.lib.auburn.edu/special

Dwayne Cox, Department Head
Lynn Williams, Librarian

Houses published and unpublished materials which, because of their uniqueness or condition, require special care and handling.

11309 Houston-Love Memorial Library
212 W Burdeshaw Street
Dothan, AL 36303
334-793-9767
Fax: 334-793-6645
e-mail: houstonlove@houstonlovelibrary.org
http://http://www.houstonlovelibrary.org

Myrtis Merrow, Librarian
Bettye Forbus, Executive Director

Offers an extensive selection of reading material via cassette recordings and brochures for various activities; braille is also available if requested. The cassette recordings are provided along with cassette players if the patron qualifies for the services.

11310 Huntsville Subregional Library for the Blind
915 Monroe St
Huntsville, AL 35801
205-532-5940
Fax: 205-532-5994
http://hpl.lib.al.us/

Joyce Smith, Librarian

Talking books for people who are blind or disabled offering reference materials on the blind and other disabilities, large-print photocopier, thermaform duplicator and more.

11311 Library for the Blind & Handicapped: Public Library-Anniston/Calhoun Counties
PO Box 308
Anniston, AL 36202-308
205-237-8501
Fax: 205-238-0474
e-mail: library@quicklink.net
http://www.anniston.lib.al.us/bandph.htm

Deenie Culver, Librarian

Reference materials on blindness, cassettes, large print books and discs.

11312 Samford University Library Special Collections
800 Lakeshore Drive
Birmingham, AL 35229
205-726-2748
Fax: 205-870-2642
e-mail: ecwelis@samford.edu
http://library.samford.edu

Elizabeth C Wells, Special Collections Librarian
Becky Strickland, Special Collections Assistant

The mission of the Special Collection is: to collect and preserve special materials through providing a secure and protected environment for the conservation and use of the sources; to provide access and organization for manuscripts and other archival materials; to promote and support the research, teaching programs and scholarship of the University; to project the image of Samford University as an institution of higher learning; and to serve asas the repository for the Samford University archives and for the Alabama Baptist Historical Collection.

1957

11313 US Deptartment of Veterans Affairs: Central Alabama Veterans Health Care System
215 Perry Hill Road
Montgomery, AL 36109-3725
334-272-4670
Fax: 334-260-4125
http://www.centralalabama.va.gov

Scieva Holland, Library Manager
Susan J Helms, Library Technician-In-Charge
Kenneth Ruyle, Executive Director

Medicine, allied health sciences.

11314 US Deptartment of Veterans Affairs: Medical Center Library
700 19th Street S
Birmingham, AL 35233-1927
205-933-8101
Fax: 205-933-4484
http://www.birmingham.va.gov

Y.C Parris, Director

Medicine, nursing, hospital administration.

11315 US Deptartment of Veterans Affairs: Alabama Veterns Health Care System
2400 Hospital Road
Tuskegee, AL 36083-5001
334-727-0550
800-214-8387
Fax: 334-724-2793
http://www.centeralalabama.va.gov

Inez C Pinkard, Library Manager

Medicine, patient education, psychiatry, geriarics.

Alaska

11316 Alaska State Library Talking Book Center
344 W 3rd Avenue
Suite 125
Anchorage, AK 99501-2338
907-269-6575
Fax: 907-269-6580
e-mail: patience_frederiksen@eed.state.ak.us
http://www.library.state.ak.us/dev/tbc.html

Patience Frederiksen, Regional Librarian
Beverly Griffin, Manager

The Talking Book Center provides library service and special materials to Alaskans whose visual or physical handicaps prevent them from reading standard print materials. The center provides books and magazines on tape and Braille, as well as necessary playback equipment, to eligible patrons.

Arizona

11317 Arizona State Braille and Talking Book Library
1030 N 32nd Street
Phoenix, AZ 85008-5108
602-255-5578
800-255-5578
Fax: 602-286-0444
e-mail: btbl@lib.az.us
http://www.dlapr.lib.az.us
Linda A Montgomery, Administrative Librarian
Linda Montgomery, Executive Director

Cassette and braille books, for blind, visually impaired and physically disabled who are unable to use standard print books.

11318 Flagstaff City-Coconino County Library for the Visually & Physically Impaired
300 W Aspen Avenue
Flagstaff, AZ 86001-5304
928-779-7670
Fax: 928-774-9573
http://www.flagstaffpubliclibrary.org
Kay Whitaker, Executive Director

Reference materials on blindness and other handicaps, braille writer, magnifiers and kurzweil reading machine.

11319 Fountain Hills Lioness Braille Service
PO Box 18332
Fountain Hills, AZ 85269-8332
480-837-1555
Jean Hauck, Chairperson
Gary Curtis, Manager

Braille and large print books on the subjects of recreation, career and vocations, religion, novels and cookbooks for the visually impaired.

11320 Mesa Arizona Regional Family History Center
41 South Hobson
Mesa, AZ 85204
480-964-1200
Fax: 480-964-7137
http://www.mesarfhc.org/
Glenn E Scott, Director

The Mesa Arizona Regional Family History Center is a branch of the Family History Library in Salt Lake City, Utah that offers patrons a variety of resources including free Internet access, workshops and classes in addition to having commercial CD's with genealogical research data.
1923

11321 Phoenix Public Library: Special Needs Center
1221 N Central Avenue
Phoenix, AZ 85004-1867
602-261-8690
Fax: 602-261-8836
e-mail: contactus@phxlib.org
http://www.ci.phoenix.az.us
Mimi McCain, Supervisor

Offers services and resources of the Phoenix Public Library accessible to people with disabilities. Books and periodicals in large print, sign language, braille, resource directories and disability information. Information also available on video and DVS.

11322 Pima Council on Aging
8467 E Broadway Boulevard
Tucson, AZ 85710-4009
520-790-7262
Fax: 520-790-7577
e-mail: help@pcoa.org
http://www.pcoa.org
Marian Lupu, Executive Director
Doris Goldstein, Public Relations Director
Melissa Morgan, Information Specialist

Serves as an advocate, planner, developer and provider of services and programs for Pima County's older citizens and their families. Since 1967, individuals, regardless of background or income, have turned to the council for relevant information about how to prepare for events and chantes that accompany their maturity.

11323 Prescott Talking Book Library
215 E Goodwin Street
Prescott, AZ 86303-3911
928-777-1500
http://www.prescottlibrary.info
Toni Kaus, Library Director

Home visits, book discussion groups, magnifiers, braille writers and reference materials on blindness and other handicaps.

11324 Travis L Williams Family Services Center
4732 South Central Avenue
Phoenix, AZ 85040
602-634-4732
Fax: 602-534-2785
http://phoenix.gov/CITZASST/famtlw.html
Joseph Kress, Executive Director

Travis L. Williams Family Services Center operates in partnership with public and private agencies to provide a comprehensive array of onsite services to meet the emergency needs of low-income Phoenix residents. Examples of assistance provided include: budgeting, education and job training referrals, social and life-skills development, client advocacy, technical assistance, resource development, counseling and direct services to become self-sufficient/self-supporting. Services may include information and referral, emergency financial assistance for eligible clients experiencing a crisis with utilities and rent. Emergency food boxes and bus tickets are available for qualifying individuals.

11325 Tucson Family History Center
500 South Langley Avenue
Tucson, AZ 85741
520-298-0905
Fax: 520-298-2339
e-mail: kcwebb@gci-net.com
http://www.lib.ci.tucson.az.us/research/
Kimberly C Webb, Director Family History Center
Nancy Ledeboer, Library Director
Pat Corella, Deputy Director

Family History Centers are branch facilities of the Family History Library in Salt Lake City. Centers provide access to most of the microfilms and microfiche in the Family History Library to help patrons identify their ancestors.
1968

11326 US Department of Veterans Affairs: Northern Arizona VA Health Care System
500 Highway 89 N
Prescott, AZ 86313
928-445-4860
800-949-1005
Fax: 928-776-6094
http://www.prescott.va.gov
Thomas Hogan, Deputy Assistant Secretary
R Allen Pittman, Administration Assist Secretary

Medicine, nursing, surgery, dentistry, allied health sciences, administration.

11327 US Department of Veterans Affairs: Phoenix Medical Center Library
650 E Indian School Road
Phoenix, AZ 85012-1839
602-277-5551
800-554-7174
Fax: 602-222-6472
http://www.phoenix.va.gov
Judith Alfred, Chair Library Department

Medicine, nursing, allied health sciences.

11328 US Department of Veterans Affairs: Tucson Medical Center Library
3601 S 6th Avenue
Tucson, AZ 85723
520-792-1450
800-470-8262
Fax: 520-629-4638
e-mail: flance.lynn@forum.va.gov
http://www.tucson.va.gov
Lynn Flance, Chief Library Service

Medicine, nursing, surgery, neurology, psychiatry, radiology, management, patient health education.

Arkansas

11329 Arkansas Aging Foundation Information Center
706 S Pulaski Street
Little Rock, AR 72201-3927   501-376-6083
Ann Wasson, Manager

Health promotion; seniors - enhancing and independent living, health issues, activities.

11330 Arkansas Regional Library for the Blind and Physically Handicapped
1 Capitol Mall
Little Rock, AR 72201-1013   501-682-1155
                                Fax: 501-682-1529
                        e-mail: jhall@asl.lib.ar.us
                                TDD 501-682-1002
John D Hall, Director

Public library books in recorded or braille format. Popular fiction and nonfiction books for all ages, books and players are on free loan, sent to patrons by mail and may be returned postage free. Anyone who cannot see well enough to read regular print with glasses on or who has a disability that makes it difficult to hold a book or turn the pages is eligible.

11331 Educational Services for the Visually Impaired
PO Box 668
Little Rock, AR 72203   501-296-1815
Jame Caton, Director

Offers textbooks, braille books and more to the visually impaired grades K-12 in the Arizona area.

11332 Northwest Ozarks Regional Library for the Blind and Handicapped
217 E Dickson Street
Fayetteville, AR 72701-4296   501-442-6253
                                Fax: 501-442-6254
                    http://www.blind.net/g3600002.htm
Rachel Anne Ames, Librarian

Offers a summer reading program, closed-circuit TV, magnifiers, braille writers and large print books.

11333 US Department of Veterans Affairs Hospital Libraries
4300 W 7th Street
Little Rock, AR 72205-5446   501-324-5234
                                Fax: 501-671-2528
George M Zumwalt, Learning Reseach Services

Medicine, surgery, nursing, psychiatry, psychology, social work, dietetics.

11334 US Department of Veterans Affairs Medical Center Library Service
1100 N College Avenue
Fayetteville, AR 72703-1944   479-443-4301
                        http://www.fayettevill.va.gov
Connie Wilson, Library Consultant
Tim Hoover, Manager

Medicine, nursing, allied health sciences, and psychology.

California

11335 Books Aloud Library
PO Box 5731
San Jose, CA 95150-5731   408-808-2613
                                Fax: 408-808-2625
                        http://www.booksaloud.org
Joyce Meurer, Executive Director

Blind, braille, talking books.

11336 Broadcast Services for the Blind
1155 Mission Street
San Francisco, CA 94103-1514   415-431-1481
Randy Scott, Director
Anita Aaron, Executive Director

Offers radio broadcasting, braille books, cassettes, records, and more for the visually handicapped in the nine San Francisco Bay Area major cities.

11337 California State Library: Braille & Talking Book Library
PO Box 942837
1115 P St
Sacramento, CA 95814   916-654-0640
Aimee Sgourakis, Manager

Blind; braille; talking books.

11338 Eureka Ward Family History Center
Church of Jesus Christ of Latter Day Saints
3441 Edgewood Road
Eureka, CA 95501-2756   707-443-7411
                                Fax: 707-443-7411
                        e-mail: eurekafhc@juno.com
                                http://www.lds.org/
Alan Cookson, Director

Family search computer programs, all Microfilms and Microfiche available for a small rental fee. Assists patrons with their family histories through a collection of films, microfiche, books and periodicals of family history subjects.

11339 Fresno County Free Library: Talking Book Library for the Blind
770 N San Pablo Avenue
Fresno, CA 93728-3640   559-488-3217
                                Fax: 559-488-1971
Wendy Eisenberg, Manager

Blind; braille; talking books.

11340 House Ear Institute: Athalie Irvine Clarke Library
2100 W 3rd Street
5th Floor
Los Angeles, CA 90057-1922   213-483-4431
                                Fax: 213-483-8789
             http://secure.netsdhost.com/hei.org/education/
Liz Gnerre, Director Library Services
Howard House, MD

Otology, otolaryngology, psychoacoustics, audiology, hearing rehabilitation, neurosurgery, biomedical engineering, molecular and cellular biology.

11341 House Ear Institute: Care Center Parent Resource Library
Parent Resource Library
2100 W 3rd Street
5th Floor
Los Angeles, CA 90057-1922   213-483-4431
                                Fax: 213-483-8789
             http://www.hei.org/about/contact/contact4.htm
Liz Gnerre, Librarian
Howard House, MD

Deafness; social problems, special education, sign language, communication, child rearing.

11342 Northern California State Library: Braille and Talking Book Library
PO Box 942837
Sacramento, CA 94237   916-654-0261
                                Fax: 916-654-1119
                        e-mail: btbl@library.ca.gov
              http://www.library.ca.gov/html/pubser05.cfm
Aimee Sgourakis, Manager

Loans braille, cassette and talking books, magazines and playback equipment to northern Californians unable to read conventional print.

Libraries & Information Centers/California

11343 Oakland Public Library
125 14th Street
Oakland, CA 94612-4397
510-238-3134
Fax: 510-238-2125
e-mail: lcutler@oaklandlibrary.org
http://www.oaklandlibrary.org
Lynne Cutler, Disablity Services Advocate

Services and materials for people that are deaf, hard of hearing or have speech disorders.

11344 Salk Institute for Biological Studies Library
PO Box 85800
San Diego, CA 92186-5800
858-453-4100
Fax: 858-452-7472
e-mail: library@salk.edu; antrim@salk.edu
http://www.salk.edu
Kimberlee K Antrim, Librarian

Molecular biology, genetics, neuroscience, AIDS, Alzheimer's disease, biochemistry, cancer, neurobiology, plant biology, structural biology, virology.

11345 San Francisco Public Library for the Blind and Print Handicapped
100 Larkin Street
San Francisco, CA 94102-4733
415-557-4400
e-mail: lbphmgr@sfpl.lib.ca.us
Martin Maqid, Librarian
Luis Herrera, Manager

Foreign-language books on cassette, children's books on cassettes and more.

11346 San Francisco Public Library: Talking Books Program & Blind Services Center
100 Larkin Street
San Francisco, CA 94102-4733
415-557-4400
Luis Herrera, Manager

Blind; braille; talking books.

11347 San Jose State University Library
1 Washington Square
San Jose, CA 95192
408-924-1000
http://www.sjlibrary.org
Donna Pontau, Reference Librarian
Don Kassing, President

Information on physical disabilities, accessibility and learning disabilities.

11348 Southern California State Library: Braille and Talking Book Library
741 N Vermont Avenue
Los Angeles, CA 90029
323-660-3880
800-808-2555
e-mail: bils@brailib.org
http://www.library.ca.gov/html/pubser05.cfm
Susan Hildreth, State Librarian
Cameron Robertson, Deputy State Librarian

Loans braille, cassette and talking books, magazines and playback equipment to northern Californians unable to read conventional print.

11349 US Department of Veteran Affairs: Palo Alto Health Care and Medical Information Service
3801 Miranda Avenue
Palo Alto, CA 94304-1207
650-493-5000
800-455-0057
Fax: 650-852-3228
Susan Shyshka, Chief Medical Information Svcs
Mel Neise, CFO

Medicine, behavioral sciences.

11350 US Department of Veterans Affairs: H Earl Gordon Medical Library
W142-D
Los Angeles, CA 90073
310-235-7421
Fax: 310-268-4919
Nina Hull, Acting Chief

Clinical medicine, surgery, dentistry, nursing, epilepsy, geriatrics, nutrition, social work.

11351 US Department of Veterans Affairs: LomaLinda Medical Center Library Service
11201 Benton Street
Loma Linda, CA 92357-1000
909-825-7084
800-741-8387
Fax: 909-422-3106
http://www.va.gov
Kathleen M Puffer, Chief

Medicine.

11352 US Department of Veterans Affairs: LongBeach Medical Center Library Service
5901 E 7th Street
Long Beach, CA 90822-5201
562-826-8000
888-769-8387
Fax: 310-494-5447
e-mail: www.va.gov
Karen Vogel, Chief Library Service

Medicine and allied health sciences, patient education.

11353 US Department of Veterans Affairs: San Diego Medical Center Library Service
3350 La Jolla Village Drive
San Diego, CA 92161
858-552-8585
Fax: 858-552-7452
e-mail: drew.chris@forum.va.gov
http://www.va.gov
Chris Drew, Chief Library Service

Medicine, patient education, management, self development, EEO, ethics.

11354 US Department of Veterans Affairs: San Francisco Medical Center Library Service
4150 Clement Street
San Francisco, CA 94121-1545
415-221-4810
Fax: 415-750-6919
http://www.va.gov
William Koch, Chief Learning Resource Service
Susan Ferris, Manager

Health sciences.

11355 University of California: Mount Zion Medical Center
Harris M Fishbon Memorial Library
1600 Divisadero Street
San Francisco, CA 94115-3010
415-567-6600
Fax: 415-776-0689
e-mail: fishbon@itsa.ucsf.edu
http://mountzion.ucsfmedicalcenter.org
Gail Sorrough, Director

Medicine, geriatrics, cardiology, pediatrics, and psychiatry.

11356 University of California: San Francisco Center on Deafness Library
3333 California Street
Suite 10
San Francisco, CA 94118
415-476-4980
415-476-4980
Fax: 415-476-7113
e-mail: info@uccd.org
http://www.uccd.org
Nancy Moser, Executive Director

Mental health, psychosocial, and linguistic aspects of deafness.

Libraries & Information Centers/Colorado

11357 VA Central California Health Care System
Heartland Regional Network Library
2615 E Clinton Avenue
Fresno, CA 93703-2223
559-228-5341
Fax: 559-228-6924
e-mail: jmisakian@direcway.com
http://www.heartlandlibraries.org/
Jo Ellen Misakian, Executive Director
Cynthia Meyer

Medicine, nursing, allied health sciences.

11358 Vacaville Public Library: Town Square
1 Town Square Place
Vacaville, CA 95688
707-469-4590
http://www.solanolibrary.com
Provides senior programs and services to Californians.

Colorado

11359 AMC Cancer Research Center Medical Library
Medical Library
1600 Pierce Street
Lakewood, CO 80214-1897
303-239-3422
800-525-3777
Fax: 303-233-9562
http://www.cancer.org
Doris Borchert, Librarian
David Silberberg, President

Cancer - research, prevention, control.

11360 Colorado Department of Social Service
Library
1575 Sherman Street
Denver, CO 80203-1702
303-866-5700
Fax: 303-866-4047
http://www.cdhs.state.co.us
Karen L Beye, Executive Director

Social work, public and social welfare, psychology, sociology, child welfare, adoption, foster care, aged, child development, handicapped, crime and juvenile delinquency, group work and community organizations.

11361 Colorado School for the Deaf and Blind
Media Center
33 N Institute Street
Colorado Springs, CO 80903-3599
719-578-2102
Fax: 719-578-2258
e-mail: csdbsupt@csdb.org
http://www.csdb.org
Mr David Ek, Chairperson

Books of interest to deaf and blind children; professional books on deafness and blindness for staff and parents.

11362 Colorado Talking Book Library
201 East Colfax Avenue
Denver, CO 80203-1799
303-830-6600
Fax: 303-830-0793
e-mail: ctbl@info@cde.state.co.us
http://www.cde.state.co.us
Barbara Goral, Supervisor
Debbie Macleod, Manager

A free service to Coloradans of all ages who are unable to read standard print material due to visual, physical or learning disabilities whether permanent or temporary. CTBL provides recorded, Braille and large-print books and magazines as well as a small collection of descriptive videos.

11363 Museum of Western Colorado: Research Center & Special Library
462 Ute Avenue
PO Box 20000
Grand Junction, CO 81501
970-242-0971
Fax: 970-242-3960
e-mail: kfiegel@westcomuseum.org
http://www.westcomuseum.org
Mike Perry, Executive Director

From fossils to man-made artifacts and photographs, we capture our region's rich prehistoric past and decades of post-settlement history. The Museum of Western Colorado is headquartered in Grand Junction and is accredited by the American Association of Museums. We have several major facilities: The Museum of the West, Cross Orchards Historic Farm, Dinosaur Journey, History Museum/ Smith Educational Tower and the Whitman Education Center. The Loyd Files Research Library and the administrative offices are located in the Museum of the West. Riggs Hill, Dinosaur Hill and the Rabbit Valley Research Natural Area are the Museum's outdoor sites. In addition, the Museum of Western Colorado offers summer Dinosaur Excavations for youngsters and their families in the dinosaur-rich Morrison Formation near Fruita, Colorado. We are also home of the Western Investigations Team, solving some of the West's most interesting mysteries and questions.

1965

11364 Penrose Hospital: Webb Memorial Library
Margery Reed Professional Building
2222 N Nevada Avenue
Colorado Springs, CO 80907-6736
719-776-5288
Fax: 719-776-5028
e-mail: webblibrary@centura.org
http://www.penrosestfrancis.orgwww.penrosestfra
Rick O'Connell, President/CEO

Consumer health collection with materials for health related issues.

11365 US Department of Veterans Affairs: Denver Medical Center Library
1055 Clermont Street
Denver, CO 80220-3808
303-393-2821
888-336-8262
Fax: 303-393-4647
e-mail: coden@forum.va.gov
http://www.denver.va.gov
Elizabeth Alme, Manager

Medicine and allied clinical sciences.

11366 US Department of Veterans Affairs: Grand Junction Medical Center Library Service
2121 North Avenue
Grand Junction, CO 81501-6428
970-242-0731
866-206-6415
Fax: 970-244-1303
e-mail: lbragdon@colosys.net
http://www.grandjunction.va.gov
Michael W Murphey, Medical Center Director

Medicine, surgery.

11367 US Department of Veterans Affairs: Southern Colorado Healthcare System
Va Medical Center 567/142d
Fort Lyon, CO 81038
303-761-0117
Fax: 303-781-9378
http://www.va.gov
Helen S Scalzi, Library Coordinator

Psychiatry, nursing, geriatrics, psychology.

11368 University of Colorado: Science Libaray
Campus
Box 184
Boulder, CO 80309
303-492-5136
Fax: 303-492-1881
e-mail: david.fagerstrom@spot.colorado.edu
David M Fagerstrom, Contact

General science; botany; chemistry; biochemistry; biology - molecular, cellular, developmental, environmental, organismic, population; psychology; pharmacy; speech pathology; audiology; artificial intelligence; exercise physiology; nutrition; zoology.

11369 Weld Library District: Lincoln Park Branch Library
919 7th Street
Greeley, CO 80631-3967   970-506-8460
Fax: 970-506-8461
http://www.mylibrary.us/

Charlene Parker, Library Branch Manager
Janine Reid, Executive Director

Located in historic downtown Greeley, the Lincoln Park Branch Library serves as a neighborhood library with an emphasis on popular materials. The Lincoln Park Branch features the largest collection of large print books in the District plus the largest collection of books and media in Spanish. The 14,000 square foot facility maintains an up-to-date selection of popular, high-demand fiction known as Express Books, that are available for immediate checkout. In addition, the Branch also has strong collections of books and media for children and teens. The Lincoln Park Branch offers a wide variety of quality programs for children, adults, and teens that encourage reading, literacy, education, and cultural diversity.

Connecticut

11370 Connecticut Braille Association
107 Vanderbilt Avenue
West Hartford, CT 06110-1514   203-227-5243

Anne Murphy, Executive Secretary
Yolanda Rossi, Manager

Offers textbooks, cassettes, large print books, braille books and more.

11371 Connecticut Society to Prevent Blindness
24 Wall Street
Madison, CT 06443-3142   203-245-4700

David Rowland, Executive Director
Joan Davis Clarke, Manager

Offers braille and large print books, large-print photocopiers, cassettes, talking books, home services and more for the visually impaired.

11372 Connecticut State Library for the Blind and Physically Handicapped
198 West Street
Rocky Hill, CT 06067-3598   860-721-2020
800-842-4516
Fax: 860-721-2056
e-mail: lbph@cslib.org
http://www.cslib.org/lbph.htm

Carol Taylor, Director/Librarian
Gordon Reddick, Deputy Director/Librarian
Kendall Wiggin, State Librarian

This service lends books and magazines in braille or recorded formats along with the necessary playback equipment, FREE, for any Connecticut adult or child who is unable to read regular print due to a visual or physical disability. All materials are mailed to and from library patrons by postage-free mail.

11373 Hartford Hospital Health Science Libraries
80 Seymour Street
Hartford, CT 06102-8000   860-545-2861
Fax: 860-545-2572
e-mail: kaplan@harthosp.org
http://www.harthosp.org

Janice J Kaplan, Director
Denise Taylor, Manager

Clinical medicine, nursing, education, administration, gerontology, allied health specialties.

11374 Hartford Hospital: Gerontology Resource Center
Hartford Hospital, Jefferson House
1 John H Stewart Drive
Newington, CT 06111-3126   860-667-4453
Fax: 860-667-4459
http://www.harthosp.org

Arlene Freed, Gerontologist Librarian
Alan Laites, Administrator

Geriatrics, gerontology.

11375 US Department of Veterans Affairs, Health & Science Library
555 Willard Avenue
Newington, CT 06111-2631   860-667-6702
Fax: 860-667-6767
http://www.vba.va.gov/ro/hartford/index.htm

Lynn A Lloyd, Contact

Medicine, geriatrics.

11376 US Department of Veterans Affairs: Healthcare System in West Haven
950 Campbell Avenue
West Haven, CT 06516-2770   203-932-5711
Fax: 203-937-3868
http://www.visn1.med.va.gov

Roger L Johnson, Director
Jeanette Diaz, Associate Director

Patient-centered integrated health care organization for American's veterans.

11377 University of Connecticut Health Center: Center on Aging
263 Farmington Avenue
Farmington, CT 06030-5215   860-679-3956
Fax: 860-679-1867
e-mail: gnadeau@uchc.edu
http://http://www.uconn-aging.uchc.edu/

George A Kuchel MD, Director
Cherell A Curtis, Admininstrative Manager

Committed to providing high quality comprehensive care for older adults. Consultative, specialty services are available along with educational activities.

11378 University of Connecticut in Storrs: Homer Babbidge Library
369 Fairfield Road
Storrs, CT 06269-9016   860-486-2518
Fax: 860-486-0584
http://www.lib.uconn.edu

Paul Kobulnicky, Director

Resource section for the aging on health information, nutrition and drug information.

Delaware

11379 Delaware Division of Libraries for the Blind and Physically Handicapped
43 S Dupont Highway
Dover, DE 19901-7430   302-736-4748
Fax: 302-736-6787
e-mail: debph@lib.de.us
http://www.state.lib.de.us

Lee Steele, Librarian

Provides books in Braille and audio books on record and cassette for the blind and physically handicapped residents of Delaware.

11380 US Department of Veterans Affairs: Health Administration Medical Center
1601 Kirkwood Highway
Wilmington, DE 19805-4917   302-994-2511
Fax: 302-633-5516
http://www.hud.gov/offices/

Donald A Passidomo, Chief Librarian

Libraries & Information Centers/District of Columbia

General medicine, surgery, dentistry, nursing, allied health sciences.

District of Columbia

11381 American Association of Homes and Services for the Aging: Research and Information Center
2519 Connecticut Ave, NW
Washington, DC 20008-1520
202-783-2242
Fax: 202-783-2255
e-mail: headmod@spaceworks.com
http://www2.aahsa.org/contact/default.asp
Daniel Smith, Vice President

Geriatrics and gerontology, government regulation, health and health care, housing, nonprofit management, Medicare.

11382 American Association of Retired Persons: Research Information Center
601 E Street NW
B-3
Washington, DC 20049
202-434-2277
http://www.aarp.org
William D Novelli, CEO

Social gerontology, retirement, pre-retirement planning, voluntarism, and association management.

11383 American Council of the Blind
1155 15th Street NW
Suite 1004
Washington, DC 20005-2706
202-467-5081
800-424-8666
Fax: 202-467-5085
http://http://www.acb.org/
Mitch Pomerantz, President
Melanie Brunson, Executive Director
Kim Charlson, First VP

Offers a forum for support and outreach, sharing of experiences and educational and cultural information to people who are blind and visually impaired.

11384 American Health Care Association: Information Resource Center
1201 L Street NW
Washington, DC 20005-4046
202-842-4444
Fax: 202-842-3860
Dave Kyllo, Vice President

Geriatrics and gerontology, health and health care, Medicaid, Medicare, nursing, nursing homes, assisted living.

11385 Association for Gerontology in Higher Education
1220 L St. NW
Suite 901
Washington, DC 20005-4018
202-289-9806
Fax: 202-289-9824
e-mail: dstepp@capaccess.org
http://www.aghe.org
Cathy J Tompkins, PhD Executive Director
Derek Stepp, Manager

Aging - education, training programs, courses.

11386 District of Columbia Public Library
901 G Street NW
Washington, DC 20001-4531
202-727-0321
Fax: 202-727-2399
e-mail: commentssuggestions.dcpl@dc.gov
http://www.dclibrary.org
Angelisa Hawes, Senior Services Outreach Manager
Phillip Long-Cross, Manager

Senior Services provides programs and services to adults over 50. The Senior Bookmobile provides a book collection and reference services on sites in D.C. Senior Computer Classes are also offered for adults over 50.

11387 District of Columbia Public Library: Blind and Physically Handicapped
901 G Street NW
Room 215
Washington, DC 20001-4531
202-727-2142
Fax: 202-727-1129
e-mail: lbph.dcpl@dc.gov
http://www.dclibrary.org
TDD 202-727-2145
TTY 202-727-2255
Grace J Lyons, Contact
Phillip Long-Cross, Manager

Senior Mobile Service Bookmobile serves 18 senior residential complexes with programs, large and regular print book collection. Washington Lifelong Learning Center serves as educational clearinghouse for low or no cost programs for seniors

11388 District of Columbia Public Library: Librarian for the Deaf Community
901 G Street NW
Room 410
Washington, DC 20001-4531
202-727-2142
Fax: 202-727-1129
e-mail: LibrDeafDC@aol.com
http://www.dclibrary.org
Janice Rosen, Librarian Service to the Deaf
Phillip Long-Cross, Manager

Offers reference services through TDD, portable TDD for public use at pay phone, signers for library programs, sign language classes, information about deafness, print and non-print materials for persons who are deaf.

11389 Employee Benefit Research Institute
Library
1100 13th St, NW
Suite 878
Washington, DC 20005
202-659-0670
Fax: 202-775-6312
e-mail: info@ebri.org
http://www.ebri.org
Jeanette B Hull, Head Librarian
Dallas Salisbury, President

Pension plans, health care benefits, employee benefits, retirement income.

11390 Gallaudet University Library Deaf Collection
800 Florida Avenue NE
Washington, DC 20002-3600
202-651-5220
Fax: 202-651-5213
e-mail: library@gallua.gallaudet.edu
http://www.gallaudet.edu
John M Day, University Librarian
Dr. Robert R Davila, President

Deaf culture and history, deaf community, sign language and audiology.

11391 Howard University Social Work Library
500 Howard Place NW
Washington, DC 20059
202-806-7234
Fax: 202-806-4622
e-mail: mcmillan@cldc.Howard.edu
http://www.howard.edu/library
Gary McMillan, Librarian
Cudore Snell, Manager

Social work theory and practice; social policy, planning, administration; social welfare problems of black community; urban-oriented problems; human development; women's issues; gerontology.

11392 Ivins, Phillips, Barker Library
1700 Pennsylvania Avenue NW
Washington, DC 20006-4704
202-393-7600
Fax: 202-393-7601
http://www.ipbtax.com/cm/custom
Eric Fox, Manager

Pensions, taxation.

Libraries & Information Centers/District of Columbia

11393 John F Germany Public Library: Special Collections
Tampa-Hillsborough County Public Library System
900 North Ashley Drive
Tampa, FL 33602-3788
813-273-3652
Fax: 813-273-5640
e-mail: sinnotta@co.st-lucie.fl.us
http://www.thpl.org/hcplc/liblocales/jfg/
Joe R Stines, Libraries Director
Jim Shelton, Head Spec. Coll. Dept.
James Johnson, Chairman

A major focal point of the John F. Germany Public Library is its genealogy collection - one of the largest in the southeastern United States. The wide array of print, microform and electronic resources benefit both new and long time family history researchers. With a geographic emphasis on Florida, the southeast region, original thirteen colonies and all other states bordering on the Mississippi River, the collection includes numerous magazines and journals as well as extensive Federal census and Soundex holdings. It also covers a wide range of topics including how-to guides, county and local histories and indexes of records such as marriage, death, cemetery, probate, military, pension and passenger arrival.

1917

11394 Judge David L Bazelon Center for Mental Health Law
1101 15th Street NW
Suite 1212
Washington, DC 20005
202-467-5730
Fax: 202-223-0409
e-mail: info@bazelon.org
http://www.bazelon.org
TDD 202-467-4232
Robert Bernstein, Executive Director
Jennifer Mathis, Deputy Legal Director
Chris Koyanagi, Policy Director

National litigation and support center for people with mental disabilities. Offers a variety of publications, handbooks, issue papers and manuals to help advocate for, implement, enforce and comply with federal laws and court orders on early intervention, discrimination based on a label of mental illness, fair housing, cultural competence of service systems, SSI for children, children's mental health care, rights of elders, and other legal issues.

11395 Laurent Clerc National Deaf Education Center
800 Florida Avenue NE
Washington, DC 20002
202-651-5031
Fax: 202-651-5101
http://clerccenter.gallaudet.edu
TTY 202-651-5636
Margaret Halau, PhD, Director Outreach & Research
Janne M Harrelson, Drctr National Mission Planning
Nicole Sutliffe, Manager Reporting and Projects

Provides information and assistance on hearing disability related problems. Operates a legal clinic for deaf and hard of hearing persons.

11396 National Academy of Social Insurance
1776 Massachusetts Avenue NW
Suite 615
Washington, DC 20036-1912
202-452-8097
Fax: 202-452-8111
e-mail: nasi@nasi.org
http://www.nasi.org

Nonprofit, nonpartisan organization made up of the nation's leading experts on social insurance. Its mission is to promote understanding and informed policymaking on social insurance and related programs through research, public education, training, and the open exchange of ideas.

11397 National Alliance of Senior Citizens Library
1744 Riggs Plaza NW
Washington, DC 20009-6113
Peter Luciano, CEO

Aging, terminal illness, economics, political theory, reference, legal services, taxation, national defense, housing, welfare services, Social Security, Medicare, crime, criminal justice reform, women's equity.

11398 National Association of the Deaf: Legal Defense Fund
800 Florida Avenue NE
PO Box 2304
Washington, DC 20002
202-651-5343
e-mail: NADlaw@nad.org
http://www.nad.org
Nancy J Bloch, CEO

Represents deaf and hearing-impaired persons with discrimination complaints in the areas of employment, education, housing, health, welfare, and social services.

11399 National Civil Rights Clearinghouse Library
US Commission on Civil Rights
624 9th Street NW
Room 600
Washington, DC 20425
202-376-7700
Fax: 202-376-7597
http://www.usccr.gov
Barbara J Fontana, Librarian
Kenneth L Marcus, Executive Director

Civil rights, economics, education, sex discrimination, law, equal employment, fair housing.

11400 National Council on Aging: Ollie A Randall Library
409 3rd Street SW
2nd Floor
Washington, DC 20024-3212
202-479-1200
Fax: 202-479-0735
Janette K Hoisington, Librarian
James P Firman, CEO

Aging, retirement, economics, employment, community organization, legislation, nursing homes, senior centers, health care.

11401 National Graduate University LibraryCapitol Hill Campus
1325 D Street SE
Washington, DC 20003-2304
202-544-1555
Fax: 202-547-8819
http://www.nationlgraduateuniv.com
Dr Jean K Boek, Lib.Communication Chairperson
Joesph Burrow, Registar
Dr. James Hammond, Academic Dean

On this campus are graduate studies and training in the fields Of managment science and supervision, human service and Gerontology, Democracy, Worl history and the american election process, Organizational and Community Participation and Leadership, and Computer and Language Skills.

11402 National Information Center on Deafness
Gallaudet University
800 Florida Ave, NE
Washington, DC 20002
202-651-5000
Fax: 202-651-5054
e-mail: nicd@gallux.gallaudet.edu
http://www.gallaudet.edu
Loraine DiPietro, Director
Susan Ripley, Manager

Deafness, hearing loss.

11403 National Library Service for the Blind and Physically Handicapped
US Library of Congress
1291 Taylor Street NW
Washington, DC 20542
202-707-5100
888-657-7323
Fax: 202-707-0712
e-mail: nls@loc.gov
http://www.loc.gov/nls
Frank Cylke, Executive Director

Libraries & Information Centers/Florida

To provide library service (books and magazines on cassette and in braille) to the blind and physically handicapped residents of the United States and its territories, and to American citizens living abroad. An applicant must provide a certificate, from a competent authority, of his inability to read or manipulate convential printed material. Program is free. See Libraries chapter for state listings.

11404 Pension Benefit Guaranty Corporation, Office of the General Counsel Library
1200 K Street NW
Suite 340
Washington, DC 20005-4026
202-326-4020
Fax: 202-326-4111
e-mail: librarystaff2@pbgc.gov/artabane.lynn@pbgc.gov
http://www.pbgc.gov

Lynn Artabane, Documents Librarian
Vince Snowbarger, Deputy Executive Director
Richard Macy, Chief Operating Officer

Pension law, pensions.

11405 US Department of Veterans Affairs, Medical Center Library Section
50 Irving Street NW
Washington, DC 20422
202-745-8000
888-553-0242
Fax: 202-745-8530
http://www.washingtondc.va.gov

Iris Renner, Administrative Librarian

General medicine, surgery.

11406 US Equal Employment Opportunity Commission
Library
1801 L Street NW
Room 6502
Washington, DC 20507
202-366-4070
Fax: 202-663-4629
http://www.eeoc.gov

Susan D Taylor, Library Director

Employment discrimination, minorities, women, aged, persons with disabilities, labor law, civil rights.

11407 US Social Security Administration: Washington Library
500 E Street SW
9th Floor
Washington, DC 20254
202-358-6276
Fax: 202-358-6193
e-mail: concepcion.mcneace@ssa.gov
http://www.ssa.gov

US and international Social Security programs, retirement, economics, disability insurance, income maintenance, pension benefits, health insurance, medical care.

11408 Volta Bureau Library
Alexander Graham Bell Association for the Deaf
3417 Volta Place, NW
Washington, DC 20007-2753
202-337-5220
Fax: 202-337-8314
e-mail: info@agbell.org
http://www.agbell.org
TTY 202-337-5220

Todd Houston, Executive Director

Contains one of the world's largest historical collections of publications, documents and information on deafness. In addition to the main collection, which includes books, periodicals and indexed clipping files dating from the turn of the century, the library also houses a significant archival collection dealing with the history of deafness since the 16th century.

Florida

11409 Broward County Talking Book Library
115 S Andrews Avenue
Fort Lauderdale, FL 33301-1830
954-831-4000
http://www.broward.org

Barbara Kelly, Librarian
Marianne Caldron, Executive Director

Reference materials on blindness and other handicaps, films, closed-circuit TV, discs, cassettes and a book discussion group is offered.

11410 Florida Department of Labor and Employment Security
Bureau of Braille & Talking Book Library Services
420 Platt Street
Daytona Beach, FL 32114-2804
386-239-6000
800-226-6075
Fax: 386-239-6069

Recreational reading material for people with print disabilities, blindness, physical disabilities, rehabilitation.

11411 Florida Division of Blind Services
Regional Library
420 Platt Street
Daytona Beach, FL 32114-2824
386-239-6000
Fax: 850-239-6069
TDD 800-226-6079

Mike Gunde, Librarian
Jane Karp, Administrator

Discs, cassettes, closed-circuit TV, large-print photocopier, films, children's books on cassettes and more.

11412 Florida Instructional Materials Center for the Visually Impaired
4210 West Bay Villa Avenue
Tampa, FL 33611-1206
813-837-7826
Fax: 813-837-7979
http://www.fimcvi.org

Suzanne Dalton, Supervisor

Operates a clearinghouse depository and production center for braille, large print and recorded texts. Provides assistance in assessment of materials and specialized apparatus, organizes volunteers for material production and more for the visually handicapped.

11413 Florida School for the Deaf and Blind
Library for the Deaf
207 San Marco Avenue
St Augustine, FL 32084-2799
904-827-2200
Fax: 386-865-4203
http://www.fsdb.k12.fl.us

Linda L Zimmerman, Head Librarian
E Dillingham, Administrator

Education of the deaf (pre-kindergarten through high school), sign language and the deaf, fiction and nonfiction (low level, high interest).

11414 Focus: Library Service to Older Adults: People With Disabilities
Ruth O'Donnel
3509 Trillium Court
Tallahassee, FL 32312-1716
850-942-4869
Fax: 850-668-6911

Ruth O'Donnell, Editor/Mailing Contact

2 pages Frequency: Monthly

11415 Hillsborough County Talking Book Library
Tampa-Hillsborough County Public Library
900 N Ashley Drive
Tampa, FL 33602-3704
813-273-3652
Fax: 813-272-5728
e-mail: tbluser@scfn.thpi.lib.fl.us
http://www.hcplc.org/hcplc/liblocales
TDD 813-273-3610

Kurt Jasielonis, Contact
Joe Stines, Executive Director

Libraries & Information Centers/Florida

Books on cassette tape free on loan to people with print disablities. A branch of the National Library Service for the Blind and Handicapped.

11416 Jacksonville Public Library
2809 Commonwealth Avenue
Jacksonville, FL 32254-2599
904-384-7424
http://jpl.coj.net

Gloria Zittrauer, Librarian
Anthony Jackson, Manager

Discs, cassettes, reference materials on blindness and other handicaps and children's books on cassettes.

11417 Jacksonville Subregional Talking Book Library
Jacksonville Public Libraries
1755 Edgewood Avenue W
Suite 1
Jacksonville, FL 32208-3224
904-384-7424
e-mail: jerryr@coj.net
TDD 904-768-7822

Jerry Reynolds, Librarian

11418 Lee County Subregional Library for the Blind and Physically Handicapped
13240 N Cleveland Avenue
5-6
North Fort Myers, FL 33903-4855
239-995-2665
Fax: 239-995-1681

Karin Delgado, Manager

Offers a braille writer, closed-circuit TV and magnifiers for the visually impaired.

11419 Miami-Dade Public Library: Genealogy Collection
101 West Flagler Street
Miami, FL 33130-1504
305-375-2665
Fax: 305-375-3048
e-mail: florida@mdpls.org
http://www.mdpls.org

Sam Boldrick, Librarian IV

A complete collection of the U.S. Census for all states and for all available years is housed in this extensive reference department. Other important microfilm holdings include the U.S. City Directories covering major cities from 1860 through 1935, and immigration lists. The Family Search Database worldwide is also available. The book collection, with publications on nearly every state in the Union, emphasizes the Eastern Atlantic States.
1913

11420 Orange County Library System Audio-Visual Department
101 E Central Boulevard
Orlando, FL 32801-2429
407-835-7323
TDD 407-425-5668

Sally Fry, Contact
Maryann Hodel, Manager

11421 Orange County Library System: Genealogy Department
101 East Central Boulevard
Orlando, FL 32801-2429
407-835-7323
Fax: 407-425-6779
e-mail: comments@ocls.info
http://www.ocls.lib.fl.us

Mary Anne Hodel, Library Director/CEO
Gregg Gronlund, Genealogy Director

The core of the Genealogy Collection, located on the fourth floor of the Orlando Public Library, was a 1923 gift of Captain Charles Albertson, an avid genealogist. In 1929, the Library became the official repository of the Florida State Society of the Daughters of the American Revolution. The collection now contains more than 25,000 books and bound periodicals, 10,000 microfiche and over 15,000 reels of microfilm.
1923

11422 Sylvester Comprehensive Cancer Center, Cancer Information Service
1550 NW 10th Avenue
Suite 200a
Miami, FL 33136-1013
305-243-4821
Fax: 305-243-6678
http://www.cancer.gov

Jo Beth Speyer, Director
Julie Kornfeld, Executive Director

Information on treatment prevention screening and clinical trials.

11423 Talking Book Library, Miami and Dade Public Library System
2455 NW 183rd Street
Miami Gardens, FL 33056-3641
305-751-8687
800-451-9544
Fax: 305-757-8401
e-mail: talkingbooks@mdpls.org
http://www.mdpls.org

Barbara Moyer, Librarian

Library services for people with visual or physical disabilities.

11424 Talking Books Library for the Blind and Physically Handicapped
Palm Beach County Library Annex
7950 Central Industrial Drive
Suite 104
Riviera Beach, FL 33404-3439
561-996-9644
Fax: 561-845-4640

Pat Mistretta, Librarian

Library services for people with disabilities.

11425 US Department of Veterans Affairs Medical Library
1201 NW 16th Street
Miami, FL 33125-1624
305-575-3150
Fax: 305-324-3118
e-mail: harker.susan@forum.va.gov
http://www.va.gov

Susan Harker, Chief Librarian
Stephen Lucas, CEO

Medicine, nursing, psychology, allied health sciences.

11426 US Department of Veterans Affairs and Center Learning Resources Service Library
801 S Marion Street
Lake City, FL 32025
386-755-3016
Fax: 386-758-3218
e-mail: byrd.j@forum.va.gov
http://www.va.gov

Susan Lescenski, Chief LRS

Medicine, surgery, nursing, and allied health sciences; hospital administration; patient education; ambulatory care.

11427 US Department of Veterans Affairs, Hospital Library
1601 SW Archer Road
Gainesville, FL 32608-1135
352-376-1611
Fax: 352-374-6148
http://www.va.gov

Marylyn E Gresser, Chief Library Service
Frederick L Malphurs, CEO

Health education, neurology, surgery, internal medicine, nursing, pathology, pharmacology, ophthalmology, psychiatry, radiology.

11428 US Department of Veterans Affairs: Medical Library
PO Box 5005
Bay Pines, FL 33744-5005
727-398-9366
Fax: 727-398-9366
http://www.va.gov

Diana F Akins, Chief Library Service

Medicine, surgery, psychiatry, nursing, radiology, consumer health.

Libraries & Information Centers/Georgia

11429 US Department of Veterans Affairs: Medical Library
James a Haley Veterans Hospit
Tampa, FL 33612
813-972-7531
Fax: 813-978-5917
http://www.va.gov

Nancy Bernal, Chief Librarian

Internal medicine, psychiatry, nursing, surgery, geriatrics, allied health.

11430 University of Florida: Center for Governmental Responsibility
PO Box 117621
Gainesville, FL 32611-7621
352-273-0835
Fax: 352-392-1457
e-mail: jlmills@nervm.nerdc.ufl.edu
http://www.law.ufl.edu

Jon Mills, Director
JoAnn Klein, Development Director
Timothy McLendon, Staff Attorney

Florida's oldest legal and public policy research institute. Provides students with the opportunity to conduct research with staff attorneys on issues of state, national, and international importance.

11431 West Florida Regional Library
200 W Gregory Street
Pensacola, FL 32502-4822
850-436-5060
Fax: 850-436-5039
http://www.cityofpensacola.com

Martha Lazor, Librarian
Eugene Fischer, Manager

Offers children's print/braille books.

Georgia

11432 Augusta-Richmond County Public Library
425 James Brown Boulevard
Augusta, GA 30901-2241
706-821-2625
Fax: 706-724-5403
e-mail: gswint@csra,net

Gary Swint, Librarian
Audrey Bell, Manager

Discs, cassettes, braille writer, films, large print books, summer reading program, magnifiers and reference materials on blindness and other handicaps.

11433 Bainbridge Subregional Library for theBlind
SW Georgia Regional Library
301 S Monroe Street
Bainbridge, GA 39819-4029
229-248-2680
Fax: 229-248-2670
e-mail: lb[h@swgrl.org
http://www.swgrl.org

Susan Whittle, Subregional Librarian/Director

Discs, cassettes, summer reading programs, closed-circuit TV, magnifiers and more.

11434 CEL Regional Library
2002 Bull Street
Savannah, GA 31401-8564
912-232-4316
Fax: 912-652-3638
e-mail: lstokes@cel.co.chatman.ga.us

Linda Stokes, Librarian
Kenneth H Cail Jr, Owner

Summer reading programs, braille writer, magnifiers, closed-circuit TV, large-print photocopier, cassette books and magazines, children's books on cassette, home visits and other reference materials on blindness and other handicaps.

11435 Cave Spring Library
17 Cedartown Street
Cave Spring, GA 30124-2702
706-777-3346
Fax: 706-777-0947
http://www.cavespringlibrary.org

Katie Faught, Branch Manager
Steve Head, Manager

Summer reading programs, braille writer, magnifiers, closed-circuit TV, large-print photocopier, cassette books and magazines, children's books on cassette, home visits and other reference materials on blindness and other handicaps.

11436 Cedartown Library
245 East Avenue
Cedartown, GA 30125-3001
770-748-5644
Fax: 770-748-4399
http://www.cedartownlibrary.org

Sharon Cleveland, Branch Manager

Summer reading programs, braille writer, magnifiers, closed-circuit TV, large-print photocopier, cassette books and magazines, children's books on cassette, home visits and other reference materials on blindness and other handicaps.

11437 Fulton Public Library Learning Center
1 Margaret Mitchell Square NW
Atlanta, GA 30303-1022
404-730-1700
Fax: 404-730-1959
e-mail: ecnujiok@af.public.lib.ga.us
http://www.af.public.lib.ga.us

John Szabo, Executive Director

Literacy program, visually impaired assistance, hearing impaired assistance, test preparation materials.

11438 Georgia Regional Library
1150 Murphy Avenue SW
Atlanta, GA 30310-3843
404-756-4619
Fax: 404-756-4618

Lindaey Koldenhoven, Librarian
Stella Cone, Executive Director

Discs, cassettes, braille, films, closed-circuit TV, braille writer, large-print photocopier, cassette books and magazines.

11439 Hall County Library System
127 N Main Street
Gainesville, GA 30501
770-532-3311
Fax: 770-532-4305

Adrian Mixson, Director

Summer reading programs, braille writer, magnifiers, closed-circuit TV, large-print photocopier, cassette books and magazines, children's books on cassette, home visits and other reference materials on blindness and other handicaps.

11440 La Fayette Subregional Library for the Blind and Physically Disabled
301 S Duke Street
La Fayette, GA 30728-2936
706-638-2342
Fax: 706-638-4028

Charles Stubblefield, Librarian
David Friend, Principal

Summer reading programs, braille writer, magnifiers, closed-circuit TV, large-print photocopier, cassette books and magazines, children's books on cassette, home visits and other reference materials on blindness and other handicaps.

11441 Macon Library for the Blind and Physically Handicapped
Washington Memorial Library
1180 Washington Avenue
Macon, GA 31201-1762
478-744-0877
Fax: 478-742-3161

Rebecca Sherrill, Librarian
Judy Harrington, Manager

Summer reading programs, braille writer, magnifiers, closed-circuit TV, large-print photocopier, cassette books and magazines, children's books on cassette, home visits and other reference materials on blindness and other handicaps.

11442 Oconee Regional Library
801 Bellevue Avenue
Dublin, GA 31021
478-272-5710
Fax: 478-275-5381
http://www.laurens.public.lib.ga.us
Susan Williams, Librarian

Summer reading programs, braille writer, magnifiers, closed-circuit TV, large-print photocopier, cassette books and magazines, children's books on cassette, home visits and other reference materials on blindness and other handicaps.

11443 Rockmart Library
134 W Elm Street
Rockmart, GA 30153-2938
770-684-3022
Fax: 770-684-7876
http://www.rockmartlibrary.org
Ann Wheeler, Branch Manager

Summer reading programs, braille writer, magnifiers, closed-circuit TV, large-print photocopier, cassette books and magazines, children's books on cassette, home visits and other reference materials on blindness and other handicaps.

11444 Rome Subregional Library Service for People with Disabilities
205 Riverside Parkway
2nd Floor
Rome, GA 30161-2922
706-236-4618
800-201-5757
Fax: 706-236-4631
e-mail: wallacdo@mail.floyd.public.lib.ga
http://www.rome-lpd.org
Deana Wallace, Coordinator
Susan Sexton Cooley, Executive Director

Patrons may borrow all types of popular interest books. Readers may also receive over 40 popular magazines and local newspapers recorded on cassette. Special equipment needed to play cassettes is loaned indefinitely to readers as long as they continue to be active readers. Equipment is repaired at no charge to the patron.

11445 US Department of Veterans Affairs Medical Center Library
1 Freedom Way
Augusta, GA 30904-6285
706-823-2238
Fax: 706-823-3920
http://www.va.gov
Elizabeth Northington, Chief Library Section
Earl Payne, Manager

Medicine, nursing, psychiatry, allied health sciences.

11446 US Department of Veterans Affairs: CarlVinson Medical Center Library
1826 Veterans Boulevard
Dublin, GA 31021-3620
478-272-1210
800-595-5229
Fax: 478-277-2717
http://www.dublin.va.gov
Steve Toepper, Chief Library Service
Benjamin Harrell, Manager

Medicine, nursing and allied health sciences.

11447 US Department of Veterans Affairs: Medical Center Medical Library
1670 Clairmont Road
Decatur, GA 30033-4004
404-321-6111
Fax: 404-728-7781
http://www1.va.gov/atlanta/
Rita L Clifton, Manager Medical Library
Thomas Cappello, CEO

Medicine, health and social sciences.

Idaho

11448 Eli M. Oboler Library: Health Services
Idaho State University
850 S 9th Avenue
Pocatello, ID 83209-8089
208-282-2958
Fax: 208-282-5847
e-mail: ihsl@isu.edu
http://www.isu.edu/library/home.htm
Marcia Francis, Director
Ruiling Guo, Health Services Librarian

11449 US Department of Veterans Affairs: Medical Center Library
500 W Fort Street
Boise, ID 83702-4501
208-334-1707
Fax: 208-422-1390
e-mail: gordon.carlson@med.va.gov
http://www.va.gov
Gordon Carlson, Chief Librarian

Clinical medicine.

Illinois

11450 Adler School of Professional Psychology
Sol and Elaine Mosak Library
65 E Wacker Place
Suite 2100
Chicago, IL 60601-7298
312-201-5900
Fax: 312-201-8756
http://www.adler.edu
Karen Drescher, Director
Raymond Crossman, President

Psychology, psychotherapy, substance abuse, gerontology, marriage and family, gender and culture, psychiatry, education.

11451 Alzheimer's Association: Green-Field Library
252 N Michigan Avenue
Floor 17
Chicago, IL 60601-7633
312-335-9602
800-272-3900
Fax: 866-699-1238
e-mail: greenfield@alz.org
http://www.alz.org
Patricia Penkowski, Manager

Alzheimer's disease, gerontology, aging.

11452 BroMenn Healthcare
AE Livingston Health Sciences Library
Virginia and Franklin Avenue
Normal, IL 61761
309-454-1400
Fax: 309-829-0707
e-mail: brom@darkstar.rsa.lib.il.us
http://www.bromenn.org
Toni Tucker, Director
Roger S Hunt, CEO

Health sciences, nursing.

11453 Catholic Guild for the Blind
180 N Michigan Avenue
Suite 1700
Chicago, IL 60601-7463
312-236-8569
Fax: 312-236-8128
David Tabak, Executive Director

Offers books in braille and large print, cassettes and a lending library.

11454 Chicago Library Service for the Blind
1055 W Roosevelt Road
Chicago, IL 60608-1559
312-746-9210
Carol Pellish, Librarian

Libraries & Information Centers/Illinois

Summer reading programs, braille writer, magnifiers, closed-circuit TV, large-print photocopier, cassette books and magazines, children's books on cassette, home visits and other reference materials on blindness and other handicaps.

11455 Du Page Library
System Center
127 S 1st Street
Geneva, IL 60134-2771
630-232-8457
Fax: 603-232-0699
e-mail: dls@dupagels.lib.il.us
http://www.dupagels.lib.il.us
Pamela Feather, Executive Director
Shirley May Byrnes, Executive Director

Library science.

11456 Hopedale Medical Complex: Medical Library
107 Tremont Avenue
Hopedale, IL 61747
309-449-3321
Fax: 309-449-5441
http://www.hopedalmedicalcomplex.com
Karen J Nordstrom, DDS

Geriatrics, substance abuse, rehabilitation.

11457 Illinois Institute of Technology: Chicago Kent Law School Information Center
565 W Adams Street
Chicago, IL 60661-3652
312-906-5600
Fax: 312-906-5685
http://www.kentlaw.edu
Prof. Mickie Voges Piatt, Director
Keith Ann Stiverson, Executive Director

Federal and Illinois law, law and aging, international relations law, financial services law, business and management, environmental law.

11458 Illinois School for the Deaf Media Center
125 S Webster Avenue
Jacksonville, IL 62650-1877
217-479-4200
Fax: 217-479-4209
e-mail: isdf@darkstar.rsa.lib.il.us
http://www.morgan.k12.il.us
David Adams, Media Center Director
Marybeth Lauderdale, Executive Director

Deafness and deaf education, curriculum supporting AV programs, high interest/low vocabulary materials, audiology, children's and adult books.

11459 Illinois School for the Visually Impaired Library
658 E State Street
Jacksonville, IL 62650-2183
217-479-4400
Fax: 217-479-4508
Bev Sanderson, Contact
Margie Olson, Administrator

Blindness, education, child psychology, exceptional children, social work.

11460 Illinois School of Professional Psychology Meadows Campus Library
Library
1701 Golf Road
Suite 101
Rolling Meadows, IL 60008-4227
847-290-7400
Janan Reyna, Director Library Service

Psychology, psychiatry, family therapy, substance abuse, aging.

11461 McDermott, Will & Emery Library
227 W Monroe Street
46th Floor
Chicago, IL 60606-5096
312-984-3289
Fax: 312-984-2094
http://www.mwe.com
Louis J Covotsos, Director Legal Information
Harvey W Freishtat, CEO

Federal, state, foreign taxation; American and English probate law; litigation; pension; real estate.

11462 Mid-Illinois Talking Book Center
600 High Point Lane
Suite 2
East Peoria, IL 61611-9397
309-353-5444
800-426-0709
Fax: 309-353-8281
e-mail: lbell@alliancelibrarysystem.com
http://www.mitbc.org
Lori Bell, Librarian

Summer reading programs, cassette books and magazines, children's books on cassette, reference materials on blindness and other handicaps.

11463 Provena-Mercy Center Medical Library
1325 N Highland Avenue
Aurora, IL 60506-1449
630-801-2582
Fax: 630-801-2687
Janet Leach, Library Manager

Medicine, psychiatry, nursing, hospital administration.

11464 Shawnee Library System
607 S Greenbriar Road
Carterville, IL 62918-1600
618-985-3711
Fax: 618-985-4211
e-mail: kgorden@shawnet.shawls.lib.il
http://www.shawls.lib.il.us
Kristi Gorden, Librarian
Thomas Joe Harris, Executive Director

Summer reading programs, braille writer, magnifiers, closed-circuit TV, large-print photocopier, cassette books and magazines, children's books on cassette, home visits and other reference materials on blindness and other handicaps.

11465 Skokie Accessible Library Services
Skokie Public Library
5215 Oakton Street
Skokie, IL 60077-3680
847-673-7774
Fax: 847-673-7797
http://www.skokielibrary.info
Carolyn Anthony, Executive Director

Library services for people with disabilities, including electronic aids, materials in special formats, programs and special services, and access to the North Suburban Library System.

11466 Suburban Audio Visual Service
920 Barnsdale Road
La Grange Park, IL 60526-1609
630-352-7671
Leon Drolet Jr, Librarian

Summer reading programs, braille writer, magnifiers, closed-circuit TV, large-print photocopier, cassette books and magazines, children's books on cassette, home visits and other reference materials on blindness and other handicaps.

11467 US Department of Veterans Affairs: Chicago Health Care System-West Side Division
820 S Damen Avenue
Chicago, IL 60612-3728
312-886-6503
Fax: 312-633-2110
http://www.va.org
Susan L Thompson, Deputy Chief Library Service
Christopher Fox, Manager

Medicine and allied health sciences.

11468 US Department of Veterans Affairs: Hospital Library
W Main Street, 142-D
Marion, IL 62959
618-993-4114
Fax: 618-993-4176
http://www.va.org
Arlene M Dueker, Chief Library Service

Medicine, surgery.

Libraries & Information Centers/Indiana

11469 **US Department of Veterans Affairs: Library Services**
Edward Hines Jr Medical Cente
5000 South 5th Avenue
Hines, IL 60141　　　　　　　　　708-202-8387
　　　　　　　　　　　　　　　Fax: 708-202-7998
　　　　　　　　　　http://www.hines.med.va.gov
John Cline, Acting Chief

Hospital administration, medicine, nursing, allied health sciences.

11470 **US Department of Veterans Affairs: Medical Library**
3001 Green Bay Road
North Chicago, IL 60064-3048　　　847-688-1900
　　　　　　　　　　　　　　　　800-393-0865
　　　　　　　　　　　　　　Fax: 224-610-3806
　　　　　　http://www.visn12.med.va.gov/northchicago
William E Nielsen, Chief Library Service

Psychiatry, psychology, medicine, allied health sciences.

11471 **University of Chicago Social Services Administration Library**
1100 E 57th Street
Chicago, IL 60637-2677　　　　　　773-702-8740
　　　　　　　　　　　　　　Fax: 773-702-0874
　　　　　　　　　　　http://www.lib.uchicago.edu
Eileen Libby, Librarian

Social services, American and foreign social work, public welfare, mental health, social and urban policy, social problems, child welfare, health care, aged, psychotherapy.

11472 **Voices of Vision Talking Book Center**
Dupage Library System Building
127 S 1st Street
Geneva, IL 60134-2771　　　　　　630-232-8457
　　　　　　　　　　　　　　Fax: 630-232-0699
　　　　　　　　e-mail: kodean@dupagels.lib.il.us
　　　　　　　　　http://www.dupagels.lib.il.us
Karen Odean, Manager

Large Print, audio cassette, or computer diskette.

Indiana

11473 **Allen County Public Library**
900 Library Plaza
Fort Wayne, IN 46802　　　　　　　260-421-1252
　　　　　　　　　　　　　　Fax: 260-421-1386
　　　　　　　　　　　　e-mail: ask@acpl.info
　　　　　　　　　　　http://www.acpl.lib.in.us
Joyce Misner, Librarian
Mark Allen, Vice President

Summer reading programs, braille writer, magnifiers, closed-circuit TV, large-print photocopier, cassette books and magazines, children's books on cassette, home visits and other reference materials on blindness and other handicaps.

11474 **Allen County Public Library of New Haven**
648 Green Street
New Haven, IN 46774-1681　　　　260-421-1345
　　　　　　　　　　　　　　Fax: 260-493-0130
　　　　　　　　　　　　e-mail: ask@acpl.info
　　　　　　　　　http://www.acpl.lib.in.us/newhaven
Linda Jeffrey, Manager

Magazines, large print books, educational videos, books on tape, and books on CD.

11475 **Allen County Public Library of Woodburn**
4701 State Road 101 North
Woodburn, IN 46797　　　　　　　260-421-1370
　　　　　　　　　　　　　　Fax: 260-632-0101
　　　　　　　　　　　　e-mail: ask@acpl.info
　　　　　　　　　http://www.acpl.lib.in.us/woodburn
Genie Bishop, Manager

Books on tape, educational videos, software; CDRoms.

11476 **Allen County Public Library, Aboite Branch**
5630 Coventry Lane
Fort Wayne, IN 46804-7140　　　　260-421-1310
　　　　　　　　　　　　　　Fax: 260-432-2394
　　　　　　　　　　　　e-mail: ask@acpl.info
　　　　　　　　　　http://www.acpl.lib.in.us/aboite
Susan Hunt, Manager

Collection of books and other materials such as magazines, large print books and books on cassette and CD.

11477 **Allen County Public Library, Pontiac Branch**
2215 S Hanna Street
Fort Wayne, IN 46803-2431　　　　260-421-1350
　　　　　　　　　　　　　　Fax: 260-744-5372
　　　　　　　　　　　　e-mail: ask@acpl.info
　　　　　　　　　　http://www.acpl.lib.in.us/pontiac
Ann Hoehn, Manager

Large print books, books on tape and CD, educational videos, movies on DVD, music CDs, and CD-ROMs.

11478 **American Legion**
National Headquarters Library
700 N Pennsylvania Street
Indianapolis, IN 46204-1172　　　　317-630-1200
　　　　　　　　　　　　　　Fax: 317-630-1223
　　　　　　　　　　e-mail: jhovish@legion.org
　　　　　　　　　　　　http://www.legion.org
Joseph J Hovish, Librarian
Daniel S Wheeler, CEO

Veterans' affairs, children and youth, national defense, patriotism, American Legion.

11479 **American United Life Insurance Company**
Library
1 American Square
Po Box 368
Indianapolis, IN 46282　　　　　　317-285-1877
　　　　　　　　　　　　　　Fax: 317-263-1979
　　　　　　　　　　　　　http://www.aul.com
Dayton H Molendorp, CEO

Insurance on life and health; pensions.

11480 **Bartholomew County Public Library**
536 5th St
Columbus, IN 47201　　　　　　　812-379-1255
　　　　　　　　　　　　http://www.barth.lib.in.us
Sharon Thompson, Librarian
Beth Poor, Executive Director

Summer reading programs, braille writer, magnifiers, closed-circuit TV, large-print photocopier, cassette books and magazines, children's books on cassette, home visits and other reference materials on blindness and other handicaps.

11481 **Evansville-Vanderburgh County Public Library**
Allen County Public Library
PO Box 2270
Fort Wayne, IN 46801-2270　　　　219-424-7241
Joyce Misner, Contact

Offers books on disc and cassette.

11482 **Indiana School for the Deaf: Alumni Hall Library**
1200 E 42nd Street
Indianapolis, IN 46205-2004　　　　317-924-4374
　　　　　　　　　　　　　　Fax: 317-923-2853
　　　　　　　　　　e-mail: lkesterke@isd.k12.in.us
Laura Kesterke, Librarian
David Geeslin III, Superintendent/CEO

American sign language, deaf studies, Bi-Bi education.

Libraries & Information Centers/Iowa

11483 Michigan City Public Library: Indiana Rooom/Genealogy
100 East 4th Street
Michigan City, IN 46360-3302
219-873-3044
Fax: 219-873-3068
e-mail: reference@mclib.org
http://www.mclib.org

Don Glossinger, Director

Provides a center for information, education, culture, and recreation for all patrons throughout thier life span.

11484 Northwest Indiana Subregional Library for Blind and Physically Handicapped
1919 W Lincoln Highway
Merrillville, IN 46410-5332
219-769-3541
Fax: 219-756-9358
http://www.lakeco.lib.in.us/talkingbooks.htm

Renee Lewis, Contact
Larry Acheff, Manager

Summer reading programs, braille writer, magnifiers, closed-circuit TV, large-print photocopier, cassette books and magazines, children's books on cassette, home visits and other reference materials on blindness and other handicaps.

11485 Purdue University: Humanities, Social Science, Education Library
Purdue University
504 West State St
West Lafayette, IN 47907
765-494-4600
800-825-4264
Fax: 765-494-0156
e-mail: libhsse@omni.cc.purdue.edu
http://www.lib.purdue.edu/hssc/

J Mark Tucker, Librarian

English and American literature, US history, North American Indians, education.

11486 Special Services Division: Indiana State Library
140 N Senate Avenue
Indianapolis, IN 46204-2207
317-232-3684
800-622-
Fax: 317-232-3728

Lissa Shanahan, Librarian

Circulates a collection of forty thousand titles in braille, large print and on cassette and the special equipment needed to play the recorded materials to anyone in Indiana who cannot read regular print due to a visual or physical disability. This is a free library service. The Division maintains a small reference collection and provides reference and referral services on disabilities and services available to people with disabilities

11487 Talking Books Service: Evansville Vanderburgh County Public Library
200 SE Martin Luther King Jr Blvd
Evansville, IN 47713
812-428-8200
Fax: 812-428-8215
e-mail: tbs@evans.evcpl.lib.in.us
http://www.evpl.org/contatus/index.html

Barbara Shanks, Contact

11488 US Department of Veterans Affairs, Medical Center Library Service
2121 Lake Avenue
Fort Wayne, IN 46805-5100
219-460-1490
Fax: 219-460-1364
e-mail: diem.laveta@forum.va.gov

Laveta J Diem, Librarian

Medicine, nursing, patient education.

11489 US Department of Veterans Affairs: Indiana Health Care System
1700 E 38th Street
Marion, IN 46953-4568
765-677-3120
Fax: 765-677-3111
e-mail: fletcha@netusa1.net

Scott Pierce, Manager Education
Patrick H Lau, DO

Medicine, with special emphasis on psychiatry and psychology.

11490 US Deprtment of Veterans Affairs: Center Library
1481 W 10th Street
Indianapolis, IN 46202-2803
317-554-0000

Linda J Bennett, Chief Library Service

General medicine, surgery, nursing, psychiatry, allied health sciences.

Iowa

11491 Ames Public Library Ames and Iowa History Collection
515 Douglas Avenue
Ames, IA 50010-6291
515-239-5630
Fax: 515-232-4571
http://www.ames.lib.ia.us

Gina Millsap, Executive Director

11492 Calhoun County Historical Museum Library
858 Lake Street
Rockwell City, IA 50579-1221
712-297-8139

11493 Iowa Library For The Blind And Physically Handicapped
524 4th Street
Des Moines, IA 50309-2364
515-281-1333
Fax: 515-281-1263
e-mail: library@blind.state.ia.us

Karen Keninger, Librarian
Allen C Harris, Executive Director

Summer reading programs, braille writer, magnifiers, closed-circuit TV, cassette books and magazines, children's books on cassette, home visits and other reference materials on blindness and other handicaps.

11494 US Department of Veterans Affairs: Central Iowa Health Care System
1515 W Pleasant Street
Knoxville, IA 50138-3399
641-828-5127

Judy Gottshall, Manager

Psychiatry, psychology, medicine, nursing.

Kansas

11495 Bukovina Society of the Americas Library
PO Box 81
Ellis, KS 67637
785-625-9492
e-mail: info@bukovinasociety.org
http://www.bukovinasoiety.org

Martha McLelland, President

11496 Cherokee County Genealogical Historical Society
PO Box 33
100 S Tennessee
Columbus, KS 66725
620-429-2992
http://skyways.lib.ks.us

Marilyn Schmidt, Manager

Libraries & Information Centers/Kansas

11497 Kansas State Historical Society: Library & Archives Division
6425 SW 6th Avenue
Topeka, KS 66615-1099
785-272-8681
785-272-8682
e-mail: referenc@hspo.wpo.state.ks.us
http://www.kshs.org
Patricia A Michaelis, Division Director
Margaret Knecht, Librarian Section Head
Susan Forbes, Western Hist. Cat.
1975

11498 Kansas State Library Talking Book Service
ESU Memorial Union
1200 Commercial Street
Emporia, KS 66801-5057
620-343-7124
Fax: 620-343-7124
http://www.kslib.info/talking
Toni Harrell, Librarian

Summer reading programs, braille, cassette books and magazines, children's books on cassette, home visits and other reference materials on blindness and other handicaps.

11499 Leavenworth County Genealogical Society Library
PO Box 362
Leavenworth, KS 66048
913-682-8181
e-mail: greyink@idir.net
Nettie Graden, Book Community Chairman
1984

11500 Manhattan Public Library
629 Poyntz Avenue
Manhattan, KS 66502-6131
785-776-4741
800-432-2796
Fax: 785-776-1545
e-mail: marionr@manhattan.lib.ks.us
http://www.manhattan.lib.ks.us
Marion Rice, Librarian
Fred Atchison, Manager

Cassette books and magazines, children books on cassette, summer reading program braille writer, magnifiers, closed-circuit TV, large-print photocopier, Community Assistive Technology Center, home visits and other reference materials aon blindness and other disabilities.

11501 Northwest Kansas Library System Talking Books
PO Box 446
Norton, KS 67654
785-877-5148
Fax: 785-877-5697
e-mail: tbook@ruraltel.net
Clarice Howard, Librarian
Leslie Bell, Executive Director

Offers books on cassette and DVS videos to qualified individuals.

11502 Old Fort Genealogical Society Of Southeastern Kansas Inc
At 3rd And National
Po Box 786
Fort Scott, KS 66701
620-223-3300
Fax: 913-367-2717
e-mail: ofgs@pbxmail.com
http://skyways.lib.ks.us
Roxanna Tosterud, President
P J Capps, Manager
Cova Chambers, VP

A non profit volunteer organization to explore and research family ancestry.

11503 South Central Kansas Library System
321 A North Main St
South Hutchinson, KS 67505
620-663-5441
800-234-0529
Fax: 620-663-9797
e-mail: ksocha@hplsck.org
http://www.sckls.info
Karen Socha, Talking Books
Cheryl Canfield, Reference Librarian
Leroy Gattin, Director

Summer reading programs, braille writer, magnifiers, closed-circuit TV, large-print books, photocopier, cassette books and magazines, children's books on cassette, home visits and other reference materials on blindness and other handicaps.

11504 Talking Books Service
1515 SW 10th Avenue
Topeka, KS 66604-1304
785-231-0574
Fax: 785-231-0579
e-mail: tbooks@tscpl.lib.ks.us
Suzanne Bundy, Librarian

Summer reading programs, braille writer, magnifiers, closed-circuit TV, large-print photocopier, cassette books and magazines, children's books on cassette, home visits and other reference materials on blindness and other handicaps.

11505 US Department of Veterans Affairs: Dr Karl Menninger Medical Library
2200 SW Gage Boulevard
Topeka, KS 66622
785-350-3111
Fax: 785-350-3111

Psychiatry, internal medicine, pathology, neurology, surgery, rehabilitation medicine, psychology, social service.

11506 US Department of Veterans Affairs: Dwight D. Eisenhower Center Medical Library
4101 S 4th Street
Leavenworth, KS 66048-5014
913-682-2000
e-mail: gosselin.jan@forum.va.gov
http://www.va.gov
Jan Gosselin, Medical Librarian
Edgar Tucker, Manager

Medicine, allied health sciences, psychology.

11507 US Department of Veterans Affairs: Medical & Regional Office Center Library Service
5500 E Kellogg Drive
Wichita, KS 67218-1607
e-mail: kswic@forum.va.gov
http://www.va.gov
Alice H Schad, Chief Library Service

Medicine, nursing, allied health sciences, patient health education, veterans affairs.

11508 Wichita Public Library
223 S Main Street
Wichita, KS 67202-3795
316-261-8500
Fax: 316-262-4540
e-mail: admin@whichita.lib.ks.us
http://www.wichita.lib.ks.us
Roger Woods, President

Offers a variety of programs and services to older adults and their caregivers. Nine convenient locations throughout the Wichita community.

11509 Young Historical Library
PO Box 55
Little River, KS 67457
620-897-6236
Doris Cory, Librarian
Lillie Whiteman, Manager
1990

Libraries & Information Centers/Kentucky

Kentucky

11510 Kentucky Historical Society-Thomas DClark Research Library
100 W Broadway Street
Frankfort, KY 40601-1931
502-564-1792
Fax: 502-696-3846
e-mail: jim.kastner@ky.gov
http://http://history.ky.gov
Kent Whitworth, Executive Director
Shirley Ackerman, Technical Services Librarian

The Thomas D Clark Research Library of the Kentucky Historical Society houses over 90,000 published works, dealing primarily with history and genealogy, as well as over 12,000 reels of microfilm, and over 20,000 vertical files of collected and contributed research.

11511 Kentucky Talking Book Library
PO Box 537
Frankfort, KY 40602-0537
502-564-8300
Fax: 502-564-5773
e-mail: richard.feindel@kdld.net
http://kdla.ky.gov/collectionsktbl.htm
Barbara Penegor, Head Librarian

Children's and adult cassette books and magazines, Braille books, and descriptive videos and DVDs for the blind and physically handicapped.

11512 Louisville Talking Book Library
Louisville Free Public Library
301 York Street
Louisville, KY 40203-2257
502-574-1625
http://www.lfpl.org/tbl.tbl.asp
Linda Atzinger, Head Librarian

Braille transcription, computer workstation with magnifier, children's and adult cassette books and magazines, Braille books, and descriptive videos and DVDs for the blind and physically handicapped.

11513 Northern Kentucky Talking Book Library
502 Scott Street
Covington, KY 41011-1530
859-962-4095
Fax: 859-655-7960
http://www.kentonlibrary.org
Clif Mayhew, Head Librarian

Children's and adult cassette books and magazines and Braille books for the blind and physically handicapped.

11514 US Department of Veterans Affairs: Hospital Library
800 Zorn Avenue
Louisville, KY 40206-1433
502-894-6240
Fax: 502-894-6134
http://www.louisville.va.gov
James F Kastner, Chief Librarian

Clinical medicine, surgery, nursing, psychiatry, social work.

11515 US Department of Veterans Affairs: Medical Center Libraries
142d-Cdd
Lexington, KY 40511
859-281-4916
Fax: 859-281-4808
http://www.va.gov
Robert Bradley, Contact

Psychology, psychiatry, nursing, medicine, surgery, social sciences, patient health education.

Louisiana

11516 Mary Bird Perkins Cancer Center Community Library
4950 Essen Lane
Baton Rouge, LA 70809-3432
225-767-0847
Fax: 225-215-1215
http://www.marybird.org
Todd Stevens, CEO/President
Tom J Meek, Secretary
Randolph Waes, Treasurer

Cancer; coping.

11517 New Orleans Public Library: Louisiana Division
219 Loyola Avenue
New Orleans, LA 70112-2007
504-596-2610
Fax: 504-596-2609
e-mail: nopl@gnofn.org
http://www.nutrias.org/~nopl/welcome.htm
Stephen Kuehling, Louisiana Division Librarian
Greg Osborn, Louisiana Division Librarian
Irene Wainwright, Louisiana Division Archivist

The Louisiana Division is a reference division which collects all types of printed, manuscript, graphic, and oral resources relating to the study of Louisiana and its citizens and to the city of New Orleans and New Orleanians. Other areas of concentration are the Mississippi River, the Gulf of Mexico, and the South. Included within the Division's collections are books by or about Louisianians; city, regional, and state documents; manuscripts, maps, newspapers, periodicals, microfilms, photographs, slides, motion pictures, sound recordings, video tapes, postcards, and ephemera of every sort.
1946

11518 State Library of Louisiana
701 N 4th Street
Baton Rouge, LA 70802-5345
225-342-4923
Fax: 225-219-4804
e-mail: sbph@pelican.state.lib.la.us
http://www.state.lib.la.us
Sharilynn Aucoin, Special Services Coordinator
Rebecca Hamilton, Manager

Summer reading programs, braille writer, magnifiers, closed-circuit TV, large-print photocopier, cassette books and magazines, children's books on cassette, and other reference materials on blindness and other handicaps.

11519 Tulane University: Howard-Tilton Memorial Library-Louisiana Collection
Tulane Libraries, Jones Hall
Tulane University
New Orleans, LA 70118
504-865-5685
Fax: 504-865-5761
e-mail: meneray@tulane.edu
http://http://specialcollections.tulane.edu/
Wilbur E Meneray, Special Collections Librarian
Jessica Jones, Special Collections Librarian
Kenneth Owen, Special Collections Librarian

The Library houses nearly 2 million print volumes, more than 7,750 current serials, nearly a million government documents, more than three linear miles of manuscripts, hundreds of thousands of microforms, as well as collections of photographs and recordings. In addition, the Library is serving a new role as a gateway to digital resources. Located within the Howard-Tilton building are many important departments and collections with librarians andstaff who work to maintain the library's resources and to provide an array of useful library services. The general collections of the Library, its Latin American Library, the Maxwell Music Library, and a federal Government Documents depository reside in the main building. Special Collections includes the Hogan Jazz Archive, Louisiana collections, Manuscripts, Rare Books, University Archives, and the Southeastern Architectural Archive. The Special Collections were moved to the adjacent Jones Hall building in 1999.

11520 US Deparment of Veterans Affairs: Center Library
1601 Perdido Street
New Orleans, LA 70112-1262
504-589-5272
Fax: 504-589-5916
http://www.va.gov
Mark Petersen, Manager

Medicine, nursing, dentistry, surgery, allied health sciences.

11521 US Department of Veterans Affairs: Medical Center Medical Library
PO Box 69004
Alexandria, LA 71306-9004
318-473-0010
Fax: 318-473-9491
http://www.va.gov
Charles T Cooker, Library Manager

Medicine, employee development, patient education and recreation.

11522 US Department of Veterans Affairs: Overton Brooks Medical Center Library
510 E Stoner Avenue
Shreveport, LA 71101-4243
318-221-8411
800-863-7441
Fax: 318-424-6156
http://www.shreveport.va.gov
Dixie Jones, Manager

General medicine.

11523 University of Southwestern Louisiana: Jefferson Caffery Louisana Room-Southwestern Archives and Manuscripts Collection
302 East Saint Mary Boulevard
Lafayette, LA 70503-2038
337-482-5702
Fax: 337-482-5702
e-mail: BTurner@usc.usl.edu
http://www.usl.edu/Departments/Library
Dr. I Bruce Turner, Special Collections Director
Jean S Kiesel, Louisiana Room Librarian
Jane Vidrine, Archives Specialist

The Special Collections department is composed of the Louisiana Room, the Rare Book Collection, the University Archives and Acadiana Manuscripts Collection, the Cajun and Creole Music Collection, the University Records Management Program, and the Microforms Room. The Louisiana Room provides access to materials pertaining to Louisiana, including books, periodicals, state government documents, genealogical materials, rare books, newspapers, and other special collections. Most Louisiana newspapers are housed in the Louisiana Room. The University Archives and Acadiana Manuscripts Collection houses the archival records of the University starting in 1900. There are also over 300 collections of personal or family papers, business or organizational records, photograph collections, and much more related to the Acadiana region.

1962

Maine

11524 Bangor Public Library
145 Harlow Street
Bangor, ME 04401-4900
207-947-8336
Fax: 207-945-6694
http://www.bpl.lib.me.us
Judith Leighton, Librarian
Barbara McDade, Manager

Summer reading programs, braille writer, magnifiers, closed-circuit TV, large-print photocopier, cassette books and magazines, children's books on cassette, home visits and other reference materials on blindness and other handicaps.

11525 Governor Baxter School for the Deaf Library
PO Box 799
One Mackworth Island
Falmouth, ME 04105
207-781-6237
Fax: 207-781-6240
http://www.gbsd.org/pages/MEDHH_library/index
Leone Anderson, Manager

Deafness, sign language, deaf education, professional education.

11526 Jackson Laboratory: Joan Staats Library
600 Main Street
Bar Harbor, ME 04609-1523
207-288-6000
Fax: 207-288-6079
e-mail: library@jax.org
http://www.jax.org/library
Douglas T Macbeth, Librarian
Rick Woychik, Executive Director

Inbred strains of mice, genetics, cancer, growth, animal health and husbandry, immunology, aging, cell biology, molecular genetics.

11527 Lewiston Public Library
200 Lisbon St
Lewiston, ME 04240-7203
207-513-3004
Fax: 207-784-0135
http://lplonline.org
Richard Speer, Director

Summer reading programs, braille writer, magnifiers, closed-circuit TV, large-print photocopier, cassette books and magazines, children's books on cassette, home visits and other reference materials on blindness and other handicaps.

11528 Maine State Library
64 State House Station
230 State St
Augusta, ME 04333-0064
207-287-5600
Fax: 207-287-5624
e-mail: benitad@ursus3.ursus.maine.edu
http://maine.gov/msl/index.shtml
J Gary Nichols, Librarian

Summer reading programs, braille writer, magnifiers, closed-circuit TV, large-print photocopier, cassette books and magazines, children's books on cassette, home visits and other reference materials on blindness and other handicaps.

11529 Portland Public Library
5 Monument Square
Portland, ME 04101-4072
207-871-1700
Fax: 207-871-1703
Janice Littlefield, Librarian
Claire Hannan, Manager

Summer reading programs, braille writer, magnifiers, closed-circuit TV, large-print photocopier, cassette books and magazines, children's books on cassette, home visits and other reference materials on blindness and other handicaps.

11530 US Department of Veterans Affairs: Medical & Regional Office Center
Togus, ME 04330
207-623-5773
Fax: 207-623-5766
e-mail: Vatogus@class.org
http://www.va.gov
Judy Littlefield, Team Leader

Social sciences/psychiatry, medicine, alcoholism, nursing, dentistry, hospital administration.

11531 Voices for the Blind
PO Box 837
Bethel, ME 04217
207-824-2920
Connie Hindman, Director

Tape library and depository for people with visual and learning disabilities. Recording services available by request.

Libraries & Information Centers/Maryland

11532 Waterville Public Library
73 Elm Street
Waterville, ME 04901-6078
207-872-5433
Fax: 207-873-4779
http://www.waterville.lib.me.us
Meta Vigue, Librarian
Sarah Sugden, Executive Director

Summer reading programs, braille writer, magnifiers, closed-circuit TV, large-print photocopier, cassette books and magazines, children's books on cassette, home visits and other reference materials on blindness and other handicaps.

Maryland

11533 American College of Cardiology
2400 N Street NW
Washington, DC 20037
202-375-6000
Fax: 202-375-7000
http://www.acc.org
James T Dove MD, FACC, President

Cardiovascular disease and surgery.

11534 Friends of Libraries for Deaf Action
2930 Craiglawn Road
Silver Spring, MD 20904-1816
301-572-5168
e-mail: folda86@aol.com
http://www.folda.net/
Alice Hagemeyer, Founder/President

Library services for people that are deaf impaired.

11535 Maryland State Library for the Blind and Physically Handicapped
415 Park Avenue
Baltimore, MD 21201-3638
410-230-2424
800-964-9209
Fax: 410-333-2095
e-mail: recept@lbta.lib.md.us
http://www.lbph.lib.md.us
TDD 410-333-8679
Sharron McFarland, Librarian
Nancy Grasmick, Manager

Summer reading programs, braille writer, magnifiers, large-print photocopier, cassette books and magazines, children's books on cassette, and other reference materials on blindness and other handicaps.

11536 National Heart, Lung, and Blood Institute Information Center
Building 31 Room 5a 48
31 Center Drive MSC 2486
Bethesda, MD 20824
301-592-8573
800-575-WELL
Fax: 240-629-3246
e-mail: nhlbiic@dgsys.com
http://www.nhlbi.nih.gov/nhlbi/nhlbi
Elizabeth G Nagel, MD, Director
Margot Raphael, Information Center Manager

High blood pressure, cholesterol, sleep disorders, health education, cardiovascular risk reduction, asthma, heart attacks, obesity and exercise.

11537 Special Needs Library Montgomery County Department of Public Libraries
6400 Cemocracy Boulevard
Bethesda, MD 20817
301-897-2212
TDD 301-897-2217
Charlette Stinnett, Contact

11538 Spring Dell Center
6040 Radio Station Road
La Plata, MD 20646-3368
301-934-4561
Fax: 301-870-2439
http://www.springdellcenter.org
Reed Walker, Transportation Director
Donna Retzlaff, Executive Director

Since 1967, Spring Dell center has been, 'bridging the gap' to enhance the lives of developmentally disabled people. Spring Dell's goal is to empower people in every aspect of their lives through the implementation of two programs, employment/vocational services and residential services including transportation. Spring Dell offers transportation door-to-door for persons with developmental disabilities, including day care programs, supportive envvironment, residential and other transportation.

11539 US Army: Medical Command Center for Health Promotion & Preventive Medicine
Aberdeen Proving Ground
Building E1570
Aberdeen, MD 21001
410-671-4236
Fax: 410-671-3665
e-mail: KGOEL@AEHA1.Army.mil
Krishan S Goel, Librarian

Occupational medicine, safety and health; chemistry and toxicology; audiology; medical entomology; laser, microwave, and radiological safety and health; air and water pollution; sanitary engineering.

11540 US Department of Veterans Affairs Hospitl: Fort Howard Hospital Library
9600 N Point Road
Fort Howard, MD 21052-3050
410-477-1800
Fax: 410-477-7207
http://www.maryland.va.gov
Joanne M Bennett, Chief Librarian
Dennis H Smith, Executive Director

Medicine.

11541 US Department of Veterans Affairs: Baltimore Medical Center Library Service
10 N Greene Street
Baltimore, MD 21201-1524
410-605-7092
Fax: 410-605-7905
e-mail: stout.deborah@baltimore.va.gov
http://www.maryland.va.gov
Deborah A Stout, Chief Library Service
Joanna Lin, Manager

Medicine, surgery, nursing.

11542 US National Institutes of Health: National Cancer Institute-Scientific Library
PO Box B
Frederick, MD 21702-1124
301-846-1093
Fax: 301-846-6332
Susan W Wilson, Director

Cancer biology, biological and chemical carcinogenesis, acquired immunodeficiency syndrome, biomedical research.

11543 US Social Security Administration Library & Records Management Branch
Altmeyer Building
Room 570
Baltimore, MD 21235
410-962-3311
Fax: 410-966-2027
Bill Vitek, Director/Librarian

Social insurance, medical and hospital economics, operations research, management, personnel administration, supervision and training, electronic data processing, law, health insurance, business and management.

Libraries & Information Centers/Massachusetts

Massachusetts

11544 Boston College: Social Work Library
McGuinn Hall
Room B38
Chestnut Hill, MA 02467   617-552-3233
Fax: 617-552-3199
Donna L Ferullo, Head Librarian

Clinical social work; child welfare and families, individuals, and groups; ethnic studies and special populations; gerontology; human behavior; mental health; social policy; administration and research; social planning.

11545 Caption Center
125 Western Avenue
Boston, MA 02134-1008   617-300-3600
Fax: 617-300-3600
http://www.icdri.org/dhhi/ccowgbh.htm
Lori Kay, Co-Director
Tom Apone, Co-Director

Provides closed captioning for videos, including training, safety, instructional and educational films. Maintains a consumer information service for overcoming communications barriers in the workplace.

11546 Caritas Southwood Hospital Medical Library
111 Dedham Street
Norfolk, MA 02056-1666   508-668-0385
Fax: 508-668-1481
e-mail: schnvha@ma.ultranet.com

11547 Dana-Farber Cancer Institute Library
44 Binney Street
Boston, MA 02115-6084   617-632-3000
Fax: 617-632-2488
http://www.dana-farber.org
Christine W Fleuriel, Librarian
Edward Benz, President

Cancer research, AIDS research.

11548 Deaconess Hospital Horrax Library
185 Pilgrim Road
Boston, MA 02215-5324   617-632-9202
Paul Vaiginas, Librarian
Carl A Rasumssen, Manager

General medicine, diabetes, cancer, renal disease, cardiology, surgery.

11549 Framingham Public Library: Framingham Room
49 Lexington Street
Framingham, MA 01702-8218   508-532-5570
Fax: 508-820-7210
e-mail: fpi\lreg@min.lib.ma.us
http://www.mln.lib.ma.us
Tom Gilchrist, Contact
1955

11550 Laboure College Library
2120 Dorchester Avenue
Dorchester Center, MA 02124-5698   617-296-8300
http://www.laboure.edu
Maryann O'Toole, Director
Andrew Callo, Manager

Offers information on physical disabilities, independent living, peer counseling and advocacy.

11551 New England Corporate Library
501 Boylston Street
Boston, MA 02116-3738   617-578-2307
Fax: 617-578-5523
e-mail: pgollis@ncfn.com
Pamela Gollis, Library Manager

Life insurance, employee benefit plans, pensions, financial products, business and finance.

11552 Perkins School for the Blind: Samuel P Hayes Research Library
175 N Beacon Street
Watertown, MA 02472-2751   617-924-3434
Fax: 617-923-8076
http://www.perkins.org/researchlibrary/
June Tulikangas, Research Librarian
Steven Rothstein, President

Nonmedical aspects of blindness and deaf-blindness, including education, rehabilitation, welfare.

11553 US Department of Veterans Affairs Bedford: Edith Nourse Rogers Memorial Veterans Hospital Medical Library
200 Springs Road
Bedford, MA 01730-1114   781-687-2000
Fax: 781-687-2102
http://www.bedford.va.gov
Arlene Devlin, Chief Library Service

Psychiatry, geriatrics.

11554 US Department of Veterans Affairs Medical Center Library
N Main Street
Northampton, MA 01060   413-584-4040
Fax: 413-582-3039
Dorothy E Young, Chief Library Service
Joanne Carney, Manager

Neurology, psychiatry, psychology, nursing, medicine, gerontology.

11555 US Department of Veterans Affairs Outpatient Clinic Learning Resources Service
251 Causeway Street
Boston, MA 02114-2148   617-248-1170
Fax: 617-248-1406
http://www.boston.va.gov/bwropc_caus.asp
Irmeli Kilburn, Acting Chief Library Service

Health sciences, patient health education.

11556 US Department of Veterans Affairs: Boston Hospital Medical Library
150 S Huntington Avenue
Boston, MA 02130-4817   617-232-9500
Fax: 617-278-4508
http://www.va.gov
Irmeli Kilburn, Contact
Michael Lawson, President

General medicine, surgery, allied health sciences, patient education.

11557 US Department of Veterans Affairs: Medical Center Library
940 Belmont Street
Brockton, MA 02301-5596   508-583-4500
Fax: 508-895-0074
http://www.boston.va.gov
Suzanne N Noyes, Chief Library Service
Christine Croteau, Manager

Psychiatry, psychology, hospital administration, nursing, alcoholism, drug abuse.

11558 Worcester Public Library
3 Salem Square
Worcester, MA 01608-2074   508-799-1655
Fax: 508-799-1652
e-mail: jizatt@site.cwmars.org
http://www.worcpublib.org
Penelope B Johnson, Head Librarian

Libraries & Information Centers/Michigan

Summer reading programs, braille writer, magnifiers, closed-circuit TV, large-print photocopier, cassette books and magazines, children's books on cassette, home visits and other reference materials on blindness and other handicaps.

Michigan

11559 Area Agency on Aging Library
29100 Northwestern Highway
Southfield, MI 48034-1046
248-213-6704
800-852-7795
Fax: 248-948-9691
http://www.aaa1b.org

Jenny Jarvis, Director of Communications
Sandra Reminga, Executive Director

Older adult issues.

11560 Downtown Detroit Subregional Library for the Blind
121 Gratiot Avenue
Detroit, MI 48226-2203
313-965-3830
Fax: 313-965-1977
e-mail: deveans@cms.xx.wayne.edu
http://www.detroit.lib.mi.us
TDD 313-224-0584

Deborah Evans, Librarian
George Saad, Owner

Summer reading programs, braille writer, magnifiers, closed-circuit TV, large-print photocopier, cassette books and magazines, children's books on cassette, home visits and other reference materials on blindness and other handicaps.

11561 Grand Traverse Area Library for the Blind and Physically Handicapped
322 6th Street
Traverse City, MI 49684-2414
231-995-0313
Fax: 616-922-0904
TDD 616-922-0901

Evelyn Welty, Contact
Daniel Truckey, Manager

11562 Herman Miller Research Corporation
3971 Research Park Drive
Ann Arbor, MI 48108-2219
734-994-0200

Dallas Moore, Librarian
Robert Logeman, Partner

Library on aging and disability.

11563 Karmanos Cancer Institute Research Library
4100 John R
Detroit, MI 48201-1312
313-833-0710
Fax: 313-831-8714
e-mail: glodekc@kci.wayne.edu

CJ Glodek, Head Librarian
April Allen, Manager

Cancer research, allied health sciences.

11564 Kent County Library for the Blind
775 Ball Avenue NE
Grand Rapids, MI 49503-1397
616-336-3265
Fax: 616-336-3256
e-mail: kdlcm@lakeland.lib.mi.us

Claudya Muller, Librarian

Summer reading programs, braille writer, magnifiers, closed-circuit TV, large-print photocopier, cassette books and magazines, children's books on cassette, home visits and other reference materials on blindness and other handicaps.

11565 Library of Michigan Service for the Blind
PO Box 30007
Lansing, MI 48909-7507
517-373-5614
Fax: 517-373-5865
e-mail: info@sbph.libomich.lib.mi.us

Nancy Robertson, Manager

Summer reading programs, braille writer, magnifiers, closed-circuit TV, large-print photocopier, cassette books and magazines, children's books on cassette, home visits and other reference materials on blindness and other handicaps.

11566 Macomb Library for the Blind and Physically Handicapped
16480 Hall Road
Clinton Township, MI 48038-1132
586-286-1580
Fax: 810-286-0634
e-mail: macbld@libcoop.net
http://www.libcoop.net/macspe/

Linda Champion, Librarian
Beverlee Babcock, Executive Director

Summer reading programs, braille writer, magnifiers, closed-circuit TV, large-print photocopier, cassette books and magazines, children's books on cassette, home visits and other reference materials on blindness and other handicaps.

11567 Mideastern Michigan Library Co-op
G-4195 W Pasadena Avenue
Flint, MI 48504
810-732-1120
Fax: 810-732-1715
e-mail: cnash@genesse.freeret.org
http://mideastern.lib.mi.us

Carolyn Nash, Librarian
Deloris King, Manager

Summer reading programs, braille writer, magnifiers, closed-circuit TV, large-print photocopier, cassette books and magazines, children's books on cassette, home visits and other reference materials on blindness and other handicaps.

11568 Northland Library Cooperative
316 E Chisholm Street
Alpena, MI 49707-2892
989-356-1622
Fax: 989-354-3939
http://www.nlc.lib.m.us

Catherine Glomski, Librarian
Christine Johnston, Executive Director

Summer reading programs, braille writer, magnifiers, closed-circuit TV, large-print photocopier, cassette books and magazines, children's books on cassette, home visits and other reference materials on blindness and other handicaps.

11569 Oakland County Library for the Blind and Physically Handicapped
1200 N Telegraph Road
Dept 482
Pontiac, MI 48341
248-858-5050
Fax: 248-452-9145
e-mail: oakllbph@oakland.lib.mi.us
http://www.oakland.lib.mi.us/oakllbph.htm

Betty Ramey, Contact
David Conklin, Manager

11570 Senior Alliance Area Agency on Aging
3850 2nd Street
Suite 201
Wayne, MI 48184-1755
734-722-2830
Fax: 734-722-2836
e-mail: info@tsalink.org
http://www.thesenioralliance.org

Bob Brown, Executive Director
Lori Vail, Program Manager

To coordinate a comprehensive network of services in Western and Southern Wayne County to enable older persons to function as independently as possible in the community environment which best suits their needs. To provide the advocacy, programming, planning, contracting, funding, and personnel necessary to accomplish the foregoing purpose.

11571 St Clark County Library for the Blind and Physically Handicapped
210 McMorran Boulevard
Port Huron, MI 48060-4098
810-987-7323
Fax: 810-987-7327
Jackie Skinner, Librarian
James Warwick, Executive Director
Offers library services to the blind and visually impaired.

11572 US Department of Veterans Affairs: Ann Arbor Hospital Library
2215 Fuller Road
Ann Arbor, MI 48105-2335
734-769-7100
800-361-8387
Fax: 734-845-3260
e-mail: smith.vickie@forum.va.gov
http://www.va.gov
Vickie Smith, Chief Librarian
Aishe Haimour, Manager
Medicine, patient education.

11573 US Department of Veterans Affairs: Battle Creek Medical Center Library Service
5500 Armstrong Road
Battle Creek, MI 49016
269-966-5600
Fax: 269-966-5483
http://www.va.gov
Linda S Polardin, Contact
Psychiatry, neurology, psychology, post traumatic stress disorder, substance abuse, geropsychiatry.

11574 US Department of Veterans Affairs: Detroit Medical Center Library Service
4646 John R Street
Detroit, MI 48201-1916
313-576-1000
Fax: 313-576-1025
e-mail: tubolino.karen_m@forun.va.gov
http://www.va.gov
Karen M Tubolino, Librarian Head
Surgery, oncology, internal medicine, psychiatry, psychology, health management.

11575 US Department of Veterans Affairs: Iron Mountain Medical Center Library
325 E H Street
Iron Mountain, MI 49801
906-774-3300
Fax: 906-779-3188
e-mail: Durocher.Jeanne@Iron-Mtn.VA.gov
http://www.va.gov
Jeanne M Durocher, Chief Library Service
Medicine, surgery, nursing, patient education, allied health.

11576 US Department of Veterans Affairs: Saginaw Aleda E Lutz Medical Center Library
1500 Weiss Street
Saginaw, MI 48602-5251
989-497-2500
800-406-5143
Fax: 989-321-4903
http://www.saginaw.va.gov
Debbie Zapolski, Program Specialist
Medicine, surgery, nursing, health education.

11577 Washtenaw County Library
PO Box 8645
4135 Washtenaw Avenue
Ann Arbor, MI 48107-8645
734-973-4359
Fax: 734-973-4963
e-mail: lbpd@ewashtenaw.org
http://www.ewashtenaw.org
Margoret Wolfe, Librarian
Julie McClellan, Manager
Summer reading programs, braille writer, magnifiers, closed-circuit TV, large-print photocopier, cassette books and magazines, children's books on cassette, home visits and other reference materials on blindness and other handicaps.

11578 Wayne County Regional Library for the Blind
33030 Van Born Road
Wayne, MI 48184-2453
734-727-7088
Fax: 734-326-3008
e-mail: werlbph@tln.lib.mi.us
http://www.tln.lib.mi.us.
TDD 313-326-3008
Pat Klemans, Librarian
Betty McCoy, Manager
Summer reading programs, braille writer, magnifiers, closed-circuit TV, large-print photocopier, cassette books and magazines, children's books on cassette, home visits and other reference materials on blindness and other handicaps.

Minnesota

11579 Duluth Public Library
520 W Superior Street
Duluth, MN 55802-1578
218-730-4200
Dean Casperson, President
Adapted access to Apple computer, adapted toys and adapted library equipment.

11580 Minnesota Department of Human Services Library & Resource Center
Human Services Building
Saint Paul, MN 55155-3821
651-297-8708
Fax: 952-282-5340
e-mail: kate.o.nelson@state.mn.us
Kate Nelson, Librarian
Psychiatry, geriatrics, social issues, training.

11581 Minnesota Library for the Blind
388 6th Avenue SE
Faribault, MN 55021-6300
507-333-4828
800-722-0550
Fax: 507-333-4832
http://www.msab.state.mn.us
Catherine Durivage, Library Program Director
Summer reading programs, braille writer, magnifiers, closed-circuit TV, large-print photocopier, cassette books and magazines, children's books on cassette, home visits and other reference materials on blindness and other handicaps.

11582 US Department of Veterans Affairs: Minneapolis Medical Center Library Service
1 Veterans Drive
Minneapolis, MN 55417-2309
612-725-2000
866-414-5058
Fax: 612-725-2049
http://www.va.gov
A Sinha, Chief
Howard Ansel, MD
General medicine, psychology, geriatrics, biomedical research, biomedical ethics, nursing, brain science, neuroscience.

Mississippi

11583 Mississippi (State) Department of Mental Health Library and Division of Professional Development
1101 Robert East Lee Bldg
239 North Lamar Street
Jackson, MS 39201-1325
601-359-1288
Fax: 601-359-6295
http://www.dmh.state.ms.us/
Margueritte Ransom, Librarian

Libraries & Information Centers/Missouri

The Mental Health Library lending service was established primarily for use by the personnel of the Department of Mental Health, and other mental health/mental retardation service agencies, but its holdings are also available to the public through the Interlibrary Loan service of any public library. Information about this service can be obtained from the Mississippi Department of Mental Health Library.
1975

11584 Mississippi Library Commission
3881 Eastwood Drive
Jackson, MS 39211-6439
601-354-7208
Fax: 601-432-4484
e-mail: mslib@mlc.lib.ms.us
http://www.mlc.lib.ms.us
TDD 601-354-6411

Blair Booker, Reference Librarian

Summer reading programs, braille writer, magnifiers, closed-circuit TV, large-print photocopier, cassette books and magazines, children's books on cassette, home visits and other reference materials on blindness and other handicaps.

11585 US Department of Veterans Affairs: Jackson Medical Center Library
1500 E Woodrow Wilson Avenue
Jackson, MS 39216-5116
601-364-1273

Carol Sistrunk, Chief Librarian
Mary Prottsman, Manager

Medicine and allied health sciences.

Missouri

11586 Bonne Terre Memorial Library
5 Southwest Main Street
Bonne Terre, MO 63628-1741
573-358-2260
Fax: 573-358-5941
e-mail: btml@bonneterre.net
http://library.bonneterre.net/

Doris Smither, Librarian

The mission of the Bonne Terre Memorial Library is to provide access to informational, educational, cultural and recreational library materials and services in a variety of formats and technologies; to be responsive to the public library needs of the community; and to uphold the public's freedom of access to information. Community needs drive our services and we take a personal interest in ensuring that they are delivered in a welcoming, convenient and responsive manner.

11587 Central Institute for the Deaf Professional Library
818 S Euclid Avenue
Saint Louis, MO 63110-1504
314-977-0132
Fax: 314-977-0030
e-mail: csarli@cid.wustl.edu

Cathy Sarli, Librarian
Jo Ellen Epstein, Principal

Audiology, early childhood education, behavioral sciences, speech pathology, physiology, otolaryngology, education of the deaf, noise control, electroacoustics, digital instrumentation, aural rehabilitation, neurophysiology.

11588 Lutheran Library for the Blind
1333 S Kirkwood Road
Saint Louis, MO 63122-7226
314-965-9000

Offers braille and large print books and cassettes for the blind and visually impaired.

11589 US Department of Veterans Affairs, John Cochran Division Library
915 N Grand Boulevard
Saint Louis, MO 63106-1621
314-652-4100
800-228-5459
Fax: 314-289-6557
e-mail: repetto@inlink.com
http://www.stlouis.va.gov

Donna S Locke, Contact
Ann Repetto, Manager

Medicine and allied health sciences.

11590 US Department of Veterans Affairs: Kansas Medical Center Library
4801 E Linwood Boulevard
Kansas City, MO 64128-2226
816-861-4700
800-525-1483
Fax: 816-922-3303
e-mail: g.library@kansas_city.va.gov
http://www.va.gov

Shirley C Ting, Chief Library Service
John McDonald, Manager

Medicine, surgery, neurology, nursing, psychology, psychiatry.

11591 US Department of Veterans Affairs: Poplar Bluff Library Service
Medical Center
1500 N Westwood Blvd
Poplar Bluff, MO 63901
573-686-4151
Fax: 573-778-4559
http://www.visn15.med.va.gov

Genise E Denton, Chief Lirary Service
Nancy Arnold, Manager

Medicine.

11592 US Department of Veterans Affairs:, Columbus Hospital Library
800 Hospital Drive
Columbia, MO 65201-5275
573-443-2511
Fax: 573-443-2511
e-mail: mocol@forum.va.gov

Mark Fleetwood, Chief Learning Research Service

Medicine, surgery.

11593 Wolfner Memorial Library for the Blind
PO Box 387
Jefferson City, MO 65102
573-751-8720
800-392-2614
Fax: 573-526-2985
e-mail: beckles@mail.sos.state.mo.us
http://www.sos.mo.gov
TDD 800-347-1379

Elizabeth Eckles, Librarian
Richard J Smith, Executive Director

Summer reading programs, braille writer, magnifiers, closed-circuit TV, large-print photocopier, cassette books and magazines, children's books on cassette, home visits and other reference materials on blindness and other handicaps.

Montana

11594 Montana State Library
1515 E 6th Avenue
Po Box 201800
Helena, MT 59620-1800
406-444-3115
Fax: 406-444-5612
TDD 406-444-5431

Darlene Staffeldt, State Librarian

Summer reading programs, braille writer, magnifiers, closed-circuit TV, large-print photocopier, cassette books and magazines, children's books on cassette, home visits and other reference materials on blindness and other handicaps.

11595 St. Patrick Hospital and Health Sciences Center: Library Center
500 W Broadway
Missoula, MT 59802
406-543-7271
Fax: 406-329-5688
e-mail: library@saintpatrick.org
http://www.saintpatrick.org
Marianne Farr, Medical Librarian

Access to medical and consumer health related information.

11596 US Department of Veterans Affairs: Fort Harrison Medical Center Library
Library Services 142d
Fort Harrison, MT 59636
406-442-6410
Fax: 406-447-7948
e-mail: grasmick.charles@forum.va.gov
http://www.va.gov
Charles Grasmick, Chief Library Service

Medicine, internal medicine, surgery.

11597 US Department of Veterans Affairs: Miles City Medical Center Library
210 S Winchester Avenue
Miles City, MT 59301-4742
406-874-5600
Fax: 406-232-8297
e-mail: wilkerson.gail@forum.va.gov
Gail Shaw Wilkerson, Chief Library Service

Medicine; nursing; geriatrics.

11598 William K. Kohrs Memorial Library
501 Missouri Avenue
Deer Lodge, MT 59722
406-846-2622
888-872-2622
e-mail: nsillima@mtlib.org
http://http://kohrslibrary.org/
Nancy Silliman, Library Director

Materials and resources on adult education and classes that the library sponsors.

Nebraska

11599 Nebraska Library Commission: Talking Book & Braille Service
1200 N Street
Suite 120
Lincoln, NE 68508-2020
402-471-4038
Fax: 402-471-6244
e-mail: talkingbook@nlc.state.ne.us
http://www.nlc.state.ne.us/tbbs
David Oerti, Librarian

Summer reading programs, braille writer, magnifiers, closed-circuit TV, large-print photocopier, cassette books and magazines, children's books on cassette, home visits and other reference materials on blindness and other handicaps.

11600 Nebraska School for the Visually Handicapped Library
824 10th Avenue
Nebraska City, NE 68410-1370
402-873-5513
Fax: 402-873-3463
Sally Giittinger, Administrator

Education, the blind and visually impaired.

11601 North Platte Public Library
120 W 4th Street
North Platte, NE 69101-3901
308-535-8036
Fax: 308-535-8296
e-mail: library@ci.north-platte.ne.us
http://www.ci.north-platte.ne.us/library
Brenda Behsman, Librarian
Cecelia Lawrence, Executive Director

Summer reading programs, braille writer, magnifiers, closed-circuit TV, large-print photocopier, cassette books and magazines, children's books on cassette, home visits and other reference materials on blindness and other handicaps.

11602 US Department of Veterans Affairs: Grand Island Greater Nebraska Health Care System Library
2201 N Broadwell Avenue
Grand Island, NE 68803-2153
308-382-3660
866-580-1810
Fax: 308-389-5148
http://www.nebraska.va.gov
Patricia Petersen, Technician

Medicine, nursing.

11603 US Department of Veterans Affairs: Omaha Hospital Library
4101 Woolworth Avenue
Omaha, NE 68105-1850
402-346-8800
800-451-5796
Fax: 402-449-0692
http://www.nebraska.va.gov

Medicine and allied health sciences.

Nevada

11604 Las Vegas-Clark County Library District
833 Las Vegas Blvd N
Las Vegas, NV 89101
702-734-7323
Fax: 702-733-1567
http://www.lvccld.org
Mary Anne Morton, Librarian
Laura Golod, Manager

Summer reading programs, braille writer, magnifiers, closed-circuit TV, large-print photocopier, cassette books and magazines, children's books on cassette, home visits and other reference materials on blindness and other handicaps.

11605 Nevada State Library and Archives
Capitol Complex
100 North Stewart Street
Carson City, NV 89710
775-684-3360
Fax: 775-684-3330
e-mail: nslref@clan.lib.nv.us
http://dmla.clan.lib..nv.us/docs/nsla
TDD 702-687-8338
Kevin E Putnam, Librarian

Summer reading programs, braille writer, magnifiers, closed-circuit TV, large-print photocopier, cassette books and magazines, children's books on cassette, home visits and other reference materials on blindness and other handicaps.

11606 Nevada State Library: Talking Book Services
100 N Stewart Street
Carson City, NV 89701-4285
775-684-3310
Fax: 775-684-3330
e-mail: nslref@clan.lib.nv.us
http://dmla.clan.lib.nv.us
TDD 775-687-8338
Keri E Putnam, Regional Librarian

Services to blind, visually or physically handicapped individuals. Books and magazines are available on cassette, disc or in Braille. Recorded books and magazines and special playback equipment are loaned to eligible readers free of charge.

11607 US Department of Veterans Affairs: Reno Medical Center Library Services
1000 Locust Street
Reno, NV 89502-2597
775-786-7200
Fax: 775-328-1464
e-mail: simpson@equinox.unr.edu
Christine J Simpson, Chief Library Service

Clinical medicine, gerontology.

Libraries & Information Centers/New Hampshire

New Hampshire

11608 Dartmouth College Biomedical Libraries: Dana Biomedical Library
6168 Dana Biomedical Library
Hanover, NH 03755-3880
603-646-1110
Fax: 603-650-1354
e-mail: contact@dartmouth.edu
http://www.dartmouth.edu
William F Garrity, Director Biomedical Librarie

Medicine, life sciences, nursing.

11609 New Hampshire Hospital: Dorothy M Breene Memorial Library
36 Clinton Street
Concord, NH 03301-2359
603-271-5420
Fax: 603-271-5395
e-mail: breenelibrary@dhhs.state.nh.us
Marion L Allen, Librarian
Chester G Batchelder, CEO

Psychiatry, psychology, geriatrics, nursing, neurology, social work, training.

11610 New Hampshire State Library
117 Pleasant Street
Concord, NH 03301-3852
603-271-3429
e-mail: talking@lilac.nhsh.lib.nh.us
http://www.nh.gov/nhsl
Betty Clark, Library Technician

Summer reading programs, braille writer, magnifiers, closed-circuit TV, large-print photocopier, cassette books and magazines, children's books on cassette, home visits and other reference materials on blindness and other handicaps.

11611 US Department of Veterans Affairs: Manchester Medical Center Library
718 Smyth Road
Manchester, NH 03104-7004
603-624-4366
800-892-8384
Fax: 603-626-6579
http://www.manchester.va.gov
Martha Roberts, Chief Library Service

Medicine, surgery, nursing.

New Jersey

11612 Cytogen Corporation R&D Library
307 College Road E
Princeton, NJ 08540-6608
609-750-8200
Fax: 609-987-8640
Michael D Becker, CEO

Cancer research, biotechnology.

11613 New Jersey Department of Environmental Protection
PO Box 402
Trenton, NJ 08625-0402
609-984-2249
Fax: 609-292-3298
e-mail: mbarattn@dep.state.nj.us
http://www.nj.gov
Maria Baratta, Library Manager
Mary Kearns-Kaplan, Manager

Toxic substances; hazardous waste; pollution - water, air, soil; carcinogens; drinking water; water resources.

11614 New Jersey Library for the Blind and Physically Handicapped
2300 Stuyvesant Avenue
Trenton, NJ 08618-3226
609-530-4000
800-792-8322
Fax: 609-530-6384
e-mail: njlbh@njstatelib.org
http://www.njlbh.org
TDD 609-633-7250
Vianne Connor, Librarian

Summer reading programs, braille writer, magnifiers, closed-circuit TV, large-print photocopier, cassette books and magazines, children's books on cassette, home visits and other reference materials on blindness and other handicaps.

11615 Princeton University Industrial Relations Library
Firestone Library
Princeton, NJ 08544
609-258-1470
Fax: 609-258-4105
e-mail: kpbarry@princeton.edu
http://www.princeton.edu
Kevin P Barry, Librarian
Andrew Golden, President

Industrial relations, labor legislation, labor unions, human resource planning, labor economics, social insurance, benefit plans, personnel administration.

11616 Sandoz Pharmaceuticals Corporate Library
Rr 10
East Hanover, NJ 07936
973-503-7500
Fax: 973-503-6357

Medicine, chemistry, oncology, pharmacology, toxicology, biochemistry, business, management.

11617 UMDNJ and Coriell Research Library
401 Haddon Avenue
Camden, NJ 08103-1505
856-757-7740
Fax: 856-757-7713
e-mail: swartz@umdnj.edu
http://www.umdnj.edu
Betty Jean Swartz, Librarian

Cancer, immunology, genetics, microbiology, cell biology, cytogenetics, molecular biology.

11618 US Department of Veterans Affairs: East Orange Medical Center Library
385 Tremont Avenue
East Orange, NJ 07018-1023
973-676-1000
Fax: 973-395-7062
http://www.eastorange.va.gov
Sophie Winston, Chief Library Service
Samuel Greene, President

General medicine.

11619 US Department of Veterans Affairs: Lyon New Jersey Health Care System - Lyons Campus Hospital Library
151 Knollcroft Road
Lyons, NJ 07939-5001
908-647-0180
Fax: 908-647-3452
http://www.lyons.va.gov
James G Delo, Learning Research Service

Psychiatry, neurology, psychology, medicine, nursing, patient health education.

New Mexico

11620 Capitan Public Library
101 E 2nd Street
PO Box 1169
Capitan, NM 88316
505-354-3035
Fax: 505-354-3223
e-mail: cpl@valornet.com
http://www.capitanlibrary.org

Pat Sullivan, President
George Hinch, VP

For the older adults there is a speaker once a month that talks about issues pertaining to seniors, free computer classes are offered and there is a literacy program.

11621 New Mexico State Library: Blind and Physically Handicapped
1209 Camino Carlos Rey
Santa Fe, NM 87503
505-476-9700
Fax: 505-476-9701
e-mail: lbph@state.nm.us
http://www.stlib.state.nm.us

Glee Wenzel, Librarian

Books, magazines, and other material in alternate format (cassette, Braille, and electronic text), playback equipment, and some production of print materials in alternative media.

11622 Roswell Public Library
301 N Pennsylvania
Roswell, NM 88201
505-622-7101
e-mail: rplref@roswellpubliclibrary.org
http://www.roswellpubliclibrary.org

Variety of books and other materials to inform and entertain adults. Audio books are available on cassette and CD. Video cassettes and DVD's cover a wide range of topics, including how-to, history, drama and travel.

11623 US Department of Veterans Affairs: Albuquerque Medical Center Library
2100 Ridgecrest Drive SE
Albuquerque, NM 87108-5128
505-256-2786
Fax: 505-256-2870

Phyllis L Kregstein, Contact

Medicine, surgery, nursing, psychiatry.

New York

11624 Albany Talking Book Center
300 Pine Avenue
Albany, NY 10103
229-431-2900
Fax: 229-430-4020

Kathryn Sinquefield, Librarian

Offers discs, cassettes, reference materials on blindness and other handicaps, large-print photocopiers, summer reading programs, cassette books and more.

11625 Beth Israel Medical Center: Seymour J Phillips Health Sciences Library
1st Avenue At 16th Street
New York, NY 10003
212-844-1505
Fax: 212-420-4640
e-mail: libraryservices@bethisraelny.org

Valerie La Rocca, Manager

11626 Braille Book Bank
3 Townline Circle
Rochester, NY 14623-2537
585-427-8260
Fax: 585-427-0263
e-mail: nbaoffice@nationalbraille.org
http://www.nationalbraille.org

David Shaffer, Executive Director
Diane Spence, President

Contains over 1,800 titles and braille music scores which are constantly updated and enlarged by transcriptions from BTAS and RTR.

11627 Calvary Hospital Medical Library
1740 Eastchester Road
Bronx, NY 10461-2392
718-518-2229
Fax: 718-518-2686

Dorothy M Maucione, Medical Librarian
Irina Pulatova, Manager

Medicine, cancer, nutrition, nursing.

11628 Center for Thanatology Research Library
391 Atlantic Avenue
Brooklyn, NY 11217-1701
718-858-3026
Fax: 718-852-1846
e-mail: thanatology@pipeline.nyc.com
http://www.thanatology.org

Roberta Halporn, Executive Director

Aging, dying, death, bereavement, gravestone studies.

11629 Center for the Study of Aging Library
706 Madison Avenue
Albany, NY 12208-3695
518-462-1331
Fax: 518-462-1339
e-mail: iapaas@aol.com

Sara Harris, Executive Director

Gerontology and geriatrics, physical activity and aging, mental health and illness, environment, social work, housing, medicine, social sciences, caregiving, nutrition, housing, prevention, long term care.

11630 Cold Spring Harbor Laboratory
1 Bungtown Road
Cold Spring Harbor, NY 11724-2209
516-367-8800
Fax: 516-367-6843
e-mail: henderso@cshl.org; stolen@cshl.org
http://www.cshl.org/library

Bruce Stillman, President

Biological sciences, genetics, cancer research, cell biology, molecular biology, neurobiology, virology.

11631 Columbia University Oral History Research Office
801 Butler Library Box 20
535 W 114th St MC1129
New York, NY 10027
212-854-7083
Fax: 212-854-5378
http://www.columbia.edu/cu/lweb/indiv/oral/

Ronald J Grele, Director

National affairs, New York history, international relations, culture and the arts, social welfare, business and labor, philanthropy, African-American community, law, medicine, education, journalism, religion.

11632 Columbia University: Augustus C Long Health Sciences Library
701 West 168th Street
New York, NY 10032-2704
212-305-3605
Fax: 212-234-0595
e-mail: hs-library@columbia.edu
http://http://library.cpmc.columbia.edu/hsl/

Mel Rodriguez, Administrative Director
Pat Molholt, Associate Vice President
Idelsi Botex, Administrative Coordinator

The Augustus C. Long Health Sciences Library serves Columbia University's Schools of Medicine, Dental and Oral Surgery, Nursing, and Public Health, the Presbyterian Hospital, and other health care, instructional and research programs in the Columbia-Presbyterian Medical Center. The Library is one of the largest academic health sciences libraries in the country. Its collection includes over 500,000 volumes, 4,400 current periodical subscriptions, and extensive holdings of media, electronic resources, rare books and archival materials.

Libraries & Information Centers/New York

11633 Columbia University: Whitney M Young, Jr Memorial Library of Social Work
535 West 114th Street
New York, NY 10027
212-854-2271
Fax: 212-854-9099
http://www.columbia.edu

Social work; community organization; social policy development and administration; health, mental health, mental retardation; social services - family and children, day care, legal; aging; corrections and court services - probation, parole, diversionary treatment; alcoholism and drug addiction; psychoanalysis; industrial social welfare; intergroup relations; social and physical rehabilitation.

11634 Cornell University School of Industrial and Labor Relations
309 Ives Hall
Ithaca, NY 14853
607-254-7250
Fax: 607-255-2741
http://www.ilr.cornell.edu

Gordon Law, Director

Labor-management relations, labor law and legislation, labor organization, industrial and labor conditions, labor economics, human resources, social security, personnel administration, supervision, occupational safety and health, international labor conditions and problems, organizational behavior.

11635 Goldwater Memorial Hospital: Medical Center Health Sciences Library
900 Main Street
New York, NY 10044
212-318-8000
Fax: 212-318-4460

Martin M Leibovici, Library Director
Muni H Shah, MD

General medicine, rehabilitation medicine, geriatrics, chronic disease.

11636 Hasting Center Library
Rr 9d
21 Malcolm Gordon Road
Garrison, NY 10524
845-424-4040
Fax: 845-424-4545
e-mail: mail@thehastingcenter.org
http://www.thehastingcenter.org

Thomas H Murray, President/CEO

Hasting Center pursues interdisciplinary research and education that includes both theory and practice. The center, as a private not-for-profit institute addresses fundamental ethical issues in the area of health, medicine and the environment as they affect individuals, communities and societies. Publishes The Hastings Center Report.

11637 Highland Hospital: John R Williams, Sr Health Sciences Library
1000 South Avenue
Rochester, NY 14620-2733
585-341-6761
Fax: 716-758-1796
e-mail: adixon@highland.rochester.edu
http://www.urmc.rochester.edu

Angela Dixon, Head Science Librarian
Yvonne Thorne, Executive Director

Medicine, surgery, family medicine, nursing, hematology/oncology, radiation therapy, obstetrics, gynecology.

11638 Hunter College of the City University of New York: Health Professional Library
425 E 25th Street
New York, NY 10010-2547
Fax: 212-481-5116
e-mail: vconant@shiva.hunter.cuny.edu
http://library.wexler.hunter.cuny.edu

Laura Cobus, Head
Yat Ping Wong, Deputy Head

Nursing, medicine, speech and hearing pathology, physical therapy, dance therapy, medical laboratory sciences, environmental health sciences, allied health services administration, community health education, nutrition, occupational health.

11639 Institute for Socioeconomic Studies Library
10 New King Street
White Plains, NY 10604-1271
914-686-7112
Fax: 914-686-0581
e-mail: mail@socioeconomic.org
http://www.socioeconomic.org

Allan T Ostergren, Senior Research Associate

Quality of life, economic development, social motivation, poverty, urban regeneration, problems of the elderly.

11640 International Ladies' Garment Workers Union Research Department Library
1710 Broadway
New York, NY 10019-5254
212-265-7000
Fax: 212-489-7238

Walter Mankoff, Associate Director Research
Bruce Raynor, President

Earnings and hours, employment and payrolls, fringe benefits, labor and labor statistics, old-age insurance, social insurance, trade unions, unemployment insurance, union agreements, wearing apparel industry, women's clothing industry.

11641 JGB Cassette Library International
15 W 65th Street
New York, NY 10023-6601
212-769-6331
Fax: 212-769-6266
e-mail: bemass@aol.com

Bruce Massis, Contact
Peter Williamson, Executive Director

Summer reading programs, braille writer, magnifiers, closed-circuit TV, large-print photocopier, cassette books and magazines, children's books on cassette, home visits and other reference materials on blindness and other handicaps.

11642 Lexington School for the Deaf Library Media Center
30th Avenue & 75th Street
Jackson Heights, NY 11370
718-350-3300
Fax: 718-899-9846

Gerard J Buckley, President

Audiology, behavior modification, deafness, education, language, child study, exceptional children, psychology, reading, speech, parenting.

11643 Lighthouse: Ruth M Shellens Library
111 E 59th Street
New York, NY 10022-1202
212-821-9200
800-829-0500
Fax: 212-821-9707
e-mail: vstepchyshyn@lighthouse.org
http://www.lighthouse.org

Tara A Cortes, President/CEO

Blindness and visual impairment, handicaps.

11644 MC Migel Memorial Library and Helen Keller Archives
11 Penn Plaza
Suite 300
New York, NY 10001-2006
212-502-7600
Fax: 212-502-7777
e-mail: afbinfo@afb.net
http://www.afb.org

Carl R Augusto, President/CEO

The history, education, sociology and rehabilitation of individuals who are blind or visually impaired; Helen Keller's papers, personal library, memorabilia and photography collection.

Libraries & Information Centers/New York

11645 Masonic Medical Research Laboratory: Max L Kamiel Library
2150 Bleecker Street
Utica, NY 13501-1738
315-735-2217
Fax: 315-735-5648
e-mail: lib@mmrl.edu

David F Schneeweiss, President

Cardiac arrhythmias, cardiovascular pharmacology, immunology, molecular biology.

11646 Monroe Community Hospital: TF Williams Health Sciences Library
435 E Henrietta Road
Rochester, NY 14620-4684
585-760-6500
Fax: 585-760-6066
e-mail: mch@rrlc.rochester.lib.ny.us
http://www.monroehosp.org

Marilyn Rosen, Library Director
Frank Tripodi, CEO

Geriatrics, gerontology, long-term care, medicine, nursing, administration.

11647 Montefiore Medical Center Health Sciences Library: Tishman Learning Center
111 E 210th Street
Bronx, NY 10467-2401
718-920-4321
Fax: 212-920-4658
http://www.montefiore.org

Steven M Safyer, President/CEO

Medicine, health sciences administration, geriatrics, psychology, psychiatry, nursing.

11648 Nassau Library System
900 Jerusalem Avenue
Uniondale, NY 11553
516-292-8920
Fax: 516-481-4777
e-mail: outreach@nassaulibrary.org
http://www.nassaulibrary.org

Jackie Tresher, Director

Information about public library services in Nassau County, including services for people with disabilities and the Senior Connections volunteer project (information and referral for seniors and their families). Co-sponsor of the Long Island Talking Book Library.

11649 National Association for Visually Handicapped Library
22 W 21st Street
New York, NY 10010-6904
212-889-3141
Fax: 212-727-2931
e-mail: staff@navh.org
http://www.navh.org

Lorianie Marchi, CEO

General collection for the visually impaired.

11650 New York Office of Mental Health Binghamton Psychiatric Center Library Services Department
425 Robinson Street
Binghamton, NY 13904-1775
607-724-1391
Fax: 607-773-4387
e-mail: bpcmason@pppmail.appliedtheory.com
http://www.omh.state.ny.us

Psychiatry, adolescent psychiatry, community mental health, psychology, child psychology, group psychotherapy, mental illness, general medicine, psychoanalysis, social services, family therapy, gerontology, geriatric nursing, geriatric psychiatry, quality improvement, managed mental health care.

11651 New York Public Library
40 W 20th Street
New York, NY 10011-4211
212-206-5400
Fax: 212-206-5418
http://www.nypl.org
TDD 212-206-5458

Bonnie Birdman, Librarian
Kevin Winkler, Manager

Offers assistive devices for the visually impaired and books on cassette.

11652 New York Public Library General Reference & Advisory Services: Accessibility Services
455 5th Avenue
New York, NY 10016
212-340-0849
Fax: 212-576-0048
http://www.nypl.org
TDD 212-340-0931

Wol Sue Lee, Department Head
Fu Mei Yang, Supervising Librarian

The disabled - vision impaired, hearing impaired, learning and mobility impaired.

11653 New York State Talking Book & Braille Library
Empire State Plaza CEC
Albany, NY 12230
518-474-5935
Fax: 518-474-5786
e-mail: TBBL@mail.nyscd.gov
http://www.nypl.org
TDD 518-474-7121

Jane Somers, Director

Books on audio cassette, cassette players, braille books, summer reading programs, braille writer, magnifiers, closed-circuit TV, large-print photocopier, cassette books and magazines, children's books on cassette, reference materials on blindness and other handicaps.

11654 Oxford Gerontology Center Library
New York State Veterans' Home
Oxford, NY 13830
607-843-6991
Fax: 607-843-6991

Long-term care, gerontology.

11655 Program Planners: Library/Information Center
230 W 41st Street
Floor 19
New York, NY 10036-7207
212-840-2609
Fax: 212-764-4094
e-mail: ppi@bway.net

Burt Lazarin, Resources Director

Collective bargaining, public employee pensions/retirement systems, local government, urban affairs, health care, insurance, sanitation.

11656 Rochester Institute of Technology Library
90 Lomb Memorial Drive
Rochester, NY 14623-5604
585-475-2562
Fax: 585-475-7007
http://wally.rit.edu

Chandra V McKenzie, Director
Albert J Simone, President

Academic library for art, business, criminal justice, printing, micro-optics, computer science, imaging science, photography, social work, engineering, science, liberal arts, food, hotel tourism.

11657 Rochester Technical Institute for the Deaf Resource Center
L B J Building
Room 2490
Rochester, NY 14623
585-482-8100
Fax: 585-475-6500
e-mail: GLK9638@RIT.EDU

Gail Kovalik, Research Specialist
Bradley Weaver, President

Deafness.

11658 Roosevelt Hospital Medical Library
428 W 59th Street
New York, NY 10019-1105
212-523-8500
Fax: 212-523-6108

Paul E Barth, Librarian

Medicine, surgery, gerontology, geriatrics, hospital administration, pediatrics, anesthesia.

Libraries & Information Centers/New York

11659 Sea View Hospital Rehabilitation Center Health Sciences Library
460 Brielle Avenue
Staten Island, NY 10314-6427
718-317-3000
Fax: 718-980-7182
Danial Mulligan, Director Education
Thomas Matteo, Executive Director

Medicine, nursing, geriatrics, hospital administration, social service, rehabilitation, dentistry.

11660 Sisters of Life: Dr Joseph R Stanton Human Life Issues Library and Resource Center
1955 Needham Avenue
Bronx, NY 10466-5824
718-881-7286
Fax: 718-881-7287
http://www.sistersoflife.org
Josamarie Perpetua, SV Director

A library and resource center providing books, videos, audiotapes, pamphlets and other information about the threat posed by assisted suicide and euthansia to the chronically ill, the frial, and the vulnerable. Also covers abortion and beginnng of life issues. Also contains the archives of the pro life movement in America, and many resources from around the world.
1970

11661 St Mary's School for the Deaf Library Information Center
2253 Main Street
Buffalo, NY 14214-2392
716-834-7200
Fax: 716-834-2720
http://www.smsdk12.org
Bill Johnson, Superintendent Of The School
Pat Brant, Administrative Assistant

Deafness, audiology, speech, special education, ASL, sign language, deaf culture, deaf history.

11662 Suffolk Cooperative Library System
627 Sunrise Service Road N
Bellport, NY 11713-1554
631-286-1600
Fax: 631-286-1647
http://www.suffolk.lib.ny.us
Kevin Verbesey, Director

Talking Books Plus provides specialized resources, services, and information to help member libraries serve people with disabilities, their family members, and service providers. Some of these resources, like talking books, are provided directly to patrons by mail or in person. Other materials, such as print books, videotapes, programming kits, and TTYs, are loaned through member libraries

11663 Syracuse University Center for Policy Research
426 Eggers Hall
Syracuse, NY 13244-1020
315-443-3114
Fax: 315-443-1081
e-mail: ctrpol@syr.edu
http://www.pr.maxwell.syr.edu/index.htm
Timothy M Smeeding, Director

Aging and long-term care, development studies, domestic urban and regional studies, public finance, social welfare, poverty, income security and microsimulation.

11664 Teachers College Milbank Memorial Library
Columbia University
525 W 120th St
New York, NY 10027
212-678-3494
Fax: 212-678-3092
e-mail: DaVinci@edunet.tc.columbia.edu
http://library.tc.columbia.edu
Jane P Franck, Director
Gary Natriello, Executive Director

Education, psychology, health sciences, nutrition, nursing, communications, computing, technology, speech and language pathology, audiology.

11665 Teachers Insurance and Annuity Association Business Library
730 3rd Avenue
New York, NY 10017-3206
212-916-1700
Fax: 212-916-6032
Margaret A Beirne, Corporate Librarian
Herbert Allison, CEO

Insurance, pensions, annuities, law, higher education.

11666 Towers Perrin Corporate Information Center
100 Summit Lake Drive
Valhalla, NY 10595-1339
914-745-4000
Fax: 914-745-4555
http://www.towerspervin.com
Jack Borbely, Director Information Service
Ann Farquhar, Manager

Compensation, retirement/pensions, employee benefits, US companies and industries, international business, insurance.

11667 US Department of Veterans Affairs: Albany Medical Center Library
113 Holland Avenue
Albany, NY 12208-3410
518-626-5000
Fax: 518-626-5500
e-mail: Korhun@FORUM.VA.GOV
http://www1.va.gov/visn02/albany.cfm
Halyna L Korhun, Contact

Medicine, social services, nursing, mental health.

11668 US Department of Veterans Affairs: Batavia Western New York Healthcare System Library
222 Richmond Avenue
Batavia, NY 14020-1227
585-297-1000
Fax: 888-798-2302
http://www.va.gov
Betty A Withrow, Chief Librarian
Mary Olix, Manager

General medicine, nursing, pathology, radiology.

11669 US Department of Veterans Affairs: Bath Medical Center Library Service
76 Veterans Avenue
Bath, NY 14810
607-664-4000
Fax: 877-845-3247
http://www.va.gov
Sally Ann Hillegas, Chief Librarian

Geriatrics, chronic diseases, general internal medicine, long term care.

11670 US Department of Veterans Affairs: Bronx Medical Center Library
130 W Kingsbridge Road
Bronx, NY 10468-3904
718-584-9000
800-877-6976
Fax: 718-741-4269
http://www.bronx.va.gov
Sumitte De Soyza, Chief Librarian

Medicine and allied health sciences.

11671 US Department of Veterans Affairs: Brooklyn Medical Center Library
800 Poly Place
Brooklyn, NY 11209-7104
718-836-6600
Fax: 718-630-3573
e-mail: tidona@medlo.hscbklyn.edu
http://www.brooklyn.va.gov
Francine Tidona, Library Service

Medicine, surgery, psychiatry, psychology, nursing, social work.

Libraries & Information Centers/North Carolina

11672 **US Department of Veterans Affairs: Buffalo Medical Center Library Service**
3495 Bailey Avenue
Buffalo, NY 14215-1129
716-834-9200
Fax: 716-862-8759
http://www.va.gov

Betty A Withrow, Chief Librarian

Medicine, surgery, nursing, management.

11673 **US Department of Veterans Affairs: Castle Point Department of Medicine and Surgery Library Service**
Rt 9D
Castle Point, NY 12511
845-831-2000
Fax: 845-838-5193
http://www.hudsonvalley.va.gov

Jeffrey Nicholas, Chief Library Service

Spinal cord injuries, surgery, nursing education, geriatric medicine, dentistry.

11674 **US Department of Veterans Affairs: Montrose Medical Library**
Veterans Medical Center
2094 Albany Post Rd. Rt 9A Po Box 100
Montrose, NY 10548
914-737-4400
Fax: 914-788-4244
http://www.hudsonvalley.va.gov

Bruce S Delman, PhD Chief Library Service

Psychiatry, psychology, medicine, social work, nursing, geriatrics.

11675 **US Department of Veterans Affairs: New York Harbour Healthcare System, New York Campus Library**
423 E 23rd Street
New York, NY 10010-5011
212-686-7500
Fax: 212-951-3487
http://www.manhattan.va.gov

Karin Wiseman, Chief Librarian
Tom Waugh, Librarian
Judy Steerle, Librarian

Medicine, surgery, neurology, psychiatry, nursing.

11676 **US Department of Veterans Affairs: Northport Medical Center-Medical Library**
79 Middleville Road
Northport, NY 11768-2200
631-261-4400
800-551-3996
Fax: 631-754-7992
http://www.northport.va.gov

Caryl Kazen, Chief Library Service

Medicine, allied health sciences, psychiatry, and dentistry.

11677 **W Alton Jones Cell Science Center: George and Margaret Gey Library**
10 Old Barn Road
Lake Placid, NY 12946-1009
518-523-1267
Fax: 518-523-4385
e-mail: wilmes@northnet.org

Teresa B Wilmes, MLIS

Cell culture, organ culture, cytology, cancer research, virology, biochemistry, immunology.

11678 **Wallace Memorial Library**
90 Lomb Memorial Drive
Rochester, NY 14623-5604
585-424-4606
Fax: 585-475-7007
e-mail: srrwml@rit.edu
http://wally.rit.edu

Melanie Norton, Reference Librarian
Dwight Wallace, Manager

Information on physical disabilities and deafness.

11679 **William and Mercer Research Library**
1166 Avenue of the Americas
New York, NY 10036-2708
212-000-1111
Fax: 212-574-9122

Patrick Sweeney, Librarian
David Morrison, President

Health care, pensions, Social Security, and group insurance.

11680 **Xavier Society for the Blind**
154 E 23rd Street
New York, NY 10010-4595
212-473-7800
Fax: 212-473-7801
http://www.visionaware.org

Rev. Alfred Caruana SJ, Executive Director
Margie Montenegro, Client Services Representative
Kathleen Lynch, Manager

Provides spiritual and inspirational reading material to visually impaired persons in suitable format: braille, large print and cassette, throughout the USA and Canada. Services provided by way of regular periodicals which are non-returnable, and through our lending library where books are returned. All services are provided free of charge, and interested persons can write or phone.

North Carolina

11681 **Duke University Center for Demographic Studies Library**
2117 Campus Drive
Durham, NC 27708
919-477-9292
Fax: 919-684-3861
http://www.duke.edu

Sue P Hicks, Librarian
Michael Duke, Owner

Demography; human ecology; census, vital statistics, other data sources; methods of research and analysis; population dynamics; urban and regional studies; economics of population size and distribution; migration studies; gerontology.

11682 **Family Health International**
PO Box 13950
Research Triangle Park, NC 27709-3950
919-544-7040
Fax: 919-544-7261
e-mail: broinson@fhi.org
http://www.fhi.org

Dr. Willard Cates Jr, President
Albert J Siemens, Chairman/CEO

Reproductive medicine, family planning, contraception, population, developing countries.

11683 **North Carolina Library for the Blind**
1811 Capital Boulevard
Raleigh, NC 27635
919-733-4376
888-388-2460
Fax: 919-733-6910
e-mail: nclbph@ncmail.net
http://statelibrary.dcr.state.nc.us/bph.htm
TDD 919-733-1462

Francine Martin, Librarian

Free laon of books on tape, in braille, and in large print to north Carolinians who caanot read standard print due to a visual or physical disability. Materials mailed to and from library via Free Matter for the Blind mailing privileges. Certified application required.

11684 **US Department of Veterans Affairs: Asheville Medical Center Library**
1100 Tunnel Road
Asheville, NC 28805-2043
828-298-7911
800-932-6408
Fax: 828-299-2502
http://www.visn6.va.gov

Peggy Patterson, Acting Chief
Dan Potter, Manager

Libraries & Information Centers/North Dakota

General and cardiopulmonary medicine, thoracic surgery, nursing.

11685 US Department of Veterans Affairs: Durham Medical Center Library
508 Fulton Street
Durham, NC 27705-3875
919-286-0411
888-878-6890
Fax: 919-286-6859
e-mail: kager.durham@ncdur.va.gov
http://www.durham.va.gov
Jeffrey F Kager, Chief Library Service

Clinical medicine, pre-clinical sciences, allied health sciences, management, research, patient health education.

11686 US Department of Veterans Affairs: Fayettville Medical Center Library Service
2300 Ramsey Street
Fayetteville, NC 28301-3856
910-488-2120
800-771-6106
Fax: 910-822-7093
http://www.visn6.va.gov
Pamela A Jackson, Chief Library Service
Karen March, Manager

Medicine, nursing, dentistry, patient education, allied health sciences.

11687 US Department of Veterans Affairs: Salisbury Medical Center Library
1601 Brenner Avenue
Salisbury, NC 28144-2515
704-638-9000
800-469-8262
Fax: 704-638-3395
e-mail: medical@interpath.com
http://www.visn6.va.gov
Nancy J Stine, Learning Research Service

Psychology, psychiatry, nursing, internal medicine, alcoholism, surgery, gerontology, dentistry.

North Dakota

11688 Alzheimer Early Stages, 2nd Edition
Hunter House Publisher
PO Box 2914
Alameda, CA 94501
510-865-5282
800-266-5592
Fax: 510-865-4295
e-mail: ordering@hunterhouse.com
http://www.hunterhouse.com
Christina Sverdrup, Customer Service Manager
Daniel Kuhn MSW, Author

First steps in caring and treatments. This book is for family memebrs and friends of those recently diagnosed with Alzheimer's Disease.

320 pages Frequency: Paperback

11689 Art of Getting Well
Hunter House Publisher
PO Box 2914
Alameda, CA 94501
510-865-5282
800-266-5592
Fax: 510-865-4295
e-mail: ordering@hunterhouse.com
http://www.hunterhouse.com
Christina Sverdrup, Customer Service Manager
David Spero RN, Author

A five step plan for maximazing health when you have a chronic illness.

224 pages Frequency: Paperback

11690 Chiropractor's Self-Help Back and Body Book
Hunter House Publisher
PO Box 2914
Alameda, CA 94501
510-865-5282
800-266-5592
Fax: 510-865-4295
e-mail: ordering@hunterhouse.com
http://www.hunterhouse.com
Christina Sverdrup, Customer Service Manager
Samuel Homola DC, Author

How to relieve common aches and pains at home and on the job.

320 pages Frequency: Paperback

11691 Get Fit While You Sit
Hunter House Publisher
PO Box 2914
Alameda, CA 94501
510-865-5282
800-266-5592
Fax: 510-865-4295
e-mail: ordering@hunterhouse.com
http://www.hunterhouse.com
Christina Sverdrup, Customer Service Manager
Charlene Torkelson, Author

Easy workouts from your chair, three total body workout programs that can be done from your chair-anywhere. $17.95 for Spiral Bound.

160 pages Frequency: Paperback

11692 I Can't Chew Cookbook
Hunter House Publisher
PO Box 2914
Alameda, CA 94501
510-865-5282
800-266-5592
Fax: 510-865-4295
e-mail: ordering@hunterhouse.com
http://www.hunterhouse.com
Christina Sverdrup, Customer Service Manager
J Randy Wilson, Author

Delicious soft-diet recipes for people with chewing, swallowing and Dry-Mouth Disorders. $22.95 Spiral Bound.

224 pages Frequency: Paperback

11693 Journey to Pain Relief
Hunter House Publisher
PO Box 2914
Alameda, CA 94501
510-865-5282
800-266-5592
Fax: 510-865-4295
e-mail: ordering@hunterhouse.com
http://www.hunterhouse.com
Christina Sverdrup, Customer Service Manager
Phyllis Berger, Author

Hands-on guide to breakthroughs in pain treatment.

288 pages Frequency: Paperback

11694 Joy of Laziness
Hunter House Publisher
PO Box 2914
Alameda, CA 94501
510-865-5282
800-266-5592
Fax: 510-865-4295
e-mail: ordering@hunterhouse.com
http://www.hunterhouse.com
Christina Sverdrup, Customer Service Manager
Peter Axt PhD, Author
Michaela Axt Gadermann MD, Author

Why life is better slower-and how to get there.

160 pages Frequency: Paperback

Libraries & Information Centers/Ohio

11695 Living Well in a Nursing Home
Hunter House Publisher
PO Box 2914
Alameda, CA 94501
510-865-5282
800-266-5592
Fax: 510-865-4295
e-mail: ordering@hunterhouse.com
http://www.hunterhouse.com

Christina Sverdrup, Customer Service Manager
Lynn Dickinson MA, Author
Xenia Vosen PhD, Author

Positive aspects of nursing homes. How to recognize signs that a family member needs extra support. How to identify and select the best facility.

288 pages Frequency: Paperback

11696 Menopause Without Medicine
Hunter House Publisher
PO Box 2914
Alameda, CA 94501
510-865-5282
800-266-5592
Fax: 510-865-4295
e-mail: ordering@hunterhouse.com
http://www.hunterhouse.com

Christina Sverdrup, Customer Service Manager
Linda Ojeda PhD, Author

Menopause Without Medicine, 5th Editon. Non medical approach to menopause. Covers Heart Disease, mood swings, cognitive decline, osteoporosis, weight control, insomnia.

400 pages Frequency: Paperback

11697 North Dakota State Library: Disability Services
604 E Boulevard Avenue
Bismarck, ND 58505
701-328-2492
800-472-2104
Fax: 701-328-2040
e-mail: tbooks@state.nd.us
http://ndsl.lib.state.nd.us/

Stella Cone, Head Local Library Disability
Sue Bicknell, Department Manager

Provides talking book and radio reading service the citizens of North Dakota are print impaired. Radio reading service limited to western half of North Dakota.

11698 Prostate Health Workbook
Hunter House Publisher
PO Box 2914
Alameda, CA 94501
510-865-5282
800-266-5592
Fax: 510-865-4295
e-mail: ordering@hunterhouse.com
http://www.hunterhouse.com

Christina Sverdrup, Customer Service Manager
Newton Malerman, Author

A practical guide for the prostate cancer patients.

160 pages Frequency: Paperback

11699 Services for the Visually Impaired: Department of Public Instruction
PO Box 8117
Grand Forks, ND 58202
701-777-2604

Betty Bender, Contact

Eligible readers of North Dakota receive library service from the regional library in Pierre, South Dakota.

11700 ShapeWalking
Hunter House Publishing
PO Box 2914
Alameda, CA 94501
510-865-5282
800-266-5592
Fax: 510-865-4295
e-mail: ordering@hunterhouse.com
http://www.hunterhouse.com

Christina Sverdrup, Customer Service Manager
Marilyn Bach PhD, Author

ShapeWalking, 2nd Edition. Six easy steps to your best body.

144 pages Frequency: Paperback

11701 Strength Training for Seniors
Hunter House Publisher
PO Box 2914
Alameda, CA 94501
510-865-5282
800-266-5592
Fax: 510-865-4295
e-mail: ordering@hunterhouse.com
http://www.hunterhouse.com

Christina Sverdrup, Customer Service Manager
Michael Fekete CSCS, ACE, Author

How to rewind your biological clock. Reduce a person's biological age by 10-20 years.

160 pages Frequency: Paperback

11702 US Department of Veterans Affairs: Fargo Medical Center Library
2101 Elm Street N
Fargo, ND 58102-2417
701-451-4600
Fax: 701-451-4690
e-mail: nicholas.j@fargo.va.gov
http://www.va.gov

Diane Nordeng, Manager

Medicine, dentistry, nursing, social work, hospital administration.

11703 Writing from Within
Hunter House Publisher
PO Box 2914
Alameda, CA 94501
510-865-5282
800-266-5592
Fax: 510-865-4295
e-mail: ordering@hunterhouse.com
http://www.hunterhouse.com

Christina Sverdrup, Customer Service Manager
Bernard Selling, Author

Writing from Within, 3rd Edition. A guide to creativity and life story writing.

320 pages Frequency: Paperback

Ohio

11704 Benjamin Rose Institute Library
11900 Fairhill Road
300
Cleveland, OH 44120-1053
216-791-8000
Fax: 216-231-7323
e-mail: kbensing@bbs2.net
http://www.benrose.org

Karen Bensing, Librarian

Aged - research, home care, long-term care, nursing homes, social work, nursing.

11705 Case Western Reserve University Elderly Care Research Center
Library
Mather Memorial
Room 226
Cleveland, OH 44106
216-368-3280
Fax: 216-368-2676
e-mail: exk@po.cwru.edu

Eva Kahana, PhD Director Research Center
Gerald Korngold, Administrator

Sociology of aging, gerontology, medical sociology, environmental psychology/sociology.

11706 Cleveland Public Library
325 Superior Ave
Cleveland, OH 44114
216-623-2800
Fax: 330-623-7036
e-mail: lbphmgr1@library.cpl.org
http://www.cpl.org/index.php?q=node/17

Barbara Mates, Librarian

Summer reading programs, braille writer, magnifiers, closed-circuit TV, large-print photocopier, cassette books and magazines, children's books on cassette, home visits and other reference materials on blindness and other handicaps.

11707 Frank Reed Memorial Library
PO Box 760
Steubenville, OH 43952-5760
740-282-3810
Fax: 740-282-0769
e-mail: info@iaetf.org

Rita Marker, Executive Director

11708 Harris Library, MSASS, Case Western Reserve University
Mandel School of Applied of Applied Social Sciences
11235 Belliflower Road
Cleveland, OH 44106-7164
216-368-2302
Fax: 216-368-2106
e-mail: harrisref@case.edu
http://www.msass.case.ed/harrislibrary

Samantha C Skutnik, Library Director

Social work, social welfare, poverty, alcoholism, aging, child welfare, minorities, community organization, mental health.

11709 Lourdes College Duns Scotus Library
6832 Convent Boulevard
Sylvania, OH 43560-4805
419-885-3211
Fax: 419-882-3786
e-mail: truffing@lourdes.edu
http://www.lourdes.edu/library

Mary Tho Ruffing, Library Director
Robert Helmer, President

Religious studies, health sciences, psychology, occupational therapy, gerontology, art.

11710 Miami University Humanities and Social Sciences Department
King Library
Oxford, OH 45056
513-529-1809
Fax: 513-529-1682
e-mail: quayrch@lib.muohio.edu
http://www.lib.muohio.edu

Richard H Quay, Head Hum/Social Science Dept

Business, history, education, American literature, political science, geography, sociology, anthropology, gerontology, military and naval science, foreign language, theater, economics, philosophy, psychology, religion, area studies, black world studies, women's studies, American studies.

11711 Ohio Regional Library for the Blind and Physically Handicapped
800 Vine Street Library Square
Cincinnati, OH 45202
513-369-6900
Fax: 513-369-3111
http://www.cincinnatilibrary.org
TDD 513-665-3384

Deliaan A Gettler, President

Summer reading programs, braille writer, magnifiers, closed-circuit TV, large-print photocopier, cassette books and magazines, children's books on cassette, home visits and other reference materials on blindness and other handicaps.

11712 Ohio School for the Deaf Library
500 Morse Road
Columbus, OH 43214-1899
614-995-1566
Fax: 614-995-1567
e-mail: A.Kent@freenet.columbus.oh.us
http://www.ohioschoolforthedeaf.org

Ada Kent, Manager

General collection, deafness, professional education.

11713 Public Library of Cincinnati and Hamilton Outreach Services Department
800 Vine Street
Cincinnati, OH 45202-2071
513-369-6900
Fax: 513-369-4586
e-mail: os@cincinnatilibrary.org
http://www.cincinnatilibrary.org

Elizabeth Zuelke, Head Outreach Services
Kimber L Fender, Executive Director

Programs and materials for children with special needs, books by mail for the homebound, delivery service to nursing homes and other facilities, extensive collection of large print books.

11714 State Library of Ohio: Talking Book Program
274 E 1st Avenue
Suite 100
Columbus, OH 43201-3692
614-644-7061
800-686-1531
Fax: 614-995-2186
e-mail: jbow@sloma.state.oh.us
http://winslo.state.oh.us

Roger Verny, Deputy State Librarian
Jo Budler, Librarian

A machine-lending agency for the visually and physically impaired.

11715 US Department of Veterans Affairs: Brecksville Medical Center Library
10000 Brecksville Road
Brecksville, OH 44141-3204
440-526-3030
Fax: 440-838-6045
http://www.va.gov

Janet Monk Gillette, Chief Regional Library Service

Psychology, nursing, psychiatry, social work, clinical medicine.

11716 US Department of Veterans Affairs: Chillicothe Medical Library
17273 State Route 104
Chillicothe, OH 45601-8608
740-773-1141
800-358-8262
Fax: 740-773-1141
e-mail: mlibrary@bright.net
http://www.chillicothe.va.gov

Jennifer Gray, Chief Library Service
Douglas Moorman, Executive Director

Psychiatry, nursing, medicine, allied health.

11717 US Department of Veterans Affairs: Cincinati Learning Resources Service
3200 Vine Street
Cincinnati, OH 45220-2213
513-861-3100
888-267-7873
Fax: 513-475-6500
e-mail: ohcin@forum.va.gov; mason.sandra@cincinnati.v
http://www.cincinnati.va.gov

Sandra Mason, Chief

Medicine, mental health, nursing, surgery.

11718 US Department of Veterans Affairs: Dayton Medical Center Library Service
4100 W 3rd Street
Dayton, OH 45428-9000
937-268-6511
800-368-8262
Fax: 937-262-2179
http://www.dayton.va.gov

Niki B Conca, Chief Library Service
Kathleen Mannix, Manager

Medicine, nursing, hospital administration, patient education, local VA history.

Libraries & Information Centers/Oklahoma

11719 University of Cincinnati Medical Center Libraries
3110 Vine Street
Po Box 210033
Cincinnati, OH 45221-0033
513-556-1424
Fax: 513-558-9102
http://libraries.uc.edu

Doris A Haag, Director

Nursing, clinical medicine, gerontology, education, sociology.

Oklahoma

11720 Hillcrest Medical Center Library
1120 S Utica Avenue
Tulsa, OK 74104-4090
918-579-1000
Fax: 918-579-8388
e-mail: pcook@hillcrest.com

Peggy Cook, Librarian
Steve Dobbs, CEO

Medicine, nursing, aging and health.

11721 Integris Baptist Medical Center: Wann Langston Memorial Library
3300 NW Expressway
Oklahoma City, OK 73112-4999
405-949-3011
Fax: 405-945-3883
e-mail: suttem@integris.health.com
http://www.integris-health.com

Cheryl Suttles, Director Medical Library
Stanley F Hupfeld, CEO

Geriatrics, medicine, nursing, hospital management.

11722 Oklahoma Library for the Blind & Physically Handicapped
300 NE 18th Street
Oklahoma City, OK 73105-3212
405-521-3514
Fax: 405-521-4582
e-mail: library@drs.state.ok.us
http://www.library.state.ok.us

Geraldine Adams, Librarian

Summer reading programs, braille writer, magnifiers, closed-circuit TV, large-print photocopier, cassette books and magazines, children's books on cassette, home visits and other reference materials on blindness and other handicaps.

11723 Tulsa City-County Library System
400 Civic Center
Tulsa, OK 74103-3830
918-596-7977
http://www.tulsalibrary.org

Ellen Ontko, Librarian
Linda Saferite, Executive Director

Summer reading programs, braille writer, magnifiers, closed-circuit TV, large-print photocopier, cassette books and magazines, children's books on cassette, home visits and other reference materials on blindness and other handicaps.

11724 US Department of Veterans Affairs: Oklahoma City Medical Center Library
921 NE 13th Street
Oklahoma City, OK 73104-5007
405-270-0501
866-835-5273
Fax: 405-270-1560
e-mail: okokc@forum.va.gov
http://www.oklahoma.va.gov

Charles T Coker, Chief
Tom Duchene, Plant Manager

Medicine, patient health education.

Oregon

11725 Oregon School for the Blind Media Center
700 Church Street SE
Salem, OR 97301-3714
503-378-3820
Fax: 503-373-7537
http://www.ode.state.or.us

Margie C Jordan, Media Specialists

Visual and hearing impairment; multihandicapped.

11726 Oregon State Library
250 Winter Street NW
Salem, OR 97310
503-378-4243
Fax: 503-585-8059
e-mail: mary.c.mohr@state.or.us
http://www.oregon.gov
TDD 503-378-4276

Mary Mohr, Librarian
Jim Scheppke, Manager

Summer reading programs, braille writer, magnifiers, closed-circuit TV, large-print photocopier, cassette books and magazines, children's books on cassette, home visits and other reference materials on blindness and other handicaps.

11727 US Department of Veterans Affairs: Portland Medical Library
PO Box 1034
3710 SW US Veterans Hospital Rd
Portland, OR 97239
503-220-8262
800-949-1004
Fax: 503-273-5319
e-mail: Jordan.Cathy@forum.va.gov
http://www.visn20.med.va.gov/portland

Mara R Wilhelm, Chief Library Service
Kim Winn, Manager

Medicine, nursing, allied health sciences, psychology, basic sciences.

11728 US Department of Veterans Affairs: Roseburg Medical Center Library Service
913 NW Garden Valley Boulevard
Roseburg, OR 97470-6523
541-440-1000
800-549-8387
Fax: 541-440-1225
e-mail: slemmer@forum.va.gov
http://www.visn20.med.va.gov/roseburg/index.asp

Anna Slemmer, Acting Librarian
George Marnell, Manager

Medicine, patient education, management, nursing.

11729 US Department of Veterans Affairs: WhiteCity Library
8495 Crater Lake Highway
White City, OR 97503-3011
541-826-2111
Fax: 541-830-3500
e-mail: sarah.fitzpatrick@med.va.gov
http://www.va.gov

Sarah Fitzpatrick, Chief Library Service
George Andries, Executive Director

Medicine; general.

Pennsylvania

11730 Alzheimer Treatment Research Center Library
161 N Dithridge Street
Pittsburgh, PA 15213-2646
412-683-1181
Fax: 412-683-1181

Alzheimer's Disease, dementias, schizophrenia, brain circulation.

Libraries & Information Centers/Pennsylvania

11731 Behan Health Science Library
Coal Valley Road
Pittsburgh, PA 15236
412-469-5786
Fax: 412-469-5468
e-mail: shhmedlib@hslc.org

Ann Ferrari, Librarian

Medicine, nursing, and allied health sciences.

11732 Berks Deaf & Hard of Hearing Services Library
223 N 6th Street
Reading, PA 19601-3307
610-373-6992
Fax: 610-374-0379

Deafness.

11733 Carnegie Library of Pittsburgh
4400 Forbes Ave
Pittsburgh, PA 15213-1389
412-622-3114
Fax: 412-687-2442
e-mail: clbph@clpgh.org
http://www.carnegielibrary.org

Barbara Mistick, President/Director

Provides on loan recorded books and magazines, large print books, and described videos to Western Pennsylvannia residents unable to use standard printed materials due to visual, physical, or physically-based reading disabilities. Also loans special cassette and disc machines; does not loan equipment to play described videos. Information about disabilities and related agencies is also available.

11734 Center for Information Resources
4025 Chestnut Street
Floor 3
Philadelphia, PA 19104-3046
215-898-8108

Kristen MacLeod, Publications Coordinator

Information on physical disabilities and computer-related vocational rehabilitation.

11735 Fair Acres Center
Medical Library
340 N Middletown Road
Lima, PA 19037-0496
610-891-5700
Fax: 610-891-2705
Joseph Doughterty, Administrator

Medicine, nursing, geriatrics, allied health sciences.

11736 Free Library of Philadelphia
1901 Vine Street
Philadelphia, PA 19103
215-686-5322
Fax: 215-928-0856
e-mail: flpblind@library.phila.gov

Vickie Lange Collins, Librarian

Summer reading programs, braille writer, magnifiers, closed-circuit TV, large-print photocopier, cassette books and magazines, children's books on cassette, home visits and other reference materials on blindness and other handicaps.

11737 Overbrook School for the Blind Library
6333 Malvern Avenue
Philadelphia, PA 19151-2597
215-877-0313
Fax: 215-877-2709
http://www.obs.org

Julia A Flinchbaugh, Librarian
Bernadette Kappen, Executive Director

Standard, large print, and braille books for kindergarten through high school; general library of braille, tape, and print titles for primary, elementary, and high school; library of print for faculty members.

11738 Pennsylvania Department of Public Welfare Norristown State Hospital
Building 11
Norristown, PA 19401
610-313-5369
Fax: 610-313-5370
http://www.dpw.state.pa.us

Frieda Liem, Librarian

Psychiatry and neurology; clinical psychology; psychiatric nursing; psychiatric and clinical social work; activities therapy - recreational, music, occupational, vocational; aging; geriatrics; gerontology.

11739 Pennsylvania State University: Human Development Collection
201 Henderson Building
University Park, PA 16802-6506
814-865-1428
Fax: 814-865-3282
e-mail: healthhd@psu.edu
http://www.hhdev.psu.edu

Gerontology, adolescent and child psychology, marriage and family.

11740 Philadelphia Corporation for Aging Library
642 N Broad Street
Philadelphia, PA 19130-3049
215-765-9000
Fax: 215-765-9066
e-mail: sspencer@pcaphl.com
http://www.pcacares.org

Scott Spencer, Librarian
Rodney Williams, President

Gerontology, gerontological literature, programs for the aging.

11741 Polisher Research Institute Library: Philadelphia Geriatric Center
5301 Old York Road
Philadelphia, PA 19141-2912
215-456-2981
Fax: 215-456-2017
http://www.pgc.org

Sheryl Panka-Bryman, Librarian
Mary McCaffrey, Library Assistant

Gerontology, geriatrics, long-term care industry, psychology, sociology, housing, long-term care administration, anthropology, research methods, death and dying.

11742 Talbot Cancer Research Library
Fox Chase Cancer Center
Philadelphia, PA 19111
215-728-2710
Fax: 215-728-3655
e-mail: ALBERT@HSLC.ORG
http://www.fccc.edu/facilities/library/talbot

Karen M Albert, Librarian

Biochemistry, cancer, cell biology, chemistry, clinical research, experimental pathology, genetics.

11743 US Deparment of Veterans Affairs: Philadelphia Medical Center Library
University & Woodland Avenues
Philadelphia, PA 19104
215-823-5860
Fax: 215-823-5108
http://www.va.gov

Mark Marchino, Chief Library Service
Bob Lye, Manager

Medicine and allied health sciences.

11744 US Department of Veterans Affairs: Altoona James E Van Zandt Medical Center Library Service
2907 Pleasant Valley Boulevard
Altoona, PA 16602-4305
814-943-8164
Fax: 814-940-7895

Gerald Williams, Executive Director

Medicine, patient education, management.

11745 US Department of Veterans Affairs: Butler Medical Center Library
325 New Castle Road
Butler, PA 16001-2480
724-287-4781
800-362-8262
Fax: 724-282-4408
http://www.butler.va.gov

Mary Ann Wagner, Library Technician
David Wood, Executive Director

Nursing, general medicine.

Libraries & Information Centers/Rhode Island

11746 US Department of Veterans Affairs: Coatesville Medical Center Library
1400 Blackhorse Hill Road
Coatesville, PA 19320-2096
610-394-7711
Fax: 610-860-2135
e-mail: vamc@hslc.org
http://www.coatesville.va.gov

Andrew Henry, Librarian

Psychiatry, neurology, medicine, nursing, psychology, geriatrics.

11747 US Department of Veterans Affairs: Erie Medical Center Library
135 E 38th Street
Erie, PA 16504-1559
814-868-8661
800-274-8387
Fax: 814-860-2135
http://www1.va.gov/erie

Mary Nourse, Director

Medicine, nursing, geriatrics, quality assurance.

11748 US Department of Veterans Affairs: Lebanon Medical Center Library
1700 S Lincoln Avenue
Lebanon, PA 17042-7529
717-272-6621
800-409-8771
Fax: 717-228-6045
http://www.va.gov/lebanonvamc/

Medicine, aging and geriatrics, psychiatry.

11749 US Department of Veterans Affairs: Pittsburgh Education, Media and Reference Service
University Drive
Pittsburgh, PA 15240
866-482-7488
Fax: 412-688-6121
http://www.va.gov/pittsburgh/

Terrie R Wheeler, Chief MLS

Medicine, surgery, gerontology, and allied health sciences.

11750 US Department of Veterans Affairs: Wilkes-Barre Medical Center Library
1111 E End Boulevard
Wilkes Barre, PA 18711
570-824-3521
http://www.va.gov

Jay Suffren, Librarian
Roland Moore, CEO

Medicine, allied health sciences.

11751 Wistar Institute of Anatomy & Biology Library
3601 Spruce Streets
Philadelphia, PA 19104
215-898-3700
http://www.wistar.upenn.edu

Russel E Kaufman, President/CEO

Cancer, virus diseases, molecular immunology, molecular genetics, biochemistry.

Rhode Island

11752 Drug & Alcohol Treatment Association of Rhode Island: In-Rhodes Resource Center Library
90 Dean Street
Providence, RI 02903-1504
401-273-3731
Fax: 401-273-6349
e-mail: jdipippo@efortess.com

11753 Rhode Island Department of State Library for the Blind and Physically Handicapped
1 Capitol Hl
Providence, RI 02908-5816
401-222-2000
Fax: 401-277-4195
e-mail: richard@dsl.rhilinet.gov

Richard Ledue, Librarian
Robert L Carl Jr, Executive Director

Offers information and services for the visually impaired including reference materials, braille printers, braille writers, large-print books and more.

11754 US Department of Veterans Affairs: Providence Health Sciences Library
830 Chalkstone Avenue
Providence, RI 02908-4799
401-273-7100
866-590-2976
Fax: 401-457-3097
e-mail: pallotti.nicola@forum.va.gov
http://www.providence.gov

Nicola F Pallotti, Contact
Kipp Hartmann, Executive Director

Medicine, nursing, and allied health sciences.

South Carolina

11755 Captioned Media Program: National Association of the Deaf
1447 E Main Street
Spartanburg, SC 29307-2240
864-585-1778
Fax: 864-585-2611
e-mail: info@dcmp.org
http://www.dcmp.org
TTY 864-585-2617

Max Duckler, President/Founder Of Caption Max

Free loans of educational and entertainment captioned films and videos for deaf and hard of hearing people.

11756 South Carolina State Library
PO Box 11469
Columbia, SC 29202
803-734-8666
Fax: 803-734-8676
e-mail: reference@statelibrary.sc.gov
http://www.statelibrary.sc.gov
TDD 803-734-7298

David S Goble, Director/State Librarian

Summer reading programs, braille writer, magnifiers, closed-circuit TV, large-print photocopier, cassette books and magazines, children's books on cassette, home visits and other reference materials on blindness and other handicaps.

11757 US Deparment of Veterans Affairs: Columbia William Jennings Bryan-Dorn Veterans Hospital Library
Va Medical Center
6439 Garners Ferry Road
Columbia, SC 29209-1639
803-776-4000
Fax: 803-695-6739
http://www.va.gov/columbia/sc

Florence D Mays, Staff Librarian

Medicine, surgery, nursing, dentistry, psychiatry.

South Dakota

11758 South Dakota Human Services Center Medical Library
PO Box 76
Yankton, SD 57078
605-668-3165
Fax: 605-668-3222

Mary Lou Kostel, Librarian

Psychiatry, psychology, psychiatric nursing, gerontology, social work, medicine.

Libraries & Information Centers/Tennessee

11759 South Dakota State Library: Braille and Talking Book Program
800 Governors Drive
Pierre, SD 57501-2235
605-773-3131
800-423-6665
Fax: 605-773-6962
e-mail: library@state.sd.us
http://library.sd.gov
TDD 605-773-4950

Dan Siebersma, State Librarian
Quynn Verhelst, Sr. Secretary
Barb Templeton, Support Staff

Summer reading programs, braille writer, magnifiers, closed-circuit TV, large-print books, scripture videos, cassette books and magazines, children's books on cassette, home visits and other reference materials on blindness and other handicaps. Publishes quarterly newsletter for adults and children.

11760 US Department of Veterans Affairs: For Meade VA Black Hills Health Care System Medical Library
113 Comanche Road
Fort Meade, SD 57741-1002
605-347-2511
800-743-1070
Fax: 605-720-7171
http://www.blackhills.va.gov

Gene Stevens, Chief Librarian

Medicine and allied health sciences.

Tennessee

11761 LRC for Students with Disabilities: MSU Library Reference Department
Memphis State University
Memphis, TN 38152
901-678-2208

Ross Johnson, Reference Librarian

Information on physical disabilities, blindness and visual impairments.

11762 Tennessee Library for the Blind and Physically Handicapped
403 7th Avenue N
Nashville, TN 37243-1409
615-741-7996
800-342-3308
Fax: 615-532-9293
e-mail: jeanne.sugg@state.tn.us
http://www.tennessee.gov/tsla/

Ruth Hemphill, Director
Donna Cirenza, Assistant Director

Offers free public library services to those unable to hold, read or turn the pages of ordinary books and magazines due to physical or visual impairment. Special library materials are provided by the Library of Congress, and free mailing privileges for these materials is provided through the US Post Office. Playback equipment is also provided.

11763 US Department of Veterans Affairs: Johnson City Medical Center Library
Corner Of Lamont And Sydney Streets
Mountain Home, TN 37684
423-926-1171
Fax: 423-979-3519
http://www.mountainhome.va.gov

Medicine and allied health sciences.

11764 US Department of Veterans Affairs: Memphis Medical Center Library
1030 Jefferson Avenue
Memphis, TN 38104-2127
901-523-8990
800-636-8262
Fax: 901-577-7251
e-mail: Taylor.Mary_Virginia@forum.va.gov
http://www.memphis.va.gov

Patricia Pittman, Director/CEO

Medicine, dentistry, nursing.

11765 US Department of Veterans Affairs: Murfreesboro Medical Center Library Service
3400 Lebanon Pike
Murfreesboro, TN 37129
615-867-6000
800-876-7093
Fax: 615-867-5768
http://www.tennesseevalley.va.gov

Pamela Howell, Chief Librarian Services

Psychiatry, medicine, nursing, geriatrics.

11766 US Department of Veterans Affairs: Nashville Medical Center Library Service
1310 24th Avenue South
Nashville, TN 37212-2637
615-327-4751
Fax: 615-321-6350
http://www.tennesseevalley.va.gov

Medicine, nursing, dentistry, surgery.

11767 University of Memphis Libraries: Audiology, Speech Language, Pathology Branch
807 Jefferson Avenue
Memphis, TN 38105-5042
901-678-5846
Fax: 901-525-1282
http://exlibris.memphis.edu

John Swearengen, Library Assistant

Audiology, speech pathology.

Texas

11768 American Heart Association National Center Library
National Center Library
7272 Greenville Avenue
Dallas, TX 75231-4596
214-373-6300
Fax: 214-706-1211
e-mail: vanessap@heart.org
http://www.americanheart.org

Vanessa S Perez, Reference Consultant
M Cass Wheeler, CEO

Cardiovascular and cerebrovascular diseases.

11769 Center for the Rights of the Terminally Ill Resource Library
3308 Glade Creek Drive
PO Box 54246
Hurst, TX 76054-2064
817-656-5143
Fax: 817-788-1658
e-mail: crti@eaze.net

Offers information and publications.

11770 Christian Education for the Blind
4200 S Freeway Drive
Suite 702
Fort Worth, TX 76115
817-920-0444
Fax: 817-920-0777
e-mail: rdyer@bcebonline.com
http://www.bcebonline.org

Rodger Dyer, Executive Director

Offers braille and large print books and cassettes for the visually impaired.

11771 Houston Public Library: Access Center
500 McKinney Street
Houston, TX 77002-5000
713-236-1313
http://www.houstonlibrary.org

Mary Crocker, Supervisor

Offers Kurzweil Reading Machine 400, closed-circuit TV, braille writer, reference materials on visual impairments and other handicaps.

11772 Houston Public Library: Acres Homes Branch
8501 W Montgomery Road
Houston, TX 77088-7118
832-393-1700
Fax: 832-393-1701

Johnson Dweban, Manager

Libraries & Information Centers/Texas

11773 Houston Public Library: Bracewell Branch
10115 Kleckley Drive
Houston, TX 77075-3409
832-393-2580
Fax: 832-393-2581

11774 Houston Public Library: Carnegie Branch
1050 Quitman Street
Houston, TX 77009-7858
832-393-1720
Fax: 832-393-1721

11775 Houston Public Library: Collier Regional Branch
6200 Pinemont Drive
Houston, TX 77092-3204
832-393-1740
Fax: 832-393-1741

T R Lynch, Manager

11776 Houston Public Library: Dixon Branch
8002 Hirsch Road
Houston, TX 77016-5602
832-393-1760
Fax: 832-393-1768

Chris Hu, Manager

11777 Houston Public Library: Flores Branch
110 N Milby Street
Houston, TX 77003-1931
832-393-1780
Fax: 832-393-3178

Elvia Pillado, Manager

11778 Houston Public Library: Hillendahl Branch
2436 Gessner Drive
Houston, TX 77080-5012
832-393-1940
Fax: 832-393-1941

11779 Houston Public Library: Moody Branch
9525 Irvington Boulevard
Houston, TX 77076-5247
832-393-1950
Fax: 832-393-1951

Sergio Tineda, Manager

11780 Houston Public Library: Park Place Regional Branch
8145 Park Place Boulevard
Houston, TX 77017-3032
832-393-1970
Fax: 832-393-1971

Regina Stemmer, Manager

11781 Houston Public Library: Pleasantville Branch
1520 Gellhorn
Houston, TX 77029
832-393-2330
Fax: 832-393-2331

11782 Houston Public Library: Robinson-Westchase Branch
3223 Wilcrest Drive
Houston, TX 77042-3349
832-393-2011
Fax: 832-393-2021

11783 Houston Public Library: Scenic Woods Regional Branch
10677 Homestead Road
Houston, TX 77016-2703
832-393-2030
Fax: 832-393-2031

Ande Tensae, Manager

11784 Houston Public Library: Smith Branch
3624 Scott Street
Houston, TX 77004-4744
832-393-2050
Fax: 713-747-1924

Lori Smith, Manager

11785 Houston Public Library: Tuttle Branch
702 Kress Street
Houston, TX 77020-4912
832-393-2100
Fax: 713-674-0093

Beatriz Deangulo, Manager

11786 Houston Public Library: Young Branch
5260 Griggs Road Palm Center
Houston, TX 77021
832-393-2140
Fax: 832-393-2141

11787 Kerrville State Hospital Professional Library
721 Thompson Drive
Kerrville, TX 78028-5199
512-458-7111
http://www.dshs.state.tx.us

Geriatrics, psychology, medicine, nursing, social studies.

11788 Mind Science Foundation Library
117 W El Prado Drive
San Antonio, TX 78212-2024
210-821-6094
Fax: 210-821-6199
e-mail: info@mindscience.org
http://www.mindscience.org

Joseph Dial, Executive Director

Parapsychology, psychology, mind-made health, creativity, traditional healing, self-esteem, brain mapping.

11789 REACH/Resource Center on Independent Living
1205 Lake Street
Fort Worth, TX 76102-4501
817-870-9082
Fax: 817-877-1622
e-mail: reachftw@reachcils.org
http://www.reachcils.org

Charlotte Stewart, Director
Anne Ancy, Case Manager

Information and referral services, peer counseling, independent living skills training, loaner equipment, advocacy assistance, ADA technical assistance and social/recreational activities.

11790 Texas Department of Health Library
1100 W 49th Street
Austin, TX 78756-3101
512-458-7355
888-963-7111
Fax: 512-458-7474
e-mail: avlibrary@tdh.state.tx.us
http://www.dshs.state.tx.us
TDD 512-458-7708

Cindy Milam Faries, Program Administrator
Lesa Walker, MD

Public health, infectious diseases, laboratory methods, environmental health, dental health, pediatrics, nursing, hospitals, heart, cancer, health promotion, health funding.

11791 Texas State Library
PO Box 12927
Austin, TX 78711-2927
800-252-9605
Fax: 512-936-0685
e-mail: tbp.services@tsl.state.tx.us
http://www.texastalkingbooks.org
TDD 512-463-5449

Ava Smith, Director

Reading materials (recorded cassette, large print, braille) and equipment for persons who cannot read standard print, Talking Book Program is part of the national library service. Patrons must meet eligibility requirements.

11792 Texas State Library Talking Book Program
PO Box 12927
Austin, TX 78711-2927
512-463-5458
800-252-9605
Fax: 512-936-0685
e-mail: tbp.services@tsl.state.tx.us
http://www.texastalkingbooks.org

Ava M Smith, Director

Libraries & Information Centers/Utah

Free library services to Texas residents for persons with vision, physical and learning impairments.

11793 Texas State Technical College: Waco Library
3801 Campus Drive
Waco, TX 76705-1696
254-799-3611
800-792-8784
e-mail: lkoepf@tstc.edu
http://walib.tstc.edu

Linda S Koepf, Library Director
Elton Stuckly, President

Laser electro-optics, electronics, air pilot training, aviation maintenance, automotive mechanics, biomedical equipment operation.

11794 US Department of Veterans Affairs Medical Center Library Service
7400 Merton Minter Street
San Antonio, TX 78229-4404
210-617-5300
888-686-6350
Fax: 210-617-5246
e-mail: janean.garreto@med.na.gov
http://www.vasthcs.med.va.gov

Janean Garrett, Medical Librarian
Charles Sepich, CEO

Medicine, allied health sciences.

11795 US Department of Veterans Affairs: Temple Medical Center Medical Library
Olin E Teague Veterans Admini
1901 Veterans Memorial Drive
Temple, TX 76504
254-778-4811
Fax: 254-743-2338
http://www.va.gov

Joann Greenwood, Chief Library Service

Medicine, surgery, nursing, dentistry.

11796 US Department of Veterans Affairs: Amarillo Hospital Library
6010 Amarillo Blvd, West
Amarillo, TX 79106
806-355-9703
800-687-8262
Fax: 806-354-7860
http://www.amarillo.va.gov

General medicine, surgery, nursing, dentistry.

11797 US Department of Veterans Affairs: Big Spring Hospital Library
300 Veterans Blvd
Big Spring, TX 79720
915-263-7361
800-472-1365
Fax: 915-264-4834
http://www.bigsprings.va.gov

Samie Pequeno, Contact

General medicine, surgery.

11798 US Department of Veterans Affairs: Bonham North Texas Health Care System
1201 E 9th Street
Bonham, TX 75418-4059
903-583-2111
800-924-8387
Fax: 903-583-6694
e-mail: scott.nancy@bva.gov
http://www.north-texas.med.va.gov

Nancy Clark, Contact
Deann Hicks, Manager

Medicine and allied health sciences.

11799 US Department of Veterans Affairs: Dallas Library Service
4500 S Lancaster Road
Dallas, TX 75216-7167
214-742-8387
800-849-3597
Fax: 214-857-1171
e-mail: clark.nancy@forum.va.gov; campbell.shirley@da
http://www.north-texas.med.va.gov

Nancy A Clark, Chief Library Service
Kathy Posh, Manager

Medicine, surgery, allied health sciences, management.

11800 US Department of Veterans Affairs: Houston Medical Center Library
2002 Holcombe Boulevard
Houston, TX 77030-4211
713-791-1414
800-553-2278
Fax: 713-794-7218
http://www.houston.med.va.gov

Jerry E Barrett, Librarian
Edgar Tucker, CEO

Medicine.

11801 US Department of Veterans Affairs: Kerrville South Texas Veterans Health Care System
3600 Memorial Boulevard
Kerrville, TX 78028-5768
830-896-2020
http://www.vasthcs.med.va.gov

Lois A Johnson, Division Manager Library Service

Medicine and allied health sciences.

11802 US Department of Veterans Affairs: Waco Medical Center Library
4800 Memorial Drive
Waco, TX 76711-1329
254-752-6581
800-423-2111
Fax: 254-297-3161
http://www.central-texas.med.va.gov

JoAnn Greenwood, Site Manager
Paul Batterton, CEO

Psychiatry, neurology, psychology, nursing, gerontology, posttraumatic stress.

Utah

11803 US Department of Veterans Affairs: Salt Lake City Hospital Medical Library
500 Foothill Drive
Salt Lake City, UT 84148
801-582-1565
800-613-4012
Fax: 801-584-1289
http://www.saltlakecity.va.gov

Carl Worstell, Chief Librarian
Kirk Davis, Manager

Medicine, surgery, psychiatry, emergency medicine, research, allied health sciences.

11804 Utah State Library: Blind and DisabledServices
250 N 1950 West
Suite A
Salt Lake City, UT 84116-7901
801-715-6789
800-662-5540
e-mail: blind@utah.gov
http://www.blindlibrary.utah.gov
TDD 801-715-6721

Bessie Oakes, Program Manager
Julie Anderson, Executive Secretary

Braille, large print, and audio books; specialized playback equipment, and a radio will be loaned by the library to eligible registered readers without charge.

Vermont

11805 Austine School: Library Media Center
209 Austine Drive
Brattleboro, VT 05301-6818   802-258-9500
                                   Fax: 802-254-3921
                       e-mail: joan@austine.pvt.kiz.vt.us
                                   http://vcdhh.org
Anne Potter, Director
Education of the deaf.

11806 Brattleboro Retreat: Asa Keyes Medical Library
Anna Marsh Lane
PO Box 803
Brattleboro, VT 50301   802-257-7785
                                   Fax: 802-258-3791
                       e-mail: jmulhall@retreathealthcare.org
Robert E Simpson, President/CEO

Retreat Healthcare was founded as the Brattleboro Retreat in 1834, by a $10,000 donation by Anna Marsh as attested to in her will. In addition to its regular services, Retreat Healthcare offers numerous programs to the community free of charge, including The Wellness in Windham County series, co-sponsored with Brattleboro Memorial Hospital, Brattleboro Area Hospice & Brooks Memorial Library, and various lectures, films, forums, and special educatational events open to the community. No registration necessary unless otherwise noted.

11807 US Department of Veterans Affairs: White River Junction Medical & Regional Office CenterLibrary Service
215 North Main Street
White River Junction, VT 05009
                                   800-827-1000
                                   Fax: 802-296-5150
                                   http://www.va.gov
Richard Haver, Chief Library Service
Medicine, surgery, psychiatry, nursing.

11808 Vermont Department of Libraries
PO Box 1870
109 State Street
Montpelier, VT 05602   802-828-3261
                                   Fax: 802-828-2199
                                   e-mail: ssu@dol.state.vt.us
                                   http://dol.state.vt.us

Summer reading programs, braille writer, magnifiers, closed-circuit TV, large-print photocopier, cassette books and magazines, children's books on cassette, home visits and other reference materials on blindness and other handicaps.

Virginia

11809 Alexandria Library Talking Book Service
5005 Duke Street
Alexandria, VA 22314-1220   703-519-5911
                                   e-mail: emccaffr@lea.eda
                                   http://www.alexandria.lib.va.vs
                                   TDD 703-838-4568
Patricia Bates, Librarian
Luis Labra, Manager

Summer reading programs, braille writer, magnifiers, closed-circuit TV, large-print photocopier, cassette books and magazines, children's books on cassette, home visits and other reference materials on blindness and other handicaps.

11810 Alexandria Library: Special Collections
717 Queen Street
Alexandria, VA 22314-2420   703-838-4555
                                   Fax: 703-838-5021
                                   http://www.alexandria.lib.va.us
Joyce A McMullin, Librarian
Leslie Morales, Reference Librarian
Luis Labra, Manager
1994

11811 Amelia Historical Society: Amelia Historical Library
PO Box 113
Amelia Court House, VA 23002   804-561-3180
                                   http://www.ameliava.com
Dorothy Eppes, President
Jerry Morris, VP
1957

11812 American College of Health Care Administrators: Information Center
12100 Sunset Hills Road
Suite 130
Reston, VA 20190   703-739-7900
                                   Fax: 703-435-4390
                                   e-mail: info@achca.org
                                   http://www.achca.org
Marianna Kern Grachek, President/CEO
Long-term care, gerontology.

11813 American Life League Library
PO Box 1350
Stafford, VA 22555-1350   540-659-4171
                                   Fax: 540-659-2586
                                   e-mail: sysop@all.org
                                   http://www.all.org
Judie Brown, President

11814 Arlington County Department of Libraries
1015 N Quincy Street
Arlington, VA 22201-4603   703-358-5990
                                   Fax: 703-358-5962
                                   TDD 703-358-6320
Roxanne Barnes, Librarian

Summer reading programs, braille writer, magnifiers, closed-circuit TV, large-print photocopier, cassette books and magazines, children's books on cassette, home visits and other reference materials on blindness and other handicaps.

11815 Bedford Research Consultants
PO Box 3074
Falls Church, VA 22043   703-560-8998
                                   Fax: 703-560-8999
                                   e-mail: deansr@sprintmail.com
Lorna M Dailey, President

Foreign social security and pensions, institutional investments, international business.

11816 Central Rappahannock Regional Library
1201 Caroline Street
Fredericksburg, VA 22401-3701   540-372-1144
                                   Fax: 540-373-9411
                                   e-mail: nschiff@hq.crrl.org
                                   TDD 540-371-9165
Nancy Schiff, Librarian
Donna Cote, Executive Director

Offers reference materials on blindness and other disabilities.

11817 Division for the Visually Handicapped
1920 Association Drive
Reston, VA 20191-1500   703-359-1100
                                   Fax: 703-359-1111
Kay Ferrell, President

Members are teachers, college faculty members, administrators, supervisors and others concerned with the education and welfare of visually handicapped and blind children and youth. This is a division of the Council For Exceptional Children.

Libraries & Information Centers/Washington

11818 Fairfax County Public Library
12000 Government Center Parkway
Suite 324
Fairfax, VA 22035
703-324-3185
Fax: 703-765-5893
e-mail: sjapikse@leo.vsla.edu
http://www.fairfaxcounty.gov/library
TDD 703-660-8524

Jeanette Studley, Librarian
Lindsey Culin, Manager

Summer reading programs, braille writer, magnifiers, closed-circuit TV, large-print photocopier, cassette books and magazines, children's books on cassette, home visits and other reference materials on blindness and other handicaps.

11819 Newport News Public Library System
112 Main Street
Newport News, VA 23601-4105
757-597-2917
Fax: 757-591-7425
e-mail: shalswin@leo.vsla.edu
http://www.nngov.com/library/front-page

Sue Balswin, Librarian

Summer reading programs, braille writer, magnifiers, closed-circuit TV, large-print photocopier, cassette books and magazines, children's books on cassette, home visits and other reference materials on blindness and other handicaps.

11820 Roanoke City Public Library System
706 South Jefferson St
Roanoke, VA 24017-5333
540-853-2473
Fax: 540-853-1030
e-mail: main.library@roanokeva.org

Rebecca Cooper, Librarian
Wendy Allen, Manager

Summer reading programs, braille writer, magnifiers, closed-circuit TV, large-print photocopier, cassette books and magazines, children's books on cassette, home visits and other reference materials on blindness and other handicaps.

11821 Staunton Public Library Talking Book Center
1 Churchville Avenue
Staunton, VA 24401-3229
540-332-3902
Fax: 540-332-3906
e-mail: talkingbook@ci.staunton.via.us
http://www.staunton.va.us

Oakley Pearson, Librarian

Sub-regional library for those who are unable to use standard print materials due to visual, physical, or reading disability.

11822 Thomas Balch Library
208 W Market Street
Leesburg, VA 20176-2709
703-737-7195
Fax: 703-737-7150
e-mail: balchlib@leesburgva.gov
http://www.leesburgva.com/library/balch.html

Jane Sullivan, Librarian Manager
Alexandra Gressitt, Manager

11823 US Department of Veterans Affairs: Hampton Medical Center Library and Educational Resources
100 Emancipation Drive
Hampton, VA 23667
757-722-9961
Fax: 757-723-6620
http://www.visn6.va.gov

Jacqueline Bird, Director
Joseph Williams Jr, Executive Director

Surgery, medicine, nursing, psychology, patient education.

11824 US Department of Veterans Affairs: Richmond Hospital Library
1201 Broad Rock Boulevard
Richmond, VA 23249
804-675-5000
Fax: 804-675-5142
http://www.richmond.va.gov

Eleanor Rollins, Chief Library Service
Paul Phillips, Manager

Medicine, psychology, sociology.

11825 US Department of Veterans Affairs: Salem Medical Center Library
1970 Roanoke Boulevard
Salem, VA 24153-6404
540-982-2463
888-982-2463
Fax: 540-983-1079
http://www.salem.va.gov

Jean A Kennedy, Chief Librarian

Medicine, psychiatry, nursing, allied health sciences.

11826 University Library Services
901 Park Avenue
2033
Richmond, VA 23284-9056
804-828-1116

Sally Jacobs, Reference Librarian
John E Ulmschneider, Executive Director

Library services for the visually disabled.

11827 Virginia Commonwealth University Virginia Center on Aging Information Resources Center
PO Box 980229
Richmond, VA 23298
804-828-1166
Fax: 804-828-7905
e-mail: jarachel@vcu.edu

Jason Rachel, Public Relations Specialist
Edward F Ansello PhD, Director
John Guthmiller, Executive Director

Gerontology, mental health, sociology and the politics of aging, geriatrics, family relationships, long-term care.

11828 Virginia State Library for the Visually and Physically Handicapped
1901 Roane Street
Richmond, VA 23222-4826
804-692-3976
Fax: 804-692-3976

Mary Ruth Halapatz, Librarian

Summer reading programs, braille writer, magnifiers, closed-circuit TV, large-print photocopier, cassette books and magazines, children's books on cassette, home visits and other reference materials on blindness and other handicaps.

Washington

11829 Fred Hutchinson Cancer Research Center: Arnold Digital Library
1100 Fairview Ave North
Seattle, WA 98109
206-288-7222
Fax: 206-667-5826
e-mail: aclark@fhcrc.org
http://www.fhcrc.org/library

Leukemia, immunology, molecular biology, cancer research, genetics, cancer prevention, soft tissue tumors, biostatistics, epidemiology.

11830 Lutheran Bible Institute of Seattle Library
4221 228th Avenue SE
Issaquah, WA 98029-9299
425-392-0400
Fax: 425-392-0404
e-mail: lbi-libr@lbi.edu; lbi-cats@lbi.edu
http://www.tlc.edu

Irene A Hausken, Head Librarian
John Stamm, President

Bible; theology - doctrinal, moral, pastoral, devotional; religion and philosophy; Christian church; missions; psychology; social sciences; Christian education; youth work; gerontology; Pacific Northwest Indians.

11831 Northwest Geriatric Education Center
PO Box 358123
1910 Fairview Ave E, Suite 203
Seattle, WA 98195-8123
206-685-7478
Fax: 206-685-3436
e-mail: sgural@u.washington.edu
http://depts.washington.edu

Susan Guralnick, Associate Director

Geriatrics.

11832 US Department of Veterans Affairs: Seattle Puget Sound Health Care System
1660 S Columbian Way
Seattle, WA 98108-1532
206-764-1010
800-329-8387
Fax: 206-764-2224
http://www.puget-sound.med.va.gov

Elizabeth L Serha, Chief Library Service

Medicine.

11833 US Department of Veterans Affairs: Spokane Medical Center Library
4815 N Assembly Street
Spokane, WA 99205-6185
509-434-7000
800-325-7940
Fax: 509-434-7119
e-mail: curtis-kellett.mary@forum.va.gov
http://www.visn20.med.va.gov

Mary Curtis-Kellett, Chief Library Service

Medicine and allied health sciences.

11834 US Department of Veterans Affairs: Tacoma/Puget Sound Health Care System
96000 Veterans Drive
Tacoma, WA 98493
253-582-8440
800-329-8387
Fax: 253-589-4029
e-mail: dupree.karen@forum.va.gov
http://www.va.gov

Elizabeth L Serha, Chief Library Service

Psychiatry, psychology, general medicine, nursing, patient health.

11835 US Department of Veterans Affairs: Walla Walla Jonathan M Wainwright Memorial VA Medical Library
77 Wainwright Drive
Walla Walla, WA 99362-3975
509-525-5200
888-687-8863
Fax: 509-527-3452
http://www.va.gov

Max J Merrell, Chief Librarian

Medicine, surgery, nursing, allied health sciences.

11836 Washington Library for the Blind and Physically Handicapped
821 Lenora Street
Seattle, WA 98129
206-464-6930
Fax: 206-464-0247
e-mail: wtbbl@spl.lib.wa.us
http://www.spl.lib.wa.us

Jan Ames, Librarian

Summer reading programs, braille writer, magnifiers, closed-circuit TV, large-print photocopier, cassette books and magazines, children's books on cassette, home visits and other reference materials on blindness and other handicaps.

West Virginia

11837 Kanawha County Public Library
123 Capitol Street
Charleston, WV 25301-2686
304-343-4646
Fax: 304-348-6530
http://kanawha.lib.wv.us

Dixie Smith, Librarian
Linda Wright, Manager

Summer reading programs, braille writer, magnifiers, closed-circuit TV, large-print photocopier, cassette books and magazines, children's books on cassette, home visits and other reference materials on blindness and other handicaps.

11838 Ohio County Public Library Services for the Blind and Physically Handicapped
52 16th Street
Wheeling, WV 26003-3671
304-232-0244
Fax: 304-232-6848

Lori Nicholson, Contact
Dorothy Thomas, Manager

11839 Parkersburg and Wood County Public Library
3100 Emerson Avenue
Parkersburg, WV 26104-2414
304-420-4587
Fax: 304-420-4589

Michael Hickman, Contact
Brian E Raitz, Manager

Services for the bind and physically handicapped.

11840 US Department of Veterans Affairs: Beckley Library Service
200 Veterans Avenue
Beckley, WV 25801-6444
304-255-2121
Fax: 304-255-2431
http://www.beckley.va.gov

Lois M Watson, Chief Library Service
Debbie Coloski, Manager

Medicine, nursing, surgery.

11841 US Department of Veterans Affairs: Clarkburg Loouis A Johnson VA Medical Center Library
1 Med Center Drive
Clarksburg, WV 26301-4155
304-623-3461
Fax: 304-626-7026
http://www.va.gov

Wanda F Kincaid, Chief Library Service
Mary McCloud, Manager

Medicine.

11842 US Department of Veterans Affairs: Huntinington Learning Resource Center
1540 Spring Valley Drive
Huntington, WV 25704-9300
304-429-6741
800-827-8244
Fax: 304-429-6713
http://www.hungington.va.gov

Ronald Maynard, Chief LRC
Philip S Elkins, Executive Director

Clinical medicine.

11843 US Department of Veterans Affairs: Martinsburg Learning Resources Service
510 Butler Ave
Martinsburg, WV 25401
304-263-0811
800-817-3807
Fax: 304-262-7433
http://www.martinsburg.va.gov

Eric Vance, Cheif Learning Resources Service

Medicine, surgery, allied health sciences.

Libraries & Information Centers/Wisconsin

11844 West Virginia Library Commission
1900 Kanawha Boulevard E
Charleston, WV 25305
304-558-2041
Fax: 304-558-2044
e-mail: fesenmf@mars.wr1c.wvnet.edu
http://librarycommission.lib.wv.us
J.D. Waggoner, State Librarian

Summer reading programs, braille writer, magnifiers, closed-circuit TV, large-print photocopier, cassette books and magazines, children's books on cassette, home visits and other reference materials on blindness and other handicaps.

11845 West Virginia School for the Blind
301 E Main Street
Romney, WV 26757-1828
304-822-4800
Fax: 304-822-3370
e-mail: cjohn@access.mountain.net
http://wvsdb2.state.k12.wv.us
Cynthia Johnson, Librarian
Jane McBride, Administrator

Summer reading programs, braille writer, magnifiers, closed-circuit TV, large-print photocopier, cassette books and magazines, children's books on cassette, home visits and other reference materials on blindness and other handicaps.

Wisconsin

11846 Gateway Technical College Learning Resource Center
3520 30th Avenue
Kenosha, WI 53144-1690
262-564-2200
Fax: 262-656-8768
e-mail: peronaj@gateway.tec.wi.us
http://www.gtc.edu
Gerald F Perona, Distribution Librarian
Samuel Borden, President

Office education, law enforcement, nursing and allied health sciences, horticulture, aeronautics, electronics, physical therapy, data processing.

11847 Marquette University Libraries Special Collections and University Archives
1415 W Wisconsin Avenue
Milwaukee, WI 53233-2287
414-288-7214
Fax: 414-288-6709
e-mail: elstonc@vms.csd.mu.edu
Charles B Elston, Head Master
Nicholas Burckel, Executive Director

Catholic social thought and action, Catholic Indian ministry, Marquette University history, recent US political history, Catholic religious formation and vocation ministries.

11848 Rock County Health Care Center Staff Library
PO Box 351
Janesville, WI 53547
608-757-5150
Fax: 608-757-5010
Ruth Beyer, Inservice Director

Psychiatry, psychiatric social work, geriatrics and nursing.

11849 Sentry Insurance Company Library
1800 N Point Drive
Stevens Point, WI 54481-1283
715-346-6000
Fax: 715-346-6405
John Carlson, Library Services Coordinator
Dale Schuh, CEO

Insurance - property/casualty and life; pensions; law; business management.

11850 US Department of Veterans Affairs: Tomah Health Sciences Library
500 E Veterans Street
Tomah, WI 54660-3105
608-372-3971
800-872-8662
Fax: 608-372-1670
http://www.va.gov
Phyllis Goetz, Manager

Psychiatry, neurology, general medicine, psychology, nursing, geriatrics, gerontology.

11851 University of Wisconsin Laboratory for Cancer Research Library
Madison, WI 53706
608-263-2400
Fax: 608-262-2824

Cancer, molecular biology, virology.

11852 Wisconsin Regional Library for the Blind: Talking Book Program
813 W Wells Street
Milwaukee, WI 53233-1436
414-286-3045
800-242-8822
Fax: 414-286-3102
e-mail: lbph@milwaukee.gov
TDD 414-286-3548
Marsha Valance, Regional Librarian
Judith Glover, Assistant Librarian

Circulates recorded materials, playback equipment and braille materials to print-handicapped Wisconsin residents.

11853 Wisconsin Veterans Museum & Research Center
30 W Mifflin Street
Madison, WI 53703-2589
608-267-1790
Fax: 608-264-7615
e-mail: veterans.museum@dva.state.wi.us
http://http://museum.dva.state.wi.us/
Dr Richard Zeitlin, Director
Came Bohman, Reference Archivist
Gayle Martinson, Manager

Military and veterans history.

Wyoming

11854 US Department of Veterans Affairs: Cheyenne Medical and Regional Office Center
Learning Resources
2360 E Pershing Boulevard
Cheyenne, WY 82001-5356
800-827-1000
e-mail: skidmore.kerry@forum.va.gov
http://www.va.gov
Kerry Skidmore, Chief LRS

Medicine, nursing.

11855 US Department of Veterans Affairs: Sheridan Medical Center Library
1898 Fort Road
Sheridan, WY 82801
307-672-3473
866-822-6714
Fax: 307-672-1900
http://www.sheridan.va.gov
Pat Carlson, Chief Library Service

Psychiatry, psychology, medicine, nursing, administration, post-traumatic stress disorder.

11856 Wyoming Services for the Visually Disabled
State Department of Education
2300 Capitol Avenue
Cheyenne, WY 82002
307-777-7690
Fax: 307-777-6234
http://www.k12.wy.us
Kent Jensen, Contact

Eligible readers of Wyoming receive library service from the regional library in Salt Lake City, Utah.

Print Resources for Older Americans/Publishers

Publishers

11857 Activity Factory
2227 Rock Island Court
Roswell, GA 30278
770-979-5727
Fax: 770-979-7010
Dennis Goodwin, Owner

Publishes books on recreation ideas for nursing home activity programs.

11858 Alliance Press
3911 5th Avenue
Suite 202
San Diego, CA 92103-3146
858-454-3610
Fax: 858-454-2432
Joe Casciani PhD, President

Self-publishes a book on aging and mental health. Offers audio cassettes. Reaches market through direct mail. Presently inactive.

11859 American Association of Homes and Services for the Aging
901 E Street NW
Suite 500
Washington, DC 20004-2037
202-661-5700
Fax: 202-783-2255
Patricia A McGinn, Contact
Daniel Smith, Vice President

Publishes paperback books about homes for the aging. Offers video cassettes. Does not accept unsolicited manuscripts.

11860 American Foundation for the Blind
11 Penn Plaza
Suite 300
New York, NY 10001-2018
212-502-7600
Fax: 212-620-2105
Carl Augusto, President

Publishes pamphlets, books, and other informational materials pertaining to the blind and visually impaired.

11861 Association for Gerontology in Higher Education
1001 Connecticut Avenue NW
Suite 410
Washington, DC 20036-5529
202-289-9806
Fax: 202-429-6097
e-mail: aghe@mnsinc.com
Derek Stepp, Manager

Nonprofit association of 320 institutions of higher education committed to gerontology education, training, and research. Publishes a national directory, a series of brief bibliographies, research reports, and annual meeting abstracts. Offers a quarterly newsletter, AGH Exchange, and a national database on gerontology. Reaches market through direct mail.

11862 Beverly Cracom Publications
12131 Dorsett Road
Suite 109
Maryland Heights, MO 63043-2418
314-291-3988
800-880-3988
Fax: 314-291-3829
Laura Plummer, Marketing

Publishes medical and trade books on aging and long-term care. Accepts unsolicited manuscripts. Reaches market through wholesalers and distributors, including Majors Co., JA, Matthews Book Co., and Rittenhouse Book Distributors.

11863 Braille Documents
Metrolina Sight Services
704 Louise Avenue
Charlotte, NC 28204-2128
704-372-3870
Fax: 704-372-3872
Robert Scheffel, Manager

This production shop creates Braille and large-print documents.

11864 Briggs Corporation
PO Box 1698
Des Moines, IA 50306-1698
515-327-6400
800-247-2343
Fax: 800-222-1996
Kristin Keeline, Prof. Resources Product Manager
Merwyn Dan, CEO

Publishes on health care related subjects. Reaches market through direct mail and telephone sales.

11865 Calyx Books & Calyx Journal
PO Box B
Corvallis, OR 97339
541-753-9384
Fax: 541-753-0515
e-mail: calyx@proaxis.com
http://www.calyxpress.org
Margarita Donnelly, Director

Publishes books by women query for guidelines. Distributed by Consortium Book Sales and Distributes small press, Distributors, and others.

11866 Caresource Healthcare Communications
426 Yale Avenue N
Seattle, WA 98109-5431
800-448-5213
Fax: 206-682-2901
e-mail: service@caresource.com
http://www.caresource.com
Diane Kenny, Contact

Specializes in print and electronic publications for senior care and healthcare. We serve consumers and senior care and healthcare professionals and provider organizations. Products and services include: healthy aging books, booklets, and brochures; videotapes; websites; web based education; and custom publishing.

11867 Center for Bio-Gerontology
PO Box 11097
Pensacola, FL 32524-1097
904-484-0595
Fax: 850-474-5255
e-mail: drdean@bis.win.net
Kum-Ja Chae, Marketing Director

Publishes books related to biological aging, aging retardation, and life extension. Accepts unsolicited manuscripts. Reaches market through direct mail and wholesalers.

11868 Center for Public Representation
PO Box 260049
Madison, WI 53726
608-251-4008
800-369-0388
Fax: 608-251-1263
Melissa Hoberg, Publications Assistant

Publishes materials relevant to the elderly and health care providers, and consumer publications on guardianship and health care.

11869 Center for Thanatology Research & Education
391 Atlantic Avenue
Brooklyn, NY 11217-1701
718-858-3026
Fax: 718-858-3026
e-mail: hdporn@mindspring.com
Roberto Halton, Contact

Objective is to distribute and promote all publications on aging, dying, and death and gravestones studies, and release relevant titles in these subjects. Offers audio cassettes, video cassettes, a newsletter and a journal. Reaches market through direct mail and trade sales. Does not accept unsolicited manuscripts.

11870 Center for the Study of Human Rights
1108 Iab
New York, NY 10027
212-854-2479
Fax: 212-316-4578
e-mail: cshr@columbia.edu
J Paul Martin, Executive Director

Print Resources for Older Americans/Publishers

Promotes teaching and research in international human rights. Publishes occasional papers, reports, proceedings, and course syllabi. Reports and documents copyrighted.

11871 Educare Press
PO Box 75086
Seattle, WA 98175
206-781-2665
Fax: 206-784-7556

Kieran O'Mahony, Publisher

Publishes educational, geography and aging titles. Reaches market through direct mail and trade sales. Does not accept unsolicited manuscripts.

11872 Edward Feil Productions
4614 Prospect Avenue
Cleveland, OH 44103-4394
216-881-0040
Fax: 216-751-6434
e-mail: naomifeil@aol.com
http://www.vfvalidation.org

Edward R Feil, President

Publishes a book helping the aging using the Validation Method. Also offers films and video cassettes. Reaches market through direct mail and telephone sales. Produces Videos (VHS) helping caregivers communicate with older people who are diagnosed with a dementia.

11873 Elder Book Store
Elder Books
2115 Elliston Place
Nashville, TN 37203-5289
615-327-1867
Fax: 415-488-4720

Randy Elder, Manager

11874 Elder Books
PO Box 490
Forest Knolls, CA 94933
415-488-9002
800-909-COPE
Fax: 415-488-4720

Susan Sullivan, Director

Publishes how-to books for families and caregivers looking after Alzheimer's patients and books of Celtic interest. Accepts unsolicited manuscripts. Reaches market through direct mail, trade sales, and wholesalers.

11875 Employee Benefit Research Institute
2121 K Street NW
Suite 600
Washington, DC 20037-1800
202-659-0670
Fax: 202-775-6312
e-mail: publications@ebri.org
http://www.ebri.org

Cheri Meyer, Contact
Dallas Salisbury, President

Publishes to contribute to the development of effective and responsible public policy in the employee benefit field. Also publishes newsletters, abstracts, journals, and speeches. Reaches market through direct mail.

11876 Gateway Books
2023 Clemens Road
Oakland, CA 94602-1915
510-530-0299
Fax: 510-530-0497

Judith Merwin, Publisher

Publishes a series of books aimed at those interested in retirement living in the US and abroad. Accepts proposals for manuscripts. Reaches market through direct mail and Publishers Group West.

11877 Gerontological Society of America
1275 K Street NW
Suite 350
Washington, DC 20005-4083
202-842-1275
Fax: 202-842-1150
e-mail: geron@geron.org

Jennifer Campi, Production Editor
Carol Schutz, Executive Director

Publishes five print journals on aging. Offers a database, a calendar online only, and both a print and an online newsletter. Accepts unsolicited manuscripts. Reaches market through trade sales.

11878 Gibbs Associates
PO Box 706
Boulder, CO 80306
303-444-6032
800-378-5089
Fax: 303-444-6032
e-mail: bgibbs@bigtreemurphy.com
http://www.bigtreemurphy.com

Betty Gibbs, President

Publishes a book on Alzheimer's disease, and a book of poetry. Reaches market through direct mail and internet.

11879 Golden Aspen Publishing
PO Box 370333
Denver, CO 80237
303-694-6555
800-639-9664
Fax: 303-694-0737
e-mail: GAPub@concentric.net

Jo Peddicord, Publisher

Publishes books on image and health tips for women over age 50. Does not accept unsolicited manuscripts. Reaches market through direct mail, trade sales, and wholesalers and distributors, including Ingram Book Co., Baker & Taylor Books, and Quality Books.

11880 Golden Horizons
5238 Pullman Avenue NE
Seattle, WA 98105-2140
206-525-8160
Fax: 206-525-8160

Publishes retirement housing guides and information directories for seniors and children of aging parents. Reaches market through direct mail, telephone sales, and Slawson Communications.

11881 Human Growth & Development Associates
6780 S Adams Way
Centennial, CO 80122-1802
303-771-8424
Fax: 303-773-1264

Mary K Kouri, Co-Owner

Self-publisher of workbook for life planning for older adults. Presently inactive.

11882 Idyll Arbor
PO Box 720
Ravensdale, WA 98051
360-825-7797
Fax: 425-432-3726
e-mail: sales@idyllarbor.com
http://www.IdyllArbor.com

Tom Blaschko, Contact

Publishes books for activity professionals, recreational therapists and allied therapists. Reaches market through direct mail, catalogs, reviews and listings, professional conferences and general book stores. Accepts unsolicited manuscripts from experienced professionals in health care. Catalog of approximately 200 books, assessments and games are available.

11883 Impact Publishers
PO Box 910
San Luis Obispo, CA 93406
805-543-5911
Fax: 805-543-4093
e-mail: bookswithimpact@compuserve.com

Connie Magee, Marketing Manager

Publishes books on human development. Accepts unsolicited manuscripts from human service professionals. Reaches market through direct mail and trade sales.

11884 John Muir Publications
PO Box 613
Santa Fe, NM 87504
505-982-4078
800-285-4078
Fax: 505-988-1680
e-mail: marketing@muir.com

Publishes general nonfiction on travel, young reader nonfiction, and auto manuals. Accepts unsolicited manuscripts. Reaches market through direct mail, trade sales, wholesalers, and distributors.

11885 Key Publications
827 2nd Street
Apt 104
Santa Monica, CA 90403-1048
818-224-4344
800-735-0015
Fax: 818-224-4343
e-mail: keypubs@aol.com
http://www.knowledgetree.com
Phil Ferguson, General Manager

Reaches market through Baker & Taylor Books, Ingram Book Co. Does not accept unsolicited manuscripts. Offers books, newsletters, colums, and more.

11886 Legal Counsel for the Elderly
601 E Street NW
Washington, DC 20049
202-434-2170
Fax: 202-434-6464
Sally Balch Hurme, Publications Coordinator
Jan May, Manager

Disseminates legal information on the problems of the elderly to attorneys, paralegals, other advocates, and consumers. Offers two newsletters, the bimonthly Elder Law Forum and a quarterly, Trainingworks. Reaches market through direct mail. Does not accept unsolicited manuscripts.

11887 Leisure Living
2445 S Laurel Avenue
Springfield, MO 65807-8152
417-886-0101
Fax: 417-887-9250
Robert S Tillman, President

Publishes video cassettes of retirement locations throughout the US Reaches market through direct mail, Quality Books, New Age Video, Unique Books, and Edu-Tech Corp. Accepts unsolicited manuscripts.

11888 National Citizens' Coalition for Nursing Home Reform
1828 L Street NW
Suite 801
Washington, DC 20036-5104
202-332-2275
Fax: 202-332-2949
Laurie Demsey, Contact
Alice Hedt, Executive Director

Publishes on nursing home reform.

11889 National Interfaith Coalition on Aging
300 D Street SW
Suite 801
Washington, DC 20024-4709
202-479-1200
Fax: 202-479-6674
James P Firman, CEO

Publishes information on resources in the field of aging for church and synagogue leaders, and other professionals. Offers conferences and workshops. Reaches market through direct mail.

11890 Northern Expressions Publishing
PO Box 136
Maple City, MI 49664
616-334-3360
Fax: 616-334-3360
Lynn McAndrews, President

Publishes on Alzheimer's disease. Reaches market through direct mail.

11891 Otterbein Homes Program Department
585 N Street
Route 741
Lebanon, OH 45036
513-932-7218
Fax: 513-932-5159
Charles W Peckham, Author/Educator

Publishes books on and for the elderly. Reaches market through direct mail. Does not accept unsolicited manuscripts.

11892 Palomino Press
10420 Queens Boulevard
Apt 9p
Forest Hills, NY 11375-3619
718-297-5053
Fax: 718-297-5053
e-mail: palomino@aol.com
Josephine Pender, Manager

Publishes nonfiction books. Reaches market through direct mail, trade sales, distributors, and wholesalers. Does not accept unsolicited manuscripts.

11893 Papier-Mache Press
627 Walker Street
Watsonville, CA 95076-4119
831-763-1420
800-927-5913
Fax: 831-763-1421
e-mail: papierma@sprynet.com
Shirley Coe, Acquisitions Editor

Publishes theme anthologies by, for, and about women. Query for guidelines with self-addressed, stamped envelope. Reaches market through direct mail, trade sales, and wholesalers, including Bookpeople, Baker & Taylor Books, Ingram Book Co., Moving Books, and New Leaf Distributing Co.

11894 Potentials Development
40 Hazelwood Drive
Suite 101
Amherst, NY 14228-2230
716-691-6601
800-691-6602
Fax: 716-691-6620
Patricia Maurer, Administrative Associate

Established by two occupational therapists who had seen the need for educational materials in the field of aging. Their philosophy is that age is not an event, it is an ongoing process. Provides resources to the elderly, their families and caregivers. Materials on Alzheimer's, resources for social workers, family support groups, etc.

11895 Resources for Rehabilitation
33 Bedford Street
Suite 19a
Lexington, MA 02420-4330
781-862-6455
Fax: 781-861-7517
e-mail: orders@rfr.org
Susan L Greenblatt, Treasurer

Publishes books and large print brochures designed to help seniors and people with disabilities function independently. Offers desk references for professionals. Reaches market through direct mail. Does not accept unsolicited manuscripts.

11896 Richard W. Waring
845 Heathermoor Lane
Perrysburg, OH 43551-2980
419-244-6711
Fax: 419-244-4791

Provides financial and estate planning resource materials for individuals, professional, financial, and estate planners, and pre-retirement programs. Conducts seminars for nonprofit organizations. Offers The Collection Basket, a fund raising newsletter, and Presenting and Extending Our Catholic Heritage, a pamphlet. Reaches market through direct mail and trade sales.

11897 SCENE
Braille Institute
741 N Vermont Avenue
Los Angeles, CA 90029-3514
310-234-0339
800-BRA-ILLE
Serial Beccai, Owner

Offers information on the organization, question and answer column, articles on the newest technology and more for visually impaired persons.

Print Resources for Older Americans/Publishers

11898 Scripps Ranch Publications
10301 Scripps Lake Drive
San Diego, CA 92131-1258
858-538-8158
Fax: 858-538-8154

Nancy Assaf, Manager

Publishes for working adults who are concerned about their future retirement. Presently inactive.

11899 Senior Fitness Productions
1780 Penfield Road
Penfield, NY 14526-2104
585-586-7548
800-306-3137
Fax: 585-385-9581
e-mail: bpc@senior-fitness.com
http://www.senior-fitness.com

Betty Perkins-Carpenter, President

Publishes books and guides for senior citizens. Does not accept unsolicited manuscripts. Reaches market through direct mail trade sales and workshops/keynotes.

11900 Sequoia Retirement Services
1911 San Ysidro Drive
Beverly Hills, CA 90210-1520
310-859-1961
Fax: 310-859-7077
e-mail: sequoiaretire@juno.com

T Lan, Owner

Publishes materials on retirement and retirement planning. Offers a personal computer-based program that is used in conjunction with the materials. Accepts unsolicited manuscripts. Reaches market through seminar sales.

11901 Southern California Senior Life
6500 Wilshire Boulevard
Suite 1200
Los Angeles, CA 90048-4932
213-427-3200
Fax: 323-933-9261
e-mail: seniorlife@aol.com
http://www.seniorlifeusa.com

Micheal Carpernter, Advertising Director
Laurence Vittes, Editor
Dirk Stoehr, Manager

Publishes a directory of special services, help lines, medical care, legal and financial information, etc., for seniors. Offers a monthly newspaper, Southern California Senior Life. Reaches market through direct mail. Does not accept unsolicited manuscripts.

11902 Springer Publishing Company
536 Broadway
New York, NY 10012-3915
212-431-4370
Fax: 212-941-7842
e-mail: springer@springerpub.com
http://www.springerpub.com

Ursula Springer, President

Publishers of scholarly books and journals in fields of psychology, social work, medicine/public health, gerontology and geriatrics, nursing, and rehabilitation. Reaches market through direct mail, Baker & Taylor, Login Brothers, and J. A. Majors. Does not accept unsolicited manuscripts.

11903 Tattersall Press
1920 Grant Street
Elkhart, IN 46514-4018
219-264-6692
800-652-7027
Fax: 219-262-0201

Paula Lochmandy, Owner

Publishes a book on cosmetic surgery. Accepts unsolicited manuscripts. Reaches market through commission representatives, direct mail, trade sales, radio, television and wholesalers and distributors, including Baker & Taylor Books.

11904 Third Age Press
1075 NW Murray Road
Suite 277
Portland, OR 97229-5501
503-690-3251
Fax: 503-669-5325

Al Tauber, VP

Publishes on aging and discrimination against the aged. Does not accept unsolicited manuscripts. Reaches market through trade sales and wholesalers, including Bookpeople, Quality Books, Unique Books, Pacific Pipeline, Baker & Taylor Books, and Upper Access.

11905 Thornapple Publishing Company
PO Box 256
Ada, MI 49301
616-676-1583
Fax: 616-676-1583

Robert Redd, President

Publishes on retirement and non royalty short plays. Does not accept unsolicited manuscripts. Distributes for Gateway Books, Bristol, Contemporary Books, and Goldfish. Reaches market through direct mail.

11906 Tide Book Publishing Company
PO Box 101
York Harbor, ME 03911
207-363-4534

Rose Safran, President

Publishes on social science, health, aging, women, and the arts. Accepts unsolicited manuscripts.

11907 Tiresias Press
116 Pinehurst Avenue
New York, NY 10033-1755
212-568-9570
Fax: 212-568-9570

Dorothy Lewis, President

Publishes books in the health field and for nurses. Accepts unsolicited manuscripts. Reaches market through direct mail, reviews and listings, plus wholesalers and distributors.

11908 Transaction Publishers
390 Campus Drive
Somerset, NJ 08873-1102
732-445-1245
888-999-6778
Fax: 732-748-9801
http://www.transactionpub.com

Periodic updates on new large print titles.

11909 University of Texas at Austin Association for Mental Health
PO Box 7998
Austin, TX 78713-7998
512-471-5940
Fax: 512-471-9608

Susan Lowrance, Contact

Publishes materials on mental health. Offers audio cassettes of radio interviews, proccedings of seminars, and quarterly newsletters. Reaches market through direct mail and trade sales.

Travel & Recreation/Transportation

Transportation

11910 Access Travel: Airports
Airport Council International - North America
1775 K Street NW
Suite 500
Washington, DC 20006-1529 202-293-8500
Fax: 202-331-1362
Gregory Principato, President

About 553 airports worldwide; dot matrix tabulation. Entries include: Airport name, location, TDD and toll free numbers of hotels and rental cars, indication of presence or absence of about 60 facilities and services of special importance to persons in wheelchairs and to blind, deaf, and elderly persons.

50 pages Frequency: Irregular

11911 Access to Travel Magazine
Admix Publishing
29 Bartlett Lane
Delmar, NY 12054-1105 518-439-4146
888-439-4146
Fax: 518-439-9004
e-mail: will@accesstravelmag.com
Will DeRuve, President
Connie Mayer, Editor

Focusing on travel for people with disabilities.

Frequency: Bimonthly

11912 America West Airlines/US Airways
4000 E Sky Harbor Blvd.y
Phoenix, AZ 85034 480-693-0800
800-235-9292
http://www.usairways.com
J Scott Kirby, Executive VP Sales/Marketing
Tom Cartwright, Manager

Senior saver pack: book of 4 or 8 one way coupons. Tickets require 14 day advance purchase; other restrictions apply. 10% off regular priced air fares for people 62 years and older.

11913 American Airlines
PO Box 619616
dFW Airport
Fort Worth, TX 75261-9616 817-963-1234
Fax: 817-967-4162
http://www.aa.com
TDD 800-543-1586
Greg Clark, Managing Director
Gerard J Arpey, CEO

Senior Traveler Coupon Books contain either four or eight one-way tickets for anywhere in the 48 continental states or the Carribean. Tickets are good for 1 year, are nontransferable, and must be reserved 14 days in advance; and there is a $25 fee to change reservations. There is also a 10% discount on regular priced fares. For people 62 years and older.

11914 Amtrak Railways
PO Box 2709
Washington, DC 20013-2709 800-872-7245
http://www.amtrak.com
David L Gunn, President/CEO

15% off travel Monday through Thursday for people 62 years and older.

11915 Avis Rent A Car
6 Sylvan Way
Parsippany, NJ 07054-3826 973-496-3500
800-230-4898
http://www.avis.com
TDD 800-331-2323
Ronald L Nelson, Chairman/CEO
F Robert Salerno, President/COO
Larry De Shon, Executive VP Operations

Requires 24-hour notice for hand control vehicles, available in any location across the US. 5-15% off car rentals fo people of 50 years and older.

11916 British Airways
7520 Astoria Boulevard
Flushing, NY 11370-1190 718-335-0464
800-403-0882
Fax: 718-397-4204
http://www.britishairways.com
John Lampl, VP Communications

Privileged Traveler Program: 10% off regular priced air fares, cars, hotels, etc., also includes other benefits. For people 60 years and older. Companion must be 50 years or older.

11917 CEH
4457 63rd Circle
Pinellas Park, FL 33781-5981 727-522-0364
866-244-1150
Fax: 727-522-9024
http://www.liftsandramps.com
Andrew E Manatos, President
Phillip Faas, Owner

New vans, used vans, rental vans; specializing in quad conversions, all types of handicap equipment. Celebrating 25 years in business.

11918 Continental Airlines
1600 Smith Street
Houston, TX 77002-7362 713-324-5000
800-525-0280
http://www.continental.com
Lawrence W Kellner, President/CEO

Check website for occasional Senior discounts.

11919 Continental Airlines - Senior Programs
http://www.contnental.com/
General information about special discounts for senior citizens flying with Continental Airlines are available on this site.

11920 Delta Shuttle
Po Box 20706
Atlanta, GA 30320 404-715-2600
800-933-5935
http://www.delta-air.com
Gerald Grinstein, CEO

Senior Pass: half-price tickets to and from New York, Washington D.C., and Boston. Flight times and days vary: Monday through Friday 10:00 a.m. to 2:30 p.m.; 7:30 p.m. to 11:59 p.m.; all day Saturday and Sunday. For people 65 years and older.

11921 Directory of Accessible Van Rentals
Twin Peaks Press
PO Box 129
Vancouver, WA 98666 360-694-2462
800-637-2256
Fax: 360-696-3210
e-mail: twinpeak@pacifier.com
http://www.netm.com

Rental companies in the US and Canada that provide vans that are accessible to disabled travelers. Entries include: Company name, address, phone, location, name and title of contact, geographical area served, description of services.

11922 Disabled Driver's Mobility Guide
AAA
1000 AAA Drive
Heathrow, FL 32746-5060 407-444-7961
Fax: 407-444-7956
e-mail: khamada@national.aaa.com
Kay Hamada, Mailing Contact/Editor

Travel & Recreation/Transportation

Approximately 550 driving aid manufacturers, driving schools, publishers, government agencies, universities, and other organizations and companies offering services and products to the disabled driver; over 20 VA-approved hand control and lift manufacturers, and augmented driving systems. Entries include: Organization, publisher, or manufacturer name, address, phone, code for products or services; travel tips and state insurance commissioners.

210 pages Frequency: Biennial

11923 Dollar Rent-a-Car
5330 E 31st Street
Tulsa, OK 74153-1167
918-669-3000
800-800-4000
Fax: 918-669-8563
http://www.dollar.com

Gary Paxton, President/CEO
Steven Hildebrand, Senior Executive VP

Discounts vary among locations.

11924 El Al Israel Airlines
15 E 26th Street
New York, NY 10010
212-768-9200
800-223-6700
Fax: 212-852-0793
http://www.elal.com

David Hermesh, President
Michael Mayer, Manager

Golden Age fare: 15% off regular apex fare to Israel. Must purchase tickets 14 days in advance. For people 60 years and older.

11925 Greyhound Bus Info Senior Discounts
http://www.greyhound.com/
Greyhound Bus Senior Discounts.

11926 Greyhound Buslines
PO Box 660362
Dallas, TX 75266-0362
972-789-7000
800-231-2222
e-mail: kplaske@greyhound.com
http://www.greyhound.com

Craig Lenzh, President/CEO
Jack W Haugsland, Executive VP/COO

Five percent discount to Seniors on all fares.

11927 Hawaiian Airlines
3375 Koapaka Street
Honolulu, HI 96819-1800
808-835-3700
800-367-5320
Fax: 808-835-3690
http://www.hawaiianair.com

Mark B Dunkerley, President/CEO
Keoni Wagner, VP Public Affairs

10% off excursion fares from the islands to the mainland. No discounts for flights between islands. For people 60 years and older.

11928 Horizon Air
19521 Pacific Highway S
Seattle, WA 98188-5499
206-241-6757
800-547-9308
Fax: 203-248-6200
http://www.horizonair.com

Jeff Pinneo, President/CEO
Cheryl Temple, Public Affairs
Dan Russo, Director Mktging/Communications

Book of four or eight one way coupons. 14 day advance purchase required; other restrictions apply. For people 62 years and older.

11929 Housing and Transportation of the Handicapped
William Hein & Company
1285 Main Street
Buffalo, NY 14209-1911
716-882-2600
800-828-7571
Fax: 716-883-8100
e-mail: mail@wshein.com
http://www.wshein.com

Kevin Marmion, President

National laws, recognizing the problems encountered by the handicapped in the areas of Housing and Transportation and providing assistance in an effort to surmount those problems. Microfilm.

11930 Iberia Airlines of Spain
6100 Blue Lagoon Drive
Miami, FL 33126-2079
305-267-7747
800-772-4642
Fax: 305-262-8763
e-mail: iberiaus@iberia.com
http://www.iberia.com

Fernando Conte, President
Luis Tirad, Plant Manager

10% off regular priced fares. Must belong to the United Silver Wings Plus travel club.

11931 KLM Royal Dutch/Northwest Airlines
565 Taxter Road
Elmsford, NY 10523-2312
914-784-2000
800-374-7747
Fax: 612-726-0776
http://www.klm.com

L M Van Wijk, President/CEO

Discount varies. Call for details. For people 60 years and older and spouses. Must be a member of the United Silver Wings Plus travel club.

11932 Mesa Airlines
2325 E 30th Street
Farmington, NM 87401-8900
505-326-3338
800-326-3338
Fax: 505-326-4485
http://www.mesa-air.com

John Ornstein, Chairman/CEO
Michael J Lotz, President/COO
Brian S Gillman, Executive Vice President

Discount varies depending on time of year and destination. For people 62 years and older.

11933 Midwest Express Airlines
6744 S Howell Avenue
Oak Creek, WI 53154-1402
414-570-4000
800-452-2022
Fax: 414-570-9922
http://www.midwestexpress.com

Timothy E Hocksema, Chairman/President/CEO
Scott R Dickson, Senior VP/CMO

10% off regular fares. For people 62 years and older.

11934 Mobile Care
6201 Riverdale Road
Suite 101
Riverdale, MD 20737-2174
301-649-0564
Fax: 301-699-1865
e-mail: jaklimo@aol.com

Jeffery A Koch, President

Specializing in non-emergency wheelchair service for the elderly and physically challenged.

Travel & Recreation/Transportation

11935 National Car Rental
6929 North Lakewood Avenue
Suite 100
Tulsa, OK 74117-1808
918-401-6000
800-468-3334
Fax: 843-767-5526
http://www.nationalcar.com

Bill Lobeck, Executive Director
Howard Schwartz, General Counsel

Discounts vary among locations, usually 5 to 10 percent for Seniors.

11936 National Car Rental System
208 Saint James Avenue
Goose Creek, SC 29445-2987
843-572-0829
800-227-7368

Accommodates special requests subject to availability. Offers hand controls, bench seats, extra mirrors and vans with lifts at many major locations. 10% off car rentals for AARP members.

11937 Northwest Limousine Service
9950 Lawrence Avenue
Schiller Park, IL 60176-1310
847-671-5482
Fax: 847-671-5482
e-mail: nwlimo@aol.com

Kathleen Maloney, Manager
Ann Walsh, Office Reservations

Offers wheelchair accessible mini vans, sedans, stretch and super stretch limousines for hourly or daily rental.

11938 PALAESTRA
Challenge Publications
PO Box 508
Macomb, IL 61455
309-833-1902
Fax: 309-833-1902
e-mail: challpub@macomb.com
http://www.palaestra.com

David P Beaver, Editor in Cheif

Journal focusing on sports, physical education, and recreation for persons with disabilities.

60 pages Frequency: Quarterly

11939 Rollx Vans
6591 Highway 13 W
Savage, MN 55378-1177
952-890-7851
800-956-6668
Fax: 952-890-1903
e-mail: questions@rollxvans.com
http://www.rollxvans.com

Mike Harris, President
Scott Andrews, Marketing

Luxury wheelchair conversion vans equipped with fully automatic liffts with tie-downs. Trade ins accepted for vehicles of all types, conversions and long term leasing available.

11940 Spa
Waterfront Press Company
5305 Shilshole Avenue NW
Suite 200
Seattle, WA 98107-4021
206-826-4000
Fax: 206-789-9193
e-mail: wfpress@wolfenet.com

Janet Thomas, Editor
Laurie Munnis, Advertising Director

Magazine containing articles on travel, well-being, and renewal.

Frequency: Quarterly

11941 Swiss International Airlines
445 Broadhollow Road
Suite 419
Melville, NY 11747
888-715-5551
Fax: 631-956-9200
http://www.swiss.com

Pieter Bouw, CEO
Daniel Wede, Marketing/Services

Some Senior discounts available, please inquire for specifics.

11942 Thrifty Rent-a-Car
5330 E 31st Street
Tulsa, OK 74135-5028
918-660-7700
800-367-2277
Fax: 918-669-2060
http://www.thrifty.com

Gary L Paxton, CEO

Discounts vary by location, usually 5% for those over 55 years of age.

11943 USAir
2345 Crystal Drive
Arlington, VA 22227
703-418-7000
800-428-4322
Fax: 336-661-8031
http://www.usairways.com

Bruce Lakefield, President/CEO

Senior Discount Books contain four or eight one-way coupons. Tickets are transferable to grandchildren between the ages of 2-17. There is a $25 penalty to change reservations. Other restrictions apply. For people 62 years and older.

11944 USAirways Shuttle
PO Box 1501
Winston Salem, NC 27102-1501
336-661-0061
800-428-4322
Fax: 336-661-8031
http://www.usairways.com

Bruce Lakefield, CEO USAirways Group

Senior discounts vary by market, also works with AARP for discounts. Call for your best rate.

11945 United Airlines
PO Box 66100
Chicago, IL 60666
773-601-5180
877-228-1327
http://www.united.com

Glenn Tilton, CEO
Diane Soucy Bergan, Director Customer Relations

Silver Wings Plus: pay $75 and receive a three-year membership that includes three $25 coupons, or pay $150 for a lifetime membership and receive three $50 coupons. Membership also includes discounts for hotels, car rentals, and more. Receive 10% off regular priced fares. Silver Travel Pac Program: book of four or eight one-way coupons. Some restrictions apply. For people 62 years and older.

11946 Wheelchair Getaways Accessible Van Rentals
PO Box 5591
Lynnwood, WA 98046
859-873-4973
800-536-5518
Fax: 859-873-8039
e-mail: corporate@wheelchair-getaways.com
http://www.wheelchair-getaways.com

Richard Gatewood, President/CEO

Rents wheelchair/scooter accessible vans by the day, week, month or longer and offers delivery to major airports and other convenient locations in more than 200 cities in 42 states. Also offers full size and mini vans with automatic lifts and ramps. Some vans are equipped with hand controls, six-way power seats and remote controls for powered door operation and lifts. Discount may apply depending on location.

1921

11947 Wheeler's Accessible Van Rentals
6614 W Sweetwater Avenue
Glendale, AZ 85304-1040
623-878-3540
456-137-

Judy Jordan, Reservations Manager
Gery King, Operations Developer

Offers customized van rentals to the disabled persons allowing them freedom and independence in their travel.

Travel & Recreation/State Programs

11948 Wheelers Accessible Van Rentals
6614 West Sweetwater
Glendale, AZ 85304
800-456-1371
Fax: 623-412-9920
e-mail: info@wheelersvanrentals.com
http://www.wheelersvanrentals.com
Offers delivery to airports at 60 locations throughout the country. Wheelers offers a variety of van configurations with capacity for up to three wheelchairs, automatic ramps or lifts and nylon tie-downs, hand controls or other modifications.
1987

State Programs

11949 Alabama Bureau of Tourism and Travel
401 Adams Avenue Suite 126
Po Box 4927
Montgomery, AL 36103-4927
334-242-4169
800-252-2262
Fax: 334-242-4554
e-mail: info@touralabama.org
http://www.touralabama.org
Lee Sentell, Director
Frances Smiley, Welcome Center Manager

11950 Alaska Division of Tourism
2600 Cordova Street
Suite 201
Anchorage, AK 99503
907-465-2017
Fax: 907-465-3767
http://www.travelalaska.com
Tom Gerrett, Manager

11951 Arizona Office of Tourism
1110 W Washington St.
Suite 155
Phoenix, AZ 85007
800-842-8257
Fax: 602-240-5432
http://www.arizonaguide.com

11952 Arkansas Department of Parks & Tourism
1 Capitol Mall
Little Rock, AR 72201-1087
501-682-7777
800-NAT-URAL
Fax: 501-682-1364
http://www.1800natural.com
Richard Davies, Executive Director

11953 California Division of Tourism
Po Box 1499
Sacramento, CA 95812-1499
916-444-4429
800-862-2543
Fax: 916-322-3402
http://www.gocalif.ca.gov

11954 Colorado Travel & Tourism Authority
1127 Pennsylvania Street
Denver, CO 80203-2502
800-COL-ORAD
Fax: 303-832-6174
http://www.colorado.com

11955 Connecticut Office of Tourism
One Financial Plaza
755 Main Street
Hartford, CT 06106-7107
860-256-2800
888-288-4748
Fax: 860-270-8077
e-mail: ct.travelinfo@ct.gov
http://www.tourism.state.ct.us
Ed Dombroskas, Executive Director

11956 Delaware Tourism Office
99 Kings Highway
Dover, DE 19901-7305
302-739-4271
866-284-7483
Fax: 302-739-5749
http://www.visitdelaware.com
Tim Morgan, Manager

11957 District of Columbia
DC Committee to Promote Washington
901 7th Street NW
4th Floor
Washington, DC 20001
202-789-9000
Fax: 202-789-7037
http://http://mp.washington.org
The Golden Washingtonian Club provides discounts to residents from about 1,800 merchants listed in the Gold Mine. The directory includes restaurants, hotels, and retail stores. Call for a free copy. For people 60 years and older.

11958 Georgia Department of Industry Trade & Tourism
75 Fifth Street NW
Suite 1200
Atlanta, GA 30308
404-962-4000
800-847-4842
Fax: 404-651-9063
http://www.georgia.org/itt/tourism

11959 Golden Buckeye Program
Ohio Department of Aging
50 W Broad Street
9th Floor
Columbus, OH 43215-3363
614-466-6191
800-266-4346
Fax: 614-466-5741
e-mail: ODAMail@age.state.oh.us
http://www.goldenbuckeye.com
Cindy Clark, Golden Buckeye Program Manager

The Golden Buckeye Card provides holders discounts on goods and services from over 20,000 participating businesses throughout the state. The program also provides cardholders with significant discounts on prescription drugs. For Ohio residents 60 years and older. For people 18-59 with total and permanent disabilities.

11960 Hawaii Tourism Office
2270 Kalakaua Avenue
Suite 801
Honolulu, HI 96815-1513
808-973-2255
800-464-2924
Fax: 808-973-2253
http://www.gohawaii.com
Rex Johnson, Manager

11961 Idaho Division of Tourism Development
700 West State Street
Po Box 83720
Boise, ID 83720-0093
208-334-2470
800-406-6418
Fax: 208-334-2631
e-mail: ceo.enjoyillinois@enjoyillinois.gov
http://www.visitid.org
Carl Wilgus, Administrator

Dedicated to the growth of the tourism industry in Idaho and provides information for consumers and assistance to our tourism partner businesses across the state. We market the state's travel opportunitites throughout the West and the world with a variety of programs and partnerships.

11962 Illinois Bureau of Tourism
100 W Randolph Street
Chicago, IL 60601-3218
312-814-4732
800-406-6418
Fax: 312-814-6581
e-mail: ceo.enjoyillinois@illinois.gov
http://www.enjoyillinois.com
Jan Kostner, Manager

Travel & Recreation/State Programs

11963 Indiana Tourism Division
1 N Capitol Avenue
Suite 600
Indianapolis, IN 46204-2040
317-232-8860
888-ENJ-OYIN
Fax: 317-233-6887
http://www.ai.org/tourism

Anicia Richardson, Marketing & Tourism Sales Mgr.
Juana Johnson, Administrations Manager
Carrie Lambert, Marketing Director

11964 Iowa Tourism Office/Iowa Travel Guide
200 E Grand Avenue
Des Moines, IA 50309
515-242-4700
888-472-6035
Fax: 515-242-4809
e-mail: info@iowalifechanging.com
http://www.traveliowa.com

Mike Tramontina, Director

The Travel Guide lists Iowa destinations, attractions, lodging and campling.
184 pages Frequency: Annually

11965 Kansas Travel & Tourism
534 S Kansas Avenue
Suite 1210
Topeka, KS 66603
785-296-2009
800-452-6727
Fax: 785-296-5563
http://www.state.ks.us
TDD 785-296-3487

Scott D Allegrucci, Executive Director

11966 Kentucky Department of Travel
500 Mero Street
22nd Floor
Frankfort, KY 40601-1957
502-564-4930
800-225-8747
Fax: 502-564-5695
http://www.kentuckytourism.com

11967 Louisiana Office of Tourism
1051 N 3rd Street
Baton Rouge, LA 70802-5239
225-342-8100
800-334-9626
Fax: 225-342-8390
http://www.lousianatravel.com

Darienne Wilson, Manager

11968 Maine Office of Tourism
59 State House Station
Augusta, ME 04333-0059
207-287-5710
888-624-6345
Fax: 207-287-8070
http://www.visitmaine.com

11969 Maryland Office of Tourism Development
217 E Redwood Street
9th Floor
Baltimore, MD 21202-3316
410-767-3400
866-639-3526
Fax: 410-333-6643
e-mail: info@mdisfun.org
http://www.mdisfun.org

Dennis Castleman, Manager

11970 Massachusetts Office of Travel & Tourism
10 Park Plaza
Suite 4510
Boston, MA 02116-3981
617-973-8500
800-277-6277
Fax: 617-973-8525
e-mail: vacationinfo@state.ma.us
http://www.mass-vacation.com

Mary Jane McKenna, Executive Director

11971 Michigan Travel Bureau
PO Box 30226
Lansing, MI 48909-7726
517-373-0670
800-543-2937
Fax: 517-373-0059
http://www.michigan.org

11972 Minnesota Office of Tourism
121 7th Place E
Metro Square Suite 100
Saint Paul, MN 55101
651-296-5029
800-868-7476
Fax: 651-296-2800
e-mail: explore@state.mn.us
http://www.exploreminnesota.com

John Edman, Executive Director

11973 Mississippi Division of Tourism Development
PO Box 849
Jackson, MI 39205
601-359-3297
800-927-6378
Fax: 601-359-5757
e-mail: tourdiv@mississippi.org
http://www.dccd.state.ms.us

11974 Missouri Division of Tourism
PO Box 1055
Jefferson City, MO 65102-1055
573-751-4133
800-877-1234
Fax: 573-751-5160
e-mail: tourism@dcd.mo.gov
http://www.visitmo.com

Becky Hereen, Marketing Executive

11975 Nebraska Division of Travel & Tourism
301 Centennial Mall South, 4th Floor
Lincoln, NE 68509-8907
402-471-3796
877-632-7275
Fax: 402-471-3026
e-mail: tourism@visitnebraska.org
http://www.visitnebraska.org

Sarah Baker, PR Coordinator

Free vacation guide The Nebraska Traveler. The Traveler includes a listing of all accomodations for hotels, motels, bed and breakfasts, guest ranches, and campgrounds. Outfitters and attractions.....more than 140 pages.

11976 Nevada Commission on Tourism
401 N Carson Street
Carson City, NV 89701-4221
775-687-4322
800-638-2328
Fax: 702-687-6779
e-mail: ncot@travelnevada.com
http://www.travelnevada.com

Bruce Bommarito, Executive Director

11977 New Hampshire Office of Travel & Tourism Development
PO Box 1856
172 Pembroke Road
Concord, NH 03302-1856
603-271-2343
800-FUN-INNH
Fax: 603-271-6870
e-mail: travel@dred.state.nh.us
http://www.visitnh.gov

11978 New Jersey Tourism Division
20 W State Street
Trenton, NJ 08608-1206
609-292-2470
800-JER-SEY7
Fax: 609-633-7418
http://www.state.nj.us/travel

Nancy Bryne, Executive Director

Travel & Recreation/State Programs

11979 New Mexico Department of Tourism
491 Old Santa Fe Trl
Santa Fe, NM 87503
505-827-7400
800-545-2040
Fax: 505-827-7402
http://www.newmexico.org

Michael Cerletti, Manager

11980 New York Division of Tourism
1 Commerce Plaza
Albany, NY 12245
518-474-4116
800-225-5697
Fax: 518-486-6416
http://www.iloveny.com

11981 North Carolina Division of Tourism
301 N Wilmington Street
Raleigh, NC 27601-1058
919-733-4171
800-847-4863
Fax: 919-715-3097
http://www.visitnc.com

Gordon Clapp, Executive Director

11982 Ohio Division of Travel and Tourism
PO Box 1001
Columbus, OH 43216-1001
614-466-8844
800-282-5393
Fax: 614-466-6744
http://www.ohiotourism.com

11983 Oklahoma Tourism & Recreation Department
120 N Robinson Avenue
6th Floor
Oklahoma City, OK 73102-5405
405-230-8400
800-652-6552
Fax: 405-522-5257
http://www.otrd.state.ok.us

Hardy Watkins, Executive Director

11984 Oregon Tourism Commission
775 Summer Street NE
Salem, OR 97310
503-986-0000
800-547-7842
Fax: 503-986-0001
http://www.traveloregon.com

11985 Pennsylvania Center for Travel, Tourism & Film
400 North Street
4th Floor
Harrisburg, PA 17120-0225
717-787-5453
800-847-4872
Fax: 717-787-0687
http://www.visitpa.com

11986 South Carolina Department of Parks, Transportation & Tourism
1205 Pendleton Street
Columbia, SC 29201-3756
803-734-1700
866-224-9339
Fax: 803-734-0133
http://www.scpit.com

11987 South Dakota Department of Tourism
711 E Wells Avenue
Pierre, SD 57501-3385
605-773-3301
800-732-5682
Fax: 605-773-3256
e-mail: travelsd@state.sd.us
http://www.travelsd.com

Billie Jo Waara, Manager

11988 State of Florida
Greater Ft Lauderdale Convention &
1850 Eller Drive
Fort Lauderdale, FL 33316-4202
954-765-4466
800-22S-UNNY
Fax: 954-765-4467
http://www.sunny.org

Nicki Grossman, President

Write for the complete Greater Fort Lauderdale Super Senior Savers. Information includes lodging discounts, attraction discounts, calander of events, and visitors guide.

11989 State of Illinois
Department of Commerce & Community Affairs
620 E Adams Street
Springfield, IL 62701-1615
217-782-7500
800-226-6632
Fax: 217-785-6336
http://www.commerce.state.il.us
TDD 800-785-6055

The Golden Age Hunting and Fishing License provides free hunting and fishing. For people 65 years and older.

11990 State of Michigan Travel Resources
License Control
PO Box 30028
Lansing, MI 48909-7528
517-373-1204
Fax: 517-373-0784

Senior fishing and hunting licenses at a significant discount. Also discounts for state park vehicle entrance permits for people 65 years and over.

11991 State of Missouri
Missouri Department of Social Services
221 West High Street
Po Box 1527
Jefferson City, MO 65102-1337
573-634-5165
800-235-5503
Fax: 573-751-4386
http://www.dss.mo.gov

Josh Campbell, Manager

Silver Citizen Discount Card entitles holders to discounts at restaurants, stores, services, and other businesses throughout the state. For people 60 years and older.

11992 State of Rhode Island
Department of Elderly Affairs
160 Pine Street
Providence, RI 02903-3708
401-462-4000
Fax: 401-222-1490
e-mail: larry@dea.state.ri.us
http://www.dea.ri.gov

Noreen Shawcross, Executive Director

Free admission to state parks. For people 65 years and older.

11993 State of Texas Office of the Governor Economic Development and Tourism
PO Box 12428
Austin, TX 78711-2428
512-936-0100
Fax: 512-936-0450
http://www.governor.state.tx.us

David Teel, Executive Director

11994 State of Utah
Park City Convention & Visitors Bureau
1910 Prospector Avenue
Park City, UT 84060-7211
435-649-6100
800-453-1360
Fax: 801-649-4132
http://www.2chambers.com/utah_state

William Malone, Executive Director

The Silver Card entitles holders to special discounts May through September. Restrictions do apply. Call for details. For people 50 years and older.

Travel & Recreation/Tours & Services

11995 **State of Vermont**
Vermont Deptartment of Aging
103 S Main Street
Weeks Building
Waterbury, VT 05671-1601
802-241-2388
Fax: 802-241-1363
http://www.vermont.gov/dial

Patrick Flood, Manager

The Green Mountain Passport entitles Vermont residents free day use admission to any state park and its programs. Other benefits are included. For people 62 years and older.

11996 **State of West Virginia**
West Virginia Commission on Aging
1900 Kanawha Blvd East
Charleston, WV 25305
304-558-3317
Fax: 304-558-5609
http://www.wvseniorservices.gov

The Golden Mountaineer Discount Card provides discounts to over 3,500 participating merchants and professionals in the state. For people 60 years and older.

11997 **Tennessee Department of Tourist Development**
312 8th Avenue North
25th Floor
Nashville, TN 37243
615-741-2159
888-836-6200
Fax: 615-741-7225
e-mail: tourdev@state.tn.us
http://http://state.tn.us/tourdev

Susan Whitaker, Commissioner
Laura Heatherly, Exec. Assistant To Commissioner
Cindy Dupree, Public Information Officer

11998 **Utah Travel Council**
300 N State Street
Council Hall/Capitol Hill
Salt Lake City, UT 84114
801-538-1030
800-200-1160
Fax: 801-538-1399
e-mail: travel@utah.com
http://www.utah.com

Leigh Von Der Esch, Managing Director
David Williams, Deputy Dir./Marketing Research
Tracie Cayford, Dep. Dir./ Comm. & Operations

The Utah Office of Tourism promotes tourism into the state through advertising and media contacts. We are an office within the Governor's office of Economic Development. Our mission is to improve the quality of life of Utah citizens through revenue and tax relief, by increasing the quality and quantity of tourism visits and spending.

11999 **Virginia Department of Economic Development Division of Tourism**
901 E Byrd Street
Richmond, VA 23219-4052
804-771-9500
800-847-4882
Fax: 804-786-1919
e-mail: vainfo@helloinc.com
http://www.virginia.org

Gina M Burgin

12000 **Washington State Tourism**
PO Box 42500
Olympia, WA 98504-2500
360-753-5601
800-544-1800
Fax: 360-753-4470
e-mail: tourism@cted.wa.gov
http://www.tourism.wa.gov

Kristin Jacobson, Public Relations

12001 **West Virginia Division of Tourism**
90 MacCorkle Ave. SW
Charleston, WV 25305-2216
304-558-2200
800-225-5982
Fax: 304-558-0108
http://www.state.wv.us/tourism

Mission is to cultivate a world-class travel and tourism industry in West Virginia through creation of jobs, stimulation of investment, expansion of current tourism attractions and promotion of a postive state image, thereby improving the way of life for West Virginians.

12002 **Wisconsin Department of Tourism**
201 W Washington Avenue
Po Box 8690
Madison, WI 53708-8690
608-266-2161
800-432-8747
Fax: 608-266-3403
e-mail: tourinfo@travelwisconsin.com
http://www.tourism.state.wi.us

Mary Burke, Manager

12003 **Wyoming Division of Tourism**
I-25 & College Drive
Cheyenne, WY 82002
307-777-7777
800-225-5996
Fax: 307-777-2877
http://www.wyomingtourism.org

Alan Dibberley, Manager

Tours & Services

12004 **Accessible Journeys**
35 West Sellers Avenue
Ridley Park, PA 19078-2113
610-521-0339
800-846-4537
Fax: 610-521-6959
e-mail: sales@accessiblejourneys.com
http://www.disabilitytravel.com

Howard Mccoy III, Director
Deborah Hoover, Associate Director

Tour operator for slow walker and wheelchair travelers offering tours to culturally intriguing destinations like Africa, China, Brazil, Alaska and Hawaii. Also offers a quarterly newsletter.

12005 **Addie's You & I Travel Service**
7545 NE Sandy Boulevard
Portland, OR 97213-6461
503-282-7545
800-342-5500
Fax: 503-828-2479
http://www.addiesyouanditravel.com

Addie Lindstrom, Contact

Arrange travel for all special needs.

12006 **America West/US Airways Airline**
4000 E Sky Harbor Boulevard
Phoenix, AZ 85034-3802
480-693-0800
http://www.usairways.com

Diana Lawson, Contact
W Douglas Parker, CEO

This airline trains employees to make sure that passengers with disabilities enjoy convenient, safe and comfortable travel.

12007 **American Hotel and Motel Association**
1201 New York Avenue NW
Washington, DC 20005-3931
202-289-3100
Fax: 202-289-3199
e-mail: comments@ahma.com
http://www.ahla.com

Joseph McInerney, President/CEO
Pam Inman, Executive VP/COO
Joori Jeon, Executive VP/CFO

Will disseminate information, develop and conduct a series of seminars for the hotel and motel industry at state-level association conferences, and develop and distribute an ADA Compliance handbook for use by the lodging industry.

Travel & Recreation/Tours & Services

12008 Anglo California Travel Service
4250 Williams Road
San Jose, CA 95129-3344
408-257-2257
Fax: 408-257-2664
Helen Jones, Contact
Audrey Cooper, President
Plans for one and two week accessible tours.

12009 B&A Travel
701 S University Avenue
Carbondale, IL 62901-2894
618-549-7347
Fax: 618-457-0241
Dave Coracy, Contact
Arranges wheelchair travel.

12010 Bill Dvorak Kayak & Rafting
17921 Us Highway 285
Nathrop, CO 81236-9701
719-539-6851
800-824-3795
Fax: 719-539-3378
e-mail: info@dvorakexpeditions.com
http://www.dvorakexpeditions.com
Bill Dvorak, Contact
Jaci Dvorak, Contact
Rafting and kayak trips for mobility limitations.

12011 Charlie Brown's Goodtime Travel
1465 North Union Blvd.
Colorado Springs, CO 80909
719-635-8992
Fax: 719-635-0045
http://www.cbgt.com
Sandy Stern, Contact
Charlie Brown, Owner
Arranges travel for all limitations.

12012 Classic Hawaii
5893 Rue Ferrari
San Jose, CA 95138
408-287-4550
800-635-1333
Fax: 408-287-9272
http://www.classicvacations.com
Paula Schneider, Contact
Greg Brockway, President
Offer accessible tours to Hawaii.

12013 Dell Rapids Sportsmen's Club
24693 Dells Drive
Dell Rapids, SD 57022-1344
605-428-5501
Fax: 605-428-5502
Dan Anderson, CEO
A club offering education and experience in planning, designing or using accessible shooting or gun club.

12014 Diabetic Cruise Desk
Hartford Holiday Travel
129 Hillside Avenue
Williston Park, NY 11596
516-746-6670
800-828-4813
Fax: 516-746-6690
http://www.hartfordholidays.com
Offers a seven-day cruise to Alaska for people with diabetes. Includes seminars on diabetes, self management, planning, special guidance for exercise classes and individual dietary advice.

12015 Easter Seals Project ACTION
1425 K Street NW
Suite 200
Washington, DC 20005-3956
202-347-3066
800-659-6428
Fax: 202-737-7914
e-mail: project_action@easterseals.com
http://www.projectaction.org
TDD 202-347-7385
TTY 202-347-7385
Alan Abeson, Director
Liz Moore, Communication/Mktging Mgr
Joseph Romer, Vice President
A national technical assistance program designed to improve access to transportation services for people with disabilities and assist transit providers in implementing the Americans with Disabilities Act.

12016 Elderhostel
11 Avenue de Lafayette
Boston, MA 02111
877-426-8056
800-454-5768
Fax: 877-426-2166
http://www.elderhostel.org
Non-profit organization dedicated to providing exceptional learning opportunities to adults at a remarkable value. As the nation's first, and the world's largest, edcuational travel organiztion primarily for adults, we believe that learning is an integral part of a healthy and fulfilling life.

12017 Elderhostel Institute Network
PO Box 1959
Wakefield, MA 01880-5959
617-426-7788
Fax: 617-426-0549
e-mail: publicity@elderhostel.org
http://www.elderhostel.org
Elderhostel Institute Network is a voluntary association of over 200 Institutes for Learning in Retirement (I.L.R.). An I.L.R. is a community based organization of retirement age learners dedicated to meeting the educational interests of its members.

12018 Empress Directions Unlimited(AcccessibleTours)
123 Green La
Bedford Hills, NY 10507-1534
914-241-1700
800-533-5343
Fax: 914-241-0243
e-mail: lawebmaster@la.gov
Lois Bonanni, Director
Arranges vacations throughout the world for all disabilities including accessible cruises, African safari, rafting and scuba diving.

12019 Environmental Traveling Companions
Fort Mason Center Building
San Francisco, CA 94123
415-474-7662
Fax: 415-474-3919
e-mail: info@etctrips.org
http://www.etctrips.org
Diane Poslosky, Executive Director
Deb Glazer, Development Director
Davido Crow, River Program Manager
Aids travelers regardless of physical or financial limitations to experience the beauty and challenge of the wilderness.

12020 Flying Wheels Travel
143 W Bridge Street
Owatonna, MN 55060-2917
507-451-5005
800-535-6790
e-mail: bjacobson@ll.net
http://www.flyingwheelstravel.com
Barbara Jacobson, Contact
Arranges travel for persons with mobility limitations.

12021 Galludet University/Alumni House
800 Florida Avenue NE
Washington, DC 20002-3600
202-651-5000
Fax: 202-651-5062
Erving King Jordan, President
Offers tours with ASL interpreters for the deaf and hearing-impaired.

12022 General Motors Mobility Program for Travelers with Disabilities
GM Mobility Program
PO Box 09011
Detroit, MI 48209
800-323-9935

Travel & Recreation/Tours & Services

12023 Green Tortoise Adventure Travel
494 Broadway
San Francisco, CA 94133-4515
415-834-1000
800-867-8647
Fax: 415-956-4900
Gardner Kent, Owner

Bus travel with experience for travelers who have mobility impairments.

12024 Handi-Cabs of the Pacific
PO Box 22428
Honolulu, HI 96823-2428
808-946-6666
Fax: 808-946-6676
e-mail: info@handicabs.com
http://www.handicabs.com
Craig Kimura, General Manager
Nick Comsa, Owner

Wheelchair taxi and tour company. All vehicles have ramps.

12025 Hinsdale Travel Service
201 E Ogden Avenue
Hinsdale, IL 60521-3633
630-325-1335
888-325-1357
Fax: 630-325-1342
e-mail: inquiries@hinsdaletravel.com
http://www.hindsdaletravel.com
Laurie Karhun, Owner
Cindy Kovacik, Agent

Offers specialized assistance for independent travel or tours for persons with disabilities including cruises and travel in the USA and abroad.

12026 House of Travel
1107 L Street
Sacramento, CA 95814-3995
916-442-0743
800-444-9996
Fax: 916-442-5656
Ann Hilderbrand, Contact
Anita Van Der Zanden, Owner

Arranges travel for all limitations.

12027 Journeys East
2443 Fillmore Street
289k
San Francisco, CA 94115-1814
415-647-9565
800-527-2612
Fax: 510-601-1977
Davis Everett, Co-Director

Specializes in backcountry trips to Japan with hands on experience staying in Japanese inns and temples. All trips open to persons with disabilities but type of disability may preclude joining certain trips.

12028 Kayak and Rafting Expeditions
17921 U.S. Highway 285
Nathrop, CO 81236
719-539-6851
800-824-3795
Fax: 719-539-3378
e-mail: info@dvorakexpeditions.com
http://www.dvorakexpeditions.com
Bill Dvorak, President
Jaci Dvorak, VP

This organization does river trips for people who are deaf, visually impaired, physically or mentally disabled. Rafting trips with groups and families and whitewater instruction.

12029 Kon Tiki Travel Agency
7906 5th Avenue
Brooklyn, NY 11209-4510
718-748-7400
800-822-5838
Fax: 718-238-3604
e-mail: gerd@kontiki-travel.com
http://www.norhouse.com/kontiki.asp
Mary Mosleh, Contact
Gerd Bjorgan, Owner

Tours for hearing-impaired. Interpreters available.

12030 MedEscort International
ABE International Airport
PO Box 8766
Allentown, PA 18105-8766
610-791-3111
800-255-7182
Fax: 610-791-9189
e-mail: medescort@fast.net
http://www.medescort.com
Diane Horvath, Director
Craig Poliner, President

Offers specially trained escorts for individuals who cannot travel alone due to age or disability.

12031 Melwood Access Adventures
9035 Ironsides Road
Nanjemoy, MD 20662-3432
301-870-3226
Fax: 301-870-2620
e-mail: accessadventures@erols.com
http://www.melwood.org
Andrew V Colevas, Chairman Of The Board
Frank O Coombs, Business Executive
Stanley J Botts, Director

A year round recreation facility that serves mentally and physically disabled individuals, offers a variety of vacations, outdoor recreation, travel and respite care.

12032 Monte Travel
4127 Hylan Boulevard
Staten Island, NY 10308-3308
718-987-6900
Fax: 718-980-2158
Ann Marie Colombo, Owner

Arranges travel for all special needs.

12033 Nantahala Outdoor Center
13077 Highway 19 W
Bryson City, NC 28713-9165
828-488-2176
800-232-7238
Fax: 828-488-2498
e-mail: rafting@noc.com
http://www.noc.com
Jennifer Petosz, Advertising Coordinator
Payson Kennedy, CEO

Nantahala Outdoor Center, the leader in outdoor recreation and education for over 27 years, strongly encourages and supports participants with disabilities. We offer whitewater rafting adventures on six rivers in the Southeast for all skill and thrill levels, also kayak and canoe adaptive instruction. NOC will tailor a whitewater program to your skill and ability level, modify the gear, and pace instruction for you.

12034 National Association of Traveling Nurses
PO Box 35189
Chicago, IL 60707-189
708-453-0080
Fax: 708-453-0083
Richard Johnson, President

Members of the medical profession. Provides travel information. Offers substantial discounts for members at major hotels, resorts, and car rental agencies. Provides members with complete list of approved travel industry suppliers, including travel agents, vendors, airlines, cruise ship companies, and hotels.

12035 National Tour Association: Travel Division
546 East Main Street
Lexington, KY 40508-2342
859-226-4444
800-682-8886
Fax: 859-226-4414
e-mail: joinnta@ntastaff.com
http://www.ntaonline.com

Provides callers with a list of tour companies who can accomodate the disabled on their escorted tours. Hours: 8:00 a.m. to 5:00 p.m. Monday-Friday.

Travel & Recreation/Tours & Services

12036 Northridge Travel
9700 Reseda Boulevard
Northridge, CA 91324-2099
818-886-2000
800-842-8880
Fax: 818-885-8229
http://www.northridgetravel.com
Helen Reiter, Contact
Teresa Tsent, Owner

One of the leading Travel Management Companies in the San Fernando Valley. It was established in 1962 and has grown from 2 to more than 48 employees.

12037 Odyssey Club
2950 SE Stark Street
Portland, OR 97214-3082
503-233-9961
800-452-4100

Provides tours all over the world for people over age 55. Member of the Society for the Advancement of Travel for the Handicapped.

12038 Outback Ranch Outfitters
34828 Wallowa Lake Highway
Joseph, OR 97846-269
541-886-2029
http://www.oregonelkhunter.com

Licensed guides and outfitters. Summer horseback trips for riders with disabilities.

12039 Over the Rainbow
186 Mehani Circle
Kihei, HI 96753-8072
808-879-5521
800-303-3750
Fax: 808-817-7536
David R McKown, Contact

All disabilities. Adventure activities including scuba diving.

12040 Professional Respite Care
Act for Health
1385 S Colorado Boulevard
Denver, CO 80222-3304
303-757-4808
Fax: 303-757-3821
Kevin Volmer, Owner

Offers travel accompaniment services for disabled persons or senior citizens.

12041 Reid & Hurley Travel
710 West Street
Braintree, MA 02184-3833
617-380-8778
Fax: 617-380-7809
Susan Packenham, Contact

Annual tour for those with severe breathing disorders.

12042 River Odysseys West (Row)
314 E Garden Avenue
Po Box 579
Coeur D Alene, ID 83814
208-765-0841
800-451-6034
Fax: 208-667-6506
e-mail: info@rowadventures.com
http://www.rowadventures.com
Peter Grubb, Owner

Offers one to six day rafting trips to physically disadvantaged people. Designs custom itineraries, or trips with a special focus for small groups. For those with special dietary needs, they prepare special meals. Free brochure upon request.

12043 Rodeway Inns
10750 Columbia Pike
Silver Spring, MD 20901-4427
301-592-5000
800-228-2000
Marni Altschuler, Contact
Charles A Ledsinger Jr, CEO

This organization has a limited number of rooms for the handicapped with extra wide doors and special bathroom assist bars.

12044 Sheridan Travel Service
7200 W Alameda Avenue
W4
Lakewood, CO 80226-3210
303-238-7111
800-444-4334
e-mail: sheridantravel@vacation.com
http://www.sheridantravel.com
TDD 303-936-8599
Tuttles Manley, Contact
Thea Foley, Owner

Travel and tours for hearing-impaired.

12045 Shilo Inns & Resorts
11707 NE Airport Way
Portland, OR 97220-1075
503-252-7500
800-222-2244
Fax: 503-254-0794
http://www.shiloinns.com

Offers handicapped-assist rooms including larger bathrooms equipped with assistance railings and wheelchair access. Please call for property specifics.

12046 Sports 'n Spokes
Paralyzed Veterans of America
2111 E Highland Avenue
Suite 180
Phoenix, AZ 85016-4756
602-224-0500
888-888-2201
Fax: 602-224-0507
Cliff Crase, Editor
Sherri Shea, Advertising Manager

Magazine covering wheelchair sports and recreation news.
Frequency: Bimonthly

12047 Sue Smith Travel Service
3806 Jfk Boulevard
North Little Rock, AR 72116-8248
501-771-0987
Fax: 501-771-0563
Donna Brown, Owner
Mike Wilkinson, Owner

Established library service for disabled travelers in the area.

12048 Sundial Special Vacations
Sundial Tours
2609 Highway 101 N
Suite 103
Seaside, OR 97138-6845
503-738-3324
800-547-9198
Fax: 503-738-3369
e-mail: ssv@sundail-travel.com
http://www.sundialtour.com
Jill Conner Ross, Tour Operations Director/Owner
Patsy Conner, Owner
Nancy Wyse, Tour Leader

Provides special vacations for developmentally disabled persons. Provides quality vacations for persons with developmental disabilities. Ratio is 1 for 7 or 1 for 5 depending on tour. Only two people to a room. Exciting destinations. 3 to 4 star properties.

12049 Ticket Counter
6900 Wisconsin Avenue
Suite 706
Chevy Chase, MD 20815-6103
301-986-0790
Fax: 301-913-0166
Tracey Bullan Rattner, Contact

Offers airlines, train, vacation and honeymoon packages, leisure and business, cruises, skiing, horseback riding and other interest tickets to persons with or without disabilities.

12050 Travel Companion Exchange
PO Box 633
Amityville, NY 11701-633
631-454-0880
e-mail: tce@travelcompanions.com
http://www.whytravelalone.com
Eul Lee, Contact

Travel & Recreation/Tours & Services

Networks divorced, widowed and single individuals in the US and Canada for leisure activities and travel.

12051 Travel Trends
9500 Topega Boulevard
Chatsworth, CA 91311
818-576-0500
Fax: 818-576-0520
TDD 818-993-5250

Kevin Mills, Contact

Tours for hearing-impaired.

12052 Travelers Aid Society
1612 K Street NW
Suite 506
Washington, DC 20006-2849
202-546-1127
Fax: 202-546-1625
http://www.travelersaid.org

Raymond M Flint, President
Michael S Oring Esq., VP Local Programs
Martha A Morris, Dir. Development & Comm.

Provides crisis intervention and casework services, limited financial assistance, protective travel assistance and information and referrals for travelers, transients and newcomers.

12053 Travelfair
320 Main Street
Islip, NY 11751-3414
631-581-4040
Fax: 631-581-4044

Kenneth Reinert, Contact

Arranges travel for all disabilities.

12054 Travelin' Talk Newsletter
PO Box 3534
Clarksville, TN 37043-3534
931-552-6670
Fax: 931-552-1182

Rick Crowder, Founder

Updates members on the progress of the Travelin' Talk network. A network which introduces numerous sources to travelers, shares tips and stories of ways people are helping travelers with disabilities, and helps members get to know each other better and establish new-found friendships.

8 pages Frequency: Quarterly

12055 US SERVAS
1125 16th Street
Suite 201
Arcata, CA 95521-5585
707-825-1714
Fax: 707-825-1762
e-mail: info@usservas.org
http://www.usservas.org

Nancy Mitchell, Board Chair
Judy Sears, Office Staff

International network that links travelers with hosts in 130+ countries with the hope of building world peace through understanding and friendship.

12056 US Travel Systems
2903 E Grant Road
Tucson, AZ 85716-2717
520-322-7300
Fax: 602-322-5914
TDD 602-495-1523

Frances Rubiner, Contact

Specializes in senior travel.

12057 Ventures
A Service of Friendship Ventures
10509 108th Street NW
Annandale, MN 55302-2912
952-852-0101
Fax: 651-274-3238

A travel service for fun, excitement and adventure for persons with disabilities. Whether persons in group homes, belonging to a local ARC, or any other special group, Ventures travel service takes care of every aspect of vacation planning and servicing.

12058 Weston Travel Agency
134 N Cass Avenue
Westmont, IL 60559-1687
630-968-2513
Fax: 630-968-2539

Michael Wolinski, Contact

Arranges travel for all physical limitations.

12059 Wheelchair Getaways
7276 Narcoossee Rd
Orlando, FL 32822
407-281-8369
800-536-5518
http://www.wheelchairgetaways.com

Mike Nilan, Contact
Joe Bobalik, Owner

Van rentals.

12060 Wilderness Inquiry
808 14th Ave SE
Minneapolis, MN 55414-1516
612-676-9400
800-728-0719
Fax: 612-676-9401
e-mail: info@wildernessinquiry.org
http://www.wildernessinquiry.org

Greg Lais, Executive Director
Greta Arnquist, Registration Manager

Allows people of all ages and abilities to share the adventure of wilderness travel. This nonprofit organization was formed in 1978 and conducts tours to some of the most beautiful and remote parts of the world.

Glossary of Health & Medical Terms

DISEASES

Abnormal PAP Smear: The Papanicolaou (Pap) smear is the most effective screening test for cervical cancer. The Pap smear is usually performed by a physician during a gynecologic examination. A wooden instrument is used to collect brushings from the cervix, which are then analyzed for abnormal cells that could be early signs of cervical cancer. An abnormal pap smear is one that has cells on it that are suspicious for infection, inflammation, or cancer.

Acute Stress Reaction: An Acute Stress Reaction or Nervous Breakdown is an emotional event that causes a significant, and at times prolonged, physiologic response felt by the body. Constant Stress can contribute to and create medical illness and physical consequences.

Asthma: Asthma or Reactive Airway Disease is a medical disease that is caused by airway inflammation and hyperactivity in the lungs. Reactive Airway Disease is a more general category that includes allergic and occupational triggers for this airway inflammation and reactivity.

Breast Cancer: A common disease of women where a portion of the breast tissue transforms into cancer, and then the cancer can spread to other parts of the body. Breast cancer can be detected early with routine physical examination and surveillance mammograms.

Cervical Cancer: Cervical cancer is a condition where a cancerous growth (also called a malignancy) arises on of the lower portion of the uterus. Cervical cancer only occurs in women. Cervical cancer can be prevented through screening Pap Smears.

Colon Cancer: Colon cancer is a condition where a cancerous growth (also called a malignancy) arises out of the large intestine. Colon cancer is a common cancer in both men and women. Screening tests for Colon cancer include colonoscopies, flexible sigmoidoscopies, and fecal occult blood cards. Colon cancer is many cases can be prevented by identifying precancerous colon polyps and removing them.

Colon Polyps: Colon polyps are growths that form in the large intestine that can be precancerous. There are many types of polyps and not all of them are the type that lead to colon cancer. Colon polyps are quite often hereditary and can cause microscopic bleeding into the bowels.

Coronary Artery Disease: A disease where cholesterol-like plaque builds up in the heart blood vessels leading to restricted blood flow and oxygen delivery and thus resulting in heart attacks. The predominate risk factors for CAD are high blood pressure, smoking, diabetes, family history of CAD, and elevated cholesterol levels.

Depression: Depression or Mood-related disorder is a medical disease of mood problems stemming from changes in brain chemistry resulting in significant relationship, occupational, and lifestyle consequences. Other mood disorders are bipolar disorder and mania.

Diabetes: A disease where the body loses the ability to control blood sugar levels. Diabetics are at high risk for heart attacks, blindness, kidney failure, and nerve damage. Diabetics can control their disease with diet, exercise, and medications.

Diabetes of Pregnancy: A condition of abnormal blood sugar regulation that occurs only during pregnancy. Individuals with this diagnosis during pregnancy are at higher risk to develop adult onset diabetes in the future.

Diabetic Protein loss in urine: Diabetes is a condition where the blood sugar is not regulated appropriately by the body resulting in increased blood glucose levels. Overtime, diabetes can cause eye disease, kidney disease, and nerve disease. An early sign of diabetic kidney disease is protein loss in the urine. This can be tested on a routine urinalysis.

Gastric Cancer: Gastric cancer is a condition where a cancerous growth (also called a malignancy) arises in the stomach. Gastric cancer risk factors include both dietary and infectious causes.

Glaucoma: Glaucoma is a condition of increased pressure in the eye. More specifically, the Intraocular pressure is elevated, which can lead to nerve damage and blindness. Glaucoma does run in families. Glaucoma can be treated to reduce the eye pressures and prevent vision loss.

Hearing Deficiency: Hearing deficiency is a common, under diagnosed condition. Routine audiogram tests can

APPENDIX 1: Glossary of Health & Medical Terms

measure baseline hearing ability. Hearing loss can result from infection, age, trauma, and noise exposure.

Heavy Menstrual Flow: Heavy menstrual flow is a difficult condition to measure. Every woman's monthly cycle is different in frequency and amount of blood flow. Heavy menstrual flow is defined as bleeding for more than 6 days straight and more than 4-6 pads per day, but a physician's judgment of the flow pattern defines it more subjectively as light, moderate, or heavy.

High Blood Pressure: High blood pressure (also called Hypertension) is a condition of elevated pressures in the blood vessels. The blood pressure measurement is composed of a systolic (top number) and a diastolic (bottom number). High blood pressure is defined as a pressure above 140/90. High blood pressure is a significant risk factor for heart disease.

High Cholesterol: High cholesterol (also called Hyperlipidemia) is a condition of elevated cholesterol in the blood. The blood total cholesterol panel is composed of the LDL-cholesterol (bad cholesterol), the HDL-cholesterol (good cholesterol), the cholesterol ratio (Total cholesterol/HDL), and the triglycerides. The goal cholesterol value depends on the medical history, family history, and health status, but is generally accepted as an LDL-cholesterol of less than 130.

High Risk Pregnancy: A pregnancy, where because of a specific health history of the mother or child, the risk of birth defects or complications is increased. Prenatal interventions can lessen this risk in some cases.

Hypogonadal: Hypogonadism is a condition where the body does not produce adequate amounts of sex hormone. For example, men that have a testosterone deficiency are hypogonadal. Women can also suffer from hypogonadism.

Iron Deficiency Anemia: Anemia is a condition where the body's red blood cell count is low. The most common cause of anemia is Iron Deficiency. This condition is much more common in women than men. Women with heavy menstrual flows are at risk for developing Iron Deficiency Anemia.

Medically Overweight: Medically overweight is defined as being more than 10% above your ideal body weight. A formula called the Body Mass Index (BMI) offers a numeric BMI score based on height and weight variables. BMI scores over 26 are suggestive of being medically overweight.

Melanoma: Melanoma is a dangerous cancer arising from cells in the skin, usually from a nevus (also called a mole). Pigmented skin lesions that change in size, color, borders, or shape should be evaluated by a physician.

Osteoporosis: Osteoporosis is a condition where an excessive loss of calcium from the bones results in an increased risk of fractures. Osteoporosis usually affects the hips and spine of both men and women. Exercise, calcium supplements, and some medications can help prevent osteoporosis.

Prostate Cancer: A common disease of men where the prostate gland transforms into cancerous tissue, and then the cancer can spread to other parts of the body. Prostate cancer can be detected early by screening strategies with digital rectal exams (DRE) and prostate specific antigen (PSA) testing.

Skin Cancer: Skin cancer is a condition where a cancerous growth arises out of the skin. The most common type is called a basal cell carcinoma which commonly occurs on the face or back. Most Skin cancers are related directly to sun exposure. Melanoma and squamous cell carcinoma are other common skin cancers.

Stroke: A stroke (also called a cerebral vascular accident (CVA)) is a condition where an area of the brain does not get the blood flow it needs resulting in permanent brain damage in that area. Strokes can be life threatening. Smoking, diabetes, and high blood pressure increase the risk of stroke.

Testicular Cancer: Testicular cancer is a condition where a cancerous growth (also called a malignancy) arises out of the male testes. This cancer occurs usually in young men and is picked up by self examination. Testicular cancer can be cured with surgery and radiation if it is caught early.

Thyroid Disease: Thyroid disease results from too much or too little thyroid hormone. The thyroid gland manufactures all of the body's thyroid hormone. Any condition that affects the thyroid gland can also affect the secretion of thyroid hormone. Thyroid diseases can run in families.

SCREENINGS

5-Day Blood Pressure Check: A five-day blood pressure check is a series of blood pressure readings performed on 5 different days in both arms to get an average as to a person's blood pressure readings. Usually individuals, who take a high blood pressure medication, get a five-day blood pressure check done

APPENDIX 1: Glossary of Health & Medical Terms

once a year to make sure that their medication(s) work to control their blood pressure.

Blood Pressure: A qualified healthcare provider can use a blood pressure cuff and a stethoscope to measure a person's blood pressure.

Blood Thyroid Level: The TSH (Thyroid Stimulating Hormone) blood test is a measure of thyroid gland function. The TSH level helps physicians evaluate the body's overall thyroid status.

Bone Density Scan: Bone Density scanning can be performed by many different machines. These machines screen a person's bones for their calcium content and overall strength. The DXA Scan (also called Dual X-ray Absorptiometry) is the most accurate and reliable measure for osteoporosis.

Cholesterol: A fasting blood test that measures the cholesterol levels in the blood. This measurement includes the total cholesterol value as well as the break down of good (HDL) and bad (LDL) cholesterols and triglyceride level.

Clinical Breast Exam: A complete manual examination of both breasts looking for suspicious nodules or masses performed by an experienced healthcare provider. This exam includes examination of all the breast tissue and the surrounding lymph nodes.

Clinical Testicular Exam: A clinical testicular exam is a full examination of the testicles for any suspicious masses by a qualified healthcare provider.

Colonoscopy: A Colonoscopy is a procedure performed by a gastroenterologist where a fiber optic tube with a camera on the end is inserted into the large intestine. The colonoscopy helps to prevent colon cancer by identifying any polyps or lesions that could become cancerous.

Complete Blood Count: A complete blood count (CBC) is a measure of the quantity and the concentration of the white blood cells, red blood cells, hemoglobin, and platelets found in the bloodstream.

Dental Exam: A dental examination is performed by a licensed dentist who exams the mouth for cavities, injured teeth and gum disease. Often a dental x-ray Is part of this routine examination.

Diabetic Foot Exam: A frequently neglected portion of the physical examination where the soles and forefoot of diabetes are examined for signs of infection, nerve disease, or other diabetic problems.

Digital Rectal Exam: A part of the physical examination where a healthcare provider inserts a gloved finger into the anus. This exam can detect prostate nodules, prostate cancer, and also rectal polyps and hemorrhoids.

EKG: An electrocardiogram, or EKG (also called an ECG by some), is a tracing of a 12 lead electronic signature of the heart. The heart emits an electronic impulse with each contraction and this registers on the EKG tracing as a waveform. These EKG "waves" can show evidence of heart enlargement, asynchrony, and even heart attacks.

Exercise Treadmill Test: A treadmill cardiac stress test is a procedure used to diagnose coronary artery disease (CAD...also called heart disease) or measure a person's functional status. The treadmill test involves walking on a exercise treadmill while being hooked up to an EKG and vital sign monitoring.

Fasting Blood Glucose: The Fasting Blood Glucose Test (FBGT) is a measurement of the amount of sugar in the blood stream at baseline. Glucose is the primary source of energy for our body. The liver can manufacture glucose, but most sugar molecules are taken in through the diet. The muscles, brain, and other vital organs require a constant glucose source to function. Individuals with high fasting glucose levels are likely to be diabetic.

Fecal Occult Blood Test: An excellent screening test for colon cancer where a small sample of stool is examined for hidden blood content. Hidden blood loss in to the bowels could be an early sign of colon cancer or polyps.

Flexible Sigmoidoscopy: A flexible sigmoidoscopy is a procedure where a fiber optic tube with a camera on the end is inserted into the large intestine. This ""Flex Sig"" scope helps to prevent colon cancer by identifying any polyps or lesions that could become cancerous.

Hearing Test: A hearing test is a specialized audiogram performed in a hearing booth to measure bilateral hearing acuity.

Helicobacter Pylori Antibody Blood Test: The Helicobacter Pylori antibody blood test measures a person's blood for the presence of an antibody to the Helicobacter Pylori bacteria. Having this antibody suggests ongoing infection with this bacteria. Helicobacter Pylori infection has been associated with peptic ulcer disease and some forms of stomach cancer.

Hemoglobin A1C: A blood test for diabetics that reveals the average blood sugar values over the past 3

APPENDIX 1: Glossary of Health & Medical Terms

months. This test is used to monitor patients with diabetes and assess their level of disease control. The goal Hemoglobin A1C should be less than 7.

Intraocular Pressure (IOP) Test: Intraocular pressure (IOP) can be measured by the primary care physician or the eye doctor. There are several different methods of measuring the eye pressure depending on equipment. An elevated eye pressure can be a sign of glaucoma.

Mammogram: A compression X-Ray of the breast tissue looking for suspicious calcifications, lesions, masses or other early signs of breast cancer. Baseline mammograms are usually initiated on women age 35-40 years old.

Pap Smear: A gynecologic examination by a healthcare provider where the female reproductive tract is examined manually for abnormalities. At the same time, a small sample of tissue is removed from the cervix using a small wooden spatula (called the PAP Smear). This cervical tissue specimen is then examined for suspicious cell types that could be the early stages of cervical cancer.

Prostate Specific Antigen: A blood test, called a PSA (Prostate Specific Antigen), can be used to detect the presence of prostate cancer in early stages. In the right situation, this test can help to diagnose prostate cancer before it becomes life threatening.

Retinal Eye Exam: A mandatory annual examination for all diabetics where the back of the eye (Retina) is examined for diabetic changes that could lead to blindness. Diabetic eye disease is the number one cause of blindness in our country.

Self Breast Exam: A complete manual examination of both breasts looking for suspicious masses. This self-exam is to be performed each month by the individual.

Self Testicular Exam: A self testicular exam is a full examination of the testicles for any suspicious masses by the individual. Self Testicular examination should be done monthly.

Total Body Skin Exam: A full skin exam is a complete examination of all of a person's skin for suspicious skin lesions that could be skin cancer or precancerous growths. This full exam is usually performed by either a primary care physician or a dermatologist.

Urinalysis: A simple test run on a urine sample looking for the presence of glucose, protein, blood, or any signs of infection in the urine.

MEDICATIONS

ACE Inhibitor: ACE (Angiotensin Converting Enzyme) Inhibitors are a family of medications used to control high blood pressure. ACE Inhibitors have been found to be very beneficial in diabetes for preventing kidney disease and in heart disease for remodeling heart muscle after heart attacks.

Anti-Anxiety Medication: Medications in this category include Valium, Xanax, Ativan to name a few. Anti-anxiety medications assist in re-establishing ideal brain chemistry to control anxiety and counterproductive emotions of panic and fear.

Anti-Depressant Medication: Medications in this category include antidepressants, which assist in re-establishing ideal brain chemistry to aid in recovering from mood disorders, anti-anxiety medications, and other mood stabilizers (some examples include Prozac, Zoloft, Celexa, Xanax, Lithium, and Depakote).

Aspirin: Aspirin is an anti-inflammatory medication used to treat sore muscles, arthritis, and headaches. Aspirin also plays a critical role in heart disease prevention by thinning the blood for people at risk for heart attack.

Asthma Inhaler: Common Asthma medications include Albuterol, Proventil, Advair, and Asmacort meter dose inhalers (MDI's). These preparations are inhaled into the lungs periodically to dilate the airways. Some preparations include an anti-inflammatory component as well. Individuals with aggressive disease may additionally need nebulizer treatments or by mouth medications like steroids or Singular.

Calcium (1500 mg each day): Calcium is a mineral that is found in our body predominantly in our bones. Calcium is found in most dairy products and in fortified cereals and fruit juices. Men and women should take in at least 1000mg to 1500mg of calcium every day.

Contrast Dye: Iodine was a large component of contrast dye used in the past for intravenous contrast during CAT Scans and X-rays. Today, contrast dye has much less iodine and generally is very well tolerated by most people.

Folate (1mg each day): A vitamin, also known as Folic Acid, in the B vitamin family that is associated with reduced risk of birth defects, cardiac events, and improved cognitive function.

High Blood Pressure Medication: Medications used to treat hypertension. There are numerous families of high blood pressure medicines (i.e. diuretics, beta blockers, calcium blockers, ACE Inhibitors, etc.) Each family works quite well with rather few significant side effects.

High Cholesterol Medication: Medications used to control blood cholesterol levels. The family of medicines most commonly used is the STATINs of which there are several different varieties (i.e. atorvastatin, simvastatin, lovastatin, pravastatin, etc.) The goal is to have your LDL level, the bad cholesterol, under good control.

Iodine: Iodine was a large component of imaging dye used in the past for intravenous contrast during CAT Scans and X-rays. Today, these imaging dyes have much less iodine in them and generally are very well tolerated by most people. Some people, who are allergic to iodine will react to lobster, shrimp, and some shellfish.

Morphine: Morphine is a strong narcotic pain medication. This medication is usually given into the veins during a hospital stay to treat pain. Morphine can be given by injection for severe pain.

Penicillin: Penicillin is an antibiotic medication used to treat certain infections like strep throat and syphilis.

Prednisone: A steroid medication that functions as an anti-inflammatory for some specific medical conditions. It is frequently used in the short term for asthma, poison ivy, and some forms of arthritis. Long term therapy with prednisone increases the risk of diabetes, cataracts, and osteoporosis.

Sulfa Drugs: Sulfa drugs are a group of medications made up of mostly antibiotics, although a few diuretics are also in this family. Some people are allergic to sulfa, and thereby need to stay away from these sulfa based products.

Tamoxifen: A medication that is a hormonal treatment used to reduce the potential development of breast cancer in women with high-risk family histories of the disease. This medication is also used at times to treat breast cancer.

Testosterone: Testosterone is the male sex hormone. Too much or too little testosterone can cause medical problems. Women have trace amounts of testosterone manufactured in their bodies.

Tetracycline: Tetracycline is an antibiotic usually used for rosacea. Tetracycline is in the same family as doxycycline.

Vitamin D (400mg each day): Vitamin D is manufactured in our skin from a sunlight reaction. Vitamin D is found in the recommended daily allowance in most multivitamins and in conjunction with calcium supplements.

Vitamin E (400iu each day): Vitamin E is a well known anti-oxidant that is found in the recommended daily allowance in most multivitamins.

Used with permission. © 2008, eDoc4u Division, Conduit Corporation, 3212 West End Avenue, 5th Floor, Nashville, TN 37203

Glossary of Legal Terms

Activities of daily living (ADL)

Activities usually performed for oneself in the course of a normal day. Although definitions differ, ADLs are usually considered to be mobility (e.g., transfer from bed to chair), dressing, bathing, self-feeding and toileting.

People may need assistance with ADLs regardless of their living arrangements. Assistance to a person limited in his/her ADLs is customarily performed by a family member, a home health aide or attendant, or a nurse's aide in a nursing facility. The assistance is of a nonmedical nature, commonly characterized as personal care, custodial care or physical care. Assistance provided in a home setting may extend beyond ADLs and include such nonmedical activities as housekeeping (e.g., cleaning, cooking), laundry and shopping.

Medicare cannot be looked to, except to a limited extent, for coverage of assistance with ADLs. Medicare pays for acute care services and does not provide coverage for chronic personal or custodial care.

Medicaid, unlike Medicare, will cover Medicaid-eligible persons for many home care services including personal care, and in certain cases ancillary services such as housekeeping.

Adult guardian

The person appointed by a court, usually a probate court under a modern protective services statute, to perform the court-ordered tasks of caring for an incapacitated adult's financial affairs and/or personal needs.

Three different types of guardians have varying degrees of authority:

- *Plenary guardian* with total authority over personal and property matters;
- *Guardian of the person* with authority only over personal matters such as medical decisions and residential questions; and
- *Guardian of the estate* with authority over property only

Assisted living facility

Provides a combination of housing and personalized health care in a professionally managed group-living environment designed to respond to the individual needs of persons who require assistance with activities of daily living.

This type of facility is specifically designed to promote maximum independence and dignity in the most residential and homelike setting possible. It may be all or part of a building that houses a few or several hundred persons, or a distinct part of a residential campus. It traditionally serves the more frail resident who cannot or chooses not to live alone, but who does not require the 24-hour skilled or custodial care of a nursing home.

Generally, residents of this type of housing pay privately in the form of rent, rent plus service charge, and sometimes a deposit or entry fee. In some states, Medicaid will pay for certain ADL services under home and community-based service waivers. Medicaid will not pay for room and board charges. Private long-term care insurance may also be used for some of the provided services.

Licensure of this housing type varies by state, depending upon each state's own regulatory requirements. These facilities sometimes are called residential care homes, domiciliary care homes, personal care homes, adult congregate living facilities, homes for the aged, catered living facilities, or board and care homes.

Balance billing/Medicare

This term refers to health care providers charging patients for amounts above the Medicare-approved charge. By Federal law antedating the Balanced Budget Act of 1997, the maximum allowable charge (charge limit) may not exceed 115% of the Medicare-approved charge. A number of states — Connecticut, Massachusetts, Minnesota, New York, Ohio, Pennsylvania, Rhode Island and Vermont — have by state statute banned the practice of balance billing. Although the statutes have been challenged in Federal courts on preemption grounds, each has withstood the challenge.

Under the Balanced Budget Act of 1997 which created Medicare+Choice plans, health care providers may or may not be permitted to engage in the practice of balance billing — depending upon the type of plan, and whether or not the provider has a contract with the plan.

Providers under contract - Under all Medicare+Choice plans, except private fee-for-service (PFFS) plans, physicians and other health care providers who contract with a plan may not balance bill. However, a contracting physician or other health care provider under a PFFS contract that establishes a payment rate for services may balance bill (i.e., charge) for their services an amount not to exceed, including deductibles, coinsurance, copayments or other balance billing, 115% of such payment rate.

Providers not under contract - Under all Medicare+ Choice plans, except Medicare+ Choice medical savings accounts (MSA) and PFFS plans, noncontracting physicians or other health care providers may not balance bill, but must accept as payment in full from a Medicare+Choice plan enrollee, the amount that would have been paid under traditional Medicare fee-for-service arrangement. However, a noncontracting physician or other health provider under an MSA or PFFS plan may balance bill without limitation.

Bed hold/Medicaid, Medicare

Preservation of a nursing home bed when a nursing home resident is temporarily hospitalized or out of the facility on therapeutic leave. State Medicaid programs may pay for bed holds, but are not required to. Nursing facility residents on Medicaid have a right to return to the first available bed in the facility which they temporarily left, even if the state has not paid to hold their original bed.

Medicare does not itself pay to hold a bed; moreover, it prohibits facilities from taking payment from beneficiaries to hold a bed if the date of return is certain. If it is not certain, beneficiaries may pay.

Community spouse's resource allowance (CSRA)/Medicaid

The CSRA is an amount of resources that states must protect for the spouse of an institutionalized person seeking Medicaid coverage. It is determined by application of a formula, or, as explained below, through a fair hearing, or by court order. The CSRA may not be counted in determining the eligibility of an individual seeking Medicaid.

The CSRA is determined as follows:

(1) All nonexempt resources belonging to either member of the married couple will be pooled together regardless of who owns them, and regardless of marital property laws (e.g., equitable distribution laws, community property laws).

(2) The community spouse is entitled to an amount (community resource allowance), subject to paragraph 3 below, equal to the greater of:

- $19,824 (2000), as adjusted annually for inflation, or more, if a greater minimum amount is set by the state, or
- One-half the total resources of the couple to a maximum of $16,824 (2000), as adjusted annually for inflation.

(3) A state may establish a dollar amount which is both the minimum and maximum resource amount. Under the foregoing formula, $84,120 represents a maximum and $16,392 represents a minimum on the CSRA. A state, by opting to use the maximum resource amount, can establish $84,120 as both a maximum and minimum. A state may opt to select a spousal share amount which, in the alternative, is that sum (e.g., New York, $74,820) or a greater figure equal to one-half of the couple's resources, but not to exceed the maximum figure of $84,120.

(4) The CSRA amount is determined according to resources owned by the couple on the first day of a continuous period of institutionalization regardless of whether the institutionalized spouse applied for Medicaid at the time. Either spouse may ask the Medicaid agency to complete an assessment of their resources as of that time.

The CSRA can be increased above the formula amount in two ways:

- Either spouse can request a fair hearing in which to demonstrate that a larger amount of resources must be protected (i.e., transferred to the community spouse from the institutionalized spouse) to generate income needed to bring the community spouse's income up to the minimum monthly maintenance needs allowance.
- A court order granting a larger amount of resources for the community spouse; the order must be honored by the Medicaid agency.

APPENDIX 2: Glossary of Legal Terms

Continuing care retirement community (CCRC)

This type of housing alternative, sometimes called a life care community, generally requires that an individual be able to live independently upon becoming a resident in the community. As a resident begins to need more assistance, specific additional services are made available. Most CCRCs offer three basic levels of housing on an as-needed basis: fully independent living, assisted living (personal care services) and skilled nursing care.

The basic idea of a CCRC is that once an individual becomes a resident, he/she never has to move again because any housing type and personal care services he/she will probably ever need are provided within the single campus setting. A CCRC guarantees housing and care across the continuum in that one community.

Generally, a CCRC will charge an entrance fee as well as a monthly payment for its residential, leisure and nursing services. In some cases, health care and personal care services can be paid for on an as-needed basis. The entrance fee, formerly nonrefundable, now is generally refundable on departure under a variety of specified conditions.

Basically, there are three types of CCRC contracts:

- *Extensive contract* - Covers shelter and residential services, amenities (e.g., swimming pool, possibly tennis courts and other types of recreation facilities) and unlimited long-term nursing care. The entrance fees and the monthly costs are usually higher than those under modified or fee-for-service contracts.

- *Modified or fee-for-service contract* - Provides shelter, residential services and amenities, plus a specified amount of nursing care, which the resident can obtain on an unlimited basis provided he/she pays for it at a daily or monthly nursing care rate.

- *Fee-for-service continuing care contract* - Covers shelter, meals, residential services and amenities, and in addition emergency and short-term nursing care. Access to long-term nursing care is provided only upon a daily nursing care rate.

Discharge planning

This service is usually performed by a social worker on staff in connection with a discharge of a patient from a hospital, nursing home or like institution. Discharge planning involves the social worker assessing the patient's level of functioning and needs following his/her discharge, including a smooth transition in moving from one level of care to another, for example from a hospital to a nursing home or from a hospital to home care. The discharge planner also contacts home health agencies to assist the patient in connection with his/her home care.

Estate recovery/Medicaid

Federal law mandates that each state place into effect an estate recovery program which provides for recovery of medical assistance to a Medicaid recipient. Mandated recovery centers mostly around the receipt by chronically ill individuals of long-term care services, although states may opt to recover Medicaid payments for other services rendered. The individuals and the assets subject to mandated recovery are set forth below.

1. Individuals subject to recovery - Recovery must be sought by the state from the following three categories of persons:

   A. Permanently institutionalized individuals - These are individuals in nursing facilities, intermediate care facilities for the mentally retarded or other medical institutions where the state has determined that the individual cannot reasonably be discharged from the facility and return home.

   B. Individuals age 55 and over - These individuals received from the state, through Medicaid, nursing home facility care, home and community-based services and related hospital and prescription drug services.

   C. Individuals with certain state authorized insurance programs - These individuals received Medicaid assistance under provisions of a state law (not recognized by Medicaid law) that permits a disregard by Medicaid of assets because of purchase of long-term care insurance, known as a Robert Wood Johnson Foundation insurance plan. Exempted are those individuals in five states with such state laws, recognized by Medicaid law, that were in effect on May 14, 1993. These states are California, Connecticut, Indiana, Iowa and New York.

2. Assets subject to recovery - The assets of these three categories of individuals which are subject to state recovery are set forth below.

Recovery must be sought from the estates of these individuals, as the term is defined by state probate law. States may adopt a broader definition of estate than is defined in state probate laws to include jointly held property and other property in which the recipient had a legal interest at the time of death. All states, except the five states mentioned in section 1C above, are mandated to apply this broader definition to any individual who received Medicaid nursing facility and other long-term care services under a Robert Wood Johnson insurance plan.

Recovery cannot occur against an individual's assets until after the death of the surviving spouse, and until there are no blind or disabled children or children under age 21.

If a lien has been properly imposed upon a Medicaid recipient's homestead, the state must seek recovery upon the sale of the liened property, or from the estate of the recipient after he/she dies. In either case, the state may not seek recovery if the Medicaid recipient's spouse is alive, if blind or disabled children or children under age 21 are alive, nor if certain siblings or caretaker children reside in the house.

Recovery from a spouse who survived the Medicaid recipient is neither required nor authorized by Medicaid law. However, some state laws do authorize recovery from a surviving spouse's estate, though these laws have been challenged as being beyond the scope of and inconsistent with the Federal law.

In situations where recovery would work undue hardship, Federal law requires states to waive it.

Hospice care/Medicare

Hospice care is designed for terminally ill persons and is covered by Medicare Part A. Hospice programs will care for patients in a hospice facility or whenever possible in their homes and emphasize relieving pain and managing symptoms rather than undertaking curative procedures. An individual may elect to receive hospice care rather than regular Medicare benefits for the management of his/her illness. For routine home care, Medicare coverage is available for the level of care that is reasonable and necessary. For periods of crisis, Medicare will cover continuous home care, including nursing for up to 24 hours per day. The beneficiary need not be homebound. During a person's lifetime, Medicare pays for up to two 90-day periods of hospice care followed by an unlimited number of 60-day periods that the individual elects to receive hospice, provided the following four conditions are met:

- The attending physician — either in the employ of the hospice, or under contract with the hospice as an independent physician or part of an independent physicians group — and the medical director of the hospice must establish and periodically review a written plan for hospice care and at the beginning of each of the successive periods mentioned above, certify that a patient is terminally ill, i.e., that the patient's life expectancy is six months or less.

- The patient must elect to receive care from a hospice instead of standard Medicare medical benefits for the terminal illness. A patient may elect to revert to standard Medicare benefits, but will then be required to pay any applicable deductibles and copayments.

- Care must be provided by a Medicare-certified hospice program.

- The individual must be eligible for Part A benefits.

If these conditions are met, Medicare will pay for the following services:

- nursing services;

- doctors' services;

- drugs, including outpatient drugs for pain relief and symptom management;

- physical, occupational and speech-language therapy;

- home health aides and homemaker services;

- medical social services;

- medical supplies (including drugs and biologicals) and appliances;

- short-term inpatient care including respite care, procedures necessary for pain control, and acute and chronic symptom management;

- training and counseling for the patient and family members; and

- any other item or service which is specified in the plan mentioned above and for which payment may otherwise by paid by Medicare.

There is no deductible for these hospice care benefits. Copayments, however, are required for two benefits:

- prescription drugs for pain relief and symptom management, for which patients can be charged 5% of the reasonable cost, but no more than $5 per prescription; and

- respite care, for which a patient can be charged about $5 per day, depending on the area of the country.

Medicare+Choice organizations are not required to provide hospice services but may do so on a voluntary basis

Income cap states/Medicaid

Several states, referred to as income cap states, do not have a medically needy program serving nursing facility residents. In these states individuals are not allowed to spend down to the SSI income level (i.e., cap) to become eligible for Medicaid-covered nursing home care.

These states avail themselves of an optional Medicaid program termed the optional categorically needy program under which individuals are provided limited nursing facility coverage. Under this program individuals qualify for Medicaid nursing home coverage if their countable income does not exceed a cap of a prescribed percentage, usually 300%, of the SSI benefit for one person. The cap is categorically fixed and severe: one dollar of excess income above the cap will disqualify the individual. An individual is not permitted to spend down for medical expenses, nor can he/she forego collection of a pension, Social Security benefits or interest income in order to fall within the income cap.

A possible method for reducing the income of an individual seeking to qualify under the optional categorically needy program, also commonly referred to as the 300% program, is to obtain from a state court a Qualified Domestic Relations Order which allocates pension payments to the community spouse. The community spouse as the payee under such order arguably is the beneficiary of the pension, and payments to him/her would constitute his/her income under the name-on-the-check rule, not income of the institutionalized spouse who was the original pensioner.

Another method of qualifying for the optional categorically needy program is available under the provisions of OBRA '93. With this law Congress allowed individuals in income cap states to become eligible for Medicaid nursing home assistance by putting their income (e.g., pension, Social Security benefits) into a so-called Miller trust. During the Medicaid recipient's lifetime, all but a small portion of the money in the trust must go toward paying the nursing home bill. If any money remains in the trust after the recipient's death, it must be paid to the state, up to the amount of Medicaid assistance that was rendered.

The income cap states are Alabama, Alaska, Colorado, Delaware, Idaho, Mississippi, Nevada, New Mexico, Ohio, South Dakota and Wyoming.

Nursing home reform law

Sometimes referred to as OBRA '87, this Federal law regulating aspects of nursing homes is contained in the Omnibus Budget Reconciliation Act of 1987. It is the most comprehensive Federal nursing home law since the passage of Medicare and Medicaid in 1965. It sets Federal standards of care, including one stipulating that nursing homes may use physical and chemical restraints only in very specific circumstances and only after other interventions have been tried. The bill also establishes certain rights for patients and requires states and the Federal government to inspect nursing homes and to enforce standards through the use of a range of sanctions designed to promote compliance without forcing the relocation of residents due to the closing of facilities.

The resident's bill of rights, mandated in the nursing home reform law, includes a resident's rights to:

- admit and discharge oneself;

- control one's own medical care and be informed of all aspects of one's health;

- choose his/her own physician of own choice and refuse treatment;

- self-administer drugs;

- be free of restraints (physical or chemical);

- see all his/her medical records;

- receive notice of any decision to transfer or discharge or change a roommate;

- manage own financial affairs;

- receive visitors of one's choice as well as refuse visitors; and

- have access to a private telephone.

Transfers or discharges are permitted only under three situations:

- if necessary for the resident's welfare and if her/his needs cannot be met in the facility;

- if a resident's health has improved and he/she no longer needs care; or
- if a resident's presence or nonpayment of charges endangers the health and safety of other residents in the facility.

All residents, whether private pay or receiving Medicaid assistance or Medicare benefits, are entitled to due process, namely, a fair hearing. In this connection, the procedures for Medicaid fair hearings apply to nursing home transfers and discharges. The right to a pretransfer hearing is mandated except for emergency transfers subject to a resident's right to a bedhold pending a post-transfer hearing.

The law requires every resident to undergo a process known as preadmission, screening, and annual resident review. Prior to admission there is to be a functional evaluation, and at the time of admission a comprehensive care plan must be developed. This plan must be prepared annually with a physician and nursing team.

The law contains a number of other significant requirements. Nursing homes may not require as a condition for admission or for continuing stay a guarantee of payment from a third party. They must provide coverage by a registered nurse, not less than eight hours a day, seven days a week. Aides must go through a training program and pass a nursing aide registry certification. States are required to create a nursing aide registry to train, certify and maintain a listing of all approved workers.

Pourover will

The testator provides in his/her will that designated assets will be paid over and distributed to a previously established trust.

Program for all-inclusive care for the elderly (PACE)

Based on a model created by On Lok Senior Services in San Francisco, this program began as a Medicare and Medicaid demonstration project initially tested at ten sites. The Balanced Budget Act expanded PACE to become an option open to all states. PACE targets frail elderly persons living at home who are eligible for nursing home care. The program integrates health and long-term care services in an adult day care setting and uses a multidisciplinary case management team of providers, including physicians, nurses, social workers, nutritionists, occupational and speech therapists, and health and transportation personnel. PACE participants are required to attend an adult day care center regularly.

Unlike the Social Health Maintenance Organization project, PACE providers in the demonstration project receive most of their funding from Medi-caid. The funding is allocated according to a fixed monthly capitated fee for each participant based on the frailty of enrollees. The project represents a test to link acute care under Medicare and long-term care under Medicaid.

The Balanced Budget Act of 1997 established PACE as a state option to furnish comprehensive health care to persons who are enrolled with an organization that has contracted to operate the PACE program, who are eligible for Medicaid, and who receive Medicaid solely through the PACE program. The salient characteristics of PACE offered as a state option are set forth below.

PACE providers may be public or private not-for-profit entities, except for those entities (up to 10) participating in the demonstration to test the operation of PACE by private, for-profit entities. During the three-year period beginning August 5, 1997, the Secretary of HHS is required to give priority to entities operating a PACE demonstration waiver program, and then to entities that have applied to operate a program as of May 1, 1997. The number of PACE program agreements that may be effective on August 5 of each year is limited. HCFA authorized up to 80 in 1999 and has limited increases by 20 for each following year.

Persons eligible for PACE must be 55 years of age or older; require nursing facility level of care that would be covered under a state's Medicaid program; reside in the service area of the PACE program; and meet such other eligibility conditions as may be imposed under the PACE program agreement. Eligible individuals include both Medicare and Medicaid beneficiaries. Medicare participants not enrolled in the PACE program through Medicaid must pay premiums equal to Medicaid capitation. PACE enrollees will be reevaluated annually to determine if they continue to need nursing facility level of care.

Under a PACE agreement, a provider at a minimum must provide eligible persons all care and services covered under Medicare and Medicaid. The services must be provided without any limitation or condition as to amount, duration and scope and without application of deductibles, copayments, coinsurance or other cost sharing that would otherwise apply under Medicare or Medicaid. The services must be provided 24 hours per day, every day of the year through a comprehensive multi-disciplinary health and social services delivery system which integrates acute and long-term services.

Primary medical care for a PACE enrollee must be furnished by a primary care physician who serves as a gatekeeper for access to treatment by specialists. HCFA may grant waivers of this requirement. A primary care physician, registered nurse, medical director, program director, other health professionals and a governing body to guide the operation must be part of the multi-disciplinary team.

States will make a prospective monthly capitation payment for each enrollee in an amount specified in the PACE agreement. PACE agreements are for one year, but may be extended for additional contract years at the discretion of the Secretary of HHS.

Qualified long-term care insurance contract

The Health Insurance Portability and Accountability Act of 1996 extends certain tax advantages to a qualified long-term care insurance contract, sometimes informally called a tax-qualified policy. The law defines such a contract as a guaranteed renewable life insurance contract or as a rider to a life insurance contract, under which the only insurance protection provided is coverage of qualified long-term care services. A qualified LTCI contract does not pay or reimburse expenses reimbursable by Medicare, except for coinsurance or deductible amounts. Nor may a qualified LTCI contract provide for a cash surrender value or other money that can be paid, pledged or borrowed. Further, certain consumer protection provisions set forth in the Long-term Care Services Model Regulations and Model Act of the National Association of Insurance Commissioners must be part of the contract.

To be qualified, LTCI contracts sold after January 1, 1997 must meet Federal standards explained above. Policies issued prior to this date that have met existing state standards are considered qualified policies though they may not meet the Federal requirements.

Qualified long-term care services

The Health Insurance Portability and Accountability Act of 1996 defines qualified long-term services as necessary diagnostic, preventive, therapeutic, curing, treating, mitigating and rehabilitative services and maintenance or personal care services which are required by a chronically ill individual and provided pursuant to a plan of care prescribed by a licensed health care provider. The phrase "maintenance or personal care services" means any care the primary purpose of which is the provision of needed assistance with any of the disabilities as a result of which the individual is chronically ill, including severe cognitive impairment. The cost of qualified long-term services can be counted as a medical expense deduction for income tax purposes.

Remainderman

This is a person or other entity designated in a trust as the beneficiary entitled to the principal or corpus of the trust after the income-paying stage comes to an end, that is after the income beneficiary of the trust has been paid in full in accordance with the terms of the trust.

Representative payee

Under Federal laws a representative payee may act as a surrogate on behalf of an individual who is not capable of making cognitive decisions, for the purpose of receiving and handling cash benefit checks of a Social Security or Supplemental Security Income recipient. The legal authority of the surrogate is usually limited to merely managing the benefits received for the well-being of the original beneficiary. A representative payee can be a public agency, nonprofit organization, bank or an individual.

The designation of a representative payee generally is a protective arrangement for incapacitated persons. It is less restrictive, simpler and less expensive than alternative protective arrangements such as guardianship or conservatorship and does not require a judicial finding of incompetency or incapacity. The arrangement can be terminated if the recipient regains cognitive ability to handle the government benefits to which he/she is entitled.

Reverse mortgage

A reverse equity mortgage allows senior citizens who are house rich and cash poor to obtain a loan based on the equity in their home. They retain title to their home as long as they continue to live there and receive nontaxable income which they can flexibly use for their own needs. According to the terms of most mortgages currently available, the loan, interest and other costs such as origination fees do not have to be paid back until the owner vacates the property through a move or death. Almost all reverse mortgages now provide a guarantee of lifetime tenancy. Most reverse mortgages are nonrecourse loans which means the lender can look only to the value of the home for repayment.

APPENDIX 2: Glossary of Legal Terms

Payments to a home owner from a reverse mortgage can be in the form of a single lump sum of cash, regular monthly advances or a line of credit. New mortgage plans allow a combination of payment methods. The amount of the loan is seldom for the full value of the property; most lenders place minimum and maximum limits on the size of mortgages they are willing to establish. Loan periods can vary.

Some mortgages combine a reverse mortgage with an annuity, thereby guaranteeing individuals monthly income for their lifetime regardless of whether they continue to live in their homes or not. The monthly payments are considered annuity advances and thus partially taxable. For purposes of Medicaid edibility these payments may be counted as income.

Reverse mortgages are currently available in all states, except Texas, and the District of Columbia. Several different plans are available, some more widely than others. Plan features offered by the same lender can vary from state to state. The Home Equity Conversion Mortgage is federally insured through the U.S. Department of Housing and Urban Development and is the most widely available plan. In 1995 the Federal National Mortgage Association began a program called Home Keeper. The three main private for-profit plans are offered by Transamerica HomeFirst, Freedom House Equity Partners, and Household Senior Services.

Roth IRA

The Roth IRA, named after Senator Roth who created it under the Taxpayer Relief Act of 1997, is a nondeductible individual retirement account. Several significant differences exist between a traditional or deductible IRA and a Roth IRA:

- eligibility to contribute to a Roth IRA is subject to special adjusted gross income limits;
- contributions to a Roth IRA are not deductible;
- Roth IRA contributions may be made after the owner has attained the age of 70½; and,
- qualified distributions from a Roth IRA are not included in gross income or subject to the minimum distribution rules if certain conditions are met.

As with a traditional IRA, the income earned on the assets of a Roth IRA is tax free prior to distribution.

Contributions to a Roth IRA are subject to two limitations:

- *Dollar limitation* - Under this a contribution cannot exceed the maximum amount allowed after the deduction for a regular IRA (the lesser of $2,000 or 100% of an individual's compensation), reduced by any contributions that an individual may have made for a taxable year to any other individual retirement plan(s) maintained for the individual's benefit.

- *Adjusted gross income limitation* - This is based upon an individual's modified adjusted gross income. The Roth IRA contribution for a taxable year is phased out after adjusted gross income reaches certain levels. The amount an individual can contribute to a Roth IRA declines when his/her income reaches $95,000 and phases out entirely when the adjusted gross income reaches $110,000. For married individuals filing jointly, the phase out occurs when their adjusted gross income is between $150,000 and $160,000, and for married individuals filing separately, the phase out occurs when the adjusted gross income is between $0 and $10,000.

An individual may make a regular contribution to both a traditional IRA and a Roth IRA for a taxable year. In this case a maximum contribution limit for a Roth IRA is the lesser of the amount determined under the dollar limitation reduced by the amount contributed to a traditional IRA for the taxable year; or, the amount determined under the adjusted gross income limitation. Eligible taxpayers may contribute to both a Roth IRA and a deductible IRA by dividing their contribution between the two. But in no event may an individual's combined total annual contributions exceed $2,000.

Withdrawals from a Roth IRA are tax exempt only if: the account has been in existence for at least five years and the taxpayer is at least age 59½ or disabled; or a distribution of no more than $10,000 is made to finance the first-time home buying expenses of a taxpayer, his/her spouse or children, grandchildren, or ancestors of a taxpayer or spouse.

Skilled nursing care

The term refers to a level of care which must be furnished by or under direct supervision of licensed nursing personnel and under the general direction of a physician in order to assure the safety of the patient and achieve the medically desired result. The service involves observation and assessment of the total needs of the patient, planning and management of a treatment plan, and rendering direct services to the patient. As long as a patient needs skilled nursing care, it makes no difference whether his/her condition is acute, chronic or terminal.

Examples of skilled nursing care are:

- intravenous injections,
- tube feeding,
- kidney dialysis,
- colostomy care,
- the use of medical gases,
- observation and monitoring of a patient's unstable condition, and
- changing sterile dressings.

Expressly excluded from the term is any service that could be safely and effectively performed (or self-administered) by the average nonmedical personnel without the direct supervision of a licensed nurse.

In determining whether the level of care required by a patient is custodial care, which is not Medicare-covered, or skilled nursing care, which is covered by Medicare, the courts have applied several accepted legal principles:

- The primary responsibility determining a patient's need for skilled nursing care rests with the physician.
- While the opinion of a physician about the need for skilled nursing care is not binding on Medicare, when there is no conflicting evidence, his decision is required to be given great weight.
- The courts will avoid using a technical approach but rather use a common sense meaning and a consideration of the needs and underlying conditions affecting the patient as a whole.

Skilled nursing facility/Medicare

A skilled nursing facility is specially staffed and equipped to provide intensive nursing and rehabilitative care to patients. Care is provided by registered and other licensed nurses or licensed therapists under the supervision of a doctor. Medicare's requirement for admission to a skilled nursing facility, the benefits covered and the period of coverage are set forth below.

Supplemental needs trust

This type of trust, also known as a special needs trust, is an irrevocable trust, sometimes funded by assets of a third party, created for a disabled beneficiary, and intended to supplement government benefits. The trust prohibits the trustee from spending trust assets in diminution of government benefits. The beneficiary has no power to control distributions.

For SSI and generally for Medicaid, disbursements from the trust are governed by SSI income principles. If payments are made for food, clothing or shelter, or if payments are made directly to the beneficiary, the amounts are counted as income to the beneficiary for purposes of eligibility. The more common arrangement with such trusts is for the trustee to make direct payments to vendors of services or goods that are not food, clothing or shelter; such payments are not considered income to the beneficiary.

In addition to these general rules, Medicaid has special rules governing the treatment of trusts established by and for a Medicaid recipient or his/her spouse during their lifetime. These rules are discussed under the entry Trust, Medicaid eligibility rules.

Terminally ill

See also *Hospice care/Medicare*

An illness, disease or injury where recovery can no longer be reasonably expected. For purposes of Medicare-covered hospice care, a person with a terminal illness has a life expectancy of six months or less, as certified by a physician, if the illness runs a normal course. In the context of tax regulations governing accelerated benefits, a terminally ill person has a reasonable life expectancy of 24 months or less.

Testator

The person who creates a will.

The glossary is reprinted with permission and made up of selections from the Dictionary of Eldercare Terminology *by Walter Feldesman (2nd edition, National Information Services Corporation).*

Entry Name Index / A

A

AA Member - Medications and Other Drugs, 7287
AA Potter Engineering Center, 6887
AA Service Manual/Twelve Concepts for World Service, 7288
AA and the Armed Services, 7289
AA and the Gay/Lesbian Alcoholic, 7290
AA as a Resource for Health Care Professionals, 7291
AA for the Native North American, 7292
AA for the Woman, 7293
AA in Correctional Facilities, 7294
AA in Treatment Facilities, 7295
AAA, 11922
AAACE, 2671, 2675
AAAD Bulletin, 6596
AAAS Resource Directory of Scientists and Engineers with Disabilities, 3686
AAC: Augmentative and Alternative Communication, 3815
AACD Legal Series, 11279
AAHA Provider News, 3996
AAN-MA's Toll-Free Hotline, 4641
AARP, 812, 2303, 2501, 2686, 2690, 3614, 3974, 3995, 4130, 6008, 4171
AARP Bulletin, 3974
AARP Fulfillment, 3644, 3853, 3933, 3978, 4055, 4078, 4958, 6026
AARP Grief and Loss Program, 3724
AARP Legal Advocacy Group, 11039
AARP Newsletter, 3997
AARP Ohio Office, 1940
AARP Pharmacy Service, 3998
AARP Southeast Regional Office, 812
AARP Southwest Regional Office, 2303
AARP West Regional Office, 2501
AARP-Consumer Protection, 4172
AARP: Alabama-Huntsville OfficeInformation Center, 2691
AARP: Alabama-Mobile OfficeInformation Center, 2692
AARP: Alabama-Montgomery Office, 2693
AARP: Alaska-Anchorage Branch Office Information Center, 2696
AARP: Alaska-Anchorage Main Office, 2697
AARP: Arizona-Phoenix Office, 2699
AARP: Arizona-Tucson Information Center, 2700
AARP: Arkansas State Office, 2708
AARP: California-Pasadena Office, 2714
AARP: California-Sacramento Office, 2715
AARP: Colorado-Denver Office, 2735
AARP: Colorado-Pueblo Information Center, 2736
AARP: Connecticut State Office, 2739
AARP: Delaware State Office, 2744
AARP: District of Columbia State OfficeCorporate Headquarters, 2746
AARP: Florida-Miramar Office, 2749
AARP: Florida-St Petersburg Office, 2750
AARP: Florida-Tallahassee Office, 2751
AARP: Georgia State Office, 2762
AARP: Hawaii-Big IslandInformation Center, 2771
AARP: Hawaii-Honolulu Office, 2772
AARP: Hawaii-Kauai Information Center, 2773
AARP: Hawaii-Oahu Information Center, 2774
AARP: Idaho State Office, 2776
AARP: Illinois State Office, 2777
AARP: Indiana State Office, 2781
AARP: Iowa State Office, 2786
AARP: Kansas State Office, 2788
AARP: Kentucky State Office, 2799
AARP: Louisiana State Office, 2802
AARP: Maine State Office, 2804
AARP: Maryland State Office, 2806
AARP: Massachusetts State Office, 2814
AARP: Michigan-Detroit Information Cntr, 2822
AARP: Michigan-Lansing Office, 2823
AARP: Minnesota-BloomingtonInformation Center, 2826
AARP: Minnesota-St Paul Office, 2827
AARP: Mississippi State Office, 2829
AARP: Missouri Information Center North, 2830
AARP: Missouri Information Center South, 2831
AARP: Missouri-Kansas City Office, 2832
AARP: Montana State Office, 2840
AARP: Nebraska-Lincoln Office, 2841
AARP: Nebraska-Omaha Information Center, 2842
AARP: Nevada State Office, 2843
AARP: New Hampshire-ConcordInformation Center, 2844
AARP: New Hampshire-Manchester Office, 2845
AARP: New Jersey State Office, 2846
AARP: New Mexico-AlbuquerqueInformation Center, 2849
AARP: New Mexico-Sante Fe Office, 2850
AARP: New York Albany State Office, 2852
AARP: New York City State Office, 2853
AARP: North Carolina State Office, 2874
AARP: North Dakota State Office, 2884
AARP: Ohio State Office, 2885
AARP: Oklahoma-Edmond Office, 2893
AARP: Oklahoma-Oklahoma City Office, 2895
AARP: Oklahoma-Oklahoma CityInformation Center, 2894
AARP: Oregon State Office, 2897
AARP: Pennsylvania-Harrisburg Office, 2902
AARP: Pennsylvania-Philadelphia Office, 2903
AARP: Rhode Island State Office, 2912
AARP: South Carolina State Office, 2914
AARP: South Dakota-Rapid City Office, 2919
AARP: South Dakota-Sioux Falls Office, 2920
AARP: Tennessee State Office, 2921
AARP: Texas-Austin Office, 2923
AARP: Texas-Dallas Office, 2924
AARP: Texas-Houston Office, 2925
AARP: Utah State Office, 2931
AARP: Vermont State Office, 2932
AARP: Virginia State Office, 2933
AARP: Washington State Office, 2939
AARP: West Virginia State Office, 2946
AARP: Wisconsin State Office, 2948
AARP: Wyoming State Office, 2951
AASE Hougen Assisted Living, 8626
ABA Community on Legal Problems of the Elderly, 3591
ABC's of Dementia, 4946
ABC-CLIO, 4535
ABE International Airport, 12030
ABLE, 10926
ABLEDATA, 3055
ACAP Recap, 7284
ACB Government Employees, 6773, 7493, 8002
ACB Radio Amateurs, 6774, 7494, 8003
ACB Reports, 7911
ACB Social Service Providers, 6775, 7495, 8004
ACE Fitness Matters, 3816
ACS Wireless, 3056
AD LIB Incorporated, 10787
ADA & the Consumer Who is Deaf or Hard of Hearing, 6597
ADA Clinical Education Series on CD-Rom, 6256
ADA Technical Assistance Program, 813
ADA and Hearing-Impaired Consumers, 6598
ADARA, 3999, 6300
ADARA Updated, 3999
ADM Publishing, 6033
AE Livingston Health Sciences Library, 11452
AER, 3817, 7912
AER Report, 3817, 7912
AFB Directory of Services for Blind and Visually Impaired Persons in the US, 7794, 7837
AFB News, 7913
AFB Press, 7811, 6742
AFB Toll-Free Hotline, 7496
AGHE Exchange Newsletter, 4000
AHA Guide to the Health Care Field, 3687
AID Bulletin, 4544
AIDS, 4575
AIDS Action Baltimore, 4534
AIDS Action Bulletin, 4534
AIDS Alert, 4515
AIDS Community Resources, 4444
AIDS Crisis in America, 4535
AIDS Directory, 4536
AIDS For Daily Living, 3317
AIDS Funding: A Guide to Giving by Foundations & Charitable Organizations, 4516
AIDS Health Pamphlets, 4545
AIDS Info, 4577
AIDS Institute, 4489
AIDS Legal Council of Chicago, 11081
AIDS Medicines in Development, 4546
AIDS Memorial Quilt, 4478
AIDS News, 4547
AIDS Policy and Law, 4548
AIDS Prevention Program, 4513
AIDS Program, 4457, 4509
AIDS Programs, 4470
AIDS Project Los Angeles, 4551
AIDS Reader, 4517
AIDS Section, 4461
AIDS Task Force of Central New York, 4444
AIDS Treatment Data Network, 2854
AIDS and Deafness: Resource Directory, 4537, 6554
AIDS and Hemophilia: Protecting Yourself and Others, 4549

979

Entry Name Index / A

AIDS and STD Prevention Program, 4451
AIDS/HIV Program, 4511
AIDS/HIV Treatment Directory, 4538
AIDS/Sexually Transmitted Diseases Control Branch, 4462
AIDS: A Communication Perspective, 4518
AIDS: Distinguishing Between Fact and Opinion, 4519
AIDS: What We Need to Know, 4550
AIDSLAW of Louisiana, 11124
AIDSinfo, 4445
AIPHONE Intercom Systems, 3057
ALC Copper Hills House, 8110
ALDA News, 7914
ALPHA One, 10780
AMC Cancer Information and Counseling Line, 5252
AMC Cancer Research Center, 5252, 5880
AMC Cancer Research Center Medical Library, 11359
AMC: Cancer Information and Counseling Line, 5253
AMI Aquamassage, 3246
APH Catalog of Accessible Books for People Who Are Visually Impaired, 7838
APH Catalog of Accessible Books for People who are Visually Impaired, 7795
APLA, 4086
APLA Update, 4551
APT Technology, 3036, 3058, 3548
APT Technology Switches, 3058
ARC Gateway, 731
ARC's Government Report, 4001
ASHA, 6568
ASHA Magazine: ASHA Leader, 6569
ASMA Hotline, 4642
AT&T Portable Telephone Amplifier, 3059
ATA Newsletter, 6599
AUL Forum, 4002
Aarenbrooke Place: Ashley Manor, 8447
Aaron Diamond AIDS Research Center, 4584
Abbey Delray Health Center, 8329
Abbey Home Healthcare, 3293
Abbeyville Assisted Living, 8900
Abbotsford Seniors' Association, 346
Abbotswood at Irving Park Assisted Living, 9363
Aberdeene Meadows, 9364
Ability, 4003
Ability Center for Independent Living, 10856
Ability Center of Greater Toledo, 10894
Ability Research, 3060
Ability Resources, 10900
Abingdon Manor for Adults, 10551
Abington Place of Gastonia, 9365
Able Commission, 1476
Able-Phone, 3061, 3062, 3063, 3075
Able-Phone 100, 3061
Able-Phone 1900, 3062
Able-Switch SW-1, 3063
AbleNet, 3083, 3085, 3101, 3102, 3123, 3125, 3162, 3166, 3168, 3170, 3174, 3185, 3241, 3275, 3298, 3301, 3313, 3314, 3326, 3344, 3347
Abledata, 6301
Ablephone, 3152, 3191
About AIDS, 4520
About High Blood Pressure, 6916
Abstracts in Social Gerontology, 4004

Abstracts in Social Gerontology: Current Literature on Aging, 3592, 3688, 3818
Abundant Care, 10384
Abused Deaf Women's Advocacy Services, 2502, 6302
Academic Software, 3067, 3074, 3144, 3192
Academy Point at Mystic, 8252
Academy for Lifelong Learning and Community Center for Successful Aging, 2815
Academy of Dispensing Audiologists, 6555, 6303
Academy of Dispensing Audiologists Membership Directory, 6555
Academy of Lifelong Learning, 2745
Academy of Rehabilitative Audiology, 6585, 6304
Academy of Senior Professionals of Eckerd (ASPEC), 2752
Acadiana Legal Service Corporation, 11125
Acantilado Vista, 9826
Accent Books & Products, 3304, 3307, 3689
Accent Buyers Guide Edition, 3689
Accent Special Publications,Cheever Publishing,Inc, 3690
Accent on Living, 3819
Accent on Living: Buyer's Guide, 3690
Access Alaska-Anchorage, 10625
Access Alaska-Fairbanks, 10626
Access Center for Independent Living, 10709, 10895
Access II Independent Living Center, 10814
Access Industries/ThyssenKrupp Access, 3375, 3387, 3389, 3399, 3409, 3413, 3355
Access Industries/Thyssenkrupp Access, 3395
Access Living of Chicago, 10722
Access Review, 7852
Access Technologies, 2040
Access Travel: Airports, 7839, 11910
Access USA, 3454, 3065
Access to Art: A Museum Directory for Blind & Visually Impaired People, 7840
Access to Art: A Museum Directory for the Blind and Visually Impaired People, 7796
Access to Independence, 10951
Access to Independence and Mobility (AIM, 10859
Access to Independence and Mobility-Bath (AIM), 10860
Access to Independence of Cortland County, 10861
Access to Travel Magazine, 11911
Access with Ease, 3033, 3039, 3240, 3259, 3268, 3306, 3324, 3450, 3452
Access-USA, 3448
Accessibility Lift, 3356
Accessible Journeys, 12004
Achromatopsia Network, 7497
Ackerman Institute for the Family, 4258
Acorn Glen, 9741
Act Wheelchair, 3497
Act for Health, 12040
Action Products, 3233, 3194
Action Toward Independence, 10862
Action for Eastern Montana, 1526
Active Aging, 2091
Activities Keep Me Going & Going, Vol 1, 3593
Activities Keep Me Going & Going, Vol 2, 3594

Activities for the Elderly: Volume 1-A Guide to Quality Programming, 3595
Activities for the Elderly: Volume 2-Working with Residents with Significant Physical and Cognitive Diseases, 3596
Activities in Action, 3597
Activities with Developmentally Disabled Elderly and Older Adults, 3598
Activity Factory, 11857
Activity Programming for Persons with Dementia: A Sourcebook, 4947
Adams Community Center, 1265
Adams Council on Aging, 1265
Adams County Council on Aging, 963
Adams County Office for Aging, 2092
Adams County RSVP, 898
Adams House, 10050
Adamsplace Assisted Living, 10339
Adapted Physical Activity Quarterly, 3820
Adaptivation, 3066
Adaptive Design Shop, 3000
Adaptive Device Locator System, 3067
Adaptive Driving Conversions, 2953
Adaptive Golf Car Model 4850, 3287
Adaptive Resources Guide, 7057
Adaptive Vans for the Physically Challenged, 2954
Addiction and Responsibility, 7235
Addictions Counseling, 7236
Addictive Personality, 7237
Addictive Thinking Understanding Self-Deception, 7238
Addie's You & I Travel Service, 12005
Addison-Wesley, 5148, 5150, 5154, 5155
Addison-Wesley Publishing Company, 4976
Addolorata Villa, 8579
Address Book, 3446
Address List: Regional and Subregional Libraries for the Blind and Physically Handicapped, 7841
Adjustable Bed, 3034
Adjustable Clear Acrylic Tray, 3318
Adjustable Incline Board, 3473
Adjustable Raised Toilet Seat, 3001
Adjustable Rigid Chair, 3042
Adjustable Toilet Safety Rails, 3002
Adjustment, Adaptation and Accomodation: Psychological Approaches, 6085
Adler School of Professional Psychology, 11450
Administration for Children and Families, 294
Administration on Aging, 4173
Administration on Aging (AoA), 1
Administration on Aging/Statistical Information, 4174
Administration on Aging: Office of Field Operations, 2
Administration on Aging: Office of Program Development, 3
Administration on Aging: Office of State and Community Programs, 4
Administration on Developmental Disabilities, 5
Administrative Advocacy Clinic/Advocates for Older People, 11040
Admix Publishing, 11911
Adult Bible Lessons for the Deaf, 6600
Adult Children & Aging Parents, 3599
Adult Congenital Heart Disease: A Practical Guide, 6848

Entry Name Index / A

Adult Residential Care Home, 8448
Advance Directive and Living Will Resources, 4175
Advanced Cancer: Living Each Day, 5810
Advanced Sign Language Vocabulary, 6464
Advanced Technology Corporation, 3424
Advanced Temporary Services, 3565
Advances, 4979
Advances in Cardiac and PulmonaryRehabilitation, 6849
Advancing Gerontological Social Work Education, 3600
Advent Residential Care, 10385
Advice From Your Allergist, 4664
Advocacy, 2385
Advocacy & Access, 6601
Advocacy Center for the Elderly and Disabled, 1173
Advocacy Centre for the Elderly, 347
Advocado Press, 3847
Advocates for Medicare Patients (AMP's), 11131
Advocates for the Disabled, 10978
Aegis Escondido, 8130
Aegis Gardens, 8131
Aegis Lodge, 10577
Aegis Senior Living of Shoreline, 10578
Aegis at Northgate, 10579
Aegis at Shadowridge, 8132
Aegis of Aptos, 8133
Aegis of Bothell, 10580
Aegis of Carmichael, 8134
Aegis of Chino Hills, 8135
Aegis of Concord, 8136
Aegis of Corte Madera, 8137
Aegis of Dana Point, 8138
Aegis of Edmonds, 10581
Aegis of Fremont, 8139
Aegis of Granada Hills, 8140
Aegis of Issaquah, 10582
Aegis of Kent, 10583
Aegis of Kirkland, 10584
Aegis of Laguna Niguel, 8141
Aegis of Las Vegas, 9735
Aegis of Lynnwood, 10585
Aegis of Moraga, 8142
Aegis of Napa, 8143
Aegis of Pleasant Hill, 8144
Aegis of Redmond, 10586
Aegis of San Francisco, 8145
Aegis of San Rafael, 8146
Aegis of Shoreline (Callahan House), 10587
Aegis of Ventura, 8147
Aeroquip Wheelchair Securement System, 2955
Affectionate Care, 10386
African American Family Services, 7276, 7316, 7340
African-Americans and Stroke, 7080
After a Stroke: 300 Tips to Making LifeEasier, 7058
Afton Oaks Assisted Living, 8627
Agape Senior Homes, 9091
Age & Opportunity Inc., 348
Age Base, 4132
Age Care Sourcebook: A Resource Guide for the Aging and Their Families, 3691
Age of Reason, 4176
Age-Related Macular Degeneration, 7797, 7915
AgeAdvantAge Area Agency on Aging: Madison, 11294

AgeAdvantAge Area: Agency on Aging Western Office, 2568
Ageing, Spirituality and Well-Being, 3601
Agency for Health Care Research and Quality, 4585
Agency of Human Services, 2441
Aging & Adult Admin\AZ Dept of Economic Security, 3683
Aging & Vision News, 7853
Aging Alert, 4005
Aging And Community Service Of South CenTral Indiana, 964
Aging Children & Aging Parents, 3602
Aging Comes of Age, 3603
Aging Eye and Low Vision, 7798
Aging International, 3821
Aging Network News, 4006
Aging News Alert, 3822
Aging Office of Western Nebraska, 1565
Aging Research & Training News, 3823
Aging Research Institute, 4259
Aging Research and Training News, 4007
Aging Research: National Institute on Aging, Public Health Service, 4260
Aging Services, 2093
Aging Services Division, 2002
Aging Services for the Upper Cumberlands, 11256
Aging Today, 3975
Aging and Adult Administration, 10980
Aging and Community Services, 979
Aging and Disabilities, 2439
Aging and Hearing Loss: Some Commonly Asked Questions, 6602
Aging and In Home Services of Northeast Indiana, 11097
Aging and In-Home Services, 965
Aging and Long Term Care of Eastern Washington, 2503
Aging and Society, 3824
Aging and Vision, 7916
Aging and Vision News, 7917
Aging and Vision: Declarations of Independence, 7854
Aging in America, 4261
Aging in Stride: A Practical Guide forOlder Adults & Their Families, 3604
Aging in the Designed Environment, 3605
Aging, Physical Activity, and Health, 3606
Aging, Rights and Quality of Life: Prospects for Older People with Developmental Disabilities, 3607
Agitation... It's a Sign, 5026
Ahnafield Corporation, 2978, 3302, 3552
Ahoskie House, 9366
Aids for Arthritis, 5165
Aiken Area Council on Aging, 2223
Air Force Aid Society, 6
Air Lift Unlimited, 3544
Air Liftunlimited, 3544
AirLift Toileting System from Mobility, 3003
Airphone Corporation, 3113
Airport Council International - North America, 7839, 11910
Akathisia in Parkinson's Disease, 6989
Akron Blind Center and Workshop, 7498
Akron Resources, 3068
Al-Anon, 7438
Al-Anon Fact File, 7296
Al-Anon Family Group Headquarters, 6513, 7239, 7241, 7255, 7263, 7266, 7296, 7297, 7298, 7299, 7300, 7301, 7302, 7303, 7304, 7319, 7320, 7321, 7322, 7327, 7334
Al-Anon Family Groups - Classic Edition, 7239
Al-Anon Focus, 7297
Al-Anon Is for Men, 7298
Al-Anon Newcomer Packet, 7299
Al-Anon Spoken Here, 7300
Al-Anon and Professionals, 7301
Al-Anon, Newcomer's Packet, 7302
Al-Anon, You, and the Alcoholic, 7303
Alabama Bureau of Tourism and Travel, 11949
Alabama Chapter Office, 5081
Alabama Chapter of the Arthritis Foundation, 5081
Alabama Client Assistance Program, 358
Alabama Department of Education: Disability Determination Service, 359
Alabama Department of Public Health, 360, 4446
Alabama Department of Rehabilitation Services, 361
Alabama Department of Retirement Systems, 362
Alabama Department of Revenue, 363
Alabama Department of Senior Services, 364, 10968
Alabama Department of Veteran Affairs, 365
Alabama Developmental Disability Council, 366
Alabama Disabilities Advocacy Program, 367
Alabama Disabilities Advocacy Program (ADAP), 10969
Alabama Division of Mental Illness and Substance Abuse Community Programs, 7127
Alabama Industries for the Blind, 7499
Alabama Institute for Deaf and Blind, 11306
Alabama Protection & Advocacy for Persons with Mental Illness, 368
Alabama Protection and Advocacy Agency, 10969
Alabama Public Library Service, 11307
Alabama Radio Reading Service Network, 369
Alabama Regional Library for the Blind and Physically Handicapped, 11307
Alabama State Bar: Elder Law, 10970
Alabama State Department of Human Resources, 370
Alabama Tombigbee Regional Commission, 371
Alabama Workers Compensation Division, 372
Alameda County Area: Agency on Aging, 489
Alamo Area: Agency on Aging, 2304
Alaska Client Assistance Program (CAP), 404
Alaska Commission on Aging, 405
Alaska Commission on Aging: Alaska Department of Health & Social Services, 10974
Alaska Department of Health and Social Services-AIDS/STD Program, 4447
Alaska Department of Military and Veterans Affairs, 406
Alaska Department of Revenue, 407

Entry Name Index / A

Alaska Disability Law Center, 408
Alaska Division of Mental Health and Developmental Disabilities, 409
Alaska Division of Retirement & Benefits, 410
Alaska Division of Tourism, 11950
Alaska Division of Vocational Rehabilitation, 411
Alaska Governor's Committee on Employment and Rehabilitation of People with Disabilities, 412
Alaska Legal Services Corporation: Senior Legal Services Project, 10975
Alaska State Library Talking Book Center, 11316
Alaska Statewide Independent Living Council, 413
Alaska Welcomes You, 414
Alaska Workers Compensation Board, 415
Alaskans Commission on Aging, 416
Alateen Talks Back on Higher Power, 7304
Albany Avenue Adult Congregate Living Facility, 8330
Albany County Department for Aging and the Handicapped, 1748
Albany Medical College: Joint Center for Cancer and Blood Disorders, 5881
Albany Talking Book Center, 11624
Albemarle Commission, 1885
Albert Einstein College of Medicine, 4443, 5080
Alcohol & Drug Abuse Services Administration, 7128
Alcohol Alert #11: Estimating the Cost of Alcohol Abuse, 7305
Alcohol Alert #15: Alcohol and AIDS, 7306
Alcohol Alert #16: Moderate Drinking, 7307
Alcohol Alert #17: Treatment Outcome Research, 7308
Alcohol Alert #18: The Genetics of Alcoholism, 7309
Alcohol Alert #21: Alcohol and Cancer, 7310
Alcohol Alert #23: Alcohol and Minorities, 7311
Alcohol Alert #24: Animal Models in Alcohol Research, 7312
Alcohol Alert #25: Alcohol-Related Impairment, 7313
Alcohol Alert #26: Alcohol and Hormones, 7314
Alcohol Alert #27: Alcohol Medication Interactions, 7315
Alcohol Rehabilitation for the Elderly, 7129
Alcohol Research Group: Public Health Institute, 7130
Alcohol Research Information Service, 7369
Alcohol and Drug Abuse in Black America: A Guide for Community Action, 7316
Alcohol-Drug Treatment Referral, 7131
Alcoholics Anonymous, 7243, 7287, 7288, 7289, 7290, 7291, 7292, 7293, 7294, 7295, 7317, 7336, 7356, 7361, 7362, 7363, 7364, 7365, 7367, 7370, 7378
Alcoholics Anonymous and Employee Assistance Program, 7317
Alcoholics Anonymous, The Big Book, 7240
Alcoholics Anonymous: An Inside View, 7431
Alcoholism Information and Treatment Directory, 7280
Alcoholism Tends to Run in Families, 7318
Alcoholism, a Merry-Go-Round Named Denial, 7319
Alcoholism: The Family Disease, 7320
Alden Place, 8931
Alderman Oaks Retirement Center, 8331
Alderwood Assisted Living, 10051
Alerter, 5168
Alerting and Communication Devices for Deaf & Hard of Hearing People, 6603
Alexander Graham Bell Association for the Deaf: Kentucky Chapter, 6305
Alexander Graham Bell Association for the Deaf, 3635, 6483, 6488, 6489, 6490, 6499, 6503, 6507, 6509, 6520, 6523, 6528, 6560, 6593, 6597, 6598, 6620, 6623, 6644, 6645, 6648
Alexander Graham Bell Association for the Deaf and Hard of Hearing, 6776
Alexander Graham Bell Association forthe Deaf and Hard of Hearing, 6306
Alexandria Library Talking Book Service, 11809
Alexandria Library: Special Collections, 11810
Alexandria Office of Aging and Adult Services, 2447
Alexandria Volunteer Bureau, 2448
Alhambra Retirement Community, 8148
Alice B. Silver Size Clothing Designs for Senior Women, 4177
Alison Health Care Center, 8628
All About the New Generation of Hearing Aids, 6604
All-Purpose Openers, 3319
Allegany County Area: Agency on Aging, 1224
Allegany County Office for the Aging, 1749
Allegheny County Area Agency on Aging, 11235
Allegheny County Department of Aging, 2094
Allen County Public Library, 11481, 11473
Allen County Public Library of New Haven, 11474
Allen County Public Library of Woodburn, 11475
Allen County Public Library, Aboite Branch, 11476
Allen County Public Library, Pontiac Branch, 11477
Allen House, 8629
Allen Morgan Health Center at Trezevant Manor, 10340
Allendale Community for Mature Living, 9742
Allergies A to Z, 4652
Allergies and You, 4665
Allergy Control Products, 4662
Allergy Plants That Cause Sneezing and Wheezing, 4653
Allergy Products Directory: Allergy/Asthma, Finding Help (Volume Three), 4663
Allergy Publications, 4663
Allergy Research Foundation, 4679
Allergy and Asthma Network Mothers ofAsthmatics, 4643, 4674
Allergy and Asthma Network/Mothers of Asthmatics, 4670
Allergy-Free Garening: The Revolutionary Guide to Healthy Landscaping, 4654
Allerton House at Central Park, 8932
Allerton House at Hancock Park, 8933
Allerton House at Harbor Park, 8934
Allerton House at the Village at Duxbury, 8935
Alliance Assisted Living Services, 9092
Alliance Newspaper, 3976
Alliance Press, 11858
Alliance for Aging, 732
Alliance for Aging Research, 4262
Alliance for Disabled in Action, 10848
Alliance for Lung Cancer Advocacy Support and Education, 5254
Alliance of People With Disabilities, 11286
Alliance on Aging and Vision Loss, 7500
Almond House, 9093
Alpena Regional Medical Center Auxiliary, 1339
Alpine Area Agency on Aging, 627
Alpine House Assisted Living, 10052
Alpine Springs Assisted Living and Cottages, 10053
Alpine View Lodge, 8149
Alta Mira Press, 3761
Altera Sterling House of Fargo, 9554
Alternative Medicine Magazine's Definitive Guide to Cancer, 5789
Alternative Publications, 3985
Alterra Clare Bridge Cottage of Monroe, 9743
Alterra Clare Bridge Cottage of Oklahoma City, 9979
Alterra Clare Bridge Cottage of Raleigh, 9367
Alterra Clare Bridge Cottage of Richland, 10387
Alterra Clare Bridge Cottage of West St Paul, 9094
Alterra Clare Bridge Cottage-Coon Rapids, 9095
Alterra Clare Bridge Cottage-Owatonna, 9096
Alterra Clare Bridge Oklahoma City, 9980
Alterra Clare Bridge of Asheville, 9368
Alterra Clare Bridge of Bradenton, 8332
Alterra Clare Bridge of Brick, 9744
Alterra Clare Bridge of Cary, 9369
Alterra Clare Bridge of Charlotte, 9370
Alterra Clare Bridge of Eagan, 9097
Alterra Clare Bridge of Galloway, 9745
Alterra Clare Bridge of Greensboro, 9371
Alterra Clare Bridge of Hamilton, 9746
Alterra Clare Bridge of North Oaks, 9098
Alterra Clare Bridge of Plymouth, 9099
Alterra Clare Bridge of Richardson, 10388
Alterra Clare Bridge of South Park, 9372
Alterra Clare Bridge of Southern Pines, 9373
Alterra Clare Bridge of Westhampton, 9747
Alterra Clare Bridge of Wilmington, 9374
Alterra Clare Bridge of Winston Salem, 9375
Alterra Sterling House of Abilene, 8756
Alterra Sterling House of Abilene II, 8757
Alterra Sterling House of Alliance, 9858
Alterra Sterling House of Apple Valley, 9100
Alterra Sterling House of Arkansas, 8758
Alterra Sterling House of Augusta, 8759
Alterra Sterling House of Bartlesville, 9981
Alterra Sterling House of Bethany, 9982
Alterra Sterling House of Blaine, 9101

Entry Name Index / A

Alterra Sterling House of Broken Arrow, 9983
Alterra Sterling House of Cedar Hill, 10389
Alterra Sterling House of Claremore, 9984
Alterra Sterling House of Coon Rapids, 9102
Alterra Sterling House of Derby, 8760
Alterra Sterling House of Desoto, 10390
Alterra Sterling House of Dodge City, 8761
Alterra Sterling House of Durant, 9985
Alterra Sterling House of Edmond, 9986
Alterra Sterling House of Emporia, 8762
Alterra Sterling House of Enid, 9987
Alterra Sterling House of Fairdale, 8763
Alterra Sterling House of Faribault, 9103
Alterra Sterling House of Florence, 9748
Alterra Sterling House of Georgetown, 10391
Alterra Sterling House of Goldsboro, 9376
Alterra Sterling House of Great Bend, 8764
Alterra Sterling House of Greenville, 9377
Alterra Sterling House of Hays, 8765
Alterra Sterling House of Hickory, 9378
Alterra Sterling House of Inver Grove Heights, 9104
Alterra Sterling House of Jacksonville, 8333
Alterra Sterling House of Junction, 8766
Alterra Sterling House of Lancaster, 10392
Alterra Sterling House of Lawrence, 8767
Alterra Sterling House of Lawton, 9988
Alterra Sterling House of Leawood, 8768
Alterra Sterling House of Lenexa I, 8769
Alterra Sterling House of Lenexa II, 8770
Alterra Sterling House of Maltsberger, 10393
Alterra Sterling House of McPherson, 8771
Alterra Sterling House of Midwest City, 9989
Alterra Sterling House of Muskogee, 9990
Alterra Sterling House of Nacogdoches, 10394
Alterra Sterling House of New Bern, 9379
Alterra Sterling House of Norman, 9991
Alterra Sterling House of Oklahoma City, 9992
Alterra Sterling House of Olathe, 8772
Alterra Sterling House of Olathe II, 8773
Alterra Sterling House of Ponca City, 9993
Alterra Sterling House of Punta Gorda, 8334
Alterra Sterling House of Raleigh, 9380
Alterra Sterling House of Rocky Mount, 9381
Alterra Sterling House of Salina, 8774
Alterra Sterling House of Shawnee, 9994
Alterra Sterling House of Shelby, 9382
Alterra Sterling House of Southern Pines, 9383
Alterra Sterling House of Springfield, 9859
Alterra Sterling House of Tavares, 8335
Alterra Sterling House of Topeka, 8775
Alterra Sterling House of Tulsa, 9995
Alterra Sterling House of Tulsa South, 9996
Alterra Sterling House of Venice, 8336
Alterra Sterling House of Waxahachie, 10395
Alterra Sterling House of Weatherford, 9997
Alterra Sterling House of West St Paul, 9105
Alterra Sterling House of Wichita, 8776
Alterra Sterling House of Woodland, 8777
Alterra Sterling House-Brooklyn Center, 9106
Alterra Sterling House-Mankato, 9107
Alterra Sterling House-Sauk Rapids, 9108
Alterra Sterling House-Willmar, 9109
Alterra Sterling House-Winona, 9110
Alterra Sterling of ADA, 9998
Alterra Sterling-Owatonna, 9111
Alterra Wynnwood of Northampton Manor, 10191
Alterra Wynwood at Riverplace, 8449
Alterra Wynwood at Twin Falls, 8450
Alterra Wynwood of Albany, 10054
Alterra Wynwood of Boynton Beach East, 8337
Alterra Wynwood of Chapel Hill, 9384
Alterra Wynwood of Charlotte, 9385
Alterra Wynwood of Dunedin, 8338
Alterra Wynwood of Emerson, 9749
Alterra Wynwood of Galloway, 9750
Alterra Wynwood of Greensboro, 9386
Alterra Wynwood of McMinnville, 10055
Alterra Wynwood of Rochester, 9112
Alterra Wynwood of Wayne, 9751
Altier & Maynard Communications, 3977
Altimate Medica, 3371
Alton Ochsner Medical Foundation, 6918
Altria Plainview, 9827
Altria Windsor Woods, 8339
AlumiRamp, 3357
Aluminum Adjustable Support Canes for the Blind, 3474
Aluminum Crutches, 3475
Aluminum Walking Canes, 3476
Alzheimer Association: Boise/Treasure Valley Chapter, 4701
Alzheimer Association: Greater Idaho Region, 4702
Alzheimer Disease and Associated Disorders, 4980
Alzheimer Early Stages, 2nd Edition, 11688
Alzheimer Research Forum, 5038
Alzheimer Support, 5039
Alzheimer Treatment Research Center Library, 11730
Alzheimer's Advocates Handbook, 4981
Alzheimer's Alliance: Northeast Texas, 4703
Alzheimer's Assocation: South Central Michigan Chapter, 4704
Alzheimer's Association, 2780, 4156, 4710, 4944, 4947, 4948, 4960, 4961, 4965, 4966, 4978, 4979, 4981, 4982, 4986, 4987, 4988, 4990, 4991, 4992, 4994
Alzheimer's Association Autopsy Assistance Network, 4706
Alzheimer's Association Greater Baton Rouge Chapter, 4707
Alzheimer's Association Greater Richmond Chapter, 4708
Alzheimer's Association Greater Youngstown Chapter, 4709
Alzheimer's Association Hotline, 4710, 5040
Alzheimer's Association Middle Tennessee Chapter, 4711
Alzheimer's Association NW Florida Chapter, 4712
Alzheimer's Association National Brochure, 4982
Alzheimer's Association Newsletter, 4983
Alzheimer's Association North Alabama Regional Office, 4713
Alzheimer's Association Tarrant County Chapter, 4984
Alzheimer's Association of Ashland, 4714
Alzheimer's Association of Greater Wisconsin: Eau Claire, 4716
Alzheimer's Association of Greater Wisconsin: Fox Valley, 4717
Alzheimer's Association of Greater Wisconsin-Wausau Regional Office, 4715
Alzheimer's Association of Hayward Wisconsin, 4718
Alzheimer's Association of Southern Minnesota Chapter, 4719
Alzheimer's Association of Superior, 4720
Alzheimer's Association, STAR Chapter, 5041
Alzheimer's Association: Alaska Chapter, 4722
Alzheimer's Association: Aloha Chapter, 4723
Alzheimer's Association: Augusta Chapter, 4724
Alzheimer's Association: California Central Coast Chapter, 4725
Alzheimer's Association: California Southland Chapter, 4726
Alzheimer's Association: Carolina Piemont Chapter, 4727
Alzheimer's Association: Central Georgia Chapter, 4728
Alzheimer's Association: Central Illinois Chapter, 4729
Alzheimer's Association: Central Indiana Chapter, 4730
Alzheimer's Association: Central Maryland Chapter, 4731
Alzheimer's Association: Central New York Chapter, 4732
Alzheimer's Association: Central Ohio Chapter, 4733
Alzheimer's Association: Central Virginia Chapter, 4734
Alzheimer's Association: Central and North Florida Chapter, 4735
Alzheimer's Association: Central and Western Kansas, 4736
Alzheimer's Association: Charleston Office, 4737
Alzheimer's Association: Charlotte/DeSoto Counties Chapter, 4738
Alzheimer's Association: Clark-Champaign-Logan Chapter, 4739
Alzheimer's Association: Cleveland Area Chapter, 4740
Alzheimer's Association: Coastal Bend Chapter, 4741
Alzheimer's Association: Colorado Chapter, 4742
Alzheimer's Association: Connecticut Chapter, 4743
Alzheimer's Association: Corn Belt Chapter, 4744
Alzheimer's Association: Dallas Chapter, 4745
Alzheimer's Association: Delaware Valley, 4746
Alzheimer's Association: Desert Southwest Chapter, 4747
Alzheimer's Association: Detroit Area Chapter, 4748
Alzheimer's Association: Dubuque Branch, Mississippi Valley Chapter, 4750

Entry Name Index / A

Alzheimer's Association: Dubuque BranchMississippi Valley Chapter, 4749
Alzheimer's Association: East Central Florida Chapter, 4752
Alzheimer's Association: East Central Michigan Chapter, 4753
Alzheimer's Association: East Central Ohio Chapter, 4754
Alzheimer's Association: East CentralIowa Chapter, 4751
Alzheimer's Association: Eastern North Carolina Chapter, 4755
Alzheimer's Association: Eastern Shore Region, 4756
Alzheimer's Association: Eastern Tennessee Chapter, 4757
Alzheimer's Association: Eastern Washington Chapter, 4758
Alzheimer's Association: El Paso Chapter, 4759
Alzheimer's Association: Florida Gulf Coast Chapter, 4760
Alzheimer's Association: Four Rivers Chapter, 4761
Alzheimer's Association: Georgia Chapter, 4762
Alzheimer's Association: Great Plains Area Chapter, 4763
Alzheimer's Association: Greater Austin Chapter, 4765
Alzheimer's Association: Greater Billings Area Chapter, 4766
Alzheimer's Association: Greater Cincinnati, 1941
Alzheimer's Association: Greater Columbus Chapter, 4767
Alzheimer's Association: Greater East Texas Chapter, 4769
Alzheimer's Association: Greater Eastern Ohio Area Chapter, 4770
Alzheimer's Association: Greater Eastern Ohio Chapter, 4768
Alzheimer's Association: Greater Idaho Chapter, 4771
Alzheimer's Association: Greater Illinios Chapter, 4772
Alzheimer's Association: Greater Maryland Chapter Western Maryland Region, 4773
Alzheimer's Association: Greater Miami Chapter, 4774
Alzheimer's Association: Greater New Hampshire Chapter, 4776
Alzheimer's Association: Greater NewJersey Chapter, 4775
Alzheimer's Association: Greater North Valley Chapter, 4777
Alzheimer's Association: Greater OrlandoArea Chapter, 4778
Alzheimer's Association: Greater PalmBeach Chapter, 4779
Alzheimer's Association: Greater Pennsylvania Chapter, 4780
Alzheimer's Association: Greater Pittsburgh Chapter, 4781
Alzheimer's Association: Greater Sacramento Chapter, 4782
Alzheimer's Association: Greater Texarkana Chapter, 4783
Alzheimer's Association: Greater Wisconsin Chapter, 4784
Alzheimer's Association: GreaterCincinnati Chapter, 4764
Alzheimer's Association: Green-Field Library, 11451
Alzheimer's Association: Grover Chapter, 4785
Alzheimer's Association: Hampton Roads Chapter, 4786
Alzheimer's Association: HarrisonburgRegion, 4787
Alzheimer's Association: Heart of Iowa Chapter, 4789
Alzheimer's Association: Heart ofAmerica Chapter, 4788
Alzheimer's Association: Highland Rim Chapter, 4790
Alzheimer's Association: Houston & Southeast Texas Chapter, 4791
Alzheimer's Association: Houston andSoutheast Texas Chapter, 4792
Alzheimer's Association: Hudson Valley/Rockland/Westchester NY Chapter, 4793
Alzheimer's Association: Indianhead Chapter, 4794
Alzheimer's Association: Iowa Golden Chapter, 4795
Alzheimer's Association: Lake Superior Chapter, 4796
Alzheimer's Association: Laurel Mountains Chapter, 4797
Alzheimer's Association: Lexington/Bluegrass Chapter, 4798
Alzheimer's Association: Long IslandChapter, 4799
Alzheimer's Association: Los Angeles Chapter, 4800
Alzheimer's Association: Louisville Chapter, 4801
Alzheimer's Association: Maine Chapter, 4802
Alzheimer's Association: Manatee/Sarasoto Counties Chapter, 4803
Alzheimer's Association: Marin Chapter, 4804
Alzheimer's Association: Marquette/Alger Chapter, 4805
Alzheimer's Association: Mary's Peak Chapter, 4806
Alzheimer's Association: Massachusetts Chapter, 4808
Alzheimer's Association: MassachusettsChapter, 4807
Alzheimer's Association: Memphis Chapter, 4809
Alzheimer's Association: Miami Valley Chapter, 4810
Alzheimer's Association: Mid Missouri Chapter, 4811
Alzheimer's Association: Mid-MichiganChapter, 4812
Alzheimer's Association: Mid-Ohio ValleyRegional Office, 4813
Alzheimer's Association: Mid-State South Carolina Chapter, 4814
Alzheimer's Association: Middle Mississippi Chapter, 4815
Alzheimer's Association: Midstate Wisconsin Chapter, 4816
Alzheimer's Association: Minnesota Lakes Chapter, 4817
Alzheimer's Association: Mississippi Valley Chapter, 4818
Alzheimer's Association: Mohawk Valley Chapter, 4819
Alzheimer's Association: Monroe RegionalCenter, 4820
Alzheimer's Association: Monterey CountyChapter, 4821
Alzheimer's Association: NationalCapital Area Chapter, 4822
Alzheimer's Association: New Mexico Chapter, 4823
Alzheimer's Association: New York City Chapter, 4824
Alzheimer's Association: North Central Texas Chapter, 4825
Alzheimer's Association: North Central West Virginia Chapter, 4826
Alzheimer's Association: North Dakota Chapter, 4827
Alzheimer's Association: North New Jersey Chapter, 4828
Alzheimer's Association: Northeast Michigan Chapter, 4829
Alzheimer's Association: Northeast Pennsylvania Chapter, 4830
Alzheimer's Association: Northeast Tennessee Chapter, 4831
Alzheimer's Association: Northeast Texas Chapter, 4832
Alzheimer's Association: Northeast Wisconsin Chapter, 4833
Alzheimer's Association: Northern Alabama Chapter, 4835
Alzheimer's Association: Northern Connecticut Chapter, 4836
Alzheimer's Association: Northern Idaho Resource Center, 4837
Alzheimer's Association: Northern Indiana Chapter, 4838
Alzheimer's Association: Northern Nevada Chapter, 4839
Alzheimer's Association: Northern Virginia Chapter, 4840
Alzheimer's Association: NorthernArizona, 4834
Alzheimer's Association: Northwest Florida Chapter, 4841
Alzheimer's Association: Northwest Lousiana Chapter, 4842
Alzheimer's Association: Northwest Missouri Chapter, 4843
Alzheimer's Association: Northwest Ohio, 4844
Alzheimer's Association: Oklahoma Chapter, 4845
Alzheimer's Association: Oklahoma and Arkansas Chapter, 4846
Alzheimer's Association: Omaha/Eastern Nebraska Chapter, 4847
Alzheimer's Association: Orange County Chapter, 4848
Alzheimer's Association: Oregon Chapter, 4849
Alzheimer's Association: Oregon-Trail Chapter, 4850
Alzheimer's Association: Panhandle Area Chapter, 4851
Alzheimer's Association: Piedmont Triad North Carolina Chapter, 4852
Alzheimer's Association: Putnam County Chapter, 4853
Alzheimer's Association: Rhode Island Chapter, 4854

Entry Name Index / A

Alzheimer's Association: Riverland Chapter, 4855
Alzheimer's Association: Riverside/SanBernardino Counties Chapter, 4856
Alzheimer's Association: Rochester Chapter, 4857
Alzheimer's Association: Rocky Mountain Chapter, 4858
Alzheimer's Association: STAR Chapter, 4859, 4860
Alzheimer's Association: Salem Regional Office, 4861
Alzheimer's Association: San Diego Chapter, 4862
Alzheimer's Association: San Francisco Bay Chapter, 4863
Alzheimer's Association: Santa Barbara Chapter, 4864, 4865
Alzheimer's Association: Santa CruzLocal Office, 4866
Alzheimer's Association: Siouxland, 4867
Alzheimer's Association: Siouxland Chapter, 4868
Alzheimer's Association: South Central Michigan Chapter, 1340, 4869
Alzheimer's Association: South Central Wisconsin Chapter, 4870
Alzheimer's Association: South Dakota Office, 4871
Alzheimer's Association: South Jersey Chapter, 4872
Alzheimer's Association: South Plains Chapter, 4873
Alzheimer's Association: Southeast Florida Chapter, 4875
Alzheimer's Association: Southeast Georgia Chapter, 4876
Alzheimer's Association: Southeast Pennsylvania Chapter, 4877
Alzheimer's Association: Southeast Tennssee Chapter, 4878
Alzheimer's Association: SoutheastWisconsin Chapter, 4874
Alzheimer's Association: Southern Arizona, 4879
Alzheimer's Association: Southern Illinois Chapter, 4880
Alzheimer's Association: Southern Nevada Chapter, 4881
Alzheimer's Association: Southern Tier Chapter, 4882
Alzheimer's Association: Southside Virginia Chpater, 4883
Alzheimer's Association: Southwest Georgia Chapter, 4885
Alzheimer's Association: Southwest Montana Chapter, 4886
Alzheimer's Association: SouthwestMissouri Chapter, 4884
Alzheimer's Association: SpringfieldRegional Office, 4887
Alzheimer's Association: St Louis Chapter, 4888
Alzheimer's Association: Star Chapter West Texas Region, 4889
Alzheimer's Association: Staten Island Chapter, 4890
Alzheimer's Association: Sullivan/Delaware Chapter, 4891
Alzheimer's Association: Tarrant County Chapter, 4892

Alzheimer's Association: Topeka Regional Office Heart of America Chapter, 4893
Alzheimer's Association: Traverse CityRegional, 4894
Alzheimer's Association: Upstate South Carolina Chapter, 4895
Alzheimer's Association: Utah Chapter, 4896
Alzheimer's Association: Vermont Chapter, 4897
Alzheimer's Association: Volusia/Flagler Counties Chapter, 4898
Alzheimer's Association: West Central Florida Chapter, 4899
Alzheimer's Association: West Central Minnesota Chapter, 4900
Alzheimer's Association: West Hawaii Chapter, 4901
Alzheimer's Association: West Michigan Chapter, 4902
Alzheimer's Association: West Shore Chapter, 4903
Alzheimer's Association: West South Dakota Chapter, 4904
Alzheimer's Association: West VirginaChapter, 4905
Alzheimer's Association: Western & Central Washington Chapter, 4906
Alzheimer's Association: Western Massachusetts Chapter, 4907
Alzheimer's Association: Western New York Chapter, 4908
Alzheimer's Association: Western North Carolina Chapter, 4909
Alzheimer's Association: Western Slope, 4910
Alzheimer's Association: Wichita FallsRegional Office, 4911
Alzheimer's Association: Wyoming Chapter, 4912
Alzheimer's Association:-Michigan Great Lakes Chapter Southwest Region, 4913
Alzheimer's Association:Hudson Valley/Rockland/Westchester, NY Chapter, 4721
Alzheimer's Disease, 4975, 5027
Alzheimer's Disease & Related DisordersAssociation, Greater Iowa Chapter, 4914
Alzheimer's Disease Center, 4915, 5042
Alzheimer's Disease Education & Referral Center, 4142, 4950, 4985, 5001, 5028, 5032, 5035
Alzheimer's Disease Education and Referral (ADEAR) Center, 4916
Alzheimer's Disease International, 5043
Alzheimer's Disease Orientation Kit, 4948
Alzheimer's Disease Support Group Janesville Chapter, 4917
Alzheimer's Disease Support Group: Janesville Chapter, 4918
Alzheimer's Disease Treatment and Family Stress: Directions for Research, 4949
Alzheimer's Disease and Related Disorders Association, 4919
Alzheimer's Disease: A Guide for Families, 4976
Alzheimer's Disease: A Guide to Federal Programs, 4950, 4985
Alzheimer's Disease: A Handbook for Caregivers, 4951

Alzheimer's Disease: Activity-Focused Care, 4952
Alzheimer's Disease: An Overview, 4986
Alzheimer's Disease: Services You May Need, 4987
Alzheimer's Disease: Statistics, 4988
Alzheimer's Disease: an Educational Training Program for Social Workers, 5028
Alzheimer's Foundation of America, 4920, 5044
Alzheimer's Foundation of Staten Island, 4921
Alzheimer's Foundation of the South & Mississippi Division, 4922
Alzheimer's Handbook, 4953
Alzheimer's Research Review, 4989
Alzheimer's Resource Center, 4923
Alzheimer's Resource Center Orlando, 4924
Alzheimer's Support Groups for Family and Friends, 4925
Alzheimer's Wyoming, 4926
Alzheimer's, Stroke and 29 Other Neurological Disorders Sourcebook, 4954
Alzheimer's: The Answers You Need, 4955
Alzheimers Aid Society of Northern California, 4927
Alzheimers of Central Alabama, 4928
Alzhimer's Association of Greater Wisconsin, 4929
Amador Senior Services, 10993
Amanda House, 9860
Amazing Grace Family Living, 8080
Ambassabor Nebraska City Assisted Living, 9591
Ambassadors Courtyards, 9999
Amber Oaks, 10396
Amber Ridge, 8630
Amelia Historical Society: Amelia Historical Library, 11811
Amelia House, 8631
Amer Assoc of Homes and Services for the Aging, 3692
America West Airlines/US Airways, 11912
America West/US Airways Airline, 12006
America's Health Insurance Plans, 7
American Academy of Addiction Psychiatry, 7451
American Academy of Allergy & Immunology, 4642, 4673
American Academy of Allergy and Immunology, 4644, 4675
American Academy of Ambulatory Care Nursing, 8
American Academy of Audiology, 3892, 4015, 6308, 6777
American Academy of Dermatology, 4178
American Academy of Environmental Medicine, 4645
American Academy of Neurology, 4930, 5045, 7051
American Academy of Nurse Practitioners, 9
American Academy of Nursing, 10
American Academy of Ophthalmology, 7501
American Academy of Oral and Maxillofacial Radiology, 11
American Academy of Otolaryngology, 6749, 6755
American Academy of Otolaryngology-Head and Neck Surgery, 6309

985

Entry Name Index / A

American Academy of Otolaryngology-Head & Neck Surgery, 4179
American Academy of Otolaryngology: Head and Neck Surgery, 12
American Academy of Otolaryngology:Head and Neck Surgery, 6310
American Action Fund for Blind Children and Adults, 7502
American Aging Association, 3899, 4263
American Airlines, 11913
American Alliance for Health, Phys Ed & Dance, 3624
American Alliance for Health, Phys. Ed. & Dance, 3633
American Alliance for Health: Physical Education, Recreation and Dance, 13
American Annals of the Deaf, 6570
American Annals of the Deaf: Reference Issue, 6556
American Assembly for Men in Nursing, 14
American Assn. of Homes & Services for the Aging, 2629, 2634, 2642, 2643, 2654, 2687, 3709, 3996, 4077, 4957, 4998
American Assoc for the Advancement of Science, 3686
American Association for Active Lifestyle & Fitness, 2449
American Association for Adult and Continuing Education, 15
American Association for Geriatric Psychiatry, 3566
American Association for Respiratory Care, 16
American Association of Colleges of Nursing, 17
American Association of Colleges of Osteopathic Medicine, 18
American Association of Critical Care Nurses, 19
American Association of Diabetes Educators, 6240, 6110
American Association of Homes & Services for the Aging, 718
American Association of Homes and Services, 3707
American Association of Homes and Services for the Aging, 3692, 4180, 11381, 11859
American Association of Managed Care Nurses, 20
American Association of Nurse Anesthetists, 21
American Association of Occupational Health Nurses, 22
American Association of Office Nurses, 23
American Association of Physician Specialists, 24
American Association of Retired Persons, 3567
American Association of Retired Persons(AARP), 4181
American Association of Retired Persons: Midwest Region Office, 899
American Association of Retired Persons: Research Information Center, 11382
American Association of Retired Veterinarians, 25
American Association of Retirement Communities, 26

American Association of Suicidology, 3726, 3727
American Association of the Deaf-Blind, 6578, 6311, 7503
American Athletic Association for the Deaf, 6312
American Athletic Association of the Deaf, 6576, 6596
American Auditory Society, 6313
American Baptist Homes & Hospitals Association, 3713
American Baptist Homes and Hospitals Association, 27
American Bar Association, 113, 3931, 3932, 4012, 6094, 28
American Benefits Council, 29
American Blind Lawyers Association, 7504, 8005
American Blue Book of Funeral Directors, 3693
American Board of Internal Medicine, 30
American Board of Perianesthesia Nursing Certification, 31
American Board of Psychiatry and Neurology, 4931, 5046, 6037
American Bone Marrow Donor Registry:New England Donor Registry, 5255
American Book Company, 5149
American Business Directories, 3790, 7281
American Cancer Society: Monroe, 5256
American Cancer Society, 5759, 5777, 5792, 5257, 5875
American Cancer Society: Aberdeen, 5258
American Cancer Society: Abescon, 5259
American Cancer Society: Abingdon, 5260
American Cancer Society: Adams, 5261
American Cancer Society: Aiea, 5262
American Cancer Society: Aiken, 5263
American Cancer Society: Alachua High Five Unit, 5264
American Cancer Society: Albany, 5265
American Cancer Society: Albuquerque, 5266
American Cancer Society: Alexandria, 5267
American Cancer Society: Amador County, 5268
American Cancer Society: Amarillo, 5269
American Cancer Society: Anchorage, 5270
American Cancer Society: Anderson, 5271
American Cancer Society: Antelope Valley Eastern Sierra Unit, 5272
American Cancer Society: AshevilleAdministrative Resource Center, 5273
American Cancer Society: Ashland, 5274
American Cancer Society: Athens, 5275
American Cancer Society: Atlanta, 5276
American Cancer Society: Augusta, 5277
American Cancer Society: Austin, 5278
American Cancer Society: Baker Clay Unit, 5279
American Cancer Society: Bakersfield, 5280
American Cancer Society: Baldwin County, 5281
American Cancer Society: Barry County, 5282
American Cancer Society: Bartow West Polk Unit, 5283
American Cancer Society: Batavia Fox Valley, 5284

American Cancer Society: Baton Rouge, 5285
American Cancer Society: Bay Area, 5286
American Cancer Society: Bemidji, 5287
American Cancer Society: Billings, 5288
American Cancer Society: Birmingham, 5289
American Cancer Society: Bismark, 5290
American Cancer Society: Blackfoot, 5291
American Cancer Society: Bluefield, 5292
American Cancer Society: Bowling Green, 5293
American Cancer Society: Bradenton, 5294
American Cancer Society: Brainerd, 5295
American Cancer Society: Brawley, 5296
American Cancer Society: Brevard, 5297
American Cancer Society: Brooklyn, 5298
American Cancer Society: Broward, 5299
American Cancer Society: Brunswick, 5300
American Cancer Society: Burlington, 5301
American Cancer Society: Byfield, 5302
American Cancer Society: Cape Cod, 5303
American Cancer Society: Cape Girardeau, 5304
American Cancer Society: Carroll, 5305
American Cancer Society: Casper, 5306
American Cancer Society: Cedar Rapids, 5307
American Cancer Society: Champaign, 5308
American Cancer Society: Charlotte, 5309
American Cancer Society: Chattanooga, 5310
American Cancer Society: Cheyenne, 5311
American Cancer Society: Chicago, 5312
American Cancer Society: Citrus, 5313
American Cancer Society: Clark/Miami, 5314
American Cancer Society: Collier, 5315
American Cancer Society: Collinsville, 5316
American Cancer Society: Colorado Springs, 5317
American Cancer Society: Columbia, 5318
American Cancer Society: Columbus, 5319
American Cancer Society: Contra Costa, 5320
American Cancer Society: Corpus Christi, 5321
American Cancer Society: Council Bluffs, 5322
American Cancer Society: Covina, 5323
American Cancer Society: Culver City, 5324
American Cancer Society: Cumberland, 5325
American Cancer Society: Cuyahoga County, 5326
American Cancer Society: Dade/Miami Beach, 5327
American Cancer Society: Dallas, 5328
American Cancer Society: Dalton, 5329
American Cancer Society: Davenport, 5330
American Cancer Society: DeSoto, 5331
American Cancer Society: Denver, 5332
American Cancer Society: Des Moines, 5333
American Cancer Society: Dothan, 5334
American Cancer Society: Downey, 5335
American Cancer Society: Dubuque, 5336
American Cancer Society: Duluth, 5337
American Cancer Society: East Lansing, 5338
American Cancer Society: East Syracuse, 5339

Entry Name Index / A

American Cancer Society: Eastern Indiana, 5340
American Cancer Society: Eau Claire, 5341
American Cancer Society: El Dorado, 5342
American Cancer Society: El Paso, 5343
American Cancer Society: Eldersburg, 5344
American Cancer Society: Elizabeth, 5345
American Cancer Society: Elmira, 5346
American Cancer Society: Erie, 5347
American Cancer Society: Eugene, 5348
American Cancer Society: Eureka, 5349
American Cancer Society: Everett, 5350
American Cancer Society: Fargo, 5351
American Cancer Society: Fayetteville, 5352
American Cancer Society: Flagler, 5353
American Cancer Society: Flint, 5354
American Cancer Society: Florence, 5355
American Cancer Society: Flushing, 5356
American Cancer Society: Fords, 5357
American Cancer Society: Fort Dodge, 5358
American Cancer Society: Fort Myers, 5359
American Cancer Society: Fort Walton Beach, 5360
American Cancer Society: Fort Worth, 5361
American Cancer Society: Franklin County, 5362
American Cancer Society: Fremont, 5363
American Cancer Society: Fresno, 5364
American Cancer Society: Gainesville, 5365
American Cancer Society: Gambrills, 5366
American Cancer Society: Gladwin County, 5367
American Cancer Society: Glen Allen, 5368
American Cancer Society: Glen Ellyn, 5369
American Cancer Society: Grand Forks, 5370
American Cancer Society: Grand Junction, 5371
American Cancer Society: Grand Rapids, 5372
American Cancer Society: Greater Tampa, 5373
American Cancer Society: Greater Ventura, 5374
American Cancer Society: Green Bay, 5375
American Cancer Society: Green River, 5376
American Cancer Society: Greenville, 5377
American Cancer Society: Greenwood, 5378
American Cancer Society: Gulfport, 5379
American Cancer Society: Gwinnett, 5380
American Cancer Society: Hagerstown, 5381
American Cancer Society: Hamilton County, 5382
American Cancer Society: Hanford, 5383
American Cancer Society: Hannibal, 5384
American Cancer Society: Hattiesburg, 5385
American Cancer Society: Helena, 5386
American Cancer Society: Hilo, 5387
American Cancer Society: Hilton Head, 5388
American Cancer Society: Honolulu, 5389
American Cancer Society: Houma, 5390
American Cancer Society: Houston, 5391
American Cancer Society: Hudson Valley, 5392
American Cancer Society: Huntington, 5393
American Cancer Society: Huntsville, 5394
American Cancer Society: Huron Valley, 5395
American Cancer Society: Indian River, 5396
American Cancer Society: Indianapolis, 5397
American Cancer Society: Ionia, 5398
American Cancer Society: Iowa City, 5399
American Cancer Society: Jackson, 5400
American Cancer Society: Jacksonville, 5401
American Cancer Society: Jacksonville Beach, 5402
American Cancer Society: Jasper, 5403
American Cancer Society: Jefferson City, 5404
American Cancer Society: Jersey Shore, 5405
American Cancer Society: Johnson City, 5406
American Cancer Society: Joplin, 5407
American Cancer Society: Kaunakakai, 5408
American Cancer Society: Kearney, 5409
American Cancer Society: Kennesaw, 5410
American Cancer Society: Kennewick, 5411
American Cancer Society: Knoxville, 5412
American Cancer Society: Kokomo, 5413
American Cancer Society: Lafayette, 5414
American Cancer Society: Lake Charles, 5415
American Cancer Society: Lake County, 5416
American Cancer Society: Lakeland, 5417
American Cancer Society: Lakes Region, 5418
American Cancer Society: Lakeshore, 5419
American Cancer Society: Lancaster, 5420
American Cancer Society: Larimer County, 5421
American Cancer Society: Las Vegas, 5422
American Cancer Society: Lathrup Village, 5423
American Cancer Society: Lawton, 5424
American Cancer Society: Leesburg, 5425
American Cancer Society: Lewistown, 5426
American Cancer Society: Lexington, 5427
American Cancer Society: Lihue, 5428
American Cancer Society: Lincoln, 5429
American Cancer Society: Little Rock, 5430
American Cancer Society: Livingston, 5431
American Cancer Society: Lompoc Valley, 5432
American Cancer Society: Long Beach, 5433
American Cancer Society: Longmont, 5434
American Cancer Society: Los Angeles, 5435
American Cancer Society: Loudonville, 5436
American Cancer Society: Louisville, 5437
American Cancer Society: Lynchburg, 5438
American Cancer Society: Macon, 5439
American Cancer Society: Madison, 5440
American Cancer Society: Manhattan, 5441
American Cancer Society: Mankato, 5442
American Cancer Society: Marco Island, 5443
American Cancer Society: Marin County, 5444
American Cancer Society: Marion, 5445
American Cancer Society: Marshall, 5446
American Cancer Society: Martin, 5447
American Cancer Society: Marysville, 5448
American Cancer Society: Mason City, 5449
American Cancer Society: Medford, 5450
American Cancer Society: Memphis, 5451
American Cancer Society: Merced, 5452
American Cancer Society: Mercer, 5453
American Cancer Society: Meridian, 5454
American Cancer Society: Minot, 5455
American Cancer Society: Missoula, 5456
American Cancer Society: Mitchell, 5457
American Cancer Society: Mobile, 5458
American Cancer Society: Modesto, 5459
American Cancer Society: Monroe, 5460
American Cancer Society: Montgomery, 5461
American Cancer Society: Moorhead, 5462
American Cancer Society: Morgantown, 5463
American Cancer Society: Morongo Basin, 5464
American Cancer Society: Mountain Valley, 5465
American Cancer Society: Muncie, 5466
American Cancer Society: Muskegon, 5467
American Cancer Society: Myrtle Beach, 5468
American Cancer Society: Napa, 5469
American Cancer Society: Nashville, 5470
American Cancer Society: Nassau Region, 5471
American Cancer Society: Natick, 5472
American Cancer Society: New Castle, 5473
American Cancer Society: New England Div, 5474
American Cancer Society: New Jersey, 5475
American Cancer Society: New Orleans, 5476
American Cancer Society: Norfolk, 5477
American Cancer Society: Norman, 5478
American Cancer Society: North Central Indiana, 5479
American Cancer Society: North Charleston, 5480
American Cancer Society: North Coast Border, 5481
American Cancer Society: North Shore, 5482
American Cancer Society: North Valley Region, 5483
American Cancer Society: Northeast Indiana, 5484
American Cancer Society: Northeast New England, 5485
American Cancer Society: Northern Arizona, 5486
American Cancer Society: Northern California, 5487
American Cancer Society: Northern Idaho, 5488
American Cancer Society: Northern Kentucky, 5489
American Cancer Society: Northern Michigan, 5490
American Cancer Society: Northern Nevada, 5491
American Cancer Society: Northern New Jersey, 5492
American Cancer Society: Northern New Mexico, 5493
American Cancer Society: Northwest Illinois, 5494
American Cancer Society: Northwest Indiana, 5495

Entry Name Index / A

American Cancer Society: Northwest New England, 5496
American Cancer Society: Northwest New Jersey, 5497
American Cancer Society: Northwest Suburban Illinois, 5498
American Cancer Society: Northwest Valley, 5499
American Cancer Society: Northwest Wyoming, 5500
American Cancer Society: O'Fallon, 5501
American Cancer Society: Oakland, 5502
American Cancer Society: Ogden, 5503
American Cancer Society: Oklahoma City, 5504
American Cancer Society: Omaha, 5505
American Cancer Society: Orange County Region, 5506
American Cancer Society: Orlando Metro, 5507
American Cancer Society: Osage Beach, 5508
American Cancer Society: Overland Park, 5509
American Cancer Society: Owensboro, 5510
American Cancer Society: Oxnard, 5511
American Cancer Society: Paducah, 5512
American Cancer Society: Palm Beach, 5513
American Cancer Society: Palm Beach Benefit, 5514
American Cancer Society: Palm Desert, 5515
American Cancer Society: Panama City, 5516
American Cancer Society: Parkersburg, 5517
American Cancer Society: Pasco, 5518
American Cancer Society: Peninsula, 5519
American Cancer Society: Pensacola, 5520
American Cancer Society: Petaluma, 5521
American Cancer Society: Pewaukee, 5522
American Cancer Society: Phoenix, 5523
American Cancer Society: Pierre, 5524
American Cancer Society: Pinellas, 5525
American Cancer Society: Pittsfield, 5526
American Cancer Society: Pleasant Hill, 5527
American Cancer Society: Porter, 5528
American Cancer Society: Portland, 5529
American Cancer Society: Prairie Land, 5530
American Cancer Society: Provo, 5531
American Cancer Society: Pueblo, 5532
American Cancer Society: Putnam, 5533
American Cancer Society: Queens Region, 5534
American Cancer Society: Raleigh, 5535
American Cancer Society: Rancho Cucamonga, 5536
American Cancer Society: Rapid City, 5537
American Cancer Society: Redding, 5538
American Cancer Society: Region VI Washington, 5539
American Cancer Society: Rhode Island, 5540
American Cancer Society: Rhode Island & Eastern Connecticut, 5541
American Cancer Society: Ridgecrest, 5542
American Cancer Society: Riverside, 5543
American Cancer Society: Roanoke, 5544
American Cancer Society: Rochester, 5545
American Cancer Society: Rockford, 5546
American Cancer Society: Roseville, 5547
American Cancer Society: Rupert, 5548
American Cancer Society: Rutland, 5549
American Cancer Society: Saint Cloud, 5550
American Cancer Society: Saint George, 5551
American Cancer Society: Saint Joseph, 5552
American Cancer Society: Saint Louis, 5553
American Cancer Society: Saint Paul, 5554
American Cancer Society: Salinas, 5555
American Cancer Society: Salisbury, 5556
American Cancer Society: Salt Lake City, 5557
American Cancer Society: San Antonio, 5558
American Cancer Society: San Diego, 5559
American Cancer Society: San Fernando Valley, 5560
American Cancer Society: San Jose, 5561
American Cancer Society: San Luis Obispo, 5562
American Cancer Society: San Mateo County, 5563
American Cancer Society: Santa Barbara, 5564
American Cancer Society: Santa Clara County, 5565
American Cancer Society: Santa Clarita Valley, 5566
American Cancer Society: Santa Cruz County, 5567
American Cancer Society: Santa Maria, 5568
American Cancer Society: Santa Maria Valley, 5569
American Cancer Society: Santa Rosa, 5570
American Cancer Society: Sarasota, 5571
American Cancer Society: Savannah, 5572
American Cancer Society: Seattle, 5573
American Cancer Society: Sheboygan, 5574
American Cancer Society: Shreveport, 5575
American Cancer Society: Sierra View, 5576
American Cancer Society: Sikeston, 5577
American Cancer Society: Silicon Valley, 5578
American Cancer Society: Silver Spring, 5579
American Cancer Society: Simi Valley, 5580
American Cancer Society: Sioux City, 5581
American Cancer Society: Sioux Falls, 5582
American Cancer Society: Solano County, 5583
American Cancer Society: Somerset, 5584
American Cancer Society: South Bay, 5585
American Cancer Society: South Burlington, 5586
American Cancer Society: South Central Indiana, 5587
American Cancer Society: South Central Los Angeles, 5588
American Cancer Society: Southeast Indiana, 5589
American Cancer Society: Southeast New England, 5590
American Cancer Society: Southeastern Arizona, 5591
American Cancer Society: Southern Illinois, 5592
American Cancer Society: Southern New England, 5593
American Cancer Society: Southwest Colorado, 5594
American Cancer Society: Southwest Kansas, 5595
American Cancer Society: Southwest Michigan, 5596
American Cancer Society: Southwest New England, 5597
American Cancer Society: Southwest Ohio, 5598
American Cancer Society: Southwest Pennsylvania, 5599
American Cancer Society: Southwestern Indiana, 5600
American Cancer Society: Spokane, 5601
American Cancer Society: Springfield, 5602
American Cancer Society: Stark Area, 5603
American Cancer Society: State College, 5604
American Cancer Society: Staten Island, 5605
American Cancer Society: Statesboro, 5606
American Cancer Society: Sterling, 5607
American Cancer Society: Stockton, 5608
American Cancer Society: Storm Lake, 5609
American Cancer Society: Suburban Hillsborough, 5610
American Cancer Society: Suffolk Region, 5611
American Cancer Society: Summit Area, 5612
American Cancer Society: Tacoma, 5613
American Cancer Society: Tallahassee, 5614
American Cancer Society: Templeton, 5615
American Cancer Society: Tequesta, 5616
American Cancer Society: Texas City, 5617
American Cancer Society: Thousand Oaks, 5618
American Cancer Society: Topeka, 5619
American Cancer Society: Treasure Valley, 5620
American Cancer Society: Trenton, 5621
American Cancer Society: Tri-Valley, 5622
American Cancer Society: Tulare County, 5623
American Cancer Society: Tulsa, 5624
American Cancer Society: Tuscaloosa, 5625
American Cancer Society: Ukiah, 5626
American Cancer Society: Upper Peninsula, 5627
American Cancer Society: Upper Valley Texas, 5628
American Cancer Society: Victorville, 5629
American Cancer Society: Vincennes, 5630
American Cancer Society: Volusia East, 5631
American Cancer Society: Volusia West, 5632
American Cancer Society: Wabash Valley, 5633
American Cancer Society: Waco, 5634
American Cancer Society: Wailuku, 5635
American Cancer Society: Waterloo, 5636
American Cancer Society: Watertown, 5637
American Cancer Society: Waycross, 5638
American Cancer Society: Weld County, 5639
American Cancer Society: West Bay Region San Francisco County Unit, 5640

Entry Name Index / A

American Cancer Society: West Central Illinois, 5641
American Cancer Society: West Contra Costa County, 5642
American Cancer Society: West Hawaii, 5643
American Cancer Society: West Michigan, 5644
American Cancer Society: West Palm Beach, 5645
American Cancer Society: Westchester Region, 5646
American Cancer Society: Western New England, 5647
American Cancer Society: Western New York, 5648
American Cancer Society: Western Yavapai, 5649
American Cancer Society: White Marsh, 5650
American Cancer Society: Wichita, 5651
American Cancer Society: Willmar, 5652
American Cancer Society: Windward, 5653
American Cancer Society: Wood Area, 5654
American Cancer Society: York, 5655
American Cancer Socity: Imperial Central, 5656
American Citizens for Justice, 77
American Civil Liberties Union AIDS Project, 4552, 4448
American College Health Association, 32
American College of Allergy & Immunology, 4647, 4664
American College of Allergy and Immunology, 4680
American College of Cardiology, 11533
American College of Clinical Pharmacology, 33
American College of Health Care Administrators: Information Center, 11812
American College of Legal Medicine, 34
American College of Physicians, 4525
American College of Trust and Estate Counsel, 35
American Correctional Health Services Association, 36
American Council for Drug Education, 7133, 7439
American Council of Blind Lions, 7505, 8006
American Council of Life Insurers, 37
American Council of the Blind, 2631, 2636, 2664, 2681, 2688, 7493, 7494, 7495, 7500, 7504, 7505, 7551, 7593, 7599, 7613, 7631, 7653, 7659, 7778, 7779, 7859
American Council on Alcohol Problems, 7284, 7285, 7134
American Council on Alcoholism, 7135
American Council on Exercise, 3816
American Counseling Association, 3599, 3602, 4530, 6084, 38
American Deaf Culture, 6465
American Deaf Culture: An Anthology, 6466
American Dental Association, 2637
American Dental Society of Anesthesiology, 39
American Diabetes Association, 6179, 6182, 6183, 6186, 6188, 6190, 6191, 6204, 6205, 6206, 6210, 6211, 6220, 6221, 6223, 6226, 6228, 6229, 6230, 6231, 6232

American Diabetes Association Southern: New Jersey District Office, 6112
American Diabetes Association/Conn. Affiliate, 4147, 6234, 6257, 6259, 6260, 6261, 6262, 6265, 6266
American Diabetes Association: Alaska Area Office, 6114
American Diabetes Association: Arizona Area Office, 6115
American Diabetes Association: Arkansas, 6116
American Diabetes Association: Atlanta Metro Area Office, Georgia, 6117
American Diabetes Association: Baton Rouge District Office, 6118
American Diabetes Association: Border Area Office, 6119
American Diabetes Association: Bowling Green District Office, 6120
American Diabetes Association: California, 6121
American Diabetes Association: Cedar Rapids District Office, 6122
American Diabetes Association: Central Ohio Area Office, 6123
American Diabetes Association: Central Pennsylvania Area, 6124
American Diabetes Association: Columbus District Office, 6125
American Diabetes Association: Connecticut, 6126
American Diabetes Association: Delaware/Eastern Shore Area Office, 6127
American Diabetes Association: Districtof Columbia, 6128
American Diabetes Association: East Washington/North Idaho District Office, 6129
American Diabetes Association: Eastern Regional Office, 6130
American Diabetes Association: Eugene Branch Office, 6131
American Diabetes Association: Great Lakes and Heartland Regional Office, Wisconsin, 6132
American Diabetes Association: Greater Hampton Roads Area Office, 6133
American Diabetes Association: Hawaii Area Office, 6134
American Diabetes Association: Huntsville District Office, 6135
American Diabetes Association: Iowa Area Office, 6136
American Diabetes Association: Kansas Area Office, 6137
American Diabetes Association: KentuckyArea Office, 6138
American Diabetes Association: Madison District Office, 6139
American Diabetes Association: Maryland Area Office, 6140
American Diabetes Association: Memphis District Office, 6141
American Diabetes Association: Mid-America Regional Office, 6142
American Diabetes Association: Minnesota Area Office, 6143
American Diabetes Association: Mississippi Area Office, 6144
American Diabetes Association: Missoula District Office, 6145

American Diabetes Association: MissouriArea Office, 6146
American Diabetes Association: Montana, 6147
American Diabetes Association: Mountain States & Pacific/Northwest Regional Office, 6148
American Diabetes Association: Nebraska/South Dakota Area Office, 6149
American Diabetes Association: Nevada, 6150
American Diabetes Association: New Mexico Area Office, 6151
American Diabetes Association: New Orleans District Office, Louisiana, 6152
American Diabetes Association: New York City Area Office, 6153
American Diabetes Association: North Dakota, 6154
American Diabetes Association: Northeast Texas/North Louisiana Area Office, 6155
American Diabetes Association: Northern Ohio/Cleveland Area Office, 6156
American Diabetes Association: Oklahoma Area Office, 6157
American Diabetes Association: Oklahoma City District Office, 6113
American Diabetes Association: Oregon Area Office, 6158
American Diabetes Association: Rhode Island/Massachusetts Area Office, 6159
American Diabetes Association: Seattle Area Office, 6160
American Diabetes Association: Sioux Fallls District Office, 6161
American Diabetes Association: South Central Regional Office, 6162
American Diabetes Association: South Coastal Regional Office, Central Florida Area, 6163
American Diabetes Association: Southeast Michigan Area Office, 6164
American Diabetes Association: Southern Regional Office, Eastern North Carolina, 6165
American Diabetes Association: Tennessee Area Office, 6166
American Diabetes Association: Upstate Alabama Area Office, 6167
American Diabetes Association: Utah Area Office, 6168
American Diabetes Association: Virginia Area Office, 6169
American Diabetes Association: West Virginia/Southern Ohio, 6170
American Diabetes Association: Western Pennsylvania Area Office, 6171
American Diabetes Association: Wyoming District Office, 6172
American Dietetic Association, 6173
American Disabled for Attendant Programs, 3568
American Federation for Aging Research, 2645, 2672, 4264
American Federation of School Administrators, 40
American Federation of Teachers HIV/AIDS Education Project, 4449
American Federation of the Blind: San Francisco Chapter, 490

989

Entry Name Index / A

American Foundation for AIDS Research, 4526, 4538, 4586
American Foundation for Aging Research, 4265
American Foundation for Urologic Disease, 6943
American Foundation for Urologic Disease: Us Too Line, 5657
American Foundation for the Blind, 2655, 6244, 6742, 7496, 7794, 7796, 7809, 7817, 7826, 7829, 7833, 7837, 7840, 7875, 7913, 7916, 7930, 7932, 7954, 7966, 7967
American Foundation for the Blind Southwest, 7507
American Foundation for the Blind/AFB Press, 7792, 7793, 7799, 7801, 7802, 7803, 7804, 7812, 7823, 7824, 7827, 7832, 7835, 7836, 7854, 7857, 7879, 7880, 7887, 7890, 7908
American Foundation for the Blind: National Literacy Center, 7508
American Foundation for the Blind: Atlanta, 7509
American Foundation for the Blind: Chigago, 7510
American Foundation for the Blind: Midwest, 7511
American Foundation for the Blind: San Francisco, 7512
American Foundation for the Blind: Washington DC, 7513
American Gastroenterological Association, 6174
American Geriatrics Society, 2632, 2657, 2666, 2674, 4008, 3569
American Geriatrics Society Newsletter, 4008
American Guidance for Seniors, 3825
American Health Assistance Foundation, 4989, 8049, 3570, 4932, 5047, 6860
American Health Care Association, 41, 4009
American Health Care Association: Information Resource Center, 11384
American Health Consultants, 4044, 4515, 4010
American Hearing Research Foundation, 6606, 6618, 6649, 6711, 6605, 6794
American Hearing Research Foundation Newsletter, 6606
American Heart Association, 6857, 6858, 6859, 6916, 7094, 7095, 7103, 7918, 6838
American Heart Association Diet, 7918
American Heart Association National Center Library, 11768
American Holistic Nurses Association, 42
American Homes for the Aging: Eastern & Northeastern Regional Offices, 4933
American Horticultural Therapy Association, 3913
American Hospital Association, 317, 3687
American Hospital Publishing, 4123
American Hotel and Motel Association, 12007
American Inn at Sawmill, 8936
American Institute for Cancer Research, 5882
American Issue, 7285
American Journal of Audiology, 6571
American Journal of Speech-Language Pathology, 3826
American Kinesiotherapy Association, 43

American Legion, 11478
American Legion Auxiliary's National News, 3827
American Legion Auxillary's National News, 3827
American Legion Magazine, 3828
American Legion National Headquarters, 3828
American Licensed Practical Nurses Association, 44
American Life League Library, 11813
American Lung Association, 3994, 4021, 4028, 4033, 4037, 4054, 4057, 4058, 4075, 4076, 4090, 4102, 4108, 4114, 4120, 4129, 4665, 5824, 7270, 4182, 4646
American Massage Therapy Association, 3924
American Medical Association, 6850, 45
American Medical Association Alliance, 46
American Medical Association Guide to Preventing and Treating Heart Disease, 6850
American Medical Directors Association (AMDA), 3571
American Medical Industries, 3247
American Medical Informatics Association, 47
American Medical Rehabilitation Providers Association (AMRPA), 48
American Medical Systems, 4050
American Mental Health Counselors Association, 49
American Nephrology Nurses' Association, 50
American Neurotology Society, 6314
American Nurses Association, 51
American ORT, 2855
American Occupational Therapy Association, 4036, 52
American Optometric Association, 7993, 7514
American Orthopaedic Association, 5082
American Paralysis Association, 4126
American Parkinson Disease Association, 6980, 6993, 7001, 7004, 7005, 7015, 7029, 7032
American Parkinson Disease Association Newsletter, 6990
American Parkinson's Disease Association, 6954
American Physiological Society, 53
American Podiatric Circulatory Society, 3572
American Printing House for the Blind, 3090, 3291, 3294, 3423, 3458, 3459, 7795, 7838, 7998, 7515, 7855, 8007
American Prostate Society, 4183, 5659
American Psychiatric Association, 2646
American Psychiatric Nurses Association, 54
American Psychoanalytic Association, 6082, 55
American Psychological Society, 56
American Radiological Nurses Association, 57
American Red Cross, 4554, 4573, 4574, 7430
American Red Cross - Carolina Low County Chapter, 11250
American Registry of Pathology, 58
American Rehabilitation Services Administration (RSA), 3829

American Senior Newsletter, 4011
American Sign Language Phrase Book, 6467
American Sign Language: A Beginning Course, 6468
American Society for Deaf Children, 6647
American Society for Geriatric Dentistry, 59
American Society for Laser Medicine and Surgery, 60
American Society for Parenteral and Enteral Nutrition, 61
American Society of Colon and Rectal Surgeons, 5807, 62, 4184
American Society of Contemporary Medicine Surgery & Ophthalmology, 7516
American Society of Deaf Social Workers, 6315
American Society of General Surgeons, 63
American Society of Hypertension, 6907
American Society of Internal Medicine, 64
American Society of Maxillofacial Surgeons, 65
American Society of Neuroradiology, 66
American Society of Ophthalmic Registered Nurses, 7517
American Society of Peri-Anesthesia Nurses, 67
American Society of Plastic Surgeons, 68
American Society of Post-Anesthesia Nurses, 69
American Society of Retired Dentists, 70
American Society of Tropical Medicine and Hygiene, 71
American Society on Aging, 3864, 3865, 3975, 3573
American Speech-Language-Hearing Association, 3826, 6568, 6569, 6571, 6582, 6583, 6584, 6316
American Thoracic Society, 72
American Tinnitus Association, 6591, 6595, 6599, 6317, 6778
American United Life Insurance Company, 11479
American Urological Association, 6944
American Volkssport Association (AVA), 3830
American Walker, 3419, 3492, 3477
American Wanderer, 3830
American Yoga Association, 73
Americans United for Life, 4002
Americans with Disabilities Act Manual:State and Local Government Services, 4012
Americans with Disabilities Act Resource Manual, 4013
Americans with Disabilities Act: Selected Resources for Deaf, 6607
Americans with Disabilities Act: What It Means for People with AIDS, 4552
Americare-Creekview, 8451
Americare-Delphic, 8452
Americare-Hiland, 8453
Americare-Lomax I, 8454
Americare-Pendlebury, 8455
Ameripark at Austin, 10397
Ameripark at Kerrville, 10398
Ameriphone Hearing Assistance Telephone, 3069
Ameriphone-Wireless Notification System, 3070
Ames Public Library Ames and Iowa History Collection, 11491

Entry Name Index / A

Amherst Manor, 9861
Amigo Centra, 3416
Amigo Mobility International, 3416, 3358
Amigos del Valle, 2851
Amphibious ATV Distributors, 3417
Amplified Handsets, 3071
Amplified Phones, 3072
Amplified Portable Phone, 3073
Amtrak Railways, 11914
An Angels Touch, 9592
An Annotated Bibliography of Recent Empirical Research in Methadone, 4521
An Invisible Condition: the Human Side of Hearing Loss, 6469
An Overview of Allergy, 4647
Analog Clock Model, 3294
Analog Switch Pad, 3074
Anam Chara Homes, 8234
Ananse Press, 5802
Anatomy of Bereavement, 6017
Anchor Lodge Retirement Village, 9862
Anchorage Pioneers' Home, 8081
Andover Court Assisted Living, 8778
Andrew Jackson Building, 2295
Andrews McMeel Publishing, 5790, 5798
Andrews McMeel Publishing Company, 4969
Andrews McMeel Publishing LLC, 5799
Aneurysm Answers, 7081
Angel House Residential Assisted Living, 10000
Angela Hall Assisted Living Center, 10233
Anglo California Travel Service, 12008
Ankylosing Spondylitis, 5169
Ann Arbor Center for Independent Living, 9038, 10798
Anna Erika Home for Adults, 9828
Anna Maria of Aurora, 9863
Annabelle House, 8456
Anne Arundel Community College, 2809
Anne Arundel County Area: Agency on Aging, 1225
Anne Arundel County Department of Aging and Disabilities, 1226
Annual Report/Newsletter, 7919
Anonymity, 7321
Another Home for Mom, 5029
Answerall 100, 3075
Answers to 100 Questions About Hypertension, 6910
Anthracite Region Center for Independent Living, 10908
Anti-Aging Press/So Young Catalog/So Young Newsletter, 4014
Anxiety & Depression in Adults & Children, 6066
Anxiety Disorders Association of America, 6038
Apollo Gardens Retirement Residence, 8340
Apostolic Christian Home, 9864
Appalachian Area: Agency on Aging, 2545
Appalachian Center for Independent Living, 10952
Appalachian Independence Center, 10938
Appalachian State University, 2877
Apple Ridge Assisted Living Apartments, 8235
Apple Valley Residential Care, 8457
Aquatic Access, 3388
Aquatic Access Pool Lifts for Pools andSpas, 3359
Aquinas College, 2824

Arbor Care Assisted Living, 9387
Arbor Glen, 9752
Arbor Heights at University, 8632
Arbor House Assisted Living Center, 10001
Arbor Place, 8633
Arbor Terrace, 10341
Arbor Terrace of Asheville, 9388
Arbor Village of North Tampa, 8341
Arbor of Natchitoches, 8853
Arbor of Ruston, 8854
Arbors at Amherst, 8937
Arbors at Carriage Club of Charlotte, 9389
Arbors at Clyde Assisted Living Center, 9865
Arbors at Dayton Residential Care, 9866
Arbors at Fairlawn Residential Care, 9867
Arbors at Hop Brook, 8253
Arbors at Marietta Residential Care, 9868
Arcola Bus Sales, 2985
Arcola Mobility, 2956
Arctic Hearth Assisted Living Homes, 8082
Arden Courts Alzheimer's Assisted Living, 8254, 10399
Arden Courts Manorcare Health Services, 8305
Arden Courts of Parma, 9869
Arden Courts of Whippany, 9753
Ardenwoods, 9390
Area 1 Agency on Aging, 491
Area 1 Northwest Indiana Community ActioN Corp., 966
Area 10 Agency on Aging, 3780, 967
Area 12 Agency on Aging, 492
Area 12 Council on Aging, 968
Area 13 Agency on Aging: Older Hoosier Programs, 969
Area 14 Agency on Aging, 1016
Area 15 Hoosier Uplands Agency on Aging, 970
Area 2 Agency on Aging: Real Services, 971
Area 4 Agency on Aging, 493
Area 4 Agency on Aging and Community Services, 972
Area 5 Agency on Aging and Community Services, 973
Area 9 Agency on Aging, 974
Area Access, 3360
Area Agency on Aging, 1924, 10984
Area Agency on Aging Library, 11559
Area Agency on Aging for Lincolnland, 900
Area Agency on Aging for Tioga, Bradford, Sullivan and Susquehanna Counties, 2095
Area Agency on Aging of Dane County, 2569
Area Agency on Aging of Somerset County, 2096
Area Agency on Aging of Southeast Texas, 2305
Area Agency on Aging of Southern Mississippi, 1443
Area Agency on Aging of Western Michigan, (AAAWM), 1341
Area Agency on Aging of the Capital Area, 2306
Area Agency on Aging of the Concho Valley, 2307
Area Agency on Aging: Senior Citizens Lawyer Referral Service, 11107
Area Eight Agency on Aging, 1527
Area Five Agency on Aging, 1528
Area Four Agency on Aging, 1529
Area Nine Agency on Aging, 1530

Area One Agency on Aging, 1531
Area Seven Agency on Aging, 1532
Area Two Agency on Aging, 1533
Area Two Area: Agency on Aging, 1942
Area Two: Agency on Aging, 876
Areawide Aging Agency, 2003
Argentine Care Center, 9039
Argyle Square, 8236
Arista Home Care, 3005, 3475, 3479, 3486
Arista Surgical Supply Co, 3030
Arizona Aging and Adult Administration, 424
Arizona Alcoholism and Drug Abuse, 7136
Arizona Area Agency on Aging: Region One, 425
Arizona Bridge to Independent Living, 10633
Arizona Bureau of Alcohol and Drug Abuse, 7137
Arizona Center for Disability Law, 10979
Arizona Center for the Blind and Visually Impaired, 7518
Arizona Center on Aging, 3574
Arizona Commission for the Deaf & Hard of Hearing, 6318
Arizona Department of Aging, 426
Arizona Department of Economic Security, 427
Arizona Department of Economic Security: Division of Aging and Community Services, 10980
Arizona Department of Family Health Services, 428
Arizona Department of Health Services, 4450
Arizona Department of Revenue, 429
Arizona Department of Veterans Services, 430
Arizona Disability Determination Services, 431
Arizona Elder Abuse and Fraud Taskforce Committee, 10981
Arizona Heart Institute, 6839
Arizona Industries for the Blind, 7519
Arizona Industries for the Blind, 7520
Arizona Inter Tribal Council, 432
Arizona Office of Substance Abuse & General Mental Health, 7138
Arizona Office of Tourism, 11951
Arizona Protection and Advocacy Agency: Arizona Center for Disability Law, 10982
Arizona Public Safety Personnel Retirement System, 433
Arizona Railroad Retirement Board, 434
Arizona Rehabilitation State Services for the Blind and Visually Impaired, 7521
Arizona Retirement System, 435
Arizona State Braille and Talking Book Library, 11317
Arizona State University: Cancer Research Institute, 5883
Arizona State University: School of Health Administration & Policy, 4587
Arizona Workers Compensation Board, 436
Arjo, 3396
Ark-Tex Council of Governments Area Agency on Aging, 2308
Arkansas Advocates for Nursing Home Residents, 454
Arkansas Aging Foundation, 455
Arkansas Aging Foundation Information Center, 11329

Entry Name Index / A

Arkansas Assistive Technology Projects, 456
Arkansas Chapter of the Arthritis Foundation, 5083
Arkansas Department of Aging, 457
Arkansas Department of Finance and Administration, 458
Arkansas Department of Health, 4451, 4578
Arkansas Department of Health & Human Services: Division of Aging and Adult Services, 10988
Arkansas Department of Human Services, 10639
Arkansas Department of Human Services: Division of Aging and Adult Services, 459
Arkansas Department of Parks & Tourism, 11952
Arkansas Department of Public Employees Retired Systems, 460
Arkansas Department of Veterans Affairs, 461
Arkansas Developmental Disability Council, 462
Arkansas Disability Determinations for SSA, 463
Arkansas Division of Aging & Adult Services, 464
Arkansas Division of Alcoholism & Drug Abuse, 7139
Arkansas Division of Developmental Disabilities Services, 465
Arkansas Division of Services for the Blind, 466
Arkansas House, 10400
Arkansas Independent Living Council (AILC), 10638
Arkansas Lighthouse for the Blind, 7522
Arkansas Office of Alcoholism and Substance Abuse, 7140
Arkansas Protection and Advocacy Agency: Disability Rights Center, 10989
Arkansas Regional Library for the Blind and Physically Handicapped, 11330
Arkansas Rehabilitation Research and Training Center for Deaf Persons, 6795
Arkansas Rehabilitation Services, 467
Arkansas Teacher Retirement System, 468
Arkansas Volunteer Lawyers for the Elderly (AVLE), 10990
Arkenstone, 3076
Arlin Flack Assisted Living, 8634
Arlington Area Agency on Aging, 2450
Arlington County Bar Association: Legal Services of Northern Virginia, 11280
Arlington County Department of Libraries, 11814
Arlington Place, 9113
Arlington Place of Grundy Center, 8635
Arlington Place of Red Oak, 8636
Arm Volumeter Set, 3248
Armed Forces Benefit Association, 74
Armstrong Area: Agency on Aging, 2097
Army Distaff Foundation, 75
Army Emergency Relief, 76
Arnold Home, 9040
Aroostook Area: Agency on Aging, 1199
Arrowhead Acres Estate, 8458
Arrowhead Area: Agency on Aging, 1391
Arrowhead Senior Living Community, 9114

Art and Science of Teaching Orientation and Mobility to Persons with Visual Impairments, 7799
Art of Getting Well, 11689
Art of Living with Change: Turning Your Good Intentions Into Progress..., 7432
Arthritic's Cookbook, 5147
Arthritis Accent, 5170
Arthritis Answers: Basic Information About Arthritis, 5171
Arthritis Arizona Southwest, 5172
Arthritis Consulting Services, 5084
Arthritis Foundation, 2766, 4013, 5157, 5160, 5167, 5169, 5171, 5173, 5174, 5181, 5182, 5183, 5184, 5186, 5187, 5188, 5189, 5190, 5191, 5192, 5193
Arthritis Foundation DistributionCenter: Pool Exercise Program, 5231
Arthritis Foundation Information Line, 5086
Arthritis Foundation Mississippi Chapter, 5087
Arthritis Foundation Mississippi Gulf Coast Chapter, 5088
Arthritis Foundation North Central Chapter, 5089
Arthritis Foundation Oregon Chapter, 5090
Arthritis Foundation Services, 5173
Arthritis Foundation Southern N.E. Chapter, 5170
Arthritis Foundation, SouthernCalifornia Chapter, 5091
Arthritis Foundation: Northeastern California Chapter, 494
Arthritis Foundation: Pool Exercise Program, 5092
Arthritis Health Professionals Association, 5093
Arthritis Helpbook: A Tested Self-Management Program for Coping, 5148
Arthritis Information: Advocacy and Government Affairs, 5174
Arthritis News, 5175
Arthritis Observer, 5176
Arthritis Reporter, 5177
Arthritis Rx: A Cutting-Edge Program for a Pain-Free Life, 5149
Arthritis Self-Help Book, 5150
Arthritis Sourcebook: Everything You Need to Know, 5151
Arthritis Today, 5167
Arthritis Update of Rhode Island, 5178
Arthritis Volunteer, 5179
Arthritis and Common Sense, 5152
Arthritis and Diet, 5180
Arthritis and Employment: You Can Get the Job You Want, 5181
Arthritis and Inflammatory Bowel Disease, 5182
Arthritis and Vocational Rehabilitation, 5183
Arthritis on the Job: You Can Work With It, 5184
Arthritis, Musculoskeletal & Skin Diseases Research: Public Health Service, 5233
Arthritis, Rheumatic Diseases and Related Disorders, 5185
Arthritis, What Exercises Work: Breakthrough Even after Drugs & Surgery Have Failed, 5153
Arthritis: A Comprehensive Guide, 5154
Arthritis: Do You Know?, 5186

Arthritis: Taking Care of Yourself Health Guide for Understanding Your Arthritis, 5155
Arthur G James Cancer Hospital, 5944
Arthur M Fishberg Research Center in Neurobiology, 4266, 5049
Arthwriter, 3077
Artia in Falmouth, 8938
Artic Technologies, 3189
Artificial Larynx, 3078
Artificial Organs & Tissues Markets, 3694
Artman Lutheran Home, 10192
As Times Goes By, 4133
Asbury Acres, 10342
Asbury Center at Birdmont, 10552
Asbury Methodist Village, 8901
Ash Street Place, 10002
Ashberry Manor, 10202
Asheville Manor, 9391
Ashland Healthcare, 9392
Ashley Court at Turtle Creek, 10401
Ashley Manor Care Centers-Harmony, 8459
Ashley Manor Care Centers-Highmont, 8460
Ashley Manor Care Centers-Nampa, 8461
Ashley Manor Medley I, 9337
Ashley Manor-Beverly Hills, 8462
Ashwood Estates Retirement Center, 9393
Ashwood Retirement & Assisted Living, 10402
Asian AIDS Project, 4588
Asian American Center for Justice, 77
Ask the Doctor: Breast Cancer, 5790
Asnuntuck Community College, 2743
Aspen Court, 10056
Aspen Grove Assisted Living-Bellevue, 8463
Aspen Grove Assisted Living-Gooding, 8464
Aspen Grove Assisted Living-Idaho Falls, 8465
Aspen Grove Assisted Living-Lava Hot Sprrings, 8466
Aspen Meadows Retirement Community, 9338
Aspen Publishers, 3861, 4117
Aspen Springs Pioneer Home, 8467
Aspen Wind Assisted Living, 10607
Aspen Woodside Village, 9870
Aspirin and Other Nonsteroidal Anti-Inflammatory Drugs, 5187
Assisted Lifestyles Of KS Inc., 8779
Assisted Living Center at Azalea Trace, 8342
Assisted Living Center at St James Place, 8855
Assisted Living Chancellor Park at theWindrows, 9754
Assisted Living Federation of America, 78
Assisted Living at Spring Oak, 9755
Assisted Living at Summerplace, 10057
Assisted Living at Windsor Place, 8780
Assisted Living in Heritage Hall, 9115
Assisted Living on Shamrock, 8468
Assisted-Living Care Roster, 3695
Assistive Devices Demonstration Centers, 6557, 6608
Assistive Devices Information Network, 4134
Assistive Devices: Doorways to Independence, 6743
Assistive Software Products, 3079

Entry Name Index / B

Assistive Technology, 3080, 3831
Assistive Technology Educational Network of Florida, 733
Assistive Technology Resource Centers of Hawaii, 854
Assistive Technology Training and Information Center, 10743
Assistive Technology of Alaska, 417
Associate Administrator for Alcohol Prevention & Treatment Policy, 7141
Associated Blind, 7523
Associated Services for the Blind, 7735, 7893
Associated Services for the Blind and Visually Impaired, 7524
Association for Adult Development and Aging, 3575
Association for Assessment in Counseling, 79
Association for Continuing Higher Education (ACHE), 3696
Association for Continuing Higher Education Directory, 3696
Association for Education and Rehabilitation, 2649
Association for Gerontology in Higher Education, 2623, 2656, 3771, 4000, 80, 11385, 11861
Association for Macular Diseases, 7525
Association for Professionals in Infection Control and Epidemiology, 81
Association for Retarded Citizens, 4001
Association for Spiritual, Ethical and Religious Values in Counseling, 82
Association for the Blind & Visually Impaired of Greater Rochester, 7526
Association for the Blind and Visually Impaired, 7527
Association for the Blind of South Carolina, 7528
Association for the Cure of Cancer of the Prostate, 5660, 5876
Association of Belltel Retirees, 1750
Association of Black Nursing Faculty, 83
Association of Brethren Caregivers, 84
Association of Community Cancer Centers, 5661
Association of Former Intelligence Officers, 85
Association of Halfway House Alcoholism: Programs of North America, 7142
Association of Homes and Services for the Aging, 4024, 4127
Association of Jewish Aging Services, 3718
Association of Junior Leagues, 7230
Association of Late-Deafened Adults, 7914
Association of Mature Canadians, 349
Association of Ohio Philanthropic Homes for the Aging, 1943
Association of Personal Historians, 86
Association of Retired Americans, 87
Association of the Bar of the City of New York: Committee for Senior Volunteer Lawyers, 11201
Association of the United States Army, 88
Asst Secretary for Fair Housing Equal Opportunity, 272
Assumption Court, 9116
Assured Care, 9117
Asthma and Allergy Foundation of America, 4653, 4658, 4648, 4677
Astor House, 10058

Athenaeum Rochester Institute of Technology, 2863
Atherton Baptist Homes, 8150
Atlanta Council of Younger Lawyers: Committee on Legal Services to the Elderly, 11059
Atlanta Legal Aid Society: Atlanta, 11060
Atlanta Legal Aid Society: Decatur, 11061
Atlanta Legal Aid Society: East Point, 11062
Atlanta Legal Aid Society: Lawrenceville, 11063
Atlanta Legal Aid Society: Marietta, 11064
Atlanta Regional Commission: Aging Services Division, 814
Atlantic County Division of Intergenerational Services, Office of Aging, 1638
Atlantis Community, 10681
Atria Assisted & Retirement Living, 8781
Atria Assisted Living Riverdale, 10343
Atria Assisted Living-Cordova, 10344
Atria Assisted Living-Merrywood South, 9394
Atria Assisted Retirement LivingMerrywood, 9395
Atria Crossroads Place, 8255
Atria Eastlake Terrace, 8619
Atria Forest Hills, 9829
Atria Inn at Lakewood, 8237
Atria Tinton Falls, 9756
Atria Wekiwa Springs, 8343
Atria Weston Place, 10345
Atria at Stratford, 8256
Atria in Kingwood, 10403
Atria in West Chase, 10404
Atrial Fibrillation and Stroke, 7082
Atrium at Cardinal Drive, 8939
Atrium at Drum Hill Alzheimer's DementiaAssisted Living, 8940
Atrium at Faxon Woods, 8941
Atrium at Veronica Drive, 8942
Attorney General's Office: Disability Rights Bureau, 901
Auburn Courts, 9118
Auburn Options for Independence, 10863
Auburn University: Special Collections & Archives, 11308
Audecibel, 3832
Audio Book Contractors, 3447
Audio Induction Loops, 6609
Audio Recordings, 3448
Audiologists Directory, 6558
Audiology Express, 4015
Audiology Today, 6572
Auditory-Verbal International, 6573, 4185, 6319
Augmentative Communication Systems (AAC), 3081
Augmentative and Alternative Communication, 3833
Augusta Biomedical Research Corporation, 4267
Augusta-Richmond County Public Library, 11432
Auricle, 6573
Aurora of Central New York, 6320, 7529
Ausburg Lutheran Home Maryland, 8902
Austin Disability Determination Services, 2309
Austin Elder Care Home, 10405

Austin State School Volunteer Council, 2310
Austine School: Library Media Center, 11805
AuthorHouse, 5796, 6029
Autonomic Failure and Parkinson's Disease, 6991
Autumn Bridge at Amber Oaks, 10406
Autumn Haven I, 8469
Autumn Haven II, 8470
Autumn Leaves Adult Care, 8111
Autumn Manor, 9396
Autumn Ridge, 9330
Autumn View Gardens, 9331
Autumn West, 8344
Autumn Wind of Smithfield, 9397
Avalon at Bridgewater, 9757
Avamere at Hillsboro, 10059
Avamere at Newberg, 10060
Avamere at Sandy, 10061
Avamere at Sherwood, 10062
Avante Terrace at Boca Raton, 8345
Avera Bormann Manor, 10234
Avera Brady Assisted Living, 10235
Avera Mother Joseph Manor Retirement Community, 10236
Avera Prince of Peace Retirement Community, 10237
Avera St Benedict Assisted Living, 10238
Avery Crossing, 8943
Avery Publishing Group, 3800, 5788
Avis Rent A Car, 11915
Avoca Lodge Assisted Living, 8637
Avon Maximum Independent Living, 1944
Away with Arthritis, 5156
Awbrey House, 10063
Azalea Estates of Gonzales, 8856
Azalea Estates of Monroe, 8857
Azalea Estates of New Iberia, 8858
Azalea Estates of Shreveport, 8859
Azalea Manor, 8061
Azalea Village, 9398

B

B and C Resthome, 10239
B&A Travel, 12009
B'nai B'rith Senior Citizens Housing Committe (BBSCHC), 89
BBBOnLine, 116
BESB Industries, 7530
BESTspeech, 3082
BIGmack Communication Aid, 3083
BVA Bulletin, 7920
Baby Jogger Company, 3051
Back Machine, 3195
Back Office, 3939
Back Pain, 5188
Back-Huggar Pillow, 3196
Bagel Holder, 3320
Bahia Oaks Lodge, 8346
Bailey, 3697
Bailey House, 8860
Bailey Manufacturing Company, 3048, 3257, 3305, 3318, 3384, 3473, 3564
Bainbridge Subregional Library for theBlind, 11433
Balance Disturbances and Parkinson's Disease, 6992
Balance Your Act: A Book for Adults with Diabetes, 6181

Entry Name Index / B

Ball Bearing Spinner, 2957
Ballard Creek Community, 8638
Baltimore City Commission on Aging, 1240
Baltimore City Commission on Aging, Retirement Education: CARE, 1227
Baltimore County Department of Aging, 1228
Bangor Public Library, 11524
Bannock Street Place, 8471
Baptist Assisted Living Center, 10346
Baptist Home of Kenmare, 9555
Baptist Homes, 8839
Barbee House, 10407
Bariatric Wheelchairs Regency, 3498
Baromedical Nurses Association, 90
Barren River Area Development District, 1097
Barrett Assisted Living Community, 9119
Barrier Free Lifts, 3361
Barrington Place, 8347
Barross House, 9120
Bartholomew County Public Library, 11480
Barton Hills Assisted Living, 10408
Barton Hills Guest House, 10409
Barton House, 10410
Barton House II, 10411
Barton House at First Colony, 10412
Basic Al-Anon Program Card, 7322
Basic Books, 6074
Basic Course in American Sign Language, 6470
Basic Course in American Sign Language Videotape Package, 6744
Basic Course in Manual Communication, 6471
Basic Information About Parkinson's Disease, 6993
Basic Sign Communication: Vocabulary, 6472
Basic Wheelchair, 3499
Basics of HIV Disease: Questions and Answers, 4553
Bath Products, 3023
BathEase, 3004
Bathtub Safety Rail, 3005
Baton Rouge Advocacy Center, 11126
Baton Rouge Regional Tumor Registry, 5662
Battery Device Adapter, 3275
Baxter Retirement Village, 8107
Bay Area Legal Services, 11052
Bay Area Managers of Volunteer Services, 2570
Bay Breeze Nursing & Retirement Center, 8348
Bay County Council on Aging, 1342
Bay Gardens Retirement Village, 8349
Bay Oaks Home for the Aged, 8350
Bay Spring Village, 10203
Bay State Council of the Blind, 7531
Bay Village of Sarasota, 8351
Bayley Place, 9871
Baylor College of Medicine, 4317
Baylor College of Medicine Center for Allergy & Immunological Disorders, 5050
Baylor College of Medicine: Cullen Eye Institute, 8036
Baylor College of Medicine: DeBakey Heart Center, 6861
Baylor College of Medicine: Roy M and Phyllis Gough Center on Aging, 4268

Baylor University Institute for Gerontological Studies, 4269
Baylor University: Bone Marrow Transplantation Research Center, 5884
Baypath Senior Citizens Services, 1266
Bayside Manor, 9758
Bayview Gardens, 8352
Baywood Publishing Company, 3886
Be Smart About HIV, 4554
Be Stroke Smart, 7083
Be Stroke Smart - Communication, 7084
Be Stroke Smart - Emotional Aspects, 7085
Be Stroke Smart - Home and Work Adaptation, 7086
Be Stroke Smart - Prevention and Warning Signs, 7087
Be Stroke Smart - Rehabilitation Guidelines and Resources, 7088
Be Stroke Smart Series, 7089
Be in the Know: Communication Access Terms, 6610
BeOK Key Lever, 3295
Beach Center on Families and Disability, 1057
Beacon House, 10413
Beacon Press, 6027, 6032
Bear & Company, 5162
Bear Mountain Manor, 8083
Bear River Area: Agency on Aging, 2391
Beat the Nursing Home Trap: A Consumer's Guide to Assisted Living and Long Term Care, 3608
Beatrice Hover Assisted Living, 8238
Beauregard Council on Aging, 1137
Beaver County Association for the Blind, 7532
Beaver County Office on Aging, 2098
Beaverton Hills Assisted Living, 10064
Bebee Medical Center/Peach Tree Acres, 8306
Becky's Rest Home, 9399
Bedford Research Consultants, 11815
Bee Hive Homes of Flathead County, 9339
Bee Hive Homes of Helena, 9340
Bee Hive Homes of Yuma, 8112
Beehive Home Assisted Living, 8639
Beehive Home Assisted Living-Hawarden, 8640
Beehive Homes of Grangeville, 8472
Beehive Homes of Idaho I, 8473
Beehive Homes of Idaho II, 8474
Beehive Homes of Idaho VI, 8475
Beehive Homes of North Idaho, 8476
Beehive Homes of Rigby, 8477
Beehive Homes-Mountain Home, 8478
Beehive of Danville, 8840
Beehive of Shelbyville, 8841
Bees-Stealy Research Foundation, 6862
Beginning Reading and Sign Language Video, 6745
Behan Health Science Library, 11731
Behavior-Dementia Management, 9759
Behcet's Disease, 5189
Being in Touch, 7800
Bell, 6086
Bell House, 9400
Bell View Rehabilitation Center, 9593
Bellaire Lodge, 10414
Belle Aims Assisted Living Facility, 9594
Belle Fourche Health Care Center, 10240
The Bellettini, 10602

Bellevue Manor Assisted Living Community, 9830
Bellmarie, 8257
Belmont Village Cardiff by the Sea, 8151
Belmont Village Crown Cove, 8152
Belmont Village Westwood, 8153
Belmont Village at Buckhead, 8434
Belmont Village at Geneva Road, 8580
Belmont Village at Johns Creek, 8435
Belmont Village at Sabre Springs, 8154
Belmont Village at St Matthews, 8842
Belmont Village at West University, 10415
Belmont Village of Buffalo Grove, 8581
Belmont Village of Burbank, 8155
Belmont Village of Encino, 8156
Belmont Village of Glenview, 8582
Belmont Village of Green Hills, 10347
Belmont Village of Hollywood Hills, 8157
Belmont Village of Memphis, 10348
Belmont Village of Oak Park, 8583
Belmont Village of Rancho Palos Verdes, 8158
Belmont Village of San Jose, 8159
Belmont Village of Sunnyvale, 8160
Beltone Electronics Corporation, 6473, 6574, 6612
Beneva Park Club, 8353
Benjamin Rose Institute Library, 11704
Bennett College, 2875
Bennett County Healthcare Center, 10241
Bentley Manor, 10416
Benton House, 8354
Berea Lake Towers Retirement Community, 9872
Bergen County Division of Senior Services, 1639
Berkeley Speech Technologies, 3082
Berkley Square Retirement Community, 9873
Berks County Center for Independent Living, 10909
Berks County Senior Citizens Council, 2041
Berks Deaf & Hard of Hearing Services Library, 11732
Berks Deaf and Hard of Hearing Service, 6321
Berman-Gund Laboratory for the Study of Retinal Degenerations, 8037
Bernardston Council on Aging, 1267
Berrien County Legal Services: Senior Law Center, 11154
Berthold Lowenfeld on Blindness and Blind People, 7801
Bertram House of Swampscott, 8944
Berverly Square Franklin, 9595
Best 25 Catalog Resources for Making Life Easier, 3698
Best Guide to Allergy, 4655
Best Years Center, 4791
Bestwork Industries for the Blind, 7533
Bet Tzedek Legal Services, 10994
Beth Israel Deaconess Medical Center, 4270
Beth Israel Medical Center: Seymour J Phillips Health Sciences Library, 11625
Bethany Home, 9596
Bethany Homes, 9556
Bethany Retirement Center, 9401
Bethel College, 2795
Bethel Four Acres, 9557
Bethel Lutheran Home, 9558
Bethel Suites, 10242

Bethesda Adult Community, 8239, 8240, 8242, 8250, 8620, 9331, 9333
Bethesda Gardens, 8113
Bethesda Gardens at the Crossings, 8620
Bethesda Gardens of Fort Worth, 10417
Bethesda Home and Retirement Center, 8584
Bethesda Towne Square, 10243
Bethlehem Woods Retirement Community, 8585
Better Back, 3043
Better Days Residential, 10204
Better Hearing Institute, 6611, 6765, 6322, 6779
Better Hearing News, 6611
Better Sleep, 3231
A Better Tomorrow, 3814
Betty and Leonard Phillips Deaf Action Center, 6323
Betty's House, 9597
Betty's House-Maple Street, 9598
Between Classes, 4016
Between Friends, 6473, 6574, 6612
Between Two Worlds of Hearing and Not Hearing, 6613
Beverly Council on Aging, 1268
Beverly Cracom Publications, 11862
Beverly Foundation, 91
Beverly Health Oak Grove, 9599
Beverly Healthcare Norfolk Chateau, 9600
Beverly Square Cozad, 9601
Beverly Square Fullerton, 9602
Beverly Square Nebraska City, 9603
Beverly Square Scottsbluff, 9604
Bexar County Area: Agency on Aging, 2311
Bey Lea Village, 9760
Beyond Sight, 3449
Bickford Cottage-Davenport, 8641
Bickford Cottage-Marshalltown, 8642
Bickford Cottage-Muscatine, 8643
Bienville Area: Agency on Aging, 1138
Bieske's Country Comfort Home Care, 10608
Big Bold Timer Low Vision, 3321
Big Bounder Power Wheelchair, 3500
Big Lamp Switch, 3296
Big Number Pocket Sized Calculator, 3084
Big Print Address Book, 3450
Big Red Switch, 3085
Big Sandy Area Development District, 1098
Bike Track, 3372
Bil Jax Construction/Rental, 3501
Bill Communications, 3708
Bill Discusses the Twelve Traditions, 7433
Bill Dvorak Kayak & Rafting, 12010
Bill Wilkerson Center, 6796
Bill's Own Story, 7434
Billerica Crossings, 8945
BioMedical Life Systems, 3441
Birch Avenue Residential Care, 8479
Birchwood Assisted Living and Physical Rehabilitation, 9831
Birchwood Retirement Estate, 8480
Birchwood Volunteers In Partnership, 1751
Birmingham Independent Living Center, 10621
Black & Decker Cordless Hand Blender, 3322
Black Experience, 6175, 6257
Black Health, 3977
Black and Deaf in America, 6474

Blackhawk Center for Independent Living, 10753
Blackstone Valley Assisted Living, 10205
Blackwell Science, 4656, 6914
Blackwell's Rest Home, 9402
Blair County Association for the Blind and Visually Handicapped, 7534
Blair Senior Services, 2099
Blakey Hall Assisted Living, 9403
Blazie Engineering, 3088
Blenheim Newport Residential Retirement Community, 10206
Blind Association of Western New York, 7535
Blind Educator, 7856
Blind Enterprises of Oregon, 7536
Blind Industries and Services of Maryland, 7537
Blind Service Association, 7538
Blind Veterans Rehabilitation Centers and Clinics, 7539
Blind Work Association, 7540
Blinded Veterans Association, 2644, 2652, 7920, 7541, 8008
Blindness and Visual Impairments: National Organizations, 7842
Blindness, A Family Matter, 7857
Blindness: What it is, What it Does and How to Live with it, 7802
Blindskills, 7865
Blinker Buddy II Electronic Turn Signal, 2958
Blood Pressure Unit Auto Inflation, 3249
Blossom Hill Care Center, 9874
Blossom Place at Edenton, 8903
Blue Ridge Independent Living Center, 10939
Blue Rivers Area: Agency on Aging (BRAAAA), 1566
Blue Valley Riverside Apartments, 9605
Blue Water Center for Independent Living Center, 10799
Bluegrass Area Agency on Aging, 1099
Blueprint for Aging, 1343
Blueprint for Progress: Al-Anon's Fourth Step Inventory, 7241
Bockus Research Institute, 6863
Body, Mind and Spirit, 7242
Bodyline Comfort Systems, 3196
Boger City Rest Home, 9404
Bold Line Paper, 3451
Bon Secours Place at Healthpark, 8355
Bon Secours Place at St Petersburg, 8356
Bone Marrow Foundation, 5872, 5877, 5885
Bone Up on Arthritis, 5157
Bonne Terre Memorial Library, 11586
Book Holder, 3452
Book of Name Signs, 6475
Bookholder: Roberts, 3453
Books Aloud Library, 11335
Books are Fun for Everyone, 7921
Boone County Senior Services Foundation, 975
Bootheel Area Independent Living Services (BAILS), 10815
Bosma Industries for the Blind, 7542
Bossier Council on Aging Area: Agency on Aging, 1139
Boston Center for Independent Living, 10788
Boston College Legal Assistance Bureau, 11143

Boston College: Social Work Library, 11544
Boston Commission on Affairs of the Elderly, 1269
Boston Common Press, 3845
Boston University Cancer Research Center, 5886
Boston University Gerontology Center, 4271
Boston University Laboratory of Neuropsychology, 7452
Boston University: Arthritis Center, 5234
Boston University: General Clinical Research Center, 6864
Boston University: Robert Dawson Evans Memorial Department of Clinical Research, 5235
Boston University: Whitaker Cardiovascular Institute, 6865
Boulder County Aging Services Division, 628
Boulder County Aging Services Division: Elder Rights Program, 11017
Bounder Plus Power Wheelchair, 3502
Bounder Power Wheelchair, 3503
Bowdle Hospital Assisted Living Center, 10244
Bowman Gray School of Medicine, 6908
Box Top Opener, 3323
Bradford Village East, 9405
Bradford Village West, 9406
Braeswood Personal Care Homes, 10418
Braille Blazer Printer, 3086
Braille Book Bank, 11626
Braille Book Review, 7858, 7922
Braille Business Cards & More, 3454
Braille Catalog of General Interest Items, 7843
Braille Compass, 3087
Braille Division, 7571
Braille Documents, 11863
Braille Forum, 7859
Braille Institute, 7491, 11897
Braille Institute Desert Center, 7543
Braille Institute Press, 7860
Braille Institute Sight Center, 7544
Braille Institute of America, 7545
Braille Institute of America, 7546
Braille Institute of America Library, 7547
Braille Institute: Orange County Center, 7548
Braille Institute: Santa Barbara Center, 7549
Braille Materials Production Center, 7550
Braille Mirror, 7860
Braille Monitor, 7861
Braille N' Speak, 3088
Braille Notebook, 3455
Braille Plates for Elevator, 3362
Braille Revival League, 7551, 8009
Braille Star Theosophist, 7862
Braille Touch-Time Watches, 3089
Braille/Print Protractor, 3090
Braille: An Extraordinary Volunteer Opportunity, 7923
Brailled Desk Calendar, 3456
Braillemaster, 3091
Brain Research Institute University of California, Los Angeles, 4272
Brain at Risk: Understanding and Preventing Stroke, 7090, 7111
Brandall Estates, 9761
Brandeis University, 253, 4273
Brandeis University Institute for Health Policy, 4273

Entry Name Index / B

Brandeis University Policy Center on Aging, 4274
Branden Publishing Company, 4517, 4953
Brandywine Assisted Living at Middlebrook Cross, 9762
Brandywine Assisted Living at Moorestown, 9763
Brandywine Assisted Living at Seaside, 8307
Brandywine Assisted Living at the Gables, 9764
Brattleboro Retreat: Asa Keyes Medical Library, 11806
Braun Corporation, 3410, 3006
The Braun Corporation, 3406, 3443
Braun Mobility Products, 2959
BraunAbility, 3022
Bravo! + Three-Wheel Scooter, 3418
Breaking the Chain of Substance Abuse and Hearing Loss, 6614, 7323
Breast Cancer: Understanding Treatment Options, 5811
Breckenridge Village, 9875
Breezy, 3504
Brentwood Retirement Community, 8357
Brevard Association for Advancement of the Blind, 7552
Brevard Association for the Advancement of the Blind, 7553
Brevard County Community Services Council, 734
Briarcliff Retirement Center, 8644
Briarfield Manor Residential Care, 9876
Briarwood, 9877
Briarwood Continuing Care Retirement Community, 8946
Briarwood Manor, 9832
Brick Manor Residential Care, 10207
Brickford Cottage, 8645, 9121
Brickford Cottage II, 8646
Brickford Cottage-Ames, 8647
Brickford Cottage-Burlington, 8648
Brickford Cottage-Clinton, 8649
Brickford Cottage-Des Moines, 8650
Brickford Cottage-Fort Dodge, 8651
Brickford Cottage-Iowa City, 8652
Brickford Cottage-West Des Moines, 8653
Bridge Assisted Living at Life Care Center, 8358
Bridges Beyond Sound, 6476
Bridges at Lake Whitney, 8258
Bridges at the Green, 8259
Bridgeview Estates, 8481
Bridgewater at Waterman Village, 8359
Bridgewood Rivers, 10065
Bridging the Gap of Care, 9407
Briggs Corporation, 11864
Brigham Young University: Cancer Research Center, 5887
Brigham and Women's Hospital: Asthma & Allergic Diseases Research Center, 4681
Brigham and Women's Hospital: Robert B Brigham Arthritis Center, 5236
Brighton Court, 10588
Brighton Gardens Marriot-San Antonio, 10419
Brighton Gardens at Friendship Heights, 8904
Brighton Gardens by Marriott of Maitland, 8360
Brighton Gardens by Marriott-Greensboro, 9408

Brighton Gardens by Marriott-Raleigh, 9409
Brighton Gardens of Cherry Hill, 9765
Brighton Gardens of Columbia, 8905
Brighton Gardens of Dedham, 8947
Brighton Gardens of Edison, 9766
Brighton Gardens of Florham Park, 9767
Brighton Gardens of Middletown, 9768
Brighton Gardens of North Shore by Marriott, 8948
Brighton Gardens of Oklahoma City, 10003
Brighton Gardens of Omaha, 9606
Brighton Gardens of Paramus, 9769
Brighton Gardens of Pikesville, 8906
Brighton Gardens of Saddle River, 9770
Brighton Gardens of Tulsa, 10004
Brighton Gardens of West Orange, 9771
Brighton Gardens of Winston Salem, 9410
Brinley Professional Plaza, 4041
Bristol Elder Services, 1270, 11144
Bristol Glen, 9772
Bristol Park of Coral Springs, 8361
British Airways, 11916
British Home in California, 8161
Brittany Park, 10589
Britthaven of Kannapolis, 9411
Britthaven of La Grange, 9412
BroMenn Healthcare, 11452
Broadcast Services for the Blind, 11336
Broadmoor Court, 8239
Broadview Residential Care Center, 8162
Broadway Plaza at Pecan Park, 10420
Broadway Plaza at Westover Hills, 10421
Broadway Proper, 8114
Bromenn Life Care Center, 4744
Bronx Independent Living Services, 10864
Bronxwood Home for the Aged, 9833
Brookdale Center for Healthy Aging and Longevity of Hunter College, 3576
Brookdale Foundation Group, 4132
Brookes Publishing, 3607, 3616, 3617, 3659, 6476
Brookhaven the Lifecare Community, 9878
The Brookings Institution, 3613, 3682
Brooklyn Center for Independence of the Disabled, 10865
Brooklyn College of City University of New York: Speech & Hearing Center, 6797
Brookridge, 9122
Brookridge Retirement Community, 10005
Brooks of St Paul, 9123
Brooks/Cole Publishing Company, 7244
Brookside Assisted Living, 8782
Brookside Estates, 9879
Brookside House, 10066
Brookside Landing, 8482
Brookstone Haven Residential Care, 9413
Brookstone Rest Home & Retirement Center, 9414
Brookstone Terrace, 9415
Brookwood Community, 10422
Broome County Office for Aging, 1752
Broward County Area: Agency on Aging, 735
Broward County Talking Book Library, 11409
Broward Meals on Wheels, 736
Brown Community for Learning in Retirement, 2913
Brown University, 2913, 7453
Brown University Center for Gerontology and Health Care Research, 4275

Brown University Population Studies and Training Center, 4276
Brown University: Division of Biology and Medicine, 5888
Brown-Karhan Health Care, 10423
Bruno Independent Living Aids, 3363, 3366, 3394, 3401, 3403, 3431, 3528
Bryan County Retired and Senior Volunteer Program, 2004
Bryant House, 9124
Buckeye Hills-Hocking Valley Regional Development District, 1945
Buckinghams Choice, 8907
Bucknell University Immunobiology Research Laboratory, 5237
Buckner Retirement Services, 10424
Buckner Villas, 10425
Bucks County Area: Agency on Aging, 2100
Bucks County Legal Aid Society: Social Security Referral Panel, 11236
Buena Vida, 3834
Buffalo Hill Terrace, 9341
Buffalo Senior Center, 1753
Buffalo Trace Area Agency on Aging, 1100
Bukovina Society of the Americas Library, 11495
Bull Publishing, 4527, 5159, 6192
Bull Publishing Company, 4529
Bulletin, 3978, 7863, 7924
Bulletin on Long-Term Care Law, 4017
Buraff Publications, 4548
Burcham Hills Retirement Center, 9041
Bureau of Braille & Talking Book Library Services, 11410
Bureau of Disability Adjudication, 1598
Bureau of Disability Determination, 1946
Bureau of Elderly & Adult Services, 11184
Bureau of HIV, 2414
Bureau of Health Professions, Health Resources and Services Administration, 1229
Bureau of Naval Personnel, 92
Bureau of Naval Personnel: Bremerton Retired Affairs, 2504
Bureau of Naval Personnel: California Retired Affairs Office, 495
Bureau of Naval Personnel: Connecticut Retired Activities Office, 672
Bureau of Naval Personnel: District of Columbia Retired Affairs Office, 719
Bureau of Naval Personnel: Fleet and Family Support Center, 496
Bureau of Naval Personnel: Florida Retired Affairs Office-Jacksonville, 737
Bureau of Naval Personnel: Hawaii Retired Activities Office, 855
Bureau of Naval Personnel: Houston Retired Activities Office, 2312
Bureau of Naval Personnel: Illinois Retired Activities Office, 902
Bureau of Naval Personnel: Kingsville Retired Activities Office, 2313
Bureau of Naval Personnel: Louisiana Retired Activities Office, 1140
Bureau of Naval Personnel: Maryland Retired Activities Office, 1230
Bureau of Naval Personnel: Michigan Retired Activities Office, 1344
Bureau of Naval Personnel: Milton Retired Activities Office, 738
Bureau of Naval Personnel: Minnesota Retired Activities Office, 1392

Entry Name Index / C

Bureau of Naval Personnel: Nevada Retired Affairs Activities Office, 1599
Bureau of Naval Personnel: Oregon Retired Activities Office, 2042
Bureau of Naval Personnel: Orlando Retired Activities Office, 739
Bureau of Naval Personnel: Patuxent Retired Activities Office, 1231
Bureau of Naval Personnel: Pensacola Retired Activities Office, 740
Bureau of Naval Personnel: Retired Activities Office, 815, 1200
Bureau of Naval Personnel: Rhode Island Retired Activities Office, 2201
Bureau of Naval Personnel: San Antonio Retired Activities Center, 2314
Bureau of Naval Personnel: San Diego Retired Activities Office, 497
Bureau of Naval Personnel: Texas Retired Activities Office, 2315
Bureau of Naval Personnel: Virginia Retired Activities Center, 2451
Bureau of Naval Personnel: Washington Retired Activities Office, 2505
Bureau of Naval Personnel: Whidbey Island Retired Activities Office, 2506
Bureau of Naval Personnel: Wisconsin Retired Activities Office, 2571
Bureau of Rehabilitation Services, 7640
Bureau of Rehabilitation Services: Disability Determination Services, 673
Bureau of Survivor Benefits, 950
Burger King Cancer Caring Center, 5663
Burke, 3440
Burley Care Assisted Living, 8483
Burlington County Bar Association, 11194
Burlington County Office on Aging, 1640
Burlington County Retired and Senior Volunteer Program, 1641
Burlington Manor, 9416
Burns Braille Transcription Dictionary, 7803
Burnsdale Extended Care, 9125
Bursitis, Tendonitis and other Soft Tissue, 5190
Bus and Taxi Sign, 3457
Busch Campus, 7218
Business Publishers, 3712, 3823, 3930, 4007, 4081, 4096, 6093
Butler County Area: Agency on Aging, 2101
Butler County Community College, 2794
Butler County Department on Aging, 4011, 1058
Butler Township Senior Citizens, 2102
Butterworth-Heinemann, 4952, 7070, 7072
Button Aid, 3234
Buyer's Guide, 6226
Bye Bye Decubiti, 3197
Bye-Bye Decubiti (BBD), 3198
Bye-Bye Decubiti Air Mattress Overlay, 3035
Byron House, 8908

C

C& C Adult Care Home, 8115
C/O Center For Community Research And Services, 209
C/O Killingly Community Center, 698
CADI, 6325
CAP Darke County, 1947
CAPCOM, 6780, 6798
CAPH Independent Living Center, 10643
CAREsource Program Development, 3628, 3658
CARF Directory of Organizations with Accredited Programs, 3699
CARF..The Rehabilitation Accreditation Commission, 3699
CARP Canada's Association for the Fifty-Plus, 350
CCCIL-Central Coast Center for Independenet Living - Capitola, 10644
CD Publications, 3822, 4045, 4104, 7404
CDC National Aids Clearinghouse, 4537, 6554
CDC National Prevention Information Network, 4452
CEH, 11917
CEL Regional Library, 11434
CHOICES Center for Independent Living, 10857
CICI's Contact, 6615
CLC Tappahannock, 10553
CLEO Economy Folding Walker, 3478
CLOSE-UP 6.5, 3092
CPPD Crystal Deposition Disease, 5191
CQC Stephenson Home, 9042
CSAP State Liason Program, 7440
Cabinet for Families and Children, 1115
Cabinet for Human Resources, 1114
Cabot Reserve on the Green, 8362
Cabrini Medical Center, 6271
Cache County Retired And SeniorVolunteer Program (RSVP), 2392
Cadbury Commons at Cambridge, 8949
Caddo Council on Aging, 1141
Cajun Area: Agency on Aging, 1142
Calcasieu Council of Aging, 1143
Caldewell Parish Council on Aging, 1144
Calendars, 3458
Caleworthy, 3093
Calhoun County Historical Museum Library, 11492
California Advocates for Nursing Home Reform, 10995
California Agency of Health & Welfare: Department of Rehabilitation, 498
California Agency of Health and Welfare: Department of Aging, 499
California Aging Services, 500
California American/Asian Elderly Society, 501
California Association for Older Americans, 502
California Association of Area Agencies on Aging, 503
California Association of Homes andServices for the Aging, 504
California Client Assistance Program, 505
California Collaborative Treatment Group, 4453
California Commission on Aging, 506
California Department of Aging, 507, 10996
California Department of Aging and Adult Services, 508
California Department of Aging: Children and Community Services, 509
California Department of Alcohol and Drug Programs: Resource Center, 510
California Department of Education, 7565
California Department of Health Services Office of AIDS, 4454
California Department of Rehabilitation, 511
California Department of Social Services, 3714
California Department of Veterans Affairs, 512
California Developmental Disability Council, 513
California Division of Tourism, 11953
California Foundation for Independent Living Centers (CFILC), 10645
California Franchise Tax Board, 514
California Governor's Committee on Employment of People with Disabilities, 515
California Institute for Medical Research, 7035
California Latino Council of the Deaf and Hard of Hearing, 516, 6324
California Protection & Advocacy for Persons With Disabilities, 517
California Protection and Advocacy Agency (PAI), 10997
California Public Employees' Retirement System, 518
California School of Professional Psychology, 6436
California Seniors Council, 519
California State Bar Committee on Legal Problems of Aging, 10998
California State Board of Equalization, 520
California State Independent Living Council (SILC), 10646
California State Library: Braille & Talking Book Library, 11337
California State Teachers Retirement System, 521
California State University, 575, 6408
California State University at FullertonUniversity Extended Education, 2716
California State University of Bakersfield, 2732
California State University, Sacramento, 2729
California State University: Bakersfield Applied Research Center, 4277
California Women's Commission on Alcohol and Drug Dependencies, 7143
California Workers Compensation Board, 522
Californian Retirement Residence, 8163
Calimay Assisted Living Home, 10426
Callista Court, 9126
Calvary Hospital Medical Library, 11627
Calvin Community Assisted Living Service, 8654
Calyx Books & Calyx Journal, 11865
Cambridge Assisted Living Community, 9417
Cambridge Court, 9607
Cambridge Hills of Raleigh, 9418
Cambridge Homes, 8950
Cambridge Hospital, 7163
Cambridge Square Retirement Center, 10427
Cambridge Terrace Assisted Living, 10067
Cambridge University Press, 3824
Camden City Independent Living Center (CCILC), 10849
Camden County Senior Center, 1886
Came to Believe, 7243
Cameron Council on Aging, 1145
Cameron House, 8951

997

Entry Name Index / C

Cameron Woods, 10744
Campbell Adult Center, 8164
Can You Hear the Clapping of One Hand? Learning to Live with a Stroke, 7059
CanHelp, 5664
Cancer Care, 5665
Cancer Center of Wake Forest University: Bowman Gray School of Medicine, 5889
Cancer Control Society and Cancer Book House, 5666
Cancer Counseling Center of Ohio, 5667
Cancer Dictionary, 5791
Cancer Facts and Figures, 5792
Cancer Federation, 5668
Cancer Information Service (CIS), 5669
Cancer Institute of Brooklyn, 5670
Cancer Rates and Risks, 5793
Cancer Research Center, 5890
Cancer Research Center of Hawaii, 5786
Cancer Research Center: Albert Einstein College of Medicine, 5891
Cancer Research Committee, 5975
Cancer Research Foundation of America, 5892
Cancer Research Institute, 5893
Cancer Research Institute of New York, 5894
Cancer Sourcebook, 5794
Cancer Therapy and Research Center, 5895
Cancer Therapy: The Independant Consumer's Guide to Non-Toxic Treatment & Prevention, 5795
Cancer Victors and Friends National Headquarters, 5671
Cancer and Leukemia Group B, 5672
Cancer of the Bladder: Research Report, 5812
Cancer of the Colon and Rectum: Research Report, 5813
Cancer of the Ovary: Research Report, 5814
Cancer of the Pancreas: Research Report, 5815
Cancer of the Uterus: Research Report, 5816
Cancer-Free: Your Guide to Gentle, 5796
Cancervive, 5673, 5797
Canfield Place Retirement, 10068
Canine Assistance for the Disabled, 6325
Canine Companions for Independence, 7554
Canine Helpers for the Handicapped, 7555
Canine Listener, 6616
Canon Communicator, 3094, 3095
Canon Communicator M, 3095
Canton Christian Home, 9880
Canton Negro Oldtimers, 1948
Canton Regency Retirement Community, 9881
Canyonlands Publishing, 4946
Capable Hands Adult Care Home, 8116
Cape & Islands Senior Corps, 1271
Cape May County Department of Aging, 1642
Cape Organization for Rights of the Disabled (CORD), 10789
Capital Area Center for Independent Living, 10800
Capital Area: Agency on Aging, 1146
Capital Assistance Program for Elderly and Persons with Disabilities, 93
Capital City Assisted Living-Spaulding, 8484
Capital District Center for Independent Living, 10866
Capitan Public Library, 11620
Capscrew, 3324
Capsule Newsletter, 4018
Captain's Deck, 8308
Captek/Science Products, 3096
Caption Center, 6617, 6326, 11545
Caption Center News, 6617
Captioned Media Program, 6327
Captioned Media Program: National Association of the Deaf, 11755
Carbohydrate Counting, 4019
Carbon County Area: Agency on Aging, 2103
Card Chart, 3459
Cardiac Rehabilitation Directory, 3700
Cardinal Care Center-Hendersonville, 9419
Cardinal Grove, 8655
Cardinal Retirement Village, 9773
Cardiovascular Research and Training Center: University of Alabama, 6866
Care Concepts, 2960
Care Givers of the Elderly Support Group, 1754
Care Pointe, 9127
Care for Advanced Alzheimer's Disease, 4990
Care of the Ears and Hearing for Health, 6618
Care with Love, 8117
Care-Age Country Home, 9128
Career Perspectives: Interviews with Blind and Visually Impaired Professionals, 7804
Carefirst Seniors & Community Services Association, 351
Carefree Living America-Brainerd, 9129
Carefree Living America-Burnsville, 9130
Carefree Living of America-St Cloud, 9131
Caregiver Alliance, 94
Caregiver Stress: Signs to Watch for... Steps to Take, 4991
Caregiver Survival Series: Positive Caregiver Attitudes, 3609
Caregivers' Roller Coaster, 3610
Caregiving at Home, 4992
Carelink Community Support Services, 10690
Caresource Healthcare Communications, 3604, 3615, 4186, 11866
Carestone at Austin, 10428
Caribou County Senior Citizens Center, 877
Carillon Assisted Living of Asheboro, 9420
Carillon Assisted Living of Cramer Mountain, 9421
Carillon Assisted Living of Newton, 9422
Carillon Assisted Living of Shelby, 9423
Carillon of Salisbury, 9424
Caring Connections, 95
Caring and Sharing Center for Independent Living, 10693
Caring for Alzheimer's Patients, 4993
Caring for Ourselves: Hope for Healthy Relationships, 7435
Caring for Those You Love: A Guide to Compassionate Care for the Aged, 3611
Caring for Your Parents: The CompleteAARP Guide, 3612
Caring for the Diabetic Soul, 6182
Caring for the Disabled Elderly, 3613
Caring... Sharing: The Alzheimer's Caregiver, 5030
Caritas Southwood Hospital Medical Library, 11546
Carman Oaks Assisted Living Facility, 10069
Carmel Hills, 9425
Carmel Terrace, 8952
Carmichaels Senior Citizens, 2104
Carnegie Library of Pittsburgh, 11733
Carol Abaya Associates, 3956
Carolina Academic Division, 6912
Carolina House of Asheboro, 9426
Carolina House of Cary, 9427
Carolina House of Durham, 9428
Carolina House of Elizabeth City, 9429
Carolina House of Forest City, 9430
Carolina House of Greenville, 9431
Carolina House of Lexington, 9432
Carolina House of Pinehurst, 9433
Carolina House of Reidsville, 9434
Carolina House of Smithfield, 9435
Carolina House of Wake Forest, 9436
Carolina Inn at Village Green, 9437
Carolina Rest Home, 9438
Carolina Village, 9439
Carolinas Chapter of the Arthritis Foundatiob, 5094
Carolyn's Low Vision Solutions, 7844
Carousel Homes I, 8485
Carousel Homes II, 8486
Carousel Living Center, 10245
Carpal Tunnel Syndrome, 5192
Carpenter's Creek by Encore Senior Living, 8363
Carriage Club of Charlotte, 9440
Carriage House, 10070
Carriage House of Greensburg, 8783
Carric Manor, 9132
Carroll Center for the Blind, 7774, 7556
Carroll County Bureau of Aging, 1232
Carroll County Council on Aging, 1949
Cartens Harbour, 9133
Carter House, 9608
Caruth Haven Court, 10429
Cascade AIDS Project: Women's Phone Network, 4589
Cascade Assisted Living, 8487
Cascadia Village Retirement Community, 10071
Case Western Reserve University, 4119
Case Western Reserve University Center for Biomedical Ethics, 4278
Case Western Reserve University Elderly Care Research Center, 4279, 11705
Case Western Reserve University School of Medicine, 4280
Case Western Reserve University: University Center on Aging and Health, 4281
Casiano Communications, 3834
Cass County Council on Aging, 1393
Castle Rock Assisted Living, 10430
Castle View Assisted Living, 10246
Caswell Parish, 2876
Cataracts, 7805, 7925
Catawba Area: Agency on Aging, 2224
Catherine McGowan Senior Center, 1323
Catholic Charities USA (CCUSA), 96
Catholic Charities of the Archdiocese of New York, 7557
Catholic Eldercare at Home, 9134
Catholic Golden Age (CGA), 97
Catholic Guild for the Blind, 7557, 11453

Entry Name Index / C

Catskill Center for Independence, 10867
Cattaraugus County Department of Aging, 1755
Cave Spring Library, 11435
Cayuga County Office of the Aging, 1756
Cecil County Department of Aging, 1233
Cedar Cove at Wilmington, 9441
Cedar Crest Estate, 9135
Cedar Crest Residential Care, 8488
Cedar Draw Living Center, 8489
Cedar Lake Village, 8784
Cedar Manor Rest Home, 9442
Cedar Rock Assisted Living, 9443
Cedar Sinai Park, 10072
Cedar View Assisted Living, 10247
Cedar Village Assisted Living Community, 10073
Cedars of Austin, 9136
Cedartown Library, 11436
Cedarview Assisted Living, 8785
Cedarville Senior Citizens, 1950
Cellular Phones - Hearing Aid Wearers Can Use Them, 6619
Cengage Learning, 6031
Cenoma House, 8490
Centenary College of Louisiana, 2803
Centennial Park Retirement Village, 9609
Centennial Villa Assisted Living, 9137
The Center, 2842
Center For Independent Living-Jacksonville, 10723
Center For People With Disabilities, 10682
Center for AIDS Prevention Studies, 4560
Center for Accessible Living, 10773
Center for Accessible Living-Louisville, 10774
Center for Adult Learning and Educational Credentials, 98
Center for Aging Newsletter, 4020
Center for Alcohol & Addiction Studies, 7453
Center for Applied Prevention Research, 7454
Center for Arkansas Legal Services, 10991
Center for Bio-Gerontology, 11867
Center for Blood Research, 4590
Center for Clinical and Aging Services Research, 4282
Center for Clinical and Lifestyle Research, 4283
Center for Community and Professional Services of the PA School for the Deaf, 6328
Center for Comprehensive Services-Carbondale, 10724
Center for Disability Rights, 10685
Center for Disease Control, 4591
Center for Endocrinology, Metabolism & Nutrition, 6267
Center for Health Sciences, 6872, 6894
Center for Human Services, 4284
Center for Independence, 10683
Center for Independence of Disabled in New York (CIDNY), 10868
Center for Independence of the Disabled (CID), 10647
Center for Independence of the Disabled-North Branch, 10648
Center for Independent Living (CIL), 10649
Center for Independent Living - Central Coast/Hollister (CCCIL), 10650

Center for Independent Living Options (CILO), 10896
Center for Independent Living for Southwest Kansas, 10759
Center for Independent Living for Western Wisconsin, 10953
Center for Independent Living of Broward, 10695
Center for Independent Living of Central Nebraska, 10844
Center for Independent Living of Central Pennsylvania, 10910
Center for Independent Living of Flordia-Lecanto, 10696
Center for Independent Living of Jacksonville, 10697
Center for Independent Living of MiddleTennessee, 10923
Center for Independent Living of North Central Florida, 10694, 10698
Center for Independent Living of Northern Florida / Ability 1st, 10699
Center for Independent Living of Northwestern Connecticut, 10686
Center for Independent Living of South Florida, 10700
Center for Independent Living of SouthCentral Pennsylvania, 10911
Center for Independent Living of Southwest Florida, 10701
Center for Independent Living of Southwest Kansas, 10760
Center for Independent Living-Central Florida, 10702
Center for Independent Living-East Hawaii, 10713
Center for Independent Living-Merced Outreach, 10651
Center for Independent Living-Northwest Florida, 10703
Center for Independent Living-Oakland, 10652
Center for Independent Living-West Hawaii, 10714
Center for Information Resources, 11734
Center for Interdisciplinary Research in Immunology & Diseases at UCLA, 4592
Center for Learning in Retirement, 2904
Center for Lifelong Learning, 2316, 2905, 2940
Center for Living and Working, 10790
Center for Medical Ethics and Mediation, 99
Center for Medicare Advocacy, 11022
Center for Medicare and Medicaid Services (CMS), 11082
Center for Neural Recovery and Rehabilitation Research, 4285
Center for New Perspectivese, 2753
Center for Positive Aging, 4148, 4163, 3577
Center for Professional Development, 2317
Center for Public Representation, 3623, 3661, 11868
Center for Rehabilitation Technology, 4121
Center for Science in the Public Interest, 4080
Center for Senility Studies: Alzheimer's Disease Treatment Research, 5051
Center for Social Gerontology, 3578
Center for Study of Aging, 4286
Center for Substance Abuse Prevention, 7179, 7194, 7195, 7232, 7144, 7441
Center for Thanatology Research, 6035

Center for Thanatology Research & Education, 11869
Center for Thanatology Research Library, 11628
Center for Understanding Aging, 4287
Center for the Advancement of State Community Services Programs (CASCSP), 100
Center for the Blind and Visually Impaired, 7558
Center for the Rights of the Terminally Ill, 101
Center for the Rights of the Terminally Ill Resource Library, 11769
Center for the Study of Aging, 4288
Center for the Study of Aging Library, 11629
Center for the Study of Aging of Albany, 1757
Center for the Study of Human Rights, 11870
Center for the Study of Pharmacy and Therapeutics for the Elderly, 4289
Center on Aging Studies\Univ Missouri-Kansas City, 3716
Center on Independent Living, 10927
Centers for Disease Control, 4541
Centers for Independent Living of South Jersey (CILSJ), 10850
Centers for Medicare and Medicaid Services (CMS), 102, 4187
Central Arkansas Area: Agency on Aging, 469
Central Association for the Blind and Visually Impaired, 7559
Central California Legal Services, 10999
Central Care, 9444
Central Coast Commission for Senior Citizens, 523
Central Illinois Agency on Aging (CIAA), 903
Central Illinois Center for Independent Living, 10725
Central Indiana Council on Aging, 976
Central Institute for the Deaf, 6329
Central Institute for the Deaf Professional Library, 11587
Central Iowa Center for Independent Living, 10754
Central Maine Area: Agency on Aging, 1201
Central Massachusetts Agency on Aging, 1272
Central Michigan University: Center for Adult Longitudinal Studies, 4290
Central Minnesota Council on Aging, 1394
Central Minnesota Self-Help for Hard of Hearing, 6330
Central Mississippi Area: Agency on Aging, 1444
Central New York Chapter of the Arthritis Foundation, 5095
Central Ohio Area: Agency on Aging, 1951
Central Ohio Chapter of the Arthritis Foundation, 5096
Central Oklahoma Economic Development District: Area Agency on Aging (COEDD), 2005
Central Oregon Council on Aging, 2043
Central Pennsylvania Chapter of the Arthritis Foundation, 5097
Central Plains Area: Agency on Aging, 1059

999

Entry Name Index / C

Central Rappahannock Regional Library, 11816
Central Savannah River Regional Area:Agency on Aging, 816
Central Todd County Care Center, 9138
Central Vermont Council on Aging (CVCOA), 2426
Central Washington Disability Resources, 10947
Central Washington University, 2940
Centralina Area: Agency on Aging, 1887
Centre County Office on Aging, 2105
Centro Gerontologico Latino, 103
Cerebral Blood Flow Laboratories, 4291, 7113
Cervipillow Covers, 3199
Chagrin Plaza East, 5128
Challenge Magazine, 3835
Challenge Publications, 11938
Challenge of Choice, 4135
Chambrel at Island Lake, 8364
Champion 1000, 3505
Champion 2000, 3506
Champion 3000, 3507
Champion Oaks by Marriot, 10431
Champions at Porters Neck, 9445
Champlain Valley Area: Agency on Aging, 2427
Chancellor Gardens of Charlotte, 9446
Chancellor Gardens of Southington, 8260
Chancellor Health Care, 8165
Chancellor Park of Park Ridge, 9774
Chancellor Place at Aspen Park, 9610
Chancellor Place of Chino Hills, 8166
Chancellor Place of Lodi, 8167
Chancellor Place of Murrieta, 8168
Chancellor Place of Pasadena, 8169
Chancellor Place of Windsor, 8170
Chandler Assisted Living, 10432
Chandler Place, 9139
The Chandler Senior Center, 2389
Change for the Better, 3614
Changing the Rules, 6477
Chapion Home of Hastings, 9611
Chappys Golden Shore, 9140
Chapter - Arthritis Foundation Greater Southwest, 5172
Chapter of the Arthritis Foundation: Greater Southwest, 5098
Char-Mac Assisted Living, 8656
Charitable Trusts, 4994
Charles C Thomas Publisher, 6464, 6491, 6494, 6530, 6549, 6550, 6553, 7815
Charles County Department of Community Service Aging Division, 1234
Charles Press Publishers, 6076
Charles R Drew Hypertension Research Center, 6919
Charleston Area Senior Center, 904
Charleston Disability Determination Services, 2546
Charlevoix County Commission on Aging, 1345
Charlie Brown's Goodtime Travel, 12011
Charlotte Square, 9447
Chateau for Seniors Citizens, 9559
Chatham Creek Rest Home, 9448
Chattahoochee Flint Area: Agency on Aging, 817
Chaucer Estates-Retirement, 8786
Chautauqua County Office for the Aging, 1758

Chautauqua Program for Senior Adults, 2787
Cheese Slicer, 3325
Cheever Publishing, 3819
Chelmsford Crossings, 8953
Chelsea at East Brunswick, 9775
Chelsea at Fanwood, 9776
Chelsea at Montville, 9777
Chelsea at Tinton Falls, 9778
Chelsea-Revere-Winthrop Elder Services Area: Agency on Aging, 1273
Chelsea: The Story of a Signal Dog, 6478
Chemical Dependency Pamphlets, 7324
Chemical Dependency and the African American, 7325
Chemical Dependency: An Acceptable Disease, 7326
Chemocare, 5674
Chemotherapy Foundation, 5675
Chemotherapy and You: A Guide to Self-Help During Treatment, 5817
Chemung County Office for the Aging, 1759
Chenango County Area: Agency on Aging, 1760
Cheney's Liberty II, 3364
Cherokee County Genealogical Historical Society, 11496
Cherry Creek Village Retirement Center, 8787
Cherry Springs Village, 9449
Cherry Wood Village, 10074
Cherrywood Nursing & Living Center, 9043
Chester County Branch Pennsylvania Association for Blind, 7560
Chester County Branch, Pennsylvania Association for Blind, 7561
Chester County Services for Senior Citizens, 11237
Chester Village West, 8261
Chestnut Hill Residence, 9779
Chicago Bar Association Senior Lawyers Committee, 11093
Chicago Department of Health, 4455
Chicago Department of Senior Services, 905
Chicago Kent Law School Information Center, 11083
Chicago Lawyers' Committee For Civil Rights Under Law, 11084
Chicago Library Service for the Blind, 11454
Chicago Lighthouse for People who areBlind or Visually Impaired, 7562
Chicago Region 5 Office, 11082
Chicago Review Press, 3808
Chicago Social Security Management Association, 1346
Children of Aging Parents, 4018, 104, 4292
Children's Hospital, 4598
Chiropractor's Self-Help Back and Body Book, 11690
Choice & Challenge: Caring for Aggressive Older Adults Across Levels of Care, 4136
Choice Magazine Listening, 7864
Choices in Deafness, 6479
Cholesterol and Your Heart, 6857
Chrisoma West Assisted Living, 9612
Christian Association of PrimeTimers, 105
Christian Care Center of New Bern, 9450
Christian Care of Smithfield, 9451
Christian Care of Winston-Salem, 9452
Christian Education for the Blind, 11770

Christian Foundation for Children and Aging, 3579
Christian Homes Assisted Living Center, 9613
Christian Opportunity Center, 11116
Christian Record Service, 7877
Christian Record Services, 7563
Christopher Heights Assisted Living, 8954
Christopher Heights of Webster, 8955
Chronimed Publishing, 4019, 4031, 4032, 4061, 4062, 4063, 4083, 4094, 4095, 4115, 4135, 4149, 6185, 6189, 6198, 6200, 6203, 6207, 6208, 6209, 6212
Chugiak Senior Center, 8084
Church of Jesus Christ of Latter Day Saints, 11338
Churchhill Assisted Living Residences, 9453
Churchill Clubhouse Estates, 10075
Cigarette Holder, 3297
Cigarette Smoking, 4021
Cincinnati Area: Council on Aging, 1952
Cincinnati Association for the Blind, 7564
Circline Illuminated Magnifier, 3097
Circus House, 9614
Citizens Plaza State Office Building, 2300
Citizens for Independence and Access, 10912
Citrus Heights Terrace, 8171
City University of New York: Center for Research in Speech & Hearing, 6331
City of Albuquerque-Bernalillo County:Department of Senior Affairs, 1709
City of Hope, 106
City of Hope Clinical Cancer Research Center, 5896
City of Hope National Medical Center: Beckman Research, 4593
City of Los Angeles Department of Aging, 524
City of Richmond, Park Department, 1011
Civic Ventures, 2677
Civil Rights Compliance Activities, 107
Civil Rights Division, 328
Civil Rights of Institutionalized Persons Division, 108
Clackamas County Social Services Area: Agency on Aging, 2044
Clackamas Woods Assisted Living, 10076
Claddagh House, 9141
Claiborne Voluntary Council on Aging, 1147
Clara-Ellen House, 9615
Clare Bridge of Chapel Hill, 9454
Clare Bridge of Leesburg, 8365
Clare Bridge of Tequesta, 8366
Clarion County Area: Agency on Aging, 2106
Clarity, 3098
Clarity Products, 3158
Clark College, 2942
Clark House, 8491
Clark Jeary Home, 9616
Clark Meadows, 9834
Clark Retirement Home, 9044
Clark Tibbitts Award, 2623
Clarke Health Care Products, 3480, 3007
Clarksburg Disability Determination Services, 2547
Classic, 2961
Classic Coach Interiors, 2962

Entry Name Index / C

Classic Hawaii, 12012
Classification of Impaired Vision, 7926
Classique, 3365
Claude Pepper Award, 2624
Claude Pepper Foundation, 2624
Clayton County Alzheimer's Support Services, 4935
Clayton County Alzheimer's SupportServices, 4934
Clayton-Davis & Associates, 3982
Clearfield County Area: Agency on Aging, 2107
Clearing the Air: A Guide to Quitting Smoking, 5818
Clearinghouse for Specialized Media and Technology, 7565
Clearinghouse on Abuse and Neglect of the Elderly (CANE), 109
Clearinghouse on Disability Information (CDI), 110
Clearview Estates Assisted Living, 8657
Clearwater House Assisted Living Concept, 8492
Clearwater Suites Assisted Living, 9142
Cleburne County Aging Program, 470
Clemmons Village, 9455
Cleo Raised Toilet Seat, 3008
Cleo of New York, 3002, 3008, 3011, 3017, 3019, 3021, 3024, 3077, 3179, 3197, 3199, 3209, 3221, 3232, 3235, 3243, 3245, 3249, 3250, 3252, 3267
Cleoplast Therapeutic Putty-2 oz., 3250
Cleveland Clinic Foundation Research Institute, 6867
Cleveland Health Care Center, 9456
Cleveland Hearing and Speech Center, 6332
Cleveland Public Library, 11706
Cleveland Sight Center, 7566
Cleveland Skilled Industries, 7567
Cleveland West Chapter: Self-Help for Hard of Hearing People, 6333
Client Assistance Program: Office of Program Operations, 111
Clinical Care in the Rheumatic Disease, 5158
Clinical Diabetes, 6236
Clinical Focus, 4555
Clinical Gerontologist, 3836
Clinical Gerontologist: The Journal of Aging and Mental Health, 3837
Clinical Practice Recommendations, 6183
Clinical Presentation of the Primary Immunodeficiency Diseases, 4556
Clinical Program for Evaluating and Managing Stroke-at-Risk Patients, 7060
Clinical Research Center, 4594
Clinical Trials Participation, 7091
Clinical Update, 4557
Clinics in Geriatric Medicine, 3838
Clinton County Office for the Aging, 1761
Clinton-Sherman Industrial Airpark, 2035
Closing the Gap, 3159, 3839
Clover Ridge, 8658
Clovernook Center: Opportunities for the Blind, 7568
Clovernook Home And School For The Blind, 7898
Coalition for Barrier Free Living: Houston Center for Independent Living, 10928
Coalition for Economic Survival (CES), 112
Coalition for Independent Living Options, 741, 10704

Coalition of Wisconsin Aging Groups, 2572
Coastal Bend Area: Agency on Aging, 2318
Coastal Georgia Regional Development Center Area: Agency on Aging, 818
Coastline Elderly Services, 1274
Cocaine Anonymous, 7145, 7442
Cochlear Impants, 6620
Cochlear Implant Association, 6334
Cochlear Implant Club Association, 6615
Cochlear Implants: Comprehensive Overview, 6621
Coeur D'Alene Home, 8493
Cognition, Education and Deafness, 6480
Cohen Florence Levine Estates, 8956
Colby Community College, 1087
Cold Spring Harbor Laboratory, 11630
Cold Springs Commons, 8262
Coles County Council on Aging, 907, 915, 916, 906
Coles County Telecare, 907
Collaborative Medicine Center, 5676
College Avenue Adult CentersCollege Avenue Baptist Church Adult Ministries (CABC), 2717
College Park, 2716
College at Sixty, 2856
College of Du Page, 2779
College of Maharishi Vedic Medicine Center for Health and Aging Studies, 4293
College of Medicine, 4397, 5073, 6898
College of Notre Dame of Maryland, 2813
College of Nursing, 4638
College of Pharmacy, 7474
College of Physicians & Surgeons: Columbia University Cancer Center, 5897
College of Physicians and Surgeons, 5897
Collier County Association for the Blind, 7569
Collin Oaks Guest Home, 10433
Collins Mobile-Tech Corporation, 3378
Collinswood Manor, 9780
Collinwood, 8240
Colonial Manor Rest Home, 9457
Colonial Meals on Wheels, 2108
Colonial Oaks at First Colony, 10434
Color of Light, 4522
Colorado Aging and Adult Services, 629
Colorado Association of Homes & Services for the Aging, 630
Colorado Cancer Research Program, 5898
Colorado Client Assistance Program, 631
Colorado Department of Aging, 632
Colorado Department of Human Services: Division of Aging and Adult Services, 11018
Colorado Department of Revenue, 633
Colorado Department of Social Service, 11360
Colorado Department of Social Services: Division of Older American Programs, 634, 635
Colorado Developmental Disability Council, 636
Colorado Disability Determination Services, 637
Colorado Division of Mental Health, 638
Colorado Mountain College Senior Nutrition Program, 639
Colorado Protection & Advocacy for Persons with Disabilities, 640

Colorado Protection and Advocacy Agency:The Legal Center at Grand Junction, 11019
Colorado Public Employees Retirement Association, 641
Colorado School for the Deaf and Blind, 11361
Colorado Springs Independence Center, 10684
Colorado Talking Book Library, 11362
Colorado Travel & Tourism Authority, 11954
Colorado Workers Compensation Board, 642
Colorectal Center at St Elizabeth's Medical Center of Boston, 5899
Colton Assisted Living Center, 10248
Columbia Area Senior Center, 1477
Columbia County Council Area: Agency onAging, 2045
Columbia County Office for the Aging, 1762
Columbia Lighthouse for the Blind, 7570
Columbia River Area: Agency on Aging, 2507
Columbia University, 4294, 7200
Columbia University Alzheimer's Disease Research Center, 5052
Columbia University Comprehensive Cancer Center, 5900
Columbia University Irving Center for Clinical Research, 4294, 6868
Columbia University Oral History Research Office, 11631
Columbia University Press, 7277
Columbia University: Augustus C Long Health Sciences Library, 11632
Columbia University: Center for Geriatrics & Gerontology, 4295
Columbia University: Whitney M Young, Jr Memorial Library of Social Work, 11633
Columbia-Montour-Area: Agency on Aging, 2109
Columbus Volunteer Corps, 1953
Colville Indian Area: Agency on Aging, 2508
Comb-O-Cycle, 3419
Combined Health Information Database, 4137
Come Sign with Us, 6481
Comfortcare Homes of Nebraska, 9617
Commission for the Blind, 1299
Commission for the Deaf and Hard of Hearing, 1296
Commission on Law and Aging, 113
Commissioner Of Labor And WorkforceDeveloper, 1643
Committee for Purchase from People who are Blind or Severely Disabled, 6335
Committee of Ten Thousand, 4456
Commode Aluminum, 3009
Common Grounds, 10993
Common Mis-Information About Hearing Loss and Hearing Aid Use, 6622
Commons of Providence, 9882
Commons of Providence: Specialized Assisted Living, 9883
Commons on Marice, 9143
Commonwealth Cancer Help Program, 5677
Commonwealth of Massachusetts ExecutiveOffice of Elder Affairs, 11145
Commonwealth of Pennsylvania, 11241

Entry Name Index / C

Communicating for Seniors, 1395
Communicating with Deaf People: An Introduction, 6482
Communicating with Older Adults: A Guide for Health Care & Senior Service Professionals & Staff, 3615
Communicating with People Who Have Trouble Hearing & Seeing: A Primer, 7927
Communicating with People Who Have a Hearing Loss, 6623
Communication Access for Persons with Hearing Loss, 6483
Communication Access in Houses of Worship, 6624
Communication Access in Medical Facilities, 6625
Communication Disorders in Aging, 6484
Communication Issues Among Deaf People, 6485
Communication Issues Among Deaf People - Eyes, Hands, and Voices, 6486
Communication Issues Related to Hearing Loss, 6487
Communication Outlook: Artificial Language Laboratory, 3840
Communication Service for the Deaf, 6336
Communication Therapy for Hearing Impaired Adults, 6488
Communication Tips to Go (Movies, Restaurants, Planes, Car...), 6626
Communication Workers of America Retirees Club of Local 2011, 2548
Communication and Adult Hearing Loss, 6489
Communication-Based Learning Communities, 6490
Communications & Disabilities Action Board, 856
Communications Services for the Deaf and Hard of Hearing, 6337
Community Access Center, 10653
Community Action Commission of Cape Cod & Islands, 1275
Community Action Council: Lexington Fayette Jessamine Counties, 1101
Community Action Partnership of Mid-Nebraska Volunteer Services, 1567
Community Action Senior Corps, 2110
Community Assisted Living, 9144
Community Awards Program (CAP), 2625
Community Care of Haywood, 9458
Community Connection of Northeast Oregon, 2046
Community Health Charities of Illinois, 908
Community Legal Aid Society: Dover, 11034
Community Legal Aid Society: Georgetown, 11035
Community Legal Aid Society: Wilmington, 11036
Community Memorial Health Center, 9618
Community Mental Health Journal, 3841
Community Outreach Awards, 2626
Community Pride Care Center, 9619
Community Recreation and People with Disabilities for Inclusion, 3616
Community Resources for Independence, 10913
Community Resources for Independence (CRI) Napa, 10654

Community Resources for Independence - CRI/Santa Rosa, 10655
Community Resources for Independent Living, 10656
Community Restorium, 8494
Community Scholars Program, 2906
Community Service Building, 6127, 11036
Community Service Program of Van Nuys, 2718
Community Service Project, 7146
Community Supports for Aging Adults with Lifelong Disabilities, 3617
Community Teamwork, 1315
Community's Hearth & Home, 9884
Community's Hearth & Home at El Camino, 9885
Company of Environmental Science, 2037
Comparative Oncology, 4623
Compassion Book Service, 6018
Compassion Books, 4166, 6023, 6005
Compassion in Dying Federation, 6006
Compassionate Friends, 6007
Compax 12, 3508
Complete Directory for People with Disabilities, 3702
Complete Directory for People with Chronic Illness, 3701
Complete Directory of Large Print Books and Serials, 3703
Complete Guide to Alzheimer's Proofing Your Home, 4956
Complete Listing of Nursing Facilities and Home for the Aged Beds when Licensed as a Part of a Nursing Facility, 3704
Complete Mental Health Directory, 3705
Comprehensive AIDS Center, 4595
Comprehensive Advocacy: Boise, 11077
Comprehensive Advocacy: Moscow, 11078
Comprehensive Advocacy: Pocatello, 11079
Comprehensive Examination of Barriers to Employment Among Persons who are Blind or Impaired, 7806
Comprehensive Reference Manual for Signers and Interpreters 4th Edition, 6491
Comprehensive Signed English Dictionary, 6492
Comprehensive Stroke Center of Oregon, 7114
Compu-Lenz, 3099
Computer Paper for Brailling, 3100
Computer Switch Interface, 3101
Computer-Assisted Notetaking, 6627
Computer-Disability News, 3842
Concepts of Chemical Dependency, Third Edition, 7244
Concepts: Al-Anon's Best Kept Secret?, 7327
Concord Park Assisted Living, 8957
Concord Place, 9459
Concord Place Retirement & Assisted Living Community, 8586
Conde Nast Publications, 3955
Conf of Educational Admin Serving Deaf, 6556
Conference of Educational Administrators Serving the Deaf, 6338
Confronting Alzheimer's Disease, 4957
Congenital Heart Disease Anomalies Support Education and Resources, 6840
Connecticut Braille Association, 7571
Connecticut Association of Not-for-Profit Providers for the Aging, 674

Connecticut Bar Association: Section on Legal Problems of the Elderly, 11023
Connecticut Board of Education and Services for the Blind, 675
Connecticut Braille Association, 7572, 11370
Connecticut Client Assistance Program, 676
Connecticut Commission on Deaf and Hearing Impaired, 6339
Connecticut Commisson on Aging, 677
Connecticut Council On Developmental Disabilities, 678
Connecticut Department of Aging, 679
Connecticut Department of Health Services, 4457
Connecticut Department of Mental Health and Addiction Services, 7147
Connecticut Department of Revenue, 680
Connecticut Department of Social Services: Elderly Services Division, 11024
Connecticut Disability Determination Serices, 681
Connecticut Elder Law Program, 11027
Connecticut Lawyers' Legal Aid to the Elderly Program (CLLAEP), 11025
Connecticut Office of Tourism, 11955
Connecticut Protection & Advocacy for Persons with Disabilities, 682
Connecticut Protection and Advocacy Agency: Office of Protection and Advocacy for Persons with Disabilities, 11026
Connecticut Society to Prevent Blindness, 11371
Connecticut State Library for the Blind and Physically Handicapped, 11372
Connecticut State of Veterans Affairs Department of Rocky Hill: Hospital Services Program, 683
Connecticut Teachers Retirement Board, 684
Connecticut Tech Act Project, 10685
Connecticut Tech Art Project, 10687
Connellsville Area Senior Tigers, 2111
Conquering Hypertension: An Illustrated Guide to Understanding Treatment, 6911
Conscious Choice, 3843
Conscious Communications, 3843
Consultation and Education Unlimited, 4188
Consumer Care Products, 3204, 3485, 3491
Consumer Health Information Source Book, 3706
Consumer Health USA: Volume 2, 3618
Consumer Information Catalog, 4022
Consumer's Directory of Continuing Care Retirement Communities, 3707
Consumer's Guide for Purchasing a Hearing Aid, 6628
Contemporary Gerontology, 3844
Contemporary Long-Term Care: Sourcebook, 3708
Continental Airlines, 11918
Continental Airlines - Senior Programs, 11919
Continuing Care Accreditation Commission, 114
Continuing Care Retirement Community Directory, 3709
Continuing Education Center at RB, 2719
Contra Costa County Office on Aging, 525
Contrasting Characteristics of Blind and Visually Impaired Clients, 7807

Entry Name Index / D

Control Diabetes the Easy Way, 6184
Convaid Products, 3049, 3420, 3508, 3509
Convention of American Instructors of the Deaf, 6570, 6340
Conversational Sign Language II, 6493
Convert-Able Table, 3545
Cook's Illustrated, 3845
Cooperating with the Professional, 7328
Coping and Caring: Living with Alzheimer's Disease, 4958
Coping with Parkinson's Disease, 6980
Coping with Vision Loss: Maximizing What You See & Do, 7808
Coping with the Multi-Handicapped Hearing Impaired: A Practical Approach, 6494
Coping: Living with Cancer, 5806
Copper Ridge, 8909
Copperfield Hill Phase II, 9145
Coral Landing Assisted Living Residences, 8367
Coral Plaza Retirement Residence, 8368
Cordia Senior Living, 8172
Cordia Senior Residence, 8587
Cordless Big Red Switch, 3102
Cordless Receiver, 3298, 3326
Core Family Care Center, 9460
Coriell Institute for Medical Research, 4296
Cornell College, 2787
Cornell Communications, 3103
Cornell Estates Living Center, 10077
Cornell University, 5079
Cornell University Medical College: Departments of Neurology and Neuroscience, 7115
Cornell University School of Industrial and Labor Relations, 11634
Cornerstone, 7148
Cornerstone Assisted Living, 8659, 8788
Cornerstone Ridge Plaza, 8789
Cornerstone Village, 8861
Cornerstone Village South, 8862
Cornerstone of Eagle Hill, 7149
Cornor Cottage, 9620
Corporate Angel Network, 5678
Corporate Volunteers of New York, 1763
Corrigan Senior Center, 1568
Corticosteriod Medications, 5193
Cortland County Area: Agency on Aging, 1764
Cortland Place, 10208
Costa Mesa Senior Center, 526
Cottage Grove Place, 8660
Cottages at Fairmont Grand, 10249
Cottingham Retirement Community, 9886
Cottonwood House, 9621
Cottonwood Villa, 9622
Cotttages of Emmett, 8495
Coulston Foundation: Primate Research Center, 4596
Council for Disability Rights, 4023, 11085
Council for Exceptional Children, 3944
Council for Health & Human Services Ministries, 115
Council for Health and Human Service Ministries, 3710
Council for Health and Human Service Ministries: Directory of Services, 3710
Council for Older Adults, 1954
Council of Better Business Bureau, 116, 4189
Council of the Virginia Museum of the Fine Arts, 4122

Council on Aging of Silicon Valley, 527
Council on Aging of Sonoma County, 11000
Council on Education of the Deaf, 6341, 6781
Council on Geriatric Cardiology, 6841
Country Care Homes, 8496, 9146
Country Care at Cottonwood, 8497
Country Club Heights, 8958
Country Club Prime Time Retirement Home, 9461
Country Club Retirement Center, 9887
Country House, 8661
Country House in Westchester, 9835
Country Inn, 8498
Country Meadow Rest Home, 9462
Country Meadows, 8499
Country Neighbors, 9147
Country Neighbors-Lake Crystal, 9148
Country Neighbors-Le Center, 9149
Country Oaks Elder Care, 9150
Country Oaks Manor, 9463
The Country Place, 9305
Country Residence, 8369
Country Sunshine Rest Home, 9464
Country Villa, 9151
Country Villa Terrace Assisted Living, 8173
Country Villa West Assisted Living Center, 8174
Country Village Senior Services, 8175
Country Wood Manor Living Center, 10006
Countryside Care Center, 9045
Countryside Home, 9623
Countryside Living, 9465
Countrytime Inn, 9466
Court at Plam Aire, 8370
Courtyard, 8662
Courtyard Senior Living, 10078
Courtyard Villa Assisted Living Center, 10250
Courtyards at Pine Creek, 8176
Courtyards at River Park, 10435
Covenant Place of Waxahachie, 10436
Covenant Village of the Great Lakes, 9046
Cowles Enthusiast Media, 3967
Cowley County Community College, 2789
Crack Cocaine - The Big Lie, 7329
Crain Communications, 3782
Crane Plumbing/Fiat Products, 3010
Crater District: Area Agency on Aging, 2452
Creative Ink, 3796
Creekside Care Center, 8500
Creekside Manor, 9467
Creighton University, 5912
Creighton University Cardiac Center, 6869
Creighton University Center for Health Policy and Ethics, 4297
Creighton University Center for Healthy Aging, 4298
Creighton University: Midwest Hypertension Research Center, 6920
Crescent Point at Niantic, 8263
Crescent View Retirement Community, 9468
Critical Path AIDS Project/AIDS Library, 4543
Croasdaile Village, 9469
Cross Key Manor, 8371
Cross Road Retirement Community, 9470
Cross Wheelchair, 3510
Crossing the Line Between Social Drinking and Alcoholism, 7330

Crossroad Publishing Company, 7235, 7236
Crossroads Assisted Living, 9624
Crossroads Mall, 2894
Crow Wing Social Services, 1430
Crowell Memorial Home, 9625
Crown Colony at Mooresville, 9471
Crown Cove, 8177
Crown Point Senior Living-Anderson, 10745
Crown Pointe, 8663
Crown Pointe of Sebring, 8372
Crown Villa, 9626
Cruiser Bus Buggy 4MB, 3420
Crutch Pockets, 3235
Crystal Place Assisted Living Center, 10007
Crystalwood Assisted Living Center, 10008
Cub, SuperCub and Special EditionScooters, 3366
Cued Speech, 6629
Cumberland County Coordinating Council for Older Adults: Elderly Law Unit, 11210
Cumberland County Office of Aging, 2112
Cumberland County Office on Aging &Disabled, 1644
Cumberland Manor, 9047
Cumberland Valley Area: Agency on Aging, 1102
Cumulative Subject Index to Current Literature on Aging, 3619
Currents, 4024
Curry College, 2820
Curtis Home, 8264
Curtis Instruments, 3546
Custer Care Center, 9627
Custom Durable, 3511
Custom Earmolds, 3276
Custom Lift Residential Elevators, 3367
Custom Training and Education: LifelongLearning Program, 2701
Cycling Past 50, 3620
Cypress Court Escondido, 8178
Cypress Court at Tucson, 8118
Cypress Village, 8373
Cytogen Corporation R&D Library, 11612

D

D'Youville Manor, 10193
D.V.H. Quarterly, 7928
DARE, 10929
DBC-1 DU-IT Bed Control, 3036
DC Committee to Promote Washington, 11957
DEAF Inc., 10791
DEAS Office Park South, 1622
DHR Division of Aging Services, 819
DIRECT Independent Living Center, 10634
DK Publishing, 6506
DNA People's Legal Services, 10983
DNA-People's Legal Services, 11195
DVS Guide, 4138
DVS Senior Shepherd's Center, 2790
DW Auto & Home Mobility Specialties, 2963
Dakota Center for Independent Living, 10841
Dakota Sun Assisted Living, 10251
Dallas Association of Directors of Volunteers, 2319
Dallas Lighthouse for the Blind, 7573

Entry Name Index / D

Dallas Retirement Assisted Living Facility, 10079
Dallas Young Lawyers Association: Committee on Legal Aid to the Elderly, 11265
Dalton Community Center, 1276
Dalton Council on Aging, 1276
Damaco, 3512
Damaco D90, 3512
Dana-Farber Cancer Institute Library, 11547
Dana-Farber Cancer Institute: National Drug Discovery Group for AIDS Treatment, 4597
Dana-Farber Institute: Division of Biostistics & Epidemiology, 5901
Dancing Without Music, 6495
Darci Too, 3104
Darlington Assisted Living Centers, 10209
Dartmouth College Biomedical Libraries: Dana Biomedical Library, 11608
Dartmouth College Center for Evaluative Clinical Sciences, 4299
Dartmouth-Hitchcock Medical Center, 5768
Data Resources in Gerontology: A Directory of Selected Information Vendors, Databases, and Archives, 3711
Data on Blindness and Visual Impairment in the US: A Resource Manual, 7809
Davenport House, 10080
Davenport Lutheran Assisted Living, 8664
David T Siegel Institute for Communicative Disorders, 6799
Davie Place Residential Care, 9472
Davis Center for Hearing, Speech and Learning: Hearing Therapy, 6342
Davis Home, 10009
Davis Manor, 8959
DawnSignPress, 6518
Day at a Time Daily Reflections for Recovering People, 7245
Day by Day, 7246
Dayle McIntosh Center for the Disabled, 10657
Dayle McIntosh Center-Clubhouse, 10658
Dayle McIntosh-South County, 10659
Dazor Manufacturing Corporation, 3097, 3167, 3299
De Soto Council on Aging Area: Agency on Aging, 1148
Deaconess Hospital Horrax Library, 11548
Deaf Action Center of Central Louisiana, 6343
Deaf Adults Education Access Program, 6344
Deaf American, 6630
Deaf Artists of America, 6559, 6345, 6631
Deaf Artists of America: Artists Directory, 6559
Deaf Community Services (DCS), 420
Deaf Culture Autobiographies, 6746
Deaf Culture Series, 6747
Deaf Culture Videotapes, 6632
Deaf Culture: Suggested Readings, 6633
Deaf Episcopalian, 6634
Deaf Independent Living Association, 10783
Deaf Life, 6575
Deaf Mosaic Series, 6748
Deaf REACH, 6346
Deaf Sports Review, 6576
Deaf Studies Department, California State Univ., 6341
Deaf USA, 6577

Deaf and Hard of Hearing Entrepreneurs Council, 2627, 6347
Deaf and Hard of Hearing Services Center, 6348
Deaf in America: Voices from a Culture, 6496
Deaf-Blind American, 6578
Deaf/Hard of Hearing Entrepreneur of the Year, 2627
Deafness 1993-2013, 6497
Deafness Research Foundation, 6782, 6800
Deafness and Communicative Disorders, 117
Deafness and Communicative Disorders Branch, 6349
Deafness: A Fact Sheet, 6635
Deafpride, 6636, 6350
Deafpride Advocate, 6636
Dealing with Anger and Echoes of a Common Fate, 6637
Dean A McGee Eye Institute, 8038
Dean Foundation, 6039
Death and Dying Health Pamphlets, 6034
Death: The Final Stage of Growth, 6019
Debbie's Sunshine Home, 10437
Decatur House, 8960
Decatur Senior Center, 1569
Decker Publications, 3815
Decorator Grab Bars, 3011
Deer Meadow Assisted Living Community, 10081
Deer Meadows, 10194
Deerfield Village, 10082
Del Mar College, 2930
Delaware Assistive Technology Initiative, 702
Delaware Assistive Technology Initiative (DATI), 10692
Delaware Association for the Blind, 7574
Delaware Association for the Blind, 7575
Delaware Association of Nonprofit Homes for the Aging, 703
Delaware Bar Association Committee on Law and the Elderly, 11037
Delaware Chapter of the Arthritis Foundation, 5099
Delaware Client Assistance Program, 704
Delaware Commission of Veterans Affairs, 705
Delaware Council for Persons with Disabiities, 706
Delaware County Legal Assistance Program: Senior Citizens Office, 11238
Delaware County Office for the Aging, 1765
Delaware Court, 9888
Delaware Department of Education, 707
Delaware Department of Health and Social Services: Division of Public Health, 4458
Delaware Department of Health and Social Services: Division for the Visually Impaired, 708
Delaware Developmental Disability Council, 709
Delaware Disability Determination Services, 710
Delaware Division for the Visually Impaired, 7576
Delaware Division of Alcoholism, Drug Abuse & Mental Health, 7150
Delaware Division of Libraries for the Blind and Physically Handicapped, 11379
Delaware Division of Revenue, 711

Delaware Division of Services for Aging Adults with Physical Disabilities, 712
Delaware Division of Services for Aging and Adults with Physical Disabilities, 11038
Delaware Drug Abuse & Mental Health, 7151
Delaware Protection & Advocacy for Persons with Disabilities, 713
Delaware Tourism Office, 11956
Delaware Workers Compensation Board, 714
Dell Publishing, 4968
Dell Rapids Sportsmen's Club, 12013
Delmar Learning, 7066
Delta Center for Independent Living, 10816
Delta Shuttle, 11920
Delta Society National Service, 7577
DeltaTalker, 3105
Deluxe Bath Bench with Adjustable Legs, 3012
Deluxe Convertible Exercise Staircase, 3368
Deluxe Long Ring Low Vision Timer Tactile, 3327
Deluxe Roller Knife, 3328
Deluxe Signature Guide, 3460
Deluxe Sock and Stocking Aid, 3236
Deluxe Standard Wood Cane, 3479
Deluxe Wheelchair Pushing Cuffs, 3547
Demonstration Grants to States with Respect to Alzheimer's Disease, Health Resources & Services, 118
Demos Medical Publishing, 6985, 7058
Demos Vermande, 6981, 7791, 7813
Denial, 7331
Dental Care for the Patient with Parkinson's Disease, 6994
Dental Tips for Diabetics, 6237
Dentists Concerned for Dentists, 4190, 7152
Denver Regional Council of Governments Area Agency on Aging, 643
Department Of Human Rights, 2nd Floor, 1024
Department for Disability Determination Services, 1103
Department for the Blind & Physically Handicapped, 7929
Department of Aging & Youth, 1766
Department of Anthropology, 4399
Department of Applied Gerontology, 4419
Department of Assistive and Rehabilitative Svcs, 2309
Department of Behavioral Neuroscience, 7452
Department of Biochemistry, 4616
Department of Blind Rehabilitation, 7578
Department of Clinical Investigation, 4599
Department of Commerce & Community Affairs, 11989
Department of Comparative Medicine, 6930
Department of Disabilities and Special Needs, 1235
Department of Drug and Alcohol Programs, 7160
Department of Elderly Affairs, 11992
Department of Employment and Economic Development, 1396
Department of English, Gallaudet University, 6590
Department of Geriatrics & Adult Development, 4342
Department of Health, 7164, 7213

Entry Name Index / D

Department of Health & Rehabilitative Services, 742
Department of Health & Social Services, 7140
Department of Health Division of Addiction Service, 7198
Department of Health Services, 7136
Department of Health and Hospitals, 7177
Department of Health and Human Services, 1638, 7128
Department of Health and Social Services, 7139
Department of Human Resources, 7203
Department of Human Services, 7183
Department of Industrial Relations, 372
Department of Internal Medicine, 6283
Department of Labor, 415
Department of Medicine, 6270
Department of Medicine, Med Sci I C264, 6281
Department of Mental Health, 1491, 7171, 7184
Department of Mental Health and Mental Retardation, 7176, 7225
Department of Mental Health, Retardation and Hospitals of Rhode Island, 2202
Department of Molecular Biology and Biochemistry, 5965
Department of Neurology, 5072, 5076, 7124
Department of Ophthalmalogy, 8057
Department of Pathology, 4619, 5052, 5934
Department of Pediatrics, 4600, 4622
Department of Pharmacology, 7458
Department of Psychiatry, 5077
Department of Public Health, 7180
Department of Public Health and Human Services, 7185
Department of Public Institutions, 7196
Department of Rehabilitative Services, 2453
Department of Social & Criminal Justice, 7480
Department of Social Work, 4431
Department of Social and Rehabilitation Services, 7175
Department of Surgery, 6892
Department of Veteran Services, 1298
Department of Veterans Affairs, 119
Departments of Neurology & Neurosurgery: University of California, 7116
Depression & Antidepressents: A Guide, 6067
Depression Sourcebook, 6068
Depression and Dementia in Parkinson's Disease, 6995, 6996
Depression and Its Treatment, 6069
Depression and Recovery From Chemical Dependency, 6087, 7332
Depression for Dummies, 6070
Depression in Older Adults, 4139
Depression in the Elderly: a Multimedia Sourcebook, 6079
Depression, the Mood Disease, 6071
Depressive Illnesses: Treatments Bring New Hope, 6072
Dept of Employment, Training and Rehabilitation, 1598
Dept of Veterans Affairs\Reports & Info Services, 3715
Derek Home, 10438
Dermatology Nurses' Association, 120
Desano Place Residential Care, 8501
Descriptive Video Service, 4138

Desert Point-La Reserve, 8119
Designing for Alzheimer's Disease: Strategies for Creating Better Care Environment, 4959
Detaching with Love, 7333
Detachment, 7334
Detroit Area: Agency on Aging, 1347
Deuel County Good Samaritan Center Assisted Living Center, 10252
Developing Adult Day Care: An Approach to Maintaining Independence, 3621
Developing an Identity for People with Hearing Loss, 6638
Developmental Evaluation Center, 4598
Developments in Technology, 6639
Devils Lake Good Samaritan, 9560
Devolution and Aging Policy, 3622
Devonshire Acres, 121
Devonshire of Hoffman Estates, 8588
Diabetes, 6228
Diabetes & Exercise Video, 6258
Diabetes 101, 6185
Diabetes A to Z, 6186
Diabetes Advisor, 6238
Diabetes Annual Vol. 8, 6187
Diabetes Burnout: What To Do When You Can't Take It Anymore, 6188
Diabetes Care, 6229
Diabetes Care Made Easy, 6189
Diabetes Dateline, 6239
Diabetes Dictionary, 6227
Diabetes Education Goals, 6190
Diabetes Education and Research Center, 6268
Diabetes Educator, 6240
Diabetes Forecast, 6230
Diabetes Medical Nutrition Therapy, 6191
Diabetes Mellitus: A Practical Handbook, 6192
Diabetes Research Center, 6269
Diabetes Research and Training Center: University of Alabama at Birmingham, 6270
Diabetes Reviews, 6231
Diabetes Self-Management, 6193, 6241
Diabetes Sourcebook - Vol. 3, 6194
Diabetes Spectrum: From Research to Practice, 6232
Diabetes Teaching Guide for People Who Use Insulin, 6195
Diabetes Update - Glucose Toxicity: The Need for 24-Hour Control, 6259
Diabetes and Brief Illness, 6242
Diabetes and Exercise, 6243
Diabetes and You, 6260
Diabetes for Dummies, 6196
Diabetes in Old Age, 6197
Diabetes in the News, 6233
Diabetes, Vision Impairment and Blindness, 6244, 7930
Diabetes: A Guide to Living Well, 6198
Diabetes: A Positive Approach, 6234
Diabetes: What You Need to Know, 6261
Diabetes: Your Complete Exercise Guide, 6199
Diabetic Cruise Desk, 12014
Diabetic Foot, 6262
Diabetic Foot Care, 6245
Diabetic Low-Fat & No-Fat Meals in Minutes, 6200
Diabetic Retinopathy, 7931
Diabetic Traveler, 6246

Diabetic's Guide to Health and Fitness, 6201
Diabetic's Innovative Cookbook, 6202
Diablo Valley Foundation for the Aging, 528
Diagnosis and Treatment of Unilateral Hearing Loss, 6749
Dial-A-Ride Rural Public Transportation, 909
Dialogue, 7865
Dialysis, 3863
Did You Grow Up with a Problem Drinker?, 7335
Diet & Fitness, 3846
Diet & Heart Disease: It's Not What YouThink, 6851
Diet and Arthritis, 5194
Diet, Nutrition and Cancer Prevention: A Guide to Food Choices, 5819
Diet, Nutrition and Cancer Prevention: The Good News, 5820
Dietary Considerations for Parkinson's Disease Patients, 6997
Differential Diagnosis of Parkinsonism, 6998
Digi-Flex, 3251
Digital Battery Operated Blood Pressure, 3252
Digital Hearing Aids: An Update, 6640
Digital and Audible Family Thermometer, 3253
Dignified Home Life Care, 8085
Dignified Living, 9152
Dignified Living-Prior Lake, 9153
Diplomatic and Consular Officers, Retired, 122
Directory of Accessible Van Rentals, 11921
Directory of Aging Resources, 3712
Directory of American Baptist Retirement Homes, Nursing Homes, Children's Homes & Special Services, 3713
Directory of Auditory-Oral Programs, 6560
Directory of Community Care Facilities, 3714
Directory of Department of Veterans Affairs Facilities, 3715
Directory of Health Education Programs for Elders, 3716
Directory of Health, Medical, and Disability Sites on the World Wide Web and Internet, 3717
Directory of Interpreters for Persons who are Deaf, Hard of Hearing or Deaf-Blind, 6561, 7845
Directory of Jewish Homes and Housing for the Aged in the United States and Canada, 3718
Directory of Long Term Care Facilities, 3719
Directory of National Organizations of and for Deaf and Hard of Hearing People, 6562
Directory of Plan Sponsors, 3720
Directory of Radio Reading Services, 7846
Directory of Resources for the Blind & Visually Impaired, 7847
Directory of Retirement Facilities, 3721
Directory of Self-Help/Mutual Aid Support Groups for Older People, 3722
Directory of Service for Persons with Disabilities, 3723

Directory of Services for Blind and Visually Impaired Persons in the United States and Canada, 7932
Directory of Services for the Widowed in the United States and Canada, 3724
Directory of State Services for People with Disabilities, 3725
Directory of Suicide Prevention/Crisis Intervention Agencies in the United States, 3726
Directory of Survivors of Suicide Support Groups, 3727
Directory of Texas Long Term Care Facilities, 3728
Directory of Travel Agencies for the Disabled, 3729
Dirico (Formerly RD Butler & Company), 2992
Disabilities Law Project-Pennsylvania, 11239
Disabilities Law Project: Washington, 11286
Disability Action Center Northwest, 10718
Disability Advocates of Kent County, 10801
Disability Coalition of Northern Kentucky, 10775
Disability Compliance Bulletin, 4025
Disability Determination Branch, 857
Disability Determination Bureau, 2573
Disability Determination Division, 720, 2006, 2225
Disability Determination Section, 2549
Disability Determination Services, 418, 878, 1149, 1202, 1397, 1478, 1534, 1710, 1767, 1888, 1925, 2047, 2203, 2428, 2453, 2612
Disability Determination Services: LosAngeles West Branch, 529
Disability Determination Services: Cape Girardeau, 1479
Disability Determination Services: Central Support Services Branch, 530
Disability Determination Services: Kansas City, 1480
Disability Determination Services: La Jolla Branch, 531
Disability Determination Services: Los Angeles South Branch, 532
Disability Determination Services: Oakland Branch, 533
Disability Determination Services: Roanoke, 2454
Disability Determination Services: Roseville Branch, 534
Disability Determination Services: Sacramento Branch, 535
Disability Determination Services: Saint Louis, 1481
Disability Determination Services: San Diego Branch, 536
Disability Determination Services: Shreveport Branch, 1150
Disability Determination Services: Springfield, 1482
Disability Determination Unit, 1615
Disability Determinations, 1570, 2275
Disability Determinations Services, 2393
Disability Evaluations Division: SierraBranch, 537
Disability Law & Advocacy Center of Tennessee (DLAC), 11257
Disability Law Center (DLC), 11146
Disability Law Center Of Alaska, 10976

Disability Law Project, 2443
Disability Network-Lakeshore Center for Independent Living, 10802
Disability Notes, 4026
Disability Rag's Ragged Edge Magazine, 3847
Disability Resource Association, 10817
Disability Resource Center of Fairfield County (DRCFC), 10687
Disability Resource Center of Southwest Michigan, 10803
Disability Resource Connection, 10948
Disability Rights And Resources, 10839
Disability Rights Center Of Kansas, 1060
Disability Rights Education and Defense Fund, 3848, 4027, 11001
Disability Rights Now, 3848, 4027
Disability Statistics Report, 3849
Disability Studies Quarterly, 3850
Disability Workbook for Social Security Applicants, 7092
Disabled American Veterans, 1104
Disabled American Veterans Magazines, 3851
Disabled American Veterans National Headquarters, 3851
Disabled Americans Rally for Equality, 11086
Disabled Citizens Alliance for Independence-DCAI, 10818
Disabled Driver's Mobility Guide, 11922
Disabled People as Second Class Citizens, 3852
Disabled Sports, USA, 3835
Discovering Sign Language, 6498
Discovery Care Centre of Salmon, 8502
Discovery Circles, 7061
Discovery Program at Burlington Manor, 9473
Diseases of the Colon and Rectum, 5807
Diseases of the Macula, 7933
Distinguished Mentorship in Gerontology Award, 2628
Distinguished Service in Aging Award, 2629
District Five Area: Agency on Aging, 1955
District Seven Area: Agency on Aging, 1956
District Three Governmental Cooperative, 2455
District of Columbia, 11957
District of Columbia Association of Nonprofit Services for the Aging, 721
District of Columbia Bar: Individual Rights Section, 11041
District of Columbia Center for Independent Living (DCCIL), 10689
District of Columbia Office on Aging, 722, 11042
District of Columbia Public Library, 11386
District of Columbia Public Library: Blind and Physically Handicapped, 11387
District of Columbia Public Library: Librarian for the Deaf Community, 11388
District of Columbia Public Service Commission, 4459
District of Columbia Rehabilitation Services, 723
District of Columbia Retirement Board, 724
District of Columbia Worker Compensation Board, 725
Divine Country Manor, 9474
Division Of Disability Determinations, 800
Division for Aging Services, 1600

Division for the Visually Handicapped, 11817
A Division of AARP (NRTA), 257
Division of Aging, 563
Division of Aging & Disability Services, 1571
Division of Aging and Adult Services - Elder Choices, 10639
Division of Aging and Disability Services: Legal Services for Older Adults, 11177
Division of Alcohol, 7151
Division of Biology, 5925
Division of Biostatistics, 5977
Division of Continuing Education, 2747
Division of Developmental Disabilities, 2257
Division of Disability Determination Services, 1645, 2509
Division of Disability Determinations, 1768
Division of Disability Determinations New Brunswick, 1646
Division of Disability Determinations-Endicott, 1769
Division of Disability Determinations: Newark, 1647
Division of Disease Control, 4446
Division of Graham Fields, 3303
Division of Infectious Diseases, 4466
Division of Mental Health, 7169
Division of Mental Health & Developmental Services, 1601
Division of Oncology, 5978
Division of Public Health, 4447
Division of Public Health Services, 4485
Division of Rehabilitation Service, 374
Division of Rehabilitation Services, 822, 1905
Division of Young Enterprises, 3390
Dixie USA, 3398
Do It Now Foundation, 7153
Do You Hear Me?, 6499
Do You Hear That?, 6750
Do You Think You're Different?, 7336
Do Your Level Best: Start Controlling Your Blood Sugar Today, 6247
Do the Right Thing: Get a Mammogram, 5821
Does She Drink Too Much?, 7337
Dog Sponsorship Program, 7934
Dogs for the Deaf, 6616, 6351
Dogwood Creek Retirement Center, 10010
Dogwood Forest Adult Care Home, 9475
Dollar Rent-a-Car, 11923
Dolomite Walkers, 3480
Domestic Mistreatment of the Elderly: Towards Prevention, 3853
Dominican Hospital Educaction Center, 5567
Don Johnston, 3106
Don't Let Your Dreams Go Up in Smoke, 4028
Don't Lose Sight of Age-Related Macular Degeneration, 7935
Don't Lose Sight of Cataracts, 7936
Don't Lose Sight of Glaucoma, 7937
Don't Lose a Friend to Drugs, 7338
Donald P. Kent Award, 2630
Donnelly Place-A Classic Residence by Hyatt, 8374
Donovan Scholars Program, 2800
Door Flashing Announcement System, 3107
Doorbell Signalers, 3108
Dora Barns Residential Home, 8665

Entry Name Index / E

Dorian Place, 10083
Dorma Architectural Hardware, 3300
Dorothea Dix Hospital: Clinical Research Unit, 7455
Dosberg Manor Adult Home, 9836
Double Gong Indoor/Outdoor Ringer, 3109
Douglas County Activity Association, 2574
Douglas County Health & Disabilities Services, 2048
Douglas County Senior Services Division, 2049
Douglas House, 10084
Downtown Care, 8086
Downtown Detroit Subregional Library for the Blind, 11560
Dr. Bernstein's Diabetes Solution, 6203
Draper Place at Hopedale, 8961
Dressing Stick, 3237
Drew Karol Industries, 3254
Drive Master Company, 2968, 2975, 2981, 2982, 2996, 2997
Drive-Master, 2964
Driving Systems, 3013
Driving and the Parkinson's Disease Patient: Some Considerations, 6999
Drug & Alcohol Treatment Association of Rhode Island: In-Rhodes Resource Center Library, 11752
Drug Abuse Health Pamphlets, 7339
Drug Abuse Resistance Education of America, 7154
Drug Abuse Update, 7286
Drug Abuse and Addiction Information/Treatment Programs, 7281
Drug Fact Sheets, 4995
Drug Free Zones: A Manual, 7340
Drug-Free Workplace Hotline, 7155
Drugs Anonymous, 7156
Du Page Library, 11455
Dual Brake Control, 2965
Dual Brakes Unit, 2966
Dual Brush with Suction Base, 3329
Dual Disorders Recovery Book, 7247
Dual Switch Latch and Timer, 3301
Duke University, 2881, 4300
Duke University Center for Demographic Studies Library, 11681
Duke University Center for the Study of Aging and Human Development, 4300
Duke University Comprehensive Cancer Center, 5679
Duke University General Clinical Research Center, 4301, 5053
Duke University Medical Center, 7117
Duke University Medical Clinic, 4301
Duke University: RERC on Communication Enhancement, 6801
Duluth Lighthouse for the Blind, 7579
Duluth Public Library, 11579
Dupage Center for Independent Living, 10726
Duplex Planet, 3854
Duracell & Rayovac Hearing Aid Batteries, 3277
Durham Manor Rest Home, 9476
Durham Tecnical Community College, 2880
Durham Village, 9477
Duro-Med Industries, 3255
Durward K. McDaniel Ambassador Award, 2631
Duval Oaks, 10439
Duxbury Braille Translator, 3110

Duxbury Systems, 3110, 3137, 3111
Dwight David Eisenhower Army Medical Center, 4599
Dynamic Systems, 3229, 3200

E

EAR Foundation, 6352, 6783
EGW Publishing Company, 3969
EHOVE Ghirst Adult Career Center, 2886
EKA/ Health & Mobility Systems, 2967
EMIS Medical Publishers, 6913
ENHANCER Cushion, 3201
ESU Memorial Union, 11498
ETAC USA, 3317, 3483, 3497, 3499, 3510, 3515, 3539, 3541
EZ-Access Portable Ramps, 3369
EZBACK Recline Control, 3548
Each Day a New Beginning, 7248
Eagle Meadows Assisted Living Community, 10590
Eagle Ridge Assisted Living, 8666
Eagle Sportschairs, 3513
Ear Book, 6500
Ear and Hearing, 6641
Early Stage Alzheimer's Care: A Guide for Community Based Programs, 4977
Early/Mild Hearing Loss, 6642
East Alabama Commission: Agency on Aging, 373
East Arkansas Area: Agency on Aging, 471
East Baton Rouge Council on Aging, 1151
East Bay Manor, 10210
East Central Area: Agency on Aging, 1445
East Central Colorado: Area Agency on Aging, 644
East Central Florida Area: Agency on Aging, 743
East Central Illinois Area: Agency on Aging, 910
East Central Kansas Area: Agency on Aging, 1061
East Central Region: Helen Keller National Center, 7580
East Central Regional Development Commission Area on Aging, 1398
East Coast Assistance Dogs, 685
East Hill Woods, 8265
East Holy Avenue, 8
East Los Angeles Service Center, 538
East Orange County Center for Independent Living, 10869
East Park Retirement Community, 9889
East Park Villa, 9628
East Penn Manufacturing Company, 3549
East Ridge Retirement Village, 8375
East Tennessee Area Agencies on Aging, 2276
East Texas Area: Agency on Aging, 2320
East Texas State University at Texarkana, 2317
Easter Seals Project ACTION, 12015
Eastern Area Agency on Aging, 1203
Eastern Carolina Council Area Agency onAging, 1889
Eastern Colorado Services for the Disabled, 645
Eastern Connecticut Area: Agency on Aging, 686
Eastern Cooperative Oncology Group, 5902

Eastern Idaho Special Services Agency Area: Agency on Aging, 879
Eastern Missouri Chapter of the Arthritis Foundation, 5100
Eastern Nebraska Office on Aging, 1572
Eastern New Mexico Area: Agency on Aging, 1711
Eastern Oklahoma Development District Area: Agency on Aging (EODD), 2007
Eastern Oregon Center for Independent Living, 10905
Eastern Shore Area: Agency on Aging, Community Action Agency, 2456
Eastman Estates, 10440
Eastmont Towers, 9629
Easy Care Quad Canes, 3481
Easy Food Tips for Heart Healthy Eating, 6858
Easy Living AFC, 8087
Easy Pivot Transfer Machine, 3370
Easy Pour Locking Lid Pot, 3330
Easy Stand, 3371
Eating Hints: Recipes and Tips for Better Nutrition During Cancer Treatment, 5822
Eating Well, 3855
Eating Well Magazine, 3855
Eaton-Peabody Laboratory of Auditory Physiology, 6353
Eckerd College, 2752
EcoTraction Surface, 3372
Econo-Float Water Flotation Cushion, 3202
Econo-Float Water Flotation Mattress, 3203
Econol Stairway Lift Corporation, 3412
Economic and Social Research Institute, 4302
Economical Liberty, 3373
Ed Lindsey Industries of the Blind, 7581
Eden Estates, 9478
Eden Gardens, 10441
Eden Gardens of Statesville, 9479
Eden Home, 10442
Eden Pines, 8910
Eden Terrace of Arlington, 10443
Edenbrook of Champions, 10444
Edenbrook of the Woodlands, 10445
Edengardens of Concord, 9480
Edengardens of Kings Mountain, 9481
Edengardens of Mooresville, 9482
Edenterrace of Kingwood, 10446
Edenwald Retirement Community, 8911
Edgehill Health Center, 8266
Edgelea, 10211
Edgewood Vista, 9154, 9342
Edgewood Vista - Minot, 9561
Edgewood Vista Columbus, 9630
Edgewood Vista Grand Island, 9631
Edgewood Vista Norfolk, 9632
Edgewood Vista of Bismark, 9562
Edgewood Vista of Fremont, 9633
Edgewood Vista of Hastings, 9634
Edgewood Vista of Omaha, 9635
Edgewood Vista of Sioux Falls, 10253
Edgewood Vista-Virginia, 9155
Edmore Memorial Rest Home, 9563
Edmund S. Muskie School of Public Service, 4303
Educare Press, 11871
Educating the Deaf: Psychology, Principles and Practices, 6501
Educational Gerontology, 3856
Educational Perspective, 6643

Entry Name Index / E

Educational Services for the Visually Impaired, 11331
Edward Feil Productions, 11872
Edward Henderson Memorial Student Award, 2632
Edward and Esther Polisher Research Institute, 4304
Edwinola Retirement Community, 8376
Efficacy of Antiparkinson Medications, 7000
Egyptian Area: Agency on Aging, 911
Ehlers-Danlos Syndrome, 5195
Eiler House, 8667
El Al Israel Airlines, 11924
El Dorado County Area: Agency on Aging, 539
El Dorado Manor Nursing Home, 9636
El Paso Lighthouse for the Blind, 7582
Elastic Shoelaces, 3238
Elder Abuse: 5 Case Studies, 4140
Elder Book Store, 11873
Elder Books, 4955, 11873, 11874
Elder Care, 3623
Elder Care Alliance, 540
The Elder Care Sourcebook, 3677
Elder Craftsmen, 2857
Elder Day Eldereed Haus, 10349
Elder Fit: A Health and Fitness Guide, 3624
Elder Haven Homes, 9156
Elder Law Center: Coalition of Wisconsin Aging Groups, 11295
Elder Law of Michigan: Legal Hotline for Michigan Seniors, 11155
Elder Service Plan of the North Shore, 1277
Elder Services of Berkshire County, 1278
Elder Services of Cape Cod and the Islands, 1279
Elder Wood Village of Dover, 8309
ElderCare Advocates, 4191
ElderConnect, 4192
ElderLink, 2254
ElderNet, 4141
Elderbridge Agency on Aging, 1017
Elderbridge-Area Agency on Aging: Legal Referral Panel, 11108
Eldercare Initiative in Consumer Law (EICL), 123
Eldercare Locator, 124, 4193
Elderhaus, 646
Elderhostel, 3730, 4016, 4194, 12016
Elderhostel Catalog, 3730
Elderhostel Institute Network, 12017
Elderlaw Project, 10977
Elderly Health Services Letter, 3857
Elderly People or Persons with Disabilities Housing, 125
Elderscholar, 2934
Elderwise, 2941
Electric Can Opener & Knife Sharpener, 3331
Electric Leg Bag Emptier and Tub Slide Shower Chair, 3014
Electric Mobility Corporation, 299
Electronic Keyless Entry System, 3302
Electronic Stethoscopes, 3256
Elevette 2100, 3374
Eli M. Oboler Library: Health Services, 11448
Elim Park Baptist Home, 8267
Elite Care, 8503
Elizabeth Pierce Olmsted Center for the Visually Impaired, 7583

Elkwood Assisted Living, 10011
Ellendale Evergreen Place, 9564
Elliott Residence, 10085
Elm Crest Retirement Community, 8668
Elm Grove Estates, 8790
Elm Heights Assisted Living, 8669
Elm York Home for Adults, 9837
Elms Retirement Home, 10212
Elms Retirement Village, 9890
Elms at Tanglewood, 9483
Elms of Cranbury, 9781
Elon Village Home, 9484
Elsevier Scientific Publishing Company, 6187
Embroidery Hoop, 3288
Emerald Bay Manor, 10213
Emerald Care, 9157
Emerald Court, 9637
Emerald Ridge of Solon, 9891
Emerald Springs Retirement & Assisted Living Community, 8120
Emerald Square Assisted Living Center, 10012
Emerald Valley, 10086
Emergency Care for the Elderly, 4142
Emergency Nurses Association, 126
Emeritus College, 2775, 2824
Emmanuel House Residence, 8962
Emory University, 2770
Emory University Laboratory for Ophthalmic Research, 8039
Emory University: Georgia Center for Cancer Statistics, 5903
Emory University: National Cooperative Drug Discovery for AIDS Treatment, 4600
Emory University: Winship Cancer Center, 5904
Emory University: Yerkes Regional Primate Research Center, 4601
Empire State Association of Assisted Living, 9838
Employee Attitudes About AIDS, 4558
Employee Benefit Research Institute, 11389, 11875
Employee Benefits Security Administration, 127
Employer's Guide to Dealing with Substance Abuse, 7341
Employers of Individuals Who are Deaf and Hard of Hearing & the ADA, 6644
Employers of Individuals with Hearing Impairments & the ADA, 6645
Employment Awards, 2633
Employment Discrimination: Age, 128
Employment Discrimination: Disabled, 129
Employment Discrimination: How to Recognize it and What to Do About it, 6646
Empress Directions Unlimited(AcccessibleTours), 12018
Enabling, 7342
Enabling Technologies Company, 3112
Encyclopedia of Deafness and Hearing Disorders, 6502, 6563
Encyclopedia of Depression, 6080
End-Stage Renal Disease: Choosing A Treatment That's Right for You, 6248
Endeavor, 6647
Endependence Center, 10940
Endependence Center of Northern Virginia, 10941

Endocrinology Research Laboratory, 6271
English Rose Suites, 9158
Enrichments, 3319, 3322, 3323, 3328, 3329, 3339, 3352, 3353
Environment Control System, 3113
Environmental Alliance for Senior Involvement, 2935
Environmental Traveling Companions, 12019
Episcopal Conference of the Deaf, 6634, 6354
Epworth Villa, 10013
Epworth Village Retirement Community, 8377
Equal Employment Advisory Council, 11043
Equal Employment Opportunity Commission, 128, 129, 130
Equal Employment Opportunity: Civil Rights Division, 131
Equal Opportunity Publications, 3882
Equinox Press, 5795
Equip for Equality Central/Southern Illinois, 912
Equip for Equality Northeastern Region, 913
Equip for Equality Northwestern Region, 914
Equip for Equality: Chicago, 11087
Equip for Equality: Rock Island, 11088
Equip for Equality: Springfield, 11089
Equipment and Suggestions for Persons with Parkinson's Disease, 7001
Erie County Department of Senior Services, 1770
Ernest Gallo Clinic and Research Center, 7456
Eskaton Cameron Park Lodge, 8179
Eskaton Gold River Lodge, 8180
Especially for the Alzheimer Caregiver, 4996
Essential Allergy, 4656
Essex County Bar: Elder Law Committee, 11188
Essex County Office for the Aging, 1771
Essex House, 10554
Essex Meadows, 8268
Estate Tax Division, 1965
Estelline Nursing and Care Center, 10254
Ethan Place, 10214
Ethel Percy Andrus Gerontology Center, 4305
Ethical Considerations: Issues in Diagnostic Disclosure, 4997
Eureka Community Health Services: Assisted Living Center, 10255
Eureka Ward Family History Center, 11338
Evac + Chair Corporation, 3044
Evac + Chair Emergency Wheelchair, 3044
Evacu-Trac, 3514
Evanston Hospital, 5921
Evansville Association for the Blind, 7584
Evansville-Vanderburgh County Public Library, 11481
Everest & Jennings, 3303
Evergreen Assisted Living, 10256
Evergreen Assisted Living Center, 10257
Evergreen Assisted Living Home, 10215
Evergreen Gardens of Garden City, 8791
Evergreen Idaho Health Care Sandpoint, 8504
Evergreen Knoll, 9159
Evergreen Society, 2807

Entry Name Index / F

Evergreen Woods, 8269
Evergreens of Moorhead, 9160
Evert Conner Rights & Resources Center for Independent Living, 10755
Everybody Counts-Ruben Center for Independent Living, 10746
Everyone's Guide To Cancer Therapy, 5798
Everyone's Guide to Cancer Therapy, 5799
Evio Plastics, 3332
Excel Stair Lift, 3375
Excellence in Practice Award, 2634
Exceptional Cancer Patients, 5680
Exercise Beats Arthritis, 5159
Exercise and Your Arthritis, 5196
Exercise and Your Heart, 6859
Exercise for Older Adults, 3625
Experience Area: Agency on Aging, 2113
Experience Works, 132
Experimental Aging Research, 3858
Explorer Van Company, 2993
Explorer+ 4-Wheel Scooter, 3421
Exploring Care Options for a Relative with Alzheimer's Disease, 4998
Extensions for Independence, 7585
External Degrees in the Information Age, 3731
Extra Loud Alarm with Lighter Plug, 3114
Eye Bank Association of America, 7586
Eye Festival Communications, 6577
Eye Opener, 7249
Eye Relief Word Processing Software, 3115
Eye and Your Vision, 7810
Eye-Q Test, 7938
Eyegaze Computer System, 3116
Eyes and Parkinson's Disease, 7002
Ez International Inc./Ortho Kinetics, 3376

F

F3 Wheelchair, 3515
FAN Flashbacks, 4666
FIT Video, 5232
FIVCO Area: Agency on Aging, 1105
FM Auditory Training Systems, 6503
Facilitating Self Care Practices in theElderly, 3626
Facing Forward: A Guide for Cancer Survivors, 5823
Factor Fax, 5197
Facts About Alcohol Abuse, 7343
Facts About Hearing Aids, 6648
Facts About Lung Cancer, 5824
Facts and Fancies About Hearing Aids, 6649
Facts on File, 4652, 5791, 6080, 6563
Facts: Books for Blind and Physically Handicapped Individuals, 7939
Facts: Music for Blind and Physically Handicapped Individuals, 7940
Facts: Playback Machines and Accessories Provided On Free Loan, 7941
Facts: Sources for Purchase of Cassette& Disc Players From NLS, 7942
Fair Acres Center, 11735
Fair Haven Retirement Community, 8062
Fairbanks Senior Center, 419
Fairfax Area: Agency on Aging, 2457
Fairfax County Public Library, 11818
Fairmont Grand Manor, 10258
Fairview Home, 10555
Fairview Living Centre, 9048
Fairway Golf Cars, 3287

Fairwinds-Coeur d'Alene, 8505
Fairwinds-Ivey Ranch, 8181
Fairwinds-Redmond, 10591
Fairwinds-River's Edge, 9332
Fairwinds-Sand Creek, 8506
Fairwinds-Spokane, 10592
Fairwinds-West Hills, 8182
Fairwinds-Woodward Park, 8183
Falling in Old Age, 3627
Falls Church Senior Center, 2458
Falls at Cordingly Dam, 8963
Families Anonymous, 7157
Families USA Foundation, 133
Families and Work Institute, 4306
Family, 5198
Family Carebook, 3628
Family Caregiver Resource Center, 915
Family Circle, 3860
Family Denial, 7344
Family Group Headquarters, 7126
Family Guide - Growth & Development of the Partially Seeing Child, 7943
Family Guide for Alzheimer's Care in Residential Settings, 4999
Family Health International, 11682
Family Meds, 4195
Family Service Center, 737, 1599
Family: Making the Difference, 5199
Fanlight Productions, 4131, 4133, 4136, 4139, 4140, 4143, 4144, 4146, 4151, 4152, 4154, 4155, 4157, 4160, 4164, 4165, 5025, 5026, 5027, 5029, 5030
Farleigh Dickinson University, 2847
Farrington Court, 10593
Farthest North Club of the Deaf, 420, 6355
Father Hudson House, 9782
Faulkner & Gray, 3762, 4040, 4060
Fay Wookey Memorial Assisted Living Center, 10259
Featherspring, 3550
Featherweight Reachers, 3239
Federal Bar Association, 11044
Federal Benefits for Veterans and Dependents, 3732
Federal Consumer Information Center, 4022
Federal Council on the Aging: Office of the Secretary, 134
Federal Laws of the Mentally Handicapped: Laws, Legislative Histories and Admin. Documents, 4029
Federal Trade Commission, 135, 4196
Federal Transit Administration, 93
Feel Nifty After 50: Top Tips to Help Women Grow Young, 3629
Feil Method, VALIDATION, 3630
Female Urinary Incontinence, 6951
Ferguson Industries for the Blind, 7587
Ferguson Publishing Company, 3789
Fidelco Guide Dog Foundation, 4197, 7588
Fieldcrest Assisted Living, 8670
Fifty Five Years & Up, 744
Fifty Plus Advocate, 3979
Fifty Something Magazine, 3859
Fifty-Plus Lifelong Fitness, 136
Fight for Sight, 7589
Fighting Back, 7158
Fighting Back Against PD: One Women's Story, 7003
Fighting Blindness News, 7944
Finance Over 50, 4030
Financial Aid for Veterans, Military Personnel and Their Dependents, 3733

Financial Aid for the Disabled and Their Families, 3734
Financial Help for Hearing Aids, 6650
Financial Power of Attorney Workbook: Who Will Finance If You Can't?, 3631
Finding Wheels: A Curriculum for Nondrivers with Visual Impairments for Gaining Control, 7811
Finding the Right Aural Rehabilitation Program, 6651
Finger Lakes Independence Center, 10870
Finger Print Pen, 3461
The First Year: HIV: An Essential Guidefor the Newly Diagnosed, 4532
The First Year: Parkinson's Disease: AnEssential Guide for the Newly Diagnosed, 6987
The First Year: Type 2 Diabetes: An Essential Guide for the Newly Diagnosed, 6218
Fitness Book: For People with Diabetes, 6204
Fitness Diet and Exercise Guide, 3860
Fitness for the Aged, Disabled and Industrial Worker, 3632
Five College Learning in Retirement, 2816
Five County Area: Agency on Aging, 2394
Five County Retired Senior Volunteer Program, 2395
Five Good Food Habits for People with Diabetes, 4031
Five Star Personal Care Homes, 10447
Five Star Publications, 3779
Five Star Quality Care, 8070
50 Secrets of the Longest Living Peoplewith Diabetes, 6180
50+ Friends Club, 4169
530 West Washington Street, 957
Flagstaff City-Coconino County Library for the Visually & Physically Impaired, 11318
Flagstone Retirement & Assisted Living, 10087
Flashing Lamp Telephone Ring Alerter, 3117
Flathead County Area Nine Agency on Aging, 1535
Fleet & Family Support Center, 2506
Fleet and Family Support Center, 738, 815, 849, 855, 902, 1140, 1230, 1231, 2201, 2313, 2315, 2451, 2505
Fleur Heights Care Center, 8671
Florence Home Assisted Living, 9638
Florentine Press, 3803
Florham Institute for Lifelong Learning(FILL), 2847
Florida Association of Homes for the Aging, 745
Florida Bar Association: Lawyer Referral Service, 11053
Florida Client Assistance Program, 746
Florida Council on Aging, 747
Florida Department of Administration: State Retirement Commission, 748
Florida Department of Aging, 749
Florida Department of Children, Families and Elderly Services, 750
Florida Department of Elder Affairs Program of Aging and Adult Services, 751
Florida Department of Health & Rehabilitative Services, 4460, 7159

Entry Name Index / G

Florida Department of Labor and Employment Security, 11410
Florida Department of Mental Health and Rehabilitative Services, 752
Florida Department of Revenue, 753
Florida Department of Veterans Affairs, 754
Florida Developmental Disabilities Council, 755
Florida Division of Blind Services, 11411
Florida Division of Vocational Rehabilitation, 756
Florida Dog Guides F.T.D., 757
Florida Dog Guides for the Deaf, 6356
Florida Independent Living Council, 10705
Florida Instructional Materials Center for the Visually Impaired, 11412
Florida Language, Speech and Hearing Association, 6357
Florida Legal Services: Tallahassee Office, 11054
Florida Living Center, 8378
Florida Lutheran Retirement Center, 8379
Florida New Concepts Marketing, 3099
Florida Ophthalmic Institute, 8040
Florida Policy Exchange Center on Aging, 4307
Florida Protection & Advocacy for Persons with Disabilities, 758
Florida Retirement Division, 759
Florida School for the Deaf and Blind, 11413
Florida State University: Pepper Institute on Aging and Public Policy, 4308
Floyd House, 8672
Flying Wheels Travel, 12020
Foam Decubitus Bed Pads, 3037
Focus on Geriatric Care and Rehabilitation, 3861
Focus on Mature Learning, 2942
Focus: Library Service to Older Adults: People With Disabilities, 11414
Focus: Library Service to Older Adults; People with Disabilities, 3862
Folding Dressing Stick, 3240
Folding Reacher, 3304
Font-Tools BIGFONT, 3118
Food Allergies for Dummies, 4657
Food Allergy Anaphylaxis Network, 4649, 4678
Food Allergy Network, 4666, 4667, 4668, 4669, 4671, 4198
Food Allergy News, 4667
Food Allergy and Atopic Dermatitis, 4668
Food Allergy: A Primer for People, 4658
Food Donation Program: Food Distribution Center, 137
Food Markers/Magnets, 3333
Food Markers/Rubberbands, 3334
Food and Drug Administration, 138, 7443
Foot Care, 4032
Foot Inversion Tread, 3257
Foot Placement Ladder, 3305
Foot Steering, 2968
Foothills Assisted Living, 10260
For Dummies, 4657, 6196, 6984
For Patients Only, 3863
Fordham University Third Age Center, 4309
Fordham University at Lincoln Center, 2856
Forest Farm Assisted Living, 10216
Forest Glade Retirement Center II, 10014
Forest Grove Beehive, 10088
Forest Hills Health Care Center, 10015

Forest Plaza Assisted Living, 8673
Forest Trace at Inverrary, 8380
Forever Learning Institute, 2782
Forge Hill Senior Living Community, 8964
Forgotten Family, 6652
Forsyth Center for the Deaf and Hard of Hearing, 6358
Fort Plain Senior Center, 1772
Fort Scott Presbyterian Village, 8792
Fort Wayne EASI, 977
Forum at Tucson, 8121
Forwood Manor Assisted Living, 8310
Foster Grandparent Program, 139
Foulk Manor North, 8311
Foulk Manor South, 8312
Foundation Aiding the Elderly (FATE), 140
Foundation Center, 3735, 3737, 3738, 4516
Foundation Fighting Blindness, 7590
Foundation for Advancement in Cancer Therapy, 5681
Foundation for Glaucoma Research, 7947
Foundations of Rehabilitation Counseling with Persons who are Blind, 7812
Fountain Hills Lioness Braille Service, 11319
Fountaingrove Lodge, 8184
Fountains at Cedar Parke, 9783
Fountains at Crystal Lake-The Inn, 8589
Fountains at Franklin, 9049
Fountains at Logan Square East, 10195
Fountains at Millbrook, 9839
Fountains at Sea Bluffs, 8185
Fountains at Town Center Village, 10089
Fountains at the Albemarle Inn, 9485
Fountainview by Marriott, 8381
Four Courts Senior Center, 8843
Four Star, 9161
4222 School of Dentistry, 4413
44-2nd Avenue, 356
Fox Chase Cancer Center: Institute for Cancer Research, 5905
Fox Run Residences, 10261
Framingham Heart Study, 6870
Framingham Public Library: Framingham Room, 11549
Frances Strietel Villa, 10016
Francis Asbury Manor, 9784
Franciscan Assisted Living, 9162
Frank Reed Memorial Library, 11707
Franken Manor, 8674
Franklin County Area: Agency on Aging, 2114
Franklin County Home Care Corporation, 1280
Franklin County Office for the Aging, 1773
Franklin Medical Building, 6268
Franklin Parish Council on the Aging, 1152
Franklin Park, 10350
Franklin Publications, 3918
Franklin Watts, 4975
Fraser A Lang, 4059
Fraser Villa: A Mercy Living Center, 9050
Frat, 6653
Fred Hutchinson Cancer Research Center, 5906
Fred Hutchinson Cancer Research Center: Arnold Digital Library, 11829
Frederick County Commission on Aging, 1236
Free Library of Philadelphia, 11736
Free University for Senior Citizens: Tuition Waver Program, 2936

Free to Care, 7345
Freedom From Despair, 7346
Freedom From Smoking Flyer, 4033
Freedom Inn at Tarpon Springs, 8382
Freedom Resource Center for Independent Living, 10806, 10842
Freedom Scientific, 3076, 3086
Freedom Valley Disability Enablement, 10914
Freedom Wheelchair Lifts, 3377
Freeport Elders Association, 1204
French Alzheimer Foundation, 4936
Fresno County Free Library: Talking Book Library for the Blind, 11339
Fresno Madera Area: Agency on Aging, 541
Friday Night Live, 7160
A Friend's House Adult Day Services, 1336
A Friend's House Adult Day Services: Romeo, 1337
A Friend's House Adult Day Services: Warren, 1338
Friends Medical Science Research Center, 7457
Friends and Relatives of Institutionalized Aged, 1774
Friends for Sight, 7591
Friends of Libraries for Deaf Action, 11534
Friends of Seniors, 2575
Friends of Tennessee School of the Blind, 7592
Friends of the Pepperell Seniors, 1281
Friends of the Senior Center, 1890
Friends-In-Art, 4199, 7593
Friendship Care, 9486
From Theory to Therapy: The Development of Drugs for Alzheimer's Disease, 4960
Front Range Community College, 2737
Frontier Nursing Service, 8844
Ft Lauderdale Retirement Home, 8383
Fulton County Office for the Aging, 1775
Fulton Public Library Learning Center, 11437
Functional Fitness Assessment for Adults, 3633
Functional Forms, 3204
Fund for Assuring an Independent Retirement, 141
Funding in Aging, 3735
Funeral Consumers Alliance, 11275

G

GA and SK Etiquette, 6504
GA-SK, 3258
GASK Newsletter, 6654
GLAD Directory of Resources Available to Deaf and Hard-of-Hearing Persons, 6564
GM Mobility Program, 2969, 12022
GW Micro, 3093, 7907, 7996, 3119
Gables at Farmington, 8270
Gables at Guilford, 8271
Gables of Lake Mary, 8384
Gabriel House of Fall River, 8965
Gadabout Wheelchairs, 3516
Gale Research, 3795
Galladet University, 6655
Gallaudet Encyclopedia of Deaf People and Deafness, 6505
Gallaudet Today, 6655
Gallaudet Univ. Press c/o Chicago Distrib. Center, 3758, 6465, 6481, 6485, 6495,

Entry Name Index / G

6500, 6501, 6505, 6510, 6511, 6516, 6524, 6525, 6526, 6531, 6533, 6534, 6536, 6537, 6542, 6546
Gallaudet University, 6359
Gallaudet University Bookstore, 6414, 6471, 6475, 6478, 6482, 6502, 6504, 6515, 6521, 6538, 6545, 6552, 6607, 6753, 6761
Gallaudet University Library Deaf Collection, 11390
Gallaudet University Press, 6480, 6484, 6498
Galludet University/Alumni House, 12021
Garaventa Canada, 3514
Garden Cottage Assisted Living, 9163
Garden Square of Casper, 10609
Garden Square of Crete, 9639
Garden of Palms, 8186
Gardens Assisted Living, 9333, 10017
Gardens at Hillsborough Village, 8187
Gardens at Park Balboa, 8188
Gardens at Rivermont, 10018
Gardens at White Chapel, 8313
Gardens of Clanton, 8063
Gardens of Richardson, 10448
Gardens of Santa Monica, 8189
Gardenside Terrace, 8272
Garnett Place, 8675
Gaston Manor, 9487
Gaston Place, 9488
Gastonia Village, 9489
Gateway Area Development District, 1106
Gateway Books, 11876
Gateway Manor, 9640
Gateway Older Adult Legal Services, 11170
Gateway Technical College Learning Resource Center, 11846
Gaymar, 3205
Gaymar Industries, 3205, 3520
Gazette International Networking Institute, 3946, 3947, 4052
Gem Wheelchair and Scooter Service, 3517
Gendron, 3498, 3501, 3536, 3518
General Clinical Research Center, 4270, 4602
General Clinical Research Center at Beth Israel Hospital, 6871
General Clinical Research Center: University of California at Los Angeles, 6872
General Facts and Figures on Blindness, 7945
General Fitness, 4200
General German Aged Peoples Home, 8912
General Media, 3920
General Motors Mobility Program for Persons with Disabilities, 2969
General Motors Mobility Program for Travelers with Disabilities, 12022
General Service Office/Grand Central Station, 7132
Generations, 3864
Generations Child and Adult Day Care, 1806
Generations Online, 4201
Generations United, 726
Generations, Journal of the American Society on Aging, 3865
Genesee County Office for the Aging, 1776
Genesis Institute, 142
Genetics and Deafness, 6656
Genetics and Hearing Loss, 6657
Geneva Mathiasen Award, 2635

Genoa Retirement Village Assisted Living, 9892
Gentle Path Through the Twelve Steps, 7250
Geo-Matt for High Risk Patients, 3206
George Card Award, 2636
George H. Snyder Enterprises, 3551
George J DePontis, 4003
George Ohsawa Macrobiotic Foundation, 3921
George Washington National Cooperative Drug Discovery/AIDS Treatment, 4603
Georgetown University: International Center for Interdiciplinary Studies of Immunology, 5054
Georgetown University: Research Resources Facility, 6873
Georgetown University: Vincent T Lombardi Cancer Research Center, 5907
Georgetown Village, 8793
Georgia Advocacy Office, 820
Georgia Association of Homes and Services for the Aging, 821
Georgia Chapter of the Arthritis Foundaton, 5101
Georgia Client Assistance Program, 822
Georgia College CBX 082, 5949
Georgia Consortium on the Psychology of Aging, 4310
Georgia Department of Aging, 823
Georgia Department of Human Resources: Division of Public Health, 4461
Georgia Department of Industry Trade & Tourism, 11958
Georgia Department of Labor: Disability Adjudication Section, 824
Georgia Department of Revenue, 825
Georgia Department of Veterans Service, 826
Georgia Division for Aging Services, 11065
Georgia Division of Mental Health and Substance Abuse, 7161
Georgia Division of Mental Health: Developmental Disabilities & Addictive Diseases, 827
Georgia Employees' Retirement System, 828
Georgia Industries for the Blind, 7594
Georgia Office of Aging, 829
Georgia Protection and Advocacy Agency, 11066
Georgia Regional Library, 11438
Georgia State Board of Workers' Compansation, 830
Georgia State University Center for Mature Consumer Studies, 4311
Georgia Statewide Independent Living Council, 10710
Georgia Teachers Retirement System, 831
Geraldine Brush Cancer Research Institute, 5908
Geriatric Oral Health Care Award, 2637
Geriatric Rehabilitation Preview, 4034
Geriatrics, 3866
Geriatrics Education and Research Institute, 4312
Geronimo, 3519
Gerontological Society of America, 2628, 2630, 2639, 2660, 2679, 2682, 3711, 3867, 4035, 6083, 4202, 4313, 11877
Gerontologist, 3867
Gerontology, 3868
Gerontology & Geriatrics Education, 3869

Gerontology News, 4035
Gerontology Research Institute, 5055
Gerontology Special Interest Section Quarterly, 4036
Gerontology: Responding to an Aging Society, 3634
Get Fit While You Sit, 11691
Get Up and Go, 3870
Getting Beyond Hearing Loss: A Guide for Families, 6658
Getting Help with a Job: Exploring Vocational Rehabilitation, 6659
Getting Started in AA, 7251
Getting Through Audiotape, 6751
Getting the Most Out of Your Hearing Aids, 6752
Gianna Homes-Sursum Corda, 9164
Gibbs Associates, 11878
Gibson Creek Retirement and Assisted Living, 10090
Gift of Sight, 7946
Gilbert Residence, 9051
Gilda's Club, 5682
Gilda's Club: Metro Detroit, 5683
Gilda's Club: Quad Cities, 5684
Gilda's Club: South Florida, 5685
Gilman Park, 10091
Glacial Lakes Retired & Senior Volunteer Program, 2258
Glacier Hills Retirement Center, 9052
Glaucoma, 7947
Glaucoma - the Sneak Thief of Sight, 7948
Glaucoma Foundation, 8041
Glaucoma Research Foundation, 7595, 7866, 7959, 8042
Glaucoma Support Network, 7595
Gleams Newsletter, 7866
Glen Bollinger Humanitarian Award, 2638
Glendale Community College, 2702
Glenn Foundation Award, 2639
Glenwood Place, 8676
Gloucester County Department on Aging, 1648
Goals and Objectives, 3120
God Grant Me the Laughter: A Treasury of Twelve Step Humor, 7252
Goddard House in Brookline, 8966
Gold Crest Retirement Center, 9641
Gold Treatment, 5200
Golden Acres Manor, 9565
Golden Aspen Publishing, 3629, 3646, 4046, 11879
Golden Buckeye Program, 11959
Golden Care Home for Adults, 9840
Golden Cove Assisted Living Facility, 8385
Golden Crescent Area: Agency on Aging, 2321
Golden Horizons, 11880
Golden Manor, 9165, 10449
Golden Manor Assisted Living, 9642
Golden Oaks Residence, 9166
Golden Oaks Village, 10019
Golden Opportunities, 3736
Golden Pond, 8241
Golden Power Lift Chair, 3045
Golden Prairie Manor, 10262
Golden Ridge Retirement Community, 10263
Golden Slipper Center for Seniors, 2115
Golden Technologies, 3034, 3045, 3432, 3434, 3439
Golden Times, 3980

1011

Entry Name Index / G

Golden Times Piano Works Mall, 3980
Golden Years Magazine, 3871
Golden Years?, 4143
Goldwater Memorial Hospital: Medical Center Health Sciences Library, 11635
Good Faith, 2226
Good First Step, 7253
Good Grips Cutlery, 3335
Good Nutrition in Parkinson's Disease, 7004
Good Place Assisted Living, 10450
Good Samaritan Center, 10264
Good Samaritan Towers, 9643
Good Shepherd Home, 9566, 9893
Good Shepherd Lutheran Home, 9644
Goodwin Institute for Cancer Research, 5909
Gordon Countryside Care, 9645
Gordon House, 10556
Gordon Oaks Assisted Living, 8064
Gordon Recovery Center, 10758
Gout, 5201
Govenor's Council on Developmental Disabilities, 832
Government Grants and Loans for Seniors, 4203
Governor Baxter School for the Deaf Library, 11525
Governor's Advisory Council for Personswith Disabilities (GACPD), 11211
Governor's Commission on Disability, 1617
Governor's Commission on Senior Services (GCSS), 11230
Governor's Committee for People with Disabilities, 2576
Governor's Committee on Employment of Persons with Disabilities, 374
Governor's Council on Developmental Disabilities, 437
Governor's Policy Council on Drug & Alcohol Abuse, 7162
Grabd Island Sterling House, 9646
Grace House, 10092
Grace House of Lake Travis, 10451
Grace Manor, 9167
Grace Morgan House, 8967
Grace Place, 9168
Graceful Living Assisted Living Home, 8088
Graduate Hospital, 6863
Graduate School of Public Health, 6291
Graham-Field, 3046, 3214, 3527, 3562
Graham-Field Health Products, 3042
Gramercy Hill, 9647
Gran Villas, 8794
Gran Villas-Atchison, 8795
Gran Villas-Eureka, 8796
Gran Villas-Fredonia, 8797
Gran Villas-Hiawatha, 8798
Gran Villas-Neodesha, 8799
Gran Villas-Osage City, 8800
Gran Villas-Wamego, 8801
Grand Court, 10557
Grand Court Greatwood, 10452
Grand Court Round Rock, 10453
Grand Court Seward Retirement CommunityAssisted Living, 9648
Grand Court Seward Retirment CommunityAssisted Living, 9649
Grand Court of Overland Park II, 8802
Grand Cove, 8863
Grand Gateway Area: Agency on Aging, 2008
Grand Island Veterand Home, 9650
Grand Park Assisted Living Community, 9343
Grand Rapids Community Cancer Center, 5372
Grand Residence at Upper St. Clair, 10196
Grand Times, 4204
Grand Traverse Area Library for the Blind and Physically Handicapped, 11561
Grand Villa, 8242
Grande Ronde Retirement Residence, 10093
Grandmar, 3560
Grandparenting with Love and Logic, 3635
Grandparents Raising Grandchildren, 4144
Grandparents Rights Organization, 143
Granite Falls Senior Services, 9169
Granite State Independent Living Center, 10847
Granny Good's Sign of Christmas, 6753
Grants for Literacy, Reading & Adult/Continuing Education, 3737
Grants of Aging, 3738
Granville Assisted Living Center, 8243
Granville County Senior Center, 1891
Grateful to Have Been There, 7254
Gravity Down Platform Lift, 3378
Gray Panthers, 144
Gray Panthers Metro Detroit, 1348
Gray Panthers Metropolitan, 727
Gray Panthers of Austin, 2322
Gray Panthers of Central Contra Costa, 542
Gray Panthers of East Bay/Berkeley, 543
Gray Panthers of Huron Valley, 1349
Gray Panthers of Long Beach, 544
Gray Panthers of Marin County, 545
Gray Panthers of New York, 1777
Gray Panthers of North Dade, 760
Gray Panthers of Northern New Jersey, 1649
Gray Panthers of Orange County, 546
Gray Panthers of Pittsburgh, 2116
Gray Panthers of Portland, 2050
Gray Panthers of Rhode Island, 2204
Gray Panthers of Sacramento, 547
Gray Panthers of San Fernando Valley, 548
Gray Panthers of San Francisco, 549
Gray Panthers of Santa Barbara, 550
Gray Panthers of Seattle, 2510
Gray Panthers of South Bay, 551
Gray Panthers of South Dade, 761
Gray Panthers of Southern Alameda County, 552
Gray Panthers of Southern New Jersey, 1650
Gray Panthers of Suffolk County, 1778
Gray Panthers of Twin Cities, 1399
Grayson County College, 2929
Great Bend Homestead, 8803
Great Big Safety Tub Mat, 3015
Great Buys for People over 50, 3739
Great Plains Region Helen Keller National Center, 7596
Great River Publishing, 3953
Greater Boston Legal Services: Elderly Ofice (GBLS), 11147
Greater Chicago Chapter of the Arthritis Foundation, 5102
Greater Detroit Agency F/T Blind and Visually Impaired, 7597
Greater Erie Community Action Committee (GECAC), 2117
Greater Fall River Health Care Services, 10265
Greater Ft Lauderdale Convention &, 11988
Greater Illinois Chapter of the Arthritis Foundation, 5103
Greater Kansas City Chapter of the Arthritis Foundation, 5104
Greater Lakewood Shepherd's Center, 2323
Greater Los Angeles Council on Deafness, 6564
Greater Lynn Senior Services (GLSS), 1282
Greater Philadelphia Parkinson's Disease and Other Movement Disorders Council, 6955
Greater Rochester Area Partnership for the Elderly, 1779
Greater Springfield Senior Services, 1283
Greater St. Louis Association of the Deaf, 1483, 6360
Greater Valley Physicians Medical Group, 553
Greater Washington Urban League, 309
Greatest of Ease Company Catalog, 3740
Greeley Assisted Living, 9651
Green Acres Manor, 9785
Green County Independent Living Resource Center, 10901
Green County Village Assisted Living, 10020
Green Hill Home for Adults, 10558
Green Meadows at Dover, 8314
Green River Area: Agency on Aging, 1107
Green Tortoise Adventure Travel, 12023
Greenbrier, 9490
Greene County Aging Services, 1780
Greene County Department for Aging, 1781
Greene House, 9652
Greene Oaks Willow Place, 9894
Greenfield Manor Assisted Living, 8677
Greenhaven Press, 4519, 4545, 6034, 7324, 7339
Greenlead Assisted Living-Flandreau, 10266
Greenleaf Assisted Living, 10267
Greenleaf Assisted Living Center, 10268
Greenleaf Assisted Living-Sisseton, 10269
Greenridge Estates, 10094
Greens at the Greenwich, 8273
Greensboro Manor, 9491
Greensboro Place on Lawndale, 9492
Greensburg Bureau of Disability Determination, 2118
Greenwich Bay Manor, 10217
Greenwood Publishing Group, 3641, 3802, 6079, 6988, 11033
Gresham Driving Aids, 2966, 2970
Grey & Emil Eisenber Assisted Living Residence, 8968
Grey House Publishing, 3701, 3702, 3705, 3774
Greyhound Bus Info Senior Discounts, 11925
Greyhound Buslines, 11926
Grief Dreams: How They Help Us Heal After the Death of a Loved One, 6020
Grief and Loss Program, 6008
Grief, Dying and Death, 6021
Grieving, 7347
Grossmont Gardens, 8190
Group Development Awards, 2640
Grove Assisted Living Community, 10095
Grove Manor Estates Assisted Living, 8969
Growing Up Hearing: A Sister's Memoir, 6660
Guadalupe County Nutrition, 1712
Guardian Angels Elem HomeCare, 9170

Entry Name Index / H

Guardian Eldercare, 1651
Guardianship Services Associates, 11090
Guest Scholar Program, 2858
Guidance on Our Journeys, 7348
Guide A Knife, 3336
Guide Dog Foundation Flyer, 7949
Guide Dog Foundation for the Blind, 7867, 7934, 7949, 7979, 7598, 8010
Guide Dog Users, 7599, 8011
Guide Dogs for the Blind, 7600
Guide for Students with Hearing Loss, 6661
Guide for the Family of the Alcoholic, 7349
Guide to Effective Volunteer Lobbying, 5202
Guide to Helping Elderly Relatives Near and Far, 4145
A Guide to Independence for the Visually Impaired and Their Families, 7791
Guide to Independence for the Visually Impaired and Their Families, 7813
Guide to Living With HIV Infection, 4523
The Guide to Living with HIV Infection, 4533
Guide to Understanding Stroke, 7093
Guide to the Nation's Hospices, 3741
Guide to the Nursing Home Industry, 3742
Guidelines for Comprehensive Low Vision Care, 7950
Guidelines for Dignity, 4961, 5000
Guidelines for Helping Deaf-Blind Persons, 6662
Guidelines for Managing Diabetes During Brief Illness, 6263
Guideway, 7867
Guiding Eyes for the Blind, 7601
Guild Briefs, 7951
Guild for the Blind, 7951
Guilford Press, 6077
Gulf Coast Village Assisted Living, 8386
Gulf Coast Village Retirement Community, 8387
Gulf Winds, 8388
Gulfcoast Branch: Florida Chapter of the Arthritis Foundation, 5105
Gundersen Lutheran Medical Center Bereavement Services, 6009
Gwinnett Council for Seniors, 833

H

H2U: Health, Happiness, You, 145
HARC Mercantile, 2958, 3071, 3072, 3073, 3078, 3108, 3109, 3114, 3127, 3141, 3145, 3149, 3150, 3157, 3160, 3161, 3163, 3164, 3169, 3173, 3175
HARC Mercantile-Division of HAC ofAmerica, 3278
HCIA, 3721, 3742
HEALTH & YOU, 3981
HEAR Center, 2638, 6684, 6361
HEAR You Are, 3070
HEAR's to the ADA, 6754
HEAR: Solutions, Skills, and Sources for People with Hearing Loss, 6506
HEATH Resource Center, 146
HEATH Resource Center, National Clearinghouse on, 3743
HEATH Resource Directory, 3743
HESSCO Elder Services, 1284
HIGH PROFILE Dual Compartment Cushion, 3207
HIGH PROFILE Single Compartment Cushion, 3208
HIV Disease in People with Hemophilia: Your Questions Answered, 4559
HIV Division, 4503
HIV Frontline, 4560
HIV Infection and AIDS, 4561
HIV Treatment Information Exchange (HTIE), 4562
HIV/AIDS Prevention & Intervention Section, 1357, 4474
HIV/AIDS Program, 4508
HIV/AIDS and Older Adults: Challenges for Individuals, Families, and Communities, 4524
HIV/AIDS/STD Prevention & Services Bureau, 4488
HIV: Third Edition, 4525
HMOs4seniors.com, 4205
HSC Level T16-040, 4692
Hachette Book Group USA, 3587, 6215, 6915
Hacienda, 8191
Hahnemann University Laboratory of Human Pharmacology, 7458
Hahnemann University: Division of Surgical Research, 6921
Hair Cell Regeneration, 6663
Hall County Library System, 11439
Hallmark Care Center, 8678
Hallmark Orthopedic Company, 3230
Halstead Place, 8804
Hamilton Heights Place of West Hartford, 8274
Hamilton House, 9344
Hammatt Senior Products: Catalog for Activity Professionals, 3289
Hammonton Senior Citizens Club, 1652
Hamot Medical Center: Research Department, 7459
Hampshire Community Action Commission, 1285
Hampton Assisted Living Residence at Pinegate, 10454
Hampton Court Independent & AssistedLiving, 8389
Hampton Manor Belleview, 8390
Hampton at Post Oaks, 10455
Hampton at Spring Shadows, 10456
Hand Brake Control Only, 2971
Hand Gas & Brake Control, 2972
Hand Parking Brake, 2973
Hand/Nail Brush, 3259
A Handbook of Activities for Persons With Dementia, 4945
Handbook of Activities for Persons with Dementia, 4962
Handbook of Assistive Devices for the Handicapped Elderly, 3744
Handi Home Lift, 3379
Handi Prolift, 3380
Handi-Cabs of the Pacific, 12024
Handi-Lift, 3364, 3365, 3373, 3379, 3380, 3385
Handi-Ramp, 3381
Handicap Helpers, 3386
Handicaps, Inc., 2994
Hands Organization for the Deaf and Hard of Hearing, 6362
Handy Reacher, 3306
Handy-Helper Cutting Board, 3337
Hanley & Belfus, 5808
Happy Old Timers Senior Center, 1400
Harbor Place at Port St Lucie, 8391
Harbor Point at Centerville, 8970
Harbor-UCLA Medical Center, 4384, 6888
Harbor-UCLA Research and Education Institute, 4314
Harbours Edge Retirement Center, 9493
Harbourview Assisted Living of League City, 10457
Harcourt Brace Jovanovich Publications, 6668
Hard Manufacturing Company, 3038
Harford County Office on Aging, 1237
Harlem Independent Living Center, 10871
Harmony Elder Care, 10458
Harmony House, 9345
Harney County Senior Center, 2051
Harold W. McGraw, Jr. Prize in Education, 2641
Harolds Haaland Home, 9567
Harper & Row, 6075
Harper Collins Publishers/Basic Books, 6022
Harrington Arthritis Research Center, 5238
Harris Communications, 6492, 6493, 6746, 6747, 6748, 6771, 7825
Harris Library, MSASS, Case Western Reserve University, 11708
Harris M Fishbon Memorial Library, 11355
Harrisburg Bureau of Disability Determination, 2119
Harrisburg District Office, 7717
Hartford Area Social Security Office, 687
Hartford Consortium for Higher Education Adult Learning Program, 2740
Hartford Holiday Travel, 12014
Hartford Hospital Health Science Libraries, 11373
Hartford Hospital, Jefferson House, 11374
Hartford Hospital: Gerontology Resource Center, 11374
Harthstone at Laural Lake, 8971
Harvard Brain Tissue Resource Center, 4315
Harvard Cocaine Recovery Project, 7163
Harvard Medical Center, 6874
Harvard Square, 8244
Harvard Thorndike Laboratory, 6874
Harvard University, 2817
Harvard University Division of Health Policy Research and Education, 4316
Harvard University Press, 7073
Harvard University: Howe Laboratory of Ophthalmology, 8043
Harvest Home Personal Care Facility, 10459
Harvest Homes, 10096
Harvey County Department on Aging, 1062
Hasting Center Library, 11636
Hastings Homestead, 9653
Hausler, 8913
Have Fun! Figure Out the Smoking Puzzle, 4037
Haven Heights Rest Home, 9494
Haven Manor Assisted Living, 9654
Haven Manor College View, 9655
Haven at Holiday Manor, 9786
Haven at Windermere, 8864
Haven in the Village at Carolina Place, 9495
Haverhill Crossings, 8972
Hawaii Alcohol and Drug Abuse Division, 7164
Hawaii Center for Independent Living, 10715

Hawaii Chapter of the Arthritis Foundation, 5106
Hawaii County Office of Aging, 858
Hawaii Department of Adult Mental Health, 859
Hawaii Department of Defense: Office of Veterans Services, 860
Hawaii Department of Health: Commission on Persons with Disabilities, 861
Hawaii Department of Health: Communicable Disease Division, 4462
Hawaii Department of Health: Disability and Communication Access Board, 862
Hawaii Disability Compensation Division: Department of Labor and Indian Relations, 863
Hawaii Disability Rights Center, 864
Hawaii Disability Rights Center: Honolulu, 11067
Hawaii Executive Office on Aging, 865
Hawaii Planning Council on Developmental Disabilities, 866
Hawaii State Council on Developmental Disabilities, 867
Hawaii State Employees' Retirement System, 868
Hawaii Tourism Office, 11960
Hawaiian Airlines, 11927
Hawkeye Valley Area: Agency on Aging, 1018
Hawkins Center of Law and Services for the Disabled, 11002
Haworth Press, 3589, 3600, 3622, 3626, 3638, 3649, 3657, 3660, 3662, 3680, 3837, 3893, 3894, 3901, 3907, 3909, 3912, 6849, 7278, 7834
The Haworth Press, 3597, 3598, 3605, 3636, 3650, 3675, 3744, 3836, 3869, 3902, 3905, 3906, 3914, 3943
Hawthorne Court, 10594
Hawthorne House, 9346
Hawthorne Inn at Windmill, 8679
Hayden Country Guest Home, 8507
Hayden Country Guest Home III, 8508
Haymarket Group, 3925
Haywood Lodge & Retirement Center, 9496
Hazel I Findlay Country Manor, 9053
Hazelden, 3652, 4158, 4522, 6087, 7237, 7238, 7240, 7242, 7245, 7246, 7247, 7248, 7249, 7250, 7251, 7252, 7253, 7254, 7256, 7257, 7258
Hazelden Foundation, 7165
Hazeldon Foundation: Library and Information Resources, 7460
Headlight Dimmer Switch, 2974
Headmaster Plus, 3121
Headwaters Area: Agency on Aging, 1401
Healing Choices, 4038
Healing Light Center Church, 5686
Healing Well, 4207
Health, 3872
Health & Housing Association Mid-Atlantic Nonprofit, 1238
Health & Human Services-Regulation & Licensure, 3793
Health After 50: Johns Hopkins Medical Letter, 4039
Health Answers, 7444
Health Care Bridges, 8089
Health Care Financing Administration, 167
Health Care of the Aged, 3636
Health Division, HIV Program, 4493

Health East Residence of South St Paul, 9171
Health Education AIDS Liaison (HEAL), 4463
Health Information Network for Women and AIDS, 4464
Health Ink Communications, 3981
Health Legislation and Regulation, 4040
Health Naturally, 3873
Health Naturally Publications, 3873
Health Perspective, 3982
Health Press, 6853
Health Professions Press, 4964
Health Promotion Institute, 147
Health Promotion and Aging: Strategies for Action, 3637
Health Resource, 5687
Health Resources, 3857, 4017, 4043
Health Resources Publishing, 4041
Health Watch, 3874
Health Watch Magazine, 3874
Health World, 3875
Health, Life and Disability Insurance for People with Arthritis, 5203
HealthProInk Publishing, 6937
HealthQuest, 3876
Healtheast Care Center-Marian St Paul, 9172
Healtheast Residence on Humboldt, 9173
Healtheast Residence-White Bear Lake, 9174
Healthlink USA, 7445
Healthteam Interactive Communications, 6856
Healthy Food Choices, 6249
Hear Now, 6363, 6784
Hear You Are, 3059, 3069, 3107, 3147, 3148, 3182, 6565
Hear: Solutions, Skills, and Sources for People with Hearing Loss, 6507
Hearing Aid Batteries, 3279
Hearing Aid Battery Testers, 3280
Hearing Aid Dehumidifier, 3281
Hearing Aid Helpline, 6364
Hearing Aids and the Consumer: Current Wisdom, 6664
Hearing Alert! Informational Brochures, 6665
Hearing Dog Resource Center (HDRC), 6365
Hearing Dogs in Public, 6666
Hearing Education and Awareness for Elders, 6785
Hearing Education and Awareness for Rockers, 6366
Hearing Health, 6579
Hearing Healthcare Team, 6667
Hearing Impaired Persons of Charlotte County Florida, 6367, 6368
Hearing Industries Association, 6369
Hearing Instruments, 6668
Hearing Journal, 6580
Hearing Loss Association of America, 6334, 6370
Hearing Loss and Rehabilitation, 6755
Hearing Loss and Staying Connected: Personal Accounts, 6669
Hearing Loss: How to Get Help-A Guide for Consumers by Consumers, 6670
Hearing Loss: Information for Professionals in the Aging Network, 6671

Hearing Loss: Personal and Social Considerations, 6672
Hearing Rehabilitation Foundation, 1286
Hearing Rehabilitation for Deafened Adults: A Psychosocial Approach, 6508
Hearing in Aging, 6509
Hearing, Speech, 6712
Hearing, Speech & Deafness Center(HSDC) Newsletter, 6673
Hearling Loss Association of America, 6371
Heart Beat, 6856
Heart Disease Research Foundation, 6875
Heart Research Foundation of Sacramento, 6876
Heart Smart: A Cardiologists 5-Step Plan for Detecting, Preventing and Even Reversing Heart Disease, 6852
Heart and Stroke Facts, 7094
Heart and Stroke Risk Factors, 7095
Heart and Vascular Institute, 6877
Heart of Florida United Way Volunteer Center, 762
Heart of Georgia Altamaha AAA, 834
Heart of Georgia Area: Agency on Aging, 835
Heart of Texas Area Agency on Aging, 2374
Heart of Texas Council of Governments Area: Agency on Aging, 2324
Heart to Heart: A Guide to the Psychological Aspects of the Disease, 6853
HeartFields Assisted Living at Cary, 9497
Heartbreak of Being A Little Bit Blind, 7952
Heartfields Hall at Heartlands, 8914
Heartfields at Frederick, 8915
Hearthhomes Resedence Bay Ridge I, 8916
Hearthhomes Residence Piney Orchard, 8917
Hearthside Commons at the Job HainesHome, 9787
Hearthside at Castle Heights, 10351
Hearthstone at Arlington, 10460
Hearthstone at New Horizons, 8973
Hearthstone at Quail Springs, 10021
Hearthstone at Vista, 10461
Hearthstone at Windcrest, 10462
Hearthstone of Arlington Heights, 8590
Hearthstone of Beaverton, 10097
Heartland Care Center Assisted Living, 8680
Heartland HCC-Crestview, 9054
Heartland Regional Network Library, 11357
Heartland of Willowbrook, 10463
Heartsworth House, 10022
Heartwood Heights, 8681
Heather and Shamrock Apartments, 9656
Heatherwood Assisted Living, 8974
Heathridge Assisted Living Comunity, 10023
Heightened Independence & Progress (HIP), 10851
Heightened Independence & Progress-Hudson (HIP Hudson), 10852
Heights Assisted Living, 10098, 10464
Heights at Avery Heights, 8275
Heimlich University, 5910
Helen Keller International, 7602
Helen Keller National Center, 6372, 6662, 6737, 7999, 7603
Helen Keller National Center for Deaf & Blind Southeast Regional Office, 836
Helen Keller National Center for Deaf: North Central Region, 6372

Entry Name Index / H

Helen Keller National Center: North Central Region, 7604
Helen Keller National Center: NorthwestRegion, 7605
Helios Health, 4208
Help Legal Assistance: Senior Citizens Law Project, 11109
Help for Incontinent People: National Association for Continence, 6945
Help the Aged, 352
Help: A Guide to Community Services for Older Citizens, 3745
Helping Hand Assisted Living, 10270
Helping Handle, 3039
Helping Hands for the Blind, 7606
Helpmates, 7062
Hematology Research Laboratory: Universiy of Southern California, 4604
Hemlock Society USA, 148
Henderson Village, 8392
Henrietta Brewer House, 8975
Henry County Council on Aging, 837
Henry Ford Hospital Department of Neurology, 7050
Henry Ford Hospital: Hypertension and Vascular Research Division, 6922
Henry Holt & Company, 6202
Henry Vogt Cancer Research Institute, 5911
Herb Quarterly, 3877
Here Comes the Sun: Directory of Summer Programs for Handicapping Conditions, 3746
Hereditary Cancer Institute, 5912
Heritage Acres Assisted Living, 9347
Heritage Area: Agency on Aging, 1019
Heritage Assisted Living Center, 10024
Heritage Assisted Living at Hammonton, 9788
Heritage Court, 8682
Heritage Estates, 8192
Heritage Estates Senior Apartments, 8193
Heritage Home, 9175
Heritage House, 8683
Heritage House Assisted Living Facility, 9176
Heritage House of Bemidji, 9177
Heritage Manor, 9178
Heritage Oaks Senior Housing, 8393
Heritage Park Independent Living Apartments, 10747
Heritage Parkview, 8509
Heritage Place, 9498, 10352
Heritage Place Assisted Living, 10025, 10099
Heritage Pointe, 8194
Heritage Retirement Center-Boise, 8510
Heritage Retirement Center-Twin Falls, 8511
Heritage Retirement Home, 9348
Heritage Senior Living, 10271
Heritage Woods, 8976, 9499
Heritage at Cleveland Circle, 8977
Heritage at Danvers, 8978
Heritage at Dartmouth, 8979
Heritage at Falmouth, 8980
Heritage at Framingham, 8981
Heritage at Gaines Ranch, 10465
Heritage at Milford, 8315
Heritage at North Andover, 8982
Heritage at Tomball, 10466
Heritage at Vernon Court, 8983
Herkimer County Office for the Aging, 1782

Herman Miller Research Corporation, 11562
Hermiston Terrace Assisted Living Facility, 10100
Heron House, 8394
Heron Pointe Retirement & Assisted Living, 10101
Herreid Good Samaritan Center, 10272
Herrick House, 8984
Herrington Place, 10353
Hester Memorial Home, 9657
Hettinger Living Center, 8512
HiRider, 3520
Hiawatha Heights Assisted Living Facility, 10273
Hickory Manor, 9500
Hickory Villa, 9658
Hidden Heights Assisted Living Home, 8090
Hidden Pines Assisted Living Community, 9659
High Blood Pressure and Stroke, 7096
High Country Region D Area: Agency on Aging, 1892
High Point Manor, 9501
High Point Place, 9502
High Street UMC Older Adult Ministry, 2783
Highland County Senior Citizens, 1957
Highland Estates, 8513
Highland Hills, 8514
Highland Hospital: John R Williams, Sr Health Sciences Library, 11637
Highland House, 9660
Highland Terrace Assisted Living Community, 8395
Highland Valley Elder Services, 1287
Highlighter and Note Tape, 3462
Highwood Senior Citizens, 1536
Hilda's Heritage Home, 10274
Hill Country Care Home, 10467
Hill Country Community Action Association, 2325
Hill County Area Ten Agency on Aging, 1556
Hillcrest, 8515
Hillcrest Medical Center Library, 11720
Hillcrest Rehabilitation & Healthcare Center, 9179
Hillcrest Spring, 9841
Hillhaven Assisted Living, 8918
Hillsborough County Talking Book Library Tampa-Hillsborough County Public Library, 11415
Hillside Communities, 10102
Hillside Homes of Duluth, 9180
Hillside House Assisted Living Center, 10103
Hillside Place, 9349
Hinsdale Travel Service, 12025
Hipple Cancer Research Center, 5913
Hippocrates, 3878
Hippocrates Partners, 3878
Hispanic Deaf Teacher Training Program, 6373
History and Use of Braille, 7953
Ho'opono Services for the Blind, 7607
Ho'opono Workshop for the Blind, 7608
Hobart Jackson Social Responsibility Award, 2642
Hofstra University, 2869
Holland Home Assisted Living, 8591
Holland Township Community Seniors, 1653

Hollenbeck Palms, 8195
Holy Family Adult Foster Home, 8091
Holy Family Assisted Living Home, 8092
Holy Infant Hospital Assisted Living Center, 10275
Holy Spirit, 8684
Home Care Agencies, Hospices and Nursing Pools, 3747
Home Care Association of Alabama, 375
Home Care Guide for Cancer, 5800
Home Equity Conversion Mortgages: Office of Insured Single Family Housing, 149
Home Exercises for Stroke Survivors, 7097
Home Health Agency Report & Directory, 3748
Home Health Line, 4042
Home Health Service Directory, 3749
Home Healthcare Agency Directory, 3750
Home Healthcare Nurses Association (HHNA), 150
Home Safety for the Alzheimer's Patient, 5001
HomeAid Orange County, 554
HomeCare Magazine Buyers' Guide, 3879
Homecare Products, 3369
Homedale Senior Center, 880
Homemaker Program, 916
Homeplace of Burlington, 9503
Homeplace of Durham, 9504
Homeplace of New Bern, 9505
Homes Nursing Directory, 3751
Homestead, 9661
Homestead Acres, 8685
Homestead Assisted Living, 10276
Homestead Hills Assisted Living, 9506
Homestead Place, 9181
Homestead Village of Fairhope, 8065
Homestead of Garden City, 8805
Homewaiter, 3382
Homeward Bound, 7350
Homewood Heights Assisted Living Facility, 10104
Homewood Residence at Air Force Village, 10468
Homewood Residence at Boca Raton, 8396
Homewood Residence at Boynton Beach, 8397
Homewood Residence at Brookmont TerraceAssisted Living and Alzheimer's Care Residence, 10354
Homewood Residence at Deane Hill, 10355
Homewood Residence at Delray Beach, 8398
Homewood Residence at Freedom Plaza, 8399
Homewood Residence at Shavano Park, 10469
Homewood Residence-Richmond Heights, 9895
Homewood Residence-Rockefeller Gardens, 9896
Homewood at Crumland Farms, 8919
Homewood of Williamsport, 8920
Honeywell, 2678
Honolulu County Elderly Affairs Division, 869
Hoover Building, 1025
Hope Heart Institute, 6878
Hope: Alcoholics Anonymous, 7436
Hopedale Medical Complex: Medical Library, 11456
Horizon Air, 11928

Entry Name Index / I

Horizon Publishers, 3611
Horizons for the Blind, 7609
Horizontal Steering, 2975
Horn Control Switch, 2976
Hospice Alternative, 6022
Hospice Association of America, 151, 6010
Hospice Care for Patients with Advanced Progressive Dementia, 4963
Hospice Foundation of America (HFA), 152
Hospice House, 9662
Hospice Letter, 4043
Hospices Directory, 3752
Hospital Audiences, 153
Hospital Home Health, 4044
Hospital of the University of Pennsylvania, 7118
Houghton Mifflin, 4967
House Ear Institute, 6705, 6374, 6786
House Ear Institute: Athalie Irvine Clarke Library, 11340
House Ear Institute: Care Center Parent Resource Library, 11341
House of Travel, 12026
House of the Good Shepherd, 9789
Housing Choices and Well-Being of Older Adults: Proper Fit, 3638
Housing Options for Massachusetts Elders(HOME), 11148
Housing and Living Arrangement for the Elderly: A Selected Bibliography, 3639
Housing and Transportation of the Handicapped, 11929
Housing for Older Adults: Options and Answers, 3640
Housing for Seniors Report, 4045
Housing for the Elderly or Disabled, 154
Houston Bar Association: Judicare Program for the Elderly, 11266
Houston Department of Health and Human Services: Bureau of HIV Prevention, 4465
Houston Ear Research Foundation, 6674, 6802
Houston Harris County Area: Agency on Aging, 2326
Houston Public Library: Access Center, 11771
Houston Public Library: Acres Homes Branch, 11772
Houston Public Library: Bracewell Branch, 11773
Houston Public Library: Carnegie Branch, 11774
Houston Public Library: Collier Regional Branch, 11775
Houston Public Library: Dixon Branch, 11776
Houston Public Library: Flores Branch, 11777
Houston Public Library: Hillendahl Branch, 11778
Houston Public Library: Moody Branch, 11779
Houston Public Library: Park Place Regional Branch, 11780
Houston Public Library: Pleasantville Branch, 11781
Houston Public Library: Robinson-Westchase Branch, 11782
Houston Public Library: Scenic Woods Regional Branch, 11783
Houston Public Library: Smith Branch, 11784
Houston Public Library: Tuttle Branch, 11785
Houston Public Library: Young Branch, 11786
Houston-Galveston Area: Agency on Aging, 2327
Houston-Love Memorial Library, 11309
How Al-Anon Works for Families & Friends of Alcoholics, 7255
How Does a Blind Person Get Around?, 7954
How Drug Abuse Takes Profit Out of Buisness, 7351
How To Cook for People with Diabetes, 6205
How to Develop a Self-Help Group for Elders Losing Eyesight, 7955
How to Feel & Look Nifty After 50, 4046
How to Get the Most Out of Group Therapy, 7352
How to Get the Most Out of Your Hearing Aid, 6675
How to Interpret Your Biopsy and other Lab Reports, 5825
How to Measure and Inject Insulin, 6264
How to Start a Parkinson's Disease Support Group, 7005
How to Survive a Hearing Loss, 6510
How to Use Your Low Vision Glasses, 7956
Howard Good Samaritan Center Assited Living Center, 10277
Howard University Cancer Center, 5914
Howard University Social Work Library, 11391
Howtek, 3091
Hub, 7868
Hub City Developmental, 9182
Huckleberry Retirement Homes II, 8516
Huckleberry Retirement Homes III, 8517
Huckleberry Retirement Homes IV, 8518
Hudson County Office on Aging, 1654
Hudson Valley Branch of the Arthritis Foundation, 5107
Huerfano Las Animas: Area Agency on Aging, 647
Huffington Center on Aging, 4317
Huffman House, 10105
Human Growth & Development Associates, 11881
Human Kinetics Publishers, 3606, 3620, 3625, 3632, 3669, 3673, 3674, 3820, 3898, 6199, 6201, 7076
Human Resource Management and the Americans with Disabilities Act, 3641
Human Sciences Press, 3887
Human Services Building, 1412
Human Services Center, 2134
Humana Hospital-Michael Reese, 6799
Humana Press, 4655
Hume Home of Muskegon, 9055
Hunter College, 3576
Hunter College of City University of New York: Brookdale Center on Aging, 4318
Hunter College of the City University of New York: Health Professional Library, 11638
Hunter House Publisher, 11688, 11689, 11690, 11691, 11692, 11693, 11694, 11695, 11696, 11698, 11701, 11703
Hunter House Publishers, 7808
Hunter House Publishing, 11700
Hunterdon County Division of Senior Services, 1655
Hunters Glen at Grizzly Peak, 9350
Huntington Terrace Assisted Living, 10106
Huntington-Bedford-Fulton Area: Agency on Aging, 2120
Huntsville Subregional Library for the Blind, 11310
Hutchinson Homestead, 8806
Hutchinson Independent Living Center, 10761
Hydroxychloroquine, 5204
Hygenics Direct Company, 3260
Hypertension Center, 6908
Hypertension: An Integrated, Clinical Approach, 6912
Hyza Home, 9183

I

I Can Hear!, 6756
I Can Hear-II, 6757
I Can't Be Addicted Because..., 7353
I Can't Chew Cookbook, 11692
I Didn't Hear the Dragon Roar, 6511
I Only Hear You When I See Your Face, 6758
I See What You Say: Self Help Lipreading Program, 6759
I Think I Have a Hearing Problem! What Should I Do?, 6512
I'm Black and I'm Sober, 7256
I'm Pretty Old, 4146
IASP Secretariat, 155
ICON Group International, 6953
IDEAMATICS, 3122
IDF Patient and Family Handbook, 4047
IHS at Swan Manor, 10470
IL Resources of Contra Costa County-Fairfield, 10660
ILRU Directory of Centers, SILCs, and Related Organizations (Independent Living Research Utilization), 3753
ILRU Insights, 4048
ILRU Research/Training Center Independent Living, 4048
IMPACT, 10719
IN-SIGHT, 7610
IRA Reporter, 4049
Iberia Airlines of Spain, 11930
Ice Storm, 7354
Idaho Commission On Aging, 881
Idaho Commission for the Blind, 7611
Idaho Commission on Aging, 882, 11080
Idaho Council on Developmental Disabilities, 883
Idaho Department of Alcoholism & Substance Abuse, 7166
Idaho Developmental Disability Council, 884
Idaho Division Of Veterans Services, 885
Idaho Division of Tourism Development, 11961
Idaho Industrial Commission, 886
Idaho Mental Health Center, 887
Idaho Office on Aging, 888
Idaho State Tax Commission, 889
Idaho State University, 11448
Ideal Personal Care Assisted Living, 10471
Ideal-Phone, 3122
Idyll Arbor, 3595, 3596, 7063, 11882

Entry Name Index / I

If Blindness Comes, 7814
If Blindness Strikes; Don't Strike Out, 7815
If Someone Close to You Has a Problem with Alcohol or Other Drugs, 7355
If You Are a Professional, AA Wants to Work with You, 7356
If You Have Alzheimer's Disease: What You Should Know, What You Can Do, 5002
If You're Over 65 and Feeling Depressed..., 6088
If Your Parents Drink Too Much, 7357
Illinios Department of Revenue, 917
Illinois Assistive Technology Project, 918
Illinois Braille Messenger, 7869
Illinois Bureau of Tourism, 11962
Illinois Cancer Center, 5915
Illinois Church Action on Alcohol Problems, 7167
Illinois Client Assistance Program (CAP), 919
Illinois Council For The Blind, 7869
Illinois Council on Developmental Disability, 920
Illinois Department of Alcoholism and Substance Abuse, 7168
Illinois Department of Human Services: Office of Rehabilitation Services, 921
Illinois Department of Mental Health and Developmental Disabilities, 922
Illinois Department of Public Health, 3719, 4466
Illinois Department of Rehabilitation Services, 3725, 923
Illinois Department of Veterans Affairs, 924
Illinois Department on Aging, 3799, 925, 11091
Illinois Family & Social Services, 7169
Illinois Institute of Technology: Chicago Kent Law School Information Center, 11457
Illinois Office of Rehabilitation Services, 6561, 7845
Illinois Oncology Research Association, 5916
Illinois School for the Deaf Media Center, 11458
Illinois School for the Visually Impaired Library, 11459
Illinois School of Professional Psychology Meadows Campus Library, 11460
Illinois Society for the Prevention of Blindness, 7612
Illinois Workers Compensation Board, 926
Illinois-Iowa Center for Independent Living (IICIL), 10727
Immaculate Conception Home, II, 8093
Immanuel Lakeside Terrace, 9663
Immanuel Trinity Village, 9664
Immune Deficiency Foundation, 4047, 4467, 4555, 4556, 4557, 4567, 4568, 4576, 4209, 4650
Immune System: How it Works, 5826
Impact Publishers, 11883
Impact!, 3880
Imperial Care Center, 8519
Imperial County Area Agency on Aging, 555
Imperial Manor Nursing Home, 9665
Impotence Causes and Treatments, 4050
Impotence Information Center, 6931

Impotence Resource Center, 4150, 4167, 6939
Impotence World Association, 6932, 6940
Impotence: How to Overcome It, 6937
Impotents Anonymous, 6933
Improved Living, 9666
Improved Living House II, 9667
Improved Living II, 9668
In All Our Affairs: Making Crises Work for You, 6513
In Control, 5160
In Focus, 7957
In God's Care, 7257
In and Out of Time, 5031
In the Ear Hearing Aid Battery Extractor, 3282
In-Home Care Services Directory, 3754
InSight, 7958
Incare Of, 3881
Incarnate Word Personal Care Facility, 10472
Inclinator Company of America, 3356, 3374, 3382, 3383, 3400
Inclinette, 3383
Increasing Capabilities Access Network, 456
Independence, 10843
Independence Court of Hyattsville, 8921
Independence First, 10954
Independence Hill Assisted Living, 10473
Independence Manor at Hunterdon, 9790
Independence Now, 10784
Independence Place, 10776
Independence Resource Center, 10942
Independence Unlimited Inc., 10688
Independence, Inc., 10762
Independent Center-Southern Tier, 10872
Independent Connection, 10763
Independent Living Aids, 3026, 3084, 3089, 3117, 3136, 3180, 3183, 3312, 3463, 3464, 3468, 7969
Independent Living Center, 10622, 10819
Independent Living Center of Hudson Valley, 10873
Independent Living Center of Kern County, 10661
Independent Living Center of SouthernCalifornia (ILCSC), 10662
Independent Living Center of the North Shore & Cape Ann, 10792
Independent Living Center-Jasper, 10623
Independent Living Center-Lancaster, 10663
Independent Living Center-Santa Clarita, 10664
Independent Living Provider, 3882
Independent Living Research Utilization Program, 3753
Independent Living Resource Center, 10764, 10820
Independent Living Resource Center (ILRCSF), 10665
Independent Living Resource Contra Costa County-Antioch, 10666
Independent Living Resource Southwest Washington, 10949
Independent Living Resource of Contra Costa County, 10667
Independent Living Resources Center-Santa Barbara, 10669
Independent Living Resources Center-Santa Maria, 10668
Independent Living Resources Center-Ventura, 10670

Independent Living Resources, Inc. (ILR), 10906
Independent Living Resources-La Crosse, 10955
Independent Living Resources-Richland, 10956
Independent Living Services for Older Individuals who are Blind, 6375
Independent Living Services of Northern California, 10671
Independent Living of Northeast Kansas, 10765
Independent Living of the Hudson Valley, 10874
Independent Mobility Systems, 2990
Independent Resources-Wilmington, 10691
Independent Visually Impaired Enterprisers, 7613, 8012
Index to Alcoholics Anonymous, 7358
Indian Health Service, 7170, 7446
Indian River Estates-East, 8400
Indiana Aging Division, 978
Indiana Area Agency on Aging, 11097, 11102, 11103
Indiana Association of Area Agencies on Aging, 979
Indiana Chapter of the Arthritis Foundation, 5108
Indiana County Association for the Blind, 7614
Indiana Department of Aging and Community Services, 980
Indiana Department of Health Veteran's Home, 981
Indiana Department of Revenue, 982
Indiana Department of Veterans Affairs, 983
Indiana Developmental Disability Council, 984
Indiana Disability Determination Bureau, 985
Indiana Division of Addiction Services, 7171
Indiana Division of Aging, 11098
Indiana Family & Social Services Administration, 11098
Indiana Family Institute, 4319
Indiana Governor's Planning Council for People with Disabilities, 986
Indiana Hearing Aid Specialists Association, 6376
Indiana Legal Services: Senior Law Project, 11099
Indiana Protection & Advocacy Services, 987
Indiana Protection and Advocacy Agency, 11100
Indiana Public Employee's Retirement Fund, 988
Indiana School for the Deaf: Alumni Hall Library, 11482
Indiana Teachers Retirement Fund, 989
Indiana Tourism Division, 11963
Indiana University Bloomington Center on Aging and Aged, 4320
Indiana University Bloomington: Rural Center for the Study and Promotion of AIDS/STD Prevention (RCAP), 4605
Indiana University Human Genetics Center, 4321
Indiana University Laboratory for Experimental Oncology, 5917

Entry Name Index / I

Indiana University-Purdue University at Indianapolis: Center for Alzheimer's Disease & Related Neuropsychiatric Disorder, 5056
Indiana University: Diabetes Research and Training Center, 6272
Indiana University: General Clinical Research Center, 4322
Indiana University: Hypertension Research Center, 6923
Indiana University: Multipurpose Arthritis Center, 5109
Indiana University: Northwest Center for Medical Education, 6273
Indiana University: Pharmacology Research Laboratory, 6274
Indiana University: Purdue University at Indianapolis Hackney Dermatopathology Research Laboratory, 4323
Indianapolis Resource Center for Independent Living (IRCIL), 10748
Indianhead Estates, 8520
Individual Care of Texas, 10474
Indo-American Connection, 1656
Indoor Allergens: Assessing & Controlling Adverse Health Effects, 4659
Industrial Commission, 436
Industries for the Blind and Visually Impaired of Louisiana, 7615
Infections Linked to AIDS, 4563
Inflatable Invalid Ring, 3209
Info, Protection & Advocacy Cntr\Handicapped Indv., 3723
Info. Protection & Advocacy Ctr for Handicapped, 3746
InfoUSA, 6558
Information & Referral Services Directory Nursing Home, 3755
Information Access Project, 7870
Information Access Project: National Federation of the Blind, 7616
Information Central, 3791
Information on Glaucoma, 7959
Information on Macular Degeneration, 7960
Information, Protection & Advocacy for Persons with Disabilities, 728
Informer, 3883, 4051
Ingham Regional Assisted Living, 9056
Inheriting Hearing Loss, 6676
Inland Counties Legal Services for Seniors, 11003
Inland Point Assisted Living, 10107
Inn at Belden Village, 9897
Inn at Chestnut Hill, 9898
Inn at Cypress Village, 8401
Inn at Lakeview, 9899
Inn at Los Patios, 10475
Inn at Orchard Park, 10476
Inn at Quail Haven, 9507
Inn at Silver Lake, 8985
Inn at University Village, 8402
Inn on Westport, 10278
Innerlip Plates, 3338
Innovation Management Group, 3079
Innovation of the Year Awards, 2643
Innovations in Aging, 3884
Innovative Products Unlimited, 3521
Innoventions, Inc., 3135
Inside MS, 3885
Insight, 7617, 7871
Institute for Cancer and Blood Research, 5918

Institute for Community Inclusion, 4324
Institute for Driver Rehabilitation, 2977
Institute for Health & Aging, 3849
Institute for Learning in Retirement, 2817
Institute for Life Course and Aging, 353
Institute for Metabolic Research, 6275
Institute for Retired Persons, 2808, 2907
Institute for Retired Professionals, 2741, 2754
Institute for Retired Professionals and Executives, 2859
Institute for Retired Professionals atSyracuse, 2860
Institute for Senior Education, 2861
Institute for Senior Scholars, 2877
Institute for Socioeconomic Studies Library, 11639
Institute of Developmental Neuroscience and Aging, 4325
Institute of New Dimensions, 2755
Institute of the Neurosciences Research Program, 5057
Institute on Black Chemical Abuse, 7172
Institutions Discount Package, 7359
Institutions Service Kit, 7360
Int'l Association of Pysical Activity/Aging/Sports, 4286
Int'l Society/Argumentative/Alternative Comm., 3833
Integrated Care Communities, 8196
Integris Baptist Medical Center: Wann Langston Memorial Library, 11721
Intensive Diabetes Management, 6206
Interdisciplinary Program in Cell and Molecular Pharmacology, 7461
Interim Assisted Care, 9184
Interim Healthcare, 9185
Interlachen Senior Suites, 9186
Intermediate Conversational SignLanguage, 6514
Internal Revenue Service, US Dept of the Treasury, 322
International Association for the Study of Pain, 155
International Association of Biomedical Gerontology, 156
International Association of Eating Disorder Professionals, 4210
International Braille Research Center, 7618
International Braille and Technology Center for the Blind, 7619
International Catholic Deaf Association, 6377
International Cemetery and Funeral Association, 6011
International Center for Hearing & Speech Research, 6803
International Center for the Disabled, 4326
International Committee of Sports for the Deaf, 2683
International Communication Service for the Blind, 7620
International Deaf/Tek, Inc., 3261
International Diabetes Center: Institute for Research & Education Health System, 6276
International Directory of Libraries for the Disabled, 3756
International Directory of Research and Researchers in Comparative Gerontology, 3757

International Foundation for Bowel Dysfunction, 6946
International Health Guide for Senior Citizen Travelers, 3642
International Health Research Foundation, 4606
International Hearing Dog, 6378
International Hearing Dog (IHDI), 6587
International Hearing Society, 3832, 6364, 6738, 6379
International Hearing Society: Hearing Aid Helpline, 6380
International Holistic Center, 5688
International Journal of Aging and Human Development, 3886
International Journal of Impotence Research, 6941
International Journal of Technology and Aging, 3887
International Kaf/Tek, 6381
International Ladies' Garment Workers Union Research Department Library, 11640
International Lawyers in Alcoholics Anonymous, 7173
International Lutheran Deaf Association, 6382
International Organization for the Education of the Hearing Impaired, 6383
International Psychogeriatric Association, 157
International Psychogeriatrics, 3888
International Rehabilitation Medicine Association, 158
International Rehabilitation Review, 3889
International Society for Quality of Life Studies, 159
International Society for Sexual Medicine, 6942
International Society for Traumatic Stress Studies, 160
International Society of Psychiatric Consultation Liaison Nurses, 161
International Specialized Book Services, 6951
International Task Force on Euthanasia and Assisted Suicide, 6012
International Telephone Directory for TDD Users, 3758
International Ventilator Users Network (IVUN) News, 4052
Internet Health Coalition, 4211
Interpretation: A Sociolinguistic Model, 6515
Interpreter Views, 6581, 6677
Intertec Publishing Corporation, 3879
Intervention Practices in the Retention of Competitive Employment Among Individuals who are Blind, 7816
Interventions for Alzheimer's Disease: A Caregiver's Complete Reference, 4964
Interview with Kirsten Gonzales, 6760
Interwood Publications, 6092
Intestinal Disease Foundation, 4053, 6947
Intestinal Fortitude, 4053
Intrepid USA-Becklund, 9187
Introduction to Cochlear Implants, 6678
Introduction to Communication, 6516
Introduction to Stroke, 7063
Invacare, 3018, 3025, 3052, 3397, 3533, 3543
Invacare Corporation, 3262

Invaluable Guide to Life After Stroke: An Owner's Manual, 7064
Invisible Condition: The Human Side of Hearing Loss, 6517
Iowa Chapter of the Arthritis Foundation, 5110
Iowa Client Assistance Program, 1020
Iowa Commission of Veterans Affairs, 1021
Iowa Commission on Persons with Disabilities, 1022
Iowa Department of Elder Affairs, 11113, 11114, 11115, 1023
Iowa Department of Elder Affairs: Legal Assistance, 11110
Iowa Department of Human Rights: Deaf Services Commissions, 1024
Iowa Department of Revenue & Finance, 1025
Iowa Developmental Disability Council, 1026
Iowa Division of MHMRDD: Office of Human Services, 1027
Iowa Division of Substance Abuse & Health Promotion, 7174
Iowa Hearing Association, 6384
Iowa Legal Aid, 11109
Iowa Library For The Blind And Physically Handicapped, 11493
Iowa Lutheran Hospital, 4795
Iowa Oncology Research Association, 5919
Iowa Program for Assistive Technology, 1028
Iowa Protection & Advocacy for the Disabled, 1029
Iowa Protection and Advocacy Agency, 11111
Iowa Regional Library for the Blind & Physically Handicapped, 7621
Iowa State Bar: Young Lawyer Section Committee on Delivery of Legal Services to the Elderly, 11112
Iowa Tourism Office/Iowa Travel Guide, 11964
Iowa Workers Compensation, 1030
Ireland Cancer Center at Case Western Reserve University, 5920
Iron Workers Local 24 Retirees Club International Association of Ironworkers, 648
Iron Workers Local 25 Retirees Club of the International Association, 1350
Irving Diener Award, 2644
Irving S Wright Award of Distinction, 2645
Irvington Institute for ImmunologicalResearch, 4327
Is AA for Me?, 7361
Is AA for You?, 7362
Is There a Safe Tobacco?, 4054
Is There an Alcoholic in Your Life?, 7363
Is it Alzheimer's? Warning Signs You Should Know, 5003
Island View Manor, 9188
Isothermal Planning & Development Commission, 1893
Issues for Aging America: Employees and Eldercare: A Briefing Book, 3643
Issues in Aging and Vision: A Curriculum for University Programs and In-Service Training, 7817
It Happened to Alice, 7364
It Sure Beats Sitting in a Cell, 7365
It's All Right to Be Angry, 7961

It's Our Hearing Loss: What Families Need to Know and Do, 6679
Ivins, Phillips, Barker Library, 11392

J

JA Preston Corporation, 3248
JADARA, 3890
JADARA California, 3890
JAI Press, 3895
JBI Points, 7962
JE Stewart Teaching Tools, 3120
JEA Senior Living, 10596
JGB Cassette Library International, 11641
JHMHC, 4392
JL and Helen Kellogg Cancer Care Center, 5921
JP Tarcher, 4661
Jack Weinberg Memorial Award for Geriatric Psychiatry, 2646
Jackson Center for Independent Living, 10924
Jackson County Department on Aging, 1894
Jackson Foundation for Medical Research & Education, 6879
Jackson Friendly Home, 9057
Jackson House, 10108
Jackson Laboratory: Joan Staats Library, 11526
Jackson Park Christian Home, 10356
Jacksonville Public Libraries, 11417
Jacksonville Public Library, 11416
Jacksonville Subregional Talking Book Library, 11417
Jacobus TenBroek Award, 2647
James Graham Brown Cancer Center, 5911
James P Mills Arthritis Resource Center, 5111
Jason Aronson, 4531, 7059
Jason Aronson Publishers, 6017, 6025
Jasper Sunrise Village, 9189
Jawonio Vocational Center, 1866
Jay Cushion, 3210
Jay Medical Ltd., 3210
Jean Camper Cahn Award, 2648
Jefferson Council on Aging, 1153
Jefferson County Area: Agency on Aging, 2121
Jefferson County Office for Aging, 1783
Jefferson County Office of Senior Citizens, 376
Jefferson County Office of Senior Citizens Services (OSCS), 10971
Jefferson Industries, 3202, 3203, 3227, 3228
Jefferson Medical College, 4377
Jefferson Place Assisted Living, 10477
Jefferson's Garden, 10026
Jelly Bean Switch, 3123
Jennings McCall Center II, 10109
Jersey Ridge, 8686
Jesse M. Parker Building, 11110
Jessica Kingsley Publishers, 3601, 3634
Jewish Association for Services for the Aged, 1784
Jewish Braille Institute Of America, 7872
Jewish Braille Institute of America, 7962, 7622
Jewish Braille Review, 7872
Jewish Communal Retirees Association of Los Angeles, 556

Jewish Community Relations Council of Greater Boston, 1288
Jewish Council for the Aging, 3580
Jewish Guild for the Blind, 7963
Jewish Guild for the Blind Newsletter, 7963
Jewish Senior Life Center, 8687
Jewish Veteran, 3983
Job Opportunities for the Blind, 7623
John F Germany Public Library: Special Collections, 11393
John George Home, 9058
John H. McAulay Award, 2649
John H. Winters Human Services Complex, 11268
John Hopkins Asthma & Allergy Center, 4682
John Knox Village of Central Florida, 8403
John Knox Village of Florida, 8404
John Knox Village of Tampa Bay, 8405
John L McClellan Memorial Veterans'Hospital Research Office, 6880
John Milton Magazine, 7873
John Milton Society for the Blind, 7847, 7873
John Muir Publications, 11884
John O. Pastore Center, 11247
John P Caulfield Technology Extension Center for Cancer Treatment, 5922
John Wiley & Sons, 4959, 6070, 6197
Johns Hopkins Behavioral Pharmacology Research Unit, 7462
Johns Hopkins Oncology Center, 5923
Johns Hopkins University, 2807
Johns Hopkins University Health Services Research and Development Center, 4328
Johns Hopkins University Institute for Policy Studies, 4329
Johns Hopkins University Press, 3656, 4523, 4533, 4945, 4962, 5161, 5800, 6071, 6986, 7065
Johns Hopkins University School of Hygiene, 4330
Johns Hopkins University: Alzheimer's Disease Research Center, 5058
Johns Hopkins University: Asthma and Allergy Center, 4683
Johns Hopkins University: Center for Communication Problems, 4607
Johns Hopkins University: Center for Immunization Research, 4330
Johns Hopkins University: Dana Center for Preventive Ophthalmology, 8044
Johns Hopkins: Health After 50, 3891
Johnson Assisted Living, 10110
Johnson Assisted Living Center, 10111
Johnson County Area Agency on Aging, 1063
Johnson Park Place, 9190
Jones Harrison Residence Assisted Living, 9191
Jones and Bartlett Publishers, 4514, 6979
Jonsson Comprehensive Cancer Center, 5924
Joslin Diabetes Center, 6195, 6277
Jossey Bass Inc, 6020
Journal of AAA, 3892
Journal of Aging & Pharmacotherapy, 3893
Journal of Aging & Social Policy, 3894
Journal of Aging Studies, 3895
Journal of Aging and Ethnicity, 3896
Journal of Aging and Health, 3897

Journal of Aging and Physical Activity, 3898
Journal of American Aging Association, 3899
Journal of Cancer Education, 5808
Journal of Developmental and Physical Disabilities, 3900
Journal of Elder Abuse & Neglect: An International Journal, 3901
Journal of Elder Abuse and Neglect, 3902
Journal of Ethics, Law, and Aging, 3903
Journal of Gerontological Nursing, 3904
Journal of Gerontological Social Work, 3905
Journal of Housing for the Elderly, 3906
Journal of Intergenerational Relationships: Programs, Policy, and Research, 3907
Journal of Mental Health and Aging, 3908, 6081
Journal of Nutrition for the Elderly, 3909
Journal of Rehabilitation, 3910
Journal of Religious Gerontology, 3911
Journal of Religious Gerontology: The Interdisciplinary Journal of Practice, Theory, and Applied Research, 3912
Journal of Speech and Hearing Disorders, 6582
Journal of Speech and Hearing Research, 6583
Journal of Speech-Language-Hearing Research, 6584
Journal of Stroke and Cerebrovascular Diseases, 7079
Journal of Therapeutic Horticulture, 3913
Journal of Vision Rehabilitation, 7874
Journal of Visual Impairment and Blindness, 7875
Journal of Visual Impairments and Blindness, 7876
Journal of Women and Aging, 3914
Journal of the Academy of Rehabilitation Audiology, 6585
Journal of the American Geriatrics Society, 3915
Journal of the American Psychoanalytic Association, 6082
Journal of the Association for Persons with Severe Handicaps, 3916
Journals of Gerontology; Psychological Sciences & Social Sciences, 6083
Journey Into the DEAF-WORLD, 6518
Journey Into the World of the Deaf, 6519
Journey to Pain Relief, 11693
Journeys East, 12027
Joy of Laziness, 11694
Joy of Listening: An Auditory Training Program, 6520
Joy of Signing, 6521, 6761
Joyce's Orchard Residential Care Home, 8521
Joystick Driving Control, 2978
Judge Advocates Association, 162
Judge David L Bazelon Center for Mental Health Law, 11394
Junction Center for Independent Living, 10943
Junction City Retirement & Assisted Living Facility, 10112
Juneau Pioneers Home, 8094
Juniper House, 10113
Just Like Home, 9192
Just Like Home at Orange City, 8406
Just One Little Bite Can Hurt! Important Facts About Anaphylaxis, 4669
Just Say No International, 7146
Just the Facts & More Kit, 4965

K

K-NOPF Assisted Living Center-Matthew Building, 10279
K-NOPF Assisted Living-John Building, 10280
K-NOPF Assisted Living-Luke Building, 10281
K-NOPF Assisted Living-Mark Building, 10282
KEDDO Area: Agency on Aging, 2009
KG Saur/ A Division of RR Bowker, 3756
KI BOIS Retired Senior Volunteer Program, 2010
KLM Royal Dutch/Northwest Airlines, 11931
Kaiser Foundation Research Institute, 4608
Kaleidoscope: Exploring the Expirence of Disability through Literature & Fine Arts, 3917
Kanawha County Public Library, 11837
Kansas Alcohol and Drug Abuse Services, 7175
Kansas Association for the Blind and Visually Impaired, 7625
Kansas Association for the Blind andVisually Impaired, 7624
Kansas Association of Area Agencies on Aging, 1063
Kansas Chapter of the Arthritis Foundation, 5112
Kansas City Association for the Blind, 7626
Kansas Client Assistance Program, 1064
Kansas Commission for the Deaf and Hard of Hearing, 6385
Kansas Commission on Disability Concerns, 1065
Kansas Commission on Veterans Affairs, 1066
Kansas Cosmosphere and Space Center, 2791
Kansas Department of Aging: Legal Assistance Services for Older Adults (KDOA), 11117
Kansas Department of Health & Environment, 4468
Kansas Department of Human Resources, 1072
Kansas Department of Human Resources: Commission on Disabilities Concern, 1067
Kansas Department of Revenue, 1068
Kansas Department of Social and Rehabilitation Services, 1069
Kansas Department on Aging, 11117, 1070
Kansas Developmental Disability Council, 1071
Kansas Division of Services for the Blind, 7627
Kansas Employment Services and Job Training Program Liaison, 1072
Kansas Geriatric Education Center (KS-GEC), 2792
Kansas Hearing Aid Association, 6386
Kansas Hearing Society, 6387
Kansas Masonic Home, 8807

Kansas Mental Health & Retardation Service, 1073
Kansas Protection and Advocacy Agency &Disability Rights Center of Kansas, 11118
Kansas Public Employees Retirement System, 1074
Kansas Specialty Dog Service, 1075
Kansas State Historical Society: Library & Archives Division, 11497
Kansas State Library Talking Book Service, 11498
Kansas State University Galichia Center for Aging, 4331
Kansas State University: Center for Basic Cancer Research, 5925
Kansas Travel & Tourism, 11965
Kansas University Medical Center, 4401
Kaplan Cancer Center, 5926
Karcher Estates, 8522
Kareco International, 3522
Karmanos Cancer Institute Research Library, 11563
Karrington Commons, 9568
Karrington Cottages, 9569
Kat's Eldercare, 8095
Kates-Boylston Publications, 3693
Kathy's Place, 9351
Kauai County Office of Elderly Affairs, 870
Kayak and Rafting Expeditions, 12028
Keep It Simple, 7258
Keep Quit, 7259
Kelly's Retirement Home I, 10283
Kelly's Retirement Home II, 10284
Kenai Peninsula Independent Living Center-Homer, 10627
Kenai Peninsula Independent Living-Central Peninsula, 10628
Kenai Senior Connection, 421
Kendal at Oberlin, 9900
Kendall Communications, 3993
Kennington Pointe, 10357
Kensington, 8688
Kensington Cottages at Quail Creek, 10478
Kensington Cottages by Centex, 10479
Kensington Park Woodlands-Groves, 8922
Kent County Library for the Blind, 11564
Kent State University Exercise Physiology Lab, 4332
Kent State University Gerontology Center, 4333
Kentucky Bar Association: Committee on Legal Concerns of Elderly Clients, 11119
Kentucky Bar Association: Senior Lawyers Section, 11120
Kentucky Cabinet for Education, Arts and The Humanities: Commission for the Deaf and Hearing Impaired, 1108
Kentucky Cabinet for Health and Family Services, 11121
Kentucky Cabinet for Workforce Development: Department for the Blind, 1109
Kentucky Cancer Program, 5927
Kentucky Chapter of the Arthritis Foundation, 5230, 5113
Kentucky Chapter: Alexander Graham Bell Association for the Deaf, 6388
Kentucky Client Assistance Program, 1110
Kentucky Council on Developmental Disabilities, 1111
Kentucky Department for the Blind, 7628

Kentucky Department of Travel, 11966
Kentucky Department of Veterans Affairs, 1112
Kentucky Department of Workers Claims, 1113
Kentucky Division of Aging Services, 11121
Kentucky Division of Mental Health, 1114
Kentucky Division of Substance Abuse, 7176
Kentucky Division: Prevent Blindness America, 7629
Kentucky Historical Society-Thomas DClark Research Library, 11510
Kentucky Legal Aid, 11122
Kentucky Office of Aging Services, 1115
Kentucky Protection & Advocacy Division, 1116
Kentucky Protection and Advocacy Agency, 11123
Kentucky Retirement Systems, 1117
Kentucky Revenue Cabinet, 1118
Kentucky River Area: Agency on Aging, 1119
Kentucky State Affliate of American Academy of Audiology, 6389
Kentucky Talking Book Library, 11511
Kentucky Teachers Retirement System, 1120
Kentuckyiana Regional Planning &Development Agency (KIPDA), 1121
Kenwood Heritage Living, 9193
Kenwood Retirement Community, 9194
Kenwood of Lake View, 8592
Kern County Aging And Adult Services, 557
Kerner Ridge Assisted Living, 9508
KerrTar Regional Council of Governments Area: Agency on Aging, 1895
Kerrville State Hospital Professional Library, 11787
Key Elements of Dementia Care, 4966
Key Holder, 3307
Key Publications, 11885
Keys to Living with Hearing Loss, 6522
Keystone Award, 2650
Keystone Bluffs, 9195
Keystone Senior Suites, 8689
Kilchis House, 10114
Kilroy House, 10480
Kimball County Manor Nusing Home, 9669
Kinedyne Corporation-Engineered Products Division, 2955
Kings Manor Methodist Retirement System, 2328
Kings Manor Personal Care Home, 10481
Kings Tulare Area: Agency on Aging, 558
Kingsborough Community College, 2865
Kingsley Place at Alexandria, 8865
Kingsley Place at Lafayette, 8866
Kingsley Place at Oakwell, 10482
Kingsley Place at Shreveport, 8867
Kingsley Place at Stonebridge Ranch, 10483
Kingstar International America, 3195
Kingston Residence of Perrysburg, 9901
Kingsway Assisted Living, 9196
Kinyon Residence, 9197
Kirby Health Center, 4830
Kirkwood House, 9670
Kirkwood Manor, 10285
Kirkwood by the River, 8066
Kit Carson And Lincoln Counties RSVP, 649

Kitsap County Area: Agency on Aging, 2511
Kiva of Mount Dora, 8407
Kiva of Palatka, 8408
Kiwanis Club of Bay Minette, 383
Klamath Basin Senior Citizens' Council, 2052
Klassic-Plus, 3522
Kluwer Academic/Plenum Publishers, 3900
Knitting Needle Holder, 3290
Knock Light, 3308
Knollwood Gardens Rest Home, 9509
Knollwood Manor, 10358
Know Your Eye, 7964
Knowing Your Rights, 3644, 4055
Knowlwood Assisted Living, 8067
Knutson Place Apartments, 9198
Kobernick/Anchin, 8409
Kon Tiki Travel Agency, 12029
Korean Senior Citizens Association of Greater Philadelphia, 2122
Kosgrove Estates Assisted Living, 8690
Krannert Institute of Cardiology, 6881
Kregel Publications, 6028
Kristianna's Assisted Living Facility, 8410
Kroepke Kontrols, 2957, 2965, 2971, 2972, 2973, 2974, 2976, 2980
Kuschall of America, 3534
Kuschall of America/Graham Field Health Products, 3505, 3506, 3507
Kuzell Institute for Arthritis and Infectious Diseases, 5114

L

LC Technologies, 3116
LEVO Standing Wheelchairs, 3523
LEVO USA Inc., 3523
LIFE, 2878
LIFE Center for Independent Living, 10728
LIFE of North Mississippi, 10812
LIFE of South Mississippi, 10813
LOW PROFILE Dual Compartment Cushion, 3211
LOW PROFILE Single Compartment Cushion, 3212
LPB, 3124
LRC for Students with Disabilities: MSU Library Reference Department, 11761
LRP Publications, 3760, 4025, 4536
LS & S Products, 3263
LS&S Group, 3783
LSS/Westwind, 9199
LT Switch, 3125
La Bonnie Vie, 9200
La Casa Asperanza Assisted Living, 8122
La Fayette Subregional Library for the Blind and Physically Disabled, 11440
La Jolla Cancer Research Foundation, 5928
La Jolla Institute for Allergy andImmunology, 4684
La Palma Recreation & Community Services, 559
La Posada, 8123
La Quinta Senior Center, 560
La Siena, 8124
LaBac Systems, 3558
LaFarge Institute of Lifelong Learning, 2949
Label Reading and Shopping, 4147
Laboure College Library, 11550

Lackawanna County Area: Agency on Aging, 2123
Ladies Auxiliary to the VFW, 3965
Lafayette Advocacy Center, 11127
Lafayette Good Samartian Assisted Living, 9201
Lafourche Council on Aging, 1154
Lake Barrington Woods, 8593
Lake County Area: Agency on Aging, 2459
Lake County Center for Independent Living (LCCIL), 10729
Lake Cumberland Area Development District Area: Agency on Aging, 1122
Lake Ridge Manor at Ebenezer Covenant Home, 9202
Lake Towers Retirement Community, 8411
Lakeridge Place, 10484
Lakeshore Wedgewood, 10359
Lakeside Assisted Living Community, 10115
Lakeside Assisted Living Residence, 10286
Lakeside Manor, 9203
Lakeview Lodge, 8691
Lakeview Ranch Adult Foster Care, 9204
Lakeview Retirement Residence, 9205
Lakeview Village, 8692
Lakewood 24 Hour Personal Care, 10485
Lakewood Pine Senior Housing, 9206
Lakewood Pointe Assisted Living, 10116
Lakewood Quarters Retirement Community, 8868
Lakewood Village: Cummings Assisted Living Apartments, 10486
Lamar University Station, 6416
Lancaster Assisted Living, 10117
Lancaster County Association for the Blind, 7630
Lancaster County Council on Aging, 2227
Lancaster County Office of Aging, 2124
Lancaster Village, 10118
Lancaster Woods, 10119
Landing of Canton, 9902
Landmark Retirement Community, 8869
Landmark at Fall River, 8986
Landmark at Ocean View, 8987
Landsmeer Ridge Retirement Community, 8693
Lane Council of Governments: Senior and Disabled Services Division, 2053
Lane County Law and Advocacy Center: Senior Law Service, 11231
Laptops/Word Processors, 3126
Laramie Lyceum, 2952
Large Button Speaker Phone, 3127
Large Print Loan Library, 7818
Large Print Loan Library Catalog, 3759, 7965
Large Print Telephone Dial, 3128
Large Print Touch-Telephone Overlays, 3129
Large Print Typewriter, 3130
Large-Room Listening Systems for Hard of Hearing People, 6680
Larimer County Office on Aging (LCOA), 11020
Larkspur Land Residential & Assisted Living Center, 8523
Las Vegas-Clark County Library District, 11604
Las Villas De Carlsbad, 8197
Las Villas Del Norte, 8198
Laszlo Corporation, 3415

Entry Name Index / L

Latchloc Automatic Wheelchair Tiedown, 3552
Late-Deafened Adults: A Selected Annotated Bibliography, 6681
Laurel Gardens at Milford, 8276
Laurel Gardens of Avon, 8277
Laurel Gardens of Hamden, 8278
Laurel Gardens of Orange, 8279
Laurel Gardens of Woodbridge, 8280
Laurel Lake Retirement Community, 9903
Laurel Lodge Assisted Living Home, 9207
Laurel Park West, 9059
Laurelhurst House Assisted Living Community, 10120
Laurels Edge, 9208
Laurels in Highland Creek, 9510
Laurels in the Village at Carolina Place, 9511
Laurent Clerc National Deaf Education Center, 11395
Law and Regulatory Affairs, 11025
Lawndale Manor, 9512
Lawrence County Area Agency on Aging, 2125
Lawrence Erlbaum Associates Publishers, 4518
Lawrence Research Group, 3797
Lawyers Glen Retirement Living Center, 9513
Lazy Days RV Center, 2979
Leading National Publications of and for Deaf People, 6566
Leading National Publications of and for Deaf People, 6682
League for the Hard of Hearing, 6683, 6804
League of Human Dignity, 10757
League of Human Dignity Independent Living Center, 10845
League of Older Americans, 2460
Learning AIDS, 4526
Learning Activities for Mature People, 2926
Learning Resources, 11854
Learning Resources Network (LERN), 2793
Learning To Hear Again, 6523
Learning in Later Life, 2818
Learning in Retirement Program (LIR), 2720
Learning is Fun Together, 2833
Learning is for Everyone, 2809
Learning to Live Well with Diabetes, 6207
Learning to See: American Sign Language as a Second Language, 6524
Learning to Speak Alzheimer's A Groundbreaking Approach for Everyone Dealing with the Disease, 4967
Leavenworth County Genealogical Society Library, 11499
Leavenworth Homestead, 8808
Lebanon County Area: Agency on Aging, 2126
Lebensraum Retirement Residence, 9671
Lee County Subregional Library for the Blind and Physically Handicapped, 11418
Lee Russell Council of Governments: Area Agency on Aging, 377
Lee's Living Center, 9514
Left Foot Gas Pedal, 2980
Leg Elevation Board, 3384
Legacy, 9672
Legacy Homes Assisted Living, 10610
Legacy Link, 838
Legacy Terrace, 9673
Legal Action Center, 4056

Legal Advocate Program: Pinal-Gila Council for Senior Citizens, 10984
Legal Aid Service of Northeastern Minnesota (LASNEM): Duluth Office, 11161
Legal Aid Services of Oklahoma, 11225
Legal Aid Services of Oregon: Senior LawProject, 11232
Legal Aid Society of Hawaii, 11068
Legal Aid Society of Hawaii: Hilo, 11069
Legal Aid Society of Hawaii: Honolulu, 11070
Legal Aid Society of Hawaii: Kaunakakai, 11071
Legal Aid Society of Hawaii: Lanai City, 11072
Legal Aid Society of Hawaii: Lihu'e, 11073
Legal Aid Society of Hawaii: Maui, 11074
Legal Aid of Arkansas, 10992
Legal Aid of East Tennessee (LAET), 11258
Legal Aid of North Carolina, 11212
Legal Aid of Southeastern Pennsylvania, 11238
Legal Aid of Western Missouri: Kansas City, 11171
Legal Assistance Corporation of Central Massachusetts: Senior Citizens Advocacy Program, 11149
Legal Assistance for Elders in Connecticut, 11027
Legal Assistance to the Elderly, 11004
Legal Center for People with Disabilities, 640, 2420
The Legal Center for People with Disabilities, 631
Legal Center for People with Disabilities and Older People, 11021
Legal Center for the Elderly and Disabled, 11005
Legal Counsel for the Elderly, 11045, 11886
Legal Information and Referral Service for the Elderly, 11246
Legal Rights of Hearing-Impaired People, 6525
Legal Rights of Persons with Disabilities: An Analysis of Federal Law, 3760
Legal Services Programs for Elders: Bridgeport, 11028
Legal Services Programs for Elders: Hartford, 11029
Legal Services Programs for Elders: Waterbury, 11030
Legal Services Programs for Elders: Willimantic, 11031
Legal Services for Older Adults in Utah, 11271
Legal Services for Seniors, 11006
Legal Services for the Elderly, 11202, 11213
Legal Services for the Elderly, Disabled or Disadvantaged of Western New York, 11203
Legal Services for the Elderly: Area Agency on Aging, 10972
Legal Services for the Elderly: Augusta, 11132
Legal Services for the Elderly: Lewiston, 11133
Legal Services of New Jersey: Atlantic City, 11189
Legal Services of New Jersey: Edison, 11190
Legal Services of North Dakota, 11217

Legends Park Assisted Living Community, 8524
Lehigh University Center for Social Research, 4334
Lehigh Valley Center for Independent Living, 10915
Leisure Living, 10287, 11887
Leisure-Lift, 3426
Leominster Crossings, 8988
Lessons in Laughter: The Autobiography of a Deaf Actor, 6526
Lester Dual-Mode Battery Charger, 3553
Lester Electrical, 3553, 3554
Lestronic II, 3554
Let's Live, 3918
Let's Solve the Smokeword Puzzle, 4057
Let's Talk, 7366
Let's Talk About Depression, 6089
Letter Writing Guide, 3463
Letter to a Woman Alcoholic, 7367
Lettering Guide Value Pack, 3464
Letting Go of the Need to Control, 7368
Leukemia & Lymphoma Society, 5689
Leukemia & Lymphoma Society: Alabama Chapter, 5690
Leukemia & Lymphoma Society: Austin Office, 5691
Leukemia & Lymphoma Society: Central Florida Chapter, 5692
Leukemia & Lymphoma Society: Central New York Chapter, 5693
Leukemia & Lymphoma Society: Central Ohio Chapter, 5694
Leukemia & Lymphoma Society: Central Pennsylvania Chapter, 5695
Leukemia & Lymphoma Society: Central Valley Branch, 5696
Leukemia & Lymphoma Society: Connecticut Chapter, 5697
Leukemia & Lymphoma Society: Desert Mountain States Chapter, 5698
Leukemia & Lymphoma Society: Eastern Iowa Satellite Office, 5699
Leukemia & Lymphoma Society: Eastern Philadelphia Chapter, 5700
Leukemia & Lymphoma Society: Gateway Chapter, 5701
Leukemia & Lymphoma Society: Georgia Chapter, 5702
Leukemia & Lymphoma Society: Greater Los Angeles Chapter, 5703
Leukemia & Lymphoma Society: Greater Sacramento Area, 5704
Leukemia & Lymphoma Society: Idaho Branch Office, 5705
Leukemia & Lymphoma Society: Illinois Chapter, 5706
Leukemia & Lymphoma Society: Indiana Chapter, 5707
Leukemia & Lymphoma Society: Iowa Branch Office, 5708
Leukemia & Lymphoma Society: Kansas Chapter, 5709
Leukemia & Lymphoma Society: Kentucky Chapter, 5710
Leukemia & Lymphoma Society: Las Vegas Office, 5711
Leukemia & Lymphoma Society: Lehigh Valley Office, 5712
Leukemia & Lymphoma Society: Long Island Chapter, 5713

Entry Name Index / L

Leukemia & Lymphoma Society: Louisiana Chapter, 5714
Leukemia & Lymphoma Society: Maryland Chapter, 5715
Leukemia & Lymphoma Society: Massachusetts Chapter, 5716
Leukemia & Lymphoma Society: Michigan Chapter, 5717
Leukemia & Lymphoma Society: Mid-America Chapter, 5718
Leukemia & Lymphoma Society: Minnesota Chapter, 5719
Leukemia & Lymphoma Society: Mississippi Chapter, 5720
Leukemia & Lymphoma Society: Nebraska Chapter, 5721
Leukemia & Lymphoma Society: New Mexico Office, 5722
Leukemia & Lymphoma Society: New York City Chapter, 5723
Leukemia & Lymphoma Society: North Carolina Chapter, 5724
Leukemia & Lymphoma Society: North Texas Chapter, 5725
Leukemia & Lymphoma Society: Northern California Chapter, 5726
Leukemia & Lymphoma Society: Northern Florida Chapter, 5727
Leukemia & Lymphoma Society: Northern New Jersey Chapter, 5728
Leukemia & Lymphoma Society: Northern Ohio Chapter, 5729
Leukemia & Lymphoma Society: Oklahoma Chapter, 5730
Leukemia & Lymphoma Society: Oregon Chapter, 5731
Leukemia & Lymphoma Society: Palm Beach Chapter, 5732
Leukemia & Lymphoma Society: Raleigh Office, 5733
Leukemia & Lymphoma Society: Rhode Island Chapter, 5734
Leukemia & Lymphoma Society: Rocky Mountain Chapter, 5735
Leukemia & Lymphoma Society: San Diego & Hawaii Chapter, 5736
Leukemia & Lymphoma Society: South Carolina Chapter, 5737
Leukemia & Lymphoma Society: Southern Florida Chapter, 5738
Leukemia & Lymphoma Society: Southern New Jersey Shore Region Chapter, 5739
Leukemia & Lymphoma Society: Southern Ohio Chapter, 5740
Leukemia & Lymphoma Society: Southwest Missouri Satellite Office, 5741
Leukemia & Lymphoma Society: Southwest Texas Chapter, 5742
Leukemia & Lymphoma Society: Suncoast Chapter, 5743
Leukemia & Lymphoma Society: Tennessee Chapter, 5744
Leukemia & Lymphoma Society: Texas Gulf Coast, 5745
Leukemia & Lymphoma Society: Tri-County Chapter, 5746
Leukemia & Lymphoma Society: Upstate New York Chapter, 5747
Leukemia & Lymphoma Society: Utah Office, 5748
Leukemia & Lymphoma Society: Virginia Chapter, 5749
Leukemia & Lymphoma Society: Washington & Alaska Chapter, 5750
Leukemia & Lymphoma Society: West Virginia Branch, 5751
Leukemia & Lymphoma Society: Western New York & Finger Lakes Chapter, 5752
Leukemia & Lymphoma Society: Western Pennsylvania/West Virginia Chapter, 5753
Leukemia & Lymphoma Society: Wisconsin Chapter, 5754
Leukemia Research Foundation, 5929
Leukemia Society of America, 5713, 4212, 5755
Leukemia Society of America: Delaware Chapter, 5756
Leukemia Society of America: National Capitol Area Chapter, 5757
Leukemia Society of America: Northern Nevada Office, 5758
Levas, 3876
Lewis County Office for the Aging, 1785
Lewiston Public Library, 11527
Lexington Place, 10487
Lexington School for the Deaf, 6390
Lexington School for the Deaf Library Media Center, 11642
Lexington\Bluegrass Chapter, 4983
Liberty Arms Assisted Living Facility, 9904
Liberty Commons Assisted Living, 9515
Liberty LT, 3385
Liberty Manor Assisted Living Residence, 9791
Liberty Media, 3870
Liberty Resources, 10916
Liberty Ridge, 8845
Library, 11360, 11389, 11406, 11460, 11479, 11705
Library Outreach Reporter, 3919
Library Resources for the Blind and Physically Handicapped, 7819, 7848
Library Users of America, 7631
Library for the Blind & Handicapped: Public Library-Anniston/Calhoun Counties, 11311
Library for the Deaf, 11413
Library of Congress, 7689
Library of Michigan Service for the Blind, 11565
License Control, 11990
Life After Stroke: The Guide to Recovering, 7065
Life Care Center of Sparta, 10360
Life Care Concepts, 9209
Life Center, 2756
Life Center at Wesley Ridge, 9905
Life Enrichment Center, 2757
Life Enrichment Program of El Dorado, 2794
Life Enrichment Program of North Newton, 2795
Life Enrichment Services, 2763
Life Force: Women Fighting AIDS, 4469
Life Insurance for Veterans: Veterans Benefits Administration, 2127
Life Services Network of Illinois: Springfield, 927
Life Stream Services, 990
Life and Independence for Today, 10917
Life of My Own Daily Meditations on Hope and Acceptance, 7820
Life of My Own: Daily Meditations on Hope and Acceptance, 7260
LifeQuest of Arkansas, 2709
LifeWay, 6600
Lifeglow, 7877
Lifelong Fitness Alliance, 136
Lifelong Learners Program: Division of Special Programs, 2862
Lifelong Learning Center, 2863
Lifelong Learning Institute, 2778
Lifelong Learning Program, 2702
Lifelong Learning Society, 2937
Lifescape Community Services, 928
Lifespan, 6090
Lifesprings Eldercare I, 8923
Lifestyles of Employed Legally Blind People, 7821
Lifetime Learning Center of Seattle, 2943
Lifetime Learning Program, 2819
Lifetime Periodicals, 3846, 3961
A Lifetime of Freedom from Smoking, 3994
Lifetime of Freedom from Smoking Maintenance Manual, 4058
Lift and Carry Wheelchair Caddy, 3555
Light of Hearts Villa, 9906
Lighthouse, 3581, 3722, 7632
Lighthouse International, 7666, 7798, 7853, 7989, 8013
Lighthouse International Ruth M. Shellens Library, 1786
Lighthouse Low Vision Products, 3131
Lighthouse National Center for Vision and Aging (LNCVA), 7633
Lighthouse for the Blind of Houston, 7634
Lighthouse for the Blind of Miami, 7635
Lighthouse for the Blind of Washington, 7636
Lighthouse of Oakland, 7637
Lighthouse: Ruth M Shellens Library, 11643
Lightweight Breezy, 3524
Lilly Home, 8525
Lincoln Area: Agency on Aging (LAAA), 1573
Lincoln Council on Aging, 1155
Lincoln Court, 8526
Lincoln Court Retirement Community, 8527
Lincoln Park Manor, 9907
Lincoln Trail Area: Agency on Aging, 1123
Lincolnshire Retirement & Assisted Living, 10121
Lincolnwood Assisted Living, 8694
Linda Valley Care Center, 8199
Linda Valley Villa, 8200
Linden Place Assisted Living, 8695
Lindenwood, 9210
Lindustries, 3309
Line Dancing Video, 4148
Line-A-Timers, 3132
Linguistics of American Sign Language, 6527
Linkville House, 10122
Linstock Press, 3960
Linwood Place I & II, 8809
Lion's Club Headquarters, 7878
Lion's Club International, 4335
Lippincott-Raven Publishers, 4980
Lipreading Made Easy, 6762
Lipreading Made Easy Book and Video Tape, 6528
Lisa and Her Soundless World, 6529
Listener, 6684
Listening, 6685

Entry Name Index / L

Listening to Depression: How Understanding Your Pain Can Heal Your Life, 6073
Lithium Info. Center-Dean Foundation for Health, 6091
Lithium Information Center, 6067, 6039
Lithium and Manic Depression, 6091
Little Brothers: Friends of the Elderly, 929
Little Brown & Company, 4660
Little Flower Assisted Living Residence, 9516
Little House on Prairie, 9211
Little More About Alcohol, 7369
Little Red Book, 7261
Little Sisters of The Poor, 3959
Live Better/Live Longer Resourcebook, 3761
Live Oak Village of Slidell, 8870
Liveoak Village, 8068
Living Alone with a Hearing Loss, 6686
Living Court Assisted Living Community, 10595
Living Independence Network (LINC), 10720
Living Independence for Everyone (LIFE) Center for Independent Living, 10711
Living Independently for Everyone (LIFE), 10821
Living Independently for Today & Tomorrow (LIFTT), 10833
Living Independently in Northwest Kansas (LINK), 10766
Living Legends Retirement Center, 8412
Living Sober, 7262, 7370
Living Springs, 8528
Living Well in a Nursing Home, 11695
Living Well with Diabetes, 6265
Living Well with HIV and AIDS, 4527
Living Will Form, 4213
Living With Rheumatoid Arthritis, 5161
Living and Loving: Information About Sexuality and Intimacy, 5205
Living at Home After a Stroke, 7098
Living in a Shelter, 7371
Living in the Labyrinth: A Personal Journey Through the Maze of Alzheimers, 4968
Living with Hearing Loss: Focus Group Results, 6687
Living with Low Vision: A Resource Guide for People with Sight Loss, 7822, 7849
Living with Ovarian Cancer, 5874
Living with Parkinson's Disease, 6981
Living with Sobriety: Another Beginning, 7372
Living with Stroke: A Guide for Families, 7066
Livingston County Office for Aging, 1787
Lizzie Lift, 3386
Lloyd Hearing Aid Corporation, 3276, 3277, 3284, 3285, 3283
Local AIDS Services: The National Directory, 4539
Location Finder, 3133
Lochaven Apartments, 9908
Lock Haven Golden Age Club, 2128
Lockwood Lodge at Ashlar of Newtown, 8281
Lodge at Leon Springs, 10488
Lodge at Lone Tree Creek, 9352
Lodge at Mission River Manor, 9353
Lodge at Wood Village, 10361
Lodge of Montgomery, 9909

Login Publishers Consortium, 6911
Lois Remembers, 7263
Lone Oak Assisted Living, 10123
Long Cane News, 7879, 7966
Long Handled Bath Sponges, 3016
Long Island Alzheimer's Foundation, 4937
Long Island Center for Independent Living, 10875
Long Island Chapter of the Arthritis Foundation, 5115
Long Island Living Program Assisted Living, 9842
Long Mountain Press, 3877
Long Oven Mitts, 3339
Long Term Care Ombudsman Program, 1484
Long-Term Care: How to Plan and Pay forIt, 3645
Longevity, 3920
Longitudinal Studies of HIV Infection in Intravenous Drug Users, 4528
Longmeadow Place at Burlington, 8989
Longmont Meals on Wheels, 650
Longreach Reacher, 3310
Longs Creek Village, 9674
Longview Retirement Apartments, 8696
Longwood Place at Reading, 8990
Look Good... Feel Better, 5759
Look Like a Winner After 50 with Care, Color & Style, 3646
Look Now, Hear This: Combined Auditory Training and Speechreading Instruction, 6530
Look at Cross-Addiction, 7373
Look at Relapse, 7374
Looking Back: A Reader on the History of Deaf Communities & Sign Language, 6531
Loop Scissors, 3311
Lorelton, 8316
Los Amigos Research and Education Institute, 4336
Los Angeles County Area Agency on Aging, 561
Los Angeles County Bar Association: Elderline Public Council, 11007
Los Angeles County Department of Health Services, 4470
Los Angeles Disability Determination Services, 562
Los Angeles Valley College, 2718
Loudoun County Area: Agency on Aging, 2461
Louis de la Parte Florida Mental Health Institute, 6040
Louise B Gerrard Award, 2651
Louisiana AIDS Prevention/Surveillance Program, 4471
Louisiana Assistive Technology Access Network, 1156
Louisiana Center for the Blind, 7638
Louisiana Chapter of the Arthritis Foundation, 5116
Louisiana Client Assistance Program, 1157
Louisiana Department of Aging, 1158
Louisiana Department of Health & Hospitals: Office of Public Health, 4471
Louisiana Department of Revenue, 1159
Louisiana Department of Veterans Affairs, 1160
Louisiana Developmental Disability Council, 1161

Louisiana Division of Mental Health, 6041
Louisiana Employee's Retirement Department, 1162
Louisiana Governor's Office of Elderly Affairs, 11128
Louisiana Office of Alcohol & Drug Abuse, 7177
Louisiana Office of Tourism, 11967
Louisiana Protection & Advocacy for Persons with Disabilities, 1163
Louisiana Teachers Retirement System, 1164
Louisiana Workers Compensation Board, 1165
Louisville Free Public Library, 11512
Louisville Talking Book Library, 11512
Lourdes College Duns Scotus Library, 11709
Love You Forever, 6023
Loveland Acres, 9354
Lovin' Life After 50, 3984
Loving Care for the Elderly South, 8413
Loving Residence, 9212
Low Blood Sugar, 6250
Low Country Area: Agency on Aging, 2228
Low Effort and No Effort Braking, 2981
Low Effort and No Effort Steering, 2982
Low Vision Questions and Answers, 7967
Low Vision Questions and Answers: Definitions, Devices, Services, 7880
Low Vision: Reflections of the Past, Issues for the Future, 7823
Lowell House, 5151
Lowell House Press, 6068
Lower Rio Grande Valley Area: Agency onAging, 2329
Lower Savannah Area: Agency on Aging, 2229
Loyaton of Coeur d'Alene, 8529
Loyola University Press, 3610
Lucas County Health Center, 1031
Lucas State Office Building, 7174
Lumbo-Posture Back Support, 3213
Lumex Recliner, 3046
Lumex's Cushions and Mattresses, 3214
Luminaud, 3134
Luther Memorial Home, 9570
Luther Park Personal Assistance Community, 10197
Luther Village, 9060
Lutheran Bible Institute of Seattle Library, 11830
Lutheran Braille Evangelism Association, 7900, 7968
Lutheran Home Apartments, 8697
Lutheran Home at Toledo Assisted Living, 9910
Lutheran Home-Cedar Haven, 9213
Lutheran Library for the Blind, 11588
Lutheran Memorial Retirement Center, 9214
Lutheran Memorial Retirement Center-Brainerd, 9215
Lutheran Social Services, 9216
Lutheran Village of Columbus, 9911
Luzerne-Wyoming Bureau for the Aging, 2129
Lvaing Well with HIV & AIDS, 4529
Lycoming-Clinton Office of Aging, 2130
Lyndon Baines Johnson Building, 6440
Lyons Golden Gang, 651

M

M C P Hahnemann Orthopedic Institute, 5117
MA Report, 4670
MA427 Health Sciences Center, 5251
MAB Community Services, 1289
MAC Area: Agency on Aging, 1239
MADAMIST 50/50 PSI Air Compressor, 3264
MATP Center, 1290
MC Migel Memorial Library and Helen Keller Archives, 11644
MICA Hill Estates, 8698
MN Workforce Center, 1396
MR Imaging in Parkinson's Disease, 7006
MVP+ 3-Wheel Scooter, 3422
Mac's Lift Gate, 2983
MacDonald Residence, 10124
MacKenzie Place: Colorado Springs, 8245
MacKenzie Place: Fort Collins, 8246
MacMillan, 5153, 6024
Macklyn House, 10125
Macomb Library for the Blind and Physically Handicapped, 11566
Macon Library for the Blind and Physically Handicapped, 11441
Macrobiotics Today, 3921
Macular Degeneration Foundation, 8045
Mada Medical Products, 3264
Maddock Memorial Home, 9571
Madison Avenue Apartments, 9217
Madison Council on Aging, 1166
Madison County Office for the Aging, 1788
Madison County RSVP, 991
Madison House, 9675
Madison Square Assisted Living, 8699
Madison York Home For Adults, 9843
Madonna Assisted Living, 9676
Magazines in Special Media, 7881
Magazines in Special Media for the Handicapped, 3922
Magic Soaper, 3017
Magic Valley Manor Assisted Living, 8530
Magnetic Card Reader, 3340
Magni-Cam, 3135, 3423
Magnifier Highlights, 3312, 7969
Magnolia Gardens Assisted Living Facilities, 10126
Magnolia Place, 9355, 10489
Magnolia Ridge Residential Care, 10559
Maharishi International University: Lab for Health & Aging Studies, 4337
Mahoney House, 9677
Mail Order Division, 6018
Maine Alzheimer's Care Center, 4938
Maine Assistive Technology Projects, 1205
Maine Association of Retirees (MAR), 1206
Maine Bureau of Elder and Adult Services, 1207
Maine Center for the Blind and Visually Impaired, 7639
Maine Department of Defense, Veterans and Emergency Management, 1208
Maine Department of Human Services: Bureau of Elder and Adult Services, 1209
Maine Department of Human Services: Disease Control Division, 4472
Maine Department of Labor: Bureau of Employment Security, 1210
Maine Department of Labor: Bureau of Rehabilitation Services, 1211
Maine Department of Mental Health & Mental Retardation, 6042
Maine Developmental Disability Council, 1212
Maine Division for the Blind & Visually Impaired Services, 7640
Maine Independent Living Services, 10781
Maine Office of Elder Affairs, 11134
Maine Office of Tourism, 11968
Maine Protection & Advocacy AgencyDisability Rights Center: Bangor Office, 11135
Maine Protection and Advocacy AgencyDisability Rights Center: Augusta Office, 11136
Maine Revenue Services, 1213
Maine State Bar Association: Section on Elder Law, 11137
Maine State Library, 11528
Maine State Office of Substance Abuse: Information and Resource Center, 7463
Maine State Retirement System, 1214
Maine Worker's Compensation Board, 1215
Mainstream, 3923
Mainstream Living, 10640
Mainstream Westchester Community College, 2864
Maison Oaks Assisted Living, 8871
Major General Melvin J. Maas Achievement Award, 2652
Make Today Count, 5760
Making Life Easier, 3698
Making Life More Livable, 7824, 8000
Making New Friends, 6688
Malash Gardens, 8201
Male Sexual Dysfunction Center, 6934
Male Sexual Medicine Clinic, 6935
Mallard Crove Seniors Community, 9912
Mallory House, 8531
Mallory Institute of Pathology Foundation, 6882
Malta Park: Willwoods II, 8872
Malta Square at Sacred Heart: Willwoods II, 8873
Man's Low-Vision Quartz Watches, 3136
Managed Home Care Sourcebook, 3762
Management of Hypertension, 6913
Managing Aging and Human Services Agencies, 3647
Managing Cocaine Cravings, 7375
Managing Incontinence: A Guide to Living with Loss of Bladder Control, 6952
Managing Tuberculosis and HIV Infection in Today's General Workplace, 4564
Managing Type II Diabetes, 6208
Managing Your Activities, 5206
Managing Your Fatigue, 5207
Managing Your Gestational Diabetes, 6209
Managing Your Health Care, 5208
Managing Your Pain, 5209
Managing Your Stress, 5210
Manchester House, 10027
Manchester Manor, 10218
Mangrove Bay, 8414
Manhattan Homestead Assisted, 8810
Manhattan Public Library, 11500
Manisses Communications Group, 4059
Mankind Research Foundation, 4338
Manor House, 9218
Manor St Joesph, 9572
Manor at Autumn Hills, 9913
Manor at the Meadows, 9914
Manor on the Hill, 8991
Manorhouse Assisted Living, 9517, 10362
Manorhouse of Wilmington, 9518
Mansion at Waterford, 10028
Manual of Allergy & Immunology, 4660
Manual of Hypertension, 6914
Maple Knoll Village-Beecher Place, 9915
Maple Manor Village, 8700
Maple Ridge Assisted Living, 8701
Maple Village, 9061
Maplewood Place at Malden, 8992
Maplewood Residence, 9844
Maranatha Place, 9219
Marbridge Ranch, 10490
March of Dimes Resource Center, 4550
Margaret Place, 9220
Marian Living Center, 9916
Marian Manor, 9573
Marian Village, 8594
Marie Haug Student Award in Gerontology, 2653
Marie Louise Heins Home for Adults, 9845
Marijuana, 7376
Marillac Manor, 9574
Marin Center for Independent Living, 10672
Marin County: Area Agency on Aging, 563
Marin Institute, 7178
Marin Senior Coordinating Council(Whistlestop), 564
Marina Place at Quincy, 8993
Marion Assisted Living Center, 10288
Mariposa Education and Research Foundation, 4609
Markham House, 10127
Markham Residential Care, 8532
Markings on the Journey, 7437
Marland Place at Andover, 8994
Marlow Manor/Manor Management, 8096
Marquette University Libraries Special Collections and University Archives, 11847
Marquis Place, 8811
Marquis Vintage Suites at Forest Grove, 10128
Marriott Maple Ridge of Willoughby, 9917
Marriott Mapleridge of Plymouth, 8995
Marriott's Brighton Garden of Port St Lucie, 8415
Marriott's Brighton Gardens of Boca Raton, 8416
Marriott's Brighton Gardens of Boynton, 8417
Marriott's Brighton Gardens of Stamford, 8282
Marriott's Brighton Gardens of WPB, 8418
Marriott's Park Summit, 8419
Marriotts Brighton Gardens of Charlotte, 9519
Mars Hill Retirement Community, 9520
Marshall County Healthcare Center, 10289
Martin Boyd Christian Home, 10363
Martin Luther Manor, 9221
Martin Technology, 3490
Martina Place, 8702
Mary Bird Perkins Cancer Center Community Library, 11516
Mary Imogene Bassett Medical Research Institute, 5930
Mary Margaret Walther Center, 5931
Mary's Woods at Marylhurst, 10129
Maryfield, 9521

Entry Name Index / M

Maryland Association of Area Agencies on Aging, 1240
Maryland Blind Industries and Services, 7641
Maryland Center for Abuse Prevention, 7179
Maryland Chapter of the Arthritis Foundation, 5118
Maryland Chapter: Alexander Graham Bell Association for the Deaf, 6391
Maryland Client Assistance Program, 1241
Maryland Department of Aging, 1242
Maryland Department of Aging: Senior Legal Assistance, 11138
Maryland Department of Health and Mental Hygiene, 6043
Maryland Developmental Disability Council, 1243
Maryland Disability Determination Services, 1244
Maryland Disability Law Center, 1245, 11139
Maryland Legal Aid Bureau: Annapolis, 11140
Maryland Legal Aid Bureau: Baltimore, 11141
Maryland Medical Research Institute, 4610
Maryland Office of Tourism Development, 11969
Maryland Protection & Advocacy Agency, 1245
Maryland Society for Sight, 7642
Maryland State Bar Association of Legal Services, 11142
Maryland State Library for the Blind and Physically Handicapped, 11535
Maryland State Retirement and Pension System, 1246
Maryland Veterans Commission, 1247
Maryland Workers Compensation Board, 1248
Marymount Place, 9918
Mason City Homestead, 8703
Mason Wright Retirement Community, 8996
Masonic Home of Florida, 8420
Masonic Medical Research Laboratory: Max L Kamiel Library, 11645
Masonic Retirement Community of Lafayette Hill, 10198
Massachusetts Alzheimer's Disease Research Center, 5059
Massachusetts Assistive Technology Partnership, 1290
Massachusetts Association for the Blind, 7643
Massachusetts Bureau of Substance Abuse Services, 7180
Massachusetts Chapter of the Arthritis Foundation, 5119
Massachusetts Client Assistance Program, 1291
Massachusetts Commission for the Blind, 7644
Massachusetts Department of Elder Affairs, 1292
Massachusetts Department of Mental Health, 6044
Massachusetts Department of Public Health, 4473
Massachusetts Department of Revenue, 1293

Massachusetts Developmental Disabilities Council, 1294
Massachusetts Disability Determination Services, 1295
Massachusetts Executive Office for Administration and Finance, 1297
Massachusetts Executive Office of Health and Human Services, 1296, 1298, 1299
Massachusetts General Departments of Neurology and Neurosurgery, 7119
Massachusetts Institute of Technology General Clinical Research Center, 4339
Massachusetts Institute of Technology: Center for Cancer Research, 5932
Massachusetts Mutual Life Insurance Company Law Library, 11150
Massachusetts Office of Travel & Tourism, 11970
Massachusetts Protection & Advocacy Organization, 1300
Massachusetts Social Security Region 1 Administration, 1301
Massachusetts Statewide Independent Living Council (MASILC), 10793
Massage Therapy Journal, 3924
Massena Independent Living Center, 10876
Massillon Senior Citizens' Center, 1958
Mastectomy: A Treatment for Breast Cancer, 5827
Mat Factory, 3556
Matilda Brown Home, 8202
Matilda Ziegler Magazine for the Blind, 7882
Mattoon Area Senior Center: Coles Council on Aging, 930
Mature American, 3985
Mature Health, 3925
Mature Lifestyles, 3926
Mature Market Resource Center, 163
Mature Minglers Senior Center: Senior Adult Services and Programs, 1351
Mature Outlook, 3927
Mature Years, 3928
Maui County Office on Aging: Department of Housing and Human Concerns, 871
Max Samter Institute of Allergy and Clinical Immunology, 4685
Maxi Aid Braille Timer, 3341
Maxi Aids, 3001, 3009, 3012, 3015, 3029, 3031, 3053, 3054, 3087, 3100, 3128, 3129, 3133, 3138, 3171, 3176, 3234, 3237, 3244, 3253, 3273
Maxi Marks, 3465
Maxi Superior Cane, 3482
Maximizing the Role of Nutrition in Diabetes Management, 6210
May Creek Lodge Assisted Living, 9222
Mayfair House, 10560
Mayfair Village Retirement Community, 9919
Mayflower, 10561
Mayflower Assisted Living, 8704
Mayflower Assisted Living Facility, 8421
Mayflower Place, 8997
Mayo Clinic and Foundation-General Clinical Research Center, 4340
Mayo Clinic and Foundation: Allergy Disease Research Laboratory, 4686
Mayo Comprehensive Cancer Center, 5933
Mayor's Committee on Persons with Disabilities, 729
McAuley, 8283

McAuley Terrace, 10130
McCall's Prime Time, 3986
McCarthy Manor, 9223
McCready Manor, 8846
McDermott, Will & Emery Library, 11461
McDowell Council on Aging, 1896
McDowell Place of Danville, 8847
McDowell Village, 8125
McFarland & Company, 6527
McGraw-Hill, 2641, 3677
McGraw-Hill Companies, 5805
McKillop Residence Assisted Living Facility, 10131
McKnight Place Assisted Living, 9334
McKnight Terrace, 9920
McLaren Homewood Village, 9062
McLoughlin Place, 10132
McMinn County Senior Citizens, 2277
McMinnville Residential Care Center, 10364
McMurray Publishing, 3970
Meadow Creek Village Assisted Living Residence, 10133
Meadow Lodge at Drum Hill, 8998
Meadow View Family Service, 10491
Meadow Wind Assisted Living, 10611
Meadow Woods, 9224
Meadowbrook Place, 10134
Meadowbrook Terrance of Greensboro, 9522
Meadowland Elder Care Home, 9225
Meadowlark Home of Grangeville, 8533
Meadows, 8705, 8812, 9226, 9678
Meadows Assisted Living, 8706
Meadows at Friendship Village, 9921
Meadows at Silver Maples, 9063
Meadows of Worthington, 9227
Meadows on Main, 9228
Meal Planning with Exchange Lists, 4149
Meals on Wheels, 763
Meals on Wheels Association of America, 3763, 164
Meals on Wheels Assoiation of America Directory, 3763
Meals on Wheels of Buffalo and Erie County Foundation, 1789
Meals on Wheels of Culver Palms, 565
Meals on Wheels of Haywood County, 1897
Meals on Wheels of Rowan, 1898
Mease Manor, 8422
Mecklenburg County Bar: Volunteer Lawyers Program and Services for the Elderly, 11214
MedDev Corporation, 3265
MedEscort International, 12030
Medi-Grip, 3266
Media & Captioning for Individuals with Disabilities, 6392
Media Access Group, 7645
Media America, 5806
Media Center, 11361
Media Center on Alcohol Issues, 7181
Media Kit, 7377
Media Productions & Marketing, 7874
Media Trends Publications, 3859
Medic Alert Foundation International, 165
Medical Arts Center Hospital, 7148, 7343
Medical Center, 5053, 5679, 5973, 7056
Medical College of Toledo: Cancer Research Division, 5934
Medical College of Wisconsin Eye Institute, 8046

Entry Name Index / M

Medical Foundation of Buffalo, 5935
Medical Library, 11359, 11735
Medical Library Association, 166, 4214
Medical Management of Impotence, 4150
Medical Management of Type II Diabetes, 6211
Medical Research Institute, 5908
Medical School, Department of Biochemistry, 6286
Medical School, H6/367 CSC, 4700
Medical School, Wing D, 6828
Medical University of South Carolina, 7461
Medical University of South Carolina: Arthritis Clinical Research Center, 5239
Medical University of South Carolina: Health Services Administration, 4611
Medical Utilization Management, 4060
Medicare, 4215
Medicare Hospital Insurance, 167
Medicare Rights Center, 168
Mediconsult, 4216
Medletter Associates, 3891, 4039
MedlinePlus®, 4217
Mednet Ketronic Inc., 2984
Medpro, 3215, 3216, 3224, 3225
Medpro Static Air Chair Cushion, 3215
Medpro Static Air Mattress Overlay, 3216
Meeting Halfway in ASL, 6532
Meeting the Needs of Employees with Disabilities, 3764
MegaDots, 3137
Melanoma Newsletter, 5828
Melanoma Research Foundation, 5936
Melanoma: Research Report, 5829
Melbourne Place, 8999
Melwood Access Adventures, 12031
Member's Eye View of Alcoholics Anonymous, 7378
Members of the Clergy Ask About Alcoholics Anonymous, 7379
Membership Services Office, 6340
Memo to an Inmate Who May Be an Alcoholic, 7380
Memorial Oaks by Marriott, 10492
Memories of Love: Caring for the Caregiver, 5032
A Memory Retention Course for the Aged, 3588
Memory Retention Course for the Aged, 3648
Memory and Aging, 5004
Memphis Area Legal Services: Pro Bono Panel for Senior Citizens, 11259
Memphis Center for Independent Living, 10925
Memphis State University: Center for the Communicatively Impaired, 6805
Men's Health, 3929
Men's/Women's Low Vision Watches & Clocks, 3138
Men: Newcomer's Packet, 7381
Meniere's Disease, 6689
Meniere's Disease: Hearing Loss & Inner Ear Blood Flow, 6690
Mennonite Memorial Home, 9922
Menopause Without Medicine, 11696
Mental Health Law News, 6092
Mental Health Law Reporter, 6093
Mental Health Report, 3930
Mental Health Services for Deaf People, 6533
Mental Health and Spirituality in Later Life, 3649
Mental Retardation & Developmentally Disabled Services Directory, 3765
Mental and Physical Disability Law Reporter, 3932, 6094
Mental and Physical Disability LawDigest, 3931
Mentally Disabled and the Law, 3766
Mentally Impaired Elderly: Strategies and Interventions to Maintain Function, 3650
Merced County Area Agency for Aging, 566
Merced Senior Community Center, 567
Mercer County Area: Agency on Aging, 2131
Merck & Company, 4218
Mercy Medical Airlift, 2462
Mercy Pavilion of Battle Creek, 9064
Meridan Oaks, 8621
Meridian International, 3973
Meritorious Service Award, 2654
Merrick Manor Assisted Living, 9679
Merrill Gardens at Bossier, 8874
Merrill Gardens at Denton, an AssistedLiving Community, 10493
Merrill Gardens at Lutz, 8423
Merrill Gardens at North Richland Hills, 10494
Merrill Gardens at Orange City, 8424
Merrill Gardens at Round, 10495
Merrill Gardens at San Antonio, 10496
Merrill Gardens at San Marcos, 10497
Merrimack Place, 9000
Mesa Airlines, 11932
Mesa Arizona Regional Family History Center, 11320
Message to Correctional Facilities Administrators, 7382
MessageMate, 3139
Meth-Wick Community, 8707
Methodist Country House, 8317
Methodist Manor House, 8318
Methodist Memorial Homes, 9680
Methotrexate, 5211
Metro United Way, 1124
MetroWest Center for Independent Living, 10794
Metrolina Sight Services, 11863
Metropolitan Area Agency on Aging, 1402
Metropolitan Center for Independent Living (MCIL), 10807
Metropolitan Commission on Aging, 1790
Metropolitan Washington Chapter of the Arthritis Foundation, 5120
Metropolitan Washington Ear, 3140
Meyer Manor II, 8534
Miami Dade County Retired and Senior Volunteer Program, 764
Miami Heart Institute, 6883
Miami Lighthouse for the Blind, 7646
Miami University Humanities and Social Sciences Department, 11710
Miami-Dade Public Library: Genealogy Collection, 11419
Michael Franck Building, 11160
Michigan Association for the Deaf: Hearing and Speech Services, 6394
Michigan Association for the DeafHearing and Speech Services, 6393
Michigan Association of Area Agencies on Aging, 1352
Michigan Association of Homes and Services for the Aging, 1353
Michigan Association of Retired School Personnel, 1354
Michigan Bureau of Workers' Disability Compensation, 1355
Michigan Cancer Foundation, 5937
Michigan Center for Substance Abuse Services, 7182
Michigan Chapter of the Arthritis Foundation, 5217, 5228, 5121
Michigan Christian Home, 9065
Michigan City Public Library: Indiana Rooom/Genealogy, 11483
Michigan Client Assistance Program, 1356
Michigan Commission for the Blind, 7790
Michigan Council of the Blind and Visually Impaired (MCBVI), 7647
Michigan Department of Community Health, 1357
Michigan Department of Human Services, 1358
Michigan Department of Labor Commission for the Blind: Center for Independent Living Program for Elderly, 9066
Michigan Department of Management and Budget: Bureau of Retirement Systems, 1359
Michigan Department of Military Affairs Bureau of State Operations and Veterans' Affairs, 1360
Michigan Department of Public Health: Bureau Infectious Disease Control, 4474
Michigan Department of Treasury, 1361
Michigan Developmental Disability Council, 1362
Michigan Office of Services to the Aging, 1363
Michigan Office of Services to the Elderly, 11156
Michigan Office on Aging, 1364
Michigan Parkinson Foundation, 6965
Michigan Protection & Advocacy Service: Livonia, 11157
Michigan Protection and Advocacy Service, 1356
Michigan Protection and Advocacy Service: Lansing, 11158
Michigan Rehabilitation Services, 1365
Michigan Society of Gerontology, 1366
Michigan Speech Language Hearing Association, 6395
Michigan Speech, Language & Hearing Association, 6396
Michigan Travel Bureau, 11971
Michigan Workers Compensation Board, 1367
Micrographia, 7007
Mid-America Regional Council of Aging Services, 1485
Mid-Carolina Area: Agency on Aging, 1899
Mid-Columbia Senior and Disabled Services, 2054
Mid-East Area: Agency on Aging, 1486
Mid-East Commission Area: Agency on Aging, 1900
Mid-Illinois Talking Book Center, 11462
Mid-Minnesota Area: Agency on Aging, 1403
Middle Flint Regional Development Center Area: Agency on Aging, 839

1027

Entry Name Index / M

Middle Georgia Regional Development Center Area: Agency on Aging, 840
Middle Rio Grande Area: Agency on Aging, 2330
Middlewoods of Farmington, 8284
Middlewoods of Newington, 8285
Mideastern Michigan Library Co-op, 11567
Midland Area: Agency on Aging, 931, 1574
Midland Center for Independent Living, 10804
Midland Empire Resources for Independent Living (MERIL), 10822
Midsouth Area: Agency on Aging, 2278
Midstate Independent Living Consultants-Stevens Point, 10957
Midstate Independent Living-Rhinelander, 10958
Midway Community and Senior Citizens, 1959
Midwest Express Airlines, 11933
Midwest Geriatrics, 1575
Mifflin-Juniata Area: Agency on Aging, 2132
Migel Medal for Outstanding Service to Blind Persons, 2655
Mildred M. Seltzer Distinguished Service Recognition, 2656
Miles, 6233
Miles Community College, 1557
Military Benefit Association, 169
Military Officers Association of America (MOAA), 170
Military Order of the World Wars, 171
Military Packet, 7383
Mill Gardens at Midland Park, 9792
Mill Pond Assisted Living, 8708
Millcroft Assisted Living, 8319
Miller Memorial Community, 8286
Milo D. Leavitt Memorial Lecture Award, 2657
Milwaukee County Department on Aging, 2577
Milwaukee Young Lawyers Association: Committee on Legal Services to the Elderly, 11296
Mind Science Foundation Library, 11788
The Mindful Way through Depression:Freeing Yourself from Chronic Unhappiness, 6077
Mine Hill Senior Citizens Good Years Club, 1657
Mini Teleloop, 3141
Mini-Bus and Mini-Vans, 2985
Mini-Max Cushion, 3217
Mini-Rider, 2986
Mini-Vibrator Stress Remover, 3267
Minivator Residential Elevator, 3387
Minneapolis Age & Opportunity Center, 11162
Minneapolis Medical Research Foundation, 4341
Minnesota Academy of Audiology, 6806
Minnesota Board on Aging, 1404, 11163
Minnesota Chapter No. 1 SHHH - Self Help for Hard of Hearing People, 6397
Minnesota Chemical Dependency Program, 7183
Minnesota Council on Disability, 1405
Minnesota Department of Health: AIDS/STD Prvention Service, 4475
Minnesota Department of Human Services Library & Resource Center, 11580
Minnesota Department of Labor & Industry Workers Compensation Division, 1406
Minnesota Department of Revenue, 1407
Minnesota Department of Veterans Affairs, 1408
Minnesota Dept of Employment and Economic Dvlpment, 1397
Minnesota Governor's Council on Developmental Disabilities, 1409
Minnesota Health & Housing Alliance, 1410
Minnesota Indian Area: Agency on Aging, 1411
Minnesota Library for the Blind, 11581
Minnesota Mental Health Division, 1412
Minnesota Office of Tourism, 11972
Minnesota Public Employees Retirement Association, 1413
Minnesota STAR Program, 1414
Minnesota State Bar Association: Elder Law Section, 11164
Minnesota State Council on Disability, 1415
Minnesota State Services for the Blind, 7648
Minnesota Teachers Retirement Association, 1416
Minnestoa Retirement System, 1417
Miracle Assisted Living, 8924
Mirror Go Lightly, 3241
Missing Words: The Family Handbook on Adult Hearing Loss, 6534
Mississippi (State) Department of Mental Health Library and Division of Professional Development, 11583
Mississippi Association of Area Agencies on Aging, 1446
Mississippi Client Assistance Program: Easter Seals Society, 1447
Mississippi Commission for Veterans Affairs, 1448
Mississippi Council on Aging, 11165
Mississippi Department of Human Services, 1452
Mississippi Department of Mental Health, 1449
Mississippi Department of Public Health: AIDS/HIV Prevention Program, 4476
Mississippi Department of Rehabilitation Services, 1453
Mississippi Department of Rehabilitation Services for the Blind, 1450
Mississippi Developmental Disability Council, 1451
Mississippi Division of Aging and Adult Services, 1452
Mississippi Division of Alcohol and Drug Abuse, 7184
Mississippi Division of Tourism Development, 11973
Mississippi Industries for the Blind, 7649
Mississippi Library Commission, 11584
Mississippi Office of Disability & Determination Services, 1453
Mississippi Protection and Advocacy System, 11166
Mississippi Public Employees Retirement Systems, 1454
Mississippi State Bar Association: Young Lawyers on Legal Problems of Elderly & Handicapped, 11167
Mississippi State Tax Commission, 1455
Mississippi State University, 7806, 7816
Missoula Aging Services, 1537
Missouri Assisted Living Association, 1487
Missouri Council of the Blind, 1488, 7650
Missouri Department of Health and Senior Services, 4477
Missouri Department of Mental Health, 1489
Missouri Department of Revenue, 1490
Missouri Department of Social Services, 11991
Missouri Developmental Disability Council, 1491
Missouri Division of Senior & Disability Services, 11172
Missouri Division of Tourism, 11974
Missouri Division on Aging, 1492
Missouri Employees Retirement System, 1493
Missouri Protection & Advocacy Services, 1494
Missouri Protection and Advocacy, 11173
Missouri Rehabilitation Services for the Blind, 7651
Mitchell Hollingsworth Annex, 8069
Mobile Association for the Blind, 7652
Mobile Care, 11934
Mobilectrics Company, 3020, 3047, 3435, 3436
Mobility International USA, 3685
Mobility Works, 2954
Moceans Center for Independent Living, 10853
Models of Oral Interpreting, 6763
Modern Maturity, 3933
Modern Maturity Center, 715
Modern Signs Press, 6541
Modesto Institute for Continued Learning, 2721
Modular Wall Grab Bars, 3018
Moffit Hospital, 5968
Molded Sock and Stocking Aid, 3242
Moment to Reflect on Codependency, 7384
Moment to Reflect on Self-Esteem, 7385
Monmouth County Office on Aging, 1658
Monmouth Vans-Access and Mobility Equipment, 2987
Monroe Community Hospital: TF Williams Health Sciences Library, 11646
Monroe County Area: Agency on Aging, 2133
Monroe County Office for the Aging and Adult Services, 1791
Montana Advocacy Program, 1548, 1538, 11174
Montana Department of Administration: Teacher's Retirement Division, 1539
Montana Department of Aging, 1540
Montana Department of Military Affairs: Division of Veteran's Affairs, 1541
Montana Department of Retirement Administration, 1542
Montana Department of Revenue, 1543
Montana Department of Social and Rahabilitation Services, 1544
Montana Developmental Disability Council, 1545
Montana Division of Addictive & Mental Disorders, 7185
Montana Governor's Office on Aging, 1546
Montana Independent Living Project, 10834
Montana Legal Services Association: Helena, 11175
Montana Legal Services Developer Program & Office on Aging, 11176

Entry Name Index / N

Montana Masonic Home, 9356
Montana Office on Aging, 1547
Montana Protection & Advocacy Agency, 1548
Montana State Library, 11594
Montclair Park Assisted Living, 8875
Monte Carlo Outreach Facility, 8876
Monte Travel, 12032
Montefiore Medical Center, 6837
Montefiore Medical Center Health Sciences Library: Tishman Learning Center, 11647
Monterey Peninsula College, 2725
Montgomery Area Council on Aging, 378
Montgomery County Government: Division of Elder Affairs, 1249
Montgomery County Office for the Aging, 1792
Montgomery County Office on Aging and Adult Services, 2134
Montgomery Independent Living Center, 10624
Monticello Nursing and Rehab Center, 8709
Mood Apart, 6074
Moorhead Manor, 9229
Moorings Park, 8425
Moorings of Arlington Heights, 8595
Morehouse Council on Aging, 1167
Morningside Manor, 10498
Morningside Manor Assisted Living, 10290
Morningside Manor Assisted Living II, 10291
Morningside Paducah, 8848
Morningside of Bowling Green, 8849
Morningside of Decatur, 8070
Morningside of Gallatin, 10365
Morningstar Assisted Living, 10292
Morris County Office on Aging, 1659
Morse Code Equalizer, 3142
Mortgage Insurance and Rental Housing foe Elderly, 172
Morton House, 9681
Morton S Horowitz Oceanside Public Schools, 2866
Mosby-Year Book, 4951
Mother Lucille Leisure Living, 9230
Mother of Mercy Nursing & Retirement Center, 9231
Motion Design, 3524
Motorized Stander, 3424
Mount Carmel Personal Care, 8436
Mount Ida College: National Center for Death Education, 11151
Mount Olive Retirement Village, 9523
Mount Royal Towers, 8071
Mount Royal Villa, 9923
Mount Sinai School of Medicine of City University of New York: Alzheimer's Disease Research Center, 4342, 5060
Mount Vernon Center for Community Mental Health: Deaf Services, 6398
Mountain Empire Older Citizens, 2463
Mountview Retirement Community, 8203
Mouthsticks, 3143
Mr. Escort Manual Wheelchair Carrier, 2988
Mt Saint Joseph, 10135
Mt. Sinai Medical Center, 4266, 5049
Mt. Sinani Medical Center, 5247
Mulberry Place, 8710
Mulligan Foundation, 7036
Multi-Scan Single Switch Activity Center, 3144

Multiple District 22: Lions Vision Research Foundation, 6278
Multiple Phone/Device Switch, 3145
Multipurpose Arthritis & Musculoskeletal Center, 5240
Multipurpose Arthritis and Musculoskeletal Disease Center, 5241
Multnomah County Aging Services Division, 2055
Multnomah County Office, 11232
Murray House, 8072
Museum of Western Colorado: Research Center & Special Library, 11363
Mushroom Inserts, 3284
Music Is for Everyone, 7970
Musical Mainstream, 7883, 7971
Muskingum County Senior Services, 1960
Mustang Manor Assisted Living, 10029
My Activity Plan, 4061
My Food Plan, 4062
My Mind is Out to Get Me: Humor and Wisdom in Recovery, 7264
My Mother, My Father, 4151
My Mother, My Father: Seven Years Later, 4152
My Personal Goals, 4063
My Turn Program, 2865
Myositis, 5212
Mystic Valley Elder Services, 1302

N

NABCO Breast Cancer Resource List, 5830
NABCO News, 5831
NAD Broadcaster, 6594, 6691
NAD Deaf Awareness Kit, 6535
NAHC Report, 4064
NAMES Project Foundation, 4478
NAMSIC, National Institutes of Health, 5180, 5222, 5226
NARIC Guide to Disability and Rehabilitation Periodicals, 3767
NARIC Quarterly, 4065
NC Department of Health and Human Services, 6049
NC Dept of Human Resources, 3747
NCD Bulletin, 4066
NCNMEDD-Area Agency on Aging, 1713
NCOA Networks, 4067
NCSC Community Service Award/Certificateof Merit, 2658
NE California Chapter - Arthritis Foundation, 5197
NEXUS Wheelchair Cushioning System, 3218
NFDI Newsletter, 6095
NH DHHS Division of Community Based Care Services, 1621
NHC Place Farragut, 10366
NHCoA Noticias of Hispanic Aging Issues & News, 4068
NHI Clinical Center, 5061
NHIF Newsletter, 4069
NHO NewsLine, 4070
NIA Publishers, 4219
NIAID Office of Communications and Public Liason, 4561, 4563, 4571, 4572
NIDA Capsules, 7386
NIDRR Program Directory, 3768
NIH/National Institute of Neurological Disorders and Stroke, 7052

NIH: Environmental Health Sciences, 173
NIH: Heart, Lung & Blood Institute, 174
NIH: National Eye Institute, 175
NIH: National Institute of Dental and Cracial Research, 176
NIH: National Institute of Osteoporosis and Related Bone Diseases, 177
NIH: National Institute on Aging, 178
NIH: National Institute on Deafness and Communication Disorders, 179
NLADA Directory of Legal Aid and Defender Offices in the United States and Territories, 3769
NLS News, 7884, 7972
NLS Update, 7885, 7973
NMAC Update, 4565
NMRLS - Northern Mississippi Rural LegalServices: Clarksdale Office, 11168
NODA Area: Agency on Aging, 2011
NOLO, 3608, 3631, 3653, 3671
NSA Audio Tape Series, 7112
NSA's Guide to Stroke, 7099
NSCLC Washington Weekly, 4071
NTID at College of Rochester Technology, 6409
NUCEA Divisional Awards, 2659
NV Dept of Employment, Training & Rehabilitation, 7694
NWT Seniors' Society, 354
NYU Medical Center, 6924
Naional Federation of the Blind, 7672
Name Brand Hearing Aids, 3285
Nantahala Outdoor Center, 12033
Narcotic and Drug Research, 7464
Narcotics Anonymous, 7265
Narragansett Senior Citizens Association, 2205
Nashville Bar Association (NBA): Young Lawyers Division (YLD), 11260
Nashville Chapter Black Deaf Advocates, 6399
Nassau County Department of Senior Citizen Affairs, 1793
Nassau Library System, 11648
Nat Committee To Preserve Social Security/Medicare, 3957
Nat Lib Serv for the Blind/Physically Handicapped, 3922, 7841, 7848
Nat Lib Svc for the Blind & Physically Handicapped, 7842
Nat'l Arthritis/Skin Diseases Info. Clearinghouse, 5185
Nat'l Council of Community Mental Health Center, 3841, 6090, 6096
Natalie Warren Bryant Cancer Center, 5938
Natchez-Adams Council on Aging, 1456
Natchitoches Parish Council on Aging, 1168
Nathan Kline Institute for Psychiatric Research: Center for Alzheimer's Disease, 5062
Nathan Shock New Investigator Award, 2660
National 4th Biennial Campvention of the Deaf, 6764
National AFL-CIO Cope Retiree Program, 180
National AIDS Information Clearinghouse, 4579
The National Academies Press, 3665
National Academy Press, 4659
National Academy for Teaching and Learning About Aging, 181

1029

Entry Name Index / N

National Academy of Elder Law Attorneys, 182, 10985
National Academy of Social Insurance, 11396
National Academy on Aging, 4220
National Accreditation Council for Agencies/Blind, 7919
National Adult Day Services Association, 183
National Aging Information Center, 4221
National Allergy and Asthma Network, 4641
National Alliance for Research on Schizophrenia and Depression, 6102
National Alliance of Blind Students, 7653
National Alliance of Breast Cancer Organizations, 5830, 5831, 5761, 5878
National Alliance of Senior Citizens Library, 11397
National Anxiety Foundation, 6045
National Arthritis and Musculoskeletal and Skin Diseases Information Clearinghouse, 5242
National Association for Addiction Professionals, 7186
National Association for Continence, 4091, 4222, 6948
National Association for Hearing and Speech Action, 6400
National Association for Hispanic Elderly, 184
National Association for Home Care, 3773, 4064
National Association for Home Care and Hospice (NAHC), 185, 4223
National Association for Parents of the Visually Impaired (NAPVI), 7654
National Association for Senior Living Industries, 186
National Association for Visually Handicapped, 3759, 7797, 7805, 7810, 7818, 7851, 7863, 7892, 7895, 7910, 7924, 7926, 7927, 7931, 7933, 7938, 7943, 7948, 7950, 7952, 7955
National Association for Visually Handicapped (NAVH), 7655
National Association for Visually Handicapped Library, 11649
National Association of Activity Professionals, 187
National Association of Addiction Treatment Providers, 7187
National Association of Area Agencies on Aging, 124, 3770, 188
National Association of Area Agencies onAging, 4224
National Association of Blind Educators, 7656, 8015
National Association of Blind Lawyers, 7657, 8016
National Association of Blind Secretaries and Transcribers, 7658, 8017
National Association of Blind Teachers, 7659
National Association of Counselors, 189
National Association of County Aging Programs, 190
National Association of Directors of Nursing Administration in Long Term Care, 191
National Association of Government Communicators (NAGC), 192
National Association of Guide Dog Users, 7660, 8018

National Association of Military Widows, 193
National Association of Nutrition and Aging Services Programs (NANASP), 194
National Association of Older Worker Employment, 195
National Association of Partners in Education, 196
National Association of Perinatal Addiction Research and Education, 7465
National Association of Physician Nurses, 197
National Association of Professional Geriatric Care Managers (PGCM), 198, 4225
National Association of Radio Reading Services, 7846
National Association of Retired Federal Employees, 3954, 199
National Association of Senior Companion Project Directors, 200
National Association of State Retirement Administrators, 201
National Association of State Units on Aging, 2651, 202, 4226
National Association of State Veterans Homes, 203
National Association of Traveling Nurses, 12034
National Association of Veterans Program Administrators, 204
National Association of the Deaf, 4161, 6402, 6468, 6472, 6486, 6497, 6535, 6594, 6630, 6691, 6764, 6401, 6586, 6787
National Association of the Deaf Law, 6788
National Association of the Deaf Law Center, 6402
National Association of the Deaf: Legal Defense Fund, 11398
National Association on Drug Abuse Problems, 7188
National Association on HIV Over Fifty, 4479
National Association to Promote the Use of Braille, 7661, 8019
National Black Deaf Advocates, 6403
National Board for Certified Counselors, 205
National Braille Association, 7550, 7843, 7662, 8020
National Braille Press, 7889, 7663
National Cancer Institute, 5669, 5793, 5810, 5811, 5812, 5813, 5814, 5815, 5816, 5817, 5818, 5819, 5820, 5821, 5822, 5823, 5826, 5827, 5829, 5832, 5833
National Cancer Institute - BRS Online, 4137
National Captioning Institute, 6404, 7664, 8021
National Car Rental, 11935
National Car Rental System, 11936
National Catholic Office for the Deaf, 6551, 6685, 7903
National Catholic Office of the Deaf, 6405
National Caucus and Center on Black Aged, 2648, 206
National Center Library, 11768
National Center for Accessible Media, 6406
National Center for Chronic Disease Prevention, 7207
National Center for Sight, 7665
National Center for State Courts, 11281

National Center for Vision and Aging, 7917, 3581, 7666
National Center for Voice and Speech, 6407
National Center for Voluntary Leadership in Aging, 207
National Center on Arts and the Aging, 208
National Center on Deafness, 6408
National Center on Elder Abuse, 209, 4227
National Center on Employment for the Deaf, 6409
National Certification Board for Diabetes Educators, 6176
National Chronic Pain Outreach Association, 5762
National Citizen's Coalition for Nursing Home Reform (NCCNHR), 730
National Citizens Coalition for Nursing Home Reform, 210
National Citizens' Coalition for Nursing Home Reform, 11888
National Civil Rights Clearinghouse Library, 11399
National Clearinghouse for Alcohol and Drug Abuse, 4973
National Clearinghouse for Alcohol and Drug Info., 4521, 4528, 7155, 7216, 7282, 7305, 7306, 7307, 7308, 7309, 7310, 7311, 7312, 7313, 7314, 7315, 7318, 7329, 7341, 7351, 7355
National Coalition for Cancer Survivorship, 5763
National Coalition on Immune System Disorders, 4480
National Coalition on Rural Aging, 211
National Committee for Quality Healthcare, 212
National Committee for Responsive Philanthropy, 213
National Committee for the Prevention of Elder Abuse, 214
National Committee to Preserve Social Security and Medicare (NCPSSM), 215
National Conference of, 4103
National Conference on Drug Abuse Research & Practice, 7282
National Conference on Public Employee Retirement Systems, 216
National Congress of Jewish Deaf, 6410
National Council News, 6096
National Council of Administrators of Adult Education (NCAAE), 2866
National Council of Community Mental, 6099
National Council of Senior Citizens, 2658, 2665
National Council of Social Security Management Associations, 217
National Council on Aging: Ollie A Randall Library, 11400
National Council on Alcoholism and Drug Dependence, 7190, 7448
National Council on Child Abuse (NCCAFV), 218
National Council on Disability, 4066, 219
National Council on the Aging, 147, 195, 207, 231, 232, 233, 234, 235, 237, 2635, 2668, 3588, 3590, 3592, 3619, 3621, 3637, 3639, 3640, 3643, 3648
National Crime Prevention Council, 7338, 4228, 7191
National Cued Speech Association, 6411

Entry Name Index / N

National Depressive and Manic Depressive Association, 6046
National Development and Research Institutes: Library/Resource Center, 7467
National Diabetes Action Network for the Blind, 6177, 7667
National Diabetes Information Clearinghouse, 6227, 6237, 6239, 6247, 6248, 6255, 6178
National Directory for Eldercare Information and Referral, 3770
National Directory of Bereavement Support Groups and Services, 6033
National Directory of Drug and Alcohol Abuse Treatment and Programs, 7283
National Directory of Educational Programs in Gerontology and Geriatrics, 3771
National Directory of Healthcare and Human Service Ministries, 3772
National Directory of Hearing Assistance Technology Assistive Device Demo Centers, 6567
National Domestic Violence Hotline, 4229
National Easter Seal Communicator, 3934
National Easter Seal Society Publications, 3842, 3934, 7905
National Eczema Assocation for Science and Education, 4651
National Emergency Medicine Association, 221
National Endowment for the Arts: Office for Special Constituencies, 222
National Eye Care Project, 7668
National Eye Care Project (NECP), 7669
National Eye Health Education Program, 7670
National Eye Institute, 8047
National Eye Institute, Information Office, 7915, 7925, 7935, 7936, 7937
National Eye Research Foundation, 8048
National Families in Action, 7192
National Family Association for Deaf-Blind, 6412
National Family Caregivers Association (NFCA), 223
National Federation for Specialty Nursing Organizations, 224
National Federation of Licensed Practical Nurses, 225
National Federation of the Blind, 2647, 2661, 2667, 6177, 6235, 7619, 7623, 7656, 7657, 7658, 7660, 7661, 7667, 7678, 7679, 7680, 7682, 7683, 7684, 7685, 7687
National Federation of the Blind Merchants Division, 8022
National Federation of the Blind Scholarship Program, 2661
National Federation of the Blind in Computer Science, 7672, 8023
National Federation of the Blind of California: Santa Barbara County Chapter, 7673
National Federation of the Blind of Kansas, 1076, 7674
National Federation of the Blind of New Jersey, 7675
National Federation of the Blind of South Dakota, 7676
National Federation of the Blind of Texas: Austin Chapter, 7677

National Federation of the Blind: Blind Industrial Workers of America, 7679
National Federation of the Blind: BlindIndustrial Workers of America, 8024
National Federation of the Blind: Human Services Division, 7680
National Federation of the Blind: HumanServices Division, 8025
National Federation of the Blind: Job Opportunities for the Blind, 7681
National Federation of the Blind: Masonic Square Club, 7682, 8026
National Federation of the Blind: Music Division, 7683
National Federation of the Blind: MusicDivision, 8027
National Federation of the Blind: Public Employees Division, 7684, 8028
National Federation of the Blind: Science and Engineering Division, 7685, 8029
National Federation of the Blind: Sligo Creek Chapter, 7686
National Federation of the Blind: Writers Division, 7687, 8030
National Federation of the Blind:Blind Merchants Division, 7678
National Food Distribution Division Office, 2466
National Foundation for Cancer Research Hotline, 5764
National Foundation for Depressive Illness, 6095, 6047
National Fraternal Society of the Deaf, 6653, 6413
National Gerontological Nursing Association, 226
National Glaucoma Research, 8049
National Graduate University LibraryCapitol Hill Campus, 11401
National Head Injury Foundation, 4069
National Headquarters Library, 11478
National Health Federation, 5765
National Health Information Center, 227
National Heart, Lung & Blood Institute, 4230
National Heart, Lung and Blood Institute, 6842
National Heart, Lung, and Blood Institute Information Center, 11536
National Hemophilia Foundation, 4553, 4559, 4562
National Hemophilia Foundation: Hemophillia and AIDS/HIV Network (HANDI), 4612
National Hispanic Council on Aging, 4068, 228
National Home Care and Hospice Directory, 3773
National Hospice Helpline, 5766
National Hospice Organization, 3741, 4070, 4481, 5767, 6013
National Housing Directory for People with Disabilities, 3774
National Hypertension Association, 6910, 6917, 6909
National Indian Council on Aging, 229
National Industries For The Blind, 7888
National Industries for the Blind, 2673, 2680, 7975, 7688
National Information Center on Deafness, 6557, 6562, 6566, 6602, 6603, 6604,
6608, 6632, 6633, 6635, 6641, 6656, 6671, 6681, 6682, 6688, 6692, 6701, 6703, 6715, 6722
National Information Center on Deafness Brochure, 6692
National Information and Referral Support Center (NIRSC), 230
National Institute for Jewish Hospice (NIJH), 6014
National Institute for the Care of the Elderly, 355
National Institute of Allergy & Infectious Disease, 4672
National Institute of Allergy and Infectious Diseases, 4687
National Institute of Arthritis and Musculoskeletal and Skin Disease, 5243
National Institute of Dental and Craniofacial Research, 4231
National Institute of Diabetes & Digestive & Kidney Disease, 6279
National Institute of Mental Health, 6097
National Institute of Neurological Disorders & Stroke, 7037
National Institute of Neurological Disorders and Stroke, 4232
National Institute of Senior Housing, 231
National Institute on Adult Daycare, 232
National Institute on Age, Work and Retirement, 233
National Institute on Aging, 4233, 4343
National Institute on Aging Gerontology Research Center, 4344
National Institute on Aging: Information Center, 4345
National Institute on Community-Based Long-Term Care, 234
National Institute on Deafness & Other Communication Disorders, 6807
National Institute on Deafness and Other Communication Disorders Clearinghouse, 6790
National Institute on Disability, 3768
National Institute on Drug Abuse, 7193
National Institute on Drug Abuse Addiction Research Center Library (NIDA), 7468
National Institute on Financial Issues and Services for Elders, 235
National Institutes of Health, 6098, 6100, 6842, 8047, 236, 4234
National Institutes on Mental Health, 6088
National Interfaith Coalition on Aging, 237, 11889
National Jewish Center for Medical and Research Center, 4688
National Jewish Medical and ResearchCenter, 238
National Kidney and Urologic Diseases Information Clearinghouse, 6936
National Law Housing Project, 125
National Leadership Coalition on AIDS, 4558, 4564, 4569, 4570
National Legal Aid & Defender Association, 3769
National Legal Center for the Medically Dependent and Disabled, 11101
National Legal Support for Elderly People with Mental Disabilities Project, 239
National Library Service for the Blind, 7819, 7858, 7883, 7884, 7885, 7899, 7921, 7922, 7923, 7939, 7940, 7941, 7942,

1031

Entry Name Index / N

7970, 7971, 7972, 7973, 7981, 7982, 7984, 7991
National Library Service for the Blind and Physically Handicapped, 7689, 8031, 11403
National Library Service for the Blind/Phys. Hand., 7881
National Library Services Blind & Physically Hand., 7902
National Library of Medicine, 4153
National Long-Term Care Ombudsman Resource Center (NLTCORC), 240
National Long-Term Care Resource Center, 241
National Media Owl Awards, 2662
National Meditation Center, 4235
National Mental Health Association, 6086, 242, 6048
National Minority AIDS Council, 4565
National Multiple Sclerosis Society, 3885
National Native American AIDS Prevention Center, 4482
National Network for the Disabled, 243
National Office, 7654
National Offices, 7554
National Old Timers Auto Racing Club, 244
National Old-Time Fiddlers' Association, 245
National Organization for Albinism and Hypopigmentation, 246
National Organization for Hearing Research, 6415
National Organization for Victim Assistance, 247, 4236
National Organization for the Advancement of the Deaf, 6416
National Organization of HIV over Fifty, 248
National Organization of Social Security Claimants' Representatives, 11204
National Organization of the Senior Blind, 7690, 8032
National Organization on Disability (NOD), 249
National Osteoporosis Foundation, 250
National Ovarian Cancer Coalition, 5874, 5879
National Parkinson Foundation, 6085, 6958, 6983, 7003, 7012, 7013, 7017, 7018, 7019, 7024, 7028, 7033, 6956
National Parkinson Foundation Adult Day Care Center, 6957
National Parkinson Foundation Hotline, 6958
National Pensioners & Senior Citizens Federation, 356
National People's Action, 251
National Prevention Resource Center, 7194
National Prison Hospice Association, 252
National Prison Project: ACLU AIDS inPrison Project, 4613
National Program Office, 7158
National Program on Women and Aging, 253
National Public Policy Program to Conquer Alzheimer's Disease, 5005
National Rehabilitation Association, 3910
National Rehabilitation Information Center, 3767, 4065, 6417, 7053
National Rehabilitation Information Center (NARIC), 254

National Resource Center on Native American Aging (NRCNAA), 255
National Resource Center on Supportive Housing & Home Modifications, 256
National Retinitis Pigmentosa Foundation Helpline, 7691
National Retired Teachers Association, 257
National Right to Work Legal Defense and Education Foundation, 11282
National Rural Health Association, 258
National Senior Citizens Law Center, 4071, 4079, 259, 11008, 11046
National Senior Games Association, 260
National Senior Service Corps, 261
National Senior Service Corps Directors Associations, 262
National Senior Women's Tennis Association, 263
National Silver-Haired Congress: Kansas Department on Aging, 1077
National Society to Prevent Blindness, 7692
National Stroke Association, 3609, 4145, 7057, 7060, 7061, 7062, 7064, 7067, 7068, 7069, 7075, 7077, 7078, 7079, 7080, 7081, 7082, 7083, 7084, 7085, 7086
National Support Awards, 2663
National Tax Association, 264
National Technical Institute for the Deaf, 6418
National Theatre of the Deaf, 6419
National Tour Association: Travel Division, 12035
National Training Center for Professional AIDS Education, 4483
National University Continuing Education Assoc., 2659, 2669
National Urban League, 265
National Veterans Legal Services Program Newsletter, 4072
National Voluntary Organizations for Independent Living for the Aging, 3582
National Volunteer Training Center for Substance Abuse Prevention, 7195
National Women's Health Network, 266
National Yellow Book of Funeral Directors, 3775
Native American Consortium Protection and Advocacy Agency, 11195
Natl Citizens' Coalition for Nursing Home Reform, 4092
Natural Way Magazine, 3935
Natural Way Publications, 3935
Navajo Area Agency on Aging: Division of Health, 438
Naval Reserve Readiness Command Region Sixteen, 1392
Naval Submarine League, 267
Naval Traing Center, 739
Navy & Marine Corps, Reserve Readiness Center, 449
Navy Family Service Center, 719
Navy Fleet and Family Support Center, 2504
Navy Mutual Aid Association, 268
Navy Retired Activities Branch, 269
Navy Seabee Veterans of America, 270
Nazareth College-Speech & Language Department, 6411
Neawanna by the Sea, 10136
Nebraska Advocacy Services, 1576, 11178
Nebraska Assistive Technology Partnership, 1577

Nebraska Association of Area Agencies on Aging, 1578
Nebraska Bar Association: Elderlaw Committee, 11179
Nebraska Chapter of the Arthritis Foundation, 5122
Nebraska Client Assistance Program, 1579
Nebraska Commission For The Blind AndVisually Impaired (NCBVI), 1580
Nebraska Commission for the Blind & Visually Impaired, 7693
Nebraska Commission for the Deaf & Hard of Hearing, 6420
Nebraska Department of Aging, 1581
Nebraska Department of Health & Human Services, 11177
Nebraska Department of Revenue, 1582
Nebraska Department of Veterans Affairs, 1583
Nebraska Division of Alcoholism and Drug Abuse, 7196
Nebraska Division of Travel & Tourism, 11975
Nebraska Health & Human Services System, 1571
Nebraska Health and Human Services, 3695
Nebraska Library Commission: Talking Book & Braille Service, 11599
Nebraska School for the Visually Handicapped Library, 11600
Ned E. Freeman Excellence in Writing Award, 2664
Ned Pattison Rensselaer County, 1864
Neighborhood Family Care, 2834
Nek-Lo, Nek-Lo Hot and Cold, Pillow-Perfect, Body Buddy, 3219
Nelson Cruikshank Award, 2665
Nelson Information, 3720
Neurology Institute, 7055
Neuropsychiatric Research Institute, 4346
Neuropsychology and Parkinson's Disease, 7008
Neurotrophic Factors in Parkinson's Disease, 7009
Nevada Assistive Technology Projects, 1602
Nevada Bureau of Alcohol and Drug Abuse, 7197
Nevada Commission on Tourism, 11976
Nevada Department of Business & Industry: Governor's Committee on Employment of People with Disabilities, 1603
Nevada Department of Health & Human Services: Division for Aging Services, 11180
Nevada Department of Human Resources Rehabilitation Division: Bureau of Services to the Blind, 1604
Nevada Department of Human Resources: Health Program Section, 4484
Nevada Department of Taxation, 1605
Nevada Developmental Disability Council, 1606
Nevada Disability Advocacy & Law CenterSparks Office/Northern Nevada, 11181
Nevada Disability Advocacy and Law Center, 1608
Nevada Disability Advocacy and Law Center (NDLAC), 11182
Nevada Division for Aging Services, 1607
Nevada Protection & Advocacy Agency, 1608

Entry Name Index / N

Nevada Public Employees' Retirement System, 1609
Nevada State Library and Archives, 11605
Nevada State Library: Talking Book Services, 11606
Nevada Workers Compensation Board, 1610
Nevada's Bureau of Services to the Blind and Visually Impaired, 7694
New Bedford Council on Aging, 1303
New Bolton Center, 5985
New Breakthroughs, 3146
New Cassel Retirement Center, 9682
New Central Manor Assisted Living Progra, 9846
New Choices, 3936
New England Corporate Library, 11551
New England Deaconess Hospital, 5893
New England Deaconess Hospital: Laboratory of Cancer Biology, 5940
New England Gerontological Association, 1616
New England Region: Helen Keller National Center, 7695
New Eyes for the Needy, 7696
The New Glucose Revolution for Diabetes, 6219
New Hampshire Association for the Blind, 7697
New Hampshire Association for the Blind, 7698
New Hampshire Client Assistance Program, 1617
New Hampshire Department of Health and Human Services, 4485
New Hampshire Department of Mental Health, 1618
New Hampshire Department of Revenue, 1619
New Hampshire Developmental Disabilities Council, 1620
New Hampshire Division of Developmental Services, 1621
New Hampshire Division of Elderly and Adult Services, 1622
New Hampshire Division of Health & Human Services, 11184
New Hampshire Governor's Commission on Disability, 1623
New Hampshire Health and Human Services: Elderly and Adult Services, 1624
New Hampshire Hospital: Dorothy M Breene Memorial Library, 11609
New Hampshire Legal Assistance, 11185
New Hampshire Legal Assistance: Senior Citizens Law Project, 11186
New Hampshire Office of Travel & Tourism Development, 11977
New Hampshire Protection & Advocacy for Persons with Disabilities, 1625
New Hampshire Protection and Advocacy Agency: Disabilities Rights Center, 11187
New Hampshire Retirement System, 1626
New Hampshire State Library, 11610
New Hampshire Veterans Council, 1627
New Hampshire for Human Rights, 1628
New Harbinger, 6073
New Harbinger Publications, 3655
New Haven Legal Assistance Association (LAA), 11032
New Hope Institute, 5941
New Horizon Care Center, 8535

New Horizons, 10778
New Horizons Assisted Living Facility, 10612
New Horizons Independent Living Center - Prescott Valley, 10635
New Horizons at Choate, 9001
New Horizons at Marlboro, 9002
New Investigator Awards, 2666
New Jersey Academy of Audiology, 6421
New Jersey Association of Non-Profit Homes for the Aging, 1660
New Jersey Blind Citizens Association, 7699
New Jersey Blind Citizens' Association, 7700
New Jersey Chapter of the Arthritis Foundation, 5123
New Jersey Client Assistance Program, 1661
New Jersey Commission for the Blind and Visually Impaired, 7701
New Jersey Department of Aging, 1662
New Jersey Department of Community Affairs: Commission on Recreation for the Handicapped, 1663
New Jersey Department of Environmental Protection, 11613
New Jersey Department of Health & Senior Services, 7198
New Jersey Department of Health: Division of AIDS Prevention & Control, 4486
New Jersey Department of Human Services: Commission for the Blind, 1664
New Jersey Department of Human Services: Deaf and Heard of Hearing Division, 1665
New Jersey Department of Mental Health, 1666
New Jersey Developmental Disability Council, 1667
New Jersey Division of Aging & Community Services: Office of the Public Guardian, 11191
New Jersey Division of Taxation, 1668
New Jersey Intergenerational Network, 1669
New Jersey Library for the Blind and Physically Handicapped, 11614
New Jersey Protection & Advocacy for Persons with Disabilities, 1670
New Jersey Protection and Advocacy Agency, 11192
New Jersey State Bar Association: Committee on the Elderly, 11193
New Jersey Tourism Division, 11978
New Jersey Women and AIDS Network, 4487
New Life Living Center, 8536
New Life Outreach Boarding Home, 10499
New Living, 3937
A New Look at Community Based Respite Programs: Utilization, Satisfaction, and Development, 3589
New Medicine Man: A Different Kind of Health Care for Elders, 3651
New Mexico Aging & Long-Term Services Department: Elderly and Disability Services Division, 11196
New Mexico Behavioral Health Services, 7199
New Mexico Chapter of the Arthritis Foundation, 5124
New Mexico Client Assistance Program, 1714

New Mexico Commission for the Blind, 7702
New Mexico Committee on Concerns of the Handicapped, 1715
New Mexico Department of Aging, 1716
New Mexico Department of Taxation and Revenue, 1717
New Mexico Department of Tourism, 11979
New Mexico Educational Retirement Board, 1718
New Mexico Governor's Committee on Concern of the Handicapped, 1719
New Mexico Health Department: Public Health Division, 4488
New Mexico Protection & Advocacy for Persons with Disabilities, 1720
New Mexico Protection and Advocacy Agency, 11197
New Mexico Public Employees Retirement Board, 1721
New Mexico State Agency on Aging, 1722
New Mexico State Library: Blind and Physically Handicapped, 11621
New Mexico Technology, 1723
New Mexico Veterans Service Commission, 1724
New Mexico Workers Compensation Board, 1725
New Mobility, 3938
New Orleans Advocacy Center, 11129
New Orleans Council on Aging, 1169
New Orleans Public Library: Louisiana Division, 11517
New Perspective of Minnesota, 9232
New Pond Village, 9003
New Readers Press, 4520
New Vision Enterprises, 7703
New Vision Store, 7850
The New Vision Store, 3446, 3451
New Vistas Independent Living Center, 10858
New York Center on Alcohol and Substance Abuse, 7200
New York Chapter of the Arthritis Foundaion, 5125
New York Chapter of the Arthritis Foundation, 5134, 5177
New York City Department for the Aging, 1794
New York Client Assistance Program, 1795
New York College of Osteopathic Medicine, 7038
New York Commission on Quality of Care and Advocacy for Persons with Disabilities, 1796
New York Department of Aging, 1797
New York Department of Health: Office ofPublic Health, AIDS Institute, 4489
New York Department of Taxation & Finance, 1798
New York Developmental Disability Planning Council, 1799
New York Division of Tourism, 11980
New York Division of Veterans Affairs, 1800
New York Foundation for Otologic Research, 6808
New York Legal Aid Society, 11205
New York Office of Mental Health Binghamton Psychiatric Center Library Services Department, 11650
New York Office on Aging, 1801

1033

Entry Name Index / N

New York Public Library, 11651
New York Public Library General Reference & Advisory Services: Accessibility Services, 11652
New York Society for the Deaf, 6422
New York State Association of Area Agencies on Aging, 1802
New York State Bar Association: Elder Law Section, 11206
New York State Coalition for the Aging, 1803
New York State Commission On Quality ofCare and Advocacy for Persons with Disabilities, 11207
New York State Commission for the Blind, 1804
New York State Directory of AIDS/HIV Clinical Trials, 4540
New York State Division of Disability Determinations, 1805
New York State Independent Living Council, 10877
New York State Institute for BasicResearch in Developmental Disabilities, 4347
New York State Intergenerational Network, 1806
New York State OASIS, 7201
New York State Office for the Aging, 11208
New York State Office for the Aging: Senior Citizens Hotline, 1807
New York State Office of Advocate for Persons with Disabilities, 1808
New York State Office of Alcoholism & Substance Abuse Services, 7202
New York State Office of Mental Health, 1809
New York State Talking Book & Braille Library, 11653
New York Teachers Retirement System, 1810
New York Times Company, 3987
New York Times Large Type Weekly, 3987
New York University Medical Center, 5926
New York University Medical Rehabilitation Research and Training Center, 7120
New York University: General Clinical Research Center, 6924
New York University: Kaplan Comprehensive Cancer Center, 5942
Newcomer Asks, 7387
Newel Perry Award, 2667
Newmarket Press, 6854
Newport Beach Plaza, 8204
Newport News Public Library System, 11819
News Report, 6917
News from the Points of Light Foundation, 4073
Newseasons of Cherry Hill, 9793
Newseasons of Voorhees, 9794
Newsletter of the Central Pennsylvania Chapter, 5213
Newsletter of the Kansas Chapter of the Arthritis Foundation, 5214
Newsline, 4074
Newsline for the Blind, 7886, 7909, 7974
Next Best Place, 9357
Nexus Magazine, 3939
Niagara County Office for the Aging, 1811
Niagara Frontier Center for Independent Living (NFCIL), 10878

Nicollet Place, 9233
Nicotine Addiction and Cigarettes, 4075
Night Light: A Book of Nighttime Meditations, 3652
Nightingale Suites at Springwood, 8247
Nisonger Center for Mental Retardation and Developmental Disabilities, 4348
Nissi Care Homes, 10500
No Less a Woman, 5801
No Limits Communications, 3938
No Longer Disabled: The Federal Courts, 11033
No Longer Immune: A Counselor's Guide to AIDS, 4530
No Smoking: Lungs at Work, 4076
No-Bows Shoe Lace Fasteners, 3243
Noland Health Services, 8078
Noll Physiological Research Center, 4349
Nolo, 3645
Nolo's Guide to Social Security Disability: Getting and Keeping Your Benefits, 3653
Nomis Publications, 3775
Non-Discrimination in Federally Assisted Programs, 271
Non-Discrimination in the Community Development Block Grant Program, 272
Nonprescription Drugs: Modern Medicines for Mature Americans, 7388
Nonprofit Housing and Care Options for Older People, 4077
Noonan Good Samaritan Center, 9575
Norfolk Homestead, 9683
Norfolk Senior Center & Adult Day Health Care, 2464
Norman House Group Home, 8877
Norris Cotton Cancer Center, 5768
North American Vegetarian Society, 3968
North Atlanta Senior Services, 2764
North Bay Manor, 10219
North Carolina Area: Agency on Aging, 1901
North Carolina Assisted Living Association, 9524
North Carolina Assistive Technology Projects, 1902
North Carolina Association of Long Term Care Facilities, 1903
North Carolina Association of Nonprofit Homes for the Aging, 1904
North Carolina Center for CreativeRetirement, 2879
North Carolina Client Assistance Program, 1905
North Carolina Council on Developmental Disabilities, 1906
North Carolina Department of Administration: Advocacy Council for Persons with Disabilities, 1907
North Carolina Department of Aging, 1908
North Carolina Department of Health & Natural Resources: Communicable Disease Control Section, 4490
North Carolina Department of Human Resources: Deaf & Hard of Hearing Division, 6423
North Carolina Department of Human Resources: Services for the Blind, 1909
North Carolina Department of Revenue, 1910
North Carolina Department of the State: Treasurer Division of Retirement Systems, 1911

North Carolina Dept of Human Resources, 3704
North Carolina Division of Aging and Adult Services, 11215
North Carolina Division of Mental Health, Developmental Disabilities and Abuse Services, 6049, 7203
North Carolina Division of Tourism, 11981
North Carolina Industrial Commission, 1912
North Carolina Library for the Blind, 11683
North Carolina Retired Government Employees Association, 1913
North Carolina Senior Citizens Association, 1914
North Carolina Society to Prevent Blindness, 7704
North Carolina Workers Compensation Board, 1915
North Central Alabama Regional Council of Governments: Area Agency on Aging, 379
North Central Area Agency on Aging, 688
North Central Area: Agency on Aging, 1457
North Central Flint Hills Area: Agency on Aging, 1078
North Central Independent Living Services, 10835
North Central Regional Training Center: Canine Companions for Independence, 7705
North Central Sight Services, 7706
North Central Texas Area: Agency on Aging, 2331
North Central West Virginia Center for Independent Living, 10950
North Central-Area Agency on Aging, 1549
North Coast Opportunities: Area Agency on Aging, 568
North Country Association for the Visually Impaired, 7707
North Country Center for Independence, 10879
North County Independent Living-Ashland, 10959
North County Independent Living-Superior, 10960
North Dakota Aging Services, 1926
North Dakota Aging Services Division, 11218
North Dakota Client Assistance Program, 1927
North Dakota Department of Aging, 1928
North Dakota Department of Mental Health, 6050
North Dakota Department of Veterans Affairs, 1929
North Dakota Lawyer Referral and Information Service: Elder Law Panel, 11219
North Dakota Mental Health & Substance Abuse, 7204
North Dakota Protection & Advocacy, 1930
North Dakota Protection and Advocacy Agency, 11220
North Dakota Public Employees Retirement System, 1931
North Dakota State Council on Developmental Disabilities, 1932
North Dakota State Library: Disability Services, 11697
North Dakota State Tax Department, 1933

North Dakota Teachers Retirement Fund, 1934
North Dakota Workers Compensation, 1935
North Delta Planning and Development District Area Agency on Aging, 1458
North Delta-Area Agency on Aging, 1170
North Florida Area: Agency on Aging, 765
North Hanover Senior Citizen Club, 1671
North Idaho College Area: Agency on Aging, 890
North Kentucky Area Development District, 1125
North Mobile Retirement Center, 8073
North Oaks on Emerson, 9234
North Platte Public Library, 11601
North Shore Elder Services, 1304
North Shore Retirement Hotel, 8596
North Texas Chapter of the Arthritis Foundation, 5126
NorthEast Independent Living Services (NEILS), 10823
Northampton County Area Community College, 2908
Northampton County Area: Agency on Aging, 2135
Northeast California Chapter of the Arthritis Foundation, 5127
Northeast Florida Area: Agency on Aging, 766
Northeast Georgia Area: Agency on Aging, 841
Northeast Independent Living Program, 10795
Northeast Kansas Area: Agency on Aging, 1079
Northeast Michigan Community Services Region 9 Area: Agency on Aging, 1368
Northeast Mississippi Area: Agency on Aging, 1459
Northeast Nebraska Area: Agency on Aging, 1584
Northeast Pennsylvania Center for Independent Living, 10918
Northeast Regional Training Center: Canine Companions for Independence, 7708
Northeastern Association of the Blind at Albany, 7709
Northeastern Illinois Area: Agency on Aging, 932
Northeastern Ohio Chapter of the Arthritis Foundation, 5128
Northeastern Vermont Area: Agency on Aging, 2429
Northern Area: Agency on Aging, 2578
Northern Arizona Council of Governments Area Agency on Aging, 439
Northern California Cancer Center, 5769
Northern California Chapter of the Arthritis Foundation, 5129
Northern California Chapter of the NHF, 4547
Northern California Chapter, NHF, 4549
Northern California State Library: Braille and Talking Book Library, 11342
Northern Expressions Publishing, 11890
Northern Hills, 8711
Northern Illinois University: Research and Training Center, 6809
Northern Kentucky Talking Book Library, 11513
Northern Mississippi Rural Legal Services (NMRLS): Elder Law Project - Oxford (Administrative) Office, 11169
Northern Neck Middle Penninsula Area: Agency on Aging, 2465
Northern Nevada Center for Independent Living, 10846
Northern New England Association of Homes and Services for the Aging, 1629
Northern New England Chapter of the Arthritis Foundation, 5130
Northern Regional Center for Independent Living, 10880
Northern Rocky Mountain Retiree Association, 1550
Northern Virginia Resource Center for Deaf and Hard of Hearing Persons, 6424
Northfield Parkview, 9235
Northfield Senior Center, 1305
Northland Library Cooperative, 11568
Northpark-A Classic Residence by Hyatt, 8426
Northpointe Woods Assisted Living, 9067
Northridge Center, 10137
Northridge Retirement Community, 9684
Northridge Travel, 12036
Northside Retirement Home, 9236
Northside Shepherd's Center, 2765
Northumberland County Area: Agency onAging, 2136
Northwest Aging Association, 11113
Northwest Alabama Council of Governments: Area Agency on Aging, 380
Northwest Arkanasas Area: Agency on Aging, 472
Northwest Assistance for the Elderly Project, 11261
Northwest Geriatric Education Center, 11831
Northwest Indiana Community Action Corp, 11102
Northwest Indiana Subregional Library for Blind and Physically Handicapped, 11484
Northwest Justice Project: Olympia, 11287
Northwest Justice Project: Seattle, 11288
Northwest Justice Project: Vancouver, 11289
Northwest Kansas Area: Agency on Aging, 1080
Northwest Kansas Library System Talking Books, 11501
Northwest Limousine Service, 11937
Northwest Oaks, 10501
Northwest Ozarks Regional Library for the Blind and Handicapped, 11332
Northwest Regional Training Center: Canine Companions for Independence, 7710
Northwest Tennessee Area Agency on Aging, 11261
Northwest Tennessee Area Agency on Aging and Disability, 2279
Northwest Tennessee Development District, 2279
Northwestern Area: Agency on Aging, 2550
Northwestern Center for Clinical Research, 4594
Northwestern Connecticut AIDS Project, 4614
Northwestern Illinois Area: Agency on Aging, 933
Northwestern Illinois Center for Independent Living, 10730
Northwestern Medical Center, 4689
Northwestern Ohio Area: Agency on Aging, 1961
Northwestern Ohio Chapter of the Arthritis Foundation, 5131
Northwestern University Cancer Center, 5943
Northwestern University: Buehler Center on Aging, 4350
Northwestern University: Ernest S Bazley Asthma and Allergic Disease Center, 4689
Northwestern University: General Clinical Research Center, 4351
Northwestern University: Multipurpose Arrhitis & Musculoskeletal Center, 5244
Norton-Lambert Corporation, 3092
Norumbega Point at Weston, 9004
Norwood Park Home, 8597
Nosey Cup, 3342
Not My Home, 4154
Not Without Sight, 7887
Notes from the Underground, 4566
Nottingham House Assited Living Residenc, 9795
Nova Walker, 3483
November Days, 7067
Now What Do I Do for Fun?, 7389
Now Where Did I Put My Keys?, 4078
Nurse Healers-Professional Associates International, 273
Nurses Christian Fellowship, 274
Nursing & Convalescent Homes Directory, 3776
Nursing Home Chain Directory, 3777
Nursing Home Directory, 3778
Nursing Home Information Services, 3654
Nursing Home Law Letter, 4079
Nutrition Action Healthletter, 4080
Nutrition Education Association, 5770
Nutrition Guide to Food Allergies, 4671
Nutrition Health Review, 3940
Nutrition Services Incentive Program (NSIP), 2466
Nutrition for Patients Receiving Chemotherapy/Radiation Treatment, 5832
Nye Square Retirement Community, 9685

O

O'Connor Woods, 8205
OASIS Akron, 2887
OASIS Cleveland, 2888
OASIS Denver, 2738
OASIS Eugene, 2898
OASIS Houston, 2927
OASIS Hyattsville, 2810
OASIS Institute, 2835
OASIS Los Angeles, 2722
OASIS Montgomery County, 2811
OASIS Pittsburgh, 2909
OASIS Portland, 2899
OASIS Rochester, 2867
OASIS San Antonio, 2928
OASIS San Diego, 2723
OASIS of Escondido, 2724
OASIS of Tucson, 2703
OKDHS Aging Services Division, 2012

Entry Name Index / O

OPTIONS for Independence-Northern UtahCenter For Independent Living, 10934
ORYX Press, 3618, 3672
Oak Estates, 8712
Oak Hill Center, 10562
Oak Hill Living Center, 9525
Oak Hill Living Center Assisted Living, 9237
Oak Park Place, 9238
Oak Park Place-Albert Lea, 9239
Oak Park Retirement Center, 10502
Oak Ridge Assisted Living-Hastings, 9240
Oak Ridge Place, 9241
Oak Ridge Retirement Community, 10367
Oak Shadows Allendale, 10503
Oak Wood Acres, 10504
Oak Wood Place, 10505
Oakcrest Village, 8925
Oakenwald Terrace, 9242
Oakland & Macomb Center for IndependentLiving, 10805
Oakland County Library for the Blind and Physically Handicapped, 11569
Oakland Heights, 8713, 9686
Oakland Public Library, 11343
Oakmont Estate, 8878
Oaknoll Assisted Living, 8714
Oaks, 9243
Oaks Retirement Center, 9687
Oaks at Lebanon, 10138
Oaks of Kingsport, 10368
Oaktree Assisted Living, 10506
Oakview Assisted Living Center, 9526
Oakwood Place Assisted Living at Ridgecrest Village, 8715
Oakwood Village, 8879, 9924
Oasis Logan County Senior Center, 934
Occupation Hearing Services, 6425
Occupational Hearing Service, 6426
Ocean County Office on Aging, 1672
Ocean Crest Retirement & Assisted Living Facility, 10139
Ocean State Center for Independent Living, 10921
Oconee Regional Library, 11442
Odd Fellows Home of Idaho, 8537
Odyssey Club, 12037
Odyssey Institute Corporation, 7205
Office for Aging and Community Services: Monterey County Department of Social Services, 569
Office for American Indian, Alaskan Native and Native Hawaiian Programs: Administration on Aging, 3583
Office for Special Education & Rehab Service, 110
Office of AIDS, 4472
Office of AIDS Administration, 4459
Office of AIDS/STD, 4498
Office of Applied Studies, 7283, 7469
Office of Communications, 7477
Office of Disability: Social Security Administration, 275
Office of Disease Prevention and Health Promotion, 227
Office of Elderly Affairs, 1158
Office of Elderly and Assisted Housing, 154
Office of Fair Housing and Equal Opportunity, 271
Office of Financial Aid, 6359
Office of Human Services, 2137
Office of Independent and Employment, 2599
Office of Indian Affairs: Indian Area Agency on Aging, 1726
Office of Multifamily Development, 172
Office of Public Affairs, Social Security Administration, 570
Office of Retirement and Survivors, 1250
Office of Supplemental Security Income, 276
Office of Supplemental Security Income: Social Security Administration, 1251
Office of Women's Services, 7206
Office of the Attorney General, 10981
Office of the Attorney General: Senior Citizens Advocacy Division, 11092
Office of the Ohio Attorney General: Health, Education & Human Services Section, 11221
Office on Aging, 1260
Office on Aging: Senior Citizens Referral Panel, 11194
Office on Smoking and Health, 4237, 7207
The Official Patient's Sourcebook on Female Urinary Incontinence, 6953
The Official Pocket Guide for Diabetic Exchanges, 6220
Ohio Assisted Living Association, 9925
Ohio Association of Area Agencies onAging, 1962
Ohio Bureau on Alcohol Abuse and Recovery, 7208
Ohio Client Assistance Program, 1963
Ohio County Public Library Services for the Blind and Physically Handicapped, 11838
Ohio Department of Aging, 11959, 1964, 11222
Ohio Department of Drug and Alcohol Addiction Services: Ohio Prevention and Education Resource Center, 7470
Ohio Department of Health, 7208
Ohio Department of Health: Division of Preventive Medicine, 4491
Ohio Department of Mental Health, 6051
Ohio Department of Taxation, 1965
Ohio Developmental Disability Council, 1966
Ohio Disabled American Veterans, 1967
Ohio Division of Travel and Tourism, 11982
Ohio Governor's Council on People with Disabilities, 1968
Ohio Masonic Home, 9926
Ohio Protection & Advocacy for Persons With Disabilities, 1969
Ohio Protection and Advocacy Agency: Ohio Legal Rights Service (OLRS), 11223
Ohio Public Employees Retirement System, 1970
Ohio Regional Library for the Blind and Physically Handicapped, 11711
Ohio Rehabilitation Services Commission, 1946
Ohio River Valley Chapter of the Arthritis Foundation, 5132
Ohio School Employees Retirement System, 1971
Ohio School for the Deaf Alumni Association, 6427
Ohio School for the Deaf Library, 11712
Ohio State University, 2889, 4348
Ohio State University Comprehensive Cancer Center, 5944
Ohio State University Neuroscience Program, 4352, 5063
Ohio State University: Clinical Research Center, 5945
Ohio State University: Division of Clinical Trials, 7471
Ohio State University: Otological Research Laboratories, 6810
Ohio University: School of Hearing and Speech Science, 6811
Okada Specialty Guide Dogs, 6428
Oklahoma & Arkansas Alzheimer's Associaton, 4939
Oklahoma Aging Services Division, 11226
Oklahoma Association Area: Agencies onAging, 2013
Oklahoma Association of Homes and Services for the Aging, 2014
Oklahoma Chapter of the Arthritis Foundation, 5133
Oklahoma City Law Center, 11225
Oklahoma Client Assistance Program, 2015
Oklahoma Department of Aging, 2016
Oklahoma Department of Health and Human Services: Alzheimer's Research Advisory Council, 4940
Oklahoma Department of Health: HIV/STD Service, 4492
Oklahoma Department of Human Services, 11226
Oklahoma Department of Mental Health, 6052
Oklahoma Department of Mental Health and Substance Abuse Services, 7209
Oklahoma Department of Mental Health andSubstance Abuse Services (ODMHSAs), 11227
Oklahoma Department of Veterans Affairs, 2017
Oklahoma Developmental Disability Council, 2018
Oklahoma Disability Law Center, 2019
Oklahoma Disability Law Center: Oklahoma City, 11228
Oklahoma Disability Law Center: Tulsa, 11229
Oklahoma League for the Blind, 7711
Oklahoma Library for the Blind & Physically Handicapped, 11722
Oklahoma Medical Research Foundation, 5245
Oklahoma Medical Research Foundation: Arthritis Immunology Research, 5246
Oklahoma Medical Research Foundation: Cardiovascular Research Program, 6884
Oklahoma Medical Research Foundation: Immunology & Cancer Research, 5946
Oklahoma Methodist Manor, 10030
Oklahoma Protection & Advocacy Agecny, 2019
Oklahoma Protection and Advocacy Agency, 11228, 11229
Oklahoma School for the Blind, 2896
Oklahoma State Office of Rehabilitation Services: Visually Impaired, 7712
Oklahoma Tax Commission, 2020
Oklahoma Tourism & Recreation Department, 11983
Oklahomans For Independent Living, 10902

Old Colony Planning Council Area: Agency on Aging, 1306
Old Fellows Home, 9576
Old Fort Genealogical Society Of Southeastern Kansas Inc, 11502
Old Lesbians Organizing for Change, 277
Older & Wiser: A Workbook for Coping with Aging, 3655
Older Adult Institute, 2779
Older Adult Program, 2725
Older Adults After Treatment, 7390
Older Adults in Treatment, 7391
Older Adults with Hearing Loss, 6693
Older Americans Report, 4081
Older Americans, Vital Communities, 3656
Older People and Their Caregivers Across the Spectrum of Care, 3657
Older Than My Mother: A Nurse's Life & Triumph, 5802
Older Women's League, 278
Older Women's League of Ohlone, 571
Older Women's Network, 357
Older is Better Senior Adult Program, 2848
Olean Center, 10881
Oley Foundation for Home Parenteral and Enteral Nutrition, 279
Olive View: UCLA Education and Researchnstitute, 4353
Ollie A. Randall Award, 2668
Olmstead County Human Services Building, 1436
Olympic Alzheimers Foundation, 4941
Olympic Area: Agency on Aging, 2512
Olympics West Retirement Inn, 10596
Omaha Department of Veteran Affairs Medical Center Research Service, 6280
Omni West, 9927
Omnigraphics, 4954, 5794, 6194
On Death and Dying, 6024
On Golden Pond, 9244
On My Own, 6536, 10824
On Top of My Game: Living with Diabetes, 6266
On Your Behalf, 3658
Once a Year for a Lifetime, 5833
Oncology Nursing Society, 5771
One Day at a Time in Al-Anon, 7266
One Step at a Time Brochure, 7010
1-800-BRAILLE, 7491
10 Questions to Help You Make Sense of Health Headlines, 4168
100 Questions & Answers About Parkinson's Disease, 6979
100 Questions and Answers About AIDS and HIV, 4514
101 Tips for Improving Your Blood Sugar, 6179
121 Congressional Lane, 3565
1230 Avenue of the Americas, 5152
1B Area: Agency on Aging, 1335
Oneida County Office for the Aging, 1812
Onhealth, 4238
Onslow Coordinating Council on Aging, 11216
Ontario County Office for the Aging, 1813
Onyx Press, 3706, 3731
Operation ABLE of Greater Boston, 1307
Ophthalmic Research Laboratory Eye Institute, 8050
Opportunities for Access, 10731
Opportunity, 7888, 7975

Options Center for Independent Living, 10732
Options Interstate Resource Center for Independent Living, 10808
Options for Independent Living-Appleton, 10961
Options for Independent Living-Green Bay, 10962
Options: A Directory of Child and Senior Services, 3779
Opus Communications, 4082
Oral Cancers: Research Report, 5834
Oral Interpreters: A Communication Option, 6694
Oral Interpreters: Facts for Consumers, 6695
Orange County Area: Agency on Aging, 572
Orange County Department on Aging: Saturday School for Senior Citizens, 2880
Orange County Home for Adults, 10563
Orange County Korean Community Service Center, 573
Orange County Library System Audio-Visual Department, 11420
Orange County Library System: Genealogy Department, 11421
Orange County Office for Aging, 1814
Orchard Grove, 9928
Orchard Hill At Sudbury, 9005
Orchard Hills, 10293
Orchard Park, 9688
Orchard Valley at Wilbraham, 9006
Orchards at Bartley Assisted Living, 9796
Orchards at Southington, 8287
Oregon Advocacy Center, 2056
Oregon Advocacy Center (OAC), 11233
Oregon Alliance of Senior & Health Services, 2057
Oregon Cascades West Senior Services, 2058
Oregon Commission for the Blind, 7713
Oregon Commission on Disabilities, 2059
Oregon Council on Developmental Disabilities, 2060
Oregon Department of Aging, 2061
Oregon Department of Human Resources, 4493
Oregon Department of Human Services: Division of Senior & Disabled Services, 2062
Oregon Department of Mental Health, 6053
Oregon Department of Revenue, 2063
Oregon Department of Veterans Affairs, 2064
Oregon Health Sciences University, 7039
Oregon Health Sciences University: Oregon Hearing Research Center, 6812
Oregon Hearing Society, 2065
Oregon Office of Alcohol and Drug Abuse Programs, 7210
Oregon Protection & Advocacy for Persons with Disabilities, 2066
Oregon Protection and Advocacy Agency, 11233
Oregon Public Employees Retirement System, 2067
Oregon Research Institute, 4354
Oregon School for the Blind Media Center, 11725
Oregon Senior Citizens' Center, 1972
Oregon Senior Services, 2068
Oregon State Bar: Rights of Persons with Disabilities Section, 11234

Oregon State Commission for the Blind, 7714
Oregon State Library, 11726
Oregon Tourism Commission, 11984
Orentreich Foundation for the Advancement of Science, 4355
Orlando Lutheran Towers, 8427
Orleans County Office for the Aging, 1815
Ortho-Kinetics-EZ-International Inc., 3422
Ortho-Kinetics/EZ International, 3421
Ortho-Kinetics/EZ-International, 3418, 3437
Ortho-Kinetics/EZ-International, Inc., 3444, 3445
Orthopedic Products Corporation, 3043
Osceola County Council on Aging, 767
Osher Lifelong Learning Institute, 2748
Osher Lifelong Learning InstituteCollege of Extended Studies, 2726
Osherlifelong Learning Institutet, 2881
Osseo Gardens, 9245
Osteoarthritis, 5215
Osteonecrosis, 5216
Oswego County Office for the Aging, 1816
Other Side of Silence, 6537
Oticon Portable Telephone Amplifier, 3147
Otosclerosis, 6696
Ototoxic Medications: What You Should Know, 6697
Otsego County Office for the Aging, 1817
Otterbein Homes Program Department, 3593, 3594, 11891
Otterbein Portage Valley, 9929
Ouachita Council on Aging, 1171
Our Circle of Friends, 9246
Our Grandchild, 4239
Our Home, Your Home, 9247
Our Homes, 9689
Our House, 9248
Our House Board and Lodge, 9249
Our Immune System, 4567, 4576
Our Special, 7889
Our World Service Office, 7392
Out of Left Field, 7890
Out-N-About American Walker, 3484
Outback Ranch Outfitters, 12038
Outdoor Independence, 3425
Outdoor Loud Bell, 3148
Outliving Heart Disease, 6854
Outlook Pointe at Knoxville, 10369
Outlook Pointe at Lima, 9930
Outlook Pointe at Medina, 9931
Outlook Pointe at Morristown, 10370
Outlook Pointe at Mountain Home, 8108
Outlook Pointe at Northridge, 9527
Outlook Pointe at Oak Ridge, 10371
Outlook Pointe at Ontario, 9932
Outlook Pointe at Ravenna, 9933
Outlook Pointe at Sagamore Hills, 9934
Outlook Pointe at Xenia, 9935
Outsiders in a Hearing World, 6538
Outsmarting Diabetes, 6212
Outstanding Continuing Education Student Awards, 2669
Outstanding Newsletter Recognitions, 2670
Outstanding Service Medallion, 2671
Oval Window Audio, 3286
Over 50 Directory & Handbook, 3780
Over 50 and a Skier?, 4240
Over the Hill Gang International, 280
Over the Rainbow, 12039
Overbrook School for the Blind Library, 11737

Entry Name Index / P

Overcoming Depression, 6075
Overcoming Impotence: A Leading Urologist Tells You Everything You Need to Know, 6938
Overcoming Rheumatoid Arthritis, 5217
Overland Park Place, 8813
Oxford Gerontology Center Library, 11654
Ozark Independent Living, 10825

P

PACE II, 2766
PALAESTRA, 11938
PARI Independent Living Center, 10922
PN, 3941
PRIDE Foundation, 281
PROPATH, 6959
PSA 2 Area Agency On Aging, 574
PXE International, 1308
Pac-All Carriers, 3557
Pac-All Wheelchair Carrier, 3557
Pace Adult Resource Center, 2868
Pace Saver Plus II, 3426
Pace University, 2868
Pacific Gardens Tarzana, 8206
Pacific Health Research Institute, 5947
Padded Bathtub Transfer Bench, 3019
Paddock Kensington, 9690
Pafford Place, 10507
Pain Syndromes and Parkinson's Disease, 7011
Paisley House for Aged Women, 9936
Palm Beach County Library Annex, 11424
Palm Beach Home for Adults, 9847
Palm Beach Junior College, 2755
Palm Beach Treasure Coast Area: Agency on Aging, 768
Palmer Independence, 3427
Palmer Industries, 3425, 3427, 3428
Palmer Pioneers' Home, 8097
Palmer Twosome, 3428
Palo Alto Commons, 8207
Palomino Press, 11892
Pamplin College of Business, 159
Panhandle Area: Agency on Aging, 2332
Panic Disorder, 6098
Pap Test: It Can Save Your Life, 5835
Papier-Mache Press, 11893
Papillion Senior Citizen Center, 1585
Paragon Gardens, 8208
Paralyzed Veterans of America, 3941, 12046
Paralyzed Veterans of America (PVA), 11047
Paramount Parks at Boise, 8538
Paraquad, 10826
Parent Resource Library, 11341
Paring Boards, 3343
Park Avenue Estates, 9691
Park City Convention & Visitors Bureau, 11994
Park Lane Estates, 9250
Park Place, 9692, 10613
Park Place Assisted Living, 10294
Park Place Assisted Living Residence, 10140
Park Place Estates, 8716
Park Place Retirement, 10508
Park Place Retirement Community, 10372
Park Place Retirement Residence of Friendswood, 10509

Park Place Retirement Residence of Stafford, 10510
Park Place Senior Congregate Assisted Living, 9251
Park River Good Samaritan, 9577
Park Square Manor, 10749
Park View Assisted Living, 8814
Park Village Pines, 9068
Park at Beckett Meadows, 10511
The Park at Vernon Hills, 8615
Parke Senior Living, 10031
Parker Oaks Assisted Living, 9252
Parkersburg and Wood County Public Library, 11839
Parkhurst House, 10141
Parkinson Association of Arizona, 6960
Parkinson Association of Davenport, 6961
Parkinson Association of Florida West Coast, 6962
Parkinson Association of Greater Kansas City, 6963
Parkinson Association of Hawaii, 6964
Parkinson Association of Michigan, 6965
Parkinson Association of Minnesota, 6966
Parkinson Association of New York, 6967
Parkinson Association of Orange County, 6968
Parkinson Association of South Dakota, 6969
Parkinson Association of South West Florida, 6970
Parkinson Association of Wisconsin, 6971
Parkinson Association of the Sacramento Valley, 6972
Parkinson Assocition of Greater Daytona, 6973
Parkinson Handbook: A Guide for Patients and Their Families, 7012
Parkinson Network of Mt Diablo, 6974
Parkinson Rehabilitation Center, 6975
Parkinson Report, 7013
Parkinson's Disease & Movement Disorders, 6982
Parkinson's Disease Foundation, 7014, 7040
Parkinson's Disease Foundation Newsletter, 7014
Parkinson's Disease Handbook, 6983, 7015
Parkinson's Disease for Dummies, 6984
Parkinson's Disease: 300 Tips for Making Life Easier, 6985
Parkinson's Disease: A Complete Guide for Patients and Families, 6986
Parkinson's Disease: The Patient Experience, 7016
Parkinson's Patient: What You and Your Family Should Know, 7017
Parkinson's Support Group of Upstate New York, 6976
Parkinsons Action Network, 6977
Parkinsons Report, 7018
Parkland College, 2778
Parkland Village Assisted Living Facility, 10142
Parkside Medical Services Corporation, 7211
Parkview Apartments Assisted Living, 10295
Parkview Lodge Asssited Living, 9693
Parkway Retirement Home, 9528
Parkwood Apartments, 9253
Parkwood Meadows Assisted Living Community, 8539

Parkwood Place, 10512
Parkwood Village, 8815
Parma Living Center, 8540
Parsons House on Eagle Run, 9694
Part A Title III: Ombudsman Services for Older Individuals, 282
Part A Title VI: Grants to Indian Tribes and Part B Title VI: Grants to Native Hawaiians, 283
Part B Title III: Grants for Supportive Services and Senior Centers, 284
Part C Title III: Nutrition Services, 285
Part F Title 111: Preventive Health Services Special Programs for the Aging, 286
Part G Title 111: Prevention of Abuse, Neglect and Exploitation of Older Individuals, 287
Part of the Community: Strategies for Including Everyone, 3659
Partnership for Prescription Assistance, 4241
Partnership for a Drug-Free America, 7212
Pasadena Braille Club, 7715
Pasadena Braille Club, 7716
Passages Adult Resource Center-Area Agency on Aging, 575
Passages Through Recovery, 7267
Passaic County Office on Aging, 1673
Pathfinder House, 9695
Pathfinders for Independent Living, 10777
Pathways For the Future-Center For IndepEndent Living, 10840
Pathways: Moving Beyond Stroke and Aphasis, 7068
Patient Advocates for Advanced Cancer Treatments, 5772
Patient Perspectives on Parkinson's, 7019
Patient Services Resource Center, 5134
A Patient's Guide to Visual Aids and Illumination, 7910
Patient's Guide to Visual Aids and Illumination, 7976
Patriot Ridge Community, 9937
Pattern Control, 4083
Paul B Beeson Career Development Awardsin Aging Research Program, 2672
Pawnee Hills, 9696
Paws for Silence, 6587
Paynesville Area Senior Center, 1418
Pearlman Biomedical Research Institute, 5247
Pebble Creek Senior Care Residence, 9938
Pender Care Center, 9697
Penguin Group USA, 6855
Penguin USA, 3739
Penicillamine, 5218
Peninsula Center for Independent Living, 10944
Peninsula Hospital of Far Rockway, 7041
Peninsula Shepherd Senior Centers, 2727
Pennsylvania Association of Area Agencies on Aging Directors, 2138
Pennsylvania Association of Non-Profit Homes for the Aging, 2139
Pennsylvania Bar Association: Elder LawSection, 11240
Pennsylvania Bureau of Blindness and Visual Services, 7717
Pennsylvania Center for Travel, Tourism & Film, 11985
Pennsylvania Client Assistance Program, 2140

Entry Name Index / P

Pennsylvania College of Optometry Eye Institute, 8051
Pennsylvania Department of Aging: LegalServices and Assistance, 11241
Pennsylvania Department of Health: Bureau of HIV/AIDS, 4494, 4580
Pennsylvania Department of Labor & Industry, 2191
Pennsylvania Department of Public Welfare Norristown State Hospital, 11738
Pennsylvania Department of Revenue, 2141
Pennsylvania Department on Aging, 2142
Pennsylvania Developmental Disabilities Council, 2143
Pennsylvania Drug and Alcohol Programs, 7213
Pennsylvania Hearing Aid Alliance, 6429
Pennsylvania Protection & Advocacy for Persons with Disabilities, 2144
Pennsylvania Protection and Advocacy Agency, 11242
Pennsylvania Public School Employees' Retirement System, 2145
Pennsylvania Society for the Advancement of the Deaf and Hearing Impaired, 6430
Pennsylvania Society of Directors of Volunteer Services, 2146
Pennsylvania State University, 4349
Pennsylvania State University Center for Developmental and Health Genetics, 4356
Pennsylvania State University Gerontology Center, 4357
Pennsylvania State University: Artificial Heart Research Project, 6885
Pennsylvania State University: Human Development Collection, 11739
Pennsylvania State University: Noll Physiological Research Center, 4358
Pennsylvania Workers Compensation Board, 2147
Penrose Hospital: Webb Memorial Library, 11364
Pensacola Junior College Seniors Club, 2758
Pension & Profit Sharing Plan Companies Directory, 3781
Pension Benefit Guaranty Corporation, Office of the General Counsel Library, 11404
Pension Research Council (PRC), 288
Pension Rights Center, 289
Pension to Veterans, Surviving Spouses, and Children, 290
Pensions, 4242
Pensions & Investments: 1,000 Largest Retirement Funds, 3782
People Against Cancer, 5773
People Animals Love, 291
People vs. Noise, 6765
People with AIDS Working for Health, 4566
People's Medical Society, 292
Peralta Cancer Research Institute, 5948
Perfect Solutions, 3126
Performance Gel Cushions, 3220
Perigee Visual Dictionary of Signing, 7825
Perimeter Adult Learning and Services, 2767
Perimeter Park West, 1117
Perinton Retired Men's Club, 1818
Perioperative Management of Parkinson's Disease, 7020
Perkins School for the Blind: Samuel P Hayes Research Library, 11552

Permian Basin Area: Agency on Aging, 2333
Permobil, 3526
Permobil Max 90, 3525
Permobil Super 90, 3526
Permobil USA, 3525
Perry County Office for Aging, 2148
Perry Lutheran Home Assisted Living, 8717
Perseus Books, 4993
Perseus Books Group, 4532, 6180, 6213, 6218, 6219, 6987
Personal Census Search: Data User Services Division, 293
Personal FM Systems, 3149
Personal Infrared Listening System, 3150
Personal Reader Department, 7891, 7977
Personal Reader Update, 7891, 7977
Personals, 4155
Persons Assuming Control of their Environment (PACE), 10733
Perspective on Aging, 3942, 4084
Perspectives in Education and Deafness, 6588
Persuading Your Spouse/Relative/Friend to Acknowledge a Hearing Loss and Seek Help, 6698
Pet Scans: A New Look at Parkinson's Disease, 7021
Peter J. Salmon Award - Blind Worker of the Year, 2673
Peter Lamy Center, 4289
Peter Lamy Center for Drug Therapy and Aging, 4359, 7449
Peterson Assisted Living, 8816
Peterson's, 3736
Pfizer/AGS Postdoctoral Research Awards, 2674
Pharmaceutical Research & Manufacturers of America, 4546
Pheasant Pointe Assisted Living, 10143
Philadelphia 1 Chapter-Self Help for Hard of Hearing People, 6431
Philadelphia Biomedical Research Institute, 4615
Philadelphia Corporation for Aging, 2149
Philadelphia Corporation for Aging Library, 11740
Philadelphia Department of Public Health: AIDS Program, 4495
Philadelphia Heart Institute: Geriatrics Practice, 6843
Phillip Roy, 3151
Phillips Publishing International, 4100
Philos House, 8541
Phoenix College, 2701
Phoenix Public Library: Special Needs Center, 11321
Phyllis Newstrom c/o Sioux Valley Hospital, 6969
Physical & Occupational Therapy in Geriatrics, 3943
Physical Disabilities—Education & Related Services, 3944
Physical Environments and Aging: Critical Contributions of M Powell Lawton to Theory and Practice, 3660
Physician Answers Your Questions About Hearing Health Care, 6699
Physicians Committee for Responsible Medicine, 5774

A Picture is Worth a Thousand Words for Blind and Visually Impaired Persons Too!, 7792
Picture is Worth a Thousand Words for Blind and Visually Impaired Persons, 7826
Piedmont Christian Home, 9529
Piedmont Senior Resources Area: Agency on Aging, 2467
Piedmont Triad Council of Governments Area: Agency on Aging, 1916
Pik Stik, 3020
Pike County Area: Agency on Aging, 2150
Pikes Peak Area: Agency on Aging, 652
Pilgram Manor, 9069
Pill Splitter, 3268
Pillow Talk, 3041
Pilot Books, 3642
Pilot Rock Senior Center, 2069
Pima Community College, 2704
Pima Community College: Adult EducationPrograms, 2704
Pima Council on Aging, 440, 11322
Pinal/Gila Council for Senior Citizens, 441
Pine Brook Assisted Living Center, 8542
Pine Haven Heritage Home, 10296
Pine Lane West Assisted Living Center, 10297
Pine Lane of Hartington, 9698
Pine Tree Cottage, 10513
Pinehill at Kimball Farms, 9007
Pines, 9254
Pines Senior Care, 9255
Pines of Tewksbury, 9008
Pioneer Estates of Minnesota, 9256
Pioneer House, 8320
Pioneer Place Assisted Living, 8718
Pioneer Senior Cottages, 9257
Pioneers Memorial Hospital, 5296
Pittsburgh Branch of the Pennsylvania Association for the Blind, 7718
Pittsburgh Hearing Speech and Deaf Services, 6432
Pittsburgh Hearing, Speech and Deaf Services, 6433
Pittsburgh Vision Service, 7719
Place at Gallitan, 10373
Place at Kingsport, 10374
Place of Their Own: Creating the DeafCommunity in America, 6539
A Place to Live: Housing Alternatives for the Elderly in Arizona, 3683
Placer Independent Resource Services/PIRS, 10673
Plain Talk About Depression, 4085
Plantation House-Okmulgee, 10032
Plantation Manor Assisted Living I, 8074
Plantation Place Retirement & Assisted Living, 8543
Plantation South at Duluth, 8437
Plantation South at Dunwoody, 8438
Plantronics SP-04, 3152
Plaquemines Council on Aging, 1172
Plastic Card Holder, 3466
Plato Society of UCLA, 2728
Platte Assisted Living, 10298
Plaza at Sun Mountain, 9736
Pleasant Valley Shelter Home, 8544
Plenum Press, 4974
Plum Creek Care Center, 9699
Plum Enterprises, 3269, 3271, 3272, 2151
Plums Award Winning Protects Hip, 3269

1039

Entry Name Index / P

Plus Magazie, 3945
Plus Magazine, 3945
Plymouth Crossings, 9009
Plymouth Inn, 9070
Po Box 1682, 645
Pocasset Lodge Assisted Living, 10220
Pocatello Assisted Living Center, 8545
Pocket Otoscope, 3270
Podiatry and Parkinson's Disease, 7022
Pohl Cancer Research Laboratory, 5949
Point Frontier Retirement Community, 10614
Point Plaza W, Bldg 2, 1645
Pointe at Cedar Park, 10514
Pointe at Kirby Gate, 10375
Points of Light Foundation, 4073
The Points of Light Foundation, 3807
Polio Network News, 3946
Polisher Research Institute Library: Philadelphia Geriatric Center, 11741
Polyarteritis Nodosa and Wegener's Granulomatosis, 5219
Polymyalgia Rheumatica and Giant Cell Arthritis, 5220
Pomperaug Woods, 8288
Ponderosa Villa, 9700
Pony Express Association for the Blind, 7720
Pony Express Association of the Blind, 7721
Pool Lifts for In-Ground Pools, 3388
Population Reference Bureau, 4360
Porch-Lift Vertical Platform Lift, 3389
Port Charles Assisted Living, 8719
Porta Ramps, 3390
Porta-Ramp, 3391
PortaPower Plus, 3153
Porter Hills Presbyterian Village, 9071
Portland Public Library, 11529
Portland State University Institute on Aging, 4361
Positioning Support Seats, 3221
Positive Living, 4086
Positively Aware, 4087
Post-Polio Health International, 3947
Postural Hypotension, 7023
Posture-Glide Lounger, 3527
Potentials Development, 11894
Potomac Technology, 3154
Potter County Area: Agency on Aging, 2152
Powell Valley ASL & ALZ Care Community, 10144
Power Chairs, 3528
Power Seat Base (6-Way), 2989
Power for Off-Pavement, 3529
Power of Attorney for Health Care, 3661
PowerLink 2 Control Unit, 3313, 3344
Practical Pointers for Parkinson Patients, 7024
Practical Theology for Aging, 3662
Praire View Inn, 8720
Prairie Crossings, 10299
Prairie Crossings-Brookings, 10300
Prairie Crossings-Huron, 10301
Prairie Crossings-Mitchell, 10302
Prairie Crossings-Sioux Falls, 10303
Prairie Crossings-Watertown, 10304
Prairie Good Samaritan Center Assisted Living, 10305
Prairie Home, 9578
Prairie Homes Assisted Living, 10306
Prairie House Retirement & Assisted Community, 10145

Prairie Pines Lodge, 9701
Prairie Senior Cottages-Alexandria, 9258
Prairie Senior Cottages-Hutchinson, 9259
Prairie Senior Cottages-Willmar, 9260
Prairie Sunset Village, 10307
Prairie View Assisted Living Center, 10308
Prairie View Gardens, 9702
Prairie Village Retirement, 9703
Prairie Winds, 9704
Pratt-Stanton Manor, 8880
Precious Time, 9705
Prediabetes: What You Need to Know to Keep Diabetes Away, 6213
Premier Estates, 8721, 9706
Premier Estates Senior Living Community, 9707
Premier Suites, 8722
Prentke Romich Company, 3105, 3121, 3165, 3184, 3186, 3155
Prentke Romich Company Product Catalog, 3156
Preparing for an Aging Society: Changes and Challenges, 3663
Presbyterian Assisted Living Homecare, 9261
Presbyterian Group Home-Waynesboro, 10564
Presbyterian Hospital, 6868
Presbyterian Hospital of Dallas, 7042
Presbyterian Medical Center, 7040
Presbyterian Residential Community, 9848
Presbyterian Village Redford, 9072
Presbyterian-St. Luke's Medical Center, 5898
Prescott Place, 9708
Prescott Talking Book Library, 11323
Prescriptions for Independence, 7827
Preserve Sight Mississippi, 1460
President's Award for Exceptional andInnovative Leadership in Adult and Continuing Education, 2675
President's Committee for People with Intellectual Disabilities (PCPID), 294
Prestige Assisted Living, 8209, 9737
Prestige Assisted Living at Autumn Wind, 8546
Prestige Assisted Living at Kalispell, 9358
Prestige Assisted Living at Yorba Linda, 8210
Prestige Living Northwest Residential, 8547
Prevent Blindness America, 7665, 7945, 7958, 7978, 7722
Prevent Blindness America New York City Division, 1819
Prevent Blindness Connecticut, 7723
Prevent Blindness Iowa, 7724
Prevent Blindness Nebraska, 7725
Prevent Blindness New Jersey, 1674
Prevent Blindness News, 7978
Prevent Blindness Northern California, 7726
Prevent Blindness Ohio, 7727
Prevent Blindness Oklahoma, 7728
Prevent Blindness Tennessee, 7729
Prevent Blindness Texas, 7730
Prevent Blindness Texas Central Regional, 6434
Prevent Blindness Tri-State, 7731
Prevent Blindness Virginia, 7732
Prevent and Reverse Heart Disease: The Revolutionary, Scientifically Proven, Nutrition-Based Care, 6855

Preventing & Reversing Arthritis Naturally, 5162
Preventing Relapse, 7393
Prevention, 3948
Prevention Resource Center, 7214
Prevention Science Group, 4627
Prevention of Blindness Society of Metropolitan Washington, 7733
Preventive Medicine Research Institute, 6886
Pride Institute, 7215
Primary Immune Deficiency Diseases: A Guide for Nurses, 4568
Prime Health & Fitness, 3949
Prime Time, 3988
Prime Times, 3989
PrimeTime Media Newspaper, 3988
Primrose, 9262
Primrose Assisted Living, 10309
Primrose Place, 10310
Primrose Retirement Center, 9579
Prince George's Community College, 2812
Prince George's County Bureau of Aging, 1252
Prince William Area: Agency on Aging, 2468
Princess Anne Residential Care, 9709
Princeton University, 4441
Princeton University Industrial Relations Library, 11615
Princeton University: Cutaneous Communication Laboratory, 6813
Princeton Village, 10146
Pritchett & Hull, 6181
Priva Inc., 3040
Private Cancer Clinic Tours, 5775
Private Long-Term Care Insurance: To Buy or Not to Buy?, 5006
Pro Bono Center for Disability and Elder Law (CDEL): Lifelong Lawyers Project, 11093
Pro Literacy Worldwide, 295
Pro Seniors, 11224
Pro-Ed, 4971
Products for People With Disabilities, 3783
Professional Advisory Support Award, 2676
Professional Book Distributing, 5146, 5158, 5163
Professional Respite Care, 12040
Professionals and Executives in Retirement, 2869
Profex Medical Products, 3037
A Profile of Older Americans, 3995
Profit Sharing/401(k) Council of America, 296
Program Booklet, 4088
Program Planners: Library/Information Center, 11655
Program Sixty, 2889
Program for You, 7268
Progress Center for Independent Living, 10734
Progressive Center for Independent Living (PCIL), 10854
Progressive Independence, 10903
Project AID Resource Center, 4544
Project Inform Hotline, 4496, 4581
Prometheus Books, 6938
Promise House, 8723
Promote Real Independence for the Disabled/Elderly, 281
Promoworks, 3784

Entry Name Index / Q

Prone Support Walker, 3485
Prostate Cancer Resource Network, 5803, 5825, 5841, 5853, 5776
Prostate Cancer: A Survivor's Guide, 5803
Prostate Health Workbook, 11698
Protecta Capstet, 3271
ProtectaCap+PLUS, ProtectaHip, 3272
Protecting Adult Welfare (PAW), 297
Protection & Advocacy for People with Disabilities, 2230
Protection & Advocacy for Persons with Developmental Disabilities, 381
Protection & Advocacy of Individual Rights, 1173
Provena Fox Knoll Retirement Community, 8598
Provena-Mercy Center Medical Library, 11463
Providence Assisted Living, 8926
Providence Benedictine Orchard House, 10147
Providence Brookside Manor, 10148
Providence Speech and Hearing Center, 6435
Providing Services for People with Vision Loss: Multidisciplinary Perspective, 7828
Pseudoxanthoma Elasticum Fact Sheet, 5221
Psoriatic Arthritis, 5222
Psychological Functioning of Older People, 3664
Psychological Stress and Hearing Loss, 6700
Psychology Department, Green Hall, 6813
Psychosocial Interventions in HIV Illness, 4531
Public Education Program, 7501
Public Information Associates, 5665
Public Interest Center on Long Term Care, 4089
Public Interest Law Center of Philadelphia, 11243
Public Interest Law Center: Philadelphia, 11244
Public Library of Cincinnati and Hamilton Outreach Services Department, 11713
Public Policy Report, 6099
Publications Department, 3809
Publications from the National Information Center on Deafness, 6701
Publicist's Guide to Senior Media, 3784
Pulaski Retirement Community, 10565
Pumping Insulin, 6214
Puppy Walker Brochure, 7979
Purchase Area Development District, 1126
Purdue University, 11485
Purdue University Cancer Center, 5950
Purdue University Press, 4956
Purdue University: Center for Research on Aging, 4362
Purdue University: Humanities, Social Science, Education Library, 11485
Purdue University: William A Hillenbrand Biomedical Engineering Center, 6887
Purple Directory: National Listing of African-American Funeral Firms, 3785
Purpose Prize, 2677
Purpose and Suggestions, 7394
Push to Talk Amplified Handset, 3157
Push-Button Quad Cane, 3486
Put on the Brakes Bulletin: Take a Look at College Drinking, 7395
Putnam County Office for Aging, 1820

Putting You in the Successful Employment Picture, 6702

Q

Q&A About Smoking and Health, 4090
QUADTRO Cushion, 3222
QuackWatch, 4243
Quail Ridge Assisted Living, 8548
Quail Ridge by Encore Senior Center, 10033
Quail Run Assisted Living at MennoniteVillage, 10149
Quality Care, 4091
Quality Care Advocate, 4092
Quality Care Conference, 2780, 4156
Quality Lift Chair, 3047
Quality Living, 9710
Quality Living Services, 2768
Quality Personal Care Home, 10515
Quality Senior Services, 1727
Quality of Living Residential Home, 10516
Quarterly Update, 7892
Queen Anne Manor, 10597
Queen Anne's County Department of Aging, 1253
Queens Independent Living Center (QILC), 10882
Questions & Answers About Depression & Its Treatment, 6076
Questions and Answers About Breast Lumps, 5836
Questions and Answers About Choosing a Mammography Facility, 5837
Questions and Answers About Employment of Deaf People, 6703
Questions and Answers About Metastatic Cancer, 5838
Questions and Answers About Pain Control, 5839
Questions and Answers on Hearing Loss, 6704
Quick Clamp Tub Grab Bar, 3021
Quick List to Build Pride in Your Communities, 7396
Quickie 2, 3429
Quincy Retirement Board, 1309
Quit & Stay Quit: A Personal Program to Stop Smoking, 7269
Quit Smoking Manual, 7270

R

RA Rapaport Publishing, 6193, 6241
RADAR Network, 7216
RCP Publishing, 3881
RD Equipment, 3014, 3032
RDL Supply, 3392
REACH of Dallas Resource Center onIndependent Living, 10930
REACH/Resource Center on Independent Living, 11789
RESNA, 3831
RIDE Retired Individuals Driving Elderly, 1821
ROHO, 3201, 3207, 3208, 3211, 3212, 3217, 3218, 3222
RP Foundation Fighting Blindness, 7944, 7946
RP Foundation Fighting Blindness (RPFFB), 7734
RP Messenger, 7980

RR Bowker, 3703
RRTC on Mental Health/Late Deaf & HOH, 6436
RSA Union Building, 366
RSBP Altus, 2021
RSVP Heartland, 1495
RSVP Adams County, 1461
RSVP Adams-Arapahoe, 653
RSVP Adams-Webster Counties, 1586
RSVP Addison County, 2430
RSVP Advacapcap, 2579
RSVP Aiken County, 2231
RSVP Aiken-Carlton Counties, 1419
RSVP Akron, 1973
RSVP Alachua County, 769
RSVP Alamogordo City, 1728
RSVP Albany County, 842
RSVP Alexandria, 2469
RSVP All Peoples Christian Center, 576
RSVP Allegany County, 1254
RSVP Allegheny County, 2153
RSVP Allegheny County-Pittsburgh, 2154
RSVP Andrew County, 1496
RSVP Anoka County, 1420
RSVP Aroostook, 1216
RSVP Arrowhead County, 1421
RSVP Artesia, 1729
RSVP Athens Limestone County, 382
RSVP Athensns, 1974
RSVP Atlantic City Chapter, 1675
RSVP Atoka, 2022
RSVP Attala County, 1462
RSVP Auburn, 1822
RSVP Audubon Area, 1127
RSVP Baldwin County, 383
RSVP Baltimore City, 1255
RSVP Barton County, 1081
RSVP Baton Rouge, 1174
RSVP Beaver County, 2155
RSVP Bedford-Cambria County, 2156
RSVP Belmont County, 1975
RSVP Bennington County, 2431
RSVP Benton-Franklin Counties, 2513
RSVP Bergen County, 1676
RSVP Bergen County New Jersey, 1677
RSVP Berkshire, 1310
RSVP Bexar County, 2334
RSVP Big Bend, 770
RSVP Big Country, 2335
RSVP Big Spring, 2336
RSVP Birmingham Area, 384
RSVP Black Hawk, 1032
RSVP Blackstone Valley, 2206
RSVP Blair County, 2157
RSVP Boone County, 1497
RSVP Boston, 1311
RSVP Boulder County, 654
RSVP Brazos Valley, 2337
RSVP Brighton Center, 1128
RSVP Broome, 1823
RSVP Broward County, 771
RSVP Brown County, 2259, 2580
RSVP Buck County, 2158
RSVP Burlington County, 1678
RSVP Butler County, 1082
RSVP Butte School District No 1, 1551
RSVP Caddo-Bossier Counties, 1175
RSVP Calcasieu Parish, 1176
RSVP Calhoun County, 385
RSVP Camden County, 1679
RSVP Campbell County, 2470
RSVP Cape May Chapter, 1680

1041

Entry Name Index / R

RSVP Cape May County, 1681
RSVP Capital Region, 2207
RSVP Capitol Region, 1824, 2159
RSVP Carbon County, 2396
RSVP Carlsbad City, 1730
RSVP Carolina Low Country, 2232
RSVP Carroll County, 1033, 1630
RSVP Cascade County, 1552
RSVP Case, 2551
RSVP Cattaraugus County, 1825
RSVP Central Coast, 577
RSVP Central Connecticut, 689
RSVP Central Kentucky, 1129
RSVP Central Naugatuck Valley, 690
RSVP Central Panhandle, 772
RSVP Central Vermont, 2432
RSVP Central Wyoming, 2613
RSVP Centre County, 2160
RSVP Chadron, 1587
RSVP Champaign, 935
RSVP Chautaqua, 1826
RSVP Chaves County, 1731
RSVP Chemung County, 1827
RSVP Chenago County, 1828
RSVP Chesapeake Bay, 2471
RSVP Chester County, 2161
RSVP Chicopee-Holyoke-Ludlow, 1312
RSVP Chisholm Trail County, 2338
RSVP Chittenden County, 2433
RSVP Cincinnati Area, 1976
RSVP Citrus County, 773
RSVP City of Burbank, 578
RSVP Clallam Jefferson County, 2514
RSVP Clarinda, 1034
RSVP Clark County, 1611, 1977, 2515
RSVP Clarksdale, 1463
RSVP Clarksville County, 2280
RSVP Clearfield County, 2162
RSVP Cleveland-McClain Counties, 2023
RSVP Clinch Valley, 2472
RSVP Clinton County, 1035, 1829
RSVP Coachella Valley, 579
RSVP Collier County, 774
RSVP Colorado West, 655
RSVP Columbia County, 1830, 2070
RSVP Concho Valley, 2339
RSVP Concho Valley Texas, 2340
RSVP Coos County, 1631, 2071
RSVP Coosa Valley, 843
RSVP Corpus Christi, 2341
RSVP Cortland, 1831
RSVP Coulee Region, 2581
RSVP Cranston, 2208
RSVP Crawford, 1588
RSVP Crawford County, 2163
RSVP Crawford-Perry-Spencer, 992
RSVP Culver City, 580
RSVP Cumberland, 1682
RSVP Cumberland County Chapter, 1683
RSVP Curry County, 1732, 2072
RSVP Dallas, 2342
RSVP Dallas County, 386
RSVP Dane County, 2582
RSVP Daviess County Indiana, 993
RSVP Davis County, 2397
RSVP Dawson-Wibaux, 1553
RSVP Dearborn County, 994
RSVP Decatur, 936
RSVP Deep East Texas, 2343
RSVP Dekalb-Noble-Steuben Counties, 995
RSVP Delaware County, 2164
RSVP Deschutes County, 2073

RSVP Devils Lake Area, 1936
RSVP Douglass Community Services, 1498
RSVP Dubois-Pike-Warrick Counties, 996
RSVP Dubuque County, 1036
RSVP Dunklin County, 1499
RSVP Dutchess County, 1832
RSVP Duval County, 775
RSVP Dyer County, 2281
RSVP East Arkansas, 473
RSVP East Bay, 2209
RSVP East Central South Dakota, 2260
RSVP East Central Tennessee, 2282
RSVP East Shore, 2473
RSVP East Valley Retired & Senior Volunteer Program, 442
RSVP Eastern Fairfield County, 691
RSVP El Paso City, 2344
RSVP Eldercircle, 1422
RSVP Elk-Cameron Counties, 2165
RSVP Elkhart County, 997
RSVP Emery, 2398
RSVP Enid, 2024
RSVP Erie County, 1833
RSVP Escambia County, 387
RSVP Essex County, 1834
RSVP Essex Hudson Chapter, 1684
RSVP Etowah County, 388
RSVP Fall River-Taunton, 1313
RSVP Fallon County, 1554
RSVP Fayettevill Area, 2283
RSVP Finney County, 1083
RSVP Flagler County, 776
RSVP Florence County, 2233
RSVP Floyd County, 2474
RSVP Ford County, 1084
RSVP Fort Dodge, 1037
RSVP Franklin County, 1835, 1978
RSVP Fresno, 581
RSVP Fulton, 998
RSVP Gallia County, 1979
RSVP Galveston County, 2345
RSVP Garland County, 474
RSVP Genesee County, 1836
RSVP Genesee-Shiawassee Counties, 1369
RSVP Gila Pinal, 443
RSVP Golden Triangle, 2346
RSVP Goucester County, 1685
RSVP Grand County, 2399
RSVP Grant County, 1733
RSVP Grays Harbor Pacific County, 2516
RSVP Greater Bristol, 692
RSVP Greater East Los Angeles, 582
RSVP Greater Erie Community Action, 2166
RSVP Greater Hartford, 693
RSVP Greater Lawrence-Haverhill, 1314
RSVP Greater Texarkana Arkansas, 475
RSVP Greater Twin Cities, 1423
RSVP Greene County, 389, 1837, 2167
RSVP Greenville, 2234
RSVP Grundy/Sullivan Counties, 1500
RSVP Hagerstown, 1256
RSVP Hamilton Wright Counties, 1038
RSVP Hancock County, 1464
RSVP Hancock-Henry-Rush, 999
RSVP Harcatus, 1980
RSVP Harrison County, 1465
RSVP Harrison-Daviess Counties, 1501
RSVP Harvey County, 1085
RSVP Hawaii County, 872
RSVP Heart of Texas, 2347
RSVP Heartland, 1424, 1502

RSVP Helena, 1555
RSVP Henry County, 1039
RSVP Herkimer County, 1838
RSVP Hernando County, 777
RSVP Hickman-McCracken Counties, 1130
RSVP High County, 656
RSVP Hill County, 1556
RSVP Hillsborough County, 778
RSVP Hockley County, 2348
RSVP Houston County, 2349
RSVP Houston Henry Geneva Counties, 390
RSVP Humboldt/Del Norte Counties, 583
RSVP Inca, 2025
RSVP Indian River County, 779
RSVP Indianapolis, 1000
RSVP Ingham, 1370
RSVP Jackson County, 1371, 2074
RSVP Jackson-Platte Counties, 1503
RSVP Jasper County, 1504
RSVP Jefferson, 1981
RSVP Jefferson Area, 2475
RSVP Jefferson County, 476, 657, 1001
RSVP Jefferson Parish, 1177
RSVP Johnson County, 1040, 1086
RSVP Joliet, 937
RSVP Josephine County, 2075
RSVP Kane McHenry Counties, 938
RSVP Kauai, 873
RSVP Kenosha County Sponsored By Kenosha Area Family And Aging Services, Inc., 2583
RSVP Kent County, 1372
RSVP King County, 2517
RSVP Kings/Tulare Counties, 584
RSVP Kitsap County, 2518
RSVP Kittitas County, 2519
RSVP KnoHo, 1982
RSVP Knox County, 1002
RSVP Knoxville-Knox County, 2284
RSVP LaPorte County, 1003
RSVP Lackawanna County, 2168
RSVP Lafayette, 1178
RSVP Lafayette County, 1466
RSVP Lake County, 939, 1004, 1983
RSVP Lake County Senior Citizens Mid Florida Community Services, 780
RSVP Lake/Mendocino Counties, 585
RSVP Laredo, 2350
RSVP Laurel-Jones County, 1467
RSVP Lawton, 2026
RSVP Lebanon-Lancaster Counties, 2169
RSVP Lee & Russell Counties, 391
RSVP Lee County, 781, 1468
RSVP Lee Scott Wise Norton, 2476
RSVP Lehigh County, 2170
RSVP Lewiston, 891
RSVP Lexington-Henderson Counties, 2285
RSVP Lincoln Area, 1589
RSVP Lincoln County, 2076
RSVP Lincoln Parish, 1179
RSVP Linn Benton County, 2077
RSVP Linn County, 1041
RSVP Little Dixie, 2027
RSVP Livingston County, 1505
RSVP Long Beach, 586
RSVP Lorain County, 1984
RSVP Los Alamos, 1734
RSVP Los Angeles Parks, 587
RSVP Loudoun, 2477
RSVP Louisville Metro Community Action Partnership, 1131
RSVP Love & Marshall Counties, 2028

Entry Name Index / R

RSVP Lowell, 1315
RSVP Lower Eastern Shore, 1257
RSVP Lowndes County, 1469
RSVP Lubbock, 2351
RSVP Luna County, 1735
RSVP Luzerne-Wyoming Counties, 2171
RSVP Macomb, 1373
RSVP Madison County, 1005, 1839
RSVP Magic Valley, 892
RSVP Mahoning County, 1985
RSVP Mahube Community Council, 1425
RSVP Maimi Valley, 1986
RSVP Manatee North Sarasota Counties, 782
RSVP Manitowoc County, 2584
RSVP Maple Lawn, 940
RSVP Maricopa County, 444
RSVP Marion County, 783, 2078
RSVP Marion-Crawford Counties, 1987
RSVP Marquette County, 1374
RSVP Marshall County, 392
RSVP Martin County, 784
RSVP Mason County, 1132
RSVP Maui County, 874
RSVP Mayflower of Plymouth County, 1316
RSVP McCormick, 2235
RSVP McKean County, 2172
RSVP McKinley County, 1736
RSVP McMinnville, 2286
RSVP Mecosta/Lake/Osceola, 1375
RSVP Meigs, 1988
RSVP Mercer County, 1686
RSVP Mercer Summer Monroe Counties, 2552
RSVP Meridian-Lauderdale Counties, 1470
RSVP Merrimack County, 1632
RSVP Metro Tarrant, 2352
RSVP Metro Tarrant, 2353
RSVP Metropolitan, 1737
RSVP Mid Rio Grand, 1738
RSVP Mid State, 694
RSVP Mid-Ohio Valley, 2553
RSVP Middlesex County, 1687
RSVP Midland, 2354
RSVP Miles City, 1557
RSVP Milwaukee, 2585
RSVP Mississippi County, 1506
RSVP Mobile, 393
RSVP Monadnock, 1633
RSVP Monroe County, 1840, 2173
RSVP Monroe Owen Counties, 1006
RSVP Monroe/Cone-Cuh County, 394
RSVP Montgomery County, 1258, 1989, 2174, 2478
RSVP Morgantown, 2554
RSVP Morris County, 1688
RSVP Morris County Chapter, 1689
RSVP Mountainland, 2400
RSVP Multonamah County, 2079
RSVP Muskogee, 2029
RSVP NV Rural Counties, 1612
RSVP Nassau County, 1841
RSVP Natchitoches Parish, 1180
RSVP Nevada County, 588
RSVP New Castle County, 716
RSVP New Orleans, 1181
RSVP New York City, 1842
RSVP Newberry County, 2236
RSVP Niagara County, 1843
RSVP Norfolk County, 1317
RSVP North Central Arkansas, 477

RSVP North Central Iowa, 1042
RSVP North Central North Dakota, 1937
RSVP North Idaho, 893
RSVP North Lee County, 1043
RSVP North Texas, 2355
RSVP Northeast Georgia, 844
RSVP Northeast Iowa, 1044
RSVP Northern Arizona, 445
RSVP Northern Black Hills, 2261
RSVP Northern Fairfield County, 695
RSVP Northern Rhode Island, 2210
RSVP Northern Santa Clara County, 589
RSVP Northwest, 2586
RSVP Northwest Arkansas, 478
RSVP Northwest Kansas, 1087
RSVP Northwest Missouri/Northeast Kansas, 1507
RSVP Oahu, 875
RSVP Oakland, 590
RSVP Oakland County, 1376
RSVP Ocean County, 1690
RSVP Ocean County Chapter, 1691
RSVP Ogallala City-Keith Counties, 1590
RSVP Ojai County, 591
RSVP Okaloosa County, 785
RSVP Oneida County, 1844
RSVP Orange County, 1845
RSVP Ostego County, 1377
RSVP Otero Bent-Crowley Counties, 658
RSVP Ottumwa, 1045
RSVP Ouachita Parish, 1182
RSVP Outagamie County, 2587
RSVP Outer Houston, 2356
RSVP Oxnard County, 592
RSVP Palm Beach County, 786
RSVP Panhandle, 2555
RSVP Pasco County, 787
RSVP Passaic County, 1692
RSVP Pemiscot County, 1508
RSVP Penquis Coastal, 1217
RSVP Peoria/Tazewell Counties, 941
RSVP Perry County, 1990
RSVP Pettis-Saline Counties, 1509
RSVP Philadelphia East, 2175
RSVP Philadelphia West, 2176
RSVP Pierce County, 2520
RSVP Pike County, 395
RSVP Pinellas County, 788
RSVP Pomona Valley, 593
RSVP Ponca City and Kay County, 2030
RSVP Poplar Bluff-Altrusa Club, 1510
RSVP Portage County, 2588
RSVP Portsmouth, 1634, 2479
RSVP Pottawatomie-Seminole Counties, 2031
RSVP Pottawattamie Mills Counties, 1046
RSVP Pratt County, 1088
RSVP Prince George's County, 1259
RSVP Prince William, 2480
RSVP Program CEFA Economic Opportunity Corporation, 942
RSVP Pueblo, 659
RSVP Pulaski County, 2481
RSVP Putnam County, 1007, 1846
RSVP Quad Lakes Area of Missouri, 1511
RSVP Rapdi City Area, 2262
RSVP Rapides Parish, 1183
RSVP Rappahannock-Rapidan, 2482
RSVP Red River Valley, 1426, 2357
RSVP Reno County, 1089
RSVP Richardson County, 1591
RSVP Richland, 2237

RSVP Richland County, 1991
RSVP Richmond, 2483
RSVP Riley County, 1090
RSVP Rio Grande Valley, 2358
RSVP River Parishes, 1184
RSVP Rock County, 2589
RSVP Rock Island, 943
RSVP Rockland, 1847
RSVP Roosevelt County, 1558
RSVP Roseburg-Douglas, 2081
RSVP Roseburgburg, 2080
RSVP Runningwater Draw, 2359
RSVP Rural Resort Region, 660
RSVP Rutherford, 2287
RSVP Sacramento County, 594
RSVP Saline County, 1091
RSVP Salt Lake County, 2401
RSVP San Bernardino County, 595
RSVP San Fernando/Santa Clarita Valleys, 596
RSVP San Juan County, 1739
RSVP San Luis Valley, 661
RSVP Sandoval, 1740
RSVP Santa Barbara, 597
RSVP Santa Fe City, 1741
RSVP Santa Rosa, 789
RSVP Sarasota/Charlotte Counties, 790
RSVP Saratoga County, 1848
RSVP Savannah, 845
RSVP Schuyler County, 1849
RSVP Schuylkill County, 2177
RSVP Scioto County, 1992
RSVP Scott-Cape Counties, 1512
RSVP Semcac, 1427
RSVP Senior Care North Shore, 1318
RSVP Seven County, 2032
RSVP Shast and Tehama Counties, 598
RSVP Shelby County, 2288
RSVP Shenandoah Area, 2484
RSVP Sheriden County, 1592
RSVP Sierra County, 1742
RSVP Simpson County, 1471
RSVP Siouxland, 2263
RSVP Six County, 2402
RSVP Skagit County, 2521
RSVP Snohomish County, 2522
RSVP Somerset County, 1693, 2178
RSVP Somerset County Chapter, 1694
RSVP Sonoma County, 599
RSVP South Bay County, 600
RSVP South Central Indiana RSVP, 1008
RSVP South Central Montana, 1559
RSVP Southeast Kansas, 1092
RSVP Southeastern Arizona, 446
RSVP Southeastern Wyoming, 2614
RSVP Southern Maine, 1218
RSVP Southern New Hampshire, 1635
RSVP Southern New London, 696
RSVP Southern Tri-County, 1428
RSVP Southside, 2485
RSVP Southwest Alabama, 396
RSVP Southwest Montana, 1560
RSVP Southwestern Connecticut, 697
RSVP Spartanburg, 2238
RSVP Spokane County, 2523
RSVP Springfield, 1319, 1513
RSVP St John's County, 791
RSVP St Lucie County, 792
RSVP St. Charles-Lincoln-Warren Counties, 1514
RSVP St. Joseph County, 1009
RSVP St. Louis, 1515

Entry Name Index / R

RSVP St. Mary's County, 1260
RSVP Story Marshall Counties, 1047
RSVP Stutgart North Arkansas, 479
RSVP Suffolk County, 1850
RSVP Sullivan County, 1851
RSVP Sumter County, 2239
RSVP Superior-Douglas, 2590
RSVP Sussex County, 717
RSVP Sussex-Warren, 1695
RSVP Sussex-Warren Chapter, 1696
RSVP Swisher County, 2360
RSVP Tallapossa & Coosa Counties, 397
RSVP Texas Panhandle, 2361
RSVP Texoma, 2362
RSVP Thousand Oaks/Conejo Valley, 601
RSVP Todd-Wadena-Otter Tail-Wilkin, 1429
RSVP Tompkins County, 1852
RSVP Travis County, 2363
RSVP Treasure Valley, 894
RSVP Tri-County, 480
RSVP Triton College Volunteer Program, 944
RSVP Tucson, 447
RSVP Tulsa, 2033
RSVP Ulster County, 1853
RSVP Union County, 1697
RSVP Union County Chapter, 1698
RSVP United Way of Central Iowa, 1048
RSVP VOA Colorado Branch, 662
RSVP VOA Denver, 663
RSVP Valparaiso, 1010
RSVP Venango County, 2179
RSVP Village of Ruidoso, 1743
RSVP Visalia Volunteer, 602
RSVP Volunteer Services, 1430
RSVP Volunteer Services of United Way Palm Beach County, 793
RSVP Volusia County, 794
RSVP Walla Walla CountySenior Citizen Center, 2524
RSVP Walworth County, 2591
RSVP Warren County, 1993
RSVP Warren-Forest Counties, 2180
RSVP Washington County, 1994, 2082
RSVP Washoe County, 1613
RSVP Waukeesha County, 2592
RSVP Wayne County, 1011, 1378
RSVP Wayne-Seneca-Ontario, 1854
RSVP Weld County, 664
RSVP West Arkansas, 481
RSVP West Bay, 2211
RSVP West Central Minnesota, 1431
RSVP West Valley of San Bernardino County, 603
RSVP Western Arizona, 448
RSVP Western Riverside County, 604
RSVP Westmoreland County, 2181
RSVP Windham County, 2434
RSVP Windham-Tolland Counties, 698
RSVP Woodbury County, 1049
RSVP Worcester Area, 1320
RSVP Wyandotte County, 1093
RSVP YWCA Senior Services, 945
RSVP Yakima County, 2525
RSVP Yellowstone County, 1561
RSVP York County, 2240
RSVP and the Volunteer Center, 1636
RSVP of Central Arkansas, 482
RSVP of Central North Dakota, 1938
RSVP of Warren and Washington Counties, 1855

RTC Connection, 4093
RTC on Aging, 4034
RX Remedy, 3951
Rachel's Place Adult Day Care, 946
Racial and Ethnic Differences in the Health of Older Americans, 3665
Rackleff House, 10150
Radiation Oncology Research & Development Center, 5951
Radiation Therapy and You: A Guide To Self-Help During Treatment, 5840
Railroad Retirement Board, 2403
Railroad Retirement Board (RRB), 298
Railroad Retirement Board District Office, 1012
Railroad Retirement Board Dsitrict Office, 1321
Railroad Retirement Board-California District Office, 605
Railroad Retirement Board-New York City, 1856
Railroad Retirement Board: -Oregon District Office, 2083
Railroad Retirement Board: Alabama District Office, 398
Railroad Retirement Board: Albany District Office, 1857
Railroad Retirement Board: Altoona Pennslvania District Office, 2182
Railroad Retirement Board: Arkansas District Office, 483
Railroad Retirement Board: Bellevue, Washington District Office, 2526
Railroad Retirement Board: Buffalo New York District Office, 1858
Railroad Retirement Board: Chicago District Office, 947
Railroad Retirement Board: Cincinnati Office, 1995
Railroad Retirement Board: Cleveland District Office, 1996
Railroad Retirement Board: Colorado District Office, 665
Railroad Retirement Board: Decatur District Office, 948
Railroad Retirement Board: District Office, 1185
Railroad Retirement Board: Duluth Minnesota District Office, 1432
Railroad Retirement Board: Fort Worth, Texas District Office, 2364
Railroad Retirement Board: Georgia District Office, 846
Railroad Retirement Board: Harrisburg Pennsylvania Branch Office, 2183
Railroad Retirement Board: Houston, Texas District Office, 2365
Railroad Retirement Board: Iowa District Office, 1050
Railroad Retirement Board: JacksonvilleDistrict Office, 795
Railroad Retirement Board: Joliet District Office, 949
Railroad Retirement Board: Kansas, 1094
Railroad Retirement Board: Kansas City Missouri District Office, 1516
Railroad Retirement Board: Kentucky District Office, 1133
Railroad Retirement Board: Maryland District Office, 1261
Railroad Retirement Board: Michigan District Office, 1379

Railroad Retirement Board: Montana District Office, 1562
Railroad Retirement Board: Nebraska District Office, 1593
Railroad Retirement Board: New Jersey District Office, 1699
Railroad Retirement Board: New Mexico, 1744
Railroad Retirement Board: North Carolina District Office, 1917
Railroad Retirement Board: North Dakota District Office, 1939
Railroad Retirement Board: Philadelphia Pennsylvania District Office, 2184
Railroad Retirement Board: Pittsburgh Pennsylvania District Office, 2185
Railroad Retirement Board: Richmond, Virginia District Office, 2486
Railroad Retirement Board: Roanoke, Virginia District Office, 2487
Railroad Retirement Board: Scranton Pennsylvania District Office, 2186
Railroad Retirement Board: Spokane, Washington District Office, 2527
Railroad Retirement Board: St. Louis, 1517
Railroad Retirement Board: St. Paul Minnesota District Office, 1433
Railroad Retirement Board: Survivor Division, 950
Railroad Retirement Board: Syracuse NewYork District Office, 1859
Railroad Retirement Board: Tennessee District Office, 2289
Railroad Retirement Board: West Virginia District Office, 2556
Railroad Retirement Board: Wisconsin District Office, 2593
Rainbows for All God's Children, 6015
Raised Line Drawing Kit, 3467
Rakhma Peace Home, 9263
Rambling Oaks Assisted Living Center, 10034
Rampvan, 2990
Ramsey Foundation, 4497
Ramsey Home, 8724
Rancho Bernardo Joslyn Senior Center, 606
Rancho Los Amigos Medical Center, 4363
Rancho Vista, 8211
Rand-Scot, 3035, 3198, 3213, 3370, 3487
Randolph-Sheppard Vendors of America, 4244
Random House, 6078
Random House Trade Books, 6184
Ranger, 3430
Ranger All Seasons, 3430, 3433, 3438
Rappahannock Area: Agency on Aging, 2488
Rappahannock Westminster-Canterbury, 10566
Rappahannock-Rapidan Community Services Board and Area Agency on Aging, 2489
Rascal Insurance Services, 299
Ravalli County Council on Aging, 1563
Raynaud's Phenomenon, 5223
Reach Out Magazine, 3950
Reach Resource Center on Independent Living, 10931
Reach of Denton Resource Center on Independent Living, 10932
Reach to Recovery, 5777
Read My Lips, 6766

Reader's Digest Publications, 3971
Reading Is for Everyone, 7981
Reading with Low Vision, 7982
Ready Willing & Able, 1860
Ready Willing & Able: Gates, 1861
Rebuilding Together, 2678
Rebuilding Together with Christmas in April, 300
Reclining Power Wheelchairs, 3558
Recognizing and Treating Low Blood Sugar(Hypoglycemia), 4094
Record Book, 4095
Recorded Periodicals, 7735, 7893
Recording Service for Visually Handicapped, 7736
Recording for the Blind, 7894, 7983
Recording for the Blind & Dyslexic, 7737
Recording for the Blind Helpline, 7738
Recording for the Blind News, 7894, 7983
Recovery After a Stroke, 7100
Recovery Journal for Exploring Who I Am, 7271
Recovery from Bereavement, 6025
Recurrence: What Do I Do Now?, 5841
Recurrent Stroke, 7101
Red River Council on Aging, 1186
Red Rock Independent & Assisted Living, 9738
Redbud Plaza, 8817
Redman Apache, 3530
Redman Crow Line, 3531
Redman Powerchair, 3050, 3519, 3529, 3530, 3531
Reducing Risk and Recognizing Symptoms, 7102
Redwood Heights, 10151
Redwood Terrace, 10152
Redwood Village, 9580
Reed House, 8725
Reeds Landing, 9010
Reference Service Press, 3733, 3734
Reference and Information Services from NLS, 7984
Referring Blind and Low Vision Patients for Rehabilitation Services, 7829, 7985
Reflex Sympathetic Dystrophy Syndrome Fact Sheet, 5224
Regal Estates Senior Living, 10517
Regal Scooters, 3431
Regency House Assisted Living, 10376
Regency Park-El Molino, 8212
Regency Place, 8213, 8881
Regency Samaritan House, 10598
Regency Square Care Center, 9711
Regency at Glen Cove, 9849
Regency at Hualalai, 10716
Regency of El Paso, 10518
Regency on Whidbey, 10599
Regent, 3432
Regent at Hamilton House Assisted Living, 10519
Regent at Parmer Woods Assisted Living, 10520
Regent at Regency Park Assisted Living, 10153
Regent at Sterling Park Assisted Living, 10600
Regina Retirement Center, 9264
Region 10: Administration on Aging (AoA), 2528
Region 14 Council on Aging, 1380

Region 1: Administration on Aging (AoA), 1322
Region 2 and 3: Administration on Aging(AoA), 1862
Region 2: Administration on Aging (AoA), 1863
Region 4: Administration on Aging (AoA), 847
Region 5: Administration on Aging (AoA), 951
Region 6: Administration on Aging (AoA), 2366
Region 7: Administration on Aging (AoA), 1518
Region 8: Administration on Aging (AoA), 666
Region 9: Administration on Aging (AoA), 607
Region Four Area: Agency on Aging, 1381
Region Nine Area: Agency on Aging, 1434, 1997
Region Seven Area: Agency on Aging, 1382
Region Ten Area: Agency on Aging, 667, 1519
Region Two Area: Agency on Aging, 1383
Regional Access & Mobilization Project (RAMP), 10735
Regional Access Mobilization Project (RAMP), 10736
Regional Cancer Foundation, 5778
Regional Center for Independent Living, 10883
Regional Library, 11411
Regional Resource Center on Deafness, 6437
Registry of Interpreters for the Deaf, 6438, 6791
Registry of the Interpreters for the Deaf, 6581, 6677
Regular, 3990
Regular Veterans Association, 3990
Rehab Research & Training Center on Blindness, 7821
Rehab and Educational Aids for Living, 3545
Rehab/Training Center on Blindness and Low-Vision, 7807
Rehabilitation Counseling Bulletin, 6084
Rehabilitation Institute of Chicago, 5248
Rehabilitation International, 3889
Rehabilitation Research and Training Center on Aging With a Disability, 4363
Rehabilitation Resource Manual: Vision, 7830
Rehabilitation Services Administration, 6349
Rehabilitation Services Administration-DVDB, 117
Rehabilitation Services Directory, 3786
Rehman Retirement Resorts-Poway, 8214
Reid & Hurley Travel, 12041
Reiter's Syndrome, 5225
Relapse and the Addict, 7397
Releasing Anger, 7398
Rem Canby Senior Services, 9265
Rem Montevideo Senior Services, 9266
Rem Southview, 9267
Remedy, 3951
Remington Heights Retirement Center, 9712
Remington House, 8439
Remington House Assisted Living, 10377
Remington Park, 10521

Reminiscence Home, 9268
Remote Control Speakerphone, 3158
Renaissance Gardens at Brooksby Village, 9011
Renaissance Gardens at Charlestown, 8927
Renaissance Gardens at Greenspring, 10567
Renaissance Gardens at Henry FordVillage, 9073
Renaissance Gardens at Oak Crest, 8928
Renaissance Gardens at Riderwood, 8929
Renaissance Gardens at Seabrook, 9797
Renaissance Institue, 2813
Renaissance SocietyCenter for Learning in Retirement, 2729
Renaissance at the Gables, 8215
Renaissance of Ponca City, 10035
Renaissance of Stillwater Extended, 10036
Rensselaer County Department for the Aging, 1864
Rent-A-Van-Handicapped Driver Services, 2991
Report on Disability Programs, 4096
Report to Members, 4569
ResCare Home Care, 848
Research & Practice, 4978
Research And Training Center, 4093
Research Institute of Palo Alto Medical Foundation, 4690
Research Institute of the Hebrew Home of Greater Washington, 4364
Research Institute on Alcoholism, 7472
Research Press, 6021, 6030
Research Report: Adult Kidney Cancer and Wilms' Tumor, 5842
Research and Education Institute, 6888
Research and Training Center for Persons Who are Deaf or Hard of Hearing, 6439
Research on Aging, 3952
Research on Drugs and the Workplace, 7399
Research to Prevent Blindness, 7739
Residence, 10199
Residence at Glen Riddle, 10200
Residence of Sterling Oaks, 9939
Residential Care Today, 4097
Resisting Care... Putting Yourself in Their Shoes, 5033
Resource Center for Accessible Living, 10884
Resource Center for Independent Living, 10767, 10885
Resource Center for Independent Living (RCIL), 10886
Resource Directory of Special Education and Rehabilitation Computer Products, 3159
A Resource Guide for Drug Management for Older Persons, 7234
Resource Guide for Drug Management for Older Persons, 7272
Resource Guide for Injury Control Programs for Older Persons, 3666
A Resource Guide for Injury Control: Programs for Older Persons, 3590
Resource List for Persons with Low Vision, 7986
Resources For Enriching Adult Learning(REAL), 11103
Resources For Independent Living, 10945
Resources For Rehabilitation, 7828
Resources and Services Database, 4541
Resources for Elders with Disabilities, 3667, 3787

Entry Name Index / R

Resources for Independence, 10785
Resources for Independent Living, 10674
Resources for Independent Living - Baton Rouge, 10779
Resources for People with Disabilities and Chronic Conditions, 3788
Resources for People with Disablities: A National Directory, 3789
Resources for Rehabilitation, 3667, 3684, 3764, 3787, 3788, 6529, 7822, 7830, 7849, 11895
Respect Your Elders Tender Loving AdultCare, 8098
Respiratory Nursing Society, 301
Respite Care Guide: How to Find What's Right for You, 5007
Respite Resource Guide, 3668
Rest Haven Home, 9074
Retired & Senior Volunteer Program of Hull House Chicago, 952
Retired & Senior Volunteer Program of Northern DuPage Counties, 953
Retired Activities Branch, 92
Retired Activities Office, 608
Retired Activities Office: Phoenix Affairs Office, 449
Retired Affairs Office: Kings Bay Office, 849
Retired Enlisted Association, 4098
Retired Enlisted Association (TREA), 302
Retired Enlisted Association: Voice, 4098
Retired Military Police Association, 303, 1918
Retired Senior Volunteer Program of Rio Grande, 1745
Retired Senior Volunteer Program of Steuben County, 1865
Retired Senior Volunteer Program of Western Dairyland, 2594
Retired Teachers Association, 1998
Retired and Senior Volunteer Program, 304
Retiree Newsletter, 4099
Retirement Center, 8882
Retirement Communities & Homes Directory, 3790
Retirement Community Business, 3953
Retirement Housing & Foodservice Who's Who, 3791
Retirement Industry Trust Association, 305
Retirement Inn by Encore Senior Living, 10522
Retirement Letter, 4100
Retirement Life, 3954
Retirement Living Publishing Company, 3936
Retirement Planning, 4245
Retirement Planning Service Directory, 3792
Retirement Research Foundation, 2625, 2662, 4365
Reversing Diabetes: Reduce or Even Eliminate Your Dependence on Insulin or Oral Drugs, 6215
Reversing Hypertension: A Vital New Program to Prevent, Treat, and Reduce High Blood Pressure, 6915
Review, 6705
Rheumatoid Arthritis, 5226
Rhode Island Client Assistance Program, 2212
Rhode Island Department of Elderly Affairs, 2213, 11247

Rhode Island Department of Health: Division of Disease Control, 4498
Rhode Island Department of Human Services, 2215
Rhode Island Department of Human Services for the Blind, 7740
Rhode Island Department of Human Services: Veterans Affairs, 2214
Rhode Island Department of Mental Health, 6054
Rhode Island Department of State Library for the Blind and Physically Handicapped, 11753
Rhode Island Department of Treasury: Retirement Office, 2216
Rhode Island Developmental Disabilities Council, 2217
Rhode Island Disability Law Center, 2221
Rhode Island Division of Substance Abuse, 7217
Rhode Island Division of Taxation, 2218
Rhode Island Governor's Committee on the Disabled, 2219
Rhode Island Legal Service: Elderly Law Unit, 11248
Rhode Island Organizing Project, 2220
Rhode Island Protection & Advocacy for Persons with Disabilities, 2221
Rhode Island Protection and Advocacy Agency: Rhode Island Disability Law Center, 11249
Rhode Island Services for the Blind and Visually Impaired, 7741
Rice International Corporation, 3172
Richard Kalish Innovative Publication Award, 2679
Richard W. Waring, 11896
Richfield Senior Suites, 9269
Richmond County Council on the Aging, 1919
Ricon, 2961, 2986, 2989
Ricon Corporation, 3393
Ridge Crest Retirement, 9530
Ridge Wind Assisted Living, 8549
Ridgeview Assisted Living, 10154
Ridgeview Heights Indepedent Living Corporation, 10606
Ridgeway Place, 8726
Ridgeway on German, 9270
Ridgewood at Friendship Village, 9940
Right to Decide, 4157
Right to Life League of Southern California, 6016
Right to Life of Michigan, 1384
Rigid Aluminum Cane with Golf Grip, 3488
Rimrock Senior Center, 895
Rinz-L-O Pillow Company, 3219
Rio Grande Area: Agency on Aging, 2367
Rio Las Palmas, 8216
Rio Salado Community College, 2705
Rio Salado Community College: Adult Basic Education Program, 2705
River Birch Residence, 9271
River Hills Village, 8727
River Odysseys West (Row), 12042
River Ridge, 9359
River Road Assisted Living Residence, 10155
River's Bend Retirement Community, 8850
Rivers Edge Villa, 9272
Riverside Lodge Retirement Community, 9713

Riverview Assisted Center, 8550
Riverview Health Services, 10311
Riverview Manor, 9075
Riverview Place, 9581
Riverview Retirement Home, 10312
Riverview Terrace, 8728
Riverwood Assisted Living, 10156
Riviera, 8551
Road Ahead: A Stroke Recovery Guide, 7069
Roanoke City Public Library System, 11820
Roanoke College, 2934
Robert B. Irwin Award, 2680
Robert S. Bray Award, 2681
Robert W. Kleemeier Award, 2682
Robert Wood Johnson University Hospital, 7043
Rochester Institute of Technology Library, 11656
Rochester Institute of Technology: National Technical Institute for the Deaf, 6440
Rochester Regional Service Center for Hearing Impaired People, 6441
Rochester Technical Institute for the Deaf Resource Center, 11657
Rock County Health Care Center Staff Library, 11848
Rockefeller University Laboratory of Biology, 7473
Rockefeller University Laboratory of Neuroendocrinology, 4366
Rockefeller University: Laboratory of Cardiac Physiology, 6889
Rockefeller University: Zachary and Elizabeth M Fisher Center for Research on Alzheimer's Disease, 5064
Rockhaven Retirement Home, 8552
Rocking Knife, 3345
Rockland County Center for the Physically Handicapped, 1866
Rockland County Office for Aging, 1867
Rockland Independent Living Center, 10887
Rockland Place, 8321
Rockland/Orange Unit of the Arthritis Foundation, 5135
Rockmart Library, 11443
Rockmill Springs Assisted Living, 9941
Rocky Mountain Chapter of the Arthritis Foundation, 5176, 5136
Rocky Mountain Development Council, 1555
Rocky Mountain Heart Research Institute, 6890
Rodale Press, 3929, 3948
Rodeway Inns, 12043
Roetell Senior Housing, 10313
Roger Williams Cancer Research, 5952
Roger Williams General Hospital, 5952
Rogue Valley Council of Governments: Senior and Disability Services Division, 2084
Roland Tseng College of Extended Learning, 2730
Role of Physical Therapy in Parkinson's Disease, 7025
Roll Chair, 3048
Roll-Aid, 3532
Roll-In Shower, 3022
Rollator Wheeled Walker, 3489
Rolling Hills Assisted Living Apartments, 8818
Rolling Start, 10675

Rolls 2000 Series, 3533
Rollx Vans, 11939
Rome Subregional Library Service for People with Disabilities, 11444
Ron Jackson Company, 4030
Ronald & Nancy Reagan Research Institute: To Treat and Prevent Alzheimer's Disease, 5008
Ronald Park Place, 8930
Room Valet Visual-Tactile AlertingSystem, 3160
Roosevelt Avenue Shelter Home, 8553
Roosevelt Hospital Medical Library, 11658
Rosalind Russell Medical Research Center for Arthritis, 5249
Rose Arbor Assisted Living, 10157
Rose Cottage, 9739
Rose Garden Home, 9076
Rose Haven, 9531
Rose Hill Assisted Living, 9798
Rose Kushner Breast Cancer Advisory Center, 5779
Rose Terrace of Wendell, 9532
Rose Valley Assisted Living Facility, 10158
Rosebush Gardens, 8729
Rosedale of Glastonbury, 8289
Rosedale of Trumbull Assisted Living Community, 8290
Rosen Publishing Group, 4575
Roseview Court Care Agency, 9273
Rosewind House, 8554
Rosewood Court Assisted Living Center, 9714
Rosewood Estate-Highland, 9274
Rosewood Estate-Maplewood, 9275
Rosewood Estates-Roseville, 9276
Rosewood Park, 10159
Rosewood Retirement & Assisted Living Community, 8883
Rosholt Care Center Assisted Living Center, 10314
Roster: Boarding Homes, Licensed, 3793
Roswell Park Cancer Institute, 5953
Roswell Public Library, 11622
Round Rock Volunteer Center, 2368
Round Table at the School of Professional Development, 2870
Routledge, 5804
Royal Estates of El Paso, 10523
Royal Estates of San Angelo, 10524
Royal Villa, 8555
Royale Oaks, 9715
RsVP Clackamas County, 2085
Rubens-Alcais Challenge, 2683
Running Past 50, 3669
Rural Advocates for Independent Living (RAIL), 10827
Rush University Alzheimer's Disease Center, 5065
Rush University Neuroscience Institute, 4367
Rush University: Rush Institute for Healthy Aging, 4368
Rush-Presbyterian-St. Luke's Medical Center, 4367
Rushmore Mall, 2919
Russ House, 8884
Russellville Park, 10160
Rutgers University Institute for Health, Health Care Policy: and Aging Research, 4369

Rutgers University: Center of Alcohol Studies, 7218
Ruth E Golding Clinical Pharmacokinetics Laboratory, 7474
Ruth Homes, 9277
Ruth O'Donnel, 11414
Ruth's House, 9012
Rutherford House, 9942

S

S Karger Publshers, 3868
SAGE Newsletter, 4101
SAILS, 10933
SAVE Senior Avocational/Vocational Education, 2929
SC Vocational Rehabilitation Department, 2242
SCENE, 11897
SCORE of Tulsa, 1051
SEAGO Area: Agency on Aging, 450
SELF Magazine, 3955
SEMO Alliance for Disability Independence (SADI), 10828
SHHH Journal, 6589
SHHH News, 6706
SHHH Publications, 6469
SILC-Iowa Department for the Blind, 10756
SMG Marketing Group, 3748, 3750, 3777, 3778
SPOKES Unlimited, 7868, 10907
SPRY Foundation, 306
SUNY Farmingdale, 7708
SUNY at Buffalo: National Cooperative Drug Discovery Group for AIDS Treatment, 4616
SW Boulevard Family Health Care Services, 248
SW Georgia Regional Library, 11433
Sabine House, 10525
Saddleridge Lodge, 10526
Safari Scooter, 3433
Safari Tilt, 3049
Safe Homes, 4246
Safe Return Brochure, 5009
Safe Return Home: An Inspirational Book for Caregivers of Alzheimer's, 4969
A Safer Place, 4131
Sage Community Resources, 896
Sage Publications, 3897, 3952, 4004, 6066
Sage Society, 2730
Saginaw Geriatrics Home, 9077
Saint Andrew Life Center, 8599
Saint Augustine Assisted Living Home, 8099
Saint Augustine Assisted Living Home II, 8100
Saint Louis Altenheim, 9335
Saint Martins in the Pines, 8075
Salem County Office on Aging, 1700
Salem Deaf Fellowship, 2086
Salem Mennonite Home, 10315
Salick Health Care, 5780
Salinas-Central Coast Center for Independent Living, 10676
Salisbury Assisted Living Center, 9013
Salisbury Gardens, 9533
Salk Institute for Biological Studies Library, 5954, 11344
Salmi Homes, 9278
Salt Lake County Aging Services, 2404

Samaritan Bethany Terrace, 9279
Samaritan Place Assisted Living, 9534
Samford University Library Special Collections, 11312
Sammons Preston, 3143, 3368, 3495
Sammons Preston Rolyan, 3295
Samuel Roberts Noble Foundation: Biomedical Division, 5955
Samuel Sadin Institute on Law & Rights of Older Adults, 11209
San Antonio Cancer Institute, 5956
San Clemente Villas by the Sea, 8217
San Diego Area Chapter of the Arthritis Foundation, 5168, 5137
San Diego Community College District(SDCCD), 2731
San Diego County Area: Agency on Aging, 609
San Diego Hebrew Homes, 610
San Diego Information & Referral Center, 7044
San Diego State University, 2726
San Francisco Commission on the Aging, 611
San Francisco General Hospital, 7456
San Francisco Heart Institute, 6844
San Francisco Public Library for the Blind and Print Handicapped, 11345
San Francisco Public Library: Talking Books Program & Blind Services Center, 11346
San Francisco Regional Public Affairs Office, 570
San Jose State University Gerontology Education and Training Center, 4370
San Jose State University Library, 11347
San Juan Area: Agency on Aging, 2405
San Juan Basin Area: Agency on Aging, 668
Sanders-Brown Center on Aging, 4112
Sandoz Pharmaceuticals Corporate Library, 11616
Sandra Beasley Independent Living Center, 10904
Sandstone Manor, 10316
Sandwich Generation, 3956
Sanford Senior Center, 796
Sansum Diabetes Research Institute, 4617
Santa Barbara Breast Cancer Institute, 5957
Santa Cruz Volunteer Center, 612
Santee-Lynches Council of Governments Area Agency on Aging, 2241
Sara Moore Home, 9943
Saratoga County Office for the Aging, 1868
Sarawood Retirement Home, 9014
Saunders House, 9716
Savannah Court, 8440
Savoy at Brooklyn, 9850
Savoy at Little Neck Assusted Living Community, 9851
Sawyer House, 10161
Say What, 3244
Scandinavian Home, 10221
Scandinavian Living Center, 9015
Scenic Valley Area: Agency on Aging, 1052
Schallmo Assisted Living Center, 10037
Scharome Manor Home for Adults, 9852
Schenectady County Office for the Aging, 1869
Schepens Eye Research Institute, 8052
Schoharie County Office for the Aging, 1870

Entry Name Index / S

School of Architecture and Urban Planning, 4434
School of Dentistry, Dept. of Biologic Sciences, 4632
School of Education and Human Development Lyceum, 2871
School of Living, 2910
School of Medicine, 4321, 4378, 4422, 4442, 4694, 5917, 5961, 6899, 7462
School of Medicine, Department of Psychiatry, 6106
School of Medicine, Infectious Disease Division, 4620
School of Medicine, Rheumatology Division, 5109
School of Metaphysics, 2836
School of Pharmacy, 4406
School of Public Health, 4415
Schuyler County Office for the Aging, 1871
Schuylkill County Area: Agency on Aging, 2187
Scituate Council on Aging, 1323
Scoota Bug, 3434
Scooter Lift/Carrier, 2992
Scooter, Power Chair and WheelchairLifts, 3394
Score Card Set, 3291
Scotland Good Samaritan Center Assisted Living Center, 10317
Scott Manor, 8101
Scottdale Community Senior Citizens Club, 2188
Scottsdale Community College, 2706
Scripps Clinic and Research Foundation:Autoimmune Disease Center, 4691
Scripps Ranch Publications, 11898
Sea View Hospital Rehabilitation Center Health Sciences Library, 11659
Seaford Center Assisted Living, 8322
Sealye House, 8819
Sears Mature Outlook, 307
Seasons Residential Care Living Center, 8556
Seasons: A Classic Residence by Hyatt, 8428
Seattle King County Division on Aging, 2529
Secondhand Smoke, 4102
Secret to a Satisfied Life: The Way You Encounter Life Can Bring Happiness..., 4158
Secretariat for Pro-Life Activities, 4103
Secure Retirement, The Newsmagazine for Mature Americans, 3957
Seeing, 7987
Seeing Clearly, 7895, 7988
Seeing Eye, 7896, 7742
Seeing Eye Guide, 7896
Self Help For Hard of Hearing People, 6589
Self Help for Hard of Hearing People, 2626, 2633, 2640, 2650, 2663, 2670, 2676, 2684, 2685, 2689, 6487, 6512, 6517, 6522, 6540, 6548, 6567, 6601, 6609, 6610, 6613
Self-Help for Hard of Hearing People, 6792
Self-Help for Hard of Hearing People, Cleveland West Chapter, 6442
Self-Help for Hard of Hearing People: Rochester Chapter, 6443
Self-Help for Hard of Hearing People: South Nassau Chapter, 6444

Self-Reliance, 10706
Selling to Seniors, 4104
Seminole Community College, 797
Seminole County Volunteer Program, 797
Senate Special Committee on Aging, 308
Seneca Area Agency on Aging, 1053, 11114
Seneca County Office for the Aging, 1872
Seneca Lake Terrace Adult ResidentialCommunity, 9853
Seneca Nation of Indians Office for Aging, 1873
Seneca Sunrise, 9717
Senior Action in A Gay Environment, 4101
Senior Action in a Gay Environment, 1874
Senior Adult Activities Center of Montgomery County, 2189
Senior Adult Education, 2944
Senior Adult Education Center for Applied Gerontology, 2890
Senior Adult Educational Program, 2706
Senior Adult Growth Exchange, 2805
Senior Adult Learning Center, 2900
Senior Adults Legal Assistance (SALA), 11009
Senior Advisory Association of North Carolina, 1920
Senior Advocacy Program, 11250
Senior Alliance Area Agency on Aging, 1385, 11570
Senior Center of Sidney Shelby County, 1999
Senior Centers and the At-Risk Older Person, 3670
Senior Centers of Bethlehem, 2190
Senior Citizen News, 3991
Senior Citizen Program Packet, 6540
Senior Citizens, 2290
Senior Citizens Council of Cobb County: Enrichment of Life Movement, 2769
Senior Citizens Council of Union County, 1701
Senior Citizens Educational Program, 2930
Senior Citizens Judicare Project, 11245
Senior Citizens Law Office, 11198
Senior Citizens Law Project, 11183
Senior Citizens Law Project of Vermont Legal Aid, 11276
Senior Citizens Legal Services, 11010
Senior Citizens Service Organizations Directory, 3794
Senior Citizens Services, 3795
Senior Citizens of Earth: Springlake Area, 2369
Senior Citizens of Patagonia, 451
Senior Citizens of Shasta County, 613
Senior Citizens of Whitley County, 1134
Senior Citizens' Wills Program: Chicago Bar Association, 11094
Senior Community Center, 1268
Senior Community Service Employment Program (Title V), 954
Senior Companion Program, 309
Senior Companion Program of Macomb, 1386
Senior Connections The Capital Area: Agency, 2490
Senior Corps, 139
Senior Fitness Productions, 11899
Senior Gleaners, 614
Senior Health, 4247
Senior Home Care Services, 1324
Senior Housing Net, 4248

Senior Job Bank, 310, 4249
Senior Law Home Page, 4250
Senior Law Project, 11011
Senior Legal Center of Northern California, 11012
Senior Living Choices at Curtis, 9718
Senior Media, 4105
Senior Media Directory, 3796
Senior News Monthly, 4106
Senior News Monthly Executive Offices, 4106
Senior Options Online Guide to Senior Services, 4251
Senior Scholars, 2891
Senior Service America (SSA), 311
Senior Services, 1387
Senior Services of Boone County, 1477
Senior Services of Central Illinois, 955
Senior Services of Northern Kentucky, 1135
Senior Solutions of Southwest Florida, 798
Senior Specialists Agency on Aging, 484
Senior Spectrum, 1219
Senior Suites, 8730
Senior Suites of New Brighton, 9280
Senior Summer School, 2759, 4252
Senior Times, 3992, 4253
Senior Times Magazine, 3958
Senior University, 2770
Senior Venture, 2901
Senior Women's Travel, 4254
Senior World Newsmagazine, 3993
SeniorNet, 4107, 4371
Seniors Action Service Caring Home Aid Program, 956
Seniors First, 799
Seniors Helping Others Volunteer Program of Washington County, 2222
Seniors Plus, 1220
Seniors Program Institute for Extended Learning, 2945
Seniors Sites, 4159
Seniors for Lifelong Learning, 2820
Seniors' Law Center, 11013
Sensor Hearing Aids, 6445
Sensorineural Hearing Loss, 6707
Sensory Access Foundation, 7852
Sentry Insurance Company Library, 11849
September House, 9281
Sequoia Retirement Services, 11900
Serenity, 3959
Serenity Gardens Personal Care, 10527
Serenity Place, 9719
Sertoma Foundation, 4074
Service Center for Independent Living, 10677
Service Center for Independent Living-Covina, 10678
Service Corp of Retired Executives: Portsmouth Chapter No. 185, 1637
Service Corps of Retired Executive Association, 312
Service Corps of Retired Executives of Tulsa, 2034
Service Opportunities After Retirement (SOAR), 1325
A Service of Friendship Ventures, 12057
Services Maximizing Independent Living and Empowerment (SMILE), 10636
Services for Independent Living, 10829, 10897
Services for the Visually Impaired: Department of Public Instruction, 11699

Serving Our Seniors, 2000
Set-Ups for Speeches, 6708
Settler's Park Assisted Living & Memory Care, 10162
Seward Aging Services, 1594
Seward Independent Living Center, 10629
Sexual Function Health Council, 6943
Sexual Intimacy and the Alcoholic Relationship, 7400
Sexual and Bladder Difficulties in Parkinson's Disease, 7026
Sexuality & Aging, 4160
Shade Tree Retirement Center, 9282
Shady Oaks Assisted Living, 8291
Shallotte Assisted Living, 9535
Shallowater Senior Citizens, 2370
Shalom House, 10782
Shame Faced, 7273
Shamrock Gardens, 8622
ShapeWalking, 11700
Sharing Solutions: A Newsletter forSupport Groups, 7989
Shawnee Development Council, 957
Shawnee Heartland Assisted Living, 8820
Shawnee Library System, 11464
Shelby Good Samaritan Center Assisted Living, 10318
Shelby Manor Group Home, 10568
Shelbyville Residential Care, 10378
Shenandoah Adult Care, 10569
Shenandoah Valley Village, 10570
Shepherd House Assisted Living Community, 9536
Shepherd of the Valley Howland, 9944
Shepherd of the Valley Lutheran Retirmen, 9945
Shepherd's Center Indianapolis, 2784
Shepherd's Center Southside, 2694
Shepherd's Center Westfield, 2785
Shepherd's Center of Beebe, 2710
Shepherd's Center of Beekley, 2947
Shepherd's Center of Bluff Park, 2695
Shepherd's Center of Columbia, 2915
Shepherd's Center of Fostoria, 2892
Shepherd's Center of Gainesville, 2760
Shepherd's Center of Grandview, 2837
Shepherd's Center of Greater Winston Salem, 2882
Shepherd's Center of Hot Springs, 2711
Shepherd's Center of Kansas City, 2796
Shepherd's Center of Kansas City Central, 2838
Shepherd's Center of Kernersville, 2883
Shepherd's Center of Madison, 2922
Shepherd's Center of North Little Rock, 2712
Shepherd's Center of Orange Park, 2761
Shepherd's Center of Raytown, 2839
Shepherd's Center of Richmond, 2938
Shepherd's Center of Rock Hill, 2916
Shepherd's Center of SW Litte Rock, 2713
Shepherd's Center of Spartanburg, 2917
Shepherd's Center of Sumter, 2918
Shepherds Inn, 9283
Sheridan Memorial Home, 9582
Sheridan Press, 7876
Sheridan Travel Service, 12044
Shilo Inns & Resorts, 12045
Shipley Manor Assisted Living, 8323
Shire at Culverton Adult Home, 9854
Shirley's Assisted Living Home, 8102
Shore Pines Assisted Living, 10163

Shoreline Lake Forest Park Senior Center, 2530
Shores at Wesley Manor, 9799
Should Tobacco Advertising and Promotion Be Banned, 4108
Showboat Retirement Center, 10615
Shreveport Advocacy Center, 11130
Shrewsbury Crossing, 9016
Shrewsbury Senior Center, 1326
Shugar's Publishing, 3785
Shuttle, 3435
Sibley Manor Assisted Living, 9284
Sibley Memorial Hospital, 6461
Side-to-Side Folding Chair, 3534
Sidekick Scooter, 3436
Sidekick Walk & Ride Power Wheelchair, 3535
Sierra 3000/4000, 3437
Sierra Hills, 10616
Sight-Loss Support Group of Central Pennsylvania, 7743
Sign Language Studies, 3960
Sign Media, 6466
Signaling and Assistive Listening Devices for Hearing-Impaired People, 6709
Signature Group, 3964
Signature Pointe on the Lake, 10528
Signature and Address Self-Inking Stamps, 3468
Signing Exact English, 6541
Signing Illustrated, 6542
Signing: How to Speak with Your Hands, 6543
Signs Across America, 6544
Signs for Computing Terminology, 4161, 6545
Silent Alarm: On the Edge with a Deaf EMT, 6546
Silicon Valley Independent Living Center, 10679
Silicone Padding, 3223
Silver Creek Assisted Living, 10164
Silver Glide Stairway Lift, 3395
Silver Rose Manor, 9740
Silver Threads Residence, 10319
Silverado Senior Living-Cypresswood, 10529
Silverado Senior Living-Sugarland, 10530
Silvercrest Ames Assisted Living, 8731
Silvercrest Assisted Living: Garner Farms, 8732
Silvercrest Legacy Pointe, 8733
Silvercrest Van Dorn Assisted Living, 9720
Silvercrest at Fountain View, 9721
Silvercrest at Miracle Hills Assisted Living, 9722
Silverleaf, 10320
Simon & Schuster, 5801, 6019
Simon & Schuster Consumer Group, 3691
Simon Foundation for Continence, 4109, 6949
The Simon Foundation for Continence, 3883
Simon Foundation for Incontinence, 4051, 4162, 6952
Sinus Survival: A Self-Help Guide for Allergies, Bronchitis, Colds & Sinusitis, 4661
Siouxland Aging Services, 1054, 11115
Sister Center for Helpful Living, 8734
Sisters of Life: Dr Joseph R Stanton Human Life Issues Library and Resource Center, 11660

Situation is Serious But Not Hopeless: The Psychological Benefits of Hearing Loss, 6710
Six County Area: Agency on Aging, 2406
60 Plus Association, 4170
611 Washington Ear, 7492
635 Southwest Harrison, 11118
Sixty Plus Club, 2732
Sixty Plus Elderlaw Clinic, 11159
Skeptic's Guide to the Twelve Steps, 7274
SkiSoft Publishing Corporation, 3115
Skiff Medical Center Assisted Living, 8735
Skin Cancer Foundation, 5809, 5828, 5843, 5846, 5958
Skin Cancer Foundation Journal, 5809
Skin Cancer: Preventable and Curable, 5843
Skin Cancers: Basal Cell and Squamous Cell Carcinomas: Research Report, 5844
Skokie Accessible Library Services, 11465
Skokie Public Library, 11465
Skylark Assisted Living, 10165
Skylight Gardens, 9285
Skyline Retirement Community, 9723
Skyway, 3559
Skyway Machine, 3559
Slack, 3904
Sleep Problems with Parkinson's Disease, 7027
Slicing Aid, 3346
Sling Solutions, 3396
Small Appliance Receiver, 3314, 3347
Small Business Administration (SBA), 312
Small Business and AIDS: How AIDS can Affect Your Business, 4570
Smart Leg, 3397
Smith Farms Manor, 10750
Smith Hall Annex, 5057
Smith Kettlewell Rehabilitation Engineering Research Center, 7831
Smith Manor, 10038
Smith-Ketterwell Eye Research Institute, 8053
Smith-Kettlewell Eye Research Foundation, 7990
Smith-Kettlewell Eye Research Institute, 7831, 7897
Smith-Kettlewell Technical File, 7897, 7990
Smoker's Robot, 3315
Smooth Mover, 3398
Snake River Living Center, 8557
Snug Seat, 3023
Snugseat, 3346
So Many of My Friends Have Moved Away or Died, 6026
So You Have Had an Ear Operation...What Next?, 6711
So You Love an Alcoholic, 7401
Sober But Stuck, 7275
Sobering Thoughts, 4110
Social Policy Prevention Handbook, 7276
Social Security Admin Office of Disability, 4026
Social Security Administration, 275, 313
Social Security Bulletin, 4111
Social Security Springfield Disability Determination, 958
Social Security for Public Employees, 2191
Social Security, Medicare and Pensions, 3671
Social Security: Atlanta Disability Determination, 850

Entry Name Index / S

Social Security: Baltimore Disability Determination, 1262
Social Security: Juneau Disability Determination Services, 422
Social Security: Louisville Disability Determination, 1136
Social Security: Miami Disability Determination, 800
Social Security: Orlando Disability Determination, 801
Social Security: Retirement Insurance, 314
Social Security: Santa Fe Disability Determination, 1746
Social Security: Special Benefits for Persons Aged 72 & Older, 315
Social Security: Tallahassee Disability Determination, 802
Social Security: Tampa Disability Determination, 803
Social Security: West Columbia Disability Determination, 2242
Social Service Association, 1702
Social and Behavioral Science Division, 4391
Society for Advancement in Nursing, 316
Society for Ambulatory Care Professionals, 317
Society for Equal Access Independent Living Center, 10898
Society of Geriatric Ophthalmology, 8054
Society of Hearing Impaired Physicians, 6446
Society's Assets-Elkhorn, 10963
Society's Assets-Kenosha, 10964
Society's Assets-Racine, 10965
Sodium Information Hotline, 6845
Soft-Touch Convertible Flotation Mattress, 3224
Soft-Touch Gel Flotation Cushion, 3225
Software to Go, 6547
Sol and Elaine Mosak Library, 11450
Solano Napa: Agency on Aging, 615
Solbakken, 9286
Solo Scooter, 3438
Solution Starts with You, 4162
Somerby at Jones Farm, 8076
Somerford House, 8324
Somerford Place, 8325
Somerset Assited Living Facility, 8077
Somerset County Office on Aging, 1703
Somerset Court, 9537
Somerset Court of Mocksville, 9538
Somerset Court of Newport, 9539
Somerset Manor North, 9800
Somerset Manor South, 9801
Somerville Cambridge Elder Services, 1327
Something Should be Done About Grandma Ruthie, 5034
Something in the Air: Airborne Allergens, 4672
Sommerset Assisted Living Residences, 10039
Sonoma County Alzheimers Task Force, 5066
Sonoma County Task Force for the Homeless, 616
Sound Induction Receiver, 3161
Sounding Board, 4112
Sources for Community Independent Living Services (SOURCES), 10641
South Atlantic Division, 5257

South Carolina Assistive TechnologyProjects, 2243
South Carolina Association Area: Agencies on Aging, 2244
South Carolina Association of Nonprofit Homes for the Aging, 2245
South Carolina Association of the Deaf, 6447
South Carolina Bar Association: Elder Law Committee, 11251
South Carolina Budget and Control Board: Retirement System Division, 2246
South Carolina Centers for Equal Justice (SCCEJ), 11252
South Carolina Client Assistance Program Office of the Governor of South Carolina, 2247
South Carolina Commission for the Blind, 6055
South Carolina Commission on Aging, 2248
South Carolina Department of Aging, 2249
South Carolina Department of Alcohol & Other Drug Abuse Services, 7219
South Carolina Department of Health & Environmental Control: Bureau of Preventive Health Services, 4499
South Carolina Department of Mental Health, 6056
South Carolina Department of Parks, Transportation & Tourism, 11986
South Carolina Department of Veterans Affairs, 2250
South Carolina Developmental Disability Council, 2251
South Carolina Library, 7929
South Carolina Lieutenant Governor's Office on Aging, 11253
South Carolina Services Information System, 2252
South Carolina State Library, 11756
South Carolina Workers Compensation Commission, 2253
South Central Alabama Development Commission: Area Agency on Aging, 399
South Central Colorado Seniors, 669
South Central Connecticut Agency on Aging, 699
South Central Indiana Council for Aging and Aged, 1013
South Central Kansas Area Agency on Aging, 1095
South Central Kansas Library System, 11503
South Central Nebraska Area Agency on Aging, 1578, 1595
South Central Region: Helen Keller National Center, 7744
South Dakota Association of Homes for the Aging, 2264
South Dakota Association of the Blind, 7745
South Dakota Client Assistance Program, 2265
South Dakota Department of Aging, 2266
South Dakota Department of Mental Health, 6057
South Dakota Department of Military and Veterans Services, 2267
South Dakota Department of Revenue, 2268
South Dakota Department of Social Services: Adult Services and Aging, 2269

South Dakota Department of Social Services: Legal Services for the Elderly, 11254
South Dakota Department of Tourism, 11987
South Dakota Disability Determination Sevices, 2270
South Dakota Division of Rehabilitation, 2271
South Dakota Human Services Center Medical Library, 11758
South Dakota Office of Adult Services, 2272
South Dakota Protection Advocacy Services, 2273
South Dakota Protection and Advocacy Services, 11255
South Dakota State Library: Braille andTalking Book Program, 11759
South Dakota Workers Compensation Board, 2274
South Delta Planning and Development District, 1472
South Florida Advocacy Center for Persons with Disabilities, 11055
South Park Assisted Living, 10321
South Plains Association of GovernmentsArea: Agency on Aging, 2371
South Salem Seniors, 2087
South Seattle Community College, 2944
South Shore Elder Services, 1328
South Shores Dignified Living, 8558
South Texas Area: Agency on Aging, 2372
South Texas Lighthouse for the Blind, 7746
South Western Oklahoma Development Authority Area Agency on Aging, 2035
Southeast Alaska Independent Living (SAIL), 10630
Southeast Alaska Independent Living Center (SAIL), 10631
Southeast Alaska Living Center (SAIL), 10632
Southeast Arkansas Area: Agency on Aging, 485
Southeast Center for Independent Living, 10796
Southeast Georgia Regional Development Center Area: Agency on Aging (SEGA), 851
Southeast Idaho Council of Governments: Area Agency on Aging, 897
Southeast Iowa Area: Agency on Aging, 1055
Southeast Kansas Area: Agency on Aging, 1096
Southeast Kansas Independent Living (SKIL), 10768
Southeast Minnesota Area: Agency on Aging, 1435
Southeast Regional Center: Canine Companions for Independence, 7747
Southeast Regional Service Center for Hearing Impaired People, 1436
Southeast Senior Federation, 1437
Southeastern Illinois Area Agency on Aging, 959
Southeastern Minnesota Area: Agency on Aging, 1438
Southeastern Minnesota Center for Independent Living, 10809
Southeastern Region: Helen Keller National Center, 7748

1050

Southeastern Utah Area: Agency on Aging, 2407
Southeastern Wisconsin Area Agency on Aging, 2601
Southeastern Wisconsin Area: Agency on Aging, 2595
Southern Adirondack Independent Living, 10888
Southern Arizona Chapter of the Arthritis Foundation Newsletter, 5138, 5227
Southern Arizona Legal Aid (SALA), 10986
Southern California Research Institute, 7475
Southern California Senior Life, 11901
Southern California State Library: Braille and Talking Book Library, 11348
Southern Hills Assisted Living Community, 10166
Southern Illinois Center for Independent Living, 10737
Southern Indiana Center For IndependentLiving, 10751
Southern Knights Assisted Living Center, 10531
Southern Living Center of Lebanon, 10379
Southern Maine Area Agency on Aging, 1221
Southern Maryland Center for LIFE, 10786
Southern Minnesota IL Enterprises and Services (SMILES), 10810
Southern Mississippi Area Agency on Aging, 1473
Southern NE Chapter of the Arthritis Foundation, 5178
Southern New England Chapter of the Arthritis Foundation, 5139
Southern Oklahoma Development Association Area: Agency on Aging (SODA), 2036
Southern Plantation, 8441
Southern Tier Association for the Visually Impaired, 7749
Southgate at Shrewsbury, 9017
Southside Gardens Assisted Living Center, 8885
Southview Heights Nursing Home, 9724
Southview on Main, 9287
Southwest 8 Senior Services, 1056
Southwest Area: Agency on Aging, 1439
Southwest Arkansas Area: Agency on Aging, 486
Southwest Biomedical Research Institute, 5959
Southwest Center for Independent Living, 10811
Southwest Center for Independent Living (SCIL), 10830
Southwest Foundation for Biomedical Research, 4372
Southwest Iowa Center for Independent Living, 10757
Southwest Mississippi Area Agency on Aging, 1474
Southwest Missouri Office on Aging (SWMOA), 1520
Southwest Regional Training Center:Canine Companions for Independence, 7750
Southwest Society on Aging, 2037
Southwest Tennessee Area: Agency on Aging, 2291
Southwestern Illinois Area Agency on Aging, 960

Southwestern Indiana Mental Health Center, 11104
Southwestern Indiana Regional Council on Aging, 1014
Southwestern New Mexico Area: Agency onAging, 1747
Southwestern Pennsylvania Area Agency on Aging, 2192
Southwestern Pennsylvania Partnership for Aging, 2193
Southwestern Region: Helen Keller National Center, 7751
Southwestern Vermont Council on Aging, 2435
Sowega Council on Aging: Georgia Division of Aging Services, 852
Soyland Access to Independent Living, 10738
Spa, 11940
Spa Area Independent Living Services (SAILS), 10642
Space Coast Center for Independent Living, 10707
Span-America Medical Systems, 3206
Spatial Tilt Custom Chair, 3050
Speak Out! Tips on Speaking in Public for Individuals with a Hearing Loss, 6548
SpeakEasy Communication Aid, 3162
Speaking Off the Cuff, 6767
Speaking Our Minds: Personal Reflections from Individuals with Alzheimer's, 4970
Speaking for Them: Identifying Psychiatric Complications in Alzheimer's Patients, 5035
Special Access Vans, 2993
Special Care Dentistry, 318
Special Edition for Disabled People, 3797
Special Friend of Hearing Impaired People Award, 2684
Special Needs III, 3051
Special Needs Library Montgomery County Department of Public Libraries, 11537
Special Services Division: Indiana State Library, 11486
Specialized Center of Research in Ischemic Heart Disease, 6891
Specialty Cooking Magazine, 3961
Spectrum, 5228
Spectrum Aquatics, 3292
Spectrum Community Health, 9288
Spectrum Community Health-Minneapolis, 9289
Speech & Hearing Institute, 7486
Speech & Lip Reading, 6549
Speech & Swallowing Problems for Parkinsonians, 7028
Speech Discrimination Unit, 3163
Speech Pathology, 4113
Speech Problems & Swallowing Problems In Parkinson's Disease, 7029
Speech Simulation Research Foundation, 6448
Speech and Deafness Newsletter, 6712
Speech and Voice Impairment, 7030
Speechmaker-Personal Speech Amplifier, 3164
Speechreading for Better Communication, 6713
Speechreading: Methods and Materials, 6714
Spellman Center for HIV Related Disease, 4500

Spencer House, 10167
Spenco Medical Corporation, 3220
Spenco Medical Group, 3223, 3226
Spirit of Change Magazine, 3962
Spirit of SHHH Award, 2685
Spiritual Fitness Division (CREDO Southwest), 617
Spokane Falls Community College, 2945
Sponsorship: What It's All About, 7402
Sport Lite 4000, 3536
Sportaid, 3537
Sports 'n Spokes, 12046
Spring Arbor of Apex, 9540
Spring Arbor of Herdersonville, 9541
Spring Arbor of Kinston, 9542
Spring Arbor of Raleigh, 9543
Spring Arbor of Rocky Mount, 9544
Spring Arbor of Wilmington, 9545
Spring Arbor of Wilson, 9546
Spring Creek Manor Assisted Living, 8559
Spring Creek Manor-American Falls, 8560
Spring Creek Manor-Montpelier, 8561
Spring Creek Manor-Soda Springs, 8562
Spring Dell Center, 11538
Spring Hills, 8563
Spring Hills at Morristown, 9802
Spring Meadows, 10168
Spring Meadows Libertyville, 8600
Spring Meadows at Summit, 9803
Spring Meadows at Trumbull, 8292
Spring Valley Assisted Living Residence, 10169
Spring Valley Estates, 9290
Spring Valley Senior Assisted Living, 8736
Spring Village, 10170
Spring Wind Assisted Living, 10617
SpringBoard Plus, 3165
Springer Publishing Company, 3627, 3647, 3844, 3852, 3888, 3896, 3903, 3908, 4524, 4963, 4977, 6081, 11902
Springfield Assisted Living Center, 10322
Springfield Center for Independent Living (CIL), 10739
Springfield Place, 8218
Springhouse Assisted Living, 8126
Springhouse Retirement Community, 9018
Springmeadows, 9360
Spruce Point, 10171
St Ann's Home, 9078
St Anne's Mead Retirement Home, 9079
St Anns Residence, 9291
St Anthony Village, 10172
St Augustine Health Campus, 9946
St Benedicts Senior Community, 9292
St Catherine's Living Center, 9583
St Charles Council on Aging, 1187
St Clark County Library for the Blind and Physically Handicapped, 11571
St Francis Residence, 9584
St Francis Villa Assisted Living, 8886
St Joesph Haven, 10532
St Joesph Manor, 8887
St Joesph's Home for the Aged, 9080
St John Area: Agency on Aging, 1188
St John Parish Council on Aging, 1189
St John's New Horizons, 8821
St Joseph Assisted Residence, 9947
St Joseph Tower Assisted Living, 9725
St Joseph's Retirement Community, 9726
St Joseph's Villa, 9727
St Josephs Nursing Home, 9728
St Luke's Countryside Villa, 9729

1051

St Mary's Healthcare Center, 10323
St Mary's School for the Deaf Library Information Center, 11661
St Marys Assisted Residence at Morris Hill, 9804
St Paul Hermitage, 10752
St Paul Urban League, 9293
St Williams Foster Care, 9294
St. Bernard Council on Aging, 1190
St. Clare's Hospital, 4500
St. Francis Hospital, 5938
St. James Parish Department of Human Resources, 1191
St. James Villas, 8601
St. John's Episcopal Church, 2915
St. John's Episcopal Hospital, 7045
St. Lawrence County Office for Aging, 1875
St. Louis Area: Agency on Aging, 1521
St. Louis Society for the Blind, 7752
St. Louis Society for the Blind and Visually Impaired, 1522
St. Louis University: Department of Psychiatry, 6103
St. Luke's Assisted Living, 10571
St. Mary's County Office on Aging, 1263
St. Mary's Hospital, 4340
St. Patrick Hospital and Health Sciences Center: Library Center, 11595
St. Paul's Senior Homes & Services, 8219
St. Regis, 8220
St. Regis Mohawk Office for the Aging, 1876
St. Tammany Council on Aging, 1192
Stages of Parkinson's Disease, 7031
Stair & Glide Stairway Lift, 3399
StairClimber, 3490
StairLIFT SC & SL, 3400
Stairway Elevators, 3401
Stand Aid, 3402
Stand Aid of Iowa, 3402, 3532
Standard Finance Building, 869
Standing Aid Frame with Rear Entry, 3491
Standing By You: Family Support Groups, 5010
Standish Village at Lower Mills, 9019
Stanford Center for Research in Disease Prevention, 7476
Stanford Centre, 8429
Stanford University School of Medicine, 7476
Stanford University: General Clinical Research Center, 4618
Stanford University: Oncology Day Care Clinic, 5781
Stanford University:National Cooperative Drug Discover /AIDS Group, 4619
Stanislaus County Department of Aging and Veteran Services, 618
State Bar of Michigan: Senior Justice Committee, 11160
State Bar of New Mexico: Elder Law Section, 11199
State Bar of New Mexico: Lawyer Referral for the Elderly Program, 11200
State Bar of Texas: Texas Young Lawyers Association, 11267
State Department of Education, 11856
State Guard Association of the United States, 319
State Independent Living Council, 10966
State Library of Louisiana, 11518

State Library of Ohio: Talking Book Program, 11714
State Public Official Award for Significant Legislative Achievement, 2686
State University College at Fredonia: Youngman Center, 6814
State University College at Plattsburgh: Auditory Research Laboratory, 6815
State University College at Plattsburgh: Biochemisrty/Biophysics Program, 5067
State University of New York, 2871, 4380
State University of New York Health Science Center at Stony Brook: Asthma and Allergic Diseases Center, 4692
State University of New York at Buffalo Toxicology Research Center, 7220
State University of New York at Stony Brook: Cognitive and Behavioral Neuroscience, 5068
State University of New York: SUNY Stony Brook Drug Discovery Group, 4620
State Vocational Rehabilitation Agencies, 3798
State Vocational Rehabilitation Agency, 2299
State and Federal Programs for the Aging, 3799
State of Alaska, Department of Health &Social Services, 423
State of Florida, 11988
State of Hawaii: Department of Health &Executive Office on Aging, 11075
State of Illinois, 11989
State of Michigan Travel Resources, 11990
State of Missouri, 11991
State of Nevada Client Assistance Program, 1614
State of Rhode Island, 11992
State of Texas Office of the GovernorEconomic Development and Tourism, 11993
State of Utah, 11994
State of Vermont, 11995
State of Vermont Division of Disabilityand Aging Services, 11277
State of West Virginia, 11996
State of Wyoming Aging Division, 11302
Staten Island Center for Independent Living, 10889
Statesville Place, 9547
Statewide Independent Living Council (SILC), 10637
Statewide Independent Living Council of Kansas, 10769
Statewide Independent Living Council-Hawaii, 10717
Statewide Independent Living Council-Idaho, 10721
Statewide Services for Deaf and Hard of Hearing People, 6715
Statistical Handbook on Aging Americans, 3672
Staunton Public Library Talking Book Center, 11821
Stavros Center for Independent Living, 10797
Stay Fit Video, 4163
Staying Healthy with Type 2 Diabetes, 6251
Steady Write, 3469
Steel Food Guard, 3348
A Step-By-Step Guide to Personal Management for Blind Persons, 7793

Step-by-Step Communicator, 3166
Steps for Caregivers: Caring for Persons with Alzheimer's Disease, 5048
Steps to Enhancing Communication, 5011
Steps to Enhancing Your Home: Modifying the Environment, 5012
Steps to Finding Home Health Care, 5013
Steps to Getting a Diagnosis: Finding Out if It's Alzheimer's Disease, 5014
Steps to Planning Activities: Structuring the Day at Home, 5015
Steps to Understanding Challenging Behaviors, 5016
Steps to Understanding Legal Issues: Planning for the Future, 5017
Sterling, 3439
Sterling Assisted Living, 9730
Sterling Aventura, 8430
Sterling House at Omaha, 9731
Sterling House at Omaha II, 9732
Sterling House of Arvada, 8248
Sterling Park Commons, 9295
Sterling Park Ridgeview, 9296
Sterling Publishing Company, 3612
Steuben County Office for the Aging, 1877
Steven Motor Chair, 3538
Steven Motor Chair Company, 3538
Stevens Residence, 9297
Stevick Senior Center, 935
Stickney Manor, 10324
Sting Wheelchair, 3539
Stockley Center, 8326
Stone-Hayes Center for Independent Living, 10740
Stonecreek Lodge, 8851
Stonewall Jackson Home for Adults, 10572
Stoney Creek Living Center, 8564
Stoneybrook Suites of Watertown, 10325
Stony Brook Court, 8293
Stop Prediabetes Now: The Ultimate Planto Lose Weight and Prevent Diabetes, 6216
Stop Smoking: A Guide to Your Options, 4114
Stop the Rollercoaster, 6217
Stop-Leak Gel Flotation Cushion, 3227
Stop-Leak Gel Flotation Mattress, 3228
Straight and Custom Curved Stairlifts, 3403
Straub Pacific Health Foundation, 5947
Strength Training Past 50, 3673
Strength Training for Seniors, 3674, 11701
Stress Management, 6716
Stress in Recovery, 7403
Stretch-View Wide-View Rectangular Illuminated Magnifier, 3167
String Switch, 3168
Strobe Light Signalers, 3169
Stroke - A Clinical Approach, 7070
Stroke Book, 7071
Stroke Connection, 7103
Stroke Research and Treatment Center, 7056
Stroke Therapy, 7072
Stroke Treatment and Recovery, 7104
Stroke and the Family: A New Guide, 7073
Stroke for Dummies, 7074
Stroke is a Brain Attack!, 7105
Stroke: Clinical Updates, 7106
Stroke: Putting the Pieces Back Together, 7075
Stroke: Questions & Answers, 7107
Stroke: Reducing Your Risk (Spanish), 7108
Stroke: Your Complete Exercise Guide, 7076

Students with Cancer: A Resource for the Educator, 5845
Studies for Mature Adults, 2872
Sturgis Library, 11152
Substance Abuse & Mental Health Services Offices, 7141, 7144, 7206, 7469
Substance Abuse Funding News, 7404
Substance Abuse Intervention, Prevention, Rehabilitation and Systems Change, 7277
Substance Abuse Program, 7233
Substance Abuse and Mental Health Services Administration, 7450, 7477
Substance Abuse and Physical Disability, 7278
Suburban Audio Visual Service, 11466
Successful Models of Community Long Term Care Services for the Elderly, 3675
Suction Grater, 3349
Sue Smith Travel Service, 12047
Suffield by the River, 8294
Suffolk Cooperative Library System, 11662
Suffolk County Office for the Aging, 1878
Sugar Land Oaks Guest Home, 10533
Sugarland Ridge, 10618
Suggested Exercise Program for People with Parkinson's Disease, 7032
Sullivan County Office for the Aging, 1879
Summer Ridge Assisted Living & Retirement Community, 10534
Summer Shades Residential Care, 8103
Summer Wind, 8565
Summerville at Garden Manor, 8221
Summerville at Hillsborough, 9805
Summerville at Kenner, 8888
Summerville at Litchfield Hills, 8295
Summerville at Main Place, 8222
Summerville at Mentor Assisted Living, 9948
Summerville at Middletown, 9949
Summerville at Orange, 8223
Summerville at South Windsor, 8296
Summerville at Stafford, 9806
Summerville at Valley View, 8224
Summerville at Victorian Court, 8225
Summerville at Villa De Anza, 8226
Summerville at Voorhees, 9807
Summerville of Singing Woods, 9950
Summit Assisted Living, 10173
Summit Heights, 8737
Summit Independent Living Center-Kalispell, 10836
Summit Independent Living Center-Missoula, 10837
Summit Independent Living Center-Ronan, 10838
Summit Springs Assisted Living Facility, 10174
Summit Square of Park Ridge, 8602
Summit Villa Assisted Living, 9951
Summit at Lakeway, 10535
Summit at Northwest Hills, 10536
Sun Dial Manor, 10326
Sun Health Research Institute: Alzheimers Center, 5069
Sun Terrace Hermiston, 10175
Sun and Skin News, 5846
Sun-Mate Seat Cushions, 3229
Sunbridge Care, 8566
Sunbridge Living Center-Meridian, 8567
Sunbridge Retirement, 8568
Suncoast Center for Independent Living, 10708

Sundial Special Vacations, 12048
Sundial Tours, 12048
Sunlight, Ultraviolet Radiation and the Skin, 5847
Sunny View Manor, 8227
Sunnybrook Assisted Living, 8738
Sunnyside Manor, 9808
Sunpointe Senior Estates, 10327
Sunquest Village of Yuma, 8127
Sunrise Assisted Living, 8889, 9952
Sunrise Assisted Living East Brunswick, 9809
Sunrise Assisted Living at Bexley, 9953
Sunrise Assisted Living at Eastover, 9548
Sunrise Assisted Living at Farmington Hills, 9081
Sunrise Assisted Living at Finneytown, 9954
Sunrise Assisted Living at Gardner Park, 9020
Sunrise Assisted Living at Northville, 9082
Sunrise Assisted Living of Ann Arbor, 9083
Sunrise Assisted Living of Bath, 9955
Sunrise Assisted Living of Baton Rouge, 8890
Sunrise Assisted Living of Buffalo, 9298
Sunrise Assisted Living of Cohasset, 9021
Sunrise Assisted Living of Cuyahoga Falls, 9956
Sunrise Assisted Living of Edgewater, 9810
Sunrise Assisted Living of Edina, 9299
Sunrise Assisted Living of Englewood, 9957
Sunrise Assisted Living of Hamilton, 9958
Sunrise Assisted Living of Kenwood, 9959
Sunrise Assisted Living of Morris Plains, 9811
Sunrise Assisted Living of Mt Laurel, 9812
Sunrise Assisted Living of Naperville, 8603
Sunrise Assisted Living of Norwood, 9022
Sunrise Assisted Living of Oakwood, 9960
Sunrise Assisted Living of Paramus, 9813
Sunrise Assisted Living of Parma, 9961
Sunrise Assisted Living of Raleigh, 9549
Sunrise Assisted Living of Rochester, 9084
Sunrise Assisted Living of Shaker Heights, 9962
Sunrise Assisted Living of South Charlotte, 9550
Sunrise Assisted Living of Stamford, 8297
Sunrise Assisted Living of Troy, 9085
Sunrise Assisted Living of Wall, 9814
Sunrise Assisted Living of Wayland, 9023
Sunrise Assisted Living of West Essex, 9815
Sunrise Assisted Living of WestBloomfield, 9086
Sunrise Assisted Living of Westfield, 9816
Sunrise Assisted Living of Wilton, 8298
Sunrise Assisted Living of Wooster, 9963
Sunrise Assisted Living-Roseville, 9300
Sunrise Atrium of Boca Raton, 8431
Sunrise Cottage of Mankato, 9301
Sunrise Cottages of Rochester, 9302
Sunrise Medical/Quickie Designs, 3429, 3504
Sunrise Senior Living, 9336
Sunrise Villa, 8739
Sunrise Village, 9303
Sunrise at Tucker Creek, 9964
Sunrise of Bloomingdale, 8604
Sunrise of Boulder, 8249
Sunrise of Buffalo Grove, 8605
Sunrise of Carmel, 8623
Sunrise of Crystal Lake, 8606

Sunrise of Flossmoor, 8607
Sunrise of Gahanna, 9965
Sunrise of Glen Ellyn, 8608
Sunrise of Gurnee, 8609
Sunrise of Naperville-North, 8610
Sunrise of Old Tappan, 9817
Sunrise of Palos Park, 8611
Sunrise of Park Ridge, 8612
Sunrise of Poland, 9966
Sunrise of Providence, 9551
Sunrise of Schaumburg, 8613
Sunrise of Wayne, 9818
Sunrise of Willowbrook, 8614
Sunrise of Woodbury Lake, 9819
Sunrise on the Scioto, 9967
Sunset Court Assisted Living Center, 10328
Sunset Hall Program at Bethany Towers, 619
Sunset Park Place, 8740
Sunset View Assisted Living, 9733
Sunshine Care Mountain Vistas, 8228
Super Scout Three Wheeler, 3440
Superarm Lift, 2994
Superintendent of Documents, 4085, 4949, 6072, 6089, 6101
Support for People with Oral and Head and Neck Cancer, 5782
Support for People with Oral, Head and Neck Cancer, 5848
Supportive Older Women's Network, 320
Sure Hands International, 3404
Sure Safe Raised Toilet Seat, 3024
SureHands Lift & Care Systems, 3405
Suregrip Bathtub Rail, 3025
Surf Chair, 3540
Surgery: Information to Consider, 5229
Surnise of Woodcliff Lake, 9820
Susan G Komen Cancer Foundation, 5960
Sussex County Assistive Technology Resource Center sussex coun, 10692
Sussex County Office on Aging, 1704
Suzanne Elise Assisted Living, 10176
Swan House, 8741
Swede Elite, 3541
Sweetwater Springs, 8442
Swing-A-Way, 3406
Swiss International Airlines, 11941
Sycamore Square Assisted Living, 10040
Sylvan House, 8569
Sylvan Woods, 8742
Sylvester Comprehensive Cancer Center, 5783
Sylvester Comprehensive Cancer Center,Cancer Information Service, 11422
Symbi-Key Computer Switch Interface, 3170
Synthetic Sheep-Skin Pads, 3230
Syracuse University, 2860, 4373
Syracuse University Biological Research Laboratories, 4373
Syracuse University Center for Policy Research, 11663
Syracuse University: Gerontology Center, 4374
Syracuse University: Institute for Sensory Research, 6816
System Center, 11455
Systems 2000, 3441

Entry Name Index / T

T

TAJ Braille Typewriter, 3171
TALKBACK Wireless Doorbell Intercom, 3172
TARCOG: Area Agency on Aging, 400
TASH, 3916
TERRA-JET USA, 3442
TERRA-JET: Utility Vehicle, 3442
TIAA-CREF, 321
TJ Publishers, 6467, 6470, 6474, 6477, 6496, 6514, 6519, 6539, 6543, 6544, 6744, 6745
TTY's-Telephone Device for the Deaf, 3173
TV & VCR Remote, 3174
Tabor College, 2797
Taconic Learning Center (TLC), 2742
Taconic Resources for Independence, 10890
Tactic, 7898
Taking Care of Gestational Diabetes, 6252
Taking Care of Your Feet, 4115
Taking Time: Support for People with Cancer & People Who Care for Them, 5849
Taking the HIV (AIDS) Test: How to Help Yourself, 4571
Talbot Cancer Research Library, 11742
Talking About Death, 6027
Talking Bathroom Scale, 3026
Talking Book Library, Miami and DadePublic Library System, 11423
Talking Book Topics, 7899, 7991
Talking Books Library for the Blind and Physically Handicapped, 11424
Talking Books Service, 11504
Talking Books Service: Evansville Vanderburgh County Public Library, 11487
Talking Books for Senior Adults, 7992
Talking Clocks, 3175
Talking Desktop Calculators, 3176
Talking Thermometers, 3273
Talking Watches, 3177
Tallahassee Advocacy Center for Personswith Disabilities, 11056
Tamarack Retirement Center, 10041
Taming Asthma and Allergy by Controlling Your Environment, 4662
Tampa AIDS Network: Florida Women's AIDS Resource Movement, 4501
Tampa Advocacy Center for Persons with Disabilities, 11057
Tampa Bay Regional Planning Council-Area Agency on Aging, 804
Tampa Bay Research Institute, 4375
Tampa Lighthouse for the Blind, 7753
Tampa-Hillsborough County Public Library System, 11393
Tanglewood Manor, 9855
Tanner Spring, 10177
Tapestry House, 8443
Tapestry at Village Gate West, 10601
Taping for the Blind, 7754
Tappan Zee Manor, 9856
Tarrant County Association for the Blind, 7755
Tatnuck Park at Worcester, 9024
Tattersall Press, 11903
Tax Counseling for the Elderly: Taxpayers Services, 322
Taxes and Alzheimer's Disease, 5018
Taylor & Francis, 3856, 3858

Teacher's Retirement Board, 1297
Teachers College Milbank Memorial Library, 11664
Teachers Insurance and Annuity Association Business Library, 11665
Teaching English to the Deaf as a Second Language, 6590
Teaching Strategies for the Developmentof Auditory Verbal Communication, 6768
Technical Assistance Resource Guide, 6717
Technology Management Group, 4542
Tele-Consumer Hotline, 6449
Telecaption Adapter, 3178
Telecoil: Plugging into Sound, 6769
Telecoils in Hearing Aids, 6770
Telecommunications Access Updates, 6718
Telecommunications for the Deaf, 3258, 6654, 6450
Telephone Amplifier, 3179
Telephone Pioneer, 4116
Telephone Pioneers of America, 4116, 7756
Teller Senior Coalition, 670
Telling Stories, 6771
Temple Association for Retired Persons, 2911
Temple University FELS Institute for Cancer Research, 5961
Temple University Institute on Aging, 3676
Temple University: General Clinical Research Center, 4376
Temple University: Section of Auditory Research, 6817
Temple University: Speech and Hearing Science Laboratories, 6818
Ten Oaks at Merrill Gardens Community, 10042
Ten Speed Press, 4654, 5789
Tender Love & Company, 8891
The Tender Scar: Life After the Death of a Spouse, 6028
Tender Social Day Center for Older Adults and Alzheimer's Group Respite Program, 4942
Tennessee Association of Homes and Services for the Aging, 2292
Tennessee Bureau of Alcohol & Drug Abuse, 7221
Tennessee Chapter of the Arthritis Foundation, 5179, 5140
Tennessee Client Assistance Program, 2293
Tennessee Commission on Aging, 2294
Tennessee Commission on Aging and Disability, 11262
Tennessee Council of the Blind, 7757
Tennessee Council on Developmental Disabilities, 2295
Tennessee Department of Aging, 2296
Tennessee Department of Health: AIDS Program, 4502
Tennessee Department of Mental Health & Developmental Disabilities, 6058
Tennessee Department of Revenue, 2297
Tennessee Department of Tourist Development, 11997
Tennessee Department of Veterans Affairs, 2298
Tennessee Division of Rehabilitation Services, 2299
Tennessee Justice Center, 11263
Tennessee Library for the Blind and Physically Handicapped, 11762
Tennessee Technology Access Project, 2300

Tensas Council on Aging, 1193
Teratologies: A Cultural Study of Cancer, 5804
Terms & Tips: An Alzheimer Care Handbook, 5019
Terrace Heights, 9304
Terrace Park Senior Living, 8743
Terrace at Bluegrass, 10380
Terrace of Shreveport, 8892
Terrebonne Council on Aging, 1194
Terreboone House, 8893
Terry-Wash Mitt, 3027
Terry-Wash Mitt - Medium Size, 3028
Terwilliger Plaza, 10178
Test Positive Aware Network, 4087
Testicular Cancer: Research Report, 5850
Testicular Self-Examination, 5851
Testing Positive for HIV, 4572
Testing for HIV Infection, 4573
Texaco Retirees Club of Houston, 2373
Texas Association of 504 Coordinators and Hearing Officers, 6451
Texas Association of Area Agencies on Aging, 2374
Texas Association of Directors of Volunteer Services, 2375
Texas Association of Homes and Services for the Aging, 2376
Texas Association of Retinitis Pigmentosa, 7980, 7758
Texas Commission for the Blind, 7759
Texas Commission for the Deaf, 6452
Texas Commission on Alcohol and Drug Abuse, 7222
Texas Comptroller of Public Accountants, 2377
Texas Department of Aging and Disability Services (DAD), 2378, 11268
Texas Department of Health Library, 11790
Texas Department of Health: Bureau of HIV and STD Control, 4503
Texas Department of Mental Health & Mental Retardation, 6059
Texas Department on Aging, 2379
Texas Dept of Human Service\Long Term Care, 3728
Texas Developmental Disability Council, 2380
Texas Employees' Retirement System, 2381
Texas Geriatrics Society, 2382
Texas Governor's Committee for People With Disabilities, 2383
Texas Heart Institute, 6846
Texas Legal Services Center: Legal Hotline for Older Texans, 11269
Texas Medical Center, 6861
Texas Planning Council for Developmental Disabilities, 2384
Texas Protection & Advocacy Services for Disabled Perosns, 2385
Texas Protection and Advocacy AgencyNorth Texas Regional Office: Dallas, 11270
Texas Society to Prevent Blindness, 7760
Texas State Library, 11791
Texas State Library Talking Book Program, 11792
Texas State Technical College: Waco Library, 11793
Texas Tech University: Speech-Language-Hearing Clinic, 6819

Entry Name Index / U

Texas Tech University: Tarbox Parkinson's Disease Institute, 7046
Texas Technical University, Health Sciences, 4873
Texas Veterans Commission, 2386
Texas Workers Compensation Commission, 2387
Texoma Area: Agency on Aging, 2388
Thania's Assisted Living Home, 8104
Theosophical Book Association for the Blind, 7862
Therapeutic Activity for Persons with Alzheimer, 4971
Therapro, 3016, 3027, 3028, 3132, 3236, 3238, 3239, 3242, 3251, 3266, 3274, 3310, 3311, 3335, 3338, 3342, 3343, 3350, 3351, 3354, 3453
Therapy Putty, 3274
Therapy for Diabetes Mellitus and Related Disorders, 6221
There's A Hart, 10329
Theta Reports, 3694
Thick-n-Easy, 3350
Third Age Press, 11904
Third Opinion: International Directory to Complementary Therapy Centers, 3800
This Is AA, 7405
This Is Al-Anon, 7406
Thomas Balch Library, 11822
Thomas Hardware, 3563
Thomas Jefferson University: Center for Research in Medical Education, 4377
Thomas M. Cooley Law School, 11159
Thomas Nelson, 3814
Thompson Gardens of Garland, 9552
Thompson House Group Home, 8894
Thornapple Publishing Company, 11905
Thorne Crest Retirement Center, 9306
A Thousand Tomorrows, 5025
Three Links Center, 10603
Three Rivers Area: Agency on Aging, 1475
Three Rivers Center for Independent Living, 10758, 10919
Three Rivers Independent Living, 10770
Three Rivers-Manhattan, 10771
Three Talks to Medical Societies, 7407
Three Views of Al-Anon, 7408
36 Hour Day: A Family Guide to Caring for Persons with Alzheimer Disease, 3587
36-Hour Day, 4944
3801 Grand, 8625
3M Brailler, 3053
3M Large Printed Labeler, 3054
3rd Opinion: International Directory to Complementary Therapy Centers, 5788
Thrifty Rent-a-Car, 11942
Throndike Publishing, 7071
Thumbs Up Cup, 3351
Thurston Woods Village: The Villa, 9087
Thyroid Foundation of America, 323
Ticket Counter, 12049
Tide Book Publishing Company, 11906
Tilt 'n Tote, Roamer Riding Chair, 3407
Tim's Trim, 2995
Timberhill Place, 10179
Time Health, 3872
Time Out!, 5020
Time to Start Living, 7409
Timex Easy Reader, 3180
Tinnitus, 6719
Tinnitus Today, 6591, 6595

Tioga Opportunities Department on Aging, 1880
Tips to Remember, 4673
Tiresias Press, 11907
To Our Family Members Who Are Hard of Hearing, 6720
Tockwotten Home, 10222
Toilet Guard Rail, 3029
Tonight's the Night, 4164
Tooele County Division of Aging and Adult Services, 2408
Topeka Independent Living Resource Center, 10772
Topics in Geriatric Rehabilitation, 4117
Torso Support, 3560
Total Access Courtroom, 6721
Total Health, 3963
Total Living Center (TLC), 10855
Toth Assisted Living Facility, 9734
Touch Page Turner, 3470
Touch of Diabetes, 6222
Touch of Home, 10537
Tour of Cancer Clinics, 5784
Toward Healthy Living - A Wellness Journal, Arthritis Foundation Distribution Center, 5163
Tower Club of the Blind, 7761
Tower One Tower East, 8299
Towers Perrin Corporate Information Center, 11666
Town Hall Estates, 9307
Towne Centre, 8624
Trace Center, 6820
Tract Messenger, 7900
Tracy's House, 9308
Traditions at Bath Road, 9968
Traditions at Mill Run, 9969
Traditions of Chillicothe, 9970
Traditions of Wayland, 9025
Trail Ridge Retirement Community Assisted Living Center, 10330
Tranquility Manor, 8105
Transaction Publishers, 3821, 11908
Transfer Bench with Back, 3052
Transfer Board, 3408
Transfer Tub Bench, 3030
Transitional Senior Housing, 9309
Transportation Equipment for People with Disabilities, 2996
Travel Companion Exchange, 12050
Travel Resources for Deaf and Hard of Hearing People, 6722
Travel Trends, 12051
Travelers Aid Society, 12052
Travelfair, 12053
Travelin' Talk, 3801
Travelin' Talk Directory, 3801
Travelin' Talk Newsletter, 12054
Travis Association for the Blind, 7762
Travis County Services for the Deaf, 6453
Travis County Services for the Deaf and Hard of Hearing, 6454
Travis L Williams Family Services Center, 11324
Treasure Valley Association of the Hearing Impaired, 6455
Treasure Valley Hearing and Balance Clinics, 6456
Treatment Information Services - AmFAR, 4540
Treatment of Complicated Mourning, 6030

Treatment of Parkinson's Disease with Carbidopa-Levodopa, 7033
Trent Assisted Living Center, 10331
Tri-County Center for Independent Living, 10831
Tri-County Independent Living Center, 10899, 10935
Tri-County Office on Aging, 1388
Tri-County Partnership for Independent Living, 10920
Tri-County Retirement Home, 9585
Tri-Grip Bathtub Rail, 3031
Tri-State Blind Society, 7763
Tri-State Independent Blind Society, 7764
Tri-Walker, 3492
Tri-Wheelers, 3443
Trident Area Agency on Aging, 2254
Trinity House, 8229
Trinity Oaks Retirement Community, 9553
Trinity Towers, 10538
Tripod Captioned Filys, 6457
Triumph 3000/4000, 3444
Triumph Scooter, 3445
Troubleshooting Your Hearing Aid, 6723
Trustee of the Year Award, 2687
Tub Slide Shower Chair, 3032
Tucson Family History Center, 11325
Tuff Village, 9310
Tufte Manor, 9586
Tufts University School of Medicine: Immunology Section, 4693
Tufts University: Asthma and Allergic Diseases Cooperative Research Center, 4694
Tulane University Occupational Lung Disease Center, 4378
Tulane University: Howard-Tilton Memorial Library-Louisiana Collection, 11519
Tulsa Area: Agency on Aging, 2038
Tulsa City-County Library System, 11723
Turnabout, 7279
Turnagain Adult Foster Home, 8106
Turtle & Crane Assisted Living, 8570
Twelve Oaks Irving Assisted Living Center, 10539
Twelve Steps Illustrated, 7410
Twelve Steps and Traditions, 7411
Twelve Steps for Tobacco Users, 7412
Twin Cedars, 9821
Twin Oaks Assisted Living, 8822
Twin Peaks Press, 3717, 3729, 11921
Twin-Rest Seat Cushion & Glamour Pillow, 3231
21st Century Scientific, 3500, 3502, 3503, 3535
250 Tips for Making Life with Arthritis Easier, 5146
Type 2 Diabetes: Your Healthy Living Guide, 6223
Type II Diabetes, 6253
Type II Diabetes Prevention Pyramids, 6254
Typewriting Institute for the Handicapped, 3130

U

U-Control II, 3181
UC San Diego Extension, 2733
UCLA AIDS Clinical Research Center, 4621
UCSD Medical Center, 8203, 6895
UCSF Memory and Aging Center, 3584

1055

Entry Name Index / U

UIC Eye Center, 8056
UMDNJ and Coriell Research Library, 11617
UMKC Institute for Human Development, 1523
UPF Newsletters, 7034
URSA Institute, 4504
US Aging Policy Interest Groups, 3802
US Army: Medical Command Center for Health Promotion & Preventive Medicine, 11539
US Association of Blind Athletes, 7871
US Coast Guard Commandant (G-OPN), 4099
US Commission on Civil Rights, 11399
US Commission on Civil Rights: Civil Rights Discrimination Complaints, 324
US Conference of Mayors, 4539
US Deparment of Veterans Affairs: Center Library, 11520
US Deparment of Veterans Affairs: Columbia William Jennings Bryan-Dorn Veterans Hospital Library, 11757
US Deparment of Veterans Affairs: Philadelphia Medical Center Library, 11743
US Department Office of Civil Rights, 107
US Department of Commerce, Bureau of the Census, 293
US Department of Education, 6392
US Department of Education OSERS, 6375
US Department of Education: Office of Civil Rights, 325
US Department of Health & Human Services, 1, 5, 53, 118, 134, 173, 174, 176, 177, 178, 179, 236, 276, 282, 283, 284, 285, 286, 287, 313, 314
US Department of Health and Human Services, 1251, 4260, 5233, 6279
US Department of Health and Human Services: Office for Civil Rights, 11095
US Department of Housing & Urban Development: Fair Housing and Equal Opportunity Hotline, 327
US Department of Housing and Urban Development, 149
US Department of Justice, 108, 131, 328
US Department of Labor, 127, 11048
US Department of Labor: Office of Federal Contract Compliance Programs, 329, 11096
US Department of Transportation, 330
US Department of Veteran Affairs: Palo Alto Health Care and Medical Information Service, 11349
US Department of Veterans Affairs, 337, 338, 2127, 3732, 331
US Department of Veterans Affairs Bedford: Edith Nourse Rogers Memorial Veterans Hospital Medical Library, 11553
US Department of Veterans Affairs Hospital Libraries, 11333
US Department of Veterans Affairs Hospitl: Fort Howard Hospital Library, 11540
US Department of Veterans Affairs Medical Center Library Service, 11334, 11445, 11554, 11794
US Department of Veterans Affairs Medical Library, 11425
US Department of Veterans Affairs Outpatient Clinic Learning Resources Service, 11555
US Department of Veterans Affairs and Center Learning Resources Service Library, 11426
US Department of Veterans Affairs, Health & Science Library, 11375
US Department of Veterans Affairs, Hospital Library, 11427
US Department of Veterans Affairs, John Cochran Division Library, 11589
US Department of Veterans Affairs, Medical Center Library Service, 11405, 11488
US Department of Veterans Affairs: Albany Medical Center Library, 11667
US Department of Veterans Affairs: Albuquerque Medical Center Library, 11623
US Department of Veterans Affairs: Altoona James E Van Zandt Medical Center Library Service, 11744
US Department of Veterans Affairs: Amarillo Hospital Library, 11796
US Department of Veterans Affairs: Ann Arbor Hospital Library, 11572
US Department of Veterans Affairs: Asheville Medical Center Library, 11684
US Department of Veterans Affairs: Baltimore Medical Center Library Service, 11541
US Department of Veterans Affairs: Batavia Western New York Healthcare System Library, 11668
US Department of Veterans Affairs: Bath Medical Center Library Service, 11669
US Department of Veterans Affairs: Battle Creek Medical Center Library Service, 11573
US Department of Veterans Affairs: Beckley Library Service, 11840
US Department of Veterans Affairs: Big Spring Hospital Library, 11797
US Department of Veterans Affairs: Bonham North Texas Health Care System, 11798
US Department of Veterans Affairs: Boston Hospital Medical Library, 11556
US Department of Veterans Affairs: Brecksville Medical Center Library, 11715
US Department of Veterans Affairs: Bronx Medical Center Library, 11670
US Department of Veterans Affairs: Brooklyn Medical Center Library, 11671
US Department of Veterans Affairs: Buffalo Medical Center Library Service, 11672
US Department of Veterans Affairs: Butler Medical Center Library, 11745
US Department of Veterans Affairs: CarlVinson Medical Center Library, 11446
US Department of Veterans Affairs: Castle Point Department of Medicine and Surgery Library Service, 11673
US Department of Veterans Affairs: Central Iowa Health Care System, 11494
US Department of Veterans Affairs: Cheyenne Medical and Regional Office Center, 11854
US Department of Veterans Affairs: Chicago Health Care System-West Side Division, 11467
US Department of Veterans Affairs: Chillicothe Medical Library, 11716
US Department of Veterans Affairs: Cincinnati Learning Resources Service, 11717
US Department of Veterans Affairs: Clarkburg Loouis A Johnson VA Medical Center Library, 11841
US Department of Veterans Affairs: Coatesville Medical Center Library, 11746
US Department of Veterans Affairs: Dallas Library Service, 11799
US Department of Veterans Affairs: Dayton Medical Center Library Service, 11718
US Department of Veterans Affairs: Denver Medical Center Library, 11365
US Department of Veterans Affairs: Detroit Medical Center Library Service, 11574
US Department of Veterans Affairs: Dr Karl Menninger Medical Library, 11505
US Department of Veterans Affairs: Durham Medical Center Library, 11685
US Department of Veterans Affairs: Dwight D. Eisenhower Center Medical Library, 11506
US Department of Veterans Affairs: East Orange Medical Center Library, 11618
US Department of Veterans Affairs: Erie Medical Center Library, 11747
US Department of Veterans Affairs: Fargo Medical Center Library, 11702
US Department of Veterans Affairs: Fayettville Medical Center Library Service, 11686
US Department of Veterans Affairs: For Meade VA Black Hills Health Care System Medical Library, 11760
US Department of Veterans Affairs: Fort Harrison Medical Center Library, 11596
US Department of Veterans Affairs: Grand Island Greater Nebraska Health Care System Library, 11602
US Department of Veterans Affairs: Grand Junction Medical Center Library Service, 11366
US Department of Veterans Affairs: H Earl Gordon Medical Library, 11350
US Department of Veterans Affairs: Hampton Medical Center Library and Educational Resources, 11823
US Department of Veterans Affairs: Health Administration Medical Center, 11380
US Department of Veterans Affairs: Healthcare System in West Haven, 11376
US Department of Veterans Affairs: Hospital Library, 11468, 11514
US Department of Veterans Affairs: Houston Medical Center Library, 11800
US Department of Veterans Affairs: Huntinington Learning Resource Center, 11842
US Department of Veterans Affairs: Indiana Health Care System, 11489
US Department of Veterans Affairs: Iron Mountain Medical Center Library, 11575
US Department of Veterans Affairs: Jackson Medical Center Library, 11585
US Department of Veterans Affairs: Johnson City Medical Center Library, 11763
US Department of Veterans Affairs: Kansas Medical Center Library, 11590

Entry Name Index / U

US Department of Veterans Affairs: Kerrville South Texas Veterans Health Care System, 11801
US Department of Veterans Affairs: Lebanon Medical Center Library, 11748
US Department of Veterans Affairs: Library Services, 11469
US Department of Veterans Affairs: LomaLinda Medical Center Library Service, 11351
US Department of Veterans Affairs: LongBeach Medical Center Library Service, 11352
US Department of Veterans Affairs: Lyon New Jersey Health Care System - Lyons Campus Hospital Library, 11619
US Department of Veterans Affairs: Manchester Medical Center Library, 11611
US Department of Veterans Affairs: Martinsburg Learning Resources Service, 11843
US Department of Veterans Affairs: Medical & Regional Office Center, 11507, 11530
US Department of Veterans Affairs: Medical Center Library, 11447, 11449, 11515, 11521, 11557
US Department of Veterans Affairs: Medical Library, 11428, 11429, 11470
US Department of Veterans Affairs: Memphis Medical Center Library, 11764
US Department of Veterans Affairs: Miles City Medical Center Library, 11597
US Department of Veterans Affairs: Minneapolis Medical Center Library Service, 11582
US Department of Veterans Affairs: Montrose Medical Library, 11674
US Department of Veterans Affairs: Murfreesboro Medical Center Library Service, 11765
US Department of Veterans Affairs: Nashville Medical Center Library Service, 11766
US Department of Veterans Affairs: New York Harbour Healthcare System, New York Campus Library, 11675
US Department of Veterans Affairs: Northern Arizona VA Health Care System, 11326
US Department of Veterans Affairs: Northport Medical Center-Medical Library, 11676
US Department of Veterans Affairs: Oklahoma City Medical Center Library, 11724
US Department of Veterans Affairs: Omaha Hospital Library, 11603
US Department of Veterans Affairs: Overton Brooks Medical Center Library, 11522
US Department of Veterans Affairs: Phoenix Medical Center Library, 11327
US Department of Veterans Affairs: Pittsburgh Education, Media and Reference Service, 11749
US Department of Veterans Affairs: Poplar Bluff Library Service, 11591
US Department of Veterans Affairs: Portland Medical Library, 11727
US Department of Veterans Affairs: Providence Health Sciences Library, 11754
US Department of Veterans Affairs: Reno Medical Center Library Services, 11607
US Department of Veterans Affairs: Richmond Hospital Library, 11824
US Department of Veterans Affairs: Roseburg Medical Center Library Service, 11728
US Department of Veterans Affairs: Saginaw Aleda E Lutz Medical Center Library, 11576
US Department of Veterans Affairs: Salem Medical Center Library, 11825
US Department of Veterans Affairs: Salisbury Medical Center Library, 11687
US Department of Veterans Affairs: Salt Lake City Hospital Medical Library, 11803
US Department of Veterans Affairs: San Diego Medical Center Library Service, 11353
US Department of Veterans Affairs: San Francisco Medical Center Library Service, 11354
US Department of Veterans Affairs: Seattle Puget Sound Health Care System, 11832
US Department of Veterans Affairs: Sheridan Medical Center Library, 11855
US Department of Veterans Affairs: Southern Colorado Healthcare System, 11367
US Department of Veterans Affairs: Spokane Medical Center Library, 11833
US Department of Veterans Affairs: Tacoma/Puget Sound Health Care System, 11834
US Department of Veterans Affairs: Tomah Health Sciences Library, 11850
US Department of Veterans Affairs: Tucson Medical Center Library, 11328
US Department of Veterans Affairs: Waco Medical Center Library, 11802
US Department of Veterans Affairs: Walla Walla Jonathan M Wainwright Memorial VA Medical Library, 11835
US Department of Veterans Affairs: White River Junction Medical & Regional Office CenterLibrary Service, 11807
US Department of Veterans Affairs: WhiteCity Library, 11729
US Department of Veterans Affairs: Wilkes-Barre Medical Center Library, 11750
US Department of Veterans Affairs:, Columbus Hospital Library, 11592
US Department of Veterans Affairs:Temple Medical Center Medical Library, 11795
US Deprtment of Veterans Affairs: Center Library, 11490
US Dept of Energy, Weatherization Assist Program, 342
US Deptartment of Veterans Affairs: Central Alabama Veterans Health Care System, 11313
US Deptartment of Veterans Affairs: Medical Center Library, 11314
US Deptartment of Veterans Affairs:Alabama Veterns Health Care System, 11315
US Equal Employment Opportunity Commission, 11406
US Library of Congress, 11403
US Library of Congress Handicapped Hotline, 332
US National AIDS Hotlines and Resources, 4505
US National Institutes of Health: National Cancer Institute-Scientific Library, 11542
US Office Special Educ and Rehabilitative Serv., 3798
US Office of Personnel Management, 333
US Railroad Retirement Board: Tampa District Office, 805
US SERVAS, 12055
US Senate Special Committee on Aging, 308
US Social Security Administration, 4111
US Social Security Administration Library & Records Management Branch, 11543
US Social Security Administration: Washington Library, 11407
US Stroke Club Listing, 7078
US Travel Systems, 12056
USA Deaf Sports Federation, 6458, 6592, 6793
USA Next United Seniors Association, 334
USABA Newsletter, 7901
USAir, 11943
USAirways Shuttle, 11944
USDA Food and Nutrition Service, 137
USDA Human Nutrition Research Center on Aging, 4379
USTA Adult and Senior National Championships Booklet, 3803
Uintah Basin Area: Agency on Aging, 2409
Uintah County Area Agency on Aging, 2410
Ultra-Lite XL Hand Control, 2997
Ultratec-Auto Answer TTY, 3182
Undercounter Lid Opener, 3352
Understanding Alzheimer's Disease, 4972
Understanding Deafness Socially, 6550
Understanding Depression and Addiction, 7413
Understanding Dying, Death and Bereavement, 6031
Understanding Gestational Diabetes, 6255
Understanding Major Anxiety Disorders and and Addiction, 7414
Understanding Medicaid Long Term Care: A Primer for Alzheimer Advocates, 5021
Understanding Our Needs: Results of the SHHH Member Survey, 6724
Understanding Ourselves and Alcoholism, 7415
Understanding Panic Disorder, 6100
Understanding Parkinson's Disease: A Personal and Professional View, 6988
Understanding Personality Problems and Addiction, 7416
Understanding Post-Traumatic Stress Disorder and Addiction, 7417
Understanding Speech and Language Problems After Stroke, 7109
Uni-Turner, 3353
Uniformed Services Almanac, Inc, 3825
Union College Academy for Lifelong Learning, 2873
Union County Division on Aging, 1705
Union-Snyder Area: Agency on Aging, 2194
Unisex Low Vision Watch, 3183
United Airlines, 11945
United Cerebral Palsy, 704
United Cerebral Palsy Association, 11051
United Cerebral Palsy Associations, 4128

Entry Name Index / U

United Church of Christ, 115
United Communications Group, 4042
United Crescent Hill Ministries, 2801
United Disability Services, 3917
United Electric Workers Retirees, 2596
United Methodist Assoc Health\Welfare Ministries, 3772
United Methodist Association of Health and Welfare Ministries (UMA), 335
United Methodist Publishing House, 3928
United Methodist Retirement Center, 10223
United Ostomy Association, 4255, 5785
United Parkinson Foundation, 6989, 6991, 6992, 6994, 6995, 6996, 6997, 6998, 6999, 7000, 7002, 7006, 7007, 7008, 7009, 7010, 7011, 7016, 7020, 7021, 7022
United States Association for Blind Athletes, 7901, 7765
United States Department of the Interior: National Park Service, 4118
United States Naval Academy Alumni Association, 3804
United States Naval Academy Alumni Association: Register of Alumni, 3804
United Way 211, 1440
United Way of Central Florida, 806
United Way of Eastern Maine, 1222
Unity/128, 3184
Universal Hand Cuff, 3354
Universal Knob Turner, 3316
Universal Pensions, 4049
Universal Switch Mounting System, 3185
University Center on Aging and Health, 2653
University Center on Aging and Health Newsletter, 4119
University Continuing Education Association, 3805
University Legal Services, 11050
University Library Services, 11826
University Of Texas-El Paso, 2316
University Press of Mississippi, 4972
University at Albany: State University of New York Ringel Institute of Gerontology, 4380
University for Seniors: Continuing Education and Extension Program, 2828
University of Akron, 4381
University of Akron Institute for LifeSpan Development and Gerontology, 4381
University of Alabama, 381
University of Alabama at Birmingham, 4020
University of Alabama at Birmingham: Asthma, Allergic and Immunologic Diseases Cooperative Research Center, 4695
University of Alabama at Birmingham: Congenital Heart Disease Center, 6892
University of Alabama at Birmingham: National Cooperative Drug/AIDS, 4622
University of Alabama at Birmingham: Parkinson's Disease Center, 7047
University of Alabama at Birmingham:Comprehensive Cancer Center, 5962
University of Alabama: Center for Alcohol and Addiction Studies, 7478
University of Alabama: Speech and Hearing Center, 6821
University of Alaska Southeast Campus:Adult Education Program, 2698
University of Arizona Cancer Center, 5963

University of Arkansas At Little Rock, 7928
University of California at Berkeley, 2720
University of California at Los Angeles, 2728, 5924
University of California, Irvine: UCI Diabetes Research Program, 6281
University of California, Los AngelesAlzheimer's Disease Center, 5070
University of California, San Diego, 2733, 4453, 5241
University of California, San Francisco Center for Social and Behavioral Sciences, 4382
University of California/Davis: AIDS Virus Diagnostic Laboratory, 4623
University of California: Berkeley Cancer Research Laboratories, 5964
University of California: Cardiovascular Research Laboratory, 6894
University of California: Center for Health & Community, 4383
University of California: Institute of Health Policy Studies, 4624
University of California: Irvine Cancer Research Institute, 5965
University of California: Los Angeles Alcohol Research Center, 7479
University of California: Los Angeles Bone Marrow Transplantation Program, 5966
University of California: Los Angeles Center for Research on Aging Project, 4384
University of California: Los Angeles Clinical AIDS Research & Education, 4625
University of California: Los Angeles Department of Medicine, 7121
University of California: Los Angeles Jules Stein Eye Institute, 8055
University of California: Mount Zion Medical Center, 11355
University of California: San Diego Alzheimer's Disease Research Center, 5071
University of California: San Diego Cancer Center, 5967
University of California: San Diego Center for AIDS Research, 4626
University of California: San Diego Center for Population Research, 4385
University of California: San Diego General Clinical Research Center, 6895
University of California: San Francisco Cancer Research Institute, 5968
University of California: San Francisco Cardiovascular Research Institute, 6896
University of California: San Francisco Center for AIDS Prevention Studies, 4627
University of California: San Francisco Center on Deafness Library, 11356
University of California: San Francisco General Clinical Research Center, 6893
University of California: San Francisco Institute for Health and Aging, 4386
University of Chicago Brain Research Institute, 4387
University of Chicago Committee on Human Development, 4388
University of Chicago Social Services Administration Library, 11471
University of Chicago: Brain Research Institute, 5072

University of Chicago: Cancer Research Center, 5969
University of Chicago: Clinical Nutrition Research Unit, 5970
University of Chicago: Diabetes Research & Training Center, 6282
University of Chicago: Temporal Bone Laboratory for Ear Research, 6822
University of Cincinnati Medical Center Libraries, 11719
University of Cincinnati: Department of Pathology & Laboratory Medicine, 6897
University of Colorado Cancer Center, 5971
University of Colorado at BoulderInstitute for Behavioral Genetics, 4389
University of Colorado: Boulder Communication Disorders Clinic, 6823
University of Colorado: Immunology Center, 4696
University of Colorado: Science Libaray, 11368
University of Connecticut Health Center: Biomolecular Structure Analysis Center, 4390
University of Connecticut Health Center: Center on Aging, 11377
University of Connecticut in Storrs: Homer Babbidge Library, 11378
University of Connecticut: Center on Aging, 4391
University of Continuing Education Association: Membership Directory, 3805
University of Delaware, 702, 2745
University of Delaware: Center for Drug and Alcohol Studies, 7480
University of Florida Brain Institute, 4392
University of Florida Health Policy andEpidemiology, 4393
University of Florida: Center for Governmental Responsibility, 11430
University of Florida: Center for Health Policy Research, 4628
University of Florida: Claude D Pepper Center for Research on Oral Health in Aging, 4394
University of Florida: General Clinical Research Center, 4697
University of Florida: Institute for Gerontology, 4395
University of Georgia: Gerontology Center, 4396
University of Hawaii at Manoa, 3850
University of Hawaii at Manoa: William S Richardson School of Law, 11076
University of Hawaii: Clinical & Community Outreach Program, 5786
University of Hawaii: Hawaii AIDS Clinical Research Program, 4629
University of Illinois Health Systems Research, 4397
University of Illinois at Chicago: Lions of Illinios Eye Research Institute, 8056
University of Iowa, 6407
University of Iowa Cancer Center, 5972
University of Iowa Center for HealthServices Research, 4398
University of Iowa College of Medicine, 7122
University of Iowa: Alzheimer's Disease Research Center, 5073
University of Iowa: Diabetes Control and Complications Trial, 6283

Entry Name Index / U

University of Iowa: Diabetes Research Center, 6284
University of Iowa: Iowa Cardiovascular Center, 6898
University of Kansas, 1057
University of Kansas Cancer Center, 5973
University of Kansas Laboratory ofBiological Anthropology, 4399
University of Kansas Neurobiology Research Laboratory, 4400
University of Kansas: Center on Aging, 4401
University of Kansas: Gerontology Center, 4402
University of Kansas: Regional Diabetes Center, 6285
University of Kentucky, 2800
University of Kentucky: Alzheimer's Disease Research Center, 5074
University of Kentucky: Lucille Parker Markey Cancer Center, 5974
University of Kentucky: Sanders-Brown Center on Aging, 4403
University of Louisville Center for Research in the Special Senses, 4404
University of Maine at Augusta, 1205
University of Maryland Division of Infectious Diseases, 4405
University of Maryland School Pharmacy, 4359
University of Maryland: Center for Research, Grants & Contracts, 4630
University of Maryland: Center for the Study of Pharmacy and Therapeutics for the Elderly, 4406
University of Maryland: Center on Aging, 4407
University of Maryland: Division of Infectious Diseases, 4631
University of Massachusetts, 5255
University of Massachusetts Medical School, 4640, 6003
University of Massachusetts at Boston: Gerontology Institute and Center, 4408
University of Massachusetts: Diabetes Endocrinology Research Center, 6286
University of Memphis Libraries: Audiology, Speech Language, Pathology Branch, 11767
University of Miami, 2754
University of Miami Center for Neurological Diseases, 4409
University of Miami Medical School, 5783
University of Miami School of Medicine: Department of Neurology, 7123
University of Miami Touch Research Institute, 4410
University of Miami: Bascom Palmer Eye Institute, 8057
University of Miami: Center for Neurological Diseases, 5075
University of Miami: Center on Adult Development and Aging, 4411
University of Miami: Diabetes Research Institute, 6287
University of Michigan Alcohol Research Center, 7481
University of Michigan Cancer Center, 5975
University of Michigan Center for Human Growth and Development, 4412
University of Michigan: Alzheimer's Disease Research Center, 5076
University of Michigan: Antiviral Laboratory, 4413
University of Michigan: Communicative Disorders Clinic, 6824
University of Michigan: Division of Hypertension, 6925
University of Michigan: Institute of Gerontology, 4414
University of Michigan: Kresge Hearing Research Institute, 6825
University of Michigan: Learning inRetirement, 2825
University of Michigan: Montgomery Allergy Research Laboratory, 4698
University of Michigan: National Cooperative Drug/AIDS Group, 4632
University of Michigan: Orthopaedic Research Laboratories, 5250
University of Michigan: Stimpson Memorial Institute for Medical Research, 5976
University of Michigan: Tecumster Mental Health Study, 6104
University of Minnesota, 1426
University of Minnesota: Center for Bioethics, 6036
University of Minnesota: Center on Aging, 4415
University of Minnesota: Coordinating Centers for Biometric Research, 5977
University of Minnesota: Division of Health Services Research and Policy, 6105
University of Minnesota: Hypertensive Research Group, 6926
University of Minnesota: Masonic Cancer Center, 5978
University of Minnesota: Program on Alcohol/Drug Control, 7482
University of Missouri Kansas City: Center for Aging Studies, 4416
University of Missouri: Columbia Arthritis Center, 5251
University of Missouri: Columbia Cosmopolitan Diabetes Center, 6288
University of Missouri: Columbia Division of Cardiothoracic Surgery, 6899
University of Missouri: Kansas City Drug Information Service, 7483
University of NE Medical Center, 156
University of Nebraska at Omaha: Eppley Institute for Research in Cancer, 5979
University of Nebraska: Lincoln Barkley Memorial Center, 6826
University of Nevada Reno: Natural Products Lab, 5980
University of Nevada: Speech and Language Pathology Department, 6827
University of New Mexico Cancer Center, 5981
University of New Mexico: Center for Non-Invasive Diagnosis, 5982
University of New Mexico: General Clinical Research Center, 6289
University of New York, 5060
University of North Carolina at Chapel Hill: Divsion of Speech & Hearing, 6828
University of North Carolina: General Clinical Research Center, 4633
University of North Carolina: UNC Linebeerger Comprehensive Cancer Center, 5983
University of North Dakota: UND Centerfor Rural Health, 4417
University of North Texas, 181
University of North Texas Health, 4312
University of North Texas Health Science Center at Forth Worth: Geriatrics Education and Research Institute, 4418
University of North Texas: Center for Studies in Aging, 4419
University of North Texas: Health Science Center at Fort Worth, 8058
University of Northern Iowa: Center forSocial and Behavioral Research, 4420
University of Notre Dame Press, 3681
University of Oklahoma: Speech & Hearing Center, 6829
University of Oregon Health Sciences Center, 7114
University of Pennsylvania Cancer Center, 5984
University of Pennsylvania Institute on Aging, 4421
University of Pennsylvania: Center for Clinical Epidemiology and Biostatistics, 4422
University of Pennsylvania: Comparative Leukemia Unit, 5985
University of Pennsylvania: Depression Research Unit, 6106
University of Pennsylvania: Diabetes Research Center, 6290
University of Pittsburgh Medical Center: Clinic Western Psychiatric Institute and Clinic, 6107
University of Pittsburgh University Center for Social and Urban Research, 4423
University of Pittsburgh: Nutrition and Biochemistry Laboratory, 6291
University of Rochester: Clinical Research Center, 6900
University of San Francisco: AIDS Clinical Research Center, 4634
University of San Francisco: Fromm Institute for Lifelong Learning, 2734
University of South Carolina, 2252
University of South Dakota Social Science Research Institute, 4424
University of South Florida, 3757, 6040
University of South Florida Library: Special Collections Department, 11058
University of South Florida: Center for HIV Education & Research, 4635
University of Southern California, 4305
University of Southern California's Hematology, Hematologic Malignancy and Retroviral Research Program, 5986
University of Southern California: Comprehensive Cancer Center, 5987
University of Southern California: Coronary Care Research, 6901
University of Southern California: Division of Nephrology, 6927
University of Southern California: Institute for Health Promotion and Disease Prevention Research, 4425
University of Southern California: Kenneth T Norris Jr Comprehensive Cancer Center, 5988
University of Southern Maine, 2805, 4303
University of Southwestern Louisiana: Jefferson Caffery Louisana Room-Southwestern Archives and Manuscripts Collection, 11523

Entry Name Index / V

University of Tennessee Drug Information Center, 7484
University of Tennessee: Division of Cardiovascular Diseases, 6847
University of Tennessee: Knoxville Society for the Study of Social Problems, 4426
University of Tennessee: Memphis Cancer Center, 5989
University of Texas, 4427
University of Texas HSC at San Antonio, 7048
University of Texas Health Science Center at Houston: Speech & Hearing, 6830
University of Texas Southwestern Medical Center at Dallas: Alzheimer's Disease Center, 5077
University of Texas at Austin Association for Mental Health, 11909
University of Texas at Austin: Drug Synamics Institute, 7485
University of Texas at Dallas: Callier Center for Communication Disorders, 6831
University of Texas-Austin, 2926
University of Texas-Houston Health Science Center Mental Sciences Institute, 4427
University of Texas: General Clinical Research Center, 6292
University of Texas: Health Science Center Neurophysiology Research Center, 7486
University of Texas: MD Anderson Cancer Center, 5990
University of Texas: Medical Branch at Galveston Cancer Center, 5991
University of Texas: Southwestern Medical Center at Dallas, 4699, 6902
University of Topeka, 2798
University of Toronto, 353
University of Utah Human Performance Research Laboratory, 4428
University of Utah School of Medicine, 5995
University of Utah: Artificial Heart Research Laboratory, 6903
University of Utah: Cardiovascular Genetic Research Clinic, 6904
University of Utah: Center for Human Toxicology, 7487
University of Utah: Gerontology Center, 4429
University of Utah: Rocky Mountain Cancer Data System, 5992
University of Vermont Cancer Center, 5993
University of Vermont: Office of Health Promotion Research, 4636
University of Virginia Diabetes Center, 6269
University of Virginia: Communication Disorders Program, 6832
University of Virginia: Hypertension and Atherosclerosis Unit, 6928
University of Washington, 4915
University of Washington Northwest: Geriatric Education Center, 4430
University of Washington: Alcohol & Drug Abuse Institute Library, 7488
University of Washington: Alzheimer's Disease Research Center, 5078
University of Washington: Department of Speech & Hearing Sciences, 6833
University of Washington: Diabetes Endocrinology Research Center, 6293
University of Washington: Speech & Hearing Clinic, 6834

University of West Florida: Center on Aging, 4431
University of Wisconsin Guild for Learning, 2950
University of Wisconsin Laboratory for Cancer Research Library, 11851
University of Wisconsin-Madison, 6820
University of Wisconsin-Madison Neuropsychology Laboratory, 4432
University of Wisconsin-Milwaukee, 2950
University of Wisconsin: Allergy/Asthma Clinical Research Unit, 4700
University of Wisconsin: Auditory Physiology Center, 6835
University of Wisconsin: Comprehensive Cancer Center, 5994
University of Wisconsin: Madison Institute on Aging, 4433
University of Wisconsin: Milwaukee Institute on Aging and Environment, 4434
University of Wisconsin: Milwaukee Medicinal Chemistry Group, 7489
University of Wyoming, 2952
University of the District of Columbia, 2747
University of the Third Age of Asnuntuck, 2743
Unlimited Care-Richmond Hills, 10043
Unpuffables Promotional Brochure, 4120
Unseen Minority: A Social History of Blindness in the United States, 7832
Up Front Drug Information, 7418
Update (Library of Congress), 7902
Update on Captioning, 6725
Update: Hearing and Vision Loss, 6726
Uplands Retirement Village, 10381
Upper Arkansas Area: Agency on Aging, 671
Upper Coastal Plain Area Agency on Aging, 1921
Upper Cumberland Area: Agency on Aging, 2301
Upper Minnesota Valley Area Agency on Aging, 1441
Upper Potomac Area Agency on Aging, 2557
Upper Savannah Council of Government Area: Agency on Aging, 2255
Urban Cardiology Research Center, 6905
Urban League of Springfield, 1319
Urban Medical Group, 1329
Urbanna Professional Center, 2465
Useful Information on Alzheimer's Disease, 4973
Useful Information on Phobias and Panic, 6101
Using Assistive Listening Devices, 6727
Using Telecommunications Relay Service, 6728
Utah Assistive Technology Projects, 2411
Utah Cancer Center, 5995
Utah Chapter of the Arthritis Foundation, 5141
Utah Chapter: Alexander Graham Bell Association for the Deaf, 6836
Utah Client Assistance Program, 2412
Utah Department of Aging, 2413
Utah Department of Health Division of Community Health Services, 2414
Utah Department of Health: Division of Community Health Services, 4637
Utah Department of Human Services for People with Disabilities, 2415

Utah Department of Human Services: Aging, 2416
Utah Department of Human ServicesDivision of Aging and Adult Services, 11271
Utah Department of Mental Health, 6060
Utah Division of Services for the Disabled, 2417
Utah Division of Substance Abuse, 7223
Utah Governor's Council for People with Disabilities, 2418
Utah Independent Living Center, 10936
Utah Industries for the Blind, 7766
Utah Office of Social Services: Department of Human Services, 2419
Utah Protection & Advocacy Services for Perosns with Disabilities, 2420
Utah Protection and Advocacy Agency: Disability Law Center, 11272
Utah Retirement Board, 2421
Utah State Association of Area Agencies on Aging, 2422
Utah State Bar: Senior Legal Clinic Program Salt Lake County, 11273
Utah State Bar: Young Lawyers Section, 11274
Utah State Library: Blind and DisabledServices, 11804
Utah State Tax Commission, 2423
Utah Statewide Independent Living Council, 10937
Utah Travel Council, 11998
Utah Workers Compensation Board, 2424

V

VA Central California Health Care System, 11357
VANTAGE, 3964
VFW Auxiliary, 3965
VISION, 6551
VOCAL-New Hanover County, 1922
VPL Series Vertical Wheelchair Lift, 3409
Vacaville Public Library: Town Square, 11358
Vallejo Alzheimers Support Group, 4943
Valley Area: Agency on Aging, 1389
Valley Country Care, 9311
Valley Lodge Assisted Living, 8745
Valley Ranch Retirement Center, 10540
Valley Springs Assisted Living, 8823
Valley View Assisted Living, 8571, 10180
Valley View Estates, 9312
Valley View Heights, 9587
Valley View Manor Assisted Living, 8746
Valleyview Board and Lodge, 9313
Van Dyke Valley Assisted Living, 9822
Van Mall, 10604
Vancrest Assisted Living, 9971
VanderWyk & Burnham, 3679
Vanderbilt University: Diabetes Research and Training Center, 6294
Vanderbilt University: Specialized Center of Research in Hypertension, 6929
Vangater, Vangater II, Mini-Vangater, 3410
VantAge Point Area: Agency on Aging-Region Ten, 1524
Vantage Plus, 3186
Vantage Point: Division of Caresouth Carolina, 2256
Vantage Press, 5156

Entry Name Index / V

Varenna at Fountaingrove, 8230
Vassar Brother's Hospital, 5392
Vassar-Warner Home, 9857
Vegetarian Journal, 3966
The Vegetarian Resource Group, 3966
Vegetarian Times, 3967
Vegetarian Voice, 3968
Veggie Life, 3969
Ventura County Area Agency on Aging, 503, 620
Ventura Enterprises, 3561
Ventures, 12057
Verde Valley Senior Citizens Association, 452
Vermont Agency of Human Services Commission for the Deaf and Hearing Impaired, 6459
Vermont Assistive Technology Projects, 2436
Vermont Association for the Blind and Visually Impaired, 7767
Vermont Center for Independent Living, 10946
Vermont Client Assistance Program, 2437
Vermont Council on Aging, 2438
Vermont Department of Developmental and Mental Health Services, 6061
Vermont Department of Disabilities, Aging and Independent Living, 2439
Vermont Department of Healt: HIV/AIDS Program, 4506, 4582
Vermont Department of Libraries, 11808
Vermont Department of Taxes, 2440
Vermont Deptartment of Aging, 11995
Vermont Developmental Disabilities Council, 2441
Vermont Division for the Blind and Visually Impaired, 7768
Vermont Office of Alcohol & Drug Abuse Programs: Agency of Human Services, 7224
Vermont Protection & Advocacy for Persons with Disabilities, 2442
Vermont Protection and Advocacy Agency, 2443, 11278
Vermont State Retirement Board, 2444
Vermont Veterans Affairs, 2445
Vernon Henley Media Award, 2688
Vertical Home Lift Sales, 3411
Vertical Wheelchair Lift, 3412
Vestibular Disorders, 6729
Vestibular Disorders Association, 336
Veterans & Military Organizations Directory, 3806
Veterans Admin. Medical Center, 4291
Veterans Administration Medical Center, 7113
Veterans Administration Medical Center: Research Service, 5996, 7490
Veterans Affairs Medical Center Research Service, 4435
Veterans Affairs Medical Center-Research Service, 4436
Veterans Affairs Medical Center: Geriatric Research, Education and Clinical Center, 4437
Veterans Affairs Medical Center: Research Service, 6295
Veterans Health Administration, 7539
Veterans Information and Assistance, 337
Veterans Prosthetic Appliance, Rehabilitation and Prosthetics, 338
Veterans' Advocate, 11049
Veterans' Employment Service, 1210
Veterans' Home of Wyoming, 10619
Vibrotactile Personal Alerting System, 3187
Victoria Court, 10224
Victoria Mews Assisted Living, 9823
Victoria Villa Assisted Living, 8432
Victorian, 10332
Victorian Estates, 10044
Victorian Inn at Victorian Village, 8616
Victorian of Chatham, 9026
Vidalia House, 4745
Vietnamese Senior Citizens Association, 339
View Pointe, 8250
Viewpoint Residential Care, 8572
Viking Manor Nursing Home, 9314
Villa Capri, 8231
Villa Cottages, 8747
Villa Hermosa, 8128
Villa Santa Barbara, 8232
Villa St Vincent, 9315
Villa at St Antoine, 10225
Village East, 8824
Village Gate, 8300
Village Oaks at Hollywood Park, 10541
Village Woods, 8617
Village at Brookfield Common, 8301
Village at Buckland Court, 8302
Village at Cook Springs, 8078
Village at East Farms, 8303
Village at Elmhurst, 10226
Village at Farm Pond, 9027
Village at Green Valley, 8327
Village at Hillsgrove, 10227
Village at South Farms, 8304
Village at Willow Crossings, 9028
Village in the Oaks, 8895
Village of Lee Retirement Center, 10045
Village of Ninnescah, 8825
The Villages at Marion, 8744
Villas at St Therese Assisted Living, 9972
Ville Ste Marie Senior Living Community, 8896
Vim & Vigor Magazine, 3970
Vincennes University: Byron R Lewis Historical Library, 11105
Vintage Park of Atchison, 8826
Vintage Park of Baldwin City, 8827
Vintage Park of Gardner, 8828
Vintage Park of Louisburg, 8829
Vintage Park of Paola, 8830
Vintage Place of Derby, 8831
Vintage Place of Russell, 8832
Vintage Point of Pittsburg, 8833
Vintage Suites, 10181
Vintage Suites at Hope Village, 10182
Virginia Association for Education & Rehabilitation of the Blind & Visually Impaired, 7769
Virginia Association of Area Agencies on Aging, 2491
Virginia Association of Nonprofit Homes for the Aging, 2492
Virginia Board for People with Disabilities, 2493
Virginia Center on Aging, 3585
Virginia Chapter of the Arthritis Foundation, 5111, 5142
Virginia Client Assistance Program, 2494
Virginia Commonwealth University, 3585
Virginia Commonwealth University Virginia Center on Aging Information Resources Center, 11827
Virginia Commonwealth University: Massey Cancer Center, 5997
Virginia Department for the Aging, 2495, 11283
Virginia Department for the Blind & Vision Impaired, 7770
Virginia Department of Deaf and Hard of Hearing, 6460
Virginia Department of Economic Development Division of Tourism, 11999
Virginia Department of Health and Human Resources: Department of Aging, 2496
Virginia Department of Health: DivisionHIV/STD, 4507, 4583
Virginia Department of Mental Health Mental Retardation and Substance Abuse Services, 6062
Virginia Department of Taxation, 2497
Virginia Developmental Disability Council, 2498
Virginia Division of Substance Abuse Services, 7225
Virginia Industries for the Blind, 7771
Virginia Mason Research Center, 6296
Virginia Office for Protection andAdvocacy, 2499
Virginia Protection & Advocacy for Persons with Disabilities, 2500
Virginia Protection and Advocacy Agency, 11284
Virginia Protection and Advocacy Agency: Virginia Beach, 11285
Virginia State Library for the Visually and Physically Handicapped, 11828
Virginian Manor, 10573
Virology & Infectious Diseases, 4593
Vision, 7903
Vision Community Services, 7772
Vision Enhancement, Journal, 7904
Vision Foundation, 7994, 7773
Vision Over 50, 7993
Vision Resource Update, 7994
Vision Use in Employment (VUE), 7774
Vision World Wide, 7904, 7775, 8033
Vision and Aging: Crossroads for Service Delivery, 7833
Vision and Aging: Issues in Social Work Practice, 7834
Visions, 7905, 8001
Visions World Wide, 7995
Visions/Services for the Blind & Visually Impaired, 8001
Visiting Nurse Association of America, 340
Vista Oaks of Lakeway, 10542
Visual Aids and Informational Material, 7851
Visual Impairment and Blindness Services of Northampton County, 7776
Visual Impairment: An Overview, 7835
Visually Impaired Center, 7777
Visually Impaired Data Processors International, 7778, 8034
Visually Impaired Seniors as Senior Companions: A Reference Guide, 7836
Visually Impaired Veterans of America, 7779, 8035
Viva Vital News, 7906
VoRtechs, 4121
Vocational Rehabilitation Division, 2088

1061

Entry Name Index / W

Voice Amplified Handsets, 3188
Voice of Vision, 7907, 7996
Voice of the Diabetic, 6224, 6235
Voices for the Blind, 11531
Voices of Vision Talking Book Center, 11472
Volta Bureau Library, 11408
Volta Voices, 6593, 6730
Voluntary Action Center of Northeastern Pennsylvania, 2195
Volunteer Center, 3745, 621
Volunteer Center Directory, 3807
Volunteer Center Orange County, 622
Volunteer Center of Camden County, 1706
Volunteer Center of Centre County, 2196
Volunteer Center of Greater Durham, 1923
Volunteer Center of Kern County, 623
Volunteer Center of Monmouth County, 1707
Volunteer Center of Morgan County, 401
Volunteer Center of Racine County, 2597
Volunteer Center of United Way for Capital Area, 700
Volunteer Committees of Art Museums of Canada and the United States News, 4122
Volunteer Exchange, 624
Volunteer Jacksonville, 807
Volunteer Lawyers Project for the Elderly, 11014
Volunteer Lawyers Project of the Boston Bar Association, 11153
Volunteer Leader, 4123
Volunteer Services of Barron County, 2598
Volunteer Vacations, 3808
Volunteer Voice, 5230
Volunteer at Your Braille and Talking Book Library, 7997
Volunteer! The Comprehensive Guide to Voluntary Service in the US and Abroad, 3809
Volunteerism in Action for the Aging: A Handbook, 3678
Volunteers Of AmericaGreater New Orleans Retired Seniors Volunteer Program, 1195
Volunteers for Abused/Neglected Children, 341
Volunteers for the Visually Handicapped, 7780
Volunteers of America, 4124
Volunteers of America Bay Area, 625
Volunteers of America Southeast, 402
Volunteers of America of Minnesota, 9316
Volunteers of American GNO - North Shore Office, 1195
Vyne at Cedar Ridge, 10046
Vyne at Crestview, 8834
Vyne at Meadows Park, 8835

W

W Alton Jones Cell Science Center: George and Margaret Gey Library, 11677
WA & NEWS, 4125
WB Saunders Company, Harcourt Brace & Company, 3838
WCIB Heavy-Duty Folding Cane, 3493
WFS' New Life Program, 7226
WGBH Educational Foundation, 6326, 6406
WH Freeman and Company, 4970
WINVISION, 3189
WW Norton & Company, 5164
Wainwright House Cancer Support Programs, 5998
Wake Forest University: Arteriosclerosis Research Center, 6930
Wake Forest University: CerebrovascularResearch Center, 7124
Wal-Pil-O, 3232
Walkane, 3494
Walker Leg Support, 3495
Walker's Assisted Living, 10333
Walking, 3971
Walking Tomorrow, 4126
Wallace Memorial Library, 11678
Walter T. Ridder Award, 2689
Walther Cancer Institute, 5931
Walton County Senior Citizens Council, 853
Walton Options for Independent Living, 10712
Waltonwood of Royal Oak, 9088
Wandering: It Is a Problem?, 5036
Warner Books, 6069
Warren County Division Of Senior ServiceS, 1708
Warren Grant Magnuson Clinical Center, 5143, 5999, 6297, 6906, 8059
Warren H Green, 3810
Warren Hamilton Counties Office for the Aging, 1881
Warren House, 8573
Warren Manor I, 10228
Washburn Walkers, 2798
Washington Aging and Disability Services, 11290
Washington Association of Area Agencies on Aging, 2531
Washington Association of Houses and Services for the Aging, 2532
Washington Client Assistance Program, 2533
Washington County Area Agency on Aging, 2089
Washington County Commission on Aging, 1264
Washington County Department of Aging Services, 2090
Washington County Deptartment of Aging Services, 2089
Washington County Historical Society: Genealogy and Historical Library, 11106
Washington County Home, 9973
Washington County Office for the Aging, 1882
Washington D.C. Protection and AdvocacyAgency, 11050
Washington Department of Health: Division of AIDS/HIV/STD, 4508
Washington Department of Mental Health, 6063
Washington Department of Retirement Systems, 2534
Washington Department of Revenue, 2535
Washington Department of Services for the Blind, 7781
Washington Department of Social and Health Services Aging and Adult Services, 2536
Washington Department of Veterans Affairs, 2537
Washington Division of Alcoholism & Substance Abuse, 7227
Washington Ear, 7782
Washington Governor's Committee on Disability Issues & Employment, 2538
Washington Hearing and Speech Center, 6461
Washington Library for the Blind and Physically Handicapped, 11836
Washington Memorial Library, 11441
Washington Oakes, 10605
Washington Odd Fellows Home, 10603
Washington Protection & Advocacy for Persons with Disabilities, 2539
Washington Protection and Advocacy Agency, 11291
Washington Report, 4127
Washington State Aging & Disability Services Administration, 2540
Washington State Chapter of the Arthritis Foundation, 5144
Washington State Department Social/Health Services, 11290
Washington State Department of Services, 2541
Washington State Developmental Disabilities Council, 2542
Washington State Tourism, 12000
Washington University Center for Aging, 3586
Washington University Medical Center, 7049
Washington University School of Medicine, 7125
Washington University: Diabetes Research and Training Center, 6298
Washington Watch, 4128, 11051
Washington Workers Compensation Board, 2543
Washington-Greene County Branch of the Pennsylvania Association for Blind, 7783
Washtenaw County Library, 11577
Waterford Assisted Living, 10543
Waterford Senior Center, 1390
Waterford at All Saints, 10334
Waterford at Hardwoodgroves, 9588
Waterford at Plano, 10544
Waterford on Elizabeth Warren, 9361
Waterford on Saddle Drive, 9362
Waterford on West Century, 9589
Waterfront Inn Assisted Living, 8836
Waterfront Press Company, 11940
Waterproof Sheet-Topper Mattress andChair Pad, 3041
Waterville Public Library, 11532
Waukon Living Center, 8748
Waupaca Elevator Company, 3367
Waverly Gardens, 10382
Waves of Stone, 5037
Way We Die, 4165
Wayne County Area: Agency on Aging, 2197
Wayne County Regional Library for the Blind, 11578
Wayne State University Center for Health Research, 4438
Wayne State University Center for Molecular Biology, 6000
Wayne State University: Center for Health Research, 4638
Wayne State University: Institute of Gerontology, 4439
We Can Do It Together!, 7908
We Will Remember, 4166

Entry Name Index / W

Weatherization Assistance for Low-Income Persons: Conservation and Renewable Energy, 342
Weber-Morgan Area: Agency on Aging, 2425
Webhelp, 4256
Webster Area: Agency on Aging, 1196
Wecolator Stairway Lift, 3413
Wedgewood Assisted Living Facility, 10335
Wedgewood Estates of Mansfield, 9974
Wedgewood Terrace, 8574
Weelington at Arapaho, 10545
Weider Publications, 3949
Weighted Holders, 3471
Weitbrecht Communications, 3190
Wel-Life at Alta, 8749
Wel-Life at Spirit Lake, 8750
Welch Assisted Living Center, 10047
Weld Library District: Lincoln Park Branch Library, 11369
Weley Manor, 8852
Well Springs Assisted Living Facility, 10183
Wellfleet Council on Aging, 1330
Wellington, 9317
Wellington Court, 8233
Wellstead of Rogers, 9318
WesTest Engineering Corporation, 3104
Wesley Acres Memorial Loss Center, 8751
Wesley Residence, 9319
Wesley Village, 10546
West Alabama Planning and Development Council: Area Agency on Aging, 403
West Alabama Regional Commission's Senior Programs: Legal Counsel for the Elderly (WARC), 10973
West Bay Manor, 10229
West Carroll Council on Aging, 1197
West Central Area: Agency on Aging, 1442
West Central Florida Area: Agency on Aging, 808
West Central Illinois Area: Agency on Aging, 961
West Central Illinois Center for Independent Living (WCICIL), 10741
West Central Independent Living Solutions (WCILS), 10832
West Central Indiana Economic Development District Area Agency On Aging And Disabled, 1015
West Central Nebraska Area: Agency on Aging, 1596
West Central Texas Council of Governments-Area Agency on Aging, 2390
West Florida Regional Library, 11431
West Hollywood Senior Center: Jewish Family Service, 626
West Libery Assisted Living Residences, 8752
West Shores Retirement Community, 8109
West Suburban Elder Services, 1331
West Tennessee Legal Services (WTLS), 11264
West Tennessee Lions Blind Industries, 7784
West Texas Lighthouse for the Blind, 7785
West Virginia Advocates, 2558
West Virginia Bureau of Human Resources: Commission for the Hearing Impaired, 6462
West Virginia Bureau of Senior Services, 11303
West Virginia Commission on Aging, 11996
West Virginia Department of Aging, 2559
West Virginia Department of Health, 2560
West Virginia Department of Health & Human Resources, 4509
West Virginia Department of Health and Human Services: Human Services Bureau Commission on Aging, 2561
West Virginia Developmental Disability Plan Council, 2562
West Virginia Directors of Senior and Community Services, 2563
West Virginia Division of Alcohol and Drug Abuse, 7228
West Virginia Division of Tax and Revenue, 2564
West Virginia Division of Tourism, 12001
West Virginia Library Commission, 11844
West Virginia Protection & Advocacy for Persons with Disabilities, 2565
West Virginia Protection and Advocacy Agency, 11292
West Virginia School for the Blind, 11845
West Virginia Senior Legal Aid, 11293
West Virginia State University Metro Area Agency on Aging, 2566
West Virginia University: Mary Babb Randolph Cencer Center, 6001
West Virginia Workers Compensation Board of Review, 2567
WestMass Elder Care, 1332
Westbridge Assisted Living, 8618
Westchase Gables, 10547
Westchester County Airport, 5678
Westchester Disabled on the Move, 10891
Westchester Independent Living Center, 10892
Western Arizona Council of Governments: Area Agency on Aging, 453
Western Arkansas Area: Agency on Aging, 487
Western Arkansas Regional Center, 4939
Western Connecticut Area: Agency on Aging, 701
Western Home Assisted Living, 8753
Western Illinois Area: Agency on Aging, 962
Western Law Center for Disability Rights, 11015
Western Michigan University, 7578
Western New York Independent Living Project, 10893
Western Piedmont Council of Governments, 1924
Western Reserve Area: Agency on Aging, 2001
Western Reserve University, 2891
Western-Area Agency on Aging, 1223
Westfield Meadows, 9029
Westhills South Assisted Living Facility, 10336
Westlake Village, 9975
Westminster Towers, 8433
Westminster Village, 8079, 8328
Westminster/John Knox Press, 3603
Westmoreland County Area: Agency on Aging, 2198
Weston Travel Agency, 12058
Westown Adult Care Home, 8129
Westside Center for Independent Living, 10680
Westview Estates, 9320
Westwood Assisted Living, 10337
Westwood Center, 10574
Westwood Place, 9321
Wharton School, University of Pennsylvania, 288
What Are Clinical Trials All About?, 5852
What Are Old People For? How Elders Will Save the World, 3679
What Are TTYs? TDDs? TTs?, 6731
What Are the Signs of Alcoholism?, 7419
What Do I Do with My Old Decoder?, 6732
What Do You Do About the Alcoholics' Drinking?, 7420
What Employers Want to Know About Assistive Technology in the Workplace, 6733
What Every Family Should Know About Stroke, 7110
What Every Man Should Know About Seeding, 5853
What Happened to Joe?, 7421
What Helped Me When My Loved One Died, 6032
What Is AA ?, 7422
What Is NA ?, 7423
What You Need to Know About Bladder Cancer, 5854
What You Need to Know About Cancer, 5855
What You Need to Know About Cancer of the Colon and Rectum, 5856
What You Need to Know About Cervical Cancer, 5857
What You Need to Know About Esophagus Cancer, 5858
What You Need to Know About Kidney Cancer, 5859
What You Need to Know About Larynx Cancer, 5860
What You Need to Know About Lung Cancer, 5861
What You Need to Know About Oral Cancers, 5862
What You Need to Know About Ovarian Cancer, 5863
What You Need to Know About Pancreatic Cancer, 5864
What You Need to Know About Prostate Cancer, 5865
What You Need to Know About Skin Cancer, 5866
What You Need to Know About Testicular Cancer, 5867
What You Need to Know About Uterine Cancer, 5868
What You Need to Know About..., 5869
What You Should Know About Cochlear Implants in Adults, 6734
What to Eat if you Have Cancer, 5805
What's Your Cigarette Smoking IQ ?, 4129
Whatland Hills Retirement Center, 10575
Wheat Ridge Acres, 8837
Wheatland Terrace, 9590
Wheel Chairs & Scooters Directory, 3811
Wheel Chairs Renting Directory, 3812
Wheelchair Access, 4125
Wheelchair Aide, 3562
Wheelchair Carrier, 3407, 3414

1063

Entry Name Index / W

Wheelchair Carriers, Ramps, and Roamer Riding Chair, 3414
Wheelchair Getaways, 12059
Wheelchair Getaways Accessible Van Rentals, 11946
Wheelchair Parts & Fasteners, 3563
Wheelchair Work Table, 3564
Wheelchair and Mattress Pads, 3233
Wheelchairs of Kansas, 3542
Wheeler's Accessible Van Rentals, 2998, 11947
Wheelers Accessible Van Rentals, 11948
When Cancer Recurs: Meeting the Challenge Again, 5870
When Diabetes Complicates Your Life, 6225
When I Got Busy, I Got Better, 7424
When Memory Fails: Helping the Alzheimer's & Dementia Patient, 4974
When Someone in Your Family Has Cancer, 5871
When You Go Back to Work, 7425
When the Mind Hears, 6552
Where Do I Go From Here?, 7426
Whetstone Gardens, 9976
Whisper 2000, 3191
Whispering Knoll Assisted Living, 9824
Whispering Pines Care Center, 9322
Whitcomb House, 9030
White Bench, 3033
White Pines Assisted Living Center, 10338
White River Area: Agency on Aging, 488
Whitehall Estate, 9031
Whitehead Institute for Biomedical Research, 4639
Whitley Place, 10548
Whitman Publications, 6851
Whitman-Walker Clinic: AIDS/Medical Services Programs, 4510
Whitney Place at Natick, 9032
Whitney Place at Northbridge, 9033
Whittier Institute for Diabetes & Endocrinology, 6299
Who Is This Person Who Helped Save My Life?, 5872
Whole Life, 3972
Whole Life Enterprises, 3972
Why Do You Smoke?, 5873
Why Is Al-Anon Anonymous?, 7427
Why People Don't Acquire and/or Wear Hearing Aids, 6735
Whythebrook Terrace, 10230
Wichita Public Library, 11508
Wichita State University: Gerontology Center, 4440
Widowed Persons Service Award, 2690
Widows and Divorcees in Later Life: On Their Own Again, 3680
Wild Acre Homes, 9323
Wilder Assisted Living Programs, 9324
Wilderness Inquiry, 12060
Wildflower House, 10549
Wildflower Lodge, 9325
Wilds of Sand Prairie, 9326
Wildwood Grove, 9327
Wiley, 6216, 6508
Wiley Creek Community, 10184
Wiley Publishing, 6848, 6852, 7074
Wilkes Barre Bureau of Disability Determination, 2199
Will-Grundy Center for Independent Living, 10742
Willamette Manor, 10185
Willamette View, 10186
Willamette View Health Center, 10187
Willamsburg Senior Living Community, 8897
William Beardall Senior Center, 809
William E Morris Institute for Justice, 10987
William Hein & Company, 4029, 11929
William K. Kohrs Memorial Library, 11598
William S Hein & Company, 3766, 3813
William T Gossett Parkinson's Disease Center, 7050
William and Mercer Research Library, 11679
Williams & Wilkins, 3915, 6580, 6982
Willow Knoll Retirement Community, 9977
Willow Lake, 10201
Willow Park Assisted Living, 8575
Willow Pointe, 8754
Willowbrook Assisted Living, 8576
Willows, 8577, 8755
Willows Assisted Living, 10231
Willows at Holmdel Assisted Living Community, 9825
Willows at Meadow Branch, 10576
Wills and Bequests, 5022
Wilson College, 2907
Wilsonville, 10188
WinSCAN-The Single Switch Interface for PCs with Windows, 3192
Windsor Court Assisted Living, 10550
Windsor Manor Assisted Living, 10048
Windsor Senior Living Community, 8898
Windward Foundation, 343
Wings & Wheels, 3472
Wings & Wheels Greeting Cards, 3472
Wings for the Future, 7998
Winifred Law Opportunity Center, 11116
Winifred Masterson Burke Medical Research Institute, 5079
Winn Council on Aging, 1198
Winning Over Stroke, 7077
Winslow Court, 8251
Winston-Salem Industries for the Blind, 7786
Winter Springs Senior Center, 810
Winthrop at Buckhead, 8444
Winthrop at Tucker, 8445
Wire Walker Basket, 3496
Wireless Phones: Don't Mix Them Up, 6736
WisTech Assistive Technology Program, 2599
Wisconsin Aging and Long Term Care Board, 2600
Wisconsin Alliance of Hearing Professionals, 6463
Wisconsin Association of Area Agencies on Aging, 2601
Wisconsin Association of Homes and Services for the Aging, 2602
Wisconsin Bar Association: Elder Law, 11297
Wisconsin Bureau of Substance Abuse Services, 7229
Wisconsin Chapter of the Arthritis Foundation, 5175
Wisconsin Client Assistance Program, 2603
Wisconsin Coalition for Advocacy, 2604
Wisconsin Coalition for Advocacy: Madison, 11298
Wisconsin Coalition for Advocacy: Milwaukee, 11299
Wisconsin Coalition for Advocacy: Rice Lake, 11300
Wisconsin Council of Senior Citizens, 2605
Wisconsin Council on Developmental Disabilities, 2606
Wisconsin Department of Aging & Long-Term Care Resources, 2607
Wisconsin Department of Health and Human Services: The State Bureau on Aging, 11301
Wisconsin Department of Health and Social Services: Division of Health, 4511
Wisconsin Department of Mental Health, 6064
Wisconsin Department of Revenue, 2608
Wisconsin Department of Tourism, 12002
Wisconsin Department of Veterans Affairs, 2609
Wisconsin Regional Library for the Blind: Talking Book Program, 11852
Wisconsin Retired Educators Association, 2610
Wisconsin State Chapter of the Arthritis Foundation, 5145
Wisconsin Veterans Museum & Research Center, 11853
Wisconsin Workers Compensation Board, 2611
Wiscraft: Wisconsin Enterprises for the Blind, 7787
The Wisdom of Death: Six Paths to Understanding Loss and Grief, 6029
Wistar Institute of Anatomy & Biology Library, 11751
Without Sight and Sound, 6737, 7999
Wizz-ard, 3542
Wlllington Place of Colonial Heights, 10383
Wolfner Memorial Library for the Blind, 11593
Woman to Woman, 7230
A Woman's Guide to Coping with Disability, 3684
Women and Children's Service Program, 4512
Women for Sobriety, 4088, 4110, 7226, 7279, 7231
Women's AIDS Network, 4512
Women's Health, 4257
Women's Perspective, 4167
Women's Suffrage for Prostate Cancer Awareness, 6002
Women, Sex and HIV, 4574
Woodbine House, 6479
Woodbridge Assisted Living, 9034
Woodhaven Retirement Community, 9089
Woodland Good Samaritan Village Apartments, 9328
Woodland Heights, 10189
Woodland Manor, 9329
Woodridge Estates, 8838
Woodrow Wilson School of Public and International Affairs: Center for Health Care Strategies, 4441
Woods at Eddy Pond, 9035
Woodside Assisted Living Community, 10190
Woodside at Friendship Village, 9090
Woodstone Retirement Center, 8578
Worcester Foundation for Biomedical Research Biology, Cancer Center, 6003

Worcester Foundation for Biomedical Research: Biology/Drug Discovery/AIDS Group, 4640
Worcester Public Library, 11558
Words+, 3139, 3142, 3153, 3181, 3193
Words+ IST (Infrared, Sound, Touch), 3193
Work Options for Older Americans, 3681
Work, Health and Income Among the Elderly, 3682
Worker's Compensation Enforcement Division, 2039
Workers Compensation Board Florida, 811
Workers Compensation Board Massachusetts, 1333
Workers Compensation Board Missouri, 1525
Workers Compensation Board Montana, 1564
Workers Compensation Board Nebraska, 1597
Workers Compensation Board Vermont, 2446
Workers Compensation Division, 2302
Workers at Risk: Drugs and Alcohol on the Job, 7428
Working Age, 4130
Working With Deaf People: Accessibility and Accommodation in the Workplace, 6553
Workmen's Benefit Fund of the USA, 344
Workplace Program, 7232
World Education, 2821
World Institute on Disability, 345
World Institute on Disability (WID), 3880
World Without Alzheimer's: A Dream Within Reach, 5023
A World of Options: A Guide to International, Educational, Exchange, Community Service...for Persons with Disabilities, 3685
World of Sound, 6738
Worldwide AIDS Directory, 4542
Worldwide Mobility Products, 2988
Worthington Christian Village, 9978
Worthington Data Solutions, 3118
Wound, Ostomy and Continence Nurses Society, 6950
Wright State University Fels Research Institute Division of Human Biology, 4442
Wright-Way, 2999
Writing from Within, 11703
Wyndemere Woods, 10232
Wynhoven Living Center, 8899
Wyoming Client Assistance Program, 2615
Wyoming County Office for Aging, 1883
Wyoming Department of Aging, 2616
Wyoming Department of Health & Social Services: Medical Services Division, 4513
Wyoming Department of Health: Aging Division, 2617
Wyoming Department of Mental Health, 6065
Wyoming Department of Revenue, 2618
Wyoming Developmental Disability Council, 2619
Wyoming Division of Behavioral Health, 7233
Wyoming Division of Rehabilitation, 2620
Wyoming Division of Tourism, 12003
Wyoming Pioneer Home, 10620
Wyoming Protection & Advocacy Agency: Evanston, 11304
Wyoming Protection & Advocacy for Persons with Disabilities, 2621
Wyoming Protection and Advocacy Agency: Developmental Disabilities Protection and Advocacy Program, 11305
Wyoming Services For Independent Living, 10967
Wyoming Services for the Visually Disabled, 11856
Wyoming Workers Safety & Compensation Division, 2622

X

Xavier Society for the Blind, 11680

Y

Y&J USA Publishing, 3986
Y-Me National Organization for Breast Cancer Information & Support, 5787
YM 9000 Ride-Lite Series, 3543
YMCA Older Adult Programs, 2707
Yakama Nation Area Agency on Aging, 2544
Yale School of Medicine, 6108
Yale University: Behavioral Medicine Clinic, 6108
Yale University: Comprehensive Cancer Center, 6004
Yale University: Ribicoff Research Facilities, 6109
Yale University: Vision Research Center, 8060
Yarmouth Council on Aging, 1334
Yates County Office for the Aging, 1884
Yellow Brick House, 8446
Yeshiva University: Institute of Communication Disorders, 6837
Yeshiva University: Resnick Gerontology Center, 4443, 5080
Yoga for Arthritis: The Complete Guide, 5164
Yoga for Depression, 6078
York County Area: Agency on Aging, 2200
York Industries for the Blind: A Division of York County Blind Center, 7788
You Can Help Your Community Get Rid of Drugs, 7429
You Can Make a Difference: 10 Ways to Help an Alzheimer Family, 5024
You Don't Have to Hate Meetings: Try Computer-Assisted Notetaking Instead, 6739
You Shared the World with Me Video, 6772
You've Done Something About It! Helpful Hints to the New Hearing Aid User, 6740
You, Me and Hearing Loss Makes Three, 6741
Young Historical Library, 11509
Youngstown Radio Reading Service, 7789
Your Health, 3973
Your Job and HIV: Are There Risks?, 7430
Youville House Assisted Living Residence, 9036
Youville Place, 9037
Yuba-Sutter Legal Center for Seniors, 11016

Z

ZYGO Industries, 3081
Zebra Books, 5147
Ziggy Medi-Chair, 3415
Zipper Pull, 3245

Alabama

Alabama Bureau of Tourism and Travel, 11949
Alabama Client Assistance Program, 358
Alabama Department of Education: Disability Determination Service, 359
Alabama Department of Public Health, 360
Alabama Department of Rehabilitation Services, 361
Alabama Department of Retirement Systems, 362
Alabama Department of Revenue, 363
Alabama Department of Senior Services, 364, 10968
Alabama Department of Veteran Affairs, 365
Alabama Developmental Disability Council, 366
Alabama Disabilities Advocacy Program, 367
Alabama Disabilities Advocacy Program (ADAP), 10969
Alabama Division of Mental Illness and Substance Abuse Community Programs, 7127
Alabama Industries for the Blind, 7499
Alabama Institute for Deaf and Blind, 11306
Alabama Protection & Advocacy for Persons with Mental Illness, 368
Alabama Radio Reading Service Network, 369
Alabama Regional Library for the Blind and Physically Handicapped, 11307
Alabama State Bar: Elder Law, 10970
Alabama State Department of Human Resources, 370
Alabama Tombigbee Regional Commission, 371
Alabama Workers Compensation Division, 372
American Association of Retirement Communities, 26
American Diabetes Association: Huntsville District Office, 6135
American Diabetes Association: Mississippi Area Office, 6144
American Diabetes Association: Upstate Alabama Area Office, 6167
Auburn University: Special Collections & Archives, 11308
Azalea Manor, 8061
Birmingham Independent Living Center, 10621
Cardiovascular Research and Training Center: University of Alabama, 6866
Diabetes Research and Training Center: University of Alabama at Birmingham, 6270
East Alabama Commission: Agency on Aging, 373
Fair Haven Retirement Community, 8062
Gardens of Clanton, 8063
Gordon Oaks Assisted Living, 8064
Governor's Committee on Employment of Persons with Disabilities, 374
Home Care Association of Alabama, 375
Homestead Village of Fairhope, 8065
Houston-Love Memorial Library, 11309
Huntsville Subregional Library for the Blind, 11310
Independent Living Center-Jasper, 10623
Jefferson County Office of Senior Citizens, 376
Jefferson County Office of Senior Citizens Services (OSCS), 10971
Kirkwood by the River, 8066
Knowlwood Assisted Living, 8067
Lee Russell Council of Governments: Area Agency on Aging, 377
Legal Services for the Elderly: Area Agency on Aging, 10972
Library for the Blind & Handicapped: Public Library-Anniston/Calhoun Counties, 11311
Liveoak Village, 8068
Mitchell Hollingsworth Annex, 8069
Mobile Association for the Blind, 7652
Montgomery Area Council on Aging, 378
Montgomery Independent Living Center, 10624
Morningside of Decatur, 8070
Mount Royal Towers, 8071
Murray House, 8072
North Central Alabama Regional Council of Governments: Area Agency on Aging, 379
North Mobile Retirement Center, 8073
Northwest Alabama Council of Governments: Area Agency on Aging, 380
Plantation Manor Assisted Living I, 8074
Protection & Advocacy for Persons with Developmental Disabilities, 381
RSVP Athens Limestone County, 382
RSVP Baldwin County, 383
RSVP Birmingham Area, 384
RSVP Calhoun County, 385
RSVP Dallas County, 386
RSVP Escambia County, 387
RSVP Etowah County, 388
RSVP Houston Henry Geneva Counties, 390
RSVP Lee & Russell Counties, 391
RSVP Marshall County, 392
RSVP Mobile, 393
RSVP Monroe/Cone-Cuh County, 394
RSVP Pike County, 395
RSVP Southwest Alabama, 396
RSVP Tallapossa & Coosa Counties, 397
Railroad Retirement Board: Alabama District Office, 398
Saint Martins in the Pines, 8075
Samford University Library Special Collections, 11312
Somerby at Jones Farm, 8076
Somerset Assited Living Facility, 8077
South Central Alabama Development Commission: Area Agency on Aging, 399
Specialized Center of Research in Ischemic Heart Disease, 6891
Stroke Research and Treatment Center, 7056
TARCOG: Area Agency on Aging, 400
US Deptartment of Veterans Affairs: Central Alabama Veterans Health Care System, 11313
US Deptartment of Veterans Affairs: Medical Center Library, 11314
US Deptartment of Veterans Affairs: Alabama Veterns Health Care System, 11315
University of Alabama at Birmingham: Congenital Heart Disease Center, 6892
University of Alabama at Birmingham: Parkinson's Disease Center, 7047
University of Alabama: Speech and Hearing Center, 6821
Village at Cook Springs, 8078
Volunteer Center of Morgan County, 401
Volunteers of America Southeast, 402
West Alabama Planning and Development Council: Area Agency on Aging, 403
West Alabama Regional Commission's Senior Programs: Legal Counsel for the Elderly (WARC), 10973

Alaska

Access Alaska-Anchorage, 10625
Access Alaska-Fairbanks, 10626
Alaska Client Assistance Program (CAP), 404
Alaska Commission on Aging, 405
Alaska Commission on Aging: Alaska Department of Health & Social Services, 10974
Alaska Department of Military and Veterans Affairs, 406
Alaska Department of Revenue, 407
Alaska Disability Law Center, 408
Alaska Division of Mental Health and Developmental Disabilities, 409
Alaska Division of Retirement & Benefits, 410
Alaska Division of Tourism, 11950
Alaska Division of Vocational Rehabilitation, 411
Alaska Governor's Committee on Employment and Rehabilitation of People with Disabilities, 412
Alaska Legal Services Corporation: Senior Legal Services Project, 10975
Alaska State Library Talking Book Center, 11316
Alaska Statewide Independent Living Council, 413
Alaska Welcomes You, 414
Alaska Workers Compensation Board, 415
Alaskans Commission on Aging, 416
Amazing Grace Family Living, 8080
American Diabetes Association: Alaska Area Office, 6114
Anchorage Pioneers' Home, 8081
Arctic Hearth Assisted Living Homes, 8082
Arkansas Division of Alcoholism & Drug Abuse, 7139
Arkansas Office of Alcoholism and Substance Abuse, 7140
Assistive Technology of Alaska, 417
Bear Mountain Manor, 8083
Braille Revival League, 7551
Chugiak Senior Center, 8084
Dignified Home Life Care, 8085
Disability Law Center Of Alaska, 10976
Downtown Care, 8086
Easy Living AFC, 8087
Elderlaw Project, 10977
Fairbanks Senior Center, 419
Farthest North Club of the Deaf, 420, 6355
Graceful Living Assisted Living Home, 8088
Health Care Bridges, 8089
Hidden Heights Assisted Living Home, 8090
Holy Family Adult Foster Home, 8091
Holy Family Assisted Living Home, 8092

Geographic Index / Arizona

Immaculate Conception Home, II, 8093
Juneau Pioneers Home, 8094
Kat's Eldercare, 8095
Kenai Peninsula Independent Living Center-Homer, 10627
Kenai Peninsula Independent Living-Central Peninsula, 10628
Kenai Senior Connection, 421
Marlow Manor/Manor Management, 8096
Palmer Pioneers' Home, 8097
Respect Your Elders Tender Loving AdultCare, 8098
Saint Augustine Assisted Living Home, 8099
Saint Augustine Assisted Living Home II, 8100
Scott Manor, 8101
Seward Independent Living Center, 10629
Shirley's Assisted Living Home, 8102
Social Security: Juneau Disability Determination Services, 422
Southeast Alaska Independent Living (SAIL), 10630
Southeast Alaska Independent Living Center (SAIL), 10631
Southeast Alaska Living Center (SAIL), 10632
State of Alaska, Department of Health &Social Services, 423
Summer Shades Residential Care, 8103
Thania's Assisted Living Home, 8104
Tranquility Manor, 8105
Turnagain Adult Foster Home, 8106
University of Alabama: Center for Alcohol and Addiction Studies, 7478

Arizona

ALC Copper Hills House, 8110
Advocates for the Disabled, 10978
America West Airlines/US Airways, 11912
America West/US Airways Airline, 12006
American Council on Alcoholism, 7135
American Diabetes Association: Arizona Area Office, 6115
American Diabetes Association: Border Area Office, 6119
American Holistic Nurses Association, 42
Arizona Aging and Adult Administration, 424
Arizona Alcoholism and Drug Abuse, 7136
Arizona Area Agency on Aging: Region One, 425
Arizona Bridge to Independent Living, 10633
Arizona Center for Disability Law, 10979
Arizona Center for the Blind and Visually Impaired, 7518
Arizona Commission for the Deaf & Hard of Hearing, 6318
Arizona Department of Aging, 426
Arizona Department of Economic Security, 427
Arizona Department of Economic Security: Division of Aging and Community Services, 10980
Arizona Department of Family Health Services, 428
Arizona Department of Revenue, 429
Arizona Department of Veterans Services, 430
Arizona Disability Determination Services, 431
Arizona Elder Abuse and Fraud Taskforce Committee, 10981
Arizona Heart Institute, 6839
Arizona Industries for the Blind, 7519
Arizona Industries for the Blind, 7520
Arizona Inter Tribal Council, 432
Arizona Office of Substance Abuse & General Mental Health, 7138
Arizona Office of Tourism, 11951
Arizona Protection and Advocacy Agency: Arizona Center for Disability Law, 10982
Arizona Public Safety Personnel Retirement System, 433
Arizona Railroad Retirement Board, 434
Arizona Rehabilitation State Services for the Blind and Visually Impaired, 7521
Arizona Retirement System, 435
Arizona State Braille and Talking Book Library, 11317
Arizona Workers Compensation Board, 436
Autumn Leaves Adult Care, 8111
Bee Hive Homes of Yuma, 8112
Bethesda Gardens, 8113
Big Print Address Book, 3450
Book Holder, 3452
Broadway Proper, 8114
C& C Adult Care Home, 8115
Capable Hands Adult Care Home, 8116
Capscrew, 3324
Care Concepts, 2960
Care with Love, 8117
Cypress Court at Tucson, 8118
DIRECT Independent Living Center, 10634
DNA People's Legal Services, 10983
Desert Point-La Reserve, 8119
Do It Now Foundation, 7153
Emerald Springs Retirement & Assisted Living Community, 8120
Flagstaff City-Coconino County Library for the Visually & Physically Impaired, 11318
Folding Dressing Stick, 3240
Forum at Tucson, 8121
Fountain Hills Lioness Braille Service, 11319
Geronimo, 3519
Governor's Council on Developmental Disabilities, 437
Hand/Nail Brush, 3259
Handy Reacher, 3306
Helping Handle, 3039
La Casa Asperanza Assisted Living, 8122
La Posada, 8123
La Siena, 8124
Large Print Typewriter, 3130
Legal Advocate Program: Pinal-Gila Council for Senior Citizens, 10984
McDowell Village, 8125
Mesa Arizona Regional Family History Center, 11320
Mr. Escort Manual Wheelchair Carrier, 2988
National Academy of Elder Law Attorneys, 182, 10985
National Association of Professional Geriatric Care Managers (PGCM), 198
Navajo Area Agency on Aging: Division of Health, 438
New Horizons Independent Living Center - Prescott Valley, 10635
Northern Arizona Council of Governments Area Agency on Aging, 439
Parkinson Association of Arizona, 6960
Phoenix Public Library: Special Needs Center, 11321
Pill Splitter, 3268
Pima Council on Aging, 440, 11322
Pinal/Gila Council for Senior Citizens, 441
Power for Off-Pavement, 3529
Prescott Talking Book Library, 11323
RSVP East Valley Retired & Senior Volunteer Program, 442
RSVP Gila Pinal, 443
RSVP Maricopa County, 444
RSVP Northern Arizona, 445
RSVP Southeastern Arizona, 446
RSVP Tucson, 447
RSVP Western Arizona, 448
Redman Apache, 3530
Redman Crow Line, 3531
Retired Activities Office: Phoenix Affairs Office, 449
Ruth E Golding Clinical Pharmacokinetics Laboratory, 7474
SEAGO Area: Agency on Aging, 450
Senior Citizens of Patagonia, 451
Services Maximizing Independent Living and Empowerment (SMILE), 10636
Southern Arizona Legal Aid (SALA), 10986
Spatial Tilt Custom Chair, 3050
Sports 'n Spokes, 12046
Springhouse Assisted Living, 8126
Statewide Independent Living Council (SILC), 10637
Sunquest Village of Yuma, 8127
Travis L Williams Family Services Center, 11324
Tucson Family History Center, 11325
US Department of Veterans Affairs: Northern Arizona VA Health Care System, 11326
US Department of Veterans Affairs: Phoenix Medical Center Library, 11327
US Department of Veterans Affairs: Tucson Medical Center Library, 11328
US Travel Systems, 12056
Verde Valley Senior Citizens Association, 452
Villa Hermosa, 8128
Western Arizona Council of Governments: Area Agency on Aging, 453
Westown Adult Care Home, 8129
Wheeler's Accessible Van Rentals, 2998, 11947
Wheelers Accessible Van Rentals, 11948
White Bench, 3033
William E Morris Institute for Justice, 10987

Arkansas

American Diabetes Association: Arkansas, 6116
Arizona Bureau of Alcohol and Drug Abuse, 7137
Arkansas Advocates for Nursing Home Residents, 454
Arkansas Aging Foundation, 455
Arkansas Aging Foundation Information Center, 11329
Arkansas Assistive Technology Projects, 456

Geographic Index / California

Arkansas Department of Aging, 457
Arkansas Department of Finance and Administration, 458
Arkansas Department of Health & Human Services: Division of Aging and Adult Services, 10988
Arkansas Department of Human Services: Division of Aging and Adult Services, 459
Arkansas Department of Parks & Tourism, 11952
Arkansas Department of Public Employees Retired Systems, 460
Arkansas Department of Veterans Affairs, 461
Arkansas Developmental Disability Council, 462
Arkansas Disability Determinations for SSA, 463
Arkansas Division of Aging & Adult Services, 464
Arkansas Division of Developmental Disabilities Services, 465
Arkansas Division of Services for the Blind, 466
Arkansas Independent Living Council (AILC), 10638
Arkansas Lighthouse for the Blind, 7522
Arkansas Protection and Advocacy Agency: Disability Rights Center, 10989
Arkansas Regional Library for the Blind and Physically Handicapped, 11330
Arkansas Rehabilitation Research and Training Center for Deaf Persons, 6795
Arkansas Rehabilitation Services, 467
Arkansas Teacher Retirement System, 468
Arkansas Volunteer Lawyers for the Elderly (AVLE), 10990
Baxter Retirement Village, 8107
Center for Arkansas Legal Services, 10991
Central Arkansas Area: Agency on Aging, 469
Cleburne County Aging Program, 470
Division of Aging and Adult Services - Elder Choices, 10639
East Arkansas Area: Agency on Aging, 471
Educational Services for the Visually Impaired, 11331
John L McClellan Memorial Veterans'Hospital Research Office, 6880
Legal Aid of Arkansas, 10992
Mainstream Living, 10640
Northwest Arkansas Area: Agency on Aging, 472
Northwest Ozarks Regional Library for the Blind and Handicapped, 11332
Outlook Pointe at Mountain Home, 8108
RSVP East Arkansas, 473
RSVP Garland County, 474
RSVP Greater Texarkana Arkansas, 475
RSVP North Central Arkansas, 477
RSVP Northwest Arkansas, 478
RSVP Stutgart North Arkansas, 479
RSVP Tri-County, 480
RSVP West Arkansas, 481
RSVP of Central Arkansas, 482
Railroad Retirement Board: Arkansas District Office, 483
Research and Training Center for Persons Who are Deaf or Hard of Hearing, 6439
Senior Specialists Agency on Aging, 484
Sources for Community Independent Living Services (SOURCES), 10641
Southeast Arkansas Area: Agency on Aging, 485
Southwest Arkansas Area: Agency on Aging, 486
Spa Area Independent Living Services (SAILS), 10642
Sue Smith Travel Service, 12047
US Department of Veterans Affairs Hospital Libraries, 11333
West Shores Retirement Community, 8109
Western Arkansas Area: Agency on Aging, 487
White River Area: Agency on Aging, 488

California

1-800-BRAILLE, 7491
ACS Wireless, 3056
ADARA, 6300
Abbey Home Healthcare, 3293
Able-Phone 100, 3061
Able-Phone 1900, 3062
Able-Switch SW-1, 3063
Achromatopsia Network, 7497
Aegis Escondido, 8130
Aegis Gardens, 8131
Aegis at Shadowridge, 8132
Aegis of Aptos, 8133
Aegis of Carmichael, 8134
Aegis of Chino Hills, 8135
Aegis of Concord, 8136
Aegis of Corte Madera, 8137
Aegis of Dana Point, 8138
Aegis of Fremont, 8139
Aegis of Granada Hills, 8140
Aegis of Laguna Niguel, 8141
Aegis of Moraga, 8142
Aegis of Napa, 8143
Aegis of Pleasant Hill, 8144
Aegis of San Francisco, 8145
Aegis of San Rafael, 8146
Aegis of Ventura, 8147
AirLift Toileting System from Mobility, 3003
Akron Resources, 3068
Alameda County Area: Agency on Aging, 489
Alcohol Research Group: Public Health Institute, 7130
Alcohol-Drug Treatment Referral, 7131
Alhambra Retirement Community, 8148
Alpine View Lodge, 8149
Alzheimer Early Stages, 2nd Edition, 11688
Amador Senior Services, 10993
American Academy of Ophthalmology, 7501
American Action Fund for Blind Children and Adults, 7502
American Association of Critical Care Nurses, 19
American College of Trust and Estate Counsel, 35
American Diabetes Association: California, 6121
American Federation of the Blind: San Francisco Chapter, 490
American Foundation for the Blind: San Francisco, 7512
American Society of Ophthalmic Registered Nurses, 7517
Anglo California Travel Service, 12008
Answerall 100, 3075
Area 1 Agency on Aging, 491
Area 12 Agency on Aging, 492
Area 4 Agency on Aging, 493
Art of Getting Well, 11689
Arthritis Foundation: Northeastern California Chapter, 494
Assistive Software Products, 3079
Atherton Baptist Homes, 8150
BESTspeech, 3082
Baromedical Nurses Association, 90
Bees-Stealy Research Foundation, 6862
Belmont Village Cardiff by the Sea, 8151
Belmont Village Crown Cove, 8152
Belmont Village Westwood, 8153
Belmont Village at Sabre Springs, 8154
Belmont Village of Burbank, 8155
Belmont Village of Encino, 8156
Belmont Village of Hollywood Hills, 8157
Belmont Village of Rancho Palos Verdes, 8158
Belmont Village of San Jose, 8159
Belmont Village of Sunnyvale, 8160
Bet Tzedek Legal Services, 10994
Better Back, 3043
Beverly Foundation, 91
Books Aloud Library, 11335
Braille Institute Desert Center, 7543
Braille Institute Sight Center, 7544
Braille Institute of America, 7545
Braille Institute of America, 7546
Braille Institute of America Library, 7547
Braille Institute: Orange County Center, 7548
Braille Institute: Santa Barbara Center, 7549
Breezy, 3504
British Home in California, 8161
Broadcast Services for the Blind, 11336
Broadview Residential Care Center, 8162
Bureau of Naval Personnel: California Retired Affairs Office, 495
Bureau of Naval Personnel: Fleet and Family Support Center, 496
Bureau of Naval Personnel: San Diego Retired Activities Office, 497
CAPH Independent Living Center, 10643
CCCIL-Central Coast Center for Independenet Living - Capitola, 10644
CLOSE-UP 6.5, 3092
California Advocates for Nursing Home Reform, 10995
California Agency of Health & Welfare: Department of Rehabilitation, 498
California Agency of Health and Welfare: Department of Aging, 499
California Aging Services, 500
California American/Asian Elderly Society, 501
California Association for Older Americans, 502
California Association of Area Agencies on Aging, 503
California Association of Homes andServices for the Aging, 504
California Client Assistance Program, 505
California Commission on Aging, 506
California Department of Aging, 507, 10996
California Department of Aging and Adult Services, 508

1069

Geographic Index / California

California Department of Aging: Children and Community Services, 509
California Department of Alcohol and Drug Programs: Resource Center, 510
California Department of Rehabilitation, 511
California Department of Veterans Affairs, 512
California Developmental Disability Council, 513
California Division of Tourism, 11953
California Foundation for Independent Living Centers (CFILC), 10645
California Franchise Tax Board, 514
California Governor's Committee on Employment of People with Disabilities, 515
California Institute for Medical Research, 7035
California Latino Council of the Deaf and Hard of Hearing, 516, 6324
California Protection & Advocacy for Persons With Disabilities, 517
California Protection and Advocacy Agency (PAI), 10997
California Public Employees' Retirement System, 518
California Seniors Council, 519
California State Bar Committee on Legal Problems of Aging, 10998
California State Board of Equalization, 520
California State Independent Living Council (SILC), 10646
California State Library: Braille & Talking Book Library, 11337
California State Teachers Retirement System, 521
California Women's Commission on Alcohol and Drug Dependencies, 7143
California Workers Compensation Board, 522
Californian Retirement Residence, 8163
Campbell Adult Center, 8164
Canine Companions for Independence, 7554
Caregiver Alliance, 94
Center for Independence of the Disabled (CID), 10647
Center for Independence of the Disabled-North Branch, 10648
Center for Independent Living (CIL), 10649
Center for Independent Living - Central Coast/Hollister (CCCIL), 10650
Center for Independent Living-Merced Outreach, 10651
Center for Independent Living-Oakland, 10652
Center for Medical Ethics and Mediation, 99
Central California Legal Services, 10999
Central Coast Commission for Senior Citizens, 523
Chancellor Health Care, 8165
Chancellor Place of Chino Hills, 8166
Chancellor Place of Lodi, 8167
Chancellor Place of Murrieta, 8168
Chancellor Place of Pasadena, 8169
Chancellor Place of Windsor, 8170
Charles R Drew Hypertension Research Center, 6919
Chiropractor's Self-Help Back and Body Book, 11690
Citrus Heights Terrace, 8171
City of Hope, 106

City of Los Angeles Department of Aging, 524
Classic, 2961
Classic Hawaii, 12012
Clearinghouse for Specialized Media and Technology, 7565
Coalition for Economic Survival (CES), 112
Cocaine Anonymous, 7145
Community Access Center, 10653
Community Resources for Independence (CRI) Napa, 10654
Community Resources for Independence - CRI/Santa Rosa, 10655
Community Resources for Independent Living, 10656
Community Service Project, 7146
Compax 12, 3508
Contra Costa County Office on Aging, 525
Convaid Products, 3509
Cordia Senior Living, 8172
Costa Mesa Senior Center, 526
Council on Aging of Silicon Valley, 527
Council on Aging of Sonoma County, 11000
Council on Education of the Deaf, 6341
Country Villa Terrace Assisted Living, 8173
Country Villa West Assisted Living Center, 8174
Country Village Senior Services, 8175
Courtyards at Pine Creek, 8176
Crown Cove, 8177
Cruiser Bus Buggy 4MB, 3420
Cypress Court Escondido, 8178
Damaco D90, 3512
Dayle McIntosh Center for the Disabled, 10657
Dayle McIntosh Center-Clubhouse, 10658
Dayle McIntosh-South County, 10659
Deaf and Hard of Hearing Services Center, 6348
Departments of Neurology & Neurosurgery: University of California, 7116
Diablo Valley Foundation for the Aging, 528
Disability Determination Services: LosAngeles West Branch, 529
Disability Determination Services: Central Support Services Branch, 530
Disability Determination Services: La Jolla Branch, 531
Disability Determination Services: Los Angeles South Branch, 532
Disability Determination Services: Oakland Branch, 533
Disability Determination Services: Roseville Branch, 534
Disability Determination Services: Sacramento Branch, 535
Disability Determination Services: San Diego Branch, 536
Disability Evaluations Division: SierraBranch, 537
Disability Rights Education and Defense Fund, 11001
Driving Systems, 3013
Drug Abuse Resistance Education of America, 7154
Drugs Anonymous, 7156
East Los Angeles Service Center, 538
El Dorado County Area: Agency on Aging, 539
Elder Care Alliance, 540

Elderly People or Persons with Disabilities Housing, 125
Environmental Traveling Companions, 12019
Ernest Gallo Clinic and Research Center, 7456
Eskaton Cameron Park Lodge, 8179
Eskaton Gold River Lodge, 8180
Eureka Ward Family History Center, 11338
Extensions for Independence, 7585
Fairwinds-Ivey Ranch, 8181
Fairwinds-West Hills, 8182
Fairwinds-Woodward Park, 8183
Families Anonymous, 7157
Fifty-Plus Lifelong Fitness, 136
Font-Tools BIGFONT, 3118
Foundation Aiding the Elderly (FATE), 140
Fountaingrove Lodge, 8184
Fountains at Sea Bluffs, 8185
Fresno County Free Library: Talking Book Library for the Blind, 11339
Fresno Madera Area: Agency on Aging, 541
Friday Night Live, 7160
Garden of Palms, 8186
Gardens at Hillsborough Village, 8187
Gardens at Park Balboa, 8188
Gardens of Santa Mónica, 8189
General Clinical Research Center: University of California at Los Angeles, 6872
Get Fit While You Sit, 11691
Glaucoma Research Foundation, 8042
Glaucoma Support Network, 7595
Glen Bollinger Humanitarian Award, 2638
Governor's Policy Council on Drug & Alcohol Abuse, 7162
Gray Panthers of Central Contra Costa, 542
Gray Panthers of East Bay/Berkeley, 543
Gray Panthers of Long Beach, 544
Gray Panthers of Marin County, 545
Gray Panthers of Orange County, 546
Gray Panthers of Sacramento, 547
Gray Panthers of San Fernando Valley, 548
Gray Panthers of San Francisco, 549
Gray Panthers of Santa Barbara, 550
Gray Panthers of South Bay, 551
Gray Panthers of Southern Alameda County, 552
Greater Valley Physicians Medical Group, 553
Green Tortoise Adventure Travel, 12023
Grossmont Gardens, 8190
Guide Dogs for the Blind, 7600
HEAR Center, 6361
Hacienda, 8191
Hawkins Center of Law and Services for the Disabled, 11002
Hearing Education and Awareness for Rockers, 6366
Hearing Loss Association of America, 6370
Heart Research Foundation of Sacramento, 6876
Helping Hands for the Blind, 7606
Heritage Estates, 8192
Heritage Estates Senior Apartments, 8193
Heritage Pointe, 8194
Hollenbeck Palms, 8195
HomeAid Orange County, 554
House Ear Institute, 6374
House Ear Institute: Athalie Irvine Clarke Library, 11340

Geographic Index / California

House Ear Institute: Care Center Parent Resource Library, 11341
House of Travel, 12026
I Can't Chew Cookbook, 11692
IL Resources of Contra Costa County-Fairfield, 10660
Imperial County Area Agency on Aging, 555
Independent Living Center of Kern County, 10661
Independent Living Center of SouthernCalifornia (ILCSC), 10662
Independent Living Center-Lancaster, 10663
Independent Living Center-Santa Clarita, 10664
Independent Living Resource Center (ILRCSF), 10665
Independent Living Resource Contra Costa County-Antioch, 10666
Independent Living Resource of Contra Costa County, 10667
Independent Living Resources Center-Santa Barbara, 10669
Independent Living Resources Center-Santa Maria, 10668
Independent Living Resources Center-Ventura, 10670
Independent Living Services of Northern California, 10671
Inland Counties Legal Services for Seniors, 11003
Integrated Care Communities, 8196
Jewish Communal Retirees Association of Los Angeles, 556
Journey to Pain Relief, 11693
Journeys East, 12027
Joy of Laziness, 11694
Kern County Aging And Adult Services, 557
Kings Tulare Area: Agency on Aging, 558
La Palma Recreation & Community Services, 559
La Quinta Senior Center, 560
Las Villas De Carlsbad, 8197
Las Villas Del Norte, 8198
Legal Assistance to the Elderly, 11004
Legal Center for the Elderly and Disabled, 11005
Legal Services for Seniors, 11006
Lightweight Breezy, 3524
Linda Valley Care Center, 8199
Linda Valley Villa, 8200
Living Well in a Nursing Home, 11695
Los Angeles County Area Agency on Aging, 561
Los Angeles County Bar Association: Elderline Public Council, 11007
Los Angeles Disability Determination Services, 562
Mac's Lift Gate, 2983
Malash Gardens, 8201
Marin Center for Independent Living, 10672
Marin County: Area Agency on Aging, 563
Marin Institute, 7178
Marin Senior Coordinating Council(Whistlestop), 564
Mat Factory, 3556
Matilda Brown Home, 8202
Meals on Wheels of Culver Palms, 565
MedDev Corporation, 3265
Media Center on Alcohol Issues, 7181
Medic Alert Foundation International, 165
Menopause Without Medicine, 11696
Merced County Area Agency for Aging, 566
Merced Senior Community Center, 567
MessageMate, 3139
Mini-Rider, 2986
Morse Code Equalizer, 3142
Mountview Retirement Community, 8203
National Association for Hispanic Elderly, 184
National Center on Deafness, 6408
National Eye Care Project, 7668
National Eye Care Project (NECP), 7669
National Federation of the Blind of California: Santa Barbara County Chapter, 7673
National Federation of the Blind: Science and Engineering Division, 7685
National Network for the Disabled, 243
National Resource Center on Supportive Housing & Home Modifications, 256
Newport Beach Plaza, 8204
North Coast Opportunities: Area Agency on Aging, 568
Northern California State Library: Braille and Talking Book Library, 11342
Northridge Travel, 12036
Northwest Regional Training Center: Canine Companions for Independence, 7710
O'Connor Woods, 8205
Oakland Public Library, 11343
Office for Aging and Community Services: Monterey County Department of Social Services, 569
Office of Public Affairs, Social Security Administration, 570
Older Women's League of Ohlone, 571
Orange County Area: Agency on Aging, 572
Orange County Korean Community Service Center, 573
PROPATH, 6959
PSA 2 Area Agency On Aging, 574
Pacific Gardens Tarzana, 8206
Palo Alto Commons, 8207
Paragon Gardens, 8208
Parkinson Association of Orange County, 6968
Parkinson Association of the Sacramento Valley, 6972
Parkinson Network of Mt Diablo, 6974
Pasadena Braille Club, 7715
Pasadena Braille Club, 7716
Passages Adult Resource Center-Area Agency on Aging, 575
Placer Independent Resource Services/PIRS, 10673
Plantronics SP-04, 3152
Porta Ramps, 3390
PortaPower Plus, 3153
Power Seat Base (6-Way), 2989
Prestige Assisted Living at Yorba Linda, 8210
Prevent Blindness Northern California, 7726
Preventive Medicine Research Institute, 6886
Prostate Health Workbook, 11698
Protecting Adult Welfare (PAW), 297
Providence Speech and Hearing Center, 6435
Purpose Prize, 2677
Quickie 2, 3429
RRTC on Mental Health/Late Deaf & HOH, 6436
RSVP All Peoples Christian Center, 576
RSVP Central Coast, 577
RSVP City of Burbank, 578
RSVP Coachella Valley, 579
RSVP Culver City, 580
RSVP Fresno, 581
RSVP Greater East Los Angeles, 582
RSVP Humboldt/Del Norte Counties, 583
RSVP Kings/Tulare Counties, 584
RSVP Lake/Mendocino Counties, 585
RSVP Long Beach, 586
RSVP Los Angeles Parks, 587
RSVP Nevada County, 588
RSVP Northern Santa Clara County, 589
RSVP Oakland, 590
RSVP Ojai County, 591
RSVP Oxnard County, 592
RSVP Pomona Valley, 593
RSVP Sacramento County, 594
RSVP San Bernardino County, 595
RSVP San Fernando/Santa Clarita Valleys, 596
RSVP Santa Barbara, 597
RSVP Shast and Tehama Counties, 598
RSVP Sonoma County, 599
RSVP South Bay County, 600
RSVP Thousand Oaks/Conejo Valley, 601
RSVP Visalia Volunteer, 602
RSVP West Valley of San Bernardino County, 603
RSVP Western Riverside County, 604
Railroad Retirement Board-California District Office, 605
Rancho Bernardo Joslyn Senior Center, 606
Rancho Vista, 8211
Regency Park-El Molino, 8212
Region 9: Administration on Aging (AoA), 607
Rehman Retirement Resorts-Poway, 8214
Renaissance at the Gables, 8215
Research and Education Institute, 6888
Resources for Independent Living, 10674
Retired Activities Office, 608
Ricon Corporation, 3393
Rio Las Palmas, 8216
Rolling Start, 10675
Safari Tilt, 3049
Salinas-Central Coast Center for Independent Living, 10676
Salk Institute for Biological Studies Library, 11344
San Clemente Villas by the Sea, 8217
San Diego County Area: Agency on Aging, 609
San Diego Hebrew Homes, 610
San Diego Information & Referral Center, 7044
San Francisco Commission on the Aging, 611
San Francisco Heart Institute, 6844
San Francisco Public Library for the Blind and Print Handicapped, 11345
San Francisco Public Library: Talking Books Program & Blind Services Center, 11346
San Jose State University Library, 11347
Santa Cruz Volunteer Center, 612
Senior Adults Legal Assistance (SALA), 11009
Senior Citizens Legal Services, 11010
Senior Citizens of Shasta County, 613
Senior Gleaners, 614

1071

Geographic Index / Canada

Senior Law Project, 11011
Senior Legal Center of Northern California, 11012
Seniors' Law Center, 11013
Service Center for Independent Living, 10677
Service Center for Independent Living-Covina, 10678
ShapeWalking, 11700
Silicon Valley Independent Living Center, 10679
Skyway, 3559
Smith-Ketterwell Eye Research Institute, 8053
Society of Hearing Impaired Physicians, 6446
Solano Napa: Agency on Aging, 615
Sonoma County Task Force for the Homeless, 616
Southern California Research Institute, 7475
Southern California State Library: Braille and Talking Book Library, 11348
Southwest Regional Training Center:Canine Companions for Independence, 7750
Southwestern Region: Helen Keller National Center, 7751
Spiritual Fitness Division (CREDO Southwest), 617
Springfield Place, 8218
St. Paul's Senior Homes & Services, 8219
St. Regis, 8220
Stanford Center for Research in Disease Prevention, 7476
Stanislaus County Department of Aging and Veteran Services, 618
Steven Motor Chair, 3538
Strength Training for Seniors, 11701
Summerville at Garden Manor, 8221
Summerville at Main Place, 8222
Summerville at Orange, 8223
Summerville at Valley View, 8224
Summerville at Victorian Court, 8225
Summerville at Villa De Anza, 8226
Sunny View Manor, 8227
Sunset Hall Program at Bethany Towers, 619
Sunshine Care Mountain Vistas, 8228
Synthetic Sheep-Skin Pads, 3230
Systems 2000, 3441
Torso Support, 3560
Travel Trends, 12051
Trinity House, 8229
Tripod Captioned Filys, 6457
U-Control II, 3181
US Department of Veteran Affairs: Palo Alto Health Care and Medical Information Service, 11349
US Department of Veterans Affairs: H Earl Gordon Medical Library, 11350
US Department of Veterans Affairs: LomaLinda Medical Center Library Service, 11351
US Department of Veterans Affairs: LongBeach Medical Center Library Service, 11352
US Department of Veterans Affairs: San Diego Medical Center Library Service, 11353
US Department of Veterans Affairs: San Francisco Medical Center Library Service, 11354
US SERVAS, 12055

University of California, Irvine: UCI Diabetes Research Program, 6281
University of California: Cardiovascular Research Laboratory, 6894
University of California: Los Angeles Alcohol Research Center, 7479
University of California: Los Angeles Department of Medicine, 7121
University of California: Los Angeles Jules Stein Eye Institute, 8055
University of California: Mount Zion Medical Center, 11355
University of California: San Diego General Clinical Research Center, 6895
University of California: San Francisco Cardiovascular Research Institute, 6896
University of California: San Francisco Center on Deafness Library, 11356
University of California: San Francisco General Clinical Research Center, 6893
University of Southern California: Coronary Care Research, 6901
University of Southern California: Division of Nephrology, 6927
VA Central California Health Care System, 11357
Vacaville Public Library: Town Square, 11358
Varenna at Fountaingrove, 8230
Ventura County Area Agency on Aging, 620
Vertical Home Lift Sales, 3411
Villa Capri, 8231
Villa Santa Barbara, 8232
Visually Impaired Veterans of America, 7779
Volunteer Center, 621
Volunteer Center Orange County, 622
Volunteer Center of Kern County, 623
Volunteer Exchange, 624
Volunteer Lawyers Project for the Elderly, 11014
Volunteers of America Bay Area, 625
Weitbrecht Communications, 3190
Wellington Court, 8233
West Hollywood Senior Center: Jewish Family Service, 626
Western Law Center for Disability Rights, 11015
Westside Center for Independent Living, 10680
Whisper 2000, 3191
Whittier Institute for Diabetes & Endocrinology, 6299
Words+ IST (Infrared, Sound, Touch), 3193
World Institute on Disability, 345
Writing from Within, 11703
Yuba-Sutter Legal Center for Seniors, 11016

Canada

Abbotsford Seniors' Association, 346
Advocacy Centre for the Elderly, 347
Age & Opportunity Inc., 348
Association of Mature Canadians, 349
CARP Canada's Association for the Fifty-Plus, 350
Carefirst Seniors & Community Services Association, 351
Help the Aged, 352
Institute for Life Course and Aging, 353
NWT Seniors' Society, 354

National Institute for the Care of the Elderly, 355
National Pensioners & Senior Citizens Federation, 356
Older Women's Network, 357
Tapestry at Village Gate West, 10601

Colorado

AMC Cancer Research Center Medical Library, 11359
Air Liftunlimited, 3544
Alpine Area Agency on Aging, 627
American Diabetes Association: Mountain States & Pacific/Northwest Regional Office, 6148
American Diabetes Association: Wyoming District Office, 6172
American Society of General Surgeons, 63
Anam Chara Homes, 8234
Apple Ridge Assisted Living Apartments, 8235
Argyle Square, 8236
Atlantis Community, 10681
Atria Inn at Lakewood, 8237
Beatrice Hover Assisted Living, 8238
Beyond Sight, 3449
Bill Dvorak Kayak & Rafting, 12010
Boulder County Aging Services Division, 628
Boulder County Aging Services Division: Elder Rights Program, 11017
Broadmoor Court, 8239
Bye-Bye Decubiti (BBD), 3198
Bye-Bye Decubiti Air Mattress Overlay, 3035
Center For People With Disabilities, 10682
Center for Applied Prevention Research, 7454
Center for Independence, 10683
Charlie Brown's Goodtime Travel, 12011
Collinwood, 8240
Colorado Aging and Adult Services, 629
Colorado Association of Homes & Services for the Aging, 630
Colorado Client Assistance Program, 631
Colorado Department of Aging, 632
Colorado Department of Human Services: Division of Aging and Adult Services, 11018
Colorado Department of Revenue, 633
Colorado Department of Social Service, 11360
Colorado Department of Social Services: Division of Older American Programs, 634, 635
Colorado Developmental Disability Council, 636
Colorado Disability Determination Services, 637
Colorado Division of Mental Health, 638
Colorado Mountain College Senior Nutrition Program, 639
Colorado Protection & Advocacy for Persons with Disabilities, 640
Colorado Protection and Advocacy Agency:The Legal Center at Grand Junction, 11019
Colorado Public Employees Retirement Association, 641

Colorado School for the Deaf and Blind, 11361
Colorado Springs Independence Center, 10684
Colorado Talking Book Library, 11362
Colorado Travel & Tourism Authority, 11954
Colorado Workers Compensation Board, 642
Denver Regional Council of Governments Area Agency on Aging, 643
Devonshire Acres, 121
East Central Colorado: Area Agency on Aging, 644
Eastern Colorado Services for the Disabled, 645
Easy Pivot Transfer Machine, 3370
Elderhaus, 646
Golden Pond, 8241
Grand Villa, 8242
Granville Assisted Living Center, 8243
Harvard Square, 8244
Hear Now, 6363
Hemlock Society USA, 148
Huerfano Las Animas: Area Agency on Aging, 647
International Hearing Dog, 6378
Iron Workers Local 24 Retirees Club International Association of Ironworkers, 648
Jay Cushion, 3210
Kayak and Rafting Expeditions, 12028
Kit Carson And Lincoln Counties RSVP, 649
Larimer County Office on Aging (LCOA), 11020
Legal Center for People with Disabilities and Older People, 11021
Longmont Meals on Wheels, 650
Lumbo-Posture Back Support, 3213
Lyons Golden Gang, 651
MacKenzie Place: Colorado Springs, 8245
MacKenzie Place: Fort Collins, 8246
Museum of Western Colorado: Research Center & Special Library, 11363
National Association of Blind Lawyers, 7657
National Jewish Medical and ResearchCenter, 238
National Prison Hospice Association, 252
National Stroke Association, 7054
Nightingale Suites at Springwood, 8247
Oval Window Audio, 3286
Over the Hill Gang International, 280
Penrose Hospital: Webb Memorial Library, 11364
Pikes Peak Area: Agency on Aging, 652
Professional Respite Care, 12040
RSVP Adams-Arapahoe, 653
RSVP Boulder County, 654
RSVP Colorado West, 655
RSVP High County, 656
RSVP Otero Bent-Crowley Counties, 658
RSVP Pueblo, 659
RSVP Rural Resort Region, 660
RSVP San Luis Valley, 661
RSVP VOA Colorado Branch, 662
RSVP VOA Denver, 663
RSVP Weld County, 664
Railroad Retirement Board: Colorado District Office, 665
Rand-Scot, 3487
Reclining Power Wheelchairs, 3558
Region 8: Administration on Aging (AoA), 666
Retired Enlisted Association (TREA), 302
Rocky Mountain Heart Research Institute, 6890
San Juan Basin Area: Agency on Aging, 668
Sheridan Travel Service, 12044
South Central Colorado Seniors, 669
Sterling House of Arvada, 8248
Sunrise of Boulder, 8249
Superarm Lift, 2994
Telephone Pioneers of America, 7756
Teller Senior Coalition, 670
US Department of Veterans Affairs: Denver Medical Center Library, 11365
US Department of Veterans Affairs: Grand Junction Medical Center Library Service, 11366
US Department of Veterans Affairs: Southern Colorado Healthcare System, 11367
United States Association for Blind Athletes, 7765
University of Colorado: Boulder Communication Disorders Clinic, 6823
University of Colorado: Science Libaray, 11368
Upper Arkansas Area: Agency on Aging, 671
View Pointe, 8250
Weld Library District: Lincoln Park Branch Library, 11369
Winslow Court, 8251

Connecticut

AMI Aquamassage, 3246
Academy Point at Mystic, 8252
American Diabetes Association: Connecticut, 6126
Arbors at Hop Brook, 8253
Atria Crossroads Place, 8255
Atria at Stratford, 8256
BESB Industries, 7530
Bellmarie, 8257
Black Experience, 6175
Bridges at Lake Whitney, 8258
Bridges at the Green, 8259
Bureau of Naval Personnel: Connecticut Retired Activities Office, 672
Bureau of Rehabilitation Services: Disability Determination Services, 673
Center for Disability Rights, 10685
Center for Independent Living of Northwestern Connecticut, 10686
Center for Medicare Advocacy, 11022
Chancellor Gardens of Southington, 8260
Chester Village West, 8261
Cold Springs Commons, 8262
Connecticut Braille Association, 7571
Connecticut Association of Not-for-Profit Providers for the Aging, 674
Connecticut Bar Association: Section on Legal Problems of the Elderly, 11023
Connecticut Board of Education and Services for the Blind, 675
Connecticut Braille Association, 11370, 7572
Connecticut Client Assistance Program, 676
Connecticut Commission on Deaf and Hearing Impaired, 6339
Connecticut Commisson on Aging, 677
Connecticut Council On DevelopmentalDisabilities, 678
Connecticut Department of Aging, 679
Connecticut Department of Mental Health and Addiction Services, 7147
Connecticut Department of Revenue, 680
Connecticut Department of Social Services: Elderly Services Division, 11024
Connecticut Disability Determination Serices, 681
Connecticut Lawyers' Legal Aid to the Elderly Program (CLLAEP), 11025
Connecticut Office of Tourism, 11955
Connecticut Protection & Advocacy for Persons with Disabilities, 682
Connecticut Protection and Advocacy Agency: Office of Protection and Advocacy for Persons with Disabilities, 11026
Connecticut Society to Prevent Blindness, 11371
Connecticut State Library for the Blindand Physically Handicapped, 11372
Connecticut State of Veterans Affairs Department of Rocky Hill: Hospital Services Program, 683
Connecticut Teachers Retirement Board, 684
Cornerstone of Eagle Hill, 7149
Council on Geriatric Cardiology, 6841
Crescent Point at Niantic, 8263
Curtis Home, 8264
Disability Resource Center of Fairfield County (DRCFC), 10687
East Coast Assistance Dogs, 685
East Hill Woods, 8265
Eastern Connecticut Area: Agency on Aging, 686
Edgehill Health Center, 8266
Elim Park Baptist Home, 8267
Essex Meadows, 8268
Evergreen Woods, 8269
Fidelco Guide Dog Foundation, 7588
Gables at Farmington, 8270
Gables at Guilford, 8271
Gardenside Terrace, 8272
Greens at the Greenwich, 8273
Hamilton Heights Place of West Hartford, 8274
Hartford Area Social Security Office, 687
Hartford Hospital Health Science Libraries, 11373
Hartford Hospital: Gerontology Resource Center, 11374
Heights at Avery Heights, 8275
Independence Unlimited Inc., 10688
Laurel Gardens at Milford, 8276
Laurel Gardens of Avon, 8277
Laurel Gardens of Hamden, 8278
Laurel Gardens of Orange, 8279
Laurel Gardens of Woodbridge, 8280
Legal Assistance for Elders in Connecticut, 11027
Legal Services Programs for Elders: Bridgeport, 11028
Legal Services Programs for Elders: Hartford, 11029
Legal Services Programs for Elders: Waterbury, 11030

1073

Geographic Index / Delaware

Legal Services Programs for Elders: Willimantic, 11031
Lockwood Lodge at Ashlar of Newtown, 8281
Marriott's Brighton Gardens of Stamford, 8282
McAuley, 8283
Middlewoods of Farmington, 8284
Middlewoods of Newington, 8285
Miller Memorial Community, 8286
National Old Timers Auto Racing Club, 244
National Theatre of the Deaf, 6419
New Haven Legal Assistance Association (LAA), 11032
No Longer Disabled: The Federal Courts, 11033
North Central Area Agency on Aging, 688
Odyssey Institute Corporation, 7205
Orchards at Southington, 8287
PRIDE Foundation, 281
Pomperaug Woods, 8288
Prevent Blindness Connecticut, 7723
Prevent Blindness New Jersey, 1674
Prevent Blindness Tri-State, 7731
RSVP Central Connecticut, 689
RSVP Central Naugatuck Valley, 690
RSVP Eastern Fairfield County, 691
RSVP Greater Bristol, 692
RSVP Greater Hartford, 693
RSVP Mid State, 694
RSVP Northern Fairfield County, 695
RSVP Southern New London, 696
RSVP Southwestern Connecticut, 697
RSVP Windham-Tolland Counties, 698
Rosedale of Glastonbury, 8289
Rosedale of Trumbull Assisted Living Community, 8290
Shady Oaks Assisted Living, 8291
South Central Connecticut Agency on Aging, 699
Spring Meadows at Trumbull, 8292
State of Vermont Division of Disabilityand Aging Services, 11277
Stony Brook Court, 8293
Suffield by the River, 8294
Summerville at Litchfield Hills, 8295
Summerville at South Windsor, 8296
Sunrise Assisted Living of Stamford, 8297
Sunrise Assisted Living of Wilton, 8298
Tower One Tower East, 8299
US Department of Veterans Affairs, Health & Science Library, 11375
US Department of Veterans Affairs: Healthcare System in West Haven, 11376
University of Connecticut Health Center: Center on Aging, 11377
University of Connecticut in Storrs: Homer Babbidge Library, 11378
Village Gate, 8300
Village at Brookfield Common, 8301
Village at Buckland Court, 8302
Village at East Farms, 8303
Village at South Farms, 8304
Volunteer Center of United Way for Capital Area, 700
Western Connecticut Area: Agency on Aging, 701
Yale University: Behavioral Medicine Clinic, 6108
Yale University: Ribicoff Research Facilities, 6109
Yale University: Vision Research Center, 8060

Delaware

American Diabetes Association: Delaware/Eastern Shore Area Office, 6127
Arden Courts Manorcare Health Services, 8305
Bebee Medical Center/Peach Tree Acres, 8306
Brandywine Assisted Living at Seaside, 8307
Captain's Deck, 8308
Carelink Community Support Services, 10690
Clearinghouse on Abuse and Neglect of the Elderly (CANE), 109
Community Legal Aid Society: Dover, 11034
Community Legal Aid Society: Georgetown, 11035
Community Legal Aid Society: Wilmington, 11036
Delaware Assistive Technology Initiative, 702
Delaware Association for the Blind, 7574
Delaware Association for the Blind, 7575
Delaware Association of Nonprofit Homes for the Aging, 703
Delaware Bar Association Committee on Law and the Elderly, 11037
Delaware Client Assistance Program, 704
Delaware Commission of Veterans Affairs, 705
Delaware Council for Persons with Disabiities, 706
Delaware Department of Education, 707
Delaware Department of Health and Social Services: Division for the Visually Impaired, 708
Delaware Developmental Disability Council, 709
Delaware Disability Determination Services, 710
Delaware Division for the Visually Impaired, 7576
Delaware Division of Alcoholism, Drug Abuse & Mental Health, 7150
Delaware Division of Libraries for the Blind and Physically Handicapped, 11379
Delaware Division of Revenue, 711
Delaware Division of Services for Aging Adults with Physical Disabilities, 712
Delaware Division of Services for Aging and Adults with Physical Disabilities, 11038
Delaware Drug Abuse & Mental Health, 7151
Delaware Protection & Advocacy for Persons with Disabilities, 713
Delaware Tourism Office, 11956
Delaware Workers Compensation Board, 714
Elder Wood Village of Dover, 8309
Forwood Manor Assisted Living, 8310
Foulk Manor North, 8311
Foulk Manor South, 8312
Gardens at White Chapel, 8313
Green Meadows at Dover, 8314
Heritage at Milford, 8315
Independent Resources-Wilmington, 10691
Lorelton, 8316
Methodist Country House, 8317
Methodist Manor House, 8318
Millcroft Assisted Living, 8319
Modern Maturity Center, 715
National Center on Elder Abuse, 209
Pioneer House, 8320
RSVP New Castle County, 716
RSVP Sussex County, 717
Rockland Place, 8321
Seaford Center Assisted Living, 8322
Shipley Manor Assisted Living, 8323
Somerford House, 8324
Somerford Place, 8325
Stockley Center, 8326
Sussex County Assistive Technology Resource Center sussex coun, 10692
US Department of Veterans Affairs: Health Administration Medical Center, 11380
University of Delaware: Center for Drug and Alcohol Studies, 7480
Village at Green Valley, 8327
Westminster Village, 8079, 8328

District of Columbia

AARP Legal Advocacy Group, 11039
ACB Government Employees, 7493
ACB Radio Amateurs, 7494
ACB Social Service Providers, 7495
Access Travel: Airports, 11910
Administration on Aging (AoA), 1
Administration on Aging: Office of Field Operations, 2
Administration on Aging: Office of Program Development, 3
Administration on Aging: Office of State and Community Programs, 4
Administration on Developmental Disabilities, 5
Administrative Advocacy Clinic/Advocates for Older People, 11040
Alcohol & Drug Abuse Services Administration, 7128
Alexander Graham Bell Association for the Deaf: Kentucky Chapter, 6305
Alexander Graham Bell Association for the Deaf, 6307
Alexander Graham Bell Association forthe Deaf and Hard of Hearing, 6306
Alliance on Aging and Vision Loss, 7500
America's Health Insurance Plans, 7
American Academy of Nursing, 10
American Association of Colleges of Nursing, 17
American Association of Homes & Services for the Aging, 718
American Association of Homes and Services for the Aging: Research and Information Center, 11381
American Association of Retired Persons: Research Information Center, 11382
American Benefits Council, 29
American Blind Lawyers Association, 7504
American College of Cardiology, 11533
American Council of Life Insurers, 37
American Council of the Blind, 11383

Geographic Index / District of Columbia

American Diabetes Association: Districtof Columbia, 6128
American Federation of School Administrators, 40
American Foundation for the Blind: Washington DC, 7513
American Health Care Association, 41
American Health Care Association: Information Resource Center, 11384
American Hotel and Motel Association, 12007
American Licensed Practical Nurses Association, 44
American Medical Rehabilitation Providers Association (AMRPA), 48
American Psychological Society, 56
American Registry of Pathology, 58
American Society of Internal Medicine, 64
Amtrak Railways, 11914
Army Distaff Foundation, 75
Asian American Center for Justice, 77
Association for Gerontology in Higher Education, 80, 11385
Association for Professionals in Infection Control and Epidemiology, 81
Audio Book Contractors, 3447
B'nai B'rith Senior Citizens Housing Committe (BBSCHC), 89
Better Hearing Institute, 6322
Blind Veterans Rehabilitation Centers and Clinics, 7539
Blinded Veterans Association, 7541
Bureau of Naval Personnel: District of Columbia Retired Affairs Office, 719
CAPCOM, 6798
Capital Assistance Program for Elderly and Persons with Disabilities, 93
Center for Adult Learning and Educational Credentials, 98
Center for the Advancement of State Community Services Programs (CASCSP), 100
Civil Rights Compliance Activities, 107
Civil Rights of Institutionalized Persons Division, 108
Clark Tibbitts Award, 2623
Clearinghouse on Disability Information (CDI), 110
Client Assistance Program: Office of Program Operations, 111
Columbia Lighthouse for the Blind, 7570
Commission on Law and Aging, 113
Continuing Care Accreditation Commission, 114
Deaf REACH, 6346
Deafness and Communicative Disorders, 117
Deafness and Communicative Disorders Branch, 6349
Deafpride, 6350
Demonstration Grants to States with Respect to Alzheimer's Disease, Health Resources & Services, 118
Department of Veterans Affairs, 119
Diplomatic and Consular Officers, Retired, 122
Distinguished Mentorship in Gerontology Award, 2628
Distinguished Service in Aging Award, 2629
District of Columbia, 11957
District of Columbia Association of Nonprofit Services for the Aging, 721

District of Columbia Bar: Individual Rights Section, 11041
District of Columbia Center for Independent Living (DCCIL), 10689
District of Columbia Office on Aging, 722, 11042
District of Columbia Public Library, 11386
District of Columbia Public Library: Blind and Physically Handicapped, 11387
District of Columbia Public Library: Librarian for the Deaf Community, 11388
District of Columbia Rehabilitation Services, 723
District of Columbia Retirement Board, 724
District of Columbia Worker Compensation Board, 725
Donald P. Kent Award, 2630
Durward K. McDaniel Ambassador Award, 2631
Easter Seals Project ACTION, 12015
Eldercare Locator, 124
Employee Benefit Research Institute, 11389
Employee Benefits Security Administration, 127
Employment Discrimination: Age, 128
Employment Discrimination: Disabled, 129
Equal Employment Advisory Council, 11043
Equal Employment Opportunity Commission, 130
Equal Employment Opportunity: Civil Rights Division, 131
Excellence in Practice Award, 2634
Eye Bank Association of America, 7586
Families USA Foundation, 133
Federal Bar Association, 11044
Federal Council on the Aging: Office of the Secretary, 134
Federal Trade Commission, 135
Foster Grandparent Program, 139
Friends-In-Art, 7593
Fund for Assuring an Independent Retirement, 141
Gallaudet University, 6359
Gallaudet University Library Deaf Collection, 11390
Galludet University/Alumni House, 12021
Generations United, 726
Geneva Mathiasen Award, 2635
George Card Award, 2636
Georgetown University: Research Resources Facility, 6873
Glenn Foundation Award, 2639
Gray Panthers, 144
Gray Panthers Metropolitan, 727
Guide Dog Users, 7599
HEATH Resource Center, 146
Health Promotion Institute, 147
Hearing Industries Association, 6369
Hobart Jackson Social Responsibility Award, 2642
Home Equity Conversion Mortgages: Office of Insured Single Family Housing, 149
Hospice Association of America, 151
Hospice Foundation of America (HFA), 152
Housing for the Elderly or Disabled, 154
Howard University Social Work Library, 11391
Independent Living Services for Older Individuals who are Blind, 6375
Independent Visually Impaired Enterprisers, 7613

Information, Protection & Advocacy for Persons with Disabilities, 728
Innovation of the Year Awards, 2643
International Organization for the Education of the Hearing Impaired, 6383
Irving Diener Award, 2644
Ivins, Phillips, Barker Library, 11392
Jean Camper Cahn Award, 2648
Judge David L Bazelon Center for Mental Health Law, 11394
Kentucky Chapter: Alexander Graham Bell Association for the Deaf, 6388
Laurent Clerc National Deaf Education Center, 11395
Legal Counsel for the Elderly, 11045
Library Users of America, 7631
Louise B Gerrard Award, 2651
Major General Melvin J. Maas Achievement Award, 2652
Mayor's Committee on Persons with Disabilities, 729
Media & Captioning for Individuals with Disabilities, 6392
Medicare Hospital Insurance, 167
Meritorious Service Award, 2654
Mildred M. Seltzer Distinguished Service Recognition, 2656
Mortgage Insurance and Rental Housing foe Elderly, 172
NUCEA Divisional Awards, 2659
Nathan Shock New Investigator Award, 2660
National AFL-CIO Cope Retiree Program, 180
National Academy of Social Insurance, 11396
National Adult Day Services Association, 183
National Alliance of Blind Students, 7653
National Alliance of Senior Citizens Library, 11397
National Association for Home Care and Hospice (NAHC), 185
National Association of Area Agencies on Aging, 188
National Association of Blind Teachers, 7659
National Association of County Aging Programs, 190
National Association of Nutrition and Aging Services Programs (NANASP), 194
National Association of Older Worker Employment, 195
National Association of State Units on Aging, 202
National Association of the Deaf: Legal Defense Fund, 11398
National Caucus and Center on Black Aged, 206
National Center for Voluntary Leadership in Aging, 207
National Center on Arts and the Aging, 208
National Citizen's Coalition for Nursing Home Reform (NCCNHR), 730
National Citizens Coalition for Nursing Home Reform, 210
National Civil Rights Clearinghouse Library, 11399
National Coalition on Rural Aging, 211
National Committee for Quality Healthcare, 212

1075

National Committee for Responsive Philanthropy, 213
National Committee for the Prevention of Elder Abuse, 214
National Committee to Preserve Social Security and Medicare (NCPSSM), 215
National Conference on Public Employee Retirement Systems, 216
National Council of Social Security Management Associations, 217
National Council on Aging: Ollie A Randall Library, 11400
National Council on Child Abuse (NCCAFV), 218
National Council on Disability, 219
National Council on the Aging, 220
National Crime Prevention Council, 7191
National Endowment for the Arts: Office for Special Constituencies, 222
National Graduate University LibraryCapitol Hill Campus, 11401
National Health Information Center, 227
National Hispanic Council on Aging, 228
National Information Center on Deafness, 11402, 6414
National Information and Referral Support Center (NIRSC), 230
National Institute of Senior Housing, 231
National Institute on Adult Daycare, 232
National Institute on Age, Work and Retirement, 233
National Institute on Community-Based Long-Term Care, 234
National Institute on Financial Issues and Services for Elders, 235
National Interfaith Coalition on Aging, 237
National Legal Support for Elderly People with Mental Disabilities Project, 239
National Library Service for the Blind and Physically Handicapped, 11403, 7689
National Long-Term Care Ombudsman Resource Center (NLTCORC), 240
National Organization on Disability (NOD), 249
National Osteoporosis Foundation, 250
National Retired Teachers Association, 257
National Senior Citizens Law Center, 259, 11008, 11046, 11046
National Senior Service Corps, 261
National Senior Service Corps Directors Associations, 262
National Tax Association, 264
National Women's Health Network, 266
Ned E. Freeman Excellence in Writing Award, 2664
Non-Discrimination in Federally Assisted Programs, 271
Non-Discrimination in the Community Development Block Grant Program, 272
Ollie A. Randall Award, 2668
Outstanding Continuing Education Student Awards, 2669
PXE International, 1308
Paralyzed Veterans of America (PVA), 11047
Parkinson Association of South Dakota, 6969
Parkinsons Action Network, 6977
Part A Title III: Ombudsman Services for Older Individuals, 282

Part A Title VI: Grants to Indian Tribes and Part B Title VI: Grants to Native Hawaiians, 283
Part B Title III: Grants for Supportive Services and Senior Centers, 284
Part C Title III: Nutrition Services, 285
Part F Title 111: Preventive Health Services Special Programs for the Aging, 286
Part G Title 111: Prevention of Abuse, Neglect and Exploitation of Older Individuals, 287
Pension Benefit Guaranty Corporation, Office of the General Counsel Library, 11404
Pension Rights Center, 289
Pension to Veterans, Surviving Spouses, and Children, 290
People Animals Love, 291
President's Committee for People with Intellectual Disabilities (PCPID), 294
Prevention of Blindness Society of Metropolitan Washington, 7733
Rebuilding Together with Christmas in April, 300
Retired and Senior Volunteer Program, 304
Richard Kalish Innovative Publication Award, 2679
Robert S. Bray Award, 2681
Robert W. Kleemeier Award, 2682
Senate Special Committee on Aging, 308
Senior Companion Program, 309
Small Business Administration (SBA), 312
Speech Simulation Research Foundation, 6448
State Public Official Award for Significant Legislative Achievement, 2686
Tax Counseling for the Elderly: Taxpayers Services, 322
Tele-Consumer Hotline, 6449
Travelers Aid Society, 12052
Trustee of the Year Award, 2687
US Commission on Civil Rights: Civil Rights Discrimination Complaints, 324
US Department of Education: Office of Civil Rights, 325
US Department of Health & Human Services, 326
US Department of Housing & Urban Development: Fair Housing and Equal Opportunity Hotline, 327
US Department of Justice, 328
US Department of Labor, 11048
US Department of Transportation, 330
US Department of Veterans Affairs, 331
US Equal Employment Opportunity Commission, 11406
US Library of Congress Handicapped Hotline, 332
US Office of Personnel Management, 333
US Social Security Administration: Washington Library, 11407
Vernon Henley Media Award, 2688
Veterans Information and Assistance, 337
Veterans Prosthetic Appliance, Rehabilitation and Prosthetics, 338
Veterans' Advocate, 11049
Visiting Nurse Association of America, 340
Visually Impaired Data Processors International, 7778
Volta Bureau Library, 11408
Volunteers for Abused/Neglected Children, 341

Washington D.C. Protection and AdvocacyAgency, 11050
Washington Hearing and Speech Center, 6461
Washington University Medical Center, 7049
Washington Watch, 11051
Weatherization Assistance for Low-Income Persons: Conservation and Renewable Energy, 342
Widowed Persons Service Award, 2690

Florida

ARC Gateway, 731
Abbey Delray Health Center, 8329
Albany Avenue Adult Congregate Living Facility, 8330
Alderman Oaks Retirement Center, 8331
Alliance for Aging, 732
Alterra Clare Bridge of Bradenton, 8332
Alterra Sterling House of Jacksonville, 8333
Alterra Sterling House of Punta Gorda, 8334
Alterra Sterling House of Tavares, 8335
Alterra Sterling House of Venice, 8336
Alterra Wynwood of Boynton Beach East, 8337
Alterra Wynwood of Dunedin, 8338
Altria Windsor Woods, 8339
American Association of Physician Specialists, 24
American Diabetes Association: South Coastal Regional Office, Central Florida Area, 6163
American Neurotology Society, 6314
American Radiological Nurses Association, 57
American Society of Deaf Social Workers, 6315
American Society of Retired Dentists, 70
American Yoga Association, 73
Amphibious ATV Distributors, 3417
Apollo Gardens Retirement Residence, 8340
Arbor Village of North Tampa, 8341
Arkenstone, 3076
Assisted Living Center at Azalea Trace, 8342
Assistive Technology Educational Network of Florida, 733
Atria Wekiwa Springs, 8343
Autumn West, 8344
Avante Terrace at Boca Raton, 8345
Back-Huggar Pillow, 3196
Bahia Oaks Lodge, 8346
Barrington Place, 8347
BathEase, 3004
Bay Area Legal Services, 11052
Bay Breeze Nursing & Retirement Center, 8348
Bay County Council on Aging, 1342
Bay Gardens Retirement Village, 8349
Bay Oaks Home for the Aged, 8350
Bay Village of Sarasota, 8351
Bayview Gardens, 8352
Beneva Park Club, 8353
Benton House, 8354
Bon Secours Place at Healthpark, 8355
Bon Secours Place at St Petersburg, 8356
Braille Blazer Printer, 3086
Brentwood Retirement Community, 8357

Geographic Index / Florida

Brevard Association for Advancement of the Blind, 7552
Brevard Association for the Advancement of the Blind, 7553
Brevard County Community Services Council, 734
Bridge Assisted Living at Life Care Center, 8358
Bridgewater at Waterman Village, 8359
Brighton Gardens by Marriott of Maitland, 8360
Bristol Park of Coral Springs, 8361
Broward County Area: Agency on Aging, 735
Broward County Talking Book Library, 11409
Broward Meals on Wheels, 736
Bureau of Naval Personnel: Florida Retired Affairs Office-Jacksonville, 737
Bureau of Naval Personnel: Milton Retired Activities Office, 738
Bureau of Naval Personnel: Orlando Retired Activities Office, 739
Bureau of Naval Personnel: Pensacola Retired Activities Office, 740
CEH, 11917
Cabot Reserve on the Green, 8362
Caring and Sharing Center for Independent Living, 10693
Carpenter's Creek by Encore Senior Living, 8363
Center for Independent Living of Broward, 10695
Center for Independent Living of Flordia-Lecanto, 10696
Center for Independent Living of Jacksonville, 10697
Center for Independent Living of North Central Florida, 10694, 10698
Center for Independent Living of Northern Florida / Ability 1st, 10699
Center for Independent Living of South Florida, 10700
Center for Independent Living of Southwest Florida, 10701
Center for Independent Living-Central Florida, 10702
Center for Independent Living-Northwest Florida, 10703
Chambrel at Island Lake, 8364
Clare Bridge of Leesburg, 8365
Clare Bridge of Tequesta, 8366
Claude Pepper Award, 2624
Coalition for Independent Living Options, 741, 10704
Collier County Association for the Blind, 7569
Compu-Lenz, 3099
Conference of Educational Administrators Serving the Deaf, 6338
Coral Landing Assisted Living Residences, 8367
Coral Plaza Retirement Residence, 8368
Country Residence, 8369
Court at Plam Aire, 8370
Cross Key Manor, 8371
Crown Pointe of Sebring, 8372
Cypress Village, 8373
Department of Health & Rehabilitative Services, 742
Disabled Driver's Mobility Guide, 11922

Donnelly Place-A Classic Residence by Hyatt, 8374
East Central Florida Area: Agency on Aging, 743
East Ridge Retirement Village, 8375
Edwinola Retirement Community, 8376
Enabling Technologies Company, 3112
Epworth Village Retirement Community, 8377
Fifty Five Years & Up, 744
Florida Association of Homes for the Aging, 745
Florida Bar Association: Lawyer Referral Service, 11053
Florida Client Assistance Program, 746
Florida Council on Aging, 747
Florida Department of Administration: State Retirement Commission, 748
Florida Department of Aging, 749
Florida Department of Children, Families and Elderly Services, 750
Florida Department of Elder Affairs Program of Aging and Adult Services, 751
Florida Department of Health & Rehabilitative Services, 7159
Florida Department of Labor and Employment Security, 11410
Florida Department of Mental Health and Rehabilitative Services, 752
Florida Department of Revenue, 753
Florida Department of Veterans Affairs, 754
Florida Developmental Disabilities Council, 755
Florida Division of Blind Services, 11411
Florida Division of Vocational Rehabilitation, 756
Florida Dog Guides F.T.D., 757
Florida Dog Guides for the Deaf, 6356
Florida Independent Living Council, 10705
Florida Instructional Materials Center for the Visually Impaired, 11412
Florida Language, Speech and Hearing Association, 6357
Florida Legal Services: Tallahassee Office, 11054
Florida Living Center, 8378
Florida Lutheran Retirement Center, 8379
Florida Ophthalmic Institute, 8040
Florida Protection & Advocacy for Persons with Disabilities, 758
Florida Retirement Division, 759
Florida School for the Deaf and Blind, 11413
Focus: Library Service to Older Adults: People With Disabilities, 11414
Forest Trace at Inverrary, 8380
Fountainview by Marriott, 8381
Freedom Inn at Tarpon Springs, 8382
Ft Lauderdale Retirement Home, 8383
Gables of Lake Mary, 8384
George H. Snyder Enterprises, 3551
Golden Cove Assisted Living Facility, 8385
Gray Panthers of North Dade, 760
Gray Panthers of South Dade, 761
Gulf Coast Village Assisted Living, 8386
Gulf Coast Village Retirement Community, 8387
Gulf Winds, 8388
Hampton Court Independent & AssistedLiving, 8389
Hampton Manor Belleview, 8390

Harbor Place at Port St Lucie, 8391
Hearing Impaired Persons of Charlotte County Florida, 6367, 6368
Heart of Florida United Way Volunteer Center, 762
Henderson Village, 8392
Heritage Oaks Senior Housing, 8393
Heron House, 8394
Highland Terrace Assisted Living Community, 8395
Hillsborough County Talking Book Library Tampa-Hillsborough County Public Library, 11415
Home Healthcare Nurses Association (HHNA), 150
Homewood Residence at Boca Raton, 8396
Homewood Residence at Boynton Beach, 8397
Homewood Residence at Delray Beach, 8398
Homewood Residence at Freedom Plaza, 8399
Hygenics Direct Company, 3260
Iberia Airlines of Spain, 11930
Indian River Estates-East, 8400
Inn at Cypress Village, 8401
Inn at University Village, 8402
Jacksonville Public Library, 11416
Jacksonville Subregional Talking Book Library, 11417
John F Germany Public Library: Special Collections, 11393
John Knox Village of Central Florida, 8403
John Knox Village of Florida, 8404
John Knox Village of Tampa Bay, 8405
Just Like Home at Orange City, 8406
Kiva of Mount Dora, 8407
Kiva of Palatka, 8408
Kobernick/Anchin, 8409
Kristianna's Assisted Living Facility, 8410
Lake Towers Retirement Community, 8411
Laptops/Word Processors, 3126
Lazy Days RV Center, 2979
Lee County Subregional Library for the Blind and Physically Handicapped, 11418
Lighthouse for the Blind of Miami, 7635
Living Legends Retirement Center, 8412
Louis de la Parte Florida Mental Health Institute, 6040
Loving Care for the Elderly South, 8413
Mangrove Bay, 8414
Marriott's Brighton Garden of Port St Lucie, 8415
Marriott's Brighton Gardens of Boca Raton, 8416
Marriott's Brighton Gardens of Boynton, 8417
Marriott's Brighton Gardens of WPB, 8418
Marriott's Park Summit, 8419
Masonic Home of Florida, 8420
Mayflower Assisted Living Facility, 8421
Meals on Wheels, 763
Mease Manor, 8422
Merrill Gardens at Lutz, 8423
Merrill Gardens at Orange City, 8424
Miami Dade County Retired and Senior Volunteer Program, 764
Miami Heart Institute, 6883
Miami Lighthouse for the Blind, 7646
Miami-Dade Public Library: Genealogy Collection, 11419
Moorings Park, 8425

Geographic Index / Georgia

National Association of Veterans Program Administrators, 204
National Gerontological Nursing Association, 226
National Parkinson Foundation, 6956
National Parkinson Foundation Adult Day Care Center, 6957
National Parkinson Foundation Hotline, 6958
North Florida Area: Agency on Aging, 765
Northeast Florida Area: Agency on Aging, 766
Northpark-A Classic Residence by Hyatt, 8426
Okada Specialty Guide Dogs, 6428
Orange County Library System Audio-Visual Department, 11420
Orange County Library System: Genealogy Department, 11421
Orlando Lutheran Towers, 8427
Osceola County Council on Aging, 767
Pac-All Wheelchair Carrier, 3557
Palm Beach Treasure Coast Area: Agency on Aging, 768
Parkinson Association of Florida West Coast, 6962
Parkinson Association of South West Florida, 6970
Parkinson Association of Greater Daytona, 6973
Parkinson Rehabilitation Center, 6975
Phillip Roy, 3151
RSVP Alachua County, 769
RSVP Big Bend, 770
RSVP Broward County, 771
RSVP Central Panhandle, 772
RSVP Citrus County, 773
RSVP Collier County, 774
RSVP Duval County, 775
RSVP Flagler County, 776
RSVP Hernando County, 777
RSVP Hillsborough County, 778
RSVP Indian River County, 779
RSVP Lake County Senior Citizens Mid Florida Community Services, 780
RSVP Manatee North Sarasota Counties, 782
RSVP Martin County, 784
RSVP Okaloosa County, 785
RSVP Palm Beach County, 786
RSVP Pasco County, 787
RSVP Pinellas County, 788
RSVP Santa Rosa, 789
RSVP Sarasota/Charlotte Counties, 790
RSVP St John's County, 791
RSVP St Lucie County, 792
RSVP Volunteer Services of United Way Palm Beach County, 793
RSVP Volusia County, 794
Railroad Retirement Board: JacksonvilleDistrict Office, 795
Sanford Senior Center, 796
Seasons: A Classic Residence by Hyatt, 8428
Self-Reliance, 10706
Seminole County Volunteer Program, 797
Senior Solutions of Southwest Florida, 798
Seniors First, 799
Social Security: Miami Disability Determination, 800
Social Security: Orlando Disability Determination, 801
Social Security: Tallahassee Disability Determination, 802
Social Security: Tampa Disability Determination, 803
Sodium Information Hotline, 6845
South Florida Advocacy Center for Persons with Disabilities, 11055
Southeast Regional Center: Canine Companions for Independence, 7747
Space Coast Center for Independent Living, 10707
Stanford Centre, 8429
State of Florida, 11988
Sterling Aventura, 8430
Suncoast Center for Independent Living, 10708
Sunrise Atrium of Boca Raton, 8431
Surf Chair, 3540
Sylvester Comprehensive Cancer Center,Cancer Information Service, 11422
TALKBACK Wireless Doorbell Intercom, 3172
Talking Book Library, Miami and DadePublic Library System, 11423
Talking Books Library for the Blind and Physically Handicapped, 11424
Tallahassee Advocacy Center for Personswith Disabilities, 11056
Tampa Advocacy Center for Persons with Disabilities, 11057
Tampa Bay Regional Planning Council-Area Agency on Aging, 804
Tampa Lighthouse for the Blind, 7753
US Department of Veterans Affairs Medical Library, 11425
US Department of Veterans Affairs and Center Learning Resources Service Library, 11426
US Department of Veterans Affairs, Hospital Library, 11427
US Railroad Retirement Board: Tampa District Office, 805
United Way of Central Florida, 806
University of Florida: Center for Governmental Responsibility, 11430
University of Miami School of Medicine: Department of Neurology, 7123
University of Miami: Bascom Palmer Eye Institute, 8057
University of Miami: Diabetes Research Institute, 6287
University of South Florida Library: Special Collections Department, 11058
Victoria Villa Assisted Living, 8432
Volunteer Jacksonville, 807
West Central Florida Area: Agency on Aging, 808
West Florida Regional Library, 11431
Westminster Towers, 8433
Wheelchair Getaways, 12059
William Beardall Senior Center, 809
Winter Springs Senior Center, 810
Workers Compensation Board Florida, 811

Georgia

AARP Southeast Regional Office, 812
ADA Technical Assistance Program, 813
Adjustable Rigid Chair, 3042
American Academy of Oral and Maxillofacial Radiology, 11
American Association of Occupational Health Nurses, 22
American Correctional Health Services Association, 36
American Diabetes Association: Atlanta Metro Area Office, Georgia, 6117
American Diabetes Association: Columbus District Office, 6125
American Foundation for the Blind: National Literacy Center, 7508
American Foundation for the Blind: Atlanta, 7509
Atlanta Council of Younger Lawyers: Committee on Legal Services to the Elderly, 11059
Atlanta Legal Aid Society: Atlanta, 11060
Atlanta Legal Aid Society: Decatur, 11061
Atlanta Legal Aid Society: East Point, 11062
Atlanta Legal Aid Society: Lawrenceville, 11063
Atlanta Legal Aid Society: Marietta, 11064
Atlanta Regional Commission: Aging Services Division, 814
Augusta-Richmond County Public Library, 11432
Bainbridge Subregional Library for theBlind, 11433
Belmont Village at Buckhead, 8434
Belmont Village at Johns Creek, 8435
CEL Regional Library, 11434
Canine Assistance for the Disabled, 6325
Cave Spring Library, 11435
Cedartown Library, 11436
Central Savannah River Regional Area:Agency on Aging, 816
Champion 1000, 3505
Champion 2000, 3506
Champion 3000, 3507
Chattahoochee Flint Area: Agency on Aging, 817
Coastal Georgia Regional Development Center Area: Agency on Aging, 818
DHR Division of Aging Services, 819
Delta Shuttle, 11920
Duro-Med Industries, 3255
Eagle Sportschairs, 3513
Emory University Laboratory for Ophthalmic Research, 8039
Fulton Public Library Learning Center, 11437
Georgia Advocacy Office, 820
Georgia Association of Homes and Services for the Aging, 821
Georgia Client Assistance Program, 822
Georgia Department of Aging, 823
Georgia Department of Industry Trade & Tourism, 11958
Georgia Department of Labor: Disability Adjudication Section, 824
Georgia Department of Revenue, 825
Georgia Department of Veterans Service, 826
Georgia Division for Aging Services, 11065
Georgia Division of Mental Health and Substance Abuse, 7161
Georgia Division of Mental Health: Developmental Disabilities & Addictive Diseases, 827

Geographic Index / Hawaii

Georgia Employees' Retirement System, 828
Georgia Industries for the Blind, 7594
Georgia Office of Aging, 829
Georgia Protection and Advocacy Agency, 11066
Georgia Regional Library, 11438
Georgia State Board of Workers' Compansation, 830
Georgia Statewide Independent Living Council, 10710
Georgia Teachers Retirement System, 831
Govenor's Council on Developmental Disabilities, 832
Gwinnett Council for Seniors, 833
Hall County Library System, 11439
Heart of Georgia Altamaha AAA, 834
Heart of Georgia Area: Agency on Aging, 835
Helen Keller National Center for Deaf & Blind Southeast Regional Office, 836
Henry County Council on Aging, 837
LEVO Standing Wheelchairs, 3523
La Fayette Subregional Library for the Blind and Physically Disabled, 11440
Legacy Link, 838
Living Independence for Everyone (LIFE) Center for Independent Living, 10711
Lumex Recliner, 3046
Lumex's Cushions and Mattresses, 3214
Macon Library for the Blind and Physically Handicapped, 11441
Middle Flint Regional Development Center Area: Agency on Aging, 839
Middle Georgia Regional Development Center Area: Agency on Aging, 840
Mount Carmel Personal Care, 8436
National Families in Action, 7192
Northeast Georgia Area: Agency on Aging, 841
Oconee Regional Library, 11442
Office on Smoking and Health, 7207
Plantation South at Duluth, 8437
Plantation South at Dunwoody, 8438
Posture-Glide Lounger, 3527
RSVP Albany County, 842
RSVP Coosa Valley, 843
RSVP Northeast Georgia, 844
RSVP Savannah, 845
Railroad Retirement Board: Georgia District Office, 846
Region 4: Administration on Aging (AoA), 847
Remington House, 8439
Rent-A-Van-Handicapped Driver Services, 2991
ResCare Home Care, 848
Retired Affairs Office: Kings Bay Office, 849
Rockmart Library, 11443
Rome Subregional Library Service for People with Disabilities, 11444
Savannah Court, 8440
Senior Job Bank, 310
Social Security: Atlanta Disability Determination, 850
Southeast Georgia Regional Development Center Area: Agency on Aging (SEGA), 851
Southeastern Region: Helen Keller National Center, 7748
Southern Plantation, 8441

Sowega Council on Aging: Georgia Division of Aging Services, 852
Sportaid, 3537
State Guard Association of the United States, 319
Sweetwater Springs, 8442
Tapestry House, 8443
US Department of Veterans Affairs: CarlVinson Medical Center Library, 11446
Walton County Senior Citizens Council, 853
Walton Options for Independent Living, 10712
Wheelchair Aide, 3562
Winthrop at Buckhead, 8444
Winthrop at Tucker, 8445
Yellow Brick House, 8446

Hawaii

American Diabetes Association: Hawaii Area Office, 6134
Assistive Technology Resource Centers of Hawaii, 854
Bureau of Naval Personnel: Hawaii Retired Activities Office, 855
Center for Independent Living-East Hawaii, 10713
Center for Independent Living-West Hawaii, 10714
Communications & Disabilities Action Board, 856
Disability Determination Branch, 857
Handi-Cabs of the Pacific, 12024
Hawaii Alcohol and Drug Abuse Division, 7164
Hawaii Center for Independent Living, 10715
Hawaii County Office of Aging, 858
Hawaii Department of Adult Mental Health, 859
Hawaii Department of Defense: Office of Veterans Services, 860
Hawaii Department of Health: Commission on Persons with Disabilities, 861
Hawaii Department of Health: Disability and Communication Access Board, 862
Hawaii Disability Compensation Division: Department of Labor and Indian Relations, 863
Hawaii Disability Rights Center, 864
Hawaii Disability Rights Center: Honolulu, 11067
Hawaii Executive Office on Aging, 865
Hawaii Planning Council on Developmental Disabilities, 866
Hawaii State Council on Developmental Disabilities, 867
Hawaii State Employees' Retirement System, 868
Hawaii Tourism Office, 11960
Hawaiian Airlines, 11927
Ho'opono Services for the Blind, 7607
Ho'opono Workshop for the Blind, 7608
Honolulu County Elderly Affairs Division, 869
Kauai County Office of Elderly Affairs, 870
Legal Aid Society of Hawaii, 11068
Legal Aid Society of Hawaii: Hilo, 11069
Legal Aid Society of Hawaii: Honolulu, 11070

Legal Aid Society of Hawaii: Kaunakakai, 11071
Legal Aid Society of Hawaii: Lanai City, 11072
Legal Aid Society of Hawaii: Lihu'e, 11073
Legal Aid Society of Hawaii: Maui, 11074
Maui County Office on Aging: Department of Housing and Human Concerns, 871
Over the Rainbow, 12039
Parkinson Association of Hawaii, 6964
RSVP Hawaii County, 872
RSVP Kauai, 873
RSVP Maui County, 874
RSVP Oahu, 875
Regency at Hualalai, 10716
State of Hawaii: Department of Health &Executive Office on Aging, 11075
Statewide Independent Living Council-Hawaii, 10717
University of Hawaii at Manoa: William S Richardson School of Law, 11076

Idaho

Aarenbrooke Place: Ashley Manor, 8447
Adult Residential Care Home, 8448
Alterra Wynwood at Riverplace, 8449
Alterra Wynwood at Twin Falls, 8450
Americare-Creekview, 8451
Americare-Delphic, 8452
Americare-Hiland, 8453
Americare-Lomax I, 8454
Americare-Pendlebury, 8455
Annabelle House, 8456
Apple Valley Residential Care, 8457
Area Two: Agency on Aging, 876
Arrowhead Acres Estate, 8458
Ashley Manor Care Centers-Harmony, 8459
Ashley Manor Care Centers-Highmont, 8460
Ashley Manor Care Centers-Nampa, 8461
Ashley Manor-Beverly Hills, 8462
Aspen Grove Assisted Living-Bellevue, 8463
Aspen Grove Assisted Living-Gooding, 8464
Aspen Grove Assisted Living-Idaho Falls, 8465
Aspen Grove Assisted Living-Lava Hot Sprrings, 8466
Aspen Springs Pioneer Home, 8467
Assisted Living on Shamrock, 8468
Autumn Haven I, 8469
Autumn Haven II, 8470
Bannock Street Place, 8471
Beehive Homes of Grangeville, 8472
Beehive Homes of Idaho I, 8473
Beehive Homes of Idaho II, 8474
Beehive Homes of Idaho VI, 8475
Beehive Homes of North Idaho, 8476
Beehive Homes of Rigby, 8477
Beehive Homes-Mountain Home, 8478
Big Bounder Power Wheelchair, 3500
Birch Avenue Residential Care, 8479
Birchwood Retirement Estate, 8480
Bounder Plus Power Wheelchair, 3502
Bounder Power Wheelchair, 3503
Bridgeview Estates, 8481
Brookside Landing, 8482
Burley Care Assisted Living, 8483

Capital City Assisted Living-Spaulding, 8484
Caribou County Senior Citizens Center, 877
Carousel Homes I, 8485
Carousel Homes II, 8486
Cascade Assisted Living, 8487
Cedar Crest Residential Care, 8488
Cedar Draw Living Center, 8489
Cenoma House, 8490
Clark House, 8491
Clearwater House Assisted Living Concept, 8492
Coeur D'Alene Home, 8493
Community Restorium, 8494
Comprehensive Advocacy: Boise, 11077
Comprehensive Advocacy: Moscow, 11078
Comprehensive Advocacy: Pocatello, 11079
Cotttages of Emmett, 8495
Country Care at Cottonwood, 8497
Country Inn, 8498
Country Meadows, 8499
Creekside Care Center, 8500
Desano Place Residential Care, 8501
Disability Action Center Northwest, 10718
Discovery Care Centre of Salmon, 8502
Eastern Idaho Special Services Agency Area: Agency on Aging, 879
Eli M. Oboler Library: Health Services, 11448
Elite Care, 8503
Evergreen Idaho Health Care Sandpoint, 8504
Fairwinds-Coeur d'Alene, 8505
Fairwinds-Sand Creek, 8506
Hayden Country Guest Home, 8507
Hayden Country Guest Home III, 8508
Heritage Parkview, 8509
Heritage Retirement Center-Boise, 8510
Heritage Retirement Center-Twin Falls, 8511
Hettinger Living Center, 8512
Highland Estates, 8513
Highland Hills, 8514
Hillcrest, 8515
Homedale Senior Center, 880
Huckleberry Retirement Homes II, 8516
Huckleberry Retirement Homes III, 8517
Huckleberry Retirement Homes IV, 8518
Idaho Commission On Aging, 881
Idaho Commission for the Blind, 7611
Idaho Commission on Aging, 882, 11080
Idaho Council on Developmental Disabilities, 883
Idaho Department of Alcoholism & Substance Abuse, 7166
Idaho Developmental Disability Council, 884
Idaho Division Of Veterans Services, 885
Idaho Division of Tourism Development, 11961
Idaho Industrial Commission, 886
Idaho Mental Health Center, 887
Idaho Office on Aging, 888
Idaho State Tax Commission, 889
Imperial Care Center, 8519
Indianhead Estates, 8520
Joyce's Orchard Residential Care Home, 8521
Karcher Estates, 8522
Larkspur Land Residential & Assisted Living Center, 8523

Legends Park Assisted Living Community, 8524
Lilly Home, 8525
Lincoln Court, 8526
Lincoln Court Retirement Community, 8527
Living Independence Network (LINC), 10720
Living Springs, 8528
Loyaton of Coeur d'Alene, 8529
Magic Valley Manor Assisted Living, 8530
Mallory House, 8531
Markham Residential Care, 8532
Meadowlark Home of Grangeville, 8533
Meyer Manor II, 8534
National Old-Time Fiddlers' Association, 245
New Horizon Care Center, 8535
New Life Living Center, 8536
North Idaho College Area: Agency on Aging, 890
Odd Fellows Home of Idaho, 8537
Paramount Parks at Boise, 8538
Parkwood Meadows Assisted Living Community, 8539
Parma Living Center, 8540
Philos House, 8541
Pine Brook Assisted Living Center, 8542
Plantation Place Retirement & Assisted Living, 8543
Pleasant Valley Shelter Home, 8544
Pocatello Assisted Living Center, 8545
Prestige Assisted Living at Autumn Wind, 8546
Prestige Living Northwest Residential, 8547
Quail Ridge Assisted Living, 8548
RSVP Lewiston, 891
RSVP Magic Valley, 892
RSVP North Idaho, 893
RSVP Treasure Valley, 894
Ridge Wind Assisted Living, 8549
Rimrock Senior Center, 895
River Odysseys West (Row), 12042
Riverview Assisted Center, 8550
Riviera, 8551
Rockhaven Retirement Home, 8552
Roosevelt Avenue Shelter Home, 8553
Rosewind House, 8554
Royal Villa, 8555
Sage Community Resources, 896
Seasons Residential Care Living Center, 8556
Sidekick Walk & Ride Power Wheelchair, 3535
Snake River Living Center, 8557
South Shores Dignified Living, 8558
Southeast Idaho Council of Governments: Area Agency on Aging, 897
Spring Creek Manor Assisted Living, 8559
Spring Creek Manor-American Falls, 8560
Spring Creek Manor-Montpelier, 8561
Spring Creek Manor-Soda Springs, 8562
Spring Hills, 8563
Statewide Independent Living Council-Idaho, 10721
Stoney Creek Living Center, 8564
Summer Wind, 8565
Sunbridge Care, 8566
Sunbridge Living Center-Meridian, 8567
Sunbridge Retirement, 8568
Sylvan House, 8569
Treasure Valley Association of the Hearing Impaired, 6455

Treasure Valley Hearing and Balance Clinics, 6456
Turtle & Crane Assisted Living, 8570
Viewpoint Residential Care, 8572
Warren House, 8573
Wedgewood Terrace, 8574
Willow Park Assisted Living, 8575
Willowbrook Assisted Living, 8576
Woodstone Retirement Center, 8578

Illinois

AIDS Legal Council of Chicago, 11081
Academy of Dispensing Audiologists, 6303
Access Living of Chicago, 10722
Adams County RSVP, 898
Addolorata Villa, 8579
Adler School of Professional Psychology, 11450
Alcohol Rehabilitation for the Elderly, 7129
All-Purpose Openers, 3319
Alzheimer's Association: Green-Field Library, 11451
American Association of Diabetes Educators, 6110
American Association of Nurse Anesthetists, 21
American Association of Retired Persons: Midwest Region Office, 899
American Bar Association, 28
American Board of Psychiatry and Neurology, 6037
American College of Legal Medicine, 34
American Dental Society of Anesthesiology, 39
American Dietetic Association, 6173
American Foundation for the Blind: Chigago, 7510
American Foundation for the Blind: Midwest, 7511
American Hearing Research Foundation, 6794
American Medical Association, 45
American Medical Association Alliance, 46
American Society for Geriatric Dentistry, 59
American Society of Colon and Rectal Surgeons, 62
American Society of Contemporary Medicine Surgery & Ophthalmology, 7516
American Society of Maxillofacial Surgeons, 65
American Society of Neuroradiology, 66
American Society of Plastic Surgeons, 68
American Society of Tropical Medicine and Hygiene, 71
Area Agency on Aging for Lincolnland, 900
Association of Black Nursing Faculty, 83
Association of Brethren Caregivers, 84
Attorney General's Office: Disability Rights Bureau, 901
B&A Travel, 12009
Back Machine, 3195
BeOK Key Lever, 3295
Belmont Village at Geneva Road, 8580
Belmont Village of Buffalo Grove, 8581
Belmont Village of Glenview, 8582
Belmont Village of Oak Park, 8583
Bethesda Home and Retirement Center, 8584

Geographic Index / Illinois

Bethlehem Woods Retirement Community, 8585
Black & Decker Cordless Hand Blender, 3322
Blind Service Association, 7538
Box Top Opener, 3323
BroMenn Healthcare, 11452
Bureau of Naval Personnel: Illinois Retired Activities Office, 902
Center For Independent Living-Jacksonville, 10723
Center for Comprehensive Services-Carbondale, 10724
Center for Endocrinology, Metabolism & Nutrition, 6267
Center for Medicare and Medicaid Services (CMS), 11082
Central Illinois Agency on Aging (CIAA), 903
Central Illinois Center for Independent Living, 10725
Charleston Area Senior Center, 904
Chicago Department of Senior Services, 905
Chicago Kent Law School Information Center, 11083
Chicago Lawyers' Committee For Civil Rights Under Law, 11084
Chicago Library Service for the Blind, 11454
Chicago Lighthouse for People who areBlind or Visually Impaired, 7562
Christian Association of PrimeTimers, 105
Classic Coach Interiors, 2962
Coles County Council on Aging, 906
Coles County Telecare, 907
Community Awards Program (CAP), 2625
Community Health Charities of Illinois, 908
Concord Place Retirement & Assisted Living Community, 8586
Cordia Senior Residence, 8587
Council for Disability Rights, 11085
Crane Plumbing/Fiat Products, 3010
Custom Earmolds, 3276
David T Siegel Institute for Communicative Disorders, 6799
Deaf Adults Education Access Program, 6344
Deluxe Convertible Exercise Staircase, 3368
Deluxe Roller Knife, 3328
Devonshire of Hoffman Estates, 8588
Dial-A-Ride Rural Public Transportation, 909
Disabled Americans Rally for Equality, 11086
Don Johnston, 3106
Du Page Library, 11455
Dual Brush with Suction Base, 3329
Dupage Center for Independent Living, 10726
Duracell & Rayovac Hearing Aid Batteries, 3277
ENHANCER Cushion, 3201
East Central Illinois Area: Agency on Aging, 910
Egyptian Area: Agency on Aging, 911
Emergency Nurses Association, 126
Equip for Equality Central/Southern Illinois, 912
Equip for Equality Northeastern Region, 913
Equip for Equality Northwestern Region, 914
Equip for Equality: Chicago, 11087

Equip for Equality: Rock Island, 11088
Equip for Equality: Springfield, 11089
Family Caregiver Resource Center, 915
Folding Reacher, 3304
Fountains at Crystal Lake-The Inn, 8589
Geriatric Oral Health Care Award, 2637
Guardianship Services Associates, 11090
HIGH PROFILE Dual Compartment Cushion, 3207
HIGH PROFILE Single Compartment Cushion, 3208
Handi-Ramp, 3381
Hands Organization for the Deaf and Hard of Hearing, 6362
Hearthstone of Arlington Heights, 8590
Helen Keller National Center for Deaf: North Central Region, 6372
Helen Keller National Center: North Central Region, 7604
Hinsdale Travel Service, 12025
Holland Home Assisted Living, 8591
Homemaker Program, 916
Hopedale Medical Complex: Medical Library, 11456
Horizons for the Blind, 7609
IMPACT, 10719
Illinios Department of Revenue, 917
Illinois Assistive Technology Project, 918
Illinois Bureau of Tourism, 11962
Illinois Church Action on Alcohol Problems, 7167
Illinois Client Assistance Program (CAP), 919
Illinois Council on Developmental Disability, 920
Illinois Department of Alcoholism and Substance Abuse, 7168
Illinois Department of Human Services: Office of Rehabilitation Services, 921
Illinois Department of Mental Health and Developmental Disabilities, 922
Illinois Department of Rehabilitation Services, 923
Illinois Department of Veterans Affairs, 924
Illinois Department on Aging, 925, 11091
Illinois Institute of Technology: Chicago Kent Law School Information Center, 11457
Illinois School for the Deaf Media Center, 11458
Illinois School for the Visually Impaired Library, 11459
Illinois School of Professional Psychology Meadows Campus Library, 11460
Illinois Society for the Prevention of Blindness, 7612
Illinois Workers Compensation Board, 926
Illinois-Iowa Center for Independent Living (IICIL), 10727
International Psychogeriatric Association, 157
International Society for Traumatic Stress Studies, 160
Kenwood of Lake View, 8592
Key Holder, 3307
LIFE Center for Independent Living, 10728
LOW PROFILE Dual Compartment Cushion, 3211
LOW PROFILE Single Compartment Cushion, 3212
LS & S Products, 3263
Lake Barrington Woods, 8593

Lake County Center for Independent Living (LCCIL), 10729
Life Services Network of Illinois: Springfield, 927
Lifescape Community Services, 928
Little Brothers: Friends of the Elderly, 929
Lloyd Hearing Aid Corporation, 3283
Long Oven Mitts, 3339
Male Sexual Medicine Clinic, 6935
Marian Village, 8594
Mattoon Area Senior Center: Coles Council on Aging, 930
Mature Market Resource Center, 163
McDermott, Will & Emery Library, 11461
Medical Library Association, 166
Mid-Illinois Talking Book Center, 11462
Mini-Max Cushion, 3217
Moorings of Arlington Heights, 8595
Mouthsticks, 3143
Mushroom Inserts, 3284
NEXUS Wheelchair Cushioning System, 3218
Name Brand Hearing Aids, 3285
National Association of Perinatal Addiction Research and Education, 7465
National Association of Traveling Nurses, 12034
National Center for Sight, 7665
National Certification Board for Diabetes Educators, 6176
National Depressive and Manic Depressive Association, 6046
National Eye Research Foundation, 8048
National Fraternal Society of the Deaf, 6413
National Media Owl Awards, 2662
National People's Action, 251
National Society to Prevent Blindness, 7692
Navy Seabee Veterans of America, 270
North Shore Retirement Hotel, 8596
Northeastern Illinois Area: Agency on Aging, 932
Northern Illinois University: Research and Training Center, 6809
Northwest Limousine Service, 11937
Northwestern Illinois Area: Agency on Aging, 933
Northwestern Illinois Center for Independent Living, 10730
Norwood Park Home, 8597
Oasis Logan County Senior Center, 934
Office of the Attorney General: Senior Citizens Advocacy Division, 11092
Opportunities for Access, 10731
Options Center for Independent Living, 10732
PALAESTRA, 11938
Parkside Medical Services Corporation, 7211
Persons Assuming Control of their Environment (PACE), 10733
Prevent Blindness America, 7722
Pro Bono Center for Disability and Elder Law (CDEL): Lifelong Lawyers Project, 11093
Profit Sharing/401(k) Council of America, 296
Progress Center for Independent Living, 10734
Provena Fox Knoll Retirement Community, 8598
Provena-Mercy Center Medical Library, 11463

1081

Geographic Index / Indiana

QUADTRO Cushion, 3222
RSVP Champaign, 935
RSVP Decatur, 936
RSVP Joliet, 937
RSVP Kane McHenry Counties, 938
RSVP Maple Lawn, 940
RSVP Peoria/Tazewell Counties, 941
RSVP Program CEFA Economic Opportunity Corporation, 942
RSVP Rock Island, 943
RSVP Triton College Volunteer Program, 944
RSVP YWCA Senior Services, 945
Rachel's Place Adult Day Care, 946
Railroad Retirement Board (RRB), 298
Railroad Retirement Board: Chicago District Office, 947
Railroad Retirement Board: Decatur District Office, 948
Railroad Retirement Board: Joliet District Office, 949
Railroad Retirement Board: Survivor Division, 950
Region 5: Administration on Aging (AoA), 951
Regional Access & Mobilization Project (RAMP), 10735
Regional Access Mobilization Project (RAMP), 10736
Retired & Senior Volunteer Program of Hull House Chicago, 952
Retired & Senior Volunteer Program of Northern DuPage Counties, 953
Saint Andrew Life Center, 8599
Senior Citizens' Wills Program: Chicago Bar Association, 11094
Senior Community Service Employment Program (Title V), 954
Senior Services of Central Illinois, 955
Seniors Action Service Caring Home Aid Program, 956
Shawnee Development Council, 957
Shawnee Library System, 11464
Simon Foundation for Continence, 6949
Skokie Accessible Library Services, 11465
Sling Solutions, 3396
Social Security Springfield Disability Determination, 958
Society for Ambulatory Care Professionals, 317
Southeastern Illinois Area Agency on Aging, 959
Southern Illinois Center for Independent Living, 10737
Southwestern Illinois Area Agency on Aging, 960
Soyland Access to Independent Living, 10738
Special Care Dentistry, 318
Spectrum Aquatics, 3292
Spring Meadows Libertyville, 8600
Springfield Center for Independent Living (CIL), 10739
St. James Villas, 8601
State of Illinois, 11989
Stone-Hayes Center for Independent Living, 10740
Suburban Audio Visual Service, 11466
Summit Square of Park Ridge, 8602
Sunrise Assisted Living of Naperville, 8603
Sunrise of Bloomingdale, 8604
Sunrise of Buffalo Grove, 8605
Sunrise of Crystal Lake, 8606
Sunrise of Flossmoor, 8607
Sunrise of Glen Ellyn, 8608
Sunrise of Gurnee, 8609
Sunrise of Naperville-North, 8610
Sunrise of Palos Park, 8611
Sunrise of Park Ridge, 8612
Sunrise of Schaumburg, 8613
Sunrise of Willowbrook, 8614
The Park at Vernon Hills, 8615
US Department of Health and Human Services: Office for Civil Rights, 11095
US Department of Labor: Office of Federal Contract Compliance Programs, 329, 11096
US Department of Veterans Affairs: Chicago Health Care System-West Side Division, 11467
US Department of Veterans Affairs: Library Services, 11469
US Department of Veterans Affairs: Medical Library, 11428, 11429, 11470, 11470
Undercounter Lid Opener, 3352
Uni-Turner, 3353
United Airlines, 11945
United Parkinson Foundation, 6978
University of Chicago Social Services Administration Library, 11471
University of Chicago: Diabetes Research & Training Center, 6282
University of Chicago: Temporal Bone Laboratory for Ear Research, 6822
University of Illinois at Chicago: Lions of Illinios Eye Research Institute, 8056
Veterans Administration Medical Center: Research Service, 7490
Victorian Inn at Victorian Village, 8616
Village Woods, 8617
Voices of Vision Talking Book Center, 11472
Walker Leg Support, 3495
West Central Illinois Area: Agency on Aging, 961
West Central Illinois Center for Independent Living (WCICIL), 10741
Westbridge Assisted Living, 8618
Western Illinois Area: Agency on Aging, 962
Weston Travel Agency, 12058
Will-Grundy Center for Independent Living, 10742

Indiana

Adams County Council on Aging, 963
Aging And Community Service Of South CenTral Indiana, 964
Aging and In Home Services of Northeast Indiana, 11097
Aging and In-Home Services, 965
Allen County Public Library, 11473
Allen County Public Library of New Haven, 11474
Allen County Public Library of Woodburn, 11475
Allen County Public Library, Aboite Branch, 11476
Allen County Public Library, Pontiac Branch, 11477
American Legion, 11478
American United Life Insurance Company, 11479
Area 1 Northwest Indiana Community ActioN Corp., 966
Area 10 Agency on Aging, 967
Area 12 Council on Aging, 968
Area 13 Agency on Aging: Older Hoosier Programs, 969
Area 15 Hoosier Uplands Agency on Aging, 970
Area 2 Agency on Aging: Real Services, 971
Area 4 Agency on Aging and Community Services, 972
Area 5 Agency on Aging and Community Services, 973
Area 9 Agency on Aging, 974
Assistive Technology Training and Information Center, 10743
Association of Retired Americans, 87
Atria Eastlake Terrace, 8619
Bartholomew County Public Library, 11480
Bethesda Gardens at the Crossings, 8620
Boone County Senior Services Foundation, 975
Bosma Industries for the Blind, 7542
Braun Corporation, 3006
Braun Mobility Products, 2959
Caleworthy, 3093
Cameron Woods, 10744
Central Indiana Council on Aging, 976
Crown Point Senior Living-Anderson, 10745
Custom Durable, 3511
Electronic Keyless Entry System, 3302
Evansville Association for the Blind, 7584
Evansville-Vanderburgh County Public Library, 11481
Everybody Counts-Ruben Center for Independent Living, 10746
Fort Wayne EASI, 977
GW Micro, 3119
Heritage Park Independent Living Apartments, 10747
Illinois Family & Social Services, 7169
Indiana Aging Division, 978
Indiana Association of Area Agencies on Aging, 979
Indiana Department of Aging and Community Services, 980
Indiana Department of Health Veteran's Home, 981
Indiana Department of Revenue, 982
Indiana Department of Veterans Affairs, 983
Indiana Developmental Disability Council, 984
Indiana Disability Determination Bureau, 985
Indiana Division of Addiction Services, 7171
Indiana Division of Aging, 11098
Indiana Governor's Planning Council for People with Disabilities, 986
Indiana Hearing Aid Specialists Association, 6376
Indiana Legal Services: Senior Law Project, 11099
Indiana Protection & Advocacy Services, 987
Indiana Protection and Advocacy Agency, 11100
Indiana Public Employee's Retirement Fund, 988

Geographic Index / Iowa

ndiana School for the Deaf: Alumni Hall Library, 11482
ndiana Teachers Retirement Fund, 989
ndiana Tourism Division, 11963
ndiana University: Diabetes Research and Training Center, 6272
ndiana University: Hypertension Research Center, 6923
ndiana University: Northwest Center for Medical Education, 6273
ndiana University: Pharmacology Research Laboratory, 6274
ndianapolis Resource Center for Independent Living (IRCIL), 10748
Joystick Driving Control, 2978
Krannert Institute of Cardiology, 6881
Latchloc Automatic Wheelchair Tiedown, 3552
Life Stream Services, 990
Madison County RSVP, 991
Meridan Oaks, 8621
Michigan City Public Library: Indiana Rooom/Genealogy, 11483
National Legal Center for the Medically Dependent and Disabled, 11101
Northwest Indiana Community Action Corp, 11102
Northwest Indiana Subregional Library for Blind and Physically Handicapped, 11484
Park Square Manor, 10749
Purdue University: Humanities, Social Science, Education Library, 11485
Purdue University: William A Hillenbrand Biomedical Engineering Center, 6887
RSVP Crawford-Perry-Spencer, 992
RSVP Daviess County Indiana, 993
RSVP Dearborn County, 994
RSVP Dekalb-Noble-Steuben Counties, 995
RSVP Dubois-Pike-Warrick Counties, 996
RSVP Elkhart County, 997
RSVP Fulton, 998
RSVP Hancock-Henry-Rush, 999
RSVP Indianapolis, 1000
RSVP Jefferson County, 476, 657, 1001, 1001
RSVP Knox County, 1002
RSVP LaPorte County, 1003
RSVP Monroe Owen Counties, 1006
RSVP South Central Indiana RSVP, 1008
RSVP St. Joseph County, 1009
RSVP Valparaiso, 1010
Railroad Retirement Board District Office, 1012
Resources For Enriching Adult Learning(REAL), 11103
Roll-In Shower, 3022
Shamrock Gardens, 8622
Smith Farms Manor, 10750
South Central Indiana Council for Aging and Aged, 1013
Southern Indiana Center For IndependentLiving, 10751
Southwestern Indiana Mental Health Center, 11104
Southwestern Indiana Regional Council on Aging, 1014
Special Access Vans, 2993
Special Services Division: Indiana State Library, 11486
St Paul Hermitage, 10752
Sunrise of Carmel, 8623
Swing-A-Way, 3406

Talking Books Service: Evansville Vanderburgh County Public Library, 11487
Towne Centre, 8624
Tri-Wheelers, 3443
US Department of Veterans Affairs, Medical Center Library Service, 11405, 11488
US Department of Veterans Affairs: Indiana Health Care System, 11489
US Deprtment of Veterans Affairs: Center Library, 11490
Vangater, Vangater II, Mini-Vangater, 3410
Ventura Enterprises, 3561
Vincennes University: Byron R Lewis Historical Library, 11105
Vision World Wide, 7775
Washington County Historical Society: Genealogy and Historical Library, 11106
West Central Indiana Economic Development District Area Agency On Aging And Disabled, 1015

Iowa

3801 Grand, 8625
AASE Hougen Assisted Living, 8626
Afton Oaks Assisted Living, 8627
Alison Health Care Center, 8628
Allen House, 8629
Amber Ridge, 8630
Amelia House, 8631
American Diabetes Association: Cedar Rapids District Office, 6122
American Diabetes Association: Iowa Area Office, 6136
Ames Public Library Ames and Iowa History Collection, 11491
Arbor Heights at University, 8632
Arbor Place, 8633
Area 14 Agency on Aging, 1016
Area Agency on Aging: Senior Citizens Lawyer Referral Service, 11107
Arlin Flack Assisted Living, 8634
Arlington Place of Grundy Center, 8635
Arlington Place of Red Oak, 8636
Avoca Lodge Assisted Living, 8637
Ballard Creek Community, 8638
Beehive Home Assisted Living, 8639
Beehive Home Assisted Living-Hawarden, 8640
Bickford Cottage-Davenport, 8641
Bickford Cottage-Marshalltown, 8642
Bickford Cottage-Muscatine, 8643
Blackhawk Center for Independent Living, 10753
Briarcliff Retirement Center, 8644
Brickford Cottage II, 8646
Brickford Cottage-Ames, 8647
Brickford Cottage-Burlington, 8648
Brickford Cottage-Clinton, 8649
Brickford Cottage-Des Moines, 8650
Brickford Cottage-Fort Dodge, 8651
Brickford Cottage-Iowa City, 8652
Brickford Cottage-West Des Moines, 8653
Calhoun County Historical Museum Library, 11492
Calvin Community Assisted Living Service, 8654
Cardinal Grove, 8655
Central Iowa Center for Independent Living, 10754

Char-Mac Assisted Living, 8656
Clearview Estates Assisted Living, 8657
Clover Ridge, 8658
Cottage Grove Place, 8660
Country House, 8661
Courtyard, 8662
Crown Pointe, 8663
Davenport Lutheran Assisted Living, 8664
Dora Barns Residential Home, 8665
Eagle Ridge Assisted Living, 8666
Eiler House, 8667
Elderbridge Agency on Aging, 1017
Elderbridge-Area Agency on Aging: Legal Referral Panel, 11108
Elm Crest Retirement Community, 8668
Elm Heights Assisted Living, 8669
Evert Conner Rights & Resources Center for Independent Living, 10755
Fieldcrest Assisted Living, 8670
Fleur Heights Care Center, 8671
Floyd House, 8672
Forest Plaza Assisted Living, 8673
Franken Manor, 8674
Garnett Place, 8675
Glenwood Place, 8676
Greenfield Manor Assisted Living, 8677
Hallmark Care Center, 8678
Hawkeye Valley Area: Agency on Aging, 1018
Hawthorne Inn at Windmill, 8679
Heartland Care Center Assisted Living, 8680
Heartwood Heights, 8681
Help Legal Assistance: Senior Citizens Law Project, 11109
Heritage Area: Agency on Aging, 1019
Heritage Court, 8682
Heritage House, 8683
Holy Spirit, 8684
Homestead Acres, 8685
Iowa Client Assistance Program, 1020
Iowa Commission of Veterans Affairs, 1021
Iowa Commission on Persons with Disabilities, 1022
Iowa Department of Elder Affairs, 1023
Iowa Department of Elder Affairs: Legal Assistance, 11110
Iowa Department of Human Rights: Deaf Services Commissions, 1024
Iowa Department of Revenue & Finance, 1025
Iowa Developmental Disability Council, 1026
Iowa Division of MHMRDD: Office of Human Services, 1027
Iowa Division of Substance Abuse & Health Promotion, 7174
Iowa Hearing Association, 6384
Iowa Library For The Blind And Physically Handicapped, 11493
Iowa Program for Assistive Technology, 1028
Iowa Protection & Advocacy for the Disabled, 1029
Iowa Protection and Advocacy Agency, 11111
Iowa Regional Library for the Blind & Physically Handicapped, 7621
Iowa State Bar: Young Lawyer Section Committee on Delivery of Legal Services to the Elderly, 11112
Iowa Tourism Office/Iowa Travel Guide, 11964

Geographic Index / Kansas

Iowa Workers Compensation, 1030
Jersey Ridge, 8686
Jewish Senior Life Center, 8687
Kensington, 8688
Keystone Senior Suites, 8689
Kosgrove Estates Assisted Living, 8690
Lakeview Lodge, 8691
Lakeview Village, 8692
Landsmeer Ridge Retirement Community, 8693
Lincolnwood Assisted Living, 8694
Linden Place Assisted Living, 8695
Longview Retirement Apartments, 8696
Lucas County Health Center, 1031
Lutheran Home Apartments, 8697
MICA Hill Estates, 8698
Madison Square Assisted Living, 8699
Maple Manor Village, 8700
Maple Ridge Assisted Living, 8701
Martina Place, 8702
Mason City Homestead, 8703
Mayflower Assisted Living, 8704
Meadows Assisted Living, 8706
Meth-Wick Community, 8707
Mill Pond Assisted Living, 8708
Monticello Nursing and Rehab Center, 8709
Mulberry Place, 8710
National Center for Voice and Speech, 6407
National Federation of the Blind in Computer Science, 7672
Northern Hills, 8711
Northwest Aging Association, 11113
Oak Estates, 8712
Oaknoll Assisted Living, 8714
Oakwood Place Assisted Living at Ridgecrest Village, 8715
Park Place Estates, 8716
Parkinson Association of Davenport, 6961
Perry Lutheran Home Assisted Living, 8717
Pioneer Place Assisted Living, 8718
Port Charles Assisted Living, 8719
Praire View Inn, 8720
Premier Suites, 8722
Prevent Blindness Iowa, 7724
Promise House, 8723
RSVP Black Hawk, 1032
RSVP Clarinda, 1034
RSVP Dubuque County, 1036
RSVP Fort Dodge, 1037
RSVP Hamilton Wright Counties, 1038
RSVP Henry County, 1039
RSVP Linn County, 1041
RSVP North Central Iowa, 1042
RSVP North Lee County, 1043
RSVP Northeast Iowa, 1044
RSVP Ottumwa, 1045
RSVP Pottawattamie Mills Counties, 1046
RSVP Story Marshall Counties, 1047
RSVP United Way of Central Iowa, 1048
RSVP Woodbury County, 1049
Railroad Retirement Board: Iowa District Office, 1050
Ramsey Home, 8724
Ranger, 3430
Reed House, 8725
Ridgeway Place, 8726
River Hills Village, 8727
Riverview Terrace, 8728
Roll-Aid, 3532
Rosebush Gardens, 8729
SCORE of Tulsa, 1051
SILC-Iowa Department for the Blind, 10756
Safari Scooter, 3433
Scenic Valley Area: Agency on Aging, 1052
Sears Mature Outlook, 307
Seneca Area Agency on Aging, 1053, 11114
Senior Suites, 8730
Silvercrest Ames Assisted Living, 8731
Silvercrest Assisted Living: Garner Farms, 8732
Silvercrest Legacy Pointe, 8733
Siouxland Aging Services, 1054, 11115
Sister Center for Helpful Living, 8734
Skiff Medical Center Assisted Living, 8735
Solo Scooter, 3438
Southeast Iowa Area: Agency on Aging, 1055
Southwest 8 Senior Services, 1056
Southwest Iowa Center for Independent Living, 10757
Spring Valley Senior Assisted Living, 8736
Stand Aid, 3402
Summit Heights, 8737
Sunnybrook Assisted Living, 8738
Sunrise Villa, 8739
Sunset Park Place, 8740
Swan House, 8741
Sylvan Woods, 8742
Terrace Park Senior Living, 8743
The Villages at Marion, 8744
Tri-State Blind Society, 7763
Tri-State Independent Blind Society, 7764
US Department of Veterans Affairs: Central Iowa Health Care System, 11494
University of Iowa College of Medicine, 7122
University of Iowa: Diabetes Control and Complications Trial, 6283
University of Iowa: Diabetes Research Center, 6284
University of Iowa: Iowa Cardiovascular Center, 6898
Valley Lodge Assisted Living, 8745
Valley View Manor Assisted Living, 8746
Vertical Wheelchair Lift, 3412
Villa Cottages, 8747
Waukon Living Center, 8748
Wel-Life at Alta, 8749
Wel-Life at Spirit Lake, 8750
Wesley Acres Memorial Loss Center, 8751
West Libery Assisted Living Residences, 8752
Western Home Assisted Living, 8753
Willow Pointe, 8754
Willows, 8577, 8755
Winifred Law Opportunity Center, 11116

Kansas

Aeroquip Wheelchair Securement System, 2955
Alterra Sterling House of Abilene, 8756
Alterra Sterling House of Abilene II, 8757
Alterra Sterling House of Arkansas, 8758
Alterra Sterling House of Augusta, 8759
Alterra Sterling House of Derby, 8760
Alterra Sterling House of Dodge City, 8761
Alterra Sterling House of Emporia, 8762
Alterra Sterling House of Fairdale, 8763
Alterra Sterling House of Great Bend, 8764
Alterra Sterling House of Hays, 8765
Alterra Sterling House of Junction, 8766
Alterra Sterling House of Lawrence, 8767
Alterra Sterling House of Leawood, 8768
Alterra Sterling House of Lenexa I, 8769
Alterra Sterling House of Lenexa II, 8770
Alterra Sterling House of McPherson, 8771
Alterra Sterling House of Olathe, 8772
Alterra Sterling House of Olathe II, 8773
Alterra Sterling House of Salina, 8774
Alterra Sterling House of Topeka, 8775
Alterra Sterling House of Wichita, 8776
Alterra Sterling House of Woodland, 8777
American Academy of Addiction Psychiatry, 7451
American Diabetes Association: Kansas Area Office, 6137
Andover Court Assisted Living, 8778
Assisted Lifestyles Of KS Inc., 8779
Assisted Living at Windsor Place, 8780
Atria Assisted & Retirement Living, 8781
Beach Center on Families and Disability, 1057
Brookside Assisted Living, 8782
Bukovina Society of the Americas Library, 11495
Butler County Department on Aging, 1058
Carriage House of Greensburg, 8783
Cedar Lake Village, 8784
Cedarview Assisted Living, 8785
Center for Independent Living for Southwest Kansas, 10759
Center for Independent Living of Southwest Kansas, 10760
Central Plains Area: Agency on Aging, 1059
Chaucer Estates-Retirement, 8786
Cherokee County Genealogical Historical Society, 11496
Cherry Creek Village Retirement Center, 8787
Cornerstone Assisted Living, 8659, 8788
Cornerstone Ridge Plaza, 8789
Disability Rights Center Of Kansas, 1060
East Central Kansas Area: Agency on Aging, 1061
Elm Grove Estates, 8790
Evergreen Gardens of Garden City, 8791
Fort Scott Presbyterian Village, 8792
Georgetown Village, 8793
Gran Villas, 8794
Gran Villas-Atchison, 8795
Gran Villas-Eureka, 8796
Gran Villas-Fredonia, 8797
Gran Villas-Hiawatha, 8798
Gran Villas-Neodesha, 8799
Gran Villas-Osage City, 8800
Gran Villas-Wamego, 8801
Grand Court of Overland Park II, 8802
Gravity Down Platform Lift, 3378
Great Bend Homestead, 8803
Great Plains Region Helen Keller National Center, 7596
Halstead Place, 8804
Harvey County Department on Aging, 1062
Homestead of Garden City, 8805
Hutchinson Homestead, 8806
Hutchinson Independent Living Center, 10761
Independence, Inc., 10762
Independent Connection, 10763
Independent Living of Northeast Kansas, 10765
Kansas Alcohol and Drug Abuse Services, 7175

Kansas Association for the Blind and Visually Impaired, 7625
Kansas Association for the Blind andVisually Impaired, 7624
Kansas Association of Area Agencies on Aging, 1063
Kansas Client Assistance Program, 1064
Kansas Commission for the Deaf and Hard of Hearing, 6385
Kansas Commission on Disability Concerns, 1065
Kansas Commission on Veterans Affairs, 1066
Kansas Department of Aging: Legal Assistance Services for Older Adults (KDOA), 11117
Kansas Department of Human Resources: Commission on Disabilities Concern, 1067
Kansas Department of Revenue, 1068
Kansas Department of Social and Rehabilitation Services, 1069
Kansas Department on Aging, 1070
Kansas Developmental Disability Council, 1071
Kansas Division of Services for the Blind, 7627
Kansas Employment Services and Job Training Program Liaison, 1072
Kansas Hearing Aid Association, 6386
Kansas Hearing Society, 6387
Kansas Masonic Home, 8807
Kansas Mental Health & Retardation Service, 1073
Kansas Protection and Advocacy Agency &Disability Rights Center of Kansas, 11118
Kansas Public Employees Retirement System, 1074
Kansas Specialty Dog Service, 1075
Kansas State Historical Society: Library & Archives Division, 11497
Kansas State Library Talking Book Service, 11498
Kansas Travel & Tourism, 11965
Leavenworth County Genealogical Society Library, 11499
Leavenworth Homestead, 8808
Linwood Place I & II, 8809
Living Independently in Northwest Kansas (LINK), 10766
Manhattan Homestead Assisted, 8810
Manhattan Public Library, 11500
Marquis Place, 8811
National Federation of the Blind of Kansas, 1076, 7674
National Organization of HIV over Fifty, 248
National Silver-Haired Congress: Kansas Department on Aging, 1077
North Central Flint Hills Area: Agency on Aging, 1078
Northeast Kansas Area: Agency on Aging, 1079
Northwest Kansas Area: Agency on Aging, 1080
Northwest Kansas Library System Talking Books, 11501
Old Fort Genealogical Society Of Southeastern Kansas Inc, 11502
Overland Park Place, 8813
Pace Saver Plus II, 3426
Park View Assisted Living, 8814
Parkinson Association of Greater Kansas City, 6963
Parkwood Village, 8815
Peterson Assisted Living, 8816
RSVP Barton County, 1081
RSVP Butler County, 1082
RSVP Finney County, 1083
RSVP Ford County, 1084
RSVP Harvey County, 1085
RSVP Johnson County, 1040, 1086
RSVP Northwest Kansas, 1087
RSVP Pratt County, 1088
RSVP Reno County, 1089
RSVP Riley County, 1090
RSVP Saline County, 1091
RSVP Southeast Kansas, 1092
RSVP Wyandotte County, 1093
Railroad Retirement Board: Kansas, 1094
Redbud Plaza, 8817
Rolling Hills Assisted Living Apartments, 8818
Sealye House, 8819
Shawnee Heartland Assisted Living, 8820
South Central Kansas Area Agency on Aging, 1095
South Central Kansas Library System, 11503
Southeast Kansas Area: Agency on Aging, 1096
Southeast Kansas Independent Living (SKIL), 10768
St John's New Horizons, 8821
Statewide Independent Living Council of Kansas, 10769
Super Scout Three Wheeler, 3440
Talking Books Service, 11504
Three Rivers Independent Living, 10770
Three Rivers-Manhattan, 10771
Topeka Independent Living Resource Center, 10772
Twin Oaks Assisted Living, 8822
US Department of Veterans Affairs: Dr Karl Menninger Medical Library, 11505
US Department of Veterans Affairs: Dwight D. Eisenhower Center Medical Library, 11506
University of Kansas: Regional Diabetes Center, 6285
Valley Springs Assisted Living, 8823
Village East, 8824
Village of Ninnescah, 8825
Vintage Park of Atchison, 8826
Vintage Park of Baldwin City, 8827
Vintage Park of Gardner, 8828
Vintage Park of Louisburg, 8829
Vintage Park of Paola, 8830
Vintage Place of Derby, 8831
Vintage Place of Russell, 8832
Vintage Point of Pittsburg, 8833
Vyne at Crestview, 8834
Vyne at Meadows Park, 8835
Waterfront Inn Assisted Living, 8836
Wheat Ridge Acres, 8837
Wichita Public Library, 11508
Wizz-ard, 3542
Woodridge Estates, 8838
Young Historical Library, 11509

Kentucky

Adaptive Device Locator System, 3067
American Council of Blind Lions, 7505
American Diabetes Association: Bowling Green District Office, 6120
American Diabetes Association: KentuckyArea Office, 6138
American Printing House for the Blind, 7515
Analog Clock Model, 3294
Analog Switch Pad, 3074
Aquatic Access Pool Lifts for Pools andSpas, 3359
Baptist Homes, 8839
Barren River Area Development District, 1097
Beehive of Danville, 8840
Beehive of Shelbyville, 8841
Belmont Village at St Matthews, 8842
Big Sandy Area Development District, 1098
Bluegrass Area Agency on Aging, 1099
Braille/Print Protractor, 3090
Buffalo Trace Area Agency on Aging, 1100
Calendars, 3458
Card Chart, 3459
Center for Accessible Living, 10773
Center for Accessible Living-Louisville, 10774
Community Action Council: Lexington Fayette Jessamine Counties, 1101
Cumberland Valley Area: Agency on Aging, 1102
Department for Disability Determination Services, 1103
Disability Coalition of Northern Kentucky, 10775
Disabled American Veterans, 1104
FIVCO Area: Agency on Aging, 1105
Four Courts Senior Center, 8843
Frontier Nursing Service, 8844
Gateway Area Development District, 1106
Green River Area: Agency on Aging, 1107
Independence Place, 10776
Kentucky Bar Association: Committee on Legal Concerns of Elderly Clients, 11119
Kentucky Bar Association: Senior Lawyers Section, 11120
Kentucky Cabinet for Education, Arts and The Humanities: Commission for the Deaf and Hearing Impaired, 1108
Kentucky Cabinet for Workforce Development: Department for the Blind, 1109
Kentucky Client Assistance Program, 1110
Kentucky Council on Developmental Disabilities, 1111
Kentucky Department for the Blind, 7628
Kentucky Department of Travel, 11966
Kentucky Department of Veterans Affairs, 1112
Kentucky Department of Workers Claims, 1113
Kentucky Division of Aging Services, 11121
Kentucky Division of Mental Health, 1114
Kentucky Division of Substance Abuse, 7176
Kentucky Division: Prevent Blindness America, 7629
Kentucky Historical Society-Thomas DClark Research Library, 11510
Kentucky Legal Aid, 11122

Geographic Index / Louisiana

Kentucky Office of Aging Services, 1115
Kentucky Protection & Advocacy Division, 1116
Kentucky Protection and Advocacy Agency, 11123
Kentucky Retirement Systems, 1117
Kentucky Revenue Cabinet, 1118
Kentucky River Area: Agency on Aging, 1119
Kentucky State Affliate of American Academy of Audiology, 6389
Kentucky Talking Book Library, 11511
Kentucky Teachers Retirement System, 1120
Kentuckyiana Regional Planning &Development Agency (KIPDA), 1121
Lake Cumberland Area Development District Area: Agency on Aging, 1122
Liberty Ridge, 8845
Lincoln Trail Area: Agency on Aging, 1123
Louisville Talking Book Library, 11512
Magni-Cam, 3135, 3423
McCready Manor, 8846
McDowell Place of Danville, 8847
Metro United Way, 1124
Morningside Paducah, 8848
Morningside of Bowling Green, 8849
Multi-Scan Single Switch Activity Center, 3144
National Anxiety Foundation, 6045
National Tour Association: Travel Division, 12035
New Vision Enterprises, 7703
North Kentucky Area Development District, 1125
Northern Kentucky Talking Book Library, 11513
Pathfinders for Independent Living, 10777
Pik Stik, 3020
Pool Lifts for In-Ground Pools, 3388
Purchase Area Development District, 1126
Quality Lift Chair, 3047
RSVP Audubon Area, 1127
RSVP Brighton Center, 1128
RSVP Central Kentucky, 1129
RSVP Hickman-McCracken Counties, 1130
RSVP Louisville Metro Community Action Partnership, 1131
RSVP Mason County, 1132
Railroad Retirement Board: Kentucky District Office, 1133
River's Bend Retirement Community, 8850
Score Card Set, 3291
Senior Citizens of Whitley County, 1134
Senior Services of Northern Kentucky, 1135
Shuttle, 3435
Sidekick Scooter, 3436
Social Security: Louisville Disability Determination, 1136
Stonecreek Lodge, 8851
US Department of Veterans Affairs: Hospital Library, 11468, 11514
Weley Manor, 8852
WinSCAN-The Single Switch Interface forPCs with Windows, 3192

Louisiana

AIDSLAW of Louisiana, 11124
Acadiana Legal Service Corporation, 11125
Alton Ochsner Medical Foundation, 6918
American Diabetes Association: Baton Rouge District Office, 6118
American Diabetes Association: New Orleans District Office, Louisiana, 6152
Arbor of Natchitoches, 8853
Arbor of Ruston, 8854
Assisted Living Center at St James Place, 8855
Azalea Estates of Gonzales, 8856
Azalea Estates of Monroe, 8857
Azalea Estates of New Iberia, 8858
Azalea Estates of Shreveport, 8859
Bailey House, 8860
Baton Rouge Advocacy Center, 11126
Beauregard Council on Aging, 1137
Betty and Leonard Phillips Deaf Action Center, 6323
Bienville Area: Agency on Aging, 1138
Bossier Council on Aging Area: Agency on Aging, 1139
Bureau of Naval Personnel: Louisiana Retired Activities Office, 1140
Caddo Council on Aging, 1141
Cajun Area: Agency on Aging, 1142
Calcasieu Council of Aging, 1143
Caldewell Parish Council on Aging, 1144
Cameron Council on Aging, 1145
Capital Area: Agency on Aging, 1146
Claiborne Voluntary Council on Aging, 1147
Cornerstone Village, 8861
Cornerstone Village South, 8862
De Soto Council on Aging Area: Agency on Aging, 1148
Deaf Action Center of Central Louisiana, 6343
Disability Determination Services: Shreveport Branch, 1150
East Baton Rouge Council on Aging, 1151
Franklin Parish Council on the Aging, 1152
Grand Cove, 8863
Haven at Windermere, 8864
Industries for the Blind and Visually Impaired of Louisiana, 7615
Jefferson Council on Aging, 1153
Kingsley Place at Alexandria, 8865
Kingsley Place at Lafayette, 8866
Kingsley Place at Shreveport, 8867
Lafayette Advocacy Center, 11127
Lafourche Council on Aging, 1154
Lakewood Quarters Retirement Community, 8868
Landmark Retirement Community, 8869
Lincoln Council on Aging, 1155
Live Oak Village of Slidell, 8870
Louisiana Assistive Technology Access Network, 1156
Louisiana Center for the Blind, 7638
Louisiana Client Assistance Program, 1157
Louisiana Department of Aging, 1158
Louisiana Department of Revenue, 1159
Louisiana Department of Veterans Affairs, 1160
Louisiana Developmental Disability Council, 1161
Louisiana Division of Mental Health, 6041
Louisiana Employee's Retirement Department, 1162
Louisiana Governor's Office of Elderly Affairs, 11128
Louisiana Office of Alcohol & Drug Abuse, 7177
Louisiana Office of Tourism, 11967
Louisiana Protection & Advocacy for Persons with Disabilities, 1163
Louisiana Teachers Retirement System, 1164
Louisiana Workers Compensation Board, 1165
Madison Council on Aging, 1166
Maison Oaks Assisted Living, 8871
Malta Park: Willwoods II, 8872
Malta Square at Sacred Heart: Willwoods II, 8873
Mary Bird Perkins Cancer Center Community Library, 11516
Merrill Gardens at Bossier, 8874
Montclair Park Assisted Living, 8875
Monte Carlo Outreach Facility, 8876
Morehouse Council on Aging, 1167
Natchitoches Parish Council on Aging, 1168
National Senior Games Association, 260
New Horizons, 10778
New Orleans Advocacy Center, 11129
New Orleans Council on Aging, 1169
New Orleans Public Library: Louisiana Division, 11517
Norman House Group Home, 8877
North Delta-Area Agency on Aging, 1170
Oakmont Estate, 8878
Ouachita Council on Aging, 1171
Plaquemines Council on Aging, 1172
Pratt-Stanton Manor, 8880
Protection & Advocacy of Individual Rights, 1173
RSVP Baton Rouge, 1174
RSVP Caddo-Bossier Counties, 1175
RSVP Calcasieu Parish, 1176
RSVP Jefferson Parish, 1177
RSVP Lafayette, 1178
RSVP Lincoln Parish, 1179
RSVP Natchitoches Parish, 1180
RSVP New Orleans, 1181
RSVP Ouachita Parish, 1182
RSVP Rapides Parish, 1183
RSVP River Parishes, 1184
Railroad Retirement Board: District Office, 1185
Red River Council on Aging, 1186
Regency Place, 8213, 8881
Resources for Independent Living - Baton Rouge, 10779
Retirement Center, 8882
Rosewood Retirement & Assisted Living Community, 8883
Russ House, 8884
Shreveport Advocacy Center, 11130
Southside Gardens Assisted Living Center, 8885
St Charles Council on Aging, 1187
St Francis Villa Assisted Living, 8886
St Joesph Manor, 8887
St John Area: Agency on Aging, 1188
St John Parish Council on Aging, 1189
St. Bernard Council on Aging, 1190
St. James Parish Department of Human Resources, 1191
St. Tammany Council on Aging, 1192
State Library of Louisiana, 11518
Summerville at Kenner, 8888
Sunrise Assisted Living of Baton Rouge, 8890
TERRA-JET: Utility Vehicle, 3442
Tender Love & Company, 8891

Geographic Index / Maine

Tensas Council on Aging, 1193
Terrace of Shreveport, 8892
Terrebonne Council on Aging, 1194
Terreboone House, 8893
Thompson House Group Home, 8894
Tulane University: Howard-Tilton Memorial Library-Louisiana Collection, 11519
US Department of Veterans Affairs: Center Library, 11520
US Department of Veterans Affairs: Overton Brooks Medical Center Library, 11522
University of Southwestern Louisiana: Jefferson Caffery Louisana Room-Southwestern Archives and Manuscripts Collection,
Village in the Oaks, 8895
Ville Ste Marie Senior Living Community, 8896
Volunteers Of AmericaGreater New Orleans Retired Seniors Volunteer Program, 1195
Webster Area: Agency on Aging, 1196
West Carroll Council on Aging, 1197
Willamsburg Senior Living Community, 8897
Windsor Senior Living Community, 8898
Winn Council on Aging, 1198
Wynhoven Living Center, 8899

Maine

ALPHA One, 10780
Advocates for Medicare Patients (AMP's), 11131
Aroostook Area: Agency on Aging, 1199
Bangor Public Library, 11524
Bureau of Naval Personnel: Retired Activities Office, 815, 1200
Central Maine Area: Agency on Aging, 1201
Eastern Area Agency on Aging, 1203
Freeport Elders Association, 1204
Governor Baxter School for the Deaf Library, 11525
Jackson Laboratory: Joan Staats Library, 11526
Legal Services for the Elderly: Augusta, 11132
Legal Services for the Elderly: Lewiston, 11133
Lewiston Public Library, 11527
Maine Assistive Technology Projects, 1205
Maine Association of Retirees (MAR), 1206
Maine Bureau of Elder and Adult Services, 1207
Maine Center for the Blind and Visually Impaired, 7639
Maine Department of Defense, Veterans and Emergency Management, 1208
Maine Department of Human Services: Bureau of Elder and Adult Services, 1209
Maine Department of Labor: Bureau of Employment Security, 1210
Maine Department of Labor: Bureau of Rehabilitation Services, 1211
Maine Department of Mental Health & Mental Retardation, 6042
Maine Developmental Disability Council, 1212
Maine Division for the Blind & Visually Impaired Services, 7640
Maine Independent Living Services, 10781

Maine Office of Elder Affairs, 11134
Maine Office of Tourism, 11968
Maine Protection & Advocacy AgencyDisability Rights Center: Bangor Office, 11135
Maine Protection and Advocacy AgencyDisability Rights Center: Augusta Office, 11136
Maine Revenue Services, 1213
Maine State Bar Association: Section on Elder Law, 11137
Maine State Library, 11528
Maine State Office of Substance Abuse: Information and Resource Center, 7463
Maine State Retirement System, 1214
Maine Worker's Compensation Board, 1215
Portland Public Library, 11529
RSVP Aroostook, 1216
RSVP Penquis Coastal, 1217
RSVP Southern Maine, 1218
Senior Spectrum, 1219
Seniors Plus, 1220
Shalom House, 10782
Southern Maine Area Agency on Aging, 1221
US Department of Veterans Affairs: Medical & Regional Office Center, 11507, 11530
United Way of Eastern Maine, 1222
Voices for the Blind, 11531
Waterville Public Library, 11532
Western-Area Agency on Aging, 1223

Maryland

611 Washington Ear, 7492
ABLEDATA, 3055
Abbeyville Assisted Living, 8900
Abledata, 6301
Action Products, 3194
Allegany County Area: Agency on Aging, 1224
American Association for Adult and Continuing Education, 15
American Association of Colleges of Osteopathic Medicine, 18
American Association of the Deaf-Blind, 6311, 7503
American College Health Association, 32
American Diabetes Association: Maryland Area Office, 6140
American Gastroenterological Association, 6174
American Health Assistance Foundation, 6860
American Medical Informatics Association, 47
American Nurses Association, 51
American Occupational Therapy Association, 52
American Physiological Society, 53
American Society for Parenteral and Enteral Nutrition, 61
American Speech-Language-Hearing Association, 6316
American Urological Association, 6944
Anne Arundel County Area: Agency on Aging, 1225
Anne Arundel County Department of Aging and Disabilities, 1226
Anxiety Disorders Association of America, 6038

Asbury Methodist Village, 8901
Associate Administrator for Alcohol Prevention & Treatment Policy, 7141
Ausburg Lutheran Home Maryland, 8902
Baltimore City Commission on Aging, Retirement Education: CARE, 1227
Baltimore County Department of Aging, 1228
Blind Industries and Services of Maryland, 7537
Blossom Place at Edenton, 8903
Braille N' Speak, 3088
Brighton Gardens at Friendship Heights, 8904
Brighton Gardens of Columbia, 8905
Brighton Gardens of Pikesville, 8906
Buckinghams Choice, 8907
Bureau of Health Professions, Health Resources and Services Administration, 1229
Bureau of Naval Personnel: Maryland Retired Activities Office, 1230
Bureau of Naval Personnel: Patuxent Retired Activities Office, 1231
Byron House, 8908
Carroll County Bureau of Aging, 1232
Cecil County Department of Aging, 1233
Center for Substance Abuse Prevention, 7144
Centers for Medicare and Medicaid Services (CMS), 102
Charles County Department of Community Service Aging Division, 1234
Community Outreach Awards, 2626
Copper Ridge, 8909
Deaf Independent Living Association, 10783
Deaf and Hard of Hearing Entrepreneurs Council, 6347
Deaf/Hard of Hearing Entrepreneur of the Year, 2627
Department of Disabilities and Special Needs, 1235
Drug-Free Workplace Hotline, 7155
EKA/ Health & Mobility Systems, 2967
East Central Region: Helen Keller National Center, 7580
Eden Pines, 8910
Edenwald Retirement Community, 8911
Employment Awards, 2633
Food and Drug Administration, 138
Foundation Fighting Blindness, 7590
Frederick County Commission on Aging, 1236
Friends Medical Science Research Center, 7457
Friends of Libraries for Deaf Action, 11534
GA-SK, 3258
General German Aged Peoples Home, 8912
Group Development Awards, 2640
Harford County Office on Aging, 1237
Hausler, 8913
Health & Housing Association Mid-Atlantic Nonprofit, 1238
Hearling Loss Association of America, 6371
Heartfields Hall at Heartlands, 8914
Heartfields at Frederick, 8915
Hearthhomes Resedence Bay Ridge I, 8916
Hearthhomes Residence Piney Orchard, 8917
Hillhaven Assisted Living, 8918
Homewood at Crumland Farms, 8919
Homewood of Williamsport, 8920

1087

Geographic Index / Maryland

Impotence World Association, 6932
Impotents Anonymous, 6933
Independence Court of Hyattsville, 8921
Independence Now, 10784
Indian Health Service, 7170
Information Access Project: National Federation of the Blind, 7616
International Braille Research Center, 7618
International Braille and Technology Center for the Blind, 7619
Jacobus TenBroek Award, 2647
Job Opportunities for the Blind, 7623
Johns Hopkins Behavioral Pharmacology Research Unit, 7462
Johns Hopkins University: Dana Center for Preventive Ophthalmology, 8044
Kensington Park Woodlands-Groves, 8922
Keystone Award, 2650
Lifesprings Eldercare I, 8923
MAC Area: Agency on Aging, 1239
Maryland Association of Area Agencies on Aging, 1240
Maryland Blind Industries and Services, 7641
Maryland Center for Abuse Prevention, 7179
Maryland Chapter: Alexander Graham Bell Association for the Deaf, 6391
Maryland Client Assistance Program, 1241
Maryland Department of Aging, 1242
Maryland Department of Aging: Senior Legal Assistance, 11138
Maryland Department of Health and Mental Hygiene, 6043
Maryland Developmental Disability Council, 1243
Maryland Disability Determination Services, 1244
Maryland Disability Law Center, 11139
Maryland Legal Aid Bureau: Annapolis, 11140
Maryland Legal Aid Bureau: Baltimore, 11141
Maryland Office of Tourism Development, 11969
Maryland Protection & Advocacy Agency, 1245
Maryland Society for Sight, 7642
Maryland State Bar Association of Legal Services, 11142
Maryland State Library for the Blind and Physically Handicapped, 11535
Maryland State Retirement and Pension System, 1246
Maryland Veterans Commission, 1247
Maryland Workers Compensation Board, 1248
Melwood Access Adventures, 12031
Metropolitan Washington Ear, 3140
Miracle Assisted Living, 8924
Mobile Care, 11934
Montgomery County Government: Division of Elder Affairs, 1249
Multiple District 22: Lions Vision Research Foundation, 6278
NCSC Community Service Award/Certificateof Merit, 2658
NIH/National Institute of Neurological Disorders and Stroke, 7052
NIH: Heart, Lung & Blood Institute, 174
NIH: National Eye Institute, 175
NIH: National Institute of Dental and Cracial Research, 176
NIH: National Institute of Osteoporosis and Related Bone Diseases, 177
NIH: National Institute on Aging, 178
NIH: National Institute on Deafness and Communication Disorders, 179
National Association for Hearing and Speech Action, 6400
National Association for Senior Living Industries, 186
National Association of State Veterans Homes, 203
National Association of the Deaf, 6401
National Association of the Deaf Law Center, 6402
National Catholic Office of the Deaf, 6405
National Clearinghouse for Alcohol and Drug Information Library (NCADI), 7189, 7466
National Diabetes Action Network for the Blind, 6177, 7667
National Diabetes Information Clearinghouse, 6178
National Emergency Medicine Association, 221
National Eye Health Education Program, 7670
National Eye Institute, 8047
National Family Caregivers Association (NFCA), 223
National Federation of the Blind, 7671
National Federation of the Blind Scholarship Program, 2661
National Federation of the Blind of South Dakota, 7676
National Federation of the Blind: Blind Industrial Workers of America, 7679
National Federation of the Blind: Human Services Division, 7680
National Federation of the Blind: Job Opportunities for the Blind, 7681
National Federation of the Blind: Masonic Square Club, 7682
National Federation of the Blind: Sligo Creek Chapter, 7686
National Federation of the Blind:Blind Merchants Division, 7678
National Glaucoma Research, 8049
National Heart, Lung and Blood Institute, 6842
National Heart, Lung, and Blood Institute Information Center, 11536
National Institute of Diabetes & Digestive & Kidney Disease, 6279
National Institute of Neurological Disorders & Stroke, 7037
National Institute on Deafness & Other Communication Disorders, 6807
National Institute on Drug Abuse, 7193
National Institute on Drug Abuse Addiction Research Center Library (NIDA), 7468
National Institutes of Health, 236
National Kidney and Urologic Diseases Information Clearinghouse, 6936
National Prevention Resource Center, 7194
National Rehabilitation Information Center, 6417, 7053
National Rehabilitation Information Center (NARIC), 254
National Support Awards, 2663
National Volunteer Training Center for Substance Abuse Prevention, 7195
Nelson Cruikshank Award, 2665
Neurology Institute, 7055
Newel Perry Award, 2667
Oakcrest Village, 8925
Office of Applied Studies, 7469
Office of Disability: Social Security Administration, 275
Office of Retirement and Survivors, 1250
Office of Supplemental Security Income, 276
Office of Supplemental Security Income: Social Security Administration, 1251
Office of Women's Services, 7206
Outstanding Newsletter Recognitions, 2670
Outstanding Service Medallion, 2671
Personal Census Search: Data User Services Division, 293
Potomac Technology, 3154
President's Award for Exceptional andInnovative Leadership in Adult and Continuing Education, 2675
Prince George's County Bureau of Aging, 1252
Professional Advisory Support Award, 2676
Providence Assisted Living, 8926
Queen Anne's County Department of Aging, 1253
RADAR Network, 7216
RP Foundation Fighting Blindness (RPFFB), 7734
RSVP Allegany County, 1254
RSVP Baltimore City, 1255
RSVP Hagerstown, 1256
RSVP Lower Eastern Shore, 1257
RSVP Prince George's County, 1259
RSVP St. Mary's County, 1260
Railroad Retirement Board: Maryland District Office, 1261
Renaissance Gardens at Charlestown, 8927
Renaissance Gardens at Oak Crest, 8928
Renaissance Gardens at Riderwood, 8929
Resources for Independence, 10785
Retirement Industry Trust Association, 305
Rodeway Inns, 12043
Ronald Park Place, 8930
Rubens-Alcais Challenge, 2683
SPRY Foundation, 306
Senior Service America (SSA), 311
Sexual Function Health Council, 6943
Social Security Administration, 313
Social Security: Baltimore Disability Determination, 1262
Social Security: Retirement Insurance, 314
Social Security: Special Benefits for Persons Aged 72 & Older, 315
Southern Maryland Center for LIFE, 10786
Special Friend of Hearing Impaired People Award, 2684
Special Needs Library Montgomery County Department of Public Libraries, 11537
Spirit of SHHH Award, 2685
Spring Dell Center, 11538
St. Mary's County Office on Aging, 1263
Substance Abuse and Mental Health Services Administration, 7477
Telecommunications for the Deaf, 6450
Ticket Counter, 12049
US Army: Medical Command Center for Health Promotion & Preventive Medicine, 11539

US Department of Veterans Affairs Hospitl: Fort Howard Hospital Library, 11540
US Department of Veterans Affairs: Baltimore Medical Center Library Service, 11541
US National Institutes of Health: National Cancer Institute-Scientific Library, 11542
US Social Security Administration Library & Records Management Branch, 11543
Urban Cardiology Research Center, 6905
Volunteers for the Visually Handicapped, 7780
Walter T. Ridder Award, 2689
Warren Grant Magnuson Clinical Center, 6297, 6906, 8059, 8059
Washington County Commission on Aging, 1264
Washington Ear, 7782
Wheelchair and Mattress Pads, 3233
Workplace Program, 7232

Massachusetts

AD LIB Incorporated, 10787
Adams Council on Aging, 1265
Alden Place, 8931
Allerton House at Central Park, 8932
Allerton House at Hancock Park, 8933
Allerton House at Harbor Park, 8934
Allerton House at the Village at Duxbury, 8935
American Inn at Sawmill, 8936
Arbors at Amherst, 8937
Artia in Falmouth, 8938
Assistive Technology, 3080
Atrium at Cardinal Drive, 8939
Atrium at Drum Hill Alzheimer's DementiaAssisted Living, 8940
Atrium at Faxon Woods, 8941
Atrium at Veronica Drive, 8942
Avery Crossing, 8943
Bay State Council of the Blind, 7531
Baypath Senior Citizens Services, 1266
Berman-Gund Laboratory for the Study of Retinal Degenerations, 8037
Bernardston Council on Aging, 1267
Bertram House of Swampscott, 8944
Beverly Council on Aging, 1268
Billerica Crossings, 8945
Bookholder: Roberts, 3453
Boston Center for Independent Living, 10788
Boston College Legal Assistance Bureau, 11143
Boston College: Social Work Library, 11544
Boston Commission on Affairs of the Elderly, 1269
Boston University Laboratory of Neuropsychology, 7452
Boston University: General Clinical Research Center, 6864
Boston University: Whitaker Cardiovascular Institute, 6865
Briarwood Continuing Care Retirement Community, 8946
Brighton Gardens of Dedham, 8947
Brighton Gardens of North Shore by Marriott, 8948
Bristol Elder Services, 1270, 11144
Cadbury Commons at Cambridge, 8949
Cambridge Homes, 8950
Cameron House, 8951
Cape & Islands Senior Corps, 1271
Cape Organization for Rights of the Disabled (CORD), 10789
Caption Center, 11545, 6326
Caritas Southwood Hospital Medical Library, 11546
Carmel Terrace, 8952
Carroll Center for the Blind, 7556
Center for Living and Working, 10790
Central Massachusetts Agency on Aging, 1272
Chelmsford Crossings, 8953
Chelsea-Revere-Winthrop Elder Services Area: Agency on Aging, 1273
Christopher Heights Assisted Living, 8954
Christopher Heights of Webster, 8955
Coastline Elderly Services, 1274
Cohen Florence Levine Estates, 8956
Commonwealth of Massachusetts ExecutiveOffice of Elder Affairs, 11145
Community Action Commission of Cape Cod & Islands, 1275
Concord Park Assisted Living, 8957
Country Club Heights, 8958
DEAF Inc., 10791
Dalton Council on Aging, 1276
Dana-Farber Cancer Institute Library, 11547
Davis Manor, 8959
Deaconess Hospital Horrax Library, 11548
Decatur House, 8960
Deluxe Sock and Stocking Aid, 3236
Digi-Flex, 3251
Disability Law Center (DLC), 11146
Draper Place at Hopedale, 8961
Duxbury Braille Translator, 3110
Duxbury Systems, 3111
Eaton-Peabody Laboratory of Auditory Physiology, 6353
Elastic Shoelaces, 3238
Elder Service Plan of the North Shore, 1277
Elder Services of Berkshire County, 1278
Elder Services of Cape Cod and the Islands, 1279
Eldercare Initiative in Consumer Law (EICL), 123
Elderhostel, 12016
Elderhostel Institute Network, 12017
Electric Leg Bag Emptier and Tub Slide Shower Chair, 3014
Emmanuel House Residence, 8962
Eye Relief Word Processing Software, 3115
Falls at Cordingly Dam, 8963
Featherweight Reachers, 3239
Ferguson Industries for the Blind, 7587
Finger Print Pen, 3461
Forge Hill Senior Living Community, 8964
Framingham Heart Study, 6870
Framingham Public Library: Framingham Room, 11549
Franklin County Home Care Corporation, 1280
Friends of the Pepperell Seniors, 1281
Gabriel House of Fall River, 8965
General Clinical Research Center at Beth Israel Hospital, 6871
Goddard House in Brookline, 8966
Good Grips Cutlery, 3335
Grace Morgan House, 8967
Greater Boston Legal Services: Elderly Ofice (GBLS), 11147
Greater Lynn Senior Services (GLSS), 1282
Greater Springfield Senior Services, 1283
Grey & Emil Eisenber Assisted Living Residence, 8968
Grove Manor Estates Assisted Living, 8969
HESSCO Elder Services, 1284
Hampshire Community Action Commission, 1285
Harbor Point at Centerville, 8970
Harthstone at Laural Lake, 8971
Harvard Cocaine Recovery Project, 7163
Harvard Thorndike Laboratory, 6874
Harvard University: Howe Laboratory of Ophthalmology, 8043
Haverhill Crossings, 8972
Hearing Rehabilitation Foundation, 1286
Hearthstone at New Horizons, 8973
Heatherwood Assisted Living, 8974
Henrietta Brewer House, 8975
Heritage at Cleveland Circle, 8977
Heritage at Danvers, 8978
Heritage at Dartmouth, 8979
Heritage at Falmouth, 8980
Heritage at Framingham, 8981
Heritage at North Andover, 8982
Heritage at Vernon Court, 8983
Herrick House, 8984
Highland Valley Elder Services, 1287
Highlighter and Note Tape, 3462
Housing Options for Massachusetts Elders(HOME), 11148
Independent Living Center of the North Shore & Cape Ann, 10792
Inn at Silver Lake, 8985
Innerlip Plates, 3338
Jewish Community Relations Council of Greater Boston, 1288
Joslin Diabetes Center, 6277
Laboure College Library, 11550
Landmark at Fall River, 8986
Landmark at Ocean View, 8987
Legal Assistance Corporation of Central Massachusetts: Senior Citizens Advocacy Program, 11149
Leominster Crossings, 8988
Lindustries, 3309
Line-A-Timers, 3132
Long Handled Bath Sponges, 3016
Longmeadow Place at Burlington, 8989
Longreach Reacher, 3310
Longwood Place at Reading, 8990
Loop Scissors, 3311
MAB Community Services, 1289
Macular Degeneration Foundation, 8045
Mallory Institute of Pathology Foundation, 6882
Manor on the Hill, 8991
Maplewood Place at Malden, 8992
Marina Place at Quincy, 8993
Marland Place at Andover, 8994
Marriott Mapleridge of Plymouth, 8995
Mason Wright Retirement Community, 8996
Massachusetts Assistive Technology Partnership, 1290
Massachusetts Association for the Blind, 7643
Massachusetts Bureau of Substance Abuse Services, 7180
Massachusetts Client Assistance Program, 1291
Massachusetts Commission for the Blind, 7644

Geographic Index / Michigan

Massachusetts Department of Elder Affairs, 1292
Massachusetts Department of Mental Health, 6044
Massachusetts Department of Revenue, 1293
Massachusetts Developmental Disabilities Council, 1294
Massachusetts Disability Determination Services, 1295
Massachusetts Executive Office for Administration and Finance, 1297
Massachusetts Executive Office of Health and Human Services, 1296, 1298, 1299, 1299
Massachusetts General Departments of Neurology and Neurosurgery, 7119
Massachusetts Mutual Life Insurance Company Law Library, 11150
Massachusetts Office of Travel & Tourism, 11970
Massachusetts Protection & Advocacy Organization, 1300
Massachusetts Social Security Region 1 Administration, 1301
Massachusetts Statewide Independent Living Council (MASILC), 10793
Mayflower Place, 8997
Meadow Lodge at Drum Hill, 8998
Medi-Grip, 3266
Media Access Group, 7645
MegaDots, 3137
Melbourne Place, 8999
Merrimack Place, 9000
MetroWest Center for Independent Living, 10794
Molded Sock and Stocking Aid, 3242
Mount Ida College: National Center for Death Education, 11151
Mystic Valley Elder Services, 1302
National Association for Parents of the Visually Impaired (NAPVI), 7654
National Association of Guide Dog Users, 7660
National Braille Press, 7663
National Center for Accessible Media, 6406
National Program on Women and Aging, 253
New Bedford Council on Aging, 1303
New England Corporate Library, 11551
New England Region: Helen Keller National Center, 7695
New Horizons at Choate, 9001
New Horizons at Marlboro, 9002
New Pond Village, 9003
North Shore Elder Services, 1304
Northeast Independent Living Program, 10795
Northfield Senior Center, 1305
Norumbega Point at Weston, 9004
Nosey Cup, 3342
Old Colony Planning Council Area: Agency on Aging, 1306
Operation ABLE of Greater Boston, 1307
Orchard Hill At Sudbury, 9005
Orchard Valley at Wilbraham, 9006
Paring Boards, 3343
Perkins School for the Blind: Samuel P Hayes Research Library, 11552
Pinehill at Kimball Farms, 9007
Pines of Tewksbury, 9008
Plastic Card Holder, 3466

Plymouth Crossings, 9009
Quincy Retirement Board, 1309
RSVP Berkshire, 1310
RSVP Boston, 1311
RSVP Chicopee-Holyoke-Ludlow, 1312
RSVP Fall River-Taunton, 1313
RSVP Greater Lawrence-Haverhill, 1314
RSVP Lowell, 1315
RSVP Mayflower of Plymouth County, 1316
RSVP Norfolk County, 1317
RSVP Senior Care North Shore, 1318
RSVP Worcester Area, 1320
Railroad Retirement Board Dsitrict Office, 1321
Reeds Landing, 9010
Region 1: Administration on Aging (AoA), 1322
Reid & Hurley Travel, 12041
Renaissance Gardens at Brooksby Village, 9011
Ruth's House, 9012
Salisbury Assisted Living Center, 9013
Sarawood Retirement Home, 9014
Scandinavian Living Center, 9015
Schepens Eye Research Institute, 8052
Scituate Council on Aging, 1323
Scooter Lift/Carrier, 2992
Senior Home Care Services, 1324
Service Opportunities After Retirement (SOAR), 1325
Shrewsbury Crossing, 9016
Shrewsbury Senior Center, 1326
Somerville Cambridge Elder Services, 1327
South Shore Elder Services, 1328
Southeast Center for Independent Living, 10796
Southgate at Shrewsbury, 9017
Springhouse Retirement Community, 9018
Standish Village at Lower Mills, 9019
Stavros Center for Independent Living, 10797
Sturgis Library, 11152
Sunrise Assisted Living at Gardner Park, 9020
Sunrise Assisted Living of Cohasset, 9021
Sunrise Assisted Living of Norwood, 9022
Sunrise Assisted Living of Wayland, 9023
Tatnuck Park at Worcester, 9024
Terry-Wash Mitt, 3027
Terry-Wash Mitt - Medium Size, 3028
Therapy Putty, 3274
Thick-n-Easy, 3350
Thumbs Up Cup, 3351
Thyroid Foundation of America, 323
Traditions of Wayland, 9025
Tub Slide Shower Chair, 3032
US Department of Veterans Affairs Bedford: Edith Nourse Rogers Memorial Veterans Hospital Medical Library, 11553
US Department of Veterans Affairs Outpatient Clinic Learning Resources Service, 11555
US Department of Veterans Affairs: Boston Hospital Medical Library, 11556
US Department of Veterans Affairs: Medical Center Library, 11447, 11449, 11515, 11515, 11521, 11557
Universal Hand Cuff, 3354
University of Massachusetts: Diabetes Endocrinology Research Center, 6286
Urban Medical Group, 1329

Victorian of Chatham, 9026
Village at Farm Pond, 9027
Village at Willow Crossings, 9028
Vision Community Services, 7772
Vision Foundation, 7773
Vision Use in Employment (VUE), 7774
Volunteer Lawyers Project of the Boston Bar Association, 11153
Weighted Holders, 3471
Wellfleet Council on Aging, 1330
West Suburban Elder Services, 1331
WestMass Elder Care, 1332
Westfield Meadows, 9029
Whitcomb House, 9030
Whitehall Estate, 9031
Whitney Place at Natick, 9032
Whitney Place at Northbridge, 9033
Woodbridge Assisted Living, 9034
Woods at Eddy Pond, 9035
Worcester Public Library, 11558
Workers Compensation Board Massachusetts, 1333
Yarmouth Council on Aging, 1334
Youville House Assisted Living Residence, 9036
Youville Place, 9037

Michigan

1B Area: Agency on Aging, 1335
A Friend's House Adult Day Services, 1336
A Friend's House Adult Day Services: Romeo, 1337
A Friend's House Adult Day Services: Warren, 1338
Alpena Regional Medical Center Auxiliary, 1339
AlumiRamp, 3357
Alzheimer's Association: South Central Michigan Chapter, 1340
American Diabetes Association: Southeast Michigan Area Office, 6164
Amigo Centra, 3416
Amigo Mobility International, 3358
Amplified Handsets, 3071
Amplified Phones, 3072
Amplified Portable Phone, 3073
Ann Arbor Center for Independent Living, 9038, 10798
Area Agency on Aging Library, 11559
Area Agency on Aging of Western Michigan, (AAAWM), 1341
Argentine Care Center, 9039
Artificial Larynx, 3078
Association for the Blind and Visually Impaired, 7527
Berrien County Legal Services: Senior Law Center, 11154
Blinker Buddy II Electronic Turn Signal, 2958
Blue Water Center for Independent Living Center, 10799
Blueprint for Aging, 1343
Burcham Hills Retirement Center, 9041
Bureau of Naval Personnel: Michigan Retired Activities Office, 1344
CQC Stephenson Home, 9042
Capital Area Center for Independent Living, 10800
Charlevoix County Commission on Aging, 1345

Geographic Index / Michigan

Cherrywood Nursing & Living Center, 9043
Chicago Social Security Management Association, 1346
Clark Retirement Home, 9044
Countryside Care Center, 9045
Covenant Village of the Great Lakes, 9046
Cumberland Manor, 9047
Department of Blind Rehabilitation, 7578
Detroit Area: Agency on Aging, 1347
Disability Advocates of Kent County, 10801
Disability Network-Lakeshore Center for Independent Living, 10802
Disability Resource Center of Southwest Michigan, 10803
Doorbell Signalers, 3108
Double Gong Indoor/Outdoor Ringer, 3109
Downtown Detroit Subregional Library for the Blind, 11560
Dual Brakes Unit, 2966
Elder Law of Michigan: Legal Hotline for Michigan Seniors, 11155
Electronic Stethoscopes, 3256
Extra Loud Alarm with Lighter Plug, 3114
Fairview Living Centre, 9048
Fountains at Franklin, 9049
Fraser Villa: A Mercy Living Center, 9050
General Motors Mobility Program for Persons with Disabilities, 2969
General Motors Mobility Program for Travelers with Disabilities, 12022
Gilbert Residence, 9051
Glacier Hills Retirement Center, 9052
Grand Traverse Area Library for the Blind and Physically Handicapped, 11561
Grandparents Rights Organization, 143
Gray Panthers Metro Detroit, 1348
Gray Panthers of Huron Valley, 1349
Greater Detroit Agency F/T Blind and Visually Impaired, 7597
Gresham Driving Aids, 2970
HARC Mercantile-Division of HAC ofAmerica, 3278
Hazel I Findlay Country Manor, 9053
Hearing Aid Batteries, 3279
Hearing Aid Battery Testers, 3280
Hearing Aid Dehumidifier, 3281
Hearing Aid Helpline, 6364
Heart and Vascular Institute, 6877
Heartland HCC-Crestview, 9054
Henry Ford Hospital: Hypertension and Vascular Research Division, 6922
Herman Miller Research Corporation, 11562
Hume Home of Muskegon, 9055
In the Ear Hearing Aid Battery Extractor, 3282
Ingham Regional Assisted Living, 9056
Innovative Products Unlimited, 3521
International Hearing Society, 6379
International Hearing Society: Hearing Aid Helpline, 6380
Iron Workers Local 25 Retirees Club of the International Association, 1350
Jackson Friendly Home, 9057
John George Home, 9058
Karmanos Cancer Institute Research Library, 11563
Kent County Library for the Blind, 11564
Knock Light, 3308
Large Button Speaker Phone, 3127
Laurel Park West, 9059
Library of Michigan Service for the Blind, 11565

Lighthouse of Oakland, 7637
Luther Village, 9060
Macomb Library for the Blind and Physically Handicapped, 11566
Maple Village, 9061
Mature Minglers Senior Center: Senior Adult Services and Programs, 1351
McLaren Homewood Village, 9062
Meadows at Silver Maples, 9063
Mednet Ketronic Inc., 2984
Mercy Pavilion of Battle Creek, 9064
Michigan Association for the Deaf: Hearing and Speech Services, 6394
Michigan Association for the DeafHearing and Speech Services, 6393
Michigan Association of Area Agencies on Aging, 1352
Michigan Association of Homes and Services for the Aging, 1353
Michigan Association of Retired School Personnel, 1354
Michigan Bureau of Workers' Disability Compensation, 1355
Michigan Center for Substance Abuse Services, 7182
Michigan Christian Home, 9065
Michigan Client Assistance Program, 1356
Michigan Commission for the Blind, 7790
Michigan Council of the Blind and Visually Impaired (MCBVI), 7647
Michigan Department of Community Health, 1357
Michigan Department of Human Services, 1358
Michigan Department of Labor Commission for the Blind: Center for Independent Living Program for Elderly, 9066
Michigan Department of Management and Budget: Bureau of Retirement Systems, 1359
Michigan Department of Military Affairs Bureau of State Operations and Veterans' Affairs, 1360
Michigan Department of Treasury, 1361
Michigan Developmental Disability Council, 1362
Michigan Office of Services to the Aging, 1363
Michigan Office of Services to the Elderly, 11156
Michigan Office on Aging, 1364
Michigan Protection & Advocacy Service: Livonia, 11157
Michigan Protection and Advocacy Service: Lansing, 11158
Michigan Rehabilitation Services, 1365
Michigan Society of Gerontology, 1366
Michigan Speech Language Hearing Association, 6395
Michigan Speech, Language & Hearing Association, 6396
Michigan Travel Bureau, 11971
Michigan Workers Compensation Board, 1367
Mideastern Michigan Library Co-op, 11567
Midland Center for Independent Living, 10804
Mini Teleloop, 3141
Mississippi Division of Tourism Development, 11973
Mulligan Foundation, 7036
Multiple Phone/Device Switch, 3145

Nek-Lo, Nek-Lo Hot and Cold, Pillow-Perfect, Body Buddy, 3219
Northeast Michigan Community Services Region 9 Area: Agency on Aging, 1368
Northland Library Cooperative, 11568
Northpointe Woods Assisted Living, 9067
Oakland & Macomb Center for IndependentLiving, 10805
Oakland County Library for the Blind and Physically Handicapped, 11569
Park Village Pines, 9068
Parkinson Association of Michigan, 6965
Personal FM Systems, 3149
Personal Infrared Listening System, 3150
Pilgram Manor, 9069
Plymouth Inn, 9070
Pocket Otoscope, 3270
Porter Hills Presbyterian Village, 9071
Presbyterian Village Redford, 9072
Push to Talk Amplified Handset, 3157
RSVP Genesee-Shiawassee Counties, 1369
RSVP Ingham, 1370
RSVP Kent County, 1372
RSVP Macomb, 1373
RSVP Marquette County, 1374
RSVP Mecosta/Lake/Osceola, 1375
RSVP Oakland County, 1376
RSVP Ostego County, 1377
RSVP Wayne County, 1011, 1378
Railroad Retirement Board: Michigan District Office, 1379
Region 14 Council on Aging, 1380
Region Four Area: Agency on Aging, 1381
Region Seven Area: Agency on Aging, 1382
Region Two Area: Agency on Aging, 1383
Renaissance Gardens at Henry FordVillage, 9073
Rest Haven Home, 9074
Right to Life of Michigan, 1384
Riverview Manor, 9075
Room Valet Visual-Tactile AlertingSystem, 3160
Rose Garden Home, 9076
Saginaw Geriatrics Home, 9077
Senior Alliance Area Agency on Aging, 1385, 11570
Senior Companion Program of Macomb, 1386
Senior Services, 1387
Sixty Plus Elderlaw Clinic, 11159
Sound Induction Receiver, 3161
Speech Discrimination Unit, 3163
Speechmaker-Personal Speech Amplifier, 3164
St Ann's Home, 9078
St Anne's Mead Retirement Home, 9079
St Clark County Library for the Blind and Physically Handicapped, 11571
St Joesph's Home for the Aged, 9080
State Bar of Michigan: Senior Justice Committee, 11160
State of Michigan Travel Resources, 11990
Strobe Light Signalers, 3169
Sunrise Assisted Living at Farmington Hills, 9081
Sunrise Assisted Living at Northville, 9082
Sunrise Assisted Living of Ann Arbor, 9083
Sunrise Assisted Living of Rochester, 9084
Sunrise Assisted Living of Troy, 9085
Sunrise Assisted Living of WestBloomfield, 9086
TTY's-Telephone Device for the Deaf, 3173

Geographic Index / Minnesota

Talking Clocks, 3175
Talking Watches, 3177
Telecaption Adapter, 3178
Thurston Woods Village: The Villa, 9087
Tri-County Office on Aging, 1388
US Department of Veterans Affairs: Ann Arbor Hospital Library, 11572
US Department of Veterans Affairs: Battle Creek Medical Center Library Service, 11573
US Department of Veterans Affairs: Detroit Medical Center Library Service, 11574
US Department of Veterans Affairs: Iron Mountain Medical Center Library, 11575
US Department of Veterans Affairs: Saginaw Aleda E Lutz Medical Center Library, 11576
University of Michigan Alcohol Research Center, 7481
University of Michigan: Communicative Disorders Clinic, 6824
University of Michigan: Division of Hypertension, 6925
University of Michigan: Kresge Hearing Research Institute, 6825
University of Michigan: Tecumster Mental Health Study, 6104
Valley Area: Agency on Aging, 1389
Vibrotactile Personal Alerting System, 3187
Visually Impaired Center, 7777
Voice Amplified Handsets, 3188
WINVISION, 3189
Waltonwood of Royal Oak, 9088
Washtenaw County Library, 11577
Waterford Senior Center, 1390
Wayne County Regional Library for the Blind, 11578
William T Gossett Parkinson's Disease Center, 7050
Woodhaven Retirement Community, 9089
Woodside at Friendship Village, 9090

Minnesota

Ability Research, 3060
AbleNet, 3064
Academy of Rehabilitative Audiology, 6304
Agape Senior Homes, 9091
Alliance Assisted Living Services, 9092
Almond House, 9093
Alterra Clare Bridge Cottage of West St Paul, 9094
Alterra Clare Bridge Cottage-Coon Rapids, 9095
Alterra Clare Bridge Cottage-Owatonna, 9096
Alterra Clare Bridge of Eagan, 9097
Alterra Clare Bridge of North Oaks, 9098
Alterra Clare Bridge of Plymouth, 9099
Alterra Sterling House of Apple Valley, 9100
Alterra Sterling House of Blaine, 9101
Alterra Sterling House of Coon Rapids, 9102
Alterra Sterling House of Faribault, 9103
Alterra Sterling House of Inver Grove Heights, 9104
Alterra Sterling House of West St Paul, 9105
Alterra Sterling House-Brooklyn Center, 9106
Alterra Sterling House-Mankato, 9107
Alterra Sterling House-Sauk Rapids, 9108
Alterra Sterling House-Willmar, 9109
Alterra Sterling House-Winona, 9110
Alterra Sterling-Owatonna, 9111
Alterra Wynwood of Rochester, 9112
American Academy of Neurology, 7051
American Diabetes Association: Minnesota Area Office, 6143
Arlington Place, 9113
Arrowhead Area: Agency on Aging, 1391
Arrowhead Senior Living Community, 9114
Assisted Living in Heritage Hall, 9115
Association of Halfway House Alcoholism: Programs of North America, 7142
Assumption Court, 9116
Assured Care, 9117
Auburn Courts, 9118
BIGmack Communication Aid, 3083
Barrett Assisted Living Community, 9119
Barross House, 9120
Battery Device Adapter, 3275
Big Red Switch, 3085
Brickford Cottage, 8645, 9121
Brookridge, 9122
Brooks of St Paul, 9123
Bryant House, 9124
Bureau of Naval Personnel: Minnesota Retired Activities Office, 1392
Burnsdale Extended Care, 9125
Callista Court, 9126
Care Pointe, 9127
Care-Age Country Home, 9128
Carefree Living America-Brainerd, 9129
Carefree Living America-Burnsville, 9130
Carefree Living of America-St Cloud, 9131
Carric Manor, 9132
Cartens Harbour, 9133
Cass County Council on Aging, 1393
Catholic Eldercare at Home, 9134
Cedar Crest Estate, 9135
Cedars of Austin, 9136
Centennial Villa Assisted Living, 9137
Central Minnesota Council on Aging, 1394
Central Minnesota Self-Help for Hard of Hearing, 6330
Central Todd County Care Center, 9138
Chandler Place, 9139
Chappys Golden Shore, 9140
Claddagh House, 9141
Clearwater Suites Assisted Living, 9142
Commons on Marice, 9143
Communicating for Seniors, 1395
Community Assisted Living, 9144
Computer Switch Interface, 3101
Copperfield Hill Phase II, 9145
Cordless Big Red Switch, 3102
Cordless Receiver, 3298, 3326
Country Care Homes, 8496, 9146
Country Neighbors, 9147
Country Neighbors-Lake Crystal, 9148
Country Neighbors-Le Center, 9149
Country Oaks Elder Care, 9150
Country Villa, 9151
Dentists Concerned for Dentists, 7152
Department of Employment and Economic Development, 1396
Dignified Living, 9152
Dignified Living-Prior Lake, 9153
Dual Switch Latch and Timer, 3301
Duluth Lighthouse for the Blind, 7579
Duluth Public Library, 11579
East Central Regional Development Commission Area on Aging, 1398
Easy Stand, 3371
Edgewood Vista-Virginia, 9155
Elder Haven Homes, 9156
Emerald Care, 9157
English Rose Suites, 9158
Evergreen Knoll, 9159
Evergreens of Moorhead, 9160
Flying Wheels Travel, 12020
Four Star, 9161
Franciscan Assisted Living, 9162
Garden Cottage Assisted Living, 9163
Gianna Homes-Sursum Corda, 9164
Golden Oaks Residence, 9166
Grace Manor, 9167
Grace Place, 9168
Granite Falls Senior Services, 9169
Gray Panthers of Twin Cities, 1399
Guardian Angels Elem HomeCare, 9170
Happy Old Timers Senior Center, 1400
Hazelden Foundation, 7165
Hazeldon Foundation: Library and Information Resources, 7460
Headwaters Area: Agency on Aging, 1401
Health East Residence of South St Paul, 9171
Healtheast Care Center-Marian St Paul, 9172
Healtheast Residence on Humboldt, 9173
Healtheast Residence-White Bear Lake, 9174
Heritage Home, 9175
Heritage House Assisted Living Facility, 9176
Heritage House of Bemidji, 9177
Heritage Manor, 9178
Hillcrest Rehabilitation & Healthcare Center, 9179
Hillside Homes of Duluth, 9180
Homestead Place, 9181
Hub City Developmental, 9182
Hyza Home, 9183
Impotence Information Center, 6931
Institute on Black Chemical Abuse, 7172
Interim Assisted Care, 9184
Interim Healthcare, 9185
Interlachen Senior Suites, 9186
International Diabetes Center: Institute for Research & Education Health System, 6276
Intrepid USA-Becklund, 9187
Island View Manor, 9188
Jasper Sunrise Village, 9189
Jelly Bean Switch, 3123
Johnson Park Place, 9190
Jones Harrison Residence Assisted Living, 9191
Just Like Home, 9192
Kenwood Heritage Living, 9193
Kenwood Retirement Community, 9194
Keystone Bluffs, 9195
Kingsway Assisted Living, 9196
Kinyon Residence, 9197
Knutson Place Apartments, 9198
LSS/Westwind, 9199
LT Switch, 3125
La Bonnie Vie, 9200
Lafayette Good Samartian Assisted Living, 9201
Lake Ridge Manor at Ebenezer Covenant Home, 9202

Geographic Index / Minnesota

Lakeside Manor, 9203
Lakeview Ranch Adult Foster Care, 9204
Lakeview Retirement Residence, 9205
Lakewood Pine Senior Housing, 9206
Laurel Lodge Assisted Living Home, 9207
Laurels Edge, 9208
Legal Aid Service of Northeastern Minnesota (LASNEM): Duluth Office, 11161
Life Care Concepts, 9209
Lindenwood, 9210
Little House on Prairie, 9211
Loving Residence, 9212
Lutheran Home-Cedar Haven, 9213
Lutheran Memorial Retirement Center, 9214
Lutheran Memorial Retirement Center-Brainerd, 9215
Lutheran Social Services, 9216
Madison Avenue Apartments, 9217
Manor House, 9218
Maranatha Place, 9219
Margaret Place, 9220
Martin Luther Manor, 9221
May Creek Lodge Assisted Living, 9222
McCarthy Manor, 9223
Meadow Woods, 9224
Meadowland Elder Care Home, 9225
Meadows of Worthington, 9227
Meadows on Main, 9228
Metropolitan Area Agency on Aging, 1402
Metropolitan Center for Independent Living (MCIL), 10807
Mid-Minnesota Area: Agency on Aging, 1403
Minneapolis Age & Opportunity Center, 11162
Minnesota Academy of Audiology, 6806
Minnesota Board on Aging, 1404, 11163
Minnesota Chapter No. 1 SHHH - Self Help for Hard of Hearing People, 6397
Minnesota Chemical Dependency Program, 7183
Minnesota Council on Disability, 1405
Minnesota Department of Human Services Library & Resource Center, 11580
Minnesota Department of Labor & Industry Workers Compensation Division, 1406
Minnesota Department of Revenue, 1407
Minnesota Department of Veterans Affairs, 1408
Minnesota Governor's Council on Developmental Disabilities, 1409
Minnesota Health & Housing Alliance, 1410
Minnesota Indian Area: Agency on Aging, 1411
Minnesota Library for the Blind, 11581
Minnesota Mental Health Division, 1412
Minnesota Office of Tourism, 11972
Minnesota Public Employees Retirement Association, 1413
Minnesota STAR Program, 1414
Minnesota State Bar Association: Elder Law Section, 11164
Minnesota State Council on Disability, 1415
Minnesota State Services for the Blind, 7648
Minnesota Teachers Retirement Association, 1416
Minnestoa Retirement System, 1417
Mirror Go Lightly, 3241
Moorhead Manor, 9229
Mother Lucille Leisure Living, 9230
Mother of Mercy Nursing & Retirement Center, 9231
National Association of Blind Educators, 7656
National Association to Promote the Use of Braille, 7661
National Long-Term Care Resource Center, 241
New Perspective of Minnesota, 9232
Nicollet Place, 9233
North Oaks on Emerson, 9234
Northfield Parkview, 9235
Northside Retirement Home, 9236
Oak Hill Living Center Assisted Living, 9237
Oak Park Place, 9238
Oak Park Place-Albert Lea, 9239
Oak Ridge Assisted Living-Hastings, 9240
Oak Ridge Place, 9241
Oakenwald Terrace, 9242
Oaks, 9243
On Golden Pond, 9244
Options Interstate Resource Center for Independent Living, 10808
Osseo Gardens, 9245
Our Circle of Friends, 9246
Our Home, Your Home, 9247
Our House, 9248
Our House Board and Lodge, 9249
Park Lane Estates, 9250
Park Place Senior Congregate Assisted Living, 9251
Parker Oaks Assisted Living, 9252
Parkinson Association of Minnesota, 6966
Parkwood Apartments, 9253
Paynesville Area Senior Center, 1418
Pines, 9254
Pines Senior Care, 9255
Pioneer Estates of Minnesota, 9256
Pioneer Senior Cottages, 9257
PowerLink 2 Control Unit, 3313, 3344
Prairie Senior Cottages-Alexandria, 9258
Prairie Senior Cottages-Hutchinson, 9259
Prairie Senior Cottages-Willmar, 9260
Presbyterian Assisted Living Homecare, 9261
Pride Institute, 7215
Primrose, 9262
RSVP Aiken-Carlton Counties, 1419
RSVP Anoka County, 1420
RSVP Arrowhead County, 1421
RSVP Eldercircle, 1422
RSVP Greater Twin Cities, 1423
RSVP Mahube Community Council, 1425
RSVP Semcac, 1427
RSVP Southern Tri-County, 1428
RSVP Todd-Wadena-Otter Tail-Wilkin, 1429
RSVP Volunteer Services, 1430
RSVP West Central Minnesota, 1431
Railroad Retirement Board: Duluth Minnesota District Office, 1432
Railroad Retirement Board: St. Paul Minnesota District Office, 1433
Rakhma Peace Home, 9263
Regina Retirement Center, 9264
Rem Canby Senior Services, 9265
Rem Montevideo Senior Services, 9266
Rem Southview, 9267
Reminiscence Home, 9268
Resource Directory of Special Education and Rehabilitation Computer Products, 3159
Richfield Senior Suites, 9269
Ridgeway on German, 9270
River Birch Residence, 9271
Rivers Edge Villa, 9272
Rochester Regional Service Center for Hearing Impaired People, 6441
Rollx Vans, 11939
Roseview Court Care Agency, 9273
Rosewood Estate-Highland, 9274
Rosewood Estate-Maplewood, 9275
Rosewood Estates-Roseville, 9276
Ruth Homes, 9277
Salmi Homes, 9278
Samaritan Bethany Terrace, 9279
Senior Suites of New Brighton, 9280
September House, 9281
Shade Tree Retirement Center, 9282
Shepherds Inn, 9283
Sibley Manor Assisted Living, 9284
Skylight Gardens, 9285
Small Appliance Receiver, 3314, 3347
Solbakken, 9286
Southeast Minnesota Area: Agency on Aging, 1435
Southeast Regional Service Center for Hearing Impaired People, 1436
Southeast Senior Federation, 1437
Southeastern Minnesota Area: Agency on Aging, 1438
Southeastern Minnesota Center for Independent Living, 10809
Southern Minnesota IL Enterprises and Services (SMILES), 10810
Southview on Main, 9287
Southwest Area: Agency on Aging, 1439
Southwest Center for Independent Living, 10811
SpeakEasy Communication Aid, 3162
Spectrum Community Health, 9288
Spectrum Community Health-Minneapolis, 9289
Spring Valley Estates, 9290
St Anns Residence, 9291
St Benedicts Senior Community, 9292
St Paul Urban League, 9293
St Williams Foster Care, 9294
Step-by-Step Communicator, 3166
Sterling Park Commons, 9295
Sterling Park Ridgeview, 9296
Stevens Residence, 9297
String Switch, 3168
Sunrise Assisted Living of Buffalo, 9298
Sunrise Assisted Living of Edina, 9299
Sunrise Assisted Living-Roseville, 9300
Sunrise Cottage of Mankato, 9301
Sunrise Cottages of Rochester, 9302
Sunrise Village, 9303
Symbi-Key Computer Switch Interface, 3170
TV & VCR Remote, 3174
Terrace Heights, 9304
The Country Place, 9305
Thorne Crest Retirement Center, 9306
Town Hall Estates, 9307
Tracy's House, 9308
Transitional Senior Housing, 9309
Tuff Village, 9310

Geographic Index / Mississippi

US Department of Veterans Affairs: Minneapolis Medical Center Library Service, 11582
United Way 211, 1440
Universal Switch Mounting System, 3185
University of Minnesota: Center for Bioethics, 6036
University of Minnesota: Division of Health Services Research and Policy, 6105
University of Minnesota: Hypertensive Research Group, 6926
University of Minnesota: Program on Alcohol/Drug Control, 7482
Upper Minnesota Valley Area Agency on Aging, 1441
Valley Country Care, 9311
Valley View Estates, 9312
Valleyview Board and Lodge, 9313
Ventures, 12057
Viking Manor Nursing Home, 9314
Villa St Vincent, 9315
Volunteers of America of Minnesota, 9316
Wellington, 9317
Wellstead of Rogers, 9318
Wesley Residence, 9319
West Central Area: Agency on Aging, 1442
Westview Estates, 9320
Westwood Place, 9321
Whispering Pines Care Center, 9322
Wild Acre Homes, 9323
Wilder Assisted Living Programs, 9324
Wilderness Inquiry, 12060
Wildflower Lodge, 9325
Wilds of Sand Prairie, 9326
Wildwood Grove, 9327
Woodland Good Samaritan Village Apartments, 9328
Woodland Manor, 9329

Mississippi

American Kinesiotherapy Association, 43
Area Agency on Aging of Southern Mississippi, 1443
Central Mississippi Area: Agency on Aging, 1444
Drew Karol Industries, 3254
East Central Area: Agency on Aging, 1445
LIFE of North Mississippi, 10812
LIFE of South Mississippi, 10813
Mississippi (State) Department of Mental Health Library and Division of Professional Development, 11583
Mississippi Association of Area Agencies on Aging, 1446
Mississippi Client Assistance Program: Easter Seals Society, 1447
Mississippi Commission for Veterans Affairs, 1448
Mississippi Council on Aging, 11165
Mississippi Department of Mental Health, 1449
Mississippi Department of Rehabilitation Services for the Blind, 1450
Mississippi Developmental Disability Council, 1451
Mississippi Division of Aging and Adult Services, 1452
Mississippi Division of Alcohol and Drug Abuse, 7184
Mississippi Industries for the Blind, 7649
Mississippi Library Commission, 11584
Mississippi Office of Disability & Determination Services, 1453
Mississippi Protection and Advocacy System, 11166
Mississippi Public Employees Retirement Systems, 1454
Mississippi State Bar Association: Young Lawyers on Legal Problems of Elderly & Handicapped, 11167
Mississippi State Tax Commission, 1455
NMRLS - Northern Mississippi Rural LegalServices: Clarksdale Office, 11168
Natchez-Adams Council on Aging, 1456
North Central Area: Agency on Aging, 1457
North Delta Planning and Development District Area Agency on Aging, 1458
Northeast Mississippi Area: Agency on Aging, 1459
Northern Mississippi Rural Legal Services (NMRLS): Elder Law Project - Oxford (Administrative) Office, 11169
Preserve Sight Mississippi, 1460
RSVP Adams County, 1461
RSVP Attala County, 1462
RSVP Clarksdale, 1463
RSVP Hancock County, 1464
RSVP Harrison County, 1465
RSVP Lafayette County, 1466
RSVP Laurel-Jones County, 1467
RSVP Lee County, 781, 1468
RSVP Lowndes County, 1469
RSVP Meridian-Lauderdale Counties, 1470
RSVP Simpson County, 1471
South Delta Planning and Development District, 1472
Southern Mississippi Area Agency on Aging, 1473
Southwest Mississippi Area Agency on Aging, 1474
Three Rivers Area: Agency on Aging, 1475
US Department of Veterans Affairs: Jackson Medical Center Library, 11585

Missouri

Able Commission, 1476
Access II Independent Living Center, 10814
Access Industries/ThyssenKrupp Access, 3355
American Council on Alcohol Problems, 7134
American Diabetes Association: Mid-America Regional Office, 6142
American Diabetes Association: MissouriArea Office, 6146
American Optometric Association, 7514
Autumn Ridge, 9330
Autumn View Gardens, 9331
Bonne Terre Memorial Library, 11586
Bootheel Area Independent Living Services (BAILS), 10815
Central Institute for the Deaf, 6329
Central Institute for the Deaf Professional Library, 11587
Circline Illuminated Magnifer, 3097
Columbia Area Senior Center, 1477
DW Auto & Home Mobility Specialties, 2963
Dazor Manufacturing Corporation, 3299
Delta Center for Independent Living, 10816
Disability Determination Services: Cape Girardeau, 1479
Disability Determination Services: Kansas City, 1480
Disability Determination Services: Saint Louis, 1481
Disability Determination Services: Springfield, 1482
Disability Resource Association, 10817
Disabled Citizens Alliance for Independence-DCAI, 10818
Everest & Jennings, 3303
Excel Stair Lift, 3375
Fairwinds-River's Edge, 9332
Foam Decubitus Bed Pads, 3037
Gateway Older Adult Legal Services, 11170
Greater St. Louis Association of the Deaf, 1483, 6360
Independent Living Center, 10622, 10819
Independent Living Resource Center, 10764, 10820
International Lutheran Deaf Association, 6382
Kansas City Association for the Blind, 7626
Legal Aid of Western Missouri: Kansas City, 11171
Living Independently for Everyone (LIFE), 10821
Long Term Care Ombudsman Program, 1484
Lutheran Library for the Blind, 11588
McKnight Place Assisted Living, 9334
Mid-America Regional Council of Aging Services, 1485
Mid-East Area: Agency on Aging, 1486
Midland Empire Resources for Independent Living (MERIL), 10822
Minivator Residential Elevator, 3387
Missouri Assisted Living Association, 1487
Missouri Council of the Blind, 1488, 7650
Missouri Department of Mental Health, 1489
Missouri Department of Revenue, 1490
Missouri Developmental Disability Council, 1491
Missouri Division of Senior & Disability Services, 11172
Missouri Division of Tourism, 11974
Missouri Division on Aging, 1492
Missouri Employees Retirement System, 1493
Missouri Protection & Advocacy Services, 1494
Missouri Protection and Advocacy, 11173
Missouri Rehabilitation Services for the Blind, 7651
National Rural Health Association, 258
NorthEast Independent Living Services (NEILS), 10823
On My Own, 10824
Ozark Independent Living, 10825
Paraquad, 10826
Pony Express Association for the Blind, 7720
Pony Express Association of the Blind, 7721
Porch-Lift Vertical Platform Lift, 3389
RSVP Heartland, 1495
RSVP Andrew County, 1496
RSVP Boone County, 1497
RSVP Douglass Community Services, 1498
RSVP Dunklin County, 1499
RSVP Grundy/Sullivan Counties, 1500

Geographic Index / Montana

RSVP Harrison-Daviess Counties, 1501
RSVP Heartland, 1424, 1502
RSVP Jackson-Platte Counties, 1503
RSVP Jasper County, 1504
RSVP Livingston County, 1505
RSVP Mississippi County, 1506
RSVP Northwest Missouri/Northeast Kansas, 1507
RSVP Pemiscot County, 1508
RSVP Pettis-Saline Counties, 1509
RSVP Poplar Bluff-Altrusa Club, 1510
RSVP Quad Lakes Area of Missouri, 1511
RSVP Scott-Cape Counties, 1512
RSVP Springfield, 1319, 1513
RSVP St. Charles-Lincoln-Warren Counties, 1514
RSVP St. Louis, 1515
Railroad Retirement Board: Kansas City Missouri District Office, 1516
Railroad Retirement Board: St. Louis, 1517
Region 7: Administration on Aging (AoA), 1518
Region Ten Area: Agency on Aging, 667, 1519
Rural Advocates for Independent Living (RAIL), 10827
SEMO Alliance for Disability Independence (SADI), 10828
Saint Louis Altenheim, 9335
Side-to-Side Folding Chair, 3534
Silver Glide Stairway Lift, 3395
Southwest Center for Independent Living (SCIL), 10830
Southwest Missouri Office on Aging (SWMOA), 1520
St. Louis Area: Agency on Aging, 1521
St. Louis Society for the Blind, 7752
St. Louis Society for the Blind and Visually Impaired, 1522
St. Louis University: Department of Psychiatry, 6103
Stair & Glide Stairway Lift, 3399
State of Missouri, 11991
Stretch-View Wide-View Rectangular Illuminated Magnifier, 3167
Sunrise Senior Living, 9336
Tower Club of the Blind, 7761
Tri-County Center for Independent Living, 10831
UMKC Institute for Human Development, 1523
US Department of Veterans Affairs, John Cochran Division Library, 11589
US Department of Veterans Affairs: Kansas Medical Center Library, 11590
US Department of Veterans Affairs: Poplar Bluff Library Service, 11591
US Department of Veterans Affairs:, Columbus Hospital Library, 11592
University of Missouri: Columbia Cosmopolitan Diabetes Center, 6288
University of Missouri: Columbia Division of Cardiothoracic Surgery, 6899
University of Missouri: Kansas City Drug Information Service, 7483
VPL Series Vertical Wheelchair Lift, 3409
VantAge Point Area: Agency on Aging-Region Ten, 1524
Washington University School of Medicine, 7125
Washington University: Diabetes Research and Training Center, 6298
Wecolator Stairway Lift, 3413
West Central Independent Living Solutions (WCILS), 10832
Wolfner Memorial Library for the Blind, 11593
Workers Compensation Board Missouri, 1525
Ziggy Medi-Chair, 3415

Montana

Action for Eastern Montana, 1526
American Diabetes Association: Missoula District Office, 6145
American Diabetes Association: Montana, 6147
Area Eight Agency on Aging, 1527
Area Five Agency on Aging, 1528
Area Four Agency on Aging, 1529
Area Nine Agency on Aging, 1530
Area One Agency on Aging, 1531
Area Seven Agency on Aging, 1532
Area Two Agency on Aging, 1533
Ashley Manor Medley I, 9337
Aspen Meadows Retirement Community, 9338
Bee Hive Homes of Flathead County, 9339
Bee Hive Homes of Helena, 9340
Buffalo Hill Terrace, 9341
Edgewood Vista, 9154, 9342
Flathead County Area Nine Agency on Aging, 1535
Grand Park Assisted Living Community, 9343
Hamilton House, 9344
Harmony House, 9345
Hawthorne House, 9346
Heritage Acres Assisted Living, 9347
Heritage Retirement Home, 9348
Highwood Senior Citizens, 1536
Hillside Place, 9349
Hunters Glen at Grizzly Peak, 9350
Kathy's Place, 9351
Living Independently for Today & Tomorrow (LIFTT), 10833
Lodge at Lone Tree Creek, 9352
Lodge at Mission River Manor, 9353
Loveland Acres, 9354
Missoula Aging Services, 1537
Montana Advocacy Program, 1538, 11174
Montana Department of Administration: Teacher's Retirement Division, 1539
Montana Department of Aging, 1540
Montana Department of Military Affairs: Division of Veteran's Affairs, 1541
Montana Department of Retirement Administration, 1542
Montana Department of Revenue, 1543
Montana Department of Social and Rehabilitation Services, 1544
Montana Developmental Disability Council, 1545
Montana Division of Addictive & Mental Disorders, 7185
Montana Governor's Office on Aging, 1546
Montana Independent Living Project, 10834
Montana Legal Services Association: Helena, 11175
Montana Legal Services Developer Program & Office on Aging, 11176
Montana Masonic Home, 9356
Montana Office on Aging, 1547
Montana Protection & Advocacy Agency, 1548
Montana State Library, 11594
Next Best Place, 9357
North Central Independent Living Services, 10835
North Central-Area Agency on Aging, 1549
Northern Rocky Mountain Retiree Association, 1550
Prestige Assisted Living at Kalispell, 9358
Prevention Resource Center, 7214
RSVP Butte School District No 1, 1551
RSVP Cascade County, 1552
RSVP Dawson-Wibaux, 1553
RSVP Fallon County, 1554
RSVP Helena, 1555
RSVP Hill County, 1556
RSVP Miles City, 1557
RSVP Roosevelt County, 1558
RSVP South Central Montana, 1559
RSVP Southwest Montana, 1560
RSVP Yellowstone County, 1561
Railroad Retirement Board: Montana District Office, 1562
Ravalli County Council on Aging, 1563
River Ridge, 9359
Springmeadows, 9360
St. Patrick Hospital and Health Sciences Center: Library Center, 11595
Summit Independent Living Center-Kalispell, 10836
Summit Independent Living Center-Missoula, 10837
Summit Independent Living Center-Ronan, 10838
US Department of Veterans Affairs: Fort Harrison Medical Center Library, 11596
US Department of Veterans Affairs: Miles City Medical Center Library, 11597
Waterford on Elizabeth Warren, 9361
Waterford on Saddle Drive, 9362
William K. Kohrs Memorial Library, 11598
Workers Compensation Board Montana, 1564

Nebraska

Aging Office of Western Nebraska, 1565
Ambassabor Nebraska City Assisted Living, 9591
American Diabetes Association: Nebraska/South Dakota Area Office, 6149
An Angels Touch, 9592
Bell View Rehabilitation Center, 9593
Belle Aims Assisted Living Facility, 9594
Berverly Square Franklin, 9595
Bethany Home, 9596
Betty's House, 9597
Betty's House-Maple Street, 9598
Beverly Health Oak Grove, 9599
Beverly Healthcare Norfolk Chateau, 9600
Beverly Square Cozad, 9601
Beverly Square Fullerton, 9602
Beverly Square Nebraska City, 9603
Beverly Square Scottsbluff, 9604
Blue Rivers Area: Agency on Aging (BRAAAA), 1566
Blue Valley Riverside Apartments, 9605
Brighton Gardens of Omaha, 9606

1095

Geographic Index / Nebraska

Cambridge Court, 9607
Carter House, 9608
Centennial Park Retirement Village, 9609
Center for Independent Living of Central Nebraska, 10844
Chancellor Place at Aspen Park, 9610
Chapion Home of Hastings, 9611
Chrisoma West Assisted Living, 9612
Christian Homes Assisted Living Center, 9613
Christian Record Services, 7563
Circus House, 9614
Clara-Ellen House, 9615
Clark Jeary Home, 9616
Comfortcare Homes of Nebraska, 9617
Community Action Partnership of Mid-Nebraska Volunteer Services, 1567
Community Memorial Health Center, 9618
Community Pride Care Center, 9619
Cornor Cottage, 9620
Corrigan Senior Center, 1568
Cottonwood House, 9621
Cottonwood Villa, 9622
Countryside Home, 9623
Creighton University Cardiac Center, 6869
Creighton University: Midwest Hypertension Research Center, 6920
Crossroads Assisted Living, 9624
Crowell Memorial Home, 9625
Crown Villa, 9626
Custer Care Center, 9627
Decatur Senior Center, 1569
Division of Aging & Disability Services, 1571
Division of Aging and Disability Services: Legal Services for Older Adults, 11177
East Park Villa, 9628
Eastern Nebraska Office on Aging, 1572
Eastmont Towers, 9629
Edgewood Vista Columbus, 9630
Edgewood Vista Grand Island, 9631
Edgewood Vista Norfolk, 9632
Edgewood Vista of Fremont, 9633
Edgewood Vista of Hastings, 9634
Edgewood Vista of Omaha, 9635
El Dorado Manor Nursing Home, 9636
Emerald Court, 9637
Florence Home Assisted Living, 9638
Garden Square of Crete, 9639
Gateway Manor, 9640
Gold Crest Retirement Center, 9641
Golden Manor Assisted Living, 9642
Good Samaritan Towers, 9643
Good Shepherd Lutheran Home, 9644
Gordon Countryside Care, 9645
Grabd Island Sterling House, 9646
Gramercy Hill, 9647
Grand Court Seward Retirement CommunityAssisted Living, 9648
Grand Court Seward Retirment CommunityAssisted Living, 9649
Grand Island Veterand Home, 9650
Greeley Assisted Living, 9651
Greene House, 9652
Hastings Homestead, 9653
Haven Manor Assisted Living, 9654
Haven Manor College View, 9655
Heather and Shamrock Apartments, 9656
Hester Memorial Home, 9657
Hickory Villa, 9658
Hidden Pines Assisted Living Community, 9659
Highland House, 9660
Homestead, 9661
Hospice House, 9662
Immanuel Lakeside Terrace, 9663
Immanuel Trinity Village, 9664
Imperial Manor Nursing Home, 9665
Improved Living, 9666
Improved Living House II, 9667
Improved Living II, 9668
International Association of Biomedical Gerontology, 156
Kimball County Manor Nusing Home, 9669
Kirkwood House, 9670
League of Human Dignity Independent Living Center, 10845
Lebensraum Retirement Residence, 9671
Legacy, 9672
Legacy Terrace, 9673
Lester Dual-Mode Battery Charger, 3553
Lestronic II, 3554
Lincoln Area: Agency on Aging (LAAA), 1573
Longs Creek Village, 9674
Madison House, 9675
Madonna Assisted Living, 9676
Mahoney House, 9677
Meadows, 8705, 8812, 9226, 9226, 9678
Merrick Manor Assisted Living, 9679
Methodist Memorial Homes, 9680
Midland Area: Agency on Aging, 931, 1574
Midwest Geriatrics, 1575
Morton House, 9681
National Federation of the Blind: Writers Division, 7687
National Organization of the Senior Blind, 7690
Nebraska Advocacy Services, 1576, 11178
Nebraska Assistive Technology Partnership, 1577
Nebraska Association of Area Agencies on Aging, 1578
Nebraska Bar Association: Elderlaw Committee, 11179
Nebraska Client Assistance Program, 1579
Nebraska Commission For The Blind AndVisually Impaired (NCBVI), 1580
Nebraska Commission for the Blind & Visually Impaired, 7693
Nebraska Commission for the Deaf & Hard of Hearing, 6420
Nebraska Department of Aging, 1581
Nebraska Department of Revenue, 1582
Nebraska Department of Veterans Affairs, 1583
Nebraska Division of Alcoholism and Drug Abuse, 7196
Nebraska Division of Travel & Tourism, 11975
Nebraska Library Commission: Talking Book & Braille Service, 11599
Nebraska School for the Visually Handicapped Library, 11600
New Cassel Retirement Center, 9682
Norfolk Homestead, 9683
North Platte Public Library, 11601
Northeast Nebraska Area: Agency on Aging, 1584
Northridge Retirement Community, 9684
Nye Square Retirement Community, 9685
Oakland Heights, 8713, 9686
Oaks Retirement Center, 9687
Omaha Department of Veteran Affairs Medical Center Research Service, 6280
Orchard Park, 9688
Our Homes, 9689
Paddock Kensington, 9690
Papillion Senior Citizen Center, 1585
Park Avenue Estates, 9691
Parkview Lodge Asssited Living, 9693
Parsons House on Eagle Run, 9694
Pathfinder House, 9695
Pawnee Hills, 9696
Pender Care Center, 9697
Pine Lane of Hartington, 9698
Plum Creek Care Center, 9699
Ponderosa Villa, 9700
Prairie Pines Lodge, 9701
Prairie View Gardens, 9702
Prairie Village Retirement, 9703
Prairie Winds, 9704
Precious Time, 9705
Premier Estates, 8721, 9706
Premier Estates Senior Living Community, 9707
Prescott Place, 9708
Prevent Blindness Nebraska, 7725
Princess Anne Residential Care, 9709
Quality Living, 9710
RSVP Adams-Webster Counties, 1586
RSVP Chadron, 1587
RSVP Crawford, 1588
RSVP Lincoln Area, 1589
RSVP Ogallala City-Keith Counties, 1590
RSVP Richardson County, 1591
RSVP Sheriden County, 1592
Railroad Retirement Board: Nebraska District Office, 1593
Regency Square Care Center, 9711
Remington Heights Retirement Center, 9712
Riverside Lodge Retirement Community, 9713
Rosewood Court Assisted Living Center, 9714
Royale Oaks, 9715
Saunders House, 9716
Seneca Sunrise, 9717
Senior Living Choices at Curtis, 9718
Serenity Place, 9719
Seward Aging Services, 1594
Silvercrest Van Dorn Assisted Living, 9720
Silvercrest at Fountain View, 9721
Silvercrest at Miracle Hills Assisted Living, 9722
Skyline Retirement Community, 9723
South Central Nebraska Area Agency on Aging, 1595
Southview Heights Nursing Home, 9724
St Joseph Tower Assisted Living, 9725
St Joseph's Retirement Community, 9726
St Joseph's Villa, 9727
St Josephs Nursing Home, 9728
St Luke's Countryside Villa, 9729
Sterling Assisted Living, 9730
Sterling House at Omaha, 9731
Sterling House at Omaha II, 9732
Sunset View Assited Living, 9733
US Department of Veterans Affairs: Grand Island Greater Nebraska Health Care System Library, 11602
US Department of Veterans Affairs: Omaha Hospital Library, 11603
University of Nebraska: Lincoln Barkley Memorial Center, 6826

West Central Nebraska Area: Agency on Aging, 1596
Workers Compensation Board Nebraska, 1597

Nevada

Aegis of Las Vegas, 9735
American Diabetes Association: Nevada, 6150
Bureau of Disability Adjudication, 1598
Bureau of Naval Personnel: Nevada Retired Affairs Activities Office, 1599
Division for Aging Services, 1600
Division of Mental Health & Developmental Services, 1601
Greater Philadelphia Parkinson's Disease and Other Movement Disorders Council, 6955
International Catholic Deaf Association, 6377
Las Vegas-Clark County Library District, 11604
National Association of State Retirement Administrators, 201
Nevada Assistive Technology Projects, 1602
Nevada Bureau of Alcohol and Drug Abuse, 7197
Nevada Commission on Tourism, 11976
Nevada Department of Business & Industry: Governor's Committee on Employment of People with Disabilities, 1603
Nevada Department of Health & Human Services: Division for Aging Services, 11180
Nevada Department of Human Resources Rehabilitation Division: Bureau of Services to the Blind, 1604
Nevada Department of Taxation, 1605
Nevada Developmental Disability Council, 1606
Nevada Disability Advocacy & Law CenterSparks Office/Northern Nevada, 11181
Nevada Disability Advocacy and Law Center (NDLAC), 11182
Nevada Division for Aging Services, 1607
Nevada Protection & Advocacy Agency, 1608
Nevada Public Employees' Retirement System, 1609
Nevada State Library and Archives, 11605
Nevada State Library: Talking Book Services, 11606
Nevada Workers Compensation Board, 1610
Nevada's Bureau of Services to the Blind and Visually Impaired, 7694
Northern Nevada Center for Independent Living, 10846
Plaza at Sun Mountain, 9736
Prestige Assisted Living, 8209, 9737
RSVP NV Rural Counties, 1612
RSVP Washoe County, 1613
Red Rock Independent & Assisted Living, 9738
Rose Cottage, 9739
Senior Citizens Law Project, 11183
Silver Rose Manor, 9740
State of Nevada Client Assistance Program, 1614

US Department of Veterans Affairs: Reno Medical Center Library Services, 11607
University of Nevada: Speech and Language Pathology Department, 6827

New Hampshire

Braillemaster, 3091
Bureau of Elderly & Adult Services, 11184
Dartmouth College Biomedical Libraries: Dana Biomedical Library, 11608
Disability Determination Unit, 1615
Granite State Independent Living Center, 10847
National Organization for Albinism and Hypopigmentation, 246
New England Gerontological Association, 1616
New Hampshire Association for the Blind, 7697
New Hampshire Association for the Blind, 7698
New Hampshire Client Assistance Program, 1617
New Hampshire Department of Mental Health, 1618
New Hampshire Department of Revenue, 1619
New Hampshire Developmental Disabilities Council, 1620
New Hampshire Division of Developmental Services, 1621
New Hampshire Division of Elderly and Adult Services, 1622
New Hampshire Governor's Commission on Disability, 1623
New Hampshire Health and Human Services: Elderly and Adult Services, 1624
New Hampshire Hospital: Dorothy M Breene Memorial Library, 11609
New Hampshire Legal Assistance, 11185
New Hampshire Legal Assistance: Senior Citizens Law Project, 11186
New Hampshire Office of Travel & Tourism Development, 11977
New Hampshire Protection & Advocacy for Persons with Disabilities, 1625
New Hampshire Protection and Advocacy Agency: Disabilities Rights Center, 11187
New Hampshire Retirement System, 1626
New Hampshire State Library, 11610
New Hampshire Veterans Council, 1627
New Hampshire for Human Rights, 1628
Northern New England Association of Homes and Services for the Aging, 1629
RSVP Carroll County, 1033, 1630
RSVP Merrimack County, 1632
RSVP Monadnock, 1633
RSVP Southern New Hampshire, 1635
RSVP and the Volunteer Center, 1636
Service Corp of Retired Executives: Portsmouth Chapter No. 185, 1637
US Department of Veterans Affairs: Manchester Medical Center Library, 11611

New Jersey

AT&T Portable Telephone Amplifier, 3059
Acorn Glen, 9741

Adaptive Driving Conversions, 2953
Allendale Community for Mature Living, 9742
Alliance for Disabled in Action, 10848
Alterra Clare Bridge Cottage of Monroe, 9743
Alterra Clare Bridge of Brick, 9744
Alterra Clare Bridge of Galloway, 9745
Alterra Clare Bridge of Hamilton, 9746
Alterra Clare Bridge of Westhampton, 9747
Alterra Sterling House of Florence, 9748
Alterra Wynwood of Emerson, 9749
Alterra Wynwood of Galloway, 9750
Alterra Wynwood of Wayne, 9751
American Academy of Ambulatory Care Nursing, 8
American Association of Office Nurses, 23
American Diabetes Association Southern: New Jersey District Office, 6112
American Nephrology Nurses' Association, 50
American Society of Peri-Anesthesia Nurses, 67
American Society of Post-Anesthesia Nurses, 69
Ameriphone Hearing Assistance Telephone, 3069
Ameriphone-Wireless Notification System, 3070
Arbor Glen, 9752
Arcola Mobility, 2956
Arden Courts of Whippany, 9753
Arm Volumeter Set, 3248
Assisted Living Chancellor Park at theWindrows, 9754
Assisted Living at Spring Oak, 9755
Atlantic County Division of Intergenerational Services, Office of Aging, 1638
Atria Tinton Falls, 9756
Avalon at Bridgewater, 9757
Avis Rent A Car, 11915
Bayside Manor, 9758
Behavior-Dementia Management, 9759
Bergen County Division of Senior Services, 1639
Bestwork Industries for the Blind, 7533
Bey Lea Village, 9760
Brandall Estates, 9761
Brandywine Assisted Living at Middlebrook Cross, 9762
Brandywine Assisted Living at Moorestown, 9763
Brandywine Assisted Living at the Gables, 9764
Brighton Gardens of Cherry Hill, 9765
Brighton Gardens of Edison, 9766
Brighton Gardens of Florham Park, 9767
Brighton Gardens of Middletown, 9768
Brighton Gardens of Paramus, 9769
Brighton Gardens of Saddle River, 9770
Brighton Gardens of West Orange, 9771
Bristol Glen, 9772
Burlington County Office on Aging, 1640
Burlington County Retired and Senior Volunteer Program, 1641
Camden City Independent Living Center (CCILC), 10849
Cape May County Department of Aging, 1642
Cardinal Retirement Village, 9773

1097

Geographic Index / New Jersey

Centers for Independent Living of South Jersey (CILSJ), 10850
Chancellor Park of Park Ridge, 9774
Chelsea at East Brunswick, 9775
Chelsea at Fanwood, 9776
Chelsea at Montville, 9777
Chelsea at Tinton Falls, 9778
Cheney's Liberty II, 3364
Chestnut Hill Residence, 9779
Classique, 3365
Collinswood Manor, 9780
Commissioner Of Labor And WorkforceDeveloper, 1643
Cumberland County Office on Aging &Disabled, 1644
Cytogen Corporation R&D Library, 11612
Davis Center for Hearing, Speech and Learning: Hearing Therapy, 6342
Dermatology Nurses' Association, 120
Division of Disability Determinations New Brunswick, 1646
Division of Disability Determinations: Newark, 1647
Door Flashing Announcment System, 3107
Drive-Master, 2964
Econo-Float Water Flotation Cushion, 3202
Econo-Float Water Flotation Mattress, 3203
Economical Liberty, 3373
Elms of Cranbury, 9781
Essex County Bar: Elder Law Committee, 11188
Father Hudson House, 9782
Foot Steering, 2968
Fountains at Cedar Parke, 9783
Francis Asbury Manor, 9784
Gloucester County Department on Aging, 1648
Gray Panthers of Northern New Jersey, 1649
Gray Panthers of Southern New Jersey, 1650
Green Acres Manor, 9785
Guardian Eldercare, 1651
Hammonton Senior Citizens Club, 1652
Handi Home Lift, 3379
Handi Prolift, 3380
Haven at Holiday Manor, 9786
Hearthside Commons at the Job HainesHome, 9787
Heightened Independence & Progress (HIP), 10851
Heightened Independence & Progress-Hudson (HIP Hudson), 10852
Heritage Assisted Living at Hammonton, 9788
Holland Township Community Seniors, 1653
Horizontal Steering, 2975
House of the Good Shepherd, 9789
Hudson County Office on Aging, 1654
Hunterdon County Division of Senior Services, 1655
Independence Manor at Hunterdon, 9790
Indo-American Connection, 1656
Institute for Driver Rehabilitation, 2977
Klassic-Plus, 3522
Legal Services of New Jersey: Atlantic City, 11189
Legal Services of New Jersey: Edison, 11190
Liberty LT, 3385
Liberty Manor Assisted Living Residence, 9791
Low Effort and No Effort Braking, 2981
Low Effort and No Effort Steering, 2982
MADAMIST 50/50 PSI Air Compressor, 3264
Medpro Static Air Chair Cushion, 3215
Medpro Static Air Mattress Overlay, 3216
Mill Gardens at Midland Park, 9792
Mine Hill Senior Citizens Good Years Club, 1657
Mini-Bus and Mini-Vans, 2985
Moceans Center for Independent Living, 10853
Monmouth County Office on Aging, 1658
Monmouth Vans-Access and Mobility Equipment, 2987
Morris County Office on Aging, 1659
National Federation for Specialty Nursing Organizations, 224
National Federation of the Blind of New Jersey, 7675
National Industries for the Blind, 7688
New Eyes for the Needy, 7696
New Jersey Academy of Audiology, 6421
New Jersey Association of Non-Profit Homes for the Aging, 1660
New Jersey Blind Citizens Association, 7699
New Jersey Blind Citizens' Association, 7700
New Jersey Client Assistance Program, 1661
New Jersey Commission for the Blind and Visually Impaired, 7701
New Jersey Department of Aging, 1662
New Jersey Department of Community Affairs: Commission on Recreation for the Handicapped, 1663
New Jersey Department of Environmental Protection, 11613
New Jersey Department of Health & Senior Services, 7198
New Jersey Department of Human Services: Commission for the Blind, 1664
New Jersey Department of Human Services: Deaf and Heard of Hearing Division, 1665
New Jersey Department of Mental Health, 1666
New Jersey Developmental Disability Council, 1667
New Jersey Division of Aging & Community Services: Office of the Public Guardian, 11191
New Jersey Division of Taxation, 1668
New Jersey Intergenerational Network, 1669
New Jersey Library for the Blind and Physically Handicapped, 11614
New Jersey Protection & Advocacy for Persons with Disabilities, 1670
New Jersey Protection and Advocacy Agency, 11192
New Jersey State Bar Association: Committee on the Elderly, 11193
New Jersey Tourism Division, 11978
Newseasons of Cherry Hill, 9793
Newseasons of Voorhees, 9794
North Hanover Senior Citizen Club, 1671
Nottingham House Astited Living Residenc, 9795
Nurse Healers-Professional Associates International, 273
Ocean County Office on Aging, 1672
Office on Aging: Senior Citizens Referral Panel, 11194
Orchards at Bartley Assisted Living, 9796
Oticon Portable Telephone Amplifier, 3147
Outdoor Loud Bell, 3148
Passaic County Office on Aging, 1673
Princeton University Industrial Relations Library, 11615
Princeton University: Cutaneous Communication Laboratory, 6813
Progressive Center for Independent Living (PCIL), 10854
RSVP Atlantic City Chapter, 1675
RSVP Bergen County, 1676
RSVP Bergen County New Jersey, 1677
RSVP Burlington County, 1678
RSVP Camden County, 1679
RSVP Cape May Chapter, 1680
RSVP Cape May County, 1681
RSVP Cumberland, 1682
RSVP Cumberland County Chapter, 1683
RSVP Essex Hudson Chapter, 1684
RSVP Goucester County, 1685
RSVP Mercer County, 1686
RSVP Middlesex County, 1687
RSVP Morris County, 1688
RSVP Morris County Chapter, 1689
RSVP Ocean County, 1690
RSVP Ocean County Chapter, 1691
RSVP Passaic County, 1692
RSVP Somerset County Chapter, 1694
RSVP Sussex-Warren, 1695
RSVP Sussex-Warren Chapter, 1696
RSVP Union County, 1697
RSVP Union County Chapter, 1698
Railroad Retirement Board: New Jersey District Office, 1699
Rascal Insurance Services, 299
Rebuilding Together, 2678
Recording for the Blind & Dyslexic, 7737
Recording for the Blind Helpline, 7738
Renaissance Gardens at Seabrook, 9797
Robert Wood Johnson University Hospital, 7043
Rose Hill Assisted Living, 9798
Rutgers University: Center of Alcohol Studies, 7218
Salem County Office on Aging, 1700
Sandoz Pharmaceuticals Corporate Library, 11616
Seeing Eye, 7742
Senior Citizens Council of Union County, 1701
Shores at Wesley Manor, 9799
Social Service Association, 1702
Society of Geriatric Ophthalmology, 8054
Soft-Touch Convertible Flotation Mattress, 3224
Soft-Touch Gel Flotation Cushion, 3225
Somerset County Office on Aging, 1703
Somerset Manor North, 9800
Somerset Manor South, 9801
Spring Hills at Morristown, 9802
Spring Meadows at Summit, 9803
St Marys Assisted Residence at Morris Hill, 9804
Stop-Leak Gel Flotation Cushion, 3227
Stop-Leak Gel Flotation Mattress, 3228
Summerville at Hillsborough, 9805
Summerville at Stafford, 9806
Summerville at Voorhees, 9807
Sunnyside Manor, 9808
Sunrise Assisted Living East Brunswick, 9809

Geographic Index / New Mexico

Sunrise Assisted Living of Edgewater, 9810
Sunrise Assisted Living of Morris Plains, 9811
Sunrise Assisted Living of Mt Laurel, 9812
Sunrise Assisted Living of Paramus, 9813
Sunrise Assisted Living of Wall, 9814
Sunrise Assisted Living of West Essex, 9815
Sunrise Assisted Living of Westfield, 9816
Sunrise of Old Tappan, 9817
Sunrise of Wayne, 9818
Sunrise of Woodbury Lake, 9819
Sunrise of Woodcliff Lake, 9820
Sussex County Office on Aging, 1704
Total Living Center (TLC), 10855
Transportation Equipment for People with Disabilities, 2996
Twin Cedars, 9821
Twin-Rest Seat Cushion & Glamour Pillow, 3231
UMDNJ and Coriell Research Library, 11617
US Department of Veterans Affairs: East Orange Medical Center Library, 11618
US Department of Veterans Affairs: Lyon New Jersey Health Care System - Lyons Campus Hospital Library, 11619
Ultra-Lite XL Hand Control, 2997
Ultratec-Auto Answer TTY, 3182
Union County Division on Aging, 1705
Van Dyke Valley Assisted Living, 9822
Victoria Mews Assisted Living, 9823
Volunteer Center of Camden County, 1706
Volunteer Center of Monmouth County, 1707
Warren County Division Of Senior ServiceS, 1708
Waterproof Sheet-Topper Mattress andChair Pad, 3041
Whispering Knoll Assisted Living, 9824
Willows at Holmdel Assisted Living Community, 9825
Wings & Wheels Greeting Cards, 3472
Wound, Ostomy and Continence Nurses Society, 6950

New Mexico

Ability Center for Independent Living, 10856
Acantilado Vista, 9826
American Diabetes Association: New Mexico Area Office, 6151
CHOICES Center for Independent Living, 10857
Capitan Public Library, 11620
City of Albuquerque-Bernalillo County:Department of Senior Affairs, 1709
Eastern New Mexico Area: Agency on Aging, 1711
Guadalupe County Nutrition, 1712
Mesa Airlines, 11932
NCNMEDD-Area Agency on Aging, 1713
National Indian Council on Aging, 229
Native American Consortium Protection and Advocacy Agency, 11195
New Mexico Aging & Long-Term Services Department: Elderly and Disability Services Division, 11196
New Mexico Behavioral Health Services, 7199
New Mexico Client Assistance Program, 1714
New Mexico Commission for the Blind, 7702
New Mexico Committee on Concerns of the Handicapped, 1715
New Mexico Department of Aging, 1716
New Mexico Department of Taxation and Revenue, 1717
New Mexico Department of Tourism, 11979
New Mexico Educational Retirement Board, 1718
New Mexico Governor's Committee on Concern of the Handicapped, 1719
New Mexico Protection & Advocacy for Persons with Disabilities, 1720
New Mexico Protection and Advocacy Agency, 11197
New Mexico Public Employees Retirement Board, 1721
New Mexico State Agency on Aging, 1722
New Mexico State Library: Blind and Physically Handicapped, 11621
New Mexico Technology, 1723
New Mexico Veterans Service Commission, 1724
New Mexico Workers Compensation Board, 1725
New Vistas Independent Living Center, 10858
Office of Indian Affairs: Indian Area Agency on Aging, 1726
Quality Senior Services, 1727
RSVP Alamogordo City, 1728
RSVP Artesia, 1729
RSVP Carlsbad City, 1730
RSVP Chaves County, 1731
RSVP Grant County, 1733
RSVP Los Alamos, 1734
RSVP Luna County, 1735
RSVP McKinley County, 1736
RSVP Metropolitan, 1737
RSVP Mid Rio Grand, 1738
RSVP San Juan County, 1739
RSVP Sandoval, 1740
RSVP Santa Fe City, 1741
RSVP Sierra County, 1742
RSVP Village of Ruidoso, 1743
Railroad Retirement Board: New Mexico, 1744
Rampvan, 2990
Retired Senior Volunteer Program of Rio Grande, 1745
Roswell Public Library, 11622
Senior Citizens Law Office, 11198
Social Security: Santa Fe Disability Determination, 1746
Southwestern New Mexico Area: Agency onAging, 1747
State Bar of New Mexico: Elder Law Section, 11199
State Bar of New Mexico: Lawyer Referral for the Elderly Program, 11200
US Department of Veterans Affairs: Albuquerque Medical Center Library, 11623
University of New Mexico: General Clinical Research Center, 6289

New York

3M Brailler, 3053
3M Large Printed Labeler, 3054
AFB Toll-Free Hotline, 7496
Access USA, 3065
Access to Independence and Mobility (AIM, 10859
Access to Independence and Mobility-Bath (AIM), 10860
Access to Independence of Cortland County, 10861
Access to Travel Magazine, 11911
Action Toward Independence, 10862
Adjustable Raised Toilet Seat, 3001
Adjustable Toilet Safety Rails, 3002
Albany County Department for Aging and the Handicapped, 1748
Albany Talking Book Center, 11624
Alcoholics Anonymous, 7132
Allegany County Office for the Aging, 1749
Altria Plainview, 9827
Aluminum Adjustable Support Canes for the Blind, 3474
Aluminum Crutches, 3475
Aluminum Walking Canes, 3476
American Assembly for Men in Nursing, 14
American Association of Retired Veterinarians, 25
American Board of Perianesthesia Nursing Certification, 31
American College of Clinical Pharmacology, 33
American Council for Drug Education, 7133
American Diabetes Association: Eastern Regional Office, 6130
American Diabetes Association: New York City Area Office, 6153
American Foundation for the Blind, 7506
American Parkinson's Disease Association, 6954
American Psychoanalytic Association, 55
American Society of Hypertension, 6907
American Thoracic Society, 72
Anna Erika Home for Adults, 9828
Arthwriter, 3077
Associated Blind, 7523
Association for Macular Diseases, 7525
Association for the Blind & Visually Impaired of Greater Rochester, 7526
Association of Belltel Retirees, 1750
Association of Personal Historians, 86
Association of the Bar of the City of New York: Committee for Senior Volunteer Lawyers, 11201
Atria Forest Hills, 9829
Auburn Options for Independence, 10863
Audio Recordings, 3448
Aurora of Central New York, 6320, 7529
Bagel Holder, 3320
Ball Bearing Spinner, 2957
Bathtub Safety Rail, 3005
Bellevue Manor Assisted Living Community, 9830
Beth Israel Medical Center: Seymour J Phillips Health Sciences Library, 11625
Big Bold Timer Low Vision, 3321
Big Lamp Switch, 3296
Big Number Pocket Sized Calculator, 3084
Birchwood Assisted Living and Physical Rehabilitation, 9831
Birchwood Volunteers In Partnership, 1751

1099

Geographic Index / New York

Blind Association of Western New York, 7535
Blind Work Association, 7540
Blood Pressure Unit Auto Inflation, 3249
Braille Book Bank, 11626
Braille Business Cards & More, 3454
Braille Compass, 3087
Braille Materials Production Center, 7550
Braille Notebook, 3455
Braille Plates for Elevator, 3362
Braille Touch-Time Watches, 3089
Brailled Desk Calendar, 3456
Briarwood Manor, 9832
British Airways, 11916
Bronx Independent Living Services, 10864
Bronxwood Home for the Aged, 9833
Brooklyn Center for Independence of the Disabled, 10865
Brooklyn College of City University of New York: Speech & Hearing Center, 6797
Broome County Office for Aging, 1752
Buffalo Senior Center, 1753
Bus and Taxi Sign, 3457
Button Aid, 3234
Bye Bye Decubiti, 3197
CLEO Economy Folding Walker, 3478
Calvary Hospital Medical Library, 11627
Canine Helpers for the Handicapped, 7555
Canon Communicator, 3094
Canon Communicator M, 3095
Capital District Center for Independent Living, 10866
Care Givers of the Elderly Support Group, 1754
Catholic Guild for the Blind, 11453, 7557
Catskill Center for Independence, 10867
Cattaraugus County Department of Aging, 1755
Cayuga County Office of the Aging, 1756
Center for Independence of Disabled in New York (CIDNY), 10868
Center for Thanatology Research, 6035
Center for Thanatology Research Library, 11628
Center for the Study of Aging Library, 11629
Center for the Study of Aging of Albany, 1757
Central Association for the Blind and Visually Impaired, 7559
Centro Gerontologico Latino, 103
Cervipillow Covers, 3199
Chautauqua County Office for the Aging, 1758
Cheese Slicer, 3325
Chemung County Office for the Aging, 1759
Chenango County Area: Agency on Aging, 1760
Cigarette Holder, 3297
City University of New York: Center for Research in Speech & Hearing, 6331
Clark Meadows, 9834
Cleo Raised Toilet Seat, 3008
Cleoplast Therapeutic Putty-2 oz., 3250
Clinton County Office for the Aging, 1761
Cochlear Implant Association, 6334
Cold Spring Harbor Laboratory, 11630
Columbia County Office for the Aging, 1762
Columbia University Irving Center for Clinical Research, 6868

Columbia University Oral History Research Office, 11631
Columbia University: Augustus C Long Health Sciences Library, 11632
Columbia University: Whitney M Young, Jr Memorial Library of Social Work, 11633
Commode Aluminum, 3009
Computer Paper for Brailling, 3100
Convert-Able Table, 3545
Cornell University Medical College: Departments of Neurology and Neuroscience, 7115
Cornell University School of Industrial and Labor Relations, 11634
Cornerstone, 7148
Corporate Volunteers of New York, 1763
Cortland County Area: Agency on Aging, 1764
Country House in Westchester, 9835
Crutch Pockets, 3235
Curtis Instruments, 3546
Deaf Artists of America, 6345
Deafness Research Foundation, 6800
Decorator Grab Bars, 3011
Delaware County Office for the Aging, 1765
Deluxe Bath Bench with Adjustable Legs, 3012
Deluxe Long Ring Low Vision Timer Tactile, 3327
Deluxe Signature Guide, 3460
Deluxe Standard Wood Cane, 3479
Deluxe Wheelchair Pushing Cuffs, 3547
Department of Aging & Youth, 1766
Diabetic Cruise Desk, 12014
Digital Battery Operated Blood Pressure, 3252
Digital and Audible Family Thermometer, 3253
Division of Disability Determinations, 1768
Division of Disability Determinations-Endicott, 1769
Dosberg Manor Adult Home, 9836
Dressing Stick, 3237
Dual Brake Control, 2965
East Orange County Center for Independent Living, 10869
Easy Care Quad Canes, 3481
Easy Pour Locking Lid Pot, 3330
Edward Henderson Memorial Student Award, 2632
El Al Israel Airlines, 11924
Electric Can Opener & Knife Sharpener, 3331
Elizabeth Pierce Olmsted Center for the Visually Impaired, 7583
Elm York Home for Adults, 9837
Embroidery Hoop, 3288
Empire State Association of Assisted Living, 9838
Empress Directions Unlimited(AcccessibleTours), 12018
Endocrinology Research Laboratory, 6271
Erie County Department of Senior Services, 1770
Essex County Office for the Aging, 1771
Evac + Chair Emergency Wheelchair, 3044
Fight for Sight, 7589
Finger Lakes Independence Center, 10870
Flashing Lamp Telephone Ring Alerter, 3117
Food Markers/Magnets, 3333
Food Markers/Rubberbands, 3334

Fort Plain Senior Center, 1772
Fountains at Millbrook, 9839
Franklin County Office for the Aging, 1773
Friends and Relatives of Institutionalized Aged, 1774
Fulton County Office for the Aging, 1775
Gadabout Wheelchairs, 3516
Gaymar, 3205
Gem Wheelchair and Scooter Service, 3517
Genesee County Office for the Aging, 1776
Glaucoma Foundation, 8041
Golden Care Home for Adults, 9840
Goldwater Memorial Hospital: Medical Center Health Sciences Library, 11635
Gray Panthers of New York, 1777
Gray Panthers of Suffolk County, 1778
Great Big Safety Tub Mat, 3015
Greater Rochester Area Partnership for the Elderly, 1779
Greene County Aging Services, 1780
Greene County Department for Aging, 1781
Guide A Knife, 3336
Guide Dog Foundation for the Blind, 7598
Guiding Eyes for the Blind, 7601
Hand Brake Control Only, 2971
Hand Gas & Brake Control, 2972
Hand Parking Brake, 2973
Handy-Helper Cutting Board, 3337
Hard Manufacturing Company, 3038
Harlem Independent Living Center, 10871
Harold W. McGraw, Jr. Prize in Education, 2641
Hasting Center Library, 11636
Headlight Dimmer Switch, 2974
Heart Disease Research Foundation, 6875
Helen Keller International, 7602
Helen Keller National Center, 7603
Herkimer County Office for the Aging, 1782
HiRider, 3520
Highland Hospital: John R Williams, Sr Health Sciences Library, 11637
Hillcrest Spring, 9841
Horn Control Switch, 2976
Hospital Audiences, 153
Housing and Transportation of the Handicapped, 11929
Hunter College of the City University of New York: Health Professional Library, 11638
Independent Center-Southern Tier, 10872
Independent Living Center of Hudson Valley, 10873
Independent Living of the Hudson Valley, 10874
Inflatable Invalid Ring, 3209
Institute for Socioeconomic Studies Library, 11639
International Center for Hearing & Speech Research, 6803
International Communication Service for the Blind, 7620
International Ladies' Garment Workers Union Research Department Library, 11640
International Lawyers in Alcoholics Anonymous, 7173
Irving S Wright Award of Distinction, 2645
JGB Cassette Library International, 11641
Jefferson County Office for Aging, 1783
Jewish Association for Services for the Aged, 1784
Jewish Braille Institute of America, 7622

Geographic Index / New York

KLM Royal Dutch/Northwest Airlines, 11931
Knitting Needle Holder, 3290
Kon Tiki Travel Agency, 12029
Large Print Telephone Dial, 3128
Large Print Touch-Telephone Overlays, 3129
League for the Hard of Hearing, 6804
Left Foot Gas Pedal, 2980
Legal Services for the Elderly, Disabled or Disadvantaged of Western New York, 11203
Letter Writing Guide, 3463
Lettering Guide Value Pack, 3464
Lewis County Office for the Aging, 1785
Lexington School for the Deaf, 6390
Lexington School for the Deaf Library Media Center, 11642
Lift and Carry Wheelchair Caddy, 3555
Lighthouse, 7632
Lighthouse International Ruth M. Shellens Library, 1786
Lighthouse Low Vision Products, 3131
Lighthouse National Center for Vision and Aging (LNCVA), 7633
Lighthouse: Ruth M Shellens Library, 11643
Livingston County Office for Aging, 1787
Location Finder, 3133
Long Island Center for Independent Living, 10875
Long Island Living Program Assisted Living, 9842
MC Migel Memorial Library and Helen Keller Archives, 11644
Madison County Office for the Aging, 1788
Madison York Home For Adults, 9843
Magic Soaper, 3017
Magnetic Card Reader, 3340
Magnifier Highlights, 3312
Male Sexual Dysfunction Center, 6934
Man's Low-Vision Quartz Watches, 3136
Maplewood Residence, 9844
Marie Louise Heins Home for Adults, 9845
Masonic Medical Research Laboratory: Max L Kamiel Library, 11645
Massena Independent Living Center, 10876
Maxi Aid Braille Timer, 3341
Maxi Marks, 3465
Maxi Superior Cane, 3482
Meals on Wheels of Buffalo and Erie County Foundation, 1789
Medicare Rights Center, 168
Men's/Women's Low Vision Watches & Clocks, 3138
Metropolitan Commission on Aging, 1790
Migel Medal for Outstanding Service to Blind Persons, 2655
Milo D. Leavitt Memorial Lecture Award, 2657
Mini-Vibrator Stress Remover, 3267
Monroe Community Hospital: TF Williams Health Sciences Library, 11646
Monroe County Office for the Aging and Adult Services, 1791
Monte Travel, 12032
Montefiore Medical Center Health Sciences Library: Tishman Learning Center, 11647
Montgomery County Office for the Aging, 1792
Narcotic and Drug Research, 7464
Nassau County Department of Senior Citizen Affairs, 1793

Nassau Library System, 11648
National Alliance for Research on Schizophrenia and Depression, 6102
National Association for Visually Handicapped (NAVH), 11649, 7655
National Association on Drug Abuse Problems, 7188
National Braille Association, 7662
National Center for Vision and Aging, 7666
National Center on Employment for the Deaf, 6409
National Congress of Jewish Deaf, 6410
National Council on Alcoholism and Drug Dependence, 7190
National Cued Speech Association, 6411
National Development and Research Institutes: Library/Resource Center, 7467
National Family Association for Deaf-Blind, 6412
National Foundation for Depressive Illness, 6047
National Hypertension Association, 6909
National Organization of Social Security Claimants' Representatives, 11204
National Senior Women's Tennis Association, 263
National Technical Institute for the Deaf, 6418
National Urban League, 265
New Central Manor Assisted Living Progra, 9846
New Investigator Awards, 2666
New York Center on Alcohol and Substance Abuse, 7200
New York City Department for the Aging, 1794
New York Client Assistance Program, 1795
New York Commission on Quality of Care and Advocacy for Persons with Disabilities, 1796
New York Department of Aging, 1797
New York Department of Taxation & Finance, 1798
New York Developmental Disability Planning Council, 1799
New York Division of Tourism, 11980
New York Division of Veterans Affairs, 1800
New York Foundation for Otologic Research, 6808
New York Legal Aid Society, 11205
New York Office of Mental Health Binghamton Psychiatric Center Library Services Department, 11650
New York Office on Aging, 1801
New York Public Library, 11651
New York Public Library General Reference & Advisory Services: Accessibility Services, 11652
New York Society for the Deaf, 6422
New York State Association of Area Agencies on Aging, 1802
New York State Bar Association: Elder Law Section, 11206
New York State Coalition for the Aging, 1803
New York State Commission On Quality ofCare and Advocacy for Persons with Disabilities, 11207
New York State Commission for the Blind, 1804

New York State Division of Disability Determinations, 1805
New York State Independent Living Council, 10877
New York State Intergenerational Network, 1806
New York State OASIS, 7201
New York State Office for the Aging, 11208
New York State Office for the Aging: Senior Citizens Hotline, 1807
New York State Office of Advocate for Persons with Disabilities, 1808
New York State Office of Alcoholism & Substance Abuse Services, 7202
New York State Office of Mental Health, 1809
New York State Talking Book & Braille Library, 11653
New York Teachers Retirement System, 1810
New York University Medical Rehabilitation Research and Training Center, 7120
New York University: General Clinical Research Center, 6924
Niagara County Office for the Aging, 1811
Niagara Frontier Center for Independent Living (NFCIL), 10878
No-Bows Shoe Lace Fasteners, 3243
North Country Association for the Visually Impaired, 7707
North Country Center for Independence, 10879
Northeast Regional Training Center: Canine Companions for Independence, 7708
Northeastern Association of the Blind at Albany, 7709
Northern Regional Center for Independent Living, 10880
Olean Center, 10881
Oley Foundation for Home Parenteral and Enteral Nutrition, 279
Oneida County Office for the Aging, 1812
Ontario County Office for the Aging, 1813
Orange County Office for Aging, 1814
Orleans County Office for the Aging, 1815
Oswego County Office for the Aging, 1816
Otsego County Office for the Aging, 1817
Outdoor Independence, 3425
Oxford Gerontology Center Library, 11654
Padded Bathtub Transfer Bench, 3019
Palm Beach Home for Adults, 9847
Palmer Independence, 3427
Palmer Twosome, 3428
Parkinson Association of New York, 6967
Parkinson's Disease Foundation, 7040
Parkinson's Support Group of Upstate New York, 6976
Partnership for a Drug-Free America, 7212
Paul B Beeson Career Development Awardsin Aging Research Program, 2672
Peninsula Hospital of Far Rockway, 7041
Perinton Retired Men's Club, 1818
Pfizer/AGS Postdoctoral Research Awards, 2674
Porta-Ramp, 3391
Positioning Support Seats, 3221
Presbyterian Residential Community, 9848
Prevent Blindness America New York City Division, 1819
Priva Inc., 3040
Pro Literacy Worldwide, 295

Geographic Index / New York

Program Planners: Library/Information Center, 11655
Push-Button Quad Cane, 3486
Putnam County Office for Aging, 1820
Queens Independent Living Center (QILC), 10882
Quick Clamp Tub Grab Bar, 3021
RIDE Retired Individuals Driving Elderly, 1821
RSVP Auburn, 1822
RSVP Broome, 1823
RSVP Cattaraugus County, 1825
RSVP Chautaqua, 1826
RSVP Chemung County, 1827
RSVP Chenago County, 1828
RSVP Clinton County, 1035, 1829
RSVP Cortland, 1831
RSVP Dutchess County, 1832
RSVP Erie County, 1833
RSVP Essex County, 1834
RSVP Genesee County, 1836
RSVP Herkimer County, 1838
RSVP Madison County, 1005, 1839
RSVP Nassau County, 1841
RSVP New York City, 1842
RSVP Niagara County, 1843
RSVP Oneida County, 1844
RSVP Orange County, 1845
RSVP Putnam County, 1007, 1846
RSVP Rockland, 1847
RSVP Saratoga County, 1848
RSVP Schuyler County, 1849
RSVP Suffolk County, 1850
RSVP Sullivan County, 1851
RSVP Tompkins County, 1852
RSVP Ulster County, 1853
RSVP Wayne-Seneca-Ontario, 1854
RSVP of Warren and Washington Counties, 1855
Railroad Retirement Board-New York City, 1856
Railroad Retirement Board: Albany District Office, 1857
Railroad Retirement Board: Buffalo New York District Office, 1858
Railroad Retirement Board: Syracuse NewYork District Office, 1859
Raised Line Drawing Kit, 3467
Ready Willing & Able, 1860
Ready Willing & Able: Gates, 1861
Regency at Glen Cove, 9849
Region 2 and 3: Administration on Aging(AoA), 1862
Region 2: Administration on Aging (AoA), 1863
Regional Center for Independent Living, 10883
Rensselaer County Department for the Aging, 1864
Research Institute on Alcoholism, 7472
Research to Prevent Blindness, 7739
Resource Center for Accessible Living, 10884
Resource Center for Independent Living, 10767, 10885
Resource Center for Independent Living (RCIL), 10886
Retired Senior Volunteer Program of Steuben County, 1865
Rigid Aluminum Cane with Golf Grip, 3488
Rochester Institute of Technology Library, 11656
Rochester Institute of Technology: National Technical Institute for the Deaf, 6440
Rochester Technical Institute for the Deaf Resource Center, 11657
Rockefeller University Laboratory of Biology, 7473
Rockefeller University: Laboratory of Cardiac Physiology, 6889
Rocking Knife, 3345
Rockland County Center for the Physically Handicapped, 1866
Rockland County Office for Aging, 1867
Rockland Independent Living Center, 10887
Rollator Wheeled Walker, 3489
Roosevelt Hospital Medical Library, 11658
Samuel Sadin Institute on Law & Rights of Older Adults, 11209
Saratoga County Office for the Aging, 1868
Savoy at Brooklyn, 9850
Savoy at Little Neck Assusted Living Community, 9851
Say What, 3244
Scharome Manor Home for Adults, 9852
Schenectady County Office for the Aging, 1869
Schoharie County Office for the Aging, 1870
Schuyler County Office for the Aging, 1871
Sea View Hospital Rehabilitation Center Health Sciences Library, 11659
Self-Help for Hard of Hearing People: Rochester Chapter, 6443
Self-Help for Hard of Hearing People: South Nassau Chapter, 6444
Seneca County Office for the Aging, 1872
Seneca Lake Terrace Adult ResidentialCommunity, 9853
Seneca Nation of Indians Office for Aging, 1873
Senior Action in a Gay Environment, 1874
Shire at Culverton Adult Home, 9854
Signature and Address Self-Inking Stamps, 3468
Sisters of Life: Dr Joseph R Stanton Human Life Issues Library and Resource Center, 11660
Smoker's Robot, 3315
Society for Advancement in Nursing, 316
South Central Region: Helen Keller National Center, 7744
Southern Adirondack Independent Living, 10888
Southern Tier Association for the Visually Impaired, 7749
St Mary's School for the Deaf Library Information Center, 11661
St. John's Episcopal Hospital, 7045
St. Lawrence County Office for Aging, 1875
St. Regis Mohawk Office for the Aging, 1876
StairClimber, 3490
State University College at Fredonia: Youngman Center, 6814
State University College at Plattsburgh: Auditory Research Laboratory, 6815
State University of New York at Buffalo Toxicology Research Center, 7220
Staten Island Center for Independent Living, 10889
Steady Write, 3469
Steel Food Guard, 3348
Steuben County Office for the Aging, 1877
Suction Grater, 3349
Suffolk Cooperative Library System, 11662
Suffolk County Office for the Aging, 1878
Sullivan County Office for the Aging, 1879
Sure Hands International, 3404
Sure Safe Raised Toilet Seat, 3024
SureHands Lift & Care Systems, 3405
Swiss International Airlines, 11941
Syracuse University Center for Policy Research, 11663
Syracuse University: Institute for Sensory Research, 6816
TAJ Braille Typewriter, 3171
TIAA-CREF, 321
Taconic Resources for Independence, 10890
Talking Bathroom Scale, 3026
Talking Desktop Calculators, 3176
Talking Thermometers, 3273
Tanglewood Manor, 9855
Tappan Zee Manor, 9856
Teachers College Milbank Memorial Library, 11664
Teachers Insurance and Annuity Association Business Library, 11665
Telephone Amplifier, 3179
Tim's Trim, 2995
Timex Easy Reader, 3180
Tioga Opportunities Department on Aging, 1880
Toilet Guard Rail, 3029
Touch Page Turner, 3470
Towers Perrin Corporate Information Center, 11666
Transfer Board, 3408
Transfer Tub Bench, 3030
Travel Companion Exchange, 12050
Travelfair, 12053
Tri-Grip Bathtub Rail, 3031
US Department of Veterans Affairs: Albany Medical Center Library, 11667
US Department of Veterans Affairs: Batavia Western New York Healthcare System Library, 11668
US Department of Veterans Affairs: Bath Medical Center Library Service, 11669
US Department of Veterans Affairs: Bronx Medical Center Library, 11670
US Department of Veterans Affairs: Brooklyn Medical Center Library, 11671
US Department of Veterans Affairs: Buffalo Medical Center Library Service, 11672
US Department of Veterans Affairs: Castle Point Department of Medicine and Surgery Library Service, 11673
US Department of Veterans Affairs: Montrose Medical Library, 11674
US Department of Veterans Affairs: New York Harbour Healthcare System, New York Campus Library, 11675
US Department of Veterans Affairs: Northport Medical Center-Medical Library, 11676
Unisex Low Vision Watch, 3183
Universal Knob Turner, 3316
University of Rochester: Clinical Research Center, 6900
Vassar-Warner Home, 9857
W Alton Jones Cell Science Center: George and Margaret Gey Library, 11677
WCIB Heavy-Duty Folding Cane, 3493
Wal-Pil-O, 3232
Walkane, 3494

Wallace Memorial Library, 11678
Warren Hamilton Counties Office for the Aging, 1881
Washington County Office for the Aging, 1882
Westchester Disabled on the Move, 10891
Westchester Independent Living Center, 10892
Western New York Independent Living Project, 10893
William and Mercer Research Library, 11679
Wire Walker Basket, 3496
Woman to Woman, 7230
Workmen's Benefit Fund of the USA, 344
Wyoming County Office for Aging, 1883
Xavier Society for the Blind, 11680
Yates County Office for the Aging, 1884
Yeshiva University: Institute of Communication Disorders, 6837
Zipper Pull, 3245

North Carolina

Abbotswood at Irving Park Assisted Living, 9363
Aberdeene Meadows, 9364
Abington Place of Gastonia, 9365
Ahoskie House, 9366
Albemarle Commission, 1885
Alterra Clare Bridge Cottage of Raleigh, 9367
Alterra Clare Bridge of Asheville, 9368
Alterra Clare Bridge of Cary, 9369
Alterra Clare Bridge of Charlotte, 9370
Alterra Clare Bridge of Greensboro, 9371
Alterra Clare Bridge of South Park, 9372
Alterra Clare Bridge of Southern Pines, 9373
Alterra Clare Bridge of Wilmington, 9374
Alterra Clare Bridge of Winston Salem, 9375
Alterra Sterling House of Goldsboro, 9376
Alterra Sterling House of Greenville, 9377
Alterra Sterling House of Hickory, 9378
Alterra Sterling House of New Bern, 9379
Alterra Sterling House of Raleigh, 9380
Alterra Sterling House of Rocky Mount, 9381
Alterra Sterling House of Shelby, 9382
Alterra Sterling House of Southern Pines, 9383
Alterra Wynwood of Chapel Hill, 9384
Alterra Wynwood of Charlotte, 9385
Alterra Wynwood of Greensboro, 9386
American Diabetes Association: Southern Regional Office, Eastern North Carolina, 6165
Arbor Care Assisted Living, 9387
Arbor Terrace of Asheville, 9388
Arbors at Carriage Club of Charlotte, 9389
Ardenwoods, 9390
Asheville Manor, 9391
Ashland Healthcare, 9392
Ashwood Estates Retirement Center, 9393
Atria Assisted Living-Merrywood South, 9394
Atria Assisted Retirement LivingMerrywood, 9395
Autumn Manor, 9396
Autumn Wind of Smithfield, 9397
Azalea Village, 9398
Becky's Rest Home, 9399
Bell House, 9400
Bethany Retirement Center, 9401
Blackwell's Rest Home, 9402
Blakey Hall Assisted Living, 9403
Boger City Rest Home, 9404
Bradford Village East, 9405
Bradford Village West, 9406
Bridging the Gap of Care, 9407
Brighton Gardens by Marriott-Greensboro, 9408
Brighton Gardens by Marriott-Raleigh, 9409
Brighton Gardens of Winston Salem, 9410
Britthaven of Kannapolis, 9411
Britthaven of La Grange, 9412
Brookstone Haven Residential Care, 9413
Brookstone Rest Home & Retirement Center, 9414
Brookstone Terrace, 9415
Burlington Manor, 9416
Cambridge Assisted Living Community, 9417
Cambridge Hills of Raleigh, 9418
Camden County Senior Center, 1886
Cardinal Care Center-Hendersonville, 9419
Carillon Assisted Living of Asheboro, 9420
Carillon Assisted Living of Cramer Mountain, 9421
Carillon Assisted Living of Newton, 9422
Carillon Assisted Living of Shelby, 9423
Carillon of Salisbury, 9424
Carmel Hills, 9425
Carolina House of Asheboro, 9426
Carolina House of Cary, 9427
Carolina House of Durham, 9428
Carolina House of Elizabeth City, 9429
Carolina House of Forest City, 9430
Carolina House of Greenville, 9431
Carolina House of Lexington, 9432
Carolina House of Pinehurst, 9433
Carolina House of Reidsville, 9434
Carolina House of Smithfield, 9435
Carolina House of Wake Forest, 9436
Carolina Inn at Village Green, 9437
Carolina Rest Home, 9438
Carolina Village, 9439
Carriage Club of Charlotte, 9440
Cedar Cove at Wilmington, 9441
Cedar Manor Rest Home, 9442
Cedar Rock Assisted Living, 9443
Central Care, 9444
Centralina Area: Agency on Aging, 1887
Champions at Porters Neck, 9445
Chancellor Gardens of Charlotte, 9446
Charlotte Square, 9447
Chatham Creek Rest Home, 9448
Cherry Springs Village, 9449
Christian Care Center of New Bern, 9450
Christian Care of Smithfield, 9451
Christian Care of Winston-Salem, 9452
Churchhill Assisted Living Residences, 9453
Clare Bridge of Chapel Hill, 9454
Clemmons Village, 9455
Cleveland Health Care Center, 9456
Colonial Manor Rest Home, 9457
Communications Services for the Deaf and Hard of Hearing, 6337
Community Care of Haywood, 9458
Concord Place, 9459
Core Family Care Center, 9460
Country Club Prime Time Retirement Home, 9461
Country Meadow Rest Home, 9462
Country Oaks Manor, 9463
Country Sunshine Rest Home, 9464
Countryside Living, 9465
Countrytime Inn, 9466
Creekside Manor, 9467
Crescent View Retirement Community, 9468
Croasdaile Village, 9469
Cross Road Retirement Community, 9470
Crown Colony at Mooresville, 9471
Cumberland County Coordinating Council for Older Adults: Elderly Law Unit, 11210
Davie Place Residential Care, 9472
Disability Rights And Resources, 10839
Discovery Program at Burlington Manor, 9473
Divine Country Manor, 9474
Dogwood Forest Adult Care Home, 9475
Dorothea Dix Hospital: Clinical Research Unit, 7455
Duke University Center for Demographic Studies Library, 11681
Duke University Medical Center, 7117
Duke University: RERC on Communication Enhancement, 6801
Durham Manor Rest Home, 9476
Durham Village, 9477
Dynamic Systems, 3200
Eastern Carolina Council Area Agency onAging, 1889
Eden Estates, 9478
Eden Gardens of Statesville, 9479
Edengardens of Concord, 9480
Edengardens of Kings Mountain, 9481
Edengardens of Mooresville, 9482
Elms at Tanglewood, 9483
Elon Village Home, 9484
Family Health International, 11682
Forsyth Center for the Deaf and Hard of Hearing, 6358
Fountains at the Albemarle Inn, 9485
Friends of the Senior Center, 1890
Friendship Care, 9486
Gaston Manor, 9487
Gaston Place, 9488
Gastonia Village, 9489
Governor's Advisory Council for Personswith Disabilities (GACPD), 11211
Granville County Senior Center, 1891
Greenbrier, 9490
Greensboro Manor, 9491
Greensboro Place on Lawndale, 9492
Harbours Edge Retirement Center, 9493
Haven Heights Rest Home, 9494
Haven in the Village at Carolina Place, 9495
Haywood Lodge & Retirement Center, 9496
HeartFields Assisted Living at Cary, 9497
Heritage Woods, 8976, 9499
Hickory Manor, 9500
High Country Region D Area: Agency on Aging, 1892
High Point Manor, 9501
High Point Place, 9502
Homeplace of Burlington, 9503
Homeplace of Durham, 9504
Homeplace of New Bern, 9505
Homestead Hills Assisted Living, 9506
Hypertension Center, 6908

Geographic Index / North Dakota

Inn at Quail Haven, 9507
Isothermal Planning & Development Commission, 1893
Jackson County Department on Aging, 1894
Kerner Ridge Assisted Living, 9508
KerrTar Regional Council of Governments Area: Agency on Aging, 1895
Knollwood Gardens Rest Home, 9509
Laurels in Highland Creek, 9510
Laurels in the Village at Carolina Place, 9511
Lawndale Manor, 9512
Lawyers Glen Retirement Living Center, 9513
Lee's Living Center, 9514
Legal Aid of North Carolina, 11212
Legal Services for the Elderly, 11202, 11213
Liberty Commons Assisted Living, 9515
Little Flower Assisted Living Residence, 9516
Manorhouse of Wilmington, 9518
Marriotts Brighton Gardens of Charlotte, 9519
Mars Hill Retirement Community, 9520
Maryfield, 9521
McDowell Council on Aging, 1896
Meadowbrook Terrance of Greensboro, 9522
Meals on Wheels of Haywood County, 1897
Meals on Wheels of Rowan, 1898
Mecklenburg County Bar: Volunteer Lawyers Program and Services for the Elderly, 11214
Mid-Carolina Area: Agency on Aging, 1899
Mid-East Commission Area: Agency on Aging, 1900
Mount Olive Retirement Village, 9523
NIH: Environmental Health Sciences, 173
Nantahala Outdoor Center, 12033
National Black Deaf Advocates, 6403
National Board for Certified Counselors, 205
National Federation of Licensed Practical Nurses, 225
North Carolina Area: Agency on Aging, 1901
North Carolina Assisted Living Association, 9524
North Carolina Assistive Technology Projects, 1902
North Carolina Association of Long Term Care Facilities, 1903
North Carolina Association of Nonprofit Homes for the Aging, 1904
North Carolina Client Assistance Program, 1905
North Carolina Council on Developmental Disabilities, 1906
North Carolina Department of Administration: Advocacy Council for Persons with Disabilities, 1907
North Carolina Department of Aging, 1908
North Carolina Department of Human Resources: Deaf & Hard of Hearing Division, 1909, 6423
North Carolina Department of Revenue, 1910
North Carolina Department of the State: Treasurer Division of Retirement Systems, 1911
North Carolina Division of Aging and Adult Services, 11215

North Carolina Division of Mental Health, Developmental Disabilities and Abuse Services, 6049, 7203
North Carolina Division of Tourism, 11981
North Carolina Industrial Commission, 1912
North Carolina Library for the Blind, 11683
North Carolina Retired Government Employees Association, 1913
North Carolina Senior Citizens Association, 1914
North Carolina Society to Prevent Blindness, 7704
North Carolina Workers Compensation Board, 1915
Oak Hill Living Center, 9525
Oakview Assisted Living Center, 9526
Onslow Coordinating Council on Aging, 11216
Outlook Pointe at Northridge, 9527
Parkway Retirement Home, 9528
Pathways For the Future-Center For IndepEndent Living, 10840
Piedmont Christian Home, 9529
Piedmont Triad Council of Governments Area: Agency on Aging, 1916
Railroad Retirement Board: North Carolina District Office, 1917
Retired Military Police Association, 303, 1918
Richmond County Council on the Aging, 1919
Ridge Crest Retirement, 9530
Rose Haven, 9531
Rose Terrace of Wendell, 9532
Salisbury Gardens, 9533
Samaritan Place Assisted Living, 9534
Senior Advisory Association of North Carolina, 1920
Shallotte Assisted Living, 9535
Shepherd House Assisted Living Community, 9536
Slicing Aid, 3346
Snug Seat, 3023
Somerset Court, 9537
Somerset Court of Mocksville, 9538
Somerset Court of Newport, 9539
Spring Arbor of Apex, 9540
Spring Arbor of Herdersonville, 9541
Spring Arbor of Kinston, 9542
Spring Arbor of Raleigh, 9543
Spring Arbor of Rocky Mount, 9544
Spring Arbor of Wilmington, 9545
Spring Arbor of Wilson, 9546
Statesville Place, 9547
Sun-Mate Seat Cushions, 3229
Sunrise Assisted Living at Eastover, 9548
Sunrise Assisted Living of Raleigh, 9549
Sunrise Assisted Living of South Charlotte, 9550
Sunrise of Providence, 9551
Thompson Gardens of Garland, 9552
Trinity Oaks Retirement Community, 9553
US Department of Veterans Affairs: Asheville Medical Center Library, 11684
US Department of Veterans Affairs: Durham Medical Center Library, 11685
US Department of Veterans Affairs: Fayettville Medical Center Library Service, 11686
US Department of Veterans Affairs: Salisbury Medical Center Library, 11687
USAirways Shuttle, 11944

University of North Carolina at Chapel Hill Divsion of Speech & Hearing, 6828
Upper Coastal Plain Area Agency on Aging 1921
VOCAL-New Hanover County, 1922
Volunteer Center of Greater Durham, 1923
Wake Forest University: Arteriosclerosis Research Center, 6930
Wake Forest University: CerebrovascularResearch Center, 7124
Western Piedmont Council of Governments, 1924
Winston-Salem Industries for the Blind, 7786

North Dakota

Altera Sterling House of Fargo, 9554
American Diabetes Association: North Dakota, 6154
Baptist Home of Kenmare, 9555
Bethany Homes, 9556
Bethel Four Acres, 9557
Bethel Lutheran Home, 9558
Chateau for Seniors Citizens, 9559
Dakota Center for Independent Living, 10841
Devils Lake Good Samaritan, 9560
Edgewood Vista - Minot, 9561
Edgewood Vista of Bismark, 9562
Edmore Memorial Rest Home, 9563
Ellendale Evergreen Place, 9564
Freedom Resource Center for Independent Living, 10806, 10842
Golden Acres Manor, 9565
Harolds Haaland Home, 9567
Independence, 10843
Karrington Commons, 9568
Karrington Cottages, 9569
Legal Services of North Dakota, 11217
Luther Memorial Home, 9570
Maddock Memorial Home, 9571
Manor St Joesph, 9572
Marian Manor, 9573
Marillac Manor, 9574
National Resource Center on Native American Aging (NRCNAA), 255
Noonan Good Samaritan Center, 9575
North Dakota Aging Services, 1926
North Dakota Aging Services Division, 11218
North Dakota Client Assistance Program, 1927
North Dakota Department of Aging, 1928
North Dakota Department of Mental Health, 6050
North Dakota Department of Veterans Affairs, 1929
North Dakota Lawyer Referral and Information Service: Elder Law Panel, 11219
North Dakota Mental Health & Substance Abuse, 7204
North Dakota Protection & Advocacy, 1930
North Dakota Protection and Advocacy Agency, 11220
North Dakota Public Employees Retirement System, 1931
North Dakota State Council on Developmental Disabilities, 1932

1104

Geographic Index / Ohio

North Dakota State Library: Disability Services, 11697
North Dakota State Tax Department, 1933
North Dakota Teachers Retirement Fund, 1934
North Dakota Workers Compensation, 1935
Old Fellows Home, 9576
Park River Good Samaritan, 9577
Prairie Home, 9578
Primrose Retirement Center, 9579
RSVP Devils Lake Area, 1936
RSVP North Central North Dakota, 1937
RSVP of Central North Dakota, 1938
Railroad Retirement Board: North Dakota District Office, 1939
Redwood Village, 9580
Riverview Place, 9581
Services for the Visually Impaired: Department of Public Instruction, 11699
Sheridan Memorial Home, 9582
St Catherine's Living Center, 9583
St Francis Residence, 9584
Tri-County Retirement Home, 9585
Tufte Manor, 9586
US Department of Veterans Affairs: Fargo Medical Center Library, 11702
Valley View Heights, 9587
Waterford at Hardwoodgroves, 9588
Waterford on West Century, 9589
Wheatland Terrace, 9590

Ohio

AARP Ohio Office, 1940
APT Technology Switches, 3058
Ability Center of Greater Toledo, 10894
Access Center for Independent Living, 10709, 10895
Adaptive Vans for the Physically Challenged, 2954
Adjustable Clear Acrylic Tray, 3318
Adjustable Incline Board, 3473
Akron Blind Center and Workshop, 7498
Alterra Sterling House of Alliance, 9858
Alterra Sterling House of Springfield, 9859
Alzheimer's Association: Greater Cincinnati, 1941
Amanda House, 9860
American Diabetes Association: Central Ohio Area Office, 6123
American Diabetes Association: Northern Ohio/Cleveland Area Office, 6156
Amherst Manor, 9861
Anchor Lodge Retirement Village, 9862
Anna Maria of Aurora, 9863
Apostolic Christian Home, 9864
Arbors at Clyde Assisted Living Center, 9865
Arbors at Dayton Residential Care, 9866
Arbors at Fairlawn Residential Care, 9867
Arbors at Marietta Residential Care, 9868
Arden Courts of Parma, 9869
Area Two Area: Agency on Aging, 1942
Aspen Woodside Village, 9870
Association of Ohio Philanthropic Homes for the Aging, 1943
Avon Maximum Independent Living, 1944
Bariatric Wheelchairs Regency, 3498
Bayley Place, 9871
Benjamin Rose Institute Library, 11704

Berea Lake Towers Retirement Community, 9872
Berkley Square Retirement Community, 9873
Bil Jax Construction/Rental, 3501
Blossom Hill Care Center, 9874
Breckenridge Village, 9875
Briarfield Manor Residential Care, 9876
Briarwood, 9877
Brookhaven the Lifecare Community, 9878
Brookside Estates, 9879
Buckeye Hills-Hocking Valley Regional Development District, 1945
Bureau of Disability Determination, 1946
CAP Darke County, 1947
Canton Christian Home, 9880
Canton Negro Oldtimers, 1948
Canton Regency Retirement Community, 9881
Carroll County Council on Aging, 1949
Case Western Reserve University Elderly Care Research Center, 11705
Cedarville Senior Citizens, 1950
Center for Independent Living Options (CILO), 10896
Central Ohio Area: Agency on Aging, 1951
Cincinnati Area: Council on Aging, 1952
Cincinnati Association for the Blind, 7564
Cleveland Clinic Foundation Research Institute, 6867
Cleveland Hearing and Speech Center, 6332
Cleveland Public Library, 11706
Cleveland Sight Center, 7566
Cleveland Skilled Industries, 7567
Cleveland West Chapter: Self-Help for Hard of Hearing People, 6333
Clovernook Center: Opportunities for the Blind, 7568
Columbus Volunteer Corps, 1953
Commons of Providence, 9882
Commons of Providence: Specialized Assisted Living, 9883
Community's Hearth & Home, 9884
Community's Hearth & Home at El Camino, 9885
Congenital Heart Disease Anomalies Support Education and Resources, 6840
Cottingham Retirement Community, 9886
Council for Health & Human Services Ministries, 115
Council for Older Adults, 1954
Country Club Retirement Center, 9887
DBC-1 DU-IT Bed Control, 3036
Delaware Court, 9888
DeltaTalker, 3105
District Five Area: Agency on Aging, 1955
District Seven Area: Agency on Aging, 1956
EZBACK Recline Control, 3548
East Park Retirement Community, 9889
Elms Retirement Village, 9890
Emerald Ridge of Solon, 9891
Evio Plastics, 3332
Foot Inversion Tread, 3257
Foot Placement Ladder, 3305
Frank Reed Memorial Library, 11707
Gendron, 3518
Genoa Retirement Village Assisted Living, 9892
Golden Buckeye Program, 11959
Good Shepherd Home, 9566, 9893
Greene Oaks Willow Place, 9894

Harris Library, MSASS, Case Western Reserve University, 11708
Headmaster Plus, 3121
Highland County Senior Citizens, 1957
Homewood Residence-Richmond Heights, 9895
Homewood Residence-Rockefeller Gardens, 9896
Inn at Belden Village, 9897
Inn at Chestnut Hill, 9898
Inn at Lakeview, 9899
Invacare Corporation, 3262
Kendal at Oberlin, 9900
Kingston Residence of Perrysburg, 9901
Landing of Canton, 9902
Laurel Lake Retirement Community, 9903
Leg Elevation Board, 3384
Liberty Arms Assisted Living Facility, 9904
Life Center at Wesley Ridge, 9905
Light of Hearts Villa, 9906
Lincoln Park Manor, 9907
Lochaven Apartments, 9908
Lodge of Montgomery, 9909
Lourdes College Duns Scotus Library, 11709
Luminaud, 3134
Lutheran Home at Toledo Assisted Living, 9910
Lutheran Village of Columbus, 9911
Mallard Crove Seniors Community, 9912
Manor at Autumn Hills, 9913
Manor at the Meadows, 9914
Maple Knoll Village-Beecher Place, 9915
Marian Living Center, 9916
Marie Haug Student Award in Gerontology, 2653
Marriott Maple Ridge of Willoughby, 9917
Marymount Place, 9918
Massillon Senior Citizens' Center, 1958
Mayfair Village Retirement Community, 9919
McKnight Terrace, 9920
Meadows at Friendship Village, 9921
Mennonite Memorial Home, 9922
Miami University Humanities and Social Sciences Department, 11710
Midway Community and Senior Citizens, 1959
Modular Wall Grab Bars, 3018
Mount Royal Villa, 9923
Muskingum County Senior Services, 1960
National Association of Blind Secretaries and Transcribers, 7658
National Association of Directors of Nursing Administration in Long Term Care, 191
North Central Regional Training Center: Canine Companions for Independence, 7705
Northwestern Ohio Area: Agency on Aging, 1961
Oakwood Village, 8879, 9924
Office of the Ohio Attorney General: Health, Education & Human Services Section, 11221
Ohio Assisted Living Association, 9925
Ohio Association of Area Agencies onAging, 1962
Ohio Bureau on Alcohol Abuse and Recovery, 7208
Ohio Client Assistance Program, 1963
Ohio Department of Aging, 1964, 11222

1105

Geographic Index / Oklahoma

Ohio Department of Drug and Alcohol Addiction Services: Ohio Prevention and Education Resource Center, 7470
Ohio Department of Mental Health, 6051
Ohio Department of Taxation, 1965
Ohio Developmental Disability Council, 1966
Ohio Disabled American Veterans, 1967
Ohio Division of Travel and Tourism, 11982
Ohio Governor's Council on People with Disabilities, 1968
Ohio Masonic Home, 9926
Ohio Protection & Advocacy for Persons With Disabilities, 1969
Ohio Public Employees Retirement System, 1970
Ohio Regional Library for the Blind and Physically Handicapped, 11711
Ohio School Employees Retirement System, 1971
Ohio School for the Deaf Alumni Association, 6427
Ohio School for the Deaf Library, 11712
Ohio State University: Division of Clinical Trials, 7471
Ohio State University: Otological Research Laboratories, 6810
Ohio University: School of Hearing and Speech Science, 6811
Old Lesbians Organizing for Change, 277
Omni West, 9927
Orchard Grove, 9928
Oregon Senior Citizens' Center, 1972
Otterbein Portage Valley, 9929
Outlook Pointe at Lima, 9930
Outlook Pointe at Medina, 9931
Outlook Pointe at Ontario, 9932
Outlook Pointe at Ravenna, 9933
Outlook Pointe at Sagamore Hills, 9934
Outlook Pointe at Xenia, 9935
Paisley House for Aged Women, 9936
Patriot Ridge Community, 9937
Pebble Creek Senior Care Residence, 9938
Prentke Romich Company, 3155
Prentke Romich Company Product Catalog, 3156
Prevent Blindness Ohio, 7727
Pro Seniors, 11224
Public Library of Cincinnati and Hamilton Outreach Services Department, 11713
RSVP Akron, 1973
RSVP Athensns, 1974
RSVP Belmont County, 1975
RSVP Cincinnati Area, 1976
RSVP Franklin County, 1835, 1978
RSVP Gallia County, 1979
RSVP Harcatus, 1980
RSVP Jefferson, 1981
RSVP KnoHo, 1982
RSVP Lake County, 939, 1004, 1983, 1983
RSVP Lorain County, 1984
RSVP Mahoning County, 1985
RSVP Maimi Valley, 1986
RSVP Marion-Crawford Counties, 1987
RSVP Meigs, 1988
RSVP Perry County, 1990
RSVP Richland County, 1991
RSVP Scioto County, 1992
RSVP Warren County, 1993
Railroad Retirement Board: Cincinnati Office, 1995

Railroad Retirement Board: Cleveland District Office, 1996
Region Nine Area: Agency on Aging, 1434, 1997
Residence of Sterling Oaks, 9939
Retired Teachers Association, 1998
Ridgewood at Friendship Village, 9940
Rockmill Springs Assisted Living, 9941
Roll Chair, 3048
Rutherford House, 9942
Sara Moore Home, 9943
Self-Help for Hard of Hearing People, Cleveland West Chapter, 6442
Senior Center of Sidney Shelby County, 1999
Services for Independent Living, 10829, 10897
Serving Our Seniors, 2000
Shepherd of the Valley Howland, 9944
Shepherd of the Valley Lutheran Retirmen, 9945
Smart Leg, 3397
Society for Equal Access Independent Living Center, 10898
Sport Lite 4000, 3536
SpringBoard Plus, 3165
St Augustine Health Campus, 9946
St Joseph Assisted Residence, 9947
State Library of Ohio: Talking Book Program, 11714
Summerville at Mentor Assisted Living, 9948
Summerville at Middletown, 9949
Summerville of Singing Woods, 9950
Summit Villa Assisted Living, 9951
Sunrise Assisted Living, 8889, 9952
Sunrise Assisted Living at Bexley, 9953
Sunrise Assisted Living at Finneytown, 9954
Sunrise Assisted Living of Bath, 9955
Sunrise Assisted Living of Cuyahoga Falls, 9956
Sunrise Assisted Living of Englewood, 9957
Sunrise Assisted Living of Hamilton, 9958
Sunrise Assisted Living of Kenwood, 9959
Sunrise Assisted Living of Oakwood, 9960
Sunrise Assisted Living of Parma, 9961
Sunrise Assisted Living of Shaker Heights, 9962
Sunrise Assisted Living of Wooster, 9963
Sunrise at Tucker Creek, 9964
Sunrise of Gahanna, 9965
Sunrise of Poland, 9966
Sunrise on the Scioto, 9967
Suregrip Bathtub Rail, 3025
Tilt 'n Tote, Roamer Riding Chair, 3407
Traditions at Bath Road, 9968
Traditions at Mill Run, 9969
Traditions of Chillicothe, 9970
Transfer Bench with Back, 3052
US Department of Veterans Affairs: Brecksville Medical Center Library, 11715
US Department of Veterans Affairs: Chillicothe Medical Library, 11716
US Department of Veterans Affairs: Cincinnati Learning Resources Service, 11717
US Department of Veterans Affairs: Dayton Medical Center Library Service, 11718
United Methodist Association of Health and Welfare Ministries (UMA), 335
Unity/128, 3184

University of Cincinnati Medical Center Libraries, 11719
University of Cincinnati: Department of Pathology & Laboratory Medicine, 6897
Vancrest Assisted Living, 9971
Vantage Plus, 3186
Villas at St Therese Assisted Living, 9972
Washington County Home, 9973
Wedgewood Estates of Mansfield, 9974
Western Reserve Area: Agency on Aging, 2001
Westlake Village, 9975
Wheelchair Carriers, Ramps, and Roamer Riding Chair, 3414
Wheelchair Work Table, 3564
Whetstone Gardens, 9976
Willow Knoll Retirement Community, 9977
Worthington Christian Village, 9978
YM 9000 Ride-Lite Series, 3543
Youngstown Radio Reading Service, 7789

Oklahoma

Ability Resources, 10900
Aging Services Division, 2002
Alterra Clare Bridge Cottage of Oklahoma City, 9979
Alterra Clare Bridge Oklahoma City, 9980
Alterra Sterling House of Bartlesville, 9981
Alterra Sterling House of Bethany, 9982
Alterra Sterling House of Broken Arrow, 9983
Alterra Sterling House of Claremore, 9984
Alterra Sterling House of Durant, 9985
Alterra Sterling House of Edmond, 9986
Alterra Sterling House of Enid, 9987
Alterra Sterling House of Lawton, 9988
Alterra Sterling House of Midwest City, 9989
Alterra Sterling House of Muskogee, 9990
Alterra Sterling House of Norman, 9991
Alterra Sterling House of Oklahoma City, 9992
Alterra Sterling House of Ponca City, 9993
Alterra Sterling House of Shawnee, 9994
Alterra Sterling House of Tulsa, 9995
Alterra Sterling House of Tulsa South, 9996
Alterra Sterling House of Weatherford, 9997
Alterra Sterling of ADA, 9998
Ambassadors Courtyards, 9999
American Diabetes Association: Oklahoma Area Office, 6157
American Diabetes Association: Oklahoma City District Office, 6113
Angel House Residential Assisted Living, 10000
Arbor House Assisted Living Center, 10001
Areawide Aging Agency, 2003
Ash Street Place, 10002
Brighton Gardens of Oklahoma City, 10003
Brighton Gardens of Tulsa, 10004
Brookridge Retirement Community, 10005
Bryan County Retired and Senior Volunteer Program, 2004
Central Oklahoma Economic Development District: Area Agency on Aging (COEDD), 2005
Country Wood Manor Living Center, 10006
Crystal Place Assisted Living Center, 10007
Crystalwood Assisted Living Center, 10008
Davis Home, 10009

Dean A McGee Eye Institute, 8038
Dogwood Creek Retirement Center, 10010
Dollar Rent-a-Car, 11923
Eastern Oklahoma Development District Area: Agency on Aging (EODD), 2007
Elkwood Assisted Living, 10011
Emerald Square Assisted Living Center, 10012
Epworth Villa, 10013
Forest Glade Retirement Center II, 10014
Forest Hills Health Care Center, 10015
Frances Strietel Villa, 10016
Gardens Assisted Living, 9333, 10017
Gardens at Rivermont, 10018
Golden Oaks Village, 10019
Grand Gateway Area: Agency on Aging, 2008
Green County Independent Living Resource Center, 10901
Green County Village Assisted Living, 10020
Hearthstone at Quail Springs, 10021
Heartsworth House, 10022
Heathridge Assisted Living Comunity, 10023
Heritage Assisted Living Center, 10024
Herrington Place, 10353
Hillcrest Medical Center Library, 11720
Integris Baptist Medical Center: Wann Langston Memorial Library, 11721
Jefferson's Garden, 10026
KEDDO Area: Agency on Aging, 2009
KI BOIS Retired Senior Volunteer Program, 2010
Legal Aid Services of Oklahoma, 11225
Manchester House, 10027
Mansion at Waterford, 10028
Mustang Manor Assisted Living, 10029
NODA Area: Agency on Aging, 2011
National Car Rental, 11935
OKDHS Aging Services Division, 2012
Oklahoma Aging Services Division, 11226
Oklahoma Association Area: Agencies onAging, 2013
Oklahoma Association of Homes and Services for the Aging, 2014
Oklahoma Client Assistance Program, 2015
Oklahoma Department of Aging, 2016
Oklahoma Department of Mental Health, 6052
Oklahoma Department of Mental Health and Substance Abuse Services, 7209
Oklahoma Department of Mental Health andSubstance Abuse Services (ODMHSAs), 11227
Oklahoma Department of Veterans Affairs, 2017
Oklahoma Developmental Disability Council, 2018
Oklahoma Disability Law Center: Oklahoma City, 11228
Oklahoma Disability Law Center: Tulsa, 11229
Oklahoma League for the Blind, 7711
Oklahoma Library for the Blind & Physically Handicapped, 11722
Oklahoma Medical Research Foundation: Cardiovascular Research Program, 6884
Oklahoma Methodist Manor, 10030
Oklahoma Protection & Advocacy Agecny, 2019
Oklahoma State Office of Rehabilitation Services: Visually Impaired, 7712
Oklahoma Tax Commission, 2020
Oklahoma Tourism & Recreation Department, 11983
Oklahomans For Independent Living, 10902
Parke Senior Living, 10031
Plantation House-Okmulgee, 10032
Prevent Blindness Oklahoma, 7728
Progressive Independence, 10903
Quail Ridge by Encore Senior Center, 10033
RSBP Altus, 2021
RSVP Atoka, 2022
RSVP Cleveland-McClain Counties, 2023
RSVP Enid, 2024
RSVP Inca, 2025
RSVP Lawton, 2026
RSVP Little Dixie, 2027
RSVP Love & Marshall Counties, 2028
RSVP Muskogee, 2029
RSVP Ponca City and Kay County, 2030
RSVP Pottawatomie-Seminole Counties, 2031
RSVP Seven County, 2032
RSVP Tulsa, 2033
Rambling Oaks Assisted Living Center, 10034
Renaissance of Ponca City, 10035
Renaissance of Stillwater Extended, 10036
Sandra Beasley Independent Living Center, 10904
Schallmo Assisted Living Center, 10037
Service Corps of Retired Executives of Tulsa, 2034
Smith Manor, 10038
Sommerset Assisted Living Residences, 10039
South Western Oklahoma Development Authority Area Agency on Aging, 2035
Southern Oklahoma Development Association Area: Agency on Aging (SODA), 2036
Southwest Society on Aging, 2037
Sycamore Square Assisted Living, 10040
Tamarack Retirement Center, 10041
Ten Oaks at Merrill Gardens Community, 10042
Thrifty Rent-a-Car, 11942
Tulsa Area: Agency on Aging, 2038
Tulsa City-County Library System, 11723
US Department of Veterans Affairs: Oklahoma City Medical Center Library, 11724
University of Oklahoma: Speech & Hearing Center, 6829
Unlimited Care-Richmond Hills, 10043
Victorian Estates, 10044
Village of Lee Retirement Center, 10045
Vyne at Cedar Ridge, 10046
Welch Assisted Living Center, 10047
Windsor Manor Assisted Living, 10048
Worker's Compensation Enforcement Division, 2039
the Retirement Village at Copper Lake, 10049

Oregon

Access Technologies, 2040
Adams House, 10050
Addie's You & I Travel Service, 12005
Alderwood Assisted Living, 10051
Alpine House Assisted Living, 10052
Alpine Springs Assisted Living and Cottages, 10053
Alterra Wynwood of Albany, 10054
Alterra Wynwood of McMinnville, 10055
American Diabetes Association, 6111
American Diabetes Association: Eugene Branch Office, 6131
American Diabetes Association: Oregon Area Office, 6158
American Tinnitus Association, 6317
Aspen Court, 10056
Assisted Living at Summerplace, 10057
Astor House, 10058
Augmentative Communication Systems (AAC), 3081
Avamere at Hillsboro, 10059
Avamere at Newberg, 10060
Avamere at Sandy, 10061
Avamere at Sherwood, 10062
Awbrey House, 10063
Beaverton Hills Assisted Living, 10064
Blind Enterprises of Oregon, 7536
Bridgewood Rivers, 10065
Brookside House, 10066
Bureau of Naval Personnel: Oregon Retired Activities Office, 2042
Cambridge Terrace Assisted Living, 10067
Canfield Place Retirement, 10068
Carman Oaks Assisted Living Facility, 10069
Carriage House, 10070
Cascadia Village Retirement Community, 10071
Cedar Sinai Park, 10072
Cedar Village Assisted Living Community, 10073
Central Oregon Council on Aging, 2043
Cherry Wood Village, 10074
Churchill Clubhouse Estates, 10075
Clackamas County Social Services Area: Agency on Aging, 2044
Clackamas Woods Assisted Living, 10076
Columbia County Council Area: Agency onAging, 2045
Community Connection of Northeast Oregon, 2046
Comprehensive Stroke Center of Oregon, 7114
Cornell Estates Living Center, 10077
Courtyard Senior Living, 10078
Dallas Retirement Assisted Living Facility, 10079
Davenport House, 10080
Deer Meadow Assisted Living Community, 10081
Deerfield Village, 10082
Dogs for the Deaf, 6351
Dorian Place, 10083
Douglas County Health & Disabilities Services, 2048
Douglas County Senior Services Division, 2049
Douglas House, 10084
Eastern Oregon Center for Independent Living, 10905
Elliott Residence, 10085
Emerald Valley, 10086
Flagstone Retirement & Assisted Living, 10087
Forest Grove Beehive, 10088

1107

Geographic Index / Oregon

Fountains at Town Center Village, 10089
Gibson Creek Retirement and Assisted Living, 10090
Gilman Park, 10091
Governor's Commission on Senior Services (GCSS), 11230
Grace House, 10092
Grande Ronde Retirement Residence, 10093
Gray Panthers of Portland, 2050
Greenridge Estates, 10094
Grove Assisted Living Community, 10095
Harney County Senior Center, 2051
Harvest Homes, 10096
Hearthstone of Beaverton, 10097
Heritage Place Assisted Living, 10025, 10099
Hermiston Terrace Assisted Living Facility, 10100
Heron Pointe Retirement & Assisted Living, 10101
Hillside Communities, 10102
Hillside House Assisted Living Center, 10103
Homewood Heights Assisted Living Facility, 10104
Huffman House, 10105
Huntington Terrace Assisted Living, 10106
Independent Living Resources, Inc. (ILR), 10906
Inland Point Assisted Living, 10107
Jackson House, 10108
Jennings McCall Center II, 10109
Johnson Assisted Living, 10110
Johnson Assisted Living Center, 10111
Junction City Retirement & Assisted Living Facility, 10112
Juniper House, 10113
Kilchis House, 10114
Klamath Basin Senior Citizens' Council, 2052
Lakeside Assisted Living Community, 10115
Lakewood Pointe Assisted Living, 10116
Lancaster Assisted Living, 10117
Lancaster Village, 10118
Lancaster Woods, 10119
Lane Council of Governments: Senior and Disabled Services Division, 2053
Lane County Law and Advocacy Center: Senior Law Service, 11231
Laurelhurst House Assisted Living Community, 10120
Legal Aid Services of Oregon: Senior LawProject, 11232
Lincolnshire Retirement & Assisted Living, 10121
Linkville House, 10122
Lone Oak Assisted Living, 10123
MacDonald Residence, 10124
Macklyn House, 10125
Magnolia Gardens Assisted Living Facilities, 10126
Markham House, 10127
Marquis Vintage Suites at Forest Grove, 10128
Mary's Woods at Marylhurst, 10129
McAuley Terrace, 10130
McKillop Residence Assisted Living Facility, 10131
McLoughlin Place, 10132
Meadow Creek Village Assisted Living Residence, 10133

Meadowbrook Place, 10134
Mid-Columbia Senior and Disabled Services, 2054
Mt Saint Joseph, 10135
Multnomah County Aging Services Division, 2055
Neawanna by the Sea, 10136
New Breakthroughs, 3146
Northridge Center, 10137
Oaks at Lebanon, 10138
Ocean Crest Retirement & Assisted Living Facility, 10139
Odyssey Club, 12037
Oregon Advocacy Center, 2056
Oregon Advocacy Center (OAC), 11233
Oregon Alliance of Senior & Health Services, 2057
Oregon Cascades West Senior Services, 2058
Oregon Commission for the Blind, 7713
Oregon Commission on Disabilities, 2059
Oregon Council on Developmental Disabilities, 2060
Oregon Department of Aging, 2061
Oregon Department of Human Services: Division of Senior & Disabled Services, 2062
Oregon Department of Mental Health, 6053
Oregon Department of Revenue, 2063
Oregon Department of Veterans Affairs, 2064
Oregon Health Sciences University, 7039
Oregon Health Sciences University: Oregon Hearing Research Center, 6812
Oregon Hearing Society, 2065
Oregon Office of Alcohol and Drug Abuse Programs, 7210
Oregon Protection & Advocacy for Persons with Disabilities, 2066
Oregon Public Employees Retirement System, 2067
Oregon School for the Blind Media Center, 11725
Oregon Senior Services, 2068
Oregon State Bar: Rights of Persons with Disabilities Section, 11234
Oregon State Commission for the Blind, 7714
Oregon State Library, 11726
Oregon Tourism Commission, 11984
Outback Ranch Outfitters, 12038
Park Place Assisted Living Residence, 10140
Parkhurst House, 10141
Parkland Village Assisted Living Facility, 10142
Pheasant Pointe Assisted Living, 10143
Pilot Rock Senior Center, 2069
Powell Valley ASL & ALZ Care Community, 10144
Prairie House Retirement & Assisted Community, 10145
Princeton Village, 10146
Providence Benedictine Orchard House, 10147
Providence Brookside Manor, 10148
Quail Run Assisted Living at MennoniteVillage, 10149
RSVP Columbia County, 1830, 2070
RSVP Coos County, 1631, 2071
RSVP Curry County, 1732, 2072
RSVP Deschutes County, 2073

RSVP Jackson County, 1371, 2074
RSVP Josephine County, 2075
RSVP Lincoln County, 2076
RSVP Linn Benton County, 2077
RSVP Marion County, 783, 2078
RSVP Multonamah County, 2079
RSVP Roseburg-Douglas, 2081
RSVP Roseburgburg, 2080
RSVP Washington County, 1994, 2082
Rackleff House, 10150
Railroad Retirement Board: -Oregon District Office, 2083
Redwood Heights, 10151
Redwood Terrace, 10152
Regent at Regency Park Assisted Living, 10153
Regional Resource Center on Deafness, 6437
Ridgeview Assisted Living, 10154
River Road Assisted Living Residence, 10155
Riverwood Assisted Living, 10156
Rogue Valley Council of Governments: Senior and Disability Services Division, 2084
Rose Arbor Assisted Living, 10157
Rose Valley Assisted Living Facility, 10158
Rosewood Park, 10159
RsVP Clackamas County, 2085
Russellville Park, 10160
SPOKES Unlimited, 10907
Salem Deaf Fellowship, 2086
Sawyer House, 10161
Settler's Park Assisted Living & Memory Care, 10162
Shilo Inns & Resorts, 12045
Shore Pines Assisted Living, 10163
Silver Creek Assisted Living, 10164
Skylark Assisted Living, 10165
South Salem Seniors, 2087
Southern Hills Assisted Living Community, 10166
Spencer House, 10167
Spring Meadows, 10168
Spring Valley Assisted Living Residence, 10169
Spring Village, 10170
Spruce Point, 10171
St Anthony Village, 10172
Summit Assisted Living, 10173
Summit Springs Assisted Living Facility, 10174
Sun Terrace Hermiston, 10175
Sundial Special Vacations, 12048
Suzanne Elise Assisted Living, 10176
Tanner Spring, 10177
Terwilliger Plaza, 10178
Timberhill Place, 10179
US Department of Veterans Affairs: Portland Medical Library, 11727
US Department of Veterans Affairs: Roseburg Medical Center Library Service, 11728
US Department of Veterans Affairs: WhiteCity Library, 11729
Valley View Assisted Living, 8571, 10180
Vestibular Disorders Association, 336
Vintage Suites, 10181
Vintage Suites at Hope Village, 10182
Vocational Rehabilitation Division, 2088
Washington County Area Agency on Aging, 2089

Geographic Index / Pennsylvania

Washington County Department of Aging Services, 2090
Well Springs Assisted Living Facility, 10183
Wiley Creek Community, 10184
Willamette Manor, 10185
Willamette View, 10186
Willamette View Health Center, 10187
Wilsonville, 10188
Woodland Heights, 10189
Woodside Assisted Living Community, 10190

Pennsylvania

Accessibility Lift, 3356
Accessible Journeys, 12004
Active Aging, 2091
Adams County Office for Aging, 2092
Address Book, 3446
Adjustable Bed, 3034
Aging Services, 2093
Allegheny County Area Agency on Aging, 11235
Allegheny County Department of Aging, 2094
Alterra Wynnwood of Northampton Manor, 10191
Alzheimer Treatment Research Center Library, 11730
American Baptist Homes and Hospitals Association, 27
American Board of Internal Medicine, 30
American Diabetes Association: Central Pennsylvania Area, 6124
American Diabetes Association: Western Pennsylvania Area Office, 6171
Anthracite Region Center for Independent Living, 10908
Area Agency on Aging for Tioga, Bradford, Sullivan and Susquehanna Counties, 2095
Area Agency on Aging of Somerset County, 2096
Armstrong Area: Agency on Aging, 2097
Artman Lutheran Home, 10192
Associated Services for the Blind and Visually Impaired, 7524
Beaver County Association for the Blind, 7532
Beaver County Office on Aging, 2098
Behan Health Science Library, 11731
Berks County Center for Independent Living, 10909
Berks County Senior Citizens Council, 2041
Berks Deaf & Hard of Hearing Services Library, 11732
Berks Deaf and Hard of Hearing Service, 6321
Blair County Association for the Blind and Visually Handicapped, 7534
Blair Senior Services, 2099
Bockus Research Institute, 6863
Bold Line Paper, 3451
Bucks County Area: Agency on Aging, 2100
Bucks County Legal Aid Society: Social Security Referral Panel, 11236
Butler County Area: Agency on Aging, 2101
Butler Township Senior Citizens, 2102
Captek/Science Products, 3096
Carbon County Area: Agency on Aging, 2103

Carmichaels Senior Citizens, 2104
Carnegie Library of Pittsburgh, 11733
Catholic Golden Age (CGA), 97
Center for Community and Professional Services of the PA School for the Deaf, 6328
Center for Independent Living of Central Pennsylvania, 10910
Center for Independent Living of SouthCentral Pennsylvania, 10911
Center for Information Resources, 11734
Center for the Blind and Visually Impaired, 7558
Centre County Office on Aging, 2105
Chester County Branch Pennsylvania Association for Blind, 7560
Chester County Branch, Pennsylvania Association for Blind, 7561
Chester County Services for Senior Citizens, 11237
Children of Aging Parents, 104
Citizens for Independence and Access, 10912
Clarion County Area: Agency on Aging, 2106
Clarke Health Care Products, 3007
Clearfield County Area: Agency on Aging, 2107
Colonial Meals on Wheels, 2108
Columbia-Montour-Area: Agency on Aging, 2109
Community Action Senior Corps, 2110
Community Resources for Independence, 10913
Connellsville Area Senior Tigers, 2111
Cumberland County Office of Aging, 2112
D'Youville Manor, 10193
Deer Meadows, 10194
Delaware County Legal Assistance Program: Senior Citizens Office, 11238
Diabetes Education and Research Center, 6268
Disabilities Law Project-Pennsylvania, 11239
Dolomite Walkers, 3480
Dorma Architectural Hardware, 3300
East Penn Manufacturing Company, 3549
Elevette 2100, 3374
Episcopal Conference of the Deaf, 6354
Experience Area: Agency on Aging, 2113
Fair Acres Center, 11735
Fountains at Logan Square East, 10195
Franklin County Area: Agency on Aging, 2114
Free Library of Philadelphia, 11736
Freedom Valley Disability Enablement, 10914
Golden Power Lift Chair, 3045
Golden Slipper Center for Seniors, 2115
Grand Residence at Upper St. Clair, 10196
Gray Panthers of Pittsburgh, 2116
Greater Erie Community Action Committee (GECAC), 2117
Greensburg Bureau of Disability Determination, 2118
Hahnemann University Laboratory of Human Pharmacology, 7458
Hahnemann University: Division of Surgical Research, 6921
Hamot Medical Center: Research Department, 7459

Harrisburg Bureau of Disability Determination, 2119
Homewaiter, 3382
Hospital of the University of Pennsylvania, 7118
Huntington-Bedford-Fulton Area: Agency on Aging, 2120
Inclinette, 3383
Indiana County Association for the Blind, 7614
Institute for Metabolic Research, 6275
Intestinal Disease Foundation, 6947
Jefferson County Area: Agency on Aging, 2121
Korean Senior Citizens Association of Greater Philadelphia, 2122
LPB, 3124
Lackawanna County Area: Agency on Aging, 2123
Lancaster County Association for the Blind, 7630
Lancaster County Office of Aging, 2124
Lawrence County Area Agency on Aging, 2125
Lebanon County Area: Agency on Aging, 2126
Lehigh Valley Center for Independent Living, 10915
Liberty Resources, 10916
Life Insurance for Veterans: Veterans Benefits Administration, 2127
Life and Independence for Today, 10917
Lock Haven Golden Age Club, 2128
Luther Park Personal Assistance Community, 10197
Luzerne-Wyoming Bureau for the Aging, 2129
Lycoming-Clinton Office of Aging, 2130
Masonic Retirement Community of Lafayette Hill, 10198
MedEscort International, 12030
Mercer County Area: Agency on Aging, 2131
Mifflin-Juniata Area: Agency on Aging, 2132
Monroe County Area: Agency on Aging, 2133
Montgomery County Office on Aging and Adult Services, 2134
National Association of Addiction Treatment Providers, 7187
National Organization for Hearing Research, 6415
North Central Sight Services, 7706
Northampton County Area: Agency on Aging, 2135
Northeast Pennsylvania Center for Independent Living, 10918
Northumberland County Area: Agency onAging, 2136
Occupation Hearing Services, 6425
Occupational Hearing Service, 6426
Office of Human Services, 2137
Overbrook School for the Blind Library, 11737
Pennsylvania Association of Area Agencies on Aging Directors, 2138
Pennsylvania Association of Non-Profit Homes for the Aging, 2139
Pennsylvania Bar Association: Elder LawSection, 11240

1109

Geographic Index / Rhode Island

Pennsylvania Bureau of Blindness and Visual Services, 7717
Pennsylvania Center for Travel, Tourism & Film, 11985
Pennsylvania Client Assistance Program, 2140
Pennsylvania College of Optometry Eye Institute, 8051
Pennsylvania Department of Aging: LegalServices and Assistance, 11241
Pennsylvania Department of Public Welfare Norristown State Hospital, 11738
Pennsylvania Department of Revenue, 2141
Pennsylvania Department on Aging, 2142
Pennsylvania Developmental Disabilities Council, 2143
Pennsylvania Drug and Alcohol Programs, 7213
Pennsylvania Hearing Aid Alliance, 6429
Pennsylvania Protection & Advocacy for Persons with Disabilities, 2144
Pennsylvania Protection and Advocacy Agency, 11242
Pennsylvania Public School Employees' Retirement System, 2145
Pennsylvania Society for the Advancement of the Deaf and Hearing Impaired, 6430
Pennsylvania Society of Directors of Volunteer Services, 2146
Pennsylvania State University: Artificial Heart Research Project, 6885
Pennsylvania State University: Human Development Collection, 11739
Pennsylvania Workers Compensation Board, 2147
Pension Research Council (PRC), 288
People's Medical Society, 292
Perry County Office for Aging, 2148
Philadelphia 1 Chapter-Self Help for Hard of Hearing People, 6431
Philadelphia Corporation for Aging, 2149
Philadelphia Corporation for Aging Library, 11740
Philadelphia Heart Institute: Geriatrics Practice, 6843
Pike County Area: Agency on Aging, 2150
Pittsburgh Branch of the Pennsylvania Association for the Blind, 7718
Pittsburgh Hearing Speech and Deaf Services, 6432
Pittsburgh Hearing, Speech and Deaf Services, 6433
Pittsburgh Vision Service, 7719
Plum Enterprises, 2151
Plums Award Winning Protects Hip, 3269
Polisher Research Institute Library: Philadelphia Geriatric Center, 11741
Potter County Area: Agency on Aging, 2152
Protecta Capstet, 3271
ProtectaCap+PLUS, ProtectaHip, 3272
Public Interest Law Center of Philadelphia, 11243
Public Interest Law Center: Philadelphia, 11244
RSVP Allegheny County, 2153
RSVP Allegheny County-Pittsburgh, 2154
RSVP Beaver County, 2155
RSVP Bedford-Cambria County, 2156
RSVP Blair County, 2157
RSVP Buck County, 2158
RSVP Capitol Region, 1824, 2159
RSVP Centre County, 2160
RSVP Chester County, 2161
RSVP Clearfield County, 2162
RSVP Crawford County, 2163
RSVP Delaware County, 2164
RSVP Elk-Cameron Counties, 2165
RSVP Greater Erie Community Action, 2166
RSVP Greene County, 389, 1837, 2167, 2167
RSVP Lackawanna County, 2168
RSVP Lebanon-Lancaster Counties, 2169
RSVP Lehigh County, 2170
RSVP Luzerne-Wyoming Counties, 2171
RSVP McKean County, 2172
RSVP Monroe County, 1840, 2173
RSVP Philadelphia East, 2175
RSVP Philadelphia West, 2176
RSVP Schuylkill County, 2177
RSVP Somerset County, 1693, 2178
RSVP Venango County, 2179
RSVP Warren-Forest Counties, 2180
RSVP Westmoreland County, 2181
Railroad Retirement Board: Altoona Pennslvania District Office, 2182
Railroad Retirement Board: Harrisburg Pennsylvania Branch Office, 2183
Railroad Retirement Board: Philadelphia Pennsylvania District Office, 2184
Railroad Retirement Board: Pittsburgh Pennsylvania District Office, 2185
Railroad Retirement Board: Scranton Pennsylvania District Office, 2186
Recorded Periodicals, 7735
Regent, 3432
Residence, 10199
Residence at Glen Riddle, 10200
Schuylkill County Area: Agency on Aging, 2187
Scoota Bug, 3434
Scottdale Community Senior Citizens Club, 2188
Senior Adult Activities Center of Montgomery County, 2189
Senior Centers of Bethlehem, 2190
Senior Citizens Judicare Project, 11245
Sensor Hearing Aids, 6445
Sight-Loss Support Group of Central Pennsylvania, 7743
Social Security for Public Employees, 2191
Southwestern Pennsylvania Area Agency on Aging, 2192
Southwestern Pennsylvania Partnership for Aging, 2193
StairLIFT SC & SL, 3400
Sterling, 3439
Supportive Older Women's Network, 320
Talbot Cancer Research Library, 11742
Temple University: Section of Auditory Research, 6817
Temple University: Speech and Hearing Science Laboratories, 6818
Three Rivers Center for Independent Living, 10758, 10919
Tri-County Partnership for Independent Living, 10920
US Deparment of Veterans Affairs: Philadelphia Medical Center Library, 11743
US Department of Veterans Affairs: Altoona James E Van Zandt Medical Center Library Service, 11744
US Department of Veterans Affairs: Butler Medical Center Library, 11745
US Department of Veterans Affairs: Coatesville Medical Center Library, 11746
US Department of Veterans Affairs: Erie Medical Center Library, 11747
US Department of Veterans Affairs: Lebanon Medical Center Library, 11748
US Department of Veterans Affairs: Pittsburgh Education, Media and Reference Service, 11749
US Department of Veterans Affairs: Wilkes-Barre Medical Center Library, 11750
Union-Snyder Area: Agency on Aging, 2194
University of Pennsylvania: Depression Research Unit, 6106
University of Pennsylvania: Diabetes Research Center, 6290
University of Pittsburgh Medical Center: Clinic Western Psychiatric Institute and Clinic, 6107
University of Pittsburgh: Nutrition and Biochemistry Laboratory, 6291
Visual Impairment and Blindness Services of Northampton County, 7776
Voluntary Action Center of Northeastern Pennsylvania, 2195
Volunteer Center of Centre County, 2196
WFS' New Life Program, 7226
Washington-Greene County Branch of the Pennsylvania Association for Blind, 7783
Wayne County Area: Agency on Aging, 2197
Westmoreland County Area: Agency on Aging, 2198
Wheelchair Parts & Fasteners, 3563
Wilkes Barre Bureau of Disability Determination, 2199
Willow Lake, 10201
Wistar Institute of Anatomy & Biology Library, 11751
Women for Sobriety, 7231
York County Area: Agency on Aging, 2200
York Industries for the Blind: A Division of York County Blind Center, 7788

Rhode Island

American Diabetes Association: Rhode Island/Massachusetts Area Office, 6159
Ashberry Manor, 10202
Bay Spring Village, 10203
Better Days Residential, 10204
Blackstone Valley Assisted Living, 10205
Blenheim Newport Residential Retirement Community, 10206
Brick Manor Residential Care, 10207
Bureau of Naval Personnel: Rhode Island Retired Activities Office, 2201
Center for Alcohol & Addiction Studies, 7453
Cortland Place, 10208
Darlington Assisted Living Centers, 10209
Department of Mental Health, Retardation and Hospitals of Rhode Island, 2202
Drug & Alcohol Treatment Association of Rhode Island: In-Rhodes Resource Center Library, 11752
East Bay Manor, 10210

Edgelea, 10211
Elms Retirement Home, 10212
Emerald Bay Manor, 10213
Ethan Place, 10214
Evergreen Assisted Living Home, 10215
Forest Farm Assisted Living, 10216
Gray Panthers of Rhode Island, 2204
Greenwhich Bay Manor, 10217
IN-SIGHT, 7610
Insight, 7617
Legal Information and Referral Service for the Elderly, 11246
Manchester Manor, 10218
Narragansett Senior Citizens Association, 2205
North Bay Manor, 10219
Ocean State Center for Independent Living, 10921
PARI Independent Living Center, 10922
Pocasset Lodge Assisted Living, 10220
RSVP Blackstone Valley, 2206
RSVP Capital Region, 2207
RSVP Cranston, 2208
RSVP East Bay, 2209
RSVP Northern Rhode Island, 2210
RSVP West Bay, 2211
Rhode Island Client Assistance Program, 2212
Rhode Island Department of Elderly Affairs, 2213, 11247
Rhode Island Department of Human Services, 2215
Rhode Island Department of Human Services for the Blind, 7740
Rhode Island Department of Human Services: Veterans Affairs, 2214
Rhode Island Department of Mental Health, 6054
Rhode Island Department of State Library for the Blind and Physically Handicapped, 11753
Rhode Island Department of Treasury: Retirement Office, 2216
Rhode Island Developmental Disabilities Council, 2217
Rhode Island Division of Substance Abuse, 7217
Rhode Island Division of Taxation, 2218
Rhode Island Governor's Committee on the Disabled, 2219
Rhode Island Legal Service: Elderly Law Unit, 11248
Rhode Island Organizing Project, 2220
Rhode Island Protection & Advocacy for Persons with Disabilities, 2221
Rhode Island Protection and Advocacy Agency: Rhode Island Disability Law Center, 11249
Rhode Island Services for the Blind and Visually Impaired, 7741
Scandinavian Home, 10221
Seniors Helping Others Volunteer Program of Washington County, 2222
State of Rhode Island, 11992
Tockwotten Home, 10222
US Department of Veterans Affairs: Providence Health Sciences Library, 11754
United Methodist Retirement Center, 10223
Victoria Court, 10224
Villa at St Antoine, 10225
Village at Elmhurst, 10226

Village at Hillsgrove, 10227
Warren Manor I, 10228
West Bay Manor, 10229
Whythebrook Terrace, 10230
Willows Assisted Living, 10231
Wyndemere Woods, 10232

South Carolina

Aiken Area Council on Aging, 2223
Association for the Blind of South Carolina, 7528
Captioned Media Program, 6327
Captioned Media Program: National Association of the Deaf, 11755
Catawba Area: Agency on Aging, 2224
Disability Determination Division, 720, 2006, 2225, 2225
Geo-Matt for High Risk Patients, 3206
Good Faith, 2226
Help for Incontinent People: National Association for Continence, 6945
Interdisciplinary Program in Cell and Molecular Pharmacology, 7461
International Deaf/Tek, Inc., 3261
International Kaf/Tek, 6381
Lancaster County Council on Aging, 2227
Low Country Area: Agency on Aging, 2228
Lower Savannah Area: Agency on Aging, 2229
National Association for Continence, 6948
National Car Rental System, 11936
Protection & Advocacy for People with Disabilities, 2230
RSVP Aiken County, 2231
RSVP Carolina Low Country, 2232
RSVP Florence County, 2233
RSVP Greenville, 2234
RSVP McCormick, 2235
RSVP Newberry County, 2236
RSVP Richland, 2237
RSVP Spartanburg, 2238
RSVP Sumter County, 2239
RSVP York County, 2240
Santee-Lynches Council of Governments Area Agency on Aging, 2241
Senior Advocacy Program, 11250
Social Security: West Columbia Disability Determination, 2242
South Carolina Assistive TechnologyProjects, 2243
South Carolina Association Area: Agencies on Aging, 2244
South Carolina Association of Nonprofit Homes for the Aging, 2245
South Carolina Association of the Deaf, 6447
South Carolina Bar Association: Elder Law Committee, 11251
South Carolina Budget and Control Board: Retirement System Division, 2246
South Carolina Centers for Equal Justice (SCCEJ), 11252
South Carolina Client Assistance Program Office of the Governor of South Carolina, 2247
South Carolina Commission for the Blind, 6055
South Carolina Commission on Aging, 2248
South Carolina Department of Aging, 2249

South Carolina Department of Alcohol & Other Drug Abuse Services, 7219
South Carolina Department of Mental Health, 6056
South Carolina Department of Parks, Transportation & Tourism, 11986
South Carolina Department of Veterans Affairs, 2250
South Carolina Developmental Disability Council, 2251
South Carolina Lieutenant Governor's Office on Aging, 11253
South Carolina Services Information System, 2252
South Carolina State Library, 11756
South Carolina Workers Compensation Commission, 2253
Trident Area Agency on Aging, 2254
US Department of Veterans Affairs: Columbia William Jennings Bryan-Dorn Veterans Hospital Library, 11757
Upper Savannah Council of Government Area: Agency on Aging, 2255
Vantage Point: Division of Caresouth Carolina, 2256

South Dakota

Adaptivation, 3066
American Diabetes Association: Sioux Fallls District Office, 6161
American Medical Industries, 3247
Angela Hall Assisted Living Center, 10233
Avera Bormann Manor, 10234
Avera Brady Assisted Living, 10235
Avera Mother Joseph Manor Retirement Community, 10236
Avera Prince of Peace Retirement Community, 10237
Avera St Benedict Assisted Living, 10238
B and C Resthome, 10239
Belle Fourche Health Care Center, 10240
Bennett County Healthcare Center, 10241
Bethel Suites, 10242
Bethesda Towne Square, 10243
Bowdle Hospital Assisted Living Center, 10244
Carousel Living Center, 10245
Castle View Assisted Living, 10246
Cedar View Assisted Living, 10247
Colton Assisted Living Center, 10248
Communication Service for the Deaf, 6336
Cottages at Fairmont Grand, 10249
Courtyard Villa Assisted Living Center, 10250
Dakota Sun Assisted Living, 10251
Dell Rapids Sportsmen's Club, 12013
Deuel County Good Samaritan Center Assisted Living Center, 10252
Division of Developmental Disabilities, 2257
Edgewood Vista of Sioux Falls, 10253
Estelline Nursing and Care Center, 10254
Eureka Community Health Services: Assisted Living Center, 10255
Evergreen Assisted Living, 10256
Evergreen Assisted Living Center, 10257
Fairmont Grand Manor, 10258
Fay Wookey Memorial Assisted Living Center, 10259
Foothills Assisted Living, 10260
Fox Run Residences, 10261

1111

Geographic Index / Tennessee

Glacial Lakes Retired & Senior Volunteer Program, 2258
Golden Prairie Manor, 10262
Golden Ridge Retirement Community, 10263
Good Samaritan Center, 10264
Greater Fall River Health Care Services, 10265
Greenlead Assisted Living-Flandreau, 10266
Greenleaf Assisted Living, 10267
Greenleaf Assisted Living Center, 10268
Greenleaf Assisted Living-Sisseton, 10269
Helping Hand Assisted Living, 10270
Heritage Senior Living, 10271
Herreid Good Samaritan Center, 10272
Hiawatha Heights Assisted Living Facility, 10273
Hilda's Heritage Home, 10274
Holy Infant Hospital Assisted Living Center, 10275
Homestead Assisted Living, 10276
Howard Good Samaritan Center Assisted Living Center, 10277
Inn on Westport, 10278
K-NOPF Assisted Living Center-Matthew Building, 10279
K-NOPF Assisted Living-John Building, 10280
K-NOPF Assisted Living-Luke Building, 10281
K-NOPF Assisted Living-Mark Building, 10282
Kelly's Retirement Home I, 10283
Kelly's Retirement Home II, 10284
Kirkwood Manor, 10285
Lakeside Assisted Living Residence, 10286
Leisure Living, 10287
Marion Assisted Living Center, 10288
Marshall County Healthcare Center, 10289
Morningside Manor Assisted Living, 10290
Morningside Manor Assisted Living II, 10291
Morningstar Assisted Living, 10292
Orchard Hills, 10293
Park Place Assisted Living, 10294
Parkview Apartments Assisted Living, 10295
Pine Haven Heritage Home, 10296
Pine Lane West Assisted Living Center, 10297
Platte Assisted Living, 10298
Prairie Crossings, 10299
Prairie Crossings-Brookings, 10300
Prairie Crossings-Huron, 10301
Prairie Crossings-Mitchell, 10302
Prairie Crossings-Sioux Falls, 10303
Prairie Crossings-Watertown, 10304
Prairie Good Samaritan Center Assisted Living, 10305
Prairie Homes Assisted Living, 10306
Prairie Sunset Village, 10307
Prairie View Assisted Living Center, 10308
Primrose Assisted Living, 10309
Primrose Place, 10310
RSVP East Central South Dakota, 2260
RSVP Northern Black Hills, 2261
RSVP Rapdi City Area, 2262
RSVP Siouxland, 2263
Riverview Health Services, 10311
Riverview Retirement Home, 10312
Roetell Senior Housing, 10313
Rosholt Care Center Assisted Living Center, 10314
Salem Mennonite Home, 10315
Sandstone Manor, 10316
Scotland Good Samaritan Center Assisted Living Center, 10317
Shelby Good Samaritan Center Assisted Living, 10318
Silver Threads Residence, 10319
Silverleaf, 10320
South Dakota Association of Homes for the Aging, 2264
South Dakota Association of the Blind, 7745
South Dakota Client Assistance Program, 2265
South Dakota Department of Aging, 2266
South Dakota Department of Mental Health, 6057
South Dakota Department of Military and Veterans Services, 2267
South Dakota Department of Revenue, 2268
South Dakota Department of Social Services: Adult Services and Aging, 2269
South Dakota Department of Social Services: Legal Services for the Elderly, 11254
South Dakota Department of Tourism, 11987
South Dakota Disability Determination Sevices, 2270
South Dakota Division of Rehabilitation, 2271
South Dakota Human Services Center Medical Library, 11758
South Dakota Office of Adult Services, 2272
South Dakota Protection Advocacy Services, 2273
South Dakota Protection and Advocacy Services, 11255
South Dakota State Library: Braille andTalking Book Program, 11759
South Dakota Workers Compensation Board, 2274
South Park Assisted Living, 10321
Springfield Assisted Living Center, 10322
St Mary's Healthcare Center, 10323
Stickney Manor, 10324
Stoneybrook Suites of Watertown, 10325
Sun Dial Manor, 10326
Sunpointe Senior Estates, 10327
Sunset Court Assisted Living Center, 10328
There's A Hart, 10329
Trail Ridge Retirement Community Assisted Living Center, 10330
Trent Assisted Living Center, 10331
US Department of Veterans Affairs: For Meade VA Black Hills Health Care System Medical Library, 11760
USA Deaf Sports Federation, 6458
Victorian, 10332
Walker's Assisted Living, 10333
Waterford at All Saints, 10334
Wedgewood Assisted Living Facility, 10335
Westhills South Assisted Living Facility, 10336
Westwood Assisted Living, 10337
White Pines Assisted Living Center, 10338

Tennessee

Adamsplace Assisted Living, 10339
Aging Services for the Upper Cumberlands, 11256
Allen Morgan Health Center at Trezevant Manor, 10340
American Diabetes Association: Memphis District Office, 6141
American Diabetes Association: Tennessee Area Office, 6166
Arbor Terrace, 10341
Arnold Home, 9040
Asbury Acres, 10342
Atria Assisted Living Riverdale, 10343
Atria Assisted Living-Cordova, 10344
Atria Weston Place, 10345
Baptist Assisted Living Center, 10346
Belmont Village of Green Hills, 10347
Belmont Village of Memphis, 10348
Bill Wilkerson Center, 6796
Bureau of Naval Personnel, 92
Center for Independent Living of MiddleTennessee, 10923
Clarity, 3098
Disability Determinations, 1570, 2275
Disability Law & Advocacy Center of Tennessee (DLAC), 11257
EAR Foundation, 6352
East Tennessee Area Agencies on Aging, 2276
Ed Lindsey Industries of the Blind, 7581
Elder Day Eldereed Haus, 10349
Fighting Back, 7158
Franklin Park, 10350
Friends of Tennessee School of the Blind, 7592
H2U: Health, Happiness, You, 145
Hearthside at Castle Heights, 10351
Heritage Place, 9498, 10352
Homewood Residence at Brookmont TerraceAssisted Living and Alzheimer's Care Residence, 10354
Homewood Residence at Deane Hill, 10355
Jackson Center for Independent Living, 10924
Jackson Park Christian Home, 10356
Kennington Pointe, 10357
Knollwood Manor, 10358
LRC for Students with Disabilities: MSU Library Reference Department, 11761
Lakeshore Wedgewood, 10359
Legal Aid of East Tennessee (LAET), 11258
Life Care Center of Sparta, 10360
Lodge at Wood Village, 10361
Manorhouse Assisted Living, 9517, 10362
Martin Boyd Christian Home, 10363
McMinn County Senior Citizens, 2277
McMinnville Residential Care Center, 10364
Memphis Area Legal Services: Pro Bono Panel for Senior Citizens, 11259
Memphis Center for Independent Living, 10925
Memphis State University: Center for the Communicatively Impaired, 6805
Midsouth Area: Agency on Aging, 2278
Morningside of Gallatin, 10365
Motorized Stander, 3424
NHC Place Farragut, 10366
Nashville Bar Association (NBA): Young Lawyers Division (YLD), 11260
Nashville Chapter Black Deaf Advocates, 6399

1112

Geographic Index / Texas

National Association of Activity Professionals, 187
Navy Retired Activities Branch, 269
Northwest Assistance for the Elderly Project, 11261
Northwest Tennessee Area Agency on Aging and Disability, 2279
Oak Ridge Retirement Community, 10367
Oaks of Kingsport, 10368
Outlook Pointe at Knoxville, 10369
Outlook Pointe at Morristown, 10370
Outlook Pointe at Oak Ridge, 10371
Park Place Retirement Community, 10372
Permobil Max 90, 3525
Permobil Super 90, 3526
Place at Gallitan, 10373
Place at Kingsport, 10374
Pointe at Kirby Gate, 10375
Prevent Blindness Tennessee, 7729
RSVP Clarksville County, 2280
RSVP Dyer County, 2281
RSVP East Central Tennessee, 2282
RSVP Fayettevill Area, 2283
RSVP Knoxville-Knox County, 2284
RSVP Lexington-Henderson Counties, 2285
RSVP McMinnville, 2286
RSVP Rutherford, 2287
RSVP Shelby County, 2288
Railroad Retirement Board: Tennessee District Office, 2289
Regency House Assisted Living, 10376
Remington House Assisted Living, 10377
Remote Control Speakerphone, 3158
Respiratory Nursing Society, 301
Senior Citizens, 2290
Shelbyville Residential Care, 10378
Southern Living Center of Lebanon, 10379
Southwest Tennessee Area: Agency on Aging, 2291
Tennessee Association of Homes and Services for the Aging, 2292
Tennessee Bureau of Alcohol & Drug Abuse, 7221
Tennessee Client Assistance Program, 2293
Tennessee Commission on Aging, 2294
Tennessee Commission on Aging and Disability, 11262
Tennessee Council of the Blind, 7757
Tennessee Council on Developmental Disabilities, 2295
Tennessee Department of Aging, 2296
Tennessee Department of Mental Health & Developmental Disabilities, 6058
Tennessee Department of Revenue, 2297
Tennessee Department of Tourist Development, 11997
Tennessee Department of Veterans Affairs, 2298
Tennessee Division of Rehabilitation Services, 2299
Tennessee Justice Center, 11263
Tennessee Library for the Blind and Physically Handicapped, 11762
Tennessee Technology Access Project, 2300
Terrace at Bluegrass, 10380
Travelin' Talk Newsletter, 12054
US Department of Veterans Affairs: Johnson City Medical Center Library, 11763
US Department of Veterans Affairs: Memphis Medical Center Library, 11764
US Department of Veterans Affairs: Murfreesboro Medical Center Library Service, 11765
US Department of Veterans Affairs: Nashville Medical Center Library Service, 11766
University of Memphis Libraries: Audiology, Speech Language, Pathology Branch, 11767
University of Tennessee Drug Information Center, 7484
University of Tennessee: Division of Cardiovascular Diseases, 6847
Uplands Retirement Village, 10381
Upper Cumberland Area: Agency on Aging, 2301
Vanderbilt University: Diabetes Research and Training Center, 6294
Vanderbilt University: Specialized Center of Research in Hypertension, 6929
Waverly Gardens, 10382
West Tennessee Legal Services (WTLS), 11264
West Tennessee Lions Blind Industries, 7784
Wlllington Place of Colonial Heights, 10383
Workers Compensation Division, 2302

Texas

AARP Southwest Regional Office, 2303
ABLE, 10926
Abundant Care, 10384
Advent Residential Care, 10385
Affectionate Care, 10386
Alamo Area: Agency on Aging, 2304
Alterra Clare Bridge Cottage of Richland, 10387
Alterra Clare Bridge of Richardson, 10388
Alterra Sterling House of Cedar Hill, 10389
Alterra Sterling House of Desoto, 10390
Alterra Sterling House of Georgetown, 10391
Alterra Sterling House of Lancaster, 10392
Alterra Sterling House of Maltsberger, 10393
Alterra Sterling House of Nacogdoches, 10394
Alterra Sterling House of Waxahachie, 10395
Amber Oaks, 10396
American Academy of Nurse Practitioners, 9
American Airlines, 11913
American Association for Respiratory Care, 16
American Diabetes Association: Northeast Texas/North Louisiana Area Office, 6155
American Diabetes Association: South Central Regional Office, 6162
American Foundation for the Blind Southwest, 7507
American Heart Association, 6838
American Heart Association National Center Library, 11768
Ameripark at Austin, 10397
Ameripark at Kerrville, 10398
Arden Courts Alzheimer's Assisted Living, 8254, 10399
Area Agency on Aging of Southeast Texas, 2305
Area Agency on Aging of the Capital Area, 2306
Area Agency on Aging of the Concho Valley, 2307
Ark-Tex Council of Governments Area Agency on Aging, 2308
Arkansas House, 10400
Ashley Court at Turtle Creek, 10401
Ashwood Retirement & Assisted Living, 10402
Atria in Kingwood, 10403
Atria in West Chase, 10404
Austin Disability Determination Services, 2309
Austin Elder Care Home, 10405
Austin State School Volunteer Council, 2310
Autumn Bridge at Amber Oaks, 10406
Barbee House, 10407
Barton Hills Assisted Living, 10408
Barton Hills Guest House, 10409
Barton House, 10410
Barton House II, 10411
Barton House at First Colony, 10412
Baylor College of Medicine: Cullen Eye Institute, 8036
Baylor College of Medicine: DeBakey Heart Center, 6861
Beacon House, 10413
Bellaire Lodge, 10414
Belmont Village at West University, 10415
Bentley Manor, 10416
Bethesda Gardens of Fort Worth, 10417
Bexar County Area: Agency on Aging, 2311
Braeswood Personal Care Homes, 10418
Brighton Gardens Marriot-San Antonio, 10419
Broadway Plaza at Pecan Park, 10420
Broadway Plaza at Westover Hills, 10421
Brookwood Community, 10422
Brown-Karhan Health Care, 10423
Buckner Retirement Services, 10424
Buckner Villas, 10425
Bureau of Naval Personnel: Houston Retired Activities Office, 2312
Bureau of Naval Personnel: Kingsville Retired Activities Office, 2313
Bureau of Naval Personnel: San Antonio Retired Activities Center, 2314
Bureau of Naval Personnel: Texas Retired Activities Office, 2315
Calimay Assisted Living Home, 10426
Cambridge Square Retirement Center, 10427
Carestone at Austin, 10428
Caruth Haven Court, 10429
Castle Rock Assisted Living, 10430
Center for Lifelong Learning, 2316
Center for Professional Development, 2317
Center for the Rights of the Terminally Ill, 101
Center for the Rights of the Terminally Ill Resource Library, 11769
Center on Independent Living, 10927
Cerebral Blood Flow Laboratories, 7113
Champion Oaks by Marriot, 10431
Chandler Assisted Living, 10432
Christian Education for the Blind, 11770
Coalition for Barrier Free Living: Houston Center for Independent Living, 10928
Coastal Bend Area: Agency on Aging, 2318
Collin Oaks Guest Home, 10433

1113

Geographic Index / Texas

Colonial Oaks at First Colony, 10434
Continental Airlines, 11918
Convention of American Instructors of the Deaf, 6340
Courtyards at River Park, 10435
Covenant Place of Waxahachie, 10436
DARE, 10929
Dallas Association of Directors of Volunteers, 2319
Dallas Lighthouse for the Blind, 7573
Dallas Young Lawyers Association: Committee on Legal Aid to the Elderly, 11265
Debbie's Sunshine Home, 10437
Derek Home, 10438
Duval Oaks, 10439
East Texas Area: Agency on Aging, 2320
Eastman Estates, 10440
Eden Gardens, 10441
Eden Home, 10442
Eden Terrace of Arlington, 10443
Edenbrook of Champions, 10444
Edenbrook of the Woodlands, 10445
Edenterrace of Kingwood, 10446
El Paso Lighthouse for the Blind, 7582
Five Star Personal Care Homes, 10447
Freedom Wheelchair Lifts, 3377
Gardens of Richardson, 10448
Golden Crescent Area: Agency on Aging, 2321
Golden Manor, 9165, 10449
Good Place Assisted Living, 10450
Grace House of Lake Travis, 10451
Grand Court Greatwood, 10452
Grand Court Round Rock, 10453
Gray Panthers of Austin, 2322
Greater Lakewood Shepherd's Center, 2323
Greyhound Buslines, 11926
Hampton Assisted Living Residence at Pinegate, 10454
Hampton at Post Oaks, 10455
Hampton at Spring Shadows, 10456
Harbourview Assisted Living of League City, 10457
Harmony Elder Care, 10458
Harvest Home Personal Care Facility, 10459
Heart of Texas Council of Governments Area: Agency on Aging, 2324
Hearthstone at Arlington, 10460
Hearthstone at Vista, 10461
Hearthstone at Windcrest, 10462
Heartland of Willowbrook, 10463
Heights Assisted Living, 10098, 10464
Heritage at Gaines Ranch, 10465
Heritage at Tomball, 10466
Hill Country Care Home, 10467
Hill Country Community Action Association, 2325
Hispanic Deaf Teacher Training Program, 6373
Homewood Residence at Air Force Village, 10468
Homewood Residence at Shavano Park, 10469
Houston Bar Association: Judicare Program for the Elderly, 11266
Houston Ear Research Foundation, 6802
Houston Harris County Area: Agency on Aging, 2326
Houston Public Library: Access Center, 11771
Houston Public Library: Acres Homes Branch, 11772
Houston Public Library: Bracewell Branch, 11773
Houston Public Library: Carnegie Branch, 11774
Houston Public Library: Collier Regional Branch, 11775
Houston Public Library: Dixon Branch, 11776
Houston Public Library: Flores Branch, 11777
Houston Public Library: Hillendahl Branch, 11778
Houston Public Library: Moody Branch, 11779
Houston Public Library: Park Place Regional Branch, 11780
Houston Public Library: Pleasantville Branch, 11781
Houston Public Library: Robinson-Westchase Branch, 11782
Houston Public Library: Scenic Woods Regional Branch, 11783
Houston Public Library: Smith Branch, 11784
Houston Public Library: Tuttle Branch, 11785
Houston Public Library: Young Branch, 11786
Houston-Galveston Area: Agency on Aging, 2327
IHS at Swan Manor, 10470
Ideal Personal Care Assisted Living, 10471
Incarnate Word Personal Care Facility, 10472
Independence Hill Assisted Living, 10473
Individual Care of Texas, 10474
Inn at Los Patios, 10475
Inn at Orchard Park, 10476
International Rehabilitation Medicine Association, 158
Jefferson Place Assisted Living, 10477
Kensington Cottages at Quail Creek, 10478
Kensington Cottages by Centex, 10479
Kerrville State Hospital Professional Library, 11787
Kilroy House, 10480
Kings Manor Methodist Retirement System, 2328
Kings Manor Personal Care Home, 10481
Kingsley Place at Oakwell, 10482
Kingsley Place at Stonebridge Ranch, 10483
Lakeridge Place, 10484
Lakewood 24 Hour Personal Care, 10485
Lakewood Village: Cummings Assisted Living Apartments, 10486
Lexington Place, 10487
Lighthouse for the Blind of Houston, 7634
Lodge at Leon Springs, 10488
Lower Rio Grande Valley Area: Agency onAging, 2329
Magnolia Place, 9355, 10489
Marbridge Ranch, 10490
Meadow View Family Service, 10491
Memorial Oaks by Marriott, 10492
Merrill Gardens at Denton, an AssistedLiving Community, 10493
Merrill Gardens at North Richland Hills, 10494
Merrill Gardens at Round, 10495
Merrill Gardens at San Antonio, 10496
Merrill Gardens at San Marcos, 10497
Middle Rio Grande Area: Agency on Aging, 2330
Mind Science Foundation Library, 11788
Morningside Manor, 10498
National Academy for Teaching and Learning About Aging, 181
National Association of Counselors, 189
National Federation of the Blind of Texas: Austin Chapter, 7677
National Organization for the Advancement of the Deaf, 6416
New Life Outreach Boarding Home, 10499
Nissi Care Homes, 10500
North Central Texas Area: Agency on Aging, 2331
Northwest Oaks, 10501
Oak Park Retirement Center, 10502
Oak Shadows Allendale, 10503
Oak Wood Acres, 10504
Oak Wood Place, 10505
Oaktree Assisted Living, 10506
Pafford Place, 10507
Panhandle Area: Agency on Aging, 2332
Park Place Retirement, 10508
Park Place Retirement Residence of Friendswood, 10509
Park Place Retirement Residence of Stafford, 10510
Park at Beckett Meadows, 10511
Parkwood Place, 10512
Performance Gel Cushions, 3220
Permian Basin Area: Agency on Aging, 2333
Pine Tree Cottage, 10513
Pointe at Cedar Park, 10514
Presbyterian Hospital of Dallas, 7042
Prevent Blindness Texas, 7730
Prevent Blindness Texas Central Regional, 6434
Quality Personal Care Home, 10515
Quality of Living Residential Home, 10516
RDL Supply, 3392
REACH of Dallas Resource Center onIndependent Living, 10930
REACH/Resource Center on Independent Living, 11789
RSVP Bexar County, 2334
RSVP Big Country, 2335
RSVP Big Spring, 2336
RSVP Brazos Valley, 2337
RSVP Chisholm Trail County, 2338
RSVP Concho Valley, 2339
RSVP Concho Valley Texas, 2340
RSVP Corpus Christi, 2341
RSVP Dallas, 2342
RSVP Deep East Texas, 2343
RSVP El Paso City, 2344
RSVP Galveston County, 2345
RSVP Golden Triangle, 2346
RSVP Heart of Texas, 2347
RSVP Hockley County, 2348
RSVP Houston County, 2349
RSVP Laredo, 2350
RSVP Lubbock, 2351
RSVP Metro Tarrant, 2352
RSVP Metro Tarrant County, 2353
RSVP Midland, 2354
RSVP North Texas, 2355
RSVP Outer Houston, 2356
RSVP Red River Valley, 1426, 2357
RSVP Rio Grande Valley, 2358

Geographic Index / Utah

RSVP Runningwater Draw, 2359
RSVP Swisher County, 2360
RSVP Texas Panhandle, 2361
RSVP Texoma, 2362
RSVP Travis County, 2363
Railroad Retirement Board: Fort Worth, Texas District Office, 2364
Railroad Retirement Board: Houston, Texas District Office, 2365
Reach Resource Center on Independent Living, 10931
Reach of Denton Resource Center on Independent Living, 10932
Regal Estates Senior Living, 10517
Regency of El Paso, 10518
Regent at Hamilton House Assisted Living, 10519
Regent at Parmer Woods Assisted Living, 10520
Region 6: Administration on Aging (AoA), 2366
Remington Park, 10521
Retirement Inn by Encore Senior Living, 10522
Rio Grande Area: Agency on Aging, 2367
Round Rock Volunteer Center, 2368
Royal Estates of El Paso, 10523
Royal Estates of San Angelo, 10524
SAILS, 10933
Sabine House, 10525
Saddleridge Lodge, 10526
Senior Citizens of Earth: Springlake Area, 2369
Serenity Gardens Personal Care, 10527
Shallowater Senior Citizens, 2370
Signature Pointe on the Lake, 10528
Silicone Padding, 3223
Silverado Senior Living-Cypresswood, 10529
Silverado Senior Living-Sugarland, 10530
Smooth Mover, 3398
South Plains Association of GovernmentsArea: Agency on Aging, 2371
South Texas Area: Agency on Aging, 2372
South Texas Lighthouse for the Blind, 7746
Southern Knights Assisted Living Center, 10531
Spenco Medical Group, 3226
St Joesph Haven, 10532
State Bar of Texas: Texas Young Lawyers Association, 11267
State of Texas Office of the GovernorEconomic Development and Tourism, 11993
Sugar Land Oaks Guest Home, 10533
Summer Ridge Assisted Living & Retirement Community, 10534
Summit at Lakeway, 10535
Summit at Northwest Hills, 10536
Taping for the Blind, 7754
Tarrant County Association for the Blind, 7755
Texaco Retirees Club of Houston, 2373
Texas Association of 504 Coordinators and Hearing Officers, 6451
Texas Association of Area Agencies on Aging, 2374
Texas Association of Directors of Volunteer Services, 2375
Texas Association of Homes and Services for the Aging, 2376

Texas Association of Retinitis Pigmentosa, 7758
Texas Commission for the Blind, 7759
Texas Commission for the Deaf, 6452
Texas Commission on Alcohol and Drug Abuse, 7222
Texas Comptroller of Public Accountants, 2377
Texas Department of Aging and Disability Services (DAD), 2378, 11268
Texas Department of Health Library, 11790
Texas Department of Mental Health & Mental Retardation, 6059
Texas Department on Aging, 2379
Texas Developmental Disability Council, 2380
Texas Employees' Retirement System, 2381
Texas Geriatrics Society, 2382
Texas Governor's Committee for People With Disabilities, 2383
Texas Heart Institute, 6846
Texas Legal Services Center: Legal Hotline for Older Texans, 11269
Texas Planning Council for Developmental Disabilities, 2384
Texas Protection & Advocacy Services for Disabled Perosns, 2385
Texas Protection and Advocacy AgencyNorth Texas Regional Office: Dallas, 11270
Texas Society to Prevent Blindness, 7760
Texas State Library, 11791
Texas State Library Talking Book Program, 11792
Texas State Technical College: Waco Library, 11793
Texas Tech University: Speech-Language-Hearing Clinic, 6819
Texas Tech University: Tarbox Parkinson's Disease Institute, 7046
Texas Veterans Commission, 2386
Texas Workers Compensation Commission, 2387
Texoma Area: Agency on Aging, 2388
The Chandler Senior Center, 2389
Touch of Home, 10537
Travis Association for the Blind, 7762
Travis County Services for the Deaf, 6453
Travis County Services for the Deaf and Hard of Hearing, 6454
Trinity Towers, 10538
Twelve Oaks Irving Assisted Living Center, 10539
US Department of Veterans Affairs Medical Center Library Service, 11334, 11445, 11554, 11554, 11794
US Department of Veterans Affairs: Amarillo Hospital Library, 11796
US Department of Veterans Affairs: Big Spring Hospital Library, 11797
US Department of Veterans Affairs: Bonham North Texas Health Care System, 11798
US Department of Veterans Affairs: Dallas Library Service, 11799
US Department of Veterans Affairs: Houston Medical Center Library, 11800
US Department of Veterans Affairs: Kerrville South Texas Veterans Health Care System, 11801
US Department of Veterans Affairs: Waco Medical Center Library, 11802

US Department of Veterans Affairs:Temple Medical Center Medical Library, 11795
University of North Texas: Health Science Center at Fort Worth, 8058
University of Texas HSC at San Antonio, 7048
University of Texas Health Science Center at Houston: Speech & Hearing, 6830
University of Texas at Austin: Drug Synamics Institute, 7485
University of Texas at Dallas: Callier Center for Communication Disorders, 6831
University of Texas: General Clinical Research Center, 6292
University of Texas: Health Science Center Neurophysiology Research Center, 7486
University of Texas: Southwestern Medical Center at Dallas, 6902
Valley Ranch Retirement Center, 10540
Village Oaks at Hollywood Park, 10541
Vista Oaks of Lakeway, 10542
Waterford Assisted Living, 10543
Waterford at Plano, 10544
Weelington at Arapaho, 10545
Wesley Village, 10546
West Central Texas Council of Governments-Area Agency on Aging, 2390
West Texas Lighthouse for the Blind, 7785
Westchase Gables, 10547
Whitley Place, 10548
Wildflower House, 10549
Windsor Court Assisted Living, 10550
Wright-Way, 2999

Utah

American Athletic Association for the Deaf, 6312
American Auditory Society, 6313
American Diabetes Association: Utah Area Office, 6168
Bear River Area: Agency on Aging, 2391
Cache County Retired And SeniorVolunteer Program (RSVP), 2392
Darci Too, 3104
Disability Determinations Services, 2393
Five County Area: Agency on Aging, 2394
Five County Retired Senior Volunteer Program, 2395
Friends for Sight, 7591
National Association of Senior Companion Project Directors, 200
OPTIONS for Independence-Northern UtahCenter For Independent Living, 10934
RSVP Carbon County, 2396
RSVP Davis County, 2397
RSVP Emery, 2398
RSVP Grand County, 2399
RSVP Mountainland, 2400
RSVP Salt Lake County, 2401
RSVP Six County, 2402
Railroad Retirement Board, 2403
Salt Lake County Aging Services, 2404
San Juan Area: Agency on Aging, 2405
Six County Area: Agency on Aging, 2406
Southeastern Utah Area: Agency on Aging, 2407
State of Utah, 11994

1115

Geographic Index / Vermont

Tooele County Division of Aging and Adult Services, 2408
Tri-County Independent Living Center, 10899, 10935
US Department of Veterans Affairs: Salt Lake City Hospital Medical Library, 11803
Uintah Basin Area: Agency on Aging, 2409
Uintah County Area Agency on Aging, 2410
University of Utah: Artificial Heart Research Laboratory, 6903
University of Utah: Cardiovascular Genetic Research Clinic, 6904
University of Utah: Center for Human Toxicology, 7487
Utah Assistive Technology Projects, 2411
Utah Chapter: Alexander Graham Bell Association for the Deaf, 6836
Utah Client Assistance Program, 2412
Utah Department of Aging, 2413
Utah Department of Health Division of Community Health Services, 2414
Utah Department of Human Services for People with Disabilities, 2415
Utah Department of Human Services: Aging, 2416
Utah Department of Human ServicesDivision of Aging and Adult Services, 11271
Utah Department of Mental Health, 6060
Utah Division of Services for the Disabled, 2417
Utah Division of Substance Abuse, 7223
Utah Governor's Council for People with Disabilities, 2418
Utah Independent Living Center, 10936
Utah Industries for the Blind, 7766
Utah Office of Social Services: Department of Human Services, 2419
Utah Protection & Advocacy Services for Perosns with Disabilities, 2420
Utah Protection and Advocacy Agency: Disability Law Center, 11272
Utah Retirement Board, 2421
Utah State Association of Area Agencies on Aging, 2422
Utah State Bar: Senior Legal Clinic Program Salt Lake County, 11273
Utah State Bar: Young Lawyers Section, 11274
Utah State Library: Blind and DisabledServices, 11804
Utah State Tax Commission, 2423
Utah Statewide Independent Living Council, 10937
Utah Travel Council, 11998
Utah Workers Compensation Board, 2424
Veterans Affairs Medical Center: Research Service, 6295
Weber-Morgan Area: Agency on Aging, 2425

Vermont

Austine School: Library Media Center, 11805
Brattleboro Retreat: Asa Keyes Medical Library, 11806
Central Vermont Council on Aging (CVCOA), 2426
Champlain Valley Area: Agency on Aging, 2427
EcoTraction Surface, 3372
Funeral Consumers Alliance, 11275
Northeastern Vermont Area: Agency on Aging, 2429
RSVP Addison County, 2430
RSVP Bennington County, 2431
RSVP Central Vermont, 2432
RSVP Chittenden County, 2433
RSVP Windham County, 2434
Senior Citizens Law Project of Vermont Legal Aid, 11276
Southwestern Vermont Council on Aging, 2435
State of Vermont, 11995
US Department of Veterans Affairs: White River Junction Medical & Regional Office CenterLibrary Service, 11807
Vermont Agency of Human Services Commission for the Deaf and Hearing Impaired, 6459
Vermont Assistive Technology Projects, 2436
Vermont Association for the Blind and Visually Impaired, 7767
Vermont Center for Independent Living, 10946
Vermont Client Assistance Program, 2437
Vermont Council on Aging, 2438
Vermont Department of Developmental and Mental Health Services, 6061
Vermont Department of Disabilities, Aging and Independent Living, 2439
Vermont Department of Libraries, 11808
Vermont Department of Taxes, 2440
Vermont Developmental Disabilities Council, 2441
Vermont Division for the Blind and Visually Impaired, 7768
Vermont Office of Alcohol & Drug Abuse Programs: Agency of Human Services, 7224
Vermont Protection & Advocacy for Persons with Disabilities, 2442
Vermont Protection and Advocacy Agency, 2443, 11278
Vermont State Retirement Board, 2444
Vermont Veterans Affairs, 2445
Workers Compensation Board Vermont, 2446

Virginia

AACD Legal Series, 11279
Abingdon Manor for Adults, 10551
Adaptive Design Shop, 3000
Air Force Aid Society, 6
Al-Anon Family Group Headquarters, 7126
Alexandria Library Talking Book Service, 11809
Alexandria Library: Special Collections, 11810
Alexandria Office of Aging and Adult Services, 2447
Alexandria Volunteer Bureau, 2448
Amelia Historical Society: Amelia Historical Library, 11811
American Academy of Audiology, 6308
American Academy of Otolaryngology-Head and Neck Surgery, 6309
American Academy of Otolaryngology: Head and Neck Surgery, 12
American Academy of Otolaryngology:Head and Neck Surgery, 6310
American Alliance for Health: Physical Education, Recreation and Dance, 13
American Association for Active Lifestyle & Fitness, 2449
American Association of Managed Care Nurses, 20
American College of Health Care Administrators: Information Center, 11812
American Counseling Association, 38
American Diabetes Association: Greater Hampton Roads Area Office, 6133
American Diabetes Association: Virginia Area Office, 6169
American Life League Library, 11813
American Mental Health Counselors Association, 49
American Psychiatric Nurses Association, 54
Appalachian Independence Center, 10938
Area Access, 3360
Arlington Area Agency on Aging, 2450
Arlington County Bar Association: Legal Services of Northern Virginia, 11280
Arlington County Department of Libraries, 11814
Armed Forces Benefit Association, 74
Army Emergency Relief, 76
Asbury Center at Birdmont, 10552
Assisted Living Federation of America, 78
Association for Assessment in Counseling, 79
Association for Spiritual, Ethical and Religious Values in Counseling, 82
Association of Former Intelligence Officers, 85
Association of the United States Army, 88
Auditory-Verbal International, 6319
Barrier Free Lifts, 3361
Bedford Research Consultants, 11815
Blue Ridge Independent Living Center, 10939
Bureau of Naval Personnel: Virginia Retired Activities Center, 2451
CLC Tappahannock, 10553
Caring Connections, 95
Catholic Charities USA (CCUSA), 96
Central Rappahannock Regional Library, 11816
Committee for Purchase from People who are Blind or Severely Disabled, 6335
Council of Better Business Bureau, 116
Crater District: Area Agency on Aging, 2452
Diabetes Research Center, 6269
Disability Determination Services: Roanoke, 2454
District Three Governmental Cooperative, 2455
Division for the Visually Handicapped, 11817
Eastern Shore Area: Agency on Aging, Community Action Agency, 2456
Endependence Center, 10940

Geographic Index / Washington

Independence Center of Northern Virginia, 10941
Essex House, 10554
Experience Works, 132
Eyegaze Computer System, 3116
Fairfax Area: Agency on Aging, 2457
Fairfax County Public Library, 11818
Fairview Home, 10555
Falls Church Senior Center, 2458
Food Donation Program: Food Distribution Center, 137
Gordon House, 10556
Grand Court, 10557
Green Hill Home for Adults, 10558
Ideal-Phone, 3122
Independence Resource Center, 10942
International Society for Quality of Life Studies, 159
Jack Weinberg Memorial Award for Geriatric Psychiatry, 2646
John H. McAulay Award, 2649
Judge Advocates Association, 162
Junction Center for Independent Living, 10943
Lake County Area: Agency on Aging, 2459
League of Older Americans, 2460
Lizzie Lift, 3386
Loudoun County Area: Agency on Aging, 2461
Magnolia Ridge Residential Care, 10559
Mayfair House, 10560
Mayflower, 10561
Meals on Wheels Association of America, 164
Mercy Medical Airlift, 2462
Military Benefit Association, 169
Military Officers Association of America (MOAA), 170
Military Order of the World Wars, 171
Mount Vernon Center for Community Mental Health: Deaf Services, 6398
Mountain Empire Older Citizens, 2463
National Association for Addiction Professionals, 7186
National Association of Government Communicators (NAGC), 192
National Association of Military Widows, 193
National Association of Partners in Education, 196
National Association of Physician Nurses, 197
National Association of Retired Federal Employees, 199
National Captioning Institute, 6404, 7664
National Center for State Courts, 11281
National Mental Health Association, 242, 6048
National Organization for Victim Assistance, 247
National Right to Work Legal Defense and Education Foundation, 11282
Naval Submarine League, 267
Navy Mutual Aid Association, 268
Newport News Public Library System, 11819
Norfolk Senior Center & Adult Day Health Care, 2464
Northern Neck Middle Penninsula Area: Agency on Aging, 2465
Northern Virginia Resource Center for Deaf and Hard of Hearing Persons, 6424
Nutrition Services Incentive Program (NSIP), 2466
Oak Hill Center, 10562
Older Women's League, 278
Orange County Home for Adults, 10563
Peninsula Center for Independent Living, 10944
Peter J. Salmon Award - Blind Worker of the Year, 2673
Piedmont Senior Resources Area: Agency on Aging, 2467
Presbyterian Group Home-Waynesboro, 10564
Prevent Blindness Virginia, 7732
Prince William Area: Agency on Aging, 2468
Pulaski Retirement Community, 10565
RSVP Alexandria, 2469
RSVP Campbell County, 2470
RSVP Chesapeake Bay, 2471
RSVP Clinch Valley, 2472
RSVP East Shore, 2473
RSVP Floyd County, 2474
RSVP Jefferson Area, 2475
RSVP Lee Scott Wise Norton, 2476
RSVP Loudoun, 2477
RSVP Montgomery County, 1258, 1989, 2174, 2174, 2478
RSVP Portsmouth, 1634, 2479
RSVP Prince William, 2480
RSVP Pulaski County, 2481
RSVP Rappahannock-Rapidan, 2482
RSVP Richmond, 2483
RSVP Shenandoah Area, 2484
RSVP Southside, 2485
Railroad Retirement Board: Richmond, Virginia District Office, 2486
Railroad Retirement Board: Roanoke, Virginia District Office, 2487
Rappahannock Area: Agency on Aging, 2488
Rappahannock Westminster-Canterbury, 10566
Rappahannock-Rapidan Community Services Board and Area Agency on Aging, 2489
Recording Service for Visually Handicapped, 7736
Registry of Interpreters for the Deaf, 6438
Renaissance Gardens at Greenspring, 10567
Resources For Independent Living, 10945
Roanoke City Public Library System, 11820
Robert B. Irwin Award, 2680
Senior Connections The Capital Area: Agency, 2490
Shelby Manor Group Home, 10568
Shenandoah Adult Care, 10569
Shenandoah Valley Village, 10570
Special Needs III, 3051
St. Luke's Assisted Living, 10571
Staunton Public Library Talking Book Center, 11821
Stonewall Jackson Home for Adults, 10572
Thomas Balch Library, 11822
US Department of Veterans Affairs: Hampton Medical Center Library and Educational Resources, 11823
US Department of Veterans Affairs: Richmond Hospital Library, 11824
US Department of Veterans Affairs: Salem Medical Center Library, 11825
USA Next United Seniors Association, 334
USAir, 11943
University Library Services, 11826
University of Virginia: Communication Disorders Program, 6832
University of Virginia: Hypertension and Atherosclerosis Unit, 6928
Vietnamese Senior Citizens Association, 339
Virginia Association for Education & Rehabilitation of the Blind & Visually Impaired, 7769
Virginia Association of Area Agencies on Aging, 2491
Virginia Association of Nonprofit Homes for the Aging, 2492
Virginia Board for People with Disabilities, 2493
Virginia Client Assistance Program, 2494
Virginia Commonwealth University Virginia Center on Aging Information Resources Center, 11827
Virginia Department for the Aging, 2495, 11283
Virginia Department for the Blind & Vision Impaired, 7770
Virginia Department of Deaf and Hard of Hearing, 6460
Virginia Department of Economic Development Division of Tourism, 11999
Virginia Department of Health and Human Resources: Department of Aging, 2496
Virginia Department of Mental Health Mental Retardation and Substance Abuse Services, 6062
Virginia Department of Taxation, 2497
Virginia Developmental Disability Council, 2498
Virginia Division of Substance Abuse Services, 7225
Virginia Industries for the Blind, 7771
Virginia Office for Protection and Advocacy, 2499
Virginia Protection & Advocacy for Persons with Disabilities, 2500
Virginia Protection and Advocacy Agency, 11284
Virginia Protection and Advocacy Agency: Virginia Beach, 11285
Virginia State Library for the Visually and Physically Handicapped, 11828
Virginian Manor, 10573
Westwood Center, 10574
Whatland Hills Retirement Center, 10575
Willows at Meadow Branch, 10576

Washington

AARP West Regional Office, 2501
AIPHONE Intercom Systems, 3057
Abused Deaf Women's Advocacy Services, 2502, 6302
Aegis Lodge, 10577
Aegis Senior Living of Shoreline, 10578
Aegis at Northgate, 10579
Aegis of Bothell, 10580
Aegis of Edmonds, 10581
Aegis of Issaquah, 10582
Aegis of Kent, 10583
Aegis of Kirkland, 10584
Aegis of Lynnwood, 10585
Aegis of Redmond, 10586

1117

Geographic Index / West Virginia

Aegis of Shoreline (Callahan House), 10587
Aging and Long Term Care of Eastern Washington, 2503
American Diabetes Association: East Washington/North Idaho District Office, 6129
American Diabetes Association: Seattle Area Office, 6160
Brighton Court, 10588
Brittany Park, 10589
Bureau of Naval Personnel: Bremerton Retired Affairs, 2504
Bureau of Naval Personnel: Washington Retired Activities Office, 2505
Bureau of Naval Personnel: Whidbey Island Retired Activities Office, 2506
Central Washington Disability Resources, 10947
Columbia River Area: Agency on Aging, 2507
Colville Indian Area: Agency on Aging, 2508
Delta Society National Service, 7577
Directory of Accessible Van Rentals, 11921
Disabilities Law Project: Washington, 11286
Disability Resource Connection, 10948
Division of Disability Determination Services, 1645, 2509
EZ-Access Portable Ramps, 3369
Eagle Meadows Assisted Living Community, 10590
Environment Control System, 3113
Evacu-Trac, 3514
Fairwinds-Redmond, 10591
Fairwinds-Spokane, 10592
Farrington Court, 10593
Featherspring, 3550
Fred Hutchinson Cancer Research Center: Arnold Digital Library, 11829
Genesis Institute, 142
Goals and Objectives, 3120
Gray Panthers of Seattle, 2510
Hammatt Senior Products: Catalog for Activity Professionals, 3289
Hawthorne Court, 10594
Hearing Dog Resource Center (HDRC), 6365
Helen Keller National Center: NorthwestRegion, 7605
Hope Heart Institute, 6878
Horizon Air, 11928
Independent Living Resource Southwest Washington, 10949
International Association for the Study of Pain, 155
Kitsap County Area: Agency on Aging, 2511
Lighthouse for the Blind of Washington, 7636
Living Court Assisted Living Community, 10595
Lutheran Bible Institute of Seattle Library, 11830
National Federation of the Blind: Public Employees Division, 7684
Northwest Geriatric Education Center, 11831
Northwest Justice Project: Olympia, 11287
Northwest Justice Project: Seattle, 11288
Northwest Justice Project: Vancouver, 11289
Olympic Area: Agency on Aging, 2512

Olympics West Retirement Inn, 10596
Ophthalmic Research Laboratory Eye Institute, 8050
Queen Anne Manor, 10597
RSVP Benton-Franklin Counties, 2513
RSVP Clallam Jefferson County, 2514
RSVP Clark County, 1611, 1977, 2515, 2515
RSVP Grays Harbor Pacific County, 2516
RSVP King County, 2517
RSVP Kitsap County, 2518
RSVP Kittitas County, 2519
RSVP Pierce County, 2520
RSVP Skagit County, 2521
RSVP Snohomish County, 2522
RSVP Spokane County, 2523
RSVP Walla Walla CountySenior Citizen Center, 2524
RSVP Yakima County, 2525
Railroad Retirement Board: Bellevue, Washington District Office, 2526
Railroad Retirement Board: Spokane, Washington District Office, 2527
Regency Samaritan House, 10598
Regency on Whidbey, 10599
Regent at Sterling Park Assisted Living, 10600
Region 10: Administration on Aging (AoA), 2528
Seattle King County Division on Aging, 2529
Shoreline Lake Forest Park Senior Center, 2530
Spa, 11940
The Bellettini, 10602
Three Links Center, 10603
US Department of Veterans Affairs: Seattle Puget Sound Health Care System, 11832
US Department of Veterans Affairs: Spokane Medical Center Library, 11833
US Department of Veterans Affairs: Tacoma/Puget Sound Health Care System, 11834
US Department of Veterans Affairs: Walla Walla Jonathan M Wainwright Memorial VA Medical Library, 11835
University of Washington: Alcohol & Drug Abuse Institute Library, 7488
University of Washington: Department of Speech & Hearing Sciences, 6833
University of Washington: Diabetes Endocrinology Research Center, 6293
University of Washington: Speech & Hearing Clinic, 6834
Van Mall, 10604
Virginia Mason Research Center, 6296
Washington Aging and Disability Services, 11290
Washington Association of Area Agencies on Aging, 2531
Washington Association of Houses and Services for the Aging, 2532
Washington Client Assistance Program, 2533
Washington Department of Mental Health, 6063
Washington Department of Retirement Systems, 2534
Washington Department of Revenue, 2535
Washington Department of Services for the Blind, 7781

Washington Department of Social and Health Services Aging and Adult Services, 2536
Washington Department of Veterans Affairs, 2537
Washington Division of Alcoholism & Substance Abuse, 7227
Washington Governor's Committee on Disability Issues & Employment, 2538
Washington Library for the Blind and Physically Handicapped, 11836
Washington Oakes, 10605
Washington Protection & Advocacy for Persons with Disabilities, 2539
Washington Protection and Advocacy Agency, 11291
Washington State Aging & Disability Services Administration, 2540
Washington State Department of Services, 2541
Washington State Developmental Disabilitities Council, 2542
Washington State Tourism, 12000
Washington Workers Compensation Board, 2543
Wheelchair Getaways Accessible Van Rentals, 11946
Windward Foundation, 343
Yakama Nation Area Agency on Aging, 2544

West Virginia

American Diabetes Association: West Virginia/Southern Ohio, 6170
Appalachian Area: Agency on Aging, 2545
Appalachian Center for Independent Living, 10952
Charleston Disability Determination Services, 2546
Clarksburg Disability Determination Services, 2547
Communication Workers of America Retirees Club of Local 2011, 2548
Disability Determination Section, 2549
Kanawha County Public Library, 11837
North Central West Virginia Center for Independent Living, 10950
Northwestern Area: Agency on Aging, 2550
Ohio County Public Library Services for the Blind and Physically Handicapped, 11838
Parkersburg and Wood County Public Library, 11839
RSVP Case, 2551
RSVP Mercer Summer Monroe Counties, 2552
RSVP Mid-Ohio Valley, 2553
RSVP Morgantown, 2554
RSVP Panhandle, 2555
Railroad Retirement Board: West Virginia District Office, 2556
State of West Virginia, 11996
US Department of Veterans Affairs: Beckley Library Service, 11840
US Department of Veterans Affairs: Clarkburg Loouis A Johnson VA Medical Center Library, 11841
US Department of Veterans Affairs: Huntington Learning Resource Center, 11842

Geographic Index / Wisconsin

US Department of Veterans Affairs: Martinsburg Learning Resources Service, 11843
Upper Potomac Area Agency on Aging, 2557
West Virginia Advocates, 2558
West Virginia Bureau of Human Resources: Commission for the Hearing Impaired, 6462
West Virginia Bureau of Senior Services, 11303
West Virginia Department of Aging, 2559
West Virginia Department of Health, 2560
West Virginia Department of Health and Human Services: Human Services Bureau Commission on Aging, 2561
West Virginia Developmental Disability Plan Council, 2562
West Virginia Directors of Senior and Community Services, 2563
West Virginia Division of Alcohol and Drug Abuse, 7228
West Virginia Division of Tax and Revenue, 2564
West Virginia Division of Tourism, 12001
West Virginia Library Commission, 11844
West Virginia Protection & Advocacy for Persons with Disabilities, 2565
West Virginia Protection and Advocacy Agency, 11292
West Virginia School for the Blind, 11845
West Virginia Senior Legal Aid, 11293
West Virginia State University Metro Area Agency on Aging, 2566
West Virginia Workers Compensation Board of Review, 2567

Wisconsin

AIDS For Daily Living, 3317
Access to Independence, 10951
Act Wheelchair, 3497
Adaptive Golf Car Model 4850, 3287
AgeAdvantAge Area Agency on Aging: Madison, 11294
AgeAdvantAge Area: Agency on Aging Western Office, 2568
American Diabetes Association: Great Lakes and Heartland Regional Office, Wisconsin, 6132
American Diabetes Association: Madison District Office, 6139
American Society for Laser Medicine and Surgery, 60
American Walker, 3477
Area Agency on Aging of Dane County, 2569
Basic Wheelchair, 3499
Bay Area Managers of Volunteer Services, 2570
Bravo! + Three-Wheel Scooter, 3418
Bruno Independent Living Aids, 3363
Bureau of Naval Personnel: Wisconsin Retired Activities Office, 2571
Center for Independent Living for Western Wisconsin, 10953
Coalition of Wisconsin Aging Groups, 2572
Comb-O-Cycle, 3419
Cornell Communications, 3103
Cross Wheelchair, 3510

Cub, SuperCub and Special EditionScooters, 3366
Custom Lift Residential Elevators, 3367
Disability Determination Bureau, 2573
Douglas County Activity Association, 2574
Elder Law Center: Coalition of Wisconsin Aging Groups, 11295
Explorer+ 4-Wheel Scooter, 3421
Ez International Inc./Ortho Kinetics, 3376
F3 Wheelchair, 3515
Friends of Seniors, 2575
Functional Forms, 3204
Gateway Technical College Learning Resource Center, 11846
Governor's Committee for People with Disabilities, 2576
Independence First, 10954
Independent Living Resources-La Crosse, 10955
Independent Living Resources-Richland, 10956
International Foundation for Bowel Dysfunction, 6946
International Society of Psychiatric Consultation Liaison Nurses, 161
Jackson Foundation for Medical Research & Education, 6879
Lithium Information Center, 6039
MVP+ 3-Wheel Scooter, 3422
Marquette University Libraries Special Collections and University Archives, 11847
Medical College of Wisconsin Eye Institute, 8046
Midstate Independent Living Consultants-Stevens Point, 10957
Midstate Independent Living-Rhinelander, 10958
Midwest Express Airlines, 11933
Milwaukee County Department on Aging, 2577
Milwaukee Young Lawyers Association: Committee on Legal Services to the Elderly, 11296
National Federation of the Blind: Music Division, 7683
North County Independent Living-Ashland, 10959
North County Independent Living-Superior, 10960
Northern Area: Agency on Aging, 2578
Nova Walker, 3483
Nurses Christian Fellowship, 274
Options for Independent Living-Appleton, 10961
Options for Independent Living-Green Bay, 10962
Out-N-About American Walker, 3484
Parkinson Association of Wisconsin, 6971
Power Chairs, 3528
Prone Support Walker, 3485
RSVP Advacapcap, 2579
RSVP Brown County, 2259, 2580
RSVP Coulee Region, 2581
RSVP Dane County, 2582
RSVP Kenosha CountySponsored By Kenosha Area Family And Aging Services, Inc., 2583
RSVP Manitowoc County, 2584
RSVP Milwaukee, 2585
RSVP Northwest, 2586
RSVP Outagamie County, 2587

RSVP Portage County, 2588
RSVP Rock County, 2589
RSVP Superior-Douglas, 2590
RSVP Walworth County, 2591
RSVP Waukeesha County, 2592
Railroad Retirement Board: Wisconsin District Office, 2593
Regal Scooters, 3431
Retired Senior Volunteer Program of Western Dairyland, 2594
Ridgeview Heights Indeped Living Corporation, 10606
Rock County Health Care Center Staff Library, 11848
Scooter, Power Chair and WheelchairLifts, 3394
Sentry Insurance Company Library, 11849
Sierra 3000/4000, 3437
Society's Assets-Elkhorn, 10963
Society's Assets-Kenosha, 10964
Society's Assets-Racine, 10965
Southeastern Wisconsin Area: Agency on Aging, 2595
Stairway Elevators, 3401
Standing Aid Frame with Rear Entry, 3491
State Independent Living Council, 10966
Sting Wheelchair, 3539
Straight and Custom Curved Stairlifts, 3403
Swede Elite, 3541
Trace Center, 6820
Tri-Walker, 3492
Triumph 3000/4000, 3444
Triumph Scooter, 3445
US Department of Veterans Affairs: Tomah Health Sciences Library, 11850
United Electric Workers Retirees, 2596
University of Wisconsin Laboratory for Cancer Research Library, 11851
University of Wisconsin: Auditory Physiology Center, 6835
University of Wisconsin: Milwaukee Medicinal Chemistry Group, 7489
Volunteer Center of Racine County, 2597
Volunteer Services of Barron County, 2598
WisTech Assistive Technology Program, 2599
Wisconsin Aging and Long Term Care Board, 2600
Wisconsin Alliance of Hearing Professionals, 6463
Wisconsin Association of Area Agencies on Aging, 2601
Wisconsin Association of Homes and Services for the Aging, 2602
Wisconsin Bar Association: Elder Law, 11297
Wisconsin Bureau of Substance Abuse Services, 7229
Wisconsin Client Assistance Program, 2603
Wisconsin Coalition for Advocacy, 2604
Wisconsin Coalition for Advocacy: Madison, 11298
Wisconsin Coalition for Advocacy: Milwaukee, 11299
Wisconsin Coalition for Advocacy: Rice Lake, 11300
Wisconsin Council of Senior Citizens, 2605
Wisconsin Council on Developmental Disabilities, 2606
Wisconsin Department of Aging & Long-Term Care Resources, 2607

Geographic Index / Wyoming

Wisconsin Department of Health and HumanServices: The State Bureau on Aging, 11301
Wisconsin Department of Mental Health, 6064
Wisconsin Department of Revenue, 2608
Wisconsin Department of Tourism, 12002
Wisconsin Department of Veterans Affairs, 2609
Wisconsin Regional Library for the Blind: Talking Book Program, 11852
Wisconsin Retired Educators Association, 2610
Wisconsin Veterans Museum & Research Center, 11853
Wisconsin Workers Compensation Board, 2611
Wiscraft: Wisconsin Enterprises for theBlind, 7787

Wyoming

Aspen Wind Assisted Living, 10607
Bieske's Country Comfort Home Care, 10608
Disability Determination Services, 418, 878, 1149, 1149, 1202, 1397, 1478, 1534, 1710, 1767, 1888, 1925, 2047, 2203, 2428, 2453, 2612
Garden Square of Casper, 10609
Legacy Homes Assisted Living, 10610
Meadow Wind Assisted Living, 10611
New Horizons Assisted Living Facility, 10612
Park Place, 9692, 10613
Point Frontier Retirement Community, 10614
RSVP Central Wyoming, 2613
RSVP Southeastern Wyoming, 2614
Showboat Retirement Center, 10615
Sierra Hills, 10616
Spring Wind Assisted Living, 10617
State of Wyoming Aging Division, 11302
Sugarland Ridge, 10618
US Department of Veterans Affairs: Cheyenne Medical and Regional Office Center, 11854
US Department of Veterans Affairs: Sheridan Medical Center Library, 11855
Veterans' Home of Wyoming, 10619
Wyoming Client Assistance Program, 2615
Wyoming Department of Aging, 2616
Wyoming Department of Health: Aging Division, 2617
Wyoming Department of Mental Health, 6065
Wyoming Department of Revenue, 2618
Wyoming Developmental Disability Council, 2619
Wyoming Division of Behavioral Health, 7233
Wyoming Division of Rehabilitation, 2620
Wyoming Division of Tourism, 12003
Wyoming Pioneer Home, 10620
Wyoming Protection & Advocacy Agency: Evanston, 11304
Wyoming Protection & Advocacy for Persons with Disabilities, 2621
Wyoming Protection and Advocacy Agency:Developmental Disabilities Protection and Advocacy Program, 11305
Wyoming Services For Independent Living, 10967
Wyoming Services for the Visually Disabled, 11856
Wyoming Workers Safety & Compensation Division, 2622

AIDS

AIDS Action Bulletin, 4534
AIDS Alert, 4515
AIDS Crisis in America, 4535
AIDS Funding: A Guide to Giving by Foundations & Charitable Organizations, 4516
AIDS Health Pamphlets, 4545
AIDS Legal Council of Chicago, 11081
AIDS News, 4547
AIDS Policy and Law, 4548
AIDS Reader, 4517
AIDS Treatment Data Network, 2854
AIDS/HIV Treatment Directory, 4538
AIDS: A Communication Perspective, 4518
AIDS: What We Need to Know, 4550
AIDSLAW of Louisiana, 11124
APLA Update, 4551
Aaron Diamond AIDS Research Center, 4584
About AIDS, 4520
American Civil Liberties Union AIDS Project, 4448
American Foundation for AIDS Research, 4586
An Annotated Bibliography of Recent Empirical Research in Methadone, 4521
Arkansas Department of Health, 4578
Asian AIDS Project, 4588
Color of Light, 4522
Comprehensive AIDS Center, 4595
Critical Path AIDS Project/AIDS Library, 4543
District of Columbia Public Service Commission, 4459
Employee Attitudes About AIDS, 4558
HIV Infection and AIDS, 4561
Infections Linked to AIDS, 4563
Learning AIDS, 4526
Living Well with HIV and AIDS, 4527
Local AIDS Services: The National Directory, 4539
Longitudinal Studies of HIV Infection in Intravenous Drug Users, 4528
Los Angeles County Department of Health Services, 4470
Managing Tuberculosis and HIV Infection in Today's General Workplace, 4564
Massachusetts Department of Public Health, 4473
National AIDS Information Clearinghouse, 4579
National Association on HIV Over Fifty, 4479
National Prison Project: ACLU AIDS inPrison Project, 4613
New York State Directory of AIDS/HIV Clinical Trials, 4540
Notes from the Underground, 4566
Oklahoma Department of Health: HIV/STD Service, 4492
Report to Members, 4569
Taking the HIV (AIDS) Test: How to Help Yourself, 4571
UCLA AIDS Clinical Research Center, 4621
University of California/Davis: AIDS Virus Diagnostic Laboratory, 4623
University of Hawaii: Hawaii AIDS Clinical Research Program, 4629
University of Michigan: National Cooperative Drug/AIDS Group, 4632
University of San Francisco: AIDS Clinical Research Center, 4634
West Virginia Department of Health & Human Resources, 4509
Whitman-Walker Clinic: AIDS/Medical Services Programs, 4510
Worldwide AIDS Directory, 4542
Wyoming Department of Health & Social Services: Medical Services Division, 4513

Abuse, Elder

Arizona Elder Abuse and Fraud Taskforce Committee, 10981
Clearinghouse on Abuse and Neglect of the Elderly (CANE), 109
Journal of Elder Abuse and Neglect, 3902

Active Elderly

ACE Fitness Matters, 3816
American Association for Active Lifestyle & Fitness, 2449
Assisted Living Federation of America, 78
Buena Vida, 3834
Deluxe Convertible Exercise Staircase, 3368
Diabetic's Guide to Health and Fitness, 6201
Diet & Fitness, 3846
Digi-Flex, 3251
Elder Fit: A Health and Fitness Guide, 3624
Exercise and Your Heart, 6859
Fitness Diet and Exercise Guide, 3860
Functional Fitness Assessment for Adults, 3633
General Fitness, 4200
Gentle Path Through the Twelve Steps, 7250
Intermediate Conversational SignLanguage, 6514
Jefferson's Garden, 10026
Mini-Max Cushion, 3217
National Association for Hispanic Elderly, 184
National Senior Games Association, 260
National Urban League, 265
Specialty Cooking Magazine, 3961
Stay Fit Video, 4163
Suggested Exercise Program for People with Parkinson's Disease, 7032
Therapy Putty, 3274
Total Health, 3963

Adult Children

Advanced Sign Language Vocabulary, 6464
Aging Children & Aging Parents, 3602
Al-Anon Family Groups - Classic Edition, 7239
Alabama Developmental Disability Council, 366
Alexander Graham Bell Association for the Deaf: Kentucky Chapter, 6305
Allergy and Asthma Network Mothers ofAsthmatics, 4643, 4674
Children of Aging Parents, 104, 4292
Choices in Deafness, 6479
Colorado School for the Deaf and Blind, 11361
Congenital Heart Disease Anomalies Support Education and Resources, 6840
Disability Rights Education and Defense Fund, 11001
Endeavor, 6647
Family Guide - Growth & Development of the Partially Seeing Child, 7943
Food Allergy and Atopic Dermatitis, 4668
Golden Horizons, 11880
If Your Parents Drink Too Much, 7357
Immune Deficiency Foundation, 4467
Kentucky Chapter: Alexander Graham Bell Association for the Deaf, 6388
Legal Center for People with Disabilities and Older People, 11021
Lessons in Laughter: The Autobiography of a Deaf Actor, 6526
Lisa and Her Soundless World, 6529
My Mother, My Father, 4151
NAD Broadcaster, 6594
National Association for Parents of the Visually Impaired (NAPVI), 7654
National Crime Prevention Council, 4228, 7191
National Network for the Disabled, 243
National Organization for the Advancement of the Deaf, 6416
Prevention Resource Center, 7214
Standing Aid Frame with Rear Entry, 3491
Treasure Valley Association of the Hearing Impaired, 6455
Treasure Valley Hearing and Balance Clinics, 6456

Aging

Aging Research Institute, 4259
Aging in America, 4261
Alliance for Aging Research, 4262
American Academy of Oral and Maxillofacial Radiology, 11
American Aging Association, 4263
American Association of Colleges of Nursing, 17
American Bar Association, 28
American Federation for Aging Research, 4264
American Foundation for Aging Research, 4265
American Holistic Nurses Association, 42
American Medical Informatics Association, 47
American Nurses Association, 51
American Registry of Pathology, 58
American Society on Aging, 3573
Arizona Center on Aging, 3574
Art of Getting Well, 11689
Association for Adult Development and Aging, 3575
Brookdale Center for Healthy Aging and Longevity of Hunter College, 3576
Butler County Department on Aging, 1058
Center for Study of Aging, 4286
Elderhostel, 12016
Experimental Aging Research, 3858
Genesis Institute, 142
Indiana University: Pharmacology Research Laboratory, 6274
Intestinal Disease Foundation, 6947
Journal of American Aging Association, 3899
Journey to Pain Relief, 11693
League for the Hard of Hearing, 6804

1121

Subject Index / Allergies

Lighthouse National Center for Vision and Aging (LNCVA), 7633
M C P Hahnemann Orthopedic Institute, 5117
National Association of Nutrition and Aging Services Programs (NANASP), 194
National Hispanic Council on Aging, 228
National Indian Council on Aging, 229
National Program on Women and Aging, 253
National Resource Center on Native American Aging (NRCNAA), 255
Preparing for an Aging Society: Changes and Challenges, 3663
Research on Aging, 3952
Temple University Institute on Aging, 3676
University of Kansas: Center on Aging, 4401
Virginia Center on Aging, 3585
Washington University Center for Aging, 3586

Allergies

Advice From Your Allergist, 4664
Allergies A to Z, 4652
Allergies and You, 4665
Allergy Research Foundation, 4679
American Academy of Allergy and Immunology, 4644, 4675
American College of Allergy and Immunology, 4680
Asthma and Allergy Foundation of America, 4648, 4677
John Hopkins Asthma & Allergy Center, 4682
Johns Hopkins University: Asthma and Allergy Center, 4683
MA Report, 4670
Mayo Clinic and Foundation: Allergy Disease Research Laboratory, 4686
National Institute of Allergy and Infectious Diseases, 4687
Something in the Air: Airborne Allergens, 4672
Tips to Remember, 4673
University of Florida: General Clinical Research Center, 4697

Alzheimer's Disease, See also Dementia

Alzheimer Association: Boise/Treasure Valley Chapter, 4701
Alzheimer Disease and Associated Disorders, 4980
Alzheimer Early Stages, 2nd Edition, 11688
Alzheimer Research Forum, 5038
Alzheimer Support, 5039
Alzheimer Treatment Research Center Library, 11730
Alzheimer's Advocates Handbook, 4981
Alzheimer's Alliance: Northeast Texas, 4703
Alzheimer's Assocation: South Central Michigan Chapter, 4704
Alzheimer's Association Autopsy Assistance Network, 4706
Alzheimer's Association Greater Baton Rouge Chapter, 4707
Alzheimer's Association Greater RichmondChapter, 4708
Alzheimer's Association Greater Youngstown Chapter, 4709
Alzheimer's Association Middle Tennessee Chapter, 4711
Alzheimer's Association NW Florida Chapter, 4712
Alzheimer's Association National Brochure, 4982
Alzheimer's Association Newsletter, 4983
Alzheimer's Association North AlabamaRegional Office, 4713
Alzheimer's Association of Ashland, 4714
Alzheimer's Association of Greater Wisconsin: Eau Claire, 4716
Alzheimer's Association of Greater Wisconsin: Fox Valley, 4717
Alzheimer's Association of GreaterWisconsin-Wausau Regional Office, 4715
Alzheimer's Association of Hayward Wisconsin, 4718
Alzheimer's Association of Superior, 4720
Alzheimer's Association: Alaska Chapter, 4722
Alzheimer's Association: Aloha Chapter, 4723
Alzheimer's Association: Augusta Chapter, 4724
Alzheimer's Association: Carolina Piemont Chapter, 4727
Alzheimer's Association: Central GeorgiaChapter, 4728
Alzheimer's Association: Central Illinois Chapter, 4729
Alzheimer's Association: Central Indiana Chapter, 4730
Alzheimer's Association: Central Maryland Chapter, 4731
Alzheimer's Association: Central New York Chapter, 4732
Alzheimer's Association: Central Ohio Chapter, 4733
Alzheimer's Association: Central Virginia Chapter, 4734
Alzheimer's Association: Central and North Florida Chapter, 4735
Alzheimer's Association: Central and Western Kansas, 4736
Alzheimer's Association: CharlestonOffice, 4737
Alzheimer's Association: Charlotte/DeSoto Counties Chapter, 4738
Alzheimer's Association: Clark-Champaign-Logan Chapter, 4739
Alzheimer's Association: Cleveland Area Chapter, 4740
Alzheimer's Association: Coastal Bend Chapter, 4741
Alzheimer's Association: Connecticut Chapter, 4743
Alzheimer's Association: Corn Belt Chapter, 4744
Alzheimer's Association: Dallas Chapter, 4745
Alzheimer's Association: Delaware Valley, 4746
Alzheimer's Association: Desert Southwest Chapter, 4747
Alzheimer's Association: Detroit Area Chapter, 4748
Alzheimer's Association: East Central Florida Chapter, 4752
Alzheimer's Association: East Central Michigan Chapter, 4753
Alzheimer's Association: East Central Ohio Chapter, 4754
Alzheimer's Association: East CentralIowa Chapter, 4751
Alzheimer's Association: Eastern North Carolina Chapter, 4755
Alzheimer's Association: Eastern Shore Region, 4756
Alzheimer's Association: Eastern Tennessee Chapter, 4757
Alzheimer's Association: Eastern Washington Chapter, 4758
Alzheimer's Association: El Paso Chapter, 4759
Alzheimer's Association: Florida Gulf Coast Chapter, 4760
Alzheimer's Association: Four Rivers Chapter, 4761
Alzheimer's Association: Georgia Chapter, 4762
Alzheimer's Association: Great Plains Area Chapter, 4763
Alzheimer's Association: Greater Austin Chapter, 4765
Alzheimer's Association: Greater Billings Area Chapter, 4766
Alzheimer's Association: Greater Columbus Chapter, 4767
Alzheimer's Association: Greater East Texas Chapter, 4769
Alzheimer's Association: Greater Eastern Ohio Area Chapter, 4770
Alzheimer's Association: Greater Eastern Ohio Chapter, 4768
Alzheimer's Association: Greater Idaho Chapter, 4771
Alzheimer's Association: Greater Illinios Chapter, 4772
Alzheimer's Association: Greater New Hampshire Chapter, 4776
Alzheimer's Association: Greater North Valley Chapter, 4777
Alzheimer's Association: Greater OrlandoArea Chapter, 4778
Alzheimer's Association: Greater PalmBeach Chapter, 4779
Alzheimer's Association: Greater Pennsylvania Chapter, 4780
Alzheimer's Association: Greater Pittsburgh Chapter, 4781
Alzheimer's Association: Greater Sacramento Chapter, 4782
Alzheimer's Association: Greater Texarkana Chapter, 4783
Alzheimer's Association: Greater Wisconsin Chapter, 4784
Alzheimer's Association: GreaterCincinnati Chapter, 4764
Alzheimer's Association: Hampton Roads Chapter, 4786
Alzheimer's Association: HarrisonburgRegion, 4787
Alzheimer's Association: Heart of Iowa Chapter, 4789
Alzheimer's Association: Heart ofAmerica Chapter, 4788
Alzheimer's Association: Highland Rim Chapter, 4790

Subject Index / Alzheimer's Disease, See also Dementia

Alzheimer's Association: Houston andSoutheast Texas Chapter, 4792
Alzheimer's Association: Hudson Valley/Rockland/Westchester NY Chapter, 4793
Alzheimer's Association: Indianhead Chapter, 4794
Alzheimer's Association: Iowa Golden Chapter, 4795
Alzheimer's Association: Lake Superior Chapter, 4796
Alzheimer's Association: Lexington/Bluegrass Chapter, 4798
Alzheimer's Association: Long IslandChapter, 4799
Alzheimer's Association: Los Angeles Chapter, 4800
Alzheimer's Association: Louisville Chapter, 4801
Alzheimer's Association: Maine Chapter, 4802
Alzheimer's Association: Manatee/Sarasoto Counties Chapter, 4803
Alzheimer's Association: Marin Chapter, 4804
Alzheimer's Association: Marquette/Alger Chapter, 4805
Alzheimer's Association: Mary's Peak Chapter, 4806
Alzheimer's Association: Massachusetts Chapter, 4808
Alzheimer's Association: MassachusettsChapter, 4807
Alzheimer's Association: Memphis Chapter, 4809
Alzheimer's Association: Miami Valley Chapter, 4810
Alzheimer's Association: Mid Missouri Chapter, 4811
Alzheimer's Association: Mid-MichiganChapter, 4812
Alzheimer's Association: Mid-Ohio ValleyRegional Office, 4813
Alzheimer's Association: Mid-State South Carolina Chapter, 4814
Alzheimer's Association: Middle Mississippi Chapter, 4815
Alzheimer's Association: Midstate Wiconsin Chapter, 4816
Alzheimer's Association: Minnesota Lakes Chapter, 4817
Alzheimer's Association: Mississippi Valley Chapter, 4818
Alzheimer's Association: Mohawk Valley Chapter, 4819
Alzheimer's Association: Monroe RegionalCenter, 4820
Alzheimer's Association: Monterey CountyChapter, 4821
Alzheimer's Association: NationalCapital Area Chapter, 4822
Alzheimer's Association: New Mexico Chapter, 4823
Alzheimer's Association: New York City Chapter, 4824
Alzheimer's Association: North Central Texas Chapter, 4825
Alzheimer's Association: North Central West Virginia Chapter, 4826
Alzheimer's Association: North Dakota Chapter, 4827

Alzheimer's Association: North New Jersey Chapter, 4828
Alzheimer's Association: Northeast Michigan Chapter, 4829
Alzheimer's Association: Northeast Pennsylvania Chapter, 4830
Alzheimer's Association: Northeast Tennessee Chapter, 4831
Alzheimer's Association: Northeast Texas Chapter, 4832
Alzheimer's Association: Northeast Wisconsin Chapter, 4833
Alzheimer's Association: Northern Alabama Chapter, 4835
Alzheimer's Association: Northern Connecticut Chapter, 4836
Alzheimer's Association: Northern Idaho Resource Center, 4837
Alzheimer's Association: Northern Indiana Chapter, 4838
Alzheimer's Association: Northern Nevada Chapter, 4839
Alzheimer's Association: Northern Virginia Chapter, 4840
Alzheimer's Association: NorthernArizona, 4834
Alzheimer's Association: Northwest Florida Chapter, 4841
Alzheimer's Association: Northwest Lousiana Chapter, 4842
Alzheimer's Association: Northwest Missouri Chapter, 4843
Alzheimer's Association: Northwest Ohio, 4844
Alzheimer's Association: Oklahoma Chapter, 4845
Alzheimer's Association: Oklahoma and Arkansas Chapter, 4846
Alzheimer's Association: Orange County Chapter, 4848
Alzheimer's Association: Oregon Chapter, 4849
Alzheimer's Association: Oregon-Trail Chapter, 4850
Alzheimer's Association: Panhandle Area Chapter, 4851
Alzheimer's Association: Piedmont Triad North Carolina Chapter, 4852
Alzheimer's Association: Putnam County Chapter, 4853
Alzheimer's Association: Rhode Island Chapter, 4854
Alzheimer's Association: Riverland Chapter, 4855
Alzheimer's Association: Riverside/SanBernardino Counties Chapter, 4856
Alzheimer's Association: Rochester Chapter, 4857
Alzheimer's Association: Rocky Mountain Chapter, 4858
Alzheimer's Association: STAR Chapter, 4859, 4860
Alzheimer's Association: Salem Regional Office, 4861
Alzheimer's Association: San Diego Chapter, 4862
Alzheimer's Association: San Francisco Bay Chapter, 4863
Alzheimer's Association: Santa CruzLocal Office, 4866
Alzheimer's Association: Siouxland, 4867

Alzheimer's Association: Siouxland Chapter, 4868
Alzheimer's Association: South Central Michigan Chapter, 1340, 4869
Alzheimer's Association: South Central Wisconsin Chapter, 4870
Alzheimer's Association: South Dakota Office, 4871
Alzheimer's Association: South Jersey Chapter, 4872
Alzheimer's Association: South Plains Chapter, 4873
Alzheimer's Association: Southeast Florida Chapter, 4875
Alzheimer's Association: Southeast Georgia Chapter, 4876
Alzheimer's Association: Southeast Pennsylvania Chapter, 4877
Alzheimer's Association: Southeast Tennssee Chapter, 4878
Alzheimer's Association: SoutheastWisconsin Chapter, 4874
Alzheimer's Association: Southern Arizona, 4879
Alzheimer's Association: Southern Illinois Chapter, 4880
Alzheimer's Association: Southern Nevada Chapter, 4881
Alzheimer's Association: Southern Tier Chapter, 4882
Alzheimer's Association: Southside Virginia Chpater, 4883
Alzheimer's Association: Southwest Georgia Chapter, 4885
Alzheimer's Association: Southwest Montana Chapter, 4886
Alzheimer's Association: SouthwestMissouri Chapter, 4884
Alzheimer's Association: SpringfieldRegional Office, 4887
Alzheimer's Association: St Louis Chapter, 4888
Alzheimer's Association: Star Chapter West Texas Region, 4889
Alzheimer's Association: Sullivan/Delaware Chapter, 4891
Alzheimer's Association: Traverse CityRegional, 4894
Alzheimer's Association: Upstate South Carolina Chapter, 4895
Alzheimer's Association: Utah Chapter, 4896
Alzheimer's Association: Vermont Chapter, 4897
Alzheimer's Association: Volusia/Flagler Counties Chapter, 4898
Alzheimer's Association: West Central Florida Chapter, 4899
Alzheimer's Association: West Central Minnesota Chapter, 4900
Alzheimer's Association: West Hawaii Chapter, 4901
Alzheimer's Association: West Michigan Chapter, 4902
Alzheimer's Association: West Shore Chapter, 4903
Alzheimer's Association: West South Dakota Chapter, 4904
Alzheimer's Association: West VirginaChapter, 4905
Alzheimer's Association: Western & Central Washington Chapter, 4906

Alzheimer's Association: Western Massachusetts Chapter, 4907
Alzheimer's Association: Western New York Chapter, 4908
Alzheimer's Association: Western North Carolina Chapter, 4909
Alzheimer's Association: Western Slope, 4910
Alzheimer's Association: Wichita FallsRegional Office, 4911
Alzheimer's Association:-Michigan Great Lakes Chapter Southwest Region, 4913
Alzheimer's Association:Hudson Valley/Rockland/Westchester, NY Chapter, 4721
Alzheimer's Disease & Related DisordersAssociation, Greater Iowa Chapter, 4914
Alzheimer's Disease Center, 4915, 5042
Alzheimer's Disease Education and Referral (ADEAR) Center, 4916
Alzheimer's Disease International, 5043
Alzheimer's Disease Treatment and Family Stress: Directions for Research, 4949
Alzheimer's Disease and Related Disorders Association, 4919
Alzheimer's Disease: A Guide for Families, 4976
Alzheimer's Disease: A Guide to Federal Programs, 4950, 4985
Alzheimer's Disease: A Handbook for Caregivers, 4951
Alzheimer's Disease: An Overview, 4986
Alzheimer's Disease: Statistics, 4988
Alzheimer's Foundation of America, 4920, 5044
Alzheimer's Foundation of the South & Mississippi Division, 4922
Alzheimer's Handbook, 4953
Alzheimer's Research Review, 4989
Alzheimer's Resource Center, 4923
Alzheimer's Wyoming, 4926
Alzheimer's: The Answers You Need, 4955
Alzheimers of Central Alabama, 4928
Alzhimer's Association of Greater Wisconsin, 4929
Another Home for Mom, 5029
Arden Courts Alzheimer's Assisted Living, 8254, 10399
Care for Advanced Alzheimer's Disease, 4990
Caring for Alzheimer's Patients, 4993
Caring... Sharing: The Alzheimer's Caregiver, 5030
Case Western Reserve University School of Medicine, 4280
Clayton County Alzheimer's Support Services, 4935
Clayton County Alzheimer's SupportServices, 4934
Columbia University Alzheimer's Disease Research Center, 5052
Complete Guide to Alzheimer's Proofing Your Home, 4956
Coping and Caring: Living with Alzheimer's Disease, 4958
Coping with Vision Loss: Maximizing What You See & Do, 7808
Early Stage Alzheimer's Care: A Guide for Community Based Programs, 4977
Especially for the Alzheimer Caregiver, 4996

French Alzheimer Foundation, 4936
From Theory to Therapy: The Development of Drugs for Alzheimer's Disease, 4960
In and Out of Time, 5031
Interventions for Alzheimer's Disease: A Caregiver's Complete Reference, 4964
Is it Alzheimer's? Warning Signs You Should Know, 5003
Johns Hopkins University: Alzheimer's Disease Research Center, 5058
Long Island Alzheimer's Foundation, 4937
Maine Alzheimer's Care Center, 4938
Memories of Love: Caring for the Caregiver, 5032
Northern Expressions Publishing, 11890
Ohio State University Neuroscience Program, 4352, 5063
Okada Specialty Guide Dogs, 6428
Oklahoma & Arkansas Alzheimer's Associaton, 4939
Olympic Alzheimers Foundation, 4941
Palo Alto Commons, 8207
Research & Practice, 4978
Rockefeller University: Zachary and Elizabeth M Fisher Center for Research on Alzheimer's Disease, 5064
Rush University Alzheimer's Disease Center, 5065
Safe Return Home: An Inspirational Book for Caregivers of Alzheimer's, 4969
Sonoma County Alzheimers Task Force, 5066
Speaking Our Minds: Personal Reflections from Individuals with Alzheimer's, 4970
Speaking for Them: Identifying Psychiatric Complications in Alzheimer's Patients, 5035
Steps to Planning Activities: Structuring the Day at Home, 5015
Sun Health Research Institute: Alzheimers Center, 5069
Tender Social Day Center for Older Adults and Alzheimer's Group Respite Program, 4942
Understanding Alzheimer's Disease, 4972
University of California, Los AngelesAlzheimer's Disease Center, 5070
University of Iowa: Alzheimer's Disease Research Center, 5073
University of Kansas Neurobiology Research Laboratory, 4400
University of Kentucky: Alzheimer's Disease Research Center, 5074
University of Texas Southwestern Medical Center at Dallas: Alzheimer's Disease Center, 5077
University of Washington: Alzheimer's Disease Research Center, 5078
Useful Information on Alzheimer's Disease, 4973
Vallejo Alzheimers Support Group, 4943
Wandering: It Is a Problem?, 5036
When Memory Fails: Helping the Alzheimer's& Dementia Patient, 4974
World Without Alzheimer's: A Dream Within Reach, 5023

Art

ATA Newsletter, 6599
Aging Network News, 4006
Aging News Alert, 3822
American Deaf Culture, 6465
American Podiatric Circulatory Society, 3572
Arthritis Foundation, SouthernCalifornia Chapter, 5091
Audecibel, 3832
Augmentative and Alternative Communication, 3833
Blind Service Association, 7538
Central New York Chapter of the Arthritis Foundation, 5095
Combined Health Information Database, 4137
Communication Issues Among Deaf People - Eyes, Hands, and Voices, 6486
Communication Outlook: Artificial Language Laboratory, 3840
Convert-Able Table, 3545
Cooperating with the Professional, 7328
Cumulative Subject Index to Current Literature on Aging, 3619
Deaf Artists of America, 6345, 6631
Deaf Artists of America: Artists Directory, 6559
Deaf Culture Series, 6747
Deaf-Blind American, 6578
Disability Studies Quarterly, 3850
Eastern Missouri Chapter of the Arthritis Foundation, 5100
Fifty Something Magazine, 3859
Florida Legal Services: Tallahassee Office, 11054
Friends-In-Art, 4199, 7593
Gleams Newsletter, 7866
Greater Illinois Chapter of the Arthritis Foundation, 5103
Hearing Industries Association, 6369
Hearing Instruments, 6668
Interview with Kirsten Gonzales, 6760
Jean Camper Cahn Award, 2648
Journal of Therapeutic Horticulture, 3913
Kaleidoscope: Exploring the Expirence of Disability through Literature & Fine Arts, 3917
Kansas Cosmosphere and Space Center, 2791
Late-Deafened Adults: A Selected Annotated Bibliography, 6681
Legal Counsel for the Elderly, 11045, 11886
Matilda Ziegler Magazine for the Blind, 7882
McCall's Prime Time, 3986
Models of Oral Interpreting, 6763
NHIF Newsletter, 4069
National Endowment for the Arts: Office for Special Constituencies, 222
National Theatre of the Deaf, 6419
Nevada Assistive Technology Projects, 1602
Northeastern Ohio Chapter of the Arthritis Foundation, 5128
Northwestern Ohio Chapter of the Arthritis Foundation, 5131
Ohio River Valley Chapter of the Arthritis Foundation, 5132
Pennsylvania State University: Artificial Heart Research Project, 6885
Perspective on Aging, 3942, 4084
Prime Times, 3989
Reach Out Magazine, 3950
Region Nine Area: Agency on Aging, 1434
Sears Mature Outlook, 307

Subject Index / Arthritis

tate of West Virginia, 11996
Vietnamese Senior Citizens Association, 339

Arthritis

Aids for Arthritis, 5165
Alabama Chapter of the Arthritis Foundation, 5081
Alerter, 5168
Arkansas Chapter of the Arthritis Foundation, 5083
Arthritis Accent, 5170
Arthritis Answers: Basic Information About Arthritis, 5171
Arthritis Arizona Southwest, 5172
Arthritis Consulting Services, 5084
Arthritis Foundation Information Line, 5086
Arthritis Foundation North Central Chapter, 5089
Arthritis Foundation Services, 5173
Arthritis Health Professionals Association, 5093
Arthritis Helpbook: A Tested Self-Management Program for Coping, 5148
Arthritis Information: Advocacy and Government Affairs, 5174
Arthritis News, 5175
Arthritis Observer, 5176
Arthritis Reporter, 5177
Arthritis Rx: A Cutting-Edge Program for a Pain-Free Life, 5149
Arthritis Self-Help Book, 5150
Arthritis Sourcebook: Everything You Need to Know, 5151
Arthritis Today, 5167
Arthritis Update of Rhode Island, 5178
Arthritis and Common Sense, 5152
Arthritis and Employment: You Can Get the Job You Want, 5181
Arthritis and Inflammatory Bowel Disease, 5182
Arthritis on the Job: You Can Work With It, 5184
Arthritis, Musculoskeletal & Skin Diseases Research: Public Health Service, 5233
Arthritis, Rheumatic Diseases and Related Disorders, 5185
Arthritis, What Exercises Work: Breakthrough Even after Drugs & Surgery Have Failed, 5153
Arthritis: A Comprehensive Guide, 5154
Arthritis: Do You Know?, 5186
Arthritis: Taking Care of Yourself Health Guide for Understanding Your Arthritis, 5155
Arthwriter, 3077
Away with Arthritis, 5156
Big Lamp Switch, 3296
Boston University: Arthritis Center, 5234
Boston University: Robert Dawson Evans Memorial Department of Clinical Research, 5235
Bucknell University Immunobiology Research Laboratory, 5237
Carolinas Chapter of the Arthritis Foundatiob, 5094
Central Pennsylvania Chapter of the Arthritis Foundation, 5097
Chapter of the Arthritis Foundation: Greater Southwest, 5098
Delaware Chapter of the Arthritis Foundation, 5099
Depression for Dummies, 6070
Diet and Arthritis, 5194
Exercise and Your Arthritis, 5196
Factor Fax, 5197
Greater Kansas City Chapter of the Arthritis Foundation, 5104
Gulfcoast Branch: Florida Chapter of the Arthritis Foundation, 5105
Harrington Arthritis Research Center, 5238
Hawaii Chapter of the Arthritis Foundation, 5106
Hudson Valley Branch of the Arthritis Foundation, 5107
In Control, 5160
Indiana Chapter of the Arthritis Foundation, 5108
Indiana University: Multipurpose Arthritis Center, 5109
Iowa Chapter of the Arthritis Foundation, 5110
Kuzell Institute for Arthritis and Infectious Diseases, 5114
Listening to Depression: How Understanding Your Pain Can Heal Your Life, 6073
Long Island Chapter of the Arthritis Foundation, 5115
Louisiana Chapter of the Arthritis Foundation, 5116
Maryland Chapter of the Arthritis Foundation, 5118
Massachusetts Chapter of the Arthritis Foundation, 5119
Michigan Chapter of the Arthritis Foundation, 5121
Multipurpose Arthritis & Musculoskeletal Center, 5240
Multipurpose Arthritis and Musculoskeletal Disease Center, 5241
NIH: National Institute of Osteoporosis and Related Bone Diseases, 177
National Arthritis and Musculoskeletal and Skin Diseases Information Clearinghouse, 5242
National Institute of Arthritis and Musculoskeletal and Skin Disease, 5243
Nebraska Chapter of the Arthritis Foundation, 5122
New Jersey Chapter of the Arthritis Foundation, 5123
North Texas Chapter of the Arthritis Foundation, 5126
Northern California Chapter of the Arthritis Foundation, 5129
Northern New England Chapter of the Arthritis Foundation, 5130
Oklahoma Chapter of the Arthritis Foundation, 5133
Osteoarthritis, 5215
Overcoming Rheumatoid Arthritis, 5217
Patient Services Resource Center, 5134
Preventing & Reversing Arthritis Naturally, 5162
Psoriatic Arthritis, 5222
Rheumatoid Arthritis, 5226
Rockland/Orange Unit of the Arthritis Foundation, 5135
Rocky Mountain Chapter of the Arthritis Foundation, 5136
San Diego Area Chapter of the Arthritis Foundation, 5137
Southern Arizona Chapter of the Arthritis Foundation Newsletter, 5138, 5227
Southern New England Chapter of the Arthritis Foundation, 5139
Spectrum, 5228
Tennessee Chapter of the Arthritis Foundation, 5140
Thumbs Up Cup, 3351
250 Tips for Making Life with Arthritis Easier, 5146
University of Michigan: Orthopaedic Research Laboratories, 5250
Utah Chapter of the Arthritis Foundation, 5141
Virginia Chapter of the Arthritis Foundation, 5142
Washington State Chapter of the Arthritis Foundation, 5144
Yoga for Arthritis: The Complete Guide, 5164
Yoga for Depression, 6078

Awards, See also Honors, Prizes

Employment Awards, 2633
Innovation of the Year Awards, 2643
National Media Owl Awards, 2662
National Support Awards, 2663
Naval Submarine League, 267
Rebuilding Together, 2678

Bereavement, See also Grief and Death & Dying

Anatomy of Bereavement, 6017
Compassion Book Service, 6018
Grief Dreams: How They Help Us Heal After the Death of a Loved One, 6020
Gundersen Lutheran Medical Center Bereavement Services, 6009
Recovery from Bereavement, 6025
Understanding Dying, Death and Bereavement, 6031

Braille, See also Visually Impaired

APH Catalog of Accessible Books for People Who Are Visually Impaired, 7838
APH Catalog of Accessible Books for People who are Visually Impaired, 7795
Access USA, 3065
Braille Blazer Printer, 3086
Braille Book Bank, 11626
Braille Book Review, 7858, 7922
Braille Business Cards & More, 3454
Braille Documents, 11863
Braille Forum, 7859
Braille Institute: Santa Barbara Center, 7549
Braille Materials Production Center, 7550
Braille Mirror, 7860
Braille Monitor, 7861
Braille N' Speak, 3088
Braille Notebook, 3455

Braille Plates for Elevator, 3362
Braille Star Theosophist, 7862
Brailled Desk Calendar, 3456
Braillemaster, 3091
Burns Braille Transcription Dictionary, 7803
Calendars, 3458
Card Chart, 3459
Computer Paper for Brailling, 3100
Enabling Technologies Company, 3112
History and Use of Braille, 7953
Horizons for the Blind, 7609
Illinois Braille Messenger, 7869
Jewish Braille Review, 7872
Lutheran Braille Evangelism Association, 7968
Maxi Marks, 3465
MegaDots, 3137
Mid-Illinois Talking Book Center, 11462
National Braille Association, 7662, 8020
National Braille Press, 7663
New York State Talking Book & Braille Library, 11653
Say What, 3244
Suburban Audio Visual Service, 11466
TAJ Braille Typewriter, 3171
Talking Books Service, 11504
Tract Messenger, 7900
West Virginia School for the Blind, 11845

Cancer

AMC Cancer Information and Counseling Line, 5252
AMC Cancer Research Center, 5880
AMC Cancer Research Center Medical Library, 11359
AMC: Cancer Information and Counseling Line, 5253
Advanced Cancer: Living Each Day, 5810
Albany Medical College: Joint Center for Cancer and Blood Disorders, 5881
Alcohol Alert #21: Alcohol and Cancer, 7310
Alliance for Lung Cancer Advocacy Support and Education, 5254
Alternative Medicine Magazine's Definitive Guide to Cancer, 5789
American Cancer Soceity: Monroe, 5256
American Cancer Society, 5257, 5875
American Cancer Society: Aberdeen, 5258
American Cancer Society: Abescon, 5259
American Cancer Society: Abingdon, 5260
American Cancer Society: Adams, 5261
American Cancer Society: Aiea, 5262
American Cancer Society: Aiken, 5263
American Cancer Society: Alachua High Five Unit, 5264
American Cancer Society: Albany, 5265
American Cancer Society: Albuquerque, 5266
American Cancer Society: Alexandria, 5267
American Cancer Society: Amador County, 5268
American Cancer Society: Amarillo, 5269
American Cancer Society: Anchorage, 5270
American Cancer Society: Anderson, 5271
American Cancer Society: Antelope Valley Eastern Sierra Unit, 5272
American Cancer Society: AshevilleAdministrative Resource Center, 5273
American Cancer Society: Ashland, 5274
American Cancer Society: Athens, 5275
American Cancer Society: Atlanta, 5276
American Cancer Society: Augusta, 5277
American Cancer Society: Austin, 5278
American Cancer Society: Baker Clay Unit, 5279
American Cancer Society: Bakersfield, 5280
American Cancer Society: Baldwin County, 5281
American Cancer Society: Barry County, 5282
American Cancer Society: Bartow West Polk Unit, 5283
American Cancer Society: Batavia Fox Valley, 5284
American Cancer Society: Baton Rouge, 5285
American Cancer Society: Bay Area, 5286
American Cancer Society: Bemidji, 5287
American Cancer Society: Billings, 5288
American Cancer Society: Birmingham, 5289
American Cancer Society: Bismark, 5290
American Cancer Society: Blackfoot, 5291
American Cancer Society: Bluefield, 5292
American Cancer Society: Bowling Green, 5293
American Cancer Society: Bradenton, 5294
American Cancer Society: Brainerd, 5295
American Cancer Society: Brawley, 5296
American Cancer Society: Brevard, 5297
American Cancer Society: Brooklyn, 5298
American Cancer Society: Broward, 5299
American Cancer Society: Brunswick, 5300
American Cancer Society: Burlington, 5301
American Cancer Society: Byfield, 5302
American Cancer Society: Cape Cod, 5303
American Cancer Society: Cape Girardeau, 5304
American Cancer Society: Carroll, 5305
American Cancer Society: Casper, 5306
American Cancer Society: Cedar Rapids, 5307
American Cancer Society: Champaign, 5308
American Cancer Society: Charlotte, 5309
American Cancer Society: Chattanooga, 5310
American Cancer Society: Cheyenne, 5311
American Cancer Society: Chicago, 5312
American Cancer Society: Citrus, 5313
American Cancer Society: Clark/Miami, 5314
American Cancer Society: Collier, 5315
American Cancer Society: Collinsville, 5316
American Cancer Society: Colorado Springs, 5317
American Cancer Society: Columbia, 5318
American Cancer Society: Columbus, 5319
American Cancer Society: Contra Costa, 5320
American Cancer Society: Corpus Christi, 5321
American Cancer Society: Council Bluffs, 5322
American Cancer Society: Covina, 5323
American Cancer Society: Culver City, 5324
American Cancer Society: Cumberland, 5325
American Cancer Society: Cuyahoga County, 5326
American Cancer Society: Dade/Miami Beach, 5327
American Cancer Society: Dallas, 5328
American Cancer Society: Dalton, 5329
American Cancer Society: Davenport, 5330
American Cancer Society: DeSoto, 5331
American Cancer Society: Denver, 5332
American Cancer Society: Des Moines, 5333
American Cancer Society: Dothan, 5334
American Cancer Society: Downey, 5335
American Cancer Society: Dubuque, 5336
American Cancer Society: Duluth, 5337
American Cancer Society: East Lansing, 5338
American Cancer Society: East Syracuse, 5339
American Cancer Society: Eastern Indiana, 5340
American Cancer Society: Eau Claire, 5341
American Cancer Society: El Dorado, 5342
American Cancer Society: El Paso, 5343
American Cancer Society: Eldersburg, 5344
American Cancer Society: Elizabeth, 5345
American Cancer Society: Elmira, 5346
American Cancer Society: Erie, 5347
American Cancer Society: Eugene, 5348
American Cancer Society: Eureka, 5349
American Cancer Society: Everett, 5350
American Cancer Society: Fargo, 5351
American Cancer Society: Fayetteville, 5352
American Cancer Society: Flagler, 5353
American Cancer Society: Flint, 5354
American Cancer Society: Florence, 5355
American Cancer Society: Flushing, 5356
American Cancer Society: Fords, 5357
American Cancer Society: Fort Dodge, 5358
American Cancer Society: Fort Myers, 5359
American Cancer Society: Fort Walton Beach, 5360
American Cancer Society: Fort Worth, 5361
American Cancer Society: Franklin County, 5362
American Cancer Society: Fremont, 5363
American Cancer Society: Fresno, 5364
American Cancer Society: Gainesville, 5365
American Cancer Society: Gambrills, 5366
American Cancer Society: Gladwin County, 5367
American Cancer Society: Glen Allen, 5368
American Cancer Society: Glen Ellyn, 5369
American Cancer Society: Grand Forks, 5370
American Cancer Society: Grand Junction, 5371
American Cancer Society: Grand Rapids, 5372
American Cancer Society: Greater Tampa, 5373
American Cancer Society: Greater Ventura, 5374
American Cancer Society: Green Bay, 5375
American Cancer Society: Green River, 5376
American Cancer Society: Greenville, 5377
American Cancer Society: Greenwood, 5378
American Cancer Society: Gulfport, 5379
American Cancer Society: Gwinnett, 5380
American Cancer Society: Hagerstown, 5381
American Cancer Society: Hamilton County, 5382

Subject Index / Cancer

American Cancer Society: Hanford, 5383
American Cancer Society: Hannibal, 5384
American Cancer Society: Hattiesburg, 5385
American Cancer Society: Helena, 5386
American Cancer Society: Hilo, 5387
American Cancer Society: Hilton Head, 5388
American Cancer Society: Honolulu, 5389
American Cancer Society: Houma, 5390
American Cancer Society: Houston, 5391
American Cancer Society: Hudson Valley, 5392
American Cancer Society: Huntington, 5393
American Cancer Society: Huntsville, 5394
American Cancer Society: Huron Valley, 5395
American Cancer Society: Indian River, 5396
American Cancer Society: Indianapolis, 5397
American Cancer Society: Ionia, 5398
American Cancer Society: Iowa City, 5399
American Cancer Society: Jackson, 5400
American Cancer Society: Jacksonville, 5401
American Cancer Society: Jacksonville Beach, 5402
American Cancer Society: Jasper, 5403
American Cancer Society: Jefferson City, 5404
American Cancer Society: Jersey Shore, 5405
American Cancer Society: Johnson City, 5406
American Cancer Society: Joplin, 5407
American Cancer Society: Kaunakakai, 5408
American Cancer Society: Kearney, 5409
American Cancer Society: Kennesaw, 5410
American Cancer Society: Kennewick, 5411
American Cancer Society: Knoxville, 5412
American Cancer Society: Kokomo, 5413
American Cancer Society: Lafayette, 5414
American Cancer Society: Lake Charles, 5415
American Cancer Society: Lake County, 5416
American Cancer Society: Lakeland, 5417
American Cancer Society: Lakes Region, 5418
American Cancer Society: Lakeshore, 5419
American Cancer Society: Lancaster, 5420
American Cancer Society: Larimer County, 5421
American Cancer Society: Las Vegas, 5422
American Cancer Society: Lathrup Village, 5423
American Cancer Society: Lawton, 5424
American Cancer Society: Leesburg, 5425
American Cancer Society: Lewistown, 5426
American Cancer Society: Lexington, 5427
American Cancer Society: Lihue, 5428
American Cancer Society: Lincoln, 5429
American Cancer Society: Little Rock, 5430
American Cancer Society: Livingston, 5431
American Cancer Society: Lompoc Valley, 5432
American Cancer Society: Long Beach, 5433
American Cancer Society: Longmont, 5434
American Cancer Society: Los Angeles, 5435
American Cancer Society: Loudonville, 5436
American Cancer Society: Louisville, 5437
American Cancer Society: Lynchburg, 5438
American Cancer Society: Macon, 5439
American Cancer Society: Madison, 5440
American Cancer Society: Manhattan, 5441
American Cancer Society: Mankato, 5442
American Cancer Society: Marco Island, 5443
American Cancer Society: Marin County, 5444
American Cancer Society: Marion, 5445
American Cancer Society: Marshall, 5446
American Cancer Society: Martin, 5447
American Cancer Society: Marysville, 5448
American Cancer Society: Mason City, 5449
American Cancer Society: Medford, 5450
American Cancer Society: Memphis, 5451
American Cancer Society: Merced, 5452
American Cancer Society: Mercer, 5453
American Cancer Society: Meridian, 5454
American Cancer Society: Minot, 5455
American Cancer Society: Missoula, 5456
American Cancer Society: Mitchell, 5457
American Cancer Society: Mobile, 5458
American Cancer Society: Modesto, 5459
American Cancer Society: Monroe, 5460
American Cancer Society: Montgomery, 5461
American Cancer Society: Moorhead, 5462
American Cancer Society: Morgantown, 5463
American Cancer Society: Morongo Basin, 5464
American Cancer Society: Mountain Valley, 5465
American Cancer Society: Muncie, 5466
American Cancer Society: Muskegon, 5467
American Cancer Society: Myrtle Beach, 5468
American Cancer Society: Napa, 5469
American Cancer Society: Nashville, 5470
American Cancer Society: Nassau Region, 5471
American Cancer Society: Natick, 5472
American Cancer Society: New Castle, 5473
American Cancer Society: New England Div, 5474
American Cancer Society: New Jersey, 5475
American Cancer Society: New Orleans, 5476
American Cancer Society: Norfolk, 5477
American Cancer Society: Norman, 5478
American Cancer Society: North Central Indiana, 5479
American Cancer Society: North Charleston, 5480
American Cancer Society: North Coast Border, 5481
American Cancer Society: North Shore, 5482
American Cancer Society: North Valley Region, 5483
American Cancer Society: Northeast Indiana, 5484
American Cancer Society: Northeast New England, 5485
American Cancer Society: Northern Arizona, 5486
American Cancer Society: Northern California, 5487
American Cancer Society: Northern Idaho, 5488
American Cancer Society: Northern Kentucky, 5489
American Cancer Society: Northern Michigan, 5490
American Cancer Society: Northern Nevada, 5491
American Cancer Society: Northern New Jersey, 5492
American Cancer Society: Northern New Mexico, 5493
American Cancer Society: Northwest Illinois, 5494
American Cancer Society: Northwest Indiana, 5495
American Cancer Society: Northwest New England, 5496
American Cancer Society: Northwest New Jersey, 5497
American Cancer Society: Northwest Suburban Illinois, 5498
American Cancer Society: Northwest Valley, 5499
American Cancer Society: Northwest Wyoming, 5500
American Cancer Society: O'Fallon, 5501
American Cancer Society: Oakland, 5502
American Cancer Society: Ogden, 5503
American Cancer Society: Oklahoma City, 5504
American Cancer Society: Omaha, 5505
American Cancer Society: Orange County Region, 5506
American Cancer Society: Orlando Metro, 5507
American Cancer Society: Osage Beach, 5508
American Cancer Society: Overland Park, 5509
American Cancer Society: Owensboro, 5510
American Cancer Society: Oxnard, 5511
American Cancer Society: Paducah, 5512
American Cancer Society: Palm Beach, 5513
American Cancer Society: Palm Beach Benefit, 5514
American Cancer Society: Palm Desert, 5515
American Cancer Society: Panama City, 5516
American Cancer Society: Parkersburg, 5517
American Cancer Society: Pasco, 5518
American Cancer Society: Peninsula, 5519
American Cancer Society: Pensacola, 5520
American Cancer Society: Petaluma, 5521
American Cancer Society: Pewaukee, 5522
American Cancer Society: Phoenix, 5523
American Cancer Society: Pierre, 5524
American Cancer Society: Pinellas, 5525
American Cancer Society: Pittsfield, 5526
American Cancer Society: Pleasant Hill, 5527
American Cancer Society: Porter, 5528
American Cancer Society: Portland, 5529
American Cancer Society: Prairie Land, 5530
American Cancer Society: Provo, 5531
American Cancer Society: Pueblo, 5532
American Cancer Society: Putnam, 5533

Subject Index / Cancer

American Cancer Society: Queens Region, 5534
American Cancer Society: Raleigh, 5535
American Cancer Society: Rancho Cucamonga, 5536
American Cancer Society: Rapid City, 5537
American Cancer Society: Redding, 5538
American Cancer Society: Region VI Washington, 5539
American Cancer Society: Rhode Island, 5540
American Cancer Society: Rhode Island &Eastern Connecticut, 5541
American Cancer Society: Ridgecrest, 5542
American Cancer Society: Riverside, 5543
American Cancer Society: Roanoke, 5544
American Cancer Society: Rochester, 5545
American Cancer Society: Rockford, 5546
American Cancer Society: Roseville, 5547
American Cancer Society: Rupert, 5548
American Cancer Society: Rutland, 5549
American Cancer Society: Saint Cloud, 5550
American Cancer Society: Saint George, 5551
American Cancer Society: Saint Joseph, 5552
American Cancer Society: Saint Louis, 5553
American Cancer Society: Saint Paul, 5554
American Cancer Society: Salinas, 5555
American Cancer Society: Salisbury, 5556
American Cancer Society: Salt Lake City, 5557
American Cancer Society: San Antonio, 5558
American Cancer Society: San Diego, 5559
American Cancer Society: San Fernando Valley, 5560
American Cancer Society: San Jose, 5561
American Cancer Society: San Luis Obispo, 5562
American Cancer Society: San Mateo County, 5563
American Cancer Society: Santa Barbara, 5564
American Cancer Society: Santa Clara County, 5565
American Cancer Society: Santa Clarita Valley, 5566
American Cancer Society: Santa Cruz County, 5567
American Cancer Society: Santa Maria, 5568
American Cancer Society: Santa Maria Valley, 5569
American Cancer Society: Santa Rosa, 5570
American Cancer Society: Sarasota, 5571
American Cancer Society: Savannah, 5572
American Cancer Society: Seattle, 5573
American Cancer Society: Sheboygan, 5574
American Cancer Society: Shreveport, 5575
American Cancer Society: Sierra View, 5576
American Cancer Society: Sikeston, 5577
American Cancer Society: Silicon Valley, 5578
American Cancer Society: Silver Spring, 5579
American Cancer Society: Simi Valley, 5580
American Cancer Society: Sioux City, 5581
American Cancer Society: Sioux Falls, 5582
American Cancer Society: Solano County, 5583
American Cancer Society: Somerset, 5584
American Cancer Society: South Bay, 5585
American Cancer Society: South Burlington, 5586
American Cancer Society: South Central Indiana, 5587
American Cancer Society: South Central Los Angeles, 5588
American Cancer Society: Southeast Indiana, 5589
American Cancer Society: Southeast New England, 5590
American Cancer Society: Southeastern Arizona, 5591
American Cancer Society: Southern Illinois, 5592
American Cancer Society: Southern New England, 5593
American Cancer Society: Southwest Colorado, 5594
American Cancer Society: Southwest Kansas, 5595
American Cancer Society: Southwest Michigan, 5596
American Cancer Society: Southwest New England, 5597
American Cancer Society: Southwest Ohio, 5598
American Cancer Society: Southwest Pennsylvania, 5599
American Cancer Society: Southwestern Indiana, 5600
American Cancer Society: Spokane, 5601
American Cancer Society: Springfield, 5602
American Cancer Society: Stark Area, 5603
American Cancer Society: State College, 5604
American Cancer Society: Staten Island, 5605
American Cancer Society: Statesboro, 5606
American Cancer Society: Sterling, 5607
American Cancer Society: Stockton, 5608
American Cancer Society: Storm Lake, 5609
American Cancer Society: Suburban Hillsborough, 5610
American Cancer Society: Suffolk Region, 5611
American Cancer Society: Summit Area, 5612
American Cancer Society: Tacoma, 5613
American Cancer Society: Tallahassee, 5614
American Cancer Society: Templeton, 5615
American Cancer Society: Tequesta, 5616
American Cancer Society: Texas City, 5617
American Cancer Society: Thousand Oaks, 5618
American Cancer Society: Topeka, 5619
American Cancer Society: Treasure Valley, 5620
American Cancer Society: Trenton, 5621
American Cancer Society: Tri-Valley, 5622
American Cancer Society: Tulare County, 5623
American Cancer Society: Tulsa, 5624
American Cancer Society: Tuscaloosa, 5625
American Cancer Society: Ukiah, 5626
American Cancer Society: Upper Peninsula, 5627
American Cancer Society: Upper Valley Texas, 5628
American Cancer Society: Victorville, 5629
American Cancer Society: Vincennes, 5630
American Cancer Society: Volusia East, 5631
American Cancer Society: Volusia West, 5632
American Cancer Society: Wabash Valley, 5633
American Cancer Society: Waco, 5634
American Cancer Society: Wailuku, 5635
American Cancer Society: Waterloo, 5636
American Cancer Society: Watertown, 5637
American Cancer Society: Waycross, 5638
American Cancer Society: Weld County, 5639
American Cancer Society: West Bay Region San Francisco County Unit, 5640
American Cancer Society: West Central Illinois, 5641
American Cancer Society: West Contra Costa County, 5642
American Cancer Society: West Hawaii, 5643
American Cancer Society: West Michigan, 5644
American Cancer Society: West Palm Beach, 5645
American Cancer Society: Westchester Region, 5646
American Cancer Society: Western New England, 5647
American Cancer Society: Western New York, 5648
American Cancer Society: Western Yavapai, 5649
American Cancer Society: White Marsh, 5650
American Cancer Society: Wichita, 5651
American Cancer Society: Willmar, 5652
American Cancer Society: Windward, 5653
American Cancer Society: Wood Area, 5654
American Cancer Society: York, 5655
American Cancer Socity: Imperial Central, 5656
American Institute for Cancer Research, 5882
American Prostate Society, 4183, 5659
American Society of Colon and Rectal Surgeons, 62
Arizona State University: Cancer Research Institute, 5883
Ask the Doctor: Breast Cancer, 5790
Association for the Cure of Cancer of the Prostate, 5660, 5876
Association of Community Cancer Centers, 5661
Boston University Cancer Research Center, 5886
Breast Cancer: Understanding Treatment Options, 5811
Brigham Young University: Cancer Research Center, 5887
Brown University: Division of Biology and Medicine, 5888
Burger King Cancer Caring Center, 5663
California Institute for Medical Research, 7035
Calvary Hospital Medical Library, 11627
CanHelp, 5664
Cancer Care, 5665
Cancer Center of Wake Forest University: Bowman Gray School of Medicine, 5889

Subject Index / Cancer

Cancer Control Society and Cancer Book House, 5666
Cancer Counseling Center of Ohio, 5667
Cancer Dictionary, 5791
Cancer Facts and Figures, 5792
Cancer Federation, 5668
Cancer Information Service (CIS), 5669
Cancer Institute of Brooklyn, 5670
Cancer Rates and Risks, 5793
Cancer Research Center, 5890
Cancer Research Center: Albert Einstein College of Medicine, 5891
Cancer Research Foundation of America, 5892
Cancer Research Institute, 5893
Cancer Research Institute of New York, 5894
Cancer Sourcebook, 5794
Cancer Therapy and Research Center, 5895
Cancer Therapy: The Independant Consumer's Guide to Non-Toxic Treatment & Prevention, 5795
Cancer Victors and Friends National Headquarters, 5671
Cancer and Leukemia Group B, 5672
Cancer of the Bladder: Research Report, 5812
Cancer of the Colon and Rectum: Research Report, 5813
Cancer of the Ovary: Research Report, 5814
Cancer of the Pancreas: Research Report, 5815
Cancer of the Uterus: Research Report, 5816
Cancer-Free: Your Guide to Gentle, 5796
Cancervive, 5673, 5797
Center for Blood Research, 4590
Chemotherapy Foundation, 5675
City of Hope, 106
City of Hope Clinical Cancer Research Center, 5896
Clearing the Air: A Guide to Quitting Smoking, 5818
Cold Spring Harbor Laboratory, 11630
Collaborative Medicine Center, 5676
Colorado Cancer Research Program, 5898
Columbia University Comprehensive Cancer Center, 5900
Commonwealth Cancer Help Program, 5677
Complete Directory for People withChronic Illness, 3701
Coping: Living with Cancer, 5806
Coriell Institute for Medical Research, 4296
Corporate Angel Network, 5678
Dana-Farber Cancer Institute Library, 11547
Dana-Farber Cancer Institute: National Drug Discovery Group for AIDS Treatment, 4597
Deaconess Hospital Horrax Library, 11548
Diet, Nutrition and Cancer Prevention: A Guide to Food Choices, 5819
Diet, Nutrition and Cancer Prevention: The Good News, 5820
Do the Right Thing: Get a Mammogram, 5821
Duke University Comprehensive Cancer Center, 5679
Eastern Cooperative Oncology Group, 5902
Emory University: Georgia Center for Cancer Statistics, 5903
Emory University: Winship Cancer Center, 5904
Everyone's Guide To Cancer Therapy, 5798

Everyone's Guide to Cancer Therapy, 5799
Exceptional Cancer Patients, 5680
Facing Forward: A Guide for Cancer Survivors, 5823
Facts About Lung Cancer, 5824
Foundation for Advancement in Cancer Therapy, 5681
Fox Chase Cancer Center: Institute for Cancer Research, 5905
Fred Hutchinson Cancer Research Center, 5906
Fred Hutchinson Cancer Research Center: Arnold Digital Library, 11829
Geraldine Brush Cancer Research Institute, 5908
Gilda's Club, 5682
Gilda's Club: Metro Detroit, 5683
Gilda's Club: Quad Cities, 5684
Gilda's Club: South Florida, 5685
Goodwin Institute for Cancer Research, 5909
Healing Choices, 4038
Health Resource, 5687
Heimlich University, 5910
Henry Vogt Cancer Research Institute, 5911
Hereditary Cancer Institute, 5912
Hipple Cancer Research Center, 5913
Home Care Guide for Cancer, 5800
How to Interpret Your Biopsy and other Lab Reports, 5825
Howard University Cancer Center, 5914
Illinois Cancer Center, 5915
Illinois Oncology Research Association, 5916
Immune System: How it Works, 5826
Indiana University: Purdue University at Indianapolis Hackney Dermatopathology Research Laboratory, 4323
Institute for Cancer and Blood Research, 5918
Iowa Oncology Research Association, 5919
Ireland Cancer Center at Case Western Reserve University, 5920
Irvington Institute for ImmunologicalResearch, 4327
JL and Helen Kellogg Cancer Care Center, 5921
Jackson Laboratory: Joan Staats Library, 11526
John P Caulfield Technology Extension Center for Cancer Treatment, 5922
Jonsson Comprehensive Cancer Center, 5924
Journal of Cancer Education, 5808
Kaplan Cancer Center, 5926
Karmanos Cancer Institute Research Library, 11563
Kentucky Cancer Program, 5927
La Jolla Cancer Research Foundation, 5928
Leukemia & Lymphoma Society: Alabama Chapter, 5690
Leukemia & Lymphoma Society: Central Florida Chapter, 5692
Leukemia & Lymphoma Society: Central New York Chapter, 5693
Leukemia & Lymphoma Society: Central Ohio Chapter, 5694
Leukemia & Lymphoma Society: Connecticut Chapter, 5697
Leukemia & Lymphoma Society: Desert Mountain States Chapter, 5698

Leukemia & Lymphoma Society: Eastern Iowa Satellite Office, 5699
Leukemia & Lymphoma Society: Eastern Philadelphia Chapter, 5700
Leukemia & Lymphoma Society: Georgia Chapter, 5702
Leukemia & Lymphoma Society: Greater Los Angeles Chapter, 5703
Leukemia & Lymphoma Society: Greater Sacramento Area, 5704
Leukemia & Lymphoma Society: Idaho Branch Office, 5705
Leukemia & Lymphoma Society: Illinois Chapter, 5706
Leukemia & Lymphoma Society: Indiana Chapter, 5707
Leukemia & Lymphoma Society: Iowa Branch Office, 5708
Leukemia & Lymphoma Society: Kansas Chapter, 5709
Leukemia & Lymphoma Society: Louisiana Chapter, 5714
Leukemia & Lymphoma Society: Maryland Chapter, 5715
Leukemia & Lymphoma Society: Mid-America Chapter, 5718
Leukemia & Lymphoma Society: Minnesota Chapter, 5719
Leukemia & Lymphoma Society: New Mexico Office, 5722
Leukemia & Lymphoma Society: New York City Chapter, 5723
Leukemia & Lymphoma Society: North Carolina Chapter, 5724
Leukemia & Lymphoma Society: North Texas Chapter, 5725
Leukemia & Lymphoma Society: Northern Florida Chapter, 5727
Leukemia & Lymphoma Society: Northern New Jersey Chapter, 5728
Leukemia & Lymphoma Society: Northern Ohio Chapter, 5729
Leukemia & Lymphoma Society: Oklahoma Chapter, 5730
Leukemia & Lymphoma Society: Oregon Chapter, 5731
Leukemia & Lymphoma Society: Palm Beach Chapter, 5732
Leukemia & Lymphoma Society: Raleigh Office, 5733
Leukemia & Lymphoma Society: Rocky Mountain Chapter, 5735
Leukemia & Lymphoma Society: San Diego & Hawaii Chapter, 5736
Leukemia & Lymphoma Society: Southern New Jersey Shore Region Chapter, 5739
Leukemia & Lymphoma Society: Southern Ohio Chapter, 5740
Leukemia & Lymphoma Society: Southwest Missouri Satellite Office, 5741
Leukemia & Lymphoma Society: Southwest Texas Chapter, 5742
Leukemia & Lymphoma Society: Texas Gulf Coast, 5745
Leukemia & Lymphoma Society: Tri-County Chapter, 5746
Leukemia & Lymphoma Society: Upstate New York Chapter, 5747
Leukemia & Lymphoma Society: Virginia Chapter, 5749
Leukemia & Lymphoma Society: Washington & Alaska Chapter, 5750

Subject Index / Caregivers

Leukemia & Lymphoma Society: Western New York & Finger Lakes Chapter, 5752
Leukemia & Lymphoma Society: Western Pennsylvania/West Virginia Chapter, 5753
Leukemia Society of America, 5755
Leukemia Society of America: Delaware Chapter, 5756
Living with Ovarian Cancer, 5874
Look Good... Feel Better, 5759
Make Today Count, 5760
Mary Bird Perkins Cancer Center Community Library, 11516
Mary Margaret Walther Center, 5931
Mayo Comprehensive Cancer Center, 5933
Medical College of Toledo: Cancer Research Division, 5934
Medical Foundation of Buffalo, 5935
Melanoma: Research Report, 5829
Michigan Cancer Foundation, 5937
NABCO Breast Cancer Resource List, 5830
NABCO News, 5831
Natalie Warren Bryant Cancer Center, 5938
National Alliance of Breast Cancer Organizations, 5761, 5878
National Cancer Institute, 5939
National Chronic Pain Outreach Association, 5762
National Coalition for Cancer Survivorship, 5763
National Foundation for Cancer Research Hotline, 5764
National Ovarian Cancer Coalition, 5879
No Less a Woman, 5801
Norris Cotton Cancer Center, 5768
Northern California Cancer Center, 5769
Northwestern University Cancer Center, 5943
Nutrition Action Healthletter, 4080
Nutrition Education Association, 5770
Ohio State University: Clinical Research Center, 5945
Older Than My Mother: A Nurse's Life & Triumph, 5802
Once a Year for a Lifetime, 5833
Oncology Nursing Society, 5771
Oral Cancers: Research Report, 5834
Patient Advocates for Advanced Cancer Treatments, 5772
People Against Cancer, 5773
Peralta Cancer Research Institute, 5948
Pohl Cancer Research Laboratory, 5949
Private Cancer Clinic Tours, 5775
Prostate Cancer Resource Network, 5776
Prostate Cancer: A Survivor's Guide, 5803
Purdue University Cancer Center, 5950
Questions and Answers About Breast Lumps, 5836
Radiation Oncology Research & Development Center, 5951
Reach to Recovery, 5777
Recurrence: What Do I Do Now?, 5841
Regional Cancer Foundation, 5778
Research Report: Adult Kidney Cancer and Wilms' Tumor, 5842
Roger Williams Cancer Research, 5952
Rose Kushner Breast Cancer Advisory Center, 5779
Roswell Park Cancer Institute, 5953
Salick Health Care, 5780
Salk Institute for Biological Studies Library, 5954, 11344

San Antonio Cancer Institute, 5956
Santa Barbara Breast Cancer Institute, 5957
Skin Cancer Foundation, 5958
Skin Cancer Foundation Journal, 5809
Skin Cancer: Preventable and Curable, 5843
Skin Cancers: Basal Cell and Squamous Cell Carcinomas: Research Report, 5844
Stanford University: Oncology Day Care Clinic, 5781
Students with Cancer: A Resource for the Educator, 5845
Sun and Skin News, 5846
Support for People with Oral and Head and Neck Cancer, 5782
Susan G Komen Cancer Foundation, 5960
Sylvester Comprehensive Cancer Center, 5783
Sylvester Comprehensive Cancer Center, Cancer Information Service, 11422
Taking Time: Support for People with Cancer & People Who Care for Them, 5849
Talbot Cancer Research Library, 11742
The Tender Scar: Life After the Death of a Spouse, 6028
Teratologies: A Cultural Study of Cancer, 5804
Testicular Cancer: Research Report, 5850
Testicular Self-Examination, 5851
Texas Department of Health Library, 11790
Third Opinion: International Directory to Complementary Therapy Centers, 3800
3rd Opinion: International Directory to Complementary Therapy Centers, 5788
Tour of Cancer Clinics, 5784
University of Arizona Cancer Center, 5963
University of California: Berkeley Cancer Research Laboratories, 5964
University of California: Irvine Cancer Research Institute, 5965
University of Chicago: Cancer Research Center, 5969
University of Colorado Cancer Center, 5971
University of Iowa Cancer Center, 5972
University of Kansas Cancer Center, 5973
University of Miami Touch Research Institute, 4410
University of Michigan Cancer Center, 5975
University of Michigan: Stimpson Memorial Institute for Medical Research, 5976
University of Minnesota: Masonic Cancer Center, 5978
University of Nebraska at Omaha: Eppley Institute for Research in Cancer, 5979
University of New Mexico Cancer Center, 5981
University of New Mexico: Center for Non-Invasive Diagnosis, 5982
University of Pennsylvania Cancer Center, 5984
University of Pennsylvania: Center for Clinical Epidemiology and Biostatistics, 4422
University of Tennessee: Memphis Cancer Center, 5989
University of Texas: MD Anderson Cancer Center, 5990
University of Utah: Rocky Mountain Cancer Data System, 5992
University of Vermont Cancer Center, 5993
Utah Cancer Center, 5995

Veterans Affairs Medical Center Research Service, 4435
Veterans Affairs Medical Center-Research Service, 4436
Veterans Affairs Medical Center: Research Service, 6295
Virginia Commonwealth University: Massey Cancer Center, 5997
W Alton Jones Cell Science Center: George and Margaret Gey Library, 11677
Wainwright House Cancer Support Programs, 5998
Wayne State University Center for Molecular Biology, 6000
What Are Clinical Trials All About?, 5852
What You Need to Know About Cancer, 5855
What You Need to Know About Cancer of the Colon and Rectum, 5856
What You Need to Know About Larynx Cancer, 5860
What You Need to Know About Lung Cancer, 5861
What You Need to Know About Oral Cancers, 5862
What You Need to Know About Prostate Cancer, 5865
What You Need to Know About Skin Cancer, 5866
What You Need to Know About Testicular Cancer, 5867
What You Need to Know About Uterine Cancer, 5868
What You Need to Know About..., 5869
What to Eat if you Have Cancer, 5805
When Cancer Recurs: Meeting the Challenge Again, 5870
When Someone in Your Family Has Cancer, 5871
Why Do You Smoke?, 5873
The Wisdom of Death: Six Paths to Understanding Loss and Grief, 6029
Women's Suffrage for Prostate Cancer Awareness, 6002
Y-Me National Organization for Breast Cancer Information & Support, 5787
Yale University: Comprehensive Cancer Center, 6004

Caregivers

Agitation... It's a Sign, 5026
Alzheimer's Association: Houston & Southeast Texas Chapter, 4791
Alzheimer's Disease, 4975, 5027
Alzheimer's Disease: Services You May Need, 4987
American Guidance for Seniors, 3825
Area Two Area: Agency on Aging, 1942
Association of Brethren Caregivers, 84
Best 25 Catalog Resources for Making Life Easier, 3698
Caregiver Survival Series: Positive Caregiver Attitudes, 3609
Confronting Alzheimer's Disease, 4957
Elder Books, 11874
Helpmates, 7062
High Country Region D Area: Agency on Aging, 1892
Just the Facts & More Kit, 4965
On Your Behalf, 3658

Orleans County Office for the Aging, 1815
Resisting Care... Putting Yourself in Their Shoes, 5033
Seniors Sites, 4159
Steps for Caregivers: Caring for Persons with Alzheimer's Disease, 5048
Steps to Enhancing Communication, 5011
Steps to Enhancing Your Home: Modifying the Environment, 5012
Way We Die, 4165

Civil Rights, See also Legal Aid

Chicago Lawyers' Committee For Civil Rights Under Law, 11084
National Right to Work Legal Defense and Education Foundation, 11282

Community Services

Beverly Council on Aging, 1268
Boulder County Aging Services Division: Elder Rights Program, 11017
Camden County Senior Center, 1886
Catholic Charities USA (CCUSA), 96
Catholic Golden Age (CGA), 97
Center for the Advancement of State Community Services Programs (CASCSP), 100
Friendship Care, 9486
Help: A Guide to Community Services for Older Citizens, 3745
Jefferson County Office of Senior Citizens Services (OSCS), 10971
La Palma Recreation & Community Services, 559
Larimer County Office on Aging (LCOA), 11020
Little Brothers: Friends of the Elderly, 929
Meadows at Friendship Village, 9921
Merced Senior Community Center, 567
National Information and Referral Support Center (NIRSC), 230
National Rural Health Association, 258
New Horizons Independent Living Center - Prescott Valley, 10635
Northeast Michigan Community Services Region 9 Area: Agency on Aging, 1368
Office for Aging and Community Services: Monterey County Department of Social Services, 569
Ridgewood at Friendship Village, 9940
Senior Companion Program of Macomb, 1386
West Alabama Regional Commission's Senior Programs: Legal Counsel for the Elderly (WARC), 10973

Computer Hardware, Software

Assistive Software Products, 3079
Dorma Architectural Hardware, 3300
Duxbury Braille Translator, 3110
GW Micro, 3119
Gibbs Associates, 11878
Goals and Objectives, 3120
Vantage Plus, 3186
Wheelchair Parts & Fasteners, 3563

Consumer Rights, Protection

Eldercare Initiative in Consumer Law (EICL), 123
Senior Citizens Law Office, 11198
Vision World Wide, 7775, 8033

Continuing Education, See also Education

AARP: Alabama-Huntsville OfficeInformation Center, 2691
AARP: Alabama-Mobile OfficeInformation Center, 2692
AARP: Alabama-Montgomery Office, 2693
AARP: Alaska-Anchorage Branch Office Information Center, 2696
AARP: Alaska-Anchorage Main Office, 2697
AARP: Arizona-Phoenix Office, 2699
AARP: Arizona-Tucson Information Center, 2700
AARP: Arkansas State Office, 2708
AARP: California-Pasadena Office, 2714
AARP: California-Sacramento Office, 2715
AARP: Colorado-Denver Office, 2735
AARP: Colorado-Pueblo Information Center, 2736
AARP: Connecticut State Office, 2739
AARP: Delaware State Office, 2744
AARP: District of Columbia State OfficeCorporate Headquarters, 2746
AARP: Florida-Miramar Office, 2749
AARP: Florida-St Petersburg Office, 2750
AARP: Florida-Tallahassee Office, 2751
AARP: Georgia State Office, 2762
AARP: Hawaii-Big IslandInformation Center, 2771
AARP: Hawaii-Honolulu Office, 2772
AARP: Hawaii-Kauai Information Center, 2773
AARP: Hawaii-Oahu Information Center, 2774
AARP: Idaho State Office, 2776
AARP: Illinois State Office, 2777
AARP: Indiana State Office, 2781
AARP: Iowa State Office, 2786
AARP: Kansas State Office, 2788
AARP: Kentucky State Office, 2799
AARP: Louisiana State Office, 2802
AARP: Maine State Office, 2804
AARP: Maryland State Office, 2806
AARP: Massachusetts State Office, 2814
AARP: Michigan-Detroit Information Cntr, 2822
AARP: Michigan-Lansing Office, 2823
AARP: Minnesota-BloomingtonInformation Center, 2826
AARP: Minnesota-St Paul Office, 2827
AARP: Mississippi State Office, 2829
AARP: Missouri Information Center North, 2830
AARP: Missouri Information Center South, 2831
AARP: Missouri-Kansas City Office, 2832
AARP: Montana State Office, 2840
AARP: Nebraska-Lincoln Office, 2841
AARP: Nebraska-Omaha Information Center, 2842
AARP: Nevada State Office, 2843
AARP: New Hampshire-ConcordInformation Center, 2844
AARP: New Hampshire-Manchester Office, 2845
AARP: New Jersey State Office, 2846
AARP: New Mexico-AlbuquerqueInformation Center, 2849
AARP: New Mexico-Sante Fe Office, 2850
AARP: New York Albany State Office, 2852
AARP: New York City State Office, 2853
AARP: North Carolina State Office, 2874
AARP: North Dakota State Office, 2884
AARP: Ohio State Office, 2885
AARP: Oklahoma-Edmond Office, 2893
AARP: Oklahoma-Oklahoma City Office, 2895
AARP: Oklahoma-Oklahoma CityInformation Center, 2894
AARP: Oregon State Office, 2897
AARP: Pennsylvania-Harrisburg Office, 2902
AARP: Pennsylvania-Philadelphia Office, 2903
AARP: Rhode Island State Office, 2912
AARP: South Carolina State Office, 2914
AARP: South Dakota-Rapid City Office, 2919
AARP: South Dakota-Sioux Falls Office, 2920
AARP: Tennessee State Office, 2921
AARP: Texas-Austin Office, 2923
AARP: Texas-Dallas Office, 2924
AARP: Texas-Houston Office, 2925
AARP: Utah State Office, 2931
AARP: Vermont State Office, 2932
AARP: Virginia State Office, 2933
AARP: Washington State Office, 2939
AARP: West Virginia State Office, 2946
AARP: Wisconsin State Office, 2948
AARP: Wyoming State Office, 2951
American Association of Nurse Anesthetists, 21
Association for Gerontology in Higher Education, 80, 11385, 11861
Grandparents Rights Organization, 143
University of Alaska Southeast Campus:Adult Education Program, 2698

Crime Victims

Office of the Attorney General: Senior Citizens Advocacy Division, 11092

Day Care Centers

Developing Adult Day Care: An Approach to Maintaining Independence, 3621
Division of Aging and Adult Services - Elder Choices, 10639
Rachel's Place Adult Day Care, 946
Senior Services of Northern Kentucky, 1135

Death & Dying, See also Bereavement and Grief

Compassion in Dying Federation, 6006
Compassionate Friends, 6007
Death: The Final Stage of Growth, 6019

1131

On Death and Dying, 6024
Rainbows for All God's Children, 6015
Talking About Death, 6027
United States Naval Academy Alumni Association: Register of Alumni, 3804

Dementia, See also Alzheimer's Disease

ABC's of Dementia, 4946
Activities for the Elderly: Volume 2-Working with Residents with Significant Physical and Cognitive,
Activity Programming for Persons with Dementia: A Sourcebook, 4947
Aegis at Shadowridge, 8132
Aegis of Carmichael, 8134
Aegis of Concord, 8136
Aegis of Pleasant Hill, 8144
Alzheimer's Association, STAR Chapter, 5041
Broadview Residential Care Center, 8162
Copper Ridge, 8909
Edward Feil Productions, 11872
Feil Method, VALIDATION, 3630
Garden of Palms, 8186
Gardens at Park Balboa, 8188
Guidelines for Dignity, 4961, 5000
Harvard Brain Tissue Resource Center, 4315
Key Elements of Dementia Care, 4966
Marlow Manor/Manor Management, 8096
University of Wisconsin-Madison Neuropsychology Laboratory, 4432

Depression

Anxiety & Depression in Adults & Children, 6066
Depression & Antidepressents: A Guide, 6067
Depression Sourcebook, 6068
Depression and Recovery From Chemical Dependency, 6087, 7332
Depression in Older Adults, 4139
Depression in the Elderly: a Multimedia Sourcebook, 6079
Encyclopedia of Depression, 6080
If You're Over 65 and Feeling Depressed..., 6088
Lithium and Manic Depression, 6091
The Mindful Way through Depression:Freeing Yourself from Chronic Unhappiness, 6077
Mood Apart, 6074
National Depressive and Manic Depressive Association, 6046
Overcoming Depression, 6075
Plain Talk About Depression, 4085
Questions & Answers About Depression & Its Treatment, 6076
Understanding Depression and Addiction, 7413

Diabetes

American Diabetes Association, 6111
American Diabetes Association Southern: New Jersey District Office, 6112
American Diabetes Association: Alaska Area Office, 6114
American Diabetes Association: Arizona Area Office, 6115
American Diabetes Association: Arkansas, 6116
American Diabetes Association: Atlanta Metro Area Office, Georgia, 6117
American Diabetes Association: Baton Rouge District Office, 6118
American Diabetes Association: Border Area Office, 6119
American Diabetes Association: Bowling Green District Office, 6120
American Diabetes Association: California, 6121
American Diabetes Association: Cedar Rapids District Office, 6122
American Diabetes Association: Central Ohio Area Office, 6123
American Diabetes Association: Central Pennsylvania Area, 6124
American Diabetes Association: Columbus District Office, 6125
American Diabetes Association: Connecticut, 6126
American Diabetes Association: Delaware/Eastern Shore Area Office, 6127
American Diabetes Association: Districtof Columbia, 6128
American Diabetes Association: East Washington/North Idaho District Office, 6129
American Diabetes Association: Eastern Regional Office, 6130
American Diabetes Association: Eugene Branch Office, 6131
American Diabetes Association: Great Lakes and Heartland Regional Office, Wisconsin, 6132
American Diabetes Association: Greater Hampton Roads Area Office, 6133
American Diabetes Association: Hawaii Area Office, 6134
American Diabetes Association: Huntsville District Office, 6135
American Diabetes Association: Iowa Area Office, 6136
American Diabetes Association: Kansas Area Office, 6137
American Diabetes Association: KentuckyArea Office, 6138
American Diabetes Association: Madison District Office, 6139
American Diabetes Association: Maryland Area Office, 6140
American Diabetes Association: Memphis District Office, 6141
American Diabetes Association: Mid-America Regional Office, 6142
American Diabetes Association: Minnesota Area Office, 6143
American Diabetes Association: Mississippi Area Office, 6144
American Diabetes Association: Missoula District Office, 6145
American Diabetes Association: MissouriArea Office, 6146
American Diabetes Association: Montana, 6147
American Diabetes Association: Mountain States & Pacific/Northwest Regional Office, 6148
American Diabetes Association: Nebraska/South Dakota Area Office, 6149
American Diabetes Association: Nevada, 6150
American Diabetes Association: New Mexico Area Office, 6151
American Diabetes Association: New Orleans District Office, Louisiana, 6152
American Diabetes Association: New York City Area Office, 6153
American Diabetes Association: North Dakota, 6154
American Diabetes Association: Northeast Texas/North Louisiana Area Office, 6155
American Diabetes Association: Northern Ohio/Cleveland Area Office, 6156
American Diabetes Association: Oklahoma Area Office, 6157
American Diabetes Association: Oklahoma City District Office, 6113
American Diabetes Association: Oregon Area Office, 6158
American Diabetes Association: Rhode Island/Massachusetts Area Office, 6159
American Diabetes Association: Seattle Area Office, 6160
American Diabetes Association: Sioux Fallls District Office, 6161
American Diabetes Association: South Central Regional Office, 6162
American Diabetes Association: South Coastal Regional Office, Central Florida Area, 6163
American Diabetes Association: Southeast Michigan Area Office, 6164
American Diabetes Association: Southern Regional Office, Eastern North Carolina, 6165
American Diabetes Association: Tennessee Area Office, 6166
American Diabetes Association: Upstate Alabama Area Office, 6167
American Diabetes Association: Utah Area Office, 6168
American Diabetes Association: Virginia Area Office, 6169
American Diabetes Association: West Virginia/Southern Ohio, 6170
American Diabetes Association: Western Pennsylvania Area Office, 6171
American Diabetes Association: Wyoming District Office, 6172
Black Experience, 6175, 6257
Clinical Diabetes, 6236
Clinical Practice Recommendations, 6183
Control Diabetes the Easy Way, 6184
Diabetes, 6228
Diabetes & Exercise Video, 6258
Diabetes 101, 6185
Diabetes A to Z, 6186
Diabetes Advisor, 6238
Diabetes Annual Vol. 8, 6187
Diabetes Care, 6229
Diabetes Care Made Easy, 6189
Diabetes Dateline, 6239
Diabetes Dictionary, 6227
Diabetes Education and Research Center, 6268
Diabetes Educator, 6240
Diabetes Forecast, 6230

Diabetes Mellitus: A Practical Handbook, 6192
Diabetes Research Center, 6269
Diabetes Research and Training Center: University of Alabama at Birmingham, 6270
Diabetes Reviews, 6231
Diabetes Self-Management, 6193, 6241
Diabetes Sourcebook - Vol. 3, 6194
Diabetes Spectrum: From Research to Practice, 6232
Diabetes Teaching Guide for People Who Use Insulin, 6195
Diabetes Update - Glucose Toxicity: The Need for 24-Hour Control, 6259
Diabetes and Brief Illness, 6242
Diabetes and Exercise, 6243
Diabetes and You, 6260
Diabetes in Old Age, 6197
Diabetes in the News, 6233
Diabetes: What You Need to Know, 6261
Diabetes: Your Complete Exercise Guide, 6199
Diabetic Cruise Desk, 12014
Diabetic's Innovative Cookbook, 6202
Do Your Level Best: Start Controlling Your Blood Sugar Today, 6247
Dr. Bernstein's Diabetes Solution, 6203
Fitness Book: For People with Diabetes, 6204
How To Cook for People with Diabetes, 6205
Indiana University: Diabetes Research and Training Center, 6272
Intensive Diabetes Management, 6206
International Diabetes Center: Institute for Research & Education Health System, 6276
Joslin Diabetes Center, 6277
Learning to Live Well with Diabetes, 6207
Living Well with Diabetes, 6265
Managing Type II Diabetes, 6208
Managing Your Gestational Diabetes, 6209
Meal Planning with Exchange Lists, 4149
Medical Management of Type II Diabetes, 6211
My Personal Goals, 4063
National Diabetes Action Network for the Blind, 6177, 7667
National Diabetes Information Clearinghouse, 6178
National Institute of Diabetes & Digestive & Kidney Disease, 6279
On Top of My Game: Living with Diabetes, 6266
Outsmarting Diabetes, 6212
Sansum Diabetes Research Institute, 4617
Staying Healthy with Type 2 Diabetes, 6251
Stop the Rollercoaster, 6217
Taking Care of Gestational Diabetes, 6252
Therapy for Diabetes Mellitus and Related Disorders, 6221
Touch of Diabetes, 6222
Type II Diabetes, 6253
University of Chicago: Diabetes Research & Training Center, 6282
University of Iowa: Diabetes Control and Complications Trial, 6283
University of Iowa: Diabetes Research Center, 6284
University of Kansas: Regional Diabetes Center, 6285
University of Massachusetts: Diabetes Endocrinology Research Center, 6286
University of Miami: Diabetes Research Institute, 6287
University of Pennsylvania: Diabetes Research Center, 6290
University of Washington: Diabetes Endocrinology Research Center, 6293
Vanderbilt University: Diabetes Research and Training Center, 6294
Voice of the Diabetic, 6235
Washington University: Diabetes Research and Training Center, 6298
When Diabetes Complicates Your Life, 6225
Whittier Institute for Diabetes & Endocrinology, 6299

Disabled, See also Handicapped

AAAS Resource Directory of Scientists and Engineers with Disabilities, 3686
AIPHONE Intercom Systems, 3057
Ability, 4003
Accent Buyers Guide Edition, 3689
Accent on Living: Buyer's Guide, 3690
Adaptive Vans for the Physically Challenged, 2954
Advocates for the Disabled, 10978
Aging And Community Service Of South CenTral Indiana, 964
Alabama Disabilities Advocacy Program, 367
Alabama Disabilities Advocacy Program (ADAP), 10969
Alliance for Disabled in Action, 10848
American Disabled for Attendant Programs, 3568
Arkenstone, 3076
Canine Assistance for the Disabled, 6325
Caring for the Disabled Elderly, 3613
Colonial Meals on Wheels, 2108
Crane Plumbing/Fiat Products, 3010
Cumberland County Office on Aging &Disabled, 1644
Dayle McIntosh Center for the Disabled, 10657
Dial-A-Ride Rural Public Transportation, 909
Disability Law Center Of Alaska, 10976
Disabled Americans Rally for Equality, 11086
Disabled Citizens Alliance for Independence-DCAI, 10818
Disabled People as Second Class Citizens, 3852
Douglas County Health & Disabilities Services, 2048
Easy Pivot Transfer Machine, 3370
Evac + Chair Emergency Wheelchair, 3044
Fitness for the Aged, Disabled and Industrial Worker, 3632
Foot Placement Ladder, 3305
Guardianship Services Associates, 11090
Headlight Dimmer Switch, 2974
ILRU Directory of Centers, SILCs, and Related Organizations (Independent Living Research Utilization, 3753
International Center for the Disabled, 4326
Left Foot Gas Pedal, 2980
Legal Services for the Elderly, Disabled or Disadvantaged of Western New York, 11203
Meals on Wheels Association of America, 164
Mental and Physical Disability Law Reporter, 3932
Mental and Physical Disability LawDigest, 3931
Mid-Columbia Senior and Disabled Services, 2054
Mini-Bus and Mini-Vans, 2985
Montana Department of Social and Rahabilitation Services, 1544
NLADA Directory of Legal Aid and Defender Offices in the United States and Territories, 3769
National Legal Center for the Medically Dependent and Disabled, 11101
New Breakthroughs, 3146
New Hampshire Developmental Disabilities Council, 1620
No Longer Disabled: The Federal Courts, 11033
Office of Supplemental Security Income, 276
Office of Supplemental Security Income: Social Security Administration, 1251
Rand-Scot, 3487
Spectrum Aquatics, 3292
Spring Dell Center, 11538
Vision and Aging: Issues in Social Work Practice, 7834
Washington State Department of Services, 2541
Weatherization Assistance for Low-Income Persons: Conservation and Renewable Energy, 342
Westchester Disabled on the Move, 10891
Wright-Way, 2999

Discrimination

ADA & the Consumer Who is Deaf or Hard of Hearing, 6597
ADA and Hearing-Impaired Consumers, 6598
Asian American Center for Justice, 77
Employment Discrimination: Age, 128
Employment Discrimination: Disabled, 129
Employment Discrimination: How to Recognize it and What to Do About it, 6646
Equip for Equality Central/Southern Illinois, 912
Equip for Equality Northeastern Region, 913
Equip for Equality Northwestern Region, 914
Gray Panthers, 144
Joy of Listening: An Auditory Training Program, 6520
National Association of Guide Dog Users, 7660, 8018
Old Lesbians Organizing for Change, 277
Speech Discrimination Unit, 3163
Third Age Press, 11904
US Department of Education: Office of Civil Rights, 325
US Department of Transportation, 330
Unseen Minority: A Social History of Blindness in the United States, 7832

Subject Index / Education, See also Continuing Education

Virginia Office for Protection and Advocacy, 2499

Education, See also Continuing Education

ADA Clinical Education Series on CD-Rom, 6256
Air Force Aid Society, 6
Alabama Department of Education: Disability Determination Service, 359
Alabama Department of Public Health, 4446
Alexander Graham Bell Association for the Deaf and Hard of Hearing, 6306
Alzheimer's Association Tarrant County Chapter, 4984
Alzheimer's Association of Southern Minnesota Chapter, 4719
Alzheimer's Association: Dubuque Branch, Mississippi Valley Chapter, 4750
Alzheimer's Association: Dubuque Branch Mississippi Valley Chapter, 4749
Alzheimer's Association: Greater Maryland Chapter Western Maryland Region, 4773
Alzheimer's Disease Support Group Janesville Chapter, 4917
Alzheimer's Disease Support Group: Janesville Chapter, 4918
Alzheimer's Disease: an Educational Training Program for Social Workers, 5028
American Academy of Ambulatory Care Nursing, 8
American Academy of Otolaryngology: Head and Neck Surgery, 12
American Academy of Otolaryngology:Head and Neck Surgery, 6310
American Association of Critical Care Nurses, 19
American Association of Diabetes Educators, 6110
American Association of Occupational Health Nurses, 22
American Association of Office Nurses, 23
American Association of Physician Specialists, 24
American Association of Retired Persons, 3567
American Association of the Deaf-Blind, 7503
American Baptist Homes and Hospitals Association, 27
American College Health Association, 32
American College of Clinical Pharmacology, 33
American Council for Drug Education, 7133, 7439
American Deaf Culture: An Anthology, 6466
American Federation of Teachers HIV/AIDS Education Project, 4449
American Foundation for the Blind Southwest, 7507
American Foundation for the Blind: Chigago, 7510
American Foundation for the Blind: Washington DC, 7513
American Licensed Practical Nurses Association, 44
American Medical Association, 45
American Nephrology Nurses' Association, 50
American ORT, 2855
American Society for Geriatric Dentistry, 59
American Society of Contemporary Medicine Surgery & Ophthalmology, 7516
American Urological Association, 6944
Arizona Department of Health Services, 4450
Arlington County Bar Association: Legal Services of Northern Virginia, 11280
Army Emergency Relief, 76
Arthritis Foundation Oregon Chapter, 5090
Arthritis Foundation: Northeastern California Chapter, 494
Association for Continuing Higher Education Directory, 3696
Association of Black Nursing Faculty, 83
Berthold Lowenfeld on Blindness and Blind People, 7801
Black and Deaf in America, 6474
Bone Up on Arthritis, 5157
Braille Revival League, 7551, 8009
CDC National Prevention Information Network, 4452
Captioned Media Program, 6327
Captioned Media Program: National Association of the Deaf, 11755
Caresource Healthcare Communications, 4186, 11866
Center for Adult Learning and Educational Credentials, 98
Center for Learning in Retirement, 2904
Central Ohio Chapter of the Arthritis Foundation, 5096
Chicago Department of Health, 4455
Coalition of Wisconsin Aging Groups, 2572
Cochlear Implant Association, 6334
Community Health Charities of Illinois, 908
Connecticut Bar Association: Section on Legal Problems of the Elderly, 11023
Connecticut Board of Education and Services for the Blind, 675
Consultation and Education Unlimited, 4188
Continuing Education Center at RB, 2719
Convention of American Instructors of the Deaf, 6340
D.V.H. Quarterly, 7928
Deaf Adults Education Access Program, 6344
Deaf and Hard of Hearing Entrepreneurs Council, 6347
Delaware Bar Association Committee on Law and the Elderly, 11037
Delaware Department of Health and Social Services: Division of Public Health, 4458
Dell Rapids Sportsmen's Club, 12013
Diabetes Education Goals, 6190
Directory of Health Education Programs for Elders, 3716
Disability Rights Now, 3848, 4027
Division of Continuing Education, 2747
Donovan Scholars Program, 2800
Douglas County Activity Association, 2574
Drug Abuse Resistance Education of America, 7154
EAR Foundation, 6352
EHOVE Ghirst Adult Career Center, 2886
Educare Press, 11871
Educational Perspective, 6643
Elderhostel Catalog, 3730
Elderhostel Institute Network, 12017
Elderscholar, 2934
End-Stage Renal Disease: Choosing A Treatment That's Right for You, 6248
Experience Works, 132
Federal Bar Association, 11044
Florham Institute for Lifelong Learning (FILL), 2847
Florida Association of Homes for the Aging 745
Florida Department of Health & Rehabilitative Services: AIDS Program, 4460
Florida School for the Deaf and Blind, 11413
Fountains at Millbrook, 9839
Fountains at Sea Bluffs, 8185
Friends for Sight, 7591
Georgia Department of Human Resources: Division of Public Health, 4461
Governor Baxter School for the Deaf Library, 11525
Grants for Literacy, Reading & Adult/Continuing Education, 3737
Greater Chicago Chapter of the Arthritis Foundation, 5102
Guide Dogs for the Blind, 7600
HEATH Resource Center, 146
HEATH Resource Directory, 3743
Hartford Consortium for Higher Education Adult Learning Program, 2740
Healing Light Center Church, 5686
Health Education AIDS Liaison (HEAL), 4463
Hearing Education and Awareness for Elders, 6785
Hearing Education and Awareness for Rockers, 6366
Hearling Loss Association of America, 6371
Hemlock Society USA, 148
House Ear Institute: Care Center Parent Resource Library, 11341
Illinois Church Action on Alcohol Problems, 7167
Illinois Department of Public Health, 4466
Illinois School for the Deaf Media Center, 11458
Illinois School for the Visually Impaired Library, 11459
Indiana School for the Deaf: Alumni Hall Library, 11482
Institute for Senior Education, 2861
International Hearing Society, 6379
International Organization for the Education of the Hearing Impaired, 6383
Jewish Council for the Aging, 3580
Kansas Commission on Disability Concerns, 1065
Kansas Department of Health & Environment, 4468
Kansas Geriatric Education Center (KS-GEC), 2792
Kentucky Cabinet for Education, Arts and The Humanities: Commission for the Deaf and Hearing Impaire, 1108
Kentucky Chapter of the Arthritis Foundation, 5113
Legal Action Center, 4056
Legal Rights of Persons with Disabilities: An Analysis of Federal Law, 3760

Subject Index / Electronic Resources

Life Enrichment Program of El Dorado, 2794
Maine Department of Human Services: Disease Control Division, 4472
Maine State Bar Association: Section on Elder Law, 11137
Maryland Society for Sight, 7642
Media Access Group, 7645
Military Order of the World Wars, 171
Missouri Department of Health and Senior Services, 4477
Mount Vernon Center for Community Mental Health: Deaf Services, 6398
National Academy of Elder Law Attorneys, 182
National Association for Continence, 4222, 6948
National Association for Senior Living Industries, 186
National Association for Visually Handicapped, 8014
National Association for Visually Handicapped (NAVH), 7655
National Association of Blind Educators, 7656
National Association of Counselors, 189
National Association of Senior Companion Project Directors, 200
National Association of the Deaf Law, 6788
National Black Deaf Advocates, 6403
National Catholic Office of the Deaf, 6405
National Center on Arts and the Aging, 208
National Center on Deafness, 6408
National Certification Board for Diabetes Educators, 6176
National Council of Administrators of Adult Education (NCAAE), 2866
National Council on Alcoholism and Drug Dependence, 7190, 7448
National Federation of Licensed Practical Nurses, 225
National Federation of the Blind: Sligo Creek Chapter, 7686
National Heart, Lung, and Blood Institute Information Center, 11536
National Native American AIDS Prevention Center, 4482
National Technical Institute for the Deaf, 6418
Nebraska Bar Association: Elderlaw Committee, 11179
Nevada Department of Human Resources: Health Program Section, 4484
New Hampshire Department of Health and Human Services, 4485
New Jersey Academy of Audiology, 6421
New Mexico Educational Retirement Board, 1718
North Atlanta Senior Services, 2764
North Carolina Assistive Technology Projects, 1902
North Carolina Department of Health & Natural Resources: Communicable Disease Control Section, 4490
Northeast Kansas Area: Agency on Aging, 1079
Northwest Geriatric Education Center, 11831
Northwestern Connecticut AIDS Project, 4614
Nurses Christian Fellowship, 274
OASIS Akron, 2887

OASIS Houston, 2927
OASIS of Escondido, 2724
Oasis Logan County Senior Center, 934
Osher Lifelong Learning InstituteCollege of Extended Studies, 2726
Osherlifelong Learning Institutet, 2881
Outstanding Continuing Education Student Awards, 2669
Outstanding Newsletter Recognitions, 2670
Outstanding Service Medallion, 2671
Perspectives in Education and Deafness, 6588
Population Reference Bureau, 4360
President's Award for Exceptional andInnovative Leadership in Adult and Continuing Education, 2675
Prince George's Community College, 2812
Purdue University: Humanities, Social Science, Education Library, 11485
Resource Directory of Special Education and Rehabilitation Computer Products, 3159
Resources For Enriching Adult Learning(REAL), 11103
Resources and Services Database, 4541
Retirement Industry Trust Association, 305
Rhode Island Department of Health: Division of Disease Control, 4498
Rochester Institute of Technology: National Technical Institute for the Deaf, 6440
SCORE of Tulsa, 1051
SHHH Journal, 6589
School of Living, 2910
School of Metaphysics, 2836
Self-Help for Hard of Hearing People: Rochester Chapter, 6443
Self-Help for Hard of Hearing People: South Nassau Chapter, 6444
Senior Adult Education, 2944
Senior Adult Education Center for Applied Gerontology, 2890
Senior Citizens Educational Program, 2930
Senior Summer School, 2759, 4252
Society for Advancement in Nursing, 316
South Carolina Department of Health & Environmental Control: Bureau of Preventive Health Services, 4499
State Bar of Michigan: Senior Justice Committee, 11160
Teaching Strategies for the Developmentof Auditory Verbal Communication, 6768
Tennessee Department of Health: AIDS Program, 4502
Texas Association of Area Agencies on Aging, 2374
Texas Department of Health: Bureau of HIV and STD Control, 4503
University of Continuting Education Association: Membership Directory, 3805
University of San Francisco: Fromm Institute for Lifelong Learning, 2734
University of South Florida: Center for HIV Education & Research, 4635
University of Washington Northwest: Geriatric Education Center, 4430
Utah Department of Health Division of Community Health Services, 2414
Utah Department of Health: Division of Community Health Services, 4637
Vermont Department of Healt: HIV/AIDS Program, 4506, 4582

Washington Department of Health: Division of AIDS/HIV/STD, 4508
Wisconsin Bar Association: Elder Law, 11297
Wisconsin State Chapter of the ArthritisFoundation, 5145

Electronic Resources

AARP, 4171
AARP-Consumer Protection, 4172
Council of Better Business Bureau, 116, 4189
Federal Trade Commission, 135, 4196
Food and Drug Administration, 138, 7443
Generations Online, 4201
Internet Health Coalition, 4211
Medical Library Association, 166, 4214
Medicare, 4215
MedlinePlus®, 4217
NIA Publishers, 4219
National Center on Elder Abuse, 209, 4227
National Domestic Violence Hotline, 4229
National Institute of Dental and Craniofacial Research, 4231
National Organization for Victim Assistance, 247, 4236
10 Questions to Help You Make Sense of Health Headlines, 4168
Partnership for Prescription Assistance, 4241
Peter Lamy Center for Drug Therapy and Aging, 4359, 7449
QuackWatch, 4243
Senior Health, 4247

Employment

ADARA Updated, 3999
Equal Employment Advisory Council, 11043
Florida Division of Vocational Rehabilitation, 756
Governor's Committee on Employment of Persons with Disabilities, 374
Independent Living Services for Older Individuals who are Blind, 6375
Job Opportunities for the Blind, 7623
Kansas Employment Services and Job Training Program Liaison, 1072
Meeting the Needs of Employees with Disabilities, 3764
National Association of Blind Lawyers, 7657, 8016
National Center on Employment for the Deaf, 6409
National Federation of the Blind: Music Division, 7683
National Federation of the Blind: Public Employees Division, 7684, 8028
Ohio Governor's Council on People with Disabilities, 1968
Putting You in the Successful Employment Picture, 6702
Questions and Answers About Employment of Deaf People, 6703
Robert B. Irwin Award, 2680
Senior Job Bank, 310
Senior Service America (SSA), 311
Seniors Action Service Caring Home Aid Program, 956

Statistical Handbook on Aging Americans, 3672
Vision Use in Employment (VUE), 7774
Work, Health and Income Among the Elderly, 3682

Excercise, See also Physical Therapy

Get Fit While You Sit, 11691
MedDev Corporation, 3265
ShapeWalking, 11700
Strength Training for Seniors, 3674, 11701

Family Relations

Al-Anon Family Group Headquarters, 7126
Alcoholism, a Merry-Go-Round Named Denial, 7319
Alcoholism: The Family Disease, 7320
Alzheimer's Association: Laurel Mountains Chapter, 4797
Alzheimer's Association: Topeka Regional Office Heart of America Chapter, 4893
Alzheimer's Disease Orientation Kit, 4948
Alzheimer's Disease: Activity-Focused Care, 4952
Alzheimer's Resource Center Orlando, 4924
Alzheimer's Support Groups for Family and Friends, 4925
Amazing Grace Family Living, 8080
American Foundation for Urologic Disease: Us Too Line, 5657
Amphibious ATV Distributors, 3417
Arizona Department of Family Health Services, 428
Arkansas Division of Developmental Disabilities Services, 465
Assistive Technology Educational Network of Florida, 733
Baylor University Institute forGerontological Studies, 4269
Bernardston Council on Aging, 1267
Brown University Population Studies and Training Center, 4276
Bureau of Naval Personnel: Fleet and Family Support Center, 496
Caregiver Alliance, 94
Caring for Those You Love: A Guide to Compassionate Care for the Aged, 3611
Caring for the Diabetic Soul, 6182
Core Family Care Center, 9460
Depressive Illnesses: Treatments Bring New Hope, 6072
Digital and Audible Family Thermometer, 3253
Do You Hear Me?, 6499
Eastern Colorado Services for the Disabled, 645
Elder Abuse: 5 Case Studies, 4140
Enabling, 7342
Ethical Considerations: Issues in Diagnostic Disclosure, 4997
Eureka Ward Family History Center, 11338
Facts About Alcohol Abuse, 7343
Family, 5198
Family Carebook, 3628
Family Denial, 7344
Family Guide for Alzheimer's Care in Residential Settings, 4999
Family: Making the Difference, 5199

Financial Aid for the Disabled and Their Families, 3734
Forgotten Family, 6652
Forsyth Center for the Deaf and Hard of Hearing, 6358
Free to Care, 7345
Guide for the Family of the Alcoholic, 7349
Guide to Helping Elderly Relatives Near and Far, 4145
Healing Well, 4207
Helen Keller National Center for Deaf & Blind Southeast Regional Office, 836
Holy Family Adult Foster Home, 8091
Holy Family Assisted Living Home, 8092
Homeward Bound, 7350
IDF Patient and Family Handbook, 4047
Illinois Family & Social Services, 7169
Missing Words: The Family Handbook on Adult Hearing Loss, 6534
Mountain Empire Older Citizens, 2463
My Mother, My Father: Seven Years Later, 4152
National Council on Child Abuse (NCCAFV), 218
National Family Association for Deaf-Blind, 6412
National Family Caregivers Association (NFCA), 223
Neighborhood Family Care, 2834
North Carolina Association of Long Term Care Facilities, 1903
Older Adults After Treatment, 7390
Potentials Development, 11894
Something Should be Done About Grandma Ruthie, 5034
Southern Plantation, 8441
Standing By You: Family Support Groups, 5010
TERRA-JET: Utility Vehicle, 3442
Terms & Tips: An Alzheimer Care Handbook, 5019
36-Hour Day, 4944
To Our Family Members Who Are Hard of Hearing, 6720
Travis L Williams Family Services Center, 11324
Tucson Family History Center, 11325
United Methodist Association of Health and Welfare Ministries (UMA), 335
University of Akron Institute for LifeSpan Development and Gerontology, 4381
Washington County Historical Society: Genealogy and Historical Library, 11106
What Every Family Should Know About Stroke, 7110
Yellow Brick House, 8446
You Can Make a Difference: 10 Ways to Help an Alzheimer Family, 5024

Financial Assistance

Capital Assistance Program for Elderly and Persons with Disabilities, 93
Civil Rights Compliance Activities, 107
Fund for Assuring an Independent Retirement, 141
Leukemia & Lymphoma Society: Tennessee Chapter, 5744
National Institute on Financial Issues and Services for Elders, 235

Non-Discrimination in Federally Assisted Programs, 271
Pension Research Council (PRC), 288
SPRY Foundation, 306

Food, See also Nutrition

AIDS: Distinguishing Between Fact and Opinion, 4519
Best Guide to Allergy, 4655
Black & Decker Cordless Hand Blender, 3322
California Association for Older Americans, 502
Carbohydrate Counting, 4019
Deluxe Roller Knife, 3328
Easy Food Tips for Heart Healthy Eating, 6858
FAN Flashbacks, 4666
Food Allergy Anaphylaxis Network, 4649, 4678
Food Allergy Network, 4198
Food Allergy: A Primer for People, 4658
Food Donation Program: Food Distribution Center, 137
Great Buys for People over 50, 3739
Guide A Knife, 3336
Guidelines for Managing Diabetes During Brief Illness, 6263
Handy-Helper Cutting Board, 3337
I Can't Chew Cookbook, 11692
Innerlip Plates, 3338
Magnetic Card Reader, 3340
Meals on Wheels Assoiation of America Directory, 3763
Paring Boards, 3343
Senior Gleaners, 614
Steel Food Guard, 3348
Vegetarian Times, 3967

Frail Elderly

City of Albuquerque-Bernalillo County:Department of Senior Affairs, 1709
Hospital Audiences, 153
Integrated Care Communities, 8196
Lake Cumberland Area Development District Area: Agency on Aging, 1122
Ohio Department of Aging, 1964

Funeral

American Blue Book of Funeral Directors, 3693
Funeral Consumers Alliance, 11275
International Cemetery and Funeral Association, 6011
National Yellow Book of Funeral Directors, 3775
Purple Directory: National Listing of African-American Funeral Firms, 3785

Generations

Aging and Vision, 7916
All About the New Generation of Hearing Aids, 6604
Generations, 3864
Generations United, 726
Love You Forever, 6023

National Academy for Teaching and
Learning About Aging, 181
National Silver-Haired Congress: Kansas
Department on Aging, 1077
Prevention of Blindness Society of
Metropolitan Washington, 7733
RP Foundation Fighting Blindness (RPFFB),
7734
Sandwich Generation, 3956
University of North Texas: Health Science
Center at Fort Worth, 8058

Gerontology

Abstracts in Social Gerontology, 4004
Abstracts in Social Gerontology: Current
Literature on Aging, 3592, 3688, 3818
Aging and Society, 3824
Alzheimer's Association: Green-Field
Library, 11451
American Association of Retired Persons:
Research Information Center, 11382
American Orthopaedic Association, 5082
American Physiological Society, 53
Boston University Gerontology Center, 4271
Case Western Reserve University Elderly
Care Research Center, 4279, 11705
Center for Bio-Gerontology, 11867
Contemporary Gerontology, 3844
Data Resources in Gerontology: A Directory
of Selected Information Vendors,
Databases, and Archives, 3711
Distinguished Mentorship in Gerontology
Award, 2628
Gerontology, 3868
Gerontology & Geriatrics Education, 3869
Gerontology News, 4035
Gerontology Special Interest Section
Quarterly, 4036
Gerontology: Responding to an Aging
Society, 3634
Hartford Hospital: Gerontology Resource
Center, 11374
Issues in Aging and Vision: A Curriculum
for University Programs and In-Service
Training, 7817
National Directory of Educational Programs
in Gerontology and Geriatrics, 3771
National Gerontological Nursing
Association, 226
Pennsylvania State University: Human
Development Collection, 11739
Philadelphia Corporation for Aging Library,
11740
San Jose State University Gerontology
Education and Training Center, 4370
Syracuse University: Gerontology Center,
4374
University of Georgia: Gerontology Center,
4396
University of Maryland: Center for the
Study of Pharmacy and Therapeutics for
the Elderly, 4406
University of North Texas: Center for
Studies in Aging, 4419
Wichita State University: Gerontology
Center, 4440
Yeshiva University: Resnick Gerontology
Center, 5080

Grandparenting

Grandparents Raising Grandchildren, 4144
Our Grandchild, 4239

Grief, See also Bereavement and Death & Dying

Compassion Books, 6005
Death and Dying Health Pamphlets, 6034
Grief and Loss Program, 6008
Grief, Dying and Death, 6021
No Longer Immune: A Counselor's Guide to
AIDS, 4530
Treatment of Complicated Mourning, 6030

Handicapped, See also Disabled

Accent on Living, 3819
Alabama Radio Reading Service Network,
369
Broadcast Services for the Blind, 11336
Canine Helpers for the Handicapped, 7555
Capital Area Center for Independent Living,
10800
Colorado Department of Social Service,
11360
Connecticut Braille Association, 7571
Coping with the Multi-Handicapped Hearing
Impaired: A Practical Approach, 6494
Delaware Department of Education, 707
Division for the Visually Handicapped,
11817
Federal Laws of the Mentally Handicapped:
Laws, Legislative Histories and Admin.
Documents, 4029
Good Faith, 2226
Handbook of Assistive Devices for the
Handicapped Elderly, 3744
Indiana University Bloomington Center on
Aging and Aged, 4320
Ohio School for the Deaf Alumni
Association, 6427
Options: A Directory of Child and Senior
Services, 3779
Oregon School for the Blind Media Center,
11725
Parkersburg and Wood County Public
Library, 11839
Recording Service for Visually
Handicapped, 7736
Recording for the Blind News, 7894, 7983
Rent-A-Van-Handicapped Driver Services,
2991
Rodeway Inns, 12043
Shilo Inns & Resorts, 12045
Verde Valley Senior Citizens Association,
452
Western Law Center for Disability Rights,
11015
Youngstown Radio Reading Service, 7789

Health Care

AA as a Resource for Health Care
Professionals, 7291
Alliance Newspaper, 3976
American Association of Colleges of
Osteopathic Medicine, 18
American Association of Managed Care
Nurses, 20
American College of Health Care
Administrators: Information Center,
11812
American Correctional Health Services
Association, 36
American Geriatrics Society, 3569
American Health Care Association, 41, 4009
American Radiological Nurses Association,
57
American Society of Neuroradiology, 66
American Society of Peri-Anesthesia
Nurses, 67
American Society of Plastic Surgeons, 68
American Society of Post-Anesthesia
Nurses, 69
Association for Professionals in Infection
Control and Epidemiology, 81
Briggs Corporation, 11864
Bureau of Health Professions, Health
Resources and Services Administration,
1229
Center for Public Representation, 11868
Clarke Health Care Products, 3007
Cleveland Health Care Center, 9456
Creighton University Center for Healthy
Aging, 4298
Dermatology Nurses' Association, 120
Emergency Nurses Association, 126
Evergreen Idaho Health Care Sandpoint,
8504
Facilitating Self Care Practices in
theElderly, 3626
Families USA Foundation, 133
Frontier Nursing Service, 8844
Geriatric Oral Health Care Award, 2637
Gray Panthers Metropolitan, 727
Gray Panthers of Austin, 2322
Hawaii Disability Compensation Division:
Department of Labor and Indian
Relations, 863
Health Care Bridges, 8089
Health Care of the Aged, 3636
Health Watch, 3874
Hearing Health, 6579
Hearing Journal, 6580
Home Health Service Directory, 3749
Independent Living Provider, 3882
International Holistic Center, 5688
James P Mills Arthritis Resource Center,
5111
Managing Your Health Care, 5208
Medicare Hospital Insurance, 167
NIH: Environmental Health Sciences, 173
NIH: National Institute of Dental and
Cracial Research, 176
National Committee for Quality Healthcare,
212
National Council on Aging: Ollie A Randall
Library, 11400
National Health Federation, 5765
National Organization of HIV over Fifty,
248
National Training Center for Professional
AIDS Education, 4483
National Voluntary Organizations for
Independent Living for the Aging, 3582
Norfolk Senior Center & Adult Day Health
Care, 2464
Ohio Department of Health: Division of
Preventive Medicine, 4491

Subject Index / Health Insurance, See also Insurance

People's Medical Society, 292
Power of Attorney for Health Care, 3661
Rock County Health Care Center Staff Library, 11848
Society for Ambulatory Care Professionals, 317
South Dakota Association of Homes for the Aging, 2264
Special Care Dentistry, 318
Type 2 Diabetes: Your Healthy Living Guide, 6223
University of Minnesota: Division of Health Services Research and Policy, 6105
Wayne State University: Institute of Gerontology, 4439
Wisconsin Department of Health and Social Services: Division of Health, 4511

Health Insurance, See also Insurance

America's Health Insurance Plans, 7
Rascal Insurance Services, 299
Small Business and AIDS: How AIDS can Affect Your Business, 4570
Southeast Minnesota Area: Agency on Aging, 1435
Taxes and Alzheimer's Disease, 5018
World Institute on Disability, 345

Hearing Aids, See also Hearing Impaired

Cleveland Hearing and Speech Center, 6332
Cognition, Education and Deafness, 6480
Deafness 1993-2013, 6497
Developments in Technology, 6639
Digital Hearing Aids: An Update, 6640
Facts About Hearing Aids, 6648
Facts and Fancies About Hearing Aids, 6649
Financial Help for Hearing Aids, 6650
Getting the Most Out of Your Hearing Aids, 6752
Hearing Aids and the Consumer: Current Wisdom, 6664
Sensor Hearing Aids, 6445
Telecoils in Hearing Aids, 6770

Hearing Impaired

Adult Bible Lessons for the Deaf, 6600
Alexander Graham Bell Association for the Deaf, 6307
Alexander Graham Bell Association for the Deaf and Hard of Hearing, 6776
American Annals of the Deaf, 6570
American Annals of the Deaf: Reference Issue, 6556
American Hearing Research Foundation, 6605, 6794
American Hearing Research Foundation Newsletter, 6606
American Tinnitus Association, 6317
Ameriphone Hearing Assistance Telephone, 3069
Brooklyn College of City University of New York: Speech & Hearing Center, 6797
Central Institute for the Deaf, 6329
Cleveland West Chapter: Self-Help for Hard of Hearing People, 6333
Communication Therapy for Hearing Impaired Adults, 6488
Communications Services for the Deaf and Hard of Hearing, 6337
Council on Education of the Deaf, 6341, 6781
Deaf Culture Autobiographies, 6746
Deaf/Hard of Hearing Entrepreneur of the Year, 2627
Deafness Research Foundation, 6782, 6800
Directory of Interpreters for Persons who are Deaf, Hard of Hearing or Deaf-Blind, 6561, 7845
Duracell & Rayovac Hearing Aid Batteries, 3277
Educating the Deaf: Psychology, Principles and Practices, 6501
Gallaudet Encyclopedia of Deaf People and Deafness, 6505
Hear You Are, 6565
Hearing Aid Batteries, 3279
Hearing Aid Battery Testers, 3280
Hearing Aid Dehumidifier, 3281
Hearing Impaired Persons of Charlotte County Florida, 6367, 6368
Hearing Rehabilitation Foundation, 1286
House Ear Institute, 6374, 6786
How to Survive a Hearing Loss, 6510
I Can Hear!, 6756
I Only Hear You When I See Your Face, 6758
In the Ear Hearing Aid Battery Extractor, 3282
International Center for Hearing & Speech Research, 6803
Journal of Speech and Hearing Research, 6583
Lexington School for the Deaf, 6390
Lloyd Hearing Aid Corporation, 3283
Looking Back: A Reader on the History of Deaf Communities & Sign Language, 6531
Minnesota Academy of Audiology, 6806
Name Brand Hearing Aids, 3285
National Association of the Deaf, 6401, 6586
National Institute on Deafness & Other Communication Disorders, 6807
National Organization for Hearing Research, 6415
Oregon Hearing Society, 2065
Products for People With Disabilities, 3783
Self-Help for Hard of Hearing People, Cleveland West Chapter, 6442
Society of Hearing Impaired Physicians, 6446
Software to Go, 6547
South Carolina Association of the Deaf, 6447
Special Friend of Hearing Impaired People Award, 2684
Teaching English to the Deaf as a Second Language, 6590
Telecaption Adapter, 3178
Understanding Deafness Socially, 6550
VISION, 6551
Wisconsin Alliance of Hearing Professionals, 6463
You Shared the World with Me Video, 6772

Heart Disease

Boston University: Whitaker Cardiovascular Institute, 6865
Cardiovascular Research and Training Center: University of Alabama, 6866
Heart Disease Research Foundation, 6875
Heart Research Foundation of Sacramento, 6876
Hope Heart Institute, 6878
Miami Heart Institute, 6883
NIH: Heart, Lung & Blood Institute, 174
National Heart, Lung & Blood Institute, 4230
National Heart, Lung and Blood Institute, 6842
Rockefeller University: Laboratory of Cardiac Physiology, 6889
Rocky Mountain Heart Research Institute, 6890
University of Rochester: Clinical Research Center, 6900
University of Tennessee: Division of Cardiovascular Diseases, 6847
University of Utah: Artificial Heart Research Laboratory, 6903
University of Utah: Cardiovascular Genetic Research Clinic, 6904
Urban Cardiology Research Center, 6905

Hobbies, See also Recreation, Sports

Butler Township Senior Citizens, 2102
Dazor Manufacturing Corporation, 3299
Wheelchair Aide, 3562
Writing from Within, 11703

Home Care

Advanced Temporary Services, 3565
American Association for Respiratory Care, 16
Arizona Area Agency on Aging: Region One, 425
Bieske's Country Comfort Home Care, 10608
Buffalo Senior Center, 1753
Caregiving at Home, 4992
Central Arkansas Area: Agency on Aging, 469
Franklin County Home Care Corporation, 1280
A Friend's House Adult Day Services, 1336
Homemaker Program, 916
Hospice Foundation of America (HFA), 152
In-Home Care Services Directory, 3754
Managed Home Care Sourcebook, 3762
National Association for Home Care and Hospice (NAHC), 185, 4223
National Association of Activity Professionals, 187
1B Area: Agency on Aging, 1335
Senior Home Care Services, 1324
Steps to Finding Home Health Care, 5013

Honors, See also Awards, Prizes

Aegis Escondido, 8130
Aegis of Dana Point, 8138

Subject Index / Hospices

American Association for Adult and Continuing Education, 15
Armed Forces Benefit Association, 74
Clark Tibbitts Award, 2623
Claude Pepper Award, 2624
Donald P. Kent Award, 2630
Geneva Mathiasen Award, 2635
Glen Bollinger Humanitarian Award, 2638
Group Development Awards, 2640
Jacobus TenBroek Award, 2647
Mildred M. Seltzer Distinguished Service Recognition, 2656
Newel Perry Award, 2667
Ollie A. Randall Award, 2668
Professional Advisory Support Award, 2676
Vernon Henley Media Award, 2688

Hospices

Caring Connections, 95
Guide to the Nation's Hospices, 3741
Hospice Alternative, 6022
Hospice Association of America, 151, 6010
Hospice Care for Patients with Advanced Progressive Dementia, 4963
Hospices Directory, 3752
National Home Care and Hospice Directory, 3773
National Hospice Helpline, 5766
National Institute for Jewish Hospice (NIJH), 6014
National Prison Hospice Association, 252
Senior Options Online Guide to Senior Services, 4251

Hot Lines

AAN-MA's Toll-Free Hotline, 4641
AARP Legal Advocacy Group, 11039
AFB Toll-Free Hotline, 7496
AIDS Community Resources, 4444
AIDS and Deafness: Resource Directory, 4537, 6554
ASMA Hotline, 4642
Allergy Products Directory: Allergy/Asthma, Finding Help (Volume Three), 4663
Alzheimer's Association Hotline, 4710, 5040
Canine Listener, 6616
Drug-Free Workplace Hotline, 7155
Michigan Department of Community Health, 1357
Michigan Department of Public Health: Bureau Infectious Disease Control, 4474
Mississippi Department of Public Health: AIDS/HIV Prevention Program, 4476
New Hampshire Legal Assistance, 11185
New Mexico Health Department: Public Health Division, 4488
Northeast California Chapter of the Arthritis Foundation, 5127
Oregon Department of Human Resources, 4493
Pennsylvania Department of Health: Bureau of HIV/AIDS, 4494, 4580
Profit Sharing/401(k) Council of America, 296
Project Inform Hotline, 4496, 4581
Sodium Information Hotline, 6845
Tele-Consumer Hotline, 6449
Texas Legal Services Center: Legal Hotline for Older Texans, 11269
US National AIDS Hotlines and Resources, 4505
Virginia Department of Health: DivisionHIV/STD, 4507, 4583

Housing

Army Distaff Foundation, 75
Association of Ohio Philanthropic Homes for the Aging, 1943
B'nai B'rith Senior Citizens Housing Committe (BBSCHC), 89
Burnsdale Extended Care, 9125
California Association of Homes andServices for the Aging, 504
Center for Lifelong Learning, 2905, 2940
Chugiak Senior Center, 8084
Coalition for Economic Survival (CES), 112
Consumer's Directory of Continuing Care Retirement Communities, 3707
Deaf REACH, 6346
Directory of Jewish Homes and Housing for the Aged in the United States and Canada, 3718
ElderNet, 4141
Elderly People or Persons with Disabilities Housing, 125
Encyclopedia of Deafness and Hearing Disorders, 6563
Excellence in Practice Award, 2634
Florida Policy Exchange Center on Aging, 4307
Fulton County Office for the Aging, 1775
Georgia Association of Homes and Services for the Aging, 821
Gray Panthers of Central Contra Costa, 542
Gray Panthers of Long Beach, 544
Gray Panthers of Marin County, 545
Gray Panthers of New York, 1777
Gray Panthers of Orange County, 546
Gray Panthers of Sacramento, 547
Gray Panthers of San Fernando Valley, 548
Gray Panthers of Santa Barbara, 550
Gray Panthers of South Bay, 551
Gray Panthers of Southern Alameda County, 552
Heritage Oaks Senior Housing, 8393
Housing Options for Massachusetts Elders(HOME), 11148
Housing and Living Arrangement for the Elderly: A Selected Bibliography, 3639
Housing and Transportation of the Handicapped, 11929
Housing for Older Adults: Options and Answers, 3640
Housing for Seniors Report, 4045
Housing for the Elderly or Disabled, 154
Johns Hopkins University Institute for Policy Studies, 4329
Journal of Housing for the Elderly, 3906
Lakewood Pine Senior Housing, 9206
Meritorious Service Award, 2654
Minnesota Health & Housing Alliance, 1410
Mortgage Insurance and Rental Housing foe Elderly, 172
National Association of the Deaf: Legal Defense Fund, 11398
National Caucus and Center on Black Aged, 206
National Housing Directory for People with Disabilities, 3774
National People's Action, 251
National Resource Center on Supportive Housing & Home Modifications, 256
New Hampshire for Human Rights, 1628
Non-Discrimination in the Community Development Block Grant Program, 272
Nonprofit Housing and Care Options for Older People, 4077
Pennsylvania Association of Non-Profit Homes for the Aging, 2139
A Place to Live: Housing Alternatives for the Elderly in Arizona, 3683
Regal Estates Senior Living, 10517
Residential Care Today, 4097
Retirement Housing & Foodservice Who's Who, 3791
Roetell Senior Housing, 10313
San Diego Hebrew Homes, 610
Senior Housing Net, 4248
Seniors Program Institute for Extended Learning, 2945
Seniors' Law Center, 11013
Sonoma County Task Force for the Homeless, 616
Southeast Arkansas Area: Agency on Aging, 485
Sunset Hall Program at Bethany Towers, 619
Transitional Senior Housing, 9309
US Department of Housing & Urban Development: Fair Housing and Equal Opportunity Hotline, 327
University of Connecticut: Center on Aging, 4391
University of Kansas: Gerontology Center, 4402
University of West Florida: Center on Aging, 4431
Utah State Bar: Young Lawyers Section, 11274
Vermont Protection and Advocacy Agency, 2443

Hypertension

American Society of Hypertension, 6907
Answers to 100 Questions About Hypertension, 6910
Conquering Hypertension: An Illustrated Guide to Understanding Treatment, 6911
Creighton University: Midwest Hypertension Research Center, 6920
Hahnemann University: Division of Surgical Research, 6921
Henry Ford Hospital: Hypertension and Vascular Research Division, 6922
Hypertension: An Integrated, Clinical Approach, 6912
Indiana University: Hypertension Research Center, 6923
Management of Hypertension, 6913
Manual of Hypertension, 6914
National Hypertension Association, 6909
New York University: General Clinical Research Center, 6924
News Report, 6917
University of Virginia: Hypertension and Atherosclerosis Unit, 6928

Impotence

Family Meds, 4195
Impotence Causes and Treatments, 4050
Impotence Resource Center, 6939
Impotence World Association, 6932, 6940
Impotence: How to Overcome It, 6937
Impotents Anonymous, 6933
Medical Management of Impotence, 4150

Incontinence

Alzheimer's Association: Tarrant County Chapter, 4892
Basic Wheelchair, 3499
Female Urinary Incontinence, 6951
Help for Incontinent People: National Association for Continence, 6945
Hygenics Direct Company, 3260
Informer, 3883, 4051
International Foundation for Bowel Dysfunction, 6946
Managing Incontinence: A Guide to Living with Loss of Bladder Control, 6952
Pennsylvania State University Gerontology Center, 4357
Priva Inc., 3040
Quality Care, 4091
Simon Foundation for Continence, 4109, 6949
Solution Starts with You, 4162
Waterproof Sheet-Topper Mattress andChair Pad, 3041

Independence

Abbotswood at Irving Park Assisted Living, 9363
Access to Independence, 10951
Access to Independence of Cortland County, 10861
Action Toward Independence, 10862
Administration on Aging/Statistical Information, 4174
Aegis of Napa, 8143
Aging in Stride: A Practical Guide forOlder Adults & Their Families, 3604
Aiken Area Council on Aging, 2223
Alaska Commission on Aging, 405
American Printing House for the Blind, 7515, 7855, 8007
Appalachian Independence Center, 10938
Area Agency on Aging of Southeast Texas, 2305
Arkansas Aging Foundation, 455
Auburn Options for Independence, 10863
Bethlehem Woods Retirement Community, 8585
Brooklyn Center for Independence of the Disabled, 10865
Canine Companions for Independence, 7554
Catskill Center for Independence, 10867
Center for Disability Rights, 10685
Center for Independence, 10683
Center for Independence of Disabled in New York (CIDNY), 10868
Center for Independence of the Disabled (CID), 10647
Center for Independence of the Disabled-North Branch, 10648
Center for Independent Living of Southwest Florida, 10701
Citizens for Independence and Access, 10912
Clarity, 3098
Colorado Springs Independence Center, 10684
Community Resources for Independence, 10913
Community Resources for Independence (CRI) Napa, 10654
Community Resources for Independence - CRI/Santa Rosa, 10655
Country House in Westchester, 9835
Cumberland County Office of Aging, 2112
DBC-1 DU-IT Bed Control, 3036
Elder Services of Berkshire County, 1278
Elderwise, 2941
Electric Leg Bag Emptier and Tub Slide Shower Chair, 3014
Extensions for Independence, 7585
Finger Lakes Independence Center, 10870
Fountains at Crystal Lake-The Inn, 8589
Fountains at the Albemarle Inn, 9485
Gadabout Wheelchairs, 3516
Gardens at Hillsborough Village, 8187
Georgia Chapter of the Arthritis Foundaton, 5101
Grand Residence at Upper St. Clair, 10196
Greatest of Ease Company Catalog, 3740
Hand Parking Brake, 2973
Harvey County Department on Aging, 1062
Heightened Independence & Progress (HIP), 10851
Heightened Independence & Progress-Hudson (HIP Hudson), 10852
IMPACT, 10719
Illinois Department on Aging, 925
Independence, 10843
Independence Court of Hyattsville, 8921
Independence First, 10954
Independence Hill Assisted Living, 10473
Independence Manor at Hunterdon, 9790
Independence Now, 10784
Independence Place, 10776
Independence Resource Center, 10942
Independence Unlimited Inc., 10688
Independence, Inc., 10762
Life Stream Services, 990
Life and Independence for Today, 10917
Lighthouse, 7632
Living Independence for Everyone (LIFE) Center for Independent Living, 10711
Lizzie Lift, 3386
Lumex's Cushions and Mattresses, 3214
Malash Gardens, 8201
Maryfield, 9521
Matilda Brown Home, 8202
Michigan Department of Human Services, 1358
National Association to Promote the Use of Braille, 7661, 8019
North Carolina Council on Developmental Disabilities, 1906
North Country Center for Independence, 10879
North Florida Area: Agency on Aging, 765
Northampton County Area: Agency on Aging, 2135
OPTIONS for Independence-Northern UtahCenter For Independent Living, 10934
Oak Park Place-Albert Lea, 9239
Oklahoma Developmental Disability Council, 2018
Outdoor Independence, 3425
Palm Beach Treasure Coast Area: Agency on Aging, 768
Palmer Independence, 3427
Plantation South at Duluth, 8437
Progressive Independence, 10903
Provena Fox Knoll Retirement Community, 8598
Push-Button Quad Cane, 3486
Regency at Glen Cove, 9849
Residence at Glen Riddle, 10200
Seniors First, 799
Southern Maine Area Agency on Aging, 1221
Sure Hands International, 3404
Taconic Resources for Independence, 10890
Texas Governor's Committee for People With Disabilities, 2383
Utah Statewide Independent Living Council, 10937
Waterford Senior Center, 1390
West Central Illinois Center for Independent Living (WCICIL), 10741
Woodside at Friendship Village, 9090
Wyoming Services For Independent Living, 10967

Information Centers, See also Libraries

Alzheimer Association: Greater Idaho Region, 4702
Alzheimer's Association: Colorado Chapter, 4742
Alzheimers Aid Society of Northern California, 4927
Arkansas Aging Foundation Information Center, 11329
Delaware Assistive Technology Initiative, 702
Impotence Information Center, 6931
Lithium Information Center, 6039
National Aging Information Center, 4221
National Information Center on Deafness, 6414, 6789, 11402
National Information Center on Deafness Brochure, 6692
Occupation Hearing Services, 6425
Occupational Hearing Service, 6426
RADAR Network, 7216

Insurance, See also Health Insurance

American Council of Life Insurers, 37
Attorney General's Office: Disability Rights Bureau, 901
Center for Community and Professional Services of the PA School for the Deaf, 6328
Centre County Office on Aging, 2105
East Central Area: Agency on Aging, 1445
Frat, 6653
Health, Life and Disability Insurance for People with Arthritis, 5203
Lifespan, 6090
Military Benefit Association, 169
National Fraternal Society of the Deaf, 6413

Navy Mutual Aid Association, 268
Office of Retirement and Survivors, 1250
Princeton University Industrial Relations Library, 11615
Private Long-Term Care Insurance: To Buy or Not to Buy?, 5006
Railroad Retirement Board (RRB), 298
Workmen's Benefit Fund of the USA, 344

Large Print

Alabama Institute for Deaf and Blind, 11306
Audio Recordings, 3448
Captek/Science Products, 3096
Career Perspectives: Interviews with Blind and Visually Impaired Professionals, 7804
Clearinghouse for Specialized Media and Technology, 7565
Complete Directory of Large Print Books and Serials, 3703
Connecticut Braille Association, 7572, 11370
Jewish Braille Institute of America, 7622
John Milton Magazine, 7873
Large Print Telephone Dial, 3128
Large Print Touch-Telephone Overlays, 3129
Large Print Typewriter, 3130
Lifeglow, 7877
New Vision Store, 7850
One Day at a Time in Al-Anon, 7266
Recorded Periodicals, 7735, 7893
Resources for Rehabilitation, 11895
Sight-Loss Support Group of Central Pennsylvania, 7743
3M Large Printed Labeler, 3054
Transaction Publishers, 11908
Vision Enhancement, Journal, 7904
Visual Aids and Informational Material, 7851
Voice of Vision, 7907, 7996

Legal Aid, See also Civil Rights

Acadiana Legal Service Corporation, 11125
Atlanta Legal Aid Society: Atlanta, 11060
Atlanta Legal Aid Society: Decatur, 11061
Atlanta Legal Aid Society: East Point, 11062
Atlanta Legal Aid Society: Lawrenceville, 11063
Atlanta Legal Aid Society: Marietta, 11064
Boston College Legal Assistance Bureau, 11143
Center for Arkansas Legal Services, 10991
Central California Legal Services, 10999
Chicago Kent Law School Information Center, 11083
Colorado Protection and Advocacy Agency:The Legal Center at Grand Junction, 11019
Community Legal Aid Society: Dover, 11034
Community Legal Aid Society: Georgetown, 11035
Division of Aging and Disability Services: Legal Services for Older Adults, 11177
Inland Counties Legal Services for Seniors, 11003
Iowa Department of Elder Affairs: Legal Assistance, 11110
Kentucky Legal Aid, 11122
Lane County Law and Advocacy Center: Senior Law Service, 11231
Legal Aid Service of Northeastern Minnesota (LASNEM): Duluth Office, 11161
Legal Aid Services of Oklahoma, 11225
Legal Aid of Arkansas, 10992
Legal Aid of East Tennessee (LAET), 11258
Legal Aid of North Carolina, 11212
Legal Aid of Western Missouri: Kansas City, 11171
Legal Assistance for Elders in Connecticut, 11027
Legal Assistance to the Elderly, 11004
Legal Services Programs for Elders: Bridgeport, 11028
Legal Services Programs for Elders: Hartford, 11029
Legal Services Programs for Elders: Waterbury, 11030
Legal Services Programs for Elders: Willimantic, 11031
Legal Services for the Elderly: Lewiston, 11133
Legal Services of New Jersey: Atlantic City, 11189
Legal Services of New Jersey: Edison, 11190
Legal Services of North Dakota, 11217
Maryland Department of Aging: Senior Legal Assistance, 11138
Maryland Legal Aid Bureau: Annapolis, 11140
Maryland Legal Aid Bureau: Baltimore, 11141
Montana Legal Services Association: Helena, 11175
Montana Legal Services Developer Program & Office on Aging, 11176
NMRLS - Northern Mississippi Rural LegalServices: Clarksdale Office, 11168
Native American Consortium Protection and Advocacy Agency, 11195
Nevada Disability Advocacy & Law CenterSparks Office/Northern Nevada, 11181
Nevada Disability Advocacy and Law Center (NDLAC), 11182
New Hampshire Legal Assistance: Senior Citizens Law Project, 11186
New Haven Legal Assistance Association (LAA), 11032
New York Legal Aid Society, 11205
Northern Mississippi Rural Legal Services (NMRLS): Elder Law Project - Oxford (Administrative) Offic, 11169
Northwest Justice Project: Olympia, 11287
Northwest Justice Project: Seattle, 11288
Northwest Justice Project: Vancouver, 11289
Ohio Protection and Advocacy Agency: Ohio Legal Rights Service (OLRS), 11223
Oklahoma Disability Law Center: Oklahoma City, 11228
Oklahoma Disability Law Center: Tulsa, 11229
Pennsylvania Department of Aging: LegalServices and Assistance, 11241
Rhode Island Protection and Advocacy Agency: Rhode Island Disability Law Center, 11249
Richard W. Waring, 11896
South Dakota Department of Social Services: Legal Services for the Elderly, 11254
Tennessee Justice Center, 11263
Utah Protection and Advocacy Agency: Disability Law Center, 11272
West Tennessee Legal Services (WTLS), 11264
West Virginia Senior Legal Aid, 11293
William E Morris Institute for Justice, 10987

Libraries, See also Information Centers

Address List: Regional and Subregional Libraries for the Blind and Physically Handicapped, 7841
Alabama Regional Library for the Blind and Physically Handicapped, 11307
Alaska State Library Talking Book Center, 11316
Alcohol Research Group: Public Health Institute, 7130
Alexandria Library Talking Book Service, 11809
Alexandria Library: Special Collections, 11810
Allen County Public Library, 11473
Allen County Public Library of New Haven, 11474
Allen County Public Library of Woodburn, 11475
Allen County Public Library, Aboite Branch, 11476
Allen County Public Library, Pontiac Branch, 11477
Alzheimer's Association: Omaha/Eastern Nebraska Chapter, 4847
American Life League Library, 11813
Ames Public Library Ames and Iowa History Collection, 11491
Area Agency on Aging Library, 11559
Arkansas Regional Library for the Blind and Physically Handicapped, 11330
Arlington County Department of Libraries, 11814
Augusta-Richmond County Public Library, 11432
Austine School: Library Media Center, 11805
Bainbridge Subregional Library for theBlind, 11433
Bangor Public Library, 11524
Bartholomew County Public Library, 11480
Benjamin Rose Institute Library, 11704
Berks Deaf & Hard of Hearing Services Library, 11732
Berks Deaf and Hard of Hearing Service, 6321
Bonne Terre Memorial Library, 11586
Books Aloud Library, 11335
Braille Institute of America Library, 7547
Broward County Talking Book Library, 11409
Bukovina Society of the Americas Library, 11495
CEL Regional Library, 11434

1141

Subject Index / Libraries, See also Information Centers

Calhoun County Historical Museum Library, 11492
California State Library: Braille & Talking Book Library, 11337
Capitan Public Library, 11620
Carnegie Library of Pittsburgh, 11733
Catholic Guild for the Blind, 7557, 11453
Cave Spring Library, 11435
Cedartown Library, 11436
Center for Thanatology Research Library, 11628
Central Rappahannock Regional Library, 11816
Chicago Library Service for the Blind, 11454
Christian Record Services, 7563
Cleveland Public Library, 11706
Colorado Talking Book Library, 11362
Connecticut State Library for the Blind and Physically Handicapped, 11372
Cytogen Corporation R&D Library, 11612
Delaware Division of Libraries for the Blind and Physically Handicapped, 11379
Delta Society National Service, 7577
District of Columbia Public Library, 11386
District of Columbia Public Library: Blind and Physically Handicapped, 11387
District of Columbia Public Library: Librarian for the Deaf Community, 11388
Downtown Detroit Subregional Library for the Blind, 11560
Du Page Library, 11455
Duluth Public Library, 11579
Fairfax County Public Library, 11818
Family Caregiver Resource Center, 915
Flagstaff City-Coconino County Library for the Visually & Physically Impaired, 11318
Focus: Library Service to Older Adults: People With Disabilities, 11414
Focus: Library Service to Older Adults; People with Disabilities, 3862
Framingham Public Library: Framingham Room, 11549
Frank Reed Memorial Library, 11707
Free Library of Philadelphia, 11736
Fresno County Free Library: Talking Book Library for the Blind, 11339
Friends of Libraries for Deaf Action, 11534
Gallaudet University Library Deaf Collection, 11390
Georgia Regional Library, 11438
Grand Traverse Area Library for the Blind and Physically Handicapped, 11561
Hall County Library System, 11439
Hazeldon Foundation: Library and Information Resources, 7460
Herman Miller Research Corporation, 11562
Hillsborough County Talking Book Library Tampa-Hillsborough County Public Library, 11415
Houston Public Library: Access Center, 11771
Houston Public Library: Acres Homes Branch, 11772
Houston Public Library: Bracewell Branch, 11773
Houston Public Library: Carnegie Branch, 11774
Houston Public Library: Collier Regional Branch, 11775
Houston Public Library: Dixon Branch, 11776
Houston Public Library: Flores Branch, 11777
Houston Public Library: Hillendahl Branch, 11778
Houston Public Library: Moody Branch, 11779
Houston Public Library: Park Place Regional Branch, 11780
Houston Public Library: Pleasantville Branch, 11781
Houston Public Library: Robinson-Westchase Branch, 11782
Houston Public Library: Scenic Woods Regional Branch, 11783
Houston Public Library: Smith Branch, 11784
Houston Public Library: Tuttle Branch, 11785
Houston Public Library: Young Branch, 11786
Houston-Love Memorial Library, 11309
Huntsville Subregional Library for the Blind, 11310
International Directory of Libraries for the Disabled, 3756
Iowa Library For The Blind And Physically Handicapped, 11493
Ivins, Phillips, Barker Library, 11392
JGB Cassette Library International, 11641
Jacksonville Public Library, 11416
Jacksonville Subregional Talking Book Library, 11417
John F Germany Public Library: Special Collections, 11393
Kanawha County Public Library, 11837
Kansas State Historical Society: Library & Archives Division, 11497
Kansas State Library Talking Book Service, 11498
Kent County Library for the Blind, 11564
Kentucky Historical Society-Thomas D Clark Research Library, 11510
Kentucky Talking Book Library, 11511
La Fayette Subregional Library for the Blind and Physically Disabled, 11440
Laboure College Library, 11550
Large Print Loan Library Catalog, 3759, 7965
Las Vegas-Clark County Library District, 11604
Lewiston Public Library, 11527
Library Outreach Reporter, 3919
Library Resources for the Blind and Physically Handicapped, 7819, 7848
Library for the Blind & Handicapped: Public Library-Anniston/Calhoun Counties, 11311
Library of Michigan Service for the Blind, 11565
Lighthouse: Ruth M Shellens Library, 11643
Louisville Talking Book Library, 11512
Lourdes College Duns Scotus Library, 11709
Macomb Library for the Blind and Physically Handicapped, 11566
Macon Library for the Blind and Physically Handicapped, 11441
Maine State Library, 11528
Manhattan Public Library, 11500
Marquette University Libraries Special Collections and University Archives, 11847
Maryland State Library for the Blind and Physically Handicapped, 11535
Mesa Arizona Regional Family History Center, 11320
Miami-Dade Public Library: Genealogy Collection, 11419
Michigan Association for the Deaf: Hearing and Speech Services, 6394
Michigan Association for the Deaf Hearing and Speech Services, 6393
Mideastern Michigan Library Co-op, 11567
Mind Science Foundation Library, 11788
Minnesota Library for the Blind, 11581
Mississippi Library Commission, 11584
Montana State Library, 11594
Multi-Scan Single Switch Activity Center, 3144
Nassau Library System, 11648
National Graduate University Library Capitol Hill Campus, 11401
National Library Service for the Blind and Physically Handicapped, 7689, 8031, 11403
Nebraska Library Commission: Talking Book & Braille Service, 11599
Nevada State Library and Archives, 11605
Nevada State Library: Talking Book Services, 11606
New England Corporate Library, 11551
New Hampshire State Library, 11610
New Jersey Library for the Blind and Physically Handicapped, 11614
New Mexico Chapter of the Arthritis Foundation, 5124
New Mexico State Library: Blind and Physically Handicapped, 11621
New Orleans Public Library: Louisiana Division, 11517
New York Chapter of the Arthritis Foundaion, 5125
Newport News Public Library System, 11819
North Carolina Library for the Blind, 11683
North Dakota State Library: Disability Services, 11697
North Platte Public Library, 11601
Northern California State Library: Braille and Talking Book Library, 11342
Northern Kentucky Talking Book Library, 11513
Northland Library Cooperative, 11568
Northwest Indiana Subregional Library for Blind and Physically Handicapped, 11484
Northwest Kansas Library System Talking Books, 11501
Northwest Ozarks Regional Library for the Blind and Handicapped, 11332
Oakland County Library for the Blind and Physically Handicapped, 11569
Oakland Public Library, 11343
Oconee Regional Library, 11442
Ohio County Public Library Services for the Blind and Physically Handicapped, 11838
Ohio Regional Library for the Blind and Physically Handicapped, 11711
Ohio School for the Deaf Library, 11712
Orange County Library System Audio-Visual Department, 11420

Subject Index / Long Term Care

Orange County Library System: Genealogy Department, 11421
Oregon State Library, 11726
Overbrook School for the Blind Library, 11737
Oxford Gerontology Center Library, 11654
Pima Council on Aging, 11322
Polisher Research Institute Library: Philadelphia Geriatric Center, 11741
Portland Public Library, 11529
Prescott Talking Book Library, 11323
Program Planners: Library/Information Center, 11655
Public Library of Cincinnati and Hamilton Outreach Services Department, 11713
Recording for the Blind & Dyslexic, 7737
Roanoke City Public Library System, 11820
Robert S. Bray Award, 2681
Rockmart Library, 11443
Rome Subregional Library Service for People with Disabilities, 11444
Roswell Public Library, 11622
San Francisco Public Library for the Blind and Print Handicapped, 11345
San Francisco Public Library: Talking Books Program & Blind Services Center, 11346
San Jose State University Library, 11347
Senior Citizens of Shasta County, 613
Sentry Insurance Company Library, 11849
Shawnee Library System, 11464
Skokie Accessible Library Services, 11465
South Carolina State Library, 11756
South Central Kansas Library System, 11503
South Dakota State Library: Braille andTalking Book Program, 11759
Southern California State Library: Braille and Talking Book Library, 11348
Special Needs Library Montgomery County Department of Public Libraries, 11537
Special Services Division: Indiana State Library, 11486
St Mary's School for the Deaf Library Information Center, 11661
St. Patrick Hospital and Health Sciences Center: Library Center, 11595
State Library of Louisiana, 11518
State Library of Ohio: Talking Book Program, 11714
Staunton Public Library Talking Book Center, 11821
Sturgis Library, 11152
Suffolk Cooperative Library System, 11662
Support for People with Oral, Head and Neck Cancer, 5848
Talking Book Library, Miami and DadePublic Library System, 11423
Talking Books Library for the Blind and Physically Handicapped, 11424
Taping for the Blind, 7754
Tennessee Library for the Blind and Physically Handicapped, 11762
Texas State Library, 11791
Texas State Library Talking Book Program, 11792
Thomas Balch Library, 11822
Tulsa City-County Library System, 11723
UMDNJ and Coriell Research Library, 11617
US Library of Congress Handicapped Hotline, 332
University Library Services, 11826
University of Memphis Libraries: Audiology, Speech Language, Pathology Branch, 11767
University of South Florida Library: Special Collections Department, 11058
Update (Library of Congress), 7902
Utah State Library: Blind and DisabledServices, 11804
Vermont Department of Libraries, 11808
Virginia State Library for the Visually and Physically Handicapped, 11828
Voices for the Blind, 11531
Volta Bureau Library, 11408
Wallace Memorial Library, 11678
Washington Library for the Blind and Physically Handicapped, 11836
Washtenaw County Library, 11577
Waterville Public Library, 11532
Wayne County Regional Library for the Blind, 11578
Weld Library District: Lincoln Park Branch Library, 11369
West Florida Regional Library, 11431
West Virginia Library Commission, 11844
Wichita Public Library, 11508
William K. Kohrs Memorial Library, 11598
Windward Foundation, 343
Wisconsin Regional Library for the Blind: Talking Book Program, 11852
Wistar Institute of Anatomy & Biology Library, 11751
Wolfner Memorial Library for the Blind, 11593
Worcester Public Library, 11558
Wyoming Services for the Visually Disabled, 11856
Young Historical Library, 11509

Long Term Care

Aging and Long Term Care of Eastern Washington, 2503
American Medical Directors Association (AMDA), 3571
Directory of Long Term Care Facilities, 3719
Directory of Texas Long Term Care Facilities, 3728
ElderCare Advocates, 4191
Florida Department of Elder Affairs Program of Aging and Adult Services, 751
Geriatrics Education and Research Institute, 4312
Indiana Legal Services: Senior Law Project, 11099
Long Term Care Ombudsman Program, 1484
National Association of Directors of Nursing Administration in Long Term Care, 191
National Long-Term Care Ombudsman Resource Center (NLTCORC), 240
National Long-Term Care Resource Center, 241
New England Gerontological Association, 1616
Older Americans Report, 4081
Public Interest Center on Long Term Care, 4089
Successful Models of Community Long Term Care Services for the Elderly, 3675
Washington State Aging & Disability Services Administration, 2540
Wisconsin Aging and Long Term Care Board, 2600

Lung Disease

American Lung Association, 4182, 4646, 4676, 5658
Cigarette Smoking, 4021
Tulane University Occupational Lung Disease Center, 4378

Marketing

Georgia State University Center for Mature Consumer Studies, 4311
NUCEA Divisional Awards, 2659
Senior Media Directory, 3796
Visiting Nurse Association of America, 340

Medicaid

Lee Russell Council of Governments: Area Agency on Aging, 377
Understanding Medicaid Long Term Care: A Primer for Alzheimer Advocates, 5021

Medicare

Advocates for Medicare Patients (AMP's), 11131
American Association of Homes and Services for the Aging: Research and Information Center, 4180, 11381
American Health Care Association: Information Resource Center, 11384
Beat the Nursing Home Trap: A Consumer's Guide to Assisted Living and Long Term Care, 3608
Bulletin on Long-Term Care Law, 4017
Center for Medicare Advocacy, 11022
Center for Medicare and Medicaid Services (CMS), 11082
Centers for Medicare and Medicaid Services (CMS), 102, 4187
Communicating for Seniors, 1395
Complete Listing of Nursing Facilities and Home for the Aged Beds when Licensed as a Part of a Nursi, 3704
Gem Wheelchair and Scooter Service, 3517
HMOs4seniors.com, 4205
Home Care Agencies, Hospices and Nursing Pools, 3747
Knowing Your Rights, 3644, 4055
Medicare Rights Center, 168
Nelson Cruikshank Award, 2665
Report on Disability Programs, 4096
SEAGO Area: Agency on Aging, 450
Senior Law Home Page, 4250
Southeastern Minnesota Area: Agency on Aging, 1438
USA Next United Seniors Association, 334
Vision Over 50, 7993

Medicine

AIDS Medicines in Development, 4546
Aging, Physical Activity, and Health, 3606

Subject Index / Men's Issues, Organizations

American Academy of Environmental Medicine, 4645
American Academy of Otolaryngology-Head and Neck Surgery, 6309
American Association of Retired Veterinarians, 25
American Board of Internal Medicine, 30
American College of Legal Medicine, 34
American Gastroenterological Association, 6174
American Psychoanalytic Association, 55
American Society for Laser Medicine and Surgery, 60
American Society of Internal Medicine, 64
American Society of Maxillofacial Surgeons, 65
American Thoracic Society, 72
Baromedical Nurses Association, 90
Baylor College of Medicine Center for Allergy & Immunological Disorders, 5050
Baylor College of Medicine: DeBakey Heart Center, 6861
Baylor College of Medicine: Roy M and Phyllis Gough Center on Aging, 4268
Behan Health Science Library, 11731
Beth Israel Deaconess Medical Center, 4270
Clinics in Geriatric Medicine, 3838
Columbia University Oral History Research Office, 11631
Cook's Illustrated, 3845
Dartmouth College Biomedical Libraries: Dana Biomedical Library, 11608
Fair Acres Center, 11735
Family Health International, 11682
Goldwater Memorial Hospital: Medical Center Health Sciences Library, 11635
Hartford Hospital Health Science Libraries, 11373
Hasting Center Library, 11636
Health, 3872
Hillcrest Medical Center Library, 11720
Hippocrates, 3878
Huffington Center on Aging, 4317
Integris Baptist Medical Center: Wann Langston Memorial Library, 11721
International Rehabilitation Medicine Association, 158
Journal of Visual Impairments and Blindness, 7876
Journal of the American Geriatrics Society, 3915
Journal of the American Psychoanalytic Association, 6082
Journals of Gerontology; Psychological Sciences & Social Sciences, 6083
Kent State University Gerontology Center, 4333
Kerrville State Hospital Professional Library, 11787
Montefiore Medical Center Health Sciences Library: Tishman Learning Center, 11647
Mount Sinai School of Medicine of City University of New York: Alzheimer's Disease Research Center, 4342, 5060
National Emergency Medicine Association, 221
National Library of Medicine, 4153
New Living, 3937
New Medicine Man: A Different Kind of Health Care for Elders, 3651
New York College of Osteopathic Medicine, 7038
Nonprescription Drugs: Modern Medicines for Mature Americans, 7388
Pearlman Biomedical Research Institute, 5247
Penrose Hospital: Webb Memorial Library, 11364
Physicians Committee for Responsible Medicine, 5774
Prevention, 3948
Preventive Medicine Research Institute, 6886
Provena-Mercy Center Medical Library, 11463
Roosevelt Hospital Medical Library, 11658
Sandoz Pharmaceuticals Corporate Library, 11616
Sea View Hospital Rehabilitation Center Health Sciences Library, 11659
South Dakota Human Services Center Medical Library, 11758
Springer Publishing Company, 11902
Three Talks to Medical Societies, 7407
Tufts University School of Medicine: Immunology Section, 4693
University of California: Mount Zion Medical Center, 11355
University of Cincinnati Medical Center Libraries, 11719
University of Iowa College of Medicine, 7122
University of Kansas Laboratory of Biological Anthropology, 4399
University of Miami School of Medicine: Department of Neurology, 7123
University of Minnesota: Center for Bioethics, 6036
Upper Minnesota Valley Area Agency on Aging, 1441
Washington University School of Medicine, 7125
Wound, Ostomy and Continence Nurses Society, 6950
Yale University: Behavioral Medicine Clinic, 6108

Men's Issues, Organizations

Al-Anon Is for Men, 7298
American Assembly for Men in Nursing, 14
Families and Work Institute, 4306
Men: Newcomer's Packet, 7381
NIH: National Institute on Aging, 178
National Institute on Aging: Information Center, 4345
Pride Institute, 7215
Prime Health & Fitness, 3949
Prostate Health Workbook, 11698

Mental Health

Alaska Division of Mental Health and Developmental Disabilities, 409
Alliance Press, 11858
American Academy of Addiction Psychiatry, 7451
American Association for Geriatric Psychiatry, 3566
American Counseling Association, 38
American Mental Health Counselors Association, 49
American Psychiatric Nurses Association, 54
American Society of Retired Dentists, 70
Bell, 6086
Brandeis University Policy Center on Aging, 4274
Center for the Study of Aging Library, 11629
Clinical Gerontologist, 3836
Colorado Division of Mental Health, 638
Columbia University: Whitney M Young, Jr Memorial Library of Social Work, 11633
Community Mental Health Journal, 3841
Connecticut Department of Mental Health and Addiction Services, 7147
Delaware Drug Abuse & Mental Health, 7151
Department of Mental Health, Retardation and Hospitals of Rhode Island, 2202
Depression and Its Treatment, 6069
Division of Mental Health & Developmental Services, 1601
Edmund S. Muskie School of Public Service, 4303
Florida Department of Mental Health and Rehabilitative Services, 752
A Friend's House Adult Day Services: Romeo, 1337
A Friend's House Adult Day Services: Warren, 1338
Georgia Division of Mental Health and Substance Abuse, 7161
Georgia Division of Mental Health: Developmental Disabilities & Addictive Diseases, 827
HIV Frontline, 4560
Harris Library, MSASS, Case Western Reserve University, 11708
Hawaii Department of Adult Mental Health, 859
Hunter College of the City University of New York: Health Professional Library, 11638
Idaho Mental Health Center, 887
Illinois Department of Mental Health and Developmental Disabilities, 922
International Society of Psychiatric Consultation Liaison Nurses, 161
Journal of Mental Health and Aging, 3908, 6081
Judge David L Bazelon Center for Mental Health Law, 11394
Kansas Mental Health & Retardation Service, 1073
Kentucky Division of Mental Health, 1114
Louis de la Parte Florida Mental Health Institute, 6040
Louisiana Division of Mental Health, 6041
Maine Department of Mental Health & Mental Retardation, 6042
Maryland Department of Health and Mental Hygiene, 6043
Massachusetts Department of Mental Health, 6044
Mental Health Law News, 6092
Mental Health Report, 3930
Mental Health Services for Deaf People, 6533
Minnesota Mental Health Division, 1412

Subject Index / Mobility Aids

Mississippi Department of Mental Health, 1449
Missouri Department of Mental Health, 1489
National Council News, 6096
National Institute of Mental Health, 6097
National Legal Support for Elderly People with Mental Disabilities Project, 239
National Mental Health Association, 242, 6048
New Hampshire Department of Mental Health, 1618
New Jersey Department of Mental Health, 1666
New York Office of Mental Health Binghamton Psychiatric Center Library Services Department, 11650
New York State Office of Mental Health, 1809
North Carolina Division of Mental Health, Developmental Disabilities and Abuse Services, 6049, 7203
North Dakota Department of Mental Health, 6050
Ohio Department of Mental Health, 6051
Oklahoma Department of Mental Health, 6052
Oklahoma Department of Mental Health and Substance Abuse Services, 7209
Oregon Department of Mental Health, 6053
Pittsburgh Hearing Speech and Deaf Services, 6432
Pittsburgh Hearing, Speech and Deaf Services, 6433
Providing Services for People with Vision Loss: Multidisciplinary Perspective, 7828
RRTC on Mental Health/Late Deaf & HOH, 6436
Rhode Island Department of Mental Health, 6054
South Carolina Department of Mental Health, 6056
South Dakota Department of Mental Health, 6057
Southwestern Indiana Mental Health Center, 11104
Tennessee Bureau of Alcohol & Drug Abuse, 7221
Tennessee Department of Mental Health & Developmental Disabilities, 6058
Texas Department of Mental Health & Mental Retardation, 6059
University of California: San Francisco Center on Deafness Library, 11356
University of Chicago Committee on Human Development, 4388
University of Chicago Social Services Administration Library, 11471
University of Pennsylvania: Depression Research Unit, 6106
University of Pittsburgh Medical Center: Clinic Western Psychiatric Institute and Clinic, 6107
University of Texas at Austin Association for Mental Health, 11909
Utah Department of Mental Health, 6060
Virginia Commonwealth University Virginia Center on Aging Information Resources Center, 11827
Virginia Department of Mental Health Mental Retardation and Substance Abuse Services, 6062
Washington Department of Mental Health, 6063
Wisconsin Department of Mental Health, 6064
Wyoming Department of Mental Health, 6065

Mobility Aids

Access to Independence and Mobility (AIM, 10859
Access to Independence and Mobility-Bath (AIM), 10860
Accessibility Lift, 3356
AirLift Toileting System from Mobility, 3003
Amigo Centra, 3416
Arcola Mobility, 2956
Art and Science of Teaching Orientation and Mobility to Persons with Visual Impairments, 7799
Bill Dvorak Kayak & Rafting, 12010
Blindness: What it is, What it Does and How to Live with it, 7802
Braun Mobility Products, 2959
Bravo! + Three-Wheel Scooter, 3418
Champion 1000, 3505
DW Auto & Home Mobility Specialties, 2963
Dallas Lighthouse for the Blind, 7573
Dolomite Walkers, 3480
Drive-Master, 2964
EKA/ Health & Mobility Systems, 2967
Environment Control System, 3113
Explorer+ 4-Wheel Scooter, 3421
Ez International Inc./Ortho Kinetics, 3376
Finger Print Pen, 3461
Gendron, 3518
General Motors Mobility Program for Persons with Disabilities, 2969
General Motors Mobility Program for Travelers with Disabilities, 12022
Guide Dog Foundation for the Blind, 8010
HiRider, 3520
Idaho Commission for the Blind, 7611
Ideal-Phone, 3122
Invacare Corporation, 3262
Lighthouse International Ruth M. Shellens Library, 1786
Line Dancing Video, 4148
Monmouth Vans-Access and Mobility Equipment, 2987
Motorized Stander, 3424
New Mobility, 3938
New York Public Library General Reference & Advisory Services: Accessibility Services, 11652
Prone Support Walker, 3485
Ricon Corporation, 3393
Roll-Aid, 3532
Scooter Lift/Carrier, 2992
Snug Seat, 3023
Speech Problems & Swallowing Problems In Parkinson's Disease, 7029
Stand Aid, 3402
Sterling, 3439
Tilt 'n Tote, Roamer Riding Chair, 3407
Triumph Scooter, 3445
Ventura Enterprises, 3561
We Can Do It Together!, 7908
Wheelchair Carriers, Ramps, and Roamer Riding Chair, 3414

Money Management

Christian Association of PrimeTimers, 105
Diablo Valley Foundation for the Aging, 528

Myths, Aging

Center for Understanding Aging, 4287
NFDI Newsletter, 6095
Telling Stories, 6771

Nursing Homes

Friends and Relatives of Institutionalized Aged, 1774
Guide to the Nursing Home Industry, 3742
Living Well in a Nursing Home, 11695
National Citizen's Coalition for Nursing Home Reform (NCCNHR), 730
Nursing Home Chain Directory, 3777
Nursing Home Directory, 3778

Nutrition, See also Food

American Society for Parenteral and Enteral Nutrition, 61
Area 10 Agency on Aging, 967
Arthritis and Diet, 5180
Baltimore County Department of Aging, 1228
Boulder County Aging Services Division, 628
Broward Meals on Wheels, 736
Challenge of Choice, 4135
Colorado Mountain College Senior Nutrition Program, 639
Community Action Commission of Cape Cod & Islands, 1275
Conscious Choice, 3843
Dallas Young Lawyers Association: Committee on Legal Aid to the Elderly, 11265
Diabetes Medical Nutrition Therapy, 6191
Diabetic Low-Fat & No-Fat Meals in Minutes, 6200
Eating Hints: Recipes and Tips for Better Nutrition During Cancer Treatment, 5822
Eating Well Magazine, 3855
Guadalupe County Nutrition, 1712
Health Naturally, 3873
Health World, 3875
Healthy Food Choices, 6249
Let's Live, 3918
Living With Rheumatoid Arthritis, 5161
Macrobiotics Today, 3921
Michigan Office of Services to the Aging, 1363
My Food Plan, 4062
Nutrition Guide to Food Allergies, 4671
Nutrition Health Review, 3940
Nutrition Services Incentive Program (NSIP), 2466
Nutrition for Patients Receiving Chemotherapy/Radiation Treatment, 5832
Oley Foundation for Home Parenteral and Enteral Nutrition, 279
Part C Title III: Nutrition Services, 285

Subject Index / Older Americans Act

Ravalli County Council on Aging, 1563
Seneca Area Agency on Aging, 1053
Teachers College Milbank Memorial Library, 11664
Type II Diabetes Prevention Pyramids, 6254
University of Chicago: Clinical Nutrition Research Unit, 5970
University of Colorado: Science Libaray, 11368
University of Florida: Institute for Gerontology, 4395
Veggie Life, 3969
Winifred Masterson Burke Medical Research Institute, 5079
World Education, 2821
Your Health, 3973

Older Americans Act

Administration on Aging (AoA), 1
Bet Tzedek Legal Services, 10994
National Association of Area Agencies on Aging, 188
National Association of Area Agencies onAging, 4224
Northwestern Area: Agency on Aging, 2550
Part A Title VI: Grants to Indian Tribes and Part B Title VI: Grants to Native Hawaiians, 283

Orthopedics

Chiropractor's Self-Help Back and Body Book, 11690

Osteoporosis

National Osteoporosis Foundation, 250
University of Wisconsin: Madison Institute on Aging, 4433

Parkinson's Disease

Adjustment, Adaptation and Accomodation: Psychological Approaches, 6085
Akathisia in Parkinson's Disease, 6989
American Parkinson Disease Association Newsletter, 6990
American Parkinson's Disease Association, 6954
Autonomic Failure and Parkinson's Disease, 6991
Balance Disturbances and Parkinson's Disease, 6992
Basic Information About Parkinson's Disease, 6993
Coping with Parkinson's Disease, 6980
Depression and Dementia in Parkinson's Disease, 6995, 6996
Dietary Considerations for Parkinson's Disease Patients, 6997
Driving and the Parkinson's Disease Patient: Some Considerations, 6999
Good Nutrition in Parkinson's Disease, 7004
Greater Philadelphia Parkinson's Disease and Other Movement Disorders Council, 6955
How to Start a Parkinson's Disease Support Group, 7005
Living with Parkinson's Disease, 6981
MR Imaging in Parkinson's Disease, 7006
National Parkinson Foundation Adult Day Care Center, 6957
National Parkinson Foundation Hotline, 6958
Neuropsychology and Parkinson's Disease, 7008
Neurotrophic Factors in Parkinson's Disease, 7009
One Step at a Time Brochure, 7010
PROPATH, 6959
Pain Syndromes and Parkinson's Disease, 7011
Parkinson Association of Arizona, 6960
Parkinson Association of Davenport, 6961
Parkinson Association of Florida West Coast, 6962
Parkinson Association of Greater Kansas City, 6963
Parkinson Association of Hawaii, 6964
Parkinson Association of Minnesota, 6966
Parkinson Association of Orange County, 6968
Parkinson Association of South Dakota, 6969
Parkinson Association of South West Florida, 6970
Parkinson Association of Wisconsin, 6971
Parkinson Association of the Sacramento Valley, 6972
Parkinson Assocition of Greater Daytona, 6973
Parkinson Network of Mt Diablo, 6974
Parkinson Report, 7013
Parkinson's Disease & Movement Disorders, 6982
Parkinson's Disease Foundation, 7040
Parkinson's Disease Foundation Newsletter, 7014
Parkinson's Disease Handbook, 6983, 7015
Parkinson's Disease: The Patient Experiance, 7016
Parkinson's Patient: What You and Your Family Should Know, 7017
Parkinsons Action Network, 6977
Parkinsons Report, 7018
Perioperative Management of Parkinson's Disease, 7020
Pet Scans: A New Look at Parkinson's Disease, 7021
Podiatry and Parkinson's Disease, 7022
Sleep Problems with Parkinson's Disease, 7027
Stages of Parkinson's Disease, 7031
Texas Tech University: Tarbox Parkinson's Disease Institute, 7046
Treatment of Parkinson's Disease with Carbidopa-Levodopa, 7033
United Parkinson Foundation, 6978
University of Michigan: Alzheimer's Disease Research Center, 5076

Pensions

American Benefits Council, 29
American United Life Insurance Company, 11479
Directory of Plan Sponsors, 3720
Employee Benefits Security Administration, 127
Hawaii State Employees' Retirement System, 868
Massachusetts Mutual Life Insurance Company Law Library, 11150
National Association of State Retirement Administrators, 201
National Conference on Public Employee Retirement Systems, 216
Pension & Profit Sharing Plan Companies Directory, 3781
Pension Benefit Guaranty Corporation, Office of the General Counsel Library, 11404
Pension Rights Center, 289
Pensions, 4242
Pensions & Investments: 1,000 Largest Retirement Funds, 3782
TIAA-CREF, 321
Teachers Insurance and Annuity Association Business Library, 11665
Towers Perrin Corporate Information Center, 11666
Triumph 3000/4000, 3444

Physical Therapy, See also Exercise

American Occupational Therapy Association, 52
Gateway Technical College Learning Resource Center, 11846
Role of Physical Therapy in Parkinson's Disease, 7025

Poverty

Eastern Shore Area: Agency on Aging, Community Action Agency, 2456
Institute for Socioeconomic Studies Library, 11639
Syracuse University Center for Policy Research, 11663

Prizes, See also Awards, Honors

Community Awards Program (CAP), 2625
Harold W. McGraw, Jr. Prize in Education, 2641
Marie Haug Student Award in Gerontology, 2653
Ned E. Freeman Excellence in Writing Award, 2664

Probate, See also Wills

American College of Trust and Estate Counsel, 35
Los Angeles County Bar Association: Elderline Public Council, 11007

Recreation, See also Sports, Hobbies

Activities Keep Me Going & Going, Vol 1, 3593
Activities Keep Me Going & Going, Vol 2, 3594
REACH/Resource Center on Independent Living, 11789

Subject Index / Rehabilitation

Rehabilitation

ABLEDATA, 3055
ADARA, 6300
Advances in Cardiac and PulmonaryRehabilitation, 6849
Alabama Department of Rehabilitation Services, 361
Alcohol Rehabilitation for the Elderly, 7129
American Kinesiotherapy Association, 43
American Medical Rehabilitation Providers Association (AMRPA), 48
American Rehabilitation Services Administration (RSA), 3829
Arizona Department of Economic Security, 427
Arthritis and Vocational Rehabilitation, 5183
Assistive Technology Resource Centers of Hawaii, 854
Bailey, 3697
Better Hearing Institute, 6322, 6779
Blindness and Visual Impairments: National Organizations, 7842
Blindness, A Family Matter, 7857
California Department of Rehabilitation, 511
Cardiac Rehabilitation Directory, 3700
Center for Information Resources, 11734
Cleoplast Therapeutic Putty-2 oz., 3250
Client Assistance Program: Office of Program Operations, 111
Cornerstone, 7148
Cornerstone of Eagle Hill, 7149
Deafness and Communicative Disorders, 117
Deafness and Communicative Disorders Branch, 6349
Delaware Client Assistance Program, 704
Department of Blind Rehabilitation, 7578
Department of Health & Rehabilitative Services, 742
Directory of Self-Help/Mutual Aid Support Groups for Older People, 3722
Directory of State Services for People with Disabilities, 3725
ElderConnect, 4192
Finding the Right Aural Rehabilitation Program, 6651
Florida Department of Labor and Employment Security, 11410
Fountains at Logan Square East, 10195
Georgia Client Assistance Program, 822
HEAR Center, 6361
Hearing Loss and Rehabilitation, 6755
Heights at Avery Heights, 8275
Helen Keller National Center, 7603
Helen Keller National Center for Deaf: North Central Region, 6372
Hillcrest Rehabilitation & Healthcare Center, 9179
HomeCare Magazine Buyers' Guide, 3879
House Ear Institute: Athalie Irvine Clarke Library, 11340
Hub, 7868
Idaho Industrial Commission, 886
Illinois Department of Rehabilitation Services, 923
Institute for Driver Rehabilitation, 2977
International Rehabilitation Review, 3889
Intervention Practices in the Retention of Competitive Employment Among Individuals who are Blind, 7816
Introduction to Cochlear Implants, 6678
Journal of Rehabilitation, 3910
Journal of Vision Rehabilitation, 7874
Journal of the Academy of Rehabilitation Audiology, 6585
Kentucky Client Assistance Program, 1110
Kentucky Department for the Blind, 7628
Learning To Hear Again, 6523
Lighthouse International, 8013
Louisiana Center for the Blind, 7638
Maine Division for the Blind & Visually Impaired Services, 7640
Maryland Client Assistance Program, 1241
Michigan Commission for the Blind, 7790
Michigan Rehabilitation Services, 1365
Montana Advocacy Program, 1538
National Adult Day Services Association, 183
National Association of the Deaf Law Center, 6402
National Federation of the Blind: Human Services Division, 7680
National Federation of the Blind: HumanServices Division, 8025
National Rehabilitation Information Center (NARIC), 254
New Jersey Client Assistance Program, 1661
North Carolina Client Assistance Program, 1905
Parkinson Rehabilitation Center, 6975
Perkins School for the Blind: Samuel P Hayes Research Library, 11552
Physical & Occupational Therapy in Geriatrics, 3943
Post-Polio Health International, 3947
Referring Blind and Low Vision Patients for Rehabilitation Services, 7829, 7985
Regional Resource Center on Deafness, 6437
Rehabilitation Counseling Bulletin, 6084
Rehabilitation Institute of Chicago, 5248
Rehabilitation Services Directory, 3786
Resources for People with Disabilities and Chronic Conditions, 3788
Rhode Island Client Assistance Program, 2212
Rochester Regional Service Center for Hearing Impaired People, 6441
Smith Kettlewell Rehabilitation Engineering Research Center, 7831
South Carolina Client Assistance Program Office of the Governor of South Carolina, 2247
South Dakota Division of Rehabilitation, 2271
Southeast Regional Service Center for Hearing Impaired People, 1436
State Vocational Rehabilitation Agencies, 3798
State of Nevada Client Assistance Program, 1614
Tennessee Division of Rehabilitation Services, 2299
US Department of Health and Human Services: Office for Civil Rights, 11095
US Department of Justice, 328
US Department of Labor: Office of Federal Contract Compliance Programs, 329, 11096
University of Texas Health Science Center at Houston: Speech & Hearing, 6830
Vision Foundation, 7773
VoRtechs, 4121
Vocational Rehabilitation Division, 2088
Washington Client Assistance Program, 2533
Wyoming Division of Rehabilitation, 2620

Relationships

Alcohol Alert #15: Alcohol and AIDS, 7306
American Academy of Nursing, 10
An Overview of Allergy, 4647
CAPCOM, 6780
Dental Tips for Diabetics, 6237
Genetics and Deafness, 6656
Grandparenting with Love and Logic, 3635
Guidance on Our Journeys, 7348
Journal of Aging and Physical Activity, 3898
Life of My Own Daily Meditations on Hope and Acceptance, 7820
Life of My Own: Daily Meditations on Hope and Acceptance, 7260
Mentally Disabled and the Law, 3766
New York Department of Health: Office ofPublic Health, AIDS Institute, 4489
Personal Census Search: Data User Services Division, 293
Shame Faced, 7273
University of Missouri Kansas City: Center for Aging Studies, 4416
When the Mind Hears, 6552

Relaxation

American Yoga Association, 73
In God's Care, 7257
Joy of Laziness, 11694

Religion

Association for Spiritual, Ethical and Religious Values in Counseling, 82
Civil Rights of Institutionalized Persons Division, 108
Fordham University Third Age Center, 4309
Jewish Community Relations Council of Greater Boston, 1288
Lutheran Bible Institute of Seattle Library, 11830

Respite

Alzheimer's Association: California Central Coast Chapter, 4725
Alzheimer's Association: Greater Cincinnati, 1941
Alzheimer's Association: Greater Miami Chapter, 4774
Alzheimer's Association: Grover Chapter, 4785
Alzheimer's Association: Santa Barbara Chapter, 4864, 4865
Center for Clinical and Aging Services Research, 4282
Center for the Study of Aging, 4288
Cleburne County Aging Program, 470
Cordia Senior Living, 8172
Demonstration Grants to States with Respect to Alzheimer's Disease, Health Resources & Services, 118

Subject Index / Restaurant Discounts

Massachusetts Commission for the Blind, 7644
Norwood Park Home, 8597
Respite Resource Guide, 3668
Senior Spectrum, 1219
St. Paul's Senior Homes & Services, 8219
Time Out!, 5020
University of Utah: Gerontology Center, 4429
Ventura County Area Agency on Aging, 620

Restaurant Discounts

Alaska Welcomes You, 414
District of Columbia, 11957
State of Missouri, 11991

Romance

AIDS, 4575
AIDS and Hemophilia: Protecting Yourself and Others, 4549
Abused Deaf Women's Advocacy Services, 2502, 6302
Alzheimer's Association: Greater NewJersey Chapter, 4775
American Federation of School Administrators, 40
As Times Goes By, 4133
Central Massachusetts Agency on Aging, 1272
Directory of Community Care Facilities, 3714
Equal Employment Opportunity Commission, 130
Equal Employment Opportunity: Civil Rights Division, 131
Gray Panthers Metro Detroit, 1348
HIV Disease in People with Hemophilia: Your Questions Answered, 4559
Hematology Research Laboratory: Universiy of Southern California, 4604
Houston Department of Health and Human Services: Bureau of HIV Prevention, 4465
International Society for Sexual Medicine, 6942
Living and Loving: Information About Sexuality and Intimacy, 5205
Male Sexual Dysfunction Center, 6934
Male Sexual Medicine Clinic, 6935
Minnesota Department of Health: AIDS/STD Prvention Service, 4475
National Civil Rights Clearinghouse Library, 11399
Patient Perspectives on Parkinson's, 7019
Philadelphia Department of Public Health: AIDS Program, 4495
Protection & Advocacy for People with Disabilities, 2230
Selling to Seniors, 4104
Sexual Function Health Council, 6943
Sexual Intimacy and the Alcoholic Relationship, 7400
Sexual and Bladder Difficulties in Parkinson's Disease, 7026
Sexuality & Aging, 4160
Special Edition for Disabled People, 3797
A Thousand Tomorrows, 5025
Tonight's the Night, 4164
US Commission on Civil Rights: Civil Rights Discrimination Complaints, 324
US Office of Personnel Management, 333
Unisex Low Vision Watch, 3183
University of North Carolina: General Clinical Research Center, 4633
Women, Sex and HIV, 4574

Safety

Adjustable Bed, 3034
Adjustable Toilet Safety Rails, 3002
Alabama State Department of Human Resources, 370
Aluminum Walking Canes, 3476
Arizona Public Safety Personnel Retirement System, 433
Bathtub Safety Rail, 3005
Caption Center, 6326, 11545
Cornell Communications, 3103
Easy Pour Locking Lid Pot, 3330
Evacu-Trac, 3514
Great Big Safety Tub Mat, 3015
Home Safety for the Alzheimer's Patient, 5001
Illinois Society for the Prevention of Blindness, 7612
Just One Little Bite Can Hurt! Important Facts About Anaphylaxis, 4669
Luminaud, 3134
Mat Factory, 3556
Mr. Escort Manual Wheelchair Carrier, 2988
National Center for Sight, 7665
National Committee for the Prevention of Elder Abuse, 214
Plums Award Winning Protects Hip, 3269
PowerLink 2 Control Unit, 3313, 3344
Prevent Blindness Connecticut, 7723
Prevent Blindness News, 7978
Prevent Blindness Northern California, 7726
Prevent Blindness Texas, 7730
Prevent Blindness Tri-State, 7731
ProtectaCap+PLUS, ProtectaHip, 3272
Savannah Court, 8440
Schoharie County Office for the Aging, 1870
Shuttle, 3435
Sierra 3000/4000, 3437
Transfer Bench with Back, 3052
US Army: Medical Command Center for Health Promotion & Preventive Medicine, 11539
Wyoming Workers Safety & Compensation Division, 2622
Ziggy Medi-Chair, 3415

Social Issues

Addiction and Responsibility, 7235
Addictive Personality, 7237
Aging Research: National Institute on Aging, Public Health Service, 4260
Alaska Department of Health and Social Services-AIDS/STD Program, 4447
Alzheimer's Association, 4705
American Association of Retirement Communities, 26
American Psychological Society, 56
Boston College: Social Work Library, 11544
Brain Research Institute University ofCalifornia, Los Angeles, 4272
CARF Directory of Organizations with Accredited Programs, 3699
Center for the Study of Aging of Albany, 1757
Central Institute for the Deaf Professional Library, 11587
Central Michigan University: Center for Adult Longitudinal Studies, 4290
Choice & Challenge: Caring for Aggressive Older Adults Across Levels of Care, 4136
Clinical Program for Evaluating and Managing Stroke-at-Risk Patients, 7060
College of Maharishi Vedic Medicine Center for Health and Aging Studies, 4293
Complete Mental Health Directory, 3705
Cornell University School of Industrial and Labor Relations, 11634
Dartmouth College Center for Evaluative Clinical Sciences, 4299
David T Siegel Institute for Communicative Disorders, 6799
Duke University Center for the Study of Aging and Human Development, 4300
Educational Gerontology, 3856
Ethel Percy Andrus Gerontology Center, 4305
Families Anonymous, 7157
Five Good Food Habits for People with Diabetes, 4031
Georgia Consortium on the Psychology of Aging, 4310
Hazelden, 4206
Hazelden Foundation, 7165
ILRU Insights, 4048
Institute for Retired Professionals atSyracuse, 2860
International Psychogeriatric Association, 157
Journal of Aging and Health, 3897
Kent State University Exercise Physiology Lab, 4332
Lehigh University Center for Social Research, 4334
Lexington School for the Deaf Library Media Center, 11642
Massachusetts Alzheimer's Disease Research Center, 5059
Massachusetts Institute of Technology General Clinical Research Center, 4339
Maximizing the Role of Nutrition in Diabetes Management, 6210
Minnesota Department of Human Services Library & Resource Center, 11580
National Institute on Age, Work and Retirement, 233
National Institute on Aging, 4233, 4343
National Institute on Aging Gerontology Research Center, 4344
New York State Institute for BasicResearch in Developmental Disabilities, 4347
Oregon Research Institute, 4354
Pennsylvania State University Center for Developmental and Health Genetics, 4356
Portland State University Institute on Aging, 4361
Quality Care Conference, 2780, 4156
RSVP Scott-Cape Counties, 1512
Research Institute of the Hebrew Home of Greater Washington, 4364
Richard Kalish Innovative Publication Award, 2679

Subject Index / Social Security

Rockefeller University Laboratory of Neuroendocrinology, 4366
Rutgers University Institute for Health, Health Care Policy: and Aging Research, 4369
Southern California Research Institute, 7475
St. Louis University: Department of Psychiatry, 6103
Steps to Understanding Challenging Behaviors, 5016
US Department of Veteran Affairs: Palo Alto Health Care and Medical Information Service, 11349
University of California, San Francisco Center for Social and Behavioral Sciences, 4382
University of Colorado at Boulder Institute for Behavioral Genetics, 4389
University of Kentucky: Sanders-Brown Center on Aging, 4403
University of Miami: Center on Adult Development and Aging, 4411
University of Michigan Center for Human Growth and Development, 4412
University of Michigan: Institute of Gerontology, 4414
University of Tennessee: Knoxville Society for the Study of Social Problems, 4426
University of Texas at Dallas: Callier Center for Communication Disorders, 6831
University of Texas-Houston Health Science Center Mental Sciences Institute, 4427
University of Wisconsin: Milwaukee Institute on Aging and Environment, 4434
Wayne State University Center for Health Research, 4438
Workers at Risk: Drugs and Alcohol on the Job, 7428

Social Security

Arizona Disability Determination Services, 431
Austin Disability Determination Services, 2309
Bedford Research Consultants, 11815
Bureau of Disability Adjudication, 1598
Bureau of Disability Determination, 1946
Bureau of Rehabilitation Services: Disability Determination Services, 673
Charleston Disability Determination Services, 2546
Chicago Social Security Management Association, 1346
Delaware Disability Determination Services, 710
Department for Disability Determination Services, 1103
Disability Determination Branch, 857
Disability Determination Bureau, 2573
Disability Determination Division, 2006
Disability Determination Services, 418, 878, 1149, 1202, 1397, 1478, 1534, 1767, 1888, 1925, 2047, 2203, 2428, 2612
Disability Determination Services: Los Angeles South Branch, 532
Disability Determination Services: Sacramento Branch, 535
Disability Determination Services: San Diego Branch, 536
Disability Determination Unit, 1615
Disability Determinations, 1570, 2275
Disability Determinations Services, 2393
Disability Evaluations Division: Sierra Branch, 537
Disability Workbook for Social Security Applicants, 7092
Division of Disability Determination Services, 1645, 2509
Gray Panthers of San Francisco, 549
Hartford Area Social Security Office, 687
Legal Center for the Elderly and Disabled, 11005
Los Angeles Disability Determination Services, 562
Massachusetts Disability Determination Services, 1295
Massachusetts Social Security Region 1 Administration, 1301
Mental Health Law Reporter, 6093
National Academy of Social Insurance, 11396
National Committee to Preserve Social Security and Medicare (NCPSSM), 215
National Council of Social Security Management Associations, 217
National Federation of the Blind Merchants Division, 8022
National Federation of the Blind: Blind Merchants Division, 7678
National Organization of Social Security Claimants' Representatives, 11204
Nolo's Guide to Social Security Disability: Getting and Keeping Your Benefits, 3653
Office of Disability: Social Security Administration, 275
Office of Public Affairs, Social Security Administration, 570
Social Security Administration, 313
Social Security Bulletin, 4111
Social Security Springfield Disability Determination, 958
Social Security for Public Employees, 2191
Social Security, Medicare and Pensions, 3671
Social Security: Atlanta Disability Determination, 850
Social Security: Baltimore Disability Determination, 1262
Social Security: Juneau Disability Determination Services, 422
Social Security: Louisville Disability Determination, 1136
Social Security: Miami Disability Determination, 800
Social Security: Orlando Disability Determination, 801
Social Security: Retirement Insurance, 314
Social Security: Santa Fe Disability Determination, 1746
Social Security: Special Benefits for Persons Aged 72 & Older, 315
Social Security: Tallahassee Disability Determination, 802
Social Security: Tampa Disability Determination, 803
Social Security: West Columbia Disability Determination, 2242
South Dakota Disability Determination Sevices, 2270
State of Alaska, Department of Health & Social Services, 423
US Social Security Administration Library & Records Management Branch, 11543
US Social Security Administration: Washington Library, 11407
University of Pennsylvania Institute on Aging, 4421

Speech Impairments

Memphis State University: Center for the Communicatively Impaired, 6805
Ohio University: School of Hearing and Speech Science, 6811
Parkinson Handbook: A Guide for Patients and Their Families, 7012
Phoenix Public Library: Special Needs Center, 11321
Providence Speech and Hearing Center, 6435
University of Alabama: Speech and Hearing Center, 6821
University of Nevada: Speech and Language Pathology Department, 6827
Washington Hearing and Speech Center, 6461

Sports, See also Hobbies, Recreation

Activities with Developmentally Disabled Elderly and Older Adults, 3598
Activity Factory, 11857
American Alliance for Health: Physical Education, Recreation and Dance, 13
American Athletic Association for the Deaf, 6312
Center for Positive Aging, 3577
Community Recreation and People with Disabilities for Inclusion, 3616
Community Service Program of Van Nuys, 2718
Eagle Sportschairs, 3513
Eskaton Cameron Park Lodge, 8179
Eskaton Gold River Lodge, 8180
Exercise for Older Adults, 3625
Falls Church Senior Center, 2458
Functional Forms, 3204
Idyll Arbor, 11882
Jewish Association for Services for the Aged, 1784
Jewish Communal Retirees Association of Los Angeles, 556
Lazy Days RV Center, 2979
Marin Senior Coordinating Council (Whistlestop), 564
Massillon Senior Citizens' Center, 1958
Mattoon Area Senior Center: Coles Council on Aging, 930
Mature Health, 3925
Michigan City Public Library: Indiana Rooom/Genealogy, 11483
Mine Hill Senior Citizens Good Years Club, 1657
Minnesota Chapter No. 1 SHHH - Self Help for Hard of Hearing People, 6397
Modern Maturity, 3933
Modern Maturity Center, 715
Nantahala Outdoor Center, 12033
Nashville Chapter Black Deaf Advocates, 6399
New Bedford Council on Aging, 1303

Subject Index / Stroke

Northern Rocky Mountain Retiree Association, 1550
PALAESTRA, 11938
Pennsylvania Department of Public Welfare Norristown State Hospital, 11738
Ranger, 3430
Regency Place, 8213
Scooter, Power Chair and WheelchairLifts, 3394
Scottdale Community Senior Citizens Club, 2188
Senior Action in a Gay Environment, 1874
Senior Adult Activities Center of Montgomery County, 2189
Senior Centers of Bethlehem, 2190
Senior Citizens of Patagonia, 451
Senior Times Magazine, 3958
Southern Mississippi Area Agency on Aging, 1473
Sports 'n Spokes, 12046
SureHands Lift & Care Systems, 3405
Travis County Services for the Deaf, 6453
Travis County Services for the Deaf and Hard of Hearing, 6454
USA Deaf Sports Federation, 6458, 6592, 6793
University of Connecticut in Storrs: Homer Babbidge Library, 11378
Walton County Senior Citizens Council, 853
West Hollywood Senior Center: Jewish Family Service, 626
William Beardall Senior Center, 809
WinSCAN-The Single Switch Interface forPCs with Windows, 3192

Stroke

Adaptive Resources Guide, 7057
African-Americans and Stroke, 7080
Alzheimer's, Stroke and 29 Other Neurological Disorders Sourcebook, 4954
American Heart Association, 6838
Atrial Fibrillation and Stroke, 7082
Be Stroke Smart, 7083
Be Stroke Smart - Communication, 7084
Be Stroke Smart - Emotional Aspects, 7085
Be Stroke Smart - Home and Work Adaptation, 7086
Be Stroke Smart - Prevention and Warning Signs, 7087
Be Stroke Smart - Rehabilitation Guidelines and Resources, 7088
Be Stroke Smart Series, 7089
Brain at Risk: Understanding and Preventing Stroke, 7111
Cerebral Blood Flow Laboratories, 4291, 7113
Clinical Trials Participation, 7091
Columbia University Irving Center for Clinical Research, 4294
Comprehensive Stroke Center of Oregon, 7114
Consumer Health USA: Volume 2, 3618
Discovery Circles, 7061
Guide to Understanding Stroke, 7093
Heart and Stroke Facts, 7094
Heart and Stroke Risk Factors, 7095
High Blood Pressure and Stroke, 7096
Home Exercises for Stroke Survivors, 7097
Introduction to Stroke, 7063
Invaluable Guide to Life After Stroke: An Owner's Manual, 7064
Journal of Stroke and Cerebrovascular Diseases, 7079
Living at Home After a Stroke, 7098
Living with Stroke: A Guide for Families, 7066
Los Amigos Research and Education Institute, 4336
NIH/National Institute of Neurological Disorders and Stroke, 7052
NSA Audio Tape Series, 7112
NSA's Guide to Stroke, 7099
National Institute of Neurological Disorders and Stroke, 4232
National Rehabilitation Information Center, 6417, 7053
National Stroke Association, 7054
Neurology Institute, 7055
New York University Medical Rehabilitation Research and Training Center, 7120
November Days, 7067
Pathways: Moving Beyond Stroke and Aphasis, 7068
Recovery After a Stroke, 7100
Recurrent Stroke, 7101
Resources for Elders with Disabilities, 3667, 3787
Road Ahead: A Stroke Recovery Guide, 7069
Rush University Neuroscience Institute, 4367
Stroke - A Clinical Approach, 7070
Stroke Book, 7071
Stroke Connection, 7103
Stroke Research and Treatment Center, 7056
Stroke Therapy, 7072
Stroke Treatment and Recovery, 7104
Stroke is a Brain Attack!, 7105
Stroke: Clinical Updates, 7106
Stroke: Putting the Pieces Back Together, 7075
Stroke: Questions & Answers, 7107
Stroke: Reducing Your Risk (Spanish), 7108
Stroke: Your Complete Exercise Guide, 7076
Symbi-Key Computer Switch Interface, 3170
US Stroke Club Listing, 7078
University of Chicago Brain Research Institute, 4387
University of Florida Brain Institute, 4392
University of Miami Center for Neurological Diseases, 4409
Winning Over Stroke, 7077

Substance Abuse

AHA Guide to the Health Care Field, 3687
AID Bulletin, 4544
Adler School of Professional Psychology, 11450
Alcohol Alert #17: Treatment Outcome Research, 7308
American Council on Alcoholism, 7135
Arizona Office of Substance Abuse & General Mental Health, 7138
Arkansas Office of Alcoholism and Substance Abuse, 7140
Art of Living with Change: Turning Your Good Intentions Into Progress..., 7432
Augusta Biomedical Research Corporation, 4267
Brandeis University Institute for Health Policy, 4273
Breaking the Chain of Substance Abuse and Hearing Loss, 6614, 7323
Caring for Ourselves: Hope for Healthy Relationships, 7435
Center for Alcohol & Addiction Studies, 7453
Center for Substance Abuse Prevention, 7144, 7441
Dual Disorders Recovery Book, 7247
Getting Started in AA, 7251
God Grant Me the Laughter: A Treasury of Twelve Step Humor, 7252
Good First Step, 7253
Grateful to Have Been There, 7254
Health Answers, 7444
Hopedale Medical Complex: Medical Library, 11456
How Drug Abuse Takes Profit Out of Buisness, 7351
Illinois School of Professional Psychology Meadows Campus Library, 11460
Indian Health Service, 7170, 7446
Iowa Division of Substance Abuse & Health Promotion, 7174
Kentucky Division of Substance Abuse, 7176
Maine State Office of Substance Abuse: Information and Resource Center, 7463
Massachusetts Bureau of Substance Abuse Services, 7180
Michigan Center for Substance Abuse Services, 7182
National Association for Addiction Professionals, 7186
National Directory of Drug and Alcohol Abuse Treatment and Programs, 7283
National Prevention Resource Center, 7194
Nevada Bureau of Alcohol and Drug Abuse, 7197
New Mexico Behavioral Health Services, 7199
New York Center on Alcohol and Substance Abuse, 7200
New York State Office of Alcoholism & Substance Abuse Services, 7202
Night Light: A Book of Nighttime Meditations, 3652
Office of Applied Studies, 7469
Office of Women's Services, 7206
Parkside Medical Services Corporation, 7211
Passages Through Recovery, 7267
Research Institute on Alcoholism, 7472
Rhode Island Division of Substance Abuse, 7217
Skeptic's Guide to the Twelve Steps, 7274
Spiritual Fitness Division (CREDO Southwest), 617
Substance Abuse Funding News, 7404
Substance Abuse and Mental Health Services Administration, 7450, 7477
Substance Abuse and Physical Disability, 7278
URSA Institute, 4504
University of Alabama: Center for Alcohol and Addiction Studies, 7478

Subject Index / Suicide

University of Delaware: Center for Drug and Alcohol Studies, 7480
University of Illinois Health Systems Research, 4397
University of Michigan Alcohol Research Center, 7481
University of Northern Iowa: Center forSocial and Behavioral Research, 4420
Utah Division of Substance Abuse, 7223
Virginia Division of Substance Abuse Services, 7225
Washington Division of Alcoholism & Substance Abuse, 7227
Wisconsin Bureau of Substance Abuse Services, 7229

Suicide

Adult Children & Aging Parents, 3599
Center for the Rights of the Terminally Ill, 101
Directory of Suicide Prevention/Crisis Intervention Agencies in the United States, 3726
Directory of Survivors of Suicide Support Groups, 3727
National Directory of Bereavement Support Groups and Services, 6033
Sisters of Life: Dr Joseph R Stanton Human Life Issues Library and Resource Center, 11660

Travel Agencies, Clubs, Tours

AIDS For Daily Living, 3317
AMI Aquamassage, 3246
Access Travel: Airports, 7839, 11910
Access to Art: A Museum Directory for Blind & Visually Impaired People, 7840
Access to Art: A Museum Directory for the Blind and Visually Impaired People, 7796
Access to Travel Magazine, 11911
Accessible Journeys, 12004
Adaptive Device Locator System, 3067
Adaptive Driving Conversions, 2953
Addie's You & I Travel Service, 12005
Aging Comes of Age, 3603
Alabama Bureau of Tourism and Travel, 11949
Alaska Division of Tourism, 11950
America West/US Airways Airline, 12006
American Society of Tropical Medicine and Hygiene, 71
Amtrak Railways, 11914
Anglo California Travel Service, 12008
Arizona Office of Tourism, 11951
Arkansas Department of Parks & Tourism, 11952
Association of Retired Americans, 87
B&A Travel, 12009
British Airways, 11916
California Division of Tourism, 11953
Charlevoix County Commission on Aging, 1345
Charlie Brown's Goodtime Travel, 12011
Classic Hawaii, 12012
Colorado Travel & Tourism Authority, 11954
Complete Directory for People with Disabilities, 3702
Connecticut Office of Tourism, 11955
Consumer Information Catalog, 4022
Continental Airlines, 11918
Council for Disability Rights, 11085
Cross Wheelchair, 3510
Delaware Tourism Office, 11956
Diabetic Traveler, 6246
Directory of Accessible Van Rentals, 11921
Directory of Travel Agencies for the Disabled, 3729
Disabled Driver's Mobility Guide, 11922
Empress Directions Unlimited(AcccessibleTours), 12018
Environmental Traveling Companions, 12019
Flying Wheels Travel, 12020
Food Allergy News, 4667
Galludet University/Alumni House, 12021
Green Tortoise Adventure Travel, 12023
Greyhound Buslines, 11926
Handi-Cabs of the Pacific, 12024
Hawaii Tourism Office, 11960
Hinsdale Travel Service, 12025
Homewaiter, 3382
House of Travel, 12026
Iberia Airlines of Spain, 11930
Idaho Division of Tourism Development, 11961
Illinois Bureau of Tourism, 11962
Indiana Tourism Division, 11963
International Braille and Technology Center for the Blind, 7619
International Ventilator Users Network (IVUN) News, 4052
Iowa Tourism Office/Iowa Travel Guide, 11964
John Muir Publications, 11884
KLM Royal Dutch/Northwest Airlines, 11931
Kansas Travel & Tourism, 11965
Kentucky Department of Travel, 11966
Kon Tiki Travel Agency, 12029
Liberty LT, 3385
Lifelong Learning Institute, 2778
Live Better/Live Longer Resourcebook, 3761
Louisiana Office of Tourism, 11967
Maine Office of Tourism, 11968
Maryland Office of Tourism Development, 11969
Massachusetts Office of Travel & Tourism, 11970
MedEscort International, 12030
Melwood Access Adventures, 12031
Michigan Travel Bureau, 11971
Military Officers Association of America (MOAA), 170
Minnesota Office of Tourism, 11972
Mississippi Division of Tourism Development, 11973
Missouri Division of Tourism, 11974
Monte Travel, 12032
NEXUS Wheelchair Cushioning System, 3218
National Association of Traveling Nurses, 12034
National Tour Association: Travel Division, 12035
Nebraska Division of Travel & Tourism, 11975
Nevada Commission on Tourism, 11976
New Hampshire Office of Travel & Tourism Development, 11977
New Jersey Tourism Division, 11978
New Mexico Department of Tourism, 11979
New York Division of Tourism, 11980
North Carolina Division of Tourism, 11981
Northridge Travel, 12036
Odyssey Club, 12037
Ohio Division of Travel and Tourism, 11982
Oklahoma Tourism & Recreation Department, 11983
Oregon Tourism Commission, 11984
Over the Hill Gang International, 280
Pennsylvania Center for Travel, Tourism & Film, 11985
Permobil Super 90, 3526
Professional Respite Care, 12040
RSVP High County, 656
Reid & Hurley Travel, 12041
Rochester Institute of Technology Library, 11656
Safari Tilt, 3049
Senior News Monthly, 4106
Senior Women's Travel, 4254
Sheridan Travel Service, 12044
Silver Glide Stairway Lift, 3395
South Dakota Department of Tourism, 11987
Spa, 11940
State of Michigan Travel Resources, 11990
State of Texas Office of the GovernorEconomic Development and Tourism, 11993
Sue Smith Travel Service, 12047
Sun-Mate Seat Cushions, 3229
Sundial Special Vacations, 12048
Suregrip Bathtub Rail, 3025
Tennessee Department of Tourist Development, 11997
Travel Companion Exchange, 12050
Travel Resources for Deaf and Hard of Hearing People, 6722
Travel Trends, 12051
Travelers Aid Society, 12052
Travelfair, 12053
Travelin' Talk Directory, 3801
Travelin' Talk Newsletter, 12054
Tub Slide Shower Chair, 3032
US SERVAS, 12055
US Travel Systems, 12056
United Airlines, 11945
United States Department of the Interior: National Park Service, 4118
University of Connecticut Health Center: Center on Aging, 11377
Utah Travel Council, 11998
Ventures, 12057
Walking, 3971
Washington State Tourism, 12000
West Virginia Division of Tourism, 12001
Weston Travel Agency, 12058
Wheeler's Accessible Van Rentals, 2998, 11947
Wilderness Inquiry, 12060
Wisconsin Department of Tourism, 12002
A World of Options: A Guide to International, Educational, Exchange, Community Service...for Persons,
Wyoming Division of Tourism, 12003

Subject Index / Veterans

Veterans

Alabama Department of Veteran Affairs, 365
American Legion, 11478
American Legion Magazine, 3828
Arizona Department of Veterans Services, 430
Arkansas Department of Veterans Affairs, 461
Blind Veterans Rehabilitation Centers and Clinics, 7539
Blinded Veterans Association, 7541, 8008
California Department of Veterans Affairs, 512
Connecticut State of Veterans Affairs Department of Rocky Hill: Hospital Services Program, 683
Delaware Commission of Veterans Affairs, 705
Department of Veterans Affairs, 119
Directory of Department of Veterans Affairs Facilities, 3715
Disabled American Veterans, 1104
Disabled American Veterans Magazines, 3851
Eli M. Oboler Library: Health Services, 11448
Federal Benefits for Veterans and Dependents, 3732
Financial Aid for Veterans, Military Personnel and Their Dependents, 3733
Florida Department of Veterans Affairs, 754
Georgia Department of Veterans Service, 826
Illinois Department of Veterans Affairs, 924
Indiana Department of Health Veteran's Home, 981
Indiana Department of Veterans Affairs, 983
Iowa Commission of Veterans Affairs, 1021
Irving Diener Award, 2644
Jewish Veteran, 3983
John L McClellan Memorial Veterans' Hospital Research Office, 6880
Kansas Commission on Veterans Affairs, 1066
Kentucky Department of Veterans Affairs, 1112
Life Insurance for Veterans: Veterans Benefits Administration, 2127
Living with Low Vision: A Resource Guide for People with Sight Loss, 7822, 7849
Louisiana Department of Veterans Affairs, 1160
Maine Department of Defense, Veterans and Emergency Management, 1208
Major General Melvin J. Maas Achievement Award, 2652
Maryland Veterans Commission, 1247
Minnesota Department of Veterans Affairs, 1408
Mississippi Commission for Veterans Affairs, 1448
Montana Office on Aging, 1547
National Association of Military Widows, 193
National Association of State Veterans Homes, 203
National Association of Veterans Program Administrators, 204
Navy Seabee Veterans of America, 270

Nebraska Department of Veterans Affairs, 1583
New Hampshire Veterans Council, 1627
New Mexico Veterans Service Commission, 1724
New York Division of Veterans Affairs, 1800
North Dakota Department of Veterans Affairs, 1929
Ohio Disabled American Veterans, 1967
Oklahoma Department of Veterans Affairs, 2017
Omaha Department of Veteran Affairs Medical Center Research Service, 6280
Oregon Department of Veterans Affairs, 2064
Paralyzed Veterans of America (PVA), 11047
Pension to Veterans, Surviving Spouses, and Children, 290
Regular, 3990
South Carolina Department of Veterans Affairs, 2250
Tennessee Department of Veterans Affairs, 2298
Texas Veterans Commission, 2386
US Deparment of Veterans Affairs: Center Library, 11520
US Deparment of Veterans Affairs: Columbia William Jennings Bryan-Dorn Veterans Hospital Library, 11757
US Deparment of Veterans Affairs: Philadelphia Medical Center Library, 11743
US Department of Veterans Affairs, 331
US Department of Veterans Affairs Bedford: Edith Nourse Rogers Memorial Veterans Hospital Medical Li, 11553
US Department of Veterans Affairs Hospital Libraries, 11333
US Department of Veterans Affairs Hospitl: Fort Howard Hospital Library, 11540
US Department of Veterans Affairs Medical Center Library Service, 11334, 11445, 11554, 11794
US Department of Veterans Affairs Medical Library, 11425
US Department of Veterans Affairs Outpatient Clinic Learning Resources Service, 11555
US Department of Veterans Affairs and Center Learning Resources Service Library, 11426
US Department of Veterans Affairs, Health & Science Library, 11375
US Department of Veterans Affairs, Hospital Library, 11427
US Department of Veterans Affairs, John Cochran Division Library, 11589
US Department of Veterans Affairs, Medical Center Library Service, 11405, 11488
US Department of Veterans Affairs: Albany Medical Center Library, 11667
US Department of Veterans Affairs: Albuquerque Medical Center Library, 11623
US Department of Veterans Affairs: Altoona James E Van Zandt Medical Center Library Service, 11744
US Department of Veterans Affairs: Amarillo Hospital Library, 11796

US Department of Veterans Affairs: Ann Arbor Hospital Library, 11572
US Department of Veterans Affairs: Asheville Medical Center Library, 11684
US Department of Veterans Affairs: Baltimore Medical Center Library Service, 11541
US Department of Veterans Affairs: Batavia Western New York Healthcare System Library, 11668
US Department of Veterans Affairs: Bath Medical Center Library Service, 11669
US Department of Veterans Affairs: Battle Creek Medical Center Library Service, 11573
US Department of Veterans Affairs: Beckley Library Service, 11840
US Department of Veterans Affairs: Big Spring Hospital Library, 11797
US Department of Veterans Affairs: Bonham North Texas Health Care System, 11798
US Department of Veterans Affairs: Boston Hospital Medical Library, 11556
US Department of Veterans Affairs: Brecksville Medical Center Library, 11715
US Department of Veterans Affairs: Bronx Medical Center Library, 11670
US Department of Veterans Affairs: Brooklyn Medical Center Library, 11671
US Department of Veterans Affairs: Buffalo Medical Center Library Service, 11672
US Department of Veterans Affairs: Butler Medical Center Library, 11745
US Department of Veterans Affairs: CarlVinson Medical Center Library, 11446
US Department of Veterans Affairs: Castle Point Department of Medicine and Surgery Library Service, 11673
US Department of Veterans Affairs: Central Iowa Health Care System, 11494
US Department of Veterans Affairs: Cheyenne Medical and Regional Office Center, 11854
US Department of Veterans Affairs: Chicago Health Care System-West Side Division, 11467
US Department of Veterans Affairs: Chillicothe Medical Library, 11716
US Department of Veterans Affairs: Cincinati Learning Resources Service, 11717
US Department of Veterans Affairs: Clarkburg Loouis A Johnson VA Medical Center Library, 11841
US Department of Veterans Affairs: Coatesville Medical Center Library, 11746
US Department of Veterans Affairs: Dallas Library Service, 11799
US Department of Veterans Affairs: Dayton Medical Center Library Service, 11718
US Department of Veterans Affairs: Denver Medical Center Library, 11365
US Department of Veterans Affairs: Detroit Medical Center Library Service, 11574
US Department of Veterans Affairs: Dr Karl Menninger Medical Library, 11505
US Department of Veterans Affairs: Durham Medical Center Library, 11685

Subject Index / Veterans

US Department of Veterans Affairs: Dwight D. Eisenhower Center Medical Library, 11506
US Department of Veterans Affairs: East Orange Medical Center Library, 11618
US Department of Veterans Affairs: Erie Medical Center Library, 11747
US Department of Veterans Affairs: Fargo Medical Center Library, 11702
US Department of Veterans Affairs: Fayettville Medical Center Library Service, 11686
US Department of Veterans Affairs: For Meade VA Black Hills Health Care System Medical Library, 11760
US Department of Veterans Affairs: Fort Harrison Medical Center Library, 11596
US Department of Veterans Affairs: Grand Island Greater Nebraska Health Care System Library, 11602
US Department of Veterans Affairs: Grand Junction Medical Center Library Service, 11366
US Department of Veterans Affairs: H Earl Gordon Medical Library, 11350
US Department of Veterans Affairs: Hampton Medical Center Library and Educational Resources, 11823
US Department of Veterans Affairs: Health Administration Medical Center, 11380
US Department of Veterans Affairs: Healthcare System in West Haven, 11376
US Department of Veterans Affairs: Hospital Library, 11468, 11514
US Department of Veterans Affairs: Houston Medical Center Library, 11800
US Department of Veterans Affairs: Huntinington Learning Resource Center, 11842
US Department of Veterans Affairs: Indiana Health Care System, 11489
US Department of Veterans Affairs: Iron Mountain Medical Center Library, 11575
US Department of Veterans Affairs: Jackson Medical Center Library, 11585
US Department of Veterans Affairs: Johnson City Medical Center Library, 11763
US Department of Veterans Affairs: Kansas Medical Center Library, 11590
US Department of Veterans Affairs: Kerrville South Texas Veterans Health Care System, 11801
US Department of Veterans Affairs: Lebanon Medical Center Library, 11748
US Department of Veterans Affairs: Library Services, 11469
US Department of Veterans Affairs: LomaLinda Medical Center Library Service, 11351
US Department of Veterans Affairs: LongBeach Medical Center Library Service, 11352
US Department of Veterans Affairs: Lyon New Jersey Health Care System - Lyons Campus Hospital Librar, 11619
US Department of Veterans Affairs: Manchester Medical Center Library, 11611
US Department of Veterans Affairs: Martinsburg Learning Resources Service, 11843
US Department of Veterans Affairs: Medical & Regional Office Center, 11507, 11530
US Department of Veterans Affairs: Medical Center Library, 11447, 11449, 11515, 11521, 11557
US Department of Veterans Affairs: Medical Library, 11428, 11429, 11470
US Department of Veterans Affairs: Memphis Medical Center Library, 11764
US Department of Veterans Affairs: Miles City Medical Center Library, 11597
US Department of Veterans Affairs: Minneapolis Medical Center Library Service, 11582
US Department of Veterans Affairs: Montrose Medical Library, 11674
US Department of Veterans Affairs: Murfreesboro Medical Center Library Service, 11765
US Department of Veterans Affairs: Nashville Medical Center Library Service, 11766
US Department of Veterans Affairs: New York Harbour Healthcare System, New York Campus Library, 11675
US Department of Veterans Affairs: Northern Arizona VA Health Care System, 11326
US Department of Veterans Affairs: Northport Medical Center-Medical Library, 11676
US Department of Veterans Affairs: Oklahoma City Medical Center Library, 11724
US Department of Veterans Affairs: Omaha Hospital Library, 11603
US Department of Veterans Affairs: Overton Brooks Medical Center Library, 11522
US Department of Veterans Affairs: Phoenix Medical Center Library, 11327
US Department of Veterans Affairs: Pittsburgh Education, Media and Reference Service, 11749
US Department of Veterans Affairs: Poplar Bluff Library Service, 11591
US Department of Veterans Affairs: Portland Medical Library, 11727
US Department of Veterans Affairs: Providence Health Sciences Library, 11754
US Department of Veterans Affairs: Reno Medical Center Library Services, 11607
US Department of Veterans Affairs: Richmond Hospital Library, 11824
US Department of Veterans Affairs: Roseburg Medical Center Library Service, 11728
US Department of Veterans Affairs: Saginaw Aleda E Lutz Medical Center Library, 11576
US Department of Veterans Affairs: Salem Medical Center Library, 11825
US Department of Veterans Affairs: Salisbury Medical Center Library, 11687
US Department of Veterans Affairs: Salt Lake City Hospital Medical Library, 11803
US Department of Veterans Affairs: San Diego Medical Center Library Service, 11353
US Department of Veterans Affairs: San Francisco Medical Center Library Service, 11354
US Department of Veterans Affairs: Seattle Puget Sound Health Care System, 11832
US Department of Veterans Affairs: Sheridan Medical Center Library, 11855
US Department of Veterans Affairs: Southern Colorado Healthcare System, 11367
US Department of Veterans Affairs: Spokane Medical Center Library, 11833
US Department of Veterans Affairs: Tacoma/Puget Sound Health Care System, 11834
US Department of Veterans Affairs: Tomah Health Sciences Library, 11850
US Department of Veterans Affairs: Tucson Medical Center Library, 11328
US Department of Veterans Affairs: Waco Medical Center Library, 11802
US Department of Veterans Affairs: Walla Walla Jonathan M Wainwright Memorial VA Medical Library, 11835
US Department of Veterans Affairs: White River Junction Medical & Regional Office CenterLibrary Serv, 11807
US Department of Veterans Affairs: WhiteCity Library, 11729
US Department of Veterans Affairs: Wilkes-Barre Medical Center Library, 11750
US Department of Veterans Affairs:, Columbus Hospital Library, 11592
US Department of Veterans Affairs:Temple Medical Center Medical Library, 11795
US Deprtment of Veterans Affairs: Center Library, 11490
US Deptartment of Veterans Affairs: Central Alabama Veterans Health Care System, 11313
US Deptartment of Veterans Affairs: Medical Center Library, 11314
US Deptartment of Veterans Affairs:Alabama Veterns Health Care System, 11315
VA Central California Health Care System, 11357
Vermont Veterans Affairs, 2445
Veterans & Military Organizations Directory, 3806
Veterans Administration Medical Center: Research Service, 5996, 7490
Veterans Affairs Medical Center: Geriatric Research, Education and Clinical Center, 4437
Veterans Information and Assistance, 337
Veterans Prosthetic Appliance, Rehabilitation and Prosthetics, 338
Veterans' Home of Wyoming, 10619
Viva Vital News, 7906
Warren H Green, 3810
Washington Department of Veterans Affairs, 2537
Wisconsin Department of Veterans Affairs, 2609
Wisconsin Veterans Museum & Research Center, 11853

Visually Impaired, See also Braille

ACB Government Employees, 6773, 7493, 8002
ACB Radio Amateurs, 6774, 7494, 8003
ACB Social Service Providers, 6775, 7495, 8004
AER Report, 3817, 7912
AFB Directory of Services for Blind and Visually Impaired Persons in the US, 7794, 7837
AFB Press, 6742
After a Stroke: 300 Tips to Making LifeEasier, 7058
Aging Eye and Low Vision, 7798
Aluminum Adjustable Support Canes for the Blind, 3474
American Action Fund for Blind Children and Adults, 7502
American Blind Lawyers Association, 7504, 8005
American Council of the Blind, 11383
American Federation of the Blind: San Francisco Chapter, 490
American Foundation for the Blind, 7506, 11860
Arizona Center for the Blind and Visually Impaired, 7518
Arizona Rehabilitation State Services for the Blind and Visually Impaired, 7521
Arizona State Braille and Talking Book Library, 11317
Associated Blind, 7523
Associated Services for the Blind and Visually Impaired, 7524
Association for Macular Diseases, 7525
Association for the Blind & Visually Impaired of Greater Rochester, 7526
Association for the Blind and Visually Impaired, 7527
Baylor College of Medicine: Cullen Eye Institute, 8036
Beaver County Association for the Blind, 7532
Beyond Sight, 3449
Blair County Association for the Blind and Visually Handicapped, 7534
Blind Association of Western New York, 7535
Blind Work Association, 7540
Braille Catalog of General InterestItems, 7843
Braille Compass, 3087
Braille Institute Desert Center, 7543
Braille Institute Sight Center, 7544
Braille Institute of America, 7545
Braille Institute of America, 7546
Braille Institute: Orange County Center, 7548
Braille Touch-Time Watches, 3089
Braille/Print Protractor, 3090
Bulletin, 7863, 7924
Carolyn's Low Vision Solutions, 7844
Carroll Center for the Blind, 7556
Chester County Branch Pennsylvania Association for Blind, 7560
Chester County Branch, Pennsylvania Association for Blind, 7561
Chicago Lighthouse for People who areBlind or Visually Impaired, 7562

Choice Magazine Listening, 7864
Christian Education for the Blind, 11770
Clovernook Center: Opportunities for the Blind, 7568
Collier County Association for the Blind, 7569
Connecticut Society to Prevent Blindness, 11371
Contrasting Characteristics of Blind and Visually Impaired Clients, 7807
DVS Guide, 4138
Dean A McGee Eye Institute, 8038
Delaware Association for the Blind, 7574
Delaware Association for the Blind, 7575
Delaware Division for the Visually Impaired, 7576
Diabetes, Vision Impairment and Blindness, 6244, 7930
Dialogue, 7865
Directory of Resources for the Blind & Visually Impaired, 7847
District of Columbia Rehabilitation Services, 723
Durward K. McDaniel Ambassador Award, 2631
Duxbury Systems, 3111
Educational Services for the Visually Impaired, 11331
El Paso Lighthouse for the Blind, 7582
Elizabeth Pierce Olmsted Center for the Visually Impaired, 7583
Eye Bank Association of America, 7586
Eye Opener, 7249
Eye Relief Word Processing Software, 3115
Eye and Your Vision, 7810
Eye-Q Test, 7938
Eyegaze Computer System, 3116
Eyes and Parkinson's Disease, 7002
Fidelco Guide Dog Foundation, 4197
Finding Wheels: A Curriculum for Nondrivers with Visual Impairments for Gaining Control, 7811
Food Markers/Magnets, 3333
Food Markers/Rubberbands, 3334
Foundation Fighting Blindness, 7590
Foundations of Rehabilitation Counseling with Persons who are Blind, 7812
Fountain Hills Lioness Braille Service, 11319
Fulton Public Library Learning Center, 11437
George Card Award, 2636
Greater Detroit Agency F/T Blind and Visually Impaired, 7597
A Guide to Independence for the Visually Impaired and Their Families, 7791
Guide to Independence for the Visually Impaired and Their Families, 7813
Guiding Eyes for the Blind, 7601
Ho'opono Services for the Blind, 7607
If Blindness Strikes; Don't Strike Out, 7815
Independent Visually Impaired Enterprisers, 7613, 8012
Information Access Project, 7870
Information Access Project: National Federation of the Blind, 7616
Insight, 7617
Iowa Regional Library for the Blind & Physically Handicapped, 7621
Journal of Visual Impairment and Blindness, 7875

Kansas Division of Services for the Blind, 7627
Kansas Specialty Dog Service, 1075
Kayak and Rafting Expeditions, 12028
Kentucky Division: Prevent Blindness America, 7629
Know Your Eye, 7964
LS & S Products, 3263
Large Print Loan Library, 7818
Lee County Subregional Library for the Blind and Physically Handicapped, 11418
Library Users of America, 7631
Lifestyles of Employed Legally Blind People, 7821
Lighthouse for the Blind of Miami, 7635
Low Vision: Reflections of the Past, Issues for the Future, 7823
Lutheran Library for the Blind, 11588
MC Migel Memorial Library and Helen Keller Archives, 11644
Magazines in Special Media for the Handicapped, 3922
Making Life More Livable, 7824, 8000
Maxi Aid Braille Timer, 3341
Maxi Aids, 5166
Medical College of Wisconsin Eye Institute, 8046
Member's Eye View of Alcoholics Anonymous, 7378
Miami Lighthouse for the Blind, 7646
Michigan Council of the Blind and Visually Impaired (MCBVI), 7647
Minnesota State Services for the Blind, 7648
Mississippi Industries for the Blind, 7649
Missouri Council of the Blind, 1488, 7650
Missouri Rehabilitation Services for the Blind, 7651
Mobile Association for the Blind, 7652
Morse Code Equalizer, 3142
NIH: National Eye Institute, 175
National Association for Visually Handicapped Library, 11649
National Association of Blind Teachers, 7659
National Eye Care Project, 7668
National Eye Care Project (NECP), 7669
National Eye Health Education Program, 7670
National Eye Institute, 8047
National Eye Research Foundation, 8048
National Federation of the Blind of California: Santa Barbara County Chapter, 7673
National Federation of the Blind of South Dakota, 7676
National Federation of the Blind of Texas: Austin Chapter, 7677
National Industries for the Blind, 7688
Nebraska Commission For The Blind AndVisually Impaired (NCBVI), 1580
Nebraska Commission for the Blind & Visually Impaired, 7693
Nebraska School for the Visually Handicapped Library, 11600
Nevada's Bureau of Services to the Blind and Visually Impaired, 7694
New Eyes for the Needy, 7696
New Hampshire Association for the Blind, 7697
New Hampshire Association for the Blind, 7698

Subject Index / Volunteerism

New Jersey Commission for the Blind and Visually Impaired, 7701
New Mexico Commission for the Blind, 7702
New York Public Library, 11651
New York State Commission for the Blind, 1804
North Country Association for the Visually Impaired, 7707
Northeastern Association of the Blind at Albany, 7709
Oklahoma Library for the Blind & Physically Handicapped, 11722
Oklahoma State Office of Rehabilitation Services: Visually Impaired, 7712
Ophthalmic Research Laboratory Eye Institute, 8050
Opportunity, 7888, 7975
Oregon Commission for the Blind, 7713
Oregon State Commission for the Blind, 7714
Out of Left Field, 7890
Pasadena Braille Club, 7715
Pasadena Braille Club, 7716
A Patient's Guide to Visual Aids and Illumination, 7910
Patient's Guide to Visual Aids and Illumination, 7976
Pennsylvania Bureau of Blindness and Visual Services, 7717
Pennsylvania College of Optometry Eye Institute, 8051
A Picture is Worth a Thousand Words for Blind and Visually Impaired Persons Too!, 7792
Picture is Worth a Thousand Words for Blind and Visually Impaired Persons, 7826
Pony Express Association for the Blind, 7720
Pony Express Association of the Blind, 7721
Prescriptions for Independence, 7827
Prevent Blindness America, 7722
Prevent Blindness America New York City Division, 1819
Prevent Blindness New Jersey, 1674
Prevent Blindness Oklahoma, 7728
Prevent Blindness Tennessee, 7729
Prevent Blindness Texas Central Regional, 6434
Quarterly Update, 7892
Rehabilitation Resource Manual: Vision, 7830
Research to Prevent Blindness, 7739
Rhode Island Department of Human Services, 2215
Rhode Island Department of State Library for the Blind and Physically Handicapped, 11753
Rhode Island Services for the Blind and Visually Impaired, 7741
Rigid Aluminum Cane with Golf Grip, 3488
SCENE, 11897
Schepens Eye Research Institute, 8052
Seeing, 7987
Seeing Clearly, 7895
Seeing Eye, 7742
Seeing Eye Guide, 7896
Services for the Visually Impaired: Department of Public Instruction, 11699
611 Washington Ear, 7492

Smith-Ketterwell Eye Research Institute, 8053
Smith-Kettlewell Technical File, 7897
South Carolina Commission for the Blind, 6055
St Clark County Library for the Blind and Physically Handicapped, 11571
St. Louis Society for the Blind, 7752
St. Louis Society for the Blind and Visually Impaired, 1522
Tampa Lighthouse for the Blind, 7753
Texas Commission for the Blind, 7759
3M Brailler, 3053
Tower Club of the Blind, 7761
Tri-State Blind Society, 7763
Tri-State Independent Blind Society, 7764
United States Association for Blind Athletes, 7765
University of Miami: Bascom Palmer Eye Institute, 8057
Utah Division of Services for the Disabled, 2417
Utah Industries for the Blind, 7766
Vermont Division for the Blind and Visually Impaired, 7768
Virginia Association for Education & Rehabilitation of the Blind & Visually Impaired, 7769
Virginia Department for the Blind & Vision Impaired, 7770
Visions, 8001
Visual Impairment and Blindness Services of Northampton County, 7776
Visually Impaired Data Processors International, 7778, 8034
Visually Impaired Seniors as Senior Companions: A Reference Guide, 7836
Visually Impaired Veterans of America, 7779, 8035
Washington Ear, 7782
West Texas Lighthouse for the Blind, 7785
Xavier Society for the Blind, 11680

Volunteerism

Able Commission, 1476
Adams County RSVP, 898
Alexandria Volunteer Bureau, 2448
Alpena Regional Medical Center Auxiliary, 1339
Alzheimer's Association: California Southland Chapter, 4726
Alzheimer's Association: Staten Island Chapter, 4890
Alzheimer's Foundation of Staten Island, 4921
Amador Senior Services, 10993
American Association of Retired Persons(AARP), 4181
American Medical Association Alliance, 46
Anne Arundel County Department of Aging and Disabilities, 1226
Arkansas Volunteer Lawyers for the Elderly (AVLE), 10990
Arthritis Foundation, 5085
Arthritis Foundation Mississippi Chapter, 5087
Arthritis Foundation Mississippi Gulf Coast Chapter, 5088
Arthritis Volunteer, 5179

Austin State School Volunteer Council, 2310
Bay Area Managers of Volunteer Services, 2570
Berks County Senior Citizens Council, 2041
Birchwood Volunteers In Partnership, 1751
Blueprint for Aging, 1343
Braille: An Extraordinary Volunteer Opportunity, 7923
Brevard Association for Advancement of the Blind, 7552
Brevard Association for the Advancement of the Blind, 7553
Brevard County Community Services Council, 734
Bryan County Retired and Senior Volunteer Program, 2004
Cache County Retired And SeniorVolunteer Program (RSVP), 2392
California Collaborative Treatment Group, 4453
Cape & Islands Senior Corps, 1271
Cass County Council on Aging, 1393
Charleston Area Senior Center, 904
Christian Foundation for Children and Aging, 3579
Columbia Lighthouse for the Blind, 7570
Columbus Volunteer Corps, 1953
Community Action Council: Lexington Fayette Jessamine Counties, 1101
Community Action Partnership of Mid-Nebraska Volunteer Services, 1567
Connecticut Lawyers' Legal Aid to the Elderly Program (CLLAEP), 11025
Corporate Volunteers of New York, 1763
Cortland County Area: Agency on Aging, 1764
Dallas Association of Directors of Volunteers, 2319
Department of Employment and Economic Development, 1396
Elder Law Center: Coalition of Wisconsin Aging Groups, 11295
Environmental Alliance for Senior Involvement, 2935
Fairbanks Senior Center, 419
Five County Retired Senior Volunteer Program, 2395
Florida Instructional Materials Center for the Visually Impaired, 11412
Fort Wayne EASI, 977
Foster Grandparent Program, 139
Gateway Older Adult Legal Services, 11170
Glacial Lakes Retired & Senior Volunteer Program, 2258
Golden Opportunities, 3736
Guide to Effective Volunteer Lobbying, 5202
Hampshire Community Action Commission, 1285
Harbor-UCLA Research and Education Institute, 4314
Hearing Loss Association of America, 6370
Heart of Florida United Way Volunteer Center, 762
Hill Country Community Action Association, 2325
Hospice Letter, 4043
Houston Bar Association: Judicare Program for the Elderly, 11266
KI BOIS Retired Senior Volunteer Program, 2010

1155

Subject Index / Volunteerism

Kansas Chapter of the Arthritis Foundation, 5112
Kit Carson And Lincoln Counties RSVP, 649
Legacy Link, 838
Legal Aid Services of Oregon: Senior LawProject, 11232
Lifescape Community Services, 928
Lucas County Health Center, 1031
MAB Community Services, 1289
Madison County RSVP, 991
Massachusetts Association for the Blind, 7643
McMinn County Senior Citizens, 2277
Meals on Wheels of Haywood County, 1897
Meals on Wheels of Rowan, 1898
Mecklenburg County Bar: Volunteer Lawyers Program and Services for the Elderly, 11214
Melanoma Research Foundation, 5936
Memphis Area Legal Services: Pro Bono Panel for Senior Citizens, 11259
Metro United Way, 1124
Miami Dade County Retired and Senior Volunteer Program, 764
Migel Medal for Outstanding Service to Blind Persons, 2655
Montgomery Area Council on Aging, 378
NLS Update, 7885, 7973
National Association of Partners in Education, 196
National Center for Voluntary Leadership in Aging, 207
National Council on the Aging, 220
National Hospice Organization, 4481, 5767, 6013
National Meditation Center, 4235
National Senior Service Corps, 261
National Veterans Legal Services Program Newsletter, 4072
National Volunteer Training Center for Substance Abuse Prevention, 7195
Newsletter of the Kansas Chapter of the Arthritis Foundation, 5214
North Carolina Society to Prevent Blindness, 7704
OASIS Cleveland, 2888
OASIS Denver, 2738
OASIS Eugene, 2898
OASIS Hyattsville, 2810
OASIS Institute, 2835
OASIS Los Angeles, 2722
OASIS Montgomery County, 2811
OASIS Portland, 2899
OASIS Rochester, 2867
OASIS San Diego, 2723
OASIS of Tucson, 2703
Old Fort Genealogical Society Of Southeastern Kansas Inc, 11502
Osceola County Council on Aging, 767
Pennsylvania Society of Directors of Volunteer Services, 2146
People Animals Love, 291
Prevent Blindness Nebraska, 7725
Prevent Blindness Ohio, 7727
Puppy Walker Brochure, 7979
RIDE Retired Individuals Driving Elderly, 1821
RSBP Altus, 2021
RSVP Heartland, 1495
RSVP Adams County, 1461
RSVP Adams-Arapahoe, 653
RSVP Adams-Webster Counties, 1586
RSVP Addison County, 2430
RSVP Advacapcap, 2579
RSVP Aiken County, 2231
RSVP Aiken-Carlton Counties, 1419
RSVP Akron, 1973
RSVP Alachua County, 769
RSVP Alamogordo City, 1728
RSVP Albany County, 842
RSVP Alexandria, 2469
RSVP All Peoples Christian Center, 576
RSVP Allegany County, 1254
RSVP Allegheny County, 2153
RSVP Allegheny County-Pittsburgh, 2154
RSVP Andrew County, 1496
RSVP Anoka County, 1420
RSVP Aroostook, 1216
RSVP Arrowhead County, 1421
RSVP Artesia, 1729
RSVP Athens Limestone County, 382
RSVP Athensns, 1974
RSVP Atlantic City Chapter, 1675
RSVP Atoka, 2022
RSVP Attala County, 1462
RSVP Auburn, 1822
RSVP Audubon Area, 1127
RSVP Baldwin County, 383
RSVP Baltimore City, 1255
RSVP Barton County, 1081
RSVP Baton Rouge, 1174
RSVP Beaver County, 2155
RSVP Bedford-Cambria County, 2156
RSVP Belmont County, 1975
RSVP Bennington County, 2431
RSVP Benton-Franklin Counties, 2513
RSVP Bergen County, 1676
RSVP Bergen County New Jersey, 1677
RSVP Berkshire, 1310
RSVP Bexar County, 2334
RSVP Big Bend, 770
RSVP Big Country, 2335
RSVP Big Spring, 2336
RSVP Birmingham Area, 384
RSVP Black Hawk, 1032
RSVP Blackstone Valley, 2206
RSVP Blair County, 2157
RSVP Boone County, 1497
RSVP Boston, 1311
RSVP Boulder County, 654
RSVP Brazos Valley, 2337
RSVP Brighton Center, 1128
RSVP Broome, 1823
RSVP Broward County, 771
RSVP Brown County, 2259, 2580
RSVP Buck County, 2158
RSVP Burlington County, 1678
RSVP Butler County, 1082
RSVP Butte School District No 1, 1551
RSVP Caddo-Bossier Counties, 1175
RSVP Calcasieu Parish, 1176
RSVP Calhoun County, 385
RSVP Camden County, 1679
RSVP Campbell County, 2470
RSVP Cape May Chapter, 1680
RSVP Cape May County, 1681
RSVP Capital Region, 2207
RSVP Capitol Region, 1824, 2159
RSVP Carbon County, 2396
RSVP Carlsbad City, 1730
RSVP Carolina Low Country, 2232
RSVP Carroll County, 1033, 1630
RSVP Cascade County, 1552
RSVP Case, 2551
RSVP Cattaraugus County, 1825
RSVP Central Coast, 577
RSVP Central Connecticut, 689
RSVP Central Kentucky, 1129
RSVP Central Naugatuck Valley, 690
RSVP Central Panhandle, 772
RSVP Central Vermont, 2432
RSVP Central Wyoming, 2613
RSVP Centre County, 2160
RSVP Chadron, 1587
RSVP Champaign, 935
RSVP Chautauqua, 1826
RSVP Chaves County, 1731
RSVP Chemung County, 1827
RSVP Chenago County, 1828
RSVP Chesapeake Bay, 2471
RSVP Chester County, 2161
RSVP Chicopee-Holyoke-Ludlow, 1312
RSVP Chisholm Trail County, 2338
RSVP Chittenden County, 2433
RSVP Cincinnati Area, 1976
RSVP Citrus County, 773
RSVP City of Burbank, 578
RSVP Clallam Jefferson County, 2514
RSVP Clarinda, 1034
RSVP Clark County, 1611, 1977, 2515
RSVP Clarksdale, 1463
RSVP Clarksville County, 2280
RSVP Clearfield County, 2162
RSVP Cleveland-McClain Counties, 2023
RSVP Clinch Valley, 2472
RSVP Clinton County, 1035, 1829
RSVP Coachella Valley, 579
RSVP Collier County, 774
RSVP Colorado West, 655
RSVP Columbia County, 1830, 2070
RSVP Concho Valley Texas, 2340
RSVP Coos County, 1631, 2071
RSVP Coosa Valley, 843
RSVP Corpus Christi, 2341
RSVP Cortland, 1831
RSVP Coulee Region, 2581
RSVP Cranston, 2208
RSVP Crawford, 1588
RSVP Crawford County, 2163
RSVP Crawford-Perry-Spencer, 992
RSVP Culver City, 580
RSVP Cumberland, 1682
RSVP Cumberland County Chapter, 1683
RSVP Curry County, 1732, 2072
RSVP Dallas, 2342
RSVP Dallas County, 386
RSVP Dane County, 2582
RSVP Daviess County Indiana, 993
RSVP Davis County, 2397
RSVP Dawson-Wibaux, 1553
RSVP Dearborn County, 994
RSVP Decatur, 936
RSVP Deep East Texas, 2343
RSVP Dekalb-Noble-Steuben Counties, 995
RSVP Delaware County, 2164
RSVP Deschutes County, 2073
RSVP Devils Lake Area, 1936
RSVP Douglass Community Services, 1498
RSVP Dubois-Pike-Warrick Counties, 996
RSVP Dubuque County, 1036
RSVP Dunklin County, 1499
RSVP Dutchess County, 1832
RSVP Duval County, 775
RSVP Dyer County, 2281
RSVP East Arkansas, 473

Subject Index / Volunteerism

RSVP East Bay, 2209
RSVP East Central South Dakota, 2260
RSVP East Central Tennessee, 2282
RSVP East Shore, 2473
RSVP East Valley Retired & Senior Volunteer Program, 442
RSVP Eastern Fairfield County, 691
RSVP El Paso City, 2344
RSVP Eldercircle, 1422
RSVP Elk-Cameron Counties, 2165
RSVP Elkhart County, 997
RSVP Emery, 2398
RSVP Enid, 2024
RSVP Erie County, 1833
RSVP Escambia County, 387
RSVP Essex County, 1834
RSVP Essex Hudson Chapter, 1684
RSVP Etowah County, 388
RSVP Fall River-Taunton, 1313
RSVP Fallon County, 1554
RSVP Fayettevill Area, 2283
RSVP Finney County, 1083
RSVP Flagler County, 776
RSVP Florence County, 2233
RSVP Floyd County, 2474
RSVP Ford County, 1084
RSVP Fort Dodge, 1037
RSVP Franklin County, 1835, 1978
RSVP Fresno, 581
RSVP Fulton, 998
RSVP Gallia County, 1979
RSVP Galveston County, 2345
RSVP Garland County, 474
RSVP Genesee County, 1836
RSVP Genesee-Shiawassee Counties, 1369
RSVP Gila Pinal, 443
RSVP Golden Triangle, 2346
RSVP Goucester County, 1685
RSVP Grand County, 2399
RSVP Grant County, 1733
RSVP Grays Harbor Pacific County, 2516
RSVP Greater Bristol, 692
RSVP Greater East Los Angeles, 582
RSVP Greater Erie Community Action, 2166
RSVP Greater Hartford, 693
RSVP Greater Lawrence-Haverhill, 1314
RSVP Greater Texarkana Arkansas, 475
RSVP Greater Twin Cities, 1423
RSVP Greene County, 389, 1837, 2167
RSVP Greenville, 2234
RSVP Grundy/Sullivan Counties, 1500
RSVP Hagerstown, 1256
RSVP Hamilton Wright Counties, 1038
RSVP Hancock County, 1464
RSVP Hancock-Henry-Rush, 999
RSVP Harcatus, 1980
RSVP Harrison County, 1465
RSVP Harrison-Daviess Counties, 1501
RSVP Harvey County, 1085
RSVP Hawaii County, 872
RSVP Heart of Texas, 2347
RSVP Heartland, 1424, 1502
RSVP Helena, 1555
RSVP Henry County, 1039
RSVP Herkimer County, 1838
RSVP Hernando County, 777
RSVP Hickman-McCracken Counties, 1130
RSVP Hill County, 1556
RSVP Hillsborough County, 778
RSVP Hockley County, 2348
RSVP Houston County, 2349

RSVP Houston Henry Geneva Counties, 390
RSVP Humboldt/Del Norte Counties, 583
RSVP Inca, 2025
RSVP Indian River County, 779
RSVP Indianapolis, 1000
RSVP Ingham, 1370
RSVP Jackson County, 1371, 2074
RSVP Jackson-Platte Counties, 1503
RSVP Jasper County, 1504
RSVP Jefferson, 1981
RSVP Jefferson Area, 2475
RSVP Jefferson County, 476, 657, 1001
RSVP Jefferson Parish, 1177
RSVP Johnson County, 1040, 1086
RSVP Joliet, 937
RSVP Josephine County, 2075
RSVP Kane McHenry Counties, 938
RSVP Kauai, 873
RSVP Kenosha County Sponsored By Kenosha Area Family And Aging Services, Inc., 2583
RSVP Kent County, 1372
RSVP King County, 2517
RSVP Kings/Tulare Counties, 584
RSVP Kitsap County, 2518
RSVP Kittitas County, 2519
RSVP KnoHo, 1982
RSVP Knox County, 1002
RSVP Knoxville-Knox County, 2284
RSVP LaPorte County, 1003
RSVP Lackawanna County, 2168
RSVP Lafayette, 1178
RSVP Lafayette County, 1466
RSVP Lake County, 939, 1004, 1983
RSVP Lake County Senior Citizens Mid Florida Community Services, 780
RSVP Lake/Mendocino Counties, 585
RSVP Laredo, 2350
RSVP Laurel-Jones County, 1467
RSVP Lawton, 2026
RSVP Lebanon-Lancaster Counties, 2169
RSVP Lee & Russell Counties, 391
RSVP Lee County, 781, 1468
RSVP Lee Scott Wise Norton, 2476
RSVP Lehigh County, 2170
RSVP Lewiston, 891
RSVP Lexington-Henderson Counties, 2285
RSVP Lincoln Area, 1589
RSVP Lincoln County, 2076
RSVP Lincoln Parish, 1179
RSVP Linn Benton County, 2077
RSVP Linn County, 1041
RSVP Little Dixie, 2027
RSVP Livingston County, 1505
RSVP Long Beach, 586
RSVP Lorain County, 1984
RSVP Los Alamos, 1734
RSVP Los Angeles Parks, 587
RSVP Loudoun, 2477
RSVP Louisville Metro Community Action Partnership, 1131
RSVP Love & Marshall Counties, 2028
RSVP Lowell, 1315
RSVP Lower Eastern Shore, 1257
RSVP Lowndes County, 1469
RSVP Lubbock, 2351
RSVP Luna County, 1735
RSVP Luzerne-Wyoming Counties, 2171
RSVP Macomb, 1373
RSVP Madison County, 1005, 1839
RSVP Magic Valley, 892
RSVP Mahoning County, 1985

RSVP Mahube Community Council, 1425
RSVP Maimi Valley, 1986
RSVP Manatee North Sarasota Counties, 782
RSVP Manitowoc County, 2584
RSVP Maple Lawn, 940
RSVP Maricopa County, 444
RSVP Marion County, 783, 2078
RSVP Marion-Crawford Counties, 1987
RSVP Marquette County, 1374
RSVP Marshall County, 392
RSVP Martin County, 784
RSVP Mason County, 1132
RSVP Maui County, 874
RSVP Mayflower of Plymouth County, 1316
RSVP McCormick, 2235
RSVP McKean County, 2172
RSVP McKinley County, 1736
RSVP McMinnville, 2286
RSVP Mecosta/Lake/Osceola, 1375
RSVP Meigs, 1988
RSVP Mercer County, 1686
RSVP Mercer Summer Monroe Counties, 2552
RSVP Meridian-Lauderdale Counties, 1470
RSVP Merrimack County, 1632
RSVP Metro Tarrant, 2352
RSVP Metro Tarrant County, 2353
RSVP Metropolitan, 1737
RSVP Mid Rio Grand, 1738
RSVP Mid State, 694
RSVP Mid-Ohio Valley, 2553
RSVP Middlesex County, 1687
RSVP Midland, 2354
RSVP Miles City, 1557
RSVP Milwaukee, 2585
RSVP Mississippi County, 1506
RSVP Mobile, 393
RSVP Monadnock, 1633
RSVP Monroe County, 1840, 2173
RSVP Monroe Owen County, 1006
RSVP Monroe/Cone-Cuh County, 394
RSVP Montgomery County, 1258, 1989, 2174, 2478
RSVP Morgantown, 2554
RSVP Morris County, 1688
RSVP Morris County Chapter, 1689
RSVP Mountainland, 2400
RSVP Multonamah County, 2079
RSVP Muskogee, 2029
RSVP NV Rural Counties, 1612
RSVP Nassau County, 1841
RSVP Natchitoches Parish, 1180
RSVP Nevada County, 588
RSVP New Castle County, 716
RSVP New Orleans, 1181
RSVP New York City, 1842
RSVP Newberry County, 2236
RSVP Niagara County, 1843
RSVP Norfolk County, 1317
RSVP North Central Arkansas, 477
RSVP North Central Iowa, 1042
RSVP North Central North Dakota, 1937
RSVP North Idaho, 893
RSVP North Lee County, 1043
RSVP North Texas, 2355
RSVP Northeast Georgia, 844
RSVP Northeast Iowa, 1044
RSVP Northern Arizona, 445
RSVP Northern Black Hills, 2261
RSVP Northern Fairfield County, 695

1157

Subject Index / Volunteerism

RSVP Northern Rhode Island, 2210
RSVP Northern Santa Clara County, 589
RSVP Northwest, 2586
RSVP Northwest Arkansas, 478
RSVP Northwest Kansas, 1087
RSVP Northwest Missouri/Northeast Kansas, 1507
RSVP Oahu, 875
RSVP Oakland, 590
RSVP Oakland County, 1376
RSVP Ocean County, 1690
RSVP Ocean County Chapter, 1691
RSVP Ogallala City-Keith Counties, 1590
RSVP Ojai County, 591
RSVP Okaloosa County, 785
RSVP Oneida County, 1844
RSVP Orange County, 1845
RSVP Ostego County, 1377
RSVP Otero Bent-Crowley Counties, 658
RSVP Ottumwa, 1045
RSVP Ouachita Parish, 1182
RSVP Outagamie County, 2587
RSVP Outer Houston, 2356
RSVP Oxnard County, 592
RSVP Palm Beach County, 786
RSVP Panhandle, 2555
RSVP Pasco County, 787
RSVP Passaic County, 1692
RSVP Pemiscot County, 1508
RSVP Penquis Coastal, 1217
RSVP Peoria/Tazewell Counties, 941
RSVP Perry County, 1990
RSVP Pettis-Saline Counties, 1509
RSVP Philadelphia East, 2175
RSVP Philadelphia West, 2176
RSVP Pierce County, 2520
RSVP Pike County, 395
RSVP Pinellas County, 788
RSVP Pomona Valley, 593
RSVP Ponca City and Kay County, 2030
RSVP Poplar Bluff-Altrusa Club, 1510
RSVP Portage County, 2588
RSVP Portsmouth, 1634, 2479
RSVP Pottawatomie-Seminole Counties, 2031
RSVP Pottawattamie Mills Counties, 1046
RSVP Pratt County, 1088
RSVP Prince George's County, 1259
RSVP Prince William, 2480
RSVP Program CEFA Economic Opportunity Corporation, 942
RSVP Pueblo, 659
RSVP Pulaski County, 2481
RSVP Putnam County, 1007, 1846
RSVP Quad Lakes Area of Missouri, 1511
RSVP Rapdi City Area, 2262
RSVP Rapides Parish, 1183
RSVP Rappahannock-Rapidan, 2482
RSVP Red River Valley, 1426, 2357
RSVP Reno County, 1089
RSVP Richardson County, 1591
RSVP Richland, 2237
RSVP Richland County, 1991
RSVP Richmond, 2483
RSVP Riley County, 1090
RSVP Rio Grande Valley, 2358
RSVP River Parishes, 1184
RSVP Rock County, 2589
RSVP Rock Island, 943
RSVP Rockland, 1847
RSVP Roosevelt County, 1558
RSVP Roseburg-Douglas, 2081

RSVP Roseburgburg, 2080
RSVP Runningwater Draw, 2359
RSVP Rural Resort Region, 660
RSVP Rutherford, 2287
RSVP Sacramento County, 594
RSVP Saline County, 1091
RSVP Salt Lake County, 2401
RSVP San Bernardino County, 595
RSVP San Fernando/Santa Clarita Valleys, 596
RSVP San Juan County, 1739
RSVP San Luis Valley, 661
RSVP Sandoval, 1740
RSVP Santa Barbara, 597
RSVP Santa Fe City, 1741
RSVP Santa Rosa, 789
RSVP Sarasota/Charlotte Counties, 790
RSVP Saratoga County, 1848
RSVP Savannah, 845
RSVP Schuyler County, 1849
RSVP Schuylkill County, 2177
RSVP Scioto County, 1992
RSVP Semcac, 1427
RSVP Senior Care North Shore, 1318
RSVP Seven County, 2032
RSVP Shast and Tehama Counties, 598
RSVP Shelby County, 2288
RSVP Shenandoah Area, 2484
RSVP Sheriden County, 1592
RSVP Sierra County, 1742
RSVP Simpson County, 1471
RSVP Siouxland, 2263
RSVP Six County, 2402
RSVP Skagit County, 2521
RSVP Snohomish County, 2522
RSVP Somerset County, 1693, 2178
RSVP Somerset County Chapter, 1694
RSVP Sonoma County, 599
RSVP South Bay County, 600
RSVP South Central Indiana RSVP, 1008
RSVP South Central Montana, 1559
RSVP Southeast Kansas, 1092
RSVP Southeastern Arizona, 446
RSVP Southeastern Wyoming, 2614
RSVP Southern Maine, 1218
RSVP Southern New Hampshire, 1635
RSVP Southern New London, 696
RSVP Southern Tri-County, 1428
RSVP Southside, 2485
RSVP Southwest Alabama, 396
RSVP Southwest Montana, 1560
RSVP Southwestern Connecticut, 697
RSVP Spartanburg, 2238
RSVP Spokane County, 2523
RSVP Springfield, 1319, 1513
RSVP St John's County, 791
RSVP St Lucie County, 792
RSVP St. Charles-Lincoln-Warren Counties, 1514
RSVP St. Joseph County, 1009
RSVP St. Louis, 1515
RSVP St. Mary's County, 1260
RSVP Story Marshall Counties, 1047
RSVP Stutgart North Arkansas, 479
RSVP Suffolk County, 1850
RSVP Sullivan County, 1851
RSVP Sumter County, 2239
RSVP Superior-Douglas, 2590
RSVP Sussex County, 717
RSVP Sussex-Warren, 1695
RSVP Sussex-Warren Chapter, 1696
RSVP Swisher County, 2360

RSVP Tallapossa & Coosa Counties, 397
RSVP Texas Panhandle, 2361
RSVP Texoma, 2362
RSVP Thousand Oaks/Conejo Valley, 601
RSVP Todd-Wadena-Otter Tail-Wilkin, 1429
RSVP Tompkins County, 1852
RSVP Travis County, 2363
RSVP Treasure Valley, 894
RSVP Tri-County, 480
RSVP Triton College Volunteer Program, 944
RSVP Tucson, 447
RSVP Tulsa, 2033
RSVP Ulster County, 1853
RSVP Union County, 1697
RSVP Union County Chapter, 1698
RSVP United Way of Central Iowa, 1048
RSVP VOA Colorado Branch, 662
RSVP VOA Denver, 663
RSVP Valparaiso, 1010
RSVP Venango County, 2179
RSVP Village of Ruidoso, 1743
RSVP Visalia Volunteer, 602
RSVP Volunteer Services, 1430
RSVP Volunteer Services of United Way Palm Beach County, 793
RSVP Volusia County, 794
RSVP Walla Walla CountySenior Citizen Center, 2524
RSVP Walworth County, 2591
RSVP Warren County, 1993
RSVP Warren-Forest Counties, 2180
RSVP Washington County, 1994
RSVP Washoe County, 1613
RSVP Waukeesha County, 2592
RSVP Wayne County, 1011, 1378
RSVP Wayne-Seneca-Ontario, 1854
RSVP Weld County, 664
RSVP West Arkansas, 481
RSVP West Bay, 2211
RSVP West Central Minnesota, 1431
RSVP West Valley of San Bernardino County, 603
RSVP Western Arizona, 448
RSVP Western Riverside County, 604
RSVP Westmoreland County, 2181
RSVP Windham County, 2434
RSVP Windham-Tolland Counties, 698
RSVP Woodbury County, 1049
RSVP Worcester Area, 1320
RSVP Wyandotte County, 1093
RSVP YWCA Senior Services, 945
RSVP Yakima County, 2525
RSVP Yellowstone County, 1561
RSVP York County, 2240
RSVP and the Volunteer Center, 1636
RSVP of Central Arkansas, 482
RSVP of Central North Dakota, 1938
RSVP of Warren and Washington Counties, 1855
Retired & Senior Volunteer Program of Hull House Chicago, 952
Retired & Senior Volunteer Program of Northern DuPage Counties, 953
Retired Military Police Association, 303
Retired Senior Volunteer Program of Rio Grande, 1745
Retired Senior Volunteer Program of Steuben County, 1865
Retired Senior Volunteer Program of Western Dairyland, 2594

Subject Index / Wills, See also Probate

Retired and Senior Volunteer Program, 304
Round Rock Volunteer Center, 2368
RsVP Clackamas County, 2085
Santa Cruz Volunteer Center, 612
School of Education and Human Development Lyceum, 2871
Seminole County Volunteer Program, 797
Senior Citizens, 2290
Senior Companion Program, 309
Senior Connections The Capital Area: Agency, 2490
Senior Services, 1387
Senior Services of Central Illinois, 955
Senior Specialists Agency on Aging, 484
Seniors Helping Others Volunteer Program of Washington County, 2222
Service Corps of Retired Executives of Tulsa, 2034
Service Opportunities After Retirement (SOAR), 1325
Shawnee Development Council, 957
Shepherd's Center of Kernersville, 2883
Shepherd's Center of Richmond, 2938
Social Service Association, 1702
South Central Connecticut Agency on Aging, 699
Southwestern Indiana Regional Council on Aging, 1014
Tax Counseling for the Elderly: Taxpayers Services, 322
Texas Association of Directors of Volunteer Services, 2375
Trustee of the Year Award, 2687
United Way 211, 1440
United Way of Central Florida, 806
United Way of Eastern Maine, 1222
University of Maryland: Center on Aging, 4407
Vacaville Public Library: Town Square, 11358
Veterans' Advocate, 11049
Vision Community Services, 7772
Visually Impaired Center, 7777
Voluntary Action Center of Northeastern Pennsylvania, 2195
Volunteer Center, 621
Volunteer Center Directory, 3807
Volunteer Center Orange County, 622
Volunteer Center of Camden County, 1706
Volunteer Center of Centre County, 2196
Volunteer Center of Greater Durham, 1923
Volunteer Center of Kern County, 623
Volunteer Center of Monmouth County, 1707
Volunteer Center of Morgan County, 401
Volunteer Center of Racine County, 2597
Volunteer Center of United Way for Capital Area, 700
Volunteer Committees of Art Museums of Canada and the United States News, 4122
Volunteer Exchange, 624
Volunteer Jacksonville, 807
Volunteer Lawyers Project for the Elderly, 11014
Volunteer Lawyers Project of the Boston Bar Association, 11153
Volunteer Leader, 4123
Volunteer Services of Barron County, 2598
Volunteer Vacations, 3808
Volunteer Voice, 5230
Volunteer at Your Braille and Talking Book Library, 7997

Volunteer! The Comprehensive Guide to Voluntary Service in the US and Abroad, 3809
Volunteerism in Action for the Aging: A Handbook, 3678
Volunteers Of AmericaGreater New Orleans Retired Seniors Volunteer Program, 1195
Volunteers for the Visually Handicapped, 7780
Volunteers of America, 4124
Volunteers of America Bay Area, 625
Volunteers of America Southeast, 402
Volunteers of America of Minnesota, 9316

Wills, See also Probate

AIDS Info, 4577
AIDSinfo, 4445
Access Industries/ThyssenKrupp Access, 3355
Access Technologies, 2040
Administrative Advocacy Clinic/Advocates for Older People, 11040
Advance Directive and Living Will Resources, 4175
Age Care Sourcebook: A Resource Guide for the Aging and Their Families, 3691
Alaska Legal Services Corporation: Senior Legal Services Project, 10975
Alterra Sterling House-Willmar, 9109
American Hotel and Motel Association, 12007
American Walker, 3477
Arkansas Rehabilitation Services, 467
Arthritis Foundation DistributionCenter: Pool Exercise Program, 5231
Arthritis Foundation: Pool Exercise Program, 5092
Association for Assessment in Counseling, 79
Back Machine, 3195
Bronxwood Home for the Aged, 9833
Change for the Better, 3614
Community Outreach Awards, 2626
Depression, the Mood Disease, 6071
Diabetes: A Guide to Living Well, 6198
Diabetes: A Positive Approach, 6234
Disability Compliance Bulletin, 4025
Elder Law of Michigan: Legal Hotline for Michigan Seniors, 11155
Elderlaw Project, 10977
Elderly Health Services Letter, 3857
Essex County Bar: Elder Law Committee, 11188
Exercise Beats Arthritis, 5159
Flashing Lamp Telephone Ring Alerter, 3117
Golden Buckeye Program, 11959
Greene Oaks Willow Place, 9894
Hear: Solutions, Skills, and Sources for People with Hearing Loss, 6507
Heartland of Willowbrook, 10463
Helen Keller National Center: NorthwestRegion, 7605
Highland Hospital: John R Williams, Sr Health Sciences Library, 11637
Homewood of Williamsport, 8920
If You Have Alzheimer's Disease: What You Should Know, What You Can Do, 5002
Illinois Assistive Technology Project, 918

Kansas Hearing Aid Association, 6386
Kansas Hearing Society, 6387
Keep It Simple, 7258
Legal Aid Society of Hawaii, 11068
Legal Aid Society of Hawaii: Hilo, 11069
Legal Aid Society of Hawaii: Honolulu, 11070
Legal Aid Society of Hawaii: Kaunakakai, 11071
Legal Aid Society of Hawaii: Lanai City, 11072
Legal Aid Society of Hawaii: Lihu'e, 11073
Legal Aid Society of Hawaii: Maui, 11074
Let's Solve the Smokeword Puzzle, 4057
Let's Talk About Depression, 6089
Living Will Form, 4213
Location Finder, 3133
Malta Park: Willwoods II, 8872
Malta Square at Sacred Heart: Willwoods II, 8873
Marriott Maple Ridge of Willoughby, 9917
Maryland State Bar Association of Legal Services, 11142
McDermott, Will & Emery Library, 11461
Mid-Minnesota Area: Agency on Aging, 1403
Milwaukee Young Lawyers Association: Committee on Legal Services to the Elderly, 11296
Monroe Community Hospital: TF Williams Health Sciences Library, 11646
National Institute on Community-Based Long-Term Care, 234
National Institutes of Health, 236, 4234
National Organization for Albinism and Hypopigmentation, 246
Northern Virginia Resource Center for Deaf and Hard of Hearing Persons, 6424
OASIS Pittsburgh, 2909
Oral Interpreters: Facts for Consumers, 6695
PRIDE Foundation, 281
Parkinson's Support Group of Upstate New York, 6976
Prairie Senior Cottages-Willmar, 9260
Prince William Area: Agency on Aging, 2468
Purdue University: William A Hillenbrand Biomedical Engineering Center, 6887
Ready Willing & Able, 1860
Ready Willing & Able: Gates, 1861
Residence, 10199
Respite Care Guide: How to Find What's Right for You, 5007
Safe Homes, 4246
Senior Citizens' Wills Program: Chicago Bar Association, 11094
Serving Our Seniors, 2000
Signs for Computing Terminology, 6545
St Williams Foster Care, 9294
Steps to Understanding Legal Issues: Planning for the Future, 5017
Sunrise of Willowbrook, 8614
Sure Safe Raised Toilet Seat, 3024
TV & VCR Remote, 3174
Talking Bathroom Scale, 3026
Thick-n-Easy, 3350
Toward Healthy Living - A Wellness Journal, Arthritis Foundation Distribution Center, 5163
University of Hawaii at Manoa: William S Richardson School of Law, 11076

1159

Subject Index / Women's Issues

Useful Information on Phobias and Panic, 6101
Village at Willow Crossings, 9028
WA & NEWS, 4125
Walter T. Ridder Award, 2689
We Will Remember, 4166
Will-Grundy Center for Independent Living, 10742
Willamette Manor, 10185
Willamette View, 10186
Willamette View Health Center, 10187
Williamsburg Senior Living Community, 8897
William S Hein & Company, 3813
William T Gossett Parkinson's Disease Center, 7050
William and Mercer Research Library, 11679
Willow Knoll Retirement Community, 9977
Willow Lake, 10201
Willow Park Assisted Living, 8575
Willow Pointe, 8754
Willowbrook Assisted Living, 8576
Willows, 8577, 8755
Willows Assisted Living, 10231
Willows at Holmdel Assisted Living Community, 9825
Willows at Meadow Branch, 10576
Wills and Bequests, 5022

Women's Issues

AA and the Armed Services, 7289
AA for the Woman, 7293
Alcoholics Anonymous, 7132
Alcoholics Anonymous, The Big Book, 7240
Alice B. Silver Size Clothing Designs for Senior Women, 4177
Brigham and Women's Hospital: Asthma & Allergic Diseases Research Center, 4681
Brigham and Women's Hospital: Robert B Brigham Arthritis Center, 5236
California Women's Commission on Alcohol and Drug Dependencies, 7143
Calyx Books & Calyx Journal, 11865
Caregivers' Roller Coaster, 3610
Cascade AIDS Project: Women's Phone Network, 4589
Center for Clinical and Lifestyle Research, 4283
Chemical Dependency Pamphlets, 7324
Cocaine Anonymous, 7145
College at Sixty, 2856
Creighton University Center for Health Policy and Ethics, 4297
Directory of Health, Medical, and Disability Sites on the World Wide Web and Internet, 3717
Does She Drink Too Much?, 7337
Elder Craftsmen, 2857
Feel Nifty After 50: Top Tips to Help Women Grow Young, 3629
Fifty-Plus Lifelong Fitness, 136
Fighting Back Against PD: One Women's Story, 7003
Golden Aspen Publishing, 11879
HIV Treatment Information Exchange (HTIE), 4562
Health Information Network for Women and AIDS, 4464
How to Feel & Look Nifty After 50, 4046
Howard University Social Work Library, 11391
I Didn't Hear the Dragon Roar, 6511
I'm Black and I'm Sober, 7256
I'm Pretty Old, 4146
International Ladies' Garment Workers Union Research Department Library, 11640
It Happened to Alice, 7364
Journal of Women and Aging, 3914
Letter to a Woman Alcoholic, 7367
Life Force: Women Fighting AIDS, 4469
Look Like a Winner After 50 with Care, Color & Style, 3646
Men's/Women's Low Vision Watches & Clocks, 3138
Menopause Without Medicine, 11696
Miami University Humanities and Social Sciences Department, 11710
Narcotics Anonymous, 7265
National Alliance of Senior Citizens Library, 11397
National Committee for Responsive Philanthropy, 213
National Institute of Senior Housing, 231
National Parkinson Foundation, 6956
National Senior Citizens Law Center, 11008, 11046
National Senior Women's Tennis Association, 263
National Women's Health Network, 266
New Jersey Blind Citizens Association, 7699
New Jersey Blind Citizens' Association, 7700
New Jersey Women and AIDS Network, 4487
Older Women's League, 278
Older Women's League of Ohlone, 571
Operation ABLE of Greater Boston, 1307
Our Special, 7889
Paisley House for Aged Women, 9936
Pap Test: It Can Save Your Life, 5835
Papier-Mache Press, 11893
A Resource Guide for Drug Management for Older Persons, 7234
Resource Guide for Drug Management for Older Persons, 7272
SELF Magazine, 3955
Senior Scholars, 2891
Sober But Stuck, 7275
Sobering Thoughts, 4110
Supportive Older Women's Network, 320
Tampa AIDS Network: Florida Women's AIDS Resource Movement, 4501
Temple Association for Retired Persons, 2911
Tide Book Publishing Company, 11906
Time to Start Living, 7409
Turnabout, 7279
US Equal Employment Opportunity Commission, 11406
Understanding Gestational Diabetes, 6255
University of Massachusetts at Boston: Gerontology Institute and Center, 4408
University of Utah Human Performance Research Laboratory, 4428
WFS' New Life Program, 7226
Woman to Woman, 7230
A Woman's Guide to Coping with Disability, 3684
Women for Sobriety, 7231
Women's AIDS Network, 4512
Women's Health, 4257
Women's Perspective, 4167

Business Information ♦ Ratings Guides ♦ General Reference ♦ Education ♦ Statistics ♦ Demographics ♦ Health Information ♦ Canadian Information

The Directory of Business Information Resources, 2008

With 100% verification, over 1,000 new listings and more than 12,000 updates, *The Directory of Business Information Resources* is the most up-to-date source for contacts in over 98 business areas – from advertising and agriculture to utilities and wholesalers. This carefully researched volume details: the Associations representing each industry; the Newsletters that keep members current; the Magazines and Journals - with their "Special Issues" - that are important to the trade, the Conventions that are "must attends," Databases, Directories and Industry Web Sites that provide access to must-have marketing resources. Includes contact names, phone & fax numbers, web sites and e-mail addresses. This one-volume resource is a gold mine of information and would be a welcome addition to any reference collection.

> "This is a most useful and easy-to-use addition to any researcher's library." –The Information Professionals Institute

Softcover ISBN 978-1-59237-193-8, 2,500 pages, $195.00 | Online Database $495.00

Hudson's Washington News Media Contacts Directory, 2008

With 100% verification of data, Hudson's Washington News Media Contacts Directory is the most accurate, most up-to-date source for media contacts in our nation's capital. With the largest concentration of news media in the world, having access to Washington's news media will get your message heard by these key media outlets. Published for over 40 years, Hudson's Washington News Media Contacts Directory brings you immediate access to: News Services & Newspapers, News Service Syndicates, DC Newspapers, Foreign Newspapers, Radio & TV, Magazines & Newsletters, and Freelance Writers & Photographers. The easy-to-read entries include contact names, phone & fax numbers, web sites and e-mail and more. For easy navigation, Hudson's Washington News Media Contacts Directory contains two indexes: Entry Index and Executive Index. This kind of comprehensive and up-to-date information would cost thousands of dollars to replicate or countless hours of searching to find. Don't miss this opportunity to have this important resource in your collection, and start saving time and money today. Hudson's Washington News Media Contacts Directory is the perfect research tool for Public Relations, Marketing, Networking and so much more. This resource is a gold mine of information and would be a welcome addition to any reference collection.

Softcover ISBN 978-1-59237-393-2, 800 pages, $289.00

Nations of the World, 2007/08 A Political, Economic and Business Handbook

This completely revised edition covers all the nations of the world in an easy-to-use, single volume. Each nation is profiled in a single chapter that includes Key Facts, Political & Economic Issues, a Country Profile and Business Information. In this fast-changing world, it is extremely important to make sure that the most up-to-date information is included in your reference collection. This edition is just the answer. Each of the 200+ country chapters have been carefully reviewed by a political expert to make sure that the text reflects the most current information on Politics, Travel Advisories, Economics and more. You'll find such vital information as a Country Map, Population Characteristics, Inflation, Agricultural Production, Foreign Debt, Political History, Foreign Policy, Regional Insecurity, Economics, Trade & Tourism, Historical Profile, Political Systems, Ethnicity, Languages, Media, Climate, Hotels, Chambers of Commerce, Banking, Travel Information and more. Five Regional Chapters follow the main text and include a Regional Map, an Introductory Article, Key Indicators and Currencies for the Region. As an added bonus, an all-inclusive CD-ROM is available as a companion to the printed text. Noted for its sophisticated, up-to-date and reliable compilation of political, economic and business information, this brand new edition will be an important acquisition to any public, academic or special library reference collection.

> "A useful addition to both general reference collections and business collections." –RUSQ

Softcover ISBN 978-1-59237-177-8, 1,700 pages, $155.00

The Directory of Venture Capital & Private Equity Firms, 2008

This edition has been extensively updated and broadly expanded to offer direct access to over 2,800 Domestic and International Venture Capital Firms, including address, phone & fax numbers, e-mail addresses and web sites for both primary and branch locations. Entries include details on the firm's Mission Statement, Industry Group Preferences, Geographic Preferences, Average and Minimum Investments and Investment Criteria. You'll also find details that are available nowhere else, including the Firm's Portfolio Companies and extensive information on each of the firm's Managing Partners, such as Education, Professional Background and Directorships held, along with the Partner's E-mail Address. *The Directory of Venture Capital & Private Equity Firms* offers five important indexes: Geographic Index, Executive Name Index, Portfolio Company Index, Industry Preference Index and College & University Index. With its comprehensive coverage and detailed, extensive information on each company, The Directory of Venture Capital & Private Equity Firms is an important addition to any finance collection.

> "The sheer number of listings, the descriptive information and the outstanding indexing make this directory a better value than …Pratt's Guide to Venture Capital Sources. Recommended for business collections in large public, academic and business libraries." –Choice

Softcover ISBN 978-1-59237-272-0, 1,300 pages, $565/$450 Library | Online Database $889.00

To preview any of our Directories Risk-Free for 30 days, call (800) 562-2139 or fax (518) 789-0556
www.greyhouse.com books@greyhouse.com

Business Information ♦ Ratings Guides ♦ General Reference ♦ Education ♦ Statistics ♦ Demographics ♦ Health Information ♦ Canadian Information

The Encyclopedia of Emerging Industries
*Published under an exclusive license from the Gale Group, Inc.

The fifth edition of the *Encyclopedia of Emerging Industries* details the inception, emergence, and current status of nearly 120 flourishing U.S. industries and industry segments. These focused essays unearth for users a wealth of relevant, current, factual data previously accessible only through a diverse variety of sources. This volume provides broad-based, highly-readable, industry information under such headings as Industry Snapshot, Organization & Structure, Background & Development, Industry Leaders, Current Conditions, America and the World, Pioneers, and Research & Technology. Essays in this new edition, arranged alphabetically for easy use, have been completely revised, with updated statistics and the most current information on industry trends and developments. In addition, there are new essays on some of the most interesting and influential new business fields, including Application Service Providers, Concierge Services, Entrepreneurial Training, Fuel Cells, Logistics Outsourcing Services, Pharmacogenomics, and Tissue Engineering. Two indexes, General and Industry, provide immediate access to this wealth of information. Plus, two conversion tables for SIC and NAICS codes, along with Suggested Further Readings, are provided to aid the user. *The Encyclopedia of Emerging Industries* pinpoints emerging industries while they are still in the spotlight. This important resource will be an important acquisition to any business reference collection.

"This well-designed source…should become another standard business source, nicely complementing Standard & Poor's Industry Surveys. It contains more information on each industry than Hoover's Handbook of Emerging Companies, is broader in scope than The Almanac of American Employers 1998-1999, but is less expansive than the Encyclopedia of Careers & Vocational Guidance. Highly recommended for all academic libraries and specialized business collections." –Library Journal

Hardcover ISBN 978-1-59237-242-3, 1,400 pages, $325.00

Encyclopedia of American Industries
*Published under an exclusive license from the Gale Group, Inc.

The Encyclopedia of American Industries is a major business reference tool that provides detailed, comprehensive information on a wide range of industries in every realm of American business. A two volume set, Volume I provides separate coverage of nearly 500 manufacturing industries, while Volume II presents nearly 600 essays covering the vast array of services and other non-manufacturing industries in the United States. Combined, these two volumes provide individual essays on every industry recognized by the U.S. Standard Industrial Classification (SIC) system. Both volumes are arranged numerically by SIC code, for easy use. Additionally, each entry includes the corresponding NAICS code(s). The *Encyclopedia's* business coverage includes information on historical events of consequence, as well as current trends and statistics. Essays include an Industry Snapshot, Organization & Structure, Background & Development, Current Conditions, Industry Leaders, Workforce, America and the World, Research & Technology along with Suggested Further Readings. Both SIC and NAICS code conversion tables and an all-encompassing Subject Index, with cross-references, complete the text. With its detailed, comprehensive information on a wide range of industries, this resource will be an important tool for both the industry newcomer and the seasoned professional.

"Encyclopedia of American Industries contains detailed, signed essays on virtually every industry in contemporary society. … Highly recommended for all but the smallest libraries." -American Reference Books Annual

Two Volumes, Hardcover ISBN 978-1-59237-244-7, 3,000 pages, $650.00

Encyclopedia of Global Industries
*Published under an exclusive license from the Gale Group, Inc.

This fourth edition of the acclaimed *Encyclopedia of Global Industries* presents a thoroughly revised and expanded look at more than 125 business sectors of global significance. Detailed, insightful articles discuss the origins, development, trends, key statistics and current international character of the world's most lucrative, dynamic and widely researched industries – including hundreds of profiles of leading international corporations. Beginning researchers will gain from this book a solid understanding of how each industry operates and which countries and companies are significant participants, while experienced researchers will glean current and historical figures for comparison and analysis. The industries profiled in previous editions have been updated, and in some cases, expanded to reflect recent industry trends. Additionally, this edition provides both SIC and NAICS codes for all industries profiled. As in the original volumes, *The Encyclopedia of Global Industries* offers thorough studies of some of the biggest and most frequently researched industry sectors, including Aircraft, Biotechnology, Computers, Internet Services, Motor Vehicles, Pharmaceuticals, Semiconductors, Software and Telecommunications. An SIC and NAICS conversion table and an all-encompassing Subject Index, with cross-references, are provided to ensure easy access to this wealth of information. These and many others make the *Encyclopedia of Global Industries* the authoritative reference for studies of international industries.

"Provides detailed coverage of the history, development, and current status of 115 of "the world's most lucrative and high-profile industries." It far surpasses the Department of Commerce's U.S. Global Trade Outlook 1995-2000 (GPO, 1995) in scope and coverage. Recommended for comprehensive public and academic library business collections." -Booklist

Hardcover ISBN 978-1-59237-243-0, 1,400 pages, $495.00

To preview any of our Directories Risk-Free for 30 days, call (800) 562-2139 or fax (518) 789-0556
www.greyhouse.com books@greyhouse.com

Business Information ♦ Ratings Guides ♦ General Reference ♦ Education ♦ Statistics ♦ Demographics ♦ Health Information ♦ Canadian Information

The Directory of Mail Order Catalogs, 2008

Published since 1981, *The Directory of Mail Order Catalogs* is the premier source of information on the mail order catalog industry. It is the source that business professionals and librarians have come to rely on for the thousands of catalog companies in the US. Since the 2007 edition, *The Directory of Mail Order Catalogs* has been combined with its companion volume, *The Directory of Business to Business Catalogs*, to offer all 13,000 catalog companies in one easy-to-use volume. Section I: Consumer Catalogs, covers over 9,000 consumer catalog companies in 44 different product chapters from Animals to Toys & Games. Section II: Business to Business Catalogs, details 5,000 business catalogs, everything from computers to laboratory supplies, building construction and much more. Listings contain detailed contact information including mailing address, phone & fax numbers, web sites, e-mail addresses and key contacts along with important business details such as product descriptions, employee size, years in business, sales volume, catalog size, number of catalogs mailed and more. Three indexes are included for easy access to information: Catalog & Company Name Index, Geographic Index and Product Index. *The Directory of Mail Order Catalogs*, now with its expanded business to business catalogs, is the largest and most comprehensive resource covering this billion-dollar industry. It is the standard in its field. This important resource is a useful tool for entrepreneurs searching for catalogs to pick up their product, vendors looking to expand their customer base in the catalog industry, market researchers, small businesses investigating new supply vendors, along with the library patron who is exploring the available catalogs in their areas of interest.

"This is a godsend for those looking for information." –Reference Book Review

Softcover ISBN 978-1-59237-202-7, 1,700 pages, $350/$250 Library | Online Database $495.00

Sports Market Place Directory, 2008

For over 20 years, this comprehensive, up-to-date directory has offered direct access to the Who, What, When & Where of the Sports Industry. With over 20,000 updates and enhancements, the *Sports Market Place Directory* is the most detailed, comprehensive and current sports business reference source available. In 1,800 information-packed pages, *Sports Market Place Directory* profiles contact information and key executives for: Single Sport Organizations, Professional Leagues, Multi-Sport Organizations, Disabled Sports, High School & Youth Sports, Military Sports, Olympic Organizations, Media, Sponsors, Sponsorship & Marketing Event Agencies, Event & Meeting Calendars, Professional Services, College Sports, Manufacturers & Retailers, Facilities and much more. The Sports Market Place Directory provides organization's contact information with detailed descriptions including: Key Contacts, physical, mailing, email and web addresses plus phone and fax numbers. *Sports Market Place Directory* provides a one-stop resources for this billion-dollar industry. This will be an important resource for large public libraries, university libraries, university athletic programs, career services or job placement organizations, and is a must for anyone doing research on or marketing to the US and Canadian sports industry.

"Grey House is the new publisher and has produced an excellent edition...highly recommended for public libraries and academic libraries with sports management programs or strong interest in athletics." -Booklist

Softcover ISBN 978-1-59237-348-2, 1,800 pages, $225.00 | Online Database $479.00

Food and Beverage Market Place, 2008

Food and Beverage Market Place is bigger and better than ever with thousands of new companies, thousands of updates to existing companies and two revised and enhanced product category indexes. This comprehensive directory profiles over 18,000 Food & Beverage Manufacturers, 12,000 Equipment & Supply Companies, 2,200 Transportation & Warehouse Companies, 2,000 Brokers & Wholesalers, 8,000 Importers & Exporters, 900 Industry Resources and hundreds of Mail Order Catalogs. Listings include detailed Contact Information, Sales Volumes, Key Contacts, Brand & Product Information, Packaging Details and much more. *Food and Beverage Market Place* is available as a three-volume printed set, a subscription-based Online Database via the Internet, on CD-ROM, as well as mailing lists and a licensable database.

"An essential purchase for those in the food industry but will also be useful in public libraries where needed. Much of the information will be difficult and time consuming to locate without this handy three-volume ready-reference source." –ARBA

3 Vol Set, Softcover ISBN 978-1-59237-198-3, 8,500 pages, $595 | Online Database $795 | Online Database & 3 Vol Set Combo, $995

The Grey House Performing Arts Directory, 2007

The Grey House Performing Arts Directory is the most comprehensive resource covering the Performing Arts. This important directory provides current information on over 8,500 Dance Companies, Instrumental Music Programs, Opera Companies, Choral Groups, Theater Companies, Performing Arts Series and Performing Arts Facilities. Plus, this edition now contains a brand new section on Artist Management Groups. In addition to mailing address, phone & fax numbers, e-mail addresses and web sites, dozens of other fields of available information include mission statement, key contacts, facilities, seating capacity, season, attendance and more. This directory also provides an important Information Resources section that covers hundreds of Performing Arts Associations, Magazines, Newsletters, Trade Shows, Directories, Databases and Industry Web Sites. Five indexes provide immediate access to this wealth of information: Entry Name, Executive Name, Performance Facilities, Geographic and Information Resources. *The Grey House Performing Arts Directory* pulls together thousands of Performing Arts Organizations, Facilities and Information Resources into an easy-to-use source – this kind of comprehensiveness and extensive detail is not available in any resource on the market place today.

"Immensely useful and user-friendly ... recommended for public, academic and certain special library reference collections." –Booklist

To preview any of our Directories Risk-Free for 30 days, call (800) 562-2139 or fax (518) 789-0556
www.greyhouse.com   books@greyhouse.com

Business Information • Ratings Guides • General Reference • Education • Statistics • Demographics • Health Information • Canadian Information

Softcover ISBN 978-1-59237-138-9, 1,500 pages, $185.00 | Online Database $335.00

New York State Directory, 2007/08

The New York State Directory, published annually since 1983, is a comprehensive and easy-to-use guide to accessing public officials and private sector organizations and individuals who influence public policy in the state of New York. *The New York State Directory* includes important information on all New York state legislators and congressional representatives, including biographies and key committee assignments. It also includes staff rosters for all branches of New York state government and for federal agencies and departments that impact the state policy process. Following the state government section are 25 chapters covering policy areas from agriculture through veterans' affairs. Each chapter identifies the state, local and federal agencies and officials that formulate or implement policy. In addition, each chapter contains a roster of private sector experts and advocates who influence the policy process. The directory also offers appendices that include statewide party officials; chambers of commerce; lobbying organizations; public and private universities and colleges; television, radio and print media; and local government agencies and officials.

"This comprehensive directory covers not only New York State government offices and key personnel but pertinent U.S. government agencies and non-governmental entities. This directory is all encompassing... recommended." -Choice

New York State Directory - Softcover ISBN 978-1-59237-190-7, 800 pages, $145.00
New York State Directory with *Profiles of New York* – 2 Volumes, Softcover ISBN 978-1-59237-191-4, 1,600 pages, $225.00

The Grey House Homeland Security Directory, 2008

This updated edition features the latest contact information for government and private organizations involved with Homeland Security along with the latest product information and provides detailed profiles of nearly 1,000 Federal & State Organizations & Agencies and over 3,000 Officials and Key Executives involved with Homeland Security. These listings are incredibly detailed and include Mailing Address, Phone & Fax Numbers, Email Addresses & Web Sites, a complete Description of the Agency and a complete list of the Officials and Key Executives associated with the Agency. Next, *The Grey House Homeland Security Directory* provides the go-to source for Homeland Security Products & Services. This section features over 2,000 Companies that provide Consulting, Products or Services. With this Buyer's Guide at their fingertips, users can locate suppliers of everything from Training Materials to Access Controls, from Perimeter Security to BioTerrorism Countermeasures and everything in between – complete with contact information and product descriptions. A handy Product Locator Index is provided to quickly and easily locate suppliers of a particular product. This comprehensive, information-packed resource will be a welcome tool for any company or agency that is in need of Homeland Security information and will be a necessary acquisition for the reference collection of all public libraries and large school districts.

"Compiles this information in one place and is discerning in content. A useful purchase for public and academic libraries." –Booklist

Softcover ISBN 978-1-59237-196-6, 800 pages, $195.00 | Online Database $385.00

The Grey House Safety & Security Directory, 2008

The Grey House Safety & Security Directory is the most comprehensive reference tool and buyer's guide for the safety and security industry. Arranged by safety topic, each chapter begins with OSHA regulations for the topic, followed by Training Articles written by top professionals in the field and Self-Inspection Checklists. Next, each topic contains Buyer's Guide sections that feature related products and services. Topics include Administration, Insurance, Loss Control & Consulting, Protective Equipment & Apparel, Noise & Vibration, Facilities Monitoring & Maintenance, Employee Health Maintenance & Ergonomics, Retail Food Services, Machine Guards, Process Guidelines & Tool Handling, Ordinary Materials Handling, Hazardous Materials Handling, Workplace Preparation & Maintenance, Electrical Lighting & Safety, Fire & Rescue and Security. Six important indexes make finding information and product manufacturers quick and easy: Geographical Index of Manufacturers and Distributors, Company Profile Index, Brand Name Index, Product Index, Index of Web Sites and Index of Advertisers. This comprehensive, up-to-date reference will provide every tool necessary to make sure a business is in compliance with OSHA regulations and locate the products and services needed to meet those regulations.

"Presents industrial safety information for engineers, plant managers, risk managers, and construction site supervisors..." –Choice

Softcover ISBN 978-1-59237-205-8, 1,500 pages, $165.00

To preview any of our Directories Risk-Free for 30 days, call (800) 562-2139 or fax (518) 789-0556
www.greyhouse.com   books@greyhouse.com

Business Information ♦ Ratings Guides ♦ General Reference ♦ Education ♦ Statistics ♦ Demographics ♦ Health Information ♦ Canadian Information

The Grey House Transportation Security Directory & Handbook

This is the only reference of its kind that brings together current data on Transportation Security. With information on everything from Regulatory Authorities to Security Equipment, this top-flight database brings together the relevant information necessary for creating and maintaining a security plan for a wide range of transportation facilities. With this current, comprehensive directory at the ready you'll have immediate access to: Regulatory Authorities & Legislation; Information Resources; Sample Security Plans & Checklists; Contact Data for Major Airports, Seaports, Railroads, Trucking Companies and Oil Pipelines; Security Service Providers; Recommended Equipment & Product Information and more. Using the *Grey House Transportation Security Directory & Handbook*, managers will be able to quickly and easily assess their current security plans; develop contacts to create and maintain new security procedures; and source the products and services necessary to adequately maintain a secure environment. This valuable resource is a must for all Security Managers at Airports, Seaports, Railroads, Trucking Companies and Oil Pipelines.

> "Highly recommended. Library collections that support all levels of readers, including professionals/practitioners; and schools/organizations offering education and training in transportation security." -Choice

Softcover ISBN 978-1-59237-075-7, 800 pages, $195.00

The Grey House Biometric Information Directory

This edition offers a complete, current overview of biometric companies and products – one of the fastest growing industries in today's economy. Detailed profiles of manufacturers of the latest biometric technology, including Finger, Voice, Face, Hand, Signature, Iris, Vein and Palm Identification systems. Data on the companies include key executives, company size and a detailed, indexed description of their product line. Information in the directory includes: Editorial on Advancements in Biometrics; Profiles of 700+ companies listed with contact information; Organizations, Trade & Educational Associations, Publications, Conferences, Trade Shows and Expositions Worldwide; Web Site Index; Biometric & Vendors Services Index by Types of Biometrics; and a Glossary of Biometric Terms. This resource will be an important source for anyone who is considering the use of a biometric product, investing in the development of biometric technology, support existing marketing and sales efforts and will be an important acquisition for the business reference collection for large public and business libraries.

> "This book should prove useful to agencies or businesses seeking companies that deal with biometric technology. Summing Up: Recommended. Specialized collections serving researchers/faculty and professionals/practitioners." -Choice

Softcover ISBN 978-1-59237-121-1, 800 pages, $225.00

The Environmental Resource Handbook, 2007/08

The Environmental Resource Handbook is the most up-to-date and comprehensive source for Environmental Resources and Statistics. Section I: Resources provides detailed contact information for thousands of information sources, including Associations & Organizations, Awards & Honors, Conferences, Foundations & Grants, Environmental Health, Government Agencies, National Parks & Wildlife Refuges, Publications, Research Centers, Educational Programs, Green Product Catalogs, Consultants and much more. Section II: Statistics, provides statistics and rankings on hundreds of important topics, including Children's Environmental Index, Municipal Finances, Toxic Chemicals, Recycling, Climate, Air & Water Quality and more. This kind of up-to-date environmental data, all in one place, is not available anywhere else on the market place today. This vast compilation of resources and statistics is a must-have for all public and academic libraries as well as any organization with a primary focus on the environment.

> "…the intrinsic value of the information make it worth consideration by libraries with environmental collections and environmentally concerned users." –Booklist

Softcover ISBN 978-1-59237-195-2, 1,000 pages, $155.00 | Online Database $300.00

To preview any of our Directories Risk-Free for 30 days, call (800) 562-2139 or fax (518) 789-0556
www.greyhouse.com   books@greyhouse.com

Business Information ♦ Ratings Guides ♦ General Reference ♦ Education ♦ Statistics ♦ Demographics ♦ Health Information ♦ Canadian Information

The Rauch Guide to the US Adhesives & Sealants, Cosmetics & Toiletries, Ink, Paint, Plastics, Pulp & Paper and Rubber Industries

The Rauch Guides save time and money by organizing widely scattered information and providing estimates for important business decisions, some of which are available nowhere else. Within each Guide, after a brief introduction, the ECONOMICS section provides data on industry shipments; long-term growth and forecasts; prices; company performance; employment, expenditures, and productivity; transportation and geographical patterns; packaging; foreign trade; and government regulations. Next, TECHNOLOGY & RAW MATERIALS provide market, technical, and raw material information for chemicals, equipment and related materials, including market size and leading suppliers, prices, end uses, and trends. PRODUCTS & MARKETS provide information for each major industry product, including market size and historical trends, leading suppliers, five-year forecasts, industry structure, and major end uses. Next, the COMPANY DIRECTORY profiles major industry companies, both public and private. Information includes complete contact information, web address, estimated total and domestic sales, product description, and recent mergers and acquisitions. *The Rauch Guides* will prove to be an invaluable source of market information, company data, trends and forecasts that anyone in these fast-paced industries.

"An invaluable and affordable publication. The comprehensive nature of the data and text offers considerable insights into the industry, market sizes, company activities, and applications of the products of the industry. The additions that have been made have certainly enhanced the value of the Guide." –Adhesives & Sealants Newsletter of the Rauch Guide to the US Adhesives & Sealants Industry

Paint Industry: Softcover ISBN 978-1-59237-127-3 $595 | Plastics Industry: Softcover ISBN 978-1-59237-128-0 $595 | Adhesives and Sealants Industry: Softcover ISBN 978-1-59237-129-7 $595 | Ink Industry: Softcover ISBN 978-1-59237-126-6 $595 | Rubber Industry: Softcover ISBN 978-1-59237-130-3 $595 | Pulp and Paper Industry: Softcover ISBN 978-1-59237-131-0 $595 | Cosmetic & Toiletries Industry: Softcover ISBN 978-1-59237-132-7 $895

Research Services Directory: Commercial & Corporate Research Centers

This ninth edition provides access to well over 8,000 independent Commercial Research Firms, Corporate Research Centers and Laboratories offering contract services for hands-on, basic or applied research. Research Services Directory covers the thousands of types of research companies, including Biotechnology & Pharmaceutical Developers, Consumer Product Research, Defense Contractors, Electronics & Software Engineers, Think Tanks, Forensic Investigators, Independent Commercial Laboratories, Information Brokers, Market & Survey Research Companies, Medical Diagnostic Facilities, Product Research & Development Firms and more. Each entry provides the company's name, mailing address, phone & fax numbers, key contacts, web site, e-mail address, as well as a company description and research and technical fields served. Four indexes provide immediate access to this wealth of information: Research Firms Index, Geographic Index, Personnel Name Index and Subject Index.

"An important source for organizations in need of information about laboratories, individuals and other facilities." –ARBA

Softcover ISBN 978-1-59237-003-0, 1,400 pages, $465.00

International Business and Trade Directories

Completely updated, the Third Edition of *International Business and Trade Directories* now contains more than 10,000 entries, over 2,000 more than the last edition, making this directory the most comprehensive resource of the worlds business and trade directories. Entries include content descriptions, price, publisher's name and address, web site and e-mail addresses, phone and fax numbers and editorial staff. Organized by industry group, and then by region, this resource puts over 10,000 industry-specific business and trade directories at the reader's fingertips. Three indexes are included for quick access to information: Geographic Index, Publisher Index and Title Index. Public, college and corporate libraries, as well as individuals and corporations seeking critical market information will want to add this directory to their marketing collection.

"Reasonably priced for a work of this type, this directory should appeal to larger academic, public and corporate libraries with an international focus." –Library Journal

Softcover ISBN 978-1-930956-63-6, 1,800 pages, $225.00

To preview any of our Directories Risk-Free for 30 days, call (800) 562-2139 or fax (518) 789-0556
www.greyhouse.com books@greyhouse.com

Business Information ♦ <u>Ratings Guides</u> ♦ General Reference ♦ Education ♦ Statistics ♦ Demographics ♦ Health Information ♦ Canadian Information

TheStreet.com Ratings Guide to Health Insurers

TheStreet.com Ratings Guide to Health Insurers is the first and only source to cover the financial stability of the nation's health care system, rating the financial safety of more than 6,000 health insurance providers, health maintenance organizations (HMOs) and all of the Blue Cross Blue Shield plans – updated quarterly to ensure the most accurate information. The Guide also provides a complete listing of all the major health insurers, including all Long-Term Care and Medigap insurers. Our *Guide to Health Insurers* includes comprehensive, timely coverage on the financial stability of HMOs and health insurers; the most accurate insurance company ratings available–the same quality ratings heralded by the U.S. General Accounting Office; separate listings for those companies offering Medigap and long-term care policies; the number of serious consumer complaints filed against most HMOs so you can see who is actually providing the best (or worst) service and more. The easy-to-use layout gives you a one-line summary analysis for each company that we track, followed by an in-depth, detailed analysis of all HMOs and the largest health insurers. The guide also includes a list of TheStreet.com Ratings Recommended Companies with information on how to contact them, and the reasoning behind any rating upgrades or downgrades.

> *"With 20 years behind its insurance-advocacy research [the rating guide] continues to offer a wealth of information that helps consumers weigh their healthcare options now and in the future." -Today's Librarian*

Issues published quarterly, Softcover, 550 pages, $499.00 for four quarterly issues, $249.00 for a single issue

TheStreet.com Ratings Guide to Life & Annuity Insurers

TheStreet.com Safety Ratings are the most reliable source for evaluating an insurer's financial solvency risk. Consequently, policyholders have come to rely on TheStreet.com's flagship publication, *TheStreet.com Ratings Guide to Life & Annuity Insurers*, to help them identify the safest companies to do business with. Each easy-to-use edition delivers TheStreet.com's independent ratings and analyses on more than 1,100 insurers, updated every quarter. Plus, your patrons will find a complete list of TheStreet.com Recommended Companies, including contact information, and the reasoning behind any rating upgrades or downgrades. This guide is perfect for those who are considering the purchase of a life insurance policy, placing money in an annuity, or advising clients about insurance and annuities. A life or health insurance policy or annuity is only as secure as the insurance company issuing it. Therefore, make sure your patrons have what they need to periodically monitor the financial condition of the companies with whom they have an investment. The TheStreet.com Ratings product line is designed to help them in their evaluations.

> *"Weiss has an excellent reputation and this title is held by hundreds of libraries. This guide is recommended for public and academic libraries." -ARBA*

Issues published quarterly, Softcover, 360 pages, $499.00 for four quarterly issues, $249.00 for a single issue

TheStreet.com Ratings Guide to Property & Casualty Insurers

TheStreet.com Ratings Guide to Property and Casualty Insurers provides the most extensive coverage of insurers writing policies, helping consumers and businesses avoid financial headaches. Updated quarterly, this easy-to-use publication delivers the independent, unbiased TheStreet.com Safety Ratings and supporting analyses on more than 2,800 U.S. insurance companies, offering auto & homeowners insurance, business insurance, worker's compensation insurance, product liability insurance, medical malpractice and other professional liability insurance. Each edition includes a list of TheStreet.com Recommended Companies by type of insurance, including a contact number, plus helpful information about the coverage provided by the State Guarantee Associations.

> *"In contrast to the other major insurance rating agencies...Weiss does not have a financial relationship worth the companies it rates. A GAO study found that Weiss identified financial vulnerability earlier than the other rating agencies." -ARBA*

Issues published quarterly, Softcover, 455 pages, $499.00 for four quarterly issues, $249.00 for a single issue

TheStreet.com Ratings Consumer Box Set

Deliver the critical information your patrons need to safeguard their personal finances with *TheStreet.com Ratings' Consumer Guide Box Set*. Each of the eight guides is packed with accurate, unbiased information and recommendations to help your patrons make sound financial decisions. TheStreet.com Ratings Consumer Guide Box Set provides your patrons with easy to understand guidance on important personal finance topics, including: *Consumer Guide to Variable Annuities, Consumer Guide to Medicare Supplement Insurance, Consumer Guide to Elder Care Choices, Consumer Guide to Automobile Insurance, Consumer Guide to Long-Term Care Insurance, Consumer Guide to Homeowners Insurance, Consumer Guide to Term Life Insurance,* and *Consumer Guide to Medicare Prescription Drug Coverage*. Each guide provides an easy-to-read overview of the topic, what to look out for when selecting a company or insurance plan to do business with, who are the recommended companies to work with and how to navigate through these often-times difficult decisions. Custom worksheets and step-by-step directions make these resources accessible to all types of users. Packaged in a handy custom display box, these helpful guides will prove to be a much-used addition to any reference collection.

Issues published twice per year, Softcover, 600 pages, $499.00 for two biennial issues

---

**To preview any of our Directories Risk-Free for 30 days, call (800) 562-2139 or fax (518) 789-0556
www.greyhouse.com   books@greyhouse.com**

Business Information ♦ Ratings Guides ♦ General Reference ♦ Education ♦ Statistics ♦ Demographics ♦ Health Information ♦ Canadian Information

TheStreet.com Ratings Guide to Stock Mutual Funds

TheStreet.com Ratings Guide to Stock Mutual Funds offers ratings and analyses on more than 8,800 equity mutual funds – more than any other publication. The exclusive TheStreet.com Investment Ratings combine an objective evaluation of each fund's performance and risk to provide a single, user-friendly, composite rating, giving your patrons a better handle on a mutual fund's risk-adjusted performance. Each edition identifies the top-performing mutual funds based on risk category, type of fund, and overall risk-adjusted performance. TheStreet.com's unique investment rating system makes it easy to see exactly which stocks are on the rise and which ones should be avoided. For those investors looking to tailor their mutual fund selections based on age, income, and tolerance for risk, we've also assigned two component ratings to each fund: a performance rating and a risk rating. With these, you can identify those funds that are best suited to meet your - or your client's – individual needs and goals. Plus, we include a handy Risk Profile Quiz to help you assess your personal tolerance for risk. So whether you're an investing novice or professional, the *Guide to Stock Mutual Funds* gives you everything you need to find a mutual fund that is right for you.

> *"There is tremendous need for information such as that provided by this Weiss publication. This reasonably priced guide is recommended for public and academic libraries serving investors."* -ARBA

Issues published quarterly, Softcover, 655 pages, $499 for four quarterly issues, $249 for a single issue

TheStreet.com Ratings Guide to Exchange-Traded Funds

TheStreet.com Ratings editors analyze hundreds of mutual funds each quarter, condensing all of the available data into a single composite opinion of each fund's risk-adjusted performance. The intuitive, consumer-friendly ratings allow investors to instantly identify those funds that have historically done well and those that have under-performed the market. Each quarterly edition identifies the top-performing exchange-traded funds based on risk category, type of fund, and overall risk-adjusted performance. The rating scale, A through F, gives you a better handle on an exchange-traded fund's risk-adjusted performance. Other features include Top & Bottom 200 Exchange-Traded Funds; Performance and Risk: 100 Best and Worst Exchange- Traded Funds; Investor Profile Quiz; Performance Benchmarks and Fund Type Descriptions. With the growing popularity of mutual fund investing, consumers need a reliable source to help them track and evaluate the performance of their mutual fund holdings. Plus, they need a way of identifying and monitoring other funds as potential new investments. Unfortunately, the hundreds of performance and risk measures available, multiplied by the vast number of mutual fund investments on the market today, can make this a daunting task for even the most sophisticated investor. This Guide will serve as a useful tool for both the first-time and seasoned investor.

Editions published quarterly, Softcover, 440 pages, $499.00 for four quarterly issues, $249.00 for a single issue

TheStreet.com Ratings Guide to Bond & Money Market Mutual Funds

TheStreet.com Ratings Guide to Bond & Money Market Mutual Funds has everything your patrons need to easily identify the top-performing fixed income funds on the market today. Each quarterly edition contains TheStreet.com's independent ratings and analyses on more than 4,600 fixed income funds – more than any other publication, including corporate bond funds, high-yield bond funds, municipal bond funds, mortgage security funds, money market funds, global bond funds and government bond funds. In addition, the fund's risk rating is combined with its three-year performance rating to get an overall picture of the fund's risk-adjusted performance. The resulting TheStreet.com Investment Rating gives a single, user-friendly, objective evaluation that makes it easy to compare one fund to another and select the right fund based on the level of risk tolerance. Most investors think of fixed income mutual funds as "safe" investments. That's not always the case, however, depending on the credit risk, interest rate risk, and prepayment risk of the securities owned by the fund. TheStreet.com Ratings assesses each of these risks and assigns each fund a risk rating to help investors quickly evaluate the fund's risk component. Plus, we include a handy Risk Profile Quiz to help you assess your personal tolerance for risk. So whether you're an investing novice or professional, the *Guide to Bond and Money Market Mutual Funds* gives you everything you need to find a mutual fund that is right for you.

> *"Comprehensive... It is easy to use and consumer-oriented, and can be recommended for larger public and academic libraries."* -ARBA

Issues published quarterly, Softcover, 470 pages, $499.00 for four quarterly issues, $249.00 for a single issue

TheStreet.com Ratings Guide to Banks & Thrifts

Updated quarterly, for the most up-to-date information, *TheStreet.com Ratings Guide to Banks and Thrifts* offers accurate, intuitive safety ratings your patrons can trust; supporting ratios and analyses that show an institution's strong & weak points; identification of the TheStreet.com Recommended Companies with branches in your area; a complete list of institutions receiving upgrades/downgrades; and comprehensive coverage of every bank and thrift in the nation – more than 9,000. TheStreet.com Safety Ratings are then based on the analysts' review of publicly available information collected by the federal banking regulators. The easy-to-use layout gives you: the institution's TheStreet.com Safety Rating for the last 3 years; the five key indexes used to evaluate each institution; along with the primary ratios and statistics used in determining the company's rating. *TheStreet.com Ratings Guide to Banks & Thrifts* will be a must for individuals who are concerned about the safety of their CD or savings account; need to be sure that an existing line of credit will be there when they need it; or simply want to avoid the hassles of dealing with a failing or troubled institution.

> *"Large public and academic libraries most definitely need to acquire the work. Likewise, special libraries in large corporations will find this title indispensable."* -ARBA

Issues published quarterly, Softcover, 370 pages, $499.00 for four quarterly issues, $249.00 for a single issue

To preview any of our Directories Risk-Free for 30 days, call (800) 562-2139 or fax (518) 789-0556
www.greyhouse.com books@greyhouse.com

Business Information ♦ Ratings Guides ♦ General Reference ♦ Education ♦ Statistics ♦ Demographics ♦ Health Information ♦ Canadian Information

TheStreet.com Ratings Guide to Common Stocks

TheStreet.com Ratings Guide to Common Stocks gives your patrons reliable insight into the risk-adjusted performance of common stocks listed on the NYSE, AMEX, and Nasdaq – over 5,800 stocks in all – more than any other publication. TheStreet.com's unique investment rating system makes it easy to see exactly which stocks are on the rise and which ones should be avoided. In addition, your patrons also get supporting analysis showing growth trends, profitability, debt levels, valuation levels, the top-rated stocks within each industry, and more. Plus, each stock is ranked with the easy-to-use buy-hold-sell equivalents commonly used by Wall Street. Whether they're selecting their own investments or checking up on a broker's recommendation, TheStreet.com Ratings can help them in their evaluations.

"Users... will find the information succinct and the explanations readable, easy to understand, and helpful to a novice." -Library Journal

Issues published quarterly, Softcover, 440 pages, $499.00 for four quarterly issues, $249.00 for a single issue

TheStreet.com Ratings Ultimate Guided Tour of Stock Investing

This important reference guide from TheStreet.com Ratings is just what librarians around the country have asked for: a step-by-step introduction to stock investing for the beginning to intermediate investor. This easy-to-navigate guide explores the basics of stock investing and includes the intuitive TheStreet.com Investment Rating on more than 5,800 stocks, complete with real-world investing information that can be put to use immediately with stocks that fit the concepts discussed in the guide; informative charts, graphs and worksheets; easy-to-understand explanations on topics like P/E, compound interest, marked indices, diversifications, brokers, and much more; along with financial safety ratings for every stock on the NYSE, American Stock Exchange and the Nasdaq. This consumer-friendly guide offers complete how-to information on stock investing that can be put to use right away; a friendly format complete with our "Wise Guide" who leads the reader on a safari to learn about the investing jungle; helpful charts, graphs and simple worksheets; the intuitive TheStreet.com Investment rating on over 6,000 stocks — every stock found on the NYSE, American Stock Exchange and the NASDAQ; and much more.

"Provides investors with an alternative to stock broker recommendations, which recently have been tarnished by conflicts of interest. In summary, the guide serves as a welcome addition for all public library collections." -ARBA

Issues published quarterly, Softcover, 370 pages, $499.00 for four quarterly issues, $249.00 for a single issue

TheStreet.com Ratings' Reports & Services

- Ratings Online — An on-line summary covering an individual company's TheStreet.com Financial Strength Rating or an investment's unique TheStreet.com Investment Rating with the factors contributing to that rating; available 24 hours a day by visiting www.thestreet.com/tscratings or calling (800) 289-9222.
- Unlimited Ratings Research — The ultimate research tool providing fast, easy online access to the very latest TheStreet.com Financial Strength Ratings and Investment Ratings. Price: $559 per industry.

Contact TheStreet.com for more information about Reports & Services at www.thestreet.com/tscratings or call (800) 289-9222

TheStreet.com Ratings' Custom Reports

TheStreet.com Ratings is pleased to offer two customized options for receiving ratings data. Each taps into TheStreet.com's vast data repositories and is designed to provide exactly the data you need. Choose from a variety of industries, companies, data variables, and delivery formats including print, Excel, SQL, Text or Access.

- Customized Reports - get right to the heart of your company's research and data needs with a report customized to your specifications.
- Complete Database Download – TheStreet.com will design and deliver the database; from there you can sort it, recalculate it, and format your results to suit your specific needs.

Contact TheStreet.com for more information about Custom Reports at www.thestreet.com/tscratings or call (800) 289-9222

**To preview any of our Directories Risk-Free for 30 days, call (800) 562-2139 or fax (518) 789-0556
www.greyhouse.com   books@greyhouse.com**

**Business Information ♦ Ratings Guides ♦ <u>General Reference</u> ♦ Education ♦
Statistics ♦ Demographics ♦ Health Information ♦ Canadian Information**

The Value of a Dollar 1600-1859, The Colonial Era to The Civil War
Following the format of the widely acclaimed, *The Value of a Dollar, 1860-2004*, *The Value of a Dollar 1600-1859, The Colonial Era to The Civil War* records the actual prices of thousands of items that consumers purchased from the Colonial Era to the Civil War. Our editorial department had been flooded with requests from users of our *Value of a Dollar* for the same type of information, just from an earlier time period. This new volume is just the answer – with pricing data from 1600 to 1859. Arranged into five-year chapters, each 5-year chapter includes a Historical Snapshot, Consumer Expenditures, Investments, Selected Income, Income/Standard Jobs, Food Basket, Standard Prices and Miscellany. There is also a section on Trends. This informative section charts the change in price over time and provides added detail on the reasons prices changed within the time period, including industry developments, changes in consumer attitudes and important historical facts. This fascinating survey will serve a wide range of research needs and will be useful in all high school, public and academic library reference collections.

"The Value of a Dollar: Colonial Era to the Civil War, 1600-1865 will find a happy audience among students, researchers, and general browsers. It offers a fascinating and detailed look at early American history from the viewpoint of everyday people trying to make ends meet. This title and the earlier publication, The Value of a Dollar, 1860-2004, complement each other very well, and readers will appreciate finding them side-by-side on the shelf." -Booklist

Hardcover ISBN 978-1-59237-094-8, 600 pages, $145.00 | Ebook ISBN 978-1-59237-169-3 www.gale.com/gvrl/partners/grey.htm

The Value of a Dollar 1860-2004, Third Edition
A guide to practical economy, *The Value of a Dollar* records the actual prices of thousands of items that consumers purchased from the Civil War to the present, along with facts about investment options and income opportunities. This brand new Third Edition boasts a brand new addition to each five-year chapter, a section on Trends. This informative section charts the change in price over time and provides added detail on the reasons prices changed within the time period, including industry developments, changes in consumer attitudes and important historical facts. Plus, a brand new chapter for 2000-2004 has been added. Each 5-year chapter includes a Historical Snapshot, Consumer Expenditures, Investments, Selected Income, Income/Standard Jobs, Food Basket, Standard Prices and Miscellany. This interesting and useful publication will be widely used in any reference collection.

"Business historians, reporters, writers and students will find this source... very helpful for historical research. Libraries will want to purchase it." –ARBA

Hardcover ISBN 978-1-59237-074-0, 600 pages, $145.00 | Ebook ISBN 978-1-59237-173-0 www.gale.com/gvrl/partners/grey.htm

Working Americans 1880-1999
Volume I: The Working Class, Volume II: The Middle Class, Volume III: The Upper Class
Each of the volumes in the *Working Americans* series focuses on a particular class of Americans, The Working Class, The Middle Class and The Upper Class over the last 120 years. Chapters in each volume focus on one decade and profile three to five families. Family Profiles include real data on Income & Job Descriptions, Selected Prices of the Times, Annual Income, Annual Budgets, Family Finances, Life at Work, Life at Home, Life in the Community, Working Conditions, Cost of Living, Amusements and much more. Each chapter also contains an Economic Profile with Average Wages of other Professions, a selection of Typical Pricing, Key Events & Inventions, News Profiles, Articles from Local Media and Illustrations. The *Working Americans* series captures the lifestyles of each of the classes from the last twelve decades, covers a vast array of occupations and ethnic backgrounds and travels the entire nation. These interesting and useful compilations of portraits of the American Working, Middle and Upper Classes during the last 120 years will be an important addition to any high school, public or academic library reference collection.

"These interesting, unique compilations of economic and social facts, figures and graphs will support multiple research needs. They will engage and enlighten patrons in high school, public and academic library collections." –Booklist

Volume I: The Working Class Hardcover ISBN 978-1-891482-81-6, 558 pages, $145.00 | Volume II: The Middle Class Hardcover ISBN 978-1-891482-72-4, 591 pages, $145.00 | Volume III: The Upper Class Hardcover ISBN 978-1-930956-38-4, 567 pages, $145.00 | Ebooks www.gale.com/gvrl/partners/grey.htm

Working Americans 1880-1999 Volume IV: Their Children
This Fourth Volume in the highly successful *Working Americans* series focuses on American children, decade by decade from 1880 to 1999. This interesting and useful volume introduces the reader to three children in each decade, one from each of the Working, Middle and Upper classes. Like the first three volumes in the series, the individual profiles are created from interviews, diaries, statistical studies, biographies and news reports. Profiles cover a broad range of ethnic backgrounds, geographic area and lifestyles – everything from an orphan in Memphis in 1882, following the Yellow Fever epidemic of 1878 to an eleven-year-old nephew of a beer baron and owner of the New York Yankees in New York City in 1921. Chapters also contain important supplementary materials including News Features as well as information on everything from Schools to Parks, Infectious Diseases to Childhood Fears along with Entertainment, Family Life and much more to provide an informative overview of the lifestyles of children from each decade. This interesting account of what life was like for Children in the Working, Middle and Upper Classes will be a welcome addition to the reference collection of any high school, public or academic library.

Hardcover ISBN 978-1-930956-35-3, 600 pages, $145.00 | Ebook ISBN 978-1-59237-166-2 www.gale.com/gvrl/partners/grey.htm

**To preview any of our Directories Risk-Free for 30 days, call (800) 562-2139 or fax (518) 789-0556
www.greyhouse.com books@greyhouse.com**

Business Information ♦ Ratings Guides ♦ <u>General Reference</u> ♦ Education ♦
Statistics ♦ Demographics ♦ Health Information ♦ Canadian Information

Working Americans 1880-2003 Volume V: Americans At War

Working Americans 1880-2003 Volume V: Americans At War is divided into 11 chapters, each covering a decade from 1880-2003 and examines the lives of Americans during the time of war, including declared conflicts, one-time military actions, protests, and preparations for war. Each decade includes several personal profiles, whether on the battlefield or on the homefront, that tell the stories of civilians, soldiers, and officers during the decade. The profiles examine: Life at Home; Life at Work; and Life in the Community. Each decade also includes an Economic Profile with statistical comparisons, a Historical Snapshot, News Profiles, local News Articles, and Illustrations that provide a solid historical background to the decade being examined. Profiles range widely not only geographically, but also emotionally, from that of a girl whose leg was torn off in a blast during WWI, to the boredom of being stationed in the Dakotas as the Indian Wars were drawing to a close. As in previous volumes of the *Working Americans* series, information is presented in narrative form, but hard facts and real-life situations back up each story. The basis of the profiles come from diaries, private print books, personal interviews, family histories, estate documents and magazine articles. For easy reference, *Working Americans 1880-2003 Volume V: Americans At War* includes an in-depth Subject Index. The Working Americans series has become an important reference for public libraries, academic libraries and high school libraries. This fifth volume will be a welcome addition to all of these types of reference collections.

Hardcover ISBN 978-1-59237-024-5, 600 pages, $145.00 | Ebook ISBN 978-1-59237-167-9 www.gale.com/gvrl/partners/grey.htm

Working Americans 1880-2005 Volume VI: Women at Work

Unlike any other volume in the *Working Americans* series, this Sixth Volume, is the first to focus on a particular gender of Americans. *Volume VI: Women at Work*, traces what life was like for working women from the 1860's to the present time. Beginning with the life of a maid in 1890 and a store clerk in 1900 and ending with the life and times of the modern working women, this text captures the struggle, strengths and changing perception of the American woman at work. Each chapter focuses on one decade and profiles three to five women with real data on Income & Job Descriptions, Selected Prices of the Times, Annual Income, Annual Budgets, Family Finances, Life at Work, Life at Home, Life in the Community, Working Conditions, Cost of Living, Amusements and much more. For even broader access to the events, economics and attitude towards women throughout the past 130 years, each chapter is supplemented with News Profiles, Articles from Local Media, Illustrations, Economic Profiles, Typical Pricing, Key Events, Inventions and more. This important volume illustrates what life was like for working women over time and allows the reader to develop an understanding of the changing role of women at work. These interesting and useful compilations of portraits of women at work will be an important addition to any high school, public or academic library reference collection.

Hardcover ISBN 978-1-59237-063-4, 600 pages, $145.00 | Ebook ISBN 978-1-59237-168-6 www.gale.com/gvrl/partners/grey.htm

Working Americans 1880-2005 Volume VII: Social Movements

Working Americans series, Volume VII: Social Movements explores how Americans sought and fought for change from the 1880s to the present time. Following the format of previous volumes in the Working Americans series, the text examines the lives of 34 individuals who have worked -- often behind the scenes --- to bring about change. Issues include topics as diverse as the Anti-smoking movement of 1901 to efforts by Native Americans to reassert their long lost rights. Along the way, the book will profile individuals brave enough to demand suffrage for Kansas women in 1912 or demand an end to lynching during a March on Washington in 1923. Each profile is enriched with real data on Income & Job Descriptions, Selected Prices of the Times, Annual Incomes & Budgets, Life at Work, Life at Home, Life in the Community, along with News Features, Key Events, and Illustrations. The depth of information contained in each profile allow the user to explore the private, financial and public lives of these subjects, deepening our understanding of how calls for change took place in our society. A must-purchase for the reference collections of high school libraries, public libraries and academic libraries.

Hardcover ISBN 978-1-59237-101-3, 600 pages, $145.00 | Ebook ISBN 978-1-59237-174-7 www.gale.com/gvrl/partners/grey.htm

Working Americans 1880-2005 Volume VIII: Immigrants

Working Americans 1880-2007 Volume VIII: Immigrants illustrates what life was like for families leaving their homeland and creating a new life in the United States. Each chapter covers one decade and introduces the reader to three immigrant families. Family profiles cover what life was like in their homeland, in their community in the United States, their home life, working conditions and so much more. As the reader moves through these pages, the families and individuals come to life, painting a picture of why they left their homeland, their experiences in setting roots in a new country, their struggles and triumphs, stretching from the 1800s to the present time. Profiles include a seven-year-old Swedish girl who meets her father for the first time at Ellis Island; a Chinese photographer's assistant; an Armenian who flees the genocide of his country to build Ford automobiles in Detroit; a 38-year-old German bachelor cigar maker who settles in Newark NJ, but contemplates tobacco farming in Virginia; a 19-year-old Irish domestic servant who is amazed at the easy life of American dogs; a 19-year-old Filipino who came to Hawaii against his parent's wishes to farm sugar cane; a French-Canadian who finds success as a boxer in Maine and many more. As in previous volumes, information is presented in narrative form, but hard facts and real-life situations back up each story. With the topic of immigration being so hotly debated in this country, this timely resource will prove to be a useful source for students, researchers, historians and library patrons to discover the issues facing immigrants in the United States. This title will be a useful addition to reference collections of public libraries, university libraries and high schools.

Hardcover ISBN 978-1-59237-197-6, 600 pages, $145.00 | Ebook ISBN 978-1-59237-232-4 www.gale.com/gvrl/partners/grey.htm

To preview any of our Directories Risk-Free for 30 days, call (800) 562-2139 or fax (518) 789-0556
www.greyhouse.com   books@greyhouse.com

Business Information ♦ Ratings Guides ♦ <u>**General Reference**</u> ♦ Education ♦
Statistics ♦ Demographics ♦ Health Information ♦ Canadian Information

The Encyclopedia of Warrior Peoples & Fighting Groups

Many military groups throughout the world have excelled in their craft either by fortuitous circumstances, outstanding leadership, or intense training. This new second edition of *The Encyclopedia of Warrior Peoples and Fighting Groups* explores the origins and leadership of these outstanding combat forces, chronicles their conquests and accomplishments, examines the circumstances surrounding their decline or disbanding, and assesses their influence on the groups and methods of warfare that followed. Readers will encounter ferocious tribes, charismatic leaders, and daring militias, from ancient times to the present, including Amazons, Buffalo Soldiers, Green Berets, Iron Brigade, Kamikazes, Peoples of the Sea, Polish Winged Hussars, Teutonic Knights, and Texas Rangers. With over 100 alphabetical entries, numerous cross-references and illustrations, a comprehensive bibliography, and index, the *Encyclopedia of Warrior Peoples and Fighting Groups* is a valuable resource for readers seeking insight into the bold history of distinguished fighting forces.

"Especially useful for high school students, undergraduates, and general readers with an interest in military history." –Library Journal

Hardcover ISBN 978-1-59237-116-7, 660 pages, $135.00 | Ebook ISBN 978-1-59237-172-3 www.gale.com/gvrl/partners/grey.htm

The Encyclopedia of Invasions & Conquests, From the Ancient Times to the Present

This second edition of the popular *Encyclopedia of Invasions & Conquests*, a comprehensive guide to over 150 invasions, conquests, battles and occupations from ancient times to the present, takes readers on a journey that includes the Roman conquest of Britain, the Portuguese colonization of Brazil, and the Iraqi invasion of Kuwait, to name a few. New articles will explore the late 20th and 21st centuries, with a specific focus on recent conflicts in Afghanistan, Kuwait, Iraq, Yugoslavia, Grenada and Chechnya. In addition to covering the military aspects of invasions and conquests, entries cover some of the political, economic, and cultural aspects, for example, the effects of a conquest on the invade country's political and monetary system and in its language and religion. The entries on leaders – among them Sargon, Alexander the Great, William the Conqueror, and Adolf Hitler – deal with the people who sought to gain control, expand power, or exert religious or political influence over others through military means. Revised and updated for this second edition, entries are arranged alphabetically within historical periods. Each chapter provides a map to help readers locate key areas and geographical features, and bibliographical references appear at the end of each entry. Other useful features include cross-references, a cumulative bibliography and a comprehensive subject index. This authoritative, well-organized, lucidly written volume will prove invaluable for a variety of readers, including high school students, military historians, members of the armed forces, history buffs and hobbyists.

"Engaging writing, sensible organization, nice illustrations, interesting and obscure facts, and useful maps make this book a pleasure to read." –ARBA

Hardcover ISBN 978-1-59237-114-3, 598 pages, $135.00 | Ebook ISBN 978-1-59237-171-6 www.gale.com/gvrl/partners/grey.htm

Encyclopedia of Prisoners of War & Internment

This authoritative second edition provides a valuable overview of the history of prisoners of war and interned civilians, from earliest times to the present. Written by an international team of experts in the field of POW studies, this fascinating and thought-provoking volume includes entries on a wide range of subjects including the Crusades, Plains Indian Warfare, concentration camps, the two world wars, and famous POWs throughout history, as well as atrocities, escapes, and much more. Written in a clear and easily understandable style, this informative reference details over 350 entries, 30% larger than the first edition, that survey the history of prisoners of war and interned civilians from the earliest times to the present, with emphasis on the 19th and 20th centuries. Medical conditions, international law, exchanges of prisoners, organizations working on behalf of POWs, and trials associated with the treatment of captives are just some of the themes explored. Entries are arranged alphabetically, plus illustrations and maps are provided for easy reference. The text also includes an introduction, bibliography, appendix of selected documents, and end-of-entry reading suggestions. This one-of-a-kind reference will be a helpful addition to the reference collections of all public libraries, high schools, and university libraries and will prove invaluable to historians and military enthusiasts.

"Thorough and detailed yet accessible to the lay reader. Of special interest to subject specialists and historians; recommended for public and academic libraries." - Library Journal

Hardcover ISBN 978-1-59237-120-4, 676 pages, $135.00 | Ebook ISBN 978-1-59237-170-9 www.gale.com/gvrl/partners/grey.htm

The Encyclopedia of Rural America: the Land & People

History, sociology, anthropology, and public policy are combined to deliver the encyclopedia destined to become the standard reference work in American rural studies. From irrigation and marriage to games and mental health, this encyclopedia is the first to explore the contemporary landscape of rural America, placed in historical perspective. With over 300 articles prepared by leading experts from across the nation, this timely encyclopedia documents and explains the major themes, concepts, industries, concerns, and everyday life of the people and land who make up rural America. Entries range from the industrial sector and government policy to arts and humanities and social and family concerns. Articles explore every aspect of life in rural America. *Encyclopedia of Rural America*, with its broad range of coverage, will appeal to high school and college students as well as graduate students, faculty, scholars, and people whose work pertains to rural areas.

"This exemplary encyclopedia is guaranteed to educate our highly urban society about the uniqueness of rural America. Recommended for public and academic libraries." -Library Journal

Two Volumes, Hardcover, ISBN 978-1-59237-115-0, 800 pages, $195.00

To preview any of our Directories Risk-Free for 30 days, call (800) 562-2139 or fax (518) 789-0556
www.greyhouse.com   books@greyhouse.com

Business Information ♦ Ratings Guides ♦ General Reference ♦ Education ♦ Statistics ♦ Demographics ♦ Health Information ♦ Canadian Information

The Religious Right, A Reference Handbook

Timely and unbiased, this third edition updates and expands its examination of the religious right and its influence on our government, citizens, society, and politics. From the fight to outlaw the teaching of Darwin's theory of evolution to the struggle to outlaw abortion, the religious right is continually exerting an influence on public policy. This text explores the influence of religion on legislation and society, while examining the alignment of the religious right with the political right. A historical survey of the movement highlights the shift to "hands-on" approach to politics and the struggle to present a unified front. The coverage offers a critical historical survey of the religious right movement, focusing on its increased involvement in the political arena, attempts to forge coalitions, and notable successes and failures. The text offers complete coverage of biographies of the men and women who have advanced the cause and an up to date chronology illuminate the movement's goals, including their accomplishments and failures. This edition offers an extensive update to all sections along with several brand new entries. Two new sections complement this third edition, a chapter on legal issues and court decisions and a chapter on demographic statistics and electoral patterns. To aid in further research, *The Religious Right*, offers an entire section of annotated listings of print and non-print resources, as well as of organizations affiliated with the religious right, and those opposing it. Comprehensive in its scope, this work offers easy-to-read, pertinent information for those seeking to understand the religious right and its evolving role in American society. A must for libraries of all sizes, university religion departments, activists, high schools and for those interested in the evolving role of the religious right.

" Recommended for all public and academic libraries." - Library Journal

Hardcover ISBN 978-1-59237-113-6, 600 pages, $135.00 | Ebook ISBN 978-1-59237-226-3 www.gale.com/gvrl/partners/grey.htm

From Suffrage to the Senate, America's Political Women

From Suffrage to the Senate is a comprehensive and valuable compendium of biographies of leading women in U.S. politics, past and present, and an examination of the wide range of women's movements. Up to date through 2006, this dynamically illustrated reference work explores American women's path to political power and social equality from the struggle for the right to vote and the abolition of slavery to the first African American woman in the U.S. Senate and beyond. This new edition includes over 150 new entries and a brand new section on trends and demographics of women in politics. The in-depth coverage also traces the political heritage of the abolition, labor, suffrage, temperance, and reproductive rights movements. The alphabetically arranged entries include biographies of every woman from across the political spectrum who has served in the U.S. House and Senate, along with women in the Judiciary and the U.S. Cabinet and, new to this edition, biographies of activists and political consultants. Bibliographical references follow each entry. For easy reference, a handy chronology is provided detailing 150 years of women's history. This up-to-date reference will be a must-purchase for women's studies departments, high schools and public libraries and will be a handy resource for those researching the key players in women's politics, past and present.

"An engaging tool that would be useful in high school, public, and academic libraries looking for an overview of the political history of women in the US." –Booklist

Two Volumes, Hardcover ISBN 978-1-59237-117-4, 1,160 pages, $195.00 | Ebook ISBN 978-1-59237-227-0 www.gale.com/gvrl/partners/grey.htm

An African Biographical Dictionary

This landmark second edition is the only biographical dictionary to bring together, in one volume, cultural, social and political leaders – both historical and contemporary – of the sub-Saharan region. Over 800 biographical sketches of prominent Africans, as well as foreigners who have affected the continent's history, are featured, 150 more than the previous edition. The wide spectrum of leaders includes religious figures, writers, politicians, scientists, entertainers, sports personalities and more. Access to these fascinating individuals is provided in a user-friendly format. The biographies are arranged alphabetically, cross-referenced and indexed. Entries include the country or countries in which the person was significant and the commonly accepted dates of birth and death. Each biographical sketch is chronologically written; entries for cultural personalities add an evaluation of their work. This information is followed by a selection of references often found in university and public libraries, including autobiographies and principal biographical works. Appendixes list each individual by country and by field of accomplishment – rulers, musicians, explorers, missionaries, businessmen, physicists – nearly thirty categories in all. Another convenient appendix lists heads of state since independence by country. Up-to-date and representative of African societies as a whole, An African Biographical Dictionary provides a wealth of vital information for students of African culture and is an indispensable reference guide for anyone interested in African affairs.

"An unquestionable convenience to have these concise, informative biographies gathered into one source, indexed, and analyzed by appendixes listing entrants by nation and occupational field." –Wilson Library Bulletin

Hardcover ISBN 978-1-59237-112-9, 667 pages, $135.00 | Ebook ISBN 978-1-59237-229-4 www.gale.com/gvrl/partners/grey.htm

To preview any of our Directories Risk-Free for 30 days, call (800) 562-2139 or fax (518) 789-0556
www.greyhouse.com books@greyhouse.com

**Business Information ♦ Ratings Guides ♦ <u>General Reference</u> ♦ Education ♦
Statistics ♦ Demographics ♦ Health Information ♦ Canadian Information**

American Environmental Leaders, From Colonial Times to the Present

A comprehensive and diverse award winning collection of biographies of the most important figures in American environmentalism. Few subjects arouse the passions the way the environment does. How will we feed an ever-increasing population and how can that food be made safe for consumption? Who decides how land is developed? How can environmental policies be made fair for everyone, including multiethnic groups, women, children, and the poor? *American Environmental Leaders* presents more than 350 biographies of men and women who have devoted their lives to studying, debating, and organizing these and other controversial issues over the last 200 years. In addition to the scientists who have analyzed how human actions affect nature, we are introduced to poets, landscape architects, presidents, painters, activists, even sanitation engineers, and others who have forever altered how we think about the environment. The easy to use A–Z format provides instant access to these fascinating individuals, and frequent cross references indicate others with whom individuals worked (and sometimes clashed). End of entry references provide users with a starting point for further research.

"Highly recommended for high school, academic, and public libraries needing environmental biographical information." –Library Journal/Starred Review

Two Volumes, Hardcover ISBN 978-1-59237-119-8, 900 pages $195.00 | Ebook ISBN 978-1-59237-230-0
www.gale.com/gvrl/partners/grey.htm

World Cultural Leaders of the Twentieth & Twenty-First Centuries

World Cultural Leaders of the Twentieth & Twenty-First Centuries is a window into the arts, performances, movements, and music that shaped the world's cultural development since 1900. A remarkable around-the-world look at one-hundred-plus years of cultural development through the eyes of those that set the stage and stayed to play. This second edition offers over 120 new biographies along with a complete update of existing biographies. To further aid the reader, a handy fold-out timeline traces important events in all six cultural categories from 1900 through the present time. Plus, a new section of detailed material and resources for 100 selected individuals is also new to this edition, with further data on museums, homesteads, websites, artwork and more. This remarkable compilation will answer a wide range of questions. Who was the originator of the term "documentary"? Which poet married the daughter of the famed novelist Thomas Mann in order to help her escape Nazi Germany? Which British writer served as an agent in Russia against the Bolsheviks before the 1917 revolution? A handy two-volume set that makes it easy to look up 450 worldwide cultural icons: novelists, poets, playwrights, painters, sculptors, architects, dancers, choreographers, actors, directors, filmmakers, singers, composers, and musicians. *World Cultural Leaders of the Twentieth & Twenty-First Centuries* provides entries (many of them illustrated) covering the person's works, achievements, and professional career in a thorough essay and offers interesting facts and statistics. Entries are fully cross-referenced so that readers can learn how various individuals influenced others. An index of leaders by occupation, a useful glossary and a thorough general index complete the coverage. This remarkable resource will be an important acquisition for the reference collections of public libraries, university libraries and high schools.

"Fills a need for handy, concise information on a wide array of international cultural figures."-ARBA

Two Volumes, Hardcover ISBN 978-1-59237-118-1, 900 pages, $195.00 | Ebook ISBN 978-1-59237-231-7
www.gale.com/gvrl/partners/grey.htm

Political Corruption in America: An Encyclopedia of Scandals, Power, and Greed

The complete scandal-filled history of American political corruption, focusing on the infamous people and cases, as well as society's electoral and judicial reactions. Since colonial times, there has been no shortage of politicians willing to take a bribe, skirt campaign finance laws, or act in their own interests. Corruption like the Whiskey Ring, Watergate, and Whitewater cases dominate American life, making political scandal a leading U.S. industry. From judges to senators, presidents to mayors, *Political Corruption in America* discusses the infamous people throughout history who have been accused of and implicated in crooked behavior. In this new second edition, more than 250 A–Z entries explore the people, crimes, investigations, and court cases behind 200 years of American political scandals. This unbiased volume also delves into the issues surrounding Koreagate, the Chinese campaign scandal, and other ethical lapses. Relevant statutes and terms, including the Independent Counsel Statute and impeachment as a tool of political punishment, are examined as well. Students, scholars, and other readers interested in American history, political science, and ethics will appreciate this survey of a wide range of corrupting influences. This title focuses on how politicians from all parties have fallen because of their greed and hubris, and how society has used electoral and judicial means against those who tested the accepted standards of political conduct. A full range of illustrations including political cartoons, photos of key figures such as Abe Fortas and Archibald Cox, graphs of presidential pardons, and tables showing the number of expulsions and censures in both the House and Senate round out the text. In addition, a comprehensive chronology of major political scandals in U.S. history from colonial times until the present. For further reading, an extensive bibliography lists sources including archival letters, newspapers, and private manuscript collections from the United States and Great Britain. With its comprehensive coverage of this interesting topic, *Political Corruption in America: An Encyclopedia of Scandals, Power, and Greed* will prove to be a useful addition to the reference collections of all public libraries, university libraries, history collections, political science collections and high schools.

"...this encyclopedia is a useful contribution to the field. Highly recommended." - CHOICE
"Political Corruption should be useful in most academic, high school, and public libraries." Booklist

Hardcover ISBN 978-1-59237-297-3, 500 pages, $135.00

**To preview any of our Directories Risk-Free for 30 days, call (800) 562-2139 or fax (518) 789-0556
www.greyhouse.com books@greyhouse.com**

Business Information ✦ Ratings Guides ✦ **General Reference** ✦ Education ✦
Statistics ✦ Demographics ✦ Health Information ✦ Canadian Information

Religion and Law: A Dictionary

This informative, easy-to-use reference work covers a wide range of legal issues that affect the roles of religion and law in American society. Extensive A–Z entries provide coverage of key court decisions, case studies, concepts, individuals, religious groups, organizations, and agencies shaping religion and law in today's society. This *Dictionary* focuses on topics involved with the constitutional theory and interpretation of religion and the law; terms providing a historical explanation of the ways in which America's ever increasing ethnic and religious diversity contributed to our current understanding of the mandates of the First and Fourteenth Amendments; terms and concepts describing the development of religion clause jurisprudence; an analytical examination of the distinct vocabulary used in this area of the law; the means by which American courts have attempted to balance religious liberty against other important individual and social interests in a wide variety of physical and regulatory environments, including the classroom, the workplace, the courtroom, religious group organization and structure, taxation, the clash of "secular" and "religious" values, and the relationship of the generalized idea of individual autonomy of the specific concept of religious liberty. Important legislation and legal cases affecting religion and society are thoroughly covered in this timely volume, including a detailed Table of Cases and Table of Statutes for more detailed research. A guide to further reading and an index are also included. This useful resource will be an important acquisition for the reference collections of all public libraries, university libraries, religion reference collections and high schools.

Hardcover ISBN 978-1-59237-298-0, 500 pages, $135.00

Human Rights in the United States: A Dictionary and Documents

This two volume set offers easy to grasp explanations of the basic concepts, laws, and case law in the field, with emphasis on human rights in the historical, political, and legal experience of the United States. Human rights is a term not fully understood by many Americans. Addressing this gap, the new second edition of *Human Rights in the United States: A Dictionary and Documents* offers a comprehensive introduction that places the history of human rights in the United States in an international context. It surveys the legal protection of human dignity in the United States, examines the sources of human rights norms, cites key legal cases, explains the role of international governmental and non-governmental organizations, and charts global, regional, and U.N. human rights measures. Over 240 dictionary entries of human rights terms are detailed—ranging from asylum and cultural relativism to hate crimes and torture. Each entry discusses the significance of the term, gives examples, and cites appropriate documents and court decisions. In addition, a Documents section is provided that contains 59 conventions, treaties, and protocols related to the most up to date international action on ethnic cleansing; freedom of expression and religion; violence against women; and much more. A bibliography, extensive glossary, and comprehensive index round out this indispensable volume. This comprehensive, timely volume is a must for large public libraries, university libraries and social science departments, along with high school libraries.

> *"...invaluable for anyone interested in human rights issues ... highly recommended for all reference collections."*
> *- American Reference Books Annual*

Two Volumes, Hardcover ISBN 978-1-59237-290-4, 750 pages, $225.00

**To preview any of our Directories Risk-Free for 30 days, call (800) 562-2139 or fax (518) 789-0556
www.greyhouse.com books@greyhouse.com**

Business Information ♦ Ratings Guides ♦ General Reference ♦ **Education** ♦
Statistics ♦ Demographics ♦ Health Information ♦ Canadian Information

The Comparative Guide to American Elementary & Secondary Schools, 2008

The only guide of its kind, this award winning compilation offers a snapshot profile of every public school district in the United States serving 1,500 or more students – more than 5,900 districts are covered. Organized alphabetically by district within state, each chapter begins with a Statistical Overview of the state. Each district listing includes contact information (name, address, phone number and web site) plus Grades Served, the Numbers of Students and Teachers and the Number of Regular, Special Education, Alternative and Vocational Schools in the district along with statistics on Student/Classroom Teacher Ratios, Drop Out Rates, Ethnicity, the Numbers of Librarians and Guidance Counselors and District Expenditures per student. As an added bonus, *The Comparative Guide to American Elementary and Secondary Schools* provides important ranking tables, both by state and nationally, for each data element. For easy navigation through this wealth of information, this handbook contains a useful City Index that lists all districts that operate schools within a city. These important comparative statistics are necessary for anyone considering relocation or doing comparative research on their own district and would be a perfect acquisition for any public library or school district library.

"This straightforward guide is an easy way to find general information. Valuable for academic and large public library collections." –ARBA

Softcover ISBN 978-1-59237-223-2, 2,400 pages, $125.00 | Ebook ISBN 978-1-59237-238-6 www.gale.com/gvrl/partners/grey.htm

The Complete Learning Disabilities Directory, 2008

The Complete Learning Disabilities Directory is the most comprehensive database of Programs, Services, Curriculum Materials, Professional Meetings & Resources, Camps, Newsletters and Support Groups for teachers, students and families concerned with learning disabilities. This information-packed directory includes information about Associations & Organizations, Schools, Colleges & Testing Materials, Government Agencies, Legal Resources and much more. For quick, easy access to information, this directory contains four indexes: Entry Name Index, Subject Index and Geographic Index. With every passing year, the field of learning disabilities attracts more attention and the network of caring, committed and knowledgeable professionals grows every day. This directory is an invaluable research tool for these parents, students and professionals.

"Due to its wealth and depth of coverage, parents, teachers and others… should find this an invaluable resource." -Booklist

Softcover ISBN 978-1-59237-207-2, 900 pages, $145.00 | Online Database $195.00 | Online Database & Directory Combo $280.00

Educators Resource Directory, 2007/08

Educators Resource Directory is a comprehensive resource that provides the educational professional with thousands of resources and statistical data for professional development. This directory saves hours of research time by providing immediate access to Associations & Organizations, Conferences & Trade Shows, Educational Research Centers, Employment Opportunities & Teaching Abroad, School Library Services, Scholarships, Financial Resources, Professional Consultants, Computer Software & Testing Resources and much more. Plus, this comprehensive directory also includes a section on Statistics and Rankings with over 100 tables, including statistics on Average Teacher Salaries, SAT/ACT scores, Revenues & Expenditures and more. These important statistics will allow the user to see how their school rates among others, make relocation decisions and so much more. For quick access to information, this directory contains four indexes: Entry & Publisher Index, Geographic Index, a Subject & Grade Index and Web Sites Index. *Educators Resource Directory* will be a well-used addition to the reference collection of any school district, education department or public library.

"Recommended for all collections that serve elementary and secondary school professionals." –Choice

Softcover ISBN 978-1-59237-179-2, 800 pages, $145.00 | Online Database $195.00 | Online Database & Directory Combo $280.00

To preview any of our Directories Risk-Free for 30 days, call (800) 562-2139 or fax (518) 789-0556
www.greyhouse.com   books@greyhouse.com

Business Information ♦ Ratings Guides ♦ General Reference ♦ Education ♦
Statistics ♦ Demographics ♦ Health Information ♦ Canadian Information

Profiles of New York | Profiles of Florida | Profiles of Texas | Profiles of Illinois | Profiles of Michigan | Profiles of Ohio | Profiles of New Jersey | Profiles of Massachusetts | Profiles of Pennsylvania | Profiles of Wisconsin | Profiles of Connecticut & Rhode Island | Profiles of Indiana | Profiles of North Carolina & South Carolina | Profiles of Virginia | Profiles of California

The careful layout gives the user an easy-to-read snapshot of every single place and county in the state, from the biggest metropolis to the smallest unincorporated hamlet. The richness of each place or county profile is astounding in its depth, from history to weather, all packed in an easy-to-navigate, compact format. Each profile contains data on History, Geography, Climate, Population, Vital Statistics, Economy, Income, Taxes, Education, Housing, Health & Environment, Public Safety, Newspapers, Transportation, Presidential Election Results, Information Contacts and Chambers of Commerce. As an added bonus, there is a section on Selected Statistics, where data from the 100 largest towns and cities is arranged into easy-to-use charts. Each of 22 different data points has its own two-page spread with the cities listed in alpha order so researchers can easily compare and rank cities. A remarkable compilation that offers overviews and insights into each corner of the state, each volume goes beyond Census statistics, beyond metro area coverage, beyond the 100 best places to live. Drawn from official census information, other government statistics and original research, you will have at your fingertips data that's available nowhere else in one single source.

"The publisher claims that this is the 'most comprehensive portrait of the state of Florida ever published,' and this reviewer is inclined to believe it...Recommended. All levels." –Choice on Profiles of Florida

Each Profiles of... title ranges from 400-800 pages, priced at $149.00 each

America's Top-Rated Cities, 2008

America's Top-Rated Cities provides current, comprehensive statistical information and other essential data in one easy-to-use source on the 100 "top" cities that have been cited as the best for business and living in the U.S. This handbook allows readers to see, at a glance, a concise social, business, economic, demographic and environmental profile of each city, including brief evaluative comments. In addition to detailed data on Cost of Living, Finances, Real Estate, Education, Major Employers, Media, Crime and Climate, city reports now include Housing Vacancies, Tax Audits, Bankruptcy, Presidential Election Results and more. This outstanding source of information will be widely used in any reference collection.

"The only source of its kind that brings together all of this information into one easy-to-use source. It will be beneficial to many business and public libraries." –ARBA

Four Volumes, Softcover ISBN 978-1-59237-349-9, 2,500 pages, $195.00 | Ebook ISBN 978-1-59237-233-1
www.gale.com/gvrl/partners/grey.htm

America's Top-Rated Smaller Cities, 2008/09

A perfect companion to *America's Top-Rated Cities*, *America's Top-Rated Smaller Cities* provides current, comprehensive business and living profiles of smaller cities (population 25,000-99,999) that have been cited as the best for business and living in the United States. Sixty cities make up this 2004 edition of America's Top-Rated Smaller Cities, all are top-ranked by Population Growth, Median Income, Unemployment Rate and Crime Rate. City reports reflect the most current data available on a wide-range of statistics, including Employment & Earnings, Household Income, Unemployment Rate, Population Characteristics, Taxes, Cost of Living, Education, Health Care, Public Safety, Recreation, Media, Air & Water Quality and much more. Plus, each city report contains a Background of the City, and an Overview of the State Finances. *America's Top-Rated Smaller Cities* offers a reliable, one-stop source for statistical data that, before now, could only be found scattered in hundreds of sources. This volume is designed for a wide range of readers: individuals considering relocating a residence or business; professionals considering expanding their business or changing careers; general and market researchers; real estate consultants; human resource personnel; urban planners and investors.

"Provides current, comprehensive statistical information in one easy-to-use source... Recommended for public and academic libraries and specialized collections." –Library Journal

Two Volumes, Softcover ISBN 978-1-59237-284-3, 1,100 pages, $195.00 | Ebook ISBN 978-1-59237-234-8
www.gale.com/gvrl/partners/grey.htm

Profiles of America: Facts, Figures & Statistics for Every Populated Place in the United States

Profiles of America is the only source that pulls together, in one place, statistical, historical and descriptive information about every place in the United States in an easy-to-use format. This award winning reference set, now in its second edition, compiles statistics and data from over 20 different sources – the latest census information has been included along with more than nine brand new statistical topics. This Four-Volume Set details over 40,000 places, from the biggest metropolis to the smallest unincorporated hamlet, and provides statistical details and information on over 50 different topics including Geography, Climate, Population, Vital Statistics, Economy, Income, Taxes, Education, Housing, Health & Environment, Public Safety, Newspapers, Transportation, Presidential Election Results and Information Contacts or Chambers of Commerce. Profiles are arranged, for ease-of-use, by state and then by county. Each county begins with a County-Wide Overview and is followed by information for each Community in that particular county. The Community Profiles within the county are arranged alphabetically. *Profiles of America* is a virtual snapshot of America at your fingertips and a unique compilation of information that will be widely used in any reference collection.

A Library Journal Best Reference Book "An outstanding compilation." –Library Journal

Four Volumes, Softcover ISBN 978-1-891482-80-9, 10,000 pages, $595.00

To preview any of our Directories Risk-Free for 30 days, call (800) 562-2139 or fax (518) 789-0556
www.greyhouse.com   books@greyhouse.com

Business Information ♦ Ratings Guides ♦ General Reference ♦ Education ♦ Statistics ♦ Demographics ♦ Health Information ♦ Canadian Information

The Comparative Guide to American Suburbs, 2007/08

The Comparative Guide to American Suburbs is a one-stop source for Statistics on the 2,000+ suburban communities surrounding the 50 largest metropolitan areas – their population characteristics, income levels, economy, school system and important data on how they compare to one another. Organized into 50 Metropolitan Area chapters, each chapter contains an overview of the Metropolitan Area, a detailed Map followed by a comprehensive Statistical Profile of each Suburban Community, including Contact Information, Physical Characteristics, Population Characteristics, Income, Economy, Unemployment Rate, Cost of Living, Education, Chambers of Commerce and more. Next, statistical data is sorted into Ranking Tables that rank the suburbs by twenty different criteria, including Population, Per Capita Income, Unemployment Rate, Crime Rate, Cost of Living and more. *The Comparative Guide to American Suburbs* is the best source for locating data on suburbs. Those looking to relocate, as well as those doing preliminary market research, will find this an invaluable timesaving resource.

"Public and academic libraries will find this compilation useful…The work draws together figures from many sources and will be especially helpful for job relocation decisions." – Booklist

Softcover ISBN 978-1-59237-180-8, 1,700 pages, $130.00 | Ebook ISBN 978-1-59237-235-5 www.gale.com/gvrl/partners/grey.htm

The American Tally: Statistics & Comparative Rankings for U.S. Cities with Populations over 10,000

This important statistical handbook compiles, all in one place, comparative statistics on all U.S. cities and towns with a 10,000+ population. *The American Tally* provides statistical details on over 4,000 cities and towns and profiles how they compare with one another in Population Characteristics, Education, Language & Immigration, Income & Employment and Housing. Each section begins with an alphabetical listing of cities by state, allowing for quick access to both the statistics and relative rankings of any city. Next, the highest and lowest cities are listed in each statistic. These important, informative lists provide quick reference to which cities are at both extremes of the spectrum for each statistic. Unlike any other reference, *The American Tally* provides quick, easy access to comparative statistics – a must-have for any reference collection.

"A solid library reference." -Bookwatch

Softcover ISBN 978-1-930956-29-2, 500 pages, $125.00 | Ebook ISBN 978-1-59237-241-6 www.gale.com/gvrl/partners/grey.htm

The Asian Databook: Statistics for all US Counties & Cities with Over 10,000 Population

This is the first-ever resource that compiles statistics and rankings on the US Asian population. *The Asian Databook* presents over 20 statistical data points for each city and county, arranged alphabetically by state, then alphabetically by place name. Data reported for each place includes Population, Languages Spoken at Home, Foreign-Born, Educational Attainment, Income Figures, Poverty Status, Homeownership, Home Values & Rent, and more. Next, in the Rankings Section, the top 75 places are listed for each data element. These easy-to-access ranking tables allow the user to quickly determine trends and population characteristics. This kind of comparative data can not be found elsewhere, in print or on the web, in a format that's as easy-to-use or more concise. A useful resource for those searching for demographics data, career search and relocation information and also for market research. With data ranging from Ancestry to Education, *The Asian Databook* presents a useful compilation of information that will be a much-needed resource in the reference collection of any public or academic library along with the marketing collection of any company whose primary focus in on the Asian population.

"This useful resource will help those searching for demographics data, and market research or relocation information… Accurate and clearly laid out, the publication is recommended for large public library and research collections." -Booklist

Softcover ISBN 978-1-59237-044-3, 1,000 pages, $150.00

The Hispanic Databook: Statistics for all US Counties & Cities with Over 10,000 Population

Previously published by Toucan Valley Publications, this second edition has been completely updated with figures from the latest census and has been broadly expanded to include dozens of new data elements and a brand new Rankings section. The Hispanic population in the United States has increased over 42% in the last 10 years and accounts for 12.5% of the total US population. For ease-of-use, *The Hispanic Databook* presents over 20 statistical data points for each city and county, arranged alphabetically by state, then alphabetically by place name. Data reported for each place includes Population, Languages Spoken at Home, Foreign-Born, Educational Attainment, Income Figures, Poverty Status, Homeownership, Home Values & Rent, and more. Next, in the Rankings Section, the top 75 places are listed for each data element. These easy-to-access ranking tables allow the user to quickly determine trends and population characteristics. This kind of comparative data can not be found elsewhere, in print or on the web, in a format that's as easy-to-use or more concise. A useful resource for those searching for demographics data, career search and relocation information and also for market research. With data ranging from Ancestry to Education, *The Hispanic Databook* presents a useful compilation of information that will be a much-needed resource in the reference collection of any public or academic library along with the marketing collection of any company whose primary focus in on the Hispanic population.

"This accurate, clearly presented volume of selected Hispanic demographics is recommended for large public libraries and research collections."-Library Journal

Softcover ISBN 978-1-59237-008-5, 1,000 pages, $150.00

**To preview any of our Directories Risk-Free for 30 days, call (800) 562-2139 or fax (518) 789-0556
www.greyhouse.com books@greyhouse.com**

Business Information ♦ Ratings Guides ♦ General Reference ♦ Education ♦ Statistics ♦ Demographics ♦ Health Information ♦ Canadian Information

Ancestry in America: A Comparative Guide to Over 200 Ethnic Backgrounds

This brand new reference work pulls together thousands of comparative statistics on the Ethnic Backgrounds of all populated places in the United States with populations over 10,000. Never before has this kind of information been reported in a single volume. Section One, Statistics by Place, is made up of a list of over 200 ancestry and race categories arranged alphabetically by each of the 5,000 different places with populations over 10,000. The population number of the ancestry group in that city or town is provided along with the percent that group represents of the total population. This informative city-by-city section allows the user to quickly and easily explore the ethnic makeup of all major population bases in the United States. Section Two, Comparative Rankings, contains three tables for each ethnicity and race. In the first table, the top 150 populated places are ranked by population number for that particular ancestry group, regardless of population. In the second table, the top 150 populated places are ranked by the percent of the total population for that ancestry group. In the third table, those top 150 populated places with 10,000 population are ranked by population number for each ancestry group. These easy-to-navigate tables allow users to see ancestry population patterns and make city-by-city comparisons as well. This brand new, information-packed resource will serve a wide-range or research requests for demographics, population characteristics, relocation information and much more. *Ancestry in America: A Comparative Guide to Over 200 Ethnic Backgrounds* will be an important acquisition to all reference collections.

"This compilation will serve a wide range of research requests for population characteristics … it offers much more detail than other sources." –Booklist

Softcover ISBN 978-1-59237-029-0, 1,500 pages, $225.00

Weather America, A Thirty-Year Summary of Statistical Weather Data and Rankings

This valuable resource provides extensive climatological data for over 4,000 National and Cooperative Weather Stations throughout the United States. Weather America begins with a new Major Storms section that details major storm events of the nation and a National Rankings section that details rankings for several data elements, such as Maximum Temperature and Precipitation. The main body of Weather America is organized into 50 state sections. Each section provides a Data Table on each Weather Station, organized alphabetically, that provides statistics on Maximum and Minimum Temperatures, Precipitation, Snowfall, Extreme Temperatures, Foggy Days, Humidity and more. State sections contain two brand new features in this edition – a City Index and a narrative Description of the climatic conditions of the state. Each section also includes a revised Map of the State that includes not only weather stations, but cities and towns.

"Best Reference Book of the Year." –Library Journal

Softcover ISBN 978-1-891482-29-8, 2,013 pages, $175.00 | Ebook ISBN 978-1-59237-237-9 www.gale.com/gvrl/partners/grey.htm

Crime in America's Top-Rated Cities

This volume includes over 20 years of crime statistics in all major crime categories: violent crimes, property crimes and total crime. *Crime in America's Top-Rated Cities* is conveniently arranged by city and covers 76 top-rated cities. Crime in America's Top-Rated Cities offers details that compare the number of crimes and crime rates for the city, suburbs and metro area along with national crime trends for violent, property and total crimes. Also, this handbook contains important information and statistics on Anti-Crime Programs, Crime Risk, Hate Crimes, Illegal Drugs, Law Enforcement, Correctional Facilities, Death Penalty Laws and much more. A much-needed resource for people who are relocating, business professionals, general researchers, the press, law enforcement officials and students of criminal justice.

"Data is easy to access and will save hours of searching." –Global Enforcement Review

Softcover ISBN 978-1-891482-84-7, 832 pages, $155.00

**Business Information ♦ Ratings Guides ♦ General Reference ♦ Education ♦
Statistics ♦ Demographics ♦ <u>Health Information</u> ♦ Canadian Information**

The Complete Directory for People with Disabilities, 2008
A wealth of information, now in one comprehensive sourcebook. Completely updated, this edition contains more information than ever before, including thousands of new entries and enhancements to existing entries and thousands of additional web sites and e-mail addresses. This up-to-date directory is the most comprehensive resource available for people with disabilities, detailing Independent Living Centers, Rehabilitation Facilities, State & Federal Agencies, Associations, Support Groups, Periodicals & Books, Assistive Devices, Employment & Education Programs, Camps and Travel Groups. Each year, more libraries, schools, colleges, hospitals, rehabilitation centers and individuals add *The Complete Directory for People with Disabilities* to their collections, making sure that this information is readily available to the families, individuals and professionals who can benefit most from the amazing wealth of resources cataloged here.

"No other reference tool exists to meet the special needs of the disabled in one convenient resource for information." –Library Journal

Softcover ISBN 978-1-59237-194-5, 1,200 pages, $165.00 | Online Database $215.00 | Online Database & Directory Combo $300.00

The Complete Learning Disabilities Directory, 2008
The Complete Learning Disabilities Directory is the most comprehensive database of Programs, Services, Curriculum Materials, Professional Meetings & Resources, Camps, Newsletters and Support Groups for teachers, students and families concerned with learning disabilities. This information-packed directory includes information about Associations & Organizations, Schools, Colleges & Testing Materials, Government Agencies, Legal Resources and much more. For quick, easy access to information, this directory contains four indexes: Entry Name Index, Subject Index and Geographic Index. With every passing year, the field of learning disabilities attracts more attention and the network of caring, committed and knowledgeable professionals grows every day. This directory is an invaluable research tool for these parents, students and professionals.

"Due to its wealth and depth of coverage, parents, teachers and others… should find this an invaluable resource." -Booklist

Softcover ISBN 978-1-59237-207-2, 900 pages, $145.00 | Online Database $195.00 | Online Database & Directory Combo $280.00

The Complete Directory for People with Chronic Illness, 2007/08
Thousands of hours of research have gone into this completely updated edition – several new chapters have been added along with thousands of new entries and enhancements to existing entries. Plus, each chronic illness chapter has been reviewed by a medical expert in the field. This widely-hailed directory is structured around the 90 most prevalent chronic illnesses – from Asthma to Cancer to Wilson's Disease – and provides a comprehensive overview of the support services and information resources available for people diagnosed with a chronic illness. Each chronic illness has its own chapter and contains a brief description in layman's language, followed by important resources for National & Local Organizations, State Agencies, Newsletters, Books & Periodicals, Libraries & Research Centers, Support Groups & Hotlines, Web Sites and much more. This directory is an important resource for health care professionals, the collections of hospital and health care libraries, as well as an invaluable tool for people with a chronic illness and their support network.

"A must purchase for all hospital and health care libraries and is strongly recommended for all public library reference departments." –ARBA

Softcover ISBN 978-1-59237-183-9, 1,200 pages, $165.00 | Online Database $215.00 | Online Database & Directory Combo $300.00

The Complete Mental Health Directory, 2008/09
This is the most comprehensive resource covering the field of behavioral health, with critical information for both the layman and the mental health professional. For the layman, this directory offers understandable descriptions of 25 Mental Health Disorders as well as detailed information on Associations, Media, Support Groups and Mental Health Facilities. For the professional, The Complete Mental Health Directory offers critical and comprehensive information on Managed Care Organizations, Information Systems, Government Agencies and Provider Organizations. This comprehensive volume of needed information will be widely used in any reference collection.

"… the strength of this directory is that it consolidates widely dispersed information into a single volume." –Booklist

Softcover ISBN 978-1-59237-285-0, 800 pages, $165.00 | Online Database $215.00 | Online & Directory Combo $300.00

**To preview any of our Directories Risk-Free for 30 days, call (800) 562-2139 or fax (518) 789-0556
www.greyhouse.com books@greyhouse.com**

Business Information ♦ Ratings Guides ♦ General Reference ♦ Education ♦
Statistics ♦ Demographics ♦ **Health Information** ♦ Canadian Information

The Comparative Guide to American Hospitals, Second Edition

This new second edition compares all of the nation's hospitals by 24 measures of quality in the treatment of heart attack, heart failure, pneumonia, and, new to this edition, surgical procedures and pregnancy care. Plus, this second edition is now available in regional volumes, to make locating information about hospitals in your area quicker and easier than ever before. The Comparative Guide to American Hospitals provides a snapshot profile of each of the nations 4,200+ hospitals. These informative profiles illustrate how the hospital rates when providing 24 different treatments within four broad categories: Heart Attack Care, Heart Failure Care, Surgical Infection Prevention (NEW), and Pregnancy Care measures (NEW). Each profile includes the raw percentage for that hospital, the state average, the US average and data on the top hospital. For easy access to contact information, each profile includes the hospital's address, phone and fax numbers, email and web addresses, type and accreditation along with 5 top key administrations. These profiles will allow the user to quickly identify the quality of the hospital and have the necessary information at their fingertips to make contact with that hospital. Most importantly, The Comparative Guide to American Hospitals provides easy-to-use Regional State by State Statistical Summary Tables for each of the data elements to allow the user to quickly locate hospitals with the best level of service. Plus, a new 30-Day Mortality Chart, Glossary of Terms and Regional Hospital Profile Index make this a must-have source. This new, expanded edition will be a must for the reference collection at all public, medical and academic libraries.

"These data will help those with heart conditions and pneumonia make informed decisions about their healthcare and encourage hospitals to improve the quality of care they provide. Large medical, hospital, and public libraries are most likely to benefit from this weighty resource."-Library Journal

Four Volumes Softcover ISBN 978-1-59237-182-2, 3,500 pages, $325.00 | Regional Volumes $135.00 |
Ebook ISBN 978-1-59237-239-3 www.gale.com/gvrl/partners/grey.htm

Older Americans Information Directory, 2007

Completely updated for 2007, this sixth edition has been completely revised and now contains 1,000 new listings, over 8,000 updates to existing listings and over 3,000 brand new e-mail addresses and web sites. You'll find important resources for Older Americans including National, Regional, State & Local Organizations, Government Agencies, Research Centers, Libraries & Information Centers, Legal Resources, Discount Travel Information, Continuing Education Programs, Disability Aids & Assistive Devices, Health, Print Media and Electronic Media. Three indexes: Entry Index, Subject Index and Geographic Index make it easy to find just the right source of information. This comprehensive guide to resources for Older Americans will be a welcome addition to any reference collection.

"Highly recommended for academic, public, health science and consumer libraries…" –Choice

1,200 pages; Softcover ISBN 978-1-59237-136-5, $165.00 | Online Database $215.00 | Online Database & Directory Combo $300.00

The Complete Directory for Pediatric Disorders, 2008

This important directory provides parents and caregivers with information about Pediatric Conditions, Disorders, Diseases and Disabilities, including Blood Disorders, Bone & Spinal Disorders, Brain Defects & Abnormalities, Chromosomal Disorders, Congenital Heart Defects, Movement Disorders, Neuromuscular Disorders and Pediatric Tumors & Cancers. This carefully written directory offers: understandable Descriptions of 15 major bodily systems; Descriptions of more than 200 Disorders and a Resources Section, detailing National Agencies & Associations, State Associations, Online Services, Libraries & Resource Centers, Research Centers, Support Groups & Hotlines, Camps, Books and Periodicals. This resource will provide immediate access to information crucial to families and caregivers when coping with children's illnesses.

"Recommended for public and consumer health libraries." –Library Journal

Softcover ISBN 978-1-59237-150-1, 1,200 pages, $165.00 | Online Database $215.00 | Online Database & Directory Combo $300.00

The Directory of Drug & Alcohol Residential Rehabilitation Facilities

This brand new directory is the first-ever resource to bring together, all in one place, data on the thousands of drug and alcohol residential rehabilitation facilities in the United States. The Directory of Drug & Alcohol Residential Rehabilitation Facilities covers over 1,000 facilities, with detailed contact information for each one, including mailing address, phone and fax numbers, email addresses and web sites, mission statement, type of treatment programs, cost, average length of stay, numbers of residents and counselors, accreditation, insurance plans accepted, type of environment, religious affiliation, education components and much more. It also contains a helpful chapter on General Resources that provides contact information for Associations, Print & Electronic Media, Support Groups and Conferences. Multiple indexes allow the user to pinpoint the facilities that meet very specific criteria. This time-saving tool is what so many counselors, parents and medical professionals have been asking for. The Directory of Drug & Alcohol Residential Rehabilitation Facilities will be a helpful tool in locating the right source for treatment for a wide range of individuals. This comprehensive directory will be an important acquisition for all reference collections: public and academic libraries, case managers, social workers, state agencies and many more.

"This is an excellent, much needed directory that fills an important gap…" –Booklist

Softcover ISBN 978-1-59237-031-3, 300 pages, $135.00

**To preview any of our Directories Risk-Free for 30 days, call (800) 562-2139 or fax (518) 789-0556
www.greyhouse.com books@greyhouse.com**

Business Information ♦ Ratings Guides ♦ General Reference ♦ Education ♦
Statistics ♦ Demographics ♦ <u>Health Information</u> ♦ Canadian Information

The Directory of Hospital Personnel, 2008

The Directory of Hospital Personnel is the best resource you can have at your fingertips when researching or marketing a product or service to the hospital market. A "Who's Who" of the hospital universe, this directory puts you in touch with over 150,000 key decision-makers. With 100% verification of data you can rest assured that you will reach the right person with just one call. Every hospital in the U.S. is profiled, listed alphabetically by city within state. Plus, three easy-to-use, cross-referenced indexes put the facts at your fingertips faster and more easily than any other directory: Hospital Name Index, Bed Size Index and Personnel Index. *The Directory of Hospital Personnel* is the only complete source for key hospital decision-makers by name. Whether you want to define or restructure sales territories... locate hospitals with the purchasing power to accept your proposals... keep track of important contacts or colleagues... or find information on which insurance plans are accepted, *The Directory of Hospital Personnel* gives you the information you need – easily, efficiently, effectively and accurately.

"Recommended for college, university and medical libraries." -ARBA

Softcover ISBN 978-1-59237-286-7, 2,500 pages, $325.00 | Online Database $545.00 | Online Database & Directory Combo, $650.00

The Directory of Health Care Group Purchasing Organizations, 2008

This comprehensive directory provides the important data you need to get in touch with over 800 Group Purchasing Organizations. By providing in-depth information on this growing market and its members, *The Directory of Health Care Group Purchasing Organizations* fills a major need for the most accurate and comprehensive information on over 800 GPOs – Mailing Address, Phone & Fax Numbers, E-mail Addresses, Key Contacts, Purchasing Agents, Group Descriptions, Membership Categorization, Standard Vendor Proposal Requirements, Membership Fees & Terms, Expanded Services, Total Member Beds & Outpatient Visits represented and more. Five Indexes provide a number of ways to locate the right GPO: Alphabetical Index, Expanded Services Index, Organization Type Index, Geographic Index and Member Institution Index. With its comprehensive and detailed information on each purchasing organization, *The Directory of Health Care Group Purchasing Organizations* is the go-to source for anyone looking to target this market.

"The information is clearly arranged and easy to access...recommended for those needing this very specialized information." –ARBA

1,000 pages; Softcover ISBN 978-1-59237-287-4, $325.00 | Online Database, $650.00 | Online Database & Directory Combo, $750.00

The HMO/PPO Directory, 2008

The HMO/PPO Directory is a comprehensive source that provides detailed information about Health Maintenance Organizations and Preferred Provider Organizations nationwide. This comprehensive directory details more information about more managed health care organizations than ever before. Over 1,100 HMOs, PPOs, Medicare Advantage Plans and affiliated companies are listed, arranged alphabetically by state. Detailed listings include Key Contact Information, Prescription Drug Benefits, Enrollment, Geographical Areas served, Affiliated Physicians & Hospitals, Federal Qualifications, Status, Year Founded, Managed Care Partners, Employer References, Fees & Payment Information and more. Plus, five years of historical information is included related to Revenues, Net Income, Medical Loss Ratios, Membership Enrollment and Number of Patient Complaints. Five easy-to-use, cross-referenced indexes will put this vast array of information at your fingertips immediately: HMO Index, PPO Index, Other Providers Index, Personnel Index and Enrollment Index. *The HMO/PPO Directory* provides the most comprehensive data on the most companies available on the market place today.

"Helpful to individuals requesting certain HMO/PPO issues such as co-payment costs, subscription costs and patient complaints. Individuals concerned (or those with questions) about their insurance may find this text to be of use to them." -ARBA

Softcover ISBN 978-1-59237-204-1, 600 pages, $325.00 | Online Database, $495.00 | Online Database & Directory Combo, $600.00

Medical Device Register, 2008

The only one-stop resource of every medical supplier licensed to sell products in the US. This award-winning directory offers immediate access to over 13,000 companies - and more than 65,000 products – in two information-packed volumes. This comprehensive resource saves hours of time and trouble when searching for medical equipment and supplies and the manufacturers who provide them. Volume I: The Product Directory, provides essential information for purchasing or specifying medical supplies for every medical device, supply, and diagnostic available in the US. Listings provide FDA codes & Federal Procurement Eligibility, Contact information for every manufacturer of the product along with Prices and Product Specifications. Volume 2 - Supplier Profiles, offers the most complete and important data about Suppliers, Manufacturers and Distributors. Company Profiles detail the number of employees, ownership, method of distribution, sales volume, net income, key executives detailed contact information medical products the company supplies, plus the medical specialties they cover. Four indexes provide immediate access to this wealth of information: Keyword Index, Trade Name Index, Supplier Geographical Index and OEM (Original Equipment Manufacturer) Index. *Medical Device Register* is the only one-stop source for locating suppliers and products; looking for new manufacturers or hard-to-find medical devices; comparing products and companies; know who's selling what and who to buy from cost effectively. This directory has become the standard in its field and will be a welcome addition to the reference collection of any medical library, large public library, university library along with the collections that serve the medical community.

"A wealth of information on medical devices, medical device companies... and key personnel in the industry is provide in this comprehensive reference work... A valuable reference work, one of the best hardcopy compilations available." -Doody Publishing

Two Volumes, Hardcover ISBN 978-1-59237-206-5, 3,000 pages, $325.00

To preview any of our Directories Risk-Free for 30 days, call (800) 562-2139 or fax (518) 789-0556
www.greyhouse.com books@greyhouse.com

Business Information ♦ Ratings Guides ♦ General Reference ♦ Education ♦
Statistics ♦ Demographics ♦ Health Information ♦ **Canadian Information**

Canadian Almanac & Directory, 2008
The Canadian Almanac & Directory contains sixteen directories in one – giving you all the facts and figures you will ever need about Canada. No other single source provides users with the quality and depth of up-to-date information for all types of research. This national directory and guide gives you access to statistics, images and over 100,000 names and addresses for everything from Airlines to Zoos - updated every year. It's Ten Directories in One! Each section is a directory in itself, providing robust information on business and finance, communications, government, associations, arts and culture (museums, zoos, libraries, etc.), health, transportation, law, education, and more. Government information includes federal, provincial and territorial - and includes an easy-to-use quick index to find key information. A separate municipal government section includes every municipality in Canada, with full profiles of Canada's largest urban centers. A complete legal directory lists judges and judicial officials, court locations and law firms across the country. A wealth of general information, the *Canadian Almanac & Directory* also includes national statistics on population, employment, imports and exports, and more. National awards and honors are presented, along with forms of address, Commonwealth information and full color photos of Canadian symbols. Postal information, weights, measures, distances and other useful charts are also incorporated. Complete almanac information includes perpetual calendars, five-year holiday planners and astronomical information. Published continuously for 160 years, *The Canadian Almanac & Directory* is the best single reference source for business executives, managers and assistants; government and public affairs executives; lawyers; marketing, sales and advertising executives; researchers, editors and journalists.

Hardcover ISBN 978-1-59237-220-1, 1,600 pages, $315.00

Associations Canada, 2008
The Most Powerful Fact-Finder to Business, Trade, Professional and Consumer Organizations
Associations Canada covers Canadian organizations and international groups including industry, commercial and professional associations, registered charities, special interest and common interest organizations. This annually revised compendium provides detailed listings and abstracts for nearly 20,000 regional, national and international organizations. This popular volume provides the most comprehensive picture of Canada's non-profit sector. Detailed listings enable users to identify an organization's budget, founding date, scope of activity, licensing body, sources of funding, executive information, full address and complete contact information, just to name a few. Powerful indexes help researchers find information quickly and easily. The following indexes are included: subject, acronym, geographic, budget, executive name, conferences & conventions, mailing list, defunct and unreachable associations and registered charitable organizations. In addition to annual spending of over $1 billion on transportation and conventions alone, Canadian associations account for many millions more in pursuit of membership interests. *Associations Canada* provides complete access to this highly lucrative market. *Associations Canada* is a strong source of prospects for sales and marketing executives, tourism and convention officials, researchers, government officials - anyone who wants to locate non-profit interest groups and trade associations.

Hardcover ISBN 978-1-59237-277-5, 1,600 pages, $315.00

Financial Services Canada, 2008/09
Financial Services Canada is the only master file of current contacts and information that serves the needs of the entire financial services industry in Canada. With over 18,000 organizations and hard-to-find business information, Financial Services Canada is the most up-to-date source for names and contact numbers of industry professionals, senior executives, portfolio managers, financial advisors, agency bureaucrats and elected representatives. Financial Services Canada incorporates the latest changes in the industry to provide you with the most current details on each company, including: name, title, organization, telephone and fax numbers, e-mail and web addresses. *Financial Services Canada* also includes private company listings never before compiled, government agencies, association and consultant services - to ensure that you'll never miss a client or a contact. Current listings include: banks and branches, non-depository institutions, stock exchanges and brokers, investment management firms, insurance companies, major accounting and law firms, government agencies and financial associations. Powerful indexes assist researchers with locating the vital financial information they need. The following indexes are included: alphabetic, geographic, executive name, corporate web site/e-mail, government quick reference and subject. *Financial Services Canada* is a valuable resource for financial executives, bankers, financial planners, sales and marketing professionals, lawyers and chartered accountants, government officials, investment dealers, journalists, librarians and reference specialists.

Hardcover ISBN 978-1-59237-278-2, 900 pages, $315.00

Directory of Libraries in Canada, 2008/09
The Directory of Libraries in Canada brings together almost 7,000 listings including libraries and their branches, information resource centers, archives and library associations and learning centers. The directory offers complete and comprehensive information on Canadian libraries, resource centers, business information centers, professional associations, regional library systems, archives, library schools and library technical programs. *The Directory of Libraries in Canada* includes important features of each library and service, including library information; personnel details, including contact names and e-mail addresses; collection information; services available to users; acquisitions budgets; and computers and automated systems. Useful information on each library's electronic access is also included, such as Internet browser, connectivity and public Internet/CD-ROM/subscription database access. The directory also provides powerful indexes for subject, location, personal name and Web site/e-mail to assist researchers with locating the crucial information they need. *The Directory of Libraries in Canada* is a vital reference tool for publishers, advocacy groups, students, research institutions, computer hardware suppliers, and other diverse groups that provide products and services to this unique market.

Hardcover ISBN 978-1-59237-279-9, 850 pages, $315.00

To preview any of our Directories Risk-Free for 30 days, call (800) 562-2139 or fax (518) 789-0556
www.greyhouse.com books@greyhouse.com

Business Information ♦ Ratings Guides ♦ General Reference ♦ Education ♦ Statistics ♦ Demographics ♦ Health Information ♦ <u>Canadian Information</u>

Canadian Environmental Directory, 2008 /09

The Canadian Environmental Directory is Canada's most complete and only national listing of environmental associations and organizations, government regulators and purchasing groups, product and service companies, special libraries, and more! The extensive Products and Services section provides detailed listings enabling users to identify the company name, address, phone, fax, e-mail, Web address, firm type, contact names (and titles), product and service information, affiliations, trade information, branch and affiliate data. The Government section gives you all the contact information you need at every government level – federal, provincial and municipal. We also include descriptions of current environmental initiatives, programs and agreements, names of environment-related acts administered by each ministry or department PLUS information and tips on who to contact and how to sell to governments in Canada. The Associations section provides complete contact information and a brief description of activities. Included are Canadian environmental organizations and international groups including industry, commercial and professional associations, registered charities, special interest and common interest organizations. All the Information you need about the Canadian environmental industry: directory of products and services, special libraries and resource, conferences, seminars and tradeshows, chronology of environmental events, law firms and major Canadian companies, *The Canadian Environmental Directory* is ideal for business, government, engineers and anyone conducting research on the environment.

Softcover ISBN 978-1-59237-224-9, 900 pages, $315.00

Canadian Parliamentary Guide, 2008

An indispensable guide to government in Canada, the annual *Canadian Parliamentary Guide* provides information on both federal and provincial governments, courts, and their elected and appointed members. The Guide is completely bilingual, with each record appearing both in English and then in French. The Guide contains biographical sketches of members of the Governor General's Household, the Privy Council, members of Canadian legislatures (federal, including both the House of Commons and the Senate, provincial and territorial), members of the federal superior courts (Supreme, Federal, Federal Appeal, Court Martial Appeal and Tax Courts) and the senior staff for these institutions. Biographies cover personal data, political career, private career and contact information. In addition, the Guide provides descriptions of each of the institutions, including brief historical information in text and chart format and significant facts (i.e. number of members and their salaries). The Guide covers the results of all federal general elections and by-elections from Confederations to the present and the results of the most recent provincial elections. A complete name index rounds out the text, making information easy to find. No other resources presents a more up-to-date, more complete picture of Canadian government and her political leaders. A must-have resource for all Canadian reference collections.

Hardcover ISBN 978-1-59237-310-9, 800 pages, $184.00